Plumbing Costs with RSMeans data

Jake MacDonald, Senior Editor

2023
46th annual edition

Chief Technology Officer
Chris Gaudreau

Chief Product Officer
Ted Kail

Director, Data Operations
Sam Giffin

Principal Engineer
Bob Mewis

Engineering and Research
Matthew Doheny, Sr. Manager

Engineers: Architectural Divisions
1, 3, 4, 5, 6, 7, 8, 9, 10, 11, 12, 13, 41
Sam Babbitt
Stephen Bell
Sergeleen Edouard
Richard Goldin
Scott Keller
Thomas Lane

Engineers: Civil Divisions and Wages
2, 31, 32, 33, 34, 35, 44, 46
Derrick Hale, PE
Christopher Babbitt
Michael Lynch
Elisa Mello
Giles Munyard
David Yazbek

Engineers: Mechanical, Electrical, Plumbing & Conveying Divisions
14, 21, 22, 23, 25, 26, 27, 28, 48
Joseph Kelble
Brian Adams
Michelle Curran
Antonio D'Aulerio
Thomas Lyons
Jake MacDonald

Contributing Engineers
John Melin, PE, Manager
Paul Cowan
Barry Hutchinson
Gerard Lafond, PE
Matthew Sorrentino

Production
Debra Panarelli, Manager
Jonathan Forgit
Sheryl Rose
Janice Thalin

Data Quality
Patrice Bruesch, QA Lead and Testing Strategist, Technology
David Byars
Ellen D'Amico

Cover Design
Blaire Collins

Data Management Ecosystem
Audrey Considine
Kedar Gaikwad
Todd Glowac
Srini Narla

RSMeans data from Gordian
Construction Publishers & Consultants
30 Patewood Dr., Suite 350
Greenville, SC 29615
United States of America
1.800.448.8182
rsmeans.com

Copyright 2022 by The Gordian Group Inc.
All rights reserved.
Cover photo © iStock/DenBoma

Printed in the United States of America
ISSN 1537-8411
ISBN 978-1-955341-65-3

Gordian's authors, editors, and engineers apply diligence and judgment in locating and using reliable sources for the information published. However, Gordian makes no express or implied warranty or guarantee in connection with the content of the information contained herein, including the accuracy, correctness, value, sufficiency, or completeness of the data, methods, and other information contained herein. Gordian makes no express or implied warranty of merchantability or fitness for a particular purpose. Gordian shall have no liability to any customer or third party for any loss, expense, or damage, including consequential, incidental, special, or punitive damage, including lost profits or lost revenue, caused directly or indirectly by any error or omission, or arising out of, or in connection with, the information contained herein. For the purposes of this paragraph, "Gordian" shall include The Gordian Group, Inc., and its divisions, subsidiaries, successors, parent companies, and their employees, partners, principals, agents and representatives, and any third-party providers or sources of information or data. Gordian grants the purchaser of this publication limited license to use the cost data contained herein for purchaser's internal business purposes in connection with construction estimating and related work. The publication, and all cost data contained herein, may not be reproduced, integrated into any software or computer program, developed into a database or other electronic compilation, stored in an information storage or retrieval system, or transmitted or distributed to anyone in any form or by any means, electronic or mechanical, including photocopying or scanning, without prior written permission of Gordian. This publication is subject to protection under copyright law, trade secret law and other intellectual property laws of the United States, Canada and other jurisdictions. Gordian and its affiliates exclusively own and retain all rights, title and interest in and to this publication and the cost data contained herein including, without limitation, all copyright, patent, trademark and trade secret rights. Except for the limited license contained herein, your purchase of this publication does not grant you any intellectual property rights in the publication or the cost data.

0213 $380.00 per copy (in United States)
Price is subject to change without prior notice.

Related Data and Services

Our engineers recommend the following products and services to complement *Plumbing Costs with RSMeans data*:

Annual Cost Data Books
2023 Assemblies Costs with RSMeans data
2023 Square Foot Costs with RSMeans data

Reference Books
Estimating Building Costs
RSMeans Estimating Handbook
Green Building: Project Planning & Estimating
How to Estimate with RSMeans data
Plan Reading & Material Takeoff
Project Scheduling & Management for Construction
Universal Design Ideas for Style, Comfort & Safety

Virtual, Instructor-led & On-site Training Offerings
Unit Price Estimating
Training for Our Online Estimating Solution
Practical Project Management for Construction Professionals
Mechanical & Electrical Estimating

RSMeans data
For access to the latest cost data, an intuitive search, and an easy-to-use estimate builder, take advantage of the time savings available from our online application.

To learn more visit: **RSMeans.com/online**

Enterprise Solutions
Building owners, facility managers, building product manufacturers and attorneys across the public and private sectors engage with RSMeans data Enterprise to solve unique challenges where trusted construction cost data is critical.

To learn more visit: **RSMeans.com/Enterprise**

Custom Built Data Sets
Building and Space Models: Quickly plan construction costs across multiple locations based on geography, project size, building system component, product options and other variables for precise budgeting and cost control.

Predictive Analytics: Accurately plan future builds with custom graphical interactive dashboards, negotiate future costs of tenant build-outs and identify and compare national account pricing.

Consulting
Building Product Manufacturing Analytics: Validate your claims and assist with new product launches.

Third-Party Legal Resources: Used in cases of construction cost or estimate disputes, construction product failure vs. installation failure, eminent domain, class action construction product liability and more.

API
For resellers or internal application integration, RSMeans data is offered via API. Deliver Unit, Assembly and Square Foot Model data within your interface. To learn more about how you can provide your customers with the latest in localized construction cost data visit:
RSMeans.com/API

Table of Contents

Foreword	iv
How the Cost Data Is Built: An Overview	v
Estimating with RSMeans data: Unit Prices	vii
How to Use the Cost Data: The Details	ix
Unit Price Section	1
RSMeans data: Unit Prices—How They Work	2
Assemblies Section	471
RSMeans data: Assemblies—How They Work	472
Reference Section	581
Construction Equipment Rental Costs	583
Crew Listings	595
Historical Cost Indexes	632
City Cost Indexes	633
Location Factors	676
Reference Tables	682
Change Orders	720
Project Costs	723
Abbreviations	728
Index	732
Training Class Options	754
Labor Trade Rates including Overhead & Profit	Inside Back Cover

Foreword

The Value of RSMeans data from Gordian

Since 1942, RSMeans data has been the industry-standard materials, labor, and equipment cost information database for contractors, facility owners and managers, architects, engineers and anyone else that requires the latest localized construction cost information. More than 75 years later, the objective remains the same: to provide facility and construction professionals with the most current and comprehensive construction cost database possible.

With the constant influx of new construction methods and materials, in addition to ever-changing labor and material costs, last year's cost data is not reliable for today's designs, estimates or budgets. Gordian's cost engineers apply real-world construction experience to identify and quantify new building products and methodologies, adjust productivity rates and adjust costs to local market conditions across the nation. This adds up to more than 30,000 hours in cost research annually. This unparalleled construction cost expertise is why so many facility and construction professionals rely on RSMeans data year over year.

About Gordian

Gordian is the leading provider of facility and construction cost data, software, and services for all phases of the building lifecycle. From planning to design, procurement, construction, and operations, Gordian delivers groundbreaking solutions to contractors, architects, engineers, business and financial officers, and facility owners in local, state, and federal governments, education, healthcare, and other industries. A pioneer of Job Order Contracting (JOC), Gordian's offerings also include our proprietary RSMeans data and Facility Intelligence solutions. We develop and maintain the largest collection of labor, material, and equipment data and associated costs for all areas of construction. Gordian's solutions are accessed through our innovative software platforms and supported by a team of industry experts proven to help clients maximize efficiency, optimize cost savings, and increase building quality.

Our Commitment

At Gordian, we do more than talk about the quality of our data and the usefulness of its application. We stand behind all of our RSMeans data — from historical cost indexes to construction materials and techniques — to craft current costs and predict future trends. If you have any questions about our products or services, please call us toll-free at 800.448.8182 or visit our website at gordian.com.

How the Cost Data Is Built: An Overview

Unit Prices*
All cost data have been divided into 50 divisions according to the MasterFormat® system of classification and numbering.

Assemblies*
The cost data in this section have been organized in an "Assemblies" format. These assemblies are the functional elements of a building and are arranged according to the seven elements of the UNIFORMAT II classification system. For a complete explanation of a typical "Assembly", see "RSMeans data: Assemblies—How They Work."

Residential Models*
Model buildings for four classes of construction — economy, average, custom, and luxury — are developed and shown with complete costs per square foot.

Commercial/Industrial/Institutional Models*
This section contains complete costs for 77 typical model buildings expressed as costs per square foot.

Green Commercial/Industrial/Institutional Models*
This section contains complete costs for 25 green model buildings expressed as costs per square foot.

References*
This section includes information on Equipment Rental Costs, Crew Listings, Historical Cost Indexes, City Cost Indexes, Location Factors, Reference Tables and Change Orders, as well as a listing of abbreviations.

- **Equipment Rental Costs:** Included are the average costs to rent and operate hundreds of pieces of construction equipment.
- **Crew Listings:** This section lists all the crews referenced in the cost data. A crew is composed of more than one trade classification and/or the addition of power equipment to any trade classification. Power equipment is included in the cost of the crew. Costs are shown both with bare labor rates and with the installing contractor's overhead and profit added. For each, the total crew cost per eight-hour day and the composite cost per labor-hour are listed.

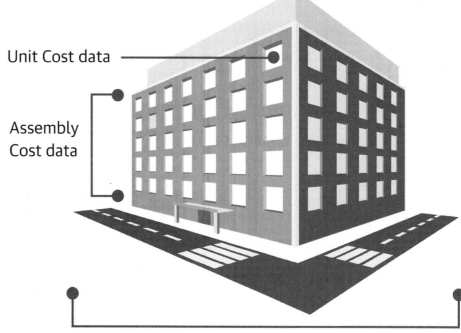

Square Foot Models

- **Historical Cost Indexes:** These indexes provide you with data to adjust construction costs over time.
- **City Cost Indexes:** All costs in this data set are U.S. national averages. Costs vary by region. You can adjust for this by CSI Division to over 730 cities in 900+ 3-digit zip codes throughout the U.S. and Canada by using this data.
- **Location Factors:** You can adjust total project costs to over 730 cities in 900+ 3-digit zip codes throughout the U.S. and Canada by using the weighted number, which applies across all divisions.
- **Reference Tables:** At the beginning of selected major classifications in the Unit Prices are reference numbers indicators. These numbers refer you to related information in the Reference Section. In this section, you'll find reference tables, explanations and estimating information that support how we develop the unit price data, technical data and estimating procedures.
- **Change Orders:** This section includes information on the factors that influence the pricing of change orders.
- **Abbreviations:** A listing of abbreviations used throughout this information, along with the terms they represent, is included.

Index (printed versions only)
A comprehensive listing of all terms and subjects will help you quickly find what you need when you are not sure where it occurs in MasterFormat®.

Conclusion
This information is designed to be as comprehensive and easy to use as possible.

The Construction Specifications Institute (CSI) and Construction Specifications Canada (CSC) have produced the 2018 edition of MasterFormat®, a system of titles and numbers used extensively to organize construction information.

All unit prices in the RSMeans cost data are now arranged in the 50-division MasterFormat® 2018 system.

---

* Not all information is available in all data sets

Note: The material prices in RSMeans cost data are "contractor's prices." They are the prices that contractors can expect to pay at the lumberyards, suppliers'/distributors' warehouses, etc. Small orders of specialty items would be higher than the costs shown, while very large orders, such as truckload lots, would be less. The variation would depend on the size, timing, and negotiating power of the contractor. The labor costs are primarily for new construction or major renovation rather than repairs or minor alterations. With reasonable exercise of judgment, the figures can be used for any building work.

Estimating with RSMeans data: Unit Prices

Following these steps will allow you to complete an accurate estimate using RSMeans data: Unit Prices.

1. Scope Out the Project
- Think through the project and identify the CSI divisions needed in your estimate.
- Identify the individual work tasks that will need to be covered in your estimate.
- The Unit Price data have been divided into 50 divisions according to CSI MasterFormat® 2018.
- In printed versions, the Unit Price Section Table of Contents on page 1 may also be helpful when scoping out your project.
- Experienced estimators find it helpful to begin with Division 2 and continue through completion. Division 1 can be estimated after the full project scope is known.

2. Quantify
- Determine the number of units required for each work task that you identified.
- Experienced estimators include an allowance for waste in their quantities. (Waste is not included in our Unit Price line items unless otherwise stated.)

3. Price the Quantities
- Use the search tools available to locate individual Unit Price line items for your estimate.
- Reference Numbers indicated within a Unit Price section refer to additional information that you may find useful.
- The crew indicates who is performing the work for that task. Crew codes are expanded in the Crew Listings in the Reference Section to include all trades and equipment that comprise the crew.
- The Daily Output is the amount of work the crew is expected to complete in one day.
- The Labor-Hours value is the amount of time it will take for the crew to install one unit of work.
- The abbreviated Unit designation indicates the unit of measure upon which the crew, productivity, and prices are based.
- Bare Costs are shown for materials, labor and equipment needed to complete the Unit Price line item. Bare costs do not include waste, project overhead, payroll insurance, payroll taxes, main office overhead or profit.
- The Total Incl O&P cost is the billing rate or invoice amount of the installing contractor or subcontractor who performs the work for the Unit Price line item.

4. Multiply
- Multiply the total number of units needed for your project by the Total Incl O&P cost for each Unit Price line item.
- Be careful that your take off unit of measure matches the unit of measure in the Unit column.
- The price you calculate is an estimate for a completed item of work.
- Keep scoping individual tasks, determining the number of units required for those tasks, matching each task with individual Unit Price line items and multiplying quantities by Total Incl O&P costs.
- An estimate completed in this manner is priced as if a subcontractor, or set of subcontractors, is performing the work. The estimate does not yet include Project Overhead or Estimate Summary components such as general contractor markups on subcontracted work, general contractor office overhead and profit, contingency and location factors.

5. Project Overhead
- Include project overhead items from Division 1-General Requirements.
- These items are needed to make the job run. They are typically, but not always, provided by the general contractor. Items include, but are not limited to, field personnel, insurance, performance bond, permits, testing, temporary utilities, field office and storage facilities, temporary scaffolding and platforms, equipment mobilization and demobilization, temporary roads and sidewalks, winter protection, temporary barricades and fencing, temporary security, temporary signs, field engineering and layout, final cleaning and commissioning.
- Each item should be quantified and matched to individual Unit Price line items in Division 1, then priced and added to your estimate.
- An alternate method of estimating project overhead costs is to apply a percentage of the total project cost — usually 5% to 15% with an average of 10% (see General Conditions).
- Include other project related expenses in your estimate such as:
  - Rented equipment not itemized in the Crew Listings
  - Rubbish handling throughout the project (see section 02 41 19.19)

6. Estimate Summary
- Include sales tax as required by laws of your state or county.
- Include the general contractor's markup on self-performed work, usually 5% to 15% with an average of 10%.
- Include the general contractor's markup on subcontracted work, usually 5% to 15% with an average of 10%.
- Include the general contractor's main office overhead and profit:
  - RSMeans data provides general guidelines on the general contractor's main office overhead (see section 01 31 13.60 and Reference Number R013113-50).
  - Markups will depend on the size of the general contractor's operations, projected annual revenue, the level of risk and the level of competition in the local area and for this project in particular.
- Include a contingency, usually 3% to 5%, if appropriate.
- Adjust your estimate to the project's location by using the City Cost Indexes or the Location Factors in the Reference Section:
  - Look at the rules in "How to Use the City Cost Indexes" to see how to apply the Indexes for your location.
  - When the proper Index or Factor has been identified for the project's location, convert it to a multiplier by dividing it by 100, then multiply that multiplier by your estimated total cost. The original estimated total cost will now be adjusted up or down from the national average to a total that is appropriate for your location.

Editors' Note:
We urge you to spend time reading and understanding the supporting material. An accurate estimate requires experience, knowledge, and careful calculation. The more you know about how we at RSMeans developed the data, the more accurate your estimate will be. In addition, it is important to take into consideration the reference material such as Equipment Listings, Crew Listings, City Cost Indexes, Location Factors, and Reference Tables.

How to Use the Cost Data: The Details

What's Behind the Numbers? The Development of Cost Data

RSMeans data engineers continually monitor developments in the construction industry to ensure reliable, thorough and up-to-date cost information. While overall construction costs may vary relative to general economic conditions, price fluctuations within the industry are dependent upon many factors. Individual price variations may, in fact, be opposite to overall economic trends. Therefore, costs are constantly tracked and complete updates are performed yearly. Also, new items are frequently added in response to changes in materials and methods.

Costs in U.S. Dollars

All costs represent U.S. national averages and are given in U.S. dollars. The City Cost Index (CCI) with RSMeans data can be used to adjust costs to a particular location. The CCI for Canada can be used to adjust U.S. national averages to local costs in Canadian dollars. No exchange rate conversion is necessary because it has already been factored in.

G The processes or products identified by the green symbol in our publications have been determined to be environmentally responsible and/or resource-efficient solely by RSMeans data engineering staff. The inclusion of the green symbol does not represent compliance with any specific industry association or standard.

Material Costs

RSMeans data engineers contact manufacturers, dealers, distributors and contractors all across the U.S. and Canada to determine national average material costs. If you have access to current material costs for your specific location, you may wish to make adjustments to reflect differences from the national average. Included within material costs are fasteners for a normal installation. RSMeans data engineers use manufacturers' recommendations, written specifications and/or standard construction practices for the sizing and spacing of fasteners. Adjustments to material costs may be required for your specific application or location. The manufacturer's warranty is assumed. Extended warranties are not included in the material costs. **Material costs do not include sales tax.**

Labor Costs

Labor costs are based upon a mathematical average of trade-specific wages in 30 major U.S. cities. The type of wage (union, open shop or residential) is identified on the inside back cover of printed publications or selected by the estimator when using the electronic products. Markups for the wages can also be found on the inside back cover of printed publications and/or under the labor references found in the electronic products.

- If wage rates in your area vary from those used, or if rate increases are expected within a given year, labor costs should be adjusted accordingly.

Labor costs reflect productivity based on actual working conditions. In addition to actual installation, these figures include time spent during a normal weekday on tasks, such as material receiving and handling, mobilization at the site, site movement, breaks and cleanup.

Productivity data is developed over an extended period so as not to be influenced by abnormal variations and reflects a typical average.

Equipment Costs

Equipment costs include not only rental but also operating costs for equipment under normal use. The operating costs include parts and labor for routine servicing, such as the repair and replacement of pumps, filters and worn lines. Normal operating expendables, such as fuel, lubricants, tires and electricity (where applicable) are also included. Extraordinary operating expendables with highly variable wear patterns, such as diamond bits and blades, are excluded. These costs are included under materials. Equipment rental rates are obtained from industry sources throughout North America — contractors, suppliers, dealers, manufacturers and distributors.

Rental rates can also be treated as reimbursement costs for contractor-owned equipment. Owned equipment costs include depreciation, loan payments, interest, taxes, insurance, storage and major repairs.

Equipment costs do not include operators' wages.

Equipment Cost/Day—The cost of equipment required for each crew is included in the Crew Listings in the Reference Section (small tools that are considered essential everyday tools are not listed out separately). The Crew Listings itemize specialized tools and heavy equipment along with labor trades. The daily cost of itemized equipment included in a crew is based on dividing the weekly bare rental rate by five (5) (number of working days per week), then adding the hourly operating cost times eight (8) (the number of hours per day). This Equipment Cost/Day is shown in the last column of the Equipment Rental Costs in the Reference Section.

Mobilization, Demobilization—The cost to move construction equipment from an equipment yard or rental company to the job site and back again is not included in equipment costs. Mobilization (to the site) and demobilization (from the site) costs can be found in the Unit Price Section. If a piece of equipment is already at the job site, it is not appropriate to utilize mobilization or demobilization costs again in an estimate.

Overhead and Profit

Total Cost including O&P for the installing contractor is shown in the last column of the Unit Price and/or Assemblies. This figure is the sum of the bare material cost plus 10% for profit, the bare labor cost plus total overhead and profit, and the bare equipment cost plus 10% for profit. Details for the calculation of overhead and profit on labor are shown on the inside back cover of the printed product and in the Reference Section of the electronic product.

General Conditions

Cost data in this dataset are presented in two ways: Bare Costs and Total Cost including O&P (Overhead and Profit). General Conditions, or General Requirements, of the contract should also be added to the Total Cost including O&P when applicable. Costs for General Conditions are listed in Division 1 of the Unit Price Section and in the Reference Section.

General Conditions for the installing contractor may range from 0% to 10% of the Total Cost including O&P. For the general or prime contractor, costs for General Conditions may range from 5% to 15% of the Total Cost including O&P, with a figure of 10% as the most typical allowance. If applicable, the Assemblies and Models sections use costs that include the installing contractor's overhead and profit (O&P).

Factors Affecting Costs

Costs can vary depending upon a number of variables. Here's a listing of some factors that affect costs and points to consider.

Quality: The prices for materials and the workmanship upon which productivity is based represent sound construction work. They are also in line with industry standard and manufacturer specifications and are frequently used by federal, state and local governments.

Overtime: We have made no allowance for overtime. If you anticipate premium time or work beyond normal working hours, be sure to make an appropriate adjustment to your labor costs.

Productivity: The productivity, daily output and labor-hour figures for each line item are based on an eight-hour work day in daylight hours in moderate temperatures and up to a 14' working height unless otherwise indicated. For work that extends beyond normal work hours or is performed under adverse conditions, productivity may decrease.

Size of Project: The size, scope of work and type of construction project will have a significant impact on cost. Economies of scale can reduce costs for large projects. Unit costs can often run higher for small projects.

Location: Material prices are for metropolitan areas. However, in dense urban areas, traffic and site storage limitations may increase costs. Beyond a 20-mile radius of metropolitan areas, extra trucking or transportation charges may also increase the material costs slightly. On the other hand, lower wage rates may be in effect. Be sure to consider both of these factors when preparing an estimate, particularly if the job site is located in a central city or remote rural location. In addition, highly specialized subcontract items may require travel and per-diem expenses for mechanics.

Other Factors
- Season of year
- Contractor management
- Weather conditions
- Local union restrictions
- Building code requirements
- Availability of:
  - adequate energy
  - skilled labor
  - building materials
- Owner's special requirements/restrictions
- Safety requirements
- Environmental considerations
- Access

Unpredictable Factors: General business conditions influence "in-place" costs of all items. Substitute materials and construction methods may have to be employed. These may affect the installed cost and/or life cycle costs. Such factors may be difficult to evaluate and cannot necessarily be predicted on the basis of the job's location in a particular section of the country. Thus, where these factors apply, you may find significant but unavoidable cost variations for which you will have to apply a measure of judgment to your estimate.

Rounding of Costs

In printed publications only, all unit prices in excess of $5.00 have been rounded to make them easier to use and still maintain adequate precision of the results.

How Subcontracted Items Affect Costs

A considerable portion of all large construction jobs is usually subcontracted. In fact, the percentage done by subcontractors is constantly increasing and may run over 90%. Since the workers employed by these companies do nothing else but install their particular products, they soon become experts in that line. As a result, installation by these firms is accomplished so efficiently that the total in-place cost, even with the general contractor's overhead and profit, is no more, and often less, than if the principal contractor had handled the installation. Companies that deal with construction specialties are anxious to have their products perform well and, consequently, the installation will be the best possible.

Contingencies

The allowance for contingencies generally provides for unforeseen construction difficulties. On alterations or repair jobs, 20% is not too much. If drawings are final and only field contingencies are being considered, 2% or 3% is probably sufficient and often nothing needs to be added. Contractually, changes in plans will be covered by extras. The contractor should consider inflationary price trends and possible material shortages during the course of the job. These escalation factors are dependent upon both economic conditions and the anticipated time between the estimate and actual construction. If drawings are not complete or approved, or a budget cost is wanted, it is wise to add 5% to 10%. Contingencies, then, are a matter of judgment.

Important Estimating Considerations

The productivity, or daily output, of each craftsman or crew assumes a well-managed job where tradesmen with the proper tools and equipment, along with the appropriate construction materials, are present. Included are daily set-up and cleanup time, break time and plan layout time. Unless otherwise indicated, time for material movement on site (for items that can be transported by hand) of up to 200' into the building and to the first or second floor is also included. If material has to be transported by other means, over greater distances or to higher floors, an additional allowance should be considered by the estimator.

While horizontal movement is typically a sole function of distances, vertical transport introduces other variables that can significantly impact productivity. In an occupied building, the use of elevators (assuming access, size and required protective measures are acceptable) must be understood at the time of the estimate. For new construction, hoist wait and cycle times can easily be 15 minutes and may result in scheduled access extending beyond the normal work day. Finally, all vertical transport will impose strict weight limits likely to preclude the use of any motorized material handling.

The productivity, or daily output, also assumes installation that meets manufacturer/designer/standard specifications. A time allowance for quality control checks, minor adjustments and any task required to ensure proper function or operation is also included. For items that require connections to services, time is included for positioning, leveling, securing the unit and making all the necessary connections (and start up where applicable) to ensure a complete installation. Estimating of the services themselves (electrical, plumbing, water, steam, hydraulics, dust collection, etc.) is separate.

In some cases, the estimator must consider the use of a crane and an appropriate crew for the installation of large or heavy items. For those situations where a crane is not included in the assigned crew and as part of the line item cost, then equipment rental costs, mobilization and demobilization costs, and operator and support personnel costs must be considered.

Labor-Hours

The labor-hours expressed in this publication are derived by dividing the total daily labor-hours for the crew by the daily output. Based on average installation time and the assumptions listed above, the labor-hours include: direct labor, indirect labor and nonproductive time. A typical day for a craftsman might include but is not limited to:

- Direct Work
  - Measuring and layout
  - Preparing materials
  - Actual installation
  - Quality assurance/quality control
- Indirect Work
  - Reading plans or specifications
  - Preparing space
  - Receiving materials
  - Material movement
  - Giving or receiving instruction
  - Miscellaneous
- Non-Work
  - Chatting
  - Personal issues
  - Breaks
  - Interruptions (i.e., sickness, weather, material or equipment shortages, etc.)

If any of the items for a typical day do not apply to the particular work or project situation, the estimator should make any necessary adjustments.

Final Checklist

Estimating can be a straightforward process provided you remember the basics. Here's a checklist of some of the steps you should remember to complete before finalizing your estimate.

Did you remember to:

- Factor in the City Cost Index for your locale?
- Take into consideration which items have been marked up and by how much?
- Mark up the entire estimate sufficiently for your purposes?
- Read the background information on techniques and technical matters that could impact your project time span and cost?
- Include all components of your project in the final estimate?
- Double check your figures for accuracy?
- Call RSMeans data engineers if you have any questions about your estimate or the data you've used? Remember, Gordian stands behind all of our products, including our extensive RSMeans data solutions. If you have any questions about your estimate, about the costs you've used from our data or even about the technical aspects of the job that may affect your estimate, feel free to call the Gordian RSMeans editors at 800.448.8182.

Save Time. Go Online.

For access to the latest cost data, an intuitive search and pre-calculated location costs, take advantage of the time savings available from our online application.

rsmeans.com/online

Unit Price Section

Table of Contents

Sect. No.		Page
	General Requirements	
01 11	Summary of Work	8
01 21	Allowances	8
01 31	Project Management and Coordination	10
01 32	Construction Progress Documentation	12
01 41	Regulatory Requirements	12
01 51	Temporary Utilities	12
01 52	Construction Facilities	13
01 54	Construction Aids	13
01 55	Vehicular Access and Parking	16
01 56	Temporary Barriers and Enclosures	16
01 57	Temporary Controls	18
01 58	Project Identification	18
01 66	Product Storage and Handling Requirements	18
01 74	Cleaning and Waste Management	18
01 91	Commissioning	19
01 93	Facility Maintenance	19
	Existing Conditions	
02 21	Surveys	22
02 41	Demolition	22
02 65	Underground Storage Tank Removal	24
02 81	Transportation and Disposal of Hazardous Materials	24
02 82	Asbestos Remediation	25
02 87	Biohazard Remediation	28
	Concrete	
03 11	Concrete Forming	32
03 15	Concrete Accessories	32
03 21	Reinforcement Bars	35
03 22	Fabric and Grid Reinforcing	36
03 30	Cast-In-Place Concrete	36
03 31	Structural Concrete	37
03 35	Concrete Finishing	38
03 63	Epoxy Grouting	38
03 82	Concrete Boring	39
	Metals	
05 05	Common Work Results for Metals	42
05 12	Structural Steel Framing	46
05 54	Metal Floor Plates	46
	Wood, Plastics & Composites	
06 11	Wood Framing	48
06 16	Sheathing	48
	Thermal & Moisture Protection	
07 65	Flexible Flashing	50
07 71	Roof Specialties	51
07 72	Roof Accessories	51
07 76	Roof Pavers	51
07 84	Firestopping	52
07 91	Preformed Joint Seals	53
07 92	Joint Sealants	54
	Finishes	
09 22	Supports for Plaster and Gypsum Board	58
09 91	Painting	58
	Specialties	
10 21	Compartments and Cubicles	62
10 28	Toilet, Bath, and Laundry Accessories	64
10 44	Fire Protection Specialties	66
	Equipment	
11 11	Vehicle Service Equipment	70
11 21	Retail and Service Equipment	70
11 30	Residential Equipment	71
11 32	Unit Kitchens	72
11 41	Foodservice Storage Equipment	73
11 44	Food Cooking Equipment	73
11 46	Food Dispensing Equipment	73

Sect. No.		Page
11 48	Foodservice Cleaning and Disposal Equipment	73
11 53	Laboratory Equipment	73
11 71	Medical Sterilizing Equipment	74
11 73	Patient Care Equipment	75
11 74	Dental Equipment	75
11 76	Operating Room Equipment	75
11 78	Mortuary Equipment	76
11 81	Facility Maintenance Equipment	76
11 91	Religious Equipment	76
11 98	Detention Equipment	76
	Furnishings	
12 32	Manufactured Wood Casework	78
	Special Construction	
13 11	Swimming Pools	80
13 12	Fountains	81
13 17	Tubs and Pools	81
13 24	Special Activity Rooms	81
13 34	Fabricated Engineered Structures	82
13 42	Building Modules	82
13 47	Facility Protection	83
	Conveying Equipment	
14 45	Vehicle Lifts	86
	Fire Suppression	
21 05	Common Work Results for Fire Suppression	88
21 11	Facility Fire-Suppression Water-Service Piping	89
21 12	Fire-Suppression Standpipes	96
21 13	Fire-Suppression Sprinkler Systems	100
21 21	Carbon-Dioxide Fire-Extinguishing Systems	103
21 22	Clean-Agent Fire-Extinguishing Systems	103
21 31	Centrifugal Fire Pumps	104
	Plumbing	
22 01	Operation and Maintenance of Plumbing	108
22 05	Common Work Results for Plumbing	109
22 07	Plumbing Insulation	132
22 11	Facility Water Distribution	151
22 12	Facility Potable-Water Storage Tanks	261
22 13	Facility Sanitary Sewerage	261
22 14	Facility Storm Drainage	283
22 15	General Service Compressed-Air Systems	286
22 31	Domestic Water Softeners	287
22 32	Domestic Water Filtration Equipment	288
22 33	Electric Domestic Water Heaters	288
22 34	Fuel-Fired Domestic Water Heaters	290
22 35	Domestic Water Heat Exchangers	291
22 41	Residential Plumbing Fixtures	292
22 42	Commercial Plumbing Fixtures	299
22 43	Healthcare Plumbing Fixtures	304
22 45	Emergency Plumbing Fixtures	305
22 46	Security Plumbing Fixtures	306
22 47	Drinking Fountains and Water Coolers	307
22 51	Swimming Pool Plumbing Systems	309
22 52	Fountain Plumbing Systems	309
22 62	Vacuum Systems for Laboratory and Healthcare Facilities	310
22 63	Gas Systems for Laboratory and Healthcare Facilities	311
22 66	Chemical-Waste Systems for Lab. and Healthcare Facilities	314
	Heating Ventilation Air Conditioning	
23 05	Common Work Results for HVAC	322
23 07	HVAC Insulation	331

Sect. No.		Page
23 09	Instrumentation and Control for HVAC	332
23 11	Facility Fuel Piping	335
23 12	Facility Fuel Pumps	337
23 13	Facility Fuel-Storage Tanks	337
23 21	Hydronic Piping and Pumps	340
23 23	Refrigerant Piping	349
23 34	HVAC Fans	349
23 35	Special Exhaust Systems	350
23 38	Ventilation Hoods	352
23 51	Breechings, Chimneys, and Stacks	353
23 52	Heating Boilers	359
23 54	Furnaces	361
23 55	Fuel-Fired Heaters	362
23 56	Solar Energy Heating Equipment	363
23 57	Heat Exchangers for HVAC	365
23 72	Air-to-Air Energy Recovery Equipment	366
23 81	Decentralized Unitary HVAC Equipment	366
23 82	Convection Heating and Cooling Units	368
23 83	Radiant Heating Units	369
23 91	Prefabricated Equipment Supports	374
	Electrical	
26 05	Common Work Results for Electrical	376
26 24	Switchboards and Panelboards	383
26 29	Low-Voltage Controllers	384
	Electronic Safety & Security	
28 31	Intrusion Detection	386
28 42	Gas Detection and Alarm	386
28 46	Fire Detection and Alarm	386
	Earthwork	
31 23	Excavation and Fill	390
	Exterior Improvements	
32 12	Flexible Paving	406
32 84	Planting Irrigation	407
	Utilities	
33 01	Operation and Maintenance of Utilities	412
33 05	Common Work Results for Utilities	417
33 11	Groundwater Sources	419
33 14	Water Utility Transmission and Distribution	421
33 16	Water Utility Storage Tanks	430
33 31	Sanitary Sewerage Piping	431
33 34	Onsite Wastewater Disposal	431
33 41	Subdrainage	433
33 42	Stormwater Conveyance	434
33 52	Hydrocarbon Transmission and Distribution	438
33 61	Hydronic Energy Distribution	455
33 63	Steam Energy Distribution	457
	Material Processing & Handling Equipment	
41 22	Cranes and Hoists	462
	Pollution Control Equipment	
44 11	Particulate Control Equipment	464
	Water and Wastewater Equipment	
46 07	Packaged Water and Wastewater Treatment Equipment	468
46 23	Grit Removal And Handling Equipment	468
46 25	Oil and Grease Separation and Removal Equipment	469

RSMeans data: Unit Prices—How They Work

All RSMeans data: Unit Prices are organized in the same way.

03 30 Cast-In-Place Concrete

03 30 53 – Miscellaneous Cast-In-Place Concrete

03 30 53.40 Concrete In Place

		Crew	Daily Output	Labor-Hours	Unit	Material	2023 Bare Costs Labor	2023 Bare Costs Equipment	Total	Total Incl O&P
0010	**CONCRETE IN PLACE**									
0020	Including forms (4 uses), Grade 60 rebar, concrete (Portland cement									
0050	Type I), placement and finishing unless otherwise indicated									
3540	Equipment pad (3000 psi), 3' x 3' x 6" thick	C-14H	45	1.067	Ea.	83	61.50	.66	145.16	183
3550	4' x 4' x 6" thick		30	1.600		120	92	.99	212.99	270
3560	5' x 5' x 8" thick		18	2.667		216	153	1.65	370.65	470
3570	6' x 6' x 8" thick		14	3.429		284	197	2.13	483.13	610
3580	8' x 8' x 10" thick		8	6		590	345	3.72	938.72	1,175
3590	10' x 10' x 12" thick		5	9.600		980	550	5.95	1,535.95	1,900
3800	Footings (3000 psi), spread under 1 C.Y.	C-14C	28	4	C.Y.	257	224	1.08	482.08	620
3825	1 C.Y. to 5 C.Y.		43	2.605		330	146	.70	476.70	580
3850	Over 5 C.Y. R033053-60		75	1.493		315	84	.40	399.40	470
3900	Footings, strip (3000 psi), 18" x 9", unreinforced	C-14L	40	2.400		211	131	.74	342.74	430
3920	18" x 9", reinforced	C-14C	35	3.200		245	179	.86	424.86	540

It is important to understand the structure of RSMeans data: Unit Prices so that you can find information easily and use it correctly.

❶ Line Numbers

Line Numbers consist of 12 characters, which identify a unique location in the database for each task. The first six (6) or eight (8) digits conform to the Construction Specifications Institute MasterFormat® 2018. The remainder of the digits are a further breakdown in order to arrange items in understandable groups of similar tasks. Line numbers are consistent across all of our publications, so a line number in any of our products will always refer to the same item of work.

❷ Descriptions

Descriptions are shown in a hierarchical structure to make them readable. In order to read a complete description, read up through the indents to the top of the section. Include everything that is above and to the left that is not contradicted by information below. For instance, the complete description for line 03 30 53.40 3550 is "Concrete in place, including forms (4 uses), Grade 60 rebar, concrete (Portland cement Type 1), placement and finishing unless otherwise indicated; Equipment pad (3,000 psi), 4' × 4' × 6" thick."

❸ RSMeans data

When using **RSMeans data**, it is important to read through an entire section to ensure that you use the data that most closely matches your work. Note that sometimes there is additional information shown in the section that may improve your price. There are frequently lines that further describe, add to or adjust data for specific situations.

❹ Reference Information

Gordian's engineers have created **reference** information to assist you in your estimate. **If** there is information that applies to a section, it will be indicated at the start of the section. The Reference Section is located in the back of the data set.

❺ Crews

Crews include labor and/or equipment necessary to accomplish each task. In this case, Crew C-14H is used. Gordian's staff selects a crew to represent the workers and equipment that are typically used for that task. In this case, Crew C-14H consists of one carpenter foreperson (outside), two carpenters, one rodman, one laborer, one cement finisher and one gas engine vibrator. Details of all crews can be found in the Reference Section.

Crews - Standard

Crew No.	Bare Costs		Incl. Subs O&P		Cost Per Labor-Hour	
Crew C-14H	Hr.	Daily	Hr.	Daily	Bare Costs	Incl. O&P
1 Carpenter Foreman (outside)	$60.60	$484.80	$90.20	$721.60	$57.43	$85.32
2 Carpenters	58.60	937.60	87.25	1396.00		
1 Rodman (reinf.)	64.55	516.40	96.40	771.20		
1 Laborer	47.25	378.00	70.35	562.80		
1 Cement Finisher	55.00	440.00	80.45	643.60		
1 Gas Engine Vibrator		29.68		32.65	.62	.68
48 L.H., Daily Totals		$2786.48		$4127.85	$58.05	$86.00

6 Daily Output
The **Daily Output** is the amount of work that the crew can do in a normal 8-hour workday, including mobilization, layout, movement of materials and cleanup. In this case, crew C-14H can install thirty 4' × 4' × 6" thick concrete pads in a day. Daily output is variable and based on many factors, including the size of the job, location and environmental conditions. RSMeans data represents work done in daylight (or adequate lighting) and temperate conditions.

7 Labor-Hours
The figure in the **Labor-Hours** column is the amount of labor required to perform one unit of work—in this case the amount of labor required to construct one 4' × 4' equipment pad. This figure is calculated by dividing the number of hours of labor in the crew by the daily output (48 labor-hours divided by 30 pads = 1.6 hours of labor per pad). Multiply 1.6 times 60 to see the value in minutes: 60 × 1.6 = 96 minutes. Note: The labor-hour figure is not dependent on the crew size. A change in crew size will result in a corresponding change in daily output, but the labor-hours per unit of work will not change.

8 Unit of Measure
Unit Prices include the typical **Unit of Measure** used for estimating that item. For concrete-in-place the typical unit is cubic yards (C.Y.) or each (Ea.). For installing broadloom carpet it is square yard and for gypsum board it is square foot. The estimator needs to take special care that the unit in the data matches the unit in the take-off. Unit conversions may be found in the Reference Section.

9 Bare Costs
Bare Costs are the costs of materials, labor, and equipment that the installing contractor pays. They represent the cost, in U.S. dollars, for one unit of work. They do not include any markups for profit or labor burden.

10 Bare Total
The **Total column** represents the total bare cost for the installing contractor in U.S. dollars. In this case, the sum of $120 for material + $92 for labor + $.99 for equipment is $212.99.

11 Total Incl O&P
The **Total Incl O&P column** is the total cost, including overhead and profit, that the installing contractor will charge the customer. This represents the cost of materials plus 10% profit, the cost of labor plus labor burden and 10% profit, and the cost of equipment plus 10% profit. It does not include the general contractor's overhead and profit. Note: See the inside back cover of the printed product or the Reference Section of the electronic product for details on how the labor burden is calculated.

National Average

The RSMeans data in our print publications represent a "national average" cost. This data should be modified to the project location using the **City Cost Indexes** or **Location Factors** tables found in the Reference Section. Use the Location Factors to adjust estimate totals if the project covers multiple trades. Use the City Cost Indexes (CCI) for single trade projects or projects where a more detailed analysis is required. All figures in the two tables are derived from the same research. The last row of data in the CCI — the weighted average — is the same as the numbers reported for each location in the location factor table.

RSMeans data: Unit Prices— How They Work (Continued)

**① **

Project Name: Pre-Engineered Steel Building		Architect: As Shown					01/01/23	STD
Location:	Anywhere, USA							
Line Number	Description	Qty	Unit	Material	Labor	Equipment	SubContract	Estimate Total
03 30 53.40 3940	Strip footing, 12" x 24", reinforced	15	C.Y.	$3,345.00	$1,965.00	$9.45	$0.00	
03 30 53.40 3950	Strip footing, 12" x 36", reinforced	34	C.Y.	$7,140.00	$3,570.00	$17.00	$0.00	
03 11 13.65 3000	Concrete slab edge forms	500	L.F.	$415.00	$1,485.00	$0.00	$0.00	
03 22 11.10 0200	Welded wire fabric reinforcing	150	C.S.F.	$9,225.00	$5,025.00	$0.00	$0.00	
03 31 13.35 0300	Ready mix concrete, 4000 psi for slab on grade	278	C.Y.	$45,036.00	$0.00	$0.00	$0.00	
03 31 13.70 4300	Place, strike off & consolidate concrete slab	278	C.Y.	$0.00	$5,977.00	$150.12	$0.00	
03 35 13.30 0250	Machine float & trowel concrete slab	15,000	S.F.	$0.00	$10,950.00	$750.00	$0.00	
03 15 16.20 0140	Cut control joints in concrete slab	950	L.F.	$38.00	$465.50	$95.00	$0.00	
03 39 23.13 0300	Sprayed concrete curing membrane	150	C.S.F.	$2,400.00	$1,192.50	$0.00	$0.00	
Division 03	**Subtotal**			**$67,599.00**	**$30,630.00**	**$1,021.57**	**$0.00**	**$99,250.57**
08 36 13.10 2650	Manual 10' x 10' steel sectional overhead door	8	Ea.	$14,200.00	$4,160.00	$0.00	$0.00	
08 36 13.10 2860	Insulation and steel back panel for OH door	800	S.F.	$5,360.00	$0.00	$0.00	$0.00	
Division 08	**Subtotal**			**$19,560.00**	**$4,160.00**	**$0.00**	**$0.00**	**$23,720.00**
13 34 19.50 1100	Pre-Engineered Steel Building, 100' x 150' x 24'	15,000	SF Flr.	$0.00	$0.00	$0.00	$420,000.00	
13 34 19.50 6050	Framing for PESB door opening, 3' x 7'	4	Opng.	$0.00	$0.00	$0.00	$2,600.00	
13 34 19.50 6100	Framing for PESB door opening, 10' x 10'	8	Opng.	$0.00	$0.00	$0.00	$10,800.00	
13 34 19.50 6200	Framing for PESB window opening, 4' x 3'	6	Opng.	$0.00	$0.00	$0.00	$3,870.00	
13 34 19.50 5750	PESB door, 3' x 7', single leaf	4	Opng.	$3,320.00	$828.00	$0.00	$0.00	
13 34 19.50 7750	PESB sliding window, 4' x 3' with screen	6	Opng.	$3,120.00	$702.00	$67.80	$0.00	
13 34 19.50 6550	PESB gutter, eave type, 26 ga., painted	300	L.F.	$2,670.00	$969.00	$0.00	$0.00	
13 34 19.50 8650	PESB roof vent, 12" wide x 10' long	15	Ea.	$750.00	$3,870.00	$0.00	$0.00	
13 34 19.50 6900	PESB insulation, vinyl faced, 4" thick	27,400	S.F.	$42,470.00	$11,234.00	$0.00	$0.00	
Division 13	**Subtotal**			**$52,330.00**	**$17,603.00**	**$67.80**	**$437,270.00**	**$507,270.80**
	Subtotal			$139,489.00	$52,393.00	$1,089.37	$437,270.00	$630,241.37
Division 01 ②	General Requirements @ 7%			9,764.23	3,667.51	76.26	30,608.90	
	Estimate Subtotal			$149,253.23	$56,060.51	$1,165.63	$467,878.90	$630,241.37
	③ Sales Tax @ 5%			7,462.66		58.28	11,696.97	
	Subtotal A			156,715.89	56,060.51	1,223.91	479,575.87	
	④ GC O & P			15,671.59	28,142.38	122.39	47,957.59	
	Subtotal B			172,387.48	84,202.89	1,346.30	527,533.46	$785,470.12
	⑤ Contingency @ 5%							39,273.51
	Subtotal C							$824,743.63
	⑥ Bond @ $12/1000 +10% O&P							10,886.62
	Subtotal D							$835,630.25
	⑦ Location Adjustment Factor				112.50			104,453.78
	Grand Total							**$940,084.03**

This estimate is based on an interactive spreadsheet. You are free to download it and adjust it to your methodology. A copy of this spreadsheet is available at **RSMeans.com/2023books**.

Sample Estimate

This sample demonstrates the elements of an estimate, including a tally of the RSMeans data lines and a summary of the markups on a contractor's work to arrive at a total cost to the owner. The Location Factor with RSMeans data is added at the bottom of the estimate to adjust the cost of the work to a specific location.

❶ Work Performed

The body of the estimate shows the RSMeans data selected, including the line number, a brief description of each item, its take-off unit and quantity, and the bare costs of materials, labor and equipment. This estimate also includes a column titled "SubContract." This data is taken from the column "Total Incl O&P" and represents the total that a subcontractor would charge a general contractor for the work, including the sub's markup for overhead and profit.

❷ Division 1, General Requirements

This is the first division numerically but the last division estimated. Division 1 includes project-wide needs provided by the general contractor. These requirements vary by project but may include temporary facilities and utilities, security, testing, project cleanup, etc. For small projects a percentage can be used — typically between 5% and 15% of project cost. For large projects the costs may be itemized and priced individually.

❸ Sales Tax

If the work is subject to state or local sales taxes, the amount must be added to the estimate. Sales tax may be added to material costs, equipment costs and subcontracted work. In this case, sales tax was added in all three categories. It was assumed that approximately half the subcontracted work would be material cost, so the tax was applied to 50% of the subcontract total.

❹ GC O&P

This entry represents the general contractor's markup on material, labor, equipment and subcontractor costs. Our standard markup on materials, equipment and subcontracted work is 10%. In this estimate, the markup on the labor performed by the GC's workers uses "Skilled Workers Average" shown in Column F on the table "Installing Contractor's Overhead & Profit," which can be found on the inside back cover of the printed product or in the Reference Section of the electronic product.

❺ Contingency

A factor for contingency may be added to any estimate to represent the cost of unknowns that may occur between the time that the estimate is performed and the time the project is constructed. The amount of the allowance will depend on the stage of design at which the estimate is done and the contractor's assessment of the risk involved. Refer to section 01 21 16.50 for contingency allowances.

❻ Bonds

Bond costs should be added to the estimate. The figures here represent a typical performance bond, ensuring the owner that if the general contractor does not complete the obligations in the construction contract the bonding company will pay the cost for completion of the work.

❼ Location Adjustment

Published prices are based on national average costs. If necessary, adjust the total cost of the project using a location factor from the "Location Factor" table or the "City Cost Index" table. Use location factors if the work is general, covering multiple trades. If the work is by a single trade (e.g., masonry) use the more specific data found in the "City Cost Indexes."

Division 1 — General Requirements

Estimating Tips

01 20 00 Price and Payment Procedures
- Allowances that should be added to estimates to cover contingencies and job conditions that are not included in the national average material and labor costs are shown in Section 01 21.
- When estimating historic preservation projects (depending on the condition of the existing structure and the owner's requirements), a 15–20% contingency or allowance is recommended, regardless of the stage of the drawings.

01 30 00 Administrative Requirements
- Before determining a final cost estimate, it is good practice to review all the items listed in Subdivisions 01 31 and 01 32 to make final adjustments for items that may need customizing to specific job conditions.
- Requirements for initial and periodic submittals can represent a significant cost to the General Requirements of a job. Thoroughly check the submittal specifications when estimating a project to determine any costs that should be included.

01 40 00 Quality Requirements
- All projects will require some degree of quality control. This cost is not included in the unit cost of construction listed in each division. Depending upon the terms of the contract, the various costs of inspection and testing can be the responsibility of either the owner or the contractor. Be sure to include the required costs in your estimate.

01 50 00 Temporary Facilities and Controls
- Barricades, access roads, safety nets, scaffolding, security, and many more requirements for the execution of a safe project are elements of direct cost. These costs can easily be overlooked when preparing an estimate. When looking through the major classifications of this subdivision, determine which items apply to each division in your estimate.
- Construction equipment rental costs can be found in the Reference Section in Section 01 54 33. Operators' wages are not included in equipment rental costs.
- Equipment mobilization and demobilization costs are not included in equipment rental costs and must be considered separately.
- The cost of small tools provided by the installing contractor for his workers is covered in the "Overhead" column on the "Installing Contractor's Overhead and Profit" table that lists labor trades, base rates, and markups. Therefore, it is included in the "Total Incl. O&P" cost of any unit price line item.

01 70 00 Execution and Closeout Requirements
- When preparing an estimate, thoroughly read the specifications to determine the requirements for Contract Closeout. Final cleaning, record documentation, operation and maintenance data, warranties and bonds, and spare parts and maintenance materials can all be elements of cost for the completion of a contract. Do not overlook these in your estimate.

Reference Numbers
Reference numbers are shown at the beginning of some major classifications. These numbers refer to related items in the Reference Section. The reference information may be an estimating procedure, an alternate pricing method, or technical information.

Note: Not all subdivisions listed here necessarily appear. ∎

Same Data. Simplified.
Enjoy the convenience and efficiency of accessing your costs anywhere:
- **Skip the multiplier** by setting your location
- **Quickly search,** edit, favorite and share costs
- **Stay on top of price changes** with automatic updates

Discover more at rsmeans.com/online

No part of this cost data may be reproduced, stored in a retrieval system, or transmitted in any form or by any means without prior written permission of Gordian.

01 11 Summary of Work

01 11 31 – Professional Consultants

01 11 31.10 Architectural Fees

	Crew	Daily Output	Labor-Hours	Unit	Material	2023 Bare Costs Labor	Equipment	Total	Total Incl O&P
0010 **ARCHITECTURAL FEES**									
0020　For new construction									
0060　　Minimum				Project				4.90%	4.90%
0090　　Maximum								16%	16%
0100　For alteration work, to $500,000, minimum								7.35%	7.35%
0125　　Maximum								24%	24%
0150　For alteration work, over $500,000, minimum								6.13%	6.13%
0175　　Maximum								20%	20%

01 11 31.20 Construction Management Fees

	Crew	Daily Output	Labor-Hours	Unit	Material	Labor	Equipment	Total	Total Incl O&P
0010 **CONSTRUCTION MANAGEMENT FEES**									
0020　$1,000,000 job, minimum				Project				4.50%	4.50%
0050　　Maximum								7.50%	7.50%
0300　$50,000,000 job, minimum								2.50%	2.50%
0350　　Maximum								4%	4%

01 11 31.30 Engineering Fees

	Crew	Daily Output	Labor-Hours	Unit	Material	Labor	Equipment	Total	Total Incl O&P
0010 **ENGINEERING FEES** R011110-30									
0020　Educational planning consultant, minimum				Project				.50%	.50%
0100　　Maximum				"				2.50%	2.50%
0200　Electrical, minimum				Contrct				4.10%	4.10%
0300　　Maximum								10.10%	10.10%
0400　Elevator & conveying systems, minimum								2.50%	2.50%
0500　　Maximum								5%	5%
0600　Food service & kitchen equipment, minimum								8%	8%
0700　　Maximum								12%	12%
0800　Landscaping & site development, minimum								2.50%	2.50%
0900　　Maximum								6%	6%
1000　Mechanical (plumbing & HVAC), minimum								4.10%	4.10%
1100　　Maximum								10.10%	10.10%
1200　Structural, minimum				Project				1%	1%
1300　　Maximum				"				2.50%	2.50%

01 21 Allowances

01 21 16 – Contingency Allowances

01 21 16.50 Contingencies

	Crew	Daily Output	Labor-Hours	Unit	Material	Labor	Equipment	Total	Total Incl O&P
0010 **CONTINGENCIES**, Add to estimate									
0020　Conceptual stage				Project				20%	20%
0050　Schematic stage								15%	15%
0100　Preliminary working drawing stage (Design Dev.)								10%	10%
0150　Final working drawing stage								3%	3%

01 21 53 – Factors Allowance

01 21 53.50 Factors

	Crew	Daily Output	Labor-Hours	Unit	Material	Labor	Equipment	Total	Total Incl O&P
0010 **FACTORS** Cost adjustments R012153-10									
0100　Add to construction costs for particular job requirements									
0500　　Cut & patch to match existing construction, add, minimum				Costs	2%	3%			
0550　　　Maximum					5%	9%			
0800　　Dust protection, add, minimum					1%	2%			
0850　　　Maximum					4%	11%			
1100　　Equipment usage curtailment, add, minimum					1%	1%			
1150　　　Maximum					3%	10%			
1400　　Material handling & storage limitation, add, minimum					1%	1%			

01 21 Allowances

01 21 53 – Factors Allowance

01 21 53.50 Factors

		Crew	Daily Output	Labor-Hours	Unit	Material	2023 Bare Costs Labor	Equipment	Total	Total Incl O&P
1450	Maximum				Costs	6%	7%			
1700	Protection of existing work, add, minimum					2%	2%			
1750	Maximum					5%	7%			
2000	Shift work requirements, add, minimum						5%			
2050	Maximum						30%			
2300	Temporary shoring and bracing, add, minimum					2%	5%			
2350	Maximum				↓	5%	12%			

01 21 53.60 Security Factors

0010	**SECURITY FACTORS** R012153-60									
0100	Additional costs due to security requirements									
0110	Daily search of personnel, supplies, equipment and vehicles									
0120	Physical search, inventory and doc of assets, at entry				Costs		30%			
0130	At entry and exit						50%			
0140	Physical search, at entry						6.25%			
0150	At entry and exit						12.50%			
0160	Electronic scan search, at entry						2%			
0170	At entry and exit						4%			
0180	Visual inspection only, at entry						.25%			
0190	At entry and exit						.50%			
0200	ID card or display sticker only, at entry						.12%			
0210	At entry and exit				↓		.25%			
0220	Day 1 as described below, then visual only for up to 5 day job duration									
0230	Physical search, inventory and doc of assets, at entry				Costs		5%			
0240	At entry and exit						10%			
0250	Physical search, at entry						1.25%			
0260	At entry and exit						2.50%			
0270	Electronic scan search, at entry						.42%			
0280	At entry and exit				↓		.83%			
0290	Day 1 as described below, then visual only for 6-10 day job duration									
0300	Physical search, inventory and doc of assets, at entry				Costs		2.50%			
0310	At entry and exit						5%			
0320	Physical search, at entry						.63%			
0330	At entry and exit						1.25%			
0340	Electronic scan search, at entry						.21%			
0350	At entry and exit				↓		.42%			
0360	Day 1 as described below, then visual only for 11-20 day job duration									
0370	Physical search, inventory and doc of assets, at entry				Costs		1.25%			
0380	At entry and exit						2.50%			
0390	Physical search, at entry						.31%			
0400	At entry and exit						.63%			
0410	Electronic scan search, at entry						.10%			
0420	At entry and exit				↓		.21%			
0430	Beyond 20 days, costs are negligible									
0440	Escort required to be with tradesperson during work effort				Costs		6.25%			

01 21 53.65 Infectious Disease Precautions

0010	**INFECTIOUS DISEASE PRECAUTIONS** R012153-65									
0100	Additional costs due to infectious disease precautions									
0120	Daily temperature checks				Costs		1%			
0130	Donning & doffing masks and gloves						1%			
0140	Washing hands						1%			
0150	Informational meetings						2%			
0160	Maintaining social distance				↓		1%			

01 21 Allowances

01 21 53 – Factors Allowance

01 21 53.65 Infectious Disease Precautions

		Crew	Daily Output	Labor-Hours	Unit	Material	2023 Bare Costs Labor	Equipment	Total	Total Incl O&P
0170	Disinfecting tools or equipment				Costs		3%			
0200	N95 rated masks				Ea.	2.33			2.33	2.56
0210	Surgical masks				"	.74			.74	.82
0220	Black nitrile disposable gloves				Pair	.70			.70	.77
0250	Hand washing station & 2 x weekly service				Week				158	174

01 21 55 – Job Conditions Allowance

01 21 55.50 Job Conditions

		Crew	Daily Output	Labor-Hours	Unit	Material	2023 Bare Costs Labor	Equipment	Total	Total Incl O&P
0010	**JOB CONDITIONS** Modifications to applicable									
0020	cost summaries									
0100	Economic conditions, favorable, deduct				Project				2%	2%
0200	Unfavorable, add								5%	5%
0300	Hoisting conditions, favorable, deduct								2%	2%
0400	Unfavorable, add								5%	5%
0700	Labor availability, surplus, deduct								1%	1%
0800	Shortage, add								10%	10%
0900	Material storage area, available, deduct								1%	1%
1000	Not available, add								2%	2%
1100	Subcontractor availability, surplus, deduct								5%	5%
1200	Shortage, add								12%	12%
1300	Work space, available, deduct								2%	2%
1400	Not available, add								5%	5%

01 21 57 – Overtime Allowance

01 21 57.50 Overtime

		Crew	Daily Output	Labor-Hours	Unit	Material	2023 Bare Costs Labor	Equipment	Total	Total Incl O&P
0010	**OVERTIME** for early completion of projects or where	R012909-90								
0020	labor shortages exist, add to usual labor, up to				Costs		100%			

01 21 63 – Taxes

01 21 63.10 Taxes

		Crew	Daily Output	Labor-Hours	Unit	Material	2023 Bare Costs Labor	Equipment	Total	Total Incl O&P
0010	**TAXES**	R012909-80								
0020	Sales tax, State, average				%	5.08%				
0050	Maximum	R012909-85				7.50%				
0200	Social Security, on first $118,500 of wages						7.65%			
0300	Unemployment, combined Federal and State, minimum	R012909-86					.60%			
0350	Average						9.60%			
0400	Maximum						12%			

01 31 Project Management and Coordination

01 31 13 – Project Coordination

01 31 13.20 Field Personnel

		Crew	Daily Output	Labor-Hours	Unit	Material	2023 Bare Costs Labor	Equipment	Total	Total Incl O&P
0010	**FIELD PERSONNEL**									
0020	Clerk, average				Week		500		500	750
0100	Field engineer, junior engineer						1,700		1,700	2,549
0120	Engineer						2,180		2,180	3,269
0140	Senior engineer						2,660		2,660	3,989
0160	General purpose laborer, average	1 Clab	.20	40			1,900		1,900	2,825
0180	Project manager, minimum						2,175		2,175	3,262
0200	Average						2,500		2,500	3,749
0220	Maximum						2,850		2,850	4,274
0240	Superintendent, minimum						2,150		2,150	3,224
0260	Average						2,325		2,325	3,525

01 31 Project Management and Coordination

01 31 13 – Project Coordination

01 31 13.20 Field Personnel		Crew	Daily Output	Labor-Hours	Unit	Material	2023 Bare Costs Labor	Equipment	Total	Total Incl O&P
0280	Maximum				Week		2,650		2,650	4,025
0290	Timekeeper, average				↓		1,350		1,350	2,050
01 31 13.30 Insurance										
0010	**INSURANCE** R013113-40									
0020	Builders risk, standard, minimum				Job				.24%	.24%
0050	Maximum R013113-50								.80%	.80%
0200	All-risk type, minimum								.25%	.25%
0250	Maximum R013113-60				↓				.62%	.62%
0400	Contractor's equipment floater, minimum				Value				.50%	.50%
0450	Maximum				"				1.50%	1.50%
0600	Public liability, average				Job				2.02%	2.02%
0800	Workers' compensation & employer's liability, average									
0850	by trade, carpentry, general				Payroll		8.92%			
1000	Electrical						3.92%			
1150	Insulation						8.13%			
1450	Plumbing						4.42%			
1550	Sheet metal work (HVAC)				↓		5.86%			
01 31 13.50 General Contractor's Mark-Up										
0010	**GENERAL CONTRACTOR'S MARK-UP** on Change Orders									
0200	Extra work, by subcontractors, add				%				10%	10%
0250	By General Contractor, add								15%	15%
0400	Omitted work, by subcontractors, deduct all but								5%	5%
0450	By General Contractor, deduct all but								7.50%	7.50%
0600	Overtime work, by subcontractors, add								15%	15%
0650	By General Contractor, add				↓				10%	10%
01 31 13.80 Overhead and Profit										
0010	**OVERHEAD & PROFIT** Allowance to add to items in this R013113-50									
0020	book that do not include Subs O&P, average				%				25%	
0100	Allowance to add to items in this book that R013113-55									
0110	do include Subs O&P, minimum				%				5%	5%
0150	Average								10%	10%
0200	Maximum								15%	15%
0300	Typical, by size of project, under $100,000								30%	
0350	$500,000 project								25%	
0400	$2,000,000 project								20%	
0450	Over $10,000,000 project				↓				15%	
01 31 13.90 Performance Bond										
0010	**PERFORMANCE BOND** R013113-80									
0020	For buildings, minimum				Job				.60%	.60%
0100	Maximum				"				2.50%	2.50%

01 31 14 – Facilities Services Coordination

01 31 14.20 Lock Out/Tag Out		Crew	Daily Output	Labor-Hours	Unit	Material	Labor	Equipment	Total	Total Incl O&P
0010	**LOCK OUT/TAG OUT**									
0020	Miniature circuit breaker lock out device	1 Elec	220	.036	Ea.	38	2.45		40.45	45
0030	Miniature pin circuit breaker lock out device		220	.036		33	2.45		35.45	40
0040	Single circuit breaker lock out device		220	.036		36	2.45		38.45	43
0050	Multi-pole circuit breaker lock out device (15 to 225 Amp)		210	.038		32.50	2.57		35.07	39.50
0060	Large 3 pole circuit breaker lock out device (over 225 Amp)		210	.038		37	2.57		39.57	44.50
0080	Square D I-Line circuit breaker lock out device		210	.038		112	2.57		114.57	127
0090	Lock out disconnect switch, 30 to 100 Amp		330	.024		23	1.63		24.63	28
0100	100 to 400 Amp		330	.024	↓	23	1.63		24.63	28

01 31 Project Management and Coordination

01 31 14 – Facilities Services Coordination

01 31 14.20 Lock Out/Tag Out		Crew	Daily Output	Labor-Hours	Unit	Material	2023 Bare Costs Labor	Equipment	Total	Total Incl O&P
0110	Over 400 Amp	1 Elec	330	.024	Ea.	23	1.63		24.63	28
0120	Lock out hasp for multiple lockout tags		200	.040		7.40	2.69		10.09	12.10
0130	Electrical cord plug lock out device		220	.036		11.90	2.45		14.35	16.75
0140	Electrical plug prong lock out device (3-wire grounding plug)		220	.036		7.90	2.45		10.35	12.30
0150	Wall switch lock out		200	.040		34.50	2.69		37.19	41.50
0160	Fire alarm pull station lock out	1 Stpi	200	.040		32	2.90		34.90	39.50
0170	Sprinkler valve tamper and flow switch lock out device	1 Skwk	220	.036		30.50	2.23		32.73	37
0180	Lock out sign		330	.024		18.80	1.48		20.28	22.50
0190	Lock out tag		440	.018		5.70	1.11		6.81	7.90

01 32 Construction Progress Documentation

01 32 33 – Photographic Documentation

01 32 33.50 Photographs		Crew	Daily Output	Labor-Hours	Unit	Material	2023 Bare Costs Labor	Equipment	Total	Total Incl O&P
0010	**PHOTOGRAPHS**									
0020	8" x 10", 4 shots, 2 prints ea., std. mounting				Set	570			570	625
0100	Hinged linen mounts					580			580	635
0200	8" x 10", 4 shots, 2 prints each, in color					600			600	660
0300	For I.D. slugs, add to all above					5.35			5.35	5.85
1500	Time lapse equipment, camera and projector, buy				Ea.	2,725			2,725	2,975
1550	Rent per month				"	1,375			1,375	1,525
1700	Cameraman and processing, black & white				Day	1,350			1,350	1,500
1720	Color				"	1,600			1,600	1,750

01 41 Regulatory Requirements

01 41 26 – Permit Requirements

01 41 26.50 Permits		Crew	Daily Output	Labor-Hours	Unit	Material	2023 Bare Costs Labor	Equipment	Total	Total Incl O&P
0010	**PERMITS**									
0020	Rule of thumb, most cities, minimum				Job				.50%	.50%
0100	Maximum				"				2%	2%

01 51 Temporary Utilities

01 51 13 – Temporary Electricity

01 51 13.80 Temporary Utilities		Crew	Daily Output	Labor-Hours	Unit	Material	2023 Bare Costs Labor	Equipment	Total	Total Incl O&P
0010	**TEMPORARY UTILITIES**									
0350	Lighting, lamps, wiring, outlets, 40,000 S.F. building, 8 strings	1 Elec	34	.235	CSF Flr	3.58	15.85		19.43	27.50
0360	16 strings	"	17	.471		7.15	31.50		38.65	55
0400	Power for temp lighting only, 6.6 KWH, per month								.92	1.01
0430	11.8 KWH, per month								1.65	1.82
0450	23.6 KWH, per month								3.30	3.63
0600	Power for job duration incl. elevator, etc., minimum								53	58
0650	Maximum								110	121
0675	Temporary cooling				Ea.	1,100			1,100	1,225

01 52 Construction Facilities

01 52 13 – Field Offices and Sheds

01 52 13.20 Office and Storage Space	Crew	Daily Output	Labor-Hours	Unit	Material	2023 Bare Costs Labor	Equipment	Total	Total Incl O&P
0010 **OFFICE AND STORAGE SPACE**									
0020 Office trailer, furnished, no hookups, 20' x 8', buy	2 Skwk	1	16	Ea.	10,500	980		11,480	13,000
0250 Rent per month						201		201	221
0300 32' x 8', buy	2 Skwk	.70	22.857		15,800	1,400		17,200	19,400
0350 Rent per month						255		255	280
0400 50' x 10', buy	2 Skwk	.60	26.667		31,900	1,625		33,525	37,600
0450 Rent per month						370		370	405
0500 50' x 12', buy	2 Skwk	.50	32		27,100	1,950		29,050	32,800
0550 Rent per month						475		475	520
0700 For air conditioning, rent per month, add						55.50		55.50	61
0800 For delivery, add per mile				Mile		12.55		12.55	13.80
0900 Bunk house trailer, 8' x 40' duplex dorm with kitchen, no hookups, buy	2 Carp	1	16	Ea.	93,500	940		94,440	104,500
0910 9 man with kitchen and bath, no hookups, buy		1	16		95,500	940		96,440	106,500
0920 18 man sleeper with bath, no hookups, buy		1	16		103,000	940		103,940	115,000
1000 Portable buildings, prefab, on skids, economy, 8' x 8'		265	.060	S.F.	105	3.54		108.54	121
1100 Deluxe, 8' x 12'		150	.107	"	90.50	6.25		96.75	109
1200 Storage boxes, 20' x 8', buy	2 Skwk	1.80	8.889	Ea.	5,025	545		5,570	6,350
1250 Rent per month						126		126	138
1300 40' x 8', buy	2 Skwk	1.40	11.429		7,925	700		8,625	9,775
1350 Rent per month						155		155	170

01 54 Construction Aids

01 54 16 – Temporary Hoists

01 54 16.50 Weekly Forklift Crew

	Crew	Daily Output	Labor-Hours	Unit	Material	Labor	Equipment	Total	Total Incl O&P
0010 **WEEKLY FORKLIFT CREW**									
0100 All-terrain forklift, 45' lift, 35' reach, 9000 lb. capacity	A-3P	.20	40	Week		2,400	3,375	5,775	7,250

01 54 19 – Temporary Cranes

01 54 19.50 Daily Crane Crews

	Crew	Daily Output	Labor-Hours	Unit	Material	Labor	Equipment	Total	Total Incl O&P
0010 **DAILY CRANE CREWS** for small jobs, portal to portal R015433-15									
0100 12-ton truck-mounted hydraulic crane	A-3H	1	8	Day		530	2,150	2,680	3,175
0200 25-ton	A-3I	1	8			530	2,275	2,805	3,300
0300 40-ton	A-3J	1	8			530	2,450	2,980	3,500
0400 55-ton	A-3K	1	16			980	2,625	3,605	4,325
0500 80-ton	A-3L	1	16			980	2,800	3,780	4,525
0900 If crane is needed on a Saturday, Sunday or Holiday									
0910 At time-and-a-half, add				Day		50%			
0920 At double time, add				"		100%			

01 54 19.60 Monthly Tower Crane Crew

	Crew	Daily Output	Labor-Hours	Unit	Material	Labor	Equipment	Total	Total Incl O&P
0010 **MONTHLY TOWER CRANE CREW**, excludes concrete footing									
0100 Static tower crane, 130' high, 106' jib, 6200 lb. capacity	A-3N	.05	176	Month		11,700	41,600	53,300	63,000

01 54 23 – Temporary Scaffolding and Platforms

01 54 23.70 Scaffolding

	Crew	Daily Output	Labor-Hours	Unit	Material	Labor	Equipment	Total	Total Incl O&P
0010 **SCAFFOLDING** R015423-10									
0015 Steel tube, regular, no plank, labor only to erect & dismantle									
0090 Building exterior, wall face, 1 to 5 stories, 6'-4" x 5' frames	3 Carp	8	3	C.S.F.		176		176	262
0200 6 to 12 stories	4 Carp	8	4			234		234	350
0301 13 to 20 stories	5 Clab	8	5			236		236	350
0460 Building interior, wall face area, up to 16' high	3 Carp	12	2			117		117	175
0560 16' to 40' high		10	2.400			141		141	209
0800 Building interior floor area, up to 30' high		150	.160	C.C.F.		9.40		9.40	13.95

For customer support on your Plumbing Costs with RSMeans data, call 800.448.8182.

01 54 Construction Aids

01 54 23 – Temporary Scaffolding and Platforms

01 54 23.70 Scaffolding

		Crew	Daily Output	Labor-Hours	Unit	Material	2023 Bare Costs Labor	Equipment	Total	Total Incl O&P
0900	Over 30' high	4 Carp	160	.200	C.C.F.		11.70		11.70	17.45
0906	Complete system for face of walls, no plank, material only rent/mo				C.S.F.	95.50			95.50	105
0908	Interior spaces, no plank, material only rent/mo				C.C.F.	6.30			6.30	6.95
0910	Steel tubular, heavy duty shoring, buy									
0920	Frames 5' high 2' wide				Ea.	83			83	91.50
0925	5' high 4' wide					99.50			99.50	110
0930	6' high 2' wide					100			100	110
0935	6' high 4' wide					124			124	136
0940	Accessories									
0945	Cross braces				Ea.	21			21	23
0950	U-head, 8" x 8"					18.40			18.40	20.50
0955	J-head, 4" x 8"					17.05			17.05	18.75
0960	Base plate, 7" x 7"					15.45			15.45	17
0965	Leveling jack					19.25			19.25	21
1000	Steel tubular, regular, buy									
1100	Frames 3' high 5' wide				Ea.	92			92	101
1150	5' high 5' wide					111			111	122
1200	6'-4" high 5' wide					119			119	131
1350	7'-6" high 6' wide					98.50			98.50	108
1500	Accessories, cross braces					17.20			17.20	18.95
1550	Guardrail post					17.05			17.05	18.75
1600	Guardrail 7' section					10.75			10.75	11.80
1650	Screw jacks & plates					20.50			20.50	22.50
1700	Sidearm brackets					14.50			14.50	15.95
1750	8" casters					34			34	37.50
1800	Plank 2" x 10" x 16'-0"					77.50			77.50	85.50
1900	Stairway section					360			360	395
1910	Stairway starter bar					18.15			18.15	20
1920	Stairway inside handrail					102			102	112
1930	Stairway outside handrail					112			112	123
1940	Walk-thru frame guardrail					51.50			51.50	56.50
2000	Steel tubular, regular, rent/mo.									
2100	Frames 3' high 5' wide				Ea.	10.70			10.70	11.75
2150	5' high 5' wide					10.70			10.70	11.75
2200	6'-4" high 5' wide					7			7	7.70
2250	7'-6" high 6' wide					12.10			12.10	13.30
2500	Accessories, cross braces					3			3	3.30
2550	Guardrail post					3.60			3.60	3.96
2600	Guardrail 7' section					13.55			13.55	14.90
2650	Screw jacks & plates					4.50			4.50	4.95
2700	Sidearm brackets					12			12	13.20
2750	8" casters					10			10	11
2800	Outrigger for rolling tower					12.75			12.75	14.05
2850	Plank 2" x 10" x 16'-0"					12.10			12.10	13.30
2900	Stairway section					39			39	43
2940	Walk-thru frame guardrail					10.80			10.80	11.90
3000	Steel tubular, heavy duty shoring, rent/mo.									
3250	5' high 2' & 4' wide				Ea.	10.30			10.30	11.30
3300	6' high 2' & 4' wide					10.30			10.30	11.30
3500	Accessories, cross braces					1.11			1.11	1.22
3600	U-head, 8" x 8"					3.03			3.03	3.33
3650	J-head, 4" x 8"					3.03			3.03	3.33
3700	Base plate, 8" x 8"					1.11			1.11	1.22

01 54 Construction Aids

01 54 23 – Temporary Scaffolding and Platforms

01 54 23.70 Scaffolding

		Crew	Daily Output	Labor-Hours	Unit	Material	2023 Bare Costs Labor	2023 Bare Costs Equipment	Total	Total Incl O&P
3750	Leveling jack				Ea.	3.01			3.01	3.31
5700	Planks, 2" x 10" x 16'-0", labor only to erect & remove to 50' H	3 Carp	72	.333			19.55		19.55	29
5800	Over 50' high	4 Carp	80	.400			23.50		23.50	35
6000	Heavy duty shoring for elevated slab forms to 8'-2" high, floor area									
6100	Labor only to erect & dismantle	4 Carp	16	2	C.S.F.		117		117	175
6110	Materials only, rent/mo.				"	53			53	58.50
6500	To 14'-8" high									
6600	Labor only to erect & dismantle	4 Carp	10	3.200	C.S.F.		188		188	279
6610	Materials only, rent/mo				"	77.50			77.50	85.50

01 54 23.75 Scaffolding Specialties

		Crew	Daily Output	Labor-Hours	Unit	Material	Labor	Equipment	Total	Total Incl O&P
0010	**SCAFFOLDING SPECIALTIES**									
1200	Sidewalk bridge, heavy duty steel posts & beams, including									
1210	parapet protection & waterproofing (material cost is rent/month)									
1220	8' to 10' wide, 2 posts	3 Carp	15	1.600	L.F.	69.50	94		163.50	216
1230	3 posts	"	10	2.400	"	101	141		242	320
1500	Sidewalk bridge using tubular steel scaffold frames including									
1510	planking (material cost is rent/month)	3 Carp	45	.533	L.F.	11.40	31.50		42.90	59
1600	For 2 uses per month, deduct from all above					50%				
1700	For 1 use every 2 months, add to all above					100%				
1900	Catwalks, 20" wide, no guardrails, 7' span, buy				Ea.	229			229	252
2000	10' span, buy					291			291	320
3720	Putlog, standard, 8' span, with hangers, buy					49			49	54
3730	Rent per month					17.15			17.15	18.85
3750	12' span, buy					106			106	116
3755	Rent per month					21.50			21.50	23.50
3760	Trussed type, 16' span, buy					545			545	600
3770	Rent per month					25.50			25.50	28
3790	22' span, buy					550			550	605
3795	Rent per month					34			34	37.50
3800	Rolling ladders with handrails, 30" wide, buy, 2 step					296			296	325
4000	7 step					900			900	990
4050	10 step					1,275			1,275	1,400
4100	Rolling towers, buy, 5' wide, 7' long, 10' high					1,425			1,425	1,550
4200	For additional 5' high sections, to buy					257			257	283
4300	Complete incl. wheels, railings, outriggers,									
4350	21' high, to buy				Ea.	2,175			2,175	2,400
4400	Rent/month = 5% of purchase cost				"	109			109	119

01 54 36 – Equipment Mobilization

01 54 36.50 Mobilization

		Crew	Daily Output	Labor-Hours	Unit	Material	Labor	Equipment	Total	Total Incl O&P
0010	**MOBILIZATION** (Use line item again for demobilization) R015436-50									
0015	Up to 25 mi. haul dist. (50 mi. RT for mob/demob crew)									
1200	Small equipment, placed in rear of, or towed by pickup truck	A-3A	4	2	Ea.		119	48	167	231
1300	Equipment hauled on 3-ton capacity towed trailer	A-3Q	2.67	3			179	101	280	380
1400	20-ton capacity	B-34U	2	8			460	245	705	955
1500	40-ton capacity	B-34N	2	8			475	375	850	1,125
1600	50-ton capacity	B-34V	1	24			1,450	1,200	2,650	3,500
1700	Crane, truck-mounted, up to 75 ton (driver only)	1 Eqhv	4	2			133		133	197
1800	Over 75 ton (with chase vehicle)	A-3E	2.50	6.400			390	76.50	466.50	665
2400	Crane, large lattice boom, requiring assembly	B-34W	.50	144			8,375	8,450	16,825	21,800
2500	For each additional 5 miles haul distance, add						10%	10%		
3000	For large pieces of equipment, allow for assembly/knockdown									
3100	For mob/demob of micro-tunneling equip, see Section 33 05 07.36									

01 55 Vehicular Access and Parking

01 55 23 – Temporary Roads

01 55 23.50 Roads and Sidewalks

		Daily Output	Labor-Hours	Unit	Material	2023 Bare Costs Labor	2023 Bare Costs Equipment	Total	Total Incl O&P
0010	**ROADS AND SIDEWALKS** Temporary								
0050	Roads, gravel fill, no surfacing, 4" gravel depth	B-14	715	.067	S.Y.	8.25	3.33	.39	11.97	14.45
0100	8" gravel depth	"	615	.078	"	16.45	3.88	.45	20.78	24.50
1000	Ramp, 3/4" plywood on 2" x 6" joists, 16" OC	2 Carp	300	.053	S.F.	3.56	3.13		6.69	8.55
1100	On 2" x 10" joists, 16" OC	"	275	.058	"	5.25	3.41		8.66	10.85

01 56 Temporary Barriers and Enclosures

01 56 13 – Temporary Air Barriers

01 56 13.60 Tarpaulins

		Crew	Daily Output	Labor-Hours	Unit	Material	Labor	Equipment	Total	Total Incl O&P
0010	**TARPAULINS**									
0020	Cotton duck, 10-13.13 oz./S.Y., 6' x 8'				S.F.	.81			.81	.89
0050	30' x 30'					.60			.60	.66
0100	Polyvinyl coated nylon, 14-18 oz., minimum					1.14			1.14	1.25
0150	Maximum					1.38			1.38	1.52
0200	Reinforced polyethylene 3 mils thick, white					.25			.25	.28
0300	4 mils thick, white, clear or black					.11			.11	.12
0400	5.5 mils thick, clear					.11			.11	.12
0500	White, fire retardant					.50			.50	.55
0600	12 mils, oil resistant, fire retardant					.49			.49	.54
0700	8.5 mils, black					.41			.41	.45
0710	Woven polyethylene, 6 mils thick					.07			.07	.08
0730	Polyester reinforced w/integral fastening system, 11 mils thick					.16			.16	.18
0740	Polyethylene, reflective, 23 mils thick					1.30			1.30	1.43

01 56 13.90 Winter Protection

		Crew	Daily Output	Labor-Hours	Unit	Material	Labor	Equipment	Total	Total Incl O&P
0010	**WINTER PROTECTION**									
0100	Framing to close openings	2 Clab	500	.032	S.F.	1.19	1.51		2.70	3.56
0200	Tarpaulins hung over scaffolding, 8 uses, not incl. scaffolding		1500	.011		.24	.50		.74	1.01
0250	Tarpaulin polyester reinf. w/integral fastening system, 11 mils thick		1600	.010		.20	.47		.67	.92
0300	Prefab fiberglass panels, steel frame, 8 uses		1200	.013		3.19	.63		3.82	4.45

01 56 16 – Temporary Dust Barriers

01 56 16.10 Dust Barriers, Temporary

		Crew	Daily Output	Labor-Hours	Unit	Material	Labor	Equipment	Total	Total Incl O&P
0010	**DUST BARRIERS, TEMPORARY**, erect and dismantle									
0020	Spring loaded telescoping pole & head, to 12', erect and dismantle	1 Clab	240	.033	Ea.		1.58		1.58	2.35
0025	Cost per day (based upon 250 days)				Day	.61			.61	.67
0030	To 21', erect and dismantle	1 Clab	240	.033	Ea.		1.58		1.58	2.35
0035	Cost per day (based upon 250 days)				Day	1.21			1.21	1.33
0040	Accessories, caution tape reel, erect and dismantle	1 Clab	480	.017	Ea.		.79		.79	1.17
0045	Cost per day (based upon 250 days)				Day	.31			.31	.34
0060	Foam rail and connector, erect and dismantle	1 Clab	240	.033	Ea.		1.58		1.58	2.35
0065	Cost per day (based upon 250 days)				Day	.26			.26	.29
0070	Caution tape	1 Clab	384	.021	C.L.F.	1.99	.98		2.97	3.66
0080	Zipper, standard duty		60	.133	Ea.	16.15	6.30		22.45	27
0090	Heavy duty		48	.167	"	23.50	7.90		31.40	38
0100	Polyethylene sheet, 4 mil		37	.216	Sq.	5.35	10.20		15.55	21
0110	6 mil		37	.216	"	6.85	10.20		17.05	22.50
1000	Dust partition, 6 mil polyethylene, 1" x 3" frame	2 Carp	2000	.008	S.F.	.39	.47		.86	1.13
1080	2" x 4" frame	"	2000	.008	"	.91	.47		1.38	1.70
1085	Negative air machine, 1800 CFM				Ea.	990			990	1,100
1090	Adhesive strip application, 2" width	1 Clab	192	.042	C.L.F.	13.50	1.97		15.47	17.80
4000	Dust & infectious control partition, adj. to 10' high, obscured, 4' panel	2 Carp	90	.178	Ea.	595	10.40		605.40	670

01 56 Temporary Barriers and Enclosures

01 56 16 – Temporary Dust Barriers

01 56 16.10 Dust Barriers, Temporary

		Crew	Daily Output	Labor-Hours	Unit	Material	2023 Bare Costs Labor	Equipment	Total	Total Incl O&P
4010	3' panel	2 Carp	90	.178	Ea.	560	10.40		570.40	635
4020	2' panel	↓	90	.178		440	10.40		450.40	500
4030	1' panel	1 Carp	90	.089		292	5.20		297.20	330
4040	6" panel	"	90	.089		270	5.20		275.20	305
4050	2' panel with HEPA filtered discharge port	2 Carp	90	.178		510	10.40		520.40	575
4060	3' panel with 32" door		90	.178		920	10.40		930.40	1,025
4070	4' panel with 36" door		90	.178		1,025	10.40		1,035.40	1,150
4080	4'-6" panel with 44" door		90	.178		1,225	10.40		1,235.40	1,375
4090	Hinged corner		80	.200		188	11.70		199.70	223
4100	Outside corner		80	.200		156	11.70		167.70	188
4110	T post		80	.200		166	11.70		177.70	199
4120	Accessories, ceiling grid clip		360	.044		7.25	2.60		9.85	11.90
4130	Panel locking clip		360	.044		5	2.60		7.60	9.40
4140	Panel joint closure strip		360	.044		8.30	2.60		10.90	13
4150	Screw jack	↓	360	.044		7.15	2.60		9.75	11.80
4160	Digital pressure difference gauge					290			290	320
4180	Combination lockset	1 Carp	13	.615	↓	205	36		241	279
4185	Sealant tape, 2" wide	1 Clab	192	.042	C.L.F.	13.50	1.97		15.47	17.80
4190	System in place, including door and accessories									
4200	Based upon 25 uses	2 Carp	51	.314	L.F.	10.05	18.40		28.45	38.50
4210	Based upon 50 uses		51	.314		5.05	18.40		23.45	33
4230	Based upon 100 uses	↓	51	.314	↓	2.51	18.40		20.91	30.50

01 56 23 – Temporary Barricades

01 56 23.10 Barricades

		Crew	Daily Output	Labor-Hours	Unit	Material	Labor	Equipment	Total	Total Incl O&P
0010	**BARRICADES**									
0020	5' high, 3 rail @ 2" x 8", fixed	2 Carp	20	.800	L.F.	13.45	47		60.45	85
0150	Movable		30	.533		12.15	31.50		43.65	60
1000	Guardrail, wooden, 3' high, 1" x 6" on 2" x 4" posts		200	.080		2.48	4.69		7.17	9.75
1100	2" x 6" on 4" x 4" posts	↓	165	.097		4.26	5.70		9.96	13.15
1200	Portable metal with base pads, buy					17.25			17.25	18.95
1250	Typical installation, assume 10 reuses	2 Carp	600	.027	↓	2.87	1.56		4.43	5.50
1300	Barricade tape, polyethylene, 7 mil, 3" wide x 300' long roll	1 Clab	128	.063	Ea.	5.95	2.95		8.90	10.95
3000	Detour signs, set up and remove									
3010	Reflective aluminum, MUTCD, 24" x 24", post mounted	1 Clab	20	.400	Ea.	4.26	18.90		23.16	32.50
4000	Roof edge portable barrier stands and warning flags, 50 uses	1 Rohe	9100	.001	L.F.	.10	.03		.13	.17
4010	100 uses	"	9100	.001	"	.05	.03		.08	.12

01 56 26 – Temporary Fencing

01 56 26.50 Temporary Fencing

		Crew	Daily Output	Labor-Hours	Unit	Material	Labor	Equipment	Total	Total Incl O&P
0010	**TEMPORARY FENCING**									
0020	Chain link, 11 ga., 4' high	2 Clab	400	.040	L.F.	2.20	1.89		4.09	5.25
0100	6' high		300	.053		5.35	2.52		7.87	9.65
0200	Rented chain link, 6' high, to 1000' (up to 12 mo.)		400	.040		3.16	1.89		5.05	6.30
0250	Over 1000' (up to 12 mo.)	↓	300	.053		3.73	2.52		6.25	7.85
0350	Plywood, painted, 2" x 4" frame, 4' high	A-4	135	.178		9.60	9.90		19.50	25.50
0400	4" x 4" frame, 8' high	"	110	.218		18.30	12.15		30.45	38
0500	Wire mesh on 4" x 4" posts, 4' high	2 Carp	100	.160		13.05	9.40		22.45	28.50
0550	8' high	"	80	.200	↓	19.65	11.70		31.35	39

01 56 Temporary Barriers and Enclosures

01 56 29 – Temporary Protective Walkways

01 56 29.50 Protection		Crew	Daily Output	Labor-Hours	Unit	Material	2023 Bare Costs Labor	Equipment	Total	Total Incl O&P
0010	**PROTECTION**									
0020	Stair tread, 2" x 12" planks, 1 use	1 Carp	75	.107	Tread	12.75	6.25		19	23.50
0100	Exterior plywood, 1/2" thick, 1 use		65	.123		3.47	7.20		10.67	14.55
0200	3/4" thick, 1 use		60	.133		5.15	7.80		12.95	17.30
2200	Sidewalks, 2" x 12" planks, 2 uses		350	.023	S.F.	2.12	1.34		3.46	4.33
2300	Exterior plywood, 2 uses, 1/2" thick		750	.011		.58	.63		1.21	1.57
2400	5/8" thick		650	.012		.69	.72		1.41	1.82
2500	3/4" thick		600	.013		.86	.78		1.64	2.10

01 57 Temporary Controls

01 57 33 – Temporary Security

01 57 33.50 Watchman		Crew	Daily Output	Labor-Hours	Unit	Material	2023 Bare Costs Labor	Equipment	Total	Total Incl O&P
0010	**WATCHMAN**									
0020	Service, monthly basis, uniformed person, minimum				Hr.				27.65	30.40
0100	Maximum								56	61.62
0200	Person and command dog, minimum								31	34
0300	Maximum								60	65

01 58 Project Identification

01 58 13 – Temporary Project Signage

01 58 13.50 Signs		Crew	Daily Output	Labor-Hours	Unit	Material	2023 Bare Costs Labor	Equipment	Total	Total Incl O&P
0010	**SIGNS**									
0020	High intensity reflectorized, no posts, buy				Ea.	16.35			16.35	17.95

01 66 Product Storage and Handling Requirements

01 66 19 – Material Handling

01 66 19.10 Material Handling		Crew	Daily Output	Labor-Hours	Unit	Material	2023 Bare Costs Labor	Equipment	Total	Total Incl O&P
0010	**MATERIAL HANDLING**									
0020	Above 2nd story, via stairs, per C.Y. of material per floor	2 Clab	145	.110	C.Y.		5.20		5.20	7.75
0030	Via elevator, per C.Y. of material		240	.067			3.15		3.15	4.69
0050	Distances greater than 200', per C.Y. of material per each addl 200'		300	.053			2.52		2.52	3.75

01 74 Cleaning and Waste Management

01 74 13 – Progress Cleaning

01 74 13.20 Cleaning Up		Crew	Daily Output	Labor-Hours	Unit	Material	2023 Bare Costs Labor	Equipment	Total	Total Incl O&P
0010	**CLEANING UP**									
0020	After job completion, allow, minimum				Job				.30%	.30%
0040	Maximum				"				1%	1%
0050	Cleanup of floor area, continuous, per day, during const.	A-5	24	.750	M.S.F.	4.56	36	3.77	44.33	62.50
0100	Final by GC at end of job	"	11.50	1.565	"	4.82	75	7.85	87.67	126

01 91 Commissioning

01 91 13 – General Commissioning Requirements

01 91 13.50 Building Commissioning		Crew	Daily Output	Labor-Hours	Unit	Material	2023 Bare Costs Labor	Equipment	Total	Total Incl O&P
0010	**BUILDING COMMISSIONING**									
0100	Systems operation and verification during turnover				%				.25%	.25%
0150	Including all systems subcontractors								.50%	.50%
0200	Systems design assistance, operation, verification and training								.50%	.50%
0250	Including all systems subcontractors								1%	1%

01 93 Facility Maintenance

01 93 13 – Facility Maintenance Procedures

01 93 13.15 Mechanical Facilities Maintenance

			Crew	Daily Output	Labor-Hours	Unit	Material	Labor	Equipment	Total	Total Incl O&P
0010	**MECHANICAL FACILITIES MAINTENANCE**										
0100	Air conditioning system maintenance										
0130	Belt, replace		1 Stpi	15	.533	Ea.		38.50		38.50	57.50
0170	Fan, clean			16	.500			36.50		36.50	54
0180	Filter, remove, clean, replace			12	.667			48.50		48.50	72
0190	Flexible coupling alignment, inspect			40	.200			14.50		14.50	21.50
0200	Gas leak, locate and repair			4	2			145		145	216
0250	Pump packing gland, remove and replace			11	.727			53		53	78.50
0270	Tighten			32	.250			18.15		18.15	27
0290	Pump, disassemble and assemble			4	2			145		145	216
0300	Air pressure regulator, disassemble, clean, assemble		1 Skwk	4	2			123		123	184
0310	Repair or replace part		"	6	1.333			81.50		81.50	123
0320	Purging system		1 Stpi	16	.500			36.50		36.50	54
0400	Compressor, air, remove or install fan wheel		1 Skwk	20	.400			24.50		24.50	37
0410	Disassemble or assemble 2 cylinder, 2 stage			4	2			123		123	184
0420	4 cylinder, 4 stage			1	8			490		490	735
0430	Repair or replace part			2	4			245		245	370
0700	Demolition, for mech. demolition see Section 23 05 05.10 or 22 05 05.10										
0800	Ductwork, clean										
0810	Rectangular										
0820	6"	G	1 Shee	187.50	.043	L.F.		2.99		2.99	4.51
0830	8"	G		140.63	.057			3.99		3.99	6
0840	10"	G		112.50	.071			4.99		4.99	7.50
0850	12"	G		93.75	.085			6		6	9
0860	14"	G		80.36	.100			7		7	10.50
0870	16"	G		70.31	.114			8		8	12.05
0900	Round										
0910	4"	G	1 Shee	358.10	.022	L.F.		1.57		1.57	2.36
0920	6"	G		238.73	.034			2.35		2.35	3.54
0930	8"	G		179.05	.045			3.13		3.13	4.72
0940	10"	G		143.24	.056			3.92		3.92	5.90
0950	12"	G		119.37	.067			4.70		4.70	7.10
0960	16"	G		89.52	.089			6.25		6.25	9.45
1000	Expansion joint, not screwed, install or remove		1 Stpi	3	2.667	Ea.		193		193	289
1010	Repack		"	6	1.333	"		96.50		96.50	144
1200	Fire protection equipment										
1220	Fire hydrant, replace		Q-1	3	5.333	Ea.		345		345	515
1230	Service, lubricate, inspect, flush, clean		1 Plum	7	1.143			82.50		82.50	123
1240	Test		"	11	.727			52.50		52.50	78
1310	Inspect valves, pressure, nozzle		1 Spri	4	2	System		142		142	211
1800	Plumbing fixtures, for installation see Section 22 41 00										
1801	Plumbing fixtures										

For customer support on your Plumbing Costs with RSMeans data, call 800.448.8182.

01 93 Facility Maintenance

01 93 13 – Facility Maintenance Procedures

01 93 13.15 Mechanical Facilities Maintenance		Crew	Daily Output	Labor-Hours	Unit	Material	2023 Bare Costs Labor	2023 Bare Costs Equipment	Total	Total Incl O&P
1850	Open drain with toilet auger	1 Plum	16	.500	Ea.		36		36	53.50
1870	Plaster trap, clean	"	6	1.333			96		96	143
1881	Clean commode	1 Clab	20	.400		.27	18.90		19.17	28.50
1882	Clean commode seat		48	.167		.13	7.90		8.03	11.90
1884	Clean double sink		20	.400		.27	18.90		19.17	28.50
1886	Clean bathtub		12	.667		.53	31.50		32.03	47.50
1888	Clean fiberglass tub/shower		8	1		.67	47.50		48.17	71
1889	Clean faucet set		32	.250		.11	11.80		11.91	17.70
1891	Clean shower head		80	.100		.01	4.73		4.74	7.05
1893	Clean water heater	↓	16	.500		.93	23.50		24.43	36
1900	Relief valve, test and adjust	1 Stpi	20	.400			29		29	43.50
1910	Clean pump, heater, or motor for whirlpool	1 Clab	16	.500		.13	23.50		23.63	35
1920	Clean thermal cover for whirlpool	"	16	.500		1.33	23.50		24.83	36.50
2000	Repair or replace, steam trap	1 Stpi	8	1			72.50		72.50	108
2020	Y-type or bell strainer		6	1.333			96.50		96.50	144
2040	Water trap or vacuum breaker, screwed joints	↓	13	.615			44.50		44.50	66.50
2100	Steam specialties, clean									
2120	Air separator with automatic trap, 1" fittings	1 Stpi	12	.667	Ea.		48.50		48.50	72
2130	Bucket trap, 2" pipe		7	1.143			83		83	124
2150	Drip leg, 2" fitting		45	.178			12.90		12.90	19.25
2200	Thermodynamic trap, 1" fittings		50	.160			11.60		11.60	17.30
2210	Thermostatic		65	.123			8.95		8.95	13.30
2240	Screen and seat in Y-type strainer, plug type		25	.320			23		23	34.50
2242	Screen and seat in Y-type strainer, flange type		12	.667			48.50		48.50	72
2500	Valve, replace broken handwheel	↓	24	.333	↓		24		24	36
3000	Valve, overhaul, regulator, relief, flushometer, mixing									
3040	Cold water, gas	1 Stpi	5	1.600	Ea.		116		116	173
3050	Hot water, steam		3	2.667			193		193	289
3080	Globe, gate, check up to 4" cold water, gas		10	.800			58		58	86.50
3090	Hot water, steam		5	1.600			116		116	173
3100	Over 4" ID hot or cold line	↓	1.40	5.714			415		415	620
3120	Remove and replace, gate, globe or check up to 4"	Q-5	6	2.667			174		174	260
3130	Over 4"	"	2	8			520		520	780
3150	Repack up to 4"	1 Stpi	13	.615			44.50		44.50	66.50
3160	Over 4"	"	4	2	↓		145		145	216

Division 2 Existing Conditions

Estimating Tips
02 30 00 Subsurface Investigation
In preparing estimates on structures involving earthwork or foundations, all information concerning soil characteristics should be obtained. Look particularly for hazardous waste, evidence of prior dumping of debris, and previous stream beds.

02 40 00 Demolition and Structure Moving
The costs shown for selective demolition do not include rubbish handling or disposal. These items should be estimated separately using RSMeans data or other sources.

- Historic preservation often requires that the contractor remove materials from the existing structure, rehab them, and replace them. The estimator must be aware of any related measures and precautions that must be taken when doing selective demolition and cutting and patching. Requirements may include special handling and storage, as well as security.
- In addition to Subdivision 02 41 00, you can find selective demolition items in each division. Example: Roofing demolition is in Division 7.
- Absent of any other specific reference, an approximate demolish-in-place cost can be obtained by halving the new-install labor cost. To remove for reuse, allow the entire new-install labor figure.

02 40 00 Building Deconstruction
This section provides costs for the careful dismantling and recycling of most low-rise building materials.

02 50 00 Containment of Hazardous Waste
This section addresses on-site hazardous waste disposal costs.

02 80 00 Hazardous Material Disposal/Remediation
This subdivision includes information on hazardous waste handling, asbestos remediation, lead remediation, and mold remediation. See reference numbers R028213-20 and R028319-60 for further guidance in using these unit price lines.

02 90 00 Monitoring Chemical Sampling, Testing Analysis
This section provides costs for on-site sampling and testing hazardous waste.

Reference Numbers
Reference numbers are shown at the beginning of some major classifications. These numbers refer to related items in the Reference Section. The reference information may be an estimating procedure, an alternate pricing method, or technical information.

Note: Not all subdivisions listed here necessarily appear. ∎

Same Data. Simplified.
Enjoy the convenience and efficiency of accessing your costs anywhere:
- **Skip the multiplier** by setting your location
- **Quickly search,** edit, favorite and share costs
- **Stay on top of price changes** with automatic updates

Discover more at rsmeans.com/online

No part of this cost data may be reproduced, stored in a retrieval system, or transmitted in any form or by any means without prior written permission of Gordian.

02 21 Surveys
02 21 13 – Site Surveys

02 21 13.09 Topographical Surveys

		Crew	Daily Output	Labor-Hours	Unit	Material	2023 Bare Costs Labor	Equipment	Total	Total Incl O&P
0010	**TOPOGRAPHICAL SURVEYS**									
0020	Topographical surveying, conventional, minimum	A-7	3.30	7.273	Acre	56.50	460	10.20	526.70	760
0050	Average	"	1.95	12.308		84.50	775	17.25	876.75	1,250
0100	Maximum	A-8	.60	53.333		113	3,275	56	3,444	5,050

02 21 13.13 Boundary and Survey Markers

		Crew	Daily Output	Labor-Hours	Unit	Material	Labor	Equipment	Total	Total Incl O&P
0010	**BOUNDARY AND SURVEY MARKERS**									
0300	Lot location and lines, large quantities, minimum	A-7	2	12	Acre	35.50	755	16.80	807.30	1,175
0320	Average	"	1.25	19.200		71.50	1,200	27	1,298.50	1,900
0400	Small quantities, maximum	A-8	1	32		71.50	1,950	33.50	2,055	3,050
0600	Monuments, 3' long	A-7	10	2.400	Ea.	39	151	3.36	193.36	273
0800	Property lines, perimeter, cleared land	"	1000	.024	L.F.	.10	1.51	.03	1.64	2.41
0900	Wooded land	A-8	875	.037	"	.13	2.24	.04	2.41	3.52

02 21 13.16 Aerial Surveys

		Crew	Daily Output	Labor-Hours	Unit	Material	Labor	Equipment	Total	Total Incl O&P
0010	**AERIAL SURVEYS**									
1500	Aerial surveying, including ground control, minimum fee, 10 acres				Total				4,700	4,700
1510	100 acres								9,400	9,400
1550	From existing photography, deduct								1,625	1,625
1600	2' contours, 10 acres				Acre				470	470
1850	100 acres								94	94
2000	1000 acres								90	90
2050	10,000 acres								85	85

02 41 Demolition
02 41 13 – Selective Site Demolition

02 41 13.17 Demolish, Remove Pavement and Curb

		Crew	Daily Output	Labor-Hours	Unit	Material	Labor	Equipment	Total	Total Incl O&P
0010	**DEMOLISH, REMOVE PAVEMENT AND CURB** R024119-10									
5010	Pavement removal, bituminous roads, up to 3" thick	B-38	690	.058	S.Y.		3.09	1.93	5.02	6.70
5050	4"-6" thick	"	420	.095	"		5.10	3.17	8.27	11.05

02 41 13.23 Utility Line Removal

		Crew	Daily Output	Labor-Hours	Unit	Material	Labor	Equipment	Total	Total Incl O&P
0010	**UTILITY LINE REMOVAL**									
0015	No hauling, abandon catch basin or manhole	B-6	7	3.429	Ea.		176	39.50	215.50	305
0020	Remove existing catch basin or manhole, masonry		4	6			310	69.50	379.50	535
0030	Catch basin or manhole frames and covers, stored		13	1.846			95	21.50	116.50	165
0040	Remove and reset		7	3.429			176	39.50	215.50	305
0900	Hydrants, fire, remove only	B-21A	5	8			470	128	598	835
0950	Remove and reset	"	2	20			1,175	320	1,495	2,100
2900	Pipe removal, sewer/water, no excavation, 12" diameter	B-6	175	.137	L.F.		7.05	1.58	8.63	12.25
2930	15"-18" diameter	B-12Z	150	.160			8.60	11.20	19.80	25
2960	21"-24" diameter		120	.200			10.70	14.05	24.75	31.50
3000	27"-36" diameter		90	.267			14.30	18.70	33	42
3200	Steel, welded connections, 4" diameter	B-6	160	.150			7.70	1.73	9.43	13.40
3300	10" diameter	"	80	.300			15.40	3.47	18.87	27

02 41 13.30 Minor Site Demolition

		Crew	Daily Output	Labor-Hours	Unit	Material	Labor	Equipment	Total	Total Incl O&P
0010	**MINOR SITE DEMOLITION** R024119-10									
4000	Sidewalk removal, bituminous, 2" thick	B-6	350	.069	S.Y.		3.52	.79	4.31	6.10
4010	2-1/2" thick		325	.074			3.80	.85	4.65	6.60
4100	Concrete, plain, 4"		160	.150			7.70	1.73	9.43	13.40
4110	Plain, 5"		140	.171			8.80	1.98	10.78	15.30
4120	Plain, 6"		120	.200			10.30	2.31	12.61	17.85

02 41 Demolition

02 41 19 – Selective Demolition

02 41 19.19 Selective Demolition

		Crew	Daily Output	Labor-Hours	Unit	Material	2023 Bare Costs Labor	2023 Bare Costs Equipment	Total	Total Incl O&P
0010	**SELECTIVE DEMOLITION**, Rubbish Handling R024119-10									
0020	The following are to be added to the demolition prices									
0600	Dumpster, weekly rental, 1 dump/week, 6 C.Y. capacity (2 tons)				Week	415			415	455
0700	10 C.Y. capacity (3 tons)					480			480	530
0725	20 C.Y. capacity (5 tons) R024119-20					565			565	625
0800	30 C.Y. capacity (7 tons)					730			730	800
0840	40 C.Y. capacity (10 tons)					775			775	850
2000	Load, haul, dump and return, 0'-50' haul, hand carried	2 Clab	24	.667	C.Y.		31.50		31.50	47
2005	Wheeled		37	.432			20.50		20.50	30.50
2040	0'-100' haul, hand carried		16.50	.970			46		46	68
2045	Wheeled		25	.640			30		30	45
2050	Forklift	A-3R	25	.320			19.10	12.45	31.55	42
2080	Haul and return, add per each extra 100' haul, hand carried	2 Clab	35.50	.451			21.50		21.50	31.50
2085	Wheeled		54	.296			14		14	21
2120	For travel in elevators, up to 10 floors, add		140	.114			5.40		5.40	8.05
2130	0'-50' haul, incl. up to 5 riser stairs, hand carried		23	.696			33		33	49
2135	Wheeled		35	.457			21.50		21.50	32
2140	6-10 riser stairs, hand carried		22	.727			34.50		34.50	51
2145	Wheeled		34	.471			22		22	33
2150	11-20 riser stairs, hand carried		20	.800			38		38	56.50
2155	Wheeled		31	.516			24.50		24.50	36.50
2160	21-40 riser stairs, hand carried		16	1			47.50		47.50	70.50
2165	Wheeled		24	.667			31.50		31.50	47
2170	0'-100' haul, incl. 5 riser stairs, hand carried		15	1.067			50.50		50.50	75
2175	Wheeled		23	.696			33		33	49
2180	6-10 riser stairs, hand carried		14	1.143			54		54	80.50
2185	Wheeled		21	.762			36		36	53.50
2190	11-20 riser stairs, hand carried		12	1.333			63		63	94
2195	Wheeled		18	.889			42		42	62.50
2200	21-40 riser stairs, hand carried		8	2			94.50		94.50	141
2205	Wheeled		12	1.333			63		63	94
2210	Haul and return, add per each extra 100' haul, hand carried		35.50	.451			21.50		21.50	31.50
2215	Wheeled		54	.296			14		14	21
2220	For each additional flight of stairs, up to 5 risers, add		550	.029	Flight		1.37		1.37	2.05
2225	6-10 risers, add		275	.058			2.75		2.75	4.09
2230	11-20 risers, add		138	.116			5.50		5.50	8.15
2235	21-40 risers, add		69	.232			10.95		10.95	16.30
3000	Loading & trucking, including 2 mile haul, chute loaded	B-16	45	.711	C.Y.		35.50	17.60	53.10	72.50
3040	Hand loading truck, 50' haul	"	48	.667			33	16.50	49.50	67.50
3080	Machine loading truck	B-17	120	.267			14	5.80	19.80	27.50
5000	Haul, per mile, up to 8 C.Y. truck	B-34B	1165	.007			.38	.68	1.06	1.32
5100	Over 8 C.Y. truck	"	1550	.005			.29	.51	.80	.99

02 41 19.20 Selective Demolition, Dump Charges

		Crew	Daily Output	Labor-Hours	Unit	Material	Labor	Equipment	Total	Total Incl O&P
0010	**SELECTIVE DEMOLITION, DUMP CHARGES** R024119-10									
0100	Building construction materials				Ton	74			74	81
0300	Rubbish only					63			63	69.50
0500	Reclamation station, usual charge					74			74	81

02 41 19.27 Selective Demolition, Torch Cutting

		Crew	Daily Output	Labor-Hours	Unit	Material	Labor	Equipment	Total	Total Incl O&P
0010	**SELECTIVE DEMOLITION, TORCH CUTTING** R024119-10									
0020	Steel, 1" thick plate	E-25	333	.024	L.F.	2.91	1.60	.04	4.55	5.70
0040	1" diameter bar	"	600	.013	Ea.	.48	.89	.02	1.39	1.93
1000	Oxygen lance cutting, reinforced concrete walls									

02 41 Demolition

02 41 19 – Selective Demolition

02 41 19.27 Selective Demolition, Torch Cutting

		Crew	Daily Output	Labor-Hours	Unit	Material	2023 Bare Costs Labor	2023 Bare Costs Equipment	Total	Total Incl O&P
1040	12"-16" thick walls	1 Clab	10	.800	L.F.		38		38	56.50
1080	24" thick walls	"	6	1.333	"		63		63	94

02 65 Underground Storage Tank Removal

02 65 10 – Underground Tank and Contaminated Soil Removal

02 65 10.30 Removal of Underground Storage Tanks

			Crew	Daily Output	Labor-Hours	Unit	Material	Labor	Equipment	Total	Total Incl O&P
0010	**REMOVAL OF UNDERGROUND STORAGE TANKS** R026510-20										
0011	Petroleum storage tanks, non-leaking										
0100	Excavate & load onto trailer										
0110	3,000 gal. to 5,000 gal. tank	G	B-14	4	12	Ea.		595	69	664	960
0120	6,000 gal. to 8,000 gal. tank	G	B-3A	3	13.333			670	395	1,065	1,425
0130	9,000 gal. to 12,000 gal. tank	G	"	2	20			1,000	595	1,595	2,150
0190	Known leaking tank, add					%				100%	100%
0200	Remove sludge, water and remaining product from bottom										
0201	of tank with vacuum truck										
0300	3,000 gal. to 5,000 gal. tank	G	A-13	5	1.600	Ea.		95.50	164	259.50	320
0310	6,000 gal. to 8,000 gal. tank	G		4	2			119	205	324	405
0320	9,000 gal. to 12,000 gal. tank	G		3	2.667			159	273	432	535
0390	Dispose of sludge off-site, average					Gal.				6.25	6.80
0400	Insert inert solid CO_2 "dry ice" into tank										
0401	For cleaning/transporting tanks (1.5 lb./100 gal. cap)	G	1 Clab	500	.016	Lb.	1.35	.76		2.11	2.62
1020	Haul tank to certified salvage dump, 100 miles round trip										
1023	3,000 gal. to 5,000 gal. tank					Ea.				760	830
1026	6,000 gal. to 8,000 gal. tank									880	960
1029	9,000 gal. to 12,000 gal. tank									1,050	1,150
1100	Disposal of contaminated soil to landfill										
1110	Minimum					C.Y.				145	160
1111	Maximum					"				400	440
1120	Disposal of contaminated soil to										
1121	bituminous concrete batch plant										
1130	Minimum					C.Y.				80	88
1131	Maximum					"				115	125
2010	Decontamination of soil on site incl poly tarp on top/bottom										
2011	Soil containment berm and chemical treatment										
2020	Minimum	G	B-11C	100	.160	C.Y.	8.45	8.80	2.77	20.02	25.50
2021	Maximum	G	"	100	.160		10.95	8.80	2.77	22.52	28.50
2050	Disposal of decontaminated soil, minimum									135	150
2055	Maximum									400	440

02 81 Transportation and Disposal of Hazardous Materials

02 81 20 – Hazardous Waste Handling

02 81 20.10 Hazardous Waste Cleanup/Pickup/Disposal

		Crew	Daily Output	Labor-Hours	Unit	Material	Labor	Equipment	Total	Total Incl O&P
0010	**HAZARDOUS WASTE CLEANUP/PICKUP/DISPOSAL**									
0100	For contractor rental equipment, i.e., dozer,									
0110	Front end loader, dump truck, etc., see 01 54 33 Reference Section									
1000	Solid pickup									
1100	55 gal. drums				Ea.				240	265
1120	Bulk material, minimum				Ton				190	210
1130	Maximum				"				595	655

02 81 Transportation and Disposal of Hazardous Materials

02 81 20 – Hazardous Waste Handling

02 81 20.10 Hazardous Waste Cleanup/Pickup/Disposal	Crew	Daily Output	Labor-Hours	Unit	Material	2023 Bare Costs Labor	Equipment	Total	Total Incl O&P
1200 Transportation to disposal site									
1220 Truckload = 80 drums or 25 C.Y. or 18 tons									
1260 Minimum				Mile				3.95	4.45
1270 Maximum				"				7.25	7.98
3000 Liquid pickup, vacuum truck, stainless steel tank									
3100 Minimum charge, 4 hours									
3110 1 compartment, 2200 gallon				Hr.				140	155
3120 2 compartment, 5000 gallon				"				200	225
3400 Transportation in 6900 gallon bulk truck				Mile				7.95	8.75
3410 In teflon lined truck				"				10.20	11.25
5000 Heavy sludge or dry vacuumable material				Hr.				140	155
6000 Dumpsite disposal charge, minimum				Ton				140	155
6020 Maximum				"				415	455

02 82 Asbestos Remediation

02 82 13 – Asbestos Abatement

02 82 13.39 Asbestos Remediation Plans and Methods

		Crew	Daily Output	Labor-Hours	Unit	Material	Labor	Equipment	Total	Total Incl O&P
0010	**ASBESTOS REMEDIATION PLANS AND METHODS**									
0100	Building Survey-Commercial Building				Ea.				2,200	2,400
0200	Asbestos Abatement Remediation Plan				"				1,350	1,475

02 82 13.41 Asbestos Abatement Equipment

		Crew	Daily Output	Labor-Hours	Unit	Material	Labor	Equipment	Total	Total Incl O&P
0010	**ASBESTOS ABATEMENT EQUIPMENT** R028213-20									
0011	Equipment and supplies, buy									
0200	Air filtration device, 2000 CFM				Ea.	1,050			1,050	1,150
0250	Large volume air sampling pump, minimum					291			291	320
0260	Maximum					1,450			1,450	1,600
0300	Airless sprayer unit, 2 gun					2,600			2,600	2,850
0350	Light stand, 500 watt					31.50			31.50	34.50
0400	Personal respirators									
0410	Negative pressure, 1/2 face, dual operation, minimum				Ea.	28			28	31
0420	Maximum					28.50			28.50	31.50
0450	P.A.P.R., full face, minimum					840			840	925
0460	Maximum					1,075			1,075	1,175
0470	Supplied air, full face, including air line, minimum					254			254	279
0480	Maximum					1,025			1,025	1,125
0500	Personnel sampling pump					310			310	340
1500	Power panel, 20 unit, including GFI					675			675	745
1600	Shower unit, including pump and filters					965			965	1,050
1700	Supplied air system (type C)					3,925			3,925	4,325
1750	Vacuum cleaner, HEPA, 16 gal., stainless steel, wet/dry					1,450			1,450	1,600
1760	55 gallon					1,850			1,850	2,050
1800	Vacuum loader, 9-18 ton/hr.					135,500			135,500	149,000
1900	Water atomizer unit, including 55 gal. drum					283			283	310
2000	Worker protection, whole body, foot, head cover & gloves, plastic					10.60			10.60	11.65
2500	Respirator, single use					2			2	2.20
2550	Cartridge for respirator					14.50			14.50	15.95
2570	Glove bag, 7 mil, 50" x 64"					12.50			12.50	13.75
2580	10 mil, 44" x 60"					12.65			12.65	13.90
2590	6 mil, 44" x 60"					7.75			7.75	8.55
6000	Disposable polyethylene bags, 6 mil, 3 C.F.					1.20			1.20	1.32
6300	Disposable fiber drums, 55gal					29			29	31.50

02 82 Asbestos Remediation

02 82 13 – Asbestos Abatement

02 82 13.41 Asbestos Abatement Equipment

		Crew	Daily Output	Labor-Hours	Unit	Material	2023 Bare Costs Labor	Equipment	Total	Total Incl O&P
6400	Pressure sensitive caution labels, 3" x 5"				Ea.	3.26			3.26	3.59
6450	11" x 17"					17.60			17.60	19.35
6500	Negative air machine, 1800 CFM					990			990	1,100

02 82 13.42 Preparation of Asbestos Containment Area

		Crew	Daily Output	Labor-Hours	Unit	Material	Labor	Equipment	Total	Total Incl O&P
0010	**PREPARATION OF ASBESTOS CONTAINMENT AREA** R028213-20									
0100	Pre-cleaning, HEPA vacuum and wet wipe, flat surfaces	A-9	12000	.005	S.F.	.02	.35		.37	.56
0200	Protect carpeted area, 2 layers 6 mil poly on 3/4" plywood	"	1000	.064		2.82	4.18		7	9.50
0300	Separation barrier, 2" x 4" @ 16", 1/2" plywood ea. side, 8' high	2 Carp	400	.040		4.99	2.34		7.33	9
0310	12' high		320	.050		4.85	2.93		7.78	9.70
0320	16' high		200	.080		4.78	4.69		9.47	12.25
0400	Personnel decontam. chamber, 2" x 4" @ 16", 3/4" ply ea. side		280	.057		5.95	3.35		9.30	11.55
0450	Waste decontam. chamber, 2" x 4" studs @ 16", 3/4" ply ea. side		360	.044		5.95	2.60		8.55	10.45
0500	Cover surfaces with polyethylene sheeting									
0501	Including glue and tape									
0550	Floors, each layer, 6 mil	A-9	8000	.008	S.F.	.07	.52		.59	.88
0551	4 mil		9000	.007		.06	.46		.52	.77
0560	Walls, each layer, 6 mil		6000	.011		.07	.70		.77	1.15
0561	4 mil		7000	.009		.06	.60		.66	.97
0570	For heights above 14', add						20%			
0575	For heights above 20', add						30%			
0580	For fire retardant poly, add					100%				
0590	For large open areas, deduct					10%	20%			
0600	Seal floor penetrations with foam firestop to 36 sq. in.	2 Carp	200	.080	Ea.	20.50	4.69		25.19	29.50
0610	36 sq. in. to 72 sq. in.		125	.128		41	7.50		48.50	56
0615	72 sq. in. to 144 sq. in.		80	.200		82	11.70		93.70	107
0620	Wall penetrations, to 36 sq. in.		180	.089		20.50	5.20		25.70	30.50
0630	36 sq. in. to 72 sq. in.		100	.160		41	9.40		50.40	59
0640	72 sq. in. to 144 sq. in.		60	.267		82	15.65		97.65	114
0800	Caulk seams with latex	1 Carp	230	.035	L.F.	.21	2.04		2.25	3.26
0900	Set up neg. air machine, 1-2k CFM/25 M.C.F. volume	1 Asbe	4.30	1.860	Ea.		121		121	186
0950	Set up and remove portable shower unit	2 Asbe	4	4	"		261		261	400

02 82 13.43 Bulk Asbestos Removal

		Crew	Daily Output	Labor-Hours	Unit	Material	Labor	Equipment	Total	Total Incl O&P
0010	**BULK ASBESTOS REMOVAL**									
0020	Includes disposable tools and 2 suits and 1 respirator filter/day/worker									
0200	Boiler insulation	A-9	480	.133	S.F.	.75	8.70		9.45	14.15
0210	With metal lath, add				%				50%	50%
0300	Boiler breeching or flue insulation	A-9	520	.123	S.F.	.55	8.05		8.60	12.90
0310	For active boiler, add				%				100%	100%
0400	Duct or AHU insulation	A-10B	440	.073	S.F.	.32	4.75		5.07	7.60
0500	Duct vibration isolation joints, up to 24 sq. in. duct	A-9	56	1.143	Ea.	5.10	74.50		79.60	120
0520	25 sq. in. to 48 sq. in. duct		48	1.333		5.95	87		92.95	140
0530	49 sq. in. to 76 sq. in. duct		40	1.600		7.15	105		112.15	168
0600	Pipe insulation, air cell type, up to 4" diameter pipe		900	.071	L.F.	.32	4.64		4.96	7.45
0610	4" to 8" diameter pipe		800	.080		.36	5.20		5.56	8.40
0620	10" to 12" diameter pipe		700	.091		.41	5.95		6.36	9.60
0630	14" to 16" diameter pipe		550	.116		.52	7.60		8.12	12.15
0650	Over 16" diameter pipe		650	.098	S.F.	.44	6.45		6.89	10.35
0700	With glove bag up to 3" diameter pipe		200	.320	L.F.	.79	21		21.79	33
1000	Pipe fitting insulation up to 4" diameter pipe		320	.200	Ea.	.89	13.05		13.94	21
1100	6" to 8" diameter pipe		304	.211		.94	13.75		14.69	22
1110	10" to 12" diameter pipe		192	.333		1.49	22		23.49	35
1120	14" to 16" diameter pipe		128	.500		2.23	32.50		34.73	52.50

02 82 Asbestos Remediation

02 82 13 – Asbestos Abatement

02 82 13.43 Bulk Asbestos Removal		Crew	Daily Output	Labor-Hours	Unit	Material	2023 Bare Costs Labor	2023 Bare Costs Equipment	Total	Total Incl O&P
1130	Over 16" diameter pipe	A-9	176	.364	S.F.	1.62	24		25.62	38.50
1200	With glove bag, up to 8" diameter pipe		75	.853	L.F.	9.15	55.50		64.65	95.50
2000	Scrape foam fireproofing from flat surface		2400	.027	S.F.	.12	1.74		1.86	2.79
2100	Irregular surfaces		1200	.053		.24	3.48		3.72	5.60
3000	Remove cementitious material from flat surface		1800	.036		.16	2.32		2.48	3.72
3100	Irregular surface		1000	.064		.20	4.18		4.38	6.60
6000	Remove contaminated soil from crawl space by hand		400	.160	C.F.	.71	10.45		11.16	16.80
6100	With large production vacuum loader	A-12	700	.091	"	.41	5.95	1.17	7.53	10.90
7000	Radiator backing, not including radiator removal	A-9	1200	.053	S.F.	.24	3.48		3.72	5.60
9000	For type B (supplied air) respirator equipment, add				%				10%	10%

02 82 13.44 Demolition In Asbestos Contaminated Area		Crew	Daily Output	Labor-Hours	Unit	Material	Labor	Equipment	Total	Total Incl O&P
0010	**DEMOLITION IN ASBESTOS CONTAMINATED AREA**									
0200	Ceiling, including suspension system, plaster and lath	A-9	2100	.030	S.F.	.14	1.99		2.13	3.19
0210	Finished plaster, leaving wire lath		585	.109		.49	7.15		7.64	11.50
0220	Suspended acoustical tile		3500	.018		.08	1.19		1.27	1.92
0230	Concealed tile grid system		3000	.021		.10	1.39		1.49	2.23
0240	Metal pan grid system		1500	.043		.19	2.79		2.98	4.47
0250	Gypsum board		2500	.026		.11	1.67		1.78	2.69
0260	Lighting fixtures up to 2' x 4'		72	.889	Ea.	3.97	58		61.97	93.50
0400	Partitions, non load bearing									
0410	Plaster, lath, and studs	A-9	690	.093	S.F.	.91	6.05		6.96	10.25
0450	Gypsum board and studs	"	1390	.046	"	.21	3.01		3.22	4.83
9000	For type B (supplied air) respirator equipment, add				%				10%	10%

02 82 13.45 OSHA Testing		Crew	Daily Output	Labor-Hours	Unit	Material	Labor	Equipment	Total	Total Incl O&P
0010	**OSHA TESTING**									
0100	Certified technician, minimum				Day		340		340	340
0110	Maximum						670		670	670
0121	Industrial hygienist, minimum						385		385	385
0130	Maximum						755		755	755
0200	Asbestos sampling and PCM analysis, NIOSH 7400, minimum	1 Asbe	8	1	Ea.	20.50	65.50		86	123
0210	Maximum		4	2		27.50	131		158.50	230
1000	Cleaned area samples		8	1		20.50	65.50		86	123
1100	PCM air sample analysis, NIOSH 7400, minimum		8	1		20.50	65.50		86	123
1110	Maximum		4	2		27.50	131		158.50	230
1200	TEM air sample analysis, NIOSH 7402, minimum								80	106
1210	Maximum								360	450

02 82 13.46 Decontamination of Asbestos Containment Area		Crew	Daily Output	Labor-Hours	Unit	Material	Labor	Equipment	Total	Total Incl O&P
0010	**DECONTAMINATION OF ASBESTOS CONTAINMENT AREA**									
0100	Spray exposed substrate with surfactant (bridging)									
0200	Flat surfaces	A-9	6000	.011	S.F.	.45	.70		1.15	1.57
0250	Irregular surfaces		4000	.016	"	.50	1.04		1.54	2.15
0300	Pipes, beams, and columns		2000	.032	L.F.	.50	2.09		2.59	3.75
1000	Spray encapsulate polyethylene sheeting		8000	.008	S.F.	.50	.52		1.02	1.35
1100	Roll down polyethylene sheeting		8000	.008	"		.52		.52	.80
1500	Bag polyethylene sheeting		400	.160	Ea.	1.42	10.45		11.87	17.55
2000	Fine clean exposed substrate, with nylon brush		2400	.027	S.F.		1.74		1.74	2.66
2500	Wet wipe substrate		4800	.013			.87		.87	1.33
2600	Vacuum surfaces, fine brush		6400	.010			.65		.65	1
3000	Structural demolition									
3100	Wood stud walls	A-9	2800	.023	S.F.		1.49		1.49	2.28
3500	Window manifolds, not incl. window replacement		4200	.015			1		1	1.52
3600	Plywood carpet protection		2000	.032			2.09		2.09	3.20

02 82 Asbestos Remediation

02 82 13 – Asbestos Abatement

02 82 13.46 Decontamination of Asbestos Containment Area

		Crew	Daily Output	Labor-Hours	Unit	Material	2023 Bare Costs Labor	Equipment	Total	Total Incl O&P
4000	Remove custom decontamination facility	A-10A	8	3	Ea.	18.55	196		214.55	320
4100	Remove portable decontamination facility	3 Asbe	12	2	"	17.05	131		148.05	219
5000	HEPA vacuum, shampoo carpeting	A-9	4800	.013	S.F.	.14	.87		1.01	1.48
9000	Final cleaning of protected surfaces	A-10A	8000	.003	"		.20		.20	.30

02 82 13.47 Asbestos Waste Pkg., Handling, and Disp.

		Crew	Daily Output	Labor-Hours	Unit	Material	Labor	Equipment	Total	Total Incl O&P
0010	**ASBESTOS WASTE PACKAGING, HANDLING, AND DISPOSAL**									
0100	Collect and bag bulk material, 3 C.F. bags, by hand	A-9	400	.160	Ea.	1.20	10.45		11.65	17.30
0200	Large production vacuum loader	A-12	880	.073		1.75	4.75	.93	7.43	10.20
1000	Double bag and decontaminate	A-9	960	.067		1.20	4.35		5.55	7.95
2000	Containerize bagged material in drums, per 55gal drum	"	800	.080		29	5.20		34.20	39.50
3000	Cart bags 50' to dumpster	2 Asbe	400	.040	↓		2.61		2.61	3.99
5000	Disposal charges, not including haul, minimum				C.Y.				61	67
5020	Maximum				"				355	395
9000	For type B (supplied air) respirator equipment, add				%				10%	10%

02 82 13.48 Asbestos Encapsulation With Sealants

		Crew	Daily Output	Labor-Hours	Unit	Material	Labor	Equipment	Total	Total Incl O&P
0010	**ASBESTOS ENCAPSULATION WITH SEALANTS**									
0100	Ceilings and walls, minimum	A-9	21000	.003	S.F.	.61	.20		.81	.97
0110	Maximum		10600	.006	"	.66	.39		1.05	1.33
0300	Pipes to 12" diameter including minor repairs, minimum		800	.080	L.F.	.74	5.20		5.94	8.80
0310	Maximum	↓	400	.160	"	1.44	10.45		11.89	17.60

02 87 Biohazard Remediation

02 87 13 – Mold Remediation

02 87 13.16 Mold Remediation Preparation and Containment

		Crew	Daily Output	Labor-Hours	Unit	Material	Labor	Equipment	Total	Total Incl O&P
0010	**MOLD REMEDIATION PREPARATION AND CONTAINMENT**									
6010	Preparation of mold containment area									
6100	Pre-cleaning, HEPA vacuum and wet wipe, flat surfaces	A-9	12000	.005	S.F.	.02	.35		.37	.56
6300	Separation barrier, 2" x 4" @ 16", 1/2" plywood ea. side, 8' high	2 Carp	333	.048		5.80	2.82		8.62	10.60
6310	12' high		320	.050		6.55	2.93		9.48	11.55
6320	16' high		200	.080		2.69	4.69		7.38	9.95
6400	Personnel decontam. chamber, 2" x 4" @ 16", 3/4" ply ea. side		280	.057		5.45	3.35		8.80	11
6450	Waste decontam. chamber, 2" x 4" studs @ 16", 3/4" ply each side	↓	360	.044	↓	22	2.60		24.60	28
6500	Cover surfaces with polyethylene sheeting									
6501	Including glue and tape									
6550	Floors, each layer, 6 mil	A-9	8000	.008	S.F.	.07	.52		.59	.88
6551	4 mil		9000	.007		.06	.46		.52	.77
6560	Walls, each layer, 6 mil		6000	.011		.07	.70		.77	1.15
6561	4 mil	↓	7000	.009	↓	.06	.60		.66	.97
6570	For heights above 14', add						20%			
6575	For heights above 20', add						30%			
6580	For fire retardant poly, add					100%				
6590	For large open areas, deduct					10%	20%			
6600	Seal floor penetrations with foam firestop to 36 sq. in.	2 Carp	200	.080	Ea.	20.50	4.69		25.19	29.50
6610	36 sq. in. to 72 sq. in.		125	.128		41	7.50		48.50	56
6615	72 sq. in. to 144 sq. in.		80	.200		82	11.70		93.70	107
6620	Wall penetrations, to 36 sq. in.		180	.089		20.50	5.20		25.70	30.50
6630	36 sq. in. to 72 sq. in.		100	.160		41	9.40		50.40	59
6640	72 sq. in. to 144 sq. in.	↓	60	.267		82	15.65		97.65	114
6800	Caulk seams with latex caulk	1 Carp	230	.035	L.F.	.21	2.04		2.25	3.26
6900	Set up neg. air machine, 1-2k CFM/25 M.C.F. volume	1 Asbe	4.30	1.860	Ea.		121		121	186

02 87 Biohazard Remediation

02 87 13 – Mold Remediation

02 87 13.33 Removal and Disposal of Materials With Mold

		Crew	Daily Output	Labor-Hours	Unit	Material	2023 Bare Costs Labor	2023 Bare Costs Equipment	Total	Total Incl O&P
0010	**REMOVAL AND DISPOSAL OF MATERIALS WITH MOLD**									
0015	Demolition in mold contaminated area									
0200	Ceiling, including suspension system, plaster and lath	A-9	2100	.030	S.F.	.14	1.99		2.13	3.19
0210	Finished plaster, leaving wire lath		585	.109		.49	7.15		7.64	11.50
0220	Suspended acoustical tile		3500	.018		.08	1.19		1.27	1.92
0230	Concealed tile grid system		3000	.021		.10	1.39		1.49	2.23
0240	Metal pan grid system		1500	.043		.19	2.79		2.98	4.47
0250	Gypsum board		2500	.026		.11	1.67		1.78	2.69
0255	Plywood		2500	.026		.11	1.67		1.78	2.69
0260	Lighting fixtures up to 2' x 4'		72	.889	Ea.	3.97	58		61.97	93.50
0400	Partitions, non load bearing									
0410	Plaster, lath, and studs	A-9	690	.093	S.F.	.91	6.05		6.96	10.25
0450	Gypsum board and studs		1390	.046		.21	3.01		3.22	4.83
0465	Carpet & pad		1390	.046		.21	3.01		3.22	4.83
0600	Pipe insulation, air cell type, up to 4" diameter pipe		900	.071	L.F.	.32	4.64		4.96	7.45
0610	4" to 8" diameter pipe		800	.080		.36	5.20		5.56	8.40
0620	10" to 12" diameter pipe		700	.091		.41	5.95		6.36	9.60
0630	14" to 16" diameter pipe		550	.116		.52	7.60		8.12	12.15
0650	Over 16" diameter pipe		650	.098	S.F.	.44	6.45		6.89	10.35
9000	For type B (supplied air) respirator equipment, add				%				10%	10%

02 87 19 – Bio-Hazard and Infectious Disease Control Remediation

02 87 19.10 Temporary Barriers, Including Ppe

		Crew	Daily Output	Labor-Hours	Unit	Material	2023 Bare Costs Labor	2023 Bare Costs Equipment	Total	Total Incl O&P
0010	**TEMPORARY BARRIERS, including PPE**									
0100	Infectious control partition, adjustable to 10' high, obscured, 4' panel	2 Carp	75	.213	Ea.	595	12.50		607.50	675
0110	3' panel		75	.213		565	12.50		577.50	640
0120	2' panel		75	.213		440	12.50		452.50	505
0130	1' panel	1 Carp	75	.107		293	6.25		299.25	330
0140	6" panel	"	75	.107		271	6.25		277.25	305
0150	2' panel with HEPA filtered discharge port	2 Carp	75	.213		515	12.50		527.50	585
0160	3' panel with 32" door		75	.213		920	12.50		932.50	1,050
0170	4' panel with 36" door		75	.213		1,025	12.50		1,037.50	1,150
0180	4'-6" panel with 44" door		75	.213		1,225	12.50		1,237.50	1,375
0190	Hinged corner		68	.235		189	13.80		202.80	229
0200	Outside corner		68	.235		157	13.80		170.80	194
0210	T post		68	.235		167	13.80		180.80	205
0220	Accessories, ceiling grid clip		300	.053		7.60	3.13		10.73	13
0230	Panel locking clip		300	.053		5.35	3.13		8.48	10.55
0240	Panel joint closure strip		300	.053		8.60	3.13		11.73	14.15
0250	Screw jack		300	.053		7.50	3.13		10.63	12.90
0260	Digital pressure difference gauge					290			290	320
0280	Combination lockset	1 Carp	11	.727		209	42.50		251.50	294
0285	Sealant tape, 2" wide	1 Clab	165	.048	C.L.F.	13.80	2.29		16.09	18.55
0290	System in place, including door and accessories									
0300	Based upon 25 uses	2 Carp	43	.372	L.F.	12.40	22		34.40	46
0310	Based upon 50 uses		43	.372		7.35	22		29.35	40.50
0330	Based upon 100 uses		43	.372		4.85	22		26.85	38
0400	Separation barrier, 2" x 4" @ 16" O.C., 1/2" plywood each side, 8' high		340	.047	S.F.	5.30	2.76		8.06	9.90
0410	12' high		275	.058		5.20	3.41		8.61	10.85
0420	16' high		170	.094		5.35	5.50		10.85	14.10
0430	5/8" FR GWB each side, 8' high		290	.055		3.51	3.23		6.74	8.65
0440	12' high		235	.068		3.37	3.99		7.36	9.65
0450	16' high		144	.111		3.30	6.50		9.80	13.35

02 87 Biohazard Remediation

02 87 19 – Bio-Hazard and Infectious Disease Control Remediation

02 87 19.20 Temporary Protection, Including Ppe

		Crew	Daily Output	Labor-Hours	Unit	Material	2023 Bare Costs Labor	Equipment	Total	Total Incl O&P
0010	**TEMPORARY PROTECTION, including PPE**									
0100	Infectious control protection, 6 mil plastic sheeting, applied to floors	1 Skwk	1900	.004	S.F.	.07	.26		.33	.47
0110	Applied to walls		1400	.006		.07	.35		.42	.61
0120	Applied to ceilings		1000	.008		.07	.49		.56	.82
0130	Sealant tape, 2" wide	1 Clab	165	.048	C.L.F.	13.80	2.29		16.09	18.55
0140	Floor covering, 1/8" tempered hardboard	2 Carp	878	.018	S.F.	.73	1.07		1.80	2.39
0150	1/2" CDX		878	.018		1.42	1.07		2.49	3.15
0160	3/4" CDX		755	.021		1.98	1.24		3.22	4.02

02 87 19.30 Infectious Control Equipment and Supplies

		Crew	Daily Output	Labor-Hours	Unit	Material	Labor	Equipment	Total	Total Incl O&P
0010	**INFECTIOUS CONTROL EQUIPMENT AND SUPPLIES**									
0100	Entry/exit decontamination chamber, portable, 10 uses	A-10C	12	2	Ea.	259	131	30	420	520
0105	Negative air machine, 1800 CFM					990			990	1,100
0110	Disposable polyethylene bags, 6 mil, 3 C.F.					1.20			1.20	1.32
0130	Paper towels, carton of 12, 350' rolls					77			77	85
0140	Heavy duty wipes, 160 per box					38.50			38.50	42
0200	Tent, including frame, weights, roof, walls, 5' x 5'	2 Skwk	32	.500		2,150	30.50		2,180.50	2,425
0205	5' x 10'		24	.667		2,500	41		2,541	2,800
0210	10' x 10'		24	.667		3,125	41		3,166	3,475
0220	13' x 26'		12	1.333		7,475	81.50		7,556.50	8,350
0230	13' x 26', flat roof infirmary		12	1.333		7,600	81.50		7,681.50	8,475
0240	13' x 26', drive through screening		12	1.333		8,800	81.50		8,881.50	9,800
0242	LED light kit for tents, 15 watt	1 Elec	48	.167		199	11.25		210.25	236
0244	Halogen heating kit, 1500 watt	"	48	.167		500	11.25		511.25	565
0250	Medical partition system, including frame, drapes, 5' x 5'	2 Skwk	48	.333		1,300	20.50		1,320.50	1,450

02 87 19.40 Infectious Control Cleaning, Includes Ppe

		Crew	Daily Output	Labor-Hours	Unit	Material	Labor	Equipment	Total	Total Incl O&P
0010	**INFECTIOUS CONTROL CLEANING, Includes PPE**									
0100	Infectious control cleaning, including PPE and antimicrobial spray, floors	1 Skwk	3600	.002	S.F.	.06	.14		.20	.27
0110	Walls		3000	.003		.06	.16		.22	.32
0120	Ceilings		2700	.003		.07	.18		.25	.34
0130	Countertops		3300	.002		.06	.15		.21	.29
0140	Other surfaces		2600	.003		.07	.19		.26	.35
0150	Plumbing fixtures		14	.571	Ea.	4.07	35		39.07	57
0160	Bathroom accessories		30	.267		1.87	16.35		18.22	26.50
0170	Kitchen appliance		9	.889		7	54.50		61.50	89.50
0180	Electrical switches and receptacles		140	.057		.41	3.50		3.91	5.70
0190	Work station		9	.889		7.50	54.50		62	90.50
0200	Door and window hardware		88	.091		.62	5.55		6.17	9.05
0250	Supply / return ductwork, up to 2 S.F. cross section		240	.033	L.F.	.50	2.04		2.54	3.62
0260	2 to 4 S.F. cross section		192	.042		.74	2.55		3.29	4.65
0270	4 to 8 S.F. cross section		144	.056		.92	3.40		4.32	6.10
0280	8 SF cross section		102	.078		1.40	4.80		6.20	8.75
0300	Duct coil		5	1.600	Ea.	11.95	98		109.95	160
0310	Duct damper and vane set		77	.104		1.61	6.35		7.96	11.30
0320	Fan coil unit or VAV box		8	1		7.25	61.50		68.75	100
0330	Air handling unit and coil		2	4		29	245		274	400
0340	Grill / diffuser or register		32	.250		2.14	15.30		17.44	25.50

Division 3 — Concrete

Estimating Tips

General

- Carefully check all the plans and specifications. Concrete often appears on drawings other than structural drawings, including mechanical and electrical drawings for equipment pads. The cost of cutting and patching is often difficult to estimate. See Subdivision 03 81 for Concrete Cutting, Subdivision 02 41 19.16 for Cutout Demolition, Subdivision 03 05 05.10 for Concrete Demolition, and Subdivision 02 41 19.19 for Rubbish Handling (handling, loading, and hauling of debris).
- Always obtain concrete prices from suppliers near the job site. A volume discount can often be negotiated, depending upon competition in the area. Remember to add for waste, particularly for slabs and footings on grade.

03 10 00 Concrete Forming and Accessories

- A primary cost for concrete construction is forming. Most jobs today are constructed with prefabricated forms. The selection of the forms best suited for the job and the total square feet of forms required for efficient concrete forming and placing are key elements in estimating concrete construction. Enough forms must be available for erection to make efficient use of the concrete placing equipment and crew.
- Concrete accessories for forming and placing depend upon the systems used. Study the plans and specifications to ensure that all special accessory requirements have been included in the cost estimate, such as anchor bolts, inserts, and hangers.
- Included within costs for forms-in-place are all necessary bracing and shoring.

03 20 00 Concrete Reinforcing

- Ascertain that the reinforcing steel supplier has included all accessories, cutting, bending, and an allowance for lapping, splicing, and waste. A good rule of thumb is 10% for lapping, splicing, and waste. Also, 10% waste should be allowed for welded wire fabric.
- The unit price items in the subdivisions for Reinforcing In Place, Glass Fiber Reinforcing, and Welded Wire Fabric include the labor to install accessories such as beam and slab bolsters, high chairs, and bar ties and tie wire. The material cost for these accessories is not included; they may be obtained from the Accessories Subdivisions.

03 30 00 Cast-In-Place Concrete

- When estimating structural concrete, pay particular attention to requirements for concrete additives, curing methods, and surface treatments. Special consideration for climate, hot or cold, must be included in your estimate. Be sure to include requirements for concrete placing equipment and concrete finishing.
- For accurate concrete estimating, the estimator must consider each of the following major components individually: forms, reinforcing steel, ready-mix concrete, placement of the concrete, and finishing of the top surface. For faster estimating, Subdivision 03 30 53.40 for Concrete-In-Place can be used; here, various items of concrete work are presented that include the costs of all five major components (unless specifically stated otherwise).

03 40 00 Precast Concrete
03 50 00 Cast Decks and Underlayment

- The cost of hauling precast concrete structural members is often an important factor. For this reason, it is important to get a quote from the nearest supplier. It may become economically feasible to set up precasting beds on the site if the hauling costs are prohibitive.

Reference Numbers

Reference numbers are shown at the beginning of some major classifications. These numbers refer to related items in the Reference Section. The reference information may be an estimating procedure, an alternate pricing method, or technical information.

Note: Not all subdivisions listed here necessarily appear. ∎

Same Data. Simplified.

Enjoy the convenience and efficiency of accessing your costs anywhere:

- **Skip the multiplier** by setting your location
- **Quickly search,** edit, favorite and share costs
- **Stay on top of price changes** with automatic updates

Discover more at rsmeans.com/online

No part of this cost data may be reproduced, stored in a retrieval system, or transmitted in any form or by any means without prior written permission of Gordian.

03 11 Concrete Forming

03 11 13 – Structural Cast-In-Place Concrete Forming

03 11 13.40 Forms In Place, Equipment Foundations

		Crew	Daily Output	Labor-Hours	Unit	Material	2023 Bare Costs Labor	Equipment	Total	Total Incl O&P
0010	**FORMS IN PLACE, EQUIPMENT FOUNDATIONS**									
0020	1 use	C-2	160	.300	SFCA	8.05	17.10		25.15	34.50
0050	2 use		190	.253		4.43	14.40		18.83	26.50
0100	3 use		200	.240		3.22	13.70		16.92	24
0150	4 use		205	.234		2.63	13.35		15.98	23

03 11 13.45 Forms In Place, Footings

		Crew	Daily Output	Labor-Hours	Unit	Material	Labor	Equipment	Total	Total Incl O&P
0010	**FORMS IN PLACE, FOOTINGS**									
0020	Continuous wall, plywood, 1 use	C-1	375	.085	SFCA	14.35	4.76		19.11	23
0050	2 use		440	.073		7.90	4.06		11.96	14.75
0100	3 use		470	.068		5.75	3.80		9.55	11.95
0150	4 use		485	.066		4.67	3.68		8.35	10.65
5000	Spread footings, job-built lumber, 1 use		305	.105		5.85	5.85		11.70	15.15
5050	2 use		371	.086		3.24	4.81		8.05	10.70
5100	3 use		401	.080		2.34	4.45		6.79	9.20
5150	4 use		414	.077		1.90	4.31		6.21	8.50

03 11 13.65 Forms In Place, Slab On Grade

		Crew	Daily Output	Labor-Hours	Unit	Material	Labor	Equipment	Total	Total Incl O&P
0010	**FORMS IN PLACE, SLAB ON GRADE**									
3000	Edge forms, wood, 4 use, on grade, to 6" high	C-1	600	.053	L.F.	.83	2.97		3.80	5.35
6000	Trench forms in floor, wood, 1 use		160	.200	SFCA	5.40	11.15		16.55	22.50
6050	2 use		175	.183		2.96	10.20		13.16	18.45
6100	3 use		180	.178		2.15	9.90		12.05	17.10
6150	4 use		185	.173		1.75	9.65		11.40	16.25

03 15 Concrete Accessories

03 15 05 – Concrete Forming Accessories

03 15 05.75 Sleeves and Chases

			Crew	Daily Output	Labor-Hours	Unit	Material	Labor	Equipment	Total	Total Incl O&P
0010	**SLEEVES AND CHASES**										
0100	Plastic, 1 use, 12" long, 2" diameter		1 Carp	100	.080	Ea.	3.41	4.69		8.10	10.75
0150	4" diameter			90	.089		.91	5.20		6.11	8.75
0200	6" diameter			75	.107		17.45	6.25		23.70	28.50
0250	12" diameter			60	.133		50.50	7.80		58.30	67.50
5000	Sheet metal, 2" diameter	G		100	.080		3.30	4.69		7.99	10.65
5100	4" diameter	G		90	.089		4.12	5.20		9.32	12.30
5150	6" diameter	G		75	.107		5.20	6.25		11.45	15
5200	12" diameter	G		60	.133		9.80	7.80		17.60	22.50
6000	Steel pipe, 2" diameter	G		100	.080		17.45	4.69		22.14	26
6100	4" diameter	G		90	.089		49	5.20		54.20	62
6150	6" diameter	G		75	.107		90	6.25		96.25	108
6200	12" diameter	G		60	.133		136	7.80		143.80	162

03 15 16 – Concrete Construction Joints

03 15 16.20 Control Joints, Saw Cut

		Crew	Daily Output	Labor-Hours	Unit	Material	Labor	Equipment	Total	Total Incl O&P
0010	**CONTROL JOINTS, SAW CUT**									
0100	Sawcut control joints in green concrete									
0120	1" depth	C-27	2000	.008	L.F.	.03	.44	.09	.56	.77
0140	1-1/2" depth		1800	.009		.04	.49	.10	.63	.88
0160	2" depth		1600	.010		.06	.55	.11	.72	.98
0180	Sawcut joint reservoir in cured concrete									
0182	3/8" wide x 3/4" deep, with single saw blade	C-27	1000	.016	L.F.	.04	.88	.18	1.10	1.53
0184	1/2" wide x 1" deep, with double saw blades		900	.018		.08	.98	.20	1.26	1.74
0186	3/4" wide x 1-1/2" deep, with double saw blades		800	.020		.17	1.10	.22	1.49	2.04

03 15 Concrete Accessories

03 15 16 – Concrete Construction Joints

03 15 16.20 Control Joints, Saw Cut		Crew	Daily Output	Labor-Hours	Unit	Material	2023 Bare Costs Labor	Equipment	Total	Total Incl O&P
0190	Water blast joint to wash away laitance, 2 passes	C-29	2500	.003	L.F.		.15	.04	.19	.28
0200	Air blast joint to blow out debris and air dry, 2 passes	C-28	2000	.004	↓		.22	.02	.24	.34
0300	For backer rod, see Section 07 91 23.10									
0342	For joint sealant, see Section 07 92 13.20									

03 15 19 – Cast-In Concrete Anchors

03 15 19.10 Anchor Bolts

	03 15 19.10 Anchor Bolts		Crew	Daily Output	Labor-Hours	Unit	Material	Labor	Equipment	Total	Total Incl O&P
0010	**ANCHOR BOLTS**										
0015	Made from recycled materials										
0025	Single bolts installed in fresh concrete, no templates										
0030	Hooked w/nut and washer, 1/2" diameter, 8" long	G	1 Carp	132	.061	Ea.	2.23	3.55		5.78	7.75
0040	12" long	G		131	.061		2.48	3.58		6.06	8.10
0050	5/8" diameter, 8" long	G		129	.062		4.02	3.63		7.65	9.85
0060	12" long	G		127	.063		4.95	3.69		8.64	10.95
0070	3/4" diameter, 8" long	G		127	.063		4.95	3.69		8.64	10.95
0080	12" long	G	↓	125	.064	↓	6.20	3.75		9.95	12.40
0090	2-bolt pattern, including job-built 2-hole template, per set										
0100	J-type, incl. hex nut & washer, 1/2" diameter x 6" long	G	1 Carp	21	.381	Set	8	22.50		30.50	42
0110	12" long	G		21	.381		9	22.50		31.50	43
0120	18" long	G		21	.381		10.50	22.50		33	44.50
0130	3/4" diameter x 8" long	G		20	.400		13.95	23.50		37.45	50.50
0140	12" long	G		20	.400		16.40	23.50		39.90	53
0150	18" long	G		20	.400		20	23.50		43.50	57
0160	1" diameter x 12" long	G		19	.421		41	24.50		65.50	81.50
0170	18" long	G		19	.421		48.50	24.50		73	90
0180	24" long	G		19	.421		58	24.50		82.50	101
0190	36" long	G		18	.444		78	26		104	125
0200	1-1/2" diameter x 18" long	G		17	.471		54.50	27.50		82	101
0210	24" long	G		16	.500		64	29.50		93.50	114
0300	L-type, incl. hex nut & washer, 3/4" diameter x 12" long	G		20	.400		19.05	23.50		42.55	56
0310	18" long	G		20	.400		23.50	23.50		47	60.50
0320	24" long	G		20	.400		27.50	23.50		51	65
0330	30" long	G		20	.400		34	23.50		57.50	72
0340	36" long	G		20	.400		38	23.50		61.50	77
0350	1" diameter x 12" long	G		19	.421		31.50	24.50		56	71
0360	18" long	G		19	.421		38	24.50		62.50	78.50
0370	24" long	G		19	.421		46	24.50		70.50	87
0380	30" long	G		19	.421		53.50	24.50		78	95.50
0390	36" long	G		18	.444		61	26		87	106
0400	42" long	G		18	.444		73	26		99	120
0410	48" long	G		18	.444		81.50	26		107.50	129
0420	1-1/4" diameter x 18" long	G		18	.444		57	26		83	102
0430	24" long	G		18	.444		67	26		93	113
0440	30" long	G		17	.471		77	27.50		104.50	126
0450	36" long	G	↓	17	.471		87	27.50		114.50	137
0460	42" long	G	2 Carp	32	.500		97.50	29.50		127	152
0470	48" long	G		32	.500		111	29.50		140.50	166
0480	54" long	G		31	.516		130	30.50		160.50	188
0490	60" long	G		31	.516		143	30.50		173.50	202
0500	1-1/2" diameter x 18" long	G		33	.485		82.50	28.50		111	134
0510	24" long	G		32	.500		95.50	29.50		125	149
0520	30" long	G		31	.516		108	30.50		138.50	163
0530	36" long	G	↓	30	.533	↓	123	31.50		154.50	182

03 15 Concrete Accessories

03 15 19 – Cast-In Concrete Anchors

03 15 19.10 Anchor Bolts			Crew	Daily Output	Labor-Hours	Unit	Material	2023 Bare Costs Labor	Equipment	Total	Total Incl O&P
0540	42" long	G	2 Carp	30	.533	Set	140	31.50		171.50	201
0550	48" long	G		29	.552		156	32.50		188.50	220
0560	54" long	G		28	.571		190	33.50		223.50	259
0570	60" long	G		28	.571		208	33.50		241.50	278
0580	1-3/4" diameter x 18" long	G		31	.516		113	30.50		143.50	170
0590	24" long	G		30	.533		132	31.50		163.50	193
0600	30" long	G		29	.552		153	32.50		185.50	217
0610	36" long	G		28	.571		175	33.50		208.50	242
0620	42" long	G		27	.593		196	34.50		230.50	267
0630	48" long	G		26	.615		215	36		251	290
0640	54" long	G		26	.615		265	36		301	345
0650	60" long	G		25	.640		286	37.50		323.50	370
0660	2" diameter x 24" long	G		27	.593		159	34.50		193.50	226
0670	30" long	G		27	.593		178	34.50		212.50	248
0680	36" long	G		26	.615		195	36		231	269
0690	42" long	G		25	.640		218	37.50		255.50	295
0700	48" long	G		24	.667		249	39		288	330
0710	54" long	G		23	.696		296	41		337	385
0720	60" long	G		23	.696		320	41		361	410
0730	66" long	G		22	.727		340	42.50		382.50	440
0740	72" long	G		21	.762		370	44.50		414.50	475
1000	4-bolt pattern, including job-built 4-hole template, per set										
1100	J-type, incl. hex nut & washer, 1/2" diameter x 6" long	G	1 Carp	19	.421	Set	11.95	24.50		36.45	49.50
1110	12" long	G		19	.421		13.95	24.50		38.45	52
1120	18" long	G		18	.444		16.95	26		42.95	57.50
1130	3/4" diameter x 8" long	G		17	.471		24	27.50		51.50	67
1140	12" long	G		17	.471		29	27.50		56.50	72.50
1150	18" long	G		17	.471		36	27.50		63.50	81
1160	1" diameter x 12" long	G		16	.500		77.50	29.50		107	129
1170	18" long	G		15	.533		93	31.50		124.50	149
1180	24" long	G		15	.533		112	31.50		143.50	171
1190	36" long	G		15	.533		152	31.50		183.50	215
1200	1-1/2" diameter x 18" long	G		13	.615		105	36		141	169
1210	24" long	G		12	.667		124	39		163	194
1300	L-type, incl. hex nut & washer, 3/4" diameter x 12" long	G		17	.471		34	27.50		61.50	78.50
1310	18" long	G		17	.471		42.50	27.50		70	87.50
1320	24" long	G		17	.471		51	27.50		78.50	97
1330	30" long	G		16	.500		63.50	29.50		93	114
1340	36" long	G		16	.500		72	29.50		101.50	123
1350	1" diameter x 12" long	G		16	.500		58.50	29.50		88	108
1360	18" long	G		15	.533		72	31.50		103.50	126
1370	24" long	G		15	.533		88	31.50		119.50	144
1380	30" long	G		15	.533		103	31.50		134.50	161
1390	36" long	G		15	.533		118	31.50		149.50	176
1400	42" long	G		14	.571		142	33.50		175.50	206
1410	48" long	G		14	.571		159	33.50		192.50	225
1420	1-1/4" diameter x 18" long	G		14	.571		110	33.50		143.50	171
1430	24" long	G		14	.571		130	33.50		163.50	193
1440	30" long	G		13	.615		150	36		186	219
1450	36" long	G		13	.615		170	36		206	241
1460	42" long	G	2 Carp	25	.640		191	37.50		228.50	267
1470	48" long	G		24	.667		218	39		257	298
1480	54" long	G		23	.696		256	41		297	345

03 15 Concrete Accessories

03 15 19 – Cast-In Concrete Anchors

03 15 19.10 Anchor Bolts

			Crew	Daily Output	Labor-Hours	Unit	Material	2023 Bare Costs Labor	Equipment	Total	Total Incl O&P
1490	60" long	G	2 Carp	23	.696	Set	281	41		322	370
1500	1-1/2" diameter x 18" long	G		25	.640		161	37.50		198.50	233
1510	24" long	G		24	.667		187	39		226	264
1520	30" long	G		23	.696		211	41		252	293
1530	36" long	G		22	.727		242	42.50		284.50	330
1540	42" long	G		22	.727		275	42.50		317.50	370
1550	48" long	G		21	.762		310	44.50		354.50	405
1560	54" long	G		20	.800		375	47		422	485
1570	60" long	G		20	.800		410	47		457	520
1580	1-3/4" diameter x 18" long	G		22	.727		223	42.50		265.50	310
1590	24" long	G		21	.762		261	44.50		305.50	355
1600	30" long	G		21	.762		305	44.50		349.50	400
1610	36" long	G		20	.800		345	47		392	450
1620	42" long	G		19	.842		385	49.50		434.50	500
1630	48" long	G		18	.889		425	52		477	550
1640	54" long	G		18	.889		525	52		577	660
1650	60" long	G		17	.941		570	55		625	705
1660	2" diameter x 24" long	G		19	.842		315	49.50		364.50	420
1670	30" long	G		18	.889		350	52		402	470
1680	36" long	G		18	.889		385	52		437	505
1690	42" long	G		17	.941		430	55		485	555
1700	48" long	G		16	1		495	58.50		553.50	635
1710	54" long	G		15	1.067		590	62.50		652.50	740
1720	60" long	G		15	1.067		630	62.50		692.50	790
1730	66" long	G		14	1.143		675	67		742	845
1740	72" long	G		14	1.143		740	67		807	915
1990	For galvanized, add					Ea.	75%				

03 15 19.45 Machinery Anchors

			Crew	Daily Output	Labor-Hours	Unit	Material	Labor	Equipment	Total	Total Incl O&P
0010	**MACHINERY ANCHORS**, heavy duty, incl. sleeve, floating base nut,										
0020	lower stud & coupling nut, fiber plug, connecting stud, washer & nut.										
0030	For flush mounted embedment in poured concrete heavy equip. pads.										
0200	Stud & bolt, 1/2" diameter	G	E-16	40	.400	Ea.	89	26	3.68	118.68	142
0300	5/8" diameter	G		35	.457		104	30	4.20	138.20	165
0500	3/4" diameter	G		30	.533		126	35	4.90	165.90	197
0600	7/8" diameter	G		25	.640		141	42	5.90	188.90	226
0800	1" diameter	G		20	.800		154	52.50	7.35	213.85	258
0900	1-1/4" diameter	G		15	1.067		204	70	9.80	283.80	345

03 21 Reinforcement Bars

03 21 11 – Plain Steel Reinforcement Bars

03 21 11.60 Reinforcing In Place

			Crew	Daily Output	Labor-Hours	Unit	Material	Labor	Equipment	Total	Total Incl O&P
0010	**REINFORCING IN PLACE**, 50-60 ton lots, A615 Grade 60										
0020	Includes labor, but not material cost, to install accessories										
0030	Made from recycled materials										
0502	Footings, #4 to #7	G	4 Rodm	4200	.008	Lb.	.71	.49		1.20	1.51
0552	#8 to #18	G		7200	.004		.71	.29		1	1.21
0602	Slab on grade, #3 to #7	G		4200	.008		.71	.49		1.20	1.51
0900	For other than 50-60 ton lots										
1000	Under 10 ton job, #3 to #7, add						25%	10%			
1010	#8 to #18, add						20%	10%			
1050	10-50 ton job, #3 to #7, add						10%				

For customer support on your Plumbing Costs with RSMeans data, call 800.448.8182.

03 21 Reinforcement Bars

03 21 11 – Plain Steel Reinforcement Bars

03 21 11.60 Reinforcing In Place	Crew	Daily Output	Labor-Hours	Unit	Material	2023 Bare Costs Labor	Equipment	Total	Total Incl O&P
1060 #8 to #18, add					5%				
1100 60-100 ton job, #3 to #7, deduct					5%				
1110 #8 to #18, deduct					10%				
1150 Over 100 ton job, #3 to #7, deduct					10%				
1160 #8 to #18, deduct					15%				

03 22 Fabric and Grid Reinforcing

03 22 11 – Plain Welded Wire Fabric Reinforcing

03 22 11.10 Plain Welded Wire Fabric

		Crew	Daily Output	Labor-Hours	Unit	Material	Labor	Equipment	Total	Total Incl O&P
0010	**PLAIN WELDED WIRE FABRIC** ASTM A185									
0020	Includes labor, but not material cost, to install accessories									
0030	Made from recycled materials									
0050	Sheets									
0100	6 x 6 - W1.4 x W1.4 (10 x 10) 21 lb./C.S.F. G	2 Rodm	35	.457	C.S.F.	37.50	29.50		67	85.50

03 22 13 – Galvanized Welded Wire Fabric Reinforcing

03 22 13.10 Galvanized Welded Wire Fabric

		Unit	Material				Total Incl O&P
0010	**GALVANIZED WELDED WIRE FABRIC**						
0100	Add to plain welded wire pricing for galvanized welded wire	Lb.	.28			.28	.31

03 22 16 – Epoxy-Coated Welded Wire Fabric Reinforcing

03 22 16.10 Epoxy-Coated Welded Wire Fabric

		Unit	Material				Total Incl O&P
0010	**EPOXY-COATED WELDED WIRE FABRIC**						
0100	Add to plain welded wire pricing for epoxy-coated welded wire	Lb.	.56			.56	.61

03 30 Cast-In-Place Concrete

03 30 53 – Miscellaneous Cast-In-Place Concrete

03 30 53.40 Concrete In Place

		Crew	Daily Output	Labor-Hours	Unit	Material	Labor	Equipment	Total	Total Incl O&P
0010	**CONCRETE IN PLACE**									
0020	Including forms (4 uses), Grade 60 rebar, concrete (Portland cement									
0050	Type I), placement and finishing unless otherwise indicated									
3540	Equipment pad (3000 psi), 3' x 3' x 6" thick	C-14H	45	1.067	Ea.	83	61.50	.66	145.16	183
3550	4' x 4' x 6" thick		30	1.600		120	92	.99	212.99	270
3560	5' x 5' x 8" thick		18	2.667		216	153	1.65	370.65	470
3570	6' x 6' x 8" thick		14	3.429		284	197	2.13	483.13	610
3580	8' x 8' x 10" thick		8	6		590	345	3.72	938.72	1,175
3590	10' x 10' x 12" thick		5	9.600		980	550	5.95	1,535.95	1,900
3800	Footings (3000 psi), spread under 1 C.Y.	C-14C	28	4	C.Y.	257	224	1.08	482.08	620
3825	1 C.Y. to 5 C.Y.		43	2.605		330	146	.70	476.70	580
3850	Over 5 C.Y. R033053-60		75	1.493		315	84	.40	399.40	470
3900	Footings, strip (3000 psi), 18" x 9", unreinforced	C-14L	40	2.400		211	131	.74	342.74	430
3920	18" x 9", reinforced	C-14C	35	3.200		245	179	.86	424.86	540
3925	20" x 10", unreinforced	C-14L	45	2.133		202	117	.66	319.66	395
3930	20" x 10", reinforced	C-14C	40	2.800		229	157	.76	386.76	485
3935	24" x 12", unreinforced	C-14L	55	1.745		194	95.50	.54	290.04	355
3940	24" x 12", reinforced	C-14C	48	2.333		223	131	.63	354.63	440
3945	36" x 12", unreinforced	C-14L	70	1.371		184	75	.43	259.43	315
3950	36" x 12", reinforced	C-14C	60	1.867		210	105	.50	315.50	390
4000	Foundation mat (3000 psi), under 10 C.Y.	"	38.67	2.896		310	162	.78	472.78	585
4650	Slab on grade (3500 psi), not including finish, 4" thick	C-14E	60.75	1.449		204	83.50	.49	287.99	350

03 30 Cast-In-Place Concrete

03 30 53 – Miscellaneous Cast-In-Place Concrete

03 30 53.40 Concrete In Place

		Crew	Daily Output	Labor-Hours	Unit	Material	2023 Bare Costs Labor	Equipment	Total	Total Incl O&P
4700	6" thick	C-14E	92	.957	C.Y.	191	55	.33	246.33	292
4701	Thickened slab edge (3500 psi), for slab on grade poured									
4702	monolithically with slab; depth is in addition to slab thickness;									
4703	formed vertical outside edge, earthen bottom and inside slope									
4705	8" deep x 8" wide bottom, unreinforced	C-14L	2190	.044	L.F.	6.10	2.40	.01	8.51	10.25
4710	8" x 8", reinforced	C-14C	1670	.067		9.45	3.76	.02	13.23	16
4715	12" deep x 12" wide bottom, unreinforced	C-14L	1800	.053		11.80	2.92	.02	14.74	17.35
4720	12" x 12", reinforced	C-14C	1310	.086		17.95	4.80	.02	22.77	27
4725	16" deep x 16" wide bottom, unreinforced	C-14L	1440	.067		19.30	3.65	.02	22.97	26.50
4730	16" x 16", reinforced	C-14C	1120	.100		26.50	5.60	.03	32.13	38
4735	20" deep x 20" wide bottom, unreinforced	C-14L	1150	.083		28.50	4.56	.03	33.09	38.50
4740	20" x 20", reinforced	C-14C	920	.122		38	6.85	.03	44.88	52
4745	24" deep x 24" wide bottom, unreinforced	C-14L	930	.103		40	5.65	.03	45.68	52.50
4750	24" x 24", reinforced	C-14C	740	.151		52	8.50	.04	60.54	70

03 31 Structural Concrete

03 31 13 – Heavyweight Structural Concrete

03 31 13.35 Heavyweight Concrete, Ready Mix

		Crew	Daily Output	Labor-Hours	Unit	Material	Labor	Equipment	Total	Total Incl O&P
0010	**HEAVYWEIGHT CONCRETE, READY MIX**, delivered									
0012	Includes local aggregate, sand, Portland cement (Type I) and water									
0015	Excludes all additives and treatments									
0020	2000 psi				C.Y.	148			148	163
0100	2500 psi					151			151	166
0150	3000 psi					154			154	170
0200	3500 psi					158			158	174
0300	4000 psi					162			162	178
1000	For high early strength (Portland cement Type III), add					10%				
1300	For winter concrete (hot water), add					8.50			8.50	9.35
1410	For mid-range water reducer, add					6.40			6.40	7.05
1420	For high-range water reducer/superplasticizer, add					8.50			8.50	9.35
1430	For retarder, add					6.05			6.05	6.65
1440	For non-Chloride accelerator, add					9.50			9.50	10.45
1450	For Chloride accelerator, per 1%, add					5			5	5.50
1460	For fiber reinforcing, synthetic (1 lb./C.Y.), add					10.40			10.40	11.45
1500	For Saturday delivery, add					15			15	16.50
1510	For truck holding/waiting time past 1st hour per load, add				Hr.	143			143	157
1520	For short load (less than 4 C.Y.), add per load				Ea.	125			125	138
2000	For all lightweight aggregate, add				C.Y.	45%				

03 31 13.70 Placing Concrete

		Crew	Daily Output	Labor-Hours	Unit	Material	Labor	Equipment	Total	Total Incl O&P
0010	**PLACING CONCRETE**									
0020	Includes labor and equipment to place, level (strike off) and consolidate									
1200	Duct bank, direct chute	C-6	155	.310	C.Y.		15.15	.38	15.53	23
1900	Footings, continuous, shallow, direct chute	"	120	.400			19.55	.50	20.05	29.50
1950	Pumped	C-20	150	.427			21.50	5.90	27.40	38.50
2000	With crane and bucket	C-7	90	.800			41	28.50	69.50	92
2100	Footings, continuous, deep, direct chute	C-6	140	.343			16.75	.43	17.18	25.50
2150	Pumped	C-20	160	.400			20	5.55	25.55	36
2200	With crane and bucket	C-7	110	.655			33.50	23.50	57	75
2400	Footings, spread, under 1 C.Y., direct chute	C-6	55	.873			42.50	1.08	43.58	64.50
2450	Pumped	C-20	65	.985			49.50	13.65	63.15	89
2500	With crane and bucket	C-7	45	1.600			82	57	139	184

03 31 Structural Concrete

03 31 13 – Heavyweight Structural Concrete

03 31 13.70 Placing Concrete

		Crew	Daily Output	Labor-Hours	Unit	Material	2023 Bare Costs Labor	2023 Bare Costs Equipment	Total	Total Incl O&P
2600	Over 5 C.Y., direct chute	C-6	120	.400	C.Y.		19.55	.50	20.05	29.50
2650	Pumped	C-20	150	.427			21.50	5.90	27.40	38.50
2700	With crane and bucket	C-7	100	.720			37	25.50	62.50	83
2900	Foundation mats, over 20 C.Y., direct chute	C-6	350	.137			6.70	.17	6.87	10.15
2950	Pumped	C-20	400	.160			8.05	2.22	10.27	14.45
3000	With crane and bucket	C-7	300	.240			12.25	8.55	20.80	27.50

03 35 Concrete Finishing

03 35 13 – High-Tolerance Concrete Floor Finishing

03 35 13.30 Finishing Floors, High Tolerance

		Crew	Daily Output	Labor-Hours	Unit	Material	2023 Bare Costs Labor	2023 Bare Costs Equipment	Total	Total Incl O&P
0010	**FINISHING FLOORS, HIGH TOLERANCE**									
0012	Finishing of fresh concrete flatwork requires that concrete									
0013	first be placed, struck off & consolidated									
0015	Basic finishing for various unspecified flatwork									
0100	Bull float only	C-10	4000	.006	S.F.		.31		.31	.46
0125	Bull float & manual float		2000	.012			.63		.63	.92
0150	Bull float, manual float & broom finish, w/edging & joints		1850	.013			.68		.68	1
0200	Bull float, manual float & manual steel trowel		1265	.019			.99		.99	1.46
0210	For specified Random Access Floors in ACI Classes 1, 2, 3 and 4 to achieve									
0215	Composite Overall Floor Flatness and Levelness values up to FF35/FL25									
0250	Bull float, machine float & machine trowel (walk-behind)	C-10C	1715	.014	S.F.		.73	.05	.78	1.13
0300	Power screed, bull float, machine float & trowel (walk-behind)	C-10D	2400	.010			.52	.07	.59	.85
0350	Power screed, bull float, machine float & trowel (ride-on)	C-10E	4000	.006			.31	.08	.39	.55
0352	For specified Random Access Floors in ACI Classes 5, 6, 7 and 8 to achieve									
0354	Composite Overall Floor Flatness and Levelness values up to FF50/FL50									
0356	Add for two-dimensional restraightening after power float	C-10	6000	.004	S.F.		.21		.21	.31
0358	For specified Random or Defined Access Floors in ACI Class 9 to achieve									
0360	Composite Overall Floor Flatness and Levelness values up to FF100/FL100									
0362	Add for two-dimensional restraightening after bull float & power float	C-10	3000	.008	S.F.		.42		.42	.62
0364	For specified Superflat Defined Access Floors in ACI Class 9 to achieve									
0366	Minimum Floor Flatness and Levelness values of FF100/FL100									
0368	Add for 2-dim'l restraightening after bull float, power float, power trowel	C-10	2000	.012	S.F.		.63		.63	.92

03 63 Epoxy Grouting

03 63 05 – Grouting of Dowels and Fasteners

03 63 05.10 Epoxy Only

		Crew	Daily Output	Labor-Hours	Unit	Material	2023 Bare Costs Labor	2023 Bare Costs Equipment	Total	Total Incl O&P
0010	**EPOXY ONLY**									
1500	Chemical anchoring, epoxy cartridge, excludes layout, drilling, fastener									
1530	For fastener 3/4" diam. x 6" embedment	2 Skwk	72	.222	Ea.	4.69	13.60		18.29	25.50
1535	1" diam. x 8" embedment		66	.242		7.05	14.85		21.90	30.50
1540	1-1/4" diam. x 10" embedment		60	.267		14.05	16.35		30.40	40
1545	1-3/4" diam. x 12" embedment		54	.296		23.50	18.15		41.65	53.50
1550	14" embedment		48	.333		28	20.50		48.50	61.50
1555	2" diam. x 12" embedment		42	.381		37.50	23.50		61	76.50
1560	18" embedment		32	.500		47	30.50		77.50	97.50

03 82 Concrete Boring

03 82 13 – Concrete Core Drilling

03 82 13.10 Core Drilling

		Crew	Daily Output	Labor-Hours	Unit	Material	2023 Bare Costs Labor	2023 Bare Costs Equipment	Total	Total Incl O&P
0010	**CORE DRILLING**									
0015	Includes bit cost, layout and set-up time									
0020	Reinforced concrete slab, up to 6" thick									
0100	1" diameter core	B-89A	17	.941	Ea.	.22	51	6.95	58.17	84.50
0150	For each additional inch of slab thickness in same hole, add		1440	.011		.04	.60	.08	.72	1.03
0200	2" diameter core		16.50	.970		.30	52.50	7.15	59.95	86.50
0250	For each additional inch of slab thickness in same hole, add		1080	.015		.05	.80	.11	.96	1.38
0300	3" diameter core		16	1		.43	54.50	7.40	62.33	89.50
0350	For each additional inch of slab thickness in same hole, add		720	.022		.07	1.21	.16	1.44	2.06
0500	4" diameter core		15	1.067		.57	58	7.85	66.42	96
0550	For each additional inch of slab thickness in same hole, add		480	.033		.10	1.81	.25	2.16	3.08
0700	6" diameter core		14	1.143		.91	62	8.45	71.36	103
0750	For each additional inch of slab thickness in same hole, add		360	.044		.15	2.41	.33	2.89	4.14
0900	8" diameter core		13	1.231		1.32	67	9.10	77.42	111
0950	For each additional inch of slab thickness in same hole, add		288	.056		.22	3.01	.41	3.64	5.20
1100	10" diameter core		12	1.333		1.62	72.50	9.85	83.97	121
1150	For each additional inch of slab thickness in same hole, add		240	.067		.27	3.62	.49	4.38	6.25
1300	12" diameter core		11	1.455		1.85	79	10.75	91.60	132
1350	For each additional inch of slab thickness in same hole, add		206	.078		.31	4.21	.57	5.09	7.25
1500	14" diameter core		10	1.600		2.29	87	11.80	101.09	146
1550	For each additional inch of slab thickness in same hole, add		180	.089		.38	4.82	.66	5.86	8.35
1700	18" diameter core		9	1.778		2.98	96.50	13.10	112.58	162
1750	For each additional inch of slab thickness in same hole, add		144	.111		.50	6.05	.82	7.37	10.45
1754	24" diameter core		8	2		4.73	109	14.75	128.48	183
1756	For each additional inch of slab thickness in same hole, add		120	.133		.79	7.25	.98	9.02	12.75
1760	For horizontal holes, add to above						20%	20%		
1770	Prestressed hollow core plank, 8" thick									
1780	1" diameter core	B-89A	17.50	.914	Ea.	.30	49.50	6.75	56.55	81.50
1790	For each additional inch of plank thickness in same hole, add		3840	.004		.04	.23	.03	.30	.41
1794	2" diameter core		17.25	.928		.40	50.50	6.85	57.75	83.50
1796	For each additional inch of plank thickness in same hole, add		2880	.006		.05	.30	.04	.39	.56
1800	3" diameter core		17	.941		.57	51	6.95	58.52	85
1810	For each additional inch of plank thickness in same hole, add		1920	.008		.07	.45	.06	.58	.83
1820	4" diameter core		16.50	.970		.76	52.50	7.15	60.41	87
1830	For each additional inch of plank thickness in same hole, add		1280	.013		.10	.68	.09	.87	1.21
1840	6" diameter core		15.50	1.032		1.21	56	7.60	64.81	93.50
1850	For each additional inch of plank thickness in same hole, add		960	.017		.15	.90	.12	1.17	1.66
1860	8" diameter core		15	1.067		1.76	58	7.85	67.61	97
1870	For each additional inch of plank thickness in same hole, add		768	.021		.22	1.13	.15	1.50	2.10
1880	10" diameter core		14	1.143		2.16	62	8.45	72.61	105
1890	For each additional inch of plank thickness in same hole, add		640	.025		.27	1.36	.18	1.81	2.53
1900	12" diameter core		13.50	1.185		2.47	64.50	8.75	75.72	108
1910	For each additional inch of plank thickness in same hole, add		548	.029		.31	1.58	.22	2.11	2.95

03 82 16 – Concrete Drilling

03 82 16.10 Concrete Impact Drilling

		Crew	Daily Output	Labor-Hours	Unit	Material	Labor	Equipment	Total	Total Incl O&P
0010	**CONCRETE IMPACT DRILLING**									
0020	Includes bit cost, layout and set-up time, no anchors									
0050	Up to 4" deep in concrete/brick floors/walls									
0100	Holes, 1/4" diameter	1 Carp	75	.107	Ea.	.04	6.25		6.29	9.35
0150	For each additional inch of depth in same hole, add		430	.019		.01	1.09		1.10	1.63
0200	3/8" diameter		63	.127		.03	7.45		7.48	11.15
0250	For each additional inch of depth in same hole, add		340	.024		.01	1.38		1.39	2.06

03 82 Concrete Boring

03 82 16 – Concrete Drilling

03 82 16.10 Concrete Impact Drilling		Crew	Daily Output	Labor-Hours	Unit	Material	2023 Bare Costs Labor	Equipment	Total	Total Incl O&P
0300	1/2" diameter	1 Carp	50	.160	Ea.	.04	9.40		9.44	14
0350	For each additional inch of depth in same hole, add		250	.032		.01	1.88		1.89	2.80
0400	5/8" diameter		48	.167		.05	9.75		9.80	14.60
0450	For each additional inch of depth in same hole, add		240	.033		.01	1.95		1.96	2.92
0500	3/4" diameter		45	.178		.08	10.40		10.48	15.60
0550	For each additional inch of depth in same hole, add		220	.036		.02	2.13		2.15	3.19
0600	7/8" diameter		43	.186		.07	10.90		10.97	16.35
0650	For each additional inch of depth in same hole, add		210	.038		.02	2.23		2.25	3.34
0700	1" diameter		40	.200		.16	11.70		11.86	17.65
0750	For each additional inch of depth in same hole, add		190	.042		.04	2.47		2.51	3.72
0800	1-1/4" diameter		38	.211		.23	12.35		12.58	18.60
0850	For each additional inch of depth in same hole, add		180	.044		.06	2.60		2.66	3.94
0900	1-1/2" diameter		35	.229		.35	13.40		13.75	20.50
0950	For each additional inch of depth in same hole, add	▼	165	.048	▼	.09	2.84		2.93	4.33
1000	For ceiling installations, add						40%			

Estimating Tips

05 05 00 Common Work Results for Metals

- Nuts, bolts, washers, connection angles, and plates can add a significant amount to both the tonnage of a structural steel job and the estimated cost. As a rule of thumb, add 10% to the total weight to account for these accessories.
- Type 2 steel construction, commonly referred to as "simple construction," consists generally of field-bolted connections with lateral bracing supplied by other elements of the building, such as masonry walls or x-bracing. The estimator should be aware, however, that shop connections may be accomplished by welding or bolting. The method may be particular to the fabrication shop and may have an impact on the estimated cost.

05 10 00 Structural Steel

- Steel items can be obtained from two sources: a fabrication shop or a metals service center. Fabrication shops can fabricate items under more controlled conditions than crews in the field can. They are also more efficient and can produce items more economically. Metal service centers serve as a source of long mill shapes to both fabrication shops and contractors.
- Most line items in this structural steel subdivision, and most items in 05 50 00 Metal Fabrications, are indicated as being shop fabricated. The bare material cost for these shop fabricated items is the "Invoice Cost" from the shop and includes the mill base price of steel plus mill extras, transportation to the shop, shop drawings and detailing where warranted, shop fabrication and handling, sandblasting and a shop coat of primer paint, all necessary structural bolts, and delivery to the job site. The bare labor cost and bare equipment cost for these shop fabricated items are for field installation or erection.
- Line items in Subdivision 05 12 23.40 Lightweight Framing, and other items scattered in Division 5, are indicated as being field fabricated. The bare material cost for these field fabricated items is the "Invoice Cost" from the metals service center and includes the mill base price of steel plus mill extras, transportation to the metals service center, material handling, and delivery of long lengths of mill shapes to the job site. Material costs for structural bolts and welding rods should be added to the estimate. The bare labor cost and bare equipment cost for these items are for both field fabrication and field installation or erection, and include time for cutting, welding, and drilling in the fabricated metal items. Drilling into concrete and fasteners to fasten field fabricated items to other work is not included and should be added to the estimate.

05 20 00 Steel Joist Framing

- In any given project the total weight of open web steel joists is determined by the loads to be supported and the design. However, economies can be realized in minimizing the amount of labor used to place the joists. This is done by maximizing the joist spacing and therefore minimizing the number of joists required to be installed on the job. Certain spacings and locations may be required by the design, but in other cases maximizing the spacing and keeping it as uniform as possible will keep the costs down.

05 30 00 Steel Decking

- The takeoff and estimating of a metal deck involve more than the area of the floor or roof and the type of deck specified or shown on the drawings. Many different sizes and types of openings may exist. Small openings for individual pipes or conduits may be drilled after the floor/roof is installed, but larger openings may require special deck lengths as well as reinforcing or structural support. The estimator should determine who will be supplying this reinforcing. Additionally, some deck terminations are part of the deck package, such as screed angles and pour stops, and others will be part of the steel contract, such as angles attached to structural members and cast-in-place angles and plates. The estimator must ensure that all pieces are accounted for in the complete estimate.

05 50 00 Metal Fabrications

- The most economical steel stairs are those that use common materials, standard details, and most importantly, a uniform and relatively simple method of field assembly. Commonly available A36/A992 channels and plates are very good choices for the main stringers of the stairs, as are angles and tees for the carrier members. Risers and treads are usually made by specialty shops, and it is most economical to use a typical detail in as many places as possible. The stairs should be pre-assembled and shipped directly to the site. The field connections should be simple and straightforward enough to be accomplished efficiently, and with minimum equipment and labor.

Reference Numbers

Reference numbers are shown at the beginning of some major classifications. These numbers refer to related items in the Reference Section. The reference information may be an estimating procedure, an alternate pricing method, or technical information.

Note: Not all subdivisions listed here necessarily appear. ■

Same Data. Simplified.

Enjoy the convenience and efficiency of accessing your costs anywhere:

- **Skip the multiplier** by setting your location
- **Quickly search,** edit, favorite and share costs
- **Stay on top of price changes** with automatic updates

Discover more at rsmeans.com/online

No part of this cost data may be reproduced, stored in a retrieval system, or transmitted in any form or by any means without prior written permission of Gordian.

05 05 Common Work Results for Metals

05 05 19 – Post-Installed Concrete Anchors

05 05 19.10 Chemical Anchors

		Crew	Daily Output	Labor-Hours	Unit	Material	2023 Bare Costs Labor	Equipment	Total	Total Incl O&P
0010	**CHEMICAL ANCHORS**									
0020	Includes layout & drilling									
1430	Chemical anchor, w/rod & epoxy cartridge, 3/4" diameter x 9-1/2" long	B-89A	27	.593	Ea.	9.55	32	4.37	45.92	63.50
1435	1" diameter x 11-3/4" long		24	.667		17.10	36	4.92	58.02	78
1440	1-1/4" diameter x 14" long		21	.762		33.50	41.50	5.60	80.60	105
1445	1-3/4" diameter x 15" long		20	.800		67.50	43.50	5.90	116.90	146
1450	18" long		17	.941		81	51	6.95	138.95	174
1455	2" diameter x 18" long		16	1		123	54.50	7.40	184.90	224
1460	24" long		15	1.067		160	58	7.85	225.85	271

05 05 19.20 Expansion Anchors

			Crew	Daily Output	Labor-Hours	Unit	Material	Labor	Equipment	Total	Total Incl O&P
0010	**EXPANSION ANCHORS**										
0100	Anchors for concrete, brick or stone, no layout and drilling										
0200	Expansion shields, zinc, 1/4" diameter, 1-5/16" long, single	G	1 Carp	90	.089	Ea.	.57	5.20		5.77	8.40
0300	1-3/8" long, double	G		85	.094		.75	5.50		6.25	9.05
0400	3/8" diameter, 1-1/2" long, single	G		85	.094		.92	5.50		6.42	9.20
0500	2" long, double	G		80	.100		1.60	5.85		7.45	10.50
0600	1/2" diameter, 2-1/16" long, single	G		80	.100		1.60	5.85		7.45	10.50
0700	2-1/2" long, double	G		75	.107		1.98	6.25		8.23	11.50
0800	5/8" diameter, 2-5/8" long, single	G		75	.107		2.56	6.25		8.81	12.10
0900	2-3/4" long, double	G		70	.114		3.57	6.70		10.27	13.90
1000	3/4" diameter, 2-3/4" long, single	G		70	.114		4.07	6.70		10.77	14.45
1100	3-15/16" long, double	G		65	.123		6.20	7.20		13.40	17.60
2100	Hollow wall anchors for gypsum wall board, plaster or tile										
2300	1/8" diameter, short	G	1 Carp	160	.050	Ea.	.43	2.93		3.36	4.83
2400	Long	G		150	.053		.37	3.13		3.50	5.05
2500	3/16" diameter, short	G		150	.053		.85	3.13		3.98	5.60
2600	Long	G		140	.057		.97	3.35		4.32	6.05
2700	1/4" diameter, short	G		140	.057		1.18	3.35		4.53	6.30
2800	Long	G		130	.062		.97	3.61		4.58	6.40
3000	Toggle bolts, bright steel, 1/8" diameter, 2" long	G		85	.094		.30	5.50		5.80	8.55
3100	4" long	G		80	.100		.29	5.85		6.14	9.05
3200	3/16" diameter, 3" long	G		80	.100		.34	5.85		6.19	9.10
3300	6" long	G		75	.107		.57	6.25		6.82	9.95
3400	1/4" diameter, 3" long	G		75	.107		.46	6.25		6.71	9.80
3500	6" long	G		70	.114		.69	6.70		7.39	10.70
3600	3/8" diameter, 3" long	G		70	.114		1.18	6.70		7.88	11.25
3700	6" long	G		60	.133		1.91	7.80		9.71	13.75
3800	1/2" diameter, 4" long	G		60	.133		2.70	7.80		10.50	14.60
3900	6" long	G		50	.160		3.29	9.40		12.69	17.55
4000	Nailing anchors										
4100	Nylon nailing anchor, 1/4" diameter, 1" long		1 Carp	3.20	2.500	C	16.65	147		163.65	236
4200	1-1/2" long			2.80	2.857		19.10	167		186.10	270
4300	2" long			2.40	3.333		23	195		218	315
4400	Metal nailing anchor, 1/4" diameter, 1" long	G		3.20	2.500		14.85	147		161.85	234
4500	1-1/2" long	G		2.80	2.857		19	167		186	270
4600	2" long	G		2.40	3.333		22.50	195		217.50	315
5000	Screw anchors for concrete, masonry,										
5100	stone & tile, no layout or drilling included										
5700	Lag screw shields, 1/4" diameter, short	G	1 Carp	90	.089	Ea.	.31	5.20		5.51	8.10
5800	Long	G		85	.094		.40	5.50		5.90	8.65
5900	3/8" diameter, short	G		85	.094		.68	5.50		6.18	8.95
6000	Long	G		80	.100		.83	5.85		6.68	9.65

05 05 Common Work Results for Metals

05 05 19 – Post-Installed Concrete Anchors

05 05 19.20 Expansion Anchors

			Crew	Daily Output	Labor-Hours	Unit	Material	2023 Bare Costs Labor	Equipment	Total	Total Incl O&P
6100	1/2" diameter, short	G	1 Carp	80	.100	Ea.	.84	5.85		6.69	9.65
6200	Long	G		75	.107		1.30	6.25		7.55	10.75
6300	5/8" diameter, short	G		70	.114		1.25	6.70		7.95	11.35
6400	Long	G		65	.123		1.95	7.20		9.15	12.90
6600	Lead, #6 & #8, 3/4" long	G		260	.031		.32	1.80		2.12	3.03
6700	#10 - #14, 1-1/2" long	G		200	.040		.69	2.34		3.03	4.25
6800	#16 & #18, 1-1/2" long	G		160	.050		.99	2.93		3.92	5.45
6900	Plastic, #6 & #8, 3/4" long			260	.031		.03	1.80		1.83	2.71
7000	#8 & #10, 7/8" long			240	.033		.03	1.95		1.98	2.94
7100	#10 & #12, 1" long			220	.036		.05	2.13		2.18	3.23
7200	#14 & #16, 1-1/2" long			160	.050		.08	2.93		3.01	4.45
8000	Wedge anchors, not including layout or drilling										
8050	Carbon steel, 1/4" diameter, 1-3/4" long	G	1 Carp	150	.053	Ea.	.86	3.13		3.99	5.60
8100	3-1/4" long	G		140	.057		1.14	3.35		4.49	6.25
8150	3/8" diameter, 2-1/4" long	G		145	.055		.46	3.23		3.69	5.30
8200	5" long	G		140	.057		.81	3.35		4.16	5.90
8250	1/2" diameter, 2-3/4" long	G		140	.057		1	3.35		4.35	6.10
8300	7" long	G		125	.064		1.71	3.75		5.46	7.50
8350	5/8" diameter, 3-1/2" long	G		130	.062		2.45	3.61		6.06	8.05
8400	8-1/2" long	G		115	.070		5.20	4.08		9.28	11.80
8450	3/4" diameter, 4-1/4" long	G		115	.070		3.97	4.08		8.05	10.40
8500	10" long	G		95	.084		9	4.93		13.93	17.30
8550	1" diameter, 6" long	G		100	.080		9.05	4.69		13.74	16.95
8575	9" long	G		85	.094		11.75	5.50		17.25	21
8600	12" long	G		75	.107		12.70	6.25		18.95	23.50
8650	1-1/4" diameter, 9" long	G		70	.114		55	6.70		61.70	70.50
8700	12" long	G		60	.133		70.50	7.80		78.30	89
8750	For type 303 stainless steel, add						350%				
8800	For type 316 stainless steel, add						450%				
8950	Self-drilling concrete screw, hex washer head, 3/16" diam. x 1-3/4" long	G	1 Carp	300	.027	Ea.	.25	1.56		1.81	2.61
8960	2-1/4" long	G		250	.032		.26	1.88		2.14	3.08
8970	Phillips flat head, 3/16" diam. x 1-3/4" long	G		300	.027		.20	1.56		1.76	2.55
8980	2-1/4" long	G		250	.032		.21	1.88		2.09	3.02

05 05 21 – Fastening Methods for Metal

05 05 21.15 Drilling Steel

			Crew	Daily Output	Labor-Hours	Unit	Material	2023 Bare Costs Labor	Equipment	Total	Total Incl O&P
0010	**DRILLING STEEL**										
1910	Drilling & layout for steel, up to 1/4" deep, no anchor										
1920	Holes, 1/4" diameter		1 Sswk	112	.071	Ea.	.06	4.61		4.67	7.15
1925	For each additional 1/4" depth, add			336	.024		.06	1.54		1.60	2.43
1930	3/8" diameter			104	.077		.04	4.97		5.01	7.70
1935	For each additional 1/4" depth, add			312	.026		.04	1.66		1.70	2.60
1940	1/2" diameter			96	.083		.07	5.40		5.47	8.40
1945	For each additional 1/4" depth, add			288	.028		.07	1.79		1.86	2.84
1950	5/8" diameter			88	.091		.07	5.85		5.92	9.15
1955	For each additional 1/4" depth, add			264	.030		.07	1.96		2.03	3.09
1960	3/4" diameter			80	.100		.13	6.45		6.58	10.10
1965	For each additional 1/4" depth, add			240	.033		.13	2.15		2.28	3.45
1970	7/8" diameter			72	.111		.11	7.15		7.26	11.15
1975	For each additional 1/4" depth, add			216	.037		.11	2.39		2.50	3.80
1980	1" diameter			64	.125		.24	8.05		8.29	12.70
1985	For each additional 1/4" depth, add			192	.042		.24	2.69		2.93	4.40
1990	For drilling up, add							40%			

05 05 Common Work Results for Metals

05 05 21 – Fastening Methods for Metal

05 05 21.90 Welding Steel

		Crew	Daily Output	Labor-Hours	Unit	Material	2023 Bare Costs Labor	Equipment	Total	Total Incl O&P
0010	**WELDING STEEL**, Structural R050521-20									
0020	Field welding, 1/8" E6011, cost per welder, no operating engineer	E-14	8	1	Hr.	8	66.50	18.40	92.90	132
0200	With 1/2 operating engineer	E-13	8	1.500		8	96.50	18.40	122.90	176
0300	With 1 operating engineer	E-12	8	2		8	126	18.40	152.40	220
0500	With no operating engineer, 2# weld rod per ton	E-14	8	1	Ton	8	66.50	18.40	92.90	132
0600	8# E6011 per ton	"	2	4		32	266	73.50	371.50	525
0800	With one operating engineer per welder, 2# E6011 per ton	E-12	8	2		8	126	18.40	152.40	220
0900	8# E6011 per ton	"	2	8		32	505	73.50	610.50	880
1200	Continuous fillet, down welding									
1300	Single pass, 1/8" thick, 0.1#/L.F.	E-14	150	.053	L.F.	.40	3.55	.98	4.93	6.95
1400	3/16" thick, 0.2#/L.F.		75	.107		.80	7.10	1.96	9.86	14
1500	1/4" thick, 0.3#/L.F.		50	.160		1.20	10.65	2.94	14.79	21
1610	5/16" thick, 0.4#/L.F.		38	.211		1.60	14	3.87	19.47	27.50
1800	3 passes, 3/8" thick, 0.5#/L.F.		30	.267		2	17.75	4.90	24.65	35
2010	4 passes, 1/2" thick, 0.7#/L.F.		22	.364		2.80	24	6.70	33.50	48
2200	5 to 6 passes, 3/4" thick, 1.3#/L.F.		12	.667		5.20	44.50	12.25	61.95	87.50
2400	8 to 11 passes, 1" thick, 2.4#/L.F.		6	1.333		9.60	88.50	24.50	122.60	175
2600	For vertical joint welding, add						20%			
2700	Overhead joint welding, add						300%			
2900	For semi-automatic welding, obstructed joints, deduct						5%			
3000	Exposed joints, deduct						15%			
4000	Cleaning and welding plates, bars, or rods									
4010	to existing beams, columns, or trusses	E-14	12	.667	L.F.	2	44.50	12.25	58.75	84

05 05 23 – Metal Fastenings

05 05 23.30 Lag Screws

			Crew	Daily Output	Labor-Hours	Unit	Material	Labor	Equipment	Total	Total Incl O&P
0010	**LAG SCREWS**										
0020	Steel, 1/4" diameter, 2" long	G	1 Carp	200	.040	Ea.	.15	2.34		2.49	3.66
0100	3/8" diameter, 3" long	G		150	.053		.51	3.13		3.64	5.20
0200	1/2" diameter, 3" long	G		130	.062		1.15	3.61		4.76	6.60
0300	5/8" diameter, 3" long	G		120	.067		1.83	3.91		5.74	7.80

05 05 23.35 Machine Screws

			Crew	Daily Output	Labor-Hours	Unit	Material	Labor	Equipment	Total	Total Incl O&P
0010	**MACHINE SCREWS**										
0020	Steel, round head, #8 x 1" long	G	1 Carp	4.80	1.667	C	5.05	97.50		102.55	151
0110	#8 x 2" long	G		2.40	3.333		8.40	195		203.40	300
0200	#10 x 1" long	G		4	2		7.10	117		124.10	183
0300	#10 x 2" long	G		2	4		12	234		246	365

05 05 23.50 Powder Actuated Tools and Fasteners

			Crew	Daily Output	Labor-Hours	Unit	Material	Labor	Equipment	Total	Total Incl O&P
0010	**POWDER ACTUATED TOOLS & FASTENERS**										
0020	Stud driver, .22 caliber, single shot					Ea.	95.50			95.50	105
0100	.27 caliber, semi automatic, strip					"	575			575	635
0300	Powder load, single shot, .22 cal, power level 2, brown					C	7.25			7.25	8
0400	Strip, .27 cal, power level 4, red						15.05			15.05	16.60
0600	Drive pin, .300 x 3/4" long	G	1 Carp	4.80	1.667		5.40	97.50		102.90	151
0700	.300 x 3" long with washer	G	"	4	2		13.85	117		130.85	190

05 05 23.55 Rivets

			Crew	Daily Output	Labor-Hours	Unit	Material	Labor	Equipment	Total	Total Incl O&P
0010	**RIVETS**										
0100	Aluminum rivet & mandrel, 1/2" grip length x 1/8" diameter	G	1 Carp	4.80	1.667	C	3.78	97.50		101.28	149
0200	3/16" diameter	G		4	2		6.95	117		123.95	183
0300	Aluminum rivet, steel mandrel, 1/8" diameter	G		4.80	1.667		3.62	97.50		101.12	149
0400	3/16" diameter	G		4	2		6.65	117		123.65	182
0500	Copper rivet, steel mandrel, 1/8" diameter	G		4.80	1.667		9.20	97.50		106.70	155

05 05 Common Work Results for Metals

05 05 23 – Metal Fastenings

05 05 23.55 Rivets

		Crew	Daily Output	Labor-Hours	Unit	Material	2023 Bare Costs Labor	2023 Bare Costs Equipment	Total	Total Incl O&P
0800	Stainless rivet & mandrel, 1/8" diameter	G 1 Carp	4.80	1.667	C	13.40	97.50		110.90	160
0900	3/16" diameter	G	4	2		24	117		141	201
1000	Stainless rivet, steel mandrel, 1/8" diameter	G	4.80	1.667		6.95	97.50		104.45	153
1100	3/16" diameter	G	4	2		19.05	117		136.05	196
1200	Steel rivet and mandrel, 1/8" diameter	G	4.80	1.667		5.45	97.50		102.95	151
1300	3/16" diameter	G	4	2		8.75	117		125.75	185
1400	Hand riveting tool, standard				Ea.	13.25			13.25	14.60
1500	Deluxe					465			465	515
1600	Power riveting tool, standard					615			615	680
1700	Deluxe					1,625			1,625	1,800

05 05 23.70 Structural Blind Bolts

		Crew	Daily Output	Labor-Hours	Unit	Material	Labor	Equipment	Total	Total Incl O&P
0010	**STRUCTURAL BLIND BOLTS**									
0100	1/4" diameter x 1/4" grip	G 1 Sswk	240	.033	Ea.	.98	2.15		3.13	4.39
0150	1/2" grip	G	216	.037		.93	2.39		3.32	4.70
0200	3/8" diameter x 1/2" grip	G	232	.034		1.91	2.23		4.14	5.55
0250	3/4" grip	G	208	.038		2	2.48		4.48	6
0300	1/2" diameter x 1/2" grip	G	224	.036		4.14	2.31		6.45	8.10
0350	3/4" grip	G	200	.040		4.14	2.58		6.72	8.55
0400	5/8" diameter x 3/4" grip	G	216	.037		6.50	2.39		8.89	10.85
0450	1" grip	G	192	.042		6.50	2.69		9.19	11.30

05 05 23.90 Welding Rod

		Crew	Daily Output	Labor-Hours	Unit	Material	Labor	Equipment	Total	Total Incl O&P
0010	**WELDING ROD**									
0020	Steel, type 6011, 1/8" diam., less than 500#				Lb.	4			4	4.40
0100	500# to 2,000#					3.60			3.60	3.96
0200	2,000# to 5,000#					3.38			3.38	3.72
0300	5/32" diam., less than 500#					3.97			3.97	4.37
0310	500# to 2,000#					3.58			3.58	3.94
0320	2,000# to 5,000#					3.37			3.37	3.70
0400	3/16" diam., less than 500#					3.96			3.96	4.36
0500	500# to 2,000#					3.57			3.57	3.93
0600	2,000# to 5,000#					3.36			3.36	3.69
0620	Steel, type 6010, 1/8" diam., less than 500#					4.06			4.06	4.47
0630	500# to 2,000#					3.66			3.66	4.03
0640	2,000# to 5,000#					3.44			3.44	3.78
0650	Steel, type 7018 Low Hydrogen, 1/8" diam., less than 500#					3.73			3.73	4.10
0660	500# to 2,000#					3.36			3.36	3.70
0670	2,000# to 5,000#					3.16			3.16	3.47
0700	Steel, type 7024 Jet Weld, 1/8" diam., less than 500#					3.94			3.94	4.33
0710	500# to 2,000#					3.55			3.55	3.91
0720	2,000# to 5,000#					3.34			3.34	3.67
1550	Aluminum, type 4043 TIG, 1/8" diam., less than 10#					7.25			7.25	7.95
1560	10# to 60#					6.50			6.50	7.15
1570	Over 60#					6.10			6.10	6.75
1600	Aluminum, type 5356 TIG, 1/8" diam., less than 10#					7.55			7.55	8.30
1610	10# to 60#					6.80			6.80	7.50
1620	Over 60#					6.40			6.40	7.05
1900	Cast iron, type 8 Nickel, 1/8" diam., less than 500#					30.50			30.50	34
1910	500# to 1,000#					27.50			27.50	30.50
1920	Over 1,000#					26			26	28.50
2000	Stainless steel, type 316/316L, 1/8" diam., less than 500#					11.60			11.60	12.75
2100	500# to 1,000#					10.45			10.45	11.45
2220	Over 1,000#					9.80			9.80	10.80

For customer support on your Plumbing Costs with RSMeans data, call 800.448.8182.

05 12 Structural Steel Framing

05 12 23 – Structural Steel for Buildings

05 12 23.40 Lightweight Framing

			Crew	Daily Output	Labor-Hours	Unit	Material	2023 Bare Costs Labor	Equipment	Total	Total Incl O&P
0010	**LIGHTWEIGHT FRAMING**										
0015	Made from recycled materials										
0400	Angle framing, field fabricated, 4" and larger	G	E-3	440	.055	Lb.	.95	3.56	.33	4.84	6.90
0450	Less than 4" angles	G		265	.091		.99	5.90	.56	7.45	10.80
0600	Channel framing, field fabricated, 8" and larger	G		500	.048		.99	3.13	.29	4.41	6.25
0650	Less than 8" channels	G		335	.072		.99	4.67	.44	6.10	8.75
1000	Continuous slotted channel framing system, shop fab, simple framing	G	2 Sswk	2400	.007		5.10	.43		5.53	6.25
1200	Complex framing	G	"	1600	.010		5.75	.65		6.40	7.35
1250	Plate & bar stock for reinforcing beams and trusses	G					1.81			1.81	1.99
1300	Cross bracing, rods, shop fabricated, 3/4" diameter	G	E-3	700	.034		1.97	2.24	.21	4.42	5.85
1310	7/8" diameter	G		850	.028		1.97	1.84	.17	3.98	5.20
1320	1" diameter	G		1000	.024		1.97	1.57	.15	3.69	4.74
1330	Angle, 5" x 5" x 3/8"	G		2800	.009		1.97	.56	.05	2.58	3.09
1350	Hanging lintels, shop fabricated	G		850	.028		1.97	1.84	.17	3.98	5.20
1380	Roof frames, shop fabricated, 3'-0" square, 5' span	G	E-2	4200	.013		1.97	.85	.64	3.46	4.17
1400	Tie rod, not upset, 1-1/2" to 4" diameter, with turnbuckle	G	2 Sswk	800	.020		2.14	1.29		3.43	4.34
1420	No turnbuckle	G		700	.023		2.06	1.48		3.54	4.53
1500	Upset, 1-3/4" to 4" diameter, with turnbuckle	G		800	.020		2.14	1.29		3.43	4.34
1520	No turnbuckle	G		700	.023		2.06	1.48		3.54	4.53

05 12 23.60 Pipe Support Framing

0010	**PIPE SUPPORT FRAMING**										
0020	Under 10#/L.F., shop fabricated	G	E-4	3900	.008	Lb.	2.21	.53	.04	2.78	3.29
0200	10.1 to 15#/L.F.	G		4300	.007		2.17	.48	.03	2.68	3.18
0400	15.1 to 20#/L.F.	G		4800	.007		2.14	.43	.03	2.60	3.05
0600	Over 20#/L.F.	G		5400	.006		2.11	.39	.03	2.53	2.94

05 54 Metal Floor Plates

05 54 13 – Floor Plates

05 54 13.20 Checkered Plates

0010	**CHECKERED PLATES**, steel, field fabricated										
0015	Made from recycled materials										
0020	1/4" & 3/8", 2000 to 5000 S.F., bolted	G	E-4	2900	.011	Lb.	1.89	.72	.05	2.66	3.25
0100	Welded	G		4400	.007	"	1.89	.47	.03	2.39	2.85
0300	Pit or trench cover and frame, 1/4" plate, 2' to 3' wide	G		100	.320	S.F.	23.50	21	1.47	45.97	59
0400	For galvanizing, add	G				Lb.	.37			.37	.41
0500	Platforms, 1/4" plate, no handrails included, rectangular	G	E-4	4200	.008		4.39	.50	.04	4.93	5.65
0600	Circular	G	"	2500	.013		5.50	.83	.06	6.39	7.40

Division 6 — Wood, Plastics & Composites

Estimating Tips

06 05 00 Common Work Results for Wood, Plastics, and Composites

- Common to any wood-framed structure are the accessory connector items such as screws, nails, adhesives, hangers, connector plates, straps, angles, and hold-downs. For typical wood-framed buildings, such as residential projects, the aggregate total for these items can be significant, especially in areas where seismic loading is a concern. For floor and wall framing, the material cost is based on 10 to 25 lbs. of accessory connectors per MBF. Hold-downs, hangers, and other connectors should be taken off by the piece.

- Included with material costs are fasteners for a normal installation. Gordian's RSMeans engineers use manufacturers' recommendations, written specifications, and/or standard construction practice for the sizing and spacing of fasteners. Prices for various fasteners are shown for informational purposes only. Adjustments should be made if unusual fastening conditions exist.

06 10 00 Carpentry

- Lumber is a traded commodity and therefore sensitive to supply and demand in the marketplace. Even with "budgetary" estimating of wood-framed projects, it is advisable to call local suppliers for the latest market pricing.

- The common quantity unit for wood-framed projects is "thousand board feet" (MBF). A board foot is a volume of wood—1" x 1' x 1' or 144 cubic inches. Board-foot quantities are generally calculated using nominal material dimensions—dressed sizes are ignored. Board foot per lineal foot of any stick of lumber can be calculated by dividing the nominal cross-sectional area by 12. As an example, 2,000 lineal feet of 2 x 12 equates to 4 MBF by dividing the nominal area, 2 x 12, by 12, which equals 2, and multiplying that by 2,000 to give 4,000 board feet. This simple rule applies to all nominal dimensioned lumber.

- Waste is an issue of concern at the quantity takeoff for any area of construction. Framing lumber is sold in even foot lengths, i.e., 8', 10', 12', 14', 16', and depending on spans, wall heights, and the grade of lumber, waste is inevitable. A rule of thumb for lumber waste is 5–10% depending on material quality and the complexity of the framing.

- Wood in various forms and shapes is used in many projects, even where the main structural framing is steel, concrete, or masonry. Plywood as a back-up partition material and 2x boards used as blocking and cant strips around roof edges are two common examples. The estimator should ensure that the costs of all wood materials are included in the final estimate.

06 20 00 Finish Carpentry

- It is necessary to consider the grade of workmanship when estimating labor costs for erecting millwork and an interior finish. In practice, there are three grades: premium, custom, and economy. The RSMeans daily output for base and case moldings is in the range of 200 to 250 L.F. per carpenter per day. This is appropriate for most average custom-grade projects. For premium projects, an adjustment to productivity of 25–50% should be made, depending on the complexity of the job.

Reference Numbers

Reference numbers are shown at the beginning of some major classifications. These numbers refer to related items in the Reference Section. The reference information may be an estimating procedure, an alternate pricing method, or technical information.

Note: Not all subdivisions listed here necessarily appear. ∎

Same Data. Simplified.

Enjoy the convenience and efficiency of accessing your costs anywhere:
- **Skip the multiplier** by setting your location
- **Quickly search,** edit, favorite and share costs
- **Stay on top of price changes** with automatic updates

Discover more at rsmeans.com/online

No part of this cost data may be reproduced, stored in a retrieval system, or transmitted in any form or by any means without prior written permission of Gordian.

06 11 Wood Framing

06 11 10 – Framing with Dimensional, Engineered or Composite Lumber

06 11 10.24 Miscellaneous Framing

		Crew	Daily Output	Labor-Hours	Unit	Material	2023 Bare Costs Labor	Equipment	Total	Total Incl O&P
0010	**MISCELLANEOUS FRAMING**									
8500	Firestops, 2" x 4"	2 Carp	.51	31.373	M.B.F.	1,700	1,850		3,550	4,600
8505	Pneumatic nailed		.62	25.806		1,700	1,500		3,200	4,125
8520	2" x 6"		.60	26.667		1,850	1,575		3,425	4,375
8525	Pneumatic nailed		.73	21.858		1,875	1,275		3,150	3,950
8540	2" x 8"		.60	26.667		2,000	1,575		3,575	4,525
8560	2" x 12"		.70	22.857		2,150	1,350		3,500	4,350
8600	Nailers, treated, wood construction, 2" x 4"		.53	30.189		1,875	1,775		3,650	4,675
8605	Pneumatic nailed		.64	25.157		1,875	1,475		3,350	4,275
8620	2" x 6"		.75	21.333		1,575	1,250		2,825	3,575
8625	Pneumatic nailed		.90	17.778		1,575	1,050		2,625	3,300

06 16 Sheathing

06 16 36 – Wood Panel Product Sheathing

06 16 36.10 Sheathing

		Crew	Daily Output	Labor-Hours	Unit	Material	2023 Bare Costs Labor	Equipment	Total	Total Incl O&P
0010	**SHEATHING**									
0012	Plywood on roofs, CDX									
0050	3/8" thick	2 Carp	1525	.010	S.F.	1.08	.61		1.69	2.11
0055	Pneumatic nailed		1860	.009		1.08	.50		1.58	1.94
0200	5/8" thick		1300	.012		1.37	.72		2.09	2.58
0205	Pneumatic nailed		1586	.010		1.37	.59		1.96	2.39
0300	3/4" thick		1200	.013		1.71	.78		2.49	3.04
0305	Pneumatic nailed		1464	.011		1.71	.64		2.35	2.83
0500	Plywood on walls, with exterior CDX, 3/8" thick		1200	.013		1.08	.78		1.86	2.35
0505	Pneumatic nailed		1488	.011		1.08	.63		1.71	2.13
0700	5/8" thick		1050	.015		1.37	.89		2.26	2.84
0705	Pneumatic nailed		1302	.012		1.37	.72		2.09	2.58
0800	3/4" thick		975	.016		1.71	.96		2.67	3.31
0805	Pneumatic nailed		1209	.013		1.71	.78		2.49	3.03

Division 7 — Thermal & Moisture Protection

Estimating Tips

07 10 00 Dampproofing and Waterproofing
- Be sure of the job specifications before pricing this subdivision. The difference in cost between waterproofing and dampproofing can be great. Waterproofing will hold back standing water. Dampproofing prevents the transmission of water vapor. Also included in this section are vapor retarding membranes.

07 20 00 Thermal Protection
- Insulation and fireproofing products are measured by area, thickness, volume, or R-value. Specifications may give only what the specific R-value should be in a certain situation. The estimator may need to choose the type of insulation to meet that R-value.

07 30 00 Steep Slope Roofing
07 40 00 Roofing and Siding Panels
- Many roofing and siding products are bought and sold by the square. One square is equal to an area that measures 100 square feet.

  This simple change in unit of measure could create a large error if the estimator is not observant. Accessories necessary for a complete installation must be figured into any calculations for both material and labor.

07 50 00 Membrane Roofing
07 60 00 Flashing and Sheet Metal
07 70 00 Roofing and Wall Specialties and Accessories
- The items in these subdivisions compose a roofing system. No one component completes the installation, and all must be estimated. Built-up or single-ply membrane roofing systems are made up of many products and installation trades. Wood blocking at roof perimeters or penetrations, parapet coverings, reglets, roof drains, gutters, downspouts, sheet metal flashing, skylights, smoke vents, and roof hatches all need to be considered along with the roofing material. Several different installation trades will need to work together on the roofing system. Inherent difficulties in the scheduling and coordination of various trades must be accounted for when estimating labor costs.

07 90 00 Joint Protection
- To complete the weather-tight shell, the sealants and caulkings must be estimated. Where different materials meet—at expansion joints, at flashing penetrations, and at hundreds of other locations throughout a construction project—caulking and sealants provide another line of defense against water penetration. Often, an entire system is based on the proper location and placement of caulking or sealants. The detailed drawings that are included as part of a set of architectural plans show typical locations for these materials. When caulking or sealants are shown at typical locations, this means the estimator must include them for all the locations where this detail is applicable. Be careful to keep different types of sealants separate, and remember to consider backer rods and primers if necessary.

Reference Numbers
Reference numbers are shown at the beginning of some major classifications. These numbers refer to related items in the Reference Section. The reference information may be an estimating procedure, an alternate pricing method, or technical information.

Note: Not all subdivisions listed here necessarily appear. ■

Same Data. Simplified.
Enjoy the convenience and efficiency of accessing your costs anywhere:
- **Skip the multiplier** by setting your location
- **Quickly search,** edit, favorite and share costs
- **Stay on top of price changes** with automatic updates

Discover more at rsmeans.com/online

No part of this cost data may be reproduced, stored in a retrieval system, or transmitted in any form or by any means without prior written permission of Gordian.

07 65 Flexible Flashing

07 65 10 – Sheet Metal Flashing

07 65 10.10 Sheet Metal Flashing and Counter Flashing

		Crew	Daily Output	Labor-Hours	Unit	Material	2023 Bare Costs Labor	Equipment	Total	Total Incl O&P
0010	**SHEET METAL FLASHING AND COUNTER FLASHING**									
0011	Including up to 4 bends									
0020	Aluminum, mill finish, .013" thick	1 Rofc	145	.055	S.F.	1.68	2.86		4.54	6.50
0030	.016" thick		145	.055		.95	2.86		3.81	5.70
0060	.019" thick		145	.055		6.70	2.86		9.56	12
0100	.032" thick		145	.055		6.70	2.86		9.56	12
0200	.040" thick		145	.055		5.70	2.86		8.56	10.95
0300	.050" thick		145	.055		8	2.86		10.86	13.45
0325	Mill finish 5" x 7" step flashing, .016" thick		1920	.004	Ea.	.21	.22		.43	.58
0350	Mill finish 12" x 12" step flashing, .016" thick		1600	.005	"	.78	.26		1.04	1.28
0400	Painted finish, add				S.F.	.40			.40	.44
1000	Mastic-coated 2 sides, .005" thick	1 Rofc	330	.024		1.34	1.26		2.60	3.51
1100	.016" thick		330	.024		2.66	1.26		3.92	4.97
1600	Copper, 16 oz. sheets, under 1000 lb.		115	.070		20	3.60		23.60	28
1700	Over 4000 lb.		155	.052		20	2.67		22.67	26.50
1900	20 oz. sheets, under 1000 lb.		110	.073		17.50	3.77		21.27	25.50
2000	Over 4000 lb.		145	.055		16.65	2.86		19.51	23
2200	24 oz. sheets, under 1000 lb.		105	.076		20.50	3.95		24.45	29
2300	Over 4000 lb.		135	.059		19.55	3.07		22.62	26.50
2500	32 oz. sheets, under 1000 lb.		100	.080		27.50	4.14		31.64	37
2600	Over 4000 lb.		130	.062		26.50	3.19		29.69	34
5800	Lead, 2.5 lb./S.F., up to 12" wide		135	.059		8.45	3.07		11.52	14.25
5900	Over 12" wide		135	.059		8.45	3.07		11.52	14.25
8900	Stainless steel sheets, 32 ga.		155	.052		4.58	2.67		7.25	9.40
9000	28 ga.		155	.052		12.45	2.67		15.12	18.05
9100	26 ga.		155	.052		9.70	2.67		12.37	15
9200	24 ga.		155	.052		11.60	2.67		14.27	17.10
9400	Terne coated stainless steel, .015" thick, 28 ga.		155	.052		10.50	2.67		13.17	15.90
9500	.018" thick, 26 ga.		155	.052		10	2.67		12.67	15.35
9600	Zinc and copper alloy (brass), .020" thick		155	.052		11.65	2.67		14.32	17.20
9700	.027" thick		155	.052		13.75	2.67		16.42	19.45
9800	.032" thick		155	.052		16	2.67		18.67	22
9900	.040" thick		155	.052		22	2.67		24.67	28.50

07 65 13 – Laminated Sheet Flashing

07 65 13.10 Laminated Sheet Flashing

		Crew	Daily Output	Labor-Hours	Unit	Material	Labor	Equipment	Total	Total Incl O&P
0010	**LAMINATED SHEET FLASHING**, Including up to 4 bends									
0500	Aluminum, fabric-backed 2 sides, mill finish, .004" thick	1 Rofc	330	.024	S.F.	2.04	1.26		3.30	4.28
0700	.005" thick		330	.024		2.40	1.26		3.66	4.68
0750	Mastic-backed, self adhesive		460	.017		4.40	.90		5.30	6.30
0800	Mastic-coated 2 sides, .004" thick		330	.024		2.04	1.26		3.30	4.28
2800	Copper, paperbacked 1 side, 2 oz.		330	.024		2.78	1.26		4.04	5.10
2900	3 oz.		330	.024		4.05	1.26		5.31	6.50
3100	Paperbacked 2 sides, 2 oz.		330	.024		3.08	1.26		4.34	5.45
3150	3 oz.		330	.024		2.88	1.26		4.14	5.20
3200	5 oz.		330	.024		5	1.26		6.26	7.55
3250	7 oz.		330	.024		6.80	1.26		8.06	9.55
3400	Mastic-backed 2 sides, copper, 2 oz.		330	.024		2.93	1.26		4.19	5.25
3500	3 oz.		330	.024		3.32	1.26		4.58	5.70
3700	5 oz.		330	.024		5.05	1.26		6.31	7.60
3800	Fabric-backed 2 sides, copper, 2 oz.		330	.024		2.64	1.26		3.90	4.94
4000	3 oz.		330	.024		3.72	1.26		4.98	6.15
4100	5 oz.		330	.024		5.20	1.26		6.46	7.80

07 65 Flexible Flashing

07 65 13 – Laminated Sheet Flashing

07 65 13.10 Laminated Sheet Flashing		Crew	Daily Output	Labor-Hours	Unit	Material	2023 Bare Costs Labor	Equipment	Total	Total Incl O&P
4300	Copper-clad stainless steel, .015" thick, under 500 lb.	1 Rofc	115	.070	S.F.	8.90	3.60		12.50	15.65
4400	Over 2000 lb.		155	.052		8.75	2.67		11.42	14
4600	.018" thick, under 500 lb.		100	.080		10.20	4.14		14.34	17.95
4700	Over 2000 lb.		145	.055		10.50	2.86		13.36	16.20
8550	Shower pan, 3 ply copper and fabric, 3 oz.		155	.052		5.30	2.67		7.97	10.20
8600	7 oz.		155	.052		6.45	2.67		9.12	11.40
9300	Stainless steel, paperbacked 2 sides, .005" thick	▼	330	.024	▼	5.20	1.26		6.46	7.80

07 65 19 – Plastic Sheet Flashing

07 65 19.10 Plastic Sheet Flashing and Counter Flashing

		Crew	Daily Output	Labor-Hours	Unit	Material	Labor	Equipment	Total	Total Incl O&P
0010	**PLASTIC SHEET FLASHING AND COUNTER FLASHING**									
7300	Polyvinyl chloride, black, 10 mil	1 Rofc	285	.028	S.F.	.35	1.45		1.80	2.75
7400	20 mil		285	.028		.34	1.45		1.79	2.73
7600	30 mil		285	.028		.43	1.45		1.88	2.83
7700	60 mil		285	.028		1.14	1.45		2.59	3.61
7900	Black or white for exposed roofs, 60 mil	▼	285	.028	▼	5.30	1.45		6.75	8.15
8060	PVC tape, 5" x 45 mils, for joint covers, 100 L.F./roll				Ea.	150			150	165
8850	Polyvinyl chloride, 30 mil	1 Rofc	160	.050	S.F.	1.07	2.59		3.66	5.40

07 71 Roof Specialties

07 71 16 – Manufactured Counterflashing Systems

07 71 16.20 Pitch Pockets, Variable Sizes

		Crew	Daily Output	Labor-Hours	Unit	Material	Labor	Equipment	Total	Total Incl O&P
0010	**PITCH POCKETS, VARIABLE SIZES**									
0100	Adjustable, 4" to 7", welded corners, 4" deep	1 Rofc	48	.167	Ea.	46	8.65		54.65	64.50
0200	Side extenders, 6"	"	240	.033	"	4.27	1.73		6	7.50

07 72 Roof Accessories

07 72 53 – Snow Guards

07 72 53.10 Snow Guard Options

		Crew	Daily Output	Labor-Hours	Unit	Material	Labor	Equipment	Total	Total Incl O&P
0010	**SNOW GUARD OPTIONS**									
0100	Slate & asphalt shingle roofs, fastened with nails	1 Rofc	160	.050	Ea.	15.50	2.59		18.09	21.50
0200	Standing seam metal roofs, fastened with set screws		48	.167		22	8.65		30.65	38.50
0300	Surface mount for metal roofs, fastened with solder		48	.167	▼	9.65	8.65		18.30	24.50
0400	Double rail pipe type, including pipe	▼	130	.062	L.F.	44.50	3.19		47.69	54

07 76 Roof Pavers

07 76 16 – Roof Decking Pavers

07 76 16.10 Roof Pavers and Supports

		Crew	Daily Output	Labor-Hours	Unit	Material	Labor	Equipment	Total	Total Incl O&P
0010	**ROOF PAVERS AND SUPPORTS**									
1000	Roof decking pavers, concrete blocks, 2" thick, natural	1 Clab	115	.070	S.F.	1.88	3.29		5.17	6.95
1100	Colors		115	.070	"	1.88	3.29		5.17	6.95
1200	Support pedestal, bottom cap		960	.008	Ea.	3.60	.39		3.99	4.55
1300	Top cap		960	.008		6.60	.39		6.99	7.85
1400	Leveling shims, 1/16"		1920	.004		1.63	.20		1.83	2.08
1500	1/8"		1920	.004		1.99	.20		2.19	2.48
1600	Buffer pad		960	.008	▼	7.70	.39		8.09	9.05
1700	PVC legs (4" SDR 35)		2880	.003	Inch	.29	.13		.42	.52
2000	Alternate pricing method, system in place		101	.079	S.F.	8.15	3.74		11.89	14.50

07 84 Firestopping

07 84 13 – Penetration Firestopping

07 84 13.10 Firestopping		Crew	Daily Output	Labor-Hours	Unit	Material	2023 Bare Costs Labor	Equipment	Total	Total Incl O&P
0010	**FIRESTOPPING**									
0100	Metallic piping, non insulated									
0110	Through walls, 2" diameter	1 Carp	16	.500	Ea.	11.75	29.50		41.25	56.50
0120	4" diameter		14	.571		20.50	33.50		54	72.50
0130	6" diameter		12	.667		30	39		69	91
0140	12" diameter		10	.800		25.50	47		72.50	98.50
0150	Through floors, 2" diameter		32	.250		5.90	14.65		20.55	28.50
0160	4" diameter		28	.286		10.30	16.75		27.05	36.50
0170	6" diameter		24	.333		15.05	19.55		34.60	45.50
0180	12" diameter		20	.400		13.25	23.50		36.75	49.50
0190	Metallic piping, insulated									
0200	Through walls, 2" diameter	1 Carp	16	.500	Ea.	20.50	29.50		50	66
0210	4" diameter		14	.571		30	33.50		63.50	83
0220	6" diameter		12	.667		40.50	39		79.50	103
0230	12" diameter		10	.800		69	47		116	146
0240	Through floors, 2" diameter		32	.250		10.30	14.65		24.95	33.50
0250	4" diameter		28	.286		15.05	16.75		31.80	41.50
0260	6" diameter		24	.333		20	19.55		39.55	51
0270	12" diameter		20	.400		34.50	23.50		58	73
0280	Non metallic piping, non insulated									
0290	Through walls, 2" diameter	1 Carp	12	.667	Ea.	71.50	39		110.50	137
0300	4" diameter		10	.800		132	47		179	215
0310	6" diameter		8	1		252	58.50		310.50	365
0330	Through floors, 2" diameter		16	.500		45	29.50		74.50	93
0340	4" diameter		6	1.333		82.50	78		160.50	207
0350	6" diameter		6	1.333		150	78		228	280
0370	Ductwork, insulated & non insulated, round									
0380	Through walls, 6" diameter	1 Carp	12	.667	Ea.	40.50	39		79.50	103
0390	12" diameter		10	.800		69	47		116	146
0400	18" diameter		8	1		84	58.50		142.50	180
0410	Through floors, 6" diameter		16	.500		20	29.50		49.50	65.50
0420	12" diameter		14	.571		15.05	33.50		48.55	66.50
0430	18" diameter		12	.667		18.20	39		57.20	78
0440	Ductwork, insulated & non insulated, rectangular									
0450	With stiffener/closure angle, through walls, 6" x 12"	1 Carp	8	1	Ea.	53	58.50		111.50	146
0460	12" x 24"		6	1.333		106	78		184	232
0470	24" x 48"		4	2		212	117		329	410
0480	With stiffener/closure angle, through floors, 6" x 12"		10	.800		10.75	47		57.75	82
0490	12" x 24"		8	1		53	58.50		111.50	146
0500	24" x 48"		6	1.333		106	78		184	232
0510	Multi trade openings									
0520	Through walls, 6" x 12"	1 Carp	2	4	Ea.	80.50	234		314.50	440
0530	12" x 24"	"	1	8		217	470		687	940
0540	24" x 48"	2 Carp	1	16		655	940		1,595	2,125
0550	48" x 96"	"	.75	21.333		2,625	1,250		3,875	4,725
0560	Through floors, 6" x 12"	1 Carp	2	4		49.50	234		283.50	405
0570	12" x 24"	"	1	8		65.50	470		535.50	770
0580	24" x 48"	2 Carp	.75	21.333		142	1,250		1,392	2,000
0590	48" x 96"	"	.50	32		335	1,875		2,210	3,175
0600	Structural penetrations, through walls									
0610	Steel beams, W8 x 10	1 Carp	8	1	Ea.	76	58.50		134.50	171
0620	W12 x 14		6	1.333		110	78		188	237
0630	W21 x 44		5	1.600		169	94		263	325

07 84 Firestopping

07 84 13 – Penetration Firestopping

07 84 13.10 Firestopping

		Crew	Daily Output	Labor-Hours	Unit	Material	2023 Bare Costs Labor	Equipment	Total	Total Incl O&P
0640	W36 x 135	1 Carp	3	2.667	Ea.	240	156		396	495
0650	Bar joists, 18" deep		6	1.333		44	78		122	165
0660	24" deep		6	1.333		62.50	78		140.50	185
0670	36" deep		5	1.600		93.50	94		187.50	243
0680	48" deep	↓	4	2	↓	135	117		252	325
0690	Construction joints, floor slab at exterior wall									
0700	Precast, brick, block or drywall exterior									
0710	2" wide joint	1 Carp	125	.064	L.F.	11.30	3.75		15.05	18.05
0720	4" wide joint	"	75	.107	"	17.45	6.25		23.70	28.50
0730	Metal panel, glass or curtain wall exterior									
0740	2" wide joint	1 Carp	40	.200	L.F.	12.85	11.70		24.55	31.50
0750	4" wide joint	"	25	.320	"	14.60	18.75		33.35	44
0760	Floor slab to drywall partition									
0770	Flat joint	1 Carp	100	.080	L.F.	14.80	4.69		19.49	23.50
0780	Fluted joint		50	.160		17.20	9.40		26.60	33
0790	Etched fluted joint	↓	75	.107	↓	20.50	6.25		26.75	32
0800	Floor slab to concrete/masonry partition									
0810	Flat joint	1 Carp	75	.107	L.F.	17.25	6.25		23.50	28.50
0820	Fluted joint	"	50	.160	"	18.80	9.40		28.20	34.50
0830	Concrete/CMU wall joints									
0840	1" wide	1 Carp	100	.080	L.F.	21	4.69		25.69	30
0850	2" wide		75	.107		32.50	6.25		38.75	45.50
0860	4" wide	↓	50	.160	↓	37	9.40		46.40	54.50
0870	Concrete/CMU floor joints									
0880	1" wide	1 Carp	200	.040	L.F.	22	2.34		24.34	27.50
0890	2" wide		150	.053		25.50	3.13		28.63	32.50
0900	4" wide	↓	100	.080	↓	37	4.69		41.69	47.50

07 91 Preformed Joint Seals

07 91 13 – Compression Seals

07 91 13.10 Compression Seals

		Crew	Daily Output	Labor-Hours	Unit	Material	2023 Bare Costs Labor	Equipment	Total	Total Incl O&P
0010	**COMPRESSION SEALS**									
4900	O-ring type cord, 1/4"	1 Bric	472	.017	L.F.	.54	.97		1.51	2.05
4910	1/2"		440	.018		1.44	1.05		2.49	3.15
4920	3/4"		424	.019		2.88	1.08		3.96	4.80
4930	1"		408	.020		5.80	1.13		6.93	8.05
4940	1-1/4"		384	.021		13.90	1.20		15.10	17.10
4950	1-1/2"		368	.022		17.10	1.25		18.35	20.50
4960	1-3/4"		352	.023		19.95	1.31		21.26	24
4970	2"	↓	344	.023		35	1.34		36.34	40

07 91 16 – Joint Gaskets

07 91 16.10 Joint Gaskets

		Crew	Daily Output	Labor-Hours	Unit	Material	2023 Bare Costs Labor	Equipment	Total	Total Incl O&P
0010	**JOINT GASKETS**									
4400	Joint gaskets, neoprene, closed cell w/adh, 1/8" x 3/8"	1 Bric	240	.033	L.F.	.22	1.92		2.14	3.12
4500	1/4" x 3/4"		215	.037		.68	2.14		2.82	3.96
4700	1/2" x 1"		200	.040		.78	2.30		3.08	4.31
4800	3/4" x 1-1/2"	↓	165	.048	↓	1.72	2.79		4.51	6.10

07 91 Preformed Joint Seals

07 91 23 – Backer Rods

07 91 23.10 Backer Rods

		Crew	Daily Output	Labor-Hours	Unit	Material	2023 Bare Costs Labor	Equipment	Total	Total Incl O&P
0010	**BACKER RODS**									
0030	Backer rod, polyethylene, 1/4" diameter	1 Bric	4.60	1.739	C.L.F.	7	100		107	158
0050	1/2" diameter		4.60	1.739		16	100		116	168
0070	3/4" diameter		4.60	1.739		17	100		117	169
0090	1" diameter		4.60	1.739		30	100		130	183

07 91 26 – Joint Fillers

07 91 26.10 Joint Fillers

		Crew	Daily Output	Labor-Hours	Unit	Material	Labor	Equipment	Total	Total Incl O&P
0010	**JOINT FILLERS**									
4360	Butyl rubber filler, 1/4" x 1/4"	1 Bric	290	.028	L.F.	.36	1.59		1.95	2.78
4365	1/2" x 1/2"		250	.032		1.44	1.84		3.28	4.34
4370	1/2" x 3/4"		210	.038		2.16	2.19		4.35	5.65
4375	3/4" x 3/4"		230	.035		3.24	2		5.24	6.55
4380	1" x 1"		180	.044		4.31	2.56		6.87	8.60
4390	For coloring, add					12%				
4980	Polyethylene joint backing, 1/4" x 2"	1 Bric	2.08	3.846	C.L.F.	14	221		235	345
4990	1/4" x 6"		1.28	6.250	"	150	360		510	705
5600	Silicone, room temp vulcanizing foam seal, 1/4" x 1/2"		1312	.006	L.F.	.37	.35		.72	.94
5610	1/2" x 1/2"		656	.012		.74	.70		1.44	1.86
5620	1/2" x 3/4"		442	.018		1.11	1.04		2.15	2.78
5630	3/4" x 3/4"		328	.024		1.67	1.40		3.07	3.94
5640	1/8" x 1"		1312	.006		.37	.35		.72	.94
5650	1/8" x 3"		442	.018		1.11	1.04		2.15	2.78
5670	1/4" x 3"		295	.027		2.22	1.56		3.78	4.78
5680	1/4" x 6"		148	.054		4.44	3.11		7.55	9.55
5690	1/2" x 6"		82	.098		8.90	5.60		14.50	18.15
5700	1/2" x 9"		52.50	.152		13.30	8.75		22.05	28
5710	1/2" x 12"		33	.242		17.75	13.95		31.70	40.50

07 92 Joint Sealants

07 92 13 – Elastomeric Joint Sealants

07 92 13.20 Caulking and Sealant Options

		Crew	Daily Output	Labor-Hours	Unit	Material	Labor	Equipment	Total	Total Incl O&P
0010	**CAULKING AND SEALANT OPTIONS**									
0050	Latex acrylic based, bulk				Gal.	39			39	43
0055	Bulk in place 1/4" x 1/4" bead	1 Bric	300	.027	L.F.	.12	1.53		1.65	2.44
0060	1/4" x 3/8"		294	.027		.21	1.56		1.77	2.58
0065	1/4" x 1/2"		288	.028		.27	1.60		1.87	2.70
0075	3/8" x 3/8"		284	.028		.31	1.62		1.93	2.77
0080	3/8" x 1/2"		280	.029		.41	1.64		2.05	2.92
0085	3/8" x 5/8"		276	.029		.51	1.67		2.18	3.07
0095	3/8" x 3/4"		272	.029		.61	1.69		2.30	3.22
0100	1/2" x 1/2"		275	.029		.55	1.67		2.22	3.11
0105	1/2" x 5/8"		269	.030		.69	1.71		2.40	3.32
0110	1/2" x 3/4"		263	.030		.82	1.75		2.57	3.54
0115	1/2" x 7/8"		256	.031		.96	1.80		2.76	3.76
0120	1/2" x 1"		250	.032		1.10	1.84		2.94	3.97
0125	3/4" x 3/4"		244	.033		1.24	1.89		3.13	4.19
0130	3/4" x 1"		225	.036		1.65	2.04		3.69	4.88
0135	1" x 1"		200	.040		2.19	2.30		4.49	5.85
0190	Cartridges				Gal.	47			47	52
0200	11 fl. oz. cartridge				Ea.	4.06			4.06	4.47

07 92 Joint Sealants

07 92 13 – Elastomeric Joint Sealants

07 92 13.20 Caulking and Sealant Options		Crew	Daily Output	Labor-Hours	Unit	Material	2023 Bare Costs Labor	Equipment	Total	Total Incl O&P
0500	1/4" x 1/2"	1 Bric	288	.028	L.F.	.33	1.60		1.93	2.76
0600	1/2" x 1/2"		275	.029		.66	1.67		2.33	3.24
0800	3/4" x 3/4"		244	.033		1.49	1.89		3.38	4.47
0900	3/4" x 1"		225	.036		1.99	2.04		4.03	5.25
1000	1" x 1"		200	.040		2.49	2.30		4.79	6.20
1400	Butyl based, bulk				Gal.	53			53	58.50
1500	Cartridges				"	53			53	58.50
1700	1/4" x 1/2", 154 L.F./gal.	1 Bric	288	.028	L.F.	.35	1.60		1.95	2.78
1800	1/2" x 1/2", 77 L.F./gal.	"	275	.029	"	.69	1.67		2.36	3.27
2300	Polysulfide compounds, 1 component, bulk				Gal.	108			108	119
2600	1 or 2 component, in place, 1/4" x 1/4", 308 L.F./gal.	1 Bric	300	.027	L.F.	.35	1.53		1.88	2.69
2700	1/2" x 1/4", 154 L.F./gal.		288	.028		.70	1.60		2.30	3.17
2900	3/4" x 3/8", 68 L.F./gal.		272	.029		1.59	1.69		3.28	4.29
3000	1" x 1/2", 38 L.F./gal.		250	.032		2.85	1.84		4.69	5.90
3200	Polyurethane, 1 or 2 component				Gal.	70.50			70.50	77.50
3300	Cartridges				"	84			84	92.50
3500	Bulk, in place, 1/4" x 1/4"	1 Bric	300	.027	L.F.	.23	1.53		1.76	2.55
3655	1/2" x 1/4"		288	.028		.46	1.60		2.06	2.90
3800	3/4" x 3/8"		272	.029		1.04	1.69		2.73	3.68
3900	1" x 1/2"		250	.032		1.83	1.84		3.67	4.77
4100	Silicone rubber, bulk				Gal.	85			85	93.50
4200	Cartridges				"	57.50			57.50	63.50

07 92 16 – Rigid Joint Sealants

07 92 16.10 Rigid Joint Sealants

		Crew	Daily Output	Labor-Hours	Unit	Material	Labor	Equipment	Total	Total Incl O&P
0010	**RIGID JOINT SEALANTS**									
5800	Tapes, sealant, PVC foam adhesive, 1/16" x 1/4"				C.L.F.	4.83			4.83	5.30
5900	1/16" x 1/2"					8.25			8.25	9.10
5950	1/16" x 1"					15.35			15.35	16.90
6000	1/8" x 1/2"					11.65			11.65	12.80

07 92 19 – Acoustical Joint Sealants

07 92 19.10 Acoustical Sealant

		Crew	Daily Output	Labor-Hours	Unit	Material	Labor	Equipment	Total	Total Incl O&P
0010	**ACOUSTICAL SEALANT**									
0020	Acoustical sealant, elastomeric, cartridges				Ea.	5.45			5.45	5.95
0025	In place, 1/4" x 1/4"	1 Bric	300	.027	L.F.	.22	1.53		1.75	2.54
0030	1/4" x 1/2"		288	.028		.44	1.60		2.04	2.89
0035	1/2" x 1/2"		275	.029		.89	1.67		2.56	3.49
0040	1/2" x 3/4"		263	.030		1.33	1.75		3.08	4.09
0045	3/4" x 3/4"		244	.033		2	1.89		3.89	5.05
0050	1" x 1"		200	.040		3.55	2.30		5.85	7.35

Division Notes

	CREW	DAILY OUTPUT	LABOR-HOURS	UNIT	BARE COSTS				TOTAL INCL O&P
					MAT.	LABOR	EQUIP.	TOTAL	

Estimating Tips
General
- Room Finish Schedule: A complete set of plans should contain a room finish schedule. If one is not available, it would be well worth the time and effort to obtain one.

09 20 00 Plaster and Gypsum Board
- Lath is estimated by the square yard plus a 5% allowance for waste. Furring, channels, and accessories are measured by the linear foot. An extra foot should be allowed for each accessory miter or stop.
- Plaster is also estimated by the square yard. Deductions for openings vary by preference, from zero deduction to 50% of all openings over 2 feet in width. The estimator should allow one extra square foot for each linear foot of horizontal interior or exterior angle located below the ceiling level. Also, double the areas of small radius work.
- Drywall accessories, studs, track, and acoustical caulking are all measured by the linear foot. Drywall taping is figured by the square foot. Gypsum wallboard is estimated by the square foot. No material deductions should be made for door or window openings under 32 S.F.

09 60 00 Flooring
- Tile and terrazzo areas are taken off on a square foot basis. Trim and base materials are measured by the linear foot. Accent tiles are listed per each. Two basic methods of installation are used. Mud set is approximately 30% more expensive than thin set.

The cost of grout is included with tile unit price lines unless otherwise noted. In terrazzo work, be sure to include the linear footage of embedded decorative strips, grounds, machine rubbing, and power cleanup.
- Wood flooring is available in strip, parquet, or block configuration. The latter two types are set in adhesives with quantities estimated by the square foot. The laying pattern will influence labor costs and material waste. In addition to the material and labor for laying wood floors, the estimator must make allowances for sanding and finishing these areas, unless the flooring is prefinished.
- Sheet flooring is measured by the square yard. Roll widths vary, so consideration should be given to use the most economical width, as waste must be figured into the total quantity. Consider also the installation methods available—direct glue down or stretched. Direct glue-down installation is assumed with sheet carpet unit price lines unless otherwise noted.

09 70 00 Wall Finishes
- Wall coverings are estimated by the square foot. The area to be covered is measured—length by height of the wall above the baseboards—to calculate the square footage of each wall. This figure is divided by the number of square feet in the single roll which is being used. Deduct, in full, the areas of openings such as doors and windows. Where a pattern match is required allow 25–30% waste.

09 80 00 Acoustic Treatment
- Acoustical systems fall into several categories. The takeoff of these materials should be by the square foot of area with a 5% allowance for waste. Do not forget about scaffolding, if applicable, when estimating these systems.

09 90 00 Painting and Coating
- New line items created for cut-ins with reference diagram.
- A major portion of the work in painting involves surface preparation. Be sure to include cleaning, sanding, filling, and masking costs in the estimate.
- Protection of adjacent surfaces is not included in painting costs. When considering the method of paint application, an important factor is the amount of protection and masking required. These must be estimated separately and may be the determining factor in choosing the method of application.

Reference Numbers
Reference numbers are shown at the beginning of some major classifications. These numbers refer to related items in the Reference Section. The reference information may be an estimating procedure, an alternate pricing method, or technical information.

Note: Not all subdivisions listed here necessarily appear. ■

Same Data. Simplified.
Enjoy the convenience and efficiency of accessing your costs anywhere:
- **Skip the multiplier** by setting your location
- **Quickly search,** edit, favorite and share costs
- **Stay on top of price changes** with automatic updates

Discover more at rsmeans.com/online

No part of this cost data may be reproduced, stored in a retrieval system, or transmitted in any form or by any means without prior written permission of Gordian.

09 22 Supports for Plaster and Gypsum Board

09 22 03 – Fastening Methods for Finishes

09 22 03.20 Drilling Plaster/Drywall

		Crew	Daily Output	Labor-Hours	Unit	Material	2023 Bare Costs Labor	Equipment	Total	Total Incl O&P
0010	**DRILLING PLASTER/DRYWALL**									
1100	Drilling & layout for drywall/plaster walls, up to 1" deep, no anchor									
1200	Holes, 1/4" diameter	1 Carp	150	.053	Ea.	.01	3.13		3.14	4.66
1300	3/8" diameter		140	.057			3.35		3.35	4.99
1400	1/2" diameter		130	.062			3.61		3.61	5.35
1500	3/4" diameter		120	.067		.01	3.91		3.92	5.80
1600	1" diameter		110	.073		.02	4.26		4.28	6.35
1700	1-1/4" diameter		100	.080		.03	4.69		4.72	7.05
1800	1-1/2" diameter	↓	90	.089	↓	.04	5.20		5.24	7.80
1900	For ceiling installations, add						40%			

09 91 Painting

09 91 23 – Interior Painting

09 91 23.52 Miscellaneous, Interior

		Crew	Daily Output	Labor-Hours	Unit	Material	2023 Bare Costs Labor	Equipment	Total	Total Incl O&P
0010	**MISCELLANEOUS, INTERIOR**									
3800	Grilles, per side, oil base, primer coat, brushwork	1 Pord	520	.015	S.F.	.20	.76		.96	1.34
3850	Spray		1140	.007		.20	.35		.55	.74
3880	Paint 1 coat, brushwork		520	.015		.36	.76		1.12	1.52
3900	Spray		1140	.007		.40	.35		.75	.96
3920	Paint 2 coats, brushwork		325	.025		.69	1.22		1.91	2.57
3940	Spray		650	.012		.79	.61		1.40	1.78
3950	Prime & paint 1 coat		325	.025		.55	1.22		1.77	2.42
3960	Prime & paint 2 coats		270	.030		.54	1.47		2.01	2.78
4500	Louvers, 1 side, primer, brushwork		524	.015		.10	.76		.86	1.23
4520	Paint 1 coat, brushwork		520	.015		.16	.76		.92	1.31
4530	Spray		1140	.007		.18	.35		.53	.72
4540	Paint 2 coats, brushwork		325	.025		.31	1.22		1.53	2.15
4550	Spray		650	.012		.35	.61		.96	1.29
4560	Paint 3 coats, brushwork		270	.030		.46	1.47		1.93	2.69
4570	Spray	↓	500	.016	↓	.52	.79		1.31	1.75
5000	Pipe, 1"-4" diameter, primer or sealer coat, oil base, brushwork	2 Pord	1250	.013	L.F.	.10	.64		.74	1.05
5100	Spray		2165	.007		.09	.37		.46	.64
5200	Paint 1 coat, brushwork		1250	.013		.19	.64		.83	1.15
5300	Spray		2165	.007		.16	.37		.53	.72
5350	Paint 2 coats, brushwork		775	.021		.33	1.03		1.36	1.88
5400	Spray		1240	.013		.36	.64		1	1.35
5420	Paint 3 coats, brushwork		775	.021		.49	1.03		1.52	2.06
5450	5"-8" diameter, primer or sealer coat, brushwork		620	.026		.20	1.28		1.48	2.12
5500	Spray		1085	.015		.33	.73		1.06	1.44
5550	Paint 1 coat, brushwork		620	.026		.50	1.28		1.78	2.45
5600	Spray		1085	.015		.55	.73		1.28	1.69
5650	Paint 2 coats, brushwork		385	.042		.66	2.06		2.72	3.78
5700	Spray		620	.026		.73	1.28		2.01	2.70
5720	Paint 3 coats, brushwork		385	.042		.97	2.06		3.03	4.13
5750	9"-12" diameter, primer or sealer coat, brushwork		415	.039		.30	1.91		2.21	3.17
5800	Spray		725	.022		.60	1.10		1.70	2.28
5850	Paint 1 coat, brushwork		415	.039		.51	1.91		2.42	3.40
6000	Spray		725	.022		.56	1.10		1.66	2.24
6200	Paint 2 coats, brushwork		260	.062		.98	3.06		4.04	5.60
6250	Spray		415	.039		1.09	1.91		3	4.04
6270	Paint 3 coats, brushwork	↓	260	.062	↓	1.46	3.06		4.52	6.15

09 91 Painting

09 91 23 – Interior Painting

09 91 23.52 Miscellaneous, Interior		Crew	Daily Output	Labor-Hours	Unit	Material	2023 Bare Costs Labor	Equipment	Total	Total Incl O&P
6300	13"-16" diameter, primer or sealer coat, brushwork	2 Pord	310	.052	L.F.	.40	2.56		2.96	4.24
6350	Spray		540	.030		.45	1.47		1.92	2.67
6400	Paint 1 coat, brushwork		310	.052		.68	2.56		3.24	4.54
6450	Spray		540	.030		.75	1.47		2.22	3.01
6500	Paint 2 coats, brushwork		195	.082		1.31	4.07		5.38	7.50
6550	Spray		310	.052		1.46	2.56		4.02	5.40
6600	Radiators, per side, primer, brushwork	1 Pord	520	.015	S.F.	.10	.76		.86	1.24
6620	Paint, 1 coat		520	.015		.09	.76		.85	1.23
6640	2 coats		340	.024		.31	1.17		1.48	2.07
6660	3 coats		283	.028		.46	1.40		1.86	2.59

Division Notes

		CREW	DAILY OUTPUT	LABOR-HOURS	UNIT	BARE COSTS				TOTAL INCL O&P
						MAT.	LABOR	EQUIP.	TOTAL	

Estimating Tips
General
- The items in this division are usually priced per square foot or each.
- Many items in Division 10 require some type of support system or special anchors that are not usually furnished with the item. The required anchors must be added to the estimate in the appropriate division.
- Some items in Division 10, such as lockers, may require assembly before installation. Verify the amount of assembly required. Assembly can often exceed installation time.

10 20 00 Interior Specialties
- Support angles and blocking are not included in the installation of toilet compartments, shower/dressing compartments, or cubicles. Appropriate line items from Division 5 or 6 may need to be added to support the installations.
- Toilet partitions are priced by the stall. A stall consists of a side wall, pilaster, and door with hardware. Toilet tissue holders and grab bars are extra.
- The required acoustical rating of a folding partition can have a significant impact on costs. Verify the sound transmission coefficient rating of the panel priced against the specification requirements.
- Grab bar installation does not include supplemental blocking or backing to support the required load. When grab bars are installed at an existing facility, provisions must be made to attach the grab bars to a solid structure.

Reference Numbers
Reference numbers are shown at the beginning of some major classifications. These numbers refer to related items in the Reference Section. The reference information may be an estimating procedure, an alternate pricing method, or technical information.

Note: Not all subdivisions listed here necessarily appear. ∎

Same Data. Simplified.

Enjoy the convenience and efficiency of accessing your costs anywhere:
- **Skip the multiplier** by setting your location
- **Quickly search,** edit, favorite and share costs
- **Stay on top of price changes** with automatic updates

Discover more at rsmeans.com/online

No part of this cost data may be reproduced, stored in a retrieval system, or transmitted in any form or by any means without prior written permission of Gordian.

10 21 Compartments and Cubicles

10 21 13 – Toilet Compartments

10 21 13.13 Metal Toilet Compartments

		Crew	Daily Output	Labor-Hours	Unit	Material	2023 Bare Costs Labor	Equipment	Total	Total Incl O&P
0010	**METAL TOILET COMPARTMENTS**									
0110	Cubicles, ceiling hung									
0200	Powder coated steel	2 Carp	4	4	Ea.	520	234		754	920
0500	Stainless steel	"	4	4		2,100	234		2,334	2,650
0600	For handicap units, add					146			146	161
0900	Floor and ceiling anchored									
1000	Powder coated steel	2 Carp	5	3.200	Ea.	780	188		968	1,150
1300	Stainless steel	"	5	3.200		2,000	188		2,188	2,475
1400	For handicap units, add					146			146	161
1610	Floor anchored									
1700	Powder coated steel	2 Carp	7	2.286	Ea.	770	134		904	1,050
2000	Stainless steel	"	7	2.286		1,250	134		1,384	1,575
2100	For handicap units, add					146			146	161
2200	For juvenile units, deduct					55			55	60.50
2450	Floor anchored, headrail braced									
2500	Powder coated steel	2 Carp	6	2.667	Ea.	580	156		736	875
2804	Stainless steel	"	6	2.667		1,350	156		1,506	1,700
2900	For handicap units, add					239			239	263
3000	Wall hung partitions, powder coated steel	2 Carp	7	2.286	Ea.	615	134		749	880
3300	Stainless steel	"	7	2.286		445	134		579	690
3400	For handicap units, add					860			860	945
4000	Screens, entrance, floor mounted, 58" high, 48" wide									
4200	Powder coated steel	2 Carp	15	1.067	Ea.	260	62.50		322.50	380
4500	Stainless steel	"	15	1.067	"	520	62.50		582.50	665
4650	Urinal screen, 18" wide									
4704	Powder coated steel	2 Carp	6.15	2.602	Ea.	320	152		472	580
5004	Stainless steel	"	6.15	2.602	"	605	152		757	890
5100	Floor mounted, headrail braced									
5300	Powder coated steel	2 Carp	8	2	Ea.	226	117		343	425
5600	Stainless steel	"	8	2	"	445	117		562	665
5750	Pilaster, flush									
5800	Powder coated steel	2 Carp	10	1.600	Ea.	287	94		381	455
6100	Stainless steel		10	1.600		184	94		278	345
6300	Post braced, powder coated steel		10	1.600		169	94		263	325
6800	Powder coated steel		10	1.600		123	94		217	275
7800	Wedge type, powder coated steel		10	1.600		168	94		262	325
8100	Stainless steel		10	1.600		770	94		864	985

10 21 13.16 Plastic-Laminate-Clad Toilet Compartments

		Crew	Daily Output	Labor-Hours	Unit	Material	Labor	Equipment	Total	Total Incl O&P
0010	**PLASTIC-LAMINATE-CLAD TOILET COMPARTMENTS**									
0110	Cubicles, ceiling hung									
0300	Plastic laminate on particle board	2 Carp	4	4	Ea.	650	234		884	1,075
0600	For handicap units, add				"	146			146	161
0900	Floor and ceiling anchored									
1100	Plastic laminate on particle board	2 Carp	5	3.200	Ea.	690	188		878	1,050
1400	For handicap units, add				"	146			146	161
1610	Floor mounted									
1800	Plastic laminate on particle board	2 Carp	7	2.286	Ea.	925	134		1,059	1,225
2450	Floor mounted, headrail braced									
2600	Plastic laminate on particle board	2 Carp	6	2.667	Ea.	995	156		1,151	1,325
3400	For handicap units, add					860			860	945
4300	Entrance screen, floor mtd., plas. lam., 58" high, 48" wide	2 Carp	15	1.067		325	62.50		387.50	450
4800	Urinal screen, 18" wide, ceiling braced, plastic laminate		8	2		291	117		408	495

10 21 Compartments and Cubicles

10 21 13 – Toilet Compartments

10 21 13.16 Plastic-Laminate-Clad Toilet Compartments		Crew	Daily Output	Labor-Hours	Unit	Material	2023 Bare Costs Labor	Equipment	Total	Total Incl O&P
5400	Floor mounted, headrail braced	2 Carp	8	2	Ea.	233	117		350	430
5900	Pilaster, flush, plastic laminate		10	1.600		320	94		414	495
6400	Post braced, plastic laminate		10	1.600		288	94		382	455
6700	Wall hung, bracket supported									
6900	Plastic laminate on particle board	2 Carp	10	1.600	Ea.	100	94		194	250
7450	Flange supported									
7500	Plastic laminate on particle board	2 Carp	10	1.600	Ea.	120	94		214	272

10 21 13.19 Plastic Toilet Compartments

		Crew	Daily Output	Labor-Hours	Unit	Material	Labor	Equipment	Total	Total Incl O&P
0010	**PLASTIC TOILET COMPARTMENTS**									
0110	Cubicles, ceiling hung									
0250	Phenolic	2 Carp	4	4	Ea.	1,350	234		1,584	1,825
0260	Polymer plastic	"	4	4		400	234		634	790
0600	For handicap units, add					146			146	161
0900	Floor and ceiling anchored									
1050	Phenolic	2 Carp	5	3.200	Ea.	1,400	188		1,588	1,800
1060	Polymer plastic	"	5	3.200		995	188		1,183	1,375
1400	For handicap units, add					146			146	161
1610	Floor mounted									
1750	Phenolic	2 Carp	7	2.286	Ea.	1,325	134		1,459	1,650
1760	Polymer plastic	"	7	2.286		925	134		1,059	1,225
2100	For handicap units, add					146			146	161
2200	For juvenile units, deduct					55			55	60.50
2450	Floor mounted, headrail braced									
2550	Phenolic	2 Carp	6	2.667	Ea.	1,300	156		1,456	1,650
3600	Polymer plastic		6	2.667		380	156		536	655
3810	Entrance screen, polymer plastic, flr. mtd., 48" x 58"		6	2.667		320	156		476	585
3820	Entrance screen, polymer plastic, flr. to clg pilaster, 48" x 58"		6	2.667		320	156		476	585
6110	Urinal screen, polymer plastic, pilaster flush, 18" w		6	2.667		273	156		429	535
7110	Wall hung		6	2.667		147	156		303	395
7710	Flange mounted		6	2.667		153	156		309	400

10 21 13.40 Stone Toilet Compartments

		Crew	Daily Output	Labor-Hours	Unit	Material	Labor	Equipment	Total	Total Incl O&P
0010	**STONE TOILET COMPARTMENTS**									
0100	Cubicles, ceiling hung, marble	2 Marb	2	8	Ea.	2,025	455		2,480	2,900
0600	For handicap units, add					146			146	161
0800	Floor & ceiling anchored, marble	2 Marb	2.50	6.400		2,050	365		2,415	2,800
1400	For handicap units, add					146			146	161
1600	Floor mounted, marble	2 Marb	3	5.333		1,300	305		1,605	1,875
2400	Floor mounted, headrail braced, marble	"	3	5.333		1,475	305		1,780	2,075
2900	For handicap units, add					239			239	263
4100	Entrance screen, floor mounted marble, 58" high, 48" wide	2 Marb	9	1.778		885	101		986	1,125
4600	Urinal screen, 18" wide, ceiling braced, marble	D-1	6	2.667		930	139		1,069	1,225
5100	Floor mounted, headrail braced									
5200	Marble	D-1	6	2.667	Ea.	795	139		934	1,075
5700	Pilaster, flush, marble		9	1.778		1,050	92.50		1,142.50	1,300
6200	Post braced, marble		9	1.778		1,025	92.50		1,117.50	1,275

10 28 Toilet, Bath, and Laundry Accessories

10 28 13 – Toilet Accessories

10 28 13.13 Commercial Toilet Accessories		Crew	Daily Output	Labor-Hours	Unit	Material	2023 Bare Costs Labor	Equipment	Total	Total Incl O&P
0010	**COMMERCIAL TOILET ACCESSORIES**									
0200	Curtain rod, stainless steel, 5' long, 1" diameter	1 Carp	13	.615	Ea.	50	36		86	109
0300	1-1/4" diameter	"	13	.615	"	45	36		81	103
0500	Dispenser units, combined soap & towel dispensers,									
0510	Mirror and shelf, flush mounted	1 Carp	10	.800	Ea.	325	47		372	425
0600	Towel dispenser and waste receptacle,									
0610	18 gallon capacity	1 Carp	10	.800	Ea.	400	47		447	510
0800	Grab bar, straight, 1-1/4" diameter, stainless steel, 18" long		24	.333		21	19.55		40.55	52
0900	24" long		23	.348		24	20.50		44.50	57
1000	30" long		22	.364		37	21.50		58.50	72
1100	36" long		20	.400		27	23.50		50.50	64.50
1105	42" long		20	.400		51	23.50		74.50	91
1120	Corner, 36" long		20	.400		110	23.50		133.50	156
1200	1-1/2" diameter, 24" long		23	.348		33	20.50		53.50	67
1300	36" long		20	.400		43	23.50		66.50	82.50
1310	42" long		18	.444		42	26		68	85.50
1500	Tub bar, 1-1/4" diameter, 24" x 36"		14	.571		114	33.50		147.50	175
1600	Plus vertical arm		12	.667		207	39		246	286
1900	End tub bar, 1" diameter, 90° angle, 16" x 32"		12	.667		99	39		138	167
2300	Hand dryer, surface mounted, electric, 115 volt, 20 amp		4	2		475	117		592	695
2400	230 volt, 10 amp		4	2		680	117		797	925
2450	Hand dryer, touch free, 1400 watt, 81,000 rpm		4	2		1,450	117		1,567	1,775
2600	Hat and coat strip, stainless steel, 4 hook, 36" long		24	.333		73.50	19.55		93.05	110
2700	6 hook, 60" long		20	.400		106	23.50		129.50	152
3000	Mirror, with stainless steel 3/4" square frame, 18" x 24"		20	.400		51	23.50		74.50	91
3100	36" x 24"		15	.533		80	31.50		111.50	135
3200	48" x 24"		10	.800		116	47		163	198
3300	72" x 24"		6	1.333		144	78		222	274
3500	With 5" stainless steel shelf, 18" x 24"		20	.400		108	23.50		131.50	154
3600	36" x 24"		15	.533		136	31.50		167.50	197
3700	48" x 24"		10	.800		219	47		266	310
3800	72" x 24"		6	1.333		800	78		878	995
4100	Mop holder strip, stainless steel, 5 holders, 48" long		20	.400		65	23.50		88.50	107
4200	Napkin/tampon dispenser, recessed		15	.533		400	31.50		431.50	485
4220	Semi-recessed		6.50	1.231		430	72		502	575
4250	Napkin receptacle, recessed		6.50	1.231		229	72		301	360
4300	Robe hook, single, regular		96	.083		26	4.88		30.88	36
4400	Heavy duty, concealed mounting		56	.143		25.50	8.35		33.85	41
4600	Soap dispenser, chrome, surface mounted, liquid		20	.400		52.50	23.50		76	92.50
5000	Recessed stainless steel, liquid		10	.800		96.50	47		143.50	176
5600	Shelf, stainless steel, 5" wide, 18 ga., 24" long		24	.333		75	19.55		94.55	112
5700	48" long		16	.500		124	29.50		153.50	180
5800	8" wide shelf, 18 ga., 24" long		22	.364		63	21.50		84.50	101
5900	48" long		14	.571		97	33.50		130.50	157
6000	Toilet seat cover dispenser, stainless steel, recessed		20	.400		211	23.50		234.50	267
6050	Surface mounted		15	.533		36	31.50		67.50	86
6200	Double roll		24	.333		103	19.55		122.55	142
6240	Plastic, twin/jumbo dbl. roll		24	.333		57.50	19.55		77.05	92
6400	Towel bar, stainless steel, 18" long		23	.348		41	20.50		61.50	75.50
6500	30" long		21	.381		40	22.50		62.50	77
6700	Towel dispenser, stainless steel, surface mounted		16	.500		48.50	29.50		78	97
6800	Flush mounted, recessed		10	.800		118	47		165	200
6900	Plastic, touchless, battery operated		16	.500		143	29.50		172.50	201

10 28 Toilet, Bath, and Laundry Accessories

10 28 13 – Toilet Accessories

10 28 13.13 Commercial Toilet Accessories

		Crew	Daily Output	Labor-Hours	Unit	Material	2023 Bare Costs Labor	2023 Bare Costs Equipment	Total	Total Incl O&P
7000	Towel holder, hotel type, 2 guest size	1 Carp	20	.400	Ea.	76	23.50		99.50	119
7200	Towel shelf, stainless steel, 24" long, 8" wide		20	.400		39.50	23.50		63	78.50
7400	Tumbler holder, for tumbler only		30	.267		20.50	15.65		36.15	46.50
7410	Tumbler holder, recessed		20	.400		17.75	23.50		41.25	54.50
7500	Soap, tumbler & toothbrush		30	.267		6.80	15.65		22.45	31
7510	Tumbler & toothbrush holder		20	.400		9	23.50		32.50	45
8000	Waste receptacles, stainless steel, with top, 13 gallon		10	.800		415	47		462	525
8100	36 gallon		8	1		485	58.50		543.50	625
9996	Bathroom access., grab bar, straight, 1-1/2" diam., SS, 42" L install only		18	.444			26		26	39

10 28 16 – Bath Accessories

10 28 16.20 Medicine Cabinets

		Crew	Daily Output	Labor-Hours	Unit	Material	2023 Bare Costs Labor	2023 Bare Costs Equipment	Total	Total Incl O&P
0010	**MEDICINE CABINETS**									
0020	With mirror, sst frame, 16" x 22", unlighted	1 Carp	14	.571	Ea.	279	33.50		312.50	355
0100	Wood frame		14	.571		106	33.50		139.50	166
0300	Sliding mirror doors, 20" x 16" x 4-3/4", unlighted		7	1.143		165	67		232	281
0400	24" x 19" x 8-1/2", lighted		5	1.600		178	94		272	335
0600	Triple door, 30" x 32", unlighted, plywood body		7	1.143		293	67		360	420
0700	Steel body		7	1.143		225	67		292	350
0900	Oak door, wood body, beveled mirror, single door		7	1.143		189	67		256	310
1000	Double door		6	1.333		480	78		558	640
1200	Hotel cabinets, stainless, with lower shelf, unlighted		10	.800		400	47		447	510
1300	Lighted		5	1.600		350	94		444	525

10 28 19 – Tub and Shower Enclosures

10 28 19.10 Partitions, Shower

		Crew	Daily Output	Labor-Hours	Unit	Material	2023 Bare Costs Labor	2023 Bare Costs Equipment	Total	Total Incl O&P
0010	**PARTITIONS, SHOWER** floor mounted, no plumbing									
0400	Cabinet, one piece, fiberglass, 32" x 32"	2 Carp	5	3.200	Ea.	570	188		758	905
0420	36" x 36"		5	3.200		1,150	188		1,338	1,550
0440	36" x 48"		5	3.200		1,250	188		1,438	1,650
0460	Acrylic, 32" x 32"		5	3.200		256	188		444	560
0480	36" x 36"		5	3.200		1,150	188		1,338	1,550
0500	36" x 48"		5	3.200		1,275	188		1,463	1,675
0520	Shower door for above, clear plastic, 24" wide	1 Carp	8	1		111	58.50		169.50	210
0540	28" wide		8	1		315	58.50		373.50	435
0560	Tempered glass, 24" wide		8	1		176	58.50		234.50	281
0580	28" wide		8	1		223	58.50		281.50	335
2400	Glass stalls, with doors, no receptors, chrome on brass	2 Shee	3	5.333		950	375		1,325	1,625
2700	Anodized aluminum	"	4	4		865	281		1,146	1,375
2900	Marble shower stall, stock design, with shower door	2 Marb	1.20	13.333		800	760		1,560	2,025
3000	With curtain		1.30	12.308		2,450	700		3,150	3,750
3200	Receptors, precast terrazzo, 32" x 32"		14	1.143		315	65		380	445
3300	48" x 34"		9.50	1.684		410	96		506	595
3500	Plastic, simulated terrazzo receptor, 32" x 32"		14	1.143		161	65		226	275
3600	32" x 48"		12	1.333		770	76		846	960
3800	Precast concrete, colors, 32" x 32"		14	1.143		200	65		265	320
3900	48" x 48"		8	2		970	114		1,084	1,250
4100	Shower doors, economy plastic, 24" wide	1 Shee	9	.889		162	62.50		224.50	272
4200	Tempered glass door, economy		8	1		340	70		410	475
4400	Folding, tempered glass, aluminum frame		6	1.333		630	93.50		723.50	835
4500	Sliding, tempered glass, 48" opening		6	1.333		580	93.50		673.50	780
4700	Deluxe, tempered glass, chrome on brass frame, 42" to 44"		8	1		375	70		445	520
4800	39" to 48" wide		1	8		940	560		1,500	1,875
4850	On anodized aluminum frame, obscure glass		2	4		730	281		1,011	1,225

For customer support on your Plumbing Costs with RSMeans data, call 800.448.8182.

10 28 Toilet, Bath, and Laundry Accessories

10 28 19 – Tub and Shower Enclosures

10 28 19.10 Partitions, Shower

		Crew	Daily Output	Labor-Hours	Unit	Material	2023 Bare Costs Labor	Equipment	Total	Total Incl O&P
4900	Clear glass	1 Shee	1	8	Ea.	505	560		1,065	1,400
5100	Shower enclosure, tempered glass, anodized alum. frame									
5120	2 panel & door, corner unit, 32" x 32"	1 Shee	2	4	Ea.	1,475	281		1,756	2,050
5140	Neo-angle corner unit, 16" x 24" x 16"	"	2	4		1,950	281		2,231	2,575
5200	Shower surround, 3 wall, polypropylene, 32" x 32"	1 Carp	4	2		365	117		482	575
5220	PVC, 32" x 32"		4	2		495	117		612	720
5240	Fiberglass		4	2		470	117		587	695
5250	2 wall, polypropylene, 32" x 32"		4	2		375	117		492	585
5270	PVC		4	2		450	117		567	670
5290	Fiberglass		4	2		450	117		567	670
5300	Tub doors, tempered glass & frame, obscure glass	1 Shee	8	1		266	70		336	400
5400	Clear glass		6	1.333		620	93.50		713.50	820
5600	Chrome plated, brass frame, obscure glass		8	1		350	70		420	490
5700	Clear glass		6	1.333		860	93.50		953.50	1,075
5900	Tub/shower enclosure, temp. glass, alum. frame, obscure glass		2	4		475	281		756	950
6200	Clear glass		1.50	5.333		990	375		1,365	1,675
6500	On chrome-plated brass frame, obscure glass		2	4		655	281		936	1,150
6600	Clear glass		1.50	5.333		1,400	375		1,775	2,125
6800	Tub surround, 3 wall, polypropylene	1 Carp	4	2		305	117		422	510
6900	PVC		4	2		445	117		562	665
7000	Fiberglass, obscure glass		4	2		465	117		582	685
7100	Clear glass		3	2.667		790	156		946	1,100

10 44 Fire Protection Specialties

10 44 13 – Fire Protection Cabinets

10 44 13.53 Fire Equipment Cabinets

			Crew	Daily Output	Labor-Hours	Unit	Material	2023 Bare Costs Labor	Equipment	Total	Total Incl O&P
0010	**FIRE EQUIPMENT CABINETS**, not equipped, 20 ga. steel box	D4020-310									
0040	Recessed, D.S. glass in door, box size given										
1000	Portable extinguisher, single, 8" x 12" x 27", alum. door & frame		Q-12	8	2	Ea.	116	127		243	320
1100	Steel door and frame			8	2		93	127		220	292
1200	Stainless steel door and frame			8	2		161	127		288	365
2000	Portable extinguisher, large, 8" x 12" x 36", alum. door & frame			8	2		370	127		497	595
2100	Steel door and frame	D4020-330		8	2		325	127		452	545
2200	Stainless steel door and frame			8	2		535	127		662	780
2500	8" x 16" x 38", aluminum door & frame			8	2		104	127		231	305
2600	Steel door and frame			8	2		121	127		248	325
2700	Fire blanket & extinguisher cab, inc blanket, rec stl., 14" x 40" x 8"			7	2.286		355	146		501	605
2800	Fire blanket cab, inc blanket, surf mtd, stl, 15"x10"x5", w/pwdr coat fin			8	2		121	127		248	325
3000	Hose rack assy., 1-1/2" valve & 100' hose, 24" x 40" x 5-1/2"										
3100	Aluminum door and frame		Q-12	6	2.667	Ea.	915	170		1,085	1,250
3200	Steel door and frame	D4020-410		6	2.667		875	170		1,045	1,225
3300	Stainless steel door and frame			6	2.667		1,175	170		1,345	1,550
4000	Hose rack assy., 2-1/2" x 1-1/2" valve, 100' hose, 24" x 40" x 8"										
4100	Aluminum door and frame		Q-12	6	2.667	Ea.	1,050	170		1,220	1,400
4200	Steel door and frame	R211226-10		6	2.667		920	170		1,090	1,275
4300	Stainless steel door and frame			6	2.667		1,200	170		1,370	1,575
5000	Hose rack assy., 2-1/2" x 1-1/2" valve, 100' hose										
5010	and extinguisher, 30" x 40" x 8"										
5100	Aluminum door and frame		Q-12	5	3.200	Ea.	400	204		604	745
5200	Steel door and frame			5	3.200		400	204		604	745
5300	Stainless steel door and frame			5	3.200		635	204		839	1,000

10 44 Fire Protection Specialties

10 44 13 – Fire Protection Cabinets

10 44 13.53 Fire Equipment Cabinets

		Crew	Daily Output	Labor-Hours	Unit	Material	2023 Bare Costs Labor	Equipment	Total	Total Incl O&P
6000	Hose rack assy., 1-1/2" valve, 100' hose									
6010	and 2-1/2" FD valve, 24" x 44" x 8"									
6100	Aluminum door and frame	Q-12	5	3.200	Ea.	420	204		624	765
6200	Steel door and frame		5	3.200		370	204		574	710
6300	Stainless steel door and frame		5	3.200		660	204		864	1,025
7000	Hose rack assy., 1-1/2" valve & 100' hose, 2-1/2" FD valve									
7010	and extinguisher, 30" x 44" x 8"									
7100	Aluminum door and frame	Q-12	5	3.200	Ea.	395	204		599	740
7200	Steel door and frame		5	3.200		340	204		544	680
7300	Stainless steel door and frame		5	3.200		655	204		859	1,025
8000	Valve cabinet for 2-1/2" FD angle valve, 18" x 18" x 8"									
8100	Aluminum door and frame	Q-12	12	1.333	Ea.	365	85		450	525
8200	Steel door and frame		12	1.333		315	85		400	470
8300	Stainless steel door and frame		12	1.333		440	85		525	605

10 44 16 – Fire Extinguishers

10 44 16.13 Portable Fire Extinguishers

		Crew	Daily Output	Labor-Hours	Unit	Material	Labor	Equipment	Total	Total Incl O&P
0010	**PORTABLE FIRE EXTINGUISHERS**									
0140	CO_2, with hose and "H" horn, 10 lb.				Ea.	345			345	380
0160	15 lb.					420			420	460
0180	20 lb.					520			520	570
1000	Dry chemical, pressurized									
1040	Standard type, portable, painted, 2-1/2 lb.				Ea.	43			43	47.50
1060	5 lb.					60			60	66
1080	10 lb.					94			94	103
1100	20 lb.					185			185	203
1120	30 lb.					935			935	1,025
1300	Standard type, wheeled, 150 lb.					2,325			2,325	2,550
2000	ABC all purpose type, portable, 2-1/2 lb.					28			28	30.50
2060	5 lb.					35			35	38.50
2080	9-1/2 lb.					57			57	62.50
2100	20 lb.					110			110	121
5000	Pressurized water, 2-1/2 gallon, stainless steel					107			107	118
5060	With anti-freeze					190			190	209
9400	Installation of extinguishers, 12 or more, on nailable surface	1 Carp	30	.267			15.65		15.65	23.50
9420	On masonry or concrete	"	15	.533			31.50		31.50	46.50

10 44 16.16 Wheeled Fire Extinguisher Units

		Crew	Daily Output	Labor-Hours	Unit	Material	Labor	Equipment	Total	Total Incl O&P
0010	**WHEELED FIRE EXTINGUISHER UNITS**									
0350	CO_2, portable, with swivel horn									
0360	Wheeled type, cart mounted, 50 lb.				Ea.	1,950			1,950	2,125
0400	100 lb.				"	3,450			3,450	3,800
2200	ABC all purpose type									
2300	Wheeled, 45 lb.				Ea.	2,350			2,350	2,575
2360	150 lb.				"	3,500			3,500	3,850

Division Notes

	CREW	DAILY OUTPUT	LABOR-HOURS	UNIT	BARE COSTS				TOTAL INCL O&P
					MAT.	LABOR	EQUIP.	TOTAL	

Division 11 Equipment

Estimating Tips
General
- The items in this division are usually priced per square foot or each. Many of these items are purchased by the owner for installation by the contractor. Check the specifications for responsibilities and include time for receiving, storage, installation, and mechanical and electrical hookups in the appropriate divisions.
- Many items in Division 11 require some type of support system that is not usually furnished with the item. Examples of these systems include blocking for the attachment of casework and support angles/blocking for ceiling-hung projection screens. The required blocking or supports must be added to the estimate in the appropriate division.
- Some items in Division 11 may require assembly or electrical hookups. Verify the amount of assembly required or the need for a hard electrical connection and add the appropriate costs.

Reference Numbers
Reference numbers are shown at the beginning of some major classifications. These numbers refer to related items in the Reference Section. The reference information may be an estimating procedure, an alternate pricing method, or technical information.

Same Data. Simplified.

Enjoy the convenience and efficiency of accessing your costs anywhere:
- **Skip the multiplier** by setting your location
- **Quickly search,** edit, favorite and share costs
- **Stay on top of price changes** with automatic updates

Discover more at rsmeans.com/online

No part of this cost data may be reproduced, stored in a retrieval system, or transmitted in any form or by any means without prior written permission of Gordian.

11 11 Vehicle Service Equipment

11 11 13 – Compressed-Air Vehicle Service Equipment

11 11 13.10 Compressed Air Equipment		Crew	Daily Output	Labor-Hours	Unit	Material	2023 Bare Costs Labor	2023 Bare Costs Equipment	Total	Total Incl O&P
0010	COMPRESSED AIR EQUIPMENT									
0030	Compressors, electric, 1-1/2 HP, standard controls	L-4	1.50	16	Ea.	1,100	895		1,995	2,575
0550	Dual controls		1.50	16		1,050	895		1,945	2,525
0600	5 HP, 115/230 volt, standard controls		1	24		1,600	1,350		2,950	3,800
0650	Dual controls		1	24		1,600	1,350		2,950	3,800

11 11 19 – Vehicle Lubrication Equipment

11 11 19.10 Lubrication Equipment		Crew	Daily Output	Labor-Hours	Unit	Material	Labor	Equipment	Total	Total Incl O&P
0010	LUBRICATION EQUIPMENT									
3000	Lube equipment, 3 reel type, with pumps, not including piping	L-4	.50	48	Set	11,700	2,675		14,375	16,900
3700	Pump lubrication, pneumatic, not incl. air compressor									
3710	Oil/gear lube	Q-1	9.60	1.667	Ea.	1,100	108		1,208	1,350
3720	Grease	"	9.60	1.667	"	194	108		302	375

11 11 33 – Vehicle Spray Painting Equipment

11 11 33.10 Spray Painting Equipment		Crew	Daily Output	Labor-Hours	Unit	Material	Labor	Equipment	Total	Total Incl O&P
0010	SPRAY PAINTING EQUIPMENT									
4000	Spray painting booth, 26' long, complete	L-4	.40	60	Ea.	24,600	3,350		27,950	32,200

11 21 Retail and Service Equipment

11 21 53 – Barber and Beauty Shop Equipment

11 21 53.10 Barber Equipment		Crew	Daily Output	Labor-Hours	Unit	Material	Labor	Equipment	Total	Total Incl O&P
0010	BARBER EQUIPMENT									
0020	Chair, hydraulic, movable, minimum	1 Carp	24	.333	Ea.	770	19.55		789.55	880
0050	Maximum	"	16	.500		4,800	29.50		4,829.50	5,325
0500	Sink, hair washing basin, rough plumbing not incl.	1 Plum	8	1		299	72		371	435
1000	Sterilizer, liquid solution for tools					198			198	218

11 21 73 – Commercial Laundry and Dry Cleaning Equipment

11 21 73.16 Drying and Conditioning Equipment		Crew	Daily Output	Labor-Hours	Unit	Material	Labor	Equipment	Total	Total Incl O&P
0010	DRYING AND CONDITIONING EQUIPMENT									
0100	Dryers, not including rough-in									
1500	Industrial, 30 lb. capacity	1 Plum	2	4	Ea.	1,650	288		1,938	2,250
1600	50 lb. capacity	"	1.70	4.706	"	5,275	340		5,615	6,325

11 21 73.26 Commercial Washers and Extractors		Crew	Daily Output	Labor-Hours	Unit	Material	Labor	Equipment	Total	Total Incl O&P
0010	COMMERCIAL WASHERS AND EXTRACTORS, not including rough-in									
6000	Combination washer/extractor, 20 lb. capacity	L-6	1.50	8	Ea.	5,950	565		6,515	7,400
6100	30 lb. capacity		.80	15		12,700	1,050		13,750	15,500
6200	50 lb. capacity		.68	17.647		16,000	1,250		17,250	19,500
6300	75 lb. capacity		.30	40		15,800	2,825		18,625	21,600
6350	125 lb. capacity		.16	75		34,800	5,275		40,075	46,200

11 21 73.33 Coin-Operated Laundry Equipment		Crew	Daily Output	Labor-Hours	Unit	Material	Labor	Equipment	Total	Total Incl O&P
0010	COIN-OPERATED LAUNDRY EQUIPMENT									
0990	Dryer, gas fired									
1000	Commercial, 30 lb. capacity, coin operated, single	1 Plum	3	2.667	Ea.	1,750	192		1,942	2,200
1100	Double stacked	"	2	4	"	2,125	288		2,413	2,750
5290	Clothes washer									
5300	Commercial, coin operated, average	1 Plum	3	2.667	Ea.	1,575	192		1,767	2,000

11 21 Retail and Service Equipment

11 21 83 – Photo Processing Equipment

11 21 83.13 Darkroom Equipment

		Crew	Daily Output	Labor-Hours	Unit	Material	2023 Bare Costs Labor	2023 Bare Costs Equipment	Total	Total Incl O&P
0010	DARKROOM EQUIPMENT									
0020	Developing sink, 5" deep, 24" x 48"	Q-1	2	8	Ea.	405	520		925	1,225
0050	48" x 52"		1.70	9.412		970	610		1,580	1,975
0200	10" deep, 24" x 48"		1.70	9.412		1,775	610		2,385	2,875
0250	24" x 108"	↓	1.50	10.667	↓	5,175	690		5,865	6,725

11 30 Residential Equipment

11 30 13 – Residential Appliances

11 30 13.15 Cooking Equipment

		Crew	Daily Output	Labor-Hours	Unit	Material	Labor	Equipment	Total	Total Incl O&P
0010	COOKING EQUIPMENT									
0020	Cooking range, 30" free standing, 1 oven, minimum	2 Clab	10	1.600	Ea.	700	75.50		775.50	885
0050	Maximum		4	4		935	189		1,124	1,300
0150	2 oven, minimum		10	1.600		3,500	75.50		3,575.50	3,975
0200	Maximum	↓	10	1.600	↓	4,475	75.50		4,550.50	5,050

11 30 13.16 Refrigeration Equipment

		Crew	Daily Output	Labor-Hours	Unit	Material	Labor	Equipment	Total	Total Incl O&P
0010	REFRIGERATION EQUIPMENT									
5200	Icemaker, automatic, 20 lbs./day	1 Plum	7	1.143	Ea.	1,400	82.50		1,482.50	1,675
5350	51 lbs./day	"	2	4	"	2,650	288		2,938	3,350

11 30 13.17 Kitchen Cleaning Equipment

		Crew	Daily Output	Labor-Hours	Unit	Material	Labor	Equipment	Total	Total Incl O&P
0010	KITCHEN CLEANING EQUIPMENT									
2750	Dishwasher, built-in, 2 cycles, minimum	L-1	4	4	Ea.	500	279		779	965
2800	Maximum		2	8		980	560		1,540	1,900
2950	4 or more cycles, minimum		4	4		680	279		959	1,150
2960	Average		4	4		905	279		1,184	1,400
3000	Maximum	↓	2	8	↓	790	560		1,350	1,700

11 30 13.18 Waste Disposal Equipment

		Crew	Daily Output	Labor-Hours	Unit	Material	Labor	Equipment	Total	Total Incl O&P
0010	WASTE DISPOSAL EQUIPMENT									
3300	Garbage disposal, sink type, minimum	L-1	10	1.600	Ea.	124	112		236	300
3350	Maximum	"	10	1.600	"	256	112		368	445

11 30 13.19 Kitchen Ventilation Equipment

		Crew	Daily Output	Labor-Hours	Unit	Material	Labor	Equipment	Total	Total Incl O&P
0010	KITCHEN VENTILATION EQUIPMENT									
4150	Hood for range, 2 speed, vented, 30" wide, minimum	L-3	5	3.200	Ea.	110	204		314	425
4200	Maximum		3	5.333		1,150	340		1,490	1,750
4300	42" wide, minimum		5	3.200		175	204		379	495
4330	Custom		5	3.200		167	204		371	490
4350	Maximum	↓	3	5.333		204	340		544	730
4500	For ventless hood, 2 speed, add					70			70	77
4650	For vented 1 speed, deduct from maximum				↓	130			130	143

11 30 13.24 Washers

		Crew	Daily Output	Labor-Hours	Unit	Material	Labor	Equipment	Total	Total Incl O&P
0010	WASHERS									
5000	Residential, 4 cycle, average	1 Plum	3	2.667	Ea.	1,150	192		1,342	1,550
6650	Washing machine, automatic, minimum		3	2.667		665	192		857	1,025
6700	Maximum	↓	1	8	↓	700	575		1,275	1,625

11 30 13.25 Dryers

		Crew	Daily Output	Labor-Hours	Unit	Material	Labor	Equipment	Total	Total Incl O&P
0010	DRYERS									
0500	Gas fired residential, 16 lb. capacity, average	1 Plum	3	2.667	Ea.	1,300	192		1,492	1,725
7450	Vent kits for dryers	1 Carp	10	.800	"	64	47		111	141

11 30 Residential Equipment

11 30 15 – Miscellaneous Residential Appliances

11 30 15.13 Sump Pumps

		Crew	Daily Output	Labor-Hours	Unit	Material	2023 Bare Costs Labor	2023 Bare Costs Equipment	Total	Total Incl O&P
0010	**SUMP PUMPS**									
6400	Cellar drainer, pedestal, 1/3 HP, molded PVC base	1 Plum	3	2.667	Ea.	138	192		330	440
6450	Solid brass	"	2	4	"	251	288		539	705
6460	Sump pump, see also Section 22 14 29.16									

11 30 15.23 Water Heaters

		Crew	Daily Output	Labor-Hours	Unit	Material	Labor	Equipment	Total	Total Incl O&P
0010	**WATER HEATERS**									
6900	Electric, glass lined, 30 gallon, minimum	L-1	5	3.200	Ea.	750	223		973	1,150
6950	Maximum		3	5.333		1,050	370		1,420	1,700
7100	80 gallon, minimum		2	8		2,100	560		2,660	3,125
7150	Maximum		1	16		2,900	1,125		4,025	4,850
7180	Gas, glass lined, 30 gallon, minimum	2 Plum	5	3.200		1,900	231		2,131	2,450
7220	Maximum		3	5.333		2,650	385		3,035	3,475
7260	50 gallon, minimum		2.50	6.400		740	460		1,200	1,500
7300	Maximum		1.50	10.667		1,025	770		1,795	2,275
7310	Water heater, see also Section 22 33 30.13									

11 30 15.43 Air Quality

		Crew	Daily Output	Labor-Hours	Unit	Material	Labor	Equipment	Total	Total Incl O&P
0010	**AIR QUALITY**									
2450	Dehumidifier, portable, automatic, 15 pint	1 Elec	4	2	Ea.	184	135		319	400
2550	40 pint		3.75	2.133		330	144		474	580
3550	Heater, electric, built-in, 1250 watt, ceiling type, minimum		4	2		136	135		271	350
3600	Maximum		3	2.667		258	180		438	550
3700	Wall type, minimum		4	2		117	135		252	330
3750	Maximum		3	2.667		135	180		315	415
3900	1500 watt wall type, with blower		4	2		227	135		362	450
3950	3000 watt		3	2.667		224	180		404	515
4850	Humidifier, portable, 8 gallons/day					170			170	187
5000	15 gallons/day					276			276	305

11 32 Unit Kitchens

11 32 13 – Metal Unit Kitchens

11 32 13.10 Commercial Unit Kitchens

		Crew	Daily Output	Labor-Hours	Unit	Material	Labor	Equipment	Total	Total Incl O&P
0010	**COMMERCIAL UNIT KITCHENS**									
1500	Combination range, refrigerator and sink, 30" wide, minimum	L-1	2	8	Ea.	1,300	560		1,860	2,250
1550	Maximum		1	16		1,525	1,125		2,650	3,325
1570	60" wide, average		1.40	11.429		2,075	795		2,870	3,450
1590	72" wide, average		1.20	13.333		2,075	930		3,005	3,650
1600	Office model, 48" wide		2	8		3,300	560		3,860	4,450
1620	Refrigerator and sink only		2.40	6.667		3,425	465		3,890	4,475
1640	Combination range, refrigerator, sink, microwave									
1660	Oven and ice maker	L-1	.80	20	Ea.	5,925	1,400		7,325	8,600

11 41 Foodservice Storage Equipment

11 41 13 – Refrigerated Food Storage Cases

11 41 13.20 Refrigerated Food Storage Equipment		Crew	Daily Output	Labor-Hours	Unit	Material	2023 Bare Costs Labor	Equipment	Total	Total Incl O&P
0010	**REFRIGERATED FOOD STORAGE EQUIPMENT**									
2350	Cooler, reach-in, beverage, 6' long	Q-1	6	2.667	Ea.	3,875	173		4,048	4,525
4300	Freezers, reach-in, 44 C.F.	↓	4	4		2,950	259		3,209	3,600
4500	68 C.F.		3	5.333	↓	8,525	345		8,870	9,900

11 44 Food Cooking Equipment

11 44 13 – Commercial Ranges

11 44 13.10 Cooking Equipment

		Crew	Daily Output	Labor-Hours	Unit	Material	Labor	Equipment	Total	Total Incl O&P
0010	**COOKING EQUIPMENT**									
0020	Bake oven, gas, one section	Q-1	8	2	Ea.	4,400	130		4,530	5,050
0300	Two sections		7	2.286		9,875	148		10,023	11,100
0600	Three sections	↓	6	2.667		13,600	173		13,773	15,200
0900	Electric convection, single deck	L-7	4	7		15,300	395		15,695	17,500
6350	Kettle, w/steam jacket, tilting, w/positive lock, SS, 20 gallons		7	4		16,500	226		16,726	18,400
6600	60 gallons	↓	6	4.667	↓	23,000	264		23,264	25,700

11 46 Food Dispensing Equipment

11 46 83 – Ice Machines

11 46 83.10 Commercial Ice Equipment

		Crew	Daily Output	Labor-Hours	Unit	Material	Labor	Equipment	Total	Total Incl O&P
0010	**COMMERCIAL ICE EQUIPMENT**									
5800	Ice cube maker, 50 lbs./day	Q-1	6	2.667	Ea.	2,075	173		2,248	2,525
6050	500 lbs./day	"	4	4	"	2,975	259		3,234	3,650

11 48 Foodservice Cleaning and Disposal Equipment

11 48 13 – Commercial Dishwashers

11 48 13.10 Dishwashers

			Crew	Daily Output	Labor-Hours	Unit	Material	Labor	Equipment	Total	Total Incl O&P
0010	**DISHWASHERS**										
2700	Dishwasher, commercial, rack type										
2720	10 to 12 racks/hour		Q-1	3.20	5	Ea.	38,500	325		38,825	42,900
2730	Energy star rated, 35 to 40 racks/hour	G		1.30	12.308		6,350	800		7,150	8,175
2740	50 to 60 racks/hour	G	↓	1.30	12.308		9,050	800		9,850	11,200
2800	Automatic, 190 to 230 racks/hour		L-6	.35	34.286		31,600	2,425		34,025	38,300
2820	235 to 275 racks/hour			.25	48		31,600	3,375		34,975	39,800
2840	8,750 to 12,500 dishes/hour		↓	.10	120	↓	51,500	8,450		59,950	69,000

11 53 Laboratory Equipment

11 53 13 – Laboratory Fume Hoods

11 53 13.13 Recirculating Laboratory Fume Hoods

		Crew	Daily Output	Labor-Hours	Unit	Material	Labor	Equipment	Total	Total Incl O&P
0010	**RECIRCULATING LABORATORY FUME HOODS**									
0670	Service fixtures, average				Ea.	1,950			1,950	2,150
0680	For sink assembly with hot and cold water, add	1 Plum	1.40	5.714	"	685	410		1,095	1,375

11 53 Laboratory Equipment

11 53 19 – Laboratory Sterilizers

11 53 19.13 Sterilizers

		Crew	Daily Output	Labor-Hours	Unit	Material	2023 Bare Costs Labor	Equipment	Total	Total Incl O&P
0010	**STERILIZERS**									
0700	Glassware washer, undercounter, minimum	L-1	1.80	8.889	Ea.	8,325	620		8,945	10,100
0710	Maximum	"	1	16		18,300	1,125		19,425	21,800
1850	Utensil washer-sanitizer	1 Plum	2	4		7,475	288		7,763	8,650

11 53 23 – Laboratory Refrigerators

11 53 23.13 Refrigerators

		Crew	Daily Output	Labor-Hours	Unit	Material	Labor	Equipment	Total	Total Incl O&P
0010	**REFRIGERATORS**									
1200	Blood bank, 28.6 C.F. emergency signal				Ea.	14,300			14,300	15,700
1210	Reach-in, 16.9 C.F.				"	8,250			8,250	9,075

11 53 33 – Emergency Safety Appliances

11 53 33.13 Emergency Equipment

		Crew	Daily Output	Labor-Hours	Unit	Material	Labor	Equipment	Total	Total Incl O&P
0010	**EMERGENCY EQUIPMENT**									
1400	Safety equipment, eye wash, hand held				Ea.	420			420	460
1450	Deluge shower				"	294			294	325

11 53 43 – Service Fittings and Accessories

11 53 43.13 Fittings

		Crew	Daily Output	Labor-Hours	Unit	Material	Labor	Equipment	Total	Total Incl O&P
0010	**FITTINGS**									
1600	Sink, one piece plastic, flask wash, hose, free standing	1 Plum	1.60	5	Ea.	345	360		705	915
1610	Epoxy resin sink, 25" x 16" x 10"	"	2	4	"	1,775	288		2,063	2,375
8000	Alternate pricing method: as percent of lab furniture									
8050	Installation, not incl. plumbing & duct work				% Furn.				22%	22%
8100	Plumbing, final connections, simple system								10%	10%
8110	Moderately complex system								15%	15%
8120	Complex system								20%	20%
8150	Electrical, simple system								10%	10%
8160	Moderately complex system								20%	20%
8170	Complex system								35%	35%

11 71 Medical Sterilizing Equipment

11 71 10 – Medical Sterilizers & Distillers

11 71 10.10 Sterilizers and Distillers

		Crew	Daily Output	Labor-Hours	Unit	Material	Labor	Equipment	Total	Total Incl O&P
0010	**STERILIZERS AND DISTILLERS**									
0700	Distiller, water, steam heated, 50 gal. capacity	1 Plum	1.40	5.714	Ea.	45,200	410		45,610	50,500
5600	Sterilizers, floor loading, 26" x 62" x 42", single door, steam					61,000			61,000	67,000
5650	Double door, steam					61,000			61,000	67,000
5800	General purpose, 20" x 20" x 38", single door					29,300			29,300	32,200
6000	Portable, counter top, steam, minimum					4,100			4,100	4,500
6020	Maximum					2,200			2,200	2,425
6050	Portable, counter top, gas, 17" x 15" x 32-1/2"					3,650			3,650	4,000
6150	Manual washer/sterilizer, 16" x 16" x 26"	1 Plum	2	4		3,200	288		3,488	3,950
6200	Steam generators, electric 10 kW to 180 kW, freestanding									
6250	Minimum	1 Elec	3	2.667	Ea.	6,450	180		6,630	7,375
6300	Maximum	"	.70	11.429		3,400	770		4,170	4,900
8200	Bed pan washer-sanitizer	1 Plum	2	4		7,675	288		7,963	8,875

11 73 Patient Care Equipment

11 73 10 – Patient Treatment Equipment

11 73 10.10 Treatment Equipment

		Crew	Daily Output	Labor-Hours	Unit	Material	2023 Bare Costs Labor	2023 Bare Costs Equipment	Total	Total Incl O&P
0010	**TREATMENT EQUIPMENT**									
1800	Heat therapy unit, humidified, 26" x 78" x 28"				Ea.	360			360	395
2100	Hubbard tank with accessories, stainless steel,									
2110	125 GPM at 45 psi water pressure				Ea.	28,900			28,900	31,800
2150	For electric overhead hoist, add					2,800			2,800	3,100
3600	Paraffin bath, 126°F, auto controlled					252			252	277
4600	Station, dietary, medium, with ice					635			635	700
8400	Whirlpool bath, mobile, sst, 18" x 24" x 60"					5,350			5,350	5,900
8450	Fixed, incl. mixing valves	1 Plum	2	4		8,650	288		8,938	9,950

11 74 Dental Equipment

11 74 10 – Dental Office Equipment

11 74 10.10 Diagnostic and Treatment Equipment

		Crew	Daily Output	Labor-Hours	Unit	Material	Labor	Equipment	Total	Total Incl O&P
0010	**DIAGNOSTIC AND TREATMENT EQUIPMENT**									
0020	Central suction system, minimum	1 Plum	1.20	6.667	Ea.	1,975	480		2,455	2,900
0100	Maximum	"	.90	8.889		4,725	640		5,365	6,125
0300	Air compressor, minimum	1 Skwk	.80	10		4,450	615		5,065	5,825
0400	Maximum		.50	16		10,200	980		11,180	12,700
0600	Chair, electric or hydraulic, minimum		.50	16		4,175	980		5,155	6,075
0700	Maximum		.25	32		6,775	1,950		8,725	10,400
2000	Light, ceiling mounted, minimum		8	1		940	61.50		1,001.50	1,125
2100	Maximum		8	1		3,175	61.50		3,236.50	3,600
2200	Unit light, minimum	2 Skwk	5.33	3.002		1,175	184		1,359	1,575
2210	Maximum		5.33	3.002		2,450	184		2,634	2,950
2220	Track light, minimum		3.20	5		2,700	305		3,005	3,425
2230	Maximum		3.20	5		4,200	305		4,505	5,075
2300	Sterilizers, steam portable, minimum					3,675			3,675	4,050
2350	Maximum					8,325			8,325	9,150
2600	Steam, institutional					4,225			4,225	4,650
2650	Dry heat, electric, portable, 3 trays					2,150			2,150	2,375

11 76 Operating Room Equipment

11 76 10 – Equipment for Operating Rooms

11 76 10.10 Surgical Equipment

		Crew	Daily Output	Labor-Hours	Unit	Material	Labor	Equipment	Total	Total Incl O&P
0010	**SURGICAL EQUIPMENT**									
5000	Scrub, surgical, stainless steel, single station, minimum	1 Plum	3	2.667	Ea.	1,625	192		1,817	2,050
5100	Maximum				"	14,900			14,900	16,400

11 78 Mortuary Equipment

11 78 13 – Mortuary Refrigerators

11 78 13.10 Mortuary and Autopsy Equipment

		Crew	Daily Output	Labor-Hours	Unit	Material	2023 Bare Costs Labor	2023 Bare Costs Equipment	Total	Total Incl O&P
0010	MORTUARY AND AUTOPSY EQUIPMENT									
0015	Autopsy table, standard	1 Plum	1	8	Ea.	8,550	575		9,125	10,300
0020	Deluxe	"	.60	13.333	"	3,175	960		4,135	4,925

11 81 Facility Maintenance Equipment

11 81 19 – Vacuum Cleaning Systems

11 81 19.10 Vacuum Cleaning

		Crew	Daily Output	Labor-Hours	Unit	Material	Labor	Equipment	Total	Total Incl O&P
0010	VACUUM CLEANING									
0020	Central, 3 inlet, residential	1 Skwk	.90	8.889	Total	1,200	545		1,745	2,150
0200	Commercial		.70	11.429		1,425	700		2,125	2,625
0400	5 inlet system, residential		.50	16		1,925	980		2,905	3,575
0600	7 inlet system, commercial		.40	20		1,250	1,225		2,475	3,225
0800	9 inlet system, residential	↓	.30	26.667	↓	4,400	1,625		6,025	7,300

11 91 Religious Equipment

11 91 13 – Baptisteries

11 91 13.10 Baptistry

		Crew	Daily Output	Labor-Hours	Unit	Material	Labor	Equipment	Total	Total Incl O&P
0010	BAPTISTRY									
0150	Fiberglass, 3'-6" deep, x 13'-7" long,									
0160	steps at both ends, incl. plumbing, minimum	L-8	1	20	Ea.	3,650	1,225		4,875	5,825
0200	Maximum	"	.70	28.571		11,100	1,750		12,850	14,800
0250	Add for filter, heater and lights					1,525			1,525	1,675

11 91 23 – Sanctuary Equipment

11 91 23.10 Sanctuary Furnishings

		Crew	Daily Output	Labor-Hours	Unit	Material	Labor	Equipment	Total	Total Incl O&P
0010	SANCTUARY FURNISHINGS									
0020	Altar, wood, custom design, plain	1 Carp	1.40	5.714	Ea.	2,500	335		2,835	3,250
0050	Deluxe	"	.20	40	"	12,000	2,350		14,350	16,700

11 98 Detention Equipment

11 98 30 – Detention Cell Equipment

11 98 30.10 Cell Equipment

		Crew	Daily Output	Labor-Hours	Unit	Material	Labor	Equipment	Total	Total Incl O&P
0010	CELL EQUIPMENT									
3000	Toilet apparatus including wash basin, average	L-8	1.50	13.333	Ea.	2,475	815		3,290	3,950

Estimating Tips
General
- The items in this division are usually priced per square foot or each. Most of these items are purchased by the owner and installed by the contractor. Do not assume the items in Division 12 will be purchased and installed by the contractor. Check the specifications for responsibilities and include receiving, storage, installation, and mechanical and electrical hookups in the appropriate divisions.
- Some items in this division require some type of support system that is not usually furnished with the item. Examples of these systems include blocking for the attachment of casework and heavy drapery rods. The required blocking must be added to the estimate in the appropriate division.

Reference Numbers
Reference numbers are shown at the beginning of some major classifications. These numbers refer to related items in the Reference Section. The reference information may be an estimating procedure, an alternate pricing method, or technical information.

Same Data. Simplified.
Enjoy the convenience and efficiency of accessing your costs anywhere:
- **Skip the multiplier** by setting your location
- **Quickly search**, edit, favorite and share costs
- **Stay on top of price changes** with automatic updates

Discover more at rsmeans.com/online

No part of this cost data may be reproduced, stored in a retrieval system, or transmitted in any form or by any means without prior written permission of Gordian.

12 32 Manufactured Wood Casework

12 32 23 – Hardwood Casework

12 32 23.10 Manufactured Wood Casework, Stock Units		Crew	Daily Output	Labor-Hours	Unit	Material	2023 Bare Costs Labor	Equipment	Total	Total Incl O&P
0010	**MANUFACTURED WOOD CASEWORK, STOCK UNITS**									
0700	Kitchen base cabinets, hardwood, not incl. counter tops,									
0710	24" deep, 35" high, prefinished									
0800	One top drawer, one door below, 12" wide	2 Carp	24.80	.645	Ea.	585	38		623	695
0840	18" wide		23.30	.687		435	40		475	540
0880	24" wide		22.30	.717		490	42		532	605
1000	Four drawers, 12" wide		24.80	.645		775	38		813	905
1040	18" wide		23.30	.687		810	40		850	950
1060	24" wide		22.30	.717		855	42		897	1,000
1200	Two top drawers, two doors below, 27" wide		22	.727		505	42.50		547.50	620
1260	36" wide		20.30	.788		565	46		611	695
1300	48" wide		18.90	.847		715	49.50		764.50	860
1500	Range or sink base, two doors below, 30" wide		21.40	.748		385	44		429	490
1540	36" wide		20.30	.788		425	46		471	540
1580	48" wide		18.90	.847		465	49.50		514.50	590
1800	For sink front units, deduct					186			186	205
9000	For deluxe models of all cabinets, add					40%				
9500	For custom built in place, add					25%	10%			
9558	Rule of thumb, kitchen cabinets not including									
9560	appliances & counter top, minimum	2 Carp	30	.533	L.F.	219	31.50		250.50	288
9600	Maximum	"	25	.640	"	485	37.50		522.50	590

12 32 23.30 Manufactured Wood Casework Vanities

		Crew	Daily Output	Labor-Hours	Unit	Material	Labor	Equipment	Total	Total Incl O&P
0010	**MANUFACTURED WOOD CASEWORK VANITIES**									
8000	Vanity bases, 2 doors, 30" high, 21" deep, 24" wide	2 Carp	20	.800	Ea.	475	47		522	595
8050	30" wide		16	1		505	58.50		563.50	645
8100	36" wide		13.33	1.200		425	70.50		495.50	575
8150	48" wide		11.43	1.400		555	82		637	730
9000	For deluxe models of all vanities, add to above					40%				
9500	For custom built in place, add to above					25%	10%			

Division 13 Special Construction

Estimating Tips
General
- The items and systems in this division are usually estimated, purchased, supplied, and installed as a unit by one or more subcontractors. The estimator must ensure that all parties are operating from the same set of specifications and assumptions, and that all necessary items are estimated and will be provided. Many times the complex items and systems are covered, but the more common ones, such as excavation or a crane, are overlooked for the very reason that everyone assumes nobody could miss them. The estimator should be the central focus and be able to ensure that all systems are complete.
- It is important to consider factors such as site conditions, weather, shape and size of building, as well as labor availability as they may impact the overall cost of erecting special structures and systems included in this division.
- Another area where problems can develop in this division is at the interface between systems.

The estimator must ensure, for instance, that anchor bolts, nuts, and washers are estimated and included for the air-supported structures and pre-engineered buildings to be bolted to their foundations. Utility supply is a common area where essential items or pieces of equipment can be missed or overlooked because each subcontractor may feel it is another's responsibility. The estimator should also be aware of certain items which may be supplied as part of a package but installed by others, and ensure that the installing contractor's estimate includes the cost of installation. Conversely, the estimator must also ensure that items are not costed by two different subcontractors, resulting in an inflated overall estimate.

13 30 00 Special Structures
- The foundations and floor slab, as well as rough mechanical and electrical, should be estimated, as this work is required for the assembly and erection of the structure. Generally, as noted in the data set, the pre-engineered building comes as a shell. Pricing is based on the size and structural design parameters stated in the reference section. Additional features, such as windows and doors with their related structural framing, must also be included by the estimator. Here again, the estimator must have a clear understanding of the scope of each portion of the work and all the necessary interfaces.

Reference Numbers
Reference numbers are shown at the beginning of some major classifications. These numbers refer to related items in the Reference Section. The reference information may be an estimating procedure, an alternate pricing method, or technical information.

Note: Not all subdivisions listed here necessarily appear. ■

Same Data. Simplified.
Enjoy the convenience and efficiency of accessing your costs anywhere:
- **Skip the multiplier** by setting your location
- **Quickly search,** edit, favorite and share costs
- **Stay on top of price changes** with automatic updates

Discover more at rsmeans.com/online

No part of this cost data may be reproduced, stored in a retrieval system, or transmitted in any form or by any means without prior written permission of Gordian.

13 11 Swimming Pools

13 11 13 – Below-Grade Swimming Pools

13 11 13.50 Swimming Pools

		Crew	Daily Output	Labor-Hours	Unit	Material	2023 Bare Costs Labor	2023 Bare Costs Equipment	Total	Total Incl O&P
0010	**SWIMMING POOLS** Residential in-ground, vinyl lined									
0020	Concrete sides, w/equip, sand bottom	B-52	300	.187	SF Surf	43	10.15	2.10	55.25	65
0100	Metal or polystyrene sides R131113-20	B-14	410	.117		81	5.80	.68	87.48	98.50
0200	Add for vermiculite bottom					4.09			4.09	4.50
0500	Gunite bottom and sides, white plaster finish									
0600	12' x 30' pool	B-52	145	.386	SF Surf	60.50	21	4.34	85.84	102
0720	16' x 32' pool		155	.361		54.50	19.60	4.06	78.16	93.50
0750	20' x 40' pool		250	.224		48.50	12.15	2.52	63.17	74.50
0810	Concrete bottom and sides, tile finish									
0820	12' x 30' pool	B-52	80	.700	SF Surf	61	38	7.85	106.85	132
0830	16' x 32' pool		95	.589		50.50	32	6.60	89.10	110
0840	20' x 40' pool		130	.431		40	23.50	4.84	68.34	84
1100	Motel, gunite with plaster finish, incl. medium									
1150	capacity filtration & chlorination	B-52	115	.487	SF Surf	74.50	26.50	5.45	106.45	127
1200	Municipal, gunite with plaster finish, incl. high									
1250	capacity filtration & chlorination	B-52	100	.560	SF Surf	96.50	30.50	6.30	133.30	158
1350	Add for formed gutters				L.F.	142			142	156
1360	Add for stainless steel gutters				"	420			420	460
1600	For water heating system, see Section 23 52 28.10									
1700	Filtration and deck equipment only, as % of total				Total				20%	20%
1800	Automatic vacuum, hand tools, etc., 20' x 40' pool				SF Pool				.56	.62
1900	5,000 S.F. pool				"				.11	.12
3000	Painting pools, preparation + 3 coats, 20' x 40' pool, epoxy	2 Pord	.33	48.485	Total	2,350	2,400		4,750	6,150
3100	Rubber base paint, 18 gallons	"	.33	48.485		1,250	2,400		3,650	4,950
3500	42' x 82' pool, 75 gallons, epoxy paint	3 Pord	.14	171		9,925	8,500		18,425	23,500
3600	Rubber base paint	"	.14	171		5,225	8,500		13,725	18,300

13 11 23 – On-Grade Swimming Pools

13 11 23.50 Swimming Pools

		Crew	Daily Output	Labor-Hours	Unit	Material	Labor	Equipment	Total	Total Incl O&P
0010	**SWIMMING POOLS** Residential above ground, steel construction									
0100	Round, 15' diam.	B-80A	3	8	Ea.	975	380	130	1,485	1,775
0120	18' diam.		2.50	9.600		1,025	455	156	1,636	2,000
0140	21' diam.		2	12		1,150	565	195	1,910	2,325
0160	24' diam.		1.80	13.333		1,325	630	217	2,172	2,625
0180	27' diam.		1.50	16		1,650	755	261	2,666	3,225
0200	30' diam.		1	24		1,925	1,125	390	3,440	4,225
0220	Oval, 12' x 24'		2.30	10.435		1,675	495	170	2,340	2,775
0240	15' x 30'		1.80	13.333		4,875	630	217	5,722	6,525
0260	18' x 33'		1	24		2,650	1,125	390	4,165	5,050

13 11 46 – Swimming Pool Accessories

13 11 46.50 Swimming Pool Equipment

		Crew	Daily Output	Labor-Hours	Unit	Material	Labor	Equipment	Total	Total Incl O&P
0010	**SWIMMING POOL EQUIPMENT**									
0020	Diving stand, stainless steel, 3 meter	2 Carp	.40	40	Ea.	20,300	2,350		22,650	25,800
0300	1 meter	"	2.70	5.926		17,000	345		17,345	19,200
2100	Lights, underwater, 12 volt, with transformer, 300 watt	1 Elec	1	8		291	540		831	1,125
2200	110 volt, 500 watt, standard		1	8		320	540		860	1,150
2400	Low water cutoff type		1	8		345	540		885	1,175
2800	Heaters, see Section 23 52 28.10									

13 12 Fountains

13 12 13 – Exterior Fountains

13 12 13.10 Outdoor Fountains

		Crew	Daily Output	Labor-Hours	Unit	Material	2023 Bare Costs Labor	Equipment	Total	Total Incl O&P
0010	**OUTDOOR FOUNTAINS**									
0100	Outdoor fountain, 48" high with bowl and figures	2 Clab	2	8	Ea.	430	380		810	1,050
0200	Commercial, concrete or cast stone, 40-60" H, simple		2	8		1,100	380		1,480	1,775
0220	Average		2	8		2,100	380		2,480	2,900
0240	Ornate		2	8		4,800	380		5,180	5,850
0260	Metal, 72" high		2	8		1,700	380		2,080	2,450
0280	90" high		2	8		2,450	380		2,830	3,275
0300	120" high		2	8		5,875	380		6,255	7,025
0320	Resin or fiberglass, 40-60" H, wall type		2	8		770	380		1,150	1,400
0340	Waterfall type		2	8		1,300	380		1,680	2,000

13 12 23 – Interior Fountains

13 12 23.10 Indoor Fountains

		Crew	Daily Output	Labor-Hours	Unit	Material	Labor	Equipment	Total	Total Incl O&P
0010	**INDOOR FOUNTAINS**									
0100	Commercial, floor type, resin or fiberglass, lighted, cascade type	2 Clab	2	8	Ea.	480	380		860	1,100
0120	Tiered type		2	8		720	380		1,100	1,350
0140	Waterfall type		2	8		2,475	380		2,855	3,275

13 17 Tubs and Pools

13 17 13 – Hot Tubs

13 17 13.10 Redwood Hot Tub System

		Crew	Daily Output	Labor-Hours	Unit	Material	Labor	Equipment	Total	Total Incl O&P
0010	**REDWOOD HOT TUB SYSTEM**									
7050	4' diameter x 4' deep	Q-1	1	16	Ea.	4,700	1,050		5,750	6,700
7100	5' diameter x 4' deep		1	16		5,000	1,050		6,050	7,050
7150	6' diameter x 4' deep		.80	20		6,350	1,300		7,650	8,925
7200	8' diameter x 4' deep		.80	20		9,075	1,300		10,375	11,900

13 17 33 – Whirlpool Tubs

13 17 33.10 Whirlpool Bath

		Crew	Daily Output	Labor-Hours	Unit	Material	Labor	Equipment	Total	Total Incl O&P
0010	**WHIRLPOOL BATH**									
6000	Whirlpool, bath with vented overflow, molded fiberglass									
6100	66" x 36" x 24"	Q-1	1	16	Ea.	1,475	1,050		2,525	3,175
6400	72" x 36" x 21"		1	16		1,800	1,050		2,850	3,525
6500	60" x 34" x 21"		1	16		1,700	1,050		2,750	3,400
6600	72" x 42" x 23"		1	16		1,175	1,050		2,225	2,825
6710	For color, add					10%				
6711	For designer colors and trim, add					25%				

13 24 Special Activity Rooms

13 24 16 – Saunas

13 24 16.50 Saunas and Heaters

		Crew	Daily Output	Labor-Hours	Unit	Material	Labor	Equipment	Total	Total Incl O&P
0010	**SAUNAS AND HEATERS**									
0020	Prefabricated, incl. heater & controls, 7' high, 6' x 4', C/C	L-7	2.20	12.727	Ea.	5,825	720		6,545	7,500
0050	6' x 4', C/P		2	14		4,750	795		5,545	6,400
0400	6' x 5', C/C		2	14		5,900	795		6,695	7,650
0450	6' x 5', C/P		2	14		5,675	795		6,470	7,425
0600	6' x 6', C/C		1.80	15.556		15,600	880		16,480	18,400
0650	6' x 6', C/P		1.80	15.556		6,325	880		7,205	8,275
0800	6' x 9', C/C		1.60	17.500		8,175	990		9,165	10,500
0850	6' x 9', C/P		1.60	17.500		6,425	990		7,415	8,550

13 24 Special Activity Rooms

13 24 16 – Saunas

13 24 16.50 Saunas and Heaters

		Crew	Daily Output	Labor-Hours	Unit	Material	2023 Bare Costs Labor	Equipment	Total	Total Incl O&P
1000	8' x 12', C/C	L-7	1.10	25.455	Ea.	19,800	1,450		21,250	24,000
1050	8' x 12', C/P		1.10	25.455		23,300	1,450		24,750	27,800
1200	8' x 8', C/C		1.40	20		10,800	1,125		11,925	13,500
1250	8' x 8', C/P		1.40	20		7,850	1,125		8,975	10,300
1400	8' x 10', C/C		1.20	23.333		9,975	1,325		11,300	13,000
1450	8' x 10', C/P		1.20	23.333		9,100	1,325		10,425	12,000
1600	10' x 12', C/C		1	28		15,700	1,575		17,275	19,700
1650	10' x 12', C/P		1	28		15,700	1,575		17,275	19,700
2500	Heaters only (incl. above), wall mounted, to 200 C.F.					1,125			1,125	1,250
2750	To 300 C.F.					1,275			1,275	1,400
3000	Floor standing, to 720 C.F., 10,000 watts, w/controls	1 Elec	3	2.667		3,250	180		3,430	3,850
3250	To 1,000 C.F., 16,000 watts	"	3	2.667		4,475	180		4,655	5,175

13 24 26 – Steam Baths

13 24 26.50 Steam Baths and Components

		Crew	Daily Output	Labor-Hours	Unit	Material	Labor	Equipment	Total	Total Incl O&P
0010	**STEAM BATHS AND COMPONENTS**									
0020	Heater, timer & head, single, to 140 C.F.	1 Plum	1.20	6.667	Ea.	2,375	480		2,855	3,325
0500	To 300 C.F.		1.10	7.273		6,500	525		7,025	7,900
1000	Commercial size, with blow-down assembly, to 800 C.F.		.90	8.889		6,750	640		7,390	8,375
1500	To 2,500 C.F.		.80	10		7,975	720		8,695	9,850
2000	Multiple, motels, apts., 2 baths, w/blow-down assm., 500 C.F.	Q-1	1.30	12.308		7,450	800		8,250	9,400
2500	4 baths	"	.70	22.857		11,200	1,475		12,675	14,600
2700	Conversion unit for residential tub, including door					4,575			4,575	5,025

13 34 Fabricated Engineered Structures

13 34 23 – Fabricated Structures

13 34 23.10 Comfort Stations

		Crew	Daily Output	Labor-Hours	Unit	Material	Labor	Equipment	Total	Total Incl O&P
0010	**COMFORT STATIONS** Prefab., stock, w/doors, windows & fixt.									
0100	Not incl. interior finish or electrical									
0300	Mobile, on steel frame, 2 unit				S.F.	201			201	221
0350	7 unit					320			320	350
0400	Permanent, including concrete slab, 2 unit	B-12J	50	.320		259	18.15	17.60	294.75	330
0500	6 unit	"	43	.372		221	21	20.50	262.50	297
0600	Alternate pricing method, mobile, 2 fixture				fixture	6,900			6,900	7,575
0650	7 fixture					12,000			12,000	13,200
0700	Permanent, 2 unit	B-12J	.70	22.857		21,400	1,300	1,250	23,950	26,800
0750	6 unit	"	.50	32		18,400	1,825	1,750	21,975	24,900

13 42 Building Modules

13 42 63 – Detention Cell Modules

13 42 63.16 Steel Detention Cell Modules

		Crew	Daily Output	Labor-Hours	Unit	Material	Labor	Equipment	Total	Total Incl O&P
0010	**STEEL DETENTION CELL MODULES**									
2000	Cells, prefab., 5' to 6' wide, 7' to 8' high, 7' to 8' deep,									
2010	bar front, cot, not incl. plumbing	E-4	1.50	21.333	Ea.	9,475	1,400	98	10,973	12,600

13 47 Facility Protection

13 47 13 – Cathodic Protection

13 47 13.16 Cathodic Prot. for Underground Storage Tanks

		Crew	Daily Output	Labor-Hours	Unit	Material	2023 Bare Costs Labor	Equipment	Total	Total Incl O&P
0010	**CATHODIC PROTECTION FOR UNDERGROUND STORAGE TANKS**									
1000	Anodes, magnesium type, 9 #	R-15	18.50	2.595	Ea.	45	172	18.70	235.70	325
1010	17 #		13	3.692		92.50	244	26.50	363	495
1020	32 #		10	4.800		136	320	34.50	490.50	655
1030	48 #	▼	7.20	6.667		174	440	48	662	900
1100	Graphite type w/epoxy cap, 3" x 60" (32 #)	R-22	8.40	4.438		160	274		434	580
1110	4" x 80" (68 #)		6	6.213		278	385		663	875
1120	6" x 72" (80 #)		5.20	7.169		1,675	440		2,115	2,500
1130	6" x 36" (45 #)		9.60	3.883		850	239		1,089	1,300
2000	Rectifiers, silicon type, air cooled, 28 V/10 A	R-19	3.50	5.714		2,675	385		3,060	3,500
2010	20 V/20 A		3.50	5.714		2,675	385		3,060	3,525
2100	Oil immersed, 28 V/10 A		3	6.667		2,725	450		3,175	3,675
2110	20 V/20 A	▼	3	6.667	▼	3,600	450		4,050	4,625
3000	Anode backfill, coke breeze	R-22	3850	.010	Lb.	.31	.60		.91	1.23
4000	Cable, HMWPE, No. 8		2.40	15.533	M.L.F.	975	960		1,935	2,500
4010	No. 6		2.40	15.533		1,275	960		2,235	2,850
4020	No. 4		2.40	15.533		2,075	960		3,035	3,700
4030	No. 2		2.40	15.533		3,000	960		3,960	4,725
4040	No. 1		2.20	16.945		2,250	1,050		3,300	4,050
4050	No. 1/0		2.20	16.945		4,700	1,050		5,750	6,725
4060	No. 2/0		2.20	16.945		6,000	1,050		7,050	8,150
4070	No. 4/0	▼	2	18.640	▼	9,600	1,150		10,750	12,300
5000	Test station, 7 terminal box, flush curb type w/lockable cover	R-19	12	1.667	Ea.	90	112		202	266
5010	Reference cell, 2" diam. PVC conduit, cplg., plug, set flush	"	4.80	4.167	"	179	281		460	615

Division Notes

	CREW	DAILY OUTPUT	LABOR-HOURS	UNIT	BARE COSTS				TOTAL INCL O&P
					MAT.	LABOR	EQUIP.	TOTAL	

Estimating Tips
General
- Many products in Division 14 will require some type of support or blocking for installation not included with the item itself. Examples are supports for conveyors or tube systems, attachment points for lifts, and footings for hoists or cranes. Add these supports in the appropriate division.

14 10 00 Dumbwaiters
14 20 00 Elevators
- Dumbwaiters and elevators are estimated and purchased in a method similar to buying a car. The manufacturer has a base unit with standard features. Added to this base unit price will be whatever options the owner or specifications require. Increased load capacity, additional vertical travel, additional stops, higher speed, and cab finish options are items to be considered. When developing an estimate for dumbwaiters and elevators, remember that some items needed by the installers may have to be included as part of the general contract.

Examples are:
- shaftway
- rail support brackets
- machine room
- electrical supply
- sill angles
- electrical connections
- pits
- roof penthouses
- pit ladders

Check the job specifications and drawings before pricing.
- Installation of elevators and handicapped lifts in historic structures can require significant additional costs. The associated structural requirements may involve cutting into and repairing finishes, moldings, flooring, etc. The estimator must account for these special conditions.

14 30 00 Escalators and Moving Walks
- Escalators and moving walks are specialty items installed by specialty contractors. There are numerous options associated with these items. For specific options, contact a manufacturer or contractor. In a method similar to estimating dumbwaiters and elevators, you should verify the extent of general contract work and add items as necessary.

14 40 00 Lifts
14 90 00 Other Conveying Equipment
- Products such as correspondence lifts, chutes, and pneumatic tube systems, as well as other items specified in this subdivision, may require trained installers. The general contractor might not have any choice as to who will perform the installation or when it will be performed. Long lead times are often required for these products, making early decisions in scheduling necessary.

Reference Numbers
Reference numbers are shown at the beginning of some major classifications. These numbers refer to related items in the Reference Section. The reference information may be an estimating procedure, an alternate pricing method, or technical information.

Note: Not all subdivisions listed here necessarily appear. ■

Same Data. Simplified.
Enjoy the convenience and efficiency of accessing your costs anywhere:
- **Skip the multiplier** by setting your location
- **Quickly search,** edit, favorite and share costs
- **Stay on top of price changes** with automatic updates

Discover more at rsmeans.com/online

No part of this cost data may be reproduced, stored in a retrieval system, or transmitted in any form or by any means without prior written permission of Gordian.

14 45 Vehicle Lifts

14 45 10 – Hydraulic Vehicle Lifts

14 45 10.10 Hydraulic Lifts		Crew	Daily Output	Labor-Hours	Unit	Material	2023 Bare Costs Labor	2023 Bare Costs Equipment	Total	Total Incl O&P
0010	**HYDRAULIC LIFTS**									
2200	Single post, 8,000 lb. capacity	L-4	.40	60	Ea.	6,675	3,350		10,025	12,400
2810	Double post, 6,000 lb. capacity		2.67	8.989		2,800	500		3,300	3,825
2815	9,000 lb. capacity		2.29	10.480		2,800	585		3,385	3,950
2820	15,000 lb. capacity		2	12		4,875	670		5,545	6,350
2822	Four post, 26,000 lb. capacity		1.80	13.333		22,700	745		23,445	26,000
2825	30,000 lb. capacity		1.60	15		43,400	835		44,235	49,000
2830	Ramp style, 4 post, 25,000 lb. capacity		2	12		14,200	670		14,870	16,600
2835	35,000 lb. capacity		1	24		19,000	1,350		20,350	22,900
2840	50,000 lb. capacity		1	24		106,000	1,350		107,350	118,500
2845	75,000 lb. capacity		1	24		104,500	1,350		105,850	117,000
2850	For drive thru tracks, add, minimum					1,225			1,225	1,350
2855	Maximum					2,125			2,125	2,325
2860	Ramp extensions, 3' (set of 2)					465			465	510
2865	Rolling jack platform					1,950			1,950	2,150
2870	Electric/hydraulic jacking beam					5,150			5,150	5,675
2880	Scissor lift, portable, 6,000 lb. capacity					2,300			2,300	2,525

Estimating Tips

Pipe for fire protection and all uses is located in Subdivisions 21 11 13 and 22 11 13.

The labor adjustment factors listed in Subdivision 22 01 02.20 also apply to Division 21.

Many, but not all, areas in the U.S. require backflow protection in the fire system. Insurance underwriters may have specific requirements for the type of materials to be installed or design requirements based on the hazard to be protected. Local jurisdictions may have requirements not covered by code. It is advisable to be aware of any special conditions.

For your reference, the following is a list of the most applicable Fire Codes and Standards, which may be purchased from the NFPA, 1 Batterymarch Park, Quincy, MA 02169-7471.

- NFPA 1: Uniform Fire Code
- NFPA 10: Portable Fire Extinguishers
- NFPA 11: Low-, Medium-, and High-Expansion Foam
- NFPA 12: Carbon Dioxide Extinguishing Systems (Also companion 12A)
- NFPA 13: Installation of Sprinkler Systems (Also companion 13D, 13E, and 13R)
- NFPA 14: Installation of Standpipe and Hose Systems
- NFPA 15: Water Spray Fixed Systems for Fire Protection
- NFPA 16: Installation of Foam-Water Sprinkler and Foam-Water Spray Systems
- NFPA 17: Dry Chemical Extinguishing Systems (Also companion 17A)
- NFPA 18: Wetting Agents
- NFPA 20: Installation of Stationary Pumps for Fire Protection
- NFPA 22: Water Tanks for Private Fire Protection
- NFPA 24: Installation of Private Fire Service Mains and their Appurtenances
- NFPA 25: Inspection, Testing and Maintenance of Water-Based Fire Protection

Reference Numbers

Reference numbers are shown at the beginning of some major classifications. These numbers refer to related items in the Reference Section. The reference information may be an estimating procedure, an alternate pricing method, or technical information.

Same Data. Simplified.

Enjoy the convenience and efficiency of accessing your costs anywhere:

- **Skip the multiplier** by setting your location
- **Quickly search,** edit, favorite and share costs
- **Stay on top of price changes** with automatic updates

Discover more at rsmeans.com/online

No part of this cost data may be reproduced, stored in a retrieval system, or transmitted in any form or by any means without prior written permission of Gordian.

Note: "Powered in part by CINX™, based on licensed proprietary information of Harrison Publishing House, Inc."

Note: Trade Service, in part, has been used as a reference source for some of the material prices used in Division 21.

21 05 Common Work Results for Fire Suppression

21 05 23 – General-Duty Valves for Water-Based Fire-Suppression Piping

21 05 23.50 General-Duty Valves

		Crew	Daily Output	Labor-Hours	Unit	Material	2023 Bare Costs Labor	Equipment	Total	Total Incl O&P
0010	**GENERAL-DUTY VALVES**, for water-based fire suppression									
6200	Valves and components									
6210	Wet alarm, includes									
6220	retard chamber, trim, gauges, alarm line strainer									
6260	3" size	Q-12	3	5.333	Ea.	2,475	340		2,815	3,225
6280	4" size	"	2	8		2,125	510		2,635	3,075
6300	6" size	Q-13	4	8		3,100	540		3,640	4,200
6320	8" size	"	3	10.667		3,625	720		4,345	5,075
6400	Dry alarm, includes									
6405	retard chamber, trim, gauges, alarm line strainer									
6410	1-1/2" size	Q-12	3	5.333	Ea.	3,900	340		4,240	4,800
6420	2" size		3	5.333		3,900	340		4,240	4,800
6430	3" size		3	5.333		3,900	340		4,240	4,775
6440	4" size		2	8		4,225	510		4,735	5,400
6450	6" size	Q-13	3	10.667		4,875	720		5,595	6,450
6460	8" size	"	3	10.667		7,175	720		7,895	8,975
6500	Check, swing, C.I. body, brass fittings, auto. ball drip									
6520	4" size	Q-12	3	5.333	Ea.	425	340		765	970
6540	6" size	Q-13	4	8		785	540		1,325	1,675
6580	8" size	"	3	10.667		2,175	720		2,895	3,475
6800	Check, wafer, butterfly type, C.I. body, bronze fittings									
6820	4" size	Q-12	4	4	Ea.	2,350	255		2,605	2,950
6840	6" size	Q-13	5.50	5.818		4,975	390		5,365	6,050
6860	8" size		5	6.400		1,575	430		2,005	2,375
6880	10" size		4.50	7.111		8,125	480		8,605	9,675
8700	Floor control valve, includes trim and gauges, 2" size	Q-12	6	2.667		1,225	170		1,395	1,600
8710	2-1/2" size		6	2.667		985	170		1,155	1,325
8720	3" size		6	2.667		885	170		1,055	1,225
8730	4" size		6	2.667		885	170		1,055	1,225
8740	6" size		5	3.200		885	204		1,089	1,275
8800	Flow control valve, includes trim and gauges, 2" size		2	8		5,225	510		5,735	6,475
8820	3" size		1.50	10.667		6,000	680		6,680	7,625
8840	4" size	Q-13	2.80	11.429		5,975	770		6,745	7,725
8860	6" size	"	2	16		7,075	1,075		8,150	9,400
9200	Pressure operated relief valve, brass body	1 Spri	18	.444		775	31.50		806.50	900
9600	Waterflow indicator, vane type, with recycling retard and									
9610	two single pole retard switches, 2" thru 6" pipe size	1 Spri	8	1	Ea.	161	71		232	283

21 05 53 – Identification For Fire-Suppression Piping and Equipment

21 05 53.50 Identification

		Crew	Daily Output	Labor-Hours	Unit	Material	2023 Bare Costs Labor	Equipment	Total	Total Incl O&P
0010	**IDENTIFICATION**, for fire suppression piping and equipment									
3010	Plates and escutcheons for identification of fire dept. service/connections									
3100	Wall mount, round, aluminum									
3110	4"	1 Plum	96	.083	Ea.	9.30	6		15.30	19.15
3120	6"	"	96	.083	"	68	6		74	84
3200	Wall mount, round, cast brass									
3210	2-1/2"	1 Plum	70	.114	Ea.	46.50	8.25		54.75	64
3220	3"		70	.114		34	8.25		42.25	50
3230	4"		70	.114		80.50	8.25		88.75	101
3240	6"		70	.114		115	8.25		123.25	139
3250	For polished brass, add					25%				
3260	For rough chrome, add					33%				
3270	For polished chrome, add					55%				

21 05 Common Work Results for Fire Suppression

21 05 53 – Identification For Fire-Suppression Piping and Equipment

21 05 53.50 Identification		Crew	Daily Output	Labor-Hours	Unit	Material	2023 Bare Costs Labor	Equipment	Total	Total Incl O&P
3300	Wall mount, square, cast brass									
3310	2-1/2"	1 Plum	70	.114	Ea.	78	8.25		86.25	98.50
3320	3"	"	70	.114	"	134	8.25		142.25	159
3330	For polished brass, add					15%				
3340	For rough chrome, add					25%				
3350	For polished chrome, add					33%				
3400	Wall mount, cast brass, multiple outlets									
3410	rect. 2 way	Q-1	5	3.200	Ea.	107	208		315	430
3420	rect. 3 way		4	4		253	259		512	665
3430	rect. 4 way		4	4		210	259		469	615
3440	square 4 way		4	4		315	259		574	735
3450	rect. 6 way	↓	3	5.333	↓	310	345		655	855
3460	For polished brass, add					10%				
3470	For rough chrome, add					20%				
3480	For polished chrome, add					25%				
3500	Base mount, free standing fdc, cast brass									
3510	4"	1 Plum	60	.133	Ea.	58.50	9.60		68.10	79
3520	6"	"	60	.133	"	78	9.60		87.60	100
3530	For polished brass, add					25%				
3540	For rough chrome, add					30%				
3550	For polished chrome, add					45%				

21 11 Facility Fire-Suppression Water-Service Piping

21 11 11 – Fire-Suppression, Pipe Fittings, Grooved Joint

21 11 11.05 Corrosion Monitors

		Crew	Daily Output	Labor-Hours	Unit	Material	2023 Bare Costs Labor	Equipment	Total	Total Incl O&P
0010	**CORROSION MONITORS**, pipe, in line spool									
1100	Powder coated, schedule 10									
1140	2"	1 Plum	17	.471	Ea.	297	34		331	375
1150	2-1/2"	Q-1	27	.593		305	38.50		343.50	395
1160	3"		22	.727		315	47		362	415
1170	4"	↓	17	.941		330	61		391	455
1180	6"	Q-2	17	1.412		355	95		450	530
1190	8"	"	14	1.714	↓	380	115		495	585
1200	Powder coated, schedule 40									
1240	2"	1 Plum	17	.471	Ea.	297	34		331	375
1250	2-1/2"	Q-1	27	.593		305	38.50		343.50	395
1260	3"		22	.727		315	47		362	415
1270	4"	↓	17	.941		345	61		406	470
1280	6"	Q-2	17	1.412		380	95		475	560
1290	8"	"	14	1.714	↓	415	115		530	625
1300	Galvanized, schedule 10									
1340	2"	1 Plum	17	.471	Ea.	320	34		354	405
1350	2-1/2"	Q-1	27	.593		340	38.50		378.50	430
1360	3"		22	.727		355	47		402	460
1370	4"	↓	17	.941		370	61		431	500
1380	6"	Q-2	17	1.412		395	95		490	575
1390	8"	"	14	1.714	↓	420	115		535	630
1400	Galvanized, schedule 40									
1440	2"	1 Plum	17	.471	Ea.	320	34		354	405
1450	2-1/2"	Q-1	27	.593		340	38.50		378.50	430
1460	3"	↓	22	.727		355	47		402	460

21 11 Facility Fire-Suppression Water-Service Piping

21 11 11 – Fire-Suppression, Pipe Fittings, Grooved Joint

21 11 11.05 Corrosion Monitors		Crew	Daily Output	Labor-Hours	Unit	Material	2023 Bare Costs Labor	Equipment	Total	Total Incl O&P
1470	4"	Q-1	17	.941	Ea.	390	61		451	515
1480	6"	Q-2	17	1.412		420	95		515	605
1490	8"	"	14	1.714		455	115		570	670
1500	Mechanical tee, painted									
1540	2"	1 Plum	50	.160	Ea.	247	11.55		258.55	289
1550	2-1/2"	Q-1	80	.200		255	12.95		267.95	300
1560	3"		67	.239		264	15.50		279.50	315
1570	4"		50	.320		272	21		293	330
1580	6"	Q-2	50	.480		280	32.50		312.50	360
1590	8"	"	42	.571		380	38.50		418.50	475
1600	Mechanical tee, galvanized									
1640	2"	1 Plum	50	.160	Ea.	264	11.55		275.55	305
1650	2-1/2"	Q-1	80	.200		272	12.95		284.95	320
1660	3"		67	.239		280	15.50		295.50	335
1670	4"		50	.320		288	21		309	345
1680	6"	Q-2	50	.480		297	32.50		329.50	375
1690	8"	"	42	.571		430	38.50		468.50	530

21 11 11.16 Pipe Fittings, Grooved Joint										
0010	**PIPE FITTINGS, GROOVED JOINT,** For fire-suppression									
0020	Fittings, ductile iron									
0030	Coupling required at joints not incl. in fitting price.									
0034	Add 1 coupling, material only, per joint for installed price.									
0038	For standard grooved joint materials see Div. 22 11 13.48									
0040	90° elbow									
0110	2"	1 Plum	25	.320	Ea.	22	23		45	58.50
0120	2-1/2"	Q-1	40	.400		43	26		69	85.50
0130	3"		33	.485		38	31.50		69.50	89
0140	4"		25	.640		54	41.50		95.50	122
0150	5"		20	.800		127	52		179	217
0160	6"	Q-2	25	.960		149	64.50		213.50	261
0170	8"	"	21	1.143		284	77		361	430
0200	45° elbow									
0210	2"	1 Plum	25	.320	Ea.	22	23		45	58.50
0220	2-1/2"	Q-1	40	.400		29.50	26		55.50	71
0230	3"		33	.485		40	31.50		71.50	91
0240	4"		25	.640		54.50	41.50		96	122
0250	5"		20	.800		184	52		236	280
0260	6"	Q-2	25	.960		149	64.50		213.50	261
0270	8"	"	21	1.143		286	77		363	430
0300	Tee									
0310	2"	1 Plum	17	.471	Ea.	38	34		72	92.50
0320	2-1/2"	Q-1	27	.593		45	38.50		83.50	107
0330	3"		22	.727		87	47		134	167
0340	4"		17	.941		108	61		169	210
0350	5"		13	1.231		300	80		380	450
0360	6"	Q-2	17	1.412		269	95		364	440
0370	8"	"	14	1.714		735	115		850	980
0400	Cap									
0410	1-1/4"	1 Plum	76	.105	Ea.	17.80	7.60		25.40	31
0420	1-1/2"		63	.127		18.80	9.15		27.95	34
0430	2"		47	.170		17.20	12.25		29.45	37.50
0440	2-1/2"	Q-1	76	.211		26	13.65		39.65	49

21 11 Facility Fire-Suppression Water-Service Piping

21 11 11 – Fire-Suppression, Pipe Fittings, Grooved Joint

21 11 11.16 Pipe Fittings, Grooved Joint		Crew	Daily Output	Labor-Hours	Unit	Material	2023 Bare Costs Labor	Equipment	Total	Total Incl O&P
0450	3"	Q-1	63	.254	Ea.	21.50	16.45		37.95	48
0460	4"		47	.340		44	22		66	81
0470	5"	▼	37	.432		87	28		115	138
0480	6"	Q-2	47	.511		64	34.50		98.50	122
0490	8"	"	39	.615	▼	184	41.50		225.50	264
0500	Coupling, rigid									
0510	1-1/4"	1 Plum	100	.080	Ea.	34	5.75		39.75	46
0520	1-1/2"		67	.119		50	8.60		58.60	68
0530	2"	▼	50	.160		40.50	11.55		52.05	61.50
0540	2-1/2"	Q-1	80	.200		64	12.95		76.95	89.50
0550	3"		67	.239		51	15.50		66.50	79
0560	4"		50	.320		67	21		88	105
0570	5"	▼	40	.400		130	26		156	182
0580	6"	Q-2	50	.480		98	32.50		130.50	156
0590	8"	"	42	.571	▼	249	38.50		287.50	330
0700	End of run fitting									
0710	1-1/4" x 1/2" NPT	1 Plum	76	.105	Ea.	59.50	7.60		67.10	77
0714	1-1/4" x 3/4" NPT		76	.105		59.50	7.60		67.10	77
0718	1-1/4" x 1" NPT		76	.105		44	7.60		51.60	59.50
0722	1-1/2" x 1/2" NPT		63	.127		59.50	9.15		68.65	79
0726	1-1/2" x 3/4" NPT		63	.127		59.50	9.15		68.65	79
0730	1-1/2" x 1" NPT		63	.127		59.50	9.15		68.65	79
0734	2" x 1/2" NPT		47	.170		63.50	12.25		75.75	88
0738	2" x 3/4" NPT		47	.170		63.50	12.25		75.75	88
0742	2" x 1" NPT		47	.170		63.50	12.25		75.75	88
0746	2-1/2" x 1/2" NPT		40	.200		75	14.40		89.40	104
0750	2-1/2" x 3/4" NPT		40	.200		75	14.40		89.40	104
0754	2-1/2" x 1" NPT	▼	40	.200	▼	75	14.40		89.40	104
0800	Drain elbow									
0820	2-1/2"	Q-1	40	.400	Ea.	148	26		174	201
0830	3"		33	.485		188	31.50		219.50	254
0840	4"	▼	25	.640		170	41.50		211.50	249
0850	6"	Q-2	25	.960	▼	255	64.50		319.50	375
1000	Valves, grooved joint									
1002	Coupling required at joints not incl. in fitting price.									
1004	Add 1 coupling, material only, per joint for installed price.									
1010	Ball valve with weatherproof actuator									
1020	1-1/4"	1 Plum	39	.205	Ea.	222	14.80		236.80	266
1030	1-1/2"		31	.258		263	18.60		281.60	320
1040	2"	▼	24	.333		320	24		344	385
1100	Butterfly valve, high pressure, with actuator									
1110	Supervised open									
1120	2"	1 Plum	23	.348	Ea.	590	25		615	690
1130	2-1/2"	Q-1	38	.421		615	27.50		642.50	715
1140	3"		30	.533		660	34.50		694.50	780
1150	4"		22	.727		695	47		742	835
1160	5"	▼	19	.842		1,050	54.50		1,104.50	1,225
1170	6"	Q-2	23	1.043		1,075	70		1,145	1,275
1180	8"		18	1.333		1,500	89.50		1,589.50	1,775
1190	10"		15	1.600		3,650	108		3,758	4,175
1200	12"	▼	12	2	▼	5,200	135		5,335	5,925
1300	Gate valve, OS&Y									
1310	2-1/2"	Q-1	35	.457	Ea.	650	29.50		679.50	760

21 11 Facility Fire-Suppression Water-Service Piping

21 11 11 – Fire-Suppression, Pipe Fittings, Grooved Joint

21 11 11.16 Pipe Fittings, Grooved Joint		Crew	Daily Output	Labor-Hours	Unit	Material	2023 Bare Costs Labor	Equipment	Total	Total Incl O&P
1320	3"	Q-1	28	.571	Ea.	500	37		537	605
1330	4"		20	.800		995	52		1,047	1,175
1340	6"	Q-2	21	1.143		1,175	77		1,252	1,425
1350	8"		16	1.500		1,850	101		1,951	2,200
1360	10"		13	1.846		2,800	124		2,924	3,275
1370	12"		10	2.400		4,550	161		4,711	5,250
1400	Gate valve, non-rising stem									
1410	2-1/2"	Q-1	36	.444	Ea.	685	29		714	795
1420	3"		29	.552		810	36		846	945
1430	4"		21	.762		965	49.50		1,014.50	1,125
1440	6"	Q-2	22	1.091		1,225	73.50		1,298.50	1,450
1450	8"		17	1.412		1,825	95		1,920	2,150
1460	10"		14	1.714		2,525	115		2,640	2,950
1470	12"		11	2.182		3,225	147		3,372	3,775
2000	Alarm check valve, pre-trimmed									
2010	1-1/2"	Q-1	6	2.667	Ea.	148	173		321	420
2020	2"	"	5	3.200		148	208		356	475
2030	2-1/2"	Q-2	7	3.429		173	231		404	535
2040	3"		6	4		2,475	269		2,744	3,125
2050	4"		5	4.800		222	325		547	725
2060	6"		4	6		222	405		627	845
2070	8"		2	12		222	805		1,027	1,450
2200	Dry valve, pre-trimmed									
2210	1-1/2"	Q-1	5	3.200	Ea.	3,950	208		4,158	4,650
2220	2"	"	4	4		3,950	259		4,209	4,725
2230	2-1/2"	Q-2	6	4		4,025	269		4,294	4,825
2240	3"		5	4.800		4,025	325		4,350	4,900
2250	4"		4	6		4,300	405		4,705	5,325
2260	6"		2	12		4,950	805		5,755	6,625
2270	8"		1	24		7,275	1,625		8,900	10,400
2300	Deluge valve, pre-trimmed, with electric solenoid									
2310	1-1/2"	Q-1	5	3.200	Ea.	5,625	208		5,833	6,500
2320	2"	"	4	4		5,625	259		5,884	6,575
2330	2-1/2"	Q-2	6	4		5,725	269		5,994	6,700
2340	3"		5	4.800		5,725	325		6,050	6,775
2350	4"		4	6		6,825	405		7,230	8,100
2360	6"		2	12		8,150	805		8,955	10,200
2370	8"		1	24		9,200	1,625		10,825	12,500
2400	Preaction valve									
2410	Valve has double interlock,									
2420	pneumatic/electric actuation and trim.									
2430	1-1/2"	Q-1	5	3.200	Ea.	3,575	208		3,783	4,250
2440	2"	"	4	4		3,575	259		3,834	4,325
2450	2-1/2"	Q-2	6	4		3,575	269		3,844	4,350
2460	3"		5	4.800		3,575	325		3,900	4,425
2470	4"		4	6		3,950	405		4,355	4,950
2480	6"		2	12		3,950	805		4,755	5,550
2490	8"		1	24		4,350	1,625		5,975	7,175
3000	Fittings, ductile iron, ready to install									
3010	Includes bolts & grade "E" gaskets									
3012	Add 1 coupling, material only, per joint for installed price.									
3200	90° elbow									
3210	1-1/4"	1 Plum	88	.091	Ea.	87	6.55		93.55	105

21 11 Facility Fire-Suppression Water-Service Piping

21 11 11 – Fire-Suppression, Pipe Fittings, Grooved Joint

21 11 11.16 Pipe Fittings, Grooved Joint

		Crew	Daily Output	Labor-Hours	Unit	Material	2023 Bare Costs Labor	2023 Bare Costs Equipment	Total	Total Incl O&P
3220	1-1/2"	1 Plum	72	.111	Ea.	89.50	8		97.50	110
3230	2"	↓	60	.133		90	9.60		99.60	113
3240	2-1/2"	Q-1	85	.188	↓	109	12.20		121.20	137
3300	45° elbow									
3310	1-1/4"	1 Plum	88	.091	Ea.	87	6.55		93.55	105
3320	1-1/2"		72	.111		89.50	8		97.50	110
3330	2"	↓	60	.133		90	9.60		99.60	113
3340	2-1/2"	Q-1	85	.188	↓	109	12.20		121.20	137
3400	Tee									
3410	1-1/4"	1 Plum	60	.133	Ea.	134	9.60		143.60	161
3420	1-1/2"		48	.167		138	12		150	170
3430	2"	↓	38	.211		140	15.15		155.15	177
3440	2-1/2"	Q-1	60	.267	↓	161	17.30		178.30	204
3500	Coupling									
3510	1-1/4"	1 Plum	200	.040	Ea.	29.50	2.88		32.38	36.50
3520	1-1/2"		134	.060		37	4.30		41.30	47.50
3530	2"	↓	100	.080		42	5.75		47.75	55
3540	2-1/2"	Q-1	160	.100		48	6.50		54.50	62.50
3550	3"		134	.119		54.50	7.75		62.25	71.50
3560	4"		100	.160		59.50	10.40		69.90	81
3570	5"		80	.200		101	12.95		113.95	130
3580	6"	Q-2	100	.240		78	16.15		94.15	110
3590	8"	"	84	.286	↓	78	19.20		97.20	114
4000	For seismic bracing, see Section 22 05 48.40									
5000	For hangers and supports, see Section 22 05 29.10									

21 11 13 – Facility Fire Suppression Piping

21 11 13.16 Pipe, Plastic

		Crew	Daily Output	Labor-Hours	Unit	Material	2023 Bare Costs Labor	2023 Bare Costs Equipment	Total	Total Incl O&P
0010	**PIPE, PLASTIC**									
0020	CPVC, fire suppression (C-UL-S, FM, NFPA 13, 13D & 13R)									
0030	Socket joint, no couplings or hangers									
0100	SDR 13.5 (ASTM F442)									
0120	3/4" diameter	Q-12	420	.038	L.F.	1.31	2.43		3.74	5.05
0130	1" diameter		340	.047		2.05	3		5.05	6.75
0140	1-1/4" diameter		260	.062		3.20	3.92		7.12	9.35
0150	1-1/2" diameter		190	.084		4.41	5.35		9.76	12.85
0160	2" diameter		140	.114		6.60	7.30		13.90	18.10
0170	2-1/2" diameter		130	.123		10.05	7.85		17.90	23
0180	3" diameter	↓	120	.133		15.30	8.50		23.80	29.50

21 11 13.18 Pipe Fittings, Plastic

		Crew	Daily Output	Labor-Hours	Unit	Material	2023 Bare Costs Labor	2023 Bare Costs Equipment	Total	Total Incl O&P
0010	**PIPE FITTINGS, PLASTIC**									
0020	CPVC, fire suppression (C-UL-S, FM, NFPA 13, 13D & 13R)									
0030	Socket joint									
0100	90° elbow									
0120	3/4"	1 Plum	26	.308	Ea.	1.87	22		23.87	35
0130	1"		22.70	.352		4.11	25.50		29.61	42.50
0140	1-1/4"		20.20	.396		5.20	28.50		33.70	48
0150	1-1/2"	↓	18.20	.440		7.40	31.50		38.90	55
0160	2"	Q-1	33.10	.483		9.20	31.50		40.70	56.50
0170	2-1/2"		24.20	.661		17.65	43		60.65	83.50
0180	3"	↓	20.80	.769	↓	24	50		74	101
0200	45° elbow									
0210	3/4"	1 Plum	26	.308	Ea.	2.57	22		24.57	36

21 11 Facility Fire-Suppression Water-Service Piping

21 11 13 – Facility Fire Suppression Piping

21 11 13.18 Pipe Fittings, Plastic		Crew	Daily Output	Labor-Hours	Unit	Material	2023 Bare Costs Labor	Equipment	Total	Total Incl O&P
0220	1"	1 Plum	22.70	.352	Ea.	3.02	25.50		28.52	41.50
0230	1-1/4"		20.20	.396		4.37	28.50		32.87	47.50
0240	1-1/2"	↓	18.20	.440		6.10	31.50		37.60	53.50
0250	2"	Q-1	33.10	.483		7.60	31.50		39.10	55
0260	2-1/2"		24.20	.661		13.60	43		56.60	79
0270	3"	↓	20.80	.769	↓	19.50	50		69.50	96
0300	Tee									
0310	3/4"	1 Plum	17.30	.462	Ea.	2.57	33.50		36.07	52.50
0320	1"		15.20	.526		5.05	38		43.05	62
0330	1-1/4"		13.50	.593		7.65	42.50		50.15	72
0340	1-1/2"	↓	12.10	.661		11.25	47.50		58.75	83.50
0350	2"	Q-1	20	.800		16.60	52		68.60	96
0360	2-1/2"		16.20	.988		27	64		91	125
0370	3"	↓	13.90	1.151		42	74.50		116.50	158
0400	Tee, reducing x any size									
0420	1"	1 Plum	15.20	.526	Ea.	4.31	38		42.31	61
0430	1-1/4"		13.50	.593		7.90	42.50		50.40	72
0440	1-1/2"	↓	12.10	.661		9.55	47.50		57.05	81.50
0450	2"	Q-1	20	.800		18.15	52		70.15	97.50
0460	2-1/2"		16.20	.988		21	64		85	119
0470	3"	↓	13.90	1.151	↓	24.50	74.50		99	138
0500	Coupling									
0510	3/4"	1 Plum	26	.308	Ea.	1.80	22		23.80	35
0520	1"		22.70	.352		2.38	25.50		27.88	40.50
0530	1-1/4"		20.20	.396		3.47	28.50		31.97	46.50
0540	1-1/2"	↓	18.20	.440		4.94	31.50		36.44	52.50
0550	2"	Q-1	33.10	.483		6.70	31.50		38.20	54
0560	2-1/2"		24.20	.661		10.20	43		53.20	75.50
0570	3"	↓	20.80	.769		13.30	50		63.30	89
0600	Coupling, reducing									
0610	1" x 3/4"	1 Plum	22.70	.352	Ea.	2.38	25.50		27.88	40.50
0620	1-1/4" x 1"		20.20	.396		3.60	28.50		32.10	46.50
0630	1-1/2" x 3/4"		18.20	.440		5.40	31.50		36.90	53
0640	1-1/2" x 1"		18.20	.440		5.20	31.50		36.70	52.50
0650	1-1/2" x 1-1/4"	↓	18.20	.440		4.94	31.50		36.44	52.50
0660	2" x 1"	Q-1	33.10	.483		6.95	31.50		38.45	54
0670	2" x 1-1/2"	"	33.10	.483	↓	6.70	31.50		38.20	54
0700	Cross									
0720	3/4"	1 Plum	13	.615	Ea.	4.05	44.50		48.55	70.50
0730	1"		11.30	.708		5.05	51		56.05	81.50
0740	1-1/4"		10.10	.792		7	57		64	92.50
0750	1-1/2"	↓	9.10	.879		9.70	63.50		73.20	105
0760	2"	Q-1	16.60	.964		15.80	62.50		78.30	110
0770	2-1/2"	"	12.10	1.322	↓	34.50	86		120.50	166
0800	Cap									
0820	3/4"	1 Plum	52	.154	Ea.	1.09	11.10		12.19	17.75
0830	1"		45	.178		1.55	12.80		14.35	21
0840	1-1/4"		40	.200		2.51	14.40		16.91	24.50
0850	1-1/2"	↓	36.40	.220		3.47	15.85		19.32	27.50
0860	2"	Q-1	66	.242		5.20	15.70		20.90	29
0870	2-1/2"		48.40	.331		7.50	21.50		29	40.50
0880	3"	↓	41.60	.385	↓	12.15	25		37.15	50.50
0900	Adapter, sprinkler head, female w/metal thd. insert (s x FNPT)									

21 11 Facility Fire-Suppression Water-Service Piping

21 11 13 – Facility Fire Suppression Piping

21 11 13.18 Pipe Fittings, Plastic		Crew	Daily Output	Labor-Hours	Unit	Material	2023 Bare Costs Labor	Equipment	Total	Total Incl O&P
0920	3/4" x 1/2"	1 Plum	52	.154	Ea.	4.96	11.10		16.06	22
0930	1" x 1/2"		45	.178		5.25	12.80		18.05	25
0940	1" x 3/4"		45	.178		8.25	12.80		21.05	28

21 11 16 – Facility Fire Hydrants

21 11 16.50 Fire Hydrants for Buildings

		Crew	Daily Output	Labor-Hours	Unit	Material	Labor	Equipment	Total	Total Incl O&P
0010	**FIRE HYDRANTS FOR BUILDINGS**									
3750	Hydrants, wall, w/caps, single, flush, polished brass									
3800	2-1/2" x 2-1/2"	Q-12	5	3.200	Ea.	330	204		534	670
3840	2-1/2" x 3"		5	3.200		365	204		569	705
3860	3" x 3"		4.80	3.333		570	212		782	940
3900	For polished chrome, add					20%				
3950	Double, flush, polished brass									
4000	2-1/2" x 2-1/2" x 4"	Q-12	5	3.200	Ea.	920	204		1,124	1,300
4040	2-1/2" x 2-1/2" x 6"		4.60	3.478		1,350	222		1,572	1,800
4080	3" x 3" x 4"		4.90	3.265		1,525	208		1,733	2,000
4120	3" x 3" x 6"		4.50	3.556		1,475	227		1,702	1,975
4200	For polished chrome, add					10%				
4350	Double, projecting, polished brass									
4400	2-1/2" x 2-1/2" x 4"	Q-12	5	3.200	Ea.	455	204		659	805
4450	2-1/2" x 2-1/2" x 6"	"	4.60	3.478	"	740	222		962	1,150
4460	Valve control, dbl. flush/projecting hydrant, cap &									
4470	chain, extension rod & cplg., escutcheon, polished brass	Q-12	8	2	Ea.	495	127		622	730
4480	Four-way square, flush, polished brass									
4540	2-1/2" (4) x 6"	Q-12	3.60	4.444	Ea.	6,825	283		7,108	7,925

21 11 19 – Fire-Department Connections

21 11 19.50 Connections for the Fire-Department

		Crew	Daily Output	Labor-Hours	Unit	Material	Labor	Equipment	Total	Total Incl O&P
0010	**CONNECTIONS FOR THE FIRE-DEPARTMENT**									
0020	For fire pro. cabinets, see Section 10 44 13.53									
4000	Storz type, with cap and chain									
4100	2-1/2" Storz x 2-1/2" F NPT, silver powder coat	Q-12	4.80	3.333	Ea.	85	212		297	410
4200	4" Storz x 1-1/2" F NPT, silver powder coat		4.80	3.333		164	212		376	495
4300	4" Storz x 2-1/2" F NPT, silver powder coat		4.80	3.333		170	212		382	500
4400	4" Storz x 3" F NPT, silver powder coat		4.80	3.333		183	212		395	515
4500	4" Storz x 4" F NPT, red powder coat		4.80	3.333		204	212		416	540
4600	4" Storz x 4" F NPT, silver powder coat		4.80	3.333		199	212		411	535
4700	4" Storz x 6" F NPT, red powder coat		4.80	3.333		281	212		493	625
4800	4" Storz x 6" F NPT, silver powder coat		4.80	3.333		279	212		491	620
4900	5" Storz x 2-1/2" F NPT, silver powder coat		4.80	3.333		244	212		456	585
5000	5" Storz x 3" F NPT, silver powder coat		4.80	3.333		256	212		468	595
5100	5" Storz x 4" F NPT, red powder coat		4.80	3.333		224	212		436	560
5200	5" Storz x 4" F NPT, silver powder coat		4.80	3.333		1,450	212		1,662	1,925
5300	5" Storz x 6" F NPT, red powder coat		4.80	3.333		335	212		547	685
5400	5" Storz x 6" F NPT, silver powder coat		4.80	3.333		2,025	212		2,237	2,550
6000	Roof manifold, horiz., brass, without valves & caps									
6040	2-1/2" x 2-1/2" x 4"	Q-12	4.80	3.333	Ea.	252	212		464	590
6060	2-1/2" x 2-1/2" x 6"		4.60	3.478		585	222		807	970
6080	2-1/2" x 2-1/2" x 2-1/2" x 4"		4.60	3.478		560	222		782	950
6090	2-1/2" x 2-1/2" x 2-1/2" x 6"		4.60	3.478		610	222		832	1,000
7000	Sprinkler line tester, cast brass					52			52	57.50
7140	Standpipe connections, wall, w/plugs & chains									
7160	Single, flush, brass, 2-1/2" x 2-1/2", Fire Dept Conn.	Q-12	5	3.200	Ea.	230	204		434	560
7180	2-1/2" x 3"	"	5	3.200	"	227	204		431	555

21 11 Facility Fire-Suppression Water-Service Piping

21 11 19 – Fire-Department Connections

21 11 19.50 Connections for the Fire-Department

		Crew	Daily Output	Labor-Hours	Unit	Material	2023 Bare Costs Labor	Equipment	Total	Total Incl O&P
7240	For polished chrome, add					15%				
7280	Double, flush, polished brass									
7300	2-1/2" x 2-1/2" x 4"	Q-12	5	3.200	Ea.	845	204		1,049	1,225
7330	2-1/2" x 2-1/2" x 6"		4.60	3.478		1,075	222		1,297	1,525
7340	3" x 3" x 4"		4.90	3.265		1,175	208		1,383	1,600
7370	3" x 3" x 6"		4.50	3.556		1,550	227		1,777	2,075
7400	For polished chrome, add					15%				
7440	For sill cock combination, add				Ea.	117			117	128
7580	Double projecting, polished brass									
7600	2-1/2" x 2-1/2" x 4"	Q-12	5	3.200	Ea.	605	204		809	970
7630	2-1/2" x 2-1/2" x 6"	"	4.60	3.478	"	1,000	222		1,222	1,425
7680	For polished chrome, add					15%				
7900	Three way, flush, polished brass									
7920	2-1/2" (3) x 4"	Q-12	4.80	3.333	Ea.	1,675	212		1,887	2,175
7930	2-1/2" (3) x 6"	"	4.60	3.478		3,275	222		3,497	3,925
8000	For polished chrome, add					9%				
8020	Three way, projecting, polished brass									
8040	2-1/2" (3) x 4"	Q-12	4.80	3.333	Ea.	2,025	212		2,237	2,550
8070	2-1/2" (3) x 6"	"	4.60	3.478		1,875	222		2,097	2,375
8100	For polished chrome, add					12%				
8200	Four way, square, flush, polished brass,									
8240	2-1/2" (4) x 6"	Q-12	3.60	4.444	Ea.	3,000	283		3,283	3,725
8300	For polished chrome, add				"	10%				
8550	Wall, vertical, flush, cast brass									
8600	Two way, 2-1/2" x 2-1/2" x 4"	Q-12	5	3.200	Ea.	580	204		784	945
8660	Four way, 2-1/2" (4) x 6"		3.80	4.211		4,175	268		4,443	5,000
8680	Six way, 2-1/2" (6) x 6"		3.40	4.706		2,325	300		2,625	3,000
8700	For polished chrome, add					10%				
8800	Free standing siamese unit, polished brass, two way									
8820	2-1/2" x 2-1/2" x 4"	Q-12	2.50	6.400	Ea.	875	410		1,285	1,575
8850	2-1/2" x 2-1/2" x 6"		2	8		1,400	510		1,910	2,275
8860	3" x 3" x 4"		2.50	6.400		1,225	410		1,635	1,950
8890	3" x 3" x 6"		2	8		1,775	510		2,285	2,725
8940	For polished chrome, add					12%				
9100	Free standing siamese unit, polished brass, three way									
9120	2-1/2" x 2-1/2" x 2-1/2" x 6"	Q-12	2	8	Ea.	1,700	510		2,210	2,625
9160	For polished chrome, add				"	15%				

21 12 Fire-Suppression Standpipes

21 12 13 – Fire-Suppression Hoses and Nozzles

21 12 13.50 Fire Hoses and Nozzles

0010	**FIRE HOSES AND NOZZLES**									
0200	Adapters, rough brass, straight hose threads	R211226-10								
0220	One piece, female to male, rocker lugs									
0240	1" x 1"	R211226-20			Ea.	37.50			37.50	41
0260	1-1/2" x 1"					46			46	50.50
0280	1-1/2" x 1-1/2"					55			55	60.50
0300	2" x 1-1/2"					80.50			80.50	88.50
0320	2" x 2"					114			114	126
0340	2-1/2" x 1-1/2"					35			35	38.50
0360	3" x 1-1/2"					136			136	150

21 12 Fire-Suppression Standpipes

21 12 13 – Fire-Suppression Hoses and Nozzles

21 12 13.50 Fire Hoses and Nozzles		Crew	Daily Output	Labor-Hours	Unit	Material	2023 Bare Costs Labor	Equipment	Total	Total Incl O&P
0380	2-1/2" x 2-1/2"				Ea.	122			122	134
0400	3" x 2-1/2"					88.50			88.50	97.50
0420	3" x 3"					159			159	175
0500	For polished brass, add					50%				
0520	For polished chrome, add					75%				
0700	One piece, female to male, hexagon									
0740	1-1/2" x 3/4"				Ea.	106			106	116
0760	2" x 1-1/2"					36			36	40
0780	2-1/2" x 1"					203			203	223
0800	2-1/2" x 1-1/2"					74			74	81.50
0820	2-1/2" x 2"					53.50			53.50	59
0840	3" x 2-1/2"					156			156	172
0900	For polished chrome, add					75%				
1100	Swivel, female to female, pin lugs									
1120	1-1/2" x 1-1/2"				Ea.	87.50			87.50	96
1200	2-1/2" x 2-1/2"					197			197	216
1260	For polished brass, add					50%				
1280	For polished chrome, add					75%				
1400	Couplings, sngl. & dbl. jacket, pin lug or rocker lug, cast brass									
1410	1-1/2"				Ea.	67			67	74
1420	2-1/2"				"	147			147	162
1500	For polished brass, add					20%				
1520	For polished chrome, add					40%				
1580	Reducing, F x M, interior installation, cast brass									
1590	2" x 1-1/2"				Ea.	86.50			86.50	95
1600	2-1/2" x 1-1/2"					25			25	27.50
1680	For polished brass, add					50%				
1720	For polished chrome, add					75%				
2200	Hose, less couplings									
2260	Synthetic jacket, lined, 300 lb. test, 1-1/2" diameter	Q-12	2600	.006	L.F.	3.31	.39		3.70	4.23
2270	2" diameter		2200	.007		3.16	.46		3.62	4.17
2280	2-1/2" diameter		2200	.007		5.80	.46		6.26	7.10
2290	3" diameter		2200	.007		5.60	.46		6.06	6.85
2360	High strength, 500 lb. test, 1-1/2" diameter		2600	.006		3.62	.39		4.01	4.57
2380	2-1/2" diameter		2200	.007		6.10	.46		6.56	7.40
5000	Nipples, straight hose to tapered iron pipe, brass									
5060	Female to female, 1-1/2" x 1-1/2"				Ea.	26			26	28.50
5100	2-1/2" x 2-1/2"					67			67	73.50
5190	For polished chrome, add					75%				
5200	Double male or male to female, 1" x 1"					34			34	37.50
5220	1-1/2" x 1"					17.40			17.40	19.15
5230	1-1/2" x 1-1/2"					18.05			18.05	19.85
5260	2" x 1-1/2"					96			96	106
5270	2" x 2"					146			146	160
5280	2-1/2" x 1-1/2"					134			134	147
5300	2-1/2" x 2"					57.50			57.50	63
5310	2-1/2" x 2-1/2"					57.50			57.50	63.50
5340	For polished chrome, add					75%				
5600	Nozzles, brass									
5620	Adjustable fog, 3/4" booster line				Ea.	154			154	170
5630	1" booster line					184			184	202
5640	1-1/2" leader line					120			120	132
5660	2-1/2" direct connection					280			280	310

21 12 Fire-Suppression Standpipes

21 12 13 – Fire-Suppression Hoses and Nozzles

21 12 13.50 Fire Hoses and Nozzles		Crew	Daily Output	Labor-Hours	Unit	Material	2023 Bare Costs Labor	Equipment	Total	Total Incl O&P
5680	2-1/2" playpipe nozzle				Ea.	380			380	415
5780	For chrome plated, add					8%				
5850	Electrical fire, adjustable fog, no shock									
5900	1-1/2"				Ea.	194			194	213
5920	2-1/2"					655			655	720
5980	For polished chrome, add					6%				
6200	Heavy duty, comb. adj. fog and str. stream, with handle									
6210	1" booster line				Ea.	335			335	370
6240	1-1/2"					675			675	745
6260	2-1/2", for playpipe					970			970	1,075
6280	2-1/2" direct connection					685			685	750
6300	2-1/2" playpipe combination					1,075			1,075	1,175
6480	For polished chrome, add					7%				
6500	Plain fog, polished brass, 1-1/2"					276			276	305
6540	Chrome plated, 1-1/2"					192			192	211
6700	Plain stream, polished brass, 1-1/2" x 10"					58.50			58.50	64.50
6760	2-1/2" x 15" x 7/8" or 1-1/2"					170			170	186
6860	For polished chrome, add					20%				
7000	Underwriters playpipe, 2-1/2" x 30" with 1-1/8" tip				Ea.	985			985	1,075
9200	Storage house, hose only, primed steel					2,025			2,025	2,225
9220	Aluminum					2,350			2,350	2,600
9280	Hose and hydrant house, primed steel					1,975			1,975	2,175
9300	Aluminum					2,100			2,100	2,300
9340	Tools, crowbar and brackets		1 Carp	12	.667		88	39		127	155
9360	Combination hydrant wrench and spanner						89			89	98
9380	Fire axe and brackets										
9400	6 lb.		1 Carp	12	.667	Ea.	216	39		255	295
9500	For fire equipment cabinets, Section 10 44 13.53										

21 12 16 – Fire-Suppression Hose Reels

21 12 16.50 Fire-Suppression Hose Reels

0010	**FIRE-SUPPRESSION HOSE REELS**									
2990	Hose reel, swinging, for 1-1/2" polyester neoprene lined hose									
3000	50' long	Q-12	14	1.143	Ea.	187	73		260	315
3020	100' long		14	1.143		280	73		353	420
3060	For 2-1/2" cotton rubber hose, 75' long		14	1.143		267	73		340	405
3100	150' long		14	1.143		310	73		383	455

21 12 19 – Fire-Suppression Hose Racks

21 12 19.50 Fire Hose Racks

0010	**FIRE HOSE RACKS**									
2600	Hose rack, swinging, for 1-1/2" diameter hose,									
2620	Enameled steel, 50' and 75' lengths of hose	Q-12	20	.800	Ea.	132	51		183	221
2640	100' and 125' lengths of hose		20	.800		117	51		168	205
2680	Chrome plated, 50' and 75' lengths of hose		20	.800		113	51		164	201
2700	100' and 125' lengths of hose		20	.800		182	51		233	276
2750	2-1/2" diameter, 100' hose		20	.800		143	51		194	233
2780	For hose rack nipple, 1-1/2" polished brass, add					33.50			33.50	37
2820	2-1/2" polished brass, add					107			107	118
2840	1-1/2" polished chrome, add					42.50			42.50	46.50
2860	2-1/2" polished chrome, add					118			118	130

21 12 Fire-Suppression Standpipes

21 12 23 – Fire-Suppression Hose Valves

21 12 23.70 Fire Hose Valves		Crew	Daily Output	Labor-Hours	Unit	Material	2023 Bare Costs Labor	Equipment	Total	Total Incl O&P
0010	**FIRE HOSE VALVES**									
0020	Angle, combination pressure adjust/restricting, rough brass	R211226-10								
0030	1-1/2"		1 Spri	12	.667	Ea.	132	47		179	216
0040	2-1/2"	R211226-20	"	7	1.143	"	217	81		298	360
0042	Nonpressure adjustable/restricting, rough brass									
0044	1-1/2"		1 Spri	12	.667	Ea.	127	47		174	210
0046	2-1/2"		"	7	1.143	"	205	81		286	345
0050	For polished brass, add						30%				
0060	For polished chrome, add						40%				
0080	Wheel handle, 300 lb., 1-1/2"		1 Spri	12	.667	Ea.	101	47		148	182
0090	2-1/2"		"	7	1.143	"	194	81		275	335
0100	For polished brass, add						35%				
0110	For polished chrome, add						50%				
1000	Ball drip, automatic, rough brass, 1/2"		1 Spri	20	.400	Ea.	18.30	28.50		46.80	62.50
1010	3/4"		"	20	.400	"	20.50	28.50		49	65
1100	Ball, 175 lb., sprinkler system, FM/UL, threaded, bronze										
1120	Slow close										
1150	1" size		1 Spri	19	.421	Ea.	305	30		335	380
1160	1-1/4" size			15	.533		330	38		368	420
1170	1-1/2" size			13	.615		435	43.50		478.50	545
1180	2" size			11	.727		530	51.50		581.50	655
1190	2-1/2" size		Q-12	15	1.067		715	68		783	885
1230	For supervisory switch kit, all sizes										
1240	One circuit, add		1 Spri	48	.167	Ea.	144	11.80		155.80	176
1280	Quarter turn for trim										
1300	1/2" size		1 Spri	22	.364	Ea.	54	26		80	97.50
1310	3/4" size			20	.400		57.50	28.50		86	106
1320	1" size			19	.421		64	30		94	115
1330	1-1/4" size			15	.533		105	38		143	173
1340	1-1/2" size			13	.615		132	43.50		175.50	210
1350	2" size			11	.727		157	51.50		208.50	250
1400	Caps, polished brass with chain, 3/4"						59.50			59.50	65.50
1420	1"						66.50			66.50	73
1440	1-1/2"						21			21	23.50
1460	2-1/2"						30.50			30.50	33.50
1480	3"						144			144	159
1900	Escutcheon plate, for angle valves, polished brass, 1-1/2"						23			23	25
1920	2-1/2"						38.50			38.50	42.50
1940	3"						46.50			46.50	51
1980	For polished chrome, add						15%				
2000	Foam, control valve, 3"		1 Spri	6	1.333		3,275	94.50		3,369.50	3,750
2020	Supply valve, 2-1/2"			7	1.143		218	81		299	360
2040	Proportioner, 8"			2	4		5,325	283		5,608	6,300
2060	Oscillating foam monitor with electric remote control		Q-12	5.33	3.002		24,300	191		24,491	27,000
3000	Gate, hose, wheel handle, N.R.S., rough brass, 1-1/2"		1 Spri	12	.667		166	47		213	254
3040	2-1/2", 300 lb.		"	7	1.143		235	81		316	380
3080	For polished brass, add						40%				
3090	For polished chrome, add						50%				
3800	Hydrant, screw type, crank handle, brass										
3840	2-1/2" size		Q-12	11	1.455	Ea.	585	92.50		677.50	780
3880	For chrome, same price										
4200	Hydrolator, vent and draining, rough brass, 1-1/2"		1 Spri	12	.667	Ea.	153	47		200	239

For customer support on your Plumbing Costs with RSMeans data, call 800.448.8182.

21 12 Fire-Suppression Standpipes

21 12 23 – Fire-Suppression Hose Valves

21 12 23.70 Fire Hose Valves		Crew	Daily Output	Labor-Hours	Unit	Material	2023 Bare Costs Labor	2023 Bare Costs Equipment	Total	Total Incl O&P
4280	For polished brass, add				Ea.	50%				
4290	For polished chrome, add					90%				
5000	Pressure reducing rough brass, 1-1/2"	1 Spri	12	.667		480	47		527	600
5020	2-1/2"	"	7	1.143		725	81		806	920
5080	For polished brass, add					105%				
5090	For polished chrome, add					140%				
8000	Wye, leader line, ball type, swivel female x male x male									
8040	2-1/2" x 1-1/2" x 1-1/2" polished brass				Ea.	785			785	865
8060	2-1/2" x 1-1/2" x 1-1/2" polished chrome				"	385			385	425

21 13 Fire-Suppression Sprinkler Systems

21 13 13 – Wet-Pipe Sprinkler Systems

21 13 13.50 Wet-Pipe Sprinkler System Components

			Crew	Daily Output	Labor-Hours	Unit	Material	2023 Bare Costs Labor	2023 Bare Costs Equipment	Total	Total Incl O&P
0010	**WET-PIPE SPRINKLER SYSTEM COMPONENTS**										
1100	Alarm, electric pressure switch (circuit closer)	R211313-10	1 Spri	26	.308	Ea.	153	22		175	201
1140	For explosion proof, max 20 psi, contacts close or open			26	.308		935	22		957	1,050
1220	Water motor gong			4	2		465	142		607	725
1900	Flexible sprinkler head connectors										
1910	Braided stainless steel hose with mounting bracket										
1920	1/2" and 3/4" outlet size										
1940	40" length		1 Spri	30	.267	Ea.	41	18.90		59.90	73.50
1960	60" length		"	22	.364	"	47.50	26		73.50	90.50
1982	May replace hard-pipe armovers										
1984	for wet and pre-action systems.										
2000	Release, emergency, manual, for hydraulic or pneumatic system		1 Spri	12	.667	Ea.	241	47		288	335
2060	Release, thermostatic, for hydraulic or pneumatic release line			20	.400		1,025	28.50		1,053.50	1,175
2200	Sprinkler cabinets, 6 head capacity			16	.500		53	35.50		88.50	112
2260	12 head capacity			16	.500		72	35.50		107.50	132
2340	Sprinkler head escutcheons, standard, brass tone, 1" size			40	.200		2.68	14.15		16.83	24
2360	Chrome, 1" size			40	.200		4.84	14.15		18.99	26.50
2400	Recessed type, bright brass			40	.200		12.50	14.15		26.65	35
2440	Chrome or white enamel			40	.200		3.50	14.15		17.65	25
2600	Sprinkler heads, not including supply piping										
3700	Standard spray, pendent or upright, brass, 135°F to 286°F										
3720	1/2" NPT, K2.8		1 Spri	16	.500	Ea.	36	35.50		71.50	92.50
3730	1/2" NPT, 7/16" orifice			16	.500		23.50	35.50		59	78.50
3740	1/2" NPT, K5.6			16	.500		18.80	35.50		54.30	73.50
3760	1/2" NPT, 17/32" orifice			16	.500		19.40	35.50		54.90	74.50
3780	3/4" NPT, 17/32" orifice			16	.500		12.20	35.50		47.70	66.50
3800	For open sprinklers, deduct						15%				
3840	For chrome, add					Ea.	5.30			5.30	5.85
3920	For 360°F, same cost										
3930	For 400°F		1 Spri	16	.500	Ea.	161	35.50		196.50	230
3940	For 500°F		"	16	.500	"	121	35.50		156.50	186
4200	Sidewall, vertical brass, 135°F to 286°F										
4240	1/2" NPT, 1/2" orifice		1 Spri	16	.500	Ea.	38	35.50		73.50	95
4280	3/4" NPT, 17/32" orifice		"	16	.500		127	35.50		162.50	193
4360	For satin chrome, add						6.30			6.30	6.90
4400	For 360°F, same cost										
4500	Sidewall, horizontal, brass, 135°F to 286°F										
4520	1/2" NPT, 1/2" orifice		1 Spri	16	.500	Ea.	35	35.50		70.50	91.50

21 13 Fire-Suppression Sprinkler Systems

21 13 13 – Wet-Pipe Sprinkler Systems

21 13 13.50 Wet-Pipe Sprinkler System Components		Crew	Daily Output	Labor-Hours	Unit	Material	2023 Bare Costs Labor	Equipment	Total	Total Incl O&P
4540	For 360°F, same cost									
4800	Recessed pendent, brass, 135°F to 286°F									
4820	1/2" NPT, K2.8	1 Spri	10	.800	Ea.	17.60	56.50		74.10	104
4830	1/2" NPT, 7/16" orifice		10	.800		18.65	56.50		75.15	105
4840	1/2" NPT, K5.6		10	.800		19.90	56.50		76.40	107
4860	1/2" NPT, 17/32" orifice		10	.800		23	56.50		79.50	110
4900	For satin chrome, add					14.50			14.50	15.95
5000	Recessed-vertical sidewall, brass, 135°F to 286°F									
5020	1/2" NPT, K2.8	1 Spri	10	.800	Ea.	47	56.50		103.50	137
5030	1/2" NPT, 7/16" orifice		10	.800		47	56.50		103.50	137
5040	1/2" NPT, K5.6		10	.800		47	56.50		103.50	137
5100	For bright nickel, same cost									
5600	Concealed, complete with cover plate									
5620	1/2" NPT, 1/2" orifice, 135°F to 212°F	1 Spri	9	.889	Ea.	53	63		116	152
5800	Window, brass, 1/2" NPT, 1/4" orifice		16	.500		54	35.50		89.50	112
5810	1/2" NPT, 5/16" orifice		16	.500		54	35.50		89.50	112
5820	1/2" NPT, 3/8" orifice		16	.500		53	35.50		88.50	111
5830	1/2" NPT, 7/16" orifice		16	.500		54	35.50		89.50	112
5840	1/2" NPT, 1/2" orifice		16	.500		53.50	35.50		89	112
5860	For polished chrome, add					62			62	68
5880	3/4" NPT, 5/8" orifice	1 Spri	16	.500		56	35.50		91.50	115
5890	3/4" NPT, 3/4" orifice	"	16	.500		61.50	35.50		97	121
6000	Sprinkler head guards, bright zinc, 1/2" NPT					9.75			9.75	10.75
6020	Bright zinc, 3/4" NPT					6.95			6.95	7.65
6025	Residential sprinkler components (one and two family)									
6026	Water motor alarm with strainer	1 Spri	4	2	Ea.	590	142		732	860
6027	Fast response, glass bulb, 135°F to 155°F									
6028	1/2" NPT, pendent, brass	1 Spri	16	.500	Ea.	17.30	35.50		52.80	72
6029	1/2" NPT, sidewall, brass		16	.500		50	35.50		85.50	108
6030	1/2" NPT, pendent, brass, extended coverage		16	.500		38	35.50		73.50	95
6031	1/2" NPT, sidewall, brass, extended coverage		16	.500		34	35.50		69.50	90.50
6032	3/4" NPT sidewall, brass, extended coverage		16	.500		30.50	35.50		66	86.50
6033	For chrome, add					15%				
6034	For polyester/teflon coating, add					20%				
6100	Sprinkler head wrenches, standard head				Ea.	47.50			47.50	52
6120	Recessed head					97			97	107
6160	Tamper switch (valve supervisory switch)	1 Spri	16	.500		241	35.50		276.50	320
6165	Flow switch (valve supervisory switch)	"	16	.500		241	35.50		276.50	320

21 13 16 – Dry-Pipe Sprinkler Systems

21 13 16.50 Dry-Pipe Sprinkler System Components

		Crew	Daily Output	Labor-Hours	Unit	Material	Labor	Equipment	Total	Total Incl O&P
0010	**DRY-PIPE SPRINKLER SYSTEM COMPONENTS**									
0600	Accelerator	1 Spri	8	1	Ea.	1,025	71		1,096	1,225
0800	Air compressor for dry pipe system, automatic, complete									
0820	30 gal. system capacity, 3/4 HP	1 Spri	1.30	6.154	Ea.	1,850	435		2,285	2,675
0860	30 gal. system capacity, 1 HP		1.30	6.154		1,650	435		2,085	2,475
0910	30 gal. system capacity, 1-1/2 HP		1.30	6.154		1,875	435		2,310	2,700
0920	30 gal. system capacity, 2 HP		1.30	6.154		1,875	435		2,310	2,700
0960	Air pressure maintenance control		24	.333		470	23.50		493.50	550
1600	Dehydrator package, incl. valves and nipples	R211313-20	12	.667		1,425	47		1,472	1,625
2600	Sprinkler heads, not including supply piping									
2640	Dry, pendent, 1/2" orifice, 3/4" or 1" NPT									
2660	3" to 6" length	1 Spri	14	.571	Ea.	119	40.50		159.50	192

21 13 Fire-Suppression Sprinkler Systems

21 13 16 – Dry-Pipe Sprinkler Systems

21 13 16.50 Dry-Pipe Sprinkler System Components		Crew	Daily Output	Labor-Hours	Unit	Material	2023 Bare Costs Labor	2023 Bare Costs Equipment	Total	Total Incl O&P
2670	6-1/4" to 8" length	1 Spri	14	.571	Ea.	125	40.50		165.50	198
2680	8-1/4" to 12" length		14	.571		131	40.50		171.50	205
2690	12-1/4" to 15" length		14	.571		140	40.50		180.50	215
2700	15-1/4" to 18" length		14	.571		148	40.50		188.50	224
2710	18-1/4" to 21" length		13	.615		157	43.50		200.50	238
2720	21-1/4" to 24" length		13	.615		168	43.50		211.50	249
2730	24-1/4" to 27" length		13	.615		178	43.50		221.50	260
2740	27-1/4" to 30" length		13	.615		274	43.50		317.50	365
2750	30-1/4" to 33" length		13	.615		194	43.50		237.50	279
2760	33-1/4" to 36" length		13	.615		202	43.50		245.50	288
2780	36-1/4" to 39" length		12	.667		194	47		241	284
2790	39-1/4" to 42" length		12	.667		201	47		248	292
2800	For each inch or fraction, add					2.58			2.58	2.84
6330	Valves and components									
6340	Alarm test/shut off valve, 1/2"	1 Spri	20	.400	Ea.	17.50	28.50		46	62
8000	Dry pipe air check valve, 3" size	Q-12	2	8		2,200	510		2,710	3,175
8200	Dry pipe valve, incl. trim and gauges, 3" size		2	8		3,725	510		4,235	4,850
8220	4" size		1	16		3,500	1,025		4,525	5,375
8240	6" size	Q-13	2	16		4,675	1,075		5,750	6,750
8280	For accelerator trim with gauges, add	1 Spri	8	1		365	71		436	505

21 13 19 – Preaction Sprinkler Systems

21 13 19.50 Preaction Sprinkler System Components		Crew	Daily Output	Labor-Hours	Unit	Material	Labor	Equipment	Total	Total Incl O&P
0010	**PREACTION SPRINKLER SYSTEM COMPONENTS**									
3000	Preaction valve cabinet									
3100	Single interlock, pneum. release, panel, 1/2 HP comp. regul. air trim									
3110	1-1/2"	Q-12	3	5.333	Ea.	27,300	340		27,640	30,500
3120	2"		3	5.333		27,400	340		27,740	30,600
3130	2-1/2"		3	5.333		27,900	340		28,240	31,200
3140	3"		3	5.333		27,600	340		27,940	30,800
3150	4"		2	8		28,900	510		29,410	32,500
3160	6"	Q-13	4	8		30,700	540		31,240	34,600
3200	Double interlock, pneum. release, panel, 1/2 HP comp. regul. air trim									
3210	1-1/2"	Q-12	3	5.333	Ea.	28,400	340		28,740	31,700
3220	2"		3	5.333		28,500	340		28,840	31,800
3230	2-1/2"		3	5.333		28,400	340		28,740	31,800
3240	3"		3	5.333		28,700	340		29,040	32,000
3250	4"		2	8		31,500	510		32,010	35,400
3260	6"	Q-13	4	8		32,900	540		33,440	37,000

21 13 20 – On-Off Multicycle Sprinkler System

21 13 20.50 On-Off Multicycle Fire-Suppression Sprinkler Systems		Crew	Daily Output	Labor-Hours	Unit	Material	Labor	Equipment	Total	Total Incl O&P
0010	**ON-OFF MULTICYCLE FIRE-SUPPRESSION SPRINKLER SYSTEMS**									
8400	On-off multicycle package, includes swing check									
8420	and flow control valves with required trim									
8440	2" size	Q-12	2	8	Ea.	5,775	510		6,285	7,100
8460	3" size		1.50	10.667		6,350	680		7,030	8,000
8480	4" size		1	16		7,100	1,025		8,125	9,325
8500	6" size	Q-13	1.40	22.857		8,200	1,550		9,750	11,300

21 13 Fire-Suppression Sprinkler Systems

21 13 26 – Deluge Fire-Suppression Sprinkler Systems

21 13 26.50 Deluge Fire-Suppression Sprinkler Sys. Comp.	Crew	Daily Output	Labor-Hours	Unit	Material	2023 Bare Costs Labor	Equipment	Total	Total Incl O&P
0010 **DELUGE FIRE-SUPPRESSION SPRINKLER SYSTEM COMPONENTS**									
1400 Deluge system, monitoring panel w/deluge valve & trim	1 Spri	18	.444	Ea.	23,600	31.50		23,631.50	25,900
6200 Valves and components									
7000 Deluge, assembly, incl. trim, pressure									
7020 operated relief, emergency release, gauges									
7040 2" size	Q-12	2	8	Ea.	5,200	510		5,710	6,475
7060 3" size		1.50	10.667		6,275	680		6,955	7,925
7080 4" size	↓	1	16		6,850	1,025		7,875	9,075
7100 6" size	Q-13	1.80	17.778	↓	7,450	1,200		8,650	9,975
7800 Pneumatic actuator, bronze, required on all									
7820 pneumatic release systems, any size deluge	1 Spri	18	.444	Ea.	385	31.50		416.50	470

21 13 39 – Foam-Water Systems

21 13 39.50 Foam-Water System Components

	Crew	Daily Output	Labor-Hours	Unit	Material	Labor	Equipment	Total	Total Incl O&P
0010 **FOAM-WATER SYSTEM COMPONENTS**									
2600 Sprinkler heads, not including supply piping									
3600 Foam-water, pendent or upright, 1/2" NPT	1 Spri	12	.667	Ea.	350	47		397	455

21 21 Carbon-Dioxide Fire-Extinguishing Systems

21 21 16 – Carbon-Dioxide Fire-Extinguishing Equipment

21 21 16.50 CO2 Fire Extinguishing System

	Crew	Daily Output	Labor-Hours	Unit	Material	Labor	Equipment	Total	Total Incl O&P
0010 **CO_2 FIRE EXTINGUISHING SYSTEM**									
0042 For detectors and control stations, see Section 28 31 23.50									
0100 Control panel, single zone with batteries (2 zones det., 1 suppr.)	1 Elec	1	8	Ea.	1,400	540		1,940	2,350
0150 Multizone (4) with batteries (8 zones det., 4 suppr.)	"	.50	16		3,400	1,075		4,475	5,350
1000 Dispersion nozzle, CO_2, 3" x 5"	1 Plum	18	.444		176	32		208	241
2000 Extinguisher, CO_2 system, high pressure, 75 lb. cylinder	Q-1	6	2.667		1,575	173		1,748	1,975
2100 100 lb. cylinder	"	5	3.200		2,200	208		2,408	2,725
3000 Electro/mechanical release	L-1	4	4		1,175	279		1,454	1,700
3400 Manual pull station	1 Plum	6	1.333		102	96		198	255
4000 Pneumatic damper release	"	8	1	↓	365	72		437	505

21 22 Clean-Agent Fire-Extinguishing Systems

21 22 16 – Clean-Agent Fire-Extinguishing Equipment

21 22 16.50 Clean-Agent Extinguishing Systems

	Crew	Daily Output	Labor-Hours	Unit	Material	Labor	Equipment	Total	Total Incl O&P
0010 **CLEAN-AGENT EXTINGUISHING SYSTEMS**									
0020 FM200 fire extinguishing system									
1100 Dispersion nozzle FM200, 1-1/2"	1 Plum	14	.571	Ea.	280	41		321	370
2400 Extinguisher, FM200 system, filled, with mounting bracket									
2460 26 lb. container	Q-1	8	2	Ea.	2,425	130		2,555	2,875
2480 44 lb. container		7	2.286		3,150	148		3,298	3,675
2500 63 lb. container		6	2.667		4,450	173		4,623	5,150
2520 101 lb. container		5	3.200		6,450	208		6,658	7,375
2540 196 lb. container	↓	4	4		7,775	259		8,034	8,925
6000 FM200 system, simple nozzle layout, with broad dispersion				C.F.	2.11			2.11	2.32
6010 Extinguisher, FM200 system, filled, with mounting bracket									
6020 Complex nozzle layout and/or including underfloor dispersion				C.F.	4.20			4.20	4.62
6100 20,000 C.F. 2 exits, 8' clng					2.35			2.35	2.59
6200 100,000 C.F. 4 exits, 8' clng				↓	2.13			2.13	2.34

21 22 Clean-Agent Fire-Extinguishing Systems

21 22 16 – Clean-Agent Fire-Extinguishing Equipment

21 22 16.50 Clean-Agent Extinguishing Systems		Crew	Daily Output	Labor-Hours	Unit	Material	2023 Bare Costs Labor	Equipment	Total	Total Incl O&P
6300	250,000 C.F. 6 exits, 8' clng				C.F.	1.79			1.79	1.97
7010	HFC-227ea fire extinguishing system									
7100	Cylinders with clean-agent									
7110	Does not include pallet jack/fork lift rental fees									
7120	70 lb. cyl, w/35 lb. agent, no solenoid	Q-12	14	1.143	Ea.	3,950	73		4,023	4,450
7130	70 lb. cyl w/70 lb. agent, no solenoid		10	1.600		5,200	102		5,302	5,875
7140	70 lb. cyl w/35 lb. agent, w/solenoid		14	1.143		4,650	73		4,723	5,200
7150	70 lb. cyl w/70 lb. agent, w/solenoid		10	1.600		5,875	102		5,977	6,600
7220	250 lb. cyl, w/125 lb. agent, no solenoid		8	2		9,175	127		9,302	10,300
7230	250 lb. cyl w/250 lb. agent, no solenoid		5	3.200		9,175	204		9,379	10,400
7240	250 lb. cyl, w/125 lb. agent, w/solenoid		8	2		10,000	127		10,127	11,300
7250	250 lb. cyl, w/250 lb. agent, w/solenoid		5	3.200		14,400	204		14,604	16,200
7320	560 lb. cyl, w/300 lb. agent, no solenoid		4	4		17,500	255		17,755	19,700
7330	560 lb. cyl, w/560 lb. agent, no solenoid		2.50	6.400		26,800	410		27,210	30,000
7340	560 lb. cyl, w/300 lb. agent, w/solenoid		4	4		18,600	255		18,855	20,900
7350	560 lb. cyl, w/560 lb. agent, w/solenoid		2.50	6.400		27,700	410		28,110	31,100
7420	1,200 lb. cyl, w/600 lb. agent, no solenoid	Q-13	4	8		33,400	540		33,940	37,500
7430	1,200 lb. cyl, w/1,200 lb. agent, no solenoid		3	10.667		54,500	720		55,220	61,000
7440	1,200 lb. cyl, w/600 lb. agent, w/solenoid		4	8		64,500	540		65,040	72,000
7450	1,200 lb. cyl, w/1,200 lb. agent, w/solenoid		3	10.667		101,500	720		102,220	112,500
7500	Accessories									
7510	Dispersion nozzle	1 Spri	16	.500	Ea.	151	35.50		186.50	219
7520	Agent release panel	1 Elec	4	2		102	135		237	310
7530	Maintenance switch	"	6	1.333		320	90		410	490
7540	Solenoid valve, 12v dc	1 Spri	8	1		273	71		344	405
7550	12v ac		8	1		670	71		741	840
7560	12v dc, explosion proof		8	1		705	71		776	880

21 31 Centrifugal Fire Pumps

21 31 13 – Electric-Drive, Centrifugal Fire Pumps

21 31 13.50 Electric-Drive Fire Pumps

		Crew	Daily Output	Labor-Hours	Unit	Material	Labor	Equipment	Total	Total Incl O&P
0010	**ELECTRIC-DRIVE FIRE PUMPS** Including controller, fittings and relief valve									
3100	250 GPM, 55 psi, 15 HP, 3550 RPM, 2" pump	Q-13	.70	45.714	Ea.	18,100	3,075		21,175	24,500
3200	500 GPM, 50 psi, 27 HP, 1770 RPM, 4" pump		.68	47.059		22,500	3,175		25,675	29,500
3250	500 GPM, 100 psi, 47 HP, 3550 RPM, 3" pump		.66	48.485		27,300	3,275		30,575	35,000
3300	500 GPM, 125 psi, 64 HP, 3550 RPM, 3" pump		.62	51.613		29,900	3,475		33,375	38,100
3350	750 GPM, 50 psi, 44 HP, 1770 RPM, 5" pump		.64	50		32,900	3,375		36,275	41,200
3400	750 GPM, 100 psi, 66 HP, 3550 RPM, 4" pump		.58	55.172		29,100	3,725		32,825	37,600
3450	750 GPM, 165 psi, 120 HP, 3550 RPM, 4" pump		.56	57.143		38,000	3,850		41,850	47,500
3500	1000 GPM, 50 psi, 48 HP, 1770 RPM, 5" pump		.60	53.333		32,900	3,600		36,500	41,600
3550	1000 GPM, 100 psi, 86 HP, 3550 RPM, 5" pump		.54	59.259		36,900	4,000		40,900	46,500
3600	1000 GPM, 150 psi, 142 HP, 3550 RPM, 5" pump		.50	64		41,800	4,325		46,125	52,500
3650	1000 GPM, 200 psi, 245 HP, 1770 RPM, 6" pump		.36	88.889		55,500	6,000		61,500	70,000
3660	1250 GPM, 75 psi, 75 HP, 1770 RPM, 5" pump		.55	58.182		33,800	3,925		37,725	43,000
3700	1500 GPM, 50 psi, 66 HP, 1770 RPM, 6" pump		.50	64		35,400	4,325		39,725	45,500
3750	1500 GPM, 100 psi, 139 HP, 1770 RPM, 6" pump		.46	69.565		40,100	4,700		44,800	51,000
3800	1500 GPM, 150 psi, 200 HP, 1770 RPM, 6" pump		.36	88.889		49,200	6,000		55,200	63,000
3850	1500 GPM, 200 psi, 279 HP, 1770 RPM, 6" pump		.32	100		53,000	6,750		59,750	68,000
3900	2000 GPM, 100 psi, 167 HP, 1770 RPM, 6" pump		.34	94.118		48,000	6,350		54,350	62,500
3950	2000 GPM, 150 psi, 292 HP, 1770 RPM, 6" pump		.28	114		60,000	7,700		67,700	77,500
4000	2500 GPM, 100 psi, 213 HP, 1770 RPM, 8" pump		.30	107		56,000	7,200		63,200	72,000

21 31 Centrifugal Fire Pumps

21 31 13 – Electric-Drive, Centrifugal Fire Pumps

21 31 13.50 Electric-Drive Fire Pumps

		Crew	Daily Output	Labor-Hours	Unit	Material	2023 Bare Costs Labor	Equipment	Total	Total Incl O&P
4040	2500 GPM, 135 psi, 339 HP, 1770 RPM, 8" pump	Q-13	.26	123	Ea.	80,000	8,300		88,300	100,500
4100	3000 GPM, 100 psi, 250 HP, 1770 RPM, 8" pump		.28	114		67,000	7,700		74,700	85,500
4150	3000 GPM, 140 psi, 428 HP, 1770 RPM, 10" pump		.24	133		106,500	8,975		115,475	130,500
4200	3500 GPM, 100 psi, 300 HP, 1770 RPM, 10" pump		.26	123		83,000	8,300		91,300	104,000
4250	3500 GPM, 140 psi, 450 HP, 1770 RPM, 10" pump		.24	133		106,500	8,975		115,475	130,500
5000	For jockey pump 1", 3 HP, with control, add	Q-12	2	8		4,275	510		4,785	5,450

21 31 16 – Diesel-Drive, Centrifugal Fire Pumps

21 31 16.50 Diesel-Drive Fire Pumps

		Crew	Daily Output	Labor-Hours	Unit	Material	2023 Bare Costs Labor	Equipment	Total	Total Incl O&P
0010	**DIESEL-DRIVE FIRE PUMPS** Including controller, fittings and relief valve									
0050	500 GPM, 50 psi, 27 HP, 4" pump	Q-13	.64	50	Ea.	72,500	3,375		75,875	84,500
0100	500 GPM, 100 psi, 62 HP, 4" pump		.60	53.333		76,500	3,600		80,100	90,000
0150	500 GPM, 125 psi, 78 HP, 4" pump		.56	57.143		77,500	3,850		81,350	91,500
0200	750 GPM, 50 psi, 44 HP, 5" pump		.60	53.333		77,500	3,600		81,100	90,500
0250	750 GPM, 100 psi, 80 HP, 4" pump		.56	57.143		81,000	3,850		84,850	95,000
0300	750 GPM, 165 psi, 203 HP, 5" pump		.52	61.538		83,500	4,150		87,650	98,000
0350	1000 GPM, 50 psi, 48 HP, 5" pump		.58	55.172		77,500	3,725		81,225	91,000
0400	1000 GPM, 100 psi, 89 HP, 4" pump		.56	57.143		83,000	3,850		86,850	97,000
0450	1000 GPM, 150 psi, 148 HP, 4" pump		.48	66.667		81,500	4,500		86,000	96,000
0470	1000 GPM, 200 psi, 280 HP, 5" pump		.40	80		102,500	5,400		107,900	121,000
0480	1250 GPM, 75 psi, 75 HP, 5" pump		.54	59.259		78,500	4,000		82,500	92,500
0500	1500 GPM, 50 psi, 66 HP, 6" pump		.50	64		83,500	4,325		87,825	98,500
0550	1500 GPM, 100 psi, 140 HP, 6" pump		.46	69.565		85,500	4,700		90,200	101,500
0600	1500 GPM, 150 psi, 228 HP, 6" pump		.42	76.190		96,500	5,125		101,625	114,000
0650	1500 GPM, 200 psi, 279 HP, 6" pump		.38	84.211		151,500	5,675		157,175	175,500
0700	2000 GPM, 100 psi, 167 HP, 6" pump		.34	94.118		88,000	6,350		94,350	106,000
0750	2000 GPM, 150 psi, 284 HP, 6" pump		.30	107		119,000	7,200		126,200	141,500
0800	2500 GPM, 100 psi, 213 HP, 8" pump		.32	100		112,000	6,750		118,750	133,500
0820	2500 GPM, 150 psi, 365 HP, 8" pump		.26	123		131,500	8,300		139,800	157,000
0850	3000 GPM, 100 psi, 250 HP, 8" pump		.28	114		129,500	7,700		137,200	154,000
0900	3000 GPM, 150 psi, 384 HP, 10" pump		.20	160		150,500	10,800		161,300	181,500
0950	3500 GPM, 100 psi, 300 HP, 10" pump		.24	133		154,500	8,975		163,475	183,500
1000	3500 GPM, 150 psi, 518 HP, 10" pump		.20	160		218,500	10,800		229,300	256,500

Division Notes

		CREW	DAILY OUTPUT	LABOR-HOURS	UNIT	BARE COSTS				TOTAL INCL O&P
						MAT.	LABOR	EQUIP.	TOTAL	

Division 22 Plumbing

Estimating Tips
22 10 00 Plumbing Piping and Pumps

This subdivision is primarily basic pipe and related materials. The pipe may be used by any of the mechanical disciplines, i.e., plumbing, fire protection, heating, and air conditioning.

Note: CPVC plastic piping approved for fire protection is located in 21 11 13.

- The labor adjustment factors listed in Subdivision 22 01 02.20 apply throughout Divisions 21, 22, and 23. CAUTION: the correct percentage may vary for the same items. For example, the percentage add for the basic pipe installation should be based on the maximum height that the installer must install for that particular section. If the pipe is to be located 14' above the floor but it is suspended on threaded rod from beams, the bottom flange of which is 18' high (4' rods), then the height is actually 18' and the add is 20%. The pipe cover, however, does not have to go above the 14' and so the add should be 10%.
- Most pipe is priced first as straight pipe with a joint (coupling, weld, etc.) every 10' and a hanger usually every 10'. There are exceptions with hanger spacing such as for cast iron pipe (5') and plastic pipe (3 per 10'). Following each type of pipe there are several lines listing sizes and the amount to be subtracted to delete couplings and hangers. This is for pipe that is to be buried or supported together on trapeze hangers. The reason that the couplings are deleted is that these runs are usually long, and frequently longer lengths of pipe are used. By deleting the couplings, the estimator is expected to look up and add back the correct reduced number of couplings.
- When preparing an estimate, it may be necessary to approximate the fittings. Fittings usually run between 25% and 50% of the cost of the pipe. The lower percentage is for simpler runs, and the higher number is for complex areas, such as mechanical rooms.
- For historic restoration projects, the systems must be as invisible as possible, and pathways must be sought for pipes, conduit, and ductwork. While installations in accessible spaces (such as basements and attics) are relatively straightforward to estimate, labor costs may be more difficult to determine when delivery systems must be concealed.

22 40 00 Plumbing Fixtures

- Plumbing fixture costs usually require two lines: the fixture itself and its "rough-in, supply, and waste."
- In the Assemblies Section (Plumbing D2010) for the desired fixture, the System Components Group at the center of the page shows the fixture on the first line. The rest of the list (fittings, pipe, tubing, etc.) will total up to what we refer to in the Unit Price section as "Rough-in, supply, waste, and vent." Note that for most fixtures we allow a nominal 5' of tubing to reach from the fixture to a main or riser.
- Remember that gas- and oil-fired units need venting.

Reference Numbers

Reference numbers are shown at the beginning of some major classifications. These numbers refer to related items in the Reference Section. The reference information may be an estimating procedure, an alternate pricing method, or technical information.

Note: Not all subdivisions listed here necessarily appear. ■

Same Data. Simplified.

Enjoy the convenience and efficiency of accessing your costs anywhere:
- **Skip the multiplier** by setting your location
- **Quickly search,** edit, favorite and share costs
- **Stay on top of price changes** with automatic updates

Discover more at rsmeans.com/online

No part of this cost data may be reproduced, stored in a retrieval system, or transmitted in any form or by any means without prior written permission of Gordian.

Note: "Powered in part by CINX™, based on licensed proprietary information of Harrison Publishing House, Inc."

Note: Trade Service, in part, has been used as a reference source for some of the material prices used in Division 22.

22 01 Operation and Maintenance of Plumbing

22 01 02 – Labor Adjustments

22 01 02.10 Boilers, General

		Crew	Daily Output	Labor-Hours	Unit	Material	2023 Bare Costs Labor	Equipment	Total	Total Incl O&P
0010	**BOILERS, GENERAL**, Prices do not include flue piping, elec. wiring,									
0020	gas or oil piping, boiler base, pad, or tankless unless noted									
0100	Boiler H.P.: 10 KW = 34 lb./steam/hr. = 33,475 BTU/hr.									
0150	To convert SFR to BTU rating: Hot water, 150 x SFR;									
0160	Forced hot water, 180 x SFR; steam, 240 x SFR									

22 01 02.20 Labor Adjustment Factors

		Crew	Daily Output	Labor-Hours	Unit	Material	2023 Bare Costs Labor	Equipment	Total	Total Incl O&P
0010	**LABOR ADJUSTMENT FACTORS** (For Div. 21, 22 and 23) R220102-20									
0100	Labor factors: The below are reasonable suggestions, but									
0110	each project must be evaluated for its own peculiarities, and									
0120	the adjustments be increased or decreased depending on the									
0130	severity of the special conditions.									
1000	Add to labor for elevated installation (Above floor level)									
1080	10' to 14.5' high R221113-70							10%			
1100	15' to 19.5' high							20%			
1120	20' to 24.5' high							25%			
1140	25' to 29.5' high							35%			
1160	30' to 34.5' high							40%			
1180	35' to 39.5' high							50%			
1200	40' and higher							55%			
2000	Add to labor for crawl space										
2100	3' high							40%			
2140	4' high							30%			
3000	Add to labor for multi-story building										
3010	For new construction (No elevator available)										
3100	Add for floors 3 thru 10							5%			
3110	Add for floors 11 thru 15							10%			
3120	Add for floors 16 thru 20							15%			
3130	Add for floors 21 thru 30							20%			
3140	Add for floors 31 and up							30%			
3170	For existing structure (Elevator available)										
3180	Add for work on floor 3 and above							2%			
4000	Add to labor for working in existing occupied buildings										
4100	Hospital							35%			
4140	Office building							25%			
4180	School							20%			
4220	Factory or warehouse							15%			
4260	Multi dwelling							15%			
5000	Add to labor, miscellaneous										
5100	Cramped shaft							35%			
5140	Congested area							15%			
5180	Excessive heat or cold							30%			
9000	Labor factors: The above are reasonable suggestions, but										
9010	each project should be evaluated for its own peculiarities.										
9100	Other factors to be considered are:										
9140	Movement of material and equipment through finished areas										
9180	Equipment room										
9220	Attic space										
9260	No service road										
9300	Poor unloading/storage area										
9340	Congested site area/heavy traffic										

22 05 Common Work Results for Plumbing

22 05 05 – Selective Demolition for Plumbing

22 05 05.10 Plumbing Demolition		Crew	Daily Output	Labor-Hours	Unit	Material	2023 Bare Costs Labor	Equipment	Total	Total Incl O&P
0010	**PLUMBING DEMOLITION** R220105-10									
0400	Air compressor, up thru 2 HP	Q-1	10	1.600	Ea.		104		104	155
0410	3 HP thru 7-1/2 HP R024119-10		5.60	2.857			185		185	276
0420	10 HP thru 15 HP		1.40	11.429			740		740	1,100
0430	20 HP thru 30 HP	Q-2	1.30	18.462			1,250		1,250	1,850
0500	Backflow preventer, up thru 2" diameter	1 Plum	17	.471			34		34	50.50
0510	2-1/2" thru 3" diameter	Q-1	10	1.600			104		104	155
0520	4" thru 6" diameter	"	5	3.200			208		208	310
0530	8" thru 10" diameter	Q-2	3	8			540		540	800
0700	Carriers and supports									
0710	Fountains, sinks, lavatories and urinals	1 Plum	14	.571	Ea.		41		41	61.50
0720	Water closets	"	12	.667	"		48		48	71.50
0730	Grinder pump or sewage ejector system									
0732	Simplex	Q-1	7	2.286	Ea.		148		148	221
0734	Duplex	"	2.80	5.714			370		370	555
0738	Hot water dispenser	1 Plum	36	.222			16		16	24
0740	Hydrant, wall		26	.308			22		22	33
0744	Ground		12	.667			48		48	71.50
0760	Cleanouts and drains, up thru 4" pipe diameter		10	.800			57.50		57.50	86
0764	5" thru 8" pipe diameter	Q-1	10	1.600			104		104	155
0780	Industrial safety fixtures	1 Plum	8	1			72		72	107
1020	Fixtures, including 10' piping									
1100	Bathtubs, cast iron	1 Plum	4	2	Ea.		144		144	215
1120	Fiberglass		6	1.333			96		96	143
1140	Steel		5	1.600			115		115	172
1150	Bidet	Q-1	7	2.286			148		148	221
1200	Lavatory, wall hung	1 Plum	10	.800			57.50		57.50	86
1220	Counter top		8	1			72		72	107
1300	Sink, single compartment		8	1			72		72	107
1320	Double compartment		7	1.143			82.50		82.50	123
1340	Shower, stall and receptor	Q-1	6	2.667			173		173	258
1350	Group	"	7	2.286			148		148	221
1400	Water closet, floor mounted	1 Plum	8	1			72		72	107
1420	Wall mounted	"	7	1.143			82.50		82.50	123
1440	Wash fountain, 36" diameter	Q-2	8	3			202		202	300
1442	54" diameter	"	7	3.429			231		231	345
1500	Urinal, floor mounted	1 Plum	4	2			144		144	215
1520	Wall mounted	"	7	1.143			82.50		82.50	123
1590	Whirl pool or hot tub	Q-1	2.60	6.154			400		400	595
1600	Water fountains, free standing	1 Plum	8	1			72		72	107
1620	Wall or deck mounted		6	1.333			96		96	143
1800	Medical gas specialties		8	1			72		72	107
1810	Plumbing demo, floor drain, remove		12	.667			48		48	71.50
1820	Plumbing demo, roof drain, remove		9	.889			64		64	95.50
1900	Piping fittings, single connection, up thru 1-1/2" diameter		30	.267			19.20		19.20	28.50
1910	2" thru 4" diameter		14	.571			41		41	61.50
1980	Pipe hanger/support removal		80	.100			7.20		7.20	10.75
1990	Glass pipe with fittings, 1" thru 3" diameter		200	.040	L.F.		2.88		2.88	4.30
1992	4" thru 6" diameter		150	.053			3.84		3.84	5.75
2000	Piping, metal, up thru 1-1/2" diameter		200	.040			2.88		2.88	4.30
2050	2" thru 3-1/2" diameter		150	.053			3.84		3.84	5.75
2100	4" thru 6" diameter	2 Plum	100	.160			11.55		11.55	17.20
2150	8" thru 14" diameter	"	60	.267			19.20		19.20	28.50

For customer support on your Plumbing Costs with RSMeans data, call 800.448.8182.

22 05 Common Work Results for Plumbing

22 05 05 – Selective Demolition for Plumbing

22 05 05.10 Plumbing Demolition		Crew	Daily Output	Labor-Hours	Unit	Material	2023 Bare Costs Labor	Equipment	Total	Total Incl O&P
2153	16" thru 20" diameter	Q-18	70	.343	L.F.		23	.92	23.92	35.50
2155	24" thru 26" diameter		55	.436			29.50	1.17	30.67	45.50
2156	30" thru 36" diameter	↓	40	.600			40.50	1.60	42.10	62.50
2160	Plastic pipe with fittings, up thru 1-1/2" diameter	1 Plum	250	.032			2.31		2.31	3.44
2162	2" thru 3" diameter	"	200	.040			2.88		2.88	4.30
2164	4" thru 6" diameter	Q-1	200	.080			5.20		5.20	7.75
2166	8" thru 14" diameter		150	.107			6.90		6.90	10.30
2168	16" diameter		100	.160	↓		10.40		10.40	15.45
2170	Prison fixtures, lavatory or sink		18	.889	Ea.		57.50		57.50	86
2172	Shower		5.60	2.857			185		185	276
2174	Urinal or water closet		13	1.231			80		80	119
2180	Pumps, all fractional horse-power		12	1.333			86.50		86.50	129
2184	1 HP thru 5 HP		6	2.667			173		173	258
2186	7-1/2 HP thru 15 HP	↓	2.50	6.400			415		415	620
2188	20 HP thru 25 HP	Q-2	4	6			405		405	600
2190	30 HP thru 60 HP		.80	30			2,025		2,025	3,000
2192	75 HP thru 100 HP		.60	40			2,700		2,700	4,000
2194	150 HP	↓	.50	48			3,225		3,225	4,825
2198	Pump, sump or submersible	1 Plum	12	.667			48		48	71.50
2200	Receptors and interceptors, up thru 20 GPM	"	8	1			72		72	107
2204	25 thru 100 GPM	Q-1	6	2.667			173		173	258
2208	125 thru 300 GPM	"	2.40	6.667			430		430	645
2211	325 thru 500 GPM	Q-2	2.60	9.231			620		620	925
2212	Deduct for salvage, aluminum scrap				Ton	690			690	760
2214	Brass scrap					3,325			3,325	3,650
2216	Copper scrap					5,700			5,700	6,250
2218	Lead scrap					1,400			1,400	1,550
2220	Steel scrap				↓				204	224
2230	Temperature maintenance cable	1 Plum	1200	.007	L.F.		.48		.48	.72
2240	Toilet partitions, see Section 10 21 13									
2250	Water heater, 40 gal.	1 Plum	6	1.333	Ea.		96		96	143
3100	Tanks, water heaters and liquid containers									
3110	Up thru 45 gallons	Q-1	22	.727	Ea.		47		47	70.50
3120	50 thru 120 gallons		14	1.143			74		74	111
3130	130 thru 240 gallons		7.60	2.105			137		137	204
3140	250 thru 500 gallons	↓	5.40	2.963			192		192	287
3150	600 thru 1,000 gallons	Q-2	1.60	15			1,000		1,000	1,500
3160	1,100 thru 2,000 gallons		.70	34.286			2,300		2,300	3,450
3170	2,100 thru 4,000 gallons	↓	.50	48			3,225		3,225	4,825
6000	Remove and reset fixtures, easy access	1 Plum	6	1.333			96		96	143
6100	Difficult access	"	4	2	↓		144		144	215
6500	Solar heating system									
6510	Solar panel, hot water system	1 Plum	304	.026	S.F.		1.90		1.90	2.83
7910	Solar panel for pool	"	300	.027	"		1.92		1.92	2.87
8000	Sprinkler system									
8100	Exposed wet/dry	1 Plum	2500	.003	SF Flr.		.23		.23	.34
8200	Concealed wet/dry	"	1250	.006	"		.46		.46	.69
9100	Valve, metal valves or strainers and similar, up thru 1-1/2" diameter	1 Stpi	28	.286	Ea.		20.50		20.50	31
9110	2" thru 3" diameter	Q-1	11	1.455			94.50		94.50	141
9120	4" thru 6" diameter	"	8	2			130		130	193
9130	8" thru 14" diameter	Q-2	8	3			202		202	300
9140	16" thru 20" diameter		2	12			805		805	1,200
9150	24" diameter	↓	1.20	20			1,350		1,350	2,000

22 05 Common Work Results for Plumbing

22 05 05 – Selective Demolition for Plumbing

22 05 05.10 Plumbing Demolition		Crew	Daily Output	Labor-Hours	Unit	Material	2023 Bare Costs Labor	Equipment	Total	Total Incl O&P
9200	Valve, plastic, up thru 1-1/2" diameter	1 Plum	42	.190	Ea.		13.70		13.70	20.50
9210	2" thru 3" diameter		15	.533			38.50		38.50	57.50
9220	4" thru 6" diameter		12	.667			48		48	71.50
9300	Vent flashing and caps		55	.145			10.50		10.50	15.65
9350	Water filter, commercial, 1" thru 1-1/2"	Q-1	2	8			520		520	775
9360	2" thru 2-1/2"	"	1.60	10			650		650	965
9400	Water heaters									
9410	Up thru 245 GPH	Q-1	2.40	6.667	Ea.		430		430	645
9420	250 thru 756 GPH		1.60	10			650		650	965
9430	775 thru 1,640 GPH		.80	20			1,300		1,300	1,925
9440	1,650 thru 4,000 GPH	Q-2	.50	48			3,225		3,225	4,825
9470	Water softener	Q-1	2	8			520		520	775

22 05 23 – General-Duty Valves for Plumbing Piping

22 05 23.10 Valves, Brass

		Crew	Daily Output	Labor-Hours	Unit	Material	2023 Bare Costs Labor	Equipment	Total	Total Incl O&P
0010	**VALVES, BRASS**									
0032	For motorized valves, see Section 23 09 53.10									
0500	Gas cocks, threaded									
0510	1/4"	1 Plum	26	.308	Ea.	31	22		53	67.50
0520	3/8"		24	.333		31	24		55	70.50
0530	1/2"		24	.333		40	24		64	80
0540	3/4"		22	.364		37	26		63	80
0550	1"		19	.421		57.50	30.50		88	109
0560	1-1/4"		15	.533		71	38.50		109.50	136
0570	1-1/2"		13	.615		112	44.50		156.50	189
0580	2"		11	.727		180	52.50		232.50	276
0672	For larger sizes use lubricated plug valve, Section 23 05 23.70									

22 05 23.20 Valves, Bronze

			Crew	Daily Output	Labor-Hours	Unit	Material	2023 Bare Costs Labor	Equipment	Total	Total Incl O&P
0010	**VALVES, BRONZE**	R220523-80									
1020	Angle, 150 lb., rising stem, threaded										
1030	1/8"	R220523-90	1 Plum	24	.333	Ea.	231	24		255	290
1040	1/4"			24	.333		231	24		255	290
1050	3/8"			24	.333		229	24		253	288
1060	1/2"			22	.364		229	26		255	291
1070	3/4"			20	.400		315	29		344	390
1080	1"			19	.421		435	30.50		465.50	525
1090	1-1/4"			15	.533		500	38.50		538.50	610
1100	1-1/2"			13	.615		810	44.50		854.50	955
1102	Soldered same price as threaded										
1110	2"		1 Plum	11	.727	Ea.	1,275	52.50		1,327.50	1,475
1300	Ball										
1304	Soldered										
1312	3/8"		1 Plum	21	.381	Ea.	24.50	27.50		52	68
1316	1/2"			18	.444		21.50	32		53.50	71.50
1320	3/4"			17	.471		40.50	34		74.50	95
1324	1"			15	.533		54.50	38.50		93	118
1328	1-1/4"			13	.615		84.50	44.50		129	159
1332	1-1/2"			11	.727		108	52.50		160.50	197
1336	2"			9	.889		175	64		239	288
1340	2-1/2"			7	1.143		605	82.50		687.50	790
1344	3"			5	1.600		710	115		825	950
1350	Single union end										
1358	3/8"		1 Plum	21	.381	Ea.	37.50	27.50		65	82

22 05 Common Work Results for Plumbing

22 05 23 – General-Duty Valves for Plumbing Piping

22 05 23.20 Valves, Bronze		Crew	Daily Output	Labor-Hours	Unit	Material	2023 Bare Costs Labor	Equipment	Total	Total Incl O&P
1362	1/2"	1 Plum	18	.444	Ea.	39	32		71	91
1366	3/4"		17	.471		71	34		105	129
1370	1"		15	.533		94	38.50		132.50	161
1374	1-1/4"		13	.615		112	44.50		156.50	189
1378	1-1/2"		11	.727		100	52.50		152.50	188
1382	2"		9	.889		274	64		338	395
1398	Threaded, 150 psi									
1400	1/4"	1 Plum	24	.333	Ea.	22	24		46	60
1430	3/8"		24	.333		23	24		47	61
1450	1/2"		22	.364		21.50	26		47.50	63
1460	3/4"		20	.400		35	29		64	81.50
1470	1"		19	.421		58	30.50		88.50	109
1480	1-1/4"		15	.533		69.50	38.50		108	134
1490	1-1/2"		13	.615		88	44.50		132.50	163
1500	2"		11	.727		134	52.50		186.50	226
1510	2-1/2"		9	.889		108	64		172	215
1520	3"		8	1		700	72		772	875
1522	Solder the same price as threaded									
1600	Butterfly, 175 psi, full port, solder or threaded ends									
1610	Stainless steel disc and stem									
1620	1/4"	1 Plum	24	.333	Ea.	32	24		56	71
1630	3/8"		24	.333		33.50	24		57.50	72.50
1640	1/2"		22	.364		37.50	26		63.50	80
1650	3/4"		20	.400		60.50	29		89.50	110
1660	1"		19	.421		78	30.50		108.50	131
1670	1-1/4"		15	.533		119	38.50		157.50	189
1680	1-1/2"		13	.615		162	44.50		206.50	244
1690	2"		11	.727		193	52.50		245.50	290
1750	Check, swing, class 150, regrinding disc, threaded									
1800	1/8"	1 Plum	24	.333	Ea.	101	24		125	148
1830	1/4"		24	.333		109	24		133	156
1840	3/8"		24	.333		160	24		184	212
1850	1/2"		24	.333		132	24		156	182
1860	3/4"		20	.400		186	29		215	248
1870	1"		19	.421		246	30.50		276.50	315
1880	1-1/4"		15	.533		395	38.50		433.50	495
1890	1-1/2"		13	.615		355	44.50		399.50	455
1900	2"		11	.727		600	52.50		652.50	740
1910	2-1/2"	Q-1	15	1.067		1,575	69		1,644	1,825
1920	3"	"	13	1.231		1,750	80		1,830	2,050
2000	For 200 lb., add					5%	10%			
2040	For 300 lb., add					15%	15%			
2060	Check swing, 300 lb., lead free unless noted, sweat, 3/8" size	1 Plum	24	.333	Ea.	217	24		241	275
2070	1/2"		24	.333		239	24		263	299
2080	3/4"		20	.400		320	29		349	395
2090	1"		19	.421		395	30.50		425.50	480
2100	1-1/4"		15	.533		530	38.50		568.50	645
2110	1-1/2"		13	.615		575	44.50		619.50	695
2120	2"		11	.727		1,025	52.50		1,077.50	1,225
2130	2-1/2", not lead free	Q-1	15	1.067		435	69		504	585
2140	3", not lead free	"	13	1.231		3,825	80		3,905	4,350
2850	Gate, N.R.S., soldered, 125 psi									
2900	3/8"	1 Plum	24	.333	Ea.	107	24		131	153

22 05 Common Work Results for Plumbing

22 05 23 – General-Duty Valves for Plumbing Piping

22 05 23.20 Valves, Bronze		Crew	Daily Output	Labor-Hours	Unit	Material	2023 Bare Costs Labor	Equipment	Total	Total Incl O&P
2920	1/2"	1 Plum	24	.333	Ea.	115	24		139	163
2940	3/4"		20	.400		127	29		156	182
2950	1"		19	.421		181	30.50		211.50	245
2960	1-1/4"		15	.533		277	38.50		315.50	365
2970	1-1/2"		13	.615		310	44.50		354.50	405
2980	2"		11	.727		435	52.50		487.50	560
2990	2-1/2"	Q-1	15	1.067		1,125	69		1,194	1,325
3000	3"	"	13	1.231		1,325	80		1,405	1,575
3350	Threaded, class 150									
3410	1/4"	1 Plum	24	.333	Ea.	164	24		188	217
3420	3/8"		24	.333		164	24		188	217
3430	1/2"		24	.333		168	24		192	221
3440	3/4"		20	.400		171	29		200	231
3450	1"		19	.421		235	30.50		265.50	305
3460	1-1/4"		15	.533		289	38.50		327.50	380
3470	1-1/2"		13	.615		435	44.50		479.50	540
3480	2"		11	.727		495	52.50		547.50	620
3490	2-1/2"	Q-1	15	1.067		1,150	69		1,219	1,375
3500	3"	"	13	1.231		1,775	80		1,855	2,075
3600	Gate, flanged, 150 lb.									
3610	1"	1 Plum	7	1.143	Ea.	1,775	82.50		1,857.50	2,075
3620	1-1/2"		6	1.333		2,200	96		2,296	2,575
3630	2"		5	1.600		3,250	115		3,365	3,750
3634	2-1/2"	Q-1	5	3.200		5,000	208		5,208	5,800
3640	3"	"	4.50	3.556		5,850	231		6,081	6,775
3850	Rising stem, soldered, 300 psi									
3900	3/8"	1 Plum	24	.333	Ea.	242	24		266	300
3920	1/2"		24	.333		236	24		260	296
3940	3/4"		20	.400		270	29		299	340
3950	1"		19	.421		365	30.50		395.50	445
3960	1-1/4"		15	.533		505	38.50		543.50	615
3970	1-1/2"		13	.615		615	44.50		659.50	740
3980	2"		11	.727		985	52.50		1,037.50	1,150
3990	2-1/2"	Q-1	15	1.067		2,100	69		2,169	2,400
4000	3"	"	13	1.231		3,250	80		3,330	3,700
4250	Threaded, class 150									
4310	1/4"	1 Plum	24	.333	Ea.	150	24		174	201
4320	3/8"		24	.333		150	24		174	201
4330	1/2"		24	.333		147	24		171	198
4340	3/4"		20	.400		159	29		188	218
4350	1"		19	.421		206	30.50		236.50	271
4360	1-1/4"		15	.533		279	38.50		317.50	365
4370	1-1/2"		13	.615		350	44.50		394.50	455
4380	2"		11	.727		475	52.50		527.50	600
4390	2-1/2"	Q-1	15	1.067		955	69		1,024	1,150
4400	3"	"	13	1.231		1,550	80		1,630	1,825
4500	For 300 psi, threaded, add					100%	15%			
4540	For chain operated type, add					15%				
4850	Globe, class 150, rising stem, threaded									
4920	1/4"	1 Plum	24	.333	Ea.	201	24		225	257
4940	3/8"		24	.333		198	24		222	254
4950	1/2"		24	.333		180	24		204	234
4960	3/4"		20	.400		240	29		269	305

22 05 Common Work Results for Plumbing

22 05 23 – General-Duty Valves for Plumbing Piping

22 05 23.20 Valves, Bronze		Crew	Daily Output	Labor-Hours	Unit	Material	2023 Bare Costs Labor	Equipment	Total	Total Incl O&P
4970	1"	1 Plum	19	.421	Ea.	415	30.50		445.50	500
4980	1-1/4"		15	.533		585	38.50		623.50	705
4990	1-1/2"		13	.615		700	44.50		744.50	835
5000	2"	↓	11	.727		1,200	52.50		1,252.50	1,400
5010	2-1/2"	Q-1	15	1.067		2,400	69		2,469	2,750
5020	3"	"	13	1.231	↓	3,425	80		3,505	3,900
5120	For 300 lb. threaded, add					50%	15%			
5600	Relief, pressure & temperature, self-closing, ASME, threaded									
5640	3/4"	1 Plum	28	.286	Ea.	305	20.50		325.50	365
5650	1"		24	.333		455	24		479	535
5660	1-1/4"		20	.400		805	29		834	930
5670	1-1/2"		18	.444		1,450	32		1,482	1,650
5680	2"	↓	16	.500		1,850	36		1,886	2,100
5950	Pressure, poppet type, threaded									
6000	1/2"	1 Plum	30	.267	Ea.	45	19.20		64.20	78
6040	3/4"	"	28	.286	"	111	20.50		131.50	153
6400	Pressure, water, ASME, threaded									
6440	3/4"	1 Plum	28	.286	Ea.	101	20.50		121.50	142
6450	1"		24	.333		183	24		207	237
6460	1-1/4"		20	.400		505	29		534	600
6470	1-1/2"		18	.444		1,050	32		1,082	1,225
6480	2"		16	.500		1,525	36		1,561	1,750
6490	2-1/2"	↓	15	.533		6,275	38.50		6,313.50	6,950
6900	Reducing, water pressure									
6920	300 psi to 25-75 psi, threaded or sweat									
6940	1/2"	1 Plum	24	.333	Ea.	254	24		278	315
6950	3/4"		20	.400		830	29		859	960
6960	1"		19	.421		1,275	30.50		1,305.50	1,475
6970	1-1/4"		15	.533		2,200	38.50		2,238.50	2,450
6980	1-1/2"		13	.615		1,100	44.50		1,144.50	1,275
6990	2"	↓	11	.727		5,000	52.50		5,052.50	5,575
7100	For built-in by-pass or 10-35 psi, add				↓	69.50			69.50	76.50
7700	High capacity, 250 psi to 25-75 psi, threaded									
7740	1/2"	1 Plum	24	.333	Ea.	1,325	24		1,349	1,475
7780	3/4"		20	.400		1,075	29		1,104	1,225
7790	1"		19	.421		1,550	30.50		1,580.50	1,750
7800	1-1/4"		15	.533		2,675	38.50		2,713.50	3,000
7810	1-1/2"		13	.615		3,900	44.50		3,944.50	4,375
7820	2"		11	.727		5,700	52.50		5,752.50	6,350
7830	2-1/2"		9	.889		8,150	64		8,214	9,075
7840	3"	↓	8	1		9,775	72		9,847	10,800
7850	3" flanged (iron body)	Q-1	10	1.600		8,675	104		8,779	9,675
7860	4" flanged (iron body)	"	8	2	↓	12,500	130		12,630	14,000
7920	For higher pressure, add					25%				
8000	Silent check, bronze trim									
8010	Compact wafer type, for 125 or 150 lb. flanges									
8020	1-1/2"	1 Plum	11	.727	Ea.	585	52.50		637.50	725
8021	2"	"	9	.889		620	64		684	775
8022	2-1/2"	Q-1	9	1.778		670	115		785	905
8023	3"		8	2		750	130		880	1,025
8024	4"	↓	5	3.200		1,250	208		1,458	1,675
8025	5"	Q-2	6	4		1,325	269		1,594	1,850
8026	6"	"	5	4.800	↓	1,450	325		1,775	2,075

22 05 Common Work Results for Plumbing

22 05 23 – General-Duty Valves for Plumbing Piping

22 05 23.20 Valves, Bronze

		Crew	Daily Output	Labor-Hours	Unit	Material	2023 Bare Costs Labor	Equipment	Total	Total Incl O&P
8050	For 250 or 300 lb. flanges, thru 6" no change									
8060	Full flange wafer type, 150 lb.									
8063	1-1/2"	1 Plum	11	.727	Ea.	70.50	52.50		123	156
8064	2"	"	9	.889		805	64		869	980
8065	2-1/2"	Q-1	9	1.778		104	115		219	287
8066	3"		8	2		155	130		285	365
8067	4"		5	3.200		224	208		432	555
8068	5"	Q-2	6	4		375	269		644	810
8069	6"	"	5	4.800		510	325		835	1,050
8080	For 300 lb., add					40%	10%			
8100	Globe type, 150 lb.									
8110	2"	1 Plum	9	.889	Ea.	795	64		859	965
8111	2-1/2"	Q-1	9	1.778		990	115		1,105	1,275
8112	3"		8	2		1,175	130		1,305	1,500
8113	4"		5	3.200		1,650	208		1,858	2,100
8114	5"	Q-2	6	4		2,000	269		2,269	2,600
8115	6"	"	5	4.800		2,800	325		3,125	3,550
8130	For 300 lb., add					20%	10%			
8140	Screwed end type, 250 lb.									
8141	1/2"	1 Plum	24	.333	Ea.	72	24		96	116
8142	3/4"		20	.400		72	29		101	123
8143	1"		19	.421		82.50	30.50		113	136
8144	1-1/4"		15	.533		114	38.50		152.50	183
8145	1-1/2"		13	.615		128	44.50		172.50	206
8146	2"		11	.727		172	52.50		224.50	267
8350	Tempering, water, sweat connections									
8400	1/2"	1 Plum	24	.333	Ea.	150	24		174	202
8440	3/4"	"	20	.400	"	248	29		277	315
8650	Threaded connections									
8700	1/2"	1 Plum	24	.333	Ea.	236	24		260	296
8740	3/4"		20	.400		1,675	29		1,704	1,875
8750	1"		19	.421		1,875	30.50		1,905.50	2,125
8760	1-1/4"		15	.533		2,900	38.50		2,938.50	3,225
8770	1-1/2"		13	.615		3,175	44.50		3,219.50	3,550
8780	2"		11	.727		4,750	52.50		4,802.50	5,300
8800	Water heater water & gas safety shut off									
8810	Protection against a leaking water heater									
8814	Shut off valve	1 Plum	16	.500	Ea.	196	36		232	269
8818	Water heater dam		32	.250		52.50	18		70.50	85
8822	Gas control wiring harness		32	.250		25.50	18		43.50	55
8830	Whole house flood safety shut off									
8834	Connections									
8838	3/4" NPT	1 Plum	12	.667	Ea.	1,100	48		1,148	1,275
8842	1" NPT		11	.727		1,125	52.50		1,177.50	1,300
8846	1-1/4" NPT		10	.800		1,150	57.50		1,207.50	1,350

22 05 23.40 Valves, Lined, Corrosion Resistant/High Purity

		Crew	Daily Output	Labor-Hours	Unit	Material	2023 Bare Costs Labor	Equipment	Total	Total Incl O&P
0010	**VALVES, LINED, CORROSION RESISTANT/HIGH PURITY**									
3500	Check lift, 125 lb., cast iron flanged									
3510	Horizontal PPL or SL lined									
3530	1"	1 Plum	14	.571	Ea.	845	41		886	990
3540	1-1/2"		11	.727		1,025	52.50		1,077.50	1,200
3550	2"		8	1		1,200	72		1,272	1,425

22 05 Common Work Results for Plumbing

22 05 23 – General-Duty Valves for Plumbing Piping

22 05 23.40 Valves, Lined, Corrosion Resistant/High Purity

		Crew	Daily Output	Labor-Hours	Unit	Material	2023 Bare Costs Labor	Equipment	Total	Total Incl O&P
3560	2-1/2"	Q-1	5	3.200	Ea.	1,550	208		1,758	2,000
3570	3"		4.50	3.556		1,950	231		2,181	2,500
3590	4"	↓	3	5.333		2,575	345		2,920	3,350
3610	6"	Q-2	3	8		4,375	540		4,915	5,600
3620	8"	"	2.50	9.600	↓	9,625	645		10,270	11,600
4250	Vertical PPL or SL lined									
4270	1"	1 Plum	14	.571	Ea.	805	41		846	945
4290	1-1/2"		11	.727		1,000	52.50		1,052.50	1,175
4300	2"	↓	8	1		1,175	72		1,247	1,400
4310	2-1/2"	Q-1	5	3.200		1,750	208		1,958	2,225
4320	3"		4.50	3.556		1,775	231		2,006	2,300
4340	4"	↓	3	5.333		2,450	345		2,795	3,225
4360	6"	Q-2	3	8		3,650	540		4,190	4,825
4370	8"	"	2.50	9.600	↓	7,150	645		7,795	8,850
5000	Clamp type, ductile iron, 150 lb. flanged									
5010	TFE lined									
5030	1" size, lever handle	1 Plum	9	.889	Ea.	1,675	64		1,739	1,950
5050	1-1/2" size, lever handle		6	1.333		2,200	96		2,296	2,575
5060	2" size, lever handle	↓	5	1.600		2,775	115		2,890	3,225
5080	3" size, lever handle	Q-1	4.50	3.556		3,525	231		3,756	4,225
5100	4" size, gear operated	"	3	5.333		4,825	345		5,170	5,850
5120	6" size, gear operated	Q-2	3	8		16,900	540		17,440	19,400
5130	8" size, gear operated	"	2.50	9.600	↓	20,100	645		20,745	23,100
6000	Diaphragm type, cast iron, 125 lb. flanged									
6010	PTFE or VITON, lined									
6030	1" size, handwheel operated	1 Plum	9	.889	Ea.	420	64		484	560
6050	1-1/2" size, handwheel operated		6	1.333		500	96		596	695
6060	2" size, handwheel operated	↓	5	1.600		570	115		685	800
6080	3" size, handwheel operated	Q-1	4.50	3.556		945	231		1,176	1,400
6100	4" size, handwheel operated	"	3	5.333		1,875	345		2,220	2,600
6120	6" size, handwheel operated	Q-2	3	8		2,925	540		3,465	4,025
6130	8" size, handwheel operated	"	2.50	9.600		5,900	645		6,545	7,475

22 05 23.60 Valves, Plastic

		Crew	Daily Output	Labor-Hours	Unit	Material	2023 Bare Costs Labor	Equipment	Total	Total Incl O&P
0010	**VALVES, PLASTIC** R220523-90									
1100	Angle, PVC, threaded									
1110	1/4"	1 Plum	26	.308	Ea.	65.50	22		87.50	105
1120	1/2"		26	.308		93.50	22		115.50	136
1130	3/4"		25	.320		111	23		134	157
1140	1"	↓	23	.348	↓	135	25		160	186
1150	Ball, PVC, socket or threaded, true union									
1230	1/2"	1 Plum	26	.308	Ea.	42	22		64	79.50
1240	3/4"		25	.320		50	23		73	89.50
1250	1"		23	.348		60	25		85	104
1260	1-1/4"		21	.381		96	27.50		123.50	146
1270	1-1/2"		20	.400		95.50	29		124.50	148
1280	2"	↓	17	.471		195	34		229	266
1290	2-1/2"	Q-1	26	.615		247	40		287	330
1300	3"		24	.667		305	43		348	400
1310	4"	↓	20	.800		515	52		567	650
1360	For PVC, flanged, add					100%	15%			
1450	Double union 1/2"	1 Plum	26	.308		65	22		87	105
1460	3/4"	↓	25	.320		77	23		100	119

22 05 Common Work Results for Plumbing

22 05 23 – General-Duty Valves for Plumbing Piping

22 05 23.60 Valves, Plastic		Crew	Daily Output	Labor-Hours	Unit	Material	2023 Bare Costs Labor	Equipment	Total	Total Incl O&P
1470	1"	1 Plum	23	.348	Ea.	94.50	25		119.50	142
1480	1-1/4"		21	.381		127	27.50		154.50	180
1490	1-1/2"		20	.400		167	29		196	226
1500	2"	↓	17	.471	↓	201	34		235	273
1650	CPVC, socket or threaded, single union									
1700	1/2"	1 Plum	26	.308	Ea.	66.50	22		88.50	106
1720	3/4"		25	.320		83.50	23		106.50	127
1730	1"		23	.348		99	25		124	147
1750	1-1/4"		21	.381		196	27.50		223.50	256
1760	1-1/2"		20	.400		160	29		189	219
1770	2"	↓	17	.471		220	34		254	293
1780	3"	Q-1	24	.667		640	43		683	770
1840	For CPVC, flanged, add					65%	15%			
1880	For true union, socket or threaded, add				↓	50%	5%			
2050	Polypropylene, threaded									
2100	1/4"	1 Plum	26	.308	Ea.	57.50	22		79.50	96.50
2120	3/8"		26	.308		59.50	22		81.50	98.50
2130	1/2"		26	.308		49	22		71	87
2140	3/4"		25	.320		59	23		82	99.50
2150	1"		23	.348		69	25		94	114
2160	1-1/4"		21	.381		91.50	27.50		119	142
2170	1-1/2"		20	.400		114	29		143	168
2180	2"	↓	17	.471		152	34		186	218
2190	3"	Q-1	24	.667		345	43		388	445
2200	4"	"	20	.800		610	52		662	750
2550	PVC, three way, socket or threaded									
2600	1/2"	1 Plum	26	.308	Ea.	81	22		103	123
2640	3/4"		25	.320		98	23		121	143
2650	1"		23	.348		117	25		142	167
2660	1-1/2"		20	.400		164	29		193	224
2670	2"	↓	17	.471		216	34		250	289
2680	3"	Q-1	24	.667		665	43		708	795
2740	For flanged, add				↓	60%	15%			
3150	Ball check, PVC, socket or threaded									
3200	1/4"	1 Plum	26	.308	Ea.	62.50	22		84.50	102
3220	3/8"		26	.308		62.50	22		84.50	102
3240	1/2"		26	.308		64	22		86	104
3250	3/4"		25	.320		71.50	23		94.50	113
3260	1"		23	.348		89.50	25		114.50	136
3270	1-1/4"		21	.381		150	27.50		177.50	206
3280	1-1/2"		20	.400		150	29		179	208
3290	2"	↓	17	.471		204	34		238	276
3310	3"	Q-1	24	.667		570	43		613	690
3320	4"	"	20	.800		805	52		857	965
3360	For PVC, flanged, add				↓	50%	15%			
3750	CPVC, socket or threaded									
3800	1/2"	1 Plum	26	.308	Ea.	118	22		140	163
3840	3/4"		25	.320		117	23		140	164
3850	1"		23	.348		139	25		164	191
3860	1-1/2"		20	.400		239	29		268	305
3870	2"	↓	17	.471		263	34		297	340
3880	3"	Q-1	24	.667		870	43		913	1,025
3920	4"	"	20	.800		1,175	52		1,227	1,375

For customer support on your Plumbing Costs with RSMeans data, call 800.448.8182.

22 05 Common Work Results for Plumbing

22 05 23 – General-Duty Valves for Plumbing Piping

22 05 23.60	Valves, Plastic	Crew	Daily Output	Labor-Hours	Unit	Material	2023 Bare Costs Labor	Equipment	Total	Total Incl O&P
3930	For CPVC, flanged, add				Ea.	40%	15%			
4340	Polypropylene, threaded									
4360	1/2"	1 Plum	26	.308	Ea.	106	22		128	149
4400	3/4"		25	.320		100	23		123	145
4440	1"		23	.348		134	25		159	185
4450	1-1/2"		20	.400		178	29		207	239
4460	2"	↓	17	.471		320	34		354	400
4500	For polypropylene flanged, add					200%	15%			
4850	Foot valve, PVC, socket or threaded									
4900	1/2"	1 Plum	34	.235	Ea.	73	16.95		89.95	106
4930	3/4"		32	.250		83	18		101	119
4940	1"		28	.286		109	20.50		129.50	150
4950	1-1/4"		27	.296		235	21.50		256.50	290
4960	1-1/2"		26	.308		209	22		231	263
4970	2"		24	.333		242	24		266	305
4980	3"		20	.400		580	29		609	680
4990	4"	↓	18	.444		1,025	32		1,057	1,175
5000	For flanged, add					25%	10%			
5050	CPVC, socket or threaded									
5060	1/2"	1 Plum	34	.235	Ea.	98	16.95		114.95	134
5070	3/4"		32	.250		137	18		155	177
5080	1"		28	.286		168	20.50		188.50	215
5090	1-1/4"		27	.296		255	21.50		276.50	310
5100	1-1/2"		26	.308		255	22		277	315
5110	2"		24	.333		320	24		344	385
5120	3"		20	.400		650	29		679	760
5130	4"	↓	18	.444		1,175	32		1,207	1,350
5140	For flanged, add					25%	10%			
5280	Needle valve, PVC, threaded									
5300	1/4"	1 Plum	26	.308	Ea.	91	22		113	133
5340	3/8"		26	.308		104	22		126	147
5360	1/2"	↓	26	.308		103	22		125	147
5380	For polypropylene, add					10%				
5800	Y check, PVC, socket or threaded									
5820	1/2"	1 Plum	26	.308	Ea.	93	22		115	135
5840	3/4"		25	.320		101	23		124	146
5850	1"		23	.348		109	25		134	158
5860	1-1/4"		21	.381		171	27.50		198.50	230
5870	1-1/2"		20	.400		187	29		216	249
5880	2"		17	.471		232	34		266	305
5890	2-1/2"	↓	15	.533		495	38.50		533.50	605
5900	3"	Q-1	24	.667		495	43		538	610
5910	4"	"	20	.800		810	52		862	970
5960	For PVC flanged, add					45%	15%			
6350	Y sediment strainer, PVC, socket or threaded									
6400	1/2"	1 Plum	26	.308	Ea.	64.50	22		86.50	104
6440	3/4"		24	.333		69.50	24		93.50	113
6450	1"		23	.348		82.50	25		107.50	128
6460	1-1/4"		21	.381		256	27.50		283.50	325
6470	1-1/2"		20	.400		170	29		199	230
6480	2"		17	.471		170	34		204	238
6490	2-1/2"	↓	15	.533		475	38.50		513.50	580
6500	3"	Q-1	24	.667		410	43		453	520

22 05 Common Work Results for Plumbing

22 05 23 – General-Duty Valves for Plumbing Piping

22 05 23.60 Valves, Plastic		Crew	Daily Output	Labor-Hours	Unit	Material	2023 Bare Costs Labor	Equipment	Total	Total Incl O&P
6510	4"	Q-1	20	.800	Ea.	685	52		737	835
6560	For PVC, flanged, add					55%	15%			

22 05 29 – Hangers and Supports for Plumbing Piping and Equipment

22 05 29.10 Hangers & Supp. for Plumb'g/HVAC Pipe/Equip.

		Crew	Daily Output	Labor-Hours	Unit	Material	Labor	Equipment	Total	Total Incl O&P
0010	**HANGERS AND SUPPORTS FOR PLUMB'G/HVAC PIPE/EQUIP.**									
0011	TYPE numbers per MSS-SP58									
0050	Brackets									
0060	Beam side or wall, malleable iron, TYPE 34									
0070	3/8" threaded rod size	1 Plum	48	.167	Ea.	8.40	12		20.40	27
0080	1/2" threaded rod size		48	.167		15	12		27	34.50
0090	5/8" threaded rod size		48	.167		25.50	12		37.50	46
0100	3/4" threaded rod size		48	.167		23	12		35	43
0110	7/8" threaded rod size		48	.167		25	12		37	45.50
0120	For concrete installation, add						30%			
0150	Wall, welded steel, medium, TYPE 32									
0160	0 size, 12" wide, 18" deep	1 Plum	34	.235	Ea.	695	16.95		711.95	790
0170	1 size, 18" wide, 24" deep		34	.235		825	16.95		841.95	930
0180	2 size, 24" wide, 30" deep		34	.235		1,100	16.95		1,116.95	1,225
0200	Beam attachment, welded, TYPE 22									
0202	3/8"	Q-15	80	.200	Ea.	34.50	12.95	.80	48.25	58
0203	1/2"		76	.211		21	13.65	.84	35.49	44.50
0204	5/8"		72	.222		22	14.40	.89	37.29	47
0205	3/4"		68	.235		30	15.25	.94	46.19	57
0206	7/8"		64	.250		62.50	16.20	1	79.70	94
0207	1"		56	.286		102	18.55	1.15	121.70	141
0300	Clamps									
0310	C-clamp, for mounting on steel beam flange, w/locknut, TYPE 23									
0320	3/8" threaded rod size	1 Plum	160	.050	Ea.	6.15	3.60		9.75	12.15
0330	1/2" threaded rod size		160	.050		7.65	3.60		11.25	13.80
0340	5/8" threaded rod size		160	.050		10.30	3.60		13.90	16.65
0350	3/4" threaded rod size		160	.050		6.85	3.60		10.45	12.85
0352	7/8" threaded rod size		140	.057		23.50	4.12		27.62	31.50
0400	High temperature to 1050°F, alloy steel									
0410	4" pipe size	Q-1	106	.151	Ea.	59	9.80		68.80	79.50
0420	6" pipe size		106	.151		86	9.80		95.80	109
0430	8" pipe size		97	.165		98	10.70		108.70	124
0440	10" pipe size		84	.190		125	12.35		137.35	156
0450	12" pipe size		72	.222		165	14.40		179.40	204
0460	14" pipe size		64	.250		289	16.20		305.20	345
0470	16" pipe size		56	.286		325	18.55		343.55	385
0480	Beam clamp, flange type, TYPE 25									
0482	For 3/8" bolt	1 Plum	48	.167	Ea.	18.05	12		30.05	38
0483	For 1/2" bolt		44	.182		14.30	13.10		27.40	35.50
0484	For 5/8" bolt		40	.200		14.30	14.40		28.70	37
0485	For 3/4" bolt		36	.222		14.30	16		30.30	39.50
0486	For 1" bolt		32	.250		9.60	18		27.60	37.50
0500	I-beam, for mounting on bottom flange, strap iron, TYPE 21									
0530	4" flange size	1 Plum	93	.086	Ea.	24	6.20		30.20	36
0540	5" flange size		92	.087		36.50	6.25		42.75	49.50
0550	6" flange size		90	.089		29.50	6.40		35.90	42
0560	7" flange size		88	.091		33	6.55		39.55	46.50
0570	8" flange size		86	.093		35	6.70		41.70	48.50

22 05 Common Work Results for Plumbing

22 05 29 – Hangers and Supports for Plumbing Piping and Equipment

	22 05 29.10 Hangers & Supp. for Plumb'g/HVAC Pipe/Equip.	Crew	Daily Output	Labor-Hours	Unit	Material	2023 Bare Costs Labor	Equipment	Total	Total Incl O&P
0600	One hole, vertical mounting, malleable iron									
0610	1/2" pipe size	1 Plum	160	.050	Ea.	3.38	3.60		6.98	9.05
0620	3/4" pipe size		145	.055		4.32	3.98		8.30	10.70
0630	1" pipe size		136	.059		4.60	4.24		8.84	11.35
0640	1-1/4" pipe size		128	.063		6.80	4.50		11.30	14.15
0650	1-1/2" pipe size		120	.067		7.95	4.80		12.75	15.85
0660	2" pipe size		112	.071		10.40	5.15		15.55	19.15
0670	2-1/2" pipe size		104	.077		20.50	5.55		26.05	31
0680	3" pipe size		96	.083		27.50	6		33.50	39
0690	3-1/2" pipe size		90	.089		14.65	6.40		21.05	25.50
0700	4" pipe size		84	.095		24	6.85		30.85	37
0750	Riser or extension pipe, carbon steel, TYPE 8									
0756	1/2" pipe size	1 Plum	52	.154	Ea.	6.35	11.10		17.45	23.50
0760	3/4" pipe size		48	.167		4.40	12		16.40	22.50
0770	1" pipe size		47	.170		4.54	12.25		16.79	23.50
0780	1-1/4" pipe size		46	.174		8.10	12.55		20.65	27.50
0790	1-1/2" pipe size		45	.178		6	12.80		18.80	25.50
0800	2" pipe size		43	.186		6.15	13.40		19.55	27
0810	2-1/2" pipe size		41	.195		6.40	14.05		20.45	28
0820	3" pipe size		40	.200		7.20	14.40		21.60	29.50
0830	3-1/2" pipe size		39	.205		21	14.80		35.80	45
0840	4" pipe size		38	.211		8.85	15.15		24	32.50
0850	5" pipe size		37	.216		29	15.60		44.60	54.50
0860	6" pipe size		36	.222		35.50	16		51.50	63
0870	8" pipe size		34	.235		84.50	16.95		101.45	118
0880	10" pipe size		32	.250		87.50	18		105.50	123
0890	12" pipe size		28	.286		124	20.50		144.50	167
0900	For plastic coating 3/4" to 4", add					190%				
0910	For copper plating 3/4" to 4", add					58%				
0950	Two piece, complete, carbon steel, medium weight, TYPE 4									
0960	1/2" pipe size	Q-1	137	.117	Ea.	10.50	7.55		18.05	23
0970	3/4" pipe size		134	.119		4.54	7.75		12.29	16.55
0980	1" pipe size		132	.121		4.64	7.85		12.49	16.80
0990	1-1/4" pipe size		130	.123		5.20	8		13.20	17.60
1000	1-1/2" pipe size		126	.127		5.15	8.25		13.40	17.95
1010	2" pipe size		124	.129		8.75	8.35		17.10	22
1020	2-1/2" pipe size		120	.133		17.70	8.65		26.35	32.50
1030	3" pipe size		117	.137		19.45	8.85		28.30	34.50
1040	3-1/2" pipe size		114	.140		32.50	9.10		41.60	49
1050	4" pipe size		110	.145		31.50	9.45		40.95	48.50
1060	5" pipe size		106	.151		61	9.80		70.80	81.50
1070	6" pipe size		104	.154		68	10		78	90
1080	8" pipe size		100	.160		81	10.40		91.40	104
1090	10" pipe size		96	.167		154	10.80		164.80	185
1100	12" pipe size		89	.180		187	11.65		198.65	223
1110	14" pipe size		82	.195		305	12.65		317.65	360
1120	16" pipe size		68	.235		330	15.25		345.25	390
1130	For galvanized, add					45%				
1150	Insert, concrete									
1160	Wedge type, carbon steel body, malleable iron nut, galvanized									
1170	1/4" threaded rod size	1 Plum	96	.083	Ea.	24	6		30	35
1180	3/8" threaded rod size		96	.083		2.17	6		8.17	11.35
1190	1/2" threaded rod size		96	.083		2.37	6		8.37	11.55

22 05 Common Work Results for Plumbing

22 05 29 – Hangers and Supports for Plumbing Piping and Equipment

22 05 29.10 Hangers & Supp. for Plumb'g/HVAC Pipe/Equip.		Crew	Daily Output	Labor-Hours	Unit	Material	2023 Bare Costs Labor	Equipment	Total	Total Incl O&P
1200	5/8" threaded rod size	1 Plum	96	.083	Ea.	3.24	6		9.24	12.50
1210	3/4" threaded rod size		96	.083		3.56	6		9.56	12.85
1220	7/8" threaded rod size	↓	96	.083	↓	52.50	6		58.50	67
1250	Pipe guide sized for insulation									
1260	No. 1, 1" pipe size, 1" thick insulation	1 Stpi	26	.308	Ea.	500	22.50		522.50	585
1270	No. 2, 1-1/4"-2" pipe size, 1" thick insulation		23	.348		500	25		525	590
1280	No. 3, 1-1/4"-2" pipe size, 1-1/2" thick insulation		21	.381		305	27.50		332.50	380
1290	No. 4, 2-1/2"-3-1/2" pipe size, 1-1/2" thick insulation		18	.444		345	32		377	430
1300	No. 5, 4"-5" pipe size, 1-1/2" thick insulation	↓	16	.500		360	36.50		396.50	455
1310	No. 6, 5"-6" pipe size, 2" thick insulation	Q-5	21	.762		415	50		465	535
1320	No. 7, 8" pipe size, 2" thick insulation		16	1		545	65.50		610.50	695
1330	No. 8, 10" pipe size, 2" thick insulation	↓	12	1.333		810	87		897	1,025
1340	No. 9, 12" pipe size, 2" thick insulation	Q-6	17	1.412		810	95.50		905.50	1,025
1350	No. 10, 12"-14" pipe size, 2-1/2" thick insulation		16	1.500		975	102		1,077	1,225
1360	No. 11, 16" pipe size, 2-1/2" thick insulation		10.50	2.286		975	155		1,130	1,300
1370	No. 12, 16"-18" pipe size, 3" thick insulation		9	2.667		1,375	181		1,556	1,775
1380	No. 13, 20" pipe size, 3" thick insulation		7.50	3.200		1,375	217		1,592	1,825
1390	No. 14, 24" pipe size, 3" thick insulation	↓	7	3.429	↓	1,950	232		2,182	2,500
1400	Bands									
1410	Adjustable band, carbon steel, for non-insulated pipe, TYPE 7									
1420	1/2" pipe size	Q-1	142	.113	Ea.	1.27	7.30		8.57	12.30
1430	3/4" pipe size		140	.114		1.26	7.40		8.66	12.45
1440	1" pipe size		137	.117		1.26	7.55		8.81	12.70
1450	1-1/4" pipe size		134	.119		1.13	7.75		8.88	12.80
1460	1-1/2" pipe size		131	.122		1.39	7.90		9.29	13.35
1470	2" pipe size		129	.124		1.39	8.05		9.44	13.55
1480	2-1/2" pipe size		125	.128		2.01	8.30		10.31	14.60
1490	3" pipe size		122	.131		2.65	8.50		11.15	15.60
1500	3-1/2" pipe size		119	.134		1.51	8.70		10.21	14.65
1510	4" pipe size		114	.140		4.30	9.10		13.40	18.30
1520	5" pipe size		110	.145		5.45	9.45		14.90	20
1530	6" pipe size		108	.148		6.40	9.60		16	21.50
1540	8" pipe size	↓	104	.154	↓	10.55	10		20.55	26.50
1550	For copper plated, add					50%				
1560	For galvanized, add					30%				
1570	For plastic coating, add					30%				
1600	Adjusting nut malleable iron, steel band, TYPE 9									
1610	1/2" pipe size, galvanized band	Q-1	137	.117	Ea.	9.90	7.55		17.45	22
1620	3/4" pipe size, galvanized band		135	.119		6.20	7.70		13.90	18.30
1630	1" pipe size, galvanized band		132	.121		10.20	7.85		18.05	23
1640	1-1/4" pipe size, galvanized band		129	.124		10.25	8.05		18.30	23.50
1650	1-1/2" pipe size, galvanized band		126	.127		10.60	8.25		18.85	24
1660	2" pipe size, galvanized band		124	.129		11.05	8.35		19.40	24.50
1670	2-1/2" pipe size, galvanized band		120	.133		17.45	8.65		26.10	32
1680	3" pipe size, galvanized band		117	.137		18.25	8.85		27.10	33
1690	3-1/2" pipe size, galvanized band		114	.140		8.10	9.10		17.20	22.50
1700	4" pipe size, cadmium plated band	↓	110	.145		46.50	9.45		55.95	65
1740	For plastic coated band, add					35%				
1750	For completely copper coated, add				↓	45%				
1800	Clevis, adjustable, carbon steel, for non-insulated pipe, TYPE 1									
1810	1/2" pipe size	Q-1	137	.117	Ea.	2.37	7.55		9.92	13.90
1820	3/4" pipe size		135	.119		1.85	7.70		9.55	13.50
1830	1" pipe size		132	.121		1.87	7.85		9.72	13.75

22 05 Common Work Results for Plumbing

22 05 29 – Hangers and Supports for Plumbing Piping and Equipment

22 05 29.10 Hangers & Supp. for Plumb'g/HVAC Pipe/Equip.		Crew	Daily Output	Labor-Hours	Unit	Material	2023 Bare Costs Labor	Equipment	Total	Total Incl O&P
1840	1-1/4" pipe size	Q-1	129	.124	Ea.	1.86	8.05		9.91	14.05
1850	1-1/2" pipe size		126	.127		2.18	8.25		10.43	14.70
1860	2" pipe size		124	.129		2.66	8.35		11.01	15.45
1870	2-1/2" pipe size		120	.133		4.08	8.65		12.73	17.40
1880	3" pipe size		117	.137		4.90	8.85		13.75	18.60
1890	3-1/2" pipe size		114	.140		4.89	9.10		13.99	18.95
1900	4" pipe size		110	.145		5.60	9.45		15.05	20
1910	5" pipe size		106	.151		7.20	9.80		17	22.50
1920	6" pipe size		104	.154		8.20	10		18.20	24
1930	8" pipe size		100	.160		14.70	10.40		25.10	31.50
1940	10" pipe size		96	.167		30	10.80		40.80	49.50
1950	12" pipe size		89	.180		79.50	11.65		91.15	105
1960	14" pipe size		82	.195		116	12.65		128.65	147
1970	16" pipe size		68	.235		128	15.25		143.25	164
1971	18" pipe size		54	.296		211	19.20		230.20	261
1972	20" pipe size		38	.421		410	27.50		437.50	495
1980	For galvanized, add					66%				
1990	For copper plated 1/2" to 4", add					77%				
2000	For light weight 1/2" to 4", deduct					13%				
2010	Insulated pipe type, 3/4" to 12" pipe, add					180%				
2020	Insulated pipe type, chrome-moly U-strap, add					530%				
2250	Split ring, malleable iron, for non-insulated pipe, TYPE 11									
2260	1/2" pipe size	Q-1	137	.117	Ea.	17.80	7.55		25.35	31
2270	3/4" pipe size		135	.119		17.95	7.70		25.65	31
2280	1" pipe size		132	.121		19	7.85		26.85	32.50
2290	1-1/4" pipe size		129	.124		23.50	8.05		31.55	38
2300	1-1/2" pipe size		126	.127		28.50	8.25		36.75	44
2310	2" pipe size		124	.129		32.50	8.35		40.85	48
2320	2-1/2" pipe size		120	.133		47	8.65		55.65	64.50
2330	3" pipe size		117	.137		58.50	8.85		67.35	77.50
2340	3-1/2" pipe size		114	.140		25.50	9.10		34.60	41.50
2350	4" pipe size		110	.145		61	9.45		70.45	81
2360	5" pipe size		106	.151		81	9.80		90.80	104
2370	6" pipe size		104	.154		181	10		191	214
2380	8" pipe size		100	.160		266	10.40		276.40	305
2390	For copper plated, add					8%				
2400	Channels, steel, 3/4" x 1-1/2"	1 Plum	80	.100	L.F.	7.20	7.20		14.40	18.65
2404	1-1/2" x 1-1/2"		70	.114		8.15	8.25		16.40	21.50
2408	1-7/8" x 1-1/2"		60	.133		51	9.60		60.60	70.50
2412	3" x 1-1/2"		50	.160		43	11.55		54.55	64.50
2416	Hangers, trapeze channel support, 12 ga. 1-1/2" x 1-1/2", 12" wide, steel		8.80	.909	Ea.	57.50	65.50		123	161
2418	18" wide, steel		8.30	.964		61.50	69.50		131	172
2430	Spring nuts, long, 1/4"		120	.067		.73	4.80		5.53	7.95
2432	3/8"		100	.080		1.16	5.75		6.91	9.90
2434	1/2"		80	.100		1.04	7.20		8.24	11.90
2436	5/8"		80	.100		6.45	7.20		13.65	17.85
2438	3/4"		75	.107		8.60	7.70		16.30	21
2440	Spring nuts, short, 1/4"		120	.067		1.99	4.80		6.79	9.35
2442	3/8"		100	.080		2.08	5.75		7.83	10.90
2444	1/2"		80	.100		3.04	7.20		10.24	14.10
2500	Washer, flat steel									
2502	3/8"	1 Plum	240	.033	Ea.	.07	2.40		2.47	3.66
2503	1/2"		220	.036		.22	2.62		2.84	4.15

22 05 Common Work Results for Plumbing

22 05 29 – Hangers and Supports for Plumbing Piping and Equipment

	22 05 29.10 Hangers & Supp. for Plumb'g/HVAC Pipe/Equip.	Crew	Daily Output	Labor-Hours	Unit	Material	2023 Bare Costs Labor	Equipment	Total	Total Incl O&P
2504	5/8"	1 Plum	200	.040	Ea.	.10	2.88		2.98	4.41
2505	3/4"		180	.044		.21	3.20		3.41	5
2506	7/8"		160	.050		.96	3.60		4.56	6.40
2507	1"		140	.057		1.03	4.12		5.15	7.30
2508	1-1/4"		120	.067		1.60	4.80		6.40	8.90
2520	Nut, steel, hex									
2522	3/8"	1 Plum	200	.040	Ea.	.22	2.88		3.10	4.54
2523	1/2"		180	.044		.53	3.20		3.73	5.35
2524	5/8"		160	.050		.85	3.60		4.45	6.30
2525	3/4"		140	.057		1.42	4.12		5.54	7.70
2526	7/8"		120	.067		2.28	4.80		7.08	9.65
2527	1"		100	.080		3.15	5.75		8.90	12.05
2528	1-1/4"		80	.100		7.85	7.20		15.05	19.40
2532	Turnbuckle, TYPE 13									
2534	3/8"	1 Plum	80	.100	Ea.	24.50	7.20		31.70	38
2535	1/2"		72	.111		31	8		39	46
2536	5/8"		64	.125		32.50	9		41.50	49
2537	3/4"		56	.143		44	10.30		54.30	64
2538	7/8"		48	.167		60	12		72	84
2539	1"		40	.200		73.50	14.40		87.90	102
2540	1-1/4"		32	.250		131	18		149	171
2650	Rods, carbon steel									
2660	Continuous thread									
2670	1/4" thread size	1 Plum	144	.056	L.F.	.43	4		4.43	6.40
2680	3/8" thread size		144	.056		.46	4		4.46	6.45
2690	1/2" thread size		144	.056		.72	4		4.72	6.75
2700	5/8" thread size		144	.056		1.03	4		5.03	7.10
2710	3/4" thread size		144	.056		1.81	4		5.81	7.95
2720	7/8" thread size		144	.056		2.27	4		6.27	8.45
2721	1" thread size	Q-1	160	.100		3.86	6.50		10.36	13.90
2722	1-1/8" thread size	"	120	.133		32.50	8.65		41.15	49
2725	1/4" thread size, bright finish	1 Plum	144	.056		1.94	4		5.94	8.10
2726	1/2" thread size, bright finish	"	144	.056		9.95	4		13.95	16.90
2730	For galvanized, add					40%				
2820	Rod couplings									
2821	3/8"	1 Plum	60	.133	Ea.	1.57	9.60		11.17	16.10
2822	1/2"		54	.148		8.60	10.65		19.25	25.50
2823	5/8"		48	.167		10.55	12		22.55	29.50
2824	3/4"		44	.182		13.65	13.10		26.75	34.50
2825	7/8"		40	.200		23	14.40		37.40	46.50
2826	1"		34	.235		32.50	16.95		49.45	61
2827	1-1/8"		30	.267		77.50	19.20		96.70	114
2860	Pipe hanger assy, adj. clevis, saddle, rod, clamp, insul. allowance									
2864	1/2" pipe size	Q-5	35	.457	Ea.	72	30		102	124
2866	3/4" pipe size		34.80	.460		70.50	30		100.50	123
2868	1" pipe size		34.60	.462		60.50	30		90.50	112
2869	1-1/4" pipe size		34.30	.466		60.50	30.50		91	113
2870	1-1/2" pipe size		33.90	.472		69	31		100	122
2872	2" pipe size		33.30	.480		75	31.50		106.50	130
2874	2-1/2" pipe size		32.30	.495		95.50	32.50		128	153
2876	3" pipe size		31.20	.513		101	33.50		134.50	161
2880	4" pipe size		30.70	.521		105	34		139	166
2884	6" pipe size		29.80	.537		153	35		188	222

22 05 Common Work Results for Plumbing

22 05 29 – Hangers and Supports for Plumbing Piping and Equipment

	22 05 29.10 Hangers & Supp. for Plumb'g/HVAC Pipe/Equip.	Crew	Daily Output	Labor-Hours	Unit	Material	2023 Bare Costs Labor	Equipment	Total	Total Incl O&P
2888	8" pipe size	Q-5	28	.571	Ea.	170	37.50		207.50	243
2892	10" pipe size		25.20	.635		299	41.50		340.50	390
2896	12" pipe size	↓	23.20	.690	↓	360	45		405	465
2900	Rolls									
2910	Adjustable yoke, carbon steel with CI roll, TYPE 43									
2918	2" pipe size	Q-1	140	.114	Ea.	17.40	7.40		24.80	30
2920	2-1/2" pipe size		137	.117		15.60	7.55		23.15	28.50
2930	3" pipe size		131	.122		40	7.90		47.90	56
2940	3-1/2" pipe size		124	.129		51	8.35		59.35	68.50
2950	4" pipe size		117	.137		50	8.85		58.85	68
2960	5" pipe size		110	.145		58.50	9.45		67.95	78
2970	6" pipe size		104	.154		24.50	10		34.50	41.50
2980	8" pipe size		96	.167		34	10.80		44.80	53
2990	10" pipe size		80	.200		60	12.95		72.95	85.50
3000	12" pipe size		68	.235		110	15.25		125.25	144
3010	14" pipe size		56	.286		495	18.55		513.55	570
3020	16" pipe size	↓	48	.333		605	21.50		626.50	695
3050	Chair, carbon steel with CI roll									
3060	2" pipe size	1 Plum	68	.118	Ea.	43	8.50		51.50	59.50
3070	2-1/2" pipe size		65	.123		46.50	8.85		55.35	64
3080	3" pipe size		62	.129		47.50	9.30		56.80	66.50
3090	3-1/2" pipe size		60	.133		36	9.60		45.60	54.50
3100	4" pipe size		58	.138		61	9.95		70.95	82
3110	5" pipe size		56	.143		67	10.30		77.30	89.50
3120	6" pipe size		53	.151		93.50	10.90		104.40	119
3130	8" pipe size		50	.160		126	11.55		137.55	156
3140	10" pipe size		48	.167		159	12		171	192
3150	12" pipe size	↓	46	.174		238	12.55		250.55	280
3170	Single pipe roll (see line 2650 for rods), TYPE 41, 1" pipe size	Q-1	137	.117		29.50	7.55		37.05	44
3180	1-1/4" pipe size		131	.122		16.25	7.90		24.15	29.50
3190	1-1/2" pipe size		129	.124		31	8.05		39.05	46
3200	2" pipe size		124	.129		32	8.35		40.35	48
3210	2-1/2" pipe size		118	.136		34.50	8.80		43.30	51
3220	3" pipe size		115	.139		36.50	9		45.50	53.50
3230	3-1/2" pipe size		113	.142		38.50	9.20		47.70	56
3240	4" pipe size		112	.143		45	9.25		54.25	63.50
3250	5" pipe size		110	.145		46	9.45		55.45	64.50
3260	6" pipe size		101	.158		76.50	10.25		86.75	99.50
3270	8" pipe size		90	.178		102	11.55		113.55	129
3280	10" pipe size		80	.200		125	12.95		137.95	156
3290	12" pipe size	↓	68	.235	↓	187	15.25		202.25	228
3300	Saddles (add vertical pipe riser, usually 3" diameter)									
3310	Pipe support, complete, adjust., CI saddle, TYPE 36									
3320	2-1/2" pipe size	1 Plum	96	.083	Ea.	288	6		294	325
3330	3" pipe size		88	.091		238	6.55		244.55	272
3340	3-1/2" pipe size		79	.101		310	7.30		317.30	350
3350	4" pipe size		68	.118		345	8.50		353.50	390
3360	5" pipe size		64	.125		265	9		274	305
3370	6" pipe size		59	.136		370	9.75		379.75	420
3380	8" pipe size		53	.151		400	10.90		410.90	455
3390	10" pipe size		50	.160		425	11.55		436.55	485
3400	12" pipe size	↓	48	.167	↓	445	12		457	510
3450	For standard pipe support, one piece, CI, deduct					34%				

22 05 Common Work Results for Plumbing

22 05 29 – Hangers and Supports for Plumbing Piping and Equipment

22 05 29.10 Hangers & Supp. for Plumb'g/HVAC Pipe/Equip.		Crew	Daily Output	Labor-Hours	Unit	Material	2023 Bare Costs Labor	Equipment	Total	Total Incl O&P
3460	For stanchion support, CI with steel yoke, deduct					60%				
3550	Insulation shield 1" thick, 1/2" pipe size, TYPE 40	1 Asbe	100	.080	Ea.	15.90	5.20		21.10	25.50
3560	3/4" pipe size		100	.080		16.90	5.20		22.10	26.50
3570	1" pipe size		98	.082		18.40	5.35		23.75	28
3580	1-1/4" pipe size		98	.082		19.35	5.35		24.70	29.50
3590	1-1/2" pipe size		96	.083		24	5.45		29.45	35
3600	2" pipe size		96	.083		20.50	5.45		25.95	31
3610	2-1/2" pipe size		94	.085		32	5.55		37.55	43.50
3620	3" pipe size		94	.085		30	5.55		35.55	41.50
3630	2" thick, 3-1/2" pipe size		92	.087		38.50	5.65		44.15	50.50
3640	4" pipe size		92	.087		43.50	5.65		49.15	56.50
3650	5" pipe size		90	.089		62.50	5.80		68.30	77.50
3660	6" pipe size		90	.089		64.50	5.80		70.30	80
3670	8" pipe size		88	.091		107	5.95		112.95	127
3680	10" pipe size		88	.091		114	5.95		119.95	134
3690	12" pipe size		86	.093		199	6.05		205.05	228
3700	14" pipe size		86	.093		225	6.05		231.05	256
3710	16" pipe size		84	.095		239	6.20		245.20	273
3720	18" pipe size		84	.095		284	6.20		290.20	320
3730	20" pipe size		82	.098		298	6.35		304.35	340
3732	24" pipe size		80	.100		325	6.55		331.55	370
3750	Covering protection saddle, TYPE 39									
3760	1" covering size									
3770	3/4" pipe size	1 Plum	68	.118	Ea.	22.50	8.50		31	37
3780	1" pipe size		68	.118		22.50	8.50		31	37
3790	1-1/4" pipe size		68	.118		19	8.50		27.50	33.50
3800	1-1/2" pipe size		66	.121		24	8.75		32.75	39.50
3810	2" pipe size		66	.121		19.95	8.75		28.70	35
3820	2-1/2" pipe size		64	.125		24	9		33	40
3830	3" pipe size		64	.125		28	9		37	44
3840	3-1/2" pipe size		62	.129		30.50	9.30		39.80	47.50
3850	4" pipe size		62	.129		27	9.30		36.30	44
3860	5" pipe size		60	.133		37	9.60		46.60	55
3870	6" pipe size		60	.133		44	9.60		53.60	63
3900	1-1/2" covering size									
3910	3/4" pipe size	1 Plum	68	.118	Ea.	17.35	8.50		25.85	32
3920	1" pipe size		68	.118		29	8.50		37.50	44.50
3930	1-1/4" pipe size		68	.118		11.50	8.50		20	25.50
3940	1-1/2" pipe size		66	.121		29	8.75		37.75	45
3950	2" pipe size		66	.121		16.30	8.75		25.05	31
3960	2-1/2" pipe size		64	.125		37.50	9		46.50	54.50
3970	3" pipe size		64	.125		37.50	9		46.50	54.50
3980	3-1/2" pipe size		62	.129		52.50	9.30		61.80	72
3990	4" pipe size		62	.129		38.50	9.30		47.80	56
4000	5" pipe size		60	.133		38.50	9.60		48.10	56.50
4010	6" pipe size		60	.133		54	9.60		63.60	74
4020	8" pipe size		58	.138		71	9.95		80.95	93
4022	10" pipe size		56	.143		71	10.30		81.30	93.50
4024	12" pipe size		54	.148		120	10.65		130.65	148
4028	2" covering size									
4029	2-1/2" pipe size	1 Plum	62	.129	Ea.	36	9.30		45.30	53.50
4032	3" pipe size		60	.133		38	9.60		47.60	56.50
4033	4" pipe size		58	.138		26.50	9.95		36.45	44

22 05 Common Work Results for Plumbing
22 05 29 – Hangers and Supports for Plumbing Piping and Equipment

22 05 29.10 Hangers & Supp. for Plumb'g/HVAC Pipe/Equip.		Crew	Daily Output	Labor-Hours	Unit	Material	2023 Bare Costs Labor	Equipment	Total	Total Incl O&P
4034	6" pipe size	1 Plum	56	.143	Ea.	63.50	10.30		73.80	85.50
4035	8" pipe size		54	.148		75	10.65		85.65	98.50
4080	10" pipe size		58	.138		79.50	9.95		89.45	102
4090	12" pipe size		56	.143		134	10.30		144.30	163
4100	14" pipe size		56	.143		134	10.30		144.30	163
4110	16" pipe size		54	.148		182	10.65		192.65	216
4120	18" pipe size		54	.148		182	10.65		192.65	216
4130	20" pipe size		52	.154		164	11.10		175.10	197
4150	24" pipe size		50	.160		236	11.55		247.55	277
4160	30" pipe size		48	.167		260	12		272	305
4180	36" pipe size	▼	45	.178	▼	280	12.80		292.80	330
4186	2-1/2" covering size									
4187	3" pipe size	1 Plum	58	.138	Ea.	42.50	9.95		52.45	62
4188	4" pipe size		56	.143		44	10.30		54.30	64
4189	6" pipe size		52	.154		70.50	11.10		81.60	94
4190	8" pipe size		48	.167		83	12		95	109
4191	10" pipe size		44	.182		91	13.10		104.10	120
4192	12" pipe size		40	.200		140	14.40		154.40	176
4193	14" pipe size		36	.222		80.50	16		96.50	113
4194	16" pipe size		32	.250		155	18		173	197
4195	18" pipe size	▼	28	.286	▼	173	20.50		193.50	221
4200	Sockets									
4210	Rod end, malleable iron, TYPE 16									
4220	1/4" thread size	1 Plum	240	.033	Ea.	5.80	2.40		8.20	9.95
4230	3/8" thread size		240	.033		2.64	2.40		5.04	6.50
4240	1/2" thread size		230	.035		3.40	2.51		5.91	7.50
4250	5/8" thread size		225	.036		14.30	2.56		16.86	19.55
4260	3/4" thread size		220	.036		20	2.62		22.62	26
4270	7/8" thread size	▼	210	.038		28	2.74		30.74	35
4290	Strap, 1/2" pipe size, TYPE 26	Q-1	142	.113		4.61	7.30		11.91	15.95
4300	3/4" pipe size		140	.114		5.70	7.40		13.10	17.35
4310	1" pipe size		137	.117		7.15	7.55		14.70	19.15
4320	1-1/4" pipe size		134	.119		7.20	7.75		14.95	19.50
4330	1-1/2" pipe size		131	.122		7.70	7.90		15.60	20.50
4340	2" pipe size		129	.124		8.50	8.05		16.55	21.50
4350	2-1/2" pipe size		125	.128		13.25	8.30		21.55	27
4360	3" pipe size		122	.131		17.20	8.50		25.70	31.50
4370	3-1/2" pipe size		119	.134		19	8.70		27.70	34
4380	4" pipe size	▼	114	.140	▼	17.95	9.10		27.05	33.50
4400	U-bolt, carbon steel									
4410	Standard, with nuts, TYPE 42									
4420	1/2" pipe size	1 Plum	160	.050	Ea.	2.56	3.60		6.16	8.15
4430	3/4" pipe size		158	.051		3.32	3.65		6.97	9.10
4450	1" pipe size		152	.053		3.52	3.79		7.31	9.50
4460	1-1/4" pipe size		148	.054		4.01	3.89		7.90	10.20
4470	1-1/2" pipe size		143	.056		4.33	4.03		8.36	10.75
4480	2" pipe size		139	.058		4.66	4.15		8.81	11.35
4490	2-1/2" pipe size		134	.060		7.80	4.30		12.10	14.95
4500	3" pipe size		128	.063		8.20	4.50		12.70	15.70
4510	3-1/2" pipe size		122	.066		8.55	4.72		13.27	16.50
4520	4" pipe size		117	.068		8.80	4.93		13.73	17.05
4530	5" pipe size		114	.070		7.20	5.05		12.25	15.50
4540	6" pipe size	▼	111	.072		14.95	5.20		20.15	24

22 05 Common Work Results for Plumbing

22 05 29 – Hangers and Supports for Plumbing Piping and Equipment

22 05 29.10 Hangers & Supp. for Plumb'g/HVAC Pipe/Equip.		Crew	Daily Output	Labor-Hours	Unit	Material	2023 Bare Costs Labor	Equipment	Total	Total Incl O&P
4550	8" pipe size	1 Plum	109	.073	Ea.	17.75	5.30		23.05	27.50
4560	10" pipe size		107	.075		32	5.40		37.40	43
4570	12" pipe size		104	.077		42.50	5.55		48.05	55.50
4580	For plastic coating on 1/2" thru 6" size, add					150%				
4700	U-hook, carbon steel, requires mounting screws or bolts									
4710	3/4" thru 2" pipe size									
4720	6" long	1 Plum	96	.083	Ea.	1.77	6		7.77	10.90
4730	8" long		96	.083		1.92	6		7.92	11.05
4740	10" long		96	.083		2.26	6		8.26	11.45
4750	12" long		96	.083		2.98	6		8.98	12.25
4760	For copper plated, add					50%				
7000	Roof supports									
7006	Duct									
7010	Rectangular, open, 12" off roof									
7020	To 18" wide	Q-9	26	.615	Ea.	263	39		302	350
7030	To 24" wide	"	22	.727		305	46		351	410
7040	To 36" wide	Q-10	30	.800		350	52.50		402.50	465
7050	To 48" wide		28	.857		395	56		451	520
7060	To 60" wide		24	1		440	65.50		505.50	580
7100	Equipment									
7120	Equipment support	Q-5	20	.800	Ea.	115	52		167	205
7300	Pipe									
7310	Roller type									
7320	Up to 2-1/2" diam. pipe									
7324	3-1/2" off roof	Q-5	24	.667	Ea.	19.75	43.50		63.25	87
7326	Up to 10" off roof	"	20	.800	"	45	52		97	128
7340	2-1/2" to 3-1/2" diam. pipe									
7342	Up to 16" off roof	Q-5	18	.889	Ea.	80	58		138	175
7360	4" to 5" diam. pipe									
7362	Up to 12" off roof	Q-5	16	1	Ea.	114	65.50		179.50	223
7400	Strut/channel type									
7410	Up to 2-1/2" diam. pipe									
7424	3-1/2" off roof	Q-5	24	.667	Ea.	18.95	43.50		62.45	86
7426	Up to 10" off roof	"	20	.800	"	49.50	52		101.50	133
7440	Strut and roller type									
7452	2-1/2" to 3-1/2" diam. pipe									
7454	Up to 16" off roof	Q-5	18	.889	Ea.	115	58		173	214
7460	Strut and hanger type									
7470	Up to 3" diam. pipe									
7474	Up to 8" off roof	Q-5	19	.842	Ea.	73	55		128	163
8000	Pipe clamp, plastic, 1/2" CTS	1 Plum	80	.100		.27	7.20		7.47	11.05
8010	3/4" CTS		73	.110		.28	7.90		8.18	12.10
8020	1" CTS		68	.118		.69	8.50		9.19	13.40
8080	Economy clamp, 1/4" CTS		175	.046		.08	3.29		3.37	5
8090	3/8" CTS		168	.048		.08	3.43		3.51	5.20
8100	1/2" CTS		160	.050		.08	3.60		3.68	5.45
8110	3/4" CTS		145	.055		.08	3.98		4.06	6.05
8200	Half clamp, 1/2" CTS		80	.100		.09	7.20		7.29	10.85
8210	3/4" CTS		73	.110		.15	7.90		8.05	11.95
8300	Suspension clamp, 1/2" CTS		80	.100		.27	7.20		7.47	11.05
8310	3/4" CTS		73	.110		.28	7.90		8.18	12.10
8320	1" CTS		68	.118		.61	8.50		9.11	13.30
8400	Insulator, 1/2" CTS		80	.100		.40	7.20		7.60	11.20

22 05 Common Work Results for Plumbing

22 05 29 – Hangers and Supports for Plumbing Piping and Equipment

22 05 29.10 Hangers & Supp. for Plumb'g/HVAC Pipe/Equip.		Crew	Daily Output	Labor-Hours	Unit	Material	2023 Bare Costs Labor	Equipment	Total	Total Incl O&P
8410	3/4" CTS	1 Plum	73	.110	Ea.	.41	7.90		8.31	12.25
8420	1" CTS		68	.118		.43	8.50		8.93	13.10
8500	J hook clamp with nail, 1/2" CTS		240	.033		.13	2.40		2.53	3.72
8501	3/4" CTS		240	.033		.14	2.40		2.54	3.73
8800	Wire cable support system									
8810	Cable with hook terminal and locking device									
8830	2 mm (.079") diam. cable (100 lb. cap.)									
8840	1 m (3.3') length, with hook	1 Shee	96	.083	Ea.	5.90	5.85		11.75	15.30
8850	2 m (6.6') length, with hook		84	.095		7	6.70		13.70	17.75
8860	3 m (9.9') length, with hook		72	.111		7.80	7.80		15.60	20.50
8870	5 m (16.4') length, with hook	Q-9	60	.267		9.55	16.85		26.40	36
8880	10 m (32.8') length, with hook	"	30	.533		13.70	33.50		47.20	65.50
8900	3 mm (.118") diam. cable (200 lb. cap.)									
8910	1 m (3.3') length, with hook	1 Shee	96	.083	Ea.	17.15	5.85		23	27.50
8920	2 m (6.6') length, with hook		84	.095		.85	6.70		7.55	11
8930	3 m (9.9') length, with hook		72	.111		21	7.80		28.80	35
8940	5 m (16.4') length, with hook	Q-9	60	.267		18.20	16.85		35.05	45.50
8950	10 m (32.8') length, with hook	"	30	.533		16.30	33.50		49.80	68.50
9000	Cable system accessories									
9010	Anchor bolt, 3/8", with nut	1 Shee	140	.057	Ea.	3.85	4.01		7.86	10.30
9020	Air duct corner protector		160	.050		1.70	3.51		5.21	7.15
9030	Air duct support attachment		140	.057		3.56	4.01		7.57	9.95
9040	Flange clip, hammer-on style									
9044	For flange thickness 3/32"-9/64", 160 lb. cap.	1 Shee	180	.044	Ea.	.88	3.12		4	5.65
9048	For flange thickness 1/8"-1/4", 200 lb. cap.		160	.050		.98	3.51		4.49	6.40
9052	For flange thickness 5/16"-1/2", 200 lb. cap.		150	.053		2.10	3.74		5.84	7.95
9056	For flange thickness 9/16"-3/4", 200 lb. cap.		140	.057		2.62	4.01		6.63	8.95
9060	Wire insulation protection tube		180	.044	L.F.	.89	3.12		4.01	5.70
9070	Wire cutter				Ea.	140			140	154

22 05 33 – Heat Tracing for Plumbing Piping

22 05 33.20 Temperature Maintenance Cable

		Crew	Daily Output	Labor-Hours	Unit	Material	Labor	Equipment	Total	Total Incl O&P
0010	**TEMPERATURE MAINTENANCE CABLE**									
0040	Components									
0080	Heating cable									
0100	208 V									
0150	140°F	Q-1	1060.80	.015	L.F.	15.90	.98		16.88	18.95
0200	120 V									
0220	125°F	Q-1	1060.80	.015	L.F.	7.10	.98		8.08	9.25
0300	Power kit w/1 end seal	1 Elec	48.80	.164	Ea.	253	11.05		264.05	295
0310	Splice kit		35.50	.225		262	15.20		277.20	310
0320	End seal		160	.050		19.80	3.37		23.17	27
0330	Tee kit w/1 end seal		26.80	.299		272	20		292	330
0340	Powered splice w/2 end seals		20	.400		225	27		252	288
0350	Powered tee kit w/3 end seals		18	.444		289	30		319	365
0360	Cross kit w/2 end seals		18.60	.430		298	29		327	375
0500	Recommended thickness of fiberglass insulation									
0510	Pipe size									
0520	1/2" to 1" use 1" insulation									
0530	1-1/4" to 2" use 1-1/2" insulation									
0540	2-1/2" to 6" use 2" insulation									
0560	NOTE: For pipe sizes 1-1/4" and smaller use 1/4" larger diameter									
0570	insulation to allow room for installation over cable.									

22 05 Common Work Results for Plumbing

22 05 48 – Vibration and Seismic Controls for Plumbing Piping and Equipment

22 05 48.40 Vibration Absorbers	Crew	Daily Output	Labor-Hours	Unit	Material	2023 Bare Costs Labor	Equipment	Total	Total Incl O&P
0010 **VIBRATION ABSORBERS**									
0100 Hangers, neoprene flex									
0200 10-120 lb. capacity				Ea.	26.50			26.50	29
0220 75-550 lb. capacity					44			44	48.50
0240 250-1,100 lb. capacity					92.50			92.50	102
0260 1,000-4,000 lb. capacity					144			144	158
0500 Spring flex, 60 lb. capacity					41			41	45
0520 450 lb. capacity					63.50			63.50	69.50
0540 900 lb. capacity					92.50			92.50	102
0560 1,100-1,300 lb. capacity					92.50			92.50	102
0600 Rubber in shear									
0610 45-340 lb., up to 1/2" rod size	1 Stpi	22	.364	Ea.	25	26.50		51.50	67
0620 130-700 lb., up to 3/4" rod size		20	.400		53.50	29		82.50	102
0630 50-1,000 lb., up to 3/4" rod size		18	.444		70.50	32		102.50	126
1000 Mounts, neoprene, 45-380 lb. capacity					18.90			18.90	21
1020 250-1,100 lb. capacity					60			60	66
1040 1,000-4,000 lb. capacity					117			117	129
1100 Spring flex, 60 lb. capacity					76			76	84
1120 165 lb. capacity					78.50			78.50	86
1140 260 lb. capacity					93.50			93.50	103
1160 450 lb. capacity					96			96	105
1180 600 lb. capacity					99.50			99.50	109
1200 750 lb. capacity					161			161	177
1220 900 lb. capacity					158			158	174
1240 1,100 lb. capacity					194			194	213
1260 1,300 lb. capacity					194			194	213
1280 1,500 lb. capacity					211			211	232
1300 1,800 lb. capacity					262			262	289
1320 2,200 lb. capacity					330			330	360
1340 2,600 lb. capacity					330			330	360
1399 Spring type									
1400 2 piece									
1410 50-1,000 lb.	1 Stpi	12	.667	Ea.	225	48.50		273.50	320
1420 1,100-1,600 lb.	"	12	.667	"	267	48.50		315.50	365
1500 Double spring open									
1510 150-450 lb.	1 Stpi	24	.333	Ea.	154	24		178	205
1520 500-1,000 lb.		24	.333		171	24		195	224
1530 1,100-1,600 lb.		24	.333		171	24		195	224
1540 1,700-2,400 lb.		24	.333		167	24		191	220
1550 2,500-3,400 lb.		24	.333		285	24		309	350
2000 Pads, cork rib, 18" x 18" x 1", 10-50 psi					174			174	192
2020 18" x 36" x 1", 10-50 psi					330			330	365
2100 Shear flexible pads, 18" x 18" x 3/8", 20-70 psi					70.50			70.50	77.50
2120 18" x 36" x 3/8", 20-70 psi					165			165	182
2150 Laminated neoprene and cork									
2160 1" thick	1 Stpi	16	.500	S.F.	89.50	36.50		126	153
2200 Neoprene elastomer isolation bearing pad									
2230 464 psi, 5/8" x 19-11/16" x 39-3/8"	1 Stpi	16	.500	Ea.	68	36.50		104.50	129
3000 Note overlap in capacities due to deflections									

22 05 Common Work Results for Plumbing

22 05 53 – Identification for Plumbing Piping and Equipment

22 05 53.10 Piping System Identification Labels

		Crew	Daily Output	Labor-Hours	Unit	Material	2023 Bare Costs Labor	Equipment	Total	Total Incl O&P
0010	**PIPING SYSTEM IDENTIFICATION LABELS**									
0100	Indicate contents and flow direction									
0106	Pipe markers									
0110	Plastic snap around									
0114	1/2" pipe	1 Plum	80	.100	Ea.	3.98	7.20		11.18	15.15
0116	3/4" pipe		80	.100		5.05	7.20		12.25	16.35
0118	1" pipe		80	.100		4.93	7.20		12.13	16.15
0120	2" pipe		75	.107		6.10	7.70		13.80	18.20
0122	3" pipe		70	.114		11.45	8.25		19.70	25
0124	4" pipe		60	.133		11.45	9.60		21.05	27
0126	6" pipe		60	.133		12.75	9.60		22.35	28.50
0128	8" pipe		56	.143		17.40	10.30		27.70	34.50
0130	10" pipe		56	.143		17.40	10.30		27.70	34.50
0200	Over 10" pipe size	↓	50	.160	↓	19.80	11.55		31.35	39
1110	Self adhesive									
1114	1" pipe	1 Plum	80	.100	Ea.	3	7.20		10.20	14.05
1116	2" pipe		75	.107		3	7.70		10.70	14.75
1118	3" pipe		70	.114		4.17	8.25		12.42	16.90
1120	4" pipe		60	.133		4.17	9.60		13.77	18.95
1122	6" pipe		60	.133		5.10	9.60		14.70	19.95
1124	8" pipe		56	.143		6.35	10.30		16.65	22.50
1126	10" pipe		56	.143		10.20	10.30		20.50	26.50
1200	Over 10" pipe size	↓	50	.160	↓	10.20	11.55		21.75	28.50
2000	Valve tags									
2010	Numbered plus identifying legend									
2100	Brass, 2" diameter	1 Plum	40	.200	Ea.	5	14.40		19.40	27
2200	Plastic, 1-1/2" diameter	"	40	.200	"	3.93	14.40		18.33	26

22 05 76 – Facility Drainage Piping Cleanouts

22 05 76.10 Cleanouts

		Crew	Daily Output	Labor-Hours	Unit	Material	Labor	Equipment	Total	Total Incl O&P
0010	**CLEANOUTS**									
0060	Floor type									
0080	Round or square, scoriated nickel bronze top									
0100	2" pipe size	1 Plum	10	.800	Ea.	300	57.50		357.50	415
0120	3" pipe size		8	1		325	72		397	465
0140	4" pipe size		6	1.333		440	96		536	625
0160	5" pipe size	↓	4	2		1,300	144		1,444	1,650
0180	6" pipe size	Q-1	6	2.667		765	173		938	1,100
0200	8" pipe size	"	4	4	↓	435	259		694	865
0340	Recessed for tile, same price									
0980	Round top, recessed for terrazzo									
1000	2" pipe size	1 Plum	9	.889	Ea.	204	64		268	320
1080	3" pipe size		6	1.333		355	96		451	540
1100	4" pipe size	↓	4	2		223	144		367	460
1120	5" pipe size	Q-1	6	2.667		830	173		1,003	1,175
1140	6" pipe size		5	3.200		875	208		1,083	1,275
1160	8" pipe size	↓	4	4	↓	640	259		899	1,075
2000	Round scoriated nickel bronze top, extra heavy duty									
2060	2" pipe size	1 Plum	9	.889	Ea.	296	64		360	420
2080	3" pipe size		6	1.333		215	96		311	380
2100	4" pipe size	↓	4	2		465	144		609	725
2120	5" pipe size	Q-1	6	2.667		605	173		778	925
2140	6" pipe size	↓	5	3.200		700	208		908	1,075

22 05 Common Work Results for Plumbing

22 05 76 – Facility Drainage Piping Cleanouts

	22 05 76.10 Cleanouts	Crew	Daily Output	Labor-Hours	Unit	Material	2023 Bare Costs Labor	Equipment	Total	Total Incl O&P
2160	8" pipe size	Q-1	4	4	Ea.	710	259		969	1,175
4000	Wall type, square smooth cover, over wall frame									
4060	2" pipe size	1 Plum	14	.571	Ea.	310	41		351	405
4080	3" pipe size		12	.667		500	48		548	620
4100	4" pipe size		10	.800		345	57.50		402.50	460
4120	5" pipe size		9	.889		505	64		569	650
4140	6" pipe size	↓	8	1		715	72		787	895
4160	8" pipe size	Q-1	11	1.455	↓	760	94.50		854.50	975
5000	Extension, CI; bronze countersunk plug, 8" long									
5040	2" pipe size	1 Plum	16	.500	Ea.	133	36		169	200
5060	3" pipe size		14	.571		206	41		247	289
5080	4" pipe size		13	.615		156	44.50		200.50	237
5100	5" pipe size		12	.667		277	48		325	375
5120	6" pipe size	↓	11	.727		490	52.50		542.50	615
	22 05 76.20 Cleanout Tees									
0010	**CLEANOUT TEES**									
0100	Cast iron, B&S, with countersunk plug									
0200	2" pipe size	1 Plum	4	2	Ea.	53	144		197	273
0220	3" pipe size		3.60	2.222		72.50	160		232.50	320
0240	4" pipe size	↓	3.30	2.424		129	175		304	400
0260	5" pipe size	Q-1	5.50	2.909		980	189		1,169	1,350
0280	6" pipe size	"	5	3.200		410	208		618	765
0300	8" pipe size	Q-3	5	6.400	↓	1,975	440		2,415	2,825
0500	For round smooth access cover, same price									
0600	For round scoriated access cover, same price									
0700	For square smooth access cover, add				Ea.	60%				
2000	Cast iron, no hub									
2010	Cleanout tee, with 2 couplings									
2012	2"	Q-1	22	.727	Ea.	56	47		103	132
2014	3"		19	.842		76.50	54.50		131	166
2016	4"	↓	16.50	.970		114	63		177	219
2018	6"	Q-2	20	1.200	↓	274	80.50		354.50	420
2040	Cleanout plug, no hub, with 1 coupling									
2042	2"	Q-1	44	.364	Ea.	24.50	23.50		48	62
2046	3"		38	.421		38	27.50		65.50	82.50
2048	4"	↓	33	.485		45	31.50		76.50	96.50
2050	6"	Q-2	40	.600		228	40.50		268.50	310
2052	8"	"	33	.727	↓	315	49		364	425
4000	Plastic, tees and adapters. Add plugs									
4010	ABS, DWV									
4020	Cleanout tee, 1-1/2" pipe size	1 Plum	15	.533	Ea.	69	38.50		107.50	134
4030	2" pipe size	Q-1	27	.593		59.50	38.50		98	123
4040	3" pipe size		21	.762		142	49.50		191.50	230
4050	4" pipe size	↓	16	1		310	65		375	435
4100	Cleanout plug, 1-1/2" pipe size	1 Plum	32	.250		14.35	18		32.35	43
4110	2" pipe size	Q-1	56	.286		15.70	18.55		34.25	45
4120	3" pipe size		36	.444		25.50	29		54.50	71
4130	4" pipe size	↓	30	.533		44	34.50		78.50	100
4180	Cleanout adapter fitting, 1-1/2" pipe size	1 Plum	32	.250		21	18		39	50.50
4190	2" pipe size	Q-1	56	.286		29.50	18.55		48.05	60
4200	3" pipe size		36	.444		74	29		103	125
4210	4" pipe size	↓	30	.533		139	34.50		173.50	205

22 05 Common Work Results for Plumbing

22 05 76 – Facility Drainage Piping Cleanouts

22 05 76.20 Cleanout Tees

		Crew	Daily Output	Labor-Hours	Unit	Material	2023 Bare Costs Labor	2023 Bare Costs Equipment	Total	Total Incl O&P
5000	PVC, DWV									
5010	Cleanout tee, 1-1/2" pipe size	1 Plum	15	.533	Ea.	45.50	38.50		84	108
5020	2" pipe size	Q-1	27	.593		53.50	38.50		92	116
5030	3" pipe size		21	.762		103	49.50		152.50	188
5040	4" pipe size	↓	16	1		184	65		249	300
5090	Cleanout plug, 1-1/2" pipe size	1 Plum	32	.250		10.70	18		28.70	39
5100	2" pipe size	Q-1	56	.286		12.05	18.55		30.60	41
5110	3" pipe size		36	.444		21.50	29		50.50	66.50
5120	4" pipe size		30	.533		31.50	34.50		66	86.50
5130	6" pipe size	↓	24	.667		101	43		144	176
5170	Cleanout adapter fitting, 1-1/2" pipe size	1 Plum	32	.250		14.40	18		32.40	43
5180	2" pipe size	Q-1	56	.286		19.30	18.55		37.85	48.50
5190	3" pipe size		36	.444		42.50	29		71.50	89.50
5200	4" pipe size		30	.533		85	34.50		119.50	145
5210	6" pipe size	↓	24	.667		292	43		335	385
5300	Cleanout tee, with plug									
5310	4"	Q-1	14	1.143	Ea.	216	74		290	350
5320	6"	"	8	2		209	130		339	425
5330	8"	Q-2	11	2.182		415	147		562	675
5340	12"	"	10	2.400	↓	1,175	161		1,336	1,525
5400	Polypropylene, Schedule 40									
5410	Cleanout tee with plug									
5420	1-1/2"	1 Plum	10	.800	Ea.	35	57.50		92.50	125
5430	2"	Q-1	17	.941		33	61		94	128
5440	3"		11	1.455		74.50	94.50		169	223
5450	4"	↓	9	1.778	↓	101	115		216	283

22 07 Plumbing Insulation

22 07 16 – Plumbing Equipment Insulation

22 07 16.10 Insulation for Plumbing Equipment

			Crew	Daily Output	Labor-Hours	Unit	Material	Labor	Equipment	Total	Total Incl O&P
0010	**INSULATION FOR PLUMBING EQUIPMENT**										
2900	Domestic water heater wrap kit										
2920	1-1/2" with vinyl jacket, 20 to 60 gal.	G	1 Plum	8	1	Ea.	26.50	72		98.50	136
2925	50 to 80 gal.	G	"	8	1	"	40.50	72		112.50	152

22 07 19 – Plumbing Piping Insulation

22 07 19.10 Piping Insulation

		Crew	Daily Output	Labor-Hours	Unit	Material	Labor	Equipment	Total	Total Incl O&P
0010	**PIPING INSULATION**									
0110	Insulation req'd. is based on the surface size/area to be covered										
0230	Insulated protectors (ADA)										
0235	For exposed piping under sinks or lavatories										
0240	Vinyl coated foam, velcro tabs										
0245	P Trap, 1-1/4" or 1-1/2"	1 Plum	32	.250	Ea.	18.80	18		36.80	47.50
0260	Valve and supply cover										
0265	1/2", 3/8", and 7/16" pipe size	1 Plum	32	.250	Ea.	18.50	18		36.50	47.50
0280	Tailpiece offset (wheelchair)										
0285	1-1/4" pipe size	1 Plum	32	.250	Ea.	15.35	18		33.35	44
0600	Pipe covering (price copper tube one size less than IPS)										
1000	Mineral wool										
1010	Preformed, 1200°F, plain										
1014	1" wall										

22 07 Plumbing Insulation

22 07 19 – Plumbing Piping Insulation

22 07 19.10 Piping Insulation		Crew	Daily Output	Labor-Hours	Unit	Material	2023 Bare Costs Labor	Equipment	Total	Total Incl O&P
1016	1/2" iron pipe size G	Q-14	230	.070	L.F.	2.60	4.09		6.69	9.10
1018	3/4" iron pipe size G		220	.073		8.35	4.27		12.62	15.75
1022	1" iron pipe size G		210	.076		2.78	4.47		7.25	9.90
1024	1-1/4" iron pipe size G		205	.078		2.85	4.58		7.43	10.15
1026	1-1/2" iron pipe size G		205	.078		2.70	4.58		7.28	9.95
1028	2" iron pipe size G		200	.080		3.66	4.70		8.36	11.25
1030	2-1/2" iron pipe size G		190	.084		3.75	4.95		8.70	11.70
1032	3" iron pipe size G		180	.089		4	5.20		9.20	12.40
1034	4" iron pipe size G		150	.107		4.93	6.25		11.18	15
1036	5" iron pipe size G		140	.114		5.60	6.70		12.30	16.40
1038	6" iron pipe size G		120	.133		5.95	7.85		13.80	18.55
1040	7" iron pipe size G		110	.145		6.95	8.55		15.50	20.50
1042	8" iron pipe size G		100	.160		9.60	9.40		19	25
1044	9" iron pipe size G		90	.178		10.15	10.45		20.60	27
1046	10" iron pipe size G	↓	90	.178	↓	11.45	10.45		21.90	28.50
1050	1-1/2" wall									
1052	1/2" iron pipe size G	Q-14	225	.071	L.F.	4.43	4.18		8.61	11.25
1054	3/4" iron pipe size G		215	.074		13.05	4.37		17.42	21
1056	1" iron pipe size G		205	.078		4.61	4.58		9.19	12.05
1058	1-1/4" iron pipe size G		200	.080		4.70	4.70		9.40	12.35
1060	1-1/2" iron pipe size G		200	.080		4.93	4.70		9.63	12.60
1062	2" iron pipe size G		190	.084		5.25	4.95		10.20	13.30
1064	2-1/2" iron pipe size G		180	.089		5.70	5.20		10.90	14.25
1066	3" iron pipe size G		165	.097		5.95	5.70		11.65	15.25
1068	4" iron pipe size G		140	.114		7.10	6.70		13.80	18.10
1070	5" iron pipe size G		130	.123		7.60	7.25		14.85	19.40
1072	6" iron pipe size G		110	.145		7.85	8.55		16.40	21.50
1074	7" iron pipe size G		100	.160		9.25	9.40		18.65	24.50
1076	8" iron pipe size G		90	.178		10.30	10.45		20.75	27.50
1078	9" iron pipe size G		85	.188		11.85	11.05		22.90	30
1080	10" iron pipe size G		80	.200		13	11.75		24.75	32.50
1082	12" iron pipe size G		75	.213		14.85	12.55		27.40	35.50
1084	14" iron pipe size G		70	.229		17	13.40		30.40	39
1086	16" iron pipe size G		65	.246		18.75	14.45		33.20	42.50
1088	18" iron pipe size G		60	.267		22	15.65		37.65	48
1090	20" iron pipe size G		55	.291		23	17.10		40.10	51.50
1092	22" iron pipe size G		50	.320		26.50	18.80		45.30	58
1094	24" iron pipe size G	↓	45	.356	↓	28.50	21		49.50	63
1100	2" wall									
1102	1/2" iron pipe size G	Q-14	220	.073	L.F.	5.75	4.27		10.02	12.85
1104	3/4" iron pipe size G		210	.076		5.95	4.47		10.42	13.40
1106	1" iron pipe size G		200	.080		6.30	4.70		11	14.15
1108	1-1/4" iron pipe size G		190	.084		6.75	4.95		11.70	15
1110	1-1/2" iron pipe size G		190	.084		7.05	4.95		12	15.30
1112	2" iron pipe size G		180	.089		7.40	5.20		12.60	16.15
1114	2-1/2" iron pipe size G		170	.094		8.35	5.55		13.90	17.65
1116	3" iron pipe size G		160	.100		8.95	5.85		14.80	18.80
1118	4" iron pipe size G		130	.123		10.40	7.25		17.65	22.50
1120	5" iron pipe size G		120	.133		11.55	7.85		19.40	24.50
1122	6" iron pipe size G		100	.160		12	9.40		21.40	27.50
1124	8" iron pipe size G		80	.200		14.60	11.75		26.35	34
1126	10" iron pipe size G		70	.229		17.80	13.40		31.20	40
1128	12" iron pipe size G		65	.246		19.75	14.45		34.20	43.50

22 07 Plumbing Insulation

22 07 19 – Plumbing Piping Insulation

22 07 19.10 Piping Insulation		Crew	Daily Output	Labor-Hours	Unit	Material	2023 Bare Costs Labor	Equipment	Total	Total Incl O&P
1130	14" iron pipe size G	Q-14	60	.267	L.F.	22	15.65		37.65	48.50
1132	16" iron pipe size G		55	.291		25	17.10		42.10	53.50
1134	18" iron pipe size G		50	.320		27	18.80		45.80	59
1136	20" iron pipe size G		45	.356		31	21		52	66
1138	22" iron pipe size G		45	.356		34	21		55	69
1140	24" iron pipe size G		40	.400		35.50	23.50		59	75
1150	4" wall									
1152	1-1/4" iron pipe size G	Q-14	170	.094	L.F.	18.20	5.55		23.75	28.50
1154	1-1/2" iron pipe size G		165	.097		18.95	5.70		24.65	29.50
1156	2" iron pipe size G		155	.103		19.30	6.05		25.35	30.50
1158	4" iron pipe size G		105	.152		24.50	8.95		33.45	40.50
1160	6" iron pipe size G		75	.213		29	12.55		41.55	50.50
1162	8" iron pipe size G		60	.267		32.50	15.65		48.15	60
1164	10" iron pipe size G		50	.320		39.50	18.80		58.30	72.50
1166	12" iron pipe size G		45	.356		43	21		64	79.50
1168	14" iron pipe size G		40	.400		46.50	23.50		70	87
1170	16" iron pipe size G		35	.457		52	27		79	98.50
1172	18" iron pipe size G		32	.500		56.50	29.50		86	107
1174	20" iron pipe size G		30	.533		60.50	31.50		92	115
1176	22" iron pipe size G		28	.571		68	33.50		101.50	126
1178	24" iron pipe size G		26	.615		72	36		108	135
4280	Cellular glass, closed cell foam, all service jacket, sealant,									
4281	working temp. (-450°F to +900°F), 0 water vapor transmission									
4284	1" wall									
4286	1/2" iron pipe size G	Q-14	120	.133	L.F.	8.80	7.85		16.65	21.50
4300	1-1/2" wall									
4301	1" iron pipe size G	Q-14	105	.152	L.F.	16.80	8.95		25.75	32
4304	2-1/2" iron pipe size G		90	.178		29	10.45		39.45	47.50
4306	3" iron pipe size G		85	.188		28	11.05		39.05	48
4308	4" iron pipe size G		70	.229		31.50	13.40		44.90	55
4310	5" iron pipe size G		65	.246		37	14.45		51.45	62.50
4320	2" wall									
4322	1" iron pipe size G	Q-14	100	.160	L.F.	24	9.40		33.40	41
4324	2-1/2" iron pipe size G		85	.188		35.50	11.05		46.55	56
4326	3" iron pipe size G		80	.200		37.50	11.75		49.25	59
4328	4" iron pipe size G		65	.246		40.50	14.45		54.95	66.50
4330	5" iron pipe size G		60	.267		52.50	15.65		68.15	81.50
4332	6" iron pipe size G		50	.320		49	18.80		67.80	83
4336	8" iron pipe size G		40	.400		56	23.50		79.50	97.50
4338	10" iron pipe size G		35	.457		64.50	27		91.50	112
4350	2-1/2" wall									
4360	12" iron pipe size G	Q-14	32	.500	L.F.	98	29.50		127.50	153
4362	14" iron pipe size G	"	28	.571	"	96	33.50		129.50	158
4370	3" wall									
4378	6" iron pipe size G	Q-14	48	.333	L.F.	68.50	19.60		88.10	106
4380	8" iron pipe size G		38	.421		84	24.50		108.50	131
4382	10" iron pipe size G		33	.485		99	28.50		127.50	153
4384	16" iron pipe size G		25	.640		139	37.50		176.50	211
4386	18" iron pipe size G		22	.727		157	42.50		199.50	239
4388	20" iron pipe size G		20	.800		158	47		205	246
4400	3-1/2" wall									
4412	12" iron pipe size G	Q-14	27	.593	L.F.	93	35		128	155
4414	14" iron pipe size G	"	25	.640	"	119	37.50		156.50	189

22 07 Plumbing Insulation

22 07 19 – Plumbing Piping Insulation

22 07 19.10 Piping Insulation		Crew	Daily Output	Labor-Hours	Unit	Material	2023 Bare Costs Labor	Equipment	Total	Total Incl O&P
4430	4" wall									
4446	16" iron pipe size	G	Q-14	22	.727	L.F.	137	42.50		179.50	217
4448	18" iron pipe size	G		20	.800		136	47		183	221
4450	20" iron pipe size	G	↓	18	.889	↓	197	52		249	297
4480	Fittings, average with fabric and mastic										
4484	1" wall										
4486	1/2" iron pipe size	G	1 Asbe	40	.200	Ea.	15.05	13.05		28.10	36.50
4500	1-1/2" wall										
4502	1" iron pipe size	G	1 Asbe	38	.211	Ea.	23.50	13.75		37.25	46.50
4504	2-1/2" iron pipe size	G		32	.250		43.50	16.30		59.80	73
4506	3" iron pipe size	G		30	.267		45.50	17.40		62.90	76.50
4508	4" iron pipe size	G		28	.286		58.50	18.65		77.15	93
4510	5" iron pipe size	G	↓	24	.333	↓	76	22		98	117
4520	2" wall										
4522	1" iron pipe size	G	1 Asbe	36	.222	Ea.	28.50	14.50		43	53.50
4524	2-1/2" iron pipe size	G		30	.267		56.50	17.40		73.90	89
4526	3" iron pipe size	G		28	.286		53.50	18.65		72.15	87
4528	4" iron pipe size	G		24	.333		68	22		90	109
4530	5" iron pipe size	G		22	.364		92	23.50		115.50	138
4532	6" iron pipe size	G		20	.400		117	26		143	169
4536	8" iron pipe size	G		12	.667		169	43.50		212.50	253
4538	10" iron pipe size	G	↓	8	1	↓	238	65.50		303.50	360
4550	2-1/2" wall										
4560	12" iron pipe size	G	1 Asbe	6	1.333	Ea.	280	87		367	445
4562	14" iron pipe size	G	"	4	2	"	315	131		446	545
4570	3" wall										
4578	6" iron pipe size	G	1 Asbe	16	.500	Ea.	124	32.50		156.50	187
4580	8" iron pipe size	G		10	.800		143	52		195	238
4582	10" iron pipe size	G	↓	6	1.333	↓	192	87		279	345
4900	Calcium silicate, with 8 oz. canvas cover										
5100	1" wall, 1/2" iron pipe size	G	Q-14	170	.094	L.F.	6.30	5.55		11.85	15.40
5130	3/4" iron pipe size	G		170	.094		3.12	5.55		8.67	11.90
5140	1" iron pipe size	G		170	.094		6.05	5.55		11.60	15.10
5150	1-1/4" iron pipe size	G		165	.097		6.15	5.70		11.85	15.45
5160	1-1/2" iron pipe size	G		165	.097		6.20	5.70		11.90	15.55
5170	2" iron pipe size	G		160	.100		3.55	5.85		9.40	12.90
5180	2-1/2" iron pipe size	G		160	.100		3.74	5.85		9.59	13.10
5190	3" iron pipe size	G		150	.107		8.10	6.25		14.35	18.55
5200	4" iron pipe size	G		140	.114		10.15	6.70		16.85	21.50
5210	5" iron pipe size	G		135	.119		11.15	6.95		18.10	23
5220	6" iron pipe size	G		130	.123		11.80	7.25		19.05	24
5280	1-1/2" wall, 1/2" iron pipe size	G		150	.107		6.90	6.25		13.15	17.15
5310	3/4" iron pipe size	G		150	.107		3.34	6.25		9.59	13.25
5320	1" iron pipe size	G		150	.107		7.60	6.25		13.85	18
5330	1-1/4" iron pipe size	G		145	.110		8.20	6.50		14.70	18.90
5340	1-1/2" iron pipe size	G		145	.110		4.23	6.50		10.73	14.55
5350	2" iron pipe size	G		140	.114		9.70	6.70		16.40	21
5360	2-1/2" iron pipe size	G		140	.114		10.55	6.70		17.25	22
5370	3" iron pipe size	G		135	.119		11.10	6.95		18.05	23
5380	4" iron pipe size	G		125	.128		12.85	7.50		20.35	25.50
5390	5" iron pipe size	G		120	.133		14.50	7.85		22.35	28
5400	6" iron pipe size	G		110	.145		14.95	8.55		23.50	29.50
5460	2" wall, 1/2" iron pipe size	G	↓	135	.119	↓	10.65	6.95		17.60	22.50

22 07 Plumbing Insulation

22 07 19 – Plumbing Piping Insulation

22 07 19.10 Piping Insulation

		Crew	Daily Output	Labor-Hours	Unit	Material	2023 Bare Costs Labor	Equipment	Total	Total Incl O&P
5490	3/4" iron pipe size	Q-14 G	135	.119	L.F.	11.15	6.95		18.10	23
5500	1" iron pipe size	G	135	.119		11.75	6.95		18.70	23.50
5510	1-1/4" iron pipe size	G	130	.123		12.60	7.25		19.85	25
5520	1-1/2" iron pipe size	G	130	.123		13.15	7.25		20.40	25.50
5530	2" iron pipe size	G	125	.128		13.90	7.50		21.40	27
5540	2-1/2" iron pipe size	G	125	.128		16.45	7.50		23.95	29.50
5550	3" iron pipe size	G	120	.133		8.20	7.85		16.05	21
5560	4" iron pipe size	G	115	.139		19.20	8.15		27.35	33.50
5570	5" iron pipe size	G	110	.145		22	8.55		30.55	37
5580	6" iron pipe size	G	105	.152		11.80	8.95		20.75	26.50
5600	Calcium silicate, no cover									
5720	1" wall, 1/2" iron pipe size	Q-14 G	180	.089	L.F.	6.30	5.20		11.50	14.95
5740	3/4" iron pipe size	G	180	.089		6.30	5.20		11.50	14.95
5750	1" iron pipe size	G	180	.089		6.05	5.20		11.25	14.65
5760	1-1/4" iron pipe size	G	175	.091		6.15	5.35		11.50	14.95
5770	1-1/2" iron pipe size	G	175	.091		6.35	5.35		11.70	15.15
5780	2" iron pipe size	G	170	.094		7.15	5.55		12.70	16.30
5790	2-1/2" iron pipe size	G	170	.094		7.55	5.55		13.10	16.75
5800	3" iron pipe size	G	160	.100		8.10	5.85		13.95	17.95
5810	4" iron pipe size	G	150	.107		10.15	6.25		16.40	21
5820	5" iron pipe size	G	145	.110		10.55	6.50		17.05	21.50
5830	6" iron pipe size	G	140	.114		11.10	6.70		17.80	22.50
5900	1-1/2" wall, 1/2" iron pipe size	G	160	.100		6.65	5.85		12.50	16.30
5920	3/4" iron pipe size	G	160	.100		6.75	5.85		12.60	16.45
5930	1" iron pipe size	G	160	.100		7.40	5.85		13.25	17.15
5940	1-1/4" iron pipe size	G	155	.103		7.95	6.05		14	18
5950	1-1/2" iron pipe size	G	155	.103		8.55	6.05		14.60	18.65
5960	2" iron pipe size	G	150	.107		9.40	6.25		15.65	19.95
5970	2-1/2" iron pipe size	G	150	.107		10.30	6.25		16.55	21
5980	3" iron pipe size	G	145	.110		10.75	6.50		17.25	22
5990	4" iron pipe size	G	135	.119		12.45	6.95		19.40	24.50
6000	5" iron pipe size	G	130	.123		14	7.25		21.25	26.50
6010	6" iron pipe size	G	120	.133		14.30	7.85		22.15	28
6020	7" iron pipe size	G	115	.139		16.80	8.15		24.95	31
6030	8" iron pipe size	G	105	.152		18.95	8.95		27.90	34.50
6040	9" iron pipe size	G	100	.160		23	9.40		32.40	39.50
6050	10" iron pipe size	G	95	.168		25	9.90		34.90	42.50
6060	12" iron pipe size	G	90	.178		28	10.45		38.45	47
6070	14" iron pipe size	G	85	.188		33.50	11.05		44.55	54
6080	16" iron pipe size	G	80	.200		37.50	11.75		49.25	59.50
6090	18" iron pipe size	G	75	.213		41.50	12.55		54.05	65
6120	2" wall, 1/2" iron pipe size	G	145	.110		9.65	6.50		16.15	20.50
6140	3/4" iron pipe size	G	145	.110		10.20	6.50		16.70	21
6150	1" iron pipe size	G	145	.110		10.75	6.50		17.25	21.50
6160	1-1/4" iron pipe size	G	140	.114		11.50	6.70		18.20	23
6170	1-1/2" iron pipe size	G	140	.114		6.45	6.70		13.15	17.35
6180	2" iron pipe size	G	135	.119		6.80	6.95		13.75	18.10
6190	2-1/2" iron pipe size	G	135	.119		8.15	6.95		15.10	19.65
6200	3" iron pipe size	G	130	.123		16.55	7.25		23.80	29.50
6210	4" iron pipe size	G	125	.128		19.15	7.50		26.65	32.50
6220	5" iron pipe size	G	120	.133		10.80	7.85		18.65	24
6230	6" iron pipe size	G	115	.139		24	8.15		32.15	39
6240	7" iron pipe size	G	110	.145		24	8.55		32.55	39

For customer support on your Plumbing Costs with RSMeans data, call 800.448.8182.

22 07 Plumbing Insulation

22 07 19 – Plumbing Piping Insulation

22 07 19.10 Piping Insulation		Crew	Daily Output	Labor-Hours	Unit	Material	2023 Bare Costs Labor	Equipment	Total	Total Incl O&P
6250	8" iron pipe size [G]	Q-14	105	.152	L.F.	14.10	8.95		23.05	29
6260	9" iron pipe size [G]		100	.160		29.50	9.40		38.90	47
6270	10" iron pipe size [G]		95	.168		33	9.90		42.90	51
6280	12" iron pipe size [G]		90	.178		36.50	10.45		46.95	56
6290	14" iron pipe size [G]		85	.188		40	11.05		51.05	61
6300	16" iron pipe size [G]		80	.200		44	11.75		55.75	66.50
6310	18" iron pipe size [G]		75	.213		48	12.55		60.55	72
6320	20" iron pipe size [G]		65	.246		59.50	14.45		73.95	87.50
6330	22" iron pipe size [G]		60	.267		65.50	15.65		81.15	96.50
6340	24" iron pipe size [G]		55	.291		67	17.10		84.10	100
6360	3" wall, 1/2" iron pipe size [G]		115	.139		17.50	8.15		25.65	32
6380	3/4" iron pipe size [G]		115	.139		17.60	8.15		25.75	32
6390	1" iron pipe size [G]		115	.139		17.75	8.15		25.90	32
6400	1-1/4" iron pipe size [G]		110	.145		18	8.55		26.55	33
6410	1-1/2" iron pipe size [G]		110	.145		18.05	8.55		26.60	33
6420	2" iron pipe size [G]		105	.152		18.70	8.95		27.65	34
6430	2-1/2" iron pipe size [G]		105	.152		22	8.95		30.95	37.50
6440	3" iron pipe size [G]		100	.160		22	9.40		31.40	39
6450	4" iron pipe size [G]		95	.168		28.50	9.90		38.40	46
6460	5" iron pipe size [G]		90	.178		30.50	10.45		40.95	50
6470	6" iron pipe size [G]		90	.178		34.50	10.45		44.95	54
6480	7" iron pipe size [G]		85	.188		38.50	11.05		49.55	59.50
6490	8" iron pipe size [G]		85	.188		7.50	11.05		18.55	25
6500	9" iron pipe size [G]		80	.200		46.50	11.75		58.25	69.50
6510	10" iron pipe size [G]		75	.213		49.50	12.55		62.05	73.50
6520	12" iron pipe size [G]		70	.229		55	13.40		68.40	81
6530	14" iron pipe size [G]		65	.246		61.50	14.45		75.95	90
6540	16" iron pipe size [G]		60	.267		68	15.65		83.65	99
6550	18" iron pipe size [G]		55	.291		75	17.10		92.10	109
6560	20" iron pipe size [G]		50	.320		89	18.80		107.80	127
6570	22" iron pipe size [G]		45	.356		96.50	21		117.50	138
6580	24" iron pipe size [G]		40	.400		104	23.50		127.50	150
6600	Fiberglass, with all service jacket									
6640	1/2" wall, 1/2" iron pipe size [G]	Q-14	250	.064	L.F.	1.50	3.76		5.26	7.40
6660	3/4" iron pipe size [G]		240	.067		1.74	3.92		5.66	7.90
6670	1" iron pipe size [G]		230	.070		2	4.09		6.09	8.45
6680	1-1/4" iron pipe size [G]		220	.073		1.90	4.27		6.17	8.65
6690	1-1/2" iron pipe size [G]		220	.073		2.20	4.27		6.47	8.95
6700	2" iron pipe size [G]		210	.076		2.36	4.47		6.83	9.45
6710	2-1/2" iron pipe size [G]		200	.080		2.57	4.70		7.27	10.05
6840	1" wall, 1/2" iron pipe size [G]		240	.067		1.86	3.92		5.78	8.05
6860	3/4" iron pipe size [G]		230	.070		2.04	4.09		6.13	8.50
6870	1" iron pipe size [G]		220	.073		2.18	4.27		6.45	8.95
6880	1-1/4" iron pipe size [G]		210	.076		2.36	4.47		6.83	9.45
6890	1-1/2" iron pipe size [G]		210	.076		2.82	4.47		7.29	9.95
6900	2" iron pipe size [G]		200	.080		2.75	4.70		7.45	10.25
6910	2-1/2" iron pipe size [G]		190	.084		3.13	4.95		8.08	11
6920	3" iron pipe size [G]		180	.089		3.36	5.20		8.56	11.70
6930	3-1/2" iron pipe size [G]		170	.094		3.45	5.55		9	12.25
6940	4" iron pipe size [G]		150	.107		4.44	6.25		10.69	14.50
6950	5" iron pipe size [G]		140	.114		5	6.70		11.70	15.75
6960	6" iron pipe size [G]		120	.133		5.30	7.85		13.15	17.85
6970	7" iron pipe size [G]		110	.145		7.60	8.55		16.15	21.50

22 07 Plumbing Insulation

22 07 19 – Plumbing Piping Insulation

22 07 19.10 Piping Insulation

		Crew	Daily Output	Labor-Hours	Unit	Material	2023 Bare Costs Labor	Equipment	Total	Total Incl O&P
6980	8" iron pipe size G	Q-14	100	.160	L.F.	8.65	9.40		18.05	24
6990	9" iron pipe size G		90	.178		9.45	10.45		19.90	26.50
7000	10" iron pipe size G		90	.178		9.45	10.45		19.90	26.50
7010	12" iron pipe size G		80	.200		10.40	11.75		22.15	29.50
7020	14" iron pipe size G		80	.200		11.20	11.75		22.95	30.50
7030	16" iron pipe size G		70	.229		21	13.40		34.40	44
7040	18" iron pipe size G		70	.229		16.75	13.40		30.15	39
7050	20" iron pipe size G		60	.267		18.75	15.65		34.40	44.50
7060	24" iron pipe size G		60	.267		23	15.65		38.65	49
7080	1-1/2" wall, 1/2" iron pipe size G		230	.070		3.52	4.09		7.61	10.10
7100	3/4" iron pipe size G		220	.073		3.52	4.27		7.79	10.40
7110	1" iron pipe size G		210	.076		3.77	4.47		8.24	11
7120	1-1/4" iron pipe size G		200	.080		4.24	4.70		8.94	11.85
7130	1-1/2" iron pipe size G		200	.080		4.42	4.70		9.12	12.05
7140	2" iron pipe size G		190	.084		4.84	4.95		9.79	12.85
7150	2-1/2" iron pipe size G		180	.089		5.25	5.20		10.45	13.75
7160	3" iron pipe size G		170	.094		5.45	5.55		11	14.45
7170	3-1/2" iron pipe size G		160	.100		5.45	5.85		11.30	15
7180	4" iron pipe size G		140	.114		6.25	6.70		12.95	17.10
7190	5" iron pipe size G		130	.123		9.25	7.25		16.50	21.50
7200	6" iron pipe size G		110	.145		7.35	8.55		15.90	21
7210	7" iron pipe size G		100	.160		10.30	9.40		19.70	25.50
7220	8" iron pipe size G		90	.178		10.30	10.45		20.75	27.50
7230	9" iron pipe size G		85	.188		11.10	11.05		22.15	29
7240	10" iron pipe size G		80	.200		11.10	11.75		22.85	30
7250	12" iron pipe size G		75	.213		12.75	12.55		25.30	33
7260	14" iron pipe size G		70	.229		15.30	13.40		28.70	37.50
7270	16" iron pipe size G		65	.246		18.90	14.45		33.35	43
7280	18" iron pipe size G		60	.267		28.50	15.65		44.15	55.50
7290	20" iron pipe size G		55	.291		21.50	17.10		38.60	50
7300	24" iron pipe size G		50	.320		52	18.80		70.80	86
7320	2" wall, 1/2" iron pipe size G		220	.073		5.60	4.27		9.87	12.70
7340	3/4" iron pipe size G		210	.076		5.80	4.47		10.27	13.20
7350	1" iron pipe size G		200	.080		6.15	4.70		10.85	13.95
7360	1-1/4" iron pipe size G		190	.084		6.50	4.95		11.45	14.70
7370	1-1/2" iron pipe size G		190	.084		6.80	4.95		11.75	15.05
7380	2" iron pipe size G		180	.089		7.15	5.20		12.35	15.90
7390	2-1/2" iron pipe size G		170	.094		7.70	5.55		13.25	16.95
7400	3" iron pipe size G		160	.100		8.15	5.85		14	18
7410	3-1/2" iron pipe size G		150	.107		8.15	6.25		14.40	18.60
7420	4" iron pipe size G		130	.123		9.55	7.25		16.80	21.50
7430	5" iron pipe size G		120	.133		10.90	7.85		18.75	24
7440	6" iron pipe size G		100	.160		9.30	9.40		18.70	24.50
7450	7" iron pipe size G		90	.178		13.70	10.45		24.15	31
7460	8" iron pipe size G		80	.200		13.70	11.75		25.45	33
7470	9" iron pipe size G		75	.213		14.30	12.55		26.85	35
7480	10" iron pipe size G		70	.229		16.40	13.40		29.80	38.50
7490	12" iron pipe size G		65	.246		18.70	14.45		33.15	42.50
7500	14" iron pipe size G		60	.267		24	15.65		39.65	50.50
7510	16" iron pipe size G		55	.291		35	17.10		52.10	64.50
7520	18" iron pipe size G		50	.320		58	18.80		76.80	92.50
7530	20" iron pipe size G		45	.356		42.50	21		63.50	78.50
7540	24" iron pipe size G		40	.400		47.50	23.50		71	88.50

22 07 Plumbing Insulation

22 07 19 – Plumbing Piping Insulation

22 07 19.10 Piping Insulation		Crew	Daily Output	Labor-Hours	Unit	Material	2023 Bare Costs Labor	Equipment	Total	Total Incl O&P
7560	2-1/2" wall, 1/2" iron pipe size	G	Q-14	210	.076	L.F.	6.35	4.47		10.82	13.80
7562	3/4" iron pipe size	G		200	.080		9.20	4.70		13.90	17.35
7564	1" iron pipe size	G		190	.084		9.60	4.95		14.55	18.15
7566	1-1/4" iron pipe size	G		185	.086		12.60	5.10		17.70	21.50
7568	1-1/2" iron pipe size	G		180	.089		15.45	5.20		20.65	25
7570	2" iron pipe size	G		170	.094		8.30	5.55		13.85	17.55
7572	2-1/2" iron pipe size	G		160	.100		9.50	5.85		15.35	19.45
7574	3" iron pipe size	G		150	.107		13.30	6.25		19.55	24
7576	3-1/2" iron pipe size	G		140	.114		10.40	6.70		17.10	21.50
7578	4" iron pipe size	G		120	.133		11.50	7.85		19.35	24.50
7580	5" iron pipe size	G		110	.145		7.60	8.55		16.15	21.50
7582	6" iron pipe size	G		90	.178		16.50	10.45		26.95	34
7584	7" iron pipe size	G		80	.200		22	11.75		33.75	42
7586	8" iron pipe size	G		70	.229		23.50	13.40		36.90	46
7588	9" iron pipe size	G		65	.246		18.45	14.45		32.90	42.50
7590	10" iron pipe size	G		60	.267		20	15.65		35.65	46
7592	12" iron pipe size	G		55	.291		24.50	17.10		41.60	53
7594	14" iron pipe size	G		50	.320		29	18.80		47.80	60.50
7596	16" iron pipe size	G		45	.356		33	21		54	68.50
7598	18" iron pipe size	G		40	.400		36	23.50		59.50	75.50
7602	24" iron pipe size	G		30	.533		47.50	31.50		79	100
7620	3" wall, 1/2" iron pipe size	G		200	.080		11.30	4.70		16	19.60
7622	3/4" iron pipe size	G		190	.084		11.90	4.95		16.85	20.50
7624	1" iron pipe size	G		180	.089		13.25	5.20		18.45	22.50
7626	1-1/4" iron pipe size	G		175	.091		15.60	5.35		20.95	25.50
7628	1-1/2" iron pipe size	G		170	.094		13.45	5.55		19	23.50
7630	2" iron pipe size	G		160	.100		14.40	5.85		20.25	25
7632	2-1/2" iron pipe size	G		150	.107		14.95	6.25		21.20	26
7634	3" iron pipe size	G		140	.114		12.15	6.70		18.85	23.50
7636	3-1/2" iron pipe size	G		130	.123		18.65	7.25		25.90	31.50
7638	4" iron pipe size	G		110	.145		14.40	8.55		22.95	29
7640	5" iron pipe size	G		100	.160		16.30	9.40		25.70	32.50
7642	6" iron pipe size	G		80	.200		17.45	11.75		29.20	37
7644	7" iron pipe size	G		70	.229		19.05	13.40		32.45	41.50
7646	8" iron pipe size	G		60	.267		22	15.65		37.65	48
7648	9" iron pipe size	G		55	.291		22.50	17.10		39.60	50.50
7650	10" iron pipe size	G		50	.320		25.50	18.80		44.30	57
7652	12" iron pipe size	G		45	.356		32	21		53	67
7654	14" iron pipe size	G		40	.400		72	23.50		95.50	115
7656	16" iron pipe size	G		35	.457		55	27		82	102
7658	18" iron pipe size	G		32	.500		59	29.50		88.50	110
7660	20" iron pipe size	G		30	.533		46	31.50		77.50	98.50
7662	24" iron pipe size	G		28	.571		98	33.50		131.50	160
7664	26" iron pipe size	G		26	.615		64.50	36		100.50	127
7666	30" iron pipe size	G		24	.667		67	39		106	134
7800	For fiberglass with standard canvas jacket, deduct						5%				
7802	For fittings, add 3 L.F. for each fitting										
7804	plus 4 L.F. for each flange of the fitting										
7820	Polyethylene tubing flexible closed cell foam, UV resistant										
7828	Standard temperature (-90°F to +212°F)										
7830	3/8" wall, 1/8" iron pipe size	G	1 Asbe	130	.062	L.F.	.47	4.02		4.49	6.65
7831	1/4" iron pipe size	G		130	.062		.48	4.02		4.50	6.70
7832	3/8" iron pipe size	G		130	.062		.45	4.02		4.47	6.65

22 07 Plumbing Insulation

22 07 19 – Plumbing Piping Insulation

22 07 19.10 Piping Insulation

			Crew	Daily Output	Labor-Hours	Unit	Material	2023 Bare Costs Labor	Equipment	Total	Total Incl O&P
7833	1/2" iron pipe size	G	1 Asbe	126	.063	L.F.	.62	4.14		4.76	7.05
7834	3/4" iron pipe size	G		122	.066		.61	4.28		4.89	7.20
7835	1" iron pipe size	G		120	.067		.78	4.35		5.13	7.50
7836	1-1/4" iron pipe size	G		118	.068		.99	4.42		5.41	7.85
7837	1-1/2" iron pipe size	G		118	.068		1.03	4.42		5.45	7.90
7838	2" iron pipe size	G		116	.069		1.64	4.50		6.14	8.70
7839	2-1/2" iron pipe size	G		114	.070		1.58	4.58		6.16	8.75
7840	3" iron pipe size	G		112	.071		3.22	4.66		7.88	10.70
7842	1/2" wall, 1/8" iron pipe size	G		120	.067		.56	4.35		4.91	7.25
7843	1/4" iron pipe size	G		120	.067		.74	4.35		5.09	7.45
7844	3/8" iron pipe size	G		120	.067		.78	4.35		5.13	7.50
7845	1/2" iron pipe size	G		118	.068		.90	4.42		5.32	7.75
7846	3/4" iron pipe size	G		116	.069		.92	4.50		5.42	7.90
7847	1" iron pipe size	G		114	.070		.96	4.58		5.54	8.05
7848	1-1/4" iron pipe size	G		112	.071		1.11	4.66		5.77	8.35
7849	1-1/2" iron pipe size	G		110	.073		1.22	4.75		5.97	8.60
7850	2" iron pipe size	G		108	.074		2.31	4.83		7.14	9.95
7851	2-1/2" iron pipe size	G		106	.075		2.98	4.92		7.90	10.85
7852	3" iron pipe size	G		104	.077		3.89	5		8.89	12
7853	3-1/2" iron pipe size	G		102	.078		4.35	5.10		9.45	12.65
7854	4" iron pipe size	G		100	.080		5.15	5.20		10.35	13.70
7855	3/4" wall, 1/8" iron pipe size	G		110	.073		.85	4.75		5.60	8.20
7856	1/4" iron pipe size	G		110	.073		.92	4.75		5.67	8.25
7857	3/8" iron pipe size	G		108	.074		1.29	4.83		6.12	8.80
7858	1/2" iron pipe size	G		106	.075		1.53	4.92		6.45	9.25
7859	3/4" iron pipe size	G		104	.077		1.81	5		6.81	9.70
7860	1" iron pipe size	G		102	.078		2.13	5.10		7.23	10.20
7861	1-1/4" iron pipe size	G		100	.080		2.36	5.20		7.56	10.60
7862	1-1/2" iron pipe size	G		100	.080		2.99	5.20		8.19	11.30
7863	2" iron pipe size	G		98	.082		4.10	5.35		9.45	12.65
7864	2-1/2" iron pipe size	G		96	.083		5.15	5.45		10.60	14
7865	3" iron pipe size	G		94	.085		5.10	5.55		10.65	14.10
7866	3-1/2" iron pipe size	G		92	.087		7.30	5.65		12.95	16.75
7867	4" iron pipe size	G		90	.089		8.15	5.80		13.95	17.80
7868	1" wall, 1/4" iron pipe size	G		100	.080		2.23	5.20		7.43	10.45
7869	3/8" iron pipe size	G		98	.082		2.10	5.35		7.45	10.45
7870	1/2" iron pipe size	G		96	.083		2.82	5.45		8.27	11.40
7871	3/4" iron pipe size	G		94	.085		3.22	5.55		8.77	12.05
7872	1" iron pipe size	G		92	.087		3.94	5.65		9.59	13.05
7873	1-1/4" iron pipe size	G		90	.089		4.46	5.80		10.26	13.75
7874	1-1/2" iron pipe size	G		90	.089		5.50	5.80		11.30	14.90
7875	2" iron pipe size	G		88	.091		6.60	5.95		12.55	16.30
7876	2-1/2" iron pipe size	G		86	.093		9.15	6.05		15.20	19.40
7877	3" iron pipe size	G		84	.095		9.90	6.20		16.10	20.50
7878	Contact cement, quart can	G				Ea.	16.50			16.50	18.15
7879	Rubber tubing, flexible closed cell foam										
7880	3/8" wall, 1/4" iron pipe size	G	1 Asbe	120	.067	L.F.	.70	4.35		5.05	7.40
7900	3/8" iron pipe size	G		120	.067		.75	4.35		5.10	7.50
7910	1/2" iron pipe size	G		115	.070		.87	4.54		5.41	7.90
7920	3/4" iron pipe size	G		115	.070		.96	4.54		5.50	8
7930	1" iron pipe size	G		110	.073		1.09	4.75		5.84	8.45
7940	1-1/4" iron pipe size	G		110	.073		1.24	4.75		5.99	8.60
7950	1-1/2" iron pipe size	G		110	.073		1.53	4.75		6.28	8.95

22 07 Plumbing Insulation

22 07 19 – Plumbing Piping Insulation

22 07 19.10 Piping Insulation		Crew	Daily Output	Labor-Hours	Unit	Material	2023 Bare Costs Labor	Equipment	Total	Total Incl O&P
8100	1/2" wall, 1/4" iron pipe size G	1 Asbe	90	.089	L.F.	1.14	5.80		6.94	10.10
8120	3/8" iron pipe size G		90	.089		1.13	5.80		6.93	10.10
8130	1/2" iron pipe size G		89	.090		1.25	5.85		7.10	10.35
8140	3/4" iron pipe size G		89	.090		1.30	5.85		7.15	10.40
8150	1" iron pipe size G		88	.091		2.48	5.95		8.43	11.80
8160	1-1/4" iron pipe size G		87	.092		1.72	6		7.72	11.10
8170	1-1/2" iron pipe size G		87	.092		1.97	6		7.97	11.35
8180	2" iron pipe size G		86	.093		2.52	6.05		8.57	12.05
8190	2-1/2" iron pipe size G		86	.093		4.37	6.05		10.42	14.10
8200	3" iron pipe size G		85	.094		5.15	6.15		11.30	15.05
8210	3-1/2" iron pipe size G		85	.094		6.50	6.15		12.65	16.55
8220	4" iron pipe size G		80	.100		7.10	6.55		13.65	17.80
8230	5" iron pipe size G		80	.100		9.05	6.55		15.60	19.95
8240	6" iron pipe size G		75	.107		9.05	6.95		16	20.50
8300	3/4" wall, 1/4" iron pipe size G		90	.089		1.60	5.80		7.40	10.60
8320	3/8" iron pipe size G		90	.089		1.74	5.80		7.54	10.75
8330	1/2" iron pipe size G		89	.090		1.90	5.85		7.75	11.05
8340	3/4" iron pipe size G		89	.090		2.28	5.85		8.13	11.45
8350	1" iron pipe size G		88	.091		2.77	5.95		8.72	12.10
8360	1-1/4" iron pipe size G		87	.092		3.17	6		9.17	12.70
8370	1-1/2" iron pipe size G		87	.092		4.21	6		10.21	13.85
8380	2" iron pipe size G		86	.093		5.10	6.05		11.15	14.95
8390	2-1/2" iron pipe size G		86	.093		5.70	6.05		11.75	15.55
8400	3" iron pipe size G		85	.094		6.35	6.15		12.50	16.35
8410	3-1/2" iron pipe size G		85	.094		7.05	6.15		13.20	17.15
8420	4" iron pipe size G		80	.100		8.10	6.55		14.65	18.90
8430	5" iron pipe size G		80	.100		13.85	6.55		20.40	25.50
8440	6" iron pipe size G		80	.100		19	6.55		25.55	31
8444	1" wall, 1/2" iron pipe size G		86	.093		3.40	6.05		9.45	13.05
8445	3/4" iron pipe size G		84	.095		4.19	6.20		10.39	14.10
8446	1" iron pipe size G		84	.095		5.10	6.20		11.30	15.10
8447	1-1/4" iron pipe size G		82	.098		5.90	6.35		12.25	16.25
8448	1-1/2" iron pipe size G		82	.098		6.55	6.35		12.90	16.95
8449	2" iron pipe size G		80	.100		7.85	6.55		14.40	18.65
8450	2-1/2" iron pipe size G		80	.100	L.F.	7.70	6.55		14.25	18.50
8456	Rubber insulation tape, 1/8" x 2" x 30' G				Ea.	25			25	27.50
8460	Polyolefin tubing, flexible closed cell foam, UV stabilized, work									
8462	temp. -165°F to +210°F, 0 water vapor transmission									
8464	3/8" wall, 1/8" iron pipe size G	1 Asbe	140	.057	L.F.	.48	3.73		4.21	6.25
8466	1/4" iron pipe size G		140	.057		.50	3.73		4.23	6.25
8468	3/8" iron pipe size G		140	.057		.56	3.73		4.29	6.30
8470	1/2" iron pipe size G		136	.059		.62	3.84		4.46	6.55
8472	3/4" iron pipe size G		132	.061		.62	3.95		4.57	6.75
8474	1" iron pipe size G		130	.062		.83	4.02		4.85	7.05
8476	1-1/4" iron pipe size G		128	.063		1.02	4.08		5.10	7.35
8478	1-1/2" iron pipe size G		128	.063		1.24	4.08		5.32	7.60
8480	2" iron pipe size G		126	.063		1.50	4.14		5.64	8
8482	2-1/2" iron pipe size G		123	.065		2.18	4.24		6.42	8.90
8484	3" iron pipe size G		121	.066		2.42	4.31		6.73	9.25
8486	4" iron pipe size G		118	.068		5.80	4.42		10.22	13.15
8500	1/2" wall, 1/8" iron pipe size G		130	.062		.70	4.02		4.72	6.90
8502	1/4" iron pipe size G		130	.062		.76	4.02		4.78	7
8504	3/8" iron pipe size G		130	.062		.82	4.02		4.84	7.05

22 07 Plumbing Insulation

22 07 19 – Plumbing Piping Insulation

22 07 19.10 Piping Insulation

			Crew	Daily Output	Labor-Hours	Unit	Material	2023 Bare Costs Labor	2023 Bare Costs Equipment	Total	Total Incl O&P
8506	1/2" iron pipe size	G	1 Asbe	128	.063	L.F.	.88	4.08		4.96	7.20
8508	3/4" iron pipe size	G		126	.063		1.03	4.14		5.17	7.50
8510	1" iron pipe size	G		123	.065		1.18	4.24		5.42	7.80
8512	1-1/4" iron pipe size	G		121	.066		1.39	4.31		5.70	8.15
8514	1-1/2" iron pipe size	G		119	.067		1.67	4.39		6.06	8.55
8516	2" iron pipe size	G		117	.068		2.11	4.46		6.57	9.10
8518	2-1/2" iron pipe size	G		114	.070		2.86	4.58		7.44	10.15
8520	3" iron pipe size	G		112	.071		3.72	4.66		8.38	11.25
8522	4" iron pipe size	G		110	.073		5.15	4.75		9.90	12.90
8534	3/4" wall, 1/8" iron pipe size	G		120	.067		1.08	4.35		5.43	7.85
8536	1/4" iron pipe size	G		120	.067		1.14	4.35		5.49	7.90
8538	3/8" iron pipe size	G		117	.068		1.31	4.46		5.77	8.25
8540	1/2" iron pipe size	G		114	.070		1.45	4.58		6.03	8.60
8542	3/4" iron pipe size	G		112	.071		1.57	4.66		6.23	8.90
8544	1" iron pipe size	G		110	.073		2.20	4.75		6.95	9.65
8546	1-1/4" iron pipe size	G		108	.074		2.94	4.83		7.77	10.65
8548	1-1/2" iron pipe size	G		108	.074		3.44	4.83		8.27	11.20
8550	2" iron pipe size	G		106	.075		4.35	4.92		9.27	12.35
8552	2-1/2" iron pipe size	G		104	.077		5.50	5		10.50	13.75
8554	3" iron pipe size	G		102	.078		6.85	5.10		11.95	15.35
8556	4" iron pipe size	G		100	.080		9	5.20		14.20	17.90
8570	1" wall, 1/8" iron pipe size	G		110	.073		1.95	4.75		6.70	9.40
8572	1/4" iron pipe size	G		108	.074		3.54	4.83		8.37	11.30
8574	3/8" iron pipe size	G		106	.075		2.04	4.92		6.96	9.80
8576	1/2" iron pipe size	G		104	.077		2.16	5		7.16	10.10
8578	3/4" iron pipe size	G		102	.078		2.75	5.10		7.85	10.90
8580	1" iron pipe size	G		100	.080		3.27	5.20		8.47	11.60
8582	1-1/4" iron pipe size	G		97	.082		3.72	5.40		9.12	12.35
8584	1-1/2" iron pipe size	G		97	.082		4.25	5.40		9.65	12.95
8586	2" iron pipe size	G		95	.084		6	5.50		11.50	15
8588	2-1/2" iron pipe size	G		93	.086		7.85	5.60		13.45	17.20
8590	3" iron pipe size	G		91	.088		9.55	5.75		15.30	19.25
8606	Contact adhesive (R-320)	G				Qt.	26			26	28.50
8608	Contact adhesive (R-320)	G				Gal.	104			104	114
8610	NOTE: Preslit/preglued vs. unslit, same price										

22 07 19.30 Piping Insulation Protective Jacketing, PVC

0010	**PIPING INSULATION PROTECTIVE JACKETING, PVC**										
0100	PVC, white, 48" lengths cut from roll goods										
0120	20 mil thick										
0140	Size based on OD of insulation										
0150	1-1/2" ID		Q-14	270	.059	L.F.	3.47	3.48		6.95	9.10
0152	2" ID			260	.062		2.17	3.61		5.78	7.95
0154	2-1/2" ID			250	.064		.61	3.76		4.37	6.40
0156	3" ID			240	.067		4.24	3.92		8.16	10.65
0158	3-1/2" ID			230	.070		2.65	4.09		6.74	9.15
0160	4" ID			220	.073		2.83	4.27		7.10	9.65
0162	4-1/2" ID			210	.076		3.17	4.47		7.64	10.35
0164	5" ID			200	.080		5.45	4.70		10.15	13.15
0166	5-1/2" ID			190	.084		1.23	4.95		6.18	8.90
0168	6" ID			180	.089		6.30	5.20		11.50	14.95
0170	6-1/2" ID			175	.091		1.28	5.35		6.63	9.60
0172	7" ID			170	.094		6.85	5.55		12.40	16

22 07 Plumbing Insulation

22 07 19 – Plumbing Piping Insulation

22 07 19.30 Piping Insulation Protective Jacketing, PVC		Crew	Daily Output	Labor-Hours	Unit	Material	2023 Bare Costs Labor	Equipment	Total	Total Incl O&P
0174	7-1/2" ID	Q-14	164	.098	L.F.	1.48	5.75		7.23	10.40
0176	8" ID		161	.099		3.90	5.85		9.75	13.25
0178	8-1/2" ID		158	.101		1.87	5.95		7.82	11.15
0180	9" ID		155	.103		1.97	6.05		8.02	11.40
0182	9-1/2" ID		152	.105		1.85	6.20		8.05	11.50
0184	10" ID		149	.107		2.17	6.30		8.47	12.05
0186	10-1/2" ID		146	.110		2.30	6.45		8.75	12.40
0188	11" ID		143	.112		2.40	6.55		8.95	12.70
0190	11-1/2" ID		140	.114		2.20	6.70		8.90	12.65
0192	12" ID		137	.117		2.61	6.85		9.46	13.35
0194	12-1/2" ID		134	.119		2.68	7		9.68	13.70
0195	13" ID		132	.121		2.82	7.10		9.92	14
0196	13-1/2" ID		132	.121		2.91	7.10		10.01	14.10
0198	14" ID		130	.123		3.02	7.25		10.27	14.35
0200	15" ID		128	.125		3.20	7.35		10.55	14.75
0202	16" ID		126	.127		3.43	7.45		10.88	15.15
0204	17" ID		124	.129		3.62	7.60		11.22	15.60
0206	18" ID		122	.131		3.84	7.70		11.54	16
0208	19" ID		120	.133		4.05	7.85		11.90	16.45
0210	20" ID		118	.136		4.33	7.95		12.28	16.95
0212	21" ID		116	.138		4.49	8.10		12.59	17.35
0214	22" ID		114	.140		4.73	8.25		12.98	17.80
0216	23" ID		112	.143		4.94	8.40		13.34	18.30
0218	24" ID		110	.145		5.15	8.55		13.70	18.70
0220	25" ID		108	.148		5.35	8.70		14.05	19.20
0222	26" ID		106	.151		5.60	8.85		14.45	19.70
0224	27" ID		104	.154		5.80	9.05		14.85	20
0226	28" ID		102	.157		6	9.20		15.20	20.50
0228	29" ID		100	.160		6.20	9.40		15.60	21
0230	30" ID		98	.163		6.45	9.60		16.05	22
0300	For colors, add				Ea.	10%				
1000	30 mil thick									
1010	Size based on OD of insulation									
1020	2" ID	Q-14	260	.062	L.F.	.74	3.61		4.35	6.35
1022	2-1/2" ID		250	.064		3.72	3.76		7.48	9.85
1024	3" ID		240	.067		2.63	3.92		6.55	8.90
1026	3-1/2" ID		230	.070		1.23	4.09		5.32	7.60
1028	4" ID		220	.073		4.09	4.27		8.36	11.05
1030	4-1/2" ID		210	.076		1.54	4.47		6.01	8.55
1032	5" ID		200	.080		1.69	4.70		6.39	9.05
1034	5-1/2" ID		190	.084		1.87	4.95		6.82	9.60
1036	6" ID		180	.089		1.99	5.20		7.19	10.20
1038	6-1/2" ID		175	.091		2.18	5.35		7.53	10.60
1040	7" ID		170	.094		2.33	5.55		7.88	11
1042	7-1/2" ID		164	.098		2.51	5.75		8.26	11.50
1044	8" ID		161	.099		2.64	5.85		8.49	11.85
1046	8-1/2" ID		158	.101		2.82	5.95		8.77	12.20
1048	9" ID		155	.103		2.97	6.05		9.02	12.50
1050	9-1/2" ID		152	.105		3.14	6.20		9.34	12.90
1052	10" ID		149	.107		5.05	6.30		11.35	15.25
1054	10-1/2" ID		146	.110		3.45	6.45		9.90	13.65
1056	11" ID		143	.112		3.63	6.55		10.18	14.05
1058	11-1/2" ID		140	.114		3.78	6.70		10.48	14.40

22 07 Plumbing Insulation

22 07 19 – Plumbing Piping Insulation

22 07 19.30 Piping Insulation Protective Jacketing, PVC		Crew	Daily Output	Labor-Hours	Unit	Material	2023 Bare Costs Labor	Equipment	Total	Total Incl O&P
1060	12" ID	Q-14	137	.117	L.F.	3.93	6.85		10.78	14.80
1062	12-1/2" ID		134	.119		4.09	7		11.09	15.25
1063	13" ID		132	.121		4.24	7.10		11.34	15.55
1064	13-1/2" ID		132	.121		4.43	7.10		11.53	15.75
1066	14" ID		130	.123		4.55	7.25		11.80	16.05
1068	15" ID		128	.125		4.88	7.35		12.23	16.60
1070	16" ID		126	.127		5.20	7.45		12.65	17.15
1072	17" ID		124	.129		5.55	7.60		13.15	17.70
1074	18" ID		122	.131		5.85	7.70		13.55	18.20
1076	19" ID		120	.133		6.15	7.85		14	18.75
1078	20" ID		118	.136		6.45	7.95		14.40	19.30
1080	21" ID		116	.138		6.80	8.10		14.90	19.85
1082	22" ID		114	.140		7.10	8.25		15.35	20.50
1084	23" ID		112	.143		7.45	8.40		15.85	21
1086	24" ID		110	.145		7.75	8.55		16.30	21.50
1088	25" ID		108	.148		8.10	8.70		16.80	22
1090	26" ID		106	.151		8.40	8.85		17.25	23
1092	27" ID		104	.154		8.75	9.05		17.80	23.50
1094	28" ID		102	.157		9.05	9.20		18.25	24
1096	29" ID		100	.160		9.35	9.40		18.75	24.50
1098	30" ID		98	.163		9.70	9.60		19.30	25.50
1300	For colors, add				Ea.	10%				
2000	PVC, white, fitting covers									
2020	Fiberglass insulation inserts included with sizes 1-3/4" thru 9-3/4"									
2030	Size is based on OD of insulation									
2040	90° elbow fitting									
2060	1-3/4"	Q-14	135	.119	Ea.	.61	6.95		7.56	11.30
2062	2"		130	.123		.76	7.25		8.01	11.90
2064	2-1/4"		128	.125		.88	7.35		8.23	12.20
2068	2-1/2"		126	.127		.93	7.45		8.38	12.40
2070	2-3/4"		123	.130		1.10	7.65		8.75	12.90
2072	3"		120	.133		5.60	7.85		13.45	18.20
2074	3-3/8"		116	.138		1.26	8.10		9.36	13.80
2076	3-3/4"		113	.142		1.34	8.30		9.64	14.15
2078	4-1/8"		110	.145		1.77	8.55		10.32	15
2080	4-3/4"		105	.152		2.14	8.95		11.09	16.05
2082	5-1/4"		100	.160		2.50	9.40		11.90	17.10
2084	5-3/4"		95	.168		3.16	9.90		13.06	18.65
2086	6-1/4"		90	.178		5.25	10.45		15.70	22
2088	6-3/4"		87	.184		5.55	10.80		16.35	22.50
2090	7-1/4"		85	.188		6.90	11.05		17.95	24.50
2092	7-3/4"		83	.193		7.30	11.30		18.60	25.50
2094	8-3/4"		80	.200		9.35	11.75		21.10	28.50
2096	9-3/4"		77	.208		12.50	12.20		24.70	32.50
2098	10-7/8"		74	.216		13.95	12.70		26.65	35
2100	11-7/8"		71	.225		16	13.25		29.25	37.50
2102	12-7/8"		68	.235		22	13.80		35.80	45.50
2104	14-1/8"		66	.242		23	14.25		37.25	47.50
2106	15-1/8"		64	.250		25	14.70		39.70	50
2108	16-1/8"		63	.254		27	14.90		41.90	53
2110	17-1/8"		62	.258		30	15.15		45.15	56
2112	18-1/8"		61	.262		40.50	15.40		55.90	68
2114	19-1/8"		60	.267		52.50	15.65		68.15	82

22 07 Plumbing Insulation

22 07 19 – Plumbing Piping Insulation

22 07 19.30 Piping Insulation Protective Jacketing, PVC		Crew	Daily Output	Labor-Hours	Unit	Material	2023 Bare Costs Labor	Equipment	Total	Total Incl O&P
2116	20-1/8"	Q-14	59	.271	Ea.	67.50	15.95		83.45	99
2200	45° elbow fitting									
2220	1-3/4" thru 9-3/4" same price as 90° elbow fitting									
2320	10-7/8"	Q-14	74	.216	Ea.	13.95	12.70		26.65	35
2322	11-7/8"		71	.225		15.40	13.25		28.65	37
2324	12-7/8"		68	.235		17.15	13.80		30.95	40
2326	14-1/8"		66	.242		19.60	14.25		33.85	43.50
2328	15-1/8"		64	.250		21	14.70		35.70	45.50
2330	16-1/8"		63	.254		24	14.90		38.90	49.50
2332	17-1/8"		62	.258		27	15.15		42.15	53
2334	18-1/8"		61	.262		33	15.40		48.40	60
2336	19-1/8"		60	.267		45	15.65		60.65	73.50
2338	20-1/8"		59	.271		51	15.95		66.95	80.50
2400	Tee fitting									
2410	1-3/4"	Q-14	96	.167	Ea.	1.15	9.80		10.95	16.20
2412	2"		94	.170		1.31	10		11.31	16.75
2414	2-1/4"		91	.176		1.41	10.35		11.76	17.35
2416	2-1/2"		88	.182		1.54	10.70		12.24	18.05
2418	2-3/4"		85	.188		1.70	11.05		12.75	18.75
2420	3"		82	.195		10.10	11.45		21.55	28.50
2422	3-3/8"		79	.203		2.12	11.90		14.02	20.50
2424	3-3/4"		76	.211		2.63	12.35		14.98	22
2426	4-1/8"		73	.219		2.85	12.85		15.70	23
2428	4-3/4"		70	.229		3.54	13.40		16.94	24.50
2430	5-1/4"		67	.239		4.26	14.05		18.31	26
2432	5-3/4"		63	.254		5.65	14.90		20.55	29.50
2434	6-1/4"		60	.267		7.45	15.65		23.10	32
2436	6-3/4"		59	.271		9.20	15.95		25.15	34.50
2438	7-1/4"		57	.281		14.85	16.50		31.35	41.50
2440	7-3/4"		54	.296		16.30	17.40		33.70	44.50
2442	8-3/4"		52	.308		19.80	18.05		37.85	49.50
2444	9-3/4"		50	.320		23.50	18.80		42.30	54.50
2446	10-7/8"		48	.333		23.50	19.60		43.10	56
2448	11-7/8"		47	.340		26.50	20		46.50	59.50
2450	12-7/8"		46	.348		29	20.50		49.50	63.50
2452	14-1/8"		45	.356		31.50	21		52.50	66.50
2454	15-1/8"		44	.364		34	21.50		55.50	70
2456	16-1/8"		43	.372		37	22		59	74
2458	17-1/8"		42	.381		39.50	22.50		62	77.50
2460	18-1/8"		41	.390		43.50	23		66.50	82.50
2462	19-1/8"		40	.400		47.50	23.50		71	88
2464	20-1/8"		39	.410		52.50	24		76.50	94.50
4000	Mechanical grooved fitting cover, including insert									
4020	90° elbow fitting									
4030	3/4" & 1"	Q-14	140	.114	Ea.	5.95	6.70		12.65	16.80
4040	1-1/4" & 1-1/2"		135	.119		7.50	6.95		14.45	18.90
4042	2"		130	.123		9.55	7.25		16.80	21.50
4044	2-1/2"		125	.128		10.65	7.50		18.15	23
4046	3"		120	.133		11.90	7.85		19.75	25
4048	3-1/2"		115	.139		13.80	8.15		21.95	27.50
4050	4"		110	.145		15.35	8.55		23.90	30
4052	5"		100	.160		19.10	9.40		28.50	35.50
4054	6"		90	.178		28.50	10.45		38.95	47.50

For customer support on your Plumbing Costs with RSMeans data, call 800.448.8182.

22 07 Plumbing Insulation

22 07 19 – Plumbing Piping Insulation

22 07 19.30 Piping Insulation Protective Jacketing, PVC

		Crew	Daily Output	Labor-Hours	Unit	Material	2023 Bare Costs Labor	Equipment	Total	Total Incl O&P
4056	8"	Q-14	80	.200	Ea.	30.50	11.75		42.25	52
4058	10"		75	.213		39.50	12.55		52.05	62.50
4060	12"		68	.235		56.50	13.80		70.30	83
4062	14"		65	.246		84	14.45		98.45	114
4064	16"		63	.254		114	14.90		128.90	148
4066	18"	↓	61	.262	↓	157	15.40		172.40	196
4100	45° elbow fitting									
4120	3/4" & 1"	Q-14	140	.114	Ea.	5.35	6.70		12.05	16.15
4130	1-1/4" & 1-1/2"		135	.119		6.85	6.95		13.80	18.15
4140	2"		130	.123		9.35	7.25		16.60	21.50
4142	2-1/2"		125	.128		10.40	7.50		17.90	23
4144	3"		120	.133		10.65	7.85		18.50	23.50
4146	3-1/2"		115	.139		14.25	8.15		22.40	28
4148	4"		110	.145		17.50	8.55		26.05	32.50
4150	5"		100	.160		18.60	9.40		28	35
4152	6"		90	.178		26	10.45		36.45	44.50
4154	8"		80	.200		27.50	11.75		39.25	48
4156	10"		75	.213		35	12.55		47.55	57.50
4158	12"		68	.235		52.50	13.80		66.30	79
4160	14"		65	.246		72	14.45		86.45	101
4162	16"		63	.254		87	14.90		101.90	119
4164	18"	↓	61	.262	↓	139	15.40		154.40	176
4200	Tee fitting									
4220	3/4" & 1"	Q-14	93	.172	Ea.	7.80	10.10		17.90	24
4230	1-1/4" & 1-1/2"		90	.178		9.90	10.45		20.35	27
4240	2"		87	.184		15.95	10.80		26.75	34
4242	2-1/2"		84	.190		17.75	11.20		28.95	36.50
4244	3"		80	.200		19.05	11.75		30.80	39
4246	3-1/2"		77	.208		20.50	12.20		32.70	41
4248	4"		73	.219		25.50	12.85		38.35	47.50
4250	5"		67	.239		31.50	14.05		45.55	56
4252	6"		60	.267		42	15.65		57.65	70
4254	8"		54	.296		45.50	17.40		62.90	76.50
4256	10"		50	.320		51.50	18.80		70.30	85.50
4258	12"		46	.348		78.50	20.50		99	118
4260	14"		43	.372		114	22		136	159
4262	16"		42	.381		117	22.50		139.50	163
4264	18"	↓	41	.390	↓	174	23		197	226

22 07 19.40 Pipe Insulation Protective Jacketing, Aluminum

		Crew	Daily Output	Labor-Hours	Unit	Material	2023 Bare Costs Labor	Equipment	Total	Total Incl O&P
0010	**PIPE INSULATION PROTECTIVE JACKETING, ALUMINUM**									
0100	Metal roll jacketing									
0120	Aluminum with polykraft moisture barrier									
0140	Smooth, based on OD of insulation, .016" thick									
0180	1/2" ID	Q-14	220	.073	L.F.	.36	4.27		4.63	6.95
0190	3/4" ID		215	.074		.46	4.37		4.83	7.20
0200	1" ID		210	.076		.56	4.47		5.03	7.45
0210	1-1/4" ID		205	.078		2.74	4.58		7.32	10
0220	1-1/2" ID		202	.079		2.74	4.65		7.39	10.10
0230	1-3/4" ID		199	.080		.98	4.72		5.70	8.30
0240	2" ID		195	.082		1.47	4.82		6.29	8.95
0250	2-1/4" ID		191	.084		1.22	4.92		6.14	8.90
0260	2-1/2" ID	↓	187	.086		1.21	5.05		6.26	9.05

22 07 Plumbing Insulation

22 07 19 – Plumbing Piping Insulation

22 07 19.40 Pipe Insulation Protective Jacketing, Aluminum		Crew	Daily Output	Labor-Hours	Unit	Material	2023 Bare Costs Labor	Equipment	Total	Total Incl O&P
0270	2-3/4" ID	Q-14	184	.087	L.F.	1.47	5.10		6.57	9.40
0280	3" ID		180	.089		1.64	5.20		6.84	9.80
0290	3-1/4" ID		176	.091		1.64	5.35		6.99	9.95
0300	3-1/2" ID		172	.093		1.80	5.45		7.25	10.35
0310	3-3/4" ID		169	.095		1.75	5.55		7.30	10.45
0320	4" ID		165	.097		1.97	5.70		7.67	10.85
0330	4-1/4" ID		161	.099		2.16	5.85		8.01	11.35
0340	4-1/2" ID		157	.102		4.32	6		10.32	13.90
0350	4-3/4" ID		154	.104		2.39	6.10		8.49	12
0360	5" ID		150	.107		4.99	6.25		11.24	15.10
0370	5-1/4" ID		146	.110		2.63	6.45		9.08	12.75
0380	5-1/2" ID		143	.112		2.51	6.55		9.06	12.80
0390	5-3/4" ID		139	.115		2.88	6.75		9.63	13.50
0400	6" ID		135	.119		2.77	6.95		9.72	13.70
0410	6-1/4" ID		133	.120		3.11	7.05		10.16	14.20
0420	6-1/2" ID		131	.122		5.65	7.15		12.80	17.20
0430	7" ID		128	.125		3.13	7.35		10.48	14.70
0440	7-1/4" ID		125	.128		3.24	7.50		10.74	15.05
0450	7-1/2" ID		123	.130		3.34	7.65		10.99	15.35
0460	8" ID		121	.132		3.52	7.75		11.27	15.75
0470	8-1/2" ID		119	.134		3.75	7.90		11.65	16.25
0480	9" ID		116	.138		3.96	8.10		12.06	16.75
0490	9-1/2" ID		114	.140		4.20	8.25		12.45	17.20
0500	10" ID		112	.143		4.28	8.40		12.68	17.55
0510	10-1/2" ID		110	.145		5.05	8.55		13.60	18.65
0520	11" ID		107	.150		4.81	8.80		13.61	18.75
0530	11-1/2" ID		105	.152		5.05	8.95		14	19.25
0540	12" ID		103	.155		5	9.10		14.10	19.45
0550	12-1/2" ID		100	.160		5.45	9.40		14.85	20.50
0560	13" ID		99	.162		5.65	9.50		15.15	21
0570	14" ID		98	.163		6.10	9.60		15.70	21.50
0580	15" ID		96	.167		6.55	9.80		16.35	22
0590	16" ID		95	.168		6.95	9.90		16.85	23
0600	17" ID		93	.172		7.35	10.10		17.45	23.50
0610	18" ID		92	.174		7.65	10.20		17.85	24
0620	19" ID		90	.178		8.25	10.45		18.70	25
0630	20" ID		89	.180		8.65	10.55		19.20	25.50
0640	21" ID		87	.184		9.10	10.80		19.90	26.50
0650	22" ID		86	.186		9.50	10.95		20.45	27
0660	23" ID		84	.190		9.95	11.20		21.15	28
0670	24" ID		83	.193		10.35	11.30		21.65	28.50
0710	For smooth .020" thick, add					27%	10%			
0720	For smooth .024" thick, add					52%	20%			
0730	For smooth .032" thick, add					104%	33%			
0800	For stucco embossed, add					1%				
0820	For corrugated, add					2.50%				
0900	White aluminum with polysurlyn moisture barrier									
0910	Smooth, % is an add to polykraft lines of same thickness									
0940	For smooth .016" thick, add				L.F.	35%				
0960	For smooth .024" thick, add				"	22%				
1000	Aluminum fitting covers									
1010	Size is based on OD of insulation									
1020	90° LR elbow, 2 piece									

22 07 Plumbing Insulation

22 07 19 – Plumbing Piping Insulation

22 07 19.40 Pipe Insulation Protective Jacketing, Aluminum		Crew	Daily Output	Labor-Hours	Unit	Material	2023 Bare Costs Labor	Equipment	Total	Total Incl O&P
1100	1-1/2"	Q-14	140	.114	Ea.	5.45	6.70		12.15	16.25
1110	1-3/4"		135	.119		5.45	6.95		12.40	16.65
1120	2"		130	.123		6.90	7.25		14.15	18.65
1130	2-1/4"		128	.125		6.90	7.35		14.25	18.85
1140	2-1/2"		126	.127		4.90	7.45		12.35	16.80
1150	2-3/4"		123	.130		6.90	7.65		14.55	19.30
1160	3"		120	.133		7.50	7.85		15.35	20.50
1170	3-1/4"		117	.137		7.50	8.05		15.55	20.50
1180	3-1/2"		115	.139		8.85	8.15		17	22
1190	3-3/4"		113	.142		9.05	8.30		17.35	22.50
1200	4"		110	.145		6.75	8.55		15.30	20.50
1210	4-1/4"		108	.148		9.75	8.70		18.45	24
1220	4-1/2"		106	.151		9.75	8.85		18.60	24.50
1230	4-3/4"		104	.154		9.75	9.05		18.80	24.50
1240	5"		102	.157		11	9.20		20.20	26
1250	5-1/4"		100	.160		12.70	9.40		22.10	28.50
1260	5-1/2"		97	.165		15.80	9.70		25.50	32
1270	5-3/4"		95	.168		15.80	9.90		25.70	32.50
1280	6"		92	.174		13.45	10.20		23.65	30.50
1290	6-1/4"		90	.178		13.45	10.45		23.90	31
1300	6-1/2"		87	.184		16.20	10.80		27	34.50
1310	7"		85	.188		19.70	11.05		30.75	38.50
1320	7-1/4"		84	.190		19.70	11.20		30.90	38.50
1330	7-1/2"		83	.193		29	11.30		40.30	49.50
1340	8"		82	.195		23	11.45		34.45	42.50
1350	8-1/2"		80	.200		40	11.75		51.75	62
1360	9"		78	.205		40	12.05		52.05	62.50
1370	9-1/2"		77	.208		29.50	12.20		41.70	51
1380	10"		76	.211		31	12.35		43.35	53.50
1390	10-1/2"		75	.213		30	12.55		42.55	52
1400	11"		74	.216		30	12.70		42.70	52.50
1410	11-1/2"		72	.222		34	13.05		47.05	57.50
1420	12"		71	.225		34	13.25		47.25	57.50
1430	12-1/2"		69	.232		60.50	13.60		74.10	88
1440	13"		68	.235		60.50	13.80		74.30	88
1450	14"		66	.242		81.50	14.25		95.75	112
1460	15"		64	.250		85	14.70		99.70	116
1470	16"		63	.254		93	14.90		107.90	125
2000	45° elbow, 2 piece									
2010	2-1/2"	Q-14	126	.127	Ea.	5.70	7.45		13.15	17.65
2020	2-3/4"		123	.130		5.70	7.65		13.35	17.95
2030	3"		120	.133		6.45	7.85		14.30	19.10
2040	3-1/4"		117	.137		6.45	8.05		14.50	19.40
2050	3-1/2"		115	.139		7.35	8.15		15.50	20.50
2060	3-3/4"		113	.142		7.35	8.30		15.65	21
2070	4"		110	.145		7.45	8.55		16	21.50
2080	4-1/4"		108	.148		8.50	8.70		17.20	22.50
2090	4-1/2"		106	.151		8.50	8.85		17.35	23
2100	4-3/4"		104	.154		8.50	9.05		17.55	23
2110	5"		102	.157		10	9.20		19.20	25
2120	5-1/4"		100	.160		10	9.40		19.40	25.50
2130	5-1/2"		97	.165		10.50	9.70		20.20	26.50
2140	6"		92	.174		10.50	10.20		20.70	27

22 07 Plumbing Insulation

22 07 19 – Plumbing Piping Insulation

22 07 19.40 Pipe Insulation Protective Jacketing, Aluminum		Crew	Daily Output	Labor-Hours	Unit	Material	2023 Bare Costs Labor	Equipment	Total	Total Incl O&P
2150	6-1/2"	Q-14	87	.184	Ea.	14.45	10.80		25.25	32.50
2160	7"		85	.188		14.45	11.05		25.50	33
2170	7-1/2"		83	.193		14.65	11.30		25.95	33.50
2180	8"		82	.195		14.65	11.45		26.10	33.50
2190	8-1/2"		80	.200		18.20	11.75		29.95	38
2200	9"		78	.205		18.20	12.05		30.25	38.50
2210	9-1/2"		77	.208		25	12.20		37.20	46
2220	10"		76	.211		25	12.35		37.35	46.50
2230	10-1/2"		75	.213		23.50	12.55		36.05	45
2240	11"		74	.216		23.50	12.70		36.20	45.50
2250	11-1/2"		72	.222		28.50	13.05		41.55	51
2260	12"		71	.225		28.50	13.25		41.75	51
2270	13"		68	.235		33.50	13.80		47.30	57.50
2280	14"		66	.242		41	14.25		55.25	67
2290	15"		64	.250		63	14.70		77.70	91.50
2300	16"		63	.254		68	14.90		82.90	98
2310	17"		62	.258		66.50	15.15		81.65	96.50
2320	18"		61	.262		76	15.40		91.40	107
2330	19"		60	.267		93	15.65		108.65	126
2340	20"		59	.271		89.50	15.95		105.45	123
2350	21"		58	.276		97	16.20		113.20	132
3000	Tee, 4 piece									
3010	2-1/2"	Q-14	88	.182	Ea.	36	10.70		46.70	56
3020	2-3/4"		86	.186		36	10.95		46.95	56
3030	3"		84	.190		40.50	11.20		51.70	61.50
3040	3-1/4"		82	.195		40.50	11.45		51.95	62
3050	3-1/2"		80	.200		42.50	11.75		54.25	64.50
3060	4"		78	.205		43	12.05		55.05	65.50
3070	4-1/4"		76	.211		45	12.35		57.35	68.50
3080	4-1/2"		74	.216		45	12.70		57.70	69
3090	4-3/4"		72	.222		45	13.05		58.05	69.50
3100	5"		70	.229		46.50	13.40		59.90	72
3110	5-1/4"		68	.235		46.50	13.80		60.30	72.50
3120	5-1/2"		66	.242		48.50	14.25		62.75	75.50
3130	6"		64	.250		48.50	14.70		63.20	76
3140	6-1/2"		60	.267		53.50	15.65		69.15	83
3150	7"		58	.276		53.50	16.20		69.70	84
3160	7-1/2"		56	.286		59.50	16.80		76.30	91
3170	8"		54	.296		59.50	17.40		76.90	92
3180	8-1/2"		52	.308		61	18.05		79.05	94.50
3190	9"		50	.320		61	18.80		79.80	96
3200	9-1/2"		49	.327		45.50	19.20		64.70	79.50
3210	10"		48	.333		45.50	19.60		65.10	80
3220	10-1/2"		47	.340		48.50	20		68.50	83.50
3230	11"		46	.348		48.50	20.50		69	84.50
3240	11-1/2"		45	.356		51	21		72	88
3250	12"		44	.364		51	21.50		72.50	88.50
3260	13"		43	.372		53.50	22		75.50	92.50
3270	14"		42	.381		56	22.50		78.50	95.50
3280	15"		41	.390		60.50	23		83.50	102
3290	16"		40	.400		62	23.50		85.50	105
3300	17"		39	.410		71.50	24		95.50	116
3310	18"		38	.421		74	24.50		98.50	120

22 07 Plumbing Insulation

22 07 19 – Plumbing Piping Insulation

22 07 19.40 Pipe Insulation Protective Jacketing, Aluminum

		Crew	Daily Output	Labor-Hours	Unit	Material	2023 Bare Costs Labor	Equipment	Total	Total Incl O&P
3320	19"	Q-14	37	.432	Ea.	82	25.50		107.50	130
3330	20"		36	.444		84	26		110	133
3340	22"		35	.457		107	27		134	158
3350	23"		34	.471		110	27.50		137.50	164
3360	24"		31	.516		113	30.50		143.50	171

22 07 19.50 Pipe Insulation Protective Jacketing, St. Stl.

		Crew	Daily Output	Labor-Hours	Unit	Material	Labor	Equipment	Total	Total Incl O&P
0010	**PIPE INSULATION PROTECTIVE JACKETING, STAINLESS STEEL**									
0100	Metal roll jacketing									
0120	Type 304 with moisture barrier									
0140	Smooth, based on OD of insulation, .010" thick									
0260	2-1/2" ID	Q-14	250	.064	L.F.	4.74	3.76		8.50	10.95
0270	2-3/4" ID		245	.065		3.73	3.84		7.57	9.95
0280	3" ID		240	.067		4.03	3.92		7.95	10.45
0290	3-1/4" ID		235	.068		4.38	4		8.38	10.90
0300	3-1/2" ID		230	.070		4.64	4.09		8.73	11.35
0310	3-3/4" ID		225	.071		4.99	4.18		9.17	11.90
0320	4" ID		220	.073		5.25	4.27		9.52	12.35
0330	4-1/4" ID		215	.074		5.55	4.37		9.92	12.80
0340	4-1/2" ID		210	.076		5.85	4.47		10.32	13.30
0350	5" ID		200	.080		6.50	4.70		11.20	14.35
0360	5-1/2" ID		190	.084		7.10	4.95		12.05	15.35
0370	6" ID		180	.089		7.70	5.20		12.90	16.45
0380	6-1/2" ID		175	.091		8.30	5.35		13.65	17.35
0390	7" ID		170	.094		8.95	5.55		14.50	18.25
0400	7-1/2" ID		164	.098		9.50	5.75		15.25	19.20
0410	8" ID		161	.099		10.10	5.85		15.95	20
0420	8-1/2" ID		158	.101		10.75	5.95		16.70	21
0430	9" ID		155	.103		11.35	6.05		17.40	22
0440	9-1/2" ID		152	.105		11.95	6.20		18.15	22.50
0450	10" ID		149	.107		12.55	6.30		18.85	23.50
0460	10-1/2" ID		146	.110		13.20	6.45		19.65	24.50
0470	11" ID		143	.112		13.80	6.55		20.35	25
0480	12" ID		137	.117		15	6.85		21.85	27
0490	13" ID		132	.121		16.20	7.10		23.30	29
0500	14" ID		130	.123		17.40	7.25		24.65	30
0700	For smooth .016" thick, add					45%	33%			
1000	Stainless steel, Type 316, fitting covers									
1010	Size is based on OD of insulation									
1020	90° LR elbow, 2 piece									
1100	1-1/2"	Q-14	126	.127	Ea.	14.30	7.45		21.75	27
1110	2-3/4"		123	.130		14.95	7.65		22.60	28
1120	3"		120	.133		15.60	7.85		23.45	29
1130	3-1/4"		117	.137		15.60	8.05		23.65	29.50
1140	3-1/2"		115	.139		16.40	8.15		24.55	30.50
1150	3-3/4"		113	.142		17.35	8.30		25.65	32
1160	4"		110	.145		19.05	8.55		27.60	34
1170	4-1/4"		108	.148		25.50	8.70		34.20	41.50
1180	4-1/2"		106	.151		25.50	8.85		34.35	41.50
1190	5"		102	.157		26	9.20		35.20	42.50
1200	5-1/2"		97	.165		38.50	9.70		48.20	57.50
1210	6"		92	.174		42.50	10.20		52.70	62
1220	6-1/2"		87	.184		58.50	10.80		69.30	80.50

For customer support on your Plumbing Costs with RSMeans data, call 800.448.8182.

22 07 Plumbing Insulation

22 07 19 – Plumbing Piping Insulation

22 07 19.50 Pipe Insulation Protective Jacketing, St. Stl.

		Crew	Daily Output	Labor-Hours	Unit	Material	2023 Bare Costs Labor	2023 Bare Costs Equipment	Total	Total Incl O&P
1230	7"	Q-14	85	.188	Ea.	58.50	11.05		69.55	81
1240	7-1/2"		83	.193		68	11.30		79.30	92.50
1250	8"		80	.200		68	11.75		79.75	93
1260	8-1/2"		80	.200		70.50	11.75		82.25	95.50
1270	9"		78	.205		107	12.05		119.05	136
1280	9-1/2"		77	.208		105	12.20		117.20	135
1290	10"		76	.211		105	12.35		117.35	135
1300	10-1/2"		75	.213		126	12.55		138.55	158
1310	11"		74	.216		120	12.70		132.70	151
1320	12"		71	.225		136	13.25		149.25	170
1330	13"		68	.235		189	13.80		202.80	229
1340	14"		66	.242		190	14.25		204.25	231
2000	45° elbow, 2 piece									
2010	2-1/2"	Q-14	126	.127	Ea.	12.45	7.45		19.90	25
2020	2-3/4"		123	.130		12.45	7.65		20.10	25.50
2030	3"		120	.133		13.35	7.85		21.20	26.50
2040	3-1/4"		117	.137		13.35	8.05		21.40	27
2050	3-1/2"		115	.139		13.55	8.15		21.70	27.50
2060	3-3/4"		113	.142		13.55	8.30		21.85	27.50
2070	4"		110	.145		17.40	8.55		25.95	32
2080	4-1/4"		108	.148		24.50	8.70		33.20	40.50
2090	4-1/2"		106	.151		24.50	8.85		33.35	40.50
2100	4-3/4"		104	.154		24.50	9.05		33.55	41
2110	5"		102	.157		25	9.20		34.20	41.50
2120	5-1/2"		97	.165		25	9.70		34.70	42.50
2130	6"		92	.174		29.50	10.20		39.70	48
2140	6-1/2"		87	.184		29.50	10.80		40.30	49
2150	7"		85	.188		50	11.05		61.05	72
2160	7-1/2"		83	.193		51	11.30		62.30	73.50
2170	8"		82	.195		51	11.45		62.45	73.50
2180	8-1/2"		80	.200		59.50	11.75		71.25	83.50
2190	9"		78	.205		59.50	12.05		71.55	84
2200	9-1/2"		77	.208		70	12.20		82.20	95.50
2210	10"		76	.211		70	12.35		82.35	96
2220	10-1/2"		75	.213		84	12.55		96.55	112
2230	11"		74	.216		84	12.70		96.70	112
2240	12"		71	.225		91.50	13.25		104.75	121
2250	13"		68	.235		108	13.80		121.80	139

22 11 Facility Water Distribution

22 11 13 – Facility Water Distribution Piping

22 11 13.14 Pipe, Brass

		Crew	Daily Output	Labor-Hours	Unit	Material	2023 Bare Costs Labor	2023 Bare Costs Equipment	Total	Total Incl O&P
0010	**PIPE, BRASS**, Plain end									
0900	Field threaded, coupling & clevis hanger assembly 10' OC									
0920	Regular weight									
1120	1/2" diameter	1 Plum	48	.167	L.F.	12.70	12		24.70	32
1140	3/4" diameter		46	.174		14.60	12.55		27.15	35
1160	1" diameter		43	.186		8	13.40		21.40	29
1180	1-1/4" diameter	Q-1	72	.222		24.50	14.40		38.90	48.50
1200	1-1/2" diameter		65	.246		32	15.95		47.95	59
1220	2" diameter		53	.302		39.50	19.60		59.10	72.50

22 11 Facility Water Distribution

22 11 13 – Facility Water Distribution Piping

22 11 13.14 Pipe, Brass

		Crew	Daily Output	Labor-Hours	Unit	Material	2023 Bare Costs Labor	Equipment	Total	Total Incl O&P
1240	2-1/2" diameter	Q-1	41	.390	L.F.	61.50	25.50		87	105
1260	3" diameter	▼	31	.516		64	33.50		97.50	121
1300	4" diameter	Q-2	37	.649	▼	198	43.50		241.50	283
1930	To delete coupling & hanger, subtract									
1940	1/2" diam.					40%	46%			
1950	3/4" diam. to 1-1/2" diam.					39%	39%			
1960	2" diam. to 4" diam.					48%	35%			

22 11 13.16 Pipe Fittings, Brass

		Crew	Daily Output	Labor-Hours	Unit	Material	2023 Bare Costs Labor	Equipment	Total	Total Incl O&P
0010	**PIPE FITTINGS, BRASS**, Rough bronze, threaded, lead free.									
1000	Standard wt., 90° elbow									
1040	1/8"	1 Plum	13	.615	Ea.	37	44.50		81.50	107
1060	1/4"		13	.615		37	44.50		81.50	107
1080	3/8"		13	.615		37	44.50		81.50	107
1100	1/2"		12	.667		37	48		85	112
1120	3/4"		11	.727		49.50	52.50		102	133
1140	1"	▼	10	.800		80.50	57.50		138	175
1160	1-1/4"	Q-1	17	.941		130	61		191	234
1180	1-1/2"		16	1		189	65		254	305
1200	2"		14	1.143		282	74		356	420
1220	2-1/2"		11	1.455		625	94.50		719.50	830
1240	3"	▼	8	2		955	130		1,085	1,250
1260	4"	Q-2	11	2.182		1,950	147		2,097	2,350
1280	5"		8	3		4,225	202		4,427	4,950
1300	6"	▼	7	3.429		7,900	231		8,131	9,050
1500	45° elbow, 1/8"	1 Plum	13	.615		45.50	44.50		90	116
1540	1/4"		13	.615		45.50	44.50		90	116
1560	3/8"		13	.615		45.50	44.50		90	116
1580	1/2"		12	.667		45.50	48		93.50	122
1600	3/4"		11	.727		64.50	52.50		117	149
1620	1"	▼	10	.800		110	57.50		167.50	207
1640	1-1/4"	Q-1	17	.941		174	61		235	283
1660	1-1/2"		16	1		220	65		285	340
1680	2"		14	1.143		355	74		429	500
1700	2-1/2"		11	1.455		680	94.50		774.50	885
1720	3"	▼	8	2		830	130		960	1,100
1740	4"	Q-2	11	2.182		1,850	147		1,997	2,250
1760	5"		8	3		3,450	202		3,652	4,100
1780	6"	▼	7	3.429		4,775	231		5,006	5,600
2000	Tee, 1/8"	1 Plum	9	.889		43.50	64		107.50	143
2040	1/4"		9	.889		43.50	64		107.50	143
2060	3/8"		9	.889		52	64		116	153
2080	1/2"		8	1		45	72		117	157
2100	3/4"		7	1.143		61.50	82.50		144	191
2120	1"	▼	6	1.333		128	96		224	284
2140	1-1/4"	Q-1	10	1.600		191	104		295	365
2160	1-1/2"		9	1.778		216	115		331	410
2180	2"		8	2		360	130		490	590
2200	2-1/2"		7	2.286		855	148		1,003	1,150
2220	3"	▼	5	3.200		1,300	208		1,508	1,725
2240	4"	Q-2	7	3.429		3,225	231		3,456	3,900
2260	5"		5	4.800		5,075	325		5,400	6,050
2280	6"	▼	4	6		8,350	405		8,755	9,775

22 11 Facility Water Distribution

22 11 13 – Facility Water Distribution Piping

22 11 13.16 Pipe Fittings, Brass		Crew	Daily Output	Labor-Hours	Unit	Material	2023 Bare Costs Labor	Equipment	Total	Total Incl O&P
2500	Coupling, 1/8"	1 Plum	26	.308	Ea.	31	22		53	67
2540	1/4"		22	.364		31	26		57	73
2560	3/8"		18	.444		31	32		63	82
2580	1/2"		15	.533		31	38.50		69.50	91.50
2600	3/4"		14	.571		43.50	41		84.50	109
2620	1"		13	.615		74	44.50		118.50	148
2640	1-1/4"	Q-1	22	.727		123	47		170	207
2660	1-1/2"		20	.800		161	52		213	255
2680	2"		18	.889		265	57.50		322.50	380
2700	2-1/2"		14	1.143		450	74		524	605
2720	3"		10	1.600		625	104		729	845
2740	4"	Q-2	12	2		1,300	135		1,435	1,625
2760	5"		10	2.400		2,375	161		2,536	2,850
2780	6"		9	2.667		3,400	179		3,579	4,025
3000	Union, 125 lb.									
3020	1/8"	1 Plum	12	.667	Ea.	50.50	48		98.50	127
3040	1/4"		12	.667		61.50	48		109.50	139
3060	3/8"		12	.667		61.50	48		109.50	139
3080	1/2"		11	.727		61.50	52.50		114	146
3100	3/4"		10	.800		84.50	57.50		142	179
3120	1"		9	.889		127	64		191	236
3140	1-1/4"	Q-1	16	1		184	65		249	300
3160	1-1/2"		15	1.067		220	69		289	345
3180	2"		13	1.231		296	80		376	445
3200	2-1/2"		10	1.600		1,100	104		1,204	1,350
3220	3"		7	2.286		1,375	148		1,523	1,750
3240	4"	Q-2	10	2.400		4,100	161		4,261	4,750

22 11 13.23 Pipe/Tube, Copper

			Crew	Daily Output	Labor-Hours	Unit	Material	2023 Bare Costs Labor	Equipment	Total	Total Incl O&P
0010	**PIPE/TUBE, COPPER**, Solder joints	R221113-50									
0100	Solder										
0120	Solder, lead free, roll					Lb.	45			45	49.50
1000	Type K tubing, couplings & clevis hanger assemblies 10' OC										
1100	1/4" diameter	R221113-70	1 Plum	84	.095	L.F.	7.10	6.85		13.95	18.10
1120	3/8" diameter			82	.098		5.15	7.05		12.20	16.20
1140	1/2" diameter			78	.103		5.45	7.40		12.85	17
1160	5/8" diameter			77	.104		8.10	7.50		15.60	20
1180	3/4" diameter			74	.108		7.75	7.80		15.55	20
1200	1" diameter			66	.121		7.65	8.75		16.40	21.50
1220	1-1/4" diameter			56	.143		10.10	10.30		20.40	26.50
1240	1-1/2" diameter			50	.160		13.05	11.55		24.60	31.50
1260	2" diameter			40	.200		20	14.40		34.40	43.50
1280	2-1/2" diameter		Q-1	60	.267		57.50	17.30		74.80	89.50
1300	3" diameter			54	.296		45	19.20		64.20	78
1320	3-1/2" diameter			42	.381		66.50	24.50		91	110
1330	4" diameter			38	.421		85	27.50		112.50	134
1340	5" diameter			32	.500		158	32.50		190.50	222
1360	6" diameter		Q-2	38	.632		246	42.50		288.50	335
1380	8" diameter		"	34	.706		365	47.50		412.50	470
1390	For other than full hard temper, add						13%				
1440	For silver solder, add							15%			
1800	For medical clean (oxygen class), add						12%				
1950	To delete cplgs. & hngrs., 1/4"-1" pipe, subtract						27%	60%			

22 11 Facility Water Distribution

22 11 13 – Facility Water Distribution Piping

22 11 13.23 Pipe/Tube, Copper		Crew	Daily Output	Labor-Hours	Unit	Material	2023 Bare Costs Labor	Equipment	Total	Total Incl O&P
1960	1-1/4"-3" pipe, subtract					14%	52%			
1970	3-1/2"-5" pipe, subtract					10%	60%			
1980	6"-8" pipe, subtract					19%	53%			
2000	Type L tubing, couplings & clevis hanger assemblies 10' OC									
2100	1/4" diameter	1 Plum	88	.091	L.F.	4.02	6.55		10.57	14.15
2120	3/8" diameter		84	.095		4.59	6.85		11.44	15.30
2140	1/2" diameter		81	.099		4.92	7.10		12.02	16
2160	5/8" diameter		79	.101		6.15	7.30		13.45	17.70
2180	3/4" diameter		76	.105		6.40	7.60		14	18.35
2200	1" diameter		68	.118		6.25	8.50		14.75	19.55
2220	1-1/4" diameter		58	.138		8.85	9.95		18.80	24.50
2240	1-1/2" diameter		52	.154		11.40	11.10		22.50	29
2260	2" diameter	▼	42	.190		24	13.70		37.70	47
2280	2-1/2" diameter	Q-1	62	.258		29	16.75		45.75	57
2300	3" diameter		56	.286		40	18.55		58.55	71.50
2320	3-1/2" diameter		43	.372		60.50	24		84.50	103
2340	4" diameter		39	.410		75	26.50		101.50	122
2360	5" diameter	▼	34	.471		136	30.50		166.50	196
2380	6" diameter	Q-2	40	.600		206	40.50		246.50	287
2400	8" diameter	"	36	.667		292	45		337	385
2410	For other than full hard temper, add				▼	21%				
2590	For silver solder, add						15%			
2900	For medical clean (oxygen class), add					12%				
2940	To delete cplgs. & hngrs., 1/4"-1" pipe, subtract					37%	63%			
2960	1-1/4"-3" pipe, subtract					12%	53%			
2970	3-1/2"-5" pipe, subtract					12%	63%			
2980	6"-8" pipe, subtract					24%	55%			
3000	Type M tubing, couplings & clevis hanger assemblies 10' OC									
3100	1/4" diameter	1 Plum	90	.089	L.F.	5.40	6.40		11.80	15.45
3120	3/8" diameter		87	.092		5.95	6.65		12.60	16.45
3140	1/2" diameter		84	.095		4.42	6.85		11.27	15.10
3160	5/8" diameter		81	.099		4.60	7.10		11.70	15.65
3180	3/4" diameter		78	.103		5.55	7.40		12.95	17.15
3200	1" diameter		70	.114		5.25	8.25		13.50	18.10
3220	1-1/4" diameter		60	.133		7.90	9.60		17.50	23
3240	1-1/2" diameter		54	.148		10.60	10.65		21.25	27.50
3260	2" diameter	▼	44	.182		16.60	13.10		29.70	38
3280	2-1/2" diameter	Q-1	64	.250		27	16.20		43.20	54
3300	3" diameter		58	.276		36.50	17.90		54.40	66.50
3320	3-1/2" diameter		45	.356		57	23		80	97
3340	4" diameter		40	.400		72	26		98	118
3360	5" diameter	▼	36	.444		137	29		166	194
3370	6" diameter	Q-2	42	.571		208	38.50		246.50	286
3380	8" diameter	"	38	.632	▼	293	42.50		335.50	390
3440	For silver solder, add						15%			
3960	To delete cplgs. & hngrs., 1/4"-1" pipe, subtract					35%	65%			
3970	1-1/4"-3" pipe, subtract					19%	56%			
3980	3-1/2"-5" pipe, subtract					13%	65%			
3990	6"-8" pipe, subtract					28%	58%			
4000	Type DWV tubing, couplings & clevis hanger assemblies 10' OC									
4100	1-1/4" diameter	1 Plum	60	.133	L.F.	9.45	9.60		19.05	25
4120	1-1/2" diameter		54	.148		11.90	10.65		22.55	29
4140	2" diameter	▼	44	.182	▼	16.80	13.10		29.90	38

22 11 Facility Water Distribution

22 11 13 – Facility Water Distribution Piping

22 11 13.23 Pipe/Tube, Copper		Crew	Daily Output	Labor-Hours	Unit	Material	2023 Bare Costs Labor	Equipment	Total	Total Incl O&P
4160	3" diameter	Q-1	58	.276	L.F.	35	17.90		52.90	65
4180	4" diameter		40	.400		92.50	26		118.50	141
4200	5" diameter		36	.444		161	29		190	220
4220	6" diameter	Q-2	42	.571		245	38.50		283.50	330
4240	8" diameter	"	38	.632		785	42.50		827.50	925
4730	To delete cplgs. & hngrs., 1-1/4"-2" pipe, subtract					16%	53%			
4740	3"-4" pipe, subtract					13%	60%			
4750	5"-8" pipe, subtract					23%	58%			
5200	ACR tubing, type L, hard temper, cleaned and									
5220	capped, no couplings or hangers									
5240	3/8" OD				L.F.	.90			.90	.99
5250	1/2" OD					1.36			1.36	1.50
5260	5/8" OD					1.75			1.75	1.93
5270	3/4" OD					2.35			2.35	2.59
5280	7/8" OD					2.80			2.80	3.08
5290	1-1/8" OD					4.02			4.02	4.42
5300	1-3/8" OD					5.30			5.30	5.85
5310	1-5/8" OD					6.90			6.90	7.60
5320	2-1/8" OD					10.50			10.50	11.55
5330	2-5/8" OD					15.10			15.10	16.60
5340	3-1/8" OD					20.50			20.50	22.50
5350	3-5/8" OD					41.50			41.50	46
5360	4-1/8" OD					36			36	40
5380	ACR tubing, type L, hard, cleaned and capped									
5381	No couplings or hangers									
5384	3/8"	1 Stpi	160	.050	L.F.	.90	3.63		4.53	6.40
5385	1/2"		160	.050		1.36	3.63		4.99	6.90
5386	5/8"		160	.050		1.75	3.63		5.38	7.35
5387	3/4"		130	.062		2.35	4.46		6.81	9.25
5388	7/8"		130	.062		2.80	4.46		7.26	9.75
5389	1-1/8"		115	.070		4.02	5.05		9.07	11.95
5390	1-3/8"		100	.080		5.30	5.80		11.10	14.50
5391	1-5/8"		90	.089		6.90	6.45		13.35	17.20
5392	2-1/8"		80	.100		10.50	7.25		17.75	22.50
5393	2-5/8"	Q-5	125	.128		15.10	8.35		23.45	29
5394	3-1/8"		105	.152		20.50	9.95		30.45	37.50
5395	4-1/8"		95	.168		36	11		47	56.50
5800	Refrigeration tubing, dryseal, 50' coils									
5840	1/8" OD				Coil	21.50			21.50	24
5850	3/16" OD					52.50			52.50	57.50
5860	1/4" OD					29			29	32
5870	5/16" OD					88			88	97
5880	3/8" OD					41			41	45
5890	1/2" OD					58.50			58.50	64.50
5900	5/8" OD					78			78	86
5910	3/4" OD					93.50			93.50	103
5920	7/8" OD					139			139	152
5930	1-1/8" OD					202			202	222
5940	1-3/8" OD					350			350	385
5950	1-5/8" OD					440			440	485

22 11 Facility Water Distribution

22 11 13 – Facility Water Distribution Piping

22 11 13.25 Pipe/Tube Fittings, Copper		Crew	Daily Output	Labor-Hours	Unit	Material	2023 Bare Costs Labor	Equipment	Total	Total Incl O&P
0010	**PIPE/TUBE FITTINGS, COPPER**, Wrought unless otherwise noted									
0020	For silver solder, add						15%			
0040	Solder joints, copper x copper									
0070	90° elbow, 1/4"	1 Plum	22	.364	Ea.	8.50	26		34.50	48.50
0090	3/8"		22	.364		8.20	26		34.20	48
0100	1/2"		20	.400		2.95	29		31.95	46.50
0110	5/8"		19	.421		4.65	30.50		35.15	50
0120	3/4"		19	.421		6.50	30.50		37	52
0130	1"		16	.500		16	36		52	71
0140	1-1/4"		15	.533		23.50	38.50		62	83.50
0150	1-1/2"		13	.615		37	44.50		81.50	107
0160	2"		11	.727		66	52.50		118.50	151
0170	2-1/2"	Q-1	13	1.231		121	80		201	252
0180	3"		11	1.455		174	94.50		268.50	335
0190	3-1/2"		10	1.600		585	104		689	800
0200	4"		9	1.778		375	115		490	585
0210	5"		6	2.667		1,625	173		1,798	2,050
0220	6"	Q-2	9	2.667		2,000	179		2,179	2,475
0230	8"	"	8	3		8,000	202		8,202	9,100
0250	45° elbow, 1/4"	1 Plum	22	.364		15.05	26		41.05	55.50
0270	3/8"		22	.364		12.95	26		38.95	53.50
0280	1/2"		20	.400		2.03	29		31.03	45
0290	5/8"		19	.421		22.50	30.50		53	70
0300	3/4"		19	.421		9.05	30.50		39.55	55
0310	1"		16	.500		23	36		59	78.50
0320	1-1/4"		15	.533		30.50	38.50		69	91
0330	1-1/2"		13	.615		37.50	44.50		82	107
0340	2"		11	.727		62.50	52.50		115	147
0350	2-1/2"	Q-1	13	1.231		121	80		201	252
0360	3"		13	1.231		170	80		250	305
0370	3-1/2"		10	1.600		315	104		419	500
0380	4"		9	1.778		345	115		460	550
0390	5"		6	2.667		1,375	173		1,548	1,750
0400	6"	Q-2	9	2.667		2,000	179		2,179	2,475
0410	8"	"	8	3		9,450	202		9,652	10,700
0450	Tee, 1/4"	1 Plum	14	.571		16.90	41		57.90	80
0470	3/8"		14	.571		13.55	41		54.55	76.50
0480	1/2"		13	.615		1.89	44.50		46.39	68
0490	5/8"		12	.667		31	48		79	106
0500	3/4"		12	.667		11.95	48		59.95	84.50
0510	1"		10	.800		14.05	57.50		71.55	101
0520	1-1/4"		9	.889		49.50	64		113.50	150
0530	1-1/2"		8	1		74.50	72		146.50	189
0540	2"		7	1.143		118	82.50		200.50	253
0550	2-1/2"	Q-1	8	2		217	130		347	430
0560	3"		7	2.286		315	148		463	565
0570	3-1/2"		6	2.667		990	173		1,163	1,325
0580	4"		5	3.200		735	208		943	1,125
0590	5"		4	4		2,450	259		2,709	3,050
0600	6"	Q-2	6	4		3,325	269		3,594	4,075
0610	8"	"	5	4.800		12,900	325		13,225	14,700
0612	Tee, reducing on the outlet, 1/4"	1 Plum	15	.533		51	38.50		89.50	114

22 11 Facility Water Distribution

22 11 13 – Facility Water Distribution Piping

22 11 13.25 Pipe/Tube Fittings, Copper		Crew	Daily Output	Labor-Hours	Unit	Material	2023 Bare Costs Labor	Equipment	Total	Total Incl O&P
0613	3/8"	1 Plum	15	.533	Ea.	43.50	38.50		82	105
0614	1/2"		14	.571		40	41		81	106
0615	5/8"		13	.615		81	44.50		125.50	155
0616	3/4"		12	.667		18.45	48		66.45	92
0617	1"		11	.727		87.50	52.50		140	175
0618	1-1/4"		10	.800		86.50	57.50		144	181
0619	1-1/2"		9	.889		92	64		156	197
0620	2"		8	1		150	72		222	272
0621	2-1/2"	Q-1	9	1.778		415	115		530	625
0622	3"		8	2		470	130		600	710
0623	4"		6	2.667		845	173		1,018	1,200
0624	5"		5	3.200		3,650	208		3,858	4,300
0625	6"	Q-2	7	3.429		6,425	231		6,656	7,400
0626	8"	"	6	4		24,800	269		25,069	27,600
0630	Tee, reducing on the run, 1/4"	1 Plum	15	.533		58	38.50		96.50	121
0631	3/8"		15	.533		65.50	38.50		104	130
0632	1/2"		14	.571		55	41		96	122
0633	5/8"		13	.615		22.50	44.50		67	91
0634	3/4"		12	.667		44.50	48		92.50	121
0635	1"		11	.727		70.50	52.50		123	156
0636	1-1/4"		10	.800		114	57.50		171.50	211
0637	1-1/2"		9	.889		196	64		260	310
0638	2"		8	1		250	72		322	385
0639	2-1/2"	Q-1	9	1.778		535	115		650	760
0640	3"		8	2		740	130		870	1,000
0641	4"		6	2.667		1,600	173		1,773	2,000
0642	5"		5	3.200		4,450	208		4,658	5,200
0643	6"	Q-2	7	3.429		6,775	231		7,006	7,800
0644	8"	"	6	4		17,200	269		17,469	19,400
0650	Coupling, 1/4"	1 Plum	24	.333		3.29	24		27.29	39.50
0670	3/8"		24	.333		4.29	24		28.29	40.50
0680	1/2"		22	.364		3.54	26		29.54	43
0690	5/8"		21	.381		9.35	27.50		36.85	51.50
0700	3/4"		21	.381		7.10	27.50		34.60	49
0710	1"		18	.444		14.20	32		46.20	63.50
0715	1-1/4"		17	.471		25	34		59	78
0716	1-1/2"		15	.533		33	38.50		71.50	93.50
0718	2"		13	.615		55	44.50		99.50	127
0721	2-1/2"	Q-1	15	1.067		112	69		181	227
0722	3"		13	1.231		153	80		233	287
0724	3-1/2"		8	2		287	130		417	510
0726	4"		7	2.286		335	148		483	590
0728	5"		6	2.667		700	173		873	1,025
0731	6"	Q-2	8	3		1,175	202		1,377	1,575
0732	8"	"	7	3.429		3,775	231		4,006	4,500
0741	Coupling, reducing, concentric									
0743	1/2"	1 Plum	23	.348	Ea.	8.20	25		33.20	46.50
0745	3/4"		21.50	.372		12.40	27		39.40	53.50
0747	1"		19.50	.410		19.40	29.50		48.90	65.50
0748	1-1/4"		18	.444		35.50	32		67.50	87
0749	1-1/2"		16	.500		45	36		81	103
0751	2"		14	.571		85	41		126	155
0752	2-1/2"		13	.615		157	44.50		201.50	239

22 11 Facility Water Distribution

22 11 13 – Facility Water Distribution Piping

22 11 13.25 Pipe/Tube Fittings, Copper

		Crew	Daily Output	Labor-Hours	Unit	Material	2023 Bare Costs Labor	Equipment	Total	Total Incl O&P
0753	3"	Q-1	14	1.143	Ea.	190	74		264	320
0755	4"	"	8	2		385	130		515	620
0757	5"	Q-2	7.50	3.200		2,100	215		2,315	2,625
0759	6"		7	3.429		3,350	231		3,581	4,025
0761	8"	↓	6.50	3.692	↓	8,900	248		9,148	10,200
0771	Cap, sweat									
0773	1/2"	1 Plum	40	.200	Ea.	3.45	14.40		17.85	25.50
0775	3/4"		38	.211		6.40	15.15		21.55	29.50
0777	1"		32	.250		14.95	18		32.95	43.50
0778	1-1/4"		29	.276		19.80	19.90		39.70	51.50
0779	1-1/2"		26	.308		29	22		51	65
0781	2"	↓	22	.364	↓	53.50	26		79.50	98
0791	Flange, sweat									
0793	3"	Q-1	22	.727	Ea.	725	47		772	865
0795	4"		18	.889		1,000	57.50		1,057.50	1,175
0797	5"	↓	12	1.333		1,900	86.50		1,986.50	2,200
0799	6"	Q-2	18	1.333		1,975	89.50		2,064.50	2,300
0801	8"	"	16	1.500		3,775	101		3,876	4,300
0850	Unions, 1/4"	1 Plum	21	.381		109	27.50		136.50	161
0870	3/8"		21	.381		110	27.50		137.50	162
0880	1/2"		19	.421		64.50	30.50		95	116
0890	5/8"		18	.444		250	32		282	325
0900	3/4"		18	.444		80.50	32		112.50	137
0910	1"		15	.533		126	38.50		164.50	197
0920	1-1/4"		14	.571		207	41		248	290
0930	1-1/2"		12	.667		273	48		321	370
0940	2"		10	.800		465	57.50		522.50	595
0950	2-1/2"	Q-1	12	1.333		1,025	86.50		1,111.50	1,250
0960	3"	"	10	1.600		2,650	104		2,754	3,050
0980	Adapter, copper x male IPS, 1/4"	1 Plum	20	.400		46	29		75	93.50
0990	3/8"		20	.400		23	29		52	68
1000	1/2"		18	.444		9.85	32		41.85	59
1010	3/4"		17	.471		16.50	34		50.50	68.50
1020	1"		15	.533		42	38.50		80.50	104
1030	1-1/4"		13	.615		60.50	44.50		105	133
1040	1-1/2"		12	.667		71	48		119	150
1050	2"	↓	11	.727		120	52.50		172.50	210
1060	2-1/2"	Q-1	10.50	1.524		420	99		519	605
1070	3"		10	1.600		525	104		629	730
1080	3-1/2"		9	1.778		360	115		475	565
1090	4"		8	2		685	130		815	945
1200	5", cast		6	2.667		3,000	173		3,173	3,550
1210	6", cast	Q-2	8.50	2.824	↓	3,400	190		3,590	4,000
1214	Adapter, copper x female IPS									
1216	1/2"	1 Plum	18	.444	Ea.	15.65	32		47.65	65
1218	3/4"		17	.471		21.50	34		55.50	74
1220	1"		15	.533		49	38.50		87.50	112
1221	1-1/4"		13	.615		71	44.50		115.50	144
1222	1-1/2"		12	.667		111	48		159	194
1224	2"		11	.727		151	52.50		203.50	244
1250	Cross, 1/2"		10	.800		75	57.50		132.50	169
1260	3/4"		9.50	.842		146	60.50		206.50	251
1270	1"	↓	8	1	↓	248	72		320	380

22 11 Facility Water Distribution

22 11 13 − Facility Water Distribution Piping

22 11 13.25 Pipe/Tube Fittings, Copper		Crew	Daily Output	Labor-Hours	Unit	Material	2023 Bare Costs Labor	Equipment	Total	Total Incl O&P
1280	1-1/4"	1 Plum	7.50	1.067	Ea.	355	77		432	505
1290	1-1/2"		6.50	1.231		505	88.50		593.50	690
1300	2"	▼	5.50	1.455		960	105		1,065	1,200
1310	2-1/2"	Q-1	6.50	2.462		2,225	160		2,385	2,675
1320	3"	"	5.50	2.909	▼	1,225	189		1,414	1,625
1500	Tee fitting, mechanically formed (Type 1, 'branch sizes up to 2 in.')									
1520	1/2" run size, 3/8" to 1/2" branch size	1 Plum	80	.100	Ea.		7.20		7.20	10.75
1530	3/4" run size, 3/8" to 3/4" branch size		60	.133			9.60		9.60	14.35
1540	1" run size, 3/8" to 1" branch size		54	.148			10.65		10.65	15.90
1550	1-1/4" run size, 3/8" to 1-1/4" branch size		48	.167			12		12	17.90
1560	1-1/2" run size, 3/8" to 1-1/2" branch size		40	.200			14.40		14.40	21.50
1570	2" run size, 3/8" to 2" branch size		35	.229			16.45		16.45	24.50
1580	2-1/2" run size, 1/2" to 2" branch size		32	.250			18		18	27
1590	3" run size, 1" to 2" branch size		26	.308			22		22	33
1600	4" run size, 1" to 2" branch size	▼	24	.333	▼		24		24	36
1640	Tee fitting, mechanically formed (Type 2, branches 2-1/2" thru 4")									
1650	2-1/2" run size, 2-1/2" branch size	1 Plum	12.50	.640	Ea.		46		46	69
1660	3" run size, 2-1/2" to 3" branch size		12	.667			48		48	71.50
1670	3-1/2" run size, 2-1/2" to 3-1/2" branch size		11	.727			52.50		52.50	78
1680	4" run size, 2-1/2" to 4" branch size		10.50	.762			55		55	82
1698	5" run size, 2" to 4" branch size		9.50	.842			60.50		60.50	90.50
1700	6" run size, 2" to 4" branch size		8.50	.941			68		68	101
1710	8" run size, 2" to 4" branch size	▼	7	1.143	▼		82.50		82.50	123
1800	ACR fittings, OD size									
1802	Tee, straight									
1808	5/8"	1 Stpi	12	.667	Ea.	2.08	48.50		50.58	74.50
1810	3/4"		12	.667		12.95	48.50		61.45	86
1812	7/8"		10	.800		5	58		63	92
1813	1"		10	.800		138	58		196	238
1814	1-1/8"		10	.800		58	58		116	151
1816	1-3/8"		9	.889		20.50	64.50		85	119
1818	1-5/8"		8	1		89.50	72.50		162	207
1820	2-1/8"	▼	7	1.143		49.50	83		132.50	179
1822	2-5/8"	Q-5	8	2		91.50	131		222.50	295
1824	3-1/8"		7	2.286		131	149		280	370
1826	4-1/8"	▼	5	3.200	▼	305	209		514	650
1830	90° elbow									
1836	5/8"	1 Stpi	19	.421	Ea.	17.10	30.50		47.60	64.50
1838	3/4"		19	.421		2.27	30.50		32.77	48
1840	7/8"		16	.500		12.45	36.50		48.95	67.50
1842	1-1/8"		16	.500		8.35	36.50		44.85	63
1844	1-3/8"		15	.533		44.50	38.50		83	106
1846	1-5/8"		13	.615		37.50	44.50		82	108
1848	2-1/8"	▼	11	.727		28	53		81	110
1850	2-5/8"	Q-5	13	1.231		51.50	80.50		132	177
1852	3-1/8"		11	1.455		73	95		168	222
1854	4-1/8"	▼	9	1.778	▼	160	116		276	350
1860	Coupling									
1866	5/8"	1 Stpi	21	.381	Ea.	.91	27.50		28.41	42
1868	3/4"		21	.381		2.41	27.50		29.91	43.50
1870	7/8"		18	.444		1.84	32		33.84	50
1871	1"		18	.444		24.50	32		56.50	75
1872	1-1/8"		18	.444		3.66	32		35.66	52

22 11 Facility Water Distribution

22 11 13 – Facility Water Distribution Piping

22 11 13.25 Pipe/Tube Fittings, Copper		Crew	Daily Output	Labor-Hours	Unit	Material	2023 Bare Costs Labor	Equipment	Total	Total Incl O&P
1874	1-3/8"	1 Stpi	17	.471	Ea.	6.40	34		40.40	58
1876	1-5/8"		15	.533		8.45	38.50		46.95	67
1878	2-1/8"	↓	13	.615		14.15	44.50		58.65	82
1880	2-5/8"	Q-5	15	1.067		29	69.50		98.50	136
1882	3-1/8"		13	1.231		39.50	80.50		120	164
1884	4-1/8"	↓	7	2.286	↓	250	149		399	500
2000	DWV, solder joints, copper x copper									
2030	90° elbow, 1-1/4"	1 Plum	13	.615	Ea.	50	44.50		94.50	121
2050	1-1/2"		12	.667		66.50	48		114.50	145
2070	2"	↓	10	.800		107	57.50		164.50	203
2090	3"	Q-1	10	1.600		258	104		362	440
2100	4"	"	9	1.778		1,250	115		1,365	1,550
2150	45° elbow, 1-1/4"	1 Plum	13	.615		41	44.50		85.50	111
2170	1-1/2"		12	.667		38.50	48		86.50	114
2180	2"	↓	10	.800		78	57.50		135.50	172
2190	3"	Q-1	10	1.600		175	104		279	350
2200	4"	"	9	1.778		158	115		273	345
2250	Tee, sanitary, 1-1/4"	1 Plum	9	.889		88	64		152	193
2270	1-1/2"		8	1		109	72		181	227
2290	2"	↓	7	1.143		150	82.50		232.50	288
2310	3"	Q-1	7	2.286		630	148		778	915
2330	4"	"	6	2.667		1,400	173		1,573	1,775
2400	Coupling, 1-1/4"	1 Plum	14	.571		21	41		62	84.50
2420	1-1/2"		13	.615		26	44.50		70.50	94.50
2440	2"	↓	11	.727		36	52.50		88.50	118
2460	3"	Q-1	11	1.455		83.50	94.50		178	233
2480	4"	"	10	1.600	↓	184	104		288	355
2602	Traps, see Section 22 13 16.60									
3500	Compression joint fittings									
3510	As used for plumbing and oil burner work									
3520	Fitting price includes nuts and sleeves									
3540	Sleeve, 1/8"				Ea.	.33			.33	.36
3550	3/16"					.33			.33	.36
3560	1/4"					.07			.07	.08
3570	5/16"					.19			.19	.21
3580	3/8"					.68			.68	.75
3600	1/2"					.90			.90	.99
3620	Nut, 1/8"					.29			.29	.32
3630	3/16"					.51			.51	.56
3640	1/4"					.50			.50	.55
3650	5/16"					.50			.50	.55
3660	3/8"					.81			.81	.89
3670	1/2"					1.41			1.41	1.55
3710	Union, 1/8"	1 Plum	26	.308		2.02	22		24.02	35
3720	3/16"		24	.333		1.92	24		25.92	38
3730	1/4"		24	.333		3.88	24		27.88	40.50
3740	5/16"		23	.348		4.52	25		29.52	42.50
3750	3/8"		22	.364		2.75	26		28.75	42
3760	1/2"		22	.364		7.70	26		33.70	47.50
3780	5/8"		21	.381		4.69	27.50		32.19	46
3820	Union tee, 1/8"		17	.471		7.65	34		41.65	59
3830	3/16"		16	.500		4.40	36		40.40	58.50
3840	1/4"	↓	15	.533		7.70	38.50		46.20	66

22 11 Facility Water Distribution

22 11 13 – Facility Water Distribution Piping

22 11 13.25 Pipe/Tube Fittings, Copper

		Crew	Daily Output	Labor-Hours	Unit	Material	2023 Bare Costs Labor	Equipment	Total	Total Incl O&P
3850	5/16"	1 Plum	15	.533	Ea.	5.60	38.50		44.10	63.50
3860	3/8"		15	.533		11.05	38.50		49.55	69.50
3870	1/2"		15	.533		16.90	38.50		55.40	76
3910	Union elbow, 1/4"		24	.333		2.61	24		26.61	39
3920	5/16"		23	.348		4	25		29	42
3930	3/8"		22	.364		8.10	26		34.10	48
3940	1/2"		22	.364		12	26		38	52
3980	Female connector, 1/8"		26	.308		1.64	22		23.64	35
4000	3/16" x 1/8"		24	.333		1.97	24		25.97	38
4010	1/4" x 1/8"		24	.333		3.07	24		27.07	39.50
4020	1/4"		24	.333		4.55	24		28.55	41
4030	3/8" x 1/4"		22	.364		4.12	26		30.12	43.50
4040	1/2" x 3/8"		22	.364		6.55	26		32.55	46
4050	5/8" x 1/2"		21	.381		9.25	27.50		36.75	51
4090	Male connector, 1/8"		26	.308		1.16	22		23.16	34.50
4100	3/16" x 1/8"		24	.333		1.29	24		25.29	37.50
4110	1/4" x 1/8"		24	.333		1.37	24		25.37	37.50
4120	1/4"		24	.333		1.37	24		25.37	37.50
4130	5/16" x 1/8"		23	.348		3.05	25		28.05	41
4140	5/16" x 1/4"		23	.348		1.79	25		26.79	39.50
4150	3/8" x 1/8"		22	.364		3.29	26		29.29	42.50
4160	3/8" x 1/4"		22	.364		4.16	26		30.16	43.50
4170	3/8"		22	.364		4.16	26		30.16	43.50
4180	3/8" x 1/2"		22	.364		5.70	26		31.70	45.50
4190	1/2" x 3/8"		22	.364		5.50	26		31.50	45
4200	1/2"		22	.364		6.20	26		32.20	46
4210	5/8" x 1/2"		21	.381		7.15	27.50		34.65	49
4240	Male elbow, 1/8"		26	.308		4.98	22		26.98	38.50
4250	3/16" x 1/8"		24	.333		2.83	24		26.83	39
4260	1/4" x 1/8"		24	.333		2.91	24		26.91	39
4270	1/4"		24	.333		3.45	24		27.45	40
4280	3/8" x 1/4"		22	.364		6	26		32	45.50
4290	3/8"		22	.364		10.30	26		36.30	50.50
4300	1/2" x 1/4"		22	.364		9.95	26		35.95	50
4310	1/2" x 3/8"		22	.364		15.65	26		41.65	56
4340	Female elbow, 1/8"		26	.308		5.55	22		27.55	39
4350	1/4" x 1/8"		24	.333		6.05	24		30.05	42.50
4360	1/4"		24	.333		7.25	24		31.25	44
4370	3/8" x 1/4"		22	.364		7.15	26		33.15	47
4380	1/2" x 3/8"		22	.364		6.95	26		32.95	46.50
4390	1/2"		22	.364		9.40	26		35.40	49.50
4420	Male run tee, 1/4" x 1/8"		15	.533		7.45	38.50		45.95	65.50
4430	5/16" x 1/8"		15	.533		7.40	38.50		45.90	65.50
4440	3/8" x 1/4"		15	.533		11.50	38.50		50	70
4480	Male branch tee, 1/4" x 1/8"		15	.533		8.60	38.50		47.10	67
4490	1/4"		15	.533		8.40	38.50		46.90	67
4500	3/8" x 1/4"		15	.533		5.60	38.50		44.10	63.50
4510	1/2" x 3/8"		15	.533		8.70	38.50		47.20	67
4520	1/2"		15	.533		13.95	38.50		52.45	73
4800	Flare joint fittings									
4810	Refrigeration fittings									
4820	Flare joint nuts and labor not incl. in price. Add 1 nut per jnt.									
4830	90° elbow, 1/4"				Ea.	3.44			3.44	3.78

22 11 Facility Water Distribution

22 11 13 – Facility Water Distribution Piping

22 11 13.25 Pipe/Tube Fittings, Copper		Crew	Daily Output	Labor-Hours	Unit	Material	2023 Bare Costs Labor	Equipment	Total	Total Incl O&P
4840	3/8"				Ea.	2.97			2.97	3.27
4850	1/2"					3.82			3.82	4.20
4860	5/8"					5.60			5.60	6.20
4870	3/4"					9.85			9.85	10.85
5030	Tee, 1/4"					4.04			4.04	4.44
5040	5/16"					5.30			5.30	5.85
5050	3/8"					4.06			4.06	4.47
5060	1/2"					7.40			7.40	8.15
5070	5/8"					7.50			7.50	8.25
5080	3/4"					9.85			9.85	10.85
5140	Union, 3/16"					2.03			2.03	2.23
5150	1/4"					1.27			1.27	1.40
5160	5/16"					1.90			1.90	2.09
5170	3/8"					1.11			1.11	1.22
5180	1/2"					1.64			1.64	1.80
5190	5/8"					3.81			3.81	4.19
5200	3/4"					15.65			15.65	17.20
5260	Long flare nut, 3/16"	1 Stpi	42	.190		.44	13.80		14.24	21
5270	1/4"		41	.195		1.42	14.15		15.57	22.50
5280	5/16"		40	.200		2.59	14.50		17.09	24.50
5290	3/8"		39	.205		2.42	14.90		17.32	24.50
5300	1/2"		38	.211		2.95	15.25		18.20	26.50
5310	5/8"		37	.216		9	15.70		24.70	33.50
5320	3/4"		34	.235		18.90	17.05		35.95	46.50
5380	Short flare nut, 3/16"		42	.190		6.25	13.80		20.05	27.50
5390	1/4"		41	.195		1	14.15		15.15	22
5400	5/16"		40	.200		1.20	14.50		15.70	23
5410	3/8"		39	.205		.68	14.90		15.58	23
5420	1/2"		38	.211		2.89	15.25		18.14	26
5430	5/8"		36	.222		3.66	16.10		19.76	28
5440	3/4"		34	.235		9.90	17.05		26.95	36.50
5500	90° elbow flare by MIPS, 1/4"					3.79			3.79	4.17
5510	3/8"					4.62			4.62	5.10
5520	1/2"					7.40			7.40	8.10
5530	5/8"					9.40			9.40	10.30
5540	3/4"					13.60			13.60	14.95
5600	Flare by FIPS, 1/4"					7			7	7.70
5610	3/8"					6.90			6.90	7.60
5620	1/2"					9.90			9.90	10.90
5670	Flare by sweat, 1/4"					3.01			3.01	3.31
5680	3/8"					5.90			5.90	6.50
5690	1/2"					6.75			6.75	7.40
5700	5/8"					17.90			17.90	19.70
5760	Tee flare by IPS, 1/4"					3.94			3.94	4.33
5770	3/8"					8.90			8.90	9.80
5780	1/2"					14.95			14.95	16.45
5790	5/8"					11.80			11.80	13
5850	Connector, 1/4"					1.52			1.52	1.67
5860	3/8"					2.26			2.26	2.49
5870	1/2"					2.76			2.76	3.04
5880	5/8"					5.50			5.50	6.05
5890	3/4"					7.55			7.55	8.35
5950	Seal cap, 1/4"					.39			.39	.43

22 11 Facility Water Distribution

22 11 13 – Facility Water Distribution Piping

22 11 13.25 Pipe/Tube Fittings, Copper		Crew	Daily Output	Labor-Hours	Unit	Material	2023 Bare Costs Labor	Equipment	Total	Total Incl O&P
5960	3/8"				Ea.	.31			.31	.34
5970	1/2"					.93			.93	1.02
5980	5/8"					2.63			2.63	2.89
5990	3/4"				↓	8.55			8.55	9.45
6000	Water service fittings									
6010	Flare joints nut and labor are included in the fitting price.									
6020	90° elbow, C x C, 3/8"	1 Plum	19	.421	Ea.	97	30.50		127.50	152
6030	1/2"		18	.444		186	32		218	253
6040	3/4"		16	.500		237	36		273	315
6050	1"		15	.533		251	38.50		289.50	335
6080	2"		10	.800		1,625	57.50		1,682.50	1,875
6090	90° elbow, C x MPT, 3/8"		19	.421		73.50	30.50		104	126
6100	1/2"		18	.444		141	32		173	203
6110	3/4"		16	.500		164	36		200	234
6120	1"		15	.533		445	38.50		483.50	550
6130	1-1/4"		13	.615		620	44.50		664.50	745
6140	1-1/2"		12	.667		920	48		968	1,100
6150	2"		10	.800		525	57.50		582.50	665
6160	90° elbow, C x FPT, 3/8"		19	.421		79	30.50		109.50	132
6170	1/2"		18	.444		152	32		184	215
6180	3/4"		16	.500		188	36		224	261
6190	1"		15	.533		435	38.50		473.50	540
6200	1-1/4"		13	.615		213	44.50		257.50	300
6210	1-1/2"		12	.667		820	48		868	970
6220	2"		10	.800		1,175	57.50		1,232.50	1,375
6230	Tee, C x C x C, 3/8"		13	.615		156	44.50		200.50	238
6240	1/2"		12	.667		272	48		320	370
6250	3/4"		11	.727		211	52.50		263.50	310
6260	1"		10	.800		320	57.50		377.50	435
6330	Tube nut, C x nut seat, 3/8"		40	.200		28.50	14.40		42.90	52.50
6340	1/2"		38	.211		28.50	15.15		43.65	53.50
6350	3/4"		34	.235		55	16.95		71.95	86
6360	1"		32	.250		100	18		118	137
6380	Coupling, C x C, 3/8"		19	.421		95.50	30.50		126	150
6390	1/2"		18	.444		167	32		199	232
6400	3/4"		16	.500		212	36		248	287
6410	1"		15	.533		390	38.50		428.50	490
6420	1-1/4"		12	.667		630	48		678	765
6430	1-1/2"		12	.667		960	48		1,008	1,125
6440	2"		10	.800		1,450	57.50		1,507.50	1,650
6450	Adapter, C x FPT, 3/8"		19	.421		72	30.50		102.50	124
6460	1/2"		18	.444		126	32		158	187
6470	3/4"		16	.500		153	36		189	222
6480	1"		15	.533		325	38.50		363.50	420
6490	1-1/4"		13	.615		188	44.50		232.50	273
6500	1-1/2"		12	.667		690	48		738	830
6510	2"		10	.800		500	57.50		557.50	635
6520	Adapter, C x MPT, 3/8"		19	.421		59	30.50		89.50	110
6530	1/2"		18	.444		113	32		145	172
6540	3/4"		16	.500		155	36		191	225
6550	1"		15	.533		275	38.50		313.50	360
6560	1-1/4"		13	.615		395	44.50		439.50	500
6570	1-1/2"		12	.667		690	48		738	825

22 11 Facility Water Distribution

22 11 13 – Facility Water Distribution Piping

22 11 13.25 Pipe/Tube Fittings, Copper

		Crew	Daily Output	Labor-Hours	Unit	Material	2023 Bare Costs Labor	2023 Bare Costs Equipment	Total	Total Incl O&P
6580	2"	1 Plum	10	.800	Ea.	930	57.50		987.50	1,100
6992	Tube connector fittings, See Section 22 11 13.76 for plastic ftng.									
7000	Insert type brass/copper, 100 psi @ 180°F, CTS									
7010	Adapter MPT 3/8" x 1/2" CTS	1 Plum	29	.276	Ea.	4.16	19.90		24.06	34
7020	1/2" x 1/2"		26	.308		4.35	22		26.35	38
7030	3/4" x 1/2"		26	.308		7.75	22		29.75	41.50
7040	3/4" x 3/4"		25	.320		3.55	23		26.55	38.50
7050	Adapter CTS 1/2" x 1/2" sweat		24	.333		3.03	24		27.03	39.50
7060	3/4" x 3/4" sweat		22	.364		.97	26		26.97	40
7070	Coupler center set 3/8" CTS		25	.320		1.98	23		24.98	36.50
7080	1/2" CTS		23	.348		1.58	25		26.58	39
7090	3/4" CTS		22	.364		1.98	26		27.98	41
7100	Elbow 90°, copper 3/8"		25	.320		3.94	23		26.94	39
7110	1/2" CTS		23	.348		2.76	25		27.76	40.50
7120	3/4" CTS		22	.364		7.65	26		33.65	47.50
7130	Tee copper 3/8" CTS		17	.471		5.10	34		39.10	56
7140	1/2" CTS		15	.533		3.62	38.50		42.12	61.50
7150	3/4" CTS		14	.571		5.55	41		46.55	67.50
7160	3/8" x 3/8" x 1/2"		16	.500		6.55	36		42.55	60.50
7170	1/2" x 3/8" x 1/2"		15	.533		4.22	38.50		42.72	62
7180	3/4" x 1/2" x 3/4"		14	.571		5.30	41		46.30	67.50

22 11 13.27 Pipe/Tube, Grooved Joint for Copper

		Crew	Daily Output	Labor-Hours	Unit	Material	2023 Bare Costs Labor	2023 Bare Costs Equipment	Total	Total Incl O&P
0010	**PIPE/TUBE, GROOVED JOINT FOR COPPER**									
4000	Fittings: coupling material required at joints not incl. in fitting price.									
4001	Add 1 selected coupling, material only, per joint for installed price.									
4010	Coupling, rigid style									
4018	2" diameter	1 Plum	50	.160	Ea.	46	11.55		57.55	67.50
4020	2-1/2" diameter	Q-1	80	.200		51	12.95		63.95	75.50
4022	3" diameter		67	.239		57	15.50		72.50	86
4024	4" diameter		50	.320		85.50	21		106.50	125
4026	5" diameter		40	.400		143	26		169	196
4028	6" diameter	Q-2	50	.480		188	32.50		220.50	255
4100	Elbow, 90° or 45°									
4108	2" diameter	1 Plum	25	.320	Ea.	78	23		101	121
4110	2-1/2" diameter	Q-1	40	.400		84.50	26		110.50	132
4112	3" diameter		33	.485		118	31.50		149.50	176
4114	4" diameter		25	.640		269	41.50		310.50	360
4116	5" diameter		20	.800		760	52		812	915
4118	6" diameter	Q-2	25	.960		1,225	64.50		1,289.50	1,425
4200	Tee									
4208	2" diameter	1 Plum	17	.471	Ea.	127	34		161	190
4210	2-1/2" diameter	Q-1	27	.593		135	38.50		173.50	207
4212	3" diameter		22	.727		201	47		248	292
4214	4" diameter		17	.941		440	61		501	570
4216	5" diameter		13	1.231		1,225	80		1,305	1,475
4218	6" diameter	Q-2	17	1.412		1,525	95		1,620	1,825
4300	Reducer, concentric									
4310	3" x 2-1/2" diameter	Q-1	35	.457	Ea.	112	29.50		141.50	167
4312	4" x 2-1/2" diameter		32	.500		227	32.50		259.50	299
4314	4" x 3" diameter		29	.552		227	36		263	305
4316	5" x 3" diameter		25	.640		635	41.50		676.50	760
4318	5" x 4" diameter		22	.727		635	47		682	770

22 11 Facility Water Distribution

22 11 13 – Facility Water Distribution Piping

22 11 13.27 Pipe/Tube, Grooved Joint for Copper

		Crew	Daily Output	Labor-Hours	Unit	Material	2023 Bare Costs Labor	Equipment	Total	Total Incl O&P
4320	6" x 3" diameter	Q-2	28	.857	Ea.	690	57.50		747.50	845
4322	6" x 4" diameter		26	.923		690	62		752	855
4324	6" x 5" diameter		24	1		690	67.50		757.50	860
4350	Flange, w/groove gasket									
4351	ANSI class 125 and 150									
4355	2" diameter	1 Plum	23	.348	Ea.	350	25		375	425
4356	2-1/2" diameter	Q-1	37	.432		365	28		393	445
4358	3" diameter		31	.516		385	33.50		418.50	475
4360	4" diameter		23	.696		420	45		465	535
4362	5" diameter		19	.842		565	54.50		619.50	700
4364	6" diameter	Q-2	23	1.043		615	70		685	780

22 11 13.29 Pipe, Fittings and Valves, Copper, Pressed-Joint

		Crew	Daily Output	Labor-Hours	Unit	Material	2023 Bare Costs Labor	Equipment	Total	Total Incl O&P
0010	**PIPE, FITTINGS AND VALVES, COPPER, PRESSED-JOINT**									
0040	Pipe/tube includes coupling & clevis type hanger assy's, 10' OC									
0120	Type K									
0130	1/2" diameter	1 Plum	78	.103	L.F.	5.55	7.40		12.95	17.10
0134	3/4" diameter		74	.108		7.70	7.80		15.50	20
0138	1" diameter		66	.121		7.55	8.75		16.30	21.50
0142	1-1/4" diameter		56	.143		9.30	10.30		19.60	25.50
0146	1-1/2" diameter		50	.160		12.85	11.55		24.40	31.50
0150	2" diameter		40	.200		18.55	14.40		32.95	42
0154	2-1/2" diameter	Q-1	60	.267		58.50	17.30		75.80	90
0158	3" diameter		54	.296		44.50	19.20		63.70	77.50
0162	4" diameter		38	.421		72.50	27.50		100	120
0180	To delete cplgs. & hngrs., 1/2" pipe, subtract					19%	48%			
0184	3/4"-2" pipe, subtract					14%	46%			
0186	2-1/2"-4" pipe, subtract					24%	34%			
0220	Type L									
0230	1/2" diameter	1 Plum	81	.099	L.F.	5	7.10		12.10	16.10
0234	3/4" diameter		76	.105		6.35	7.60		13.95	18.30
0238	1" diameter		68	.118		6.20	8.50		14.70	19.45
0242	1-1/4" diameter		58	.138		8.10	9.95		18.05	23.50
0246	1-1/2" diameter		52	.154		11.20	11.10		22.30	29
0250	2" diameter		42	.190		22.50	13.70		36.20	45.50
0254	2-1/2" diameter	Q-1	62	.258		30	16.75		46.75	58
0258	3" diameter		56	.286		40	18.55		58.55	71.50
0262	4" diameter		39	.410		62.50	26.50		89	109
0280	To delete cplgs. & hngrs., 1/2" pipe, subtract					21%	52%			
0284	3/4"-2" pipe, subtract					17%	46%			
0286	2-1/2"-4" pipe, subtract					23%	35%			
0320	Type M									
0330	1/2" diameter	1 Plum	84	.095	L.F.	4.50	6.85		11.35	15.20
0334	3/4" diameter		78	.103		5.50	7.40		12.90	17.05
0338	1" diameter		70	.114		5.15	8.25		13.40	17.95
0342	1-1/4" diameter		60	.133		7.15	9.60		16.75	22
0346	1-1/2" diameter		54	.148		10.45	10.65		21.10	27.50
0350	2" diameter		44	.182		15.10	13.10		28.20	36
0354	2-1/2" diameter	Q-1	64	.250		28	16.20		44.20	54.50
0358	3" diameter		58	.276		36	17.90		53.90	66
0362	4" diameter		40	.400		59.50	26		85.50	104
0380	To delete cplgs. & hngrs., 1/2" pipe, subtract					32%	49%			
0384	3/4"-2" pipe, subtract					21%	46%			

22 11 Facility Water Distribution
22 11 13 – Facility Water Distribution Piping

22 11 13.29 Pipe, Fittings and Valves, Copper, Pressed-Joint		Crew	Daily Output	Labor-Hours	Unit	Material	2023 Bare Costs Labor	Equipment	Total	Total Incl O&P
0386	2-1/2"-4" pipe, subtract					25%	36%			
1600	Fittings									
1610	Press joints, copper x copper									
1620	Note: Reducing fittings show most expensive size combination.									
1800	90° elbow, 1/2"	1 Plum	36.60	.219	Ea.	5.85	15.75		21.60	30
1810	3/4"		27.50	.291		5.70	21		26.70	38
1820	1"		25.90	.309		15.60	22.50		38.10	50
1830	1-1/4"		20.90	.383		24.50	27.50		52	68
1840	1-1/2"		18.30	.437		59.50	31.50		91	113
1850	2"		15.70	.510		57.50	36.50		94	118
1860	2-1/2"	Q-1	25.90	.618		238	40		278	320
1870	3"		22	.727		300	47		347	400
1880	4"		16.30	.982		355	63.50		418.50	485
2000	45° elbow, 1/2"	1 Plum	36.60	.219		5.45	15.75		21.20	29.50
2010	3/4"		27.50	.291		6.90	21		27.90	39
2020	1"		25.90	.309		22	22.50		44.50	57
2030	1-1/4"		20.90	.383		29.50	27.50		57	73.50
2040	1-1/2"		18.30	.437		51	31.50		82.50	103
2050	2"		15.70	.510		70.50	36.50		107	133
2060	2-1/2"	Q-1	25.90	.618		153	40		193	228
2070	3"		22	.727		214	47		261	305
2080	4"		16.30	.982		305	63.50		368.50	430
2200	Tee, 1/2"	1 Plum	27.50	.291		7.40	21		28.40	39.50
2210	3/4"		20.70	.386		12.95	28		40.95	56
2220	1"		19.40	.412		23.50	29.50		53	70.50
2230	1-1/4"		15.70	.510		41	36.50		77.50	100
2240	1-1/2"		13.80	.580		78	42		120	148
2250	2"		11.80	.678		96	49		145	179
2260	2-1/2"	Q-1	19.40	.825		286	53.50		339.50	395
2270	3"		16.50	.970		350	63		413	480
2280	4"		12.20	1.311		500	85		585	675
2400	Tee, reducing on the outlet									
2410	3/4"	1 Plum	20.70	.386	Ea.	10.55	28		38.55	53
2420	1"		19.40	.412		26	29.50		55.50	73
2430	1-1/4"		15.70	.510		37.50	36.50		74	96.50
2440	1-1/2"		13.80	.580		79	42		121	149
2450	2"		11.80	.678		123	49		172	209
2460	2-1/2"	Q-1	19.40	.825		370	53.50		423.50	485
2470	3"		16.50	.970		460	63		523	600
2480	4"		12.20	1.311		555	85		640	735
2600	Tee, reducing on the run									
2610	3/4"	1 Plum	20.70	.386	Ea.	21	28		49	64.50
2620	1"		19.40	.412		40	29.50		69.50	88.50
2630	1-1/4"		15.70	.510		79.50	36.50		116	143
2640	1-1/2"		13.80	.580		121	42		163	197
2650	2"		11.80	.678		134	49		183	220
2660	2-1/2"	Q-1	19.40	.825		430	53.50		483.50	555
2670	3"		16.50	.970		515	63		578	665
2680	4"		12.20	1.311		645	85		730	835
2800	Coupling, 1/2"	1 Plum	36.60	.219		4.37	15.75		20.12	28.50
2810	3/4"		27.50	.291		6.60	21		27.60	39
2820	1"		25.90	.309		13.25	22.50		35.75	47.50
2830	1-1/4"		20.90	.383		17.10	27.50		44.60	60

22 11 Facility Water Distribution

22 11 13 – Facility Water Distribution Piping

22 11 13.29 Pipe, Fittings and Valves, Copper, Pressed-Joint		Crew	Daily Output	Labor-Hours	Unit	Material	2023 Bare Costs Labor	Equipment	Total	Total Incl O&P
2840	1-1/2"	1 Plum	18.30	.437	Ea.	31	31.50		62.50	81.50
2850	2"		15.70	.510		40	36.50		76.50	99
2860	2-1/2"	Q-1	25.90	.618		119	40		159	191
2870	3"		22	.727		151	47		198	237
2880	4"		16.30	.982		214	63.50		277.50	330
3000	Union, 1/2"	1 Plum	36.60	.219		27.50	15.75		43.25	53.50
3010	3/4"		27.50	.291		34.50	21		55.50	69.50
3020	1"		25.90	.309		55.50	22.50		78	94
3030	1-1/4"		20.90	.383		106	27.50		133.50	158
3040	1-1/2"		18.30	.437		139	31.50		170.50	200
3050	2"		15.70	.510		223	36.50		259.50	300
3200	Adapter, tube to MPT									
3210	1/2"	1 Plum	15.10	.530	Ea.	5.35	38		43.35	63
3220	3/4"		13.60	.588		9.65	42.50		52.15	73.50
3230	1"		11.60	.690		20.50	49.50		70	96.50
3240	1-1/4"		9.90	.808		38.50	58		96.50	129
3250	1-1/2"		9	.889		41.50	64		105.50	141
3260	2"		7.90	1.013		109	73		182	228
3270	2-1/2"	Q-1	13.40	1.194		231	77.50		308.50	370
3280	3"		10.60	1.509		291	98		389	465
3290	4"		7.70	2.078		355	135		490	590
3400	Adapter, tube to FPT									
3410	1/2"	1 Plum	15.10	.530	Ea.	6.65	38		44.65	64.50
3420	3/4"		13.60	.588		10.35	42.50		52.85	74.50
3430	1"		11.60	.690		19.80	49.50		69.30	96
3440	1-1/4"		9.90	.808		45.50	58		103.50	137
3450	1-1/2"		9	.889		63.50	64		127.50	166
3460	2"		7.90	1.013		106	73		179	226
3470	2-1/2"	Q-1	13.40	1.194		261	77.50		338.50	400
3480	3"		10.60	1.509		430	98		528	615
3490	4"		7.70	2.078		550	135		685	805
3600	Flange									
3620	1"	1 Plum	36.20	.221	Ea.	195	15.90		210.90	239
3630	1-1/4"		29.30	.273		278	19.65		297.65	335
3640	1-1/2"		25.60	.313		305	22.50		327.50	375
3650	2"		22	.364		345	26		371	420
3660	2-1/2"	Q-1	36.20	.442		345	28.50		373.50	425
3670	3"		30.80	.519		420	33.50		453.50	515
3680	4"		22.80	.702		470	45.50		515.50	590
3800	Cap, 1/2"	1 Plum	53.10	.151		9.25	10.85		20.10	26.50
3810	3/4"		39.80	.201		14.85	14.50		29.35	38
3820	1"		37.50	.213		24.50	15.35		39.85	50
3830	1-1/4"		30.40	.263		27.50	18.95		46.45	58.50
3840	1-1/2"		26.60	.301		42.50	21.50		64	79
3850	2"		22.80	.351		51.50	25.50		77	94.50
3860	2-1/2"	Q-1	37.50	.427		160	27.50		187.50	218
3870	3"		31.90	.502		202	32.50		234.50	271
3880	4"		23.60	.678		236	44		280	325
4000	Reducer									
4010	3/4"	1 Plum	27.50	.291	Ea.	20	21		41	53.50
4020	1"		25.90	.309		37	22.50		59.50	73.50
4030	1-1/4"		20.90	.383		51	27.50		78.50	97
4040	1-1/2"		18.30	.437		65	31.50		96.50	119

22 11 Facility Water Distribution

22 11 13 – Facility Water Distribution Piping

22 11 13.29 Pipe, Fittings and Valves, Copper, Pressed-Joint

		Crew	Daily Output	Labor-Hours	Unit	Material	2023 Bare Costs Labor	Equipment	Total	Total Incl O&P
4050	2"	1 Plum	15.70	.510	Ea.	90.50	36.50		127	155
4060	2-1/2"	Q-1	25.90	.618		228	40		268	310
4070	3"		22	.727		310	47		357	410
4080	4"	↓	16.30	.982		400	63.50		463.50	535
4100	Stub out, 1/2"	1 Plum	50	.160		13.55	11.55		25.10	32
4110	3/4"		35	.229		24.50	16.45		40.95	51.50
4120	1"	↓	30	.267		26.50	19.20		45.70	57.50
6000	Valves									
6200	Ball valve									
6210	1/2"	1 Plum	25.60	.313	Ea.	41.50	22.50		64	79
6220	3/4"		19.20	.417		48.50	30		78.50	98.50
6230	1"		18.10	.442		67.50	32		99.50	122
6240	1-1/4"		14.70	.544		127	39		166	199
6250	1-1/2"		12.80	.625		146	45		191	227
6260	2"	↓	11	.727	↓	269	52.50		321.50	375
6400	Check valve									
6410	1/2"	1 Plum	30	.267	Ea.	42	19.20		61.20	74.50
6420	3/4"		22.50	.356		53.50	25.50		79	97
6430	1"		21.20	.377		34.50	27		61.50	78.50
6440	1-1/4"		17.20	.465		89.50	33.50		123	149
6450	1-1/2"		15	.533		127	38.50		165.50	198
6460	2"	↓	12.90	.620	↓	133	44.50		177.50	213
6600	Butterfly valve, lug type									
6660	2-1/2"	Q-1	9	1.778	Ea.	197	115		312	390
6670	3"		8	2		242	130		372	460
6680	4"	↓	5	3.200	↓	300	208		508	640

22 11 13.44 Pipe, Steel

		Crew	Daily Output	Labor-Hours	Unit	Material	2023 Bare Costs Labor	Equipment	Total	Total Incl O&P
0010	**PIPE, STEEL**	R221113-50								
0020	All pipe sizes are to Spec. A-53 unless noted otherwise	R221113-70								
0032	Schedule 10, see Line 22 11 13.48 0500									
0050	Schedule 40, threaded, with couplings, and clevis hanger									
0060	assemblies sized for covering, 10' OC									
0540	Black, 1/4" diameter	1 Plum	66	.121	L.F.	9.70	8.75		18.45	23.50
0550	3/8" diameter		65	.123		12.75	8.85		21.60	27.50
0560	1/2" diameter		63	.127		5.60	9.15		14.75	19.80
0570	3/4" diameter		61	.131		7.05	9.45		16.50	22
0580	1" diameter	↓	53	.151		9.70	10.90		20.60	27
0590	1-1/4" diameter	Q-1	89	.180		12.80	11.65		24.45	31.50
0600	1-1/2" diameter		80	.200		15.25	12.95		28.20	36
0610	2" diameter		64	.250		20.50	16.20		36.70	46.50
0620	2-1/2" diameter		50	.320		34	21		55	68
0630	3" diameter		43	.372		44	24		68	84.50
0640	3-1/2" diameter		40	.400		63	26		89	108
0650	4" diameter	↓	36	.444	↓	64.50	29		93.50	114
0809	A-106, gr. A/B, seamless w/cplgs. & clevis hanger assemblies									
0811	1/4" diameter	1 Plum	66	.121	L.F.	5.95	8.75		14.70	19.55
0812	3/8" diameter		65	.123		5.95	8.85		14.80	19.70
0813	1/2" diameter		63	.127		4.89	9.15		14.04	19.05
0814	3/4" diameter		61	.131		5.70	9.45		15.15	20.50
0815	1" diameter		53	.151		6.85	10.90		17.75	24
0816	1-1/4" diameter	Q-1	89	.180		8.80	11.65		20.45	27
0817	1-1/2" diameter		80	.200		10.40	12.95		23.35	31

22 11 Facility Water Distribution

22 11 13 – Facility Water Distribution Piping

22 11 13.44 Pipe, Steel		Crew	Daily Output	Labor-Hours	Unit	Material	2023 Bare Costs Labor	Equipment	Total	Total Incl O&P
0819	2" diameter	Q-1	64	.250	L.F.	12.25	16.20		28.45	37.50
0821	2-1/2" diameter		50	.320		10.10	21		31.10	42
0822	3" diameter		43	.372		23	24		47	61.50
0823	4" diameter	↓	36	.444	↓	37.50	29		66.50	84.50
1220	To delete coupling & hanger, subtract									
1230	1/4" diam. to 3/4" diam.					31%	56%			
1240	1" diam. to 1-1/2" diam.					23%	51%			
1250	2" diam. to 4" diam.					23%	41%			
1280	All pipe sizes are to Spec. A-53 unless noted otherwise									
1281	Schedule 40, threaded, with couplings and clevis hanger									
1282	assemblies sized for covering, 10' OC									
1290	Galvanized, 1/4" diameter	1 Plum	66	.121	L.F.	13.50	8.75		22.25	28
1300	3/8" diameter		65	.123		17.80	8.85		26.65	33
1310	1/2" diameter		63	.127		6.60	9.15		15.75	21
1320	3/4" diameter		61	.131		8.30	9.45		17.75	23.50
1330	1" diameter	↓	53	.151		11.35	10.90		22.25	28.50
1340	1-1/4" diameter	Q-1	89	.180		15.05	11.65		26.70	34
1350	1-1/2" diameter		80	.200		17.90	12.95		30.85	39
1360	2" diameter		64	.250		24	16.20		40.20	50.50
1370	2-1/2" diameter		50	.320		39	21		60	74
1380	3" diameter		43	.372		51	24		75	92
1390	3-1/2" diameter		40	.400		41.50	26		67.50	84.50
1400	4" diameter	↓	36	.444	↓	76	29		105	127
1750	To delete coupling & hanger, subtract									
1760	1/4" diam. to 3/4" diam.					31%	56%			
1770	1" diam. to 1-1/2" diam.					23%	51%			
1780	2" diam. to 4" diam.					23%	41%			
1900	Pipe nipple std black 2" long, 1/2" diameter	1 Plum	19	.421	Ea.	1.95	30.50		32.45	47
1910	Pipe nipple std black 2" long, 1" diameter	"	15	.533		2.91	38.50		41.41	60.50
1920	3" long, 2-1/2" diameter	Q-1	16	1	↓	22	65		87	121
2000	Welded, sch. 40, on yoke & roll hanger assy's, sized for covering, 10' OC									
2040	Black, 1" diameter	Q-15	93	.172	L.F.	12.40	11.15	.69	24.24	31
2050	1-1/4" diameter		84	.190		16.30	12.35	.76	29.41	37
2060	1-1/2" diameter		76	.211		18.45	13.65	.84	32.94	42
2070	2" diameter		61	.262		23	17	1.05	41.05	51.50
2080	2-1/2" diameter		47	.340		32.50	22	1.37	55.87	70.50
2090	3" diameter		43	.372		41	24	1.49	66.49	82.50
2100	3-1/2" diameter		39	.410		44.50	26.50	1.65	72.65	90.50
2110	4" diameter		37	.432		52	28	1.73	81.73	101
2120	5" diameter	↓	32	.500		27	32.50	2.01	61.51	80
2130	6" diameter	Q-16	36	.667		94	45	1.78	140.78	172
2140	8" diameter		29	.828		109	55.50	2.21	166.71	205
2150	10" diameter		24	1		139	67.50	2.67	209.17	256
2160	12" diameter		19	1.263		191	85	3.37	279.37	340
2170	14" diameter (two rod roll type hanger for 14" diam. and up)		15	1.600		192	108	4.27	304.27	375
2180	16" diameter (two rod roll type hanger)		13	1.846		277	124	4.93	405.93	495
2190	18" diameter (two rod roll type hanger)		11	2.182		264	147	5.85	416.85	515
2200	20" diameter (two rod roll type hanger)		9	2.667		297	179	7.10	483.10	600
2220	24" diameter (two rod roll type hanger)	↓	8	3	↓	395	202	8	605	745
2560	To delete hanger, subtract									
2570	1" diam. to 1-1/2" diam.					15%	34%			
2580	2" diam. to 3-1/2" diam.					9%	21%			
2590	4" diam. to 12" diam.					5%	12%			

22 11 Facility Water Distribution

22 11 13 – Facility Water Distribution Piping

22 11 13.44 Pipe, Steel		Crew	Daily Output	Labor-Hours	Unit	Material	2023 Bare Costs Labor	Equipment	Total	Total Incl O&P
2596	14" diam. to 24" diam.					3%	10%			
3250	Flanged, 150 lb. weld neck, on yoke & roll hangers									
3260	sized for covering, 10' OC									
3290	Black, 1" diameter	Q-15	70	.229	L.F.	21	14.80	.92	36.72	46.50
3300	1-1/4" diameter		64	.250		27	16.20	1	44.20	54.50
3310	1-1/2" diameter		58	.276		25	17.90	1.11	44.01	55
3320	2" diameter		45	.356		30	23	1.43	54.43	69
3330	2-1/2" diameter		36	.444		40.50	29	1.78	71.28	89.50
3340	3" diameter		32	.500		49.50	32.50	2.01	84.01	105
3350	3-1/2" diameter		29	.552		55.50	36	2.21	93.71	117
3360	4" diameter		26	.615		63	40	2.47	105.47	131
3370	5" diameter	▼	21	.762		47	49.50	3.06	99.56	129
3380	6" diameter	Q-16	25	.960		117	64.50	2.56	184.06	227
3390	8" diameter		19	1.263		135	85	3.37	223.37	280
3400	10" diameter		16	1.500		221	101	4.01	326.01	395
3410	12" diameter	▼	14	1.714	▼	264	115	4.58	383.58	470
3470	For 300 lb. flanges, add					63%				
3480	For 600 lb. flanges, add					310%				
3960	To delete flanges & hanger, subtract									
3970	1" diam. to 2" diam.					76%	65%			
3980	2-1/2" diam. to 4" diam.					62%	59%			
3990	5" diam. to 12" diam.					60%	46%			
4750	Schedule 80, threaded, with couplings, and clevis hanger assemblies									
4760	sized for covering, 10' OC									
4790	Black, 1/4" diameter	1 Plum	54	.148	L.F.	10.60	10.65		21.25	27.50
4800	3/8" diameter		53	.151		13.35	10.90		24.25	31
4810	1/2" diameter		52	.154		7.75	11.10		18.85	25
4820	3/4" diameter		50	.160		9.60	11.55		21.15	28
4830	1" diameter	▼	45	.178		13.05	12.80		25.85	33.50
4840	1-1/4" diameter	Q-1	75	.213		18.10	13.85		31.95	40.50
4850	1-1/2" diameter		69	.232		21	15.05		36.05	46
4860	2" diameter		56	.286		28.50	18.55		47.05	59
4870	2-1/2" diameter		44	.364		40	23.50		63.50	79
4880	3" diameter		38	.421		52.50	27.50		80	98
4890	3-1/2" diameter		35	.457		39.50	29.50		69	87.50
4900	4" diameter	▼	32	.500	▼	47	32.50		79.50	100
5430	To delete coupling & hanger, subtract									
5440	1/4" diam. to 1/2" diam.					31%	54%			
5450	3/4" diam. to 1-1/2" diam.					28%	49%			
5460	2" diam. to 4" diam.					21%	40%			
5510	Galvanized, 1/4" diameter	1 Plum	54	.148	L.F.	17.05	10.65		27.70	34.50
5520	3/8" diameter		53	.151		18.45	10.90		29.35	36.50
5530	1/2" diameter		52	.154		5.45	11.10		16.55	22.50
5540	3/4" diameter		50	.160		6.60	11.55		18.15	24.50
5550	1" diameter	▼	45	.178		7.95	12.80		20.75	28
5560	1-1/4" diameter	Q-1	75	.213		11.05	13.85		24.90	32.50
5570	1-1/2" diameter		69	.232		12.65	15.05		27.70	36.50
5580	2" diameter		56	.286		17.60	18.55		36.15	47
5590	2-1/2" diameter		44	.364		28	23.50		51.50	66
5600	3" diameter		38	.421		36	27.50		63.50	80.50
5610	3-1/2" diameter		35	.457		42	29.50		71.50	90.50
5620	4" diameter	▼	32	.500		53.50	32.50		86	108
5930	To delete coupling & hanger, subtract									

22 11 Facility Water Distribution

22 11 13 – Facility Water Distribution Piping

22 11 13.44 Pipe, Steel

		Crew	Daily Output	Labor-Hours	Unit	Material	2023 Bare Costs Labor	Equipment	Total	Total Incl O&P
5940	1/4" diam. to 1/2" diam.					31%	54%			
5950	3/4" diam. to 1-1/2" diam.					28%	49%			
5960	2" diam. to 4" diam.					21%	40%			
6000	Welded, on yoke & roller hangers									
6010	sized for covering, 10' OC									
6040	Black, 1" diameter	Q-15	85	.188	L.F.	14.85	12.20	.75	27.80	35.50
6050	1-1/4" diameter		79	.203		19.95	13.15	.81	33.91	42.50
6060	1-1/2" diameter		72	.222		23	14.40	.89	38.29	48
6070	2" diameter		57	.281		29	18.20	1.13	48.33	60
6080	2-1/2" diameter		44	.364		39	23.50	1.46	63.96	79.50
6090	3" diameter		40	.400		50	26	1.60	77.60	95.50
6100	3-1/2" diameter		34	.471		31	30.50	1.89	63.39	81.50
6110	4" diameter		33	.485		37	31.50	1.94	70.44	89.50
6120	5" diameter, A-106B		26	.615		66.50	40	2.47	108.97	135
6130	6" diameter, A-106B	Q-16	30	.800		135	54	2.14	191.14	231
6140	8" diameter, A-106B		25	.960		159	64.50	2.56	226.06	274
6150	10" diameter, A-106B		20	1.200		415	80.50	3.20	498.70	580
6160	12" diameter, A-106B		15	1.600		640	108	4.27	752.27	865
6540	To delete hanger, subtract									
6550	1" diam. to 1-1/2" diam.					30%	14%			
6560	2" diam. to 3" diam.					23%	9%			
6570	3-1/2" diam. to 5" diam.					12%	6%			
6580	6" diam. to 12" diam.					10%	4%			
7250	Flanged, 300 lb. weld neck, on yoke & roll hangers									
7260	sized for covering, 10' OC									
7290	Black, 1" diameter	Q-15	66	.242	L.F.	24	15.70	.97	40.67	51
7300	1-1/4" diameter		61	.262		29	17	1.05	47.05	58.50
7310	1-1/2" diameter		54	.296		32.50	19.20	1.19	52.89	65.50
7320	2" diameter		42	.381		38	24.50	1.53	64.03	80.50
7330	2-1/2" diameter		33	.485		51.50	31.50	1.94	84.94	106
7340	3" diameter		29	.552		62.50	36	2.21	100.71	125
7350	3-1/2" diameter		24	.667		48.50	43	2.67	94.17	120
7360	4" diameter		23	.696		54	45	2.79	101.79	130
7370	5" diameter		19	.842		99	54.50	3.38	156.88	194
7380	6" diameter	Q-16	23	1.043		170	70	2.79	242.79	295
7390	8" diameter		17	1.412		210	95	3.77	308.77	380
7400	10" diameter		14	1.714		510	115	4.58	629.58	735
7410	12" diameter		12	2		760	135	5.35	900.35	1,050
7470	For 600 lb. flanges, add					100%				
7940	To delete flanges & hanger, subtract									
7950	1" diam. to 1-1/2" diam.					75%	66%			
7960	2" diam. to 3" diam.					62%	60%			
7970	3-1/2" diam. to 5" diam.					54%	66%			
7980	6" diam. to 12" diam.					55%	62%			
9000	Threading pipe labor, one end, all schedules through 80									
9010	1/4" through 3/4" pipe size	1 Plum	80	.100	Ea.		7.20		7.20	10.75
9020	1" through 2" pipe size		73	.110			7.90		7.90	11.80
9030	2-1/2" pipe size		53	.151			10.90		10.90	16.20
9040	3" pipe size		50	.160			11.55		11.55	17.20
9050	3-1/2" pipe size	Q-1	89	.180			11.65		11.65	17.40
9060	4" pipe size		73	.219			14.20		14.20	21
9070	5" pipe size		53	.302			19.60		19.60	29
9080	6" pipe size		46	.348			22.50		22.50	33.50

22 11 Facility Water Distribution

22 11 13 – Facility Water Distribution Piping

22 11 13.44 Pipe, Steel

		Crew	Daily Output	Labor-Hours	Unit	Material	2023 Bare Costs Labor	Equipment	Total	Total Incl O&P
9090	8" pipe size	Q-1	29	.552	Ea.		36		36	53.50
9100	10" pipe size		21	.762			49.50		49.50	73.50
9110	12" pipe size	↓	13	1.231	↓		80		80	119
9120	Cutting pipe labor, one cut									
9124	Shop fabrication, machine cut									
9126	Schedule 40, straight pipe									
9128	2" pipe size or less	1 Stpi	62	.129	Ea.		9.35		9.35	13.95
9130	2-1/2" pipe size		56	.143			10.35		10.35	15.45
9132	3" pipe size		42	.190			13.80		13.80	20.50
9134	4" pipe size		31	.258			18.70		18.70	28
9136	5" pipe size		26	.308			22.50		22.50	33.50
9138	6" pipe size		19	.421			30.50		30.50	45.50
9140	8" pipe size		14	.571			41.50		41.50	62
9142	10" pipe size		10	.800			58		58	86.50
9144	12" pipe size	↓	7	1.143			83		83	124
9146	14" pipe size	Q-5	10.50	1.524			99.50		99.50	148
9148	16" pipe size		8.60	1.860			121		121	181
9150	18" pipe size		7	2.286			149		149	223
9152	20" pipe size		5.80	2.759			180		180	269
9154	24" pipe size	↓	4	4	↓		261		261	390
9160	Schedule 80, straight pipe									
9164	2" pipe size or less	1 Stpi	42	.190	Ea.		13.80		13.80	20.50
9166	2-1/2" pipe size		37	.216			15.70		15.70	23.50
9168	3" pipe size		31	.258			18.70		18.70	28
9170	4" pipe size		23	.348			25		25	37.50
9172	5" pipe size		18	.444			32		32	48
9174	6" pipe size		14.60	.548			40		40	59.50
9176	8" pipe size	↓	10	.800			58		58	86.50
9178	10" pipe size	Q-5	14	1.143			74.50		74.50	111
9180	12" pipe size	"	10	1.600	↓		104		104	156
9200	Welding labor per joint									
9210	Schedule 40									
9230	1/2" pipe size	Q-15	32	.500	Ea.		32.50	2.01	34.51	50.50
9240	3/4" pipe size		27	.593			38.50	2.38	40.88	60
9250	1" pipe size		23	.696			45	2.79	47.79	70.50
9260	1-1/4" pipe size		20	.800			52	3.21	55.21	81
9270	1-1/2" pipe size		19	.842			54.50	3.38	57.88	85
9280	2" pipe size		16	1			65	4.01	69.01	101
9290	2-1/2" pipe size		13	1.231			80	4.94	84.94	124
9300	3" pipe size		12	1.333			86.50	5.35	91.85	135
9310	4" pipe size		10	1.600			104	6.40	110.40	162
9320	5" pipe size		9	1.778			115	7.15	122.15	180
9330	6" pipe size		8	2			130	8	138	202
9340	8" pipe size		5	3.200			208	12.85	220.85	325
9350	10" pipe size		4	4			259	16.05	275.05	405
9360	12" pipe size		3	5.333			345	21.50	366.50	540
9370	14" pipe size		2.60	6.154			400	24.50	424.50	620
9380	16" pipe size		2.20	7.273			470	29	499	735
9390	18" pipe size		2	8			520	32	552	810
9400	20" pipe size		1.80	8.889			575	35.50	610.50	900
9410	22" pipe size		1.70	9.412			610	37.50	647.50	950
9420	24" pipe size	↓	1.50	10.667			690	43	733	1,075
9450	Schedule 80									

22 11 Facility Water Distribution

22 11 13 – Facility Water Distribution Piping

22 11 13.44 Pipe, Steel

		Crew	Daily Output	Labor-Hours	Unit	Material	2023 Bare Costs Labor	Equipment	Total	Total Incl O&P
9460	1/2" pipe size	Q-15	27	.593	Ea.	38.50	2.38		40.88	60
9470	3/4" pipe size		23	.696		45	2.79		47.79	70.50
9480	1" pipe size		20	.800		52	3.21		55.21	81
9490	1-1/4" pipe size		19	.842		54.50	3.38		57.88	85
9500	1-1/2" pipe size		18	.889		57.50	3.56		61.06	90
9510	2" pipe size		15	1.067		69	4.28		73.28	108
9520	2-1/2" pipe size		12	1.333		86.50	5.35		91.85	135
9530	3" pipe size		11	1.455		94.50	5.85		100.35	147
9540	4" pipe size		8	2		130	8		138	202
9550	5" pipe size		6	2.667		173	10.70		183.70	270
9560	6" pipe size		5	3.200		208	12.85		220.85	325
9570	8" pipe size		4	4		259	16.05		275.05	405
9580	10" pipe size		3	5.333		345	21.50		366.50	540
9590	12" pipe size	▼	2	8		520	32		552	810
9600	14" pipe size	Q-16	2.60	9.231		620	24.50		644.50	950
9610	16" pipe size		2.30	10.435		700	28		728	1,075
9620	18" pipe size		2	12		805	32		837	1,225
9630	20" pipe size		1.80	13.333		895	35.50		930.50	1,375
9640	22" pipe size		1.60	15		1,000	40		1,040	1,550
9650	24" pipe size	▼	1.50	16	▼	1,075	42.50		1,117.50	1,650

22 11 13.45 Pipe Fittings, Steel, Threaded

		Crew	Daily Output	Labor-Hours	Unit	Material	2023 Bare Costs Labor	Equipment	Total	Total Incl O&P
0010	**PIPE FITTINGS, STEEL, THREADED**									
0020	Cast iron									
0040	Standard weight, black									
0060	90° elbow, straight									
0070	1/4"	1 Plum	16	.500	Ea.	17.05	36		53.05	72.50
0080	3/8"		16	.500		24.50	36		60.50	80.50
0090	1/2"		15	.533		10.80	38.50		49.30	69.50
0100	3/4"		14	.571		11.25	41		52.25	74
0110	1"	▼	13	.615		13.35	44.50		57.85	80.50
0120	1-1/4"	Q-1	22	.727		18.95	47		65.95	91.50
0130	1-1/2"		20	.800		26	52		78	107
0140	2"		18	.889		41	57.50		98.50	131
0150	2-1/2"		14	1.143		98	74		172	219
0160	3"		10	1.600		161	104		265	330
0170	3-1/2"		8	2		435	130		565	675
0180	4"	▼	6	2.667	▼	298	173		471	590
0250	45° elbow, straight									
0260	1/4"	1 Plum	16	.500	Ea.	22	36		58	78
0270	3/8"		16	.500		23.50	36		59.50	79.50
0280	1/2"		15	.533		16.55	38.50		55.05	76
0300	3/4"		14	.571		16.65	41		57.65	80
0320	1"	▼	13	.615		19.55	44.50		64.05	87.50
0330	1-1/4"	Q-1	22	.727		26.50	47		73.50	99.50
0340	1-1/2"		20	.800		43.50	52		95.50	126
0350	2"		18	.889		50	57.50		107.50	141
0360	2-1/2"		14	1.143		131	74		205	255
0370	3"		10	1.600		207	104		311	385
0380	3-1/2"		8	2		510	130		640	755
0400	4"	▼	6	2.667	▼	430	173		603	735
0500	Tee, straight									
0510	1/4"	1 Plum	10	.800	Ea.	28	57.50		85.50	117

22 11 Facility Water Distribution

22 11 13 – Facility Water Distribution Piping

22 11 13.45 Pipe Fittings, Steel, Threaded		Crew	Daily Output	Labor-Hours	Unit	Material	2023 Bare Costs Labor	Equipment	Total	Total Incl O&P
0520	3/8"	1 Plum	10	.800	Ea.	26	57.50		83.50	115
0530	1/2"		9	.889		16.85	64		80.85	114
0540	3/4"		9	.889		19.65	64		83.65	117
0550	1"		8	1		17.50	72		89.50	126
0560	1-1/4"	Q-1	14	1.143		32	74		106	146
0570	1-1/2"		13	1.231		41.50	80		121.50	165
0580	2"		11	1.455		58	94.50		152.50	205
0590	2-1/2"		9	1.778		150	115		265	335
0600	3"		6	2.667		231	173		404	510
0610	3-1/2"		5	3.200		465	208		673	820
0620	4"	▼	4	4	▼	450	259		709	880
0660	Tee, reducing, run or outlet									
0661	1/2"	1 Plum	9	.889	Ea.	43.50	64		107.50	144
0662	3/4"		9	.889		27.50	64		91.50	126
0663	1"		8	1		23.50	72		95.50	133
0664	1-1/4"	Q-1	14	1.143		31.50	74		105.50	146
0665	1-1/2"		13	1.231		58.50	80		138.50	184
0666	2"		11	1.455		69	94.50		163.50	217
0667	2-1/2"		9	1.778		170	115		285	360
0668	3"		6	2.667		297	173		470	585
0669	3-1/2"		5	3.200		750	208		958	1,125
0670	4"	▼	4	4	▼	580	259		839	1,025
0674	Reducer, concentric									
0675	3/4"	1 Plum	18	.444	Ea.	30.50	32		62.50	81.50
0676	1"	"	15	.533		20.50	38.50		59	80
0677	1-1/4"	Q-1	26	.615		53	40		93	118
0678	1-1/2"		24	.667		75	43		118	147
0679	2"		21	.762		98.50	49.50		148	182
0680	2-1/2"		18	.889		140	57.50		197.50	240
0681	3"		14	1.143		232	74		306	365
0682	3-1/2"		12	1.333		475	86.50		561.50	655
0683	4"	▼	10	1.600	▼	475	104		579	680
0687	Reducer, eccentric									
0688	3/4"	1 Plum	16	.500	Ea.	63.50	36		99.50	124
0689	1"	"	14	.571		68.50	41		109.50	137
0690	1-1/4"	Q-1	25	.640		102	41.50		143.50	175
0691	1-1/2"		22	.727		139	47		186	224
0692	2"		20	.800		184	52		236	280
0693	2-1/2"		16	1		281	65		346	405
0694	3"		12	1.333		440	86.50		526.50	615
0695	3-1/2"		10	1.600		675	104		779	900
0696	4"	▼	9	1.778	▼	885	115		1,000	1,150
0700	Standard weight, galvanized cast iron									
0720	90° elbow, straight									
0730	1/4"	1 Plum	16	.500	Ea.	23.50	36		59.50	79.50
0740	3/8"		16	.500		23.50	36		59.50	79.50
0750	1/2"		15	.533		29.50	38.50		68	90
0760	3/4"		14	.571		23	41		64	86.50
0770	1"	▼	13	.615		30.50	44.50		75	99.50
0780	1-1/4"	Q-1	22	.727		41	47		88	116
0790	1-1/2"		20	.800		64.50	52		116.50	149
0800	2"		18	.889		82.50	57.50		140	177
0810	2-1/2"	▼	14	1.143		170	74		244	298

22 11 Facility Water Distribution

22 11 13 – Facility Water Distribution Piping

22 11 13.45 Pipe Fittings, Steel, Threaded

		Crew	Daily Output	Labor-Hours	Unit	Material	2023 Bare Costs Labor	Equipment	Total	Total Incl O&P
0820	3"	Q-1	10	1.600	Ea.	258	104		362	440
0830	3-1/2"		8	2		410	130		540	650
0840	4"		6	2.667		475	173		648	780
0900	45° elbow, straight									
0910	1/4"	1 Plum	16	.500	Ea.	32	36		68	89
0920	3/8"		16	.500		28	36		64	84.50
0930	1/2"		15	.533		23	38.50		61.50	83
0940	3/4"		14	.571		26.50	41		67.50	90.50
0950	1"		13	.615		52	44.50		96.50	123
0960	1-1/4"	Q-1	22	.727		76.50	47		123.50	155
0970	1-1/2"		20	.800		90	52		142	177
0980	2"		18	.889		126	57.50		183.50	225
0990	2-1/2"		14	1.143		190	74		264	320
1000	3"		10	1.600		395	104		499	590
1010	3-1/2"		8	2		735	130		865	1,000
1020	4"		6	2.667		690	173		863	1,025
1100	Tee, straight									
1110	1/4"	1 Plum	10	.800	Ea.	28.50	57.50		86	117
1120	3/8"		10	.800		24.50	57.50		82	113
1130	1/2"		9	.889		39.50	64		103.50	139
1140	3/4"		9	.889		37.50	64		101.50	137
1150	1"		8	1		35.50	72		107.50	146
1160	1-1/4"	Q-1	14	1.143		62	74		136	179
1170	1-1/2"		13	1.231		82	80		162	209
1180	2"		11	1.455		102	94.50		196.50	254
1190	2-1/2"		9	1.778		210	115		325	405
1200	3"		6	2.667		690	173		863	1,025
1210	3-1/2"		5	3.200		585	208		793	955
1220	4"		4	4		810	259		1,069	1,275
1300	Extra heavy weight, black									
1310	Couplings, steel straight									
1320	1/4"	1 Plum	19	.421	Ea.	8.60	30.50		39.10	54.50
1330	3/8"		19	.421		9.35	30.50		39.85	55.50
1340	1/2"		19	.421		12.65	30.50		43.15	59
1350	3/4"		18	.444		13.55	32		45.55	63
1360	1"		15	.533		17.20	38.50		55.70	76.50
1370	1-1/4"	Q-1	26	.615		27.50	40		67.50	90
1380	1-1/2"		24	.667		27.50	43		70.50	95
1390	2"		21	.762		42	49.50		91.50	120
1400	2-1/2"		18	.889		62.50	57.50		120	155
1410	3"		14	1.143		74.50	74		148.50	193
1420	3-1/2"		12	1.333		100	86.50		186.50	239
1430	4"		10	1.600		117	104		221	284
1510	90° elbow, straight									
1520	1/2"	1 Plum	15	.533	Ea.	58.50	38.50		97	122
1530	3/4"		14	.571		59.50	41		100.50	127
1540	1"		13	.615		72	44.50		116.50	145
1550	1-1/4"	Q-1	22	.727		107	47		154	189
1560	1-1/2"		20	.800		133	52		185	224
1580	2"		18	.889		164	57.50		221.50	266
1590	2-1/2"		14	1.143		380	74		454	525
1600	3"		10	1.600		535	104		639	745
1610	4"		6	2.667		1,175	173		1,348	1,525

22 11 Facility Water Distribution

22 11 13 – Facility Water Distribution Piping

22 11 13.45 Pipe Fittings, Steel, Threaded		Crew	Daily Output	Labor-Hours	Unit	Material	2023 Bare Costs Labor	Equipment	Total	Total Incl O&P
1650	45° elbow, straight									
1660	1/2"	1 Plum	15	.533	Ea.	79.50	38.50		118	145
1670	3/4"		14	.571		80.50	41		121.50	150
1680	1"		13	.615		96.50	44.50		141	172
1690	1-1/4"	Q-1	22	.727		159	47		206	246
1700	1-1/2"		20	.800		175	52		227	270
1710	2"		18	.889		249	57.50		306.50	360
1720	2-1/2"		14	1.143		405	74		479	555
1800	Tee, straight									
1810	1/2"	1 Plum	9	.889	Ea.	91	64		155	196
1820	3/4"		9	.889		91	64		155	196
1830	1"		8	1		110	72		182	228
1840	1-1/4"	Q-1	14	1.143		164	74		238	291
1850	1-1/2"		13	1.231		211	80		291	350
1860	2"		11	1.455		262	94.50		356.50	430
1870	2-1/2"		9	1.778		575	115		690	805
1880	3"		6	2.667		780	173		953	1,125
1890	4"		4	4		1,525	259		1,784	2,050
4000	Standard weight, black									
4010	Couplings, steel straight, merchants									
4030	1/4"	1 Plum	19	.421	Ea.	2.31	30.50		32.81	47.50
4040	3/8"		19	.421		2.78	30.50		33.28	48
4050	1/2"		19	.421		2.95	30.50		33.45	48.50
4060	3/4"		18	.444		3.77	32		35.77	52
4070	1"		15	.533		5.25	38.50		43.75	63.50
4080	1-1/4"	Q-1	26	.615		6.75	40		46.75	67
4090	1-1/2"		24	.667		8.50	43		51.50	74
4100	2"		21	.762		12.20	49.50		61.70	87
4110	2-1/2"		18	.889		37	57.50		94.50	127
4120	3"		14	1.143		52	74		126	169
4130	3-1/2"		12	1.333		92.50	86.50		179	231
4140	4"		10	1.600		92.50	104		196.50	257
4166	Plug, 1/4"	1 Plum	38	.211		5	15.15		20.15	28
4167	3/8"		38	.211		4.16	15.15		19.31	27
4168	1/2"		38	.211		4.81	15.15		19.96	28
4169	3/4"		32	.250		12.90	18		30.90	41
4170	1"		30	.267		13.75	19.20		32.95	43.50
4171	1-1/4"	Q-1	52	.308		15.80	19.95		35.75	47.50
4172	1-1/2"		48	.333		22.50	21.50		44	56.50
4173	2"		42	.381		29	24.50		53.50	69
4176	2-1/2"		36	.444		43	29		72	90
4180	4"		20	.800		93	52		145	180
4200	Standard weight, galvanized									
4210	Couplings, steel straight, merchants									
4230	1/4"	1 Plum	19	.421	Ea.	2.66	30.50		33.16	48
4240	3/8"		19	.421		3.40	30.50		33.90	48.50
4250	1/2"		19	.421		3.61	30.50		34.11	49
4260	3/4"		18	.444		4.53	32		36.53	53
4270	1"		15	.533		6.35	38.50		44.85	64.50
4280	1-1/4"	Q-1	26	.615		8.10	40		48.10	68.50
4290	1-1/2"		24	.667		10.05	43		53.05	75.50
4300	2"		21	.762		15.05	49.50		64.55	90
4310	2-1/2"		18	.889		34.50	57.50		92	124

22 11 Facility Water Distribution

22 11 13 – Facility Water Distribution Piping

22 11 13.45 Pipe Fittings, Steel, Threaded

		Crew	Daily Output	Labor-Hours	Unit	Material	2023 Bare Costs Labor	Equipment	Total	Total Incl O&P
4320	3"	Q-1	14	1.143	Ea.	49.50	74		123.50	166
4330	3-1/2"		12	1.333		107	86.50		193.50	247
4340	4"	↓	10	1.600	↓	107	104		211	273
4370	Plug, galvanized, square head									
4374	1/2"	1 Plum	38	.211	Ea.	13	15.15		28.15	37
4375	3/4"		32	.250		11.65	18		29.65	40
4376	1"	↓	30	.267		11.65	19.20		30.85	41.50
4377	1-1/4"	Q-1	52	.308		19.40	19.95		39.35	51.50
4378	1-1/2"		48	.333		26	21.50		47.50	61
4379	2"		42	.381		32.50	24.50		57	73
4380	2-1/2"		36	.444		68.50	29		97.50	119
4381	3"		28	.571		88	37		125	153
4382	4"		20	.800		242	52		294	345
4385	8"		20	.800		178	52		230	274
4700	Nipple, black									
4710	1/2" x 4" long	1 Plum	19	.421	Ea.	5.90	30.50		36.40	51.50
4712	3/4" x 4" long		18	.444		7.10	32		39.10	56
4714	1" x 4" long	↓	15	.533		9.90	38.50		48.40	68.50
4716	1-1/4" x 4" long	Q-1	26	.615		12.35	40		52.35	73
4718	1-1/2" x 4" long		24	.667		14.55	43		57.55	80.50
4720	2" x 4" long		21	.762		20.50	49.50		70	96
4722	2-1/2" x 4" long		18	.889		55	57.50		112.50	147
4724	3" x 4" long		14	1.143		70	74		144	188
4726	4" x 4" long	↓	10	1.600	↓	94.50	104		198.50	259
4800	Nipple, galvanized									
4810	1/2" x 4" long	1 Plum	19	.421	Ea.	7.20	30.50		37.70	53
4812	3/4" x 4" long		18	.444		8.95	32		40.95	58
4814	1" x 4" long	↓	15	.533		12	38.50		50.50	70.50
4816	1-1/4" x 4" long	Q-1	26	.615		14.70	40		54.70	75.50
4818	1-1/2" x 4" long		24	.667		18.60	43		61.60	85
4820	2" x 4" long		21	.762		23.50	49.50		73	99.50
4822	2-1/2" x 4" long		18	.889		62	57.50		119.50	155
4824	3" x 4" long		14	1.143		82.50	74		156.50	202
4826	4" x 4" long	↓	10	1.600	↓	111	104		215	277
5000	Malleable iron, 150 lb.									
5020	Black									
5040	90° elbow, straight									
5060	1/4"	1 Plum	16	.500	Ea.	8.40	36		44.40	63
5070	3/8"		16	.500		8.40	36		44.40	63
5080	1/2"		15	.533		5.80	38.50		44.30	64
5090	3/4"		14	.571		7	41		48	69
5100	1"	↓	13	.615		12.20	44.50		56.70	79.50
5110	1-1/4"	Q-1	22	.727		20	47		67	92.50
5120	1-1/2"		20	.800		26.50	52		78.50	107
5130	2"		18	.889		45.50	57.50		103	136
5140	2-1/2"		14	1.143		102	74		176	223
5150	3"		10	1.600		149	104		253	320
5160	3-1/2"		8	2		430	130		560	665
5170	4"	↓	6	2.667	↓	283	173		456	570
5250	45° elbow, straight									
5270	1/4"	1 Plum	16	.500	Ea.	12.65	36		48.65	67.50
5280	3/8"		16	.500		12.65	36		48.65	67.50
5290	1/2"		15	.533		9.60	38.50		48.10	68

For customer support on your Plumbing Costs with RSMeans data, call 800.448.8182.

22 11 Facility Water Distribution

22 11 13 – Facility Water Distribution Piping

22 11 13.45 Pipe Fittings, Steel, Threaded		Crew	Daily Output	Labor-Hours	Unit	Material	2023 Bare Costs Labor	Equipment	Total	Total Incl O&P
5300	3/4"	1 Plum	14	.571	Ea.	11.90	41		52.90	74.50
5310	1"	▼	13	.615		14.95	44.50		59.45	82.50
5320	1-1/4"	Q-1	22	.727		26.50	47		73.50	99.50
5330	1-1/2"		20	.800		33	52		85	114
5340	2"		18	.889		49.50	57.50		107	141
5350	2-1/2"		14	1.143		143	74		217	269
5360	3"		10	1.600		186	104		290	360
5370	3-1/2"		8	2		340	130		470	570
5380	4"	▼	6	2.667	▼	365	173		538	660
5450	Tee, straight									
5470	1/4"	1 Plum	10	.800	Ea.	12.20	57.50		69.70	99.50
5480	3/8"		10	.800		12.20	57.50		69.70	99.50
5490	1/2"		9	.889		7.80	64		71.80	104
5500	3/4"		9	.889		11.20	64		75.20	108
5510	1"	▼	8	1		19.10	72		91.10	128
5520	1-1/4"	Q-1	14	1.143		31	74		105	145
5530	1-1/2"		13	1.231		38.50	80		118.50	162
5540	2"		11	1.455		65.50	94.50		160	213
5550	2-1/2"		9	1.778		142	115		257	330
5560	3"		6	2.667		209	173		382	485
5570	3-1/2"		5	3.200		505	208		713	865
5580	4"	▼	4	4	▼	505	259		764	940
5601	Tee, reducing, on outlet									
5602	1/2"	1 Plum	9	.889	Ea.	13.25	64		77.25	110
5603	3/4"		9	.889		17.25	64		81.25	115
5604	1"	▼	8	1		22	72		94	131
5605	1-1/4"	Q-1	14	1.143		38	74		112	153
5606	1-1/2"		13	1.231		54.50	80		134.50	179
5607	2"		11	1.455		115	94.50		209.50	267
5608	2-1/2"		9	1.778		184	115		299	375
5609	3"		6	2.667		292	173		465	580
5610	3-1/2"		5	3.200		650	208		858	1,025
5611	4"	▼	4	4	▼	595	259		854	1,050
5650	Coupling									
5670	1/4"	1 Plum	19	.421	Ea.	10.45	30.50		40.95	56.50
5680	3/8"		19	.421		10.45	30.50		40.95	56.50
5690	1/2"		19	.421		8.05	30.50		38.55	54
5700	3/4"		18	.444		9.45	32		41.45	58.50
5710	1"	▼	15	.533		14.10	38.50		52.60	73
5720	1-1/4"	Q-1	26	.615		16.20	40		56.20	77.50
5730	1-1/2"		24	.667		22	43		65	88.50
5740	2"		21	.762		32.50	49.50		82	109
5750	2-1/2"		18	.889		89.50	57.50		147	185
5760	3"		14	1.143		121	74		195	244
5770	3-1/2"		12	1.333		239	86.50		325.50	390
5780	4"	▼	10	1.600		244	104		348	425
5840	Reducer, concentric, 1/4"	1 Plum	19	.421		11	30.50		41.50	57
5850	3/8"		19	.421		11	30.50		41.50	57
5860	1/2"		19	.421		9.45	30.50		39.95	55.50
5870	3/4"		16	.500		10.60	36		46.60	65
5880	1"	▼	15	.533		16.45	38.50		54.95	75.50
5890	1-1/4"	Q-1	26	.615		21	40		61	83
5900	1-1/2"	▼	24	.667		27	43		70	94

22 11 Facility Water Distribution

22 11 13 — Facility Water Distribution Piping

22 11 13.45	Pipe Fittings, Steel, Threaded	Crew	Daily Output	Labor-Hours	Unit	Material	2023 Bare Costs Labor	Equipment	Total	Total Incl O&P
5910	2"	Q-1	21	.762	Ea.	39	49.50		88.50	116
5911	2-1/2"		18	.889		89	57.50		146.50	184
5912	3"		14	1.143		135	74		209	259
5913	3-1/2"		12	1.333		460	86.50		546.50	640
5914	4"	▼	10	1.600		440	104		544	640
5981	Bushing, 1/4"	1 Plum	19	.421		1.63	30.50		32.13	47
5982	3/8"		19	.421		1.94	30.50		32.44	47
5983	1/2"		19	.421		8.65	30.50		39.15	54.50
5984	3/4"		16	.500		9.45	36		45.45	64
5985	1"		15	.533		9.95	38.50		48.45	68.50
5986	1-1/4"	Q-1	26	.615		12.95	40		52.95	74
5987	1-1/2"		24	.667		16.45	43		59.45	82.50
5988	2"	▼	21	.762		20.50	49.50		70	96.50
5989	Cap, 1/4"	1 Plum	38	.211		9.75	15.15		24.90	33
5991	3/8"		38	.211		9.25	15.15		24.40	32.50
5992	1/2"		38	.211		5.85	15.15		21	29
5993	3/4"		32	.250		7.95	18		25.95	36
5994	1"		30	.267		9.65	19.20		28.85	39
5995	1-1/4"	Q-1	52	.308		12.70	19.95		32.65	44
5996	1-1/2"		48	.333		17.45	21.50		38.95	51
5997	2"	▼	42	.381		25.50	24.50		50	65
6000	For galvanized elbows, tees, and couplings, add				▼	20%				
6058	For galvanized reducers, caps and bushings, add					20%				
6100	90° elbow, galvanized, 150 lb., reducing									
6110	3/4" x 1/2"	1 Plum	15.40	.519	Ea.	16.75	37.50		54.25	74.50
6112	1" x 3/4"		14	.571		21.50	41		62.50	85
6114	1" x 1/2"	▼	14.50	.552		23	40		63	84.50
6116	1-1/4" x 1"	Q-1	24.20	.661		36	43		79	104
6118	1-1/4" x 3/4"		25.40	.630		43	41		84	109
6120	1-1/4" x 1/2"		26.20	.611		46	39.50		85.50	110
6122	1-1/2" x 1-1/4"		21.60	.741		57.50	48		105.50	135
6124	1-1/2" x 1"		23.50	.681		57.50	44		101.50	130
6126	1-1/2" x 3/4"		24.60	.650		57.50	42		99.50	127
6128	2" x 1-1/2"		20.50	.780		67	50.50		117.50	150
6130	2" x 1-1/4"		21	.762		77	49.50		126.50	158
6132	2" x 1"		22.80	.702		80	45.50		125.50	156
6134	2" x 3/4"		23.90	.669		81.50	43.50		125	154
6136	2-1/2" x 2"		12.30	1.301		228	84.50		312.50	375
6138	2-1/2" x 1-1/2"		12.50	1.280		254	83		337	405
6140	3" x 2-1/2"		8.60	1.860		415	121		536	635
6142	3" x 2"		11.80	1.356		360	88		448	525
6144	4" x 3"	▼	8.20	1.951	▼	935	127		1,062	1,225
6160	90° elbow, black, 150 lb., reducing									
6170	1" x 3/4"	1 Plum	14	.571	Ea.	14.65	41		55.65	77.50
6174	1-1/2" x 1"	Q-1	23.50	.681		35	44		79	104
6178	1-1/2" x 3/4"		24.60	.650		40	42		82	107
6182	2" x 1-1/2"		20.50	.780		50.50	50.50		101	131
6186	2" x 1"		22.80	.702		57	45.50		102.50	131
6190	2" x 3/4"		23.90	.669		60.50	43.50		104	131
6194	2-1/2" x 2"	▼	12.30	1.301	▼	138	84.50		222.50	278
7000	Union, with brass seat									
7010	1/4"	1 Plum	15	.533	Ea.	43.50	38.50		82	106
7020	3/8"	▼	15	.533		30	38.50		68.50	90.50

22 11 Facility Water Distribution

22 11 13 – Facility Water Distribution Piping

22 11 13.45 Pipe Fittings, Steel, Threaded

		Crew	Daily Output	Labor-Hours	Unit	Material	2023 Bare Costs Labor	Equipment	Total	Total Incl O&P
7030	1/2"	1 Plum	14	.571	Ea.	27	41		68	91.50
7040	3/4"		13	.615		31.50	44.50		76	101
7050	1"		12	.667		40.50	48		88.50	117
7060	1-1/4"	Q-1	21	.762		58.50	49.50		108	138
7070	1-1/2"		19	.842		73	54.50		127.50	162
7080	2"		17	.941		84.50	61		145.50	184
7090	2-1/2"		13	1.231		252	80		332	395
7100	3"		9	1.778		305	115		420	505
7120	Union, galvanized									
7124	1/2"	1 Plum	14	.571	Ea.	36	41		77	101
7125	3/4"		13	.615		41.50	44.50		86	112
7126	1"		12	.667		54.50	48		102.50	131
7127	1-1/4"	Q-1	21	.762		78.50	49.50		128	160
7128	1-1/2"		19	.842		95	54.50		149.50	187
7129	2"		17	.941		109	61		170	211
7130	2-1/2"		13	1.231		380	80		460	540
7131	3"		9	1.778		530	115		645	755
7500	Malleable iron, 300 lb.									
7520	Black									
7540	90° elbow, straight, 1/4"	1 Plum	16	.500	Ea.	29.50	36		65.50	86
7560	3/8"		16	.500		26	36		62	82.50
7570	1/2"		15	.533		35.50	38.50		74	96.50
7580	3/4"		14	.571		38.50	41		79.50	104
7590	1"		13	.615		49	44.50		93.50	120
7600	1-1/4"	Q-1	22	.727		71.50	47		118.50	149
7610	1-1/2"		20	.800		84.50	52		136.50	171
7620	2"		18	.889		121	57.50		178.50	219
7630	2-1/2"		14	1.143		315	74		389	455
7640	3"		10	1.600		360	104		464	550
7650	4"		6	2.667		935	173		1,108	1,275
7700	45° elbow, straight, 1/4"	1 Plum	16	.500		44	36		80	102
7720	3/8"		16	.500		44	36		80	102
7730	1/2"		15	.533		49	38.50		87.50	111
7740	3/4"		14	.571		54.50	41		95.50	122
7750	1"		13	.615		60	44.50		104.50	132
7760	1-1/4"	Q-1	22	.727		96.50	47		143.50	177
7770	1-1/2"		20	.800		126	52		178	216
7780	2"		18	.889		190	57.50		247.50	295
7790	2-1/2"		14	1.143		445	74		519	600
7800	3"		10	1.600		585	104		689	795
7810	4"		6	2.667		1,325	173		1,498	1,700
7850	Tee, straight, 1/4"	1 Plum	10	.800		37	57.50		94.50	127
7870	3/8"		10	.800		39.50	57.50		97	129
7880	1/2"		9	.889		50	64		114	151
7890	3/4"		9	.889		54	64		118	155
7900	1"		8	1		65	72		137	179
7910	1-1/4"	Q-1	14	1.143		93	74		167	213
7920	1-1/2"		13	1.231		109	80		189	239
7930	2"		11	1.455		160	94.50		254.50	315
7940	2-1/2"		9	1.778		410	115		525	620
7950	3"		6	2.667		555	173		728	870
7960	4"		4	4		1,650	259		1,909	2,200
8050	Couplings, straight, 1/4"	1 Plum	19	.421		26.50	30.50		57	74.50

22 11 Facility Water Distribution

22 11 13 – Facility Water Distribution Piping

22 11 13.45 Pipe Fittings, Steel, Threaded		Crew	Daily Output	Labor-Hours	Unit	Material	2023 Bare Costs Labor	Equipment	Total	Total Incl O&P
8070	3/8"	1 Plum	19	.421	Ea.	26.50	30.50		57	74.50
8080	1/2"		19	.421		29.50	30.50		60	77.50
8090	3/4"		18	.444		34	32		66	85.50
8100	1"		15	.533		39	38.50		77.50	101
8110	1-1/4"	Q-1	26	.615		46.50	40		86.50	111
8120	1-1/2"		24	.667		69.50	43		112.50	141
8130	2"		21	.762		100	49.50		149.50	184
8140	2-1/2"		18	.889		193	57.50		250.50	298
8150	3"		14	1.143		278	74		352	415
8160	4"		10	1.600		525	104		629	730
8162	6"		10	1.600		525	104		629	730
8200	Galvanized									
8220	90° elbow, straight, 1/4"	1 Plum	16	.500	Ea.	53	36		89	112
8222	3/8"		16	.500		54	36		90	113
8224	1/2"		15	.533		64	38.50		102.50	128
8226	3/4"		14	.571		72	41		113	141
8228	1"		13	.615		92.50	44.50		137	168
8230	1-1/4"	Q-1	22	.727		145	47		192	230
8232	1-1/2"		20	.800		157	52		209	251
8234	2"		18	.889		264	57.50		321.50	375
8236	2-1/2"		14	1.143		590	74		664	755
8238	3"		10	1.600		695	104		799	915
8240	4"		6	2.667		2,175	173		2,348	2,625
8280	45° elbow, straight									
8282	1/2"	1 Plum	15	.533	Ea.	103	38.50		141.50	172
8284	3/4"		14	.571		110	41		151	183
8286	1"		13	.615		120	44.50		164.50	198
8288	1-1/4"	Q-1	22	.727		187	47		234	276
8290	1-1/2"		20	.800		242	52		294	345
8292	2"		18	.889		335	57.50		392.50	455
8310	Tee, straight, 1/4"	1 Plum	10	.800		75	57.50		132.50	169
8312	3/8"		10	.800		76.50	57.50		134	170
8314	1/2"		9	.889		96	64		160	201
8316	3/4"		9	.889		105	64		169	212
8318	1"		8	1		130	72		202	250
8320	1-1/4"	Q-1	14	1.143		186	74		260	315
8322	1-1/2"		13	1.231		193	80		273	330
8324	2"		11	1.455		310	94.50		404.50	480
8326	2-1/2"		9	1.778		975	115		1,090	1,250
8328	3"		6	2.667		1,100	173		1,273	1,475
8330	4"		4	4		2,975	259		3,234	3,650
8380	Couplings, straight, 1/4"	1 Plum	19	.421		34.50	30.50		65	83
8382	3/8"		19	.421		50	30.50		80.50	100
8384	1/2"		19	.421		51	30.50		81.50	101
8386	3/4"		18	.444		57.50	32		89.50	112
8388	1"		15	.533		76.50	38.50		115	142
8390	1-1/4"	Q-1	26	.615		99.50	40		139.50	170
8392	1-1/2"		24	.667		141	43		184	220
8394	2"		21	.762		170	49.50		219.50	261
8396	2-1/2"		18	.889		470	57.50		527.50	600
8398	3"		14	1.143		560	74		634	725
8399	4"		10	1.600		920	104		1,024	1,175
8529	Black									

22 11 Facility Water Distribution

22 11 13 – Facility Water Distribution Piping

22 11 13.45 Pipe Fittings, Steel, Threaded

		Crew	Daily Output	Labor-Hours	Unit	Material	2023 Bare Costs Labor	Equipment	Total	Total Incl O&P
8530	Reducer, concentric, 1/4"	1 Plum	19	.421	Ea.	36.50	30.50		67	85.50
8531	3/8"		19	.421		35	30.50		65.50	83.50
8532	1/2"		17	.471		42.50	34		76.50	97
8533	3/4"		16	.500		43.50	36		79.50	101
8534	1"		15	.533		51.50	38.50		90	115
8535	1-1/4"	Q-1	26	.615		68	40		108	135
8536	1-1/2"		24	.667		106	43		149	182
8537	2"		21	.762		134	49.50		183.50	221
8550	Cap, 1/4"	1 Plum	38	.211		27.50	15.15		42.65	52.50
8551	3/8"		38	.211		27.50	15.15		42.65	52.50
8552	1/2"		34	.235		27	16.95		43.95	55
8553	3/4"		32	.250		34	18		52	64.50
8554	1"		30	.267		45	19.20		64.20	78
8555	1-1/4"	Q-1	52	.308		49.50	19.95		69.45	84.50
8556	1-1/2"		48	.333		72.50	21.50		94	112
8557	2"		42	.381		101	24.50		125.50	148
8570	Plug, 1/4"	1 Plum	38	.211		5.50	15.15		20.65	28.50
8571	3/8"		38	.211		5.75	15.15		20.90	29
8572	1/2"		34	.235		6	16.95		22.95	32
8573	3/4"		32	.250		7.50	18		25.50	35.50
8574	1"		30	.267		11.50	19.20		30.70	41
8575	1-1/4"	Q-1	52	.308		23.50	19.95		43.45	56
8576	1-1/2"		48	.333		27	21.50		48.50	61.50
8577	2"		42	.381		42.50	24.50		67	84
9500	Union with brass seat, 1/4"	1 Plum	15	.533		63.50	38.50		102	128
9530	3/8"		15	.533		64.50	38.50		103	129
9540	1/2"		14	.571		52	41		93	119
9550	3/4"		13	.615		57.50	44.50		102	130
9560	1"		12	.667		75.50	48		123.50	155
9570	1-1/4"	Q-1	21	.762		123	49.50		172.50	209
9580	1-1/2"		19	.842		129	54.50		183.50	224
9590	2"		17	.941		159	61		220	266
9600	2-1/2"		13	1.231		515	80		595	685
9610	3"		9	1.778		665	115		780	900
9620	4"		5	3.200		2,325	208		2,533	2,850
9630	Union, all iron, 1/4"	1 Plum	15	.533		98.50	38.50		137	166
9650	3/8"		15	.533		98.50	38.50		137	166
9660	1/2"		14	.571		104	41		145	176
9670	3/4"		13	.615		111	44.50		155.50	189
9680	1"		12	.667		137	48		185	222
9690	1-1/4"	Q-1	21	.762		210	49.50		259.50	305
9700	1-1/2"		19	.842		128	54.50		182.50	223
9710	2"		17	.941		108	61		169	210
9720	2-1/2"		13	1.231		144	80		224	277
9730	3"		9	1.778		218	115		333	410
9750	For galvanized unions, add					15%				
9757	Forged steel, 3000 lb.									
9758	Black									
9760	90° elbow, 1/4"	1 Plum	16	.500	Ea.	32.50	36		68.50	89
9761	3/8"		16	.500		32.50	36		68.50	89
9762	1/2"		15	.533		25	38.50		63.50	84.50
9763	3/4"		14	.571		31	41		72	95.50
9764	1"		13	.615		46	44.50		90.50	117

22 11 Facility Water Distribution
22 11 13 – Facility Water Distribution Piping

22 11 13.45 Pipe Fittings, Steel, Threaded		Crew	Daily Output	Labor-Hours	Unit	Material	2023 Bare Costs Labor	Equipment	Total	Total Incl O&P
9765	1-1/4"	Q-1	22	.727	Ea.	88	47		135	167
9766	1-1/2"		20	.800		113	52		165	203
9767	2"	▼	18	.889		137	57.50		194.50	237
9780	45° elbow, 1/4"	1 Plum	16	.500		41	36		77	98.50
9781	3/8"		16	.500		41	36		77	98.50
9782	1/2"		15	.533		40.50	38.50		79	102
9783	3/4"		14	.571		46.50	41		87.50	113
9784	1"	▼	13	.615		63.50	44.50		108	136
9785	1-1/4"	Q-1	22	.727		88	47		135	168
9786	1-1/2"		20	.800		126	52		178	217
9787	2"	▼	18	.889		174	57.50		231.50	278
9800	Tee, 1/4"	1 Plum	10	.800		39.50	57.50		97	129
9801	3/8"		10	.800		39.50	57.50		97	129
9802	1/2"		9	.889		35.50	64		99.50	135
9803	3/4"		9	.889		47.50	64		111.50	148
9804	1"	▼	8	1		63	72		135	176
9805	1-1/4"	Q-1	14	1.143		122	74		196	245
9806	1-1/2"		13	1.231		142	80		222	276
9807	2"	▼	11	1.455		184	94.50		278.50	345
9820	Reducer, concentric, 1/4"	1 Plum	19	.421		19.75	30.50		50.25	66.50
9821	3/8"		19	.421		20.50	30.50		51	67.50
9822	1/2"		17	.471		20.50	34		54.50	73
9823	3/4"		16	.500		24.50	36		60.50	80.50
9824	1"	▼	15	.533		32	38.50		70.50	92.50
9825	1-1/4"	Q-1	26	.615		56	40		96	121
9826	1-1/2"		24	.667		60.50	43		103.50	131
9827	2"	▼	21	.762		88	49.50		137.50	170
9840	Cap, 1/4"	1 Plum	38	.211		12.15	15.15		27.30	36
9841	3/8"		38	.211		12.15	15.15		27.30	36
9842	1/2"		34	.235		11.80	16.95		28.75	38.50
9843	3/4"		32	.250		16.45	18		34.45	45
9844	1"	▼	30	.267		25.50	19.20		44.70	56.50
9845	1-1/4"	Q-1	52	.308		40.50	19.95		60.45	74.50
9846	1-1/2"		48	.333		48.50	21.50		70	85.50
9847	2"	▼	42	.381		70	24.50		94.50	114
9860	Plug, 1/4"	1 Plum	38	.211		4.53	15.15		19.68	27.50
9861	3/8"		38	.211		5.90	15.15		21.05	29
9862	1/2"		34	.235		4.90	16.95		21.85	31
9863	3/4"		32	.250		6.20	18		24.20	34
9864	1"	▼	30	.267		9.50	19.20		28.70	39
9865	1-1/4"	Q-1	52	.308		22.50	19.95		42.45	54.50
9866	1-1/2"		48	.333		29.50	21.50		51	64.50
9867	2"	▼	42	.381		47	24.50		71.50	88.50
9880	Union, bronze seat, 1/4"	1 Plum	15	.533		89.50	38.50		128	156
9881	3/8"		15	.533		89.50	38.50		128	156
9882	1/2"		14	.571		86	41		127	156
9883	3/4"		13	.615		115	44.50		159.50	192
9884	1"	▼	12	.667		130	48		178	215
9885	1-1/4"	Q-1	21	.762		252	49.50		301.50	350
9886	1-1/2"		19	.842		260	54.50		314.50	370
9887	2"	▼	17	.941		355	61		416	480
9900	Coupling, 1/4"	1 Plum	19	.421		12.55	30.50		43.05	59
9901	3/8"	▼	19	.421		12.55	30.50		43.05	59

22 11 Facility Water Distribution

22 11 13 – Facility Water Distribution Piping

22 11 13.45 Pipe Fittings, Steel, Threaded

		Crew	Daily Output	Labor-Hours	Unit	Material	2023 Bare Costs Labor	Equipment	Total	Total Incl O&P
9902	1/2"	1 Plum	17	.471	Ea.	10.35	34		44.35	62
9903	3/4"		16	.500		13.45	36		49.45	68.50
9904	1"	↓	15	.533		23.50	38.50		62	83.50
9905	1-1/4"	Q-1	26	.615		39	40		79	103
9906	1-1/2"		24	.667		50.50	43		93.50	120
9907	2"		21	.762		63	49.50		112.50	143

22 11 13.47 Pipe Fittings, Steel

		Crew	Daily Output	Labor-Hours	Unit	Material	2023 Bare Costs Labor	Equipment	Total	Total Incl O&P
0010	**PIPE FITTINGS, STEEL**, flanged, welded & special									
0020	Flanged joints, CI, standard weight, black. One gasket & bolt									
0040	set, mat'l only, required at each joint, not included (see line 0620)									
0060	90° elbow, straight, 1-1/2" pipe size	Q-1	14	1.143	Ea.	1,025	74		1,099	1,225
0080	2" pipe size		13	1.231		570	80		650	745
0090	2-1/2" pipe size		12	1.333		615	86.50		701.50	805
0100	3" pipe size		11	1.455		515	94.50		609.50	705
0110	4" pipe size		8	2		635	130		765	895
0120	5" pipe size	↓	7	2.286		1,500	148		1,648	1,875
0130	6" pipe size	Q-2	9	2.667		995	179		1,174	1,375
0140	8" pipe size		8	3		1,725	202		1,927	2,200
0150	10" pipe size		7	3.429		3,775	231		4,006	4,500
0160	12" pipe size	↓	6	4	↓	7,575	269		7,844	8,725
0171	90° elbow, reducing									
0172	2-1/2" by 2" pipe size	Q-1	12	1.333	Ea.	2,000	86.50		2,086.50	2,325
0173	3" by 2-1/2" pipe size		11	1.455		1,900	94.50		1,994.50	2,250
0174	4" by 3" pipe size		8	2		1,400	130		1,530	1,750
0175	5" by 3" pipe size	↓	7	2.286		3,775	148		3,923	4,375
0176	6" by 4" pipe size	Q-2	9	2.667		1,750	179		1,929	2,200
0177	8" by 6" pipe size		8	3		2,550	202		2,752	3,100
0178	10" by 8" pipe size		7	3.429		4,850	231		5,081	5,700
0179	12" by 10" pipe size	↓	6	4		9,300	269		9,569	10,600
0200	45° elbow, straight, 1-1/2" pipe size	Q-1	14	1.143		1,450	74		1,524	1,700
0220	2" pipe size		13	1.231		825	80		905	1,025
0230	2-1/2" pipe size		12	1.333		880	86.50		966.50	1,100
0240	3" pipe size		11	1.455		855	94.50		949.50	1,075
0250	4" pipe size		8	2		965	130		1,095	1,250
0260	5" pipe size	↓	7	2.286		2,300	148		2,448	2,750
0270	6" pipe size	Q-2	9	2.667		1,575	179		1,754	2,000
0280	8" pipe size		8	3		2,300	202		2,502	2,825
0290	10" pipe size		7	3.429		4,875	231		5,106	5,700
0300	12" pipe size	↓	6	4	↓	7,425	269		7,694	8,575
0310	Cross, straight									
0311	2-1/2" pipe size	Q-1	6	2.667	Ea.	2,225	173		2,398	2,675
0312	3" pipe size		5	3.200		1,900	208		2,108	2,400
0313	4" pipe size		4	4		2,475	259		2,734	3,100
0314	5" pipe size	↓	3	5.333		6,550	345		6,895	7,750
0315	6" pipe size	Q-2	5	4.800		5,200	325		5,525	6,200
0316	8" pipe size		4	6		955	405		1,360	1,650
0317	10" pipe size		3	8		1,875	540		2,415	2,875
0318	12" pipe size	↓	2	12		2,125	805		2,930	3,550
0350	Tee, straight, 1-1/2" pipe size	Q-1	10	1.600		1,200	104		1,304	1,450
0370	2" pipe size		9	1.778		625	115		740	855
0380	2-1/2" pipe size		8	2		910	130		1,040	1,200
0390	3" pipe size	↓	7	2.286		635	148		783	920

22 11 Facility Water Distribution

22 11 13 – Facility Water Distribution Piping

22 11 13.47 Pipe Fittings, Steel		Crew	Daily Output	Labor-Hours	Unit	Material	2023 Bare Costs Labor	Equipment	Total	Total Incl O&P
0400	4" pipe size	Q-1	5	3.200	Ea.	970	208		1,178	1,375
0410	5" pipe size	↓	4	4		2,600	259		2,859	3,225
0420	6" pipe size	Q-2	6	4		1,400	269		1,669	1,950
0430	8" pipe size		5	4.800		2,400	325		2,725	3,125
0440	10" pipe size		4	6		6,450	405		6,855	7,700
0450	12" pipe size	↓	3	8	↓	10,100	540		10,640	12,000
0459	Tee, reducing on outlet									
0460	2-1/2" by 2" pipe size	Q-1	8	2	Ea.	520	130		650	765
0461	3" by 2-1/2" pipe size		7	2.286		266	148		414	515
0462	4" by 3" pipe size		5	3.200		2,000	208		2,208	2,500
0463	5" by 4" pipe size	↓	4	4		850	259		1,109	1,325
0464	6" by 4" pipe size	Q-2	6	4		1,925	269		2,194	2,500
0465	8" by 6" pipe size		5	4.800		3,000	325		3,325	3,775
0466	10" by 8" pipe size		4	6		6,850	405		7,255	8,125
0467	12" by 10" pipe size	↓	3	8		1,700	540		2,240	2,675
0476	Reducer, concentric									
0477	3" by 2-1/2"	Q-1	12	1.333	Ea.	1,150	86.50		1,236.50	1,375
0478	4" by 3"		9	1.778		1,275	115		1,390	1,575
0479	5" by 4"	↓	8	2		1,975	130		2,105	2,375
0480	6" by 4"	Q-2	10	2.400		1,725	161		1,886	2,125
0481	8" by 6"		9	2.667		2,150	179		2,329	2,650
0482	10" by 8"		8	3		4,450	202		4,652	5,200
0483	12" by 10"	↓	7	3.429	↓	7,675	231		7,906	8,800
0492	Reducer, eccentric									
0493	4" by 3"	Q-1	8	2	Ea.	2,075	130		2,205	2,475
0494	5" by 4"	"	7	2.286		3,400	148		3,548	3,975
0495	6" by 4"	Q-2	9	2.667		1,975	179		2,154	2,425
0496	8" by 6"		8	3		2,500	202		2,702	3,025
0497	10" by 8"		7	3.429		6,350	231		6,581	7,325
0498	12" by 10"	↓	6	4		975	269		1,244	1,475
0500	For galvanized elbows and tees, add					100%				
0520	For extra heavy weight elbows and tees, add					140%				
0620	Gasket and bolt set, 150 lb., 1/2" pipe size	1 Plum	20	.400		5.95	29		34.95	49.50
0622	3/4" pipe size		19	.421		5.05	30.50		35.55	50.50
0624	1" pipe size		18	.444		7.90	32		39.90	56.50
0626	1-1/4" pipe size		17	.471		9.55	34		43.55	61
0628	1-1/2" pipe size		15	.533		8	38.50		46.50	66.50
0630	2" pipe size		13	.615		14.95	44.50		59.45	82.50
0640	2-1/2" pipe size		12	.667		14.25	48		62.25	87
0650	3" pipe size		11	.727		13.50	52.50		66	93
0660	3-1/2" pipe size		9	.889		24.50	64		88.50	123
0670	4" pipe size		8	1		22	72		94	131
0680	5" pipe size		7	1.143		37.50	82.50		120	165
0690	6" pipe size		6	1.333		73.50	96		169.50	224
0700	8" pipe size		5	1.600		39.50	115		154.50	215
0710	10" pipe size		4.50	1.778		77	128		205	276
0720	12" pipe size		4.20	1.905		98	137		235	315
0730	14" pipe size		4	2		114	144		258	340
0740	16" pipe size		3	2.667		141	192		333	440
0750	18" pipe size		2.70	2.963		147	213		360	480
0760	20" pipe size		2.30	3.478		340	251		591	750
0780	24" pipe size		1.90	4.211		425	305		730	920
0790	26" pipe size		1.60	5		580	360		940	1,175

22 11 Facility Water Distribution

22 11 13 – Facility Water Distribution Piping

22 11 13.47 Pipe Fittings, Steel		Crew	Daily Output	Labor-Hours	Unit	Material	2023 Bare Costs Labor	Equipment	Total	Total Incl O&P
0810	30" pipe size	1 Plum	1.40	5.714	Ea.	1,125	410		1,535	1,875
0830	36" pipe size	↓	1.10	7.273	↓	2,100	525		2,625	3,100
0850	For 300 lb. gasket set, add					40%				
2000	Flanged unions, 125 lb., black, 1/2" pipe size	1 Plum	17	.471	Ea.	169	34		203	237
2040	3/4" pipe size		17	.471		202	34		236	274
2050	1" pipe size		16	.500		196	36		232	270
2060	1-1/4" pipe size	Q-1	28	.571		232	37		269	310
2070	1-1/2" pipe size		27	.593		214	38.50		252.50	293
2080	2" pipe size		26	.615		252	40		292	335
2090	2-1/2" pipe size		24	.667		340	43		383	440
2100	3" pipe size		22	.727		385	47		432	495
2110	3-1/2" pipe size		18	.889		655	57.50		712.50	805
2120	4" pipe size		16	1		525	65		590	670
2130	5" pipe size	↓	14	1.143		1,225	74		1,299	1,450
2140	6" pipe size	Q-2	19	1.263		1,150	85		1,235	1,375
2150	8" pipe size	"	16	1.500		2,775	101		2,876	3,200
2200	For galvanized unions, add				↓	150%				
2290	Threaded flange									
2300	Cast iron									
2310	Black, 125 lb., per flange									
2320	1" pipe size	1 Plum	27	.296	Ea.	73.50	21.50		95	113
2330	1-1/4" pipe size	Q-1	44	.364		99.50	23.50		123	144
2340	1-1/2" pipe size		40	.400		81.50	26		107.50	128
2350	2" pipe size		36	.444		91.50	29		120.50	144
2360	2-1/2" pipe size		28	.571		107	37		144	174
2370	3" pipe size		20	.800		138	52		190	230
2380	3-1/2" pipe size		16	1		207	65		272	325
2390	4" pipe size		12	1.333		165	86.50		251.50	310
2400	5" pipe size	↓	10	1.600		263	104		367	445
2410	6" pipe size	Q-2	14	1.714		297	115		412	495
2420	8" pipe size		12	2		470	135		605	715
2430	10" pipe size		10	2.400		830	161		991	1,150
2440	12" pipe size	↓	8	3	↓	1,975	202		2,177	2,475
2460	For galvanized flanges, add					95%				
2490	Blind flange									
2492	Cast iron									
2494	Black, 125 lb., per flange									
2496	1" pipe size	1 Plum	27	.296	Ea.	132	21.50		153.50	177
2500	1-1/2" pipe size	Q-1	40	.400		148	26		174	202
2502	2" pipe size		36	.444		167	29		196	227
2504	2-1/2" pipe size		28	.571		184	37		221	258
2506	3" pipe size		20	.800		221	52		273	320
2508	4" pipe size		12	1.333		283	86.50		369.50	440
2510	5" pipe size	↓	10	1.600		460	104		564	660
2512	6" pipe size	Q-2	14	1.714		500	115		615	720
2514	8" pipe size		12	2		785	135		920	1,050
2516	10" pipe size		10	2.400		1,150	161		1,311	1,525
2518	12" pipe size	↓	8	3	↓	2,350	202		2,552	2,875
2520	For galvanized flanges, add					80%				
2570	Threaded flange									
2580	Forged steel									
2590	Black, 150 lb., per flange									
2600	1/2" pipe size	1 Plum	30	.267	Ea.	37	19.20		56.20	69

22 11 Facility Water Distribution

22 11 13 – Facility Water Distribution Piping

22 11 13.47 Pipe Fittings, Steel		Crew	Daily Output	Labor-Hours	Unit	Material	2023 Bare Costs Labor	Equipment	Total	Total Incl O&P
2610	3/4" pipe size	1 Plum	28	.286	Ea.	37	20.50		57.50	71
2620	1" pipe size	↓	27	.296		37	21.50		58.50	72.50
2630	1-1/4" pipe size	Q-1	44	.364		37	23.50		60.50	75.50
2640	1-1/2" pipe size		40	.400		37	26		63	79
2650	2" pipe size		36	.444		37	29		66	84
2660	2-1/2" pipe size		28	.571		60.50	37		97.50	122
2670	3" pipe size		20	.800		45	52		97	127
2690	4" pipe size		12	1.333		59.50	86.50		146	195
2700	5" pipe size	↓	10	1.600		111	104		215	277
2710	6" pipe size	Q-2	14	1.714		124	115		239	310
2720	8" pipe size		12	2		209	135		344	430
2730	10" pipe size	↓	10	2.400	↓	380	161		541	660
2860	Black, 300 lb., per flange									
2870	1/2" pipe size	1 Plum	30	.267	Ea.	41	19.20		60.20	73.50
2880	3/4" pipe size		28	.286		42	20.50		62.50	77
2890	1" pipe size	↓	27	.296		42	21.50		63.50	78.50
2900	1-1/4" pipe size	Q-1	44	.364		42	23.50		65.50	81.50
2910	1-1/2" pipe size		40	.400		42	26		68	85
2920	2" pipe size		36	.444		47.50	29		76.50	95.50
2930	2-1/2" pipe size		28	.571		79.50	37		116.50	143
2940	3" pipe size		20	.800		71.50	52		123.50	156
2960	4" pipe size	↓	12	1.333		103	86.50		189.50	242
2970	6" pipe size	Q-2	14	1.714	↓	192	115		307	385
3000	Weld joint, butt, carbon steel, standard weight									
3040	90° elbow, long radius									
3050	1/2" pipe size	Q-15	16	1	Ea.	15	65	4.01	84.01	117
3060	3/4" pipe size		16	1		15	65	4.01	84.01	117
3070	1" pipe size		16	1		15	65	4.01	84.01	117
3080	1-1/4" pipe size		14	1.143		15	74	4.58	93.58	133
3090	1-1/2" pipe size		13	1.231		15	80	4.94	99.94	141
3100	2" pipe size		10	1.600		28	104	6.40	138.40	193
3110	2-1/2" pipe size		8	2		23.50	130	8	161.50	227
3120	3" pipe size		7	2.286		55	148	9.15	212.15	292
3130	4" pipe size		5	3.200		48.50	208	12.85	269.35	375
3136	5" pipe size	↓	4	4		147	259	16.05	422.05	565
3140	6" pipe size	Q-16	5	4.800		102	325	12.80	439.80	605
3150	8" pipe size		3.75	6.400		198	430	17.10	645.10	875
3160	10" pipe size		3	8		380	540	21.50	941.50	1,250
3170	12" pipe size		2.50	9.600		565	645	25.50	1,235.50	1,625
3180	14" pipe size		2	12		1,200	805	32	2,037	2,550
3190	16" pipe size		1.50	16		1,100	1,075	42.50	2,217.50	2,875
3191	18" pipe size		1.25	19.200		1,475	1,300	51.50	2,826.50	3,575
3192	20" pipe size		1.15	20.870		2,025	1,400	55.50	3,480.50	4,375
3194	24" pipe size	↓	1.02	23.529	↓	2,900	1,575	63	4,538	5,600
3200	45° elbow, long									
3210	1/2" pipe size	Q-15	16	1	Ea.	95	65	4.01	164.01	206
3220	3/4" pipe size		16	1		95	65	4.01	164.01	206
3230	1" pipe size		16	1		20	65	4.01	89.01	123
3240	1-1/4" pipe size		14	1.143		20	74	4.58	98.58	138
3250	1-1/2" pipe size		13	1.231		20	80	4.94	104.94	146
3260	2" pipe size		10	1.600		27	104	6.40	137.40	192
3270	2-1/2" pipe size		8	2		24.50	130	8	162.50	229
3280	3" pipe size		7	2.286		24.50	148	9.15	181.65	258

22 11 Facility Water Distribution

22 11 13 – Facility Water Distribution Piping

22 11 13.47 Pipe Fittings, Steel		Crew	Daily Output	Labor-Hours	Unit	Material	2023 Bare Costs Labor	Equipment	Total	Total Incl O&P
3290	4" pipe size	Q-15	5	3.200	Ea.	42	208	12.85	262.85	370
3296	5" pipe size	▼	4	4		92.50	259	16.05	367.55	505
3300	6" pipe size	Q-16	5	4.800		120	325	12.80	457.80	625
3310	8" pipe size		3.75	6.400		200	430	17.10	647.10	880
3320	10" pipe size		3	8		400	540	21.50	961.50	1,275
3330	12" pipe size		2.50	9.600		565	645	25.50	1,235.50	1,625
3340	14" pipe size		2	12		760	805	32	1,597	2,075
3341	16" pipe size		1.50	16		1,350	1,075	42.50	2,467.50	3,150
3342	18" pipe size		1.25	19.200		1,925	1,300	51.50	3,276.50	4,075
3343	20" pipe size		1.15	20.870		2,000	1,400	55.50	3,455.50	4,325
3345	24" pipe size		1.05	22.857		3,025	1,525	61	4,611	5,700
3346	26" pipe size		.85	28.235		4,125	1,900	75.50	6,100.50	7,425
3347	30" pipe size		.45	53.333		4,525	3,575	142	8,242	10,500
3349	36" pipe size	▼	.38	63.158	▼	4,975	4,250	169	9,394	12,000
3350	Tee, straight									
3352	For reducing tees and concentrics see starting line 4600									
3360	1/2" pipe size	Q-15	10	1.600	Ea.	47.50	104	6.40	157.90	215
3370	3/4" pipe size		10	1.600		47.50	104	6.40	157.90	215
3380	1" pipe size		10	1.600		62.50	104	6.40	172.90	231
3390	1-1/4" pipe size		9	1.778		62.50	115	7.15	184.65	249
3400	1-1/2" pipe size		8	2		62.50	130	8	200.50	271
3410	2" pipe size		6	2.667		59.50	173	10.70	243.20	335
3420	2-1/2" pipe size		5	3.200		62.50	208	12.85	283.35	395
3430	3" pipe size		4	4		69.50	259	16.05	344.55	480
3440	4" pipe size		3	5.333		98	345	21.50	464.50	645
3446	5" pipe size	▼	2.50	6.400		239	415	25.50	679.50	910
3450	6" pipe size	Q-16	3	8		168	540	21.50	729.50	1,000
3460	8" pipe size		2.50	9.600		435	645	25.50	1,105.50	1,475
3470	10" pipe size		2	12		855	805	32	1,692	2,175
3480	12" pipe size		1.60	15		805	1,000	40	1,845	2,425
3481	14" pipe size		1.30	18.462		2,100	1,250	49.50	3,399.50	4,200
3482	16" pipe size		1	24		1,575	1,625	64	3,264	4,200
3483	18" pipe size		.80	30		3,750	2,025	80	5,855	7,225
3484	20" pipe size		.75	32		5,850	2,150	85.50	8,085.50	9,725
3486	24" pipe size		.70	34.286		7,550	2,300	91.50	9,941.50	11,900
3487	26" pipe size		.55	43.636		10,300	2,925	117	13,342	15,800
3488	30" pipe size		.30	80		11,300	5,375	214	16,889	20,700
3490	36" pipe size	▼	.25	96		12,500	6,450	256	19,206	23,600
3491	Eccentric reducer, 1-1/2" pipe size	Q-15	14	1.143		69.50	74	4.58	148.08	193
3492	2" pipe size		11	1.455		80.50	94.50	5.85	180.85	236
3493	2-1/2" pipe size		9	1.778		88.50	115	7.15	210.65	277
3494	3" pipe size		8	2		116	130	8	254	330
3495	4" pipe size	▼	6	2.667		234	173	10.70	417.70	525
3496	6" pipe size	Q-16	5	4.800		350	325	12.80	687.80	880
3497	8" pipe size		4	6		405	405	16	826	1,075
3498	10" pipe size		3	8		695	540	21.50	1,256.50	1,575
3499	12" pipe size		2.50	9.600		1,025	645	25.50	1,695.50	2,125
3501	Cap, 1-1/2" pipe size	Q-15	28	.571		23.50	37	2.29	62.79	83.50
3502	2" pipe size		22	.727		29	47	2.92	78.92	106
3503	2-1/2" pipe size		18	.889		30.50	57.50	3.56	91.56	123
3504	3" pipe size		16	1		30.50	65	4.01	99.51	134
3505	4" pipe size	▼	12	1.333		38	86.50	5.35	129.85	176
3506	6" pipe size	Q-16	10	2.400		76	161	6.40	243.40	330

22 11 Facility Water Distribution

22 11 13 — Facility Water Distribution Piping

22 11 13.47 Pipe Fittings, Steel

		Crew	Daily Output	Labor-Hours	Unit	Material	2023 Bare Costs Labor	Equipment	Total	Total Incl O&P
3507	8" pipe size	Q-16	8	3	Ea.	107	202	8	317	425
3508	10" pipe size		6	4		208	269	10.70	487.70	640
3509	12" pipe size		5	4.800		315	325	12.80	652.80	840
3511	14" pipe size		4	6		385	405	16	806	1,050
3512	16" pipe size		4	6		445	405	16	866	1,100
3513	18" pipe size		3	8		665	540	21.50	1,226.50	1,550
3517	Weld joint, butt, carbon steel, extra strong									
3519	90° elbow, long									
3520	1/2" pipe size	Q-15	13	1.231	Ea.	132	80	4.94	216.94	269
3530	3/4" pipe size		12	1.333		132	86.50	5.35	223.85	280
3540	1" pipe size		11	1.455		132	94.50	5.85	232.35	292
3550	1-1/4" pipe size		10	1.600		132	104	6.40	242.40	305
3560	1-1/2" pipe size		9	1.778		132	115	7.15	254.15	325
3570	2" pipe size		8	2		33.50	130	8	171.50	239
3580	2-1/2" pipe size		7	2.286		47	148	9.15	204.15	283
3590	3" pipe size		6	2.667		60.50	173	10.70	244.20	335
3600	4" pipe size		4	4		99	259	16.05	374.05	510
3606	5" pipe size		3.50	4.571		237	296	18.35	551.35	720
3610	6" pipe size	Q-16	4.50	5.333		251	360	14.25	625.25	825
3620	8" pipe size		3.50	6.857		475	460	18.30	953.30	1,225
3630	10" pipe size		2.50	9.600		1,000	645	25.50	1,670.50	2,100
3640	12" pipe size		2.25	10.667		1,225	715	28.50	1,968.50	2,450
3650	45° elbow, long									
3660	1/2" pipe size	Q-15	13	1.231	Ea.	94	80	4.94	178.94	228
3670	3/4" pipe size		12	1.333		94	86.50	5.35	185.85	239
3680	1" pipe size		11	1.455		26.50	94.50	5.85	126.85	176
3690	1-1/4" pipe size		10	1.600		26.50	104	6.40	136.90	191
3700	1-1/2" pipe size		9	1.778		26.50	115	7.15	148.65	209
3710	2" pipe size		8	2		35	130	8	173	240
3720	2-1/2" pipe size		7	2.286		78	148	9.15	235.15	315
3730	3" pipe size		6	2.667		45	173	10.70	228.70	320
3740	4" pipe size		4	4		71	259	16.05	346.05	480
3746	5" pipe size		3.50	4.571		169	296	18.35	483.35	645
3750	6" pipe size	Q-16	4.50	5.333		195	360	14.25	569.25	765
3760	8" pipe size		3.50	6.857		335	460	18.30	813.30	1,075
3770	10" pipe size		2.50	9.600		650	645	25.50	1,320.50	1,700
3780	12" pipe size		2.25	10.667		965	715	28.50	1,708.50	2,150
3800	Tee, straight									
3810	1/2" pipe size	Q-15	9	1.778	Ea.	207	115	7.15	329.15	410
3820	3/4" pipe size		8.50	1.882		35	122	7.55	164.55	229
3830	1" pipe size		8	2		105	130	8	243	315
3840	1-1/4" pipe size		7	2.286		62.50	148	9.15	219.65	300
3850	1-1/2" pipe size		6	2.667		35	173	10.70	218.70	310
3860	2" pipe size		5	3.200		74	208	12.85	294.85	405
3870	2-1/2" pipe size		4	4		123	259	16.05	398.05	540
3880	3" pipe size		3.50	4.571		195	296	18.35	509.35	675
3890	4" pipe size		2.50	6.400		185	415	25.50	625.50	850
3896	5" pipe size		2.25	7.111		405	460	28.50	893.50	1,175
3900	6" pipe size	Q-16	2.25	10.667		355	715	28.50	1,098.50	1,500
3910	8" pipe size		2	12		700	805	32	1,537	2,000
3920	10" pipe size		1.75	13.714		1,050	920	36.50	2,006.50	2,575
3930	12" pipe size		1.50	16		1,525	1,075	42.50	2,642.50	3,325
4000	Eccentric reducer, 1-1/2" pipe size	Q-15	10	1.600		46.50	104	6.40	156.90	213

22 11 Facility Water Distribution

22 11 13 – Facility Water Distribution Piping

22 11 13.47 Pipe Fittings, Steel

		Crew	Daily Output	Labor-Hours	Unit	Material	2023 Bare Costs Labor	2023 Bare Costs Equipment	Total	Total Incl O&P
4010	2" pipe size	Q-15	9	1.778	Ea.	60	115	7.15	182.15	246
4020	2-1/2" pipe size		8	2		90	130	8	228	300
4030	3" pipe size		7	2.286		74.50	148	9.15	231.65	315
4040	4" pipe size		5	3.200		116	208	12.85	336.85	450
4046	5" pipe size	↓	4.70	3.404		500	221	13.65	734.65	895
4050	6" pipe size	Q-16	4.50	5.333		480	360	14.25	854.25	1,075
4060	8" pipe size		3.50	6.857		495	460	18.30	973.30	1,250
4070	10" pipe size		2.50	9.600		840	645	25.50	1,510.50	1,925
4080	12" pipe size		2.25	10.667		1,075	715	28.50	1,818.50	2,275
4090	14" pipe size		2.10	11.429		1,875	770	30.50	2,675.50	3,225
4100	16" pipe size	↓	1.90	12.632		2,325	850	33.50	3,208.50	3,875
4151	Cap, 1-1/2" pipe size	Q-15	24	.667		29	43	2.67	74.67	99.50
4152	2" pipe size		18	.889		29	57.50	3.56	90.06	122
4153	2-1/2" pipe size		16	1		40	65	4.01	109.01	145
4154	3" pipe size		14	1.143		44.50	74	4.58	123.08	165
4155	4" pipe size	↓	10	1.600		60.50	104	6.40	170.90	229
4156	6" pipe size	Q-16	9	2.667		123	179	7.10	309.10	410
4157	8" pipe size		7	3.429		184	231	9.15	424.15	560
4158	10" pipe size		5	4.800		283	325	12.80	620.80	805
4159	12" pipe size	↓	4	6	↓	380	405	16	801	1,025
4190	Weld fittings, reducing, standard weight									
4200	Welding ring w/spacer pins, 2" pipe size				Ea.	4.33			4.33	4.76
4210	2-1/2" pipe size					3.63			3.63	3.99
4220	3" pipe size					4.59			4.59	5.05
4230	4" pipe size					5.10			5.10	5.65
4236	5" pipe size					6.35			6.35	7
4240	6" pipe size					6.65			6.65	7.35
4250	8" pipe size					7.35			7.35	8.10
4260	10" pipe size					8.55			8.55	9.40
4270	12" pipe size					9.95			9.95	10.90
4280	14" pipe size					10.10			10.10	11.10
4290	16" pipe size					11.80			11.80	12.95
4300	18" pipe size					13.20			13.20	14.50
4310	20" pipe size					15			15	16.50
4330	24" pipe size					21			21	23.50
4340	26" pipe size					25.50			25.50	28
4350	30" pipe size					29			29	32
4370	36" pipe size				↓	35.50			35.50	39
4600	Tee, reducing on outlet									
4601	2-1/2" x 2" pipe size	Q-15	5	3.200	Ea.	75.50	208	12.85	296.35	405
4602	3" x 2-1/2" pipe size		4	4		73.50	259	16.05	348.55	485
4604	4" x 3" pipe size		3	5.333		93.50	345	21.50	460	640
4605	5" x 4" pipe size	↓	2.50	6.400		202	415	25.50	642.50	870
4606	6" x 5" pipe size	Q-16	3	8		182	540	21.50	743.50	1,025
4607	8" x 6" pipe size		2.50	9.600		345	645	25.50	1,015.50	1,375
4608	10" x 8" pipe size		2	12		640	805	32	1,477	1,950
4609	12" x 10" pipe size		1.60	15		800	1,000	40	1,840	2,425
4610	16" x 12" pipe size		1.50	16		3,625	1,075	42.50	4,742.50	5,650
4611	14" x 12" pipe size	↓	1.52	15.789		1,425	1,050	42	2,517	3,200
4618	Reducer, concentric									
4619	2-1/2" by 2" pipe size	Q-15	10	1.600	Ea.	61	104	6.40	171.40	229
4620	3" by 2-1/2" pipe size		9	1.778		26.50	115	7.15	148.65	209
4621	3-1/2" by 3" pipe size	↓	8	2		76	130	8	214	285

22 11 Facility Water Distribution

22 11 13 – Facility Water Distribution Piping

22 11 13.47 Pipe Fittings, Steel		Crew	Daily Output	Labor-Hours	Unit	Material	2023 Bare Costs Labor	Equipment	Total	Total Incl O&P
4622	4" by 2-1/2" pipe size	Q-15	7	2.286	Ea.	41.50	148	9.15	198.65	277
4623	5" by 3" pipe size		7	2.286		209	148	9.15	366.15	460
4624	6" by 4" pipe size	Q-16	6	4		71	269	10.70	350.70	490
4625	8" by 6" pipe size		5	4.800		93	325	12.80	430.80	595
4626	10" by 8" pipe size		4	6		180	405	16	601	815
4627	12" by 10" pipe size		3	8		425	540	21.50	986.50	1,300
4660	Reducer, eccentric									
4662	3" x 2" pipe size	Q-15	8	2	Ea.	44.50	130	8	182.50	251
4664	4" x 3" pipe size		6	2.667		132	173	10.70	315.70	415
4666	4" x 2" pipe size		6	2.667		66	173	10.70	249.70	345
4670	6" x 4" pipe size	Q-16	5	4.800		111	325	12.80	448.80	615
4672	6" x 3" pipe size		5	4.800		175	325	12.80	512.80	685
4676	8" x 6" pipe size		4	6		350	405	16	771	1,000
4678	8" x 4" pipe size		4	6		260	405	16	681	905
4682	10" x 8" pipe size		3	8		310	540	21.50	871.50	1,175
4684	10" x 6" pipe size		3	8		550	540	21.50	1,111.50	1,425
4688	12" x 10" pipe size		2.50	9.600		485	645	25.50	1,155.50	1,525
4690	12" x 8" pipe size		2.50	9.600		765	645	25.50	1,435.50	1,825
4691	14" x 12" pipe size		2.20	10.909		855	735	29	1,619	2,075
4693	16" x 14" pipe size		1.80	13.333		1,300	895	35.50	2,230.50	2,800
4694	16" x 12" pipe size		2	12		1,725	805	32	2,562	3,125
4696	18" x 16" pipe size		1.60	15		2,350	1,000	40	3,390	4,150
5000	Weld joint, socket, forged steel, 3000 lb., schedule 40 pipe									
5010	90° elbow, straight									
5020	1/4" pipe size	Q-15	22	.727	Ea.	40	47	2.92	89.92	118
5030	3/8" pipe size		22	.727		40	47	2.92	89.92	118
5040	1/2" pipe size		20	.800		19.35	52	3.21	74.56	103
5050	3/4" pipe size		20	.800		23	52	3.21	78.21	107
5060	1" pipe size		20	.800		32	52	3.21	87.21	117
5070	1-1/4" pipe size		18	.889		57	57.50	3.56	118.06	152
5080	1-1/2" pipe size		16	1		66.50	65	4.01	135.51	174
5090	2" pipe size		12	1.333		97.50	86.50	5.35	189.35	242
5100	2-1/2" pipe size		10	1.600		305	104	6.40	415.40	495
5110	3" pipe size		8	2		495	130	8	633	745
5120	4" pipe size		6	2.667		1,275	173	10.70	1,458.70	1,675
5130	45° elbow, straight									
5134	1/4" pipe size	Q-15	22	.727	Ea.	40	47	2.92	89.92	118
5135	3/8" pipe size		22	.727		40	47	2.92	89.92	118
5136	1/2" pipe size		20	.800		29.50	52	3.21	84.71	114
5137	3/4" pipe size		20	.800		34.50	52	3.21	89.71	119
5140	1" pipe size		20	.800		34.50	52	3.21	89.71	119
5150	1-1/4" pipe size		18	.889		61.50	57.50	3.56	122.56	158
5160	1-1/2" pipe size		16	1		75.50	65	4.01	144.51	184
5170	2" pipe size		12	1.333		122	86.50	5.35	213.85	269
5180	2-1/2" pipe size		10	1.600		320	104	6.40	430.40	510
5190	3" pipe size		8	2		540	130	8	678	795
5200	4" pipe size		6	2.667		1,100	173	10.70	1,283.70	1,475
5250	Tee, straight									
5254	1/4" pipe size	Q-15	15	1.067	Ea.	44	69	4.28	117.28	156
5255	3/8" pipe size		15	1.067		44	69	4.28	117.28	156
5256	1/2" pipe size		13	1.231		27.50	80	4.94	112.44	155
5257	3/4" pipe size		13	1.231		33.50	80	4.94	118.44	161
5260	1" pipe size		13	1.231		45.50	80	4.94	130.44	175

22 11 Facility Water Distribution

22 11 13 – Facility Water Distribution Piping

22 11 13.47 Pipe Fittings, Steel

		Crew	Daily Output	Labor-Hours	Unit	Material	2023 Bare Costs Labor	Equipment	Total	Total Incl O&P
5270	1-1/4" pipe size	Q-15	12	1.333	Ea.	70	86.50	5.35	161.85	212
5280	1-1/2" pipe size		11	1.455		93	94.50	5.85	193.35	249
5290	2" pipe size		8	2		134	130	8	272	350
5300	2-1/2" pipe size		6	2.667		385	173	10.70	568.70	695
5310	3" pipe size		5	3.200		920	208	12.85	1,140.85	1,350
5320	4" pipe size		4	4		1,475	259	16.05	1,750.05	2,025
5350	For reducing sizes, add					60%				
5450	Couplings									
5451	1/4" pipe size	Q-15	23	.696	Ea.	25.50	45	2.79	73.29	98.50
5452	3/8" pipe size		23	.696		4.42	45	2.79	52.21	75.50
5453	1/2" pipe size		21	.762		6	49.50	3.06	58.56	83.50
5454	3/4" pipe size		21	.762		10.65	49.50	3.06	63.21	88.50
5460	1" pipe size		20	.800		7.10	52	3.21	62.31	89
5470	1-1/4" pipe size		20	.800		14.90	52	3.21	70.11	97.50
5480	1-1/2" pipe size		18	.889		15.50	57.50	3.56	76.56	107
5490	2" pipe size		14	1.143		20	74	4.58	98.58	138
5500	2-1/2" pipe size		12	1.333		50	86.50	5.35	141.85	190
5510	3" pipe size		9	1.778		170	115	7.15	292.15	365
5520	4" pipe size		7	2.286		154	148	9.15	311.15	400
5570	Union, 1/4" pipe size		21	.762		87	49.50	3.06	139.56	172
5571	3/8" pipe size		21	.762		87	49.50	3.06	139.56	172
5572	1/2" pipe size		19	.842		79.50	54.50	3.38	137.38	173
5573	3/4" pipe size		19	.842		127	54.50	3.38	184.88	225
5574	1" pipe size		19	.842		28.50	54.50	3.38	86.38	117
5575	1-1/4" pipe size		17	.941		221	61	3.77	285.77	340
5576	1-1/2" pipe size		15	1.067		249	69	4.28	322.28	380
5577	2" pipe size		11	1.455		315	94.50	5.85	415.35	490
5600	Reducer, 1/4" pipe size		23	.696		64.50	45	2.79	112.29	142
5601	3/8" pipe size		23	.696		68	45	2.79	115.79	146
5602	1/2" pipe size		21	.762		41.50	49.50	3.06	94.06	122
5603	3/4" pipe size		21	.762		41.50	49.50	3.06	94.06	122
5604	1" pipe size		21	.762		58	49.50	3.06	110.56	141
5605	1-1/4" pipe size		19	.842		74	54.50	3.38	131.88	167
5607	1-1/2" pipe size		17	.941		79.50	61	3.77	144.27	183
5608	2" pipe size		13	1.231		87.50	80	4.94	172.44	221
5612	Cap, 1/4" pipe size		46	.348		24	22.50	1.39	47.89	61.50
5613	3/8" pipe size		46	.348		24	22.50	1.39	47.89	61.50
5614	1/2" pipe size		42	.381		14.70	24.50	1.53	40.73	55
5615	3/4" pipe size		42	.381		17.75	24.50	1.53	43.78	58
5616	1" pipe size		42	.381		26	24.50	1.53	52.03	67
5617	1-1/4" pipe size		38	.421		30.50	27.50	1.69	59.69	76
5618	1-1/2" pipe size		34	.471		15.55	30.50	1.89	47.94	64.50
5619	2" pipe size		26	.615		68	40	2.47	110.47	137
5630	T-O-L, 1/4" pipe size, nozzle		23	.696		12.75	45	2.79	60.54	84.50
5631	3/8" pipe size, nozzle		23	.696		13.15	45	2.79	60.94	85
5632	1/2" pipe size, nozzle		22	.727		5.30	47	2.92	55.22	79.50
5633	3/4" pipe size, nozzle		21	.762		6.10	49.50	3.06	58.66	83.50
5634	1" pipe size, nozzle		20	.800		7.10	52	3.21	62.31	89
5635	1-1/4" pipe size, nozzle		18	.889		11.30	57.50	3.56	72.36	102
5636	1-1/2" pipe size, nozzle		16	1		11.30	65	4.01	80.31	113
5637	2" pipe size, nozzle		12	1.333		12.85	86.50	5.35	104.70	149
5638	2-1/2" pipe size, nozzle		10	1.600		104	104	6.40	214.40	276
5639	4" pipe size, nozzle		6	2.667		97	173	10.70	280.70	375

22 11 Facility Water Distribution

22 11 13 – Facility Water Distribution Piping

22 11 13.47 Pipe Fittings, Steel		Crew	Daily Output	Labor-Hours	Unit	Material	2023 Bare Costs Labor	Equipment	Total	Total Incl O&P
5640	W-O-L, 1/4" pipe size, nozzle	Q-15	23	.696	Ea.	32	45	2.79	79.79	106
5641	3/8" pipe size, nozzle		23	.696		26.50	45	2.79	74.29	99.50
5642	1/2" pipe size, nozzle		22	.727		26.50	47	2.92	76.42	103
5643	3/4" pipe size, nozzle		21	.762		13.85	49.50	3.06	66.41	92
5644	1" pipe size, nozzle		20	.800		14.50	52	3.21	69.71	97
5645	1-1/4" pipe size, nozzle		18	.889		33.50	57.50	3.56	94.56	127
5646	1-1/2" pipe size, nozzle		16	1		34.50	65	4.01	103.51	139
5647	2" pipe size, nozzle		12	1.333		35	86.50	5.35	126.85	173
5648	2-1/2" pipe size, nozzle		10	1.600		80	104	6.40	190.40	250
5649	3" pipe size, nozzle		8	2		43.50	130	8	181.50	250
5650	4" pipe size, nozzle		6	2.667		111	173	10.70	294.70	390
5651	5" pipe size, nozzle		5	3.200		273	208	12.85	493.85	625
5652	6" pipe size, nozzle		4	4		305	259	16.05	580.05	740
5653	8" pipe size, nozzle		3	5.333		880	345	21.50	1,246.50	1,500
5654	10" pipe size, nozzle		2.60	6.154		825	400	24.50	1,249.50	1,525
5655	12" pipe size, nozzle		2.20	7.273		1,575	470	29	2,074	2,450
5674	S-O-L, 1/4" pipe size, outlet		23	.696		15.80	45	2.79	63.59	88
5675	3/8" pipe size, outlet		23	.696		15.80	45	2.79	63.59	88
5676	1/2" pipe size, outlet		22	.727		15.85	47	2.92	65.77	91
5677	3/4" pipe size, outlet		21	.762		8.45	49.50	3.06	61.01	86
5678	1" pipe size, outlet		20	.800		9.40	52	3.21	64.61	91.50
5679	1-1/4" pipe size, outlet		18	.889		29.50	57.50	3.56	90.56	122
5680	1-1/2" pipe size, outlet		16	1		29.50	65	4.01	98.51	133
5681	2" pipe size, outlet		12	1.333		31	86.50	5.35	122.85	169
6000	Weld-on flange, forged steel									
6020	Slip-on, 150 lb. flange (welded front and back)									
6050	1/2" pipe size	Q-15	18	.889	Ea.	24.50	57.50	3.56	85.56	117
6060	3/4" pipe size		18	.889		24.50	57.50	3.56	85.56	117
6070	1" pipe size		17	.941		24.50	61	3.77	89.27	122
6080	1-1/4" pipe size		16	1		24.50	65	4.01	93.51	128
6090	1-1/2" pipe size		15	1.067		24.50	69	4.28	97.78	135
6100	2" pipe size		12	1.333		19.85	86.50	5.35	111.70	157
6110	2-1/2" pipe size		10	1.600		34.50	104	6.40	144.90	200
6120	3" pipe size		9	1.778		33	115	7.15	155.15	216
6130	3-1/2" pipe size		7	2.286		42	148	9.15	199.15	277
6140	4" pipe size		6	2.667		42	173	10.70	225.70	315
6150	5" pipe size		5	3.200		76	208	12.85	296.85	410
6160	6" pipe size	Q-16	6	4		69.50	269	10.70	349.20	490
6170	8" pipe size		5	4.800		105	325	12.80	442.80	610
6180	10" pipe size		4	6		178	405	16	599	815
6190	12" pipe size		3	8		215	540	21.50	776.50	1,050
6191	14" pipe size		2.50	9.600		350	645	25.50	1,020.50	1,375
6192	16" pipe size		1.80	13.333		560	895	35.50	1,490.50	1,975
6200	300 lb. flange									
6210	1/2" pipe size	Q-15	17	.941	Ea.	33	61	3.77	97.77	131
6220	3/4" pipe size		17	.941		33	61	3.77	97.77	131
6230	1" pipe size		16	1		33	65	4.01	102.01	137
6240	1-1/4" pipe size		13	1.231		33	80	4.94	117.94	160
6250	1-1/2" pipe size		12	1.333		33	86.50	5.35	124.85	171
6260	2" pipe size		11	1.455		39	94.50	5.85	139.35	190
6270	2-1/2" pipe size		9	1.778		44	115	7.15	166.15	228
6280	3" pipe size		7	2.286		50	148	9.15	207.15	287
6290	4" pipe size		6	2.667		71	173	10.70	254.70	350

22 11 Facility Water Distribution

22 11 13 – Facility Water Distribution Piping

22 11 13.47 Pipe Fittings, Steel

		Crew	Daily Output	Labor-Hours	Unit	Material	2023 Bare Costs Labor	Equipment	Total	Total Incl O&P
6300	5" pipe size	Q-15	4	4	Ea.	116	259	16.05	391.05	530
6310	6" pipe size	Q-16	5	4.800		121	325	12.80	458.80	625
6320	8" pipe size		4	6		203	405	16	624	840
6330	10" pipe size		3.40	7.059		345	475	18.85	838.85	1,100
6340	12" pipe size		2.80	8.571		435	575	23	1,033	1,375
6400	Welding neck, 150 lb. flange									
6410	1/2" pipe size	Q-15	40	.400	Ea.	36	26	1.60	63.60	80
6420	3/4" pipe size		36	.444		36	29	1.78	66.78	84.50
6430	1" pipe size		32	.500		41.50	32.50	2.01	76.01	96
6440	1-1/4" pipe size		29	.552		50.50	36	2.21	88.71	111
6450	1-1/2" pipe size		26	.615		31	40	2.47	73.47	96.50
6460	2" pipe size		20	.800		29	52	3.21	84.21	113
6470	2-1/2" pipe size		16	1		31.50	65	4.01	100.51	135
6480	3" pipe size		14	1.143		36	74	4.58	114.58	156
6500	4" pipe size		10	1.600		43.50	104	6.40	153.90	210
6510	5" pipe size		8	2		83	130	8	221	293
6520	6" pipe size	Q-16	10	2.400		63	161	6.40	230.40	320
6530	8" pipe size		7	3.429		111	231	9.15	351.15	475
6540	10" pipe size		6	4		179	269	10.70	458.70	610
6550	12" pipe size		5	4.800		260	325	12.80	597.80	780
6551	14" pipe size		4.50	5.333		470	360	14.25	844.25	1,075
6552	16" pipe size		3	8		740	540	21.50	1,301.50	1,650
6553	18" pipe size		2.50	9.600		1,000	645	25.50	1,670.50	2,100
6554	20" pipe size		2.30	10.435		1,225	700	28	1,953	2,425
6556	24" pipe size		2	12		1,625	805	32	2,462	3,025
6557	26" pipe size		1.70	14.118		2,150	950	37.50	3,137.50	3,850
6558	30" pipe size		.90	26.667		2,475	1,800	71	4,346	5,475
6559	36" pipe size		.75	32		2,850	2,150	85.50	5,085.50	6,425
6560	300 lb. flange									
6570	1/2" pipe size	Q-15	36	.444	Ea.	43.50	29	1.78	74.28	92.50
6580	3/4" pipe size		34	.471		43.50	30.50	1.89	75.89	95
6590	1" pipe size		30	.533		43.50	34.50	2.14	80.14	101
6600	1-1/4" pipe size		28	.571		43.50	37	2.29	82.79	106
6610	1-1/2" pipe size		24	.667		43.50	43	2.67	89.17	115
6620	2" pipe size		18	.889		39.50	57.50	3.56	100.56	133
6630	2-1/2" pipe size		14	1.143		55.50	74	4.58	134.08	177
6640	3" pipe size		12	1.333		56.50	86.50	5.35	148.35	197
6650	4" pipe size		8	2		74	130	8	212	283
6660	5" pipe size		7	2.286		144	148	9.15	301.15	390
6670	6" pipe size	Q-16	9	2.667		148	179	7.10	334.10	440
6680	8" pipe size		6	4		248	269	10.70	527.70	685
6690	10" pipe size		5	4.800		440	325	12.80	777.80	980
6700	12" pipe size		4	6		565	405	16	986	1,250
7740	Plain ends for plain end pipe, mechanically coupled									
7750	Cplg. & labor required at joints not included, add 1 per									
7760	joint for installed price, see line 9180									
7770	Malleable iron, painted, unless noted otherwise									
7800	90° elbow, 1"				Ea.	221			221	243
7810	1-1/2"					261			261	287
7820	2"					390			390	430
7830	2-1/2"					455			455	500
7840	3"					470			470	520
7860	4"					535			535	590

22 11 Facility Water Distribution

22 11 13 – Facility Water Distribution Piping

22 11 13.47 Pipe Fittings, Steel

		Crew	Daily Output	Labor-Hours	Unit	Material	2023 Bare Costs Labor	Equipment	Total	Total Incl O&P
7870	5" welded steel				Ea.	615			615	675
7880	6"					775			775	855
7890	8" welded steel					1,450			1,450	1,600
7900	10" welded steel					1,850			1,850	2,025
7910	12" welded steel					2,050			2,050	2,275
7970	45° elbow, 1"					133			133	146
7980	1-1/2"					197			197	217
7990	2"					410			410	455
8000	2-1/2"					410			410	455
8010	3"					470			470	520
8030	4"					490			490	540
8040	5" welded steel					615			615	675
8050	6"					705			705	775
8060	8"					825			825	905
8070	10" welded steel					850			850	935
8080	12" welded steel					1,525			1,525	1,700
8140	Tee, straight 1"					247			247	271
8150	1-1/2"					320			320	350
8160	2"					320			320	350
8170	2-1/2"					415			415	455
8180	3"					635			635	700
8200	4"					910			910	1,000
8210	5" welded steel					1,250			1,250	1,375
8220	6"					1,075			1,075	1,200
8230	8" welded steel					1,550			1,550	1,725
8240	10" welded steel					3,050			3,050	3,350
8250	12" welded steel					2,850			2,850	3,150
8340	Segmentally welded steel, painted									
8390	Wye 2"				Ea.	450			450	495
8400	2-1/2"					450			450	495
8410	3"					540			540	595
8430	4"					585			585	640
8440	5"					1,025			1,025	1,125
8450	6"					1,250			1,250	1,375
8460	8"					1,825			1,825	2,000
8470	10"					2,825			2,825	3,100
8480	12"					2,550			2,550	2,825
8540	Wye, lateral 2"					430			430	470
8550	2-1/2"					495			495	540
8560	3"					585			585	645
8580	4"					805			805	885
8590	5"					1,375			1,375	1,500
8600	6"					1,400			1,400	1,550
8610	8"					2,350			2,350	2,600
8620	10"					2,350			2,350	2,600
8630	12"					4,325			4,325	4,775
8690	Cross, 2"					273			273	300
8700	2-1/2"					273			273	300
8710	3"					325			325	360
8730	4"					685			685	755
8740	5"					1,025			1,025	1,125
8750	6"					1,075			1,075	1,175
8760	8"					1,550			1,550	1,700

22 11 Facility Water Distribution

22 11 13 – Facility Water Distribution Piping

22 11 13.47 Pipe Fittings, Steel		Crew	Daily Output	Labor-Hours	Unit	Material	2023 Bare Costs Labor	Equipment	Total	Total Incl O&P
8770	10"				Ea.	2,650			2,650	2,900
8780	12"					2,775			2,775	3,075
8800	Tees, reducing 2" x 1"					365			365	405
8810	2" x 1-1/2"					365			365	405
8820	3" x 1"					365			365	400
8830	3" x 1-1/2"					272			272	299
8840	3" x 2"					365			365	405
8850	4" x 1"					540			540	595
8860	4" x 1-1/2"					540			540	595
8870	4" x 2"					395			395	435
8880	4" x 2-1/2"					245			245	270
8890	4" x 3"					405			405	445
8900	6" x 2"					560			560	620
8910	6" x 3"					690			690	755
8920	6" x 4"					575			575	630
8930	8" x 2"					1,000			1,000	1,100
8940	8" x 3"					890			890	980
8950	8" x 4"					1,225			1,225	1,350
8960	8" x 5"					705			705	780
8970	8" x 6"					915			915	1,000
8980	10" x 4"					795			795	875
8990	10" x 6"					820			820	900
9000	10" x 8"					1,275			1,275	1,400
9010	12" x 6"					2,125			2,125	2,325
9020	12" x 8"					1,575			1,575	1,750
9030	12" x 10"				↓	1,575			1,575	1,725
9080	Adapter nipples 3" long									
9090	1"				Ea.	30			30	33
9100	1-1/2"					39.50			39.50	43.50
9110	2"					39.50			39.50	43.50
9120	2-1/2"					45			45	49.50
9130	3"					55			55	60.50
9140	4"					88.50			88.50	97
9150	6"				↓	231			231	254
9180	Coupling, mechanical, plain end pipe to plain end pipe or fitting									
9190	1"	Q-1	29	.552	Ea.	134	36		170	201
9200	1-1/2"		28	.571		134	37		171	203
9210	2"		27	.593		134	38.50		172.50	205
9220	2-1/2"		26	.615		134	40		174	207
9230	3"		25	.640		195	41.50		236.50	277
9240	3-1/2"		24	.667		226	43		269	315
9250	4"	↓	22	.727		226	47		273	320
9260	5"	Q-2	28	.857		320	57.50		377.50	435
9270	6"		24	1		390	67.50		457.50	530
9280	8"		19	1.263		690	85		775	880
9290	10"		16	1.500		890	101		991	1,125
9300	12"	↓	12	2	↓	1,125	135		1,260	1,425
9310	Outlets for precut holes through pipe wall									
9331	Strapless type, with gasket									
9332	4" to 8" pipe x 1/2"	1 Plum	13	.615	Ea.	147	44.50		191.50	227
9333	4" to 8" pipe x 3/4"		13	.615		156	44.50		200.50	238
9334	10" pipe and larger x 1/2"		11	.727		147	52.50		199.50	239
9335	10" pipe and larger x 3/4"	↓	11	.727		156	52.50		208.50	250

22 11 Facility Water Distribution

22 11 13 – Facility Water Distribution Piping

22 11 13.47 Pipe Fittings, Steel

		Crew	Daily Output	Labor-Hours	Unit	Material	2023 Bare Costs Labor	Equipment	Total	Total Incl O&P
9341	Thermometer wells with gasket									
9342	4" to 8" pipe, 6" stem	1 Plum	14	.571	Ea.	219	41		260	305
9343	8" pipe and larger, 6" stem	"	13	.615	"	219	44.50		263.50	305
9800	Mech. tee, cast iron, grooved or threaded, w/nuts and bolts									
9805	2" x 1"	1 Plum	50	.160	Ea.	166	11.55		177.55	199
9810	2" x 1-1/4"		50	.160		194	11.55		205.55	230
9815	2" x 1-1/2"		50	.160		201	11.55		212.55	238
9820	2-1/2" x 1"	Q-1	80	.200		173	12.95		185.95	209
9825	2-1/2" x 1-1/4"		80	.200		255	12.95		267.95	299
9830	2-1/2" x 1-1/2"		80	.200		255	12.95		267.95	299
9835	2-1/2" x 2"		80	.200		173	12.95		185.95	209
9840	3" x 1"		80	.200		188	12.95		200.95	225
9845	3" x 1-1/4"		80	.200		244	12.95		256.95	287
9850	3" x 1-1/2"		80	.200		244	12.95		256.95	287
9852	3" x 2"		80	.200		298	12.95		310.95	345
9856	4" x 1"		67	.239		233	15.50		248.50	279
9858	4" x 1-1/4"		67	.239		305	15.50		320.50	360
9860	4" x 1-1/2"		67	.239		310	15.50		325.50	365
9862	4" x 2"		67	.239		320	15.50		335.50	375
9864	4" x 2-1/2"		67	.239		330	15.50		345.50	385
9866	4" x 3"		67	.239		330	15.50		345.50	390
9870	6" x 1-1/2"	Q-2	50	.480		385	32.50		417.50	475
9872	6" x 2"		50	.480		390	32.50		422.50	480
9874	6" x 2-1/2"		50	.480		390	32.50		422.50	480
9876	6" x 3"		50	.480		445	32.50		477.50	540
9878	6" x 4"		50	.480		495	32.50		527.50	595
9880	8" x 2"		42	.571		665	38.50		703.50	795
9882	8" x 2-1/2"		42	.571		665	38.50		703.50	795
9884	8" x 3"		42	.571		700	38.50		738.50	830
9886	8" x 4"		42	.571		1,425	38.50		1,463.50	1,625
9940	For galvanized fittings for plain end pipe, add					20%				

22 11 13.48 Pipe, Fittings and Valves, Steel, Grooved-Joint

		Crew	Daily Output	Labor-Hours	Unit	Material	2023 Bare Costs Labor	Equipment	Total	Total Incl O&P
0010	**PIPE, FITTINGS AND VALVES, STEEL, GROOVED-JOINT** R221113-70									
0012	Fittings are ductile iron. Steel fittings noted.									
0020	Pipe includes coupling & clevis type hanger assemblies, 10' OC									
0500	Schedule 10, black									
0550	2" diameter	1 Plum	43	.186	L.F.	9.75	13.40		23.15	31
0560	2-1/2" diameter	Q-1	61	.262		12.10	17		29.10	39
0570	3" diameter		55	.291		13.95	18.85		32.80	43.50
0580	3-1/2" diameter		53	.302		20	19.60		39.60	51
0590	4" diameter		49	.327		19.05	21		40.05	52.50
0600	5" diameter		40	.400		24	26		50	65
0610	6" diameter	Q-2	46	.522		30.50	35		65.50	86
0620	8" diameter	"	41	.585		44	39.50		83.50	107
0700	To delete couplings & hangers, subtract									
0710	2" diam. to 5" diam.					25%	20%			
0720	6" diam. to 8" diam.					27%	15%			
1000	Schedule 40, black									
1040	3/4" diameter	1 Plum	71	.113	L.F.	10.25	8.10		18.35	23.50
1050	1" diameter		63	.127		12.15	9.15		21.30	27
1060	1-1/4" diameter		58	.138		16.05	9.95		26	32.50
1070	1-1/2" diameter		51	.157		18.65	11.30		29.95	37.50

22 11 Facility Water Distribution

22 11 13 – Facility Water Distribution Piping

22 11 13.48 Pipe, Fittings and Valves, Steel, Grooved-Joint		Crew	Daily Output	Labor-Hours	Unit	Material	2023 Bare Costs Labor	Equipment	Total	Total Incl O&P
1080	2" diameter	1 Plum	40	.200	L.F.	23.50	14.40		37.90	47.50
1090	2-1/2" diameter	Q-1	57	.281		33.50	18.20		51.70	64
1100	3" diameter		50	.320		42.50	21		63.50	77.50
1110	4" diameter		45	.356		60.50	23		83.50	101
1120	5" diameter	↓	37	.432		39	28		67	85
1130	6" diameter	Q-2	42	.571		109	38.50		147.50	178
1140	8" diameter		37	.649		129	43.50		172.50	206
1150	10" diameter		31	.774		178	52		230	274
1160	12" diameter		27	.889		203	60		263	315
1170	14" diameter		20	1.200		222	80.50		302.50	365
1180	16" diameter		17	1.412		320	95		415	495
1190	18" diameter		14	1.714		325	115		440	530
1200	20" diameter		12	2		410	135		545	650
1210	24" diameter	↓	10	2.400	↓	445	161		606	730
1740	To delete coupling & hanger, subtract									
1750	3/4" diam. to 2" diam.					65%	27%			
1760	2-1/2" diam. to 5" diam.					41%	18%			
1770	6" diam. to 12" diam.					31%	13%			
1780	14" diam. to 24" diam.					35%	10%			
1800	Galvanized									
1840	3/4" diameter	1 Plum	71	.113	L.F.	11.45	8.10		19.55	24.50
1850	1" diameter		63	.127		13.75	9.15		22.90	29
1860	1-1/4" diameter		58	.138		18.15	9.95		28.10	35
1870	1-1/2" diameter		51	.157		21	11.30		32.30	40.50
1880	2" diameter	↓	40	.200		27	14.40		41.40	51
1890	2-1/2" diameter	Q-1	57	.281		21.50	18.20		39.70	50.50
1900	3" diameter		50	.320		26.50	21		47.50	60
1910	4" diameter		45	.356		38	23		61	76
1920	5" diameter	↓	37	.432		39.50	28		67.50	85
1930	6" diameter	Q-2	42	.571		51.50	38.50		90	115
1940	8" diameter		37	.649		78	43.50		121.50	151
1950	10" diameter		31	.774		176	52		228	271
1960	12" diameter	↓	27	.889	↓	217	60		277	325
2540	To delete coupling & hanger, subtract									
2550	3/4" diam. to 2" diam.					36%	27%			
2560	2-1/2" diam. to 5" diam.					19%	18%			
2570	6" diam. to 12" diam.					14%	13%			
2600	Schedule 80, black									
2610	3/4" diameter	1 Plum	65	.123	L.F.	11.80	8.85		20.65	26
2650	1" diameter		61	.131		14.70	9.45		24.15	30.50
2660	1-1/4" diameter		55	.145		19.75	10.50		30.25	37
2670	1-1/2" diameter		49	.163		23.50	11.75		35.25	43
2680	2" diameter	↓	38	.211		29.50	15.15		44.65	55
2690	2-1/2" diameter	Q-1	54	.296		40	19.20		59.20	72.50
2700	3" diameter		48	.333		51.50	21.50		73	89
2710	4" diameter		44	.364		45	23.50		68.50	84.50
2720	5" diameter	↓	35	.457		79	29.50		108.50	131
2730	6" diameter	Q-2	40	.600		146	40.50		186.50	220
2740	8" diameter		35	.686		176	46		222	263
2750	10" diameter		29	.828		415	55.50		470.50	540
2760	12" diameter	↓	24	1	↓	640	67.50		707.50	800
3240	To delete coupling & hanger, subtract									
3250	3/4" diam. to 2" diam.					30%	25%			

22 11 Facility Water Distribution

22 11 13 – Facility Water Distribution Piping

22 11 13.48 Pipe, Fittings and Valves, Steel, Grooved-Joint	Crew	Daily Output	Labor-Hours	Unit	Material	2023 Bare Costs Labor	Equipment	Total	Total Incl O&P
3260 2-1/2" diam. to 5" diam.					14%	17%			
3270 6" diam. to 12" diam.					12%	12%			
3300 Galvanized									
3310 3/4" diameter	1 Plum	65	.123	L.F.	8.85	8.85		17.70	23
3350 1" diameter		61	.131		9.55	9.45		19	24.50
3360 1-1/4" diameter		55	.145		12.70	10.50		23.20	29.50
3370 1-1/2" diameter		46	.174		14.70	12.55		27.25	35
3380 2" diameter	↓	38	.211		19.45	15.15		34.60	44
3390 2-1/2" diameter	Q-1	54	.296		28.50	19.20		47.70	60
3400 3" diameter		48	.333		37	21.50		58.50	72.50
3410 4" diameter		44	.364		53	23.50		76.50	93
3420 5" diameter	↓	35	.457		59	29.50		88.50	109
3430 6" diameter	Q-2	40	.600		80	40.50		120.50	148
3440 8" diameter		35	.686		210	46		256	300
3450 10" diameter		29	.828		370	55.50		425.50	490
3460 12" diameter	↓	24	1	↓	1,025	67.50		1,092.50	1,225
3920 To delete coupling & hanger, subtract									
3930 3/4" diam. to 2" diam.					30%	25%			
3940 2-1/2" diam. to 5" diam.					15%	17%			
3950 6" diam. to 12" diam.					11%	12%			
3990 Fittings: coupling material required at joints not incl. in fitting price.									
3994 Add 1 selected coupling, material only, per joint for installed price.									
4000 Elbow, 90° or 45°, painted									
4030 3/4" diameter	1 Plum	50	.160	Ea.	119	11.55		130.55	148
4040 1" diameter		50	.160		64	11.55		75.55	87.50
4050 1-1/4" diameter		40	.200		64	14.40		78.40	92
4060 1-1/2" diameter		33	.242		64	17.45		81.45	96.50
4070 2" diameter	↓	25	.320		64	23		87	105
4080 2-1/2" diameter	Q-1	40	.400		64	26		90	109
4090 3" diameter		33	.485		112	31.50		143.50	170
4100 4" diameter		25	.640		122	41.50		163.50	196
4110 5" diameter	↓	20	.800		288	52		340	395
4120 6" diameter	Q-2	25	.960		340	64.50		404.50	465
4130 8" diameter		21	1.143		700	77		777	885
4140 10" diameter		18	1.333		1,300	89.50		1,389.50	1,550
4150 12" diameter		15	1.600		1,425	108		1,533	1,725
4170 14" diameter		12	2		1,300	135		1,435	1,650
4180 16" diameter	↓	11	2.182		1,700	147		1,847	2,100
4190 18" diameter	Q-3	14	2.286		2,150	157		2,307	2,600
4200 20" diameter		12	2.667		2,850	183		3,033	3,400
4210 24" diameter	↓	10	3.200		4,125	219		4,344	4,850
4250 For galvanized elbows, add				↓	26%				
4690 Tee, painted									
4700 3/4" diameter	1 Plum	38	.211	Ea.	127	15.15		142.15	163
4740 1" diameter		33	.242		98.50	17.45		115.95	134
4750 1-1/4" diameter		27	.296		98.50	21.50		120	140
4760 1-1/2" diameter		22	.364		98.50	26		124.50	147
4770 2" diameter	↓	17	.471		98.50	34		132.50	159
4780 2-1/2" diameter	Q-1	27	.593		98.50	38.50		137	166
4790 3" diameter		22	.727		134	47		181	219
4800 4" diameter		17	.941		204	61		265	315
4810 5" diameter	↓	13	1.231		475	80		555	640
4820 6" diameter	Q-2	17	1.412		545	95		640	740

22 11 Facility Water Distribution

22 11 13 – Facility Water Distribution Piping

22 11 13.48 Pipe, Fittings and Valves, Steel, Grooved-Joint		Crew	Daily Output	Labor-Hours	Unit	Material	2023 Bare Costs Labor	Equipment	Total	Total Incl O&P
4830	8" diameter	Q-2	14	1.714	Ea.	1,200	115		1,315	1,500
4840	10" diameter		12	2		1,550	135		1,685	1,900
4850	12" diameter		10	2.400		2,025	161		2,186	2,475
4851	14" diameter		9	2.667		1,650	179		1,829	2,100
4852	16" diameter	↓	8	3		1,875	202		2,077	2,350
4853	18" diameter	Q-3	10	3.200		2,350	219		2,569	2,900
4854	20" diameter		9	3.556		3,350	244		3,594	4,050
4855	24" diameter	↓	8	4	↓	5,100	274		5,374	6,025
4900	For galvanized tees, add					24%				
4906	Couplings, rigid style, painted									
4908	1" diameter	1 Plum	100	.080	Ea.	49.50	5.75		55.25	63
4909	1-1/4" diameter		100	.080		46.50	5.75		52.25	59.50
4910	1-1/2" diameter		67	.119		49.50	8.60		58.10	67.50
4912	2" diameter	↓	50	.160		63.50	11.55		75.05	86.50
4914	2-1/2" diameter	Q-1	80	.200		71.50	12.95		84.45	98.50
4916	3" diameter		67	.239		83	15.50		98.50	115
4918	4" diameter		50	.320		115	21		136	157
4920	5" diameter	↓	40	.400		148	26		174	201
4922	6" diameter	Q-2	50	.480		195	32.50		227.50	263
4924	8" diameter		42	.571		305	38.50		343.50	395
4926	10" diameter		35	.686		595	46		641	725
4928	12" diameter		32	.750		665	50.50		715.50	805
4930	14" diameter		24	1		580	67.50		647.50	740
4931	16" diameter		20	1.200		620	80.50		700.50	805
4932	18" diameter		18	1.333		720	89.50		809.50	925
4933	20" diameter		16	1.500		980	101		1,081	1,225
4934	24" diameter	↓	13	1.846	↓	1,250	124		1,374	1,550
4940	Flexible, standard, painted									
4950	3/4" diameter	1 Plum	100	.080	Ea.	36.50	5.75		42.25	49
4960	1" diameter		100	.080		36.50	5.75		42.25	49
4970	1-1/4" diameter		80	.100		47	7.20		54.20	62.50
4980	1-1/2" diameter		67	.119		51	8.60		59.60	69.50
4990	2" diameter	↓	50	.160		55	11.55		66.55	77.50
5000	2-1/2" diameter	Q-1	80	.200		63.50	12.95		76.45	89.50
5010	3" diameter		67	.239		70	15.50		85.50	100
5020	3-1/2" diameter		57	.281		100	18.20		118.20	137
5030	4" diameter		50	.320		101	21		122	142
5040	5" diameter	↓	40	.400		151	26		177	205
5050	6" diameter	Q-2	50	.480		179	32.50		211.50	244
5070	8" diameter		42	.571		289	38.50		327.50	380
5090	10" diameter		35	.686		470	46		516	585
5110	12" diameter		32	.750		535	50.50		585.50	665
5120	14" diameter		24	1		765	67.50		832.50	940
5130	16" diameter		20	1.200		1,000	80.50		1,080.50	1,225
5140	18" diameter		18	1.333		1,175	89.50		1,264.50	1,425
5150	20" diameter		16	1.500		1,850	101		1,951	2,175
5160	24" diameter	↓	13	1.846	↓	2,025	124		2,149	2,400
5176	Lightweight style, painted									
5178	1-1/2" diameter	1 Plum	67	.119	Ea.	45	8.60		53.60	62.50
5180	2" diameter	"	50	.160		55	11.55		66.55	77.50
5182	2-1/2" diameter	Q-1	80	.200		63.50	12.95		76.45	89.50
5184	3" diameter		67	.239		70	15.50		85.50	100
5186	3-1/2" diameter		57	.281		84	18.20		102.20	120

22 11 Facility Water Distribution

22 11 13 – Facility Water Distribution Piping

	22 11 13.48 Pipe, Fittings and Valves, Steel, Grooved-Joint	Crew	Daily Output	Labor-Hours	Unit	Material	2023 Bare Costs Labor	Equipment	Total	Total Incl O&P
5188	4" diameter	Q-1	50	.320	Ea.	101	21		122	142
5190	5" diameter		40	.400		151	26		177	205
5192	6" diameter	Q-2	50	.480		179	32.50		211.50	244
5194	8" diameter		42	.571		289	38.50		327.50	380
5196	10" diameter		35	.686		590	46		636	720
5198	12" diameter		32	.750		655	50.50		705.50	795
5200	For galvanized couplings, add					33%				
5220	Tee, reducing, painted									
5225	2" x 1-1/2" diameter	Q-1	38	.421	Ea.	206	27.50		233.50	268
5226	2-1/2" x 2" diameter		28	.571		206	37		243	283
5227	3" x 2-1/2" diameter		23	.696		182	45		227	268
5228	4" x 3" diameter		18	.889		245	57.50		302.50	355
5229	5" x 4" diameter		15	1.067		520	69		589	680
5230	6" x 4" diameter	Q-2	18	1.333		575	89.50		664.50	765
5231	8" x 6" diameter		15	1.600		1,200	108		1,308	1,475
5232	10" x 8" diameter		13	1.846		1,325	124		1,449	1,650
5233	12" x 10" diameter		11	2.182		1,675	147		1,822	2,050
5234	14" x 12" diameter		10	2.400		1,750	161		1,911	2,150
5235	16" x 12" diameter		9	2.667		1,500	179		1,679	1,925
5236	18" x 12" diameter	Q-3	12	2.667		1,800	183		1,983	2,250
5237	18" x 16" diameter		11	2.909		2,275	200		2,475	2,800
5238	20" x 16" diameter		10	3.200		2,950	219		3,169	3,575
5239	24" x 20" diameter		9	3.556		4,675	244		4,919	5,500
5240	Reducer, concentric, painted									
5241	2-1/2" x 2" diameter	Q-1	43	.372	Ea.	74.50	24		98.50	118
5242	3" x 2-1/2" diameter		35	.457		89.50	29.50		119	143
5243	4" x 3" diameter		29	.552		108	36		144	173
5244	5" x 4" diameter		22	.727		148	47		195	234
5245	6" x 4" diameter	Q-2	26	.923		172	62		234	282
5246	8" x 6" diameter		23	1.043		440	70		510	590
5247	10" x 8" diameter		20	1.200		865	80.50		945.50	1,075
5248	12" x 10" diameter		16	1.500		1,550	101		1,651	1,850
5255	Eccentric, painted									
5256	2-1/2" x 2" diameter	Q-1	42	.381	Ea.	154	24.50		178.50	206
5257	3" x 2-1/2" diameter		34	.471		176	30.50		206.50	239
5258	4" x 3" diameter		28	.571		214	37		251	291
5259	5" x 4" diameter		21	.762		290	49.50		339.50	395
5260	6" x 4" diameter	Q-2	25	.960		335	64.50		399.50	465
5261	8" x 6" diameter		22	1.091		680	73.50		753.50	855
5262	10" x 8" diameter		19	1.263		1,775	85		1,860	2,100
5263	12" x 10" diameter		15	1.600		2,450	108		2,558	2,850
5270	Coupling, reducing, painted									
5272	2" x 1-1/2" diameter	1 Plum	52	.154	Ea.	72	11.10		83.10	95.50
5274	2-1/2" x 2" diameter	Q-1	82	.195		93	12.65		105.65	121
5276	3" x 2" diameter		69	.232		105	15.05		120.05	139
5278	4" x 2" diameter		52	.308		166	19.95		185.95	212
5280	5" x 4" diameter		42	.381		186	24.50		210.50	242
5282	6" x 4" diameter	Q-2	52	.462		280	31		311	355
5284	8" x 6" diameter	"	44	.545		420	36.50		456.50	515
5290	Outlet coupling, painted									
5294	1-1/2" x 1" pipe size	1 Plum	65	.123	Ea.	95	8.85		103.85	118
5296	2" x 1" pipe size	"	48	.167		96.50	12		108.50	124
5298	2-1/2" x 1" pipe size	Q-1	78	.205		148	13.30		161.30	182

22 11 Facility Water Distribution

22 11 13 – Facility Water Distribution Piping

22 11 13.48 Pipe, Fittings and Valves, Steel, Grooved-Joint

		Crew	Daily Output	Labor-Hours	Unit	Material	2023 Bare Costs Labor	Equipment	Total	Total Incl O&P
5300	2-1/2" x 1-1/4" pipe size	Q-1	70	.229	Ea.	166	14.80		180.80	205
5302	3" x 1" pipe size		65	.246		188	15.95		203.95	231
5304	4" x 3/4" pipe size		48	.333		208	21.50		229.50	261
5306	4" x 1-1/2" pipe size		46	.348		294	22.50		316.50	360
5308	6" x 1-1/2" pipe size	Q-2	44	.545		415	36.50		451.50	510
5320	Outlet, strap-on T, painted									
5324	Threaded female branch									
5330	2" pipe x 1-1/2" branch size	1 Plum	50	.160	Ea.	68.50	11.55		80.05	92.50
5334	2-1/2" pipe x 1-1/2" branch size	Q-1	80	.200		83	12.95		95.95	111
5338	3" pipe x 1-1/2" branch size		67	.239		86	15.50		101.50	118
5342	3" pipe x 2" branch size		59	.271		99	17.60		116.60	135
5346	4" pipe x 2" branch size		50	.320		104	21		125	145
5350	4" pipe x 2-1/2" branch size		47	.340		108	22		130	152
5354	4" pipe x 3" branch size		43	.372		115	24		139	163
5358	5" pipe x 3" branch size		40	.400		142	26		168	195
5362	6" pipe x 2" branch size	Q-2	50	.480		130	32.50		162.50	191
5366	6" pipe x 3" branch size		47	.511		148	34.50		182.50	214
5370	6" pipe x 4" branch size		44	.545		164	36.50		200.50	236
5374	8" pipe x 2-1/2" branch size		42	.571		226	38.50		264.50	305
5378	8" pipe x 4" branch size		38	.632		245	42.50		287.50	335
5390	Grooved branch									
5394	2" pipe x 1-1/4" branch size	1 Plum	78	.103	Ea.	68.50	7.40		75.90	86.50
5398	2" pipe x 1-1/2" branch size	"	50	.160		68.50	11.55		80.05	92.50
5402	2-1/2" pipe x 1-1/2" branch size	Q-1	80	.200		83	12.95		95.95	111
5406	3" pipe x 1-1/2" branch size		67	.239		86	15.50		101.50	118
5410	3" pipe x 2" branch size		59	.271		99	17.60		116.60	135
5414	4" pipe x 2" branch size		50	.320		104	21		125	145
5418	4" pipe x 2-1/2" branch size		47	.340		108	22		130	152
5422	4" pipe x 3" branch size		43	.372		115	24		139	163
5426	5" pipe x 3" branch size		40	.400		142	26		168	195
5430	6" pipe x 2" branch size	Q-2	50	.480		130	32.50		162.50	191
5434	6" pipe x 3" branch size		47	.511		148	34.50		182.50	214
5438	6" pipe x 4" branch size		44	.545		164	36.50		200.50	236
5442	8" pipe x 2-1/2" branch size		42	.571		226	38.50		264.50	305
5446	8" pipe x 4" branch size		38	.632		245	42.50		287.50	335
5750	Flange, w/groove gasket, black steel									
5754	See Line 22 11 13.47 0620 for gasket & bolt set									
5760	ANSI class 125 and 150, painted									
5780	2" pipe size	1 Plum	23	.348	Ea.	209	25		234	267
5790	2-1/2" pipe size	Q-1	37	.432		259	28		287	325
5800	3" pipe size		31	.516		279	33.50		312.50	355
5820	4" pipe size		23	.696		370	45		415	480
5830	5" pipe size		19	.842		430	54.50		484.50	555
5840	6" pipe size	Q-2	23	1.043		470	70		540	625
5850	8" pipe size		17	1.412		530	95		625	725
5860	10" pipe size		14	1.714		840	115		955	1,100
5870	12" pipe size		12	2		1,100	135		1,235	1,400
5880	14" pipe size		10	2.400		1,900	161		2,061	2,350
5890	16" pipe size		9	2.667		2,200	179		2,379	2,700
5900	18" pipe size		6	4		2,725	269		2,994	3,400
5910	20" pipe size		5	4.800		3,275	325		3,600	4,075
5920	24" pipe size		4.50	5.333		4,200	360		4,560	5,125
5940	ANSI class 350, painted									

22 11 Facility Water Distribution

22 11 13 – Facility Water Distribution Piping

22 11 13.48 Pipe, Fittings and Valves, Steel, Grooved-Joint	Crew	Daily Output	Labor-Hours	Unit	Material	2023 Bare Costs Labor	Equipment	Total	Total Incl O&P
5946	2" pipe size	1 Plum	23	.348	Ea.	261	25		286	325
5948	2-1/2" pipe size	Q-1	37	.432		300	28		328	370
5950	3" pipe size		31	.516		410	33.50		443.50	500
5952	4" pipe size		23	.696		545	45		590	670
5954	5" pipe size		19	.842		620	54.50		674.50	765
5956	6" pipe size	Q-2	23	1.043		720	70		790	900
5958	8" pipe size		17	1.412		830	95		925	1,050
5960	10" pipe size		14	1.714		1,325	115		1,440	1,625
5962	12" pipe size		12	2		1,400	135		1,535	1,750
6100	Cross, painted									
6110	2" diameter	1 Plum	12.50	.640	Ea.	174	46		220	261
6112	2-1/2" diameter	Q-1	20	.800		174	52		226	270
6114	3" diameter		15.50	1.032		310	67		377	440
6116	4" diameter		12.50	1.280		510	83		593	690
6118	6" diameter	Q-2	12.50	1.920		1,325	129		1,454	1,675
6120	8" diameter		10.50	2.286		1,750	154		1,904	2,150
6122	10" diameter		9	2.667		2,875	179		3,054	3,450
6124	12" diameter		7.50	3.200		4,175	215		4,390	4,900
7400	Suction diffuser									
7402	Grooved end inlet x flanged outlet									
7410	3" x 3"	Q-1	27	.593	Ea.	1,675	38.50		1,713.50	1,900
7412	4" x 4"		19	.842		2,275	54.50		2,329.50	2,575
7414	5" x 5"		14	1.143		2,675	74		2,749	3,025
7416	6" x 6"	Q-2	20	1.200		3,350	80.50		3,430.50	3,825
7418	8" x 8"		15	1.600		6,250	108		6,358	7,025
7420	10" x 10"		12	2		8,500	135		8,635	9,550
7422	12" x 12"		9	2.667		14,000	179		14,179	15,700
7424	14" x 14"		7	3.429		13,000	231		13,231	14,600
7426	16" x 14"		6	4		13,300	269		13,569	15,100
7500	Strainer, tee type, painted									
7506	2" pipe size	1 Plum	21	.381	Ea.	1,125	27.50		1,152.50	1,275
7508	2-1/2" pipe size	Q-1	30	.533		1,175	34.50		1,209.50	1,350
7510	3" pipe size		28	.571		1,325	37		1,362	1,500
7512	4" pipe size		20	.800		1,500	52		1,552	1,725
7514	5" pipe size		15	1.067		2,175	69		2,244	2,475
7516	6" pipe size	Q-2	23	1.043		2,350	70		2,420	2,675
7518	8" pipe size		16	1.500		3,600	101		3,701	4,125
7520	10" pipe size		13	1.846		5,300	124		5,424	6,000
7522	12" pipe size		10	2.400		6,800	161		6,961	7,750
7524	14" pipe size		8	3		17,500	202		17,702	19,500
7526	16" pipe size		7	3.429		21,700	231		21,931	24,200
7570	Expansion joint, max. 3" travel									
7572	2" diameter	1 Plum	24	.333	Ea.	1,425	24		1,449	1,575
7574	3" diameter	Q-1	31	.516		1,625	33.50		1,658.50	1,825
7576	4" diameter	"	23	.696		2,150	45		2,195	2,425
7578	6" diameter	Q-2	38	.632		3,325	42.50		3,367.50	3,725
7790	Valves: coupling material required at joints not incl. in valve price.									
7794	Add 1 selected coupling, material only, per joint for installed price.									
7800	Ball valve w/handle, carbon steel trim									
7810	1-1/2" pipe size	1 Plum	31	.258	Ea.	252	18.60		270.60	305
7812	2" pipe size	"	24	.333		280	24		304	345
7814	2-1/2" pipe size	Q-1	38	.421		610	27.50		637.50	710
7816	3" pipe size		31	.516		985	33.50		1,018.50	1,125

22 11 Facility Water Distribution

22 11 13 – Facility Water Distribution Piping

22 11 13.48 Pipe, Fittings and Valves, Steel, Grooved-Joint

		Crew	Daily Output	Labor-Hours	Unit	Material	2023 Bare Costs Labor	2023 Bare Costs Equipment	Total	Total Incl O&P
7818	4" pipe size	Q-1	23	.696	Ea.	1,525	45		1,570	1,750
7820	6" pipe size	Q-2	24	1		4,650	67.50		4,717.50	5,225
7830	With gear operator									
7834	2-1/2" pipe size	Q-1	38	.421	Ea.	1,225	27.50		1,252.50	1,400
7836	3" pipe size		31	.516		1,750	33.50		1,783.50	1,975
7838	4" pipe size	↓	23	.696		2,225	45		2,270	2,525
7840	6" pipe size	Q-2	24	1	↓	5,225	67.50		5,292.50	5,850
7870	Check valve									
7874	2-1/2" pipe size	Q-1	38	.421	Ea.	540	27.50		567.50	630
7876	3" pipe size		31	.516		635	33.50		668.50	745
7878	4" pipe size		23	.696		670	45		715	805
7880	5" pipe size	↓	18	.889		1,125	57.50		1,182.50	1,300
7882	6" pipe size	Q-2	24	1		1,325	67.50		1,392.50	1,550
7884	8" pipe size		19	1.263		1,800	85		1,885	2,100
7886	10" pipe size		16	1.500		4,825	101		4,926	5,450
7888	12" pipe size	↓	13	1.846	↓	5,700	124		5,824	6,450
7900	Plug valve, balancing, w/lever operator									
7906	3" pipe size	Q-1	31	.516	Ea.	1,100	33.50		1,133.50	1,250
7908	4" pipe size	"	23	.696		1,350	45		1,395	1,575
7909	6" pipe size	Q-2	24	1	↓	2,075	67.50		2,142.50	2,375
7916	With gear operator									
7920	3" pipe size	Q-1	31	.516	Ea.	2,075	33.50		2,108.50	2,350
7922	4" pipe size	"	23	.696		2,150	45		2,195	2,450
7924	6" pipe size	Q-2	24	1		2,925	67.50		2,992.50	3,300
7926	8" pipe size		19	1.263		4,475	85		4,560	5,050
7928	10" pipe size		16	1.500		5,650	101		5,751	6,375
7930	12" pipe size	↓	13	1.846	↓	8,625	124		8,749	9,650
8000	Butterfly valve, 2 position handle, with standard trim									
8010	1-1/2" pipe size	1 Plum	30	.267	Ea.	505	19.20		524.20	585
8020	2" pipe size	"	23	.348		505	25		530	595
8030	3" pipe size	Q-1	30	.533		725	34.50		759.50	845
8050	4" pipe size	"	22	.727		795	47		842	945
8070	6" pipe size	Q-2	23	1.043		1,600	70		1,670	1,875
8080	8" pipe size		18	1.333		2,150	89.50		2,239.50	2,500
8090	10" pipe size	↓	15	1.600	↓	3,550	108		3,658	4,050
8200	With stainless steel trim									
8240	1-1/2" pipe size	1 Plum	30	.267	Ea.	640	19.20		659.20	735
8250	2" pipe size	"	23	.348		640	25		665	745
8270	3" pipe size	Q-1	30	.533		860	34.50		894.50	995
8280	4" pipe size	"	22	.727		935	47		982	1,100
8300	6" pipe size	Q-2	23	1.043		1,750	70		1,820	2,025
8310	8" pipe size		18	1.333		4,300	89.50		4,389.50	4,850
8320	10" pipe size		15	1.600		7,175	108		7,283	8,050
8322	12" pipe size		12	2		8,250	135		8,385	9,275
8324	14" pipe size		10	2.400		10,600	161		10,761	11,800
8326	16" pipe size	↓	9	2.667		17,600	179		17,779	19,600
8328	18" pipe size	Q-3	12	2.667		18,800	183		18,983	21,000
8330	20" pipe size		10	3.200		23,100	219		23,319	25,700
8332	24" pipe size	↓	9	3.556	↓	30,900	244		31,144	34,400
8336	Note: sizes 8" up w/manual gear operator									
9000	Cut one groove, labor									
9010	3/4" pipe size	Q-1	152	.105	Ea.		6.85		6.85	10.20
9020	1" pipe size	↓	140	.114	↓		7.40		7.40	11.05

22 11 Facility Water Distribution

22 11 13 – Facility Water Distribution Piping

22 11 13.48 Pipe, Fittings and Valves, Steel, Grooved-Joint

		Crew	Daily Output	Labor-Hours	Unit	Material	2023 Bare Costs Labor	2023 Bare Costs Equipment	Total	Total Incl O&P
9030	1-1/4" pipe size	Q-1	124	.129	Ea.		8.35		8.35	12.50
9040	1-1/2" pipe size		114	.140			9.10		9.10	13.55
9050	2" pipe size		104	.154			10		10	14.90
9060	2-1/2" pipe size		96	.167			10.80		10.80	16.10
9070	3" pipe size		88	.182			11.80		11.80	17.60
9080	3-1/2" pipe size		83	.193			12.50		12.50	18.65
9090	4" pipe size		78	.205			13.30		13.30	19.85
9100	5" pipe size		72	.222			14.40		14.40	21.50
9110	6" pipe size		70	.229			14.80		14.80	22
9120	8" pipe size		54	.296			19.20		19.20	28.50
9130	10" pipe size		38	.421			27.50		27.50	40.50
9140	12" pipe size		30	.533			34.50		34.50	51.50
9150	14" pipe size		20	.800			52		52	77.50
9160	16" pipe size		19	.842			54.50		54.50	81.50
9170	18" pipe size		18	.889			57.50		57.50	86
9180	20" pipe size		17	.941			61		61	91
9190	24" pipe size	↓	15	1.067	↓		69		69	103
9210	Roll one groove									
9220	3/4" pipe size	Q-1	266	.060	Ea.		3.90		3.90	5.80
9230	1" pipe size		228	.070			4.55		4.55	6.80
9240	1-1/4" pipe size		200	.080			5.20		5.20	7.75
9250	1-1/2" pipe size		178	.090			5.85		5.85	8.70
9260	2" pipe size		116	.138			8.95		8.95	13.35
9270	2-1/2" pipe size		110	.145			9.45		9.45	14.05
9280	3" pipe size		100	.160			10.40		10.40	15.45
9290	3-1/2" pipe size		94	.170			11.05		11.05	16.45
9300	4" pipe size		86	.186			12.05		12.05	18
9310	5" pipe size		84	.190			12.35		12.35	18.40
9320	6" pipe size		80	.200			12.95		12.95	19.35
9330	8" pipe size		66	.242			15.70		15.70	23.50
9340	10" pipe size		58	.276			17.90		17.90	26.50
9350	12" pipe size		46	.348			22.50		22.50	33.50
9360	14" pipe size		30	.533			34.50		34.50	51.50
9370	16" pipe size		28	.571			37		37	55.50
9380	18" pipe size		27	.593			38.50		38.50	57.50
9390	20" pipe size		25	.640			41.50		41.50	62
9400	24" pipe size	↓	23	.696	↓		45		45	67.50

22 11 13.60 Tubing, Stainless Steel

		Crew	Daily Output	Labor-Hours	Unit	Material	2023 Bare Costs Labor	2023 Bare Costs Equipment	Total	Total Incl O&P
0010	**TUBING, STAINLESS STEEL**									
5000	Tubing									
5010	Type 304, no joints, no hangers									
5020	.035 wall									
5021	1/4"	1 Plum	160	.050	L.F.	11.10	3.60		14.70	17.55
5022	3/8"		160	.050		4.61	3.60		8.21	10.40
5023	1/2"		160	.050		11.90	3.60		15.50	18.40
5024	5/8"		160	.050		7.30	3.60		10.90	13.35
5025	3/4"		133	.060		8.75	4.33		13.08	16.10
5026	7/8"		133	.060		9.25	4.33		13.58	16.65
5027	1"		114	.070		10.20	5.05		15.25	18.75
5040	.049 wall									
5041	1/4"	1 Plum	160	.050	L.F.	4.29	3.60		7.89	10.05
5042	3/8"	↓	160	.050	↓	5.95	3.60		9.55	11.90

22 11 Facility Water Distribution

22 11 13 – Facility Water Distribution Piping

22 11 13.60 Tubing, Stainless Steel		Crew	Daily Output	Labor-Hours	Unit	Material	2023 Bare Costs Labor	Equipment	Total	Total Incl O&P
5043	1/2"	1 Plum	160	.050	L.F.	6.60	3.60		10.20	12.60
5044	5/8"		160	.050		8.90	3.60		12.50	15.15
5045	3/4"		133	.060		9.45	4.33		13.78	16.85
5046	7/8"		133	.060		14.30	4.33		18.63	22
5047	1"	↓	114	.070	↓	10.50	5.05		15.55	19.10
5060	.065 wall									
5061	1/4"	1 Plum	160	.050	L.F.	4.81	3.60		8.41	10.65
5062	3/8"		160	.050		6.65	3.60		10.25	12.65
5063	1/2"		160	.050		8.05	3.60		11.65	14.20
5064	5/8"		160	.050		9.75	3.60		13.35	16.10
5065	3/4"		133	.060		10.35	4.33		14.68	17.85
5066	7/8"		133	.060		11.90	4.33		16.23	19.50
5067	1"	↓	114	.070		11.60	5.05		16.65	20.50
5210	Type 316									
5220	.035 wall									
5221	1/4"	1 Plum	160	.050	L.F.	5.30	3.60		8.90	11.15
5222	3/8"		160	.050		6.90	3.60		10.50	12.95
5223	1/2"		160	.050		10.95	3.60		14.55	17.40
5224	5/8"		160	.050		8.35	3.60		11.95	14.50
5225	3/4"		133	.060		19.50	4.33		23.83	28
5226	7/8"		133	.060		17.55	4.33		21.88	26
5227	1"	↓	114	.070		13.95	5.05		19	23
5240	.049 wall									
5241	1/4"	1 Plum	160	.050	L.F.	6.30	3.60		9.90	12.30
5242	3/8"		160	.050		10.40	3.60		14	16.80
5243	1/2"		160	.050		10.80	3.60		14.40	17.20
5244	5/8"		160	.050		13.30	3.60		16.90	19.95
5245	3/4"		133	.060		17.15	4.33		21.48	25.50
5246	7/8"		133	.060		15.80	4.33		20.13	24
5247	1"	↓	114	.070		14.30	5.05		19.35	23.50
5260	.065 wall									
5261	1/4"	1 Plum	160	.050	L.F.	6.40	3.60		10	12.40
5262	3/8"		160	.050		10.65	3.60		14.25	17.05
5263	1/2"		160	.050		9.25	3.60		12.85	15.55
5264	5/8"		160	.050		10.75	3.60		14.35	17.15
5265	3/4"		133	.060		11.25	4.33		15.58	18.85
5266	7/8"		133	.060		18.50	4.33		22.83	27
5267	1"	↓	114	.070		17.60	5.05		22.65	27

22 11 13.61 Tubing Fittings, Stainless Steel		Crew	Daily Output	Labor-Hours	Unit	Material	2023 Bare Costs Labor	Equipment	Total	Total Incl O&P
0010	**TUBING FITTINGS, STAINLESS STEEL**									
8200	Tube fittings, compression type									
8202	Type 316									
8204	90° elbow									
8206	1/4"	1 Plum	24	.333	Ea.	27.50	24		51.50	66.50
8207	3/8"		22	.364		34	26		60	76.50
8208	1/2"		22	.364		55.50	26		81.50	101
8209	5/8"		21	.381		62.50	27.50		90	110
8210	3/4"		21	.381		98.50	27.50		126	149
8211	7/8"		20	.400		152	29		181	210
8212	1"	↓	20	.400	↓	188	29		217	250
8220	Union tee									
8222	1/4"	1 Plum	15	.533	Ea.	39	38.50		77.50	101

22 11 Facility Water Distribution

22 11 13 − Facility Water Distribution Piping

22 11 13.61 Tubing Fittings, Stainless Steel		Crew	Daily Output	Labor-Hours	Unit	Material	2023 Bare Costs Labor	Equipment	Total	Total Incl O&P
8224	3/8"	1 Plum	15	.533	Ea.	50.50	38.50		89	113
8225	1/2"		15	.533		77.50	38.50		116	143
8226	5/8"		14	.571		87	41		128	158
8227	3/4"		14	.571		116	41		157	190
8228	7/8"		13	.615		227	44.50		271.50	315
8229	1"		13	.615		249	44.50		293.50	340
8234	Union									
8236	1/4"	1 Plum	24	.333	Ea.	19.15	24		43.15	57
8237	3/8"		22	.364		27	26		53	69
8238	1/2"		22	.364		40.50	26		66.50	83.50
8239	5/8"		21	.381		53	27.50		80.50	99
8240	3/4"		21	.381		66	27.50		93.50	114
8241	7/8"		20	.400		108	29		137	162
8242	1"		20	.400		114	29		143	168
8250	Male connector									
8252	1/4" x 1/4"	1 Plum	24	.333	Ea.	12.25	24		36.25	49.50
8253	3/8" x 3/8"		22	.364		19.15	26		45.15	60
8254	1/2" x 1/2"		22	.364		28.50	26		54.50	70
8256	3/4" x 3/4"		21	.381		43.50	27.50		71	88.50
8258	1" x 1"		20	.400		75.50	29		104.50	126

22 11 13.64 Pipe, Stainless Steel

		Crew	Daily Output	Labor-Hours	Unit	Material	Labor	Equipment	Total	Total Incl O&P
0010	**PIPE, STAINLESS STEEL** R221113-70									
0020	Welded, with clevis type hanger assemblies, 10' OC									
0500	Schedule 5, type 304									
0540	1/2" diameter	Q-15	128	.125	L.F.	8.55	8.10	.50	17.15	22
0550	3/4" diameter		116	.138		10.45	8.95	.55	19.95	25.50
0560	1" diameter		103	.155		10.90	10.05	.62	21.57	27.50
0570	1-1/4" diameter		93	.172		16.90	11.15	.69	28.74	36
0580	1-1/2" diameter		85	.188		20.50	12.20	.75	33.45	41.50
0590	2" diameter		69	.232		35	15.05	.93	50.98	62
0600	2-1/2" diameter		53	.302		31	19.60	1.21	51.81	65
0610	3" diameter		48	.333		97	21.50	1.34	119.84	140
0620	4" diameter		44	.364		167	23.50	1.46	191.96	220
0630	5" diameter		36	.444		73.50	29	1.78	104.28	125
0640	6" diameter	Q-16	42	.571		440	38.50	1.53	480.03	540
0650	8" diameter		34	.706		675	47.50	1.88	724.38	820
0660	10" diameter		26	.923		86.50	62	2.46	150.96	190
0670	12" diameter		21	1.143		530	77	3.05	610.05	705
0700	To delete hangers, subtract									
0710	1/2" diam. to 1-1/2" diam.					8%	19%			
0720	2" diam. to 5" diam.					4%	9%			
0730	6" diam. to 12" diam.					3%	4%			
0750	For small quantities, add				L.F.	10%				
1250	Schedule 5, type 316									
1290	1/2" diameter	Q-15	128	.125	L.F.	9.80	8.10	.50	18.40	23.50
1300	3/4" diameter		116	.138		11.75	8.95	.55	21.25	27
1310	1" diameter		103	.155		18.05	10.05	.62	28.72	35.50
1320	1-1/4" diameter		93	.172		22.50	11.15	.69	34.34	42.50
1330	1-1/2" diameter		85	.188		31	12.20	.75	43.95	53
1340	2" diameter		69	.232		43	15.05	.93	58.98	70.50
1350	2-1/2" diameter		53	.302		114	19.60	1.21	134.81	156
1360	3" diameter		48	.333		146	21.50	1.34	168.84	193

22 11 Facility Water Distribution

22 11 13 – Facility Water Distribution Piping

22 11 13.64 Pipe, Stainless Steel		Crew	Daily Output	Labor-Hours	Unit	Material	2023 Bare Costs Labor	Equipment	Total	Total Incl O&P
1370	4" diameter	Q-15	44	.364	L.F.	181	23.50	1.46	205.96	236
1380	5" diameter	▼	36	.444		207	29	1.78	237.78	273
1390	6" diameter	Q-16	42	.571		246	38.50	1.53	286.03	330
1400	8" diameter		34	.706		370	47.50	1.88	419.38	485
1410	10" diameter		26	.923		440	62	2.46	504.46	580
1420	12" diameter	▼	21	1.143		156	77	3.05	236.05	290
1490	For small quantities, add					10%				
1940	To delete hanger, subtract				▼					
1950	1/2" diam. to 1-1/2" diam.					5%	19%			
1960	2" diam. to 5" diam.					3%	9%			
1970	6" diam. to 12" diam.					2%	4%			
2000	Schedule 10, type 304									
2040	1/4" diameter	Q-15	131	.122	L.F.	13.60	7.90	.49	21.99	27.50
2050	3/8" diameter		128	.125		11.40	8.10	.50	20	25
2060	1/2" diameter		125	.128		8.80	8.30	.51	17.61	22.50
2070	3/4" diameter		113	.142		10.45	9.20	.57	20.22	26
2080	1" diameter		100	.160		11.90	10.40	.64	22.94	29.50
2090	1-1/4" diameter		91	.176		18.10	11.40	.71	30.21	37.50
2100	1-1/2" diameter		83	.193		20.50	12.50	.77	33.77	42
2110	2" diameter		67	.239		18.85	15.50	.96	35.31	45
2120	2-1/2" diameter		51	.314		35	20.50	1.26	56.76	71
2130	3" diameter		46	.348		41.50	22.50	1.39	65.39	80.50
2140	4" diameter		42	.381		52.50	24.50	1.53	78.53	96.50
2150	5" diameter	▼	35	.457		118	29.50	1.83	149.33	176
2160	6" diameter	Q-16	40	.600		83	40.50	1.60	125.10	153
2170	8" diameter		33	.727		91.50	49	1.94	142.44	175
2180	10" diameter		25	.960		137	64.50	2.56	204.06	250
2190	12" diameter	▼	21	1.143		107	77	3.05	187.05	236
2250	For small quantities, add				▼	10%				
2650	To delete hanger, subtract									
2660	1/4" diam. to 3/4" diam.					9%	22%			
2670	1" diam. to 2" diam.					4%	15%			
2680	2-1/2" diam. to 5" diam.					3%	8%			
2690	6" diam. to 12" diam.					3%	4%			
2750	Schedule 10, type 316									
2790	1/4" diameter	Q-15	131	.122	L.F.	10.10	7.90	.49	18.49	23.50
2800	3/8" diameter		128	.125		12.05	8.10	.50	20.65	26
2810	1/2" diameter		125	.128		7.80	8.30	.51	16.61	21.50
2820	3/4" diameter		113	.142		9.20	9.20	.57	18.97	24.50
2830	1" diameter		100	.160		13.80	10.40	.64	24.84	31.50
2840	1-1/4" diameter		91	.176		16.70	11.40	.71	28.81	36
2850	1-1/2" diameter		83	.193		21	12.50	.77	34.27	42.50
2860	2" diameter		67	.239		24	15.50	.96	40.46	50.50
2870	2-1/2" diameter		51	.314		35.50	20.50	1.26	57.26	71
2880	3" diameter		46	.348		41	22.50	1.39	64.89	80
2890	4" diameter		42	.381		55.50	24.50	1.53	81.53	99.50
2900	5" diameter	▼	35	.457		74	29.50	1.83	105.33	127
2910	6" diameter	Q-16	40	.600		84	40.50	1.60	126.10	154
2920	8" diameter		33	.727		84.50	49	1.94	135.44	168
2930	10" diameter		25	.960		112	64.50	2.56	179.06	223
2940	12" diameter	▼	21	1.143		127	77	3.05	207.05	257
2990	For small quantities, add				▼	10%				
3430	To delete hanger, subtract									

22 11 Facility Water Distribution

22 11 13 – Facility Water Distribution Piping

22 11 13.64 Pipe, Stainless Steel		Crew	Daily Output	Labor-Hours	Unit	Material	2023 Bare Costs Labor	Equipment	Total	Total Incl O&P
3440	1/4" diam. to 3/4" diam.					6%	22%			
3450	1" diam. to 2" diam.					3%	15%			
3460	2-1/2" diam. to 5" diam.					2%	8%			
3470	6" diam. to 12" diam.					2%	4%			
3500	Threaded, couplings and clevis hanger assemblies, 10' OC									
3520	Schedule 40, type 304									
3540	1/4" diameter	1 Plum	54	.148	L.F.	7	10.65		17.65	23.50
3550	3/8" diameter		53	.151		7.85	10.90		18.75	25
3560	1/2" diameter		52	.154		8.90	11.10		20	26.50
3570	3/4" diameter		51	.157		12.05	11.30		23.35	30
3580	1" diameter	↓	45	.178		18.20	12.80		31	39
3590	1-1/4" diameter	Q-1	76	.211		24	13.65		37.65	47
3600	1-1/2" diameter		69	.232		30	15.05		45.05	55.50
3610	2" diameter		57	.281		43	18.20		61.20	74
3620	2-1/2" diameter		44	.364		71	23.50		94.50	113
3630	3" diameter	↓	38	.421		92	27.50		119.50	142
3640	4" diameter	Q-2	51	.471		131	31.50		162.50	191
3740	For small quantities, add				↓	10%				
4200	To delete couplings & hangers, subtract									
4210	1/4" diam. to 3/4" diam.					15%	56%			
4220	1" diam. to 2" diam.					18%	49%			
4230	2-1/2" diam. to 4" diam.					34%	40%			
4250	Schedule 40, type 316									
4290	1/4" diameter	1 Plum	54	.148	L.F.	15.25	10.65		25.90	32.50
4300	3/8" diameter		53	.151		15.95	10.90		26.85	34
4310	1/2" diameter		52	.154		17.50	11.10		28.60	36
4320	3/4" diameter		51	.157		22	11.30		33.30	41
4330	1" diameter	↓	45	.178		32	12.80		44.80	54
4340	1-1/4" diameter	Q-1	76	.211		43.50	13.65		57.15	68.50
4350	1-1/2" diameter		69	.232		44	15.05		59.05	71
4360	2" diameter		57	.281		68.50	18.20		86.70	103
4370	2-1/2" diameter		44	.364		122	23.50		145.50	169
4380	3" diameter	↓	38	.421		162	27.50		189.50	219
4390	4" diameter	Q-2	51	.471		215	31.50		246.50	283
4490	For small quantities, add				↓	10%				
4900	To delete couplings & hangers, subtract									
4910	1/4" diam. to 3/4" diam.					12%	56%			
4920	1" diam. to 2" diam.					14%	49%			
4930	2-1/2" diam. to 4" diam.					27%	40%			
5000	Schedule 80, type 304									
5040	1/4" diameter	1 Plum	53	.151	L.F.	22	10.90		32.90	40
5050	3/8" diameter		52	.154		27	11.10		38.10	46
5060	1/2" diameter		51	.157		27.50	11.30		38.80	47.50
5070	3/4" diameter		48	.167		26.50	12		38.50	47
5080	1" diameter	↓	43	.186		34.50	13.40		47.90	57.50
5090	1-1/4" diameter	Q-1	73	.219		72	14.20		86.20	100
5100	1-1/2" diameter		67	.239		56.50	15.50		72	85.50
5110	2" diameter	↓	54	.296		74	19.20		93.20	110
5190	For small quantities, add				↓	10%				
5700	To delete couplings & hangers, subtract									
5710	1/4" diam. to 3/4" diam.					10%	53%			
5720	1" diam. to 2" diam.					14%	47%			
5750	Schedule 80, type 316									

For customer support on your Plumbing Costs with RSMeans data, call 800.448.8182.

22 11 Facility Water Distribution

22 11 13 – Facility Water Distribution Piping

22 11 13.64 Pipe, Stainless Steel

		Crew	Daily Output	Labor-Hours	Unit	Material	2023 Bare Costs Labor	Equipment	Total	Total Incl O&P
5790	1/4" diameter	1 Plum	53	.151	L.F.	26.50	10.90		37.40	45.50
5800	3/8" diameter		52	.154		32	11.10		43.10	52
5810	1/2" diameter		51	.157		29	11.30		40.30	49
5820	3/4" diameter		48	.167		32.50	12		44.50	54
5830	1" diameter		43	.186		48.50	13.40		61.90	73
5840	1-1/4" diameter	Q-1	73	.219		45	14.20		59.20	71
5850	1-1/2" diameter		67	.239		64.50	15.50		80	94
5860	2" diameter		54	.296		84.50	19.20		103.70	122
5950	For small quantities, add					10%				
7000	To delete couplings & hangers, subtract									
7010	1/4" diam. to 3/4" diam.					9%	53%			
7020	1" diam. to 2" diam.					14%	47%			
8000	Weld joints with clevis type hanger assemblies, 10' OC									
8010	Schedule 40, type 304									
8050	1/8" pipe size	Q-15	126	.127	L.F.	5.30	8.25	.51	14.06	18.65
8060	1/4" pipe size		125	.128		5.65	8.30	.51	14.46	19.20
8070	3/8" pipe size		122	.131		6.25	8.50	.53	15.28	20
8080	1/2" pipe size		118	.136		6.70	8.80	.54	16.04	21
8090	3/4" pipe size		109	.147		9.10	9.50	.59	19.19	25
8100	1" pipe size		95	.168		13.55	10.90	.68	25.13	32
8110	1-1/4" pipe size		86	.186		16.70	12.05	.75	29.50	37
8120	1-1/2" pipe size		78	.205		22	13.30	.82	36.12	45
8130	2" pipe size		62	.258		29.50	16.75	1.03	47.28	58.50
8140	2-1/2" pipe size		49	.327		40.50	21	1.31	62.81	77.50
8150	3" pipe size		44	.364		50.50	23.50	1.46	75.46	92
8160	3-1/2" pipe size		44	.364		119	23.50	1.46	143.96	168
8170	4" pipe size		39	.410		71	26.50	1.65	99.15	119
8180	5" pipe size		32	.500		118	32.50	2.01	152.51	180
8190	6" pipe size	Q-16	37	.649		115	43.50	1.73	160.23	194
8191	6" pipe size		37	.649		114	43.50	1.73	159.23	192
8200	8" pipe size		29	.828		164	55.50	2.21	221.71	266
8210	10" pipe size		24	1		495	67.50	2.67	565.17	650
8220	12" pipe size		20	1.200		680	80.50	3.20	763.70	875
8300	Schedule 40, type 316									
8310	1/8" pipe size	Q-15	126	.127	L.F.	20.50	8.25	.51	29.26	35.50
8320	1/4" pipe size		125	.128		13.65	8.30	.51	22.46	28
8330	3/8" pipe size		122	.131		14	8.50	.53	23.03	28.50
8340	1/2" pipe size		118	.136		14.90	8.80	.54	24.24	30
8350	3/4" pipe size		109	.147		18.40	9.50	.59	28.49	35
8360	1" pipe size		95	.168		26.50	10.90	.68	38.08	46
8370	1-1/4" pipe size		86	.186		34.50	12.05	.75	47.30	57
8380	1-1/2" pipe size		78	.205		34	13.30	.82	48.12	58.50
8390	2" pipe size		62	.258		52.50	16.75	1.03	70.28	84
8400	2-1/2" pipe size		49	.327		85.50	21	1.31	107.81	127
8410	3" pipe size		44	.364		112	23.50	1.46	136.96	160
8420	3-1/2" pipe size		44	.364		146	23.50	1.46	170.96	197
8430	4" pipe size		39	.410		143	26.50	1.65	171.15	199
8440	5" pipe size		32	.500		275	32.50	2.01	309.51	355
8450	6" pipe size	Q-16	37	.649		160	43.50	1.73	205.23	243
8460	8" pipe size		29	.828		282	55.50	2.21	339.71	395
8470	10" pipe size		24	1		795	67.50	2.67	865.17	980
8480	12" pipe size		20	1.200		690	80.50	3.20	773.70	885
8500	Schedule 80, type 304									

22 11 Facility Water Distribution

22 11 13 – Facility Water Distribution Piping

22 11 13.64 Pipe, Stainless Steel		Crew	Daily Output	Labor-Hours	Unit	Material	2023 Bare Costs Labor	Equipment	Total	Total Incl O&P
8510	1/4" pipe size	Q-15	110	.145	L.F.	18.70	9.45	.58	28.73	35
8520	3/8" pipe size		109	.147		23.50	9.50	.59	33.59	41
8530	1/2" pipe size		106	.151		24.50	9.80	.61	34.91	42.50
8540	3/4" pipe size		96	.167		22	10.80	.67	33.47	41.50
8550	1" pipe size		87	.184		28.50	11.95	.74	41.19	49.50
8560	1-1/4" pipe size		81	.198		58.50	12.80	.79	72.09	84.50
8570	1-1/2" pipe size		74	.216		44.50	14	.87	59.37	71
8580	2" pipe size		58	.276		56	17.90	1.11	75.01	89.50
8590	2-1/2" pipe size		46	.348		130	22.50	1.39	153.89	178
8600	3" pipe size		41	.390		91	25.50	1.56	118.06	139
8610	4" pipe size		33	.485		111	31.50	1.94	144.44	172
8630	6" pipe size	Q-16	30	.800		198	54	2.14	254.14	300
8640	Schedule 80, type 316									
8650	1/4" pipe size	Q-15	110	.145	L.F.	24.50	9.45	.58	34.53	41.50
8660	3/8" pipe size		109	.147		30	9.50	.59	40.09	48
8670	1/2" pipe size		106	.151		26.50	9.80	.61	36.91	44.50
8680	3/4" pipe size		96	.167		29	10.80	.67	40.47	49
8690	1" pipe size		87	.184		43	11.95	.74	55.69	66
8700	1-1/4" pipe size		81	.198		34.50	12.80	.79	48.09	58
8710	1-1/2" pipe size		74	.216		54.50	14	.87	69.37	82
8720	2" pipe size		58	.276		68	17.90	1.11	87.01	102
8730	2-1/2" pipe size		46	.348		89.50	22.50	1.39	113.39	133
8740	3" pipe size		41	.390		107	25.50	1.56	134.06	156
8760	4" pipe size		33	.485		141	31.50	1.94	174.44	204
8770	6" pipe size	Q-16	30	.800		255	54	2.14	311.14	360
9100	Threading pipe labor, sst, one end, schedules 40 & 80									
9110	1/4" through 3/4" pipe size	1 Plum	61.50	.130	Ea.		9.35		9.35	14
9120	1" through 2" pipe size		55.90	.143			10.30		10.30	15.40
9130	2-1/2" pipe size		41.50	.193			13.90		13.90	20.50
9140	3" pipe size		38.50	.208			14.95		14.95	22.50
9150	3-1/2" pipe size	Q-1	68.40	.234			15.15		15.15	22.50
9160	4" pipe size		73	.219			14.20		14.20	21
9170	5" pipe size		40.70	.393			25.50		25.50	38
9180	6" pipe size		35.40	.452			29.50		29.50	43.50
9190	8" pipe size		22.30	.717			46.50		46.50	69.50
9200	10" pipe size		16.10	.994			64.50		64.50	96
9210	12" pipe size		12.30	1.301			84.50		84.50	126
9250	Welding labor per joint for stainless steel									
9260	Schedule 5 and 10									
9270	1/4" pipe size	Q-15	36	.444	Ea.		29	1.78	30.78	45
9280	3/8" pipe size		35	.457			29.50	1.83	31.33	46
9290	1/2" pipe size		35	.457			29.50	1.83	31.33	46
9300	3/4" pipe size		28	.571			37	2.29	39.29	58
9310	1" pipe size		25	.640			41.50	2.57	44.07	65
9320	1-1/4" pipe size		22	.727			47	2.92	49.92	73.50
9330	1-1/2" pipe size		21	.762			49.50	3.06	52.56	77
9340	2" pipe size		18	.889			57.50	3.56	61.06	90
9350	2-1/2" pipe size		12	1.333			86.50	5.35	91.85	135
9360	3" pipe size		9.73	1.644			107	6.60	113.60	166
9370	4" pipe size		7.37	2.171			141	8.70	149.70	220
9380	5" pipe size		6.15	2.602			169	10.45	179.45	263
9390	6" pipe size		5.71	2.802			182	11.25	193.25	283
9400	8" pipe size		3.69	4.336			281	17.40	298.40	440

22 11 Facility Water Distribution

22 11 13 – Facility Water Distribution Piping

22 11 13.64 Pipe, Stainless Steel

		Crew	Daily Output	Labor-Hours	Unit	Material	2023 Bare Costs Labor	2023 Bare Costs Equipment	Total	Total Incl O&P
9410	10" pipe size	Q-15	2.91	5.498	Ea.		355	22	377	555
9420	12" pipe size		2.31	6.926			450	28	478	700
9500	Schedule 40									
9510	1/4" pipe size	Q-15	28	.571	Ea.		37	2.29	39.29	58
9520	3/8" pipe size		27	.593			38.50	2.38	40.88	60
9530	1/2" pipe size		25.40	.630			41	2.53	43.53	64
9540	3/4" pipe size		22.22	.720			46.50	2.89	49.39	72.50
9550	1" pipe size		20.25	.790			51	3.17	54.17	80
9560	1-1/4" pipe size		18.82	.850			55	3.41	58.41	86
9570	1-1/2" pipe size		17.78	.900			58.50	3.61	62.11	91
9580	2" pipe size		15.09	1.060			69	4.25	73.25	108
9590	2-1/2" pipe size		7.96	2.010			130	8.05	138.05	203
9600	3" pipe size		6.43	2.488			161	10	171	252
9610	4" pipe size		4.88	3.279			213	13.15	226.15	330
9620	5" pipe size		4.26	3.756			244	15.05	259.05	380
9630	6" pipe size		3.77	4.244			275	17	292	430
9640	8" pipe size		2.44	6.557			425	26.50	451.50	665
9650	10" pipe size		1.92	8.333			540	33.50	573.50	840
9660	12" pipe size		1.52	10.526			685	42	727	1,075
9750	Schedule 80									
9760	1/4" pipe size	Q-15	21.55	.742	Ea.		48	2.98	50.98	75.50
9770	3/8" pipe size		20.75	.771			50	3.09	53.09	78
9780	1/2" pipe size		19.54	.819			53	3.28	56.28	82.50
9790	3/4" pipe size		17.09	.936			60.50	3.75	64.25	94.50
9800	1" pipe size		15.58	1.027			66.50	4.12	70.62	104
9810	1-1/4" pipe size		14.48	1.105			71.50	4.43	75.93	112
9820	1-1/2" pipe size		13.68	1.170			76	4.69	80.69	118
9830	2" pipe size		11.61	1.378			89.50	5.55	95.05	139
9840	2-1/2" pipe size		6.12	2.614			170	10.50	180.50	265
9850	3" pipe size		4.94	3.239			210	13	223	330
9860	4" pipe size		3.75	4.267			277	17.10	294.10	435
9870	5" pipe size		3.27	4.893			315	19.60	334.60	495
9880	6" pipe size		2.90	5.517			360	22	382	560
9890	8" pipe size		1.87	8.556			555	34.50	589.50	865
9900	10" pipe size		1.48	10.811			700	43.50	743.50	1,100
9910	12" pipe size		1.17	13.675			885	55	940	1,375
9920	Schedule 160, 1/2" pipe size		17	.941			61	3.77	64.77	95
9930	3/4" pipe size		14.81	1.080			70	4.33	74.33	109
9940	1" pipe size		13.50	1.185			77	4.75	81.75	120
9950	1-1/4" pipe size		12.55	1.275			82.50	5.10	87.60	129
9960	1-1/2" pipe size		11.85	1.350			87.50	5.40	92.90	137
9970	2" pipe size		10	1.600			104	6.40	110.40	162
9980	3" pipe size		4.28	3.738			242	15	257	375
9990	4" pipe size		3.25	4.923			320	19.75	339.75	495

22 11 13.66 Pipe Fittings, Stainless Steel

		Crew	Daily Output	Labor-Hours	Unit	Material	2023 Bare Costs Labor	2023 Bare Costs Equipment	Total	Total Incl O&P
0010	**PIPE FITTINGS, STAINLESS STEEL**									
0100	Butt weld joint, schedule 5, type 304									
0120	90° elbow, long									
0140	1/2"	Q-15	17.50	.914	Ea.	28	59.50	3.67	91.17	123
0150	3/4"		14	1.143		28	74	4.58	106.58	147
0160	1"		12.50	1.280		29.50	83	5.15	117.65	162
0170	1-1/4"		11	1.455		40	94.50	5.85	140.35	192

22 11 Facility Water Distribution

22 11 13 – Facility Water Distribution Piping

22 11 13.66 Pipe Fittings, Stainless Steel

		Crew	Daily Output	Labor-Hours	Unit	Material	2023 Bare Costs Labor	Equipment	Total	Total Incl O&P
0180	1-1/2"	Q-15	10.50	1.524	Ea.	34	99	6.10	139.10	191
0190	2"		9	1.778		40	115	7.15	162.15	224
0200	2-1/2"		6	2.667		93	173	10.70	276.70	370
0210	3"		4.86	3.292		86.50	214	13.20	313.70	430
0220	3-1/2"		4.27	3.747		255	243	15.05	513.05	660
0230	4"		3.69	4.336		145	281	17.40	443.40	600
0240	5"		3.08	5.195		540	335	21	896	1,125
0250	6"	Q-16	4.29	5.594		420	375	14.95	809.95	1,025
0260	8"		2.76	8.696		880	585	23	1,488	1,875
0270	10"		2.18	11.009		1,350	740	29.50	2,119.50	2,625
0280	12"		1.73	13.873		1,925	935	37	2,897	3,575
0320	For schedule 5, type 316, add					30%				
0600	45° elbow, long									
0620	1/2"	Q-15	17.50	.914	Ea.	28	59.50	3.67	91.17	123
0630	3/4"		14	1.143		28	74	4.58	106.58	147
0640	1"		12.50	1.280		29.50	83	5.15	117.65	162
0650	1-1/4"		11	1.455		40	94.50	5.85	140.35	192
0660	1-1/2"		10.50	1.524		34	99	6.10	139.10	191
0670	2"		9	1.778		40	115	7.15	162.15	224
0680	2-1/2"		6	2.667		93	173	10.70	276.70	370
0690	3"		4.86	3.292		69.50	214	13.20	296.70	410
0700	3-1/2"		4.27	3.747		255	243	15.05	513.05	660
0710	4"		3.69	4.336		118	281	17.40	416.40	570
0720	5"		3.08	5.195		435	335	21	791	1,000
0730	6"	Q-16	4.29	5.594		294	375	14.95	683.95	900
0740	8"		2.76	8.696		620	585	23	1,228	1,575
0750	10"		2.18	11.009		1,075	740	29.50	1,844.50	2,325
0760	12"		1.73	13.873		1,350	935	37	2,322	2,950
0800	For schedule 5, type 316, add					25%				
1100	Tee, straight									
1130	1/2"	Q-15	11.66	1.372	Ea.	83.50	89	5.50	178	231
1140	3/4"		9.33	1.715		83.50	111	6.90	201.40	266
1150	1"		8.33	1.921		88	125	7.70	220.70	291
1160	1-1/4"		7.33	2.183		71	142	8.75	221.75	299
1170	1-1/2"		7	2.286		69.50	148	9.15	226.65	310
1180	2"		6	2.667		73	173	10.70	256.70	350
1190	2-1/2"		4	4		175	259	16.05	450.05	595
1200	3"		3.24	4.938		128	320	19.80	467.80	640
1210	3-1/2"		2.85	5.614		365	365	22.50	752.50	970
1220	4"		2.46	6.504		198	420	26	644	875
1230	5"		2	8		630	520	32	1,182	1,500
1240	6"	Q-16	2.85	8.421		495	565	22.50	1,082.50	1,425
1250	8"		1.84	13.043		1,050	875	35	1,960	2,500
1260	10"		1.45	16.552		1,700	1,125	44	2,869	3,575
1270	12"		1.15	20.870		2,375	1,400	55.50	3,830.50	4,750
1320	For schedule 5, type 316, add					25%				
2000	Butt weld joint, schedule 10, type 304									
2020	90° elbow, long									
2040	1/2"	Q-15	17	.941	Ea.	7.45	61	3.77	72.22	103
2050	3/4"		14	1.143		7.60	74	4.58	86.18	124
2060	1"		12.50	1.280		8.50	83	5.15	96.65	139
2070	1-1/4"		11	1.455		13	94.50	5.85	113.35	162
2080	1-1/2"		10.50	1.524		10.60	99	6.10	115.70	165

For customer support on your Plumbing Costs with RSMeans data, call 800.448.8182.

22 11 Facility Water Distribution

22 11 13 – Facility Water Distribution Piping

22 11 13.66 Pipe Fittings, Stainless Steel		Crew	Daily Output	Labor-Hours	Unit	Material	2023 Bare Costs Labor	Equipment	Total	Total Incl O&P
2090	2"	Q-15	9	1.778	Ea.	12.75	115	7.15	134.90	194
2100	2-1/2"		6	2.667		23	173	10.70	206.70	295
2110	3"		4.86	3.292		27.50	214	13.20	254.70	365
2120	3-1/2"		4.27	3.747		253	243	15.05	511.05	655
2130	4"		3.69	4.336		45.50	281	17.40	343.90	490
2140	5"		3.08	5.195		535	335	21	891	1,125
2150	6"	Q-16	4.29	5.594		121	375	14.95	510.95	710
2160	8"		2.76	8.696		201	585	23	809	1,125
2170	10"		2.18	11.009		500	740	29.50	1,269.50	1,675
2180	12"		1.73	13.873		770	935	37	1,742	2,300
2500	45° elbow, long									
2520	1/2"	Q-15	17.50	.914	Ea.	9.45	59.50	3.67	72.62	103
2530	3/4"		14	1.143		9.65	74	4.58	88.23	127
2540	1"		12.50	1.280		10.70	83	5.15	98.85	141
2550	1-1/4"		11	1.455		17.90	94.50	5.85	118.25	167
2560	1-1/2"		10.50	1.524		10.90	99	6.10	116	166
2570	2"		9	1.778		13	115	7.15	135.15	194
2580	2-1/2"		6	2.667		20.50	173	10.70	204.20	292
2590	3"		4.86	3.292		23.50	214	13.20	250.70	360
2600	3-1/2"		4.27	3.747		253	243	15.05	511.05	655
2610	4"		3.69	4.336		38	281	17.40	336.40	480
2620	5"		3.08	5.195		248	335	21	604	795
2630	6"	Q-16	4.29	5.594		82	375	14.95	471.95	665
2640	8"		2.76	8.696		146	585	23	754	1,050
2650	10"		2.18	11.009		360	740	29.50	1,129.50	1,525
2660	12"		1.73	13.873		550	935	37	1,522	2,050
2670	Reducer, concentric									
2674	1" x 3/4"	Q-15	13.25	1.208	Ea.	20	78.50	4.84	103.34	144
2676	2" x 1-1/2"	"	9.75	1.641		14.55	106	6.60	127.15	182
2678	6" x 4"	Q-16	4.91	4.888		36.50	330	13.05	379.55	545
2680	Caps									
2682	1"	Q-15	25	.640	Ea.	22.50	41.50	2.57	66.57	89.50
2684	1-1/2"		21	.762		24.50	49.50	3.06	77.06	103
2685	2"		18	.889		21	57.50	3.56	82.06	113
2686	4"		7.38	2.168		33.50	141	8.70	183.20	256
2687	6"	Q-16	8.58	2.797		54.50	188	7.45	249.95	350
3000	Tee, straight									
3030	1/2"	Q-15	11.66	1.372	Ea.	26.50	89	5.50	121	168
3040	3/4"		9.33	1.715		26.50	111	6.90	144.40	203
3050	1"		8.33	1.921		27	125	7.70	159.70	224
3060	1-1/4"		7.33	2.183		41.50	142	8.75	192.25	266
3070	1-1/2"		7	2.286		27	148	9.15	184.15	261
3080	2"		6	2.667		29	173	10.70	212.70	300
3090	2-1/2"		4	4		76	259	16.05	351.05	485
3100	3"		3.24	4.938		53.50	320	19.80	393.30	560
3110	3-1/2"		2.85	5.614		201	365	22.50	588.50	790
3120	4"		2.46	6.504		80	420	26	526	745
3130	5"		2	8		620	520	32	1,172	1,500
3140	6"	Q-16	2.85	8.421		183	565	22.50	770.50	1,075
3150	8"		1.84	13.043		375	875	35	1,285	1,750
3151	10"		1.45	16.552		470	1,125	44	1,639	2,225
3152	12"		1.15	20.870		1,075	1,400	55.50	2,530.50	3,325
3154	For schedule 10, type 316, add					25%				

22 11 Facility Water Distribution

22 11 13 – Facility Water Distribution Piping

22 11 13.66 Pipe Fittings, Stainless Steel		Crew	Daily Output	Labor-Hours	Unit	Material	2023 Bare Costs Labor	Equipment	Total	Total Incl O&P
3281	Butt weld joint, schedule 40, type 304									
3284	90° elbow, long, 1/2"	Q-15	12.70	1.260	Ea.	8.30	81.50	5.05	94.85	137
3288	3/4"		11.10	1.441		8.45	93.50	5.80	107.75	155
3289	1"		10.13	1.579		9.60	102	6.35	117.95	171
3290	1-1/4"		9.40	1.702		14.30	110	6.85	131.15	188
3300	1-1/2"		8.89	1.800		11.35	117	7.20	135.55	194
3310	2"		7.55	2.119		15.75	137	8.50	161.25	232
3320	2-1/2"		3.98	4.020		33.50	261	16.10	310.60	445
3330	3"		3.21	4.984		42.50	325	20	387.50	550
3340	3-1/2"		2.83	5.654		460	365	22.50	847.50	1,075
3350	4"		2.44	6.557		79	425	26.50	530.50	750
3360	5"	▼	2.13	7.512		720	485	30	1,235	1,550
3370	6"	Q-16	2.83	8.481		215	570	22.50	807.50	1,100
3380	8"		1.83	13.115		390	880	35	1,305	1,800
3390	10"		1.44	16.667		1,500	1,125	44.50	2,669.50	3,375
3400	12"	▼	1.14	21.053	▼	2,750	1,425	56	4,231	5,175
3410	For schedule 40, type 316, add					25%				
3460	45° elbow, long, 1/2"	Q-15	12.70	1.260	Ea.	11.45	81.50	5.05	98	140
3470	3/4"		11.10	1.441		11.55	93.50	5.80	110.85	158
3480	1"		10.13	1.579		11.65	102	6.35	120	173
3490	1-1/4"		9.40	1.702		16.90	110	6.85	133.75	191
3500	1-1/2"		8.89	1.800		13.15	117	7.20	137.35	196
3510	2"		7.55	2.119		16.35	137	8.50	161.85	232
3520	2-1/2"		3.98	4.020		33.50	261	16.10	310.60	445
3530	3"		3.21	4.984		30.50	325	20	375.50	535
3540	3-1/2"		2.83	5.654		460	365	22.50	847.50	1,075
3550	4"		2.44	6.557		55	425	26.50	506.50	725
3560	5"	▼	2.13	7.512		505	485	30	1,020	1,325
3570	6"	Q-16	2.83	8.481		138	570	22.50	730.50	1,025
3580	8"		1.83	13.115		272	880	35	1,187	1,675
3590	10"		1.44	16.667		1,500	1,125	44.50	2,669.50	3,375
3600	12"	▼	1.14	21.053	▼	855	1,425	56	2,336	3,100
3610	For schedule 40, type 316, add					25%				
3660	Tee, straight 1/2"	Q-15	8.46	1.891	Ea.	27.50	123	7.60	158.10	221
3670	3/4"		7.40	2.162		27.50	140	8.65	176.15	249
3680	1"		6.74	2.374		28	154	9.50	191.50	271
3690	1-1/4"		6.27	2.552		46.50	165	10.25	221.75	310
3700	1-1/2"		5.92	2.703		28.50	175	10.85	214.35	305
3710	2"		5.03	3.181		30.50	206	12.75	249.25	360
3720	2-1/2"		2.65	6.038		76	390	24	490	695
3730	3"		2.14	7.477		61.50	485	30	576.50	825
3740	3-1/2"		1.88	8.511		335	550	34	919	1,225
3750	4"		1.62	9.877		87.50	640	39.50	767	1,100
3760	5"	▼	1.42	11.268		775	730	45	1,550	2,000
3770	6"	Q-16	1.88	12.766		197	860	34	1,091	1,525
3780	8"		1.22	19.672		575	1,325	52.50	1,952.50	2,675
3790	10"		.96	25		2,375	1,675	67	4,117	5,200
3800	12"	▼	.76	31.579	▼	2,575	2,125	84.50	4,784.50	6,125
3810	For schedule 40, type 316, add					25%				
3820	Tee, reducing on outlet, 3/4" x 1/2"	Q-15	7.73	2.070	Ea.	95.50	134	8.30	237.80	315
3822	1" x 1/2"		7.24	2.210		120	143	8.85	271.85	355
3824	1" x 3/4"		6.96	2.299		110	149	9.20	268.20	355
3826	1-1/4" x 1"		6.43	2.488	▼	270	161	10	441	550

22 11 Facility Water Distribution

22 11 13 – Facility Water Distribution Piping

22 11 13.66 Pipe Fittings, Stainless Steel		Crew	Daily Output	Labor-Hours	Unit	Material	2023 Bare Costs Labor	Equipment	Total	Total Incl O&P
3828	1-1/2" x 1/2"	Q-15	6.58	2.432	Ea.	162	158	9.75	329.75	425
3830	1-1/2" x 3/4"		6.35	2.520		152	163	10.10	325.10	420
3832	1-1/2" x 1"		6.18	2.589		116	168	10.40	294.40	390
3834	2" x 1"		5.50	2.909		208	189	11.65	408.65	525
3836	2" x 1-1/2"		5.30	3.019		175	196	12.10	383.10	495
3838	2-1/2" x 2"		3.15	5.079		264	330	20.50	614.50	805
3840	3" x 1-1/2"		2.72	5.882		267	380	23.50	670.50	890
3842	3" x 2"		2.65	6.038		222	390	24	636	855
3844	4" x 2"		2.10	7.619		131	495	30.50	656.50	915
3846	4" x 3"		1.77	9.040		405	585	36.50	1,026.50	1,350
3848	5" x 4"	↓	1.48	10.811		930	700	43.50	1,673.50	2,125
3850	6" x 3"	Q-16	2.19	10.959		1,025	735	29.50	1,789.50	2,250
3852	6" x 4"		2.04	11.765		890	790	31.50	1,711.50	2,200
3854	8" x 4"		1.46	16.438		2,075	1,100	44	3,219	3,975
3856	10" x 8"		.69	34.783		3,500	2,350	93	5,943	7,450
3858	12" x 10"	↓	.55	43.636		4,675	2,925	117	7,717	9,650
3950	Reducer, concentric, 3/4" x 1/2"	Q-15	11.85	1.350		18.65	87.50	5.40	111.55	157
3952	1" x 3/4"		10.60	1.509		21.50	98	6.05	125.55	177
3954	1-1/4" x 3/4"		10.19	1.570		64	102	6.30	172.30	229
3956	1-1/4" x 1"		9.76	1.639		31	106	6.55	143.55	200
3958	1-1/2" x 3/4"		9.88	1.619		54.50	105	6.50	166	224
3960	1-1/2" x 1"		9.47	1.690		107	110	6.80	223.80	288
3962	2" x 1"		8.65	1.850		20.50	120	7.40	147.90	210
3964	2" x 1-1/2"		8.16	1.961		16.35	127	7.85	151.20	217
3966	2-1/2" x 1"		5.71	2.802		93.50	182	11.25	286.75	385
3968	2-1/2" x 2"		5.21	3.071		73	199	12.30	284.30	390
3970	3" x 1"		4.88	3.279		64	213	13.15	290.15	400
3972	3" x 1-1/2"		4.72	3.390		29	220	13.60	262.60	375
3974	3" x 2"		4.51	3.548		26.50	230	14.25	270.75	390
3976	4" x 2"		3.69	4.336		38	281	17.40	336.40	480
3978	4" x 3"		2.77	5.776		29	375	23	427	620
3980	5" x 3"		2.56	6.250		485	405	25	915	1,175
3982	5" x 4"	↓	2.27	7.048		390	455	28.50	873.50	1,150
3984	6" x 3"	Q-16	3.57	6.723		112	450	17.95	579.95	820
3986	6" x 4"		3.19	7.524		76	505	20	601	860
3988	8" x 4"		2.44	9.836		246	660	26.50	932.50	1,275
3990	8" x 6"		2.22	10.811		172	725	29	926	1,300
3992	10" x 6"		1.91	12.565		730	845	33.50	1,608.50	2,100
3994	10" x 8"		1.61	14.907		605	1,000	40	1,645	2,200
3995	12" x 6"		1.63	14.724		1,375	990	39.50	2,404.50	3,050
3996	12" x 8"		1.41	17.021		1,025	1,150	45.50	2,220.50	2,875
3997	12" x 10"	↓	1.27	18.898	↓	725	1,275	50.50	2,050.50	2,750
4000	Socket weld joint, 3,000 lb., type 304									
4100	90° elbow									
4140	1/4"	Q-15	13.47	1.188	Ea.	41	77	4.76	122.76	165
4150	3/8"		12.97	1.234		53	80	4.95	137.95	183
4160	1/2"		12.21	1.310		56	85	5.25	146.25	194
4170	3/4"		10.68	1.498		68	97	6	171	226
4180	1"		9.74	1.643		102	107	6.60	215.60	279
4190	1-1/4"		9.05	1.768		305	115	7.10	427.10	515
4200	1-1/2"		8.55	1.871		218	121	7.50	346.50	430
4210	2"	↓	7.26	2.204	↓	345	143	8.85	496.85	605
4300	45° elbow									

22 11 Facility Water Distribution

22 11 13 – Facility Water Distribution Piping

22 11 13.66 Pipe Fittings, Stainless Steel		Crew	Daily Output	Labor-Hours	Unit	Material	2023 Bare Costs Labor	Equipment	Total	Total Incl O&P
4340	1/4"	Q-15	13.47	1.188	Ea.	74	77	4.76	155.76	202
4350	3/8"		12.97	1.234		74.50	80	4.95	159.45	206
4360	1/2"		12.21	1.310		74.50	85	5.25	164.75	215
4370	3/4"		10.68	1.498		84.50	97	6	187.50	245
4380	1"		9.74	1.643		122	107	6.60	235.60	300
4390	1-1/4"		9.05	1.768		360	115	7.10	482.10	575
4400	1-1/2"		8.55	1.871		207	121	7.50	335.50	415
4410	2"		7.26	2.204		370	143	8.85	521.85	635
4500	Tee									
4540	1/4"	Q-15	8.97	1.784	Ea.	93	116	7.15	216.15	282
4550	3/8"		8.64	1.852		111	120	7.45	238.45	310
4560	1/2"		8.13	1.968		90.50	128	7.90	226.40	298
4570	3/4"		7.12	2.247		104	146	9	259	340
4580	1"		6.48	2.469		141	160	9.90	310.90	405
4590	1-1/4"		6.03	2.653		375	172	10.65	557.65	685
4600	1-1/2"		5.69	2.812		415	182	11.30	608.30	740
4610	2"		4.83	3.313		595	215	13.30	823.30	990
5000	Socket weld joint, 3,000 lb., type 316									
5100	90° elbow									
5140	1/4"	Q-15	13.47	1.188	Ea.	86.50	77	4.76	168.26	215
5150	3/8"		12.97	1.234		101	80	4.95	185.95	235
5160	1/2"		12.21	1.310		80.50	85	5.25	170.75	222
5170	3/4"		10.68	1.498		106	97	6	209	269
5180	1"		9.74	1.643		151	107	6.60	264.60	330
5190	1-1/4"		9.05	1.768		405	115	7.10	527.10	625
5200	1-1/2"		8.55	1.871		355	121	7.50	483.50	580
5210	2"		7.26	2.204		570	143	8.85	721.85	850
5300	45° elbow									
5340	1/4"	Q-15	13.47	1.188	Ea.	174	77	4.76	255.76	310
5350	3/8"		12.97	1.234		174	80	4.95	258.95	315
5360	1/2"		12.21	1.310		116	85	5.25	206.25	260
5370	3/4"		10.68	1.498		128	97	6	231	293
5380	1"		9.74	1.643		230	107	6.60	343.60	420
5390	1-1/4"		9.05	1.768		415	115	7.10	537.10	640
5400	1-1/2"		8.55	1.871		360	121	7.50	488.50	590
5410	2"		7.26	2.204		540	143	8.85	691.85	820
5500	Tee									
5540	1/4"	Q-15	8.97	1.784	Ea.	117	116	7.15	240.15	310
5550	3/8"		8.64	1.852		143	120	7.45	270.45	345
5560	1/2"		8.13	1.968		106	128	7.90	241.90	315
5570	3/4"		7.12	2.247		131	146	9	286	370
5580	1"		6.48	2.469		237	160	9.90	406.90	510
5590	1-1/4"		6.03	2.653		480	172	10.65	662.65	795
5600	1-1/2"		5.69	2.812		505	182	11.30	698.30	840
5610	2"		4.83	3.313		790	215	13.30	1,018.30	1,200
5700	For socket weld joint, 6,000 lb., type 304 and 316, add					100%				
6000	Threaded companion flange									
6010	Stainless steel, 150 lb., type 304									
6020	1/2" diam.	1 Plum	30	.267	Ea.	30	19.20		49.20	61
6030	3/4" diam.		28	.286		34.50	20.50		55	68
6040	1" diam.		27	.296		37.50	21.50		59	73.50
6050	1-1/4" diam.	Q-1	44	.364		48.50	23.50		72	88.50
6060	1-1/2" diam.		40	.400		49	26		75	92.50

22 11 Facility Water Distribution

22 11 13 – Facility Water Distribution Piping

22 11 13.66 Pipe Fittings, Stainless Steel		Crew	Daily Output	Labor-Hours	Unit	Material	2023 Bare Costs Labor	Equipment	Total	Total Incl O&P
6070	2" diam.	Q-1	36	.444	Ea.	64	29		93	114
6080	2-1/2" diam.		28	.571		96	37		133	162
6090	3" diam.		20	.800		96.50	52		148.50	184
6110	4" diam.	▼	12	1.333		133	86.50		219.50	275
6130	6" diam.	Q-2	14	1.714		231	115		346	425
6140	8" diam.	"	12	2	▼	430	135		565	675
6150	For type 316, add					40%				
6260	Weld flanges, stainless steel, type 304									
6270	Slip on, 150 lb. (welded, front and back)									
6280	1/2" diam.	Q-15	12.70	1.260	Ea.	28	81.50	5.05	114.55	159
6290	3/4" diam.		11.11	1.440		29	93.50	5.75	128.25	177
6300	1" diam.		10.13	1.579		31.50	102	6.35	139.85	195
6310	1-1/4" diam.		9.41	1.700		44	110	6.80	160.80	220
6320	1-1/2" diam.		8.89	1.800		44	117	7.20	168.20	230
6330	2" diam.		7.55	2.119		53.50	137	8.50	199	273
6340	2-1/2" diam.		3.98	4.020		77	261	16.10	354.10	490
6350	3" diam.		3.21	4.984		85	325	20	430	595
6370	4" diam.	▼	2.44	6.557		114	425	26.50	565.50	790
6390	6" diam.	Q-16	1.89	12.698		174	855	34	1,063	1,500
6400	8" diam.	"	1.22	19.672	▼	315	1,325	52.50	1,692.50	2,375
6410	For type 316, add					40%				
6530	Weld neck 150 lb.									
6540	1/2" diam.	Q-15	25.40	.630	Ea.	30.50	41	2.53	74.03	97.50
6550	3/4" diam.		22.22	.720		36	46.50	2.89	85.39	112
6560	1" diam.		20.25	.790		39.50	51	3.17	93.67	123
6570	1-1/4" diam.		18.82	.850		62.50	55	3.41	120.91	154
6580	1-1/2" diam.		17.78	.900		56	58.50	3.61	118.11	152
6590	2" diam.		15.09	1.060		59	69	4.25	132.25	172
6600	2-1/2" diam.		7.96	2.010		95.50	130	8.05	233.55	310
6610	3" diam.		6.43	2.488		96.50	161	10	267.50	360
6630	4" diam.		4.88	3.279		145	213	13.15	371.15	490
6640	5" diam.	▼	4.26	3.756		207	244	15.05	466.05	610
6650	6" diam.	Q-16	5.66	4.240		211	285	11.30	507.30	670
6652	8" diam.		3.65	6.575		375	440	17.55	832.55	1,100
6654	10" diam.		2.88	8.333		430	560	22.50	1,012.50	1,325
6656	12" diam.	▼	2.28	10.526	▼	530	710	28	1,268	1,650
6670	For type 316, add					23%				
7000	Threaded joint, 150 lb., type 304									
7030	90° elbow									
7040	1/8"	1 Plum	13	.615	Ea.	27.50	44.50		72	96.50
7050	1/4"		13	.615		27.50	44.50		72	96.50
7070	3/8"		13	.615		32.50	44.50		77	102
7080	1/2"		12	.667		30	48		78	105
7090	3/4"		11	.727		37	52.50		89.50	119
7100	1"	▼	10	.800		51.50	57.50		109	143
7110	1-1/4"	Q-1	17	.941		83	61		144	182
7120	1-1/2"		16	1		98	65		163	205
7130	2"		14	1.143		137	74		211	261
7140	2-1/2"		11	1.455		320	94.50		414.50	490
7150	3"	▼	8	2		450	130		580	690
7160	4"	Q-2	11	2.182	▼	765	147		912	1,075
7180	45° elbow									
7190	1/8"	1 Plum	13	.615	Ea.	40	44.50		84.50	110

22 11 Facility Water Distribution

22 11 13 – Facility Water Distribution Piping

22 11 13.66 Pipe Fittings, Stainless Steel

		Crew	Daily Output	Labor-Hours	Unit	Material	2023 Bare Costs Labor	Equipment	Total	Total Incl O&P
7200	1/4"	1 Plum	13	.615	Ea.	40	44.50		84.50	110
7210	3/8"		13	.615		41	44.50		85.50	111
7220	1/2"		12	.667		42	48		90	118
7230	3/4"		11	.727		48.50	52.50		101	132
7240	1"		10	.800		57	57.50		114.50	149
7250	1-1/4"	Q-1	17	.941		82	61		143	181
7260	1-1/2"		16	1		104	65		169	211
7270	2"		14	1.143		147	74		221	273
7280	2-1/2"		11	1.455		435	94.50		529.50	620
7290	3"		8	2		630	130		760	890
7300	4"	Q-2	11	2.182		1,075	147		1,222	1,425
7320	Tee, straight									
7330	1/8"	1 Plum	9	.889	Ea.	42	64		106	142
7340	1/4"		9	.889		42	64		106	142
7350	3/8"		9	.889		46	64		110	147
7360	1/2"		8	1		44.50	72		116.50	156
7370	3/4"		7	1.143		52	82.50		134.50	180
7380	1"		6.50	1.231		66.50	88.50		155	205
7390	1-1/4"	Q-1	11	1.455		117	94.50		211.50	269
7400	1-1/2"		10	1.600		148	104		252	320
7410	2"		9	1.778		186	115		301	375
7420	2-1/2"		7	2.286		455	148		603	720
7430	3"		5	3.200		685	208		893	1,050
7440	4"	Q-2	7	3.429		1,525	231		1,756	2,050
7460	Coupling, straight									
7470	1/8"	1 Plum	19	.421	Ea.	11.50	30.50		42	57.50
7480	1/4"		19	.421		13.65	30.50		44.15	60
7490	3/8"		19	.421		16.20	30.50		46.70	63
7500	1/2"		19	.421		22	30.50		52.50	69
7510	3/4"		18	.444		29.50	32		61.50	80.50
7520	1"		15	.533		46.50	38.50		85	109
7530	1-1/4"	Q-1	26	.615		75	40		115	142
7540	1-1/2"		24	.667		83	43		126	156
7550	2"		21	.762		133	49.50		182.50	220
7560	2-1/2"		18	.889		305	57.50		362.50	420
7570	3"		14	1.143		415	74		489	570
7580	4"	Q-2	16	1.500		595	101		696	805
7600	Reducer, concentric, 1/2"	1 Plum	12	.667		36.50	48		84.50	112
7610	3/4"		11	.727		47	52.50		99.50	130
7612	1"		10	.800		78	57.50		135.50	172
7614	1-1/4"	Q-1	17	.941		165	61		226	273
7616	1-1/2"		16	1		181	65		246	296
7618	2"		14	1.143		282	74		356	420
7620	2-1/2"		11	1.455		740	94.50		834.50	955
7622	3"		8	2		825	130		955	1,100
7624	4"	Q-2	11	2.182		1,375	147		1,522	1,725
7710	Union									
7720	1/8"	1 Plum	12	.667	Ea.	54.50	48		102.50	132
7730	1/4"		12	.667		56.50	48		104.50	134
7740	3/8"		12	.667		63	48		111	141
7750	1/2"		11	.727		75.50	52.50		128	161
7760	3/4"		10	.800		102	57.50		159.50	198
7770	1"		9	.889		149	64		213	260

22 11 Facility Water Distribution

22 11 13 – Facility Water Distribution Piping

22 11 13.66 Pipe Fittings, Stainless Steel

		Crew	Daily Output	Labor-Hours	Unit	Material	2023 Bare Costs Labor	Equipment	Total	Total Incl O&P
7780	1-1/4"	Q-1	16	1	Ea.	350	65		415	480
7790	1-1/2"		15	1.067		380	69		449	525
7800	2"		13	1.231		480	80		560	650
7810	2-1/2"		10	1.600		935	104		1,039	1,175
7820	3"		7	2.286		1,225	148		1,373	1,575
7830	4"	Q-2	10	2.400		1,700	161		1,861	2,125
7838	Caps									
7840	1/2"	1 Plum	24	.333	Ea.	10.05	24		34.05	47
7841	3/4"		22	.364		26	26		52	67.50
7842	1"		20	.400		23.50	29		52.50	69
7843	1-1/2"	Q-1	32	.500		97	32.50		129.50	156
7844	2"	"	28	.571		115	37		152	183
7845	4"	Q-2	22	1.091		660	73.50		733.50	840
7850	For 150 lb., type 316, add					25%				

22 11 13.74 Pipe, Plastic

		Crew	Daily Output	Labor-Hours	Unit	Material	2023 Bare Costs Labor	Equipment	Total	Total Incl O&P
0010	**PIPE, PLASTIC** R221113-70									
0020	Fiberglass reinforced, couplings 10' OC, clevis hanger assy's, 3 per 10'									
0080	General service									
0120	2" diameter	Q-1	59	.271	L.F.	22	17.60		39.60	50.50
0140	3" diameter		52	.308		30.50	19.95		50.45	63.50
0150	4" diameter		48	.333		39.50	21.50		61	75.50
0160	6" diameter		39	.410		47	26.50		73.50	91.50
0170	8" diameter	Q-2	49	.490		79.50	33		112.50	137
0180	10" diameter		41	.585		123	39.50		162.50	194
0190	12" diameter		36	.667		170	45		215	254
0600	PVC, high impact/pressure, cplgs. 10' OC, clevis hanger assy's, 3 per 10'									
1020	Schedule 80									
1070	1/2" diameter	1 Plum	50	.160	L.F.	10.20	11.55		21.75	28.50
1080	3/4" diameter		47	.170		10.85	12.25		23.10	30
1090	1" diameter		43	.186		5.20	13.40		18.60	25.50
1100	1-1/4" diameter		39	.205		6.70	14.80		21.50	29.50
1110	1-1/2" diameter		34	.235		8.05	16.95		25	34.50
1120	2" diameter	Q-1	55	.291		10	18.85		28.85	39
1140	3" diameter		50	.320		19.30	21		40.30	52
1150	4" diameter		46	.348		26	22.50		48.50	62.50
1170	6" diameter		38	.421		57	27.50		84.50	103
1730	To delete coupling & hangers, subtract									
1740	1/2" diam.					62%	80%			
1750	3/4" diam. to 1-1/4" diam.					58%	73%			
1760	1-1/2" diam. to 6" diam.					40%	57%			
1800	PVC, couplings 10' OC, clevis hanger assemblies, 3 per 10'									
1820	Schedule 40									
1860	1/2" diameter	1 Plum	54	.148	L.F.	9.90	10.65		20.55	27
1870	3/4" diameter		51	.157		10.25	11.30		21.55	28
1880	1" diameter		46	.174		4.44	12.55		16.99	23.50
1890	1-1/4" diameter		42	.190		5.35	13.70		19.05	26.50
1900	1-1/2" diameter		36	.222		6.75	16		22.75	31.50
1910	2" diameter	Q-1	59	.271		8.05	17.60		25.65	35
1920	2-1/2" diameter		56	.286		12.20	18.55		30.75	41
1930	3" diameter		53	.302		15.15	19.60		34.75	45.50
1940	4" diameter		48	.333		11.30	21.50		32.80	44.50
1950	5" diameter		43	.372		31.50	24		55.50	70.50

22 11 Facility Water Distribution

22 11 13 – Facility Water Distribution Piping

22 11 13.74 Pipe, Plastic

		Crew	Daily Output	Labor-Hours	Unit	Material	2023 Bare Costs Labor	Equipment	Total	Total Incl O&P
1960	6" diameter	Q-1	39	.410	L.F.	37.50	26.50		64	80.50
1970	8" diameter	Q-2	48	.500		69.50	33.50		103	127
1980	10" diameter		43	.558		104	37.50		141.50	171
1990	12" diameter		42	.571		162	38.50		200.50	236
2000	14" diameter		31	.774		270	52		322	375
2010	16" diameter		23	1.043		365	70		435	505
2340	To delete coupling & hangers, subtract									
2360	1/2" diam. to 1-1/4" diam.					65%	74%			
2370	1-1/2" diam. to 6" diam.					44%	57%			
2380	8" diam. to 12" diam.					41%	53%			
2390	14" diam. to 16" diam.					48%	45%			
2420	Schedule 80									
2440	1/4" diameter	1 Plum	58	.138	L.F.	8.95	9.95		18.90	24.50
2450	3/8" diameter		55	.145		8.95	10.50		19.45	25.50
2460	1/2" diameter		50	.160		9.95	11.55		21.50	28
2470	3/4" diameter		47	.170		10.60	12.25		22.85	30
2480	1" diameter		43	.186		4.80	13.40		18.20	25.50
2490	1-1/4" diameter		39	.205		6.15	14.80		20.95	29
2500	1-1/2" diameter		34	.235		8.15	16.95		25.10	34.50
2510	2" diameter	Q-1	55	.291		9.05	18.85		27.90	38
2520	2-1/2" diameter		52	.308		12.55	19.95		32.50	44
2530	3" diameter		50	.320		20.50	21		41.50	53.50
2540	4" diameter		46	.348		27.50	22.50		50	63.50
2550	5" diameter		42	.381		32.50	24.50		57	72.50
2560	6" diameter		38	.421		53	27.50		80.50	99
2570	8" diameter	Q-2	47	.511		93	34.50		127.50	153
2580	10" diameter		42	.571		114	38.50		152.50	184
2590	12" diameter		38	.632		177	42.50		219.50	258
2830	To delete coupling & hangers, subtract									
2840	1/4" diam. to 1/2" diam.					66%	80%			
2850	3/4" diam. to 1-1/4" diam.					61%	73%			
2860	1-1/2" diam. to 6" diam.					41%	57%			
2870	8" diam. to 12" diam.					31%	50%			
2900	Schedule 120									
2910	1/2" diameter	1 Plum	50	.160	L.F.	10.85	11.55		22.40	29
2950	3/4" diameter		47	.170		11.80	12.25		24.05	31.50
2960	1" diameter		43	.186		6.60	13.40		20	27.50
2970	1-1/4" diameter		39	.205		8.75	14.80		23.55	31.50
2980	1-1/2" diameter		33	.242		10.50	17.45		27.95	37.50
2990	2" diameter	Q-1	54	.296		13.90	19.20		33.10	44
3000	2-1/2" diameter		52	.308		21.50	19.95		41.45	53.50
3010	3" diameter		49	.327		42	21		63	77.50
3020	4" diameter		45	.356		38.50	23		61.50	77
3030	6" diameter		37	.432		102	28		130	154
3240	To delete coupling & hangers, subtract									
3250	1/2" diam. to 1-1/4" diam.					52%	74%			
3260	1-1/2" diam. to 4" diam.					30%	57%			
3270	6" diam.					17%	50%			
3300	PVC, pressure, couplings 10' OC, clevis hanger assy's, 3 per 10'									
3310	SDR 26, 160 psi									
3350	1-1/4" diameter	1 Plum	42	.190	L.F.	5.10	13.70		18.80	26
3360	1-1/2" diameter	"	36	.222		6.55	16		22.55	31
3370	2" diameter	Q-1	59	.271		7.85	17.60		25.45	34.50

22 11 Facility Water Distribution

22 11 13 – Facility Water Distribution Piping

22 11 13.74 Pipe, Plastic

		Crew	Daily Output	Labor-Hours	Unit	Material	2023 Bare Costs Labor	Equipment	Total	Total Incl O&P
3380	2-1/2" diameter	Q-1	56	.286	L.F.	11.75	18.55		30.30	40.50
3390	3" diameter		53	.302		15.60	19.60		35.20	46
3400	4" diameter		48	.333		22.50	21.50		44	57
3420	6" diameter		39	.410		43.50	26.50		70	87.50
3430	8" diameter	Q-2	48	.500		77	33.50		110.50	135
3660	To delete coupling & clevis hanger assy's, subtract									
3670	1-1/4" diam.					63%	68%			
3680	1-1/2" diam. to 4" diam.					48%	57%			
3690	6" diam. to 8" diam.					60%	54%			
3720	SDR 21, 200 psi, 1/2" diameter	1 Plum	54	.148	L.F.	9.80	10.65		20.45	26.50
3740	3/4" diameter		51	.157		9.85	11.30		21.15	27.50
3750	1" diameter		46	.174		3.63	12.55		16.18	22.50
3760	1-1/4" diameter		42	.190		5.35	13.70		19.05	26.50
3770	1-1/2" diameter		36	.222		4.99	16		20.99	29.50
3780	2" diameter	Q-1	59	.271		6.80	17.60		24.40	33.50
3790	2-1/2" diameter		56	.286		9.85	18.55		28.40	38.50
3800	3" diameter		53	.302		10.95	19.60		30.55	41
3810	4" diameter		48	.333		14.70	21.50		36.20	48
3830	6" diameter		39	.410		29.50	26.50		56	72
3840	8" diameter	Q-2	48	.500		58.50	33.50		92	114
4000	To delete coupling & hangers, subtract									
4010	1/2" diam. to 3/4" diam.					71%	77%			
4020	1" diam. to 1-1/4" diam.					63%	70%			
4030	1-1/2" diam. to 6" diam.					44%	57%			
4040	8" diam.					46%	54%			
4100	DWV type, schedule 40, couplings 10' OC, clevis hanger assy's, 3 per 10'									
4210	ABS, schedule 40, foam core type									
4212	Plain end black									
4214	1-1/2" diameter	1 Plum	39	.205	L.F.	5.55	14.80		20.35	28
4216	2" diameter	Q-1	62	.258		7	16.75		23.75	32.50
4218	3" diameter		56	.286		14.60	18.55		33.15	43.50
4220	4" diameter		51	.314		22	20.50		42.50	54.50
4222	6" diameter		42	.381		65	24.50		89.50	109
4240	To delete coupling & hangers, subtract									
4244	1-1/2" diam. to 6" diam.					43%	48%			
4400	PVC									
4410	1-1/4" diameter	1 Plum	42	.190	L.F.	8.50	13.70		22.20	30
4420	1-1/2" diameter	"	36	.222		4.77	16		20.77	29.50
4460	2" diameter	Q-1	59	.271		6.10	17.60		23.70	32.50
4470	3" diameter		53	.302		12.85	19.60		32.45	43
4480	4" diameter		48	.333		18	21.50		39.50	52
4490	6" diameter		39	.410		48	26.50		74.50	92
4500	8" diameter	Q-2	48	.500		76	33.50		109.50	134
4510	To delete coupling & hangers, subtract									
4520	1-1/4" diam. to 1-1/2" diam.					48%	60%			
4530	2" diam. to 8" diam.					42%	54%			
4532	to delete hangers, 2" diam. to 8" diam.	Q-1	50	.320	L.F.	3.12	21		24.12	34.50
4550	PVC, schedule 40, foam core type									
4552	Plain end, white									
4554	1-1/2" diameter	1 Plum	39	.205	L.F.	3.27	14.80		18.07	25.50
4556	2" diameter	Q-1	62	.258		5.65	16.75		22.40	31
4558	3" diameter		56	.286		11.55	18.55		30.10	40
4560	4" diameter		51	.314		16.80	20.50		37.30	49

22 11 Facility Water Distribution

22 11 13 – Facility Water Distribution Piping

22 11 13.74 Pipe, Plastic

		Crew	Daily Output	Labor-Hours	Unit	Material	2023 Bare Costs Labor	Equipment	Total	Total Incl O&P
4562	6" diameter	Q-1	42	.381	L.F.	38.50	24.50		63	79.50
4564	8" diameter	Q-2	51	.471		61	31.50		92.50	114
4568	10" diameter		48	.500		78.50	33.50		112	137
4570	12" diameter	↓	46	.522	↓	93	35		128	155
4580	To delete coupling & hangers, subtract									
4582	1-1/2" diam. to 2" diam.					58%	54%			
4584	3" diam. to 12" diam.					46%	42%			
4800	PVC, clear pipe, cplgs. 10' OC, clevis hanger assy's 3 per 10', Sched. 40									
4840	1/4" diameter	1 Plum	59	.136	L.F.	9.30	9.75		19.05	25
4850	3/8" diameter		56	.143		9.70	10.30		20	26
4860	1/2" diameter		54	.148		10.45	10.65		21.10	27.50
4870	3/4" diameter		51	.157		11.20	11.30		22.50	29
4880	1" diameter		46	.174		6.30	12.55		18.85	25.50
4890	1-1/4" diameter		42	.190		8	13.70		21.70	29.50
4900	1-1/2" diameter	↓	36	.222		9.40	16		25.40	34.50
4910	2" diameter	Q-1	59	.271		12.35	17.60		29.95	39.50
4920	2-1/2" diameter		56	.286		18.35	18.55		36.90	47.50
4930	3" diameter		53	.302		25	19.60		44.60	56.50
4940	3-1/2" diameter		50	.320		38.50	21		59.50	73
4950	4" diameter	↓	48	.333	↓	37	21.50		58.50	72.50
5250	To delete coupling & hangers, subtract									
5260	1/4" diam. to 3/8" diam.					60%	81%			
5270	1/2" diam. to 3/4" diam.					41%	77%			
5280	1" diam. to 1-1/2" diam.					26%	67%			
5290	2" diam. to 4" diam.					16%	58%			
5300	CPVC, socket joint, couplings 10' OC, clevis hanger assemblies, 3 per 10'									
5302	Schedule 40									
5304	1/2" diameter	1 Plum	54	.148	L.F.	10.75	10.65		21.40	28
5305	3/4" diameter		51	.157		12	11.30		23.30	30
5306	1" diameter		46	.174		13.35	12.55		25.90	33.50
5307	1-1/4" diameter		42	.190		9.50	13.70		23.20	31
5308	1-1/2" diameter	↓	36	.222		11.45	16		27.45	36.50
5309	2" diameter	Q-1	59	.271		17.95	17.60		35.55	46
5310	2-1/2" diameter		56	.286		22.50	18.55		41.05	52
5311	3" diameter		53	.302		40	19.60		59.60	73
5312	4" diameter		48	.333		54	21.50		75.50	91.50
5314	6" diameter	↓	43	.372	↓	97.50	24		121.50	143
5318	To delete coupling & hangers, subtract									
5319	1/2" diam. to 3/4" diam.					37%	77%			
5320	1" diam. to 1-1/4" diam.					27%	70%			
5321	1-1/2" diam. to 3" diam.					21%	57%			
5322	4" diam. to 6" diam.					16%	57%			
5324	Schedule 80									
5325	1/2" diameter	1 Plum	50	.160	L.F.	19.25	11.55		30.80	38
5326	3/4" diameter		47	.170		20.50	12.25		32.75	41
5327	1" diameter		43	.186		14.30	13.40		27.70	36
5328	1-1/4" diameter		39	.205		9.70	14.80		24.50	32.50
5329	1-1/2" diameter	↓	34	.235		17.75	16.95		34.70	45
5330	2" diameter	Q-1	55	.291		19.95	18.85		38.80	50
5331	2-1/2" diameter		52	.308		26.50	19.95		46.45	59.50
5332	3" diameter		50	.320		45	21		66	80.50
5333	4" diameter		46	.348		62	22.50		84.50	102
5334	6" diameter	↓	38	.421		122	27.50		149.50	175

22 11 Facility Water Distribution

22 11 13 – Facility Water Distribution Piping

22 11 13.74 Pipe, Plastic		Crew	Daily Output	Labor-Hours	Unit	Material	2023 Bare Costs Labor	Equipment	Total	Total Incl O&P
5335	8" diameter	Q-2	47	.511	L.F.	234	34.50		268.50	310
5339	To delete couplings & hangers, subtract									
5340	1/2" diam. to 3/4" diam.					44%	77%			
5341	1" diam. to 1-1/4" diam.					32%	71%			
5342	1-1/2" diam. to 4" diam.					25%	58%			
5343	6" diam. to 8" diam.					20%	53%			
5360	CPVC, threaded, couplings 10' OC, clevis hanger assemblies, 3 per 10'									
5380	Schedule 40									
5460	1/2" diameter	1 Plum	54	.148	L.F.	12.30	10.65		22.95	29.50
5470	3/4" diameter		51	.157		14.70	11.30		26	33
5480	1" diameter		46	.174		16.15	12.55		28.70	36.50
5490	1-1/4" diameter		42	.190		11.75	13.70		25.45	33.50
5500	1-1/2" diameter		36	.222		13.35	16		29.35	38.50
5510	2" diameter	Q-1	59	.271		20	17.60		37.60	48
5520	2-1/2" diameter		56	.286		25	18.55		43.55	55
5530	3" diameter		53	.302		40.50	19.60		60.10	73.50
5540	4" diameter		48	.333		61.50	21.50		83	100
5550	6" diameter		43	.372		102	24		126	148
5730	To delete coupling & hangers, subtract									
5740	1/2" diam. to 3/4" diam.					37%	77%			
5750	1" diam. to 1-1/4" diam.					27%	70%			
5760	1-1/2" diam. to 3" diam.					21%	57%			
5770	4" diam. to 6" diam.					16%	57%			
5800	Schedule 80									
5860	1/2" diameter	1 Plum	50	.160	L.F.	21	11.55		32.55	40
5870	3/4" diameter		47	.170		23	12.25		35.25	44
5880	1" diameter		43	.186		17.10	13.40		30.50	39
5890	1-1/4" diameter		39	.205		11.90	14.80		26.70	35
5900	1-1/2" diameter		34	.235		19.65	16.95		36.60	47
5910	2" diameter	Q-1	55	.291		22	18.85		40.85	52.50
5920	2-1/2" diameter		52	.308		29	19.95		48.95	62
5930	3" diameter		50	.320		45.50	21		66.50	81
5940	4" diameter		46	.348		69.50	22.50		92	110
5950	6" diameter		38	.421		126	27.50		153.50	180
5960	8" diameter	Q-2	47	.511		226	34.50		260.50	299
6060	To delete couplings & hangers, subtract									
6070	1/2" diam. to 3/4" diam.					44%	77%			
6080	1" diam. to 1-1/4" diam.					32%	71%			
6090	1-1/2" diam. to 4" diam.					25%	58%			
6100	6" diam. to 8" diam.					20%	53%			
6240	CTS, 1/2" diameter	1 Plum	54	.148	L.F.	8.75	10.65		19.40	25.50
6250	3/4" diameter		51	.157		5.75	11.30		17.05	23
6260	1" diameter		46	.174		11.50	12.55		24.05	31.50
6270	1-1/4" diameter		42	.190		18.90	13.70		32.60	41.50
6280	1-1/2" diameter		36	.222		25	16		41	51.50
6290	2" diameter	Q-1	59	.271		41	17.60		58.60	71
6370	To delete coupling & hangers, subtract									
6380	1/2" diam.					51%	79%			
6390	3/4" diam.					40%	76%			
6392	1" thru 2" diam.					72%	68%			
6500	Residential installation, plastic pipe									
6510	Couplings 10' OC, strap hangers 3 per 10'									
6520	PVC, Schedule 40									

22 11 Facility Water Distribution

22 11 13 – Facility Water Distribution Piping

22 11 13.74 Pipe, Plastic		Crew	Daily Output	Labor-Hours	Unit	Material	2023 Bare Costs Labor	Equipment	Total	Total Incl O&P
6530	1/2" diameter	1 Plum	138	.058	L.F.	2.40	4.18		6.58	8.90
6540	3/4" diameter		128	.063		2.90	4.50		7.40	9.90
6550	1" diameter		119	.067		4.03	4.84		8.87	11.65
6560	1-1/4" diameter		111	.072		4.49	5.20		9.69	12.70
6570	1-1/2" diameter		104	.077		5.10	5.55		10.65	13.85
6580	2" diameter	Q-1	197	.081		6.30	5.25		11.55	14.80
6590	2-1/2" diameter		162	.099		10.40	6.40		16.80	21
6600	4" diameter		123	.130		8.05	8.45		16.50	21.50
6700	PVC, DWV, Schedule 40									
6720	1-1/4" diameter	1 Plum	100	.080	L.F.	9.25	5.75		15	18.80
6730	1-1/2" diameter	"	94	.085		5.55	6.15		11.70	15.25
6740	2" diameter	Q-1	178	.090		6.95	5.85		12.80	16.35
6760	4" diameter	"	110	.145		20.50	9.45		29.95	36.50
7280	PEX, flexible, no couplings or hangers									
7282	Note: For labor costs add 25% to the couplings and fittings labor total.									
7285	For fittings see section 23 83 16.10 7000									
7300	Non-barrier type, hot/cold tubing rolls									
7310	1/4" diameter x 100'				L.F.	.49			.49	.54
7350	3/8" diameter x 100'					.63			.63	.69
7360	1/2" diameter x 100'					.52			.52	.57
7370	1/2" diameter x 500'					.70			.70	.77
7380	1/2" diameter x 1000'					.52			.52	.57
7400	3/4" diameter x 100'					.88			.88	.97
7410	3/4" diameter x 500'					.87			.87	.96
7420	3/4" diameter x 1000'					1.90			1.90	2.09
7460	1" diameter x 100'					1.56			1.56	1.72
7470	1" diameter x 300'					1.54			1.54	1.69
7480	1" diameter x 500'					1.90			1.90	2.09
7500	1-1/4" diameter x 100'					4.13			4.13	4.54
7510	1-1/4" diameter x 300'					3.76			3.76	4.14
7540	1-1/2" diameter x 100'					4.29			4.29	4.72
7550	1-1/2" diameter x 300'					4.10			4.10	4.51
7596	Most sizes available in red or blue									
7700	Non-barrier type, hot/cold tubing straight lengths									
7710	1/2" diameter x 20'				L.F.	.73			.73	.80
7750	3/4" diameter x 20'					2.15			2.15	2.37
7760	1" diameter x 20'					2.24			2.24	2.46
7770	1-1/4" diameter x 20'					5.20			5.20	5.70
7780	1-1/2" diameter x 20'					5.80			5.80	6.40
7790	2" diameter					14.75			14.75	16.25
7796	Most sizes available in red or blue									
9000	Polypropylene pipe									
9002	For fusion weld fittings and accessories see line 22 11 13.76 9400									
9004	Note: sizes 1/2" thru 4" use socket fusion									
9005	Sizes 6" thru 10" use butt fusion									
9010	SDR 7.4 (domestic hot water piping)									
9011	Enhanced to minimize thermal expansion and high temperature life									
9016	13' lengths, size is ID, includes joints 13' OC and hangers 3 per 10'									
9020	3/8" diameter	1 Plum	53	.151	L.F.	3.87	10.90		14.77	20.50
9022	1/2" diameter		52	.154		4.65	11.10		15.75	21.50
9024	3/4" diameter		50	.160		5.65	11.55		17.20	23.50
9026	1" diameter		45	.178		7.15	12.80		19.95	27
9028	1-1/4" diameter		40	.200		10.65	14.40		25.05	33

22 11 Facility Water Distribution

22 11 13 – Facility Water Distribution Piping

22 11 13.74 Pipe, Plastic

		Crew	Daily Output	Labor-Hours	Unit	Material	2023 Bare Costs Labor	Equipment	Total	Total Incl O&P
9030	1-1/2" diameter	1 Plum	35	.229	L.F.	15.55	16.45		32	41.50
9032	2" diameter	Q-1	58	.276		20.50	17.90		38.40	49
9034	2-1/2" diameter		55	.291		28.50	18.85		47.35	59.50
9036	3" diameter		52	.308		38	19.95		57.95	71.50
9038	3-1/2" diameter		49	.327		57.50	21		78.50	94.50
9040	4" diameter		46	.348		58.50	22.50		81	98
9042	6" diameter	↓	39	.410		87	26.50		113.50	135
9044	8" diameter	Q-2	48	.500		133	33.50		166.50	196
9046	10" diameter	"	43	.558		211	37.50		248.50	288
9050	To delete joint & hangers, subtract									
9052	3/8" diam. to 1" diam.					45%	65%			
9054	1-1/4" diam. to 4" diam.					15%	45%			
9056	6" diam. to 10" diam.					5%	24%			
9060	SDR 11 (domestic cold water piping)									
9062	13' lengths, size is ID, includes joints 13' OC and hangers 3 per 10'									
9064	1/2" diameter	1 Plum	57	.140	L.F.	4.22	10.10		14.32	19.75
9066	3/4" diameter		54	.148		4.67	10.65		15.32	21
9068	1" diameter		49	.163		5.80	11.75		17.55	24
9070	1-1/4" diameter		45	.178		8	12.80		20.80	28
9072	1-1/2" diameter	↓	40	.200		11	14.40		25.40	33.50
9074	2" diameter	Q-1	62	.258		15.90	16.75		32.65	42.50
9076	2-1/2" diameter		59	.271		21	17.60		38.60	49.50
9078	3" diameter		56	.286		28.50	18.55		47.05	59
9080	3-1/2" diameter		53	.302		41.50	19.60		61.10	75
9082	4" diameter		50	.320		46	21		67	81.50
9084	6" diameter	↓	47	.340		58.50	22		80.50	97.50
9086	8" diameter	Q-2	51	.471		91	31.50		122.50	147
9088	10" diameter	"	46	.522		139	35		174	205
9090	To delete joint & hangers, subtract									
9092	1/2" diam. to 1" diam.					45%	65%			
9094	1-1/4" diam. to 4" diam.					15%	45%			
9096	6" diam. to 10" diam.					5%	24%			

22 11 13.76 Pipe Fittings, Plastic

		Crew	Daily Output	Labor-Hours	Unit	Material	Labor	Equipment	Total	Total Incl O&P
0010	**PIPE FITTINGS, PLASTIC**									
0030	Epoxy resin, fiberglass reinforced, general service									
0100	3"	Q-1	20.80	.769	Ea.	179	50		229	272
0110	4"		16.50	.970		192	63		255	305
0120	6"	↓	10.10	1.584		355	103		458	545
0130	8"	Q-2	9.30	2.581		655	174		829	980
0140	10"		8.50	2.824		825	190		1,015	1,200
0150	12"	↓	7.60	3.158		1,175	212		1,387	1,625
0170	Elbow, 90°, flanged									
0172	2"	Q-1	23	.696	Ea.	410	45		455	520
0173	3"		16	1		470	65		535	610
0174	4"		13	1.231		610	80		690	790
0176	6"	↓	8	2		1,100	130		1,230	1,425
0177	8"	Q-2	9	2.667		2,000	179		2,179	2,475
0178	10"		7	3.429		2,725	231		2,956	3,350
0179	12"	↓	5	4.800		3,675	325		4,000	4,525
0186	Elbow, 45°, flanged									
0188	2"	Q-1	23	.696	Ea.	410	45		455	520
0189	3"	↓	16	1		470	65		535	610

22 11 Facility Water Distribution

22 11 13 – Facility Water Distribution Piping

22 11 13.76 Pipe Fittings, Plastic

		Crew	Daily Output	Labor-Hours	Unit	Material	2023 Bare Costs Labor	Equipment	Total	Total Incl O&P
0190	4"	Q-1	13	1.231	Ea.	610	80		690	790
0192	6"		8	2		1,100	130		1,230	1,425
0193	8"	Q-2	9	2.667		2,025	179		2,204	2,500
0194	10"		7	3.429		2,825	231		3,056	3,450
0195	12"		5	4.800		3,825	325		4,150	4,700
0352	Tee, flanged									
0354	2"	Q-1	17	.941	Ea.	555	61		616	700
0355	3"		10	1.600		730	104		834	960
0356	4"		8	2		820	130		950	1,100
0358	6"		5	3.200		1,400	208		1,608	1,850
0359	8"	Q-2	6	4		2,675	269		2,944	3,325
0360	10"		5	4.800		3,875	325		4,200	4,750
0361	12"		4	6		5,350	405		5,755	6,475
0365	Wye, flanged									
0367	2"	Q-1	17	.941	Ea.	1,100	61		1,161	1,300
0368	3"		10	1.600		1,500	104		1,604	1,800
0369	4"		8	2		2,000	130		2,130	2,400
0371	6"		5	3.200		2,850	208		3,058	3,425
0372	8"	Q-2	6	4		4,625	269		4,894	5,500
0373	10"		5	4.800		7,200	325		7,525	8,400
0374	12"		4	6		10,500	405		10,905	12,100
0380	Couplings									
0410	2"	Q-1	33.10	.483	Ea.	27	31.50		58.50	76
0420	3"		20.80	.769		35.50	50		85.50	114
0430	4"		16.50	.970		50	63		113	149
0440	6"		10.10	1.584		63.50	103		166.50	223
0450	8"	Q-2	9.30	2.581		107	174		281	375
0460	10"		8.50	2.824		380	190		570	700
0470	12"		7.60	3.158		540	212		752	910
0473	High corrosion resistant couplings, add					30%				
0474	Reducer, concentric, flanged									
0475	2" x 1-1/2"	Q-1	30	.533	Ea.	1,050	34.50		1,084.50	1,225
0476	3" x 2"		24	.667		1,150	43		1,193	1,350
0477	4" x 3"		19	.842		1,300	54.50		1,354.50	1,500
0479	6" x 4"		15	1.067		1,300	69		1,369	1,525
0480	8" x 6"	Q-2	16	1.500		2,125	101		2,226	2,500
0481	10" x 8"		13	1.846		1,975	124		2,099	2,350
0482	12" x 10"		11	2.182		3,050	147		3,197	3,600
0486	Adapter, bell x male or female									
0488	2"	Q-1	28	.571	Ea.	54	37		91	115
0489	3"		20	.800		81.50	52		133.50	167
0491	4"		17	.941		96.50	61		157.50	197
0492	6"		12	1.333		222	86.50		308.50	375
0493	8"	Q-2	15	1.600		320	108		428	510
0494	10"	"	11	2.182		460	147		607	725
0528	Flange									
0532	2"	Q-1	46	.348	Ea.	71	22.50		93.50	112
0533	3"		32	.500		98.50	32.50		131	158
0534	4"		26	.615		125	40		165	197
0536	6"		16	1		148	65		213	260
0537	8"	Q-2	18	1.333		365	89.50		454.50	535
0538	10"		14	1.714		515	115		630	735
0539	12"		10	2.400		645	161		806	950

22 11 Facility Water Distribution

22 11 13 – Facility Water Distribution Piping

22 11 13.76 Pipe Fittings, Plastic		Crew	Daily Output	Labor-Hours	Unit	Material	2023 Bare Costs Labor	Equipment	Total	Total Incl O&P
2100	PVC schedule 80, socket joint									
2110	90° elbow, 1/2"	1 Plum	30.30	.264	Ea.	4.74	19		23.74	33.50
2130	3/4"		26	.308		6.10	22		28.10	39.50
2140	1"		22.70	.352		9.80	25.50		35.30	49
2150	1-1/4"		20.20	.396		12.75	28.50		41.25	56.50
2160	1-1/2"	↓	18.20	.440		14.05	31.50		45.55	62.50
2170	2"	Q-1	33.10	.483		16.95	31.50		48.45	65
2180	3"		20.80	.769		43.50	50		93.50	122
2190	4"		16.50	.970		68	63		131	169
2200	6"	↓	10.10	1.584		193	103		296	365
2210	8"	Q-2	9.30	2.581		530	174		704	845
2250	45° elbow, 1/2"	1 Plum	30.30	.264		8.95	19		27.95	38.50
2270	3/4"		26	.308		13.65	22		35.65	48
2280	1"		22.70	.352		20.50	25.50		46	60.50
2290	1-1/4"		20.20	.396		25.50	28.50		54	70.50
2300	1-1/2"	↓	18.20	.440		31	31.50		62.50	81
2310	2"	Q-1	33.10	.483		40	31.50		71.50	90.50
2320	3"		20.80	.769		99.50	50		149.50	184
2330	4"		16.50	.970		184	63		247	297
2340	6"	↓	10.10	1.584		232	103		335	410
2350	8"	Q-2	9.30	2.581		505	174		679	815
2400	Tee, 1/2"	1 Plum	20.20	.396		13.40	28.50		41.90	57.50
2420	3/4"		17.30	.462		14.05	33.50		47.55	65
2430	1"		15.20	.526		17.60	38		55.60	76
2440	1-1/4"		13.50	.593		47	42.50		89.50	115
2450	1-1/2"	↓	12.10	.661		48.50	47.50		96	124
2460	2"	Q-1	20	.800		60.50	52		112.50	144
2470	3"		13.90	1.151		80	74.50		154.50	199
2480	4"		11	1.455		95	94.50		189.50	246
2490	6"	↓	6.70	2.388		325	155		480	585
2500	8"	Q-2	6.20	3.871		755	260		1,015	1,225
2510	Flange, socket, 150 lb., 1/2"	1 Plum	55.60	.144		35	10.35		45.35	54
2514	3/4"		47.60	.168		37	12.10		49.10	59
2518	1"		41.70	.192		41.50	13.80		55.30	66
2522	1-1/2"	↓	33.30	.240		43.50	17.30		60.80	74
2526	2"	Q-1	60.60	.264		62.50	17.10		79.60	94.50
2530	4"		30.30	.528		135	34		169	200
2534	6"	↓	18.50	.865		213	56		269	320
2538	8"	Q-2	17.10	1.404		350	94.50		444.50	525
2550	Coupling, 1/2"	1 Plum	30.30	.264		8.95	19		27.95	38.50
2570	3/4"		26	.308		12.40	22		34.40	46.50
2580	1"		22.70	.352		12.95	25.50		38.45	52.50
2590	1-1/4"		20.20	.396		17.75	28.50		46.25	62
2600	1-1/2"	↓	18.20	.440		27	31.50		58.50	76.50
2610	2"	Q-1	33.10	.483		28.50	31.50		60	78
2620	3"		20.80	.769		58	50		108	139
2630	4"		16.50	.970		72.50	63		135.50	174
2640	6"	↓	10.10	1.584		156	103		259	325
2650	8"	Q-2	9.30	2.581		212	174		386	495
2660	10"		8.50	2.824		400	190		590	725
2670	12"	↓	7.60	3.158		700	212		912	1,075
2700	PVC (white), schedule 40, socket joints									
2760	90° elbow, 1/2"	1 Plum	33.30	.240	Ea.	.90	17.30		18.20	27

22 11 Facility Water Distribution

22 11 13 – Facility Water Distribution Piping

22 11 13.76 Pipe Fittings, Plastic		Crew	Daily Output	Labor-Hours	Unit	Material	2023 Bare Costs Labor	2023 Bare Costs Equipment	Total	Total Incl O&P
2770	3/4"	1 Plum	28.60	.280	Ea.	1.02	20		21.02	31
2780	1"		25	.320		1.84	23		24.84	36.50
2790	1-1/4"		22.20	.360		3.04	26		29.04	42
2800	1-1/2"		20	.400		3.56	29		32.56	47
2810	2"	Q-1	36.40	.440		5.40	28.50		33.90	48.50
2820	2-1/2"		26.70	.599		18.10	39		57.10	78
2830	3"		22.90	.699		21.50	45.50		67	91.50
2840	4"		18.20	.879		38.50	57		95.50	128
2850	5"		12.10	1.322		79	86		165	215
2860	6"		11.10	1.441		123	93.50		216.50	274
2870	8"	Q-2	10.30	2.330		315	157		472	585
2980	45° elbow, 1/2"	1 Plum	33.30	.240		1.64	17.30		18.94	28
2990	3/4"		28.60	.280		2.55	20		22.55	33
3000	1"		25	.320		3.04	23		26.04	38
3010	1-1/4"		22.20	.360		4.33	26		30.33	43.50
3020	1-1/2"		20	.400		5.30	29		34.30	49
3030	2"	Q-1	36.40	.440		6.95	28.50		35.45	50
3040	2-1/2"		26.70	.599		18.15	39		57.15	78
3050	3"		22.90	.699		28.50	45.50		74	99
3060	4"		18.20	.879		50.50	57		107.50	141
3070	5"		12.10	1.322		102	86		188	240
3080	6"		11.10	1.441		125	93.50		218.50	276
3090	8"	Q-2	10.30	2.330		300	157		457	565
3180	Tee, 1/2"	1 Plum	22.20	.360		1.22	26		27.22	40
3190	3/4"		19	.421		1.28	30.50		31.78	46.50
3200	1"		16.70	.479		2.24	34.50		36.74	54
3210	1-1/4"		14.80	.541		3.57	39		42.57	62
3220	1-1/2"		13.30	.602		4.58	43.50		48.08	69.50
3230	2"	Q-1	24.20	.661		6.70	43		49.70	71.50
3240	2-1/2"		17.80	.899		19.90	58.50		78.40	109
3250	3"		15.20	1.053		32.50	68.50		101	138
3260	4"		12.10	1.322		51	86		137	184
3270	5"		8.10	1.975		141	128		269	345
3280	6"		7.40	2.162		170	140		310	395
3290	8"	Q-2	6.80	3.529		450	237		687	850
3380	Coupling, 1/2"	1 Plum	33.30	.240		.65	17.30		17.95	26.50
3390	3/4"		28.60	.280		.90	20		20.90	31
3400	1"		25	.320		1.57	23		24.57	36
3410	1-1/4"		22.20	.360		1.88	26		27.88	40.50
3420	1-1/2"		20	.400		2.32	29		31.32	45.50
3430	2"	Q-1	36.40	.440		3.56	28.50		32.06	46.50
3440	2-1/2"		26.70	.599		7.85	39		46.85	66.50
3450	3"		22.90	.699		12.25	45.50		57.75	81
3460	4"		18.20	.879		17.75	57		74.75	105
3470	5"		12.10	1.322		33	86		119	165
3480	6"		11.10	1.441		56	93.50		149.50	201
3490	8"	Q-2	10.30	2.330		107	157		264	350
3600	Cap, schedule 40, PVC socket 1/2"	1 Plum	60.60	.132		.90	9.50		10.40	15.20
3610	3/4"		51.90	.154		1.04	11.10		12.14	17.70
3620	1"		45.50	.176		1.64	12.65		14.29	20.50
3630	1-1/4"		40.40	.198		2.36	14.25		16.61	24
3640	1-1/2"		36.40	.220		2.55	15.85		18.40	26.50
3650	2"	Q-1	66.10	.242		3.04	15.70		18.74	27

22 11 Facility Water Distribution

22 11 13 – Facility Water Distribution Piping

22 11 13.76 Pipe Fittings, Plastic

		Crew	Daily Output	Labor-Hours	Unit	Material	2023 Bare Costs Labor	2023 Bare Costs Equipment	Total	Total Incl O&P
3660	2-1/2"	Q-1	48.50	.330	Ea.	9.90	21.50		31.40	43
3670	3"		41.60	.385		10.80	25		35.80	49
3680	4"		33.10	.483		24	31.50		55.50	73
3690	6"	↓	20.20	.792		58	51.50		109.50	141
3700	8"	Q-2	18.60	1.290	↓	146	87		233	289
3710	Reducing insert, schedule 40, socket weld									
3712	3/4"	1 Plum	31.50	.254	Ea.	1.04	18.30		19.34	28.50
3713	1"		27.50	.291		1.88	21		22.88	33.50
3715	1-1/2"	↓	22	.364		2.68	26		28.68	42
3716	2"	Q-1	40	.400		4.44	26		30.44	43.50
3717	4"		20	.800		23.50	52		75.50	104
3718	6"	↓	12.20	1.311		58	85		143	191
3719	8"	Q-2	11.30	2.124	↓	216	143		359	450
3730	Reducing insert, socket weld x female/male thread									
3732	1/2"	1 Plum	38.30	.209	Ea.	4.78	15.05		19.83	28
3733	3/4"		32.90	.243		2.95	17.50		20.45	29.50
3734	1"		28.80	.278		4.13	20		24.13	34.50
3736	1-1/2"	↓	23	.348		7.45	25		32.45	45.50
3737	2"	Q-1	41.90	.382		7.95	25		32.95	46
3738	4"	"	20.90	.766	↓	76	49.50		125.50	158
3742	Male adapter, socket weld x male thread									
3744	1/2"	1 Plum	38.30	.209	Ea.	.90	15.05		15.95	23.50
3745	3/4"		32.90	.243		.99	17.50		18.49	27
3746	1"		28.80	.278		1.78	20		21.78	32
3748	1-1/2"	↓	23	.348		2.66	25		27.66	40.50
3749	2"	Q-1	41.90	.382		3.81	25		28.81	41
3750	4"	"	20.90	.766	↓	21	49.50		70.50	97
3754	Female adapter, socket weld x female thread									
3756	1/2"	1 Plum	38.30	.209	Ea.	1.12	15.05		16.17	23.50
3757	3/4"		32.90	.243		1.41	17.50		18.91	27.50
3758	1"		28.80	.278		1.64	20		21.64	32
3760	1-1/2"	↓	23	.348		2.91	25		27.91	40.50
3761	2"	Q-1	41.90	.382		3.89	25		28.89	41.50
3762	4"	"	20.90	.766	↓	22	49.50		71.50	98
3800	PVC, schedule 80, socket joints									
3810	Reducing insert									
3812	3/4"	1 Plum	28.60	.280	Ea.	3.02	20		23.02	33.50
3813	1"		25	.320		8.65	23		31.65	44
3815	1-1/2"	↓	20	.400		18.45	29		47.45	63.50
3816	2"	Q-1	36.40	.440		26.50	28.50		55	71.50
3817	4"		18.20	.879		100	57		157	196
3818	6"	↓	11.10	1.441		140	93.50		233.50	293
3819	8"	Q-2	10.20	2.353		805	158		963	1,125
3830	Reducing insert, socket weld x female/male thread									
3832	1/2"	1 Plum	34.80	.230	Ea.	18.90	16.55		35.45	45.50
3833	3/4"		29.90	.268		11.60	19.30		30.90	42
3834	1"		26.10	.307		18.15	22		40.15	53
3836	1-1/2"	↓	20.90	.383		23	27.50		50.50	66
3837	2"	Q-1	38	.421		33.50	27.50		61	77.50
3838	4"	"	19	.842		162	54.50		216.50	260
3844	Adapter, male socket x male thread									
3846	1/2"	1 Plum	34.80	.230	Ea.	7.30	16.55		23.85	32.50
3847	3/4"	↓	29.90	.268		8.05	19.30		27.35	38

22 11 Facility Water Distribution

22 11 13 – Facility Water Distribution Piping

22 11 13.76	Pipe Fittings, Plastic	Crew	Daily Output	Labor-Hours	Unit	Material	2023 Bare Costs Labor	Equipment	Total	Total Incl O&P
3848	1"	1 Plum	26.10	.307	Ea.	13.95	22		35.95	48.50
3850	1-1/2"	▼	20.90	.383		23.50	27.50		51	67
3851	2"	Q-1	38	.421		34	27.50		61.50	78
3852	4"	"	19	.842	▼	76	54.50		130.50	165
3860	Adapter, female socket x female thread									
3862	1/2"	1 Plum	34.80	.230	Ea.	8.75	16.55		25.30	34
3863	3/4"		29.90	.268		13.05	19.30		32.35	43.50
3864	1"		26.10	.307		19.20	22		41.20	54
3866	1-1/2"	▼	20.90	.383		38	27.50		65.50	83
3867	2"	Q-1	38	.421		66.50	27.50		94	114
3868	4"	"	19	.842	▼	203	54.50		257.50	305
3872	Union, socket joints									
3874	1/2"	1 Plum	25.80	.310	Ea.	19.20	22.50		41.70	54.50
3875	3/4"		22.10	.362		24.50	26		50.50	66
3876	1"		19.30	.415		28	30		58	75
3878	1-1/2"	▼	15.50	.516		62.50	37		99.50	125
3879	2"	Q-1	28.10	.569	▼	85	37		122	149
3888	Cap									
3890	1/2"	1 Plum	54.50	.147	Ea.	9.15	10.60		19.75	26
3891	3/4"		46.70	.171		9.70	12.35		22.05	29
3892	1"		41	.195		17.20	14.05		31.25	40
3894	1-1/2"	▼	32.80	.244		20.50	17.55		38.05	49
3895	2"	Q-1	59.50	.269		54.50	17.45		71.95	86
3896	4"		30	.533		165	34.50		199.50	233
3897	6"		18.20	.879		410	57		467	535
3898	8"	Q-2	16.70	1.437	▼	525	96.50		621.50	725
4500	DWV, ABS, non pressure, socket joints									
4540	1/4 bend, 1-1/4"	1 Plum	20.20	.396	Ea.	25.50	28.50		54	70.50
4560	1-1/2"	"	18.20	.440		19.90	31.50		51.40	69
4570	2"	Q-1	33.10	.483		18.75	31.50		50.25	67
4580	3"		20.80	.769		77	50		127	159
4590	4"		16.50	.970		158	63		221	268
4600	6"	▼	10.10	1.584	▼	675	103		778	895
4650	1/8 bend, same as 1/4 bend									
4800	Tee, sanitary									
4820	1-1/4"	1 Plum	13.50	.593	Ea.	34	42.50		76.50	101
4830	1-1/2"	"	12.10	.661		29.50	47.50		77	104
4840	2"	Q-1	20	.800		45.50	52		97.50	128
4850	3"		13.90	1.151		123	74.50		197.50	246
4860	4"		11	1.455		219	94.50		313.50	380
4862	Tee, sanitary, reducing, 2" x 1-1/2"		22	.727		39.50	47		86.50	114
4864	3" x 2"		15.30	1.046		98	68		166	209
4868	4" x 3"	▼	12.10	1.322		220	86		306	370
4870	Combination Y and 1/8 bend									
4872	1-1/2"	1 Plum	12.10	.661	Ea.	76.50	47.50		124	155
4874	2"	Q-1	20	.800		77.50	52		129.50	163
4876	3"		13.90	1.151		185	74.50		259.50	315
4878	4"		11	1.455		385	94.50		479.50	565
4880	3" x 1-1/2"		15.50	1.032		209	67		276	330
4882	4" x 3"		12.10	1.322		277	86		363	435
4900	Wye, 1-1/4"	1 Plum	13.50	.593		39	42.50		81.50	107
4902	1-1/2"	"	12.10	.661		48.50	47.50		96	125
4904	2"	Q-1	20	.800		63.50	52		115.50	148

22 11 Facility Water Distribution

22 11 13 – Facility Water Distribution Piping

22 11 13.76 Pipe Fittings, Plastic

		Crew	Daily Output	Labor-Hours	Unit	Material	2023 Bare Costs Labor	Equipment	Total	Total Incl O&P
4906	3"	Q-1	13.90	1.151	Ea.	137	74.50		211.50	262
4908	4"		11	1.455		278	94.50		372.50	445
4910	6"		6.70	2.388		835	155		990	1,150
4918	3" x 1-1/2"		15.50	1.032		121	67		188	233
4920	4" x 3"		12.10	1.322		240	86		326	390
4922	6" x 4"	▼	6.90	2.319		760	150		910	1,050
4930	Double wye, 1-1/2"	1 Plum	9.10	.879		150	63.50		213.50	260
4932	2"	Q-1	16.60	.964		179	62.50		241.50	290
4934	3"		10.40	1.538		400	100		500	590
4936	4"		8.25	1.939		785	126		911	1,050
4940	2" x 1-1/2"		16.80	.952		170	62		232	279
4942	3" x 2"		10.60	1.509		279	98		377	450
4944	4" x 3"		8.45	1.893		650	123		773	900
4946	6" x 4"		7.25	2.207		890	143		1,033	1,200
4950	Reducer bushing, 2" x 1-1/2"		36.40	.440		15.65	28.50		44.15	59.50
4952	3" x 1-1/2"		27.30	.586		68.50	38		106.50	132
4954	4" x 2"		18.20	.879		127	57		184	225
4956	6" x 4"	▼	11.10	1.441		355	93.50		448.50	530
4960	Couplings, 1-1/2"	1 Plum	18.20	.440		10.20	31.50		41.70	58
4962	2"	Q-1	33.10	.483		12.80	31.50		44.30	60.50
4963	3"		20.80	.769		38.50	50		88.50	117
4964	4"		16.50	.970		64.50	63		127.50	165
4966	6"		10.10	1.584		269	103		372	450
4970	2" x 1-1/2"		33.30	.480		27.50	31		58.50	76.50
4972	3" x 1-1/2"		21	.762		81	49.50		130.50	163
4974	4" x 3"	▼	16.70	.958		121	62		183	226
4978	Closet flange, 4"	1 Plum	32	.250		73	18		91	108
4980	4" x 3"	"	34	.235	▼	80	16.95		96.95	113
5000	DWV, PVC, schedule 40, socket joints									
5040	1/4 bend, 1-1/4"	1 Plum	20.20	.396	Ea.	53.50	28.50		82	101
5060	1-1/2"	"	18.20	.440		15.30	31.50		46.80	64
5070	2"	Q-1	33.10	.483		24	31.50		55.50	73
5080	3"		20.80	.769		71	50		121	153
5090	4"		16.50	.970		140	63		203	248
5100	6"	▼	10.10	1.584		490	103		593	695
5105	8"	Q-2	9.30	2.581		635	174		809	960
5106	10"	"	8.50	2.824		775	190		965	1,150
5110	1/4 bend, long sweep, 1-1/2"	1 Plum	18.20	.440		35.50	31.50		67	86
5112	2"	Q-1	33.10	.483		39.50	31.50		71	90
5114	3"		20.80	.769		91	50		141	175
5116	4"	▼	16.50	.970		172	63		235	283
5150	1/8 bend, 1-1/4"	1 Plum	20.20	.396		36.50	28.50		65	82.50
5170	1-1/2"	"	18.20	.440		14.95	31.50		46.45	63.50
5180	2"	Q-1	33.10	.483		22.50	31.50		54	71
5190	3"		20.80	.769		63.50	50		113.50	144
5200	4"		16.50	.970		116	63		179	222
5210	6"	▼	10.10	1.584		430	103		533	630
5215	8"	Q-2	9.30	2.581		146	174		320	420
5216	10"		8.50	2.824		725	190		915	1,075
5217	12"	▼	7.60	3.158		895	212		1,107	1,300
5250	Tee, sanitary 1-1/4"	1 Plum	13.50	.593		57	42.50		99.50	127
5254	1-1/2"	"	12.10	.661		26.50	47.50		74	101
5255	2"	Q-1	20	.800		39.50	52		91.50	121

22 11 Facility Water Distribution

22 11 13 – Facility Water Distribution Piping

22 11 13.76	Pipe Fittings, Plastic	Crew	Daily Output	Labor-Hours	Unit	Material	2023 Bare Costs Labor	Equipment	Total	Total Incl O&P
5256	3"	Q-1	13.90	1.151	Ea.	104	74.50		178.50	225
5257	4"		11	1.455		189	94.50		283.50	350
5259	6"		6.70	2.388		760	155		915	1,075
5261	8"	Q-2	6.20	3.871		1,675	260		1,935	2,250
5276	Tee, sanitary, reducing									
5281	2" x 1-1/2" x 1-1/2"	Q-1	23	.696	Ea.	34.50	45		79.50	106
5282	2" x 1-1/2" x 2"		22	.727		41.50	47		88.50	117
5283	2" x 2" x 1-1/2"		22	.727		16.80	47		63.80	89
5284	3" x 3" x 1-1/2"		15.50	1.032		36.50	67		103.50	140
5285	3" x 3" x 2"		15.30	1.046		78	68		146	187
5286	4" x 4" x 1-1/2"		12.30	1.301		198	84.50		282.50	345
5287	4" x 4" x 2"		12.20	1.311		163	85		248	305
5288	4" x 4" x 3"		12.10	1.322		107	86		193	246
5291	6" x 6" x 4"		6.90	2.319		355	150		505	615
5294	Tee, double sanitary									
5295	1-1/2"	1 Plum	9.10	.879	Ea.	59	63.50		122.50	159
5296	2"	Q-1	16.60	.964		79.50	62.50		142	181
5297	3"		10.40	1.538		222	100		322	395
5298	4"		8.25	1.939		355	126		481	585
5303	Wye, reducing									
5304	2" x 1-1/2" x 1-1/2"	Q-1	23	.696	Ea.	67	45		112	141
5305	2" x 2" x 1-1/2"		22	.727		58.50	47		105.50	135
5306	3" x 3" x 2"		15.30	1.046		191	68		259	310
5307	4" x 4" x 2"		12.20	1.311		141	85		226	282
5309	4" x 4" x 3"		12.10	1.322		191	86		277	340
5314	Combination Y & 1/8 bend, 1-1/2"	1 Plum	12.10	.661		64.50	47.50		112	142
5315	2"	Q-1	20	.800		81	52		133	167
5317	3"		13.90	1.151		178	74.50		252.50	305
5318	4"		11	1.455		350	94.50		444.50	525
5319	6"		6.70	2.388		1,325	155		1,480	1,700
5320	8"	Q-2	6.20	3.871		2,025	260		2,285	2,625
5321	10"		5.70	4.211		3,200	283		3,483	3,950
5322	12"		5.10	4.706		3,775	315		4,090	4,625
5324	Combination Y & 1/8 bend, reducing									
5325	2" x 2" x 1-1/2"	Q-1	22	.727	Ea.	91	47		138	171
5327	3" x 3" x 1-1/2"		15.50	1.032		162	67		229	278
5328	3" x 3" x 2"		15.30	1.046		122	68		190	235
5329	4" x 4" x 2"		12.20	1.311		183	85		268	330
5331	Wye, 1-1/4"	1 Plum	13.50	.593		73	42.50		115.50	144
5332	1-1/2"	"	12.10	.661		48.50	47.50		96	125
5333	2"	Q-1	20	.800		48	52		100	130
5334	3"		13.90	1.151		129	74.50		203.50	253
5335	4"		11	1.455		235	94.50		329.50	400
5336	6"		6.70	2.388		680	155		835	975
5337	8"	Q-2	6.20	3.871		1,200	260		1,460	1,700
5338	10"		5.70	4.211		1,500	283		1,783	2,075
5339	12"		5.10	4.706		2,450	315		2,765	3,150
5341	2" x 1-1/2"	Q-1	22	.727		16.80	47		63.80	89
5342	3" x 1-1/2"		15.50	1.032		25	67		92	128
5343	4" x 3"		12.10	1.322		54.50	86		140.50	188
5344	6" x 4"		6.90	2.319		148	150		298	385
5345	8" x 6"	Q-2	6.40	3.750		260	252		512	660
5347	Double wye, 1-1/2"	1 Plum	9.10	.879		109	63.50		172.50	215

22 11 Facility Water Distribution

22 11 13 – Facility Water Distribution Piping

22 11 13.76 Pipe Fittings, Plastic		Crew	Daily Output	Labor-Hours	Unit	Material	2023 Bare Costs Labor	Equipment	Total	Total Incl O&P
5348	2"	Q-1	16.60	.964	Ea.	130	62.50		192.50	236
5349	3"		10.40	1.538		254	100		354	430
5350	4"	↓	8.25	1.939	↓	545	126		671	790
5353	Double wye, reducing									
5354	2" x 2" x 1-1/2" x 1-1/2"	Q-1	16.80	.952	Ea.	111	62		173	215
5355	3" x 3" x 2" x 2"		10.60	1.509		189	98		287	355
5356	4" x 4" x 3" x 3"		8.45	1.893		405	123		528	635
5357	6" x 6" x 4" x 4"	↓	7.25	2.207		1,425	143		1,568	1,800
5374	Coupling, 1-1/4"	1 Plum	20.20	.396		34.50	28.50		63	80.50
5376	1-1/2"	"	18.20	.440		7.20	31.50		38.70	55
5378	2"	Q-1	33.10	.483		9.85	31.50		41.35	57.50
5380	3"		20.80	.769		34.50	50		84.50	113
5390	4"		16.50	.970		58.50	63		121.50	158
5400	6"	↓	10.10	1.584		191	103		294	365
5402	8"	Q-2	9.30	2.581		320	174		494	610
5404	2" x 1-1/2"	Q-1	33.30	.480		22	31		53	70.50
5406	3" x 1-1/2"		21	.762		64	49.50		113.50	144
5408	4" x 3"		16.70	.958		104	62		166	208
5410	Reducer bushing, 2" x 1-1/4"		36.50	.438		6.85	28.50		35.35	50
5411	2" x 1-1/2"		36.40	.440		12.45	28.50		40.95	56
5412	3" x 1-1/2"		27.30	.586		17.20	38		55.20	75.50
5413	3" x 2"		27.10	.590		31.50	38.50		70	91.50
5414	4" x 2"		18.20	.879		104	57		161	200
5415	4" x 3"		16.70	.958		54	62		116	152
5416	6" x 4"	↓	11.10	1.441		268	93.50		361.50	435
5418	8" x 6"	Q-2	10.20	2.353		525	158		683	810
5425	Closet flange 4"	Q-1	32	.500		90	32.50		122.50	148
5426	4" x 3"	"	34	.471	↓	96	30.50		126.50	151
5450	Solvent cement for PVC, industrial grade, per quart				Qt.	33			33	36.50
5500	CPVC, Schedule 80, threaded joints									
5540	90° elbow, 1/4"	1 Plum	32	.250	Ea.	24	18		42	53
5560	1/2"		30.30	.264		13.85	19		32.85	44
5570	3/4"		26	.308		20.50	22		42.50	56
5580	1"		22.70	.352		29	25.50		54.50	70
5590	1-1/4"		20.20	.396		56	28.50		84.50	104
5600	1-1/2"		18.20	.440		60	31.50		91.50	114
5610	2"	Q-1	33.10	.483		80.50	31.50		112	136
5620	2-1/2"		24.20	.661		251	43		294	340
5630	3"		20.80	.769		269	50		319	370
5640	4"		16.50	.970		420	63		483	560
5650	6"	↓	10.10	1.584	↓	455	103		558	655
5660	45° elbow same as 90° elbow									
5700	Tee, 1/4"	1 Plum	22	.364	Ea.	46.50	26		72.50	90
5702	1/2"		20.20	.396		46.50	28.50		75	93.50
5704	3/4"		17.30	.462		67	33.50		100.50	123
5706	1"		15.20	.526		72	38		110	136
5708	1-1/4"		13.50	.593		72.50	42.50		115	143
5710	1-1/2"		12.10	.661		76	47.50		123.50	155
5712	2"	Q-1	20	.800		84.50	52		136.50	171
5714	2-1/2"		16.20	.988		415	64		479	550
5716	3"		13.90	1.151		480	74.50		554.50	640
5718	4"		11	1.455		1,150	94.50		1,244.50	1,400
5720	6"	↓	6.70	2.388		1,200	155		1,355	1,525

22 11 Facility Water Distribution

22 11 13 – Facility Water Distribution Piping

22 11 13.76 Pipe Fittings, Plastic

		Crew	Daily Output	Labor-Hours	Unit	Material	2023 Bare Costs Labor	2023 Bare Costs Equipment	Total	Total Incl O&P
5730	Coupling, 1/4"	1 Plum	32	.250	Ea.	30.50	18		48.50	60.50
5732	1/2"		30.30	.264		25	19		44	56
5734	3/4"		26	.308		40.50	22		62.50	77.50
5736	1"		22.70	.352		46	25.50		71.50	88.50
5738	1-1/4"		20.20	.396		48.50	28.50		77	96
5740	1-1/2"		18.20	.440		52.50	31.50		84	105
5742	2"	Q-1	33.10	.483		61.50	31.50		93	115
5744	2-1/2"		24.20	.661		111	43		154	186
5746	3"		20.80	.769		97.50	50		147.50	183
5748	4"		16.50	.970		199	63		262	315
5750	6"		10.10	1.584		335	103		438	525
5752	8"	Q-2	9.30	2.581		700	174		874	1,025
5900	CPVC, Schedule 80, socket joints									
5904	90° elbow, 1/4"	1 Plum	32	.250	Ea.	22.50	18		40.50	52
5906	1/2"		30.30	.264		8.90	19		27.90	38.50
5908	3/4"		26	.308		11.35	22		33.35	45.50
5910	1"		22.70	.352		18	25.50		43.50	58
5912	1-1/4"		20.20	.396		39	28.50		67.50	85.50
5914	1-1/2"		18.20	.440		43.50	31.50		75	95
5916	2"	Q-1	33.10	.483		52.50	31.50		84	105
5918	2-1/2"		24.20	.661		121	43		164	197
5920	3"		20.80	.769		137	50		187	226
5922	4"		16.50	.970		247	63		310	365
5924	6"		10.10	1.584		495	103		598	700
5926	8"		9.30	1.720		1,225	112		1,337	1,500
5930	45° elbow, 1/4"	1 Plum	32	.250		34	18		52	64
5932	1/2"		30.30	.264		10.90	19		29.90	40.50
5934	3/4"		26	.308		15.70	22		37.70	50.50
5936	1"		22.70	.352		25	25.50		50.50	65.50
5938	1-1/4"		20.20	.396		49	28.50		77.50	96.50
5940	1-1/2"		18.20	.440		50.50	31.50		82	103
5942	2"	Q-1	33.10	.483		56.50	31.50		88	109
5944	2-1/2"		24.20	.661		116	43		159	191
5946	3"		20.80	.769		148	50		198	238
5948	4"		16.50	.970		204	63		267	320
5950	6"		10.10	1.584		630	103		733	845
5952	8"		9.30	1.720		1,300	112		1,412	1,600
5960	Tee, 1/4"	1 Plum	22	.364		21	26		47	62
5962	1/2"		20.20	.396		21	28.50		49.50	65.50
5964	3/4"		17.30	.462		21	33.50		54.50	73
5966	1"		15.20	.526		26	38		64	85
5968	1-1/4"		13.50	.593		55	42.50		97.50	124
5970	1-1/2"		12.10	.661		63	47.50		110.50	140
5972	2"	Q-1	20	.800		70	52		122	155
5974	2-1/2"		16.20	.988		178	64		242	292
5976	3"		13.90	1.151		178	74.50		252.50	305
5978	4"		11	1.455		237	94.50		331.50	400
5980	6"		6.70	2.388		615	155		770	910
5982	8"	Q-2	6.20	3.871		1,775	260		2,035	2,350
5990	Coupling, 1/4"	1 Plum	32	.250		24	18		42	53.50
5992	1/2"		30.30	.264		9.40	19		28.40	39
5994	3/4"		26	.308		13.15	22		35.15	47.50
5996	1"		22.70	.352		17.70	25.50		43.20	57.50

22 11 Facility Water Distribution

22 11 13 – Facility Water Distribution Piping

22 11 13.76 Pipe Fittings, Plastic

		Crew	Daily Output	Labor-Hours	Unit	Material	2023 Bare Costs Labor	2023 Bare Costs Equipment	Total	Total Incl O&P
5998	1-1/4"	1 Plum	20.20	.396	Ea.	26.50	28.50		55	71.50
6000	1-1/2"	↓	18.20	.440		33.50	31.50		65	83.50
6002	2"	Q-1	33.10	.483		39	31.50		70.50	89
6004	2-1/2"		24.20	.661		86.50	43		129.50	159
6006	3"		20.80	.769		94	50		144	178
6008	4"		16.50	.970		123	63		186	229
6010	6"	↓	10.10	1.584		289	103		392	475
6012	8"	Q-2	9.30	2.581	↓	780	174		954	1,125
6200	CTS, 100 psi at 180°F, hot and cold water									
6230	90° elbow, 1/2"	1 Plum	20	.400	Ea.	.59	29		29.59	43.50
6250	3/4"		19	.421		.97	30.50		31.47	46
6251	1"		16	.500		2.84	36		38.84	56.50
6252	1-1/4"		15	.533		5.65	38.50		44.15	64
6253	1-1/2"	↓	14	.571		10.20	41		51.20	73
6254	2"	Q-1	23	.696		19.60	45		64.60	89
6260	45° elbow, 1/2"	1 Plum	20	.400		.74	29		29.74	44
6280	3/4"		19	.421		1.30	30.50		31.80	46.50
6281	1"		16	.500		3.28	36		39.28	57
6282	1-1/4"		15	.533		6.95	38.50		45.45	65
6283	1-1/2"	↓	14	.571		10.10	41		51.10	72.50
6284	2"	Q-1	23	.696		21	45		66	91
6290	Tee, 1/2"	1 Plum	13	.615		.76	44.50		45.26	67
6310	3/4"		12	.667		1.42	48		49.42	73
6311	1"		11	.727		7.10	52.50		59.60	86
6312	1-1/4"		10	.800		10.95	57.50		68.45	98
6313	1-1/2"	↓	10	.800		14.20	57.50		71.70	102
6314	2"	Q-1	17	.941		23	61		84	117
6320	Coupling, 1/2"	1 Plum	22	.364		.48	26		26.48	39.50
6340	3/4"		21	.381		.77	27.50		28.27	42
6341	1"		18	.444		2.88	32		34.88	51
6342	1-1/4"		17	.471		3.71	34		37.71	54.50
6343	1-1/2"	↓	16	.500		5.25	36		41.25	59.50
6344	2"	Q-1	28	.571	↓	10	37		47	66.50
6360	Solvent cement for CPVC, commercial grade, per quart				Qt.	50.50			50.50	55.50
7340	PVC flange, slip-on, Sch 80 std., 1/2"	1 Plum	22	.364	Ea.	11.85	26		37.85	52
7350	3/4"		21	.381		12.70	27.50		40.20	55
7360	1"		18	.444		14.20	32		46.20	63.50
7370	1-1/4"		17	.471		14.65	34		48.65	66.50
7380	1-1/2"		16	.500		14.95	36		50.95	70
7390	2"	Q-1	26	.615		19.85	40		59.85	81.50
7400	2-1/2"		24	.667		29	43		72	96
7410	3"		18	.889		32	57.50		89.50	121
7420	4"		15	1.067		40	69		109	148
7430	6"	↓	10	1.600		63.50	104		167.50	225
7440	8"	Q-2	11	2.182		189	147		336	425
7550	Union, schedule 40, socket joints, 1/2"	1 Plum	19	.421		9.75	30.50		40.25	55.50
7560	3/4"		18	.444		11.05	32		43.05	60
7570	1"		15	.533		11.40	38.50		49.90	70
7580	1-1/4"		14	.571		35	41		76	100
7590	1-1/2"	↓	13	.615		38.50	44.50		83	108
7600	2"	Q-1	20	.800	↓	51.50	52		103.50	134
7992	Polybutyl/polyethyl pipe, for copper fittings see Line 22 11 13.25 7000									
8000	Compression type, PVC, 160 psi cold water									

22 11 Facility Water Distribution

22 11 13 – Facility Water Distribution Piping

22 11 13.76 Pipe Fittings, Plastic		Crew	Daily Output	Labor-Hours	Unit	Material	2023 Bare Costs Labor	Equipment	Total	Total Incl O&P
8010	Coupling, 3/4" CTS	1 Plum	21	.381	Ea.	4.06	27.50		31.56	45.50
8020	1" CTS		18	.444		5.05	32		37.05	53.50
8030	1-1/4" CTS		17	.471		7.10	34		41.10	58.50
8040	1-1/2" CTS		16	.500		9.75	36		45.75	64
8050	2" CTS		15	.533		13.50	38.50		52	72.50
8060	Female adapter, 3/4" FPT x 3/4" CTS		23	.348		9.60	25		34.60	48
8070	3/4" FPT x 1" CTS		21	.381		12.75	27.50		40.25	55
8080	1" FPT x 1" CTS		20	.400		11.20	29		40.20	55.50
8090	1-1/4" FPT x 1-1/4" CTS		18	.444		11.45	32		43.45	60.50
8100	1-1/2" FPT x 1-1/2" CTS		16	.500		13.05	36		49.05	68
8110	2" FPT x 2" CTS		13	.615		24.50	44.50		69	92.50
8130	Male adapter, 3/4" MPT x 3/4" CTS		23	.348		8	25		33	46.50
8140	3/4" MPT x 1" CTS		21	.381		10.85	27.50		38.35	53
8150	1" MPT x 1" CTS		20	.400		9.55	29		38.55	53.50
8160	1-1/4" MPT x 1-1/4" CTS		18	.444		12.85	32		44.85	62
8170	1-1/2" MPT x 1-1/2" CTS		16	.500		15.45	36		51.45	70.50
8180	2" MPT x 2" CTS		13	.615		20	44.50		64.50	88
8200	Spigot adapter, 3/4" IPS x 3/4" CTS		23	.348		2.73	25		27.73	40.50
8210	3/4" IPS x 1" CTS		21	.381		4.17	27.50		31.67	45.50
8220	1" IPS x 1" CTS		20	.400		3.34	29		32.34	46.50
8230	1-1/4" IPS x 1-1/4" CTS		18	.444		5.05	32		37.05	53.50
8240	1-1/2" IPS x 1-1/2" CTS		16	.500		5.30	36		41.30	59.50
8250	2" IPS x 2" CTS		13	.615		6.55	44.50		51.05	73
8270	Price includes insert stiffeners									
8280	250 psi is same price as 160 psi									
8300	Insert type, nylon, 160 & 250 psi, cold water									
8310	Clamp ring stainless steel, 3/4" IPS	1 Plum	115	.070	Ea.	4.47	5		9.47	12.35
8320	1" IPS		107	.075		5.40	5.40		10.80	14
8330	1-1/4" IPS		101	.079		4.60	5.70		10.30	13.55
8340	1-1/2" IPS		95	.084		6.40	6.05		12.45	16.10
8350	2" IPS		85	.094		8.35	6.80		15.15	19.25
8370	Coupling, 3/4" IPS		22	.364		1.85	26		27.85	41
8380	1" IPS		19	.421		1.94	30.50		32.44	47
8390	1-1/4" IPS		18	.444		2.87	32		34.87	51
8400	1-1/2" IPS		17	.471		3.38	34		37.38	54
8410	2" IPS		16	.500		6.40	36		42.40	60.50
8430	Elbow, 90°, 3/4" IPS		22	.364		3.70	26		29.70	43
8440	1" IPS		19	.421		4.08	30.50		34.58	49.50
8450	1-1/4" IPS		18	.444		4.58	32		36.58	53
8460	1-1/2" IPS		17	.471		5.40	34		39.40	56.50
8470	2" IPS		16	.500		7.50	36		43.50	62
8490	Male adapter, 3/4" IPS x 3/4" MPT		25	.320		1.85	23		24.85	36.50
8500	1" IPS x 1" MPT		21	.381		1.90	27.50		29.40	43
8510	1-1/4" IPS x 1-1/4" MPT		20	.400		3.02	29		32.02	46.50
8520	1-1/2" IPS x 1-1/2" MPT		18	.444		3.38	32		35.38	51.50
8530	2" IPS x 2" MPT		15	.533		6.50	38.50		45	64.50
8550	Tee, 3/4" IPS		14	.571		3.59	41		44.59	65.50
8560	1" IPS		13	.615		4.64	44.50		49.14	71
8570	1-1/4" IPS		12	.667		7.25	48		55.25	79.50
8580	1-1/2" IPS		11	.727		8.25	52.50		60.75	87
8590	2" IPS		10	.800		16.30	57.50		73.80	104
8610	Insert type, PVC, 100 psi @ 180°F, hot & cold water									
8620	Coupler, male, 3/8" CTS x 3/8" MPT	1 Plum	29	.276	Ea.	1.21	19.90		21.11	31

For customer support on your Plumbing Costs with RSMeans data, call 800.448.8182.

22 11 Facility Water Distribution

22 11 13 – Facility Water Distribution Piping

22 11 13.76 Pipe Fittings, Plastic		Crew	Daily Output	Labor-Hours	Unit	Material	2023 Bare Costs Labor	Equipment	Total	Total Incl O&P
8630	3/8" CTS x 1/2" MPT	1 Plum	28	.286	Ea.	1.21	20.50		21.71	32
8640	1/2" CTS x 1/2" MPT		27	.296		1.23	21.50		22.73	33.50
8650	1/2" CTS x 3/4" MPT		26	.308		4.79	22		26.79	38.50
8660	3/4" CTS x 1/2" MPT		25	.320		4.33	23		27.33	39.50
8670	3/4" CTS x 3/4" MPT		25	.320		1.65	23		24.65	36.50
8700	Coupling, 3/8" CTS x 1/2" CTS		25	.320		6.60	23		29.60	42
8710	1/2" CTS		23	.348		8.75	25		33.75	47
8730	3/4" CTS		22	.364		20	26		46	61
8750	Elbow 90°, 3/8" CTS		25	.320		6.45	23		29.45	41.50
8760	1/2" CTS		23	.348		8.70	25		33.70	47
8770	3/4" CTS		22	.364		11.85	26		37.85	52
8800	Rings, crimp, copper, 3/8" CTS		120	.067		.33	4.80		5.13	7.50
8810	1/2" CTS		117	.068		.34	4.93		5.27	7.70
8820	3/4" CTS		115	.070		.45	5		5.45	7.95
8850	Reducer tee, bronze, 3/8" x 3/8" x 1/2" CTS		17	.471		7.60	34		41.60	59
8860	1/2" x 1/2" x 3/4" CTS		15	.533		16.55	38.50		55.05	75.50
8870	3/4" x 1/2" x 1/2" CTS		14	.571		16.35	41		57.35	79.50
8890	3/4" x 3/4" x 1/2" CTS		14	.571		16.35	41		57.35	79.50
8900	1" x 1/2" x 1/2" CTS		14	.571		27.50	41		68.50	92
8930	Tee, 3/8" CTS		17	.471		4.81	34		38.81	56
8940	1/2" CTS		15	.533		4.45	38.50		42.95	62.50
8950	3/4" CTS		14	.571		5.60	41		46.60	67.50
8960	Copper rings included in fitting price									
9000	Flare type, assembled, acetal, hot & cold water									
9010	Coupling, 1/4" & 3/8" CTS	1 Plum	24	.333	Ea.	5.50	24		29.50	42
9020	1/2" CTS		22	.364		6.30	26		32.30	46
9030	3/4" CTS		21	.381		9.30	27.50		36.80	51.50
9040	1" CTS		18	.444		11.85	32		43.85	61
9050	Elbow 90°, 1/4" CTS		26	.308		6.10	22		28.10	39.50
9060	3/8" CTS		24	.333		6.55	24		30.55	43
9070	1/2" CTS		22	.364		7.75	26		33.75	47.50
9080	3/4" CTS		21	.381		11.85	27.50		39.35	54
9090	1" CTS		18	.444		17.15	32		49.15	67
9110	Tee, 1/4" CTS		16	.500		6.45	36		42.45	60.50
9114	3/8" CTS		15	.533		7.25	38.50		45.75	65.50
9120	1/2" CTS		14	.571		8.65	41		49.65	71
9130	3/4" CTS		13	.615		13.50	44.50		58	81
9140	1" CTS		12	.667		18.10	48		66.10	91.50
9400	Polypropylene, fittings and accessories									
9404	Fittings fusion welded, sizes are ID									
9408	Note: sizes 1/2" thru 4" use socket fusion									
9410	Sizes 6" thru 10" use butt fusion									
9416	Coupling									
9420	3/8"	1 Plum	39	.205	Ea.	1.48	14.80		16.28	23.50
9422	1/2"		37.40	.214		1.61	15.40		17.01	25
9424	3/4"		35.40	.226		1.79	16.30		18.09	26.50
9426	1"		29.70	.269		2.36	19.40		21.76	31.50
9428	1-1/4"		27.60	.290		2.83	21		23.83	34
9430	1-1/2"		24.80	.323		5.95	23		28.95	41
9432	2"	Q-1	43	.372		11.90	24		35.90	49
9434	2-1/2"		35.60	.449		13.30	29		42.30	58
9436	3"		30.90	.518		29	33.50		62.50	82
9438	3-1/2"		27.80	.576		47.50	37.50		85	108

22 11 Facility Water Distribution

22 11 13 – Facility Water Distribution Piping

22 11 13.76 Pipe Fittings, Plastic		Crew	Daily Output	Labor-Hours	Unit	Material	2023 Bare Costs Labor	Equipment	Total	Total Incl O&P
9440	4"	Q-1	25	.640	Ea.	62.50	41.50		104	131
9442	Reducing coupling, female to female									
9446	2" to 1-1/2"	Q-1	49	.327	Ea.	23.50	21		44.50	57.50
9448	2-1/2" to 2"		41.20	.388		26	25		51	66
9450	3" to 2-1/2"		33.10	.483		25.50	31.50		57	74.50
9470	Reducing bushing, female to female									
9472	1/2" to 3/8"	1 Plum	38.20	.209	Ea.	1.97	15.10		17.07	24.50
9474	3/4" to 3/8" or 1/2"		36.50	.219		2.47	15.80		18.27	26
9476	1" to 3/4" or 1/2"		33.10	.242		3.30	17.40		20.70	29.50
9478	1-1/4" to 3/4" or 1"		28.70	.279		5.10	20		25.10	35.50
9480	1-1/2" to 1/2" thru 1-1/4"		26.20	.305		8.40	22		30.40	42.50
9482	2" to 1/2" thru 1-1/2"	Q-1	43	.372		16.85	24		40.85	54.50
9484	2-1/2" to 1/2" thru 2"		41.20	.388		18.85	25		43.85	58
9486	3" to 1-1/2" thru 2-1/2"		33.10	.483		30.50	31.50		62	80
9488	3-1/2" to 2" thru 3"		29.20	.548		67	35.50		102.50	127
9490	4" to 2-1/2" thru 3-1/2"		26.20	.611		76	39.50		115.50	143
9491	6" to 4" SDR 7.4		16.50	.970		125	63		188	232
9492	6" to 4" SDR 11		16.50	.970		105	63		168	209
9493	8" to 6" SDR 7.4		10.10	1.584		185	103		288	355
9494	8" to 6" SDR 11		10.10	1.584		118	103		221	283
9495	10" to 8" SDR 7.4		7.80	2.051		253	133		386	475
9496	10" to 8" SDR 11		7.80	2.051		174	133		307	390
9500	90° elbow									
9504	3/8"	1 Plum	39	.205	Ea.	1.98	14.80		16.78	24
9506	1/2"		37.40	.214		2.37	15.40		17.77	25.50
9508	3/4"		35.40	.226		3.05	16.30		19.35	28
9510	1"		29.70	.269		3.19	19.40		22.59	32.50
9512	1-1/4"		27.60	.290		6.80	21		27.80	38.50
9514	1-1/2"		24.80	.323		14.60	23		37.60	50.50
9516	2"	Q-1	43	.372		22.50	24		46.50	60.50
9518	2-1/2"		35.60	.449		50	29		79	98
9520	3"		30.90	.518		82.50	33.50		116	141
9522	3-1/2"		27.80	.576		117	37.50		154.50	185
9524	4"		25	.640		131	41.50		172.50	206
9526	6" SDR 7.4		5.55	2.883		261	187		448	565
9528	6" SDR 11		5.55	2.883		217	187		404	515
9530	8" SDR 7.4	Q-2	8.10	2.963		500	199		699	845
9532	8" SDR 11		8.10	2.963		360	199		559	695
9534	10" SDR 7.4		7.50	3.200		670	215		885	1,050
9536	10" SDR 11		7.50	3.200		485	215		700	855
9551	45° elbow									
9554	3/8"	1 Plum	39	.205	Ea.	1.98	14.80		16.78	24
9556	1/2"		37.40	.214		2.37	15.40		17.77	25.50
9558	3/4"		35.40	.226		3.05	16.30		19.35	28
9564	1"		29.70	.269		4.41	19.40		23.81	34
9566	1-1/4"		27.60	.290		6.80	21		27.80	38.50
9568	1-1/2"		24.80	.323		14.60	23		37.60	50.50
9570	2"	Q-1	43	.372		22	24		46	60.50
9572	2-1/2"		35.60	.449		49	29		78	97.50
9574	3"		30.90	.518		90.50	33.50		124	150
9576	3-1/2"		27.80	.576		129	37.50		166.50	198
9578	4"		25	.640		199	41.50		240.50	281
9580	6" SDR 7.4		5.55	2.883		223	187		410	525

For customer support on your Plumbing Costs with RSMeans data, call 800.448.8182.

22 11 Facility Water Distribution

22 11 13 – Facility Water Distribution Piping

22 11 13.76 Pipe Fittings, Plastic		Crew	Daily Output	Labor-Hours	Unit	Material	2023 Bare Costs Labor	Equipment	Total	Total Incl O&P
9582	6" SDR 11	Q-1	5.55	2.883	Ea.	212	187		399	515
9584	8" SDR 7.4	Q-2	8.10	2.963		450	199		649	790
9586	8" SDR 11		8.10	2.963		340	199		539	670
9588	10" SDR 7.4		7.50	3.200		725	215		940	1,125
9590	10" SDR 11		7.50	3.200		450	215		665	815
9600	Tee									
9604	3/8"	1 Plum	26	.308	Ea.	2.64	22		24.64	36
9606	1/2"		24.90	.321		3.20	23		26.20	38
9608	3/4"		23.70	.338		4.41	24.50		28.91	41.50
9610	1"		19.90	.402		4.05	29		33.05	47.50
9612	1-1/4"		18.50	.432		8.55	31		39.55	56
9614	1-1/2"		16.60	.482		24.50	34.50		59	79
9616	2"	Q-1	26.80	.597		25.50	38.50		64	85.50
9618	2-1/2"		23.80	.672		42.50	43.50		86	112
9620	3"		20.60	.777		70	50.50		120.50	152
9622	3-1/2"		18.40	.870		151	56.50		207.50	250
9624	4"		16.70	.958		200	62		262	315
9626	6" SDR 7.4		3.70	4.324		276	280		556	725
9628	6" SDR 11		3.70	4.324		221	280		501	665
9630	8" SDR 7.4	Q-2	5.40	4.444		605	299		904	1,100
9632	8" SDR 11		5.40	4.444		450	299		749	940
9634	10" SDR 7.4		5	4.800		1,050	325		1,375	1,625
9636	10" SDR 11		5	4.800		700	325		1,025	1,250
9638	For reducing tee use same tee price									
9660	End cap									
9662	3/8"	1 Plum	78	.103	Ea.	2.81	7.40		10.21	14.10
9664	1/2"		74.60	.107		3.48	7.75		11.23	15.35
9666	3/4"		71.40	.112		4.41	8.05		12.46	16.90
9668	1"		59.50	.134		5.35	9.70		15.05	20.50
9670	1-1/4"		55.60	.144		8.40	10.35		18.75	24.50
9672	1-1/2"		49.50	.162		8.40	11.65		20.05	26.50
9674	2"	Q-1	80	.200		14.05	12.95		27	35
9676	2-1/2"		71.40	.224		28	14.55		42.55	52.50
9678	3"		61.70	.259		63.50	16.80		80.30	95
9680	3-1/2"		55.20	.290		76.50	18.80		95.30	112
9682	4"		50	.320		117	21		138	159
9684	6" SDR 7.4		26.50	.604		160	39		199	235
9686	6" SDR 11		26.50	.604		124	39		163	195
9688	8" SDR 7.4	Q-2	16.30	1.472		160	99		259	325
9690	8" SDR 11		16.30	1.472		134	99		233	295
9692	10" SDR 7.4		14.90	1.611		240	108		348	425
9694	10" SDR 11		14.90	1.611		164	108		272	345
9800	Accessories and tools									
9802	Pipe clamps for suspension, not including rod or beam clamp									
9804	3/8"	1 Plum	74	.108	Ea.	3.63	7.80		11.43	15.60
9805	1/2"		70	.114		4.55	8.25		12.80	17.30
9806	3/4"		68	.118		4.61	8.50		13.11	17.70
9807	1"		66	.121		5.70	8.75		14.45	19.30
9808	1-1/4"		64	.125		5.85	9		14.85	19.90
9809	1-1/2"		62	.129		5.55	9.30		14.85	19.95
9810	2"	Q-1	110	.145		7.95	9.45		17.40	23
9811	2-1/2"		104	.154		10.20	10		20.20	26
9812	3"		98	.163		11.90	10.60		22.50	29

22 11 Facility Water Distribution

22 11 13 – Facility Water Distribution Piping

22 11 13.76 Pipe Fittings, Plastic		Crew	Daily Output	Labor-Hours	Unit	Material	2023 Bare Costs Labor	Equipment	Total	Total Incl O&P
9813	3-1/2"	Q-1	92	.174	Ea.	12.05	11.30		23.35	30
9814	4"		86	.186		21.50	12.05		33.55	42
9815	6"		70	.229		16.45	14.80		31.25	40
9816	8"	Q-2	100	.240		59	16.15		75.15	89
9817	10"	"	94	.255		67.50	17.15		84.65	99.50
9820	Pipe cutter									
9822	For 3/8" thru 1-1/4"				Ea.	182			182	200
9824	For 1-1/2" thru 4"				"	174			174	191
9826	Note: Pipes may be cut with standard									
9827	iron saw with blades for plastic.									
9982	For plastic hangers see Line 22 05 29.10 8000									
9986	For copper/brass fittings see Line 22 11 13.25 7000									

22 11 13.78 Pipe, High Density Polyethylene Plastic (HDPE)

		Crew	Daily Output	Labor-Hours	Unit	Material	Labor	Equipment	Total	Total Incl O&P
0010	**PIPE, HIGH DENSITY POLYETHYLENE PLASTIC (HDPE)**									
0020	Not incl. hangers, trenching, backfill, hoisting or digging equipment.									
0030	Standard length is 40', add a weld for each joint									
0035	For HDPE weld machine see 015433401685 in equipment rental									
0040	Single wall									
0050	Straight									
0054	1" diameter DR 11				L.F.	.89			.89	.98
0058	1-1/2" diameter DR 11					1.75			1.75	1.93
0062	2" diameter DR 11					2			2	2.20
0066	3" diameter DR 11					3.66			3.66	4.03
0070	3" diameter DR 17					2.59			2.59	2.85
0074	4" diameter DR 11					5.35			5.35	5.90
0078	4" diameter DR 17					3.62			3.62	3.98
0082	6" diameter DR 11					10.50			10.50	11.55
0086	6" diameter DR 17					7.20			7.20	7.90
0090	8" diameter DR 11					18.40			18.40	20
0094	8" diameter DR 26					6.30			6.30	6.90
0098	10" diameter DR 11					27.50			27.50	30.50
0102	10" diameter DR 26					18.30			18.30	20
0106	12" diameter DR 11					39			39	43
0110	12" diameter DR 26					27.50			27.50	30
0114	16" diameter DR 11					88.50			88.50	97
0118	16" diameter DR 26					39.50			39.50	43.50
0122	18" diameter DR 11					113			113	124
0126	18" diameter DR 26					52			52	57
0130	20" diameter DR 11					137			137	151
0134	20" diameter DR 26					61			61	67
0138	22" diameter DR 11					167			167	184
0142	22" diameter DR 26					76			76	83.50
0146	24" diameter DR 11					198			198	218
0150	24" diameter DR 26					88.50			88.50	97
0154	28" diameter DR 17					183			183	201
0158	28" diameter DR 26					122			122	134
0162	30" diameter DR 21					171			171	188
0166	30" diameter DR 26					140			140	154
0170	36" diameter DR 26					140			140	154
0174	42" diameter DR 26					271			271	298
0178	48" diameter DR 26					355			355	390
0182	54" diameter DR 26					450			450	490

22 11 Facility Water Distribution

22 11 13 – Facility Water Distribution Piping

22 11 13.78 Pipe, High Density Polyethylene Plastic (HDPE)

		Crew	Daily Output	Labor-Hours	Unit	Material	2023 Bare Costs Labor	Equipment	Total	Total Incl O&P
0300	90° elbow									
0304	1" diameter DR 11				Ea.	8.80			8.80	9.65
0308	1-1/2" diameter DR 11					11.05			11.05	12.15
0312	2" diameter DR 11					9.60			9.60	10.55
0316	3" diameter DR 11					22			22	24.50
0320	3" diameter DR 17					22			22	24.50
0324	4" diameter DR 11					32.50			32.50	36
0328	4" diameter DR 17					31			31	34
0332	6" diameter DR 11					70			70	77
0336	6" diameter DR 17					70			70	77
0340	8" diameter DR 11					170			170	187
0344	8" diameter DR 26					154			154	170
0348	10" diameter DR 11					159			159	175
0352	10" diameter DR 26					600			600	660
0356	12" diameter DR 11					211			211	232
0360	12" diameter DR 26					620			620	685
0364	16" diameter DR 11					815			815	895
0368	16" diameter DR 26					800			800	880
0372	18" diameter DR 11					1,025			1,025	1,125
0376	18" diameter DR 26					965			965	1,050
0380	20" diameter DR 11					1,200			1,200	1,325
0384	20" diameter DR 26					1,175			1,175	1,275
0388	22" diameter DR 11					1,250			1,250	1,375
0392	22" diameter DR 26					1,200			1,200	1,325
0396	24" diameter DR 11					1,400			1,400	1,550
0400	24" diameter DR 26					1,375			1,375	1,500
0404	28" diameter DR 17					1,700			1,700	1,875
0408	28" diameter DR 26					1,600			1,600	1,775
0412	30" diameter DR 17					2,400			2,400	2,650
0416	30" diameter DR 26					2,200			2,200	2,425
0420	36" diameter DR 26					2,800			2,800	3,100
0424	42" diameter DR 26					3,600			3,600	3,975
0428	48" diameter DR 26					4,200			4,200	4,625
0432	54" diameter DR 26					10,000			10,000	11,000
0500	45° elbow									
0512	2" diameter DR 11				Ea.	8.85			8.85	9.70
0516	3" diameter DR 11					22			22	24.50
0520	3" diameter DR 17					22			22	24.50
0524	4" diameter DR 11					31			31	34
0528	4" diameter DR 17					31			31	34
0532	6" diameter DR 11					70.50			70.50	77.50
0536	6" diameter DR 17					70.50			70.50	77.50
0540	8" diameter DR 11					174			174	192
0544	8" diameter DR 26					101			101	112
0548	10" diameter DR 11					650			650	715
0552	10" diameter DR 26					600			600	660
0556	12" diameter DR 11					690			690	755
0560	12" diameter DR 26					620			620	685
0564	16" diameter DR 11					360			360	395
0568	16" diameter DR 26					340			340	375
0572	18" diameter DR 11					385			385	420
0576	18" diameter DR 26					350			350	385
0580	20" diameter DR 11					580			580	640

22 11 Facility Water Distribution

22 11 13 – Facility Water Distribution Piping

22 11 13.78 Pipe, High Density Polyethylene Plastic (HDPE)		Crew	Daily Output	Labor-Hours	Unit	Material	2023 Bare Costs Labor	Equipment	Total	Total Incl O&P
0584	20" diameter DR 26				Ea.	550			550	605
0588	22" diameter DR 11					800			800	880
0592	22" diameter DR 26					760			760	840
0596	24" diameter DR 11					985			985	1,075
0600	24" diameter DR 26					945			945	1,025
0604	28" diameter DR 17					1,125			1,125	1,225
0608	28" diameter DR 26					1,075			1,075	1,200
0612	30" diameter DR 17					1,375			1,375	1,525
0616	30" diameter DR 26					1,350			1,350	1,475
0620	36" diameter DR 26					1,700			1,700	1,875
0624	42" diameter DR 26					2,200			2,200	2,400
0628	48" diameter DR 26					2,375			2,375	2,625
0632	54" diameter DR 26					3,200			3,200	3,500
0700	Tee									
0704	1" diameter DR 11				Ea.	11.50			11.50	12.65
0708	1-1/2" diameter DR 11					16.15			16.15	17.75
0712	2" diameter DR 11					13.85			13.85	15.20
0716	3" diameter DR 11					25.50			25.50	28
0720	3" diameter DR 17					25.50			25.50	28
0724	4" diameter DR 11					37			37	40.50
0728	4" diameter DR 17					37			37	40.50
0732	6" diameter DR 11					92			92	101
0736	6" diameter DR 17					92			92	101
0740	8" diameter DR 11					228			228	251
0744	8" diameter DR 17					228			228	251
0748	10" diameter DR 11					680			680	750
0752	10" diameter DR 17					680			680	750
0756	12" diameter DR 11					910			910	1,000
0760	12" diameter DR 17					910			910	1,000
0764	16" diameter DR 11					480			480	525
0768	16" diameter DR 17					395			395	435
0772	18" diameter DR 11					675			675	745
0776	18" diameter DR 17					555			555	610
0780	20" diameter DR 11					825			825	910
0784	20" diameter DR 17					675			675	745
0788	22" diameter DR 11					1,050			1,050	1,175
0792	22" diameter DR 17					835			835	920
0796	24" diameter DR 11					1,300			1,300	1,450
0800	24" diameter DR 17					1,100			1,100	1,225
0804	28" diameter DR 17					2,150			2,150	2,350
0812	30" diameter DR 17					2,450			2,450	2,700
0820	36" diameter DR 17					4,050			4,050	4,450
0824	42" diameter DR 26					4,500			4,500	4,975
0828	48" diameter DR 26					4,850			4,850	5,325
1000	Flange adptr, w/back-up ring and 1/2 cost of plated bolt set									
1004	1" diameter DR 11				Ea.	44			44	48
1008	1-1/2" diameter DR 11					44			44	48
1012	2" diameter DR 11					18.85			18.85	20.50
1016	3" diameter DR 11					32.50			32.50	35.50
1020	3" diameter DR 17					32.50			32.50	35.50
1024	4" diameter DR 11					44			44	48
1028	4" diameter DR 17					44			44	48
1032	6" diameter DR 11					62.50			62.50	68.50

22 11 Facility Water Distribution

22 11 13 – Facility Water Distribution Piping

22 11 13.78 Pipe, High Density Polyethylene Plastic (HDPE)	Crew	Daily Output	Labor-Hours	Unit	Material	2023 Bare Costs Labor	Equipment	Total	Total Incl O&P
1036	6" diameter DR 17				Ea.	62.50			62.50	68.50
1040	8" diameter DR 11					90			90	99
1044	8" diameter DR 26					90			90	99
1048	10" diameter DR 11					88.50			88.50	97.50
1052	10" diameter DR 26					143			143	157
1056	12" diameter DR 11					210			210	231
1060	12" diameter DR 26					210			210	231
1064	16" diameter DR 11					450			450	495
1068	16" diameter DR 26					450			450	495
1072	18" diameter DR 11					585			585	640
1076	18" diameter DR 26					585			585	640
1080	20" diameter DR 11					810			810	890
1084	20" diameter DR 26					810			810	890
1088	22" diameter DR 11					880			880	965
1092	22" diameter DR 26					875			875	965
1096	24" diameter DR 17					955			955	1,050
1100	24" diameter DR 32.5					955			955	1,050
1104	28" diameter DR 15.5					1,300			1,300	1,425
1108	28" diameter DR 32.5					1,300			1,300	1,425
1112	30" diameter DR 11					1,500			1,500	1,650
1116	30" diameter DR 21					1,500			1,500	1,650
1120	36" diameter DR 26					1,650			1,650	1,800
1124	42" diameter DR 26					1,875			1,875	2,050
1128	48" diameter DR 26					2,275			2,275	2,500
1132	54" diameter DR 26				↓	2,775			2,775	3,050
1200	Reducer									
1208	2" x 1-1/2" diameter DR 11				Ea.	13.25			13.25	14.60
1212	3" x 2" diameter DR 11					13.25			13.25	14.60
1216	4" x 2" diameter DR 11					15.45			15.45	17
1220	4" x 3" diameter DR 11					19.85			19.85	22
1224	6" x 4" diameter DR 11					46.50			46.50	51
1228	8" x 6" diameter DR 11					70.50			70.50	77.50
1232	10" x 8" diameter DR 11					121			121	133
1236	12" x 8" diameter DR 11					199			199	218
1240	12" x 10" diameter DR 11					159			159	175
1244	14" x 12" diameter DR 11					176			176	194
1248	16" x 14" diameter DR 11					225			225	248
1252	18" x 16" diameter DR 11					274			274	300
1256	20" x 18" diameter DR 11					545			545	595
1260	22" x 20" diameter DR 11					665			665	735
1264	24" x 22" diameter DR 11					750			750	825
1268	26" x 24" diameter DR 11					880			880	970
1272	28" x 24" diameter DR 11					1,125			1,125	1,250
1276	32" x 28" diameter DR 17					1,450			1,450	1,600
1280	36" x 32" diameter DR 17				↓	1,975			1,975	2,175
4000	Welding labor per joint, not including welding machine									
4010	Pipe joint size (cost based on thickest wall for each diam.)									
4030	1" pipe size	4 Skwk	273	.117	Ea.		7.20		7.20	10.80
4040	1-1/2" pipe size		175	.183			11.20		11.20	16.80
4050	2" pipe size		128	.250			15.30		15.30	23
4060	3" pipe size		100	.320			19.60		19.60	29.50
4070	4" pipe size	↓	77	.416			25.50		25.50	38
4080	6" pipe size	5 Skwk	63	.635			39		39	58.50

22 11 Facility Water Distribution
22 11 13 – Facility Water Distribution Piping

22 11 13.78 Pipe, High Density Polyethylene Plastic (HDPE)	Crew	Daily Output	Labor-Hours	Unit	Material	2023 Bare Costs Labor	2023 Bare Costs Equipment	Total	Total Incl O&P
4090	8" pipe size	5 Skwk	48	.833	Ea.		51		51	76.50
4100	10" pipe size		40	1			61.50		61.50	92
4110	12" pipe size	6 Skwk	41	1.171			71.50		71.50	108
4120	16" pipe size		34	1.412			86.50		86.50	130
4130	18" pipe size		32	1.500			92		92	138
4140	20" pipe size	8 Skwk	37	1.730			106		106	159
4150	22" pipe size		35	1.829			112		112	168
4160	24" pipe size		34	1.882			115		115	173
4170	28" pipe size		33	1.939			119		119	178
4180	30" pipe size		32	2			123		123	184
4190	36" pipe size		31	2.065			126		126	190
4200	42" pipe size		30	2.133			131		131	196
4210	48" pipe size	9 Skwk	33	2.182			134		134	201
4220	54" pipe size	"	31	2.323			142		142	214
5000	Dual wall contained pipe									
5040	Straight									
5054	1" DR 11 x 3" DR 11				L.F.	8.35			8.35	9.15
5058	1" DR 11 x 4" DR 11					8.80			8.80	9.65
5062	1-1/2" DR 11 x 4" DR 17					9.70			9.70	10.65
5066	2" DR 11 x 4" DR 17					10.20			10.20	11.25
5070	2" DR 11 x 6" DR 17					15.45			15.45	17
5074	3" DR 11 x 6" DR 17					17.35			17.35	19.10
5078	3" DR 11 x 6" DR 26					14.80			14.80	16.30
5086	3" DR 17 x 8" DR 17					18.85			18.85	20.50
5090	4" DR 11 x 8" DR 17					26			26	29
5094	4" DR 17 x 8" DR 26					20.50			20.50	22.50
5098	6" DR 11 x 10" DR 17					40.50			40.50	44.50
5102	6" DR 17 x 10" DR 26					27.50			27.50	30.50
5106	6" DR 26 x 10" DR 26					26			26	28.50
5110	8" DR 17 x 12" DR 26					40			40	44
5114	8" DR 26 x 12" DR 32.5					36.50			36.50	40
5118	10" DR 17 x 14" DR 26					59.50			59.50	65.50
5122	10" DR 17 x 16" DR 26					42.50			42.50	47
5126	10" DR 26 x 16" DR 26					56.50			56.50	62.50
5130	12" DR 26 x 16" DR 26					59.50			59.50	65.50
5134	12" DR 17 x 18" DR 26					83			83	91
5138	12" DR 26 x 18" DR 26					78.50			78.50	86.50
5142	14" DR 26 x 20" DR 32.5					80			80	88
5146	16" DR 26 x 22" DR 32.5					88.50			88.50	97.50
5150	18" DR 26 x 24" DR 32.5					110			110	121
5154	20" DR 32.5 x 28" DR 32.5					125			125	137
5158	22" DR 32.5 x 30" DR 32.5					125			125	137
5162	24" DR 32.5 x 32" DR 32.5					130			130	143
5166	36" DR 32.5 x 42" DR 32.5					151			151	166
5300	Force transfer coupling									
5354	1" DR 11 x 3" DR 11				Ea.	288			288	315
5358	1" DR 11 x 4" DR 17					340			340	375
5362	1-1/2" DR 11 x 4" DR 17					325			325	355
5366	2" DR 11 x 4" DR 17					325			325	355
5370	2" DR 11 x 6" DR 17					555			555	610
5374	3" DR 11 x 6" DR 17					595			595	655
5378	3" DR 11 x 6" DR 26					595			595	655
5382	3" DR 11 x 8" DR 11					595			595	655

22 11 Facility Water Distribution

22 11 13 – Facility Water Distribution Piping

22 11 13.78 Pipe, High Density Polyethylene Plastic (HDPE)		Crew	Daily Output	Labor-Hours	Unit	Material	2023 Bare Costs Labor	Equipment	Total	Total Incl O&P
5386	3" DR 11 x 8" DR 17				Ea.	650			650	715
5390	4" DR 11 x 8" DR 17					665			665	730
5394	4" DR 17 x 8" DR 26					670			670	740
5398	6" DR 11 x 10" DR 17					795			795	875
5402	6" DR 17 x 10" DR 26					760			760	835
5406	6" DR 26 x 10" DR 26					1,025			1,025	1,150
5410	8" DR 17 x 12" DR 26					1,100			1,100	1,225
5414	8" DR 26 x 12" DR 32.5					1,275			1,275	1,400
5418	10" DR 17 x 14" DR 26					1,500			1,500	1,650
5422	10" DR 17 x 16" DR 26					1,525			1,525	1,675
5426	10" DR 26 x 16" DR 26					1,700			1,700	1,850
5430	12" DR 26 x 16" DR 26					2,050			2,050	2,250
5434	12" DR 17 x 18" DR 26					2,075			2,075	2,275
5438	12" DR 26 x 18" DR 26					2,275			2,275	2,500
5442	14" DR 26 x 20" DR 32.5					2,525			2,525	2,775
5446	16" DR 26 x 22" DR 32.5					2,775			2,775	3,050
5450	18" DR 26 x 24" DR 32.5					3,075			3,075	3,375
5454	20" DR 32.5 x 28" DR 32.5					3,375			3,375	3,700
5458	22" DR 32.5 x 30" DR 32.5					3,725			3,725	4,100
5462	24" DR 32.5 x 32" DR 32.5					4,100			4,100	4,525
5466	36" DR 32.5 x 42" DR 32.5					4,400			4,400	4,850
5600	90° elbow									
5654	1" DR 11 x 3" DR 11				Ea.	315			315	345
5658	1" DR 11 x 4" DR 17					375			375	410
5662	1-1/2" DR 11 x 4" DR 17					385			385	420
5666	2" DR 11 x 4" DR 17					375			375	410
5670	2" DR 11 x 6" DR 17					540			540	595
5674	3" DR 11 x 6" DR 17					585			585	645
5678	3" DR 17 x 6" DR 26					595			595	655
5682	3" DR 17 x 8" DR 11					800			800	880
5686	3" DR 17 x 8" DR 17					850			850	935
5690	4" DR 11 x 8" DR 17					720			720	795
5694	4" DR 17 x 8" DR 26					695			695	765
5698	6" DR 11 x 10" DR 17					1,250			1,250	1,375
5702	6" DR 17 x 10" DR 26					1,275			1,275	1,400
5706	6" DR 26 x 10" DR 26					1,250			1,250	1,375
5710	8" DR 17 x 12" DR 26					1,675			1,675	1,825
5714	8" DR 26 x 12" DR 32.5					1,375			1,375	1,525
5718	10" DR 17 x 14" DR 26					1,650			1,650	1,800
5722	10" DR 17 x 16" DR 26					1,600			1,600	1,750
5726	10" DR 26 x 16" DR 26					1,575			1,575	1,750
5730	12" DR 26 x 16" DR 26					1,625			1,625	1,800
5734	12" DR 17 x 18" DR 26					1,775			1,775	1,950
5738	12" DR 26 x 18" DR 26					1,800			1,800	1,975
5742	14" DR 26 x 20" DR 32.5					1,925			1,925	2,125
5746	16" DR 26 x 22" DR 32.5					2,025			2,025	2,225
5750	18" DR 26 x 24" DR 32.5					2,100			2,100	2,300
5754	20" DR 32.5 x 28" DR 32.5					2,175			2,175	2,375
5758	22" DR 32.5 x 30" DR 32.5					2,250			2,250	2,475
5762	24" DR 32.5 x 32" DR 32.5					2,325			2,325	2,550
5766	36" DR 32.5 x 42" DR 32.5					2,400			2,400	2,650
5800	45° elbow									
5804	1" DR 11 x 3" DR 11				Ea.	365			365	405

22 11 Facility Water Distribution

22 11 13 – Facility Water Distribution Piping

22 11 13.78 Pipe, High Density Polyethylene Plastic (HDPE)	Crew	Daily Output	Labor-Hours	Unit	Material	2023 Bare Costs Labor	Equipment	Total	Total Incl O&P
5808	1" DR 11 x 4" DR 17				Ea.	300			300	330
5812	1-1/2" DR 11 x 4" DR 17					305			305	335
5816	2" DR 11 x 4" DR 17					291			291	320
5820	2" DR 11 x 6" DR 17					415			415	460
5824	3" DR 11 x 6" DR 17					450			450	490
5828	3" DR 17 x 6" DR 26					450			450	495
5832	3" DR 17 x 8" DR 11					575			575	630
5836	3" DR 17 x 8" DR 17					645			645	710
5840	4" DR 11 x 8" DR 17					530			530	585
5844	4" DR 17 x 8" DR 26					540			540	590
5848	6" DR 11 x 10" DR 17					840			840	925
5852	6" DR 17 x 10" DR 26					850			850	935
5856	6" DR 26 x 10" DR 26					955			955	1,050
5860	8" DR 17 x 12" DR 26					1,125			1,125	1,250
5864	8" DR 26 x 12" DR 32.5					1,075			1,075	1,175
5868	10" DR 17 x 14" DR 26					1,200			1,200	1,325
5872	10" DR 17 x 16" DR 26					1,150			1,150	1,275
5876	10" DR 26 x 16" DR 26					1,225			1,225	1,350
5880	12" DR 26 x 16" DR 26					1,100			1,100	1,225
5884	12" DR 17 x 18" DR 26					1,575			1,575	1,725
5888	12" DR 26 x 18" DR 26					1,400			1,400	1,525
5892	14" DR 26 x 20" DR 32.5					1,525			1,525	1,675
5896	16" DR 26 x 22" DR 32.5					1,575			1,575	1,725
5900	18" DR 26 x 24" DR 32.5					1,675			1,675	1,825
5904	20" DR 32.5 x 28" DR 32.5					1,650			1,650	1,825
5908	22" DR 32.5 x 30" DR 32.5					1,725			1,725	1,900
5912	24" DR 32.5 x 32" DR 32.5					1,775			1,775	1,950
5916	36" DR 32.5 x 42" DR 32.5					1,850			1,850	2,025
6000	Access port with 4" riser									
6050	1" DR 11 x 4" DR 17				Ea.	435			435	480
6054	1-1/2" DR 11 x 4" DR 17					440			440	485
6058	2" DR 11 x 6" DR 17					535			535	590
6062	3" DR 11 x 6" DR 17					545			545	595
6066	3" DR 17 x 6" DR 26					525			525	580
6070	3" DR 17 x 8" DR 11					545			545	595
6074	3" DR 17 x 8" DR 17					565			565	620
6078	4" DR 11 x 8" DR 17					580			580	640
6082	4" DR 17 x 8" DR 26					555			555	610
6086	6" DR 11 x 10" DR 17					680			680	745
6090	6" DR 17 x 10" DR 26					620			620	680
6094	6" DR 26 x 10" DR 26					650			650	715
6098	8" DR 17 x 12" DR 26					695			695	765
6102	8" DR 26 x 12" DR 32.5					685			685	750
6200	End termination with vent plug									
6204	1" DR 11 x 3" DR 11				Ea.	148			148	163
6208	1" DR 11 x 4" DR 17					216			216	238
6212	1-1/2" DR 11 x 4" DR 17					216			216	238
6216	2" DR 11 x 4" DR 17					216			216	238
6220	2" DR 11 x 6" DR 17					440			440	480
6224	3" DR 11 x 6" DR 17					440			440	480
6228	3" DR 17 x 6" DR 26					440			440	480
6232	3" DR 17 x 8" DR 11					425			425	465
6236	3" DR 17 x 8" DR 17					475			475	520

For customer support on your Plumbing Costs with RSMeans data, call 800.448.8182.

22 11 Facility Water Distribution

22 11 13 – Facility Water Distribution Piping

22 11 13.78 Pipe, High Density Polyethylene Plastic (HDPE)		Crew	Daily Output	Labor-Hours	Unit	Material	2023 Bare Costs Labor	Equipment	Total	Total Incl O&P
6240	4" DR 11 x 8" DR 17				Ea.	565			565	620
6244	4" DR 17 x 8" DR 26					530			530	585
6248	6" DR 11 x 10" DR 17					615			615	675
6252	6" DR 17 x 10" DR 26					570			570	625
6256	6" DR 26 x 10" DR 26					830			830	910
6260	8" DR 17 x 12" DR 26					870			870	955
6264	8" DR 26 x 12" DR 32.5					1,050			1,050	1,150
6268	10" DR 17 x 14" DR 26					1,375			1,375	1,525
6272	10" DR 17 x 16" DR 26					1,300			1,300	1,425
6276	10" DR 26 x 16" DR 26					1,475			1,475	1,625
6280	12" DR 26 x 16" DR 26					1,625			1,625	1,775
6284	12" DR 17 x 18" DR 26					1,900			1,900	2,075
6288	12" DR 26 x 18" DR 26					2,075			2,075	2,275
6292	14" DR 26 x 20" DR 32.5					2,325			2,325	2,550
6296	16" DR 26 x 22" DR 32.5					2,600			2,600	2,850
6300	18" DR 26 x 24" DR 32.5					2,925			2,925	3,200
6304	20" DR 32.5 x 28" DR 32.5					3,250			3,250	3,575
6308	22" DR 32.5 x 30" DR 32.5					3,625			3,625	4,000
6312	24" DR 32.5 x 32" DR 32.5					4,075			4,075	4,475
6316	36" DR 32.5 x 42" DR 32.5					4,500			4,500	4,950
6600	Tee									
6604	1" DR 11 x 3" DR 11				Ea.	365			365	405
6608	1" DR 11 x 4" DR 17					400			400	440
6612	1-1/2" DR 11 x 4" DR 17					410			410	455
6616	2" DR 11 x 4" DR 17					375			375	410
6620	2" DR 11 x 6" DR 17					600			600	660
6624	3" DR 11 x 6" DR 17					705			705	775
6628	3" DR 17 x 6" DR 26					670			670	735
6632	3" DR 17 x 8" DR 11					820			820	905
6636	3" DR 17 x 8" DR 17					890			890	980
6640	4" DR 11 x 8" DR 17					1,075			1,075	1,175
6644	4" DR 17 x 8" DR 26					1,075			1,075	1,175
6648	6" DR 11 x 10" DR 17					1,400			1,400	1,525
6652	6" DR 17 x 10" DR 26					1,400			1,400	1,550
6656	6" DR 26 x 10" DR 26					1,725			1,725	1,900
6660	8" DR 17 x 12" DR 26					1,725			1,725	1,900
6664	8" DR 26 x 12" DR 32.5					2,225			2,225	2,450
6668	10" DR 17 x 14" DR 26					2,575			2,575	2,850
6672	10" DR 17 x 16" DR 26					2,875			2,875	3,150
6676	10" DR 26 x 16" DR 26					2,875			2,875	3,150
6680	12" DR 26 x 16" DR 26					3,250			3,250	3,600
6684	12" DR 17 x 18" DR 26					3,250			3,250	3,600
6688	12" DR 26 x 18" DR 26					3,700			3,700	4,075
6692	14" DR 26 x 20" DR 32.5					4,175			4,175	4,600
6696	16" DR 26 x 22" DR 32.5					4,725			4,725	5,200
6700	18" DR 26 x 24" DR 32.5					5,375			5,375	5,925
6704	20" DR 32.5 x 28" DR 32.5					6,075			6,075	6,675
6708	22" DR 32.5 x 30" DR 32.5					6,875			6,875	7,550
6712	24" DR 32.5 x 32" DR 32.5					7,775			7,775	8,550
6716	36" DR 32.5 x 42" DR 32.5					8,925			8,925	9,825
6800	Wye									
6816	2" DR 11 x 4" DR 17				Ea.	910			910	1,000
6820	2" DR 11 x 6" DR 17					1,125			1,125	1,250

22 11 Facility Water Distribution

22 11 13 – Facility Water Distribution Piping

22 11 13.78 Pipe, High Density Polyethylene Plastic (HDPE)		Crew	Daily Output	Labor-Hours	Unit	Material	2023 Bare Costs Labor	Equipment	Total	Total Incl O&P
6824	3" DR 11 x 6" DR 17				Ea.	1,200			1,200	1,300
6828	3" DR 17 x 6" DR 26					320			320	355
6832	3" DR 17 x 8" DR 11					1,275			1,275	1,400
6836	3" DR 17 x 8" DR 17					1,375			1,375	1,525
6840	4" DR 11 x 8" DR 17					1,525			1,525	1,675
6844	4" DR 17 x 8" DR 26					955			955	1,050
6848	6" DR 11 x 10" DR 17					595			595	655
6852	6" DR 17 x 10" DR 26					1,450			1,450	1,600
6856	6" DR 26 x 10" DR 26					2,025			2,025	2,225
6860	8" DR 17 x 12" DR 26					2,825			2,825	3,125
6864	8" DR 26 x 12" DR 32.5					2,350			2,350	2,575
6868	10" DR 17 x 14" DR 26					2,500			2,500	2,750
6872	10" DR 17 x 16" DR 26					2,700			2,700	2,975
6876	10" DR 26 x 16" DR 26					2,925			2,925	3,225
6880	12" DR 26 x 16" DR 26					3,150			3,150	3,475
6884	12" DR 17 x 18" DR 26					3,400			3,400	3,725
6888	12" DR 26 x 18" DR 26					3,675			3,675	4,025
6892	14" DR 26 x 20" DR 32.5					3,925			3,925	4,325
6896	16" DR 26 x 22" DR 32.5					4,150			4,150	4,550
6900	18" DR 26 x 24" DR 32.5					4,750			4,750	5,225
6904	20" DR 32.5 x 28" DR 32.5					4,975			4,975	5,450
6908	22" DR 32.5 x 30" DR 32.5					5,350			5,350	5,900
6912	24" DR 32.5 x 32" DR 32.5					5,775			5,775	6,350
9000	Welding labor per joint, not including welding machine									
9010	Pipe joint size, outer pipe (cost based on the thickest walls)									
9020	Straight pipe									
9050	3" pipe size	4 Skwk	96	.333	Ea.		20.50		20.50	30.50
9060	4" pipe size	"	77	.416			25.50		25.50	38
9070	6" pipe size	5 Skwk	60	.667			41		41	61.50
9080	8" pipe size	"	40	1			61.50		61.50	92
9090	10" pipe size	6 Skwk	41	1.171			71.50		71.50	108
9100	12" pipe size		39	1.231			75.50		75.50	113
9110	14" pipe size		38	1.263			77.50		77.50	116
9120	16" pipe size		35	1.371			84		84	126
9130	18" pipe size	8 Skwk	45	1.422			87		87	131
9140	20" pipe size		42	1.524			93.50		93.50	140
9150	22" pipe size		40	1.600			98		98	147
9160	24" pipe size		38	1.684			103		103	155
9170	28" pipe size		37	1.730			106		106	159
9180	30" pipe size		36	1.778			109		109	164
9190	32" pipe size		35	1.829			112		112	168
9200	42" pipe size		32	2			123		123	184

22 11 19 – Domestic Water Piping Specialties

22 11 19.10 Flexible Connectors

		Crew	Daily Output	Labor-Hours	Unit	Material	2023 Bare Costs Labor	Equipment	Total	Total Incl O&P
0010	**FLEXIBLE CONNECTORS**, Corrugated, 5/8" OD, 3/4" ID									
0050	Gas, seamless brass, steel fittings									
0200	12" long	1 Plum	36	.222	Ea.	26	16		42	52.50
0220	18" long		36	.222		32	16		48	59.50
0240	24" long		34	.235		38	16.95		54.95	67.50
0260	30" long		34	.235		41	16.95		57.95	70.50
0280	36" long		32	.250		45.50	18		63.50	77
0320	48" long		30	.267		57.50	19.20		76.70	92

22 11 Facility Water Distribution

22 11 19 – Domestic Water Piping Specialties

22 11 19.10 Flexible Connectors

		Crew	Daily Output	Labor-Hours	Unit	Material	2023 Bare Costs Labor	Equipment	Total	Total Incl O&P
0340	60" long	1 Plum	30	.267	Ea.	68.50	19.20		87.70	104
0360	72" long		30	.267		79.50	19.20		98.70	116
2000	Water, copper tubing, dielectric separators									
2100	12" long	1 Plum	36	.222	Ea.	12.85	16		28.85	38
2220	15" long		36	.222		14.30	16		30.30	39.50
2240	18" long		36	.222		13.15	16		29.15	38.50
2260	24" long		34	.235		19.10	16.95		36.05	46.50

22 11 19.14 Flexible Metal Hose

		Crew	Daily Output	Labor-Hours	Unit	Material	2023 Bare Costs Labor	Equipment	Total	Total Incl O&P
0010	**FLEXIBLE METAL HOSE**, Connectors, standard lengths									
0100	Bronze braided, bronze ends									
0120	3/8" diameter x 12"	1 Stpi	26	.308	Ea.	31.50	22.50		54	68
0140	1/2" diameter x 12"		24	.333		38	24		62	78
0160	3/4" diameter x 12"		20	.400		61	29		90	111
0180	1" diameter x 18"		19	.421		77.50	30.50		108	131
0200	1-1/2" diameter x 18"		13	.615		117	44.50		161.50	196
0220	2" diameter x 18"		11	.727		150	53		203	244
1000	Carbon steel ends									
1020	1/4" diameter x 12"	1 Stpi	28	.286	Ea.	59.50	20.50		80	96.50
1040	3/8" diameter x 12"		26	.308		39.50	22.50		62	77
1060	1/2" diameter x 12"		24	.333		53.50	24		77.50	95
1080	1/2" diameter x 24"		24	.333		74.50	24		98.50	118
1120	3/4" diameter x 12"		20	.400		73	29		102	124
1140	3/4" diameter x 24"		20	.400		87.50	29		116.50	140
1160	3/4" diameter x 36"		20	.400		99	29		128	153
1180	1" diameter x 18"		19	.421		88	30.50		118.50	143
1200	1" diameter x 30"		19	.421		101	30.50		131.50	157
1220	1" diameter x 36"		19	.421		116	30.50		146.50	174
1240	1-1/4" diameter x 18"		15	.533		310	38.50		348.50	400
1260	1-1/4" diameter x 36"		15	.533		138	38.50		176.50	210
1280	1-1/2" diameter x 18"		13	.615		157	44.50		201.50	240
1300	1-1/2" diameter x 36"		13	.615		157	44.50		201.50	240
1320	2" diameter x 24"		11	.727		177	53		230	273
1340	2" diameter x 36"		11	.727		196	53		249	294
1360	2-1/2" diameter x 24"		9	.889		340	64.50		404.50	470
1380	2-1/2" diameter x 36"		9	.889		199	64.50		263.50	315
1400	3" diameter x 24"		7	1.143		705	83		788	900
1420	3" diameter x 36"		7	1.143		1,600	83		1,683	1,900
2000	Carbon steel braid, carbon steel solid ends									
2100	1/2" diameter x 12"	1 Stpi	24	.333	Ea.	64.50	24		88.50	107
2120	3/4" diameter x 12"		20	.400		72	29		101	123
2140	1" diameter x 12"		19	.421		117	30.50		147.50	174
2160	1-1/4" diameter x 12"		15	.533		91.50	38.50		130	158
2180	1-1/2" diameter x 12"		13	.615		101	44.50		145.50	178
3000	Stainless steel braid, welded on carbon steel ends									
3100	1/2" diameter x 12"	1 Stpi	24	.333	Ea.	82	24		106	127
3120	3/4" diameter x 12"		20	.400		96	29		125	150
3140	3/4" diameter x 24"		20	.400		107	29		136	162
3160	3/4" diameter x 36"		20	.400		120	29		149	176
3180	1" diameter x 12"		19	.421		144	30.50		174.50	204
3200	1" diameter x 24"		19	.421		147	30.50		177.50	207
3220	1" diameter x 36"		19	.421		145	30.50		175.50	206
3240	1-1/4" diameter x 12"		15	.533		163	38.50		201.50	237

22 11 Facility Water Distribution

22 11 19 – Domestic Water Piping Specialties

22 11 19.14 Flexible Metal Hose

		Crew	Daily Output	Labor-Hours	Unit	Material	2023 Bare Costs Labor	Equipment	Total	Total Incl O&P
3260	1-1/4" diameter x 24"	1 Stpi	15	.533	Ea.	174	38.50		212.50	249
3280	1-1/4" diameter x 36"		15	.533		196	38.50		234.50	273
3300	1-1/2" diameter x 12"		13	.615		105	44.50		149.50	183
3320	1-1/2" diameter x 24"		13	.615		204	44.50		248.50	292
3340	1-1/2" diameter x 36"		13	.615		120	44.50		164.50	199
3400	Metal stainless steel braid, over corrugated stainless steel, flanged ends									
3410	150 psi									
3420	1/2" diameter x 12"	1 Stpi	24	.333	Ea.	100	24		124	146
3430	1" diameter x 12"		20	.400		154	29		183	213
3440	1-1/2" diameter x 12"		15	.533		100	38.50		138.50	168
3450	2-1/2" diameter x 9"		12	.667		168	48.50		216.50	257
3460	3" diameter x 9"		9	.889		168	64.50		232.50	281
3470	4" diameter x 9"		7	1.143		219	83		302	365
3480	4" diameter x 30"		5	1.600		450	116		566	670
3490	4" diameter x 36"		4.80	1.667		450	121		571	675
3500	6" diameter x 11"		5	1.600		390	116		506	605
3510	6" diameter x 36"		3.80	2.105		695	153		848	990
3520	8" diameter x 12"		4	2		605	145		750	880
3530	10" diameter x 13"		3	2.667		815	193		1,008	1,200
3540	12" diameter x 14"	Q-5	4	4		1,375	261		1,636	1,900
6000	Molded rubber with helical wire reinforcement									
6010	150 psi									
6020	1-1/2" diameter x 12"	1 Stpi	15	.533	Ea.	48	38.50		86.50	111
6030	2" diameter x 12"		12	.667		156	48.50		204.50	244
6040	3" diameter x 12"		8	1		163	72.50		235.50	287
6050	4" diameter x 12"		6	1.333		207	96.50		303.50	370
6060	6" diameter x 18"		4	2		310	145		455	555
6070	8" diameter x 24"		3	2.667		435	193		628	765
6080	10" diameter x 24"		2	4		525	290		815	1,025
6090	12" diameter x 24"	Q-5	3	5.333		600	350		950	1,175
7000	Molded teflon with stainless steel flanges									
7010	150 psi									
7020	2-1/2" diameter x 3-3/16"	Q-1	7.80	2.051	Ea.	920	133		1,053	1,225
7030	3" diameter x 3-5/8"		6.50	2.462		860	160		1,020	1,175
7040	4" diameter x 3-5/8"		5	3.200		1,100	208		1,308	1,500
7050	6" diameter x 4"		4.30	3.721		1,525	241		1,766	2,025
7060	8" diameter x 6"		3.80	4.211		2,425	273		2,698	3,050

22 11 19.18 Mixing Valve

		Crew	Daily Output	Labor-Hours	Unit	Material	2023 Bare Costs Labor	Equipment	Total	Total Incl O&P
0010	**MIXING VALVE**, Automatic, water tempering.									
0040	1/2" size	1 Stpi	19	.421	Ea.	625	30.50		655.50	730
0050	3/4" size		18	.444		535	32		567	635
0100	1" size		16	.500		995	36.50		1,031.50	1,150
0120	1-1/4" size		13	.615		1,350	44.50		1,394.50	1,550
0140	1-1/2" size		10	.800		1,325	58		1,383	1,550
0160	2" size		8	1		1,725	72.50		1,797.50	1,975
0170	2-1/2" size		6	1.333		1,725	96.50		1,821.50	2,025
0180	3" size		4	2		3,925	145		4,070	4,550
0190	4" size		3	2.667		3,925	193		4,118	4,625

22 11 Facility Water Distribution

22 11 19 – Domestic Water Piping Specialties

22 11 19.22 Pressure Reducing Valve

		Crew	Daily Output	Labor-Hours	Unit	Material	2023 Bare Costs Labor	Equipment	Total	Total Incl O&P
0010	**PRESSURE REDUCING VALVE**, Steam, pilot operated.									
0100	Threaded, iron body									
0200	1-1/2" size	1 Stpi	8	1	Ea.	2,650	72.50		2,722.50	3,000
0220	2" size	"	5	1.600	"	3,800	116		3,916	4,375
1000	Flanged, iron body, 125 lb. flanges									
1020	2" size	1 Stpi	8	1	Ea.	5,175	72.50		5,247.50	5,800
1040	2-1/2" size	"	4	2		4,050	145		4,195	4,675
1060	3" size	Q-5	4.50	3.556		4,525	232		4,757	5,325
1080	4" size	"	3	5.333		5,425	350		5,775	6,500
1500	For 250 lb. flanges, add					5%				

22 11 19.26 Pressure Regulators

		Crew	Daily Output	Labor-Hours	Unit	Material	2023 Bare Costs Labor	Equipment	Total	Total Incl O&P
0010	**PRESSURE REGULATORS**									
0100	Gas appliance regulators									
0106	Main burner and pilot applications									
0108	Rubber seat poppet type									
0109	1/8" pipe size	1 Stpi	24	.333	Ea.	29.50	24		53.50	68.50
0110	1/4" pipe size		24	.333		29.50	24		53.50	68.50
0112	3/8" pipe size		24	.333		25	24		49	63
0113	1/2" pipe size		24	.333		30	24		54	69
0114	3/4" pipe size		20	.400		30	29		59	76.50
0122	Lever action type									
0123	3/8" pipe size	1 Stpi	24	.333	Ea.	46	24		70	86.50
0124	1/2" pipe size		24	.333		24	24		48	62
0125	3/4" pipe size		20	.400		60	29		89	110
0126	1" pipe size		19	.421		60.50	30.50		91	113
0132	Double diaphragm type									
0133	3/8" pipe size	1 Stpi	24	.333	Ea.	71.50	24		95.50	115
0134	1/2" pipe size		24	.333		89.50	24		113.50	135
0135	3/4" pipe size		20	.400		148	29		177	207
0136	1" pipe size		19	.421		141	30.50		171.50	201
0137	1-1/4" pipe size		15	.533		445	38.50		483.50	550
0138	1-1/2" pipe size		13	.615		1,100	44.50		1,144.50	1,275
0139	2" pipe size		11	.727		790	53		843	950
0140	2-1/2" pipe size	Q-5	15	1.067		2,125	69.50		2,194.50	2,425
0141	3" pipe size		13	1.231		1,650	80.50		1,730.50	1,950
0142	4" pipe size (flanged)		8	2		3,200	131		3,331	3,700
0160	Main burner only									
0162	Straight-thru-flow design									
0163	1/2" pipe size	1 Stpi	24	.333	Ea.	63	24		87	106
0164	3/4" pipe size		20	.400		63	29		92	113
0165	1" pipe size		19	.421		114	30.50		144.50	171
0166	1-1/4" pipe size		15	.533		98	38.50		136.50	166
0200	Oil, light, hot water, ordinary steam, threaded									
0220	Bronze body, 1/4" size	1 Stpi	24	.333	Ea.	345	24		369	415
0230	3/8" size		24	.333		355	24		379	425
0240	1/2" size		24	.333		460	24		484	540
0250	3/4" size		20	.400		510	29		539	605
0260	1" size		19	.421		900	30.50		930.50	1,025
0270	1-1/4" size		15	.533		1,025	38.50		1,063.50	1,175
0320	Iron body, 1/4" size		24	.333		201	24		225	257
0330	3/8" size		24	.333		370	24		394	440
0340	1/2" size		24	.333		390	24		414	460

22 11 Facility Water Distribution

22 11 19 – Domestic Water Piping Specialties

22 11 19.26 Pressure Regulators

		Crew	Daily Output	Labor-Hours	Unit	Material	2023 Bare Costs Labor	2023 Bare Costs Equipment	Total	Total Incl O&P
0350	3/4" size	1 Stpi	20	.400	Ea.	470	29		499	565
0360	1" size		19	.421		610	30.50		640.50	715
0370	1-1/4" size	↓	15	.533	↓	530	38.50		568.50	645
9002	For water pressure regulators, see Section 22 05 23.20									

22 11 19.30 Pressure and Temperature Safety Plug

		Crew	Daily Output	Labor-Hours	Unit	Material	Labor	Equipment	Total	Total Incl O&P
0010	**PRESSURE & TEMPERATURE SAFETY PLUG**									
1000	3/4" external thread, 3/8" diam. element									
1020	Carbon steel									
1050	7-1/2" insertion	1 Stpi	32	.250	Ea.	78	18.15		96.15	113
1120	304 stainless steel									
1150	7-1/2" insertion	1 Stpi	32	.250	Ea.	61.50	18.15		79.65	94.50
1220	316 stainless steel									
1250	7-1/2" insertion	1 Stpi	32	.250	Ea.	110	18.15		128.15	148

22 11 19.32 Pressure and Temperature Measurement Plug

		Crew	Daily Output	Labor-Hours	Unit	Material	Labor	Equipment	Total	Total Incl O&P
0010	**PRESSURE & TEMPERATURE MEASUREMENT PLUG**									
0020	A permanent access port for insertion of									
0030	a pressure or temperature measuring probe									
0100	Plug, brass									
0110	1/4" MNPT, 1-1/2" long	1 Stpi	32	.250	Ea.	24.50	18.15		42.65	54
0120	3" long		31	.258		19.65	18.70		38.35	49.50
0140	1/2" MNPT, 1-1/2" long		30	.267		17.45	19.35		36.80	48
0150	3" long	↓	29	.276	↓	24	20		44	56
0200	Pressure gauge probe adapter									
0210	1/8" diameter, 1-1/2" probe				Ea.	25.50			25.50	28
0220	3" probe				"	32.50			32.50	36
0300	Temperature gauge, 5" stem									
0310	Analog				Ea.	17.55			17.55	19.30
0330	Digital				"	48			48	52.50
0400	Pressure gauge, compound									
0410	1/4" MNPT				Ea.	31.50			31.50	34.50
0500	Pressure and temperature test kit									
0510	Contains 2 thermometers and 2 pressure gauges									
0520	Kit				Ea.	570			570	630

22 11 19.34 Sleeves and Escutcheons

		Crew	Daily Output	Labor-Hours	Unit	Material	Labor	Equipment	Total	Total Incl O&P
0010	**SLEEVES & ESCUTCHEONS**									
0100	Pipe sleeve									
0110	Steel, w/water stop, 12" long, with link seal									
0120	2" diam. for 1/2" carrier pipe	1 Plum	8.40	.952	Ea.	116	68.50		184.50	229
0130	2-1/2" diam. for 3/4" carrier pipe		8	1		130	72		202	250
0140	2-1/2" diam. for 1" carrier pipe		8	1		123	72		195	243
0150	3" diam. for 1-1/4" carrier pipe		7.20	1.111		157	80		237	292
0160	3-1/2" diam. for 1-1/2" carrier pipe		6.80	1.176		185	85		270	330
0170	4" diam. for 2" carrier pipe		6	1.333		176	96		272	335
0180	4" diam. for 2-1/2" carrier pipe		6	1.333		174	96		270	335
0190	5" diam. for 3" carrier pipe		5.40	1.481		201	107		308	380
0200	6" diam. for 4" carrier pipe	↓	4.80	1.667		220	120		340	420
0210	10" diam. for 6" carrier pipe	Q-1	8	2		435	130		565	675
0220	12" diam. for 8" carrier pipe		7.20	2.222		605	144		749	880
0230	14" diam. for 10" carrier pipe		6.40	2.500		615	162		777	920
0240	16" diam. for 12" carrier pipe		5.80	2.759		685	179		864	1,025
0250	18" diam. for 14" carrier pipe		5.20	3.077		1,200	200		1,400	1,625
0260	24" diam. for 18" carrier pipe	↓	4	4	↓	1,800	259		2,059	2,350

22 11 Facility Water Distribution

22 11 19 – Domestic Water Piping Specialties

22 11 19.34 Sleeves and Escutcheons

		Crew	Daily Output	Labor-Hours	Unit	Material	2023 Bare Costs Labor	Equipment	Total	Total Incl O&P
0270	24" diam. for 20" carrier pipe	Q-1	4	4	Ea.	1,575	259		1,834	2,100
0280	30" diam. for 24" carrier pipe	↓	3.20	5	↓	2,050	325		2,375	2,725
0500	Wall sleeve									
0510	Ductile iron with rubber gasket seal									
0520	3"	1 Plum	8.40	.952	Ea.	330	68.50		398.50	460
0530	4"		7.20	1.111		350	80		430	505
0540	6"		6	1.333		425	96		521	615
0550	8"		4	2		1,900	144		2,044	2,300
0560	10"		3	2.667		2,300	192		2,492	2,800
0570	12"	↓	2.40	3.333	↓	2,725	240		2,965	3,325
5000	Escutcheon									
5100	Split ring, pipe									
5110	Chrome plated									
5120	1/2"	1 Plum	160	.050	Ea.	1.35	3.60		4.95	6.85
5130	3/4"		160	.050		1.48	3.60		5.08	7
5140	1"		135	.059		1.58	4.27		5.85	8.10
5150	1-1/2"		115	.070		2.23	5		7.23	9.90
5160	2"		100	.080		2.48	5.75		8.23	11.35
5170	4"		80	.100		8.10	7.20		15.30	19.65
5180	6"	↓	68	.118	↓	12.70	8.50		21.20	26.50
5400	Shallow flange type									
5410	Chrome plated steel									
5420	1/2" CTS	1 Plum	180	.044	Ea.	.53	3.20		3.73	5.35
5430	3/4" CTS		180	.044		.57	3.20		3.77	5.40
5440	1/2" IPS		180	.044		.53	3.20		3.73	5.35
5450	3/4" IPS		180	.044		.65	3.20		3.85	5.50
5460	1" IPS		175	.046		.76	3.29		4.05	5.75
5470	1-1/2" IPS		170	.047		1.24	3.39		4.63	6.40
5480	2" IPS	↓	160	.050	↓	1.51	3.60		5.11	7

22 11 19.38 Water Supply Meters

		Crew	Daily Output	Labor-Hours	Unit	Material	Labor	Equipment	Total	Total Incl O&P
0010	**WATER SUPPLY METERS**									
1000	Detector, serves dual systems such as fire and domestic or									
1020	process water, wide range cap., UL and FM approved									
1100	3" mainline x 2" by-pass, 400 GPM	Q-1	3.60	4.444	Ea.	13,100	288		13,388	14,800
1140	4" mainline x 2" by-pass, 700 GPM	"	2.50	6.400		13,100	415		13,515	15,000
1180	6" mainline x 3" by-pass, 1,600 GPM	Q-2	2.60	9.231		20,000	620		20,620	22,900
1220	8" mainline x 4" by-pass, 2,800 GPM		2.10	11.429		29,600	770		30,370	33,800
1260	10" mainline x 6" by-pass, 4,400 GPM		2	12		42,400	805		43,205	47,800
1300	10" x 12" mainlines x 6" by-pass, 5,400 GPM	↓	1.70	14.118	↓	57,500	950		58,450	64,500
2000	Domestic/commercial, bronze									
2020	Threaded									
2060	5/8" diameter, to 20 GPM	1 Plum	16	.500	Ea.	185	36		221	258
2080	3/4" diameter, to 30 GPM		14	.571		465	41		506	570
2100	1" diameter, to 50 GPM		12	.667	↓	625	48		673	760
2300	Threaded/flanged									
2340	1-1/2" diameter, to 100 GPM	1 Plum	8	1	Ea.	1,425	72		1,497	1,675
2360	2" diameter, to 160 GPM	"	6	1.333	"	2,075	96		2,171	2,425
2600	Flanged, compound									
2640	3" diameter, 320 GPM	Q-1	3	5.333	Ea.	2,200	345		2,545	2,950
2660	4" diameter, to 500 GPM		1.50	10.667		3,275	690		3,965	4,625
2680	6" diameter, to 1,000 GPM		1	16		8,225	1,050		9,275	10,600
2700	8" diameter, to 1,800 GPM	↓	.80	20	↓	9,575	1,300		10,875	12,400

22 11 Facility Water Distribution

22 11 19 – Domestic Water Piping Specialties

22 11 19.38 Water Supply Meters

		Crew	Daily Output	Labor-Hours	Unit	Material	2023 Bare Costs Labor	Equipment	Total	Total Incl O&P
7000	Turbine									
7260	Flanged									
7300	2" diameter, to 160 GPM	1 Plum	7	1.143	Ea.	1,000	82.50		1,082.50	1,225
7320	3" diameter, to 450 GPM	Q-1	3.60	4.444		1,700	288		1,988	2,300
7340	4" diameter, to 650 GPM	"	2.50	6.400		2,850	415		3,265	3,750
7360	6" diameter, to 1,800 GPM	Q-2	2.60	9.231		4,675	620		5,295	6,075
7380	8" diameter, to 2,500 GPM		2.10	11.429		8,025	770		8,795	9,975
7400	10" diameter, to 5,500 GPM		1.70	14.118		10,800	950		11,750	13,300

22 11 19.42 Backflow Preventers

		Crew	Daily Output	Labor-Hours	Unit	Material	Labor	Equipment	Total	Total Incl O&P
0010	**BACKFLOW PREVENTERS**, Includes valves									
0020	and four test cocks, corrosion resistant, automatic operation									
1000	Double check principle									
1010	Threaded, with ball valves									
1020	3/4" pipe size	1 Plum	16	.500	Ea.	254	36		290	335
1030	1" pipe size		14	.571		435	41		476	535
1040	1-1/2" pipe size		10	.800		820	57.50		877.50	985
1050	2" pipe size		7	1.143		1,225	82.50		1,307.50	1,475
1080	Threaded, with gate valves									
1100	3/4" pipe size	1 Plum	16	.500	Ea.	1,975	36		2,011	2,225
1120	1" pipe size		14	.571		2,000	41		2,041	2,250
1140	1-1/2" pipe size		10	.800		1,775	57.50		1,832.50	2,025
1160	2" pipe size		7	1.143		3,175	82.50		3,257.50	3,600
1200	Flanged, valves are gate									
1210	3" pipe size	Q-1	4.50	3.556	Ea.	2,175	231		2,406	2,725
1220	4" pipe size	"	3	5.333		2,675	345		3,020	3,475
1230	6" pipe size	Q-2	3	8		4,150	540		4,690	5,350
1240	8" pipe size		2	12		7,375	805		8,180	9,300
1250	10" pipe size		1	24		10,400	1,625		12,025	13,800
1300	Flanged, valves are OS&Y									
1370	1" pipe size	1 Plum	5	1.600	Ea.	2,175	115		2,290	2,550
1374	1-1/2" pipe size		5	1.600		1,975	115		2,090	2,325
1378	2" pipe size		4.80	1.667		3,375	120		3,495	3,875
1380	3" pipe size	Q-1	4.50	3.556		3,625	231		3,856	4,325
1400	4" pipe size	"	3	5.333		3,750	345		4,095	4,625
1420	6" pipe size	Q-2	3	8		5,675	540		6,215	7,050
1430	8" pipe size	"	2	12		17,100	805		17,905	20,000
4000	Reduced pressure principle									
4100	Threaded, bronze, valves are ball									
4120	3/4" pipe size	1 Plum	16	.500	Ea.	245	36		281	325
4140	1" pipe size		14	.571		395	41		436	495
4150	1-1/4" pipe size		12	.667		1,825	48		1,873	2,075
4160	1-1/2" pipe size		10	.800		1,500	57.50		1,557.50	1,725
4180	2" pipe size		7	1.143		620	82.50		702.50	810
5000	Flanged, bronze, valves are OS&Y									
5060	2-1/2" pipe size	Q-1	5	3.200	Ea.	5,050	208		5,258	5,850
5080	3" pipe size		4.50	3.556		5,175	231		5,406	6,050
5100	4" pipe size		3	5.333		6,700	345		7,045	7,900
5120	6" pipe size	Q-2	3	8		10,200	540		10,740	12,000
5200	Flanged, iron, valves are gate									
5210	2-1/2" pipe size	Q-1	5	3.200	Ea.	4,050	208		4,258	4,750
5220	3" pipe size		4.50	3.556		4,150	231		4,381	4,925
5230	4" pipe size		3	5.333		5,375	345		5,720	6,450

22 11 Facility Water Distribution

22 11 19 – Domestic Water Piping Specialties

22 11 19.42 Backflow Preventers

		Crew	Daily Output	Labor-Hours	Unit	Material	2023 Bare Costs Labor	Equipment	Total	Total Incl O&P
5240	6" pipe size	Q-2	3	8	Ea.	7,950	540		8,490	9,550
5250	8" pipe size		2	12		11,800	805		12,605	14,200
5260	10" pipe size	↓	1	24	↓	16,200	1,625		17,825	20,300
5600	Flanged, iron, valves are OS&Y									
5660	2-1/2" pipe size	Q-1	5	3.200	Ea.	5,050	208		5,258	5,850
5680	3" pipe size		4.50	3.556		5,175	231		5,406	6,050
5700	4" pipe size	↓	3	5.333		6,700	345		7,045	7,900
5720	6" pipe size	Q-2	3	8		10,200	540		10,740	12,000
5740	8" pipe size		2	12		18,000	805		18,805	21,000
5760	10" pipe size	↓	1	24		19,600	1,625		21,225	23,900

22 11 19.50 Vacuum Breakers

		Crew	Daily Output	Labor-Hours	Unit	Material	2023 Bare Costs Labor	Equipment	Total	Total Incl O&P
0010	**VACUUM BREAKERS** R221113-40									
0013	See also backflow preventers Section 22 11 19.42									
1000	Anti-siphon continuous pressure type									
1010	Max. 150 psi - 210°F									
1020	Bronze body									
1030	1/2" size	1 Stpi	24	.333	Ea.	345	24		369	410
1040	3/4" size		20	.400		345	29		374	420
1050	1" size		19	.421		350	30.50		380.50	430
1060	1-1/4" size		15	.533		700	38.50		738.50	830
1070	1-1/2" size		13	.615		845	44.50		889.50	990
1080	2" size	↓	11	.727	↓	550	53		603	685
1200	Max. 125 psi with atmospheric vent									
1210	Brass, in-line construction									
1220	1/4" size	1 Stpi	24	.333	Ea.	234	24		258	293
1230	3/8" size	"	24	.333		234	24		258	293
1260	For polished chrome finish, add				↓	13%				
2000	Anti-siphon, non-continuous pressure type									
2010	Hot or cold water 125 psi - 210°F									
2020	Bronze body									
2030	1/4" size	1 Stpi	24	.333	Ea.	143	24		167	193
2040	3/8" size		24	.333		143	24		167	193
2050	1/2" size		24	.333		160	24		184	212
2060	3/4" size		20	.400		192	29		221	255
2070	1" size		19	.421		296	30.50		326.50	370
2080	1-1/4" size		15	.533		520	38.50		558.50	630
2090	1-1/2" size		13	.615		575	44.50		619.50	695
2100	2" size		11	.727		945	53		998	1,125
2110	2-1/2" size		8	1		2,725	72.50		2,797.50	3,100
2120	3" size	↓	6	1.333	↓	3,600	96.50		3,696.50	4,125
2150	For polished chrome finish, add					50%				
3000	Air gap fitting									
3020	1/2" NPT size	1 Plum	19	.421	Ea.	104	30.50		134.50	160
3030	1" NPT size	"	15	.533		104	38.50		142.50	173
3040	2" NPT size	Q-1	21	.762		132	49.50		181.50	219
3050	3" NPT size		14	1.143		425	74		499	580
3060	4" NPT size	↓	10	1.600	↓	279	104		383	460

22 11 19.54 Water Hammer Arresters/Shock Absorbers

		Crew	Daily Output	Labor-Hours	Unit	Material	2023 Bare Costs Labor	Equipment	Total	Total Incl O&P
0010	**WATER HAMMER ARRESTERS/SHOCK ABSORBERS**									
0490	Copper									
0500	3/4" male IPS for 1 to 11 fixtures	1 Plum	12	.667	Ea.	44.50	48		92.50	121
0600	1" male IPS for 12 to 32 fixtures	↓	8	1		74.50	72		146.50	189

22 11 Facility Water Distribution

22 11 19 – Domestic Water Piping Specialties

22 11 19.54 Water Hammer Arresters/Shock Absorbers

		Crew	Daily Output	Labor-Hours	Unit	Material	2023 Bare Costs Labor	2023 Bare Costs Equipment	Total	Total Incl O&P
0700	1-1/4" male IPS for 33 to 60 fixtures	1 Plum	8	1	Ea.	72.50	72		144.50	187
0800	1-1/2" male IPS for 61 to 113 fixtures		8	1		105	72		177	223
0900	2" male IPS for 114 to 154 fixtures		8	1		155	72		227	278
1000	2-1/2" male IPS for 155 to 330 fixtures		4	2		445	144		589	705
4000	Bellows type									
4010	3/4" FNPT, to 11 fixture units	1 Plum	10	.800	Ea.	495	57.50		552.50	630
4020	1" FNPT, to 32 fixture units		8.80	.909		1,000	65.50		1,065.50	1,200
4030	1" FNPT, to 60 fixture units		8.80	.909		1,500	65.50		1,565.50	1,750
4040	1" FNPT, to 113 fixture units		8.80	.909		3,775	65.50		3,840.50	4,250
4050	1" FNPT, to 154 fixture units		6.60	1.212		4,250	87.50		4,337.50	4,800
4060	1-1/2" FNPT, to 300 fixture units		5	1.600		5,225	115		5,340	5,925

22 11 19.64 Hydrants

		Crew	Daily Output	Labor-Hours	Unit	Material	2023 Bare Costs Labor	2023 Bare Costs Equipment	Total	Total Incl O&P
0010	**HYDRANTS**									
0050	Wall type, moderate climate, bronze, encased									
0200	3/4" IPS connection	1 Plum	16	.500	Ea.	1,725	36		1,761	1,950
0300	1" IPS connection		14	.571		3,625	41		3,666	4,025
0500	Anti-siphon type, 3/4" connection		16	.500		1,350	36		1,386	1,525
1000	Non-freeze, bronze, exposed									
1100	3/4" IPS connection, 4" to 9" thick wall	1 Plum	14	.571	Ea.	820	41		861	965
1120	10" to 14" thick wall		12	.667		720	48		768	860
1140	15" to 19" thick wall		12	.667		915	48		963	1,075
1160	20" to 24" thick wall		10	.800		1,250	57.50		1,307.50	1,450
1200	For 1" IPS connection, add					15%	10%			
1240	For 3/4" adapter type vacuum breaker, add				Ea.	145			145	160
1280	For anti-siphon type, add				"	310			310	340
2000	Non-freeze bronze, encased, anti-siphon type									
2100	3/4" IPS connection, 5" to 9" thick wall	1 Plum	14	.571	Ea.	2,050	41		2,091	2,325
2120	10" to 14" thick wall		12	.667		2,675	48		2,723	3,025
2140	15" to 19" thick wall		12	.667		2,850	48		2,898	3,225
2160	20" to 24" thick wall		10	.800		2,950	57.50		3,007.50	3,325
2200	For 1" IPS connection, add					10%	10%			
3000	Ground box type, bronze frame, 3/4" IPS connection									
3080	Non-freeze, all bronze, polished face, set flush									
3100	2' depth of bury	1 Plum	8	1	Ea.	1,875	72		1,947	2,175
3120	3' depth of bury		8	1		1,150	72		1,222	1,350
3140	4' depth of bury		8	1		1,275	72		1,347	1,500
3160	5' depth of bury		7	1.143		1,375	82.50		1,457.50	1,625
3180	6' depth of bury		7	1.143		1,450	82.50		1,532.50	1,725
3200	7' depth of bury		6	1.333		2,775	96		2,871	3,200
3220	8' depth of bury		5	1.600		1,625	115		1,740	1,950
3240	9' depth of bury		4	2		3,100	144		3,244	3,625
3260	10' depth of bury		4	2		1,800	144		1,944	2,200
3400	For 1" IPS connection, add					15%	10%			
3450	For 1-1/4" IPS connection, add					325%	14%			
3500	For 1-1/2" IPS connection, add					370%	18%			
3550	For 2" IPS connection, add					445%	24%			
3600	For tapped drain port in box, add					177			177	194
4000	Non-freeze, CI body, bronze frame & scoriated cover									
4010	with hose storage									
4100	2' depth of bury	1 Plum	7	1.143	Ea.	3,625	82.50		3,707.50	4,125
4120	3' depth of bury		7	1.143		3,800	82.50		3,882.50	4,300
4140	4' depth of bury		7	1.143		3,900	82.50		3,982.50	4,425

22 11 Facility Water Distribution

22 11 19 – Domestic Water Piping Specialties

22 11 19.64 Hydrants

		Crew	Daily Output	Labor-Hours	Unit	Material	2023 Bare Costs Labor	Equipment	Total	Total Incl O&P
4160	5' depth of bury	1 Plum	6.50	1.231	Ea.	2,725	88.50		2,813.50	3,125
4180	6' depth of bury		6	1.333		2,425	96		2,521	2,825
4200	7' depth of bury		5.50	1.455		4,200	105		4,305	4,775
4220	8' depth of bury		5	1.600		4,300	115		4,415	4,925
4240	9' depth of bury		4.50	1.778		4,025	128		4,153	4,625
4260	10' depth of bury		4	2		4,625	144		4,769	5,325
4280	For 1" IPS connection, add					885			885	970
4300	For tapped drain port in box, add					177			177	194
5000	Moderate climate, all bronze, polished face									
5020	and scoriated cover, set flush									
5100	3/4" IPS connection	1 Plum	16	.500	Ea.	1,375	36		1,411	1,550
5120	1" IPS connection	"	14	.571		3,125	41		3,166	3,475
5200	For tapped drain port in box, add					196			196	216
6000	Ground post type, all non-freeze, all bronze, aluminum casing									
6010	guard, exposed head, 3/4" IPS connection									
6100	2' depth of bury	1 Plum	8	1	Ea.	1,850	72		1,922	2,150
6120	3' depth of bury		8	1		1,250	72		1,322	1,475
6140	4' depth of bury		8	1		2,175	72		2,247	2,475
6160	5' depth of bury		7	1.143		1,450	82.50		1,532.50	1,700
6180	6' depth of bury		7	1.143		2,475	82.50		2,557.50	2,850
6200	7' depth of bury		6	1.333		1,650	96		1,746	1,950
6220	8' depth of bury		5	1.600		1,750	115		1,865	2,100
6240	9' depth of bury		4	2		3,100	144		3,244	3,625
6260	10' depth of bury		4	2		3,275	144		3,419	3,825
6300	For 1" IPS connection, add					40%	10%			
6350	For 1-1/4" IPS connection, add					140%	14%			
6400	For 1-1/2" IPS connection, add					225%	18%			
6450	For 2" IPS connection, add					315%	24%			

22 11 23 – Domestic Water Pumps

22 11 23.10 General Utility Pumps

		Crew	Daily Output	Labor-Hours	Unit	Material	Labor	Equipment	Total	Total Incl O&P
0010	**GENERAL UTILITY PUMPS**									
2000	Single stage									
3000	Double suction,									
3140	50 HP, 5" D x 6" S	Q-2	.33	72.727	Ea.	11,300	4,900		16,200	19,700
3180	60 HP, 6" D x 8" S	Q-3	.30	107		27,300	7,325		34,625	40,900
3190	75 HP, to 2,500 GPM		.28	114		33,100	7,850		40,950	48,200
3220	100 HP, to 3,000 GPM		.26	123		42,600	8,450		51,050	59,500
3240	150 HP, to 4,000 GPM		.24	133		44,500	9,150		53,650	62,500
4000	Centrifugal, end suction, mounted on base									
4010	Horizontal mounted, with drip proof motor, rated @ 100' head									
4020	Vertical split case, single stage									
4040	100 GPM, 5 HP, 1-1/2" discharge	Q-1	1.70	9.412	Ea.	7,250	610		7,860	8,875
4050	200 GPM, 10 HP, 2" discharge		1.30	12.308		7,925	800		8,725	9,925
4060	250 GPM, 10 HP, 3" discharge		1.28	12.500		8,700	810		9,510	10,800
4070	300 GPM, 15 HP, 2" discharge	Q-2	1.56	15.385		9,800	1,025		10,825	12,400
4080	500 GPM, 20 HP, 4" discharge		1.44	16.667		12,300	1,125		13,425	15,200
4090	750 GPM, 30 HP, 4" discharge		1.20	20		13,000	1,350		14,350	16,300
4100	1,050 GPM, 40 HP, 5" discharge		1	24		11,300	1,625		12,925	14,800
4110	1,500 GPM, 60 HP, 6" discharge		.60	40		27,300	2,700		30,000	34,000
4120	2,000 GPM, 75 HP, 6" discharge		.50	48		19,500	3,225		22,725	26,200
4130	3,000 GPM, 100 HP, 8" discharge		.40	60		37,100	4,025		41,125	46,900
4200	Horizontal split case, single stage									

22 11 Facility Water Distribution

22 11 23 – Domestic Water Pumps

22 11 23.10 General Utility Pumps

		Crew	Daily Output	Labor-Hours	Unit	Material	2023 Bare Costs Labor	Equipment	Total	Total Incl O&P
4210	100 GPM, 7.5 HP, 1-1/2" discharge	Q-1	1.70	9.412	Ea.	8,325	610		8,935	10,100
4220	250 GPM, 15 HP, 2-1/2" discharge	"	1.30	12.308		9,750	800		10,550	11,900
4230	500 GPM, 20 HP, 4" discharge	Q-2	1.60	15		12,000	1,000		13,000	14,700
4240	750 GPM, 25 HP, 5" discharge		1.54	15.584		14,500	1,050		15,550	17,600
4250	1,000 GPM, 40 HP, 5" discharge		1.20	20		14,500	1,350		15,850	18,000
4260	1,500 GPM, 50 HP, 6" discharge	Q-3	1.42	22.535		19,600	1,550		21,150	23,900
4270	2,000 GPM, 75 HP, 8" discharge		1.14	28.070		25,500	1,925		27,425	31,000
4280	3,000 GPM, 100 HP, 10" discharge		.96	33.333		35,800	2,275		38,075	42,800
4290	3,500 GPM, 150 HP, 10" discharge		.86	37.209		44,500	2,550		47,050	53,000
4300	4,000 GPM, 200 HP, 10" discharge		.66	48.485		38,400	3,325		41,725	47,200
4330	Horizontal split case, two stage, 500' head									
4340	100 GPM, 40 HP, 1-1/2" discharge	Q-2	1.70	14.118	Ea.	29,400	950		30,350	33,700
4350	200 GPM, 50 HP, 1-1/2" discharge	"	1.44	16.667		31,600	1,125		32,725	36,500
4360	300 GPM, 75 HP, 2" discharge	Q-3	1.57	20.382		42,200	1,400		43,600	48,600
4370	400 GPM, 100 HP, 3" discharge		1.14	28.070		48,900	1,925		50,825	57,000
4380	800 GPM, 200 HP, 4" discharge		.86	37.209		68,000	2,550		70,550	78,500
5000	Centrifugal, in-line									
5006	Vertical mount, iron body, 125 lb. flgd, 1,800 RPM TEFC mtr									
5010	Single stage									
5012	.5 HP, 1-1/2" suction & discharge	Q-1	3.20	5	Ea.	2,425	325		2,750	3,150
5014	.75 HP, 2" suction & discharge		2.80	5.714		4,800	370		5,170	5,825
5015	1 HP, 3" suction & discharge		2.50	6.400		2,675	415		3,090	3,575
5016	1.5 HP, 3" suction & discharge		2.30	6.957		5,450	450		5,900	6,675
5018	2 HP, 4" suction & discharge		2.10	7.619		7,325	495		7,820	8,775
5020	3 HP, 5" suction & discharge		1.90	8.421		5,375	545		5,920	6,750
5030	5 HP, 6" suction & discharge		1.60	10		5,875	650		6,525	7,425
5040	7.5 HP, 6" suction & discharge		1.30	12.308		6,800	800		7,600	8,700
5050	10 HP, 8" suction & discharge	Q-2	1.80	13.333		8,000	895		8,895	10,100
5060	15 HP, 8" suction & discharge		1.70	14.118		9,425	950		10,375	11,800
5064	20 HP, 8" suction & discharge		1.60	15		11,300	1,000		12,300	13,900
5070	30 HP, 8" suction & discharge		1.50	16		22,500	1,075		23,575	26,300
5080	40 HP, 8" suction & discharge		1.40	17.143		27,000	1,150		28,150	31,400
5090	50 HP, 8" suction & discharge		1.30	18.462		27,500	1,250		28,750	32,100
5094	60 HP, 8" suction & discharge		.90	26.667		33,000	1,800		34,800	39,000
5100	75 HP, 8" suction & discharge	Q-3	.60	53.333		33,000	3,650		36,650	41,800
5110	100 HP, 8" suction & discharge	"	.50	64		23,400	4,400		27,800	32,300

22 11 23.11 Miscellaneous Pumps

		Crew	Daily Output	Labor-Hours	Unit	Material	Labor	Equipment	Total	Total Incl O&P
0010	**MISCELLANEOUS PUMPS**									
0020	Water pump, portable, gasoline powered									
0100	170 GPH, 2" discharge	Q-1	11	1.455	Ea.	1,225	94.50		1,319.50	1,500
0110	343 GPH, 3" discharge		10.50	1.524		1,125	99		1,224	1,400
0120	608 GPH, 4" discharge		10	1.600		2,550	104		2,654	2,950
0500	Pump, propylene body, housing and impeller									
0510	22 GPM, 1/3 HP, 40' HD	1 Plum	5	1.600	Ea.	810	115		925	1,050
0520	33 GPM, 1/2 HP, 40' HD	Q-1	5	3.200		645	208		853	1,025
0530	53 GPM, 3/4 HP, 40' HD	"	4	4		1,275	259		1,534	1,775
0600	Rotary pump, CI									
0614	282 GPH, 3/4 HP, 1" discharge	Q-1	4.50	3.556	Ea.	1,850	231		2,081	2,400
0618	277 GPH, 1 HP, 1" discharge		4	4		1,850	259		2,109	2,400
0624	1,100 GPH, 1.5 HP, 1-1/4" discharge		3.60	4.444		5,100	288		5,388	6,025
0628	1,900 GPH, 2 HP, 1-1/4" discharge		3.20	5		6,850	325		7,175	8,000
1000	Turbine pump, CI									

22 11 Facility Water Distribution

22 11 23 – Domestic Water Pumps

22 11 23.11 Miscellaneous Pumps

		Crew	Daily Output	Labor-Hours	Unit	Material	2023 Bare Costs Labor	2023 Bare Costs Equipment	Total	Total Incl O&P
1010	50 GPM, 2 HP, 3" discharge	Q-1	.80	20	Ea.	5,900	1,300		7,200	8,400
1020	100 GPM, 3 HP, 4" discharge	Q-2	.96	25		11,100	1,675		12,775	14,700
1030	250 GPM, 15 HP, 6" discharge	"	.94	25.532		13,800	1,725		15,525	17,800
1040	500 GPM, 25 HP, 6" discharge	Q-3	1.22	26.230		13,900	1,800		15,700	18,000
1050	1,000 GPM, 50 HP, 8" discharge		1.14	28.070		19,200	1,925		21,125	24,000
1060	2,000 GPM, 100 HP, 10" discharge		1	32		22,800	2,200		25,000	28,300
1070	3,000 GPM, 150 HP, 10" discharge		.80	40		36,600	2,750		39,350	44,400
1080	4,000 GPM, 200 HP, 12" discharge		.70	45.714		40,100	3,125		43,225	48,800
1090	6,000 GPM, 300 HP, 14" discharge		.60	53.333		61,000	3,650		64,650	72,500
1100	10,000 GPM, 300 HP, 18" discharge		.58	55.172		70,500	3,775		74,275	83,000
2000	Centrifugal stainless steel pumps									
2100	100 GPM, 100' TDH, 3 HP	Q-1	1.80	8.889	Ea.	19,900	575		20,475	22,800
2130	250 GPM, 100' TDH, 10 HP	"	1.28	12.500		27,900	810		28,710	31,900
2160	500 GPM, 100' TDH, 20 HP	Q-2	1.44	16.667		31,900	1,125		33,025	36,800
2200	Vertical turbine stainless steel pumps									
2220	100 GPM, 100' TDH, 7.5 HP	Q-2	.95	25.263	Ea.	111,500	1,700		113,200	125,500
2240	250 GPM, 100' TDH, 15 HP		.94	25.532		123,500	1,725		125,225	138,500
2260	500 GPM, 100' TDH, 20 HP		.93	25.806		135,500	1,725		137,225	151,500
2280	750 GPM, 100' TDH, 30 HP	Q-3	1.19	26.891		147,500	1,850		149,350	165,000
2300	1,000 GPM, 100' TDH, 40 HP	"	1.16	27.586		159,500	1,900		161,400	178,500
2320	100 GPM, 200' TDH, 15 HP	Q-2	.94	25.532		171,500	1,725		173,225	191,000
2340	250 GPM, 200' TDH, 25 HP	Q-3	1.22	26.230		183,500	1,800		185,300	204,000
2360	500 GPM, 200' TDH, 40 HP		1.16	27.586		195,500	1,900		197,400	218,000
2380	750 GPM, 200' TDH, 60 HP		1.13	28.319		185,000	1,950		186,950	206,500
2400	1,000 GPM, 200' TDH, 75 HP		1.12	28.571		203,000	1,950		204,950	226,500

22 11 23.13 Domestic-Water Packaged Booster Pumps

		Crew	Daily Output	Labor-Hours	Unit	Material	2023 Bare Costs Labor	2023 Bare Costs Equipment	Total	Total Incl O&P
0010	**DOMESTIC-WATER PACKAGED BOOSTER PUMPS**									
0200	Pump system, with diaphragm tank, control, press. switch									
0300	1 HP pump	Q-1	1.30	12.308	Ea.	11,800	800		12,600	14,200
0400	1-1/2 HP pump		1.25	12.800		11,900	830		12,730	14,400
0420	2 HP pump		1.20	13.333		11,200	865		12,065	13,600
0440	3 HP pump		1.10	14.545		12,400	945		13,345	15,000
0460	5 HP pump	Q-2	1.50	16		12,600	1,075		13,675	15,500
0480	7-1/2 HP pump		1.42	16.901		15,200	1,125		16,325	18,500
0500	10 HP pump		1.34	17.910		15,900	1,200		17,100	19,300
2000	Pump system, variable speed, base, controls, starter									
2010	Duplex, 100' head									
2020	400 GPM, 7-1/2 HP, 4" discharge	Q-2	.70	34.286	Ea.	71,500	2,300		73,800	82,000
2025	Triplex, 100' head									
2030	1,000 GPM, 15 HP, 6" discharge	Q-2	.50	48	Ea.	76,500	3,225		79,725	89,000
2040	1,700 GPM, 30 HP, 6" discharge	"	.30	80		114,500	5,375		119,875	133,500
0020	Chlorinator Injector, sewer, gas injected w/booster pump	Q-1	1.30	12.308		2,450	800		3,250	3,900

22 12 Facility Potable-Water Storage Tanks

22 12 21 – Facility Underground Potable-Water Storage Tanks

22 12 21.13 Fiberglass, Undrgrnd Pot.-Water Storage Tanks

	22 12 21.13 Fiberglass, Undrgrnd Pot.-Water Storage Tanks	Crew	Daily Output	Labor-Hours	Unit	Material	2023 Bare Costs Labor	Equipment	Total	Total Incl O&P
0010	**FIBERGLASS, UNDERGROUND POTABLE-WATER STORAGE TANKS**									
0020	Excludes excavation, backfill & piping									
0030	Single wall									
2000	600 gallon capacity	B-21B	3.75	10.667	Ea.	1,400	550	575	2,525	2,975
2010	1,000 gallon capacity		3.50	11.429		2,650	590	615	3,855	4,450
2020	2,000 gallon capacity		3.25	12.308		4,425	635	660	5,720	6,525
2030	4,000 gallon capacity		3	13.333		8,025	685	715	9,425	10,600
2040	6,000 gallon capacity		2.65	15.094		27,300	775	810	28,885	32,000
2050	8,000 gallon capacity		2.30	17.391		15,300	895	935	17,130	19,200
2060	10,000 gallon capacity		2	20		22,600	1,025	1,075	24,700	27,500
2070	12,000 gallon capacity		1.50	26.667		21,100	1,375	1,425	23,900	26,800
2080	15,000 gallon capacity		1	40		26,800	2,050	2,150	31,000	35,000
2090	20,000 gallon capacity		.75	53.333		37,700	2,750	2,875	43,325	48,700
2100	25,000 gallon capacity		.50	80		52,000	4,125	4,300	60,425	68,000
2110	30,000 gallon capacity		.35	114		63,000	5,875	6,150	75,025	84,500
2120	40,000 gallon capacity		.30	133		85,500	6,850	7,175	99,525	112,000

22 12 23 – Facility Indoor Potable-Water Storage Tanks

22 12 23.13 Facility Steel, Indoor Pot.-Water Storage Tanks

	22 12 23.13 Facility Steel, Indoor Pot.-Water Storage Tanks	Crew	Daily Output	Labor-Hours	Unit	Material	2023 Bare Costs Labor	Equipment	Total	Total Incl O&P
0010	**FACILITY STEEL, INDOOR POT.-WATER STORAGE TANKS**									
2000	Galvanized steel, 15 gal., 14" diam. x 26" LOA	1 Plum	12	.667	Ea.	1,025	48		1,073	1,200
2060	30 gal., 14" diam. x 49" LOA		11	.727		1,150	52.50		1,202.50	1,325
2080	80 gal., 20" diam. x 64" LOA		9	.889		1,700	64		1,764	1,975
2100	135 gal., 24" diam. x 75" LOA		6	1.333		2,525	96		2,621	2,925
2120	240 gal., 30" diam. x 86" LOA		4	2		4,675	144		4,819	5,375
2140	300 gal., 36" diam. x 76" LOA		3	2.667		6,575	192		6,767	7,500
2160	400 gal., 36" diam. x 100" LOA	Q-1	4	4		8,000	259		8,259	9,175
2180	500 gal., 36" diam. x 126" LOA	"	3	5.333		9,975	345		10,320	11,500
3000	Glass lined, P.E., 80 gal., 20" diam. x 60" LOA	1 Plum	9	.889		4,175	64		4,239	4,700
3060	140 gal., 24" diam. x 75" LOA		6	1.333		5,750	96		5,846	6,475
3080	200 gal., 30" diam. x 71" LOA		4	2		7,825	144		7,969	8,825
3100	350 gal., 36" diam. x 86" LOA		3	2.667		9,450	192		9,642	10,700
3120	450 gal., 42" diam. x 79" LOA	Q-1	4	4		12,900	259		13,159	14,500
3140	600 gal., 48" diam. x 81" LOA		3	5.333		15,700	345		16,045	17,800
3160	750 gal., 48" diam. x 105" LOA		3	5.333		17,600	345		17,945	19,900
3180	900 gal., 54" diam. x 95" LOA		2.50	6.400		24,500	415		24,915	27,600
3200	1,500 gal., 54" diam. x 153" LOA		2	8		31,500	520		32,020	35,500
3220	1,800 gal., 54" diam. x 181" LOA		1.50	10.667		35,300	690		35,990	39,800
3240	2,000 gal., 60" diam. x 165" LOA		1	16		40,400	1,050		41,450	46,100
3260	3,500 gal., 72" diam. x 201" LOA	Q-2	1.50	16		51,000	1,075		52,075	58,000

22 13 Facility Sanitary Sewerage

22 13 16 – Sanitary Waste and Vent Piping

22 13 16.20 Pipe, Cast Iron

	22 13 16.20 Pipe, Cast Iron		Crew	Daily Output	Labor-Hours	Unit	Material	2023 Bare Costs Labor	Equipment	Total	Total Incl O&P
0010	**PIPE, CAST IRON**, Soil, on clevis hanger assemblies, 5' OC	R221113-70									
0020	Single hub, service wt., lead & oakum joints 10' OC										
2120	2" diameter	R221316-10	Q-1	63	.254	L.F.	7.85	16.45		24.30	33
2140	3" diameter			60	.267		10.85	17.30		28.15	38
2160	4" diameter	R221316-20		55	.291		14	18.85		32.85	43.50
2180	5" diameter		Q-2	76	.316		39.50	21		60.50	75
2200	6" diameter		"	73	.329		23.50	22		45.50	59

For customer support on your Plumbing Costs with RSMeans data, call 800.448.8182.

22 13 Facility Sanitary Sewerage

22 13 16 – Sanitary Waste and Vent Piping

22 13 16.20 Pipe, Cast Iron

		Crew	Daily Output	Labor-Hours	Unit	Material	2023 Bare Costs Labor	Equipment	Total	Total Incl O&P
2220	8" diameter	Q-3	59	.542	L.F.	46	37		83	106
2240	10" diameter		54	.593		85.50	40.50		126	155
2260	12" diameter		48	.667		305	45.50		350.50	405
2261	15" diameter	↓	40	.800		445	55		500	570
2320	For service weight, double hub, add					10%				
2340	For extra heavy, single hub, add					48%	4%			
2360	For extra heavy, double hub, add				↓	71%	4%			
2400	Lead for caulking (1#/diam. in.)	Q-1	160	.100	Lb.	1.17	6.50		7.67	10.95
2420	Oakum for caulking (1/8#/diam. in.)	"	40	.400	"	13.85	26		39.85	53.50
2960	To delete hangers, subtract									
2970	2" diam. to 4" diam.					16%	19%			
2980	5" diam. to 8" diam.					14%	14%			
2990	10" diam. to 15" diam.					13%	19%			
3000	Single hub, service wt., push-on gasket joints 10' OC									
3010	2" diameter	Q-1	66	.242	L.F.	9.30	15.70		25	33.50
3020	3" diameter		63	.254		12.70	16.45		29.15	38.50
3030	4" diameter	↓	57	.281		16.30	18.20		34.50	45
3040	5" diameter	Q-2	79	.304		43	20.50		63.50	78
3050	6" diameter	"	75	.320		27	21.50		48.50	62
3060	8" diameter	Q-3	62	.516		54.50	35.50		90	113
3070	10" diameter		56	.571		100	39		139	169
3080	12" diameter		49	.653		325	45		370	420
3082	15" diameter	↓	40	.800	↓	465	55		520	595
3100	For service weight, double hub, add					65%				
3110	For extra heavy, single hub, add					48%	4%			
3120	For extra heavy, double hub, add					29%	4%			
3130	To delete hangers, subtract									
3140	2" diam. to 4" diam.					12%	21%			
3150	5" diam. to 8" diam.					10%	16%			
3160	10" diam. to 15" diam.					9%	21%			
4000	No hub, couplings 10' OC									
4100	1-1/2" diameter	Q-1	71	.225	L.F.	12.30	14.60		26.90	35.50
4120	2" diameter		67	.239		12.75	15.50		28.25	37
4140	3" diameter		64	.250		17.20	16.20		33.40	43
4160	4" diameter	↓	58	.276		22.50	17.90		40.40	51.50
4180	5" diameter	Q-2	83	.289		33	19.45		52.45	65
4200	6" diameter	"	79	.304		38.50	20.50		59	72.50
4220	8" diameter	Q-3	69	.464		75.50	32		107.50	131
4240	10" diameter		61	.525		120	36		156	186
4244	12" diameter		58	.552		200	38		238	277
4248	15" diameter	↓	52	.615	↓	292	42		334	385
4280	To delete hangers, subtract									
4290	1-1/2" diam. to 6" diam.					22%	47%			
4300	8" diam. to 10" diam.					21%	44%			
4310	12" diam. to 15" diam.					19%	40%			

22 13 16.30 Pipe Fittings, Cast Iron

		Crew	Daily Output	Labor-Hours	Unit	Material	2023 Bare Costs Labor	Equipment	Total	Total Incl O&P
0010	**PIPE FITTINGS, CAST IRON**, Soil									
0040	Hub and spigot, service weight, lead & oakum joints									
0080	1/4 bend, 2"	Q-1	16	1	Ea.	42.50	65		107.50	144
0120	3"		14	1.143		57	74		131	174
0140	4"	↓	13	1.231		89.50	80		169.50	218
0160	5"	Q-2	18	1.333	↓	125	89.50		214.50	271

22 13 Facility Sanitary Sewerage

22 13 16 – Sanitary Waste and Vent Piping

22 13 16.30 Pipe Fittings, Cast Iron		Crew	Daily Output	Labor-Hours	Unit	Material	2023 Bare Costs Labor	Equipment	Total	Total Incl O&P
0180	6"	Q-2	17	1.412	Ea.	155	95		250	315
0200	8"	Q-3	11	2.909		470	200		670	810
0220	10"		10	3.200		685	219		904	1,075
0224	12"		9	3.556		925	244		1,169	1,400
0226	15"		7	4.571		3,250	315		3,565	4,050
0242	Short sweep, CI, 90°, 2"	Q-1	16	1		41.50	65		106.50	143
0243	3"		14	1.143		74.50	74		148.50	193
0244	4"		13	1.231		114	80		194	245
0245	6"	Q-2	17	1.412		232	95		327	395
0246	8"	Q-3	11	2.909		505	200		705	850
0247	10"		10	3.200		1,025	219		1,244	1,450
0248	12"		9	3.556		2,400	244		2,644	3,025
0251	Long sweep elbow									
0252	2"	Q-1	16	1	Ea.	65	65		130	168
0253	3"		14	1.143		92.50	74		166.50	213
0254	4"		13	1.231		136	80		216	268
0255	6"	Q-2	17	1.412		273	95		368	440
0256	8"	Q-3	11	2.909		615	200		815	975
0257	10"		10	3.200		1,050	219		1,269	1,475
0258	12"		9	3.556		1,700	244		1,944	2,225
0259	15"		7	4.571		4,475	315		4,790	5,400
0266	Closet bend, 3" diameter with flange 10" x 16"	Q-1	14	1.143		235	74		309	370
0268	16" x 16"		12	1.333		263	86.50		349.50	420
0270	Closet bend, 4" diameter, 2-1/2" x 4" ring, 6" x 16"		13	1.231		205	80		285	345
0280	8" x 16"		13	1.231		179	80		259	315
0290	10" x 12"		12	1.333		167	86.50		253.50	310
0300	10" x 18"		11	1.455		246	94.50		340.50	410
0310	12" x 16"		11	1.455		207	94.50		301.50	370
0330	16" x 16"		10	1.600		270	104		374	450
0340	1/8 bend, 2"		16	1		30.50	65		95.50	130
0350	3"		14	1.143		47.50	74		121.50	164
0360	4"		13	1.231		69.50	80		149.50	196
0380	5"	Q-2	18	1.333		98	89.50		187.50	242
0400	6"	"	17	1.412		118	95		213	272
0420	8"	Q-3	11	2.909		355	200		555	685
0440	10"		10	3.200		505	219		724	880
0460	12"		9	3.556		960	244		1,204	1,425
0461	15"		7	4.571		2,275	315		2,590	2,975
0500	Sanitary tee, 2"	Q-1	10	1.600		59.50	104		163.50	221
0540	3"		9	1.778		96.50	115		211.50	278
0620	4"		8	2		118	130		248	325
0700	5"	Q-2	12	2		235	135		370	460
0800	6"	"	11	2.182		266	147		413	510
0880	8"	Q-3	7	4.571		705	315		1,020	1,250
0881	10"		7	4.571		1,300	315		1,615	1,900
0882	12"		6	5.333		2,300	365		2,665	3,075
0883	15"		4	8		4,675	550		5,225	5,950
0900	Sanitary tee, tapped									
0901	2" x 2"	Q-1	9	1.778	Ea.	80	115		195	260
0902	3" x 2"		8	2		89.50	130		219.50	292
0903	4" x 2"		7	2.286		146	148		294	380
0910	Sanitary cross, tapped (double tapped sanitary tee)									
0911	2" x 2"	Q-1	7	2.286	Ea.	83.50	148		231.50	315

22 13 Facility Sanitary Sewerage

22 13 16 – Sanitary Waste and Vent Piping

22 13 16.30 Pipe Fittings, Cast Iron		Crew	Daily Output	Labor-Hours	Unit	Material	2023 Bare Costs Labor	Equipment	Total	Total Incl O&P
0912	3" x 2"	Q-1	6	2.667	Ea.	158	173		331	430
0913	4" x 2"	↓	5	3.200	↓	154	208		362	480
0940	Sanitary tee, reducing									
0942	3" x 2"	Q-1	10	1.600	Ea.	83	104		187	246
0943	4" x 3"		9	1.778		108	115		223	291
0944	4" x 2"	↓	9	1.778		101	115		216	283
0945	5" x 3"	Q-2	12.50	1.920		205	129		334	420
0946	6" x 4"		10	2.400		300	161		461	570
0947	6" x 3"		11	2.182		216	147		363	455
0948	6" x 2"	↓	12.50	1.920		209	129		338	425
0949	8" x 6"	Q-3	9	3.556		595	244		839	1,025
0950	8" x 5"		9	3.556		405	244		649	810
0951	8" x 4"		10	3.200		450	219		669	820
0954	10" x 6"		8	4		1,025	274		1,299	1,525
0958	12" x 8"		7	4.571		1,850	315		2,165	2,500
0962	15" x 10"	↓	5	6.400		1,975	440		2,415	2,825
1000	Tee, 2"	Q-1	10	1.600		86	104		190	250
1060	3"		9	1.778		128	115		243	315
1120	4"	↓	8	2		165	130		295	375
1200	5"	Q-2	12	2		350	135		485	585
1300	6"	"	11	2.182		345	147		492	600
1380	8"	Q-3	7	4.571	↓	360	315		675	860
1400	Combination Y and 1/8 bend									
1420	2"	Q-1	10	1.600	Ea.	74.50	104		178.50	237
1460	3"		9	1.778		113	115		228	297
1520	4"	↓	8	2		156	130		286	365
1540	5"	Q-2	12	2		297	135		432	525
1560	6"		11	2.182		375	147		522	635
1580	8"	↓	7	3.429		925	231		1,156	1,375
1582	12"	Q-3	6	5.333	↓	1,300	365		1,665	1,975
1584	Combination Y & 1/8 bend, reducing									
1586	3" x 2"	Q-1	10	1.600	Ea.	86	104		190	250
1587	4" x 2"		9.50	1.684		116	109		225	290
1588	4" x 3"	↓	9	1.778		136	115		251	320
1589	6" x 2"	Q-2	12.50	1.920		242	129		371	460
1590	6" x 3"		12	2		258	135		393	485
1591	6" x 4"	↓	11	2.182		271	147		418	515
1592	8" x 2"	Q-3	11	2.909		510	200		710	855
1593	8" x 4"		10	3.200		450	219		669	820
1594	8" x 6"	↓	9	3.556		620	244		864	1,050
1600	Double Y, 2"	Q-1	8	2		133	130		263	340
1610	3"		7	2.286		165	148		313	405
1620	4"	↓	6.50	2.462		216	160		376	475
1630	5"	Q-2	9	2.667		415	179		594	725
1640	6"	"	8	3		565	202		767	920
1650	8"	Q-3	5.50	5.818		1,350	400		1,750	2,100
1660	10"		5	6.400		3,275	440		3,715	4,250
1670	12"	↓	4.50	7.111	↓	3,750	490		4,240	4,850
1676	Combination double Y & 1/8 bend									
1678	2"	Q-1	8	2	Ea.	153	130		283	360
1680	3"		7	2.286		196	148		344	435
1682	4"	↓	6.50	2.462		320	160		480	595
1684	6"	Q-2	8	3	↓	1,100	202		1,302	1,525

22 13 Facility Sanitary Sewerage
22 13 16 – Sanitary Waste and Vent Piping

22 13 16.30 Pipe Fittings, Cast Iron		Crew	Daily Output	Labor-Hours	Unit	Material	2023 Bare Costs Labor	Equipment	Total	Total Incl O&P
1690	Combination double Y & 1/8 bend, CI, reducing									
1692	3" x 2"	Q-1	8	2	Ea.	170	130		300	380
1694	4" x 2"		7	2.286		198	148		346	440
1696	4" x 3"		7	2.286		226	148		374	470
1698	6" x 4"	Q-2	9	2.667		725	179		904	1,075
1700	Double Y, CI, reducing									
1702	3" x 2"	Q-1	8	2	Ea.	141	130		271	350
1703	4" x 2"		7	2.286		170	148		318	410
1704	4" x 3"		7	2.286		179	148		327	420
1706	6" x 3"	Q-2	9.50	2.526		430	170		600	730
1707	6" x 4"	"	9	2.667		440	179		619	745
1708	8" x 4"	Q-3	8.50	3.765		945	258		1,203	1,425
1709	8" x 6"		8	4		970	274		1,244	1,475
1711	10" x 6"		8	4		2,075	274		2,349	2,675
1712	10" x 8"		6.50	4.923		3,175	340		3,515	3,975
1713	12" x 6"		7.50	4.267		3,825	293		4,118	4,650
1714	12" x 8"		6	5.333		3,775	365		4,140	4,700
1740	Reducer, 3" x 2"	Q-1	15	1.067		41.50	69		110.50	149
1750	4" x 2"		14.50	1.103		47.50	71.50		119	160
1760	4" x 3"		14	1.143		54.50	74		128.50	171
1770	5" x 2"		14	1.143		115	74		189	238
1780	5" x 3"		13.50	1.185		122	77		199	249
1790	5" x 4"		13	1.231		70	80		150	196
1800	6" x 2"		13.50	1.185		114	77		191	240
1810	6" x 3"		13	1.231		111	80		191	241
1830	6" x 4"		12.50	1.280		110	83		193	245
1840	6" x 5"		11	1.455		118	94.50		212.50	271
1880	8" x 3"	Q-2	13.50	1.778		213	120		333	410
1900	8" x 4"		13	1.846		183	124		307	385
1920	8" x 5"		12	2		193	135		328	415
1940	8" x 6"		12	2		188	135		323	410
1942	10" x 4"		12.50	1.920		276	129		405	500
1943	10" x 6"		11.50	2.087		310	140		450	550
1944	10" x 8"		9.50	2.526		310	170		480	595
1945	12" x 4"		11.50	2.087		450	140		590	705
1946	12" x 6"		11	2.182		480	147		627	750
1947	12" x 8"		9	2.667		495	179		674	810
1948	12" x 10"		8.50	2.824		505	190		695	840
1949	15" x 6"	Q-3	12	2.667		940	183		1,123	1,300
1950	15" x 8"		10	3.200		1,025	219		1,244	1,450
1951	15" x 10"		9.50	3.368		1,050	231		1,281	1,525
1952	15" x 12"		9	3.556		1,075	244		1,319	1,550
1960	Increaser, 2" x 3"	Q-1	15	1.067		70.50	69		139.50	181
1980	2" x 4"		14	1.143		100	74		174	221
2000	2" x 5"		13	1.231		74.50	80		154.50	201
2020	3" x 4"		13	1.231		110	80		190	240
2040	3" x 5"		13	1.231		74.50	80		154.50	201
2060	3" x 6"		12	1.333		99	86.50		185.50	238
2070	4" x 5"		13	1.231		131	80		211	263
2080	4" x 6"		12	1.333		149	86.50		235.50	293
2090	4" x 8"	Q-2	13	1.846		310	124		434	525
2100	5" x 6"	Q-1	11	1.455		221	94.50		315.50	385
2110	5" x 8"	Q-2	12	2		234	135		369	460

22 13 Facility Sanitary Sewerage

22 13 16 – Sanitary Waste and Vent Piping

22 13 16.30 Pipe Fittings, Cast Iron		Crew	Daily Output	Labor-Hours	Unit	Material	2023 Bare Costs Labor	Equipment	Total	Total Incl O&P
2120	6" x 8"	Q-2	12	2	Ea.	355	135		490	595
2130	6" x 10"		8	3		430	202		632	770
2140	8" x 10"		6.50	3.692		655	248		903	1,100
2150	10" x 12"	↓	5.50	4.364		785	293		1,078	1,300
2500	Y, 2"	Q-1	10	1.600		54.50	104		158.50	215
2510	3"		9	1.778		101	115		216	283
2520	4"	↓	8	2		135	130		265	340
2530	5"	Q-2	12	2		239	135		374	465
2540	6"	"	11	2.182		310	147		457	560
2550	8"	Q-3	7	4.571		760	315		1,075	1,300
2560	10"		6	5.333		1,225	365		1,590	1,900
2570	12"		5	6.400		3,100	440		3,540	4,050
2580	15"	↓	4	8	↓	6,175	550		6,725	7,625
2581	Y, reducing									
2582	3" x 2"	Q-1	10	1.600	Ea.	78	104		182	241
2584	4" x 2"		9.50	1.684		105	109		214	278
2586	4" x 3"	↓	9	1.778		116	115		231	299
2588	6" x 2"	Q-2	12.50	1.920		207	129		336	420
2590	6" x 3"		12.25	1.959		211	132		343	430
2592	6" x 4"	↓	12	2		209	135		344	430
2594	8" x 2"	Q-3	11	2.909		465	200		665	805
2596	8" x 3"		10.50	3.048		465	209		674	820
2598	8" x 4"		10	3.200		400	219		619	765
2600	8" x 6"		9	3.556		495	244		739	910
2602	10" x 3"		10	3.200		695	219		914	1,100
2604	10" x 4"		9.50	3.368		685	231		916	1,100
2606	10" x 6"		8	4		745	274		1,019	1,225
2608	10" x 8"		8	4		1,025	274		1,299	1,525
2610	12" x 4"		9	3.556		1,150	244		1,394	1,650
2612	12" x 6"		8.50	3.765		1,200	258		1,458	1,675
2614	12" x 8"		8	4		1,475	274		1,749	2,025
2616	12" x 10"		7.50	4.267		2,725	293		3,018	3,425
2618	15" x 4"		7	4.571		3,875	315		4,190	4,725
2620	15" x 6"		6.50	4.923		4,025	340		4,365	4,950
2622	15" x 8"		6.50	4.923		4,100	340		4,440	5,025
2624	15" x 10"		5	6.400		4,275	440		4,715	5,350
2626	15" x 12"	↓	4.50	7.111		4,350	490		4,840	5,500
3000	For extra heavy, add				↓	44%	4%			
3600	Hub and spigot, service weight gasket joint									
3605	Note: gaskets and joint labor have									
3606	been included with all listed fittings.									
3610	1/4 bend, 2"	Q-1	20	.800	Ea.	57	52		109	140
3620	3"		17	.941		75.50	61		136.50	174
3630	4"	↓	15	1.067		113	69		182	227
3640	5"	Q-2	21	1.143		161	77		238	292
3650	6"	"	19	1.263		193	85		278	340
3660	8"	Q-3	12	2.667		550	183		733	880
3670	10"		11	2.909		825	200		1,025	1,200
3680	12"		10	3.200		1,100	219		1,319	1,550
3690	15"	↓	8	4		3,450	274		3,724	4,200
3692	Short sweep, CI, 90°, 2"	Q-1	20	.800		56	52		108	139
3693	3"		17	.941		93	61		154	193
3694	4"	↓	15	1.067		137	69		206	254

22 13 Facility Sanitary Sewerage

22 13 16 – Sanitary Waste and Vent Piping

22 13 16.30 Pipe Fittings, Cast Iron		Crew	Daily Output	Labor-Hours	Unit	Material	2023 Bare Costs Labor	Equipment	Total	Total Incl O&P
3695	6"	Q-2	19	1.263	Ea.	269	85		354	425
3696	8"	Q-3	12	2.667		585	183		768	920
3697	10"		11	2.909		1,175	200		1,375	1,600
3698	12"		10	3.200		2,575	219		2,794	3,175
3700	Closet bend, 3" diameter with ring 10" x 16"	Q-1	17	.941		253	61		314	370
3710	16" x 16"		15	1.067		281	69		350	415
3730	Closet bend, 4" diameter, 1" x 4" ring, 6" x 16"		15	1.067		228	69		297	355
3740	8" x 16"		15	1.067		202	69		271	325
3750	10" x 12"		14	1.143		190	74		264	320
3760	10" x 18"		13	1.231		269	80		349	415
3770	12" x 16"		13	1.231		230	80		310	370
3780	16" x 16"		12	1.333		293	86.50		379.50	450
3786	Long sweep elbow									
3787	2"	Q-1	20	.800	Ea.	79	52		131	165
3788	3"		17	.941		111	61		172	213
3789	4"		15	1.067		159	69		228	278
3790	6"	Q-2	19	1.263		310	85		395	465
3791	8"	Q-3	12	2.667		700	183		883	1,050
3792	10"		11	2.909		1,175	200		1,375	1,600
3793	12"		10	3.200		1,875	219		2,094	2,375
3794	15"		8	4		4,700	274		4,974	5,550
3800	1/8 bend, 2"	Q-1	20	.800		44.50	52		96.50	127
3810	3"		17	.941		66	61		127	164
3820	4"		15	1.067		92.50	69		161.50	205
3830	5"	Q-2	21	1.143		134	77		211	263
3840	6"	"	19	1.263		155	85		240	298
3850	8"	Q-3	12	2.667		435	183		618	755
3860	10"		11	2.909		650	200		850	1,000
3870	12"		10	3.200		1,150	219		1,369	1,575
3880	15"		8	4		2,500	274		2,774	3,150
3882	Sanitary tee, tapped									
3884	2" x 2"	Q-1	11	1.455	Ea.	109	94.50		203.50	261
3886	3" x 2"		10	1.600		122	104		226	289
3888	4" x 2"		9	1.778		183	115		298	375
3890	Sanitary cross, tapped [double tapped sanitary tee]									
3892	2" x 2"	Q-1	9	1.778	Ea.	112	115		227	295
3894	3" x 2"		8	2		190	130		320	400
3896	4" x 2"		7	2.286		191	148		339	430
3900	Sanitary tee, 2"		12	1.333		88	86.50		174.50	226
3910	3"		10	1.600		133	104		237	300
3920	4"		9	1.778		164	115		279	355
3930	5"	Q-2	13	1.846		310	124		434	525
3940	6"	"	11	2.182		340	147		487	595
3950	8"	Q-3	8.50	3.765		870	258		1,128	1,350
3952	10"		8	4		1,575	274		1,849	2,150
3954	12"		7	4.571		2,650	315		2,965	3,400
3956	15"		6	5.333		5,100	365		5,465	6,150
3960	Sanitary tee, reducing									
3961	3" x 2"	Q-1	10.50	1.524	Ea.	115	99		214	274
3962	4" x 2"		10	1.600		138	104		242	305
3963	4" x 3"		9.50	1.684		150	109		259	330
3964	5" x 3"	Q-2	13.50	1.778		260	120		380	465
3965	6" x 2"		13	1.846		260	124		384	470

22 13 Facility Sanitary Sewerage

22 13 16 — Sanitary Waste and Vent Piping

22 13 16.30 Pipe Fittings, Cast Iron		Crew	Daily Output	Labor-Hours	Unit	Material	2023 Bare Costs Labor	Equipment	Total	Total Incl O&P
3966	6" x 3"	Q-2	12.50	1.920	Ea.	272	129		401	490
3967	6" x 4"	↓	12	2		360	135		495	600
3968	8" x 4"	Q-3	10.50	3.048		555	209		764	920
3969	8" x 5"		10	3.200		525	219		744	900
3970	8" x 6"		9.50	3.368		715	231		946	1,125
3971	10" x 6"		9	3.556		1,200	244		1,444	1,700
3972	12" x 8"		8.50	3.765		2,100	258		2,358	2,700
3973	15" x 10"	↓	6	5.333		2,350	365		2,715	3,125
3980	Tee, 2"	Q-1	12	1.333		115	86.50		201.50	255
3990	3"		10	1.600		165	104		269	335
4000	4"	↓	9	1.778		211	115		326	405
4010	5"	Q-2	13	1.846		420	124		544	650
4020	6"	"	11	2.182		420	147		567	680
4030	8"	Q-3	8	4	↓	525	274		799	985
4060	Combination Y and 1/8 bend									
4070	2"	Q-1	12	1.333	Ea.	103	86.50		189.50	243
4080	3"		10	1.600		150	104		254	320
4090	4"	↓	9	1.778		203	115		318	395
4100	5"	Q-2	13	1.846		370	124		494	590
4110	6"	"	11	2.182		450	147		597	715
4120	8"	Q-3	8	4		1,100	274		1,374	1,600
4121	12"	"	7	4.571	↓	1,675	315		1,990	2,300
4130	Combination Y & 1/8 bend, reducing									
4132	3" x 2"	Q-1	10.50	1.524	Ea.	118	99		217	277
4134	4" x 2"		10	1.600		153	104		257	325
4136	4" x 3"	↓	9.50	1.684		177	109		286	360
4138	6" x 2"	Q-2	13	1.846		294	124		418	510
4140	6" x 3"		12.50	1.920		315	129		444	540
4142	6" x 4"	↓	12	2		330	135		465	565
4144	8" x 2"	Q-3	11	2.909		630	200		830	990
4146	8" x 4"		10.50	3.048		555	209		764	920
4148	8" x 6"	↓	9.50	3.368		735	231		966	1,150
4160	Double Y, 2"	Q-1	10	1.600		175	104		279	350
4170	3"		8	2		220	130		350	435
4180	4"	↓	7	2.286		285	148		433	535
4190	5"	Q-2	10	2.400		525	161		686	820
4200	6"	"	9	2.667		675	179		854	1,000
4210	8"	Q-3	6	5.333		1,600	365		1,965	2,325
4220	10"		5	6.400		3,700	440		4,140	4,725
4230	12"	↓	4.50	7.111	↓	4,300	490		4,790	5,450
4234	Combination double Y & 1/8 bend									
4235	2"	Q-1	10	1.600	Ea.	196	104		300	370
4236	3"		8	2		251	130		381	470
4237	4"	↓	7	2.286		390	148		538	650
4238	6"	Q-2	9	2.667	↓	1,225	179		1,404	1,625
4242	Combination double Y & 1/8 bend, CI, reducing									
4243	3" x 2"	Q-1	9	1.778	Ea.	217	115		332	410
4244	4" x 2"		8	2		250	130		380	470
4245	4" x 3"	↓	7.50	2.133		285	138		423	520
4246	6" x 4"	Q-2	10	2.400	↓	810	161		971	1,125
4248	Double Y, CI, reducing									
4249	3" x 2"	Q-1	9	1.778	Ea.	188	115		303	380
4250	4" x 2"	↓	8	2	↓	221	130		351	435

22 13 Facility Sanitary Sewerage

22 13 16 – Sanitary Waste and Vent Piping

22 13 16.30 Pipe Fittings, Cast Iron		Crew	Daily Output	Labor-Hours	Unit	Material	2023 Bare Costs Labor	Equipment	Total	Total Incl O&P
4251	4" x 3"	Q-1	7.50	2.133	Ea.	220	138		358	450
4252	6" x 3"	Q-2	10.50	2.286		505	154		659	785
4253	6" x 4"	"	10	2.400		520	161		681	815
4254	8" x 4"	Q-3	9.50	3.368		1,075	231		1,306	1,525
4255	8" x 6"		9	3.556		1,125	244		1,369	1,625
4256	10" x 6"		8.50	3.765		2,275	258		2,533	2,900
4257	10" x 8"		7.50	4.267		3,475	293		3,768	4,250
4258	12" x 6"		8	4		4,100	274		4,374	4,900
4259	12" x 8"	▼	7	4.571		4,100	315		4,415	5,000
4260	Reducer, 3" x 2"	Q-1	17	.941		74.50	61		135.50	173
4270	4" x 2"		16.50	.970		85	63		148	188
4280	4" x 3"		16	1		95.50	65		160.50	202
4290	5" x 2"		16	1		166	65		231	279
4300	5" x 3"		15.50	1.032		176	67		243	294
4310	5" x 4"		15	1.067		129	69		198	245
4320	6" x 2"		15.50	1.032		165	67		232	282
4330	6" x 3"		15	1.067		167	69		236	287
4336	6" x 4"		14	1.143		170	74		244	298
4340	6" x 5"	▼	13	1.231		192	80		272	330
4360	8" x 3"	Q-2	15	1.600		315	108		423	505
4370	8" x 4"		15	1.600		288	108		396	475
4380	8" x 5"		14	1.714		310	115		425	510
4390	8" x 6"		14	1.714		305	115		420	510
4394	10" x 4"		13.50	1.778		440	120		560	665
4395	10" x 6"		13	1.846		490	124		614	720
4396	10" x 8"		12.50	1.920		535	129		664	780
4397	12" x 4"		12	2		655	135		790	920
4398	12" x 6"		11.50	2.087		700	140		840	980
4399	12" x 8"		11	2.182		760	147		907	1,050
4400	12" x 10"	▼	10.50	2.286		825	154		979	1,150
4401	15" x 6"	Q-3	13	2.462		1,200	169		1,369	1,550
4402	15" x 8"		12	2.667		1,325	183		1,508	1,725
4403	15" x 10"		11	2.909		1,425	200		1,625	1,850
4404	15" x 12"	▼	10	3.200		1,475	219		1,694	1,950
4430	Increaser, 2" x 3"	Q-1	17	.941		89	61		150	189
4440	2" x 4"		16	1		123	65		188	232
4450	2" x 5"		15	1.067		111	69		180	225
4460	3" x 4"		15	1.067		133	69		202	249
4470	3" x 5"		15	1.067		111	69		180	225
4480	3" x 6"		14	1.143		136	74		210	261
4490	4" x 5"		15	1.067		167	69		236	286
4500	4" x 6"	▼	14	1.143		186	74		260	315
4510	4" x 8"	Q-2	15	1.600		390	108		498	590
4520	5" x 6"	Q-1	13	1.231		258	80		338	405
4530	5" x 8"	Q-2	14	1.714		315	115		430	520
4540	6" x 8"		14	1.714		440	115		555	655
4550	6" x 10"		10	2.400		570	161		731	870
4560	8" x 10"		8.50	2.824		800	190		990	1,175
4570	10" x 12"	▼	7.50	3.200		965	215		1,180	1,375
4600	Y, 2"	Q-1	12	1.333		83	86.50		169.50	220
4610	3"		10	1.600		137	104		241	305
4620	4"	▼	9	1.778		181	115		296	370
4630	5"	Q-2	13	1.846		310	124		434	530

For customer support on your Plumbing Costs with RSMeans data, call 800.448.8182.

22 13 Facility Sanitary Sewerage
22 13 16 – Sanitary Waste and Vent Piping

22 13 16.30 Pipe Fittings, Cast Iron		Crew	Daily Output	Labor-Hours	Unit	Material	2023 Bare Costs Labor	Equipment	Total	Total Incl O&P
4640	6"	Q-2	11	2.182	Ea.	385	147		532	645
4650	8"	Q-3	8	4		925	274		1,199	1,425
4660	10"		7	4.571		1,500	315		1,815	2,125
4670	12"		6	5.333		3,450	365		3,815	4,350
4672	15"	↓	5	6.400	↓	6,600	440		7,040	7,925
4680	Y, reducing									
4681	3" x 2"	Q-1	10.50	1.524	Ea.	111	99		210	269
4682	4" x 2"		10	1.600		142	104		246	310
4683	4" x 3"	↓	9.50	1.684		157	109		266	335
4684	6" x 2"	Q-2	13	1.846		259	124		383	470
4685	6" x 3"		12.50	1.920		267	129		396	485
4686	6" x 4"	↓	12	2		270	135		405	500
4687	8" x 2"	Q-3	11	2.909		560	200		760	915
4688	8" x 3"		10.75	2.977		565	204		769	925
4689	8" x 4"		10.50	3.048		505	209		714	865
4690	8" x 6"		9.50	3.368		615	231		846	1,025
4691	10" x 3"		10	3.200		855	219		1,074	1,275
4692	10" x 4"		9.50	3.368		850	231		1,081	1,275
4693	10" x 6"		9	3.556		925	244		1,169	1,400
4694	10" x 8"		8.80	3.636		1,250	249		1,499	1,750
4695	12" x 4"		9.50	3.368		1,350	231		1,581	1,850
4696	12" x 6"		9	3.556		1,400	244		1,644	1,925
4697	12" x 8"		8.50	3.765		1,750	258		2,008	2,300
4698	12" x 10"		8	4		3,050	274		3,324	3,750
4699	15" x 4"		8	4		4,100	274		4,374	4,925
4700	15" x 6"		7.50	4.267		4,300	293		4,593	5,150
4701	15" x 8"		7	4.571		4,400	315		4,715	5,325
4702	15" x 10"		6	5.333		4,625	365		4,990	5,625
4703	15" x 12"	↓	5	6.400	↓	4,750	440		5,190	5,875
4900	For extra heavy, add					44%	4%			
4940	Gasket and making push-on joint									
4950	2"	Q-1	40	.400	Ea.	14.30	26		40.30	54
4960	3"		35	.457		18.35	29.50		47.85	64
4970	4"	↓	32	.500		23	32.50		55.50	74
4980	5"	Q-2	43	.558		36	37.50		73.50	96
4990	6"	"	40	.600		37.50	40.50		78	101
5000	8"	Q-3	32	1		82	68.50		150.50	192
5010	10"		29	1.103		142	75.50		217.50	270
5020	12"		25	1.280		182	88		270	330
5022	15"	↓	21	1.524	↓	217	105		322	395
5030	Note: gaskets and joint labor have									
5040	been included with all listed fittings.									
5990	No hub									
6000	Cplg. & labor required at joints not incl. in fitting									
6010	price. Add 1 coupling per joint for installed price									
6020	1/4 bend, 1-1/2"				Ea.	22			22	24
6060	2"					24			24	26.50
6080	3"					33.50			33.50	37
6120	4"					49.50			49.50	54.50
6140	5"					111			111	123
6160	6"					123			123	136
6180	8"					335			335	370
6181	10"				↓	670			670	740

22 13 Facility Sanitary Sewerage

22 13 16 – Sanitary Waste and Vent Piping

22 13 16.30 Pipe Fittings, Cast Iron		Crew	Daily Output	Labor-Hours	Unit	Material	2023 Bare Costs Labor	Equipment	Total	Total Incl O&P
6182	12"				Ea.	2,100			2,100	2,300
6183	15"					2,750			2,750	3,025
6184	1/4 bend, long sweep, 1-1/2"					56			56	61.50
6186	2"					52.50			52.50	57.50
6188	3"					63.50			63.50	69.50
6189	4"					101			101	111
6190	5"					182			182	200
6191	6"					223			223	245
6192	8"					390			390	430
6193	10"					750			750	830
6200	1/8 bend, 1-1/2"					18.25			18.25	20
6210	2"					20.50			20.50	22.50
6212	3"					27.50			27.50	30.50
6214	4"					36.50			36.50	40
6216	5"					75.50			75.50	83
6218	6"					80.50			80.50	88.50
6220	8"					231			231	255
6222	10"					440			440	485
6364	Closet flange									
6366	4"				Ea.	33.50			33.50	37
6370	Closet bend, no hub									
6376	4" x 16"				Ea.	178			178	195
6380	Sanitary tee, tapped, 1-1/2"					40.50			40.50	45
6382	2" x 1-1/2"					36			36	39.50
6384	2"					41.50			41.50	45.50
6386	3" x 2"					57.50			57.50	63.50
6388	3"					106			106	117
6390	4" x 1-1/2"					51			51	56
6392	4" x 2"					58			58	63.50
6393	4"					58			58	63.50
6394	6" x 1-1/2"					137			137	151
6396	6" x 2"					145			145	160
6459	Sanitary tee, 1-1/2"					31			31	34
6460	2"					33			33	36.50
6470	3"					40.50			40.50	45
6472	4"					77			77	85
6474	5"					180			180	198
6476	6"					184			184	202
6478	8"					745			745	820
6480	10"					580			580	635
6724	Sanitary tee, reducing									
6725	3" x 2"				Ea.	36			36	39.50
6726	4" x 3"					59.50			59.50	65
6727	5" x 4"					139			139	153
6728	6" x 3"					135			135	149
6729	8" x 4"					395			395	430
6730	Y, 1-1/2"					31			31	34.50
6740	2"					30.50			30.50	33.50
6750	3"					44.50			44.50	49
6760	4"					71.50			71.50	78.50
6762	5"					169			169	186
6764	6"					189			189	208
6768	8"					445			445	490

For customer support on your Plumbing Costs with RSMeans data, call 800.448.8182.

22 13 Facility Sanitary Sewerage
22 13 16 – Sanitary Waste and Vent Piping

22 13 16.30 Pipe Fittings, Cast Iron		Crew	Daily Output	Labor-Hours	Unit	Material	2023 Bare Costs Labor	Equipment	Total	Total Incl O&P
6769	10"				Ea.	990			990	1,100
6770	12"					1,950			1,950	2,150
6771	15"					4,525			4,525	5,000
6791	Y, reducing, 3" x 2"					33			33	36.50
6792	4" x 2"					47.50			47.50	52
6793	5" x 2"					105			105	115
6794	6" x 2"					116			116	128
6795	6" x 4"					151			151	166
6796	8" x 4"					260			260	286
6797	8" x 6"					320			320	350
6798	10" x 6"					720			720	790
6799	10" x 8"					860			860	950
6800	Double Y, 2"					48.50			48.50	53.50
6920	3"					89.50			89.50	98.50
7000	4"					182			182	200
7100	6"					320			320	355
7120	8"					945			945	1,050
7200	Combination Y and 1/8 bend									
7220	1-1/2"				Ea.	33.50			33.50	36.50
7260	2"					35			35	38.50
7320	3"					55			55	60.50
7400	4"					106			106	117
7480	5"					216			216	238
7500	6"					290			290	320
7520	8"					680			680	745
7800	Reducer, 3" x 2"					17.20			17.20	18.95
7820	4" x 2"					26			26	28.50
7840	4" x 3"					26			26	28.50
7842	6" x 3"					70			70	77
7844	6" x 4"					70			70	77
7846	6" x 5"					72			72	79
7848	8" x 2"					111			111	122
7850	8" x 3"					103			103	113
7852	8" x 4"					108			108	119
7854	8" x 5"					122			122	134
7856	8" x 6"					120			120	132
7858	10" x 4"					212			212	234
7860	10" x 6"					225			225	247
7862	10" x 8"					263			263	290
7864	12" x 4"					440			440	485
7866	12" x 6"					470			470	520
7868	12" x 8"					485			485	535
7870	12" x 10"					490			490	540
7872	15" x 4"					950			950	1,050
7874	15" x 6"					895			895	985
7876	15" x 8"					1,025			1,025	1,125
7878	15" x 10"					1,075			1,075	1,175
7880	15" x 12"					1,050			1,050	1,150
8000	Coupling, standard (by CISPI Mfrs.)									
8020	1-1/2"	Q-1	48	.333	Ea.	15.65	21.50		37.15	49
8040	2"		44	.364		17.45	23.50		40.95	54
8080	3"		38	.421		20.50	27.50		48	63
8120	4"		33	.485		27	31.50		58.50	76.50

22 13 Facility Sanitary Sewerage

22 13 16 – Sanitary Waste and Vent Piping

22 13 16.30 Pipe Fittings, Cast Iron		Crew	Daily Output	Labor-Hours	Unit	Material	2023 Bare Costs Labor	Equipment	Total	Total Incl O&P
8160	5"	Q-2	44	.545	Ea.	68	36.50		104.50	129
8180	6"	"	40	.600		69	40.50		109.50	136
8200	8"	Q-3	33	.970		113	66.50		179.50	223
8220	10"	"	26	1.231		139	84.50		223.50	279
8300	Coupling, cast iron clamp & neoprene gasket (by MG)									
8310	1-1/2"	Q-1	48	.333	Ea.	10.95	21.50		32.45	44
8320	2"		44	.364		14.70	23.50		38.20	51
8330	3"		38	.421		14.40	27.50		41.90	56.50
8340	4"		33	.485		22	31.50		53.50	71
8350	5"	Q-2	44	.545		40.50	36.50		77	99
8360	6"	"	40	.600		39	40.50		79.50	103
8380	8"	Q-3	33	.970		125	66.50		191.50	237
8400	10"	"	26	1.231		197	84.50		281.50	345
8410	Reducing, no hub									
8416	2" x 1-1/2"	Q-1	44	.364	Ea.	12.15	23.50		35.65	48.50
8600	Coupling, stainless steel, heavy duty									
8620	1-1/2"	Q-1	48	.333	Ea.	6	21.50		27.50	38.50
8630	2"		44	.364		6.50	23.50		30	42
8640	2" x 1-1/2"		44	.364		14.65	23.50		38.15	51
8650	3"		38	.421		6.80	27.50		34.30	48
8660	4"		33	.485		7.65	31.50		39.15	55.50
8670	4" x 3"		33	.485		21	31.50		52.50	70
8680	5"	Q-2	44	.545		16.75	36.50		53.25	73
8690	6"	"	40	.600		18.45	40.50		58.95	80.50
8700	8"	Q-3	33	.970		31	66.50		97.50	134
8710	10"		26	1.231		39.50	84.50		124	170
8712	12"		22	1.455		81	100		181	238
8715	15"		18	1.778		126	122		248	320

22 13 16.40 Pipe Fittings, Cast Iron for Drainage		Crew	Daily Output	Labor-Hours	Unit	Material	2023 Bare Costs Labor	Equipment	Total	Total Incl O&P
0010	**PIPE FITTINGS, CAST IRON FOR DRAINAGE**, Special									
0020	Cast iron, drainage, threaded, black									
0030	90° elbow, straight									
0031	1-1/2" pipe size	Q-1	20	.800	Ea.	65	52		117	149
0032	2" pipe size		18	.889		98	57.50		155.50	194
0033	3" pipe size		10	1.600		370	104		474	560
0034	4" pipe size		6	2.667		580	173		753	900
0040	90° long turn elbow, straight									
0041	1-1/2" pipe size	Q-1	20	.800	Ea.	91	52		143	178
0042	2" pipe size		18	.889		135	57.50		192.50	235
0043	3" pipe size		10	1.600		495	104		599	700
0044	4" pipe size		6	2.667		910	173		1,083	1,250
0050	90° street elbow, straight									
0051	1-1/2" pipe size	Q-1	20	.800	Ea.	92.50	52		144.50	180
0052	2" pipe size	"	18	.889	"	123	57.50		180.50	221
0060	45° elbow									
0061	1-1/2" pipe size	Q-1	20	.800	Ea.	63.50	52		115.50	148
0062	2" pipe size		18	.889		91.50	57.50		149	187
0063	3" pipe size		10	1.600		360	104		464	550
0064	4" pipe size		6	2.667		560	173		733	880
0070	45° street elbow									
0071	1-1/2" pipe size	Q-1	20	.800	Ea.	86.50	52		138.50	173
0072	2" pipe size	"	18	.889	"	140	57.50		197.50	240

22 13 Facility Sanitary Sewerage

22 13 16 – Sanitary Waste and Vent Piping

22 13 16.40 Pipe Fittings, Cast Iron for Drainage		Crew	Daily Output	Labor-Hours	Unit	Material	2023 Bare Costs Labor	Equipment	Total	Total Incl O&P
0092	Tees, straight									
0093	1-1/2" pipe size	Q-1	13	1.231	Ea.	107	80		187	236
0094	2" pipe size	"	11	1.455	"	177	94.50		271.50	335
0100	TY's, straight									
0101	1-1/2" pipe size	Q-1	13	1.231	Ea.	105	80		185	234
0102	2" pipe size		11	1.455		173	94.50		267.50	330
0103	3" pipe size		6	2.667		685	173		858	1,025
0104	4" pipe size	↓	4	4	↓	945	259		1,204	1,400
0120	45° Y branch, straight									
0121	1-1/2" pipe size	Q-1	13	1.231	Ea.	128	80		208	260
0122	2" pipe size		11	1.455		240	94.50		334.50	405
0123	3" pipe size		6	2.667		825	173		998	1,175
0124	4" pipe size	↓	4	4		1,225	259		1,484	1,725
0147	Double Y branch, straight									
0148	1-1/2" pipe size	Q-1	10	1.600	Ea.	345	104		449	535
0149	2" pipe size	"	7	2.286	"	291	148		439	540
0160	P trap									
0161	1-1/2" pipe size	Q-1	15	1.067	Ea.	191	69		260	315
0162	2" pipe size		13	1.231		325	80		405	480
0163	3" pipe size		7	2.286		1,075	148		1,223	1,400
0164	4" pipe size	↓	5	3.200	↓	2,375	208		2,583	2,925
0180	Tucker connection									
0181	1-1/2" pipe size	Q-1	24	.667	Ea.	198	43		241	283
0182	2" pipe size	"	21	.762	"	244	49.50		293.50	345
0205	Cast iron, drainage, threaded, galvanized									
0206	90° elbow, straight									
0207	1-1/2" pipe size	Q-1	20	.800	Ea.	96.50	52		148.50	184
0208	2" pipe size		18	.889		146	57.50		203.50	246
0209	3" pipe size		10	1.600		550	104		654	760
0210	4" pipe size	↓	6	2.667		1,075	173		1,248	1,425
0216	90° long turn elbow, straight									
0217	1-1/2" pipe size	Q-1	20	.800	Ea.	110	52		162	198
0218	2" pipe size		18	.889		188	57.50		245.50	293
0219	3" pipe size		10	1.600		510	104		614	715
0220	4" pipe size	↓	6	2.667		720	173		893	1,050
0226	90° street elbow, straight									
0227	1-1/2" pipe size	Q-1	20	.800	Ea.	122	52		174	212
0228	2" pipe size	"	18	.889	"	200	57.50		257.50	305
0236	45° elbow									
0237	1-1/2" pipe size	Q-1	20	.800	Ea.	95	52		147	183
0238	2" pipe size		18	.889		136	57.50		193.50	236
0239	3" pipe size		10	1.600		475	104		579	675
0240	4" pipe size	↓	6	2.667	↓	775	173		948	1,100
0246	45° street elbow									
0247	1-1/2" pipe size	Q-1	20	.800	Ea.	126	52		178	217
0248	2" pipe size	"	18	.889	"	194	57.50		251.50	300
0268	Tees, straight									
0269	1-1/2" pipe size	Q-1	13	1.231	Ea.	145	80		225	278
0270	2" pipe size	"	11	1.455	"	242	94.50		336.50	410
0276	TY's, straight									
0277	1-1/2" pipe size	Q-1	13	1.231	Ea.	147	80		227	280
0278	2" pipe size		11	1.455		240	94.50		334.50	405
0279	3" pipe size	↓	6	2.667		1,025	173		1,198	1,375

22 13 Facility Sanitary Sewerage

22 13 16 – Sanitary Waste and Vent Piping

22 13 16.40 Pipe Fittings, Cast Iron for Drainage

		Crew	Daily Output	Labor-Hours	Unit	Material	2023 Bare Costs Labor	Equipment	Total	Total Incl O&P
0280	4" pipe size	Q-1	4	4	Ea.	1,150	259		1,409	1,650
0296	45° Y branch, straight									
0297	1-1/2" pipe size	Q-1	13	1.231	Ea.	163	80		243	298
0298	2" pipe size		11	1.455		325	94.50		419.50	500
0299	3" pipe size		6	2.667		1,200	173		1,373	1,575
0300	4" pipe size	↓	4	4	↓	1,775	259		2,034	2,325
0323	Double Y branch, straight									
0324	1-1/2" pipe size	Q-1	10	1.600	Ea.	217	104		321	395
0325	2" pipe size	"	7	2.286	"	550	148		698	825
0336	P trap									
0337	1-1/2" pipe size	Q-1	15	1.067	Ea.	263	69		332	390
0338	2" pipe size		13	1.231		330	80		410	480
0339	3" pipe size		7	2.286		1,575	148		1,723	1,950
0340	4" pipe size	↓	5	3.200	↓	2,350	208		2,558	2,875
0356	Tucker connection									
0357	1-1/2" pipe size	Q-1	24	.667	Ea.	300	43		343	395
0358	2" pipe size	"	21	.762	"	450	49.50		499.50	575
1000	Drip pan elbow (safety valve discharge elbow)									
1010	Cast iron, threaded inlet									
1014	2-1/2"	Q-1	8	2	Ea.	2,450	130		2,580	2,900
1015	3"		6.40	2.500		2,625	162		2,787	3,150
1017	4"	↓	4.80	3.333	↓	3,550	216		3,766	4,225
1018	Cast iron, flanged inlet									
1019	6"	Q-2	3.60	6.667	Ea.	2,975	450		3,425	3,950
1020	8"	"	2.60	9.231	"	3,700	620		4,320	5,000

22 13 16.50 Shower Drains

		Crew	Daily Output	Labor-Hours	Unit	Material	Labor	Equipment	Total	Total Incl O&P
0010	**SHOWER DRAINS**									
2780	Shower, with strainer, uniform diam. trap, bronze top									
2800	2" and 3" pipe size	Q-1	8	2	Ea.	530	130		660	780
2820	4" pipe size	"	7	2.286		605	148		753	885
2840	For galvanized body, add				↓	320			320	350
2860	With strainer, backwater valve, drum trap									
2880	1-1/2", 2" & 3" pipe size	Q-1	8	2	Ea.	530	130		660	775
2890	4" pipe size	"	7	2.286		735	148		883	1,025
2900	For galvanized body, add				↓	253			253	278

22 13 16.60 Traps

		Crew	Daily Output	Labor-Hours	Unit	Material	Labor	Equipment	Total	Total Incl O&P
0010	**TRAPS**									
0030	Cast iron, service weight									
0050	Running P trap, without vent									
1100	2"	Q-1	16	1	Ea.	240	65		305	360
1140	3"		14	1.143		240	74		314	375
1150	4"	↓	13	1.231		305	80		385	460
1160	6"	Q-2	17	1.412	↓	1,350	95		1,445	1,650
1180	Running trap, single hub, with vent									
2080	3" pipe size, 3" vent	Q-1	14	1.143	Ea.	244	74		318	380
2120	4" pipe size, 4" vent	"	13	1.231		330	80		410	485
2140	5" pipe size, 4" vent	Q-2	11	2.182		530	147		677	800
2160	6" pipe size, 4" vent		10	2.400		1,425	161		1,586	1,825
2180	6" pipe size, 6" vent	↓	8	3		1,275	202		1,477	1,700
2200	8" pipe size, 4" vent	Q-3	10	3.200		6,575	219		6,794	7,550
2220	8" pipe size, 6" vent	"	8	4	↓	5,075	274		5,349	5,975
2300	For double hub, vent, add					10%	20%			

22 13 Facility Sanitary Sewerage

22 13 16 – Sanitary Waste and Vent Piping

22 13 16.60 Traps		Crew	Daily Output	Labor-Hours	Unit	Material	2023 Bare Costs Labor	Equipment	Total	Total Incl O&P
2800	S trap,									
2850	4" pipe size	Q-1	13	1.231	Ea.	123	80		203	254
3000	P trap, B&S, 2" pipe size		16	1		73	65		138	177
3040	3" pipe size		14	1.143		109	74		183	231
3060	4" pipe size		13	1.231		157	80		237	292
3080	5" pipe size	Q-2	18	1.333		390	89.50		479.50	565
3100	6" pipe size	"	17	1.412		485	95		580	670
3120	8" pipe size	Q-3	11	2.909		1,450	200		1,650	1,900
3130	10" pipe size	"	10	3.200		2,350	219		2,569	2,900
3150	P trap, no hub, 1-1/2" pipe size	Q-1	17	.941		39.50	61		100.50	135
3160	2" pipe size		16	1		37.50	65		102.50	138
3170	3" pipe size		14	1.143		82	74		156	201
3180	4" pipe size		13	1.231		145	80		225	279
3190	6" pipe size	Q-2	17	1.412		350	95		445	525
3350	Deep seal trap, B&S									
3400	1-1/4" pipe size	Q-1	14	1.143	Ea.	101	74		175	222
3410	1-1/2" pipe size		14	1.143		101	74		175	222
3420	2" pipe size		14	1.143		109	74		183	231
3440	3" pipe size		12	1.333		134	86.50		220.50	277
3460	4" pipe size		11	1.455		213	94.50		307.50	375
3500	For trap primer connection, add					1/8			178	196
3540	For trap with floor cleanout, add					70%	5%			
3580	For trap with adjustable cleanout, add	Q-1	10	1.600	Ea.	237	104		341	415
4700	Copper, drainage, drum trap									
4800	3" x 5" solid, 1-1/2" pipe size	1 Plum	16	.500	Ea.	660	36		696	780
4840	3" x 6" swivel, 1-1/2" pipe size	"	16	.500	"	1,450	36		1,486	1,650
5100	P trap, standard pattern									
5200	1-1/4" pipe size	1 Plum	18	.444	Ea.	435	32		467	525
5240	1-1/2" pipe size		17	.471		330	34		364	415
5260	2" pipe size		15	.533		510	38.50		548.50	620
5280	3" pipe size		11	.727		1,450	52.50		1,502.50	1,675
5340	With cleanout, swivel joint and slip joint									
5360	1-1/4" pipe size	1 Plum	18	.444	Ea.	197	32		229	265
5400	1-1/2" pipe size		17	.471		860	34		894	995
5420	2" pipe size		15	.533		740	38.50		778.50	870
5750	Chromed brass, tubular, P trap, without cleanout, 20 ga.									
5800	1-1/4" pipe size	1 Plum	18	.444	Ea.	22	32		54	72.50
5840	1-1/2" pipe size	"	17	.471	"	21	34		55	74
5900	With cleanout, 20 ga.									
5940	1-1/4" pipe size	1 Plum	18	.444	Ea.	38	32		70	89.50
6000	1-1/2" pipe size	"	17	.471	"	41	34		75	95.50
6350	S trap, without cleanout, 20 ga.									
6400	1-1/4" pipe size	1 Plum	18	.444	Ea.	58	32		90	112
6440	1-1/2" pipe size	"	17	.471	"	55.50	34		89.50	112
6550	With cleanout, 20 ga.									
6600	1-1/4" pipe size	1 Plum	18	.444	Ea.	98.50	32		130.50	157
6640	1-1/2" pipe size	"	17	.471		61.50	34		95.50	119
6660	Corrosion resistant, glass, P trap, 1-1/2" pipe size	Q-1	17	.941		105	61		166	207
6670	2" pipe size		16	1		138	65		203	248
6680	3" pipe size		14	1.143		282	74		356	420
6690	4" pipe size		13	1.231		420	80		500	585
6700	6" pipe size	Q-2	17	1.412		1,625	95		1,720	1,925
6710	ABS DWV P trap, solvent weld joint									

22 13 Facility Sanitary Sewerage

22 13 16 – Sanitary Waste and Vent Piping

22 13 16.60 Traps

		Crew	Daily Output	Labor-Hours	Unit	Material	2023 Bare Costs Labor	2023 Bare Costs Equipment	Total	Total Incl O&P
6720	1-1/2" pipe size	1 Plum	18	.444	Ea.	70	32		102	125
6722	2" pipe size		17	.471		85	34		119	144
6724	3" pipe size		15	.533		365	38.50		403.50	460
6726	4" pipe size		14	.571		670	41		711	795
6732	PVC DWV P trap, solvent weld joint									
6733	1-1/2" pipe size	1 Plum	18	.444	Ea.	57	32		89	111
6734	2" pipe size		17	.471		69	34		103	127
6735	3" pipe size		15	.533		233	38.50		271.50	315
6736	4" pipe size		14	.571		560	41		601	675
6760	PP DWV, dilution trap, 1-1/2" pipe size		16	.500		360	36		396	450
6770	P trap, 1-1/2" pipe size		17	.471		90	34		124	150
6780	2" pipe size		16	.500		133	36		169	200
6790	3" pipe size		14	.571		244	41		285	330
6800	4" pipe size		13	.615		410	44.50		454.50	515
6830	S trap, 1-1/2" pipe size		16	.500		74	36		110	135
6840	2" pipe size		15	.533		111	38.50		149.50	180
6850	Universal trap, 1-1/2" pipe size		14	.571		148	41		189	224
6860	PVC DWV hub x hub, basin trap, 1-1/4" pipe size		18	.444		57	32		89	111
6870	Sink P trap, 1-1/2" pipe size		18	.444		15.90	32		47.90	65.50
6880	Tubular S trap, 1-1/2" pipe size		17	.471		41	34		75	95.50
6890	PVC sch. 40 DWV, drum trap									
6900	1-1/2" pipe size	1 Plum	16	.500	Ea.	57.50	36		93.50	117
6910	P trap, 1-1/2" pipe size		18	.444		13.35	32		45.35	62.50
6920	2" pipe size		17	.471		17.95	34		51.95	70.50
6930	3" pipe size		15	.533		47	38.50		85.50	109
6940	4" pipe size		14	.571		139	41		180	214
6950	P trap w/clean out, 1-1/2" pipe size		18	.444		22.50	32		54.50	73
6960	2" pipe size		17	.471		27	34		61	80
6970	P trap adjustable, 1-1/2" pipe size		17	.471		15.25	34		49.25	67.50
6980	P trap adj. w/union & cleanout, 1-1/2" pipe size		16	.500		58.50	36		94.50	118
7000	Trap primer, flow through type, 1/2" diameter		24	.333		57.50	24		81.50	99
7100	With sediment strainer		22	.364		62	26		88	108
7450	Trap primer distribution unit									
7500	2 openings	1 Plum	18	.444	Ea.	40	32		72	92
7540	3 openings		17	.471		43	34		77	98
7560	4 openings		16	.500		45	36		81	103
7850	Trap primer manifold									
7900	2 outlet	1 Plum	18	.444	Ea.	77	32		109	133
7940	4 outlet		16	.500		122	36		158	189
7960	6 outlet		15	.533		170	38.50		208.50	245
7980	8 outlet		13	.615		219	44.50		263.50	305

22 13 16.80 Vent Flashing and Caps

		Crew	Daily Output	Labor-Hours	Unit	Material	2023 Bare Costs Labor	2023 Bare Costs Equipment	Total	Total Incl O&P
0010	**VENT FLASHING AND CAPS**									
0120	Vent caps									
0140	Cast iron									
0160	1-1/4" to 1-1/2" pipe	1 Plum	23	.348	Ea.	46.50	25		71.50	88.50
0170	2" to 2-1/8" pipe		22	.364		54	26		80	98
0180	2-1/2" to 3-5/8" pipe		21	.381		59	27.50		86.50	106
0190	4" to 4-1/8" pipe		19	.421		85	30.50		115.50	139
0200	5" to 6" pipe		17	.471		121	34		155	184
0300	PVC									
0320	1-1/4" to 1-1/2" pipe	1 Plum	24	.333	Ea.	15.80	24		39.80	53.50

For customer support on your Plumbing Costs with RSMeans data, call 800.448.8182.

22 13 Facility Sanitary Sewerage

22 13 16 – Sanitary Waste and Vent Piping

22 13 16.80 Vent Flashing and Caps

		Crew	Daily Output	Labor-Hours	Unit	Material	2023 Bare Costs Labor	Equipment	Total	Total Incl O&P
0330	2" to 2-1/8" pipe	1 Plum	23	.348	Ea.	17.85	25		42.85	57
0900	Vent flashing									
1000	Aluminum with lead ring									
1020	1-1/4" pipe	1 Plum	20	.400	Ea.	6.40	29		35.40	50
1030	1-1/2" pipe		20	.400		6.10	29		35.10	49.50
1040	2" pipe		18	.444		6.05	32		38.05	54.50
1050	3" pipe		17	.471		6.75	34		40.75	58
1060	4" pipe		16	.500		8.15	36		44.15	62.50
1350	Copper with neoprene ring									
1400	1-1/4" pipe	1 Plum	20	.400	Ea.	83.50	29		112.50	135
1430	1-1/2" pipe		20	.400		83.50	29		112.50	135
1440	2" pipe		18	.444		83.50	32		115.50	140
1450	3" pipe		17	.471		101	34		135	162
1460	4" pipe		16	.500		101	36		137	165
2000	Galvanized with neoprene ring									
2020	1-1/4" pipe	1 Plum	20	.400	Ea.	16.20	29		45.20	61
2030	1-1/2" pipe		20	.400		21.50	29		50.50	66.50
2040	2" pipe		18	.444		22	32		54	72
2050	3" pipe		17	.471		24	34		58	77
2060	4" pipe		16	.500		28	36		64	84
2980	Neoprene, one piece									
3000	1-1/4" pipe	1 Plum	24	.333	Ea.	3.64	24		27.64	40
3030	1-1/2" pipe		24	.333		3.61	24		27.61	40
3040	2" pipe		23	.348		5.60	25		30.60	43.50
3050	3" pipe		21	.381		7.55	27.50		35.05	49.50
3060	4" pipe		20	.400		11.25	29		40.25	55.50
4000	Lead, 4#, 8" skirt, vent through roof									
4100	2" pipe	1 Plum	18	.444	Ea.	49.50	32		81.50	103
4110	3" pipe		17	.471		56.50	34		90.50	113
4120	4" pipe		16	.500		64	36		100	124
4130	6" pipe		14	.571		96	41		137	167

22 13 19 – Sanitary Waste Piping Specialties

22 13 19.13 Sanitary Drains

		Crew	Daily Output	Labor-Hours	Unit	Material	2023 Bare Costs Labor	Equipment	Total	Total Incl O&P
0010	**SANITARY DRAINS**									
0400	Deck, auto park, CI, 13" top									
0440	3", 4", 5", and 6" pipe size	Q-1	8	2	Ea.	2,425	130		2,555	2,850
0480	For galvanized body, add				"	1,500			1,500	1,650
0800	Promenade, heelproof grate, CI, 14" top									
0840	2", 3", and 4" pipe size	Q-1	10	1.600	Ea.	1,075	104		1,179	1,350
0860	5" and 6" pipe size		9	1.778		1,350	115		1,465	1,675
0880	8" pipe size		8	2		1,375	130		1,505	1,700
0940	For galvanized body, add					775			775	855
0960	With polished bronze top, 2"-3"-4" diam.					1,825			1,825	2,000
1200	Promenade, heelproof grate, CI, lateral, 14" top									
1240	2", 3" and 4" pipe size	Q-1	10	1.600	Ea.	1,225	104		1,329	1,500
1260	5" and 6" pipe size		9	1.778		1,425	115		1,540	1,750
1280	8" pipe size		8	2		1,650	130		1,780	2,025
1340	For galvanized body, add					635			635	700
1360	For polished bronze top, add					1,225			1,225	1,350
1500	Promenade, slotted grate, CI, 11" top									
1540	2", 3", 4", 5", and 6" pipe size	Q-1	12	1.333	Ea.	640	86.50		726.50	830
1600	For galvanized body, add					445			445	490

22 13 Facility Sanitary Sewerage

22 13 19 – Sanitary Waste Piping Specialties

22 13 19.13 Sanitary Drains

		Crew	Daily Output	Labor-Hours	Unit	Material	2023 Bare Costs Labor	Equipment	Total	Total Incl O&P
1640	With polished bronze top				Ea.	1,300			1,300	1,425
2000	Floor, medium duty, CI, deep flange, 7" diam. top									
2040	2" and 3" pipe size	Q-1	12	1.333	Ea.	510	86.50		596.50	690
2080	For galvanized body, add					187			187	205
2120	With polished bronze top					510			510	560
2160	Heavy duty, CI, 12" diam. anti-tilt grate									
2180	2", 3", 4", 5" and 6" pipe size	Q-1	10	1.600	Ea.	1,150	104		1,254	1,400
2220	For galvanized body, add					570			570	625
2240	With polished bronze top					1,400			1,400	1,550
2300	Extra-heavy duty, CI, 15" anti-tilt grate									
2320	4", 5", 6", and 8" pipe size	Q-1	8	2	Ea.	2,100	130		2,230	2,500
2360	For galvanized body, add					930			930	1,025
2380	With polished bronze top					2,950			2,950	3,225
2400	Heavy duty, with sediment bucket, CI, 12" diam. loose grate									
2420	2", 3", 4", 5", and 6" pipe size	Q-1	9	1.778	Ea.	1,400	115		1,515	1,725
2440	For galvanized body, add					845			845	930
2460	With polished bronze top					2,075			2,075	2,300
2500	Heavy duty, cleanout & trap w/bucket, CI, 15" top									
2540	2", 3", and 4" pipe size	Q-1	6	2.667	Ea.	7,975	173		8,148	9,025
2560	For galvanized body, add					3,225			3,225	3,550
2580	With polished bronze top					12,900			12,900	14,200
2600	Medium duty, with perforated SS basket, CI, body,									
2610	18" top for refuse container washing area									
2620	2" thru 6" pipe size	Q-1	4	4	Ea.	5,425	259		5,684	6,350
2630	Acid resistant									
2638	PVC									
2640	2", 3" and 4" pipe size	Q-1	16	1	Ea.	505	65		570	655
2644	Cast iron, epoxy coated									
2646	2", 3" and 4" pipe size	Q-1	14	1.143	Ea.	1,025	74		1,099	1,225
2650	PVC or ABS thermoplastic									
2660	3" and 4" pipe size	Q-1	16	1	Ea.	545	65		610	695
2680	Extra heavy duty, oil intercepting, gas seal cone,									
2690	with cleanout, loose grate, CI, body 16" top									
2700	3" and 4" diameter outlet, 4" slab depth	Q-1	4	4	Ea.	12,000	259		12,259	13,600
2720	4" diameter outlet, 8" slab depth		3	5.333		9,925	345		10,270	11,400
2740	4" diam. outlet, 10"-12" slab depth, 16" top		2	8		15,500	520		16,020	17,800
2910	Prison cell, vandal-proof, 1-1/2", and 2" diam. pipe		12	1.333		650	86.50		736.50	845
2920	3" pipe size		10	1.600		620	104		724	835
2930	Trap drain, light duty, backwater valve CI top									
2950	8" diameter top, 2" pipe size	Q-1	12	1.333	Ea.	585	86.50		671.50	775
2960	10" diameter top, 3" pipe size		10	1.600		805	104		909	1,050
2970	12" diameter top, 4" pipe size		8	2		1,125	130		1,255	1,450

22 13 19.14 Floor Receptors

		Crew	Daily Output	Labor-Hours	Unit	Material	Labor	Equipment	Total	Total Incl O&P
0010	**FLOOR RECEPTORS**, For connection to 2", 3" & 4" diameter pipe									
0200	12-1/2" square top, 25 sq. in. open area	Q-1	10	1.600	Ea.	2,250	104		2,354	2,625
0300	For grate with 4" diameter x 3-3/4" high funnel, add					2,825			2,825	3,100
0400	For grate with 6" diameter x 6" high funnel, add					281			281	310
0500	For full hinged grate with open center, add					124			124	136
0600	For aluminum bucket, add					245			245	270
0700	For acid-resisting bucket, add					360			360	395
0900	For stainless steel mesh bucket liner, add					365			365	400
1000	For bronze antisplash dome strainer, add					174			174	192

22 13 Facility Sanitary Sewerage

22 13 19 – Sanitary Waste Piping Specialties

22 13 19.14 Floor Receptors

		Crew	Daily Output	Labor-Hours	Unit	Material	2023 Bare Costs Labor	2023 Bare Costs Equipment	Total	Total Incl O&P
1100	For partial solid cover, add				Ea.	89.50			89.50	98.50
1200	For trap primer connection, add					140			140	154
2000	12-5/8" diameter top, 40 sq. in. open area	Q-1	10	1.600		935	104		1,039	1,175
2100	For options, add same prices as square top									
3000	8" x 4" rectangular top, 7.5 sq. in. open area	Q-1	14	1.143	Ea.	1,150	74		1,224	1,350
3100	For trap primer connections, add					113			113	124
4000	24" x 16" rectangular top, 70 sq. in. open area	Q-1	4	4		6,575	259		6,834	7,600
4100	For trap primer connection, add					293			293	320

22 13 19.15 Sink Waste Treatment

		Crew	Daily Output	Labor-Hours	Unit	Material	Labor	Equipment	Total	Total Incl O&P
0010	**SINK WASTE TREATMENT**, System for commercial kitchens									
0100	includes clock timer & fittings									
0200	System less chemical, wall mounted cabinet	1 Plum	16	.500	Ea.	480	36		516	585
2000	Chemical, 1 gallon, add					48.50			48.50	53.50
2100	6 gallons, add					219			219	241
2200	15 gallons, add					595			595	655
2300	30 gallons, add					1,125			1,125	1,225
2400	55 gallons, add					1,900			1,900	2,100

22 13 19.39 Floor Drain Trap Seal

		Crew	Daily Output	Labor-Hours	Unit	Material	Labor	Equipment	Total	Total Incl O&P
0010	**FLOOR DRAIN TRAP SEAL**									
0100	Inline									
0110	2"	1 Plum	20	.400	Ea.	70	29		99	120
0120	3"		16	.500		50	36		86	109
0130	3.5"		14	.571		53.50	41		94.50	121
0140	4"		10	.800		61	57.50		118.50	154

22 13 23 – Sanitary Waste Interceptors

22 13 23.10 Interceptors

		Crew	Daily Output	Labor-Hours	Unit	Material	Labor	Equipment	Total	Total Incl O&P
0010	**INTERCEPTORS**									
0150	Grease, fabricated steel, 4 GPM, 8 lb. fat capacity	1 Plum	4	2	Ea.	2,275	144		2,419	2,725
0200	7 GPM, 14 lb. fat capacity		4	2		2,650	144		2,794	3,150
1000	10 GPM, 20 lb. fat capacity		4	2		3,700	144		3,844	4,300
1040	15 GPM, 30 lb. fat capacity		4	2		4,625	144		4,769	5,300
1060	20 GPM, 40 lb. fat capacity		3	2.667		6,700	192		6,892	7,650
1080	25 GPM, 50 lb. fat capacity	Q-1	3.50	4.571		6,350	296		6,646	7,450
1100	35 GPM, 70 lb. fat capacity		3	5.333		9,300	345		9,645	10,700
1120	50 GPM, 100 lb. fat capacity		2	8		10,400	520		10,920	12,300
1140	75 GPM, 150 lb. fat capacity		2	8		24,800	520		25,320	28,100
1160	100 GPM, 200 lb. fat capacity		2	8		27,900	520		28,420	31,500
1180	150 GPM, 300 lb. fat capacity		2	8		27,800	520		28,320	31,400
1200	200 GPM, 400 lb. fat capacity		1.50	10.667		39,200	690		39,890	44,100
1220	250 GPM, 500 lb. fat capacity		1.30	12.308		44,200	800		45,000	49,800
1240	300 GPM, 600 lb. fat capacity		1	16		52,000	1,050		53,050	59,000
1260	400 GPM, 800 lb. fat capacity	Q-2	1.20	20		45,700	1,350		47,050	52,500
1280	500 GPM, 1,000 lb. fat capacity	"	1	24		75,500	1,625		77,125	85,500
1580	For seepage pan, add					7%				
3000	Hair, cast iron, 1-1/4" and 1-1/2" pipe connection	1 Plum	8	1	Ea.	720	72		792	895
3100	For chrome-plated cast iron, add					540			540	595
3200	For polished bronze, add					1,250			1,250	1,375
3400	Lint interceptor, fabricated steel									
3410	Size based on 10 GPM per machine									
3420	30 GPM, 2" pipe size	Q-1	3	5.333	Ea.	8,400	345		8,745	9,750
3430	70 GPM, 3" pipe size		2.50	6.400		9,775	415		10,190	11,300
3440	100 GPM, 4" pipe size		2	8		11,500	520		12,020	13,400

22 13 Facility Sanitary Sewerage

22 13 23 – Sanitary Waste Interceptors

22 13 23.10 Interceptors

		Crew	Daily Output	Labor-Hours	Unit	Material	2023 Bare Costs Labor	Equipment	Total	Total Incl O&P
3450	200 GPM, 4" pipe size	Q-1	1.50	10.667	Ea.	12,300	690		12,990	14,500
3460	300 GPM, 6" pipe size		1	16		16,200	1,050		17,250	19,400
3470	400 GPM, 6" pipe size	Q-2	1.20	20		18,400	1,350		19,750	22,300
3480	500 GPM, 6" pipe size	"	1	24		18,800	1,625		20,425	23,100
4000	Oil, fabricated steel, 10 GPM, 2" pipe size	1 Plum	4	2		4,250	144		4,394	4,925
4100	15 GPM, 2" or 3" pipe size		4	2		5,850	144		5,994	6,650
4120	20 GPM, 2" or 3" pipe size		3	2.667		7,700	192		7,892	8,750
4140	25 GPM, 2" or 3" pipe size	Q-1	3.50	4.571		7,675	296		7,971	8,900
4160	35 GPM, 2", 3", or 4" pipe size		3	5.333		9,325	345		9,670	10,800
4180	50 GPM, 2", 3", or 4" pipe size		2	8		12,600	520		13,120	14,600
4200	75 GPM, 3" pipe size		2	8		23,700	520		24,220	26,900
4220	100 GPM, 3" pipe size		2	8		23,600	520		24,120	26,700
4240	150 GPM, 4" pipe size		2	8		29,200	520		29,720	32,900
4260	200 GPM, 4" pipe size		1.50	10.667		41,200	690		41,890	46,400
4280	250 GPM, 5" pipe size		1.30	12.308		47,800	800		48,600	53,500
4300	300 GPM, 5" pipe size		1	16		54,000	1,050		55,050	61,000
4320	400 GPM, 6" pipe size	Q-2	1.20	20		69,500	1,350		70,850	78,500
4340	500 GPM, 6" pipe size	"	1	24		87,500	1,625		89,125	99,000
5000	Sand interceptor, fabricated steel									
5020	20 GPM, 4" pipe size	Q-1	3	5.333	Ea.	13,100	345		13,445	14,900
5030	50 GPM, 4" pipe size		2.50	6.400		13,900	415		14,315	15,900
5040	150 GPM, 4" pipe size		2	8		42,000	520		42,520	47,000
5050	250 GPM, 6" pipe size		1.30	12.308		43,700	800		44,500	49,300
5060	500 GPM, 6" pipe size	Q-2	1	24		56,000	1,625		57,625	64,500
6000	Solids, precious metals recovery, CI, 1-1/4" to 2" pipe	1 Plum	4	2		840	144		984	1,150
6100	Dental lab., large, CI, 1-1/2" to 2" pipe	"	3	2.667		2,950	192		3,142	3,525

22 13 26 – Sanitary Waste Separators

22 13 26.10 Separators

		Crew	Daily Output	Labor-Hours	Unit	Material	2023 Bare Costs Labor	Equipment	Total	Total Incl O&P
0010	**SEPARATORS**, Entrainment eliminator, steel body, 150 PSIG									
0100	1/4" size	1 Stpi	24	.333	Ea.	335	24		359	405
0120	1/2" size		24	.333		276	24		300	340
0140	3/4" size		20	.400		282	29		311	355
0160	1" size		19	.421		360	30.50		390.50	440
0180	1-1/4" size		15	.533		380	38.50		418.50	480
0200	1-1/2" size		13	.615		420	44.50		464.50	530
0220	2" size		11	.727		470	53		523	595

22 13 29 – Sanitary Sewerage Pumps

22 13 29.13 Wet-Pit-Mounted, Vertical Sewerage Pumps

		Crew	Daily Output	Labor-Hours	Unit	Material	2023 Bare Costs Labor	Equipment	Total	Total Incl O&P
0010	**WET-PIT-MOUNTED, VERTICAL SEWERAGE PUMPS**									
0020	Controls incl. alarm/disconnect panel w/wire. Excavation not included									
0260	Simplex, 9 GPM at 60 PSIG, 91 gal. tank				Ea.	4,300			4,300	4,725
0300	Unit with manway, 26" ID, 18" high					4,775			4,775	5,250
0340	26" ID, 36" high					4,675			4,675	5,150
0380	43" ID, 4' high					4,975			4,975	5,475
0600	Simplex, 9 GPM at 60 PSIG, 150 gal. tank, indoor					5,000			5,000	5,500
0700	Unit with manway, 26" ID, 36" high					5,725			5,725	6,275
0740	26" ID, 4' high					5,875			5,875	6,475
2000	Duplex, 18 GPM at 60 PSIG, 150 gal. tank, indoor					9,250			9,250	10,200
2060	Unit with manway, 43" ID, 4' high					11,000			11,000	12,100
2400	For core only					2,325			2,325	2,550
3000	Indoor residential type installation									
3020	Simplex, 9 GPM at 60 PSIG, 91 gal. HDPE tank				Ea.	4,325			4,325	4,750

22 13 Facility Sanitary Sewerage

22 13 29 – Sanitary Sewerage Pumps

22 13 29.14 Sewage Ejector Pumps		Crew	Daily Output	Labor-Hours	Unit	Material	2023 Bare Costs Labor	2023 Bare Costs Equipment	Total	Total Incl O&P
0010	**SEWAGE EJECTOR PUMPS**, With operating and level controls									
0100	Simplex system incl. tank, cover, pump 15' head									
0500	37 gal. PE tank, 12 GPM, 1/2 HP, 2" discharge	Q-1	3.20	5	Ea.	595	325		920	1,125
0510	3" discharge		3.10	5.161		630	335		965	1,200
0530	87 GPM, .7 HP, 2" discharge		3.20	5		910	325		1,235	1,475
0540	3" discharge		3.10	5.161		990	335		1,325	1,600
0600	45 gal. coated stl. tank, 12 GPM, 1/2 HP, 2" discharge		3	5.333		1,050	345		1,395	1,700
0610	3" discharge		2.90	5.517		1,100	360		1,460	1,750
0630	87 GPM, .7 HP, 2" discharge		3	5.333		1,375	345		1,720	2,025
0640	3" discharge		2.90	5.517		1,450	360		1,810	2,100
0660	134 GPM, 1 HP, 2" discharge		2.80	5.714		1,475	370		1,845	2,175
0680	3" discharge		2.70	5.926		1,550	385		1,935	2,275
0700	70 gal. PE tank, 12 GPM, 1/2 HP, 2" discharge		2.60	6.154		1,150	400		1,550	1,850
0710	3" discharge		2.40	6.667		1,225	430		1,655	2,000
0730	87 GPM, .7 HP, 2" discharge		2.50	6.400		1,525	415		1,940	2,300
0740	3" discharge		2.30	6.957		1,575	450		2,025	2,400
0760	134 GPM, 1 HP, 2" discharge		2.20	7.273		1,600	470		2,070	2,475
0770	3" discharge		2	8		1,725	520		2,245	2,650
0800	75 gal. coated stl. tank, 12 GPM, 1/2 HP, 2" discharge		2.40	6.667		1,275	430		1,705	2,050
0810	3" discharge		2.20	7.273		1,325	470		1,795	2,150
0830	87 GPM, .7 HP, 2" discharge		2.30	6.957		1,600	450		2,050	2,425
0840	3" discharge		2.10	7.619		1,675	495		2,170	2,575
0860	134 GPM, 1 HP, 2" discharge		2	8		1,725	520		2,245	2,675
0880	3" discharge		1.80	8.889		1,800	575		2,375	2,825
1040	Duplex system incl. tank, covers, pumps									
1060	110 gal. fiberglass tank, 24 GPM, 1/2 HP, 2" discharge	Q-1	1.60	10	Ea.	2,300	650		2,950	3,500
1080	3" discharge		1.40	11.429		2,400	740		3,140	3,750
1100	174 GPM, .7 HP, 2" discharge		1.50	10.667		2,975	690		3,665	4,300
1120	3" discharge		1.30	12.308		3,100	800		3,900	4,600
1140	268 GPM, 1 HP, 2" discharge		1.20	13.333		3,225	865		4,090	4,850
1160	3" discharge		1	16		3,350	1,050		4,400	5,225
1260	135 gal. coated stl. tank, 24 GPM, 1/2 HP, 2" discharge	Q-2	1.70	14.118		2,375	950		3,325	4,025
2000	3" discharge		1.60	15		2,525	1,000		3,525	4,275
2640	174 GPM, .7 HP, 2" discharge		1.60	15		3,100	1,000		4,100	4,925
2660	3" discharge		1.50	16		3,275	1,075		4,350	5,200
2700	268 GPM, 1 HP, 2" discharge		1.30	18.462		3,375	1,250		4,625	5,550
3040	3" discharge		1.10	21.818		3,600	1,475		5,075	6,150
3060	275 gal. coated stl. tank, 24 GPM, 1/2 HP, 2" discharge		1.50	16		2,975	1,075		4,050	4,875
3080	3" discharge		1.40	17.143		3,000	1,150		4,150	5,025
3100	174 GPM, .7 HP, 2" discharge		1.40	17.143		3,825	1,150		4,975	5,925
3120	3" discharge		1.30	18.462		4,125	1,250		5,375	6,375
3140	268 GPM, 1 HP, 2" discharge		1.10	21.818		4,200	1,475		5,675	6,825
3160	3" discharge		.90	26.667		4,425	1,800		6,225	7,550
3260	Pump system accessories, add									
3300	Alarm horn and lights, 115 V mercury switch	Q-1	8	2	Ea.	117	130		247	320
3340	Switch, mag. contactor, alarm bell, light, 3 level control		5	3.200		600	208		808	965
3380	Alternator, mercury switch activated		4	4		1,075	259		1,334	1,550

22 14 Facility Storm Drainage

22 14 23 – Storm Drainage Piping Specialties

22 14 23.33 Backwater Valves

		Crew	Daily Output	Labor-Hours	Unit	Material	2023 Bare Costs Labor	2023 Bare Costs Equipment	Total	Total Incl O&P
0010	**BACKWATER VALVES**, CI Body									
6980	Bronze gate and automatic flapper valves									
7000	3" and 4" pipe size	Q-1	13	1.231	Ea.	3,075	80		3,155	3,500
7100	5" and 6" pipe size	"	13	1.231	"	4,725	80		4,805	5,325
7240	Bronze flapper valve, bolted cover									
7260	2" pipe size	Q-1	16	1	Ea.	900	65		965	1,075
7280	3" pipe size		14.50	1.103		1,400	71.50		1,471.50	1,650
7300	4" pipe size		13	1.231		1,325	80		1,405	1,575
7320	5" pipe size	Q-2	18	1.333		2,075	89.50		2,164.50	2,425
7340	6" pipe size	"	17	1.412		2,950	95		3,045	3,375
7360	8" pipe size	Q-3	10	3.200		4,200	219		4,419	4,950
7380	10" pipe size	"	9	3.556		6,875	244		7,119	7,925
7500	For threaded cover, same cost									
7540	Revolving disk type, same cost as flapper type									

22 14 26 – Facility Storm Drains

22 14 26.13 Roof Drains

		Crew	Daily Output	Labor-Hours	Unit	Material	2023 Bare Costs Labor	2023 Bare Costs Equipment	Total	Total Incl O&P
0010	**ROOF DRAINS**									
0140	Cornice, CI, 45° or 90° outlet									
0200	3" and 4" pipe size	Q-1	12	1.333	Ea.	455	86.50		541.50	635
0260	For galvanized body, add					148			148	162
0280	For polished bronze dome, add					110			110	121
3860	Roof, flat metal deck, CI body, 12" CI dome									
3880	2" pipe size	Q-1	15	1.067	Ea.	385	69		454	525
3890	3" pipe size		14	1.143		540	74		614	705
3900	4" pipe size		13	1.231		865	80		945	1,075
3910	5" pipe size		12	1.333		840	86.50		926.50	1,050
3920	6" pipe size		10	1.600		1,075	104		1,179	1,325
4280	Integral expansion joint, CI body, 12" CI dome									
4300	2" pipe size	Q-1	8	2	Ea.	710	130		840	975
4320	3" pipe size		7	2.286		710	148		858	1,000
4340	4" pipe size		6	2.667		710	173		883	1,050
4360	5" pipe size		4	4		1,100	259		1,359	1,600
4380	6" pipe size		3	5.333		710	345		1,055	1,300
4400	8" pipe size		3	5.333		1,925	345		2,270	2,625
4440	For galvanized body, add					490			490	540
4620	Main, all aluminum, 12" low profile dome									
4640	2", 3" and 4" pipe size	Q-1	14	1.143	Ea.	855	74		929	1,050
4660	5" and 6" pipe size		13	1.231		1,125	80		1,205	1,375
4680	8" pipe size		10	1.600		950	104		1,054	1,200
4690	Main, CI body, 12" poly. dome, 2", 3" & 4" pipe		8	2		745	130		875	1,025
4710	5" and 6" pipe size		6	2.667		1,025	173		1,198	1,375
4720	8" pipe size		4	4		1,075	259		1,334	1,550
4730	For underdeck clamp, add		22	.727		395	47		442	505
4740	For vandalproof dome, add					99.50			99.50	109
4750	For galvanized body, add					835			835	920
4760	Main, ABS body and dome, 2" pipe size	Q-1	14	1.143		161	74		235	288
4780	3" pipe size		14	1.143		168	74		242	295
4800	4" pipe size		14	1.143		161	74		235	288
4820	For underdeck clamp, add		24	.667		60	43		103	131
4900	Terrace planting area, with perforated overflow, CI									
4920	2", 3" and 4" pipe size	Q-1	8	2	Ea.	940	130		1,070	1,225

22 14 Facility Storm Drainage

22 14 26 – Facility Storm Drains

22 14 26.16 Facility Area Drains

		Crew	Daily Output	Labor-Hours	Unit	Material	2023 Bare Costs Labor	Equipment	Total	Total Incl O&P
0010	**FACILITY AREA DRAINS**									
4980	Scupper floor, oblique strainer, CI									
5000	6" x 7" top, 2", 3" and 4" pipe size	Q-1	16	1	Ea.	485	65		550	630
5100	8" x 12" top, 5" and 6" pipe size	"	14	1.143		940	74		1,014	1,125
5160	For galvanized body, add					40%				
5200	For polished bronze strainer, add					85%				

22 14 26.19 Facility Trench Drains

0010	**FACILITY TRENCH DRAINS**									
5980	Trench, floor, heavy duty, modular, CI, 12" x 12" top									
6000	2", 3", 4", 5" & 6" pipe size	Q-1	8	2	Ea.	1,350	130		1,480	1,700
6100	For unit with polished bronze top		8	2		2,000	130		2,130	2,400
6200	For 12" extension section, CI top		8	2		1,375	130		1,505	1,700
6240	For 12" extension section, polished bronze top		8	2		2,175	130		2,305	2,600
6600	Trench, floor, for cement concrete encasement									
6610	Not including trenching or concrete									
6640	Polyester polymer concrete									
6650	4" internal width, with grate									
6660	Light duty steel grate	Q-1	120	.133	L.F.	80	8.65		88.65	101
6670	Medium duty steel grate		115	.139		143	9		152	171
6680	Heavy duty iron grate		110	.145		142	9.45		151.45	170
6700	12" internal width, with grate									
6770	Heavy duty galvanized grate	Q-1	80	.200	L.F.	193	12.95		205.95	231
6800	Fiberglass									
6810	8" internal width, with grate									
6820	Medium duty galvanized grate	Q-1	115	.139	L.F.	130	9		139	156
6830	Heavy duty iron grate	"	110	.145	"	229	9.45		238.45	266

22 14 29 – Sump Pumps

22 14 29.13 Wet-Pit-Mounted, Vertical Sump Pumps

0010	**WET-PIT-MOUNTED, VERTICAL SUMP PUMPS**									
0400	Molded PVC base, 21 GPM at 15' head, 1/3 HP	1 Plum	5	1.600	Ea.	138	115		253	325
0800	Iron base, 21 GPM at 15' head, 1/3 HP		5	1.600		155	115		270	345
1200	Solid brass, 21 GPM at 15' head, 1/3 HP		5	1.600		251	115		366	450
2000	Sump pump, single stage									
2010	25 GPM, 1 HP, 1-1/2" discharge	Q-1	1.80	8.889	Ea.	4,000	575		4,575	5,250
2020	75 GPM, 1-1/2 HP, 2" discharge		1.50	10.667		4,225	690		4,915	5,675
2030	100 GPM, 2 HP, 2-1/2" discharge		1.30	12.308		1,575	800		2,375	2,950
2040	150 GPM, 3 HP, 3" discharge		1.10	14.545		4,300	945		5,245	6,150
2050	200 GPM, 3 HP, 3" discharge		1	16		4,575	1,050		5,625	6,575
2060	300 GPM, 10 HP, 4" discharge	Q-2	1.20	20		4,925	1,350		6,275	7,425
2070	500 GPM, 15 HP, 5" discharge		1.10	21.818		4,975	1,475		6,450	7,650
2080	800 GPM, 20 HP, 6" discharge		1	24		6,625	1,625		8,250	9,700
2090	1,000 GPM, 30 HP, 6" discharge		.85	28.235		7,275	1,900		9,175	10,800
2100	1,600 GPM, 50 HP, 8" discharge		.72	33.333		11,300	2,250		13,550	15,900
2110	2,000 GPM, 60 HP, 8" discharge	Q-3	.85	37.647		11,600	2,575		14,175	16,700
2202	For general purpose float switch, copper coated float, add	Q-1	5	3.200		120	208		328	440

22 14 Facility Storm Drainage

22 14 29 – Sump Pumps

22 14 29.16 Submersible Sump Pumps

	22 14 29.16 Submersible Sump Pumps	Crew	Daily Output	Labor-Hours	Unit	Material	2023 Bare Costs Labor	Equipment	Total	Total Incl O&P
0010	**SUBMERSIBLE SUMP PUMPS**									
1000	Elevator sump pumps, automatic									
1010	Complete systems, pump, oil detector, controls and alarm									
1020	1-1/2" discharge, does not include the sump pit/tank									
1040	1/3 HP, 115 V	1 Plum	4.40	1.818	Ea.	1,650	131		1,781	2,000
1050	1/2 HP, 115 V		4	2		1,725	144		1,869	2,125
1060	1/2 HP, 230 V		4	2		1,725	144		1,869	2,125
1070	3/4 HP, 115 V		3.60	2.222		1,825	160		1,985	2,250
1080	3/4 HP, 230 V		3.60	2.222		1,800	160		1,960	2,225
1100	Sump pump only									
1110	1/3 HP, 115 V	1 Plum	6.40	1.250	Ea.	152	90		242	300
1120	1/2 HP, 115 V		5.80	1.379		218	99.50		317.50	390
1130	1/2 HP, 230 V		5.80	1.379		253	99.50		352.50	425
1140	3/4 HP, 115 V		5.40	1.481		289	107		396	480
1150	3/4 HP, 230 V		5.40	1.481		330	107		437	520
1200	Oil detector, control and alarm only									
1210	115 V	1 Plum	8	1	Ea.	1,925	72		1,997	2,225
1220	230 V	"	8	1	"	2,025	72		2,097	2,325
7000	Sump pump, automatic									
7100	Plastic, 1-1/4" discharge, 1/4 HP	1 Plum	6.40	1.250	Ea.	149	90		239	298
7140	1/3 HP		6	1.333		197	96		293	360
7160	1/2 HP		5.40	1.481		214	107		321	395
7180	1-1/2" discharge, 1/2 HP		5.20	1.538		136	111		247	315
7500	Cast iron, 1-1/4" discharge, 1/4 HP		6	1.333		245	96		341	415
7540	1/3 HP		6	1.333		221	96		317	385
7560	1/2 HP		5	1.600		340	115		455	545

22 14 53 – Rainwater Storage Tanks

22 14 53.13 Fiberglass, Rainwater Storage Tank

		Crew	Daily Output	Labor-Hours	Unit	Material	Labor	Equipment	Total	Total Incl O&P
0010	**FIBERGLASS, RAINWATER STORAGE TANK**									
2000	600 gallon	B-21B	3.75	10.667	Ea.	1,400	550	575	2,525	2,975
2010	1,000 gallon		3.50	11.429		2,650	590	615	3,855	4,450
2020	2,000 gallon		3.25	12.308		4,425	635	660	5,720	6,525
2030	4,000 gallon		3	13.333		8,025	685	715	9,425	10,600
2040	6,000 gallon		2.65	15.094		27,300	775	810	28,885	32,000
2050	8,000 gallon		2.30	17.391		15,300	895	935	17,130	19,200
2060	10,000 gallon		2	20		22,600	1,025	1,075	24,700	27,500
2070	12,000 gallon		1.50	26.667		21,100	1,375	1,425	23,900	26,800
2080	15,000 gallon		1	40		26,800	2,050	2,150	31,000	35,000
2090	20,000 gallon		.75	53.333		37,700	2,750	2,875	43,325	48,700
2100	25,000 gallon		.50	80		52,000	4,125	4,300	60,425	68,000
2110	30,000 gallon		.35	114		63,000	5,875	6,150	75,025	84,500
2120	40,000 gallon		.30	133		85,500	6,850	7,175	99,525	112,000

22 15 General Service Compressed-Air Systems

22 15 13 – General Service Compressed-Air Piping

22 15 13.10 Compressor Accessories		Crew	Daily Output	Labor-Hours	Unit	Material	2023 Bare Costs Labor	Equipment	Total	Total Incl O&P
0010	**COMPRESSOR ACCESSORIES**									
3460	Air filter, regulator, lubricator combination									
3470	Flush mount									
3480	Adjustable range 0-140 psi									
3500	1/8" NPT, 34 SCFM	1 Stpi	17	.471	Ea.	126	34		160	190
3510	1/4" NPT, 61 SCFM		17	.471		228	34		262	300
3520	3/8" NPT, 85 SCFM		16	.500		233	36.50		269.50	310
3530	1/2" NPT, 150 SCFM		15	.533		250	38.50		288.50	335
3540	3/4" NPT, 171 SCFM		14	.571		305	41.50		346.50	400
3550	1" NPT, 150 SCFM		13	.615		490	44.50		534.50	605
4000	Couplers, air line, sleeve type									
4010	Female, connection size NPT									
4020	1/4"	1 Stpi	38	.211	Ea.	10.35	15.25		25.60	34.50
4030	3/8"		36	.222		9.20	16.10		25.30	34
4040	1/2"		35	.229		19.75	16.60		36.35	46
4050	3/4"		34	.235		24.50	17.05		41.55	52.50
4100	Male									
4110	1/4"	1 Stpi	38	.211	Ea.	7.25	15.25		22.50	31
4120	3/8"		36	.222		11.50	16.10		27.60	36.50
4130	1/2"		35	.229		20.50	16.60		37.10	47
4140	3/4"		34	.235		18.05	17.05		35.10	45.50
4150	Coupler, combined male and female halves									
4160	1/2"	1 Stpi	17	.471	Ea.	40.50	34		74.50	95.50
4170	3/4"	"	15	.533	"	42.50	38.50		81	105

22 15 19 – General Service Packaged Air Compressors and Receivers

22 15 19.10 Air Compressors

		Crew	Daily Output	Labor-Hours	Unit	Material	2023 Bare Costs Labor	Equipment	Total	Total Incl O&P
0010	**AIR COMPRESSORS**									
5250	Air, reciprocating air cooled, splash lubricated, tank mounted									
5300	Single stage, 1 phase, 140 psi									
5303	1/2 HP, 17 gal. tank	1 Stpi	3	2.667	Ea.	2,200	193		2,393	2,725
5305	3/4 HP, 30 gal. tank		2.60	3.077		1,800	223		2,023	2,325
5307	1 HP, 30 gal. tank		2.20	3.636		2,650	264		2,914	3,325
5309	2 HP, 30 gal. tank	Q-5	4	4		3,175	261		3,436	3,900
5310	3 HP, 30 gal. tank		3.60	4.444		3,500	290		3,790	4,275
5314	3 HP, 60 gal. tank		3.50	4.571		4,475	299		4,774	5,375
5320	5 HP, 60 gal. tank		3.20	5		3,875	325		4,200	4,725
5330	5 HP, 80 gal. tank		3	5.333		7,200	350		7,550	8,450
5340	7.5 HP, 80 gal. tank		2.60	6.154		5,800	400		6,200	7,000
5600	2 stage pkg., 3 phase									
5650	6 CFM at 125 psi, 1-1/2 HP, 60 gal. tank	Q-5	3	5.333	Ea.	3,100	350		3,450	3,925
5670	10.9 CFM at 125 psi, 3 HP, 80 gal. tank		1.50	10.667		6,275	695		6,970	7,950
5680	38.7 CFM at 125 psi, 10 HP, 120 gal. tank		.60	26.667		10,900	1,750		12,650	14,600
5690	105 CFM at 125 psi, 25 HP, 250 gal. tank	Q-6	.60	40		19,600	2,700		22,300	25,700
5800	With single stage pump									
5850	8.3 CFM at 125 psi, 2 HP, 80 gal. tank	Q-6	3.50	6.857	Ea.	3,325	465		3,790	4,375
5860	38.7 CFM at 125 psi, 10 HP, 120 gal. tank	"	.90	26.667	"	6,250	1,800		8,050	9,575
6000	Reciprocating, 2 stage, tank mtd, 3 ph, cap rated @ 175 PSIG									
6050	Pressure lubricated, hvy. duty, 9.7 CFM, 3 HP, 120 gal. tank	Q-5	1.30	12.308	Ea.	5,625	805		6,430	7,375
6054	5 CFM, 1-1/2 HP, 80 gal. tank		2.80	5.714		3,175	375		3,550	4,050
6056	6.4 CFM, 2 HP, 80 gal. tank		2	8		3,325	520		3,845	4,450
6058	8.1 CFM, 3 HP, 80 gal. tank		1.70	9.412		3,875	615		4,490	5,200
6059	14.8 CFM, 5 HP, 80 gal. tank		1	16		3,875	1,050		4,925	5,800

22 15 General Service Compressed-Air Systems

22 15 19 – General Service Packaged Air Compressors and Receivers

22 15 19.10 Air Compressors

		Crew	Daily Output	Labor-Hours	Unit	Material	2023 Bare Costs Labor	2023 Bare Costs Equipment	Total	Total Incl O&P
6060	16.5 CFM, 5 HP, 120 gal. tank	Q-5	1	16	Ea.	5,375	1,050		6,425	7,450
6063	13 CFM, 6 HP, 80 gal. tank		.90	17.778		5,900	1,150		7,050	8,200
6066	19.8 CFM, 7.5 HP, 80 gal. tank		.80	20		6,925	1,300		8,225	9,575
6070	25.8 CFM, 7-1/2 HP, 120 gal. tank		.80	20		5,525	1,300		6,825	8,025
6078	34.8 CFM, 10 HP, 80 gal. tank		.70	22.857		8,075	1,500		9,575	11,100
6080	34.8 CFM, 10 HP, 120 gal. tank		.60	26.667		9,050	1,750		10,800	12,600
6090	53.7 CFM, 15 HP, 120 gal. tank	Q-6	.80	30		8,250	2,025		10,275	12,100
6100	76.7 CFM, 20 HP, 120 gal. tank		.70	34.286		11,100	2,325		13,425	15,700
6104	76.7 CFM, 20 HP, 240 gal. tank		.68	35.294		13,900	2,400		16,300	18,900
6110	90.1 CFM, 25 HP, 120 gal. tank		.63	38.095		13,900	2,575		16,475	19,200
6120	101 CFM, 30 HP, 120 gal. tank		.57	42.105		12,100	2,850		14,950	17,600
6130	101 CFM, 30 HP, 250 gal. tank		.52	46.154		14,400	3,125		17,525	20,500
6200	Oil-less, 13.6 CFM, 5 HP, 120 gal. tank	Q-5	.88	18.182		15,300	1,175		16,475	18,600
6210	13.6 CFM, 5 HP, 250 gal. tank		.80	20		16,300	1,300		17,600	20,000
6220	18.2 CFM, 7.5 HP, 120 gal. tank		.73	21.918		15,200	1,425		16,625	18,800
6230	18.2 CFM, 7.5 HP, 250 gal. tank		.67	23.881		16,300	1,550		17,850	20,300
6250	30.5 CFM, 10 HP, 120 gal. tank		.57	28.070		17,900	1,825		19,725	22,400
6260	30.5 CFM, 10 HP, 250 gal. tank		.53	30.189		19,100	1,975		21,075	24,000
6270	41.3 CFM, 15 HP, 120 gal. tank	Q-6	.70	34.286		19,500	2,325		21,825	24,900
6280	41.3 CFM, 15 HP, 250 gal. tank	"	.67	35.821		20,600	2,425		23,025	26,300

22 31 Domestic Water Softeners

22 31 13 – Residential Domestic Water Softeners

22 31 13.10 Residential Water Softeners

		Crew	Daily Output	Labor-Hours	Unit	Material	2023 Bare Costs Labor	2023 Bare Costs Equipment	Total	Total Incl O&P
0010	**RESIDENTIAL WATER SOFTENERS**									
7350	Water softener, automatic, to 30 grains per gallon	2 Plum	5	3.200	Ea.	590	231		821	995
7400	To 100 grains per gallon	"	4	4	"	530	288		818	1,025

22 31 16 – Commercial Domestic Water Softeners

22 31 16.10 Water Softeners

		Crew	Daily Output	Labor-Hours	Unit	Material	2023 Bare Costs Labor	2023 Bare Costs Equipment	Total	Total Incl O&P
0010	**WATER SOFTENERS**									
5800	Softener systems, automatic, intermediate sizes									
5820	available, may be used in multiples.									
6000	Hardness capacity between regenerations and flow									
6060	40,000 grains, 14 GPM	Q-1	4	4	Ea.	5,250	259		5,509	6,150
6070	50,000 grains, 17 GPM		3.60	4.444		4,925	288		5,213	5,850
6080	90,000 grains, 25 GPM		2.80	5.714		5,900	370		6,270	7,025
6100	150,000 grains, 37 GPM cont., 51 GPM peak		1.20	13.333		10,700	865		11,565	13,000
6200	300,000 grains, 81 GPM cont., 113 GPM peak		1	16		7,825	1,050		8,875	10,200
6300	750,000 grains, 160 GPM cont., 230 GPM peak		.80	20		11,300	1,300		12,600	14,400
6400	900,000 grains, 185 GPM cont., 270 GPM peak		.70	22.857		18,300	1,475		19,775	22,300
8000	Water treatment, salts, 50 lb. bag									
8020	Salt, water softener, bag, pelletized				Lb.	.50			.50	.55
8030	Salt, water softener, bag, crystal rock salt				"	.20			.20	.22

22 32 Domestic Water Filtration Equipment

22 32 19 – Domestic-Water Off-Floor Cartridge Filters

22 32 19.10 Water Filters		Crew	Daily Output	Labor-Hours	Unit	Material	2023 Bare Costs Labor	2023 Bare Costs Equipment	Total	Total Incl O&P
0010	**WATER FILTERS**, Purification and treatment									
1000	Cartridge style, dirt and rust type	1 Plum	12	.667	Ea.	132	48		180	218
1200	Replacement cartridge		32	.250		22	18		40	51.50
1600	Taste and odor type		12	.667		151	48		199	238
1700	Replacement cartridge		32	.250		60	18		78	93
3000	Central unit, dirt/rust/odor/taste/scale		4	2		585	144		729	855
3100	Replacement cartridge, standard		20	.400		95.50	29		124.50	148
3600	Replacement cartridge, heavy duty		20	.400		99.50	29		128.50	152
8000	Commercial, fully automatic or push button automatic									
8200	Iron removal, 660 GPH, 1" pipe size	Q-1	1.50	10.667	Ea.	2,025	690		2,715	3,250
8240	1,500 GPH, 1-1/4" pipe size		1	16		3,600	1,050		4,650	5,500
8280	2,340 GPH, 1-1/2" pipe size		.80	20		3,950	1,300		5,250	6,275
8320	3,420 GPH, 2" pipe size		.60	26.667		7,300	1,725		9,025	10,600
8360	4,620 GPH, 2-1/2" pipe size		.50	32		11,600	2,075		13,675	15,900
8500	Neutralizer for acid water, 780 GPH, 1" pipe size		1.50	10.667		2,075	690		2,765	3,300
8540	1,140 GPH, 1-1/4" pipe size		1	16		2,325	1,050		3,375	4,100
8580	1,740 GPH, 1-1/2" pipe size		.80	20		3,375	1,300		4,675	5,650
8620	2,520 GPH, 2" pipe size		.60	26.667		4,375	1,725		6,100	7,400
8660	3,480 GPH, 2-1/2" pipe size		.50	32		7,300	2,075		9,375	11,100
8800	Sediment removal, 780 GPH, 1" pipe size		1.50	10.667		1,975	690		2,665	3,200
8840	1,140 GPH, 1-1/4" pipe size		1	16		2,350	1,050		3,400	4,150
8880	1,740 GPH, 1-1/2" pipe size		.80	20		3,125	1,300		4,425	5,350
8920	2,520 GPH, 2" pipe size		.60	26.667		4,525	1,725		6,250	7,550
8960	3,480 GPH, 2-1/2" pipe size		.50	32		7,100	2,075		9,175	10,900
9200	Taste and odor removal, 660 GPH, 1" pipe size		1.50	10.667		2,750	690		3,440	4,050
9240	1,500 GPH, 1-1/4" pipe size		1	16		4,725	1,050		5,775	6,750
9280	2,340 GPH, 1-1/2" pipe size		.80	20		5,400	1,300		6,700	7,850
9320	3,420 GPH, 2" pipe size		.60	26.667		8,250	1,725		9,975	11,700
9360	4,620 GPH, 2-1/2" pipe size		.50	32		11,000	2,075		13,075	15,300

22 33 Electric Domestic Water Heaters

22 33 13 – Instantaneous Electric Domestic Water Heaters

22 33 13.10 Hot Water Dispensers

		Crew	Daily Output	Labor-Hours	Unit	Material	Labor	Equipment	Total	Total Incl O&P
0010	**HOT WATER DISPENSERS**									
0160	Commercial, 100 cup, 11.3 amp	1 Plum	14	.571	Ea.	455	41		496	560
3180	Household, 60 cup	"	14	.571	"	239	41		280	325

22 33 13.20 Instantaneous Elec. Point-Of-Use Water Heaters

			Crew	Daily Output	Labor-Hours	Unit	Material	Labor	Equipment	Total	Total Incl O&P
0010	**INSTANTANEOUS ELECTRIC POINT-OF-USE WATER HEATERS**										
8965	Point of use, electric, glass lined										
8969	Energy saver										
8970	2.5 gal. single element	G	1 Plum	2.80	2.857	Ea.	238	206		444	565
8971	4 gal. single element	G		2.80	2.857		278	206		484	610
8974	6 gal. single element	G		2.50	3.200		335	231		566	715
8975	10 gal. single element	G		2.50	3.200		495	231		726	890
8976	15 gal. single element	G		2.40	3.333		515	240		755	930
8977	20 gal. single element	G		2.40	3.333		530	240		770	940
8978	30 gal. single element	G		2.30	3.478		670	251		921	1,100
8979	40 gal. single element	G		2.20	3.636		1,325	262		1,587	1,850
8988	Commercial (ASHRAE energy std. 90)										
8989	6 gallon	G	1 Plum	2.50	3.200	Ea.	1,200	231		1,431	1,675
8990	10 gallon	G		2.50	3.200		1,150	231		1,381	1,600

22 33 Electric Domestic Water Heaters

22 33 13 – Instantaneous Electric Domestic Water Heaters

22 33 13.20 Instantaneous Elec. Point-Of-Use Water Heaters		Crew	Daily Output	Labor-Hours	Unit	Material	2023 Bare Costs Labor	Equipment	Total	Total Incl O&P
8991	15 gallon	G 1 Plum	2.40	3.333	Ea.	1,150	240		1,390	1,625
8992	20 gallon	G	2.40	3.333		1,325	240		1,565	1,800
8993	30 gallon	G	2.30	3.478		2,775	251		3,026	3,425
8995	Under the sink, copper, w/bracket									
8996	2.5 gallon	G 1 Plum	4	2	Ea.	395	144		539	645

22 33 30 – Residential, Electric Domestic Water Heaters

22 33 30.13 Residential, Small-Capacity Elec. Water Heaters

			Crew	Daily Output	Labor-Hours	Unit	Material	Labor	Equipment	Total	Total Incl O&P
0010	**RESIDENTIAL, SMALL-CAPACITY ELECTRIC DOMESTIC WATER HEATERS**										
1000	Residential, electric, glass lined tank, 5 yr., 10 gal., single element	D2020-210	1 Plum	2.30	3.478	Ea.	440	251		691	860
1040	20 gallon, single element			2.20	3.636		480	262		742	920
1060	30 gallon, double element			2.20	3.636		835	262		1,097	1,300
1080	40 gallon, double element			2	4		865	288		1,153	1,375
1100	52 gallon, double element			2	4		1,500	288		1,788	2,075
1120	66 gallon, double element			1.80	4.444		2,050	320		2,370	2,725
1140	80 gallon, double element			1.60	5		2,325	360		2,685	3,075
1180	120 gallon, double element			1.40	5.714		3,200	410		3,610	4,150

22 33 33 – Light-Commercial Electric Domestic Water Heaters

22 33 33.10 Commercial Electric Water Heaters

		Crew	Daily Output	Labor-Hours	Unit	Material	Labor	Equipment	Total	Total Incl O&P
0010	**COMMERCIAL ELECTRIC WATER HEATERS**									
4000	Commercial, 100° rise. NOTE: for each size tank, a range of									
4010	heaters between the ones shown is available									
4020	Electric									
4100	5 gal., 3 kW, 12 GPH, 208 volt	1 Plum	2	4	Ea.	4,750	288		5,038	5,650
4120	10 gal., 6 kW, 25 GPH, 208 volt		2	4		5,200	288		5,488	6,125
4130	30 gal., 24 kW, 98 GPH, 208 volt		1.92	4.167		8,325	300		8,625	9,600
4136	40 gal., 36 kW, 148 GPH, 208 volt		1.88	4.255		10,600	305		10,905	12,200
4140	50 gal., 9 kW, 37 GPH, 208 volt		1.80	4.444		6,500	320		6,820	7,625
4160	50 gal., 36 kW, 148 GPH, 208 volt		1.80	4.444		11,000	320		11,320	12,600
4180	80 gal., 12 kW, 49 GPH, 208 volt		1.50	5.333		8,050	385		8,435	9,425
4200	80 gal., 36 kW, 148 GPH, 208 volt		1.50	5.333		12,500	385		12,885	14,300
4220	100 gal., 36 kW, 148 GPH, 208 volt		1.20	6.667		13,400	480		13,880	15,400
4240	120 gal., 36 kW, 148 GPH, 208 volt		1.20	6.667		13,900	480		14,380	16,000
4260	150 gal., 15 kW, 61 GPH, 480 volt		1	8		36,000	575		36,575	40,500
4280	150 gal., 120 kW, 490 GPH, 480 volt		1	8		48,900	575		49,475	55,000
4300	200 gal., 15 kW, 61 GPH, 480 volt	Q-1	1.70	9.412		38,100	610		38,710	42,900
4320	200 gal., 120 kW, 490 GPH, 480 volt		1.70	9.412		51,500	610		52,110	57,500
4340	250 gal., 15 kW, 61 GPH, 480 volt		1.50	10.667		39,500	690		40,190	44,400
4360	250 gal., 150 kW, 615 GPH, 480 volt		1.50	10.667		48,300	690		48,990	54,000
4380	300 gal., 30 kW, 123 GPH, 480 volt		1.30	12.308		43,400	800		44,200	49,000
4400	300 gal., 180 kW, 738 GPH, 480 volt		1.30	12.308		75,000	800		75,800	83,500
4420	350 gal., 30 kW, 123 GPH, 480 volt		1.10	14.545		38,600	945		39,545	43,800
4440	350 gal., 180 kW, 738 GPH, 480 volt		1.10	14.545		54,500	945		55,445	61,500
4460	400 gal., 30 kW, 123 GPH, 480 volt		1	16		53,000	1,050		54,050	59,500
4480	400 gal., 210 kW, 860 GPH, 480 volt		1	16		88,000	1,050		89,050	98,500
4500	500 gal., 30 kW, 123 GPH, 480 volt		.80	20		61,500	1,300		62,800	70,000
4520	500 gal., 240 kW, 984 GPH, 480 volt		.80	20		103,000	1,300		104,300	115,000
4540	600 gal., 30 kW, 123 GPH, 480 volt	Q-2	1.20	20		69,500	1,350		70,850	78,000
4560	600 gal., 300 kW, 1,230 GPH, 480 volt		1.20	20		121,500	1,350		122,850	135,500
4580	700 gal., 30 kW, 123 GPH, 480 volt		1	24		61,500	1,625		63,125	70,000
4600	700 gal., 300 kW, 1,230 GPH, 480 volt		1	24		92,500	1,625		94,125	104,000
4620	800 gal., 60 kW, 245 GPH, 480 volt		.90	26.667		83,000	1,800		84,800	94,000
4640	800 gal., 300 kW, 1,230 GPH, 480 volt		.90	26.667		94,500	1,800		96,300	106,000

22 33 Electric Domestic Water Heaters

22 33 33 – Light-Commercial Electric Domestic Water Heaters

22 33 33.10 Commercial Electric Water Heaters		Crew	Daily Output	Labor-Hours	Unit	Material	2023 Bare Costs Labor	Equipment	Total	Total Incl O&P
4660	1,000 gal., 60 kW, 245 GPH, 480 volt	Q-2	.70	34.286	Ea.	72,500	2,300		74,800	83,500
4680	1,000 gal., 480 kW, 1,970 GPH, 480 volt		.70	34.286		120,500	2,300		122,800	136,000
4700	1,200 gal., 60 kW, 245 GPH, 480 volt		.60	40		82,000	2,700		84,700	94,500
4720	1,200 gal., 480 kW, 1,970 GPH, 480 volt		.60	40		125,000	2,700		127,700	141,000
4740	1,500 gal., 60 kW, 245 GPH, 480 volt		.50	48		108,000	3,225		111,225	124,000
4760	1,500 gal., 480 kW, 1,970 GPH, 480 volt		.50	48		150,000	3,225		153,225	170,000
5400	Modulating step control for under 90 kW, 2-5 steps	1 Elec	5.30	1.509		955	102		1,057	1,200
5440	For above 90 kW, 1 through 5 steps beyond standard, add		3.20	2.500		256	168		424	530
5460	For above 90 kW, 6 through 10 steps beyond standard, add		2.70	2.963		570	200		770	920
5480	For above 90 kW, 11 through 18 steps beyond standard, add		1.60	5		845	335		1,180	1,425

22 34 Fuel-Fired Domestic Water Heaters

22 34 13 – Instantaneous, Tankless, Gas Domestic Water Heaters

22 34 13.10 Instantaneous, Tankless, Gas Water Heaters

			Crew	Daily Output	Labor-Hours	Unit	Material	Labor	Equipment	Total	Total Incl O&P
0010	**INSTANTANEOUS, TANKLESS, GAS WATER HEATERS**										
9410	Natural gas/propane, 3.2 GPM	G	1 Plum	2	4	Ea.	575	288		863	1,075
9420	6.4 GPM	G		1.90	4.211		625	305		930	1,150
9430	8.4 GPM	G		1.80	4.444		1,375	320		1,695	2,000
9440	9.5 GPM	G		1.60	5		970	360		1,330	1,600

22 34 30 – Residential Gas Domestic Water Heaters

22 34 30.13 Residential, Atmos, Gas Domestic Wtr Heaters

		Crew	Daily Output	Labor-Hours	Unit	Material	Labor	Equipment	Total	Total Incl O&P
0010	**RESIDENTIAL, ATMOSPHERIC, GAS DOMESTIC WATER HEATERS**									
2000	Gas fired, foam lined tank, 10 yr., vent not incl.									
2040	30 gallon	1 Plum	2	4	Ea.	2,100	288		2,388	2,750
2060	40 gallon		1.90	4.211		725	305		1,030	1,250
2080	50 gallon		1.80	4.444		825	320		1,145	1,375
2090	60 gallon		1.70	4.706		1,800	340		2,140	2,475
2100	75 gallon		1.50	5.333		1,325	385		1,710	2,050
2120	100 gallon		1.30	6.154		2,525	445		2,970	3,425
2900	Water heater, safety-drain pan, 26" round		20	.400		20	29		49	65
3000	Tank leak safety, water & gas shut off see 22 05 23.20 8800									

22 34 36 – Commercial Gas Domestic Water Heaters

22 34 36.13 Commercial, Atmos., Gas Domestic Water Htrs.

		Crew	Daily Output	Labor-Hours	Unit	Material	Labor	Equipment	Total	Total Incl O&P
0010	**COMMERCIAL, ATMOSPHERIC, GAS DOMESTIC WATER HEATERS**									
6000	Gas fired, flush jacket, std. controls, vent not incl.									
6040	75 MBH input, 73 GPH	1 Plum	1.40	5.714	Ea.	3,525	410		3,935	4,500
6060	98 MBH input, 95 GPH		1.40	5.714		8,650	410		9,060	10,100
6080	120 MBH input, 110 GPH		1.20	6.667		6,800	480		7,280	8,200
6100	120 MBH input, 115 GPH		1.10	7.273		5,000	525		5,525	6,275
6120	140 MBH input, 130 GPH		1	8		10,100	575		10,675	12,000
6140	155 MBH input, 150 GPH		.80	10		6,375	720		7,095	8,075
6160	180 MBH input, 170 GPH		.70	11.429		11,200	825		12,025	13,500
6180	200 MBH input, 192 GPH		.60	13.333		11,200	960		12,160	13,700
6200	250 MBH input, 245 GPH		.50	16		12,100	1,150		13,250	15,000
6220	260 MBH input, 250 GPH	Q-1	.80	20		7,725	1,300		9,025	10,400
6240	360 MBH input, 360 GPH		.80	20		8,825	1,300		10,125	11,600
6260	500 MBH input, 480 GPH		.70	22.857		12,400	1,475		13,875	15,900
6280	725 MBH input, 690 GPH		.60	26.667		27,200	1,725		28,925	32,500
6900	For low water cutoff, add	1 Plum	8	1		385	72		457	530
6960	For bronze body hot water circulator, add	"	4	2		2,200	144		2,344	2,625

22 34 Fuel-Fired Domestic Water Heaters

22 34 46 – Oil-Fired Domestic Water Heaters

22 34 46.10 Residential Oil-Fired Water Heaters

		Crew	Daily Output	Labor-Hours	Unit	Material	2023 Bare Costs Labor	Equipment	Total	Total Incl O&P
0010	**RESIDENTIAL OIL-FIRED WATER HEATERS**									
3000	Oil fired, glass lined tank, 5 yr., vent not included, 30 gallon D2020-260	1 Plum	2	4	Ea.	1,600	288		1,888	2,175
3040	50 gallon		1.80	4.444		1,450	320		1,770	2,075
3060	70 gallon		1.50	5.333		2,225	385		2,610	3,025

22 34 46.20 Commercial Oil-Fired Water Heaters

		Crew	Daily Output	Labor-Hours	Unit	Material	2023 Bare Costs Labor	Equipment	Total	Total Incl O&P
0010	**COMMERCIAL OIL-FIRED WATER HEATERS**									
8000	Oil fired, glass lined, UL listed, std. controls, vent not incl.									
8060	140 gal., 140 MBH input, 134 GPH	Q-1	2.13	7.512	Ea.	23,700	485		24,185	26,800
8080	140 gal., 199 MBH input, 191 GPH		2	8		24,500	520		25,020	27,800
8100	140 gal., 255 MBH input, 247 GPH		1.60	10		25,200	650		25,850	28,800
8120	140 gal., 270 MBH input, 259 GPH		1.20	13.333		31,200	865		32,065	35,600
8140	140 gal., 400 MBH input, 384 GPH		1	16		32,000	1,050		33,050	36,800
8160	140 gal., 540 MBH input, 519 GPH		.96	16.667		33,500	1,075		34,575	38,400
8180	140 gal., 720 MBH input, 691 GPH		.92	17.391		34,100	1,125		35,225	39,200
8200	221 gal., 300 MBH input, 288 GPH		.88	18.182		45,100	1,175		46,275	51,500
8220	221 gal., 600 MBH input, 576 GPH		.86	18.605		58,500	1,200		59,700	66,500
8240	221 gal., 800 MBH input, 768 GPH		.82	19.512		50,500	1,275		51,775	57,500
8260	201 gal., 1,000 MBH input, 960 GPH	Q-2	1.26	19.048		52,000	1,275		53,275	59,000
8280	201 gal., 1,250 MBH input, 1,200 GPH		1.22	19.672		52,500	1,325		53,825	60,000
8300	201 gal., 1,500 MBH input, 1,441 GPH		1.16	20.690		57,000	1,400		58,400	64,500
8320	411 gal., 600 MBH input, 576 GPH		1.12	21.429		57,500	1,450		58,950	65,000
8340	411 gal., 800 MBH input, 768 GPH		1.08	22.222		59,500	1,500		61,000	67,500
8360	411 gal., 1,000 MBH input, 960 GPH		1.04	23.077		61,000	1,550		62,550	69,500
8380	411 gal., 1,250 MBH input, 1,200 GPH		.98	24.490		62,500	1,650		64,150	71,000
8400	397 gal., 1,500 MBH input, 1,441 GPH		.92	26.087		65,500	1,750		67,250	75,000
8420	397 gal., 1,750 MBH input, 1,681 GPH		.86	27.907		68,000	1,875		69,875	78,000
8430	397 gal., 2,000 MBH input, 1,921 GPH		.82	29.268		73,500	1,975		75,475	84,000
8440	375 gal., 2,250 MBH input, 2,161 GPH		.76	31.579		75,500	2,125		77,625	86,000
8450	375 gal., 2,500 MBH input, 2,401 GPH		.82	29.268		78,500	1,975		80,475	89,500
8500	Oil fired, polymer lined									
8510	400 MBH, 125 gallon	Q-2	1	24	Ea.	37,900	1,625		39,525	44,100
8520	400 MBH, 600 gallon		.80	30		70,000	2,025		72,025	80,000
8530	800 MBH, 400 gallon		.67	35.821		63,500	2,400		65,900	73,000
8540	800 MBH, 600 gallon		.60	40		96,000	2,700		98,700	109,500
8550	1,000 MBH, 600 gallon		.50	48		85,000	3,225		88,225	98,500
8560	1,200 MBH, 900 gallon		.40	60		94,000	4,025		98,025	109,500
8900	For low water cutoff, add	1 Plum	8	1		365	72		437	505
8960	For bronze body hot water circulator, add	"	4	2		995	144		1,139	1,325

22 35 Domestic Water Heat Exchangers

22 35 30 – Water Heating by Steam

22 35 30.10 Water Heating Transfer Package

		Crew	Daily Output	Labor-Hours	Unit	Material	2023 Bare Costs Labor	Equipment	Total	Total Incl O&P
0010	**WATER HEATING TRANSFER PACKAGE**, Complete controls,									
0020	expansion tank, converter, air separator									
1000	Hot water, 180°F enter, 200°F exit, 15# steam									
1010	One pump system, 28 GPM	Q-6	.75	32	Ea.	24,000	2,175		26,175	29,600
1020	35 GPM		.70	34.286		27,400	2,325		29,725	33,600
1040	55 GPM		.65	36.923		30,700	2,500		33,200	37,500
1060	130 GPM		.55	43.636		39,000	2,950		41,950	47,300
1080	255 GPM		.40	60		51,000	4,075		55,075	62,000

22 35 Domestic Water Heat Exchangers

22 35 30 – Water Heating by Steam

22 35 30.10 Water Heating Transfer Package		Crew	Daily Output	Labor-Hours	Unit	Material	2023 Bare Costs Labor	Equipment	Total	Total Incl O&P
1100	550 GPM	Q-6	.30	80	Ea.	78,000	5,425		83,425	94,000
1120	800 GPM		.25	96		79,500	6,500		86,000	97,000
1220	Two pump system, 28 GPM		.70	34.286		32,500	2,325		34,825	39,300
1240	35 GPM		.65	36.923		40,000	2,500		42,500	47,800
1260	55 GPM		.60	40		41,200	2,700		43,900	49,500
1280	130 GPM		.50	48		54,500	3,250		57,750	64,500
1300	255 GPM		.35	68.571		71,500	4,650		76,150	85,500
1320	550 GPM		.25	96		87,000	6,500		93,500	105,000
1340	800 GPM		.20	120		105,000	8,125		113,125	127,500

22 35 43 – Domestic Water Heat Reclaimers

22 35 43.10 Drainwater Heat Recovery

		Crew	Daily Output	Labor-Hours	Unit	Material	Labor	Equipment	Total	Total Incl O&P
0010	**DRAINWATER HEAT RECOVERY**									
9005	Drainwater heat recov unit, copp coil type, for 1/2" supply, 3" waste	1 Plum	3	2.667	Ea.	510	192		702	850
9010	For 1/2" supply, 4" waste		3	2.667		810	192		1,002	1,175
9020	For 3/4" supply, 3" waste		3	2.667		595	192		787	940
9030	For 3/4" supply, 4" waste		3	2.667		760	192		952	1,125
9040	For 1" supply, 4" waste, double manifold		3	2.667		1,400	192		1,592	1,825

22 41 Residential Plumbing Fixtures

22 41 06 – Plumbing Fixtures General

22 41 06.10 Plumbing Fixture Notes

		Crew	Daily Output	Labor-Hours	Unit	Material	Labor	Equipment	Total	Total Incl O&P
0010	**PLUMBING FIXTURE NOTES**, Incl. trim fittings unless otherwise noted R224000-30									
0080	For rough-in, supply, waste, and vent, see add for each type									
0122	For electric water coolers, see Section 22 47 16.10									
0160	For color, unless otherwise noted, add				Ea.	20%				

22 41 13 – Residential Water Closets, Urinals, and Bidets

22 41 13.13 Water Closets

		Crew	Daily Output	Labor-Hours	Unit	Material	Labor	Equipment	Total	Total Incl O&P
0010	**WATER CLOSETS** D2010-110									
0022	For seats, see Section 22 41 13.44									
0032	For automatic flush, see Line 22 42 39.10 0972									
0150	Tank type, vitreous china, incl. seat, supply pipe w/stop, 1.6 gpf or noted									
0200	Wall hung R224000-30									
0400	Two piece, close coupled	Q-1	5.30	3.019	Ea.	460	196		656	795
0960	For rough-in, supply, waste, vent and carrier	"	2.73	5.861	"	1,650	380		2,030	2,400
0999	Floor mounted									
1020	One piece, low profile	Q-1	5.30	3.019	Ea.	890	196		1,086	1,275
1050	One piece		5.30	3.019		905	196		1,101	1,300
1100	Two piece, close coupled		5.30	3.019		234	196		430	550
1102	Economy		5.30	3.019		132	196		328	435
1110	Two piece, close coupled, dual flush		5.30	3.019		284	196		480	600
1140	Two piece, close coupled, 1.28 gpf, ADA G		5.30	3.019		276	196		472	595
1960	For color, add					30%				
1961	For designer colors and trim, add					55%				
1980	For rough-in, supply, waste and vent	Q-1	3.05	5.246	Ea.	565	340		905	1,125

22 41 13.19 Bidets

		Crew	Daily Output	Labor-Hours	Unit	Material	Labor	Equipment	Total	Total Incl O&P
0010	**BIDETS**									
0180	Vitreous china, with trim on fixture	Q-1	5	3.200	Ea.	700	208		908	1,075
0200	With trim for wall mounting	"	5	3.200		825	208		1,033	1,225
9590	For color, add					40%				
9591	For designer colors and trim, add					50%				

22 41 Residential Plumbing Fixtures

22 41 13 – Residential Water Closets, Urinals, and Bidets

22 41 13.19 Bidets		Crew	Daily Output	Labor-Hours	Unit	Material	2023 Bare Costs Labor	Equipment	Total	Total Incl O&P
9600	For rough-in, supply, waste and vent, add	Q-1	1.78	8.989	Ea.	555	585		1,140	1,475

22 41 13.44 Toilet Seats

		Crew	Daily Output	Labor-Hours	Unit	Material	Labor	Equipment	Total	Total Incl O&P
0010	**TOILET SEATS**									
0100	Molded composition, white									
0150	Industrial, w/o cover, open front, regular bowl	1 Plum	24	.333	Ea.	24	24		48	62.50
0200	With self-sustaining hinge		24	.333		25.50	24		49.50	64
0220	With self-sustaining check hinge		24	.333		24.50	24		48.50	63
0240	Extra heavy, with check hinge		24	.333		29	24		53	68
0260	Elongated bowl, same price									
0300	Junior size, w/o cover, open front	1 Plum	24	.333	Ea.	48	24		72	88.50
0320	Regular primary bowl, open front		24	.333		43.50	24		67.50	84
0340	Regular baby bowl, open front, check hinge		24	.333		40.50	24		64.50	80.50
0380	Open back & front, w/o cover, reg. or elongated bowl		24	.333		19.65	24		43.65	57.50
0400	Residential									
0420	Regular bowl, w/cover, closed front	1 Plum	24	.333	Ea.	40	24		64	80
0440	Open front	"	24	.333	"	28.50	24		52.50	67.50
0460	Elongated bowl, add					25%				
0500	Self-raising hinge, w/o cover, open front									
0520	Regular bowl	1 Plum	24	.333	Ea.	113	24		137	160
0540	Elongated bowl	"	24	.333	"	27.50	24		51.50	66.50
0700	Molded wood, white, with cover									
0720	Closed front, regular bowl, square back	1 Plum	24	.333	Ea.	11.05	24		35.05	48
0740	Extended back		24	.333		15.45	24		39.45	53
0780	Elongated bowl, square back		24	.333		14.70	24		38.70	52
0800	Open front		24	.333		15.50	24		39.50	53
0850	Decorator styles									
0890	Vinyl top, patterned	1 Plum	24	.333	Ea.	23.50	24		47.50	62
0900	Vinyl padded, plain colors, regular bowl		24	.333		23.50	24		47.50	62
0930	Elongated bowl		24	.333		27	24		51	66
1000	Solid plastic, white									
1030	Industrial, w/o cover, open front, regular bowl	1 Plum	24	.333	Ea.	29.50	24		53.50	68
1080	Extra heavy, concealed check hinge		24	.333		24.50	24		48.50	63
1100	Self-sustaining hinge		24	.333		27.50	24		51.50	66.50
1150	Elongated bowl		24	.333		25	24		49	63.50
1170	Concealed check		24	.333		19.25	24		43.25	57
1190	Self-sustaining hinge, concealed check		24	.333		61	24		85	103
1220	Residential, with cover, closed front, regular bowl		24	.333		42.50	24		66.50	83
1240	Elongated bowl		24	.333		54	24		78	95.50
1260	Open front, regular bowl		24	.333		45.50	24		69.50	86
1280	Elongated bowl		24	.333		58.50	24		82.50	100

22 41 16 – Residential Lavatories and Sinks

22 41 16.13 Lavatories

			Crew	Daily Output	Labor-Hours	Unit	Material	Labor	Equipment	Total	Total Incl O&P
0010	**LAVATORIES**, With trim, white unless noted otherwise	D2010-310									
0500	Vanity top, porcelain enamel on cast iron										
0600	20" x 18"	R224000-30	Q-1	6.40	2.500	Ea.	435	162		597	720
0640	33" x 19" oval			6.40	2.500		705	162		867	1,025
0680	20" x 17" oval			6.40	2.500		178	162		340	440
0720	19" round			6.40	2.500		750	162		912	1,075
0760	20" x 12" triangular bowl			6.40	2.500		300	162		462	570
0860	For color, add						25%				
0861	For designer colors and trim, add						70%				
1000	Cultured marble, 19" x 17", single bowl		Q-1	6.40	2.500	Ea.	173	162		335	430

22 41 Residential Plumbing Fixtures

22 41 16 – Residential Lavatories and Sinks

22 41 16.13 Lavatories		Crew	Daily Output	Labor-Hours	Unit	Material	2023 Bare Costs Labor	Equipment	Total	Total Incl O&P
1040	25" x 19", single bowl	Q-1	6.40	2.500	Ea.	233	162		395	500
1080	31" x 19", single bowl		6.40	2.500		201	162		363	465
1120	25" x 22", single bowl		6.40	2.500		194	162		356	455
1160	37" x 22", single bowl		6.40	2.500		268	162		430	535
1200	49" x 22", single bowl		6.40	2.500		305	162		467	575
1580	For color, same price									
1900	Stainless steel, self-rimming, 25" x 22", single bowl, ledge	Q-1	6.40	2.500	Ea.	570	162		732	865
1960	17" x 22", single bowl		6.40	2.500		550	162		712	845
2040	18-3/4" round		6.40	2.500		1,450	162		1,612	1,825
2600	Steel, enameled, 20" x 17", single bowl		5.80	2.759		205	179		384	490
2660	19" round		5.80	2.759		210	179		389	500
2720	18" round		5.80	2.759		132	179		311	410
2860	For color, add					10%				
2861	For designer colors and trim, add					20%				
2900	Vitreous china, 20" x 16", single bowl	Q-1	5.40	2.963	Ea.	263	192		455	575
2960	20" x 17", single bowl		5.40	2.963		158	192		350	460
3020	19" round, single bowl		5.40	2.963		156	192		348	460
3080	19" x 16", single bowl		5.40	2.963		273	192		465	585
3140	17" x 14", single bowl		5.40	2.963		193	192		385	500
3200	22" x 13", single bowl		5.40	2.963		268	192		460	580
3560	For color, add					50%				
3561	For designer colors and trim, add					100%				
3580	Rough-in, supply, waste and vent for all above lavatories	Q-1	2.30	6.957	Ea.	705	450		1,155	1,450
4000	Wall hung									
4040	Porcelain enamel on cast iron, 16" x 14", single bowl	Q-1	8	2	Ea.	550	130		680	805
4060	18" x 15", single bowl		8	2		365	130		495	600
4120	19" x 17", single bowl		8	2		475	130		605	720
4180	20" x 18", single bowl		8	2		330	130		460	555
4240	22" x 19", single bowl		8	2		865	130		995	1,150
4580	For color, add					30%				
4581	For designer colors and trim, add					75%				
6000	Vitreous china, 18" x 15", single bowl with backsplash	Q-1	7	2.286	Ea.	208	148		356	450
6060	19" x 17", single bowl		7	2.286		187	148		335	425
6120	20" x 18", single bowl		7	2.286		310	148		458	560
6210	27" x 20", ADA compliant		7	2.286		640	148		788	925
6500	For color, add					30%				
6501	For designer colors and trim, add					50%				
6960	Rough-in, supply, waste and vent for above lavatories	Q-1	1.66	9.639	Ea.	625	625		1,250	1,625
7000	Pedestal type									
7600	Vitreous china, 27" x 21", white	Q-1	6.60	2.424	Ea.	790	157		947	1,100
7610	27" x 21", colored		6.60	2.424		995	157		1,152	1,325
7620	27" x 21", premium color		6.60	2.424		1,125	157		1,282	1,475
7660	26" x 20", white		6.60	2.424		770	157		927	1,075
7670	26" x 20", colored		6.60	2.424		970	157		1,127	1,300
7680	26" x 20", premium color		6.60	2.424		1,175	157		1,332	1,525
7700	24" x 20", white		6.60	2.424		530	157		687	815
7710	24" x 20", colored		6.60	2.424		640	157		797	940
7720	24" x 20", premium color		6.60	2.424		705	157		862	1,000
7760	21" x 18", white		6.60	2.424		320	157		477	585
7770	21" x 18", colored		6.60	2.424		495	157		652	780
7990	Rough-in, supply, waste and vent for pedestal lavatories		1.66	9.639		625	625		1,250	1,625

22 41 Residential Plumbing Fixtures

22 41 16 – Residential Lavatories and Sinks

22 41 16.16 Sinks

		Crew	Daily Output	Labor-Hours	Unit	Material	2023 Bare Costs Labor	2023 Bare Costs Equipment	Total	Total Incl O&P
0010	**SINKS**, With faucets and drain D2010-410									
2000	Kitchen, counter top style, PE on CI, 24" x 21" single bowl	Q-1	5.60	2.857	Ea.	805	185		990	1,175
2100	31" x 22" single bowl		5.60	2.857		1,300	185		1,485	1,725
2200	32" x 21" double bowl		4.80	3.333		420	216		636	785
2310	For color, add					20%				
2311	For designer colors and trim, add					50%				
3000	Stainless steel, self rimming, 19" x 18" single bowl	Q-1	5.60	2.857	Ea.	680	185		865	1,025
3100	25" x 22" single bowl		5.60	2.857		755	185		940	1,100
3200	33" x 22" double bowl		4.80	3.333		1,100	216		1,316	1,525
3300	43" x 22" double bowl		4.80	3.333		1,275	216		1,491	1,725
3400	22" x 43" triple bowl		4.40	3.636		1,175	236		1,411	1,625
3500	Corner double bowl each 14" x 16"		4.80	3.333		845	216		1,061	1,250
4000	Steel, enameled, with ledge, 24" x 21" single bowl		5.60	2.857		520	185		705	845
4100	32" x 21" double bowl		4.80	3.333		520	216		736	895
4960	For color sinks except stainless steel, add					10%				
4961	For designer colors and trim, add					20%				
4980	For rough-in, supply, waste and vent, counter top sinks	Q-1	2.14	7.477		655	485		1,140	1,450
5000	Kitchen, raised deck, PE on CI									
5100	32" x 21", dual level, double bowl	Q-1	2.60	6.154	Ea.	525	400		925	1,175
5200	42" x 21", double bowl & disposer well	"	2.20	7.273		1,075	470		1,545	1,875
5700	For color, add					20%				
5701	For designer colors and trim, add					50%				
5790	For rough-in, supply, waste & vent, sinks	Q-1	1.85	8.649		655	560		1,215	1,550

22 41 19 – Residential Bathtubs

22 41 19.10 Baths

		Crew	Daily Output	Labor-Hours	Unit	Material	2023 Bare Costs Labor	2023 Bare Costs Equipment	Total	Total Incl O&P
0010	**BATHS** D2010-510									
0100	Tubs, recessed porcelain enamel on cast iron, with trim									
0180	48" x 42"	Q-1	4	4	Ea.	3,500	259		3,759	4,225
0220	72" x 36"	"	3	5.333	"	3,400	345		3,745	4,275
0300	Mat bottom									
0340	4'-6" long	Q-1	5	3.200	Ea.	2,375	208		2,583	2,900
0380	5' long		4.40	3.636		1,625	236		1,861	2,125
0420	5'-6" long		4	4		1,950	259		2,209	2,525
0480	Above floor drain, 5' long		4	4		1,175	259		1,434	1,650
0560	Corner 48" x 44"		4.40	3.636		3,175	236		3,411	3,850
0750	For color, add					30%				
0760	For designer colors & trim, add					60%				
2000	Enameled formed steel, 4'-6" long	Q-1	5.80	2.759	Ea.	585	179		764	905
2300	Above floor drain, 5' long	"	5.50	2.909	"	620	189		809	965
2350	For color, add					10%				
4000	Soaking, acrylic, w/pop-up drain 66" x 36" x 20" deep	Q-1	5.50	2.909	Ea.	2,425	189		2,614	2,950
4100	60" x 42" x 20" deep		5	3.200		1,400	208		1,608	1,850
4200	72" x 42" x 23" deep		4.80	3.333		2,375	216		2,591	2,950
4310	For color, add					5%				
4311	For designer colors & trim, add					20%				
4600	Module tub & showerwall surround, molded fiberglass									
4610	5' long x 34" wide x 76" high	Q-1	4	4	Ea.	895	259		1,154	1,375
4620	For color, add					10%				
4621	For designer colors and trim, add					25%				
4750	ADA compliant with 1-1/2" OD grab bar, antiskid bottom									
4760	60" x 32-3/4" x 72" high	Q-1	4	4	Ea.	645	259		904	1,100
4770	60" x 30" x 71" high with molded seat		3.50	4.571		815	296		1,111	1,325

22 41 Residential Plumbing Fixtures

22 41 19 – Residential Bathtubs

22 41 19.10 Baths

		Crew	Daily Output	Labor-Hours	Unit	Material	2023 Bare Costs Labor	2023 Bare Costs Equipment	Total	Total Incl O&P
9600	Rough-in, supply, waste and vent, for all above tubs, add	Q-1	2.07	7.729	Ea.	775	500		1,275	1,600

22 41 23 – Residential Showers

22 41 23.20 Showers

		Crew	Daily Output	Labor-Hours	Unit	Material	Labor	Equipment	Total	Total Incl O&P
0010	**SHOWERS** D2010-710									
1500	Stall, with drain only. Add for valve and door/curtain									
1510	Baked enamel, molded stone receptor, 30" square	Q-1	5.20	3.077	Ea.	1,475	200		1,675	1,925
1520	32" square		5	3.200		1,250	208		1,458	1,675
1530	36" square		4.80	3.333		3,350	216		3,566	4,000
1540	Terrazzo receptor, 32" square		5	3.200		1,450	208		1,658	1,900
1560	36" square		4.80	3.333		1,900	216		2,116	2,425
1580	36" corner angle		4.80	3.333		2,400	216		2,616	2,950
1600	For color, add					10%				
1601	For designer colors and trim, add					15%				
1604	For thermostatic valve, add				Ea.	1,300			1,300	1,425
3000	Fiberglass, one piece, with 3 walls, 32" x 32" square	Q-1	5.50	2.909		460	189		649	785
3100	36" x 36" square	"	5.50	2.909		510	189		699	840
3200	ADA compliant, 1-1/2" OD grab bars, nonskid floor									
3210	48" x 34-1/2" x 72" corner seat	Q-1	5	3.200	Ea.	690	208		898	1,075
3220	60" x 34-1/2" x 72" corner seat		4	4		830	259		1,089	1,300
3230	48" x 34-1/2" x 72" fold up seat		5	3.200		1,225	208		1,433	1,650
3250	64" x 65-3/4" x 81-1/2" fold. seat, ADA		3.80	4.211		1,525	273		1,798	2,075
3260	For thermostatic valve, add					1,300			1,300	1,425
4000	Polypropylene, stall only, w/molded-stone floor, 30" x 30"	Q-1	2	8		830	520		1,350	1,675
4100	32" x 32"	"	2	8		840	520		1,360	1,700
4110	For thermostatic valve, add					1,300			1,300	1,425
4200	Rough-in, supply, waste and vent for above showers	Q-1	2.05	7.805		750	505		1,255	1,575

22 41 23.40 Shower System Components

		Crew	Daily Output	Labor-Hours	Unit	Material	Labor	Equipment	Total	Total Incl O&P
0010	**SHOWER SYSTEM COMPONENTS**									
4500	Receptor only									
4510	For tile, 36" x 36"	1 Plum	4	2	Ea.	435	144		579	695
4520	Fiberglass receptor only, 32" x 32"		8	1		137	72		209	258
4530	34" x 34"		7.80	1.026		256	74		330	390
4540	36" x 36"		7.60	1.053		160	76		236	289
4600	Rectangular									
4620	32" x 48"	1 Plum	7.40	1.081	Ea.	190	78		268	325
4630	34" x 54"		7.20	1.111		229	80		309	370
4640	34" x 60"		7	1.143		242	82.50		324.50	390
5000	Built-in, head, arm, 2.5 GPM valve		4	2		101	144		245	325
5200	Head, arm, by-pass, integral stops, handles		3.60	2.222		330	160		490	600
5500	Head, water economizer, 1.6 GPM [G]		24	.333		32	24		56	71
5800	Mixing valve, built-in		6	1.333		80.50	96		176.50	232
5900	Exposed		6	1.333		890	96		986	1,125

22 41 36 – Residential Laundry Trays

22 41 36.10 Laundry Sinks

		Crew	Daily Output	Labor-Hours	Unit	Material	Labor	Equipment	Total	Total Incl O&P
0010	**LAUNDRY SINKS**, With trim D2010-420									
0020	Porcelain enamel on cast iron, black iron frame									
0050	24" x 21", single compartment	Q-1	6	2.667	Ea.	670	173		843	995
0100	26" x 21", single compartment		6	2.667		730	173		903	1,075
0200	48" x 20", double compartment		5	3.200		855	208		1,063	1,250
2000	Molded stone, on wall hanger or legs									
2020	22" x 23", single compartment	Q-1	6	2.667	Ea.	192	173		365	470

22 41 Residential Plumbing Fixtures

22 41 36 – Residential Laundry Trays

22 41 36.10 Laundry Sinks		Crew	Daily Output	Labor-Hours	Unit	Material	2023 Bare Costs Labor	Equipment	Total	Total Incl O&P
2100	45" x 21", double compartment	Q-1	5	3.200	Ea.	395	208		603	740
3000	Plastic, on wall hanger or legs									
3020	18" x 23", single compartment	Q-1	6.50	2.462	Ea.	157	160		317	410
3100	20" x 24", single compartment		6.50	2.462		175	160		335	430
3200	36" x 23", double compartment		5.50	2.909		232	189		421	535
3300	40" x 24", double compartment		5.50	2.909		305	189		494	615
5000	Stainless steel, counter top, 22" x 17" single compartment		6	2.667		82	173		255	350
5200	33" x 22", double compartment		5	3.200		98.50	208		306.50	420
9600	Rough-in, supply, waste and vent, for all laundry sinks		2.14	7.477		655	485		1,140	1,450

22 41 39 – Residential Faucets, Supplies and Trim

22 41 39.10 Faucets and Fittings

		Crew	Daily Output	Labor-Hours	Unit	Material	Labor	Equipment	Total	Total Incl O&P
0010	**FAUCETS AND FITTINGS**									
0150	Bath, faucets, diverter spout combination, sweat	1 Plum	8	1	Ea.	94.50	72		166.50	211
0200	For integral stops, IPS unions, add					121			121	133
0300	Three valve combinations, spout, head, arm, flange, sweat	1 Plum	6	1.333		107	96		203	260
0400	For integral stops, IPS unions, add				Pair	72.50			72.50	80
0420	Bath, press-bal mix valve w/diverter, spout, shower head, arm/flange	1 Plum	8	1	Ea.	216	72		288	345
0500	Drain, central lift, 1-1/2" IPS male		20	.400		57.50	29		86.50	106
0600	Trip lever, 1-1/2" IPS male		20	.400		65	29		94	115
0700	Pop up, 1-1/2" IPS male		18	.444		79.50	32		111.50	136
0800	Chain and stopper, 1-1/2" IPS male		24	.333		35.50	24		59.50	75.50
0810	Bidet									
0812	Fitting, over the rim, swivel spray/pop-up drain	1 Plum	8	1	Ea.	249	72		321	380
1000	Kitchen sink faucets, top mount, cast spout		10	.800		91	57.50		148.50	186
1100	For spray, add		24	.333		18.60	24		42.60	56.50
1110	For basket strainer w/tail piece, add		24	.333		16.85	24		40.85	54.50
1200	Wall type, swing tube spout		10	.800		79.50	57.50		137	174
1240	For soap dish, add					3.97			3.97	4.37
1250	For basket strainer w/tail piece, add					50			50	55
1300	Single control lever handle									
1310	With pull out spray									
1320	Polished chrome	1 Plum	10	.800	Ea.	243	57.50		300.50	355
2000	Laundry faucets, shelf type, IPS or copper unions		12	.667		65	48		113	143
2100	Lavatory faucet, centerset, without drain		10	.800		74.50	57.50		132	168
2120	With pop-up drain		6.66	1.201		94	86.50		180.50	232
2130	For acrylic handles, add					5.70			5.70	6.25
2150	Concealed, 12" centers	1 Plum	10	.800		97	57.50		154.50	193
2160	With pop-up drain	"	6.66	1.201		117	86.50		203.50	257
2210	Porcelain cross handles and pop-up drain									
2220	Polished chrome	1 Plum	6.66	1.201	Ea.	232	86.50		318.50	385
2230	Polished brass	"	6.66	1.201	"	305	86.50		391.50	465
2260	Single lever handle and pop-up drain									
2280	Satin nickel	1 Plum	6.66	1.201	Ea.	385	86.50		471.50	550
2290	Polished chrome		6.66	1.201		274	86.50		360.50	430
2600	Shelfback, 4" to 6" centers, 17 ga. tailpiece		10	.800		89.50	57.50		147	184
2650	With pop-up drain		6.66	1.201		143	86.50		229.50	286
2700	Shampoo faucet with supply tube		24	.333		50.50	24		74.50	92
2800	Self-closing, center set		10	.800		158	57.50		215.50	260
2810	Automatic sensor and operator, with faucet head		6.15	1.301		640	93.50		733.50	845
4000	Shower by-pass valve with union		18	.444		61.50	32		93.50	116
4100	Shower arm with flange and head		22	.364		20.50	26		46.50	61.50
4140	Shower, hand held, pin mount, massage action, chrome		22	.364		79.50	26		105.50	127

22 41 Residential Plumbing Fixtures

22 41 39 – Residential Faucets, Supplies and Trim

22 41 39.10 Faucets and Fittings		Crew	Daily Output	Labor-Hours	Unit	Material	2023 Bare Costs Labor	Equipment	Total	Total Incl O&P
4142	Polished brass	1 Plum	22	.364	Ea.	173	26		199	230
4144	Shower, hand held, wall mtd, adj. spray, 2 wall mounts, chrome		20	.400		124	29		153	180
4146	Polished brass		20	.400		265	29		294	335
4148	Shower, hand held head, bar mounted 24", adj. spray, chrome		20	.400		199	29		228	261
4150	Polished brass		20	.400		410	29		439	495
4200	Shower thermostatic mixing valve, concealed, with shower head trim kit		8	1		395	72		467	535
4220	Shower pressure balancing mixing valve									
4230	With shower head, arm, flange and diverter tub spout									
4240	Chrome	1 Plum	6.14	1.303	Ea.	455	94		549	640
4250	Satin nickel		6.14	1.303		595	94		689	790
4260	Polished graphite		6.14	1.303		580	94		674	780
5000	Sillcock, compact, brass, IPS or copper to hose		24	.333		19.40	24		43.40	57.50
6000	Stop and waste valves, bronze									
6100	Angle, solder end 1/2"	1 Plum	24	.333	Ea.	59	24		83	101
6110	3/4"		20	.400		68.50	29		97.50	118
6300	Straightway, solder end 3/8"		24	.333		21	24		45	59
6310	1/2"		24	.333		33	24		57	72.50
6320	3/4"		20	.400		37.50	29		66.50	84.50
6410	Straightway, threaded 1/2"		24	.333		39	24		63	79
6420	3/4"		20	.400		44	29		73	91.50
6430	1"		19	.421		23.50	30.50		54	71
7800	Water closet, wax gasket		96	.083		1.36	6		7.36	10.45
7820	Gasket toilet tank to bowl		32	.250		3.12	18		21.12	30.50
7830	Replacement diaphragm washer assy for ballcock valve		12	.667		3.12	48		51.12	75
7850	Dual flush valve		12	.667		120	48		168	204
8000	Water supply stops, polished chrome plate									
8200	Angle, 3/8"	1 Plum	24	.333	Ea.	12.25	24		36.25	49.50
8300	1/2"		22	.364		14	26		40	54.50
8400	Straight, 3/8"		26	.308		16.70	22		38.70	51.50
8500	1/2"		24	.333		12.85	24		36.85	50
8600	Water closet, angle, w/flex riser, 3/8"		24	.333		43.50	24		67.50	84
9100	Miscellaneous									
9720	Teflon tape, 1/2" x 520" roll				Ea.	1.11			1.11	1.22

22 41 39.70 Washer/Dryer Accessories

		Crew	Daily Output	Labor-Hours	Unit	Material	Labor	Equipment	Total	Total Incl O&P
0010	**WASHER/DRYER ACCESSORIES**									
1020	Valves ball type single lever									
1030	1/2" diam., IPS	1 Plum	21	.381	Ea.	56.50	27.50		84	103
1040	1/2" diam., solder	"	21	.381	"	56.50	27.50		84	103
1050	Recessed box, 16 ga., two hose valves and drain									
1060	1/2" size, 1-1/2" drain	1 Plum	18	.444	Ea.	126	32		158	187
1070	1/2" size, 2" drain	"	17	.471	"	113	34		147	175
1080	With grounding electric receptacle									
1090	1/2" size, 1-1/2" drain	1 Plum	18	.444	Ea.	153	32		185	216
1100	1/2" size, 2" drain	"	17	.471	"	149	34		183	215
1110	With grounding and dryer receptacle									
1120	1/2" size, 1-1/2" drain	1 Plum	18	.444	Ea.	171	32		203	236
1130	1/2" size, 2" drain	"	17	.471	"	172	34		206	241
1140	Recessed box, 16 ga., ball valves with single lever and drain									
1150	1/2" size, 1-1/2" drain	1 Plum	19	.421	Ea.	238	30.50		268.50	305
1160	1/2" size, 2" drain	"	18	.444	"	206	32		238	275
1170	With grounding electric receptacle									
1180	1/2" size, 1-1/2" drain	1 Plum	19	.421	Ea.	282	30.50		312.50	355

22 41 Residential Plumbing Fixtures

22 41 39 – Residential Faucets, Supplies and Trim

22 41 39.70 Washer/Dryer Accessories		Crew	Daily Output	Labor-Hours	Unit	Material	2023 Bare Costs Labor	Equipment	Total	Total Incl O&P
1190	1/2" size, 2" drain	1 Plum	18	.444	Ea.	229	32		261	300
1200	With grounding and dryer receptacles									
1210	1/2" size, 1-1/2" drain	1 Plum	19	.421	Ea.	250	30.50		280.50	320
1220	1/2" size, 2" drain	"	18	.444	"	250	32		282	325
1300	Recessed box, 20 ga., two hose valves and drain (economy type)									
1310	1/2" size, 1-1/2" drain	1 Plum	19	.421	Ea.	98.50	30.50		129	153
1320	1/2" size, 2" drain		18	.444		92	32		124	149
1330	Box with drain only		24	.333		57	24		81	98.50
1340	1/2" size, 1-1/2" ABS/PVC drain		19	.421		123	30.50		153.50	180
1350	1/2" size, 2" ABS/PVC drain		18	.444		149	32		181	212
1352	Box with drain and 15 A receptacle		24	.333		111	24		135	158
1360	1/2" size, 2" drain ABS/PVC, 15 A receptacle	↓	24	.333	↓	89	24		113	134
1400	Wall mounted									
1410	1/2" size, 1-1/2" plastic drain	1 Plum	19	.421	Ea.	30.50	30.50		61	78.50
1420	1/2" size, 2" plastic drain	"	18	.444	"	17.95	32		49.95	67.50
1500	Dryer vent kit									
1510	8' flex duct, clamps and outside hood	1 Plum	20	.400	Ea.	14.75	29		43.75	59
1980	Rough-in, supply, waste, and vent for washer boxes	"	3.46	2.310	"	750	166		916	1,075

22 42 Commercial Plumbing Fixtures

22 42 13 – Commercial Water Closets, Urinals, and Bidets

22 42 13.13 Water Closets

			Crew	Daily Output	Labor-Hours	Unit	Material	2023 Bare Costs Labor	Equipment	Total	Total Incl O&P
0010	**WATER CLOSETS**										
3000	Bowl only, with flush valve, seat, 1.6 gpf unless noted										
3100	Wall hung		Q-1	5.80	2.759	Ea.	1,050	179		1,229	1,425
3200	For rough-in, supply, waste and vent, single WC			2.56	6.250		1,700	405		2,105	2,475
3300	Floor mounted			5.80	2.759		365	179		544	665
3350	With wall outlet			5.80	2.759		610	179		789	935
3360	With floor outlet, 1.28 gpf	G		5.80	2.759		590	179		769	915
3362	With floor outlet, 1.28 gpf, ADA	G		5.80	2.759		615	179		794	945
3370	For rough-in, supply, waste and vent, single WC		↓	2.84	5.634	↓	605	365		970	1,200
3390	Floor mounted children's size, 10-3/4" high										
3392	With automatic flush sensor, 1.6 gpf		Q-1	6.20	2.581	Ea.	700	167		867	1,025
3396	With automatic flush sensor, 1.28 gpf			6.20	2.581		645	167		812	960
3400	For rough-in, supply, waste and vent, single WC		↓	2.84	5.634	↓	605	365		970	1,200
3500	Gang side by side carrier system, rough-in, supply, waste & vent										
3510	For single hook-up		Q-1	1.97	8.122	Ea.	2,000	525		2,525	2,975
3520	For each additional hook-up, add		"	2.14	7.477	"	1,850	485		2,335	2,750
3550	Gang back to back carrier system, rough-in, supply, waste & vent										
3560	For pair hook-up		Q-1	1.76	9.091	Pair	3,300	590		3,890	4,500
3570	For each additional pair hook-up, add		"	1.81	8.840	"	3,125	575		3,700	4,275

22 42 13.16 Urinals

			Crew	Daily Output	Labor-Hours	Unit	Material	2023 Bare Costs Labor	Equipment	Total	Total Incl O&P
0010	**URINALS**	D2010-210									
0102	For automatic flush see Line 22 42 39.10 0972										
3000	Wall hung, vitreous china, with self-closing valve	R224000-30									
3100	Siphon jet type		Q-1	3	5.333	Ea.	415	345		760	975
3120	Blowout type			3	5.333		635	345		980	1,200
3140	Water saving .5 gpf	G		3	5.333		660	345		1,005	1,250
3300	Rough-in, supply, waste & vent			2.83	5.654		1,325	365		1,690	2,025
5000	Stall type, vitreous china, includes valve			2.50	6.400		1,000	415		1,415	1,725
6980	Rough-in, supply, waste and vent			1.99	8.040		880	520		1,400	1,750

22 42 Commercial Plumbing Fixtures

22 42 13 – Commercial Water Closets, Urinals, and Bidets

22 42 13.16 Urinals

		Crew	Daily Output	Labor-Hours	Unit	Material	2023 Bare Costs Labor	2023 Bare Costs Equipment	Total	Total Incl O&P
8000	Waterless (no flush) urinal									
8010	Wall hung									
8014	Fiberglass reinforced polyester									
8020	Standard unit G	Q-1	21.30	.751	Ea.	610	48.50		658.50	750
8030	ADA compliant unit G	"	21.30	.751		530	48.50		578.50	660
8070	For solid color, add G					95			95	104
8080	For 2" brass flange (new const.), add G	Q-1	96	.167		23	10.80		33.80	41.50
8200	Vitreous china									
8220	ADA compliant unit, 14" G	Q-1	21.30	.751	Ea.	315	48.50		363.50	420
8250	ADA compliant unit, 15.5"	"	21.30	.751		530	48.50		578.50	660
8270	For solid color, add G					95			95	104
8290	Rough-in, supply, waste & vent G	Q-1	2.92	5.479		1,275	355		1,630	1,950
8400	Trap liquid									
8410	1 quart G				Ea.	26			26	29
8420	1 gallon G				"	92.50			92.50	102

22 42 16 – Commercial Lavatories and Sinks

22 42 16.13 Lavatories

0010	**LAVATORIES**, With trim, white unless noted otherwise									
0020	Commercial lavatories same as residential. See Section 22 41 16									

22 42 16.16 Commercial Sinks

		Crew	Daily Output	Labor-Hours	Unit	Material	Labor	Equipment	Total	Total Incl O&P
0010	**COMMERCIAL SINKS**									
5900	Scullery sink, stainless steel									
5910	1 bowl and drain board, 43" x 22" OD	Q-1	5.40	2.963	Ea.	1,550	192		1,742	1,975
5920	2 bowls and drain board, 49" x 22" OD		4.60	3.478		2,925	226		3,151	3,525
5930	3 bowls and drain board, 43" x 22" OD		4.20	3.810		5,075	247		5,322	5,950
5940	1 bowl and drain board, 50" x 28" OD, with legs		5.40	2.963		1,900	192		2,092	2,350

22 42 16.30 Classroom Sinks

		Crew	Daily Output	Labor-Hours	Unit	Material	Labor	Equipment	Total	Total Incl O&P
0010	**CLASSROOM SINKS**									
6020	Countertop, stainless steel									
6024	with faucet, bubbler and strainer, ADA compliant									
6036	25" x 17" single bowl	Q-1	5.20	3.077	Ea.	1,825	200		2,025	2,325
6040	28" x 22" single bowl		5.20	3.077		1,400	200		1,600	1,825
6044	31" x 19" single bowl		5.20	3.077		1,450	200		1,650	1,900
6070	37" x 17" double bowl		4.40	3.636		2,125	236		2,361	2,675
6100	For rough-in, supply, waste and vent, counter top classroom sinks		2.14	7.477		655	485		1,140	1,450

22 42 16.34 Laboratory Countertops and Sinks

		Crew	Daily Output	Labor-Hours	Unit	Material	Labor	Equipment	Total	Total Incl O&P
0010	**LABORATORY COUNTERTOPS AND SINKS**									
0050	Laboratory sinks, corrosion resistant									
1000	Stainless steel sink, bench mounted, with									
1020	plug & waste fitting with 1-1/2" straight threads									
1030	Single bowl, 2 drainboards, backnut & strainer									
1050	18-1/2" x 15-1/2" x 12-1/2" sink, 54" x 24" OD	Q-1	3	5.333	Ea.	1,450	345		1,795	2,125
1100	Single bowl, single drainboard, backnut & strainer									
1130	18-1/2" x 15-1/2" x 12-1/2" sink, 47" x 24" OD	Q-1	3	5.333	Ea.	1,050	345		1,395	1,700
1146	Double bowl, single drainboard, backnut & strainer									
1150	18-1/2" x 15-1/2" x 12-1/2" sink, 70" x 24" OD	Q-1	3	5.333	Ea.	1,600	345		1,945	2,300
1280	Polypropylene									
1290	Flanged 1-1/4" wide, rectangular with strainer									
1300	plug & waste fitting, 1-1/2" straight threads									
1320	12" x 12" x 8" sink, 14-1/2" x 14-1/2" OD	Q-1	4	4	Ea.	286	259		545	700
1340	16" x 16" x 8" sink, 18-1/2" x 18-1/2" OD		4	4		405	259		664	835

22 42 Commercial Plumbing Fixtures

22 42 16 – Commercial Lavatories and Sinks

22 42 16.34 Laboratory Countertops and Sinks		Crew	Daily Output	Labor-Hours	Unit	Material	2023 Bare Costs Labor	Equipment	Total	Total Incl O&P
1360	21" x 18" x 10" sink, 23-1/2" x 20-1/2" OD	Q-1	4	4	Ea.	420	259		679	845
1490	For rough-in, supply, waste & vent, add	▼	2.02	7.921	▼	435	515		950	1,250
1600	Polypropylene									
1620	Cup sink, oval, integral strainers									
1640	6" x 3" I.D., 7" x 4" OD	Q-1	6	2.667	Ea.	177	173		350	455
1660	9" x 3" I.D., 10" x 4-1/2" OD	"	6	2.667		211	173		384	490
1740	1-1/2" diam. x 11" long					48.50			48.50	53.50
1980	For rough-in, supply, waste & vent, add	Q-1	1.70	9.412	▼	480	610		1,090	1,450

22 42 16.40 Service Sinks

		Crew	Daily Output	Labor-Hours	Unit	Material	Labor	Equipment	Total	Total Incl O&P
0010	**SERVICE SINKS**									
6650	Service, floor, corner, PE on CI, 28" x 28"	Q-1	4.40	3.636	Ea.	1,575	236		1,811	2,100
6750	Vinyl coated rim guard, add					70			70	77
6755	Mop sink, molded stone, 22" x 18"	1 Plum	3.33	2.402		815	173		988	1,150
6760	Mop sink, molded stone, 24" x 36"		3.33	2.402		235	173		408	515
6770	Mop sink, molded stone, 24" x 36", w/rim 3 sides	▼	3.33	2.402		410	173		583	715
6790	For rough-in, supply, waste & vent, floor service sinks	Q-1	1.64	9.756		2,500	635		3,135	3,675
7000	Service, wall, PE on CI, roll rim, 22" x 18"		4	4		1,075	259		1,334	1,575
7100	24" x 20"	▼	4	4		1,600	259		1,859	2,125
7600	For stainless steel rim guard, two sides only, add					55			55	60.50
7800	For stainless steel rim guard, front only, add					61			61	67
8600	Vitreous china, 22" x 20"	Q-1	4	4		1,100	259		1,359	1,600
8960	For stainless steel rim guard, front or one side, add					86.50			86.50	95
8980	For rough-in, supply, waste & vent, wall service sinks	Q-1	1.30	12.308	▼	3,650	800		4,450	5,200

22 42 23 – Commercial Showers

22 42 23.30 Group Showers

		Crew	Daily Output	Labor-Hours	Unit	Material	Labor	Equipment	Total	Total Incl O&P
0010	**GROUP SHOWERS**									
6000	Group, w/pressure balancing valve, rough-in and rigging not included									
6800	Column, 6 heads, no receptors, less partitions	Q-1	3	5.333	Ea.	10,500	345		10,845	12,000
6900	With stainless steel partitions		1	16		13,900	1,050		14,950	16,900
7600	5 heads, no receptors, less partitions		3	5.333		7,175	345		7,520	8,425
7620	4 heads (1 ADA compliant) no receptors, less partitions		3	5.333		6,675	345		7,020	7,875
7700	With stainless steel partitions		1	16		7,200	1,050		8,250	9,450
8000	Wall, 2 heads, no receptors, less partitions		4	4		3,050	259		3,309	3,725
8100	With stainless steel partitions	▼	2	8	▼	6,700	520		7,220	8,150

22 42 33 – Wash Fountains

22 42 33.20 Commercial Wash Fountains

		Crew	Daily Output	Labor-Hours	Unit	Material	Labor	Equipment	Total	Total Incl O&P
0010	**COMMERCIAL WASH FOUNTAINS** D2010-610									
1900	Group, foot control									
2000	Precast terrazzo, circular, 36" diam., 5 or 6 persons	Q-2	3	8	Ea.	7,800	540		8,340	9,375
2100	54" diam. for 8 or 10 persons		2.50	9.600		11,400	645		12,045	13,500
2400	Semi-circular, 36" diam. for 3 persons		3	8		6,375	540		6,915	7,800
2500	54" diam. for 4 or 5 persons		2.50	9.600		11,700	645		12,345	13,900
2700	Quarter circle (corner), 54" diam. for 3 persons		3.50	6.857		7,650	460		8,110	9,125
3000	Stainless steel, circular, 36" diameter		3.50	6.857		6,850	460		7,310	8,250
3100	54" diameter		2.80	8.571		8,575	575		9,150	10,300
3400	Semi-circular, 36" diameter		3.50	6.857		5,625	460		6,085	6,875
3500	54" diameter		2.80	8.571		6,000	575		6,575	7,450
5000	Thermoplastic, pre-assembled, circular, 36" diameter		6	4		4,775	269		5,044	5,650
5100	54" diameter		4	6		4,575	405		4,980	5,625
5400	Semi-circular, 36" diameter		6	4		5,175	269		5,444	6,075
5600	54" diameter	▼	4	6		5,250	405		5,655	6,350

22 42 Commercial Plumbing Fixtures

22 42 33 – Wash Fountains

22 42 33.20 Commercial Wash Fountains

		Crew	Daily Output	Labor-Hours	Unit	Material	2023 Bare Costs Labor	Equipment	Total	Total Incl O&P
5610	Group, infrared control, barrier free									
5614	Precast terrazzo									
5620	Semi-circular 36" diam. for 3 persons	Q-2	3	8	Ea.	7,825	540		8,365	9,400
5630	46" diam. for 4 persons		2.80	8.571		8,475	575		9,050	10,200
5640	Circular, 54" diam. for 8 persons, button control		2.50	9.600		10,200	645		10,845	12,200
5700	Rough-in, supply, waste and vent for above wash fountains	Q-1	1.82	8.791		940	570		1,510	1,875
6200	Duo for small washrooms, stainless steel		2	8		3,450	520		3,970	4,550
6400	Bowl with backsplash		2	8		2,500	520		3,020	3,525
6500	Rough-in, supply, waste & vent for duo fountains		2.02	7.921		575	515		1,090	1,400

22 42 39 – Commercial Faucets, Supplies, and Trim

22 42 39.10 Faucets and Fittings

		Crew	Daily Output	Labor-Hours	Unit	Material	2023 Bare Costs Labor	Equipment	Total	Total Incl O&P
0010	**FAUCETS AND FITTINGS**									
0840	Flush valves, with vacuum breaker									
0850	Water closet									
0860	Exposed, rear spud	1 Plum	8	1	Ea.	164	72		236	288
0870	Top spud		8	1		214	72		286	340
0880	Concealed, rear spud		8	1		246	72		318	380
0890	Top spud		8	1		232	72		304	360
0900	Wall hung		8	1		245	72		317	375
0910	Dual flush flushometer		12	.667		257	48		305	355
0912	Flushometer retrofit kit		18	.444		19.15	32		51.15	69
0920	Urinal									
0930	Exposed, stall	1 Plum	8	1	Ea.	214	72		286	340
0940	Wall (washout)		8	1		173	72		245	298
0950	Pedestal, top spud		8	1		188	72		260	315
0960	Concealed, stall		8	1		183	72		255	310
0970	Wall (washout)		8	1		197	72		269	325
0971	Automatic flush sensor and operator for									
0972	urinals or water closets, standard	1 Plum	8	1	Ea.	605	72		677	770
0980	High efficiency water saving									
0984	Water closets, 1.28 gpf	1 Plum	8	1	Ea.	470	72		542	625
0988	Urinals, .5 gpf	"	8	1	"	470	72		542	625
2790	Faucets for lavatories									
2800	Self-closing, center set	1 Plum	10	.800	Ea.	158	57.50		215.50	260
2810	Automatic sensor and operator, with faucet head		6.15	1.301		640	93.50		733.50	845
3000	Service sink faucet, cast spout, pail hook, hose end		14	.571		81	41		122	151

22 42 39.30 Carriers and Supports

		Crew	Daily Output	Labor-Hours	Unit	Material	2023 Bare Costs Labor	Equipment	Total	Total Incl O&P
0010	**CARRIERS AND SUPPORTS**, For plumbing fixtures									
0500	Drinking fountain, wall mounted									
0600	Plate type with studs, top back plate	1 Plum	7	1.143	Ea.	61.50	82.50		144	191
0700	Top front and back plate		7	1.143		660	82.50		742.50	850
0800	Top & bottom, front & back plates, w/bearing jacks		7	1.143		1,050	82.50		1,132.50	1,275
3000	Lavatory, concealed arm									
3050	Floor mounted, single									
3100	High back fixture	1 Plum	6	1.333	Ea.	1,800	96		1,896	2,150
3200	Flat slab fixture		6	1.333		1,475	96		1,571	1,775
3220	ADA compliant		6	1.333		291	96		387	465
3250	Floor mounted, back to back									
3300	High back fixtures	1 Plum	5	1.600	Ea.	1,100	115		1,215	1,375
3400	Flat slab fixtures		5	1.600		1,350	115		1,465	1,650
3430	ADA compliant		5	1.600		370	115		485	575
3500	Wall mounted, in stud or masonry									

22 42 Commercial Plumbing Fixtures

22 42 39 – Commercial Faucets, Supplies, and Trim

22 42 39.30 Carriers and Supports		Crew	Daily Output	Labor-Hours	Unit	Material	2023 Bare Costs Labor	2023 Bare Costs Equipment	Total	Total Incl O&P
3600	High back fixture	1 Plum	6	1.333	Ea.	755	96		851	975
3700	Flat slab fixture	"	6	1.333	"	320	96		416	495
4000	Exposed arm type, floor mounted									
4100	Single high back or flat slab fixture	1 Plum	6	1.333	Ea.	1,100	96		1,196	1,350
4200	Back to back, high back or flat slab fixtures		5	1.600		1,700	115		1,815	2,050
4300	Wall mounted, high back or flat slab lavatory	↓	6	1.333	↓	755	96		851	975
4600	Sink, floor mounted									
4650	Exposed arm system									
4700	Single heavy fixture	1 Plum	5	1.600	Ea.	2,025	115		2,140	2,400
4750	Single heavy sink with slab		5	1.600		3,275	115		3,390	3,775
4800	Back to back, standard fixtures		5	1.600		3,275	115		3,390	3,775
4850	Back to back, heavy fixtures		5	1.600		3,275	115		3,390	3,775
4900	Back to back, heavy sink with slab	↓	5	1.600		2,225	115		2,340	2,600
4950	Exposed offset arm system									
5000	Single heavy deep fixture	1 Plum	5	1.600	Ea.	3,275	115		3,390	3,775
5100	Plate type system									
5200	With bearing jacks, single fixture	1 Plum	5	1.600	Ea.	1,400	115		1,515	1,725
5300	With exposed arms, single heavy fixture		5	1.600		1,225	115		1,340	1,525
5400	Wall mounted, exposed arms, single heavy fixture		5	1.600		1,250	115		1,365	1,550
6000	Urinal, floor mounted, 2" or 3" coupling, blowout type		6	1.333		1,350	96		1,446	1,650
6100	With fixture or hanger bolts, blowout or washout		6	1.333		580	96		676	785
6200	With bearing plate		6	1.333		1,075	96		1,171	1,325
6300	Wall mounted, plate type system	↓	6	1.333	↓	965	96		1,061	1,225
6980	Water closet, siphon jet									
7000	Horizontal, adjustable, caulk									
7040	Single, 4" pipe size	1 Plum	5.33	1.501	Ea.	1,425	108		1,533	1,725
7050	4" pipe size, ADA compliant		5.33	1.501		2,050	108		2,158	2,400
7060	5" pipe size		5.33	1.501		1,175	108		1,283	1,450
7100	Double, 4" pipe size		5	1.600		2,675	115		2,790	3,125
7110	4" pipe size, ADA compliant		5	1.600		1,225	115		1,340	1,525
7120	5" pipe size	↓	5	1.600	↓	1,700	115		1,815	2,050
7160	Horizontal, adjustable, extended, caulk									
7180	Single, 4" pipe size	1 Plum	5.33	1.501	Ea.	1,775	108		1,883	2,100
7200	5" pipe size		5.33	1.501		2,200	108		2,308	2,575
7240	Double, 4" pipe size		5	1.600		5,350	115		5,465	6,050
7260	5" pipe size	↓	5	1.600	↓	3,050	115		3,165	3,550
7400	Vertical, adjustable, caulk or thread									
7440	Single, 4" pipe size	1 Plum	5.33	1.501	Ea.	2,275	108		2,383	2,650
7460	5" pipe size		5.33	1.501		1,900	108		2,008	2,250
7480	6" pipe size		5	1.600		1,975	115		2,090	2,350
7520	Double, 4" pipe size		5	1.600		5,350	115		5,465	6,050
7540	5" pipe size		5	1.600		2,450	115		2,565	2,875
7560	6" pipe size	↓	4	2	↓	2,700	144		2,844	3,200
7600	Vertical, adjustable, extended, caulk									
7620	Single, 4" pipe size	1 Plum	5.33	1.501	Ea.	1,450	108		1,558	1,750
7640	5" pipe size		5.33	1.501		1,125	108		1,233	1,375
7680	6" pipe size		5	1.600		2,150	115		2,265	2,550
7720	Double, 4" pipe size		5	1.600		2,450	115		2,565	2,875
7740	5" pipe size		5	1.600		1,325	115		1,440	1,625
7760	6" pipe size	↓	4	2	↓	1,450	144		1,594	1,800
7780	Water closet, blow out									
7800	Vertical offset, caulk or thread									
7820	Single, 4" pipe size	1 Plum	5.33	1.501	Ea.	1,825	108		1,933	2,175

22 42 Commercial Plumbing Fixtures

22 42 39 – Commercial Faucets, Supplies, and Trim

22 42 39.30 Carriers and Supports

		Crew	Daily Output	Labor-Hours	Unit	Material	2023 Bare Costs Labor	2023 Bare Costs Equipment	Total	Total Incl O&P
7840	Double, 4" pipe size	1 Plum	5	1.600	Ea.	3,150	115		3,265	3,625
7880	Vertical offset, extended, caulk									
7900	Single, 4" pipe size	1 Plum	5.33	1.501	Ea.	2,300	108		2,408	2,675
7920	Double, 4" pipe size	"	5	1.600	"	3,600	115		3,715	4,150
7960	Vertical, for floor mounted back-outlet									
7980	Single, 4" thread, 2" vent	1 Plum	5.33	1.501	Ea.	3,575	108		3,683	4,075
8000	Double, 4" thread, 2" vent	"	6	1.333	"	5,350	96		5,446	6,025
8040	Vertical, for floor mounted back-outlet, extended									
8060	Single, 4" caulk, 2" vent	1 Plum	6	1.333	Ea.	7,900	96		7,996	8,825
8080	Double, 4" caulk, 2" vent	"	6	1.333	"	2,750	96		2,846	3,175
8200	Water closet, residential									
8220	Vertical centerline, floor mount									
8240	Single, 3" caulk, 2" or 3" vent	1 Plum	6	1.333	Ea.	1,475	96		1,571	1,775
8260	4" caulk, 2" or 4" vent		6	1.333		1,250	96		1,346	1,525
8280	3" copper sweat, 3" vent		6	1.333		870	96		966	1,100
8300	4" copper sweat, 4" vent		6	1.333		1,050	96		1,146	1,300
8400	Vertical offset, floor mount									
8420	Single, 3" or 4" caulk, vent	1 Plum	4	2	Ea.	1,100	144		1,244	1,450
8440	3" or 4" copper sweat, vent		5	1.600		1,100	115		1,215	1,400
8460	Double, 3" or 4" caulk, vent		4	2		1,900	144		2,044	2,300
8480	3" or 4" copper sweat, vent		5	1.600		1,900	115		2,015	2,250
9000	Water cooler (electric), floor mounted									
9100	Plate type with bearing plate, single	1 Plum	6	1.333	Ea.	1,075	96		1,171	1,325
9140	Plate type with bearing plate, back to back	"	4	2	"	1,075	144		1,219	1,400

22 43 Healthcare Plumbing Fixtures

22 43 13 – Healthcare Water Closets

22 43 13.40 Water Closets

		Crew	Daily Output	Labor-Hours	Unit	Material	2023 Bare Costs Labor	2023 Bare Costs Equipment	Total	Total Incl O&P
0010	**WATER CLOSETS**									
1000	Bowl only, 1 piece, w/seat and flush valve, ADA compliant, 18" high									
1030	Floor mounted									
1150	With wall outlet	Q-1	5.30	3.019	Ea.	355	196		551	680
1180	For rough-in, supply, waste and vent		2.84	5.634		605	365		970	1,200
1200	With floor outlet		5.30	3.019		395	196		591	725
1800	For rough-in, supply, waste and vent		3.05	5.246		565	340		905	1,125
3100	Wall hung		5.80	2.759		1,050	179		1,229	1,425
3150	Hospital type, slotted rim for bed pan									
3156	Elongated bowl, top spud	Q-1	5.80	2.759	Ea.	655	179		834	985
3160	Elongated bowl, rear spud		5.80	2.759		405	179		584	710
3200	For rough-in, supply, waste and vent, single WC		2.56	6.250		1,700	405		2,105	2,475
3300	Floor mounted									
3320	Bariatric (1,200 lb. capacity), elongated bowl, ADA compliant	Q-1	4.60	3.478	Ea.	3,000	226		3,226	3,625
3360	Hospital type, slotted rim for bed pan									
3370	Elongated bowl, top spud	Q-1	5	3.200	Ea.	380	208		588	730
3380	Elongated bowl, rear spud		5	3.200		445	208		653	800
3500	For rough-in, supply, waste and vent		3.05	5.246		565	340		905	1,125

22 43 Healthcare Plumbing Fixtures

22 43 16 – Healthcare Sinks

22 43 16.10 Sinks

		Crew	Daily Output	Labor-Hours	Unit	Material	2023 Bare Costs Labor	Equipment	Total	Total Incl O&P
0010	SINKS									
0020	Vitreous china									
6702	Hospital type, without trim (see Section 22 41 39.10)									
6710	20" x 18", contoured splash shield	Q-1	8	2	Ea.	106	130		236	310
6730	28" x 20", surgeon, side decks		8	2		765	130		895	1,050
6740	28" x 22", surgeon scrub-up, deep bowl		8	2		935	130		1,065	1,225
6750	20" x 27", patient, ADA compliant		7	2.286		640	148		788	925
6760	30" x 22", all purpose		7	2.286		775	148		923	1,075
6770	30" x 22", plaster work		7	2.286		775	148		923	1,075
6820	20" x 24" clinic service, liquid/solid waste		6	2.667		1,325	173		1,498	1,700

22 43 19 – Healthcare Bathtubs

22 43 19.10 Bathtubs

		Crew	Daily Output	Labor-Hours	Unit	Material	Labor	Equipment	Total	Total Incl O&P
0010	BATHTUBS									
5002	Hospital type, with trim, see Section 22 41 39.10									
5050	Bathing pool, porcelain enamel on cast iron, grab bars									
5060	pop-up drain, 72" x 36"	Q-1	3	5.333	Ea.	4,875	345		5,220	5,900
5100	Perineal (sitz), vitreous china		3	5.333		1,525	345		1,870	2,200
5120	For pedestal, vitreous china, add		8	2		310	130		440	535
5300	Whirlpool, porcelain enamel on cast iron, 72" x 36"		1	16		5,550	1,050		6,600	7,675
5310	For color, add					5%				
5311	For designer colors and trim, add					15%				

22 43 23 – Healthcare Showers

22 43 23.10 Showers

		Crew	Daily Output	Labor-Hours	Unit	Material	Labor	Equipment	Total	Total Incl O&P
0010	SHOWERS									
5950	Module, ADA compl, SS panel, fixed & hand held head, control									
5960	valves, grab bar, curtain & rod, folding seat	1 Plum	4	2	Ea.	1,700	144		1,844	2,100

22 43 39 – Healthcare Faucets

22 43 39.10 Faucets and Fittings

		Crew	Daily Output	Labor-Hours	Unit	Material	Labor	Equipment	Total	Total Incl O&P
0010	FAUCETS AND FITTINGS									
2850	Medical, bedpan cleanser, with pedal valve,	1 Plum	12	.667	Ea.	940	48		988	1,100
2860	With screwdriver stop valve		12	.667		490	48		538	605
2870	With self-closing spray valve		12	.667		355	48		403	460
2900	Faucet, gooseneck spout, wrist handles, grid drain		10	.800		199	57.50		256.50	305
2940	Mixing valve, knee action, screwdriver stops		4	2		525	144		669	795

22 45 Emergency Plumbing Fixtures

22 45 13 – Emergency Showers

22 45 13.10 Emergency Showers

		Crew	Daily Output	Labor-Hours	Unit	Material	Labor	Equipment	Total	Total Incl O&P
0010	EMERGENCY SHOWERS, Rough-in not included									
5000	Shower, single head, drench, ball valve, pull, freestanding	Q-1	4	4	Ea.	460	259		719	890
5200	Horizontal or vertical supply		4	4		755	259		1,014	1,225
6000	Multi-nozzle, eye/face wash combination		4	4		1,000	259		1,259	1,475
6400	Multi-nozzle, 12 spray, shower only		4	4		2,450	259		2,709	3,075
6600	For freeze-proof, add		6	2.667		620	173		793	940
8000	Walk-thru decontamination with eye-face wash		2	8		5,100	520		5,620	6,400
8200	For freeze proof, add		4	4		725	259		984	1,175

22 45 Emergency Plumbing Fixtures

22 45 16 – Eyewash Equipment

22 45 16.10 Eyewash Safety Equipment

	22 45 16.10 Eyewash Safety Equipment	Crew	Daily Output	Labor-Hours	Unit	Material	2023 Bare Costs Labor	Equipment	Total	Total Incl O&P
0010	**EYEWASH SAFETY EQUIPMENT**, Rough-in not included									
1000	Eye wash fountain									
1400	Plastic bowl, pedestal mounted	Q-1	4	4	Ea.	600	259		859	1,050
1600	Unmounted		4	4		430	259		689	855
1800	Wall mounted		4	4		220	259		479	625
2000	Stainless steel, pedestal mounted		4	4		495	259		754	930
2200	Unmounted		4	4		335	259		594	755
2400	Wall mounted		4	4		310	259		569	725

22 45 19 – Self-Contained Eyewash Equipment

22 45 19.10 Self-Contained Eyewash Safety Equipment

		Crew	Daily Output	Labor-Hours	Unit	Material	Labor	Equipment	Total	Total Incl O&P
0010	**SELF-CONTAINED EYEWASH SAFETY EQUIPMENT**									
3000	Eye wash, portable, self-contained				Ea.	1,350			1,350	1,475

22 45 26 – Eye/Face Wash Equipment

22 45 26.10 Eye/Face Wash Safety Equipment

		Crew	Daily Output	Labor-Hours	Unit	Material	Labor	Equipment	Total	Total Incl O&P
0010	**EYE/FACE WASH SAFETY EQUIPMENT**, Rough-in not included									
4000	Eye and face wash, combination fountain									
4200	Stainless steel, pedestal mounted	Q-1	4	4	Ea.	2,150	259		2,409	2,750
4400	Unmounted		4	4		360	259		619	780
4600	Wall mounted		4	4		510	259		769	950

22 46 Security Plumbing Fixtures

22 46 13 – Security Water Closets and Urinals

22 46 13.10 Security Water Closets and Urinals

		Crew	Daily Output	Labor-Hours	Unit	Material	Labor	Equipment	Total	Total Incl O&P
0010	**SECURITY WATER CLOSETS AND URINALS**, Stainless steel									
2000	Urinal, back supply and flush									
2200	Wall hung	Q-1	4	4	Ea.	1,875	259		2,134	2,450
2240	Stall		2.50	6.400		2,475	415		2,890	3,350
2300	For urinal rough-in, supply, waste and vent		1.49	10.738		450	695		1,145	1,550
3000	Water closet, integral seat, back supply and flush									
3300	Wall hung, wall outlet	Q-1	5.80	2.759	Ea.	1,075	179		1,254	1,450
3400	Floor mount, wall outlet		5.80	2.759		1,400	179		1,579	1,800
3440	Floor mount, floor outlet		5.80	2.759		1,400	179		1,579	1,825
3480	For recessed tissue holder, add					97			97	107
3500	For water closet rough-in, supply, waste and vent	Q-1	1.19	13.445		565	870		1,435	1,925
5000	Water closet and lavatory units, push button filler valves,									
5010	soap & paper holders, seat									
5300	Wall hung	Q-1	5	3.200	Ea.	2,125	208		2,333	2,650
5400	Floor mount		5	3.200		2,125	208		2,333	2,650
6300	For unit rough-in, supply, waste and vent		1	16		660	1,050		1,710	2,275

22 46 16 – Security Lavatories and Sinks

22 46 16.13 Security Lavatories

		Crew	Daily Output	Labor-Hours	Unit	Material	Labor	Equipment	Total	Total Incl O&P
0010	**SECURITY LAVATORIES**, Stainless steel									
1000	Lavatory, wall hung, push button filler valve									
1100	Rectangular bowl	Q-1	8	2	Ea.	760	130		890	1,025
1200	Oval bowl		8	2		775	130		905	1,050
1240	Oval bowl, corner mount		8	2		905	130		1,035	1,200
1300	For lavatory rough-in, supply, waste and vent		1.50	10.667		855	690		1,545	1,975

22 46 Security Plumbing Fixtures

22 46 63 – Security Service Sink

22 46 63.10 Security Service Sink	Crew	Daily Output	Labor-Hours	Unit	Material	2023 Bare Costs Labor	Equipment	Total	Total Incl O&P
0010 **SECURITY SERVICE SINK**, Stainless steel									
1700 Service sink, with soap dish									
1740 24" x 19" size	Q-1	3	5.333	Ea.	2,300	345		2,645	3,075
1790 For sink rough-in, supply, waste and vent	"	.89	17.978	"	1,800	1,175		2,975	3,725

22 46 73 – Security Shower

22 46 73.10 Security Shower	Crew	Daily Output	Labor-Hours	Unit	Material	Labor	Equipment	Total	Total Incl O&P
0010 **SECURITY SHOWER**, Stainless steel									
1800 Shower cabinet, unitized									
1840 36" x 36" x 88"	Q-1	2.20	7.273	Ea.	5,725	470		6,195	7,000
1900 Shower package for built-in									
1940 Hot & cold valves, recessed soap dish	Q-1	6	2.667	Ea.	248	173		421	530

22 47 Drinking Fountains and Water Coolers

22 47 13 – Drinking Fountains

22 47 13.10 Drinking Water Fountains		Crew	Daily Output	Labor-Hours	Unit	Material	Labor	Equipment	Total	Total Incl O&P
0010 **DRINKING WATER FOUNTAINS**, For connection to cold water supply										
0802 For remote water chiller, see Section 22 47 23.10										
1000 Wall mounted, non-recessed	R224000-30									
1200 Aluminum,										
1280 Dual bubbler type		1 Plum	3.20	2.500	Ea.	3,600	180		3,780	4,225
1400 Bronze, with no back			4	2		1,525	144		1,669	1,900
1600 Cast iron, enameled, low back, single bubbler	D2010-810		4	2		1,675	144		1,819	2,050
1640 Dual bubbler type			3.20	2.500		2,750	180		2,930	3,300
1680 Triple bubbler type			3.20	2.500		3,575	180		3,755	4,200
1800 Cast aluminum, enameled, for correctional institutions			4	2		1,750	144		1,894	2,175
2000 Fiberglass, 12" back, single bubbler unit			4	2		3,250	144		3,394	3,800
2040 Dual bubbler			3.20	2.500		3,075	180		3,255	3,675
2080 Triple bubbler			3.20	2.500		3,400	180		3,580	4,025
2200 Polymarble, no back, single bubbler			4	2		1,050	144		1,194	1,375
2240 Dual bubbler			3.20	2.500		2,800	180		2,980	3,350
2280 Triple bubbler			3.20	2.500		2,775	180		2,955	3,325
2400 Precast stone, no back			4	2		1,275	144		1,419	1,625
2700 Stainless steel, single bubbler, no back			4	2		970	144		1,114	1,300
2740 With back			4	2		1,250	144		1,394	1,600
2780 Dual handle, ADA compliant			4	2		965	144		1,109	1,275
2820 Dual level, ADA compliant			3.20	2.500		2,100	180		2,280	2,575
2840 Vandal resistant type			4	2		1,175	144		1,319	1,500
3300 Vitreous china										
3340 7" back		1 Plum	4	2	Ea.	985	144		1,129	1,300
3940 For vandal-resistant bottom plate, add						137			137	151
3960 For freeze-proof valve system, add		1 Plum	2	4		1,400	288		1,688	1,975
3980 For rough-in, supply and waste, add		"	2.21	3.620		625	261		886	1,075
4000 Wall mounted, semi-recessed										
4200 Poly-marble, single bubbler		1 Plum	4	2	Ea.	1,275	144		1,419	1,625
4600 Stainless steel, satin finish, single bubbler			4	2		1,900	144		2,044	2,325
4900 Vitreous china, single bubbler			4	2		1,425	144		1,569	1,800
5980 For rough-in, supply and waste, add			1.83	4.372		625	315		940	1,150
6000 Wall mounted, fully recessed										
6400 Poly-marble, single bubbler		1 Plum	4	2	Ea.	2,375	144		2,519	2,825
6440 For water glass filler, add						116			116	127

22 47 Drinking Fountains and Water Coolers

22 47 13 – Drinking Fountains

22 47 13.10 Drinking Water Fountains

		Crew	Daily Output	Labor-Hours	Unit	Material	2023 Bare Costs Labor	Equipment	Total	Total Incl O&P
6800	Stainless steel, single bubbler	1 Plum	4	2	Ea.	1,800	144		1,944	2,200
6900	Fountain and cuspidor combination		2	4		3,525	288		3,813	4,300
7560	For freeze-proof valve system, add		2	4		1,800	288		2,088	2,400
7580	For rough-in, supply and waste, add		1.83	4.372		625	315		940	1,150
7600	Floor mounted, pedestal type									
7700	Aluminum, architectural style, CI base	1 Plum	2	4	Ea.	3,150	288		3,438	3,900
7780	ADA compliant unit		2	4		3,000	288		3,288	3,725
8000	Bronze, architectural style		2	4		3,775	288		4,063	4,575
8040	Enameled steel cylindrical column style		2	4		3,025	288		3,313	3,750
8200	Precast stone/concrete, cylindrical column		1	8		2,525	575		3,100	3,625
8240	ADA compliant unit		1	8		4,125	575		4,700	5,375
8400	Stainless steel, architectural style		2	4		2,650	288		2,938	3,350
8600	Enameled iron, heavy duty service, 2 bubblers		2	4		3,875	288		4,163	4,700
8660	4 bubblers		2	4		5,600	288		5,888	6,600
8880	For freeze-proof valve system, add		2	4		1,400	288		1,688	1,975
8900	For rough-in, supply and waste, add		1.83	4.372		625	315		940	1,150
9100	Deck mounted									
9500	Stainless steel, circular receptor	1 Plum	4	2	Ea.	610	144		754	885
9540	14" x 9" receptor		4	2		505	144		649	770
9580	25" x 17" deep receptor, with water glass filler		3	2.667		395	192		587	720
9760	White enameled steel, 14" x 9" receptor		4	2		535	144		679	800
9860	White enameled cast iron, 24" x 16" receptor		3	2.667		695	192		887	1,050
9980	For rough-in, supply and waste, add		1.83	4.372		625	315		940	1,150

22 47 16 – Pressure Water Coolers

22 47 16.10 Electric Water Coolers

		Crew	Daily Output	Labor-Hours	Unit	Material	2023 Bare Costs Labor	Equipment	Total	Total Incl O&P
0010	**ELECTRIC WATER COOLERS** D2010-820									
0100	Wall mounted, non-recessed									
0140	4 GPH	Q-1	4	4	Ea.	970	259		1,229	1,450
0160	8 GPH, barrier free, sensor operated		4	4		1,950	259		2,209	2,525
0180	8.2 GPH		4	4		1,250	259		1,509	1,725
0220	14.3 GPH		4	4		1,325	259		1,584	1,825
0600	8 GPH hot and cold water		4	4		1,775	259		2,034	2,325
0640	For stainless steel cabinet, add					125			125	138
1000	Dual height, 8.2 GPH	Q-1	3.80	4.211		3,750	273		4,023	4,525
1040	14.3 GPH	"	3.80	4.211		2,725	273		2,998	3,400
1240	For stainless steel cabinet, add					283			283	310
2600	ADA compliant, 8 GPH	Q-1	4	4		1,275	259		1,534	1,775
3000	Simulated recessed, 8 GPH		4	4		990	259		1,249	1,475
3040	11.5 GPH		4	4		1,375	259		1,634	1,900
3200	For glass filler, add					136			136	149
3240	For stainless steel cabinet, add					117			117	129
3300	Semi-recessed, 8.1 GPH	Q-1	4	4		1,125	259		1,384	1,625
3320	12 GPH	"	4	4		1,300	259		1,559	1,800
3340	For glass filler, add					220			220	242
3360	For stainless steel cabinet, add					196			196	215
3400	Full recessed, stainless steel, 8 GPH	Q-1	3.50	4.571		2,750	296		3,046	3,475
3420	11.5 GPH	"	3.50	4.571		2,450	296		2,746	3,150
3460	For glass filler, add					267			267	294
3600	For mounting can only					294			294	325
4600	Floor mounted, flush-to-wall									
4640	4 GPH	1 Plum	3	2.667	Ea.	1,100	192		1,292	1,475
4680	8.2 GPH		3	2.667		1,150	192		1,342	1,550

22 47 Drinking Fountains and Water Coolers

22 47 16 – Pressure Water Coolers

22 47 16.10 Electric Water Coolers		Crew	Daily Output	Labor-Hours	Unit	Material	2023 Bare Costs Labor	Equipment	Total	Total Incl O&P
4720	14.3 GPH	1 Plum	3	2.667	Ea.	1,325	192		1,517	1,725
4960	14 GPH hot and cold water	↓	3	2.667		1,350	192		1,542	1,775
4980	For stainless steel cabinet, add					190			190	209
5000	Dual height, 8.2 GPH	1 Plum	2	4		1,600	288		1,888	2,200
5040	14.3 GPH	"	2	4		1,675	288		1,963	2,275
5120	For stainless steel cabinet, add					278			278	305
5600	Explosion proof, 16 GPH	1 Plum	3	2.667		3,075	192		3,267	3,650
6000	Refrigerator compartment type, 4.5 GPH		3	2.667		2,050	192		2,242	2,550
6600	Bottle supply type, 1.0 GPH		4	2		1,575	144		1,719	1,950
6640	Hot and cold, 1.0 GPH		4	2		760	144		904	1,050
9800	For supply, waste & vent, all coolers	↓	2.21	3.620	↓	625	261		886	1,075

22 47 23 – Remote Water Coolers

22 47 23.10 Remote Water Coolers		Crew	Daily Output	Labor-Hours	Unit	Material	2023 Bare Costs Labor	Equipment	Total	Total Incl O&P
0010	**REMOTE WATER COOLERS**, 80°F inlet									
0100	Air cooled, 50°F outlet, 115 V, 4.1 GPH	1 Plum	6	1.333	Ea.	740	96		836	960
0200	5.7 GPH		5.50	1.455		1,275	105		1,380	1,550
0300	8.0 GPH		5	1.600		815	115		930	1,075
0400	10.0 GPH		4.50	1.778		1,325	128		1,453	1,675
0500	13.4 GPH	↓	4	2		2,125	144		2,269	2,575
0700	29 GPH	Q-1	5	3.200		2,500	208		2,708	3,050
1000	230 V, 32 GPH	"	5	3.200	↓	2,475	208		2,683	3,025

22 51 Swimming Pool Plumbing Systems

22 51 19 – Swimming Pool Water Treatment Equipment

22 51 19.50 Swimming Pool Filtration Equipment

		Crew	Daily Output	Labor-Hours	Unit	Material	2023 Bare Costs Labor	Equipment	Total	Total Incl O&P
0010	**SWIMMING POOL FILTRATION EQUIPMENT**									
0900	Filter system, sand or diatomite type, incl. pump, 6,000 gal./hr.	2 Plum	1.80	8.889	Total	1,250	640		1,890	2,325
1020	Add for chlorination system, 800 S.F. pool		3	5.333	Ea.	143	385		528	730
1040	5,000 S.F. pool	↓	3	5.333	"	2,875	385		3,260	3,725

22 52 Fountain Plumbing Systems

22 52 16 – Fountain Pumps

22 52 16.10 Fountain Water Pumps

		Crew	Daily Output	Labor-Hours	Unit	Material	2023 Bare Costs Labor	Equipment	Total	Total Incl O&P
0010	**FOUNTAIN WATER PUMPS**									
0100	Pump w/controls									
0200	Single phase, 100' cord, 1/2 HP pump	2 Skwk	4.40	3.636	Ea.	1,675	223		1,898	2,175
0300	3/4 HP pump		4.30	3.721		1,775	228		2,003	2,300
0400	1 HP pump		4.20	3.810		2,075	233		2,308	2,625
0500	1-1/2 HP pump		4.10	3.902		2,350	239		2,589	2,925
0600	2 HP pump		4	4		5,625	245		5,870	6,550
0700	Three phase, 200' cord, 5 HP pump		3.90	4.103		8,125	251		8,376	9,300
0800	7-1/2 HP pump		3.80	4.211		15,200	258		15,458	17,100
0900	10 HP pump		3.70	4.324		17,000	265		17,265	19,100
1000	15 HP pump		3.60	4.444	↓	23,700	272		23,972	26,500
2000	DESIGN NOTE: Use two horsepower per surface acre.									

22 52 Fountain Plumbing Systems

22 52 33 – Fountain Ancillary

22 52 33.10 Fountain Miscellaneous		Crew	Daily Output	Labor-Hours	Unit	Material	2023 Bare Costs Labor	2023 Bare Costs Equipment	Total	Total Incl O&P
0010	**FOUNTAIN MISCELLANEOUS**									
1300	Lights w/mounting kits, 200 watt	2 Skwk	18	.889	Ea.	1,200	54.50		1,254.50	1,400
1400	300 watt		18	.889		1,375	54.50		1,429.50	1,600
1500	500 watt		18	.889		1,600	54.50		1,654.50	1,850
1600	Color blender	↓	12	1.333	↓	610	81.50		691.50	800

22 62 Vacuum Systems for Laboratory and Healthcare Facilities

22 62 19 – Vacuum Equipment for Laboratory and Healthcare Facilities

22 62 19.70 Healthcare Vacuum Equipment		Crew	Daily Output	Labor-Hours	Unit	Material	2023 Bare Costs Labor	2023 Bare Costs Equipment	Total	Total Incl O&P
0010	**HEALTHCARE VACUUM EQUIPMENT**									
0300	Dental oral									
0310	Duplex									
0330	165 SCFM with 77 gal. separator	Q-2	1.30	18.462	Ea.	55,500	1,250		56,750	63,000
1100	Vacuum system									
1110	Vacuum outlet alarm panel	1 Plum	3.20	2.500	Ea.	1,100	180		1,280	1,475
2000	Medical, with receiver									
2100	Rotary vane type, lubricated, with controls									
2110	Simplex									
2120	1.5 HP, 80 gal. tank	Q-1	8	2	Ea.	7,125	130		7,255	8,050
2130	2 HP, 80 gal. tank		7	2.286		7,375	148		7,523	8,350
2140	3 HP, 80 gal. tank		6.60	2.424		7,775	157		7,932	8,775
2150	5 HP, 80 gal. tank	↓	6	2.667	↓	8,475	173		8,648	9,575
2200	Duplex									
2210	1 HP, 80 gal. tank	Q-1	8.40	1.905	Ea.	11,400	124		11,524	12,700
2220	1.5 HP, 80 gal. tank		7.80	2.051		11,700	133		11,833	13,100
2230	2 HP, 80 gal. tank		6.80	2.353		12,600	153		12,753	14,100
2240	3 HP, 120 gal. tank		6	2.667		13,700	173		13,873	15,400
2250	5 HP, 120 gal. tank		5.40	2.963		15,600	192		15,792	17,500
2260	7.5 HP, 200 gal. tank	Q-2	7	3.429		22,300	231		22,531	24,900
2270	10 HP, 200 gal. tank		6.40	3.750		25,800	252		26,052	28,800
2280	15 HP, 200 gal. tank		5.80	4.138		46,100	278		46,378	51,500
2290	20 HP, 200 gal. tank		5	4.800		52,500	325		52,825	58,500
2300	25 HP, 200 gal. tank		4	6	↓	61,000	405		61,405	68,000
2400	Triplex									
2410	7.5 HP, 200 gal. tank	Q-2	6.40	3.750	Ea.	35,400	252		35,652	39,400
2420	10 HP, 200 gal. tank		5.70	4.211		41,300	283		41,583	45,800
2430	15 HP, 200 gal. tank		4.90	4.898		69,500	330		69,830	77,000
2440	20 HP, 200 gal. tank		4	6		79,500	405		79,905	88,000
2450	25 HP, 200 gal. tank	↓	3.70	6.486	↓	92,000	435		92,435	101,500
2500	Quadruplex									
2510	7.5 HP, 200 gal. tank	Q-2	5.30	4.528	Ea.	44,100	305		44,405	49,100
2520	10 HP, 200 gal. tank		4.70	5.106		51,000	345		51,345	56,500
2530	15 HP, 200 gal. tank		4	6		92,000	405		92,405	101,500
2540	20 HP, 200 gal. tank		3.60	6.667		104,500	450		104,950	115,500
2550	25 HP, 200 gal. tank	↓	3.20	7.500	↓	121,500	505		122,005	135,000
4000	Liquid ring type, water sealed, with controls									
4200	Duplex									
4210	1.5 HP, 120 gal. tank	Q-1	6	2.667	Ea.	22,500	173		22,673	25,100
4220	3 HP, 120 gal. tank	"	5.50	2.909		23,500	189		23,689	26,100
4230	4 HP, 120 gal. tank	Q-2	6.80	3.529		25,000	237		25,237	27,900

22 62 Vacuum Systems for Laboratory and Healthcare Facilities

22 62 19 – Vacuum Equipment for Laboratory and Healthcare Facilities

22 62 19.70 Healthcare Vacuum Equipment		Crew	Daily Output	Labor-Hours	Unit	Material	2023 Bare Costs Labor	Equipment	Total	Total Incl O&P
4240	5 HP, 120 gal. tank	Q-2	6.50	3.692	Ea.	26,400	248		26,648	29,500
4250	7.5 HP, 200 gal. tank		6.20	3.871		32,200	260		32,460	35,800
4260	10 HP, 200 gal. tank		5.80	4.138		40,100	278		40,378	44,500
4270	15 HP, 200 gal. tank		5.10	4.706		48,600	315		48,915	54,000
4280	20 HP, 200 gal. tank		4.60	5.217		63,000	350		63,350	69,500
4290	30 HP, 200 gal. tank	↓	4	6	↓	75,000	405		75,405	83,000

22 63 Gas Systems for Laboratory and Healthcare Facilities

22 63 13 – Gas Piping for Laboratory and Healthcare Facilities

22 63 13.70 Healthcare Gas Piping		Crew	Daily Output	Labor-Hours	Unit	Material	Labor	Equipment	Total	Total Incl O&P
0010	**HEALTHCARE GAS PIPING**									
0030	Air compressor intake filter									
0034	Rooftop									
0036	Filter/silencer									
0040	1"	1 Stpi	10	.800	Ea.	268	58		326	380
0044	1-1/4"		9.60	.833		276	60.50		336.50	395
0048	1-1/2"		9.20	.870		296	63		359	420
0052	2"		8.80	.909		296	66		362	425
0056	2-1/2"		8.40	.952		395	69		464	540
0060	3"		8	1		475	72.50		547.50	630
0064	4"		7.60	1.053		495	76.50		571.50	660
0068	5"	↓	7.40	1.081	↓	690	78.50		768.50	875
0076	Inline									
0080	Filter/silencer									
0084	2"	1 Stpi	8.20	.976	Ea.	895	71		966	1,100
0088	2-1/2"		8	1		920	72.50		992.50	1,125
0090	3"		7.60	1.053		1,025	76.50		1,101.50	1,250
0092	4"		7.20	1.111		1,200	80.50		1,280.50	1,425
0094	5"		6.80	1.176		1,300	85.50		1,385.50	1,550
0096	6"	↓	6.40	1.250	↓	1,450	90.50		1,540.50	1,725
1000	Nitrogen or oxygen system									
1010	Cylinder manifold									
1020	5 cylinder	1 Plum	.80	10	Ea.	5,900	720		6,620	7,550
1026	10 cylinder	"	.40	20		7,100	1,450		8,550	9,950
1050	Nitrogen generator, 30 LPM	Q-5	.40	40	↓	31,700	2,600		34,300	38,800
1900	Vaporizers									
1910	LOX vaporizers									
1920	Nominal capacity									
1930	1410 SCFM	Q-1	2	8	Ea.	2,025	520		2,545	3,000
1940	5650 SCFM		1.40	11.429		4,650	740		5,390	6,225
1950	12,703 SCFM	↓	.80	20	↓	7,150	1,300		8,450	9,775
1980	Removal of LOX vaporizers									
1982	Nominal capacity									
1986	1410 SCFM	Q-1	4	4	Ea.		259		259	385
1990	5650 SCFM		2.80	5.714			370		370	555
1994	12,703 SCFM	↓	1.60	10	↓		650		650	965
3000	Outlets and valves									
3010	Recessed, wall mounted									
3012	Single outlet	1 Plum	3.20	2.500	Ea.	44.50	180		224.50	320
3100	Ceiling outlet									
3190	Zone valve with box									

22 63 Gas Systems for Laboratory and Healthcare Facilities

22 63 13 – Gas Piping for Laboratory and Healthcare Facilities

22 63 13.70 Healthcare Gas Piping		Crew	Daily Output	Labor-Hours	Unit	Material	2023 Bare Costs Labor	Equipment	Total	Total Incl O&P
3192	Cleaned for oxygen service, not including gauges									
3194	1/2" valve size	1 Plum	4.60	1.739	Ea.	235	125		360	445
3196	3/4" valve size		4.30	1.860		258	134		392	485
3198	1" valve size		4	2		286	144		430	530
3202	1-1/4" valve size		3.80	2.105		320	152		472	575
3206	1-1/2" valve size		3.60	2.222		355	160		515	635
3210	2" valve size		3.20	2.500		410	180		590	725
3214	2-1/2" valve size		3.10	2.581		1,050	186		1,236	1,450
3218	3" valve size	↓	3	2.667	↓	1,475	192		1,667	1,900
3224	Gauges for zone valve box									
3226	0-100 psi (O2, air, N2, CO_2)	1 Plum	16	.500	Ea.	18.75	36		54.75	74
3228	Vacuum, WAGD (Waste Anesthesia Gas)		16	.500		18.75	36		54.75	74
3230	0-300 psi (Nitrogen)	↓	16	.500	↓	18.75	36		54.75	74
4000	Alarm panel, medical gases and vacuum									
4010	Alarm panel	1 Plum	3.20	2.500	Ea.	1,100	180		1,280	1,475
4030	Master alarm panel									
4034	Can also monitor area alarms									
4038	and communicate with PC-based alarm monitor.									
4040	10 signal	1 Elec	3.20	2.500	Ea.	1,075	168		1,243	1,425
4044	20 signal		3	2.667		1,250	180		1,430	1,625
4048	30 signal		2.80	2.857		1,650	192		1,842	2,100
4052	40 signal		2.60	3.077		1,875	207		2,082	2,350
4056	50 signal		2.40	3.333		2,000	225		2,225	2,525
4060	60 signal	↓	2.20	3.636	↓	2,350	245		2,595	2,975
4100	Area alarm panel									
4104	Does not include specific gas transducers.									
4108	3 module alarm panel									
4112	P-P-P	1 Elec	2.80	2.857	Ea.	1,450	192		1,642	1,875
4116	P-P-V		2.80	2.857		985	192		1,177	1,350
4120	D-D-D		2.80	2.857		1,075	192		1,267	1,450
4130	6 module alarm panel									
4132	4-P, 3-V	1 Elec	2.20	3.636	Ea.	1,550	245		1,795	2,075
4136	3-P, 2-V, B		2.20	3.636		1,175	245		1,420	1,675
4140	5-D, B		2.20	3.636		1,500	245		1,745	2,025
4144	6-D		2.20	3.636		2,025	245		2,270	2,600
4148	3-P, 3-V	↓	2.20	3.636	↓	1,875	245		2,120	2,425
4170	Note: P=pressure, V=vacuum, B=blank, D=dual display									
4180	Alarm transducers, gas specific									
4182	Oxygen	1 Elec	24	.333	Ea.	166	22.50		188.50	216
4184	Vacuum		24	.333		162	22.50		184.50	212
4186	Nitrous oxide		24	.333		162	22.50		184.50	212
4188	Medical air		24	.333		166	22.50		188.50	216
4190	Carbon dioxide		24	.333		166	22.50		188.50	216
4192	Nitrogen		24	.333		166	22.50		188.50	216
4194	WAGD	↓	24	.333	↓	177	22.50		199.50	229
4300	Ball valves cleaned for oxygen service									
4310	with copper extensions and gauge port									
4320	1/4" diam.	1 Plum	24	.333	Ea.	67	24		91	110
4330	1/2" diam.		22	.364		66	26		92	112
4334	3/4" diam.		20	.400		85	29		114	137
4338	1" diam.		19	.421		118	30.50		148.50	175
4342	1-1/4" diam.		15	.533		148	38.50		186.50	221
4346	1-1/2" diam.	↓	13	.615	↓	196	44.50		240.50	281

22 63 Gas Systems for Laboratory and Healthcare Facilities

22 63 13 – Gas Piping for Laboratory and Healthcare Facilities

	22 63 13.70 Healthcare Gas Piping	Crew	Daily Output	Labor-Hours	Unit	Material	2023 Bare Costs Labor	2023 Bare Costs Equipment	Total	Total Incl O&P
4350	2" diam.	1 Plum	11	.727	Ea.	325	52.50		377.50	435
4354	2-1/2" diam.	Q-1	15	1.067		890	69		959	1,075
4358	3" diam.		13	1.231		1,325	80		1,405	1,600
4362	4" diam.	↓	10	1.600	↓	2,525	104		2,629	2,925
5000	Manifold									
5010	Automatic switchover type									
5020	Note: Both a control panel and header assembly are required									
5030	Control panel									
5040	Oxygen	Q-1	4	4	Ea.	5,100	259		5,359	6,000
5060	Header assembly									
5066	Oxygen									
5070	2 x 2	Q-1	6	2.667	Ea.	835	173		1,008	1,175
5074	3 x 3		5.50	2.909		980	189		1,169	1,350
5078	4 x 4		5	3.200		1,275	208		1,483	1,725
5082	5 x 5		4.50	3.556		1,425	231		1,656	1,925
5086	6 x 6		4	4		1,800	259		2,059	2,350
5090	7 x 7	↓	3.50	4.571	↓	1,950	296		2,246	2,575
7000	Medical air compressors									
7020	Oil-less with inlet filter, duplexed dryers and aftercoolers									
7030	Duplex systems, horizontal tank, 208/230/460/575 V, 3 Ph.									
7040	1 HP, 80 gal. tank, 3.8 ACFM @50PSIG, 2.7 ACFM @100PSIG	Q-5	4	4	Ea.	31,400	261		31,661	34,900
7050	1.5 HP, 80 gal. tank, 6.8 ACFM @50PSIG, 4.5 ACFM @100PSIG		3.80	4.211		39,100	275		39,375	43,400
7060	2 HP, 80 gal. tank, 8.2 ACFM @50PSIG, 6.3 ACFM @100PSIG		3.60	4.444		39,200	290		39,490	43,600
7070	3 HP, 120 gal. tank, 11.2 ACFM @50PSIG, 9.4 ACFM @100PSIG		3.20	5		30,400	325		30,725	34,000
7080	5 HP, 120 gal. tank, 17.4 ACFM @50PSIG, 15.6 ACFM @100PSIG		2.80	5.714		50,500	375		50,875	56,500
7090	7.5 HP, 250 gal. tank, 31.6 ACFM @50PSIG, 25.9 ACFM @100PSIG		2.40	6.667		67,500	435		67,935	74,500
7100	10 HP, 250 gal. tank, 43 ACFM @50PSIG, 35.2 ACFM @100PSIG		2	8		73,000	520		73,520	81,000
7110	15 HP, 250 gal. tank, 69 ACFM @50PSIG, 56.5 ACFM @100PSIG	↓	1.80	8.889	↓	87,500	580		88,080	97,500
7200	Aftercooler, air-cooled									
7210	Steel manifold, copper tube, aluminum fins									
7220	35 SCFM @ 100PSIG	Q-5	4	4	Ea.	1,100	261		1,361	1,600
7300	Air dryer system									
7310	Refrigerated type									
7320	Flow @ 125 psi									
7330	20 SCFM	Q-5	6	2.667	Ea.	1,600	174		1,774	2,025
7332	25 SCFM		5.80	2.759		1,675	180		1,855	2,125
7334	35 SCFM		5.40	2.963		2,050	193		2,243	2,575
7336	50 SCFM		5	3.200		2,550	209		2,759	3,125
7338	75 SCFM		4.60	3.478		3,200	227		3,427	3,875
7340	100 SCFM		4.30	3.721		3,850	243		4,093	4,575
7342	125 SCFM	↓	4	4	↓	4,950	261		5,211	5,850
7360	Desiccant type									
7362	Flow with energy saving controls									
7366	40 SCFM	Q-5	3.60	4.444	Ea.	6,550	290		6,840	7,625
7368	60 SCFM		3.40	4.706		7,150	305		7,455	8,300
7370	90 SCFM		3.20	5		8,475	325		8,800	9,800
7372	115 SCFM		3	5.333		9,100	350		9,450	10,500
7374	165 SCFM	↓	2.90	5.517		9,800	360		10,160	11,300
7378	260 SCFM	Q-6	3.60	6.667		11,500	450		11,950	13,400
7382	370 SCFM		3.40	7.059		13,500	480		13,980	15,500
7386	590 SCFM		3.20	7.500		16,600	510		17,110	19,100
7390	1130 SCFM	↓	3	8		25,800	540		26,340	29,200
7460	Dew point monitor									

For customer support on your Plumbing Costs with RSMeans data, call 800.448.8182.

22 63 Gas Systems for Laboratory and Healthcare Facilities

22 63 13 – Gas Piping for Laboratory and Healthcare Facilities

22 63 13.70 Healthcare Gas Piping		Crew	Daily Output	Labor-Hours	Unit	Material	2023 Bare Costs Labor	2023 Bare Costs Equipment	Total	Total Incl O&P
7466	LCD readout, high dew point alarm, probe included									
7470	Monitor	1 Stpi	2	4	Ea.	3,425	290		3,715	4,200

22 66 Chemical-Waste Systems for Lab. and Healthcare Facilities

22 66 53 – Laboratory Chemical-Waste and Vent Piping

22 66 53.30 Glass Pipe

		Crew	Daily Output	Labor-Hours	Unit	Material	Labor	Equipment	Total	Total Incl O&P
0010	**GLASS PIPE**, Borosilicate, couplings & clevis hanger assemblies, 10' OC R221113-70									
0020	Drainage									
1100	1-1/2" diameter	Q-1	52	.308	L.F.	15	19.95		34.95	46.50
1120	2" diameter		44	.364		19.60	23.50		43.10	56.50
1140	3" diameter		39	.410		26.50	26.50		53	68.50
1160	4" diameter		30	.533		47.50	34.50		82	104
1180	6" diameter		26	.615		89	40		129	158
1870	To delete coupling & hanger, subtract									
1880	1-1/2" diam. to 2" diam.					19%	22%			
1890	3" diam. to 6" diam.					20%	17%			
2000	Process supply (pressure), beaded joints									
2040	1/2" diameter	1 Plum	36	.222	L.F.	10.10	16		26.10	35
2060	3/4" diameter		31	.258		11.45	18.60		30.05	40
2080	1" diameter		27	.296		28	21.50		49.50	63
2100	1-1/2" diameter	Q-1	47	.340		16.80	22		38.80	51.50
2120	2" diameter		39	.410		22.50	26.50		49	64
2140	3" diameter		34	.471		30.50	30.50		61	79
2160	4" diameter		25	.640		50.50	41.50		92	118
2180	6" diameter		21	.762		123	49.50		172.50	209
2860	To delete coupling & hanger, subtract									
2870	1/2" diam. to 1" diam.					25%	33%			
2880	1-1/2" diam. to 3" diam.					22%	21%			
2890	4" diam. to 6" diam.					23%	15%			
3800	Conical joint, transparent									
3980	6" diameter	Q-1	21	.762	L.F.	182	49.50		231.50	274
4500	To delete couplings & hangers, subtract									
4530	6" diam.					22%	26%			

22 66 53.40 Pipe Fittings, Glass

		Crew	Daily Output	Labor-Hours	Unit	Material	Labor	Equipment	Total	Total Incl O&P
0010	**PIPE FITTINGS, GLASS**									
0020	Drainage, beaded ends									
0040	Coupling & labor required at joints not incl. in fitting									
0050	price. Add 1 per joint for installed price									
0070	90° bend or sweep, 1-1/2"				Ea.	54.50			54.50	60
0090	2"					69			69	76
0100	3"					102			102	112
0110	4"					182			182	200
0120	6" (sweep only)					440			440	480
0200	45° bend or sweep same as 90°									
0350	Tee, single sanitary, 1-1/2"				Ea.	79.50			79.50	87.50
0370	2"					133			133	146
0380	3"					114			114	126
0390	4"					211			211	232
0400	6"					395			395	435
0410	Tee, straight, 1-1/2"					91.50			91.50	100
0430	2"					98			98	108

22 66 Chemical-Waste Systems for Lab. and Healthcare Facilities

22 66 53 – Laboratory Chemical-Waste and Vent Piping

22 66 53.40 Pipe Fittings, Glass

		Crew	Daily Output	Labor-Hours	Unit	Material	2023 Bare Costs Labor	Equipment	Total	Total Incl O&P
0440	3"				Ea.	136			136	150
0450	4"					195			195	215
0460	6"					610			610	670
0500	Coupling, stainless steel, TFE seal ring									
0520	1-1/2"	Q-1	32	.500	Ea.	43	32.50		75.50	95.50
0530	2"		30	.533		54	34.50		88.50	111
0540	3"		25	.640		72.50	41.50		114	142
0550	4"		23	.696		125	45		170	206
0560	6"		20	.800		281	52		333	390
0600	Coupling, stainless steel, bead to plain end									
0610	1-1/2"	Q-1	36	.444	Ea.	46	29		75	93.50
0620	2"		34	.471		66.50	30.50		97	119
0630	3"		29	.552		101	36		137	165
0640	4"		27	.593		169	38.50		207.50	243
0650	6"		24	.667		570	43		613	690
2350	Coupling, Viton liner, for temperatures to 400°F									
2370	1/2"	Q-1	40	.400	Ea.	96.50	26		122.50	145
2380	3/4"		37	.432		110	28		138	163
2390	1"		35	.457		190	29.50		219.50	253
2400	1-1/2"		32	.500		43	32.50		75.50	95.50
2410	2"		30	.533		54	34.50		88.50	111
2420	3"		25	.640		72.50	41.50		114	142
2430	4"		23	.696		125	45		170	206
2440	6"		20	.800		281	52		333	390
2550	For beaded joint armored fittings, add					200%				
2600	Conical ends. Flange set, gasket & labor not incl. in fitting									
2620	price. Add 1 per joint for installed price.									
2650	90° sweep elbow, 1"				Ea.	164			164	180
2670	1-1/2"					390			390	430
2680	2"					340			340	375
2690	3"					625			625	690
2700	4"					1,125			1,125	1,250
2710	6"					1,650			1,650	1,800
2750	Cross (straight), add					55%				
2850	Tee, add					20%				

22 66 53.60 Corrosion Resistant Pipe

			Crew	Daily Output	Labor-Hours	Unit	Material	Labor	Equipment	Total	Total Incl O&P
0010	**CORROSION RESISTANT PIPE**, No couplings or hangers	R221113-70									
0020	Iron alloy, drain, mechanical joint										
1000	1-1/2" diameter		Q-1	70	.229	L.F.	97	14.80		111.80	129
1100	2" diameter			66	.242		100	15.70		115.70	134
1120	3" diameter			60	.267		110	17.30		127.30	147
1140	4" diameter			52	.308		139	19.95		158.95	183
1980	Iron alloy, drain, B&S joint										
2000	2" diameter		Q-1	54	.296	L.F.	117	19.20		136.20	158
2100	3" diameter			52	.308		114	19.95		133.95	155
2120	4" diameter			48	.333		138	21.50		159.50	184
2140	6" diameter		Q-2	59	.407		209	27.50		236.50	270
2160	8" diameter		"	54	.444		430	30		460	515
2980	Plastic, epoxy, fiberglass filament wound, B&S joint										
3000	2" diameter		Q-1	62	.258	L.F.	15.50	16.75		32.25	42
3100	3" diameter			51	.314		18.15	20.50		38.65	50.50
3120	4" diameter			45	.356		26	23		49	63

22 66 Chemical-Waste Systems for Lab. and Healthcare Facilities

22 66 53 – Laboratory Chemical-Waste and Vent Piping

22 66 53.60 Corrosion Resistant Pipe

		Crew	Daily Output	Labor-Hours	Unit	Material	2023 Bare Costs Labor	Equipment	Total	Total Incl O&P
3140	6" diameter	Q-1	32	.500	L.F.	36.50	32.50		69	88.50
3160	8" diameter	Q-2	38	.632		57	42.50		99.50	127
3180	10" diameter		32	.750		78	50.50		128.50	161
3200	12" diameter		28	.857		94.50	57.50		152	190
3980	Polyester, fiberglass filament wound, B&S joint									
4000	2" diameter	Q-1	62	.258	L.F.	16.85	16.75		33.60	43.50
4100	3" diameter		51	.314		22	20.50		42.50	55
4120	4" diameter		45	.356		32.50	23		55.50	70
4140	6" diameter		32	.500		47.50	32.50		80	101
4160	8" diameter	Q-2	38	.632		112	42.50		154.50	187
4180	10" diameter		32	.750		150	50.50		200.50	240
4200	12" diameter		28	.857		164	57.50		221.50	266
4980	Polypropylene, acid resistant, fire retardant, Schedule 40									
5000	1-1/2" diameter	Q-1	68	.235	L.F.	24	15.25		39.25	49
5100	2" diameter		62	.258		16.75	16.75		33.50	43.50
5120	3" diameter		51	.314		26	20.50		46.50	59.50
5140	4" diameter		45	.356		33.50	23		56.50	71
5160	6" diameter		32	.500		67	32.50		99.50	123
5980	Proxylene, fire retardant, Schedule 40									
6000	1-1/2" diameter	Q-1	68	.235	L.F.	7.95	15.25		23.20	31.50
6100	2" diameter		62	.258		7.95	16.75		24.70	33.50
6120	3" diameter		51	.314		9.65	20.50		30.15	41
6140	4" diameter		45	.356		11.25	23		34.25	47
6160	6" diameter		32	.500		87	32.50		119.50	145
6820	For Schedule 80, add					35%	2%			

22 66 53.70 Pipe Fittings, Corrosion Resistant

		Crew	Daily Output	Labor-Hours	Unit	Material	2023 Bare Costs Labor	Equipment	Total	Total Incl O&P
0010	**PIPE FITTINGS, CORROSION RESISTANT**									
0030	Iron alloy									
0050	Mechanical joint									
0060	1/4 bend, 1-1/2"	Q-1	12	1.333	Ea.	170	86.50		256.50	315
0080	2"		10	1.600		279	104		383	460
0090	3"		9	1.778		335	115		450	540
0100	4"		8	2		385	130		515	620
0110	1/8 bend, 1-1/2"		12	1.333		108	86.50		194.50	248
0130	2"		10	1.600		186	104		290	360
0140	3"		9	1.778		248	115		363	445
0150	4"		8	2		330	130		460	560
0160	Tee and Y, sanitary, straight									
0170	1-1/2"	Q-1	8	2	Ea.	186	130		316	400
0180	2"		7	2.286		248	148		396	495
0190	3"		6	2.667		385	173		558	685
0200	4"		5	3.200		705	208		913	1,075
0360	Coupling, 1-1/2"		14	1.143		89	74		163	209
0380	2"		12	1.333		101	86.50		187.50	240
0390	3"		11	1.455		106	94.50		200.50	258
0400	4"		10	1.600		120	104		224	287
0500	Bell & Spigot									
0510	1/4 and 1/16 bend, 2"	Q-1	16	1	Ea.	161	65		226	274
0520	3"		14	1.143		375	74		449	525
0530	4"		13	1.231		385	80		465	545
0540	6"	Q-2	17	1.412		765	95		860	980
0550	8"	"	12	2		3,150	135		3,285	3,650

22 66 Chemical-Waste Systems for Lab. and Healthcare Facilities

22 66 53 – Laboratory Chemical-Waste and Vent Piping

22 66 53.70 Pipe Fittings, Corrosion Resistant

		Crew	Daily Output	Labor-Hours	Unit	Material	2023 Bare Costs Labor	Equipment	Total	Total Incl O&P
0620	1/8 bend, 2"	Q-1	16	1	Ea.	181	65		246	296
0640	3"		14	1.143		335	74		409	480
0650	4"	▼	13	1.231		335	80		415	485
0660	6"	Q-2	17	1.412		640	95		735	845
0680	8"	"	12	2		2,500	135		2,635	2,950
0700	Tee, sanitary, 2"	Q-1	10	1.600		345	104		449	535
0710	3"		9	1.778		1,125	115		1,240	1,400
0720	4"	▼	8	2		925	130		1,055	1,225
0730	6"	Q-2	11	2.182		1,150	147		1,297	1,500
0740	8"	"	8	3		3,175	202		3,377	3,800
1800	Y, sanitary, 2"	Q-1	10	1.600		365	104		469	555
1820	3"		9	1.778		650	115		765	885
1830	4"	▼	8	2		580	130		710	835
1840	6"	Q-2	11	2.182		1,925	147		2,072	2,350
1850	8"	"	8	3		5,350	202		5,552	6,175
3000	Epoxy, filament wound									
3030	Quick-lock joint									
3040	90° elbow, 2"	Q-1	28	.571	Ea.	132	37		169	201
3060	3"		16	1		151	65		216	263
3070	4"		13	1.231		206	80		286	345
3080	6"	▼	8	2		300	130		430	525
3090	8"	Q-2	9	2.667		550	179		729	870
3100	10"		7	3.429		695	231		926	1,100
3110	12"	▼	6	4		995	269		1,264	1,500
3120	45° elbow, 2"	Q-1	28	.571		101	37		138	167
3130	3"		16	1		156	65		221	269
3140	4"		13	1.231		166	80		246	300
3150	6"	▼	8	2		300	130		430	525
3160	8"	Q-2	9	2.667		550	179		729	870
3170	10"		7	3.429		695	231		926	1,100
3180	12"		6	4		995	269		1,264	1,500
3190	Tee, 2"	Q-1	19	.842		315	54.50		369.50	425
3200	3"		11	1.455		375	94.50		469.50	555
3210	4"		9	1.778		455	115		570	670
3220	6"	▼	5	3.200		750	208		958	1,125
3230	8"	Q-2	6	4		865	269		1,134	1,350
3240	10"		5	4.800		1,200	325		1,525	1,800
3250	12"	▼	4	6	▼	1,875	405		2,280	2,675
4000	Polypropylene, acid resistant									
4020	Non-pressure, electrofusion joints									
4050	1/4 bend, 1-1/2"	1 Plum	16	.500	Ea.	38.50	36		74.50	96
4060	2"	Q-1	28	.571		63.50	37		100.50	125
4080	3"		17	.941		97	61		158	198
4090	4"		14	1.143		137	74		211	262
4110	6"	▼	8	2	▼	325	130		455	555
4150	1/4 bend, long sweep									
4170	1-1/2"	1 Plum	16	.500	Ea.	43	36		79	101
4180	2"	Q-1	28	.571		78	37		115	141
4200	3"		17	.941		93.50	61		154.50	194
4210	4"		14	1.143		141	74		215	266
4250	1/8 bend, 1-1/2"	1 Plum	16	.500		37	36		73	94
4260	2"	Q-1	28	.571		33	37		70	91.50
4280	3"	▼	17	.941		70.50	61		131.50	169

22 66 Chemical-Waste Systems for Lab. and Healthcare Facilities

22 66 53 – Laboratory Chemical-Waste and Vent Piping

22 66 53.70 Pipe Fittings, Corrosion Resistant		Crew	Daily Output	Labor-Hours	Unit	Material	2023 Bare Costs Labor	Equipment	Total	Total Incl O&P
4290	4"	Q-1	14	1.143	Ea.	95.50	74		169.50	216
4310	6"	↓	8	2	↓	264	130		394	485
4400	Tee, sanitary									
4420	1-1/2"	1 Plum	10	.800	Ea.	50.50	57.50		108	142
4430	2"	Q-1	17	.941		57	61		118	154
4450	3"		11	1.455		118	94.50		212.50	271
4460	4"		9	1.778		171	115		286	360
4480	6"		5	3.200		1,125	208		1,333	1,550
4490	Tee, sanitary reducing, 2" x 2" x 1-1/2"		17	.941		57	61		118	154
4491	3" x 3" x 1-1/2"		11	1.455		114	94.50		208.50	266
4492	3" x 3" x 2"		11	1.455		101	94.50		195.50	253
4493	4" x 4" x 2"		10	1.600		153	104		257	325
4494	4" x 4" x 3"		9	1.778		166	115		281	355
4496	6" x 6" x 4"	↓	5	3.200		555	208		763	925
4650	Wye 45°, 1-1/2"	1 Plum	10	.800		53	57.50		110.50	144
4652	2"	Q-1	17	.941		73	61		134	172
4653	3"		11	1.455		126	94.50		220.50	280
4654	4"		9	1.778		177	115		292	365
4656	6"	↓	5	3.200	↓	475	208		683	830
4660	Wye, reducing									
4662	2" x 2" x 1-1/2"	Q-1	17	.941	Ea.	69	61		130	167
4666	3" x 3" x 2"		11	1.455		138	94.50		232.50	293
4668	4" x 4" x 2"		10	1.600		163	104		267	335
4669	4" x 4" x 3"		9	1.778		179	115		294	370
4671	6" x 6" x 2"		6	2.667		276	173		449	565
4673	6" x 6" x 3"		5.50	2.909		305	189		494	615
4675	6" x 6" x 4"	↓	5	3.200	↓	315	208		523	660
4678	Combination Y & 1/8 bend									
4681	1-1/2"	1 Plum	10	.800	Ea.	64	57.50		121.50	157
4683	2"	Q-1	17	.941		84.50	61		145.50	184
4684	3"		11	1.455		138	94.50		232.50	293
4685	4"	↓	9	1.778		190	115		305	380
4689	Combination Y & 1/8 bend, reducing									
4692	2" x 2" x 1-1/2"	Q-1	17	.941	Ea.	77	61		138	176
4694	3" x 3" x 1-1/2"		12	1.333		116	86.50		202.50	256
4695	3" x 3" x 2"		11	1.455		121	94.50		215.50	275
4697	4" x 4" x 2"		10	1.600		172	104		276	345
4699	4" x 4" x 3"	↓	9	1.778		179	115		294	370
4710	Hub adapter									
4712	1-1/2"	1 Plum	16	.500	Ea.	89.50	36		125.50	152
4713	2"	Q-1	28	.571		101	37		138	168
4714	3"		17	.941		128	61		189	231
4715	4"	↓	14	1.143	↓	166	74		240	294
4719	Mechanical joint adapter									
4721	1-1/2"	1 Plum	16	.500	Ea.	55	36		91	114
4722	2"	Q-1	28	.571		57	37		94	118
4723	3"		17	.941		81.50	61		142.50	181
4724	4"	↓	14	1.143		121	74		195	245
4728	Couplings									
4731	1-1/2"	1 Plum	16	.500	Ea.	30.50	36		66.50	87
4732	2"	Q-1	28	.571		38.50	37		75.50	98
4733	3"		17	.941		50.50	61		111.50	147
4734	4"		14	1.143		69	74		143	187

22 66 Chemical-Waste Systems for Lab. and Healthcare Facilities

22 66 53 – Laboratory Chemical-Waste and Vent Piping

22 66 53.70 Pipe Fittings, Corrosion Resistant		Crew	Daily Output	Labor-Hours	Unit	Material	2023 Bare Costs Labor	Equipment	Total	Total Incl O&P
4736	6"	Q-1	8	2	Ea.	109	130		239	315

22 66 83 – Chemical-Waste Tanks

22 66 83.13 Chemical-Waste Dilution Tanks

		Crew	Daily Output	Labor-Hours	Unit	Material	Labor	Equipment	Total	Total Incl O&P
0010	**CHEMICAL-WASTE DILUTION TANKS**									
7000	Tanks, covers included									
7800	Polypropylene									
7810	Continuous service to 200°F									
7830	2 gallon, 8" x 8" x 8"	Q-1	20	.800	Ea.	158	52		210	252
7850	7 gallon, 12" x 12" x 12"		20	.800		370	52		422	485
7870	16 gallon, 18" x 12" x 18"		17	.941		297	61		358	415
8010	33 gallon, 24" x 18" x 18"		12	1.333		550	86.50		636.50	735
8070	44 gallon, 24" x 18" x 24"		10	1.600		400	104		504	595
8080	89 gallon, 36" x 24" x 24"	↓	8	2	↓	705	130		835	970
8150	Polyethylene, heavy duty walls									
8160	Continuous service to 180°F									
8180	5 gallon, 12" x 6" x 18"	Q-1	20	.800	Ea.	41	52		93	123
8210	15 gallon, 14" I.D. x 27" deep		17	.941		92.50	61		153.50	193
8230	55 gallon, 22" I.D. x 36" deep		10	1.600		257	104		361	440
8250	100 gallon, 28" I.D. x 42" deep		8	2		420	130		550	660
8270	200 gallon, 36" I.D. x 48" deep		6	2.667		525	173		698	835
8290	360 gallon, 48" I.D. x 48" deep	↓	5	3.200	↓	855	208		1,063	1,250

Division Notes

	CREW	DAILY OUTPUT	LABOR-HOURS	UNIT	BARE COSTS				TOTAL INCL O&P
					MAT.	LABOR	EQUIP.	TOTAL	

Estimating Tips

The labor adjustment factors listed in Subdivision 22 01 02.20 also apply to Division 23.

23 10 00 Facility Fuel Systems

- The prices in this subdivision for above- and below-ground storage tanks do not include foundations or hold-down slabs, unless noted. The estimator should refer to Divisions 3 and 31 for foundation system pricing. In addition to the foundations, required tank accessories, such as tank gauges, leak detection devices, and additional manholes and piping, must be added to the tank prices.

23 50 00 Central Heating Equipment

- When estimating the cost of an HVAC system, check to see who is responsible for providing and installing the temperature control system. It is possible to overlook controls, assuming that they would be included in the electrical estimate.
- When looking up a boiler, be careful on specified capacity. Some manufacturers rate their products on output while others use input.
- Include HVAC insulation for pipe, boiler, and duct (wrap and liner).
- Be careful when looking up mechanical items to get the correct pressure rating and connection type (thread, weld, flange).

23 70 00 Central HVAC Equipment

- Combination heating and cooling units are sized by the air conditioning requirements. (See Reference No. R236000-20 for the preliminary sizing guide.)
- A ton of air conditioning is nominally 400 CFM.
- Rectangular duct is taken off by the linear foot for each size, but its cost is usually estimated by the pound. Remember that SMACNA standards now base duct on internal pressure.
- Prefabricated duct is estimated and purchased like pipe: straight sections and fittings.
- Note that cranes or other lifting equipment are not included on any lines in Division 23. For example, if a crane is required to lift a heavy piece of pipe into place high above a gym floor, or to put a rooftop unit on the roof of a four-story building, etc., it must be added. Due to the potential for extreme variation—from nothing additional required to a major crane or helicopter—we feel that including a nominal amount for "lifting contingency" would be useless and detract from the accuracy of the estimate. When using equipment rental cost data from RSMeans, do not forget to include the cost of the operator(s).

Reference Numbers

Reference numbers are shown at the beginning of some major classifications. These numbers refer to related items in the Reference Section. The reference information may be an estimating procedure, an alternate pricing method, or technical information.

Note: Not all subdivisions listed here necessarily appear. ■

Same Data. Simplified.

Enjoy the convenience and efficiency of accessing your costs anywhere:

- **Skip the multiplier** by setting your location
- **Quickly search,** edit, favorite and share costs
- **Stay on top of price changes** with automatic updates

Discover more at rsmeans.com/online

No part of this cost data may be reproduced, stored in a retrieval system, or transmitted in any form or by any means without prior written permission of Gordian.

Note: "Powered in part by CINX™, based on licensed proprietary information of Harrison Publishing House, Inc."

Note: Trade Service, in part, has been used as a reference source for some of the material prices used in Division 23.

23 05 Common Work Results for HVAC

23 05 02 – HVAC General

23 05 02.10 Air Conditioning, General

		Crew	Daily Output	Labor-Hours	Unit	Material	2023 Bare Costs Labor	2023 Bare Costs Equipment	Total	Total Incl O&P
0010	**AIR CONDITIONING, GENERAL** Prices are for standard efficiencies (SEER 13)									
0020	for upgrade to SEER 14 add					10%				

23 05 05 – Selective Demolition for HVAC

23 05 05.10 HVAC Demolition

			Crew	Daily Output	Labor-Hours	Unit	Material	Labor	Equipment	Total	Total Incl O&P
0010	**HVAC DEMOLITION**	R220105-10									
0100	Air conditioner, split unit, 3 ton		Q-5	2	8	Ea.		520		520	780
0150	Package unit, 3 ton	R024119-10	Q-6	3	8			540		540	810
0190	Rooftop, self contained, up to 5 ton		1 Plum	1.20	6.667			480		480	715
0250	Air curtain		Q-9	20	.800	L.F.		50.50		50.50	76
0254	Air filters, up thru 16,000 CFM			20	.800	Ea.		50.50		50.50	76
0256	20,000 thru 60,000 CFM			16	1			63		63	95
0297	Boiler blowdown		Q-5	8	2			131		131	195
0298	Boilers										
0300	Electric, up thru 148 kW		Q-19	2	12	Ea.		790		790	1,175
0310	150 thru 518 kW		"	1	24			1,575		1,575	2,350
0320	550 thru 2,000 kW		Q-21	.40	80			5,400		5,400	8,050
0330	2,070 kW and up		"	.30	107			7,225		7,225	10,700
0340	Gas and/or oil, up thru 150 MBH		Q-7	2.20	14.545			1,000		1,000	1,500
0350	160 thru 2,000 MBH			.80	40			2,750		2,750	4,125
0360	2,100 thru 4,500 MBH			.50	64			4,425		4,425	6,600
0370	4,600 thru 7,000 MBH			.30	107			7,375		7,375	11,000
0380	7,100 thru 12,000 MBH			.16	200			13,800		13,800	20,600
0390	12,200 thru 25,000 MBH			.12	267			18,400		18,400	27,500
0400	Central station air handler unit, up thru 15 ton		Q-5	1.60	10			655		655	975
0410	17.5 thru 30 ton		"	.80	20			1,300		1,300	1,950
0430	Computer room unit										
0434	Air cooled split, up thru 10 ton		Q-5	.67	23.881	Ea.		1,550		1,550	2,325
0436	12 thru 23 ton			.53	30.189			1,975		1,975	2,950
0440	Chilled water, up thru 10 ton			1.30	12.308			805		805	1,200
0444	12 thru 23 ton			1	16			1,050		1,050	1,550
0450	Glycol system, up thru 10 ton			.53	30.189			1,975		1,975	2,950
0454	12 thru 23 ton			.40	40			2,600		2,600	3,900
0460	Water cooled, not including condenser, up thru 10 ton			.80	20			1,300		1,300	1,950
0464	12 thru 23 ton			.60	26.667			1,750		1,750	2,600
0600	Condenser, up thru 50 ton			1	16			1,050		1,050	1,550
0610	51 thru 100 ton		Q-6	.90	26.667			1,800		1,800	2,700
0620	101 thru 1,000 ton		"	.70	34.286			2,325		2,325	3,450
0660	Condensing unit, up thru 10 ton		Q-5	1.25	12.800			835		835	1,250
0670	11 thru 50 ton		"	.40	40			2,600		2,600	3,900
0680	60 thru 100 ton		Q-6	.30	80			5,425		5,425	8,075
0700	Cooling tower, up thru 400 ton			.80	30			2,025		2,025	3,025
0710	450 thru 600 ton			.53	45.283			3,075		3,075	4,575
0720	700 thru 1,300 ton			.40	60			4,075		4,075	6,050
0780	Dehumidifier, up thru 155 lb./hr.		Q-1	8	2			130		130	193
0790	240 lb./hr. and up		"	2	8			520		520	775
1560	Ductwork										
1570	Metal, steel, sst, fabricated		Q-9	1000	.016	Lb.		1.01		1.01	1.52
1580	Aluminum, fabricated			485	.033	"		2.08		2.08	3.14
1590	Spiral, prefabricated			400	.040	L.F.		2.53		2.53	3.80
1600	Fiberglass, prefabricated			400	.040			2.53		2.53	3.80
1610	Flex, prefabricated			500	.032			2.02		2.02	3.04
1620	Glass fiber reinforced plastic, prefabricated			280	.057			3.61		3.61	5.45

23 05 Common Work Results for HVAC

23 05 05 – Selective Demolition for HVAC

23 05 05.10 HVAC Demolition

		Crew	Daily Output	Labor-Hours	Unit	Material	2023 Bare Costs Labor	2023 Bare Costs Equipment	Total	Total Incl O&P
1630	Diffusers, registers or grills, up thru 20" max dimension	1 Shee	50	.160	Ea.		11.20		11.20	16.90
1640	21 thru 36" max dimension		36	.222			15.60		15.60	23.50
1650	Above 36" max dimension		30	.267			18.70		18.70	28
1700	Evaporator, up thru 12,000 BTUH	Q-5	5.30	3.019			197		197	294
1710	12,500 thru 30,000 BTUH	"	2.70	5.926			385		385	575
1720	31,000 BTUH and up	Q-6	1.50	16			1,075		1,075	1,625
1730	Evaporative cooler, up thru 5 HP	Q-9	2.70	5.926			375		375	565
1740	10 thru 30 HP	"	.67	23.881			1,500		1,500	2,275
1750	Exhaust systems									
1760	Exhaust components	1 Shee	8	1	System		70		70	106
1770	Weld fume hoods	"	20	.400	Ea.		28		28	42.50
2120	Fans, up thru 1 HP or 2,000 CFM	Q-9	8	2			126		126	190
2124	1-1/2 thru 10 HP or 20,000 CFM		5.30	3.019			191		191	287
2128	15 thru 30 HP or above 20,000 CFM		4	4			253		253	380
2150	Fan coil air conditioner, chilled water, up thru 7.5 ton	Q-5	14	1.143			74.50		74.50	111
2154	Direct expansion, up thru 10 ton		8	2			131		131	195
2158	11 thru 30 ton		2	8			520		520	780
2170	Flue shutter damper	Q-9	8	2			126		126	190
2200	Furnace, electric	Q-20	2	10			640		640	960
2300	Gas or oil, under 120 MBH	Q-9	4	4			253		253	380
2340	Over 120 MBH	"	3	5.333			335		335	505
2730	Heating and ventilating unit	Q-5	2.70	5.926			385		385	575
2740	Heater, electric, wall, baseboard and quartz	1 Elec	10	.800			54		54	80
2750	Heater, electric, unit, cabinet, fan and convector	"	8	1			67.50		67.50	100
2760	Heat exchanger, shell and tube type	Q-5	1.60	10			655		655	975
2770	Plate type	Q-6	.60	40			2,700		2,700	4,050
2810	Heat pump									
2820	Air source, split, 4 thru 10 ton	Q-5	.90	17.778	Ea.		1,150		1,150	1,725
2830	15 thru 25 ton	Q-6	.80	30			2,025		2,025	3,025
2850	Single package, up thru 12 ton	Q-5	1	16			1,050		1,050	1,550
2860	Water source, up thru 15 ton	"	.90	17.778			1,150		1,150	1,725
2870	20 thru 50 ton	Q-6	.80	30			2,025		2,025	3,025
2910	Heat recovery package, up thru 20,000 CFM	Q-5	2	8			520		520	780
2920	25,000 CFM and up		1.20	13.333			870		870	1,300
2930	Heat transfer package, up thru 130 GPM		.80	20			1,300		1,300	1,950
2934	255 thru 800 GPM		.42	38.095			2,500		2,500	3,700
2940	Humidifier		10.60	1.509			98.50		98.50	147
2961	Hydronic unit heaters, up thru 200 MBH		14	1.143			74.50		74.50	111
2962	Above 200 MBH		8	2			131		131	195
2964	Valance units		32	.500			32.50		32.50	48.50
2966	Radiant floor heating									
2967	System valves, controls, manifolds	Q-5	16	1	Ea.		65.50		65.50	97.50
2968	Per room distribution		8	2			131		131	195
2970	Hydronic heating, baseboard radiation		16	1			65.50		65.50	97.50
2976	Convectors and free standing radiators		18	.889			58		58	86.50
2980	Induced draft fan, up thru 1 HP	Q-9	4.60	3.478			220		220	330
2984	1-1/2 HP thru 7-1/2 HP	"	2.20	7.273			460		460	690
2988	Infrared unit	Q-5	16	1			65.50		65.50	97.50
2992	Louvers	1 Shee	46	.174	S.F.		12.20		12.20	18.40
3000	Mechanical equipment, light items. Unit is weight, not cooling.	Q-5	.90	17.778	Ton		1,150		1,150	1,725
3600	Heavy items		1.10	14.545	"		950		950	1,425
3720	Make-up air unit, up thru 6,000 CFM		3	5.333	Ea.		350		350	520
3730	6,500 thru 30,000 CFM		1.60	10			655		655	975

23 05 Common Work Results for HVAC

23 05 05 – Selective Demolition for HVAC

23 05 05.10 HVAC Demolition

		Crew	Daily Output	Labor-Hours	Unit	Material	2023 Bare Costs Labor	2023 Bare Costs Equipment	Total	Total Incl O&P
3740	35,000 thru 75,000 CFM	Q-6	1	24	Ea.		1,625		1,625	2,425
3800	Mixing boxes, constant and VAV	Q-9	18	.889			56		56	84.50
4000	Packaged terminal air conditioner, up thru 18,000 BTUH	Q-5	8	2			131		131	195
4010	24,000 thru 48,000 BTUH	"	2.80	5.714	↓		375		375	555
5000	Refrigerant compressor, reciprocating or scroll									
5010	Up thru 5 ton	1 Stpi	6	1.333	Ea.		96.50		96.50	144
5020	5.08 thru 10 ton	Q-5	6	2.667			174		174	260
5030	15 thru 50 ton	"	3	5.333			350		350	520
5040	60 thru 130 ton	Q-6	2.80	8.571	↓		580		580	865
5090	Remove refrigerant from system	1 Stpi	40	.200	Lb.		14.50		14.50	21.50
5100	Rooftop air conditioner, up thru 10 ton	Q-5	1.40	11.429	Ea.		745		745	1,125
5110	12 thru 40 ton	Q-6	1	24			1,625		1,625	2,425
5120	50 thru 140 ton		.50	48			3,250		3,250	4,850
5130	150 thru 300 ton	↓	.30	80			5,425		5,425	8,075
6000	Self contained single package air conditioner, up thru 10 ton	Q-5	1.60	10			655		655	975
6010	15 thru 60 ton	Q-6	1.20	20			1,350		1,350	2,025
6100	Space heaters, up thru 200 MBH	Q-5	10	1.600			104		104	156
6110	Over 200 MBH		5	3.200			209		209	310
6200	Split ductless, both sections	↓	8	2			131		131	195
6300	Steam condensate meter	1 Stpi	11	.727			53		53	78.50
6600	Thru-the-wall air conditioner	L-2	8	2			104		104	155
7000	Vent chimney, prefabricated, up thru 12" diameter	Q-9	94	.170	V.L.F.		10.75		10.75	16.20
7010	14" thru 36" diameter		40	.400			25.50		25.50	38
7020	38" thru 48" diameter	↓	32	.500			31.50		31.50	47.50
7030	54" thru 60" diameter	Q-10	14	1.714	↓		112		112	169
7400	Ventilators, up thru 14" neck diameter	Q-9	58	.276	Ea.		17.40		17.40	26
7410	16" thru 50" neck diameter		40	.400			25.50		25.50	38
7450	Relief vent, up thru 24" x 96"		22	.727			46		46	69
7460	48" x 60" thru 96" x 144"	↓	10	1.600			101		101	152
8000	Water chiller up thru 10 ton	Q-5	2.50	6.400			420		420	625
8010	15 thru 100 ton	Q-6	.48	50			3,375		3,375	5,050
8020	110 thru 500 ton	Q-7	.29	110			7,625		7,625	11,400
8030	600 thru 1000 ton		.23	139			9,600		9,600	14,300
8040	1100 ton and up		.20	160			11,000		11,000	16,500
8041	Absorption Chiller		.02	1600			110,500		110,500	165,000
8042	HVAC demo, water chiller plant	↓	.01	4571			315,500		315,500	471,000
8400	Window air conditioner	1 Carp	16	.500	↓		29.50		29.50	43.50
8401	HVAC demo, water chiller, 1100 ton and up	"	12	.667	Ton		39		39	58

23 05 23 – General-Duty Valves for HVAC Piping

23 05 23.20 Valves, Bronze/Brass

		Crew	Daily Output	Labor-Hours	Unit	Material	2023 Bare Costs Labor	2023 Bare Costs Equipment	Total	Total Incl O&P
0010	**VALVES, BRONZE/BRASS**									
0020	Brass									
1300	Ball combination valves, shut-off and union									
1310	Solder, with strainer, drain and PT ports									
1320	1/2"	1 Stpi	17	.471	Ea.	118	34		152	181
1330	3/4"		16	.500		129	36.50		165.50	196
1340	1"		14	.571		174	41.50		215.50	253
1350	1-1/4"		12	.667		224	48.50		272.50	320
1360	1-1/2"		10	.800		330	58		388	445
1370	2"	↓	8	1	↓	415	72.50		487.50	565
1410	Threaded, with strainer, drain and PT ports									
1420	1/2"	1 Stpi	20	.400	Ea.	118	29		147	174

23 05 Common Work Results for HVAC

23 05 23 – General-Duty Valves for HVAC Piping

23 05 23.20 Valves, Bronze/Brass

		Crew	Daily Output	Labor-Hours	Unit	Material	2023 Bare Costs Labor	Equipment	Total	Total Incl O&P
1430	3/4"	1 Stpi	18	.444	Ea.	129	32		161	190
1440	1"		17	.471		174	34		208	242
1450	1-1/4"		12	.667		224	48.50		272.50	320
1460	1-1/2"		11	.727		330	53		383	440
1470	2"		9	.889		415	64.50		479.50	550

23 05 23.30 Valves, Iron Body

		Crew	Daily Output	Labor-Hours	Unit	Material	Labor	Equipment	Total	Total Incl O&P
0010	**VALVES, IRON BODY** R220523-90									
0022	For grooved joint, see Section 22 11 13.48									
0100	Angle, 125 lb.									
0110	Flanged									
0116	2"	1 Plum	5	1.600	Ea.	2,700	115		2,815	3,150
0118	4"	Q-1	3	5.333		4,475	345		4,820	5,450
0120	6"	Q-2	3	8		8,900	540		9,440	10,600
0122	8"	"	2.50	9.600		15,700	645		16,345	18,200
1020	Butterfly, wafer type, gear actuator, 200 lb.									
1030	2"	1 Plum	14	.571	Ea.	118	41		159	192
1040	2-1/2"	Q-1	9	1.778		120	115		235	305
1050	3"		8	2		124	130		254	330
1060	4"		5	3.200		138	208		346	460
1070	5"	Q-2	5	4.800		155	325		480	650
1080	6"		5	4.800		176	325		501	675
1090	8"		4.50	5.333		219	360		579	775
1100	10"		4	6		294	405		699	925
1110	12"		3	8		725	540		1,265	1,600
1200	Wafer type, lever actuator, 200 lb.									
1220	2"	1 Plum	14	.571	Ea.	330	41		371	425
1230	2-1/2"	Q-1	9	1.778		292	115		407	490
1240	3"		8	2		310	130		440	535
1250	4"		5	3.200		375	208		583	720
1260	5"	Q-2	5	4.800		780	325		1,105	1,325
1270	6"		5	4.800		630	325		955	1,175
1280	8"		4.50	5.333		1,125	360		1,485	1,775
1290	10"		4	6		715	405		1,120	1,375
1300	12"		3	8		1,575	540		2,115	2,550
1650	Gate, 125 lb., N.R.S.									
2150	Flanged									
2200	2"	1 Plum	5	1.600	Ea.	1,225	115		1,340	1,500
2240	2-1/2"	Q-1	5	3.200		1,250	208		1,458	1,675
2260	3"		4.50	3.556		1,400	231		1,631	1,875
2280	4"		3	5.333		2,150	345		2,495	2,900
2290	5"	Q-2	3.40	7.059		3,400	475		3,875	4,450
2300	6"		3	8		2,300	540		2,840	3,325
2320	8"		2.50	9.600		5,400	645		6,045	6,925
2340	10"		2.20	10.909		8,150	735		8,885	10,100
2360	12"		1.70	14.118		13,100	950		14,050	15,800
2420	For 250 lb. flanged, add					200%	10%			
3550	OS&Y, 125 lb., flanged									
3600	2"	1 Plum	5	1.600	Ea.	1,025	115		1,140	1,325
3640	2-1/2"	Q-1	5	3.200		935	208		1,143	1,325
3660	3"		4.50	3.556		1,025	231		1,256	1,475
3670	3-1/2"		3	5.333		1,125	345		1,470	1,775
3680	4"		3	5.333		1,500	345		1,845	2,175

23 05 Common Work Results for HVAC

23 05 23 – General-Duty Valves for HVAC Piping

23 05 23.30 Valves, Iron Body		Crew	Daily Output	Labor-Hours	Unit	Material	2023 Bare Costs Labor	Equipment	Total	Total Incl O&P
3690	5"	Q-2	3.40	7.059	Ea.	2,375	475		2,850	3,325
3700	6"		3	8		2,375	540		2,915	3,425
3720	8"		2.50	9.600		4,900	645		5,545	6,350
3740	10"		2.20	10.909		8,950	735		9,685	11,000
3760	12"		1.70	14.118		12,200	950		13,150	14,800
3900	For 175 lb., flanged, add					200%	10%			
4350	Globe, OS&Y									
4540	Class 125, flanged									
4550	2"	1 Plum	5	1.600	Ea.	2,075	115		2,190	2,450
4560	2-1/2"	Q-1	5	3.200		2,075	208		2,283	2,600
4570	3"		4.50	3.556		2,200	231		2,431	2,750
4580	4"		3	5.333		3,625	345		3,970	4,525
4590	5"	Q-2	3.40	7.059		6,600	475		7,075	7,975
4600	6"		3	8		6,600	540		7,140	8,075
4610	8"		2.50	9.600		12,900	645		13,545	15,200
4612	10"		2.20	10.909		20,200	735		20,935	23,300
4614	12"		1.70	14.118		11,200	950		12,150	13,800
5040	Class 250, flanged									
5050	2"	1 Plum	4.50	1.778	Ea.	3,300	128		3,428	3,850
5060	2-1/2"	Q-1	4.50	3.556		3,900	231		4,131	4,650
5070	3"		4	4		4,450	259		4,709	5,275
5080	4"		2.70	5.926		6,525	385		6,910	7,750
5090	5"	Q-2	3	8		11,700	540		12,240	13,700
5100	6"		2.70	8.889		11,700	600		12,300	13,800
5110	8"		2.20	10.909		19,800	735		20,535	22,900
5120	10"		2	12		17,500	805		18,305	20,400
5130	12"		1.60	15		26,200	1,000		27,200	30,400
5240	Valve sprocket rim w/chain, for 2" valve	1 Stpi	30	.267		289	19.35		308.35	350
5250	2-1/2" valve		27	.296		217	21.50		238.50	270
5260	3-1/2" valve		25	.320		455	23		478	535
5270	6" valve		20	.400		217	29		246	282
5280	8" valve		18	.444		605	32		637	715
5290	12" valve		16	.500		405	36.50		441.50	500
5300	16" valve		12	.667		900	48.50		948.50	1,075
5310	20" valve		10	.800		900	58		958	1,075
5320	36" valve		8	1		585	72.50		657.50	755
5450	Swing check, 125 lb., threaded									
5500	2"	1 Plum	11	.727	Ea.	285	52.50		337.50	395
5540	2-1/2"	Q-1	15	1.067		355	69		424	495
5550	3"		13	1.231		380	80		460	540
5560	4"		10	1.600		520	104		624	730
5950	Flanged									
5994	1"	1 Plum	7	1.143	Ea.	455	82.50		537.50	625
5998	1-1/2"		6	1.333		760	96		856	980
6000	2"		5	1.600		900	115		1,015	1,175
6040	2-1/2"	Q-1	5	3.200		725	208		933	1,100
6050	3"		4.50	3.556		750	231		981	1,175
6060	4"		3	5.333		1,175	345		1,520	1,825
6070	6"	Q-2	3	8		2,350	540		2,890	3,400
6080	8"		2.50	9.600		3,975	645		4,620	5,325
6090	10"		2.20	10.909		7,575	735		8,310	9,425
6100	12"		1.70	14.118		12,600	950		13,550	15,300
6102	14"		1.55	15.484		16,600	1,050		17,650	19,900

23 05 Common Work Results for HVAC

23 05 23 – General-Duty Valves for HVAC Piping

23 05 23.30 Valves, Iron Body

		Crew	Daily Output	Labor-Hours	Unit	Material	2023 Bare Costs Labor	Equipment	Total	Total Incl O&P
6104	16"	Q-2	1.40	17.143	Ea.	29,400	1,150		30,550	34,100
6110	18"		1.30	18.462		33,600	1,250		34,850	38,900
6112	20"		1	24		53,500	1,625		55,125	61,500
6114	24"	↓	.75	32	↓	60,000	2,150		62,150	69,000
6160	For 250 lb. flanged, add					200%	20%			
6600	Silent check, bronze trim									
6610	Compact wafer type, for 125 or 150 lb. flanges									
6630	1-1/2"	1 Plum	11	.727	Ea.	163	52.50		215.50	258
6640	2"	"	9	.889		199	64		263	315
6650	2-1/2"	Q-1	9	1.778		217	115		332	410
6660	3"		8	2		231	130		361	445
6670	4"	↓	5	3.200		295	208		503	635
6680	5"	Q-2	6	4		390	269		659	830
6690	6"		6	4		520	269		789	970
6700	8"		4.50	5.333		880	360		1,240	1,500
6710	10"		4	6		1,525	405		1,930	2,275
6720	12"	↓	3	8	↓	2,900	540		3,440	4,000
6740	For 250 or 300 lb. flanges, thru 6" no change									
6741	For 8" and 10", add				Ea.	11%	10%			
6750	Twin disc									
6752	2"	1 Plum	9	.889	Ea.	790	64		854	965
6754	4"	Q-1	5	3.200		1,300	208		1,508	1,725
6756	6"	Q-2	5	4.800		1,925	325		2,250	2,575
6758	8"		4.50	5.333		2,950	360		3,310	3,750
6760	10"		4	6		4,700	405		5,105	5,750
6762	12"		3	8		6,100	540		6,640	7,500
6764	18"		1.50	16		26,300	1,075		27,375	30,500
6766	24"	↓	.75	32	↓	37,000	2,150		39,150	43,900
6800	Full flange type, 150 lb.									
6900	Globe type, 125 lb.									
6911	2-1/2"	Q-1	9	1.778	Ea.	485	115		600	705
6912	3"		8	2		430	130		560	670
6913	4"	↓	5	3.200		770	208		978	1,150
6914	5"	Q-2	6	4		1,075	269		1,344	1,575
6915	6"		5	4.800		1,350	325		1,675	1,950
6916	8"		4.50	5.333		2,450	360		2,810	3,225
6917	10"		4	6		3,100	405		3,505	4,000
6918	12"	↓	3	8		5,350	540		5,890	6,675
6940	For 250 lb., add				↓	40%	10%			
6980	Screwed end type, 125 lb.									
6981	1"	1 Plum	19	.421	Ea.	174	30.50		204.50	236
6982	1-1/4"		15	.533		229	38.50		267.50	310
6983	1-1/2"		13	.615		278	44.50		322.50	370
6984	2"	↓	11	.727		380	52.50		432.50	500

23 05 23.70 Valves, Semi-Steel

		Crew	Daily Output	Labor-Hours	Unit	Material	Labor	Equipment	Total	Total Incl O&P
0010	**VALVES, SEMI-STEEL** R220523-90									
1020	Lubricated plug valve, threaded, 200 psi									
1030	1/2"	1 Plum	18	.444	Ea.	134	32		166	196
1040	3/4"		16	.500		169	36		205	240
1050	1"		14	.571		193	41		234	274
1060	1-1/4"		12	.667		169	48		217	258
1070	1-1/2"		11	.727		201	52.50		253.50	299

23 05 Common Work Results for HVAC

23 05 23 – General-Duty Valves for HVAC Piping

23 05 23.70 Valves, Semi-Steel

		Crew	Daily Output	Labor-Hours	Unit	Material	2023 Bare Costs Labor	Equipment	Total	Total Incl O&P
1080	2"	1 Plum	8	1	Ea.	615	72		687	785
1090	2-1/2"	Q-1	5	3.200		675	208		883	1,050
1100	3"	"	4.50	3.556		315	231		546	690
6990	Flanged, 200 psi									
7000	2"	1 Plum	8	1	Ea.	605	72		677	770
7010	2-1/2"	Q-1	5	3.200		905	208		1,113	1,300
7020	3"		4.50	3.556		1,125	231		1,356	1,600
7030	4"		3	5.333		1,550	345		1,895	2,225
7036	5"		2.50	6.400		970	415		1,385	1,700
7040	6"	Q-2	3	8		1,275	540		1,815	2,200
7050	8"		2.50	9.600		2,275	645		2,920	3,475
7060	10"		2.20	10.909		3,800	735		4,535	5,275
7070	12"		1.70	14.118		6,175	950		7,125	8,200

23 05 23.90 Valves, Stainless Steel

		Crew	Daily Output	Labor-Hours	Unit	Material	2023 Bare Costs Labor	Equipment	Total	Total Incl O&P
0010	**VALVES, STAINLESS STEEL** R220523-90									
1700	Check, 200 lb., threaded									
1710	1/4"	1 Plum	24	.333	Ea.	144	24		168	195
1720	1/2"		22	.364		69.50	26		95.50	116
1730	3/4"		20	.400		143	29		172	201
1750	1"		19	.421		163	30.50		193.50	224
1760	1-1/2"		13	.615		360	44.50		404.50	465
1770	2"		11	.727		615	52.50		667.50	755
1800	150 lb., flanged									
1810	2-1/2"	Q-1	5	3.200	Ea.	1,375	208		1,583	1,800
1820	3"		4.50	3.556		2,000	231		2,231	2,550
1830	4"		3	5.333		3,000	345		3,345	3,825
1840	6"	Q-2	3	8		5,300	540		5,840	6,625
1850	8"	"	2.50	9.600		10,800	645		11,445	12,900
2100	Gate, OS&Y, 150 lb., flanged									
2120	1/2"	1 Plum	18	.444	Ea.	510	32		542	610
2140	3/4"		16	.500		490	36		526	595
2150	1"		14	.571		615	41		656	740
2160	1-1/2"		11	.727		1,200	52.50		1,252.50	1,375
2170	2"		8	1		1,425	72		1,497	1,650
2180	2-1/2"	Q-1	5	3.200		1,825	208		2,033	2,300
2190	3"		4.50	3.556		1,825	231		2,056	2,350
2200	4"		3	5.333		2,700	345		3,045	3,500
2205	5"		2.80	5.714		5,550	370		5,920	6,650
2210	6"	Q-2	3	8		5,050	540		5,590	6,350
2220	8"		2.50	9.600		8,775	645		9,420	10,600
2230	10"		2.30	10.435		15,200	700		15,900	17,800
2240	12"		1.90	12.632		20,300	850		21,150	23,700
2260	For 300 lb., flanged, add					120%	15%			
2600	600 lb., flanged									
2620	1/2"	1 Plum	16	.500	Ea.	188	36		224	261
2640	3/4"		14	.571		203	41		244	285
2650	1"		12	.667		244	48		292	340
2660	1-1/2"		10	.800		390	57.50		447.50	515
2670	2"		7	1.143		535	82.50		617.50	715
2680	2-1/2"	Q-1	4	4		6,675	259		6,934	7,700
2690	3"	"	3.60	4.444		6,675	288		6,963	7,750
3100	Globe, OS&Y, 150 lb., flanged									

23 05 Common Work Results for HVAC

23 05 23 – General-Duty Valves for HVAC Piping

23 05 23.90 Valves, Stainless Steel

		Crew	Daily Output	Labor-Hours	Unit	Material	2023 Bare Costs Labor	2023 Bare Costs Equipment	Total	Total Incl O&P
3120	1/2"	1 Plum	18	.444	Ea.	485	32		517	585
3140	3/4"		16	.500		525	36		561	635
3150	1"		14	.571		690	41		731	815
3160	1-1/2"		11	.727		1,075	52.50		1,127.50	1,250
3170	2"		8	1		1,425	72		1,497	1,650
3180	2-1/2"	Q-1	5	3.200		3,100	208		3,308	3,700
3190	3"		4.50	3.556		3,100	231		3,331	3,750
3200	4"		3	5.333		4,950	345		5,295	5,975
3210	6"	Q-2	3	8		8,325	540		8,865	9,975

23 05 23.94 Hospital Type Valves

		Crew	Daily Output	Labor-Hours	Unit	Material	Labor	Equipment	Total	Total Incl O&P
0010	**HOSPITAL TYPE VALVES**									
0300	Chiller valves									
0330	Manual operation balancing valve									
0340	2-1/2" line size	Q-1	9	1.778	Ea.	785	115		900	1,025
0350	3" line size		8	2		805	130		935	1,075
0360	4" line size		5	3.200		1,175	208		1,383	1,575
0370	5" line size	Q-2	5	4.800		1,475	325		1,800	2,075
0380	6" line size		5	4.800		1,825	325		2,150	2,475
0390	8" line size		4.50	5.333		4,050	360		4,410	4,975
0400	10" line size		4	6		6,600	405		7,005	7,875
0410	12" line size		3	8		8,725	540		9,265	10,400
0600	Automatic flow limiting valve									
0620	2-1/2" line size	Q-1	8	2	Ea.	445	130		575	685
0630	3" line size		7	2.286		705	148		853	995
0640	4" line size		6	2.667		1,000	173		1,173	1,350
0645	5" line size	Q-2	5	4.800		1,350	325		1,675	1,975
0650	6" line size		5	4.800		1,675	325		2,000	2,300
0660	8" line size		4.50	5.333		2,550	360		2,910	3,325
0670	10" line size		4	6		4,050	405		4,455	5,075
0680	12" line size		3	8		6,775	540		7,315	8,250

23 05 93 – Testing, Adjusting, and Balancing for HVAC

23 05 93.10 Balancing, Air

		Crew	Daily Output	Labor-Hours	Unit	Material	Labor	Equipment	Total	Total Incl O&P
0010	**BALANCING, AIR** (Subcontractor's quote incl. material and labor)									
0900	Heating and ventilating equipment									
1000	Centrifugal fans, utility sets				Ea.				420	420
1100	Heating and ventilating unit								630	630
1200	In-line fan								630	630
1300	Propeller and wall fan								119	119
1400	Roof exhaust fan								280	280
2000	Air conditioning equipment, central station								910	910
2100	Built-up low pressure unit								840	840
2200	Built-up high pressure unit								980	980
2300	Built-up high pressure dual duct								1,550	1,550
2400	Built-up variable volume								1,825	1,825
2500	Multi-zone A.C. and heating unit								630	630
2600	For each zone over one, add								140	140
2700	Package A.C. unit								350	350
2800	Rooftop heating and cooling unit								490	490
3000	Supply, return, exhaust, registers & diffusers, avg. height ceiling								84	84
3100	High ceiling								126	126
3200	Floor height								70	70
3300	Off mixing box								56	56

23 05 Common Work Results for HVAC

23 05 93 – Testing, Adjusting, and Balancing for HVAC

23 05 93.10 Balancing, Air

		Crew	Daily Output	Labor-Hours	Unit	Material	2023 Bare Costs Labor	Equipment	Total	Total Incl O&P
3500	Induction unit				Ea.				91	91
3600	Lab fume hood								420	420
3700	Linear supply								210	210
3800	Linear supply high								245	245
4000	Linear return								70	70
4100	Light troffers								84	84
4200	Moduline - master								84	84
4300	Moduline - slaves								42	42
4400	Regenerators								560	560
4500	Taps into ceiling plenums								105	105
4600	Variable volume boxes								84	84

23 05 93.20 Balancing, Water

		Crew	Daily Output	Labor-Hours	Unit	Material	Labor	Equipment	Total	Total Incl O&P
0010	**BALANCING, WATER** (Subcontractor's quote incl. material and labor)									
0050	Air cooled condenser				Ea.				256	256
0080	Boiler								515	515
0100	Cabinet unit heater								88	88
0200	Chiller								620	620
0300	Convector								73	73
0400	Converter								365	365
0500	Cooling tower								475	475
0600	Fan coil unit, unit ventilator								132	132
0700	Fin tube and radiant panels								146	146
0800	Main and duct re-heat coils								135	135
0810	Heat exchanger								135	135
0900	Main balancing cocks								110	110
1000	Pumps								320	320
1100	Unit heater								102	102

23 05 93.50 Piping, Testing

		Crew	Daily Output	Labor-Hours	Unit	Material	Labor	Equipment	Total	Total Incl O&P
0010	**PIPING, TESTING**									
0100	Nondestructive testing									
0110	Nondestructive hydraulic pressure test, isolate & 1 hr. hold									
0120	1" - 4" pipe									
0140	0-250 L.F.	1 Stpi	1.33	6.015	Ea.		435		435	650
0160	250-500 L.F.	"	.80	10			725		725	1,075
0180	500-1000 L.F.	Q-5	1.14	14.035			915		915	1,375
0200	1000-2000 L.F.		.80	20			1,300		1,300	1,950
0320	0-250 L.F.		1	16			1,050		1,050	1,550
0340	250-500 L.F.		.73	21.918			1,425		1,425	2,125
0360	500-1000 L.F.		.53	30.189			1,975		1,975	2,950
0380	1000-2000 L.F.		.38	42.105			2,750		2,750	4,100
1000	Pneumatic pressure test, includes soaping joints									
1120	1" - 4" pipe									
1140	0-250 L.F.	Q-5	2.67	5.993	Ea.	14.40	390		404.40	600
1160	250-500 L.F.		1.33	12.030		29	785		814	1,200
1180	500-1000 L.F.		.80	20		43	1,300		1,343	2,000
1200	1000-2000 L.F.		.50	32		57.50	2,100		2,157.50	3,200
1300	6" - 10" pipe									
1320	0-250 L.F.	Q-5	1.33	12.030	Ea.	14.40	785		799.40	1,200
1340	250-500 L.F.		.67	23.881		29	1,550		1,579	2,350
1360	500-1000 L.F.		.40	40		57.50	2,600		2,657.50	3,975
1380	1000-2000 L.F.		.25	64		72	4,175		4,247	6,300
2110	2" diam.	1 Stpi	8	1		22.50	72.50		95	133

23 05 Common Work Results for HVAC

23 05 93 – Testing, Adjusting, and Balancing for HVAC

23 05 93.50 Piping, Testing

		Crew	Daily Output	Labor-Hours	Unit	Material	2023 Bare Costs Labor	Equipment	Total	Total Incl O&P
2120	3" diam.	1 Stpi	8	1	Ea.	22.50	72.50		95	133
2130	4" diam.		8	1		34	72.50		106.50	146
2140	6" diam.		8	1		34	72.50		106.50	146
2150	8" diam.		6.60	1.212		34	88		122	169
2160	10" diam.		6	1.333		45.50	96.50		142	194
3000	Liquid penetration of welds									
3110	2" diam.	1 Stpi	14	.571	Ea.	15.50	41.50		57	79
3120	3" diam.		13.60	.588		15.50	42.50		58	80.50
3130	4" diam.		13.40	.597		15.50	43.50		59	81.50
3140	6" diam.		13.20	.606		15.50	44		59.50	82.50
3150	8" diam.		13	.615		23.50	44.50		68	92
3160	10" diam.		12.80	.625		23.50	45.50		69	93

23 07 HVAC Insulation

23 07 13 – Duct Insulation

23 07 13.10 Duct Thermal Insulation

			Crew	Daily Output	Labor-Hours	Unit	Material	2023 Bare Costs Labor	Equipment	Total	Total Incl O&P
0010	**DUCT THERMAL INSULATION**										
0110	Insulation req'd. is based on the surface size/area to be covered										
3730	Sheet insulation										
3760	Polyethylene foam, closed cell, UV resistant										
3770	Standard temperature (-90°F to +212°F)										
3771	1/4" thick	G	Q-14	450	.036	S.F.	2.54	2.09		4.63	6
3772	3/8" thick	G		440	.036		3.63	2.14		5.77	7.25
3773	1/2" thick	G		420	.038		4.44	2.24		6.68	8.30
3774	3/4" thick	G		400	.040		6.35	2.35		8.70	10.60
3775	1" thick	G		380	.042		8.60	2.47		11.07	13.25
3776	1-1/2" thick	G		360	.044		13.55	2.61		16.16	18.95
3777	2" thick	G		340	.047		17.95	2.76		20.71	24
3778	2-1/2" thick	G		320	.050		23	2.94		25.94	30
3779	Adhesive (see line 7878)										
3780	Foam, rubber										
3782	1" thick	G	1 Stpi	50	.160	S.F.	5.90	11.60		17.50	24
7000	Board insulation										
7020	Mineral wool, 1200° F										
7022	6 lb. density, plain										
7024	1" thick	G	Q-14	370	.043	S.F.	1.05	2.54		3.59	5.05
7026	1-1/2" thick	G		350	.046		.48	2.68		3.16	4.64
7028	2" thick	G		330	.048		.63	2.85		3.48	5.05
7030	3" thick	G		300	.053		.78	3.13		3.91	5.65
7032	4" thick	G		280	.057		1.28	3.36		4.64	6.55
7038	8 lb. density, plain										
7040	1" thick	G	Q-14	360	.044	S.F.	.39	2.61		3	4.42
7042	1-1/2" thick	G		340	.047		.57	2.76		3.33	4.86
7044	2" thick	G		320	.050		.77	2.94		3.71	5.35
7046	3" thick	G		290	.055		1.16	3.24		4.40	6.25
7048	4" thick	G		270	.059		1.52	3.48		5	6.95
7060	10 lb. density, plain										
7062	1" thick	G	Q-14	350	.046	S.F.	.54	2.68		3.22	4.70
7064	1-1/2" thick	G		330	.048		.81	2.85		3.66	5.25
7066	2" thick	G		310	.052		1.08	3.03		4.11	5.85
7068	3" thick	G		280	.057		1.63	3.36		4.99	6.95

23 07 HVAC Insulation

23 07 13 – Duct Insulation

23 07 13.10 Duct Thermal Insulation

		Crew	Daily Output	Labor-Hours	Unit	Material	2023 Bare Costs Labor	Equipment	Total	Total Incl O&P
7070	4" thick G	Q-14	260	.062	S.F.	2.07	3.61		5.68	7.85
7878	Contact cement, quart can				Ea.	16.50			16.50	18.15

23 07 16 – HVAC Equipment Insulation

23 07 16.10 HVAC Equipment Thermal Insulation

		Crew	Daily Output	Labor-Hours	Unit	Material	Labor	Equipment	Total	Total Incl O&P
0010	**HVAC EQUIPMENT THERMAL INSULATION**									
0110	Insulation req'd. is based on the surface size/area to be covered									
1000	Boiler, 1-1/2" calcium silicate only G	Q-14	110	.145	S.F.	8.95	8.55		17.50	23
1020	Plus 2" fiberglass G	"	80	.200	"	14.55	11.75		26.30	34
2000	Breeching, 2" calcium silicate									
2020	Rectangular G	Q-14	42	.381	S.F.	10.15	22.50		32.65	45
2040	Round G	"	38.70	.413	"	10.15	24.50		34.65	48
2300	Calcium silicate block, +200°F to +1,200°F									
2310	On irregular surfaces, valves and fittings									
2340	1" thick G	Q-14	30	.533	S.F.	5.65	31.50		37.15	54.50
2360	1-1/2" thick G		25	.640		6.25	37.50		43.75	64.50
2380	2" thick G		22	.727		7.95	42.50		50.45	74
2400	3" thick G	↓	18	.889	↓	12.60	52		64.60	94
2410	On plane surfaces									
2420	1" thick G	Q-14	126	.127	S.F.	5.65	7.45		13.10	17.65
2430	1-1/2" thick G		120	.133		6.25	7.85		14.10	18.90
2440	2" thick G		100	.160		7.95	9.40		17.35	23
2450	3" thick G	↓	70	.229	↓	12.60	13.40		26	34.50

23 09 Instrumentation and Control for HVAC

23 09 13 – Instrumentation and Control Devices for HVAC

23 09 13.60 Water Level Controls

		Crew	Daily Output	Labor-Hours	Unit	Material	Labor	Equipment	Total	Total Incl O&P
0010	**WATER LEVEL CONTROLS**									
3000	Low water cut-off for hot water boiler, 50 psi maximum									
3100	1" top & bottom equalizing pipes, manual reset	1 Stpi	14	.571	Ea.	705	41.50		746.50	835
3200	1" top & bottom equalizing pipes		14	.571		560	41.50		601.50	675
3300	2-1/2" side connection for nipple-to-boiler	↓	14	.571	↓	630	41.50		671.50	755

23 09 23 – Direct-Digital Control System for HVAC

23 09 23.10 Control Components/DDC Systems

		Crew	Daily Output	Labor-Hours	Unit	Material	Labor	Equipment	Total	Total Incl O&P
0010	**CONTROL COMPONENTS/DDC SYSTEMS** (Sub's quote incl. M & L)									
0100	Analog inputs									
0110	Sensors (avg. 50' run in 1/2" EMT)									
0120	Duct temperature				Ea.				465	465
0130	Space temperature								665	665
0140	Duct humidity, +/- 3%								595	595
0150	Space humidity, +/- 2%								1,150	1,150
0160	Duct static pressure								680	680
0170	CFM/transducer								920	920
0172	Water temperature								940	940
0174	Water flow								3,450	3,450
0176	Water pressure differential								975	975
0177	Steam flow								2,400	2,400
0178	Steam pressure								1,025	1,025
0180	KW/transducer								1,350	1,350
0182	KWH totalization (not incl. elec. meter pulse xmtr.)								625	625
0190	Space static pressure				↓				1,075	1,075

23 09 Instrumentation and Control for HVAC

23 09 23 – Direct-Digital Control System for HVAC

23 09 23.10 Control Components/DDC Systems		Crew	Daily Output	Labor-Hours	Unit	Material	2023 Bare Costs Labor	Equipment	Total	Total Incl O&P
1000	Analog outputs (avg. 50' run in 1/2" EMT)									
1010	P/I transducer				Ea.				635	635
1020	Analog output, matl. in MUX								305	305
1030	Pneumatic (not incl. control device)								645	645
1040	Electric (not incl. control device)				↓				380	380
2000	Status (alarms)									
2100	Digital inputs (avg. 50' run in 1/2" EMT)									
2110	Freeze				Ea.				435	435
2120	Fire								395	395
2130	Differential pressure (air)		2 Elec	3	5.333		385	360		745	960
2140	Differential pressure (water)								975	975
2150	Current sensor								435	435
2160	Duct high temperature thermostat								570	570
2170	Duct smoke detector				↓				705	705
2200	Digital output (avg. 50' run in 1/2" EMT)									
2210	Start/stop				Ea.				340	340
2220	On/off (maintained contact)				"				585	585
3000	Controller MUX panel, incl. function boards									
3100	48 point				Ea.				5,275	5,275
3110	128 point				"				7,225	7,225
3200	DDC controller (avg. 50' run in conduit)									
3210	Mechanical room									
3214	16 point controller (incl. 120 volt/1 phase power supply)				Ea.				3,275	3,275
3229	32 point controller (incl. 120 volt/1 phase power supply)				"				5,425	5,425
3230	Includes software programming and checkout									
3260	Space									
3266	VAV terminal box (incl. space temp. sensor)				Ea.				840	840
3280	Host computer (avg. 50' run in conduit)									
3281	Package complete with PC, keyboard,									
3282	printer, monitor, basic software				Ea.				3,150	3,150
4000	Front end costs									
4100	Computer (P.C.) with software program				Ea.				6,350	6,350
4200	Color graphics software								3,925	3,925
4300	Color graphics slides								490	490
4350	Additional printer				↓				980	980
4400	Communications trunk cable				L.F.				3.80	3.80
4500	Engineering labor (not incl. dftg.)				Point				94	94
4600	Calibration labor								120	120
4700	Start-up, checkout labor				↓				120	120
4800	Programming labor, as req'd									
5000	Communications bus (data transmission cable)									
5010	#18 twisted shielded pair in 1/2" EMT conduit				C.L.F.				380	380
8000	Applications software									
8050	Basic maintenance manager software (not incl. data base entry)				Ea.				1,950	1,950
8100	Time program				Point				6.85	6.85
8120	Duty cycle								13.65	13.65
8140	Optimum start/stop								41.50	41.50
8160	Demand limiting								20.50	20.50
8180	Enthalpy program				↓				41.50	41.50
8200	Boiler optimization				Ea.				1,225	1,225
8220	Chiller optimization				"				1,625	1,625
8240	Custom applications									
8260	Cost varies with complexity									

23 09 Instrumentation and Control for HVAC

23 09 53 – Pneumatic and Electric Control System for HVAC

23 09 53.10 Control Components		Crew	Daily Output	Labor-Hours	Unit	Material	2023 Bare Costs Labor	Equipment	Total	Total Incl O&P
0010	**CONTROL COMPONENTS** R230500-10									
0680	Controller for VAV box, includes actuator	1 Stpi	7.30	1.096	Ea.	535	79.50		614.50	710
2000	Gauges, pressure or vacuum									
2100	2" diameter dial	1 Stpi	32	.250	Ea.	12.40	18.15		30.55	40.50
2200	2-1/2" diameter dial		32	.250		15.35	18.15		33.50	44
2300	3-1/2" diameter dial		32	.250		33	18.15		51.15	63
2400	4-1/2" diameter dial		32	.250		37.50	18.15		55.65	68
2700	Flanged iron case, black ring									
2800	3-1/2" diameter dial	1 Stpi	32	.250	Ea.	175	18.15		193.15	220
2900	4-1/2" diameter dial		32	.250		158	18.15		176.15	200
3000	6" diameter dial		32	.250		250	18.15		268.15	300
3010	Steel case, 0-300 psi									
3012	2" diameter dial	1 Stpi	16	.500	Ea.	8.80	36.50		45.30	63.50
3014	4" diameter dial	"	16	.500	"	24	36.50		60.50	80.50
3020	Aluminum case, 0-300 psi									
3022	3-1/2" diameter dial	1 Stpi	16	.500	Ea.	21	36.50		57.50	77.50
3024	4-1/2" diameter dial		16	.500		35	36.50		71.50	92.50
3026	6" diameter dial		16	.500		284	36.50		320.50	365
3028	8-1/2" diameter dial		16	.500		495	36.50		531.50	600
3030	Brass case, 0-300 psi									
3032	2" diameter dial	1 Stpi	16	.500	Ea.	27	36.50		63.50	84
3034	4-1/2" diameter dial	"	16	.500	"	128	36.50		164.50	195
3040	Steel case, high pressure, 0-10,000 psi									
3042	4-1/2" diameter dial	1 Stpi	16	.500	Ea.	300	36.50		336.50	385
3044	6-1/2" diameter dial		16	.500		228	36.50		264.50	305
3046	8-1/2" diameter dial		16	.500		590	36.50		626.50	705
3080	Pressure gauge, differential, magnehelic									
3084	0-2" W.C., with air filter kit	1 Stpi	6	1.333	Ea.	42.50	96.50		139	191
3300	For compound pressure-vacuum, add					18%				
4000	Thermometers									
4100	Dial type, 3-1/2" diameter, vapor type, union connection	1 Stpi	32	.250	Ea.	226	18.15		244.15	276
4120	Liquid type, union connection		32	.250		435	18.15		453.15	505
4500	Stem type, 6-1/2" case, 2" stem, 1/2" NPT		32	.250		60	18.15		78.15	93
4520	4" stem, 1/2" NPT		32	.250		73.50	18.15		91.65	108
4600	9" case, 3-1/2" stem, 3/4" NPT		28	.286		48	20.50		68.50	84
4620	6" stem, 3/4" NPT		28	.286		57.50	20.50		78	94.50
4640	8" stem, 3/4" NPT		28	.286		192	20.50		212.50	242
4660	12" stem, 1" NPT		26	.308		188	22.50		210.50	241
4670	Bi-metal, dial type, steel case brass stem									
4672	2" dial, 4" - 9" stem	1 Stpi	16	.500	Ea.	45.50	36.50		82	105
4673	2-1/2" dial, 4" - 9" stem		16	.500		45.50	36.50		82	105
4674	3-1/2" dial, 4" - 9" stem		16	.500		56.50	36.50		93	116
4680	Mercury filled, industrial, union connection type									
4682	Angle stem, 7" scale	1 Stpi	16	.500	Ea.	61.50	36.50		98	122
4683	9" scale		16	.500		170	36.50		206.50	241
4684	12" scale		16	.500		218	36.50		254.50	293
4686	Straight stem, 7" scale		16	.500		166	36.50		202.50	237
4687	9" scale		16	.500		217	36.50		253.50	292
4688	12" scale		16	.500		261	36.50		297.50	340
4690	Mercury filled, industrial, separable socket type, with well									
4692	Angle stem, with socket, 7" scale	1 Stpi	16	.500	Ea.	200	36.50		236.50	274
4693	9" scale		16	.500		200	36.50		236.50	274

23 09 Instrumentation and Control for HVAC

23 09 53 – Pneumatic and Electric Control System for HVAC

23 09 53.10 Control Components		Crew	Daily Output	Labor-Hours	Unit	Material	2023 Bare Costs Labor	Equipment	Total	Total Incl O&P
4694	12" scale	1 Stpi	16	.500	Ea.	237	36.50		273.50	315
4696	Straight stem, with socket, 7" scale		16	.500		156	36.50		192.50	226
4697	9" scale		16	.500		156	36.50		192.50	226
4698	12" scale		16	.500		192	36.50		228.50	265
6000	Valves, motorized zone									
6100	Sweat connections, 1/2" C x C	1 Stpi	20	.400	Ea.	107	29		136	162
6110	3/4" C x C		20	.400		107	29		136	162
6120	1" C x C		19	.421		140	30.50		170.50	200
6140	1/2" C x C, with end switch, 2 wire		20	.400		106	29		135	160
6150	3/4" C x C, with end switch, 2 wire		20	.400		106	29		135	160
6160	1" C x C, with end switch, 2 wire		19	.421		130	30.50		160.50	190

23 11 Facility Fuel Piping

23 11 13 – Facility Fuel-Oil Piping

23 11 13.10 Fuel Oil Specialties		Crew	Daily Output	Labor-Hours	Unit	Material	2023 Bare Costs Labor	Equipment	Total	Total Incl O&P
0010	**FUEL OIL SPECIALTIES**									
0020	Foot valve, single poppet, metal to metal construction									
0040	Bevel seat, 1/2" diameter	1 Stpi	20	.400	Ea.	151	29		180	210
0060	3/4" diameter		18	.444		77.50	32		109.50	134
1000	Oil filters, 3/8" IPT, 20 gal. per hour		20	.400		27.50	29		56.50	73.50
2000	Remote tank gauging system, self contained									
3000	Valve, ball check, globe type, 3/8" diameter	1 Stpi	24	.333	Ea.	16.25	24		40.25	54
3500	Fusible, 3/8" diameter		24	.333		33.50	24		57.50	72.50
3600	1/2" diameter		24	.333		80	24		104	124
3610	3/4" diameter		20	.400		183	29		212	245
3620	1" diameter		19	.421		495	30.50		525.50	585
4000	Nonfusible, 3/8" diameter		24	.333		33	24		57	72.50
4500	Shutoff, gate type, lever handle, spring-fusible kit									
4520	1/4" diameter	1 Stpi	14	.571	Ea.	34.50	41.50		76	100
4540	3/8" diameter		12	.667		83.50	48.50		132	164
4560	1/2" diameter		10	.800		122	58		180	222
4570	3/4" diameter		8	1		142	72.50		214.50	264
5000	Vent alarm, whistling signal					45.50			45.50	50
5500	Vent protector/breather, 1-1/4" diameter	1 Stpi	32	.250		27.50	18.15		45.65	57.50

23 11 23 – Facility Natural-Gas Piping

23 11 23.10 Gas Meters		Crew	Daily Output	Labor-Hours	Unit	Material	2023 Bare Costs Labor	Equipment	Total	Total Incl O&P
0010	**GAS METERS**									
4000	Residential									
4010	Gas meter, residential, 3/4" pipe size	1 Plum	14	.571	Ea.	365	41		406	465
4020	Gas meter, residential, 1" pipe size		12	.667		370	48		418	480
4030	Gas meter, residential, 1-1/4" pipe size		10	.800		335	57.50		392.50	455

23 11 23.20 Gas Piping, Flexible (Csst)		Crew	Daily Output	Labor-Hours	Unit	Material	2023 Bare Costs Labor	Equipment	Total	Total Incl O&P
0010	**GAS PIPING, FLEXIBLE (CSST)**									
0100	Tubing with lightning protection									
0110	3/8"	1 Stpi	65	.123	L.F.	4.25	8.95		13.20	18
0120	1/2"		62	.129		4.77	9.35		14.12	19.20
0130	3/4"		60	.133		6.20	9.65		15.85	21.50
0140	1"		55	.145		8.85	10.55		19.40	25.50
0150	1-1/4"		50	.160		11.05	11.60		22.65	29.50
0160	1-1/2"		45	.178		19.50	12.90		32.40	41

23 11 Facility Fuel Piping

23 11 23 – Facility Natural-Gas Piping

23 11 23.20 Gas Piping, Flexible (Csst)		Crew	Daily Output	Labor-Hours	Unit	Material	2023 Bare Costs Labor	Equipment	Total	Total Incl O&P
0170	2"	1 Stpi	40	.200	L.F.	28	14.50		42.50	52
0200	Tubing for underground/underslab burial									
0210	3/8"	1 Stpi	65	.123	L.F.	5.90	8.95		14.85	19.80
0220	1/2"		62	.129		6.70	9.35		16.05	21.50
0230	3/4"		60	.133		10.05	9.65		19.70	25.50
0240	1"		55	.145		11.50	10.55		22.05	28.50
0250	1-1/4"		50	.160		15.45	11.60		27.05	34.50
0260	1-1/2"		45	.178		29	12.90		41.90	51.50
0270	2"	↓	40	.200	↓	34.50	14.50		49	59.50
3000	Fittings									
3010	Straight									
3100	Tube to NPT									
3110	3/8"	1 Stpi	29	.276	Ea.	17.40	20		37.40	49
3120	1/2"		27	.296		19.45	21.50		40.95	53.50
3130	3/4"		25	.320		26.50	23		49.50	63.50
3140	1"		23	.348		41	25		66	82.50
3150	1-1/4"		20	.400		91	29		120	144
3160	1-1/2"		17	.471		187	34		221	257
3170	2"	↓	15	.533	↓	320	38.50		358.50	410
3200	Coupling									
3210	3/8"	1 Stpi	29	.276	Ea.	34	20		54	67.50
3220	1/2"		27	.296		36	21.50		57.50	71.50
3230	3/4"		25	.320		49	23		72	88.50
3240	1"		23	.348		84	25		109	130
3250	1-1/4"		20	.400		186	29		215	249
3260	1-1/2"		17	.471		355	34		389	440
3270	2"	↓	15	.533	↓	605	38.50		643.50	725
3300	Flange fitting									
3310	3/8"	1 Stpi	25	.320	Ea.	23.50	23		46.50	60.50
3320	1/2"		22	.364		24.50	26.50		51	66.50
3330	3/4"		19	.421		31	30.50		61.50	80
3340	1"		16	.500		45.50	36.50		82	104
3350	1-1/4"	↓	12	.667	↓	101	48.50		149.50	183
3400	90° flange valve									
3410	3/8"	1 Stpi	25	.320	Ea.	39	23		62	77
3420	1/2"		22	.364		46	26.50		72.50	90
3430	3/4"	↓	19	.421	↓	65	30.50		95.50	117
4000	Tee									
4120	1/2"	1 Stpi	20.50	.390	Ea.	62	28.50		90.50	111
4130	3/4"		19	.421		67.50	30.50		98	120
4140	1"	↓	17.50	.457		130	33		163	193
5000	Reducing									
5110	Tube to NPT									
5120	3/4" to 1/2" NPT	1 Stpi	26	.308	Ea.	28.50	22.50		51	65
5130	1" to 3/4" NPT	"	24	.333	"	44	24		68	84.50
5200	Reducing tee									
5210	1/2" x 3/8" x 3/8"	1 Stpi	21	.381	Ea.	74.50	27.50		102	123
5220	3/4" x 1/2" x 1/2"		20	.400		70	29		99	121
5230	1" x 3/4" x 1/2"		18	.444		116	32		148	175
5240	1-1/4" x 1-1/4" x 1"		15.60	.513		310	37		347	395
5250	1-1/2" x 1-1/2" x 1-1/4"		13.30	.602		470	43.50		513.50	585
5260	2" x 2" x 1-1/2"		11.80	.678		710	49		759	855
5300	Manifold with four ports and mounting bracket									

23 11 Facility Fuel Piping

23 11 23 – Facility Natural-Gas Piping

23 11 23.20 Gas Piping, Flexible (Csst)

		Crew	Daily Output	Labor-Hours	Unit	Material	2023 Bare Costs Labor	Equipment	Total	Total Incl O&P
5302	Labor to mount manifold does not include making pipe									
5304	connections which are included in fitting labor.									
5310	3/4" x 1/2" x 1/2" (4)	1 Stpi	76	.105	Ea.	54.50	7.65		62.15	71.50
5330	1-1/4" x 1" x 3/4" (4)		72	.111		78.50	8.05		86.55	98.50
5350	2" x 1-1/2" x 1" (4)	↓	68	.118	↓	98.50	8.55		107.05	121
5600	Protective striker plate									
5610	Quarter plate, 3" x 2"	1 Stpi	88	.091	Ea.	1.26	6.60		7.86	11.25
5620	Half plate, 3" x 7"		82	.098		2.71	7.10		9.81	13.55
5630	Full plate, 3" x 12"	↓	78	.103	↓	5.10	7.45		12.55	16.70

23 12 Facility Fuel Pumps

23 12 13 – Facility Fuel-Oil Pumps

23 12 13.10 Pump and Motor Sets

		Crew	Daily Output	Labor-Hours	Unit	Material	Labor	Equipment	Total	Total Incl O&P
0010	**PUMP AND MOTOR SETS**									
1810	Light fuel and diesel oils									
1820	20 GPH, 1/3 HP	Q-5	6	2.667	Ea.	2,000	174		2,174	2,450
1850	145 GPH, 1/2 HP	"	4	4	"	2,100	261		2,361	2,725

23 13 Facility Fuel-Storage Tanks

23 13 13 – Facility Underground Fuel-Oil, Storage Tanks

23 13 13.09 Single-Wall Steel Fuel-Oil Tanks

		Crew	Daily Output	Labor-Hours	Unit	Material	Labor	Equipment	Total	Total Incl O&P
0010	**SINGLE-WALL STEEL FUEL-OIL TANKS**									
5000	Tanks, steel ugnd., sti-p3, not incl. hold-down bars									
5500	Excavation, pad, pumps and piping not included									
5510	Single wall, 500 gallon capacity, 7 ga. shell	Q-5	2.70	5.926	Ea.	2,475	385		2,860	3,300
5520	1,000 gallon capacity, 7 ga. shell	"	2.50	6.400		3,575	420		3,995	4,550
5530	2,000 gallon capacity, 1/4" thick shell	Q-7	4.60	6.957		5,150	480		5,630	6,400
5535	2,500 gallon capacity, 7 ga. shell	Q-5	3	5.333		6,950	350		7,300	8,150
5540	5,000 gallon capacity, 1/4" thick shell	Q-7	3.20	10		16,300	690		16,990	18,900
5560	10,000 gallon capacity, 1/4" thick shell		2	16		13,300	1,100		14,400	16,300
5580	15,000 gallon capacity, 5/16" thick shell		1.70	18.824		13,700	1,300		15,000	17,000
5600	20,000 gallon capacity, 5/16" thick shell		1.50	21.333		33,300	1,475		34,775	38,800
5610	25,000 gallon capacity, 3/8" thick shell		1.30	24.615		38,200	1,700		39,900	44,500
5620	30,000 gallon capacity, 3/8" thick shell		1.10	29.091		42,900	2,000		44,900	50,000
5630	40,000 gallon capacity, 3/8" thick shell		.90	35.556		56,000	2,450		58,450	65,000
5640	50,000 gallon capacity, 3/8" thick shell	↓	.80	40	↓	63,500	2,750		66,250	74,000

23 13 13.13 Dbl-Wall Steel, Undrgrnd Fuel-Oil, Stor. Tanks

		Crew	Daily Output	Labor-Hours	Unit	Material	Labor	Equipment	Total	Total Incl O&P
0010	**DOUBLE-WALL STEEL, UNDERGROUND FUEL-OIL, STORAGE TANKS**									
6200	Steel, underground, 360°, double wall, UL listed,									
6210	with sti-P3 corrosion protection,									
6220	(dielectric coating, cathodic protection, electrical									
6230	isolation) 30 year warranty,									
6240	not incl. manholes or hold-downs.									
6250	500 gallon capacity	Q-5	2.40	6.667	Ea.	4,400	435		4,835	5,475
6260	1,000 gallon capacity	"	2.25	7.111		4,775	465		5,240	5,975
6270	2,000 gallon capacity	Q-7	4.16	7.692		6,325	530		6,855	7,750
6280	3,000 gallon capacity		3.90	8.205		9,100	565		9,665	10,800
6290	4,000 gallon capacity		3.64	8.791		10,700	605		11,305	12,700
6300	5,000 gallon capacity		2.91	10.997		11,500	760		12,260	13,800

23 13 Facility Fuel-Storage Tanks

23 13 13 – Facility Underground Fuel-Oil, Storage Tanks

23 13 13.13 Dbl-Wall Steel, Undrgrnd Fuel-Oil, Stor. Tanks

		Crew	Daily Output	Labor-Hours	Unit	Material	2023 Bare Costs Labor	Equipment	Total	Total Incl O&P
6310	6,000 gallon capacity	Q-7	2.42	13.223	Ea.	14,800	915		15,715	17,700
6320	8,000 gallon capacity		2.08	15.385		14,600	1,050		15,650	17,700
6330	10,000 gallon capacity		1.82	17.582		18,200	1,225		19,425	21,800
6340	12,000 gallon capacity		1.70	18.824		20,300	1,300		21,600	24,300
6350	15,000 gallon capacity		1.33	24.060		27,200	1,650		28,850	32,400
6360	20,000 gallon capacity		1.33	24.060		44,900	1,650		46,550	52,000
6370	25,000 gallon capacity		1.16	27.586		53,500	1,900		55,400	62,000
6380	30,000 gallon capacity		1.03	31.068		49,600	2,150		51,750	57,500
6390	40,000 gallon capacity		.80	40		167,000	2,750		169,750	187,500
6395	50,000 gallon capacity		.73	43.836		203,000	3,025		206,025	227,500
6400	For hold-downs 500-2,000 gal., add		16	2	Set	265	138		403	500
6410	For hold-downs 3,000-6,000 gal., add		12	2.667		460	184		644	780
6420	For hold-downs 8,000-12,000 gal., add		11	2.909		655	201		856	1,025
6430	For hold-downs 15,000 gal., add		9	3.556		895	246		1,141	1,350
6440	For hold-downs 20,000 gal., add		8	4		1,025	276		1,301	1,525
6450	For hold-downs 20,000 gal. plus, add		6	5.333		1,250	370		1,620	1,925
6500	For manways, add				Ea.	1,475			1,475	1,625
6600	In place with hold-downs									
6652	550 gallon capacity	Q-5	1.84	8.696	Ea.	4,650	570		5,220	5,975

23 13 13.23 Glass-Fiber-Reinfcd-Plastic, Fuel-Oil, Storage

		Crew	Daily Output	Labor-Hours	Unit	Material	2023 Bare Costs Labor	Equipment	Total	Total Incl O&P
0010	**GLASS-FIBER-REINFCD-PLASTIC, UNDERGRND. FUEL-OIL, STORAGE**									
0210	Fiberglass, underground, single wall, UL listed, not including									
0220	manway or hold-down strap									
0225	550 gallon capacity	Q-5	2.67	5.993	Ea.	5,225	390		5,615	6,325
0230	1,000 gallon capacity	"	2.46	6.504		6,725	425		7,150	8,025
0240	2,000 gallon capacity	Q-7	4.57	7.002		10,800	485		11,285	12,600
0245	3,000 gallon capacity		3.90	8.205		10,900	565		11,465	12,800
0250	4,000 gallon capacity		3.55	9.014		14,600	620		15,220	16,900
0255	5,000 gallon capacity		3.20	10		13,300	690		13,990	15,600
0260	6,000 gallon capacity		2.67	11.985		12,500	830		13,330	14,900
0270	8,000 gallon capacity		2.29	13.974		19,500	965		20,465	22,900
0280	10,000 gallon capacity		2	16		19,600	1,100		20,700	23,300
0282	12,000 gallon capacity		1.88	17.021		20,800	1,175		21,975	24,700
0284	15,000 gallon capacity		1.68	19.048		30,000	1,325		31,325	35,000
0290	20,000 gallon capacity		1.45	22.069		41,800	1,525		43,325	48,300
0300	25,000 gallon capacity		1.28	25		72,000	1,725		73,725	81,500
0320	30,000 gallon capacity		1.14	28.070		108,500	1,950		110,450	122,000
0340	40,000 gallon capacity		.89	35.955		154,000	2,475		156,475	173,000
0360	48,000 gallon capacity		.81	39.506		228,500	2,725		231,225	255,500
0500	For manway, fittings and hold-downs, add					20%	15%			
0600	For manways, add					3,525			3,525	3,875
1000	For helical heating coil, add	Q-5	2.50	6.400		6,950	420		7,370	8,275
1020	Fiberglass, underground, double wall, UL listed									
1030	includes manways, not incl. hold-down straps									
1040	600 gallon capacity	Q-5	2.42	6.612	Ea.	11,500	430		11,930	13,200
1050	1,000 gallon capacity	"	2.25	7.111		15,700	465		16,165	18,000
1060	2,500 gallon capacity	Q-7	4.16	7.692		21,700	530		22,230	24,700
1070	3,000 gallon capacity		3.90	8.205		24,300	565		24,865	27,500
1080	4,000 gallon capacity		3.64	8.791		25,400	605		26,005	28,800
1090	6,000 gallon capacity		2.42	13.223		31,500	915		32,415	36,100
1100	8,000 gallon capacity		2.08	15.385		40,100	1,050		41,150	45,700
1110	10,000 gallon capacity		1.82	17.582		48,500	1,225		49,725	55,500

23 13 Facility Fuel-Storage Tanks

23 13 13 – Facility Underground Fuel-Oil, Storage Tanks

23 13 13.23 Glass-Fiber-Reinfcd-Plastic, Fuel-Oil, Storage

		Crew	Daily Output	Labor-Hours	Unit	Material	2023 Bare Costs Labor	Equipment	Total	Total Incl O&P
1120	12,000 gallon capacity	Q-7	1.70	18.824	Ea.	50,500	1,300		51,800	57,500
1122	15,000 gallon capacity		1.52	21.053		90,000	1,450		91,450	101,000
1124	20,000 gallon capacity		1.33	24.060		97,000	1,650		98,650	109,000
1126	25,000 gallon capacity		1.16	27.586		112,000	1,900		113,900	126,500
1128	30,000 gallon capacity		1.03	31.068		134,500	2,150		136,650	151,000
1140	For hold-down straps, add					2%	10%			
1150	For hold-downs 500-4,000 gal., add	Q-7	16	2	Set	560	138		698	820
1160	For hold-downs 5,000-15,000 gal., add		8	4		1,125	276		1,401	1,625
1170	For hold-downs 20,000 gal., add		5.33	6.004		1,675	415		2,090	2,475
1180	For hold-downs 25,000 gal., add		4	8		2,225	550		2,775	3,275
1190	For hold-downs 30,000 gal., add		2.60	12.308		3,350	850		4,200	4,950
2210	Fiberglass, underground, single wall, UL listed, including									
2220	hold-down straps, no manways									
2225	550 gallon capacity	Q-5	2	8	Ea.	5,775	520		6,295	7,125
2230	1,000 gallon capacity	"	1.88	8.511		7,275	555		7,830	8,825
2240	2,000 gallon capacity	Q-7	3.55	9.014		11,300	620		11,920	13,400
2250	4,000 gallon capacity		2.90	11.034		15,100	760		15,860	17,700
2260	6,000 gallon capacity		2	16		13,600	1,100		14,700	16,600
2270	8,000 gallon capacity		1.78	17.978		20,600	1,250		21,850	24,500
2280	10,000 gallon capacity		1.60	20		20,800	1,375		22,175	24,900
2282	12,000 gallon capacity		1.52	21.053		21,900	1,450		23,350	26,300
2284	15,000 gallon capacity		1.39	23.022		31,100	1,600		32,700	36,600
2290	20,000 gallon capacity		1.14	28.070		43,500	1,950		45,450	50,500
2300	25,000 gallon capacity		.96	33.333		74,000	2,300		76,300	85,000
2320	30,000 gallon capacity		.80	40		111,500	2,750		114,250	127,000
3020	Fiberglass, underground, double wall, UL listed									
3030	includes manways and hold-down straps									
3040	600 gallon capacity	Q-5	1.86	8.602	Ea.	12,000	560		12,560	14,000
3050	1,000 gallon capacity	"	1.70	9.412		16,300	615		16,915	18,800
3060	2,500 gallon capacity	Q-7	3.29	9.726		22,200	670		22,870	25,500
3070	3,000 gallon capacity		3.13	10.224		24,800	705		25,505	28,400
3080	4,000 gallon capacity		2.93	10.922		25,900	755		26,655	29,600
3090	6,000 gallon capacity		1.86	17.204		32,600	1,200		33,800	37,700
3100	8,000 gallon capacity		1.65	19.394		41,200	1,350		42,550	47,300
3110	10,000 gallon capacity		1.48	21.622		49,700	1,500		51,200	56,500
3120	12,000 gallon capacity		1.40	22.857		51,500	1,575		53,075	59,000
3122	15,000 gallon capacity		1.28	25		91,000	1,725		92,725	102,500
3124	20,000 gallon capacity		1.06	30.189		98,500	2,075		100,575	111,500
3126	25,000 gallon capacity		.90	35.556		114,500	2,450		116,950	129,500
3128	30,000 gallon capacity		.74	43.243		138,000	2,975		140,975	156,500

23 13 23 – Facility Aboveground Fuel-Oil, Storage Tanks

23 13 23.16 Horizontal, Stl, Abvgrd Fuel-Oil, Storage Tanks

		Crew	Daily Output	Labor-Hours	Unit	Material	2023 Bare Costs Labor	Equipment	Total	Total Incl O&P
0010	**HORIZONTAL, STEEL, ABOVEGROUND FUEL-OIL, STORAGE TANKS**									
3000	Steel, storage, aboveground, including cradles, coating,									
3020	fittings, not including foundation, pumps or piping									
3040	Single wall, 275 gallon	Q-5	5	3.200	Ea.	1,875	209		2,084	2,375
3060	550 gallon	"	2.70	5.926		7,150	385		7,535	8,450
3080	1,000 gallon	Q-7	5	6.400		12,000	440		12,440	13,900
3100	1,500 gallon		4.75	6.737		18,400	465		18,865	20,900
3120	2,000 gallon		4.60	6.957		17,700	480		18,180	20,200
3320	Double wall, 500 gallon capacity	Q-5	2.40	6.667		3,925	435		4,360	4,950
3330	2,000 gallon capacity	Q-7	4.15	7.711		6,925	530		7,455	8,400

23 13 Facility Fuel-Storage Tanks

23 13 23 – Facility Aboveground Fuel-Oil, Storage Tanks

23 13 23.16 Horizontal, Stl, Abvgrd Fuel-Oil, Storage Tanks		Crew	Daily Output	Labor-Hours	Unit	Material	2023 Bare Costs Labor	Equipment	Total	Total Incl O&P
3340	4,000 gallon capacity	Q-7	3.60	8.889	Ea.	14,800	615		15,415	17,100
3350	6,000 gallon capacity		2.40	13.333		41,600	920		42,520	47,200
3360	8,000 gallon capacity		2	16		48,800	1,100		49,900	55,000
3370	10,000 gallon capacity		1.80	17.778		57,000	1,225		58,225	65,000
3380	15,000 gallon capacity		1.50	21.333		79,000	1,475		80,475	89,000
3390	20,000 gallon capacity		1.30	24.615		95,500	1,700		97,200	107,500
3400	25,000 gallon capacity		1.15	27.826		90,500	1,925		92,425	102,500
3410	30,000 gallon capacity		1	32		122,500	2,200		124,700	138,500

23 13 23.26 Horizontal, Conc., Abvgrd Fuel-Oil, Stor. Tanks

		Crew	Daily Output	Labor-Hours	Unit	Material	Labor	Equipment	Total	Total Incl O&P
0010	**HORIZONTAL, CONCRETE, ABOVEGROUND FUEL-OIL, STORAGE TANKS**									
0050	Concrete, storage, aboveground, including pad & pump									
0100	500 gallon	F-3	2	20	Ea.	13,700	1,200	1,075	15,975	18,100
0200	1,000 gallon	"	2	20		19,200	1,200	1,075	21,475	24,200
0300	2,000 gallon	F-4	2	24		24,700	1,425	1,225	27,350	30,700

23 21 Hydronic Piping and Pumps

23 21 20 – Hydronic HVAC Piping Specialties

23 21 20.10 Air Control

		Crew	Daily Output	Labor-Hours	Unit	Material	Labor	Equipment	Total	Total Incl O&P
0010	**AIR CONTROL**									
0030	Air separator, with strainer									
0040	2" diameter	Q-5	6	2.667	Ea.	1,775	174		1,949	2,200
0080	2-1/2" diameter		5	3.200		1,975	209		2,184	2,475
0100	3" diameter		4	4		3,050	261		3,311	3,750
1000	Micro-bubble separator for total air removal, closed loop system									
1010	Requires bladder type tank in system.									
1020	Water (hot or chilled) or glycol system									
1030	Threaded									
1040	3/4" diameter	1 Stpi	20	.400	Ea.	95.50	29		124.50	149
1050	1" diameter		19	.421		111	30.50		141.50	168
1060	1-1/4" diameter		16	.500		147	36.50		183.50	215
1070	1-1/2" diameter		13	.615		195	44.50		239.50	281
1080	2" diameter		11	.727		1,325	53		1,378	1,525
1090	2-1/2" diameter	Q-5	15	1.067		1,575	69.50		1,644.50	1,825
1100	3" diameter		13	1.231		2,125	80.50		2,205.50	2,450
1110	4" diameter		10	1.600		2,350	104		2,454	2,750
1800	With drain/dismantle/cleaning access flange									
1810	Flanged									
1820	2" diameter	Q-5	4.60	3.478	Ea.	3,750	227		3,977	4,450
1830	2-1/2" diameter		4	4		4,050	261		4,311	4,850
1840	3" diameter		3.60	4.444		4,950	290		5,240	5,875
1850	4" diameter		2.50	6.400		5,650	420		6,070	6,850
1860	5" diameter	Q-6	2.80	8.571		10,400	580		10,980	12,300
1870	6" diameter	"	2.60	9.231		13,400	625		14,025	15,600

23 21 20.14 Air Purging Scoop

		Crew	Daily Output	Labor-Hours	Unit	Material	Labor	Equipment	Total	Total Incl O&P
0010	**AIR PURGING SCOOP**, With tappings.									
0020	For air vent and expansion tank connection									
0100	1" pipe size, threaded	1 Stpi	19	.421	Ea.	26	30.50		56.50	74
0110	1-1/4" pipe size, threaded		15	.533		36.50	38.50		75	98
0120	1-1/2" pipe size, threaded		13	.615		80.50	44.50		125	155
0130	2" pipe size, threaded		11	.727		91.50	53		144.50	180

23 21 Hydronic Piping and Pumps

23 21 20 – Hydronic HVAC Piping Specialties

23 21 20.18 Automatic Air Vent

		Crew	Daily Output	Labor-Hours	Unit	Material	2023 Bare Costs Labor	2023 Bare Costs Equipment	Total	Total Incl O&P
0010	**AUTOMATIC AIR VENT**									
0020	Cast iron body, stainless steel internals, float type									
0180	1/2" NPT inlet, 250 psi	1 Stpi	10	.800	Ea.	370	58		428	490
0220	3/4" NPT inlet, 250 psi	"	10	.800	"	370	58		428	490
0600	Forged steel body, stainless steel internals, float type									
0640	1/2" NPT inlet, 750 psi	1 Stpi	12	.667	Ea.	1,225	48.50		1,273.50	1,425
0680	3/4" NPT inlet, 750 psi	"	12	.667	"	1,225	48.50		1,273.50	1,425
1100	Formed steel body, noncorrosive									
1110	1/8" NPT inlet, 150 psi	1 Stpi	32	.250	Ea.	19.35	18.15		37.50	48.50
1120	1/4" NPT inlet, 150 psi		32	.250		65	18.15		83.15	98.50
1130	3/4" NPT inlet, 150 psi		32	.250		65	18.15		83.15	98.50
1300	Chrome plated brass, automatic/manual, for radiators									
1310	1/8" NPT inlet, nickel plated brass	1 Stpi	32	.250	Ea.	11.30	18.15		29.45	39.50

23 21 20.26 Circuit Setter

		Crew	Daily Output	Labor-Hours	Unit	Material	Labor	Equipment	Total	Total Incl O&P
0010	**CIRCUIT SETTER**, Balance valve									
0018	Threaded									
0019	1/2" pipe size	1 Stpi	22	.364	Ea.	104	26.50		130.50	155
0020	3/4" pipe size	"	20	.400	"	111	29		140	167

23 21 20.30 Cocks, Drains and Specialties

		Crew	Daily Output	Labor-Hours	Unit	Material	Labor	Equipment	Total	Total Incl O&P
0010	**COCKS, DRAINS AND SPECIALTIES**									
1000	Boiler drain									
1010	Pipe thread to hose									
1020	Bronze									
1030	1/2" size	1 Stpi	36	.222	Ea.	23	16.10		39.10	49.50
1040	3/4" size	"	34	.235	"	28	17.05		45.05	56.50
1100	Solder to hose									
1110	Bronze									
1120	1/2" size	1 Stpi	46	.174	Ea.	23.50	12.60		36.10	45
1130	3/4" size	"	44	.182	"	25.50	13.20		38.70	47.50
1600	With built-in vacuum breaker									
1610	1/2" I.P. or solder	1 Stpi	36	.222	Ea.	34.50	16.10		50.60	62
1630	With tamper proof vacuum breaker									
1640	1/2" I.P. or solder	1 Stpi	36	.222	Ea.	76	16.10		92.10	108
1650	3/4" I.P. or solder	"	34	.235	"	73	17.05		90.05	106
3000	Cocks									
3010	Air, lever or tee handle									
3020	Bronze, single thread									
3030	1/8" size	1 Stpi	52	.154	Ea.	15.65	11.15		26.80	34
3040	1/4" size		46	.174		13.80	12.60		26.40	34
3050	3/8" size		40	.200		17.05	14.50		31.55	40.50
3060	1/2" size		36	.222		20	16.10		36.10	46
3100	Bronze, double thread									
3110	1/8" size	1 Stpi	26	.308	Ea.	20	22.50		42.50	55.50
3120	1/4" size		22	.364		17.45	26.50		43.95	58.50
3130	3/8" size		18	.444		22	32		54	72
3140	1/2" size		15	.533		26.50	38.50		65	87
4500	Gauge cock, brass									
4510	1/4" FPT	1 Stpi	24	.333	Ea.	13.80	24		37.80	51
4512	1/4" MPT	"	24	.333	"	17.70	24		41.70	55.50
4600	Pigtail, steam syphon									
4604	1/4"	1 Stpi	24	.333	Ea.	30	24		54	69
4650	Snubber valve									

23 21 Hydronic Piping and Pumps

23 21 20 – Hydronic HVAC Piping Specialties

23 21 20.30 Cocks, Drains and Specialties	Crew	Daily Output	Labor-Hours	Unit	Material	2023 Bare Costs Labor	Equipment	Total	Total Incl O&P
4654	1/4"	1 Stpi	22	.364	Ea.	5.75	26.50		32.25	46
4660	Nipple, black steel									
4664	1/4" x 3"	1 Stpi	37	.216	Ea.	6.10	15.70		21.80	30

23 21 20.34 Dielectric Unions

		Crew	Daily Output	Labor-Hours	Unit	Material	Labor	Equipment	Total	Total Incl O&P
0010	**DIELECTRIC UNIONS**, Standard gaskets for water and air									
0020	250 psi maximum pressure									
0280	Female IPT to sweat, straight									
0300	1/2" pipe size	1 Plum	24	.333	Ea.	9.95	24		33.95	47
0340	3/4" pipe size		20	.400		11.05	29		40.05	55
0360	1" pipe size		19	.421		14.90	30.50		45.40	61.50
0380	1-1/4" pipe size		15	.533		17.95	38.50		56.45	77
0400	1-1/2" pipe size		13	.615		34.50	44.50		79	104
0420	2" pipe size		11	.727		47	52.50		99.50	130
0580	Female IPT to brass pipe thread, straight									
0600	1/2" pipe size	1 Plum	24	.333	Ea.	21.50	24		45.50	59.50
0640	3/4" pipe size		20	.400		23.50	29		52.50	68.50
0660	1" pipe size		19	.421		43.50	30.50		74	92.50
0680	1-1/4" pipe size		15	.533		43	38.50		81.50	105
0700	1-1/2" pipe size		13	.615		62.50	44.50		107	135
0720	2" pipe size		11	.727		113	52.50		165.50	202
0780	Female IPT to female IPT, straight									
0800	1/2" pipe size	1 Plum	24	.333	Ea.	25	24		49	63.50
0840	3/4" pipe size		20	.400		29	29		58	75
0860	1" pipe size		19	.421		38	30.50		68.50	86.50
0880	1-1/4" pipe size		15	.533		51	38.50		89.50	114
0900	1-1/2" pipe size		13	.615		77	44.50		121.50	151
0920	2" pipe size		11	.727		115	52.50		167.50	205
2000	175 psi maximum pressure									
2180	Female IPT to sweat									
2240	2" pipe size	1 Plum	9	.889	Ea.	231	64		295	350
2260	2-1/2" pipe size	Q-1	15	1.067		279	69		348	410
2280	3" pipe size		14	1.143		385	74		459	535
2300	4" pipe size		11	1.455		1,000	94.50		1,094.50	1,275
2480	Female IPT to brass pipe									
2500	1-1/2" pipe size	1 Plum	11	.727	Ea.	310	52.50		362.50	420
2540	2" pipe size	"	9	.889		325	64		389	450
2560	2-1/2" pipe size	Q-1	15	1.067		360	69		429	500
2580	3" pipe size		14	1.143		360	74		434	505
2600	4" pipe size		11	1.455		510	94.50		604.50	705

23 21 20.42 Expansion Joints

		Crew	Daily Output	Labor-Hours	Unit	Material	Labor	Equipment	Total	Total Incl O&P
0010	**EXPANSION JOINTS**									
0100	Bellows type, neoprene cover, flanged spool									
0140	6" face to face, 1-1/4" diameter	1 Stpi	11	.727	Ea.	390	53		443	510
0160	1-1/2" diameter	"	10.60	.755		390	55		445	510
0180	2" diameter	Q-5	13.30	1.203		395	78.50		473.50	550
0190	2-1/2" diameter		12.40	1.290		410	84.50		494.50	575
0200	3" diameter		11.40	1.404		460	91.50		551.50	640
0210	4" diameter		8.40	1.905		495	124		619	730
0220	5" diameter		7.60	2.105		605	137		742	870
0230	6" diameter		6.80	2.353		625	154		779	915
0240	8" diameter		5.40	2.963		725	193		918	1,075
0250	10" diameter		5	3.200		1,000	209		1,209	1,400

23 21 Hydronic Piping and Pumps

23 21 20 – Hydronic HVAC Piping Specialties

23 21 20.42 Expansion Joints

		Crew	Daily Output	Labor-Hours	Unit	Material	2023 Bare Costs Labor	Equipment	Total	Total Incl O&P
0260	12" diameter	Q-5	4.60	3.478	Ea.	1,150	227		1,377	1,600
0480	10" face to face, 2" diameter		13	1.231		570	80.50		650.50	745
0500	2-1/2" diameter		12	1.333		600	87		687	790
0520	3" diameter		11	1.455		610	95		705	810
0540	4" diameter		8	2		695	131		826	960
0560	5" diameter		7	2.286		830	149		979	1,125
0580	6" diameter		6	2.667		855	174		1,029	1,200
0600	8" diameter		5	3.200		1,025	209		1,234	1,425
0620	10" diameter		4.60	3.478		1,125	227		1,352	1,600
0640	12" diameter		4	4		1,400	261		1,661	1,950
0660	14" diameter		3.80	4.211		1,725	275		2,000	2,300
0680	16" diameter		2.90	5.517		2,000	360		2,360	2,725
0700	18" diameter		2.50	6.400		2,250	420		2,670	3,100
0720	20" diameter		2.10	7.619		2,350	500		2,850	3,350
0740	24" diameter		1.80	8.889		2,775	580		3,355	3,925
0760	26" diameter		1.40	11.429		3,075	745		3,820	4,525
0780	30" diameter		1.20	13.333		3,450	870		4,320	5,100
0800	36" diameter	↓	1	16	↓	3,950	1,050		5,000	5,900

23 21 20.46 Expansion Tanks

		Crew	Daily Output	Labor-Hours	Unit	Material	2023 Bare Costs Labor	Equipment	Total	Total Incl O&P
0010	**EXPANSION TANKS**									
1502	Plastic, corrosion resistant, see Section 22 66 83.13									
1505	Aboveground fuel-oil, storage tanks, see Section 23 13 23									
1507	Underground fuel-oil storage tanks, see Section 23 13 13									
1512	Tank leak detection systems, see Section 28 33 33.50									
2000	Steel, liquid expansion, ASME, painted, 15 gallon capacity	Q-5	17	.941	Ea.	935	61.50		996.50	1,125
2020	24 gallon capacity		14	1.143		780	74.50		854.50	965
2040	30 gallon capacity		12	1.333		1,125	87		1,212	1,350
2060	40 gallon capacity	↓	10	1.600	↓	1,300	104		1,404	1,575
2360	Galvanized									
2370	15 gallon capacity	Q-5	17	.941	Ea.	1,500	61.50		1,561.50	1,750
2380	24 gallon capacity		14	1.143		1,625	74.50		1,699.50	1,900
2390	30 gallon capacity		12	1.333		1,675	87		1,762	1,975
3000	Steel ASME expansion, rubber diaphragm, 19 gal. cap. accept.		12	1.333		3,550	87		3,637	4,025
3020	31 gallon capacity		8	2		3,950	131		4,081	4,550
3040	61 gallon capacity	↓	6	2.667	↓	5,925	174		6,099	6,775

23 21 20.50 Float Valves

		Crew	Daily Output	Labor-Hours	Unit	Material	2023 Bare Costs Labor	Equipment	Total	Total Incl O&P
0010	**FLOAT VALVES**									
0020	With ball and bracket									
0030	Single seat, threaded									
0040	Brass body									
0050	1/2"	1 Stpi	11	.727	Ea.	101	53		154	190
0060	3/4"		9	.889		114	64.50		178.50	222
0070	1"		7	1.143		203	83		286	345
0080	1-1/2"		4.50	1.778		278	129		407	495
0090	2"	↓	3.60	2.222	↓	297	161		458	565
0300	For condensate receivers, CI, in-line mount									
0320	1" inlet	1 Stpi	7	1.143	Ea.	185	83		268	325
0360	For condensate receiver, CI, external float, flanged tank mount									
0370	3/4" inlet	1 Stpi	5	1.600	Ea.	114	116		230	299

23 21 Hydronic Piping and Pumps

23 21 20 – Hydronic HVAC Piping Specialties

23 21 20.54 Flow Check Control

		Crew	Daily Output	Labor-Hours	Unit	Material	2023 Bare Costs Labor	Equipment	Total	Total Incl O&P
0010	**FLOW CHECK CONTROL**									
0100	Bronze body, soldered									
0110	3/4" size	1 Stpi	20	.400	Ea.	90	29		119	143
0120	1" size	"	19	.421	"	109	30.50		139.50	165
0200	Cast iron body, threaded									
0210	3/4" size	1 Stpi	20	.400	Ea.	47	29		76	95
0220	1" size		19	.421		48	30.50		78.50	98.50
0230	1-1/4" size		15	.533		74	38.50		112.50	139
0240	1-1/2" size		13	.615		144	44.50		188.50	225
0250	2" size		11	.727		206	53		259	305

23 21 20.58 Hydronic Heating Control Valves

		Crew	Daily Output	Labor-Hours	Unit	Material	Labor	Equipment	Total	Total Incl O&P
0010	**HYDRONIC HEATING CONTROL VALVES**									
0050	Hot water, nonelectric, thermostatic									
0100	Radiator supply, 1/2" diameter	1 Stpi	24	.333	Ea.	42	24		66	82
0120	3/4" diameter	"	20	.400	"	48	29		77	96
1000	Manual, radiator supply									
1010	1/2" pipe size, angle union	1 Stpi	24	.333	Ea.	106	24		130	153
1020	3/4" pipe size, angle union	"	20	.400	"	133	29		162	191
1100	Radiator, balancing, straight, sweat connections									
1110	1/2" pipe size	1 Stpi	24	.333	Ea.	35	24		59	74.50
1120	3/4" pipe size	"	20	.400	"	48.50	29		77.50	97
1200	Steam, radiator, supply									
1210	1/2" pipe size, angle union	1 Stpi	24	.333	Ea.	108	24		132	154
1220	3/4" pipe size, angle union	"	20	.400	"	117	29		146	172
8000	System balancing and shut-off									
8020	Butterfly, quarter turn, calibrated, threaded or solder									
8040	Bronze, -30°F to +350°F, pressure to 175 psi									
8060	1/2" size	1 Stpi	22	.364	Ea.	37.50	26.50		64	80.50
8070	3/4" size	"	20	.400	"	60.50	29		89.50	110

23 21 20.66 Monoflow Tee Fitting

		Crew	Daily Output	Labor-Hours	Unit	Material	Labor	Equipment	Total	Total Incl O&P
0010	**MONOFLOW TEE FITTING**									
1100	For one pipe hydronic, supply and return									
1110	Copper, soldered									
1120	3/4" x 1/2" size	1 Stpi	13	.615	Ea.	27	44.50		71.50	96

23 21 20.74 Strainers, Basket Type

		Crew	Daily Output	Labor-Hours	Unit	Material	Labor	Equipment	Total	Total Incl O&P
0010	**STRAINERS, BASKET TYPE**, Perforated stainless steel basket									
0100	Brass or monel available									
2000	Simplex style									
2300	Bronze body									
2320	Screwed, 3/8" pipe size	1 Stpi	22	.364	Ea.	246	26.50		272.50	310
2340	1/2" pipe size		20	.400		275	29		304	345
2360	3/4" pipe size		17	.471		315	34		349	400
2380	1" pipe size		15	.533		350	38.50		388.50	445
2400	1-1/4" pipe size		13	.615		530	44.50		574.50	645
2420	1-1/2" pipe size		12	.667		495	48.50		543.50	615
2440	2" pipe size		10	.800		605	58		663	750
2460	2-1/2" pipe size	Q-5	15	1.067		1,350	69.50		1,419.50	1,575
2480	3" pipe size	"	14	1.143		2,000	74.50		2,074.50	2,300
2600	Flanged, 2" pipe size	1 Stpi	6	1.333		1,175	96.50		1,271.50	1,450
2620	2-1/2" pipe size	Q-5	4.50	3.556		2,050	232		2,282	2,600
2640	3" pipe size		3.50	4.571		2,300	299		2,599	2,975

23 21 Hydronic Piping and Pumps

23 21 20 – Hydronic HVAC Piping Specialties

23 21 20.74 Strainers, Basket Type

		Crew	Daily Output	Labor-Hours	Unit	Material	2023 Bare Costs Labor	Equipment	Total	Total Incl O&P
2660	4" pipe size	Q-5	3	5.333	Ea.	3,525	350		3,875	4,400
2680	5" pipe size	Q-6	3.40	7.059		5,625	480		6,105	6,925
2700	6" pipe size		3	8		6,875	540		7,415	8,350
2710	8" pipe size	↓	2.50	9.600	↓	11,200	650		11,850	13,300
3600	Iron body									
3700	Screwed, 3/8" pipe size	1 Stpi	22	.364	Ea.	214	26.50		240.50	275
3720	1/2" pipe size		20	.400		238	29		267	305
3740	3/4" pipe size		17	.471		300	34		334	380
3760	1" pipe size		15	.533		310	38.50		348.50	400
3780	1-1/4" pipe size		13	.615		405	44.50		449.50	510
3800	1-1/2" pipe size		12	.667		445	48.50		493.50	560
3820	2" pipe size	↓	10	.800		530	58		588	670
3840	2-1/2" pipe size	Q-5	15	1.067		710	69.50		779.50	885
3860	3" pipe size	"	14	1.143		860	74.50		934.50	1,050
4000	Flanged, 2" pipe size	1 Stpi	6	1.333		820	96.50		916.50	1,050
4020	2-1/2" pipe size	Q-5	4.50	3.556		1,100	232		1,332	1,575
4040	3" pipe size		3.50	4.571		1,150	299		1,449	1,725
4060	4" pipe size	↓	3	5.333		1,775	350		2,125	2,475
4080	5" pipe size	Q-6	3.40	7.059		2,675	480		3,155	3,675
4100	6" pipe size		3	8		3,425	540		3,965	4,575
4120	8" pipe size		2.50	9.600		6,200	650		6,850	7,800
4140	10" pipe size	↓	2.20	10.909	↓	13,600	740		14,340	16,100
7000	Stainless steel body									
7200	Screwed, 1" pipe size	1 Stpi	15	.533	Ea.	660	38.50		698.50	785
7210	1-1/4" pipe size		13	.615		1,025	44.50		1,069.50	1,200
7220	1-1/2" pipe size		12	.667		1,025	48.50		1,073.50	1,200
7240	2" pipe size	↓	10	.800		1,525	58		1,583	1,750
7260	2-1/2" pipe size	Q-5	15	1.067		2,150	69.50		2,219.50	2,475
7280	3" pipe size	"	14	1.143		2,975	74.50		3,049.50	3,375
7400	Flanged, 2" pipe size	1 Stpi	6	1.333		4,825	96.50		4,921.50	5,475
7420	2-1/2" pipe size	Q-5	4.50	3.556		4,725	232		4,957	5,550
7440	3" pipe size		3.50	4.571		4,825	299		5,124	5,775
7460	4" pipe size	↓	3	5.333		7,600	350		7,950	8,875
7480	6" pipe size	Q-6	3	8		15,200	540		15,740	17,500
7500	8" pipe size	"	2.50	9.600	↓	22,100	650		22,750	25,300
8100	Duplex style									
8200	Bronze body									
8240	Screwed, 3/4" pipe size	1 Stpi	16	.500	Ea.	1,825	36.50		1,861.50	2,050
8260	1" pipe size		14	.571		1,825	41.50		1,866.50	2,050
8280	1-1/4" pipe size		12	.667		3,075	48.50		3,123.50	3,475
8300	1-1/2" pipe size		11	.727		3,075	53		3,128	3,475
8320	2" pipe size	↓	9	.889		5,800	64.50		5,864.50	6,475
8340	2-1/2" pipe size	Q-5	14	1.143		7,475	74.50		7,549.50	8,325
8420	Flanged, 2" pipe size	1 Stpi	6	1.333		7,125	96.50		7,221.50	8,000
8440	2-1/2" pipe size	Q-5	4.50	3.556		9,850	232		10,082	11,100
8460	3" pipe size		3.50	4.571		10,700	299		10,999	12,200
8480	4" pipe size	↓	3	5.333		14,600	350		14,950	16,500
8500	5" pipe size	Q-6	3.40	7.059		35,300	480		35,780	39,500
8520	6" pipe size	"	3	8	↓	34,300	540		34,840	38,500
8700	Iron body									
8740	Screwed, 3/4" pipe size	1 Stpi	16	.500	Ea.	2,425	36.50		2,461.50	2,725
8760	1" pipe size		14	.571		2,425	41.50		2,466.50	2,725
8780	1-1/4" pipe size	↓	12	.667		2,700	48.50		2,748.50	3,050

23 21 Hydronic Piping and Pumps

23 21 20 – Hydronic HVAC Piping Specialties

23 21 20.74 Strainers, Basket Type

		Crew	Daily Output	Labor-Hours	Unit	Material	2023 Bare Costs Labor	Equipment	Total	Total Incl O&P
8800	1-1/2" pipe size	1 Stpi	11	.727	Ea.	2,700	53		2,753	3,050
8820	2" pipe size	↓	9	.889		4,575	64.50		4,639.50	5,125
8840	2-1/2" pipe size	Q-5	14	1.143		5,050	74.50		5,124.50	5,650
9000	Flanged, 2" pipe size	1 Stpi	6	1.333		4,875	96.50		4,971.50	5,525
9020	2-1/2" pipe size	Q-5	4.50	3.556		5,225	232		5,457	6,100
9040	3" pipe size		3.50	4.571		5,675	299		5,974	6,700
9060	4" pipe size	↓	3	5.333		9,600	350		9,950	11,100
9080	5" pipe size	Q-6	3.40	7.059		20,900	480		21,380	23,700
9100	6" pipe size		3	8		20,900	540		21,440	23,800
9120	8" pipe size		2.50	9.600		41,500	650		42,150	46,600
9140	10" pipe size		2.20	10.909		59,000	740		59,740	66,000
9160	12" pipe size		1.70	14.118		65,500	955		66,455	73,500
9170	14" pipe size		1.40	17.143		77,000	1,150		78,150	86,000
9180	16" pipe size	↓	1	24	↓	94,500	1,625		96,125	106,500
9700	Stainless steel body									
9740	Screwed, 1" pipe size	1 Stpi	14	.571	Ea.	4,425	41.50		4,466.50	4,925
9760	1-1/2" pipe size		11	.727		6,650	53		6,703	7,375
9780	2" pipe size	↓	9	.889		9,375	64.50		9,439.50	10,400
9860	Flanged, 2" pipe size	↓	6	1.333		10,100	96.50		10,196.50	11,200
9880	2-1/2" pipe size	Q-5	4.50	3.556		16,900	232		17,132	18,900
9900	3" pipe size		3.50	4.571		18,500	299		18,799	20,700
9920	4" pipe size	↓	3	5.333		24,000	350		24,350	26,900
9940	6" pipe size	Q-6	3	8		36,700	540		37,240	41,200
9960	8" pipe size	"	2.50	9.600	↓	91,500	650		92,150	102,000

23 21 20.76 Strainers, Y Type, Bronze Body

		Crew	Daily Output	Labor-Hours	Unit	Material	2023 Bare Costs Labor	Equipment	Total	Total Incl O&P
0010	**STRAINERS, Y TYPE, BRONZE BODY**									
0050	Screwed, 125 lb., 1/4" pipe size	1 Stpi	24	.333	Ea.	63	24		87	105
0070	3/8" pipe size		24	.333		63	24		87	105
0100	1/2" pipe size		20	.400		52	29		81	101
0120	3/4" pipe size		19	.421		77.50	30.50		108	131
0140	1" pipe size		17	.471		115	34		149	177
0150	1-1/4" pipe size		15	.533		182	38.50		220.50	258
0160	1-1/2" pipe size		14	.571		246	41.50		287.50	330
0180	2" pipe size		13	.615		320	44.50		364.50	420
0182	3" pipe size	↓	12	.667		2,150	48.50		2,198.50	2,450
0200	300 lb., 2-1/2" pipe size	Q-5	17	.941		1,225	61.50		1,286.50	1,450
0220	3" pipe size		16	1		1,525	65.50		1,590.50	1,775
0240	4" pipe size	↓	15	1.067	↓	2,800	69.50		2,869.50	3,175
0500	For 300 lb. rating 1/4" thru 2", add					15%				
1000	Flanged, 150 lb., 1-1/2" pipe size	1 Stpi	11	.727	Ea.	650	53		703	795
1020	2" pipe size	"	8	1		795	72.50		867.50	985
1030	2-1/2" pipe size	Q-5	5	3.200		1,325	209		1,534	1,775
1040	3" pipe size		4.50	3.556		1,650	232		1,882	2,150
1060	4" pipe size	↓	3	5.333		2,525	350		2,875	3,300
1080	5" pipe size	Q-6	3.40	7.059		3,625	480		4,105	4,700
1100	6" pipe size		3	8		4,850	540		5,390	6,150
1106	8" pipe size	↓	2.60	9.231	↓	5,275	625		5,900	6,725
1500	For 300 lb. rating, add					40%				

23 21 20.78 Strainers, Y Type, Iron Body

		Crew	Daily Output	Labor-Hours	Unit	Material	2023 Bare Costs Labor	Equipment	Total	Total Incl O&P
0010	**STRAINERS, Y TYPE, IRON BODY**									
0050	Screwed, 250 lb., 1/4" pipe size	1 Stpi	20	.400	Ea.	26.50	29		55.50	72.50
0070	3/8" pipe size	↓	20	.400		26.50	29		55.50	72.50

23 21 Hydronic Piping and Pumps

23 21 20 – Hydronic HVAC Piping Specialties

23 21 20.78 Strainers, Y Type, Iron Body

		Crew	Daily Output	Labor-Hours	Unit	Material	2023 Bare Costs Labor	Equipment	Total	Total Incl O&P
0100	1/2" pipe size	1 Stpi	20	.400	Ea.	26.50	29		55.50	72.50
0120	3/4" pipe size		18	.444		30.50	32		62.50	82
0140	1" pipe size		16	.500		40	36.50		76.50	98
0150	1-1/4" pipe size		15	.533		56.50	38.50		95	120
0160	1-1/2" pipe size		12	.667		76.50	48.50		125	157
0180	2" pipe size	▼	8	1		115	72.50		187.50	234
0200	2-1/2" pipe size	Q-5	12	1.333		475	87		562	650
0220	3" pipe size		11	1.455		510	95		605	700
0240	4" pipe size	▼	5	3.200	▼	865	209		1,074	1,275
0500	For galvanized body, add					50%				
1000	Flanged, 125 lb., 1-1/2" pipe size	1 Stpi	11	.727	Ea.	360	53		413	475
1020	2" pipe size	"	8	1		253	72.50		325.50	385
1030	2-1/2" pipe size	Q-5	5	3.200		228	209		437	560
1040	3" pipe size		4.50	3.556		335	232		567	710
1060	4" pipe size	▼	3	5.333		550	350		900	1,125
1080	5" pipe size	Q-6	3.40	7.059		660	480		1,140	1,450
1100	6" pipe size		3	8		1,100	540		1,640	2,025
1120	8" pipe size		2.50	9.600		1,850	650		2,500	3,025
1140	10" pipe size		2	12		3,375	815		4,190	4,925
1160	12" pipe size		1.70	14.118		5,075	955		6,030	7,000
1170	14" pipe size		1.30	18.462		9,350	1,250		10,600	12,200
1180	16" pipe size	▼	1	24	▼	13,300	1,625		14,925	17,000
1500	For 250 lb. rating, add					20%				
2000	For galvanized body, add					50%				
2500	For steel body, add					40%				

23 21 20.80 Suction Diffusers

		Crew	Daily Output	Labor-Hours	Unit	Material	Labor	Equipment	Total	Total Incl O&P
0010	**SUCTION DIFFUSERS**									
0100	Cast iron body with integral straightening vanes, strainer									
1000	Flanged									
1010	2" inlet, 1-1/2" pump side	1 Stpi	6	1.333	Ea.	350	96.50		446.50	530
1020	2" pump side	"	5	1.600		475	116		591	700
1030	3" inlet, 2" pump side	Q-5	6.50	2.462	▼	440	161		601	725

23 21 20.84 Thermoflo Indicator

		Crew	Daily Output	Labor-Hours	Unit	Material	Labor	Equipment	Total	Total Incl O&P
0010	**THERMOFLO INDICATOR**, For balancing									
1000	Sweat connections, 1-1/4" pipe size	1 Stpi	12	.667	Ea.	955	48.50		1,003.50	1,125
1020	1-1/2" pipe size	"	10	.800	"	970	58		1,028	1,150

23 21 20.88 Venturi Flow

		Crew	Daily Output	Labor-Hours	Unit	Material	Labor	Equipment	Total	Total Incl O&P
0010	**VENTURI FLOW**, Measuring device									
0050	1/2" diameter	1 Stpi	24	.333	Ea.	335	24		359	405
0100	3/4" diameter		20	.400		305	29		334	385
0120	1" diameter		19	.421		330	30.50		360.50	405
0140	1-1/4" diameter		15	.533		410	38.50		448.50	510
0160	1-1/2" diameter		13	.615		410	44.50		454.50	515
0180	2" diameter	▼	11	.727		440	53		493	560
0200	2-1/2" diameter	Q-5	16	1		600	65.50		665.50	760
0220	3" diameter		14	1.143		620	74.50		694.50	790
0240	4" diameter		11	1.455		925	95		1,020	1,175
0260	5" diameter	Q-6	4	6		1,225	405		1,630	1,925
0280	6" diameter		3.50	6.857		1,350	465		1,815	2,175
0300	8" diameter		3	8		1,725	540		2,265	2,700
0320	10" diameter		2	12		4,100	815		4,915	5,700
0330	12" diameter		1.80	13.333		5,800	905		6,705	7,725

23 21 Hydronic Piping and Pumps

23 21 20 – Hydronic HVAC Piping Specialties

23 21 20.88 Venturi Flow		Crew	Daily Output	Labor-Hours	Unit	Material	2023 Bare Costs Labor	Equipment	Total	Total Incl O&P
0340	14" diameter	Q-6	1.60	15	Ea.	6,575	1,025		7,600	8,775
0350	16" diameter	↓	1.40	17.143		7,550	1,150		8,700	10,000
0500	For meter, add				↓	2,800			2,800	3,075

23 21 23 – Hydronic Pumps

23 21 23.13 In-Line Centrifugal Hydronic Pumps

		Crew	Daily Output	Labor-Hours	Unit	Material	Labor	Equipment	Total	Total Incl O&P
0010	**IN-LINE CENTRIFUGAL HYDRONIC PUMPS**									
0600	Bronze, sweat connections, 1/40 HP, in line									
0640	3/4" size	Q-1	16	1	Ea.	335	65		400	465
1000	Flange connection, 3/4" to 1-1/2" size									
1040	1/12 HP	Q-1	6	2.667	Ea.	770	173		943	1,100
1060	1/8 HP		6	2.667		1,550	173		1,723	1,975
1100	1/3 HP		6	2.667		1,750	173		1,923	2,175
1140	2" size, 1/6 HP		5	3.200		2,250	208		2,458	2,775
1180	2-1/2" size, 1/4 HP		5	3.200		2,425	208		2,633	2,950
1220	3" size, 1/4 HP		4	4		2,675	259		2,934	3,325
1260	1/3 HP		4	4		3,100	259		3,359	3,775
1300	1/2 HP		4	4		3,175	259		3,434	3,850
1340	3/4 HP		4	4		2,925	259		3,184	3,600
1380	1 HP	↓	4	4		4,575	259		4,834	5,400
2000	Cast iron, flange connection									
2040	3/4" to 1-1/2" size, in line, 1/12 HP	Q-1	6	2.667	Ea.	615	173		788	940
2060	1/8 HP		6	2.667		980	173		1,153	1,325
2100	1/3 HP		6	2.667		1,100	173		1,273	1,450
2140	2" size, 1/6 HP		5	3.200		1,200	208		1,408	1,625
2180	2-1/2" size, 1/4 HP		5	3.200		1,150	208		1,358	1,550
2220	3" size, 1/4 HP		4	4		1,125	259		1,384	1,600
2260	1/3 HP		4	4		1,425	259		1,684	1,950
2300	1/2 HP		4	4		1,475	259		1,734	2,000
2340	3/4 HP		4	4		1,725	259		1,984	2,250
2380	1 HP	↓	4	4		2,475	259		2,734	3,100
2600	For nonferrous impeller, add					3%				
3000	High head, bronze impeller									
3030	1-1/2" size, 1/2 HP	Q-1	5	3.200	Ea.	1,300	208		1,508	1,725
3040	1-1/2" size, 3/4 HP		5	3.200		1,800	208		2,008	2,275
3050	2" size, 1 HP		4	4		2,175	259		2,434	2,775
3090	2" size, 1-1/2 HP	↓	4	4		2,550	259		2,809	3,175
4000	Close coupled, end suction, bronze impeller									
4040	1-1/2" size, 1-1/2 HP, to 40 GPM	Q-1	3	5.333	Ea.	3,100	345		3,445	3,925
4090	2" size, 2 HP, to 50 GPM		3	5.333		3,400	345		3,745	4,250
4100	2" size, 3 HP, to 90 GPM		2.30	6.957		3,000	450		3,450	3,975
4190	2-1/2" size, 3 HP, to 150 GPM		2	8		4,375	520		4,895	5,575
4300	3" size, 5 HP, to 225 GPM		1.80	8.889		4,575	575		5,150	5,900
4410	3" size, 10 HP, to 350 GPM		1.60	10		7,925	650		8,575	9,700
4420	4" size, 7-1/2 HP, to 350 GPM	↓	1.60	10		5,475	650		6,125	7,000
4520	4" size, 10 HP, to 600 GPM	Q-2	1.70	14.118		8,450	950		9,400	10,700
4530	5" size, 15 HP, to 1,000 GPM		1.70	14.118		5,975	950		6,925	7,975
4610	5" size, 20 HP, to 1,350 GPM		1.50	16		6,750	1,075		7,825	9,025
4620	5" size, 25 HP, to 1,550 GPM	↓	1.50	16	↓	10,800	1,075		11,875	13,500
5000	Base mounted, bronze impeller, coupling guard									
5040	1-1/2" size, 1-1/2 HP, to 40 GPM	Q-1	2.30	6.957	Ea.	8,650	450		9,100	10,200
5090	2" size, 2 HP, to 50 GPM		2.30	6.957		9,700	450		10,150	11,400
5100	2" size, 3 HP, to 90 GPM	↓	2	8		9,600	520		10,120	11,400

23 21 Hydronic Piping and Pumps

23 21 23 – Hydronic Pumps

23 21 23.13 In-Line Centrifugal Hydronic Pumps

		Crew	Daily Output	Labor-Hours	Unit	Material	2023 Bare Costs Labor	Equipment	Total	Total Incl O&P
5190	2-1/2" size, 3 HP, to 150 GPM	Q-1	1.80	8.889	Ea.	11,400	575		11,975	13,400
5300	3" size, 5 HP, to 225 GPM		1.60	10		14,000	650		14,650	16,400
5410	4" size, 5 HP, to 350 GPM		1.50	10.667		14,300	690		14,990	16,700
5420	4" size, 7-1/2 HP, to 350 GPM	↓	1.50	10.667		13,500	690		14,190	15,900
5520	5" size, 10 HP, to 600 GPM	Q-2	1.60	15		17,100	1,000		18,100	20,300
5530	5" size, 15 HP, to 1,000 GPM		1.60	15		18,300	1,000		19,300	21,700
5610	6" size, 20 HP, to 1,350 GPM		1.40	17.143		29,100	1,150		30,250	33,700
5620	6" size, 25 HP, to 1,550 GPM	↓	1.40	17.143	↓	23,400	1,150		24,550	27,500
5800	The above pump capacities are based on 1,800 RPM,									
5810	at a 60' head. Increasing the RPM									
5820	or decreasing the head will increase the GPM.									

23 21 29 – Automatic Condensate Pump Units

23 21 29.10 Condensate Removal Pump System

			Crew	Daily Output	Labor-Hours	Unit	Material	Labor	Equipment	Total	Total Incl O&P
0010	**CONDENSATE REMOVAL PUMP SYSTEM**										
0020	Pump with 1 gal. ABS tank										
0100	115 V										
0120	1/50 HP, 200 GPH	G	1 Stpi	12	.667	Ea.	233	48.50		281.50	330
0140	1/18 HP, 270 GPH	G		10	.800		232	58		290	345
0160	1/5 HP, 450 GPH	G	↓	8	1	↓	243	72.50		315.50	375
0200	230 V										
0240	1/18 HP, 270 GPH		1 Stpi	10	.800	Ea.	258	58		316	370
0260	1/5 HP, 450 GPH	G	"	8	1	"	625	72.50		697.50	795

23 23 Refrigerant Piping

23 23 23 – Refrigerants

23 23 23.10 Anti-Freeze

		Crew	Daily Output	Labor-Hours	Unit	Material	Labor	Equipment	Total	Total Incl O&P
0010	**ANTI-FREEZE**, Inhibited									
0900	Ethylene glycol concentrated									
1000	55 gallon drums, small quantities				Gal.	15.20			15.20	16.70
1200	Large quantities					11.85			11.85	13
2000	Propylene glycol, for solar heat, small quantities					25.50			25.50	28
2100	Large quantities				↓	13.20			13.20	14.50

23 34 HVAC Fans

23 34 14 – Blower HVAC Fans

23 34 14.10 Blower Type HVAC Fans

		Crew	Daily Output	Labor-Hours	Unit	Material	Labor	Equipment	Total	Total Incl O&P
0010	**BLOWER TYPE HVAC FANS**									
2500	Ceiling fan, right angle, extra quiet, 0.10" S.P.									
2520	95 CFM	Q-20	20	1	Ea.	300	64		364	425
2540	210 CFM		19	1.053		355	67.50		422.50	490
2560	385 CFM	↓	18	1.111		455	71		526	605
2640	For wall or roof cap, add	1 Shee	16	.500		300	35		335	385
2660	For straight thru fan, add					10%				
2680	For speed control switch, add	1 Elec	16	.500	↓	165	33.50		198.50	231

23 34 HVAC Fans

23 34 23 – HVAC Power Ventilators

23 34 23.10 HVAC Power Circulators and Ventilators	Crew	Daily Output	Labor-Hours	Unit	Material	2023 Bare Costs Labor	Equipment	Total	Total Incl O&P
0010 **HVAC POWER CIRCULATORS AND VENTILATORS**									
6650 Residential, bath exhaust, grille, back draft damper									
6660 50 CFM	Q-20	24	.833	Ea.	50	53.50		103.50	135
6670 110 CFM		22	.909		111	58		169	210
6680 Light combination, squirrel cage, 100 watt, 70 CFM	↓	24	.833	↓	153	53.50		206.50	248
6700 Light/heater combination, ceiling mounted									
6710 70 CFM, 1,450 watt	Q-20	24	.833	Ea.	189	53.50		242.50	288
6800 Heater combination, recessed, 70 CFM		24	.833		85.50	53.50		139	174
6820 With 2 infrared bulbs	↓	23	.870	↓	101	55.50		156.50	195
6940 Residential roof jacks and wall caps									
6944 Wall cap with back draft damper									
6946 3" & 4" diam. round duct	1 Shee	11	.727	Ea.	25	51		76	105
6948 6" diam. round duct	"	11	.727	"	60	51		111	143
6958 Roof jack with bird screen and back draft damper									
6960 3" & 4" diam. round duct	1 Shee	11	.727	Ea.	31	51		82	112
6962 3-1/4" x 10" rectangular duct	"	10	.800	"	39.50	56		95.50	128
6980 Transition									
6982 3-1/4" x 10" to 6" diam. round	1 Shee	20	.400	Ea.	26.50	28		54.50	72

23 35 Special Exhaust Systems

23 35 16 – Engine Exhaust Systems

23 35 16.10 Engine Exhaust Removal Systems

	Crew	Daily Output	Labor-Hours	Unit	Material	Labor	Equipment	Total	Total Incl O&P
0010 **ENGINE EXHAUST REMOVAL SYSTEMS** D3090-320									
0500 Engine exhaust, garage, in-floor system									
0510 Single tube outlet assemblies									
0520 For transite pipe ducting, self-storing tube									
0530 3" tubing adapter plate	1 Shee	16	.500	Ea.	310	35		345	395
0540 4" tubing adapter plate		16	.500		315	35		350	400
0550 5" tubing adapter plate	↓	16	.500	↓	310	35		345	400
0600 For vitrified tile ducting									
0610 3" tubing adapter plate, self-storing tube	1 Shee	16	.500	Ea.	305	35		340	395
0620 4" tubing adapter plate, self-storing tube		16	.500		315	35		350	400
0660 5" tubing adapter plate, self-storing tube	↓	16	.500		315	35		350	400
0800 Two tube outlet assemblies									
0810 For transite pipe ducting, self-storing tube									
0820 3" tubing, dual exhaust adapter plate	1 Shee	16	.500	Ea.	315	35		350	405
0850 For vitrified tile ducting									
0860 3" tubing, dual exhaust, self-storing tube	1 Shee	16	.500	Ea.	345	35		380	435
0870 3" tubing, double outlet, non-storing tubes	"	16	.500	"	345	35		380	435
0900 Accessories for metal tubing (overhead systems also)									
0910 Adapters, for metal tubing end									
0920 3" tail pipe type				Ea.	60			60	66
0930 4" tail pipe type					66.50			66.50	73
0940 5" tail pipe type					67.50			67.50	74.50
0990 5" diesel stack type					355			355	390
1000 6" diesel stack type				↓	420			420	465
1100 Bullnose (guide) required for in-floor assemblies									
1110 3" tubing size				Ea.	36			36	39.50
1120 4" tubing size					37			37	41
1130 5" tubing size					39.50			39.50	43.50

23 35 Special Exhaust Systems

23 35 16 – Engine Exhaust Systems

23 35 16.10 Engine Exhaust Removal Systems		Crew	Daily Output	Labor-Hours	Unit	Material	2023 Bare Costs Labor	Equipment	Total	Total Incl O&P
1150	Plain rings, for tubing end									
1160	3" tubing size				Ea.	25.50			25.50	28
1170	4" tubing size				"	42.50			42.50	47
1200	Tubing, galvanized, flexible (for overhead systems also)									
1210	3" ID				L.F.	12.15			12.15	13.35
1220	4" ID					14.85			14.85	16.35
1230	5" ID					17.50			17.50	19.25
1240	6" ID					20.50			20.50	22.50
1250	Stainless steel, flexible (for overhead system also)									
1260	3" ID				L.F.	24.50			24.50	27
1270	4" ID					33.50			33.50	37
1280	5" ID					38			38	42
1290	6" ID					44.50			44.50	48.50
1500	Engine exhaust, garage, overhead components, for neoprene tubing									
1510	Alternate metal tubing & accessories see above									
1550	Adapters, for neoprene tubing end									
1560	3" tail pipe, adjustable, neoprene				Ea.	71			71	78
1570	3" tail pipe, heavy wall neoprene					80			80	88
1580	4" tail pipe, heavy wall neoprene					118			118	130
1590	5" tail pipe, heavy wall neoprene					140			140	154
1650	Connectors, tubing									
1660	3" interior, aluminum				Ea.	25.50			25.50	28.50
1670	4" interior, aluminum					42.50			42.50	47
1710	5" interior, neoprene					67			67	73.50
1750	3" spiralock, neoprene					25.50			25.50	28
1760	4" spiralock, neoprene					42.50			42.50	47
1780	Y for 3" ID tubing, neoprene, dual exhaust					240			240	264
1790	Y for 4" ID tubing, aluminum, dual exhaust					190			190	208
1850	Elbows, aluminum, splice into tubing for strap									
1860	3" neoprene tubing size				Ea.	64.50			64.50	71
1870	4" neoprene tubing size					45.50			45.50	50
1900	Flange assemblies, connect tubing to overhead duct						81			81	89
2000	Hardware and accessories									
2020	Cable, galvanized, 1/8" diameter				L.F.	.60			.60	.66
2040	Cleat, tie down cable or rope				Ea.	6.20			6.20	6.80
2060	Pulley					8.55			8.55	9.40
2080	Pulley hook, universal					6.20			6.20	6.80
2100	Rope, nylon, 1/4" diameter				L.F.	.43			.43	.47
2120	Winch, 1" diameter				Ea.	125			125	138
2150	Lifting strap, mounts on neoprene									
2160	3" tubing size				Ea.	31			31	34
2170	4" tubing size					31			31	34
2180	5" tubing size					31			31	34
2190	6" tubing size					31			31	34
2200	Tubing, neoprene, 11' lengths									
2210	3" ID				L.F.	14.55			14.55	16
2220	4" ID					19			19	21
2230	5" ID					34.50			34.50	38
2500	Engine exhaust, thru-door outlet									
2510	3" tube size	1 Carp	16	.500	Ea.	75.50	29.50		105	127
2530	4" tube size	"	16	.500	"	66	29.50		95.50	116
3000	Tubing, exhaust, flex hose, with									
3010	coupler, damper and tail pipe adapter									

23 35 Special Exhaust Systems

23 35 16 – Engine Exhaust Systems

23 35 16.10 Engine Exhaust Removal Systems

		Crew	Daily Output	Labor-Hours	Unit	Material	2023 Bare Costs Labor	2023 Bare Costs Equipment	Total	Total Incl O&P
3020	Neoprene									
3040	3" x 20'	1 Shee	6	1.333	Ea.	430	93.50		523.50	610
3050	4" x 15'		5.40	1.481		480	104		584	680
3060	4" x 20'		5	1.600		575	112		687	800
3070	5" x 15'	↓	4.40	1.818	↓	760	128		888	1,025
3100	Galvanized									
3110	3" x 20'	1 Shee	6	1.333	Ea.	360	93.50		453.50	535
3120	4" x 17'		5.60	1.429		395	100		495	585
3130	4" x 20'		5	1.600		440	112		552	655
3140	5" x 17'	↓	4.60	1.739	↓	470	122		592	700

23 35 43 – Welding Fume Elimination Systems

23 35 43.10 Welding Fume Elimination System Components

		Crew	Daily Output	Labor-Hours	Unit	Material	Labor	Equipment	Total	Total Incl O&P
0010	**WELDING FUME ELIMINATION SYSTEM COMPONENTS**									
7500	Welding fume elimination accessories for garage exhaust systems									
7600	Cut off (blast gate)									
7610	3" tubing size, 3" x 6" opening	1 Shee	24	.333	Ea.	32.50	23.50		56	71
7620	4" tubing size, 4" x 8" opening		24	.333		33.50	23.50		57	71.50
7630	5" tubing size, 5" x 10" opening		24	.333		37.50	23.50		61	76.50
7640	6" tubing size		24	.333		41.50	23.50		65	81
7650	8" tubing size	↓	24	.333	↓	54	23.50		77.50	94
7700	Hoods, magnetic, with handle & screen									
7710	3" tubing size, 3" x 6" opening	1 Shee	24	.333	Ea.	121	23.50		144.50	168
7720	4" tubing size, 4" x 8" opening		24	.333		107	23.50		130.50	152
7730	5" tubing size, 5" x 10" opening	↓	24	.333	↓	107	23.50		130.50	152

23 38 Ventilation Hoods

23 38 13 – Commercial-Kitchen Hoods

23 38 13.10 Hood and Ventilation Equipment

		Crew	Daily Output	Labor-Hours	Unit	Material	Labor	Equipment	Total	Total Incl O&P
0010	**HOOD AND VENTILATION EQUIPMENT**									
2970	Exhaust hood, sst, gutter on all sides, 4' x 4' x 2'	1 Carp	1.80	4.444	Ea.	2,825	260		3,085	3,525
2980	4' x 4' x 7'	"	1.60	5		2,450	293		2,743	3,125
7800	Vent hood, wall canopy with fire protection, 30"	L-3A	9	1.333		112	85		197	250
7810	Without fire protection, 36"		10	1.200		98.50	76.50		175	222
7820	Island canopy with fire protection, 30"		7	1.714		780	109		889	1,025
7830	Without fire protection, 36"		8	1.500		800	95.50		895.50	1,025
7840	Back shelf with fire protection, 30"		11	1.091		415	69.50		484.50	560
7850	Without fire protection, black, 36"		12	1		475	64		539	620
7852	Without fire protection, stainless steel, 36"	↓	12	1		480	64		544	625
7860	Range hood & CO_2 system, 30"	1 Carp	2.50	3.200		4,875	188		5,063	5,625
7950	Hood fire protection system, electric stove	Q-1	3	5.333		2,000	345		2,345	2,725
7952	Hood fire protection system, gas stove	"	3	5.333	↓	2,400	345		2,745	3,175

23 51 Breechings, Chimneys, and Stacks

23 51 13 – Draft Control Devices

23 51 13.16 Vent Dampers

		Crew	Daily Output	Labor-Hours	Unit	Material	2023 Bare Costs Labor	2023 Bare Costs Equipment	Total	Total Incl O&P
0010	**VENT DAMPERS**									
5000	Vent damper, bi-metal, gas, 3" diameter	Q-9	24	.667	Ea.	97.50	42		139.50	171
5010	4" diameter	"	24	.667	"	73.50	42		115.50	145

23 51 13.19 Barometric Dampers

		Crew	Daily Output	Labor-Hours	Unit	Material	Labor	Equipment	Total	Total Incl O&P
0010	**BAROMETRIC DAMPERS**									
1000	Barometric, gas fired system only, 6" size for 5" and 6" pipes	1 Shee	20	.400	Ea.	148	28		176	206
1020	7" size, for 6" and 7" pipes		19	.421		158	29.50		187.50	219
1040	8" size, for 7" and 8" pipes		18	.444		205	31		236	272
1060	9" size, for 8" and 9" pipes		16	.500		230	35		265	305
2000	All fuel, oil, oil/gas, coal									
2020	10" for 9" and 10" pipes	1 Shee	15	.533	Ea.	345	37.50		382.50	430
2040	12" for 11" and 12" pipes		15	.533		450	37.50		487.50	545
2060	14" for 13" and 14" pipes		14	.571		580	40		620	700
2080	16" for 15" and 16" pipes		13	.615		815	43		858	960
2100	18" for 17" and 18" pipes		12	.667		1,075	47		1,122	1,275
2120	20" for 19" and 21" pipes		10	.800		1,300	56		1,356	1,500
2140	24" for 22" and 25" pipes	Q-9	12	1.333		1,575	84		1,659	1,875
2160	28" for 26" and 30" pipes		10	1.600		1,975	101		2,076	2,300
2180	32" for 31" and 34" pipes		8	2		2,525	126		2,651	2,975
3260	For thermal switch for above, add	1 Shee	24	.333		134	23.50		157.50	183

23 51 23 – Gas Vents

23 51 23.10 Gas Chimney Vents

		Crew	Daily Output	Labor-Hours	Unit	Material	Labor	Equipment	Total	Total Incl O&P
0010	**GAS CHIMNEY VENTS**, Prefab metal, UL listed									
0020	Gas, double wall, galvanized steel									
0080	3" diameter	Q-9	72	.222	V.L.F.	10.90	14.05		24.95	33
0100	4" diameter		68	.235		13.50	14.85		28.35	37.50
0120	5" diameter		64	.250		15.30	15.80		31.10	41
0140	6" diameter		60	.267		18.25	16.85		35.10	45.50
0160	7" diameter		56	.286		35	18.05		53.05	65.50
0180	8" diameter		52	.308		37	19.40		56.40	70.50
0200	10" diameter		48	.333		71	21		92	110
0220	12" diameter		44	.364		84.50	23		107.50	128
0240	14" diameter		42	.381		141	24		165	191
0260	16" diameter		40	.400		203	25.50		228.50	261
0280	18" diameter		38	.421		250	26.50		276.50	315
0300	20" diameter	Q-10	36	.667		295	43.50		338.50	390
0320	22" diameter		34	.706		375	46		421	480
0340	24" diameter		32	.750		465	49		514	585
0600	For 4", 5" and 6" oval, add					50%				
0650	Gas, double wall, galvanized steel, fittings									
0660	Elbow 45°, 3" diameter	Q-9	36	.444	Ea.	19.25	28		47.25	63.50
0670	4" diameter		34	.471		23	29.50		52.50	70.50
0680	5" diameter		32	.500		27	31.50		58.50	77.50
0690	6" diameter		30	.533		33.50	33.50		67	87.50
0700	7" diameter		28	.571		53.50	36		89.50	114
0710	8" diameter		26	.615		71.50	39		110.50	137
0720	10" diameter		24	.667		152	42		194	231
0730	12" diameter		22	.727		162	46		208	247
0740	14" diameter		21	.762		254	48		302	355
0750	16" diameter		20	.800		330	50.50		380.50	440
0760	18" diameter		19	.842		435	53		488	555
0770	20" diameter	Q-10	18	1.333		485	87.50		572.50	660

23 51 Breechings, Chimneys, and Stacks

23 51 23 – Gas Vents

23 51 23.10 Gas Chimney Vents		Crew	Daily Output	Labor-Hours	Unit	Material	2023 Bare Costs Labor	Equipment	Total	Total Incl O&P
0780	22" diameter	Q-10	17	1.412	Ea.	775	92.50		867.50	990
0790	24" diameter	↓	16	1.500	↓	985	98		1,083	1,225
0916	Adjustable length									
0918	3" diameter, to 12"	Q-9	36	.444	Ea.	24.50	28		52.50	69.50
0920	4" diameter, to 12"		34	.471		28.50	29.50		58	76.50
0924	6" diameter, to 12"		30	.533		36.50	33.50		70	91
0928	8" diameter, to 12"		26	.615		69	39		108	134
0930	10" diameter, to 18"		24	.667		212	42		254	297
0932	12" diameter, to 18"		22	.727		215	46		261	305
0936	16" diameter, to 18"		20	.800		435	50.50		485.50	555
0938	18" diameter, to 18"	↓	19	.842		500	53		553	630
0944	24" diameter, to 18"	Q-10	16	1.500		950	98		1,048	1,200
0950	Elbow 90°, adjustable, 3" diameter	Q-9	36	.444		32.50	28		60.50	78.50
0960	4" diameter		34	.471		38.50	29.50		68	87
0970	5" diameter		32	.500		45.50	31.50		77	98
0980	6" diameter		30	.533		55.50	33.50		89	112
0990	7" diameter		28	.571		95.50	36		131.50	160
1010	8" diameter		26	.615		97	39		136	166
1020	Wall thimble, 4 to 7" adjustable, 3" diameter		36	.444		20.50	28		48.50	65
1022	4" diameter		34	.471		23	29.50		52.50	70.50
1024	5" diameter		32	.500		28	31.50		59.50	78.50
1026	6" diameter		30	.533		29	33.50		62.50	82
1028	7" diameter		28	.571		59.50	36		95.50	120
1030	8" diameter		26	.615		73.50	39		112.50	140
1040	Roof flashing, 3" diameter		36	.444		11.30	28		39.30	55
1050	4" diameter		34	.471		13.10	29.50		42.60	59.50
1060	5" diameter		32	.500		32.50	31.50		64	83
1070	6" diameter		30	.533		31	33.50		64.50	85
1080	7" diameter		28	.571		41.50	36		77.50	100
1090	8" diameter		26	.615		44	39		83	107
1100	10" diameter		24	.667		59.50	42		101.50	129
1110	12" diameter		22	.727		83.50	46		129.50	161
1120	14" diameter		20	.800		189	50.50		239.50	284
1130	16" diameter		18	.889		220	56		276	325
1140	18" diameter	↓	16	1		310	63		373	440
1150	20" diameter	Q-10	18	1.333		415	87.50		502.50	585
1160	22" diameter		14	1.714		515	112		627	735
1170	24" diameter	↓	12	2		600	131		731	850
1200	Tee, 3" diameter	Q-9	27	.593		50	37.50		87.50	112
1210	4" diameter		26	.615		54	39		93	118
1220	5" diameter		25	.640		57	40.50		97.50	124
1230	6" diameter		24	.667		65	42		107	135
1240	7" diameter		23	.696		93	44		137	168
1250	8" diameter		22	.727		102	46		148	181
1260	10" diameter		21	.762		271	48		319	370
1270	12" diameter		20	.800		278	50.50		328.50	380
1280	14" diameter		18	.889		495	56		551	630
1290	16" diameter		16	1		735	63		798	905
1300	18" diameter	↓	14	1.143		885	72		957	1,075
1310	20" diameter	Q-10	17	1.412		1,225	92.50		1,317.50	1,475
1320	22" diameter		13	1.846		1,550	121		1,671	1,900
1330	24" diameter	↓	12	2		1,800	131		1,931	2,175
1460	Tee cap, 3" diameter	Q-9	45	.356		3.36	22.50		25.86	37.50

23 51 Breechings, Chimneys, and Stacks

23 51 23 – Gas Vents

23 51 23.10 Gas Chimney Vents		Crew	Daily Output	Labor-Hours	Unit	Material	2023 Bare Costs Labor	2023 Bare Costs Equipment	Total	Total Incl O&P
1470	4" diameter	Q-9	42	.381	Ea.	3.61	24		27.61	40
1480	5" diameter		40	.400		4.63	25.50		30.13	43
1490	6" diameter		37	.432		6.75	27.50		34.25	48.50
1500	7" diameter		35	.457		11.30	29		40.30	56
1510	8" diameter		34	.471		12.35	29.50		41.85	58.50
1520	10" diameter		32	.500		99.50	31.50		131	158
1530	12" diameter		30	.533		99.50	33.50		133	160
1540	14" diameter		28	.571		104	36		140	169
1550	16" diameter		25	.640		106	40.50		146.50	177
1560	18" diameter	↓	24	.667		125	42		167	202
1570	20" diameter	Q-10	27	.889		141	58		199	244
1580	22" diameter		22	1.091		136	71.50		207.50	257
1590	24" diameter	↓	21	1.143		160	75		235	289
1750	Top, 3" diameter	Q-9	46	.348		25.50	22		47.50	61
1760	4" diameter		44	.364		27	23		50	64
1770	5" diameter		42	.381		25	24		49	63.50
1780	6" diameter		40	.400		33.50	25.50		59	74.50
1790	7" diameter		38	.421		74	26.50		100.50	121
1800	8" diameter		36	.444		91	28		119	143
1810	10" diameter		34	.471		149	29.50		178.50	209
1820	12" diameter		32	.500		182	31.50		213.50	248
1830	14" diameter		30	.533		291	33.50		324.50	370
1840	16" diameter		28	.571		375	36		411	465
1850	18" diameter	↓	26	.615		515	39		554	625
1860	20" diameter	Q-10	28	.857		780	56		836	945
1870	22" diameter		22	1.091		1,200	71.50		1,271.50	1,425
1880	24" diameter	↓	20	1.200	↓	1,500	78.50		1,578.50	1,775
1900	Gas, double wall, galvanized steel, oval									
1904	4" x 1'	Q-9	68	.235	V.L.F.	22	14.85		36.85	46.50
1906	5" x 1'		64	.250		138	15.80		153.80	176
1908	5"/6" x 1'	↓	60	.267		53.50	16.85		70.35	84.50
1910	Oval fittings									
1912	Adjustable length									
1914	4" diameter to 12" long	Q-9	34	.471	Ea.	22.50	29.50		52	69.50
1916	5" diameter to 12" long		32	.500		29.50	31.50		61	80
1918	5"/6" diameter to 12" long	↓	30	.533	↓	33	33.50		66.50	86.50
1920	Elbow 45°									
1922	4"	Q-9	34	.471	Ea.	46.50	29.50		76	96
1924	5"		32	.500		93.50	31.50		125	151
1926	5"/6"	↓	30	.533	↓	95.50	33.50		129	156
1930	Elbow 45°, flat									
1932	4"	Q-9	34	.471	Ea.	46.50	29.50		76	96
1934	5"		32	.500		93.50	31.50		125	151
1936	5"/6"	↓	30	.533		95.50	33.50		129	156
1940	Top									
1942	4"	Q-9	44	.364	Ea.	41	23		64	79.50
1944	5"		42	.381		36.50	24		60.50	76
1946	5"/6"	↓	40	.400	↓	47	25.50		72.50	90
1950	Adjustable flashing									
1952	4"	Q-9	34	.471	Ea.	19.65	29.50		49.15	66.50
1954	5"		32	.500		57.50	31.50		89	111
1956	5"/6"	↓	30	.533		62	33.50		95.50	119
1960	Tee									

23 51 Breechings, Chimneys, and Stacks

23 51 23 – Gas Vents

23 51 23.10 Gas Chimney Vents

		Crew	Daily Output	Labor-Hours	Unit	Material	2023 Bare Costs Labor	Equipment	Total	Total Incl O&P
1962	4"	Q-9	26	.615	Ea.	69	39		108	135
1964	5"		25	.640		141	40.50		181.50	216
1966	5"/6"	↓	24	.667	↓	144	42		186	222
1970	Tee with short snout									
1972	4"	Q-9	26	.615	Ea.	57.50	39		96.50	122

23 51 26 – All-Fuel Vent Chimneys

23 51 26.10 All-Fuel Vent Chimneys, Press. Tight, Dbl. Wall

		Crew	Daily Output	Labor-Hours	Unit	Material	Labor	Equipment	Total	Total Incl O&P
0010	**ALL-FUEL VENT CHIMNEYS, PRESSURE TIGHT, DOUBLE WALL**									
3200	All fuel, pressure tight, double wall, 1" insulation, UL listed, 1,400°F.									
3210	304 stainless steel liner, aluminized steel outer jacket									
3220	6" diameter	Q-9	60	.267	L.F.	86	16.85		102.85	121
3221	8" diameter		52	.308		106	19.40		125.40	147
3222	10" diameter		48	.333		145	21		166	192
3223	12" diameter		44	.364		90	23		113	134
3224	14" diameter		42	.381		274	24		298	335
3225	16" diameter		40	.400		123	25.50		148.50	173
3226	18" diameter	↓	38	.421		109	26.50		135.50	160
3227	20" diameter	Q-10	36	.667		158	43.50		201.50	239
3228	24" diameter	"	32	.750		196	49		245	290
3260	For 316 stainless steel liner, add				↓	30%				
3280	All fuel, pressure tight, double wall fittings									
3284	304 stainless steel inner, aluminized steel jacket									
3288	Adjustable 20"/29" section									
3292	6" diameter	Q-9	30	.533	Ea.	225	33.50		258.50	298
3293	8" diameter		26	.615		254	39		293	340
3294	10" diameter		24	.667		290	42		332	385
3295	12" diameter		22	.727		325	46		371	425
3296	14" diameter		21	.762		280	48		328	385
3297	16" diameter		20	.800		375	50.50		425.50	485
3298	18" diameter	↓	19	.842		455	53		508	580
3299	20" diameter	Q-10	18	1.333		480	87.50		567.50	655
3300	24" diameter	"	16	1.500	↓	615	98		713	825
3350	Elbow 90° fixed									
3354	6" diameter	Q-9	30	.533	Ea.	460	33.50		493.50	555
3355	8" diameter		26	.615		520	39		559	630
3356	10" diameter		24	.667		590	42		632	710
3357	12" diameter		22	.727		665	46		711	805
3358	14" diameter		21	.762		755	48		803	905
3359	16" diameter		20	.800		855	50.50		905.50	1,025
3360	18" diameter	↓	19	.842		965	53		1,018	1,125
3361	20" diameter	Q-10	18	1.333		1,100	87.50		1,187.50	1,325
3362	24" diameter	"	16	1.500		1,400	98		1,498	1,675
3380	For 316 stainless steel liner, add					30%				
3400	Elbow 45°									
3404	6" diameter	Q-9	30	.533	Ea.	231	33.50		264.50	305
3405	8" diameter		26	.615		276	39		315	365
3406	10" diameter		24	.667		296	42		338	390
3407	12" diameter		22	.727		335	46		381	440
3408	14" diameter		21	.762		405	48		453	520
3409	16" diameter		20	.800		455	50.50		505.50	575
3410	18" diameter	↓	19	.842		515	53		568	645
3411	20" diameter	Q-10	18	1.333		605	87.50		692.50	795

23 51 Breechings, Chimneys, and Stacks

23 51 26 – All-Fuel Vent Chimneys

	23 51 26.10 All-Fuel Vent Chimneys, Press. Tight, Dbl. Wall	Crew	Daily Output	Labor-Hours	Unit	Material	2023 Bare Costs Labor	Equipment	Total	Total Incl O&P
3412	24" diameter	Q-10	16	1.500	Ea.	775	98		873	1,000
3430	For 316 stainless steel liner, add					30%				
3450	Tee 90°									
3454	6" diameter	Q-9	24	.667	Ea.	278	42		320	370
3455	8" diameter		22	.727		300	46		346	400
3456	10" diameter		21	.762		335	48		383	445
3457	12" diameter		20	.800		390	50.50		440.50	500
3458	14" diameter		18	.889		470	56		526	600
3459	16" diameter		16	1		535	63		598	680
3460	18" diameter		14	1.143		625	72		697	800
3461	20" diameter	Q-10	17	1.412		705	92.50		797.50	915
3462	24" diameter	"	12	2		830	131		961	1,100
3480	For tee cap, add					35%	20%			
3500	For 316 stainless steel liner, add					30%				
3520	Plate support, galvanized									
3524	6" diameter	Q-9	26	.615	Ea.	138	39		177	210
3525	8" diameter		22	.727		162	46		208	247
3526	10" diameter		20	.800		176	50.50		226.50	270
3527	12" diameter		18	.889		185	56		241	289
3528	14" diameter		17	.941		219	59.50		278.50	330
3529	16" diameter		16	1		232	63		295	350
3530	18" diameter		15	1.067		244	67.50		311.50	370
3531	20" diameter	Q-10	16	1.500		253	98		351	425
3532	24" diameter	"	14	1.714		264	112		376	460
3570	Bellows, lined									
3574	6" diameter	Q-9	30	.533	Ea.	1,700	33.50		1,733.50	1,925
3575	8" diameter		26	.615		1,750	39		1,789	1,975
3576	10" diameter		24	.667		1,775	42		1,817	2,025
3577	12" diameter		22	.727		1,800	46		1,846	2,075
3578	14" diameter		21	.762		1,450	48		1,498	1,675
3579	16" diameter		20	.800		1,900	50.50		1,950.50	2,150
3580	18" diameter		19	.842		1,950	53		2,003	2,225
3581	20" diameter	Q-10	18	1.333		1,975	87.50		2,062.50	2,300
3590	For all 316 stainless steel construction, add					55%				
3600	Ventilated roof thimble, 304 stainless steel									
3620	6" diameter	Q-9	26	.615	Ea.	297	39		336	385
3624	8" diameter		22	.727		288	46		334	385
3625	10" diameter		20	.800		287	50.50		337.50	390
3626	12" diameter		18	.889		330	56		386	445
3627	14" diameter		17	.941		345	59.50		404.50	465
3628	16" diameter		16	1		380	63		443	515
3629	18" diameter		15	1.067		410	67.50		477.50	550
3630	20" diameter	Q-10	16	1.500		420	98		518	610
3631	24" diameter	"	14	1.714		465	112		577	680
3650	For 316 stainless steel, add					30%				
3670	Exit cone, 316 stainless steel only									
3674	6" diameter	Q-9	46	.348	Ea.	218	22		240	273
3675	8" diameter		42	.381		223	24		247	281
3676	10" diameter		40	.400		221	25.50		246.50	281
3677	12" diameter		38	.421		251	26.50		277.50	315
3678	14" diameter		37	.432		248	27.50		275.50	315
3679	16" diameter		36	.444		275	28		303	350
3680	18" diameter		35	.457		335	29		364	410

23 51 Breechings, Chimneys, and Stacks

23 51 26 – All-Fuel Vent Chimneys

23 51 26.10 All-Fuel Vent Chimneys, Press. Tight, Dbl. Wall		Crew	Daily Output	Labor-Hours	Unit	Material	2023 Bare Costs Labor	Equipment	Total	Total Incl O&P
3681	20" diameter	Q-10	28	.857	Ea.	400	56		456	525
3682	24" diameter	"	26	.923		535	60.50		595.50	680
3720	Roof guide, 304 stainless steel									
3724	6" diameter	Q-9	25	.640	Ea.	109	40.50		149.50	181
3725	8" diameter		21	.762		127	48		175	212
3726	10" diameter		19	.842		138	53		191	232
3727	12" diameter		17	.941		143	59.50		202.50	248
3728	14" diameter		16	1		167	63		230	279
3729	16" diameter		15	1.067		177	67.50		244.50	295
3730	18" diameter		14	1.143		187	72		259	315
3731	20" diameter	Q-10	15	1.600		197	105		302	375
3732	24" diameter	"	13	1.846		206	121		327	410
3750	For 316 stainless steel, add					30%				
3770	Rain cap with bird screen									
3774	6" diameter	Q-9	46	.348	Ea.	330	22		352	400
3775	8" diameter		42	.381		385	24		409	460
3776	10" diameter		40	.400		450	25.50		475.50	535
3777	12" diameter		38	.421		520	26.50		546.50	610
3778	14" diameter		37	.432		600	27.50		627.50	700
3779	16" diameter		36	.444		680	28		708	795
3780	18" diameter		35	.457		775	29		804	895
3781	20" diameter	Q-10	28	.857		880	56		936	1,050
3782	24" diameter	"	26	.923		1,050	60.50		1,110.50	1,275

23 51 26.30 All-Fuel Vent Chimneys, Double Wall, St. Stl.

		Crew	Daily Output	Labor-Hours	Unit	Material	Labor	Equipment	Total	Total Incl O&P
0010	**ALL-FUEL VENT CHIMNEYS, DOUBLE WALL, STAINLESS STEEL**									
7780	All fuel, pressure tight, double wall, 4" insulation, UL listed, 1,400°F.									
7790	304 stainless steel liner, aluminized steel outer jacket									
7800	6" diameter	Q-9	60	.267	V.L.F.	60.50	16.85		77.35	92
7804	8" diameter		52	.308		88	19.40		107.40	126
7806	10" diameter		48	.333		100	21		121	142
7808	12" diameter		44	.364		117	23		140	164
7810	14" diameter		42	.381		131	24		155	180
7880	For 316 stainless steel liner, add				L.F.	30%				
8000	All fuel, double wall, stainless steel fittings									
8010	Roof support, 6" diameter	Q-9	30	.533	Ea.	135	33.50		168.50	200
8030	8" diameter		26	.615		142	39		181	216
8040	10" diameter		24	.667		170	42		212	251
8050	12" diameter		22	.727		178	46		224	265
8060	14" diameter		21	.762		191	48		239	284
8100	Elbow 45°, 6" diameter		30	.533		276	33.50		309.50	355
8140	8" diameter		26	.615		315	39		354	405
8160	10" diameter		24	.667		380	42		422	485
8180	12" diameter		22	.727		410	46		456	520
8200	14" diameter		21	.762		475	48		523	595
8300	Insulated tee, 6" diameter		30	.533		350	33.50		383.50	430
8360	8" diameter		26	.615		365	39		404	460
8380	10" diameter		24	.667		390	42		432	495
8400	12" diameter		22	.727		475	46		521	595
8420	14" diameter		20	.800		560	50.50		610.50	690
8500	Boot tee, 6" diameter		28	.571		790	36		826	925
8520	8" diameter		24	.667		845	42		887	990
8530	10" diameter		22	.727		955	46		1,001	1,125

23 51 Breechings, Chimneys, and Stacks

23 51 26 – All-Fuel Vent Chimneys

23 51 26.30 All-Fuel Vent Chimneys, Double Wall, St. Stl.

		Crew	Daily Output	Labor-Hours	Unit	Material	2023 Bare Costs Labor	Equipment	Total	Total Incl O&P
8540	12" diameter	Q-9	20	.800	Ea.	1,125	50.50		1,175.50	1,300
8550	14" diameter		18	.889		1,150	56		1,206	1,350
8600	Rain cap with bird screen, 6" diameter		30	.533		355	33.50		388.50	440
8640	8" diameter		26	.615		385	39		424	485
8660	10" diameter		24	.667		395	42		437	500
8680	12" diameter		22	.727		555	46		601	680
8700	14" diameter		21	.762		585	48		633	720
8800	Flat roof flashing, 6" diameter		30	.533		130	33.50		163.50	194
8840	8" diameter		26	.615		132	39		171	205
8860	10" diameter		24	.667		142	42		184	220
8880	12" diameter		22	.727		159	46		205	244
8900	14" diameter		21	.762		167	48		215	257

23 52 Heating Boilers

23 52 13 – Electric Boilers

23 52 13.10 Electric Boilers, ASME

			Crew	Daily Output	Labor-Hours	Unit	Material	Labor	Equipment	Total	Total Incl O&P
0010	**ELECTRIC BOILERS, ASME**, Standard controls and trim	D3020-102									
1000	Steam, 6 KW, 20.5 MBH		Q-19	1.20	20	Ea.	4,525	1,325		5,850	6,950
1040	9 KW, 30.7 MBH			1.20	20		4,350	1,325		5,675	6,750
1060	18 KW, 61.4 MBH			1.20	20		4,475	1,325		5,800	6,900
1080	24 KW, 81.8 MBH			1.10	21.818		5,175	1,450		6,625	7,850
1120	36 KW, 123 MBH			1.10	21.818		5,725	1,450		7,175	8,450
2000	Hot water, 7.5 KW, 25.6 MBH			1.30	18.462		5,150	1,225		6,375	7,500
2020	15 KW, 51.2 MBH			1.30	18.462		5,450	1,225		6,675	7,825
2040	30 KW, 102 MBH			1.20	20		5,550	1,325		6,875	8,075
2060	45 KW, 164 MBH			1.20	20		5,425	1,325		6,750	7,925
2070	60 KW, 205 MBH			1.20	20		5,800	1,325		7,125	8,350
2080	75 KW, 256 MBH			1.10	21.818		6,125	1,450		7,575	8,900

23 52 16 – Condensing Boilers

23 52 16.24 Condensing Boilers

			Crew	Daily Output	Labor-Hours	Unit	Material	Labor	Equipment	Total	Total Incl O&P
0010	**CONDENSING BOILERS**, Cast iron, high efficiency										
0020	Packaged with standard controls, circulator and trim										
0030	Intermittent (spark) pilot, natural or LP gas										
0040	Hot water, DOE MBH output (AFUE %)										
0100	42 MBH (84.0%)	G	Q-5	1.80	8.889	Ea.	2,075	580		2,655	3,150
0120	57 MBH (84.3%)	G		1.60	10		2,250	655		2,905	3,450
0140	85 MBH (84.0%)	G		1.40	11.429		2,525	745		3,270	3,900
0160	112 MBH (83.7%)	G		1.20	13.333		2,850	870		3,720	4,425
0180	140 MBH (83.3%)	G	Q-6	1.60	15		3,175	1,025		4,200	5,025
0200	167 MBH (83.0%)	G		1.40	17.143		3,900	1,150		5,050	6,025
0220	194 MBH (82.7%)	G		1.20	20		3,975	1,350		5,325	6,375

23 52 19 – Pulse Combustion Boilers

23 52 19.20 Pulse Type Combustion Boilers

			Crew	Daily Output	Labor-Hours	Unit	Material	Labor	Equipment	Total	Total Incl O&P
0010	**PULSE TYPE COMBUSTION BOILERS**, High efficiency										
7990	Special feature gas fired boilers										
8000	Pulse combustion, standard controls/trim										
8010	Hot water, DOE MBH output (AFUE %)										
8030	71 MBH (95.2%)		Q-5	1.60	10	Ea.	4,050	655		4,705	5,425
8050	94 MBH (95.3%)	G		1.40	11.429		4,475	745		5,220	6,050
8080	139 MBH (95.6%)	G		1.20	13.333		5,025	870		5,895	6,825

23 52 Heating Boilers

23 52 19 – Pulse Combustion Boilers

23 52 19.20 Pulse Type Combustion Boilers		Crew	Daily Output	Labor-Hours	Unit	Material	2023 Bare Costs Labor	Equipment	Total	Total Incl O&P
8090	207 MBH (95.4%)	Q-5	1.16	13.793	Ea.	5,675	900		6,575	7,600
8120	270 MBH (96.4%)		1.12	14.286		7,850	935		8,785	10,100
8130	365 MBH (91.7%)	↓	1.07	14.953	↓	8,875	975		9,850	11,200

23 52 23 – Cast-Iron Boilers

23 52 23.20 Gas-Fired Boilers

0010	**GAS-FIRED BOILERS**, Natural or propane, standard controls, packaged									
1000	Cast iron, with insulated jacket									
2000	Steam, gross output, 81 MBH	Q-7	1.40	22.857	Ea.	3,150	1,575		4,725	5,825
2020	102 MBH		1.30	24.615		2,600	1,700		4,300	5,400
2040	122 MBH		1	32		3,450	2,200		5,650	7,100
2060	163 MBH		.90	35.556		3,450	2,450		5,900	7,425
2080	203 MBH		.90	35.556		4,150	2,450		6,600	8,200
2100	240 MBH		.85	37.647		4,225	2,600		6,825	8,525
2120	280 MBH		.80	40		4,500	2,750		7,250	9,075
2140	320 MBH		.70	45.714		4,825	3,150		7,975	10,000
3000	Hot water, gross output, 80 MBH		1.46	21.918		2,875	1,525		4,400	5,400
3020	100 MBH		1.35	23.704		2,800	1,625		4,425	5,550
3040	122 MBH		1.10	29.091		3,050	2,000		5,050	6,350
3060	163 MBH		1	32		3,575	2,200		5,775	7,225
3080	203 MBH		1	32		4,175	2,200		6,375	7,875
3100	240 MBH		.95	33.684		4,275	2,325		6,600	8,200
3120	280 MBH		.90	35.556		3,875	2,450		6,325	7,925
3140	320 MBH		.80	40		4,250	2,750		7,000	8,800
7000	For tankless water heater, add					10%				
7050	For additional zone valves up to 312 MBH, add				↓	200			200	220

23 52 23.40 Oil-Fired Boilers

0010	**OIL-FIRED BOILERS**, Standard controls, flame retention burner, packaged									
1000	Cast iron, with insulated flush jacket									
2000	Steam, gross output, 109 MBH	Q-7	1.20	26.667	Ea.	2,500	1,850		4,350	5,500
2020	144 MBH		1.10	29.091		2,800	2,000		4,800	6,075
2040	173 MBH		1	32		3,175	2,200		5,375	6,800
2060	207 MBH	↓	.90	35.556	↓	3,400	2,450		5,850	7,375
3000	Hot water, same price as steam									
4000	For tankless coil in smaller sizes, add				Ea.	15%				

23 52 26 – Steel Boilers

23 52 26.40 Oil-Fired Boilers

0010	**OIL-FIRED BOILERS**, Standard controls, flame retention burner									
5000	Steel, with insulated flush jacket									
7000	Hot water, gross output, 103 MBH	Q-6	1.60	15	Ea.	2,225	1,025		3,250	3,975
7020	122 MBH		1.45	16.506		2,125	1,125		3,250	4,000
7040	137 MBH		1.36	17.595		2,875	1,200		4,075	4,925
7060	168 MBH		1.30	18.405		2,800	1,250		4,050	4,950
7080	225 MBH	↓	1.22	19.704		4,300	1,325		5,625	6,750
7340	For tankless coil in steam or hot water, add					7%				

23 52 28 – Swimming Pool Boilers

23 52 28.10 Swimming Pool Heaters

0010	**SWIMMING POOL HEATERS**, Not including wiring, external									
0020	piping, base or pad									
0160	Gas fired, input, 155 MBH	Q-6	1.50	16	Ea.	1,875	1,075		2,950	3,675
0200	199 MBH		1	24		2,025	1,625		3,650	4,650
0220	250 MBH	↓	.70	34.286	↓	2,200	2,325		4,525	5,850

23 52 Heating Boilers

23 52 28 – Swimming Pool Boilers

23 52 28.10 Swimming Pool Heaters		Crew	Daily Output	Labor-Hours	Unit	Material	2023 Bare Costs Labor	Equipment	Total	Total Incl O&P
0240	300 MBH	Q-6	.60	40	Ea.	2,300	2,700		5,000	6,575
0260	399 MBH		.50	48		2,575	3,250		5,825	7,675
0280	500 MBH		.40	60		7,375	4,075		11,450	14,200
0300	650 MBH		.35	68.571		7,850	4,650		12,500	15,600
0320	750 MBH		.33	72.727		8,575	4,925		13,500	16,800
0360	990 MBH		.22	109		11,500	7,400		18,900	23,700
0370	1,260 MBH		.21	114		17,600	7,750		25,350	30,900
0380	1,440 MBH		.19	126		19,500	8,550		28,050	34,300
0400	1,800 MBH		.14	171		20,900	11,600		32,500	40,300
0410	2,070 MBH	↓	.13	185		24,600	12,500		37,100	45,700
2000	Electric, 12 KW, 4,800 gallon pool	Q-19	3	8		2,450	530		2,980	3,475
2020	15 KW, 7,200 gallon pool		2.80	8.571		2,575	565		3,140	3,700
2040	24 KW, 9,600 gallon pool		2.40	10		3,300	660		3,960	4,625
2060	30 KW, 12,000 gallon pool		2	12		3,375	790		4,165	4,875
2080	36 KW, 14,400 gallon pool		1.60	15		3,925	990		4,915	5,800
2100	57 KW, 24,000 gallon pool	↓	1.20	20	↓	4,375	1,325		5,700	6,800
9000	To select pool heater: 12 BTUH x S.F. pool area									
9010	X temperature differential = required output									
9050	For electric, KW = gallons x 2.5 divided by 1,000									
9100	For family home type pool, double the									
9110	Rated gallon capacity = 1/2°F rise per hour									

23 52 88 – Burners

23 52 88.10 Replacement Type Burners		Crew	Daily Output	Labor-Hours	Unit	Material	Labor	Equipment	Total	Total Incl O&P
0010	**REPLACEMENT TYPE BURNERS**									
0990	Residential, conversion, gas fired, LP or natural									
1000	Gun type, atmospheric input 50 to 225 MBH	Q-1	2.50	6.400	Ea.	1,725	415		2,140	2,525
1020	100 to 400 MBH	"	2	8	"	2,875	520		3,395	3,950
3000	Flame retention oil fired assembly, input									
3020	.50 to 2.25 GPH	Q-1	2.40	6.667	Ea.	365	430		795	1,050
3040	2.0 to 5.0 GPH	"	2	8		340	520		860	1,150
4600	Gas safety, shut off valve, 3/4" threaded	1 Stpi	20	.400		193	29		222	256
4610	1" threaded		19	.421		186	30.50		216.50	251
4620	1-1/4" threaded		15	.533		210	38.50		248.50	289
4630	1-1/2" threaded		13	.615		227	44.50		271.50	315
4640	2" threaded	↓	11	.727		254	53		307	360
4650	2-1/2" threaded	Q-1	15	1.067		291	69		360	425
4660	3" threaded		13	1.231		580	80		660	755
4670	4" flanged	↓	3	5.333		2,850	345		3,195	3,650
4680	6" flanged	Q-2	3	8	↓	6,375	540		6,915	7,800

23 54 Furnaces

23 54 16 – Fuel-Fired Furnaces

23 54 16.14 Condensing Furnaces		Crew	Daily Output	Labor-Hours	Unit	Material	Labor	Equipment	Total	Total Incl O&P
0010	**CONDENSING FURNACES**, High efficiency									
0020	Oil fired, packaged, complete									
0030	Upflow									
0040	Output @ 95% A.F.U.E.									
0100	49 MBH @ 1,000 CFM	Q-9	3.70	4.324	Ea.	8,350	273		8,623	9,575
0110	73.5 MBH @ 2,000 CFM		3.60	4.444		8,725	281		9,006	10,000
0120	96 MBH @ 2,000 CFM	↓	3.40	4.706	↓	8,725	297		9,022	10,100

23 54 Furnaces

23 54 16 – Fuel-Fired Furnaces

23 54 16.14 Condensing Furnaces

		Crew	Daily Output	Labor-Hours	Unit	Material	2023 Bare Costs Labor	Equipment	Total	Total Incl O&P
0130	115.6 MBH @ 2,000 CFM	Q-9	3.40	4.706	Ea.	8,725	297		9,022	10,100
0140	147 MBH @ 2,000 CFM		3.30	4.848		20,000	305		20,305	22,400
0150	192 MBH @ 4,000 CFM		2.60	6.154		20,700	390		21,090	23,400
0170	231.5 MBH @ 4,000 CFM		2.30	6.957		20,700	440		21,140	23,500
0260	For variable speed motor, add					810			810	895
0270	Note: Also available in horizontal, counterflow and lowboy configurations.									

23 55 Fuel-Fired Heaters

23 55 23 – Gas-Fired Radiant Heaters

23 55 23.10 Infrared Type Heating Units

		Crew	Daily Output	Labor-Hours	Unit	Material	Labor	Equipment	Total	Total Incl O&P
0010	**INFRARED TYPE HEATING UNITS**									
0020	Gas fired, unvented, electric ignition, 100% shutoff.									
0030	Piping and wiring not included									
0100	Input, 30 MBH	Q-5	6	2.667	Ea.	1,050	174		1,224	1,400
0120	45 MBH		5	3.200		1,375	209		1,584	1,800
0140	50 MBH		4.50	3.556		1,400	232		1,632	1,900
0160	60 MBH		4	4		2,050	261		2,311	2,650
0180	75 MBH		3	5.333		1,400	350		1,750	2,075
0200	90 MBH		2.50	6.400		2,150	420		2,570	2,975
0220	105 MBH		2	8		1,650	520		2,170	2,575
0240	120 MBH		2	8		2,450	520		2,970	3,475
1000	Gas fired, vented, electric ignition, tubular									
1020	Piping and wiring not included, 20' to 80' lengths									
1030	Single stage, input, 60 MBH	Q-6	4.50	5.333	Ea.	1,950	360		2,310	2,700
1040	80 MBH		3.90	6.154		1,750	415		2,165	2,550
1050	100 MBH		3.40	7.059		1,975	480		2,455	2,900
1060	125 MBH		2.90	8.276		1,850	560		2,410	2,850
1070	150 MBH		2.70	8.889		2,425	600		3,025	3,575
1080	170 MBH		2.50	9.600		1,725	650		2,375	2,875
1090	200 MBH		2.20	10.909		2,525	740		3,265	3,875
1100	Note: Final pricing may vary due to									
1110	tube length and configuration package selected									
1130	Two stage, input, 60 MBH high, 45 MBH low	Q-6	4.50	5.333	Ea.	2,150	360		2,510	2,900
1140	80 MBH high, 60 MBH low		3.90	6.154		2,150	415		2,565	2,975
1150	100 MBH high, 65 MBH low		3.40	7.059		2,150	480		2,630	3,075
1160	125 MBH high, 95 MBH low		2.90	8.276		2,175	560		2,735	3,200
1170	150 MBH high, 100 MBH low		2.70	8.889		2,175	600		2,775	3,275
1180	170 MBH high, 125 MBH low		2.50	9.600		2,400	650		3,050	3,625
1190	200 MBH high, 150 MBH low		2.20	10.909		3,225	740		3,965	4,625
1220	Note: Final pricing may vary due to									
1230	tube length and configuration package selected									

23 56 Solar Energy Heating Equipment

23 56 16 – Packaged Solar Heating Equipment

23 56 16.40 Solar Heating Systems

			Crew	Daily Output	Labor-Hours	Unit	Material	2023 Bare Costs Labor	2023 Bare Costs Equipment	Total	Total Incl O&P
0010	**SOLAR HEATING SYSTEMS**	D2020-265									
0020	System/package prices, not including connecting										
0030	pipe, insulation, or special heating/plumbing fixtures	D2020-270									
0152	For solar ultraviolet pipe insulation see Section 22 07 19.10										
0500	Hot water, standard package, low temperature	D2020-275									
0540	1 collector, circulator, fittings, 65 gal. tank	G	Q-1	.50	32	Ea.	5,525	2,075		7,600	9,175
0580	2 collectors, circulator, fittings, 120 gal. tank	D2020-280 G		.40	40		5,500	2,600		8,100	9,925
0620	3 collectors, circulator, fittings, 120 gal. tank	G		.34	47.059		8,850	3,050		11,900	14,300
0700	Medium temperature package	D2020-285									
0720	1 collector, circulator, fittings, 80 gal. tank	G	Q-1	.50	32	Ea.	5,175	2,075		7,250	8,800
0740	2 collectors, circulator, fittings, 120 gal. tank	D2020-290 G		.40	40		8,250	2,600		10,850	13,000
0780	3 collectors, circulator, fittings, 120 gal. tank	G		.30	53.333		8,975	3,450		12,425	15,000
0980	For each additional 120 gal. tank, add	D2020-295 G					1,825			1,825	2,000

23 56 19 – Solar Heating Components

23 56 19.50 Solar Heating Ancillary

			Crew	Daily Output	Labor-Hours	Unit	Material	Labor	Equipment	Total	Total Incl O&P
0010	**SOLAR HEATING ANCILLARY**										
2300	Circulators, air	D3010-650									
2310	Blowers										
2330	100-300 S.F. system, 1/10 HP	D3010-660 G	Q-9	16	1	Ea.	272	63		335	395
2340	300-500 S.F. system, 1/5 HP	G		15	1.067		365	67.50		432.50	500
2350	Two speed, 100-300 S.F., 1/10 HP	D3010-675 G		14	1.143		149	72		221	273
2400	Reversible fan, 20" diameter, 2 speed	G		18	.889		117	56		173	214
2550	Booster fan 6" diameter, 120 CFM	G		16	1		38	63		101	137
2570	6" diameter, 225 CFM	G		16	1		47	63		110	147
2580	8" diameter, 150 CFM	G		16	1		43	63		106	143
2590	8" diameter, 310 CFM	G		14	1.143		66	72		138	182
2600	8" diameter, 425 CFM	G		14	1.143		74	72		146	191
2650	Rheostat	G		32	.500		16.10	31.50		47.60	65
2660	Shutter/damper	G		12	1.333		59.50	84		143.50	193
2670	Shutter motor	G		16	1		148	63		211	258
2800	Circulators, liquid, 1/25 HP, 5.3 GPM	G	Q-1	14	1.143		210	74		284	340
2820	1/20 HP, 17 GPM	G		12	1.333		310	86.50		396.50	470
2850	1/20 HP, 17 GPM, stainless steel	G		12	1.333		264	86.50		350.50	420
2870	1/12 HP, 30 GPM	G		10	1.600		360	104		464	550
3000	Collector panels, air with aluminum absorber plate										
3010	Wall or roof mount										
3040	Flat black, plastic glazing										
3080	4' x 8'	G	Q-9	6	2.667	Ea.	690	168		858	1,025
3100	4' x 10'	G		5	3.200	"	850	202		1,052	1,250
3200	Flush roof mount, 10' to 16' x 22" wide	G		96	.167	L.F.	183	10.50		193.50	218
3210	Manifold, by L.F. width of collectors	G		160	.100	"	152	6.30		158.30	177
3300	Collector panels, liquid with copper absorber plate										
3320	Black chrome, tempered glass glazing										
3330	Alum. frame, 4' x 8', 5/32" single glazing	G	Q-1	9.50	1.684	Ea.	1,050	109		1,159	1,350
3390	Alum. frame, 4' x 10', 5/32" single glazing	G		6	2.667		1,225	173		1,398	1,575
3450	Flat black, alum. frame, 3.5' x 7.5'	G		9	1.778		770	115		885	1,025
3500	4' x 8'	G		5.50	2.909		935	189		1,124	1,300
3520	4' x 10'	G		10	1.600		1,150	104		1,254	1,425
3540	4' x 12.5'	G		5	3.200		1,250	208		1,458	1,675
3550	Liquid with fin tube absorber plate										
3560	Alum. frame 4' x 8' tempered glass	G	Q-1	10	1.600	Ea.	585	104		689	800
3580	Liquid with vacuum tubes, 4' x 6'-10"	G		9	1.778		960	115		1,075	1,225

23 56 Solar Energy Heating Equipment

23 56 19 – Solar Heating Components

23 56 19.50 Solar Heating Ancillary		Crew	Daily Output	Labor-Hours	Unit	Material	2023 Bare Costs Labor	Equipment	Total	Total Incl O&P
3600	Liquid, full wetted, plastic, alum. frame, 4' x 10'	G Q-1	5	3.200	Ea.	330	208		538	675
3650	Collector panel mounting, flat roof or ground rack	G	7	2.286		268	148		416	515
3670	Roof clamps	G	70	.229	Set	3.59	14.80		18.39	26
3700	Roof strap, teflon	G 1 Plum	205	.039	L.F.	25	2.81		27.81	31.50
3900	Differential controller with two sensors									
3930	Thermostat, hard wired	G 1 Plum	8	1	Ea.	116	72		188	234
3950	Line cord and receptacle	G	12	.667		234	48		282	330
4050	Pool valve system	G	2.50	3.200		188	231		419	550
4070	With 12 VAC actuator	G	2	4		335	288		623	795
4080	Pool pump system, 2" pipe size	G	6	1.333		202	96		298	365
4100	Five station with digital read-out	G	3	2.667		280	192		472	595
4150	Sensors									
4200	Brass plug, 1/2" MPT	G 1 Plum	32	.250	Ea.	15.50	18		33.50	44
4210	Brass plug, reversed	G	32	.250		30	18		48	60
4220	Freeze prevention	G	32	.250		26	18		44	56
4240	Screw attached	G	32	.250		18	18		36	47
4250	Brass, immersion	G	32	.250		18	18		36	47
4300	Heat exchanger									
4315	includes coil, blower, circulator									
4316	and controller for DHW and space hot air									
4330	Fluid to air coil, up flow, 45 MBH	G Q-1	4	4	Ea.	335	259		594	755
4380	70 MBH	G	3.50	4.571		380	296		676	860
4400	80 MBH	G	3	5.333		505	345		850	1,075
4580	Fluid to fluid package includes two circulating pumps									
4590	expansion tank, check valve, relief valve									
4600	controller, high temperature cutoff and sensors	G Q-1	2.50	6.400	Ea.	790	415		1,205	1,500
4650	Heat transfer fluid									
4700	Propylene glycol, inhibited anti-freeze	G 1 Plum	28	.286	Gal.	25.50	20.50		46	58.50
4800	Solar storage tanks, knocked down									
4810	Air, galvanized steel clad, double wall, 4" fiberglass insulation									
5120	45 mil reinforced polypropylene lining,									
5140	4' high, 4' x 4' = 64 C.F./450 gallons	G Q-9	2	8	Ea.	3,000	505		3,505	4,050
5150	4' x 8' = 128 C.F./900 gallons	G	1.50	10.667		4,800	675		5,475	6,300
5160	4' x 12' = 190 C.F./1,300 gallons	G	1.30	12.308		6,000	775		6,775	7,775
5170	8' x 8' = 250 C.F./1,700 gallons	G	1	16		7,625	1,000		8,625	9,900
5190	6'-3" high, 7' x 7' = 306 C.F./2,000 gallons	G Q-10	1.20	20		14,100	1,300		15,400	17,500
5200	7' x 10'-6" = 459 C.F./3,000 gallons	G	.80	30		17,500	1,975		19,475	22,200
5210	7' x 14' = 613 C.F./4,000 gallons	G	.60	40		22,200	2,625		24,825	28,500
5220	10'-6" x 10'-6" = 689 C.F./4,500 gallons	G	.50	48		21,000	3,150		24,150	27,700
5230	10'-6" x 14' = 919 C.F./6,000 gallons	G	.40	60		24,400	3,925		28,325	32,800
5240	14' x 14' = 1,225 C.F./8,000 gallons	G Q-11	.40	80		29,300	5,350		34,650	40,300
5250	14' x 17'-6" = 1,531 C.F./10,000 gallons	G	.30	107		31,700	7,125		38,825	45,500
5260	17'-6" x 17'-6" = 1,914 C.F./12,500 gallons	G	.25	128		43,500	8,550		52,050	60,500
5270	17'-6" x 21' = 2,297 C.F./15,000 gallons	G	.20	160		40,700	10,700		51,400	61,000
5280	21' x 21' = 2,756 C.F./18,000 gallons	G	.18	178		43,100	11,900		55,000	65,500
5290	30 mil reinforced Hypalon lining, add					.02%				
7000	Solar control valves and vents									
7050	Air purger, 1" pipe size	G 1 Plum	12	.667	Ea.	53	48		101	130
7070	Air eliminator, automatic 3/4" size	G	32	.250		31	18		49	61
7090	Air vent, automatic, 1/8" fitting	G	32	.250		16.05	18		34.05	44.50
7100	Manual, 1/8" NPT	G	32	.250		3.33	18		21.33	30.50
7120	Backflow preventer, 1/2" pipe size	G	16	.500		89.50	36		125.50	152
7130	3/4" pipe size	G	16	.500		74.50	36		110.50	136

23 56 Solar Energy Heating Equipment

23 56 19 – Solar Heating Components

23 56 19.50 Solar Heating Ancillary

			Crew	Daily Output	Labor-Hours	Unit	Material	2023 Bare Costs Labor	2023 Bare Costs Equipment	Total	Total Incl O&P
7150	Balancing valve, 3/4" pipe size	G	1 Plum	20	.400	Ea.	56.50	29		85.50	105
7180	Draindown valve, 1/2" copper tube	G		9	.889		221	64		285	340
7200	Flow control valve, 1/2" pipe size	G		22	.364		144	26		170	197
7220	Expansion tank, up to 5 gal.	G		32	.250		66	18		84	99.50
7250	Hydronic controller (aquastat)	G		8	1		155	72		227	278
7400	Pressure gauge, 2" dial	G		32	.250		25.50	18		43.50	55
7450	Relief valve, temp. and pressure 3/4" pipe size	G		30	.267		27	19.20		46.20	58
7500	Solenoid valve, normally closed										
7520	Brass, 3/4" NPT, 24V	G	1 Plum	9	.889	Ea.	174	64		238	288
7530	1" NPT, 24V	G		9	.889		274	64		338	395
7750	Vacuum relief valve, 3/4" pipe size	G		32	.250		31.50	18		49.50	61.50
7800	Thermometers										
7820	Digital temperature monitoring, 4 locations	G	1 Plum	2.50	3.200	Ea.	168	231		399	530
7900	Upright, 1/2" NPT	G		8	1		59	72		131	172
7970	Remote probe, 2" dial	G		8	1		35	72		107	146
7990	Stem, 2" dial, 9" stem	G		16	.500		23	36		59	78.50
8250	Water storage tank with heat exchanger and electric element										
8270	66 gal. with 2" x 2 lb. density insulation	G	1 Plum	1.60	5	Ea.	2,100	360		2,460	2,825
8300	80 gal. with 2" x 2 lb. density insulation	G		1.60	5		1,800	360		2,160	2,525
8380	120 gal. with 2" x 2 lb. density insulation	G		1.40	5.714		1,750	410		2,160	2,550
8400	120 gal. with 2" x 2 lb. density insul., 40 S.F. heat coil	G		1.40	5.714		2,600	410		3,010	3,500
8500	Water storage module, plastic										
8600	Tubular, 12" diameter, 4' high	G	1 Carp	48	.167	Ea.	102	9.75		111.75	127
8610	12" diameter, 8' high	G		40	.200		160	11.70		171.70	193
8620	18" diameter, 5' high	G		38	.211		180	12.35		192.35	216
8630	18" diameter, 10' high	G		32	.250		264	14.65		278.65	310
8640	58" diameter, 5' high	G	2 Carp	32	.500		860	29.50		889.50	995
8650	Cap, 12" diameter	G					20.50			20.50	22.50
8660	18" diameter	G					26			26	28.50

23 57 Heat Exchangers for HVAC

23 57 16 – Steam-to-Water Heat Exchangers

23 57 16.10 Shell/Tube Type Steam-to-Water Heat Exch.

		Crew	Daily Output	Labor-Hours	Unit	Material	Labor	Equipment	Total	Total Incl O&P
0010	**SHELL AND TUBE TYPE STEAM-TO-WATER HEAT EXCHANGERS**									
0016	Shell & tube type, 2 or 4 pass, 3/4" OD copper tubes,									
0020	C.I. heads, C.I. tube sheet, steel shell									
0100	Hot water 40°F to 180°F, by steam at 10 psi									
0120	8 GPM	Q-5	6	2.667	Ea.	3,050	174		3,224	3,600
0140	10 GPM		5	3.200		4,575	209		4,784	5,325
0160	40 GPM		4	4		7,050	261		7,311	8,175
0500	For bronze head and tube sheet, add					50%				

23 57 19 – Liquid-to-Liquid Heat Exchangers

23 57 19.13 Plate-Type, Liquid-to-Liquid Heat Exchangers

		Crew	Daily Output	Labor-Hours	Unit	Material	Labor	Equipment	Total	Total Incl O&P
0010	**PLATE-TYPE, LIQUID-TO-LIQUID HEAT EXCHANGERS**									
3000	Plate type,									
3100	400 GPM	Q-6	.80	30	Ea.	52,000	2,025		54,025	60,500
3120	800 GPM	"	.50	48		90,000	3,250		93,250	104,000
3140	1,200 GPM	Q-7	.34	94.118		133,500	6,500		140,000	156,500
3160	1,800 GPM	"	.24	133		177,000	9,200		186,200	208,500

23 57 Heat Exchangers for HVAC

23 57 19 – Liquid-to-Liquid Heat Exchangers

23 57 19.16 Shell-Type, Liquid-to-Liquid Heat Exchangers	Crew	Daily Output	Labor-Hours	Unit	Material	2023 Bare Costs Labor	Equipment	Total	Total Incl O&P
0010 **SHELL-TYPE, LIQUID-TO-LIQUID HEAT EXCHANGERS**									
1000 Hot water 40°F to 140°F, by water at 200°F									
1020 7 GPM	Q-5	6	2.667	Ea.	13,500	174		13,674	15,200
1040 16 GPM		5	3.200		20,000	209		20,209	22,200
1060 34 GPM		4	4		29,500	261		29,761	32,900
1080 55 GPM		3	5.333		41,900	350		42,250	46,600
1100 74 GPM		1.50	10.667		54,000	695		54,695	60,500
1120 86 GPM		1.40	11.429		71,000	745		71,745	79,000
1140 112 GPM	Q-6	2	12		88,000	815		88,815	98,000
1160 126 GPM		1.80	13.333		110,000	905		110,905	122,500
1180 152 GPM		1	24		87,000	1,625		88,625	98,000

23 72 Air-to-Air Energy Recovery Equipment

23 72 16 – Heat-Pipe Air-To-Air Energy-Recovery Equipment

23 72 16.10 Heat Pipes

	Crew	Daily Output	Labor-Hours	Unit	Material	Labor	Equipment	Total	Total Incl O&P
0010 **HEAT PIPES**									
8000 Heat pipe type, glycol, 50% efficient									
8010 100 MBH, 1,700 CFM	1 Stpi	.80	10	Ea.	5,275	725		6,000	6,900
8020 160 MBH, 2,700 CFM		.60	13.333		7,100	965		8,065	9,250
8030 620 MBH, 4,000 CFM		.40	20		10,700	1,450		12,150	14,000

23 81 Decentralized Unitary HVAC Equipment

23 81 13 – Packaged Terminal Air-Conditioners

23 81 13.10 Packaged Cabinet Type Air-Conditioners

	Crew	Daily Output	Labor-Hours	Unit	Material	Labor	Equipment	Total	Total Incl O&P
0010 **PACKAGED CABINET TYPE AIR-CONDITIONERS**, Cabinet, wall sleeve,									
0100 louver, electric heat, thermostat, manual changeover, 208 V									
0200 6,000 BTUH cooling, 8,800 BTU heat	Q-5	6	2.667	Ea.	1,200	174		1,374	1,550
0220 9,000 BTUH cooling, 13,900 BTU heat		5	3.200		3,475	209		3,684	4,125
0240 12,000 BTUH cooling, 13,900 BTU heat		4	4		3,800	261		4,061	4,575
0260 15,000 BTUH cooling, 13,900 BTU heat		3	5.333		1,950	350		2,300	2,675

23 81 19 – Self-Contained Air-Conditioners

23 81 19.10 Window Unit Air Conditioners

	Crew	Daily Output	Labor-Hours	Unit	Material	Labor	Equipment	Total	Total Incl O&P
0010 **WINDOW UNIT AIR CONDITIONERS**									
4000 Portable/window, 15 amp, 125 V grounded receptacle required									
4060 5,000 BTUH	1 Carp	8	1	Ea.	330	58.50		388.50	455
4340 6,000 BTUH		8	1		370	58.50		428.50	500
4480 8,000 BTUH		6	1.333		410	78		488	565
4500 10,000 BTUH		6	1.333		540	78		618	710
4520 12,000 BTUH	L-2	8	2		2,300	104		2,404	2,675
4600 Window/thru-the-wall, 15 amp, 230 V grounded receptacle required									
4780 18,000 BTUH	L-2	6	2.667	Ea.	1,150	138		1,288	1,475
4940 25,000 BTUH		4	4		2,475	207		2,682	3,025
4960 29,000 BTUH		4	4		1,475	207		1,682	1,925

23 81 Decentralized Unitary HVAC Equipment

23 81 43 – Air-Source Unitary Heat Pumps

23 81 43.10 Air-Source Heat Pumps

		Crew	Daily Output	Labor-Hours	Unit	Material	2023 Bare Costs Labor	2023 Bare Costs Equipment	Total	Total Incl O&P
0010	**AIR-SOURCE HEAT PUMPS**, Not including interconnecting tubing									
1000	Air to air, split system, not including curbs, pads, fan coil and ductwork									
1010	For curbs/pads see Section 23 91 10									
1012	Outside condensing unit only, for fan coil see Section 23 82 19.10									
1015	1.5 ton cooling, 7 MBH heat @ 0°F	Q-5	2.40	6.667	Ea.	1,575	435		2,010	2,375
1020	2 ton cooling, 8.5 MBH heat @ 0°F		2	8		1,700	520		2,220	2,650
1030	2.5 ton cooling, 10 MBH heat @ 0°F		1.60	10		1,875	655		2,530	3,050
1040	3 ton cooling, 13 MBH heat @ 0°F		1.20	13.333		2,075	870		2,945	3,575
1050	3.5 ton cooling, 18 MBH heat @ 0°F		1	16		2,225	1,050		3,275	3,975
1054	4 ton cooling, 24 MBH heat @ 0°F		.80	20		2,400	1,300		3,700	4,600
1060	5 ton cooling, 27 MBH heat @ 0°F	↓	.50	32	↓	2,625	2,100		4,725	6,000
1500	Single package, not including curbs, pads, or plenums									
1502	0.5 ton cooling, supplementary heat included	Q-5	8	2	Ea.	2,925	131		3,056	3,425
1504	0.75 ton cooling, supplementary heat included		6	2.667		3,100	174		3,274	3,650
1506	1 ton cooling, supplementary heat included		4	4		4,000	261		4,261	4,800
1510	1.5 ton cooling, 5 MBH heat @ 0°F		1.55	10.323		3,500	675		4,175	4,850
1520	2 ton cooling, 6.5 MBH heat @ 0°F		1.50	10.667		3,550	695		4,245	4,950
1540	2.5 ton cooling, 8 MBH heat @ 0°F		1.40	11.429		3,450	745		4,195	4,900
1560	3 ton cooling, 10 MBH heat @ 0°F		1.20	13.333		3,950	870		4,820	5,650
1570	3.5 ton cooling, 11 MBH heat @ 0°F		1	16		4,400	1,050		5,450	6,375
1580	4 ton cooling, 13 MBH heat @ 0°F		.96	16.667		4,725	1,100		5,825	6,825
1620	5 ton cooling, 27 MBH heat @ 0°F		.65	24.615		5,350	1,600		6,950	8,275
1640	7.5 ton cooling, 35 MBH heat @ 0°F	↓	.40	40	↓	8,200	2,600		10,800	12,900
6000	Air to water, single package, excluding storage tank and ductwork									
6010	Includes circulating water pump, air duct connections, digital temperature									
6020	controller with remote tank temp. probe and sensor for storage tank.									
6040	Water heating - air cooling capacity									
6110	35.5 MBH heat water, 2.3 ton cool air	Q-5	1.60	10	Ea.	17,800	655		18,455	20,600
6120	58 MBH heat water, 3.8 ton cool air		1.10	14.545		20,300	950		21,250	23,800
6130	76 MBH heat water, 4.9 ton cool air		.87	18.391		24,300	1,200		25,500	28,500
6140	98 MBH heat water, 6.5 ton cool air		.62	25.806		31,400	1,675		33,075	37,000
6150	113 MBH heat water, 7.4 ton cool air		.59	27.119		34,400	1,775		36,175	40,500
6160	142 MBH heat water, 9.2 ton cool air		.52	30.769		41,700	2,000		43,700	48,900
6170	171 MBH heat water, 11.1 ton cool air	↓	.49	32.653	↓	49,000	2,125		51,125	57,000

23 81 46 – Water-Source Unitary Heat Pumps

23 81 46.10 Water Source Heat Pumps

		Crew	Daily Output	Labor-Hours	Unit	Material	Labor	Equipment	Total	Total Incl O&P
0010	**WATER SOURCE HEAT PUMPS**, Not incl. connecting tubing or water source									
2000	Water source to air, single package									
2100	1 ton cooling, 13 MBH heat @ 75°F	Q-5	2	8	Ea.	2,225	520		2,745	3,200
2120	1.5 ton cooling, 17 MBH heat @ 75°F		1.80	8.889		2,050	580		2,630	3,125
2140	2 ton cooling, 19 MBH heat @ 75°F		1.70	9.412		2,450	615		3,065	3,600
2160	2.5 ton cooling, 25 MBH heat @ 75°F		1.60	10		6,600	655		7,255	8,225
2180	3 ton cooling, 27 MBH heat @ 75°F		1.40	11.429		6,900	745		7,645	8,725
2190	3.5 ton cooling, 29 MBH heat @ 75°F		1.30	12.308		2,950	805		3,755	4,450
2200	4 ton cooling, 31 MBH heat @ 75°F		1.20	13.333		3,400	870		4,270	5,050
2220	5 ton cooling, 29 MBH heat @ 75°F	↓	.90	17.778	↓	3,575	1,150		4,725	5,650
3960	For supplementary heat coil, add					10%				

23 82 Convection Heating and Cooling Units

23 82 19 – Fan Coil Units

23 82 19.10 Fan Coil Air Conditioning

		Crew	Daily Output	Labor-Hours	Unit	Material	2023 Bare Costs Labor	2023 Bare Costs Equipment	Total	Total Incl O&P
0010	**FAN COIL AIR CONDITIONING**									
0030	Fan coil AC, cabinet mounted, filters and controls									
0320	1 ton cooling	Q-5	6	2.667	Ea.	2,025	174		2,199	2,475
0940	Direct expansion, for use w/air cooled condensing unit, 1-1/2 ton cooling		5	3.200		785	209		994	1,175
0950	2 ton cooling		4.80	3.333		770	218		988	1,175
0960	2-1/2 ton cooling		4.40	3.636		900	237		1,137	1,350
0970	3 ton cooling		3.80	4.211		1,100	275		1,375	1,600
0980	3-1/2 ton cooling		3.60	4.444		1,125	290		1,415	1,675
0990	4 ton cooling		3.40	4.706		1,075	305		1,380	1,650
1000	5 ton cooling	↓	3	5.333	↓	1,425	350		1,775	2,075
1500	For hot water coil, add					40%	10%			

23 82 29 – Radiators

23 82 29.10 Hydronic Heating

		Crew	Daily Output	Labor-Hours	Unit	Material	2023 Bare Costs Labor	2023 Bare Costs Equipment	Total	Total Incl O&P
0010	**HYDRONIC HEATING**, Terminal units, not incl. main supply pipe									
1000	Radiation									
1100	Panel, baseboard, C.I., including supports, no covers	Q-5	46	.348	L.F.	54.50	22.50		77	94
3000	Radiators, cast iron									
3100	Free standing or wall hung, 6 tube, 25" high	Q-5	96	.167	Section	72	10.90		82.90	95.50
3150	4 tube, 25" high		96	.167		53.50	10.90		64.40	75.50
3200	4 tube, 19" high	↓	96	.167	↓	50	10.90		60.90	71.50
3250	Adj. brackets, 2 per wall radiator up to 30 sections	1 Stpi	32	.250	Ea.	52	18.15		70.15	84.50
3500	Recessed, 20" high x 5" deep, without grille	Q-5	60	.267	Section	59.50	17.40		76.90	91.50
3525	Free standing or wall hung, 30" high	"	60	.267		47	17.40		64.40	77.50
3600	For inlet grille, add					6.55			6.55	7.20
9500	To convert SFR to BTU rating: Hot water, 150 x SFR									
9510	Forced hot water, 180 x SFR; steam, 240 x SFR									

23 82 33 – Convectors

23 82 33.10 Convector Units

		Crew	Daily Output	Labor-Hours	Unit	Material	2023 Bare Costs Labor	2023 Bare Costs Equipment	Total	Total Incl O&P
0010	**CONVECTOR UNITS**, Terminal units, not incl. main supply pipe									
2204	Convector, multifin, 2 pipe w/cabinet									
2210	17" H x 24" L	Q-5	10	1.600	Ea.	111	104		215	278
2214	17" H x 36" L		8.60	1.860		167	121		288	365
2218	17" H x 48" L		7.40	2.162		222	141		363	455
2222	21" H x 24" L		9	1.778		124	116		240	310
2228	21" H x 48" L	↓	6.80	2.353	↓	248	154		402	500
2240	For knob operated damper, add					140%				
2241	For metal trim strips, add	Q-5	64	.250	Ea.	6.70	16.35		23.05	32
2243	For snap-on inlet grille, add					10%	10%			
2245	For hinged access door, add	Q-5	64	.250	Ea.	40	16.35		56.35	68
2246	For air chamber, auto-venting, add	"	58	.276	"	8.65	18		26.65	36.50

23 82 36 – Finned-Tube Radiation Heaters

23 82 36.10 Finned Tube Radiation

		Crew	Daily Output	Labor-Hours	Unit	Material	2023 Bare Costs Labor	2023 Bare Costs Equipment	Total	Total Incl O&P
0010	**FINNED TUBE RADIATION**, Terminal units, not incl. main supply pipe									
1310	Baseboard, pkgd, 1/2" copper tube, alum. fin, 7" high	Q-5	60	.267	L.F.	11.80	17.40		29.20	39
1320	3/4" copper tube, alum. fin, 7" high	"	58	.276	"	7.85	18		25.85	35.50
1381	Rough in baseboard panel & fin tube, supply & balance valves	1 Stpi	1.06	7.547	Ea.	445	550		995	1,300
1500	Note: fin tube may also require corners, caps, etc.									

23 83 Radiant Heating Units

23 83 16 – Radiant-Heating Hydronic Piping

23 83 16.10 Radiant Floor Heating

		Crew	Daily Output	Labor-Hours	Unit	Material	2023 Bare Costs Labor	Equipment	Total	Total Incl O&P
0010	**RADIANT FLOOR HEATING**									
0100	Tubing, PEX (cross-linked polyethylene)									
0110	Oxygen barrier type for systems with ferrous materials									
0120	1/2"	Q-5	800	.020	L.F.	1.14	1.31		2.45	3.20
0130	3/4"		535	.030		1.61	1.95		3.56	4.68
0140	1"	↓	400	.040	↓	2.52	2.61		5.13	6.65
0200	Non barrier type for ferrous free systems									
0210	1/2"	Q-5	800	.020	L.F.	.63	1.31		1.94	2.64
0220	3/4"		535	.030		1.15	1.95		3.10	4.18
0230	1"	↓	400	.040	↓	1.97	2.61		4.58	6.05
1000	Manifolds									
1110	Brass									
1120	With supply and return valves, flow meter, thermometer,									
1122	auto air vent and drain/fill valve.									
1130	1", 2 circuit	Q-5	14	1.143	Ea.	370	74.50		444.50	515
1140	1", 3 circuit		13.50	1.185		420	77.50		497.50	580
1150	1", 4 circuit		13	1.231		460	80.50		540.50	625
1154	1", 5 circuit		12.50	1.280		545	83.50		628.50	725
1158	1", 6 circuit		12	1.333		595	87		682	785
1162	1", 7 circuit		11.50	1.391		650	91		741	850
1166	1", 8 circuit		11	1.455		720	95		815	930
1172	1", 9 circuit		10.50	1.524		775	99.50		874.50	1,000
1174	1", 10 circuit		10	1.600		830	104		934	1,075
1178	1", 11 circuit		9.50	1.684		865	110		975	1,125
1182	1", 12 circuit	↓	9	1.778	↓	955	116		1,071	1,225
1610	Copper manifold header (cut to size)									
1620	1" header, 12 circuit 1/2" sweat outlets	Q-5	3.33	4.805	Ea.	134	315		449	615
1630	1-1/4" header, 12 circuit 1/2" sweat outlets		3.20	5		155	325		480	655
1640	1-1/4" header, 12 circuit 3/4" sweat outlets		3	5.333		167	350		517	705
1650	1-1/2" header, 12 circuit 3/4" sweat outlets		3.10	5.161		201	335		536	725
1660	2" header, 12 circuit 3/4" sweat outlets	↓	2.90	5.517	↓	295	360		655	860
3000	Valves									
3110	Thermostatic zone valve actuator with end switch	Q-5	40	.400	Ea.	55.50	26		81.50	100
3114	Thermostatic zone valve actuator	"	36	.444	"	105	29		134	159
3120	Motorized straight zone valve with operator complete									
3130	3/4"	Q-5	35	.457	Ea.	171	30		201	233
3140	1"		32	.500		185	32.50		217.50	253
3150	1-1/4"	↓	29.60	.541	↓	236	35.50		271.50	315
3500	4 way mixing valve, manual, brass									
3530	1"	Q-5	13.30	1.203	Ea.	245	78.50		323.50	385
3540	1-1/4"		11.40	1.404		265	91.50		356.50	430
3550	1-1/2"		11	1.455		340	95		435	515
3560	2"		10.60	1.509		480	98.50		578.50	675
3800	Mixing valve motor, 4 way for valves, 1" and 1-1/4"		34	.471		405	30.50		435.50	490
3810	Mixing valve motor, 4 way for valves, 1-1/2" and 2"	↓	30	.533	↓	465	35		500	565
5000	Radiant floor heating, zone control panel									
5120	4 zone actuator valve control, expandable	Q-5	20	.800	Ea.	157	52		209	251
5130	6 zone actuator valve control, expandable		18	.889		292	58		350	405
6070	Thermal track, straight panel for long continuous runs, 5.333 S.F.		40	.400		38.50	26		64.50	81
6080	Thermal track, utility panel, for direction reverse at run end, 5.333 S.F.		40	.400		38.50	26		64.50	81
6090	Combination panel, for direction reverse plus straight run, 5.333 S.F.		40	.400		38.50	26		64.50	81
7000	PEX tubing fittings									
7100	Compression type									

23 83 Radiant Heating Units

23 83 16 – Radiant-Heating Hydronic Piping

23 83 16.10 Radiant Floor Heating		Crew	Daily Output	Labor-Hours	Unit	Material	2023 Bare Costs Labor	Equipment	Total	Total Incl O&P
7116	Coupling									
7120	1/2" x 1/2"	1 Stpi	27	.296	Ea.	7.30	21.50		28.80	40
7124	3/4" x 3/4"	"	23	.348	"	17.60	25		42.60	57
7130	Adapter									
7132	1/2" x female sweat 1/2"	1 Stpi	27	.296	Ea.	4.75	21.50		26.25	37.50
7134	1/2" x female sweat 3/4"		26	.308		5.30	22.50		27.80	39.50
7136	5/8" x female sweat 3/4"		24	.333		7.60	24		31.60	44.50
7140	Elbow									
7142	1/2" x female sweat 1/2"	1 Stpi	27	.296	Ea.	7.25	21.50		28.75	40
7144	1/2" x female sweat 3/4"		26	.308		8.50	22.50		31	43
7146	5/8" x female sweat 3/4"		24	.333		9.50	24		33.50	46.50
7200	Insert type									
7206	PEX x male NPT									
7210	1/2" x 1/2"	1 Stpi	29	.276	Ea.	3.38	20		23.38	33.50
7220	3/4" x 3/4"		27	.296		4.98	21.50		26.48	37.50
7230	1" x 1"		26	.308		8.40	22.50		30.90	43
7300	PEX coupling									
7310	1/2" x 1/2"	1 Stpi	30	.267	Ea.	1.28	19.35		20.63	30.50
7320	3/4" x 3/4"		29	.276		1.93	20		21.93	32
7330	1" x 1"		28	.286		2.99	20.50		23.49	34.50
7400	PEX stainless crimp ring									
7410	1/2" x 1/2"	1 Stpi	86	.093	Ea.	.61	6.75		7.36	10.70
7420	3/4" x 3/4"		84	.095		.83	6.90		7.73	11.20
7430	1" x 1"		82	.098		1.19	7.10		8.29	11.85

23 83 33 – Electric Radiant Heaters

23 83 33.10 Electric Heating		Crew	Daily Output	Labor-Hours	Unit	Material	Labor	Equipment	Total	Total Incl O&P
0010	**ELECTRIC HEATING**, not incl. conduit or feed wiring									
1100	Rule of thumb: Baseboard units, including control	1 Elec	4.40	1.818	KW	138	122		260	335
1300	Baseboard heaters, 2' long, 350 watt		8	1	Ea.	41.50	67.50		109	146
1400	3' long, 750 watt		8	1		44.50	67.50		112	149
1600	4' long, 1,000 watt		6.70	1.194		54	80.50		134.50	179
1800	5' long, 935 watt		5.70	1.404		64.50	94.50		159	211
2000	6' long, 1,500 watt		5	1.600		72.50	108		180.50	240
2200	7' long, 1,310 watt		4.40	1.818		74	122		196	264
2400	8' long, 2,000 watt		4	2		89.50	135		224.50	299
2600	9' long, 1,680 watt		3.60	2.222		99.50	150		249.50	330
2800	10' long, 1,875 watt		3.30	2.424		97.50	163		260.50	350
2950	Wall heaters with fan, 120 to 277 volt									
3160	Recessed, residential, 750 watt	1 Elec	6	1.333	Ea.	96.50	90		186.50	239
3170	1,000 watt		6	1.333		385	90		475	560
3180	1,250 watt		5	1.600		132	108		240	305
3190	1,500 watt		4	2		415	135		550	660
3600	Thermostats, integral		16	.500		34	33.50		67.50	87.50
3800	Line voltage, 1 pole		8	1		34.50	67.50		102	138
3810	2 pole		8	1		27	67.50		94.50	130
4000	Heat trace system, 400 degree									
4020	115 V, 2.5 watts/L.F.	1 Elec	530	.015	L.F.	11.70	1.02		12.72	14.35
4030	5 watts/L.F.		530	.015		11.70	1.02		12.72	14.35
4050	10 watts/L.F.		530	.015		8.60	1.02		9.62	11
4060	208 V, 5 watts/L.F.		530	.015		11.70	1.02		12.72	14.35
4080	480 V, 8 watts/L.F.		530	.015		11.70	1.02		12.72	14.35
4200	Heater raceway									

23 83 Radiant Heating Units

23 83 33 – Electric Radiant Heaters

23 83 33.10 Electric Heating		Crew	Daily Output	Labor-Hours	Unit	Material	2023 Bare Costs Labor	2023 Bare Costs Equipment	Total	Total Incl O&P
4260	Heat transfer cement									
4280	1 gallon				Ea.	96.50			96.50	106
4300	5 gallon				"	283			283	310
4320	Cable tie									
4340	3/4" pipe size	1 Elec	470	.017	Ea.	.03	1.15		1.18	1.73
4360	1" pipe size		444	.018		.03	1.21		1.24	1.83
4380	1-1/4" pipe size		400	.020		.03	1.35		1.38	2.03
4400	1-1/2" pipe size		355	.023		.03	1.52		1.55	2.29
4420	2" pipe size		320	.025		.02	1.68		1.70	2.52
4440	3" pipe size		160	.050		.02	3.37		3.39	5
4460	4" pipe size		100	.080		.07	5.40		5.47	8.10
4480	Thermostat NEMA 3R, 22 amp, 0-150 degree, 10' cap.		8	1		210	67.50		277.50	330
4500	Thermostat NEMA 4X, 25 amp, 40 degree, 5-1/2' cap.		7	1.143		210	77		287	345
4520	Thermostat NEMA 4X, 22 amp, 25-325 degree, 10' cap.		7	1.143		575	77		652	750
4540	Thermostat NEMA 4X, 22 amp, 15-140 degree		6	1.333		470	90		560	655
4580	Thermostat NEMA 4, 7, 9, 22 amp, 25-325 degree, 10' cap.		3.60	2.222		690	150		840	980
4600	Thermostat NEMA 4, 7, 9, 22 amp, 15-140 degree		3	2.667		645	180		825	975
4720	Fiberglass application tape, 36 yard roll		11	.727		58	49		107	137
5000	Radiant heating ceiling panels, 2' x 4', 500 watt		16	.500		325	33.50		358.50	405
5050	750 watt		16	.500		320	33.50		353.50	400
5200	For recessed plaster frame, add		32	.250		138	16.85		154.85	176
5300	Infrared quartz heaters, 120 volts, 1,000 watt		6.70	1.194		300	80.50		380.50	450
5350	1,500 watt		5	1.600		315	108		423	510
5400	240 volts, 1,500 watt		5	1.600		282	108		390	470
5450	2,000 watt		4	2		320	135		455	555
5500	3,000 watt		3	2.667		345	180		525	645
5550	4,000 watt		2.60	3.077		370	207		577	715
5570	Modulating control		.80	10		156	675		831	1,175
5600	Unit heaters, heavy duty, with fan & mounting bracket									
5650	Single phase, 208-240-277 volt, 3 kW	1 Elec	6	1.333	Ea.	610	90		700	805
5750	5 kW		5.50	1.455		640	98		738	845
5800	7 kW		5	1.600		855	108		963	1,100
5850	10 kW		4	2		1,200	135		1,335	1,525
5950	15 kW		3.80	2.105		2,025	142		2,167	2,425
6000	480 volt, 3 kW		6	1.333		525	90		615	715
6020	4 kW		5.80	1.379		365	93		458	545
6040	5 kW		5.50	1.455		375	98		473	560
6060	7 kW		5	1.600		580	108		688	800
6080	10 kW		4	2		1,200	135		1,335	1,525
6100	13 kW		3.80	2.105		2,150	142		2,292	2,575
6120	15 kW		3.70	2.162		1,075	146		1,221	1,400
6140	20 kW		3.50	2.286		2,925	154		3,079	3,450
6300	3 phase, 208-240 volt, 5 kW		5.50	1.455		535	98		633	735
6320	7 kW		5	1.600		860	108		968	1,100
6340	10 kW		4	2		885	135		1,020	1,175
6360	15 kW		3.70	2.162		1,675	146		1,821	2,075
6380	20 kW		3.50	2.286		2,975	154		3,129	3,500
6400	25 kW		3.30	2.424		3,150	163		3,313	3,700
6500	480 volt, 5 kW		5.50	1.455		760	98		858	980
6520	7 kW		5	1.600		1,075	108		1,183	1,325
6540	10 kW		4	2		1,025	135		1,160	1,350
6560	13 kW		3.80	2.105		1,775	142		1,917	2,150
6580	15 kW		3.70	2.162		1,675	146		1,821	2,050

23 83 Radiant Heating Units

23 83 33 – Electric Radiant Heaters

23 83 33.10 Electric Heating		Crew	Daily Output	Labor-Hours	Unit	Material	2023 Bare Costs Labor	Equipment	Total	Total Incl O&P
6600	20 kW	1 Elec	3.50	2.286	Ea.	2,475	154		2,629	2,950
6800	Vertical discharge heaters, with fan									
6820	Single phase, 208-240-277 volt, 10 kW	1 Elec	4	2	Ea.	1,050	135		1,185	1,350
6840	15 kW		3.70	2.162		1,750	146		1,896	2,175
6900	3 phase, 208-240 volt, 10 kW		4	2		1,125	135		1,260	1,450
6920	15 kW		3.70	2.162		1,750	146		1,896	2,150
6940	20 kW		3.50	2.286		3,225	154		3,379	3,775
7100	480 volt, 10 kW		4	2		1,325	135		1,460	1,650
7120	15 kW		3.70	2.162		2,150	146		2,296	2,600
7140	20 kW		3.50	2.286		2,950	154		3,104	3,475
7160	25 kW		3.30	2.424		3,875	163		4,038	4,500
7900	Cabinet convector heaters, 240 volt, three phase,									
7920	3' long, 2,000 watt	1 Elec	5.30	1.509	Ea.		102		102	151
7940	3,000 watt		5.30	1.509		1,925	102		2,027	2,250
7960	4,000 watt		5.30	1.509		1,975	102		2,077	2,325
7980	6,000 watt		4.60	1.739		2,050	117		2,167	2,425
8000	8,000 watt		4.60	1.739		2,125	117		2,242	2,500
8020	4' long, 4,000 watt		4.60	1.739		1,850	117		1,967	2,200
8040	6,000 watt		4	2		1,925	135		2,060	2,300
8060	8,000 watt		4	2		2,025	135		2,160	2,425
8080	10,000 watt		4	2		2,050	135		2,185	2,450
8100	Available also in 208 or 277 volt									
8200	Cabinet unit heaters, 120 to 277 volt, 1 pole,									
8220	wall mounted, 2 kW	1 Elec	4.60	1.739	Ea.	1,850	117		1,967	2,200
8230	3 kW		4.60	1.739		1,925	117		2,042	2,275
8240	4 kW		4.40	1.818		1,975	122		2,097	2,350
8250	5 kW		4.40	1.818		2,025	122		2,147	2,400
8260	6 kW		4.20	1.905		2,050	128		2,178	2,450
8270	8 kW		4	2		2,125	135		2,260	2,525
8280	10 kW		3.80	2.105		2,050	142		2,192	2,450
8290	12 kW		3.50	2.286		1,950	154		2,104	2,375
8300	13.5 kW		2.90	2.759		2,125	186		2,311	2,600
8310	16 kW		2.70	2.963		2,175	200		2,375	2,675
8320	20 kW		2.30	3.478		3,300	234		3,534	3,975
8330	24 kW		1.90	4.211		3,350	284		3,634	4,100
8350	Recessed, 2 kW		4.40	1.818		2,050	122		2,172	2,425
8370	3 kW		4.40	1.818		2,125	122		2,247	2,500
8380	4 kW		4.20	1.905		2,175	128		2,303	2,575
8390	5 kW		4.20	1.905		2,225	128		2,353	2,650
8400	6 kW		4	2		2,025	135		2,160	2,425
8410	8 kW		3.80	2.105		2,125	142		2,267	2,550
8420	10 kW		3.50	2.286		2,650	154		2,804	3,150
8430	12 kW		2.90	2.759		2,675	186		2,861	3,225
8440	13.5 kW		2.70	2.963		2,700	200		2,900	3,250
8450	16 kW		2.30	3.478		2,700	234		2,934	3,325
8460	20 kW		1.90	4.211		3,225	284		3,509	3,975
8470	24 kW		1.60	5		3,275	335		3,610	4,100
8490	Ceiling mounted, 2 kW		3.20	2.500		2,050	168		2,218	2,500
8510	3 kW		3.20	2.500		2,125	168		2,293	2,575
8520	4 kW		3	2.667		2,175	180		2,355	2,650
8530	5 kW		3	2.667		2,225	180		2,405	2,725
8540	6 kW		2.80	2.857		2,250	192		2,442	2,750
8550	8 kW		2.40	3.333		2,325	225		2,550	2,875

23 83 Radiant Heating Units

23 83 33 – Electric Radiant Heaters

23 83 33.10 Electric Heating

		Crew	Daily Output	Labor-Hours	Unit	Material	Labor	Equipment	Total	Total Incl O&P
8560	10 kW	1 Elec	2.20	3.636	Ea.	2,150	245		2,395	2,725
8570	12 kW		2	4		2,175	269		2,444	2,800
8580	13.5 kW		1.50	5.333		2,225	360		2,585	2,975
8590	16 kW		1.30	6.154		2,275	415		2,690	3,125
8600	20 kW		.90	8.889		3,225	600		3,825	4,450
8610	24 kW		.60	13.333		3,275	900		4,175	4,925
8630	208 to 480 V, 3 pole									
8650	Wall mounted, 2 kW	1 Elec	4.60	1.739	Ea.	2,050	117		2,167	2,425
8670	3 kW		4.60	1.739		1,925	117		2,042	2,275
8680	4 kW		4.40	1.818		1,975	122		2,097	2,350
8690	5 kW		4.40	1.818		2,025	122		2,147	2,400
8700	6 kW		4.20	1.905		2,050	128		2,178	2,450
8710	8 kW		4	2		2,125	135		2,260	2,525
8720	10 kW		3.80	2.105		2,050	142		2,192	2,450
8730	12 kW		3.50	2.286		2,075	154		2,229	2,525
8740	13.5 kW		2.90	2.759		2,125	186		2,311	2,600
8750	16 kW		2.70	2.963		2,175	200		2,375	2,675
8760	20 kW		2.30	3.478		3,100	234		3,334	3,750
8770	24 kW		1.90	4.211		3,350	284		3,634	4,100
8790	Recessed, 2 kW		4.40	1.818		2,050	122		2,172	2,425
8810	3 kW		4.40	1.818		2,125	122		2,247	2,500
8820	4 kW		4.20	1.905		2,175	128		2,303	2,575
8830	5 kW		4.20	1.905		2,225	128		2,353	2,650
8840	6 kW		4	2		2,250	135		2,385	2,675
8850	8 kW		3.80	2.105		2,325	142		2,467	2,750
8860	10 kW		3.50	2.286		2,150	154		2,304	2,575
8870	12 kW		2.90	2.759		2,175	186		2,361	2,675
8880	13.5 kW		2.70	2.963		2,225	200		2,425	2,750
8890	16 kW		2.30	3.478		3,400	234		3,634	4,075
8900	20 kW		1.90	4.211		3,450	284		3,734	4,225
8920	24 kW		1.60	5		3,500	335		3,835	4,350
8940	Ceiling mount, 2 kW		3.20	2.500		2,050	168		2,218	2,500
8950	3 kW		3.20	2.500		2,125	168		2,293	2,575
8960	4 kW		3	2.667		2,175	180		2,355	2,650
8970	5 kW		3	2.667		2,225	180		2,405	2,725
8980	6 kW		2.80	2.857		2,250	192		2,442	2,750
8990	8 kW		2.40	3.333		2,125	225		2,350	2,675
9000	10 kW		2.20	3.636		2,650	245		2,895	3,300
9020	13.5 kW		1.50	5.333		2,700	360		3,060	3,475
9030	16 kW		1.30	6.154		3,400	415		3,815	4,350
9040	20 kW		.90	8.889		3,450	600		4,050	4,700
9060	24 kW		.60	13.333		3,275	900		4,175	4,925
9230	13.5 kW, 40,956 BTU		2.20	3.636		2,150	245		2,395	2,725
9250	24 kW, 81,912 BTU		2	4		2,375	269		2,644	3,000

23 91 Prefabricated Equipment Supports

23 91 10 – Prefabricated Curbs, Pads and Stands

23 91 10.10 Prefabricated Pads and Stands	Crew	Daily Output	Labor-Hours	Unit	Material	2023 Bare Costs Labor	Equipment	Total	Total Incl O&P
0010 **PREFABRICATED PADS AND STANDS**									
6000 Pad, fiberglass reinforced concrete with polystyrene foam core									
6220 30" x 36"	1 Shee	8	1	Ea.	78	70		148	192
6340 36" x 54"	Q-9	6	2.667	"	141	168		309	410

Division 26 Electrical

Estimating Tips

26 05 00 Common Work Results for Electrical

- Conduit should be taken off in three main categories—power distribution, branch power, and branch lighting—so the estimator can concentrate on systems and components, therefore making it easier to ensure all items have been accounted for.
- For cost modifications for elevated conduit installation, add the percentages to labor according to the height of installation and only to the quantities exceeding the different height levels, not to the total conduit quantities. Refer to subdivision 26 01 02.20 for labor adjustment factors.
- Remember that aluminum wiring of equal ampacity is larger in diameter than copper and may require larger conduit.
- If more than three wires at a time are being pulled, deduct percentages from the labor hours of that grouping of wires.
- When taking off grounding systems, identify separately the type and size of wire, and list each unique type of ground connection.
- The estimator should take the weights of materials into consideration when completing a takeoff. Topics to consider include: How will the materials be supported? What methods of support are available? How high will the support structure have to reach? Will the final support structure be able to withstand the total burden? Is the support material included or separate from the fixture, equipment, and material specified?
- Do not overlook the costs for equipment used in the installation. If scaffolding or highlifts are available in the field, contractors may use them in lieu of the proposed ladders and rolling staging.

26 20 00 Low-Voltage Electrical Transmission

- Supports and concrete pads may be shown on drawings for the larger equipment, or the support system may be only a piece of plywood for the back of a panelboard. In either case, they must be included in the costs.

26 40 00 Electrical and Cathodic Protection

- When taking off cathodic protection systems, identify the type and size of cable, and list each unique type of anode connection.

26 50 00 Lighting

- Fixtures should be taken off room by room using the fixture schedule, specifications, and the ceiling plan. For large concentrations of lighting fixtures in the same area, deduct the percentages from labor hours.

Reference Numbers

Reference numbers are shown at the beginning of some major classifications. These numbers refer to related items in the Reference Section. The reference information may be an estimating procedure, an alternate pricing method, or technical information.

Note: Not all subdivisions listed here necessarily appear. ∎

Same Data. Simplified.

Enjoy the convenience and efficiency of accessing your costs anywhere:

- **Skip the multiplier** by setting your location
- **Quickly search,** edit, favorite and share costs
- **Stay on top of price changes** with automatic updates

Discover more at rsmeans.com/online

No part of this cost data may be reproduced, stored in a retrieval system, or transmitted in any form or by any means without prior written permission of Gordian.

Note: "Powered in part by CINX™, based on licensed proprietary information of Harrison Publishing House, Inc."

Note: The following companies, in part, have been used as a reference source for some of the material prices used in Division 26:

Electriflex

Trade Service

26 05 Common Work Results for Electrical

26 05 33 – Raceway and Boxes for Electrical Systems

26 05 33.95 Cutting and Drilling		Crew	Daily Output	Labor-Hours	Unit	Material	2023 Bare Costs Labor	Equipment	Total	Total Incl O&P
0010	**CUTTING AND DRILLING**									
0100	Hole drilling to 10' high, concrete wall									
0110	8" thick, 1/2" pipe size	R-31	12	.667	Ea.	.30	45	5.10	50.40	72.50
0120	3/4" pipe size		12	.667		.30	45	5.10	50.40	72.50
0130	1" pipe size		9.50	.842		.40	56.50	6.45	63.35	92
0140	1-1/4" pipe size		9.50	.842		.40	56.50	6.45	63.35	92
0150	1-1/2" pipe size		9.50	.842		.40	56.50	6.45	63.35	92
0160	2" pipe size		4.40	1.818		.57	122	13.95	136.52	198
0170	2-1/2" pipe size		4.40	1.818		.57	122	13.95	136.52	198
0180	3" pipe size		4.40	1.818		.57	122	13.95	136.52	198
0190	3-1/2" pipe size		3.30	2.424		.76	163	18.60	182.36	264
0200	4" pipe size		3.30	2.424		.76	163	18.60	182.36	264
0500	12" thick, 1/2" pipe size		9.40	.851		.44	57.50	6.55	64.49	92.50
0520	3/4" pipe size		9.40	.851		.44	57.50	6.55	64.49	92.50
0540	1" pipe size		7.30	1.096		.61	74	8.40	83.01	120
0560	1-1/4" pipe size		7.30	1.096		.61	74	8.40	83.01	120
0570	1-1/2" pipe size		7.30	1.096		.61	74	8.40	83.01	120
0580	2" pipe size		3.60	2.222		.86	150	17.05	167.91	242
0590	2-1/2" pipe size		3.60	2.222		.86	150	17.05	167.91	242
0600	3" pipe size		3.60	2.222		.86	150	17.05	167.91	242
0610	3-1/2" pipe size		2.80	2.857		1.15	192	22	215.15	310
0630	4" pipe size		2.50	3.200		1.15	216	24.50	241.65	350
0650	16" thick, 1/2" pipe size		7.60	1.053		.59	71	8.10	79.69	115
0670	3/4" pipe size		7	1.143		.59	77	8.80	86.39	124
0690	1" pipe size		6	1.333		.81	90	10.25	101.06	145
0710	1-1/4" pipe size		5.50	1.455		.81	98	11.15	109.96	159
0730	1-1/2" pipe size		5.50	1.455		.81	98	11.15	109.96	159
0750	2" pipe size		3	2.667		1.15	180	20.50	201.65	291
0770	2-1/2" pipe size		2.70	2.963		1.15	200	23	224.15	325
0790	3" pipe size		2.50	3.200		1.15	216	24.50	241.65	350
0810	3-1/2" pipe size		2.30	3.478		1.53	234	26.50	262.03	380
0830	4" pipe size		2	4		1.53	269	30.50	301.03	435
0850	20" thick, 1/2" pipe size		6.40	1.250		.74	84	9.60	94.34	136
0870	3/4" pipe size		6	1.333		.74	90	10.25	100.99	145
0890	1" pipe size		5	1.600		1.01	108	12.30	121.31	175
0910	1-1/4" pipe size		4.80	1.667		1.01	112	12.80	125.81	182
0930	1-1/2" pipe size		4.60	1.739		1.01	117	13.35	131.36	190
0950	2" pipe size		2.70	2.963		1.43	200	23	224.43	325
0970	2-1/2" pipe size		2.40	3.333		1.43	225	25.50	251.93	365
0990	3" pipe size		2.20	3.636		1.43	245	28	274.43	395
1010	3-1/2" pipe size		2	4		1.91	269	30.50	301.41	435
1030	4" pipe size		1.70	4.706		1.91	315	36	352.91	510
1050	24" thick, 1/2" pipe size		5.50	1.455		.89	98	11.15	110.04	159
1070	3/4" pipe size		5.10	1.569		.89	106	12.05	118.94	171
1090	1" pipe size		4.30	1.860		1.21	125	14.30	140.51	203
1110	1-1/4" pipe size		4	2		1.21	135	15.35	151.56	218
1130	1-1/2" pipe size		4	2		1.21	135	15.35	151.56	218
1150	2" pipe size		2.40	3.333		1.72	225	25.50	252.22	365
1170	2-1/2" pipe size		2.20	3.636		1.72	245	28	274.72	395
1190	3" pipe size		2	4		1.72	269	30.50	301.22	435
1210	3-1/2" pipe size		1.80	4.444		2.29	299	34	335.29	485
1230	4" pipe size		1.50	5.333		2.29	360	41	403.29	585
1500	Brick wall, 8" thick, 1/2" pipe size		18	.444		.30	30	3.41	33.71	48.50

26 05 Common Work Results for Electrical

26 05 33 – Raceway and Boxes for Electrical Systems

26 05 33.95 Cutting and Drilling		Crew	Daily Output	Labor-Hours	Unit	Material	2023 Bare Costs Labor	Equipment	Total	Total Incl O&P
1520	3/4" pipe size	R-31	18	.444	Ea.	.30	30	3.41	33.71	48.50
1540	1" pipe size		13.30	.602		.40	40.50	4.62	45.52	65.50
1560	1-1/4" pipe size		13.30	.602		.40	40.50	4.62	45.52	65.50
1580	1-1/2" pipe size		13.30	.602		.40	40.50	4.62	45.52	65.50
1600	2" pipe size		5.70	1.404		.57	94.50	10.80	105.87	152
1620	2-1/2" pipe size		5.70	1.404		.57	94.50	10.80	105.87	152
1640	3" pipe size		5.70	1.404		.57	94.50	10.80	105.87	152
1660	3-1/2" pipe size		4.40	1.818		.76	122	13.95	136.71	198
1680	4" pipe size		4	2		.76	135	15.35	151.11	218
1700	12" thick, 1/2" pipe size		14.50	.552		.44	37	4.24	41.68	60
1720	3/4" pipe size		14.50	.552		.44	37	4.24	41.68	60
1740	1" pipe size		11	.727		.61	49	5.60	55.21	80
1760	1-1/4" pipe size		11	.727		.61	49	5.60	55.21	80
1780	1-1/2" pipe size		11	.727		.61	49	5.60	55.21	80
1800	2" pipe size		5	1.600		.86	108	12.30	121.16	174
1820	2-1/2" pipe size		5	1.600		.86	108	12.30	121.16	174
1840	3" pipe size		5	1.600		.86	108	12.30	121.16	174
1860	3-1/2" pipe size		3.80	2.105		1.15	142	16.15	159.30	230
1880	4" pipe size		3.30	2.424		1.15	163	18.60	182.75	265
1900	16" thick, 1/2" pipe size		12.30	.650		.59	44	5	49.59	71
1920	3/4" pipe size		12.30	.650		.59	44	5	49.59	71
1940	1" pipe size		9.30	.860		.81	58	6.60	65.41	94
1960	1-1/4" pipe size		9.30	.860		.81	58	6.60	65.41	94
1980	1-1/2" pipe size		9.30	.860		.81	58	6.60	65.41	94
2000	2" pipe size		4.40	1.818		1.15	122	13.95	137.10	199
2010	2-1/2" pipe size		4.40	1.818		1.15	122	13.95	137.10	199
2030	3" pipe size		4.40	1.818		1.15	122	13.95	137.10	199
2050	3-1/2" pipe size		3.30	2.424		1.53	163	18.60	183.13	265
2070	4" pipe size		3	2.667		1.53	180	20.50	202.03	291
2090	20" thick, 1/2" pipe size		10.70	.748		.74	50.50	5.75	56.99	82
2110	3/4" pipe size		10.70	.748		.74	50.50	5.75	56.99	82
2130	1" pipe size		8	1		1.01	67.50	7.70	76.21	110
2150	1-1/4" pipe size		8	1		1.01	67.50	7.70	76.21	110
2170	1-1/2" pipe size		8	1		1.01	67.50	7.70	76.21	110
2190	2" pipe size		4	2		1.43	135	15.35	151.78	218
2210	2-1/2" pipe size		4	2		1.43	135	15.35	151.78	218
2230	3" pipe size		4	2		1.43	135	15.35	151.78	218
2250	3-1/2" pipe size		3	2.667		1.91	180	20.50	202.41	292
2270	4" pipe size		2.70	2.963		1.91	200	23	224.91	325
2290	24" thick, 1/2" pipe size		9.40	.851		.89	57.50	6.55	64.94	93
2310	3/4" pipe size		9.40	.851		.89	57.50	6.55	64.94	93
2330	1" pipe size		7.10	1.127		1.21	76	8.65	85.86	124
2350	1-1/4" pipe size		7.10	1.127		1.21	76	8.65	85.86	124
2370	1-1/2" pipe size		7.10	1.127		1.21	76	8.65	85.86	124
2390	2" pipe size		3.60	2.222		1.72	150	17.05	168.77	243
2410	2-1/2" pipe size		3.60	2.222		1.72	150	17.05	168.77	243
2430	3" pipe size		3.60	2.222		1.72	150	17.05	168.77	243
2450	3-1/2" pipe size		2.80	2.857		2.29	192	22	216.29	315
2470	4" pipe size		2.50	3.200		2.29	216	24.50	242.79	350
3000	Knockouts to 8' high, metal boxes & enclosures									
3020	With hole saw, 1/2" pipe size	1 Elec	53	.151	Ea.		10.15		10.15	15.10
3040	3/4" pipe size		47	.170			11.45		11.45	17.05
3050	1" pipe size		40	.200			13.45		13.45	20

For customer support on your Plumbing Costs with RSMeans data, call 800.448.8182.

26 05 Common Work Results for Electrical

26 05 33 – Raceway and Boxes for Electrical Systems

26 05 33.95 Cutting and Drilling

		Crew	Daily Output	Labor-Hours	Unit	Material	2023 Bare Costs Labor	Equipment	Total	Total Incl O&P
3060	1-1/4" pipe size	1 Elec	36	.222	Ea.		14.95		14.95	22
3070	1-1/2" pipe size		32	.250			16.85		16.85	25
3080	2" pipe size		27	.296			19.95		19.95	29.50
3090	2-1/2" pipe size		20	.400			27		27	40
4010	3" pipe size		16	.500			33.50		33.50	50
4030	3-1/2" pipe size		13	.615			41.50		41.50	61.50
4050	4" pipe size		11	.727			49		49	73

26 05 83 – Wiring Connections

26 05 83.10 Motor Connections

		Crew	Daily Output	Labor-Hours	Unit	Material	Labor	Equipment	Total	Total Incl O&P
0010	**MOTOR CONNECTIONS**									
0020	Flexible conduit and fittings, 115 volt, 1 phase, up to 1 HP motor	1 Elec	8	1	Ea.	6.60	67.50		74.10	107
0050	2 HP motor		6.50	1.231		13.85	83		96.85	138
0100	3 HP motor		5.50	1.455		12.10	98		110.10	159
0110	230 volt, 3 phase, 3 HP motor		6.78	1.180		8	79.50		87.50	127
0112	5 HP motor		5.47	1.463		6.85	98.50		105.35	154
0114	7-1/2 HP motor		4.61	1.735		12.05	117		129.05	187
0120	10 HP motor		4.20	1.905		21.50	128		149.50	215
0150	15 HP motor		3.30	2.424		21.50	163		184.50	267
0200	25 HP motor		2.70	2.963		32	200		232	330
0400	50 HP motor		2.20	3.636		66.50	245		311.50	440
0600	100 HP motor		1.50	5.333		151	360		511	700

26 05 90 – Residential Applications

26 05 90.10 Residential Wiring

		Crew	Daily Output	Labor-Hours	Unit	Material	Labor	Equipment	Total	Total Incl O&P
0010	**RESIDENTIAL WIRING**									
0020	20' avg. runs and #14/2 wiring incl. unless otherwise noted									
1000	Service & panel, includes 24' SE-AL cable, service eye, meter,									
1010	Socket, panel board, main bkr., ground rod, 15 or 20 amp									
1020	1-pole circuit breakers, and misc. hardware									
1100	100 amp, with 10 branch breakers	1 Elec	1.19	6.723	Ea.	605	455		1,060	1,350
1110	With PVC conduit and wire		.92	8.696		695	585		1,280	1,625
1120	With RGS conduit and wire		.73	10.959		975	740		1,715	2,175
1150	150 amp, with 14 branch breakers		1.03	7.767		915	525		1,440	1,775
1170	With PVC conduit and wire		.82	9.756		1,075	655		1,730	2,175
1180	With RGS conduit and wire		.67	11.940		1,650	805		2,455	3,025
1200	200 amp, with 18 branch breakers	2 Elec	1.80	8.889		1,550	600		2,150	2,600
1220	With PVC conduit and wire		1.46	10.959		1,725	740		2,465	2,975
1230	With RGS conduit and wire		1.24	12.903		2,400	870		3,270	3,925
1800	Lightning surge suppressor	1 Elec	32	.250		93	16.85		109.85	128
2000	Switch devices									
2100	Single pole, 15 amp, ivory, with a 1-gang box, cover plate,									
2110	Type NM (Romex) cable	1 Elec	17.10	.468	Ea.	12.90	31.50		44.40	61
2120	Type MC cable		14.30	.559		23	37.50		60.50	81
2130	EMT & wire		5.71	1.401		54.50	94.50		149	200
2150	3-way, #14/3, type NM cable		14.55	.550		15.70	37		52.70	72.50
2170	Type MC cable		12.31	.650		30.50	44		74.50	98.50
2180	EMT & wire		5	1.600		59.50	108		167.50	225
2200	4-way, #14/3, type NM cable		14.55	.550		24	37		61	81.50
2220	Type MC cable		12.31	.650		38.50	44		82.50	108
2230	EMT & wire		5	1.600		67.50	108		175.50	234
2250	S.P., 20 amp, #12/2, type NM cable		13.33	.600		19.25	40.50		59.75	81
2270	Type MC cable		11.43	.700		27.50	47		74.50	100
2280	EMT & wire		4.85	1.649		59	111		170	230

26 05 Common Work Results for Electrical

26 05 90 – Residential Applications

26 05 90.10 Residential Wiring		Crew	Daily Output	Labor-Hours	Unit	Material	2023 Bare Costs Labor	Equipment	Total	Total Incl O&P
2290	S.P. rotary dimmer, 600 W, no wiring	1 Elec	17	.471	Ea.	30.50	31.50		62	80.50
2300	S.P. rotary dimmer, 600 W, type NM cable		14.55	.550		40	37		77	99
2320	Type MC cable		12.31	.650		50	44		94	120
2330	EMT & wire		5	1.600		86	108		194	255
2350	3-way rotary dimmer, type NM cable		13.33	.600		42.50	40.50		83	107
2370	Type MC cable		11.43	.700		52.50	47		99.50	128
2380	EMT & wire		4.85	1.649		88.50	111		199.50	262
2400	Interval timer wall switch, 20 amp, 1-30 min., #12/2									
2410	Type NM cable	1 Elec	14.55	.550	Ea.	91	37		128	155
2420	Type MC cable		12.31	.650		92	44		136	166
2430	EMT & wire		5	1.600		131	108		239	305
2500	Decorator style									
2510	S.P., 15 amp, type NM cable	1 Elec	17.10	.468	Ea.	19.40	31.50		50.90	68.50
2520	Type MC cable		14.30	.559		29.50	37.50		67	88.50
2530	EMT & wire		5.71	1.401		61	94.50		155.50	207
2550	3-way, #14/3, type NM cable		14.55	.550		22	37		59	79.50
2570	Type MC cable		12.31	.650		37	44		81	106
2580	EMT & wire		5	1.600		66	108		174	233
2600	4-way, #14/3, type NM cable		14.55	.550		30.50	37		67.50	88.50
2620	Type MC cable		12.31	.650		45	44		89	115
2630	EMT & wire		5	1.600		74	108		182	242
2650	S.P., 20 amp, #12/2, type NM cable		13.33	.600		26	40.50		66.50	88.50
2670	Type MC cable		11.43	.700		34	47		81	107
2680	EMT & wire		4.85	1.649		65.50	111		176.50	237
2700	S.P., slide dimmer, type NM cable		17.10	.468		44	31.50		75.50	95.50
2720	Type MC cable		14.30	.559		54.50	37.50		92	116
2730	EMT & wire		5.71	1.401		90	94.50		184.50	239
2750	S.P., touch dimmer, type NM cable		17.10	.468		38	31.50		69.50	88.50
2770	Type MC cable		14.30	.559		48	37.50		85.50	109
2780	EMT & wire		5.71	1.401		84	94.50		178.50	232
2800	3-way touch dimmer, type NM cable		13.33	.600		40	40.50		80.50	104
2820	Type MC cable		11.43	.700		50	47		97	125
2830	EMT & wire		4.85	1.649		86	111		197	260
3000	Combination devices									
3100	S.P. switch/15 amp recpt., ivory, 1-gang box, plate									
3110	Type NM cable	1 Elec	11.43	.700	Ea.	28	47		75	101
3120	Type MC cable		10	.800		38	54		92	122
3130	EMT & wire		4.40	1.818		74	122		196	263
3150	S.P. switch/pilot light, type NM cable		11.43	.700		29.50	47		76.50	103
3170	Type MC cable		10	.800		39.50	54		93.50	124
3180	EMT & wire		4.43	1.806		75.50	122		197.50	264
3190	2-S.P. switches, 2-#14/2, no wiring		14	.571		5.35	38.50		43.85	63
3200	2-S.P. switches, 2-#14/2, type NM cables		10	.800		34.50	54		88.50	118
3220	Type MC cable		8.89	.900		43	60.50		103.50	138
3230	EMT & wire		4.10	1.951		84	131		215	288
3250	3-way switch/15 amp recpt., #14/3, type NM cable		10	.800		37.50	54		91.50	122
3270	Type MC cable		8.89	.900		52.50	60.50		113	148
3280	EMT & wire		4.10	1.951		81.50	131		212.50	285
3300	2-3 way switches, 2-#14/3, type NM cables		8.89	.900		49	60.50		109.50	144
3320	Type MC cable		8	1		67	67.50		134.50	174
3330	EMT & wire		4	2		94	135		229	305
3350	S.P. switch/20 amp recpt., #12/2, type NM cable		10	.800		41.50	54		95.50	126
3370	Type MC cable		8.89	.900		42.50	60.50		103	137

26 05 Common Work Results for Electrical

26 05 90 – Residential Applications

26 05 90.10 Residential Wiring		Crew	Daily Output	Labor-Hours	Unit	Material	2023 Bare Costs Labor	Equipment	Total	Total Incl O&P
3380	EMT & wire	1 Elec	4.10	1.951	Ea.	81.50	131		212.50	285
3400	Decorator style									
3410	S.P. switch/15 amp recpt., type NM cable	1 Elec	11.43	.700	Ea.	34.50	47		81.50	108
3420	Type MC cable		10	.800		44.50	54		98.50	129
3430	EMT & wire		4.40	1.818		80.50	122		202.50	271
3450	S.P. switch/pilot light, type NM cable		11.43	.700		36	47		83	110
3470	Type MC cable		10	.800		46	54		100	131
3480	EMT & wire		4.40	1.818		82	122		204	273
3500	2-S.P. switches, 2-#14/2, type NM cables		10	.800		41	54		95	125
3520	Type MC cable		8.89	.900		49.50	60.50		110	145
3530	EMT & wire		4.10	1.951		90.50	131		221.50	295
3550	3-way/15 amp recpt., #14/3, type NM cable		10	.800		44.50	54		98.50	129
3570	Type MC cable		8.89	.900		59	60.50		119.50	155
3580	EMT & wire		4.10	1.951		88	131		219	292
3650	2-3 way switches, 2-#14/3, type NM cables		8.89	.900		55.50	60.50		116	151
3670	Type MC cable		8	1		73.50	67.50		141	181
3680	EMT & wire		4	2		101	135		236	310
3700	S.P. switch/20 amp recpt., #12/2, type NM cable		10	.800		48	54		102	133
3720	Type MC cable		8.89	.900		49	60.50		109.50	144
3730	EMT & wire		4.10	1.951		88	131		219	292
4000	Receptacle devices									
4010	Duplex outlet, 15 amp recpt., ivory, 1-gang box, plate									
4015	Type NM cable	1 Elec	14.55	.550	Ea.	13.45	37		50.45	70
4020	Type MC cable		12.31	.650		23.50	44		67.50	91
4030	EMT & wire		5.33	1.501		55	101		156	211
4050	With #12/2, type NM cable		12.31	.650		16.55	44		60.55	83
4070	Type MC cable		10.67	.750		24.50	50.50		75	102
4080	EMT & wire		4.71	1.699		56.50	114		170.50	232
4100	20 amp recpt., #12/2, type NM cable		12.31	.650		28	44		72	95.50
4120	Type MC cable		10.67	.750		36	50.50		86.50	115
4130	EMT & wire		4.71	1.699		68	114		182	245
4140	For GFI see Section 26 05 90.10 line 4300 below									
4150	Decorator style, 15 amp recpt., type NM cable	1 Elec	14.55	.550	Ea.	19.95	37		56.95	77
4170	Type MC cable		12.31	.650		30	44		74	98
4180	EMT & wire		5.33	1.501		61.50	101		162.50	218
4200	With #12/2, type NM cable		12.31	.650		23	44		67	90.50
4220	Type MC cable		10.67	.750		31	50.50		81.50	109
4230	EMT & wire		4.71	1.699		63	114		177	239
4250	20 amp recpt., #12/2, type NM cable		12.31	.650		34.50	44		78.50	103
4270	Type MC cable		10.67	.750		42.50	50.50		93	122
4280	EMT & wire		4.71	1.699		74.50	114		188.50	252
4300	GFI, 15 amp recpt., type NM cable		12.31	.650		32.50	44		76.50	101
4320	Type MC cable		10.67	.750		43	50.50		93.50	122
4330	EMT & wire		4.71	1.699		74.50	114		188.50	252
4350	GFI with #12/2, type NM cable		10.67	.750		36	50.50		86.50	115
4370	Type MC cable		9.20	.870		44	58.50		102.50	135
4380	EMT & wire		4.21	1.900		75.50	128		203.50	273
4400	20 amp recpt., #12/2, type NM cable		10.67	.750		53.50	50.50		104	134
4420	Type MC cable		9.20	.870		61.50	58.50		120	155
4430	EMT & wire		4.21	1.900		93.50	128		221.50	293
4500	Weather-proof cover for above receptacles, add		32	.250		4.48	16.85		21.33	30
4550	Air conditioner outlet, 20 amp-240 volt recpt.									
4560	30' of #12/2, 2 pole circuit breaker									

26 05 Common Work Results for Electrical

26 05 90 – Residential Applications

26 05 90.10 Residential Wiring

		Crew	Daily Output	Labor-Hours	Unit	Material	2023 Bare Costs Labor	2023 Bare Costs Equipment	Total	Total Incl O&P
4570	Type NM cable	1 Elec	10	.800	Ea.	94.50	54		148.50	184
4580	Type MC cable		9	.889		101	60		161	200
4590	EMT & wire		4	2		133	135		268	345
4600	Decorator style, type NM cable		10	.800		101	54		155	191
4620	Type MC cable		9	.889		108	60		168	207
4630	EMT & wire	↓	4	2	↓	140	135		275	355
4650	Dryer outlet, 30 amp-240 volt recpt., 20' of #10/3									
4660	2 pole circuit breaker									
4670	Type NM cable	1 Elec	6.41	1.248	Ea.	90.50	84		174.50	225
4680	Type MC cable		5.71	1.401		79.50	94.50		174	228
4690	EMT & wire	↓	3.48	2.299	↓	128	155		283	370
4700	Range outlet, 50 amp-240 volt recpt., 30' of #8/3									
4710	Type NM cable	1 Elec	4.21	1.900	Ea.	163	128		291	370
4720	Type MC cable		4	2		141	135		276	355
4730	EMT & wire		2.96	2.703		174	182		356	460
4750	Central vacuum outlet, type NM cable		6.40	1.250		93	84		177	227
4770	Type MC cable		5.71	1.401		90	94.50		184.50	240
4780	EMT & wire	↓	3.48	2.299	↓	145	155		300	390
4800	30 amp-110 volt locking recpt., #10/2 circ. bkr.									
4810	Type NM cable	1 Elec	6.20	1.290	Ea.	114	87		201	255
4830	EMT & wire	"	3.20	2.500	"	173	168		341	440
4900	Low voltage outlets									
4910	Telephone recpt., 20' of 4/C phone wire	1 Elec	26	.308	Ea.	10.55	20.50		31.05	42.50
4920	TV recpt., 20' of RG59U coax wire, F type connector	"	16	.500	"	18.75	33.50		52.25	70.50
4950	Door bell chime, transformer, 2 buttons, 60' of bellwire									
4970	Economy model	1 Elec	11.50	.696	Ea.	72	47		119	149
4980	Custom model		11.50	.696		120	47		167	202
4990	Luxury model, 3 buttons	↓	9.50	.842	↓	208	56.50		264.50	315
6000	Lighting outlets									
6050	Wire only (for fixture), type NM cable	1 Elec	32	.250	Ea.	13.45	16.85		30.30	40
6070	Type MC cable		24	.333		13	22.50		35.50	48
6080	EMT & wire		10	.800		43.50	54		97.50	128
6100	Box (4") and wire (for fixture), type NM cable		25	.320		23	21.50		44.50	57
6120	Type MC cable		20	.400		22.50	27		49.50	64.50
6130	EMT & wire	↓	11	.727	↓	53	49		102	132
6200	Fixtures (use with line 6050 or 6100 above)									
6210	Canopy style, economy grade	1 Elec	40	.200	Ea.	24.50	13.45		37.95	47
6220	Custom grade		40	.200		63.50	13.45		76.95	89.50
6250	Dining room chandelier, economy grade		19	.421		101	28.50		129.50	153
6260	Custom grade		19	.421		385	28.50		413.50	460
6270	Luxury grade		15	.533		3,200	36		3,236	3,575
6310	Kitchen fixture (fluorescent), economy grade		30	.267		90.50	17.95		108.45	126
6320	Custom grade		25	.320		220	21.50		241.50	274
6350	Outdoor, wall mounted, economy grade		30	.267		45	17.95		62.95	75.50
6360	Custom grade		30	.267		139	17.95		156.95	180
6370	Luxury grade		25	.320		248	21.50		269.50	305
6410	Outdoor PAR floodlights, 1 lamp, 150 watt		20	.400		17.85	27		44.85	59.50
6420	2 lamp, 150 watt each		20	.400		28.50	27		55.50	71.50
6430	For infrared security sensor, add		32	.250		114	16.85		130.85	150
6450	Outdoor, quartz-halogen, 300 watt flood		20	.400		48	27		75	93
6600	Recessed downlight, round, pre-wired, 50 or 75 watt trim		30	.267		56.50	17.95		74.45	89
6610	With shower light trim		30	.267		86.50	17.95		104.45	122
6620	With wall washer trim		28	.286		87	19.25		106.25	124

26 05 Common Work Results for Electrical

26 05 90 – Residential Applications

26 05 90.10 Residential Wiring		Crew	Daily Output	Labor-Hours	Unit	Material	2023 Bare Costs Labor	Equipment	Total	Total Incl O&P
6630	With eye-ball trim	1 Elec	28	.286	Ea.	36	19.25		55.25	68.50
6700	Porcelain lamp holder		40	.200		3.12	13.45		16.57	23.50
6710	With pull switch		40	.200		13.55	13.45		27	35
6750	Fluorescent strip, 2-20 watt tube, wrap around diffuser, 24"		24	.333		52	22.50		74.50	90.50
6770	2-34 watt tubes, 48"		20	.400		149	27		176	204
6800	Bathroom heat lamp, 1-250 watt		28	.286		41	19.25		60.25	73.50
6810	2-250 watt lamps	↓	28	.286	↓	72	19.25		91.25	108
6820	For timer switch, see Section 26 05 90.10 line 2400									
6900	Outdoor post lamp, incl. post, fixture, 35' of #14/2									
6910	Type NM cable	1 Elec	3.50	2.286	Ea.	405	154		559	675
6920	Photo-eye, add		27	.296		15.20	19.95		35.15	46
6950	Clock dial time switch, 24 hr., w/enclosure, type NM cable		11.43	.700		93	47		140	173
6970	Type MC cable		11	.727		103	49		152	187
6980	EMT & wire	↓	4.85	1.649	↓	135	111		246	315
7000	Alarm systems									
7050	Smoke detectors, box, #14/3, type NM cable	1 Elec	14.55	.550	Ea.	40.50	37		77.50	99.50
7070	Type MC cable		12.31	.650		47.50	44		91.50	118
7080	EMT & wire	↓	5	1.600	↓	76.50	108		184.50	244
7090	For relay output to security system, add					10.70			10.70	11.75
8000	Residential equipment									
8050	Disposal hook-up, incl. switch, outlet box, 3' of flex									
8060	20 amp-1 pole circ. bkr., and 25' of #12/2									
8070	Type NM cable	1 Elec	10	.800	Ea.	40	54		94	124
8080	Type MC cable		8	1		47.50	67.50		115	152
8090	EMT & wire	↓	5	1.600	↓	86	108		194	255
8100	Trash compactor or dishwasher hook-up, incl. outlet box,									
8110	3' of flex, 15 amp-1 pole circ. bkr., and 25' of #14/2									
8120	Type NM cable	1 Elec	10	.800	Ea.	34	54		88	117
8130	Type MC cable		8	1		45	67.50		112.50	150
8140	EMT & wire	↓	5	1.600	↓	79.50	108		187.50	248
8150	Hot water sink dispenser hook-up, use line 8100									
8200	Vent/exhaust fan hook-up, type NM cable	1 Elec	32	.250	Ea.	13.45	16.85		30.30	40
8220	Type MC cable		24	.333		13	22.50		35.50	48
8230	EMT & wire	↓	10	.800	↓	43.50	54		97.50	128
8250	Bathroom vent fan, 50 CFM (use with above hook-up)									
8260	Economy model	1 Elec	15	.533	Ea.	23.50	36		59.50	79
8270	Low noise model		15	.533		60	36		96	120
8280	Custom model	↓	12	.667	↓	120	45		165	199
8300	Bathroom or kitchen vent fan, 110 CFM									
8310	Economy model	1 Elec	15	.533	Ea.	75	36		111	136
8320	Low noise model	"	15	.533	"	121	36		157	187
8350	Paddle fan, variable speed (w/o lights)									
8360	Economy model (AC motor)	1 Elec	10	.800	Ea.	157	54		211	253
8362	With light kit		10	.800		201	54		255	300
8370	Custom model (AC motor)		10	.800		385	54		439	500
8372	With light kit		10	.800		425	54		479	550
8380	Luxury model (DC motor)		8	1		299	67.50		366.50	430
8382	With light kit		8	1		340	67.50		407.50	475
8390	Remote speed switch for above, add	↓	12	.667	↓	48.50	45		93.50	120
8500	Whole house exhaust fan, ceiling mount, 36", variable speed									
8510	Remote switch, incl. shutters, 20 amp-1 pole circ. bkr.									
8520	30' of #12/2, type NM cable	1 Elec	4	2	Ea.	1,675	135		1,810	2,025
8530	Type MC cable	↓	3.50	2.286		1,675	154		1,829	2,075

26 05 Common Work Results for Electrical

26 05 90 – Residential Applications

26 05 90.10 Residential Wiring

		Crew	Daily Output	Labor-Hours	Unit	Material	2023 Bare Costs Labor	Equipment	Total	Total Incl O&P
8540	EMT & wire	1 Elec	3	2.667	Ea.	1,725	180		1,905	2,175
8600	Whirlpool tub hook-up, incl. timer switch, outlet box									
8610	3' of flex, 20 amp-1 pole GFI circ. bkr.									
8620	30' of #12/2, type NM cable	1 Elec	5	1.600	Ea.	266	108		374	455
8630	Type MC cable		4.20	1.905		268	128		396	485
8640	EMT & wire	↓	3.40	2.353	↓	300	158		458	565
8650	Hot water heater hook-up, incl. 1-2 pole circ. bkr., box;									
8660	3' of flex, 20' of #10/2, type NM cable	1 Elec	5	1.600	Ea.	48.50	108		156.50	213
8670	Type MC cable		4.20	1.905		51	128		179	247
8680	EMT & wire	↓	3.40	2.353		78.50	158		236.50	320
9000	Heating/air conditioning									
9050	Furnace/boiler hook-up, incl. firestat, local on-off switch									
9060	Emergency switch, and 40' of type NM cable	1 Elec	4	2	Ea.	82	135		217	290
9070	Type MC cable		3.50	2.286		90.50	154		244.50	330
9080	EMT & wire	↓	1.50	5.333	↓	155	360		515	705
9100	Air conditioner hook-up, incl. local 60 amp disc. switch									
9110	3' sealtite, 40 amp, 2 pole circuit breaker									
9130	40' of #8/2, type NM cable	1 Elec	3.50	2.286	Ea.	239	154		393	490
9140	Type MC cable		3	2.667		224	180		404	515
9150	EMT & wire	↓	1.30	6.154		285	415		700	930
9200	Heat pump hook-up, 1-40 & 1-100 amp 2 pole circ. bkr.									
9210	Local disconnect switch, 3' sealtite									
9220	40' of #8/2 & 30' of #3/2									
9230	Type NM cable	1 Elec	1.30	6.154	Ea.	810	415		1,225	1,500
9240	Type MC cable		1.08	7.407		525	500		1,025	1,325
9250	EMT & wire	↓	.94	8.511	↓	765	575		1,340	1,700
9500	Thermostat hook-up, using low voltage wire									
9520	Heating only, 25' of #18-3	1 Elec	24	.333	Ea.	14	22.50		36.50	49
9530	Heating/cooling, 25' of #18-4	"	20	.400	"	15.05	27		42.05	56.50

26 24 Switchboards and Panelboards

26 24 19 – Motor-Control Centers

26 24 19.40 Motor Starters and Controls

		Crew	Daily Output	Labor-Hours	Unit	Material	2023 Bare Costs Labor	Equipment	Total	Total Incl O&P
0010	**MOTOR STARTERS AND CONTROLS**									
0050	Magnetic, FVNR, with enclosure and heaters, 480 volt									
0080	2 HP, size 00	1 Elec	3.50	2.286	Ea.	151	154		305	395
0100	5 HP, size 0		2.30	3.478		460	234		694	855
0200	10 HP, size 1	↓	1.60	5		214	335		549	735
0300	25 HP, size 2	2 Elec	2.20	7.273		425	490		915	1,200
0400	50 HP, size 3		1.80	8.889		705	600		1,305	1,675
0500	100 HP, size 4		1.20	13.333		1,600	900		2,500	3,075
0600	200 HP, size 5		.90	17.778		3,650	1,200		4,850	5,800
0610	400 HP, size 6	↓	.80	20		10,600	1,350		11,950	13,600
0620	NEMA 7, 5 HP, size 0	1 Elec	1.60	5		2,575	335		2,910	3,350
0630	10 HP, size 1	"	1.10	7.273		2,700	490		3,190	3,700
0640	25 HP, size 2	2 Elec	1.80	8.889		4,350	600		4,950	5,700
0650	50 HP, size 3		1.20	13.333		6,550	900		7,450	8,525
0660	100 HP, size 4		.90	17.778		8,450	1,200		9,650	11,100
0670	200 HP, size 5	↓	.50	32		13,700	2,150		15,850	18,300
0700	Combination, with motor circuit protectors, 5 HP, size 0	1 Elec	1.80	4.444		1,475	299		1,774	2,075
0800	10 HP, size 1	"	1.30	6.154	↓	1,550	415		1,965	2,325

26 24 Switchboards and Panelboards

26 24 19 – Motor-Control Centers

26 24 19.40 Motor Starters and Controls		Crew	Daily Output	Labor-Hours	Unit	Material	2023 Bare Costs Labor	Equipment	Total	Total Incl O&P
0900	25 HP, size 2	2 Elec	2	8	Ea.	2,150	540		2,690	3,150
1000	50 HP, size 3	"	1.32	12.121		3,125	815		3,940	4,650
1200	100 HP, size 4	↓	.80	20		6,850	1,350		8,200	9,525
1220	NEMA 7, 5 HP, size 0	1 Elec	1.30	6.154		3,450	415		3,865	4,425
1230	10 HP, size 1	"	1	8		3,550	540		4,090	4,700
1240	25 HP, size 2	2 Elec	1.32	12.121		4,725	815		5,540	6,425
1250	50 HP, size 3		.80	20		7,800	1,350		9,150	10,600
1260	100 HP, size 4		.60	26.667		12,200	1,800		14,000	16,100
1270	200 HP, size 5	↓	.40	40		26,400	2,700		29,100	33,000
1400	Combination, with fused switch, 5 HP, size 0	1 Elec	1.80	4.444		1,400	299		1,699	1,975
1600	10 HP, size 1	"	1.30	6.154		1,400	415		1,815	2,150
1800	25 HP, size 2	2 Elec	2	8		2,300	540		2,840	3,325
2000	50 HP, size 3		1.32	12.121		3,725	815		4,540	5,325
2200	100 HP, size 4	↓	.80	20		7,400	1,350		8,750	10,200
3500	Magnetic FVNR with NEMA 12, enclosure & heaters, 480 volt									
3600	5 HP, size 0	1 Elec	2.20	3.636	Ea.	260	245		505	650
3700	10 HP, size 1	"	1.50	5.333		390	360		750	965
3800	25 HP, size 2	2 Elec	2	8		735	540		1,275	1,600
3900	50 HP, size 3		1.60	10		1,125	675		1,800	2,250
4000	100 HP, size 4		1	16		2,700	1,075		3,775	4,575
4100	200 HP, size 5	↓	.80	20		6,475	1,350		7,825	9,125
4200	Combination, with motor circuit protectors, 5 HP, size 0	1 Elec	1.70	4.706		860	315		1,175	1,425
4300	10 HP, size 1	"	1.20	6.667		895	450		1,345	1,650
4400	25 HP, size 2	2 Elec	1.80	8.889		1,350	600		1,950	2,375
4500	50 HP, size 3		1.20	13.333		2,175	900		3,075	3,725
4600	100 HP, size 4	↓	.74	21.622		4,925	1,450		6,375	7,600
4700	Combination, with fused switch, 5 HP, size 0	1 Elec	1.70	4.706		710	315		1,025	1,250
4800	10 HP, size 1	"	1.20	6.667		735	450		1,185	1,475
4900	25 HP, size 2	2 Elec	1.80	8.889		1,125	600		1,725	2,125
5000	50 HP, size 3		1.20	13.333		1,800	900		2,700	3,300
5100	100 HP, size 4		.74	21.622	↓	3,650	1,450		5,100	6,200
5200	Factory installed controls, adders to size 0 thru 5									
5300	Start-stop push button	1 Elec	32	.250	Ea.	54.50	16.85		71.35	85
5400	Hand-off-auto-selector switch		32	.250		54.50	16.85		71.35	85
5500	Pilot light		32	.250		102	16.85		118.85	137
5600	Start-stop-pilot		32	.250		157	16.85		173.85	197
5700	Auxiliary contact, NO or NC		32	.250		75	16.85		91.85	108
5800	NO-NC	↓	32	.250		150	16.85		166.85	190

26 29 Low-Voltage Controllers

26 29 13 – Enclosed Controllers

26 29 13.20 Control Stations		Crew	Daily Output	Labor-Hours	Unit	Material	2023 Bare Costs Labor	Equipment	Total	Total Incl O&P
0010	**CONTROL STATIONS**									
0050	NEMA 1, heavy duty, stop/start	1 Elec	8	1	Ea.	335	67.50		402.50	470
0100	Stop/start, pilot light		6.20	1.290		370	87		457	540
0200	Hand/off/automatic		6.20	1.290		375	87		462	540
0400	Stop/start/reverse		5.30	1.509		485	102		587	685
0500	NEMA 7, heavy duty, stop/start		6	1.333		470	90		560	650
0600	Stop/start, pilot light	↓	4	2		680	135		815	950

Division 28 Electronic Safety & Security

Estimating Tips

- When estimating material costs for electronic safety and security systems, it is always prudent to obtain manufacturers' quotations for equipment prices and special installation requirements that may affect the total cost.
- Fire alarm systems consist of control panels, annunciator panels, batteries with rack, charger, and fire alarm actuating and indicating devices. Some fire alarm systems include speakers, telephone lines, door closer controls, and other components. Be careful not to overlook the costs related to installation for these items. Also be aware of costs for integrated automation instrumentation and terminal devices, control equipment, control wiring, and programming. Insurance underwriters may have specific requirements for the type of materials to be installed or design requirements based on the hazard to be protected. Local jurisdictions may have requirements not covered by code. It is advisable to be aware of any special conditions.
- Security equipment includes items such as CCTV, access control, and other detection and identification systems to perform alert and alarm functions. Be sure to consider the costs related to installation for this security equipment, such as for integrated automation instrumentation and terminal devices, control equipment, control wiring, and programming.

Reference Numbers

Reference numbers are shown at the beginning of some major classifications. These numbers refer to related items in the Reference Section. The reference information may be an estimating procedure, an alternate pricing method, or technical information.

Same Data. Simplified.

Enjoy the convenience and efficiency of accessing your costs anywhere:

- **Skip the multiplier** by setting your location
- **Quickly search,** edit, favorite and share costs
- **Stay on top of price changes** with automatic updates

Discover more at rsmeans.com/online

No part of this cost data may be reproduced, stored in a retrieval system, or transmitted in any form or by any means without prior written permission of Gordian.

Note: Trade Service, in part, has been used as a reference source for some of the material prices used in Division 28.

28 31 Intrusion Detection

28 31 16 – Intrusion Detection Systems Infrastructure

28 31 16.50 Intrusion Detection	Crew	Daily Output	Labor-Hours	Unit	Material	2023 Bare Costs Labor	Equipment	Total	Total Incl O&P
0010 **INTRUSION DETECTION**, not including wires & conduits									
0100 Burglar alarm, battery operated, mechanical trigger	1 Elec	4	2	Ea.	283	135		418	510
0200 Electrical trigger		4	2		340	135		475	570
0400 For outside key control, add		8	1		87	67.50		154.50	196
0600 For remote signaling circuitry, add		8	1		144	67.50		211.50	259
0800 Card reader, flush type, standard		2.70	2.963		680	200		880	1,050
1000 Multi-code	↓	2.70	2.963	↓	620	200		820	975

28 42 Gas Detection and Alarm

28 42 15 – Gas Detection Sensors

28 42 15.50 Tank Leak Detection Systems

	Crew	Daily Output	Labor-Hours	Unit	Material	Labor	Equipment	Total	Total Incl O&P
0010 **TANK LEAK DETECTION SYSTEMS** Liquid and vapor									
0100 For hydrocarbons and hazardous liquids/vapors									
0120 Controller, data acquisition, incl. printer, modem, RS232 port									
0140 24 channel, for use with all probes				Ea.	6,325			6,325	6,975
0160 9 channel, for external monitoring				"	2,125			2,125	2,325
0200 Probes									
0210 Well monitoring									
0220 Liquid phase detection				Ea.	845			845	930
0230 Hydrocarbon vapor, fixed position					1,025			1,025	1,125
0240 Hydrocarbon vapor, float mounted					775			775	855
0250 Both liquid and vapor hydrocarbon				↓	1,025			1,025	1,125
0300 Secondary containment, liquid phase									
0310 Pipe trench/manway sump				Ea.	875			875	965
0320 Double wall pipe and manual sump					735			735	810
0330 Double wall fiberglass annular space					525			525	580
0340 Double wall steel tank annular space				↓	320			320	350
0500 Accessories									
0510 Modem, non-dedicated phone line				Ea.	405			405	445
0600 Monitoring, internal									
0610 Automatic tank gauge, incl. overfill				Ea.	1,575			1,575	1,750
0620 Product line				"	1,650			1,650	1,800
0700 Monitoring, special									
0710 Cathodic protection				Ea.	895			895	985
0720 Annular space chemical monitor				"	1,225			1,225	1,350

28 46 Fire Detection and Alarm

28 46 11 – Fire Sensors and Detectors

28 46 11.27 Other Sensors

	Crew	Daily Output	Labor-Hours	Unit	Material	Labor	Equipment	Total	Total Incl O&P
0010 **OTHER SENSORS**									
5200 Smoke detector, ceiling type	1 Elec	6.20	1.290	Ea.	155	87		242	300
5240 Smoke detector, addressable type		6	1.333		241	90		331	400
5400 Duct type		3.20	2.500		330	168		498	615
5420 Duct addressable type	↓	3.20	2.500	↓	202	168		370	470

28 46 11.50 Fire and Heat Detectors

	Crew	Daily Output	Labor-Hours	Unit	Material	Labor	Equipment	Total	Total Incl O&P
0010 **FIRE & HEAT DETECTORS**									
5000 Detector, rate of rise	1 Elec	8	1	Ea.	33	67.50		100.50	137
5100 Fixed temp fire alarm	"	7	1.143	"	44	77		121	162

28 46 Fire Detection and Alarm

28 46 20 – Fire Alarm

28 46 20.50 Alarm Panels and Devices		Crew	Daily Output	Labor-Hours	Unit	Material	2023 Bare Costs Labor	Equipment	Total	Total Incl O&P
0010	**ALARM PANELS AND DEVICES**, not including wires & conduits									
3600	4 zone	2 Elec	2	8	Ea.	490	540		1,030	1,350
3700	5 zone		1.50	10.667		645	720		1,365	1,775
3800	8 zone		1	16		660	1,075		1,735	2,325
3900	10 zone		1.25	12.800		1,050	860		1,910	2,425
4000	12 zone		.67	23.988		2,875	1,625		4,500	5,550
4020	Alarm device, tamper, flow	1 Elec	8	1		227	67.50		294.50	350
4025	Fire alarm, loop expander card		16	.500		670	33.50		703.50	790
4050	Actuating device		8	1		370	67.50		437.50	505
4200	Battery and rack		4	2		520	135		655	770
4400	Automatic charger		8	1		590	67.50		657.50	750
4600	Signal bell		8	1		56.50	67.50		124	163
4610	Fire alarm signal bell 10" red 20-24 V P		8	1		205	67.50		272.50	325
4800	Trouble buzzer or manual station		8	1		85	67.50		152.50	194
5425	Duct smoke and heat detector 2 wire		8	1		179	67.50		246.50	296
5430	Fire alarm duct detector controller		3	2.667		222	180		402	510
5435	Fire alarm duct detector sensor kit		8	1		86	67.50		153.50	195
5440	Remote test station for smoke detector duct type		5.30	1.509		59	102		161	216
5460	Remote fire alarm indicator light		5.30	1.509		30.50	102		132.50	185
5600	Strobe and horn		5.30	1.509		105	102		207	267
5610	Strobe and horn (ADA type)		5.30	1.509		132	102		234	296
5620	Visual alarm (ADA type)		6.70	1.194		116	80.50		196.50	247
5800	electric bell		6.70	1.194		56.50	80.50		137	182
6000	Door holder, electro-magnetic		4	2		106	135		241	315
6200	Combination holder and closer		3.20	2.500		176	168		344	445
6600	Drill switch		8	1		545	67.50		612.50	700
6800	Master box		2.70	2.963		6,575	200		6,775	7,550
7000	Break glass station		8	1		65	67.50		132.50	172
7800	Remote annunciator, 8 zone lamp		1.80	4.444		345	299		644	825
8000	12 zone lamp	2 Elec	2.60	6.154		455	415		870	1,125
8200	16 zone lamp	"	2.20	7.273		440	490		930	1,225

Division Notes

	CREW	DAILY OUTPUT	LABOR-HOURS	UNIT	BARE COSTS				TOTAL INCL O&P
					MAT.	LABOR	EQUIP.	TOTAL	

Division 31 Earthwork

Estimating Tips
31 05 00 Common Work Results for Earthwork

- Estimating the actual cost of performing earthwork requires careful consideration of the variables involved. This includes items such as type of soil, whether water will be encountered, dewatering, whether banks need bracing, disposal of excavated earth, and length of haul to fill or spoil sites, etc. If the project has large quantities of cut or fill, consider raising or lowering the site to reduce costs, while paying close attention to the effect on site drainage and utilities.
- If the project has large quantities of fill, creating a borrow pit on the site can significantly lower the costs.
- It is very important to consider what time of year the project is scheduled for completion. Bad weather can create large cost overruns from dewatering, site repair, and lost productivity from cold weather.

Reference Numbers
Reference numbers are shown at the beginning of some major classifications. These numbers refer to related items in the Reference Section. The reference information may be an estimating procedure, an alternate pricing method, or technical information.

Note: Not all subdivisions listed here necessarily appear. ■

Same Data. Simplified.

Enjoy the convenience and efficiency of accessing your costs anywhere:
- **Skip the multiplier** by setting your location
- **Quickly search,** edit, favorite and share costs
- **Stay on top of price changes** with automatic updates

Discover more at rsmeans.com/online

No part of this cost data may be reproduced, stored in a retrieval system, or transmitted in any form or by any means without prior written permission of Gordian.

31 23 Excavation and Fill

31 23 16 – Excavation

31 23 16.13 Excavating, Trench

		Crew	Daily Output	Labor-Hours	Unit	Material	2023 Bare Costs Labor	2023 Bare Costs Equipment	Total	Total Incl O&P
0010	**EXCAVATING, TRENCH** G1030-805									
0011	Or continuous footing									
0020	Common earth with no sheeting or dewatering included									
0050	1' to 4' deep, 3/8 C.Y. excavator	B-11C	150	.107	B.C.Y.		5.90	1.85	7.75	10.80
0060	1/2 C.Y. excavator	B-11M	200	.080			4.41	1.79	6.20	8.50
0090	4' to 6' deep, 1/2 C.Y. excavator	"	200	.080			4.41	1.79	6.20	8.50
0100	5/8 C.Y. excavator	B-12Q	250	.064			3.63	3.25	6.88	9
0300	1/2 C.Y. excavator, truck mounted	B-12J	200	.080			4.54	4.40	8.94	11.60
0500	6' to 10' deep, 3/4 C.Y. excavator	B-12F	225	.071			4.04	4.07	8.11	10.50
0600	1 C.Y. excavator, truck mounted	B-12K	400	.040			2.27	3.80	6.07	7.55
0900	10' to 14' deep, 3/4 C.Y. excavator	B-12F	200	.080			4.54	4.58	9.12	11.80
1000	1-1/2 C.Y. excavator	B-12B	540	.030			1.68	2.19	3.87	4.91
1300	14' to 20' deep, 1 C.Y. excavator	B-12A	320	.050			2.84	3.08	5.92	7.60
1340	20' to 24' deep, 1 C.Y. excavator	"	288	.056			3.15	3.43	6.58	8.45
1352	4' to 6' deep, 1/2 C.Y. excavator w/trench box	B-13H	188	.085			4.83	5.40	10.23	13.10
1354	5/8 C.Y. excavator	"	235	.068			3.87	4.31	8.18	10.50
1362	6' to 10' deep, 3/4 C.Y. excavator w/trench box	B-13G	212	.075			4.29	4.94	9.23	11.85
1374	10' to 14' deep, 3/4 C.Y. excavator w/trench box	"	188	.085			4.83	5.55	10.38	13.35
1376	1-1/2 C.Y. excavator	B-13E	508	.032			1.79	2.59	4.38	5.50
1381	14' to 20' deep, 1 C.Y. excavator w/trench box	B-13D	301	.053			3.02	3.71	6.73	8.60
1386	20' to 24' deep, 1 C.Y. excavator w/trench box	"	271	.059			3.35	4.13	7.48	9.55
1400	By hand with pick and shovel 2' to 6' deep, light soil	1 Clab	8	1			47.50		47.50	70.50
1500	Heavy soil	"	4	2			94.50		94.50	141
1700	For tamping backfilled trenches, air tamp, add	A-1G	100	.080			3.78	.88	4.66	6.60
1900	Vibrating plate, add	B-18	180	.133			6.40	.81	7.21	10.40
2100	Trim sides and bottom for concrete pours, common earth		1500	.016	S.F.		.77	.10	.87	1.25
2300	Hardpan		600	.040	"		1.92	.24	2.16	3.12
5020	Loam & sandy clay with no sheeting or dewatering included									
5050	1' to 4' deep, 3/8 C.Y. tractor loader/backhoe	B-11C	162	.099	B.C.Y.		5.45	1.71	7.16	10
5060	1/2 C.Y. excavator	B-11M	216	.074			4.09	1.66	5.75	7.90
5080	4' to 6' deep, 1/2 C.Y. excavator	"	216	.074			4.09	1.66	5.75	7.90
5090	5/8 C.Y. excavator	B-12Q	276	.058			3.29	2.95	6.24	8.15
5130	1/2 C.Y. excavator, truck mounted	B-12J	216	.074			4.21	4.08	8.29	10.75
5140	6' to 10' deep, 3/4 C.Y. excavator	B-12F	243	.066			3.74	3.77	7.51	9.70
5160	1 C.Y. excavator, truck mounted	B-12K	432	.037			2.10	3.52	5.62	7
5190	10' to 14' deep, 3/4 C.Y. excavator	B-12F	216	.074			4.21	4.24	8.45	10.90
5210	1-1/2 C.Y. excavator	B-12B	583	.027			1.56	2.03	3.59	4.56
5250	14' to 20' deep, 1 C.Y. excavator	B-12A	346	.046			2.63	2.85	5.48	7.05
5300	20' to 24' deep, 1 C.Y. excavator	"	311	.051			2.92	3.17	6.09	7.85
5352	4' to 6' deep, 1/2 C.Y. excavator w/trench box	B-13H	205	.078			4.43	4.94	9.37	12.05
5354	5/8 C.Y. excavator	"	257	.062			3.53	3.94	7.47	9.60
5362	6' to 10' deep, 3/4 C.Y. excavator w/trench box	B-13G	231	.069			3.93	4.53	8.46	10.85
5370	10' to 14' deep, 3/4 C.Y. excavator w/trench box	"	205	.078			4.43	5.10	9.53	12.20
5374	1-1/2 C.Y. excavator	B-13E	554	.029			1.64	2.38	4.02	5.05
5382	14' to 20' deep, 1 C.Y. excavator w/trench box	B-13D	329	.049			2.76	3.40	6.16	7.85
5392	20' to 24' deep, 1 C.Y. excavator w/trench box	"	295	.054			3.08	3.79	6.87	8.75
6020	Sand & gravel with no sheeting or dewatering included									
6050	1' to 4' deep, 3/8 C.Y. excavator	B-11C	165	.097	B.C.Y.		5.35	1.68	7.03	9.80
6060	1/2 C.Y. excavator	B-11M	220	.073			4.01	1.63	5.64	7.75
6080	4' to 6' deep, 1/2 C.Y. excavator	"	220	.073			4.01	1.63	5.64	7.75
6090	5/8 C.Y. excavator	B-12Q	275	.058			3.30	2.96	6.26	8.15
6130	1/2 C.Y. excavator, truck mounted	B-12J	220	.073			4.13	4	8.13	10.55
6140	6' to 10' deep, 3/4 C.Y. excavator	B-12F	248	.065			3.66	3.69	7.35	9.50

31 23 Excavation and Fill

31 23 16 – Excavation

31 23 16.13 Excavating, Trench

		Crew	Daily Output	Labor-Hours	Unit	Material	2023 Bare Costs Labor	2023 Bare Costs Equipment	Total	Total Incl O&P
6160	1 C.Y. excavator, truck mounted	B-12K	440	.036	B.C.Y.		2.06	3.46	5.52	6.85
6190	10' to 14' deep, 3/4 C.Y. excavator	B-12F	220	.073			4.13	4.16	8.29	10.75
6210	1-1/2 C.Y. excavator	B-12B	594	.027			1.53	2	3.53	4.48
6250	14' to 20' deep, 1 C.Y. excavator	B-12A	352	.045			2.58	2.80	5.38	6.90
6300	20' to 24' deep, 1 C.Y. excavator	"	317	.050			2.87	3.11	5.98	7.70
6352	4' to 6' deep, 1/2 C.Y. excavator w/trench box	B-13H	209	.077			4.35	4.84	9.19	11.80
6354	5/8 C.Y. excavator	"	261	.061			3.48	3.88	7.36	9.45
6362	6' to 10' deep, 3/4 C.Y. excavator w/trench box	B-13G	236	.068			3.85	4.44	8.29	10.65
6370	10' to 14' deep, 3/4 C.Y. excavator w/trench box	"	209	.077			4.35	5	9.35	11.95
6374	1-1/2 C.Y. excavator	B-13E	564	.028			1.61	2.33	3.94	4.97
6382	14' to 20' deep, 1 C.Y. excavator w/trench box	B-13D	334	.048			2.72	3.35	6.07	7.75
6392	20' to 24' deep, 1 C.Y. excavator w/trench box	"	301	.053			3.02	3.71	6.73	8.60
7020	Dense hard clay with no sheeting or dewatering included									
7050	1' to 4' deep, 3/8 C.Y. excavator	B-11C	132	.121	B.C.Y.		6.70	2.10	8.80	12.25
7060	1/2 C.Y. excavator	B-11M	176	.091			5	2.03	7.03	9.70
7080	4' to 6' deep, 1/2 C.Y. excavator	"	176	.091			5	2.03	7.03	9.70
7090	5/8 C.Y. excavator	B-12Q	220	.073			4.13	3.70	7.83	10.20
7130	1/2 C.Y. excavator, truck mounted	B-12J	176	.091			5.15	5	10.15	13.20
7140	6' to 10' deep, 3/4 C.Y. excavator	B-12F	198	.081			4.59	4.62	9.21	11.95
7160	1 C.Y. excavator, truck mounted	B-12K	352	.045			2.58	4.32	6.90	8.60
7190	10' to 14' deep, 3/4 C.Y. excavator	B-12F	176	.091			5.15	5.20	10.35	13.40
7210	1-1/2 C.Y. excavator	B-12B	475	.034			1.91	2.50	4.41	5.60
7250	14' to 20' deep, 1 C.Y. excavator	B-12A	282	.057			3.22	3.50	6.72	8.65
7300	20' to 24' deep, 1 C.Y. excavator	"	254	.063			3.58	3.88	7.46	9.55

31 23 16.14 Excavating, Utility Trench

		Crew	Daily Output	Labor-Hours	Unit	Material	2023 Bare Costs Labor	2023 Bare Costs Equipment	Total	Total Incl O&P
0010	**EXCAVATING, UTILITY TRENCH** G1030-805									
0011	Common earth									
0050	Trenching with chain trencher, 12 HP, operator walking									
0100	4" wide trench, 12" deep	B-53	800	.010	L.F.		.60	.25	.85	1.17
0150	18" deep		750	.011			.64	.27	.91	1.25
0200	24" deep		700	.011			.68	.29	.97	1.34
0300	6" wide trench, 12" deep		650	.012			.73	.31	1.04	1.43
0350	18" deep		600	.013			.80	.34	1.14	1.55
0400	24" deep		550	.015			.87	.37	1.24	1.69
0450	36" deep		450	.018			1.06	.45	1.51	2.07
0600	8" wide trench, 12" deep		475	.017			1.01	.43	1.44	1.97
0650	18" deep		400	.020			1.19	.51	1.70	2.34
0700	24" deep		350	.023			1.36	.58	1.94	2.67
0750	36" deep		300	.027			1.59	.67	2.26	3.11
1000	Backfill by hand including compaction, add									
1050	4" wide trench, 12" deep	A-1G	800	.010	L.F.		.47	.11	.58	.82
1100	18" deep		530	.015			.71	.17	.88	1.24
1150	24" deep		400	.020			.95	.22	1.17	1.65
1300	6" wide trench, 12" deep		540	.015			.70	.16	.86	1.22
1350	18" deep		405	.020			.93	.22	1.15	1.63
1400	24" deep		270	.030			1.40	.33	1.73	2.44
1450	36" deep		180	.044			2.10	.49	2.59	3.67
1600	8" wide trench, 12" deep		400	.020			.95	.22	1.17	1.65
1650	18" deep		265	.030			1.43	.33	1.76	2.49
1700	24" deep		200	.040			1.89	.44	2.33	3.29
1750	36" deep		135	.059			2.80	.65	3.45	4.89
2000	Chain trencher, 40 HP operator riding									

31 23 Excavation and Fill

31 23 16 – Excavation

31 23 16.14 Excavating, Utility Trench

		Crew	Daily Output	Labor-Hours	Unit	Material	2023 Bare Costs Labor	Equipment	Total	Total Incl O&P
2050	6" wide trench and backfill, 12" deep	B-54	1200	.007	L.F.		.40	.32	.72	.94
2100	18" deep		1000	.008			.48	.39	.87	1.14
2150	24" deep		975	.008			.49	.40	.89	1.17
2200	36" deep		900	.009			.53	.43	.96	1.26
2250	48" deep		750	.011			.64	.52	1.16	1.52
2300	60" deep		650	.012			.73	.59	1.32	1.74
2400	8" wide trench and backfill, 12" deep		1000	.008			.48	.39	.87	1.14
2450	18" deep		950	.008			.50	.41	.91	1.20
2500	24" deep		900	.009			.53	.43	.96	1.26
2550	36" deep		800	.010			.60	.48	1.08	1.42
2600	48" deep		650	.012			.73	.59	1.32	1.74
2700	12" wide trench and backfill, 12" deep		975	.008			.49	.40	.89	1.17
2750	18" deep		860	.009			.56	.45	1.01	1.32
2800	24" deep		800	.010			.60	.48	1.08	1.42
2850	36" deep		725	.011			.66	.53	1.19	1.57
3000	16" wide trench and backfill, 12" deep		835	.010			.57	.46	1.03	1.36
3050	18" deep		750	.011			.64	.52	1.16	1.52
3100	24" deep	▼	700	.011	▼		.68	.55	1.23	1.63
3200	Compaction with vibratory plate, add								35%	35%
5100	Hand excavate and trim for pipe bells after trench excavation									
5200	8" pipe	1 Clab	155	.052	L.F.		2.44		2.44	3.63
5300	18" pipe	"	130	.062	"		2.91		2.91	4.33

31 23 19 – Dewatering

31 23 19.20 Dewatering Systems

		Crew	Daily Output	Labor-Hours	Unit	Material	2023 Bare Costs Labor	Equipment	Total	Total Incl O&P
0010	**DEWATERING SYSTEMS**									
0020	Excavate drainage trench, 2' wide, 2' deep	B-11C	90	.178	C.Y.		9.80	3.08	12.88	18
0100	2' wide, 3' deep, with backhoe loader	"	135	.119			6.55	2.05	8.60	12
0200	Excavate sump pits by hand, light soil	1 Clab	7.10	1.127			53		53	79.50
0300	Heavy soil	"	3.50	2.286	▼		108		108	161
0500	Pumping 8 hrs., attended 2 hrs./day, incl. 20 L.F.									
0550	of suction hose & 100 L.F. discharge hose									
0600	2" diaphragm pump used for 8 hrs.	B-10H	4	3	Day		173	18.65	191.65	279
0650	4" diaphragm pump used for 8 hrs.	B-10I	4	3			173	49.50	222.50	315
0800	8 hrs. attended, 2" diaphragm pump	B-10H	1	12			695	74.50	769.50	1,100
0900	3" centrifugal pump	B-10J	1	12			695	101	796	1,125
1000	4" diaphragm pump	B-10I	1	12			695	198	893	1,250
1100	6" centrifugal pump	B-10K	1	12	▼		695	455	1,150	1,525
1300	CMP, incl. excavation 3' deep, 12" diameter	B-6	115	.209	L.F.	13.90	10.75	2.41	27.06	34
1400	18" diameter		100	.240	"	21.50	12.35	2.77	36.62	45.50
1600	Sump hole construction, incl. excavation and gravel, pit		1250	.019	C.F.	1.08	.99	.22	2.29	2.90
1700	With 12" gravel collar, 12" pipe, corrugated, 16 ga.		70	.343	L.F.	22.50	17.60	3.96	44.06	55.50
1800	15" pipe, corrugated, 16 ga.		55	.436		29.50	22.50	5.05	57.05	71.50
1900	18" pipe, corrugated, 16 ga.		50	.480		34.50	24.50	5.55	64.55	80
2000	24" pipe, corrugated, 14 ga.		40	.600	▼	41	31	6.95	78.95	99
2200	Wood lining, up to 4' x 4', add	▼	300	.080	SFCA	15.30	4.11	.92	20.33	24
9950	See Section 31 23 19.40 for wellpoints									
9960	See Section 31 23 19.30 for deep well systems									

31 23 19.30 Wells

		Crew	Daily Output	Labor-Hours	Unit	Material	2023 Bare Costs Labor	Equipment	Total	Total Incl O&P
0010	**WELLS**									
0011	For dewatering 10' to 20' deep, 2' diameter									
0020	with steel casing, minimum	B-6	165	.145	V.L.F.	36	7.50	1.68	45.18	53
0050	Average	▼	98	.245		44	12.60	2.83	59.43	70.50

31 23 Excavation and Fill

31 23 19 – Dewatering

31 23 19.30 Wells

		Crew	Daily Output	Labor-Hours	Unit	Material	2023 Bare Costs Labor	2023 Bare Costs Equipment	Total	Total Incl O&P
0100	Maximum	B-6	49	.490	V.L.F.	50	25	5.65	80.65	98.50
0300	For dewatering pumps see 01 54 33 in Reference Section									
0500	For domestic water wells, see Section 33 21 13.10									

31 23 19.40 Wellpoints

		Crew	Daily Output	Labor-Hours	Unit	Material	Labor	Equipment	Total	Total Incl O&P
0010	**WELLPOINTS** R312319-90									
0011	For equipment rental, see 01 54 33 in Reference Section									
0100	Installation and removal of single stage system									
0110	Labor only, 0.75 labor-hours per L.F.	1 Clab	10.70	.748	LF Hdr		35.50		35.50	52.50
0200	2.0 labor-hours per L.F.	"	4	2	"		94.50		94.50	141
0400	Pump operation, 4 @ 6 hr. shifts									
0410	Per 24 hr. day	4 Eqlt	1.27	25.197	Day		1,500		1,500	2,250
0500	Per 168 hr. week, 160 hr. straight, 8 hr. double time		.18	178	Week		10,600		10,600	15,800
0550	Per 4.3 week month		.04	800	Month		47,800		47,800	71,000
0600	Complete installation, operation, equipment rental, fuel &									
0610	removal of system with 2" wellpoints 5' OC									
0700	100' long header, 6" diameter, first month	4 Eqlt	3.23	9.907	LF Hdr	154	590		744	1,050
0800	Thereafter, per month		4.13	7.748		123	465		588	825
1000	200' long header, 8" diameter, first month		6	5.333		147	320		467	635
1100	Thereafter, per month		8.39	3.814		69	228		297	415
1300	500' long header, 8" diameter, first month		10.63	3.010		54	180		234	325
1400	Thereafter, per month		20.91	1.530		38.50	91.50		130	179
1600	1,000' long header, 10" diameter, first month		11.62	2.754		46	164		210	296
1700	Thereafter, per month		41.81	.765		23	45.50		68.50	93.50
1900	Note: above figures include pumping 168 hrs. per week,									
1910	the pump operator, and one stand-by pump.									

31 23 23 – Fill

31 23 23.15 Borrow, Loading and/or Spreading

		Crew	Daily Output	Labor-Hours	Unit	Material	Labor	Equipment	Total	Total Incl O&P
0010	**BORROW, LOADING AND/OR SPREADING**									
0020	Material only, bank run gravel				Ton	32.50			32.50	35.50
0500	Haul 2 mi. spread, 200 HP dozer, bank run gravel	B-15	1100	.025			1.44	2.70	4.14	5.10
1000	Hand spread, bank run gravel	A-5	33	.545			26	2.74	28.74	42
1800	Delivery charge, minimum 20 tons, 1 hr. round trip, add	B-34B	130	.062			3.41	6.10	9.51	11.80
1820	1-1/2 hr. round trip, add		93	.086			4.77	8.50	13.27	16.50
1840	2 hr. round trip, add		65	.123			6.80	12.15	18.95	23.50

31 23 23.16 Fill By Borrow and Utility Bedding

		Crew	Daily Output	Labor-Hours	Unit	Material	Labor	Equipment	Total	Total Incl O&P
0010	**FILL BY BORROW AND UTILITY BEDDING**									
0049	Utility bedding, for pipe & conduit, not incl. compaction G1030–805									
0050	Crushed or screened bank run gravel	B-6	150	.160	L.C.Y.	51.50	8.20	1.85	61.55	71
0100	Crushed stone 3/4" to 1/2"		150	.160		38.50	8.20	1.85	48.55	57
0200	Sand, dead or bank		150	.160		13.85	8.20	1.85	23.90	29.50
0500	Compacting bedding in trench	A-1D	90	.089	B.C.Y.		4.20	1.60	5.80	8
0600	If material source exceeds 2 miles, add for extra mileage.									
0610	See Section 31 23 23.20 for hauling mileage add.									

31 23 23.17 General Fill

		Crew	Daily Output	Labor-Hours	Unit	Material	Labor	Equipment	Total	Total Incl O&P
0010	**GENERAL FILL**									
0011	Spread dumped material, no compaction									
0020	By dozer	B-10B	1000	.012	L.C.Y.		.69	1.38	2.07	2.55
0100	By hand	1 Clab	12	.667	"		31.50		31.50	47
0500	Gravel fill, compacted, under floor slabs, 4" deep	B-37	10000	.005	S.F.	.52	.24	.03	.79	.95
0600	6" deep		8600	.006		.77	.28	.03	1.08	1.30
0700	9" deep		7200	.007		1.29	.33	.04	1.66	1.95

31 23 Excavation and Fill

31 23 23 – Fill

31 23 23.17 General Fill		Crew	Daily Output	Labor-Hours	Unit	Material	2023 Bare Costs Labor	Equipment	Total	Total Incl O&P
0800	12" deep	B-37	6000	.008	S.F.	1.81	.40	.05	2.26	2.63
1000	Alternate pricing method, 4" deep		120	.400	B.C.Y.	38.50	19.85	2.40	60.75	74.50
1100	6" deep		160	.300		38.50	14.90	1.80	55.20	66.50
1200	9" deep		200	.240		38.50	11.90	1.44	51.84	62
1300	12" deep		220	.218		38.50	10.85	1.31	50.66	60
1400	Granular fill				L.C.Y.	26			26	28.50

31 23 23.20 Hauling

		Crew	Daily Output	Labor-Hours	Unit	Material	Labor	Equipment	Total	Total Incl O&P
0010	**HAULING**									
0011	Excavated or borrow, loose cubic yards									
0012	no loading equipment, including hauling, waiting, loading/dumping									
0013	time per cycle (wait, load, travel, unload or dump & return)									
0014	8 C.Y. truck, 15 MPH avg., cycle 0.5 miles, 10 min. wait/ld./uld.	B-34A	320	.025	L.C.Y.		1.39	1.30	2.69	3.51
0016	cycle 1 mile		272	.029			1.63	1.54	3.17	4.13
0018	cycle 2 miles		208	.038			2.13	2.01	4.14	5.40
0020	cycle 4 miles		144	.056			3.08	2.90	5.98	7.80
0022	cycle 6 miles		112	.071			3.96	3.73	7.69	10
0024	cycle 8 miles		88	.091			5.05	4.74	9.79	12.75
0026	20 MPH avg., cycle 0.5 mile		336	.024			1.32	1.24	2.56	3.34
0028	cycle 1 mile		296	.027			1.50	1.41	2.91	3.79
0030	cycle 2 miles		240	.033			1.85	1.74	3.59	4.67
0032	cycle 4 miles		176	.045			2.52	2.37	4.89	6.40
0034	cycle 6 miles		136	.059			3.26	3.07	6.33	8.25
0036	cycle 8 miles		112	.071			3.96	3.73	7.69	10
0044	25 MPH avg., cycle 4 miles		192	.042			2.31	2.17	4.48	5.85
0046	cycle 6 miles		160	.050			2.77	2.61	5.38	7
0048	cycle 8 miles		128	.063			3.47	3.26	6.73	8.80
0050	30 MPH avg., cycle 4 miles		216	.037			2.05	1.93	3.98	5.20
0052	cycle 6 miles		176	.045			2.52	2.37	4.89	6.40
0054	cycle 8 miles		144	.056			3.08	2.90	5.98	7.80
0114	15 MPH avg., cycle 0.5 mile, 15 min. wait/ld./uld.		224	.036			1.98	1.86	3.84	5
0116	cycle 1 mile		200	.040			2.22	2.09	4.31	5.60
0118	cycle 2 miles		168	.048			2.64	2.49	5.13	6.70
0120	cycle 4 miles		120	.067			3.70	3.48	7.18	9.35
0122	cycle 6 miles		96	.083			4.62	4.35	8.97	11.70
0124	cycle 8 miles		80	.100			5.55	5.20	10.75	14.05
0126	20 MPH avg., cycle 0.5 mile		232	.034			1.91	1.80	3.71	4.84
0128	cycle 1 mile		208	.038			2.13	2.01	4.14	5.40
0130	cycle 2 miles		184	.043			2.41	2.27	4.68	6.10
0132	cycle 4 miles		144	.056			3.08	2.90	5.98	7.80
0134	cycle 6 miles		112	.071			3.96	3.73	7.69	10
0136	cycle 8 miles		96	.083			4.62	4.35	8.97	11.70
0144	25 MPH avg., cycle 4 miles		152	.053			2.92	2.75	5.67	7.40
0146	cycle 6 miles		128	.063			3.47	3.26	6.73	8.80
0148	cycle 8 miles		112	.071			3.96	3.73	7.69	10
0150	30 MPH avg., cycle 4 miles		168	.048			2.64	2.49	5.13	6.70
0152	cycle 6 miles		144	.056			3.08	2.90	5.98	7.80
0154	cycle 8 miles		120	.067			3.70	3.48	7.18	9.35
0214	15 MPH avg., cycle 0.5 mile, 20 min. wait/ld./uld.		176	.045			2.52	2.37	4.89	6.40
0216	cycle 1 mile		160	.050			2.77	2.61	5.38	7
0218	cycle 2 miles		136	.059			3.26	3.07	6.33	8.25
0220	cycle 4 miles		104	.077			4.27	4.01	8.28	10.75
0222	cycle 6 miles		88	.091			5.05	4.74	9.79	12.75

31 23 Excavation and Fill

31 23 23 – Fill

31 23 23.20 Hauling

		Crew	Daily Output	Labor-Hours	Unit	Material	2023 Bare Costs Labor	Equipment	Total	Total Incl O&P
0224	cycle 8 miles	B-34A	72	.111	L.C.Y.		6.15	5.80	11.95	15.60
0226	20 MPH avg., cycle 0.5 mile		176	.045			2.52	2.37	4.89	6.40
0228	cycle 1 mile		168	.048			2.64	2.49	5.13	6.70
0230	cycle 2 miles		144	.056			3.08	2.90	5.98	7.80
0232	cycle 4 miles		120	.067			3.70	3.48	7.18	9.35
0234	cycle 6 miles		96	.083			4.62	4.35	8.97	11.70
0236	cycle 8 miles		88	.091			5.05	4.74	9.79	12.75
0244	25 MPH avg., cycle 4 miles		128	.063			3.47	3.26	6.73	8.80
0246	cycle 6 miles		112	.071			3.96	3.73	7.69	10
0248	cycle 8 miles		96	.083			4.62	4.35	8.97	11.70
0250	30 MPH avg., cycle 4 miles		136	.059			3.26	3.07	6.33	8.25
0252	cycle 6 miles		120	.067			3.70	3.48	7.18	9.35
0254	cycle 8 miles		104	.077			4.27	4.01	8.28	10.75
0314	15 MPH avg., cycle 0.5 mile, 25 min. wait/ld./uld.		144	.056			3.08	2.90	5.98	7.80
0316	cycle 1 mile		128	.063			3.47	3.26	6.73	8.80
0318	cycle 2 miles		112	.071			3.96	3.73	7.69	10
0320	cycle 4 miles		96	.083			4.62	4.35	8.97	11.70
0322	cycle 6 miles		80	.100			5.55	5.20	10.75	14.05
0324	cycle 8 miles		64	.125			6.95	6.50	13.45	17.55
0326	20 MPH avg., cycle 0.5 mile		144	.056			3.08	2.90	5.98	7.80
0328	cycle 1 mile		136	.059			3.26	3.07	6.33	8.25
0330	cycle 2 miles		120	.067			3.70	3.48	7.18	9.35
0332	cycle 4 miles		104	.077			4.27	4.01	8.28	10.75
0334	cycle 6 miles		88	.091			5.05	4.74	9.79	12.75
0336	cycle 8 miles		80	.100			5.55	5.20	10.75	14.05
0344	25 MPH avg., cycle 4 miles		112	.071			3.96	3.73	7.69	10
0346	cycle 6 miles		96	.083			4.62	4.35	8.97	11.70
0348	cycle 8 miles		88	.091			5.05	4.74	9.79	12.75
0350	30 MPH avg., cycle 4 miles		112	.071			3.96	3.73	7.69	10
0352	cycle 6 miles		104	.077			4.27	4.01	8.28	10.75
0354	cycle 8 miles		96	.083			4.62	4.35	8.97	11.70
0414	15 MPH avg., cycle 0.5 mile, 30 min. wait/ld./uld.		120	.067			3.70	3.48	7.18	9.35
0416	cycle 1 mile		112	.071			3.96	3.73	7.69	10
0418	cycle 2 miles		96	.083			4.62	4.35	8.97	11.70
0420	cycle 4 miles		80	.100			5.55	5.20	10.75	14.05
0422	cycle 6 miles		72	.111			6.15	5.80	11.95	15.60
0424	cycle 8 miles		64	.125			6.95	6.50	13.45	17.55
0426	20 MPH avg., cycle 0.5 mile		120	.067			3.70	3.48	7.18	9.35
0428	cycle 1 mile		112	.071			3.96	3.73	7.69	10
0430	cycle 2 miles		104	.077			4.27	4.01	8.28	10.75
0432	cycle 4 miles		88	.091			5.05	4.74	9.79	12.75
0434	cycle 6 miles		80	.100			5.55	5.20	10.75	14.05
0436	cycle 8 miles		72	.111			6.15	5.80	11.95	15.60
0444	25 MPH avg., cycle 4 miles		96	.083			4.62	4.35	8.97	11.70
0446	cycle 6 miles		88	.091			5.05	4.74	9.79	12.75
0448	cycle 8 miles		80	.100			5.55	5.20	10.75	14.05
0450	30 MPH avg., cycle 4 miles		96	.083			4.62	4.35	8.97	11.70
0452	cycle 6 miles		88	.091			5.05	4.74	9.79	12.75
0454	cycle 8 miles		80	.100			5.55	5.20	10.75	14.05
0514	15 MPH avg., cycle 0.5 mile, 35 min. wait/ld./uld.		104	.077			4.27	4.01	8.28	10.75
0516	cycle 1 mile		96	.083			4.62	4.35	8.97	11.70
0518	cycle 2 miles		88	.091			5.05	4.74	9.79	12.75
0520	cycle 4 miles		72	.111			6.15	5.80	11.95	15.60

31 23 Excavation and Fill

31 23 23 – Fill

31 23 23.20 Hauling

		Crew	Daily Output	Labor-Hours	Unit	Material	2023 Bare Costs Labor	2023 Bare Costs Equipment	Total	Total Incl O&P
0522	cycle 6 miles	B-34A	64	.125	L.C.Y.		6.95	6.50	13.45	17.55
0524	cycle 8 miles		56	.143			7.90	7.45	15.35	20
0526	20 MPH avg., cycle 0.5 mile		104	.077			4.27	4.01	8.28	10.75
0528	cycle 1 mile		96	.083			4.62	4.35	8.97	11.70
0530	cycle 2 miles		96	.083			4.62	4.35	8.97	11.70
0532	cycle 4 miles		80	.100			5.55	5.20	10.75	14.05
0534	cycle 6 miles		72	.111			6.15	5.80	11.95	15.60
0536	cycle 8 miles		64	.125			6.95	6.50	13.45	17.55
0544	25 MPH avg., cycle 4 miles		88	.091			5.05	4.74	9.79	12.75
0546	cycle 6 miles		80	.100			5.55	5.20	10.75	14.05
0548	cycle 8 miles		72	.111			6.15	5.80	11.95	15.60
0550	30 MPH avg., cycle 4 miles		88	.091			5.05	4.74	9.79	12.75
0552	cycle 6 miles		80	.100			5.55	5.20	10.75	14.05
0554	cycle 8 miles		72	.111			6.15	5.80	11.95	15.60
1014	12 C.Y. truck, cycle 0.5 mile, 15 MPH avg., 15 min. wait/ld./uld.	B-34B	336	.024			1.32	2.36	3.68	4.56
1016	cycle 1 mile		300	.027			1.48	2.64	4.12	5.10
1018	cycle 2 miles		252	.032			1.76	3.14	4.90	6.10
1020	cycle 4 miles		180	.044			2.46	4.40	6.86	8.50
1022	cycle 6 miles		144	.056			3.08	5.50	8.58	10.65
1024	cycle 8 miles		120	.067			3.70	6.60	10.30	12.75
1025	cycle 10 miles		96	.083			4.62	8.25	12.87	15.95
1026	20 MPH avg., cycle 0.5 mile		348	.023			1.27	2.27	3.54	4.40
1028	cycle 1 mile		312	.026			1.42	2.54	3.96	4.91
1030	cycle 2 miles		276	.029			1.61	2.87	4.48	5.55
1032	cycle 4 miles		216	.037			2.05	3.66	5.71	7.10
1034	cycle 6 miles		168	.048			2.64	4.71	7.35	9.15
1036	cycle 8 miles		144	.056			3.08	5.50	8.58	10.65
1038	cycle 10 miles		120	.067			3.70	6.60	10.30	12.75
1040	25 MPH avg., cycle 4 miles		228	.035			1.95	3.47	5.42	6.75
1042	cycle 6 miles		192	.042			2.31	4.12	6.43	8
1044	cycle 8 miles		168	.048			2.64	4.71	7.35	9.15
1046	cycle 10 miles		144	.056			3.08	5.50	8.58	10.65
1050	30 MPH avg., cycle 4 miles		252	.032			1.76	3.14	4.90	6.10
1052	cycle 6 miles		216	.037			2.05	3.66	5.71	7.10
1054	cycle 8 miles		180	.044			2.46	4.40	6.86	8.50
1056	cycle 10 miles		156	.051			2.84	5.05	7.89	9.85
1060	35 MPH avg., cycle 4 miles		264	.030			1.68	3	4.68	5.80
1062	cycle 6 miles		228	.035			1.95	3.47	5.42	6.75
1064	cycle 8 miles		204	.039			2.17	3.88	6.05	7.50
1066	cycle 10 miles		180	.044			2.46	4.40	6.86	8.50
1068	cycle 20 miles		120	.067			3.70	6.60	10.30	12.75
1069	cycle 30 miles		84	.095			5.30	9.40	14.70	18.25
1070	cycle 40 miles		72	.111			6.15	11	17.15	21.50
1072	40 MPH avg., cycle 6 miles		240	.033			1.85	3.30	5.15	6.40
1074	cycle 8 miles		216	.037			2.05	3.66	5.71	7.10
1076	cycle 10 miles		192	.042			2.31	4.12	6.43	8
1078	cycle 20 miles		120	.067			3.70	6.60	10.30	12.75
1080	cycle 30 miles		96	.083			4.62	8.25	12.87	15.95
1082	cycle 40 miles		72	.111			6.15	11	17.15	21.50
1084	cycle 50 miles		60	.133			7.40	13.20	20.60	25.50
1094	45 MPH avg., cycle 8 miles		216	.037			2.05	3.66	5.71	7.10
1096	cycle 10 miles		204	.039			2.17	3.88	6.05	7.50
1098	cycle 20 miles		132	.061			3.36	6	9.36	11.60

31 23 Excavation and Fill

31 23 23 – Fill

31 23 23.20 Hauling		Crew	Daily Output	Labor-Hours	Unit	Material	2023 Bare Costs Labor	2023 Bare Costs Equipment	Total	Total Incl O&P
1100	cycle 30 miles	B-34B	108	.074	L.C.Y.		4.11	7.35	11.46	14.20
1102	cycle 40 miles		84	.095			5.30	9.40	14.70	18.25
1104	cycle 50 miles		72	.111			6.15	11	17.15	21.50
1106	50 MPH avg., cycle 10 miles		216	.037			2.05	3.66	5.71	7.10
1108	cycle 20 miles		144	.056			3.08	5.50	8.58	10.65
1110	cycle 30 miles		108	.074			4.11	7.35	11.46	14.20
1112	cycle 40 miles		84	.095			5.30	9.40	14.70	18.25
1114	cycle 50 miles		72	.111			6.15	11	17.15	21.50
1214	15 MPH avg., cycle 0.5 mile, 20 min. wait/ld./uld.		264	.030			1.68	3	4.68	5.80
1216	cycle 1 mile		240	.033			1.85	3.30	5.15	6.40
1218	cycle 2 miles		204	.039			2.17	3.88	6.05	7.50
1220	cycle 4 miles		156	.051			2.84	5.05	7.89	9.85
1222	cycle 6 miles		132	.061			3.36	6	9.36	11.60
1224	cycle 8 miles		108	.074			4.11	7.35	11.46	14.20
1225	cycle 10 miles		96	.083			4.62	8.25	12.87	15.95
1226	20 MPH avg., cycle 0.5 mile		264	.030			1.68	3	4.68	5.80
1228	cycle 1 mile		252	.032			1.76	3.14	4.90	6.10
1230	cycle 2 miles		216	.037			2.05	3.66	5.71	7.10
1232	cycle 4 miles		180	.044			2.46	4.40	6.86	8.50
1234	cycle 6 miles		144	.056			3.08	5.50	8.58	10.65
1236	cycle 8 miles		132	.061			3.36	6	9.36	11.60
1238	cycle 10 miles		108	.074			4.11	7.35	11.46	14.20
1240	25 MPH avg., cycle 4 miles		192	.042			2.31	4.12	6.43	8
1242	cycle 6 miles		168	.048			2.64	4.71	7.35	9.15
1244	cycle 8 miles		144	.056			3.08	5.50	8.58	10.65
1246	cycle 10 miles		132	.061			3.36	6	9.36	11.60
1250	30 MPH avg., cycle 4 miles		204	.039			2.17	3.88	6.05	7.50
1252	cycle 6 miles		180	.044			2.46	4.40	6.86	8.50
1254	cycle 8 miles		156	.051			2.84	5.05	7.89	9.85
1256	cycle 10 miles		144	.056			3.08	5.50	8.58	10.65
1260	35 MPH avg., cycle 4 miles		216	.037			2.05	3.66	5.71	7.10
1262	cycle 6 miles		192	.042			2.31	4.12	6.43	8
1264	cycle 8 miles		168	.048			2.64	4.71	7.35	9.15
1266	cycle 10 miles		156	.051			2.84	5.05	7.89	9.85
1268	cycle 20 miles		108	.074			4.11	7.35	11.46	14.20
1269	cycle 30 miles		72	.111			6.15	11	17.15	21.50
1270	cycle 40 miles		60	.133			7.40	13.20	20.60	25.50
1272	40 MPH avg., cycle 6 miles		192	.042			2.31	4.12	6.43	8
1274	cycle 8 miles		180	.044			2.46	4.40	6.86	8.50
1276	cycle 10 miles		156	.051			2.84	5.05	7.89	9.85
1278	cycle 20 miles		108	.074			4.11	7.35	11.46	14.20
1280	cycle 30 miles		84	.095			5.30	9.40	14.70	18.25
1282	cycle 40 miles		72	.111			6.15	11	17.15	21.50
1284	cycle 50 miles		60	.133			7.40	13.20	20.60	25.50
1294	45 MPH avg., cycle 8 miles		180	.044			2.46	4.40	6.86	8.50
1296	cycle 10 miles		168	.048			2.64	4.71	7.35	9.15
1298	cycle 20 miles		120	.067			3.70	6.60	10.30	12.75
1300	cycle 30 miles		96	.083			4.62	8.25	12.87	15.95
1302	cycle 40 miles		72	.111			6.15	11	17.15	21.50
1304	cycle 50 miles		60	.133			7.40	13.20	20.60	25.50
1306	50 MPH avg., cycle 10 miles		180	.044			2.46	4.40	6.86	8.50
1308	cycle 20 miles		132	.061			3.36	6	9.36	11.60
1310	cycle 30 miles		96	.083			4.62	8.25	12.87	15.95

31 23 Excavation and Fill

31 23 23 – Fill

31 23 23.20 Hauling		Crew	Daily Output	Labor-Hours	Unit	Material	2023 Bare Costs Labor	Equipment	Total	Total Incl O&P
1312	cycle 40 miles	B-34B	84	.095	L.C.Y.		5.30	9.40	14.70	18.25
1314	cycle 50 miles		72	.111			6.15	11	17.15	21.50
1414	15 MPH avg., cycle 0.5 mile, 25 min. wait/ld./uld.		204	.039			2.17	3.88	6.05	7.50
1416	cycle 1 mile		192	.042			2.31	4.12	6.43	8
1418	cycle 2 miles		168	.048			2.64	4.71	7.35	9.15
1420	cycle 4 miles		132	.061			3.36	6	9.36	11.60
1422	cycle 6 miles		120	.067			3.70	6.60	10.30	12.75
1424	cycle 8 miles		96	.083			4.62	8.25	12.87	15.95
1425	cycle 10 miles		84	.095			5.30	9.40	14.70	18.25
1426	20 MPH avg., cycle 0.5 mile		216	.037			2.05	3.66	5.71	7.10
1428	cycle 1 mile		204	.039			2.17	3.88	6.05	7.50
1430	cycle 2 miles		180	.044			2.46	4.40	6.86	8.50
1432	cycle 4 miles		156	.051			2.84	5.05	7.89	9.85
1434	cycle 6 miles		132	.061			3.36	6	9.36	11.60
1436	cycle 8 miles		120	.067			3.70	6.60	10.30	12.75
1438	cycle 10 miles		96	.083			4.62	8.25	12.87	15.95
1440	25 MPH avg., cycle 4 miles		168	.048			2.64	4.71	7.35	9.15
1442	cycle 6 miles		144	.056			3.08	5.50	8.58	10.65
1444	cycle 8 miles		132	.061			3.36	6	9.36	11.60
1446	cycle 10 miles		108	.074			4.11	7.35	11.46	14.20
1450	30 MPH avg., cycle 4 miles		168	.048			2.64	4.71	7.35	9.15
1452	cycle 6 miles		156	.051			2.84	5.05	7.89	9.85
1454	cycle 8 miles		132	.061			3.36	6	9.36	11.60
1456	cycle 10 miles		120	.067			3.70	6.60	10.30	12.75
1460	35 MPH avg., cycle 4 miles		180	.044			2.46	4.40	6.86	8.50
1462	cycle 6 miles		156	.051			2.84	5.05	7.89	9.85
1464	cycle 8 miles		144	.056			3.08	5.50	8.58	10.65
1466	cycle 10 miles		132	.061			3.36	6	9.36	11.60
1468	cycle 20 miles		96	.083			4.62	8.25	12.87	15.95
1469	cycle 30 miles		72	.111			6.15	11	17.15	21.50
1470	cycle 40 miles		60	.133			7.40	13.20	20.60	25.50
1472	40 MPH avg., cycle 6 miles		168	.048			2.64	4.71	7.35	9.15
1474	cycle 8 miles		156	.051			2.84	5.05	7.89	9.85
1476	cycle 10 miles		144	.056			3.08	5.50	8.58	10.65
1478	cycle 20 miles		96	.083			4.62	8.25	12.87	15.95
1480	cycle 30 miles		84	.095			5.30	9.40	14.70	18.25
1482	cycle 40 miles		60	.133			7.40	13.20	20.60	25.50
1484	cycle 50 miles		60	.133			7.40	13.20	20.60	25.50
1494	45 MPH avg., cycle 8 miles		156	.051			2.84	5.05	7.89	9.85
1496	cycle 10 miles		144	.056			3.08	5.50	8.58	10.65
1498	cycle 20 miles		108	.074			4.11	7.35	11.46	14.20
1500	cycle 30 miles		84	.095			5.30	9.40	14.70	18.25
1502	cycle 40 miles		72	.111			6.15	11	17.15	21.50
1504	cycle 50 miles		60	.133			7.40	13.20	20.60	25.50
1506	50 MPH avg., cycle 10 miles		156	.051			2.84	5.05	7.89	9.85
1508	cycle 20 miles		120	.067			3.70	6.60	10.30	12.75
1510	cycle 30 miles		96	.083			4.62	8.25	12.87	15.95
1512	cycle 40 miles		72	.111			6.15	11	17.15	21.50
1514	cycle 50 miles		60	.133			7.40	13.20	20.60	25.50
1614	15 MPH avg., cycle 0.5 mile, 30 min. wait/ld./uld.		180	.044			2.46	4.40	6.86	8.50
1616	cycle 1 mile		168	.048			2.64	4.71	7.35	9.15
1618	cycle 2 miles		144	.056			3.08	5.50	8.58	10.65
1620	cycle 4 miles		120	.067			3.70	6.60	10.30	12.75

31 23 Excavation and Fill

31 23 23 – Fill

31 23 23.20 Hauling		Crew	Daily Output	Labor-Hours	Unit	Material	2023 Bare Costs Labor	2023 Bare Costs Equipment	Total	Total Incl O&P
1622	cycle 6 miles	B-34B	108	.074	L.C.Y.		4.11	7.35	11.46	14.20
1624	cycle 8 miles		84	.095			5.30	9.40	14.70	18.25
1625	cycle 10 miles		84	.095			5.30	9.40	14.70	18.25
1626	20 MPH avg., cycle 0.5 mile		180	.044			2.46	4.40	6.86	8.50
1628	cycle 1 mile		168	.048			2.64	4.71	7.35	9.15
1630	cycle 2 miles		156	.051			2.84	5.05	7.89	9.85
1632	cycle 4 miles		132	.061			3.36	6	9.36	11.60
1634	cycle 6 miles		120	.067			3.70	6.60	10.30	12.75
1636	cycle 8 miles		108	.074			4.11	7.35	11.46	14.20
1638	cycle 10 miles		96	.083			4.62	8.25	12.87	15.95
1640	25 MPH avg., cycle 4 miles		144	.056			3.08	5.50	8.58	10.65
1642	cycle 6 miles		132	.061			3.36	6	9.36	11.60
1644	cycle 8 miles		108	.074			4.11	7.35	11.46	14.20
1646	cycle 10 miles		108	.074			4.11	7.35	11.46	14.20
1650	30 MPH avg., cycle 4 miles		144	.056			3.08	5.50	8.58	10.65
1652	cycle 6 miles		132	.061			3.36	6	9.36	11.60
1654	cycle 8 miles		120	.067			3.70	6.60	10.30	12.75
1656	cycle 10 miles		108	.074			4.11	7.35	11.46	14.20
1660	35 MPH avg., cycle 4 miles		156	.051			2.84	5.05	7.89	9.85
1662	cycle 6 miles		144	.056			3.08	5.50	8.58	10.65
1664	cycle 8 miles		132	.061			3.36	6	9.36	11.60
1666	cycle 10 miles		120	.067			3.70	6.60	10.30	12.75
1668	cycle 20 miles		84	.095			5.30	9.40	14.70	18.25
1669	cycle 30 miles		72	.111			6.15	11	17.15	21.50
1670	cycle 40 miles		60	.133			7.40	13.20	20.60	25.50
1672	40 MPH avg., cycle 6 miles		144	.056			3.08	5.50	8.58	10.65
1674	cycle 8 miles		132	.061			3.36	6	9.36	11.60
1676	cycle 10 miles		120	.067			3.70	6.60	10.30	12.75
1678	cycle 20 miles		96	.083			4.62	8.25	12.87	15.95
1680	cycle 30 miles		72	.111			6.15	11	17.15	21.50
1682	cycle 40 miles		60	.133			7.40	13.20	20.60	25.50
1684	cycle 50 miles		48	.167			9.25	16.50	25.75	32
1694	45 MPH avg., cycle 8 miles		144	.056			3.08	5.50	8.58	10.65
1696	cycle 10 miles		132	.061			3.36	6	9.36	11.60
1698	cycle 20 miles		96	.083			4.62	8.25	12.87	15.95
1700	cycle 30 miles		84	.095			5.30	9.40	14.70	18.25
1702	cycle 40 miles		60	.133			7.40	13.20	20.60	25.50
1704	cycle 50 miles		60	.133			7.40	13.20	20.60	25.50
1706	50 MPH avg., cycle 10 miles		132	.061			3.36	6	9.36	11.60
1708	cycle 20 miles		108	.074			4.11	7.35	11.46	14.20
1710	cycle 30 miles		84	.095			5.30	9.40	14.70	18.25
1712	cycle 40 miles		72	.111			6.15	11	17.15	21.50
1714	cycle 50 miles		60	.133			7.40	13.20	20.60	25.50
2000	Hauling, 8 C.Y. truck, small project cost per hour	B-34A	8	1	Hr.		55.50	52	107.50	141
2100	12 C.Y. truck	B-34B	8	1			55.50	99	154.50	192
2150	16.5 C.Y. truck	B-34C	8	1			55.50	87	142.50	179
2175	18 C.Y. 8 wheel truck	B-34I	8	1			55.50	98.50	154	191
2200	20 C.Y. truck	B-34D	8	1			55.50	89.50	145	182
2300	Grading at dump, or embankment if required, by dozer	B-10B	1000	.012	L.C.Y.		.69	1.38	2.07	2.55
2310	Spotter at fill or cut, if required	1 Clab	8	1	Hr.		47.50		47.50	70.50
9014	18 C.Y. truck, 8 wheels,15 min. wait/ld./uld.,15 MPH, cycle 0.5 mi.	B-34I	504	.016	L.C.Y.		.88	1.56	2.44	3.04
9016	cycle 1 mile		450	.018			.99	1.75	2.74	3.40
9018	cycle 2 miles		378	.021			1.17	2.09	3.26	4.04

31 23 Excavation and Fill

31 23 23 – Fill

31 23 23.20 Hauling		Crew	Daily Output	Labor-Hours	Unit	Material	2023 Bare Costs Labor	Equipment	Total	Total Incl O&P
9020	cycle 4 miles	B-34I	270	.030	L.C.Y.		1.64	2.92	4.56	5.65
9022	cycle 6 miles		216	.037			2.05	3.65	5.70	7.10
9024	cycle 8 miles		180	.044			2.46	4.38	6.84	8.50
9025	cycle 10 miles		144	.056			3.08	5.50	8.58	10.60
9026	20 MPH avg., cycle 0.5 mile		522	.015			.85	1.51	2.36	2.93
9028	cycle 1 mile		468	.017			.95	1.68	2.63	3.27
9030	cycle 2 miles		414	.019			1.07	1.90	2.97	3.69
9032	cycle 4 miles		324	.025			1.37	2.43	3.80	4.73
9034	cycle 6 miles		252	.032			1.76	3.13	4.89	6.05
9036	cycle 8 miles		216	.037			2.05	3.65	5.70	7.10
9038	cycle 10 miles		180	.044			2.46	4.38	6.84	8.50
9040	25 MPH avg., cycle 4 miles		342	.023			1.30	2.31	3.61	4.48
9042	cycle 6 miles		288	.028			1.54	2.74	4.28	5.30
9044	cycle 8 miles		252	.032			1.76	3.13	4.89	6.05
9046	cycle 10 miles		216	.037			2.05	3.65	5.70	7.10
9050	30 MPH avg., cycle 4 miles		378	.021			1.17	2.09	3.26	4.04
9052	cycle 6 miles		324	.025			1.37	2.43	3.80	4.73
9054	cycle 8 miles		270	.030			1.64	2.92	4.56	5.65
9056	cycle 10 miles		234	.034			1.90	3.37	5.27	6.55
9060	35 MPH avg., cycle 4 miles		396	.020			1.12	1.99	3.11	3.86
9062	cycle 6 miles		342	.023			1.30	2.31	3.61	4.48
9064	cycle 8 miles		288	.028			1.54	2.74	4.28	5.30
9066	cycle 10 miles		270	.030			1.64	2.92	4.56	5.65
9068	cycle 20 miles		162	.049			2.74	4.87	7.61	9.45
9070	cycle 30 miles		126	.063			3.52	6.25	9.77	12.15
9072	cycle 40 miles		90	.089			4.93	8.75	13.68	17
9074	40 MPH avg., cycle 6 miles		360	.022			1.23	2.19	3.42	4.25
9076	cycle 8 miles		324	.025			1.37	2.43	3.80	4.73
9078	cycle 10 miles		288	.028			1.54	2.74	4.28	5.30
9080	cycle 20 miles		180	.044			2.46	4.38	6.84	8.50
9082	cycle 30 miles		144	.056			3.08	5.50	8.58	10.60
9084	cycle 40 miles		108	.074			4.11	7.30	11.41	14.20
9086	cycle 50 miles		90	.089			4.93	8.75	13.68	17
9094	45 MPH avg., cycle 8 miles		324	.025			1.37	2.43	3.80	4.73
9096	cycle 10 miles		306	.026			1.45	2.58	4.03	5
9098	cycle 20 miles		198	.040			2.24	3.98	6.22	7.75
9100	cycle 30 miles		144	.056			3.08	5.50	8.58	10.60
9102	cycle 40 miles		126	.063			3.52	6.25	9.77	12.15
9104	cycle 50 miles		108	.074			4.11	7.30	11.41	14.20
9106	50 MPH avg., cycle 10 miles		324	.025			1.37	2.43	3.80	4.73
9108	cycle 20 miles		216	.037			2.05	3.65	5.70	7.10
9110	cycle 30 miles		162	.049			2.74	4.87	7.61	9.45
9112	cycle 40 miles		126	.063			3.52	6.25	9.77	12.15
9114	cycle 50 miles		108	.074			4.11	7.30	11.41	14.20
9214	20 min. wait/ld./uld.,15 MPH, cycle 0.5 mi.		396	.020			1.12	1.99	3.11	3.86
9216	cycle 1 mile		360	.022			1.23	2.19	3.42	4.25
9218	cycle 2 miles		306	.026			1.45	2.58	4.03	5
9220	cycle 4 miles		234	.034			1.90	3.37	5.27	6.55
9222	cycle 6 miles		198	.040			2.24	3.98	6.22	7.75
9224	cycle 8 miles		162	.049			2.74	4.87	7.61	9.45
9225	cycle 10 miles		144	.056			3.08	5.50	8.58	10.60
9226	20 MPH avg., cycle 0.5 mile		396	.020			1.12	1.99	3.11	3.86
9228	cycle 1 mile		378	.021			1.17	2.09	3.26	4.04

31 23 Excavation and Fill

31 23 23 – Fill

31 23 23.20 Hauling

		Crew	Daily Output	Labor-Hours	Unit	Material	2023 Bare Costs Labor	Equipment	Total	Total Incl O&P
9230	cycle 2 miles	B-34I	324	.025	L.C.Y.		1.37	2.43	3.80	4.73
9232	cycle 4 miles		270	.030			1.64	2.92	4.56	5.65
9234	cycle 6 miles		216	.037			2.05	3.65	5.70	7.10
9236	cycle 8 miles		198	.040			2.24	3.98	6.22	7.75
9238	cycle 10 miles		162	.049			2.74	4.87	7.61	9.45
9240	25 MPH avg., cycle 4 miles		288	.028			1.54	2.74	4.28	5.30
9242	cycle 6 miles		252	.032			1.76	3.13	4.89	6.05
9244	cycle 8 miles		216	.037			2.05	3.65	5.70	7.10
9246	cycle 10 miles		198	.040			2.24	3.98	6.22	7.75
9250	30 MPH avg., cycle 4 miles		306	.026			1.45	2.58	4.03	5
9252	cycle 6 miles		270	.030			1.64	2.92	4.56	5.65
9254	cycle 8 miles		234	.034			1.90	3.37	5.27	6.55
9256	cycle 10 miles		216	.037			2.05	3.65	5.70	7.10
9260	35 MPH avg., cycle 4 miles		324	.025			1.37	2.43	3.80	4.73
9262	cycle 6 miles		288	.028			1.54	2.74	4.28	5.30
9264	cycle 8 miles		252	.032			1.76	3.13	4.89	6.05
9266	cycle 10 miles		234	.034			1.90	3.37	5.27	6.55
9268	cycle 20 miles		162	.049			2.74	4.87	7.61	9.45
9270	cycle 30 miles		108	.074			4.11	7.30	11.41	14.20
9272	cycle 40 miles		90	.089			4.93	8.75	13.68	17
9274	40 MPH avg., cycle 6 miles		288	.028			1.54	2.74	4.28	5.30
9276	cycle 8 miles		270	.030			1.64	2.92	4.56	5.65
9278	cycle 10 miles		234	.034			1.90	3.37	5.27	6.55
9280	cycle 20 miles		162	.049			2.74	4.87	7.61	9.45
9282	cycle 30 miles		126	.063			3.52	6.25	9.77	12.15
9284	cycle 40 miles		108	.074			4.11	7.30	11.41	14.20
9286	cycle 50 miles		90	.089			4.93	8.75	13.68	17
9294	45 MPH avg., cycle 8 miles		270	.030			1.64	2.92	4.56	5.65
9296	cycle 10 miles		252	.032			1.76	3.13	4.89	6.05
9298	cycle 20 miles		180	.044			2.46	4.38	6.84	8.50
9300	cycle 30 miles		144	.056			3.08	5.50	8.58	10.60
9302	cycle 40 miles		108	.074			4.11	7.30	11.41	14.20
9304	cycle 50 miles		90	.089			4.93	8.75	13.68	17
9306	50 MPH avg., cycle 10 miles		270	.030			1.64	2.92	4.56	5.65
9308	cycle 20 miles		198	.040			2.24	3.98	6.22	7.75
9310	cycle 30 miles		144	.056			3.08	5.50	8.58	10.60
9312	cycle 40 miles		126	.063			3.52	6.25	9.77	12.15
9314	cycle 50 miles		108	.074			4.11	7.30	11.41	14.20
9414	25 min. wait/ld./uld.,15 MPH, cycle 0.5 mi.		306	.026			1.45	2.58	4.03	5
9416	cycle 1 mile		288	.028			1.54	2.74	4.28	5.30
9418	cycle 2 miles		252	.032			1.76	3.13	4.89	6.05
9420	cycle 4 miles		198	.040			2.24	3.98	6.22	7.75
9422	cycle 6 miles		180	.044			2.46	4.38	6.84	8.50
9424	cycle 8 miles		144	.056			3.08	5.50	8.58	10.60
9425	cycle 10 miles		126	.063			3.52	6.25	9.77	12.15
9426	20 MPH avg., cycle 0.5 mile		324	.025			1.37	2.43	3.80	4.73
9428	cycle 1 mile		306	.026			1.45	2.58	4.03	5
9430	cycle 2 miles		270	.030			1.64	2.92	4.56	5.65
9432	cycle 4 miles		234	.034			1.90	3.37	5.27	6.55
9434	cycle 6 miles		198	.040			2.24	3.98	6.22	7.75
9436	cycle 8 miles		180	.044			2.46	4.38	6.84	8.50
9438	cycle 10 miles		144	.056			3.08	5.50	8.58	10.60
9440	25 MPH avg., cycle 4 miles		252	.032			1.76	3.13	4.89	6.05

31 23 Excavation and Fill
31 23 23 – Fill

31 23 23.20 Hauling		Crew	Daily Output	Labor-Hours	Unit	Material	2023 Bare Costs Labor	Equipment	Total	Total Incl O&P
9442	cycle 6 miles	B-34I	216	.037	L.C.Y.		2.05	3.65	5.70	7.10
9444	cycle 8 miles		198	.040			2.24	3.98	6.22	7.75
9446	cycle 10 miles		180	.044			2.46	4.38	6.84	8.50
9450	30 MPH avg., cycle 4 miles		252	.032			1.76	3.13	4.89	6.05
9452	cycle 6 miles		234	.034			1.90	3.37	5.27	6.55
9454	cycle 8 miles		198	.040			2.24	3.98	6.22	7.75
9456	cycle 10 miles		180	.044			2.46	4.38	6.84	8.50
9460	35 MPH avg., cycle 4 miles		270	.030			1.64	2.92	4.56	5.65
9462	cycle 6 miles		234	.034			1.90	3.37	5.27	6.55
9464	cycle 8 miles		216	.037			2.05	3.65	5.70	7.10
9466	cycle 10 miles		198	.040			2.24	3.98	6.22	7.75
9468	cycle 20 miles		144	.056			3.08	5.50	8.58	10.60
9470	cycle 30 miles		108	.074			4.11	7.30	11.41	14.20
9472	cycle 40 miles		90	.089			4.93	8.75	13.68	17
9474	40 MPH avg., cycle 6 miles		252	.032			1.76	3.13	4.89	6.05
9476	cycle 8 miles		234	.034			1.90	3.37	5.27	6.55
9478	cycle 10 miles		216	.037			2.05	3.65	5.70	7.10
9480	cycle 20 miles		144	.056			3.08	5.50	8.58	10.60
9482	cycle 30 miles		126	.063			3.52	6.25	9.77	12.15
9484	cycle 40 miles		90	.089			4.93	8.75	13.68	17
9486	cycle 50 miles		90	.089			4.93	8.75	13.68	17
9494	45 MPH avg., cycle 8 miles		234	.034			1.90	3.37	5.27	6.55
9496	cycle 10 miles		216	.037			2.05	3.65	5.70	7.10
9498	cycle 20 miles		162	.049			2.74	4.87	7.61	9.45
9500	cycle 30 miles		126	.063			3.52	6.25	9.77	12.15
9502	cycle 40 miles		108	.074			4.11	7.30	11.41	14.20
9504	cycle 50 miles		90	.089			4.93	8.75	13.68	17
9506	50 MPH avg., cycle 10 miles		234	.034			1.90	3.37	5.27	6.55
9508	cycle 20 miles		180	.044			2.46	4.38	6.84	8.50
9510	cycle 30 miles		144	.056			3.08	5.50	8.58	10.60
9512	cycle 40 miles		108	.074			4.11	7.30	11.41	14.20
9514	cycle 50 miles		90	.089			4.93	8.75	13.68	17
9614	30 min. wait/ld./uld.,15 MPH, cycle 0.5 mi.		270	.030			1.64	2.92	4.56	5.65
9616	cycle 1 mile		252	.032			1.76	3.13	4.89	6.05
9618	cycle 2 miles		216	.037			2.05	3.65	5.70	7.10
9620	cycle 4 miles		180	.044			2.46	4.38	6.84	8.50
9622	cycle 6 miles		162	.049			2.74	4.87	7.61	9.45
9624	cycle 8 miles		126	.063			3.52	6.25	9.77	12.15
9625	cycle 10 miles		126	.063			3.52	6.25	9.77	12.15
9626	20 MPH avg., cycle 0.5 mile		270	.030			1.64	2.92	4.56	5.65
9628	cycle 1 mile		252	.032			1.76	3.13	4.89	6.05
9630	cycle 2 miles		234	.034			1.90	3.37	5.27	6.55
9632	cycle 4 miles		198	.040			2.24	3.98	6.22	7.75
9634	cycle 6 miles		180	.044			2.46	4.38	6.84	8.50
9636	cycle 8 miles		162	.049			2.74	4.87	7.61	9.45
9638	cycle 10 miles		144	.056			3.08	5.50	8.58	10.60
9640	25 MPH avg., cycle 4 miles		216	.037			2.05	3.65	5.70	7.10
9642	cycle 6 miles		198	.040			2.24	3.98	6.22	7.75
9644	cycle 8 miles		180	.044			2.46	4.38	6.84	8.50
9646	cycle 10 miles		162	.049			2.74	4.87	7.61	9.45
9650	30 MPH avg., cycle 4 miles		216	.037			2.05	3.65	5.70	7.10
9652	cycle 6 miles		198	.040			2.24	3.98	6.22	7.75
9654	cycle 8 miles		180	.044			2.46	4.38	6.84	8.50

31 23 Excavation and Fill

31 23 23 – Fill

31 23 23.20 Hauling		Crew	Daily Output	Labor-Hours	Unit	Material	2023 Bare Costs Labor	Equipment	Total	Total Incl O&P
9656	cycle 10 miles	B-34I	162	.049	L.C.Y.		2.74	4.87	7.61	9.45
9660	35 MPH avg., cycle 4 miles		234	.034			1.90	3.37	5.27	6.55
9662	cycle 6 miles		216	.037			2.05	3.65	5.70	7.10
9664	cycle 8 miles		198	.040			2.24	3.98	6.22	7.75
9666	cycle 10 miles		180	.044			2.46	4.38	6.84	8.50
9668	cycle 20 miles		126	.063			3.52	6.25	9.77	12.15
9670	cycle 30 miles		108	.074			4.11	7.30	11.41	14.20
9672	cycle 40 miles		90	.089			4.93	8.75	13.68	17
9674	40 MPH avg., cycle 6 miles		216	.037			2.05	3.65	5.70	7.10
9676	cycle 8 miles		198	.040			2.24	3.98	6.22	7.75
9678	cycle 10 miles		180	.044			2.46	4.38	6.84	8.50
9680	cycle 20 miles		144	.056			3.08	5.50	8.58	10.60
9682	cycle 30 miles		108	.074			4.11	7.30	11.41	14.20
9684	cycle 40 miles		90	.089			4.93	8.75	13.68	17
9686	cycle 50 miles		72	.111			6.15	10.95	17.10	21.50
9694	45 MPH avg., cycle 8 miles		216	.037			2.05	3.65	5.70	7.10
9696	cycle 10 miles		198	.040			2.24	3.98	6.22	7.75
9698	cycle 20 miles		144	.056			3.08	5.50	8.58	10.60
9700	cycle 30 miles		126	.063			3.52	6.25	9.77	12.15
9702	cycle 40 miles		108	.074			4.11	7.30	11.41	14.20
9704	cycle 50 miles		90	.089			4.93	8.75	13.68	17
9706	50 MPH avg., cycle 10 miles		198	.040			2.24	3.98	6.22	7.75
9708	cycle 20 miles		162	.049			2.74	4.87	7.61	9.45
9710	cycle 30 miles		126	.063			3.52	6.25	9.77	12.15
9712	cycle 40 miles		108	.074			4.11	7.30	11.41	14.20
9714	cycle 50 miles		90	.089			4.93	8.75	13.68	17

Division Notes

	CREW	DAILY OUTPUT	LABOR-HOURS	UNIT	BARE COSTS				TOTAL INCL O&P
					MAT.	LABOR	EQUIP.	TOTAL	

Division 32 — Exterior Improvements

Estimating Tips

32 01 00 Operations and Maintenance of Exterior Improvements

- Recycling of asphalt pavement is becoming very popular and is an alternative to removal and replacement. It can be a good value engineering proposal if removed pavement can be recycled, either at the project site or at another site that is reasonably close to the project site. Sections on repair of flexible and rigid pavement are included.

32 10 00 Bases, Ballasts, and Paving

- When estimating paving, keep in mind the project schedule. Also note that prices for asphalt and concrete are generally higher in the cold seasons. Lines for pavement markings, including tactile warning systems and fence lines, are included.

32 90 00 Planting

- The timing of planting and guarantee specifications often dictate the costs for establishing tree and shrub growth and a stand of grass or ground cover. Establish the work performance schedule to coincide with the local planting season. Maintenance and growth guarantees can add 20-100% to the total landscaping cost and can be contractually cumbersome. The cost to replace trees and shrubs can be as high as 5% of the total cost, depending on the planting zone, soil conditions, and time of year.

Reference Numbers

Reference numbers are shown at the beginning of some major classifications. These numbers refer to related items in the Reference Section. The reference information may be an estimating procedure, an alternate pricing method, or technical information.

Note: Not all subdivisions listed here necessarily appear. ■

Same Data. Simplified.

Enjoy the convenience and efficiency of accessing your costs anywhere:

- **Skip the multiplier** by setting your location
- **Quickly search**, edit, favorite and share costs
- **Stay on top of price changes** with automatic updates

Discover more at rsmeans.com/online

No part of this cost data may be reproduced, stored in a retrieval system, or transmitted in any form or by any means without prior written permission of Gordian.

32 12 Flexible Paving

32 12 16 – Asphalt Paving

32 12 16.13 Plant-Mix Asphalt Paving

		Crew	Daily Output	Labor-Hours	Unit	Material	2023 Bare Costs Labor	2023 Bare Costs Equipment	Total	Total Incl O&P
0010	**PLANT-MIX ASPHALT PAVING**									
0020	For highways and large paved areas, excludes hauling									
0025	See Section 31 23 23.20 for hauling costs									
0080	Binder course, 1-1/2" thick	B-25	7725	.011	S.Y.	5.85	.59	.40	6.84	7.70
0120	2" thick		6345	.014		7.75	.72	.49	8.96	10.15
0130	2-1/2" thick		5620	.016		9.70	.81	.55	11.06	12.50
0160	3" thick		4905	.018		11.65	.93	.64	13.22	14.90
0170	3-1/2" thick		4520	.019		13.60	1.01	.69	15.30	17.20
0200	4" thick		4140	.021		15.55	1.10	.75	17.40	19.55
0300	Wearing course, 1" thick	B-25B	10575	.009		3.85	.48	.33	4.66	5.30
0340	1-1/2" thick		7725	.012		6.45	.65	.45	7.55	8.55
0380	2" thick		6345	.015		8.70	.80	.55	10.05	11.35
0420	2-1/2" thick		5480	.018		10.70	.92	.64	12.26	13.85
0460	3" thick		4900	.020		12.80	1.03	.71	14.54	16.35
0470	3-1/2" thick		4520	.021		15	1.12	.77	16.89	19
0480	4" thick		4140	.023		17.15	1.22	.84	19.21	21.50
0600	Porous pavement, 1-1/2" open graded friction course	B-25	7725	.011		19.75	.59	.40	20.74	23
0800	Alternate method of figuring paving costs									
0810	Binder course, 1-1/2" thick	B-25	630	.140	Ton	71.50	7.25	4.95	83.70	94.50
0811	2" thick		690	.128		71.50	6.60	4.52	82.62	93.50
0812	3" thick		800	.110		71.50	5.70	3.90	81.10	91
0813	4" thick		900	.098		71.50	5.05	3.46	80.01	90
0850	Wearing course, 1" thick	B-25B	575	.167		76	8.80	6.10	90.90	104
0851	1-1/2" thick		630	.152		76	8.05	5.55	89.60	102
0852	2" thick		690	.139		76	7.35	5.05	88.40	100
0853	2-1/2" thick		765	.125		76	6.60	4.57	87.17	99
0854	3" thick		800	.120		76	6.30	4.37	86.67	98
1000	Pavement replacement over trench, 2" thick	B-17C	90	.533	S.Y.	8	28	22.50	58.50	75.50
1050	4" thick		70	.686		15.85	36	29	80.85	102
1080	6" thick		55	.873		25	45.50	37	107.50	137

32 12 16.14 Asphaltic Concrete Paving

		Crew	Daily Output	Labor-Hours	Unit	Material	2023 Bare Costs Labor	2023 Bare Costs Equipment	Total	Total Incl O&P
0011	**ASPHALTIC CONCRETE PAVING**, parking lots & driveways									
0015	No asphalt hauling included									
0018	Use 6.05 C.Y. per inch per M.S.F. for hauling									
0020	6" stone base, 2" binder course, 1" topping	B-25C	9000	.005	S.F.	2.21	.28	.30	2.79	3.18
0025	2" binder course, 2" topping		9000	.005		2.67	.28	.30	3.25	3.69
0030	3" binder course, 2" topping		9000	.005		3.11	.28	.30	3.69	4.17
0035	4" binder course, 2" topping		9000	.005		3.54	.28	.30	4.12	4.64
0040	1-1/2" binder course, 1" topping		9000	.005		2	.28	.30	2.58	2.95
0042	3" binder course, 1" topping		9000	.005		2.65	.28	.30	3.23	3.66
0045	3" binder course, 3" topping		9000	.005		3.57	.28	.30	4.15	4.68
0050	4" binder course, 3" topping		9000	.005		4	.28	.30	4.58	5.15
0055	4" binder course, 4" topping		9000	.005		4.46	.28	.30	5.04	5.65
0300	Binder course, 1-1/2" thick		35000	.001		.65	.07	.08	.80	.91
0400	2" thick		25000	.002		.84	.10	.11	1.05	1.19
0500	3" thick		15000	.003		1.30	.17	.18	1.65	1.88
0600	4" thick		10800	.004		1.70	.23	.25	2.18	2.50
0800	Sand finish course, 3/4" thick		41000	.001		.37	.06	.07	.50	.57
0900	1" thick		34000	.001		.46	.07	.08	.61	.70
1000	Fill pot holes, hot mix, 2" thick	B-16	4200	.008		.90	.38	.19	1.47	1.77
1100	4" thick		3500	.009		1.31	.46	.23	2	2.38
1120	6" thick		3100	.010		1.77	.51	.26	2.54	2.99

32 12 Flexible Paving

32 12 16 – Asphalt Paving

32 12 16.14 Asphaltic Concrete Paving		Crew	Daily Output	Labor-Hours	Unit	Material	2023 Bare Costs Labor	Equipment	Total	Total Incl O&P
1140	Cold patch, 2" thick	B-51	3000	.016	S.F.	1.34	.78	.12	2.24	2.77
1160	4" thick		2700	.018		2.56	.86	.13	3.55	4.24
1180	6" thick		1900	.025		3.97	1.23	.19	5.39	6.40

32 84 Planting Irrigation

32 84 13 – Drip Irrigation

32 84 13.10 Subsurface Drip Irrigation

			Crew	Daily Output	Labor-Hours	Unit	Material	Labor	Equipment	Total	Total Incl O&P
0010	**SUBSURFACE DRIP IRRIGATION**										
0011	Looped grid, pressure compensating										
0100	Preinserted PE emitter, line, hand bury, irregular area, small	G	3 Skwk	1200	.020	L.F.	.30	1.23		1.53	2.17
0150	Medium	G		1800	.013		.30	.82		1.12	1.56
0200	Large	G		2520	.010		.30	.58		.88	1.21
0250	Rectangular area, small	G		2040	.012		.30	.72		1.02	1.41
0300	Medium	G		2640	.009		.30	.56		.86	1.17
0350	Large	G		3600	.007		.30	.41		.71	.94
0400	Install in trench, irregular area, small	G		4050	.006		.30	.36		.66	.88
0450	Medium	G		7488	.003		.30	.20		.50	.62
0500	Large	G		16560	.001		.30	.09		.39	.46
0550	Rectangular area, small	G		8100	.003		.30	.18		.48	.60
0600	Medium	G		21960	.001		.30	.07		.37	.43
0650	Large	G		33264	.001		.30	.04		.34	.40
0700	Trenching and backfill	G	B-53	500	.016			.96	.40	1.36	1.87
0800	Vinyl tubing, 1/4", material only	G					.08			.08	.09
0850	Supply tubing, 1/2", material only, 100' coil	G					.16			.16	.18
0900	500' coil	G					.14			.14	.16
0950	Compression fittings	G	1 Skwk	90	.089	Ea.	1.85	5.45		7.30	10.25
1000	Barbed fittings, 1/4"	G		360	.022		.16	1.36		1.52	2.22
1100	Flush risers	G		60	.133		5.05	8.15		13.20	17.80
1150	Flush ends, figure eight	G		180	.044		.73	2.72		3.45	4.89
1300	Auto flush, spring loaded	G		90	.089		2.73	5.45		8.18	11.20
1350	Volumetric	G		90	.089		9.60	5.45		15.05	18.75
1400	Air relief valve, inline with compensation tee, 1/2"	G		45	.178		20	10.90		30.90	38.50
1450	1"	G		30	.267		21	16.35		37.35	47.50
1500	Round box for flush ends, 6"	G		30	.267		9.50	16.35		25.85	35
1600	Screen filter, 3/4" screen	G		12	.667		10.90	41		51.90	73.50
1650	1" disk	G		8	1		33	61.50		94.50	129
1700	1-1/2" disk	G		4	2		134	123		257	330
1750	2" disk	G		3	2.667		180	163		343	445
1800	Typical installation 18" OC, small, minimum					S.F.				1.53	2.35
1850	Maximum									1.78	2.75
1900	Large, minimum									1.48	2.28
2000	Maximum									1.71	2.64
2100	For non-pressure compensating systems, deduct									10%	10%

32 84 23 – Underground Sprinklers

32 84 23.10 Sprinkler Irrigation System

			Crew	Daily Output	Labor-Hours	Unit	Material	Labor	Equipment	Total	Total Incl O&P
0010	**SPRINKLER IRRIGATION SYSTEM**	G2050-710									
0011	For lawns										
0800	Residential system, custom, 1" supply		B-20	2000	.012	S.F.	.32	.63		.95	1.29
0900	1-1/2" supply		"	1800	.013	"	.48	.70		1.18	1.58
1020	Pop up spray head w/risers, hi-pop, full circle pattern, 4"		2 Skwk	76	.211	Ea.	10.65	12.90		23.55	31

32 84 Planting Irrigation

32 84 23 – Underground Sprinklers

32 84 23.10 Sprinkler Irrigation System		Crew	Daily Output	Labor-Hours	Unit	Material	2023 Bare Costs Labor	Equipment	Total	Total Incl O&P
1030	1/2 circle pattern, 4"	2 Skwk	76	.211	Ea.	10.65	12.90		23.55	31
1040	6", full circle pattern		76	.211		15.05	12.90		27.95	36
1050	1/2 circle pattern, 6"		76	.211		12.50	12.90		25.40	33
1060	12", full circle pattern		76	.211		21.50	12.90		34.40	43
1070	1/2 circle pattern, 12"		76	.211		21	12.90		33.90	42.50
1080	Pop up bubbler head w/risers, hi-pop bubbler head, 4"		76	.211		4.97	12.90		17.87	25
1110	Impact full/part circle sprinklers, 28'-54' @ 25-60 psi		37	.432		26.50	26.50		53	69
1120	Spaced 37'-49' @ 25-50 psi		37	.432		22	26.50		48.50	64.50
1130	Spaced 43'-61' @ 30-60 psi		37	.432		74	26.50		100.50	122
1140	Spaced 54'-78' @ 40-80 psi		37	.432		126	26.50		152.50	178
1145	Impact rotor pop-up full/part commercial circle sprinklers									
1150	Spaced 42'-65' @ 35-80 psi	2 Skwk	25	.640	Ea.	22	39		61	83
1160	Spaced 48'-76' @ 45-85 psi	"	25	.640	"	22	39		61	83
1165	Impact rotor pop-up part. circle comm., 53'-75', 55-100 psi, w/accessories									
1180	Sprinkler, premium, pop-up rotator, 50'-100'	2 Skwk	25	.640	Ea.	110	39		149	180
1250	Plastic case, 2 nozzle, metal cover		25	.640		133	39		172	206
1260	Rubber cover		25	.640		117	39		156	187
1270	Iron case, 2 nozzle, metal cover		22	.727		168	44.50		212.50	252
1280	Rubber cover		22	.727		167	44.50		211.50	250
1282	Impact rotor pop-up full circle commercial, 39'-99', 30-100 psi									
1284	Plastic case, metal cover	2 Skwk	25	.640	Ea.	106	39		145	175
1286	Rubber cover		25	.640		155	39		194	230
1288	Iron case, metal cover		22	.727		206	44.50		250.50	294
1290	Rubber cover		22	.727		209	44.50		253.50	297
1292	Plastic case, 2 nozzle, metal cover		22	.727		154	44.50		198.50	236
1294	Rubber cover		22	.727		157	44.50		201.50	240
1296	Iron case, 2 nozzle, metal cover		20	.800		180	49		229	272
1298	Rubber cover		20	.800		213	49		262	310
1305	Electric remote control valve, plastic, 3/4"		18	.889		22	54.50		76.50	106
1310	1"		18	.889		30.50	54.50		85	116
1320	1-1/2"		18	.889		107	54.50		161.50	199
1330	2"		18	.889		149	54.50		203.50	246
1335	Quick coupling valves, brass, locking cover									
1340	Inlet coupling valve, 3/4"	2 Skwk	18.75	.853	Ea.	81	52.50		133.50	168
1350	1"		18.75	.853		126	52.50		178.50	218
1360	Controller valve boxes, 6" round boxes		18.75	.853		15.30	52.50		67.80	95.50
1370	10" round boxes		14.25	1.123		20.50	69		89.50	126
1380	12" square box		9.75	1.641		43.50	101		144.50	199
1388	Electromech. control, 14 day 3-60 min., auto start to 23/day									
1390	4 station	2 Skwk	1.04	15.385	Ea.	104	940		1,044	1,550
1400	7 station		.64	25		178	1,525		1,703	2,500
1410	12 station		.40	40		355	2,450		2,805	4,075
1420	Dual programs, 18 station		.24	66.667		360	4,075		4,435	6,525
1430	23 station		.16	100		445	6,125		6,570	9,700
1435	Backflow preventer, bronze, 0-175 psi, w/valves, test cocks									
1440	3/4"	2 Skwk	6	2.667	Ea.	240	163		403	510
1450	1"		6	2.667		265	163		428	535
1460	1-1/2"		6	2.667		525	163		688	825
1470	2"		6	2.667		505	163		668	805
1475	Pressure vacuum breaker, brass, 15-150 psi									
1480	3/4"	2 Skwk	6	2.667	Ea.	133	163		296	390
1490	1"		6	2.667		163	163		326	425
1500	1-1/2"		6	2.667		740	163		903	1,050

32 84 Planting Irrigation

32 84 23 – Underground Sprinklers

32 84 23.10 Sprinkler Irrigation System	Crew	Daily Output	Labor-Hours	Unit	Material	2023 Bare Costs Labor	Equipment	Total	Total Incl O&P
1510 2"	2 Skwk	6	2.667	Ea.	850	163		1,013	1,175
6000 Riser mounted gear drive sprinkler, nozzle and case									
6200 Plastic, medium volume	1 Skwk	30	.267	Ea.	23	16.35		39.35	49.50
7000 Riser mounted impact sprinkler, body, part or full circle									
7200 Full circle plastic, low/medium volume	1 Skwk	25	.320	Ea.	22.50	19.60		42.10	54.50
7400 Brass, low/medium volume		25	.320		51	19.60		70.60	85.50
7600 Medium volume		25	.320		68	19.60		87.60	104
7800 Female thread		25	.320		121	19.60		140.60	163
8000 Riser mounted impact sprinkler, body, full circle only									
8200 Plastic, low/medium volume	1 Skwk	25	.320	Ea.	12.20	19.60		31.80	43
8400 Brass, low/medium volume		25	.320		58.50	19.60		78.10	94
8600 High volume		25	.320		104	19.60		123.60	145
8800 Very high volume		25	.320		193	19.60		212.60	243

Division Notes

		CREW	DAILY OUTPUT	LABOR-HOURS	UNIT	BARE COSTS				TOTAL INCL O&P
						MAT.	LABOR	EQUIP.	TOTAL	

33 01 Operation and Maintenance of Utilities

33 01 10 – Operation and Maintenance of Water Utilities

33 01 10.20 Pipe Repair

		Crew	Daily Output	Labor-Hours	Unit	Material	2023 Bare Costs Labor	Equipment	Total	Total Incl O&P
0180	3" diameter pipe	1 Plum	22	.364	Ea.	33.50	26		59.50	75.50
0190	3-1/2" diameter pipe	↓	21	.381		33.50	27.50		61	77.50
0200	4" diameter pipe	B-20	44	.545		36	28.50		64.50	82.50
0210	5" diameter pipe		42	.571		44.50	30		74.50	93.50
0220	6" diameter pipe		38	.632		47	33		80	102
0230	8" diameter pipe		30	.800		56	42		98	125
0240	10" diameter pipe		28	.857		385	45		430	495
0250	12" diameter pipe		24	1		405	52.50		457.50	525
0260	14" diameter pipe		22	1.091		445	57.50		502.50	575
0270	16" diameter pipe		20	1.200		480	63		543	625
0280	18" diameter pipe		18	1.333		505	70		575	660
0290	20" diameter pipe		16	1.500		535	79		614	710
0300	24" diameter pipe	↓	14	1.714		595	90		685	790
0360	For 6" long, add					100%	40%			
0370	For 9" long, add					200%	100%			
0380	For 12" long, add					300%	150%			
0390	For 18" long, add				↓	500%	200%			
0400	Pipe freezing for live repairs of systems 3/8" to 6"									
0410	Note: Pipe freezing can also be used to install a valve into a live system									
0420	Pipe freezing each side 3/8"	2 Skwk	8	2	Ea.	585	123		708	825
0425	Pipe freezing each side 3/8", second location same kit		8	2		35	123		158	223
0430	Pipe freezing each side 3/4"		8	2		585	123		708	825
0435	Pipe freezing each side 3/4", second location same kit		8	2		35	123		158	223
0440	Pipe freezing each side 1-1/2"		6	2.667		585	163		748	885
0445	Pipe freezing each side 1-1/2", second location same kit		6	2.667		35	163		198	284
0450	Pipe freezing each side 2"		6	2.667		585	163		748	885
0455	Pipe freezing each side 2", second location same kit		6	2.667		35	163		198	284
0460	Pipe freezing each side 2-1/2" to 3"		6	2.667		895	163		1,058	1,225
0465	Pipe freezing each side 2-1/2" to 3", second location same kit		6	2.667		70	163		233	320
0470	Pipe freezing each side 4"		4	4		1,600	245		1,845	2,125
0475	Pipe freezing each side 4", second location same kit		4	4		103	245		348	485
0480	Pipe freezing each side 5" to 6"		4	4		5,050	245		5,295	5,950
0485	Pipe freezing each side 5" to 6", second location same kit	↓	4	4		310	245		555	710
0490	Pipe freezing extra 20 lb. CO_2 cylinders (3/8" to 2" - 1 ea, 3" - 2 ea)					271			271	298
0500	Pipe freezing extra 50 lb. CO_2 cylinders (4" - 2 ea, 5"-6" - 6 ea)				↓	785			785	865
1000	Clamp, stainless steel, with threaded service tap									
1040	Full seal for iron, steel, PVC pipe									
1100	6" long, 2" diameter pipe	1 Plum	17	.471	Ea.	138	34		172	203
1110	2-1/2" diameter pipe		16	.500		158	36		194	227
1120	3" diameter pipe		15.60	.513		165	37		202	236
1130	3-1/2" diameter pipe	↓	15	.533		192	38.50		230.50	269
1140	4" diameter pipe	B-20	32	.750		190	39.50		229.50	268
1150	6" diameter pipe		28	.857		232	45		277	325
1160	8" diameter pipe		21	1.143		274	60		334	390
1170	10" diameter pipe		20	1.200		350	63		413	480
1180	12" diameter pipe	↓	17	1.412		400	74		474	550
1200	8" long, 2" diameter pipe	1 Plum	11.72	.683		205	49		254	300
1210	2-1/2" diameter pipe		11	.727		216	52.50		268.50	315
1220	3" diameter pipe		10.75	.744		227	53.50		280.50	330
1230	3-1/2" diameter pipe	↓	10.34	.774		237	55.50		292.50	345
1240	4" diameter pipe	B-20	22	1.091		250	57.50		307.50	360
1250	6" diameter pipe		19.31	1.243		297	65.50		362.50	425
1260	8" diameter pipe	↓	14.48	1.657	↓	345	87		432	510

33 01 Operation and Maintenance of Utilities

33 01 10 – Operation and Maintenance of Water Utilities

33 01 10.20 Pipe Repair

		Crew	Daily Output	Labor-Hours	Unit	Material	2023 Bare Costs Labor	2023 Bare Costs Equipment	Total	Total Incl O&P
1270	10" diameter pipe	B-20	13.80	1.739	Ea.	445	91.50		536.50	620
1280	12" diameter pipe	▼	11.72	2.048		495	108		603	705
1300	12" long, 2" diameter pipe	1 Plum	9.44	.847		292	61		353	410
1310	2-1/2" diameter pipe		8.89	.900		300	65		365	430
1320	3" diameter pipe		8.67	.923		315	66.50		381.50	445
1330	3-1/2" diameter pipe	▼	8.33	.960		330	69		399	465
1340	4" diameter pipe	B-20	17.78	1.350		350	71		421	490
1350	6" diameter pipe		15.56	1.542		415	81		496	575
1360	8" diameter pipe		11.67	2.057		485	108		593	695
1370	10" diameter pipe		11.11	2.160		610	114		724	845
1380	12" diameter pipe	▼	9.44	2.542		710	134		844	980
1400	20" long, 2" diameter pipe	1 Plum	8.10	.988		420	71		491	565
1410	2-1/2" diameter pipe		7.62	1.050		460	75.50		535.50	625
1420	3" diameter pipe		7.43	1.077		530	77.50		607.50	695
1430	3-1/2" diameter pipe	▼	7.14	1.120		560	80.50		640.50	735
1440	4" diameter pipe	B-20	15.24	1.575		585	83		668	765
1450	6" diameter pipe		13.33	1.800		690	94.50		784.50	900
1460	8" diameter pipe		10	2.400		800	126		926	1,075
1470	10" diameter pipe		9.52	2.521		980	133		1,113	1,275
1480	12" diameter pipe	▼	8.10	2.963	▼	1,125	156		1,281	1,475
1600	Clamp, stainless steel, single section									
1640	Full seal for iron, steel, PVC pipe									
1700	6" long, 2" diameter pipe	1 Plum	17	.471	Ea.	143	34		177	209
1710	2-1/2" diameter pipe		16	.500		152	36		188	221
1720	3" diameter pipe		15.60	.513		172	37		209	244
1730	3-1/2" diameter pipe	▼	15	.533		181	38.50		219.50	257
1740	4" diameter pipe	B-20	32	.750		190	39.50		229.50	268
1750	6" diameter pipe		27	.889		232	46.50		278.50	325
1760	8" diameter pipe		21	1.143		274	60		334	390
1770	10" diameter pipe		20	1.200		350	63		413	480
1780	12" diameter pipe		17	1.412		400	74		474	550
1800	8" long, 2" diameter pipe	1 Plum	11.72	.683		205	49		254	300
1805	2-1/2" diameter pipe		11.03	.725		219	52.50		271.50	320
1810	3" diameter pipe		10.76	.743		226	53.50		279.50	330
1815	3-1/2" diameter pipe	▼	10.34	.774		241	55.50		296.50	350
1820	4" diameter pipe	B-20	22.07	1.087		251	57		308	360
1825	6" diameter pipe		19.31	1.243		296	65.50		361.50	425
1830	8" diameter pipe		14.48	1.657		340	87		427	505
1835	10" diameter pipe		13.79	1.740		445	91.50		536.50	620
1840	12" diameter pipe		11.72	2.048		495	108		603	705
1850	12" long, 2" diameter pipe	1 Plum	9.44	.847		292	61		353	410
1855	2-1/2" diameter pipe		8.89	.900		305	65		370	430
1860	3" diameter pipe		8.67	.923		315	66.50		381.50	445
1865	3-1/2" diameter pipe	▼	8.33	.960		335	69		404	475
1870	4" diameter pipe	B-20	17.78	1.350		350	71		421	490
1875	6" diameter pipe		15.56	1.542		410	81		491	570
1880	8" diameter pipe		11.67	2.057		475	108		583	685
1885	10" diameter pipe		11.11	2.160		610	114		724	845
1890	12" diameter pipe	▼	9.44	2.542		715	134		849	985
1900	20" long, 2" diameter pipe	1 Plum	8.10	.988		375	71		446	515
1905	2-1/2" diameter pipe		7.62	1.050		415	75.50		490.50	570
1910	3" diameter pipe		7.43	1.077		475	77.50		552.50	635
1915	3-1/2" diameter pipe	▼	7.14	1.120		490	80.50		570.50	655

33 01 Operation and Maintenance of Utilities

33 01 10 – Operation and Maintenance of Water Utilities

33 01 10.20 Pipe Repair

		Crew	Daily Output	Labor-Hours	Unit	Material	2023 Bare Costs Labor	Equipment	Total	Total Incl O&P
1920	4" diameter pipe	B-20	15.24	1.575	Ea.	585	83		668	765
1925	6" diameter pipe		13.33	1.800		695	94.50		789.50	905
1930	8" diameter pipe		10	2.400		785	126		911	1,050
1935	10" diameter pipe		9.52	2.521		980	133		1,113	1,275
1940	12" diameter pipe		8.10	2.963		1,125	156		1,281	1,475
2000	Clamp, stainless steel, two section									
2040	Full seal, for iron, steel, PVC pipe									
2100	8" long, 4" diameter pipe	B-20	24	1	Ea.	360	52.50		412.50	475
2110	6" diameter pipe		20	1.200		415	63		478	550
2120	8" diameter pipe		13	1.846		475	97		572	670
2130	10" diameter pipe		12	2		420	105		525	615
2140	12" diameter pipe		10	2.400		685	126		811	945
2200	10" long, 4" diameter pipe		16	1.500		475	79		554	640
2210	6" diameter pipe		13	1.846		535	97		632	730
2220	8" diameter pipe		9	2.667		590	140		730	860
2230	10" diameter pipe		8	3		775	158		933	1,100
2240	12" diameter pipe		7	3.429		890	180		1,070	1,250
2242	Clamp, stainless steel, three section									
2244	Full seal, for iron, steel, PVC pipe									
2250	10" long, 14" diameter pipe	B-20	6.40	3.750	Ea.	1,350	197		1,547	1,800
2260	16" diameter pipe		6	4		1,250	210		1,460	1,700
2270	18" diameter pipe		5	4.800		1,675	252		1,927	2,225
2280	20" diameter pipe		4.60	5.217		1,925	274		2,199	2,525
2290	24" diameter pipe		4	6		2,175	315		2,490	2,875
2320	For 12" long, add to 10"					15%	25%			
2330	For 20" long, add to 10"					70%	55%			
8000	For internal cleaning and inspection, see Section 33 01 30.11									
8100	For pipe testing, see Section 23 05 93.50									

33 01 30 – Operation and Maintenance of Sewer Utilities

33 01 30.11 Television Inspection of Sewers

					Unit				Total	Total Incl O&P
0010	**TELEVISION INSPECTION OF SEWERS**									
0100	Pipe internal cleaning & inspection, cleaning, pressure pipe systems									
0120	Pig method, lengths 1000' to 10,000'									
0140	4" diameter thru 24" diameter, minimum				L.F.				3.60	4.14
0160	Maximum				"				18	21
6000	Sewage/sanitary systems									
6100	Power rodder with header & cutters									
6110	Mobilization charge, minimum				Total				695	800
6120	Mobilization charge, maximum				"				9,125	10,600
6140	Cleaning 4"-12" diameter				L.F.				6	6.60
6190	14"-24" diameter								8	8.80
6240	30" diameter								9.60	10.50
6250	36" diameter								12	13.20
6260	48" diameter								16	17.60
6270	60" diameter								24	26.50
6280	72" diameter								48	53
9000	Inspection, television camera with video									
9060	up to 500 linear feet				Total				715	820
9220	up to 500 linear feet				"					

33 01 Operation and Maintenance of Utilities

33 01 30 – Operation and Maintenance of Sewer Utilities

33 01 30.23 Pipe Bursting

		Crew	Daily Output	Labor-Hours	Unit	Material	2023 Bare Costs Labor	2023 Bare Costs Equipment	Total	Total Incl O&P
0010	**PIPE BURSTING**									
0011	300' runs, replace with HDPE pipe									
0020	Not including excavation, backfill, shoring, or dewatering									
0100	6" to 15" diameter, minimum				L.F.				200	220
0200	Maximum								550	605
0300	18" to 36" diameter, minimum								650	715
0400	Maximum				▼				1,050	1,150
0500	Mobilize and demobilize, minimum				Job				3,000	3,300
0600	Maximum				"				32,100	35,400

33 01 30.72 Cured-In-Place Pipe Lining

		Crew	Daily Output	Labor-Hours	Unit	Material	Labor	Equipment	Total	Total Incl O&P
0010	**CURED-IN-PLACE PIPE LINING**									
0011	Not incl. bypass or cleaning									
0020	Less than 10,000 L.F., urban, 6" to 10"	C-17E	130	.615	L.F.	13.85	38	.31	52.16	72.50
0050	10" to 12"		125	.640		17.05	39.50	.33	56.88	78.50
0070	12" to 16"		115	.696		17.45	43	.35	60.80	84
0100	16" to 20"		95	.842		20.50	52	.43	72.93	101
0200	24" to 36"		90	.889		22.50	55	.45	77.95	108
0300	48" to 72"	▼	80	1	▼	35	61.50	.51	97.01	132

33 01 30.74 Sliplining, Excludes Cleaning

		Crew	Daily Output	Labor-Hours	Unit	Material	Labor	Equipment	Total	Total Incl O&P
0010	**SLIPLINING, excludes cleaning** and video inspection									
0020	Pipe relined with one pipe size smaller than original (4" for 6")									
0100	6" diameter, original size	B-6B	600	.080	L.F.	1.97	3.83	1.80	7.60	9.85
0150	8" diameter, original size		600	.080		3.35	3.83	1.80	8.98	11.35
0200	10" diameter, original size		600	.080		10.50	3.83	1.80	16.13	19.25
0250	12" diameter, original size		400	.120		6.85	5.75	2.70	15.30	19.05
0300	14" diameter, original size	▼	400	.120		14.30	5.75	2.70	22.75	27.50
0350	16" diameter, original size	B-6C	300	.160		10.80	7.65	6.05	24.50	30
0400	18" diameter, original size	"	300	.160	▼	13.70	7.65	6.05	27.40	33
1000	Pipe HDPE lining, make service line taps	B-6	4	6	Ea.	104	310	69.50	483.50	650

33 01 30.75 Cured-In-place Pipe Lining

		Crew	Daily Output	Labor-Hours	Unit	Material	Labor	Equipment	Total	Total Incl O&P
0010	**CURED-IN-PLACE PIPE LINING**									
0050	Bypass, Sewer	C-17E	500	.160	L.F.	9.85		.08	9.93	14.90
0090	Mobilize - (Any Size) 1 Mob per Job.		1	80	Job		4,925	41	4,966	7,450
0091	Relocate - (°12") (8hrs, 3 per day)		3	26.667	Ea.		1,650	13.60	1,663.60	2,500
0092	Relocate - (12" to 24") (8hrs, 2 per day)		2	40			2,475	20.50	2,495.50	3,725
0093	Relocate - (24" to 42") (8hrs, 1.5 per day)		1.50	53.333			3,300	27	3,327	4,975
0094	Relocate - (42") (8hrs, 1.5 per day)		1	80	▼		4,925	41	4,966	7,450
0095	Additional Travel, $2.00 per Mile		3362.50	.024	Mile		1.47	.01	1.48	2.21
0096	Demobilize - (Any Size) 1 Demob per Job.		1	80	Job		4,925	41	4,966	7,450
0097	Refrigeration Truck (12", Cost per Each Location)		3	26.667	Ea.		1,650	13.60	1,663.60	2,500
0098	Refrigeration Truck (12"-24", Each Pipe/Location)		3	26.667			1,650	13.60	1,663.60	2,500
0099	Refrigeration Truck (24"-42", Each Pipe/Location)		1.50	53.333			3,300	27	3,327	4,975
0100	Refrigeration Truck (42", Each Pipe / Location)		1	80	▼		4,925	41	4,966	7,450
1210	12", 6mm, Epoxy, 250k, 2ft		6	13.333	L.F.	73.50	820	6.80	900.30	1,325
1211	12", 6mm, Epoxy, 250k, 4ft		12	6.667		73.50	410	3.40	486.90	700
1212	12", 6mm, Epoxy, 250k, 10ft		30	2.667		73.50	164	1.36	238.86	330
1213	12", 6mm, Epoxy, 250k, 20ft		60	1.333		73.50	82	.68	156.18	205
1214	12", 6mm, Epoxy, 250k, 50ft		150	.533		73.50	33	.27	106.77	131
1215	12", 6mm, Epoxy, 250k, 100ft		300	.267		73.50	16.45	.14	90.09	106
1216	12", 6mm, Epoxy, 250k, 300ft		900	.089		73.50	5.50	.05	79.05	89.50
1217	12", 6mm, Epoxy, 250k, 328ft	▼	1000	.080		73.50	4.93	.04	78.47	88.50

33 01 Operation and Maintenance of Utilities

33 01 30 – Operation and Maintenance of Sewer Utilities

33 01 30.75 Cured-In-place Pipe Lining		Crew	Daily Output	Labor-Hours	Unit	Material	2023 Bare Costs Labor	Equipment	Total	Total Incl O&P
1218	12", 6mm, Epoxy, 250k, Transitions, add				L.F.	20%				
1219	12", 6mm, Epoxy, 250k, 45 and 90 deg, add					50%				
1230	12", 5mm, Epoxy, 400k, 2ft	C-17E	6	13.333		61.50	820	6.80	888.30	1,300
1231	12", 5mm, Epoxy, 400k, 4ft		12	6.667		61.50	410	3.40	474.90	685
1232	12", 5mm, Epoxy, 400k, 10ft		30	2.667		61.50	164	1.36	226.86	315
1233	12", 5mm, Epoxy, 400k, 20ft		60	1.333		61.50	82	.68	144.18	191
1234	12", 5mm, Epoxy, 400k, 50ft		150	.533		61.50	33	.27	94.77	117
1235	12", 5mm, Epoxy, 400k, 100ft		300	.267		61.50	16.45	.14	78.09	92
1236	12", 5mm, Epoxy, 400k, 300ft		900	.089		61.50	5.50	.05	67.05	76
1237	12", 5mm, Epoxy, 400k, 328ft		1000	.080		61.50	4.93	.04	66.47	75
1238	12", 5mm, Epoxy, 400k, Transitions, add					20%				
1239	12", 5mm, Epoxy, 400k, 45 and 90 deg, add					50%				
2410	24", 12mm, Epoxy, 250k, 2ft	C-17E	4	20		295	1,225	10.20	1,530.20	2,175
2411	24", 12mm, Epoxy, 250k, 4ft		8	10		295	615	5.10	915.10	1,250
2412	24", 12mm, Epoxy, 250k, 10ft		20	4		295	247	2.04	544.04	695
2413	24", 12mm, Epoxy, 250k, 20ft		40	2		295	123	1.02	419.02	510
2414	24", 12mm, Epoxy, 250k, 50ft		100	.800		295	49.50	.41	344.91	400
2415	24", 12mm, Epoxy, 250k, 100ft		200	.400		295	24.50	.20	319.70	360
2416	24", 12mm, Epoxy, 250k, 300ft		600	.133		295	8.20	.07	303.27	335
2417	24", 12mm, Epoxy, 250k, 328ft		656	.122		295	7.50	.06	302.56	335
2418	24", 12mm, Epoxy, 250k, Transitions, add					20%				
2419	24", 12mm, Epoxy, 250k, 45 and 90 deg, add					50%				
2430	24", 10.5mm, Epoxy, 400k, 2ft	C-17E	4	20		258	1,225	10.20	1,493.20	2,150
2431	24", 10.5mm, Epoxy, 400k, 4ft		8	10		258	615	5.10	878.10	1,225
2432	24", 10.5mm, Epoxy, 400k, 10ft		20	4		258	247	2.04	507.04	655
2433	24", 10.5mm, Epoxy, 400k, 20ft		40	2		258	123	1.02	382.02	470
2434	24", 10.5mm, Epoxy, 400k, 50ft		100	.800		258	49.50	.41	307.91	360
2435	24", 10.5mm, Epoxy, 400k, 100ft		200	.400		258	24.50	.20	282.70	320
2436	24", 10.5mm, Epoxy, 400k, 300ft		600	.133		258	8.20	.07	266.27	296
2437	24", 10.5mm, Epoxy, 400k, 328ft		656	.122		258	7.50	.06	265.56	295
2438	24", 10.5mm, Epoxy, 400k, Transitions, add					20%				
2439	24", 10.5mm, Epoxy, 400k, 45 and 90 deg, add					50%				

33 05 Common Work Results for Utilities

33 05 07 – Trenchless Installation of Utility Piping

33 05 07.23 Utility Boring and Jacking

		Crew	Daily Output	Labor-Hours	Unit	Material	Labor	Equipment	Total	Total Incl O&P
0010	**UTILITY BORING AND JACKING**									
0011	Casing only, 100' minimum,									
0020	not incl. jacking pits or dewatering									
0100	Roadwork, 1/2" thick wall, 24" diameter casing	B-42	20	3.200	L.F.	163	170	143	476	590
0200	36" diameter		16	4		252	213	179	644	795
0300	48" diameter		15	4.267		350	227	191	768	935
0500	Railroad work, 24" diameter		15	4.267		163	227	191	581	730
0600	36" diameter		14	4.571		252	243	204	699	865
0700	48" diameter		12	5.333		350	284	238	872	1,075
0900	For ledge, add								20%	20%
1000	Small diameter boring, 3", sandy soil	B-82	900	.018		44.50	.95	.13	45.58	50.50
1040	Rocky soil	"	500	.032		44.50	1.71	.23	46.44	52
1100	Prepare jacking pits, incl. mobilization & demobilization, minimum				Ea.				3,225	3,700
1101	Maximum				"				22,000	25,500

33 05 Common Work Results for Utilities

33 05 07 – Trenchless Installation of Utility Piping

33 05 07.36 Microtunneling

		Crew	Daily Output	Labor-Hours	Unit	Material	2023 Bare Costs Labor	Equipment	Total	Total Incl O&P
0010	**MICROTUNNELING**									
0011	Not including excavation, backfill, shoring,									
0020	or dewatering, average 50'/day, slurry method									
0100	24" to 48" outside diameter, minimum				L.F.				965	965
0110	Adverse conditions, add				"				500	500
1000	Rent microtunneling machine, average monthly lease				Month				97,500	107,000
1010	Operating technician				Day				630	705
1100	Mobilization and demobilization, minimum				Job				41,200	45,900
1110	Maximum				"				445,500	490,500

33 05 61 – Concrete Manholes

33 05 61.10 Storm Drainage Manholes, Frames and Covers

		Crew	Daily Output	Labor-Hours	Unit	Material	Labor	Equipment	Total	Total Incl O&P
0010	**STORM DRAINAGE MANHOLES, FRAMES & COVERS**									
0020	Excludes footing, excavation, backfill (See line items for frame & cover)									
0050	Brick, 4' inside diameter, 4' deep	D-1	1	16	Ea.	1,475	835		2,310	2,875
0100	6' deep		.70	22.857		2,175	1,200		3,375	4,150
0150	8' deep		.50	32		2,825	1,675		4,500	5,625
0200	Add for 1' depth increase		4	4	V.L.F.	370	208		578	725
0400	Concrete blocks (radial), 4' ID, 4' deep		1.50	10.667	Ea.	480	555		1,035	1,350
0500	6' deep		1	16		625	835		1,460	1,925
0600	8' deep		.70	22.857		770	1,200		1,970	2,625
0700	For depths over 8', add		5.50	2.909	V.L.F.	76	152		228	310
0800	Concrete, cast in place, 4' x 4', 8" thick, 4' deep	C-14H	2	24	Ea.	785	1,375	14.90	2,174.90	2,925
0900	6' deep		1.50	32		1,150	1,850	19.85	3,019.85	4,000
1000	8' deep		1	48		1,625	2,750	30	4,405	5,925
1100	For depths over 8', add		8	6	V.L.F.	199	345	3.72	547.72	735
1110	Precast, 4' ID, 4' deep	B-22	4.10	7.317	Ea.	1,225	405	70.50	1,700.50	2,000
1120	6' deep		3	10		1,475	555	96.50	2,126.50	2,550
1130	8' deep		2	15		1,875	830	145	2,850	3,475
1140	For depths over 8', add		16	1.875	V.L.F.	167	104	18.10	289.10	360
1150	5' ID, 4' deep	B-6	3	8	Ea.	2,325	410	92.50	2,827.50	3,250
1160	6' deep		2	12		2,850	615	139	3,604	4,200
1170	8' deep		1.50	16		3,375	820	185	4,380	5,150
1180	For depths over 8', add		12	2	V.L.F.	340	103	23	466	555
1190	6' ID, 4' deep		2	12	Ea.	4,100	615	139	4,854	5,600
1200	6' deep		1.50	16		4,100	820	185	5,105	5,925
1210	8' deep		1	24		4,800	1,225	277	6,302	7,400
1220	For depths over 8', add		8	3	V.L.F.	440	154	34.50	628.50	755
1250	Slab tops, precast, 8" thick									
1300	4' diameter manhole	B-6	8	3	Ea.	285	154	34.50	473.50	585
1400	5' diameter manhole		7.50	3.200		540	164	37	741	880
1500	6' diameter manhole		7	3.429		925	176	39.50	1,140.50	1,325
3800	Steps, heavyweight cast iron, 7" x 9"	1 Bric	40	.200		21	11.50		32.50	40.50
3900	8" x 9"		40	.200		25	11.50		36.50	45
3928	12" x 10-1/2"		40	.200		86	11.50		97.50	112
4000	Standard sizes, galvanized steel		40	.200		29	11.50		40.50	49.50
4100	Aluminum		40	.200		37	11.50		48.50	58.50
4150	Polyethylene		40	.200		36	11.50		47.50	57

33 05 Common Work Results for Utilities

33 05 63 – Concrete Vaults and Chambers

33 05 63.13 Precast Concrete Utility Structures

		Crew	Daily Output	Labor-Hours	Unit	Material	2023 Bare Costs Labor	Equipment	Total	Total Incl O&P
0010	**PRECAST CONCRETE UTILITY STRUCTURES**, 6" thick									
0050	5' x 10' x 6' high, ID	B-13	2	28	Ea.	2,100	1,450	1,125	4,675	5,700
0100	6' x 10' x 6' high, ID		2	28		2,175	1,450	1,125	4,750	5,800
0150	5' x 12' x 6' high, ID		2	28		2,300	1,450	1,125	4,875	5,950
0200	6' x 12' x 6' high, ID		1.80	31.111		2,575	1,600	1,275	5,450	6,650
0250	6' x 13' x 6' high, ID		1.50	37.333		3,400	1,925	1,525	6,850	8,275
0300	8' x 14' x 7' high, ID		1	56		3,675	2,875	2,275	8,825	10,800
0350	Hand hole, precast concrete, 1-1/2" thick									
0400	1'-0" x 2'-0" x 1'-9", ID, light duty	B-1	4	6	Ea.	650	288		938	1,150
0450	4'-6" x 3'-2" x 2'-0", OD, heavy duty	B-6	3	8	"	3,525	410	92.50	4,027.50	4,575

33 05 71 – Cleanouts

33 05 71.10 Cleanout Access

		Crew	Daily Output	Labor-Hours	Unit	Material	Labor	Equipment	Total	Total Incl O&P
0010	**CLEANOUT ACCESS**									
0300	Cleanout Access Housing, X-Hvy Dty, Ductile Iron	B-20	10	2.400	Ea.	1,600	126		1,726	1,950
0306	Vandal Proof, Add					111			111	122
0313	Galvanized, Add					890			890	980

33 05 97 – Identification and Signage for Utilities

33 05 97.05 Utility Connection

		Crew	Daily Output	Labor-Hours	Unit	Material	Labor	Equipment	Total	Total Incl O&P
0010	**UTILITY CONNECTION**									
0020	Water, sanitary, stormwater, gas, single connection	B-14	1	48	Ea.	4,425	2,375	277	7,077	8,700
0030	Telecommunication	"	3	16	"	450	795	92.50	1,337.50	1,775

33 05 97.10 Utility Accessories

		Crew	Daily Output	Labor-Hours	Unit	Material	Labor	Equipment	Total	Total Incl O&P
0010	**UTILITY ACCESSORIES**									
0400	Underground tape, detectable, reinforced, alum. foil core, 2"	1 Clab	150	.053	C.L.F.	2	2.52		4.52	5.95

33 11 Groundwater Sources

33 11 13 – Potable Water Supply Wells

33 11 13.10 Wells and Accessories

		Crew	Daily Output	Labor-Hours	Unit	Material	Labor	Equipment	Total	Total Incl O&P
0010	**WELLS & ACCESSORIES**									
0011	Domestic									
0100	Drilled, 4" to 6" diameter	B-23	120	.333	L.F.		15.90	10.40	26.30	35
0200	8" diameter	"	95.20	.420	"		20	13.10	33.10	44.50
0400	Gravel pack well, 40' deep, incl. gravel & casing, complete									
0500	24" diameter casing x 18" diameter screen	B-23	.13	308	Total	51,000	14,700	9,600	75,300	89,000
0600	36" diameter casing x 18" diameter screen		.12	333	"	52,500	15,900	10,400	78,800	93,000
0800	Observation wells, 1-1/4" riser pipe		163	.245	V.L.F.	24	11.70	7.65	43.35	52.50
0900	For flush Buffalo roadway box, add	1 Skwk	16.60	.482	Ea.	69	29.50		98.50	121
1200	Test well, 2-1/2" diameter, up to 50' deep (15 to 50 GPM)	B-23	1.51	26.490	"	1,175	1,250	825	3,250	4,075
1300	Over 50' deep, add	"	121.80	.328	L.F.	31.50	15.65	10.25	57.40	69.50
1500	Pumps, installed in wells to 100' deep, 4" submersible									
1510	1/2 HP	Q-1	3.22	4.969	Ea.	965	320		1,285	1,525
1520	3/4 HP		2.66	6.015		1,000	390		1,390	1,675
1600	1 HP		2.29	6.987		1,250	455		1,705	2,050
1700	1-1/2 HP	Q-22	1.60	10		1,600	650	1,350	3,600	4,200
1800	2 HP		1.33	12.030		2,200	780	1,625	4,605	5,375
1900	3 HP		1.14	14.035		2,725	910	1,875	5,510	6,400
2000	5 HP		1.14	14.035		3,025	910	1,875	5,810	6,750
3000	Pump, 6" submersible, 25' to 150' deep, 25 HP, 103 to 400 GPM		.89	17.978		12,300	1,175	2,425	15,900	18,000
3100	25' to 500' deep, 30 HP, 104 to 400 GPM		.73	21.918		14,500	1,425	2,950	18,875	21,300

33 11 Groundwater Sources

33 11 13 – Potable Water Supply Wells

33 11 13.10 Wells and Accessories

		Crew	Daily Output	Labor-Hours	Unit	Material	2023 Bare Costs Labor	Equipment	Total	Total Incl O&P
8000	Steel well casing	B-23A	3020	.008	Lb.	1.71	.42	.32	2.45	2.87
8110	Well screen assembly, stainless steel, 2" diameter		273	.088	L.F.	126	4.68	3.59	134.27	150
8120	3" diameter		253	.095		186	5.05	3.87	194.92	216
8130	4" diameter		200	.120		240	6.40	4.89	251.29	279
8140	5" diameter		168	.143		224	7.60	5.85	237.45	265
8150	6" diameter		126	.190		252	10.15	7.75	269.90	300
8160	8" diameter		98.50	.244		335	12.95	9.95	357.90	400
8170	10" diameter		73	.329		420	17.50	13.40	450.90	500
8180	12" diameter		62.50	.384		490	20.50	15.65	526.15	590
8190	14" diameter		54.30	.442		550	23.50	18	591.50	660
8200	16" diameter		48.30	.497		605	26.50	20.50	652	725
8210	18" diameter		39.20	.612		765	32.50	25	822.50	920
8220	20" diameter		31.20	.769		870	41	31.50	942.50	1,050
8230	24" diameter		23.80	1.008		1,075	53.50	41	1,169.50	1,300
8240	26" diameter		21	1.143		1,350	61	46.50	1,457.50	1,650
8244	Well casing or drop pipe, PVC, 1/2" diameter		550	.044		1.72	2.32	1.78	5.82	7.30
8245	3/4" diameter		550	.044		1.74	2.32	1.78	5.84	7.30
8246	1" diameter		550	.044		1.79	2.32	1.78	5.89	7.40
8247	1-1/4" diameter		520	.046		2.24	2.45	1.88	6.57	8.20
8248	1-1/2" diameter		490	.049		2.38	2.60	2	6.98	8.70
8249	1-3/4" diameter		380	.063		2.43	3.36	2.58	8.37	10.50
8250	2" diameter		280	.086		2.79	4.56	3.50	10.85	13.70
8252	3" diameter		260	.092		5.50	4.91	3.76	14.17	17.50
8254	4" diameter		205	.117		5.85	6.25	4.77	16.87	21
8255	5" diameter		170	.141		5.90	7.50	5.75	19.15	24
8256	6" diameter		130	.185		11.25	9.80	7.55	28.60	35.50
8258	8" diameter		100	.240		17.15	12.75	9.80	39.70	48.50
8260	10" diameter		73	.329		27.50	17.50	13.40	58.40	71.50
8262	12" diameter		62	.387		31.50	20.50	15.80	67.80	82.50
8300	Slotted PVC, 1-1/4" diameter		521	.046		3.80	2.45	1.88	8.13	9.90
8310	1-1/2" diameter		488	.049		3.94	2.62	2.01	8.57	10.45
8320	2" diameter		273	.088		5.10	4.68	3.59	13.37	16.50
8330	3" diameter		253	.095		8.95	5.05	3.87	17.87	21.50
8340	4" diameter		200	.120		9.55	6.40	4.89	20.84	25.50
8350	5" diameter		168	.143		20.50	7.60	5.85	33.95	40.50
8360	6" diameter		126	.190		22	10.15	7.75	39.90	48
8370	8" diameter		98.50	.244		32.50	12.95	9.95	55.40	66.50
8400	Artificial gravel pack, 2" screen, 6" casing	B-23B	174	.138		5.95	7.35	7.85	21.15	26
8405	8" casing		111	.216		8.15	11.50	12.30	31.95	39.50
8410	10" casing		74.50	.322		11.25	17.15	18.35	46.75	58
8415	12" casing		60	.400		17.95	21.50	23	62.45	76.50
8420	14" casing		50.20	.478		18.35	25.50	27	70.85	88
8425	16" casing		40.70	.590		24	31.50	33.50	89	110
8430	18" casing		36	.667		29.50	35.50	38	103	127
8435	20" casing		29.50	.814		32.50	43.50	46.50	122.50	152
8440	24" casing		25.70	.934		37.50	49.50	53	140	174
8445	26" casing		24.60	.976		41.50	52	55.50	149	184
8450	30" casing		20	1.200		47.50	64	68.50	180	223
8455	36" casing		16.40	1.463		52	78	83.50	213.50	265
8500	Develop well		8	3	Hr.	400	160	171	731	870
8550	Pump test well		8	3		127	160	171	458	565
8560	Standby well	B-23A	8	3		131	160	122	413	515
8570	Standby, drill rig		8	3			160	122	282	370

33 11 Groundwater Sources

33 11 13 – Potable Water Supply Wells

33 11 13.10 Wells and Accessories

		Crew	Daily Output	Labor-Hours	Unit	Material	2023 Bare Costs Labor	Equipment	Total	Total Incl O&P
8580	Surface seal well, concrete filled	B-23A	1	24	Ea.	1,425	1,275	980	3,680	4,550
8590	Well test pump, install & remove	B-23	1	40			1,900	1,250	3,150	4,225
8600	Well sterilization, chlorine	2 Clab	1	16		82	755		837	1,225
8610	Well water pressure switch	1 Clab	12	.667		129	31.50		160.50	189
8630	Well water pressure switch with manual reset	"	12	.667	↓	171	31.50		202.50	235
9950	See Section 31 23 19.40 for wellpoints									
9960	See Section 31 23 19.30 for drainage wells									

33 11 13.20 Water Supply Wells, Pumps

		Crew	Daily Output	Labor-Hours	Unit	Material	Labor	Equipment	Total	Total Incl O&P
0010	**WATER SUPPLY WELLS, PUMPS**									
0011	With pressure control									
1000	Deep well, jet, 42 gal. galvanized tank									
1040	3/4 HP	1 Plum	.80	10	Ea.	1,500	720		2,220	2,700
3000	Shallow well, jet, 30 gal. galvanized tank									
3040	1/2 HP	1 Plum	2	4	Ea.	1,200	288		1,488	1,750

33 14 Water Utility Transmission and Distribution

33 14 13 – Public Water Utility Distribution Piping

33 14 13.15 Water Supply, Ductile Iron Pipe

		Crew	Daily Output	Labor-Hours	Unit	Material	Labor	Equipment	Total	Total Incl O&P
0010	**WATER SUPPLY, DUCTILE IRON PIPE** R331113-80									
0020	Not including excavation or backfill									
2000	Pipe, class 50 water piping, 18' lengths									
2020	Mechanical joint, 4" diameter	B-21	200	.140	L.F.	101	7.65	.96	109.61	123
2040	6" diameter		160	.175		120	9.55	1.21	130.76	148
2060	8" diameter		133.33	.210		169	11.45	1.45	181.90	204
2080	10" diameter		114.29	.245		220	13.35	1.69	235.04	264
2100	12" diameter		105.26	.266		272	14.50	1.83	288.33	325
2120	14" diameter		100	.280		141	15.25	1.93	158.18	180
2140	16" diameter		72.73	.385		143	21	2.65	166.65	192
2160	18" diameter		68.97	.406		192	22	2.80	216.80	247
2170	20" diameter		57.14	.490		194	26.50	3.38	223.88	257
2180	24" diameter		47.06	.595		213	32.50	4.10	249.60	288
3000	Push-on joint, 4" diameter		400	.070		24	3.82	.48	28.30	32.50
3020	6" diameter		333.33	.084		23.50	4.58	.58	28.66	33.50
3040	8" diameter		200	.140		33	7.65	.96	41.61	49
3060	10" diameter		181.82	.154		51	8.40	1.06	60.46	70
3080	12" diameter		160	.175		54	9.55	1.21	64.76	75
3100	14" diameter		133.33	.210		54	11.45	1.45	66.90	78
3120	16" diameter		114.29	.245		57.50	13.35	1.69	72.54	85
3140	18" diameter		100	.280		64	15.25	1.93	81.18	95
3160	20" diameter		88.89	.315		66.50	17.20	2.17	85.87	101
3180	24" diameter	↓	76.92	.364	↓	92.50	19.85	2.51	114.86	134
8000	Piping, fittings, mechanical joint, AWWA C110									
8006	90° bend, 4" diameter	B-20	16	1.500	Ea.	258	79		337	400
8020	6" diameter	"	12.80	1.875		410	98.50		508.50	600
8040	8" diameter	B-21	10.67	2.624		670	143	18.10	831.10	975
8060	10" diameter		11.43	2.450		1,075	134	16.90	1,225.90	1,425
8080	12" diameter		10.53	2.659		1,525	145	18.30	1,688.30	1,900
8100	14" diameter		10	2.800		2,350	153	19.30	2,522.30	2,825
8120	16" diameter		7.27	3.851		2,850	210	26.50	3,086.50	3,475
8140	18" diameter		6.90	4.058		4,075	221	28	4,324	4,825
8160	20" diameter		5.71	4.904		4,950	267	34	5,251	5,850

33 14 Water Utility Transmission and Distribution

33 14 13 – Public Water Utility Distribution Piping

33 14 13.15 Water Supply, Ductile Iron Pipe

		Crew	Daily Output	Labor-Hours	Unit	Material	2023 Bare Costs Labor	Equipment	Total	Total Incl O&P
8180	24" diameter	B-21	4.70	5.957	Ea.	7,250	325	41	7,616	8,500
8200	Wye or tee, 4" diameter	B-20	10.67	2.249		555	118		673	785
8220	6" diameter	"	8.53	2.814		965	148		1,113	1,300
8240	8" diameter	B-21	7.11	3.938		1,350	215	27	1,592	1,825
8260	10" diameter		7.62	3.675		1,725	200	25.50	1,950.50	2,225
8280	12" diameter		7.02	3.989		3,225	218	27.50	3,470.50	3,875
8300	14" diameter		6.67	4.198		4,775	229	29	5,033	5,625
8320	16" diameter		4.85	5.773		5,050	315	40	5,405	6,075
8340	18" diameter		4.60	6.087		8,325	330	42	8,697	9,700
8360	20" diameter		3.81	7.349		9,825	400	50.50	10,275.50	11,500
8380	24" diameter		3.14	8.917		14,600	485	61.50	15,146.50	16,900
8398	45° bend, 4" diameter	B-20	16	1.500		255	79		334	400
8400	6" diameter	"	12.80	1.875		390	98.50		488.50	575
8405	8" diameter	B-21	10.67	2.624		570	143	18.10	731.10	865
8410	12" diameter		10.53	2.659		1,200	145	18.30	1,363.30	1,550
8420	16" diameter		7.27	3.851		2,425	210	26.50	2,661.50	3,000
8430	20" diameter		5.71	4.904		3,525	267	34	3,826	4,300
8440	24" diameter		4.70	5.957		4,925	325	41	5,291	5,950
8450	Decreaser, 6" x 4" diameter	B-20	14.22	1.688		355	88.50		443.50	525
8460	8" x 6" diameter	B-21	11.64	2.406		545	131	16.55	692.55	810
8470	10" x 6" diameter		13.33	2.101		725	115	14.45	854.45	985
8480	12" x 6" diameter		12.70	2.205		1,025	120	15.20	1,160.20	1,325
8490	16" x 6" diameter		10	2.800		1,275	153	19.30	1,447.30	1,650
8500	20" x 6" diameter		8.42	3.325		5,550	181	23	5,754	6,400
8552	For water utility valves see Section 33 14 19									
8700	Joint restraint, ductile iron mechanical joints									
8710	4" diameter	B-20	32	.750	Ea.	45	39.50		84.50	109
8720	6" diameter	"	25.60	.938		54	49.50		103.50	133
8730	8" diameter	B-21	21.33	1.313		82	71.50	9.05	162.55	207
8740	10" diameter		18.28	1.532		132	83.50	10.55	226.05	282
8750	12" diameter		16.84	1.663		171	90.50	11.45	272.95	335
8760	14" diameter		16	1.750		236	95.50	12.05	343.55	415
8770	16" diameter		11.64	2.406		299	131	16.55	446.55	545
8780	18" diameter		11.03	2.539		425	138	17.50	580.50	690
8785	20" diameter		9.14	3.063		525	167	21	713	850
8790	24" diameter		7.53	3.718		725	203	25.50	953.50	1,125
9600	Steel sleeve with tap, 4" diameter	B-20	3	8		550	420		970	1,225
9620	6" diameter		2	12		590	630		1,220	1,600
9630	8" diameter		2	12		750	630		1,380	1,775

33 14 13.20 Water Supply, Polyethylene Pipe, C901

		Crew	Daily Output	Labor-Hours	Unit	Material	2023 Bare Costs Labor	Equipment	Total	Total Incl O&P
0010	**WATER SUPPLY, POLYETHYLENE PIPE, C901**									
0020	Not including excavation or backfill									
1000	Piping, 160 psi, 3/4" diameter	Q-1A	525	.019	L.F.	.69	1.38		2.07	2.82
1120	1" diameter		485	.021		.70	1.49		2.19	3
1140	1-1/2" diameter		450	.022		1.85	1.61		3.46	4.44
1160	2" diameter		365	.027		2.37	1.98		4.35	5.55
2000	Fittings, insert type, nylon, 160 & 250 psi, cold water									
2220	Clamp ring, stainless steel, 3/4" diameter	Q-1A	345	.029	Ea.	2.95	2.10		5.05	6.40
2240	1" diameter		321	.031		3.08	2.26		5.34	6.75
2260	1-1/2" diameter		285	.035		3.35	2.54		5.89	7.50
2280	2" diameter		255	.039		4.60	2.84		7.44	9.30
2300	Coupling, 3/4" diameter		66	.152		1.71	11		12.71	18.25

33 14 Water Utility Transmission and Distribution

33 14 13 – Public Water Utility Distribution Piping

33 14 13.20 Water Supply, Polyethylene Pipe, C901		Crew	Daily Output	Labor-Hours	Unit	Material	2023 Bare Costs Labor	Equipment	Total	Total Incl O&P
2320	1" diameter	Q-1A	57	.175	Ea.	2.29	12.70		14.99	21.50
2340	1-1/2" diameter		51	.196		5.55	14.20		19.75	27
2360	2" diameter		48	.208		7.05	15.10		22.15	30.50
2400	Elbow, 90°, 3/4" diameter		66	.152		2.81	11		13.81	19.45
2420	1" diameter		57	.175		3.37	12.70		16.07	22.50
2440	1-1/2" diameter		51	.196		8.70	14.20		22.90	30.50
2460	2" diameter		48	.208		11.60	15.10		26.70	35.50

33 14 13.25 Water Supply, Polyvinyl Chloride Pipe		Crew	Daily Output	Labor-Hours	Unit	Material	2023 Bare Costs Labor	Equipment	Total	Total Incl O&P
0010	**WATER SUPPLY, POLYVINYL CHLORIDE PIPE** R331113-80									
0020	Not including excavation or backfill, unless specified									
2100	PVC pipe, Class 150, 1-1/2" diameter	Q-1A	750	.013	L.F.	1.43	.97		2.40	3.01
2120	2" diameter		686	.015		1.40	1.06		2.46	3.11
2140	2-1/2" diameter		500	.020		2.37	1.45		3.82	4.77
2160	3" diameter	B-20	430	.056		3.04	2.93		5.97	7.70
3010	AWWA C905, PR 100, DR 25									
3030	14" diameter	B-21	213	.131	L.F.	18.80	7.15	.91	26.86	32
3040	16" diameter		200	.140		25.50	7.65	.96	34.11	40.50
3050	18" diameter		160	.175		31	9.55	1.21	41.76	49.50
3060	20" diameter		133	.211		38.50	11.50	1.45	51.45	61.50
3070	24" diameter		107	.262		57.50	14.25	1.80	73.55	86.50
3080	30" diameter		80	.350		96.50	19.10	2.41	118.01	137
3090	36" diameter		80	.350		149	19.10	2.41	170.51	195
3100	42" diameter		60	.467		202	25.50	3.22	230.72	264
3200	48" diameter		60	.467		257	25.50	3.22	285.72	325
3960	Pressure pipe, class 200, ASTM 2241, SDR 21, 3/4" diameter	Q-1A	1000	.010		.36	.72		1.08	1.48
3980	1" diameter		900	.011		.77	.81		1.58	2.05
4000	1-1/2" diameter		750	.013		2.46	.97		3.43	4.15
4010	2" diameter		686	.015		3.22	1.06		4.28	5.10
4020	2-1/2" diameter		500	.020		4.41	1.45		5.86	7
4030	3" diameter	B-20	430	.056		6.45	2.93		9.38	11.50
4040	4" diameter		375	.064		10.70	3.37		14.07	16.80
4050	6" diameter		316	.076		25.50	3.99		29.49	34
4060	8" diameter		260	.092		11.50	4.85		16.35	19.90
4090	Including trenching to 3' deep, 3/4" diameter	Q-1C	300	.080		.36	5.15	6.95	12.46	15.65
4100	1" diameter		280	.086		.77	5.50	7.45	13.72	17.20
4110	1-1/2" diameter		260	.092		2.46	5.95	8	16.41	20.50
4120	2" diameter		220	.109		3.22	7	9.45	19.67	24.50
4130	2-1/2" diameter		200	.120		4.41	7.70	10.40	22.51	28
4140	3" diameter		175	.137		6.45	8.80	11.90	27.15	33.50
4150	4" diameter		150	.160		10.70	10.30	13.85	34.85	42.50
4160	6" diameter		125	.192		25.50	12.35	16.65	54.50	64.50
4165	Fittings									
4170	Elbow, 90°, 3/4"	Q-1A	114	.088	Ea.	.71	6.35		7.06	10.30
4180	1"		100	.100		4.35	7.25		11.60	15.60
4190	1-1/2"		80	.125		27	9.05		36.05	43
4200	2"		72	.139		27.50	10.05		37.55	45
4210	3"	B-20	46	.522		72	27.50		99.50	120
4220	4"		36	.667		68	35		103	128
4230	6"		24	1		213	52.50		265.50	315
4240	8"		14	1.714		130	90		220	278
4250	Elbow, 45°, 3/4"	Q-1A	114	.088		1	6.35		7.35	10.60
4260	1"		100	.100		20	7.25		27.25	33

33 14 Water Utility Transmission and Distribution

33 14 13 – Public Water Utility Distribution Piping

33 14 13.25 Water Supply, Polyvinyl Chloride Pipe		Crew	Daily Output	Labor-Hours	Unit	Material	2023 Bare Costs Labor	Equipment	Total	Total Incl O&P
4270	1-1/2"	Q-1A	80	.125	Ea.	25.50	9.05		34.55	42
4280	2"		72	.139		27	10.05		37.05	44.50
4290	2-1/2"	↓	54	.185		30.50	13.40		43.90	53.50
4300	3"	B-20	46	.522		38.50	27.50		66	83.50
4310	4"		36	.667		66	35		101	126
4320	6"		24	1		121	52.50		173.50	213
4330	8"	↓	14	1.714		172	90		262	325
4340	Tee, 3/4"	Q-1A	76	.132		4.43	9.55		13.98	19.05
4350	1"		66	.152		7.85	11		18.85	25
4360	1-1/2"		54	.185		45	13.40		58.40	69.50
4370	2"		48	.208		55.50	15.10		70.60	84
4380	2-1/2"	↓	36	.278		62	20		82	98
4390	3"	B-20	30	.800		62.50	42		104.50	132
4400	4"		24	1		33	52.50		85.50	115
4410	6"		14.80	1.622		72.50	85.50		158	207
4420	8"	↓	9	2.667		128	140		268	350
4430	Coupling, 3/4"	Q-1A	114	.088		2.19	6.35		8.54	11.90
4440	1"		100	.100		7.05	7.25		14.30	18.60
4450	1-1/2"		80	.125		31	9.05		40.05	48
4460	2"		72	.139		32	10.05		42.05	50
4470	2-1/2"	↓	54	.185		34.50	13.40		47.90	57.50
4480	3"	B-20	46	.522		43.50	27.50		71	88.50
4490	4"		36	.667		79	35		114	140
4500	6"		24	1		61.50	52.50		114	146
4510	8"		14	1.714	↓	68.50	90		158.50	210
4520	Pressure pipe Class 150, SDR 18, AWWA C900, 4" diameter		380	.063	L.F.	5.20	3.32		8.52	10.65
4530	6" diameter	↓	316	.076		7.50	3.99		11.49	14.20
4540	8" diameter	B-21	264	.106		9.60	5.80	.73	16.13	20
4550	10" diameter		220	.127		13.05	6.95	.88	20.88	25.50
4560	12" diameter		186	.151	↓	17.75	8.20	1.04	26.99	33
8000	Fittings with rubber gasket									
8003	Class 150, DR 18									
8006	90° bend, 4" diameter	B-20	100	.240	Ea.	57	12.60		69.60	82
8020	6" diameter	"	90	.267		102	14		116	133
8040	8" diameter	B-21	80	.350		197	19.10	2.41	218.51	247
8060	10" diameter		50	.560		385	30.50	3.86	419.36	470
8080	12" diameter		30	.933		570	51	6.45	627.45	710
8100	Tee, 4" diameter		90	.311		165	16.95	2.14	184.09	210
8120	6" diameter		80	.350		269	19.10	2.41	290.51	325
8140	8" diameter		70	.400		490	22	2.76	514.76	575
8160	10" diameter		40	.700		1,450	38	4.82	1,492.82	1,650
8180	12" diameter	↓	20	1.400		2,075	76.50	9.65	2,161.15	2,400
8200	45° bend, 4" diameter	B-20	100	.240		73	12.60		85.60	99.50
8220	6" diameter	"	90	.267		134	14		148	168
8240	8" diameter	B-21	50	.560		335	30.50	3.86	369.36	415
8260	10" diameter		50	.560		655	30.50	3.86	689.36	770
8280	12" diameter		30	.933		1,025	51	6.45	1,082.45	1,200
8300	Reducing tee 6" x 4"		100	.280		171	15.25	1.93	188.18	213
8320	8" x 6"		90	.311		305	16.95	2.14	324.09	365
8330	10" x 6"		90	.311		267	16.95	2.14	286.09	320
8340	10" x 8"		90	.311		286	16.95	2.14	305.09	345
8350	12" x 6"		90	.311		360	16.95	2.14	379.09	425
8360	12" x 8"		90	.311		395	16.95	2.14	414.09	465

33 14 Water Utility Transmission and Distribution

33 14 13 – Public Water Utility Distribution Piping

33 14 13.25 Water Supply, Polyvinyl Chloride Pipe

		Crew	Daily Output	Labor-Hours	Unit	Material	2023 Bare Costs Labor	Equipment	Total	Total Incl O&P
8400	Tapped service tee (threaded type) 6" x 6" x 3/4"	B-21	100	.280	Ea.	130	15.25	1.93	147.18	168
8430	6" x 6" x 1"		90	.311		130	16.95	2.14	149.09	171
8440	6" x 6" x 1-1/2"		90	.311		130	16.95	2.14	149.09	171
8450	6" x 6" x 2"		90	.311		130	16.95	2.14	149.09	171
8460	8" x 8" x 3/4"		90	.311		191	16.95	2.14	210.09	238
8470	8" x 8" x 1"		90	.311		191	16.95	2.14	210.09	238
8480	8" x 8" x 1-1/2"		90	.311		191	16.95	2.14	210.09	238
8490	8" x 8" x 2"		90	.311		191	16.95	2.14	210.09	238
8500	Repair coupling 4"	B-20	100	.240		35.50	12.60		48.10	58
8520	6" diameter		90	.267		54.50	14		68.50	80.50
8540	8" diameter		50	.480		131	25		156	182
8560	10" diameter		50	.480		276	25		301	345
8580	12" diameter		50	.480		350	25		375	425
8600	Plug end 4"		100	.240		30.50	12.60		43.10	53
8620	6" diameter		90	.267		55.50	14		69.50	82
8640	8" diameter		50	.480		94	25		119	141
8660	10" diameter		50	.480		150	25		175	203
8680	12" diameter		50	.480		202	25		227	260
8700	PVC pipe, joint restraint									
8710	4" diameter	B-20	32	.750	Ea.	46.50	39.50		86	111
8720	6" diameter		25.60	.938		57.50	49.50		107	137
8730	8" diameter		21.33	1.125		83.50	59		142.50	181
8740	10" diameter		18.28	1.313		133	69		202	249
8750	12" diameter		16.84	1.425		140	75		215	266
8760	14" diameter		16	1.500		190	79		269	325
8770	16" diameter		11.64	2.062		256	108		364	445
8780	18" diameter		11.03	2.176		315	114		429	515
8785	20" diameter		9.14	2.626		445	138		583	695
8790	24" diameter		7.53	3.187		515	168		683	815

33 14 13.35 Water Supply, HDPE

		Crew	Daily Output	Labor-Hours	Unit	Material	2023 Bare Costs Labor	Equipment	Total	Total Incl O&P
0010	**WATER SUPPLY, HDPE**									
0011	Butt fusion joints, SDR 21 40' lengths not including excavation or backfill									
0100	4" diameter	B-22A	400	.100	L.F.	.91	5.45	1.80	8.16	11.10
0200	6" diameter		380	.105		1.97	5.70	1.89	9.56	12.75
0300	8" diameter		320	.125		3.35	6.80	2.24	12.39	16.25
0400	10" diameter		300	.133		10.50	7.25	2.39	20.14	25
0500	12" diameter		260	.154		6.85	8.35	2.76	17.96	23
0600	14" diameter	B-22B	220	.182		14.30	9.85	5.35	29.50	36.50
0700	16" diameter		180	.222		10.80	12.05	6.50	29.35	37
0800	18" diameter		140	.286		13.70	15.50	8.40	37.60	47.50
0850	20" diameter		130	.308		27	16.70	9	52.70	64.50
0900	24" diameter		100	.400		24.50	21.50	11.75	57.75	72.50
1000	Fittings									
1100	Elbows, 90 degrees									
1200	4" diameter	B-22A	32	1.250	Ea.	43	68	22.50	133.50	173
1300	6" diameter		28	1.429		37.50	77.50	25.50	140.50	185
1400	8" diameter		24	1.667		75	90.50	30	195.50	251
1500	10" diameter		18	2.222		112	121	40	273	345
1600	12" diameter		12	3.333		149	181	60	390	500
1700	14" diameter	B-22B	9	4.444		233	241	130	604	760
1800	16" diameter		6	6.667		730	360	196	1,286	1,550
1900	18" diameter		4	10		450	545	293	1,288	1,625

33 14 Water Utility Transmission and Distribution

33 14 13 – Public Water Utility Distribution Piping

33 14 13.35 Water Supply, HDPE

		Crew	Daily Output	Labor-Hours	Unit	Material	2023 Bare Costs Labor	Equipment	Total	Total Incl O&P
2000	24" diameter	B-22B	3	13.333	Ea.	940	725	390	2,055	2,525
2100	Tees									
2200	4" diameter	B-22A	30	1.333	Ea.	25	72.50	24	121.50	162
2300	6" diameter		26	1.538		43	83.50	27.50	154	203
2400	8" diameter		22	1.818		64.50	98.50	32.50	195.50	254
2500	10" diameter		15	2.667		85	145	48	278	360
2600	12" diameter		10	4		355	217	72	644	795
2700	14" diameter	B-22B	8	5		420	271	147	838	1,025
2800	16" diameter		6	6.667		495	360	196	1,051	1,300
2900	18" diameter		4	10		605	545	293	1,443	1,800
3000	24" diameter		2	20		740	1,075	585	2,400	3,075
4100	Caps									
4110	4" diameter	B-22A	34	1.176	Ea.	23	64	21	108	144
4120	6" diameter		30	1.333		28	72.50	24	124.50	165
4130	8" diameter		26	1.538		46.50	83.50	27.50	157.50	207
4150	10" diameter		20	2		115	109	36	260	330
4160	12" diameter		14	2.857		139	155	51.50	345.50	440

33 14 13.45 Water Supply, Copper Pipe

		Crew	Daily Output	Labor-Hours	Unit	Material	2023 Bare Costs Labor	Equipment	Total	Total Incl O&P
0010	**WATER SUPPLY, COPPER PIPE**									
0020	Not including excavation or backfill									
2000	Tubing, type K, 20' joints, 3/4" diameter	Q-1	400	.040	L.F.	4.41	2.59		7	8.70
2200	1" diameter		320	.050		5.75	3.24		8.99	11.15
3000	1-1/2" diameter		265	.060		9.25	3.92		13.17	16.05
3020	2" diameter		230	.070		14.05	4.51		18.56	22
3040	2-1/2" diameter		146	.110		45.50	7.10		52.60	60.50
3060	3" diameter		134	.119		28.50	7.75		36.25	43
4012	4" diameter		95	.168		50	10.90		60.90	71.50
4016	6" diameter	Q-2	80	.300		102	20		122	142
4018	8" diameter	"	80	.300		239	20		259	293
5000	Tubing, type L									
5108	2" diameter	Q-1	230	.070	L.F.	17.95	4.51		22.46	26.50
6010	3" diameter		134	.119		24	7.75		31.75	38
6012	4" diameter		95	.168		40	10.90		50.90	60.50
6016	6" diameter	Q-2	80	.300		88	20		108	127
7165	Fittings, brass, corporation stops, no lead, 3/4" diameter	1 Plum	19	.421	Ea.	109	30.50		139.50	165
7166	1" diameter		16	.500		120	36		156	186
7167	1-1/2" diameter		13	.615		276	44.50		320.50	370
7168	2" diameter		11	.727		515	52.50		567.50	645
7170	Curb stops, no lead, 3/4" diameter		19	.421		137	30.50		167.50	196
7171	1" diameter		16	.500		187	36		223	259
7172	1-1/2" diameter		13	.615		460	44.50		504.50	570
7173	2" diameter		11	.727		310	52.50		362.50	420

33 14 17 – Site Water Utility Service Laterals

33 14 17.15 Tapping, Crosses and Sleeves

		Crew	Daily Output	Labor-Hours	Unit	Material	2023 Bare Costs Labor	Equipment	Total	Total Incl O&P
0010	**TAPPING, CROSSES AND SLEEVES**									
4000	Drill and tap pressurized main (labor only)									
4100	6" main, 1" to 2" service	Q-1	3	5.333	Ea.		345		345	515
4150	8" main, 1" to 2" service	"	2.75	5.818	"		375		375	565
4500	Tap and insert gate valve									
4600	8" main, 4" branch	B-21	3.20	8.750	Ea.	475	60.50		535.50	775
4650	6" branch		2.70	10.370		565	71.50		636.50	925
4700	10" main, 4" branch		2.70	10.370		565	71.50		636.50	925

33 14 Water Utility Transmission and Distribution

33 14 17 – Site Water Utility Service Laterals

33 14 17.15 Tapping, Crosses and Sleeves		Crew	Daily Output	Labor-Hours	Unit	Material	2023 Bare Costs Labor	Equipment	Total	Total Incl O&P
4750	6" branch	B-21	2.35	11.915	Ea.		650	82	732	1,050
4800	12" main, 6" branch		2.35	11.915			650	82	732	1,050
4850	8" branch		2.35	11.915			650	82	732	1,050
7020	Crosses, 4" x 4"		37	.757		1,400	41.50	5.20	1,446.70	1,625
7030	6" x 4"		25	1.120		1,675	61	7.70	1,743.70	1,950
7040	6" x 6"		25	1.120		1,675	61	7.70	1,743.70	1,950
7060	8" x 6"		21	1.333		2,050	72.50	9.20	2,131.70	2,375
7080	8" x 8"		21	1.333		2,225	72.50	9.20	2,306.70	2,575
7100	10" x 6"		21	1.333		4,050	72.50	9.20	4,131.70	4,600
7120	10" x 10"		21	1.333		4,400	72.50	9.20	4,481.70	4,950
7140	12" x 6"		18	1.556		4,050	85	10.70	4,145.70	4,625
7160	12" x 12"		18	1.556		5,125	85	10.70	5,220.70	5,800
7180	14" x 6"		16	1.750		10,100	95.50	12.05	10,207.55	11,300
7200	14" x 14"		16	1.750		10,700	95.50	12.05	10,807.55	12,000
7220	16" x 6"		14	2		10,900	109	13.80	11,022.80	12,100
7240	16" x 10"		14	2		11,000	109	13.80	11,122.80	12,300
7260	16" x 16"		14	2		11,600	109	13.80	11,722.80	12,900
7280	18" x 6"		10	2.800		16,200	153	19.30	16,372.30	18,100
7300	18" x 12"		10	2.800		16,400	153	19.30	16,572.30	18,200
7320	18" x 18"		10	2.800		16,800	153	19.30	16,972.30	18,700
7340	20" x 6"		8	3.500		13,100	191	24	13,315	14,800
7360	20" x 12"		8	3.500		14,100	191	24	14,315	15,800
7380	20" x 20"		8	3.500		20,600	191	24	20,815	22,900
7400	24" x 6"		6	4.667		17,000	255	32	17,287	19,100
7420	24" x 12"		6	4.667		17,200	255	32	17,487	19,300
7440	24" x 18"		6	4.667		26,100	255	32	26,387	29,100
7460	24" x 24"		6	4.667		26,700	255	32	26,987	29,800
7600	Cut-in sleeves with rubber gaskets, 4"		18	1.556		735	85	10.70	830.70	950
7620	6"		12	2.333		910	127	16.10	1,053.10	1,200
7640	8"		10	2.800		1,075	153	19.30	1,247.30	1,450
7660	10"		10	2.800		1,525	153	19.30	1,697.30	1,925
7680	12"		9	3.111		2,100	170	21.50	2,291.50	2,575
7800	Cut-in valves with rubber gaskets, 4"		18	1.556		510	85	10.70	605.70	700
7820	6"		12	2.333		660	127	16.10	803.10	935
7840	8"		10	2.800		910	153	19.30	1,082.30	1,250
7860	10"		10	2.800		1,375	153	19.30	1,547.30	1,750
7880	12"		9	3.111		1,725	170	21.50	1,916.50	2,150
7900	Tapping valve 4", MJ, ductile iron		18	1.556		645	85	10.70	740.70	845
7920	6", MJ, ductile iron		12	2.333		890	127	16.10	1,033.10	1,200
7940	Tapping valve 8", MJ, ductile iron		10	2.800		1,475	153	19.30	1,647.30	1,875
7960	Tapping valve 10", MJ, ductile iron		10	2.800		1,900	153	19.30	2,072.30	2,350
7980	Tapping valve 12", MJ, ductile iron		8	3.500		2,600	191	24	2,815	3,150
8000	Sleeves with rubber gaskets, 4" x 4"		37	.757		1,125	41.50	5.20	1,171.70	1,300
8010	6" x 4"		25	1.120		1,325	61	7.70	1,393.70	1,575
8020	6" x 6"		25	1.120		1,325	61	7.70	1,393.70	1,575
8030	8" x 4"		21	1.333		1,525	72.50	9.20	1,606.70	1,800
8040	8" x 6"		21	1.333		1,575	72.50	9.20	1,656.70	1,850
8060	8" x 8"		21	1.333		1,950	72.50	9.20	2,031.70	2,250
8070	10" x 4"		21	1.333		1,425	72.50	9.20	1,506.70	1,700
8080	10" x 6"		21	1.333		1,525	72.50	9.20	1,606.70	1,800
8090	10" x 8"		21	1.333		1,925	72.50	9.20	2,006.70	2,250
8100	10" x 10"		21	1.333		2,600	72.50	9.20	2,681.70	3,000
8110	12" x 4"		18	1.556		1,500	85	10.70	1,595.70	1,800

33 14 Water Utility Transmission and Distribution

33 14 17 – Site Water Utility Service Laterals

33 14 17.15 Tapping, Crosses and Sleeves		Crew	Daily Output	Labor-Hours	Unit	Material	2023 Bare Costs Labor	Equipment	Total	Total Incl O&P
8120	12" x 6"	B-21	18	1.556	Ea.	1,650	85	10.70	1,745.70	1,950
8130	12" x 8"		18	1.556		2,100	85	10.70	2,195.70	2,450
8135	12" x 10"		18	1.556		2,800	85	10.70	2,895.70	3,225
8140	12" x 12"		18	1.556		3,100	85	10.70	3,195.70	3,550
8160	14" x 6"		16	1.750		2,275	95.50	12.05	2,382.55	2,675
8180	14" x 14"		16	1.750		5,025	95.50	12.05	5,132.55	5,675
8200	16" x 6"		14	2		2,725	109	13.80	2,847.80	3,175
8220	16" x 10"		14	2		3,150	109	13.80	3,272.80	3,625
8240	16" x 16"		14	2		5,425	109	13.80	5,547.80	6,150
8260	18" x 6"		10	2.800		2,000	153	19.30	2,172.30	2,450
8280	18" x 12"		10	2.800		3,825	153	19.30	3,997.30	4,450
8300	18" x 18"		10	2.800		6,000	153	19.30	6,172.30	6,850
8320	20" x 6"		8	3.500		2,075	191	24	2,290	2,575
8340	20" x 12"		8	3.500		3,725	191	24	3,940	4,400
8360	20" x 20"		8	3.500		6,500	191	24	6,715	7,450
8380	24" x 6"		6	4.667		2,350	255	32	2,637	3,025
8400	24" x 12"		6	4.667		4,200	255	32	4,487	5,050
8420	24" x 18"		6	4.667		6,875	255	32	7,162	7,975
8440	24" x 24"	↓	6	4.667		10,500	255	32	10,787	11,900
8800	Hydrant valve box, 6' long	B-20	20	1.200		360	63		423	495
8820	8' long		18	1.333		415	70		485	565
8830	Valve box w/lid 4' deep		14	1.714		117	90		207	264
8840	Valve box and large base w/lid	↓	14	1.714	↓	360	90		450	530

33 14 19 – Valves and Hydrants for Water Utility Service

33 14 19.10 Valves		Crew	Daily Output	Labor-Hours	Unit	Material	2023 Bare Costs Labor	Equipment	Total	Total Incl O&P
0010	**VALVES**, water distribution									
0011	See Sections 22 05 23.20 and 22 05 23.60									
3000	Butterfly valves with boxes, cast iron, mechanical joint									
3100	4" diameter	B-6	6	4	Ea.	1,050	206	46	1,302	1,500
3140	6" diameter		6	4		1,375	206	46	1,627	1,875
3180	8" diameter		6	4		1,750	206	46	2,002	2,300
3300	10" diameter		6	4		2,100	206	46	2,352	2,675
3340	12" diameter		6	4		3,275	206	46	3,527	3,950
3400	14" diameter		4	6		6,050	310	69.50	6,429.50	7,175
3440	16" diameter		4	6		9,600	310	69.50	9,979.50	11,100
3460	18" diameter		4	6		12,000	310	69.50	12,379.50	13,600
3480	20" diameter		4	6		15,800	310	69.50	16,179.50	17,900
3500	24" diameter		4	6		26,700	310	69.50	27,079.50	29,800
3510	30" diameter		4	6		16,900	310	69.50	17,279.50	19,100
3520	36" diameter		4	6		21,000	310	69.50	21,379.50	23,600
3530	42" diameter		4	6		26,600	310	69.50	26,979.50	29,800
3540	48" diameter	↓	4	6	↓	34,300	310	69.50	34,679.50	38,200
3600	With lever operator									
3610	4" diameter	B-6	6	4	Ea.	925	206	46	1,177	1,375
3614	6" diameter		6	4		1,275	206	46	1,527	1,750
3616	8" diameter		6	4		1,650	206	46	1,902	2,150
3618	10" diameter		6	4		2,000	206	46	2,252	2,525
3620	12" diameter		6	4		3,150	206	46	3,402	3,825
3622	14" diameter		4	6		5,675	310	69.50	6,054.50	6,775
3624	16" diameter		4	6		9,250	310	69.50	9,629.50	10,700
3626	18" diameter		4	6		11,600	310	69.50	11,979.50	13,300
3628	20" diameter		4	6		15,500	310	69.50	15,879.50	17,500

33 14 Water Utility Transmission and Distribution

33 14 19 – Valves and Hydrants for Water Utility Service

33 14 19.10 Valves

		Crew	Daily Output	Labor-Hours	Unit	Material	2023 Bare Costs Labor	2023 Bare Costs Equipment	Total	Total Incl O&P
3630	24" diameter	B-6	4	6	Ea.	26,300	310	69.50	26,679.50	29,400
3700	Check valves, flanged									
3710	4" diameter	B-6	6	4	Ea.	1,175	206	46	1,427	1,650
3714	6" diameter		6	4		2,350	206	46	2,602	2,950
3716	8" diameter		6	4		3,975	206	46	4,227	4,700
3718	10" diameter		6	4		7,575	206	46	7,827	8,675
3720	12" diameter		6	4		12,600	206	46	12,852	14,300
3726	18" diameter		4	6		33,600	310	69.50	33,979.50	37,500
3730	24" diameter		4	6		60,000	310	69.50	60,379.50	66,500
3800	Gate valves, C.I., 125 psi, mechanical joint, w/boxes									
3810	4" diameter	B-6	6	4	Ea.	1,600	206	46	1,852	2,125
3814	6" diameter		6	4		2,500	206	46	2,752	3,100
3816	8" diameter		6	4		5,025	206	46	5,277	5,875
3818	10" diameter		6	4		9,050	206	46	9,302	10,300
3820	12" diameter		6	4		12,300	206	46	12,552	13,900
3822	14" diameter		4	6		25,300	310	69.50	25,679.50	28,300
3824	16" diameter		4	6		35,700	310	69.50	36,079.50	39,800
3826	18" diameter		4	6		43,300	310	69.50	43,679.50	48,100
3828	20" diameter		4	6		60,000	310	69.50	60,379.50	66,500
3830	24" diameter		4	6		89,000	310	69.50	89,379.50	98,500
3831	30" diameter		4	6		58,500	310	69.50	58,879.50	65,000
3832	36" diameter		4	6		91,500	310	69.50	91,879.50	101,000
3880	Sleeve, for tapping mains, 8" x 4", add					1,525			1,525	1,675
3884	10" x 6", add					1,525			1,525	1,675
3888	12" x 6", add					1,650			1,650	1,800
3892	12" x 8", add					2,100			2,100	2,300

33 14 19.20 Valves

		Crew	Daily Output	Labor-Hours	Unit	Material	2023 Bare Costs Labor	2023 Bare Costs Equipment	Total	Total Incl O&P
0010	**VALVES**									
0011	Special trim or use									
9000	Valves, gate valve, N.R.S. PIV with post, 4" diameter	B-6	6	4	Ea.	3,375	206	46	3,627	4,050
9020	6" diameter		6	4		4,275	206	46	4,527	5,050
9040	8" diameter		6	4		6,775	206	46	7,027	7,800
9060	10" diameter		6	4		10,800	206	46	11,052	12,300
9080	12" diameter		6	4		14,100	206	46	14,352	15,900
9100	14" diameter		6	4		26,800	206	46	27,052	29,900
9120	OS&Y, 4" diameter		6	4		1,050	206	46	1,302	1,525
9140	6" diameter		6	4		1,475	206	46	1,727	1,975
9160	8" diameter		6	4		1,625	206	46	1,877	2,125
9180	10" diameter		6	4		5,125	206	46	5,377	5,975
9200	12" diameter		6	4		3,675	206	46	3,927	4,400
9220	14" diameter		4	6		5,400	310	69.50	5,779.50	6,450
9400	Check valves, rubber disc, 2-1/2" diameter		6	4		545	206	46	797	955
9420	3" diameter		6	4		670	206	46	922	1,100
9440	4" diameter		6	4		1,175	206	46	1,427	1,650
9480	6" diameter		6	4		2,350	206	46	2,602	2,950
9500	8" diameter		6	4		3,975	206	46	4,227	4,700
9520	10" diameter		6	4		7,575	206	46	7,827	8,675
9540	12" diameter		6	4		12,600	206	46	12,852	14,300
9542	14" diameter		4	6		8,675	310	69.50	9,054.50	10,100
9700	Detector check valves, reducing, 4" diameter		6	4		2,525	206	46	2,777	3,125
9720	6" diameter		6	4		4,050	206	46	4,302	4,800
9740	8" diameter		6	4		5,550	206	46	5,802	6,450

33 14 Water Utility Transmission and Distribution

33 14 19 – Valves and Hydrants for Water Utility Service

33 14 19.20 Valves

		Crew	Daily Output	Labor-Hours	Unit	Material	2023 Bare Costs Labor	Equipment	Total	Total Incl O&P
9760	10" diameter	B-6	6	4	Ea.	8,275	206	46	8,527	9,450
9800	Galvanized, 4" diameter		6	4		2,450	206	46	2,702	3,050
9820	6" diameter		6	4		3,575	206	46	3,827	4,300
9840	8" diameter		6	4		6,225	206	46	6,477	7,200
9860	10" diameter	↓	6	4		11,200	206	46	11,452	12,700

33 14 19.30 Fire Hydrants

		Crew	Daily Output	Labor-Hours	Unit	Material	2023 Bare Costs Labor	Equipment	Total	Total Incl O&P
0010	**FIRE HYDRANTS** G3010-410									
0020	Mechanical joints unless otherwise noted									
1000	Fire hydrants, two way; excavation and backfill not incl.									
1100	4-1/2" valve size, depth 2'-0"	B-21	10	2.800	Ea.	3,075	153	19.30	3,247.30	3,650
1200	4'-6"		9	3.111		3,325	170	21.50	3,516.50	3,950
1260	6'-0"		7	4		3,575	218	27.50	3,820.50	4,300
1340	8'-0"		6	4.667		3,725	255	32	4,012	4,525
1420	10'-0"		5	5.600		3,975	305	38.50	4,318.50	4,875
2000	5-1/4" valve size, depth 2'-0"		10	2.800		3,325	153	19.30	3,497.30	3,925
2080	4'-0"		9	3.111		3,650	170	21.50	3,841.50	4,300
2160	6'-0"		7	4		3,975	218	27.50	4,220.50	4,725
2240	8'-0"		6	4.667		4,350	255	32	4,637	5,225
2320	10'-0"	↓	5	5.600		4,675	305	38.50	5,018.50	5,650
2350	For threeway valves, add					7%				
2400	Lower barrel extensions with stems, 1'-0"	B-20	14	1.714		655	90		745	855
2440	2'-0"		13	1.846		800	97		897	1,025
2480	3'-0"		12	2		1,375	105		1,480	1,650
2520	4'-0"	↓	10	2.400	↓	1,500	126		1,626	1,875
5000	Indicator post									
5020	Adjustable, valve size 4" to 14", 4' bury	B-21	10	2.800	Ea.	1,650	153	19.30	1,822.30	2,050
5060	8' bury		7	4		1,875	218	27.50	2,120.50	2,425
5080	10' bury		6	4.667		2,500	255	32	2,787	3,175
5100	12' bury		5	5.600		2,050	305	38.50	2,393.50	2,750
5120	14' bury		4	7		1,950	380	48	2,378	2,775
5500	Non-adjustable, valve size 4" to 14", 3' bury		10	2.800		1,025	153	19.30	1,197.30	1,375
5520	3'-6" bury		10	2.800		1,025	153	19.30	1,197.30	1,375
5540	4' bury	↓	9	3.111	↓	1,025	170	21.50	1,216.50	1,400

33 16 Water Utility Storage Tanks

33 16 36 – Ground-Level Reinforced Concrete Water Storage Tanks

33 16 36.16 Prestressed Conc. Water Storage Tanks

		Crew	Daily Output	Labor-Hours	Unit	Material	2023 Bare Costs Labor	Equipment	Total	Total Incl O&P
0010	**PRESTRESSED CONC. WATER STORAGE TANKS**									
0020	Not including fdn., pipe or pumps, 250,000 gallons				Ea.				299,000	329,500

33 31 Sanitary Sewerage Piping

33 31 11 – Public Sanitary Sewerage Gravity Piping

33 31 11.10 Sewage Collection, Valves

	33 31 11.10 Sewage Collection, Valves	Crew	Daily Output	Labor-Hours	Unit	Material	2023 Bare Costs Labor	Equipment	Total	Total Incl O&P
0010	**SEWAGE COLLECTION, VALVES**									
1000	Backwater sewer line valve									
1010	Offset type, bronze swing check assy and bronze cover									
1020	B&S connections									
1040	2" size	2 Skwk	14	1.143	Ea.	1,075	70		1,145	1,275
1050	3" size		12.50	1.280		2,125	78.50		2,203.50	2,475
1060	4" size		11	1.455		1,525	89		1,614	1,800
1070	6" size	3 Skwk	15	1.600		2,450	98		2,548	2,850
1080	8" size	"	7.50	3.200		4,650	196		4,846	5,425
1110	Backwater drainage control									
1120	Offset type, w/bronze manually operated shear gate									
1130	B&S connections									
1160	4" size	2 Skwk	11	1.455	Ea.	4,425	89		4,514	5,000
1170	6" size	3 Skwk	15	1.600	"	6,025	98		6,123	6,775

33 31 11.25 Sewage Collection, Polyvinyl Chloride Pipe

	33 31 11.25 Sewage Collection, Polyvinyl Chloride Pipe	Crew	Daily Output	Labor-Hours	Unit	Material	Labor	Equipment	Total	Total Incl O&P
0010	**SEWAGE COLLECTION, POLYVINYL CHLORIDE PIPE**									
0020	Not including excavation or backfill									
2000	20' lengths, SDR 35, B&S, 4" diameter	B-20	375	.064	L.F.	3.44	3.37		6.81	8.85
2040	6" diameter	"	350	.069		8.15	3.61		11.76	14.35
2120	10" diameter	B-21	330	.085		12.05	4.63	.58	17.26	21
2160	12" diameter		320	.088		16.95	4.77	.60	22.32	26.50
2170	14" diameter		280	.100		33.50	5.45	.69	39.64	45.50
2200	15" diameter		240	.117		57	6.35	.80	64.15	73
2250	16" diameter		220	.127		49.50	6.95	.88	57.33	66
4000	Piping, DWV PVC, no exc./bkfill., 10' L, Sch 40, 4" diameter	B-20	375	.064		14.70	3.37		18.07	21
4010	6" diameter		350	.069		42.50	3.61		46.11	52
4020	8" diameter		335	.072		68	3.77		71.77	80.50

33 31 11.37 Centrif. Cst. Fbgs-Reinf. Polymer Mort. Util. Pipe

	33 31 11.37 Centrif. Cst. Fbgs-Reinf. Polymer Mort. Util. Pipe	Crew	Daily Output	Labor-Hours	Unit	Material	Labor	Equipment	Total	Total Incl O&P
0010	**CENTRIF. CST. FBGS-REINF. POLYMER MORT. UTIL. PIPE**									
0020	Not including excavation or backfill									
3348	48" diameter, SN 46, 25psi	B-13B	40	1.400	L.F.	208	72	61.50	341.50	405
3354	54" diameter		40	1.400		340	72	61.50	473.50	550
3363	63" diameter		20	2.800		420	144	123	687	810
3418	18" diameter, 100psi		60	.933		147	48	41	236	279
3424	24" diameter		60	.933		162	48	41	251	295
3436	36" diameter		40	1.400		183	72	61.50	316.50	375
3444	44" diameter		40	1.400		201	72	61.50	334.50	395
3448	48" diameter		40	1.400		224	72	61.50	357.50	420

33 34 Onsite Wastewater Disposal

33 34 13 – Septic Tanks

33 34 13.13 Concrete Septic Tanks

	33 34 13.13 Concrete Septic Tanks		Crew	Daily Output	Labor-Hours	Unit	Material	Labor	Equipment	Total	Total Incl O&P
0010	**CONCRETE SEPTIC TANKS**	G3020-300									
0011	Not including excavation or piping										
0015	Septic tanks, precast, 1,000 gallon		B-21	8	3.500	Ea.	985	191	24	1,200	1,375
0060	1,500 gallon			7	4		1,475	218	27.50	1,720.50	1,975
0100	2,000 gallon			5	5.600		2,400	305	38.50	2,743.50	3,125
0200	5,000 gallon		B-13	3.50	16		7,450	825	650	8,925	10,100
0300	15,000 gallon, 4 piece		B-13B	1.70	32.941		20,200	1,700	1,450	23,350	26,300
0400	25,000 gallon, 4 piece			1.10	50.909		37,300	2,625	2,225	42,150	47,400

33 34 Onsite Wastewater Disposal

33 34 13 – Septic Tanks

33 34 13.13 Concrete Septic Tanks

		Crew	Daily Output	Labor-Hours	Unit	Material	2023 Bare Costs Labor	Equipment	Total	Total Incl O&P
0500	40,000 gallon, 4 piece	B-13B	.80	70	Ea.	59,500	3,600	3,075	66,175	74,500
0520	50,000 gallon, 5 piece	B-13C	.60	93.333		68,500	4,800	2,575	75,875	85,500
0640	75,000 gallon, cast in place	C-14C	.25	448		83,500	25,100	121	108,721	129,500
0660	100,000 gallon	"	.15	747		103,500	41,900	202	145,602	176,500
1150	Leaching field chambers, 13' x 3'-7" x 1'-4", standard	B-13	16	3.500		480	180	142	802	950
1200	Heavy duty, 8' x 4' x 1'-6"		14	4		283	206	162	651	795
1300	13' x 3'-9" x 1'-6"		12	4.667		1,400	241	189	1,830	2,100
1350	20' x 4' x 1'-6"		5	11.200		1,250	575	455	2,280	2,725
1400	Leaching pit, precast concrete, 3' diameter, 3' deep	B-21	8	3.500		710	191	24	925	1,100
1500	6' diameter, 3' section		4.70	5.957		1,125	325	41	1,491	1,750
2000	Velocity reducing pit, precast conc., 6' diameter, 3' deep		4.70	5.957		1,875	325	41	2,241	2,600

33 34 13.33 Polyethylene Septic Tanks

		Crew	Daily Output	Labor-Hours	Unit	Material	Labor	Equipment	Total	Total Incl O&P
0010	**POLYETHYLENE SEPTIC TANKS**									
0011	High density polyethylene, 300 gallon	B-21	9.50	2.947	Ea.	885	161	20.50	1,066.50	1,250
0012	High density polyethylene, 500 gallon		9	3.111		1,200	170	21.50	1,391.50	1,600
0014	High density polyethylene, 750 gallon		8.50	3.294		1,500	180	22.50	1,702.50	1,950
0015	High density polyethylene, 1,000 gallon		8	3.500		2,500	191	24	2,715	3,050
0020	1,250 gallon		8	3.500		3,175	191	24	3,390	3,775
0025	1,500 gallon		7	4		3,750	218	27.50	3,995.50	4,475
0030	2,500 gallon		6	4.667		4,725	255	32	5,012	5,625
0035	3,000 gallon		5.50	5.091		6,475	278	35	6,788	7,575
0040	3,500 gallon		5	5.600		7,725	305	38.50	8,068.50	9,000

33 34 16 – Septic Tank Effluent Filters

33 34 16.13 Septic Tank Gravity Effluent Filters

		Crew	Daily Output	Labor-Hours	Unit	Material	Labor	Equipment	Total	Total Incl O&P
0010	**SEPTIC TANK GRAVITY EFFLUENT FILTERS**									
3000	Effluent filter, 4" diameter	1 Skwk	8	1	Ea.	36	61.50		97.50	132
3020	6" diameter		7	1.143		43.50	70		113.50	153
3030	8" diameter		7	1.143		254	70		324	385
3040	8" diameter, very fine		7	1.143		505	70		575	660
3050	10" diameter, very fine		6	1.333		240	81.50		321.50	385
3060	10" diameter		6	1.333		275	81.50		356.50	425
3080	12" diameter		6	1.333		660	81.50		741.50	850
3090	15" diameter		5	1.600		1,100	98		1,198	1,350

33 34 51 – Drainage Field Systems

33 34 51.10 Drainage Field Excavation and Fill

		Crew	Daily Output	Labor-Hours	Unit	Material	Labor	Equipment	Total	Total Incl O&P
0010	**DRAINAGE FIELD EXCAVATION AND FILL**									
2200	Septic tank & drainage field excavation with 3/4 C.Y. backhoe	B-12F	145	.110	C.Y.		6.25	6.30	12.55	16.25
2400	4' trench for disposal field, 3/4 C.Y. backhoe	"	335	.048	L.F.		2.71	2.73	5.44	7.05
2600	Gravel fill, run of bank	B-6	150	.160	C.Y.	41	8.20	1.85	51.05	59.50
2800	Crushed stone, 3/4"	"	150	.160	"	31.50	8.20	1.85	41.55	49

33 34 51.13 Utility Septic Tank Tile Drainage Field

		Crew	Daily Output	Labor-Hours	Unit	Material	Labor	Equipment	Total	Total Incl O&P
0010	**UTILITY SEPTIC TANK TILE DRAINAGE FIELD**									
0015	Distribution box, concrete, 5 outlets	2 Clab	20	.800	Ea.	90	38		128	156
0020	7 outlets		16	1		93.50	47.50		141	174
0025	9 outlets		8	2		530	94.50		624.50	725
0115	Distribution boxes, HDPE, 5 outlets		20	.800		75	38		113	139
0117	6 outlets		15	1.067		75	50.50		125.50	158
0118	7 outlets		15	1.067		75	50.50		125.50	158
0120	8 outlets		10	1.600		79	75.50		154.50	200
0240	Distribution boxes, outlet flow leveler	1 Clab	50	.160		3	7.55		10.55	14.55
0300	Precast concrete, galley, 4' x 4' x 4'	B-21	16	1.750		247	95.50	12.05	354.55	425

33 34 Onsite Wastewater Disposal

33 34 51 – Drainage Field Systems

33 34 51.13 Utility Septic Tank Tile Drainage Field

		Crew	Daily Output	Labor-Hours	Unit	Material	2023 Bare Costs Labor	Equipment	Total	Total Incl O&P
0350	HDPE infiltration chamber 12" H x 15" W	2 Clab	300	.053	L.F.	7.05	2.52		9.57	11.55
0351	12" H x 15" W end cap	1 Clab	32	.250	Ea.	19.10	11.80		30.90	38.50
0355	chamber 12" H x 22" W	2 Clab	300	.053	L.F.	6.70	2.52		9.22	11.15
0356	12" H x 22" W end cap	1 Clab	32	.250	Ea.	23.50	11.80		35.30	43
0360	chamber 13" H x 34" W	2 Clab	300	.053	L.F.	14.45	2.52		16.97	19.65
0361	13" H x 34" W end cap	1 Clab	32	.250	Ea.	51	11.80		62.80	74
0365	chamber 16" H x 34" W	2 Clab	300	.053	L.F.	14.90	2.52		17.42	20
0366	16" H x 34" W end cap	1 Clab	32	.250	Ea.	16.95	11.80		28.75	36
0370	chamber 8" H x 16" W	2 Clab	300	.053	L.F.	11.35	2.52		13.87	16.25
0371	8" H x 16" W end cap	1 Clab	32	.250	Ea.	11.15	11.80		22.95	30

33 41 Subdrainage

33 41 16 – Subdrainage Piping

33 41 16.25 Piping, Subdrainage, Corrugated Metal

		Crew	Daily Output	Labor-Hours	Unit	Material	2023 Bare Costs Labor	Equipment	Total	Total Incl O&P
0010	**PIPING, SUBDRAINAGE, CORRUGATED METAL** G1030-805									
0021	Not including excavation and backfill									
2010	Aluminum, perforated									
2020	6" diameter, 18 ga.	B-20	380	.063	L.F.	8.05	3.32		11.37	13.80
2200	8" diameter, 16 ga.	"	370	.065		13.20	3.41		16.61	19.60
2220	10" diameter, 16 ga.	B-21	360	.078		16.50	4.24	.54	21.28	25
2240	12" diameter, 16 ga.		285	.098		18.50	5.35	.68	24.53	29
2260	18" diameter, 16 ga.		205	.137		27.50	7.45	.94	35.89	42.50
3000	Uncoated galvanized, perforated									
3020	6" diameter, 18 ga.	B-20	380	.063	L.F.	8.55	3.32		11.87	14.35
3200	8" diameter, 16 ga.	"	370	.065		10.25	3.41		13.66	16.40
3220	10" diameter, 16 ga.	B-21	360	.078		10.90	4.24	.54	15.68	18.90
3240	12" diameter, 16 ga.		285	.098		12.10	5.35	.68	18.13	22
3260	18" diameter, 16 ga.		205	.137		18.55	7.45	.94	26.94	32.50
4000	Steel, perforated, asphalt coated									
4020	6" diameter, 18 ga.	B-20	380	.063	L.F.	7.60	3.32		10.92	13.30
4030	8" diameter, 18 ga.	"	370	.065		11.75	3.41		15.16	18.05
4040	10" diameter, 16 ga.	B-21	360	.078		11.90	4.24	.54	16.68	20
4050	12" diameter, 16 ga.		285	.098		11.90	5.35	.68	17.93	22
4060	18" diameter, 16 ga.		205	.137		21.50	7.45	.94	29.89	35.50

33 41 16.30 Piping, Subdrainage, Plastic

		Crew	Daily Output	Labor-Hours	Unit	Material	2023 Bare Costs Labor	Equipment	Total	Total Incl O&P
0010	**PIPING, SUBDRAINAGE, PLASTIC**									
0020	Not including excavation and backfill									
2100	Perforated PVC, 4" diameter	B-14	314	.153	L.F.	3.44	7.60	.88	11.92	16.05
2110	6" diameter		300	.160		8.15	7.95	.92	17.02	22
2120	8" diameter		290	.166		9	8.20	.96	18.16	23
2130	10" diameter		280	.171		11.15	8.50	.99	20.64	26
2140	12" diameter		270	.178		15.70	8.85	1.03	25.58	31.50

33 42 Stormwater Conveyance

33 42 11 – Stormwater Gravity Piping

33 42 11.40 Piping, Storm Drainage, Corrugated Metal	Crew	Daily Output	Labor-Hours	Unit	Material	2023 Bare Costs Labor	Equipment	Total	Total Incl O&P
0010 **PIPING, STORM DRAINAGE, CORRUGATED METAL**									
0020 Not including excavation or backfill									
2000 Corrugated metal pipe, galvanized									
2040 8" diameter, 16 ga.	B-14	330	.145	L.F.	8.40	7.20	.84	16.44	21
2060 10" diameter, 16 ga.		260	.185		8.75	9.15	1.07	18.97	24.50
2080 12" diameter, 16 ga.		210	.229		13.90	11.35	1.32	26.57	33.50
2100 15" diameter, 16 ga.		200	.240		14.70	11.90	1.38	27.98	35.50
2120 18" diameter, 16 ga.		190	.253		21.50	12.55	1.46	35.51	44.50
2140 24" diameter, 14 ga.	↓	160	.300		24	14.90	1.73	40.63	50.50
2160 30" diameter, 14 ga.	B-13	120	.467		30.50	24	18.95	73.45	90.50
2180 36" diameter, 12 ga.		120	.467		34	24	18.95	76.95	94.50
2200 48" diameter, 12 ga.	↓	100	.560		46	29	22.50	97.50	119
2220 60" diameter, 10 ga.	B-13B	75	.747		81	38.50	33	152.50	183
2240 72" diameter, 8 ga.	"	45	1.244	↓	84	64	54.50	202.50	248
2250 End sections, 8" diameter, 16 ga.	B-14	20	2.400	Ea.	50.50	119	13.85	183.35	248
2255 10" diameter, 16 ga.		20	2.400		59.50	119	13.85	192.35	258
2260 12" diameter, 16 ga.		18	2.667		122	132	15.40	269.40	350
2265 15" diameter, 16 ga.		18	2.667		241	132	15.40	388.40	480
2270 18" diameter, 16 ga.	↓	16	3		279	149	17.30	445.30	545
2275 24" diameter, 16 ga.	B-13	16	3.500		365	180	142	687	830
2280 30" diameter, 16 ga.		14	4		600	206	162	968	1,150
2285 36" diameter, 14 ga.		14	4		750	206	162	1,118	1,300
2290 48" diameter, 14 ga.		10	5.600		2,175	289	227	2,691	3,050
2292 60" diameter, 14 ga.	↓	6	9.333		2,150	480	380	3,010	3,500
2294 72" diameter, 14 ga.	B-13B	5	11.200		3,275	575	490	4,340	5,000
2300 Bends or elbows, 8" diameter	B-14	28	1.714		120	85	9.90	214.90	269
2320 10" diameter		25	1.920		148	95.50	11.10	254.60	315
2340 12" diameter, 16 ga.		23	2.087		175	104	12.05	291.05	360
2342 18" diameter, 16 ga.		20	2.400		250	119	13.85	382.85	465
2344 24" diameter, 14 ga.		16	3		415	149	17.30	581.30	700
2346 30" diameter, 14 ga.	↓	15	3.200		510	159	18.45	687.45	820
2348 36" diameter, 14 ga.	B-13	15	3.733		665	192	152	1,009	1,200
2350 48" diameter, 12 ga.	"	12	4.667		855	241	189	1,285	1,525
2352 60" diameter, 10 ga.	B-13B	10	5.600		1,150	289	246	1,685	1,975
2354 72" diameter, 10 ga.	"	6	9.333		1,425	480	410	2,315	2,750
2360 Wyes or tees, 8" diameter	B-14	25	1.920		169	95.50	11.10	275.60	340
2380 10" diameter		21	2.286		211	114	13.20	338.20	415
2400 12" diameter, 16 ga.		19	2.526		240	125	14.60	379.60	465
2410 18" diameter, 16 ga.		16	3		335	149	17.30	501.30	605
2412 24" diameter, 14 ga.	↓	16	3		605	149	17.30	771.30	905
2414 30" diameter, 14 ga.	B-13	12	4.667		790	241	189	1,220	1,450
2416 36" diameter, 14 ga.		11	5.091		920	262	207	1,389	1,625
2418 48" diameter, 12 ga.	↓	10	5.600		1,250	289	227	1,766	2,050
2420 60" diameter, 10 ga.	B-13B	8	7		1,825	360	310	2,495	2,875
2422 72" diameter, 10 ga.	"	5	11.200	↓	2,175	575	490	3,240	3,800
2500 Galvanized, uncoated, 20' lengths									
2520 8" diameter, 16 ga.	B-14	355	.135	L.F.	9.45	6.70	.78	16.93	21.50
2540 10" diameter, 16 ga.		280	.171		9.45	8.50	.99	18.94	24
2560 12" diameter, 16 ga.		220	.218		31.50	10.85	1.26	43.61	52
2580 15" diameter, 16 ga.		220	.218		30	10.85	1.26	42.11	50.50
2600 18" diameter, 16 ga.		205	.234		35.50	11.65	1.35	48.50	58
2620 24" diameter, 14 ga.		175	.274		40	13.60	1.58	55.18	66
2640 30" diameter, 14 ga.	B-13	130	.431		32.50	22	17.50	72	88

33 42 Stormwater Conveyance

33 42 11 – Stormwater Gravity Piping

33 42 11.40 Piping, Storm Drainage, Corrugated Metal

		Crew	Daily Output	Labor-Hours	Unit	Material	2023 Bare Costs Labor	2023 Bare Costs Equipment	Total	Total Incl O&P
2660	36" diameter, 12 ga.	B-13	130	.431	L.F.	37	22	17.50	76.50	93
2680	48" diameter, 12 ga.	↓	110	.509		54.50	26.50	20.50	101.50	122
2690	60" diameter, 10 ga.	B-13B	78	.718		90	37	31.50	158.50	189
2695	72" diameter, 10 ga.	"	60	.933		104	48	41	193	231
2711	Bends or elbows, 12" diameter, 16 ga.	B-14	30	1.600	Ea.	142	79.50	9.25	230.75	284
2712	15" diameter, 16 ga.		25.04	1.917		181	95	11.05	287.05	355
2714	18" diameter, 16 ga.		20	2.400		203	119	13.85	335.85	415
2716	24" diameter, 14 ga.		16	3		305	149	17.30	471.30	575
2718	30" diameter, 14 ga.	↓	15	3.200		410	159	18.45	587.45	710
2720	36" diameter, 14 ga.	B-13	15	3.733		545	192	152	889	1,050
2722	48" diameter, 12 ga.		12	4.667		740	241	189	1,170	1,375
2724	60" diameter, 10 ga.		10	5.600		1,150	289	227	1,666	1,950
2726	72" diameter, 10 ga.	↓	6	9.333		1,450	480	380	2,310	2,725
2728	Wyes or tees, 12" diameter, 16 ga.	B-14	22.48	2.135		182	106	12.30	300.30	375
2730	18" diameter, 16 ga.		15	3.200		283	159	18.45	460.45	570
2732	24" diameter, 14 ga.		15	3.200		490	159	18.45	667.45	800
2734	30" diameter, 14 ga.	↓	14	3.429		635	170	19.80	824.80	975
2736	36" diameter, 14 ga.	B-13	14	4		805	206	162	1,173	1,375
2738	48" diameter, 12 ga.		12	4.667		1,175	241	189	1,605	1,875
2740	60" diameter, 10 ga.		10	5.600		1,700	289	227	2,216	2,550
2742	72" diameter, 10 ga.		6	9.333		2,050	480	380	2,910	3,375
2780	End sections, 8" diameter	B-14	35	1.371		95	68	7.90	170.90	215
2785	10" diameter		35	1.371		93	68	7.90	168.90	213
2790	12" diameter		35	1.371		111	68	7.90	186.90	232
2800	18" diameter	↓	30	1.600		129	79.50	9.25	217.75	270
2810	24" diameter	B-13	25	2.240		218	115	91	424	510
2820	30" diameter		25	2.240		395	115	91	601	705
2825	36" diameter		20	2.800		525	144	114	783	915
2830	48" diameter	↓	10	5.600		1,150	289	227	1,666	1,925
2835	60" diameter	B-13B	5	11.200		2,250	575	490	3,315	3,875
2840	72" diameter	"	4	14		2,600	720	615	3,935	4,600
2850	Couplings, 12" diameter					37.50			37.50	41
2855	18" diameter					52.50			52.50	57.50
2860	24" diameter					58.50			58.50	64.50
2865	30" diameter					31			31	34
2870	36" diameter					47			47	51.50
2875	48" diameter					68.50			68.50	75.50
2880	60" diameter					65.50			65.50	72
2885	72" diameter				↓	74			74	81

33 42 11.60 Sewage/Drainage Collection, Concrete Pipe

		Crew	Daily Output	Labor-Hours	Unit	Material	Labor	Equipment	Total	Total Incl O&P
0010	**SEWAGE/DRAINAGE COLLECTION, CONCRETE PIPE**									
0020	Not including excavation or backfill									
1000	Non-reinforced pipe, extra strength, B&S or T&G joints									
1010	6" diameter	B-14	265.04	.181	L.F.	11.95	9	1.04	21.99	27.50
1020	8" diameter		224	.214		13.15	10.65	1.24	25.04	31.50
1030	10" diameter		216	.222		14.55	11.05	1.28	26.88	34
1040	12" diameter		200	.240		15.15	11.90	1.38	28.43	36
1050	15" diameter		180	.267		22	13.25	1.54	36.79	45.50
1060	18" diameter		144	.333		27.50	16.55	1.92	45.97	56.50
1070	21" diameter		112	.429		28.50	21.50	2.47	52.47	65.50
1080	24" diameter	↓	100	.480	↓	33	24	2.77	59.77	75
2000	Reinforced culvert, class 3, no gaskets									

33 42 Stormwater Conveyance

33 42 11 – Stormwater Gravity Piping

33 42 11.60 Sewage/Drainage Collection, Concrete Pipe

		Crew	Daily Output	Labor-Hours	Unit	Material	2023 Bare Costs Labor	Equipment	Total	Total Incl O&P
2010	12" diameter	B-14	150	.320	L.F.	22	15.90	1.85	39.75	50
2020	15" diameter		150	.320		26.50	15.90	1.85	44.25	54.50
2030	18" diameter		132	.364		30.50	18.05	2.10	50.65	63
2035	21" diameter		120	.400		35.50	19.85	2.31	57.66	71.50
2040	24" diameter	▼	100	.480		44	24	2.77	70.77	87
2045	27" diameter	B-13	92	.609		50.50	31.50	24.50	106.50	129
2050	30" diameter		88	.636		61	33	26	120	145
2060	36" diameter	▼	72	.778		104	40	31.50	175.50	208
2070	42" diameter	B-13B	68	.824		147	42.50	36	225.50	265
2080	48" diameter		64	.875		198	45	38.50	281.50	325
2085	54" diameter		56	1		201	51.50	44	296.50	345
2090	60" diameter		48	1.167		236	60	51.50	347.50	405
2100	72" diameter		40	1.400		340	72	61.50	473.50	550
2120	84" diameter		32	1.750		550	90	77	717	825
2140	96" diameter	▼	24	2.333		660	120	103	883	1,025
2200	With gaskets, class 3, 12" diameter	B-21	168	.167		24.50	9.10	1.15	34.75	41.50
2220	15" diameter		160	.175		29	9.55	1.21	39.76	47.50
2230	18" diameter		152	.184		33.50	10.05	1.27	44.82	53.50
2235	21" diameter		152	.184		39.50	10.05	1.27	50.82	59.50
2240	24" diameter	▼	136	.206		54	11.25	1.42	66.67	78
2260	30" diameter	B-13	88	.636		73	33	26	132	158
2270	36" diameter	"	72	.778		118	40	31.50	189.50	224
2290	48" diameter	B-13B	64	.875		217	45	38.50	300.50	350
2310	72" diameter	"	40	1.400	▼	370	72	61.50	503.50	580
2330	Flared ends, 12" diameter	B-21	31	.903	Ea.	66	49.50	6.20	121.70	153
2340	15" diameter		25	1.120		71	61	7.70	139.70	178
2400	18" diameter		20	1.400		78.50	76.50	9.65	164.65	211
2420	24" diameter	▼	14	2		93.50	109	13.80	216.30	281
2440	36" diameter	B-13	10	5.600	▼	164	289	227	680	860
3080	Radius pipe, add to pipe prices, 12" to 60" diameter				L.F.	50%				
3090	Over 60" diameter, add				"	20%				
3500	Reinforced elliptical, 8' lengths, C507 class 3									
3520	14" x 23" inside, round equivalent 18" diameter	B-21	82	.341	L.F.	43.50	18.60	2.35	64.45	78.50
3524	18" x 29" inside, round equivalent 30" diameter	B-13	58	.966		61.50	50	39	150.50	185
3525	22" x 36" inside, round equivalent 30" diameter		58	.966		81	50	39	170	206
3530	24" x 38" inside, round equivalent 30" diameter		58	.966		81	50	39	170	206
3540	29" x 45" inside, round equivalent 36" diameter		52	1.077		111	55.50	43.50	210	253
3550	38" x 60" inside, round equivalent 48" diameter		38	1.474		228	76	60	364	430
3560	48" x 76" inside, round equivalent 60" diameter		26	2.154		297	111	87.50	495.50	585
3570	58" x 91" inside, round equivalent 72" diameter	▼	22	2.545	▼	415	131	103	649	770
3780	Concrete slotted pipe, class 4 mortar joint									
3800	12" diameter	B-21	168	.167	L.F.	36.50	9.10	1.15	46.75	55
3840	18" diameter	"	152	.184	"	45.50	10.05	1.27	56.82	66.50
3900	Concrete slotted pipe, Class 4 O-ring joint									
3940	12" diameter	B-21	168	.167	L.F.	29.50	9.10	1.15	39.75	47.50
3960	18" diameter	"	152	.184	"	47	10.05	1.27	58.32	68.50

33 42 13 – Stormwater Culverts

33 42 13.15 Oval Arch Culverts

		Crew	Daily Output	Labor-Hours	Unit	Material	Labor	Equipment	Total	Total Incl O&P
0010	**OVAL ARCH CULVERTS**									
3000	Corrugated galvanized or aluminum, coated & paved									
3020	17" x 13", 16 ga., 15" equivalent	B-14	200	.240	L.F.	14.20	11.90	1.38	27.48	35
3040	21" x 15", 16 ga., 18" equivalent	▼	150	.320		14.55	15.90	1.85	32.30	41.50

33 42 Stormwater Conveyance

33 42 13 – Stormwater Culverts

33 42 13.15 Oval Arch Culverts

		Crew	Daily Output	Labor-Hours	Unit	Material	2023 Bare Costs Labor	Equipment	Total	Total Incl O&P
3060	28" x 20", 14 ga., 24" equivalent	B-14	125	.384	L.F.	22	19.05	2.22	43.27	55.50
3080	35" x 24", 14 ga., 30" equivalent	↓	100	.480		27.50	24	2.77	54.27	68.50
3100	42" x 29", 12 ga., 36" equivalent	B-13	100	.560		25.50	29	22.50	77	96
3120	49" x 33", 12 ga., 42" equivalent		90	.622		32.50	32	25.50	90	112
3140	57" x 38", 12 ga., 48" equivalent	↓	75	.747	↓	43	38.50	30.50	112	139
3160	Steel, plain oval arch culverts, plain									
3180	17" x 13", 16 ga., 15" equivalent	B-14	225	.213	L.F.	23	10.60	1.23	34.83	42
3200	21" x 15", 16 ga., 18" equivalent		175	.274		37.50	13.60	1.58	52.68	63.50
3220	28" x 20", 14 ga., 24" equivalent	↓	150	.320		16.95	15.90	1.85	34.70	44
3240	35" x 24", 14 ga., 30" equivalent	B-13	108	.519		22	26.50	21	69.50	87
3260	42" x 29", 12 ga., 36" equivalent		108	.519		39	26.50	21	86.50	106
3280	49" x 33", 12 ga., 42" equivalent		92	.609		47.50	31.50	24.50	103.50	126
3300	57" x 38", 12 ga., 48" equivalent		75	.747	↓	47.50	38.50	30.50	116.50	143
3320	End sections, 17" x 13"		22	2.545	Ea.	345	131	103	579	690
3340	42" x 29"	↓	17	3.294	"	460	170	134	764	905
3360	Multi-plate arch, steel	B-20	1690	.014	Lb.	1.08	.75		1.83	2.31

33 42 33 – Stormwater Curbside Drains and Inlets

33 42 33.13 Catch Basins

		Crew	Daily Output	Labor-Hours	Unit	Material	2023 Bare Costs Labor	Equipment	Total	Total Incl O&P
0010	**CATCH BASINS**									
0011	Not including footing & excavation									
1600	Frames & grates, C.I., 24" square, 500 lb.	B-6	7.80	3.077	Ea.	1,050	158	35.50	1,243.50	1,425
1700	26" D shape, 600 lb.		7	3.429		1,950	176	39.50	2,165.50	2,450
1800	Light traffic, 18" diameter, 100 lb.		10	2.400		895	123	27.50	1,045.50	1,200
1900	24" diameter, 300 lb.		8.70	2.759		1,000	142	32	1,174	1,350
2000	36" diameter, 900 lb.		5.80	4.138		1,425	213	48	1,686	1,950
2100	Heavy traffic, 24" diameter, 400 lb.		7.80	3.077		945	158	35.50	1,138.50	1,325
2200	36" diameter, 1,150 lb.		3	8		2,900	410	92.50	3,402.50	3,875
2300	Mass. State standard, 26" diameter, 475 lb.		7	3.429		1,225	176	39.50	1,440.50	1,650
2400	30" diameter, 620 lb.		7	3.429		455	176	39.50	670.50	805
2500	Watertight, 24" diameter, 350 lb.		7.80	3.077		2,000	158	35.50	2,193.50	2,475
2600	26" diameter, 500 lb.		7	3.429		1,600	176	39.50	1,815.50	2,050
2700	32" diameter, 575 lb.	↓	6	4	↓	1,100	206	46	1,352	1,550
2800	3 piece cover & frame, 10" deep,									
2900	1,200 lb., for heavy equipment	B-6	3	8	Ea.	1,300	410	92.50	1,802.50	2,150
3000	Raised for paving 1-1/4" to 2" high									
3100	4 piece expansion ring									
3200	20" to 26" diameter	1 Clab	3	2.667	Ea.	269	126		395	485
3300	30" to 36" diameter	"	3	2.667	"	430	126		556	665
3320	Frames and covers, existing, raised for paving, 2", including									
3340	row of brick, concrete collar, up to 12" wide frame	B-6	18	1.333	Ea.	63	68.50	15.40	146.90	188
3360	20" to 26" wide frame		11	2.182		95	112	25	232	300
3380	30" to 36" wide frame	↓	9	2.667		118	137	31	286	370
3400	Inverts, single channel brick	D-1	3	5.333		136	278		414	565
3500	Concrete		5	3.200		165	167		332	430
3600	Triple channel, brick		2	8		224	415		639	870
3700	Concrete	↓	3	5.333	↓	187	278		465	620

33 52 Hydrocarbon Transmission and Distribution

33 52 13 – Liquid Hydrocarbon Piping

33 52 13.16 Gasoline Piping

		Crew	Daily Output	Labor-Hours	Unit	Material	2023 Bare Costs Labor	Equipment	Total	Total Incl O&P
0010	**GASOLINE PIPING**									
0020	Primary containment pipe, fiberglass-reinforced									
0030	Plastic pipe 15' & 30' lengths									
0040	2" diameter	Q-6	425	.056	L.F.	6.55	3.82		10.37	12.90
0050	3" diameter		400	.060		8.90	4.06		12.96	15.85
0060	4" diameter	↓	375	.064	↓	11.55	4.33		15.88	19.15
0100	Fittings									
0110	Elbows, 90° & 45°, bell ends, 2"	Q-6	24	1	Ea.	39.50	67.50		107	145
0120	3" diameter		22	1.091		51.50	74		125.50	167
0130	4" diameter		20	1.200		64.50	81.50		146	192
0200	Tees, bell ends, 2"		21	1.143		52	77.50		129.50	172
0210	3" diameter		18	1.333		59.50	90.50		150	200
0230	Flanges bell ends, 2"		24	1		28	67.50		95.50	132
0240	3" diameter		22	1.091		35	74		109	149
0250	4" diameter		20	1.200		39	81.50		120.50	164
0260	Sleeve couplings, 2"		21	1.143		10.80	77.50		88.30	127
0270	3" diameter		18	1.333		17.05	90.50		107.55	154
0280	4" diameter		15	1.600		18.95	108		126.95	183
0290	Threaded adapters, 2"		21	1.143		17.70	77.50		95.20	134
0300	3" diameter		18	1.333		23	90.50		113.50	161
0310	4" diameter		15	1.600		33	108		141	198
0320	Reducers, 2"		27	.889		24	60		84	117
0330	3" diameter		22	1.091		24	74		98	137
0340	4" diameter	↓	20	1.200	↓	32	81.50		113.50	157
1010	Gas station product line for secondary containment (double wall)									
1100	Fiberglass reinforced plastic pipe 25' lengths									
1120	Pipe, plain end, 3" diameter	Q-6	375	.064	L.F.	32.50	4.33		36.83	42
1130	4" diameter		350	.069		26.50	4.64		31.14	36
1140	5" diameter		325	.074		29.50	5		34.50	40
1150	6" diameter	↓	300	.080	↓	33	5.40		38.40	44
1200	Fittings									
1230	Elbows, 90° & 45°, 3" diameter	Q-6	18	1.333	Ea.	137	90.50		227.50	286
1240	4" diameter		16	1.500		165	102		267	335
1250	5" diameter		14	1.714		159	116		275	345
1260	6" diameter		12	2		197	135		332	420
1270	Tees, 3" diameter		15	1.600		171	108		279	350
1280	4" diameter		12	2		163	135		298	380
1290	5" diameter		9	2.667		213	181		394	505
1300	6" diameter		6	4		300	271		571	735
1310	Couplings, 3" diameter		18	1.333		48.50	90.50		139	189
1320	4" diameter		16	1.500		110	102		212	272
1330	5" diameter		14	1.714		197	116		313	390
1340	6" diameter		12	2		310	135		445	540
1350	Cross-over nipples, 3" diameter		18	1.333		9.20	90.50		99.70	145
1360	4" diameter		16	1.500		11.25	102		113.25	163
1370	5" diameter		14	1.714		15.60	116		131.60	190
1380	6" diameter		12	2		16.30	135		151.30	220
1400	Telescoping, reducers, concentric 4" x 3"		18	1.333		39	90.50		129.50	178
1410	5" x 4"		17	1.412		84	95.50		179.50	236
1420	6" x 5"	↓	16	1.500		236	102		338	410

33 52 Hydrocarbon Transmission and Distribution

33 52 16 – Gas Hydrocarbon Piping

33 52 16.20 Piping, Gas Service and Distribution, P.E.	Crew	Daily Output	Labor-Hours	Unit	Material	2023 Bare Costs Labor	Equipment	Total	Total Incl O&P
0010 **PIPING, GAS SERVICE AND DISTRIBUTION, POLYETHYLENE**									
0020 Not including excavation or backfill									
1000 60 psi coils, compression coupling @ 100', 1/2" diameter, SDR 11	B-20A	608	.053	L.F.	.64	2.98		3.62	5.15
1010 1" diameter, SDR 11		544	.059		1.73	3.33		5.06	6.85
1040 1-1/4" diameter, SDR 11		544	.059		2.78	3.33		6.11	8
1100 2" diameter, SDR 11		488	.066		4.68	3.71		8.39	10.70
1160 3" diameter, SDR 11		408	.078		10.15	4.44		14.59	17.80
1500 60 psi 40' joints with coupling, 3" diameter, SDR 11	B-21A	408	.098		10.65	5.75	1.56	17.96	22
1540 4" diameter, SDR 11		352	.114		10.85	6.65	1.81	19.31	24
1600 6" diameter, SDR 11		328	.122		52.50	7.15	1.95	61.60	70.50
1640 8" diameter, SDR 11		272	.147		87.50	8.60	2.35	98.45	112

33 52 16.23 Medium Density Polyethylene Piping

	Crew	Daily Output	Labor-Hours	Unit	Material	Labor	Equipment	Total	Total Incl O&P
2010 **MEDIUM DENSITY POLYETHYLENE PIPING**									
2020 ASTM D2513, not including excavation or backfill									
2200 Butt fused pipe									
2205 80psi coils, butt fusion joint @ 100', 1/2" CTS diameter, SDR 7	B-22C	2050	.008	L.F.	.36	.42	.14	.92	1.18
2210 1" CTS diameter, SDR 11.5		1900	.008		.34	.46	.15	.95	1.21
2215 80psi coils, butt fusion joint @ 100', IPS 1/2" diameter, SDR 9.3		1950	.008		.37	.45	.14	.96	1.24
2220 3/4" diameter, SDR 11		1950	.008		.53	.45	.14	1.12	1.41
2225 1" diameter, SDR 11		1850	.009		.86	.47	.15	1.48	1.82
2230 1-1/4" diameter, SDR 11		1850	.009		1.63	.47	.15	2.25	2.66
2235 1-1/2" diameter, SDR 11		1750	.009		1.73	.50	.16	2.39	2.82
2240 2" diameter, SDR 11		1750	.009		3.20	.50	.16	3.86	4.44
2245 80psi 40' lengths, butt fusion joint, IPS 3" diameter, SDR 11.5	B-22A	660	.061		3.59	3.29	1.09	7.97	10.05
2250 4" diameter, SDR 11.5	"	500	.080		5.65	4.34	1.44	11.43	14.30
2400 Socket fused pipe									
2405 80psi coils, socket fusion coupling @ 100', 1/2" CTS diameter, SDR 7	B-20	1050	.023	L.F.	.39	1.20		1.59	2.22
2410 1" CTS diameter, SDR 11.5		1000	.024		.37	1.26		1.63	2.30
2415 80psi coils, socket fusion coupling @ 100', IPS 1/2" diameter, SDR 9.3		1000	.024		.39	1.26		1.65	2.32
2420 3/4" diameter, SDR 11		1000	.024		.55	1.26		1.81	2.50
2425 1" diameter, SDR 11		950	.025		.88	1.33		2.21	2.95
2430 1-1/4" diameter, SDR 11		950	.025		1.66	1.33		2.99	3.81
2435 1-1/2" diameter, SDR 11		900	.027		1.77	1.40		3.17	4.03
2440 2" diameter, SDR 11		850	.028		3.23	1.48		4.71	5.75
2445 80psi 40' lengths, socket fusion coupling, IPS 3" diameter, SDR 11.5	B-21A	340	.118		3.90	6.90	1.88	12.68	16.60
2450 4" diameter, SDR 11.5	"	260	.154		6.50	9	2.45	17.95	23.50
2600 Compression coupled pipe									
2605 80psi coils, compression coupling @ 100', 1/2" CTS diameter, SDR 7	B-20	2250	.011	L.F.	.55	.56		1.11	1.44
2610 1" CTS diameter, SDR 11.5		2175	.011		.70	.58		1.28	1.64
2615 80psi coils, compression coupling @ 100', IPS 1/2" diameter, SDR 9.3		2175	.011		.59	.58		1.17	1.52
2620 3/4" diameter, SDR 11		2100	.011		.84	.60		1.44	1.82
2625 1" diameter, SDR 11		2025	.012		1.19	.62		1.81	2.24
3000 Fittings, butt fusion									
3010 SDR 11, IPS unless noted CTS									
3100 Caps, 3/4" diameter	B-22C	28.50	.561	Ea.	4.69	30.50	9.85	45.04	61.50
3105 1" diameter		27	.593		4.32	32	10.40	46.72	64
3110 1-1/4" diameter		27	.593		6.90	32	10.40	49.30	67
3115 1-1/2" diameter		25.50	.627		4	34	11	49	67.50
3120 2" diameter		24	.667		13.80	36	11.70	61.50	82
3125 3" diameter		24	.667		19.60	36	11.70	67.30	88.50
3130 4" diameter		18	.889		35.50	48	15.60	99.10	128
3200 Reducers, 1" x 3/4" diameters		13.50	1.185		16.65	64.50	21	102.15	137

33 52 Hydrocarbon Transmission and Distribution

33 52 16 – Gas Hydrocarbon Piping

33 52 16.23 Medium Density Polyethylene Piping		Crew	Daily Output	Labor-Hours	Unit	Material	2023 Bare Costs Labor	Equipment	Total	Total Incl O&P
3205	1-1/4" x 1" diameters	B-22C	13.50	1.185	Ea.	18.55	64.50	21	104.05	140
3210	1-1/2" x 3/4" diameters		12.75	1.255		24	68	22	114	153
3215	1-1/2" x 1" diameters		12.75	1.255		20.50	68	22	110.50	149
3220	1-1/2" x 1-1/4" diameters		12.75	1.255		20.50	68	22	110.50	149
3225	2" x 1" diameters		12	1.333		21	72.50	23.50	117	157
3230	2" x 1-1/4" diameters		12	1.333		21	72.50	23.50	117	157
3235	2" x 1-1/2" diameters		12	1.333		24.50	72.50	23.50	120.50	161
3240	3" x 2" diameters		12	1.333		24.50	72.50	23.50	120.50	161
3245	4" x 2" diameters		9	1.778		39.50	96.50	31	167	222
3250	4" x 3" diameters		9	1.778		35	96.50	31	162.50	217
3300	Elbows, 90°, 3/4" diameter		14.25	1.123		5.85	61	19.70	86.55	119
3302	1" diameter		13.50	1.185		7.15	64.50	21	92.65	127
3304	1-1/4" diameter		13.50	1.185		13.75	64.50	21	99.25	134
3306	1-1/2" diameter		12.75	1.255		11.95	68	22	101.95	139
3308	2" diameter		12	1.333		15.30	72.50	23.50	111.30	150
3310	3" diameter		12	1.333		31	72.50	23.50	127	168
3312	4" diameter		9	1.778		47.50	96.50	31	175	231
3350	45°, 3" diameter		12	1.333		38.50	72.50	23.50	134.50	176
3352	4" diameter		9	1.778		47.50	96.50	31	175	231
3400	Tees, 3/4" diameter		9.50	1.684		24	91.50	29.50	145	196
3405	1" diameter		9	1.778		7.20	96.50	31	134.70	186
3410	1-1/4" diameter		9	1.778		18.55	96.50	31	146.05	199
3415	1-1/2" diameter		8.50	1.882		22.50	102	33	157.50	215
3420	2" diameter		8	2		24	109	35	168	227
3425	3" diameter		8	2		43	109	35	187	248
3430	4" diameter		6	2.667		67	145	47	259	340
3500	Tapping tees, high volume, butt fusion outlets									
3505	1-1/2" punch, 2" x 2" outlet	B-22C	11	1.455	Ea.	159	79	25.50	263.50	320
3510	1-7/8" punch, 3" x 2" outlet		11	1.455		159	79	25.50	263.50	320
3515	4" x 2" outlet		9	1.778		159	96.50	31	286.50	355
3550	For protective sleeves, add					4.11			4.11	4.52
3600	Service saddles, saddle contour x outlet, butt fusion outlets									
3602	1-1/4" x 3/4" outlet	B-22C	17	.941	Ea.	26.50	51	16.50	94	124
3604	1-1/4" x 1" outlet		17	.941		9.65	51	16.50	77.15	105
3606	1-1/4" x 1-1/4" outlet		16	1		9.65	54.50	17.55	81.70	111
3608	1-1/2" x 3/4" outlet		16	1		9.65	54.50	17.55	81.70	111
3610	1-1/2" x 1-1/4" outlet		15	1.067		25.50	58	18.70	102.20	135
3612	2" x 3/4" outlet		12	1.333		9.65	72.50	23.50	105.65	144
3614	2" x 1" outlet		12	1.333		9.65	72.50	23.50	105.65	144
3616	2" x 1-1/4" outlet		11	1.455		9.65	79	25.50	114.15	157
3618	3" x 3/4" outlet		12	1.333		9.65	72.50	23.50	105.65	144
3620	3" x 1" outlet		12	1.333		9.65	72.50	23.50	105.65	144
3622	3" x 1-1/4" outlet		11	1.455		9.65	79	25.50	114.15	157
3624	4" x 3/4" outlet		10	1.600		9.65	87	28	124.65	172
3626	4" x 1" outlet		10	1.600		9.65	87	28	124.65	172
3628	4" x 1-1/4" outlet		9	1.778		26.50	96.50	31	154	208
3685	For protective sleeves, 3/4" diameter outlets, add					1.22			1.22	1.34
3690	1" diameter outlets, add					2.04			2.04	2.24
3695	1-1/4" diameter outlets, add					3.52			3.52	3.87
3700	Branch saddles, contour x outlet, butt outlets, round base									
3702	2" x 2" outlet	B-22C	11	1.455	Ea.	25	79	25.50	129.50	174
3704	3" x 2" outlet		11	1.455		47.50	79	25.50	152	199
3706	3" x 3" outlet		11	1.455		39	79	25.50	143.50	189

33 52 Hydrocarbon Transmission and Distribution

33 52 16 – Gas Hydrocarbon Piping

	33 52 16.23 Medium Density Polyethylene Piping	Crew	Daily Output	Labor-Hours	Unit	Material	2023 Bare Costs Labor	Equipment	Total	Total Incl O&P
3708	4" x 2" outlet	B-22C	9	1.778	Ea.	47.50	96.50	31	175	231
3710	4" x 3" outlet		9	1.778		89	96.50	31	216.50	277
3712	4" x 4" outlet		9	1.778		52	96.50	31	179.50	236
3750	Rectangular base, 2" x 2" outlet		11	1.455		25	79	25.50	129.50	174
3752	3" x 2" outlet		11	1.455		27	79	25.50	131.50	176
3754	3" x 3" outlet		11	1.455		39	79	25.50	143.50	189
3756	4" x 2" outlet		9	1.778		31	96.50	31	158.50	213
3758	4" x 3" outlet		9	1.778		37	96.50	31	164.50	220
3760	4" x 4" outlet	↓	9	1.778	↓	45	96.50	31	172.50	228
4000	Fittings, socket fusion									
4010	SDR 11, IPS unless noted CTS									
4100	Caps, 1/2" CTS diameter	B-20	30	.800	Ea.	3.43	42		45.43	67
4105	1/2" diameter		28.50	.842		3.43	44.50		47.93	70
4110	3/4" diameter		28.50	.842		5.15	44.50		49.65	71.50
4115	1" CTS diameter		28	.857		5.70	45		50.70	74
4120	1" diameter		27	.889		5.70	46.50		52.20	76.50
4125	1-1/4" diameter		27	.889		6.90	46.50		53.40	77.50
4130	1-1/2" diameter		25.50	.941		8.90	49.50		58.40	84
4135	2" diameter		24	1		8.75	52.50		61.25	88
4140	3" diameter		24	1		20	52.50		72.50	101
4145	4" diameter		18	1.333		29.50	70		99.50	138
4200	Reducers, 1/2" x 1/2" CTS diameters		14.25	1.684		8.95	88.50		97.45	142
4202	3/4" x 1/2" CTS diameters		14.25	1.684		8.20	88.50		96.70	141
4204	3/4" x 1/2" diameters		14.25	1.684		8.80	88.50		97.30	142
4206	1" CTS x 1/2" diameters		14	1.714		8.60	90		98.60	144
4208	1" CTS x 3/4" diameters		13.50	1.778		8.70	93.50		102.20	150
4210	1" x 1/2" CTS diameters		13.50	1.778		8.20	93.50		101.70	149
4212	1" x 1/2" diameters		13.50	1.778		9.15	93.50		102.65	150
4214	1" x 3/4" diameters		13.50	1.778		12.70	93.50		106.20	154
4216	1" x 1" CTS diameters		13.50	1.778		7.45	93.50		100.95	148
4218	1-1/4" x 1/2" CTS diameters		13.50	1.778		8.60	93.50		102.10	149
4220	1-1/4" x 1/2" diameters		13.50	1.778		12.55	93.50		106.05	154
4222	1-1/4" x 3/4" diameters		13.50	1.778		18	93.50		111.50	160
4224	1-1/4" x 1" CTS diameters		13.50	1.778		12.55	93.50		106.05	154
4226	1-1/4" x 1" diameters		13.50	1.778		15.35	93.50		108.85	157
4228	1-1/2" x 3/4" diameters		12.75	1.882		13.75	99		112.75	163
4230	1-1/2" x 1" diameters		12.75	1.882		11.65	99		110.65	161
4232	1-1/2" x 1-1/4" diameters		12.75	1.882		13.15	99		112.15	163
4234	2" x 3/4" diameters		12	2		14.40	105		119.40	173
4236	2" x 1" CTS diameters		12	2		14.20	105		119.20	173
4238	2" x 1" diameters		12	2		15.50	105		120.50	174
4240	2" x 1-1/4" diameters		12	2		14.10	105		119.10	173
4242	2" x 1-1/2" diameters		12	2		12.30	105		117.30	171
4244	3" x 2" diameters		12	2		17	105		122	176
4246	4" x 2" diameters		9	2.667		35.50	140		175.50	249
4248	4" x 3" diameters		9	2.667		40.50	140		180.50	254
4300	Couplings, 1/2" CTS diameter		15	1.600		2.61	84		86.61	129
4305	1/2" diameter		14.25	1.684		2.17	88.50		90.67	134
4310	3/4" diameter		14.25	1.684		2.43	88.50		90.93	135
4315	1" CTS diameter		14	1.714		2.94	90		92.94	138
4320	1" diameter		13.50	1.778		2.48	93.50		95.98	143
4325	1-1/4" diameter		13.50	1.778		2.98	93.50		96.48	143
4330	1-1/2" diameter	↓	12.75	1.882	↓	3.52	99		102.52	152

33 52 Hydrocarbon Transmission and Distribution

33 52 16 – Gas Hydrocarbon Piping

33 52 16.23 Medium Density Polyethylene Piping		Crew	Daily Output	Labor-Hours	Unit	Material	2023 Bare Costs Labor	Equipment	Total	Total Incl O&P
4335	2" diameter	B-20	12	2	Ea.	3.07	105		108.07	160
4340	3" diameter		12	2		12.40	105		117.40	171
4345	4" diameter		9	2.667		33.50	140		173.50	246
4400	Elbows, 90°, 1/2" CTS diameter		15	1.600		4.94	84		88.94	131
4405	1/2" diameter		14.25	1.684		4.85	88.50		93.35	137
4410	3/4" diameter		14.25	1.684		5.75	88.50		94.25	138
4415	1" CTS diameter		14	1.714		5.50	90		95.50	141
4420	1" diameter		13.50	1.778		6.15	93.50		99.65	147
4425	1-1/4" diameter		13.50	1.778		5.85	93.50		99.35	146
4430	1-1/2" diameter		12.75	1.882		7.35	99		106.35	156
4435	2" diameter		12	2		6.05	105		111.05	164
4440	3" diameter		12	2		32	105		137	192
4445	4" diameter		9	2.667		82.50	140		222.50	300
4460	45°, 1" diameter		13.50	1.778		9.85	93.50		103.35	151
4465	2" diameter		12	2		13.20	105		118.20	172
4500	Tees, 1/2" CTS diameter		10	2.400		4.72	126		130.72	194
4505	1/2" diameter		9.50	2.526		4.19	133		137.19	203
4510	3/4" diameter		9.50	2.526		5.65	133		138.65	204
4515	1" CTS diameter		9.33	2.571		5.50	135		140.50	208
4520	1" diameter		9	2.667		6.90	140		146.90	217
4525	1-1/4" diameter		9	2.667		7.65	140		147.65	217
4530	1-1/2" diameter		8.50	2.824		12.60	148		160.60	236
4535	2" diameter		8	3		15.10	158		173.10	253
4540	3" diameter		8	3		76	158		234	320
4545	4" diameter		6	4		86.50	210		296.50	410
4600	Tapping tees, type II, 3/4" punch, socket fusion outlets									
4601	Saddle contour x outlet diameter, IPS unless noted CTS									
4602	1-1/4" x 1/2" CTS outlet	B-20	17	1.412	Ea.	17.30	74		91.30	130
4604	1-1/4" x 1/2" outlet		17	1.412		17.30	74		91.30	130
4606	1-1/4" x 3/4" outlet		17	1.412		17.30	74		91.30	130
4608	1-1/4" x 1" CTS outlet		17	1.412		18.90	74		92.90	132
4610	1-1/4" x 1" outlet		17	1.412		18.90	74		92.90	132
4612	1-1/4" x 1-1/4" outlet		16	1.500		32	79		111	153
4614	1-1/2" x 1/2" CTS outlet		16	1.500		17.30	79		96.30	137
4616	1-1/2" x 1/2" outlet		16	1.500		17.30	79		96.30	137
4618	1-1/2" x 3/4" outlet		16	1.500		17.30	79		96.30	137
4620	1-1/2" x 1" CTS outlet		16	1.500		18.90	79		97.90	139
4622	1-1/2" x 1" outlet		16	1.500		18.90	79		97.90	139
4624	1-1/2" x 1-1/4" outlet		15	1.600		32	84		116	161
4626	2" x 1/2" CTS outlet		12	2		17.30	105		122.30	176
4628	2" x 1/2" outlet		12	2		17.30	105		122.30	176
4630	2" x 3/4" outlet		12	2		17.30	105		122.30	176
4632	2" x 1" CTS outlet		12	2		18.90	105		123.90	178
4634	2" x 1" outlet		12	2		18.90	105		123.90	178
4636	2" x 1-1/4" outlet		11	2.182		32	115		147	206
4638	3" x 1/2" CTS outlet		12	2		17.30	105		122.30	176
4640	3" x 1/2" outlet		12	2		17.30	105		122.30	176
4642	3" x 3/4" outlet		12	2		17.30	105		122.30	176
4644	3" x 1" CTS outlet		12	2		18.90	105		123.90	178
4646	3" x 1" outlet		12	2		18.90	105		123.90	178
4648	3" x 1-1/4" outlet		11	2.182		32	115		147	206
4650	4" x 1/2" CTS outlet		10	2.400		17.30	126		143.30	208
4652	4" x 1/2" outlet		10	2.400		17.30	126		143.30	208

33 52 Hydrocarbon Transmission and Distribution

33 52 16 – Gas Hydrocarbon Piping

33 52 16.23 Medium Density Polyethylene Piping		Crew	Daily Output	Labor-Hours	Unit	Material	2023 Bare Costs Labor	Equipment	Total	Total Incl O&P
4654	4" x 3/4" outlet	B-20	10	2.400	Ea.	17.30	126		143.30	208
4656	4" x 1" CTS outlet		10	2.400		18.90	126		144.90	210
4658	4" x 1" outlet		10	2.400		18.90	126		144.90	210
4660	4" x 1-1/4" outlet	▼	9	2.667		32	140		172	244
4685	For protective sleeves, 1/2" CTS to 3/4" diameter outlets, add					1.22			1.22	1.34
4690	1" CTS & IPS diameter outlets, add					2.04			2.04	2.24
4695	1-1/4" diameter outlets, add				▼	3.52			3.52	3.87
4700	Tapping tees, high volume, socket fusion outlets									
4705	1-1/2" punch, 2" x 1-1/4" outlet	B-20	11	2.182	Ea.	159	115		274	345
4710	1-7/8" punch, 3" x 1-1/4" outlet		11	2.182		159	115		274	345
4715	4" x 1-1/4" outlet	▼	9	2.667		159	140		299	385
4750	For protective sleeves, add				▼	4.11			4.11	4.52
4800	Service saddles, saddle contour x outlet, socket fusion outlets									
4801	IPS unless noted CTS									
4802	1-1/4" x 1/2" CTS outlet	B-20	17	1.412	Ea.	5.35	74		79.35	117
4804	1-1/4" x 1/2" outlet		17	1.412		5.35	74		79.35	117
4806	1-1/4" x 3/4" outlet		17	1.412		5.35	74		79.35	117
4808	1-1/4" x 1" CTS outlet		17	1.412		8.85	74		82.85	121
4810	1-1/4" x 1" outlet		17	1.412		26.50	74		100.50	140
4812	1-1/4" x 1-1/4" outlet		16	1.500		14.20	79		93.20	134
4814	1-1/2" x 1/2" CTS outlet		16	1.500		5.35	79		84.35	124
4816	1-1/2" x 1/2" outlet		16	1.500		5.35	79		84.35	124
4818	1-1/2" x 3/4" outlet		16	1.500		26.50	79		105.50	147
4820	1-1/2" x 1-1/4" outlet		15	1.600		14.20	84		98.20	142
4822	2" x 1/2" CTS outlet		12	2		5.35	105		110.35	163
4824	2" x 1/2" outlet		12	2		5.35	105		110.35	163
4826	2" x 3/4" outlet		12	2		5.35	105		110.35	163
4828	2" x 1" CTS outlet		12	2		8.85	105		113.85	167
4830	2" x 1" outlet		12	2		8.85	105		113.85	167
4832	2" x 1-1/4" outlet		11	2.182		26.50	115		141.50	200
4834	3" x 1/2" CTS outlet		12	2		5.35	105		110.35	163
4836	3" x 1/2" outlet		12	2		5.35	105		110.35	163
4838	3" x 3/4" outlet		12	2		5.35	105		110.35	163
4840	3" x 1" CTS outlet		12	2		8.85	105		113.85	167
4842	3" x 1" outlet		12	2		8.85	105		113.85	167
4844	3" x 1-1/4" outlet		11	2.182		22.50	115		137.50	196
4846	4" x 1/2" CTS outlet		10	2.400		5.35	126		131.35	195
4848	4" x 1/2" outlet		10	2.400		5.35	126		131.35	195
4850	4" x 3/4" outlet		10	2.400		5.35	126		131.35	195
4852	4" x 1" CTS outlet		10	2.400		8.85	126		134.85	199
4854	4" x 1" outlet		10	2.400		8.85	126		134.85	199
4856	4" x 1-1/4" outlet	▼	9	2.667		23.50	140		163.50	235
4885	For protective sleeves, 1/2" CTS to 3/4" diameter outlets, add					1.22			1.22	1.34
4890	1" CTS & IPS diameter outlets, add					2.04			2.04	2.24
4895	1-1/4" diameter outlets, add					3.52			3.52	3.87
4900	Spigot fittings, tees, SDR 7, 1/2" CTS diameter	B-20	10	2.400		37	126		163	230
4901	SDR 9.3, 1/2" diameter		9.50	2.526		16.35	133		149.35	216
4902	SDR 10, 1-1/4" diameter		9	2.667		16.35	140		156.35	227
4903	SDR 11, 3/4" diameter		9.50	2.526		34	133		167	236
4904	2" diameter		8	3		31.50	158		189.50	271
4906	SDR 11.5, 1" CTS diameter		9.33	2.571		87	135		222	298
4907	3" diameter		8	3		88.50	158		246.50	335
4908	4" diameter		6	4		228	210		438	565

33 52 Hydrocarbon Transmission and Distribution

33 52 16 – Gas Hydrocarbon Piping

	33 52 16.23 Medium Density Polyethylene Piping	Crew	Daily Output	Labor-Hours	Unit	Material	2023 Bare Costs Labor	Equipment	Total	Total Incl O&P
4921	90° elbows, SDR 7, 1/2" CTS diameter	B-20	15	1.600	Ea.	19.45	84		103.45	148
4922	SDR 9.3, 1/2" diameter		14.25	1.684		8.35	88.50		96.85	141
4923	SDR 10, 1-1/4" diameter		13.50	1.778		8.55	93.50		102.05	149
4924	SDR 11, 3/4" diameter		14.25	1.684		9.55	88.50		98.05	143
4925	2" diameter		12	2		36	105		141	197
4927	SDR 11.5, 1" CTS diameter		14	1.714		33	90		123	172
4928	3" diameter		12	2		82	105		187	247
4929	4" diameter		9	2.667		175	140		315	400
4935	Caps, SDR 7, 1/2" CTS diameter		30	.800		6.45	42		48.45	70
4936	SDR 9.3, 1/2" diameter		28.50	.842		6.45	44.50		50.95	73
4937	SDR 10, 1-1/4" diameter		27	.889		6.70	46.50		53.20	77.50
4938	SDR 11, 3/4" diameter		28.50	.842		6.90	44.50		51.40	73.50
4939	1" diameter		27	.889		7.70	46.50		54.20	78.50
4940	2" diameter		24	1		8.20	52.50		60.70	87.50
4942	SDR 11.5, 1" CTS diameter		28	.857		27	45		72	97.50
4943	3" diameter		24	1		44	52.50		96.50	127
4944	4" diameter		18	1.333		42	70		112	152
4946	SDR 13.5, 4" diameter		18	1.333		106	70		176	222
4950	Reducers, SDR 10 x SDR 11, 1-1/4" x 3/4" diameters		13.50	1.778		22	93.50		115.50	165
4951	1-1/4" x 1" diameters		13.50	1.778		22	93.50		115.50	165
4952	SDR 10 x SDR 11.5, 1-1/4" x 1" CTS diameters		13.50	1.778		22	93.50		115.50	165
4953	SDR 11 x SDR 7, 3/4" x 1/2" CTS diameters		14.25	1.684		9.85	88.50		98.35	143
4954	SDR 11 x SDR 9.3, 3/4" x 1/2" diameters		14.25	1.684		9.85	88.50		98.35	143
4955	SDR 11 x SDR 10, 2" x 1-1/4" diameters		12	2		23	105		128	182
4956	SDR 11 x SDR 11, 1" x 3/4" diameters		13.50	1.778		11.35	93.50		104.85	153
4957	2" x 3/4" diameters		12	2		22.50	105		127.50	182
4958	2" x 1" diameters		12	2		22.50	105		127.50	182
4959	SDR 11 x SDR 11.5, 1" x 1" CTS diameters		13.50	1.778		11.55	93.50		105.05	153
4960	2" x 1" CTS diameters		12	2		22.50	105		127.50	182
4962	SDR 11.5 x SDR 11, 3" x 2" diameters		12	2		30.50	105		135.50	191
4963	4" x 2" diameters		9	2.667		46	140		186	260
4964	SDR 11.5 x SDR 11.5, 4" x 3" diameters		9	2.667		49.50	140		189.50	264
6100	Fittings, compression									
6101	MDPE gas pipe, ASTM D2513/ASTM F1924-98									
6102	Caps, SDR 7, 1/2" CTS diameter	B-20	60	.400	Ea.	18.60	21		39.60	52
6104	SDR 9.3, 1/2" IPS diameter		58	.414		32.50	22		54.50	68
6106	SDR 10, 1/2" CTS diameter		60	.400		16.40	21		37.40	49.50
6108	1-1/4" IPS diameter		54	.444		108	23.50		131.50	154
6110	SDR 11, 3/4" IPS diameter		58	.414		29	22		51	64.50
6112	1" IPS diameter		54	.444		47	23.50		70.50	86.50
6114	1-1/4" IPS diameter		54	.444		113	23.50		136.50	160
6116	1-1/2" IPS diameter		52	.462		138	24.50		162.50	188
6118	2" IPS diameter		50	.480		121	25		146	171
6120	SDR 11.5, 1" CTS diameter		56	.429		30	22.50		52.50	66.50
6122	SDR 12.5, 1" CTS diameter		56	.429		34.50	22.50		57	71.50
6202	Reducers, SDR 7 x SDR 10, 1/2" CTS x 1/2" CTS diameters		30	.800		25	42		67	90.50
6204	SDR 9.3 x SDR 7, 1/2" IPS x 1/2" CTS diameters		29	.828		72.50	43.50		116	145
6206	SDR 11 x SDR 7, 3/4" IPS x 1/2" CTS diameters		29	.828		72	43.50		115.50	144
6208	1" IPS x 1/2" CTS diameters		27	.889		87	46.50		133.50	166
6210	SDR 11 x SDR 9.3, 3/4" IPS x 1/2" IPS diameters		29	.828		70.50	43.50		114	143
6212	1" IPS x 1/2" IPS diameters		27	.889		90	46.50		136.50	169
6214	SDR 11 x SDR 10, 2" IPS x 1-1/4" IPS diameters		25	.960		138	50.50		188.50	228
6216	SDR 11 x SDR 11, 1" IPS x 3/4" IPS diameters		27	.889		87	46.50		133.50	166

33 52 Hydrocarbon Transmission and Distribution

33 52 16 – Gas Hydrocarbon Piping

	33 52 16.23 Medium Density Polyethylene Piping	Crew	Daily Output	Labor-Hours	Unit	Material	2023 Bare Costs Labor	Equipment	Total	Total Incl O&P
6218	1-1/4" IPS x 1" IPS diameters	B-20	27	.889	Ea.	82.50	46.50		129	161
6220	2" IPS x 1-1/4" IPS diameters		25	.960		138	50.50		188.50	228
6222	SDR 11 x SDR 11.5, 1" IPS x 1" CTS diameters		27	.889		67	46.50		113.50	144
6224	SDR 11 x SDR 12.5, 1" IPS x 1" CTS diameters		27	.889		81.50	46.50		128	160
6226	SDR 11.5 x SDR 7, 1" CTS x 1/2" CTS diameters		28	.857		49.50	45		94.50	122
6228	SDR 11.5 x SDR 9.3, 1" CTS x 1/2" IPS diameters		28	.857		57	45		102	130
6230	SDR 11.5 x SDR 11, 1" CTS x 3/4" IPS diameters		28	.857		79.50	45		124.50	155
6232	SDR 12.5 x SDR 7, 1" CTS x 1/2" CTS diameters		28	.857		52	45		97	125
6234	SDR 12.5 x SDR 9.3, 1" CTS x 1/2" IPS diameters		28	.857		58.50	45		103.50	132
6236	SDR 12.5 x SDR 11, 1" CTS x 3/4" IPS diameters		28	.857		50	45		95	123
6302	Couplings, SDR 7, 1/2" CTS diameter		30	.800		18.95	42		60.95	84
6304	SDR 9.3, 1/2" IPS diameter		29	.828		22.50	43.50		66	89.50
6306	SDR 10, 1/2" CTS diameter		30	.800		18	42		60	83
6308	SDR 11, 3/4" IPS diameter		29	.828		30.50	43.50		74	98.50
6310	1" IPS diameter		27	.889		33.50	46.50		80	107
6312	SDR 11.5, 1" CTS diameter		28	.857		35.50	45		80.50	107
6314	SDR 12.5, 1" CTS diameter		28	.857		40	45		85	112
6402	Repair couplings, SDR 10, 1-1/4" IPS diameter		27	.889		104	46.50		150.50	184
6404	SDR 11, 1-1/4" IPS diameter		27	.889		106	46.50		152.50	186
6406	1-1/2" IPS diameter		26	.923		114	48.50		162.50	198
6408	2" IPS diameter		25	.960		133	50.50		183.50	222
6502	Elbows, 90°, SDR 7, 1/2" CTS diameter		30	.800		33.50	42		75.50	100
6504	SDR 9.3, 1/2" IPS diameter		29	.828		57.50	43.50		101	129
6506	SDR 10, 1-1/4" IPS diameter		27	.889		142	46.50		188.50	226
6508	SDR 11, 3/4" IPS diameter		29	.828		52.50	43.50		96	123
6510	1" IPS diameter		27	.889		52.50	46.50		99	128
6512	1-1/4" IPS diameter		27	.889		141	46.50		187.50	226
6514	1-1/2" IPS diameter		26	.923		212	48.50		260.50	305
6516	2" IPS diameter		25	.960		180	50.50		230.50	274
6518	SDR 11.5, 1" CTS diameter		28	.857		53.50	45		98.50	126
6520	SDR 12.5, 1" CTS diameter		28	.857		77.50	45		122.50	153
6602	Tees, SDR 7, 1/2" CTS diameter		20	1.200		58.50	63		121.50	159
6604	SDR 9.3, 1/2" IPS diameter		19.33	1.241		65	65.50		130.50	169
6606	SDR 10, 1-1/4" IPS diameter		18	1.333		184	70		254	305
6608	SDR 11, 3/4" IPS diameter		19.33	1.241		82	65.50		147.50	188
6610	1" IPS diameter		18	1.333		89.50	70		159.50	204
6612	1-1/4" IPS diameter		18	1.333		151	70		221	271
6614	1-1/2" IPS diameter		17.33	1.385		310	73		383	455
6616	2" IPS diameter		16.67	1.440		207	75.50		282.50	340
6618	SDR 11.5, 1" CTS diameter		18.67	1.286		82.50	67.50		150	192
6620	SDR 12.5, 1" CTS diameter	↓	18.67	1.286	↓	85.50	67.50		153	195
8100	Fittings, accessories									
8105	SDR 11, IPS unless noted CTS									
8110	Protective sleeves, for high volume tapping tees, butt fusion outlets	1 Skwk	16	.500	Ea.	7.90	30.50		38.40	54.50
8120	For tapping tees, socket outlets, CTS, 1/2" diameter		18	.444		2.05	27		29.05	43.50
8122	1" diameter		18	.444		3.63	27		30.63	45
8124	IPS, 1/2" diameter		18	.444		2.84	27		29.84	44
8126	3/4" diameter		18	.444		3.63	27		30.63	45
8128	1" diameter		18	.444		4.95	27		31.95	46.50
8130	1-1/4" diameter		18	.444		6.25	27		33.25	48
8205	Tapping tee test caps, type I, yellow PE cap, "aldyl style"		45	.178		64	10.90		74.90	86.50
8210	Type II, yellow polyethylene cap		45	.178		62.50	10.90		73.40	85.50
8215	High volume, yellow polyethylene cap	↓	45	.178		82	10.90		92.90	107

33 52 Hydrocarbon Transmission and Distribution

33 52 16 – Gas Hydrocarbon Piping

33 52 16.23 Medium Density Polyethylene Piping

		Crew	Daily Output	Labor-Hours	Unit	Material	2023 Bare Costs Labor	Equipment	Total	Total Incl O&P
8250	Quick connector, female x female inlets, 1/4" N.P.T.	1 Skwk	50	.160	Ea.	26	9.80		35.80	43
8255	Test hose, 24" length, 3/8" ID, male outlets, 1/4" N.P.T.		50	.160		35.50	9.80		45.30	53.50
8260	Quick connector and test hose assembly		50	.160		61.50	9.80		71.30	82
8305	Purge point caps, butt fusion, SDR 10, 1-1/4" diameter	B-22C	27	.593		46	32	10.40	88.40	110
8310	SDR 11, 1-1/4" diameter		27	.593		46	32	10.40	88.40	110
8315	2" diameter		24	.667		47	36	11.70	94.70	118
8320	3" diameter		24	.667		65	36	11.70	112.70	138
8325	4" diameter		18	.889		63.50	48	15.60	127.10	159
8340	Socket fusion, SDR 11, 1-1/4" diameter		27	.593		11.55	32	10.40	53.95	72
8345	2" diameter		24	.667		13.90	36	11.70	61.60	82
8350	3" diameter		24	.667		85	36	11.70	132.70	160
8355	4" diameter		18	.889		62.50	48	15.60	126.10	158
8360	Purge test quick connector, female x female inlets, 1/4" N.P.T.	1 Skwk	50	.160		26	9.80		35.80	43
8365	Purge test hose, 24" length, 3/8" ID, male outlets, 1/4" N.P.T.		50	.160		35.50	9.80		45.30	53.50
8370	Purge test quick connector and test hose assembly		50	.160		61.50	9.80		71.30	82
8405	Transition fittings, MDPE x zinc plated steel, SDR 7, 1/2" CTS x 1/2" MPT	B-22C	30	.533		35.50	29	9.35	73.85	93
8410	SDR 9.3, 1/2" IPS x 3/4" MPT		28.50	.561		55.50	30.50	9.85	95.85	117
8415	SDR 10, 1-1/4" IPS x 1-1/4" MPT		27	.593		53	32	10.40	95.40	118
8420	SDR 11, 3/4" IPS x 3/4" MPT		28.50	.561		28	30.50	9.85	68.35	87.50
8425	1" IPS x 1" MPT		27	.593		34.50	32	10.40	76.90	97
8430	1-1/4" IPS x 1-1/4" MPT		17	.941		64	51	16.50	131.50	165
8435	1-1/2" IPS x 1-1/2" MPT		25.50	.627		65.50	34	11	110.50	135
8440	2" IPS x 2" MPT		24	.667		75	36	11.70	122.70	149
8445	SDR 11.5, 1" CTS x 1" MPT		28	.571		46	31	10	87	109

33 52 16.26 High Density Polyethylene Piping

		Crew	Daily Output	Labor-Hours	Unit	Material	2023 Bare Costs Labor	Equipment	Total	Total Incl O&P
2010	**HIGH DENSITY POLYETHYLENE PIPING**									
2020	ASTM D2513, not including excavation or backfill									
2200	Butt fused pipe									
2205	125psi coils, butt fusion joint @ 100', 1/2" CTS diameter, SDR 7	B-22C	2050	.008	L.F.	.20	.42	.14	.76	1
2210	160psi coils, butt fusion joint @ 100', IPS 1/2" diameter, SDR 9		1950	.008		.27	.45	.14	.86	1.13
2215	3/4" diameter, SDR 11		1950	.008		.40	.45	.14	.99	1.27
2220	1" diameter, SDR 11		1850	.009		.65	.47	.15	1.27	1.59
2225	1-1/4" diameter, SDR 11		1850	.009		.96	.47	.15	1.58	1.93
2230	1-1/2" diameter, SDR 11		1750	.009		1.79	.50	.16	2.45	2.89
2235	2" diameter, SDR 11		1750	.009		1.46	.50	.16	2.12	2.53
2240	3" diameter, SDR 11		1650	.010		2.40	.53	.17	3.10	3.62
2245	160psi 40' lengths, butt fusion joint, IPS 3" diameter, SDR 11	B-22A	660	.061		2.61	3.29	1.09	6.99	8.95
2250	4" diameter, SDR 11		500	.080		4.31	4.34	1.44	10.09	12.75
2255	6" diameter, SDR 11		500	.080		9.30	4.34	1.44	15.08	18.30
2260	8" diameter, SDR 11		420	.095		15.75	5.15	1.71	22.61	27
2265	10" diameter, SDR 11		340	.118		36.50	6.40	2.11	45.01	52
2270	12" diameter, SDR 11		300	.133		50.50	7.25	2.39	60.14	69
2400	Socket fused pipe									
2405	125psi coils, socket fusion coupling @ 100', 1/2" CTS diameter, SDR 7	B-20	1050	.023	L.F.	.23	1.20		1.43	2.05
2410	160psi coils, socket fusion coupling @ 100', IPS 1/2" diameter, SDR 9		1000	.024		.30	1.26		1.56	2.22
2415	3/4" diameter, SDR 11		1000	.024		.42	1.26		1.68	2.36
2420	1" diameter, SDR 11		950	.025		.67	1.33		2	2.72
2425	1-1/4" diameter, SDR 11		950	.025		1	1.33		2.33	3.07
2430	1-1/2" diameter, SDR 11		900	.027		1.83	1.40		3.23	4.10
2435	2" diameter, SDR 11		850	.028		1.50	1.48		2.98	3.87
2440	3" diameter, SDR 11		850	.028		2.58	1.48		4.06	5.05
2445	160psi 40' lengths, socket fusion coupling, IPS 3" diameter, SDR 11	B-21A	340	.118		3.06	6.90	1.88	11.84	15.70

33 52 Hydrocarbon Transmission and Distribution

33 52 16 – Gas Hydrocarbon Piping

33 52 16.26 High Density Polyethylene Piping		Crew	Daily Output	Labor-Hours	Unit	Material	2023 Bare Costs Labor	Equipment	Total	Total Incl O&P
2450	4" diameter, SDR 11	B-21A	260	.154	L.F.	5.15	9	2.45	16.60	22
2600	Compression coupled pipe									
2610	160psi coils, compression coupling @ 100', IPS 1/2" diameter, SDR 9	B-20	1000	.024	L.F.	.49	1.26		1.75	2.43
2615	3/4" diameter, SDR 11		1000	.024		.71	1.26		1.97	2.67
2620	1" diameter, SDR 11		950	.025		.98	1.33		2.31	3.06
2625	1-1/4" diameter, SDR 11		950	.025		2.02	1.33		3.35	4.20
2630	1-1/2" diameter, SDR 11		900	.027		2.93	1.40		4.33	5.30
2635	2" diameter, SDR 11	▼	850	.028	▼	2.79	1.48		4.27	5.30
3000	Fittings, butt fusion									
3010	SDR 11, IPS unless noted CTS									
3105	Caps, 1/2" diameter	B-22C	28.50	.561	Ea.	10.50	30.50	9.85	50.85	68
3110	3/4" diameter		28.50	.561		5.45	30.50	9.85	45.80	62.50
3115	1" diameter		27	.593		5.95	32	10.40	48.35	66
3120	1-1/4" diameter		27	.593		9.80	32	10.40	52.20	70.50
3125	1-1/2" diameter		25.50	.627		7.15	34	11	52.15	71
3130	2" diameter		24	.667		14.85	36	11.70	62.55	83
3135	3" diameter		24	.667		21	36	11.70	68.70	90
3140	4" diameter	▼	18	.889		38	48	15.60	101.60	131
3145	6" diameter	B-22A	18	2.222		112	121	40	273	345
3150	8" diameter		15	2.667		176	145	48	369	460
3155	10" diameter		12	3.333		520	181	60	761	910
3160	12" diameter	▼	10.50	3.810		560	207	68.50	835.50	1,000
3205	Reducers, 1/2" x 1/2" CTS diameters	B-22C	14.25	1.123		19.45	61	19.70	100.15	134
3210	3/4" x 1/2" CTS diameters		14.25	1.123		13.95	61	19.70	94.65	128
3215	1" x 1/2" CTS diameters		13.50	1.185		21.50	64.50	21	107	143
3220	1" x 1/2" diameters		13.50	1.185		26.50	64.50	21	112	149
3225	1" x 3/4" diameters		13.50	1.185		17.90	64.50	21	103.40	139
3230	1-1/4" x 1" diameters		13.50	1.185		20	64.50	21	105.50	141
3232	1-1/2" x 3/4" diameters		12.75	1.255		12.55	68	22	102.55	140
3233	1-1/2" x 1" diameters		12.75	1.255		12.55	68	22	102.55	140
3234	1-1/2" x 1-1/4" diameters		12.75	1.255		12.55	68	22	102.55	140
3235	2" x 1" diameters		12	1.333		22.50	72.50	23.50	118.50	159
3240	2" x 1-1/4" diameters		12	1.333		22.50	72.50	23.50	118.50	159
3245	2" x 1-1/2" diameters		12	1.333		14.35	72.50	23.50	110.35	149
3250	3" x 2" diameters		12	1.333		16.70	72.50	23.50	112.70	152
3255	4" x 2" diameters		9	1.778		23	96.50	31	150.50	204
3260	4" x 3" diameters	▼	9	1.778		24.50	96.50	31	152	206
3262	6" x 3" diameters	B-22A	9	4.444		56	241	80	377	510
3265	6" x 4" diameters		9	4.444		75	241	80	396	530
3270	8" x 6" diameters		7.50	5.333		129	289	95.50	513.50	675
3275	10" x 8" diameters		6	6.667		269	360	120	749	970
3280	12" x 8" diameters		5.25	7.619		395	415	137	947	1,200
3285	12" x 10" diameters	▼	5.25	7.619		185	415	137	737	970
3305	Elbows, 90°, 3/4" diameter	B-22C	14.25	1.123		9.25	61	19.70	89.95	123
3310	1" diameter		13.50	1.185		9.10	64.50	21	94.60	129
3315	1-1/4" diameter		13.50	1.185		10.60	64.50	21	96.10	131
3320	1-1/2" diameter		12.75	1.255		12.05	68	22	102.05	139
3325	2" diameter		12	1.333		13.05	72.50	23.50	109.05	148
3330	3" diameter		12	1.333		25.50	72.50	23.50	121.50	162
3335	4" diameter	▼	9	1.778		33	96.50	31	160.50	215
3340	6" diameter	B-22A	9	4.444		87.50	241	80	408.50	545
3345	8" diameter		7.50	5.333		261	289	95.50	645.50	820
3350	10" diameter	▼	6	6.667		630	360	120	1,110	1,350

33 52 Hydrocarbon Transmission and Distribution

33 52 16 – Gas Hydrocarbon Piping

33 52 16.26 High Density Polyethylene Piping

		Crew	Daily Output	Labor-Hours	Unit	Material	2023 Bare Costs Labor	Equipment	Total	Total Incl O&P
3355	12" diameter	B-22A	5.25	7.619	Ea.	585	415	137	1,137	1,400
3380	45°, 3/4" diameter	B-22C	14.25	1.123		10.30	61	19.70	91	124
3385	1" diameter		13.50	1.185		10.30	64.50	21	95.80	130
3390	1-1/4" diameter		13.50	1.185		10.55	64.50	21	96.05	131
3395	1-1/2" diameter		12.75	1.255		13.75	68	22	103.75	141
3400	2" diameter		12	1.333		15.35	72.50	23.50	111.35	150
3405	3" diameter		12	1.333		26	72.50	23.50	122	162
3410	4" diameter		9	1.778		32.50	96.50	31	160	215
3415	6" diameter	B-22A	9	4.444		87.50	241	80	408.50	545
3420	8" diameter		7.50	5.333		271	289	95.50	655.50	835
3425	10" diameter		6	6.667		595	360	120	1,075	1,325
3430	12" diameter		5.25	7.619		1,175	415	137	1,727	2,050
3505	Tees, 1/2" CTS diameter	B-22C	10	1.600		12.65	87	28	127.65	175
3510	1/2" diameter		9.50	1.684		14	91.50	29.50	135	185
3515	3/4" diameter		9.50	1.684		10.35	91.50	29.50	131.35	181
3520	1" diameter		9	1.778		11.20	96.50	31	138.70	191
3525	1-1/4" diameter		9	1.778		11.90	96.50	31	139.40	192
3530	1-1/2" diameter		8.50	1.882		19.55	102	33	154.55	211
3535	2" diameter		8	2		15.50	109	35	159.50	218
3540	3" diameter		8	2		28.50	109	35	172.50	232
3545	4" diameter		6	2.667		42	145	47	234	315
3550	6" diameter	B-22A	6	6.667		104	360	120	584	785
3555	8" diameter		5	8		420	435	144	999	1,275
3560	10" diameter		4	10		775	545	180	1,500	1,850
3565	12" diameter		3.50	11.429		1,025	620	205	1,850	2,275
3600	Tapping tees, type II, 3/4" punch, butt fusion outlets									
3601	Saddle contour x outlet diameter, IPS unless noted CTS									
3602	1-1/4" x 1/2" CTS outlet	B-22C	17	.941	Ea.	17.75	51	16.50	85.25	114
3604	1-1/4" x 1/2" outlet		17	.941		17.75	51	16.50	85.25	114
3606	1-1/4" x 3/4" outlet		17	.941		17.75	51	16.50	85.25	114
3608	1-1/4" x 1" outlet		17	.941		20.50	51	16.50	88	118
3610	1-1/4" x 1-1/4" outlet		16	1		37	54.50	17.55	109.05	141
3612	1-1/2" x 1/2" CTS outlet		16	1		17.75	54.50	17.55	89.80	120
3614	1-1/2" x 1/2" outlet		16	1		17.75	54.50	17.55	89.80	120
3616	1-1/2" x 3/4" outlet		16	1		17.75	54.50	17.55	89.80	120
3618	1-1/2" x 1" outlet		16	1		20.50	54.50	17.55	92.55	123
3620	1-1/2" x 1-1/4" outlet		15	1.067		37	58	18.70	113.70	148
3622	2" x 1/2" CTS outlet		12	1.333		17.75	72.50	23.50	113.75	153
3624	2" x 1/2" outlet		12	1.333		17.75	72.50	23.50	113.75	153
3626	2" x 3/4" outlet		12	1.333		17.75	72.50	23.50	113.75	153
3628	2" x 1" outlet		12	1.333		20.50	72.50	23.50	116.50	157
3630	2" x 1-1/4" outlet		11	1.455		37	79	25.50	141.50	187
3632	3" x 1/2" CTS outlet		12	1.333		17.75	72.50	23.50	113.75	153
3634	3" x 1/2" outlet		12	1.333		17.75	72.50	23.50	113.75	153
3636	3" x 3/4" outlet		12	1.333		17.75	72.50	23.50	113.75	153
3638	3" x 1" outlet		12	1.333		20.50	72.50	23.50	116.50	157
3640	3" x 1-1/4" outlet		11	1.455		20.50	79	25.50	125	169
3642	4" x 1/2" CTS outlet		10	1.600		17.75	87	28	132.75	181
3644	4" x 1/2" outlet		10	1.600		17.75	87	28	132.75	181
3646	4" x 3/4" outlet		10	1.600		17.75	87	28	132.75	181
3648	4" x 1" outlet		10	1.600		20.50	87	28	135.50	184
3650	4" x 1-1/4" outlet		9	1.778		37	96.50	31	164.50	220
3652	6" x 1/2" CTS outlet	B-22A	10	4		17.75	217	72	306.75	425

33 52 Hydrocarbon Transmission and Distribution

33 52 16 – Gas Hydrocarbon Piping

33 52 16.26 High Density Polyethylene Piping

		Crew	Daily Output	Labor-Hours	Unit	Material	2023 Bare Costs Labor	Equipment	Total	Total Incl O&P
3654	6" x 1/2" outlet	B-22A	10	4	Ea.	17.75	217	72	306.75	425
3656	6" x 3/4" outlet		10	4		17.75	217	72	306.75	425
3658	6" x 1" outlet		10	4		20.50	217	72	309.50	425
3660	6" x 1-1/4" outlet		9	4.444		37	241	80	358	490
3662	8" x 1/2" CTS outlet		8	5		17.75	271	90	378.75	525
3664	8" x 1/2" outlet		8	5		17.75	271	90	378.75	525
3666	8" x 3/4" outlet		8	5		17.75	271	90	378.75	525
3668	8" x 1" outlet		8	5		20.50	271	90	381.50	525
3670	8" x 1-1/4" outlet		7	5.714		37	310	103	450	615
3675	For protective sleeves, 1/2" to 3/4" diameter outlets, add					1.22			1.22	1.34
3680	1" diameter outlets, add					2.04			2.04	2.24
3685	1-1/4" diameter outlets, add					3.52			3.52	3.87
3700	Tapping tees, high volume, butt fusion outlets									
3705	1-1/2" punch, 2" x 2" outlet	B-22C	11	1.455	Ea.	174	79	25.50	278.50	340
3710	1-7/8" punch, 3" x 2" outlet		11	1.455		174	79	25.50	278.50	340
3715	4" x 2" outlet		9	1.778		174	96.50	31	301.50	370
3720	6" x 2" outlet	B-22A	9	4.444		212	241	80	533	680
3725	8" x 2" outlet		7	5.714		174	310	103	587	765
3730	10" x 2" outlet		6	6.667		174	360	120	654	865
3735	12" x 2" outlet		5	8		244	435	144	823	1,075
3750	For protective sleeves, add					4.11			4.11	4.52
3800	Service saddles, saddle contour x outlet, butt fusion outlets									
3801	IPS unless noted CTS									
3802	1-1/4" x 3/4" outlet	B-22C	17	.941	Ea.	10.55	51	16.50	78.05	106
3804	1-1/4" x 1" outlet		16	1		10.55	54.50	17.55	82.60	112
3806	1-1/4" x 1-1/4" outlet		16	1		11	54.50	17.55	83.05	112
3808	1-1/2" x 3/4" outlet		16	1		28.50	54.50	17.55	100.55	132
3810	1-1/2" x 1-1/4" outlet		15	1.067		28.50	58	18.70	105.20	139
3812	2" x 3/4" outlet		12	1.333		28.50	72.50	23.50	124.50	165
3814	2" x 1" outlet		11	1.455		10.55	79	25.50	115.05	158
3816	2" x 1-1/4" outlet		11	1.455		11	79	25.50	115.50	158
3818	3" x 3/4" outlet		12	1.333		28.50	72.50	23.50	124.50	165
3820	3" x 1" outlet		11	1.455		28.50	79	25.50	133	178
3822	3" x 1-1/4" outlet		11	1.455		11	79	25.50	115.50	158
3824	4" x 3/4" outlet		10	1.600		28.50	87	28	143.50	193
3826	4" x 1" outlet		9	1.778		28.50	96.50	31	156	210
3828	4" x 1-1/4" outlet		9	1.778		28.50	96.50	31	156	210
3830	6" x 3/4" outlet	B-22A	10	4		10.55	217	72	299.55	415
3832	6" x 1" outlet		9	4.444		10.55	241	80	331.55	460
3834	6" x 1-1/4" outlet		9	4.444		11	241	80	332	460
3836	8" x 3/4" outlet		8	5		28.50	271	90	389.50	535
3838	8" x 1" outlet		7	5.714		10.55	310	103	423.55	585
3840	8" x 1-1/4" outlet		7	5.714		11	310	103	424	585
3880	For protective sleeves, 3/4" diameter outlets, add					1.22			1.22	1.34
3885	1" diameter outlets, add					2.04			2.04	2.24
3890	1-1/4" diameter outlets, add					3.52			3.52	3.87
3905	Branch saddles, contour x outlet, 2" x 2" outlet	B-22C	11	1.455		29.50	79	25.50	134	179
3910	3" x 2" outlet		11	1.455		29.50	79	25.50	134	179
3915	3" x 3" outlet		11	1.455		39.50	79	25.50	144	190
3920	4" x 2" outlet		9	1.778		29.50	96.50	31	157	211
3925	4" x 3" outlet		9	1.778		39.50	96.50	31	167	222
3930	4" x 4" outlet		9	1.778		54	96.50	31	181.50	238
3935	6" x 2" outlet	B-22A	9	4.444		29.50	241	80	350.50	480

33 52 Hydrocarbon Transmission and Distribution

33 52 16 – Gas Hydrocarbon Piping

33 52 16.26 High Density Polyethylene Piping		Crew	Daily Output	Labor-Hours	Unit	Material	2023 Bare Costs Labor	Equipment	Total	Total Incl O&P
3940	6" x 3" outlet	B-22A	9	4.444	Ea.	39.50	241	80	360.50	490
3945	6" x 4" outlet		9	4.444		54	241	80	375	510
3950	6" x 6" outlet		9	4.444		130	241	80	451	590
3955	8" x 2" outlet		7	5.714		29.50	310	103	442.50	605
3960	8" x 3" outlet		7	5.714		39.50	310	103	452.50	615
3965	8" x 4" outlet		7	5.714		54	310	103	467	635
3970	8" x 6" outlet		7	5.714		130	310	103	543	715
3980	Ball valves, full port, 3/4" diameter	B-22C	14.25	1.123		91	61	19.70	171.70	213
3982	1" diameter		13.50	1.185		91	64.50	21	176.50	219
3984	1-1/4" diameter		13.50	1.185		91.50	64.50	21	177	220
3986	1-1/2" diameter		12.75	1.255		134	68	22	224	273
3988	2" diameter		12	1.333		209	72.50	23.50	305	365
3990	3" diameter		12	1.333		490	72.50	23.50	586	675
3992	4" diameter		9	1.778		645	96.50	31	772.50	890
3994	6" diameter	B-22A	9	4.444		1,725	241	80	2,046	2,350
3996	8" diameter	"	7.50	5.333		2,800	289	95.50	3,184.50	3,600
4000	Fittings, socket fusion									
4010	SDR 11, IPS unless noted CTS									
4105	Caps, 1/2" CTS diameter	B-20	30	.800	Ea.	3.76	42		45.76	67
4110	1/2" diameter		28.50	.842		3.78	44.50		48.28	70
4115	3/4" diameter		28.50	.842		4.13	44.50		48.63	70.50
4120	1" diameter		27	.889		5.25	46.50		51.75	76
4125	1-1/4" diameter		27	.889		5.45	46.50		51.95	76
4130	1-1/2" diameter		25.50	.941		6.05	49.50		55.55	80.50
4135	2" diameter		24	1		6.35	52.50		58.85	85.50
4140	3" diameter		24	1		39	52.50		91.50	121
4145	4" diameter		18	1.333		63.50	70		133.50	175
4205	Reducers, 1/2" x 1/2" CTS diameters		14.25	1.684		9.50	88.50		98	142
4210	3/4" x 1/2" CTS diameters		14.25	1.684		9.80	88.50		98.30	143
4215	3/4" x 1/2" diameters		14.25	1.684		9.80	88.50		98.30	143
4220	1" x 1/2" CTS diameters		13.50	1.778		9.45	93.50		102.95	150
4225	1" x 1/2" diameters		13.50	1.778		10	93.50		103.50	151
4230	1" x 3/4" diameters		13.50	1.778		8.20	93.50		101.70	149
4235	1-1/4" x 1/2" CTS diameters		13.50	1.778		9.45	93.50		102.95	150
4240	1-1/4" x 3/4" diameters		13.50	1.778		9.45	93.50		102.95	150
4245	1-1/4" x 1" diameters		13.50	1.778		8.95	93.50		102.45	150
4250	1-1/2" x 3/4" diameters		12.75	1.882		10.25	99		109.25	159
4252	1-1/2" x 1" diameters		12.75	1.882		12.75	99		111.75	162
4255	1-1/2" x 1-1/4" diameters		12.75	1.882		10.50	99		109.50	160
4260	2" x 3/4" diameters		12	2		13	105		118	171
4265	2" x 1" diameters		12	2		13.25	105		118.25	172
4270	2" x 1-1/4" diameters		12	2		13.60	105		118.60	172
4275	3" x 2" diameters		12	2		18.80	105		123.80	178
4280	4" x 2" diameters		9	2.667		44.50	140		184.50	258
4285	4" x 3" diameters		9	2.667		41	140		181	255
4305	Couplings, 1/2" CTS diameter		15	1.600		3.09	84		87.09	129
4310	1/2" diameter		14.25	1.684		3.09	88.50		91.59	135
4315	3/4" diameter		14.25	1.684		2.44	88.50		90.94	135
4320	1" diameter		13.50	1.778		2.41	93.50		95.91	143
4325	1-1/4" diameter		13.50	1.778		3.53	93.50		97.03	144
4330	1-1/2" diameter		12.75	1.882		3.85	99		102.85	152
4335	2" diameter		12	2		3.99	105		108.99	161
4340	3" diameter		12	2		18.15	105		123.15	177

33 52 Hydrocarbon Transmission and Distribution

33 52 16 – Gas Hydrocarbon Piping

33 52 16.26	High Density Polyethylene Piping	Crew	Daily Output	Labor-Hours	Unit	Material	2023 Bare Costs Labor	Equipment	Total	Total Incl O&P
4345	4" diameter	B-20	9	2.667	Ea.	34.50	140		174.50	247
4405	Elbows, 90°, 1/2" CTS diameter		15	1.600		5.30	84		89.30	132
4410	1/2" diameter		14.25	1.684		5.35	88.50		93.85	138
4415	3/4" diameter		14.25	1.684		4.41	88.50		92.91	137
4420	1" diameter		13.50	1.778		5.35	93.50		98.85	146
4425	1-1/4" diameter		13.50	1.778		7.35	93.50		100.85	148
4430	1-1/2" diameter		12.75	1.882		10.70	99		109.70	160
4435	2" diameter		12	2		10.90	105		115.90	169
4440	3" diameter		12	2		39.50	105		144.50	201
4445	4" diameter		9	2.667		158	140		298	385
4450	45°, 3/4" diameter		14.25	1.684		10.80	88.50		99.30	144
4455	1" diameter		13.50	1.778		12.10	93.50		105.60	153
4460	1-1/4" diameter		13.50	1.778		10.20	93.50		103.70	151
4465	1-1/2" diameter		12.75	1.882		16	99		115	166
4470	2" diameter		12	2		11.85	105		116.85	170
4475	3" diameter		12	2		65.50	105		170.50	229
4480	4" diameter		9	2.667		85	140		225	305
4505	Tees, 1/2" CTS diameter		10	2.400		4.59	126		130.59	194
4510	1/2" diameter		9.50	2.526		4.55	133		137.55	203
4515	3/4" diameter		9.50	2.526		4.54	133		137.54	203
4520	1" diameter		9	2.667		5.60	140		145.60	215
4525	1-1/4" diameter		9	2.667		7.80	140		147.80	218
4530	1-1/2" diameter		8.50	2.824		13.40	148		161.40	237
4535	2" diameter		8	3		14.35	158		172.35	252
4540	3" diameter		8	3		59.50	158		217.50	300
4545	4" diameter		6	4		115	210		325	440
4600	Tapping tees, type II, 3/4" punch, socket fusion outlets									
4601	Saddle countour x outlet diameter, IPS unless noted CTS									
4602	1-1/4" x 1/2" CTS outlet	B-20	17	1.412	Ea.	17.75	74		91.75	131
4604	1-1/4" x 1/2" outlet		17	1.412		17.75	74		91.75	131
4606	1-1/4" x 3/4" outlet		17	1.412		17.75	74		91.75	131
4608	1-1/4" x 1" outlet		17	1.412		20.50	74		94.50	134
4610	1-1/4" x 1-1/4" outlet		16	1.500		37	79		116	159
4612	1-1/2" x 1/2" CTS outlet		16	1.500		17.75	79		96.75	138
4614	1-1/2" x 1/2" outlet		16	1.500		17.75	79		96.75	138
4616	1-1/2" x 3/4" outlet		16	1.500		17.75	79		96.75	138
4618	1-1/2" x 1" outlet		16	1.500		20.50	79		99.50	141
4620	1-1/2" x 1-1/4" outlet		15	1.600		37	84		121	167
4622	2" x 1/2" CTS outlet		12	2		17.75	105		122.75	177
4624	2" x 1/2" outlet		12	2		17.75	105		122.75	177
4626	2" x 3/4" outlet		12	2		17.75	105		122.75	177
4628	2" x 1" outlet		12	2		20.50	105		125.50	180
4630	2" x 1-1/4" outlet		11	2.182		37	115		152	212
4632	3" x 1/2" CTS outlet		12	2		17.75	105		122.75	177
4634	3" x 1/2" outlet		12	2		17.75	105		122.75	177
4636	3" x 3/4" outlet		12	2		17.75	105		122.75	177
4638	3" x 1" outlet		12	2		20.50	105		125.50	180
4640	3" x 1-1/4" outlet		11	2.182		37	115		152	212
4642	4" x 1/2" CTS outlet		10	2.400		17.75	126		143.75	209
4644	4" x 1/2" outlet		10	2.400		17.75	126		143.75	209
4646	4" x 3/4" outlet		10	2.400		17.75	126		143.75	209
4648	4" x 1" outlet		10	2.400		20.50	126		146.50	212
4650	4" x 1-1/4" outlet		9	2.667		37	140		177	250

For customer support on your Plumbing Costs with RSMeans data, call 800.448.8182.

33 52 Hydrocarbon Transmission and Distribution

33 52 16 – Gas Hydrocarbon Piping

33 52 16.26 High Density Polyethylene Piping		Crew	Daily Output	Labor-Hours	Unit	Material	2023 Bare Costs Labor	Equipment	Total	Total Incl O&P
4652	6" x 1/2" CTS outlet	B-21A	10	4	Ea.	17.75	234	64	315.75	440
4654	6" x 1/2" outlet	B-20	10	2.400		17.75	126		143.75	209
4656	6" x 3/4" outlet	B-21A	10	4		17.75	234	64	315.75	440
4658	6" x 1" outlet		10	4		20.50	234	64	318.50	445
4660	6" x 1-1/4" outlet		9	4.444		37	260	71	368	505
4662	8" x 1/2" CTS outlet		8	5		17.75	293	80	390.75	540
4664	8" x 1/2" outlet		8	5		17.75	293	80	390.75	540
4666	8" x 3/4" outlet		8	5		17.75	293	80	390.75	540
4668	8" x 1" outlet		8	5		20.50	293	80	393.50	545
4670	8" x 1-1/4" outlet		7	5.714		37	335	91	463	640
4675	For protective sleeves, 1/2" to 3/4" diameter outlets, add					1.22			1.22	1.34
4680	1" diameter outlets, add					2.04			2.04	2.24
4685	1-1/4" diameter outlets, add					3.52			3.52	3.87
4700	Tapping tees, high volume, socket fusion outlets									
4705	1-1/2" punch, 2" x 1-1/4" outlet	B-20	11	2.182	Ea.	174	115		289	365
4710	1-7/8" punch, 3" x 1-1/4" outlet		11	2.182		174	115		289	365
4715	4" x 1-1/4" outlet		9	2.667		174	140		314	400
4720	6" x 1-1/4" outlet	B-21A	9	4.444		174	260	71	505	655
4725	8" x 1-1/4" outlet		7	5.714		174	335	91	600	790
4730	10" x 1-1/4" outlet		6	6.667		174	390	106	670	890
4735	12" x 1-1/4" outlet		5	8		174	470	128	772	1,025
4750	For protective sleeves, add					4.11			4.11	4.52
4800	Service saddles, saddle contour x outlet, socket fusion outlets									
4801	IPS unless noted CTS									
4802	1-1/4" x 1/2" CTS outlet	B-20	17	1.412	Ea.	9.35	74		83.35	121
4804	1-1/4" x 1/2" outlet		17	1.412		9.35	74		83.35	121
4806	1-1/4" x 3/4" outlet		17	1.412		9.35	74		83.35	121
4808	1-1/4" x 1" outlet		16	1.500		11	79		90	130
4810	1-1/4" x 1-1/4" outlet		16	1.500		15.55	79		94.55	135
4812	1-1/2" x 1/2" CTS outlet		16	1.500		9.35	79		88.35	128
4814	1-1/2" x 1/2" outlet		16	1.500		9.35	79		88.35	128
4816	1-1/2" x 3/4" outlet		16	1.500		9.35	79		88.35	128
4818	1-1/2" x 1-1/4" outlet		15	1.600		15.55	84		99.55	143
4820	2" x 1/2" CTS outlet		12	2		9.35	105		114.35	167
4822	2" x 1/2" outlet		12	2		9.35	105		114.35	167
4824	2" x 3/4" outlet		12	2		9.35	105		114.35	167
4826	2" x 1" outlet		11	2.182		11	115		126	183
4828	2" x 1-1/4" outlet		11	2.182		15.55	115		130.55	188
4830	3" x 1/2" CTS outlet		12	2		9.35	105		114.35	167
4832	3" x 1/2" outlet		12	2		9.35	105		114.35	167
4834	3" x 3/4" outlet		12	2		9.35	105		114.35	167
4836	3" x 1" outlet		11	2.182		11	115		126	183
4838	3" x 1-1/4" outlet		11	2.182		15.55	115		130.55	188
4840	4" x 1/2" CTS outlet		10	2.400		9.35	126		135.35	199
4842	4" x 1/2" outlet		10	2.400		9.35	126		135.35	199
4844	4" x 3/4" outlet		10	2.400		9.35	126		135.35	199
4846	4" x 1" outlet		9	2.667		11	140		151	221
4848	4" x 1-1/4" outlet		9	2.667		15.55	140		155.55	226
4850	6" x 1/2" CTS outlet	B-21A	10	4		9.35	234	64	307.35	430
4852	6" x 1/2" outlet		10	4		9.35	234	64	307.35	430
4854	6" x 3/4" outlet		10	4		9.35	234	64	307.35	430
4856	6" x 1" outlet		9	4.444		11	260	71	342	475
4858	6" x 1-1/4" outlet		9	4.444		15.55	260	71	346.55	480

33 52 Hydrocarbon Transmission and Distribution

33 52 16 – Gas Hydrocarbon Piping

33 52 16.26 High Density Polyethylene Piping		Crew	Daily Output	Labor-Hours	Unit	Material	2023 Bare Costs Labor	Equipment	Total	Total Incl O&P
4860	8" x 1/2" CTS outlet	B-21A	8	5	Ea.	9.35	293	80	382.35	535
4862	8" x 1/2" outlet		8	5		9.35	293	80	382.35	535
4864	8" x 3/4" outlet		8	5		9.35	293	80	382.35	535
4866	8" x 1" outlet		7	5.714		11.20	335	91	437.20	610
4868	8" x 1-1/4" outlet	▼	7	5.714		15.90	335	91	441.90	615
4880	For protective sleeves, 1/2" to 3/4" diameter outlets, add					1.22			1.22	1.34
4885	1" diameter outlets, add					2.04			2.04	2.24
4890	1-1/4" diameter outlets, add					3.52			3.52	3.87
4900	Reducer tees, 1-1/4" x 3/4" x 3/4" diameters	B-20	9	2.667		11.90	140		151.90	222
4902	1-1/4" x 3/4" x 1" diameters		9	2.667		15.35	140		155.35	226
4904	1-1/4" x 3/4" x 1-1/4" diameters		9	2.667		15.35	140		155.35	226
4906	1-1/4" x 1" x 3/4" diameters		9	2.667		15.35	140		155.35	226
4908	1-1/4" x 1" x 1" diameters		9	2.667		11.75	140		151.75	222
4910	1-1/4" x 1" x 1-1/4" diameters		9	2.667		15.35	140		155.35	226
4912	1-1/4" x 1-1/4" x 3/4" diameters		9	2.667		11.10	140		151.10	221
4914	1-1/4" x 1-1/4" x 1" diameters		9	2.667		11.75	140		151.75	222
4916	1-1/2" x 3/4" x 3/4" diameters		8.50	2.824		19.55	148		167.55	244
4918	1-1/2" x 3/4" x 1" diameters		8.50	2.824		19.55	148		167.55	244
4920	1-1/2" x 3/4" x 1-1/4" diameters		8.50	2.824		19.55	148		167.55	244
4922	1-1/2" x 3/4" x 1-1/2" diameters		8.50	2.824		19.55	148		167.55	244
4924	1-1/2" x 1" x 3/4" diameters		8.50	2.824		19.55	148		167.55	244
4926	1-1/2" x 1" x 1" diameters		8.50	2.824		19.55	148		167.55	244
4928	1-1/2" x 1" x 1-1/4" diameters		8.50	2.824		19.55	148		167.55	244
4930	1-1/2" x 1" x 1-1/2" diameters		8.50	2.824		19.55	148		167.55	244
4932	1-1/2" x 1-1/4" x 3/4" diameters		8.50	2.824		16.45	148		164.45	240
4934	1-1/2" x 1-1/4" x 1" diameters		8.50	2.824		16.20	148		164.20	240
4936	1-1/2" x 1-1/4" x 1-1/4" diameters		8.50	2.824		16.45	148		164.45	240
4938	1-1/2" x 1-1/4" x 1-1/2" diameters		8.50	2.824		19.55	148		167.55	244
4940	1-1/2" x 1-1/2" x 3/4" diameters		8.50	2.824		15.30	148		163.30	239
4942	1-1/2" x 1-1/2" x 1" diameters		8.50	2.824		15.30	148		163.30	239
4944	1-1/2" x 1-1/2" x 1-1/4" diameters		8.50	2.824		15.30	148		163.30	239
4946	2" x 1-1/4" x 3/4" diameters		8	3		17.75	158		175.75	256
4948	2" x 1-1/4" x 1" diameters		8	3		17.20	158		175.20	255
4950	2" x 1-1/4" x 1-1/4" diameters		8	3		17.90	158		175.90	256
4952	2" x 1-1/2" x 3/4" diameters		8	3		17.75	158		175.75	256
4954	2" x 1-1/2" x 1" diameters		8	3		17.20	158		175.20	255
4956	2" x 1-1/2" x 1-1/4" diameters		8	3		17.20	158		175.20	255
4958	2" x 2" x 3/4" diameters		8	3		17.70	158		175.70	255
4960	2" x 2" x 1" diameters		8	3		17.35	158		175.35	255
4962	2" x 2" x 1-1/4" diameters	▼	8	3	▼	17.80	158		175.80	256
8100	Fittings, accessories									
8105	SDR 11, IPS unless noted CTS									
8110	Flange adapters, 2" x 6" long	1 Skwk	32	.250	Ea.	24.50	15.30		39.80	50
8115	3" x 6" long		32	.250		30.50	15.30		45.80	56.50
8120	4" x 6" long	▼	24	.333		38.50	20.50		59	73
8125	6" x 8" long	2 Skwk	24	.667		60	41		101	128
8130	8" x 9" long	"	20	.800		84.50	49		133.50	167
8135	Backup flanges, 2" diameter	1 Skwk	32	.250		31.50	15.30		46.80	57.50
8140	3" diameter		32	.250		42.50	15.30		57.80	69.50
8145	4" diameter	▼	24	.333		83	20.50		103.50	122
8150	6" diameter	2 Skwk	24	.667		85.50	41		126.50	156
8155	8" diameter	"	20	.800	▼	146	49		195	235
8200	Tapping tees, test caps									

33 52 Hydrocarbon Transmission and Distribution

33 52 16 – Gas Hydrocarbon Piping

33 52 16.26 High Density Polyethylene Piping		Crew	Daily Output	Labor-Hours	Unit	Material	2023 Bare Costs Labor	Equipment	Total	Total Incl O&P
8205	Type II, yellow polyethylene cap	1 Skwk	45	.178	Ea.	62.50	10.90		73.40	85.50
8210	High volume, black polyethylene cap		45	.178		80.50	10.90		91.40	105
8215	Quick connector, female x female inlets, 1/4" N.P.T.		50	.160		26	9.80		35.80	43
8220	Test hose, 24" length, 3/8" ID, male outlets, 1/4" N.P.T.		50	.160		35.50	9.80		45.30	53.50
8225	Quick connector and test hose assembly	↓	50	.160	↓	61.50	9.80		71.30	82
8300	Threaded transition fittings									
8302	HDPE x MPT zinc plated steel, SDR 7, 1/2" CTS x 1/2" MPT	B-22C	30	.533	Ea.	48	29	9.35	86.35	107
8304	SDR 9.3, 1/2" IPS x 3/4" MPT		28.50	.561		63.50	30.50	9.85	103.85	126
8306	SDR 11, 3/4" IPS x 3/4" MPT		28.50	.561		31.50	30.50	9.85	71.85	91
8308	1" IPS x 1" MPT		27	.593		41	32	10.40	83.40	104
8310	1-1/4" IPS x 1-1/4" MPT		27	.593		65	32	10.40	107.40	131
8312	1-1/2" IPS x 1-1/2" MPT		25.50	.627		75.50	34	11	120.50	146
8314	2" IPS x 2" MPT		24	.667		86.50	36	11.70	134.20	162
8322	HDPE x MPT 316 stainless steel, SDR 11, 3/4" IPS x 3/4" MPT		28.50	.561		41.50	30.50	9.85	81.85	102
8324	1" IPS x 1" MPT		27	.593		43	32	10.40	85.40	106
8326	1-1/4" IPS x 1-1/4" MPT		27	.593		52.50	32	10.40	94.90	117
8328	2" IPS x 2" MPT		24	.667		63	36	11.70	110.70	136
8330	3" IPS x 3" MPT		24	.667		126	36	11.70	173.70	206
8332	4" IPS x 4" MPT	↓	18	.889		173	48	15.60	236.60	280
8334	6" IPS x 6" MPT	B-22A	18	2.222		320	121	40	481	580
8342	HDPE x FPT 316 stainless steel, SDR 11, 3/4" IPS x 3/4" FPT	B-22C	28.50	.561		54	30.50	9.85	94.35	116
8344	1" IPS x 1" FPT		27	.593		72.50	32	10.40	114.90	139
8346	1-1/4" IPS x 1-1/4" FPT		27	.593		117	32	10.40	159.40	188
8348	1-1/2" IPS x 1-1/2" FPT		25.50	.627		112	34	11	157	186
8350	2" IPS x 2" FPT		24	.667		148	36	11.70	195.70	230
8352	3" IPS x 3" FPT		24	.667		286	36	11.70	333.70	380
8354	4" IPS x 4" FPT		18	.889		410	48	15.60	473.60	540
8362	HDPE x MPT epoxy carbon steel, SDR 11, 3/4" IPS x 3/4" MPT		28.50	.561		31.50	30.50	9.85	71.85	91
8364	1" IPS x 1" MPT		27	.593		34.50	32	10.40	76.90	97.50
8366	1-1/4" IPS x 1-1/4" MPT		27	.593		36.50	32	10.40	78.90	99.50
8368	1-1/2" IPS x 1-1/2" MPT		25.50	.627		40	34	11	85	107
8370	2" IPS x 2" MPT		24	.667		43.50	36	11.70	91.20	114
8372	3" IPS x 3" MPT		24	.667		67	36	11.70	114.70	140
8374	4" IPS x 4" MPT		18	.889		90.50	48	15.60	154.10	189
8382	HDPE x FPT epoxy carbon steel, SDR 11, 3/4" IPS x 3/4" FPT		28.50	.561		38.50	30.50	9.85	78.85	98.50
8384	1" IPS x 1" FPT		27	.593		42	32	10.40	84.40	105
8386	1-1/4" IPS x 1-1/4" FPT		27	.593		89.50	32	10.40	131.90	158
8388	1-1/2" IPS x 1-1/2" FPT		25.50	.627		90.50	34	11	135.50	163
8390	2" IPS x 2" FPT		24	.667		96	36	11.70	143.70	173
8392	3" IPS x 3" FPT		24	.667		163	36	11.70	210.70	247
8394	4" IPS x 4" FPT		18	.889		205	48	15.60	268.60	315
8402	HDPE x MPT poly coated carbon steel, SDR 11, 1" IPS x 1" MPT		27	.593		34	32	10.40	76.40	96.50
8404	1-1/4" IPS x 1-1/4" MPT		27	.593		44	32	10.40	86.40	108
8406	1-1/2" IPS x 1-1/2" MPT		25.50	.627		52.50	34	11	97.50	121
8408	2" IPS x 2" MPT		24	.667		59.50	36	11.70	107.20	132
8410	3" IPS x 3" MPT		24	.667		115	36	11.70	162.70	193
8412	4" IPS x 4" MPT	↓	18	.889		179	48	15.60	242.60	286
8414	6" IPS x 6" MPT	B-22A	18	2.222		415	121	40	576	685
8602	Socket fused HDPE x MPT brass, SDR 11, 3/4" IPS x 3/4" MPT	B-20	28.50	.842		18.50	44.50		63	86.50
8604	1" IPS x 3/4" MPT		27	.889		22.50	46.50		69	94.50
8606	1" IPS x 1" MPT		27	.889		21.50	46.50		68	94
8608	1-1/4" IPS x 3/4" MPT		27	.889		23	46.50		69.50	95.50
8610	1-1/4" IPS x 1" MPT		27	.889		23	46.50		69.50	95.50

33 52 Hydrocarbon Transmission and Distribution

33 52 16 – Gas Hydrocarbon Piping

33 52 16.26 High Density Polyethylene Piping		Crew	Daily Output	Labor-Hours	Unit	Material	2023 Bare Costs Labor	Equipment	Total	Total Incl O&P
8612	1-1/4" IPS x 1-1/4" MPT	B-20	27	.889	Ea.	33	46.50		79.50	107
8614	1-1/2" IPS x 1-1/2" MPT		25.50	.941		45.50	49.50		95	124
8616	2" IPS x 2" MPT		24	1		46.50	52.50		99	130
8618	Socket fused HDPE x FPT brass, SDR 11, 3/4" IPS x 3/4" FPT		28.50	.842		18.50	44.50		63	86.50
8620	1" IPS x 1/2" FPT		27	.889		18.50	46.50		65	90.50
8622	1" IPS x 3/4" FPT		27	.889		22.50	46.50		69	94.50
8624	1" IPS x 1" FPT		27	.889		21.50	46.50		68	94
8626	1-1/4" IPS x 3/4" FPT		27	.889		23	46.50		69.50	95.50
8628	1-1/4" IPS x 1" FPT		27	.889		22.50	46.50		69	94.50
8630	1-1/4" IPS x 1-1/4" FPT		27	.889		33	46.50		79.50	107
8632	1-1/2" IPS x 1-1/2" FPT		25.50	.941		46.50	49.50		96	125
8634	2" IPS x 1-1/2" FPT		24	1		47	52.50		99.50	131
8636	2" IPS x 2" FPT	↓	24	1	↓	49.50	52.50		102	133

33 61 Hydronic Energy Distribution

33 61 13 – Underground Hydronic Energy Distribution

33 61 13.20 Pipe Conduit, Prefabricated/Preinsulated

		Crew	Daily Output	Labor-Hours	Unit	Material	Labor	Equipment	Total	Total Incl O&P
0010	**PIPE CONDUIT, PREFABRICATED/PREINSULATED** R221113-70									
0020	Does not include trenching, fittings or crane.									
0300	For cathodic protection, add 12 to 14%									
0310	of total built-up price (casing plus service pipe)									
0580	Polyurethane insulated system, 250°F max. temp.									
0620	Black steel service pipe, standard wt., 1/2" insulation									
0660	3/4" diam. pipe size	Q-17	54	.296	L.F.	121	19.35	1.19	141.54	163
0670	1" diam. pipe size		50	.320		133	21	1.28	155.28	179
0680	1-1/4" diam. pipe size		47	.340		149	22	1.37	172.37	199
0690	1-1/2" diam. pipe size		45	.356		161	23	1.43	185.43	213
0700	2" diam. pipe size		42	.381		167	25	1.53	193.53	223
0710	2-1/2" diam. pipe size		34	.471		170	30.50	1.89	202.39	235
0720	3" diam. pipe size		28	.571		197	37.50	2.29	236.79	275
0730	4" diam. pipe size		22	.727		248	47.50	2.92	298.42	345
0740	5" diam. pipe size	↓	18	.889		315	58	3.56	376.56	440
0750	6" diam. pipe size	Q-18	23	1.043		370	70.50	2.79	443.29	515
0760	8" diam. pipe size		19	1.263		540	85.50	3.37	628.87	725
0770	10" diam. pipe size		16	1.500		680	102	4.01	786.01	905
0780	12" diam. pipe size		13	1.846		845	125	4.93	974.93	1,125
0790	14" diam. pipe size		11	2.182		945	148	5.85	1,098.85	1,275
0800	16" diam. pipe size		10	2.400		1,075	163	6.40	1,244.40	1,450
0810	18" diam. pipe size		8	3		1,250	203	8	1,461	1,700
0820	20" diam. pipe size		7	3.429		1,375	232	9.15	1,616.15	1,875
0830	24" diam. pipe size	↓	6	4		1,700	271	10.70	1,981.70	2,300
0900	For 1" thick insulation, add					10%				
0940	For 1-1/2" thick insulation, add					13%				
0980	For 2" thick insulation, add				↓	20%				
1500	Gland seal for system, 3/4" diam. pipe size	Q-17	32	.500	Ea.	1,400	32.50	2.01	1,434.51	1,600
1510	1" diam. pipe size		32	.500		1,400	32.50	2.01	1,434.51	1,600
1540	1-1/4" diam. pipe size		30	.533		1,500	35	2.14	1,537.14	1,700
1550	1-1/2" diam. pipe size		30	.533		1,500	35	2.14	1,537.14	1,700
1560	2" diam. pipe size		28	.571		1,775	37.50	2.29	1,814.79	2,000
1570	2-1/2" diam. pipe size		26	.615		1,925	40	2.47	1,967.47	2,175
1580	3" diam. pipe size		24	.667		2,050	43.50	2.67	2,096.17	2,325

33 61 Hydronic Energy Distribution

33 61 13 − Underground Hydronic Energy Distribution

33 61 13.20 Pipe Conduit, Prefabricated/Preinsulated		Crew	Daily Output	Labor-Hours	Unit	Material	2023 Bare Costs Labor	Equipment	Total	Total Incl O&P
1590	4" diam. pipe size	Q-17	22	.727	Ea.	2,425	47.50	2.92	2,475.42	2,750
1600	5" diam. pipe size		19	.842		3,000	55	3.38	3,058.38	3,375
1610	6" diam. pipe size	Q-18	26	.923		3,175	62.50	2.46	3,239.96	3,600
1620	8" diam. pipe size		25	.960		3,700	65	2.56	3,767.56	4,150
1630	10" diam. pipe size		23	1.043		4,300	70.50	2.79	4,373.29	4,825
1640	12" diam. pipe size		21	1.143		4,750	77.50	3.05	4,830.55	5,350
1650	14" diam. pipe size		19	1.263		5,325	85.50	3.37	5,413.87	6,000
1660	16" diam. pipe size		18	1.333		6,300	90.50	3.56	6,394.06	7,075
1670	18" diam. pipe size		16	1.500		6,675	102	4.01	6,781.01	7,500
1680	20" diam. pipe size		14	1.714		7,600	116	4.58	7,720.58	8,525
1690	24" diam. pipe size		12	2		8,425	135	5.35	8,565.35	9,475
2000	Elbow, 45° for system									
2020	3/4" diam. pipe size	Q-17	14	1.143	Ea.	920	74.50	4.58	999.08	1,125
2040	1" diam. pipe size		13	1.231		945	80.50	4.94	1,030.44	1,175
2050	1-1/4" diam. pipe size		11	1.455		1,075	95	5.85	1,175.85	1,325
2060	1-1/2" diam. pipe size		9	1.778		1,075	116	7.15	1,198.15	1,350
2070	2" diam. pipe size		6	2.667		1,150	174	10.70	1,334.70	1,550
2080	2-1/2" diam. pipe size		4	4		1,275	261	16.05	1,552.05	1,800
2090	3" diam. pipe size		3.50	4.571		1,475	299	18.35	1,792.35	2,075
2100	4" diam. pipe size		3	5.333		1,700	350	21.50	2,071.50	2,425
2110	5" diam. pipe size		2.80	5.714		2,200	375	23	2,598	3,000
2120	6" diam. pipe size	Q-18	4	6		2,475	405	16	2,896	3,350
2130	8" diam. pipe size		3	8		3,600	540	21.50	4,161.50	4,800
2140	10" diam. pipe size		2.40	10		4,400	675	26.50	5,101.50	5,875
2150	12" diam. pipe size		2	12		5,800	815	32	6,647	7,625
2160	14" diam. pipe size		1.80	13.333		7,200	905	35.50	8,140.50	9,325
2170	16" diam. pipe size		1.60	15		8,575	1,025	40	9,640	11,000
2180	18" diam. pipe size		1.30	18.462		10,800	1,250	49.50	12,099.50	13,700
2190	20" diam. pipe size		1	24		13,600	1,625	64	15,289	17,400
2200	24" diam. pipe size		.70	34.286		17,000	2,325	91.50	19,416.50	22,300
2260	For elbow, 90°, add					25%				
2300	For tee, straight, add					85%	30%			
2340	For tee, reducing, add					170%	30%			
2380	For weldolet, straight, add					50%				
2400	Polyurethane insulation, 1"									
2410	FRP carrier and casing									
2420	4"	Q-5	18	.889	L.F.	71	58		129	165
2422	6"	Q-6	23	1.043		123	70.50		193.50	241
2424	8"		19	1.263		201	85.50		286.50	350
2426	10"		16	1.500		271	102		373	450
2428	12"		13	1.846		355	125		480	575
2430	FRP carrier and PVC casing									
2440	4"	Q-5	18	.889	L.F.	29.50	58		87.50	119
2444	8"	Q-6	19	1.263		63.50	85.50		149	198
2446	10"		16	1.500		91.50	102		193.50	252
2448	12"		13	1.846		125	125		250	325
2450	PVC carrier and casing									
2460	4"	Q-1	36	.444	L.F.	15.15	29		44.15	59.50
2462	6"	"	29	.552		21.50	36		57.50	77.50
2464	8"	Q-2	36	.667		30.50	45		75.50	101
2466	10"		32	.750		40	50.50		90.50	119
2468	12"		31	.774		48	52		100	131

33 63 Steam Energy Distribution

33 63 13 – Underground Steam and Condensate Distribution Piping

33 63 13.10 Calcium Silicate Insulated System		Crew	Daily Output	Labor-Hours	Unit	Material	2023 Bare Costs Labor	Equipment	Total	Total Incl O&P
0010	**CALCIUM SILICATE INSULATED SYSTEM**									
0011	High temp. (1200 degrees F)									
2840	Steel casing with protective exterior coating									
2850	6-5/8" diameter	Q-18	52	.462	L.F.	176	31.50	1.23	208.73	241
2860	8-5/8" diameter		50	.480		191	32.50	1.28	224.78	260
2870	10-3/4" diameter		47	.511		224	34.50	1.36	259.86	299
2880	12-3/4" diameter		44	.545		244	37	1.46	282.46	325
2890	14" diameter		41	.585		275	39.50	1.56	316.06	365
2900	16" diameter		39	.615		295	41.50	1.64	338.14	390
2910	18" diameter		36	.667		325	45	1.78	371.78	425
2920	20" diameter		34	.706		365	48	1.88	414.88	480
2930	22" diameter		32	.750		505	51	2	558	635
2940	24" diameter		29	.828		580	56	2.21	638.21	725
2950	26" diameter		26	.923		665	62.50	2.46	729.96	825
2960	28" diameter		23	1.043		820	70.50	2.79	893.29	1,025
2970	30" diameter		21	1.143		880	77.50	3.05	960.55	1,075
2980	32" diameter		19	1.263		985	85.50	3.37	1,073.87	1,200
2990	34" diameter		18	1.333		995	90.50	3.56	1,089.06	1,250
3000	36" diameter		16	1.500		1,075	102	4.01	1,181.01	1,325
3040	For multi-pipe casings, add					10%				
3060	For oversize casings, add					2%				
3400	Steel casing gland seal, single pipe									
3420	6-5/8" diameter	Q-18	25	.960	Ea.	2,675	65	2.56	2,742.56	3,050
3440	8-5/8" diameter		23	1.043		3,125	70.50	2.79	3,198.29	3,550
3450	10-3/4" diameter		21	1.143		3,500	77.50	3.05	3,580.55	3,975
3460	12-3/4" diameter		19	1.263		4,125	85.50	3.37	4,213.87	4,650
3470	14" diameter		17	1.412		4,575	95.50	3.77	4,674.27	5,200
3480	16" diameter		16	1.500		5,350	102	4.01	5,456.01	6,050
3490	18" diameter		15	1.600		5,950	108	4.27	6,062.27	6,725
3500	20" diameter		13	1.846		6,575	125	4.93	6,704.93	7,450
3510	22" diameter		12	2		7,400	135	5.35	7,540.35	8,325
3520	24" diameter		11	2.182		8,300	148	5.85	8,453.85	9,350
3530	26" diameter		10	2.400		9,475	163	6.40	9,644.40	10,600
3540	28" diameter		9.50	2.526		10,700	171	6.75	10,877.75	12,100
3550	30" diameter		9	2.667		10,900	181	7.10	11,088.10	12,300
3560	32" diameter		8.50	2.824		12,300	191	7.55	12,498.55	13,800
3570	34" diameter		8	3		13,300	203	8	13,511	15,000
3580	36" diameter		7	3.429		14,200	232	9.15	14,441.15	16,000
3620	For multi-pipe casings, add					5%				
4000	Steel casing anchors, single pipe									
4020	6-5/8" diameter	Q-18	8	3	Ea.	2,400	203	8	2,611	2,975
4040	8-5/8" diameter		7.50	3.200		2,500	217	8.55	2,725.55	3,075
4050	10-3/4" diameter		7	3.429		3,275	232	9.15	3,516.15	3,950
4060	12-3/4" diameter		6.50	3.692		3,500	250	9.85	3,759.85	4,225
4070	14" diameter		6	4		4,125	271	10.70	4,406.70	4,975
4080	16" diameter		5.50	4.364		4,775	296	11.65	5,082.65	5,700
4090	18" diameter		5	4.800		5,400	325	12.80	5,737.80	6,450
4100	20" diameter		4.50	5.333		5,950	360	14.25	6,324.25	7,100
4110	22" diameter		4	6		6,625	405	16	7,046	7,925
4120	24" diameter		3.50	6.857		7,225	465	18.30	7,708.30	8,625
4130	26" diameter		3	8		8,175	540	21.50	8,736.50	9,800
4140	28" diameter		2.50	9.600		9,000	650	25.50	9,675.50	10,900
4150	30" diameter		2	12		9,525	815	32	10,372	11,700

For customer support on your Plumbing Costs with RSMeans data, call 800.448.8182.

33 63 Steam Energy Distribution

33 63 13 – Underground Steam and Condensate Distribution Piping

33 63 13.10 Calcium Silicate Insulated System		Crew	Daily Output	Labor-Hours	Unit	Material	2023 Bare Costs Labor	Equipment	Total	Total Incl O&P
4160	32" diameter	Q-18	1.50	16	Ea.	11,400	1,075	42.50	12,517.50	14,200
4170	34" diameter		1	24		12,800	1,625	64	14,489	16,600
4180	36" diameter	↓	1	24		13,900	1,625	64	15,589	17,800
4220	For multi-pipe, add				↓	5%	20%			
4800	Steel casing elbow									
4820	6-5/8" diameter	Q-18	15	1.600	Ea.	3,400	108	4.27	3,512.27	3,925
4830	8-5/8" diameter		15	1.600		3,650	108	4.27	3,762.27	4,175
4850	10-3/4" diameter		14	1.714		4,400	116	4.58	4,520.58	5,025
4860	12-3/4" diameter		13	1.846		5,200	125	4.93	5,329.93	5,925
4870	14" diameter		12	2		5,600	135	5.35	5,740.35	6,350
4880	16" diameter		11	2.182		6,100	148	5.85	6,253.85	6,950
4890	18" diameter		10	2.400		6,950	163	6.40	7,119.40	7,900
4900	20" diameter		9	2.667		7,425	181	7.10	7,613.10	8,450
4910	22" diameter		8	3		8,000	203	8	8,211	9,125
4920	24" diameter		7	3.429		8,800	232	9.15	9,041.15	10,000
4930	26" diameter		6	4		9,650	271	10.70	9,931.70	11,000
4940	28" diameter		5	4.800		10,400	325	12.80	10,737.80	12,000
4950	30" diameter		4	6		10,500	405	16	10,921	12,100
4960	32" diameter		3	8		11,900	540	21.50	12,461.50	13,900
4970	34" diameter		2	12		13,100	815	32	13,947	15,600
4980	36" diameter	↓	2	12	↓	13,900	815	32	14,747	16,500
5500	Black steel service pipe, std. wt., 1" thick insulation									
5510	3/4" diameter pipe size	Q-17	54	.296	L.F.	110	19.35	1.19	130.54	150
5540	1" diameter pipe size		50	.320		113	21	1.28	135.28	156
5550	1-1/4" diameter pipe size		47	.340		142	22	1.37	165.37	192
5560	1-1/2" diameter pipe size		45	.356		149	23	1.43	173.43	200
5570	2" diameter pipe size		42	.381		162	25	1.53	188.53	217
5580	2-1/2" diameter pipe size		34	.471		169	30.50	1.89	201.39	234
5590	3" diameter pipe size		28	.571		148	37.50	2.29	187.79	221
5600	4" diameter pipe size		22	.727		155	47.50	2.92	205.42	245
5610	5" diameter pipe size	↓	18	.889		213	58	3.56	274.56	325
5620	6" diameter pipe size	Q-18	23	1.043	↓	229	70.50	2.79	302.29	360
6000	Black steel service pipe, std. wt., 1-1/2" thick insul.									
6010	3/4" diameter pipe size	Q-17	54	.296	L.F.	130	19.35	1.19	150.54	173
6040	1" diameter pipe size		50	.320		136	21	1.28	158.28	181
6050	1-1/4" diameter pipe size		47	.340		146	22	1.37	169.37	196
6060	1-1/2" diameter pipe size		45	.356		144	23	1.43	168.43	195
6070	2" diameter pipe size		42	.381		155	25	1.53	181.53	210
6080	2-1/2" diameter pipe size		34	.471		141	30.50	1.89	173.39	204
6090	3" diameter pipe size		28	.571		157	37.50	2.29	196.79	231
6100	4" diameter pipe size		22	.727		180	47.50	2.92	230.42	272
6110	5" diameter pipe size	↓	18	.889		241	58	3.56	302.56	355
6120	6" diameter pipe size	Q-18	23	1.043		252	70.50	2.79	325.29	385
6130	8" diameter pipe size		19	1.263		325	85.50	3.37	413.87	485
6140	10" diameter pipe size		16	1.500		420	102	4.01	526.01	615
6150	12" diameter pipe size	↓	13	1.846		480	125	4.93	609.93	715
6190	For 2" thick insulation, add					15%				
6220	For 2-1/2" thick insulation, add					25%				
6260	For 3" thick insulation, add				↓	30%				
6800	Black steel service pipe, ex. hvy. wt., 1" thick insul.									
6820	3/4" diameter pipe size	Q-17	50	.320	L.F.	131	21	1.28	153.28	176
6840	1" diameter pipe size		47	.340		139	22	1.37	162.37	188
6850	1-1/4" diameter pipe size		44	.364		154	24	1.46	179.46	206

33 63 Steam Energy Distribution

33 63 13 – Underground Steam and Condensate Distribution Piping

33 63 13.10 Calcium Silicate Insulated System

		Crew	Daily Output	Labor-Hours	Unit	Material	2023 Bare Costs Labor	Equipment	Total	Total Incl O&P
6860	1-1/2" diameter pipe size	Q-17	42	.381	L.F.	155	25	1.53	181.53	210
6870	2" diameter pipe size		40	.400		171	26	1.60	198.60	229
6880	2-1/2" diameter pipe size		31	.516		140	33.50	2.07	175.57	207
6890	3" diameter pipe size		27	.593		161	38.50	2.38	201.88	237
6900	4" diameter pipe size		21	.762		199	50	3.06	252.06	296
6910	5" diameter pipe size		17	.941		187	61.50	3.77	252.27	300
6920	6" diameter pipe size	Q-18	22	1.091		181	74	2.91	257.91	310
7400	Black steel service pipe, ex. hvy. wt., 1-1/2" thick insul.									
7420	3/4" diameter pipe size	Q-17	50	.320	L.F.	97	21	1.28	119.28	139
7440	1" diameter pipe size		47	.340		122	22	1.37	145.37	169
7450	1-1/4" diameter pipe size		44	.364		134	24	1.46	159.46	184
7460	1-1/2" diameter pipe size		42	.381		131	25	1.53	157.53	183
7470	2" diameter pipe size		40	.400		140	26	1.60	167.60	195
7480	2-1/2" diameter pipe size		31	.516		130	33.50	2.07	165.57	196
7490	3" diameter pipe size		27	.593		144	38.50	2.38	184.88	218
7500	4" diameter pipe size		21	.762		183	50	3.06	236.06	278
7510	5" diameter pipe size		17	.941		252	61.50	3.77	317.27	375
7520	6" diameter pipe size	Q-18	22	1.091		253	74	2.91	329.91	390
7530	8" diameter pipe size		18	1.333		415	90.50	3.56	509.06	595
7540	10" diameter pipe size		15	1.600		390	108	4.27	502.27	590
7550	12" diameter pipe size		13	1.846		465	125	4.93	594.93	700
7590	For 2" thick insulation, add					13%				
7640	For 2-1/2" thick insulation, add					18%				
7680	For 3" thick insulation, add					24%				

33 63 13.20 Combined Steam Pipe With Condensate Return

		Crew	Daily Output	Labor-Hours	Unit	Material	Labor	Equipment	Total	Total Incl O&P
0010	**COMBINED STEAM PIPE WITH CONDENSATE RETURN**									
9010	8" and 4" in 24" case	Q-18	100	.240	L.F.	595	16.25	.64	611.89	675
9020	6" and 3" in 20" case		104	.231		500	15.65	.62	516.27	575
9030	3" and 1-1/2" in 16" case		110	.218		375	14.80	.58	390.38	435
9040	2" and 1-1/4" in 12-3/4" case		114	.211		315	14.25	.56	329.81	365
9050	1-1/2" and 1-1/4" in 10-3/4" case		116	.207		370	14	.55	384.55	430
9100	Steam pipe only (no return)									
9110	6" in 18" case	Q-18	108	.222	L.F.	405	15.05	.59	420.64	475
9120	4" in 14" case		112	.214		315	14.50	.57	330.07	365
9130	3" in 14" case		114	.211		299	14.25	.56	313.81	350
9140	2-1/2" in 12-3/4" case		118	.203		278	13.75	.54	292.29	325
9150	2" in 12-3/4" case		122	.197		263	13.30	.53	276.83	310

Division Notes

		CREW	DAILY OUTPUT	LABOR-HOURS	UNIT	BARE COSTS				TOTAL INCL O&P
						MAT.	LABOR	EQUIP.	TOTAL	

Division 41 Material Processing & Handling Equipment

Estimating Tips
Products such as conveyors, material handling cranes and hoists, and other items specified in this division require trained installers. The general contractor may not have any choice as to who will perform the installation or when it will be performed. Long lead times are often required for these products, making early decisions in purchasing and scheduling necessary. The installation of this type of equipment may require the embedment of mounting hardware during the construction of floors, structural walls, or interior walls/partitions. Electrical connections will require coordination with the electrical contractor.

Reference Numbers
Reference numbers are shown at the beginning of some major classifications. These numbers refer to related items in the Reference Section. The reference information may be an estimating procedure, an alternate pricing method, or technical information.

Same Data. Simplified.

Enjoy the convenience and efficiency of accessing your costs anywhere:
- **Skip the multiplier** by setting your location
- **Quickly search,** edit, favorite and share costs
- **Stay on top of price changes** with automatic updates

Discover more at rsmeans.com/online

No part of this cost data may be reproduced, stored in a retrieval system, or transmitted in any form or by any means without prior written permission of Gordian.

41 22 Cranes and Hoists

41 22 23 – Hoists

41 22 23.10 Material Handling		Crew	Daily Output	Labor-Hours	Unit	Material	2023 Bare Costs Labor	Equipment	Total	Total Incl O&P
0010	**MATERIAL HANDLING**, cranes, hoists and lifts									
1500	Cranes, portable hydraulic, floor type, 2,000 lb. capacity				Ea.	4,250			4,250	4,675
1600	4,000 lb. capacity					6,675			6,675	7,350
1800	Movable gantry type, 12' to 15' range, 2,000 lb. capacity					3,750			3,750	4,125
1900	6,000 lb. capacity					7,625			7,625	8,375
2100	Hoists, electric overhead, chain, hook hung, 15' lift, 1 ton cap.					3,425			3,425	3,775
2200	3 ton capacity					4,675			4,675	5,150
2500	5 ton capacity					8,725			8,725	9,600
2600	For hand-pushed trolley, add					15%				
2700	For geared trolley, add					30%				
2800	For motor trolley, add					75%				
3000	For lifts over 15', 1 ton, add				L.F.	30			30	33
3100	5 ton, add				"	112			112	123
3300	Lifts, scissor type, portable, electric, 36" high, 2,000 lb.				Ea.	4,625			4,625	5,075
3400	48" high, 4,000 lb.				"	7,800			7,800	8,575

Division 44 Pollution & Waste Control Equipment

Estimating Tips
This section involves equipment and construction costs for air, noise, and odor pollution control systems. These systems may be interrelated and care must be taken that the complete systems are estimated. For example, air pollution equipment may include dust and air-entrained particles that have to be collected. The vacuum systems could be noisy, requiring silencers to reduce noise pollution, and the collected solids have to be disposed of to prevent solid pollution.

Reference Numbers
Reference numbers are shown at the beginning of some major classifications. These numbers refer to related items in the Reference Section. The reference information may be an estimating procedure, an alternate pricing method, or technical information.

Same Data. Simplified.
Enjoy the convenience and efficiency of accessing your costs anywhere:
- **Skip the multiplier** by setting your location
- **Quickly search,** edit, favorite and share costs
- **Stay on top of price changes** with automatic updates

Discover more at rsmeans.com/online

No part of this cost data may be reproduced, stored in a retrieval system, or transmitted in any form or by any means without prior written permission of Gordian.

44 11 Particulate Control Equipment

44 11 16 – Fugitive Dust Barrier Systems

44 11 16.10 Dust Collection Systems		Crew	Daily Output	Labor-Hours	Unit	Material	2023 Bare Costs Labor	Equipment	Total	Total Incl O&P
0010	**DUST COLLECTION SYSTEMS** Commercial/Industrial									
0120	Central vacuum units									
0130	Includes stand, filters and motorized shaker									
0200	500 CFM, 10" inlet, 2 HP	Q-20	2.40	8.333	Ea.	4,200	535		4,735	5,425
0220	1,000 CFM, 10" inlet, 3 HP		2.20	9.091		4,475	580		5,055	5,800
0240	1,500 CFM, 10" inlet, 5 HP		2	10		4,450	640		5,090	5,825
0260	3,000 CFM, 13" inlet, 10 HP		1.50	13.333		6,700	855		7,555	8,650
0280	5,000 CFM, 16" inlet, 2 @ 10 HP	↓	1	20	↓	15,500	1,275		16,775	18,900
1000	Vacuum tubing, galvanized									
1100	2-1/8" OD, 16 ga.	Q-9	440	.036	L.F.	3.76	2.30		6.06	7.60
1110	2-1/2" OD, 16 ga.		420	.038		4.07	2.40		6.47	8.10
1120	3" OD, 16 ga.		400	.040		4.15	2.53		6.68	8.35
1130	3-1/2" OD, 16 ga.		380	.042		6.35	2.66		9.01	11
1140	4" OD, 16 ga.		360	.044		7.30	2.81		10.11	12.25
1150	5" OD, 14 ga.		320	.050		10.35	3.16		13.51	16.10
1160	6" OD, 14 ga.		280	.057		12.50	3.61		16.11	19.20
1170	8" OD, 14 ga.		200	.080		19.35	5.05		24.40	29
1180	10" OD, 12 ga.		160	.100		56.50	6.30		62.80	71.50
1190	12" OD, 12 ga.		120	.133		53	8.40		61.40	71
1200	14" OD, 12 ga.	↓	80	.200	↓	60	12.65		72.65	85
1940	Hose, flexible wire reinforced rubber									
1956	3" diam.	Q-9	400	.040	L.F.	8.05	2.53		10.58	12.65
1960	4" diam.		360	.044		9.80	2.81		12.61	15.05
1970	5" diam.		320	.050		12.25	3.16		15.41	18.25
1980	6" diam.	↓	280	.057	↓	12.50	3.61		16.11	19.20
2000	90° elbow, slip fit									
2110	2-1/8" diam.	Q-9	70	.229	Ea.	16.75	14.45		31.20	40
2120	2-1/2" diam.		65	.246		23.50	15.55		39.05	49.50
2130	3" diam.		60	.267		32	16.85		48.85	60.50
2140	3-1/2" diam.		55	.291		39	18.35		57.35	70.50
2150	4" diam.		50	.320		48.50	20		68.50	84
2160	5" diam.		45	.356		92	22.50		114.50	135
2170	6" diam.		40	.400		127	25.50		152.50	178
2180	8" diam.	↓	30	.533	↓	242	33.50		275.50	315
2400	45° elbow, slip fit									
2410	2-1/8" diam.	Q-9	70	.229	Ea.	14.65	14.45		29.10	37.50
2420	2-1/2" diam.		65	.246		21.50	15.55		37.05	47.50
2430	3" diam.		60	.267		26	16.85		42.85	54
2440	3-1/2" diam.		55	.291		33	18.35		51.35	63.50
2450	4" diam.		50	.320		42.50	20		62.50	77.50
2460	5" diam.		45	.356		71.50	22.50		94	113
2470	6" diam.		40	.400		97	25.50		122.50	145
2480	8" diam.	↓	35	.457	↓	190	29		219	253
2800	90° TY, slip fit thru 6" diam.									
2810	2-1/8" diam.	Q-9	42	.381	Ea.	32.50	24		56.50	72
2820	2-1/2" diam.		39	.410		42.50	26		68.50	86
2830	3" diam.		36	.444		56.50	28		84.50	105
2840	3-1/2" diam.		33	.485		71.50	30.50		102	125
2850	4" diam.		30	.533		154	33.50		187.50	221
2860	5" diam.		27	.593		196	37.50		233.50	272
2870	6" diam.	↓	24	.667		267	42		309	355
2880	8" diam., butt end					565			565	625
2890	10" diam., butt end	↓			↓	655			655	720

44 11 Particulate Control Equipment

44 11 16 – Fugitive Dust Barrier Systems

44 11 16.10 Dust Collection Systems		Crew	Daily Output	Labor-Hours	Unit	Material	2023 Bare Costs Labor	Equipment	Total	Total Incl O&P
2900	12" diam., butt end				Ea.	655			655	720
2910	14" diam., butt end					2,325			2,325	2,550
2920	6" x 4" diam., butt end					163			163	179
2930	8" x 4" diam., butt end					310			310	340
2940	10" x 4" diam., butt end					405			405	445
2950	12" x 4" diam., butt end					465			465	510
3100	90° elbow, butt end, segmented									
3110	8" diam., butt end, segmented				Ea.	635			635	695
3120	10" diam., butt end, segmented					605			605	665
3130	12" diam., butt end, segmented					207			207	228
3140	14" diam., butt end, segmented					264			264	290
3200	45° elbow, butt end, segmented									
3210	8" diam., butt end, segmented				Ea.	106			106	117
3220	10" diam., butt end, segmented					218			218	239
3230	12" diam., butt end, segmented					119			119	131
3240	14" diam., butt end, segmented					810			810	890
3400	All butt end fittings require one coupling per joint.									
3410	Labor for fitting included with couplings.									
3460	Compression coupling, galvanized, neoprene gasket									
3470	2-1/8" diam.	Q-9	44	.364	Ea.	15.90	23		38.90	52
3480	2-1/2" diam.		44	.364		15.90	23		38.90	52
3490	3" diam.		38	.421		18.45	26.50		44.95	60.50
3500	3-1/2" diam.		35	.457		19.30	29		48.30	64.50
3510	4" diam.		33	.485		21	30.50		51.50	69
3520	5" diam.		29	.552		25.50	35		60.50	80.50
3530	6" diam.		26	.615		29.50	39		68.50	91
3540	8" diam.		22	.727		53	46		99	128
3550	10" diam.		20	.800		67.50	50.50		118	150
3560	12" diam.		18	.889		75	56		131	168
3570	14" diam.		16	1		113	63		176	219
3800	Air gate valves, galvanized									
3810	2-1/8" diam.	Q-9	30	.533	Ea.	110	33.50		143.50	172
3820	2-1/2" diam.		28	.571		119	36		155	186
3830	3" diam.		26	.615		127	39		166	199
3840	4" diam.		23	.696		147	44		191	228
3850	6" diam.		18	.889		205	56		261	310

Division Notes

		CREW	DAILY OUTPUT	LABOR-HOURS	UNIT	BARE COSTS				TOTAL INCL O&P
						MAT.	LABOR	EQUIP.	TOTAL	

Division 46 — Water & Wastewater Equipment

Estimating Tips

This division contains information about water and wastewater equipment and systems, which was formerly located in Division 44. The main areas of focus are total wastewater treatment plants and components of wastewater treatment plants. Also included in this section are oil/water separators for wastewater treatment.

Reference Numbers

Reference numbers are shown at the beginning of some major classifications. These numbers refer to related items in the Reference Section. The reference information may be an estimating procedure, an alternate pricing method, or technical information.

Same Data. Simplified.

Enjoy the convenience and efficiency of accessing your costs anywhere:

- **Skip the multiplier** by setting your location
- **Quickly search**, edit, favorite and share costs
- **Stay on top of price changes** with automatic updates

Discover more at rsmeans.com/online

No part of this cost data may be reproduced, stored in a retrieval system, or transmitted in any form or by any means without prior written permission of Gordian.

46 07 Packaged Water and Wastewater Treatment Equipment

46 07 53 – Packaged Wastewater Treatment Equipment

46 07 53.10 Biological Pkg. Wastewater Treatment Plants		Crew	Daily Output	Labor-Hours	Unit	Material	2023 Bare Costs Labor	Equipment	Total	Total Incl O&P
0010	BIOLOGICAL PACKAGED WASTEWATER TREATMENT PLANTS									
0011	Not including fencing or external piping									
0020	Steel packaged, blown air aeration plants									
0100	1,000 GPD				Gal.				55	60.50
0200	5,000 GPD								22	24
0300	15,000 GPD								22	24
0400	30,000 GPD								15.40	16.95
0500	50,000 GPD								11	12.10
0600	100,000 GPD								9.90	10.90
0700	200,000 GPD								8.80	9.70
0800	500,000 GPD				▼				7.70	8.45
1000	Concrete, extended aeration, primary and secondary treatment									
1010	10,000 GPD				Gal.				22	24
1100	30,000 GPD								15.40	16.95
1200	50,000 GPD								11	12.10
1400	100,000 GPD								9.90	10.90
1500	500,000 GPD				▼				7.70	8.45
1700	Municipal wastewater treatment facility									
1720	1.0 MGD				Gal.				11	12.10
1740	1.5 MGD								10.60	11.65
1760	2.0 MGD								10	11
1780	3.0 MGD								7.80	8.60
1800	5.0 MGD				▼				5.80	6.70
2000	Holding tank system, not incl. excavation or backfill									
2010	Recirculating chemical water closet	2 Plum	4	4	Ea.	525	288		813	1,000
2100	For voltage converter, add	"	16	1		264	72		336	395
2200	For high level alarm, add	1 Plum	7.80	1.026	▼	160	74		234	286

46 07 53.20 Wastewater Treatment System		Crew	Daily Output	Labor-Hours	Unit	Material	Labor	Equipment	Total	Total Incl O&P
0010	WASTEWATER TREATMENT SYSTEM									
0020	Fiberglass, 1,000 gallon	B-21	1.29	21.705	Ea.	4,100	1,175	150	5,425	6,475
0100	1,500 gallon	"	1.03	27.184	"	8,775	1,475	187	10,437	12,100

46 23 Grit Removal And Handling Equipment

46 23 23 – Vortex Grit Removal Equipment

46 23 23.10 Rainwater Filters		Crew	Daily Output	Labor-Hours	Unit	Material	Labor	Equipment	Total	Total Incl O&P
0010	RAINWATER FILTERS									
0100	42 gal./min	B-21	3.50	8	Ea.	60,000	435	55	60,490	66,500
0200	65 gal./min		3.50	8		60,000	435	55	60,490	66,500
0300	208 gal./min	▼	3.50	8	▼	60,000	435	55	60,490	66,500

46 25 Oil and Grease Separation and Removal Equipment

46 25 13 – Coalescing Oil-Water Separators

46 25 13.20 Oil/Water Separators		Crew	Daily Output	Labor-Hours	Unit	Material	2023 Bare Costs Labor	Equipment	Total	Total Incl O&P
0010	**OIL/WATER SEPARATORS**									
0020	Underground, tank only									
0030	Excludes excavation, backfill & piping									
0100	200 GPM	B-21	3.50	8	Ea.	60,000	435	55	60,490	66,500
0110	400 GPM		3.25	8.615		74,000	470	59.50	74,529.50	82,000
0120	600 GPM		2.75	10.182		107,500	555	70	108,125	119,500
0130	800 GPM		2.50	11.200		132,500	610	77	133,187	146,500
0140	1,000 GPM		2	14		138,500	765	96.50	139,361.50	154,000
0150	1,200 GPM		1.50	18.667		164,000	1,025	129	165,154	182,000
0160	1,500 GPM	B-21	1	28	Ea.	199,500	1,525	193	201,218	222,000

Assemblies Section

Table of Contents

Table No.	Page

D SERVICES

D2010 Plumbing Fixtures
D2010 110 Water Closet Systems 478
D2010 120 Water Closets, Group 479
D2010 210 Urinal Systems 480
D2010 220 Urinal Systems, Battery Mount 481
D2010 310 Lavatory Systems 482
D2010 320 Lavatory Systems, Battery Mount 483
D2010 410 Kitchen Sink Systems 484
D2010 420 Laundry Sink Systems 485
D2010 430 Laboratory Sink Systems 486
D2010 440 Service Sink Systems 487
D2010 510 Bathtub Systems 488
D2010 610 Group Wash Fountain Systems 489
D2010 710 Shower Systems 490
D2010 810 Drinking Fountain Systems 491
D2010 820 Water Cooler Systems 492
D2010 920 Two Fixture Bathroom, Two Wall Plumbing 493
D2010 922 Two Fixture Bathroom, One Wall Plumbing 493
D2010 924 Three Fixture Bathroom, One Wall Plumbing 494
D2010 926 Three Fixture Bathroom, Two Wall Plumbing 494
D2010 928 Four Fixture Bathroom, Two Wall Plumbing 495
D2010 930 Four Fixture Bathroom, Three Wall Plumbing 495
D2010 932 Five Fixture Bathroom, Two Wall Plumbing 496
D2010 934 Five Fixture Bathroom, Three Wall Plumbing 496
D2010 936 Five Fixture Bathroom, One Wall Plumbing 496
D2010 951 Plumbing Systems 20 Unit, 2 Story Apartment Building 497

D2020 Domestic Water Distribution
D2020 210 Electric Water Heaters - Residential Systems 498
D2020 220 Gas Fired Water Heaters - Residential Systems 499
D2020 230 Oil Fired Water Heaters - Residential Systems 500
D2020 240 Electric Water Heaters - Commercial Systems 501
D2020 250 Gas Fired Water Heaters - Commercial Systems 502
D2020 260 Oil Fired Water Heaters - Commercial Systems 503
D2020 265 Solar, Closed Loop, Add-On Hot Water Systems 505
D2020 270 Solar, Drainback, Hot Water Systems 507
D2020 275 Solar, Draindown, Hot Water Systems 509
D2020 280 Solar, Recirculation, Domestic Hot Water Systems .. 511
D2020 285 Thermosyphon, Hot Water 513
D2020 290 Solar, Hot Water, Air To Water Heat Exchange 515
D2020 295 Solar, Closed Loop, Hot Water Systems 517

D2040 Rain Water Drainage
D2040 210 Roof Drain Systems 518

D3010 Energy Supply
D3010 510 Apartment Building Heating - Fin Tube Radiation 520
D3010 650 Solar, Closed Loop, Space/Hot Water Systems 523
D3010 660 Solar Swimming Pool Heater Systems 525
D3010 675 Air To Water Heat Exchange 527

D3020 Heat Generating Systems
D3020 102 Small Heating Systems, Hydronic, Electric Boilers 528

D3090 Other HVAC Systems/Equip
D3090 320 Garage Exhaust Systems 529

D4010 Sprinklers
D4010 310 Dry Pipe Sprinkler Systems 530
D4010 350 Preaction Sprinkler Systems 533
D4010 370 Deluge Sprinkler Systems 536
D4010 390 On-off multicycle Sprinkler Systems 539
D4010 410 Wet Pipe Sprinkler Systems 542
D4010 412 Wet Sprinkler Seismic Components 545
D4010 413 Seismic Wet Pipe Flexible Feed Sprinkler Systems 548
D4010 414 Seismic Wet Pipe Flexible Feed Sprinkler Systems 550

D4020 Standpipes
D4020 310 Wet Standpipe Risers, Class I 552
          Wet Standpipe Risers, Class II 552
          Wet Standpipe Risers, Class III 553
D4020 330 Dry Standpipe Risers, Class I 554
          Dry Standpipe Risers, Class II 554
          Dry Standpipe Risers, Class III 555
D4020 410 Fire Hose Equipment 556

D4090 Other Fire Protection Systems
D4090 910 Fire Suppression Unit Components 557
D4090 920 FM200 Systems 557

G BUILDING SITEWORK

G1030 Site Earthwork
G1030 805 Trenching Common Earth 560
G1030 806 Trenching Loam & Sandy Clay 562
G1030 807 Trenching Sand & Gravel 564
G1030 815 Pipe Bedding 566

G2040 Site Development
G2040 920 Swimming Pools 568

G2050 Landscaping
G2050 710 Site Irrigation 569
G2050 720 Site Irrigation 572

G3010 Water Supply
G3010 121 Water Service, Lead Free 573
G3010 410 Fire Hydrants 575

G3020 Sanitary Sewer
G3020 302 Septic Systems 577

G3030 Storm Sewer
G3030 210 Manholes & Catch Basins 579

RSMeans data: Assemblies— How They Work

Assemblies estimating provides a fast and reasonably accurate way to develop construction costs. An assembly is the grouping of individual work items — with appropriate quantities — to provide a cost for a major construction component in a convenient unit of measure.

An assemblies estimate is often used during early stages of design development to compare the cost impact of various design alternatives on total building cost.

Assemblies estimates are also used as an efficient tool to verify construction estimates.

Assemblies estimates do not require a completed design or detailed drawings. Instead, they are based on the general size of the structure and other known parameters of the project. The degree of accuracy of an assemblies estimate is generally within +/- 15%.

Most assemblies consist of three major elements: a graphic, the system components, and the cost data itself. The **graphic** is a visual representation showing the typical appearance of the assembly

❶ Unique 12-Character Identifier

Our assemblies are identified by a **unique 12-character identifier**. The assemblies are numbered using UNIFORMAT II, ASTM Standard E1557. The first five characters represent this system to level three. The last seven characters represent further breakdown in order to arrange items in understandable groups of similar tasks. Line numbers are consistent across all of our publications, so a line number in any assemblies data set will always refer to the same item.

❷ Reference Box

Information is available in the Reference Section to assist the estimator with estimating procedures, alternate pricing methods, and additional technical information.

The **Reference Box** indicates the exact location of this information in the Reference Section. The "R" stands for "reference," and the remaining characters are the line numbers.

❸ Narrative Descriptions

Our assemblies descriptions appear in two formats: narrative and table. **Narrative descriptions** are shown in a hierarchical structure to make them readable. In order to read a complete description, read up through the indents to the top of the section. Include everything that is above and to the left that is not contradicted by information below.

❹ System Components

System Components are listed separately to detail what is included in the development of the total system price.

Narrative Format

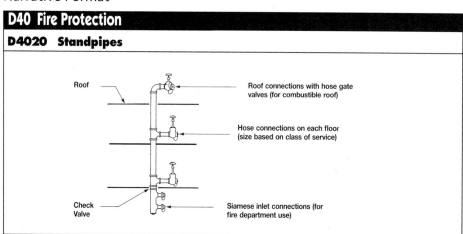

For supplemental customizable square foot estimating forms, visit: RSMeans.com/2023books

472

in question. It is frequently accompanied by additional explanatory technical information describing the class of items. The **System Components** is a listing of the individual tasks that make up the assembly, including the quantity and unit of measure for each item, along with the cost of material and installation. The **Assemblies data** below lists prices for other similar systems with dimensional and/or size variations.

All of our assemblies costs represent the cost for the installing contractor. An allowance for profit has been added to all material, labor, and equipment rental costs. A markup for labor burdens, including workers' compensation, fixed overhead, and business overhead, is included with installation costs.

The information in RSMeans cost data represents a "national average" cost. This data should be modified to the project location using the **City Cost Indexes** or **Location Factors** tables found in the Reference Section.

Table Format

D20 Plumbing
D2010 Plumbing Fixtures

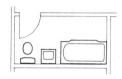

Example of Plumbing Cost Calculations: The bathroom system includes the individual fixtures such as bathtub, lavatory, shower and water closet. These fixtures are listed below as separate items merely as a checklist.

❺ Unit of Measure

All RSMeans data: Assemblies include a typical **Unit of Measure** used for estimating that item. For instance, for continuous footings or foundation walls the unit is linear feet (L.F.). For spread footings the unit is each (Ea.). The estimator needs to take special care that the unit in the data matches the unit in the takeoff. Abbreviations and unit conversions can be found in the Reference Section.

❻ Table Descriptions

Table descriptions work similar to Narrative Descriptions, except that if there is a blank in the column at a particular line number, read up to the description above in the same column.

D2010 951	Plumbing Systems 20 Unit, 2 Story Apartment Building					COST EACH		
	FIXTURE	SYSTEM	LINE	QUANTITY	UNIT	MAT.	INST.	TOTAL
0440	Bathroom	D2010 926	3640	20	Ea.	92,000	61,500	153,500
0480	Bathtub							
0520	Booster pump[1]	not req'd.						
0560	Drinking fountain							
0600	Garbage disposal[1]	not incl.						
0660								
0680	Grease interceptor							
0720	Water heater	D2020 250	2140	1	Ea.	12,800	4,175	16,975
0760	Kitchen sink	D2010 410	1960	20	Ea.	39,000	21,500	60,500
0800	Laundry sink	D2010 420	1840	4	Ea.	6,775	4,275	11,050
0840	Lavatory							
0900								
0920	Roof drain, 1 floor	D2040 210	4200	2	Ea.	3,225	2,225	5,450
0960	Roof drain, add'l floor	D2040 210	4240	20	L.F.	310	560	870
1000	Service sink	D2010 440	4300	1	Ea.	5,275	1,500	6,775
1040	Sewage ejector[1]	not req'd.						
1080	Shower							
1100								
1160	Sump pump							
1200	Urinal							
1240	Water closet							
1320								
1360	SUB TOTAL					159,500	95,500	255,000
1481	Water controls	R221113-40		10%[2]		16,000	9,550	25,550
1521	Pipe & fittings[3]	R221113-40		30%[2]		47,900	28,600	76,500
1560	Other							
1601	Quality/complexity	R221113-40		15%[2]		23,900	14,300	38,200
1680								
1720	TOTAL					247,500	148,000	395,500
1741								

[1]**Note:** Cost for items such as booster pumps, backflow preventers, sewage ejectors, water meters, etc., may be obtained from the unit price section in the front of this data set.

Water controls, pipe and fittings, and the Quality/Complexity factors come from Table R221113-40.

[2]Percentage of subtotal.

[3]Long, easily discernable runs of pipe would be more accurately priced from Unit Price Section 22 11 13. If this is done, reduce the miscellaneous percentage in proportion.

RSMeans data: Assemblies— How They Work (Continued)

Sample Estimate

This sample demonstrates the elements of an estimate, including a tally of the RSMeans data lines. Published assemblies costs include all markups for labor burden and profit for the installing contractor. This estimate adds a summary of the markups applied by a general contractor on the installing contractor's work. These figures represent the total cost to the owner. The location factor with RSMeans data is applied at the bottom of the estimate to adjust the cost of the work to a specific location.

Project Name:	Interior Fit-out, ABC Office			
Location:	Anywhere, USA	Date: 1/1/2023		STD
Assembly Number	Description	Qty.	Unit	Subtotal
❶ C1010 124 1200	Wood partition, 2 x 4 @ 16" OC w/5/8" FR gypsum board	560	S.F.	$3,656.80
C1020 114 1800	Metal door & frame, flush hollow core, 3'-0" x 7'-0"	2	Ea.	$2,370.00
C3010 230 0080	Painting, brushwork, primer & 2 coats	1,120	S.F.	$1,556.80
C3020 410 0140	Carpet, tufted, nylon, roll goods, 12' wide, 26 oz	240	S.F.	$703.20
C3030 210 6000	Acoustic ceilings, 24" x 48" tile, tee grid suspension	200	S.F.	$1,896.00
D5020 125 0560	Receptacles incl plate, box, conduit, wire, 20 A duplex	8	Ea.	$2,844.00
D5020 125 0720	Light switch incl plate, box, conduit, wire, 20 A single pole	2	Ea.	$692.00
D5020 210 0560	Fluorescent fixtures, recess mounted, 20 per 1000 SF	200	S.F.	$3,310.00
	Assembly Subtotal			**$17,028.80**
	Sales Tax @ ❷	5 %		$ 425.72
	General Requirements @ ❸	7 %		$ 1,192.02
	Subtotal A			**$18,646.54**
	GC Overhead @ ❹	5 %		$ 932.33
	Subtotal B			**$19,578.86**
	GC Profit @ ❺	5 %		$ 978.94
	Subtotal C			**$20,557.81**
	Adjusted by Location Factor ❻	112.5		$ 23,127.53
	Architects Fee @ ❼	8 %		$ 1,850.20
	Contingency @ ❽	15 %		$ 3,469.13
	Project Total Cost			**$ 28,446.86**

This estimate is based on an interactive spreadsheet. You are free to download it and adjust it to your methodology.
A copy of this spreadsheet is available at RSMeans.com/2023books.

① Work Performed
The body of the estimate shows the RSMeans data selected, including line numbers, a brief description of each item, its takeoff quantity and unit, and the total installed cost, including the installing contractor's overhead and profit.

② Sales Tax
If the work is subject to state or local sales taxes, the amount must be added to the estimate. In a conceptual estimate, it can be assumed that one half of the total represents material costs. Therefore, apply the sales tax rate to 50% of the assembly subtotal.

③ General Requirements
This item covers project-wide needs provided by the general contractor. These items vary by project but may include temporary facilities and utilities, security, testing, project cleanup, etc. In assemblies estimates a percentage is used—typically between 5% and 15% of project cost.

④ General Contractor Overhead
This entry represents the general contractor's markup on all work to cover project administration costs.

⑤ General Contractor Profit
This entry represents the General Contractor's profit on all work performed. The value included here can vary widely by project and is influenced by the General Contractor's perception of the project's financial risk and market conditions.

⑥ Location Factor
RSMeans published data are based on national average costs. If necessary, adjust the total cost of the project using a location factor from the "Location Factor" table or the "City Cost Indexes" table found in the Reference Section. Use location factors if the work is general, covering the work of multiple trades. If the work is by a single trade (e.g., masonry), use the more specific data found in the City Cost Indexes.

To adjust costs by location factors, multiply the base cost by the factor and divide by 100.

⑦ Architect's Fee
If appropriate, add the design cost to the project estimate. These fees vary based on project complexity and size. Typical design and engineering fees can be found in the Reference Section.

⑧ Contingency
A factor for contingency may be added to any estimate to represent the cost of unknowns that may occur between the time that the estimate is performed and the time the project is constructed. The amount of the allowance will depend on the stage of design at which the estimate is done, as well as the contractor's assessment of the risk involved.

D Services

Same Data. Simplified.

Enjoy the convenience and efficiency of accessing your costs anywhere:
- **Skip the multiplier** by setting your location
- **Quickly search,** edit, favorite and share costs
- **Stay on top of price changes** with automatic updates

Discover more at rsmeans.com/online

No part of this cost data may be reproduced, stored in a retrieval system, or transmitted in any form or by any means without prior written permission of Gordian.

D20 Plumbing

D2010 Plumbing Fixtures

One Piece Wall Hung

Systems are complete with trim seat and rough-in (supply, waste and vent) for connection to supply branches and waste mains.

Supply

Waste/Vent

Floor Mount

System Components	QUANTITY	UNIT	COST EACH		
			MAT.	INST.	TOTAL
SYSTEM D2010 110 1880					
WATER CLOSET, VITREOUS CHINA					
TANK TYPE, WALL HUNG, TWO PIECE					
Water closet, tank type vit china wall hung 2 pc. w/seat supply & stop	1.000	Ea.	505	292	797
Pipe Steel galvanized, schedule 40, threaded, 2" diam.	4.000	L.F.	106	96	202
Pipe, CI soil, no hub, cplg 10' OC, hanger 5' OC, 4" diam.	2.000	L.F.	50	53	103
Pipe, coupling, standard coupling, CI soil, no hub, 4" diam.	2.000	Ea.	59	94	153
Copper tubing type L solder joint, hangar 10' O.C., 1/2" diam.	6.000	L.F.	32.40	63.60	96
Wrought copper 90° elbow for solder joints 1/2" diam.	2.000	Ea.	6.50	86	92.50
Wrought copper Tee for solder joints 1/2" diam.	1.000	Ea.	2.08	66	68.08
Supports/carrier, water closet, siphon jet, horiz, single, 4" waste	1.000	Ea.	1,575	161	1,736
TOTAL			2,335.98	911.60	3,247.58

D2010 110		Water Closet Systems		COST EACH		
				MAT.	INST.	TOTAL
1800	Water closet, vitreous china					
1840		Tank type, wall hung				
1880			Close coupled two piece	2,325	910	3,235
1920			Floor mount, one piece	1,675	970	2,645
1960			One piece low profile	1,650	970	2,620
2000			Two piece close coupled	935	970	1,905
2040		Bowl only with flush valve				
2080			Wall hung	3,150	1,025	4,175
2120			Floor mount	1,125	985	2,110
2160			Floor mount, ADA compliant with 18" high bowl	1,150	1,000	2,150

Reference notes: R221113-40, R224000-30

D20 Plumbing

D2010 Plumbing Fixtures

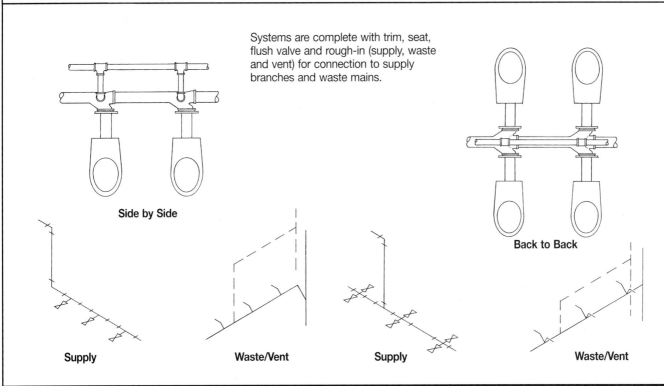

Systems are complete with trim, seat, flush valve and rough-in (supply, waste and vent) for connection to supply branches and waste mains.

System Components	QUANTITY	UNIT	COST EACH MAT.	COST EACH INST.	COST EACH TOTAL
SYSTEM D2010 120 1760					
WATER CLOSETS, BATTERY MOUNT, WALL HUNG, SIDE BY SIDE, FIRST CLOSET					
Water closet, bowl only w/flush valve, seat, wall hung	1.000	Ea.	1,150	267	1,417
Pipe, CI soil, no hub, cplg 10' OC, hanger 5' OC, 4" diam.	3.000	L.F.	75	79.50	154.50
Coupling, standard, CI, soil, no hub, 4" diam.	2.000	Ea.	59	94	153
Copper tubing, type L, solder joints, hangers 10' OC, 1" diam.	6.000	L.F.	41.40	75.90	117.30
Copper tubing, type DWV, solder joints, hangers 10'OC, 2" diam.	6.000	L.F.	111	117.30	228.30
Wrought copper 90° elbow for solder joints 1" diam.	1.000	Ea.	17.60	53.50	71.10
Wrought copper Tee for solder joints 1" diam.	1.000	Ea.	15.45	86	101.45
Support/carrier, siphon jet, horiz, adjustable single, 4" pipe	1.000	Ea.	1,575	161	1,736
Valve, gate, bronze, 125 lb, NRS, soldered 1" diam.	1.000	Ea.	200	45	245
Wrought copper, DWV, 90° elbow, 2" diam.	1.000	Ea.	117	86	203
TOTAL			3,361.45	1,065.20	4,426.65

D2010 120	Water Closets, Group		COST EACH MAT.	COST EACH INST.	COST EACH TOTAL
1760	Water closets, battery mount, wall hung, side by side, first closet	R221113 -40	3,350	1,075	4,425
1800	Each additional water closet, add		3,175	1,000	4,175
3000	Back to back, first pair of closets	R224000 -30	5,925	1,425	7,350
3100	Each additional pair of closets, back to back		5,750	1,400	7,150
9000	Back to back, first pair of closets, auto sensor flush valve, 1.28 gpf		6,425	1,525	7,950
9100	Ea additional pair of cls, back to back, auto sensor flush valve, 1.28 gpf		6,175	1,425	7,600

D20 Plumbing

D2010 Plumbing Fixtures

Systems are complete with trim, flush valve and rough-in (supply, waste and vent) for connection to supply branches and waste mains.

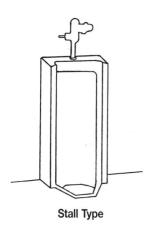
Stall Type

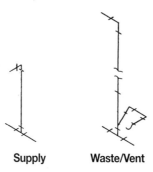
Supply   Waste/Vent

Wall Hung

System Components	QUANTITY	UNIT	COST EACH		
			MAT.	INST.	TOTAL
SYSTEM D2010 210 2000					
URINAL, VITREOUS CHINA, WALL HUNG					
Urinal, wall hung, vitreous china, incl. hanger	1.000	Ea.	460	515	975
Pipe, steel, galvanized, schedule 40, threaded, 1-1/2" diam.	5.000	L.F.	98.50	96.75	195.25
Copper tubing type DWV, solder joint, hangers 10' OC, 2" diam.	3.000	L.F.	55.50	58.65	114.15
Combination Y & 1/8 bend for CI soil pipe, no hub, 3" diam.	1.000	Ea.	45		45
Pipe, CI, no hub, cplg. 10' OC, hanger 5' OC, 3" diam.	4.000	L.F.	75.80	96	171.80
Pipe coupling standard, CI soil, no hub, 3" diam.	2.000	Ea.	45	81	126
Copper tubing type L, solder joint, hanger 10' OC 3/4" diam.	5.000	L.F.	35.25	56.50	91.75
Wrought copper 90° elbow for solder joints 3/4" diam.	1.000	Ea.	7.15	45	52.15
Wrought copper Tee for solder joints, 3/4" diam.	1.000	Ea.	13.15	71.50	84.65
TOTAL			835.35	1,020.40	1,855.75

D2010 210		Urinal Systems		COST EACH		
				MAT.	INST.	TOTAL
2000	Urinal, vitreous china, wall hung		R224000 -30	835	1,025	1,860
2001	Urinal, vitreous china, wall hung			835	1,025	1,860
2040	Stall type			2,075	1,225	3,300

For customer support on your Plumbing Costs with RSMeans data, call 800.448.8182.

D20 Plumbing

D2010 Plumbing Fixtures

Systems are complete with trim, flush valve and rough-in (supply, waste and vent) for connection to supply branches and waste mains.

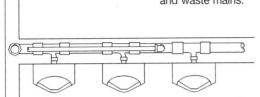
Side by Side

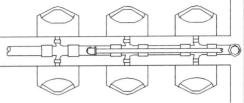
Back to Back

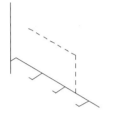
Waste/Vent

Supply

Supply

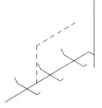
Waste/Vent

System Components	QUANTITY	UNIT	COST EACH MAT.	COST EACH INST.	COST EACH TOTAL
SYSTEM D2010 220 1760					
URINALS, BATTERY MOUNT, WALL HUNG, SIDE BY SIDE, FIRST URINAL					
Urinal, wall hung, vitreous china, with hanger & trim	1.000	Ea.	460	515	975
No hub cast iron soil pipe, 3" diameter	4.000	L.F.	75.80	96	171.80
No hub cast iron sanitary tee, 3" diameter	1.000	Ea.	45		45
No hub coupling, 3" diameter	2.000	Ea.	45	81	126
Copper tubing, type L, 3/4" diameter	5.000	L.F.	35.25	56.50	91.75
Copper tubing, type DWV, 2" diameter	2.000	L.F.	37	39.10	76.10
Copper 90° elbow, 3/4" diameter	2.000	Ea.	14.30	90	104.30
Copper 90° elbow, type DWV, 2" diameter	2.000	Ea.	234	172	406
Galvanized steel pipe, 1-1/2" diameter	5.000	L.F.	98.50	96.75	195.25
Cast iron drainage elbow, 90°, 1-1/2" diameter	1.000	Ea.	13.15	71.50	84.65
TOTAL			1,058	1,217.85	2,275.85

D2010 220	Urinal Systems, Battery Mount		MAT.	INST.	TOTAL
1760	Urinals, battery mount, side by side, first urinal	R221113 -40	1,050	1,225	2,275
1800	Each additional urinal, add		1,000	1,100	2,100
2000	Back to back, first pair of urinals	R224000 -30	1,800	1,850	3,650
2100	Each additional pair of urinals, back to back		1,250	1,475	2,725

For customer support on your Plumbing Costs with RSMeans data, call 800.448.8182.

D20 Plumbing

D2010 Plumbing Fixtures

Systems are complete with trim and rough-in (supply, waste and vent) to connect to supply branches and waste mains.

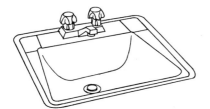
Vanity Top

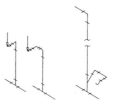
Supply   Waste/Vent

Wall Hung

System Components	QUANTITY	UNIT	COST EACH		
			MAT.	INST.	TOTAL
SYSTEM D2010 310 1560					
LAVATORY W/TRIM, VANITY TOP, P.E. ON C.I., 20" X 18"					
Lavatory w/trim, PE on CI, white, vanity top, 20" x 18" oval	1.000	Ea.	480	242	722
Pipe, steel, galvanized, schedule 40, threaded, 1-1/4" diam.	4.000	L.F.	66.20	69.60	135.80
Copper tubing type DWV, solder joint, hanger 10' OC 1-1/4" diam.	4.000	L.F.	41.60	57.40	99
Wrought copper DWV, Tee, sanitary, 1-1/4" diam.	1.000	Ea.	97	95.50	192.50
P trap w/cleanout, 20 ga., 1-1/4" diam.	1.000	Ea.	475	48	523
Copper tubing type L, solder joint, hanger 10' OC 1/2" diam.	10.000	L.F.	54	106	160
Wrought copper 90° elbow for solder joints 1/2" diam.	2.000	Ea.	6.50	86	92.50
Wrought copper Tee for solder joints, 1/2" diam.	2.000	Ea.	4.16	132	136.16
Stop, chrome, angle supply, 1/2" diam.	2.000	Ea.	30.80	78	108.80
TOTAL			1,255.26	914.50	2,169.76

D2010 310	Lavatory Systems		COST EACH		
			MAT.	INST.	TOTAL
1560	Lavatory w/trim, vanity top, PE on CI, 20" x 18", Vanity top by others.	R221113 -40	1,250	915	2,165
1600	19" x 16" oval		970	915	1,885
1640	18" round		1,600	915	2,515
1680	Cultured marble, 19" x 17"		965	915	1,880
1720	25" x 19"		1,025	915	1,940
1760	Stainless, self-rimming, 25" x 22"		1,400	915	2,315
1800	17" x 22"	R224000 -30	1,375	915	2,290
1840	Steel enameled, 20" x 17"		1,000	940	1,940
1880	19" round		1,000	940	1,940
1920	Vitreous china, 20" x 16"		1,075	960	2,035
1960	19" x 16"		1,075	960	2,035
2000	22" x 13"		1,075	960	2,035
2040	Wall hung, PE on CI, 18" x 15"		1,100	1,000	2,100
2080	19" x 17"		1,225	1,000	2,225
2120	20" x 18"		1,050	1,000	2,050
2160	Vitreous china, 18" x 15"		920	1,025	1,945
2200	19" x 17"		900	1,025	1,925
2240	24" x 20"		1,025	1,025	2,050
2300	20" x 27", handicap		1,450	1,125	2,575

For customer support on your Plumbing Costs with RSMeans data, call 800.448.8182.

D20 Plumbing

D2010 Plumbing Fixtures

Systems are complete with trim, flush valve and rough-in (supply, waste and vent) for connection to supply branches and waste mains.

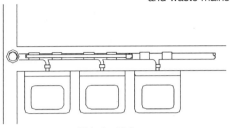
Side by Side

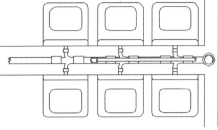
Back to Back

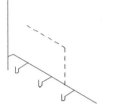
Waste/Vent

Supply
(Two supply systems required)

Supply
(Two supply systems required)

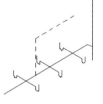
Waste/Vent

System Components	QUANTITY	UNIT	COST EACH		
			MAT.	INST.	TOTAL
SYSTEM D2010 320 1760					
LAVATORIES, BATTERY MOUNT, WALL HUNG, SIDE BY SIDE, FIRST LAVATORY					
Lavatory w/trim wall hung PE on CI 20" x 18"	1.000	Ea.	360	193	553
Stop, chrome, angle supply, 3/8" diameter	2.000	Ea.	26.90	72	98.90
Concealed arm support	1.000	Ea.	2,000	143	2,143
P trap w/cleanout, 20 ga. C.P., 1-1/4" diameter	1.000	Ea.	41.50	48	89.50
Copper tubing, type L, 1/2" diameter	10.000	L.F.	54	106	160
Copper tubing, type DWV, 1-1/4" diameter	4.000	L.F.	41.60	57.40	99
Copper 90° elbow, 1/2" diameter	2.000	Ea.	6.50	86	92.50
Copper tee, 1/2" diameter	2.000	Ea.	4.16	132	136.16
DWV copper sanitary tee, 1-1/4" diameter	2.000	Ea.	194	191	385
Galvanized steel pipe, 1-1/4" diameter	4.000	L.F.	66.20	69.60	135.80
Black cast iron 90° elbow, 1-1/4" diameter	1.000	Ea.	21	70.50	91.50
TOTAL			2,815.86	1,168.50	3,984.36

D2010 320	Lavatory Systems, Battery Mount		COST EACH		
			MAT.	INST.	TOTAL
1760	Lavatories, battery mount, side by side, first lavatory	R221113 -40	2,825	1,175	4,000
1800	Each additional lavatory, add		2,625	810	3,435
2000	Back to back, first pair of lavatories		2,575	1,850	4,425
2100	Each additional pair of lavatories, back to back		2,425	1,525	3,950

D20 Plumbing

D2010 Plumbing Fixtures

Systems are complete with trim and rough-in (supply, waste and vent) to connect to supply branches and waste mains.

Countertop Single Bowl

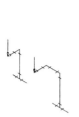
Supply

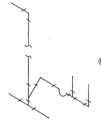
Waste/Vent

Countertop Double Bowl

System Components	QUANTITY	UNIT	COST EACH		
			MAT.	INST.	TOTAL
SYSTEM D2010 410 1720					
KITCHEN SINK W/TRIM, COUNTERTOP, P.E. ON C.I., 24" X 21", SINGLE BOWL					
Kitchen sink, counter top style, PE on CI, 24" x 21" single bowl	1.000	Ea.	890	276	1,166
Pipe, steel, galvanized, schedule 40, threaded, 1-1/4" diam.	4.000	L.F.	66.20	69.60	135.80
Copper tubing, type DWV, solder, hangers 10' OC 1-1/2" diam.	6.000	L.F.	78.60	95.40	174
Wrought copper, DWV, Tee, sanitary, 1-1/2" diam.	1.000	Ea.	120	107	227
P trap, standard, copper, 1-1/2" diam.	1.000	Ea.	365	50.50	415.50
Copper tubing, type L, solder joints, hangers 10' OC 1/2" diam.	10.000	L.F.	54	106	160
Wrought copper 90° elbow for solder joints 1/2" diam.	2.000	Ea.	6.50	86	92.50
Wrought copper Tee for solder joints, 1/2" diam.	2.000	Ea.	4.16	132	136.16
Stop, angle supply, chrome, 1/2" CTS	2.000	Ea.	30.80	78	108.80
TOTAL			1,615.26	1,000.50	2,615.76

D2010 410	Kitchen Sink Systems		COST EACH		
			MAT.	INST.	TOTAL
1720	Kitchen sink w/trim, countertop, PE on CI, 24"x21", single bowl	R221113 -40	1,625	1,000	2,625
1760	30" x 21" single bowl		2,175	1,000	3,175
1800	32" x 21" double bowl		1,225	1,075	2,300
1880	Stainless steel, 19" x 18" single bowl		1,475	1,000	2,475
1920	25" x 22" single bowl		1,550	1,000	2,550
1960	33" x 22" double bowl		1,950	1,075	3,025
2000	43" x 22" double bowl		2,175	1,100	3,275
2040	44" x 22" triple bowl		2,050	1,150	3,200
2080	44" x 24" corner double bowl		1,700	1,100	2,800
2120	Steel, enameled, 24" x 21" single bowl		1,300	1,000	2,300
2160	32" x 21" double bowl		1,325	1,075	2,400
2240	Raised deck, PE on CI, 32" x 21", dual level, double bowl		1,350	1,375	2,725
2280	42" x 21" dual level, triple bowl		1,950	1,500	3,450

D20 Plumbing

D2010 Plumbing Fixtures

Systems are complete with trim and rough-in (supply, waste and vent) to connect to supply branches and waste mains.

Single Compartment Sink

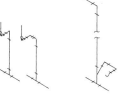

Supply   Waste/Vent

Double Compartment Sink

System Components	QUANTITY	UNIT	COST EACH MAT.	COST EACH INST.	TOTAL
SYSTEM D2010 420 1760					
LAUNDRY SINK W/TRIM, PE ON CI, BLACK IRON FRAME					
24" X 20" OD, SINGLE COMPARTMENT					
Laundry sink PE on CI w/trim & frame, 24" x 21" OD, 1 compartment	1.000	Ea.	735	258	993
Pipe, steel, galvanized, schedule 40, threaded, 1-1/4" diam	4.000	L.F.	66.20	69.60	135.80
Copper tubing, type DWV, solder joint, hanger 10' OC 1-1/2"diam	6.000	L.F.	78.60	95.40	174
Wrought copper, DWV, Tee, sanitary, 1-1/2" diam	1.000	Ea.	120	107	227
P trap, standard, copper, 1-1/2" diam	1.000	Ea.	365	50.50	415.50
Copper tubing type L, solder joints, hangers 10' OC, 1/2" diam	10.000	L.F.	54	106	160
Wrought copper 90° elbow for solder joints 1/2" diam	2.000	Ea.	6.50	86	92.50
Wrought copper Tee for solder joints, 1/2" diam	2.000	Ea.	4.16	132	136.16
Stop, angle supply, 1/2" diam	2.000	Ea.	30.80	78	108.80
TOTAL			1,460.26	982.50	2,442.76

D2010 420	Laundry Sink Systems		COST EACH MAT.	COST EACH INST.	TOTAL
1740	Laundry sink w/trim, PE on CI, black iron frame	R221113 -40			
1760	24" x 20", single compartment		1,450	985	2,435
1800	24" x 23" single compartment	R224000 -30	1,525	985	2,510
1840	48" x 21" double compartment		1,700	1,075	2,775
1920	Molded stone, on wall, 22" x 21" single compartment		935	985	1,920
1960	45"x 21" double compartment		1,175	1,075	2,250
2040	Plastic, on wall or legs, 18" x 23" single compartment		895	965	1,860
2080	20" x 24" single compartment		920	965	1,885
2120	36" x 23" double compartment		1,000	1,025	2,025
2160	40" x 24" double compartment		1,075	1,025	2,100

D20 Plumbing

D2010 Plumbing Fixtures

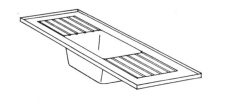
Laboratory Sink

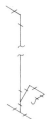
Supply   Waste/Vent

Polypropylene Cup Sink

Corrosion resistant laboratory sink systems are complete with trim and rough-in (supply, waste and vent) to connect to supply branches and waste mains.

System Components	QUANTITY	UNIT	COST EACH MAT.	COST EACH INST.	COST EACH TOTAL
SYSTEM D2010 430 1600					
LABORATORY SINK W/TRIM, STAINLESS STEEL, SINGLE BOWL					
DOUBLE DRAINBOARD, 54" X 24" O.D.					
Sink w/trim, stainless steel, 1 bowl, 2 drainboards 54" x 24" OD	1.000	Ea.	1,600	515	2,115
Pipe, polypropylene, schedule 40, acid resistant 1-1/2" diam.	10.000	L.F.	260	230	490
Tee, sanitary, polypropylene, acid resistant, 1-1/2" diam.	1.000	Ea.	55.50	86	141.50
P trap, polypropylene, acid resistant, 1-1/2" diam.	1.000	Ea.	99	50.50	149.50
Copper tubing type L, solder joint, hanger 10' O.C. 1/2" diam.	10.000	L.F.	54	106	160
Wrought copper 90° elbow for solder joints 1/2" diam.	2.000	Ea.	6.50	86	92.50
Wrought copper Tee for solder joints, 1/2" diam.	2.000	Ea.	4.16	132	136.16
Stop, angle supply, chrome, 1/2" diam.	2.000	Ea.	30.80	78	108.80
TOTAL			2,109.96	1,283.50	3,393.46

D2010 430	Laboratory Sink Systems	COST EACH MAT.	COST EACH INST.	COST EACH TOTAL
1580	Laboratory sink w/trim,			
1590	Stainless steel, single bowl,			
1600	Double drainboard, 54" x 24" O.D.	2,100	1,275	3,375
1640	Single drainboard, 47" x 24"O.D.	1,675	1,275	2,950
1670	Stainless steel, double bowl,			
1680	70" x 24" O.D.	2,275	1,275	3,550
1750	Polyethylene, single bowl,			
1760	Flanged, 14-1/2" x 14-1/2" O.D.	825	1,150	1,975
1800	18-1/2" x 18-1/2" O.D.	960	1,150	2,110
1840	23-1/2" x 20-1/2" O.D.	970	1,150	2,120
1920	Polypropylene, cup sink, oval, 7" x 4" O.D.	745	1,025	1,770
1960	10" x 4-1/2" O.D.	785	1,025	1,810

D20 Plumbing

D2010 Plumbing Fixtures

Wall Hung

Supply

Waste/Vent

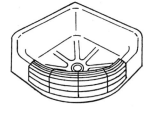
Corner, Floor

Corrosion resistant laboratory sink systems are complete with trim and rough-in (supply, waste and vent) to connect to supply branches and waste mains.

System Components	QUANTITY	UNIT	COST EACH MAT.	COST EACH INST.	COST EACH TOTAL
SYSTEM D2010 440 4260					
SERVICE SINK, PE ON CI, CORNER FLOOR, 28"X28", W/RIM GUARD & TRIM					
Service sink, corner floor, PE on CI, 28" x 28", w/rim guard & trim	1.000	Ea.	1,750	350	2,100
Copper tubing type DWV, solder joint, hanger 10'OC 3" diam.	6.000	L.F.	231	159	390
Copper tubing type DWV, solder joint, hanger 10'OC 2" diam	4.000	L.F.	74	78.20	152.20
Wrought copper DWV, Tee, sanitary, 3" diam.	1.000	Ea.	695	221	916
P trap with cleanout & slip joint, copper 3" diam	1.000	Ea.	1,600	78	1,678
Copper tubing, type L, solder joints, hangers 10' OC, 1/2" diam	10.000	L.F.	54	106	160
Wrought copper 90° elbow for solder joints 1/2" diam	2.000	Ea.	6.50	86	92.50
Wrought copper Tee for solder joints, 1/2" diam	2.000	Ea.	4.16	132	136.16
Stop, angle supply, chrome, 1/2" diam	2.000	Ea.	30.80	78	108.80
TOTAL			4,445.46	1,288.20	5,733.66

D2010 440	Service Sink Systems		COST EACH MAT.	COST EACH INST.	COST EACH TOTAL
4260	Service sink w/trim, PE on CI, corner floor, 28" x 28", w/rim guard	R221113-40	4,450	1,300	5,750
4300	Wall hung w/rim guard, 22" x 18"		5,275	1,500	6,775
4340	24" x 20"	R224000-30	5,825	1,500	7,325
4380	Vitreous china, wall hung 22" x 20"		5,300	1,500	6,800

D20 Plumbing

D2010 Plumbing Fixtures

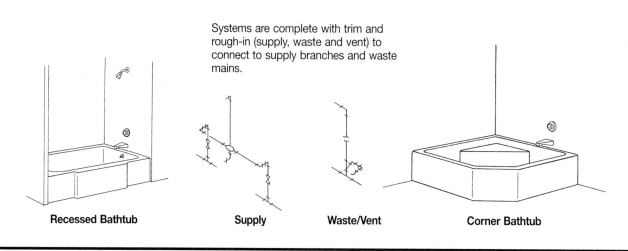

Systems are complete with trim and rough-in (supply, waste and vent) to connect to supply branches and waste mains.

Recessed Bathtub | Supply | Waste/Vent | Corner Bathtub

System Components	QUANTITY	UNIT	COST EACH		
			MAT.	INST.	TOTAL
SYSTEM D2010 510 2000					
BATHTUB, RECESSED, PORCELAIN ENAMEL ON CAST IRON,, 48" x 42"					
Bath tub, porcelain enamel on cast iron, w/fittings, 48" x 42"	1.000	Ea.	3,850	385	4,235
Pipe, steel, galvanized, schedule 40, threaded, 1-1/4" diam.	4.000	L.F.	66.20	69.60	135.80
Pipe, Cl no hub soil w/couplings 10' OC, hangers 5' OC, 4" diam.	3.000	L.F.	75	79.50	154.50
Combination Y and 1/8 bend for C.I. soil pipe, no hub, 4" pipe size	1.000	Ea.	117		117
Drum trap, 3" x 5", copper, 1-1/2" diam.	1.000	Ea.	725	53.50	778.50
Copper tubing type L, solder joints, hangers 10' OC 1/2" diam.	10.000	L.F.	54	106	160
Wrought copper 90° elbow, solder joints, 1/2" diam.	2.000	Ea.	6.50	86	92.50
Wrought copper Tee, solder joints, 1/2" diam.	2.000	Ea.	4.16	132	136.16
Stop, angle supply, 1/2" diameter	2.000	Ea.	30.80	78	108.80
Copper tubing type DWV, solder joints, hanger 10' OC 1-1/2" diam.	3.000	L.F.	39.30	47.70	87
Pipe coupling, standard, C.I. soil no hub, 4" pipe size	2.000	Ea.	59	94	153
TOTAL			5,026.96	1,131.30	6,158.26

D2010 510	Bathtub Systems		COST EACH		
			MAT.	INST.	TOTAL
2000	Bathtub, recessed, P.E. on Cl., 48" x 42"	R224000 -30	5,025	1,125	6,150
2040	72" x 36"		4,925	1,250	6,175
2080	Mat bottom, 5' long	R221113 -40	2,950	1,100	4,050
2120	5'-6" long		3,325	1,125	4,450
2160	Corner, 48" x 42"		4,675	1,100	5,775
2200	Formed steel, enameled, 4'-6" long		1,825	1,025	2,850

D20 Plumbing

D2010 Plumbing Fixtures

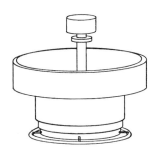
Circular Fountain

Systems are complete with trim, flush valve and rough-in (supply, waste and vent) for connection to supply branches and waste mains.

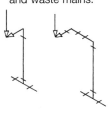
Supply

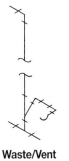
Waste/Vent

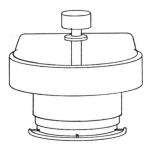
Semi-Circular Fountain

System Components	QUANTITY	UNIT	COST EACH		
			MAT.	INST.	TOTAL
SYSTEM D2010 610 1760 GROUP WASH FOUNTAIN, PRECAST TERRAZZO CIRCULAR, 36" DIAMETER					
Wash fountain, group, precast terrazzo, foot control 36" diam.	1.000	Ea.	8,575	800	9,375
Copper tubing type DWV, solder joint, hanger 10' OC, 2" diam.	10.000	L.F.	185	195.50	380.50
P trap, standard, copper, 2" diam.	1.000	Ea.	560	57.50	617.50
Wrought copper, Tee, sanitary, 2" diam.	1.000	Ea.	165	123	288
Copper tubing type L, solder joint, hanger 10' OC 1/2" diam.	20.000	L.F.	108	212	320
Wrought copper 90° elbow for solder joints 1/2" diam.	3.000	Ea.	9.75	129	138.75
Wrought copper Tee for solder joints, 1/2" diam.	2.000	Ea.	4.16	132	136.16
TOTAL			9,606.91	1,649	11,255.91

D2010 610	Group Wash Fountain Systems		COST EACH		
			MAT.	INST.	TOTAL
1740	Group wash fountain, precast terrazzo				
1760	Circular, 36" diameter	R221113 -40	9,600	1,650	11,250
1800	54" diameter		13,500	1,825	15,325
1840	Semi-circular, 36" diameter	R224000 -30	8,025	1,650	9,675
1880	54" diameter		13,900	1,825	15,725
1960	Stainless steel, circular, 36" diameter		8,575	1,550	10,125
2000	54" diameter		10,500	1,700	12,200
2040	Semi-circular, 36" diameter		7,200	1,550	8,750
2080	54" diameter		7,625	1,700	9,325
2160	Thermoplastic, circular, 36" diameter		6,275	1,250	7,525
2200	54" diameter		6,050	1,450	7,500
2240	Semi-circular, 36" diameter		6,700	1,250	7,950
2280	54" diameter		6,775	1,450	8,225

For customer support on your Plumbing Costs with RSMeans data, call 800.448.8182.

D20 Plumbing

D2010 Plumbing Fixtures

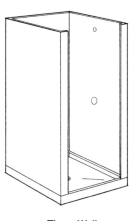

Three Wall

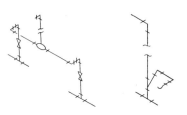

Supply   Waste/Vent

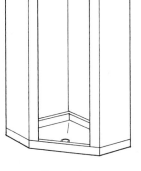

Corner Angle

Systems are complete with trim and rough-in (supply, waste and vent) for connection to supply branches and waste mains.

System Components	QUANTITY	UNIT	COST EACH MAT.	COST EACH INST.	COST EACH TOTAL
SYSTEM D2010 710 1560					
SHOWER, STALL, BAKED ENAMEL, MOLDED STONE RECEPTOR, 30" SQUARE					
Shower stall, enameled steel, molded stone receptor, 30" square	1.000	Ea.	1,625	298	1,923
Copper tubing type DWV, solder joints, hangers 10' OC, 2" diam.	6.000	L.F.	78.60	95.40	174
Wrought copper DWV, Tee, sanitary, 2" diam.	1.000	Ea.	120	107	227
Trap, standard, copper, 2" diam.	1.000	Ea.	365	50.50	415.50
Copper tubing type L, solder joint, hanger 10' OC 1/2" diam.	16.000	L.F.	86.40	169.60	256
Wrought copper 90° elbow for solder joints 1/2" diam.	3.000	Ea.	9.75	129	138.75
Wrought copper Tee for solder joints, 1/2" diam.	2.000	Ea.	4.16	132	136.16
Stop and waste, straightway, bronze, solder joint 1/2" diam.	2.000	Ea.	73	72	145
TOTAL			2,361.91	1,053.50	3,415.41

D2010 710	Shower Systems		COST EACH MAT.	COST EACH INST.	COST EACH TOTAL
1560	Shower, stall, baked enamel, molded stone receptor, 30" square		2,350	1,050	3,400
1600	32" square	R221113 -40	2,100	1,075	3,175
1640	Terrazzo receptor, 32" square		2,325	1,075	3,400
1680	36" square	R224000 -30	2,825	1,075	3,900
1720	36" corner angle		3,075	445	3,520
1800	Fiberglass one piece, three walls, 32" square		1,250	1,025	2,275
1840	36" square		1,300	1,025	2,325
1880	Polypropylene, molded stone receptor, 30" square		1,650	1,525	3,175
1920	32" square		1,650	1,525	3,175
1960	Built-in head, arm, bypass, stops and handles		148	395	543
2050	Shower, stainless steel panels, handicap				
2100	w/fixed and handheld head, control valves, grab bar, and seat		6,825	4,750	11,575
2500	Shower, group with six heads, thermostatic mix valves & balancing valve		14,100	1,150	15,250
2520	Five heads		10,100	1,050	11,150

D20 Plumbing

D2010 Plumbing Fixtures

Wall Mounted, No Back

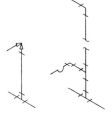
Supply   Waste/Vent

Wall Mounted, Low Back

Systems are complete with trim and rough-in (supply, waste and vent) to connect to supply branches and waste mains.

System Components	QUANTITY	UNIT	COST EACH		
			MAT.	INST.	TOTAL
SYSTEM D2010 810 1800					
DRINKING FOUNTAIN, ONE BUBBLER, WALL MOUNTED					
NON RECESSED, BRONZE, NO BACK					
Drinking fountain, wall mount, bronze, 1 bubbler	1.000	Ea.	1,675	215	1,890
Copper tubing, type L, solder joint, hanger 10' OC 3/8" diam.	5.000	L.F.	25.25	51.25	76.50
Stop, supply, straight, chrome, 3/8" diam.	1.000	Ea.	23	36	59
Wrought copper 90° elbow for solder joints 3/8" diam.	1.000	Ea.	9	39	48
Wrought copper Tee for solder joints, 3/8" diam.	1.000	Ea.	14.90	61.50	76.40
Copper tubing, type DWV, solder joint, hanger 10' OC 1-1/4" diam.	4.000	L.F.	41.60	57.40	99
P trap, standard, copper drainage, 1-1/4" diam.	1.000	Ea.	475	48	523
Wrought copper, DWV, Tee, sanitary, 1-1/4" diam.	1.000	Ea.	97	95.50	192.50
TOTAL			2,360.75	603.65	2,964.40

D2010 810	Drinking Fountain Systems	COST EACH		
		MAT.	INST.	TOTAL
1740	Drinking fountain, one bubbler, wall mounted			
1760	Non recessed			
1800	Bronze, no back	2,350	605	2,955
1840	Cast iron, enameled, low back	2,500	605	3,105
1880	Fiberglass, 12" back	4,250	605	4,855
1920	Stainless steel, no back	1,750	605	2,355
1960	Semi-recessed, poly marble	2,075	605	2,680
2040	Stainless steel	2,775	605	3,380
2080	Vitreous china	2,250	605	2,855
2120	Full recessed, poly marble	3,275	605	3,880
2200	Stainless steel	2,650	605	3,255
2240	Floor mounted, pedestal type, aluminum	4,150	820	4,970
2320	Bronze	4,825	820	5,645
2360	Stainless steel	3,600	820	4,420

D20 Plumbing

D2010 Plumbing Fixtures

Systems are complete with trim and rough-in (supply, waste and vent) for connection to supply branches and waste mains.

Wall Hung

Supply

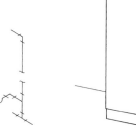
Waste/Vent

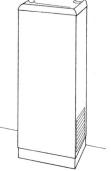
Floor Mounted

System Components	QUANTITY	UNIT	COST EACH		
			MAT.	INST.	TOTAL
SYSTEM D2010 820 1840					
WATER COOLER, ELECTRIC, SELF CONTAINED, WALL HUNG, 8.2 G.P.H.					
Water cooler, wall mounted, 8.2 GPH	1.000	Ea.	1,350	385	1,735
Copper tubing type DWV, solder joint, hanger 10' OC 1-1/4" diam.	4.000	L.F.	41.60	57.40	99
Wrought copper DWV, Tee, sanitary 1-1/4" diam.	1.000	Ea.	97	95.50	192.50
P trap, copper drainage, 1-1/4" diam.	1.000	Ea.	475	48	523
Copper tubing type L, solder joint, hanger 10' OC 3/8" diam.	5.000	L.F.	25.25	51.25	76.50
Wrought copper 90° elbow for solder joints 3/8" diam.	1.000	Ea.	9	39	48
Wrought copper Tee for solder joints, 3/8" diam.	1.000	Ea.	14.90	61.50	76.40
Stop and waste, straightway, bronze, solder, 3/8" diam.	1.000	Ea.	23	36	59
TOTAL			2,035.75	773.65	2,809.40

D2010 820		Water Cooler Systems		COST EACH		
				MAT.	INST.	TOTAL
1840	Water cooler, electric, wall hung, 8.2 G.P.H.		R221113-40	2,025	775	2,800
1880	Dual height, 14.3 G.P.H.			3,675	795	4,470
1920	Wheelchair type, 7.5 G.P.H.		R224000-30	2,075	775	2,850
1960	Semi recessed, 8.1 G.P.H.			1,925	775	2,700
2000	Full recessed, 8 G.P.H.			3,700	830	4,530
2040	Floor mounted, 14.3 G.P.H.			2,125	675	2,800
2080	Dual height, 14.3 G.P.H.			2,525	820	3,345
2120	Refrigerated compartment type, 1.5 G.P.H.			2,950	675	3,625

D20 Plumbing

D2010 Plumbing Fixtures

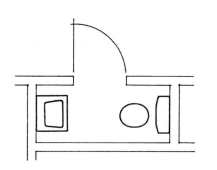

Two Fixture Bathroom Systems consisting of a lavatory, water closet, and rough-in service piping.
- Prices for plumbing and fixtures only.

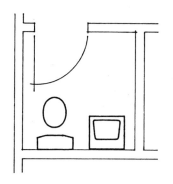

*Common wall is with an adjacent bathroom.

System Components	QUANTITY	UNIT	COST EACH MAT.	INST.	TOTAL
SYSTEM D2010 920 1180					
BATHROOM, LAVATORY & WATER CLOSET, 2 WALL PLUMBING, STAND ALONE					
Water closet, two piece, close coupled	1.000	Ea.	257	292	549
Water closet, rough-in waste & vent	1.000	Set	620	505	1,125
Lavatory w/ftngs., wall hung, white, PE on CI, 20" x 18"	1.000	Ea.	360	193	553
Lavatory, rough-in waste & vent	1.000	Set	690	930	1,620
Copper tubing type L, solder joint, hanger 10' OC 1/2" diam.	10.000	L.F.	54	106	160
Pipe, steel, galvanized, schedule 40, threaded, 2" diam.	12.000	L.F.	318	288	606
Pipe, CI soil, no hub, coupling 10' OC, hanger 5' OC, 4" diam.	7.000	L.F.	107.80	196	303.80
TOTAL			2,406.80	2,510	4,916.80

D2010 920	Two Fixture Bathroom, Two Wall Plumbing		COST EACH MAT.	INST.	TOTAL
1180	Bathroom, lavatory & water closet, 2 wall plumbing, stand alone	R221113 -40	2,400	2,500	4,900
1200	Share common plumbing wall*		2,100	2,175	4,275

D2010 922	Two Fixture Bathroom, One Wall Plumbing		COST EACH MAT.	INST.	TOTAL
2220	Bathroom, lavatory & water closet, one wall plumbing, stand alone	R221113 -40	2,200	2,250	4,450
2240	Share common plumbing wall*		1,925	1,925	3,850
2260		R224000 -30			
2280					

D20 Plumbing

D2010 Plumbing Fixtures

Three Fixture Bathroom Systems consisting of a lavatory, water closet, bathtub or shower and rough-in service piping.

- Prices for plumbing and fixtures only.

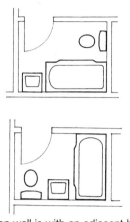
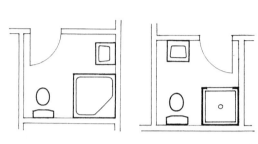
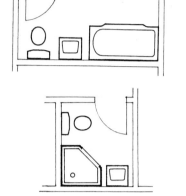

*Common wall is with an adjacent bathroom.

System Components	QUANTITY	UNIT	COST EACH MAT.	COST EACH INST.	COST EACH TOTAL
SYSTEM D2010 924 1170					
BATHROOM, LAVATORY, WATER CLOSET & BATHTUB					
ONE WALL PLUMBING, STAND ALONE					
Wtr closet, rough-in, supply, waste and vent	1.000	Set	620	505	1,125
Wtr closet, 2 pc close cpld vit china flr mntd w/seat supply & stop	1.000	Ea.	257	292	549
Lavatory w/ftngs, wall hung, white, PE on CI, 20" x 18"	1.000	Ea.	360	193	553
Lavatory, rough-in waste & vent	1.000	Set	690	930	1,620
Bathtub, white PE on CI, w/ftgs, mat bottom, recessed, 5' long	1.000	Ea.	1,775	350	2,125
Baths, rough-in waste and vent	1.000	Set	855	745	1,600
TOTAL			4,557	3,015	7,572

D2010 924		Three Fixture Bathroom, One Wall Plumbing		COST EACH MAT.	COST EACH INST.	COST EACH TOTAL
1150	Bathroom, three fixture, one wall plumbing		R221113 -40			
1160		Lavatory, water closet & bathtub				
1170		Stand alone	R224000 -30	4,550	3,025	7,575
1180		Share common plumbing wall *		3,875	2,125	6,000

D2010 926		Three Fixture Bathroom, Two Wall Plumbing		COST EACH MAT.	COST EACH INST.	COST EACH TOTAL
2130	Bathroom, three fixture, two wall plumbing		R221113 -40			
2140		Lavatory, water closet & bathtub				
2160		Stand alone		4,525	2,975	7,500
2180		Long plumbing wall common *		4,075	2,375	6,450
3610		Lavatory, bathtub & water closet				
3620		Stand alone		4,925	3,400	8,325
3640		Long plumbing wall common *		4,600	3,075	7,675
4660		Water closet, corner bathtub & lavatory				
4680		Stand alone		6,275	3,025	9,300
4700		Long plumbing wall common *		5,425	2,275	7,700
6100		Water closet, stall shower & lavatory				
6120		Stand alone		4,425	3,375	7,800
6140		Long plumbing wall common *		4,225	3,125	7,350
7060		Lavatory, corner stall shower & water closet				
7080		Stand alone		5,375	3,000	8,375
7100		Short plumbing wall common *		4,375	2,000	6,375

D20 Plumbing

D2010 Plumbing Fixtures

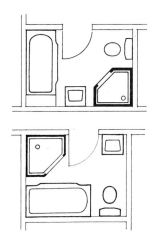
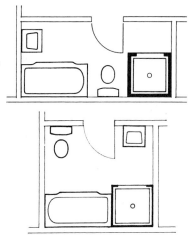

Four Fixture Bathroom Systems consisting of a lavatory, water closet, bathtub, shower and rough-in service piping.
- Prices for plumbing and fixtures only.

*Common wall is with an adjacent bathroom.

System Components	QUANTITY	UNIT	COST EACH MAT.	COST EACH INST.	COST EACH TOTAL
SYSTEM D2010 928 1160					
BATHROOM, BATHTUB, WATER CLOSET, STALL SHOWER & LAVATORY					
TWO WALL PLUMBING, STAND ALONE					
Wtr closet, 2 pc close cpld vit china flr mntd w/seat supply & stop	1.000	Ea.	257	292	549
Water closet, rough-in waste & vent	1.000	Set	620	505	1,125
Lavatory w/ftngs, wall hung, white PE on CI, 20" x 18"	1.000	Ea.	360	193	553
Lavatory, rough-in waste & vent	1.000	Set	690	930	1,620
Bathtub, white PE on CI, w/ftgs, mat bottom, recessed, 5' long	1.000	Ea.	1,775	350	2,125
Baths, rough-in waste and vent	1.000	Set	855	745	1,600
Shower stall, bkd enam, molded stone receptor, door & trim 32" sq.	1.000	Ea.	1,375	310	1,685
Shower stall, rough-in supply, waste & vent	1.000	Set	825	755	1,580
TOTAL			6,757	4,080	10,837

D2010 928	Four Fixture Bathroom, Two Wall Plumbing		MAT.	INST.	TOTAL
1140	Bathroom, four fixture, two wall plumbing	R221113-40			
1150	Bathtub, water closet, stall shower & lavatory				
1160	Stand alone	R224000-30	6,750	4,075	10,825
1180	Long plumbing wall common *		5,275	2,500	7,775
2260	Bathtub, lavatory, corner stall shower & water closet				
2280	Stand alone		7,375	3,250	10,625
2320	Long plumbing wall common *		6,525	2,500	9,025
3620	Bathtub, stall shower, lavatory & water closet				
3640	Stand alone		6,750	4,075	10,825
3660	Long plumbing wall (opp. door) common *		5,900	3,325	9,225

D2010 930	Four Fixture Bathroom, Three Wall Plumbing		MAT.	INST.	TOTAL
4680	Bathroom, four fixture, three wall plumbing	R221113-40			
4700	Bathtub, stall shower, lavatory & water closet				
4720	Stand alone		8,375	4,475	12,850
4760	Long plumbing wall (opposite door) common *		8,050	4,150	12,200

For customer support on your Plumbing Costs with RSMeans data, call 800.448.8182.

D20 Plumbing

D2010 Plumbing Fixtures

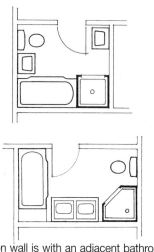
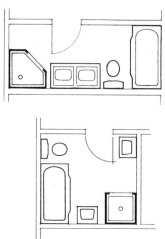

Five Fixture Bathroom Systems consisting of two lavatories, a water closet, bathtub, shower and rough-in service piping.

- Prices for plumbing and fixtures only.

*Common wall is with an adjacent bathroom.

System Components	QUANTITY	UNIT	COST EACH MAT.	INST.	TOTAL
SYSTEM D2010 932 1360					
BATHROOM, BATHTUB, WATER CLOSET, STALL SHOWER & TWO LAVATORIES					
TWO WALL PLUMBING, STAND ALONE					
Wtr closet, 2 pc close cpld vit china flr mntd incl seat, supply & stop	1.000	Ea.	257	292	549
Water closet, rough-in waste & vent	1.000	Set	620	505	1,125
Lavatory w/ftngs, wall hung, white PE on CI, 20" x 18"	2.000	Ea.	720	386	1,106
Lavatory, rough-in waste & vent	2.000	Set	1,380	1,860	3,240
Bathtub, white PE on CI, w/ftgs, mat bottom, recessed, 5' long	1.000	Ea.	1,775	350	2,125
Baths, rough-in waste and vent	1.000	Set	855	745	1,600
Shower stall, bkd enam molded stone receptor, door & ftng, 32" sq.	1.000	Ea.	1,375	310	1,685
Shower stall, rough-in supply, waste & vent	1.000	Set	825	755	1,580
TOTAL			7,807	5,203	13,010

D2010 932	Five Fixture Bathroom, Two Wall Plumbing	COST EACH MAT.	INST.	TOTAL
1320	Bathroom, five fixture, two wall plumbing			
1340	Bathtub, water closet, stall shower & two lavatories			
1360	Stand alone	7,800	5,200	13,000
1400	One short plumbing wall common *	6,950	4,450	11,400
1500	Bathtub, two lavatories, corner stall shower & water closet			
1520	Stand alone	9,050	5,225	14,275
1540	Long plumbing wall common*	8,200	4,050	12,250

D2010 934	Five Fixture Bathroom, Three Wall Plumbing	COST EACH MAT.	INST.	TOTAL
2360	Bathroom, five fixture, three wall plumbing			
2380	Water closet, bathtub, two lavatories & stall shower			
2400	Stand alone	9,050	5,225	14,275
2440	One short plumbing wall common *	8,200	4,475	12,675

D2010 936	Five Fixture Bathroom, One Wall Plumbing	COST EACH MAT.	INST.	TOTAL
4080	Bathroom, five fixture, one wall plumbing			
4100	Bathtub, two lavatories, corner stall shower & water closet			
4120	Stand alone	8,650	4,650	13,300
4160	Share common wall *	7,250	3,025	10,275

D20 Plumbing

D2010 Plumbing Fixtures

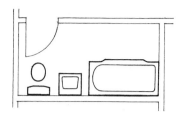

Example of Plumbing Cost Calculations: The bathroom system includes the individual fixtures such as bathtub, lavatory, shower and water closet. These fixtures are listed below as separate items merely as a checklist.

D2010 951 Plumbing Systems 20 Unit, 2 Story Apartment Building

	FIXTURE	SYSTEM	LINE	QUANTITY	UNIT	COST EACH		
						MAT.	INST.	TOTAL
0440	Bathroom	D2010 926	3640	20	Ea.	92,000	61,500	153,500
0480	Bathtub							
0520	Booster pump[1]	not req'd.						
0560	Drinking fountain							
0600	Garbage disposal[1]	not incl.						
0660								
0680	Grease interceptor							
0720	Water heater	D2020 250	2140	1	Ea.	12,800	4,175	16,975
0760	Kitchen sink	D2010 410	1960	20	Ea.	39,000	21,500	60,500
0800	Laundry sink	D2010 420	1840	4	Ea.	6,775	4,275	11,050
0840	Lavatory							
0900								
0920	Roof drain, 1 floor	D2040 210	4200	2	Ea.	3,225	2,225	5,450
0960	Roof drain, add'l floor	D2040 210	4240	20	L.F.	310	560	870
1000	Service sink	D2010 440	4300	1	Ea.	5,275	1,500	6,775
1040	Sewage ejector[1]	not req'd.						
1080	Shower							
1100								
1160	Sump pump							
1200	Urinal							
1240	Water closet							
1320								
1360	SUB TOTAL					159,500	95,500	255,000
1481	Water controls	R221113-40		10%[2]		16,000	9,550	25,550
1521	Pipe & fittings[3]	R221113-40		30%[2]		47,900	28,600	76,500
1560	Other							
1601	Quality/complexity	R221113-40		15%[2]		23,900	14,300	38,200
1680								
1720	TOTAL					247,500	148,000	395,500
1741								

[1]**Note:** Cost for items such as booster pumps, backflow preventers, sewage ejectors, water meters, etc., may be obtained from the unit price section in the front of this data set.

Water controls, pipe and fittings, and the Quality/Complexity factors come from Table R221113-40.

[2]Percentage of subtotal.

[3]Long, easily discernable runs of pipe would be more accurately priced from Unit Price Section 22 11 13. If this is done, reduce the miscellaneous percentage in proportion.

D20 Plumbing

D2020 Domestic Water Distribution

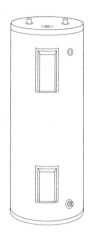

Installation includes piping and fittings within 10' of heater. Electric water heaters do not require venting.

1 Kilowatt hour will raise:			
Gallons of Water	Degrees F	Gallons of Water	Degrees F
4.1	100°	6.8	60°
4.5	90°	8.2	50°
5.1	80°	10.0	40°
5.9	70°		

System Components	QUANTITY	UNIT	COST EACH		
			MAT.	INST.	TOTAL
SYSTEM D2020 210 1780					
ELECTRIC WATER HEATER, RESIDENTIAL, 100°F RISE					
10 GALLON TANK, 7 GPH					
Water heater, residential electric, glass lined tank, 10 gal.	1.000	Ea.	485	375	860
Copper tubing, type L, solder joint, hanger 10' OC 1/2" diam.	30.000	L.F.	162	318	480
Wrought copper 90° elbow for solder joints 1/2" diam.	4.000	Ea.	13	172	185
Wrought copper Tee for solder joints, 1/2" diam.	2.000	Ea.	4.16	132	136.16
Union, wrought copper, 1/2" diam.	2.000	Ea.	142	90	232
Valve, gate, bronze, 125 lb, NRS, soldered 1/2" diam.	2.000	Ea.	254	72	326
Relief valve, bronze, press & temp, self-close, 3/4" IPS	1.000	Ea.	335	30.50	365.50
Wrought copper adapter, CTS to MPT 3/4" IPS	1.000	Ea.	18.15	50.50	68.65
Copper tubing, type L, solder joints, 3/4" diam.	1.000	L.F.	7.05	11.30	18.35
Wrought copper 90° elbow for solder joints 3/4" diam.	1.000	Ea.	7.15	45	52.15
TOTAL			1,427.51	1,296.30	2,723.81

D2020 210	Electric Water Heaters - Residential Systems	COST EACH		
		MAT.	INST.	TOTAL
1760	Electric water heater, residential, 100°F rise			
1780	10 gallon tank, 7 GPH	1,425	1,300	2,725
1820	20 gallon tank, 7 GPH	1,625	1,375	3,000
1860	30 gallon tank, 7 GPH	2,225	1,450	3,675
1900	40 gallon tank, 8 GPH	2,525	1,600	4,125
1940	52 gallon tank, 10 GPH	3,225	1,600	4,825
1980	66 gallon tank, 13 GPH	4,850	1,850	6,700
2020	80 gallon tank, 16 GPH	5,175	1,925	7,100
2060	120 gallon tank, 23 GPH	7,375	2,250	9,625

D20 Plumbing

D2020 Domestic Water Distribution

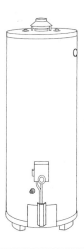

Installation includes piping and fittings within 10' of heater. Gas heaters require vent piping (not included with these units).

System Components	QUANTITY	UNIT	COST EACH MAT.	COST EACH INST.	COST EACH TOTAL
SYSTEM D2020 220 2260					
GAS FIRED WATER HEATER, RESIDENTIAL, 100°F RISE					
30 GALLON TANK, 32 GPH					
Water heater, residential, gas, glass lined tank, 30 gallon	1.000	Ea.	2,325	430	2,755
Copper tubing, type L, solder joint, hanger 10' OC, 3/4" diam	33.000	L.F.	232.65	372.90	605.55
Wrought copper 90° elbow for solder joints, 3/4" diam	5.000	Ea.	35.75	225	260.75
Wrought copper Tee for solder joints, 3/4" diam	2.000	Ea.	26.30	143	169.30
Wrought copper union for soldered joints, 3/4" diam.	2.000	Ea.	178	96	274
Valve bronze, 125 lb., NRS, soldered 3/4" diam	2.000	Ea.	278	86	364
Relief valve, press & temp, bronze, self-close, 3/4" diam	1.000	Ea.	335	30.50	365.50
Wrought copper, adapter, CTS to MPT 3/4" IPS	1.000	Ea.	18.15	50.50	68.65
Pipe steel black, schedule 40, threaded, 1/2" diam	10.000	L.F.	61.50	136.50	198
Pipe, 90° elbow, malleable iron black, 150 lb., threaded, 1/2" diam	2.000	Ea.	12.80	115	127.80
Pipe, union with brass seat, malleable iron black, 1/2" diam	1.000	Ea.	30	61.50	91.50
Valve, gas stop w/o check, brass, 1/2" IPS	1.000	Ea.	44	36	80
TOTAL			3,577.15	1,782.90	5,360.05

D2020 220	Gas Fired Water Heaters - Residential Systems		MAT.	INST.	TOTAL
2200	Gas fired water heater, residential, 100°F rise				
2260	30 gallon tank, 32 GPH	R224000-10	3,575	1,775	5,350
2300	40 gallon tank, 32 GPH		2,325	2,000	4,325
2340	50 gallon tank, 63 GPH	R224000-20	2,450	2,000	4,450
2380	75 gallon tank, 63 GPH		3,625	2,250	5,875
2420	100 gallon tank, 63 GPH		4,925	2,350	7,275

D20 Plumbing

D2020 Domestic Water Distribution

Installation includes piping and fittings within 10' of heater. Oil fired heaters require vent piping (not included in these prices).

System Components	QUANTITY	UNIT	COST EACH MAT.	COST EACH INST.	COST EACH TOTAL
SYSTEM D2020 230 2220					
OIL FIRED WATER HEATER, RESIDENTIAL, 100°F RISE					
30 GALLON TANK, 103 GPH					
Water heater, residential, oil glass lined tank, 30 Gal	1.000	Ea.	1,750	430	2,180
Copper tubing, type L, solder joint, hanger 10' O.C. 3/4" diam.	33.000	L.F.	232.65	372.90	605.55
Wrought copper 90° elbow for solder joints 3/4" diam.	5.000	Ea.	35.75	225	260.75
Wrought copper Tee for solder joints, 3/4" diam.	2.000	Ea.	26.30	143	169.30
Wrought copper union for soldered joints, 3/4" diam.	2.000	Ea.	178	96	274
Valve, gate, bronze, 125 lb, NRS, soldered 3/4" diam.	2.000	Ea.	278	86	364
Relief valve, bronze, press & temp, self-close, 3/4" IPS	1.000	Ea.	335	30.50	365.50
Wrought copper adapter, CTS to MPT, 3/4" IPS	1.000	Ea.	18.15	50.50	68.65
Copper tubing, type L, solder joint, hanger 10' OC 3/8" diam.	10.000	L.F.	50.50	102.50	153
Wrought copper 90° elbow for solder joints 3/8" diam.	2.000	Ea.	18	78	96
Valve, globe, fusible, 3/8" diam.	1.000	Ea.	36.50	36	72.50
TOTAL			2,958.85	1,650.40	4,609.25

D2020 230	Oil Fired Water Heaters - Residential Systems		MAT.	INST.	TOTAL
2200	Oil fired water heater, residential, 100°F rise				
2220	30 gallon tank, 103 GPH		2,950	1,650	4,600
2260	50 gallon tank, 145 GPH		3,075	1,850	4,925
2300	70 gallon tank, 164 GPH	R224000 -20	4,525	2,100	6,625
2340	85 gallon tank, 181 GPH		11,700	2,150	13,850

For customer support on your Plumbing Costs with RSMeans data, call 800.448.8182.

D20 Plumbing

D2020 Domestic Water Distribution

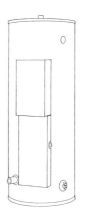

Systems below include piping and fittings within 10' of heater. Electric water heaters do not require venting.

System Components	QUANTITY	UNIT	COST EACH MAT.	COST EACH INST.	COST EACH TOTAL
SYSTEM D2020 240 1820					
ELECTRIC WATER HEATER, COMMERCIAL, 100°F RISE					
50 GALLON TANK, 9 KW, 37 GPH					
Water heater, commercial, electric, 50 Gal, 9 KW, 37 GPH	1.000	Ea.	7,150	480	7,630
Copper tubing, type L, solder joint, hanger 10' OC, 3/4" diam	34.000	L.F.	239.70	384.20	623.90
Wrought copper 90° elbow for solder joints 3/4" diam	5.000	Ea.	35.75	225	260.75
Wrought copper Tee for solder joints, 3/4" diam	2.000	Ea.	26.30	143	169.30
Wrought copper union for soldered joints, 3/4" diam.	2.000	Ea.	178	96	274
Valve, gate, bronze, 125 lb, NRS, soldered 3/4" diam	2.000	Ea.	278	86	364
Relief valve, bronze, press & temp, self-close, 3/4" IPS	1.000	Ea.	335	30.50	365.50
Wrought copper adapter, copper tubing to male, 3/4" IPS	1.000	Ea.	18.15	50.50	68.65
TOTAL			8,260.90	1,495.20	9,756.10

D2020 240	Electric Water Heaters - Commercial Systems		COST EACH MAT.	COST EACH INST.	COST EACH TOTAL
1800	Electric water heater, commercial, 100°F rise				
1820	50 gallon tank, 9 KW 37 GPH		8,250	1,500	9,750
1860	80 gal, 12 KW 49 GPH	R224000-10	10,800	1,850	12,650
1864	50 gal, 9 KW 49 GPH		9,100	1,750	10,850
1900	36 KW 147 GPH	R224000-20	16,100	2,000	18,100
1940	120 gal, 36 KW 147 GPH		17,700	2,150	19,850
1980	150 gal, 120 KW 490 GPH		56,500	2,300	58,800
2020	200 gal, 120 KW 490 GPH		59,000	2,375	61,375
2060	250 gal, 150 KW 615 GPH		57,000	2,750	59,750
2100	300 gal, 180 KW 738 GPH		86,500	2,925	89,425
2140	350 gal, 30 KW 123 GPH		46,300	3,125	49,425
2180	180 KW 738 GPH		64,000	3,125	67,125
2220	500 gal, 30 KW 123 GPH		72,000	3,675	75,675
2260	240 KW 984 GPH		117,000	3,675	120,675
2300	700 gal, 30 KW 123 GPH		72,000	4,225	76,225
2340	300 KW 1230 GPH		106,000	4,225	110,225
2380	1000 gal, 60 KW 245 GPH		88,500	5,900	94,400
2420	480 KW 1970 GPH		141,000	5,900	146,900
2460	1500 gal, 60 KW 245 GPH		127,500	7,275	134,775
2500	480 KW 1970 GPH		173,500	7,275	180,775

D20 Plumbing

D2020 Domestic Water Distribution

Units may be installed in multiples for increased capacity.

Included below is the heater with self-energizing gas controls, safety pilots, insulated jacket, hi-limit aquastat and pressure relief valve.

Installation includes piping and fittings within 10' of heater. Gas heaters require vent piping (not included in these prices).

System Components	QUANTITY	UNIT	COST EACH		
			MAT.	INST.	TOTAL
SYSTEM D2020 250 1780					
GAS FIRED WATER HEATER, COMMERCIAL, 100°F RISE					
75.5 MBH INPUT, 63 GPH					
Water heater, commercial, gas, 75.5 MBH, 63 GPH	1.000	Ea.	3,875	615	4,490
Copper tubing, type L, solder joint, hanger 10' OC, 1-1/4" diam	30.000	L.F.	292.50	444	736.50
Wrought copper 90° elbow for solder joints 1-1/4" diam	4.000	Ea.	104	230	334
Wrought copper tee for solder joints, 1-1/4" diam	2.000	Ea.	109	191	300
Wrought copper union for soldered joints, 1-1/4" diam	2.000	Ea.	456	123	579
Valve, gate, bronze, 125 lb, NRS, soldered 1-1/4" diam	2.000	Ea.	610	115	725
Relief valve, bronze, press & temp, self-close, 3/4" IPS	1.000	Ea.	335	30.50	365.50
Copper tubing, type L, solder joints, 3/4" diam	8.000	L.F.	56.40	90.40	146.80
Wrought copper 90° elbow for solder joints 3/4" diam	1.000	Ea.	7.15	45	52.15
Wrought copper, adapter, CTS to MPT, 3/4" IPS	1.000	Ea.	18.15	50.50	68.65
Pipe steel black, schedule 40, threaded, 3/4" diam	10.000	L.F.	77.50	141	218.50
Pipe, 90° elbow, malleable iron black, 150 lb threaded, 3/4" diam	2.000	Ea.	15.40	123	138.40
Pipe, union with brass seat, malleable iron black, 3/4" diam	1.000	Ea.	34.50	66	100.50
Valve, gas stop w/o check, brass, 3/4" IPS	1.000	Ea.	41	39	80
TOTAL			6,031.60	2,303.40	8,335

D2020 250	Gas Fired Water Heaters - Commercial Systems		COST EACH		
			MAT.	INST.	TOTAL
1760	Gas fired water heater, commercial, 100°F rise				
1780	75.5 MBH input, 63 GPH		6,025	2,300	8,325
1820	95 MBH input, 86 GPH	R224000 -10	11,700	2,300	14,000
1860	100 MBH input, 91 GPH		9,625	2,400	12,025
1900	115 MBH input, 110 GPH		7,675	2,475	10,150
1980	155 MBH input, 150 GPH		9,175	2,775	11,950
2020	175 MBH input, 168 GPH	R224000 -20	14,700	2,975	17,675
2060	200 MBH input, 192 GPH		15,200	3,350	18,550
2100	240 MBH input, 230 GPH		16,200	3,650	19,850
2140	300 MBH input, 278 GPH		12,800	4,175	16,975
2180	390 MBH input, 374 GPH		14,400	4,225	18,625
2220	500 MBH input, 480 GPH		18,600	4,550	23,150
2260	600 MBH input, 576 GPH		34,800	4,925	39,725

D20 Plumbing

D2020 Domestic Water Distribution

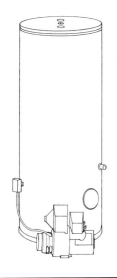

Units may be installed in multiples for increased capacity.

Included below is the heater, wired-in flame retention burners, cadmium cell primary controls, hi-limit controls, ASME pressure relief valves, draft controls, and insulated jacket.

Oil fired water heater systems include piping and fittings within 10' of heater. Oil fired heaters require vent piping (not included in these systems).

System Components	QUANTITY	UNIT	COST EACH		
			MAT.	INST.	TOTAL
SYSTEM D2020 260 1820 OIL FIRED WATER HEATER, COMMERCIAL, 100°F RISE 140 GAL., 140 MBH INPUT, 134 GPH					
Water heater, commercial, oil, 140 gal., 140 MBH input, 134 GPH	1.000	Ea.	26,100	725	26,825
Copper tubing, type L, solder joint, hanger 10' OC, 3/4" diam.	34.000	L.F.	239.70	384.20	623.90
Wrought copper 90° elbow for solder joints 3/4" diam.	5.000	Ea.	35.75	225	260.75
Wrought copper Tee for solder joints, 3/4" diam.	2.000	Ea.	26.30	143	169.30
Wrought copper union for soldered joints, 3/4" diam.	2.000	Ea.	178	96	274
Valve, bronze, 125 lb, NRS, soldered 3/4" diam.	2.000	Ea.	278	86	364
Relief valve, bronze, press & temp, self-close, 3/4" IPS	1.000	Ea.	335	30.50	365.50
Wrought copper adapter, copper tubing to male, 3/4" IPS	1.000	Ea.	18.15	50.50	68.65
Copper tubing, type L, solder joint, hanger 10' OC, 3/8" diam.	10.000	L.F.	50.50	102.50	153
Wrought copper 90° elbow for solder joints 3/8" diam.	2.000	Ea.	18	78	96
Valve, globe, fusible, 3/8" IPS	1.000	Ea.	36.50	36	72.50
TOTAL			27,315.90	1,956.70	29,272.60

D2020 260	Oil Fired Water Heaters - Commercial Systems		COST EACH		
			MAT.	INST.	TOTAL
1800	Oil fired water heater, commercial, 100°F rise				
1820	140 gal., 140 MBH input, 134 GPH		27,300	1,950	29,250
1900	140 gal., 255 MBH input, 247 GPH		29,900	2,450	32,350
1940	140 gal., 270 MBH input, 259 GPH	R224000 -10	36,400	2,825	39,225
1980	140 gal., 400 MBH input, 384 GPH		37,900	3,250	41,150
2060	140 gal., 720 MBH input, 691 GPH	R224000 -20	40,200	3,375	43,575
2100	221 gal., 300 MBH input, 288 GPH		53,500	3,700	57,200
2140	221 gal., 600 MBH input, 576 GPH		68,500	3,750	72,250
2180	221 gal., 800 MBH input, 768 GPH		60,000	3,875	63,875
2220	201 gal., 1000 MBH input, 960 GPH		61,500	3,900	65,400
2260	201 gal., 1250 MBH input, 1200 GPH		63,500	4,025	67,525
2300	201 gal., 1500 MBH input, 1441 GPH		68,000	4,125	72,125
2340	411 gal., 600 MBH input, 576 GPH		68,500	4,225	72,725
2380	411 gal., 800 MBH input, 768 GPH		71,500	4,325	75,825
2420	411 gal., 1000 MBH input, 960 GPH		76,000	5,000	81,000
2460	411 gal., 1250 MBH input, 1200 GPH		77,500	5,125	82,625
2500	397 gal., 1500 MBH input, 1441 GPH		81,500	5,300	86,800

D20 Plumbing

D2020 Domestic Water Distribution

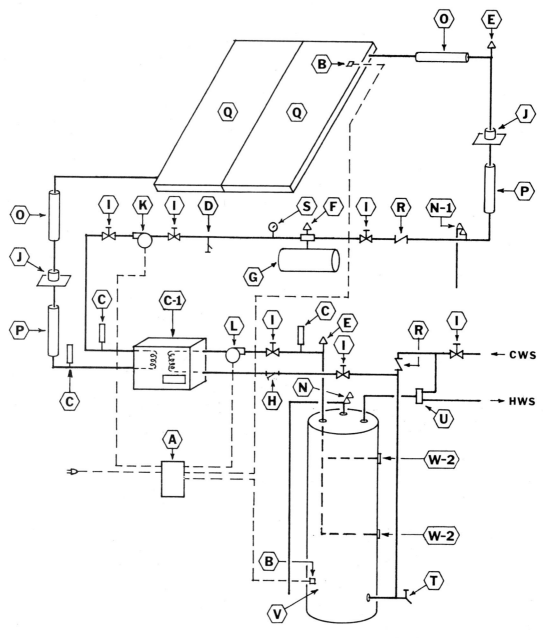

In this closed-loop indirect collection system, fluid with a low freezing temperature, such as propylene glycol, transports heat from the collectors to water storage. The transfer fluid is contained in a closed-loop consisting of collectors, supply and return piping, and a remote heat exchanger. The heat exchanger transfers heat energy from the fluid in the collector loop to potable water circulated in a storage loop. A typical two-or-three panel system contains 5 to 6 gallons of heat transfer fluid.

When the collectors become approximately 20°F warmer than the storage temperature, a controller activates the circulator on the collector and storage loops. The circulators will move the fluid and potable water through the heat exchanger until heat collection no longer occurs. At that point, the system shuts down. Since the heat transfer medium is a fluid with a very low freezing temperature, there is no need for it to be drained from the system between periods of collection.

D20 Plumbing

D2020 Domestic Water Distribution

System Components	QUANTITY	UNIT	COST EACH		
			MAT.	INST.	TOTAL
SYSTEM D2020 265 2760					
SOLAR, CLOSED LOOP, ADD-ON HOT WATER SYS., EXTERNAL HEAT EXCHANGER					
3/4" TUBING, TWO 3'X7' BLACK CHROME COLLECTORS					
A,B,G,L,K,M Heat exchanger fluid-fluid pkg incl 2 circulators, expansion tank,					
Check valve, relief valve, controller, hi temp cutoff, & 2 sensors	1.000	Ea.	870	620	1,490
C Thermometer, 2" dial	3.000	Ea.	75	160.50	235.50
D, T Fill & drain valve, brass, 3/4" connection	1.000	Ea.	21.50	36	57.50
E Air vent, manual, 1/8" fitting	2.000	Ea.	7.32	54	61.32
F Air purger	1.000	Ea.	58	71.50	129.50
H Strainer, Y type, bronze body, 3/4" IPS	1.000	Ea.	85	45.50	130.50
I Valve, gate, bronze, NRS, soldered 3/4" diam	6.000	Ea.	834	258	1,092
J Neoprene vent flashing	2.000	Ea.	24.80	86	110.80
N, N-1 Relief valve temp & press, 150 psi 210°F self-closing 3/4" IPS	1.000	Ea.	29.50	28.50	58
O Pipe covering, urethane, ultraviolet cover, 1" wall 3/4" diam	20.000	L.F.	60.60	157	217.60
P Pipe covering, fiberglass, all service jacket, 1" wall, 3/4" diam	50.000	L.F.	112	312.50	424.50
Q Collector panel solar energy blk chrome on copper, 1/8" temp glass 3'x7'	2.000	Ea.	2,350	326	2,676
Roof clamps for solar energy collector panels	2.000	Set	7.90	44	51.90
R Valve, swing check, bronze, regrinding disc, 3/4" diam	2.000	Ea.	410	86	496
S Pressure gauge, 60 psi, 2" dial	1.000	Ea.	28	27	55
U Valve, water tempering, bronze, sweat connections, 3/4" diam	1.000	Ea.	273	43	316
W-2, V Tank water storage w/heating element, drain, relief valve, existing	1.000	Ea.			
Copper tubing type L, solder joint, hanger 10' OC 3/4" diam	20.000	L.F.	141	226	367
Copper tubing, type M, solder joint, hanger 10' OC 3/4" diam	70.000	L.F.	430.50	770	1,200.50
Sensor wire, #22-2 conductor multistranded	.500	C.L.F.	10.75	40	50.75
Solar energy heat transfer fluid, propylene glycol anti-freeze	6.000	Gal.	168	183	351
Wrought copper fittings & solder, 3/4" diam	76.000	Ea.	543.40	3,420	3,963.40
TOTAL			**6,540.27**	**6,994.50**	**13,534.77**

D2020 265	Solar, Closed Loop, Add-On Hot Water Systems		COST EACH		
			MAT.	INST.	TOTAL
2550	Solar, closed loop, add-on hot water system, external heat exchanger				
2570	3/8" tubing, 3 ea. 4' x 4'-4" vacuum tube collectors		7,125	6,575	13,700
2580	1/2" tubing, 4 ea. 4 x 4'-4" vacuum tube collectors	R235616 -60	7,625	7,100	14,725
2600	2 ea. 3'x7' black chrome collectors		5,775	6,700	12,475
2620	3 ea. 3'x7' black chrome collectors		6,950	6,875	13,825
2640	2 ea. 3'x7' flat black collectors		5,125	6,725	11,850
2660	3 ea. 3'x7' flat black collectors		5,975	6,900	12,875
2700	3/4" tubing, 3 ea. 3'x7' black chrome collectors		7,725	7,175	14,900
2720	3 ea. 3'x7' flat black absorber plate collectors		6,725	7,200	13,925
2740	2 ea. 4'x9' flat black w/plastic glazing collectors		6,250	7,225	13,475
2760	2 ea. 3'x7' black chrome collectors		6,550	7,000	13,550
2780	1" tubing, 4 ea 2'x9' plastic absorber & glazing collectors		8,100	8,125	16,225
2800	4 ea. 3'x7' black chrome absorber collectors		10,200	8,175	18,375
2820	4 ea. 3'x7' flat black absorber collectors		8,900	8,200	17,100

D20 Plumbing

D2020 Domestic Water Distribution

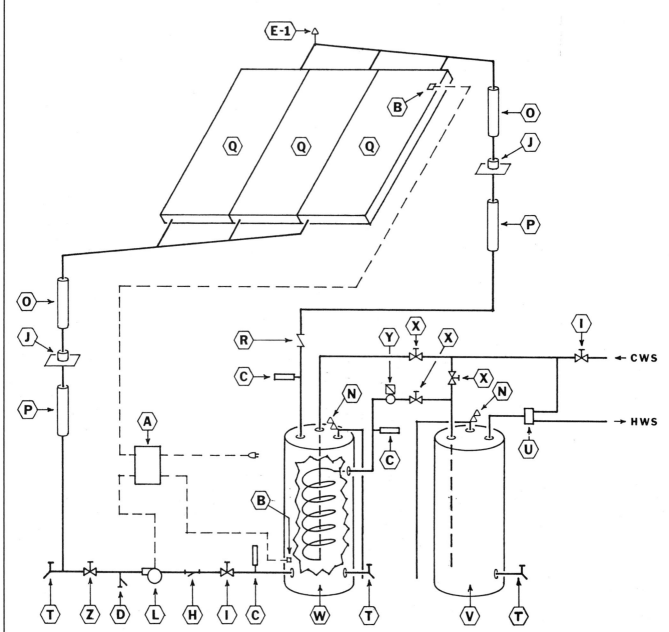

In the drainback indirect-collection system, the heat transfer fluid is distilled water contained in a loop consisting of collectors, supply and return piping, and an unpressurized holding tank. A large heat exchanger containing incoming potable water is immersed in the holding tank. When a controller activates solar collection, the distilled water is pumped through the collectors and heated and pumped back down to the holding tank. When the temperature differential between the water in the collectors and water in storage is such that collection no longer occurs, the pump turns off and gravity causes the distilled water in the collector loop to drain back to the holding tank. All the loop piping is pitched so that the water can drain out of the collectors and piping and not freeze there. As hot water is needed in the home, incoming water first flows through the holding tank with the immersed heat exchanger and is warmed and then flows through a conventional heater for any supplemental heating that is necessary.

D20 Plumbing

D2020 Domestic Water Distribution

System Components	QUANTITY	UNIT	COST EACH		
			MAT.	INST.	TOTAL
SYSTEM D2020 270 2760					
SOLAR, DRAINBACK, ADD ON, HOT WATER, IMMERSED HEAT EXCHANGER					
3/4" TUBING, THREE EA 3'X7' BLACK CHROME COLLECTOR					
A, B Differential controller 2 sensors, thermostat, solar energy system	1.000	Ea.	258	71.50	329.50
C Thermometer 2" dial	3.000	Ea.	75	160.50	235.50
D, T Fill & drain valve, brass, 3/4" connection	1.000	Ea.	21.50	36	57.50
E-1 Automatic air vent 1/8" fitting	1.000	Ea.	17.70	27	44.70
H Strainer, Y type, bronze body, 3/4" IPS	1.000	Ea.	85	45.50	130.50
I Valve, gate, bronze, NRS, soldered 3/4" diam	2.000	Ea.	278	86	364
J Neoprene vent flashing	2.000	Ea.	24.80	86	110.80
L Circulator, solar heated liquid, 1/20 HP	1.000	Ea.	340	129	469
N Relief valve temp. & press. 150 psi 210°F self-closing 3/4" IPS	1.000	Ea.	29.50	28.50	58
O Pipe covering, urethane, ultraviolet cover, 1" wall, 3/4" diam	20.000	L.F.	60.60	157	217.60
P Pipe covering, fiberglass, all service jacket, 1" wall, 3/4" diam	50.000	L.F.	112	312.50	424.50
Q Collector panel solar energy blk chrome on copper, 1/8" temp glas 3'x7'	3.000	Ea.	3,525	489	4,014
Roof clamps for solar energy collector panels	3.000	Set	11.85	66	77.85
R Valve, swing check, bronze, regrinding disc, 3/4" diam	1.000	Ea.	205	43	248
U Valve, water tempering, bronze sweat connections, 3/4" diam	1.000	Ea.	273	43	316
V Tank, water storage w/heating element, drain, relief valve, existing	1.000	Ea.			
W Tank, water storage immersed heat exchr elec 2"x1/2# insul 120 gal	1.000	Ea.	1,925	615	2,540
X Valve, globe, bronze, rising stem, 3/4" diam, soldered	3.000	Ea.	792	129	921
Y Flow control valve	1.000	Ea.	158	39	197
Z Valve, ball, bronze, solder 3/4" diam, solar loop flow control	1.000	Ea.	38.50	43	81.50
Copper tubing, type L, solder joint, hanger 10' OC 3/4" diam	20.000	L.F.	141	226	367
Copper tubing, type M, solder joint, hanger 10' OC 3/4" diam	70.000	L.F.	430.50	770	1,200.50
Sensor wire, #22-2 conductor, multistranded	.500	C.L.F.	10.75	40	50.75
Wrought copper fittings & solder, 3/4" diam	76.000	Ea.	543.40	3,420	3,963.40
TOTAL			9,356.10	7,062.50	16,418.60

D2020 270	Solar, Drainback, Hot Water Systems	COST EACH		
		MAT.	INST.	TOTAL
2550	Solar, drainback, hot water, immersed heat exchanger			
2560	3/8" tubing, 3 ea. 4' x 4'-4" vacuum tube collectors	8,825	6,375	15,200
2580	1/2" tubing, 4 ea 4' x 4'-4" vacuum tube collectors, 80 gal tank	9,250	6,925	16,175
2600	120 gal tank	9,175	7,000	16,175
2640	2 ea. 3'x7' blk chrome collectors, 80 gal tank	7,375	6,500	13,875
2660	3 ea. 3'x7' blk chrome collectors, 120 gal tank	8,475	6,775	15,250
2700	2 ea. 3'x7' flat blk collectors, 120 gal tank	6,650	6,600	13,250
2720	3 ea. 3'x7' flat blk collectors, 120 gal tank	7,500	6,800	14,300
2760	3/4" tubing, 3 ea 3'x7' black chrome collectors, 120 gal tank	9,350	7,075	16,425
2780	3 ea. 3'x7' flat black absorber collectors, 120 gal tank	8,375	7,100	15,475
2800	2 ea. 4'x9' flat blk w/plastic glazing collectors 120 gal tank	7,875	7,125	15,000
2840	1" tubing, 4 ea. 2'x9' plastic absorber & glazing collectors, 120 gal tank	10,000	8,025	18,025
2860	4 ea. 3'x7' black chrome absorber collectors, 120 gal tank	12,100	8,050	20,150
2880	4 ea. 3'x7' flat black absorber collectors, 120 gal tank	10,800	8,075	18,875

Reference: R235616-60 (at row 2580)

D20 Plumbing

D2020 Domestic Water Distribution

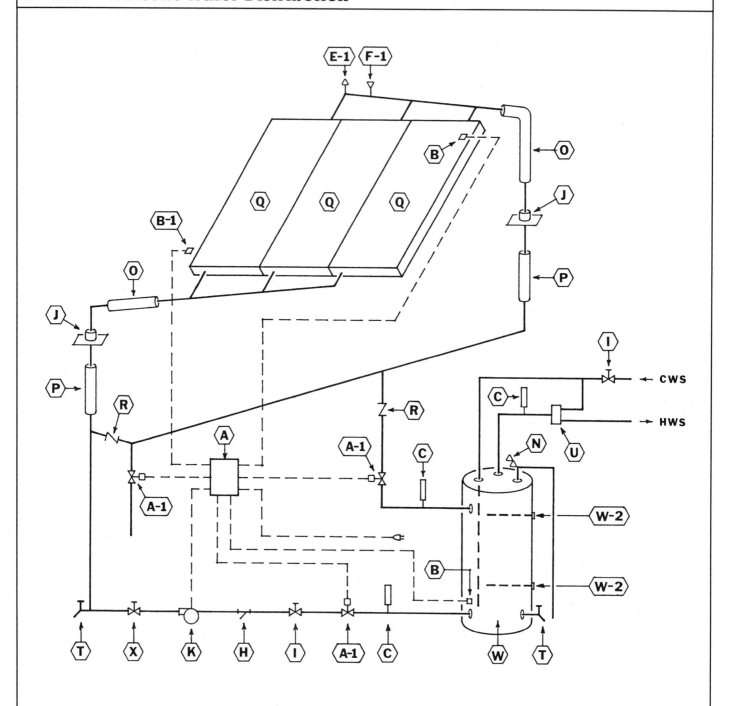

In the draindown direct-collection system, incoming domestic water is heated in the collectors. When the controller activates solar collection, domestic water is first heated as it flows through the collectors and is then pumped to storage. When conditions are no longer suitable for heat collection, the pump shuts off and the water in the loop drains down and out of the system by means of solenoid valves and properly pitched piping.

D20 Plumbing

D2020 Domestic Water Distribution

System Components	QUANTITY	UNIT	COST EACH		
			MAT.	INST.	TOTAL
SYSTEM D2020 275 2760					
SOLAR, DRAINDOWN, HOT WATER, DIRECT COLLECTION					
3/4" TUBING, THREE 3'X7' BLACK CHROME COLLECTORS					
A, B Differential controller, 2 sensors, thermostat, solar energy system	1.000	Ea.	258	71.50	329.50
A-1 Solenoid valve, solar heating loop, brass, 3/4" diam, 24 volts	3.000	Ea.	576	286.50	862.50
B-1 Solar energy sensor, freeze prevention	1.000	Ea.	29	27	56
C Thermometer, 2" dial	3.000	Ea.	75	160.50	235.50
E-1 Vacuum relief valve, 3/4" diam	1.000	Ea.	34.50	27	61.50
F-1 Air vent, automatic, 1/8" fitting	1.000	Ea.	17.70	27	44.70
H Strainer, Y type, bronze body, 3/4" IPS	1.000	Ea.	85	45.50	130.50
I Valve, gate, bronze, NRS, soldered, 3/4" diam	2.000	Ea.	278	86	364
J Vent flashing neoprene	2.000	Ea.	24.80	86	110.80
K Circulator, solar heated liquid, 1/25 HP	1.000	Ea.	231	111	342
N Relief valve temp & press 150 psi 210°F self-closing 3/4" IPS	1.000	Ea.	29.50	28.50	58
O Pipe covering, urethane, ultraviolet cover, 1" wall, 3/4" diam	20.000	L.F.	60.60	157	217.60
P Pipe covering, fiberglass, all service jacket, 1" wall, 3/4" diam	50.000	L.F.	112	312.50	424.50
Roof clamps for solar energy collector panels	3.000	Set	11.85	66	77.85
Q Collector panel solar energy blk chrome on copper, 1/8" temp glass 3'x7'	3.000	Ea.	3,525	489	4,014
R Valve, swing check, bronze, regrinding disc, 3/4" diam, soldered	2.000	Ea.	410	86	496
T Drain valve, brass, 3/4" connection	2.000	Ea.	43	72	115
U Valve, water tempering, bronze, sweat connections, 3/4" diam	1.000	Ea.	273	43	316
W, W-2 Tank, water storage elec elem 2"x1/2# insul 120 gal	1.000	Ea.	1,925	615	2,540
X Valve, globe, bronze, rising stem, 3/4" diam, soldered	1.000	Ea.	264	43	307
Copper tubing, type L, solder joints, hangers 10' OC 3/4" diam	20.000	L.F.	141	226	367
Copper tubing, type M, solder joints, hangers 10' OC 3/4" diam	70.000	L.F.	430.50	770	1,200.50
Sensor wire, #22-2 conductor, multistranded	.500	C.L.F.	10.75	40	50.75
Wrought copper fittings & solder, 3/4" diam	76.000	Ea.	543.40	3,420	3,963.40
TOTAL			9,388.60	7,296	16,684.60

D2020 275	Solar, Draindown, Hot Water Systems		COST EACH		
			MAT.	INST.	TOTAL
2550	Solar, draindown, hot water				
2560	3/8" tubing, 3 ea. 4' x 4'-4" vacuum tube collectors, 80 gal tank		8,300	6,975	15,275
2580	1/2" tubing, 4 ea. 4' x 4'-4" vacuum tube collectors, 80 gal tank		9,350	7,150	16,500
2600	120 gal tank	R235616-60	9,275	7,250	16,525
2640	2 ea. 3'x7' black chrome collectors, 80 gal tank		7,500	6,750	14,250
2660	3 ea. 3'x7' black chrome collectors, 120 gal tank		8,600	7,025	15,625
2700	2 ea. 3'x7' flat black collectors, 120 gal tank		6,775	6,850	13,625
2720	3 ea. 3'x7' flat black collectors, 120 gal tank		7,475	7,000	14,475
2760	3/4" tubing, 3 ea. 3'x7' black chrome collectors, 120 gal tank		9,400	7,300	16,700
2780	3 ea. 3'x7' flat collectors, 120 gal tank		8,400	7,325	15,725
2800	2 ea. 4'x9' flat black & plastic glazing collectors, 120 gal tank		7,900	7,350	15,250
2840	1" tubing, 4 ea. 2'x9' plastic absorber & glazing collectors, 120 gal tank		13,700	9,700	23,400
2860	4 ea. 3'x7' black chrome absorber collectors, 120 gal tank		13,300	9,175	22,475
2880	4 ea. 3'x7' flat black absorber collectors, 120 gal tank		10,800	8,325	19,125

D20 Plumbing

D2020 Domestic Water Distribution

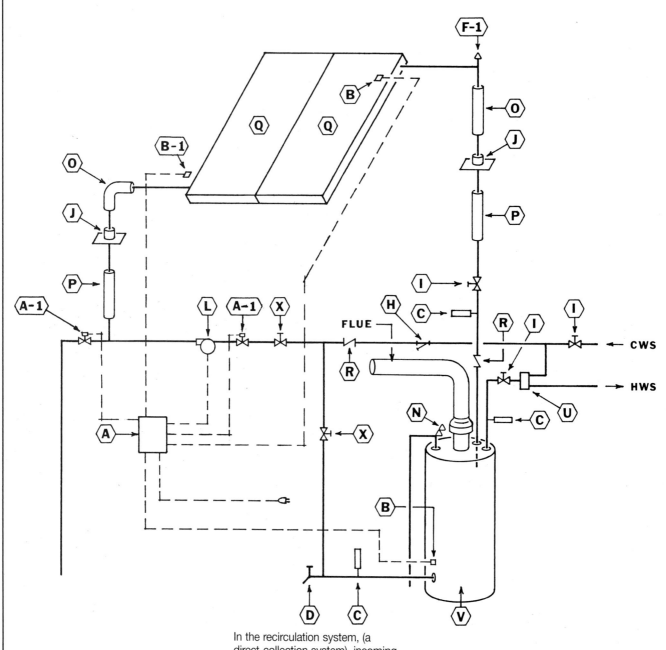

In the recirculation system, (a direct-collection system), incoming domestic water is heated in the collectors. When the controller activates solar collection, domestic water is heated as it flows through the collectors and then it flows back to storage. When conditions are not suitable for heat collection, the pump shuts off and the flow of the water stops. In this type of system, water remains in the collector loop at all times. A "frost sensor" at the collector activates the circulation of warm water from storage through the collectors when protection from freezing is required.

D20 Plumbing

D2020 Domestic Water Distribution

System Components	QUANTITY	UNIT	MAT.	INST.	TOTAL
SYSTEM D2020 280 2820					
SOLAR, RECIRCULATION, HOT WATER					
3/4" TUBING, TWO 3'X7' BLACK CHROME COLLECTORS					
A, B Differential controller 2 sensors, thermostat, for solar energy system	1.000	Ea.	258	71.50	329.50
A-1 Solenoid valve, solar heating loop, brass, 3/4" IPS, 24 volts	2.000	Ea.	384	191	575
B-1 Solar energy sensor freeze prevention	1.000	Ea.	29	27	56
C Thermometer, 2" dial	3.000	Ea.	75	160.50	235.50
D Drain valve, brass, 3/4" connection	1.000	Ea.	21.50	36	57.50
F-1 Air vent, automatic, 1/8" fitting	1.000	Ea.	17.70	27	44.70
H Strainer, Y type, bronze body, 3/4" IPS	1.000	Ea.	85	45.50	130.50
I Valve, gate, bronze, 125 lb, soldered 3/4" diam	3.000	Ea.	417	129	546
J Vent flashing, neoprene	2.000	Ea.	24.80	86	110.80
L Circulator, solar heated liquid, 1/20 HP	1.000	Ea.	340	129	469
N Relief valve, temp & press 150 psi 210° F self-closing 3/4" IPS	2.000	Ea.	59	57	116
O Pipe covering, urethane, ultraviolet cover, 1" wall, 3/4" diam	20.000	L.F.	60.60	157	217.60
P Pipe covering, fiberglass, all service jacket, 1" wall 3/4" diam	50.000	L.F.	112	312.50	424.50
Q Collector panel solar energy blk chrome on copper, 1/8" temp glass 3'x7'	2.000	Ea.	2,350	326	2,676
Roof clamps for solar energy collector panels	2.000	Set	7.90	44	51.90
R Valve, swing check, bronze, 125 lb, regrinding disc, soldered 3/4" diam	2.000	Ea.	410	86	496
U Valve, water tempering, bronze, sweat connections, 3/4" diam	1.000	Ea.	273	43	316
V Tank, water storage, w/heating element, drain, relief valve, existing	1.000	Ea.			
X Valve, globe, bronze, 125 lb, 3/4" diam	2.000	Ea.	528	86	614
Copper tubing, type L, solder joints, hangers 10' OC 3/4" diam	20.000	L.F.	141	226	367
Copper tubing, type M, solder joints, hangers 10' OC 3/4" diam	70.000	L.F.	430.50	770	1,200.50
Wrought copper fittings & solder, 3/4" diam	76.000	Ea.	543.40	3,420	3,963.40
Sensor wire, #22-2 conductor, multistranded	.500	C.L.F.	10.75	40	50.75
TOTAL			6,578.15	6,470	13,048.15

D2020 280	Solar, Recirculation, Domestic Hot Water Systems		MAT.	INST.	TOTAL
2550	Solar, recirculation, hot water				
2560	3/8" tubing, 3 ea. 4' x 4'-4" vacuum tube collectors		7,150	6,050	13,200
2580	1/2" tubing, 4 ea. 4' x 4'-4" vacuum tube collectors	R235616 -60	7,575	6,575	14,150
2640	2 ea. 3'x7' black chrome collectors		5,725	6,175	11,900
2660	3 ea. 3'x7' black chrome collectors		6,900	6,375	13,275
2700	2 ea. 3'x7' flat black collectors		5,050	6,200	11,250
2720	3 ea. 3'x7' flat black collectors		5,900	6,400	12,300
2760	3/4" tubing, 3 ea. 3'x7' black chrome collectors		7,750	6,650	14,400
2780	3 ea. 3'x7' flat black absorber plate collectors		6,775	6,675	13,450
2800	2 ea. 4'x9' flat black w/plastic glazing collectors		6,275	6,700	12,975
2820	2 ea. 3'x7' black chrome collectors		6,575	6,475	13,050
2840	1" tubing, 4 ea. 2'x9' black plastic absorber & glazing collectors		8,550	7,600	16,150
2860	4 ea. 3'x7' black chrome absorber collectors		10,700	7,650	18,350
2880	4 ea. 3'x7' flat black absorber collectors		9,350	7,675	17,025

D20 Plumbing

D2020 Domestic Water Distribution

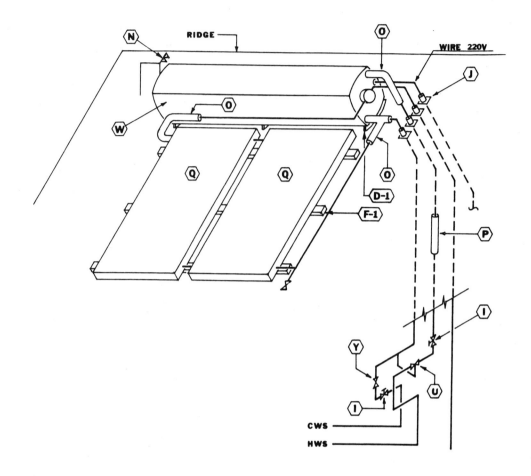

The thermosyphon domestic hot water system, a direct collection system, operates under city water pressure and does not require pumps for system operation. An insulated water storage tank is located above the collectors. As the sun heats the collectors, warm water in them rises by means of natural convection; the colder water in the storage tank flows into the collectors by means of gravity. As long as the sun is shining the water continues to flow through the collectors and to become warmer.

To prevent freezing, the system must be drained or the collectors covered with an insulated lid when the temperature drops below 32°F.

D20 Plumbing

D2020 Domestic Water Distribution

System Components	QUANTITY	UNIT	COST EACH		
			MAT.	INST.	TOTAL
SYSTEM D2020 285 0960					
SOLAR, THERMOSYPHON, WATER HEATER					
3/4" TUBING, TWO 3'X7' BLACK CHROME COLLECTORS					
D-1 Framing lumber, fir, 2" x 6" x 8', tank cradle	.008	M.B.F.	16.40	9	25.40
F-1 Framing lumber, fir, 2" x 4" x 24', sleepers	.016	M.B.F.	30	26.80	56.80
I Valve, gate, bronze, 125 lb, soldered 1/2" diam	2.000	Ea.	254	72	326
J Vent flashing, neoprene	4.000	Ea.	49.60	172	221.60
O Pipe covering, urethane, ultraviolet cover, 1" wall, 1/2"diam	40.000	L.F.	95.20	308	403.20
P Pipe covering fiberglass all service jacket 1" wall 1/2" diam	160.000	L.F.	328	960	1,288
Q Collector panel solar, blk chrome on copper, 3/16" temp glass 3'-6" x 7.5'	2.000	Ea.	1,690	344	2,034
Y Flow control valve, globe, bronze, 125#, soldered, 1/2" diam	1.000	Ea.	198	36	234
U Valve, water tempering, bronze, sweat connections, 1/2" diam	1.000	Ea.	166	36	202
W Tank, water storage, solar energy system, 80 Gal, 2" x 1/2 lb insul	1.000	Ea.	2,000	535	2,535
Copper tubing type L, solder joints, hangers 10' OC 1/2" diam	150.000	L.F.	810	1,590	2,400
Copper tubing type M, solder joints, hangers 10' OC 1/2" diam	50.000	L.F.	243	512.50	755.50
Sensor wire, #22-2 gauge multistranded	.500	C.L.F.	10.75	40	50.75
Wrought copper fittings & solder, 1/2" diam	75.000	Ea.	243.75	3,225	3,468.75
TOTAL			6,134.70	7,866.30	14,001

D2020 285	Thermosyphon, Hot Water		COST EACH		
			MAT.	INST.	TOTAL
0960	Solar, thermosyphon, hot water, two collector system	R235616-60	6,125	7,875	14,000
0970					

D20 Plumbing

D2020 Domestic Water Distribution

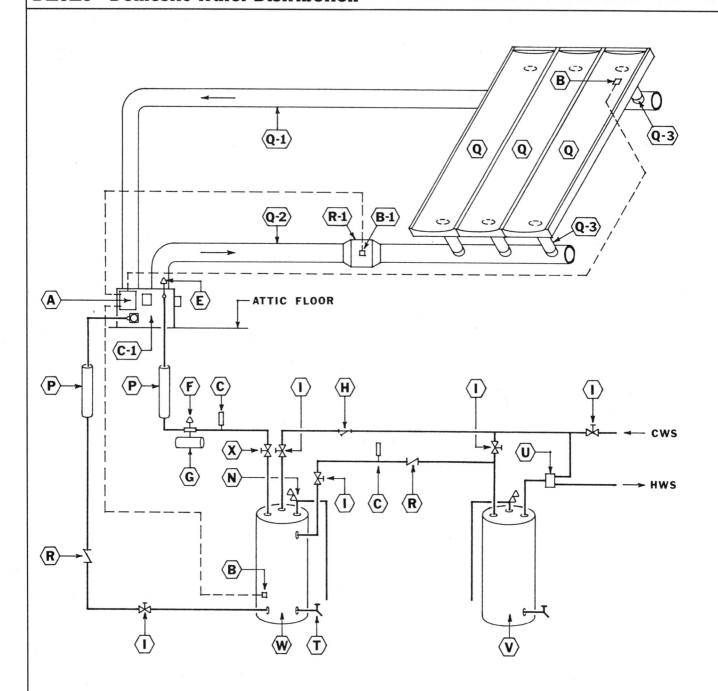

This domestic hot water pre-heat system includes heat exchanger with a circulating pump, blower, air-to-water, coil and controls, mounted in the upper collector manifold. Heat from the hot air coming out of the collectors is transferred through the heat exchanger. For each degree of DHW preheating gained, one degree less heating is needed from the fuel fired water heater. The system is simple, inexpensive to operate and can provide a substantial portion of DHW requirements for modest additional cost.

D20 Plumbing

D2020 Domestic Water Distribution

System Components	QUANTITY	UNIT	COST EACH		
			MAT.	INST.	TOTAL
SYSTEM D2020 290 2560					
SOLAR, HOT WATER, AIR TO WATER HEAT EXCHANGE					
THREE COLLECTORS, OPTICAL BLACK ON ALUM., 7.5' x 3.5', 80 GAL TANK					
A, B Differential controller, 2 sensors, thermostat, solar energy system	1.000	Ea.	258	71.50	329.50
C Thermometer, 2" dial	2.000	Ea.	50	107	157
C-1 Heat exchanger, air to fluid, up flow 70 MBH	1.000	Ea.	420	440	860
E Air vent, manual, for solar energy system 1/8" fitting	1.000	Ea.	3.66	27	30.66
F Air purger	1.000	Ea.	58	71.50	129.50
G Expansion tank	1.000	Ea.	72.50	27	99.50
H Strainer, Y type, bronze body, 1/2" IPS	1.000	Ea.	57.50	43.50	101
I Valve, gate, bronze, 125 lb, NRS, soldered 1/2" diam	5.000	Ea.	635	180	815
N Relief valve, temp & pressure solar 150 psi 210°F self-closing	1.000	Ea.	29.50	28.50	58
P Pipe covering, fiberglass, all service jacket, 1" wall, 1/2" diam	60.000	L.F.	123	360	483
Q Collector panel solar energy, air, black on alum plate, 7.5' x 3.5'	3.000	Ea.	2,535	516	3,051
B-1, R-1 Shutter damper for solar heater circulator	1.000	Ea.	65.50	127	192.50
B-1, R-1 Shutter motor for solar heater circulator	1.000	Ea.	163	95	258
R Backflow preventer, 1/2" pipe size	2.000	Ea.	197	107	304
T Drain valve, brass, 3/4" connection	1.000	Ea.	21.50	36	57.50
U Valve, water tempering, bronze, sweat connections, 1/2" diam	1.000	Ea.	166	36	202
W Tank, water storage, solar energy system, 80 Gal, 2" x 2 lb insul	1.000	Ea.	2,000	535	2,535
V Tank, water storage, w/heating element, drain, relief valve, existing	1.000	System			
X Valve, globe, bronze, 125 lb, rising stem, 1/2" diam	1.000	Ea.	198	36	234
Copper tubing type M, solder joints, hangers 10' OC, 1/2" diam	50.000	L.F.	243	512.50	755.50
Copper tubing type L, solder joints, hangers 10' OC 1/2" diam	10.000	L.F.	54	106	160
Wrought copper fittings & solder, 1/2" diam	10.000	Ea.	32.50	430	462.50
Sensor wire, #22-2 conductor multistranded	.500	C.L.F.	10.75	40	50.75
Q-1, Q-2 Ductwork, fiberglass, aluminized jacket, 1-1/2" thick, 8" diam	32.000	S.F.	332.80	270.40	603.20
Q-3 Manifold for flush mount solar energy collector panels, air	6.000	L.F.	1,002	57	1,059
TOTAL			8,728.21	4,259.90	12,988.11

D2020 290	Solar, Hot Water, Air To Water Heat Exchange		COST EACH		
			MAT.	INST.	TOTAL
2550	Solar, hot water, air to water heat exchange				
2560	Three collectors, optical black on aluminum, 7.5' x 3.5', 80 Gal tank		8,725	4,250	12,975
2580	Four collectors, optical black on aluminum, 7.5' x 3.5', 80 Gal tank	R235616 -60	9,975	4,500	14,475
2600	Four collectors, optical black on aluminum, 7.5' x 3.5', 120 Gal tank		9,900	4,600	14,500

D20 Plumbing

D2020 Domestic Water Distribution

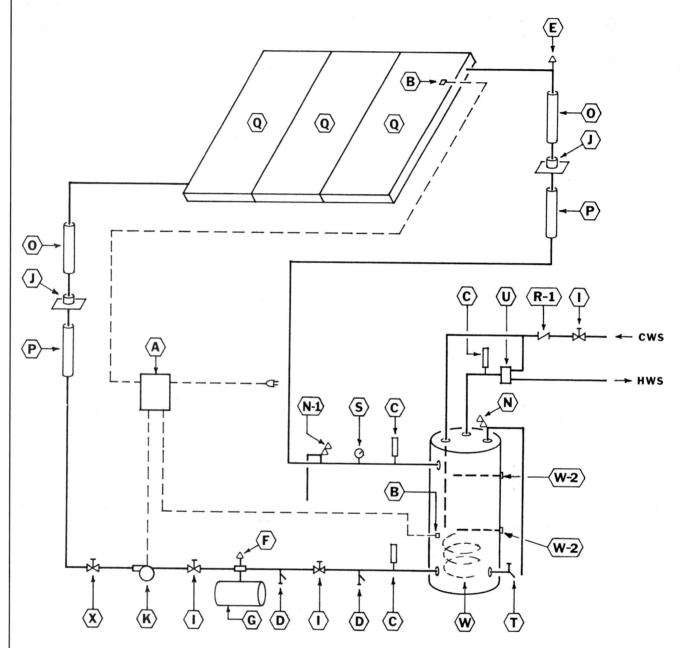

In this closed-loop indirect collection system, fluid with a low freezing temperature, such as propylene glycol, transports heat from the collectors to water storage. The transfer fluid is contained in a closed-loop consisting of collectors, supply and return piping, and a heat exchanger immersed in the storage tank. A typical two-or-three panel system contains 5 to 6 gallons of heat transfer fluid.

When the collectors become approximately 20°F warmer than the storage temperature, a controller activates the circulator. The circulator moves the fluid continuously through the collectors until the temperature difference between the collectors and storage is such that heat collection no longer occurs; at that point, the circulator shuts off. Since the heat transfer fluid has a very low freezing temperature, there is no need for it to be drained from the collectors between periods of collection.

D20 Plumbing

D2020 Domestic Water Distribution

System Components	QUANTITY	UNIT	COST EACH		
			MAT.	INST.	TOTAL
SYSTEM D2020 295 2760 **SOLAR, CLOSED LOOP, HOT WATER SYSTEM, IMMERSED HEAT EXCHANGER** **3/4" TUBING, THREE 3' X 7' BLACK CHROME COLLECTORS**					
A, B Differential controller, 2 sensors, thermostat, solar energy system	1.000	Ea.	258	71.50	329.50
C Thermometer 2" dial	3.000	Ea.	75	160.50	235.50
A, D, T Fill & drain valves, brass, 3/4" connection	3.000	Ea.	64.50	108	172.50
E Air vent, manual, 1/8" fitting	1.000	Ea.	3.66	27	30.66
F Air purger	1.000	Ea.	58	71.50	129.50
G Expansion tank	1.000	Ea.	72.50	27	99.50
I Valve, gate, bronze, NRS, soldered 3/4" diam	3.000	Ea.	417	129	546
J Neoprene vent flashing	2.000	Ea.	24.80	86	110.80
K Circulator, solar heated liquid, 1/25 HP	1.000	Ea.	231	111	342
N, N-1 Relief valve, temp & press 150 psi 210°F self-closing 3/4" IPS	2.000	Ea.	59	57	116
O Pipe covering, urethane ultraviolet cover, 1" wall, 3/4" diam	20.000	L.F.	60.60	157	217.60
P Pipe covering, fiberglass, all service jacket, 1" wall, 3/4" diam	50.000	L.F.	112	312.50	424.50
Roof clamps for solar energy collector panel	3.000	Set	11.85	66	77.85
Q Collector panel solar blk chrome on copper, 1/8" temp glass, 3'x7'	3.000	Ea.	3,525	489	4,014
R-1 Valve, swing check, bronze, regrinding disc, 3/4" diam, soldered	1.000	Ea.	205	43	248
S Pressure gauge, 60 psi, 2-1/2" dial	1.000	Ea.	28	27	55
U Valve, water tempering, bronze, sweat connections, 3/4" diam	1.000	Ea.	273	43	316
W, W-2 Tank, water storage immersed heat exchr elec elem 2"x2# insul 120 Gal	1.000	Ea.	1,925	615	2,540
X Valve, globe, bronze, rising stem, 3/4" diam, soldered	1.000	Ea.	264	43	307
Copper tubing type L, solder joint, hanger 10' OC 3/4" diam	20.000	L.F.	141	226	367
Copper tubing, type M, solder joint, hanger 10' OC 3/4" diam	70.000	L.F.	430.50	770	1,200.50
Sensor wire, #22-2 conductor multistranded	.500	C.L.F.	10.75	40	50.75
Solar energy heat transfer fluid, propylene glycol, anti-freeze	6.000	Gal.	168	183	351
Wrought copper fittings & solder, 3/4" diam	76.000	Ea.	543.40	3,420	3,963.40
TOTAL			8,961.56	7,283	16,244.56

D2020 295	Solar, Closed Loop, Hot Water Systems		COST EACH		
			MAT.	INST.	TOTAL
2550	Solar, closed loop, hot water system, immersed heat exchanger				
2560	3/8" tubing, 3 ea. 4' x 4'-4" vacuum tube collectors, 80 gal. tank		8,525	6,625	15,150
2580	1/2" tubing, 4 ea. 4' x 4'-4" vacuum tube collectors, 80 gal. tank		9,000	7,150	16,150
2600	120 gal. tank		8,925	7,225	16,150
2640	2 ea. 3'x7' black chrome collectors, 80 gal. tank	R235616 -60	7,175	6,825	14,000
2660	120 gal. tank		7,075	6,825	13,900
2700	2 ea. 3'x7' flat black collectors, 120 gal. tank		6,400	6,850	13,250
2720	3 ea. 3'x7' flat black collectors, 120 gal. tank		7,250	7,025	14,275
2760	3/4" tubing, 3 ea. 3'x7' black chrome collectors, 120 gal. tank		8,950	7,275	16,225
2780	3 ea. 3'x7' flat black collectors, 120 gal. tank		7,975	7,300	15,275
2800	2 ea. 4'x9' flat black w/plastic glazing collectors 120 gal. tank		7,475	7,325	14,800
2840	1" tubing, 4 ea. 2'x9' plastic absorber & glazing collectors 120 gal. tank		9,250	8,200	17,450
2860	4 ea. 3'x7' black chrome collectors, 120 gal. tank		11,400	8,225	19,625
2880	4 ea. 3'x7' flat black absorber collectors, 120 gal. tank		10,000	8,275	18,275

D20 Plumbing

D2040 Rain Water Drainage

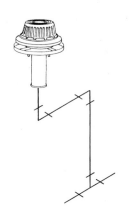

Design Assumptions: Vertical conductor size is based on a maximum rate of rainfall of 4" per hour. To convert roof area to other rates multiply "Max. S.F. Roof Area" shown by four and divide the result by desired local rate. The answer is the local roof area that may be handled by the indicated pipe diameter.

Basic cost is for roof drain, 10' of vertical leader and 10' of horizontal, plus connection to the main.

Pipe Dia.	Max. S.F. Roof Area	Gallons per Min.
2"	544	23
3"	1610	67
4"	3460	144
5"	6280	261
6"	10,200	424
8"	22,000	913

System Components	QUANTITY	UNIT	COST EACH		
			MAT.	INST.	TOTAL
SYSTEM D2040 210 1880					
ROOF DRAIN, DWV PVC PIPE, 2" DIAM., 10' HIGH					
Drain, roof, main, ABS, dome type 2" pipe size	1.000	Ea.	177	111	288
Clamp, roof drain, underdeck	1.000	Ea.	66	64.50	130.50
Pipe, Tee, PVC DWV, schedule 40, 2" pipe size	1.000	Ea.	43	77.50	120.50
Pipe, PVC, DWV, schedule 40, 2" diam.	20.000	L.F.	134	520	654
Pipe, elbow, PVC schedule 40, 2" diam.	2.000	Ea.	11.80	85	96.80
TOTAL			431.80	858	1,289.80

D2040 210	Roof Drain Systems	COST EACH		
		MAT.	INST.	TOTAL
1880	Roof drain, DWV PVC, 2" diam., piping, 10' high	430	860	1,290
1920	For each additional foot add	6.70	26	32.70
1960	3" diam., 10' high	695	1,000	1,695
2000	For each additional foot add	14.15	29	43.15
2040	4" diam., 10' high	930	1,125	2,055
2080	For each additional foot add	19.80	32	51.80
2120	5" diam., 10' high	2,050	1,300	3,350
2160	For each additional foot add	34.50	36	70.50
2200	6" diam., 10' high	2,800	1,450	4,250
2240	For each additional foot add	52.50	39.50	92
2280	8" diam., 10' high	5,100	2,450	7,550
2320	For each additional foot add	76.50	50	126.50
3940	C.I., soil, single hub, service wt., 2" diam. piping, 10' high	745	940	1,685
3980	For each additional foot add	8.65	24.50	33.15
4120	3" diam., 10' high	1,075	1,025	2,100
4160	For each additional foot add	11.95	26	37.95
4200	4" diam., 10' high	1,600	1,100	2,700
4240	For each additional foot add	15.40	28	43.40
4280	5" diam., 10' high	2,325	1,225	3,550
4320	For each additional foot add	43.50	31.50	75
4360	6" diam., 10' high	2,375	1,325	3,700
4400	For each additional foot add	26	33	59
4440	8" diam., 10' high	4,975	2,675	7,650
4480	For each additional foot add	50.50	55.50	106
6040	Steel galv. sch 40 threaded, 2" diam. piping, 10' high	1,200	910	2,110
6080	For each additional foot add	26.50	24	50.50
6120	3" diam., 10' high	2,400	1,325	3,725
6160	For each additional foot add	56	36	92

D20 Plumbing

D2040 Rain Water Drainage

D2040 210	Roof Drain Systems	COST EACH		
		MAT.	INST.	TOTAL
6200	4" diam., 10' high	3,825	1,700	5,525
6240	For each additional foot add	84	43	127
6280	5" diam., 10' high	3,000	1,400	4,400
6320	For each additional foot add	43	42	85
6360	6" diam, 10' high	3,825	1,825	5,650
6400	For each additional foot add	57	57.50	114.50
6440	8" diam, 10' high	6,875	2,625	9,500
6480	For each additional foot add	86	65	151

D30 HVAC

D3010 Energy Supply

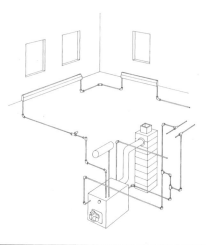

Basis for Heat Loss Estimate, Apartment Type Structures:

1. Masonry walls and flat roof are insulated. U factor is assumed at .08.
2. Window glass area taken as BOCA minimum, 1/10th of floor area. Double insulating glass with 1/4" air space, U = .65.
3. Infiltration = 0.3 C.F. per hour per S.F. of net wall.
4. Concrete floor loss is 2 BTUH per S.F.
5. Temperature difference taken as 70°F.
6. Ventilating or makeup air has not been included and must be added if desired. Air shafts are not used.

System Components	QUANTITY	UNIT	COST EACH MAT.	COST EACH INST.	COST EACH TOTAL
SYSTEM D3010 510 1760					
HEATING SYSTEM, FIN TUBE RADIATION, FORCED HOT WATER					
1,000 S.F. AREA, 10,000 C.F. VOLUME					
Boiler, oil fired, CI, burner, ctrls/insul/breech/pipe/ftng/valves, 109 MBH	1.000	Ea.	4,812.50	4,812.50	9,625
Circulating pump, CI flange connection, 1/12 HP	1.000	Ea.	680	258	938
Expansion tank, painted steel, ASME 18 Gal capacity	1.000	Ea.	855	111	966
Storage tank, steel, above ground, 275 Gal capacity w/supports	1.000	Ea.	2,075	310	2,385
Copper tubing type L, solder joint, hanger 10' OC, 3/4" diam	100.000	L.F.	705	1,130	1,835
Radiation, 3/4" copper tube w/alum fin baseboard pkg, 7" high	30.000	L.F.	259.50	810	1,069.50
Pipe covering, calcium silicate w/cover, 1' wall, 3/4' diam	100.000	L.F.	695	845	1,540
TOTAL			10,082	8,276.50	18,358.50
COST PER S.F.			10.08	8.28	18.36

D3010 510	Apartment Building Heating - Fin Tube Radiation	COST PER S.F. MAT.	COST PER S.F. INST.	COST PER S.F. TOTAL
1740	Heating systems, fin tube radiation, forced hot water			
1760	1,000 S.F. area, 10,000 C.F. volume	10.10	8.28	18.38
1800	10,000 S.F. area, 100,000 C.F. volume	4.32	4.98	9.30
1840	20,000 S.F. area, 200,000 C.F. volume	4.20	5.60	9.80
1880	30,000 S.F. area, 300,000 C.F. volume	4.10	5.40	9.50

D30 HVAC

D3010 Energy Supply

Many styles of active solar energy systems exist. Those shown on the following page represent the majority of systems now being installed in different regions of the country.

The five active domestic hot water (DHW) systems which follow are typically specified as two or three panel systems with additional variations being the type of glazing and size of the storage tanks. Various combinations have been costed for the user's evaluation and comparison. The basic specifications from which the following systems were developed satisfy the construction detail requirements specified in the HUD Intermediate Minimum Property Standards (IMPS). If these standards are not complied with, the renewable energy system's costs could be significantly lower than shown.

To develop the system's specifications and costs it was necessary to make a number of assumptions about the systems. Certain systems are more appropriate to one climatic region than another or the systems may require modifications to be usable in particular locations. Specific instances in which the systems are not appropriate throughout the country as specified, or in which modification will be needed include the following:

- The freeze protection mechanisms provided in the DHW systems vary greatly. In harsh climates, where freeze is a major concern, a closed-loop indirect collection system may be more appropriate than a direct collection system.
- The thermosyphon water heater system described cannot be used when temperatures drop below 32°F.
- In warm climates it may be necessary to modify the systems installed to prevent overheating.

For each renewable resource (solar) system a schematic diagram and descriptive summary of the system is provided along with a list of all the components priced as part of the system. The costs were developed based on these specifications.

Considerations affecting costs which may increase or decrease beyond the estimates presented here include the following:

- Special structural qualities (allowance for earthquake, future expansion, high winds, and unusual spans or shapes);
- Isolated building site or rough terrain that would affect the transportation of personnel, material, or equipment;
- Unusual climatic conditions during the construction process;
- Substitution of other materials or system components for those used in the system specifications.

D30 HVAC

D3010 Energy Supply

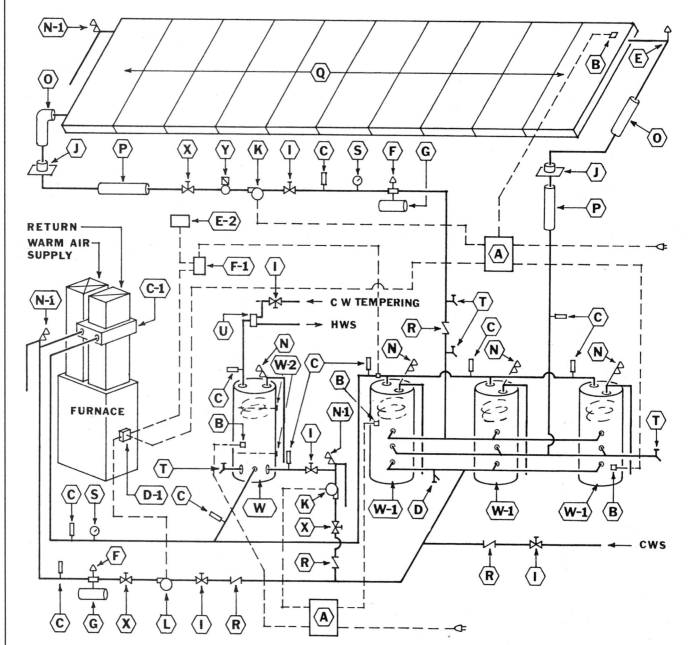

In this closed-loop indirect collection system, fluid with a low freezing temperature, propylene glycol, transports heat from the collectors to water storage. The transfer fluid is contained in a closed loop consisting of collectors, supply and return piping, and a heat exchanger immersed in the storage tank.

When the collectors become approximately 20°F warmer than the storage temperature, the controller activates the circulator. The circulator moves the fluid continuously until the temperature difference between fluid in the collectors and storage is such that the collection will no longer occur and then the circulator turns off. Since the heat transfer fluid has a very low freezing temperature, there is no need for it to be drained from the collectors between periods of collection.

D30 HVAC

D3010 Energy Supply

System Components	QUANTITY	UNIT	COST EACH		
			MAT.	INST.	TOTAL
SYSTEM D3010 650 2750					
SOLAR, CLOSED LOOP, SPACE/HOT WATER					
1" TUBING, TEN 3'X7' BLK CHROME ON COPPER ABSORBER COLLECTORS					
A, B Differential controller 2 sensors, thermostat, solar energy system	2.000	Ea.	516	143	659
C Thermometer, 2" dial	10.000	Ea.	250	535	785
C-1 Heat exchanger, solar energy system, fluid to air, up flow, 80 MBH	1.000	Ea.	555	515	1,070
D, T Fill & drain valves, brass, 3/4" connection	5.000	Ea.	107.50	180	287.50
D-1 Fan center	1.000	Ea.	212	178	390
E Air vent, manual, 1/8" fitting	1.000	Ea.	3.66	27	30.66
E-2 Thermostat, 2 stage for sensing room temperature	1.000	Ea.	276	108	384
F Air purger	2.000	Ea.	116	143	259
F-1 Controller, liquid temperature, solar energy system	1.000	Ea.	131	172	303
G Expansion tank	2.000	Ea.	145	54	199
I Valve, gate, bronze, 125 lb, soldered, 1" diam	5.000	Ea.	1,000	225	1,225
J Vent flashing, neoprene	2.000	Ea.	24.80	86	110.80
K Circulator, solar heated liquid, 1/25 HP	2.000	Ea.	462	222	684
L Circulator, solar heated liquid, 1/20 HP	1.000	Ea.	340	129	469
N Relief valve, temp & pressure 150 psi 210°F self-closing	4.000	Ea.	118	114	232
N-1 Relief valve, pressure poppet, bronze, 30 psi, 3/4" IPS	3.000	Ea.	366	91.50	457.50
O Pipe covering, urethane, ultraviolet cover, 1" wall, 1" diam	50.000	L.F.	151.50	392.50	544
P Pipe covering, fiberglass, all service jacket, 1" wall, 1" diam	60.000	L.F.	134.40	375	509.40
Q Collector panel solar energy blk chrome on copper 1/8" temp glass 3'x7'	10.000	Ea.	11,750	1,630	13,380
Roof clamps for solar energy collector panel	10.000	Set	39.50	220	259.50
R Valve, swing check, bronze, 125 lb, regrinding disc, 3/4" & 1" diam	4.000	Ea.	1,084	180	1,264
S Pressure gage, 0-60 psi, for solar energy system	2.000	Ea.	56	54	110
U Valve, water tempering, bronze, sweat connections, 3/4" diam	1.000	Ea.	273	43	316
W, W-1, W-2 Tank, water storage immersed heat xchr elec elem 2"x1/2# ins 120 gal	4.000	Ea.	7,700	2,460	10,160
X Valve, globe, bronze, 125 lb, rising stem, 1" diam	3.000	Ea.	1,365	135	1,500
Y Valve, flow control	1.000	Ea.	158	39	197
Copper tubing, type M, solder joint, hanger 10' OC 1" diam	110.000	L.F.	638	1,353	1,991
Copper tubing, type L, solder joint, hanger 10' OC 3/4" diam	20.000	L.F.	141	226	367
Wrought copper fittings & solder, 3/4" & 1" diam	121.000	Ea.	2,129.60	6,473.50	8,603.10
Sensor, wire, #22-2 conductor, multistranded	.700	C.L.F.	15.05	56	71.05
Ductwork, galvanized steel, for heat exchanger	8.000	Lb.	5.92	80.40	86.32
Solar energy heat transfer fluid propylene glycol, anti-freeze	25.000	Gal.	700	762.50	1,462.50
TOTAL			30,963.93	17,402.40	48,366.33

D3010 650	Solar, Closed Loop, Space/Hot Water Systems		COST EACH		
			MAT.	INST.	TOTAL
2540	Solar, closed loop, space/hot water				
2550	1/2" tubing, 12 ea. 4'x4'4" vacuum tube collectors		28,100	16,300	44,400
2600	3/4" tubing, 12 ea. 4'x4'4" vacuum tube collectors	R235616 -60	30,200	16,700	46,900
2650	10 ea. 3' x 7' black chrome absorber collectors		29,400	16,200	45,600
2700	10 ea. 3' x 7' flat black absorber collectors		26,100	16,300	42,400
2750	1" tubing, 10 ea. 3' x 7' black chrome absorber collectors		31,000	17,400	48,400
2800	10 ea. 3' x 7' flat black absorber collectors		27,900	17,500	45,400
2850	6 ea. 4' x 9' flat black w/plastic glazing collectors		25,600	17,400	43,000
2900	12 ea. 2' x 9' plastic absorber and glazing collectors		27,200	17,700	44,900

D30 HVAC

D3010 Energy Supply

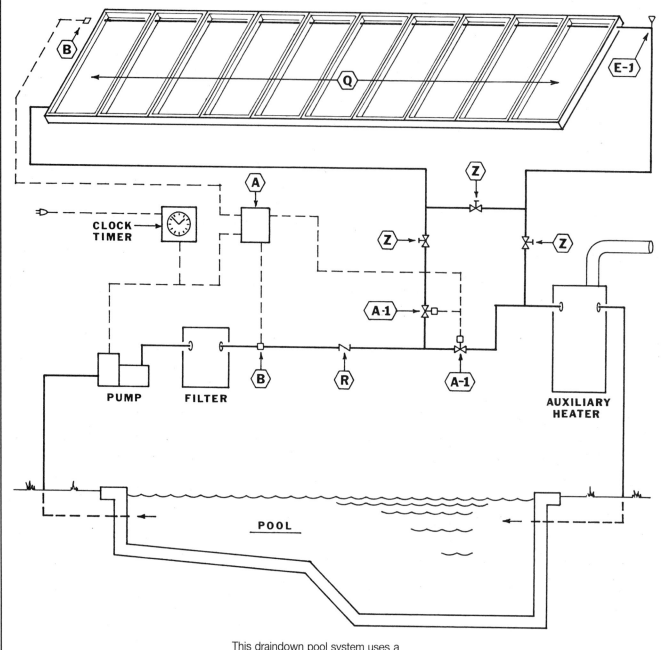

This draindown pool system uses a differential thermostat similar to those used in solar domestic hot water and space heating applications. To heat the pool, the pool water passes through the conventional pump-filter loop and then flows through the collectors. When collection is not possible, or when the pool temperature is reached, all water drains from the solar loop back to the pool through the existing piping. The modes are controlled by solenoid valves or other automatic valves in conjunction with a vacuum breaker relief valve, which facilitates draindown.

D30 HVAC

D3010 Energy Supply

System Components	QUANTITY	UNIT	COST EACH		
			MAT.	INST.	TOTAL
SYSTEM D3010 660 2640					
SOLAR SWIMMING POOL HEATER, ROOF MOUNTED COLLECTORS					
TEN 4' X 10' FULLY WETTED UNGLAZED PLASTIC ABSORBERS					
A Differential thermostat/controller, 110V, adj pool pump system	1.000	Ea.	365	430	795
A-1 Solenoid valve, PVC, normally 1 open 1 closed (included)	2.000	Ea.			
B Sensor, thermistor type (included)	2.000	Ea.			
E-1 Valve, vacuum relief	1.000	Ea.	34.50	27	61.50
Q Collector panel, solar energy, plastic, liquid full wetted, 4' x 10'	10.000	Ea.	3,650	3,100	6,750
R Valve, ball check, PVC, socket, 1-1/2" diam	1.000	Ea.	165	43	208
Z Valve, ball, PVC, socket, 1-1/2" diam	3.000	Ea.	315	129	444
Pipe, PVC, sch 40, 1-1/2" diam	80.000	L.F.	596	1,920	2,516
Pipe fittings, PVC sch 40, socket joint, 1-1/2" diam	10.000	Ea.	39.20	430	469.20
Sensor wire, #22-2 conductor, multistranded	.500	C.L.F.	10.75	40	50.75
Roof clamps for solar energy collector panels	10.000	Set	39.50	220	259.50
Roof strap, teflon for solar energy collector panels	26.000	L.F.	715	108.94	823.94
TOTAL			5,929.95	6,447.94	12,377.89

D3010 660	Solar Swimming Pool Heater Systems		COST EACH		
			MAT.	INST.	TOTAL
2530	Solar swimming pool heater systems, roof mounted collectors				
2540	10 ea. 3'x7' black chrome absorber, 1/8" temp. glass		14,000	4,975	18,975
2560	10 ea. 4'x8' black chrome absorber, 3/16" temp. glass	R235616 -60	15,500	5,925	21,425
2580	10 ea. 3'8"x6' flat black absorber, 3/16" temp. glass		10,700	5,075	15,775
2600	10 ea. 4'x9' flat black absorber, plastic glazing		12,500	6,150	18,650
2620	10 ea. 2'x9' rubber absorber, plastic glazing		15,200	6,675	21,875
2640	10 ea. 4'x10' fully wetted unglazed plastic absorber		5,925	6,450	12,375
2660	Ground mounted collectors				
2680	10 ea. 3'x7' black chrome absorber, 1/8" temp. glass		14,300	5,550	19,850
2700	10 ea. 4'x8' black chrome absorber, 3/16" temp. glass		15,800	6,500	22,300
2720	10 ea. 3'8"x6' flat blk absorber, 3/16" temp. glass		11,000	5,650	16,650
2740	10 ea. 4'x9' flat blk absorber, plastic glazing		12,800	6,750	19,550
2760	10 ea. 2'x9' rubber absorber, plastic glazing		15,400	7,025	22,425
2780	10 ea. 4'x10' fully wetted unglazed plastic absorber		6,175	7,025	13,200

D30 HVAC

D3010 Energy Supply

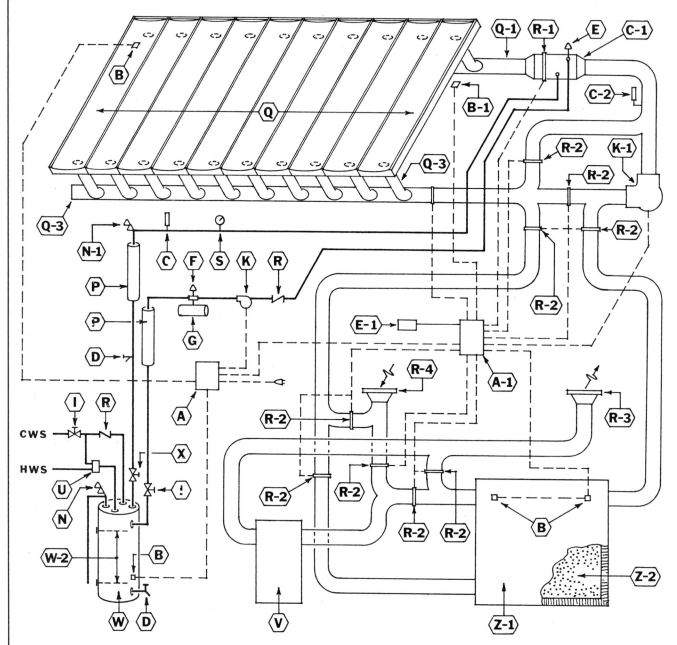

The complete Solar Air Heating System provides maximum savings of conventional fuel with both space heating and year-round domestic hot water heating. It allows for the home air conditioning to operate simultaneously and independently from the solar domestic water heating in summer. The system's modes of operation are:

Mode 1: The building is heated directly from the collectors with air circulated by the Solar Air Mover.

Mode 2: When heat is not needed in the building, the dampers change within the air mover to circulate the air from the collectors to the rock storage bin.

Mode 3: When heat is not available from the collector array and is available in rock storage, the air mover draws heated air from rock storage and directs it into the building. When heat is not available from the collectors or the rock storage bin, the auxiliary heating unit will provide heat for the building. The size of the collector array is typically 25% the size of the main floor area.

D30 HVAC

D3010 Energy Supply

System Components	QUANTITY	UNIT	COST EACH MAT.	COST EACH INST.	TOTAL
SYSTEM D3010 675 1210					
SOLAR, SPACE/HOT WATER, AIR TO WATER HEAT EXCHANGE					
A, B Differential controller 2 sensors thermos., solar energy sys liquid loop	1.000	Ea.	258	71.50	329.50
A-1, B Differential controller 2 sensors 6 station solar energy sys air loop	1.000	Ea.	310	287	597
B-1 Solar energy sensor, freeze prevention	1.000	Ea.	29	27	56
C Thermometer for solar energy system, 2" dial	2.000	Ea.	50	107	157
C-1 Heat exchanger, solar energy system, air to fluid, up flow, 70 MBH	1.000	Ea.	420	440	860
D Drain valve, brass, 3/4" connection	2.000	Ea.	43	72	115
E Air vent, manual, for solar energy system 1/8" fitting	1.000	Ea.	3.66	27	30.66
E-1 Thermostat, 2 stage for sensing room temperature	1.000	Ea.	276	108	384
F Air purger	1.000	Ea.	58	71.50	129.50
G Expansion tank, for solar energy system	1.000	Ea.	72.50	27	99.50
I Valve, gate, bronze, 125 lb, NRS, soldered 3/4" diam	2.000	Ea.	278	86	364
K Circulator, solar heated liquid, 1/25 HP	1.000	Ea.	231	111	342
N Relief valve temp & press 150 psi 210°F self-closing, 3/4" IPS	1.000	Ea.	29.50	28.50	58
N-1 Relief valve, pressure, poppet, bronze, 30 psi, 3/4" IPS	1.000	Ea.	122	30.50	152.50
P Pipe covering, fiberglass, all service jacket, 1" wall, 3/4" diam	60.000	L.F.	134.40	375	509.40
Q-3 Manifold for flush mount solar energy collector panels	20.000	L.F.	3,340	190	3,530
Q Collector panel solar energy, air, black on alum. plate, 7.5' x 3.5'	10.000	Ea.	8,450	1,720	10,170
R Valve, swing check, bronze, 125 lb, regrinding disc, 3/4" diam	2.000	Ea.	410	86	496
S Pressure gage, 2" dial, for solar energy system	1.000	Ea.	28	27	55
U Valve, water tempering, bronze, sweat connections, 3/4" diam	1.000	Ea.	273	43	316
W, W-2 Tank, water storage, solar, elec element 2"x1/2# insul, 80 Gal	1.000	Ea.	2,000	535	2,535
X Valve, globe, bronze, 125 lb, soldered, 3/4" diam	1.000	Ea.	264	43	307
Copper tubing type L, solder joints, hangers 10' OC 3/4" diam	10.000	L.F.	70.50	113	183.50
Copper tubing type M, solder joints, hangers 10' OC 3/4" diam	60.000	L.F.	369	660	1,029
Wrought copper fittings & solder, 3/4" diam	26.000	Ea.	185.90	1,170	1,355.90
Sensor wire, #22-2 conductor multistranded	1.200	C.L.F.	25.80	96	121.80
Q-1 Duct work, rigid fiberglass, rectangular	400.000	S.F.	436	2,700	3,136
Duct work, spiral preformed, steel, PVC coated both sides, 12" x 10"	8.000	Ea.	192	508	700
R-2 Shutter/damper for solar heater circulator	9.000	Ea.	589.50	1,143	1,732.50
K-1 Shutter motor for solar heater circulator blower	9.000	Ea.	1,467	855	2,322
K-1 Fan, solar energy heated air circulator, space & DHW system	1.000	Ea.	1,775	3,050	4,825
R-3, R-4, V Tank, solar energy air storage, 6'-3"H 7'x7' = 306 CF/2000 Gal	1.000	Ea.	15,500	1,975	17,475
Z-2 Crushed stone 1-1/2"	11.000	C.Y.	357.50	103.18	460.68
C-2 Thermometer, remote probe, 2" dial	1.000	Ea.	38.50	107	145.50
R-1 Solenoid valve	1.000	Ea.	192	95.50	287.50
Z-1 Furnace, supply diffusers, return grilles, existing	1.000	Ea.	15,500	1,975	17,475
TOTAL			53,778.76	19,063.68	72,842.44

D3010 675	Air To Water Heat Exchange		MAT.	INST.	TOTAL
1210	Solar, air to water heat exchange, for space/hot water heating	R235616 -60	54,000	19,100	73,100
1220					

D30 HVAC

D3020 Heat Generating Systems

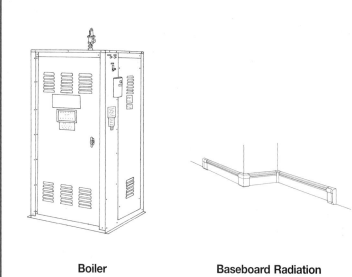

Boiler   Baseboard Radiation

Small Electric Boiler
System Considerations:
1. Terminal units are fin tube baseboard radiation rated at 720 BTU/hr with 200° water temperature or 820 BTU/hr steam.
2. Primary use being for residential or smaller supplementary areas, the floor levels are based on 7-1/2' ceiling heights.
3. All distribution piping is copper for boilers through 205 MBH. All piping for larger systems is steel pipe.

System Components	QUANTITY	UNIT	COST EACH		
			MAT.	INST.	TOTAL
SYSTEM D3020 102 1120					
SMALL HEATING SYSTEM, HYDRONIC, ELECTRIC BOILER					
1,480 S.F., 61 MBH, STEAM, 1 FLOOR					
Boiler, electric steam, std cntrls, trim, ftngs and valves, 18 KW, 61.4 MBH	1.000	Ea.	5,417.50	2,172.50	7,590
Copper tubing type L, solder joint, hanger 10'OC, 1-1/4" diam	160.000	L.F.	1,560	2,368	3,928
Radiation, 3/4" copper tube w/alum fin baseboard pkg 7" high	60.000	L.F.	519	1,620	2,139
Rough in baseboard panel or fin tube with valves & traps	10.000	Set	4,900	8,150	13,050
Pipe covering, calcium silicate w/cover, 1" wall 1-1/4" diam	160.000	L.F.	1,080	1,392	2,472
Low water cut-off, quick hookup, in gage glass tappings	1.000	Ea.	595	54	649
TOTAL			14,071.50	15,756.50	29,828
COST PER S.F.			9.85	11.03	20.88

D3020 102	Small Heating Systems, Hydronic, Electric Boilers	COST PER S.F.		
		MAT.	INST.	TOTAL
1100	Small heating systems, hydronic, electric boilers			
1120	Steam, 1 floor, 1480 S.F., 61 M.B.H.	9.87	11.06	20.93
1160	3,000 S.F., 123 M.B.H.	7.55	9.35	16.90
1200	5,000 S.F., 205 M.B.H.	6.65	8.60	15.25
1240	2 floors, 12,400 S.F., 512 M.B.H.	6.25	8.55	14.80
1280	3 floors, 24,800 S.F., 1023 M.B.H.	6.50	8.45	14.95
1360	Hot water, 1 floor, 1,000 S.F., 41 M.B.H.	14.50	5.95	20.45
1400	2,500 S.F., 103 M.B.H.	11.15	10.65	21.80
1440	2 floors, 4,850 S.F., 205 M.B.H.	11.05	12.75	23.80
1480	3 floors, 9,700 S.F., 410 M.B.H.	11.95	13.25	25.20

D30 HVAC

D3090 Other HVAC Systems/Equip

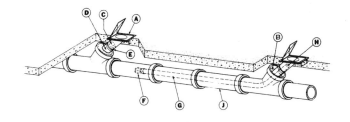

Cast Iron Garage Exhaust System

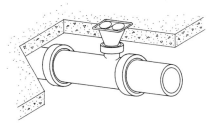

Dual Exhaust System

System Components	QUANTITY	UNIT	COST EACH		
			MAT.	INST.	TOTAL
SYSTEM D3090 320 1040					
GARAGE, EXHAUST, SINGLE 3" EXHAUST OUTLET, CARS & LIGHT TRUCKS					
A Outlet top assy, for engine exhaust system with adapters and ftngs, 3" diam	1.000	Ea.	340	53	393
F Bullnose (guide) for engine exhaust system, 3" diam	1.000	Ea.	39.50		39.50
G Galvanized flexible tubing for engine exhaust system, 3" diam	8.000	L.F.	106.80		106.80
H Adapter for metal tubing end of engine exhaust system, 3" tail pipe	1.000	Ea.	66		66
J Pipe, sewer, cast iron, push-on joint, 8" diam.	18.000	L.F.	1,071	954	2,025
Excavating utility trench, chain trencher, 8" wide, 24" deep	18.000	L.F.		48.06	48.06
Backfill utility trench by hand, incl. compaction, 8" wide 24" deep	18.000	L.F.		59.22	59.22
Stand for blower, concrete over polystyrene core, 6" high	1.000	Ea.	6.25	26.50	32.75
AC&V duct spiral reducer 10"x8"	1.000	Ea.	66	47.50	113.50
AC&V duct spiral reducer 12"x10"	1.000	Ea.	77.50	63.50	141
AC&V duct spiral preformed 45° elbow, 8" diam	1.000	Ea.	41	54.50	95.50
AC&V utility fan, belt drive, 3 phase, 2000 CFM, 1 HP	2.000	Ea.	3,450	840	4,290
Safety switch, heavy duty fused, 240V, 3 pole, 30 amp	1.000	Ea.	153	250	403
TOTAL			5,417.05	2,396.28	7,813.33

D3090 320	Garage Exhaust Systems	COST PER BAY		
		MAT.	INST.	TOTAL
1040	Garage, single 3" exhaust outlet, cars & light trucks, one bay	5,425	2,400	7,825
1060	Additional bays up to seven bays	1,150	645	1,795
1500	4" outlet, trucks, one bay	5,450	2,400	7,850
1520	Additional bays up to six bays	1,175	645	1,820
1600	5" outlet, diesel trucks, one bay	5,800	2,400	8,200
1650	Additional single bays up to six bays	1,650	760	2,410
1700	Two adjoining bays	5,800	2,400	8,200
2000	Dual exhaust, 3" outlets, pair of adjoining bays	6,550	2,975	9,525
2100	Additional pairs of adjoining bays	1,800	760	2,560

D40 Fire Protection

D4010 Sprinklers

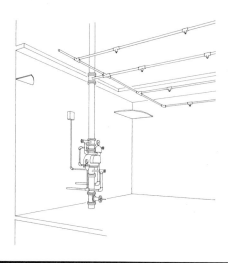

Dry Pipe System: A system employing automatic sprinklers attached to a piping system containing air under pressure, the release of which from the opening of sprinklers permits the water pressure to open a valve known as a "dry pipe valve". The water then flows into the piping system and out the opened sprinklers.

All areas are assumed to be open.

System Components	QUANTITY	UNIT	COST EACH MAT.	COST EACH INST.	COST EACH TOTAL
SYSTEM D4010 310 0580					
DRY PIPE SPRINKLER, STEEL, BLACK, SCH. 40 PIPE					
LIGHT HAZARD, ONE FLOOR, 2000 S.F.					
Valve, gate, iron body 125 lb., OS&Y, flanged, 4" pipe size	1.000	Ea.	1,650	515	2,165
4" pipe size	1.000	Ea.	4,100	515	4,615
Tamper switch (valve supervisory switch)	3.000	Ea.	795	159	954
Valve, swing check, bronze, 125 lb, regrinding disc, 2-1/2" pipe size	1.000	Ea.	1,725	103	1,828
Valve, angle, bronze, 150 lb., rising stem, threaded, 2" pipe size	1.000	Ea.	1,400	78	1,478
*Alarm valve, 2-1/2" pipe size	1.000	Ea.	2,725	505	3,230
Alarm, water motor, complete with gong	1.000	Ea.	515	211	726
Fire alarm horn, electric	1.000	Ea.	62	120	182
Valve swing check w/balldrip Cl with brass trim, 4" pipe size	1.000	Ea.	465	505	970
Pipe, steel, black, schedule 40, 4" diam.	8.000	L.F.	460	351.28	811.28
Dry pipe valve, trim & gauges, 4" pipe size	1.000	Ea.	3,850	1,525	5,375
Pipe, steel, black, schedule 40, threaded, cplg & hngr 10'OC 2-1/2" diam.	15.000	L.F.	555	465	1,020
Pipe, steel, black, schedule 40, threaded, cplg & hngr 10'OC 2" diam.	9.375	L.F.	210.94	225	435.94
Pipe, steel, black, schedule 40, threaded, cplg & hngr 10'OC 1-1/4" diam.	28.125	L.F.	396.56	489.38	885.94
Pipe, steel, black, schedule 40, threaded, cplg & hngr 10'OC 1" diam.	84.000	L.F.	894.60	1,360.80	2,255.40
Pipe Tee, malleable iron black, 150 lb. threaded, 4" pipe size	2.000	Ea.	1,110	770	1,880
Pipe Tee, malleable iron black, 150 lb. threaded, 2-1/2" pipe size	2.000	Ea.	312	344	656
Pipe Tee, malleable iron black, 150 lb. threaded, 2" pipe size	1.000	Ea.	72	141	213
Pipe Tee, malleable iron black, 150 lb. threaded, 1-1/4" pipe size	4.000	Ea.	136	444	580
Pipe Tee, malleable iron black, 150 lb. threaded, 1" pipe size	3.000	Ea.	63	321	384
Pipe 90° elbow malleable iron black, 150 lb. threaded, 1" pipe size	5.000	Ea.	67.25	330	397.25
Sprinkler head dry K5.6, 1" NPT, 3" to 6" length	12.000	Ea.	1,572	726	2,298
Air compressor, 200 Gal sprinkler system capacity, 1/3 HP	1.000	Ea.	2,025	650	2,675
*Standpipe connection, wall, flush, brs. w/plug & chain 2-1/2"x2-1/2"	1.000	Ea.	253	305	558
Valve gate bronze, 300 psi, NRS, class 150, threaded, 1" pipe size	1.000	Ea.	258	45	303
TOTAL			25,672.35	11,203.46	36,875.81
COST PER S.F.			10.27	4.48	14.75

*Not included in systems under 2000 S.F.

D4010 310	Dry Pipe Sprinkler Systems		COST PER S.F. MAT.	COST PER S.F. INST.	COST PER S.F. TOTAL
0520	Dry pipe sprinkler systems, steel, black, sch. 40 pipe				
0530	Light hazard, one floor, 500 S.F.		18.60	8	26.60
0560	1000 S.F.		12.45	4.70	17.15
0580	2000 S.F.	R211313-10	10.28	4.48	14.76

D40 Fire Protection

D4010 Sprinklers

D4010 310	Dry Pipe Sprinkler Systems		COST PER S.F.		
			MAT.	INST.	TOTAL
0600	5000 S.F.	R211313 -20	5.10	3.16	8.26
0620	10,000 S.F.		3.52	2.58	6.10
0640	50,000 S.F.		2.70	2.27	4.97
0660	Each additional floor, 500 S.F.		3.83	3.79	7.62
0680	1000 S.F.		3.40	3.09	6.49
0700	2000 S.F.		3.10	2.85	5.95
0720	5000 S.F.		2.38	2.44	4.82
0740	10,000 S.F.		2.22	2.24	4.46
0760	50,000 S.F.		2	2	4
1000	Ordinary hazard, one floor, 500 S.F.		18.80	8.05	26.85
1020	1000 S.F.		12.55	4.74	17.29
1040	2000 S.F.		10.40	4.95	15.35
1060	5000 S.F.		5.80	3.38	9.18
1080	10,000 S.F.		4.49	3.37	7.86
1100	50,000 S.F.		3.85	3.15	7
1140	Each additional floor, 500 S.F.		4.02	3.88	7.90
1160	1000 S.F.		3.82	3.46	7.28
1180	2000 S.F.		3.55	3.14	6.69
1200	5000 S.F.		3.20	2.70	5.90
1220	10,000 S.F.		2.83	2.63	5.46
1240	50,000 S.F.		2.58	2.27	4.85
1500	Extra hazard, one floor, 500 S.F.		24.50	10.05	34.55
1520	1000 S.F.		17.75	7.30	25.05
1540	2000 S.F.		11.30	6.30	17.60
1560	5000 S.F.		6.60	4.67	11.27
1580	10,000 S.F.		6.70	4.42	11.12
1600	50,000 S.F.		7.25	4.24	11.49
1660	Each additional floor, 500 S.F.		5.90	4.79	10.69
1680	1000 S.F.		5.35	4.49	9.84
1700	2000 S.F.		4.72	4.49	9.21
1720	5000 S.F.		3.98	3.93	7.91
1740	10,000 S.F.		4.62	3.59	8.21
1760	50,000 S.F.		4.65	3.45	8.10
2020	Grooved steel, black, sch. 40 pipe, light hazard, one floor, 2000 S.F.		10.30	4.12	14.42
2060	10,000 S.F.		3.77	2.24	6.01
2100	Each additional floor, 2000 S.F.		3.44	2.31	5.75
2150	10,000 S.F.		2.47	1.90	4.37
2200	Ordinary hazard, one floor, 2000 S.F.		10.65	4.35	15
2250	10,000 S.F.		4.58	2.87	7.45
2300	Each additional floor, 2000 S.F.		3.78	2.54	6.32
2350	10,000 S.F.		3.58	2.56	6.14
2400	Extra hazard, one floor, 2000 S.F.		11.80	5.40	17.20
2450	10,000 S.F.		6.40	3.71	10.11
2500	Each additional floor, 2000 S.F.		5.35	3.72	9.07
2550	10,000 S.F.		4.61	3.17	7.78
3050	Grooved steel, black, sch. 10 pipe, light hazard, one floor, 2000 S.F.		9.85	4.09	13.94
3100	10,000 S.F.		3.40	2.21	5.61
3150	Each additional floor, 2000 S.F.		3.01	2.27	5.28
3200	10,000 S.F.		2.10	1.87	3.97
3250	Ordinary hazard, one floor, 2000 S.F.		10.25	4.32	14.57
3300	10,000 S.F.		3.96	2.79	6.75
3350	Each additional floor, 2000 S.F.		3.38	2.51	5.89
3400	10,000 S.F.		2.74	2.47	5.21
3450	Extra hazard, one floor, 2000 S.F.		11.50	5.40	16.90
3500	10,000 S.F.		5.75	3.65	9.40
3550	Each additional floor, 2000 S.F.		5	3.69	8.69
3600	10,000 S.F.		4.22	3.13	7.35
4050	Copper tubing, type L, light hazard, one floor, 2000 S.F.		9.95	4.12	14.07

D40 Fire Protection

D4010 Sprinklers

D4010 310	Dry Pipe Sprinkler Systems	COST PER S.F.		
		MAT.	INST.	TOTAL
4100	10,000 S.F.	3.60	2.29	5.89
4150	Each additional floor, 2000 S.F.	3.11	2.35	5.46
4200	10,000 S.F.	2.31	1.96	4.27
4250	Ordinary hazard, one floor, 2000 S.F.	10.35	4.55	14.90
4300	10,000 S.F.	3.98	2.63	6.61
4350	Each additional floor, 2000 S.F.	3.79	2.66	6.45
4400	10,000 S.F.	2.58	2.25	4.83
4450	Extra hazard, one floor, 2000 S.F.	11.50	5.50	17
4500	10,000 S.F.	7.95	3.98	11.93
4550	Each additional floor, 2000 S.F.	4.87	3.75	8.62
4600	10,000 S.F.	5.50	3.41	8.91
5050	Copper tubing, type L, T-drill system, light hazard, one floor			
5060	2000 S.F.	9.80	3.88	13.68
5100	10,000 S.F.	3.24	1.92	5.16
5150	Each additional floor, 2000 S.F.	2.98	2.11	5.09
5200	10,000 S.F.	1.95	1.59	3.54
5250	Ordinary hazard, one floor, 2000 S.F.	9.80	3.95	13.75
5300	10,000 S.F.	3.95	2.41	6.36
5350	Each additional floor, 2000 S.F.	2.95	2.14	5.09
5400	10,000 S.F.	2.53	1.97	4.50
5450	Extra hazard, one floor, 2000 S.F.	10.50	4.62	15.12
5500	10,000 S.F.	6.05	3.01	9.06
5550	Each additional floor, 2000 S.F.	4.02	2.93	6.95
5600	10,000 S.F.	3.62	2.44	6.06

D40 Fire Protection

D4010 Sprinklers

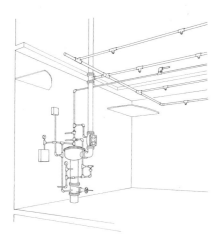

Pre-Action System: A system employing automatic sprinklers attached to a piping system containing air that may or may not be under pressure, with a supplemental heat responsive system of generally more sensitive characteristics than the automatic sprinklers themselves, installed in the same areas as the sprinklers. Actuation of the heat responsive system, as from a fire, opens a valve which permits water to flow into the sprinkler piping system and to be discharged from those sprinklers which were opened by heat from the fire.

All areas are assumed to be open.

System Components	QUANTITY	UNIT	COST EACH MAT.	INST.	TOTAL
SYSTEM D4010 350 0580					
PREACTION SPRINKLER SYSTEM, STEEL, BLACK, SCH. 40 PIPE					
LIGHT HAZARD, 1 FLOOR, 2000 S.F.					
Valve, gate, iron body 125 lb., OS&Y, flanged, 4" pipe size	1.000	Ea.	1,650	515	2,165
4" pipe size	1.000	Ea.	4,100	515	4,615
Tamper switch (valve supervisory switch)	3.000	Ea.	795	159	954
*Valve, swing check w/ball drip CI with brass trim 4" pipe size	1.000	Ea.	465	505	970
Valve, swing check, bronze, 125 lb, regrinding disc, 2-1/2" pipe size	1.000	Ea.	1,725	103	1,828
Valve, angle, bronze, 150 lb., rising stem, threaded, 2" pipe size	1.000	Ea.	1,400	78	1,478
*Alarm valve, 2-1/2" pipe size	1.000	Ea.	2,725	505	3,230
Alarm, water motor, complete with gong	1.000	Ea.	515	211	726
Fire alarm horn, electric	1.000	Ea.	62	120	182
Thermostatic release for release line	2.000	Ea.	2,250	85	2,335
Pipe, steel, black, schedule 40, 4" diam.	8.000	L.F.	460	351.28	811.28
Dry pipe valve, trim & gauges, 4" pipe size	1.000	Ea.	3,850	1,525	5,375
Pipe, steel, black, schedule 40, threaded, cplg. & hngr. 10'OC 2-1/2" diam.	15.000	L.F.	555	465	1,020
Pipe steel black, schedule 40, threaded, cplg. & hngr. 10'OC 2" diam.	9.375	L.F.	210.94	225	435.94
Pipe, steel, black, schedule 40, threaded, cplg. & hngr. 10'OC 1-1/4" diam.	28.125	L.F.	396.56	489.38	885.94
Pipe, steel, black, schedule 40, threaded, cplg. & hngr. 10'OC 1" diam.	84.000	L.F.	894.60	1,360.80	2,255.40
Pipe, Tee, malleable iron, black, 150 lb. threaded, 4" diam.	2.000	Ea.	1,110	770	1,880
Pipe, Tee, malleable iron, black, 150 lb. threaded, 2-1/2" pipe size	2.000	Ea.	312	344	656
Pipe, Tee, malleable iron, black, 150 lb. threaded, 2" pipe size	1.000	Ea.	72	141	213
Pipe, Tee, malleable iron, black, 150 lb. threaded, 1-1/4" pipe size	4.000	Ea.	136	444	580
Pipe, Tee, malleable iron, black, 150 lb. threaded, 1" pipe size	3.000	Ea.	63	321	384
Pipe, 90° elbow, malleable iron, blk., 150 lb. threaded, 1" pipe size	5.000	Ea.	67.25	330	397.25
Sprinkler head, std. spray, brass 135°-286°F 1/2" NPT, 3/8" orifice	12.000	Ea.	474	636	1,110
Air compressor auto complete 200 Gal sprinkler sys. cap., 1/3 HP	1.000	Ea.	2,025	650	2,675
*Standpipe conn.,wall, flush, brass w/plug & chain 2-1/2" x 2-1/2"	1.000	Ea.	253	305	558
Valve, gate, bronze, 300 psi, NRS, class 150, threaded, 1" pipe size	1.000	Ea.	258	45	303
TOTAL			26,824.35	11,198.46	38,022.81
COST PER S.F.			10.73	4.48	15.21

*Not included in systems under 2000 S.F.

D4010 350	Preaction Sprinkler Systems	COST PER S.F. MAT.	INST.	TOTAL
0520	Preaction sprinkler systems, steel, black, sch. 40 pipe			
0530	Light hazard, one floor, 500 S.F.	19.50	6.45	25.95

D40 Fire Protection

D4010 Sprinklers

D4010 350	Preaction Sprinkler Systems		COST PER S.F.		
			MAT.	INST.	TOTAL
0560	1000 S.F.	R211313 -10	11.20	4.77	15.97
0580	2000 S.F.		10.72	4.48	15.20
0600	5000 S.F.	R211313 -20	5.35	3.15	8.50
0620	10,000 S.F.		3.72	2.57	6.29
0640	50,000 S.F.		2.89	2.26	5.15
0660	Each additional floor, 500 S.F.		5	3.39	8.39
0680	1000 S.F.		3.83	3.09	6.92
0700	2000 S.F.		3.53	2.85	6.38
0720	5000 S.F.		3.53	2.49	6.02
0740	10,000 S.F.		2.91	2.27	5.18
0760	50,000 S.F.		2.43	2.06	4.49
1000	Ordinary hazard, one floor, 500 S.F.		20.50	6.95	27.45
1020	1000 S.F.		12.85	4.73	17.58
1040	2000 S.F.		11.10	4.96	16.06
1060	5000 S.F.		5.90	3.36	9.26
1080	10,000 S.F.		4.53	3.35	7.88
1100	50,000 S.F.		3.90	3.12	7.02
1140	Each additional floor, 500 S.F.		5.15	3.90	9.05
1160	1000 S.F.		3.81	3.12	6.93
1180	2000 S.F.		3.42	3.11	6.53
1200	5000 S.F.		3.58	2.91	6.49
1220	10,000 S.F.		3.26	3.02	6.28
1240	50,000 S.F.		2.94	2.67	5.61
1500	Extra hazard, one floor, 500 S.F.		29	8.95	37.95
1520	1000 S.F.		17.95	6.70	24.65
1540	2000 S.F.		11.30	6.25	17.55
1560	5000 S.F.		7.25	5	12.25
1580	10,000 S.F.		6.95	4.88	11.83
1600	50,000 S.F.		7.35	4.70	12.05
1660	Each additional floor, 500 S.F.		6.80	4.79	11.59
1680	1000 S.F.		5.60	4.49	10.09
1700	2000 S.F.		4.84	4.48	9.32
1720	5000 S.F.		4.04	3.96	8
1740	10,000 S.F.		4.47	3.63	8.10
1760	50,000 S.F.		4.33	3.40	7.73
2020	Grooved steel, black, sch. 40 pipe, light hazard, one floor, 2000 S.F.		10.70	4.11	14.81
2060	10,000 S.F.		3.97	2.23	6.20
2100	Each additional floor of 2000 S.F.		3.87	2.30	6.17
2150	10,000 S.F.		2.68	1.89	4.57
2200	Ordinary hazard, one floor, 2000 S.F.		10.95	4.34	15.29
2250	10,000 S.F.		4.62	2.85	7.47
2300	Each additional floor, 2000 S.F.		4.08	2.53	6.61
2350	10,000 S.F.		3.34	2.51	5.85
2400	Extra hazard, one floor, 2000 S.F.		11.85	5.40	17.25
2450	10,000 S.F.		6.30	3.66	9.96
2500	Each additional floor, 2000 S.F.		5.35	3.68	9.03
2550	10,000 S.F.		4.37	3.13	7.50
3050	Grooved steel, black, sch. 10 pipe light hazard, one floor, 2000 S.F.		10.30	4.08	14.38
3100	10,000 S.F.		3.60	2.20	5.80
3150	Each additional floor, 2000 S.F.		3.44	2.27	5.71
3200	10,000 S.F.		2.31	1.86	4.17
3250	Ordinary hazard, one floor, 2000 S.F.		10.35	4.05	14.40
3300	10,000 S.F.		3.64	2.77	6.41
3350	Each additional floor, 2000 S.F.		3.67	2.50	6.17
3400	10,000 S.F.		2.78	2.45	5.23
3450	Extra hazard, one floor, 2000 S.F.		11.50	5.35	16.85
3500	10,000 S.F.		5.50	3.60	9.10
3550	Each additional floor, 2000 S.F.		5.05	3.66	8.71

D40 Fire Protection

D4010 Sprinklers

D4010 350	Preaction Sprinkler Systems	MAT.	INST.	TOTAL
3600	10,000 S.F.	3.98	3.08	7.06
4050	Copper tubing, type L, light hazard, one floor, 2000 S.F.	10.40	4.12	14.52
4100	10,000 S.F.	3.81	2.28	6.09
4150	Each additional floor, 2000 S.F.	3.56	2.35	5.91
4200	10,000 S.F.	2.09	1.93	4.02
4250	Ordinary hazard, one floor, 2000 S.F.	10.50	4.50	15
4300	10,000 S.F.	4.02	2.61	6.63
4350	Each additional floor, 2000 S.F.	3.49	2.36	5.85
4400	10,000 S.F.	2.46	2.06	4.52
4450	Extra hazard, one floor, 2000 S.F.	11.35	5.40	16.75
4500	10,000 S.F.	7.60	3.92	11.52
4550	Each additional floor, 2000 S.F.	4.89	3.72	8.61
4600	10,000 S.F.	5.30	3.37	8.67
5050	Copper tubing, type L, T-drill system, light hazard, one floor			
5060	2000 S.F.	10.25	3.87	14.12
5100	10,000 S.F.	3.45	1.91	5.36
5150	Each additional floor, 2000 S.F.	3.41	2.11	5.52
5200	10,000 S.F.	2.16	1.58	3.74
5250	Ordinary hazard, one floor, 2000 S.F.	10.10	3.94	14.04
5300	10,000 S.F.	3.99	2.39	6.38
5350	Each additional floor, 2000 S.F.	3.26	2.14	5.40
5400	10,000 S.F.	2.71	2.05	4.76
5450	Extra hazard, one floor, 2000 S.F.	10.50	4.58	15.08
5500	10,000 S.F.	5.70	2.96	8.66
5550	Each additional floor, 2000 S.F.	4.04	2.89	6.93
5600	10,000 S.F.	3.39	2.40	5.79

D40 Fire Protection

D4010 Sprinklers

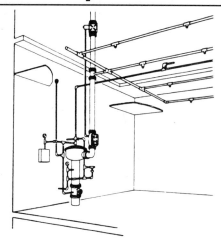

Deluge System: A system employing open sprinklers attached to a piping system connected to a water supply through a valve which is opened by the operation of a heat responsive system installed in the same areas as the sprinklers. When this valve opens, water flows into the piping system and discharges from all sprinklers attached thereto.

All areas are assumed to be open.

System Components	QUANTITY	UNIT	COST EACH MAT.	COST EACH INST.	COST EACH TOTAL
SYSTEM D4010 370 0580					
DELUGE SPRINKLER SYSTEM, STEEL BLACK SCH. 40 PIPE					
LIGHT HAZARD, 1 FLOOR, 2000 S.F.					
Valve, gate, iron body 125 lb., OS&Y, flanged, 4" pipe size	1.000	Ea.	1,650	515	2,165
4" pipe size	1.000	Ea.	4,100	515	4,615
Tamper switch (valve supervisory switch)	3.000	Ea.	795	159	954
Valve, swing check w/ball drip, CI w/brass ftngs., 4" pipe size	1.000	Ea.	465	505	970
Valve, swing check, bronze, 125 lb, regrinding disc, 2-1/2" pipe size	1.000	Ea.	1,725	103	1,828
Valve, angle, bronze, 150 lb., rising stem, threaded, 2" pipe size	1.000	Ea.	1,400	78	1,478
*Alarm valve, 2-1/2" pipe size	1.000	Ea.	2,725	505	3,230
Alarm, water motor, complete with gong	1.000	Ea.	515	211	726
Fire alarm horn, electric	1.000	Ea.	62	120	182
Thermostatic release for release line	2.000	Ea.	2,250	85	2,335
Pipe, steel, black, schedule 40, 4" diam.	8.000	L.F.	460	351.28	811.28
Deluge valve trim, pressure relief, emergency release, gauge, 4" pipe size	1.000	Ea.	7,550	1,525	9,075
Deluge system, monitoring panel w/deluge valve & trim	1.000	Ea.	25,900	47	25,947
Pipe, steel, black, schedule 40, threaded, cplg & hngr 10' OC 2-1/2" diam.	15.000	L.F.	555	465	1,020
Pipe, steel, black, schedule 40, threaded, cplg & hngr 10' OC 2" diam.	9.375	L.F.	210.94	225	435.94
Pipe, steel, black, schedule 40, threaded, cplg & hngr 10' OC 1-1/4" diam.	28.125	L.F.	396.56	489.38	885.94
Pipe, steel, black, schedule 40, threaded, cplg & hngr 10' OC 1" diam.	84.000	L.F.	894.60	1,360.80	2,255.40
Pipe, Tee, malleable iron, black, 150 lb. threaded, 4" pipe size	2.000	Ea.	1,110	770	1,880
Pipe, Tee, malleable iron, black, 150 lb. threaded, 2-1/2" pipe size	2.000	Ea.	312	344	656
Pipe, Tee, malleable iron, black, 150 lb. threaded, 2" pipe size	1.000	Ea.	72	141	213
Pipe, Tee, malleable iron, black, 150 lb. threaded, 1-1/4" pipe size	4.000	Ea.	136	444	580
Pipe, Tee, malleable iron, black, 150 lb. threaded, 1" pipe size	3.000	Ea.	63	321	384
Pipe, 90° elbow, malleable iron, black, 150 lb. threaded 1" pipe size	5.000	Ea.	67.25	330	397.25
Sprinkler head, std spray, brass 135°-286°F 1/2" NPT, 3/8" orifice	12.000	Ea.	474	636	1,110
Air compressor, auto, complete, 200 Gal sprinkler sys. cap., 1/3 HP	1.000	Ea.	2,025	650	2,675
*Standpipe connection, wall, flush w/plug & chain 2-1/2" x 2-1/2"	1.000	Ea.	253	305	558
Valve, gate, bronze, 300 psi, NRS, class 150, threaded, 1" pipe size	1.000	Ea.	258	45	303
TOTAL			56,424.35	11,245.46	67,669.81
COST PER S.F.			22.57	4.50	27.07

*Not included in systems under 2000 S.F.

D4010 370	Deluge Sprinkler Systems	COST PER S.F. MAT.	COST PER S.F. INST.	COST PER S.F. TOTAL
0520	Deluge sprinkler systems, steel, black, sch. 40 pipe			
0530	Light hazard, one floor, 500 S.F.	61	6.50	67.50

D40 Fire Protection

D4010 Sprinklers

D4010 370	Deluge Sprinkler Systems		COST PER S.F.		
			MAT.	INST.	TOTAL
0560	1000 S.F.	R211313 -10	33.50	4.63	38.13
0580	2000 S.F.		22.60	4.48	27.08
0600	5000 S.F.	R211313 -20	9.80	3.16	12.96
0620	10,000 S.F.		5.95	2.57	8.52
0640	50,000 S.F.		3.33	2.26	5.59
0660	Each additional floor, 500 S.F.		4.34	3.39	7.73
0680	1000 S.F.		3.83	3.09	6.92
0700	2000 S.F.		3.53	2.85	6.38
0720	5000 S.F.		2.62	2.43	5.05
0740	10,000 S.F.		2.43	2.23	4.66
0760	50,000 S.F.		2.41	2.06	4.47
1000	Ordinary hazard, one floor, 500 S.F.		63.50	7.40	70.90
1020	1000 S.F.		33.50	4.77	38.27
1040	2000 S.F.		22	4.97	26.97
1060	5000 S.F.		10.35	3.37	13.72
1080	10,000 S.F.		6.75	3.35	10.10
1100	50,000 S.F.		4.38	3.17	7.55
1140	Each additional floor, 500 S.F.		5.15	3.90	9.05
1160	1000 S.F.		3.81	3.12	6.93
1180	2000 S.F.		3.42	3.11	6.53
1200	5000 S.F.		3.33	2.68	6.01
1220	10,000 S.F.		3.12	2.66	5.78
1240	50,000 S.F.		2.76	2.45	5.21
1500	Extra hazard, one floor, 500 S.F.		70.50	9.05	79.55
1520	1000 S.F.		39.50	6.95	46.45
1540	2000 S.F.		22.50	6.25	28.75
1560	5000 S.F.		10.95	4.64	15.59
1580	10,000 S.F.		8.75	4.47	13.22
1600	50,000 S.F.		8.75	4.32	13.07
1660	Each additional floor, 500 S.F.		6.80	4.79	11.59
1680	1000 S.F.		5.60	4.49	10.09
1700	2000 S.F.		4.84	4.48	9.32
1720	5000 S.F.		4.04	3.96	8
1740	10,000 S.F.		4.59	3.77	8.36
1760	50,000 S.F.		4.58	3.63	8.21
2000	Grooved steel, black, sch. 40 pipe, light hazard, one floor				
2020	2000 S.F.		22	4.13	26.13
2060	10,000 S.F.		6.25	2.26	8.51
2100	Each additional floor, 2,000 S.F.		3.87	2.30	6.17
2150	10,000 S.F.		2.68	1.89	4.57
2200	Ordinary hazard, one floor, 2000 S.F.		10.95	4.34	15.29
2250	10,000 S.F.		6.85	2.85	9.70
2300	Each additional floor, 2000 S.F.		4.08	2.53	6.61
2350	10,000 S.F.		3.34	2.51	5.85
2400	Extra hazard, one floor, 2000 S.F.		23	5.40	28.40
2450	10,000 S.F.		8.45	3.68	12.13
2500	Each additional floor, 2000 S.F.		5.35	3.68	9.03
2550	10,000 S.F.		4.37	3.13	7.50
3000	Grooved steel, black, sch. 10 pipe, light hazard, one floor				
3050	2000 S.F.		20.50	3.93	24.43
3100	10,000 S.F.		5.80	2.21	8.01
3150	Each additional floor, 2000 S.F.		3.44	2.27	5.71
3200	10,000 S.F.		2.31	1.86	4.17
3250	Ordinary hazard, one floor, 2000 S.F.		21.50	4.33	25.83
3300	10,000 S.F.		5.85	2.77	8.62
3350	Each additional floor, 2000 S.F.		3.67	2.50	6.17
3400	10,000 S.F.		2.78	2.45	5.23
3450	Extra hazard, one floor, 2000 S.F.		22.50	5.35	27.85

For customer support on your Plumbing Costs with RSMeans data, call 800.448.8182.

D40 Fire Protection

D4010 Sprinklers

D4010 370	Deluge Sprinkler Systems	COST PER S.F.		
		MAT.	INST.	TOTAL
3500	10,000 S.F.	7.75	3.60	11.35
3550	Each additional floor, 2000 S.F.	5.05	3.66	8.71
3600	10,000 S.F.	3.98	3.08	7.06
4000	Copper tubing, type L, light hazard, one floor			
4050	2000 S.F.	21.50	4.13	25.63
4100	10,000 S.F.	5.95	2.28	8.23
4150	Each additional floor, 2000 S.F.	3.54	2.35	5.89
4200	10,000 S.F.	2.09	1.93	4.02
4250	Ordinary hazard, one floor, 2000 S.F.	21.50	4.56	26.06
4300	10,000 S.F.	6.40	2.67	9.07
4350	Each additional floor, 2000 S.F.	3.59	2.39	5.98
4400	10,000 S.F.	2.64	2.10	4.74
4450	Extra hazard, one floor, 2000 S.F.	22.50	5.50	28
4500	10,000 S.F.	9.85	4.01	13.86
4550	Each additional floor, 2000 S.F.	5.05	3.78	8.83
4600	10,000 S.F.	5.40	3.42	8.82
5000	Copper tubing, type L, T-drill system, light hazard, one floor			
5050	2000 S.F.	21.50	3.89	25.39
5100	10,000 S.F.	5.65	1.91	7.56
5150	Each additional floor, 2000 S.F.	3.37	2.14	5.51
5200	10,000 S.F.	2.16	1.58	3.74
5250	Ordinary hazard, one floor, 2000 S.F.	19.35	3.70	23.05
5300	10,000 S.F.	6.20	2.39	8.59
5350	Each additional floor, 2000 S.F.	3.23	2.12	5.35
5400	10,000 S.F.	2.71	2.05	4.76
5450	Extra hazard, one floor, 2000 S.F.	19.80	4.35	24.15
5500	10,000 S.F.	7.90	2.96	10.86
5550	Each additional floor, 2000 S.F.	4.04	2.89	6.93
5600	10,000 S.F.	3.39	2.40	5.79

D40 Fire Protection

D4010 Sprinklers

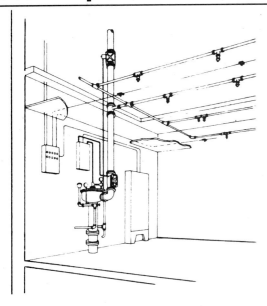

On-off multicycle sprinkler system is a fixed fire protection system utilizing water as its extinguishing agent. It is a time delayed, recycling, preaction type which automatically shuts the water off when heat is reduced below the detector operating temperature and turns the water back on when that temperature is exceeded.

The system senses a fire condition through a closed circuit electrical detector system which controls water flow to the fire automatically. Batteries supply up to 90 hour emergency power supply for system operation. The piping system is dry (until water is required) and is monitored with pressurized air. Should any leak in the system piping occur, an alarm will sound, but water will not enter the system until heat is sensed by a Firecycle detector.

All areas are assumed to be open.

System Components	QUANTITY	UNIT	COST EACH MAT.	COST EACH INST.	COST EACH TOTAL
SYSTEM D4010 390 0580					
ON-OFF MULTICYCLE SPRINKLER SYSTEM, STEEL, BLACK, SCH. 40 PIPE					
LIGHT HAZARD, ONE FLOOR, 2000 S.F.					
Valve, gate, iron body 125 lb., OS&Y, flanged, 4" pipe size	1.000	Ea.	1,650	515	2,165
4" pipe size	1.000	Ea.	4,100	515	4,615
Tamper switch (valve supervisory switch)	3.000	Ea.	795	159	954
Valve, angle, bronze, 150 lb., rising stem, threaded, 2" pipe size	1.000	Ea.	1,400	78	1,478
Valve, swing check, bronze, 125 lb, regrinding disc, 2-1/2" pipe size	1.000	Ea.	1,725	103	1,828
*Alarm valve, 2-1/2" pipe size	1.000	Ea.	2,725	505	3,230
Alarm, water motor, complete with gong	1.000	Ea.	515	211	726
Pipe, steel, black, schedule 40, 4" diam.	8.000	L.F.	460	351.28	811.28
Fire alarm, horn, electric	1.000	Ea.	62	120	182
Pipe, steel, black, schedule 40, threaded, cplg & hngr 10' OC 2-1/2" diam.	15.000	L.F.	555	465	1,020
Pipe, steel, black, schedule 40, threaded, cplg & hngr 10' OC 2" diam.	9.375	L.F.	210.94	225	435.94
Pipe, steel, black, schedule 40, threaded, cplg & hngr 10' OC 1-1/4" diam.	28.125	L.F.	396.56	489.38	885.94
Pipe, steel, black, schedule 40, threaded, cplg & hngr 10' OC 1" diam.	84.000	L.F.	894.60	1,360.80	2,255.40
Pipe, Tee, malleable iron, black, 150 lb. threaded, 4" pipe size	2.000	Ea.	1,110	770	1,880
Pipe, Tee, malleable iron, black, 150 lb. threaded, 2-1/2" pipe size	2.000	Ea.	312	344	656
Pipe, Tee, malleable iron, black, 150 lb. threaded, 2" pipe size	1.000	Ea.	72	141	213
Pipe, Tee, malleable iron, black, 150 lb. threaded, 1-1/4" pipe size	4.000	Ea.	136	444	580
Pipe, Tee, malleable iron, black, 150 lb. threaded, 1" pipe size	3.000	Ea.	63	321	384
Pipe, 90° elbow, malleable iron, black, 150 lb. threaded, 1" pipe size	5.000	Ea.	67.25	330	397.25
Sprinkler head std spray, brass 135°-286°F 1/2" NPT, 3/8" orifice	12.000	Ea.	474	636	1,110
Firecycle controls, incls panel, battery, solenoid valves, press switches	1.000	Ea.	37,000	3,225	40,225
Detector, firecycle system	2.000	Ea.	2,400	106	2,506
Firecycle pkg, swing check & flow control valves w/trim 4" pipe size	1.000	Ea.	7,800	1,525	9,325
Air compressor, auto, complete, 200 Gal sprinkler sys. cap., 1/3 HP	1.000	Ea.	2,025	650	2,675
*Standpipe connection, wall, flush, brass w/plug & chain 2-1/2"x2-1/2"	1.000	Ea.	253	305	558
Valve, gate, bronze 300 psi, NRS, class 150, threaded, 1" diam.	1.000	Ea.	258	45	303
TOTAL			67,459.35	13,939.46	81,398.81
COST PER S.F.			26.98	5.58	32.56

*Not included in systems under 2000 S.F.

D4010 390	On-off multicycle Sprinkler Systems	COST PER S.F. MAT.	COST PER S.F. INST.	COST PER S.F. TOTAL
0520	On-off multicycle sprinkler systems, steel, black, sch. 40 pipe			
0530	Light hazard, one floor, 500 S.F.	80	12.35	92.35

For customer support on your Plumbing Costs with RSMeans data, call 800.448.8182.

D40 Fire Protection

D4010 Sprinklers

D4010 390	On-off multicycle Sprinkler Systems		COST PER S.F.		
			MAT.	INST.	TOTAL
0560	1000 S.F.	R211313 -10	43	7.75	50.75
0580	2000 S.F.		27	5.56	32.56
0600	5000 S.F.	R211313 -20	11.50	3.57	15.07
0620	10,000 S.F.		6.90	2.78	9.68
0640	50,000 S.F.		3.60	2.30	5.90
0660	Each additional floor of 500 S.F.		4.46	3.40	7.86
0680	1000 S.F.		3.89	3.10	6.99
0700	2000 S.F.		3.14	2.83	5.97
0720	5000 S.F.		2.66	2.43	5.09
0740	10,000 S.F.		2.56	2.24	4.80
0760	50,000 S.F.		2.49	2.06	4.55
1000	Ordinary hazard, one floor, 500 S.F.		76.50	12.50	89
1020	1000 S.F.		43	7.65	50.65
1040	2000 S.F.		26	5.95	31.95
1060	5000 S.F.		12.05	3.77	15.82
1080	10,000 S.F.		7.70	3.56	11.26
1100	50,000 S.F.		4.85	3.54	8.39
1140	Each additional floor, 500 S.F.		5.25	3.92	9.17
1160	1000 S.F.		3.87	3.13	7
1180	2000 S.F.		3.72	2.86	6.58
1200	5000 S.F.		3.37	2.69	6.06
1220	10,000 S.F.		3	2.61	5.61
1240	50,000 S.F.		2.79	2.33	5.12
1500	Extra hazard, one floor, 500 S.F.		89	14.85	103.85
1520	1000 S.F.		47	9.60	56.60
1540	2000 S.F.		26.50	7.30	33.80
1560	5000 S.F.		12.65	5.05	17.70
1580	10,000 S.F.		9.95	5.05	15
1600	50,000 S.F.		8.85	5.55	14.40
1660	Each additional floor, 500 S.F.		6.90	4.81	11.71
1680	1000 S.F.		5.65	4.50	10.15
1700	2000 S.F.		4.90	4.49	9.39
1720	5000 S.F.		4.09	3.96	8.05
1740	10,000 S.F.		4.60	3.64	8.24
1760	50,000 S.F.		4.58	3.51	8.09
2020	Grooved steel, black, sch. 40 pipe, light hazard, one floor				
2030	2000 S.F.		24	4.89	28.89
2060	10,000 S.F.		7.85	3.38	11.23
2100	Each additional floor, 2000 S.F.		3.92	2.31	6.23
2150	10,000 S.F.		2.81	1.90	4.71
2200	Ordinary hazard, one floor, 2000 S.F.		26	5.35	31.35
2250	10,000 S.F.		8.40	3.23	11.63
2300	Each additional floor, 2000 S.F.		4.14	2.54	6.68
2350	10,000 S.F.		3.47	2.52	5.99
2400	Extra hazard, one floor, 2000 S.F.		25	6.15	31.15
2450	10,000 S.F.		9.30	3.85	13.15
2500	Each additional floor, 2000 S.F.		5.40	3.69	9.09
2550	10,000 S.F.		4.50	3.14	7.64
3050	Grooved steel, black, sch. 10 pipe, light hazard, one floor,				
3060	2000 S.F.		25.50	5.10	30.60
3100	10,000 S.F.		6.75	2.42	9.17
3150	Each additional floor, 2000 S.F.		3.50	2.28	5.78
3200	10,000 S.F.		2.44	1.87	4.31
3250	Ordinary hazard, one floor, 2000 S.F.		26	5.35	31.35
3300	10,000 S.F.		7.20	3	10.20
3350	Each additional floor, 2000 S.F.		3.73	2.51	6.24
3400	10,000 S.F.		2.91	2.46	5.37
3450	Extra hazard, one floor, 2000 S.F.		26.50	6.40	32.90

D40 Fire Protection

D4010 Sprinklers

D4010 390	On-off multicycle Sprinkler Systems	COST PER S.F.		
		MAT.	INST.	TOTAL
3500	10,000 S.F.	8.65	3.79	12.44
3550	Each additional floor, 2000 S.F.	5.10	3.67	8.77
3600	10,000 S.F.	4.11	3.09	7.20
4060	Copper tubing, type L, light hazard, one floor, 2000 S.F.	25.50	5.15	30.65
4100	10,000 S.F.	6.95	2.49	9.44
4150	Each additional floor, 2000 S.F.	3.60	2.36	5.96
4200	10,000 S.F.	2.64	1.96	4.60
4250	Ordinary hazard, one floor, 2000 S.F.	25.50	5.55	31.05
4300	10,000 S.F.	7.20	2.83	10.03
4350	Each additional floor, 2000 S.F.	3.55	2.37	5.92
4400	10,000 S.F.	2.56	2.04	4.60
4450	Extra hazard, one floor, 2000 S.F.	26.50	6.45	32.95
4500	10,000 S.F.	10.85	4.17	15.02
4550	Each additional floor, 2000 S.F.	4.94	3.73	8.67
4600	10,000 S.F.	5.40	3.38	8.78
5060	Copper tubing, type L, T-drill system, light hazard, one floor 2000 S.F.	25.50	4.90	30.40
5100	10,000 S.F.	6.50	2.11	8.61
5150	Each additional floor, 2000 S.F.	3.79	2.21	6
5200	10,000 S.F.	2.29	1.59	3.88
5250	Ordinary hazard, one floor, 2000 S.F.	25	4.92	29.92
5300	10,000 S.F.	6.90	2.55	9.45
5350	Each additional floor, 2000 S.F.	3.17	2.09	5.26
5400	10,000 S.F.	2.58	2.01	4.59
5450	Extra hazard, one floor, 2000 S.F.	25.50	5.55	31.05
5500	10,000 S.F.	8.70	3.09	11.79
5550	Each additional floor, 2000 S.F.	3.96	2.84	6.80
5600	10,000 S.F.	3.40	2.35	5.75

D40 Fire Protection

D4010 Sprinklers

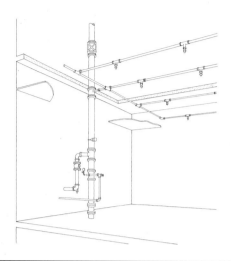

Wet Pipe System. A system employing automatic sprinklers attached to a piping system containing water and connected to a water supply so that water discharges immediately from sprinklers opened by heat from a fire.

All areas are assumed to be open.

System Components	QUANTITY	UNIT	COST EACH		
			MAT.	INST.	TOTAL
SYSTEM D4010 410 0580					
WET PIPE SPRINKLER, STEEL, BLACK, SCH. 40 PIPE					
LIGHT HAZARD, ONE FLOOR, 2000 S.F.					
Valve, gate, iron body, 125 lb., OS&Y, flanged, 4" diam.	1.000	Ea.	1,650	515	2,165
4" pipe size	1.000	Ea.	4,100	515	4,615
Tamper switch (valve supervisory switch)	3.000	Ea.	795	159	954
Valve, swing check, bronze, 125 lb, regrinding disc, 2-1/2" pipe size	1.000	Ea.	1,725	103	1,828
Valve, angle, bronze, 150 lb., rising stem, threaded, 2" diam.	1.000	Ea.	1,400	78	1,478
*Alarm valve, 2-1/2" pipe size	1.000	Ea.	2,725	505	3,230
Alarm, water motor, complete with gong	1.000	Ea.	515	211	726
Valve, swing check, w/balldrip CI with brass trim 4" pipe size	1.000	Ea.	465	505	970
Pipe, steel, black, schedule 40, 4" diam.	8.000	L.F.	460	351.28	811.28
Fire alarm horn, electric	1.000	Ea.	62	120	182
Pipe, steel, black, schedule 40, threaded, cplg & hngr 10' OC, 2-1/2" diam.	15.000	L.F.	555	465	1,020
Pipe, steel, black, schedule 40, threaded, cplg & hngr 10' OC, 2" diam.	9.375	L.F.	210.94	225	435.94
Pipe, steel, black, schedule 40, threaded, cplg & hngr 10' OC, 1-1/4" diam.	28.125	L.F.	396.56	489.38	885.94
Pipe, steel, black, schedule 40, threaded cplg & hngr 10' OC, 1" diam.	84.000	L.F.	894.60	1,360.80	2,255.40
Pipe Tee, malleable iron black, 150 lb. threaded, 4" pipe size	2.000	Ea.	1,110	770	1,880
Pipe Tee, malleable iron black, 150 lb. threaded, 2-1/2" pipe size	2.000	Ea.	312	344	656
Pipe Tee, malleable iron black, 150 lb. threaded, 2" pipe size	1.000	Ea.	72	141	213
Pipe Tee, malleable iron black, 150 lb. threaded, 1-1/4" pipe size	4.000	Ea.	136	444	580
Pipe Tee, malleable iron black, 150 lb. threaded, 1" pipe size	3.000	Ea.	63	321	384
Pipe 90° elbow, malleable iron black, 150 lb. threaded, 1" pipe size	5.000	Ea.	67.25	330	397.25
Sprinkler head, standard spray, brass 135°-286°F 1/2" NPT, 3/8" orifice	12.000	Ea.	474	636	1,110
Valve, gate, bronze, NRS, class 150, threaded, 1" pipe size	1.000	Ea.	258	45	303
*Standpipe connection, wall, single, flush w/plug & chain 2-1/2"x2-1/2"	1.000	Ea.	253	305	558
TOTAL			18,699.35	8,938.46	27,637.81
COST PER S.F.			7.48	3.58	11.06

*Not included in systems under 2000 S.F.

D4010 410		Wet Pipe Sprinkler Systems		COST PER S.F.		
				MAT.	INST.	TOTAL
0520	Wet pipe sprinkler systems, steel, black, sch. 40 pipe					
0530	Light hazard, one floor, 500 S.F.			8.60	4.25	12.85
0560	1000 S.F.		R211313 -10	7.50	3.72	11.22
0581	2000 S.F.					
0600	5000 S.F.		R211313 -20	3.80	2.80	6.60
0620	10,000 S.F.			2.69	2.38	5.07

D40 Fire Protection

D4010 Sprinklers

D4010 410	Wet Pipe Sprinkler Systems	COST PER S.F.		
		MAT.	INST.	TOTAL
0640	50,000 S.F.	2.26	2.20	4.46
0660	Each additional floor, 500 S.F.	2.72	3.40	6.12
0680	1000 S.F.	3.04	3.14	6.18
0700	2000 S.F.	2.69	2.81	5.50
0720	5000 S.F.	1.94	2.40	4.34
0740	10,000 S.F.	1.84	2.21	4.05
0760	50,000 S.F.	1.55	1.74	3.29
1000	Ordinary hazard, one floor, 500 S.F.	9.30	4.52	13.82
1020	1000 S.F.	7.45	3.64	11.09
1040	2000 S.F.	7.65	4.09	11.74
1060	5000 S.F.	4.36	3.01	7.37
1080	10,000 S.F.	3.50	3.16	6.66
1100	50,000 S.F.	3.23	3.03	6.26
1140	Each additional floor, 500 S.F.	3.47	3.84	7.31
1160	1000 S.F.	2.97	3.09	6.06
1180	2000 S.F.	3	3.10	6.10
1200	5000 S.F.	2.95	2.93	5.88
1220	10,000 S.F.	2.66	2.99	5.65
1240	50,000 S.F.	2.40	2.65	5.05
1500	Extra hazard, one floor, 500 S.F.	14	5.85	19.85
1520	1000 S.F.	10.45	5.20	15.65
1540	2000 S.F.	8.35	5.55	13.90
1560	5000 S.F.	6.20	4.95	11.15
1580	10,000 S.F.	5.75	4.75	10.50
1600	50,000 S.F.	6.40	4.54	10.94
1660	Each additional floor, 500 S.F.	5.10	4.73	9.83
1680	1000 S.F.	4.74	4.46	9.20
1700	2000 S.F.	4	4.45	8.45
1720	5000 S.F.	3.37	3.93	7.30
1740	10,000 S.F.	3.88	3.61	7.49
1760	50,000 S.F.	3.91	3.44	7.35
2020	Grooved steel, black sch. 40 pipe, light hazard, one floor, 2000 S.F.	7.65	3.27	10.92
2060	10,000 S.F.	2.94	2.05	4.99
2100	Each additional floor, 2000 S.F.	3.02	2.27	5.29
2150	10,000 S.F.	2.09	1.87	3.96
2200	Ordinary hazard, one floor, 2000 S.F.	7.90	3.49	11.39
2250	10,000 S.F.	3.59	2.66	6.25
2300	Each additional floor, 2000 S.F.	3.24	2.50	5.74
2350	10,000 S.F.	2.75	2.49	5.24
2400	Extra hazard, one floor, 2000 S.F.	6.95	4.28	11.23
2450	10,000 S.F.	4.64	3.41	8.05
2500	Each additional floor, 2000 S.F.	4.52	3.65	8.17
2550	10,000 S.F.	3.78	3.10	6.88
3050	Grooved steel, black sch. 10 pipe, light hazard, one floor, 2000 S.F.	5.40	2.98	8.38
3100	10,000 S.F.	2.57	2.02	4.59
3150	Each additional floor, 2000 S.F.	2.60	2.24	4.84
3200	10,000 S.F.	1.72	1.84	3.56
3250	Ordinary hazard, one floor, 2000 S.F.	7.50	3.46	10.96
3300	10,000 S.F.	2.97	2.59	5.56
3350	Each additional floor, 2000 S.F.	2.83	2.47	5.30
3400	10,000 S.F.	2.19	2.43	4.62
3450	Extra hazard, one floor, 2000 S.F.	8.45	4.51	12.96
3500	10,000 S.F.	4.47	3.41	7.88
3550	Each additional floor, 2000 S.F.	4.19	3.63	7.82
3600	10,000 S.F.	3.39	3.06	6.45
4050	Copper tubing, type L, light hazard, one floor, 2000 S.F.	7.35	3.27	10.62
4100	10,000 S.F.	2.77	2.09	4.86
4150	Each additional floor, 2000 S.F.	2.70	2.32	5.02

D40 Fire Protection

D4010 Sprinklers

D4010 410	Wet Pipe Sprinkler Systems	COST PER S.F.		
		MAT.	INST.	TOTAL
4200	10,000 S.F.	1.92	1.92	3.84
4250	Ordinary hazard, one floor, 2000 S.F.	7.60	3.69	11.29
4300	10,000 S.F.	3.25	2.48	5.73
4350	Each additional floor, 2000 S.F.	3.01	2.56	5.57
4400	10,000 S.F.	2.29	2.26	4.55
4450	Extra hazard, one floor, 2000 S.F.	8.45	4.62	13.07
4500	10,000 S.F.	6.70	3.80	10.50
4550	Each additional floor, 2000 S.F.	4.19	3.74	7.93
4600	10,000 S.F.	4.81	3.40	8.21
5050	Copper tubing, type L, T-drill system, light hazard, one floor			
5060	2000 S.F.	7.20	3.03	10.23
5100	10,000 S.F.	2.42	1.72	4.14
5150	Each additional floor, 2000 S.F.	2.57	2.08	4.65
5200	10,000 S.F.	1.57	1.56	3.13
5250	Ordinary hazard, one floor, 2000 S.F.	5.20	2.84	8.04
5300	10,000 S.F.	2.96	2.20	5.16
5350	Each additional floor, 2000 S.F.	2.40	2.10	4.50
5400	10,000 S.F.	2.12	2.03	4.15
5450	Extra hazard, one floor, 2000 S.F.	7.45	3.74	11.19
5500	10,000 S.F.	4.67	2.78	7.45
5550	Each additional floor, 2000 S.F.	5.65	3.20	8.85
5600	10,000 S.F.	2.79	2.37	5.16

D40 Fire Protection

D4010 Sprinklers

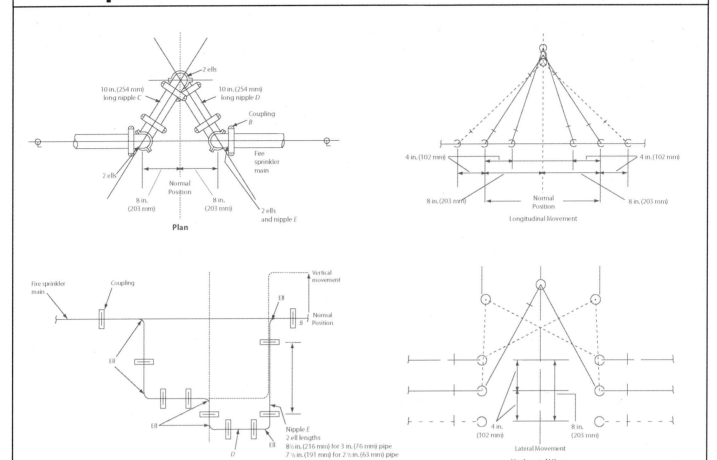

System Components	QUANTITY	UNIT	COST PER EACH		
			MAT.	INST.	TOTAL
SYSTEM D4010 412 1000					
WET SPRINKLER SYSTEM, SCHEDULE 10 BLACK STEEL GROOVED PIPE					
SEPARATION ASSEMBLY, 2 INCH DIAMETER					
Hanger support for 2 inch pipe	2.000	Ea.	165	94	259
Pipe roller support yoke	2.000	Ea.	38.30	22.10	60.40
Spool pieces 2 inch	3.000	Ea.	32.25	60	92.25
2 inch grooved elbows	6.000	Ea.	423	207	630
Coupling grooved joint 2 inch pipe	10.000	Ea.	695	172	867
Roll grooved joint labor only	8.000	Ea.		106.80	106.80
TOTAL			1,353.55	661.90	2,015.45

D4010 412	Wet Sprinkler Seismic Components	COST PER EACH		
		MAT.	INST.	TOTAL
1000	Wet sprinkler sys, Sch. 10, blk steel grooved, separation assembly, 2 inch	1,350	660	2,010
1100	2-1/2 inch	1,500	730	2,230
1200	3 inch	2,000	845	2,845
1300	4 inch	2,475	1,050	3,525
1400	6 inch	4,850	1,500	6,350
1500	8 inch	8,575	1,775	10,350
2000	Wet sprinkler sys, Sch. 10, blk steel grooved, flexible coupling, 2-1/2 inch	940	365	1,305
2100	3 inch	1,000	430	1,430
2200	4 inch	1,350	570	1,920
2300	6 inch	2,050	805	2,855

For customer support on your Plumbing Costs with RSMeans data, call 800.448.8182.

D40 Fire Protection

D4010 Sprinklers

D4010 412	Wet Sprinkler Seismic Components	COST PER EACH		
		MAT.	INST.	TOTAL
2400	8 inch	2,600	1,000	3,600
2990	Allowance for seismic movement by providing annular space in concrete wall			
2995	If additional cores are performed for the same size and at the same time reduce			
2996	price of additional cores by 50 %. If different size cores reduce by 30 %.			
3000	Wet pipe sprinkler systems, 2 inch black steel, annular space 6 inch wall	12.95	760	772.95
3010	8 inch wall	13.20	765	778.20
3020	10 inch wall	13.45	775	788.45
3030	12 inch wall	13.75	780	793.75
3100	Wet pipe sprinkler systems, 2-1/2/3 inch black steel, annular space 6" wall	12.95	780	792.95
3110	8 inch wall	13.20	790	803.20
3120	10 inch wall	13.45	795	808.45
3130	12 inch wall	13.75	805	818.75
3200	Wet pipe sprinkler systems, 4 inch black steel, annular space 6" wall	12.95	865	877.95
3210	8 inch wall	13.20	875	888.20
3220	10 inch wall	13.45	880	893.45
3230	12 inch wall	13.75	890	903.75
3300	Wet pipe sprinkler systems, 6 inch black steel, annular space 6" wall	12.95	900	912.95
3310	8 inch wall	13.20	910	923.20
3320	10 inch wall	13.45	915	928.45
3330	12 inch wall	13.75	925	938.75
3400	Wet pipe sprinkler systems, 8 inch black steel, annular space 6" wall	12.95	935	947.95
3410	8 inch wall	13.20	945	958.20
3420	10 inch wall	13.45	955	968.45
3430	12 inch wall	13.75	960	973.75
3996	Lateral, longitudinal and 4-way seismic strut braces			
4000	Wet pipe sprinkler systems, 2 inch pipe double lateral strut brace	231	355	586
4010	2 -1/2 inch	247	355	602
4020	3 inch	260	355	615
4030	4 inch	281	360	641
4040	6 inch	415	360	775
4050	8 inch	505	365	870
4100	Wet pipe sprinkler systems, 2 inch pipe longitudinal strut brace	231	355	586
4110	2 -1/2 inch	247	355	602
4120	3 inch	260	355	615
4130	4 inch	281	360	641
4140	6 inch	415	360	775
4150	8 inch	505	365	870
4200	Wet pipe sprinkler systems, 2 inch pipe single lateral strut brace	163	235	398
4210	2 -1/2 inch	179	235	414
4220	3 inch	192	236	428
4230	4 inch	210	239	449
4240	6 inch	340	240	580
4250	8 inch	435	241	676
4300	Wet pipe sprinkler systems, 2 inch pipe longitudinal wire brace	125	247	372
4310	2 -1/2 inch	141	247	388
4320	3 inch	154	247	401
4330	4 inch	219	255	474
4340	6 inch	305	253	558
4350	8 inch	400	253	653
4400	Wet pipe sprinkler systems, 2 inch pipe 4-way wire brace	155	380	535
4410	2 -1/2 inch	171	380	551
4420	3 inch	184	380	564
4430	4 inch	299	395	694
4440	6 inch	345	390	735
4450	8 inch	435	390	825
4500	Wet pipe sprinkler systems, 2 inch pipe 4-way strut brace	365	600	965
4510	2 -1/2 inch	380	600	980
4520	3 inch	395	600	995

D40 Fire Protection

D4010 Sprinklers

D4010 412	Wet Sprinkler Seismic Components	COST PER EACH		
		MAT.	INST.	TOTAL
4530	4 inch	420	605	1,025
4540	6 inch	555	605	1,160
4550	8 inch	645	605	1,250

D40 Fire Protection

D4010 Sprinklers

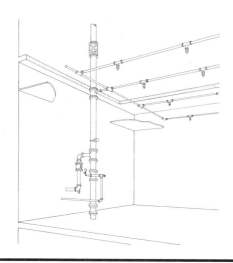

Wet Pipe System. A system employing automatic sprinklers attached to a piping system containing water and connected to a water supply so that water discharges immediately from sprinklers opened by heat from a fire.

All areas are assumed to be open.

System Components	QUANTITY	UNIT	COST PER S.F. MAT.	COST PER S.F. INST.	COST PER S.F. TOTAL
SYSTEM D4010 413 0580					
SEISMIC WET PIPE SPRINKLER, STEEL, BLACK, SCH. 40 PIPE					
LIGHT HAZARD, ONE FLOOR, 3' FLEXIBLE FEED, 2000 S.F.					
Valve, gate, iron body, 125 lb., OS&Y, flanged, 4" diam.	1.000	Ea.	.62	.19	.81
4" pipe size	1.000	Ea.	1.54	.19	1.73
Tamper switch (valve supervisory switch)	3.000	Ea.	.30	.06	.36
Valve, swing check, bronze, 125 lb, regrinding disc, 2-1/2" pipe size	1.000	Ea.	.65	.04	.69
Valve, angle, bronze, 150 lb., rising stem, threaded, 2" diam.	1.000	Ea.	.52	.03	.55
*Alarm valve, 2-1/2" pipe size	1.000	Ea.	1.02	.19	1.21
Alarm, water motor, complete with gong	1.000	Ea.	.19	.08	.27
Valve, swing check, w/balldrip CI with brass trim 4" pipe size	1.000	Ea.	.17	.19	.36
Pipe, steel, black, schedule 40, 4" diam.	8.000	L.F.	.17	.14	.31
Fire alarm horn, electric	1.000	Ea.	.02	.04	.06
Pipe, steel, black, schedule 40, threaded, cplg & hngr 10' OC, 2-1/2" diam.	15.000	L.F.	.21	.17	.38
Pipe, steel, black, schedule 40, threaded, cplg & hngr 10' OC, 2" diam.	9.375	L.F.	.08	.08	.16
Pipe, steel, black, schedule 40, threaded, cplg & hngr 10' OC, 1-1/4" diam.	28.125	L.F.	.15	.18	.33
Pipe Tee, malleable iron black, 150 lb. threaded, 4" pipe size	2.000	Ea.	.42	.29	.71
Pipe Tee, malleable iron black, 150 lb. threaded, 2-1/2" pipe size	2.000	Ea.	.12	.13	.25
Pipe Tee, malleable iron black, 150 lb. threaded, 2" pipe size	1.000	Ea.	.03	.05	.08
Pipe Tee, malleable iron black, 150 lb. threaded, 1-1/4" pipe size	4.000	Ea.	.05	.17	.22
Pipe Tee, malleable iron black, 150 lb. threaded, 1" pipe size	3.000	Ea.	.02	.12	.14
Pipe 90° elbow, malleable iron black, 150 lb. threaded, 1" pipe size	5.000	Ea.	.03	.12	.15
Sprinkler head, standard spray, brass 135°-286°F 1/2" NPT, 3/8" orifice	12.000	Ea.	.18	.24	.42
Valve, gate, bronze, NRS, class 150, threaded, 1" pipe size	1.000	Ea.	.10	.02	.12
*Standpipe connection, wall, single, flush w/plug & chain 2-1/2"x2-1/2"	1.000	Ea.	.09	.11	.20
Flexible connector 36 inches long	12.000	Ea.	.20	.13	.33
TOTAL			6.88	2.96	9.84

*Not included in systems under 2000 S.F.

D4010 413	Seismic Wet Pipe Flexible Feed Sprinkler Systems	COST PER S.F. MAT.	COST PER S.F. INST.	COST PER S.F. TOTAL
0520	Seismic wet pipe 3' flexible feed sprinkler systems, steel, black, sch. 40 pipe			
0525	Note: See D4010-412 for strut braces, flexible joints and separation assemblies			
0530	Light hazard, one floor, 3' flexible feed, 500 S.F.	8.25	3.50	11.75
0560	1000 S.F.	7.30	3.24	10.54
0580	2000 S.F.	6.90	2.97	9.87
0600	5000 S.F.	3.70	2.45	6.15

D40 Fire Protection

D4010 Sprinklers

D4010 413	Seismic Wet Pipe Flexible Feed Sprinkler Systems	COST PER S.F.		
		MAT.	INST.	TOTAL
0620	10,000 S.F.	2.70	2.22	4.92
0640	50,000 S.F.	2.18	1.92	4.10
0660	Each additional floor, 500 S.F.	2.41	2.70	5.11
0680	1000 S.F.	2.92	2.70	5.62
0700	2000 S.F.	2.45	2.26	4.71
0720	5000 S.F.	1.84	2.05	3.89
0740	10,000 S.F.	1.87	2.05	3.92
0760	50,000 S.F.	1.59	1.63	3.22
1000	Ordinary hazard, one floor, 500 S.F.	9	3.82	12.82
1020	1000 S.F.	7.25	3.12	10.37
1040	2000 S.F.	7.60	3.77	11.37
1060	5000 S.F.	4.38	2.79	7.17
1080	10,000 S.F.	3.57	3.02	6.59
1100	50,000 S.F.	3.19	2.74	5.93
1140	Each additional floor, 500 S.F.	6.95	3.40	10.35
1160	1000 S.F.	2.78	2.56	5.34
1180	2000 S.F.	2.95	2.78	5.73
1200	5000 S.F.	3.01	2.71	5.72
1220	10,000 S.F.	2.75	2.85	5.60
1240	50,000 S.F.	2.38	2.36	4.74
1500	Extra hazard, one floor, 500 S.F.	13.45	4.73	18.18
1520	1000 S.F.	9.90	4.13	14.03
1540	2000 S.F.	8.20	5.05	13.25
1560	5000 S.F.	6.15	4.63	10.78
1580	10,000 S.F.	5.80	4.50	10.30
1600	50,000 S.F.	6.45	4.27	10.72
1660	Each additional floor, 500 S.F.	4.12	3.54	7.66
1680	1000 S.F.	4.39	3.42	7.81
1700	2000 S.F.	3.95	3.96	7.91
1720	5000 S.F.	3.38	3.62	7
1740	10,000 S.F.	3.95	3.37	7.32
1760	50,000 S.F.	3.96	3.16	7.12
2020	Grooved steel, black sch. 40 pipe, light hazard, one floor, 2000 S.F.	5.50	2.57	8.07
2060	10,000 S.F.	2.77	1.85	4.62
2100	Each additional floor, 2000 S.F.	2.67	1.82	4.49
2150	10,000 S.F.	1.93	1.68	3.61
2200	Ordinary hazard, one floor, 2000 S.F.	7.75	3.25	11
2250	10,000 S.F.	3.60	2.56	6.16
2300	Each additional floor, 2000 S.F.	3.11	2.25	5.36
2350	10,000 S.F.	2.78	2.39	5.17
2400	Extra hazard, one floor, 2000 S.F.	8.50	4.14	12.64
2450	10,000 S.F.	5.10	3.31	8.41
2500	Each additional floor, 2000 S.F.	4.33	3.28	7.61
2550	10,000 S.F.	3.75	2.94	6.69
3050	Grooved steel black sch. 10 pipe, light hazard, one floor, 2000 S.F.	6.90	2.79	9.69
3100	10,000 S.F.	2.53	1.90	4.43
3150	Each additional floor, 2000 S.F.	2.24	1.79	4.03
3200	10,000 S.F.	1.56	1.64	3.20
3250	Ordinary hazard, one floor, 2000 S.F.	7.35	3.22	10.57
3300	10,000 S.F.	3.04	2.50	5.54
3350	Each additional floor, 2000 S.F.	2.60	2.21	4.81
3400	10,000 S.F.	2.18	2.33	4.51
3450	Extra hazard, one floor, 2000 S.F.	8.15	4.12	12.27
3500	10,000 S.F.	4.43	3.25	7.68
3550	Each additional floor, 2000 S.F.	4	3.26	7.26
3600	10,000 S.F.	3.36	2.90	6.26

D40 Fire Protection

D4010 Sprinklers

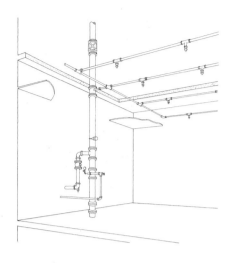

Wet Pipe System. A system employing automatic sprinklers attached to a piping system containing water and connected to a water supply so that water discharges immediately from sprinklers opened by heat from a fire.

All areas are assumed to be open.

System Components	QUANTITY	UNIT	COST PER S.F. MAT.	COST PER S.F. INST.	COST PER S.F. TOTAL
SYSTEM D4010 414 0580					
SEISMIC WET PIPE SPRINKLER, STEEL, BLACK, SCH. 40 PIPE					
LIGHT HAZARD, ONE FLOOR, 4' FLEXIBLE FEED, 2000 S.F.					
Valve, gate, iron body, 125 lb., OS&Y, flanged, 4" diam.	1.000	Ea.	.62	.19	.81
4" pipe size	1.000	Ea.	1.54	.19	1.73
Tamper switch (valve supervisory switch)	3.000	Ea.	.30	.06	.36
Valve, swing check, bronze, 125 lb, regrinding disc, 2-1/2" pipe size	1.000	Ea.	.65	.04	.69
Valve, angle, bronze, 150 lb., rising stem, threaded, 2" diam.	1.000	Ea.	.52	.03	.55
*Alarm valve, 2-1/2" pipe size	1.000	Ea.	1.02	.19	1.21
Alarm, water motor, complete with gong	1.000	Ea.	.19	.08	.27
Valve, swing check, w/balldrip CI with brass trim 4" pipe size	1.000	Ea.	.17	.19	.36
Pipe, steel, black, schedule 40, 4" diam.	8.000	L.F.	.17	.14	.31
Fire alarm horn, electric	1.000	Ea.	.02	.04	.06
Pipe, steel, black, schedule 40, threaded, cplg & hngr 10' OC, 2-1/2" diam.	15.000	L.F.	.21	.17	.38
Pipe, steel, black, schedule 40, threaded, cplg & hngr 10' OC, 2" diam.	9.375	L.F.	.08	.08	.16
Pipe, steel, black, schedule 40, threaded, cplg & hngr 10' OC, 1-1/4" diam.	28.125	L.F.	.15	.18	.33
Pipe Tee, malleable iron black, 150 lb. threaded, 4" pipe size	2.000	Ea.	.42	.29	.71
Pipe Tee, malleable iron black, 150 lb. threaded, 2-1/2" pipe size	2.000	Ea.	.12	.13	.25
Pipe Tee, malleable iron black, 150 lb. threaded, 2" pipe size	1.000	Ea.	.03	.05	.08
Pipe Tee, malleable iron black, 150 lb. threaded, 1-1/4" pipe size	4.000	Ea.	.05	.17	.22
Pipe Tee, malleable iron black, 150 lb. threaded, 1" pipe size	3.000	Ea.	.02	.12	.14
Pipe 90° elbow, malleable iron black, 150 lb. threaded, 1" pipe size	5.000	Ea.	.03	.12	.15
Sprinkler head, standard spray, brass 135°-286°F 1/2" NPT, 3/8" orifice	12.000	Ea.	.18	.24	.42
Valve, gate, bronze, NRS, class 150, threaded, 1" pipe size	1.000	Ea.	.10	.02	.12
*Standpipe connection, wall, single, flush w/plug & chain 2-1/2"x2-1/2"	1.000	Ea.	.09	.11	.20
Flexible connector 48 inches long	12.000	Ea.	.23	.17	.40
TOTAL			6.91	3	9.91

*Not included in systems under 2000 S.F.

D4010 414	Seismic Wet Pipe Flexible Feed Sprinkler Systems	COST PER S.F. MAT.	COST PER S.F. INST.	COST PER S.F. TOTAL
0520	Seismic wet pipe 4' flexible feed sprinkler systems, steel, black, sch. 40 pipe			
0525	Note: See D4010-412 for strut braces, flexible joints and separation assemblies			
0530	Light hazard, one floor, 4' flexible feed, 500 S.F.	8.30	3.55	11.85
0560	1000 S.F.	7.35	3.28	10.63
0580	2000 S.F.	6.90	3.01	9.91
0600	5000 S.F.	3.73	2.50	6.23
0620	10,000 S.F.	2.73	2.27	5
0640	50,000 S.F.	2.21	1.96	4.17

D40 Fire Protection

D4010 Sprinklers

D4010 414	Seismic Wet Pipe Flexible Feed Sprinkler Systems	COST PER S.F.		
		MAT.	INST.	TOTAL
0660	Each additional floor, 500 S.F.	2.45	2.76	5.21
0680	1000 S.F.	2.96	2.76	5.72
0700	2000 S.F.	2.47	2.31	4.78
0720	5000 S.F.	1.87	2.10	3.97
0740	10,000 S.F.	1.90	2.10	4
0760	50,000 S.F.	1.62	1.67	3.29
1000	Ordinary hazard, one floor, 500 S.F.	9.05	3.88	12.93
1020	1000 S.F.	7.30	3.18	10.48
1040	2000 S.F.	7.65	3.84	11.49
1060	5000 S.F.	4.42	2.85	7.27
1080	10,000 S.F.	3.61	3.08	6.69
1100	50,000 S.F.	3.23	2.80	6.03
1140	Each additional floor, 500 S.F.	3.21	3.20	6.41
1160	1000 S.F.	2.82	2.62	5.44
1180	2000 S.F.	2.99	2.84	5.83
1200	5000 S.F.	3.05	2.78	5.83
1220	10,000 S.F.	2.79	2.91	5.70
1240	50,000 S.F.	2.42	2.42	4.84
1500	Extra hazard, one floor, 500 S.F.	13.50	4.83	18.33
1520	1000 S.F.	9.95	4.23	14.18
1540	2000 S.F.	8.25	5.15	13.40
1560	5000 S.F.	6.20	4.71	10.91
1580	10,000 S.F.	5.85	4.60	10.45
1600	50,000 S.F.	6.55	4.37	10.92
1660	Each additional floor, 500 S.F.	4.18	3.64	7.82
1680	1000 S.F.	4.44	3.51	7.95
1700	2000 S.F.	4.01	4.06	8.07
1720	5000 S.F.	3.43	3.70	7.13
1740	10,000 S.F.	4.01	3.46	7.47
1760	50,000 S.F.	4.02	3.26	7.28
2020	Grooved steel, black sch. 40 pipe, light hazard, one floor, 2000 S.F.	7.35	2.87	10.22
2060	10,000 S.F.	2.77	1.86	4.63
2100	Each additional floor, 2000 S.F.	2.70	1.87	4.57
2150	10,000 S.F.	1.94	1.69	3.63
2200	Ordinary hazard, one floor, 2000 S.F.	7.80	3.31	11.11
2250	10,000 S.F.	3.64	2.62	6.26
2300	Each additional floor, 2000 S.F.	3.15	2.32	5.47
2350	10,000 S.F.	2.82	2.46	5.28
2400	Extra hazard, one floor, 2000 S.F.	8.55	4.24	12.79
2450	10,000 S.F.	5.15	3.40	8.55
2500	Each additional floor, 2000 S.F.	4.39	3.38	7.77
2550	10,000 S.F.	3.81	3.03	6.84
3050	Grooved steel black sch. 10 pipe, light hazard, one floor, 2000 S.F.	6.90	2.84	9.74
3100	10,000 S.F.	2.56	1.94	4.50
3150	Each additional floor, 2000 S.F.	2.27	1.84	4.11
3200	10,000 S.F.	1.57	1.66	3.23
3250	Ordinary hazard, one floor, 2000 S.F.	7.40	3.28	10.68
3300	10,000 S.F.	3.08	2.56	5.64
3350	Each additional floor, 2000 S.F.	2.74	2.29	5.03
3400	10,000 S.F.	2.26	2.40	4.66
3450	Extra hazard, one floor, 2000 S.F.	8.20	4.21	12.41
3500	10,000 S.F.	4.49	3.34	7.83
3550	Each additional floor, 2000 S.F.	4.06	3.35	7.41
3600	10,000 S.F.	3.42	2.99	6.41

D40 Fire Protection

D4020 Standpipes

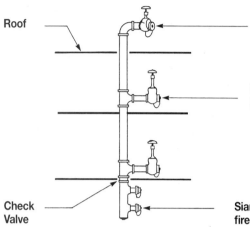

- Roof connections with hose gate valves (for combustible roof)
- Hose connections on each floor (size based on class of service)
- Siamese inlet connections (for fire department use)
- Check Valve
- Roof

System Components	QUANTITY	UNIT	COST PER FLOOR		
			MAT.	INST.	TOTAL
SYSTEM D4020 310 0560 WET STANDPIPE RISER, CLASS I, STEEL, BLACK, SCH. 40 PIPE, 10' HEIGHT 4" DIAMETER PIPE, ONE FLOOR					
Pipe, steel, black, schedule 40, threaded, 4" diam.	20.000	L.F.	1,420	860	2,280
Pipe, Tee, malleable iron, black, 150 lb. threaded, 4" pipe size	2.000	Ea.	1,110	770	1,880
Pipe, 90° elbow, malleable iron, black, 150 lb threaded, 4" pipe size	1.000	Ea.	310	258	568
Pipe, nipple, steel, black, schedule 40, 2-1/2" pipe size x 3" long	2.000	Ea.	48	193	241
Fire valve, gate, 300 lb., brass w/handwheel, 2-1/2" pipe size	1.000	Ea.	258	121	379
Fire valve, pressure reducing rgh brs, 2-1/2" pipe size	1.000	Ea.	1,600	242	1,842
Valve, swing check, w/ball drip, CI w/brs. ftngs., 4" pipe size	1.000	Ea.	465	505	970
Standpipe conn wall dble. flush brs. w/plugs & chains 2-1/2"x2-1/2"x4"	1.000	Ea.	930	305	1,235
Valve, swing check, bronze, 125 lb, regrinding disc, 2-1/2" pipe size	1.000	Ea.	1,725	103	1,828
Roof manifold, fire, w/valves & caps, horiz/vert brs 2-1/2"x2-1/2"x4"	1.000	Ea.	277	315	592
Fire, hydrolator, vent & drain, 2-1/2" pipe size	1.000	Ea.	168	70.50	238.50
Valve, gate, iron body 125 lb., OS&Y, threaded, 4" pipe size	1.000	Ea.	1,650	515	2,165
Tamper switch (valve supervisory switch)	1.000	Ea.	265	53	318
TOTAL			10,226	4,310.50	14,536.50

D4020 310	Wet Standpipe Risers, Class I		COST PER FLOOR		
			MAT.	INST.	TOTAL
0550	Wet standpipe risers, Class I, steel, black, sch. 40, 10' height				
0560	4" diameter pipe, one floor		10,200	4,300	14,500
0580	Additional floors		2,550	1,325	3,875
0600	6" diameter pipe, one floor		16,300	7,475	23,775
0620	Additional floors	R211226 -10	4,250	2,100	6,350
0640	8" diameter pipe, one floor		24,200	9,025	33,225
0660	Additional floors	R211226 -20	5,475	2,550	8,025
0680					

D4020 310	Wet Standpipe Risers, Class II	COST PER FLOOR		
		MAT.	INST.	TOTAL
1030	Wet standpipe risers, Class II, steel, black sch. 40, 10' height			
1040	2" diameter pipe, one floor	4,475	1,600	6,075
1060	Additional floors	1,275	595	1,870
1080	2-1/2" diameter pipe, one floor	6,025	2,250	8,275
1100	Additional floors	1,550	695	2,245
1120				

D40 Fire Protection

D4020 Standpipes

D4020 310	Wet Standpipe Risers, Class III	COST PER FLOOR		
		MAT.	INST.	TOTAL
1530	Wet standpipe risers, Class III, steel, black, sch. 40, 10' height			
1540	4" diameter pipe, one floor	10,500	4,300	14,800
1560	Additional floors	2,400	1,100	3,500
1580	6" diameter pipe, one floor	16,600	7,475	24,075
1600	Additional floors	4,400	2,100	6,500
1620	8" diameter pipe, one floor	24,500	9,025	33,525
1640	Additional floors	5,625	2,550	8,175

For customer support on your Plumbing Costs with RSMeans data, call 800.448.8182.

D40 Fire Protection

D4020 Standpipes

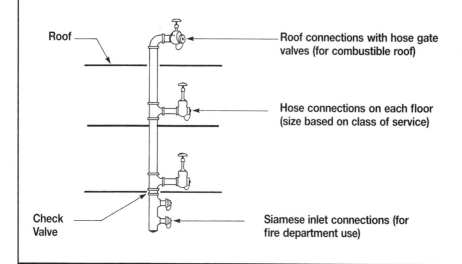

System Components	QUANTITY	UNIT	COST PER FLOOR		
			MAT.	INST.	TOTAL
SYSTEM D4020 330 0540					
DRY STANDPIPE RISER, CLASS I, PIPE, STEEL, BLACK, SCH 40, 10' HEIGHT					
4" DIAMETER PIPE, ONE FLOOR					
Pipe, steel, black, schedule 40, threaded, 4" diam.	20.000	L.F.	1,420	860	2,280
Pipe, Tee, malleable iron, black, 150 lb. threaded, 4" pipe size	2.000	Ea.	1,110	770	1,880
Pipe, 90° elbow, malleable iron, black, 150 lb threaded, 4" pipe size	1.000	Ea.	310	258	568
Pipe, nipple, steel, black, schedule 40, 2-1/2" pipe size x 3" long	2.000	Ea.	48	193	241
Fire valve gate NRS 300 lb., brass w/handwheel, 2-1/2" pipe size	1.000	Ea.	258	121	379
Tamper switch (valve supervisory switch)	1.000	Ea.	265	53	318
Fire valve, pressure reducing rgh brs, 2-1/2" pipe size	1.000	Ea.	800	121	921
Standpipe conn wall dble. flush brs. w/plugs & chains 2-1/2"x2-1/2"x4"	1.000	Ea.	930	305	1,235
Valve swing check w/ball drip CI w/brs. ftngs., 4"pipe size	1.000	Ea.	465	505	970
Roof manifold, fire, w/valves & caps, horiz/vert brs 2-1/2"x2-1/2"x4"	1.000	Ea.	277	315	592
TOTAL			5,883	3,501	9,384

D4020 330	Dry Standpipe Risers, Class I		COST PER FLOOR		
			MAT.	INST.	TOTAL
0530	Dry standpipe riser, Class I, steel, black, sch. 40, 10' height				
0540	4" diameter pipe, one floor		5,875	3,500	9,375
0560	Additional floors		2,375	1,250	3,625
0580	6" diameter pipe, one floor		11,500	5,925	17,425
0600	Additional floors	R211226 -10	4,075	2,025	6,100
0620	8" diameter pipe, one floor		16,700	7,200	23,900
0640	Additional floors	R211226 -20	5,300	2,475	7,775
0660					

D4020 330	Dry Standpipe Risers, Class II	COST PER FLOOR		
		MAT.	INST.	TOTAL
1030	Dry standpipe risers, Class II, steel, black, sch. 40, 10' height			
1040	2" diameter pipe, one floor	3,250	1,600	4,850
1060	Additional floors	1,125	520	1,645
1080	2-1/2" diameter pipe, one floor	4,825	1,875	6,700
1100	Additional floors	1,375	625	2,000
1120				

D40 Fire Protection

D4020 Standpipes

D4020 330	Dry Standpipe Risers, Class III	COST PER FLOOR		
		MAT.	INST.	TOTAL
1530	Dry standpipe risers, Class III, steel, black, sch. 40, 10' height			
1540	4" diameter pipe, one floor	5,725	3,375	9,100
1560	Additional floors	2,250	1,125	3,375
1580	6" diameter pipe, one floor	11,600	5,925	17,525
1600	Additional floors	4,225	2,025	6,250
1620	8" diameter pipe, one floor	16,900	7,200	24,100
1640	Additional floors	5,450	2,475	7,925

For customer support on your Plumbing Costs with RSMeans data, call 800.448.8182.

D40 Fire Protection

D4020 Standpipes

D4020 410 Fire Hose Equipment

		COST EACH		
		MAT.	INST.	TOTAL
0100	Adapters, reducing, 1 piece, FxM, hexagon, cast brass, 2-1/2" x 1-1/2"	81.50		81.50
0200	Pin lug, 1-1/2" x 1"	50.50		50.50
0250	3" x 2-1/2"	97.50		97.50
0300	For polished chrome, add 75% mat.			
0400	Cabinets, D.S. glass in door, recessed, steel box, not equipped			
0500	Single extinguisher, steel door & frame	102	190	292
0550	Stainless steel door & frame	177	190	367
0600	Valve, 2-1/2" angle, steel door & frame	345	127	472
0650	Aluminum door & frame	400	127	527
0700	Stainless steel door & frame	480	127	607
0750	Hose rack assy, 2-1/2" x 1-1/2" valve & 100' hose, steel door & frame	1,025	254	1,279
0800	Aluminum door & frame	1,150	254	1,404
0850	Stainless steel door & frame	1,325	254	1,579
0900	Hose rack assy & extinguisher, 2-1/2"x1-1/2" valve & hose, steel door & frame	440	305	745
0950	Aluminum	440	305	745
1000	Stainless steel	700	305	1,005
1550	Compressor, air, dry pipe system, automatic, 200 gal., 3/4 H.P.	2,025	650	2,675
1600	520 gal., 1 H.P.	1,825	650	2,475
1650	Alarm, electric pressure switch (circuit closer)	168	32.50	200.50
2500	Couplings, hose, rocker lug, cast brass, 1-1/2"	74		74
2550	2-1/2"	162		162
3000	Escutcheon plate, for angle valves, polished brass, 1-1/2"	25		25
3050	2-1/2"	42.50		42.50
3500	Fire pump, electric, w/controller, fittings, relief valve			
3550	4" pump, 30 HP, 500 GPM	24,800	4,725	29,525
3600	5" pump, 40 H.P., 1000 G.P.M.	36,200	5,375	41,575
3650	5" pump, 100 H.P., 1000 G.P.M.	40,500	5,950	46,450
3700	For jockey pump system, add	4,700	760	5,460
5000	Hose, per linear foot, synthetic jacket, lined,			
5100	300 lb. test, 1-1/2" diameter	3.64	.59	4.23
5150	2-1/2" diameter	6.40	.69	7.09
5200	500 lb. test, 1-1/2" diameter	3.98	.59	4.57
5250	2-1/2" diameter	6.70	.69	7.39
5500	Nozzle, plain stream, polished brass, 1-1/2" x 10"	64.50		64.50
5550	2-1/2" x 15" x 13/16" or 1-1/2"	186		186
5600	Heavy duty combination adjustable fog and straight stream w/handle 1-1/2"	745		745
5650	2-1/2" direct connection	750		750
6000	Rack, for 1-1/2" diameter hose 100 ft. long, steel	129	76	205
6050	Brass	200	76	276
6500	Reel, steel, for 50 ft. long 1-1/2" diameter hose	206	109	315
6550	For 75 ft. long 2-1/2" diameter hose	294	109	403
7050	Siamese, w/plugs & chains, polished brass, sidewalk, 4" x 2-1/2" x 2-1/2"	965	610	1,575
7100	6" x 2-1/2" x 2-1/2"	1,525	760	2,285
7200	Wall type, flush, 4" x 2-1/2" x 2-1/2"	930	305	1,235
7250	6" x 2-1/2" x 2-1/2"	1,200	330	1,530
7300	Projecting, 4" x 2-1/2" x 2-1/2"	665	305	970
7350	6" x 2-1/2" x 2-1/2"	1,100	330	1,430
7400	For chrome plate, add 15% mat.			
8000	Valves, angle, wheel handle, 300 Lb., rough brass, 1-1/2"	111	70.50	181.50
8050	2-1/2"	214	121	335
8100	Combination pressure restricting, 1-1/2"	145	70.50	215.50
8150	2-1/2"	238	121	359
8200	Pressure restricting, adjustable, satin brass, 1-1/2"	530	70.50	600.50
8250	2-1/2"	800	121	921
8300	Hydrolator, vent and drain, rough brass, 1-1/2"	168	70.50	238.50
8350	2-1/2"	168	70.50	238.50
8400	Cabinet assy, incls. adapter, rack, hose, and nozzle	1,825	460	2,285

D40 Fire Protection

D4090 Other Fire Protection Systems

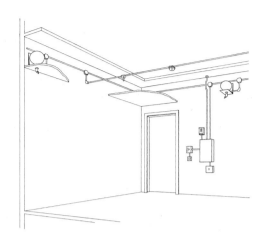

General: Automatic fire protection (suppression) systems other than water sprinklers may be desired for special environments, high risk areas, isolated locations or unusual hazards. Some typical applications would include:

Paint dip tanks
Securities vaults
Electronic data processing
Tape and data storage
Transformer rooms
Spray booths
Petroleum storage
High rack storage

Piping and wiring costs are dependent on the individual application and must be added to the component costs shown below.

All areas are assumed to be open.

D4090 910	Fire Suppression Unit Components	COST EACH		
		MAT.	INST.	TOTAL
0020	Detectors with brackets			
0040	Fixed temperature heat detector	48	114	162
0060	Rate of temperature rise detector	36.50	100	136.50
0080	Ion detector (smoke) detector	171	129	300
0200	Extinguisher agent			
0240	200 lb FM200, container	8,550	385	8,935
0280	75 lb carbon dioxide cylinder	1,725	258	1,983
0320	Dispersion nozzle			
0340	FM200 1-1/2" dispersion nozzle	310	61.50	371.50
0380	Carbon dioxide 3" x 5" dispersion nozzle	193	48	241
0420	Control station			
0440	Single zone control station with batteries	1,550	800	2,350
0470	Multizone (4) control station with batteries	3,750	1,600	5,350
0490				
0500	Electric mechanical release	1,275	415	1,690
0520				
0550	Manual pull station	112	143	255
0570				
0640	Battery standby power 10" x 10" x 17"	570	200	770
0700				
0740	Bell signalling device	62.50	100	162.50

D4090 920	FM200 Systems	COST PER C.F.		
		MAT.	INST.	TOTAL
0820	Average FM200 system, minimum	2.32		2.32
0840	Maximum	4.62		4.62

G Building Sitework

Same Data. Simplified.

Enjoy the convenience and efficiency of accessing your costs anywhere:
- **Skip the multiplier** by setting your location
- **Quickly search,** edit, favorite and share costs
- **Stay on top of price changes** with automatic updates

Discover more at rsmeans.com/online

No part of this cost data may be reproduced, stored in a retrieval system, or transmitted in any form or by any means without prior written permission of Gordian.

G10 Site Preparation

G1030 Site Earthwork

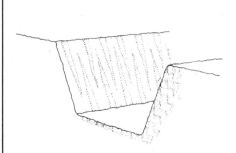

Trenching Systems are shown on a cost per linear foot basis. The systems include: excavation; backfill and removal of spoil; and compaction for various depths and trench bottom widths. The backfill has been reduced to accommodate a pipe of suitable diameter and bedding.

The slope for trench sides varies from none to 1:1.

The Expanded System Listing shows Trenching Systems that range from 2' to 12' in width. Depths range from 2' to 25'.

System Components	QUANTITY	UNIT	COST PER L.F.		
			EQUIP.	LABOR	TOTAL
SYSTEM G1030 805 1310					
TRENCHING, COMMON EARTH, NO SLOPE, 2' WIDE, 2' DP, 3/8 C.Y. BUCKET					
Excavation, trench, hyd. backhoe, track mtd., 3/8 C.Y. bucket	.148	C.Y.	.30	1.30	1.60
Backfill and load spoil, from stockpile	.153	L.C.Y.	.17	.39	.56
Compaction by vibrating plate, 6" lifts, 4 passes	.118	C.Y.	.13	.47	.60
Remove excess spoil, 8 C.Y. dump truck, 2 mile roundtrip	.040	L.C.Y.	.15	.22	.37
TOTAL			.75	2.38	3.13

G1030 805	Trenching Common Earth	COST PER L.F.		
		EQUIP.	LABOR	TOTAL
1310	Trenching, common earth, no slope, 2' wide, 2' deep, 3/8 C.Y. bucket	.75	2.38	3.14
1320	3' deep, 3/8 C.Y. bucket	1.09	3.58	4.67
1330	4' deep, 3/8 C.Y. bucket	1.43	4.77	6.20
1340	6' deep, 3/8 C.Y. bucket	2.08	6.20	8.25
1350	8' deep, 1/2 C.Y. bucket	2.80	8.20	11
1360	10' deep, 1 C.Y. bucket	5.25	9.80	15.05
1400	4' wide, 2' deep, 3/8 C.Y. bucket	1.64	4.75	6.40
1410	3' deep, 3/8 C.Y. bucket	2.31	7.15	9.45
1420	4' deep, 1/2 C.Y. bucket	3.11	7.95	11.05
1430	6' deep, 1/2 C.Y. bucket	4.22	12.80	17
1440	8' deep, 1/2 C.Y. bucket	8.50	16.60	25
1450	10' deep, 1 C.Y. bucket	10.15	20.50	30.50
1460	12' deep, 1 C.Y. bucket	13.20	26	39.50
1470	15' deep, 1-1/2 C.Y. bucket	10.55	23.50	34
1480	18' deep, 2-1/2 C.Y. bucket	15.20	32.50	48
1520	6' wide, 6' deep, 5/8 C.Y. bucket w/trench box	10.95	19.20	30
1530	8' deep, 3/4 C.Y. bucket	14.75	25	40
1540	10' deep, 1 C.Y. bucket	13.55	26	39.50
1550	12' deep, 1-1/2 C.Y. bucket	14.10	28	42
1560	16' deep, 2-1/2 C.Y. bucket	18.35	35	53
1570	20' deep, 3-1/2 C.Y. bucket	23	41.50	64.50
1580	24' deep, 3-1/2 C.Y. bucket	27.50	50	77.50
1640	8' wide, 12' deep, 1-1/2 C.Y. bucket w/trench box	19.45	35.50	55
1650	15' deep, 1-1/2 C.Y. bucket	25.50	46.50	72
1660	18' deep, 2-1/2 C.Y. bucket	26	46.50	72.50
1680	24' deep, 3-1/2 C.Y. bucket	37	64.50	101
1730	10' wide, 20' deep, 3-1/2 C.Y. bucket w/trench box	30	61.50	91.50
1740	24' deep, 3-1/2 C.Y. bucket	43.50	74	118
1780	12' wide, 20' deep, 3-1/2 C.Y. bucket w/trench box	46.50	78	125
1790	25' deep, bucket	58	99.50	157
1800	1/2 to 1 slope, 2' wide, 2' deep, 3/8 C.Y. bucket	1.09	3.58	4.67
1810	3' deep, 3/8 C.Y. bucket	1.86	6.25	8.15
1820	4' deep, 3/8 C.Y. bucket	2.79	9.55	12.35
1840	6' deep, 3/8 C.Y. bucket	5.10	15.45	20.50

G10 Site Preparation

G1030 Site Earthwork

G1030 805	Trenching Common Earth	COST PER L.F.		
		EQUIP.	LABOR	TOTAL
1860	8' deep, 1/2 C.Y. bucket	8.15	24.50	33
1880	10' deep, 1 C.Y. bucket	18.25	34.50	53
2300	4' wide, 2' deep, 3/8 C.Y. bucket	1.98	5.95	7.90
2310	3' deep, 3/8 C.Y. bucket	3.08	9.85	12.90
2320	4' deep, 1/2 C.Y. bucket	4.46	12.10	16.55
2340	6' deep, 1/2 C.Y. bucket	7.05	22.50	29.50
2360	8' deep, 1/2 C.Y. bucket	16.40	33.50	50
2380	10' deep, 1 C.Y. bucket	22.50	47	69.50
2400	12' deep, 1 C.Y. bucket	28.50	63.50	92
2430	15' deep, 1-1/2 C.Y. bucket	30	68	98
2460	18' deep, 2-1/2 C.Y. bucket	50	106	156
2840	6' wide, 6' deep, 5/8 C.Y. bucket w/trench box	16.45	28.50	45
2860	8' deep, 3/4 C.Y. bucket	24	42.50	66.50
2880	10' deep, 1 C.Y. bucket	21	43	64.50
2900	12' deep, 1-1/2 C.Y. bucket	27	56.50	83.50
2940	16' deep, 2-1/2 C.Y. bucket	42	83	125
2980	20' deep, 3-1/2 C.Y. bucket	57.50	112	169
3020	24' deep, 3-1/2 C.Y. bucket	81.50	153	234
3100	8' wide, 12' deep, 1-1/2 C.Y. bucket w/trench box	33	64.50	97.50
3120	15' deep, 1-1/2 C.Y. bucket	48.50	93.50	142
3140	18' deep, 2-1/2 C.Y. bucket	57.50	111	169
3180	24' deep, 3-1/2 C.Y. bucket	91	167	258
3270	10' wide, 20' deep, 3-1/2 C.Y. bucket w/trench box	59	129	187
3280	24' deep, 3-1/2 C.Y. bucket	100	183	283
3370	12' wide, 20' deep, 3-1/2 C.Y. bucket w/trench box	84	149	234
3380	25' deep, 3-1/2 C.Y. bucket	117	213	330
3500	1 to 1 slope, 2' wide, 2' deep, 3/8 C.Y. bucket	1.43	4.78	6.20
3520	3' deep, 3/8 C.Y. bucket	4	10.95	14.95
3540	4' deep, 3/8 C.Y. bucket	4.15	14.35	18.50
3560	6' deep, 1/2 C.Y. bucket	5.10	15.45	20.50
3580	8' deep, 1/2 C.Y. bucket	10.15	31	41
3600	10' deep, 1 C.Y. bucket	31.50	59.50	90.50
3800	4' wide, 2' deep, 3/8 C.Y. bucket	2.32	7.15	9.45
3820	3' deep, 3/8 C.Y. bucket	3.84	12.50	16.35
3840	4' deep, 1/2 C.Y. bucket	5.80	16.20	22
3860	6' deep, 1/2 C.Y. bucket	9.85	32.50	42.50
3880	8' deep, 1/2 C.Y. bucket	24.50	50.50	75
3900	10' deep, 1 C.Y. bucket	35	73.50	109
3920	12' deep, 1 C.Y. bucket	52	106	158
3940	15' deep, 1-1/2 C.Y. bucket	49.50	113	162
3960	18' deep, 2-1/2 C.Y. bucket	68.50	147	215
4030	6' wide, 6' deep, 5/8 C.Y. bucket w/trench box	21.50	38.50	60
4040	8' deep, 3/4 C.Y. bucket	32	52.50	84.50
4050	10' deep, 1 C.Y. bucket	30.50	63.50	94
4060	12' deep, 1-1/2 C.Y. bucket	41.50	86	127
4070	16' deep, 2-1/2 C.Y. bucket	66	131	197
4080	20' deep, 3-1/2 C.Y. bucket	93	182	275
4090	24' deep, 3-1/2 C.Y. bucket	136	256	390
4500	8' wide, 12' deep, 1-1/2 C.Y. bucket w/trench box	46.50	93.50	140
4550	15' deep, 1-1/2 C.Y. bucket	71	140	211
4600	18' deep, 2-1/2 C.Y. bucket	88	172	260
4650	24' deep, 3-1/2 C.Y. bucket	145	270	415
4800	10' wide, 20' deep, 3-1/2 C.Y. bucket w/trench box	87.50	196	283
4850	24' deep, 3-1/2 C.Y. bucket	154	286	440
4950	12' wide, 20' deep, 3-1/2 C.Y. bucket w/trench box	122	220	340
4980	25' deep, 3-1/2 C.Y. bucket	175	325	500

For customer support on your Plumbing Costs with RSMeans data, call 800.448.8182.

G10 Site Preparation

G1030 Site Earthwork

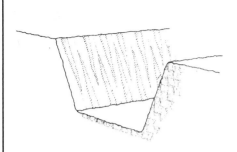

Trenching Systems are shown on a cost per linear foot basis. The systems include: excavation; backfill and removal of spoil; and compaction for various depths and trench bottom widths. The backfill has been reduced to accommodate a pipe of suitable diameter and bedding.

The slope for trench sides varies from none to 1:1.

The Expanded System Listing shows Trenching Systems that range from 2' to 12' in width. Depths range from 2' to 25'.

System Components	QUANTITY	UNIT	COST PER L.F.		
			EQUIP.	LABOR	TOTAL
SYSTEM G1030 806 1310					
TRENCHING, LOAM & SANDY CLAY, NO SLOPE, 2' WIDE, 2' DP, 3/8 C.Y. BUCKET					
Excavation, trench, hyd. backhoe, track mtd., 3/8 C.Y. bucket	.148	C.Y.	.28	1.20	1.48
Backfill and load spoil, from stockpile	.165	L.C.Y.	.18	.43	.61
Compaction by vibrating plate 18" wide, 6" lifts, 4 passes	.118	C.Y.	.13	.47	.60
Remove excess spoil, 8 C.Y. dump truck, 2 mile roundtrip	.042	L.C.Y.	.16	.23	.39
TOTAL			.75	2.33	3.08

G1030 806	Trenching Loam & Sandy Clay	COST PER L.F.		
		EQUIP.	LABOR	TOTAL
1310	Trenching, loam & sandy clay, no slope, 2' wide, 2' deep, 3/8 C.Y. bucket	.75	2.33	3.08
1320	3' deep, 3/8 C.Y. bucket	1.16	3.83	4.98
1330	4' deep, 3/8 C.Y. bucket	1.42	4.66	6.10
1340	6' deep, 3/8 C.Y. bucket	2.70	5.55	8.25
1350	8' deep, 1/2 C.Y. bucket	3.62	7.35	10.95
1360	10' deep, 1 C.Y. bucket	3.88	7.85	11.75
1400	4' wide, 2' deep, 3/8 C.Y. bucket	1.66	4.66	6.30
1410	3' deep, 3/8 C.Y. bucket	2.33	7	9.30
1420	4' deep, 1/2 C.Y. bucket	3.13	7.85	11
1430	6' deep, 1/2 C.Y. bucket	5.50	11.55	17
1440	8' deep, 1/2 C.Y. bucket	8.25	16.35	24.50
1450	10' deep, 1 C.Y. bucket	7.45	16.70	24
1460	12' deep, 1 C.Y. bucket	9.40	21	30
1470	15' deep, 1-1/2 C.Y. bucket	11.05	24	35
1480	18' deep, 2-1/2 C.Y. bucket	12.40	26.50	39
1520	6' wide, 6' deep, 5/8 C.Y. bucket w/trench box	10.50	18.85	29.50
1530	8' deep, 3/4 C.Y. bucket	14.15	24.50	39
1540	10' deep, 1 C.Y. bucket	12.40	25	37.50
1550	12' deep, 1-1/2 C.Y. bucket	13.75	28	41.50
1560	16' deep, 2-1/2 C.Y. bucket	18	35	53
1570	20' deep, 3-1/2 C.Y. bucket	21.50	41.50	63
1580	24' deep, 3-1/2 C.Y. bucket	26.50	50.50	77.50
1640	8' wide, 12' deep, 1-1/4 C.Y. bucket w/trench box	19.10	35.50	54.50
1650	15' deep, 1-1/2 C.Y. bucket	23.50	45	68.50
1660	18' deep, 2-1/2 C.Y. bucket	27	50.50	78
1680	24' deep, 3-1/2 C.Y. bucket	36	65.50	102
1730	10' wide, 20' deep, 3-1/2 C.Y. bucket w/trench box	36	66	102
1740	24' deep, 3-1/2 C.Y. bucket	45.50	81.50	127
1780	12' wide, 20' deep, 3-1/2 C.Y. bucket w/trench box	43.50	78.50	122
1790	25' deep, 3-1/2 C.Y. bucket	56.50	101	158
1800	1/2:1 slope, 2' wide, 2' deep, 3/8 C.Y. bucket	1.09	3.50	4.58
1810	3' deep, 3/8 C.Y. bucket	1.85	6.10	7.95
1820	4' deep, 3/8 C.Y. bucket	2.77	9.30	12.10
1840	6' deep, 3/8 C.Y. bucket	6.65	13.90	20.50

G10 Site Preparation

G1030 Site Earthwork

G1030 806	Trenching Loam & Sandy Clay	COST PER L.F.		
		EQUIP.	LABOR	TOTAL
1860	8' deep, 1/2 C.Y. bucket	10.60	22	33
1880	10' deep, 1 C.Y. bucket	13.45	28	41
2300	4' wide, 2' deep, 3/8 C.Y. bucket	1.99	5.85	7.85
2310	3' deep, 3/8 C.Y. bucket	3.08	9.60	12.70
2320	4' deep, 1/2 C.Y. bucket	4.45	11.90	16.35
2340	6' deep, 1/2 C.Y. bucket	9.20	20.50	29.50
2360	8' deep, 1/2 C.Y. bucket	15.90	33	49
2380	10' deep, 1 C.Y. bucket	16.45	38.50	54.50
2400	12' deep, 1 C.Y. bucket	27.50	63.50	91
2430	15' deep, 1-1/2 C.Y. bucket	31.50	70.50	102
2460	18' deep, 2-1/2 C.Y. bucket	49	108	157
2840	6' wide, 6' deep, 5/8 C.Y. bucket w/trench box	15.40	28.50	44
2860	8' deep, 3/4 C.Y. bucket	23	41.50	64.50
2880	10' deep, 1 C.Y. bucket	22.50	47	69
2900	12' deep, 1-1/2 C.Y. bucket	27	57	84
2940	16' deep, 2-1/2 C.Y. bucket	41.50	84	125
2980	20' deep, 3-1/2 C.Y. bucket	56	113	169
3020	24' deep, 3-1/2 C.Y. bucket	79.50	155	234
3100	8' wide, 12' deep, 1-1/2 C.Y. bucket w/trench box	32.50	64.50	97
3120	15' deep, 1-1/2 C.Y. bucket	44	91	135
3140	18' deep, 2-1/2 C.Y. bucket	56.50	112	169
3180	24' deep, 3-1/2 C.Y. bucket	88.50	170	259
3270	10' wide, 20' deep, 3-1/2 C.Y. bucket w/trench box	71	138	209
3280	24' deep, 3-1/2 C.Y. bucket	98	186	284
3320	12' wide, 20' deep, 3-1/2 C.Y. bucket w/trench box	78.50	150	228
3380	25' deep, 3-1/2 C.Y. bucket w/trench box	107	201	310
3500	1:1 slope, 2' wide, 2' deep, 3/8 C.Y. bucket	1.43	4.66	6.10
3520	3' deep, 3/8 C.Y. bucket	2.60	8.75	11.35
3540	4' deep, 3/8 C.Y. bucket	4.11	14	18.10
3560	6' deep, 1/2 C.Y. bucket	6.65	13.90	20.50
3580	8' deep, 1/2 C.Y. bucket	17.60	37	54.50
3600	10' deep, 1 C.Y. bucket	23	47.50	70.50
3800	4' wide, 2' deep, 3/8 C.Y. bucket	2.33	7	9.35
3820	3' deep, 1/2 C.Y. bucket	3.84	12.25	16.10
3840	4' deep, 1/2 C.Y. bucket	5.80	16	22
3860	6' deep, 1/2 C.Y. bucket	12.95	29.50	42.50
3880	8' deep, 1/2 C.Y. bucket	23.50	49.50	73.50
3900	10' deep, 1 C.Y. bucket	25.50	60	85.50
3920	12' deep, 1 C.Y. bucket	37	85	122
3940	15' deep, 1-1/2 C.Y. bucket	51.50	117	169
3960	18' deep, 2-1/2 C.Y. bucket	67.50	148	216
4030	6' wide, 6' deep, 5/8 C.Y. bucket w/trench box	20.50	38	58.50
4040	8' deep, 3/4 C.Y. bucket	31.50	58.50	90
4050	10' deep, 1 C.Y. bucket	32	69	101
4060	12' deep, 1-1/2 C.Y. bucket	40	86.50	127
4070	16' deep, 2-1/2 C.Y. bucket	64.50	132	197
4080	20' deep, 3-1/2 C.Y. bucket	91	185	276
4090	24' deep, 3-1/2 C.Y. bucket	132	259	390
4500	8' wide, 12' deep, 1-1/4 C.Y. bucket w/trench box	45.50	94	140
4550	15' deep, 1-1/2 C.Y. bucket	65	137	202
4600	18' deep, 2-1/2 C.Y. bucket	86	174	260
4650	24' deep, 3-1/2 C.Y. bucket	141	274	415
4800	10' wide, 20' deep, 3-1/2 C.Y. bucket w/trench box	106	209	315
4850	24' deep, 3-1/2 C.Y. bucket	151	290	440
4950	12' wide, 20' deep, 3-1/2 C.Y. bucket w/trench box	113	222	335
4980	25' deep, 3-1/2 C.Y. bucket	171	325	500

G10 Site Preparation

G1030 Site Earthwork

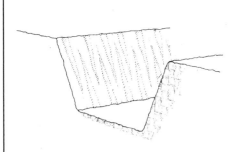

Trenching Systems are shown on a cost per linear foot basis. The systems include: excavation; backfill and removal of spoil; and compaction for various depths and trench bottom widths. The backfill has been reduced to accommodate a pipe of suitable diameter and bedding.

The slope for trench sides varies from none to 1:1.

The Expanded System Listing shows Trenching Systems that range from 2' to 12' in width. Depths range from 2' to 25'.

System Components	QUANTITY	UNIT	COST PER L.F.		
			EQUIP.	LABOR	TOTAL
SYSTEM G1030 807 1310					
TRENCHING, SAND & GRAVEL, NO SLOPE, 2' WIDE, 2' DEEP, 3/8 C.Y. BUCKET					
Excavation, trench, hyd. backhoe, track mtd., 3/8 C.Y. bucket	.148	C.Y.	.27	1.18	1.45
Backfill and load spoil, from stockpile	.140	L.C.Y.	.15	.36	.51
Compaction by vibrating plate 18" wide, 6" lifts, 4 passes	.118	C.Y.	.13	.47	.60
Remove excess spoil, 8 C.Y. dump truck, 2 mile roundtrip	.035	L.C.Y.	.14	.19	.33
TOTAL			.69	2.20	2.89

G1030 807	Trenching Sand & Gravel	COST PER L.F.		
		EQUIP.	LABOR	TOTAL
1310	Trenching, sand & gravel, no slope, 2' wide, 2' deep, 3/8 C.Y. bucket	.70	2.21	2.90
1320	3' deep, 3/8 C.Y. bucket	1.09	3.68	4.77
1330	4' deep, 3/8 C.Y. bucket	1.33	4.43	5.75
1340	6' deep, 3/8 C.Y. bucket	2.58	5.30	7.90
1350	8' deep, 1/2 C.Y. bucket	3.46	7	10.50
1360	10' deep, 1 C.Y. bucket	3.66	7.40	11.05
1400	4' wide, 2' deep, 3/8 C.Y. bucket	1.51	4.38	5.90
1410	3' deep, 3/8 C.Y. bucket	2.14	6.60	8.75
1420	4' deep, 1/2 C.Y. bucket	2.88	7.40	10.30
1430	6' deep, 1/2 C.Y. bucket	5.20	11.05	16.20
1440	8' deep, 1/2 C.Y. bucket	7.75	15.50	23.50
1450	10' deep, 1 C.Y. bucket	6.95	15.75	22.50
1460	12' deep, 1 C.Y. bucket	8.80	19.65	28.50
1470	15' deep, 1-1/2 C.Y. bucket	10.35	23	33
1480	18' deep, 2-1/2 C.Y. bucket	11.65	25	36.50
1520	6' wide, 6' deep, 5/8 C.Y. bucket w/trench box	9.95	17.85	28
1530	8' deep, 3/4 C.Y. bucket	13.40	23.50	37
1540	10' deep, 1 C.Y. bucket	11.65	23.50	35
1550	12' deep, 1-1/2 C.Y. bucket	12.90	26.50	39.50
1560	16' deep, 2 C.Y. bucket	17.05	33	50.50
1570	20' deep, 3-1/2 C.Y. bucket	19.95	39	59
1580	24' deep, 3-1/2 C.Y. bucket	25	47.50	72.50
1640	8' wide, 12' deep, 1-1/2 C.Y. bucket w/trench box	17.95	33.50	51.50
1650	15' deep, 1-1/2 C.Y. bucket	22	42.50	64.50
1660	18' deep, 2-1/2 C.Y. bucket	25.50	47.50	73
1680	24' deep, 3-1/2 C.Y. bucket	33.50	61.50	95
1730	10' wide, 20' deep, 3-1/2 C.Y. bucket w/trench box	34	61.50	95.50
1740	24' deep, 3-1/2 C.Y. bucket	42.50	76	118
1780	12' wide, 20' deep, 3-1/2 C.Y. bucket w/trench box	40.50	73	114
1790	25' deep, 3-1/2 C.Y. bucket	53	94.50	147
1800	1/2:1 slope, 2' wide, 2' deep, 3/8 C.Y. bucket	1.01	3.32	4.33
1810	3' deep, 3/8 C.Y. bucket	1.72	5.80	7.55
1820	4' deep, 3/8 C.Y. bucket	2.59	8.90	11.45
1840	6' deep, 3/8 C.Y. bucket	6.35	13.30	19.65

G10 Site Preparation

G1030 Site Earthwork

G1030 807	Trenching Sand & Gravel	COST PER L.F.		
		EQUIP.	LABOR	TOTAL
1860	8' deep, 1/2 C.Y. bucket	10.15	21	31.50
1880	10' deep, 1 C.Y. bucket	12.70	26	39
2300	4' wide, 2' deep, 3/8 C.Y. bucket	1.82	5.50	7.30
2310	3' deep, 3/8 C.Y. bucket	2.85	9.10	11.95
2320	4' deep, 1/2 C.Y. bucket	4.12	11.25	15.35
2340	6' deep, 1/2 C.Y. bucket	8.75	19.60	28.50
2360	8' deep, 1/2 C.Y. bucket	15.05	31.50	46.50
2380	10' deep, 1 C.Y. bucket	15.45	36	51.50
2400	12' deep, 1 C.Y. bucket	26	60	86
2430	15' deep, 1-1/2 C.Y. bucket	29.50	66.50	96
2460	18' deep, 2-1/2 C.Y. bucket	46	101	148
2840	6' wide, 6' deep, 5/8 C.Y. bucket w/trench box	14.60	27	41.50
2860	8' deep, 3/4 C.Y. bucket	21.50	39.50	61.50
2880	10' deep, 1 C.Y. bucket	21	44.50	65.50
2900	12' deep, 1-1/2 C.Y. bucket	25.50	54	79.50
2940	16' deep, 2 C.Y. bucket	39	79	118
2980	20' deep, 3-1/2 C.Y. bucket	52.50	106	159
3020	24' deep, 3-1/2 C.Y. bucket	74.50	146	220
3100	8' wide, 12' deep, 1-1/4 C.Y. bucket w/trench box	30.50	61	91.50
3120	15' deep, 1-1/2 C.Y. bucket	41.50	85.50	127
3140	18' deep, 2-1/2 C.Y. bucket	53.50	106	159
3180	24' deep, 3-1/2 C.Y. bucket	83.50	159	243
3270	10' wide, 20' deep, 3-1/2 C.Y. bucket w/trench box	66.50	129	195
3280	24' deep, 3-1/2 C.Y. bucket	92	174	266
3370	12' wide, 20' deep, 3-1/2 C.Y. bucket w/trench box	74.50	143	218
3380	25' deep, 3-1/2 C.Y. bucket	107	201	310
3500	1:1 slope, 2' wide, 2' deep, 3/8 C.Y. bucket	2.23	5.60	7.80
3520	3' deep, 3/8 C.Y. bucket	2.43	8.30	10.75
3540	4' deep, 3/8 C.Y. bucket	3.86	13.35	17.20
3560	6' deep, 3/8 C.Y. bucket	6.35	13.30	19.65
3580	8' deep, 1/2 C.Y. bucket	16.90	35.50	52.50
3600	10' deep, 1 C.Y. bucket	22	45	66.50
3800	4' wide, 2' deep, 3/8 C.Y. bucket	2.14	6.60	8.75
3820	3' deep, 3/8 C.Y. bucket	3.56	11.60	15.15
3840	4' deep, 1/2 C.Y. bucket	5.35	15.10	20.50
3860	6' deep, 1/2 C.Y. bucket	12.35	28	40.50
3880	8' deep, 1/2 C.Y. bucket	22.50	47.50	69.50
3900	10' deep, 1 C.Y. bucket	24	56.50	80.50
3920	12' deep, 1 C.Y. bucket	34.50	80.50	115
3940	15' deep, 1-1/2 C.Y. bucket	48.50	110	159
3960	18' deep, 2-1/2 C.Y. bucket	63.50	140	203
4030	6' wide, 6' deep, 5/8 C.Y. bucket w/trench box	19.30	36	55.50
4040	8' deep, 3/4 C.Y. bucket	30	56	86
4050	10' deep, 1 C.Y. bucket	30.50	65	95.50
4060	12' deep, 1-1/2 C.Y. bucket	38	81.50	119
4070	16' deep, 2 C.Y. bucket	61.50	125	186
4080	20' deep, 3-1/2 C.Y. bucket	85.50	173	259
4090	24' deep, 3-1/2 C.Y. bucket	124	244	370
4500	8' wide, 12' deep, 1-1/2 C.Y. bucket w/trench box	43	89	132
4550	15' deep, 1-1/2 C.Y. bucket	61	129	190
4600	18' deep, 2-1/2 C.Y. bucket	81	164	245
4650	24' deep, 3-1/2 C.Y. bucket	133	257	390
4800	10' wide, 20' deep, 3-1/2 C.Y. bucket w/trench box	99.50	196	295
4850	24' deep, 3-1/2 C.Y. bucket	141	272	415
4950	12' wide, 20' deep, 3-1/2 C.Y. bucket w/trench box	106	207	315
4980	25' deep, 3-1/2 C.Y. bucket	161	305	470

For customer support on your Plumbing Costs with RSMeans data, call 800.448.8182.

G10 Site Preparation

G1030 Site Earthwork

The Pipe Bedding System is shown for various pipe diameters. Compacted bank sand is used for pipe bedding and to fill 12" over the pipe. No backfill is included. Various side slopes are shown to accommodate different soil conditions. Pipe sizes vary from 6" to 84" diameter.

System Components	QUANTITY	UNIT	COST PER L.F.		
			MAT.	INST.	TOTAL
SYSTEM G1030 815 1440 PIPE BEDDING, SIDE SLOPE 0 TO 1, 1' WIDE, PIPE SIZE 6" DIAMETER					
Borrow, bank sand, 2 mile haul, machine spread	.086	C.Y.	1.30	.81	2.11
Compaction, vibrating plate	.086	C.Y.		.31	.31
TOTAL			1.30	1.12	2.42

G1030 815	Pipe Bedding	COST PER L.F.		
		MAT.	INST.	TOTAL
1440	Pipe bedding, side slope 0 to 1, 1' wide, pipe size 6" diameter	1.30	1.11	2.41
1460	2' wide, pipe size 8" diameter	2.81	2.40	5.21
1480	Pipe size 10" diameter	2.87	2.45	5.32
1500	Pipe size 12" diameter	2.93	2.51	5.44
1520	3' wide, pipe size 14" diameter	4.76	4.06	8.82
1540	Pipe size 15" diameter	4.80	4.10	8.90
1560	Pipe size 16" diameter	4.85	4.14	8.99
1580	Pipe size 18" diameter	4.94	4.22	9.16
1600	4' wide, pipe size 20" diameter	7	6	13
1620	Pipe size 21" diameter	7.10	6.05	13.15
1640	Pipe size 24" diameter	7.25	6.20	13.45
1660	Pipe size 30" diameter	7.35	6.30	13.65
1680	6' wide, pipe size 32" diameter	12.60	10.75	23.35
1700	Pipe size 36" diameter	12.90	11	23.90
1720	7' wide, pipe size 48" diameter	20.50	17.50	38
1740	8' wide, pipe size 60" diameter	25	21.50	46.50
1760	10' wide, pipe size 72" diameter	35	29.50	64.50
1780	12' wide, pipe size 84" diameter	46	39	85
2140	Side slope 1/2 to 1, 1' wide, pipe size 6" diameter	2.42	2.07	4.49
2160	2' wide, pipe size 8" diameter	4.12	3.52	7.64
2180	Pipe size 10" diameter	4.42	3.78	8.20
2200	Pipe size 12" diameter	4.68	4	8.68
2220	3' wide, pipe size 14" diameter	6.75	5.80	12.55
2240	Pipe size 15" diameter	6.90	5.90	12.80
2260	Pipe size 16" diameter	7.10	6.05	13.15
2280	Pipe size 18" diameter	7.45	6.35	13.80
2300	4' wide, pipe size 20" diameter	9.85	8.40	18.25
2320	Pipe size 21" diameter	10.05	8.60	18.65
2340	Pipe size 24" diameter	10.70	9.15	19.85
2360	Pipe size 30" diameter	11.85	10.15	22
2380	6' wide, pipe size 32" diameter	17.50	14.95	32.45
2400	Pipe size 36" diameter	18.60	15.90	34.50
2420	7' wide, pipe size 48" diameter	29	25	54
2440	8' wide, pipe size 60" diameter	37	31.50	68.50
2460	10' wide, pipe size 72" diameter	50.50	43	93.50
2480	12' wide, pipe size 84" diameter	66	56.50	122.50
2620	Side slope 1 to 1, 1' wide, pipe size 6" diameter	3.55	3.03	6.58
2640	2' wide, pipe size 8" diameter	5.45	4.67	10.12

G10 Site Preparation

G1030 Site Earthwork

G1030 815	Pipe Bedding	COST PER L.F.		
		MAT.	INST.	TOTAL
2660	Pipe size 10" diameter	5.95	5.10	11.05
2680	Pipe size 12" diameter	6.50	5.55	12.05
2700	3' wide, pipe size 14" diameter	8.75	7.50	16.25
2720	Pipe size 15" diameter	9.05	7.70	16.75
2740	Pipe size 16" diameter	9.35	8	17.35
2760	Pipe size 18" diameter	10	8.55	18.55
2780	4' wide, pipe size 20" diameter	12.70	10.85	23.55
2800	Pipe size 21" diameter	13.05	11.15	24.20
2820	Pipe size 24" diameter	14.15	12.05	26.20
2840	Pipe size 30" diameter	16.35	13.95	30.30
2860	6' wide, pipe size 32" diameter	22.50	19.15	41.65
2880	Pipe size 36" diameter	24.50	21	45.50
2900	7' wide, pipe size 48" diameter	37.50	32	69.50
2920	8' wide, pipe size 60" diameter	49	41.50	90.50
2940	10' wide, pipe size 72" diameter	66.50	56.50	123
2960	12' wide, pipe size 84" diameter	86.50	74	160.50

For customer support on your Plumbing Costs with RSMeans data, call 800.448.8182.

G20 Site Improvements

G2040 Site Development

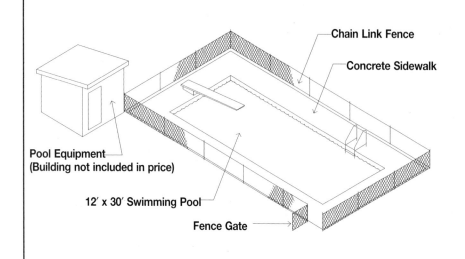

- Chain Link Fence
- Concrete Sidewalk
- Pool Equipment (Building not included in price)
- 12' x 30' Swimming Pool
- Fence Gate

The Swimming Pool System is a complete package. Everything from excavation to deck hardware is included in system costs. Below are three basic types of pool systems: residential, motel, and municipal. Systems elements include: excavation, pool materials, installation, deck hardware, pumps and filters, sidewalk, and fencing.

The Expanded System Listing shows three basic types of pools with a variety of finishes and basic materials. These systems are either vinyl lined with metal sides; gunite shell with a cement plaster finish or tile finish; or concrete sided with vinyl lining. Pool sizes listed here vary from 12' x 30' to 60' x 82.5'. All costs are on a per unit basis.

System Components	QUANTITY	UNIT	COST EACH		
			MAT.	INST.	TOTAL
SYSTEM G2040 920 1000					
SWIMMING POOL, RESIDENTIAL, CONC. SIDES, VINYL LINED, 12' X 30'					
Swimming pool, residential, in-ground including equipment	360.000	S.F.	17,100	6,249.60	23,349.60
4" thick reinforced concrete sidewalk, broom finish, no base	400.000	S.F.	1,296	1,268	2,564
Chain link fence, residential, 4' high	124.000	L.F.	1,320.60	685.72	2,006.32
Fence gate, chain link, 4' high	1.000	Ea.	119	221.50	340.50
TOTAL			19,835.60	8,424.82	28,260.42

G2040 920	Swimming Pools	COST EACH		
		MAT.	INST.	TOTAL
1000	Swimming pool, residential class, concrete sides, vinyl lined, 12' x 30'	19,800	8,425	28,225
1100	16' x 32'	22,500	9,500	32,000
1200	20' x 40'	29,000	12,100	41,100
1500	Tile finish, 12' x 30'	33,300	35,400	68,700
1600	16' x 32'	33,900	37,300	71,200
1700	20' x 40'	50,500	52,000	102,500
2000	Metal sides, vinyl lined, 12' x 30'	34,800	5,550	40,350
2100	16' x 32'	39,500	6,250	45,750
2200	20' x 40'	51,500	7,850	59,350
3000	Gunite shell, cement plaster finish, 12' x 30'	26,700	15,100	41,800
3100	16' x 32'	33,700	19,500	53,200
3200	20' x 40'	46,400	19,500	65,900
4000	Motel class, concrete sides, vinyl lined, 20' x 40'	41,600	16,700	58,300
4100	28' x 60'	58,500	23,400	81,900
4500	Tile finish, 20' x 40'	59,000	60,000	119,000
4600	28' x 60'	93,500	98,000	191,500
5000	Metal sides, vinyl lined, 20' x 40'	92,500	12,200	104,700
5100	28' x 60'	124,000	16,400	140,400
6000	Gunite shell, cement plaster finish, 20' x 40'	85,500	47,800	133,300
6100	28' x 60'	128,000	71,500	199,500
7000	Municipal class, gunite shell, cement plaster finish, 42' x 75'	340,000	168,500	508,500
7100	60' x 82.5'	437,000	216,000	653,000
7500	Concrete walls, tile finish, 42' x 75'	379,500	228,500	608,000
7600	60' x 82.5'	494,000	303,000	797,000
7700	Tile finish and concrete gutter, 42' x 75'	416,500	228,500	645,000
7800	60' x 82.5'	538,500	303,000	841,500
7900	Tile finish and stainless gutter, 42' x 75'	488,000	228,500	716,500
8000	60' x 82.5'	720,500	350,000	1,070,500

G20 Site Improvements

G2050 Landscaping

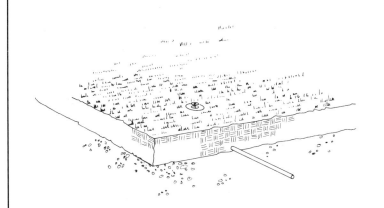

There are three basic types of Site Irrigation Systems: pop-up, riser mounted and quick coupling. Sprinkler heads are spray, impact or gear driven. Each system includes: the hardware for spraying the water; the pipe and fittings needed to deliver the water; and all other accessory equipment such as valves, couplings, nipples, and nozzles. Excavation heads and backfill costs are also included in the system.
The Expanded System Listing shows a wide variety of Site Irrigation Systems.

System Components	QUANTITY	UNIT	COST PER S.F.		
			MAT.	INST.	TOTAL
SYSTEM G2050 710 1000					
SITE IRRIGATION, POP UP SPRAY, PLASTIC, 10' RADIUS, 1000 S.F., PVC PIPE					
Excavation, chain trencher	54.000	L.F.		63.18	63.18
Pipe, fittings & nipples, PVC Schedule 40, 1" diameter	5.000	Ea.	8.65	135	143.65
Fittings, bends or elbows, 4" diameter	5.000	Ea.	94.50	307.50	402
Couplings PVC plastic, high pressure, 1" diameter	5.000	Ea.	8.65	172.50	181.15
Valves, bronze, globe, 125 lb. rising stem, threaded, 1" diameter	1.000	Ea.	455	45	500
Head & nozzle, pop-up spray, PVC plastic	5.000	Ea.	27	122.50	149.50
Backfill by hand with compaction	54.000	L.F.		44.28	44.28
Total cost per 1,000 S.F.			593.80	889.96	1,483.76
Total cost per S.F.			.59	.89	1.48

G2050 710	Site Irrigation	COST PER S.F.		
		MAT.	INST.	TOTAL
1000	Site irrigation, pop up spray, 10' radius, 1000 S.F., PVC pipe	.60	.89	1.49
1100	Polyethylene pipe	.64	.77	1.41
1200	14' radius, 8000 S.F., PVC pipe	.22	.39	.61
1300	Polyethylene pipe	.20	.35	.55
1400	18' square, 1000 S.F. PVC pipe	.64	.61	1.25
1500	Polyethylene pipe	.59	.53	1.12
1600	24' square, 8000 S.F., PVC pipe	.17	.25	.42
1700	Polyethylene pipe	.17	.24	.41
1800	4' x 30' strip, 200 S.F., PVC pipe	2.91	2.51	5.42
1900	Polyethylene pipe	2.80	2.33	5.13
2000	6' x 40' strip, 800 S.F., PVC pipe	.79	.83	1.62
2200	Economy brass, 11' radius, 1000 S.F., PVC pipe	.77	.85	1.62
2300	Polyethylene pipe	.72	.77	1.49
2400	14' radius, 8000 S.F., PVC pipe	.26	.39	.65
2500	Polyethylene pipe	.24	.35	.59
2600	3' x 28' strip, 200 S.F., PVC pipe	3.15	2.51	5.66
2700	Polyethylene pipe	3.04	2.33	5.37
2800	7' x 36' strip, 1000 S.F., PVC pipe	.69	.67	1.36
2900	Polyethylene pipe	.66	.61	1.27
3000	Hd brass, 11' radius, 1000 S.F., PVC pipe	.82	.85	1.67
3100	Polyethylene pipe	.77	.77	1.54
3200	14' radius, 8000 S.F., PVC pipe	.28	.39	.67
3300	Polyethylene pipe	.26	.35	.61
3400	Riser mounted spray, plastic, 10' radius, 1000 S.F., PVC pipe	.69	.85	1.54
3500	Polyethylene pipe	.65	.77	1.42
3600	12' radius, 5000 S.F., PVC pipe	.32	.51	.83

G20 Site Improvements

G2050 Landscaping

G2050 710	Site Irrigation	COST PER S.F.		
		MAT.	INST.	TOTAL
3700	Polyethylene pipe	.30	.47	.77
3800	19' square, 2000 S.F., PVC pipe	.31	.28	.59
3900	Polyethylene pipe	.29	.25	.54
4000	24' square, 8000 S.F., PVC pipe	.18	.25	.43
4100	Polyethylene pipe	.17	.24	.41
4200	5' x 32' strip, 300 S.F., PVC pipe	1.95	1.68	3.63
4300	Polyethylene pipe	1.88	1.56	3.44
4400	6' x 40' strip, 800 S.F., PVC pipe	.79	.83	1.62
4500	Polyethylene pipe	.75	.77	1.52
4600	Brass, 11' radius, 1000 S.F., PVC pipe	.74	.85	1.59
4700	Polyethylene pipe	.69	.77	1.46
4800	14' radius, 8000 S.F., PVC pipe	.24	.39	.63
4900	Polyethylene pipe	.22	.35	.57
5000	Pop up gear drive stream type, plastic, 30' radius, 10,000 S.F., PVC pipe	.33	.74	1.07
5020	Polyethylene pipe	.20	.22	.42
5040	40,000 S.F., PVC pipe	.30	.74	1.04
5060	Polyethylene pipe	.15	.21	.36
5080	Riser mounted gear drive stream type, plas., 30' rad., 10,000 S.F., PVC pipe	.32	.74	1.06
5100	Polyethylene pipe	.19	.22	.41
5120	40,000 S.F., PVC pipe	.29	.74	1.03
5140	Polyethylene pipe	.14	.21	.35
5200	Q.C. valve thread type w/impact head, brass, 75' rad, 20,000 S.F., PVC pipe	.13	.29	.42
5250	Polyethylene pipe	.07	.07	.14
5300	100,000 S.F., PVC pipe	.20	.46	.66
5350	Polyethylene pipe	.10	.11	.21
5400	Q.C. valve lug type w/impact head, brass, 75' rad, 20,000 S.F., PVC pipe	.13	.29	.42
5450	Polyethylene pipe	.07	.07	.14
5500	100,000 S.F. PVC pipe	.20	.46	.66
5550	Polyethylene pipe	.10	.11	.21
6000	Site irrigation, pop up impact type, plastic, 40' rad.,10000 S.F., PVC pipe	.20	.48	.68
6100	Polyethylene pipe	.11	.13	.24
6200	45,000 S.F., PVC pipe	.19	.53	.72
6300	Polyethylene pipe	.08	.14	.22
6400	High medium volume brass, 40' radius, 10000 S.F., PVC pipe	.20	.48	.68
6500	Polyethylene pipe	.11	.13	.24
6600	45,000 S.F. PVC pipe	.20	.53	.73
6700	Polyethylene pipe	.09	.14	.23
6800	High volume brass, 60' radius, 25,000 S.F., PVC pipe	.15	.37	.52
6900	Polyethylene pipe	.08	.09	.17
7000	100,000 S.F., PVC pipe	.17	.37	.54
7100	Polyethylene pipe	.09	.09	.18
7200	Riser mounted part/full impact type, plas., 40' rad., 10,000 S.F., PVC pipe	.19	.48	.67
7300	Polyethylene pipe	.11	.27	.38
7400	45,000 S.F., PVC pipe	.18	.53	.71
7500	Polyethylene pipe	.08	.14	.22
7600	Low medium volume brass, 40' radius, 10,000 S.F., PVC pipe	.20	.48	.68
7700	Polyethylene pipe	.11	.13	.24
7800	45,000 S.F., PVC pipe	.19	.53	.72
7900	Polyethylene pipe	.09	.14	.23
8000	Medium volume brass, 50' radius, 30,000 S.F., PVC pipe	.15	.39	.54
8100	Polyethylene pipe	.08	.10	.18
8200	70,000 S.F., PVC pipe	.24	.64	.88
8300	Polyethylene pipe	.11	.16	.27
8400	Riser mounted full only impact type, plas., 40' rad., 10,000 S.F., PVC pipe	.19	.48	.67
8500	Polyethylene pipe	.10	.13	.23
8600	45,000 S.F., PVC pipe	.18	.53	.71
8700	Polyethylene pipe	.07	.14	.21
8800	Low medium volume brass, 40' radius, 10,000 S.F., PVC pipe	.20	.48	.68

G20 Site Improvements

G2050 Landscaping

G2050 710	Site Irrigation	COST PER S.F.		
		MAT.	INST.	TOTAL
8900	Polyethylene pipe	.11	.13	.24
9000	45,000 S.F., PVC pipe	.20	.53	.73
9100	Polyethylene pipe	.09	.14	.23
9200	High volume brass, 80' radius, 75,000 S.F., PVC pipe	.12	.28	.40
9300	Polyethylene pipe	.06	.07	.13
9400	150,000 S.F., PVC pipe	.12	.26	.38
9500	Polyethylene pipe	.07	.06	.13
9600	Very high volume brass, 100' radius, 100,000 S.F., PVC pipe	.11	.22	.33
9700	Polyethylene pipe	.06	.05	.11
9800	200,000 S.F., PVC pipe	.11	.22	.33
9900	Polyethylene pipe	.06	.05	.11

G20 Site Improvements

G2050 Landscaping

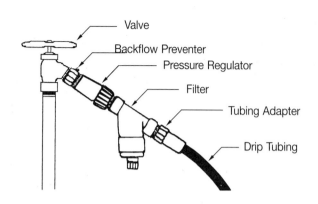

Drip irrigation systems can be for either lawns or individual plants. Shown below are drip irrigation systems for lawns. These drip type systems are most cost effective where there are water restrictions on use or the cost of water is very high. The supply uses PVC piping with the laterals polyethylene drip lines.

System Components	QUANTITY	UNIT	COST PER S.F. MAT.	COST PER S.F. INST.	COST PER S.F. TOTAL
SYSTEM G2050 720 1000					
SITE IRRIGATION, DRIP SYSTEM, 800 S.F. (20' X 40')					
Excavate supply and header lines 4" x 18" deep	50.000	L.F.		62.50	62.50
Excavate drip lines 4" x 4" deep	560.000	L.F.		1,047.20	1,047.20
Install supply manifold (stop valve, strainer, PRV, adapters)	1.000	Ea.	28	184	212
Install 3/4" PVC supply line and risers to 4" drip level	75.000	L.F.	30	183.75	213.75
Install 3/4" PVC fittings for supply line	33.000	Ea.	71.94	607.20	679.14
Install PVC to drip line adapters	14.000	Ea.	31.36	257.60	288.96
Install 1/4 inch drip lines with hose clamps	560.000	L.F.	72.80	341.60	414.40
Backfill trenches	3.180	C.Y.		162.18	162.18
Cleanup area when completed	1.000	Ea.		141	141
Total cost per 800 S.F.			234.10	2,987.03	3,221.13
Total cost per S.F.			.30	3.88	4.19

G2050 720		Site Irrigation	COST PER S.F. MAT.	COST PER S.F. INST.	COST PER S.F. TOTAL
1000	Site irrigation, drip lawn watering system, 800 S.F. (20' x 40' area)		.30	3.87	4.17
1100		1000 S.F. (20' x 50' area)	.25	3.36	3.61
1200		1600 S.F. (40' x 40' area), 2 zone	.32	3.59	3.91
1300		2000 S.F. (40' x 50' area), 2 zone	.27	3.25	3.52
1400		2400 S.F. (60' x 40' area), 3 zone	.30	3.54	3.84
1500		3000 S.F. (60' x 50' area), 3 zone	.26	3.19	3.45
1600		3200 S.F. (2 x 40' x 40'), 4 zone	.31	3.52	3.83
1700		4000 S.F. (2 x 40' x 50'), 4 zone	.26	3.19	3.45
1800		4800 S.F. (2 x 60' x 40'), 6 zone with control	.33	3.50	3.83
1900		6000 S.F. (2 x 60' x 50'), 6 zone with control	.28	3.16	3.44
2000		6400 S.F. (4 x 40' x 40'), 8 zone with control	.32	3.54	3.86
2100		8000 S.F. (4 x 40' x 50'), 8 zone with control	.27	3.21	3.48
2200		3200 S.F. (2 x 40' x 40'), 4 zone with control	.33	3.60	3.93
2300		4000 S.F. (2 x 40' x 50'), 4 zone with control	.28	3.26	3.54
2400		2400 S.F. (60' x 40'), 3 zone with control	.33	3.65	3.98
2500		3000 S.F. (60' x 50'), 3 zone with control	.28	3.28	3.56
2600		4800 S.F. (2 x 60' x 40'), 6 zone, manual	.29	3.45	3.74
2700		6000 S.F. (2 x 60' x 50'), 6 zone, manual	.25	3.12	3.37
2800		1000 S.F. (10' x 100' area)	.16	2.09	2.25
2900		2000 S.F. (2 x 10' x 100' area)	.18	2.02	2.20

G30 Site Mechanical Utilities

G3010 Water Supply

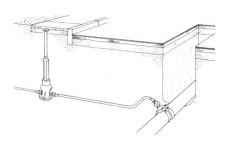

The Water Service Systems are for copper service taps from 1" to 2" diameter into pressurized mains from 6" to 8" diameter. Costs are given for two offsets with depths varying from 2' to 10'. Included in system components are excavation and backfill and required curb stops with boxes.

System Components	QUANTITY	UNIT	COST EACH MAT.	COST EACH INST.	COST EACH TOTAL
SYSTEM G3010 121 1000 WATER SERVICE, LEAD FREE, 6" MAIN, 1" COPPER SERVICE, 10' OFFSET, 2' DEEP					
Trench excavation, 1/2 C.Y. backhoe, 1 laborer	2.220	C.Y.		18.91	18.91
Drill & tap pressurized main, 6", 1" to 2" service	1.000	Ea.		515	515
Corporation stop, 1" diameter	1.000	Ea.	132	53.50	185.50
Saddles, 3/4" & 1" diameter, add	1.000	Ea.	80.50		80.50
Copper tubing, type K, 1" diameter	12.000	L.F.	75.60	58.08	133.68
Piping, curb stops, no lead, 1" diameter	1.000	Ea.	205	53.50	258.50
Curb box, cast iron, 1/2" to 1" curb stops	1.000	Ea.	44.50	71.50	116
Backfill by hand, no compaction, heavy soil	2.890	C.Y.		8.20	8.20
Compaction, vibrating plate	2.220	C.Y.		23.07	23.07
TOTAL			537.60	801.76	1,339.36

G3010 121	Water Service, Lead Free	COST EACH MAT.	COST EACH INST.	COST EACH TOTAL
1000	Water service, Lead Free, 6" main, 1" copper service, 10' offset, 2' deep	540	800	1,340
1040	4' deep	540	850	1,390
1060	6' deep	540	1,100	1,640
1080	8' deep	540	1,225	1,765
1100	10' deep	540	1,325	1,865
1200	20' offset, 2' deep	540	850	1,390
1240	4' deep	540	955	1,495
1260	6' deep	540	1,450	1,990
1280	8' deep	540	1,675	2,215
1300	10' deep	540	1,900	2,440
1400	1-1/2" copper service, 10' offset, 2' deep	1,200	875	2,075
1440	4' deep	1,200	925	2,125
1460	6' deep	1,200	1,175	2,375
1480	8' deep	1,200	1,275	2,475
1500	10' deep	1,200	1,400	2,600
1520	20' offset, 2' deep	1,200	925	2,125
1530	4' deep	1,200	1,025	2,225
1540	6' deep	1,200	1,525	2,725
1560	8' deep	1,200	1,750	2,950
1580	10' deep	1,200	1,975	3,175
1600	2" copper service, 10' offset, 2' deep	1,575	910	2,485
1610	4' deep	1,350	960	2,310
1620	6' deep	1,350	1,200	2,550
1630	8' deep	1,350	1,325	2,675
1650	10' deep	1,350	1,425	2,775
1660	20' offset, 2' deep	1,350	960	2,310
1670	4' deep	1,350	1,050	2,400
1680	6' deep	1,350	1,550	2,900

G30 Site Mechanical Utilities

G3010 Water Supply

G3010 121	Water Service, Lead Free	COST EACH		
		MAT.	INST.	TOTAL
1690	8' deep	1,350	1,775	3,125
1695	10' deep	1,350	2,000	3,350
1700	8" main, 1" copper service, 10' offset, 2' deep	540	850	1,390
1710	4' deep	540	900	1,440
1720	6' deep	540	1,150	1,690
1730	8' deep	540	1,275	1,815
1740	10' deep	540	1,375	1,915
1750	20' offset, 2' deep	540	900	1,440
1760	4' deep	540	1,000	1,540
1770	6' deep	540	1,500	2,040
1780	8' deep	540	1,725	2,265
1790	10' deep	540	1,950	2,490
1800	1-1/2" copper service, 10' offset, 2' deep	1,200	925	2,125
1810	4' deep	1,200	975	2,175
1820	6' deep	1,200	1,225	2,425
1830	8' deep	1,200	1,800	3,000
1840	10' deep	1,200	1,450	2,650
1850	20' offset, 2' deep	1,200	975	2,175
1860	4' deep	1,200	975	2,175
1870	6' deep	1,200	1,575	2,775
1880	8' deep	1,200	1,800	3,000
1890	10' deep	1,200	2,025	3,225
1900	2" copper service, 10' offset, 2' deep	1,575	960	2,535
1910	4' deep	1,350	1,000	2,350
1920	6' deep	1,350	1,250	2,600
1930	8' deep	1,350	1,375	2,725
1940	10' deep	1,350	1,475	2,825
1950	20' offset, 2' deep	1,350	1,000	2,350
1960	4' deep	1,350	1,100	2,450
1970	6' deep	1,350	1,600	2,950
1980	8' deep	1,350	1,825	3,175
1990	10' deep	1,350	2,050	3,400

G30 Site Mechanical Utilities

G3010 Water Supply

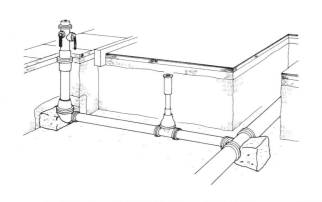

The Fire Hydrant Systems include: four different hydrants with three different lengths of offsets, at several depths of trenching. Excavation and backfill is included with each system as well as thrust blocks as necessary and pipe bedding. Finally spreading of excess material and fine grading complete the components.

System Components	QUANTITY	UNIT	COST PER EACH		
			MAT.	INST.	TOTAL
SYSTEM G3010 410 1500					
HYDRANT, 4-1/2" VALVE SIZE, TWO WAY, 10' OFFSET, 2' DEEP					
Excavation, trench, 1 C.Y. hydraulic backhoe	3.556	C.Y.		37.27	37.27
Sleeve, 12" x 6"	1.000	Ea.	1,800	138.80	1,938.80
Ductile iron pipe, 6" diameter	8.000	L.F.	1,056	124.64	1,180.64
Gate valve, 6"	1.000	Ea.	4,700	356	5,056
Hydrant valve box, 6' long	1.000	Ea.	400	94.50	494.50
4-1/2" valve size, depth 2'-0"	1.000	Ea.	3,400	249	3,649
Thrust blocks, at valve, shoe and sleeve	1.600	C.Y.	452.80	537.86	990.66
Borrow, crushed stone, 3/8"	4.089	C.Y.	177.87	38.36	216.23
Backfill and compact, dozer, air tamped	4.089	C.Y.		92.83	92.83
Spread excess excavated material	.204	C.Y.		10.40	10.40
Fine grade, hand	400.000	S.F.		329	329
TOTAL			11,986.67	2,008.66	13,995.33

G3010 410	Fire Hydrants	COST PER EACH		
		MAT.	INST.	TOTAL
1000	Hydrant, 4-1/2" valve size, two way, 0' offset, 2' deep	10,900	1,425	12,325
1100	4' deep	11,200	1,450	12,650
1200	6' deep	11,500	1,525	13,025
1300	8' deep	11,700	1,600	13,300
1400	10' deep	12,000	1,675	13,675
1500	10' offset, 2' deep	12,000	2,000	14,000
1600	4' deep	12,300	2,375	14,675
1700	6' deep	12,500	3,100	15,600
1800	8' deep	12,700	4,150	16,850
1900	10' deep	13,000	6,350	19,350
2000	20' offset, 2' deep	13,300	2,600	15,900
2100	4' deep	13,600	3,225	16,825
2200	6' deep	13,900	4,275	18,175
2300	8' deep	14,100	5,800	19,900
2400	10' deep	14,300	7,875	22,175
2500	Hydrant, 4-1/2" valve size, three way, 0' offset, 2' deep	11,200	1,425	12,625
2600	4' deep	11,500	1,450	12,950
2700	6' deep	11,800	1,550	13,350
2800	8' deep	12,000	1,625	13,625
2900	10' deep	12,300	1,700	14,000
3000	10' offset, 2' deep	12,200	2,025	14,225
3100	4' deep	12,500	2,400	14,900
3200	6' deep	12,800	3,125	15,925
3300	8' deep	13,000	4,175	17,175

G30 Site Mechanical Utilities

G3010 Water Supply

G3010 410	Fire Hydrants	COST PER EACH		
		MAT.	INST.	TOTAL
3400	10' deep	13,300	6,375	19,675
3500	20' offset, 2' deep	13,500	2,625	16,125
3600	4' deep	13,800	3,250	17,050
3700	6' deep	14,100	4,300	18,400
3800	8' deep	14,300	5,825	20,125
3900	10' deep	14,600	7,925	22,525
5000	5-1/4" valve size, two way, 0' offset, 2' deep	11,200	1,425	12,625
5100	4' deep	11,600	1,450	13,050
5200	6' deep	11,900	1,525	13,425
5300	8' deep	12,400	1,600	14,000
5400	10' deep	12,700	1,675	14,375
5500	10' offset, 2' deep	12,300	2,000	14,300
5600	4' deep	12,600	2,375	14,975
5700	6' deep	13,000	3,100	16,100
5800	8' deep	13,400	4,150	17,550
5900	10' deep	13,800	6,350	20,150
6000	20' offset, 2' deep	13,600	2,600	16,200
6100	4' deep	13,900	3,225	17,125
6200	6' deep	14,300	4,275	18,575
6300	8' deep	14,800	5,800	20,600
6400	10' deep	15,100	7,875	22,975
6500	Three way, 0' offset, 2' deep	11,500	1,425	12,925
6600	4' deep	11,800	1,450	13,250
6700	6' deep	12,200	1,550	13,750
6800	8' deep	12,700	1,625	14,325
6900	10' deep	13,100	1,700	14,800
7000	10' offset, 2' deep	12,500	2,025	14,525
7100	4' deep	12,900	2,400	15,300
7200	6' deep	13,300	3,125	16,425
7300	8' deep	13,800	4,175	17,975
7400	10' deep	14,200	6,375	20,575
7500	20' offset, 2' deep	13,800	2,625	16,425
7600	4' deep	14,200	2,925	17,125
7700	6' deep	14,600	4,300	18,900

G30 Site Mechanical Utilities

G3020 Sanitary Sewer

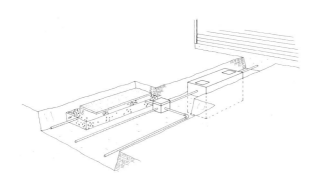

The Septic System includes: a septic tank; leaching field; concrete distribution boxes; plus excavation and gravel backfill.

The Expanded System Listing shows systems with tanks ranging from 1000 gallons to 2000 gallons. Tanks are either concrete or fiberglass. Cost is on a complete unit basis.

System Components	QUANTITY	UNIT	COST EACH		
			MAT.	INST.	TOTAL
SYSTEM G3020 302 0300					
1000 GALLON TANK, LEACHING FIELD, 600 S.F., 50′ FROM BLDG.					
Mobilization	2.000	Ea.		1,910	1,910
Septic tank, precast, 1000 gallon	1.000	Ea.	1,075	311.50	1,386.50
Effluent filter	1.000	Ea.	39.50	92	131.50
Distribution box, precast, 5 outlets	1.000	Ea.	103	70.50	173.50
Flow leveler	3.000	Ea.	9.90	33.75	43.65
Sewer pipe, PVC, SDR 35, 4″ diameter	160.000	L.F.	604.80	808	1,412.80
Tee	1.000	Ea.	21	92	113
Elbow	2.000	Ea.	37.80	123	160.80
Viewport cap	1.000	Ea.	22.50	30.50	53
Filter fabric	67.000	S.Y.	146.73	31.49	178.22
Detectable marking tape	1.600	C.L.F.	3.52	6	9.52
Excavation	160.000	C.Y.		2,600	2,600
Backfill	133.000	L.C.Y.		488.11	488.11
Spoil	55.000	L.C.Y.		428.45	428.45
Compaction	113.000	C.Y.		1,360.52	1,360.52
Stone fill, 3/4″ to 1-1/2″	39.000	C.Y.	1,345.50	556.92	1,902.42
TOTAL			3,409.25	8,942.74	12,351.99

G3020 302	Septic Systems	COST EACH		
		MAT.	INST.	TOTAL
0300	1000 gal. concrete septic tank, 600 S.F. leaching field, 50 feet from bldg.	3,400	8,950	12,350
0301	200 feet from building	3,975	11,100	15,075
0305	750 S.F. leaching field, 50 feet from building	3,875	9,725	13,600
0306	200 feet from building	4,450	11,900	16,350
0400	1250 gal. concrete septic tank, 600 S.F. leaching field, 50 feet from bldg.	3,625	9,300	12,925
0401	200 feet from building	4,200	11,500	15,700
0405	750 S.F. leaching field, 50 feet from building	4,100	10,100	14,200
0406	200 feet from building	4,675	12,300	16,975
0410	1000 S.F. leaching field, 50 feet from building	4,925	11,600	16,525
0411	200 feet from building	5,500	13,800	19,300
0500	1500 gal. concrete septic tank, 600 S.F. leaching field, 50 feet from bldg.	3,975	9,650	13,625
0501	200 feet from building	4,525	11,800	16,325
0505	750 S.F. leaching field, 50 feet from building	4,450	10,500	14,950
0506	200 feet from building	5,000	13,700	18,700
0510	1000 S.F. leaching field, 50 feet from building	5,275	11,900	17,175
0511	200 feet from building	5,825	14,100	19,925
0515	1100 S.F. leaching field, 50 feet from building	5,575	12,500	18,075
0516	200 feet from building	6,150	14,800	20,950
0600	2000 gal concrete tank, 1200 S.F. leaching field, 50 feet from building	6,925	13,200	20,125
0601	200 feet from building	7,475	15,400	22,875

G30 Site Mechanical Utilities

G3020 Sanitary Sewer

G3020 302	Septic Systems	COST EACH		
		MAT.	INST.	TOTAL
0605	1500 S.F. leaching field, 50 feet from building	7,875	14,900	22,775
0606	200 feet from building	8,450	17,100	25,550
0710	2500 gal concrete tank, 1500 S.F. leaching field, 50 feet from building	7,800	15,800	23,600
0711	200 feet from building	8,375	18,000	26,375
0715	1600 S.F. leaching field, 50 feet from building	8,150	16,400	24,550
0716	200 feet from building	8,725	18,600	27,325
0720	1800 S.F. leaching field, 50 feet from building	8,800	17,600	26,400
0721	200 feet from building	9,375	19,800	29,175
1300	1000 gal. 2 compartment tank, 600 S.F. leaching field, 50 feet from bldg.	3,100	8,950	12,050
1301	200 feet from building	3,675	11,100	14,775
1305	750 S.F. leaching field, 50 feet from building	3,575	9,725	13,300
1306	200 feet from building	4,150	11,900	16,050
1400	1250 gal. 2 compartment tank, 600 S.F. leaching field, 50 feet from bldg.	3,500	9,300	12,800
1401	200 feet from building	4,075	11,500	15,575
1405	750 S.F. leaching field, 50 feet from building	3,975	10,100	14,075
1406	200 feet from building	4,550	12,300	16,850
1410	1000 S.F. leaching field, 50 feet from building	4,800	11,600	16,400
1411	200 feet from building	5,375	13,800	19,175
1500	1500 gal. 2 compartment tank, 600 S.F. leaching field, 50 feet from bldg.	4,425	9,650	14,075
1501	200 feet from building	4,975	11,800	16,775
1505	750 S.F. leaching field, 50 feet from building	4,900	10,500	15,400
1506	200 feet from building	5,450	13,700	19,150
1510	1000 S.F. leaching field, 50 feet from building	5,725	11,900	17,625
1511	200 feet from building	6,275	14,100	20,375
1515	1100 S.F. leaching field, 50 feet from building	6,025	12,500	18,525
1516	200 feet from building	6,600	14,800	21,400
1600	2000 gal 2 compartment tank, 1200 S.F. leaching field, 50 feet from bldg.	7,125	13,200	20,325
1601	200 feet from building	7,675	15,400	23,075
1605	1500 S.F. leaching field, 50 feet from building	8,075	14,900	22,975
1606	200 feet from building	8,650	17,100	25,750
1710	2500 gal 2 compartment tank, 1500 S.F. leaching field, 50 feet from bldg.	9,150	15,800	24,950
1711	200 feet from building	9,725	18,000	27,725
1715	1600 S.F. leaching field, 50 feet from building	9,500	16,400	25,900
1716	200 feet from building	10,100	18,600	28,700
1720	1800 S.F. leaching field, 50 feet from building	10,200	17,600	27,800
1721	200 feet from building	10,700	19,800	30,500

G30 Site Mechanical Utilities

G3030 Storm Sewer

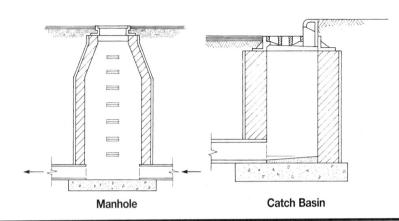

Manhole   Catch Basin

The Manhole and Catch Basin System includes: excavation with a backhoe; a formed concrete footing; frame and cover; cast iron steps and compacted backfill.

The Expanded System Listing shows manholes that have a 4', 5' and 6' inside diameter riser. Depths range from 4' to 14'. Construction material shown is either concrete, concrete block, precast concrete, or brick.

System Components	QUANTITY	UNIT	COST PER EACH MAT.	COST PER EACH INST.	COST PER EACH TOTAL
SYSTEM G3030 210 1920					
MANHOLE/CATCH BASIN, BRICK, 4' I.D. RISER, 4' DEEP					
Excavation, hydraulic backhoe, 3/8 C.Y. bucket	14.815	C.Y.		155.26	155.26
Trim sides and bottom of excavation	64.000	S.F.		80	80
Forms in place, manhole base, 4 uses	20.000	SFCA	41.80	128	169.80
Reinforcing in place footings, #4 to #7	.019	Ton	29.93	28.03	57.96
Concrete, 3000 psi	.925	C.Y.	157.25		157.25
Place and vibrate concrete, footing, direct chute	.925	C.Y.		59.84	59.84
Catch basin or MH, brick, 4' ID, 4' deep	1.000	Ea.	1,625	1,250	2,875
Catch basin or MH steps; heavy galvanized cast iron	1.000	Ea.	23	17.25	40.25
Catch basin or MH frame and cover	1.000	Ea.	1,050	274	1,324
Fill, granular	12.954	L.C.Y.	369.19		369.19
Backfill, spread with wheeled front end loader	12.954	L.C.Y.		36.79	36.79
Backfill compaction, 12" lifts, air tamp	12.954	C.Y.		144.56	144.56
TOTAL			3,296.17	2,173.73	5,469.90

G3030 210	Manholes & Catch Basins	MAT.	INST.	TOTAL
1920	Manhole/catch basin, brick, 4' I.D. riser, 4' deep	3,300	2,175	5,475
1940	6' deep	4,400	3,025	7,425
1960	8' deep	5,625	4,150	9,775
1980	10' deep	6,750	5,150	11,900
3000	12' deep	8,225	5,575	13,800
3020	14' deep	9,850	7,875	17,725
3200	Block, 4' I.D. riser, 4' deep	2,200	1,750	3,950
3220	6' deep	2,725	2,500	5,225
3240	8' deep	3,350	3,425	6,775
3260	10' deep	3,825	4,250	8,075
3280	12' deep	4,650	5,400	10,050
3300	14' deep	5,625	6,625	12,250
4620	Concrete, cast-in-place, 4' I.D. riser, 4' deep	2,525	3,000	5,525
4640	6' deep	3,275	4,000	7,275
4660	8' deep	4,300	5,775	10,075
4680	10' deep	5,050	7,175	12,225
4700	12' deep	6,150	8,925	15,075
4720	14' deep	7,400	10,700	18,100
5820	Concrete, precast, 4' I.D. riser, 4' deep	3,000	1,600	4,600
5840	6' deep	3,650	2,175	5,825

G30 Site Mechanical Utilities

G3030 Storm Sewer

G3030 210	Manholes & Catch Basins	COST PER EACH		
		MAT.	INST.	TOTAL
5860	8' deep	4,575	3,050	7,625
5880	10' deep	5,250	3,775	9,025
5900	12' deep	6,275	4,550	10,825
5920	14' deep	7,450	5,950	13,400
6000	5' I.D. riser, 4' deep	4,325	1,750	6,075
6020	6' deep	5,275	2,475	7,750
6040	8' deep	6,375	3,275	9,650
6060	10' deep	7,750	4,175	11,925
6080	12' deep	9,250	5,350	14,600
6100	14' deep	10,900	6,550	17,450
6200	6' I.D. riser, 4' deep	6,500	2,300	8,800
6220	6' deep	6,925	3,050	9,975
6240	8' deep	8,275	4,275	12,550
6260	10' deep	9,950	5,425	15,375
6280	12' deep	11,800	6,850	18,650
6300	14' deep	13,800	8,325	22,125

Reference Section

All the reference information is in one section, making it easy to find what you need to know and easy to use the data set on a daily basis. This section is visually identified by a vertical black bar on the page edges.

In this Reference Section, we've included Equipment Rental Costs, a listing of rental and operating costs; Crew Listings, a full listing of all crews and equipment, and their costs; Historical Cost Indexes for cost comparisons over time; City Cost Indexes and Location Factors for adjusting costs to the region you are in; Reference Tables, where you will find explanations, estimating information and procedures, and technical data; Change Orders, information on pricing changes to contract documents; and an explanation of all the Abbreviations in the data set.

Table of Contents

Construction Equipment Rental Costs	583
Crew Listings	595
Historical Cost Indexes	632
City Cost Indexes	633
Location Factors	676
Reference Tables	682
R01 General Requirements	682
R02 Existing Conditions	697
R03 Concrete	698
R05 Metals	699
R13 Special Construction	699
R21 Fire Suppression	699

Reference Tables (cont.)

R22 Plumbing	703
R23 Heating, Ventilating & Air Conditioning	713
R26 Electrical	716
R31 Earthwork	717
R33 Utilities	719
Change Orders	720
Project Costs	723
Abbreviations	728

Equipment Rental Costs

Estimating Tips

- This section contains the average costs to rent and operate hundreds of pieces of construction equipment. This is useful information when one is estimating the time and material requirements of any particular operation in order to establish a unit or total cost. Bare equipment costs shown on a unit cost line include, not only rental, but also operating costs for equipment under normal use.

Rental Costs

- Equipment rental rates are obtained from the following industry sources throughout North America: contractors, suppliers, dealers, manufacturers, and distributors.
- Rental rates vary throughout the country, with larger cities generally having lower rates. Lease plans for new equipment are available for periods in excess of six months, with a percentage of payments applying toward purchase.
- Monthly rental rates vary from 2% to 5% of the purchase price of the equipment depending on the anticipated life of the equipment and its wearing parts.
- Rental rates can also be treated as reimbursement costs for contractor-owned equipment. Owned equipment costs include depreciation, loan payments, interest, taxes, insurance, storage, and major repairs.

Operating Costs

- The operating costs include parts and labor for routine servicing, such as the repair and replacement of pumps, filters, and worn lines. Normal operating expendables, such as fuel, lubricants, tires, and electricity (where applicable), are also included.
- Extraordinary operating expendables with highly variable wear patterns, such as diamond bits and blades, are excluded. These costs can be found as material costs in the Unit Price section.
- The hourly operating costs listed do not include the operator's wages.

Equipment Cost/Day

- Any power equipment required by a crew is shown in the Crew Listings with a daily cost.
- This daily cost of equipment needed by a crew includes both the rental cost and the operating cost and is based on dividing the weekly rental rate by 5 (the number of working days in the week), then adding the hourly operating cost multiplied by 8 (the number of hours in a day). This "Equipment Cost/Day" is shown in the far right column of the Equipment Rental section.
- If equipment is needed for only one or two days, it is best to develop your own cost by including components for daily rent and hourly operating costs. This is important when the listed Crew for a task does not contain the equipment needed, such as a crane for lifting mechanical heating/cooling equipment up onto a roof.
- If the quantity of work is less than the crew's Daily Output shown for a Unit Price line item that includes a bare unit equipment cost, the recommendation is to estimate one day's rental cost and operating cost for equipment shown in the Crew Listing for that line item.
- Please note, in some cases the equipment description in the crew is followed by a time period in parenthesis. For example: (daily) or (monthly). In these cases the equipment cost/day is calculated by adding the rental cost per time period to the hourly operating cost multiplied by 8.

Mobilization, Demobilization Costs

- The cost to move construction equipment from an equipment yard or rental company to the job site and back again is not included in equipment rental costs listed in the Reference Section. It is also not included in the bare equipment cost of any Unit Price line item or in any equipment costs shown in the Crew Listings.
- Mobilization (to the site) and demobilization (from the site) costs can be found in the Unit Price section.
- If a piece of equipment is already at the job site, it is not appropriate to utilize mobilization or demobilization costs again in an estimate. ■

Same Data. Simplified.

Enjoy the convenience and efficiency of accessing your costs anywhere:

- **Skip the multiplier** by setting your location
- **Quickly search,** edit, favorite and share costs
- **Stay on top of price changes** with automatic updates

Discover more at rsmeans.com/online

No part of this cost data may be reproduced, stored in a retrieval system, or transmitted in any form or by any means without prior written permission of Gordian.

01 54 | Construction Aids

01 54 33 | Equipment Rental

		UNIT	HOURLY OPER. COST	RENT PER DAY	RENT PER WEEK	RENT PER MONTH	EQUIPMENT COST/DAY
10 0010	**CONCRETE EQUIPMENT RENTAL** without operators R015433-10						
0200	Bucket, concrete lightweight, 1/2 C.Y.	Ea.	.83	58.58	175.73	527.18	41.75
0300	1 C.Y.		1.08	70.61	211.82	635.46	50.97
0400	1-1/2 C.Y.		1.40	92.10	276.31	828.93	66.47
0500	2 C.Y.		1.52	107.25	321.76	965.28	76.52
0580	8 C.Y.		7.61	134.90	404.70	1,214.10	141.86
0600	Cart, concrete, self-propelled, operator walking, 10 C.F.		3.13	208.12	624.35	1,873.05	149.92
0700	Operator riding, 18 C.F.		5.27	145	402.71	965.71	122.73
0800	Conveyer for concrete, portable, gas, 16" wide, 26' long		11.64	114	342	1,026	161.50
0900	46' long		12.05	155	465	1,395	189.41
1000	56' long		12.23	161.53	484.58	1,453.73	194.76
1100	Core drill, electric, 2-1/2 H.P., 1" to 8" bit diameter		1.72	75	238.33	568.33	61.41
1150	11 H.P., 8" to 18" cores		5.92	131.80	354	895	118.14
1200	Finisher, concrete floor, gas, riding trowel, 96" wide		10.59	241	703	1,843.10	225.34
1300	Gas, walk-behind, 3 blade, 36" trowel		2.23	107.57	334.08	969.15	84.69
1400	4 blade, 48" trowel		3.37	110	293.33	710	85.62
1500	Float, hand-operated (Bull float), 48" wide		.09	13.85	43.07	124.61	9.33
1570	Curb builder, 14 H.P., gas, single screw		15.36	160	480	1,440	218.85
1590	Double screw		13.58	350	1,050	3,150	318.63
1600	Floor grinder, concrete and terrazzo, electric, 22" path		3.33	140.63	416.25	1,013.13	109.91
1700	Edger, concrete, electric, 7" path		1.30	77	211.25	513.13	52.63
1750	Vacuum pick-up system for floor grinders, wet/dry		1.78	98.78	296.67	832.78	73.53
1800	Mixer, powered, mortar and concrete, gas, 6 C.F., 18 H.P.		8.13	84.29	255.71	707.14	116.18
1900	10 C.F., 25 H.P.		9.86	122.17	354.29	859.35	149.77
2000	16 C.F.		10.26	112.50	310	812.50	144.05
2100	Concrete, stationary, tilt drum, 2 C.Y.		8.67	84	249.38	686.25	119.22
2120	Pump, concrete, truck mounted, 4" line, 80' boom		33.94	926.67	2,780	8,340	827.49
2140	5" line, 110' boom		43.44	1,203.33	3,610	10,830	1,069.53
2160	Mud jack, 50 C.F. per hr.		7.06	170	510	1,530	158.45
2180	225 C.F. per hr.		9.35	201.67	605	1,815	195.81
2190	Shotcrete pump rig, 12 C.Y./hr.		18.17	843	2,529	7,587	651.19
2200	35 C.Y./hr.		17.28	1,098.33	3,295	9,885	797.28
2600	Saw, concrete, manual, gas, 18 H.P.		6.07	107.67	320.83	832.50	112.72
2650	Self-propelled, gas, 30 H.P.		8.65	193.33	533.89	1,411.11	176
2675	V-groove crack chaser, manual, gas, 6 H.P.		1.80	138.92	361.15	1,022.75	86.61
2700	Vibrators, concrete, electric, 60 cycle, 2 H.P.		.51	41	144	425	32.92
2800	3 H.P.		.62	73.33	198.67	461.67	44.66
2900	Gas engine, 5 H.P.		1.69	18.16	56.56	164.01	24.85
3000	8 H.P.		2.28	18.37	57.14	165.08	29.68
3050	Vibrating screed, gas engine, 8 H.P.		3.08	128.75	330.13	781.25	90.64
3120	Concrete transit mixer, 6 x 4, 250 H.P., 8 C.Y., rear discharge		55.49	167	501	1,503	544.13
3200	Front discharge		64.42	102.55	307.64	922.92	576.87
3300	6 x 6, 285 H.P., 12 C.Y., rear discharge		63.61	333.33	1,000	3,000	708.92
3400	Front discharge		66.28	283.33	850	2,550	700.26
20 0010	**EARTHWORK EQUIPMENT RENTAL** without operators R015433-10						
0040	Aggregate spreader, push type, 8' to 12' wide	Ea.	2.84	74.55	223.65	670.95	67.49
0045	Tailgate type, 8' wide		2.79	56.09	168.27	504.81	55.94
0055	Earth auger, truck mounted, for fence & sign posts, utility poles		15.16	66.30	163.60	464.30	153.97
0060	For borings and monitoring wells		46.66	122.70	368.09	1,104.27	446.91
0070	Portable, trailer mounted		2.52	119.75	314.25	746.25	83.02
0075	Truck mounted, for caissons, water wells		93.42	181.47	544.40	1,633.20	856.23
0080	Horizontal boring machine, 12" to 36" diameter, 45 H.P.		24.91	231.67	695	2,085	338.28
0090	12" to 48" diameter, 65 H.P.		34.19	273.33	820	2,460	437.50
0095	Auger, for fence posts, gas engine, hand held		.49	77.79	241.44	578.16	52.21
0100	Excavator, diesel hydraulic, crawler mounted, 1/2 C.Y. cap.		23.81	977.86	2,872.14	5,938.57	764.88
0120	5/8 C.Y. capacity		31.83	1,052.44	2,792.78	6,226.11	813.17
0140	3/4 C.Y. capacity		35.80	1,195.25	3,144.88	7,524.38	915.34
0150	1 C.Y. capacity		45.17	1,160.22	3,126	7,463.89	986.56

01 54 | Construction Aids

01 54 33 | Equipment Rental

		UNIT	HOURLY OPER. COST	RENT PER DAY	RENT PER WEEK	RENT PER MONTH	EQUIPMENT COST/DAY
0200	1-1/2 C.Y. capacity	Ea.	53.25	1,479	3,796	9,465	1,185.24
0300	2 C.Y. capacity		62.02	1,000	3,000	9,000	1,096.14
0320	2-1/2 C.Y. capacity		90.57	1,868.60	4,795.50	12,022.50	1,683.69
0325	3-1/2 C.Y. capacity		131.66	2,156.63	6,705.94	19,383	2,394.44
0330	4-1/2 C.Y. capacity		166.19	3,940.50	12,294.23	35,571	3,788.37
0335	6 C.Y. capacity		210.86	3,461.25	10,785.39	31,204.50	3,843.97
0340	7 C.Y. capacity		192.03	4,450	13,350	40,050	4,206.21
0342	Excavator attachments, bucket thumbs		3.73	277.97	865.74	2,502.75	202.95
0345	Grapples		3.44	239.63	744.53	2,156.63	176.44
0346	Hydraulic hammer for boom mounting, 4000 ft lb.		14.77	958.50	2,984.15	8,626.50	715.03
0347	5000 ft lb.		17.48	1,022.40	3,185.33	9,212.25	776.94
0348	8000 ft lb.		25.80	1,304.63	4,023.57	11,608.50	1,011.13
0349	12,000 ft lb.		29.67	1,500.32	4,627.11	13,349.78	1,162.80
0350	Gradall type, truck mounted, 3 ton @ 15' radius, 5/8 C.Y.		47.61	833.33	2,500	7,500	880.91
0370	1 C.Y. capacity		65.11	1,666.67	5,000	15,000	1,520.84
0400	Backhoe-loader, 40 to 45 H.P., 5/8 C.Y. capacity		13.04	211.38	589.63	1,520.13	222.27
0450	45 H.P. to 60 H.P., 3/4 C.Y. capacity		19.75	214.56	595.78	1,565.67	277.19
0460	80 H.P., 1-1/4 C.Y. capacity		22.31	325	896	2,266.44	357.71
0470	112 H.P., 1-1/2 C.Y. capacity		36.15	660.30	2,048.91	5,937.38	699
0482	Backhoe-loader attachment, compactor, 20,000 lb.		7.06	397	1,009	2,993	258.25
0485	Hydraulic hammer, 750 ft lb.		4.03	115.02	357.84	1,033.05	103.85
0486	Hydraulic hammer, 1200 ft lb.		7.18	220.46	686.82	1,996.88	194.78
0500	Brush chipper, gas engine, 6" cutter head, 35 H.P.		10.05	276.50	920.13	2,218.13	264.41
0550	Diesel engine, 12" cutter head, 130 H.P.		25.95	512.33	1,552.78	4,121	518.12
0600	15" cutter head, 165 H.P.		29.14	548.48	1,706.31	4,925.63	574.37
0750	Bucket, clamshell, general purpose, 3/8 C.Y.		1.53	40	120	360	36.25
0800	1/2 C.Y.		1.66	40	120	360	37.28
0850	3/4 C.Y.		1.80	43.67	131	393	40.58
0900	1 C.Y.		1.86	53.33	160	480	46.89
0950	1-1/2 C.Y.		3.05	49.17	147.50	442.50	53.92
1000	2 C.Y.		3.20	168.33	505	1,515	126.58
1010	Bucket, dragline, medium duty, 1/2 C.Y.		.90	35	105	315	28.17
1020	3/4 C.Y.		.85	37.83	113.50	340.50	29.54
1030	1 C.Y.		.87	43.17	129.50	388.50	32.89
1040	1-1/2 C.Y.		1.38	43.83	131.50	394.50	37.32
1050	2 C.Y.		1.70	43.20	129.60	388.80	39.49
1070	3 C.Y.		2.28	55.83	167.50	502.50	51.71
1200	Compactor, manually guided 2-drum vibratory smooth roller, 7.5 H.P.		7.91	182.38	471	1,302.56	157.50
1250	Rammer/tamper, gas, 8"		2.42	108.50	272.50	807.50	73.84
1260	15"		2.88	104.37	324.83	755.09	88.02
1300	Vibratory plate, gas, 18" plate, 3000 lb. blow		2.33	213.97	625.83	1,586.50	143.82
1350	21" plate, 5000 lb. blow		2.87	244.63	615.88	1,715.88	146.12
1370	Curb builder/extruder, 14 H.P., gas, single screw		13.58	1,065	3,195	9,585	747.63
1390	Double screw		16.29	1,278	3,834	11,502	897.16
1500	Disc harrow attachment, for tractor		.52	372.75	1,171.50	3,514.50	238.45
1810	Feller buncher, shearing & accumulating trees, 100 H.P.		47.53	1,236.67	3,710	11,130	1,122.21
1860	Grader, self-propelled, 25,000 lb.		36.55	1,058.33	3,175	9,525	927.41
1910	30,000 lb.		46.71	1,195.83	3,587.50	10,762.50	1,091.19
1920	40,000 lb.		56.87	1,333.33	4,000	12,000	1,254.97
1930	55,000 lb.		73.36	1,666.67	5,000	15,000	1,586.87
1950	Hammer, pavement breaker, self-propelled, diesel, 1000 to 1250 lb.		31.13	600	1,800	5,400	609.02
2000	1300 to 1500 lb.		46.91	600	1,800	5,400	735.29
2050	Pile driving hammer, steam or air, 4150 ft lb. @ 225 bpm		13.32	537.83	1,676.49	4,845.75	441.85
2100	8750 ft lb. @ 145 bpm		15.72	756.15	2,347.08	6,789.38	595.21
2150	15,000 ft lb. @ 60 bpm		16.08	899.93	2,794.14	8,094	687.50
2200	24,450 ft lb. @ 111 bpm		17.19	1,043.70	3,241.21	9,372	785.80
2250	Leads, 60' high for pile driving hammers up to 20,000 ft lb.		4.02	324.83	1,005.89	2,902.13	233.36
2300	90' high for hammers over 20,000 ft lb.		5.97	580.43	1,810.61	5,245.13	409.90

01 54 | Construction Aids

01 54 33 | Equipment Rental

			UNIT	HOURLY OPER. COST	RENT PER DAY	RENT PER WEEK	RENT PER MONTH	EQUIPMENT COST/DAY	
20	2350	Diesel type hammer, 22,400 ft lb.	Ea.	19.53	527.18	1,644.90	4,765.88	485.21	20
	2400	41,300 ft lb.		28.15	665.63	2,077.77	6,017.25	640.74	
	2450	141,000 ft lb.		45.30	1,059.68	3,289.81	9,505.13	1,020.34	
	2500	Vib. elec. hammer/extractor, 200 kW diesel generator, 34 H.P.		45.34	772.13	2,395.21	6,922.50	841.80	
	2550	80 H.P.		80.04	1,118.25	3,462.95	10,011	1,332.90	
	2600	150 H.P.		148.12	2,130	6,666.18	19,276.50	2,518.21	
	2700	Hydro Excavator w/EXT boom 12 C.Y., 1200 gallons		41.44	1,730.63	5,364.76	15,549	1,404.51	
	2800	Log chipper, up to 22" diameter, 600 H.P.		48.88	492.50	1,477.50	4,432.50	686.57	
	2850	Logger, for skidding & stacking logs, 150 H.P.		47.62	141.67	425	1,275	465.97	
	2860	Mulcher, diesel powered, trailer mounted		21.79	765.50	2,296.50	6,889.50	633.63	
	2900	Rake, spring tooth, with tractor		16.13	58.20	162.50	410.60	161.55	
	3000	Roller, vibratory, tandem, smooth drum, 20 H.P.		8.56	380.83	1,095	2,632.50	287.45	
	3050	35 H.P.		11.11	496.88	1,451.88	3,263.13	379.22	
	3100	Towed type vibratory compactor, smooth drum, 50 H.P.		27.70	766.67	2,300	6,900	681.59	
	3150	Sheepsfoot, 50 H.P.		28.10	366.67	1,100	3,300	444.83	
	3170	Landfill compactor, 220 H.P.		76.59	1,798.33	5,395	16,185	1,691.72	
	3200	Pneumatic tire roller, 80 H.P.		14.16	436.65	1,356.32	3,913.88	384.55	
	3250	120 H.P.		21.25	566.67	1,700	5,100	510	
	3300	Sheepsfoot vibratory roller, 240 H.P.		68.18	366.67	1,100	3,300	765.47	
	3320	340 H.P.		91.87	1,500	4,500	13,500	1,635	
	3350	Smooth drum vibratory roller, 75 H.P.		25.58	268.33	711.67	2,012.22	346.96	
	3400	125 H.P.		30.27	479.25	1,437.75	4,206.75	529.68	
	3410	Rotary mower, brush, 60", with tractor		20.59	133	370.50	944	238.84	
	3420	Rototiller, walk-behind, gas, 5 H.P.		2.34	125	260	645	70.72	
	3422	8 H.P.		3.08	130	325	706	89.64	
	3440	Scrapers, towed type, 7 C.Y. capacity		7.06	137.39	427.10	1,224.75	141.88	
	3450	10 C.Y. capacity		7.90	183.18	571.38	1,650.75	177.45	
	3500	15 C.Y. capacity		8.11	211.94	657.96	1,890.38	196.46	
	3525	Self-propelled, single engine, 14 C.Y. capacity		146.09	1,666.67	5,000	15,000	2,168.71	
	3550	Dual engine, 21 C.Y. capacity		154.95	1,666.67	5,000	15,000	2,239.60	
	3600	31 C.Y. capacity		205.89	2,208.33	6,625	19,875	2,972.09	
	3640	44 C.Y. capacity		255.02	2,333.33	7,000	21,000	3,440.19	
	3650	Elevating type, single engine, 11 C.Y. capacity		67.81	800	2,400	7,200	1,022.46	
	3700	22 C.Y. capacity		125.63	1,666.67	5,000	15,000	2,005.03	
	3710	Screening plant, 110 H.P. w/5' x 10' screen		23.16	692.25	2,156.42	6,230.25	616.57	
	3720	5' x 16' screen		29.24	1,222.22	3,666.67	11,000	967.25	
	3850	Shovel, crawler-mounted, front-loading, 7 C.Y. capacity		239.65	4,233.38	13,159.21	38,020.50	4,549.05	
	3855	12 C.Y. capacity		369.25	5,857.50	18,238.21	52,717.50	6,601.66	
	3860	Shovel/backhoe bucket, 1/2 C.Y.		2.95	78.81	244.72	708.23	72.55	
	3870	3/4 C.Y.		2.92	88.40	274.73	793.43	78.31	
	3880	1 C.Y.		3.02	59.13	175	488.75	59.18	
	3890	1-1/2 C.Y.		3.24	115.02	357.84	1,033.05	97.47	
	3910	3 C.Y.		3.77	155.49	484.81	1,411.13	127.10	
	3950	Stump chipper, 18" deep, 30 H.P.		7.55	329.43	1,017.29	2,480.14	263.85	
	4110	Dozer, crawler, torque converter, diesel 80 H.P.		27.68	692.50	1,852	4,464	591.82	
	4150	105 H.P.		37.63	644.33	2,008.05	5,804.25	702.68	
	4200	140 H.P.		45.24	660	1,980	5,940	757.89	
	4260	200 H.P.		69.22	1,381	4,143	12,429	1,382.36	
	4310	300 H.P.		88.48	1,611.11	4,833.33	14,500	1,674.53	
	4360	410 H.P.		117.00	2,666.67	8,000	24,000	2,535.96	
	4370	500 H.P.		146.19	2,333.33	7,000	21,000	2,569.55	
	4380	700 H.P.		252.27	3,466.67	10,400	31,200	4,098.16	
	4400	Loader, crawler, torque conv., diesel, 1-1/2 C.Y., 80 H.P.		32.38	591.08	1,841.82	5,325	627.38	
	4450	1-1/2 to 1-3/4 C.Y., 95 H.P.		33.18	750.83	2,341.34	6,762.75	733.70	
	4510	1-3/4 to 2-1/4 C.Y., 130 H.P.		52.34	900	2,700	8,100	958.76	
	4530	2-1/2 to 3-1/4 C.Y., 190 H.P.		63.34	1,198.13	3,754.98	10,863	1,257.68	
	4560	3-1/2 to 5 C.Y., 275 H.P.		78.26	1,466.67	4,400	13,200	1,506.11	
	4610	Front end loader, 4WD, articulated frame, diesel, 1 to 1-1/4 C.Y., 70 H.P.		18.22	495.20	1,245.10	3,126	394.79	

01 54 | Construction Aids

01 54 33 | Equipment Rental

			UNIT	HOURLY OPER. COST	RENT PER DAY	RENT PER WEEK	RENT PER MONTH	EQUIPMENT COST/DAY	
20	4620	1-1/2 to 1-3/4 C.Y., 95 H.P.	Ea.	21.92	466.67	1,400	4,200	455.32	20
	4650	1-3/4 to 2 C.Y., 130 H.P.		23.09	497.14	1,455.50	4,235.40	475.82	
	4710	2-1/2 to 3-1/2 C.Y., 145 H.P.		32.36	666.67	2,000	6,000	658.89	
	4730	3 to 4-1/2 C.Y., 185 H.P.		35.17	879.10	2,543	5,789.50	789.98	
	4760	5-1/4 to 5-3/4 C.Y., 270 H.P.		58.30	1,200	3,600	10,800	1,186.42	
	4810	7 to 9 C.Y., 475 H.P.		99.93	2,000	6,000	18,000	1,999.44	
	4870	9 to 11 C.Y., 620 H.P.		144.59	3,470	8,530	21,500	2,862.71	
	4880	Skid-steer loader, wheeled, 10 C.F., 30 H.P. gas		10.49	295	885.40	1,880.40	260.99	
	4890	1 C.Y., 78 H.P., diesel		20.21	438.75	1,341.25	3,095	429.91	
	4892	Skid-steer attachment, auger		.82	135.67	341.11	875	74.76	
	4893	Backhoe		.81	100.29	262.86	759.29	59.06	
	4894	Broom		.78	184.60	429.20	969.60	92.04	
	4895	Forks		.17	44.63	117.75	310	24.90	
	4896	Grapple		.79	86.53	235.63	652.85	53.47	
	4897	Concrete hammer		1.15	209.29	588.57	1,515	126.94	
	4898	Tree spade		.66	335.48	1,006.43	2,415.42	206.55	
	4899	Trencher		.72	152.78	415.56	1,068.89	88.83	
	4900	Trencher, chain, boom type, gas, operator walking, 12 H.P.		4.58	277.13	829.25	2,053.88	202.47	
	4910	Operator riding, 40 H.P.		18.29	453	1,201	2,779	386.50	
	5000	Wheel type, diesel, 4' deep, 12" wide		75.31	1,038.38	3,232.08	9,345.38	1,248.89	
	5100	6' deep, 20" wide		95.99	1,268.75	2,852.50	6,592.50	1,338.44	
	5150	Chain type, diesel, 5' deep, 8" wide		17.87	388.73	1,212.03	3,514.50	385.33	
	5200	Diesel, 8' deep, 16" wide		98.27	2,076.75	6,464.18	18,744	2,079.03	
	5202	Rock trencher, wheel type, 6" wide x 18" deep		51.55	1,268.75	2,900	6,592.50	992.44	
	5206	Chain type, 18" wide x 7' deep		114.54	271.67	815	2,445	1,079.31	
	5210	Tree spade, self-propelled		14.98	415	1,245	3,735	368.85	
	5250	Truck, dump, 2-axle, 12 ton, 8 C.Y. payload, 220 H.P.		26.25	366.85	1,037.44	2,773.47	417.49	
	5300	Three axle dump, 16 ton, 12 C.Y. payload, 400 H.P.		48.92	666.67	2,000	6,000	791.36	
	5310	Four axle dump, 25 ton, 18 C.Y. payload, 450 H.P.		54.80	583.33	1,750	5,250	788.42	
	5350	Dump trailer only, rear dump, 16-1/2 C.Y.		6.30	162.95	507.90	1,464.38	151.94	
	5400	20 C.Y.		6.80	183.18	571.38	1,650.75	168.66	
	5450	Flatbed, single axle, 1-1/2 ton rating		20.88	271.58	974.48	2,556	361.95	
	5500	3 ton rating		28.19	275.83	827.50	2,482.50	391.02	
	5550	Off highway rear dump, 25 ton capacity		68.89	1,533.33	4,600	13,800	1,471.16	
	5600	35 ton capacity		73.55	1,533.33	4,600	13,800	1,508.36	
	5610	50 ton capacity		92.20	2,166.67	6,500	19,500	2,037.60	
	5620	65 ton capacity		98.46	2,156.63	6,695.04	19,383	2,126.70	
	5630	100 ton capacity		133.29	3,168.38	9,869.41	28,542	3,040.18	
	6000	Vibratory plow, 25 H.P., walking		7.43	344.35	1,033.05	3,099.15	266.08	
40	0010	**GENERAL EQUIPMENT RENTAL** without operators							40
	0020	Aerial lift, scissor type, to 20' high, 1200 lb. capacity, electric	Ea.	3.83	195.84	399.97	744.90	110.61	
	0030	To 30' high, 1200 lb. capacity		4.15	350	815	1,975	196.19	
	0040	Over 30' high, 1500 lb. capacity		5.64	410	861.25	1,817.50	217.41	
	0070	Articulating boom, to 45' high, 500 lb. capacity, diesel		13.51	561.06	1,309.50	2,950.56	369.98	
	0075	To 60' high, 500 lb. capacity		15.02	623.40	1,455	3,278.40	411.13	
	0080	To 80' high, 500 lb. capacity		17.65	918.44	2,459.44	6,057	633.06	
	0085	To 125' high, 500 lb. capacity		20.17	1,986.67	4,695	11,533.89	1,100.34	
	0100	Telescoping boom to 40' high, 500 lb. capacity, diesel		12.35	540	1,233.75	2,615	345.57	
	0105	To 45' high, 500 lb. capacity		13.75	520	1,209	2,582	351.80	
	0110	To 60' high, 500 lb. capacity		17.98	520	1,209	2,582	385.68	
	0115	To 80' high, 500 lb. capacity		23.38	1,112	2,615	5,357	710.06	
	0120	To 100' high, 500 lb. capacity		31.57	918.44	2,459.44	6,057	744.42	
	0125	To 120' high, 500 lb. capacity		32.06	1,818.33	4,756.11	11,001.67	1,207.69	
	0195	Air compressor, portable, 6.5 CFM, electric		.99	46.05	121.75	353	32.29	
	0196	Gasoline		.72	50.74	144	387.43	34.53	
	0200	Towed type, gas engine, 60 CFM		10.37	150.25	451.25	984.38	173.21	
	0300	160 CFM		11.51	250	760	1,810	244.12	

01 54 | Construction Aids

01 54 33 | Equipment Rental

		UNIT	HOURLY OPER. COST	RENT PER DAY	RENT PER WEEK	RENT PER MONTH	EQUIPMENT COST/DAY
0400	Diesel engine, rotary screw, 250 CFM	Ea.	13.29	137.50	450	1,155	196.28
0500	365 CFM		17.59	474.29	1,246.43	3,123.57	389.99
0550	450 CFM		21.93	357.78	966.67	2,764.44	368.76
0600	600 CFM		37.49	267.32	831.10	2,396.25	466.11
0700	750 CFM		38.06	690	1,757	4,224	655.87
0915	Air purifier		.77	10.53	24.89	69.11	11.12
0917	Air scrubber, 500 - 700 CFM, 110 V		.76	86.80	270.58	782.78	60.20
0919	200 - 1200 CFM, 110 V		.76	102.77	320.28	926.55	70.14
0930	Air tools, breaker, pavement, 60 lb.		.62	52	147.50	381.67	34.47
0940	80 lb.		.62	49.80	154	389	35.75
0950	Drills, hand (jackhammer), 65 lb.		.74	66	184.29	465	42.75
0960	Track or wagon, swing boom, 4" drifter		67.89	1,080	3,240	9,720	1,191.15
0970	5" drifter		67.89	1,080	3,240	9,720	1,191.15
0975	Track mounted quarry drill, 6" diameter drill		111.83	798.33	2,395	7,185	1,373.61
0980	Dust control per drill		1.14	10.67	32	96	15.54
0990	Hammer, chipping, 12 lb.		.66	39	109.50	270	27.16
1000	Hose, air with couplings, 50' long, 3/4" diameter		.07	14.40	37.83	95.83	8.16
1100	1" diameter		.09	17.18	43.13	127.25	9.31
1200	1-1/2" diameter		.24	43.87	108.33	304.44	23.60
1300	2" diameter		.26	61.50	151.25	419.38	32.35
1400	2-1/2" diameter		.39	65.78	183.56	534.56	39.86
1410	3" diameter		.46	83	215.50	636	46.76
1450	Drill, steel, 7/8" x 2'		.09	14.47	35	104.22	7.74
1460	7/8" x 6'		.13	21.14	65.80	190.64	14.17
1520	Moil points		.03	8.98	20.88	61.13	4.42
1525	Pneumatic nailer w/accessories		.52	25	75	150	19.20
1530	Sheeting driver for 60 lb. breaker		.05	8.36	25.98	75.08	5.58
1540	For 90 lb. breaker		.14	11.34	35.21	101.71	8.19
1550	Spade, 25 lb.		.55	7.99	24.81	71.89	9.37
1560	Tamper, single, 35 lb.		.65	96	259.20	701.70	57.02
1570	Triple, 140 lb.		.97	56.43	155	402.86	38.79
1580	Wrenches, impact, air powered, up to 3/4" bolt		.47	41.82	110.22	305.89	25.78
1590	Up to 1-1/4" bolt		.63	79.33	206.11	581.11	46.28
1600	Barricades, barrels, reflectorized, 1 to 99 barrels		.04	4.70	11.80	35	2.64
1610	100 to 200 barrels		.03	5.33	12.67	40.11	2.75
1620	Barrels with flashers, 1 to 99 barrels		.04	5.33	12.67	40.11	2.84
1630	100 to 200 barrels		.03	5.33	12.67	40.11	2.78
1640	Barrels with steady burn type C lights		.05	5.33	12.67	40.11	2.94
1650	Illuminated board, trailer mounted, with generator		3.60	91	288.57	734.14	86.53
1670	Portable barricade, stock, with flashers, 1 to 6 units		.04	4.29	12.14	39	2.73
1680	25 to 50 units		.04	4.29	12.14	39	2.72
1685	Butt fusion machine, wheeled, 1.5 HP electric, 2" - 8" diameter pipe		2.89	429	1,287	3,861	280.48
1690	Tracked, 20 HP diesel, 4"-12" diameter pipe		10.91	408.33	1,225	3,675	332.25
1695	83 HP diesel, 8" - 24" diameter pipe		56.31	561.67	1,685	5,055	787.50
1700	Carts, brick, gas engine, 1000 lb. capacity		3.23	32.22	84.52	215.66	42.77
1800	1500 lb., 7-1/2' lift		3.21	74.55	232.47	670.95	72.14
1822	Dehumidifier, medium, 6 lb./hr., 150 CFM		1.31	45.86	159.86	487.43	42.42
1824	Large, 18 lb./hr., 600 CFM		2.41	257.50	1,795	5,382.50	378.29
1830	Distributor, asphalt, trailer mounted, 2000 gal., 38 H.P. diesel		12.09	378.08	1,183.17	3,434.63	333.32
1840	3000 gal., 38 H.P. diesel		14.14	410.03	1,269.75	3,674.25	367.10
1850	Drill, rotary hammer, electric		1.22	36	126	378	34.98
1860	Carbide bit, 1-1/2" diameter, add to electric rotary hammer		.03	51.98	131.70	385.50	26.61
1865	Rotary, crawler, 250 H.P.		149.26	2,458.33	7,375	22,125	2,669.07
1870	Emulsion sprayer, 65 gal., 5 H.P. gas engine		3.04	115.02	357.84	1,033.05	95.90
1880	200 gal., 5 H.P. engine		7.94	192.77	600.24	1,730.63	183.58
1900	Floor auto-scrubbing machine, walk-behind, 28" path		6.18	222.67	728.67	1,475	195.20
1930	Floodlight, mercury vapor, or quartz, on tripod, 1000 watt		.50	43.10	108.70	293.30	25.76
1940	2000 watt		.65	45.60	124.50	343	30.09

01 54 | Construction Aids

01 54 33 | Equipment Rental

		UNIT	HOURLY OPER. COST	RENT PER DAY	RENT PER WEEK	RENT PER MONTH	EQUIPMENT COST/DAY
1950	Floodlights, trailer mounted with generator, 1 - 300 watt light	Ea.	3.90	185	413.33	916.67	113.84
1960	2 - 1000 watt lights		4.93	185	413.33	916.67	122.12
2000	4 - 300 watt lights		4.67	185	413.33	916.67	119.99
2005	Foam spray rig, incl. box trailer, compressor, generator, proportioner		27.99	575.10	1,789.19	5,165.25	581.75
2015	Forklift, pneumatic tire, rough terr, straight mast, 5000 lb, 12' lift, gas		20.44	535.67	1,292.78	2,935.11	422.09
2025	8000 lb, 12' lift		24.93	687.78	1,678.33	3,556.11	535.15
2030	5000 lb, 12' lift, diesel		16.94	427.33	1,069	2,580.17	349.30
2035	8000 lb, 12' lift, diesel		18.36	687.78	1,678.33	3,556.11	482.54
2045	All terrain, telescoping boom, diesel 5000 lb, 10' reach, 19' lift		18.91	535.67	1,292.78	2,935.11	409.81
2055	6600 lb, 29' reach, 42' lift		23.13	593.75	1,432.50	3,192.50	471.51
2065	10,000 lb, 31' reach, 45' lift		25.31	957.50	2,353.75	4,978.75	673.26
2070	Cushion tire, smooth floor, gas, 5000 lb capacity		9.04	381.11	938.89	2,223.33	260.12
2075	8000 lb capacity		12.46	435	1,057	2,638	311.06
2085	Diesel, 5000 lb capacity		8.49	327.50	823	2,002.50	232.55
2090	12,000 lb capacity		13.21	680.63	1,817.64	4,240.39	469.19
2095	20,000 lb capacity		18.91	866.79	2,460.30	6,396.21	643.35
2100	Generator, electric, gas engine, 1.5 kW to 3 kW		2.82	59.25	167.50	408.75	56.08
2200	5 kW		3.53	84.83	238.33	585.83	75.88
2300	10 kW		6.50	129.17	340.83	949.17	120.15
2400	25 kW		8.12	370.50	958.50	2,186.50	256.64
2500	Diesel engine, 20 kW		10.09	288.50	733.50	1,665	227.44
2600	50 kW		17.48	388.33	1,125	2,645	364.82
2700	100 kW		31.34	626	1,586.50	3,968	568.06
2800	250 kW		59.57	1,019.50	2,677.50	6,297.50	1,012.10
2850	Hammer, hydraulic, for mounting on boom, to 500 ft lb.		3.18	100.64	312.82	905.25	88
2860	1000 ft lb.		5.05	150.17	467.50	1,357.88	133.88
2900	Heaters, space, oil or electric, 50 MBH		1.60	93.20	284	750	69.63
3000	100 MBH		2.98	135.63	352.50	861.25	94.34
3100	300 MBH		8.69	678.50	1,928	5,358	455.08
3150	500 MBH		14.42	267.06	609.69	1,686.25	237.32
3200	Hose, water, suction with coupling, 20' long, 2" diameter		.02	8.33	21	60	4.37
3210	3" diameter		.03	15.88	43.50	124.38	8.96
3220	4" diameter		.03	30.35	93.88	271.58	19.04
3230	6" diameter		.12	43.67	135.80	394.05	28.12
3240	8" diameter		.30	57.51	178.82	516.53	38.13
3250	Discharge hose with coupling, 50' long, 2" diameter		.01	7.20	20	55.60	4.09
3260	3" diameter		.01	9.10	23.95	74.55	4.88
3270	4" diameter		.02	22.37	69.85	202.35	14.15
3280	6" diameter		.07	31.42	97.23	281.16	19.99
3290	8" diameter		.26	40.47	125.73	362.10	27.24
3295	Insulation blower		.91	125.67	390.45	1,118.25	85.38
3300	Ladders, extension type, 16' to 36' long		.20	44.05	122	347.25	25.99
3400	40' to 60' long		.70	119.03	333.67	989.67	72.33
3405	Lance for cutting concrete		2.42	103.33	310	930	81.33
3407	Lawn mower, rotary, 22", 5 H.P.		1.16	25	140	400	37.25
3408	48" self-propelled		3.18	161.20	429	1,186	111.21
3410	Level, electronic, automatic, with tripod and leveling rod		1.15	47.37	121.83	344.50	33.60
3430	Laser type, for pipe and sewer line and grade		2.38	144.37	365.14	1,111.86	92.11
3440	Rotating beam for interior control		.99	83.28	214	622.80	50.71
3460	Builder's optical transit, with tripod and rod		.11	47.37	121.83	344.50	25.23
3500	Light towers, towable, with diesel generator, 2000 watt		4.68	185	413.33	916.67	120.08
3600	4000 watt		4.95	185	413.33	916.67	122.23
3700	Mixer, powered, plaster and mortar, 6 C.F., 7 H.P.		2.26	89.29	257.86	648.57	69.62
3800	10 C.F., 9 H.P.		2.46	111	328	956	85.26
3850	Nailer, pneumatic		.53	25	75	150	19.21
3900	Paint sprayers complete, 8 CFM		.96	93.16	222.09	619.25	52.14
4000	17 CFM		1.75	169.38	403.80	1,125.90	94.79
4020	Pavers, bituminous, rubber tires, 8' wide, 50 H.P., diesel		35.10	612.38	1,904.62	5,511.38	661.71

01 54 | Construction Aids

01 54 33 | Equipment Rental

		UNIT	HOURLY OPER. COST	RENT PER DAY	RENT PER WEEK	RENT PER MONTH	EQUIPMENT COST/DAY
4030	10' wide, 150 H.P.	Ea.	105.12	2,103.38	6,521.89	18,850.50	2,145.33
4050	Crawler, 8' wide, 100 H.P., diesel		96.29	1,200	3,560	9,240	1,482.34
4060	10' wide, 150 H.P.		114.29	1,425	4,225	10,975	1,759.34
4070	Concrete paver, 12' to 24' wide, 250 H.P.		96.32	1,810.50	5,656.15	16,401	1,901.82
4080	Placer-spreader-trimmer, 24' wide, 300 H.P.		129.19	2,742.38	8,570.80	24,814.50	2,747.64
4100	Pump, centrifugal gas pump, 1-1/2" diam., 65 GPM		4.31	58.04	181.23	521.85	70.74
4200	2" diameter, 130 GPM		5.47	44.44	140	368.80	71.79
4300	3" diameter, 250 GPM		5.62	62.94	187	521	82.39
4400	6" diameter, 1500 GPM		24.40	366.90	956.30	2,400.30	386.48
4500	Submersible electric pump, 1-1/4" diameter, 55 GPM		.44	47.70	125.17	331.50	28.54
4600	1-1/2" diameter, 83 GPM		.49	59.23	160.43	428.57	35.99
4700	2" diameter, 120 GPM		1.81	58.58	182.23	527.18	50.89
4800	3" diameter, 300 GPM		3.33	132.11	347.80	976.83	96.23
4900	4" diameter, 560 GPM		16.19	80.76	242.29	726.86	177.96
5000	6" diameter, 1590 GPM		24.22	225.43	676.28	2,028.83	329.05
5100	Diaphragm pump, gas, single, 1-1/2" diameter		1.24	40	120	360	33.88
5200	2" diameter		4.37	45	135	405	61.92
5300	3" diameter		4.44	79.40	243.40	614.20	84.23
5400	Double, 4" diameter		6.62	218.19	488.77	1,246.91	150.72
5450	Pressure washer 5 GPM, 3000 psi		4.25	109.50	351	838	104.23
5460	7 GPM, 3000 psi		5.43	112	350	847	113.42
5470	High Pressure Water Jet 10 KSI		43.48	777.45	2,414.14	6,975.75	830.66
5480	40 KSI		30.65	1,054.35	3,285.92	9,505.13	902.38
5500	Trash pump, self-priming, gas, 2" diameter		4.19	82.50	247.50	742.50	83
5600	Diesel, 4" diameter		7.33	275	717.22	1,955.56	202.06
5650	Diesel, 6" diameter		18.49	366.90	956.30	2,400.30	339.17
5655	Grout Pump		20.55	302.46	940.77	2,715.75	352.58
5700	Salamanders, L.P. gas fired, 100,000 Btu		3.17	60.10	169.40	451.90	59.23
5705	50,000 Btu		1.83	28.20	72.30	192	29.07
5720	Sandblaster, portable, open top, 3 C.F. capacity		.66	131.67	395	1,185	84.26
5730	6 C.F. capacity		1.10	263.33	790	2,370	166.82
5740	Accessories for above		.15	25.56	79.65	230.04	17.14
5750	Sander, floor		.84	75.68	215	521.49	49.75
5760	Edger		.57	33	109	319	26.35
5800	Saw, chain, gas engine, 18" long		1.93	46.25	160.88	426.25	47.58
5900	Hydraulic powered, 36" long		.86	77.92	233.77	701.30	53.61
5950	60" long		.86	86.98	260.93	782.78	59.04
6000	Masonry, table mounted, 14" diameter, 5 H.P.		1.45	86.87	297.65	723.88	71.14
6050	Portable cut-off, 8 H.P.		1.99	81.25	262.50	590	68.42
6100	Circular, hand held, electric, 7-1/4" diameter		.25	23	50	125	11.99
6200	12" diameter		.26	48.14	126.43	331.43	27.37
6250	Wall saw, w/hydraulic power, 10 H.P.		3.61	137.74	413.22	1,239.66	111.53
6275	Shot blaster, walk-behind, 20" wide		5.20	302.46	940.77	2,715.75	229.79
6280	Sidewalk broom, walk-behind		2.46	88.93	277.04	804.08	75.10
6300	Steam cleaner, 100 gallons per hour		3.67	88.93	277.04	804.08	84.77
6310	200 gallons per hour		4.76	107.57	334.75	969.15	105.05
6340	Tar Kettle/Pot, 400 gallons		18.08	126.67	380	1,140	220.65
6350	Torch, cutting, acetylene-oxygen, 150' hose, excludes gases		.50	16.51	51.36	149.10	14.24
6360	Hourly operating cost includes tips and gas		23.00	7.56	23.45	67.63	188.67
6410	Toilet, portable chemical		.14	25.03	77.34	223.65	16.63
6420	Recycle flush type		.18	30.89	95.81	276.90	20.58
6430	Toilet, fresh water flush, garden hose,		.21	36.74	114.27	330.15	24.56
6440	Hoisted, non-flush, for high rise		.17	29.82	93.50	270.51	20.08
6465	Tractor, farm with attachment		19.09	342.50	984	2,422	349.52
6480	Trailers, platform, flush deck, 2 axle, 3 ton capacity		1.86	102.24	317.41	915.90	78.34
6500	25 ton capacity		6.85	154.43	479.04	1,384.50	150.61
6600	40 ton capacity		8.84	219.39	681.05	1,970.25	206.92
6700	3 axle, 50 ton capacity		9.59	433.33	1,300	3,900	336.69

01 54 | Construction Aids

01 54 33 | Equipment Rental

			UNIT	HOURLY OPER. COST	RENT PER DAY	RENT PER WEEK	RENT PER MONTH	EQUIPMENT COST/DAY	
40	6800	75 ton capacity	Ea.	12.18	324.83	1,002.39	2,902.13	297.90	40
	6810	Trailer mounted cable reel for high voltage line work		6.46	252.67	758	2,274	203.26	
	6820	Trailer mounted cable tensioning rig		12.81	83.33	250	750	152.47	
	6830	Cable pulling rig		80.95	156.67	470	1,410	741.56	
	6850	Portable cable/wire puller, 8000 lb max pulling capacity		4.06	170.69	428.86	1,132.86	118.26	
	6900	Water tank trailer, engine driven discharge, 5000 gallons		7.87	170.40	530.99	1,544.25	169.14	
	6925	10,000 gallons		10.72	232.17	721.45	2,076.75	230.04	
	6950	Water truck, off highway, 6000 gallons		78.88	1,333.33	4,000	12,000	1,431.03	
	7010	Tram car for high voltage line work, powered, 2 conductor		7.55	31.33	94	282	79.21	
	7020	Transit (builder's level) with tripod		.11	47.37	121.83	344.50	25.23	
	7030	Trench box, 3000 lb., 6' x 8'		.61	103.84	323.76	937.20	69.67	
	7040	7200 lb., 6' x 20'		.79	201.29	625.89	1,810.50	131.49	
	7050	8000 lb., 8' x 16'		1.18	218.33	679.21	1,970.25	145.31	
	7060	9500 lb., 8' x 20'		1.32	250.28	779.16	2,263.13	166.41	
	7065	11,000 lb., 8' x 24'		1.39	235.37	732.99	2,130	157.70	
	7070	12,000 lb., 10' x 20'		1.64	284.36	883.06	2,556	189.71	
	7100	Truck, pickup, 3/4 ton, 2 wheel drive		10.15	66.56	206.62	596.40	122.56	
	7200	4 wheel drive		10.42	185.73	541.70	1,602.98	191.73	
	7250	Crew carrier, 9 passenger		13.91	116.09	362.57	1,049.03	183.83	
	7290	Flat bed truck, 20,000 lb. GVW		16.78	142.71	444.41	1,278	223.10	
	7300	Tractor, 4 x 2, 220 H.P.		24.46	232.17	721.45	2,076.75	339.98	
	7410	330 H.P.		35.54	317.37	986.95	2,848.88	481.71	
	7500	6 x 4, 380 H.P.		39.68	367.43	1,142.78	3,301.50	545.98	
	7600	450 H.P.		48.63	447.30	1,385.18	4,020.38	666.04	
	7610	Tractor, with A frame, boom and winch, 225 H.P.		27.20	315.24	979.34	2,822.25	413.43	
	7620	Vacuum truck, hazardous material, 2500 gallons		14.06	335.48	1,038.89	3,008.63	320.26	
	7625	5,000 gallons		14.32	473.93	1,471.76	4,260	408.90	
	7650	Vacuum, HEPA, 16 gallon, wet/dry		.93	126	362	959.50	79.88	
	7655	55 gallon, wet/dry		.93	126	362	959	79.84	
	7660	Water tank, portable		.80	156.99	453.41	1,153.82	97.09	
	7690	Sewer/catch basin vacuum, 14 C.Y., 1500 gallons		19.03	713.55	2,222.06	6,416.63	596.69	
	7700	Welder, electric, 200 amp		4.19	35.40	81.80	236.50	49.91	
	7800	300 amp		6.10	29.96	76.90	198.50	64.17	
	7900	Gas engine, 200 amp		9.83	107.10	290.20	681.10	136.72	
	8000	300 amp		11.13	107.10	290.20	681.10	147.09	
	8100	Wheelbarrow, any size		.07	12	32	93	6.97	
	8200	Wrecking ball, 4000 lb.		2.75	68.33	205	615	62.98	
50	0010	**HIGHWAY EQUIPMENT RENTAL** without operators	R015433 -10						50
	0050	Asphalt batch plant, portable drum mixer, 100 ton/hr.	Ea.	97.19	1,650.75	5,165.57	14,910	1,810.63	
	0060	200 ton/hr.		112.12	1,783.88	5,511.86	15,975	1,999.31	
	0070	300 ton/hr.		131.76	2,076.75	6,464.18	18,744	2,346.93	
	0100	Backhoe attachment, long stick, up to 185 H.P., 10.5' long		.41	27.69	85.42	247.08	20.33	
	0140	Up to 250 H.P., 12' long		.45	30.89	95.81	276.90	22.78	
	0180	Over 250 H.P., 15' long		.62	42.07	130.44	378.08	31.05	
	0200	Special dipper arm, up to 100 H.P., 32' long		1.27	85.73	266.64	772.13	63.50	
	0240	Over 100 H.P., 33' long		1.59	107.57	334.75	969.15	79.65	
	0280	Catch basin/sewer cleaning truck, 3 ton, 9 C.Y., 1000 gal.		38.90	452.63	1,414.04	4,100.25	594.04	
	0300	Concrete batch plant, portable, electric, 200 C.Y./hr.		26.59	601.73	1,875.76	5,431.50	587.85	
	0520	Grader/dozer attachment, ripper/scarifier, rear mounted, up to 135 H.P.		3.46	68.16	212.39	612.38	70.18	
	0540	Up to 180 H.P.		4.55	103.31	320.90	926.55	100.54	
	0580	Up to 250 H.P.		6.43	165.08	513.67	1,491	154.19	
	0700	Pvmt. removal bucket, for hyd. excavator, up to 90 H.P.		2.37	62.84	195.08	564.45	58	
	0740	Up to 200 H.P.		2.53	80.41	249.33	718.88	70.14	
	0780	Over 200 H.P.		2.77	98.51	305.89	883.95	83.32	
	0900	Aggregate spreader, self-propelled, 187 H.P.		55.63	798.75	2,481.78	7,188.75	941.36	
	1000	Chemical spreader, 3 C.Y.		3.48	99.67	299	897	87.61	
	1900	Hammermill, traveling, 250 H.P.		73.90	358.67	1,076	3,228	806.43	

01 54 | Construction Aids

01 54 33 | Equipment Rental

		UNIT	HOURLY OPER. COST	RENT PER DAY	RENT PER WEEK	RENT PER MONTH	EQUIPMENT COST/DAY	
50	2000	Horizontal borer, 3" diameter, 13 H.P. gas driven	Ea.	5.94	111.67	335	1,005	114.54	50
	2150	Horizontal directional drill, 20,000 lb. thrust, 78 H.P. diesel		30.26	738.67	2,216	6,648	685.30	
	2160	30,000 lb. thrust, 115 H.P.		37.20	738.67	2,216	6,648	740.76	
	2170	50,000 lb. thrust, 170 H.P.		53.33	738.67	2,216	6,648	869.81	
	2190	Mud trailer for HDD, 1500 gallons, 175 H.P., gas		27.98	787.17	2,361.50	7,084.50	696.17	
	2200	Hydromulcher, diesel, 3000 gallon, for truck mounting		19.13	986.90	2,960.70	8,882.10	745.16	
	2300	Gas, 600 gallon		8.22	281.67	845	2,535	234.78	
	2400	Joint & crack cleaner, walk behind, 25 H.P.		3.47	232.67	698	2,094	167.33	
	2500	Filler, trailer mounted, 400 gallons, 20 H.P.		9.16	213.33	640	1,920	201.26	
	3000	Paint striper, self-propelled, 40 gallon, 22 H.P.		7.42	24	72	216	73.74	
	3100	120 gallon, 120 H.P.		19.36	155	465	1,395	247.91	
	3200	Post drivers, 6" I-Beam frame, for truck mounting		13.62	125	375	1,125	183.96	
	3400	Road sweeper, self-propelled, 8' wide, 90 H.P.		39.47	397.01	1,111.15	2,832.90	538.01	
	3450	Road sweeper, vacuum assisted, 4 C.Y., 220 gallons		64.07	3,232.28	6,938.48	13,360.43	1,900.22	
	4000	Road mixer, self-propelled, 130 H.P.		50.83	889.28	2,770.36	8,014.13	960.69	
	4100	310 H.P.		82.46	2,316.38	7,243.34	20,980.50	2,108.32	
	4220	Cold mix paver, incl. pug mill and bitumen tank, 165 H.P.		104.40	716.67	2,150	6,450	1,265.22	
	4240	Pavement brush, towed		3.77	107.57	334.75	969.15	97.08	
	4250	Paver, asphalt, wheel or crawler, 130 H.P., diesel		103.60	2,449.50	7,618.49	22,045.50	2,352.46	
	4300	Paver, road widener, gas, 1' to 6', 67 H.P.		51.29	1,049.03	3,260.94	9,425.25	1,062.55	
	4400	Diesel, 2' to 14', 88 H.P.		61.98	1,251.38	3,866.96	11,182.50	1,269.25	
	4600	Slipform pavers, curb and gutter, 2 track, 75 H.P.		63.58	910.58	2,828.08	8,173.88	1,074.23	
	4700	4 track, 165 H.P.		39.23	1,357.88	4,213.26	12,141	1,156.49	
	4800	Median barrier, 215 H.P.		64.23	1,437.75	4,501.84	12,993	1,414.24	
	4901	Trailer, low bed, 75 ton capacity		11.77	304.59	946.54	2,742.38	283.47	
	5000	Road planer, walk behind, 10" cutting width, 10 H.P.		2.69	421	1,089	2,635	239.34	
	5100	Self-propelled, 12" cutting width, 64 H.P.		9.06	347.31	934.84	2,587.95	259.43	
	5120	Traffic line remover, metal ball blaster, truck mounted, 115 H.P.		51.09	2,066.67	6,200	18,600	1,648.72	
	5140	Grinder, truck mounted, 115 H.P.		55.84	2,066.67	6,200	18,600	1,686.74	
	5160	Walk-behind, 11 H.P.		3.90	305.30	915.90	2,747.70	214.39	
	5200	Pavement profiler, 4' to 6' wide, 450 H.P.		237.65	1,125	3,375	10,125	2,576.21	
	5300	8' to 10' wide, 750 H.P.		363.84	1,283.33	3,850	11,550	3,680.74	
	5400	Roadway plate, steel, 1" x 8' x 20'		.09	65.50	203.97	591.08	41.55	
	5600	Stabilizer, self-propelled, 150 H.P.		45.14	251.67	755	2,265	512.10	
	5700	310 H.P.		83.59	313.33	940	2,820	856.73	
	5800	Striper, truck mounted, 120 gallon paint, 460 H.P.		53.49	410	1,230	3,690	673.88	
	5900	Thermal paint heating kettle, 115 gallons		8.46	170	510	1,530	169.64	
	6000	Tar kettle, 330 gallon, trailer mounted		13.47	153	459	1,377	199.54	
	7000	Tunnel locomotive, diesel, 8 to 12 ton		32.71	665.63	2,077.77	6,017.25	677.26	
	7005	Electric, 10 ton		32.15	761.48	2,366.34	6,842.63	730.48	
	7010	Muck cars, 1/2 C.Y. capacity		2.53	28.76	89.46	258.80	38.10	
	7020	1 C.Y. capacity		2.76	37.28	116.59	335.48	45.41	
	7030	2 C.Y. capacity		2.92	42.07	130.44	378.08	49.44	
	7040	Side dump, 2 C.Y. capacity		3.16	52.19	161.60	468.60	57.56	
	7050	3 C.Y. capacity		4.24	56.98	177.77	516.53	69.44	
	7060	5 C.Y. capacity		6.18	74.02	229.71	665.63	95.40	
	7100	Ventilating blower for tunnel, 7-1/2 H.P.		2.35	56.98	176.61	511.20	54.12	
	7110	10 H.P.		2.66	59.11	184.69	532.50	58.22	
	7120	20 H.P.		3.89	77.21	240.09	692.25	79.16	
	7140	40 H.P.		6.75	102.24	317.43	915.90	117.47	
	7160	60 H.P.		9.55	109.70	340.52	985.13	144.52	
	7175	75 H.P.		11.40	170.40	530.99	1,544.25	197.38	
	7180	200 H.P.		22.85	335.48	1,044.66	3,035.25	391.71	
	7800	Windrow loader, elevating		59.19	1,666.67	5,000	15,000	1,473.50	
60	0010	**LIFTING AND HOISTING EQUIPMENT RENTAL** without operators	R015433-10						60
	0150	Crane, flatbed mounted, 3 ton capacity	Ea.	15.84	815	2,348.50	5,692	596.44	
	0200	Crane, climbing, 106' jib, 6000 lb. capacity, 410 fpm	R312316-45	43.59	3,006.59	9,019.77	27,059.32	2,152.66	
	0300	101' jib, 10,250 lb. capacity, 270 fpm		50.95	3,165.64	9,496.92	28,490.76	2,306.99	

01 54 | Construction Aids

01 54 33 | Equipment Rental

		UNIT	HOURLY OPER. COST	RENT PER DAY	RENT PER WEEK	RENT PER MONTH	EQUIPMENT COST/DAY
0500	Tower, static, 130' high, 106' jib, 6200 lb. capacity at 400 fpm	Ea.	49.55	2,588.20	7,764.59	23,293.78	1,949.33
0520	Mini crawler spider crane, up to 24" wide, 1990 lb. lifting capacity		13.74	591.08	1,846.91	5,351.63	479.34
0525	Up to 30" wide, 6450 lb. lifting capacity		15.97	702.90	2,193.20	6,336.75	566.37
0530	Up to 52" wide, 6680 lb. lifting capacity		25.40	862.65	2,683.79	7,774.50	739.94
0535	Up to 55" wide, 8920 lb. lifting capacity		28.36	953.18	2,972.36	8,599.88	821.33
0540	Up to 66" wide, 13,350 lb. lifting capacity		38.39	1,491	4,617.26	13,312.50	1,230.57
0600	Crawler mounted, lattice boom, 1/2 C.Y., 15 tons at 12' radius		40.56	957.29	2,871.87	8,615.60	898.84
0700	3/4 C.Y., 20 tons at 12' radius		59.44	1,075.55	3,226.64	9,679.92	1,120.87
0800	1 C.Y., 25 tons at 12' radius		73.98	1,136.92	3,410.76	10,232.29	1,274
0900	1-1/2 C.Y., 40 tons at 12' radius		72.77	1,300.84	3,902.51	11,707.52	1,362.63
1000	2 C.Y., 50 tons at 12' radius		97.40	1,541.84	4,625.52	13,876.57	1,704.33
1100	3 C.Y., 75 tons at 12' radius		71.32	2,698.22	8,094.67	24,284	2,189.46
1200	100 ton capacity, 60' boom		94.27	1,330	3,990	11,970	1,552.12
1300	165 ton capacity, 60' boom		116.43	1,593.33	4,780	14,340	1,887.41
1400	200 ton capacity, 70' boom		151.66	1,775	5,325	15,975	2,278.25
1500	350 ton capacity, 80' boom		199.92	3,725	11,175	33,525	3,834.39
1600	Truck mounted, lattice boom, 6 x 4, 20 tons at 10' radius		43.62	1,026.25	2,595.54	7,663.02	868.10
1700	25 tons at 10' radius		46.88	2,698.11	8,094.34	24,283.02	1,993.94
1800	8 x 4, 30 tons at 10' radius		59.43	2,891.04	8,673.13	26,019.39	2,210.08
1900	40 tons at 12' radius		59.43	3,160.64	9,481.91	28,445.73	2,371.83
2000	60 tons at 15' radius		58.91	3,315.05	9,945.16	29,835.48	2,460.30
2050	82 tons at 15' radius		65.21	3,411.34	10,234.01	30,702.03	2,568.46
2100	90 tons at 15' radius		72.85	3,511.25	10,533.76	31,601.28	2,689.54
2200	115 tons at 15' radius		82.18	3,615.53	10,846.59	32,539.77	2,826.79
2300	150 tons at 18' radius		88.98	3,122.12	9,366.37	28,099.11	2,585.11
2350	165 tons at 18' radius		95.50	3,180.26	9,540.77	28,622.31	2,672.17
2400	Truck mounted, hydraulic, 12 ton capacity		32.37	3,152.78	9,458.34	28,375.03	2,150.65
2500	25 ton capacity		39.89	3,256.95	9,770.86	29,312.57	2,273.31
2550	33 ton capacity		59.43	3,256.95	9,770.86	29,312.57	2,429.62
2560	40 ton capacity		59.43	3,285.77	9,857.31	29,571.92	2,446.91
2600	55 ton capacity		59.01	3,314.96	9,944.88	29,834.63	2,461.06
2700	80 ton capacity		77.27	3,372.59	10,117.77	30,353.32	2,641.70
2720	100 ton capacity		82.25	3,517.04	10,551.13	31,653.40	2,768.24
2740	120 ton capacity		115.52	3,565.70	10,697.09	32,091.26	3,063.55
2760	150 ton capacity		123.62	3,791.37	11,374.11	34,122.32	3,263.79
2800	Self-propelled, 4 x 4, with telescoping boom, 5 ton		16.61	421.67	1,265	3,795	385.89
2900	12-1/2 ton capacity		23.50	750	2,250	6,750	637.99
3000	15 ton capacity		37.77	855	2,565	7,695	815.14
3050	20 ton capacity		24.50	941.67	2,825	8,475	760.97
3100	25 ton capacity		40.26	1,008.33	3,025	9,075	927.07
3150	40 ton capacity		49.27	1,241.67	3,725	11,175	1,139.14
3200	Derricks, guy, 20 ton capacity, 60' boom, 75' mast		24.96	1,638.39	4,915.18	14,745.54	1,182.69
3300	100' boom, 115' mast		39.55	2,312.76	6,938.29	20,814.86	1,704.04
3400	Stiffleg, 20 ton capacity, 70' boom, 37' mast		27.88	713.29	2,139.87	6,419.60	650.99
3500	100' boom, 47' mast		43.14	770.92	2,312.76	6,938.29	807.69
3550	Helicopter, small, lift to 1250 lb. maximum, w/pilot		108.79	8,233.33	24,700	74,100	5,810.29
3600	Hoists, chain type, overhead, manual, 3/4 ton		.16	15.98	40.47	79.88	9.37
3900	10 ton		.86	124	310	620	68.92
4000	Hoist and tower, 5000 lb. cap., portable electric, 40' high		5.24	163.91	491.74	1,475.23	140.24
4100	For each added 10' section, add		.13	36.67	110.02	330.07	23.02
4200	Hoist and single tubular tower, 5000 lb. electric, 100' high		7.63	121.63	364.88	1,094.63	134.03
4300	For each added 6'-6" section, add		.23	44.16	132.48	397.44	28.31
4400	Hoist and double tubular tower, 5000 lb., 100' high		8.31	139.88	419.65	1,258.95	150.40
4500	For each added 6'-6" section, add		.25	44.33	132.98	398.94	28.58
4550	Hoist and tower, mast type, 6000 lb., 100' high		10.12	519.22	1,557.67	4,673.01	392.53
4570	For each added 10' section, add		.14	36.67	110.02	330.07	23.16
4600	Hoist and tower, personnel, electric, 2000 lb., 100' @ 125 fpm		19.20	576.32	1,728.96	5,186.87	499.39
4700	3000 lb., 100' @ 200 fpm		21.97	605.14	1,815.41	5,446.22	538.83

01 54 | Construction Aids

01 54 33 | Equipment Rental

			UNIT	HOURLY OPER. COST	RENT PER DAY	RENT PER WEEK	RENT PER MONTH	EQUIPMENT COST/DAY	
60	4800	3000 lb., 150' @ 300 fpm	Ea.	24.38	817.33	2,451.98	7,355.93	685.43	60
	4900	4000 lb., 100' @ 300 fpm		25.22	845.77	2,537.30	7,611.91	709.22	
	5000	6000 lb., 100' @ 275 fpm		27.10	874.96	2,624.87	7,874.62	741.81	
	5100	For added heights up to 500', add	L.F.	.01	3.74	11.23	33.68	2.33	
	5200	Jacks, hydraulic, 20 ton	Ea.	.05	35	80	175	16.44	
	5500	100 ton		.44	27.75	68.91	142.16	17.29	
	6100	Jacks, hydraulic, climbing w/50' jackrods, control console, 30 ton cap.		2.38	35.93	107.78	323.34	40.57	
	6150	For each added 10' jackrod section, add		.05	5.61	16.84	50.52	3.81	
	6300	50 ton capacity		3.82	38.55	115.64	346.91	53.69	
	6350	For each added 10' jackrod section, add		.07	5.61	16.84	50.52	3.89	
	6500	125 ton capacity		9.99	38.55	115.64	346.91	103.05	
	6550	For each added 10' jackrod section, add		.68	5.61	16.84	50.52	8.77	
	6600	Cable jack, 10 ton capacity with 200' cable		1.74	41.17	123.50	370.49	38.60	
	6650	For each added 50' of cable, add		.24	17.21	51.64	154.93	12.27	
70	0010	**WELLPOINT EQUIPMENT RENTAL** without operators R015433-10							70
	0020	Based on 2 months rental							
	0100	Combination jetting & wellpoint pump, 60 H.P. diesel	Ea.	17.20	345.04	1,035.13	3,105.39	344.59	
	0200	High pressure gas jet pump, 200 H.P., 300 psi	"	37.12	192	576	1,728	412.18	
	0300	Discharge pipe, 8" diameter	L.F.	.01	53.25	159.75	479.25	32.03	
	0350	12" diameter		.01	56.80	170.40	511.20	34.19	
	0400	Header pipe, flows up to 150 GPM, 4" diameter		.01	31.33	94	282	18.87	
	0500	400 GPM, 6" diameter		.01	41.33	124	372	24.88	
	0600	800 GPM, 8" diameter		.01	45.67	137	411	27.51	
	0700	1500 GPM, 10" diameter		.01	57.51	172.53	517.59	34.62	
	0800	2500 GPM, 12" diameter		.03	65.32	195.96	587.88	39.41	
	0900	4500 GPM, 16" diameter		.04	55.67	167	501	33.68	
	0950	For quick coupling aluminum and plastic pipe, add		.04	10.55	31.64	94.91	6.62	
	1100	Wellpoint, 25' long, with fittings & riser pipe, 1-1/2" or 2" diameter	Ea.	.07	82.27	246.81	740.44	49.95	
	1200	Wellpoint pump, diesel powered, 4" suction, 20 H.P.		7.68	161.67	485	1,455	158.46	
	1300	6" suction, 30 H.P.		10.31	296.67	890	2,670	260.45	
	1400	8" suction, 40 H.P.		13.96	258.33	775	2,325	266.71	
	1500	10" suction, 75 H.P.		20.37	290.67	872	2,616	337.35	
	1600	12" suction, 100 H.P.		29.89	298.33	895	2,685	418.09	
	1700	12" suction, 175 H.P.		42.77	306.67	920	2,760	526.15	
80	0010	**MARINE EQUIPMENT RENTAL** without operators R015433-10							80
	0200	Barge, 400 Ton, 30' wide x 90' long	Ea.	19.38	1,278	4,011.25	11,608.50	957.33	
	0240	800 Ton, 45' wide x 90' long		24.34	1,597.50	4,934.71	14,271	1,181.66	
	2000	Tugboat, diesel, 100 H.P.		32.51	255.60	796.48	2,316.38	419.35	
	2040	250 H.P.		63.11	463.28	1,442.89	4,180.13	793.50	
	2080	380 H.P.		137.40	1,384.50	4,328.69	12,567	1,964.96	
	3000	Small work boat, gas, 16-foot, 50 H.P.		12.47	51.65	160.15	463.28	131.82	
	4000	Large, diesel, 48-foot, 200 H.P.		82.09	1,464.38	4,588.41	13,312.50	1,574.43	

Crews - Standard

Crew No.	Bare Costs Hr.	Bare Costs Daily	Incl. Subs O&P Hr.	Incl. Subs O&P Daily	Cost Per Labor-Hour Bare Costs	Cost Per Labor-Hour Incl. O&P
Crew A-1						
1 Building Laborer	$47.25	$378.00	$70.35	$562.80	$47.25	$70.35
1 Concrete Saw, Gas Manual		112.72		123.99	14.09	15.50
8 L.H., Daily Totals		$490.72		$686.79	$61.34	$85.85
Crew A-1A						
1 Skilled Worker	$61.25	$490.00	$92.00	$736.00	$61.25	$92.00
1 Shot Blaster, 20"		229.79		252.77	28.72	31.60
8 L.H., Daily Totals		$719.79		$988.77	$89.97	$123.60
Crew A-1B						
1 Building Laborer	$47.25	$378.00	$70.35	$562.80	$47.25	$70.35
1 Concrete Saw		176.00		193.60	22.00	24.20
8 L.H., Daily Totals		$554.00		$756.40	$69.25	$94.55
Crew A-1C						
1 Building Laborer	$47.25	$378.00	$70.35	$562.80	$47.25	$70.35
1 Chain Saw, Gas, 18"		47.58		52.34	5.95	6.54
8 L.H., Daily Totals		$425.58		$615.14	$53.20	$76.89
Crew A-1D						
1 Building Laborer	$47.25	$378.00	$70.35	$562.80	$47.25	$70.35
1 Vibrating Plate, Gas, 18"		143.82		158.20	17.98	19.78
8 L.H., Daily Totals		$521.82		$721.00	$65.23	$90.13
Crew A-1E						
1 Building Laborer	$47.25	$378.00	$70.35	$562.80	$47.25	$70.35
1 Vibrating Plate, Gas, 21"		146.12		160.73	18.27	20.09
8 L.H., Daily Totals		$524.12		$723.53	$65.52	$90.44
Crew A-1F						
1 Building Laborer	$47.25	$378.00	$70.35	$562.80	$47.25	$70.35
1 Rammer/Tamper, Gas, 8"		73.84		81.22	9.23	10.15
8 L.H., Daily Totals		$451.84		$644.02	$56.48	$80.50
Crew A-1G						
1 Building Laborer	$47.25	$378.00	$70.35	$562.80	$47.25	$70.35
1 Rammer/Tamper, Gas, 15"		88.02		96.82	11.00	12.10
8 L.H., Daily Totals		$466.02		$659.62	$58.25	$82.45
Crew A-1H						
1 Building Laborer	$47.25	$378.00	$70.35	$562.80	$47.25	$70.35
1 Exterior Steam Cleaner		84.77		93.25	10.60	11.66
8 L.H., Daily Totals		$462.77		$656.05	$57.85	$82.01
Crew A-1J						
1 Building Laborer	$47.25	$378.00	$70.35	$562.80	$47.25	$70.35
1 Cultivator, Walk-Behind, 5 H.P.		70.72		77.79	8.84	9.72
8 L.H., Daily Totals		$448.72		$640.59	$56.09	$80.07
Crew A-1K						
1 Building Laborer	$47.25	$378.00	$70.35	$562.80	$47.25	$70.35
1 Cultivator, Walk-Behind, 8 H.P.		89.64		98.60	11.21	12.33
8 L.H., Daily Totals		$467.64		$661.40	$58.45	$82.68
Crew A-1M						
1 Building Laborer	$47.25	$378.00	$70.35	$562.80	$47.25	$70.35
1 Snow Blower, Walk-Behind		75.10		82.61	9.39	10.33
8 L.H., Daily Totals		$453.10		$645.41	$56.64	$80.68
Crew A-2						
2 Laborers	$47.25	$756.00	$70.35	$1125.60	$49.13	$73.23
1 Truck Driver (light)	52.90	423.20	79.00	632.00		
1 Flatbed Truck, Gas, 1.5 Ton		361.95		398.14	15.08	16.59
24 L.H., Daily Totals		$1541.15		$2155.74	$64.21	$89.82
Crew A-2A						
2 Laborers	$47.25	$756.00	$70.35	$1125.60	$49.13	$73.23
1 Truck Driver (light)	52.90	423.20	79.00	632.00		
1 Flatbed Truck, Gas, 1.5 Ton		361.95		398.14		
1 Concrete Saw		176.00		193.60	22.41	24.66
24 L.H., Daily Totals		$1717.15		$2349.34	$71.55	$97.89
Crew A-2B						
1 Truck Driver (light)	$52.90	$423.20	$79.00	$632.00	$52.90	$79.00
1 Flatbed Truck, Gas, 1.5 Ton		361.95		398.14	45.24	49.77
8 L.H., Daily Totals		$785.15		$1030.15	$98.14	$128.77
Crew A-3A						
1 Equip. Oper. (light)	$59.70	$477.60	$88.85	$710.80	$59.70	$88.85
1 Pickup Truck, 4x4, 3/4 Ton		191.73		210.90	23.97	26.36
8 L.H., Daily Totals		$669.33		$921.70	$83.67	$115.21
Crew A-3B						
1 Equip. Oper. (medium)	$63.05	$504.40	$93.80	$750.40	$59.25	$88.33
1 Truck Driver (heavy)	55.45	443.60	82.85	662.80		
1 Dump Truck, 12 C.Y., 400 H.P.		791.36		870.50		
1 F.E. Loader, W.M., 2.5 C.Y.		658.89		724.78	90.64	99.70
16 L.H., Daily Totals		$2398.25		$3008.47	$149.89	$188.03
Crew A-3C						
1 Equip. Oper. (light)	$59.70	$477.60	$88.85	$710.80	$59.70	$88.85
1 Loader, Skid Steer, 78 H.P.		429.91		472.90	53.74	59.11
8 L.H., Daily Totals		$907.51		$1183.70	$113.44	$147.96
Crew A-3D						
1 Truck Driver (light)	$52.90	$423.20	$79.00	$632.00	$52.90	$79.00
1 Pickup Truck, 4x4, 3/4 Ton		191.73		210.90		
1 Flatbed Trailer, 25 Ton		150.61		165.67	42.79	47.07
8 L.H., Daily Totals		$765.54		$1008.57	$95.69	$126.07
Crew A-3E						
1 Equip. Oper. (crane)	$66.30	$530.40	$98.65	$789.20	$60.88	$90.75
1 Truck Driver (heavy)	55.45	443.60	82.85	662.80		
1 Pickup Truck, 4x4, 3/4 Ton		191.73		210.90	11.98	13.18
16 L.H., Daily Totals		$1165.73		$1662.90	$72.86	$103.93
Crew A-3F						
1 Equip. Oper. (crane)	$66.30	$530.40	$98.65	$789.20	$60.88	$90.75
1 Truck Driver (heavy)	55.45	443.60	82.85	662.80		
1 Pickup Truck, 4x4, 3/4 Ton		191.73		210.90		
1 Truck Tractor, 6x4, 380 H.P.		545.98		600.58		
1 Lowbed Trailer, 75 Ton		283.47		311.82	63.82	70.21
16 L.H., Daily Totals		$1995.18		$2575.30	$124.70	$160.96

Crews - Standard

Crew No.	Bare Costs		Incl. Subs O&P		Cost Per Labor-Hour	
Crew A-3G	Hr.	Daily	Hr.	Daily	Bare Costs	Incl. O&P
1 Equip. Oper. (crane)	$66.30	$530.40	$98.65	$789.20	$60.88	$90.75
1 Truck Driver (heavy)	55.45	443.60	82.85	662.80		
1 Pickup Truck, 4x4, 3/4 Ton		191.73		210.90		
1 Truck Tractor, 6x4, 450 H.P.		666.04		732.64		
1 Lowbed Trailer, 75 Ton		283.47		311.82	71.33	78.46
16 L.H., Daily Totals		$2115.24		$2707.36	$132.20	$169.21
Crew A-3H	Hr.	Daily	Hr.	Daily	Bare Costs	Incl. O&P
1 Equip. Oper. (crane)	$66.30	$530.40	$98.65	$789.20	$66.30	$98.65
1 Hyd. Crane, 12 Ton (Daily)		2150.65		2365.72	268.83	295.71
8 L.H., Daily Totals		$2681.05		$3154.92	$335.13	$394.36
Crew A-3I	Hr.	Daily	Hr.	Daily	Bare Costs	Incl. O&P
1 Equip. Oper. (crane)	$66.30	$530.40	$98.65	$789.20	$66.30	$98.65
1 Hyd. Crane, 25 Ton (Daily)		2273.31		2500.64	284.16	312.58
8 L.H., Daily Totals		$2803.71		$3289.84	$350.46	$411.23
Crew A-3J	Hr.	Daily	Hr.	Daily	Bare Costs	Incl. O&P
1 Equip. Oper. (crane)	$66.30	$530.40	$98.65	$789.20	$66.30	$98.65
1 Hyd. Crane, 40 Ton (Daily)		2446.91		2691.60	305.86	336.45
8 L.H., Daily Totals		$2977.31		$3480.80	$372.16	$435.10
Crew A-3K	Hr.	Daily	Hr.	Daily	Bare Costs	Incl. O&P
1 Equip. Oper. (crane)	$66.30	$530.40	$98.65	$789.20	$61.35	$91.28
1 Equip. Oper. (oiler)	56.40	451.20	83.90	671.20		
1 Hyd. Crane, 55 Ton (Daily)		2461.06		2707.17		
1 P/U Truck, 3/4 Ton (Daily)		157.41		173.15	163.65	180.02
16 L.H., Daily Totals		$3600.07		$4340.72	$225.00	$271.29
Crew A-3L	Hr.	Daily	Hr.	Daily	Bare Costs	Incl. O&P
1 Equip. Oper. (crane)	$66.30	$530.40	$98.65	$789.20	$61.35	$91.28
1 Equip. Oper. (oiler)	56.40	451.20	83.90	671.20		
1 Hyd. Crane, 80 Ton (Daily)		2641.70		2905.87		
1 P/U Truck, 3/4 Ton (Daily)		157.41		173.15	174.94	192.44
16 L.H., Daily Totals		$3780.71		$4539.42	$236.29	$283.71
Crew A-3M	Hr.	Daily	Hr.	Daily	Bare Costs	Incl. O&P
1 Equip. Oper. (crane)	$66.30	$530.40	$98.65	$789.20	$61.35	$91.28
1 Equip. Oper. (oiler)	56.40	451.20	83.90	671.20		
1 Hyd. Crane, 100 Ton (Daily)		2768.24		3045.06		
1 P/U Truck, 3/4 Ton (Daily)		157.41		173.15	182.85	201.14
16 L.H., Daily Totals		$3907.25		$4678.61	$244.20	$292.41
Crew A-3N	Hr.	Daily	Hr.	Daily	Bare Costs	Incl. O&P
1 Equip. Oper. (crane)	$66.30	$530.40	$98.65	$789.20	$66.30	$98.65
1 Tower Crane (monthly)		1891.47		2080.62	236.43	260.08
8 L.H., Daily Totals		$2421.87		$2869.82	$302.73	$358.73
Crew A-3P	Hr.	Daily	Hr.	Daily	Bare Costs	Incl. O&P
1 Equip. Oper. (light)	$59.70	$477.60	$88.85	$710.80	$59.70	$88.85
1 A.T. Forklift, 31' reach, 45' lift		673.26		740.59	84.16	92.57
8 L.H., Daily Totals		$1150.86		$1451.39	$143.86	$181.42
Crew A-3Q	Hr.	Daily	Hr.	Daily	Bare Costs	Incl. O&P
1 Equip. Oper. (light)	$59.70	$477.60	$88.85	$710.80	$59.70	$88.85
1 Pickup Truck, 4x4, 3/4 Ton		191.73		210.90		
1 Flatbed Trailer, 3 Ton		78.34		86.17	33.76	37.13
8 L.H., Daily Totals		$747.67		$1007.88	$93.46	$125.98

Crew No.	Bare Costs		Incl. Subs O&P		Cost Per Labor-Hour	
Crew A-3R	Hr.	Daily	Hr.	Daily	Bare Costs	Incl. O&P
1 Equip. Oper. (light)	$59.70	$477.60	$88.85	$710.80	$59.70	$88.85
1 Forklift, Smooth Floor, 8,000 Lb.		311.06		342.17	38.88	42.77
8 L.H., Daily Totals		$788.66		$1052.97	$98.58	$131.62
Crew A-4	Hr.	Daily	Hr.	Daily	Bare Costs	Incl. O&P
2 Carpenters	$58.60	$937.60	$87.25	$1396.00	$55.62	$82.68
1 Painter, Ordinary	49.65	397.20	73.55	588.40		
24 L.H., Daily Totals		$1334.80		$1984.40	$55.62	$82.68
Crew A-5	Hr.	Daily	Hr.	Daily	Bare Costs	Incl. O&P
2 Laborers	$47.25	$756.00	$70.35	$1125.60	$47.88	$71.31
.25 Truck Driver (light)	52.90	105.80	79.00	158.00		
.25 Flatbed Truck, Gas, 1.5 Ton		90.49		99.54	5.03	5.53
18 L.H., Daily Totals		$952.29		$1383.14	$52.90	$76.84
Crew A-6	Hr.	Daily	Hr.	Daily	Bare Costs	Incl. O&P
1 Instrument Man	$61.25	$490.00	$92.00	$736.00	$58.65	$87.65
1 Rodman/Chainman	56.05	448.40	83.30	666.40		
1 Level, Electronic		33.60		36.96	2.10	2.31
16 L.H., Daily Totals		$972.00		$1439.36	$60.75	$89.96
Crew A-7	Hr.	Daily	Hr.	Daily	Bare Costs	Incl. O&P
1 Chief of Party	$71.80	$574.40	$107.20	$857.60	$63.03	$94.17
1 Instrument Man	61.25	490.00	92.00	736.00		
1 Rodman/Chainman	56.05	448.40	83.30	666.40		
1 Level, Electronic		33.60		36.96	1.40	1.54
24 L.H., Daily Totals		$1546.40		$2296.96	$64.43	$95.71
Crew A-8	Hr.	Daily	Hr.	Daily	Bare Costs	Incl. O&P
1 Chief of Party	$71.80	$574.40	$107.20	$857.60	$61.29	$91.45
1 Instrument Man	61.25	490.00	92.00	736.00		
2 Rodmen/Chainmen	56.05	896.80	83.30	1332.80		
1 Level, Electronic		33.60		36.96	1.05	1.16
32 L.H., Daily Totals		$1994.80		$2963.36	$62.34	$92.61
Crew A-9	Hr.	Daily	Hr.	Daily	Bare Costs	Incl. O&P
1 Asbestos Foreman	$65.75	$526.00	$100.60	$804.80	$65.31	$99.90
7 Asbestos Workers	65.25	3654.00	99.80	5588.80		
64 L.H., Daily Totals		$4180.00		$6393.60	$65.31	$99.90
Crew A-10A	Hr.	Daily	Hr.	Daily	Bare Costs	Incl. O&P
1 Asbestos Foreman	$65.75	$526.00	$100.60	$804.80	$65.42	$100.07
2 Asbestos Workers	65.25	1044.00	99.80	1596.80		
24 L.H., Daily Totals		$1570.00		$2401.60	$65.42	$100.07
Crew A-10B	Hr.	Daily	Hr.	Daily	Bare Costs	Incl. O&P
1 Asbestos Foreman	$65.75	$526.00	$100.60	$804.80	$65.38	$100.00
3 Asbestos Workers	65.25	1566.00	99.80	2395.20		
32 L.H., Daily Totals		$2092.00		$3200.00	$65.38	$100.00
Crew A-10C	Hr.	Daily	Hr.	Daily	Bare Costs	Incl. O&P
3 Asbestos Workers	$65.25	$1566.00	$99.80	$2395.20	$65.25	$99.80
1 Flatbed Truck, Gas, 1.5 Ton		361.95		398.14	15.08	16.59
24 L.H., Daily Totals		$1927.95		$2793.34	$80.33	$116.39

Crews - Standard

Crew No.		Bare Costs		Incl. Subs O&P		Cost Per Labor-Hour	
Crew A-10D	Hr.	Daily	Hr.	Daily	Bare Costs	Incl. O&P
2 Asbestos Workers	$65.25	$1044.00	$99.80	$1596.80	$63.30	$95.54
1 Equip. Oper. (crane)	66.30	530.40	98.65	789.20		
1 Equip. Oper. (oiler)	56.40	451.20	83.90	671.20		
1 Hydraulic Crane, 33 Ton		2429.62		2672.58	75.93	83.52
32 L.H., Daily Totals		$4455.22		$5729.78	$139.23	$179.06
Crew A-11	Hr.	Daily	Hr.	Daily	Bare Costs	Incl. O&P
1 Asbestos Foreman	$65.75	$526.00	$100.60	$804.80	$65.31	$99.90
7 Asbestos Workers	65.25	3654.00	99.80	5588.80		
2 Chip. Hammers, 12 Lb., Elec.		54.32		59.75	.85	.93
64 L.H., Daily Totals		$4234.32		$6453.35	$66.16	$100.83
Crew A-12	Hr.	Daily	Hr.	Daily	Bare Costs	Incl. O&P
1 Asbestos Foreman	$65.75	$526.00	$100.60	$804.80	$65.31	$99.90
7 Asbestos Workers	65.25	3654.00	99.80	5588.80		
1 Trk-Mtd Vac, 14 CY, 1500 Gal.		596.69		656.36		
1 Flatbed Truck, 20,000 GVW		223.10		245.41	12.81	14.09
64 L.H., Daily Totals		$4999.79		$7295.37	$78.12	$113.99
Crew A-13	Hr.	Daily	Hr.	Daily	Bare Costs	Incl. O&P
1 Equip. Oper. (light)	$59.70	$477.60	$88.85	$710.80	$59.70	$88.85
1 Trk-Mtd Vac, 14 CY, 1500 Gal.		596.69		656.36		
1 Flatbed Truck, 20,000 GVW		223.10		245.41	102.47	112.72
8 L.H., Daily Totals		$1297.39		$1612.57	$162.17	$201.57
Crew B-1	Hr.	Daily	Hr.	Daily	Bare Costs	Incl. O&P
1 Labor Foreman (outside)	$49.25	$394.00	$73.30	$586.40	$47.92	$71.33
2 Laborers	47.25	756.00	70.35	1125.60		
24 L.H., Daily Totals		$1150.00		$1712.00	$47.92	$71.33
Crew B-1A	Hr.	Daily	Hr.	Daily	Bare Costs	Incl. O&P
1 Labor Foreman (outside)	$49.25	$394.00	$73.30	$586.40	$47.92	$71.33
2 Laborers	47.25	756.00	70.35	1125.60		
2 Cutting Torches		28.48		31.33		
2 Sets of Gases		377.34		415.07	16.91	18.60
24 L.H., Daily Totals		$1555.82		$2158.40	$64.83	$89.93
Crew B-1B	Hr.	Daily	Hr.	Daily	Bare Costs	Incl. O&P
1 Labor Foreman (outside)	$49.25	$394.00	$73.30	$586.40	$52.51	$78.16
2 Laborers	47.25	756.00	70.35	1125.60		
1 Equip. Oper. (crane)	66.30	530.40	98.65	789.20		
2 Cutting Torches		28.48		31.33		
2 Sets of Gases		377.34		415.07		
1 Hyd. Crane, 12 Ton		2150.65		2365.72	79.89	87.88
32 L.H., Daily Totals		$4236.87		$5313.32	$132.40	$166.04
Crew B-1C	Hr.	Daily	Hr.	Daily	Bare Costs	Incl. O&P
1 Labor Foreman (outside)	$49.25	$394.00	$73.30	$586.40	$47.92	$71.33
2 Laborers	47.25	756.00	70.35	1125.60		
1 Telescoping Boom Lift, to 60'		385.68		424.25	16.07	17.68
24 L.H., Daily Totals		$1535.68		$2136.25	$63.99	$89.01
Crew B-1D	Hr.	Daily	Hr.	Daily	Bare Costs	Incl. O&P
2 Laborers	$47.25	$756.00	$70.35	$1125.60	$47.25	$70.35
1 Small Work Boat, Gas, 50 H.P.		131.82		145.00		
1 Pressure Washer, 7 GPM		113.42		124.76	15.33	16.86
16 L.H., Daily Totals		$1001.24		$1395.36	$62.58	$87.21

Crew No.		Bare Costs		Incl. Subs O&P		Cost Per Labor-Hour	
Crew B-1E	Hr.	Daily	Hr.	Daily	Bare Costs	Incl. O&P
1 Labor Foreman (outside)	$49.25	$394.00	$73.30	$586.40	$47.75	$71.09
3 Laborers	47.25	1134.00	70.35	1688.40		
1 Work Boat, Diesel, 200 H.P.		1574.43		1731.87		
2 Pressure Washers, 7 GPM		226.84		249.52	56.29	61.92
32 L.H., Daily Totals		$3329.27		$4256.20	$104.04	$133.01
Crew B-1F	Hr.	Daily	Hr.	Daily	Bare Costs	Incl. O&P
2 Skilled Workers	$61.25	$980.00	$92.00	$1472.00	$56.58	$84.78
1 Laborer	47.25	378.00	70.35	562.80		
1 Small Work Boat, Gas, 50 H.P.		131.82		145.00		
1 Pressure Washer, 7 GPM		113.42		124.76	10.22	11.24
24 L.H., Daily Totals		$1603.24		$2304.56	$66.80	$96.02
Crew B-1G	Hr.	Daily	Hr.	Daily	Bare Costs	Incl. O&P
2 Laborers	$47.25	$756.00	$70.35	$1125.60	$47.25	$70.35
1 Small Work Boat, Gas, 50 H.P.		131.82		145.00	8.24	9.06
16 L.H., Daily Totals		$887.82		$1270.60	$55.49	$79.41
Crew B-1H	Hr.	Daily	Hr.	Daily	Bare Costs	Incl. O&P
2 Skilled Workers	$61.25	$980.00	$92.00	$1472.00	$56.58	$84.78
1 Laborer	47.25	378.00	70.35	562.80		
1 Small Work Boat, Gas, 50 H.P.		131.82		145.00	5.49	6.04
24 L.H., Daily Totals		$1489.82		$2179.80	$62.08	$90.83
Crew B-1J	Hr.	Daily	Hr.	Daily	Bare Costs	Incl. O&P
1 Labor Foreman (inside)	$47.75	$382.00	$71.10	$568.80	$47.50	$70.72
1 Laborer	47.25	378.00	70.35	562.80		
16 L.H., Daily Totals		$760.00		$1131.60	$47.50	$70.72
Crew B-1K	Hr.	Daily	Hr.	Daily	Bare Costs	Incl. O&P
1 Carpenter Foreman (inside)	$59.10	$472.80	$88.00	$704.00	$58.85	$87.63
1 Carpenter	58.60	468.80	87.25	698.00		
16 L.H., Daily Totals		$941.60		$1402.00	$58.85	$87.63
Crew B-2	Hr.	Daily	Hr.	Daily	Bare Costs	Incl. O&P
1 Labor Foreman (outside)	$49.25	$394.00	$73.30	$586.40	$47.65	$70.94
4 Laborers	47.25	1512.00	70.35	2251.20		
40 L.H., Daily Totals		$1906.00		$2837.60	$47.65	$70.94
Crew B-2A	Hr.	Daily	Hr.	Daily	Bare Costs	Incl. O&P
1 Labor Foreman (outside)	$49.25	$394.00	$73.30	$586.40	$47.92	$71.33
2 Laborers	47.25	756.00	70.35	1125.60		
1 Telescoping Boom Lift, to 60'		385.68		424.25	16.07	17.68
24 L.H., Daily Totals		$1535.68		$2136.25	$63.99	$89.01
Crew B-3	Hr.	Daily	Hr.	Daily	Bare Costs	Incl. O&P
1 Labor Foreman (outside)	$49.25	$394.00	$73.30	$586.40	$52.95	$78.92
2 Laborers	47.25	756.00	70.35	1125.60		
1 Equip. Oper. (medium)	63.05	504.40	93.80	750.40		
2 Truck Drivers (heavy)	55.45	887.20	82.85	1325.60		
1 Crawler Loader, 3 C.Y.		1257.68		1383.45		
2 Dump Trucks, 12 C.Y., 400 H.P.		1582.72		1740.99	59.17	65.09
48 L.H., Daily Totals		$5382.00		$6912.44	$112.13	$144.01
Crew B-3A	Hr.	Daily	Hr.	Daily	Bare Costs	Incl. O&P
4 Laborers	$47.25	$1512.00	$70.35	$2251.20	$50.41	$75.04
1 Equip. Oper. (medium)	63.05	504.40	93.80	750.40		
1 Hyd. Excavator, 1.5 C.Y.		1185.24		1303.76	29.63	32.59
40 L.H., Daily Totals		$3201.64		$4305.36	$80.04	$107.63

Crews - Standard

Crew No.	Bare Costs		Incl. Subs O&P		Cost Per Labor-Hour	
Crew B-3B	Hr.	Daily	Hr.	Daily	Bare Costs	Incl. O&P
2 Laborers	$47.25	$756.00	$70.35	$1125.60	$53.25	$79.34
1 Equip. Oper. (medium)	63.05	504.40	93.80	750.40		
1 Truck Driver (heavy)	55.45	443.60	82.85	662.80		
1 Backhoe Loader, 80 H.P.		357.71		393.48		
1 Dump Truck, 12 C.Y., 400 H.P.		791.36		870.50	35.91	39.50
32 L.H., Daily Totals		$2853.07		$3802.78	$89.16	$118.84
Crew B-3C	Hr.	Daily	Hr.	Daily	Bare Costs	Incl. O&P
3 Laborers	$47.25	$1134.00	$70.35	$1688.40	$51.20	$76.21
1 Equip. Oper. (medium)	63.05	504.40	93.80	750.40		
1 Crawler Loader, 4 C.Y.		1506.11		1656.72	47.07	51.77
32 L.H., Daily Totals		$3144.51		$4095.52	$98.27	$127.99
Crew B-4	Hr.	Daily	Hr.	Daily	Bare Costs	Incl. O&P
1 Labor Foreman (outside)	$49.25	$394.00	$73.30	$586.40	$48.95	$72.92
4 Laborers	47.25	1512.00	70.35	2251.20		
1 Truck Driver (heavy)	55.45	443.60	82.85	662.80		
1 Truck Tractor, 220 H.P.		339.98		373.98		
1 Flatbed Trailer, 40 Ton		206.92		227.61	11.39	12.53
48 L.H., Daily Totals		$2896.50		$4101.99	$60.34	$85.46
Crew B-5	Hr.	Daily	Hr.	Daily	Bare Costs	Incl. O&P
1 Labor Foreman (outside)	$49.25	$394.00	$73.30	$586.40	$52.05	$77.47
4 Laborers	47.25	1512.00	70.35	2251.20		
2 Equip. Oper. (medium)	63.05	1008.80	93.80	1500.80		
1 Air Compressor, 250 cfm		196.28		215.91		
2 Breakers, Pavement, 60 lb.		68.94		75.83		
2 -50' Air Hoses, 1.5"		47.20		51.92		
1 Crawler Loader, 3 C.Y.		1257.68		1383.45	28.04	30.84
56 L.H., Daily Totals		$4484.90		$6065.51	$80.09	$108.31
Crew B-5A	Hr.	Daily	Hr.	Daily	Bare Costs	Incl. O&P
1 Labor Foreman (outside)	$49.25	$394.00	$73.30	$586.40	$52.45	$78.13
6 Laborers	47.25	2268.00	70.35	3376.80		
2 Equip. Oper. (medium)	63.05	1008.80	93.80	1500.80		
1 Equip. Oper. (light)	59.70	477.60	88.85	710.80		
2 Truck Drivers (heavy)	55.45	887.20	82.85	1325.60		
1 Air Compressor, 365 cfm		389.99		428.99		
2 Breakers, Pavement, 60 lb.		68.94		75.83		
8 -50' Air Hoses, 1"		74.48		81.93		
2 Dump Trucks, 8 C.Y., 220 H.P.		834.98		918.48	14.25	15.68
96 L.H., Daily Totals		$6403.99		$9005.63	$66.71	$93.81
Crew B-5B	Hr.	Daily	Hr.	Daily	Bare Costs	Incl. O&P
1 Powderman	$61.25	$490.00	$92.00	$736.00	$58.95	$88.03
2 Equip. Oper. (medium)	63.05	1008.80	93.80	1500.80		
3 Truck Drivers (heavy)	55.45	1330.80	82.85	1988.40		
1 F.E. Loader, W.M., 2.5 C.Y.		658.89		724.78		
3 Dump Trucks, 12 C.Y., 400 H.P.		2374.08		2611.49		
1 Air Compressor, 365 cfm		389.99		428.99	71.31	78.44
48 L.H., Daily Totals		$6252.56		$7990.46	$130.26	$166.47

Crew No.	Bare Costs		Incl. Subs O&P		Cost Per Labor-Hour	
Crew B-5C	Hr.	Daily	Hr.	Daily	Bare Costs	Incl. O&P
3 Laborers	$47.25	$1134.00	$70.35	$1688.40	$54.80	$81.64
1 Equip. Oper. (medium)	63.05	504.40	93.80	750.40		
2 Truck Drivers (heavy)	55.45	887.20	82.85	1325.60		
1 Equip. Oper. (crane)	66.30	530.40	98.65	789.20		
1 Equip. Oper. (oiler)	56.40	451.20	83.90	671.20		
2 Dump Trucks, 12 C.Y., 400 H.P.		1582.72		1740.99		
1 Crawler Loader, 4 C.Y.		1506.11		1656.72		
1 S.P. Crane, 4x4, 25 Ton		927.07		1019.78	62.75	69.02
64 L.H., Daily Totals		$7523.10		$9642.29	$117.55	$150.66
Crew B-5D	Hr.	Daily	Hr.	Daily	Bare Costs	Incl. O&P
1 Labor Foreman (outside)	$49.25	$394.00	$73.30	$586.40	$52.48	$78.14
4 Laborers	47.25	1512.00	70.35	2251.20		
2 Equip. Oper. (medium)	63.05	1008.80	93.80	1500.80		
1 Truck Driver (heavy)	55.45	443.60	82.85	662.80		
1 Air Compressor, 250 cfm		196.28		215.91		
2 Breakers, Pavement, 60 lb.		68.94		75.83		
2 -50' Air Hoses, 1.5"		47.20		51.92		
1 Crawler Loader, 3 C.Y.		1257.68		1383.45		
1 Dump Truck, 12 C.Y., 400 H.P.		791.36		870.50	36.90	40.59
64 L.H., Daily Totals		$5719.86		$7598.81	$89.37	$118.73
Crew B-5E	Hr.	Daily	Hr.	Daily	Bare Costs	Incl. O&P
1 Labor Foreman (outside)	$49.25	$394.00	$73.30	$586.40	$52.48	$78.14
4 Laborers	47.25	1512.00	70.35	2251.20		
2 Equip. Oper. (medium)	63.05	1008.80	93.80	1500.80		
1 Truck Driver (heavy)	55.45	443.60	82.85	662.80		
1 Water Tank Trailer, 5000 Gal.		169.14		186.05		
1 High Pressure Water Jet 40 KSI		902.38		992.62		
2 -50' Air Hoses, 1.5"		47.20		51.92		
1 Crawler Loader, 3 C.Y.		1257.68		1383.45		
1 Dump Truck, 12 C.Y., 400 H.P.		791.36		870.50	49.50	54.45
64 L.H., Daily Totals		$6526.16		$8485.74	$101.97	$132.59
Crew B-6	Hr.	Daily	Hr.	Daily	Bare Costs	Incl. O&P
2 Laborers	$47.25	$756.00	$70.35	$1125.60	$51.40	$76.52
1 Equip. Oper. (light)	59.70	477.60	88.85	710.80		
1 Backhoe Loader, 48 H.P.		277.19		304.91	11.55	12.70
24 L.H., Daily Totals		$1510.79		$2141.31	$62.95	$89.22
Crew B-6A	Hr.	Daily	Hr.	Daily	Bare Costs	Incl. O&P
.5 Labor Foreman (outside)	$49.25	$197.00	$73.30	$293.20	$53.97	$80.32
1 Laborer	47.25	378.00	70.35	562.80		
1 Equip. Oper. (medium)	63.05	504.40	93.80	750.40		
1 Vacuum Truck, 5000 Gal.		408.90		449.79	20.45	22.49
20 L.H., Daily Totals		$1488.30		$2056.19	$74.42	$102.81
Crew B-6B	Hr.	Daily	Hr.	Daily	Bare Costs	Incl. O&P
2 Labor Foremen (outside)	$49.25	$788.00	$73.30	$1172.80	$47.92	$71.33
4 Laborers	47.25	1512.00	70.35	2251.20		
1 S.P. Crane, 4x4, 5 Ton		385.89		424.48		
1 Flatbed Truck, Gas, 1.5 Ton		361.95		398.14		
1 Butt Fusion Mach., 4"-12" diam.		332.25		365.48	22.50	24.75
48 L.H., Daily Totals		$3380.09		$4612.10	$70.42	$96.09

Crews - Standard

Crew No.		Bare Costs		Incl. Subs O&P	Cost Per Labor-Hour	
Crew B-6C	Hr.	Daily	Hr.	Daily	Bare Costs	Incl. O&P
2 Labor Foremen (outside)	$49.25	$788.00	$73.30	$1172.80	$47.92	$71.33
4 Laborers	47.25	1512.00	70.35	2251.20		
1 S.P. Crane, 4x4, 12 Ton		637.99		701.79		
1 Flatbed Truck, Gas, 3 Ton		391.02		430.12		
1 Butt Fusion Mach., 8"-24" diam.		787.50		866.25	37.84	41.63
48 L.H., Daily Totals		$4116.51		$5422.16	$85.76	$112.96

Crew No.		Bare Costs		Incl. Subs O&P	Cost Per Labor-Hour	
Crew B-6D	Hr.	Daily	Hr.	Daily	Bare Costs	Incl. O&P
.5 Labor Foreman (outside)	$49.25	$197.00	$73.30	$293.20	$53.97	$80.32
1 Laborer	47.25	378.00	70.35	562.80		
1 Equip. Oper. (medium)	63.05	504.40	93.80	750.40		
1 Hydro Excavator, 12 C.Y.		1404.51		1544.96	70.23	77.25
20 L.H., Daily Totals		$2483.91		$3151.36	$124.20	$157.57

Crew B-7	Hr.	Daily	Hr.	Daily	Bare Costs	Incl. O&P
1 Labor Foreman (outside)	$49.25	$394.00	$73.30	$586.40	$50.22	$74.75
4 Laborers	47.25	1512.00	70.35	2251.20		
1 Equip. Oper. (medium)	63.05	504.40	93.80	750.40		
1 Brush Chipper, 12", 130 H.P.		518.12		569.93		
1 Crawler Loader, 3 C.Y.		1257.68		1383.45		
2 Chain Saws, Gas, 36" Long		107.22		117.94	39.23	43.15
48 L.H., Daily Totals		$4293.42		$5659.32	$89.45	$117.90

Crew B-7A	Hr.	Daily	Hr.	Daily	Bare Costs	Incl. O&P
2 Laborers	$47.25	$756.00	$70.35	$1125.60	$51.40	$76.52
1 Equip. Oper. (light)	59.70	477.60	88.85	710.80		
1 Rake w/Tractor		161.55		177.71		
2 Chain Saws, Gas, 18"		95.16		104.68	10.70	11.77
24 L.H., Daily Totals		$1490.31		$2118.78	$62.10	$88.28

Crew B-7B	Hr.	Daily	Hr.	Daily	Bare Costs	Incl. O&P
1 Labor Foreman (outside)	$49.25	$394.00	$73.30	$586.40	$50.96	$75.91
4 Laborers	47.25	1512.00	70.35	2251.20		
1 Equip. Oper. (medium)	63.05	504.40	93.80	750.40		
1 Truck Driver (heavy)	55.45	443.60	82.85	662.80		
1 Brush Chipper, 12", 130 H.P.		518.12		569.93		
1 Crawler Loader, 3 C.Y.		1257.68		1383.45		
2 Chain Saws, Gas, 36" Long		107.22		117.94		
1 Dump Truck, 8 C.Y., 220 H.P.		417.49		459.24	41.08	45.19
56 L.H., Daily Totals		$5154.51		$6781.36	$92.04	$121.10

Crew B-7C	Hr.	Daily	Hr.	Daily	Bare Costs	Incl. O&P
1 Labor Foreman (outside)	$49.25	$394.00	$73.30	$586.40	$50.96	$75.91
4 Laborers	47.25	1512.00	70.35	2251.20		
1 Equip. Oper. (medium)	63.05	504.40	93.80	750.40		
1 Truck Driver (heavy)	55.45	443.60	82.85	662.80		
1 Brush Chipper, 12", 130 H.P.		518.12		569.93		
1 Crawler Loader, 3 C.Y.		1257.68		1383.45		
2 Chain Saws, Gas, 36" Long		107.22		117.94		
1 Dump Truck, 12 C.Y., 400 H.P.		791.36		870.50	47.76	52.53
56 L.H., Daily Totals		$5528.38		$7192.62	$98.72	$128.44

Crew No.		Bare Costs		Incl. Subs O&P	Cost Per Labor-Hour	
Crew B-8	Hr.	Daily	Hr.	Daily	Bare Costs	Incl. O&P
1 Labor Foreman (outside)	$49.25	$394.00	$73.30	$586.40	$54.64	$81.40
2 Laborers	47.25	756.00	70.35	1125.60		
2 Equip. Oper. (medium)	63.05	1008.80	93.80	1500.80		
1 Equip. Oper. (oiler)	56.40	451.20	83.90	671.20		
2 Truck Drivers (heavy)	55.45	887.20	82.85	1325.60		
1 Hyd. Crane, 25 Ton		2273.31		2500.64		
1 Crawler Loader, 3 C.Y.		1257.68		1383.45		
2 Dump Trucks, 12 C.Y., 400 H.P.		1582.72		1740.99	79.90	87.89
64 L.H., Daily Totals		$8610.91		$10834.68	$134.55	$169.29

Crew B-9	Hr.	Daily	Hr.	Daily	Bare Costs	Incl. O&P
1 Labor Foreman (outside)	$49.25	$394.00	$73.30	$586.40	$47.65	$70.94
4 Laborers	47.25	1512.00	70.35	2251.20		
1 Air Compressor, 250 cfm		196.28		215.91		
2 Breakers, Pavement, 60 lb.		68.94		75.83		
2 -50' Air Hoses, 1.5"		47.20		51.92	7.81	8.59
40 L.H., Daily Totals		$2218.42		$3181.26	$55.46	$79.53

Crew B-9A	Hr.	Daily	Hr.	Daily	Bare Costs	Incl. O&P
2 Laborers	$47.25	$756.00	$70.35	$1125.60	$49.98	$74.52
1 Truck Driver (heavy)	55.45	443.60	82.85	662.80		
1 Water Tank Trailer, 5000 Gal.		169.14		186.05		
1 Truck Tractor, 220 H.P.		339.98		373.98		
2 -50' Discharge Hoses, 3"		9.76		10.74	21.62	23.78
24 L.H., Daily Totals		$1718.48		$2359.17	$71.60	$98.30

Crew B-9B	Hr.	Daily	Hr.	Daily	Bare Costs	Incl. O&P
2 Laborers	$47.25	$756.00	$70.35	$1125.60	$49.98	$74.52
1 Truck Driver (heavy)	55.45	443.60	82.85	662.80		
2 -50' Discharge Hoses, 3"		9.76		10.74		
1 Water Tank Trailer, 5000 Gal.		169.14		186.05		
1 Truck Tractor, 220 H.P.		339.98		373.98		
1 Pressure Washer		104.23		114.65	25.96	28.56
24 L.H., Daily Totals		$1822.71		$2473.82	$75.95	$103.08

Crew B-9D	Hr.	Daily	Hr.	Daily	Bare Costs	Incl. O&P
1 Labor Foreman (outside)	$49.25	$394.00	$73.30	$586.40	$47.65	$70.94
4 Common Laborers	47.25	1512.00	70.35	2251.20		
1 Air Compressor, 250 cfm		196.28		215.91		
2 -50' Air Hoses, 1.5"		47.20		51.92		
2 Air Powered Tampers		114.04		125.44	8.94	9.83
40 L.H., Daily Totals		$2263.52		$3230.87	$56.59	$80.77

Crew B-9E	Hr.	Daily	Hr.	Daily	Bare Costs	Incl. O&P
1 Cement Finisher	$55.00	$440.00	$80.45	$643.60	$51.13	$75.40
1 Laborer	47.25	378.00	70.35	562.80		
1 Chip. Hammers, 12 Lb., Elec.		27.16		29.88	1.70	1.87
16 L.H., Daily Totals		$845.16		$1236.28	$52.82	$77.27

Crew B-10	Hr.	Daily	Hr.	Daily	Bare Costs	Incl. O&P
1 Equip. Oper. (medium)	$63.05	$504.40	$93.80	$750.40	$57.78	$85.98
.5 Laborer	47.25	189.00	70.35	281.40		
12 L.H., Daily Totals		$693.40		$1031.80	$57.78	$85.98

Crew B-10A	Hr.	Daily	Hr.	Daily	Bare Costs	Incl. O&P
1 Equip. Oper. (medium)	$63.05	$504.40	$93.80	$750.40	$57.78	$85.98
.5 Laborer	47.25	189.00	70.35	281.40		
1 Roller, 2-Drum, W.B., 7.5 H.P.		157.50		173.25	13.13	14.44
12 L.H., Daily Totals		$850.90		$1205.05	$70.91	$100.42

Crews - Standard

Crew No.	Bare Costs		Incl. Subs O&P		Cost Per Labor-Hour	
Crew B-10B	Hr.	Daily	Hr.	Daily	Bare Costs	Incl. O&P
1 Equip. Oper. (medium)	$63.05	$504.40	$93.80	$750.40	$57.78	$85.98
.5 Laborer	47.25	189.00	70.35	281.40		
1 Dozer, 200 H.P.		1382.36		1520.60	115.20	126.72
12 L.H., Daily Totals		$2075.76		$2552.40	$172.98	$212.70
Crew B-10C	Hr.	Daily	Hr.	Daily	Bare Costs	Incl. O&P
1 Equip. Oper. (medium)	$63.05	$504.40	$93.80	$750.40	$57.78	$85.98
.5 Laborer	47.25	189.00	70.35	281.40		
1 Dozer, 200 H.P.		1382.36		1520.60		
1 Vibratory Roller, Towed, 23 Ton		681.59		749.75	172.00	189.20
12 L.H., Daily Totals		$2757.35		$3302.15	$229.78	$275.18
Crew B-10D	Hr.	Daily	Hr.	Daily	Bare Costs	Incl. O&P
1 Equip. Oper. (medium)	$63.05	$504.40	$93.80	$750.40	$57.78	$85.98
.5 Laborer	47.25	189.00	70.35	281.40		
1 Dozer, 200 H.P.		1382.36		1520.60		
1 Sheepsft. Roller, Towed		444.83		489.31	152.27	167.49
12 L.H., Daily Totals		$2520.59		$3041.71	$210.05	$253.48
Crew B-10E	Hr.	Daily	Hr.	Daily	Bare Costs	Incl. O&P
1 Equip. Oper. (medium)	$63.05	$504.40	$93.80	$750.40	$57.78	$85.98
.5 Laborer	47.25	189.00	70.35	281.40		
1 Tandem Roller, 5 Ton		287.45		316.19	23.95	26.35
12 L.H., Daily Totals		$980.85		$1347.99	$81.74	$112.33
Crew B-10F	Hr.	Daily	Hr.	Daily	Bare Costs	Incl. O&P
1 Equip. Oper. (medium)	$63.05	$504.40	$93.80	$750.40	$57.78	$85.98
.5 Laborer	47.25	189.00	70.35	281.40		
1 Tandem Roller, 10 Ton		379.22		417.14	31.60	34.76
12 L.H., Daily Totals		$1072.62		$1448.94	$89.39	$120.75
Crew B-10G	Hr.	Daily	Hr.	Daily	Bare Costs	Incl. O&P
1 Equip. Oper. (medium)	$63.05	$504.40	$93.80	$750.40	$57.78	$85.98
.5 Laborer	47.25	189.00	70.35	281.40		
1 Sheepsfoot Roller, 240 H.P.		765.47		842.02	63.79	70.17
12 L.H., Daily Totals		$1458.87		$1873.82	$121.57	$156.15
Crew B-10H	Hr.	Daily	Hr.	Daily	Bare Costs	Incl. O&P
1 Equip. Oper. (medium)	$63.05	$504.40	$93.80	$750.40	$57.78	$85.98
.5 Laborer	47.25	189.00	70.35	281.40		
1 Diaphragm Water Pump, 2"		61.92		68.11		
1 -20' Suction Hose, 2"		4.37		4.81		
2 -50' Discharge Hoses, 2"		8.18		9.00	6.21	6.83
12 L.H., Daily Totals		$767.87		$1113.72	$63.99	$92.81
Crew B-10I	Hr.	Daily	Hr.	Daily	Bare Costs	Incl. O&P
1 Equip. Oper. (medium)	$63.05	$504.40	$93.80	$750.40	$57.78	$85.98
.5 Laborer	47.25	189.00	70.35	281.40		
1 Diaphragm Water Pump, 4"		150.72		165.79		
1 -20' Suction Hose, 4"		19.04		20.94		
2 -50' Discharge Hoses, 4"		28.30		31.13	16.50	18.16
12 L.H., Daily Totals		$891.46		$1249.67	$74.29	$104.14
Crew B-10J	Hr.	Daily	Hr.	Daily	Bare Costs	Incl. O&P
1 Equip. Oper. (medium)	$63.05	$504.40	$93.80	$750.40	$57.78	$85.98
.5 Laborer	47.25	189.00	70.35	281.40		
1 Centrifugal Water Pump, 3"		82.39		90.63		
1 -20' Suction Hose, 3"		8.96		9.86		
2 -50' Discharge Hoses, 3"		9.76		10.74	8.43	9.27
12 L.H., Daily Totals		$794.51		$1143.02	$66.21	$95.25

Crew No.	Bare Costs		Incl. Subs O&P		Cost Per Labor-Hour	
Crew B-10K	Hr.	Daily	Hr.	Daily	Bare Costs	Incl. O&P
1 Equip. Oper. (medium)	$63.05	$504.40	$93.80	$750.40	$57.78	$85.98
.5 Laborer	47.25	189.00	70.35	281.40		
1 Centr. Water Pump, 6"		386.48		425.13		
1 -20' Suction Hose, 6"		28.12		30.93		
2 -50' Discharge Hoses, 6"		39.98		43.98	37.88	41.67
12 L.H., Daily Totals		$1147.98		$1531.84	$95.67	$127.65
Crew B-10L	Hr.	Daily	Hr.	Daily	Bare Costs	Incl. O&P
1 Equip. Oper. (medium)	$63.05	$504.40	$93.80	$750.40	$57.78	$85.98
.5 Laborer	47.25	189.00	70.35	281.40		
1 Dozer, 80 H.P.		591.82		651.00	49.32	54.25
12 L.H., Daily Totals		$1285.22		$1682.80	$107.10	$140.23
Crew B-10M	Hr.	Daily	Hr.	Daily	Bare Costs	Incl. O&P
1 Equip. Oper. (medium)	$63.05	$504.40	$93.80	$750.40	$57.78	$85.98
.5 Laborer	47.25	189.00	70.35	281.40		
1 Dozer, 300 H.P.		1674.53		1841.98	139.54	153.50
12 L.H., Daily Totals		$2367.93		$2873.78	$197.33	$239.48
Crew B-10N	Hr.	Daily	Hr.	Daily	Bare Costs	Incl. O&P
1 Equip. Oper. (medium)	$63.05	$504.40	$93.80	$750.40	$57.78	$85.98
.5 Laborer	47.25	189.00	70.35	281.40		
1 F.E. Loader, T.M., 1.5 C.Y.		627.38		690.12	52.28	57.51
12 L.H., Daily Totals		$1320.78		$1721.92	$110.07	$143.49
Crew B-10O	Hr.	Daily	Hr.	Daily	Bare Costs	Incl. O&P
1 Equip. Oper. (medium)	$63.05	$504.40	$93.80	$750.40	$57.78	$85.98
.5 Laborer	47.25	189.00	70.35	281.40		
1 F.E. Loader, T.M., 2.25 C.Y.		958.76		1054.64	79.90	87.89
12 L.H., Daily Totals		$1652.16		$2086.44	$137.68	$173.87
Crew B-10P	Hr.	Daily	Hr.	Daily	Bare Costs	Incl. O&P
1 Equip. Oper. (medium)	$63.05	$504.40	$93.80	$750.40	$57.78	$85.98
.5 Laborer	47.25	189.00	70.35	281.40		
1 Crawler Loader, 3 C.Y.		1257.68		1383.45	104.81	115.29
12 L.H., Daily Totals		$1951.08		$2415.25	$162.59	$201.27
Crew B-10Q	Hr.	Daily	Hr.	Daily	Bare Costs	Incl. O&P
1 Equip. Oper. (medium)	$63.05	$504.40	$93.80	$750.40	$57.78	$85.98
.5 Laborer	47.25	189.00	70.35	281.40		
1 Crawler Loader, 4 C.Y.		1506.11		1656.72	125.51	138.06
12 L.H., Daily Totals		$2199.51		$2688.52	$183.29	$224.04
Crew B-10R	Hr.	Daily	Hr.	Daily	Bare Costs	Incl. O&P
1 Equip. Oper. (medium)	$63.05	$504.40	$93.80	$750.40	$57.78	$85.98
.5 Laborer	47.25	189.00	70.35	281.40		
1 F.E. Loader, W.M., 1 C.Y.		394.79		434.27	32.90	36.19
12 L.H., Daily Totals		$1088.19		$1466.07	$90.68	$122.17
Crew B-10S	Hr.	Daily	Hr.	Daily	Bare Costs	Incl. O&P
1 Equip. Oper. (medium)	$63.05	$504.40	$93.80	$750.40	$57.78	$85.98
.5 Laborer	47.25	189.00	70.35	281.40		
1 F.E. Loader, W.M., 1.5 C.Y.		455.32		500.85	37.94	41.74
12 L.H., Daily Totals		$1148.72		$1532.65	$95.73	$127.72
Crew B-10T	Hr.	Daily	Hr.	Daily	Bare Costs	Incl. O&P
1 Equip. Oper. (medium)	$63.05	$504.40	$93.80	$750.40	$57.78	$85.98
.5 Laborer	47.25	189.00	70.35	281.40		
1 F.E. Loader, W.M., 2.5 C.Y.		658.89		724.78	54.91	60.40
12 L.H., Daily Totals		$1352.29		$1756.58	$112.69	$146.38

Crews - Standard

Crew No.	Bare Costs		Incl. Subs O&P		Cost Per Labor-Hour	
	Hr.	Daily	Hr.	Daily	Bare Costs	Incl. O&P
Crew B-10U						
1 Equip. Oper. (medium)	$63.05	$504.40	$93.80	$750.40	$57.78	$85.98
.5 Laborer	47.25	189.00	70.35	281.40		
1 F.E. Loader, W.M., 5.5 C.Y.		1186.42		1305.06	98.87	108.76
12 L.H., Daily Totals		$1879.82		$2336.86	$156.65	$194.74
Crew B-10V	Hr.	Daily	Hr.	Daily	Bare Costs	Incl. O&P
1 Equip. Oper. (medium)	$63.05	$504.40	$93.80	$750.40	$57.78	$85.98
.5 Laborer	47.25	189.00	70.35	281.40		
1 Dozer, 700 H.P.		4098.16		4507.98	341.51	375.66
12 L.H., Daily Totals		$4791.56		$5539.78	$399.30	$461.65
Crew B-10W	Hr.	Daily	Hr.	Daily	Bare Costs	Incl. O&P
1 Equip. Oper. (medium)	$63.05	$504.40	$93.80	$750.40	$57.78	$85.98
.5 Laborer	47.25	189.00	70.35	281.40		
1 Dozer, 105 H.P.		702.68		772.95	58.56	64.41
12 L.H., Daily Totals		$1396.08		$1804.75	$116.34	$150.40
Crew B-10X	Hr.	Daily	Hr.	Daily	Bare Costs	Incl. O&P
1 Equip. Oper. (medium)	$63.05	$504.40	$93.80	$750.40	$57.78	$85.98
.5 Laborer	47.25	189.00	70.35	281.40		
1 Dozer, 410 H.P.		2535.96		2789.56	211.33	232.46
12 L.H., Daily Totals		$3229.36		$3821.36	$269.11	$318.45
Crew B-10Y	Hr.	Daily	Hr.	Daily	Bare Costs	Incl. O&P
1 Equip. Oper. (medium)	$63.05	$504.40	$93.80	$750.40	$57.78	$85.98
.5 Laborer	47.25	189.00	70.35	281.40		
1 Vibr. Roller, Towed, 12 Ton		346.96		381.66	28.91	31.80
12 L.H., Daily Totals		$1040.36		$1413.46	$86.70	$117.79
Crew B-11A	Hr.	Daily	Hr.	Daily	Bare Costs	Incl. O&P
1 Equipment Oper. (med.)	$63.05	$504.40	$93.80	$750.40	$55.15	$82.08
1 Laborer	47.25	378.00	70.35	562.80		
1 Dozer, 200 H.P.		1382.36		1520.60	86.40	95.04
16 L.H., Daily Totals		$2264.76		$2833.80	$141.55	$177.11
Crew B-11B	Hr.	Daily	Hr.	Daily	Bare Costs	Incl. O&P
1 Equipment Oper. (light)	$59.70	$477.60	$88.85	$710.80	$53.48	$79.60
1 Laborer	47.25	378.00	70.35	562.80		
1 Air Powered Tamper		57.02		62.72		
1 Air Compressor, 365 cfm		389.99		428.99		
2 -50' Air Hoses, 1.5"		47.20		51.92	30.89	33.98
16 L.H., Daily Totals		$1349.81		$1817.23	$84.36	$113.58
Crew B-11C	Hr.	Daily	Hr.	Daily	Bare Costs	Incl. O&P
1 Equipment Oper. (med.)	$63.05	$504.40	$93.80	$750.40	$55.15	$82.08
1 Laborer	47.25	378.00	70.35	562.80		
1 Backhoe Loader, 48 H.P.		277.19		304.91	17.32	19.06
16 L.H., Daily Totals		$1159.59		$1618.11	$72.47	$101.13
Crew B-11J	Hr.	Daily	Hr.	Daily	Bare Costs	Incl. O&P
1 Equipment Oper. (med.)	$63.05	$504.40	$93.80	$750.40	$55.15	$82.08
1 Laborer	47.25	378.00	70.35	562.80		
1 Grader, 30,000 Lbs.		1091.19		1200.31		
1 Ripper, Beam & 1 Shank		100.54		110.59	74.48	81.93
16 L.H., Daily Totals		$2074.13		$2624.10	$129.63	$164.01
Crew B-11K	Hr.	Daily	Hr.	Daily	Bare Costs	Incl. O&P
1 Equipment Oper. (med.)	$63.05	$504.40	$93.80	$750.40	$55.15	$82.08
1 Laborer	47.25	378.00	70.35	562.80		
1 Trencher, Chain Type, 8' D		2079.03		2286.93	129.94	142.93
16 L.H., Daily Totals		$2961.43		$3600.13	$185.09	$225.01
Crew B-11L	Hr.	Daily	Hr.	Daily	Bare Costs	Incl. O&P
1 Equipment Oper. (med.)	$63.05	$504.40	$93.80	$750.40	$55.15	$82.08
1 Laborer	47.25	378.00	70.35	562.80		
1 Grader, 30,000 Lbs.		1091.19		1200.31	68.20	75.02
16 L.H., Daily Totals		$1973.59		$2513.51	$123.35	$157.09
Crew B-11M	Hr.	Daily	Hr.	Daily	Bare Costs	Incl. O&P
1 Equipment Oper. (med.)	$63.05	$504.40	$93.80	$750.40	$55.15	$82.08
1 Laborer	47.25	378.00	70.35	562.80		
1 Backhoe Loader, 80 H.P.		357.71		393.48	22.36	24.59
16 L.H., Daily Totals		$1240.11		$1706.68	$77.51	$106.67
Crew B-11N	Hr.	Daily	Hr.	Daily	Bare Costs	Incl. O&P
1 Labor Foreman (outside)	$49.25	$394.00	$73.30	$586.40	$56.45	$84.22
2 Equipment Operators (med.)	63.05	1008.80	93.80	1500.80		
6 Truck Drivers (heavy)	55.45	2661.60	82.85	3976.80		
1 F.E. Loader, W.M., 5.5 C.Y.		1186.42		1305.06		
1 Dozer, 410 H.P.		2535.96		2789.56		
6 Dump Trucks, Off Hwy., 50 Ton		12225.60		13448.16	221.50	243.65
72 L.H., Daily Totals		$20012.38		$23606.78	$277.95	$327.87
Crew B-11Q	Hr.	Daily	Hr.	Daily	Bare Costs	Incl. O&P
1 Equipment Operator (med.)	$63.05	$504.40	$93.80	$750.40	$57.78	$85.98
.5 Laborer	47.25	189.00	70.35	281.40		
1 Dozer, 140 H.P.		757.89		833.68	63.16	69.47
12 L.H., Daily Totals		$1451.29		$1865.48	$120.94	$155.46
Crew B-11R	Hr.	Daily	Hr.	Daily	Bare Costs	Incl. O&P
1 Equipment Operator (med.)	$63.05	$504.40	$93.80	$750.40	$57.78	$85.98
.5 Laborer	47.25	189.00	70.35	281.40		
1 Dozer, 200 H.P.		1382.36		1520.60	115.20	126.72
12 L.H., Daily Totals		$2075.76		$2552.40	$172.98	$212.70
Crew B-11S	Hr.	Daily	Hr.	Daily	Bare Costs	Incl. O&P
1 Equipment Operator (med.)	$63.05	$504.40	$93.80	$750.40	$57.78	$85.98
.5 Laborer	47.25	189.00	70.35	281.40		
1 Dozer, 300 H.P.		1674.53		1841.98		
1 Ripper, Beam & 1 Shank		100.54		110.59	147.92	162.71
12 L.H., Daily Totals		$2468.47		$2984.38	$205.71	$248.70
Crew B-11T	Hr.	Daily	Hr.	Daily	Bare Costs	Incl. O&P
1 Equipment Operator (med.)	$63.05	$504.40	$93.80	$750.40	$57.78	$85.98
.5 Laborer	47.25	189.00	70.35	281.40		
1 Dozer, 410 H.P.		2535.96		2789.56		
1 Ripper, Beam & 2 Shanks		154.19		169.61	224.18	246.60
12 L.H., Daily Totals		$3383.55		$3990.97	$281.96	$332.58
Crew B-11U	Hr.	Daily	Hr.	Daily	Bare Costs	Incl. O&P
1 Equipment Operator (med.)	$63.05	$504.40	$93.80	$750.40	$57.78	$85.98
.5 Laborer	47.25	189.00	70.35	281.40		
1 Dozer, 520 H.P.		2569.55		2826.51	214.13	235.54
12 L.H., Daily Totals		$3262.95		$3858.30	$271.91	$321.53

Crews - Standard

Crew No.	Bare Costs		Incl. Subs O&P		Cost Per Labor-Hour	
Crew B-11V	Hr.	Daily	Hr.	Daily	Bare Costs	Incl. O&P
3 Laborers	$47.25	$1134.00	$70.35	$1688.40	$47.25	$70.35
1 Roller, 2-Drum, W.B., 7.5 H.P.		157.50		173.25	6.56	7.22
24 L.H., Daily Totals		$1291.50		$1861.65	$53.81	$77.57
Crew B-11W	Hr.	Daily	Hr.	Daily	Bare Costs	Incl. O&P
1 Equipment Operator (med.)	$63.05	$504.40	$93.80	$750.40	$55.40	$82.72
1 Common Laborer	47.25	378.00	70.35	562.80		
10 Truck Drivers (heavy)	55.45	4436.00	82.85	6628.00		
1 Dozer, 200 H.P.		1382.36		1520.60		
1 Vibratory Roller, Towed, 23 Ton		681.59		749.75		
10 Dump Trucks, 8 C.Y., 220 H.P.		4174.90		4592.39	64.99	71.49
96 L.H., Daily Totals		$11557.25		$14803.93	$120.39	$154.21
Crew B-11Y	Hr.	Daily	Hr.	Daily	Bare Costs	Incl. O&P
1 Labor Foreman (outside)	$49.25	$394.00	$73.30	$586.40	$52.74	$78.49
5 Common Laborers	47.25	1890.00	70.35	2814.00		
3 Equipment Operators (med.)	63.05	1513.20	93.80	2251.20		
1 Dozer, 80 H.P.		591.82		651.00		
2 Rollers, 2-Drum, W.B., 7.5 H.P.		315.00		346.50		
4 Vibrating Plates, Gas, 21"		584.48		642.93	20.71	22.78
72 L.H., Daily Totals		$5288.50		$7292.03	$73.45	$101.28
Crew B-12A	Hr.	Daily	Hr.	Daily	Bare Costs	Incl. O&P
1 Equip. Oper. (crane)	$66.30	$530.40	$98.65	$789.20	$56.77	$84.50
1 Laborer	47.25	378.00	70.35	562.80		
1 Hyd. Excavator, 1 C.Y.		986.56		1085.22	61.66	67.83
16 L.H., Daily Totals		$1894.96		$2437.22	$118.44	$152.33
Crew B-12B	Hr.	Daily	Hr.	Daily	Bare Costs	Incl. O&P
1 Equip. Oper. (crane)	$66.30	$530.40	$98.65	$789.20	$56.77	$84.50
1 Laborer	47.25	378.00	70.35	562.80		
1 Hyd. Excavator, 1.5 C.Y.		1185.24		1303.76	74.08	81.49
16 L.H., Daily Totals		$2093.64		$2655.76	$130.85	$165.99
Crew B-12C	Hr.	Daily	Hr.	Daily	Bare Costs	Incl. O&P
1 Equip. Oper. (crane)	$66.30	$530.40	$98.65	$789.20	$56.77	$84.50
1 Laborer	47.25	378.00	70.35	562.80		
1 Hyd. Excavator, 2 C.Y.		1096.14		1205.75	68.51	75.36
16 L.H., Daily Totals		$2004.54		$2557.75	$125.28	$159.86
Crew B-12D	Hr.	Daily	Hr.	Daily	Bare Costs	Incl. O&P
1 Equip. Oper. (crane)	$66.30	$530.40	$98.65	$789.20	$56.77	$84.50
1 Laborer	47.25	378.00	70.35	562.80		
1 Hyd. Excavator, 3.5 C.Y.		2394.44		2633.88	149.65	164.62
16 L.H., Daily Totals		$3302.84		$3985.88	$206.43	$249.12
Crew B-12E	Hr.	Daily	Hr.	Daily	Bare Costs	Incl. O&P
1 Equip. Oper. (crane)	$66.30	$530.40	$98.65	$789.20	$56.77	$84.50
1 Laborer	47.25	378.00	70.35	562.80		
1 Hyd. Excavator, .5 C.Y.		764.88		841.37	47.81	52.59
16 L.H., Daily Totals		$1673.28		$2193.37	$104.58	$137.09
Crew B-12F	Hr.	Daily	Hr.	Daily	Bare Costs	Incl. O&P
1 Equip. Oper. (crane)	$66.30	$530.40	$98.65	$789.20	$56.77	$84.50
1 Laborer	47.25	378.00	70.35	562.80		
1 Hyd. Excavator, .75 C.Y.		915.34		1006.87	57.21	62.93
16 L.H., Daily Totals		$1823.74		$2358.87	$113.98	$147.43

Crew No.	Bare Costs		Incl. Subs O&P		Cost Per Labor-Hour	
Crew B-12G	Hr.	Daily	Hr.	Daily	Bare Costs	Incl. O&P
1 Equip. Oper. (crane)	$66.30	$530.40	$98.65	$789.20	$56.77	$84.50
1 Laborer	47.25	378.00	70.35	562.80		
1 Crawler Crane, 15 Ton		898.84		988.72		
1 Clamshell Bucket, .5 C.Y.		37.28		41.01	58.51	64.36
16 L.H., Daily Totals		$1844.52		$2381.73	$115.28	$148.86
Crew B-12H	Hr.	Daily	Hr.	Daily	Bare Costs	Incl. O&P
1 Equip. Oper. (crane)	$66.30	$530.40	$98.65	$789.20	$56.77	$84.50
1 Laborer	47.25	378.00	70.35	562.80		
1 Crawler Crane, 25 Ton		1274.00		1401.40		
1 Clamshell Bucket, 1 C.Y.		46.89		51.58	82.56	90.81
16 L.H., Daily Totals		$2229.29		$2804.98	$139.33	$175.31
Crew B-12I	Hr.	Daily	Hr.	Daily	Bare Costs	Incl. O&P
1 Equip. Oper. (crane)	$66.30	$530.40	$98.65	$789.20	$56.77	$84.50
1 Laborer	47.25	378.00	70.35	562.80		
1 Crawler Crane, 20 Ton		1120.87		1232.96		
1 Dragline Bucket, .75 C.Y.		29.54		32.49	71.90	79.09
16 L.H., Daily Totals		$2058.81		$2617.45	$128.68	$163.59
Crew B-12J	Hr.	Daily	Hr.	Daily	Bare Costs	Incl. O&P
1 Equip. Oper. (crane)	$66.30	$530.40	$98.65	$789.20	$56.77	$84.50
1 Laborer	47.25	378.00	70.35	562.80		
1 Gradall, 5/8 C.Y.		880.91		969.00	55.06	60.56
16 L.H., Daily Totals		$1789.31		$2321.00	$111.83	$145.06
Crew B-12K	Hr.	Daily	Hr.	Daily	Bare Costs	Incl. O&P
1 Equip. Oper. (crane)	$66.30	$530.40	$98.65	$789.20	$56.77	$84.50
1 Laborer	47.25	378.00	70.35	562.80		
1 Gradall, 3 Ton, 1 C.Y.		1520.84		1672.92	95.05	104.56
16 L.H., Daily Totals		$2429.24		$3024.92	$151.83	$189.06
Crew B-12L	Hr.	Daily	Hr.	Daily	Bare Costs	Incl. O&P
1 Equip. Oper. (crane)	$66.30	$530.40	$98.65	$789.20	$56.77	$84.50
1 Laborer	47.25	378.00	70.35	562.80		
1 Crawler Crane, 15 Ton		898.84		988.72		
1 F.E. Attachment, .5 C.Y.		72.55		79.81	60.71	66.78
16 L.H., Daily Totals		$1879.79		$2420.53	$117.49	$151.28
Crew B-12M	Hr.	Daily	Hr.	Daily	Bare Costs	Incl. O&P
1 Equip. Oper. (crane)	$66.30	$530.40	$98.65	$789.20	$56.77	$84.50
1 Laborer	47.25	378.00	70.35	562.80		
1 Crawler Crane, 20 Ton		1120.87		1232.96		
1 F.E. Attachment, .75 C.Y.		78.31		86.14	74.95	82.44
16 L.H., Daily Totals		$2107.58		$2671.10	$131.72	$166.94
Crew B-12N	Hr.	Daily	Hr.	Daily	Bare Costs	Incl. O&P
1 Equip. Oper. (crane)	$66.30	$530.40	$98.65	$789.20	$56.77	$84.50
1 Laborer	47.25	378.00	70.35	562.80		
1 Crawler Crane, 25 Ton		1274.00		1401.40		
1 F.E. Attachment, 1 C.Y.		59.18		65.10	83.32	91.66
16 L.H., Daily Totals		$2241.58		$2818.50	$140.10	$176.16
Crew B-12O	Hr.	Daily	Hr.	Daily	Bare Costs	Incl. O&P
1 Equip. Oper. (crane)	$66.30	$530.40	$98.65	$789.20	$56.77	$84.50
1 Laborer	47.25	378.00	70.35	562.80		
1 Crawler Crane, 40 Ton		1362.63		1498.89		
1 F.E. Attachment, 1.5 C.Y.		97.47		107.22	91.26	100.38
16 L.H., Daily Totals		$2368.50		$2958.11	$148.03	$184.88

Crews - Standard

Crew No.	Bare Costs		Incl. Subs O&P		Cost Per Labor-Hour	
Crew B-12P	Hr.	Daily	Hr.	Daily	Bare Costs	Incl. O&P
1 Equip. Oper. (crane)	$66.30	$530.40	$98.65	$789.20	$56.77	$84.50
1 Laborer	47.25	378.00	70.35	562.80		
1 Crawler Crane, 40 Ton		1362.63		1498.89		
1 Dragline Bucket, 1.5 C.Y.		37.32		41.05	87.50	96.25
16 L.H., Daily Totals		$2308.35		$2891.95	$144.27	$180.75
Crew B-12Q	Hr.	Daily	Hr.	Daily	Bare Costs	Incl. O&P
1 Equip. Oper. (crane)	$66.30	$530.40	$98.65	$789.20	$56.77	$84.50
1 Laborer	47.25	378.00	70.35	562.80		
1 Hyd. Excavator, 5/8 C.Y.		813.17		894.49	50.82	55.91
16 L.H., Daily Totals		$1721.57		$2246.49	$107.60	$140.41
Crew B-12S	Hr.	Daily	Hr.	Daily	Bare Costs	Incl. O&P
1 Equip. Oper. (crane)	$66.30	$530.40	$98.65	$789.20	$56.77	$84.50
1 Laborer	47.25	378.00	70.35	562.80		
1 Hyd. Excavator, 2.5 C.Y.		1683.69		1852.06	105.23	115.75
16 L.H., Daily Totals		$2592.09		$3204.06	$162.01	$200.25
Crew B-12T	Hr.	Daily	Hr.	Daily	Bare Costs	Incl. O&P
1 Equip. Oper. (crane)	$66.30	$530.40	$98.65	$789.20	$56.77	$84.50
1 Laborer	47.25	378.00	70.35	562.80		
1 Crawler Crane, 75 Ton		2189.46		2408.41		
1 F.E. Attachment, 3 C.Y.		127.10		139.81	144.79	159.26
16 L.H., Daily Totals		$3224.96		$3900.22	$201.56	$243.76
Crew B-12V	Hr.	Daily	Hr.	Daily	Bare Costs	Incl. O&P
1 Equip. Oper. (crane)	$66.30	$530.40	$98.65	$789.20	$56.77	$84.50
1 Laborer	47.25	378.00	70.35	562.80		
1 Crawler Crane, 75 Ton		2189.46		2408.41		
1 Dragline Bucket, 3 C.Y.		51.71		56.88	140.07	154.08
16 L.H., Daily Totals		$3149.57		$3817.29	$196.85	$238.58
Crew B-12Y	Hr.	Daily	Hr.	Daily	Bare Costs	Incl. O&P
1 Equip. Oper. (crane)	$66.30	$530.40	$98.65	$789.20	$53.60	$79.78
2 Laborers	47.25	756.00	70.35	1125.60		
1 Hyd. Excavator, 3.5 C.Y.		2394.44		2633.88	99.77	109.75
24 L.H., Daily Totals		$3680.84		$4548.68	$153.37	$189.53
Crew B-12Z	Hr.	Daily	Hr.	Daily	Bare Costs	Incl. O&P
1 Equip. Oper. (crane)	$66.30	$530.40	$98.65	$789.20	$53.60	$79.78
2 Laborers	47.25	756.00	70.35	1125.60		
1 Hyd. Excavator, 2.5 C.Y.		1683.69		1852.06	70.15	77.17
24 L.H., Daily Totals		$2970.09		$3766.86	$123.75	$156.95
Crew B-13	Hr.	Daily	Hr.	Daily	Bare Costs	Incl. O&P
1 Labor Foreman (outside)	$49.25	$394.00	$73.30	$586.40	$51.56	$76.75
4 Laborers	47.25	1512.00	70.35	2251.20		
1 Equip. Oper. (crane)	66.30	530.40	98.65	789.20		
1 Equip. Oper. (oiler)	56.40	451.20	83.90	671.20		
1 Hyd. Crane, 25 Ton		2273.31		2500.64	40.59	44.65
56 L.H., Daily Totals		$5160.91		$6798.64	$92.16	$121.40

Crew No.	Bare Costs		Incl. Subs O&P		Cost Per Labor-Hour	
Crew B-13A	Hr.	Daily	Hr.	Daily	Bare Costs	Incl. O&P
1 Labor Foreman (outside)	$49.25	$394.00	$73.30	$586.40	$54.39	$81.04
2 Laborers	47.25	756.00	70.35	1125.60		
2 Equipment Operators (med.)	63.05	1008.80	93.80	1500.80		
2 Truck Drivers (heavy)	55.45	887.20	82.85	1325.60		
1 Crawler Crane, 75 Ton		2189.46		2408.41		
1 Crawler Loader, 4 C.Y.		1506.11		1656.72		
2 Dump Trucks, 8 C.Y., 220 H.P.		834.98		918.48	80.90	88.99
56 L.H., Daily Totals		$7576.55		$9522.00	$135.30	$170.04
Crew B-13B	Hr.	Daily	Hr.	Daily	Bare Costs	Incl. O&P
1 Labor Foreman (outside)	$49.25	$394.00	$73.30	$586.40	$51.56	$76.75
4 Laborers	47.25	1512.00	70.35	2251.20		
1 Equip. Oper. (crane)	66.30	530.40	98.65	789.20		
1 Equip. Oper. (oiler)	56.40	451.20	83.90	671.20		
1 Hyd. Crane, 55 Ton		2461.06		2707.17	43.95	48.34
56 L.H., Daily Totals		$5348.66		$7005.17	$95.51	$125.09
Crew B-13C	Hr.	Daily	Hr.	Daily	Bare Costs	Incl. O&P
1 Labor Foreman (outside)	$49.25	$394.00	$73.30	$586.40	$51.56	$76.75
4 Laborers	47.25	1512.00	70.35	2251.20		
1 Equip. Oper. (crane)	66.30	530.40	98.65	789.20		
1 Equip. Oper. (oiler)	56.40	451.20	83.90	671.20		
1 Crawler Crane, 100 Ton		1552.12		1707.33	27.72	30.49
56 L.H., Daily Totals		$4439.72		$6005.33	$79.28	$107.24
Crew B-13D	Hr.	Daily	Hr.	Daily	Bare Costs	Incl. O&P
1 Laborer	$47.25	$378.00	$70.35	$562.80	$56.77	$84.50
1 Equip. Oper. (crane)	66.30	530.40	98.65	789.20		
1 Hyd. Excavator, 1 C.Y.		986.56		1085.22		
1 Trench Box		131.49		144.64	69.88	76.87
16 L.H., Daily Totals		$2026.45		$2581.86	$126.65	$161.37
Crew B-13E	Hr.	Daily	Hr.	Daily	Bare Costs	Incl. O&P
1 Laborer	$47.25	$378.00	$70.35	$562.80	$56.77	$84.50
1 Equip. Oper. (crane)	66.30	530.40	98.65	789.20		
1 Hyd. Excavator, 1.5 C.Y.		1185.24		1303.76		
1 Trench Box		131.49		144.64	82.30	90.53
16 L.H., Daily Totals		$2225.13		$2800.40	$139.07	$175.03
Crew B-13F	Hr.	Daily	Hr.	Daily	Bare Costs	Incl. O&P
1 Laborer	$47.25	$378.00	$70.35	$562.80	$56.77	$84.50
1 Equip. Oper. (crane)	66.30	530.40	98.65	789.20		
1 Hyd. Excavator, 3.5 C.Y.		2394.44		2633.88		
1 Trench Box		131.49		144.64	157.87	173.66
16 L.H., Daily Totals		$3434.33		$4130.52	$214.65	$258.16
Crew B-13G	Hr.	Daily	Hr.	Daily	Bare Costs	Incl. O&P
1 Laborer	$47.25	$378.00	$70.35	$562.80	$56.77	$84.50
1 Equip. Oper. (crane)	66.30	530.40	98.65	789.20		
1 Hyd. Excavator, .75 C.Y.		915.34		1006.87		
1 Trench Box		131.49		144.64	65.43	71.97
16 L.H., Daily Totals		$1955.23		$2503.51	$122.20	$156.47
Crew B-13H	Hr.	Daily	Hr.	Daily	Bare Costs	Incl. O&P
1 Laborer	$47.25	$378.00	$70.35	$562.80	$56.77	$84.50
1 Equip. Oper. (crane)	66.30	530.40	98.65	789.20		
1 Gradall, 5/8 C.Y.		880.91		969.00		
1 Trench Box		131.49		144.64	63.27	69.60
16 L.H., Daily Totals		$1920.80		$2465.64	$120.05	$154.10

Crews - Standard

Crew No.	Bare Costs		Incl. Subs O&P		Cost Per Labor-Hour	
Crew B-13I	Hr.	Daily	Hr.	Daily	Bare Costs	Incl. O&P
1 Laborer	$47.25	$378.00	$70.35	$562.80	$56.77	$84.50
1 Equip. Oper. (crane)	66.30	530.40	98.65	789.20		
1 Gradall, 3 Ton, 1 C.Y.		1520.84		1672.92		
1 Trench Box		131.49		144.64	103.27	113.60
16 L.H., Daily Totals		$2560.73		$3169.56	$160.05	$198.10
Crew B-13J	Hr.	Daily	Hr.	Daily	Bare Costs	Incl. O&P
1 Laborer	$47.25	$378.00	$70.35	$562.80	$56.77	$84.50
1 Equip. Oper. (crane)	66.30	530.40	98.65	789.20		
1 Hyd. Excavator, 2.5 C.Y.		1683.69		1852.06		
1 Trench Box		131.49		144.64	113.45	124.79
16 L.H., Daily Totals		$2723.58		$3348.70	$170.22	$209.29
Crew B-13K	Hr.	Daily	Hr.	Daily	Bare Costs	Incl. O&P
2 Equip. Opers. (crane)	$66.30	$1060.80	$98.65	$1578.40	$66.30	$98.65
1 Hyd. Excavator, .75 C.Y.		915.34		1006.87		
1 Hyd. Hammer, 4000 ft-lb		715.03		786.53		
1 Hyd. Excavator, .75 C.Y.		915.34		1006.87	159.11	175.02
16 L.H., Daily Totals		$3606.51		$4378.68	$225.41	$273.67
Crew B-13L	Hr.	Daily	Hr.	Daily	Bare Costs	Incl. O&P
2 Equip. Opers. (crane)	$66.30	$1060.80	$98.65	$1578.40	$66.30	$98.65
1 Hyd. Excavator, 1.5 C.Y.		1185.24		1303.76		
1 Hyd. Hammer, 5000 ft-lb		776.94		854.63		
1 Hyd. Excavator, .75 C.Y.		915.34		1006.87	179.85	197.83
16 L.H., Daily Totals		$3938.32		$4743.67	$246.15	$296.48
Crew B-13M	Hr.	Daily	Hr.	Daily	Bare Costs	Incl. O&P
2 Equip. Opers. (crane)	$66.30	$1060.80	$98.65	$1578.40	$66.30	$98.65
1 Hyd. Excavator, 2.5 C.Y.		1683.69		1852.06		
1 Hyd. Hammer, 8000 ft-lb		1011.13		1112.24		
1 Hyd. Excavator, 1.5 C.Y.		1185.24		1303.76	242.50	266.75
16 L.H., Daily Totals		$4940.86		$5846.47	$308.80	$365.40
Crew B-13N	Hr.	Daily	Hr.	Daily	Bare Costs	Incl. O&P
2 Equip. Opers. (crane)	$66.30	$1060.80	$98.65	$1578.40	$66.30	$98.65
1 Hyd. Excavator, 3.5 C.Y.		2394.44		2633.88		
1 Hyd. Hammer, 12,000 ft-lb		1162.80		1279.08		
1 Hyd. Excavator, 1.5 C.Y.		1185.24		1303.76	296.40	326.05
16 L.H., Daily Totals		$5803.28		$6795.13	$362.70	$424.70
Crew B-14	Hr.	Daily	Hr.	Daily	Bare Costs	Incl. O&P
1 Labor Foreman (outside)	$49.25	$394.00	$73.30	$586.40	$49.66	$73.92
4 Laborers	47.25	1512.00	70.35	2251.20		
1 Equip. Oper. (light)	59.70	477.60	88.85	710.80		
1 Backhoe Loader, 48 H.P.		277.19		304.91	5.77	6.35
48 L.H., Daily Totals		$2660.79		$3853.31	$55.43	$80.28
Crew B-14A	Hr.	Daily	Hr.	Daily	Bare Costs	Incl. O&P
1 Equip. Oper. (crane)	$66.30	$530.40	$98.65	$789.20	$59.95	$89.22
.5 Laborer	47.25	189.00	70.35	281.40		
1 Hyd. Excavator, 4.5 C.Y.		3788.37		4167.21	315.70	347.27
12 L.H., Daily Totals		$4507.77		$5237.81	$375.65	$436.48
Crew B-14B	Hr.	Daily	Hr.	Daily	Bare Costs	Incl. O&P
1 Equip. Oper. (crane)	$66.30	$530.40	$98.65	$789.20	$59.95	$89.22
.5 Laborer	47.25	189.00	70.35	281.40		
1 Hyd. Excavator, 6 C.Y.		3843.97		4228.37	320.33	352.36
12 L.H., Daily Totals		$4563.37		$5298.97	$380.28	$441.58

Crew No.	Bare Costs		Incl. Subs O&P		Cost Per Labor-Hour	
Crew B-14C	Hr.	Daily	Hr.	Daily	Bare Costs	Incl. O&P
1 Equip. Oper. (crane)	$66.30	$530.40	$98.65	$789.20	$59.95	$89.22
.5 Laborer	47.25	189.00	70.35	281.40		
1 Hyd. Excavator, 7 C.Y.		4206.21		4626.83	350.52	385.57
12 L.H., Daily Totals		$4925.61		$5697.43	$410.47	$474.79
Crew B-14F	Hr.	Daily	Hr.	Daily	Bare Costs	Incl. O&P
1 Equip. Oper. (crane)	$66.30	$530.40	$98.65	$789.20	$59.95	$89.22
.5 Laborer	47.25	189.00	70.35	281.40		
1 Hyd. Shovel, 7 C.Y.		4549.05		5003.95	379.09	417.00
12 L.H., Daily Totals		$5268.45		$6074.56	$439.04	$506.21
Crew B-14G	Hr.	Daily	Hr.	Daily	Bare Costs	Incl. O&P
1 Equip. Oper. (crane)	$66.30	$530.40	$98.65	$789.20	$59.95	$89.22
.5 Laborer	47.25	189.00	70.35	281.40		
1 Hyd. Shovel, 12 C.Y.		6601.66		7261.83	550.14	605.15
12 L.H., Daily Totals		$7321.06		$8332.43	$610.09	$694.37
Crew B-14J	Hr.	Daily	Hr.	Daily	Bare Costs	Incl. O&P
1 Equip. Oper. (medium)	$63.05	$504.40	$93.80	$750.40	$57.78	$85.98
.5 Laborer	47.25	189.00	70.35	281.40		
1 F.E. Loader, 8 C.Y.		1999.44		2199.38	166.62	183.28
12 L.H., Daily Totals		$2692.84		$3231.18	$224.40	$269.27
Crew B-14K	Hr.	Daily	Hr.	Daily	Bare Costs	Incl. O&P
1 Equip. Oper. (medium)	$63.05	$504.40	$93.80	$750.40	$57.78	$85.98
.5 Laborer	47.25	189.00	70.35	281.40		
1 F.E. Loader, 10 C.Y.		2862.71		3148.98	238.56	262.42
12 L.H., Daily Totals		$3556.11		$4180.78	$296.34	$348.40
Crew B-15	Hr.	Daily	Hr.	Daily	Bare Costs	Incl. O&P
1 Equipment Oper. (med.)	$63.05	$504.40	$93.80	$750.40	$56.45	$84.19
.5 Laborer	47.25	189.00	70.35	281.40		
2 Truck Drivers (heavy)	55.45	887.20	82.85	1325.60		
2 Dump Trucks, 12 C.Y., 400 H.P.		1582.72		1740.99		
1 Dozer, 200 H.P.		1382.36		1520.60	105.90	116.49
28 L.H., Daily Totals		$4545.68		$5618.99	$162.35	$200.68
Crew B-16	Hr.	Daily	Hr.	Daily	Bare Costs	Incl. O&P
1 Labor Foreman (outside)	$49.25	$394.00	$73.30	$586.40	$49.80	$74.21
2 Laborers	47.25	756.00	70.35	1125.60		
1 Truck Driver (heavy)	55.45	443.60	82.85	662.80		
1 Dump Truck, 12 C.Y., 400 H.P.		791.36		870.50	24.73	27.20
32 L.H., Daily Totals		$2384.96		$3245.30	$74.53	$101.42
Crew B-17	Hr.	Daily	Hr.	Daily	Bare Costs	Incl. O&P
2 Laborers	$47.25	$756.00	$70.35	$1125.60	$52.41	$78.10
1 Equip. Oper. (light)	59.70	477.60	88.85	710.80		
1 Truck Driver (heavy)	55.45	443.60	82.85	662.80		
1 Backhoe Loader, 48 H.P.		277.19		304.91		
1 Dump Truck, 8 C.Y., 220 H.P.		417.49		459.24	21.71	23.88
32 L.H., Daily Totals		$2371.88		$3263.35	$74.12	$101.98
Crew B-17A	Hr.	Daily	Hr.	Daily	Bare Costs	Incl. O&P
2 Labor Foremen (outside)	$49.25	$788.00	$73.30	$1172.80	$50.65	$75.57
6 Laborers	47.25	2268.00	70.35	3376.80		
1 Skilled Worker Foreman (out)	63.25	506.00	95.00	760.00		
1 Skilled Worker	61.25	490.00	92.00	736.00		
80 L.H., Daily Totals		$4052.00		$6045.60	$50.65	$75.57

Crews - Standard

Crew No.	Bare Costs		Incl. Subs O&P		Cost Per Labor-Hour	
Crew B-17B	Hr.	Daily	Hr.	Daily	Bare Costs	Incl. O&P
2 Laborers	$47.25	$756.00	$70.35	$1125.60	$52.41	$78.10
1 Equip. Oper. (light)	59.70	477.60	88.85	710.80		
1 Truck Driver (heavy)	55.45	443.60	82.85	662.80		
1 Backhoe Loader, 48 H.P.		277.19		304.91		
1 Dump Truck, 12 C.Y., 400 H.P.		791.36		870.50	33.39	36.73
32 L.H., Daily Totals		$2745.75		$3674.61	$85.80	$114.83
Crew B-17C	Hr.	Daily	Hr.	Daily	Bare Costs	Incl. O&P
1 Labor Foreman (outside)	$49.25	$394.00	$73.30	$586.40	$52.13	$77.64
3 Laborers	47.25	1134.00	70.35	1688.40		
1 Equip. Oper. (heavy)	66.30	530.40	98.65	789.20		
1 Truck Driver (heavy)	55.45	443.60	82.85	662.80		
1 Hyd. Excavator, 2 C.Y.		1096.14		1205.75		
1 Dump Truck, 12 C.Y., 400 H.P.		791.36		870.50		
1 P/U, 3/4 ton, Tool Truck		157.41		173.15	42.60	46.86
48 L.H., Daily Totals		$4546.91		$5976.20	$94.73	$124.50
Crew B-18	Hr.	Daily	Hr.	Daily	Bare Costs	Incl. O&P
1 Labor Foreman (outside)	$49.25	$394.00	$73.30	$586.40	$47.92	$71.33
2 Laborers	47.25	756.00	70.35	1125.60		
1 Vibrating Plate, Gas, 21"		146.12		160.73	6.09	6.70
24 L.H., Daily Totals		$1296.12		$1872.73	$54.01	$78.03
Crew B-19	Hr.	Daily	Hr.	Daily	Bare Costs	Incl. O&P
1 Pile Driver Foreman (outside)	$62.50	$500.00	$96.70	$773.60	$61.69	$94.04
4 Pile Drivers	60.50	1936.00	93.60	2995.20		
2 Equip. Oper. (crane)	66.30	1060.80	98.65	1578.40		
1 Equip. Oper. (oiler)	56.40	451.20	83.90	671.20		
1 Crawler Crane, 40 Ton		1362.63		1498.89		
1 Lead, 90' High		409.90		450.89		
1 Hammer, Diesel, 22k ft-lb		485.21		533.73	35.28	38.80
64 L.H., Daily Totals		$6205.74		$8501.91	$96.96	$132.84
Crew B-19A	Hr.	Daily	Hr.	Daily	Bare Costs	Incl. O&P
1 Pile Driver Foreman (outside)	$62.50	$500.00	$96.70	$773.60	$61.69	$94.04
4 Pile Drivers	60.50	1936.00	93.60	2995.20		
2 Equip. Oper. (crane)	66.30	1060.80	98.65	1578.40		
1 Equip. Oper. (oiler)	56.40	451.20	83.90	671.20		
1 Crawler Crane, 75 Ton		2189.46		2408.41		
1 Lead, 90' High		409.90		450.89		
1 Hammer, Diesel, 41k ft-lb		640.74		704.81	50.63	55.69
64 L.H., Daily Totals		$7188.10		$9582.51	$112.31	$149.73
Crew B-19B	Hr.	Daily	Hr.	Daily	Bare Costs	Incl. O&P
1 Pile Driver Foreman (outside)	$62.50	$500.00	$96.70	$773.60	$61.69	$94.04
4 Pile Drivers	60.50	1936.00	93.60	2995.20		
2 Equip. Oper. (crane)	66.30	1060.80	98.65	1578.40		
1 Equip. Oper. (oiler)	56.40	451.20	83.90	671.20		
1 Crawler Crane, 40 Ton		1362.63		1498.89		
1 Lead, 90' High		409.90		450.89		
1 Hammer, Diesel, 22k ft-lb		485.21		533.73		
1 Barge, 400 Ton		957.33		1053.06	50.24	55.26
64 L.H., Daily Totals		$7163.07		$9554.98	$111.92	$149.30

Crew No.	Bare Costs		Incl. Subs O&P		Cost Per Labor-Hour	
Crew B-19C	Hr.	Daily	Hr.	Daily	Bare Costs	Incl. O&P
1 Pile Driver Foreman (outside)	$62.50	$500.00	$96.70	$773.60	$61.69	$94.04
4 Pile Drivers	60.50	1936.00	93.60	2995.20		
2 Equip. Oper. (crane)	66.30	1060.80	98.65	1578.40		
1 Equip. Oper. (oiler)	56.40	451.20	83.90	671.20		
1 Crawler Crane, 75 Ton		2189.46		2408.41		
1 Lead, 90' High		409.90		450.89		
1 Hammer, Diesel, 41k ft-lb		640.74		704.81		
1 Barge, 400 Ton		957.33		1053.06	65.58	72.14
64 L.H., Daily Totals		$8145.43		$10635.57	$127.27	$166.18
Crew B-20	Hr.	Daily	Hr.	Daily	Bare Costs	Incl. O&P
1 Labor Foreman (outside)	$49.25	$394.00	$73.30	$586.40	$52.58	$78.55
1 Skilled Worker	61.25	490.00	92.00	736.00		
1 Laborer	47.25	378.00	70.35	562.80		
24 L.H., Daily Totals		$1262.00		$1885.20	$52.58	$78.55
Crew B-20A	Hr.	Daily	Hr.	Daily	Bare Costs	Incl. O&P
1 Labor Foreman (outside)	$49.25	$394.00	$73.30	$586.40	$56.55	$84.26
1 Laborer	47.25	378.00	70.35	562.80		
1 Plumber	72.05	576.40	107.45	859.60		
1 Plumber Apprentice	57.65	461.20	85.95	687.60		
32 L.H., Daily Totals		$1809.60		$2696.40	$56.55	$84.26
Crew B-21	Hr.	Daily	Hr.	Daily	Bare Costs	Incl. O&P
1 Labor Foreman (outside)	$49.25	$394.00	$73.30	$586.40	$54.54	$81.42
1 Skilled Worker	61.25	490.00	92.00	736.00		
1 Laborer	47.25	378.00	70.35	562.80		
.5 Equip. Oper. (crane)	66.30	265.20	98.65	394.60		
.5 S.P. Crane, 4x4, 5 Ton		192.94		212.24	6.89	7.58
28 L.H., Daily Totals		$1720.15		$2492.04	$61.43	$89.00
Crew B-21A	Hr.	Daily	Hr.	Daily	Bare Costs	Incl. O&P
1 Labor Foreman (outside)	$49.25	$394.00	$73.30	$586.40	$58.50	$87.14
1 Laborer	47.25	378.00	70.35	562.80		
1 Plumber	72.05	576.40	107.45	859.60		
1 Plumber Apprentice	57.65	461.20	85.95	687.60		
1 Equip. Oper. (crane)	66.30	530.40	98.65	789.20		
1 S.P. Crane, 4x4, 12 Ton		637.99		701.79	15.95	17.54
40 L.H., Daily Totals		$2977.99		$4187.39	$74.45	$104.68
Crew B-21B	Hr.	Daily	Hr.	Daily	Bare Costs	Incl. O&P
1 Labor Foreman (outside)	$49.25	$394.00	$73.30	$586.40	$51.46	$76.60
3 Laborers	47.25	1134.00	70.35	1688.40		
1 Equip. Oper. (crane)	66.30	530.40	98.65	789.20		
1 Hyd. Crane, 12 Ton		2150.65		2365.72	53.77	59.14
40 L.H., Daily Totals		$4209.05		$5429.72	$105.23	$135.74
Crew B-21C	Hr.	Daily	Hr.	Daily	Bare Costs	Incl. O&P
1 Labor Foreman (outside)	$49.25	$394.00	$73.30	$586.40	$51.56	$76.75
4 Laborers	47.25	1512.00	70.35	2251.20		
1 Equip. Oper. (crane)	66.30	530.40	98.65	789.20		
1 Equip. Oper. (oiler)	56.40	451.20	83.90	671.20		
2 Cutting Torches		28.48		31.33		
2 Sets of Gases		377.34		415.07		
1 Lattice Boom Crane, 90 Ton		2689.54		2958.49	55.27	60.80
56 L.H., Daily Totals		$5982.96		$7702.90	$106.84	$137.55

Crews - Standard

Crew No.		Bare Costs		Incl. Subs O&P		Cost Per Labor-Hour	
Crew B-22	Hr.	Daily	Hr.	Daily	Bare Costs	Incl. O&P	
1 Labor Foreman (outside)	$49.25	$394.00	$73.30	$586.40	$55.33	$82.57	
1 Skilled Worker	61.25	490.00	92.00	736.00			
1 Laborer	47.25	378.00	70.35	562.80			
.75 Equip. Oper. (crane)	66.30	397.80	98.65	591.90			
.75 S.P. Crane, 4x4, 5 Ton		289.42		318.36	9.65	10.61	
30 L.H., Daily Totals		$1949.22		$2795.46	$64.97	$93.18	
Crew B-22A	Hr.	Daily	Hr.	Daily	Bare Costs	Incl. O&P	
1 Labor Foreman (outside)	$49.25	$394.00	$73.30	$586.40	$54.26	$80.93	
1 Skilled Worker	61.25	490.00	92.00	736.00			
2 Laborers	47.25	756.00	70.35	1125.60			
1 Equipment Operator, Crane	66.30	530.40	98.65	789.20			
1 S.P. Crane, 4x4, 5 Ton		385.89		424.48			
1 Butt Fusion Mach., 4"-12" diam.		332.25		365.48	17.95	19.75	
40 L.H., Daily Totals		$2888.54		$4027.15	$72.21	$100.68	
Crew B-22B	Hr.	Daily	Hr.	Daily	Bare Costs	Incl. O&P	
1 Labor Foreman (outside)	$49.25	$394.00	$73.30	$586.40	$54.26	$80.93	
1 Skilled Worker	61.25	490.00	92.00	736.00			
2 Laborers	47.25	756.00	70.35	1125.60			
1 Equip. Oper. (crane)	66.30	530.40	98.65	789.20			
1 S.P. Crane, 4x4, 5 Ton		385.89		424.48			
1 Butt Fusion Mach., 8"-24" diam.		787.50		866.25	29.33	32.27	
40 L.H., Daily Totals		$3343.79		$4527.93	$83.59	$113.20	
Crew B-22C	Hr.	Daily	Hr.	Daily	Bare Costs	Incl. O&P	
1 Skilled Worker	$61.25	$490.00	$92.00	$736.00	$54.25	$81.17	
1 Laborer	47.25	378.00	70.35	562.80			
1 Butt Fusion Mach., 2"-8" diam.		280.48		308.53	17.53	19.28	
16 L.H., Daily Totals		$1148.48		$1607.33	$71.78	$100.46	
Crew B-23	Hr.	Daily	Hr.	Daily	Bare Costs	Incl. O&P	
1 Labor Foreman (outside)	$49.25	$394.00	$73.30	$586.40	$47.65	$70.94	
4 Laborers	47.25	1512.00	70.35	2251.20			
1 Drill Rig, Truck-Mounted		856.23		941.85			
1 Flatbed Truck, Gas, 3 Ton		391.02		430.12	31.18	34.30	
40 L.H., Daily Totals		$3153.25		$4209.57	$78.83	$105.24	
Crew B-23A	Hr.	Daily	Hr.	Daily	Bare Costs	Incl. O&P	
1 Labor Foreman (outside)	$49.25	$394.00	$73.30	$586.40	$53.18	$79.15	
1 Laborer	47.25	378.00	70.35	562.80			
1 Equip. Oper. (medium)	63.05	504.40	93.80	750.40			
1 Drill Rig, Truck-Mounted		856.23		941.85			
1 Pickup Truck, 3/4 Ton		122.56		134.82	40.78	44.86	
24 L.H., Daily Totals		$2255.19		$2976.27	$93.97	$124.01	
Crew B-23B	Hr.	Daily	Hr.	Daily	Bare Costs	Incl. O&P	
1 Labor Foreman (outside)	$49.25	$394.00	$73.30	$586.40	$53.18	$79.15	
1 Laborer	47.25	378.00	70.35	562.80			
1 Equip. Oper. (medium)	63.05	504.40	93.80	750.40			
1 Drill Rig, Truck-Mounted		856.23		941.85			
1 Pickup Truck, 3/4 Ton		122.56		134.82			
1 Centr. Water Pump, 6"		386.48		425.13	56.89	62.57	
24 L.H., Daily Totals		$2641.67		$3401.40	$110.07	$141.72	
Crew B-24	Hr.	Daily	Hr.	Daily	Bare Costs	Incl. O&P	
1 Cement Finisher	$55.00	$440.00	$80.45	$643.60	$53.62	$79.35	
1 Laborer	47.25	378.00	70.35	562.80			
1 Carpenter	58.60	468.80	87.25	698.00			
24 L.H., Daily Totals		$1286.80		$1904.40	$53.62	$79.35	

Crew No.		Bare Costs		Incl. Subs O&P		Cost Per Labor-Hour	
Crew B-25	Hr.	Daily	Hr.	Daily	Bare Costs	Incl. O&P	
1 Labor Foreman (outside)	$49.25	$394.00	$73.30	$586.40	$51.74	$77.01	
7 Laborers	47.25	2646.00	70.35	3939.60			
3 Equip. Oper. (medium)	63.05	1513.20	93.80	2251.20			
1 Asphalt Paver, 130 H.P.		2352.46		2587.71			
1 Tandem Roller, 10 Ton		379.22		417.14			
1 Roller, Pneum. Whl., 12 Ton		384.55		423.01	35.41	38.95	
88 L.H., Daily Totals		$7669.43		$10205.05	$87.15	$115.97	
Crew B-25B	Hr.	Daily	Hr.	Daily	Bare Costs	Incl. O&P	
1 Labor Foreman (outside)	$49.25	$394.00	$73.30	$586.40	$52.68	$78.41	
7 Laborers	47.25	2646.00	70.35	3939.60			
4 Equip. Oper. (medium)	63.05	2017.60	93.80	3001.60			
1 Asphalt Paver, 130 H.P.		2352.46		2587.71			
2 Tandem Rollers, 10 Ton		758.44		834.28			
1 Roller, Pneum. Whl., 12 Ton		384.55		423.01	36.41	40.05	
96 L.H., Daily Totals		$8553.05		$11372.59	$89.09	$118.46	
Crew B-25C	Hr.	Daily	Hr.	Daily	Bare Costs	Incl. O&P	
1 Labor Foreman (outside)	$49.25	$394.00	$73.30	$586.40	$52.85	$78.66	
3 Laborers	47.25	1134.00	70.35	1688.40			
2 Equip. Oper. (medium)	63.05	1008.80	93.80	1500.80			
1 Asphalt Paver, 130 H.P.		2352.46		2587.71			
1 Tandem Roller, 10 Ton		379.22		417.14	56.91	62.60	
48 L.H., Daily Totals		$5268.48		$6780.45	$109.76	$141.26	
Crew B-25D	Hr.	Daily	Hr.	Daily	Bare Costs	Incl. O&P	
1 Labor Foreman (outside)	$49.25	$394.00	$73.30	$586.40	$53.12	$79.06	
3 Laborers	47.25	1134.00	70.35	1688.40			
2.130 Equip. Oper. (medium)	63.05	1074.37	93.80	1598.35			
.13 Truck Driver (heavy)	55.45	57.67	82.85	86.16			
.13 Truck Tractor, 6x4, 380 H.P.		70.98		78.08			
.13 Dist. Tanker, 3000 Gallon		47.72		52.50			
1 Asphalt Paver, 130 H.P.		2352.46		2587.71			
1 Tandem Roller, 10 Ton		379.22		417.14	56.92	62.61	
50.08 L.H., Daily Totals		$5510.42		$7094.73	$110.03	$141.67	
Crew B-25E	Hr.	Daily	Hr.	Daily	Bare Costs	Incl. O&P	
1 Labor Foreman (outside)	$49.25	$394.00	$73.30	$586.40	$53.34	$79.40	
3 Laborers	47.25	1134.00	70.35	1688.40			
2.250 Equip. Oper. (medium)	63.05	1134.90	93.80	1688.40			
.25 Truck Driver (heavy)	55.45	110.90	82.85	165.70			
.25 Truck Tractor, 6x4, 380 H.P.		136.50		150.14			
.25 Dist. Tanker, 3000 Gallon		91.78		100.95			
1 Asphalt Paver, 130 H.P.		2352.46		2587.71			
1 Tandem Roller, 10 Ton		379.22		417.14	56.92	62.61	
52 L.H., Daily Totals		$5733.75		$7384.85	$110.26	$142.02	
Crew B-26	Hr.	Daily	Hr.	Daily	Bare Costs	Incl. O&P	
1 Labor Foreman (outside)	$49.25	$394.00	$73.30	$586.40	$52.58	$78.17	
6 Laborers	47.25	2268.00	70.35	3376.80			
2 Equip. Oper. (medium)	63.05	1008.80	93.80	1500.80			
1 Rodman (reinf.)	64.55	516.40	96.40	771.20			
1 Cement Finisher	55.00	440.00	80.45	643.60			
1 Grader, 30,000 Lbs.		1091.19		1200.31			
1 Paving Mach. & Equip.		2747.64		3022.40	43.62	47.99	
88 L.H., Daily Totals		$8466.03		$11101.51	$96.20	$126.15	

Crews - Standard

Crew No.	Bare Costs		Incl. Subs O&P		Cost Per Labor-Hour	
Crew B-26A	Hr.	Daily	Hr.	Daily	Bare Costs	Incl. O&P
1 Labor Foreman (outside)	$49.25	$394.00	$73.30	$586.40	$52.58	$78.17
6 Laborers	47.25	2268.00	70.35	3376.80		
2 Equip. Oper. (medium)	63.05	1008.80	93.80	1500.80		
1 Rodman (reinf.)	64.55	516.40	96.40	771.20		
1 Cement Finisher	55.00	440.00	80.45	643.60		
1 Grader, 30,000 Lbs.		1091.19		1200.31		
1 Paving Mach. & Equip.		2747.64		3022.40		
1 Concrete Saw		176.00		193.60	45.62	50.19
88 L.H., Daily Totals		$8642.03		$11295.11	$98.20	$128.35

Crew No.	Bare Costs		Incl. Subs O&P		Cost Per Labor-Hour	
Crew B-26B	Hr.	Daily	Hr.	Daily	Bare Costs	Incl. O&P
1 Labor Foreman (outside)	$49.25	$394.00	$73.30	$586.40	$53.45	$79.47
6 Laborers	47.25	2268.00	70.35	3376.80		
3 Equip. Oper. (medium)	63.05	1513.20	93.80	2251.20		
1 Rodman (reinf.)	64.55	516.40	96.40	771.20		
1 Cement Finisher	55.00	440.00	80.45	643.60		
1 Grader, 30,000 Lbs.		1091.19		1200.31		
1 Paving Mach. & Equip.		2747.64		3022.40		
1 Concrete Pump, 110' Boom		1069.53		1176.48	51.13	56.24
96 L.H., Daily Totals		$10039.96		$13028.40	$104.58	$135.71

Crew No.	Bare Costs		Incl. Subs O&P		Cost Per Labor-Hour	
Crew B-26C	Hr.	Daily	Hr.	Daily	Bare Costs	Incl. O&P
1 Labor Foreman (outside)	$49.25	$394.00	$73.30	$586.40	$51.53	$76.61
6 Laborers	47.25	2268.00	70.35	3376.80		
1 Equip. Oper. (medium)	63.05	504.40	93.80	750.40		
1 Rodman (reinf.)	64.55	516.40	96.40	771.20		
1 Cement Finisher	55.00	440.00	80.45	643.60		
1 Paving Mach. & Equip.		2747.64		3022.40		
1 Concrete Saw		176.00		193.60	36.55	40.20
80 L.H., Daily Totals		$7046.44		$9344.40	$88.08	$116.81

Crew No.	Bare Costs		Incl. Subs O&P		Cost Per Labor-Hour	
Crew B-27	Hr.	Daily	Hr.	Daily	Bare Costs	Incl. O&P
1 Labor Foreman (outside)	$49.25	$394.00	$73.30	$586.40	$47.75	$71.09
3 Laborers	47.25	1134.00	70.35	1688.40		
1 Berm Machine		897.16		986.88	28.04	30.84
32 L.H., Daily Totals		$2425.16		$3261.68	$75.79	$101.93

Crew No.	Bare Costs		Incl. Subs O&P		Cost Per Labor-Hour	
Crew B-28	Hr.	Daily	Hr.	Daily	Bare Costs	Incl. O&P
2 Carpenters	$58.60	$937.60	$87.25	$1396.00	$54.82	$81.62
1 Laborer	47.25	378.00	70.35	562.80		
24 L.H., Daily Totals		$1315.60		$1958.80	$54.82	$81.62

Crew No.	Bare Costs		Incl. Subs O&P		Cost Per Labor-Hour	
Crew B-29	Hr.	Daily	Hr.	Daily	Bare Costs	Incl. O&P
1 Labor Foreman (outside)	$49.25	$394.00	$73.30	$586.40	$51.56	$76.75
4 Laborers	47.25	1512.00	70.35	2251.20		
1 Equip. Oper. (crane)	66.30	530.40	98.65	789.20		
1 Equip. Oper. (oiler)	56.40	451.20	83.90	671.20		
1 Gradall, 5/8 C.Y.		880.91		969.00	15.73	17.30
56 L.H., Daily Totals		$3768.51		$5267.00	$67.29	$94.05

Crew No.	Bare Costs		Incl. Subs O&P		Cost Per Labor-Hour	
Crew B-30	Hr.	Daily	Hr.	Daily	Bare Costs	Incl. O&P
1 Equip. Oper. (medium)	$63.05	$504.40	$93.80	$750.40	$57.98	$86.50
2 Truck Drivers (heavy)	55.45	887.20	82.85	1325.60		
1 Hyd. Excavator, 1.5 C.Y.		1185.24		1303.76		
2 Dump Trucks, 12 C.Y., 400 H.P.		1582.72		1740.99	115.33	126.86
24 L.H., Daily Totals		$4159.56		$5120.76	$173.32	$213.36

Crew No.	Bare Costs		Incl. Subs O&P		Cost Per Labor-Hour	
Crew B-31	Hr.	Daily	Hr.	Daily	Bare Costs	Incl. O&P
1 Labor Foreman (outside)	$49.25	$394.00	$73.30	$586.40	$49.92	$74.32
3 Laborers	47.25	1134.00	70.35	1688.40		
1 Carpenter	58.60	468.80	87.25	698.00		
1 Air Compressor, 250 cfm		196.28		215.91		
1 Sheeting Driver		8.19		9.01		
2 -50' Air Hoses, 1.5"		47.20		51.92	6.29	6.92
40 L.H., Daily Totals		$2248.47		$3249.64	$56.21	$81.24

Crew No.	Bare Costs		Incl. Subs O&P		Cost Per Labor-Hour	
Crew B-32	Hr.	Daily	Hr.	Daily	Bare Costs	Incl. O&P
1 Laborer	$47.25	$378.00	$70.35	$562.80	$59.10	$87.94
3 Equip. Oper. (medium)	63.05	1513.20	93.80	2251.20		
1 Grader, 30,000 Lbs.		1091.19		1200.31		
1 Tandem Roller, 10 Ton		379.22		417.14		
1 Dozer, 200 H.P.		1382.36		1520.60	89.15	98.06
32 L.H., Daily Totals		$4743.97		$5952.05	$148.25	$186.00

Crew No.	Bare Costs		Incl. Subs O&P		Cost Per Labor-Hour	
Crew B-32A	Hr.	Daily	Hr.	Daily	Bare Costs	Incl. O&P
1 Laborer	$47.25	$378.00	$70.35	$562.80	$57.78	$85.98
2 Equip. Oper. (medium)	63.05	1008.80	93.80	1500.80		
1 Grader, 30,000 Lbs.		1091.19		1200.31		
1 Roller, Vibratory, 25 Ton		529.68		582.65	67.54	74.29
24 L.H., Daily Totals		$3007.67		$3846.56	$125.32	$160.27

Crew No.	Bare Costs		Incl. Subs O&P		Cost Per Labor-Hour	
Crew B-32B	Hr.	Daily	Hr.	Daily	Bare Costs	Incl. O&P
1 Laborer	$47.25	$378.00	$70.35	$562.80	$57.78	$85.98
2 Equip. Oper. (medium)	63.05	1008.80	93.80	1500.80		
1 Dozer, 200 H.P.		1382.36		1520.60		
1 Roller, Vibratory, 25 Ton		529.68		582.65	79.67	87.64
24 L.H., Daily Totals		$3298.84		$4166.84	$137.45	$173.62

Crew No.	Bare Costs		Incl. Subs O&P		Cost Per Labor-Hour	
Crew B-32C	Hr.	Daily	Hr.	Daily	Bare Costs	Incl. O&P
1 Labor Foreman (outside)	$49.25	$394.00	$73.30	$586.40	$55.48	$82.57
2 Laborers	47.25	756.00	70.35	1125.60		
3 Equip. Oper. (medium)	63.05	1513.20	93.80	2251.20		
1 Grader, 30,000 Lbs.		1091.19		1200.31		
1 Tandem Roller, 10 Ton		379.22		417.14		
1 Dozer, 200 H.P.		1382.36		1520.60	59.43	65.38
48 L.H., Daily Totals		$5515.97		$7101.25	$114.92	$147.94

Crew No.	Bare Costs		Incl. Subs O&P		Cost Per Labor-Hour	
Crew B-33A	Hr.	Daily	Hr.	Daily	Bare Costs	Incl. O&P
1 Equip. Oper. (medium)	$63.05	$504.40	$93.80	$750.40	$58.54	$87.10
.5 Laborer	47.25	189.00	70.35	281.40		
.25 Equip. Oper. (medium)	63.05	126.10	93.80	187.60		
1 Scraper, Towed, 7 C.Y.		141.88		156.07		
1.25 Dozers, 300 H.P.		2093.16		2302.48	159.65	175.61
14 L.H., Daily Totals		$3054.54		$3677.95	$218.18	$262.71

Crew No.	Bare Costs		Incl. Subs O&P		Cost Per Labor-Hour	
Crew B-33B	Hr.	Daily	Hr.	Daily	Bare Costs	Incl. O&P
1 Equip. Oper. (medium)	$63.05	$504.40	$93.80	$750.40	$58.54	$87.10
.5 Laborer	47.25	189.00	70.35	281.40		
.25 Equip. Oper. (medium)	63.05	126.10	93.80	187.60		
1 Scraper, Towed, 10 C.Y.		177.45		195.19		
1.25 Dozers, 300 H.P.		2093.16		2302.48	162.19	178.41
14 L.H., Daily Totals		$3090.11		$3717.07	$220.72	$265.51

Crews - Standard

Crew No.	Bare Costs		Incl. Subs O&P		Cost Per Labor-Hour	
Crew B-33C	**Hr.**	**Daily**	**Hr.**	**Daily**	**Bare Costs**	**Incl. O&P**
1 Equip. Oper. (medium)	$63.05	$504.40	$93.80	$750.40	$58.54	$87.10
.5 Laborer	47.25	189.00	70.35	281.40		
.25 Equip. Oper. (medium)	63.05	126.10	93.80	187.60		
1 Scraper, Towed, 15 C.Y.		196.46		216.11		
1.25 Dozers, 300 H.P.		2093.16		2302.48	163.54	179.90
14 L.H., Daily Totals		$3109.12		$3737.98	$222.08	$267.00
Crew B-33D	**Hr.**	**Daily**	**Hr.**	**Daily**	**Bare Costs**	**Incl. O&P**
1 Equip. Oper. (medium)	$63.05	$504.40	$93.80	$750.40	$58.54	$87.10
.5 Laborer	47.25	189.00	70.35	281.40		
.25 Equip. Oper. (medium)	63.05	126.10	93.80	187.60		
1 S.P. Scraper, 14 C.Y.		2168.71		2385.58		
.25 Dozer, 300 H.P.		418.63		460.50	184.81	203.29
14 L.H., Daily Totals		$3406.84		$4065.48	$243.35	$290.39
Crew B-33E	**Hr.**	**Daily**	**Hr.**	**Daily**	**Bare Costs**	**Incl. O&P**
1 Equip. Oper. (medium)	$63.05	$504.40	$93.80	$750.40	$58.54	$87.10
.5 Laborer	47.25	189.00	70.35	281.40		
.25 Equip. Oper. (medium)	63.05	126.10	93.80	187.60		
1 S.P. Scraper, 21 C.Y.		2239.60		2463.56		
.25 Dozer, 300 H.P.		418.63		460.50	189.87	208.86
14 L.H., Daily Totals		$3477.73		$4143.46	$248.41	$295.96
Crew B-33F	**Hr.**	**Daily**	**Hr.**	**Daily**	**Bare Costs**	**Incl. O&P**
1 Equip. Oper. (medium)	$63.05	$504.40	$93.80	$750.40	$58.54	$87.10
.5 Laborer	47.25	189.00	70.35	281.40		
.25 Equip. Oper. (medium)	63.05	126.10	93.80	187.60		
1 Elev. Scraper, 11 C.Y.		1022.46		1124.71		
.25 Dozer, 300 H.P.		418.63		460.50	102.94	113.23
14 L.H., Daily Totals		$2260.59		$2804.60	$161.47	$200.33
Crew B-33G	**Hr.**	**Daily**	**Hr.**	**Daily**	**Bare Costs**	**Incl. O&P**
1 Equip. Oper. (medium)	$63.05	$504.40	$93.80	$750.40	$58.54	$87.10
.5 Laborer	47.25	189.00	70.35	281.40		
.25 Equip. Oper. (medium)	63.05	126.10	93.80	187.60		
1 Elev. Scraper, 22 C.Y.		2005.03		2205.53		
.25 Dozer, 300 H.P.		418.63		460.50	173.12	190.43
14 L.H., Daily Totals		$3243.16		$3885.43	$231.65	$277.53
Crew B-33H	**Hr.**	**Daily**	**Hr.**	**Daily**	**Bare Costs**	**Incl. O&P**
.5 Laborer	$47.25	$189.00	$70.35	$281.40	$58.54	$87.10
1 Equipment Operator (med.)	63.05	504.40	93.80	750.40		
.25 Equipment Operator (med.)	63.05	126.10	93.80	187.60		
1 S.P. Scraper, 44 C.Y.		3440.19		3784.21		
.25 Dozer, 410 H.P.		633.99		697.39	291.01	320.11
14 L.H., Daily Totals		$4893.68		$5701.00	$349.55	$407.21
Crew B-33J	**Hr.**	**Daily**	**Hr.**	**Daily**	**Bare Costs**	**Incl. O&P**
1 Equipment Operator (med.)	$63.05	$504.40	$93.80	$750.40	$63.05	$93.80
1 S.P. Scraper, 14 C.Y.		2168.71		2385.58	271.09	298.20
8 L.H., Daily Totals		$2673.11		$3135.98	$334.14	$392.00
Crew B-33K	**Hr.**	**Daily**	**Hr.**	**Daily**	**Bare Costs**	**Incl. O&P**
1 Equipment Operator (med.)	$63.05	$504.40	$93.80	$750.40	$58.54	$87.10
.25 Equipment Operator (med.)	63.05	126.10	93.80	187.60		
.5 Laborer	47.25	189.00	70.35	281.40		
1 S.P. Scraper, 31 C.Y.		2972.09		3269.30		
.25 Dozer, 410 H.P.		633.99		697.39	257.58	283.33
14 L.H., Daily Totals		$4425.58		$5186.09	$316.11	$370.43

Crew No.	Bare Costs		Incl. Subs O&P		Cost Per Labor-Hour	
Crew B-34A	**Hr.**	**Daily**	**Hr.**	**Daily**	**Bare Costs**	**Incl. O&P**
1 Truck Driver (heavy)	$55.45	$443.60	$82.85	$662.80	$55.45	$82.85
1 Dump Truck, 8 C.Y., 220 H.P.		417.49		459.24	52.19	57.40
8 L.H., Daily Totals		$861.09		$1122.04	$107.64	$140.25
Crew B-34B	**Hr.**	**Daily**	**Hr.**	**Daily**	**Bare Costs**	**Incl. O&P**
1 Truck Driver (heavy)	$55.45	$443.60	$82.85	$662.80	$55.45	$82.85
1 Dump Truck, 12 C.Y., 400 H.P.		791.36		870.50	98.92	108.81
8 L.H., Daily Totals		$1234.96		$1533.30	$154.37	$191.66
Crew B-34C	**Hr.**	**Daily**	**Hr.**	**Daily**	**Bare Costs**	**Incl. O&P**
1 Truck Driver (heavy)	$55.45	$443.60	$82.85	$662.80	$55.45	$82.85
1 Truck Tractor, 6x4, 380 H.P.		545.98		600.58		
1 Dump Trailer, 16.5 C.Y.		151.94		167.13	87.24	95.96
8 L.H., Daily Totals		$1141.52		$1430.51	$142.69	$178.81
Crew B-34D	**Hr.**	**Daily**	**Hr.**	**Daily**	**Bare Costs**	**Incl. O&P**
1 Truck Driver (heavy)	$55.45	$443.60	$82.85	$662.80	$55.45	$82.85
1 Truck Tractor, 6x4, 380 H.P.		545.98		600.58		
1 Dump Trailer, 20 C.Y.		168.66		185.53	89.33	98.26
8 L.H., Daily Totals		$1158.24		$1448.90	$144.78	$181.11
Crew B-34E	**Hr.**	**Daily**	**Hr.**	**Daily**	**Bare Costs**	**Incl. O&P**
1 Truck Driver (heavy)	$55.45	$443.60	$82.85	$662.80	$55.45	$82.85
1 Dump Truck, Off Hwy., 25 Ton		1471.16		1618.28	183.90	202.28
8 L.H., Daily Totals		$1914.76		$2281.08	$239.35	$285.13
Crew B-34F	**Hr.**	**Daily**	**Hr.**	**Daily**	**Bare Costs**	**Incl. O&P**
1 Truck Driver (heavy)	$55.45	$443.60	$82.85	$662.80	$55.45	$82.85
1 Dump Truck, Off Hwy., 35 Ton		1508.36		1659.20	188.54	207.40
8 L.H., Daily Totals		$1951.96		$2322.00	$244.00	$290.25
Crew B-34G	**Hr.**	**Daily**	**Hr.**	**Daily**	**Bare Costs**	**Incl. O&P**
1 Truck Driver (heavy)	$55.45	$443.60	$82.85	$662.80	$55.45	$82.85
1 Dump Truck, Off Hwy., 50 Ton		2037.60		2241.36	254.70	280.17
8 L.H., Daily Totals		$2481.20		$2904.16	$310.15	$363.02
Crew B-34H	**Hr.**	**Daily**	**Hr.**	**Daily**	**Bare Costs**	**Incl. O&P**
1 Truck Driver (heavy)	$55.45	$443.60	$82.85	$662.80	$55.45	$82.85
1 Dump Truck, Off Hwy., 65 Ton		2126.70		2339.37	265.84	292.42
8 L.H., Daily Totals		$2570.30		$3002.17	$321.29	$375.27
Crew B-34I	**Hr.**	**Daily**	**Hr.**	**Daily**	**Bare Costs**	**Incl. O&P**
1 Truck Driver (heavy)	$55.45	$443.60	$82.85	$662.80	$55.45	$82.85
1 Dump Truck, 18 C.Y., 450 H.P.		788.42		867.26	98.55	108.41
8 L.H., Daily Totals		$1232.02		$1530.06	$154.00	$191.26
Crew B-34J	**Hr.**	**Daily**	**Hr.**	**Daily**	**Bare Costs**	**Incl. O&P**
1 Truck Driver (heavy)	$55.45	$443.60	$82.85	$662.80	$55.45	$82.85
1 Dump Truck, Off Hwy., 100 Ton		3040.18		3344.20	380.02	418.02
8 L.H., Daily Totals		$3483.78		$4007.00	$435.47	$500.87
Crew B-34K	**Hr.**	**Daily**	**Hr.**	**Daily**	**Bare Costs**	**Incl. O&P**
1 Truck Driver (heavy)	$55.45	$443.60	$82.85	$662.80	$55.45	$82.85
1 Truck Tractor, 6x4, 450 H.P.		666.04		732.64		
1 Lowbed Trailer, 75 Ton		283.47		311.82	118.69	130.56
8 L.H., Daily Totals		$1393.11		$1707.26	$174.14	$213.41

Crews - Standard

Crew No.	Bare Costs		Incl. Subs O&P		Cost Per Labor-Hour	
Crew B-34L	Hr.	Daily	Hr.	Daily	Bare Costs	Incl. O&P
1 Equip. Oper. (light)	$59.70	$477.60	$88.85	$710.80	$59.70	$88.85
1 Flatbed Truck, Gas, 1.5 Ton		361.95		398.14	45.24	49.77
8 L.H., Daily Totals		$839.55		$1108.94	$104.94	$138.62
Crew B-34M	Hr.	Daily	Hr.	Daily	Bare Costs	Incl. O&P
1 Equip. Oper. (light)	$59.70	$477.60	$88.85	$710.80	$59.70	$88.85
1 Flatbed Truck, Gas, 3 Ton		391.02		430.12	48.88	53.77
8 L.H., Daily Totals		$868.62		$1140.92	$108.58	$142.62
Crew B-34N	Hr.	Daily	Hr.	Daily	Bare Costs	Incl. O&P
1 Truck Driver (heavy)	$55.45	$443.60	$82.85	$662.80	$59.25	$88.33
1 Equip. Oper. (medium)	63.05	504.40	93.80	750.40		
1 Truck Tractor, 6x4, 380 H.P.		545.98		600.58		
1 Flatbed Trailer, 40 Ton		206.92		227.61	47.06	51.76
16 L.H., Daily Totals		$1700.90		$2241.39	$106.31	$140.09
Crew B-34P	Hr.	Daily	Hr.	Daily	Bare Costs	Incl. O&P
1 Pipe Fitter	$72.55	$580.40	$108.20	$865.60	$62.83	$93.67
1 Truck Driver (light)	52.90	423.20	79.00	632.00		
1 Equip. Oper. (medium)	63.05	504.40	93.80	750.40		
1 Flatbed Truck, Gas, 3 Ton		391.02		430.12		
1 Backhoe Loader, 48 H.P.		277.19		304.91	27.84	30.63
24 L.H., Daily Totals		$2176.21		$2983.03	$90.68	$124.29
Crew B-34Q	Hr.	Daily	Hr.	Daily	Bare Costs	Incl. O&P
1 Pipe Fitter	$72.55	$580.40	$108.20	$865.60	$63.92	$95.28
1 Truck Driver (light)	52.90	423.20	79.00	632.00		
1 Equip. Oper. (crane)	66.30	530.40	98.65	789.20		
1 Flatbed Trailer, 25 Ton		150.61		165.67		
1 Dump Truck, 8 C.Y., 220 H.P.		417.49		459.24		
1 Hyd. Crane, 25 Ton		2273.31		2500.64	118.39	130.23
24 L.H., Daily Totals		$4375.41		$5412.35	$182.31	$225.51
Crew B-34R	Hr.	Daily	Hr.	Daily	Bare Costs	Incl. O&P
1 Pipe Fitter	$72.55	$580.40	$108.20	$865.60	$63.92	$95.28
1 Truck Driver (light)	52.90	423.20	79.00	632.00		
1 Equip. Oper. (crane)	66.30	530.40	98.65	789.20		
1 Flatbed Trailer, 25 Ton		150.61		165.67		
1 Dump Truck, 8 C.Y., 220 H.P.		417.49		459.24		
1 Hyd. Crane, 25 Ton		2273.31		2500.64		
1 Hyd. Excavator, 1 C.Y.		986.56		1085.22	159.50	175.45
24 L.H., Daily Totals		$5361.97		$6497.57	$223.42	$270.73
Crew B-34S	Hr.	Daily	Hr.	Daily	Bare Costs	Incl. O&P
2 Pipe Fitters	$72.55	$1160.80	$108.20	$1731.20	$66.71	$99.47
1 Truck Driver (heavy)	55.45	443.60	82.85	662.80		
1 Equip. Oper. (crane)	66.30	530.40	98.65	789.20		
1 Flatbed Trailer, 40 Ton		206.92		227.61		
1 Truck Tractor, 6x4, 380 H.P.		545.98		600.58		
1 Hyd. Crane, 80 Ton		2641.70		2905.87		
1 Hyd. Excavator, 2 C.Y.		1096.14		1205.75	140.34	154.37
32 L.H., Daily Totals		$6625.54		$8123.01	$207.05	$253.84
Crew B-34T	Hr.	Daily	Hr.	Daily	Bare Costs	Incl. O&P
2 Pipe Fitters	$72.55	$1160.80	$108.20	$1731.20	$66.71	$99.47
1 Truck Driver (heavy)	55.45	443.60	82.85	662.80		
1 Equip. Oper. (crane)	66.30	530.40	98.65	789.20		
1 Flatbed Trailer, 40 Ton		206.92		227.61		
1 Truck Tractor, 6x4, 380 H.P.		545.98		600.58		
1 Hyd. Crane, 80 Ton		2641.70		2905.87	106.08	116.69
32 L.H., Daily Totals		$5529.40		$6917.26	$172.79	$216.16

Crew No.	Bare Costs		Incl. Subs O&P		Cost Per Labor-Hour	
Crew B-34U	Hr.	Daily	Hr.	Daily	Bare Costs	Incl. O&P
1 Truck Driver (heavy)	$55.45	$443.60	$82.85	$662.80	$57.58	$85.85
1 Equip. Oper. (light)	59.70	477.60	88.85	710.80		
1 Truck Tractor, 220 H.P.		339.98		373.98		
1 Flatbed Trailer, 25 Ton		150.61		165.67	30.66	33.73
16 L.H., Daily Totals		$1411.79		$1913.25	$88.24	$119.58
Crew B-34V	Hr.	Daily	Hr.	Daily	Bare Costs	Incl. O&P
1 Truck Driver (heavy)	$55.45	$443.60	$82.85	$662.80	$60.48	$90.12
1 Equip. Oper. (crane)	66.30	530.40	98.65	789.20		
1 Equip. Oper. (light)	59.70	477.60	88.85	710.80		
1 Truck Tractor, 6x4, 450 H.P.		666.04		732.64		
1 Equipment Trailer, 50 Ton		336.69		370.36		
1 Pickup Truck, 4x4, 3/4 Ton		191.73		210.90	49.77	54.75
24 L.H., Daily Totals		$2646.06		$3476.71	$110.25	$144.86
Crew B-34W	Hr.	Daily	Hr.	Daily	Bare Costs	Incl. O&P
5 Truck Drivers (heavy)	$55.45	$2218.00	$82.85	$3314.00	$58.17	$86.74
2 Equip. Opers. (crane)	66.30	1060.80	98.65	1578.40		
1 Equip. Oper. (mechanic)	66.40	531.20	98.80	790.40		
1 Laborer	47.25	378.00	70.35	562.80		
4 Truck Tractors, 6x4, 380 H.P.		2183.92		2402.31		
2 Equipment Trailers, 50 Ton		673.38		740.72		
2 Flatbed Trailers, 40 Ton		413.84		455.22		
1 Pickup Truck, 4x4, 3/4 Ton		191.73		210.90		
1 S.P. Crane, 4x4, 20 Ton		760.97		837.07	58.66	64.53
72 L.H., Daily Totals		$8411.84		$10891.82	$116.83	$151.28
Crew B-35	Hr.	Daily	Hr.	Daily	Bare Costs	Incl. O&P
1 Labor Foreman (outside)	$49.25	$394.00	$73.30	$586.40	$60.65	$90.44
1 Skilled Worker	61.25	490.00	92.00	736.00		
2 Welders	72.05	1152.80	107.45	1719.20		
1 Laborer	47.25	378.00	70.35	562.80		
1 Equip. Oper. (crane)	66.30	530.40	98.65	789.20		
1 Equip. Oper. (oiler)	56.40	451.20	83.90	671.20		
2 Welder, Electric, 300 amp		128.34		141.17		
1 Hyd. Excavator, .75 C.Y.		915.34		1006.87	18.64	20.50
56 L.H., Daily Totals		$4440.08		$6212.85	$79.29	$110.94
Crew B-35A	Hr.	Daily	Hr.	Daily	Bare Costs	Incl. O&P
1 Labor Foreman (outside)	$49.25	$394.00	$73.30	$586.40	$57.11	$85.14
2 Laborers	47.25	756.00	70.35	1125.60		
1 Skilled Worker	61.25	490.00	92.00	736.00		
1 Welder (plumber)	72.05	576.40	107.45	859.60		
1 Equip. Oper. (crane)	66.30	530.40	98.65	789.20		
1 Equip. Oper. (oiler)	56.40	451.20	83.90	671.20		
1 Welder, Gas Engine, 300 amp		147.09		161.80		
1 Crawler Crane, 75 Ton		2189.46		2408.41	41.72	45.90
56 L.H., Daily Totals		$5534.55		$7338.20	$98.83	$131.04
Crew B-36	Hr.	Daily	Hr.	Daily	Bare Costs	Incl. O&P
1 Labor Foreman (outside)	$49.25	$394.00	$73.30	$586.40	$53.97	$80.32
2 Laborers	47.25	756.00	70.35	1125.60		
2 Equip. Oper. (medium)	63.05	1008.80	93.80	1500.80		
1 Dozer, 200 H.P.		1382.36		1520.60		
1 Aggregate Spreader		67.49		74.24		
1 Tandem Roller, 10 Ton		379.22		417.14	45.73	50.30
40 L.H., Daily Totals		$3987.87		$5224.78	$99.70	$130.62

Crews - Standard

Crew No.	Bare Costs		Incl. Subs O&P		Cost Per Labor-Hour	
Crew B-36A	Hr.	Daily	Hr.	Daily	Bare Costs	Incl. O&P
1 Labor Foreman (outside)	$49.25	$394.00	$73.30	$586.40	$56.56	$84.17
2 Laborers	47.25	756.00	70.35	1125.60		
4 Equip. Oper. (medium)	63.05	2017.60	93.80	3001.60		
1 Dozer, 200 H.P.		1382.36		1520.60		
1 Aggregate Spreader		67.49		74.24		
1 Tandem Roller, 10 Ton		379.22		417.14		
1 Roller, Pneum. Whl., 12 Ton		384.55		423.01	39.53	43.48
56 L.H., Daily Totals		$5381.22		$7148.58	$96.09	$127.65
Crew B-36B	Hr.	Daily	Hr.	Daily	Bare Costs	Incl. O&P
1 Labor Foreman (outside)	$49.25	$394.00	$73.30	$586.40	$56.42	$84.01
2 Laborers	47.25	756.00	70.35	1125.60		
4 Equip. Oper. (medium)	63.05	2017.60	93.80	3001.60		
1 Truck Driver (heavy)	55.45	443.60	82.85	662.80		
1 Grader, 30,000 Lbs.		1091.19		1200.31		
1 F.E. Loader, Crl, 1.5 C.Y.		733.70		807.07		
1 Dozer, 300 H.P.		1674.53		1841.98		
1 Roller, Vibratory, 25 Ton		529.68		582.65		
1 Truck Tractor, 6x4, 450 H.P.		666.04		732.64		
1 Water Tank Trailer, 5000 Gal.		169.14		186.05	76.00	83.60
64 L.H., Daily Totals		$8475.48		$10727.11	$132.43	$167.61
Crew B-36C	Hr.	Daily	Hr.	Daily	Bare Costs	Incl. O&P
1 Labor Foreman (outside)	$49.25	$394.00	$73.30	$586.40	$58.77	$87.51
3 Equip. Oper. (medium)	63.05	1513.20	93.80	2251.20		
1 Truck Driver (heavy)	55.45	443.60	82.85	662.80		
1 Grader, 30,000 Lbs.		1091.19		1200.31		
1 Dozer, 300 H.P.		1674.53		1841.98		
1 Roller, Vibratory, 25 Ton		529.68		582.65		
1 Truck Tractor, 6x4, 450 H.P.		666.04		732.64		
1 Water Tank Trailer, 5000 Gal.		169.14		186.05	103.26	113.59
40 L.H., Daily Totals		$6481.38		$8044.04	$162.03	$201.10
Crew B-36D	Hr.	Daily	Hr.	Daily	Bare Costs	Incl. O&P
1 Labor Foreman (outside)	$49.25	$394.00	$73.30	$586.40	$59.60	$88.67
3 Equip. Oper. (medium)	63.05	1513.20	93.80	2251.20		
1 Grader, 30,000 Lbs.		1091.19		1200.31		
1 Dozer, 300 H.P.		1674.53		1841.98		
1 Roller, Vibratory, 25 Ton		529.68		582.65	102.98	113.28
32 L.H., Daily Totals		$5202.60		$6462.54	$162.58	$201.95
Crew B-37	Hr.	Daily	Hr.	Daily	Bare Costs	Incl. O&P
1 Labor Foreman (outside)	$49.25	$394.00	$73.30	$586.40	$49.66	$73.92
4 Laborers	47.25	1512.00	70.35	2251.20		
1 Equip. Oper. (light)	59.70	477.60	88.85	710.80		
1 Tandem Roller, 5 Ton		287.45		316.19	5.99	6.59
48 L.H., Daily Totals		$2671.05		$3864.59	$55.65	$80.51
Crew B-37A	Hr.	Daily	Hr.	Daily	Bare Costs	Incl. O&P
2 Laborers	$47.25	$756.00	$70.35	$1125.60	$49.13	$73.23
1 Truck Driver (light)	52.90	423.20	79.00	632.00		
1 Flatbed Truck, Gas, 1.5 Ton		361.95		398.14		
1 Tar Kettle, T.M.		199.54		219.49	23.40	25.73
24 L.H., Daily Totals		$1740.69		$2375.24	$72.53	$98.97
Crew B-37B	Hr.	Daily	Hr.	Daily	Bare Costs	Incl. O&P
3 Laborers	$47.25	$1134.00	$70.35	$1688.40	$48.66	$72.51
1 Truck Driver (light)	52.90	423.20	79.00	632.00		
1 Flatbed Truck, Gas, 1.5 Ton		361.95		398.14		
1 Tar Kettle, T.M.		199.54		219.49	17.55	19.30
32 L.H., Daily Totals		$2118.69		$2938.04	$66.21	$91.81

Crew No.	Bare Costs		Incl. Subs O&P		Cost Per Labor-Hour	
Crew B-37C	Hr.	Daily	Hr.	Daily	Bare Costs	Incl. O&P
2 Laborers	$47.25	$756.00	$70.35	$1125.60	$50.08	$74.67
2 Truck Drivers (light)	52.90	846.40	79.00	1264.00		
2 Flatbed Trucks, Gas, 1.5 Ton		723.90		796.29		
1 Tar Kettle, T.M.		199.54		219.49	28.86	31.74
32 L.H., Daily Totals		$2525.84		$3405.38	$78.93	$106.42
Crew B-37D	Hr.	Daily	Hr.	Daily	Bare Costs	Incl. O&P
1 Laborer	$47.25	$378.00	$70.35	$562.80	$50.08	$74.67
1 Truck Driver (light)	52.90	423.20	79.00	632.00		
1 Pickup Truck, 3/4 Ton		122.56		134.82	7.66	8.43
16 L.H., Daily Totals		$923.76		$1329.62	$57.73	$83.10
Crew B-37E	Hr.	Daily	Hr.	Daily	Bare Costs	Incl. O&P
3 Laborers	$47.25	$1134.00	$70.35	$1688.40	$52.90	$78.81
1 Equip. Oper. (light)	59.70	477.60	88.85	710.80		
1 Equip. Oper. (medium)	63.05	504.40	93.80	750.40		
2 Truck Drivers (light)	52.90	846.40	79.00	1264.00		
4 Barrels w/ Flasher		11.36		12.50		
1 Concrete Saw		176.00		193.60		
1 Rotary Hammer Drill		34.98		38.48		
1 Hammer Drill Bit		26.61		29.27		
1 Loader, Skid Steer, 30 H.P.		260.99		287.09		
1 Conc. Hammer Attach.		126.94		139.63		
1 Vibrating Plate, Gas, 18"		143.82		158.20		
2 Flatbed Trucks, Gas, 1.5 Ton		723.90		796.29	26.87	29.55
56 L.H., Daily Totals		$4467.00		$6068.66	$79.77	$108.37
Crew B-37F	Hr.	Daily	Hr.	Daily	Bare Costs	Incl. O&P
3 Laborers	$47.25	$1134.00	$70.35	$1688.40	$48.66	$72.51
1 Truck Driver (light)	52.90	423.20	79.00	632.00		
4 Barrels w/ Flasher		11.36		12.50		
1 Concrete Mixer, 10 C.F.		149.77		164.75		
1 Air Compressor, 60 cfm		173.21		190.53		
1 -50' Air Hose, 3/4"		8.16		8.98		
1 Spade (Chipper)		9.37		10.31		
1 Flatbed Truck, Gas, 1.5 Ton		361.95		398.14	22.31	24.54
32 L.H., Daily Totals		$2271.02		$3105.60	$70.97	$97.05
Crew B-37G	Hr.	Daily	Hr.	Daily	Bare Costs	Incl. O&P
1 Labor Foreman (outside)	$49.25	$394.00	$73.30	$586.40	$49.66	$73.92
4 Laborers	47.25	1512.00	70.35	2251.20		
1 Equip. Oper. (light)	59.70	477.60	88.85	710.80		
1 Berm Machine		897.16		986.88		
1 Tandem Roller, 5 Ton		287.45		316.19	24.68	27.15
48 L.H., Daily Totals		$3568.21		$4851.47	$74.34	$101.07
Crew B-37H	Hr.	Daily	Hr.	Daily	Bare Costs	Incl. O&P
1 Labor Foreman (outside)	$49.25	$394.00	$73.30	$586.40	$49.66	$73.92
4 Laborers	47.25	1512.00	70.35	2251.20		
1 Equip. Oper. (light)	59.70	477.60	88.85	710.80		
1 Tandem Roller, 5 Ton		287.45		316.19		
1 Flatbed Truck, Gas, 1.5 Ton		361.95		398.14		
1 Tar Kettle, T.M.		199.54		219.49	17.69	19.45
48 L.H., Daily Totals		$3232.54		$4482.23	$67.34	$93.38

Crews - Standard

Crew No.	Bare Costs		Incl. Subs O&P		Cost Per Labor-Hour	

Crew B-37I	Hr.	Daily	Hr.	Daily	Bare Costs	Incl. O&P
3 Laborers	$47.25	$1134.00	$70.35	$1688.40	$52.90	$78.81
1 Equip. Oper. (light)	59.70	477.60	88.85	710.80		
1 Equip. Oper. (medium)	63.05	504.40	93.80	750.40		
2 Truck Drivers (light)	52.90	846.40	79.00	1264.00		
4 Barrels w/ Flasher		11.36		12.50		
1 Concrete Saw		176.00		193.60		
1 Rotary Hammer Drill		34.98		38.48		
1 Hammer Drill Bit		26.61		29.27		
1 Air Compressor, 60 cfm		173.21		190.53		
1 -50' Air Hose, 3/4"		8.16		8.98		
1 Spade (Chipper)		9.37		10.31		
1 Loader, Skid Steer, 30 H.P.		260.99		287.09		
1 Conc. Hammer Attach.		126.94		139.63		
1 Concrete Mixer, 10 C.F.		149.77		164.75		
1 Vibrating Plate, Gas, 18"		143.82		158.20		
2 Flatbed Trucks, Gas, 1.5 Ton		723.90		796.29	32.95	36.24
56 L.H., Daily Totals		$4807.51		$6443.22	$85.85	$115.06

Crew B-37J	Hr.	Daily	Hr.	Daily	Bare Costs	Incl. O&P
1 Labor Foreman (outside)	$49.25	$394.00	$73.30	$586.40	$49.66	$73.92
4 Laborers	47.25	1512.00	70.35	2251.20		
1 Equip. Oper. (light)	59.70	477.60	88.85	710.80		
1 Air Compressor, 60 cfm		173.21		190.53		
1 -50' Air Hose, 3/4"		8.16		8.98		
2 Concrete Mixers, 10 C.F.		299.54		329.49		
2 Flatbed Trucks, Gas, 1.5 Ton		723.90		796.29		
1 Shot Blaster, 20"		229.79		252.77	29.89	32.88
48 L.H., Daily Totals		$3818.20		$5126.46	$79.55	$106.80

Crew B-37K	Hr.	Daily	Hr.	Daily	Bare Costs	Incl. O&P
1 Labor Foreman (outside)	$49.25	$394.00	$73.30	$586.40	$49.66	$73.92
4 Laborers	47.25	1512.00	70.35	2251.20		
1 Equip. Oper. (light)	59.70	477.60	88.85	710.80		
1 Air Compressor, 60 cfm		173.21		190.53		
1 -50' Air Hose, 3/4"		8.16		8.98		
2 Flatbed Trucks, Gas, 1.5 Ton		723.90		796.29		
1 Shot Blaster, 20"		229.79		252.77	23.65	26.01
48 L.H., Daily Totals		$3518.66		$4796.97	$73.31	$99.94

Crew B-38	Hr.	Daily	Hr.	Daily	Bare Costs	Incl. O&P
1 Labor Foreman (outside)	$49.25	$394.00	$73.30	$586.40	$53.30	$79.33
2 Laborers	47.25	756.00	70.35	1125.60		
1 Equip. Oper. (light)	59.70	477.60	88.85	710.80		
1 Equip. Oper. (medium)	63.05	504.40	93.80	750.40		
1 Backhoe Loader, 48 H.P.		277.19		304.91		
1 Hyd. Hammer (1200 lb.)		194.78		214.26		
1 F.E. Loader, W.M., 4 C.Y.		789.98		868.98		
1 Pvmt. Rem. Bucket		70.14		77.15	33.30	36.63
40 L.H., Daily Totals		$3464.09		$4638.50	$86.60	$115.96

Crew B-39	Hr.	Daily	Hr.	Daily	Bare Costs	Incl. O&P
1 Labor Foreman (outside)	$49.25	$394.00	$73.30	$586.40	$49.66	$73.92
4 Laborers	47.25	1512.00	70.35	2251.20		
1 Equip. Oper. (light)	59.70	477.60	88.85	710.80		
1 Air Compressor, 250 cfm		196.28		215.91		
2 Breakers, Pavement, 60 lb.		68.94		75.83		
2 -50' Air Hoses, 1.5"		47.20		51.92	6.51	7.16
48 L.H., Daily Totals		$2696.02		$3892.06	$56.17	$81.08

Crew B-40	Hr.	Daily	Hr.	Daily	Bare Costs	Incl. O&P
1 Pile Driver Foreman (outside)	$62.50	$500.00	$96.70	$773.60	$61.69	$94.04
4 Pile Drivers	60.50	1936.00	93.60	2995.20		
2 Equip. Oper. (crane)	66.30	1060.80	98.65	1578.40		
1 Equip. Oper. (oiler)	56.40	451.20	83.90	671.20		
1 Crawler Crane, 40 Ton		1362.63		1498.89		
1 Vibratory Hammer & Gen.		2518.21		2770.03	60.64	66.70
64 L.H., Daily Totals		$7828.84		$10287.32	$122.33	$160.74

Crew B-40B	Hr.	Daily	Hr.	Daily	Bare Costs	Incl. O&P
1 Labor Foreman (outside)	$49.25	$394.00	$73.30	$586.40	$52.28	$77.82
3 Laborers	47.25	1134.00	70.35	1688.40		
1 Equip. Oper. (crane)	66.30	530.40	98.65	789.20		
1 Equip. Oper. (oiler)	56.40	451.20	83.90	671.20		
1 Lattice Boom Crane, 40 Ton		2371.83		2609.01	49.41	54.35
48 L.H., Daily Totals		$4881.43		$6344.21	$101.70	$132.17

Crew B-41	Hr.	Daily	Hr.	Daily	Bare Costs	Incl. O&P
1 Labor Foreman (outside)	$49.25	$394.00	$73.30	$586.40	$48.90	$72.79
4 Laborers	47.25	1512.00	70.35	2251.20		
.25 Equip. Oper. (crane)	66.30	132.60	98.65	197.30		
.25 Equip. Oper. (oiler)	56.40	112.80	83.90	167.80		
.25 Crawler Crane, 40 Ton		340.66		374.72	7.74	8.52
44 L.H., Daily Totals		$2492.06		$3577.42	$56.64	$81.31

Crew B-42	Hr.	Daily	Hr.	Daily	Bare Costs	Incl. O&P
1 Labor Foreman (outside)	$49.25	$394.00	$73.30	$586.40	$53.19	$79.58
4 Laborers	47.25	1512.00	70.35	2251.20		
1 Equip. Oper. (crane)	66.30	530.40	98.65	789.20		
1 Equip. Oper. (oiler)	56.40	451.20	83.90	671.20		
1 Welder	64.55	516.40	99.40	795.20		
1 Hyd. Crane, 25 Ton		2273.31		2500.64		
1 Welder, Gas Engine, 300 amp		147.09		161.80		
1 Horz. Boring Csg. Mch.		437.50		481.25	44.65	49.12
64 L.H., Daily Totals		$6261.90		$8236.89	$97.84	$128.70

Crew B-43	Hr.	Daily	Hr.	Daily	Bare Costs	Incl. O&P
1 Labor Foreman (outside)	$49.25	$394.00	$73.30	$586.40	$52.28	$77.82
3 Laborers	47.25	1134.00	70.35	1688.40		
1 Equip. Oper. (crane)	66.30	530.40	98.65	789.20		
1 Equip. Oper. (oiler)	56.40	451.20	83.90	671.20		
1 Drill Rig, Truck-Mounted		856.23		941.85	17.84	19.62
48 L.H., Daily Totals		$3365.83		$4677.05	$70.12	$97.44

Crew B-44	Hr.	Daily	Hr.	Daily	Bare Costs	Incl. O&P
1 Pile Driver Foreman (outside)	$62.50	$500.00	$96.70	$773.60	$60.54	$92.34
4 Pile Drivers	60.50	1936.00	93.60	2995.20		
2 Equip. Oper. (crane)	66.30	1060.80	98.65	1578.40		
1 Laborer	47.25	378.00	70.35	562.80		
1 Crawler Crane, 40 Ton		1362.63		1498.89		
1 Lead, 60' High		233.36		256.70		
1 Hammer, Diesel, 15K ft.-lbs.		687.50		756.25	35.68	39.25
64 L.H., Daily Totals		$6158.29		$8421.84	$96.22	$131.59

Crew B-45	Hr.	Daily	Hr.	Daily	Bare Costs	Incl. O&P
1 Equip. Oper. (medium)	$63.05	$504.40	$93.80	$750.40	$59.25	$88.33
1 Truck Driver (heavy)	55.45	443.60	82.85	662.80		
1 Dist. Tanker, 3000 Gallon		367.10		403.81		
1 Truck Tractor, 6x4, 380 H.P.		545.98		600.58	57.07	62.77
16 L.H., Daily Totals		$1861.08		$2417.59	$116.32	$151.10

Crews - Standard

Crew No.		Bare Costs	Incl. Subs O&P		Cost Per Labor-Hour	
Crew B-46	Hr.	Daily	Hr.	Daily	Bare Costs	Incl. O&P
1 Pile Driver Foreman (outside)	$62.50	$500.00	$96.70	$773.60	$54.21	$82.49
2 Pile Drivers	60.50	968.00	93.60	1497.60		
3 Laborers	47.25	1134.00	70.35	1688.40		
1 Chain Saw, Gas, 36" Long		53.61		58.97	1.12	1.23
48 L.H., Daily Totals		$2655.61		$4018.57	$55.33	$83.72
Crew B-47	Hr.	Daily	Hr.	Daily	Bare Costs	Incl. O&P
1 Blast Foreman (outside)	$49.25	$394.00	$73.30	$586.40	$52.07	$77.50
1 Driller	47.25	378.00	70.35	562.80		
1 Equip. Oper. (light)	59.70	477.60	88.85	710.80		
1 Air Track Drill, 4"		1191.15		1310.27		
1 Air Compressor, 600 cfm		466.11		512.72		
2 -50' Air Hoses, 3"		93.52		102.87	72.95	80.24
24 L.H., Daily Totals		$3000.38		$3785.86	$125.02	$157.74
Crew B-47A	Hr.	Daily	Hr.	Daily	Bare Costs	Incl. O&P
1 Drilling Foreman (outside)	$49.25	$394.00	$73.30	$586.40	$57.32	$85.28
1 Equip. Oper. (heavy)	66.30	530.40	98.65	789.20		
1 Equip. Oper. (oiler)	56.40	451.20	83.90	671.20		
1 Air Track Drill, 5"		1191.15		1310.27	49.63	54.59
24 L.H., Daily Totals		$2566.75		$3357.07	$106.95	$139.88
Crew B-47C	Hr.	Daily	Hr.	Daily	Bare Costs	Incl. O&P
1 Laborer	$47.25	$378.00	$70.35	$562.80	$53.48	$79.60
1 Equip. Oper. (light)	59.70	477.60	88.85	710.80		
1 Air Compressor, 750 C.F.M.		655.87		721.46		
2 -50' Air Hoses, 3"		93.52		102.87		
1 Air Track Drill, 4"		1191.15		1310.27	121.28	133.41
16 L.H., Daily Totals		$2796.14		$3408.19	$174.76	$213.01
Crew B-47E	Hr.	Daily	Hr.	Daily	Bare Costs	Incl. O&P
1 Labor Foreman (outside)	$49.25	$394.00	$73.30	$586.40	$47.75	$71.09
3 Laborers	47.25	1134.00	70.35	1688.40		
1 Flatbed Truck, Gas, 3 Ton		391.02		430.12	12.22	13.44
32 L.H., Daily Totals		$1919.02		$2704.92	$59.97	$84.53
Crew B-47G	Hr.	Daily	Hr.	Daily	Bare Costs	Incl. O&P
1 Labor Foreman (outside)	$49.25	$394.00	$73.30	$586.40	$50.86	$75.71
2 Laborers	47.25	756.00	70.35	1125.60		
1 Equip. Oper. (light)	59.70	477.60	88.85	710.80		
1 Air Track Drill, 4"		1191.15		1310.27		
1 Air Compressor, 600 cfm		466.11		512.72		
2 -50' Air Hoses, 3"		93.52		102.87		
1 Gunite Pump Rig		352.58		387.84	65.73	72.30
32 L.H., Daily Totals		$3730.96		$4736.50	$116.59	$148.02
Crew B-47H	Hr.	Daily	Hr.	Daily	Bare Costs	Incl. O&P
1 Skilled Worker Foreman (out)	$63.25	$506.00	$95.00	$760.00	$61.75	$92.75
3 Skilled Workers	61.25	1470.00	92.00	2208.00		
1 Flatbed Truck, Gas, 3 Ton		391.02		430.12	12.22	13.44
32 L.H., Daily Totals		$2367.02		$3398.12	$73.97	$106.19

Crew No.		Bare Costs	Incl. Subs O&P		Cost Per Labor-Hour	
Crew B-48	Hr.	Daily	Hr.	Daily	Bare Costs	Incl. O&P
1 Labor Foreman (outside)	$49.25	$394.00	$73.30	$586.40	$53.34	$79.39
3 Laborers	47.25	1134.00	70.35	1688.40		
1 Equip. Oper. (crane)	66.30	530.40	98.65	789.20		
1 Equip. Oper. (oiler)	56.40	451.20	83.90	671.20		
1 Equip. Oper. (light)	59.70	477.60	88.85	710.80		
1 Centr. Water Pump, 6"		386.48		425.13		
1 -20' Suction Hose, 6"		28.12		30.93		
1 -50' Discharge Hose, 6"		19.99		21.99		
1 Drill Rig, Truck-Mounted		856.23		941.85	23.05	25.36
56 L.H., Daily Totals		$4278.02		$5865.90	$76.39	$104.75
Crew B-49	Hr.	Daily	Hr.	Daily	Bare Costs	Incl. O&P
1 Labor Foreman (outside)	$49.25	$394.00	$73.30	$586.40	$56.10	$84.14
3 Laborers	47.25	1134.00	70.35	1688.40		
2 Equip. Oper. (crane)	66.30	1060.80	98.65	1578.40		
2 Equip. Oper. (oilers)	56.40	902.40	83.90	1342.40		
1 Equip. Oper. (light)	59.70	477.60	88.85	710.80		
2 Pile Drivers	60.50	968.00	93.60	1497.60		
1 Hyd. Crane, 25 Ton		2273.31		2500.64		
1 Centr. Water Pump, 6"		386.48		425.13		
1 -20' Suction Hose, 6"		28.12		30.93		
1 -50' Discharge Hose, 6"		19.99		21.99		
1 Drill Rig, Truck-Mounted		856.23		941.85	40.50	44.55
88 L.H., Daily Totals		$8500.93		$11324.54	$96.60	$128.69
Crew B-50	Hr.	Daily	Hr.	Daily	Bare Costs	Incl. O&P
2 Pile Driver Foremen (outside)	$62.50	$1000.00	$96.70	$1547.20	$58.48	$89.09
6 Pile Drivers	60.50	2904.00	93.60	4492.80		
2 Equip. Oper. (crane)	66.30	1060.80	98.65	1578.40		
1 Equip. Oper. (oiler)	56.40	451.20	83.90	671.20		
3 Laborers	47.25	1134.00	70.35	1688.40		
1 Crawler Crane, 40 Ton		1362.63		1498.89		
1 Lead, 60' High		233.36		256.70		
1 Hammer, Diesel, 15K ft.-lbs.		687.50		756.25		
1 Air Compressor, 600 cfm		466.11		512.72		
2 -50' Air Hoses, 3"		93.52		102.87		
1 Chain Saw, Gas, 36" Long		53.61		58.97	25.86	28.45
112 L.H., Daily Totals		$9446.73		$13164.40	$84.35	$117.54
Crew B-51	Hr.	Daily	Hr.	Daily	Bare Costs	Incl. O&P
1 Labor Foreman (outside)	$49.25	$394.00	$73.30	$586.40	$48.52	$72.28
4 Laborers	47.25	1512.00	70.35	2251.20		
1 Truck Driver (light)	52.90	423.20	79.00	632.00		
1 Flatbed Truck, Gas, 1.5 Ton		361.95		398.14	7.54	8.29
48 L.H., Daily Totals		$2691.15		$3867.74	$56.07	$80.58
Crew B-52	Hr.	Daily	Hr.	Daily	Bare Costs	Incl. O&P
1 Carpenter Foreman (outside)	$60.60	$484.80	$90.20	$721.60	$54.25	$80.58
1 Carpenter	58.60	468.80	87.25	698.00		
3 Laborers	47.25	1134.00	70.35	1688.40		
1 Cement Finisher	55.00	440.00	80.45	643.60		
.5 Rodman (reinf.)	64.55	258.20	96.40	385.60		
.5 Equip. Oper. (medium)	63.05	252.20	93.80	375.20		
.5 Crawler Loader, 3 C.Y.		628.84		691.72	11.23	12.35
56 L.H., Daily Totals		$3666.84		$5204.12	$65.48	$92.93
Crew B-53	Hr.	Daily	Hr.	Daily	Bare Costs	Incl. O&P
1 Equip. Oper. (light)	$59.70	$477.60	$88.85	$710.80	$59.70	$88.85
1 Trencher, Chain, 12 H.P.		202.47		222.72	25.31	27.84
8 L.H., Daily Totals		$680.07		$933.52	$85.01	$116.69

Crews - Standard

Crew No.	Bare Costs		Incl. Subs O&P		Cost Per Labor-Hour	
Crew B-54	Hr.	Daily	Hr.	Daily	Bare Costs	Incl. O&P
1 Equip. Oper. (light)	$59.70	$477.60	$88.85	$710.80	$59.70	$88.85
1 Trencher, Chain, 40 H.P.		386.50		425.15	48.31	53.14
8 L.H., Daily Totals		$864.10		$1135.95	$108.01	$141.99
Crew B-54A	Hr.	Daily	Hr.	Daily	Bare Costs	Incl. O&P
.17 Labor Foreman (outside)	$49.25	$66.98	$73.30	$99.69	$61.04	$90.82
1 Equipment Operator (med.)	63.05	504.40	93.80	750.40		
1 Wheel Trencher, 67 H.P.		1248.89		1373.78	133.43	146.77
9.36 L.H., Daily Totals		$1820.27		$2223.87	$194.47	$237.59
Crew B-54B	Hr.	Daily	Hr.	Daily	Bare Costs	Incl. O&P
.25 Labor Foreman (outside)	$49.25	$98.50	$73.30	$146.60	$60.29	$89.70
1 Equipment Operator (med.)	63.05	504.40	93.80	750.40		
1 Wheel Trencher, 150 H.P.		1338.44		1472.28	133.84	147.23
10 L.H., Daily Totals		$1941.34		$2369.28	$194.13	$236.93
Crew B-54C	Hr.	Daily	Hr.	Daily	Bare Costs	Incl. O&P
1 Laborer	$47.25	$378.00	$70.35	$562.80	$55.15	$82.08
1 Equipment Operator (med.)	63.05	504.40	93.80	750.40		
1 Wheel Trencher, 67 H.P.		1248.89		1373.78	78.06	85.86
16 L.H., Daily Totals		$2131.29		$2686.98	$133.21	$167.94
Crew B-54D	Hr.	Daily	Hr.	Daily	Bare Costs	Incl. O&P
1 Laborer	$47.25	$378.00	$70.35	$562.80	$55.15	$82.08
1 Equipment Operator (med.)	63.05	504.40	93.80	750.40		
1 Rock Trencher, 6" Width		992.44		1091.68	62.03	68.23
16 L.H., Daily Totals		$1874.84		$2404.88	$117.18	$150.31
Crew B-54E	Hr.	Daily	Hr.	Daily	Bare Costs	Incl. O&P
1 Laborer	$47.25	$378.00	$70.35	$562.80	$55.15	$82.08
1 Equipment Operator (med.)	63.05	504.40	93.80	750.40		
1 Rock Trencher, 18" Width		1079.31		1187.24	67.46	74.20
16 L.H., Daily Totals		$1961.71		$2500.44	$122.61	$156.28
Crew B-55	Hr.	Daily	Hr.	Daily	Bare Costs	Incl. O&P
2 Laborers	$47.25	$756.00	$70.35	$1125.60	$49.13	$73.23
1 Truck Driver (light)	52.90	423.20	79.00	632.00		
1 Truck-Mounted Earth Auger		446.91		491.60		
1 Flatbed Truck, Gas, 3 Ton		391.02		430.12	34.91	38.41
24 L.H., Daily Totals		$2017.13		$2679.32	$84.05	$111.64
Crew B-56	Hr.	Daily	Hr.	Daily	Bare Costs	Incl. O&P
1 Laborer	$47.25	$378.00	$70.35	$562.80	$53.48	$79.60
1 Equip. Oper. (light)	59.70	477.60	88.85	710.80		
1 Air Track Drill, 4"		1191.15		1310.27		
1 Air Compressor, 600 cfm		466.11		512.72		
1 -50' Air Hose, 3"		46.76		51.44	106.50	117.15
16 L.H., Daily Totals		$2559.62		$3148.02	$159.98	$196.75

Crew No.	Bare Costs		Incl. Subs O&P		Cost Per Labor-Hour	
Crew B-57	Hr.	Daily	Hr.	Daily	Bare Costs	Incl. O&P
1 Labor Foreman (outside)	$49.25	$394.00	$73.30	$586.40	$54.36	$80.90
2 Laborers	47.25	756.00	70.35	1125.60		
1 Equip. Oper. (crane)	66.30	530.40	98.65	789.20		
1 Equip. Oper. (light)	59.70	477.60	88.85	710.80		
1 Equip. Oper. (oiler)	56.40	451.20	83.90	671.20		
1 Crawler Crane, 25 Ton		1274.00		1401.40		
1 Clamshell Bucket, 1 C.Y.		46.89		51.58		
1 Centr. Water Pump, 6"		386.48		425.13		
1 -20' Suction Hose, 6"		28.12		30.93		
20 -50' Discharge Hoses, 6"		399.80		439.78	44.49	48.93
48 L.H., Daily Totals		$4744.49		$6232.02	$98.84	$129.83
Crew B-58	Hr.	Daily	Hr.	Daily	Bare Costs	Incl. O&P
2 Laborers	$47.25	$756.00	$70.35	$1125.60	$51.40	$76.52
1 Equip. Oper. (light)	59.70	477.60	88.85	710.80		
1 Backhoe Loader, 48 H.P.		277.19		304.91		
1 Small Helicopter, w/ Pilot		5810.29		6391.32	253.65	279.01
24 L.H., Daily Totals		$7321.08		$8532.63	$305.05	$355.53
Crew B-59	Hr.	Daily	Hr.	Daily	Bare Costs	Incl. O&P
1 Truck Driver (heavy)	$55.45	$443.60	$82.85	$662.80	$55.45	$82.85
1 Truck Tractor, 220 H.P.		339.98		373.98		
1 Water Tank Trailer, 5000 Gal.		169.14		186.05	63.64	70.00
8 L.H., Daily Totals		$952.72		$1222.83	$119.09	$152.85
Crew B-59A	Hr.	Daily	Hr.	Daily	Bare Costs	Incl. O&P
2 Laborers	$47.25	$756.00	$70.35	$1125.60	$49.98	$74.52
1 Truck Driver (heavy)	55.45	443.60	82.85	662.80		
1 Water Tank Trailer, 5000 Gal.		169.14		186.05		
1 Truck Tractor, 220 H.P.		339.98		373.98	21.21	23.33
24 L.H., Daily Totals		$1708.72		$2348.43	$71.20	$97.85
Crew B-60	Hr.	Daily	Hr.	Daily	Bare Costs	Incl. O&P
1 Labor Foreman (outside)	$49.25	$394.00	$73.30	$586.40	$55.12	$82.04
2 Laborers	47.25	756.00	70.35	1125.60		
1 Equip. Oper. (crane)	66.30	530.40	98.65	789.20		
2 Equip. Oper. (light)	59.70	955.20	88.85	1421.60		
1 Equip. Oper. (oiler)	56.40	451.20	83.90	671.20		
1 Crawler Crane, 40 Ton		1362.63		1498.89		
1 Lead, 60' High		233.36		256.70		
1 Hammer, Diesel, 15K ft.-lbs.		687.50		756.25		
1 Backhoe Loader, 48 H.P.		277.19		304.91	45.73	50.30
56 L.H., Daily Totals		$5647.48		$7410.75	$100.85	$132.33
Crew B-61	Hr.	Daily	Hr.	Daily	Bare Costs	Incl. O&P
1 Labor Foreman (outside)	$49.25	$394.00	$73.30	$586.40	$50.14	$74.64
3 Laborers	47.25	1134.00	70.35	1688.40		
1 Equip. Oper. (light)	59.70	477.60	88.85	710.80		
1 Cement Mixer, 2 C.Y.		119.22		131.14		
1 Air Compressor, 160 cfm		244.12		268.53	9.08	9.99
40 L.H., Daily Totals		$2368.94		$3385.27	$59.22	$84.63
Crew B-62	Hr.	Daily	Hr.	Daily	Bare Costs	Incl. O&P
2 Laborers	$47.25	$756.00	$70.35	$1125.60	$51.40	$76.52
1 Equip. Oper. (light)	59.70	477.60	88.85	710.80		
1 Loader, Skid Steer, 30 H.P.		260.99		287.09	10.87	11.96
24 L.H., Daily Totals		$1494.59		$2123.49	$62.27	$88.48

Crews - Standard

Crew No.		Bare Costs		Incl. Subs O&P		Cost Per Labor-Hour	
Crew B-62A	Hr.	Daily	Hr.	Daily	Bare Costs	Incl. O&P
2 Laborers	$47.25	$756.00	$70.35	$1125.60	$51.40	$76.52
1 Equip. Oper. (light)	59.70	477.60	88.85	710.80		
1 Loader, Skid Steer, 30 H.P.		260.99		287.09		
1 Trencher Attachment		88.83		97.71	14.58	16.03
24 L.H., Daily Totals		$1583.42		$2221.20	$65.98	$92.55
Crew B-63	Hr.	Daily	Hr.	Daily	Bare Costs	Incl. O&P
4 Laborers	$47.25	$1512.00	$70.35	$2251.20	$49.74	$74.05
1 Equip. Oper. (light)	59.70	477.60	88.85	710.80		
1 Loader, Skid Steer, 30 H.P.		260.99		287.09	6.52	7.18
40 L.H., Daily Totals		$2250.59		$3249.09	$56.26	$81.23
Crew B-63B	Hr.	Daily	Hr.	Daily	Bare Costs	Incl. O&P
1 Labor Foreman (inside)	$47.75	$382.00	$71.10	$568.80	$50.49	$75.16
2 Laborers	47.25	756.00	70.35	1125.60		
1 Equip. Oper. (light)	59.70	477.60	88.85	710.80		
1 Loader, Skid Steer, 78 H.P.		429.91		472.90	13.43	14.78
32 L.H., Daily Totals		$2045.51		$2878.10	$63.92	$89.94
Crew B-64	Hr.	Daily	Hr.	Daily	Bare Costs	Incl. O&P
1 Laborer	$47.25	$378.00	$70.35	$562.80	$50.08	$74.67
1 Truck Driver (light)	52.90	423.20	79.00	632.00		
1 Power Mulcher (small)		264.41		290.85		
1 Flatbed Truck, Gas, 1.5 Ton		361.95		398.14	39.15	43.06
16 L.H., Daily Totals		$1427.56		$1883.80	$89.22	$117.74
Crew B-65	Hr.	Daily	Hr.	Daily	Bare Costs	Incl. O&P
1 Laborer	$47.25	$378.00	$70.35	$562.80	$50.08	$74.67
1 Truck Driver (light)	52.90	423.20	79.00	632.00		
1 Power Mulcher (Large)		633.63		696.99		
1 Flatbed Truck, Gas, 1.5 Ton		361.95		398.14	62.22	68.45
16 L.H., Daily Totals		$1796.78		$2289.94	$112.30	$143.12
Crew B-66	Hr.	Daily	Hr.	Daily	Bare Costs	Incl. O&P
1 Equip. Oper. (light)	$59.70	$477.60	$88.85	$710.80	$59.70	$88.85
1 Loader-Backhoe, 40 H.P.		222.27		244.50	27.78	30.56
8 L.H., Daily Totals		$699.87		$955.30	$87.48	$119.41
Crew B-67	Hr.	Daily	Hr.	Daily	Bare Costs	Incl. O&P
1 Millwright	$62.85	$502.80	$90.80	$726.40	$61.27	$89.83
1 Equip. Oper. (light)	59.70	477.60	88.85	710.80		
1 R.T. Forklift, 5,000 Lb., diesel		349.30		384.23	21.83	24.01
16 L.H., Daily Totals		$1329.70		$1821.43	$83.11	$113.84
Crew B-67B	Hr.	Daily	Hr.	Daily	Bare Costs	Incl. O&P
1 Millwright Foreman (inside)	$63.35	$506.80	$91.55	$732.40	$63.10	$91.17
1 Millwright	62.85	502.80	90.80	726.40		
16 L.H., Daily Totals		$1009.60		$1458.80	$63.10	$91.17
Crew B-68	Hr.	Daily	Hr.	Daily	Bare Costs	Incl. O&P
2 Millwrights	$62.85	$1005.60	$90.80	$1452.80	$61.80	$90.15
1 Equip. Oper. (light)	59.70	477.60	88.85	710.80		
1 R.T. Forklift, 5,000 Lb., diesel		349.30		384.23	14.55	16.01
24 L.H., Daily Totals		$1832.50		$2547.83	$76.35	$106.16
Crew B-68A	Hr.	Daily	Hr.	Daily	Bare Costs	Incl. O&P
1 Millwright Foreman (inside)	$63.35	$506.80	$91.55	$732.40	$63.02	$91.05
2 Millwrights	62.85	1005.60	90.80	1452.80		
1 Forklift, Smooth Floor, 8,000 Lb.		311.06		342.17	12.96	14.26
24 L.H., Daily Totals		$1823.46		$2527.37	$75.98	$105.31

Crew No.		Bare Costs		Incl. Subs O&P		Cost Per Labor-Hour	
Crew B-68B	Hr.	Daily	Hr.	Daily	Bare Costs	Incl. O&P
1 Millwright Foreman (inside)	$63.35	$506.80	$91.55	$732.40	$66.84	$98.32
2 Millwrights	62.85	1005.60	90.80	1452.80		
2 Electricians	67.35	1077.60	100.10	1601.60		
2 Plumbers	72.05	1152.80	107.45	1719.20		
1 R.T. Forklift, 5,000 Lb., gas		422.09		464.30	7.54	8.29
56 L.H., Daily Totals		$4164.89		$5970.30	$74.37	$106.61
Crew B-68C	Hr.	Daily	Hr.	Daily	Bare Costs	Incl. O&P
1 Millwright Foreman (inside)	$63.35	$506.80	$91.55	$732.40	$66.40	$97.47
1 Millwright	62.85	502.80	90.80	726.40		
1 Electrician	67.35	538.80	100.10	800.80		
1 Plumber	72.05	576.40	107.45	859.60		
1 R.T. Forklift, 5,000 Lb., gas		422.09		464.30	13.19	14.51
32 L.H., Daily Totals		$2546.89		$3583.50	$79.59	$111.98
Crew B-68D	Hr.	Daily	Hr.	Daily	Bare Costs	Incl. O&P
1 Labor Foreman (inside)	$47.75	$382.00	$71.10	$568.80	$51.57	$76.77
1 Laborer	47.25	378.00	70.35	562.80		
1 Equip. Oper. (light)	59.70	477.60	88.85	710.80		
1 R.T. Forklift, 5,000 Lb., gas		422.09		464.30	17.59	19.35
24 L.H., Daily Totals		$1659.69		$2306.70	$69.15	$96.11
Crew B-68E	Hr.	Daily	Hr.	Daily	Bare Costs	Incl. O&P
1 Struc. Steel Foreman (inside)	$65.05	$520.40	$100.20	$801.60	$64.65	$99.56
3 Struc. Steel Workers	64.55	1549.20	99.40	2385.60		
1 Welder	64.55	516.40	99.40	795.20		
1 Forklift, Smooth Floor, 8,000 Lb.		311.06		342.17	7.78	8.55
40 L.H., Daily Totals		$2897.06		$4324.57	$72.43	$108.11
Crew B-68F	Hr.	Daily	Hr.	Daily	Bare Costs	Incl. O&P
1 Skilled Worker Foreman (out)	$63.25	$506.00	$95.00	$760.00	$61.92	$93.00
2 Skilled Workers	61.25	980.00	92.00	1472.00		
1 R.T. Forklift, 5,000 Lb., gas		422.09		464.30	17.59	19.35
24 L.H., Daily Totals		$1908.09		$2696.30	$79.50	$112.35
Crew B-68G	Hr.	Daily	Hr.	Daily	Bare Costs	Incl. O&P
2 Structural Steel Workers	$64.55	$1032.80	$99.40	$1590.40	$64.55	$99.40
1 R.T. Forklift, 5,000 Lb., gas		422.09		464.30	26.38	29.02
16 L.H., Daily Totals		$1454.89		$2054.70	$90.93	$128.42
Crew B-69	Hr.	Daily	Hr.	Daily	Bare Costs	Incl. O&P
1 Labor Foreman (outside)	$49.25	$394.00	$73.30	$586.40	$52.28	$77.82
3 Laborers	47.25	1134.00	70.35	1688.40		
1 Equip. Oper. (crane)	66.30	530.40	98.65	789.20		
1 Equip. Oper. (oiler)	56.40	451.20	83.90	671.20		
1 Hyd. Crane, 80 Ton		2641.70		2905.87	55.04	60.54
48 L.H., Daily Totals		$5151.30		$6641.07	$107.32	$138.36
Crew B-69A	Hr.	Daily	Hr.	Daily	Bare Costs	Incl. O&P
1 Labor Foreman (outside)	$49.25	$394.00	$73.30	$586.40	$51.51	$76.43
3 Laborers	47.25	1134.00	70.35	1688.40		
1 Equip. Oper. (medium)	63.05	504.40	93.80	750.40		
1 Concrete Finisher	55.00	440.00	80.45	643.60		
1 Curb/Gutter Paver, 2-Track		1074.23		1181.65	22.38	24.62
48 L.H., Daily Totals		$3546.63		$4850.45	$73.89	$101.05

Crews - Standard

Crew No.		Bare Costs		Incl. Subs O&P		Cost Per Labor-Hour	
Crew B-69B	Hr.	Daily	Hr.	Daily	Bare Costs	Incl. O&P	
1 Labor Foreman (outside)	$49.25	$394.00	$73.30	$586.40	$51.51	$76.43	
3 Laborers	47.25	1134.00	70.35	1688.40			
1 Equip. Oper. (medium)	63.05	504.40	93.80	750.40			
1 Cement Finisher	55.00	440.00	80.45	643.60			
1 Curb/Gutter Paver, 4-Track		1156.49		1272.14	24.09	26.50	
48 L.H., Daily Totals		$3628.89		$4940.94	$75.60	$102.94	

Crew No.		Bare Costs		Incl. Subs O&P		Cost Per Labor-Hour	
Crew B-70	Hr.	Daily	Hr.	Daily	Bare Costs	Incl. O&P	
1 Labor Foreman (outside)	$49.25	$394.00	$73.30	$586.40	$54.31	$80.82	
3 Laborers	47.25	1134.00	70.35	1688.40			
3 Equip. Oper. (medium)	63.05	1513.20	93.80	2251.20			
1 Grader, 30,000 Lbs.		1091.19		1200.31			
1 Ripper, Beam & 1 Shank		100.54		110.59			
1 Road Sweeper, S.P., 8' wide		538.01		591.81			
1 F.E. Loader, W.M., 1.5 C.Y.		455.32		500.85	39.02	42.92	
56 L.H., Daily Totals		$5226.26		$6929.57	$93.33	$123.74	

Crew B-70A	Hr.	Daily	Hr.	Daily	Bare Costs	Incl. O&P
1 Laborer	$47.25	$378.00	$70.35	$562.80	$59.89	$89.11
4 Equip. Oper. (medium)	63.05	2017.60	93.80	3001.60		
1 Grader, 40,000 Lbs.		1254.97		1380.47		
1 F.E. Loader, W.M., 2.5 C.Y.		658.89		724.78		
1 Dozer, 80 H.P.		591.82		651.00		
1 Roller, Pneum. Whl., 12 Ton		384.55		423.01	72.26	79.48
40 L.H., Daily Totals		$5285.83		$6743.65	$132.15	$168.59

Crew B-71	Hr.	Daily	Hr.	Daily	Bare Costs	Incl. O&P
1 Labor Foreman (outside)	$49.25	$394.00	$73.30	$586.40	$54.31	$80.82
3 Laborers	47.25	1134.00	70.35	1688.40		
3 Equip. Oper. (medium)	63.05	1513.20	93.80	2251.20		
1 Pvmt. Profiler, 750 H.P.		3680.74		4048.81		
1 Road Sweeper, S.P., 8' wide		538.01		591.81		
1 F.E. Loader, W.M., 1.5 C.Y.		455.32		500.85	83.47	91.81
56 L.H., Daily Totals		$7715.27		$9667.48	$137.77	$172.63

Crew B-72	Hr.	Daily	Hr.	Daily	Bare Costs	Incl. O&P
1 Labor Foreman (outside)	$49.25	$394.00	$73.30	$586.40	$55.40	$82.44
3 Laborers	47.25	1134.00	70.35	1688.40		
4 Equip. Oper. (medium)	63.05	2017.60	93.80	3001.60		
1 Pvmt. Profiler, 750 H.P.		3680.74		4048.81		
1 Hammermill, 250 H.P.		806.43		887.07		
1 Windrow Loader		1473.50		1620.85		
1 Mix Paver, 165 H.P.		1265.22		1391.74		
1 Roller, Pneum. Whl., 12 Ton		384.55		423.01	118.91	130.80
64 L.H., Daily Totals		$11156.04		$13647.88	$174.31	$213.25

Crew B-73	Hr.	Daily	Hr.	Daily	Bare Costs	Incl. O&P
1 Labor Foreman (outside)	$49.25	$394.00	$73.30	$586.40	$57.38	$85.38
2 Laborers	47.25	756.00	70.35	1125.60		
5 Equip. Oper. (medium)	63.05	2522.00	93.80	3752.00		
1 Road Mixer, 310 H.P.		2108.32		2319.15		
1 Tandem Roller, 10 Ton		379.22		417.14		
1 Hammermill, 250 H.P.		806.43		887.07		
1 Grader, 30,000 Lbs.		1091.19		1200.31		
.5 F.E. Loader, W.M., 1.5 C.Y.		227.66		250.43		
.5 Truck Tractor, 220 H.P.		169.99		186.99		
.5 Water Tank Trailer, 5000 Gal.		84.57		93.03	76.05	83.66
64 L.H., Daily Totals		$8539.38		$10818.12	$133.43	$169.03

Crew B-74	Hr.	Daily	Hr.	Daily	Bare Costs	Incl. O&P
1 Labor Foreman (outside)	$49.25	$394.00	$73.30	$586.40	$57.45	$85.57
1 Laborer	47.25	378.00	70.35	562.80		
4 Equip. Oper. (medium)	63.05	2017.60	93.80	3001.60		
2 Truck Drivers (heavy)	55.45	887.20	82.85	1325.60		
1 Grader, 30,000 Lbs.		1091.19		1200.31		
1 Ripper, Beam & 1 Shank		100.54		110.59		
2 Stabilizers, 310 H.P.		1713.46		1884.81		
1 Flatbed Truck, Gas, 3 Ton		391.02		430.12		
1 Chem. Spreader, Towed		87.61		96.37		
1 Roller, Vibratory, 25 Ton		529.68		582.65		
1 Water Tank Trailer, 5000 Gal.		169.14		186.05		
1 Truck Tractor, 220 H.P.		339.98		373.98	69.10	76.01
64 L.H., Daily Totals		$8099.42		$10341.28	$126.55	$161.58

Crew B-75	Hr.	Daily	Hr.	Daily	Bare Costs	Incl. O&P
1 Labor Foreman (outside)	$49.25	$394.00	$73.30	$586.40	$57.74	$85.96
1 Laborer	47.25	378.00	70.35	562.80		
4 Equip. Oper. (medium)	63.05	2017.60	93.80	3001.60		
1 Truck Driver (heavy)	55.45	443.60	82.85	662.80		
1 Grader, 30,000 Lbs.		1091.19		1200.31		
1 Ripper, Beam & 1 Shank		100.54		110.59		
2 Stabilizers, 310 H.P.		1713.46		1884.81		
1 Dist. Tanker, 3000 Gallon		367.10		403.81		
1 Truck Tractor, 6x4, 380 H.P.		545.98		600.58		
1 Roller, Vibratory, 25 Ton		529.68		582.65	77.64	85.41
56 L.H., Daily Totals		$7581.15		$9596.34	$135.38	$171.36

Crew B-76	Hr.	Daily	Hr.	Daily	Bare Costs	Incl. O&P
1 Dock Builder Foreman (outside)	$62.50	$500.00	$96.70	$773.60	$61.56	$93.99
5 Dock Builders	60.50	2420.00	93.60	3744.00		
2 Equip. Oper. (crane)	66.30	1060.80	98.65	1578.40		
1 Equip. Oper. (oiler)	56.40	451.20	83.90	671.20		
1 Crawler Crane, 50 Ton		1704.33		1874.76		
1 Barge, 400 Ton		957.33		1053.06		
1 Hammer, Diesel, 15K ft.-lbs.		687.50		756.25		
1 Lead, 60' High		233.36		256.70		
1 Air Compressor, 600 cfm		466.11		512.72		
2 -50' Air Hoses, 3"		93.52		102.87	57.53	63.28
72 L.H., Daily Totals		$8574.15		$11323.57	$119.09	$157.27

Crew B-76A	Hr.	Daily	Hr.	Daily	Bare Costs	Incl. O&P
1 Labor Foreman (outside)	$49.25	$394.00	$73.30	$586.40	$51.02	$75.95
5 Laborers	47.25	1890.00	70.35	2814.00		
1 Equip. Oper. (crane)	66.30	530.40	98.65	789.20		
1 Equip. Oper. (oiler)	56.40	451.20	83.90	671.20		
1 Crawler Crane, 50 Ton		1704.33		1874.76		
1 Barge, 400 Ton		957.33		1053.06	41.59	45.75
64 L.H., Daily Totals		$5927.26		$7788.63	$92.61	$121.70

Crew B-77	Hr.	Daily	Hr.	Daily	Bare Costs	Incl. O&P
1 Labor Foreman (outside)	$49.25	$394.00	$73.30	$586.40	$48.78	$72.67
3 Laborers	47.25	1134.00	70.35	1688.40		
1 Truck Driver (light)	52.90	423.20	79.00	632.00		
1 Crack Cleaner, 25 H.P.		167.33		184.06		
1 Crack Filler, Trailer Mtd.		201.26		221.39		
1 Flatbed Truck, Gas, 3 Ton		391.02		430.12	18.99	20.89
40 L.H., Daily Totals		$2710.81		$3742.37	$67.77	$93.56

Crews - Standard

Crew No.	Bare Costs		Incl. Subs O&P		Cost Per Labor-Hour	
Crew B-78	**Hr.**	**Daily**	**Hr.**	**Daily**	**Bare Costs**	**Incl. O&P**
1 Labor Foreman (outside)	$49.25	$394.00	$73.30	$586.40	$48.52	$72.28
4 Laborers	47.25	1512.00	70.35	2251.20		
1 Truck Driver (light)	52.90	423.20	79.00	632.00		
1 Paint Striper, S.P., 40 Gallon		73.74		81.11		
1 Flatbed Truck, Gas, 3 Ton		391.02		430.12		
1 Pickup Truck, 3/4 Ton		122.56		134.82	12.24	13.46
48 L.H., Daily Totals		$2916.52		$4115.65	$60.76	$85.74

Crew B-78A	Hr.	Daily	Hr.	Daily	Bare Costs	Incl. O&P
1 Equip. Oper. (light)	$59.70	$477.60	$88.85	$710.80	$59.70	$88.85
1 Line Rem. (Metal Balls) 115 H.P.		1648.72		1813.59	206.09	226.70
8 L.H., Daily Totals		$2126.32		$2524.39	$265.79	$315.55

Crew B-78B	Hr.	Daily	Hr.	Daily	Bare Costs	Incl. O&P
2 Laborers	$47.25	$756.00	$70.35	$1125.60	$48.63	$72.41
.25 Equip. Oper. (light)	59.70	119.40	88.85	177.70		
1 Pickup Truck, 3/4 Ton		122.56		134.82		
1 Line Rem.,11 H.P.,Walk Behind		214.39		235.83		
.25 Road Sweeper, S.P., 8' wide		134.50		147.95	26.19	28.81
18 L.H., Daily Totals		$1346.85		$1821.90	$74.83	$101.22

Crew B-78C	Hr.	Daily	Hr.	Daily	Bare Costs	Incl. O&P
1 Labor Foreman (outside)	$49.25	$394.00	$73.30	$586.40	$48.52	$72.28
4 Laborers	47.25	1512.00	70.35	2251.20		
1 Truck Driver (light)	52.90	423.20	79.00	632.00		
1 Paint Striper, T.M., 120 Gal.		673.88		741.27		
1 Flatbed Truck, Gas, 3 Ton		391.02		430.12		
1 Pickup Truck, 3/4 Ton		122.56		134.82	24.74	27.21
48 L.H., Daily Totals		$3516.66		$4775.81	$73.26	$99.50

Crew B-78D	Hr.	Daily	Hr.	Daily	Bare Costs	Incl. O&P
2 Labor Foremen (outside)	$49.25	$788.00	$73.30	$1172.80	$48.22	$71.81
7 Laborers	47.25	2646.00	70.35	3939.60		
1 Truck Driver (light)	52.90	423.20	79.00	632.00		
1 Paint Striper, T.M., 120 Gal.		673.88		741.27		
1 Flatbed Truck, Gas, 3 Ton		391.02		430.12		
3 Pickup Trucks, 3/4 Ton		367.68		404.45		
1 Air Compressor, 60 cfm		173.21		190.53		
1 -50' Air Hose, 3/4"		8.16		8.98		
1 Breaker, Pavement, 60 lb.		34.47		37.92	20.61	22.67
80 L.H., Daily Totals		$5505.62		$7557.66	$68.82	$94.47

Crew B-78E	Hr.	Daily	Hr.	Daily	Bare Costs	Incl. O&P
2 Labor Foremen (outside)	$49.25	$788.00	$73.30	$1172.80	$48.05	$71.56
9 Laborers	47.25	3402.00	70.35	5065.20		
1 Truck Driver (light)	52.90	423.20	79.00	632.00		
1 Paint Striper, T.M., 120 Gal.		673.88		741.27		
1 Flatbed Truck, Gas, 3 Ton		391.02		430.12		
4 Pickup Trucks, 3/4 Ton		490.24		539.26		
2 Air Compressors, 60 cfm		346.42		381.06		
2 -50' Air Hoses, 3/4"		16.32		17.95		
2 Breakers, Pavement, 60 lb.		68.94		75.83	20.70	22.77
96 L.H., Daily Totals		$6600.02		$9055.50	$68.75	$94.33

Crew B-78F	Hr.	Daily	Hr.	Daily	Bare Costs	Incl. O&P
2 Labor Foremen (outside)	$49.25	$788.00	$73.30	$1172.80	$47.94	$71.39
11 Laborers	47.25	4158.00	70.35	6190.80		
1 Truck Driver (light)	52.90	423.20	79.00	632.00		
1 Paint Striper, T.M., 120 Gal.		673.88		741.27		
1 Flatbed Truck, Gas, 3 Ton		391.02		430.12		
7 Pickup Trucks, 3/4 Ton		857.92		943.71		
3 Air Compressors, 60 cfm		519.63		571.59		
3 -50' Air Hoses, 3/4"		24.48		26.93		
3 Breakers, Pavement, 60 lb.		103.41		113.75	22.95	25.24
112 L.H., Daily Totals		$7939.54		$10822.97	$70.89	$96.63

Crew B-79	Hr.	Daily	Hr.	Daily	Bare Costs	Incl. O&P
1 Labor Foreman (outside)	$49.25	$394.00	$73.30	$586.40	$48.78	$72.67
3 Laborers	47.25	1134.00	70.35	1688.40		
1 Truck Driver (light)	52.90	423.20	79.00	632.00		
1 Paint Striper, T.M., 120 Gal.		673.88		741.27		
1 Heating Kettle, 115 Gallon		169.64		186.60		
1 Flatbed Truck, Gas, 3 Ton		391.02		430.12		
2 Pickup Trucks, 3/4 Ton		245.12		269.63	36.99	40.69
40 L.H., Daily Totals		$3430.86		$4534.43	$85.77	$113.36

Crew B-79A	Hr.	Daily	Hr.	Daily	Bare Costs	Incl. O&P
1.5 Equip. Oper. (light)	$59.70	$716.40	$88.85	$1066.20	$59.70	$88.85
.5 Line Remov. (Grinder) 115 H.P.		843.37		927.71		
1 Line Rem. (Metal Balls) 115 H.P.		1648.72		1813.59	207.67	228.44
12 L.H., Daily Totals		$3208.49		$3807.50	$267.37	$317.29

Crew B-79B	Hr.	Daily	Hr.	Daily	Bare Costs	Incl. O&P
1 Laborer	$47.25	$378.00	$70.35	$562.80	$47.25	$70.35
1 Set of Gases		188.67		207.54	23.58	25.94
8 L.H., Daily Totals		$566.67		$770.34	$70.83	$96.29

Crew B-79C	Hr.	Daily	Hr.	Daily	Bare Costs	Incl. O&P
1 Labor Foreman (outside)	$49.25	$394.00	$73.30	$586.40	$48.34	$72.01
5 Laborers	47.25	1890.00	70.35	2814.00		
1 Truck Driver (light)	52.90	423.20	79.00	632.00		
1 Paint Striper, T.M., 120 Gal.		673.88		741.27		
1 Heating Kettle, 115 Gallon		169.64		186.60		
1 Flatbed Truck, Gas, 3 Ton		391.02		430.12		
3 Pickup Trucks, 3/4 Ton		367.68		404.45		
1 Air Compressor, 60 cfm		173.21		190.53		
1 -50' Air Hose, 3/4"		8.16		8.98		
1 Breaker, Pavement, 60 lb.		34.47		37.92	32.47	35.71
56 L.H., Daily Totals		$4525.26		$6032.27	$80.81	$107.72

Crew B-79D	Hr.	Daily	Hr.	Daily	Bare Costs	Incl. O&P
2 Labor Foremen (outside)	$49.25	$788.00	$73.30	$1172.80	$48.46	$72.17
5 Laborers	47.25	1890.00	70.35	2814.00		
1 Truck Driver (light)	52.90	423.20	79.00	632.00		
1 Paint Striper, T.M., 120 Gal.		673.88		741.27		
1 Heating Kettle, 115 Gallon		169.64		186.60		
1 Flatbed Truck, Gas, 3 Ton		391.02		430.12		
4 Pickup Trucks, 3/4 Ton		490.24		539.26		
1 Air Compressor, 60 cfm		173.21		190.53		
1 -50' Air Hose, 3/4"		8.16		8.98		
1 Breaker, Pavement, 60 lb.		34.47		37.92	30.32	33.35
64 L.H., Daily Totals		$5041.82		$6753.48	$78.78	$105.52

Crews - Standard

Crew No.	Bare Costs		Incl. Subs O&P		Cost Per Labor-Hour	

Crew B-79E	Hr.	Daily	Hr.	Daily	Bare Costs	Incl. O&P
2 Labor Foremen (outside)	$49.25	$788.00	$73.30	$1172.80	$48.22	$71.81
7 Laborers	47.25	2646.00	70.35	3939.60		
1 Truck Driver (light)	52.90	423.20	79.00	632.00		
1 Paint Striper, T.M., 120 Gal.		673.88		741.27		
1 Heating Kettle, 115 Gallon		169.64		186.60		
1 Flatbed Truck, Gas, 3 Ton		391.02		430.12		
5 Pickup Trucks, 3/4 Ton		612.80		674.08		
2 Air Compressors, 60 cfm		346.42		381.06		
2 -50' Air Hoses, 3/4"		16.32		17.95		
2 Breakers, Pavement, 60 lb.		68.94		75.83	28.49	31.34
80 L.H., Daily Totals		$6136.22		$8251.32	$76.70	$103.14

Crew B-80	Hr.	Daily	Hr.	Daily	Bare Costs	Incl. O&P
1 Labor Foreman (outside)	$49.25	$394.00	$73.30	$586.40	$52.27	$77.88
1 Laborer	47.25	378.00	70.35	562.80		
1 Truck Driver (light)	52.90	423.20	79.00	632.00		
1 Equip. Oper. (light)	59.70	477.60	88.85	710.80		
1 Flatbed Truck, Gas, 3 Ton		391.02		430.12		
1 Earth Auger, Truck-Mtd.		153.97		169.37	17.03	18.73
32 L.H., Daily Totals		$2217.79		$3091.49	$69.31	$96.61

Crew B-80A	Hr.	Daily	Hr.	Daily	Bare Costs	Incl. O&P
3 Laborers	$47.25	$1134.00	$70.35	$1688.40	$47.25	$70.35
1 Flatbed Truck, Gas, 3 Ton		391.02		430.12	16.29	17.92
24 L.H., Daily Totals		$1525.02		$2118.52	$63.54	$88.27

Crew B-80B	Hr.	Daily	Hr.	Daily	Bare Costs	Incl. O&P
3 Laborers	$47.25	$1134.00	$70.35	$1688.40	$50.36	$74.97
1 Equip. Oper. (light)	59.70	477.60	88.85	710.80		
1 Crane, Flatbed Mounted, 3 Ton		596.44		656.08	18.64	20.50
32 L.H., Daily Totals		$2208.04		$3055.28	$69.00	$95.48

Crew B-80C	Hr.	Daily	Hr.	Daily	Bare Costs	Incl. O&P
2 Laborers	$47.25	$756.00	$70.35	$1125.60	$49.13	$73.23
1 Truck Driver (light)	52.90	423.20	79.00	632.00		
1 Flatbed Truck, Gas, 1.5 Ton		361.95		398.14		
1 Manual Fence Post Auger, Gas		52.21		57.43	17.26	18.98
24 L.H., Daily Totals		$1593.36		$2213.18	$66.39	$92.22

Crew B-81	Hr.	Daily	Hr.	Daily	Bare Costs	Incl. O&P
1 Laborer	$47.25	$378.00	$70.35	$562.80	$55.25	$82.33
1 Equip. Oper. (medium)	63.05	504.40	93.80	750.40		
1 Truck Driver (heavy)	55.45	443.60	82.85	662.80		
1 Hydromulcher, T.M., 3000 Gal.		745.16		819.68		
1 Truck Tractor, 220 H.P.		339.98		373.98	45.21	49.74
24 L.H., Daily Totals		$2411.14		$3169.65	$100.46	$132.07

Crew B-81A	Hr.	Daily	Hr.	Daily	Bare Costs	Incl. O&P
1 Laborer	$47.25	$378.00	$70.35	$562.80	$50.08	$74.67
1 Truck Driver (light)	52.90	423.20	79.00	632.00		
1 Hydromulcher, T.M., 600 Gal.		234.78		258.26		
1 Flatbed Truck, Gas, 3 Ton		391.02		430.12	39.11	43.02
16 L.H., Daily Totals		$1427.00		$1883.18	$89.19	$117.70

Crew B-82	Hr.	Daily	Hr.	Daily	Bare Costs	Incl. O&P
1 Laborer	$47.25	$378.00	$70.35	$562.80	$53.48	$79.60
1 Equip. Oper. (light)	59.70	477.60	88.85	710.80		
1 Horiz. Borer, 6 H.P.		114.54		125.99	7.16	7.87
16 L.H., Daily Totals		$970.14		$1399.59	$60.63	$87.47

Crew B-82A	Hr.	Daily	Hr.	Daily	Bare Costs	Incl. O&P
2 Laborers	$47.25	$756.00	$70.35	$1125.60	$53.48	$79.60
2 Equip. Opers. (light)	59.70	955.20	88.85	1421.60		
2 Dump Truck, 8 C.Y., 220 H.P.		834.98		918.48		
1 Flatbed Trailer, 25 Ton		150.61		165.67		
1 Horiz. Dir. Drill, 20k lb. Thrust		685.30		753.83		
1 Mud Trailer for HDD, 1500 Gal.		696.17		765.79		
1 Pickup Truck, 4x4, 3/4 Ton		191.73		210.90		
1 Flatbed Trailer, 3 Ton		78.34		86.17		
1 Loader, Skid Steer, 78 H.P.		429.91		472.90	95.84	105.43
32 L.H., Daily Totals		$4778.24		$5920.94	$149.32	$185.03

Crew B-82B	Hr.	Daily	Hr.	Daily	Bare Costs	Incl. O&P
2 Laborers	$47.25	$756.00	$70.35	$1125.60	$53.48	$79.60
2 Equip. Opers. (light)	59.70	955.20	88.85	1421.60		
2 Dump Truck, 8 C.Y., 220 H.P.		834.98		918.48		
1 Flatbed Trailer, 25 Ton		150.61		165.67		
1 Horiz. Dir. Drill, 30k lb. Thrust		740.76		814.84		
1 Mud Trailer for HDD, 1500 Gal.		696.17		765.79		
1 Pickup Truck, 4x4, 3/4 Ton		191.73		210.90		
1 Flatbed Trailer, 3 Ton		78.34		86.17		
1 Loader, Skid Steer, 78 H.P.		429.91		472.90	97.58	107.34
32 L.H., Daily Totals		$4833.70		$5981.95	$151.05	$186.94

Crew B-82C	Hr.	Daily	Hr.	Daily	Bare Costs	Incl. O&P
2 Laborers	$47.25	$756.00	$70.35	$1125.60	$53.48	$79.60
2 Equip. Opers. (light)	59.70	955.20	88.85	1421.60		
2 Dump Truck, 8 C.Y., 220 H.P.		834.98		918.48		
1 Flatbed Trailer, 25 Ton		150.61		165.67		
1 Horiz. Dir. Drill, 50k lb. Thrust		869.81		956.79		
1 Mud Trailer for HDD, 1500 Gal.		696.17		765.79		
1 Pickup Truck, 4x4, 3/4 Ton		191.73		210.90		
1 Flatbed Trailer, 3 Ton		78.34		86.17		
1 Loader, Skid Steer, 78 H.P.		429.91		472.90	101.61	111.77
32 L.H., Daily Totals		$4962.75		$6123.90	$155.09	$191.37

Crew B-82D	Hr.	Daily	Hr.	Daily	Bare Costs	Incl. O&P
1 Equip. Oper. (light)	$59.70	$477.60	$88.85	$710.80	$59.70	$88.85
1 Mud Trailer for HDD, 1500 Gal.		696.17		765.79	87.02	95.72
8 L.H., Daily Totals		$1173.77		$1476.59	$146.72	$184.57

Crew B-83	Hr.	Daily	Hr.	Daily	Bare Costs	Incl. O&P
1 Tugboat Captain	$63.05	$504.40	$93.80	$750.40	$55.15	$82.08
1 Tugboat Hand	47.25	378.00	70.35	562.80		
1 Tugboat, 250 H.P.		793.50		872.85	49.59	54.55
16 L.H., Daily Totals		$1675.90		$2186.05	$104.74	$136.63

Crew B-84	Hr.	Daily	Hr.	Daily	Bare Costs	Incl. O&P
1 Equip. Oper. (medium)	$63.05	$504.40	$93.80	$750.40	$63.05	$93.80
1 Rotary Mower/Tractor		238.84		262.72	29.86	32.84
8 L.H., Daily Totals		$743.24		$1013.12	$92.91	$126.64

Crew B-85	Hr.	Daily	Hr.	Daily	Bare Costs	Incl. O&P
3 Laborers	$47.25	$1134.00	$70.35	$1688.40	$52.05	$77.54
1 Equip. Oper. (medium)	63.05	504.40	93.80	750.40		
1 Truck Driver (heavy)	55.45	443.60	82.85	662.80		
1 Telescoping Boom Lift, to 80'		710.06		781.07		
1 Brush Chipper, 12", 130 H.P.		518.12		569.93		
1 Pruning Saw, Rotary		27.37		30.11	31.39	34.53
40 L.H., Daily Totals		$3337.55		$4482.70	$83.44	$112.07

Crews - Standard

Crew No.	Bare Costs		Incl. Subs O&P		Cost Per Labor-Hour	
Crew B-86	Hr.	Daily	Hr.	Daily	Bare Costs	Incl. O&P
1 Equip. Oper. (medium)	$63.05	$504.40	$93.80	$750.40	$63.05	$93.80
1 Stump Chipper, S.P.		263.85		290.24	32.98	36.28
8 L.H., Daily Totals		$768.25		$1040.64	$96.03	$130.08
Crew B-86A	Hr.	Daily	Hr.	Daily	Bare Costs	Incl. O&P
1 Equip. Oper. (medium)	$63.05	$504.40	$93.80	$750.40	$63.05	$93.80
1 Grader, 30,000 Lbs.		1091.19		1200.31	136.40	150.04
8 L.H., Daily Totals		$1595.59		$1950.71	$199.45	$243.84
Crew B-86B	Hr.	Daily	Hr.	Daily	Bare Costs	Incl. O&P
1 Equip. Oper. (medium)	$63.05	$504.40	$93.80	$750.40	$63.05	$93.80
1 Dozer, 200 H.P.		1382.36		1520.60	172.79	190.07
8 L.H., Daily Totals		$1886.76		$2271.00	$235.85	$283.87
Crew B-87	Hr.	Daily	Hr.	Daily	Bare Costs	Incl. O&P
1 Laborer	$47.25	$378.00	$70.35	$562.80	$59.89	$89.11
4 Equip. Oper. (medium)	63.05	2017.60	93.80	3001.60		
2 Feller Bunchers, 100 H.P.		2244.42		2468.86		
1 Log Chipper, 22" Tree		686.57		755.23		
1 Dozer, 105 H.P.		702.68		772.95		
1 Chain Saw, Gas, 36" Long		53.61		58.97	92.18	101.40
40 L.H., Daily Totals		$6082.88		$7620.41	$152.07	$190.51
Crew B-88	Hr.	Daily	Hr.	Daily	Bare Costs	Incl. O&P
1 Laborer	$47.25	$378.00	$70.35	$562.80	$60.79	$90.45
6 Equip. Oper. (medium)	63.05	3026.40	93.80	4502.40		
2 Feller Bunchers, 100 H.P.		2244.42		2468.86		
1 Log Chipper, 22" Tree		686.57		755.23		
2 Log Skidders, 50 H.P.		931.94		1025.13		
1 Dozer, 105 H.P.		702.68		772.95		
1 Chain Saw, Gas, 36" Long		53.61		58.97	82.49	90.73
56 L.H., Daily Totals		$8023.62		$10146.34	$143.28	$181.18
Crew B-89	Hr.	Daily	Hr.	Daily	Bare Costs	Incl. O&P
1 Equip. Oper. (light)	$59.70	$477.60	$88.85	$710.80	$56.30	$83.92
1 Truck Driver (light)	52.90	423.20	79.00	632.00		
1 Flatbed Truck, Gas, 3 Ton		391.02		430.12		
1 Concrete Saw		176.00		193.60		
1 Water Tank, 65 Gal.		97.09		106.80	41.51	45.66
16 L.H., Daily Totals		$1564.91		$2073.32	$97.81	$129.58
Crew B-89A	Hr.	Daily	Hr.	Daily	Bare Costs	Incl. O&P
1 Skilled Worker	$61.25	$490.00	$92.00	$736.00	$54.25	$81.17
1 Laborer	47.25	378.00	70.35	562.80		
1 Core Drill (Large)		118.14		129.95	7.38	8.12
16 L.H., Daily Totals		$986.14		$1428.75	$61.63	$89.30
Crew B-89B	Hr.	Daily	Hr.	Daily	Bare Costs	Incl. O&P
1 Equip. Oper. (light)	$59.70	$477.60	$88.85	$710.80	$56.30	$83.92
1 Truck Driver (light)	52.90	423.20	79.00	632.00		
1 Wall Saw, Hydraulic, 10 H.P.		111.53		122.68		
1 Generator, Diesel, 100 kW		568.06		624.87		
1 Water Tank, 65 Gal.		97.09		106.80		
1 Flatbed Truck, Gas, 3 Ton		391.02		430.12	72.98	80.28
16 L.H., Daily Totals		$2068.50		$2627.27	$129.28	$164.20
Crew B-89C	Hr.	Daily	Hr.	Daily	Bare Costs	Incl. O&P
1 Cement Finisher	$55.00	$440.00	$80.45	$643.60	$55.00	$80.45
1 Masonry cut-off saw, gas		68.42		75.26	8.55	9.41
8 L.H., Daily Totals		$508.42		$718.86	$63.55	$89.86

Crew No.	Bare Costs		Incl. Subs O&P		Cost Per Labor-Hour	
Crew B-90	Hr.	Daily	Hr.	Daily	Bare Costs	Incl. O&P
1 Labor Foreman (outside)	$49.25	$394.00	$73.30	$586.40	$52.66	$78.47
3 Laborers	47.25	1134.00	70.35	1688.40		
2 Equip. Oper. (light)	59.70	955.20	88.85	1421.60		
2 Truck Drivers (heavy)	55.45	887.20	82.85	1325.60		
1 Road Mixer, 310 H.P.		2108.32		2319.15		
1 Dist. Truck, 2000 Gal.		333.32		366.65	38.15	41.97
64 L.H., Daily Totals		$5812.04		$7707.80	$90.81	$120.43
Crew B-90A	Hr.	Daily	Hr.	Daily	Bare Costs	Incl. O&P
1 Labor Foreman (outside)	$49.25	$394.00	$73.30	$586.40	$56.56	$84.17
2 Laborers	47.25	756.00	70.35	1125.60		
4 Equip. Oper. (medium)	63.05	2017.60	93.80	3001.60		
2 Graders, 30,000 Lbs.		2182.38		2400.62		
1 Tandem Roller, 10 Ton		379.22		417.14		
1 Roller, Pneum. Whl., 12 Ton		384.55		423.01	52.61	57.87
56 L.H., Daily Totals		$6113.75		$7954.36	$109.17	$142.04
Crew B-90B	Hr.	Daily	Hr.	Daily	Bare Costs	Incl. O&P
1 Labor Foreman (outside)	$49.25	$394.00	$73.30	$586.40	$55.48	$82.57
2 Laborers	47.25	756.00	70.35	1125.60		
3 Equip. Oper. (medium)	63.05	1513.20	93.80	2251.20		
1 Roller, Pneum. Whl., 12 Ton		384.55		423.01		
1 Road Mixer, 310 H.P.		2108.32		2319.15	51.93	57.13
48 L.H., Daily Totals		$5156.07		$6705.36	$107.42	$139.69
Crew B-90C	Hr.	Daily	Hr.	Daily	Bare Costs	Incl. O&P
1 Labor Foreman (outside)	$49.25	$394.00	$73.30	$586.40	$53.98	$80.42
4 Laborers	47.25	1512.00	70.35	2251.20		
3 Equip. Oper. (medium)	63.05	1513.20	93.80	2251.20		
3 Truck Drivers (heavy)	55.45	1330.80	82.85	1988.40		
3 Road Mixers, 310 H.P.		6324.96		6957.46	71.87	79.06
88 L.H., Daily Totals		$11074.96		$14034.66	$125.85	$159.48
Crew B-90D	Hr.	Daily	Hr.	Daily	Bare Costs	Incl. O&P
1 Labor Foreman (outside)	$49.25	$394.00	$73.30	$586.40	$52.94	$78.87
6 Laborers	47.25	2268.00	70.35	3376.80		
3 Equip. Oper. (medium)	63.05	1513.20	93.80	2251.20		
3 Truck Drivers (heavy)	55.45	1330.80	82.85	1988.40		
3 Road Mixers, 310 H.P.		6324.96		6957.46	60.82	66.90
104 L.H., Daily Totals		$11830.96		$15160.26	$113.76	$145.77
Crew B-90E	Hr.	Daily	Hr.	Daily	Bare Costs	Incl. O&P
1 Labor Foreman (outside)	$49.25	$394.00	$73.30	$586.40	$53.65	$79.88
4 Laborers	47.25	1512.00	70.35	2251.20		
3 Equip. Oper. (medium)	63.05	1513.20	93.80	2251.20		
1 Truck Driver (heavy)	55.45	443.60	82.85	662.80		
1 Road Mixer, 310 H.P.		2108.32		2319.15	29.28	32.21
72 L.H., Daily Totals		$5971.12		$8070.75	$82.93	$112.09
Crew B-91	Hr.	Daily	Hr.	Daily	Bare Costs	Incl. O&P
1 Labor Foreman (outside)	$49.25	$394.00	$73.30	$586.40	$56.42	$84.01
2 Laborers	47.25	756.00	70.35	1125.60		
4 Equip. Oper. (medium)	63.05	2017.60	93.80	3001.60		
1 Truck Driver (heavy)	55.45	443.60	82.85	662.80		
1 Dist. Tanker, 3000 Gallon		367.10		403.81		
1 Truck Tractor, 6x4, 380 H.P.		545.98		600.58		
1 Aggreg. Spreader, S.P.		941.36		1035.50		
1 Roller, Pneum. Whl., 12 Ton		384.55		423.01		
1 Tandem Roller, 10 Ton		379.22		417.14	40.91	45.00
64 L.H., Daily Totals		$6229.41		$8256.43	$97.33	$129.01

Crews - Standard

Crew No.		Bare Costs		Incl. Subs O&P		Cost Per Labor-Hour	
Crew B-91B	Hr.	Daily	Hr.	Daily	Bare Costs	Incl. O&P
1 Laborer	$47.25	$378.00	$70.35	$562.80	$55.15	$82.08
1 Equipment Oper. (med.)	63.05	504.40	93.80	750.40		
1 Road Sweeper, Vac. Assist.		1900.22		2090.24	118.76	130.64
16 L.H., Daily Totals		$2782.62		$3403.44	$173.91	$212.72

Crew No.		Bare Costs		Incl. Subs O&P		Cost Per Labor-Hour	
Crew B-91C	Hr.	Daily	Hr.	Daily	Bare Costs	Incl. O&P
1 Laborer	$47.25	$378.00	$70.35	$562.80	$50.08	$74.67
1 Truck Driver (light)	52.90	423.20	79.00	632.00		
1 Catch Basin Cleaning Truck		594.04		653.44	37.13	40.84
16 L.H., Daily Totals		$1395.24		$1848.24	$87.20	$115.52

Crew B-91D	Hr.	Daily	Hr.	Daily	Bare Costs	Incl. O&P
1 Labor Foreman (outside)	$49.25	$394.00	$73.30	$586.40	$54.74	$81.52
5 Laborers	47.25	1890.00	70.35	2814.00		
5 Equip. Oper. (medium)	63.05	2522.00	93.80	3752.00		
2 Truck Drivers (heavy)	55.45	887.20	82.85	1325.60		
1 Aggreg. Spreader, S.P.		941.36		1035.50		
2 Truck Tractors, 6x4, 380 H.P.		1091.96		1201.16		
2 Dist. Tankers, 3000 Gallon		734.20		807.62		
2 Pavement Brushes, Towed		194.16		213.58		
2 Rollers Pneum. Whl., 12 Ton		769.10		846.01	35.87	39.46
104 L.H., Daily Totals		$9423.98		$12581.86	$90.62	$120.98

Crew B-92	Hr.	Daily	Hr.	Daily	Bare Costs	Incl. O&P
1 Labor Foreman (outside)	$49.25	$394.00	$73.30	$586.40	$47.75	$71.09
3 Laborers	47.25	1134.00	70.35	1688.40		
1 Crack Cleaner, 25 H.P.		167.33		184.06		
1 Air Compressor, 60 cfm		173.21		190.53		
1 Tar Kettle, T.M.		199.54		219.49		
1 Flatbed Truck, Gas, 3 Ton		391.02		430.12	29.10	32.01
32 L.H., Daily Totals		$2459.10		$3299.01	$76.85	$103.09

Crew B-93	Hr.	Daily	Hr.	Daily	Bare Costs	Incl. O&P
1 Equip. Oper. (medium)	$63.05	$504.40	$93.80	$750.40	$63.05	$93.80
1 Feller Buncher, 100 H.P.		1122.21		1234.43	140.28	154.30
8 L.H., Daily Totals		$1626.61		$1984.83	$203.33	$248.10

Crew B-94A	Hr.	Daily	Hr.	Daily	Bare Costs	Incl. O&P
1 Laborer	$47.25	$378.00	$70.35	$562.80	$47.25	$70.35
1 Diaphragm Water Pump, 2"		61.92		68.11		
1 -20' Suction Hose, 2"		4.37		4.81		
2 -50' Discharge Hoses, 2"		8.18		9.00	9.31	10.24
8 L.H., Daily Totals		$452.47		$644.72	$56.56	$80.59

Crew B-94B	Hr.	Daily	Hr.	Daily	Bare Costs	Incl. O&P
1 Laborer	$47.25	$378.00	$70.35	$562.80	$47.25	$70.35
1 Diaphragm Water Pump, 4"		150.72		165.79		
1 -20' Suction Hose, 4"		19.04		20.94		
2 -50' Discharge Hoses, 4"		28.30		31.13	24.76	27.23
8 L.H., Daily Totals		$576.06		$780.67	$72.01	$97.58

Crew B-94C	Hr.	Daily	Hr.	Daily	Bare Costs	Incl. O&P
1 Laborer	$47.25	$378.00	$70.35	$562.80	$47.25	$70.35
1 Centrifugal Water Pump, 3"		82.39		90.63		
1 -20' Suction Hose, 3"		8.96		9.86		
2 -50' Discharge Hoses, 3"		9.76		10.74	12.64	13.90
8 L.H., Daily Totals		$479.11		$674.02	$59.89	$84.25

Crew B-94D	Hr.	Daily	Hr.	Daily	Bare Costs	Incl. O&P
1 Laborer	$47.25	$378.00	$70.35	$562.80	$47.25	$70.35
1 Centr. Water Pump, 6"		386.48		425.13		
1 -20' Suction Hose, 6"		28.12		30.93		
2 -50' Discharge Hoses, 6"		39.98		43.98	56.82	62.50
8 L.H., Daily Totals		$832.58		$1062.84	$104.07	$132.85

Crew C-1	Hr.	Daily	Hr.	Daily	Bare Costs	Incl. O&P
3 Carpenters	$58.60	$1406.40	$87.25	$2094.00	$55.76	$83.03
1 Laborer	47.25	378.00	70.35	562.80		
32 L.H., Daily Totals		$1784.40		$2656.80	$55.76	$83.03

Crew C-2	Hr.	Daily	Hr.	Daily	Bare Costs	Incl. O&P
1 Carpenter Foreman (outside)	$60.60	$484.80	$90.20	$721.60	$57.04	$84.92
4 Carpenters	58.60	1875.20	87.25	2792.00		
1 Laborer	47.25	378.00	70.35	562.80		
48 L.H., Daily Totals		$2738.00		$4076.40	$57.04	$84.92

Crew C-2A	Hr.	Daily	Hr.	Daily	Bare Costs	Incl. O&P
1 Carpenter Foreman (outside)	$60.60	$484.80	$90.20	$721.60	$56.44	$83.79
3 Carpenters	58.60	1406.40	87.25	2094.00		
1 Cement Finisher	55.00	440.00	80.45	643.60		
1 Laborer	47.25	378.00	70.35	562.80		
48 L.H., Daily Totals		$2709.20		$4022.00	$56.44	$83.79

Crew C-3	Hr.	Daily	Hr.	Daily	Bare Costs	Incl. O&P
1 Rodman Foreman (outside)	$66.55	$532.40	$99.40	$795.20	$59.87	$89.32
4 Rodmen (reinf.)	64.55	2065.60	96.40	3084.80		
1 Equip. Oper. (light)	59.70	477.60	88.85	710.80		
2 Laborers	47.25	756.00	70.35	1125.60		
3 Stressing Equipment		51.87		57.06		
.5 Grouting Equipment		97.91		107.70	2.34	2.57
64 L.H., Daily Totals		$3981.38		$5881.15	$62.21	$91.89

Crew C-4	Hr.	Daily	Hr.	Daily	Bare Costs	Incl. O&P
1 Rodman Foreman (outside)	$66.55	$532.40	$99.40	$795.20	$65.05	$97.15
3 Rodmen (reinf.)	64.55	1549.20	96.40	2313.60		
3 Stressing Equipment		51.87		57.06	1.62	1.78
32 L.H., Daily Totals		$2133.47		$3165.86	$66.67	$98.93

Crew C-4A	Hr.	Daily	Hr.	Daily	Bare Costs	Incl. O&P
2 Rodmen (reinf.)	$64.55	$1032.80	$96.40	$1542.40	$64.55	$96.40
4 Stressing Equipment		69.16		76.08	4.32	4.75
16 L.H., Daily Totals		$1101.96		$1618.48	$68.87	$101.15

Crew C-5	Hr.	Daily	Hr.	Daily	Bare Costs	Incl. O&P
1 Rodman Foreman (outside)	$66.55	$532.40	$99.40	$795.20	$63.92	$95.36
4 Rodmen (reinf.)	64.55	2065.60	96.40	3084.80		
1 Equip. Oper. (crane)	66.30	530.40	98.65	789.20		
1 Equip. Oper. (oiler)	56.40	451.20	83.90	671.20		
1 Hyd. Crane, 25 Ton		2273.31		2500.64	40.59	44.65
56 L.H., Daily Totals		$5852.91		$7841.04	$104.52	$140.02

Crew C-6	Hr.	Daily	Hr.	Daily	Bare Costs	Incl. O&P
1 Labor Foreman (outside)	$49.25	$394.00	$73.30	$586.40	$48.88	$72.53
4 Laborers	47.25	1512.00	70.35	2251.20		
1 Cement Finisher	55.00	440.00	80.45	643.60		
2 Gas Engine Vibrators		59.36		65.30	1.24	1.36
48 L.H., Daily Totals		$2405.36		$3546.50	$50.11	$73.89

Crews - Standard

Crew No.		Bare Costs		Incl. Subs O&P		Cost Per Labor-Hour	
Crew C-6A	Hr.	Daily	Hr.	Daily	Bare Costs	Incl. O&P
2 Cement Finishers	$55.00	$880.00	$80.45	$1287.20	$55.00	$80.45
1 Concrete Vibrator, Elec, 2 HP		32.92		36.21	2.06	2.26
16 L.H., Daily Totals		$912.92		$1323.41	$57.06	$82.71
Crew C-7	Hr.	Daily	Hr.	Daily	Bare Costs	Incl. O&P
1 Labor Foreman (outside)	$49.25	$394.00	$73.30	$586.40	$51.11	$75.91
5 Laborers	47.25	1890.00	70.35	2814.00		
1 Cement Finisher	55.00	440.00	80.45	643.60		
1 Equip. Oper. (medium)	63.05	504.40	93.80	750.40		
1 Equip. Oper. (oiler)	56.40	451.20	83.90	671.20		
2 Gas Engine Vibrators		59.36		65.30		
1 Concrete Bucket, 1 C.Y.		50.97		56.07		
1 Hyd. Crane, 55 Ton		2461.06		2707.17	35.71	39.29
72 L.H., Daily Totals		$6250.99		$8294.13	$86.82	$115.20
Crew C-7A	Hr.	Daily	Hr.	Daily	Bare Costs	Incl. O&P
1 Labor Foreman (outside)	$49.25	$394.00	$73.30	$586.40	$49.55	$73.84
5 Laborers	47.25	1890.00	70.35	2814.00		
2 Truck Drivers (heavy)	55.45	887.20	82.85	1325.60		
2 Conc. Transit Mixers		1400.52		1540.57	21.88	24.07
64 L.H., Daily Totals		$4571.72		$6266.57	$71.43	$97.92
Crew C-7B	Hr.	Daily	Hr.	Daily	Bare Costs	Incl. O&P
1 Labor Foreman (outside)	$49.25	$394.00	$73.30	$586.40	$51.02	$75.95
5 Laborers	47.25	1890.00	70.35	2814.00		
1 Equipment Operator, Crane	66.30	530.40	98.65	789.20		
1 Equipment Oiler	56.40	451.20	83.90	671.20		
1 Conc. Bucket, 2 C.Y.		76.52		84.17		
1 Lattice Boom Crane, 165 Ton		2672.17		2939.39	42.95	47.24
64 L.H., Daily Totals		$6014.29		$7884.36	$93.97	$123.19
Crew C-7C	Hr.	Daily	Hr.	Daily	Bare Costs	Incl. O&P
1 Labor Foreman (outside)	$49.25	$394.00	$73.30	$586.40	$51.45	$76.58
5 Laborers	47.25	1890.00	70.35	2814.00		
2 Equipment Operators (med.)	63.05	1008.80	93.80	1500.80		
2 F.E. Loaders, W.M., 4 C.Y.		1579.96		1737.96	24.69	27.16
64 L.H., Daily Totals		$4872.76		$6639.16	$76.14	$103.74
Crew C-7D	Hr.	Daily	Hr.	Daily	Bare Costs	Incl. O&P
1 Labor Foreman (outside)	$49.25	$394.00	$73.30	$586.40	$49.79	$74.12
5 Laborers	47.25	1890.00	70.35	2814.00		
1 Equip. Oper. (medium)	63.05	504.40	93.80	750.40		
1 Concrete Conveyer		194.76		214.24	3.48	3.83
56 L.H., Daily Totals		$2983.16		$4365.04	$53.27	$77.95
Crew C-8	Hr.	Daily	Hr.	Daily	Bare Costs	Incl. O&P
1 Labor Foreman (outside)	$49.25	$394.00	$73.30	$586.40	$52.01	$77.01
3 Laborers	47.25	1134.00	70.35	1688.40		
2 Cement Finishers	55.00	880.00	80.45	1287.20		
1 Equip. Oper. (medium)	63.05	504.40	93.80	750.40		
1 Concrete Pump (Small)		827.49		910.24	14.78	16.25
56 L.H., Daily Totals		$3739.89		$5222.64	$66.78	$93.26
Crew C-8A	Hr.	Daily	Hr.	Daily	Bare Costs	Incl. O&P
1 Labor Foreman (outside)	$49.25	$394.00	$73.30	$586.40	$50.17	$74.21
3 Laborers	47.25	1134.00	70.35	1688.40		
2 Cement Finishers	55.00	880.00	80.45	1287.20		
48 L.H., Daily Totals		$2408.00		$3562.00	$50.17	$74.21

Crew No.		Bare Costs		Incl. Subs O&P		Cost Per Labor-Hour	
Crew C-8B	Hr.	Daily	Hr.	Daily	Bare Costs	Incl. O&P
1 Labor Foreman (outside)	$49.25	$394.00	$73.30	$586.40	$50.81	$75.63
3 Laborers	47.25	1134.00	70.35	1688.40		
1 Equip. Oper. (medium)	63.05	504.40	93.80	750.40		
1 Vibrating Power Screed		90.64		99.70		
1 Roller, Vibratory, 25 Ton		529.68		582.65		
1 Dozer, 200 H.P.		1382.36		1520.60	50.07	55.07
40 L.H., Daily Totals		$4035.08		$5228.15	$100.88	$130.70
Crew C-8C	Hr.	Daily	Hr.	Daily	Bare Costs	Incl. O&P
1 Labor Foreman (outside)	$49.25	$394.00	$73.30	$586.40	$51.51	$76.43
3 Laborers	47.25	1134.00	70.35	1688.40		
1 Cement Finisher	55.00	440.00	80.45	643.60		
1 Equip. Oper. (medium)	63.05	504.40	93.80	750.40		
1 Shotcrete Pump Rig, 12 C.Y./hr		651.19		716.31		
1 Air Compressor, 160 cfm		244.12		268.53		
4 -50' Air Hoses, 1"		37.24		40.96		
4 -50' Air Hoses, 2"		129.40		142.34	22.12	24.34
48 L.H., Daily Totals		$3534.35		$4836.94	$73.63	$100.77
Crew C-8D	Hr.	Daily	Hr.	Daily	Bare Costs	Incl. O&P
1 Labor Foreman (outside)	$49.25	$394.00	$73.30	$586.40	$52.80	$78.24
1 Laborer	47.25	378.00	70.35	562.80		
1 Cement Finisher	55.00	440.00	80.45	643.60		
1 Equipment Oper. (light)	59.70	477.60	88.85	710.80		
1 Air Compressor, 250 cfm		196.28		215.91		
2 -50' Air Hoses, 1"		18.62		20.48	6.72	7.39
32 L.H., Daily Totals		$1904.50		$2739.99	$59.52	$85.62
Crew C-8E	Hr.	Daily	Hr.	Daily	Bare Costs	Incl. O&P
1 Labor Foreman (outside)	$49.25	$394.00	$73.30	$586.40	$50.95	$75.61
3 Laborers	47.25	1134.00	70.35	1688.40		
1 Cement Finisher	55.00	440.00	80.45	643.60		
1 Equipment Oper. (light)	59.70	477.60	88.85	710.80		
1 Shotcrete Rig, 35 C.Y./hr		797.28		877.01		
1 Air Compressor, 250 cfm		196.28		215.91		
4 -50' Air Hoses, 1"		37.24		40.96		
4 -50' Air Hoses, 2"		129.40		142.34	24.17	26.59
48 L.H., Daily Totals		$3605.80		$4905.42	$75.12	$102.20
Crew C-9	Hr.	Daily	Hr.	Daily	Bare Costs	Incl. O&P
1 Cement Finisher	$55.00	$440.00	$80.45	$643.60	$52.30	$77.50
2 Laborers	47.25	756.00	70.35	1125.60		
1 Equipment Oper. (light)	59.70	477.60	88.85	710.80		
1 Grout Pump, 50 C.F./hr.		158.45		174.29		
1 Air Compressor, 160 cfm		244.12		268.53		
2 -50' Air Hoses, 1"		18.62		20.48		
2 -50' Air Hoses, 2"		64.70		71.17	15.18	16.70
32 L.H., Daily Totals		$2159.49		$3014.48	$67.48	$94.20
Crew C-10	Hr.	Daily	Hr.	Daily	Bare Costs	Incl. O&P
1 Laborer	$47.25	$378.00	$70.35	$562.80	$52.42	$77.08
2 Cement Finishers	55.00	880.00	80.45	1287.20		
24 L.H., Daily Totals		$1258.00		$1850.00	$52.42	$77.08
Crew C-10B	Hr.	Daily	Hr.	Daily	Bare Costs	Incl. O&P
3 Laborers	$47.25	$1134.00	$70.35	$1688.40	$50.35	$74.39
2 Cement Finishers	55.00	880.00	80.45	1287.20		
1 Concrete Mixer, 10 C.F.		149.77		164.75		
2 Trowels, 48" Walk-Behind		171.24		188.36	8.03	8.83
40 L.H., Daily Totals		$2335.01		$3328.71	$58.38	$83.22

Crews - Standard

Crew No.	Hr.	Bare Costs Daily	Hr.	Incl. Subs O&P Daily	Cost Per Labor-Hour Bare Costs	Incl. O&P
Crew C-10C						
1 Laborer	$47.25	$378.00	$70.35	$562.80	$52.42	$77.08
2 Cement Finishers	55.00	880.00	80.45	1287.20		
1 Trowel, 48" Walk-Behind		85.62		94.18	3.57	3.92
24 L.H., Daily Totals		$1343.62		$1944.18	$55.98	$81.01
Crew C-10D						
1 Laborer	$47.25	$378.00	$70.35	$562.80	$52.42	$77.08
2 Cement Finishers	55.00	880.00	80.45	1287.20		
1 Vibrating Power Screed		90.64		99.70		
1 Trowel, 48" Walk-Behind		85.62		94.18	7.34	8.08
24 L.H., Daily Totals		$1434.26		$2043.89	$59.76	$85.16
Crew C-10E						
1 Laborer	$47.25	$378.00	$70.35	$562.80	$52.42	$77.08
2 Cement Finishers	55.00	880.00	80.45	1287.20		
1 Vibrating Power Screed		90.64		99.70		
1 Cement Trowel, 96" Ride-On		225.34		247.87	13.17	14.48
24 L.H., Daily Totals		$1573.98		$2197.58	$65.58	$91.57
Crew C-10F						
1 Laborer	$47.25	$378.00	$70.35	$562.80	$52.42	$77.08
2 Cement Finishers	55.00	880.00	80.45	1287.20		
1 Telescoping Boom Lift, to 60'		385.68		424.25	16.07	17.68
24 L.H., Daily Totals		$1643.68		$2274.25	$68.49	$94.76
Crew C-11						
1 Struc. Steel Foreman (outside)	$66.55	$532.40	$102.50	$820.00	$64.06	$97.94
6 Struc. Steel Workers	64.55	3098.40	99.40	4771.20		
1 Equip. Oper. (crane)	66.30	530.40	98.65	789.20		
1 Equip. Oper. (oiler)	56.40	451.20	83.90	671.20		
1 Lattice Boom Crane, 150 Ton		2585.11		2843.62	35.90	39.49
72 L.H., Daily Totals		$7197.51		$9895.22	$99.97	$137.43
Crew C-12						
1 Carpenter Foreman (outside)	$60.60	$484.80	$90.20	$721.60	$58.33	$86.83
3 Carpenters	58.60	1406.40	87.25	2094.00		
1 Laborer	47.25	378.00	70.35	562.80		
1 Equip. Oper. (crane)	66.30	530.40	98.65	789.20		
1 Hyd. Crane, 12 Ton		2150.65		2365.72	44.81	49.29
48 L.H., Daily Totals		$4950.25		$6533.31	$103.13	$136.11
Crew C-13						
1 Struc. Steel Worker	$64.55	$516.40	$99.40	$795.20	$62.57	$95.35
1 Welder	64.55	516.40	99.40	795.20		
1 Carpenter	58.60	468.80	87.25	698.00		
1 Welder, Gas Engine, 300 amp		147.09		161.80	6.13	6.74
24 L.H., Daily Totals		$1648.69		$2450.20	$68.70	$102.09
Crew C-14						
1 Carpenter Foreman (outside)	$60.60	$484.80	$90.20	$721.60	$57.42	$85.38
5 Carpenters	58.60	2344.00	87.25	3490.00		
4 Laborers	47.25	1512.00	70.35	2251.20		
4 Rodmen (reinf.)	64.55	2065.60	96.40	3084.80		
2 Cement Finishers	55.00	880.00	80.45	1287.20		
1 Equip. Oper. (crane)	66.30	530.40	98.65	789.20		
1 Equip. Oper. (oiler)	56.40	451.20	83.90	671.20		
1 Hyd. Crane, 80 Ton		2641.70		2905.87	18.35	20.18
144 L.H., Daily Totals		$10909.70		$15201.07	$75.76	$105.56

Crew No.	Hr.	Bare Costs Daily	Hr.	Incl. Subs O&P Daily	Cost Per Labor-Hour Bare Costs	Incl. O&P
Crew C-14A						
1 Carpenter Foreman (outside)	$60.60	$484.80	$90.20	$721.60	$58.76	$87.47
16 Carpenters	58.60	7500.80	87.25	11168.00		
4 Rodmen (reinf.)	64.55	2065.60	96.40	3084.80		
2 Laborers	47.25	756.00	70.35	1125.60		
1 Cement Finisher	55.00	440.00	80.45	643.60		
1 Equip. Oper. (medium)	63.05	504.40	93.80	750.40		
1 Gas Engine Vibrator		29.68		32.65		
1 Concrete Pump (Small)		827.49		910.24	4.29	4.71
200 L.H., Daily Totals		$12608.77		$18436.89	$63.04	$92.18
Crew C-14B						
1 Carpenter Foreman (outside)	$60.60	$484.80	$90.20	$721.60	$58.61	$87.20
16 Carpenters	58.60	7500.80	87.25	11168.00		
4 Rodmen (reinf.)	64.55	2065.60	96.40	3084.80		
2 Laborers	47.25	756.00	70.35	1125.60		
2 Cement Finishers	55.00	880.00	80.45	1287.20		
1 Equip. Oper. (medium)	63.05	504.40	93.80	750.40		
1 Gas Engine Vibrator		29.68		32.65		
1 Concrete Pump (Small)		827.49		910.24	4.12	4.53
208 L.H., Daily Totals		$13048.77		$19080.49	$62.73	$91.73
Crew C-14C						
1 Carpenter Foreman (outside)	$60.60	$484.80	$90.20	$721.60	$56.09	$83.45
6 Carpenters	58.60	2812.80	87.25	4188.00		
2 Rodmen (reinf.)	64.55	1032.80	96.40	1542.40		
4 Laborers	47.25	1512.00	70.35	2251.20		
1 Cement Finisher	55.00	440.00	80.45	643.60		
1 Gas Engine Vibrator		29.68		32.65	.27	.29
112 L.H., Daily Totals		$6312.08		$9379.45	$56.36	$83.75
Crew C-14D						
1 Carpenter Foreman (outside)	$60.60	$484.80	$90.20	$721.60	$58.28	$86.74
18 Carpenters	58.60	8438.40	87.25	12564.00		
2 Rodmen (reinf.)	64.55	1032.80	96.40	1542.40		
2 Laborers	47.25	756.00	70.35	1125.60		
1 Cement Finisher	55.00	440.00	80.45	643.60		
1 Equip. Oper. (medium)	63.05	504.40	93.80	750.40		
1 Gas Engine Vibrator		29.68		32.65		
1 Concrete Pump (Small)		827.49		910.24	4.29	4.71
200 L.H., Daily Totals		$12513.57		$18290.49	$62.57	$91.45
Crew C-14E						
1 Carpenter Foreman (outside)	$60.60	$484.80	$90.20	$721.60	$57.52	$85.62
2 Carpenters	58.60	937.60	87.25	1396.00		
4 Rodmen (reinf.)	64.55	2065.60	96.40	3084.80		
3 Laborers	47.25	1134.00	70.35	1688.40		
1 Cement Finisher	55.00	440.00	80.45	643.60		
1 Gas Engine Vibrator		29.68		32.65	.34	.37
88 L.H., Daily Totals		$5091.68		$7567.05	$57.86	$85.99
Crew C-14F						
1 Labor Foreman (outside)	$49.25	$394.00	$73.30	$586.40	$52.64	$77.41
2 Laborers	47.25	756.00	70.35	1125.60		
6 Cement Finishers	55.00	2640.00	80.45	3861.60		
1 Gas Engine Vibrator		29.68		32.65	.41	.45
72 L.H., Daily Totals		$3819.68		$5606.25	$53.05	$77.86

Crews - Standard

Crew No.	Bare Costs		Incl. Subs O&P		Cost Per Labor-Hour	
Crew C-14G	Hr.	Daily	Hr.	Daily	Bare Costs	Incl. O&P
1 Labor Foreman (outside)	$49.25	$394.00	$73.30	$586.40	$51.96	$76.54
2 Laborers	47.25	756.00	70.35	1125.60		
4 Cement Finishers	55.00	1760.00	80.45	2574.40		
1 Gas Engine Vibrator		29.68		32.65	.53	.58
56 L.H., Daily Totals		$2939.68		$4319.05	$52.49	$77.13
Crew C-14H	Hr.	Daily	Hr.	Daily	Bare Costs	Incl. O&P
1 Carpenter Foreman (outside)	$60.60	$484.80	$90.20	$721.60	$57.43	$85.32
2 Carpenters	58.60	937.60	87.25	1396.00		
1 Rodman (reinf.)	64.55	516.40	96.40	771.20		
1 Laborer	47.25	378.00	70.35	562.80		
1 Cement Finisher	55.00	440.00	80.45	643.60		
1 Gas Engine Vibrator		29.68		32.65	.62	.68
48 L.H., Daily Totals		$2786.48		$4127.85	$58.05	$86.00
Crew C-14L	Hr.	Daily	Hr.	Daily	Bare Costs	Incl. O&P
1 Carpenter Foreman (outside)	$60.60	$484.80	$90.20	$721.60	$54.68	$81.30
6 Carpenters	58.60	2812.80	87.25	4188.00		
4 Laborers	47.25	1512.00	70.35	2251.20		
1 Cement Finisher	55.00	440.00	80.45	643.60		
1 Gas Engine Vibrator		29.68		32.65	.31	.34
96 L.H., Daily Totals		$5279.28		$7837.05	$54.99	$81.64
Crew C-14M	Hr.	Daily	Hr.	Daily	Bare Costs	Incl. O&P
1 Carpenter Foreman (outside)	$60.60	$484.80	$90.20	$721.60	$56.86	$84.51
2 Carpenters	58.60	937.60	87.25	1396.00		
1 Rodman (reinf.)	64.55	516.40	96.40	771.20		
2 Laborers	47.25	756.00	70.35	1125.60		
1 Cement Finisher	55.00	440.00	80.45	643.60		
1 Equip. Oper. (medium)	63.05	504.40	93.80	750.40		
1 Gas Engine Vibrator		29.68		32.65		
1 Concrete Pump (Small)		827.49		910.24	13.39	14.73
64 L.H., Daily Totals		$4496.37		$6351.29	$70.26	$99.24
Crew C-15	Hr.	Daily	Hr.	Daily	Bare Costs	Incl. O&P
1 Carpenter Foreman (outside)	$60.60	$484.80	$90.20	$721.60	$54.90	$81.45
2 Carpenters	58.60	937.60	87.25	1396.00		
3 Laborers	47.25	1134.00	70.35	1688.40		
2 Cement Finishers	55.00	880.00	80.45	1287.20		
1 Rodman (reinf.)	64.55	516.40	96.40	771.20		
72 L.H., Daily Totals		$3952.80		$5864.40	$54.90	$81.45
Crew C-16	Hr.	Daily	Hr.	Daily	Bare Costs	Incl. O&P
1 Labor Foreman (outside)	$49.25	$394.00	$73.30	$586.40	$52.01	$77.01
3 Laborers	47.25	1134.00	70.35	1688.40		
2 Cement Finishers	55.00	880.00	80.45	1287.20		
1 Equip. Oper. (medium)	63.05	504.40	93.80	750.40		
1 Gunite Pump Rig		352.58		387.84		
2 -50' Air Hoses, 3/4"		16.32		17.95		
2 -50' Air Hoses, 2"		64.70		71.17	7.74	8.52
56 L.H., Daily Totals		$3346.00		$4789.36	$59.75	$85.52
Crew C-16A	Hr.	Daily	Hr.	Daily	Bare Costs	Incl. O&P
1 Laborer	$47.25	$378.00	$70.35	$562.80	$55.08	$81.26
2 Cement Finishers	55.00	880.00	80.45	1287.20		
1 Equip. Oper. (medium)	63.05	504.40	93.80	750.40		
1 Gunite Pump Rig		352.58		387.84		
2 -50' Air Hoses, 3/4"		16.32		17.95		
2 -50' Air Hoses, 2"		64.70		71.17		
1 Telescoping Boom Lift, to 60'		385.68		424.25	25.60	28.16
32 L.H., Daily Totals		$2581.68		$3501.61	$80.68	$109.43

Crew No.	Bare Costs		Incl. Subs O&P		Cost Per Labor-Hour	
Crew C-17	Hr.	Daily	Hr.	Daily	Bare Costs	Incl. O&P
2 Skilled Worker Foremen (out)	$63.25	$1012.00	$95.00	$1520.00	$61.65	$92.60
8 Skilled Workers	61.25	3920.00	92.00	5888.00		
80 L.H., Daily Totals		$4932.00		$7408.00	$61.65	$92.60
Crew C-17A	Hr.	Daily	Hr.	Daily	Bare Costs	Incl. O&P
2 Skilled Worker Foremen (out)	$63.25	$1012.00	$95.00	$1520.00	$61.71	$92.68
8 Skilled Workers	61.25	3920.00	92.00	5888.00		
.13 Equip. Oper. (crane)	66.30	68.95	98.65	102.60		
.13 Hyd. Crane, 80 Ton		343.42		377.76	4.24	4.66
81.04 L.H., Daily Totals		$5344.37		$7888.36	$65.95	$97.34
Crew C-17B	Hr.	Daily	Hr.	Daily	Bare Costs	Incl. O&P
2 Skilled Worker Foremen (out)	$63.25	$1012.00	$95.00	$1520.00	$61.76	$92.75
8 Skilled Workers	61.25	3920.00	92.00	5888.00		
.25 Equip. Oper. (crane)	66.30	132.60	98.65	197.30		
.25 Hyd. Crane, 80 Ton		660.42		726.47		
.25 Trowel, 48" Walk-Behind		21.41		23.55	8.31	9.15
82 L.H., Daily Totals		$5746.43		$8355.31	$70.08	$101.89
Crew C-17C	Hr.	Daily	Hr.	Daily	Bare Costs	Incl. O&P
2 Skilled Worker Foremen (out)	$63.25	$1012.00	$95.00	$1520.00	$61.82	$92.82
8 Skilled Workers	61.25	3920.00	92.00	5888.00		
.38 Equip. Oper. (crane)	66.30	201.55	98.65	299.90		
.38 Hyd. Crane, 80 Ton		1003.85		1104.23	12.09	13.30
83.04 L.H., Daily Totals		$6137.40		$8812.13	$73.91	$106.12
Crew C-17D	Hr.	Daily	Hr.	Daily	Bare Costs	Incl. O&P
2 Skilled Worker Foremen (out)	$63.25	$1012.00	$95.00	$1520.00	$61.87	$92.89
8 Skilled Workers	61.25	3920.00	92.00	5888.00		
.5 Equip. Oper. (crane)	66.30	265.20	98.65	394.60		
.5 Hyd. Crane, 80 Ton		1320.85		1452.93	15.72	17.30
84 L.H., Daily Totals		$6518.05		$9255.53	$77.60	$110.18
Crew C-17E	Hr.	Daily	Hr.	Daily	Bare Costs	Incl. O&P
2 Skilled Worker Foremen (out)	$63.25	$1012.00	$95.00	$1520.00	$61.65	$92.60
8 Skilled Workers	61.25	3920.00	92.00	5888.00		
1 Hyd. Jack with Rods		40.57		44.63	.51	.56
80 L.H., Daily Totals		$4972.57		$7452.63	$62.16	$93.16
Crew C-18	Hr.	Daily	Hr.	Daily	Bare Costs	Incl. O&P
.13 Labor Foreman (outside)	$49.25	$51.22	$73.30	$76.23	$47.48	$70.69
1 Laborer	47.25	378.00	70.35	562.80		
1 Concrete Cart, 10 C.F.		149.92		164.91	16.58	18.24
9.04 L.H., Daily Totals		$579.14		$803.94	$64.06	$88.93
Crew C-19	Hr.	Daily	Hr.	Daily	Bare Costs	Incl. O&P
.13 Labor Foreman (outside)	$49.25	$51.22	$73.30	$76.23	$47.48	$70.69
1 Laborer	47.25	378.00	70.35	562.80		
1 Concrete Cart, 18 C.F.		122.73		135.00	13.58	14.93
9.04 L.H., Daily Totals		$551.95		$774.03	$61.06	$85.62
Crew C-20	Hr.	Daily	Hr.	Daily	Bare Costs	Incl. O&P
1 Labor Foreman (outside)	$49.25	$394.00	$73.30	$586.40	$50.44	$74.91
5 Laborers	47.25	1890.00	70.35	2814.00		
1 Cement Finisher	55.00	440.00	80.45	643.60		
1 Equip. Oper. (medium)	63.05	504.40	93.80	750.40		
2 Gas Engine Vibrators		59.36		65.30		
1 Concrete Pump (Small)		827.49		910.24	13.86	15.24
64 L.H., Daily Totals		$4115.25		$5769.94	$64.30	$90.16

Crews - Standard

Crew No.	Bare Costs		Incl. Subs O&P		Cost Per Labor-Hour	
Crew C-21	Hr.	Daily	Hr.	Daily	Bare Costs	Incl. O&P
1 Labor Foreman (outside)	$49.25	$394.00	$73.30	$586.40	$50.44	$74.91
5 Laborers	47.25	1890.00	70.35	2814.00		
1 Cement Finisher	55.00	440.00	80.45	643.60		
1 Equip. Oper. (medium)	63.05	504.40	93.80	750.40		
2 Gas Engine Vibrators		59.36		65.30		
1 Concrete Conveyer		194.76		214.24	3.97	4.37
64 L.H., Daily Totals		$3482.52		$5073.93	$54.41	$79.28

Crew No.	Bare Costs		Incl. Subs O&P		Cost Per Labor-Hour	
Crew C-22	Hr.	Daily	Hr.	Daily	Bare Costs	Incl. O&P
1 Rodman Foreman (outside)	$66.55	$532.40	$99.40	$795.20	$64.77	$96.72
4 Rodmen (reinf.)	64.55	2065.60	96.40	3084.80		
.13 Equip. Oper. (crane)	66.30	68.95	98.65	102.60		
.13 Equip. Oper. (oiler)	56.40	58.66	83.90	87.26		
.13 Hyd. Crane, 25 Ton		295.53		325.08	7.02	7.73
42.08 L.H., Daily Totals		$3021.14		$4394.94	$71.80	$104.44

Crew C-23	Hr.	Daily	Hr.	Daily	Bare Costs	Incl. O&P
2 Skilled Worker Foremen (out)	$63.25	$1012.00	$95.00	$1520.00	$61.67	$92.45
6 Skilled Workers	61.25	2940.00	92.00	4416.00		
1 Equip. Oper. (crane)	66.30	530.40	98.65	789.20		
1 Equip. Oper. (oiler)	56.40	451.20	83.90	671.20		
1 Lattice Boom Crane, 90 Ton		2689.54		2958.49	33.62	36.98
80 L.H., Daily Totals		$7623.14		$10354.89	$95.29	$129.44

Crew C-23A	Hr.	Daily	Hr.	Daily	Bare Costs	Incl. O&P
1 Labor Foreman (outside)	$49.25	$394.00	$73.30	$586.40	$53.29	$79.31
2 Laborers	47.25	756.00	70.35	1125.60		
1 Equip. Oper. (crane)	66.30	530.40	98.65	789.20		
1 Equip. Oper. (oiler)	56.40	451.20	83.90	671.20		
1 Crawler Crane, 100 Ton		1552.12		1707.33		
3 Conc. Buckets, 8 C.Y.		425.58		468.14	49.44	54.39
40 L.H., Daily Totals		$4109.30		$5347.87	$102.73	$133.70

Crew C-24	Hr.	Daily	Hr.	Daily	Bare Costs	Incl. O&P
2 Skilled Worker Foremen (out)	$63.25	$1012.00	$95.00	$1520.00	$61.67	$92.45
6 Skilled Workers	61.25	2940.00	92.00	4416.00		
1 Equip. Oper. (crane)	66.30	530.40	98.65	789.20		
1 Equip. Oper. (oiler)	56.40	451.20	83.90	671.20		
1 Lattice Boom Crane, 150 Ton		2585.11		2843.62	32.31	35.55
80 L.H., Daily Totals		$7518.71		$10240.02	$93.98	$128.00

Crew C-25	Hr.	Daily	Hr.	Daily	Bare Costs	Incl. O&P
2 Rodmen (reinf.)	$64.55	$1032.80	$96.40	$1542.40	$51.70	$79.67
2 Rodmen Helpers	38.85	621.60	62.95	1007.20		
32 L.H., Daily Totals		$1654.40		$2549.60	$51.70	$79.67

Crew C-27	Hr.	Daily	Hr.	Daily	Bare Costs	Incl. O&P
2 Cement Finishers	$55.00	$880.00	$80.45	$1287.20	$55.00	$80.45
1 Concrete Saw		176.00		193.60	11.00	12.10
16 L.H., Daily Totals		$1056.00		$1480.80	$66.00	$92.55

Crew C-28	Hr.	Daily	Hr.	Daily	Bare Costs	Incl. O&P
1 Cement Finisher	$55.00	$440.00	$80.45	$643.60	$55.00	$80.45
1 Portable Air Compressor, Gas		34.53		37.98	4.32	4.75
8 L.H., Daily Totals		$474.53		$681.58	$59.32	$85.20

Crew C-29	Hr.	Daily	Hr.	Daily	Bare Costs	Incl. O&P
1 Laborer	$47.25	$378.00	$70.35	$562.80	$47.25	$70.35
1 Pressure Washer		104.23		114.65	13.03	14.33
8 L.H., Daily Totals		$482.23		$677.45	$60.28	$84.68

Crew C-30	Hr.	Daily	Hr.	Daily	Bare Costs	Incl. O&P
1 Laborer	$47.25	$378.00	$70.35	$562.80	$47.25	$70.35
1 Concrete Mixer, 10 C.F.		149.77		164.75	18.72	20.59
8 L.H., Daily Totals		$527.77		$727.55	$65.97	$90.94

Crew C-31	Hr.	Daily	Hr.	Daily	Bare Costs	Incl. O&P
1 Cement Finisher	$55.00	$440.00	$80.45	$643.60	$55.00	$80.45
1 Grout Pump		352.58		387.84	44.07	48.48
8 L.H., Daily Totals		$792.58		$1031.44	$99.07	$128.93

Crew C-32	Hr.	Daily	Hr.	Daily	Bare Costs	Incl. O&P
1 Cement Finisher	$55.00	$440.00	$80.45	$643.60	$51.13	$75.40
1 Laborer	47.25	378.00	70.35	562.80		
1 Crack Chaser Saw, Gas, 6 H.P.		86.61		95.27		
1 Vacuum Pick-Up System		73.53		80.88	10.01	11.01
16 L.H., Daily Totals		$978.14		$1382.55	$61.13	$86.41

Crew D-1	Hr.	Daily	Hr.	Daily	Bare Costs	Incl. O&P
1 Bricklayer	$57.50	$460.00	$86.35	$690.80	$52.08	$78.20
1 Bricklayer Helper	46.65	373.20	70.05	560.40		
16 L.H., Daily Totals		$833.20		$1251.20	$52.08	$78.20

Crew D-2	Hr.	Daily	Hr.	Daily	Bare Costs	Incl. O&P
3 Bricklayers	$57.50	$1380.00	$86.35	$2072.40	$53.65	$80.50
2 Bricklayer Helpers	46.65	746.40	70.05	1120.80		
.5 Carpenter	58.60	234.40	87.25	349.00		
44 L.H., Daily Totals		$2360.80		$3542.20	$53.65	$80.50

Crew D-3	Hr.	Daily	Hr.	Daily	Bare Costs	Incl. O&P
3 Bricklayers	$57.50	$1380.00	$86.35	$2072.40	$53.42	$80.18
2 Bricklayer Helpers	46.65	746.40	70.05	1120.80		
.25 Carpenter	58.60	117.20	87.25	174.50		
42 L.H., Daily Totals		$2243.60		$3367.70	$53.42	$80.18

Crew D-4	Hr.	Daily	Hr.	Daily	Bare Costs	Incl. O&P
1 Bricklayer	$57.50	$460.00	$86.35	$690.80	$52.63	$78.83
2 Bricklayer Helpers	46.65	746.40	70.05	1120.80		
1 Equip. Oper. (light)	59.70	477.60	88.85	710.80		
1 Grout Pump, 50 C.F./hr.		158.45		174.29	4.95	5.45
32 L.H., Daily Totals		$1842.45		$2696.70	$57.58	$84.27

Crew D-5	Hr.	Daily	Hr.	Daily	Bare Costs	Incl. O&P
1 Bricklayer	57.50	460.00	86.35	690.80	57.50	86.35
8 L.H., Daily Totals		$460.00		$690.80	$57.50	$86.35

Crew D-6	Hr.	Daily	Hr.	Daily	Bare Costs	Incl. O&P
3 Bricklayers	$57.50	$1380.00	$86.35	$2072.40	$52.34	$78.56
3 Bricklayer Helpers	46.65	1119.60	70.05	1681.20		
.25 Carpenter	58.60	117.20	87.25	174.50		
50 L.H., Daily Totals		$2616.80		$3928.10	$52.34	$78.56

Crew D-7	Hr.	Daily	Hr.	Daily	Bare Costs	Incl. O&P
1 Tile Layer	$55.30	$442.40	$80.80	$646.40	$49.90	$72.90
1 Tile Layer Helper	44.50	356.00	65.00	520.00		
16 L.H., Daily Totals		$798.40		$1166.40	$49.90	$72.90

Crew D-8	Hr.	Daily	Hr.	Daily	Bare Costs	Incl. O&P
3 Bricklayers	$57.50	$1380.00	$86.35	$2072.40	$53.16	$79.83
2 Bricklayer Helpers	46.65	746.40	70.05	1120.80		
40 L.H., Daily Totals		$2126.40		$3193.20	$53.16	$79.83

Crews - Standard

Crew No.		Bare Costs		Incl. Subs O&P		Cost Per Labor-Hour	
Crew D-9	Hr.	Daily	Hr.	Daily	Bare Costs	Incl. O&P
3 Bricklayers	$57.50	$1380.00	$86.35	$2072.40	$52.08	$78.20
3 Bricklayer Helpers	46.65	1119.60	70.05	1681.20		
48 L.H., Daily Totals		$2499.60		$3753.60	$52.08	$78.20
Crew D-10	Hr.	Daily	Hr.	Daily	Bare Costs	Incl. O&P
1 Bricklayer Foreman (outside)	$59.50	$476.00	$89.35	$714.80	$57.49	$86.10
1 Bricklayer	57.50	460.00	86.35	690.80		
1 Bricklayer Helper	46.65	373.20	70.05	560.40		
1 Equip. Oper. (crane)	66.30	530.40	98.65	789.20		
1 S.P. Crane, 4x4, 12 Ton		637.99		701.79	19.94	21.93
32 L.H., Daily Totals		$2477.59		$3456.99	$77.42	$108.03
Crew D-11	Hr.	Daily	Hr.	Daily	Bare Costs	Incl. O&P
1 Bricklayer Foreman (outside)	$59.50	$476.00	$89.35	$714.80	$54.55	$81.92
1 Bricklayer	57.50	460.00	86.35	690.80		
1 Bricklayer Helper	46.65	373.20	70.05	560.40		
24 L.H., Daily Totals		$1309.20		$1966.00	$54.55	$81.92
Crew D-12	Hr.	Daily	Hr.	Daily	Bare Costs	Incl. O&P
1 Bricklayer Foreman (outside)	$59.50	$476.00	$89.35	$714.80	$52.58	$78.95
1 Bricklayer	57.50	460.00	86.35	690.80		
2 Bricklayer Helpers	46.65	746.40	70.05	1120.80		
32 L.H., Daily Totals		$1682.40		$2526.40	$52.58	$78.95
Crew D-13	Hr.	Daily	Hr.	Daily	Bare Costs	Incl. O&P
1 Bricklayer Foreman (outside)	$59.50	$476.00	$89.35	$714.80	$55.87	$83.62
1 Bricklayer	57.50	460.00	86.35	690.80		
2 Bricklayer Helpers	46.65	746.40	70.05	1120.80		
1 Carpenter	58.60	468.80	87.25	698.00		
1 Equip. Oper. (crane)	66.30	530.40	98.65	789.20		
1 S.P. Crane, 4x4, 12 Ton		637.99		701.79	13.29	14.62
48 L.H., Daily Totals		$3319.59		$4715.39	$69.16	$98.24
Crew D-14	Hr.	Daily	Hr.	Daily	Bare Costs	Incl. O&P
3 Bricklayers	$57.50	$1380.00	$86.35	$2072.40	$54.79	$82.28
1 Bricklayer Helper	46.65	373.20	70.05	560.40		
32 L.H., Daily Totals		$1753.20		$2632.80	$54.79	$82.28
Crew E-1	Hr.	Daily	Hr.	Daily	Bare Costs	Incl. O&P
1 Welder Foreman (outside)	$66.55	$532.40	$102.50	$820.00	$63.60	$96.92
1 Welder	64.55	516.40	99.40	795.20		
1 Equip. Oper. (light)	59.70	477.60	88.85	710.80		
1 Welder, Gas Engine, 300 amp		147.09		161.80	6.13	6.74
24 L.H., Daily Totals		$1673.49		$2487.80	$69.73	$103.66
Crew E-2	Hr.	Daily	Hr.	Daily	Bare Costs	Incl. O&P
1 Struc. Steel Foreman (outside)	$66.55	$532.40	$102.50	$820.00	$63.92	$97.52
4 Struc. Steel Workers	64.55	2065.60	99.40	3180.80		
1 Equip. Oper. (crane)	66.30	530.40	98.65	789.20		
1 Equip. Oper. (oiler)	56.40	451.20	83.90	671.20		
1 Lattice Boom Crane, 90 Ton		2689.54		2958.49	48.03	52.83
56 L.H., Daily Totals		$6269.14		$8419.69	$111.95	$150.35
Crew E-3	Hr.	Daily	Hr.	Daily	Bare Costs	Incl. O&P
1 Struc. Steel Foreman (outside)	$66.55	$532.40	$102.50	$820.00	$65.22	$100.43
1 Struc. Steel Worker	64.55	516.40	99.40	795.20		
1 Welder	64.55	516.40	99.40	795.20		
1 Welder, Gas Engine, 300 amp		147.09		161.80	6.13	6.74
24 L.H., Daily Totals		$1712.29		$2572.20	$71.35	$107.17

Crew No.		Bare Costs		Incl. Subs O&P		Cost Per Labor-Hour	
Crew E-3A	Hr.	Daily	Hr.	Daily	Bare Costs	Incl. O&P
1 Struc. Steel Foreman (outside)	$66.55	$532.40	$102.50	$820.00	$65.22	$100.43
1 Struc. Steel Worker	64.55	516.40	99.40	795.20		
1 Welder	64.55	516.40	99.40	795.20		
1 Welder, Gas Engine, 300 amp		147.09		161.80		
1 Telescoping Boom Lift, to 40'		345.57		380.13	20.53	22.58
24 L.H., Daily Totals		$2057.86		$2952.33	$85.74	$123.01
Crew E-4	Hr.	Daily	Hr.	Daily	Bare Costs	Incl. O&P
1 Struc. Steel Foreman (outside)	$66.55	$532.40	$102.50	$820.00	$65.05	$100.18
3 Struc. Steel Workers	64.55	1549.20	99.40	2385.60		
1 Welder, Gas Engine, 300 amp		147.09		161.80	4.60	5.06
32 L.H., Daily Totals		$2228.69		$3367.40	$69.65	$105.23
Crew E-5	Hr.	Daily	Hr.	Daily	Bare Costs	Incl. O&P
2 Struc. Steel Foremen (outside)	$66.55	$1064.80	$102.50	$1640.00	$64.31	$98.39
5 Struc. Steel Workers	64.55	2582.00	99.40	3976.00		
1 Equip. Oper. (crane)	66.30	530.40	98.65	789.20		
1 Welder	64.55	516.40	99.40	795.20		
1 Equip. Oper. (oiler)	56.40	451.20	83.90	671.20		
1 Lattice Boom Crane, 90 Ton		2689.54		2958.49		
1 Welder, Gas Engine, 300 amp		147.09		161.80	35.46	39.00
80 L.H., Daily Totals		$7981.43		$10991.89	$99.77	$137.40
Crew E-6	Hr.	Daily	Hr.	Daily	Bare Costs	Incl. O&P
3 Struc. Steel Foremen (outside)	$66.55	$1597.20	$102.50	$2460.00	$64.22	$98.31
9 Struc. Steel Workers	64.55	4647.60	99.40	7156.80		
1 Equip. Oper. (crane)	66.30	530.40	98.65	789.20		
1 Welder	64.55	516.40	99.40	795.20		
1 Equip. Oper. (oiler)	56.40	451.20	83.90	671.20		
1 Equip. Oper. (light)	59.70	477.60	88.85	710.80		
1 Lattice Boom Crane, 90 Ton		2689.54		2958.49		
1 Welder, Gas Engine, 300 amp		147.09		161.80		
1 Air Compressor, 160 cfm		244.12		268.53		
2 Impact Wrenches		92.56		101.82	24.79	27.27
128 L.H., Daily Totals		$11393.71		$16073.84	$89.01	$125.58
Crew E-7	Hr.	Daily	Hr.	Daily	Bare Costs	Incl. O&P
1 Struc. Steel Foreman (outside)	$66.55	$532.40	$102.50	$820.00	$64.31	$98.39
4 Struc. Steel Workers	64.55	2065.60	99.40	3180.80		
1 Equip. Oper. (crane)	66.30	530.40	98.65	789.20		
1 Equip. Oper. (oiler)	56.40	451.20	83.90	671.20		
1 Welder Foreman (outside)	66.55	532.40	102.50	820.00		
2 Welders	64.55	1032.80	99.40	1590.40		
1 Lattice Boom Crane, 90 Ton		2689.54		2958.49		
2 Welder, Gas Engine, 300 amp		294.18		323.60	37.30	41.03
80 L.H., Daily Totals		$8128.52		$11153.69	$101.61	$139.42
Crew E-8	Hr.	Daily	Hr.	Daily	Bare Costs	Incl. O&P
1 Struc. Steel Foreman (outside)	$66.55	$532.40	$102.50	$820.00	$63.99	$97.82
4 Struc. Steel Workers	64.55	2065.60	99.40	3180.80		
1 Welder Foreman (outside)	66.55	532.40	102.50	820.00		
4 Welders	64.55	2065.60	99.40	3180.80		
1 Equip. Oper. (crane)	66.30	530.40	98.65	789.20		
1 Equip. Oper. (oiler)	56.40	451.20	83.90	671.20		
1 Equip. Oper. (light)	59.70	477.60	88.85	710.80		
1 Lattice Boom Crane, 90 Ton		2689.54		2958.49		
4 Welder, Gas Engine, 300 amp		588.36		647.20	31.52	34.67
104 L.H., Daily Totals		$9933.10		$13778.49	$95.51	$132.49

Crews - Standard

Crew No.		Bare Costs	Incl. Subs O&P		Cost Per Labor-Hour	
Crew E-9	Hr.	Daily	Hr.	Daily	Bare Costs	Incl. O&P
2 Struc. Steel Foremen (outside)	$66.55	$1064.80	$102.50	$1640.00	$64.22	$98.31
5 Struc. Steel Workers	64.55	2582.00	99.40	3976.00		
1 Welder Foreman (outside)	66.55	532.40	102.50	820.00		
5 Welders	64.55	2582.00	99.40	3976.00		
1 Equip. Oper. (crane)	66.30	530.40	98.65	789.20		
1 Equip. Oper. (oiler)	56.40	451.20	83.90	671.20		
1 Equip. Oper. (light)	59.70	477.60	88.85	710.80		
1 Lattice Boom Crane, 90 Ton		2689.54		2958.49		
5 Welder, Gas Engine, 300 amp		735.45		809.00	26.76	29.43
128 L.H., Daily Totals		$11645.39		$16350.69	$90.98	$127.74

Crew E-10	Hr.	Daily	Hr.	Daily	Bare Costs	Incl. O&P
1 Welder Foreman (outside)	$66.55	$532.40	$102.50	$820.00	$65.55	$100.95
1 Welder	64.55	516.40	99.40	795.20		
1 Welder, Gas Engine, 300 amp		147.09		161.80		
1 Flatbed Truck, Gas, 3 Ton		391.02		430.12	33.63	37.00
16 L.H., Daily Totals		$1586.91		$2207.12	$99.18	$137.95

Crew E-11	Hr.	Daily	Hr.	Daily	Bare Costs	Incl. O&P
2 Painters, Struc. Steel	$51.20	$819.20	$81.75	$1308.00	$52.34	$80.67
1 Building Laborer	47.25	378.00	70.35	562.80		
1 Equip. Oper. (light)	59.70	477.60	88.85	710.80		
1 Air Compressor, 250 cfm		196.28		215.91		
1 Sandblaster, Portable, 3 C.F.		84.26		92.69		
1 Set Sand Blasting Accessories		17.14		18.85	9.30	10.23
32 L.H., Daily Totals		$1972.48		$2909.05	$61.64	$90.91

Crew E-11A	Hr.	Daily	Hr.	Daily	Bare Costs	Incl. O&P
2 Painters, Struc. Steel	$51.20	$819.20	$81.75	$1308.00	$52.34	$80.67
1 Building Laborer	47.25	378.00	70.35	562.80		
1 Equip. Oper. (light)	59.70	477.60	88.85	710.80		
1 Air Compressor, 250 cfm		196.28		215.91		
1 Sandblaster, Portable, 3 C.F.		84.26		92.69		
1 Set Sand Blasting Accessories		17.14		18.85		
1 Telescoping Boom Lift, to 60'		385.68		424.25	21.36	23.49
32 L.H., Daily Totals		$2358.16		$3333.30	$73.69	$104.17

Crew E-11B	Hr.	Daily	Hr.	Daily	Bare Costs	Incl. O&P
2 Painters, Struc. Steel	$51.20	$819.20	$81.75	$1308.00	$49.88	$77.95
1 Building Laborer	47.25	378.00	70.35	562.80		
2 Paint Sprayer, 8 C.F.M.		104.28		114.71		
1 Telescoping Boom Lift, to 60'		385.68		424.25	20.41	22.46
24 L.H., Daily Totals		$1687.16		$2409.76	$70.30	$100.41

Crew E-12	Hr.	Daily	Hr.	Daily	Bare Costs	Incl. O&P
1 Welder Foreman (outside)	$66.55	$532.40	$102.50	$820.00	$63.13	$95.67
1 Equip. Oper. (light)	59.70	477.60	88.85	710.80		
1 Welder, Gas Engine, 300 amp		147.09		161.80	9.19	10.11
16 L.H., Daily Totals		$1157.09		$1692.60	$72.32	$105.79

Crew E-13	Hr.	Daily	Hr.	Daily	Bare Costs	Incl. O&P
1 Welder Foreman (outside)	$66.55	$532.40	$102.50	$820.00	$64.27	$97.95
.5 Equip. Oper. (light)	59.70	238.80	88.85	355.40		
1 Welder, Gas Engine, 300 amp		147.09		161.80	12.26	13.48
12 L.H., Daily Totals		$918.29		$1337.20	$76.52	$111.43

Crew E-14	Hr.	Daily	Hr.	Daily	Bare Costs	Incl. O&P
1 Welder Foreman (outside)	$66.55	$532.40	$102.50	$820.00	$66.55	$102.50
1 Welder, Gas Engine, 300 amp		147.09		161.80	18.39	20.22
8 L.H., Daily Totals		$679.49		$981.80	$84.94	$122.72

Crew E-16	Hr.	Daily	Hr.	Daily	Bare Costs	Incl. O&P
1 Welder Foreman (outside)	$66.55	$532.40	$102.50	$820.00	$65.55	$100.95
1 Welder	64.55	516.40	99.40	795.20		
1 Welder, Gas Engine, 300 amp		147.09		161.80	9.19	10.11
16 L.H., Daily Totals		$1195.89		$1777.00	$74.74	$111.06

Crew E-17	Hr.	Daily	Hr.	Daily	Bare Costs	Incl. O&P
1 Struc. Steel Foreman (outside)	$66.55	$532.40	$102.50	$820.00	$65.55	$100.95
1 Structural Steel Worker	64.55	516.40	99.40	795.20		
16 L.H., Daily Totals		$1048.80		$1615.20	$65.55	$100.95

Crew E-18	Hr.	Daily	Hr.	Daily	Bare Costs	Incl. O&P
1 Struc. Steel Foreman (outside)	$66.55	$532.40	$102.50	$820.00	$64.65	$98.90
3 Structural Steel Workers	64.55	1549.20	99.40	2385.60		
1 Equipment Operator (med.)	63.05	504.40	93.80	750.40		
1 Lattice Boom Crane, 20 Ton		868.10		954.91	21.70	23.87
40 L.H., Daily Totals		$3454.10		$4910.91	$86.35	$122.77

Crew E-19	Hr.	Daily	Hr.	Daily	Bare Costs	Incl. O&P
1 Struc. Steel Foreman (outside)	$66.55	$532.40	$102.50	$820.00	$63.60	$96.92
1 Structural Steel Worker	64.55	516.40	99.40	795.20		
1 Equip. Oper. (light)	59.70	477.60	88.85	710.80		
1 Lattice Boom Crane, 20 Ton		868.10		954.91	36.17	39.79
24 L.H., Daily Totals		$2394.50		$3280.91	$99.77	$136.70

Crew E-20	Hr.	Daily	Hr.	Daily	Bare Costs	Incl. O&P
1 Struc. Steel Foreman (outside)	$66.55	$532.40	$102.50	$820.00	$64.00	$97.76
5 Structural Steel Workers	64.55	2582.00	99.40	3976.00		
1 Equip. Oper. (crane)	66.30	530.40	98.65	789.20		
1 Equip. Oper. (oiler)	56.40	451.20	83.90	671.20		
1 Lattice Boom Crane, 40 Ton		2371.83		2609.01	37.06	40.77
64 L.H., Daily Totals		$6467.83		$8865.41	$101.06	$138.52

Crew E-22	Hr.	Daily	Hr.	Daily	Bare Costs	Incl. O&P
1 Skilled Worker Foreman (out)	$63.25	$506.00	$95.00	$760.00	$61.92	$93.00
2 Skilled Workers	61.25	980.00	92.00	1472.00		
24 L.H., Daily Totals		$1486.00		$2232.00	$61.92	$93.00

Crew E-24	Hr.	Daily	Hr.	Daily	Bare Costs	Incl. O&P
3 Structural Steel Workers	$64.55	$1549.20	$99.40	$2385.60	$64.17	$98.00
1 Equipment Operator (med.)	63.05	504.40	93.80	750.40		
1 Hyd. Crane, 25 Ton		2273.31		2500.64	71.04	78.14
32 L.H., Daily Totals		$4326.91		$5636.64	$135.22	$176.15

Crew E-25	Hr.	Daily	Hr.	Daily	Bare Costs	Incl. O&P
1 Welder Foreman (outside)	$66.55	$532.40	$102.50	$820.00	$66.55	$102.50
1 Cutting Torch		14.24		15.66	1.78	1.96
8 L.H., Daily Totals		$546.64		$835.66	$68.33	$104.46

Crew E-26	Hr.	Daily	Hr.	Daily	Bare Costs	Incl. O&P
1 Struc. Steel Foreman (outside)	$66.55	$532.40	$102.50	$820.00	$65.86	$100.91
1 Struc. Steel Worker	64.55	516.40	99.40	795.20		
1 Welder	64.55	516.40	99.40	795.20		
.25 Electrician	67.35	134.70	100.10	200.20		
.25 Plumber	72.05	144.10	107.45	214.90		
1 Welder, Gas Engine, 300 amp		147.09		161.80	5.25	5.78
28 L.H., Daily Totals		$1991.09		$2987.30	$71.11	$106.69

Crews - Standard

Crew No.		Bare Costs		Incl. Subs O&P		Cost Per Labor-Hour	
Crew E-27	Hr.	Daily	Hr.	Daily	Bare Costs	Incl. O&P	
1 Struc. Steel Foreman (outside)	$66.55	$532.40	$102.50	$820.00	$64.00	$97.76	
5 Struc. Steel Workers	64.55	2582.00	99.40	3976.00			
1 Equip. Oper. (crane)	66.30	530.40	98.65	789.20			
1 Equip. Oper. (oiler)	56.40	451.20	83.90	671.20			
1 Hyd. Crane, 12 Ton		2150.65		2365.72			
1 Hyd. Crane, 80 Ton		2641.70		2905.87	74.88	82.37	
64 L.H., Daily Totals		$8888.35		$11527.99	$138.88	$180.12	
Crew F-3	Hr.	Daily	Hr.	Daily	Bare Costs	Incl. O&P	
4 Carpenters	$58.60	$1875.20	$87.25	$2792.00	$60.14	$89.53	
1 Equip. Oper. (crane)	66.30	530.40	98.65	789.20			
1 Hyd. Crane, 12 Ton		2150.65		2365.72	53.77	59.14	
40 L.H., Daily Totals		$4556.25		$5946.92	$113.91	$148.67	
Crew F-4	Hr.	Daily	Hr.	Daily	Bare Costs	Incl. O&P	
4 Carpenters	$58.60	$1875.20	$87.25	$2792.00	$59.52	$88.59	
1 Equip. Oper. (crane)	66.30	530.40	98.65	789.20			
1 Equip. Oper. (oiler)	56.40	451.20	83.90	671.20			
1 Hyd. Crane, 55 Ton		2461.06		2707.17	51.27	56.40	
48 L.H., Daily Totals		$5317.86		$6959.57	$110.79	$144.99	
Crew F-5	Hr.	Daily	Hr.	Daily	Bare Costs	Incl. O&P	
1 Carpenter Foreman (outside)	$60.60	$484.80	$90.20	$721.60	$59.10	$87.99	
3 Carpenters	58.60	1406.40	87.25	2094.00			
32 L.H., Daily Totals		$1891.20		$2815.60	$59.10	$87.99	
Crew F-6	Hr.	Daily	Hr.	Daily	Bare Costs	Incl. O&P	
2 Carpenters	$58.60	$937.60	$87.25	$1396.00	$55.60	$82.77	
2 Building Laborers	47.25	756.00	70.35	1125.60			
1 Equip. Oper. (crane)	66.30	530.40	98.65	789.20			
1 Hyd. Crane, 12 Ton		2150.65		2365.72	53.77	59.14	
40 L.H., Daily Totals		$4374.65		$5676.52	$109.37	$141.91	
Crew F-7	Hr.	Daily	Hr.	Daily	Bare Costs	Incl. O&P	
2 Carpenters	$58.60	$937.60	$87.25	$1396.00	$52.92	$78.80	
2 Building Laborers	47.25	756.00	70.35	1125.60			
32 L.H., Daily Totals		$1693.60		$2521.60	$52.92	$78.80	
Crew G-1	Hr.	Daily	Hr.	Daily	Bare Costs	Incl. O&P	
1 Roofer Foreman (outside)	$53.80	$430.40	$87.20	$697.60	$48.39	$78.41	
4 Roofers Composition	51.80	1657.60	83.95	2686.40			
2 Roofer Helpers	38.85	621.60	62.95	1007.20			
1 Application Equipment		189.41		208.35			
1 Tar Kettle/Pot		220.65		242.72			
1 Crew Truck		183.83		202.21	10.61	11.67	
56 L.H., Daily Totals		$3303.49		$5044.48	$58.99	$90.08	
Crew G-2	Hr.	Daily	Hr.	Daily	Bare Costs	Incl. O&P	
1 Plasterer	$53.35	$426.80	$79.30	$634.40	$49.38	$73.43	
1 Plasterer Helper	47.55	380.40	70.65	565.20			
1 Building Laborer	47.25	378.00	70.35	562.80			
1 Grout Pump, 50 C.F./hr.		158.45		174.29	6.60	7.26	
24 L.H., Daily Totals		$1343.65		$1936.69	$55.99	$80.70	
Crew G-2A	Hr.	Daily	Hr.	Daily	Bare Costs	Incl. O&P	
1 Roofer Composition	$51.80	$414.40	$83.95	$671.60	$45.97	$72.42	
1 Roofer Helper	38.85	310.80	62.95	503.60			
1 Building Laborer	47.25	378.00	70.35	562.80			
1 Foam Spray Rig, Trailer-Mtd.		581.75		639.92			
1 Pickup Truck, 3/4 Ton		122.56		134.82	29.35	32.28	
24 L.H., Daily Totals		$1807.51		$2512.74	$75.31	$104.70	
Crew G-3	Hr.	Daily	Hr.	Daily	Bare Costs	Incl. O&P	
2 Sheet Metal Workers	$70.15	$1122.40	$105.70	$1691.20	$58.70	$88.03	
2 Building Laborers	47.25	756.00	70.35	1125.60			
32 L.H., Daily Totals		$1878.40		$2816.80	$58.70	$88.03	
Crew G-4	Hr.	Daily	Hr.	Daily	Bare Costs	Incl. O&P	
1 Labor Foreman (outside)	$49.25	$394.00	$73.30	$586.40	$47.92	$71.33	
2 Building Laborers	47.25	756.00	70.35	1125.60			
1 Flatbed Truck, Gas, 1.5 Ton		361.95		398.14			
1 Air Compressor, 160 cfm		244.12		268.53	25.25	27.78	
24 L.H., Daily Totals		$1756.07		$2378.68	$73.17	$99.11	
Crew G-5	Hr.	Daily	Hr.	Daily	Bare Costs	Incl. O&P	
1 Roofer Foreman (outside)	$53.80	$430.40	$87.20	$697.60	$47.02	$76.20	
2 Roofers Composition	51.80	828.80	83.95	1343.20			
2 Roofer Helpers	38.85	621.60	62.95	1007.20			
1 Application Equipment		189.41		208.35	4.74	5.21	
40 L.H., Daily Totals		$2070.21		$3256.35	$51.76	$81.41	
Crew G-6A	Hr.	Daily	Hr.	Daily	Bare Costs	Incl. O&P	
2 Roofers Composition	$51.80	$828.80	$83.95	$1343.20	$51.80	$83.95	
1 Small Compressor, Electric		32.29		35.52			
2 Pneumatic Nailers		38.40		42.24	4.42	4.86	
16 L.H., Daily Totals		$899.49		$1420.96	$56.22	$88.81	
Crew G-7	Hr.	Daily	Hr.	Daily	Bare Costs	Incl. O&P	
1 Carpenter	$58.60	$468.80	$87.25	$698.00	$58.60	$87.25	
1 Small Compressor, Electric		32.29		35.52			
1 Pneumatic Nailer		19.20		21.12	6.44	7.08	
8 L.H., Daily Totals		$520.29		$754.64	$65.04	$94.33	
Crew H-1	Hr.	Daily	Hr.	Daily	Bare Costs	Incl. O&P	
2 Glaziers	$56.05	$896.80	$83.30	$1332.80	$60.30	$91.35	
2 Struc. Steel Workers	64.55	1032.80	99.40	1590.40			
32 L.H., Daily Totals		$1929.60		$2923.20	$60.30	$91.35	
Crew H-2	Hr.	Daily	Hr.	Daily	Bare Costs	Incl. O&P	
2 Glaziers	$56.05	$896.80	$83.30	$1332.80	$53.12	$78.98	
1 Building Laborer	47.25	378.00	70.35	562.80			
24 L.H., Daily Totals		$1274.80		$1895.60	$53.12	$78.98	
Crew H-3	Hr.	Daily	Hr.	Daily	Bare Costs	Incl. O&P	
1 Glazier	$56.05	$448.40	$83.30	$666.40	$50.50	$75.63	
1 Helper	44.95	359.60	67.95	543.60			
16 L.H., Daily Totals		$808.00		$1210.00	$50.50	$75.63	
Crew H-4	Hr.	Daily	Hr.	Daily	Bare Costs	Incl. O&P	
1 Carpenter	$58.60	$468.80	$87.25	$698.00	$54.89	$82.10	
1 Carpenter Helper	44.95	359.60	67.95	543.60			
.5 Electrician	67.35	269.40	100.10	400.40			
20 L.H., Daily Totals		$1097.80		$1642.00	$54.89	$82.10	

Crews - Standard

Crew No.		Bare Costs		Incl. Subs O&P	Cost Per Labor-Hour		Crew No.		Bare Costs		Incl. Subs O&P	Cost Per Labor-Hour	
Crew J-1	Hr.	Daily	Hr.	Daily	Bare Costs	Incl. O&P	**Crew K-1**	Hr.	Daily	Hr.	Daily	Bare Costs	Incl. O&P
3 Plasterers	$53.35	$1280.40	$79.30	$1903.20	$51.03	$75.84	1 Carpenter	$58.60	$468.80	$87.25	$698.00	$55.75	$83.13
2 Plasterer Helpers	47.55	760.80	70.65	1130.40			1 Truck Driver (light)	52.90	423.20	79.00	632.00		
1 Mixing Machine, 6 C.F.		116.18		127.80	2.90	3.19	1 Flatbed Truck, Gas, 3 Ton		391.02		430.12	24.44	26.88
40 L.H., Daily Totals		$2157.38		$3161.40	$53.93	$79.03	16 L.H., Daily Totals		$1283.02		$1760.12	$80.19	$110.01
Crew J-2	Hr.	Daily	Hr.	Daily	Bare Costs	Incl. O&P	**Crew K-2**	Hr.	Daily	Hr.	Daily	Bare Costs	Incl. O&P
3 Plasterers	$53.35	$1280.40	$79.30	$1903.20	$52.27	$77.42	1 Struc. Steel Foreman (outside)	$66.55	$532.40	$102.50	$820.00	$61.33	$93.63
2 Plasterer Helpers	47.55	760.80	70.65	1130.40			1 Struc. Steel Worker	64.55	516.40	99.40	795.20		
1 Lather	58.45	467.60	85.30	682.40			1 Truck Driver (light)	52.90	423.20	79.00	632.00		
1 Mixing Machine, 6 C.F.		116.18		127.80	2.42	2.66	1 Flatbed Truck, Gas, 3 Ton		391.02		430.12	16.29	17.92
48 L.H., Daily Totals		$2624.98		$3843.80	$54.69	$80.08	24 L.H., Daily Totals		$1863.02		$2677.32	$77.63	$111.56
Crew J-3	Hr.	Daily	Hr.	Daily	Bare Costs	Incl. O&P	**Crew L-1**	Hr.	Daily	Hr.	Daily	Bare Costs	Incl. O&P
1 Terrazzo Worker	$55.25	$442.00	$80.70	$645.60	$51.02	$74.53	1 Electrician	$67.35	$538.80	$100.10	$800.80	$69.70	$103.78
1 Terrazzo Helper	46.80	374.40	68.35	546.80			1 Plumber	72.05	576.40	107.45	859.60		
1 Floor Grinder, 22" Path		109.91		120.90			16 L.H., Daily Totals		$1115.20		$1660.40	$69.70	$103.78
1 Terrazzo Mixer		144.05		158.46	15.87	17.46	**Crew L-2**	Hr.	Daily	Hr.	Daily	Bare Costs	Incl. O&P
16 L.H., Daily Totals		$1070.36		$1471.76	$66.90	$91.98	1 Carpenter	$58.60	$468.80	$87.25	$698.00	$51.77	$77.60
Crew J-4	Hr.	Daily	Hr.	Daily	Bare Costs	Incl. O&P	1 Carpenter Helper	44.95	359.60	67.95	543.60		
2 Cement Finishers	$55.00	$880.00	$80.45	$1287.20	$52.42	$77.08	16 L.H., Daily Totals		$828.40		$1241.60	$51.77	$77.60
1 Laborer	47.25	378.00	70.35	562.80			**Crew L-3**	Hr.	Daily	Hr.	Daily	Bare Costs	Incl. O&P
1 Floor Grinder, 22" Path		109.91		120.90			1 Carpenter	$58.60	$468.80	$87.25	$698.00	$63.67	$95.08
1 Floor Edger, 7" Path		52.63		57.89			.5 Electrician	67.35	269.40	100.10	400.40		
1 Vacuum Pick-Up System		73.53		80.88	9.84	10.82	.5 Sheet Metal Worker	70.15	280.60	105.70	422.80		
24 L.H., Daily Totals		$1494.07		$2109.68	$62.25	$87.90	16 L.H., Daily Totals		$1018.80		$1521.20	$63.67	$95.08
Crew J-4A	Hr.	Daily	Hr.	Daily	Bare Costs	Incl. O&P	**Crew L-3A**	Hr.	Daily	Hr.	Daily	Bare Costs	Incl. O&P
2 Cement Finishers	$55.00	$880.00	$80.45	$1287.20	$51.13	$75.40	1 Carpenter Foreman (outside)	$60.60	$484.80	$90.20	$721.60	$63.78	$95.37
2 Laborers	47.25	756.00	70.35	1125.60			.5 Sheet Metal Worker	70.15	280.60	105.70	422.80		
1 Floor Grinder, 22" Path		109.91		120.90			12 L.H., Daily Totals		$765.40		$1144.40	$63.78	$95.37
1 Floor Edger, 7" Path		52.63		57.89			**Crew L-4**	Hr.	Daily	Hr.	Daily	Bare Costs	Incl. O&P
1 Vacuum Pick-Up System		73.53		80.88			2 Skilled Workers	$61.25	$980.00	$92.00	$1472.00	$55.82	$83.98
1 Floor Auto Scrubber		195.20		214.72	13.48	14.82	1 Helper	44.95	359.60	67.95	543.60		
32 L.H., Daily Totals		$2067.27		$2887.20	$64.60	$90.22	24 L.H., Daily Totals		$1339.60		$2015.60	$55.82	$83.98
Crew J-4B	Hr.	Daily	Hr.	Daily	Bare Costs	Incl. O&P	**Crew L-5**	Hr.	Daily	Hr.	Daily	Bare Costs	Incl. O&P
1 Laborer	$47.25	$378.00	$70.35	$562.80	$47.25	$70.35	1 Struc. Steel Foreman (outside)	$66.55	$532.40	$102.50	$820.00	$65.09	$99.74
1 Floor Auto Scrubber		195.20		214.72	24.40	26.84	5 Struc. Steel Workers	64.55	2582.00	99.40	3976.00		
8 L.H., Daily Totals		$573.20		$777.52	$71.65	$97.19	1 Equip. Oper. (crane)	66.30	530.40	98.65	789.20		
Crew J-6	Hr.	Daily	Hr.	Daily	Bare Costs	Incl. O&P	1 Hyd. Crane, 25 Ton		2273.31		2500.64	40.59	44.65
2 Painters	$49.65	$794.40	$73.55	$1176.80	$51.56	$76.58	56 L.H., Daily Totals		$5918.11		$8085.84	$105.68	$144.39
1 Building Laborer	47.25	378.00	70.35	562.80			**Crew L-5A**	Hr.	Daily	Hr.	Daily	Bare Costs	Incl. O&P
1 Equip. Oper. (light)	59.70	477.60	88.85	710.80			1 Struc. Steel Foreman (outside)	$66.55	$532.40	$102.50	$820.00	$65.49	$99.99
1 Air Compressor, 250 cfm		196.28		215.91			2 Structural Steel Workers	64.55	1032.80	99.40	1590.40		
1 Sandblaster, Portable, 3 C.F.		84.26		92.69			1 Equip. Oper. (crane)	66.30	530.40	98.65	789.20		
1 Set Sand Blasting Accessories		17.14		18.85	9.30	10.23	1 S.P. Crane, 4x4, 25 Ton		927.07		1019.78	28.97	31.87
32 L.H., Daily Totals		$1947.68		$2777.85	$60.87	$86.81	32 L.H., Daily Totals		$3022.67		$4219.38	$94.46	$131.86
Crew J-7	Hr.	Daily	Hr.	Daily	Bare Costs	Incl. O&P							
2 Painters	$49.65	$794.40	$73.55	$1176.80	$49.65	$73.55							
1 Floor Belt Sander		49.75		54.73									
1 Floor Sanding Edger		26.35		28.98	4.76	5.23							
16 L.H., Daily Totals		$870.50		$1260.51	$54.41	$78.78							

Crews - Standard

Crew No.		Bare Costs		Incl. Subs O&P		Cost Per Labor-Hour	
Crew L-5B	Hr.	Daily	Hr.	Daily	Bare Costs	Incl. O&P
1 Struc. Steel Foreman (outside)	$66.55	$532.40	$102.50	$820.00	$66.46	$100.05
2 Structural Steel Workers	64.55	1032.80	99.40	1590.40		
2 Electricians	67.35	1077.60	100.10	1601.60		
2 Steamfitters/Pipefitters	72.55	1160.80	108.20	1731.20		
1 Equip. Oper. (crane)	66.30	530.40	98.65	789.20		
1 Equip. Oper. (oiler)	56.40	451.20	83.90	671.20		
1 Hyd. Crane, 80 Ton		2641.70		2905.87	36.69	40.36
72 L.H., Daily Totals		$7426.90		$10109.47	$103.15	$140.41
Crew L-6	Hr.	Daily	Hr.	Daily	Bare Costs	Incl. O&P
1 Plumber	$72.05	$576.40	$107.45	$859.60	$70.48	$105.00
.5 Electrician	67.35	269.40	100.10	400.40		
12 L.H., Daily Totals		$845.80		$1260.00	$70.48	$105.00
Crew L-7	Hr.	Daily	Hr.	Daily	Bare Costs	Incl. O&P
2 Carpenters	$58.60	$937.60	$87.25	$1396.00	$56.61	$84.26
1 Building Laborer	47.25	378.00	70.35	562.80		
.5 Electrician	67.35	269.40	100.10	400.40		
28 L.H., Daily Totals		$1585.00		$2359.20	$56.61	$84.26
Crew L-8	Hr.	Daily	Hr.	Daily	Bare Costs	Incl. O&P
2 Carpenters	$58.60	$937.60	$87.25	$1396.00	$61.29	$91.29
.5 Plumber	72.05	288.20	107.45	429.80		
20 L.H., Daily Totals		$1225.80		$1825.80	$61.29	$91.29
Crew L-9	Hr.	Daily	Hr.	Daily	Bare Costs	Incl. O&P
1 Labor Foreman (inside)	$47.75	$382.00	$71.10	$568.80	$53.44	$80.28
2 Building Laborers	47.25	756.00	70.35	1125.60		
1 Struc. Steel Worker	64.55	516.40	99.40	795.20		
.5 Electrician	67.35	269.40	100.10	400.40		
36 L.H., Daily Totals		$1923.80		$2890.00	$53.44	$80.28
Crew L-10	Hr.	Daily	Hr.	Daily	Bare Costs	Incl. O&P
1 Struc. Steel Foreman (outside)	$66.55	$532.40	$102.50	$820.00	$65.80	$100.18
1 Structural Steel Worker	64.55	516.40	99.40	795.20		
1 Equip. Oper. (crane)	66.30	530.40	98.65	789.20		
1 Hyd. Crane, 12 Ton		2150.65		2365.72	89.61	98.57
24 L.H., Daily Totals		$3729.85		$4770.11	$155.41	$198.75
Crew L-11	Hr.	Daily	Hr.	Daily	Bare Costs	Incl. O&P
2 Wreckers	$47.25	$756.00	$71.35	$1141.60	$55.13	$82.55
1 Equip. Oper. (crane)	66.30	530.40	98.65	789.20		
1 Equip. Oper. (light)	59.70	477.60	88.85	710.80		
1 Hyd. Excavator, 2.5 C.Y.		1683.69		1852.06		
1 Loader, Skid Steer, 78 H.P.		429.91		472.90	66.05	72.66
32 L.H., Daily Totals		$3877.60		$4966.56	$121.18	$155.21
Crew M-1	Hr.	Daily	Hr.	Daily	Bare Costs	Incl. O&P
3 Elevator Constructors	$96.60	$2318.40	$143.00	$3432.00	$91.78	$135.86
1 Elevator Apprentice	77.30	618.40	114.45	915.60		
5 Hand Tools		344.60		379.06	10.77	11.85
32 L.H., Daily Totals		$3281.40		$4726.66	$102.54	$147.71

Crew No.		Bare Costs		Incl. Subs O&P		Cost Per Labor-Hour	
Crew M-3	Hr.	Daily	Hr.	Daily	Bare Costs	Incl. O&P
1 Electrician Foreman (outside)	$69.35	$554.80	$103.05	$824.40	$72.06	$106.89
1 Common Laborer	47.25	378.00	70.35	562.80		
.25 Equipment Operator (med.)	63.05	126.10	93.80	187.60		
1 Elevator Constructor	96.60	772.80	143.00	1144.00		
1 Elevator Apprentice	77.30	618.40	114.45	915.60		
.25 S.P. Crane, 4x4, 20 Ton		190.24		209.27	5.60	6.15
34 L.H., Daily Totals		$2640.34		$3843.67	$77.66	$113.05
Crew M-4	Hr.	Daily	Hr.	Daily	Bare Costs	Incl. O&P
1 Electrician Foreman (outside)	$69.35	$554.80	$103.05	$824.40	$71.37	$105.89
1 Common Laborer	47.25	378.00	70.35	562.80		
.25 Equipment Operator, Crane	66.30	132.60	98.65	197.30		
.25 Equip. Oper. (oiler)	56.40	112.80	83.90	167.80		
1 Elevator Constructor	96.60	772.80	143.00	1144.00		
1 Elevator Apprentice	77.30	618.40	114.45	915.60		
.25 S.P. Crane, 4x4, 40 Ton		284.79		313.26	7.91	8.70
36 L.H., Daily Totals		$2854.18		$4125.16	$79.28	$114.59
Crew Q-1	Hr.	Daily	Hr.	Daily	Bare Costs	Incl. O&P
1 Plumber	$72.05	$576.40	$107.45	$859.60	$64.85	$96.70
1 Plumber Apprentice	57.65	461.20	85.95	687.60		
16 L.H., Daily Totals		$1037.60		$1547.20	$64.85	$96.70
Crew Q-1A	Hr.	Daily	Hr.	Daily	Bare Costs	Incl. O&P
.25 Plumber Foreman (outside)	$74.05	$148.10	$110.40	$220.80	$72.45	$108.04
1 Plumber	72.05	576.40	107.45	859.60		
10 L.H., Daily Totals		$724.50		$1080.40	$72.45	$108.04
Crew Q-1C	Hr.	Daily	Hr.	Daily	Bare Costs	Incl. O&P
1 Plumber	$72.05	$576.40	$107.45	$859.60	$64.25	$95.73
1 Plumber Apprentice	57.65	461.20	85.95	687.60		
1 Equip. Oper. (medium)	63.05	504.40	93.80	750.40		
1 Trencher, Chain Type, 8' D		2079.03		2286.93	86.63	95.29
24 L.H., Daily Totals		$3621.03		$4584.53	$150.88	$191.02
Crew Q-2	Hr.	Daily	Hr.	Daily	Bare Costs	Incl. O&P
2 Plumbers	$72.05	$1152.80	$107.45	$1719.20	$67.25	$100.28
1 Plumber Apprentice	57.65	461.20	85.95	687.60		
24 L.H., Daily Totals		$1614.00		$2406.80	$67.25	$100.28
Crew Q-3	Hr.	Daily	Hr.	Daily	Bare Costs	Incl. O&P
1 Plumber Foreman (inside)	$72.55	$580.40	$108.20	$865.60	$68.58	$102.26
2 Plumbers	72.05	1152.80	107.45	1719.20		
1 Plumber Apprentice	57.65	461.20	85.95	687.60		
32 L.H., Daily Totals		$2194.40		$3272.40	$68.58	$102.26
Crew Q-4	Hr.	Daily	Hr.	Daily	Bare Costs	Incl. O&P
1 Plumber Foreman (inside)	$72.55	$580.40	$108.20	$865.60	$68.58	$102.26
1 Plumber	72.05	576.40	107.45	859.60		
1 Welder (plumber)	72.05	576.40	107.45	859.60		
1 Plumber Apprentice	57.65	461.20	85.95	687.60		
1 Welder, Electric, 300 amp		64.17		70.59	2.01	2.21
32 L.H., Daily Totals		$2258.57		$3342.99	$70.58	$104.47
Crew Q-5	Hr.	Daily	Hr.	Daily	Bare Costs	Incl. O&P
1 Steamfitter	$72.55	$580.40	$108.20	$865.60	$65.30	$97.38
1 Steamfitter Apprentice	58.05	464.40	86.55	692.40		
16 L.H., Daily Totals		$1044.80		$1558.00	$65.30	$97.38

Crews - Standard

Crew No.		Bare Costs	Incl. Subs O&P		Cost Per Labor-Hour	

Crew Q-6	Hr.	Daily	Hr.	Daily	Bare Costs	Incl. O&P
2 Steamfitters	$72.55	$1160.80	$108.20	$1731.20	$67.72	$100.98
1 Steamfitter Apprentice	58.05	464.40	86.55	692.40		
24 L.H., Daily Totals		$1625.20		$2423.60	$67.72	$100.98

Crew Q-7	Hr.	Daily	Hr.	Daily	Bare Costs	Incl. O&P
1 Steamfitter Foreman (inside)	$73.05	$584.40	$108.95	$871.60	$69.05	$102.97
2 Steamfitters	72.55	1160.80	108.20	1731.20		
1 Steamfitter Apprentice	58.05	464.40	86.55	692.40		
32 L.H., Daily Totals		$2209.60		$3295.20	$69.05	$102.97

Crew Q-8	Hr.	Daily	Hr.	Daily	Bare Costs	Incl. O&P
1 Steamfitter Foreman (inside)	$73.05	$584.40	$108.95	$871.60	$69.05	$102.97
1 Steamfitter	72.55	580.40	108.20	865.60		
1 Welder (steamfitter)	72.55	580.40	108.20	865.60		
1 Steamfitter Apprentice	58.05	464.40	86.55	692.40		
1 Welder, Electric, 300 amp		64.17		70.59	2.01	2.21
32 L.H., Daily Totals		$2273.77		$3365.79	$71.06	$105.18

Crew Q-9	Hr.	Daily	Hr.	Daily	Bare Costs	Incl. O&P
1 Sheet Metal Worker	$70.15	$561.20	$105.70	$845.60	$63.13	$95.10
1 Sheet Metal Apprentice	56.10	448.80	84.50	676.00		
16 L.H., Daily Totals		$1010.00		$1521.60	$63.13	$95.10

Crew Q-10	Hr.	Daily	Hr.	Daily	Bare Costs	Incl. O&P
2 Sheet Metal Workers	$70.15	$1122.40	$105.70	$1691.20	$65.47	$98.63
1 Sheet Metal Apprentice	56.10	448.80	84.50	676.00		
24 L.H., Daily Totals		$1571.20		$2367.20	$65.47	$98.63

Crew Q-11	Hr.	Daily	Hr.	Daily	Bare Costs	Incl. O&P
1 Sheet Metal Foreman (inside)	$70.65	$565.20	$106.45	$851.60	$66.76	$100.59
2 Sheet Metal Workers	70.15	1122.40	105.70	1691.20		
1 Sheet Metal Apprentice	56.10	448.80	84.50	676.00		
32 L.H., Daily Totals		$2136.40		$3218.80	$66.76	$100.59

Crew Q-12	Hr.	Daily	Hr.	Daily	Bare Costs	Incl. O&P
1 Sprinkler Installer	$70.80	$566.40	$105.70	$845.60	$63.73	$95.13
1 Sprinkler Apprentice	56.65	453.20	84.55	676.40		
16 L.H., Daily Totals		$1019.60		$1522.00	$63.73	$95.13

Crew Q-13	Hr.	Daily	Hr.	Daily	Bare Costs	Incl. O&P
1 Sprinkler Foreman (inside)	$71.30	$570.40	$106.45	$851.60	$67.39	$100.60
2 Sprinkler Installers	70.80	1132.80	105.70	1691.20		
1 Sprinkler Apprentice	56.65	453.20	84.55	676.40		
32 L.H., Daily Totals		$2156.40		$3219.20	$67.39	$100.60

Crew Q-14	Hr.	Daily	Hr.	Daily	Bare Costs	Incl. O&P
1 Asbestos Worker	$65.25	$522.00	$99.80	$798.40	$58.73	$89.83
1 Asbestos Apprentice	52.20	417.60	79.85	638.80		
16 L.H., Daily Totals		$939.60		$1437.20	$58.73	$89.83

Crew Q-15	Hr.	Daily	Hr.	Daily	Bare Costs	Incl. O&P
1 Plumber	$72.05	$576.40	$107.45	$859.60	$64.85	$96.70
1 Plumber Apprentice	57.65	461.20	85.95	687.60		
1 Welder, Electric, 300 amp		64.17		70.59	4.01	4.41
16 L.H., Daily Totals		$1101.77		$1617.79	$68.86	$101.11

Crew Q-16	Hr.	Daily	Hr.	Daily	Bare Costs	Incl. O&P
2 Plumbers	$72.05	$1152.80	$107.45	$1719.20	$67.25	$100.28
1 Plumber Apprentice	57.65	461.20	85.95	687.60		
1 Welder, Electric, 300 amp		64.17		70.59	2.67	2.94
24 L.H., Daily Totals		$1678.17		$2477.39	$69.92	$103.22

Crew Q-17	Hr.	Daily	Hr.	Daily	Bare Costs	Incl. O&P
1 Steamfitter	$72.55	$580.40	$108.20	$865.60	$65.30	$97.38
1 Steamfitter Apprentice	58.05	464.40	86.55	692.40		
1 Welder, Electric, 300 amp		64.17		70.59	4.01	4.41
16 L.H., Daily Totals		$1108.97		$1628.59	$69.31	$101.79

Crew Q-17A	Hr.	Daily	Hr.	Daily	Bare Costs	Incl. O&P
1 Steamfitter	$72.55	$580.40	$108.20	$865.60	$65.63	$97.80
1 Steamfitter Apprentice	58.05	464.40	86.55	692.40		
1 Equip. Oper. (crane)	66.30	530.40	98.65	789.20		
1 Hyd. Crane, 12 Ton		2150.65		2365.72		
1 Welder, Electric, 300 amp		64.17		70.59	92.28	101.51
24 L.H., Daily Totals		$3790.02		$4783.50	$157.92	$199.31

Crew Q-18	Hr.	Daily	Hr.	Daily	Bare Costs	Incl. O&P
2 Steamfitters	$72.55	$1160.80	$108.20	$1731.20	$67.72	$100.98
1 Steamfitter Apprentice	58.05	464.40	86.55	692.40		
1 Welder, Electric, 300 amp		64.17		70.59	2.67	2.94
24 L.H., Daily Totals		$1689.37		$2494.19	$70.39	$103.92

Crew Q-19	Hr.	Daily	Hr.	Daily	Bare Costs	Incl. O&P
1 Steamfitter	$72.55	$580.40	$108.20	$865.60	$65.98	$98.28
1 Steamfitter Apprentice	58.05	464.40	86.55	692.40		
1 Electrician	67.35	538.80	100.10	800.80		
24 L.H., Daily Totals		$1583.60		$2358.80	$65.98	$98.28

Crew Q-20	Hr.	Daily	Hr.	Daily	Bare Costs	Incl. O&P
1 Sheet Metal Worker	$70.15	$561.20	$105.70	$845.60	$63.97	$96.10
1 Sheet Metal Apprentice	56.10	448.80	84.50	676.00		
.5 Electrician	67.35	269.40	100.10	400.40		
20 L.H., Daily Totals		$1279.40		$1922.00	$63.97	$96.10

Crew Q-21	Hr.	Daily	Hr.	Daily	Bare Costs	Incl. O&P
2 Steamfitters	$72.55	$1160.80	$108.20	$1731.20	$67.63	$100.76
1 Steamfitter Apprentice	58.05	464.40	86.55	692.40		
1 Electrician	67.35	538.80	100.10	800.80		
32 L.H., Daily Totals		$2164.00		$3224.40	$67.63	$100.76

Crew Q-22	Hr.	Daily	Hr.	Daily	Bare Costs	Incl. O&P
1 Plumber	$72.05	$576.40	$107.45	$859.60	$64.85	$96.70
1 Plumber Apprentice	57.65	461.20	85.95	687.60		
1 Hyd. Crane, 12 Ton		2150.65		2365.72	134.42	147.86
16 L.H., Daily Totals		$3188.25		$3912.92	$199.27	$244.56

Crew Q-22A	Hr.	Daily	Hr.	Daily	Bare Costs	Incl. O&P
1 Plumber	$72.05	$576.40	$107.45	$859.60	$60.81	$90.60
1 Plumber Apprentice	57.65	461.20	85.95	687.60		
1 Laborer	47.25	378.00	70.35	562.80		
1 Equip. Oper. (crane)	66.30	530.40	98.65	789.20		
1 Hyd. Crane, 12 Ton		2150.65		2365.72	67.21	73.93
32 L.H., Daily Totals		$4096.65		$5264.92	$128.02	$164.53

Crews - Standard

Crew No.	Bare Costs		Incl. Subs O&P		Cost Per Labor-Hour	
Crew Q-23	Hr.	Daily	Hr.	Daily	Bare Costs	Incl. O&P
1 Plumber Foreman (outside)	$74.05	$592.40	$110.40	$883.20	$69.72	$103.88
1 Plumber	72.05	576.40	107.45	859.60		
1 Equip. Oper. (medium)	63.05	504.40	93.80	750.40		
1 Lattice Boom Crane, 20 Ton		868.10		954.91	36.17	39.79
24 L.H., Daily Totals		$2541.30		$3448.11	$105.89	$143.67

Crew No.	Bare Costs		Incl. Subs O&P		Cost Per Labor-Hour	
Crew R-1	Hr.	Daily	Hr.	Daily	Bare Costs	Incl. O&P
1 Electrician Foreman	$67.85	$542.80	$100.85	$806.80	$62.95	$93.56
3 Electricians	67.35	1616.40	100.10	2402.40		
2 Electrician Apprentices	53.90	862.40	80.10	1281.60		
48 L.H., Daily Totals		$3021.60		$4490.80	$62.95	$93.56

Crew R-1A	Hr.	Daily	Hr.	Daily	Bare Costs	Incl. O&P
1 Electrician	$67.35	$538.80	$100.10	$800.80	$60.63	$90.10
1 Electrician Apprentice	53.90	431.20	80.10	640.80		
16 L.H., Daily Totals		$970.00		$1441.60	$60.63	$90.10

Crew R-1B	Hr.	Daily	Hr.	Daily	Bare Costs	Incl. O&P
1 Electrician	$67.35	$538.80	$100.10	$800.80	$58.38	$86.77
2 Electrician Apprentices	53.90	862.40	80.10	1281.60		
24 L.H., Daily Totals		$1401.20		$2082.40	$58.38	$86.77

Crew R-1C	Hr.	Daily	Hr.	Daily	Bare Costs	Incl. O&P
2 Electricians	$67.35	$1077.60	$100.10	$1601.60	$60.63	$90.10
2 Electrician Apprentices	53.90	862.40	80.10	1281.60		
1 Portable cable puller, 8000 lb.		118.26		130.09	3.70	4.07
32 L.H., Daily Totals		$2058.26		$3013.29	$64.32	$94.17

Crew R-2	Hr.	Daily	Hr.	Daily	Bare Costs	Incl. O&P
1 Electrician Foreman	$67.85	$542.80	$100.85	$806.80	$63.43	$94.29
3 Electricians	67.35	1616.40	100.10	2402.40		
2 Electrician Apprentices	53.90	862.40	80.10	1281.60		
1 Equip. Oper. (crane)	66.30	530.40	98.65	789.20		
1 S.P. Crane, 4x4, 5 Ton		385.89		424.48	6.89	7.58
56 L.H., Daily Totals		$3937.89		$5704.48	$70.32	$101.87

Crew R-3	Hr.	Daily	Hr.	Daily	Bare Costs	Incl. O&P
1 Electrician Foreman	$67.85	$542.80	$100.85	$806.80	$67.34	$100.11
1 Electrician	67.35	538.80	100.10	800.80		
.5 Equip. Oper. (crane)	66.30	265.20	98.65	394.60		
.5 S.P. Crane, 4x4, 5 Ton		192.94		212.24	9.65	10.61
20 L.H., Daily Totals		$1539.74		$2214.44	$76.99	$110.72

Crew R-4	Hr.	Daily	Hr.	Daily	Bare Costs	Incl. O&P
1 Struc. Steel Foreman (outside)	$66.55	$532.40	$102.50	$820.00	$65.51	$100.16
3 Struc. Steel Workers	64.55	1549.20	99.40	2385.60		
1 Electrician	67.35	538.80	100.10	800.80		
1 Welder, Gas Engine, 300 amp		147.09		161.80	3.68	4.04
40 L.H., Daily Totals		$2767.49		$4168.20	$69.19	$104.21

Crew No.	Bare Costs		Incl. Subs O&P		Cost Per Labor-Hour	
Crew R-5	Hr.	Daily	Hr.	Daily	Bare Costs	Incl. O&P
1 Electrician Foreman	$67.85	$542.80	$100.85	$806.80	$59.25	$88.48
4 Electrician Linemen	67.35	2155.20	100.10	3203.20		
2 Electrician Operators	67.35	1077.60	100.10	1601.60		
4 Electrician Groundmen	44.95	1438.40	67.95	2174.40		
1 Crew Truck		183.83		202.21		
1 Flatbed Truck, 20,000 GVW		223.10		245.41		
1 Pickup Truck, 3/4 Ton		122.56		134.82		
.2 Hyd. Crane, 55 Ton		492.21		541.43		
.2 Hyd. Crane, 12 Ton		430.13		473.14		
.2 Earth Auger, Truck-Mtd.		30.79		33.87		
1 Tractor w/Winch		413.43		454.77	21.55	23.70
88 L.H., Daily Totals		$7110.06		$9871.66	$80.80	$112.18

Crew R-6	Hr.	Daily	Hr.	Daily	Bare Costs	Incl. O&P
1 Electrician Foreman	$67.85	$542.80	$100.85	$806.80	$59.25	$88.48
4 Electrician Linemen	67.35	2155.20	100.10	3203.20		
2 Electrician Operators	67.35	1077.60	100.10	1601.60		
4 Electrician Groundmen	44.95	1438.40	67.95	2174.40		
1 Crew Truck		183.83		202.21		
1 Flatbed Truck, 20,000 GVW		223.10		245.41		
1 Pickup Truck, 3/4 Ton		122.56		134.82		
.2 Hyd. Crane, 55 Ton		492.21		541.43		
.2 Hyd. Crane, 12 Ton		430.13		473.14		
.2 Earth Auger, Truck-Mtd.		30.79		33.87		
1 Tractor w/Winch		413.43		454.77		
3 Cable Trailers		609.78		670.76		
.5 Tensioning Rig		76.23		83.86		
.5 Cable Pulling Rig		370.78		407.86	33.56	36.91
88 L.H., Daily Totals		$8166.85		$11034.14	$92.81	$125.39

Crew R-7	Hr.	Daily	Hr.	Daily	Bare Costs	Incl. O&P
1 Electrician Foreman	$67.85	$542.80	$100.85	$806.80	$48.77	$73.43
5 Electrician Groundmen	44.95	1798.00	67.95	2718.00		
1 Crew Truck		183.83		202.21	3.83	4.21
48 L.H., Daily Totals		$2524.63		$3727.01	$52.60	$77.65

Crew R-8	Hr.	Daily	Hr.	Daily	Bare Costs	Incl. O&P
1 Electrician Foreman	$67.85	$542.80	$100.85	$806.80	$59.97	$89.51
3 Electrician Linemen	67.35	1616.40	100.10	2402.40		
2 Electrician Groundmen	44.95	719.20	67.95	1087.20		
1 Pickup Truck, 3/4 Ton		122.56		134.82		
1 Crew Truck		183.83		202.21	6.38	7.02
48 L.H., Daily Totals		$3184.79		$4633.43	$66.35	$96.53

Crew R-9	Hr.	Daily	Hr.	Daily	Bare Costs	Incl. O&P
1 Electrician Foreman	$67.85	$542.80	$100.85	$806.80	$56.21	$84.12
1 Electrician Lineman	67.35	538.80	100.10	800.80		
2 Electrician Operators	67.35	1077.60	100.10	1601.60		
4 Electrician Groundmen	44.95	1438.40	67.95	2174.40		
1 Pickup Truck, 3/4 Ton		122.56		134.82		
1 Crew Truck		183.83		202.21	4.79	5.27
64 L.H., Daily Totals		$3903.99		$5720.63	$61.00	$89.38

Crew R-10	Hr.	Daily	Hr.	Daily	Bare Costs	Incl. O&P
1 Electrician Foreman	$67.85	$542.80	$100.85	$806.80	$63.70	$94.87
4 Electrician Linemen	67.35	2155.20	100.10	3203.20		
1 Electrician Groundman	44.95	359.60	67.95	543.60		
1 Crew Truck		183.83		202.21		
3 Tram Cars		237.63		261.39	8.78	9.66
48 L.H., Daily Totals		$3479.06		$5017.21	$72.48	$104.53

Crews - Standard

Crew No.		Bare Costs		Incl. Subs O&P		Cost Per Labor-Hour	
Crew R-11	Hr.	Daily	Hr.	Daily	Bare Costs	Incl. O&P
1 Electrician Foreman	$67.85	$542.80	$100.85	$806.80	$64.40	$95.75
4 Electricians	67.35	2155.20	100.10	3203.20		
1 Equip. Oper. (crane)	66.30	530.40	98.65	789.20		
1 Common Laborer	47.25	378.00	70.35	562.80		
1 Crew Truck		183.83		202.21		
1 Hyd. Crane, 12 Ton		2150.65		2365.72	41.69	45.86
56 L.H., Daily Totals		$5940.88		$7929.93	$106.09	$141.61
Crew R-12	Hr.	Daily	Hr.	Daily	Bare Costs	Incl. O&P
1 Carpenter Foreman (inside)	$59.10	$472.80	$88.00	$704.00	$55.46	$82.87
4 Carpenters	58.60	1875.20	87.25	2792.00		
4 Common Laborers	47.25	1512.00	70.35	2251.20		
1 Equip. Oper. (medium)	63.05	504.40	93.80	750.40		
1 Steel Worker	64.55	516.40	99.40	795.20		
1 Dozer, 200 H.P.		1382.36		1520.60		
1 Pickup Truck, 3/4 Ton		122.56		134.82	17.10	18.81
88 L.H., Daily Totals		$6385.72		$8948.21	$72.56	$101.68
Crew R-13	Hr.	Daily	Hr.	Daily	Bare Costs	Incl. O&P
1 Electrician Foreman	$67.85	$542.80	$100.85	$806.80	$65.31	$97.09
3 Electricians	67.35	1616.40	100.10	2402.40		
.25 Equip. Oper. (crane)	66.30	132.60	98.65	197.30		
1 Equipment Oiler	56.40	451.20	83.90	671.20		
.25 Hydraulic Crane, 33 Ton		607.40		668.15	14.46	15.91
42 L.H., Daily Totals		$3350.41		$4745.85	$79.77	$113.00
Crew R-15	Hr.	Daily	Hr.	Daily	Bare Costs	Incl. O&P
1 Electrician Foreman	$67.85	$542.80	$100.85	$806.80	$66.16	$98.35
4 Electricians	67.35	2155.20	100.10	3203.20		
1 Equipment Oper. (light)	59.70	477.60	88.85	710.80		
1 Telescoping Boom Lift, to 40'		345.57		380.13	7.20	7.92
48 L.H., Daily Totals		$3521.17		$5100.93	$73.36	$106.27
Crew R-15A	Hr.	Daily	Hr.	Daily	Bare Costs	Incl. O&P
1 Electrician Foreman	$67.85	$542.80	$100.85	$806.80	$59.46	$88.43
2 Electricians	67.35	1077.60	100.10	1601.60		
2 Common Laborers	47.25	756.00	70.35	1125.60		
1 Equip. Oper. (light)	59.70	477.60	88.85	710.80		
1 Telescoping Boom Lift, to 40'		345.57		380.13	7.20	7.92
48 L.H., Daily Totals		$3199.57		$4624.93	$66.66	$96.35
Crew R-18	Hr.	Daily	Hr.	Daily	Bare Costs	Incl. O&P
.25 Electrician Foreman	$67.85	$135.70	$100.85	$201.70	$59.11	$87.85
1 Electrician	67.35	538.80	100.10	800.80		
2 Electrician Apprentices	53.90	862.40	80.10	1281.60		
26 L.H., Daily Totals		$1536.90		$2284.10	$59.11	$87.85
Crew R-19	Hr.	Daily	Hr.	Daily	Bare Costs	Incl. O&P
.5 Electrician Foreman	$67.85	$271.40	$100.85	$403.40	$67.45	$100.25
2 Electricians	67.35	1077.60	100.10	1601.60		
20 L.H., Daily Totals		$1349.00		$2005.00	$67.45	$100.25
Crew R-21	Hr.	Daily	Hr.	Daily	Bare Costs	Incl. O&P
1 Electrician Foreman	$67.85	$542.80	$100.85	$806.80	$67.37	$100.13
3 Electricians	67.35	1616.40	100.10	2402.40		
.1 Equip. Oper. (medium)	63.05	50.44	93.80	75.04		
.1 S.P. Crane, 4x4, 25 Ton		92.71		101.98	2.83	3.11
32.8 L.H., Daily Totals		$2302.35		$3386.22	$70.19	$103.24
Crew R-22	Hr.	Daily	Hr.	Daily	Bare Costs	Incl. O&P
.66 Electrician Foreman	$67.85	$358.25	$100.85	$532.49	$61.65	$91.62
2 Electricians	67.35	1077.60	100.10	1601.60		
2 Electrician Apprentices	53.90	862.40	80.10	1281.60		
37.28 L.H., Daily Totals		$2298.25		$3415.69	$61.65	$91.62
Crew R-30	Hr.	Daily	Hr.	Daily	Bare Costs	Incl. O&P
.25 Electrician Foreman (outside)	$69.35	$138.70	$103.05	$206.10	$55.13	$82.02
1 Electrician	67.35	538.80	100.10	800.80		
2 Laborers (Semi-Skilled)	47.25	756.00	70.35	1125.60		
26 L.H., Daily Totals		$1433.50		$2132.50	$55.13	$82.02
Crew R-31	Hr.	Daily	Hr.	Daily	Bare Costs	Incl. O&P
1 Electrician	$67.35	$538.80	$100.10	$800.80	$67.35	$100.10
1 Core Drill, Electric, 2.5 H.P.		61.41		67.55	7.68	8.44
8 L.H., Daily Totals		$600.21		$868.35	$75.03	$108.54
Crew W-41E	Hr.	Daily	Hr.	Daily	Bare Costs	Incl. O&P
.5 Plumber Foreman (outside)	$74.05	$296.20	$110.40	$441.60	$62.53	$93.20
1 Plumber	72.05	576.40	107.45	859.60		
1 Laborer	47.25	378.00	70.35	562.80		
20 L.H., Daily Totals		$1250.60		$1864.00	$62.53	$93.20

Historical Cost Indexes

The table below lists both the RSMeans® historical cost index based on Jan. 1, 1993 = 100 as well as the computed value of an index based on Jan. 1, 2023 costs. Since the Jan. 1, 2023 figure is estimated, space is left to write in the actual index figures as they become available through the quarterly *RSMeans Construction Cost Indexes*.

To compute the actual index based on Jan. 1, 2023 = 100, divide the historical cost index for a particular year by the actual Jan. 1, 2023 construction cost index. Space has been left to advance the index figures as the year progresses.

Year	Historical Cost Index Jan. 1, 1993 = 100		Current Index Based on Jan. 1, 2023 = 100		Year	Historical Cost Index Jan. 1, 1993 = 100	Current Index Based on Jan. 1, 2023 = 100		Year	Historical Cost Index Jan. 1, 1993 = 100	Current Index Based on Jan. 1, 2023 = 100	
	Est.	Actual	Est.	Actual		Actual	Est.	Actual		Actual	Est.	Actual
Oct 2023					July 2006	162.0	50.8		July 1986	84.2	26.4	
July 2023					2005	151.6	47.6		1985	82.6	25.9	
April 2023					2004	143.7	45.1		1984	82.0	25.7	
Jan 2023	318.8		100.0		2003	132.0	41.4		1983	80.2	25.1	
July 2022		297.1	93.2		2002	128.7	40.4		1982	76.1	23.9	
2021		257.5	80.8		2001	125.1	39.2		1981	70.0	22.0	
2020		234.6	73.6		2000	120.9	37.9		1980	62.9	19.7	
2019		232.2	72.8		1999	117.6	36.9		1979	57.8	18.1	
2018		222.9	69.9		1998	115.1	36.1		1978	53.5	16.8	
2017		213.6	67.0		1997	112.8	35.4		1977	49.5	15.5	
2016		207.3	65.0		1996	110.2	34.6		1976	46.9	14.7	
2015		206.2	64.7		1995	107.6	33.8		1975	44.8	14.1	
2014		204.9	64.3		1994	104.4	32.7		1974	41.4	13.0	
2013		201.2	63.1		1993	101.7	31.9		1973	37.7	11.8	
2012		194.6	61.0		1992	99.4	31.2		1972	34.8	10.9	
2011		191.2	60.0		1991	96.8	30.4		1971	32.1	10.1	
2010		183.5	57.6		1990	94.3	29.6					
2009		180.1	56.5		1989	92.1	28.9					
2008		180.4	56.6		1988	89.9	28.2					
2007		169.4	53.1		1987	87.7	27.5					

Adjustments to Costs

The "Historical Cost Index" can be used to convert national average building costs at a particular time to the approximate building costs for some other time.

Example:

Estimate and compare construction costs for different years in the same city.

To estimate the national average construction cost of a building in 1971, knowing that it cost $900,000 in 2023:

INDEX in 1970 = 32.1
INDEX in 2023 = 318.8

Note: The city cost indexes for Canada can be used to convert U.S. national averages to local costs in Canadian dollars.

Time Adjustment Using the Historical Cost Indexes:

$$\frac{\text{Index for Year A}}{\text{Index for Year B}} \times \text{Cost in Year B} = \text{Cost in Year A}$$

$$\frac{\text{INDEX 1971}}{\text{INDEX 2023}} \times \text{Cost 2023} = \text{Cost 1971}$$

$$\frac{32.1}{318.8} \times \$900,000 = .100 \times \$900,000 = \$90,000$$

The construction cost of the building in 1971 was $90,000.

Example:

To estimate and compare the cost of a building in Toronto, ON in 2023 with the known cost of $600,000 (US$) in New York, NY in 2023:

INDEX Toronto = 132.1
INDEX New York = 139.6

$$\frac{\text{INDEX Toronto}}{\text{INDEX New York}} \times \text{Cost New York} = \text{Cost Toronto}$$

$$\frac{132.1}{139.6} \times \$600,000 = .947 \times \$600,000 = \$568,200$$

The construction cost of the building in Toronto is $568,200 (CN$).

*Historical Cost Index updates and other resources are provided on the following website:
rsmeans.com/2023books

City Cost Indexes

How to Use the City Cost Indexes

What you should know before you begin

RSMeans City Cost Indexes (CCI) are an extremely useful tool for when you want to compare costs from city to city and region to region.

This publication contains average construction cost indexes for 731 U.S. and Canadian cities covering over 930 three-digit zip code locations, as listed directly under each city.

Keep in mind that a City Cost Index number is a percentage ratio of a specific city's cost to the national average cost of the same item at a stated time period.

In other words, these index figures represent relative construction factors (or, if you prefer, multipliers) for material and installation costs, as well as the weighted average for Total In Place costs for each CSI MasterFormat division. Installation costs include both labor and equipment rental costs. When estimating equipment rental rates only for a specific location, use 01 54 33 EQUIPMENT RENTAL COSTS in the Reference Section.

The 30 City Average Index is the average of 30 major U.S. cities and serves as a national average. This national average represents the baseline from which all locations are calculated.

Index figures for both material and installation are based on the 30 major city average of 100 and represent the cost relationship as of July 1, 2022. The index for each division is computed from representative material and labor quantities for that division. The weighted average for each city is a weighted total of the components listed above it. It does not include relative productivity between trades or cities.

As changes occur in local material prices, labor rates, and equipment rental rates (including fuel costs), the impact of these changes should be accurately measured by the change in the City Cost Index for each particular city (as compared to the 30 city average).

Therefore, if you know (or have estimated) building costs in one city today, you can easily convert those costs to expected building costs in another city.

In addition, by using the Historical Cost Index, you can easily convert national average building costs at a particular time to the approximate building costs for some other time. The City Cost Indexes can then be applied to calculate the costs for a particular city.

Quick calculations

Location Adjustment Using the City Cost Indexes:

$$\frac{\text{Index for City A}}{\text{Index for City B}} \times \text{Cost in City B} = \text{Cost in City A}$$

Time Adjustment for the National Average Using the Historical Cost Index:

$$\frac{\text{Index for Year A}}{\text{Index for Year B}} \times \text{Cost in Year B} = \text{Cost in Year A}$$

Adjustment from the National Average:

$$\frac{\text{Index for City A}}{100} \times \text{National Average Cost} = \text{Cost in City A}$$

Since each of the other RSMeans data sets contains many different items, any *one* item multiplied by the particular city index may give incorrect results. However, the larger the number of items compiled, the closer the results should be to actual costs for that particular city.

The City Cost Indexes for Canadian cities are calculated using Canadian material and equipment prices and labor rates in Canadian dollars. When compared to the baseline mentioned previously, the resulting index enables the user to convert baseline costs to local costs. Therefore, indexes for Canadian cities can be used to convert U.S. national average prices to local costs in Canadian dollars.

How to use this section

1. Compare costs from city to city.

In using the RSMeans Indexes, remember that an index number is not a fixed number but a ratio: It's a percentage ratio of a building component's cost at any stated time to the national average cost of that same component at the same time period. Put in the form of an equation:

$$\frac{\text{Specific City Cost}}{\text{National Average Cost}} \times 100 = \text{City Index Number}$$

Therefore, when making cost comparisons between cities, do not subtract one city's index number from the index number of another city and read the result as a percentage difference. Instead, divide one city's index number by that of the other city. The resulting number may then be used as a multiplier to calculate cost differences from city to city.

The formula used to find cost differences between cities for the purpose of comparison is as follows:

$$\frac{\text{City A Index}}{\text{City B Index}} \times \text{City B Cost (Known)} = \text{City A Cost (Unknown)}$$

In addition, you can use RSMeans CCI to calculate and compare costs division by division between cities using the same basic formula. (Just be sure that you're comparing similar divisions.)

2. Compare a specific city's construction costs with the national average.

When you're studying construction location feasibility, it's advisable to compare a prospective project's cost index with an index of the national average cost.

For example, divide the weighted average index of construction costs of a specific city by that of the 30 City Average, which = 100.

$$\frac{\text{City Index}}{100} = \% \text{ of National Average}$$

As a result, you get a ratio that indicates the relative cost of construction in that city in comparison with the national average.

3. Convert U.S. national average to actual costs in Canadian City.

$$\frac{\text{Index for Canadian City}}{100} \times \text{National Average Cost} = \text{Cost in Canadian City in \$ CAN}$$

4. Adjust construction cost data based on a national average.

When you use a source of construction cost data which is based on a national average (such as RSMeans cost data), it is necessary to adjust those costs to a specific location.

$$\frac{\text{City Index}}{100} \times \frac{\text{Cost Based on}}{\text{National Average Costs}} = \frac{\text{City Cost}}{\text{(Unknown)}}$$

5. When applying the City Cost Indexes to demolition projects, use the appropriate division installation index. For example, for removal of existing doors and windows, use the Division 8 (Openings) index.

What you might like to know about how we developed the Indexes

The information presented in the CCI is organized according to the Construction Specifications Institute (CSI) MasterFormat 2018 classification system.

To create a reliable index, RSMeans researched the building type most often constructed in the United States and Canada. Because it was concluded that no one type of building completely represented the building construction industry, nine different types of buildings were combined to create a composite model.

The exact material, labor, and equipment quantities are based on detailed analyses of these nine building types, and then each quantity is weighted in proportion to expected usage. These various material items, labor hours, and equipment rental rates are thus combined to form a composite building representing as closely as possible the actual usage of materials, labor, and equipment in the North American building construction industry.

The following structures were chosen to make up that composite model:

1. Factory, 1 story
2. Office, 2-4 stories
3. Store, Retail
4. Town Hall, 2-3 stories
5. High School, 2-3 stories
6. Hospital, 4-8 stories
7. Garage, Parking
8. Apartment, 1-3 stories
9. Hotel/Motel, 2-3 stories

For the purposes of ensuring the timeliness of the data, the components of the index for the composite model have been streamlined. They currently consist of:

- specific quantities of 66 commonly used construction materials;
- specific labor-hours for 21 building construction trades; and
- specific days of equipment rental for 6 types of construction equipment (normally used to install the 66 material items by the 21 trades.) Fuel costs and routine maintenance costs are included in the equipment cost.

Material and equipment price quotations are gathered quarterly from cities in the United States and Canada. These prices and the latest negotiated labor wage rates for 21 different building trades are used to compile the quarterly update of the City Cost Index.

The 30 major U.S. cities used to calculate the national average are:

Atlanta, GA
Baltimore, MD
Boston, MA
Buffalo, NY
Chicago, IL
Cincinnati, OH
Cleveland, OH
Columbus, OH
Dallas, TX
Denver, CO
Detroit, MI
Houston, TX
Indianapolis, IN
Kansas City, MO
Los Angeles, CA
Memphis, TN
Milwaukee, WI
Minneapolis, MN
Nashville, TN
New Orleans, LA
New York, NY
Philadelphia, PA
Phoenix, AZ
Pittsburgh, PA
St. Louis, MO
San Antonio, TX
San Diego, CA
San Francisco, CA
Seattle, WA
Washington, DC

What the CCI does not indicate

The weighted average for each city is a total of the divisional components weighted to reflect typical usage. It does not include the productivity variations between trades or cities.

In addition, the CCI does not take into consideration factors such as the following:

- managerial efficiency
- competitive conditions
- automation
- restrictive union practices
- unique local requirements
- regional variations due to specific building codes

City Cost Indexes

		UNITED STATES 30 CITY AVERAGE			ANNISTON 362			ALABAMA BIRMINGHAM 350 - 352			BUTLER 369			DECATUR 356			DOTHAN 363		
DIVISION		MAT.	INST.	TOTAL	MAT.	INST.	TOTAL	MAT.	INST.	TOTAL	MAT.	INST.	TOTAL	MAT.	INST.	TOTAL	MAT.	INST.	TOTAL
015433	CONTRACTOR EQUIPMENT		100.0	100.0		98.3	98.3		102.9	102.9		96.1	96.1		98.3	98.3		96.1	96.1
0241, 31 - 34	SITE & INFRASTRUCTURE, DEMOLITION	100.0	100.0	100.0	104.1	85.5	92.0	99.0	93.6	95.5	111.3	82.0	92.2	91.3	85.1	87.3	108.9	82.2	91.4
0310	Concrete Forming & Accessories	100.0	100.0	100.0	92.5	63.3	69.9	100.0	67.6	74.9	88.2	65.5	70.6	99.3	61.9	70.3	98.4	69.0	75.5
0320	Concrete Reinforcing	100.0	100.0	100.0	88.0	67.9	82.4	98.0	68.1	89.7	92.9	67.4	85.8	91.4	64.4	83.9	92.9	68.2	86.0
0330	Cast-in-Place Concrete	100.0	100.0	100.0	87.9	65.7	80.0	106.6	70.4	93.8	85.7	65.9	78.7	99.0	65.0	86.9	85.7	67.6	79.3
03	CONCRETE	100.0	100.0	100.0	90.5	66.7	81.1	98.4	70.1	87.2	91.5	67.7	82.1	92.2	65.2	81.5	91.5	70.0	83.0
04	MASONRY	100.0	100.0	100.0	81.2	59.8	68.2	86.2	62.3	71.7	82.5	59.8	68.7	81.8	58.8	67.8	84.4	63.1	71.5
05	METALS	100.0	100.0	100.0	104.2	92.5	101.9	104.6	90.3	101.8	103.2	92.9	101.2	105.9	90.6	102.9	103.3	94.0	101.5
06	WOOD, PLASTICS & COMPOSITES	100.0	100.0	100.0	87.0	63.5	76.4	94.5	67.8	82.5	80.8	65.9	74.1	97.8	61.6	81.6	94.5	69.6	83.3
07	THERMAL & MOISTURE PROTECTION	100.0	100.0	100.0	102.7	59.2	87.2	106.7	66.1	92.2	102.7	62.9	88.5	104.1	62.1	89.1	102.8	64.4	89.1
08	OPENINGS	100.0	100.0	100.0	102.9	65.0	94.4	103.0	67.9	95.1	102.9	66.7	94.8	106.5	63.6	96.8	103.0	68.9	95.3
0920	Plaster & Gypsum Board	100.0	100.0	100.0	92.5	63.0	73.8	93.2	67.1	76.7	90.1	65.5	74.5	92.5	61.1	72.6	101.2	69.3	81.0
0950, 0980	Ceilings & Acoustic Treatment	100.0	100.0	100.0	92.1	63.0	75.8	90.1	67.1	77.2	92.1	65.5	77.2	87.9	61.1	72.9	92.1	69.3	79.3
0960	Flooring	100.0	100.0	100.0	68.1	64.2	67.1	106.5	67.5	96.7	71.7	64.2	69.8	100.1	64.2	91.1	75.8	68.8	74.0
0970, 0990	Wall Finishes & Painting/Coating	100.0	100.0	100.0	96.2	50.1	69.2	99.2	51.1	70.5	96.2	42.4	64.1	88.5	56.4	69.4	96.2	82.0	87.7
09	FINISHES	100.0	100.0	100.0	84.6	62.0	73.3	97.9	65.6	81.7	87.4	62.6	75.0	92.8	61.4	77.0	89.9	70.3	80.0
COVERS	DIVS. 10 - 14, 25, 28, 41, 43, 44, 46	100.0	100.0	100.0	100.0	83.4	96.8	100.0	85.0	97.1	100.0	84.5	97.0	100.0	78.9	95.9	100.0	85.2	97.1
21, 22, 23	FIRE SUPPRESSION, PLUMBING & HVAC	100.0	100.0	100.0	105.5	49.6	85.5	100.0	63.5	86.9	95.9	61.3	83.5	100.0	61.3	86.1	95.9	61.8	83.7
26, 27, 3370	ELECTRICAL, COMMUNICATIONS & UTIL.	100.0	100.0	100.0	98.0	53.3	78.6	100.7	64.2	84.9	99.1	53.5	79.3	98.0	60.3	81.6	98.4	73.4	87.6
MF2018	WEIGHTED AVERAGE	100.0	100.0	100.0	99.2	64.0	86.3	100.6	70.5	89.5	97.5	66.7	86.2	99.3	66.7	87.3	97.8	71.5	88.1

		ALABAMA EVERGREEN 364			GADSDEN 359			HUNTSVILLE 357 - 358			JASPER 355			MOBILE 365 - 366			MONTGOMERY 360 - 361		
DIVISION		MAT.	INST.	TOTAL	MAT.	INST.	TOTAL	MAT.	INST.	TOTAL	MAT.	INST.	TOTAL	MAT.	INST.	TOTAL	MAT.	INST.	TOTAL
015433	CONTRACTOR EQUIPMENT		96.1	96.1		98.3	98.3		98.3	98.3		98.3	98.3		96.1	96.1		103.7	103.7
0241, 31 - 34	SITE & INFRASTRUCTURE, DEMOLITION	111.8	82.0	92.3	101.5	85.5	91.1	91.0	85.5	87.4	101.4	85.5	91.1	105.7	82.0	90.2	104.4	94.8	98.1
0310	Concrete Forming & Accessories	84.7	63.5	68.3	90.5	65.8	71.3	99.3	72.0	78.1	96.3	64.1	71.3	97.4	66.6	73.6	102.8	67.3	75.2
0320	Concrete Reinforcing	92.9	67.4	85.8	96.5	68.0	88.7	91.4	76.0	87.1	91.4	67.9	84.9	91.0	68.8	84.8	99.8	68.1	91.0
0330	Cast-in-Place Concrete	85.7	65.8	78.7	99.0	67.8	87.9	96.4	67.6	86.2	109.8	66.4	94.3	89.9	66.9	81.7	89.8	68.8	82.3
03	CONCRETE	91.6	66.8	81.8	95.6	68.6	84.9	91.1	72.7	83.8	98.5	67.3	86.2	89.0	68.9	81.1	92.2	69.4	83.2
04	MASONRY	82.5	59.8	68.7	80.4	61.8	69.1	82.7	61.5	69.8	77.9	60.8	67.5	83.9	61.3	70.2	81.4	61.4	69.3
05	METALS	103.3	92.7	101.2	102.9	93.2	101.0	105.9	96.1	103.9	102.8	92.9	100.9	106.1	93.5	103.6	105.7	90.3	102.7
06	WOOD, PLASTICS & COMPOSITES	76.4	63.5	70.6	86.2	65.7	77.0	97.8	74.1	87.2	94.5	63.5	80.6	93.3	67.5	81.7	97.9	67.8	84.4
07	THERMAL & MOISTURE PROTECTION	102.7	61.8	88.1	104.2	64.2	90.0	104.1	65.0	90.1	104.3	62.3	89.3	102.5	63.2	88.5	102.5	65.6	89.3
08	OPENINGS	102.9	65.3	94.5	103.0	66.7	94.8	106.2	73.3	98.8	102.9	65.5	94.5	105.9	67.9	97.3	104.2	67.9	96.0
0920	Plaster & Gypsum Board	89.8	63.0	72.8	83.4	65.3	71.9	92.5	73.9	80.7	87.9	63.0	72.1	98.9	67.1	78.8	101.4	67.1	79.6
0950, 0980	Ceilings & Acoustic Treatment	92.1	63.0	75.8	81.1	65.3	72.2	88.9	73.9	80.5	81.1	63.0	70.9	101.3	67.1	82.1	104.0	67.1	83.3
0960	Flooring	70.0	64.2	68.6	97.0	66.8	89.4	100.1	66.8	91.7	98.7	64.2	90.0	75.7	67.5	73.6	75.0	67.5	73.1
0970, 0990	Wall Finishes & Painting/Coating	96.2	42.4	64.1	88.5	50.1	65.6	88.5	58.8	70.8	88.5	50.1	65.6	99.8	42.4	65.6	101.2	50.1	70.7
09	FINISHES	86.9	61.2	74.0	89.3	64.0	76.6	93.1	69.8	81.4	90.3	62.2	76.2	91.6	64.2	77.8	94.1	65.3	79.6
COVERS	DIVS. 10 - 14, 25, 28, 41, 43, 44, 46	100.0	84.2	96.9	100.0	83.9	96.9	100.0	84.7	97.0	100.0	83.7	96.8	100.0	84.7	97.0	100.0	84.7	97.0
21, 22, 23	FIRE SUPPRESSION, PLUMBING & HVAC	95.9	55.4	81.4	107.1	63.7	91.5	100.0	63.4	86.9	107.1	63.3	91.4	100.1	60.2	85.8	100.1	60.3	85.8
26, 27, 3370	ELECTRICAL, COMMUNICATIONS & UTIL.	97.6	53.5	78.5	98.1	64.2	83.5	98.7	65.6	84.4	97.8	53.3	78.5	99.7	58.6	81.9	100.8	71.1	87.9
MF2018	WEIGHTED AVERAGE	97.3	65.0	85.4	100.2	69.5	88.9	99.3	71.6	89.1	100.6	67.2	88.3	99.4	67.8	87.8	99.8	70.6	89.0

		ALABAMA PHENIX CITY 368			SELMA 367			TUSCALOOSA 354			ALASKA ANCHORAGE 995 - 996			FAIRBANKS 997			JUNEAU 998		
DIVISION		MAT.	INST.	TOTAL	MAT.	INST.	TOTAL	MAT.	INST.	TOTAL	MAT.	INST.	TOTAL	MAT.	INST.	TOTAL	MAT.	INST.	TOTAL
015433	CONTRACTOR EQUIPMENT		96.1	96.1		96.1	96.1		98.3	98.3		104.7	104.7		109.1	109.1		104.7	104.7
0241, 31 - 34	SITE & INFRASTRUCTURE, DEMOLITION	115.6	81.9	93.7	108.6	81.9	91.2	91.5	85.5	87.6	137.2	112.6	121.2	133.5	118.5	123.7	149.0	112.4	125.3
0310	Concrete Forming & Accessories	92.4	65.3	71.3	89.7	63.8	69.6	99.3	66.9	74.1	96.6	113.8	110.0	100.2	113.7	110.7	96.1	113.8	109.9
0320	Concrete Reinforcing	92.8	64.2	84.9	92.9	67.9	86.0	91.4	68.0	84.9	106.6	117.1	109.5	103.7	117.1	107.4	106.5	117.1	109.4
0330	Cast-in-Place Concrete	85.8	66.2	78.8	85.7	65.9	78.7	100.4	67.5	88.7	131.6	112.9	125.0	130.4	111.0	123.5	131.5	112.9	124.9
03	CONCRETE	94.0	67.2	83.4	90.8	67.0	81.4	92.8	69.0	83.4	116.1	113.4	115.0	108.8	112.8	110.4	120.9	113.4	117.9
04	MASONRY	82.5	59.8	68.7	87.3	59.8	70.6	82.1	61.3	69.5	180.4	113.0	139.5	179.4	113.0	139.1	165.4	113.1	133.6
05	METALS	103.2	91.6	100.9	103.2	93.0	101.2	105.0	93.2	102.7	132.1	101.8	126.1	126.8	104.1	122.3	127.1	101.8	122.1
06	WOOD, PLASTICS & COMPOSITES	86.4	65.4	77.0	82.9	63.5	74.2	97.8	67.5	84.2	107.6	111.8	109.5	120.9	111.7	116.8	112.1	111.8	112.0
07	THERMAL & MOISTURE PROTECTION	103.0	63.3	88.9	102.6	62.6	88.3	104.1	64.1	89.9	119.1	111.1	116.3	119.1	109.8	115.8	114.7	111.1	113.4
08	OPENINGS	102.9	65.6	94.5	102.9	65.5	94.5	106.2	67.7	97.5	121.5	113.6	119.7	124.5	112.2	121.7	123.4	113.6	121.2
0920	Plaster & Gypsum Board	94.2	65.0	75.7	92.0	63.0	73.6	92.5	67.1	76.4	129.5	112.1	118.4	154.7	112.1	127.7	142.9	112.1	123.4
0950, 0980	Ceilings & Acoustic Treatment	92.1	65.0	76.9	92.1	63.0	75.8	88.9	67.1	76.7	112.6	112.1	112.3	103.7	112.1	108.4	123.9	112.1	117.3
0960	Flooring	73.2	64.2	70.9	72.0	64.2	70.0	100.1	66.8	91.7	112.5	109.5	111.7	101.7	109.5	103.6	108.1	109.5	108.4
0970, 0990	Wall Finishes & Painting/Coating	96.2	74.4	83.2	96.2	50.1	68.7	88.5	50.1	65.6	105.1	115.5	111.3	101.8	109.7	106.5	105.1	115.5	111.3
09	FINISHES	88.8	65.8	77.3	87.5	62.0	74.7	93.1	64.9	78.9	113.3	113.3	113.4	111.4	112.7	112.0	116.7	113.3	115.0
COVERS	DIVS. 10 - 14, 25, 28, 41, 43, 44, 46	100.0	80.3	96.2	100.0	83.4	96.8	100.0	83.9	96.9	100.0	111.3	102.2	100.0	111.2	102.2	100.0	111.3	102.2
21, 22, 23	FIRE SUPPRESSION, PLUMBING & HVAC	95.9	60.1	83.1	95.9	60.8	83.3	100.0	63.5	86.8	100.0	107.3	102.6	99.8	107.2	102.5	100.0	107.3	102.6
26, 27, 3370	ELECTRICAL, COMMUNICATIONS & UTIL.	98.8	63.0	83.3	98.3	67.7	85.0	98.5	64.2	83.6	102.4	102.2	102.3	117.4	102.2	110.8	102.4	102.2	102.3
MF2018	WEIGHTED AVERAGE	98.0	67.8	86.9	97.5	68.3	86.7	99.3	69.6	88.4	116.6	109.2	113.9	116.2	109.6	113.8	116.1	109.2	113.5

City Cost Indexes

DIVISION		ALASKA KETCHIKAN 999			ARIZONA CHAMBERS 865			ARIZONA FLAGSTAFF 860			ARIZONA GLOBE 855			ARIZONA KINGMAN 864			ARIZONA MESA/TEMPE 852		
		MAT.	INST.	TOTAL	MAT.	INST.	TOTAL	MAT.	INST.	TOTAL	MAT.	INST.	TOTAL	MAT.	INST.	TOTAL	MAT.	INST.	TOTAL
015433	CONTRACTOR EQUIPMENT		109.1	109.1		87.5	87.5		87.5	87.5		89.5	89.5		87.5	87.5		89.5	89.5
0241, 31 - 34	SITE & INFRASTRUCTURE, DEMOLITION	186.9	118.5	142.3	74.0	87.4	82.7	94.9	87.7	90.2	105.8	88.8	94.7	74.0	87.7	82.9	99.0	89.1	92.6
0310	Concrete Forming & Accessories	92.6	113.8	109.1	98.6	65.6	72.9	104.8	73.1	80.2	93.0	65.8	71.8	96.5	62.0	69.7	96.3	70.6	76.3
0320	Concrete Reinforcing	80.6	117.1	90.7	93.5	73.7	88.0	93.4	73.3	87.9	104.7	73.7	96.1	93.6	73.7	88.1	105.4	73.7	96.6
0330	Cast-in-Place Concrete	264.1	111.7	209.9	80.9	67.0	75.9	80.9	67.4	76.1	78.5	66.9	74.4	80.6	67.3	75.9	79.2	67.3	75.0
03	CONCRETE	175.7	113.1	151.0	89.4	67.6	80.8	104.5	71.2	91.4	95.1	67.8	84.3	89.1	66.2	80.1	89.9	70.1	82.1
04	MASONRY	188.4	113.0	142.6	97.3	65.2	77.8	97.5	65.1	77.8	118.6	65.1	86.1	97.3	65.3	77.9	118.8	65.2	86.3
05	METALS	127.0	104.1	122.5	98.5	72.4	93.4	99.1	73.0	94.0	95.8	73.8	91.4	99.3	73.4	94.2	96.1	74.8	91.9
06	WOOD, PLASTICS & COMPOSITES	110.6	111.7	111.1	104.3	66.3	87.3	112.5	76.2	96.2	91.7	66.5	80.4	98.6	61.2	81.8	96.4	72.7	85.8
07	THERMAL & MOISTURE PROTECTION	131.5	109.5	123.6	91.1	68.9	83.2	92.6	68.6	84.1	90.9	67.7	82.6	91.0	68.8	83.1	90.9	68.8	83.0
08	OPENINGS	120.5	113.6	118.9	100.3	63.8	92.1	100.4	72.9	94.2	90.9	63.9	84.8	100.4	62.5	91.9	91.0	68.2	85.8
0920	Plaster & Gypsum Board	138.2	112.1	121.6	104.2	65.6	79.7	109.1	75.8	88.0	101.5	65.6	78.8	94.4	60.4	72.8	105.6	72.1	84.3
0950, 0980	Ceilings & Acoustic Treatment	100.7	112.1	107.1	110.8	65.6	85.5	111.7	75.8	91.6	99.0	65.6	80.3	111.7	60.4	82.9	99.0	72.1	83.9
0960	Flooring	101.3	109.5	103.4	90.4	57.7	82.2	92.0	62.8	84.7	93.8	57.7	84.8	89.5	57.7	81.5	94.9	61.7	86.6
0970, 0990	Wall Finishes & Painting/Coating	101.8	115.5	110.0	87.5	55.2	68.2	87.5	55.2	68.2	93.3	55.2	70.6	87.5	55.2	68.2	93.3	55.2	70.6
09	FINISHES	112.7	113.3	113.0	97.4	62.6	79.9	100.3	69.4	84.8	98.6	62.8	80.6	96.0	59.7	77.7	98.4	67.3	82.8
COVERS	DIVS. 10 - 14, 25, 28, 41, 43, 44, 46	100.0	111.2	102.2	100.0	83.6	96.8	100.0	84.6	97.0	100.0	84.0	96.9	100.0	83.0	96.7	100.0	84.6	97.0
21, 22, 23	FIRE SUPPRESSION, PLUMBING & HVAC	93.2	107.2	98.2	94.2	74.1	87.0	100.4	76.2	91.7	92.8	74.2	86.1	94.2	76.2	87.8	100.4	74.2	91.0
26, 27, 3370	ELECTRICAL, COMMUNICATIONS & UTIL.	117.4	102.2	110.8	101.9	65.6	86.2	101.4	63.8	85.1	97.7	63.8	83.0	101.9	63.8	85.4	96.1	63.8	82.1
MF2018	WEIGHTED AVERAGE	124.5	109.8	119.1	96.2	70.2	86.6	100.3	71.7	89.8	96.3	70.2	86.7	96.2	69.8	86.5	97.1	71.5	87.7

DIVISION		ARIZONA PHOENIX 850,853			ARIZONA PRESCOTT 863			ARIZONA SHOW LOW 859			ARIZONA TUCSON 856 - 857			ARKANSAS BATESVILLE 725			ARKANSAS CAMDEN 717		
		MAT.	INST.	TOTAL	MAT.	INST.	TOTAL	MAT.	INST.	TOTAL	MAT.	INST.	TOTAL	MAT.	INST.	TOTAL	MAT.	INST.	TOTAL
015433	CONTRACTOR EQUIPMENT		98.6	98.6		87.5	87.5		89.5	89.5		89.5	89.5		87.3	87.3		87.3	87.3
0241, 31 - 34	SITE & INFRASTRUCTURE, DEMOLITION	99.8	97.3	98.2	83.3	87.7	86.2	108.0	88.8	95.5	95.0	89.2	91.2	73.4	82.4	79.3	78.5	82.3	81.0
0310	Concrete Forming & Accessories	101.4	71.6	78.3	100.3	68.7	75.8	100.9	65.8	73.6	97.1	77.7	82.0	86.0	56.9	63.4	83.1	57.1	62.9
0320	Concrete Reinforcing	100.7	71.7	92.6	93.4	73.7	88.0	105.4	73.7	96.6	86.5	73.4	82.8	96.2	63.6	87.2	96.0	64.6	87.3
0330	Cast-in-Place Concrete	83.4	71.7	79.2	80.9	67.4	76.1	78.5	66.9	74.4	81.5	67.3	76.5	61.7	71.7	65.2	67.1	71.2	68.6
03	CONCRETE	91.0	71.9	83.5	93.5	69.3	83.9	97.1	67.8	85.5	85.9	73.3	80.9	73.1	64.1	69.6	75.3	64.2	70.9
04	MASONRY	110.7	65.6	83.3	97.4	65.3	77.9	118.6	65.1	86.1	103.2	58.8	76.2	89.3	58.2	70.4	110.3	58.1	78.6
05	METALS	103.4	76.5	98.1	99.2	73.7	94.1	95.5	73.8	91.2	96.9	74.4	92.5	98.5	74.8	93.8	109.3	75.1	102.5
06	WOOD, PLASTICS & COMPOSITES	104.1	73.1	90.2	106.4	70.2	90.2	102.3	66.5	86.2	96.9	82.4	90.4	82.0	57.7	71.1	81.7	58.2	71.2
07	THERMAL & MOISTURE PROTECTION	91.6	71.0	84.3	91.5	70.5	84.0	91.2	67.7	82.8	91.4	68.1	83.1	106.1	58.8	89.2	100.7	59.1	85.9
08	OPENINGS	100.8	70.3	93.9	100.4	66.4	92.7	90.3	65.4	84.7	87.7	76.3	85.2	103.7	56.0	93.0	97.1	56.5	88.0
0920	Plaster & Gypsum Board	116.1	72.1	88.2	104.8	69.7	82.5	108.5	65.6	81.3	110.6	82.0	92.5	74.9	57.0	63.5	84.7	57.5	67.5
0950, 0980	Ceilings & Acoustic Treatment	115.1	72.1	91.0	109.0	69.7	86.9	99.0	65.6	80.3	101.7	82.0	90.7	98.9	57.0	75.4	103.7	57.5	77.8
0960	Flooring	100.1	66.3	91.7	91.1	61.9	83.7	95.9	57.7	86.3	85.0	62.5	79.3	91.2	66.1	84.9	92.8	67.4	86.5
0970, 0990	Wall Finishes & Painting/Coating	101.2	55.0	73.7	87.5	55.2	68.2	93.3	55.2	70.6	93.5	55.2	70.7	95.4	48.8	67.8	97.1	50.4	69.2
09	FINISHES	106.2	68.9	87.4	97.6	65.8	81.6	100.3	62.8	81.5	96.7	73.1	84.9	87.8	57.5	72.6	92.1	58.0	75.0
COVERS	DIVS. 10 - 14, 25, 28, 41, 43, 44, 46	100.0	86.1	97.3	100.0	84.0	96.9	100.0	84.0	96.9	100.0	85.7	97.2	100.0	78.4	95.8	100.0	78.2	95.8
21, 22, 23	FIRE SUPPRESSION, PLUMBING & HVAC	100.1	77.2	91.9	100.4	74.1	91.0	92.8	74.2	86.1	100.3	76.2	91.7	93.0	49.2	77.3	92.6	54.0	78.8
26, 27, 3370	ELECTRICAL, COMMUNICATIONS & UTIL.	100.1	63.8	84.4	101.2	63.8	85.0	96.3	63.8	82.2	97.3	57.9	80.2	93.8	53.8	76.5	95.6	51.7	76.6
MF2018	WEIGHTED AVERAGE	100.4	73.7	90.6	98.4	70.9	88.3	96.6	70.3	86.9	95.9	72.1	87.1	92.6	60.4	80.7	95.9	61.2	83.1

DIVISION		ARKANSAS FAYETTEVILLE 727			ARKANSAS FORT SMITH 729			ARKANSAS HARRISON 726			ARKANSAS HOT SPRINGS 719			ARKANSAS JONESBORO 724			ARKANSAS LITTLE ROCK 720 - 722		
		MAT.	INST.	TOTAL	MAT.	INST.	TOTAL	MAT.	INST.	TOTAL	MAT.	INST.	TOTAL	MAT.	INST.	TOTAL	MAT.	INST.	TOTAL
015433	CONTRACTOR EQUIPMENT		87.3	87.3		87.3	87.3		87.3	87.3		87.3	87.3		107.9	107.9		93.8	93.8
0241, 31 - 34	SITE & INFRASTRUCTURE, DEMOLITION	73.1	82.3	79.1	80.8	82.4	81.8	77.5	82.3	80.6	81.1	82.4	81.9	96.7	97.7	97.3	86.0	92.5	90.2
0310	Concrete Forming & Accessories	80.9	57.1	62.4	103.1	58.1	68.1	91.3	56.9	64.6	79.7	57.4	62.2	89.8	57.6	64.8	102.5	58.7	68.5
0320	Concrete Reinforcing	96.2	61.4	86.6	97.4	63.6	88.1	95.8	64.6	87.2	94.2	64.4	86.0	93.5	65.6	85.8	98.7	66.3	89.7
0330	Cast-in-Place Concrete	61.7	71.2	65.1	70.5	72.5	71.2	68.4	71.2	69.4	68.7	72.0	69.9	67.1	72.9	69.2	68.4	75.1	70.8
03	CONCRETE	72.7	63.7	69.1	79.3	64.9	73.6	77.9	64.1	72.5	77.0	64.6	72.1	75.9	66.1	72.0	81.8	66.5	75.7
04	MASONRY	81.6	58.1	67.3	91.8	59.0	71.9	89.7	58.1	70.5	82.9	57.4	67.4	83.3	59.7	69.0	88.8	61.6	72.3
05	METALS	98.5	74.0	93.6	101.3	74.6	96.0	100.1	74.9	95.2	109.2	74.7	102.4	95.5	89.0	94.2	101.4	74.5	96.1
06	WOOD, PLASTICS & COMPOSITES	77.1	58.2	68.6	103.4	59.3	83.7	89.1	58.2	75.2	78.1	58.2	69.2	85.9	58.5	73.6	98.1	59.6	80.8
07	THERMAL & MOISTURE PROTECTION	106.7	59.1	89.7	107.2	59.4	90.2	106.4	59.1	89.5	100.9	58.4	85.8	111.8	59.7	93.2	100.8	61.6	86.8
08	OPENINGS	103.7	55.7	92.9	105.4	56.8	94.4	104.4	56.4	93.6	97.1	56.0	87.9	109.1	56.9	97.3	98.6	57.3	89.3
0920	Plaster & Gypsum Board	73.4	57.5	63.3	81.5	58.7	67.0	81.1	57.5	66.1	83.5	57.5	67.0	83.1	57.5	66.9	93.2	58.7	71.3
0950, 0980	Ceilings & Acoustic Treatment	98.9	57.5	75.7	101.6	58.7	77.5	101.6	57.5	76.9	103.7	57.5	77.8	100.4	57.5	76.3	109.0	58.7	80.8
0960	Flooring	88.7	67.4	83.4	96.6	74.6	91.1	93.1	67.4	86.6	92.0	63.5	84.9	63.4	74.6	66.2	99.8	80.1	94.9
0970, 0990	Wall Finishes & Painting/Coating	95.8	50.4	68.7	95.8	50.1	68.6	95.8	50.4	68.7	97.1	48.4	68.1	84.3	49.5	63.6	99.1	49.5	69.6
09	FINISHES	87.0	58.0	72.4	91.3	60.4	75.7	90.2	58.0	74.1	92.0	57.4	74.6	83.5	59.9	71.6	100.7	61.6	81.1
COVERS	DIVS. 10 - 14, 25, 28, 41, 43, 44, 46	100.0	78.1	95.8	100.0	78.6	95.8	100.0	78.2	95.8	100.0	78.7	95.9	100.0	79.2	96.0	100.0	79.3	96.0
21, 22, 23	FIRE SUPPRESSION, PLUMBING & HVAC	93.1	58.1	80.6	100.7	47.7	81.7	93.0	46.8	76.4	92.6	47.7	76.5	101.2	48.6	82.4	100.2	50.1	82.2
26, 27, 3370	ELECTRICAL, COMMUNICATIONS & UTIL.	90.9	48.0	72.3	92.5	56.8	77.0	93.1	51.2	75.0	96.6	58.0	79.9	99.9	58.3	81.9	100.8	58.5	82.4
MF2018	WEIGHTED AVERAGE	91.9	61.4	80.6	96.4	61.1	83.4	93.9	59.6	81.3	95.1	60.6	82.4	95.4	64.2	83.9	97.4	63.4	84.9

City Cost Indexes

		ARKANSAS											CALIFORNIA					
	DIVISION	PINE BLUFF			RUSSELLVILLE			TEXARKANA			WEST MEMPHIS			ALHAMBRA			ANAHEIM		
		716			728			718			723			917 - 918			928		
		MAT.	INST.	TOTAL	MAT.	INST.	TOTAL	MAT.	INST.	TOTAL	MAT.	INST.	TOTAL	MAT.	INST.	TOTAL	MAT.	INST.	TOTAL
015433	CONTRACTOR EQUIPMENT		87.3	87.3		87.3	87.3		88.4	88.4		107.9	107.9		93.7	93.7		96.6	96.6
0241, 31 - 34	SITE & INFRASTRUCTURE, DEMOLITION	86.2	82.4	83.7	74.7	82.4	79.7	94.7	84.2	87.8	99.1	97.5	98.1	113.1	101.2	105.4	110.8	101.5	104.7
0310	Concrete Forming & Accessories	79.5	57.5	62.4	86.9	57.3	63.9	87.3	57.3	64.0	96.1	57.7	66.3	97.0	138.9	129.6	96.1	139.0	129.5
0320	Concrete Reinforcing	95.9	66.1	87.7	96.9	64.4	87.9	95.4	66.1	87.3	93.5	56.9	83.4	99.5	132.7	108.7	79.8	132.6	94.4
0330	Cast-in-Place Concrete	68.7	71.8	69.8	64.6	72.0	67.2	74.8	71.5	73.7	70.4	73.0	71.3	94.3	126.6	105.8	99.3	129.5	110.0
03	CONCRETE	77.7	64.8	72.6	75.3	64.5	71.1	77.4	64.7	72.4	80.5	64.7	74.3	101.6	132.4	113.7	99.9	133.5	113.1
04	MASONRY	117.5	60.2	82.7	91.1	57.4	70.6	96.6	59.6	74.1	76.2	57.3	64.7	150.7	138.1	143.0	83.0	135.6	114.9
05	METALS	110.0	75.7	103.3	98.5	74.5	93.7	100.8	75.8	95.9	94.5	85.5	92.8	95.9	114.8	99.6	110.4	114.9	111.6
06	WOOD, PLASTICS & COMPOSITES	77.6	58.2	68.9	83.7	58.2	72.3	88.1	58.2	74.7	93.4	58.5	77.7	94.2	137.6	113.6	102.8	137.8	118.5
07	THERMAL & MOISTURE PROTECTION	101.0	60.1	86.4	106.9	58.4	89.6	101.5	59.6	86.6	112.3	58.3	93.0	125.1	129.5	126.7	91.3	131.9	105.8
08	OPENINGS	98.2	56.7	88.8	103.7	56.0	93.0	102.3	56.9	92.0	107.0	54.5	95.1	92.0	136.4	102.0	99.6	136.6	107.9
0920	Plaster & Gypsum Board	83.3	57.5	66.9	74.9	57.5	63.9	87.6	57.5	68.5	85.7	57.5	67.8	140.3	139.1	139.5	120.5	139.1	132.3
0950, 0980	Ceilings & Acoustic Treatment	103.7	57.5	77.8	98.9	57.5	75.7	112.8	57.5	81.8	99.8	57.5	76.1	105.4	139.1	124.3	105.3	139.1	124.2
0960	Flooring	91.9	74.6	87.6	90.7	63.5	83.9	93.4	75.7	89.0	65.4	63.5	64.9	91.7	118.3	98.4	89.6	118.3	96.8
0970, 0990	Wall Finishes & Painting/Coating	97.1	51.1	69.7	95.8	48.4	67.6	97.1	50.4	69.2	84.3	48.4	62.9	95.3	127.1	114.2	87.9	127.1	111.2
09	FINISHES	92.0	59.8	75.8	87.9	57.4	72.6	95.9	59.8	77.8	85.0	57.7	71.2	104.3	133.9	119.1	98.5	134.0	116.3
COVERS	DIVS. 10 - 14, 25, 28, 41, 43, 44, 46	100.0	78.5	95.8	100.0	78.7	95.9	100.0	78.3	95.8	100.0	79.7	96.1	100.0	116.2	103.1	100.0	116.7	103.2
21, 22, 23	FIRE SUPPRESSION, PLUMBING & HVAC	100.3	51.1	82.7	93.1	47.2	76.7	100.3	54.8	84.0	93.7	59.4	81.4	92.5	128.4	105.4	99.8	128.4	110.1
26, 27, 3370	ELECTRICAL, COMMUNICATIONS & UTIL.	95.6	55.4	78.2	92.5	51.2	74.6	96.5	53.3	77.8	100.7	58.1	82.2	101.3	134.5	115.7	84.4	117.1	98.6
MF2018	WEIGHTED AVERAGE	98.5	61.8	85.0	92.9	59.5	80.6	96.7	62.3	84.1	94.0	65.3	83.4	100.4	128.2	110.6	99.9	125.8	109.4

		CALIFORNIA																	
	DIVISION	BAKERSFIELD			BERKELEY			EUREKA			FRESNO			INGLEWOOD			LONG BEACH		
		932 - 933			947			955			936 - 938			903 - 905			906 - 908		
		MAT.	INST.	TOTAL	MAT.	INST.	TOTAL	MAT.	INST.	TOTAL	MAT.	INST.	TOTAL	MAT.	INST.	TOTAL	MAT.	INST.	TOTAL
015433	CONTRACTOR EQUIPMENT		99.2	99.2		95.8	95.8		94.7	94.7		94.9	94.9		95.8	95.8		95.8	95.8
0241, 31 - 34	SITE & INFRASTRUCTURE, DEMOLITION	112.0	107.6	109.1	113.5	102.4	106.3	121.2	99.1	106.8	114.5	99.5	104.7	97.7	98.8	98.4	106.0	98.8	101.3
0310	Concrete Forming & Accessories	101.1	138.0	129.8	112.0	168.4	155.9	103.3	155.6	143.9	102.4	155.0	143.2	103.6	139.3	131.3	97.6	139.3	130.0
0320	Concrete Reinforcing	97.9	132.6	107.5	89.1	138.5	102.7	87.9	134.0	100.7	81.1	133.3	95.5	99.7	132.6	108.9	98.9	132.6	108.3
0330	Cast-in-Place Concrete	95.2	130.3	107.7	109.1	133.0	117.6	107.7	129.4	115.4	103.1	129.1	112.4	107.2	129.0	114.9	122.1	129.0	124.5
03	CONCRETE	101.5	133.1	114.0	106.7	148.7	123.3	110.6	141.1	122.6	99.9	140.6	115.9	105.6	133.5	116.6	114.8	133.5	122.2
04	MASONRY	111.1	137.1	126.9	105.8	152.0	133.9	101.1	153.7	133.1	116.5	143.3	132.8	84.1	138.2	117.0	94.3	138.2	121.0
05	METALS	103.9	112.3	105.6	100.2	116.6	103.5	110.4	117.4	111.8	104.8	115.8	106.9	87.4	116.6	93.2	87.3	116.6	93.1
06	WOOD, PLASTICS & COMPOSITES	101.0	136.8	117.1	136.9	174.4	153.7	117.8	159.7	136.6	109.5	159.7	132.0	98.9	137.9	116.4	90.5	137.9	111.7
07	THERMAL & MOISTURE PROTECTION	105.3	126.1	112.7	90.6	155.2	113.6	93.9	149.1	113.6	95.7	134.7	109.6	102.8	131.0	112.9	102.9	131.0	112.9
08	OPENINGS	98.5	134.9	106.7	91.6	163.2	107.8	98.8	144.0	109.0	100.7	147.5	111.2	86.8	136.6	98.0	86.8	136.6	98.0
0920	Plaster & Gypsum Board	110.5	137.9	127.9	123.1	176.3	156.9	127.6	161.6	149.2	104.4	161.6	140.7	119.8	139.1	132.0	113.2	139.1	129.6
0950, 0980	Ceilings & Acoustic Treatment	113.8	137.9	127.3	93.3	176.3	139.9	111.7	161.6	139.7	101.5	161.6	135.2	100.5	139.1	122.1	100.5	139.1	122.1
0960	Flooring	96.0	118.3	101.6	110.5	143.2	118.7	94.5	143.2	106.7	95.2	123.7	102.3	95.0	118.3	100.8	93.1	118.3	99.4
0970, 0990	Wall Finishes & Painting/Coating	99.1	110.3	105.8	98.4	165.8	138.6	90.1	134.0	116.3	105.9	121.6	115.2	99.8	127.1	116.1	99.8	127.1	116.1
09	FINISHES	104.2	131.7	118.0	104.9	165.1	135.1	105.1	152.7	129.0	100.4	148.0	124.3	101.2	134.1	117.7	100.2	134.1	117.3
COVERS	DIVS. 10 - 14, 25, 28, 41, 43, 44, 46	100.0	117.8	103.4	100.0	129.9	105.8	100.0	127.1	105.3	100.0	127.0	105.2	100.0	117.0	103.3	100.0	117.0	103.3
21, 22, 23	FIRE SUPPRESSION, PLUMBING & HVAC	100.0	128.3	110.1	92.7	167.5	119.5	92.3	130.0	105.8	100.0	132.6	111.7	91.7	128.5	104.9	91.7	128.5	104.9
26, 27, 3370	ELECTRICAL, COMMUNICATIONS & UTIL.	98.7	108.0	102.8	99.7	165.2	128.1	91.2	125.7	106.1	87.4	107.6	96.1	100.5	134.5	115.2	100.4	134.5	115.1
MF2018	WEIGHTED AVERAGE	102.0	124.3	110.2	99.5	151.1	118.6	101.7	134.0	113.6	100.7	129.9	111.4	94.6	128.5	107.0	96.1	128.5	108.0

		CALIFORNIA																	
	DIVISION	LOS ANGELES			MARYSVILLE			MODESTO			MOJAVE			OAKLAND			OXNARD		
		900 - 902			959			953			935			946			930		
		MAT.	INST.	TOTAL	MAT.	INST.	TOTAL	MAT.	INST.	TOTAL	MAT.	INST.	TOTAL	MAT.	INST.	TOTAL	MAT.	INST.	TOTAL
015433	CONTRACTOR EQUIPMENT		108.2	108.2		94.7	94.7		94.7	94.7		94.9	94.9		95.8	95.8		93.9	93.9
0241, 31 - 34	SITE & INFRASTRUCTURE, DEMOLITION	108.7	112.2	111.0	117.2	99.1	105.4	114.4	99.1	104.4	104.2	99.7	101.2	122.1	102.4	109.2	114.8	98.0	103.9
0310	Concrete Forming & Accessories	101.5	139.7	131.1	93.0	155.2	141.3	88.9	155.2	140.4	110.9	138.0	131.9	99.2	168.4	153.0	102.7	139.1	131.0
0320	Concrete Reinforcing	98.6	134.4	108.5	87.9	133.4	100.5	91.1	133.4	102.8	99.1	132.6	108.4	91.1	138.5	104.2	97.3	132.7	107.1
0330	Cast-in-Place Concrete	110.8	131.4	118.2	120.4	129.2	123.5	107.8	129.2	115.4	89.2	128.7	103.2	103.4	133.0	114.0	102.9	128.9	112.8
03	CONCRETE	112.8	135.0	121.6	111.6	140.8	123.1	103.6	140.7	118.3	95.5	132.7	110.2	107.2	148.7	123.6	102.5	133.3	114.6
04	MASONRY	102.2	138.3	124.2	102.3	144.3	127.8	106.2	144.3	129.4	114.5	137.0	128.1	113.6	152.0	136.9	117.9	137.2	129.6
05	METALS	102.5	120.4	106.1	109.8	116.2	111.1	103.1	116.1	105.6	104.3	114.5	106.3	96.1	116.6	100.1	100.3	114.8	103.1
06	WOOD, PLASTICS & COMPOSITES	102.7	138.3	118.7	102.2	159.7	128.0	96.4	159.7	124.8	110.1	136.7	122.0	120.0	174.4	144.4	103.5	137.9	118.9
07	THERMAL & MOISTURE PROTECTION	99.9	132.8	111.7	93.3	139.5	109.8	93.0	139.8	109.6	101.4	123.2	109.2	89.8	155.2	113.2	103.1	131.5	113.2
08	OPENINGS	101.4	137.2	109.5	98.2	148.4	109.5	97.3	148.4	108.8	95.3	134.8	104.2	91.7	163.2	107.8	98.0	136.6	106.7
0920	Plaster & Gypsum Board	115.4	139.1	130.4	117.6	161.6	145.5	120.5	161.6	146.6	117.1	137.9	130.3	114.3	176.3	153.7	107.9	139.1	127.7
0950, 0980	Ceilings & Acoustic Treatment	112.8	139.1	127.5	101.8	161.6	135.3	105.3	161.6	136.9	107.8	137.9	124.7	94.8	176.3	140.5	104.1	139.1	123.7
0960	Flooring	97.0	118.3	102.4	91.9	130.2	101.5	92.1	133.9	102.6	94.0	118.3	100.1	106.7	143.2	115.8	87.8	118.3	95.4
0970, 0990	Wall Finishes & Painting/Coating	99.1	127.1	115.8	90.1	134.0	116.3	90.1	130.3	114.1	90.4	110.3	102.3	98.4	165.8	138.6	90.4	127.1	112.2
09	FINISHES	105.2	134.4	119.9	102.2	150.5	126.4	100.6	150.7	125.8	101.9	131.6	116.8	103.4	165.1	134.4	98.1	134.1	116.2
COVERS	DIVS. 10 - 14, 25, 28, 41, 43, 44, 46	100.0	117.8	103.5	100.0	127.1	105.2	100.0	127.0	105.2	100.0	123.8	104.6	100.0	129.8	105.8	100.0	116.8	103.3
21, 22, 23	FIRE SUPPRESSION, PLUMBING & HVAC	100.1	128.6	110.3	92.3	130.9	106.1	99.8	132.6	111.6	92.4	128.2	105.2	100.2	167.5	124.3	99.9	128.5	110.1
26, 27, 3370	ELECTRICAL, COMMUNICATIONS & UTIL.	99.5	134.5	114.7	89.6	118.5	102.1	91.1	109.8	99.2	86.0	108.0	95.5	99.2	165.2	127.8	94.4	111.7	101.9
MF2018	WEIGHTED AVERAGE	102.9	130.2	112.9	101.1	131.6	112.3	100.3	130.8	111.5	97.8	123.9	107.4	100.5	151.3	119.2	100.6	124.8	109.5

City Cost Indexes

CALIFORNIA

DIVISION		PALM SPRINGS 922			PALO ALTO 943			PASADENA 910 - 912			REDDING 960			RICHMOND 948			RIVERSIDE 925		
		MAT.	INST.	TOTAL	MAT.	INST.	TOTAL	MAT.	INST.	TOTAL	MAT.	INST.	TOTAL	MAT.	INST.	TOTAL	MAT.	INST.	TOTAL
015433	CONTRACTOR EQUIPMENT		95.6	95.6		95.8	95.8		93.7	93.7		94.7	94.7		95.8	95.8		95.6	95.6
0241, 31 - 34	SITE & INFRASTRUCTURE, DEMOLITION	99.2	99.8	99.6	110.0	102.4	105.0	109.0	101.2	104.0	136.0	99.1	111.9	118.2	102.3	107.9	109.2	99.8	103.1
0310	Concrete Forming & Accessories	92.8	139.0	128.7	97.2	168.6	152.6	90.7	138.9	128.2	86.8	155.2	139.9	115.2	168.1	156.3	96.8	139.1	129.6
0320	Concrete Reinforcing	92.3	132.7	103.5	89.1	138.5	102.8	101.2	132.7	109.9	88.1	133.4	100.7	89.1	138.5	102.7	89.7	132.7	101.6
0330	Cast-in-Place Concrete	94.6	129.5	107.0	92.2	133.1	106.8	89.4	126.6	102.6	131.5	129.2	130.7	106.1	132.9	115.6	102.9	129.5	112.4
03	CONCRETE	96.7	133.5	111.2	97.5	148.8	117.7	98.0	132.4	111.6	116.9	140.7	126.3	109.1	148.4	124.6	101.9	133.5	114.4
04	MASONRY	80.0	137.2	114.8	91.1	152.0	128.1	132.4	138.1	135.9	112.6	144.3	131.9	105.6	152.0	133.8	81.2	137.2	115.2
05	METALS	111.1	115.0	111.8	93.7	116.7	98.3	87.3	114.8	92.8	105.3	116.1	107.4	93.8	116.2	98.2	109.0	115.1	110.2
06	WOOD, PLASTICS & COMPOSITES	96.3	137.8	114.9	116.6	174.4	142.5	84.6	137.6	108.3	100.9	159.7	127.3	141.4	174.4	156.2	102.8	137.8	118.5
07	THERMAL & MOISTURE PROTECTION	90.8	130.6	105.0	89.1	155.2	112.7	111.7	129.5	118.0	97.3	139.5	112.3	89.9	154.3	112.8	91.5	132.4	106.1
08	OPENINGS	95.8	136.6	105.0	91.7	162.3	107.6	87.7	136.4	98.7	103.8	148.4	113.8	91.7	163.2	107.8	98.4	136.6	107.0
0920	Plaster & Gypsum Board	112.3	139.1	129.3	111.9	176.3	152.8	118.0	139.1	131.4	108.5	161.6	142.2	123.7	176.3	157.1	119.1	139.1	131.8
0950, 0980	Ceilings & Acoustic Treatment	100.8	139.1	122.2	93.8	176.3	140.1	98.1	139.1	121.1	120.7	161.6	143.7	93.8	176.3	140.1	105.4	139.1	124.3
0960	Flooring	93.9	118.3	100.0	105.9	143.2	115.3	88.7	118.3	96.1	71.0	119.0	83.0	111.9	143.2	119.9	94.6	118.3	100.6
0970, 0990	Wall Finishes & Painting/Coating	86.9	127.1	110.8	98.4	165.8	138.6	94.7	127.1	114.0	96.3	134.0	118.8	98.4	165.8	138.6	86.9	127.1	110.8
09	FINISHES	96.8	134.0	115.5	101.9	165.1	133.7	97.8	133.9	115.9	99.1	148.5	123.9	106.0	165.1	135.7	99.5	134.0	116.8
COVERS	DIVS. 10 - 14, 25, 28, 41, 43, 44, 46	100.0	116.7	103.2	100.0	130.0	105.8	100.0	116.2	103.1	100.0	127.1	105.2	100.0	129.8	105.8	100.0	117.6	103.4
21, 22, 23	FIRE SUPPRESSION, PLUMBING & HVAC	92.3	128.4	105.2	92.7	168.7	119.9	92.5	128.4	105.4	99.7	130.9	110.9	92.7	157.7	116.0	99.8	128.4	110.1
26, 27, 3370	ELECTRICAL, COMMUNICATIONS & UTIL.	85.8	118.3	99.9	99.2	181.5	134.8	109.1	134.5	120.1	93.3	118.5	104.2	99.4	139.1	116.6	84.2	118.3	99.0
MF2018	WEIGHTED AVERAGE	97.1	125.9	107.7	95.8	153.9	117.2	96.8	128.2	108.4	103.9	131.4	114.0	98.5	145.5	115.8	99.6	126.0	109.3

CALIFORNIA

DIVISION		SACRAMENTO 942, 956 - 958			SALINAS 939			SAN BERNARDINO 923 - 924			SAN DIEGO 919 - 921			SAN FRANCISCO 940 - 941			SAN JOSE 951		
		MAT.	INST.	TOTAL	MAT.	INST.	TOTAL	MAT.	INST.	TOTAL	MAT.	INST.	TOTAL	MAT.	INST.	TOTAL	MAT.	INST.	TOTAL
015433	CONTRACTOR EQUIPMENT		94.8	94.8		94.9	94.9		95.6	95.6		105.6	105.6		112.4	112.4		96.2	96.2
0241, 31 - 34	SITE & INFRASTRUCTURE, DEMOLITION	102.9	107.1	105.7	127.0	99.6	109.1	84.4	99.8	94.5	119.7	112.3	114.9	122.3	117.6	119.2	148.4	94.8	113.3
0310	Concrete Forming & Accessories	98.2	157.5	144.3	107.2	158.0	146.6	100.7	139.0	130.5	101.5	137.7	129.6	101.0	168.9	153.8	94.7	168.3	151.9
0320	Concrete Reinforcing	83.5	133.5	97.3	97.9	133.9	107.9	89.7	132.7	101.6	98.6	129.0	107.0	99.3	139.6	110.4	79.7	138.5	96.0
0330	Cast-in-Place Concrete	87.5	130.2	102.6	102.6	129.5	112.2	71.0	129.5	91.8	102.5	128.4	111.7	115.6	134.7	122.4	125.3	132.1	127.7
03	CONCRETE	98.6	141.6	115.5	110.9	142.2	123.2	79.0	133.5	100.5	109.4	131.9	118.3	117.3	150.2	130.3	108.4	148.8	124.3
04	MASONRY	92.0	144.3	123.8	114.6	149.4	135.8	89.7	137.2	118.6	121.4	133.9	129.0	116.2	155.0	139.7	133.9	152.0	144.9
05	METALS	91.7	108.9	95.1	107.4	117.2	109.4	109.0	115.0	110.1	103.7	114.3	105.8	105.9	126.3	109.9	102.5	124.1	106.8
06	WOOD, PLASTICS & COMPOSITES	113.6	162.7	135.6	110.3	162.4	133.7	107.7	137.8	121.0	102.8	137.7	118.5	121.2	174.4	145.0	108.7	174.1	138.0
07	THERMAL & MOISTURE PROTECTION	98.0	141.1	113.4	102.1	145.6	117.6	90.2	132.4	105.3	105.6	121.9	111.4	95.0	157.3	117.2	90.6	155.2	113.6
08	OPENINGS	103.5	150.0	114.0	99.2	155.5	111.9	95.8	136.6	105.0	99.2	132.6	106.7	103.7	163.4	117.1	89.2	163.0	105.8
0920	Plaster & Gypsum Board	108.0	164.4	143.7	110.1	164.4	144.5	121.5	139.1	132.6	113.6	138.8	129.5	111.8	176.3	152.7	113.3	176.3	153.3
0950, 0980	Ceilings & Acoustic Treatment	93.8	164.4	133.4	107.8	164.4	139.5	105.3	139.1	124.2	105.6	138.6	124.1	113.6	176.3	148.8	99.9	176.3	142.8
0960	Flooring	105.4	130.2	111.6	90.1	143.2	103.4	95.9	118.3	101.5	97.3	118.3	102.6	104.0	142.0	113.5	84.4	143.2	99.2
0970, 0990	Wall Finishes & Painting/Coating	95.4	138.5	121.1	91.3	170.3	138.4	86.9	127.1	110.8	95.2	118.9	109.3	99.1	174.0	143.8	89.8	165.8	135.1
09	FINISHES	100.4	152.7	126.7	112.0	158.3	130.3	98.6	134.0	116.4	102.9	132.6	117.8	107.1	165.8	136.6	97.6	164.9	131.4
COVERS	DIVS. 10 - 14, 25, 28, 41, 43, 44, 46	100.0	127.9	105.4	100.0	127.4	105.3	100.0	115.1	102.9	100.0	116.9	103.2	100.0	130.2	105.8	100.0	129.4	105.7
21, 22, 23	FIRE SUPPRESSION, PLUMBING & HVAC	100.1	130.8	111.1	92.4	138.0	108.7	92.3	128.4	105.2	100.1	127.2	109.8	100.1	180.3	128.8	99.8	168.7	124.5
26, 27, 3370	ELECTRICAL, COMMUNICATIONS & UTIL.	94.3	118.4	104.8	86.9	135.3	107.8	85.8	113.5	97.8	101.0	103.0	101.9	99.7	189.6	138.7	95.5	181.5	132.8
MF2018	WEIGHTED AVERAGE	97.6	132.2	110.3	101.3	137.9	114.7	94.8	125.2	106.0	103.7	123.3	110.9	105.4	160.2	125.6	102.2	153.9	121.3

CALIFORNIA

DIVISION		SAN LUIS OBISPO 934			SAN MATEO 944			SAN RAFAEL 949			SANTA ANA 926 - 927			SANTA BARBARA 931			SANTA CRUZ 950		
		MAT.	INST.	TOTAL	MAT.	INST.	TOTAL	MAT.	INST.	TOTAL	MAT.	INST.	TOTAL	MAT.	INST.	TOTAL	MAT.	INST.	TOTAL
015433	CONTRACTOR EQUIPMENT		94.9	94.9		95.8	95.8		95.1	95.1		95.6	95.6		94.9	94.9		96.2	96.2
0241, 31 - 34	SITE & INFRASTRUCTURE, DEMOLITION	118.0	99.7	106.1	116.0	102.4	107.1	112.1	107.1	108.8	97.4	99.8	99.0	114.8	99.7	104.9	148.5	94.7	113.4
0310	Concrete Forming & Accessories	112.9	139.1	133.3	104.2	168.5	154.1	112.3	168.1	155.7	101.1	139.0	130.6	103.1	139.1	131.0	94.7	158.0	143.9
0320	Concrete Reinforcing	99.1	132.6	108.4	89.1	138.7	102.8	89.4	134.4	101.8	92.6	132.7	103.7	97.3	132.6	107.0	99.1	133.9	108.7
0330	Cast-in-Place Concrete	110.3	128.8	116.9	102.7	133.0	113.5	119.6	132.1	124.0	90.8	129.5	104.5	103.5	128.8	112.5	124.4	131.0	126.8
03	CONCRETE	109.8	133.2	119.0	105.8	148.7	122.7	125.9	147.3	134.3	94.7	133.5	110.0	102.3	133.2	114.5	113.1	143.0	124.9
04	MASONRY	116.3	136.2	128.4	105.2	154.8	135.3	86.1	154.8	127.8	77.7	137.5	114.0	114.7	136.2	127.8	138.1	149.6	145.1
05	METALS	105.7	114.7	107.5	93.6	116.8	98.2	96.6	111.6	99.6	109.0	115.0	110.2	101.9	114.7	104.5	109.1	121.1	111.5
06	WOOD, PLASTICS & COMPOSITES	112.9	137.9	124.1	127.3	174.4	148.4	126.4	174.2	147.8	109.6	137.8	122.2	103.5	137.9	118.9	108.7	162.5	132.8
07	THERMAL & MOISTURE PROTECTION	102.2	130.8	112.3	89.6	155.2	113.0	92.6	154.0	114.7	91.1	131.6	105.5	101.6	130.8	112.0	90.3	147.4	110.6
08	OPENINGS	97.3	135.4	105.9	91.6	162.3	107.6	100.9	161.2	114.5	95.1	136.6	104.5	99.1	136.6	107.6	90.0	155.6	104.8
0920	Plaster & Gypsum Board	118.0	139.1	131.4	120.3	176.3	155.9	124.3	176.3	157.3	122.9	139.1	133.2	107.9	139.1	127.7	121.6	164.4	148.7
0950, 0980	Ceilings & Acoustic Treatment	107.8	139.1	125.3	93.8	176.3	140.1	107.4	176.3	146.0	105.3	139.1	124.2	104.1	139.1	123.7	106.7	164.4	139.0
0960	Flooring	94.6	118.3	100.6	108.1	143.2	116.9	117.5	143.2	123.9	96.3	118.3	101.8	89.5	118.3	96.7	88.1	143.2	101.9
0970, 0990	Wall Finishes & Painting/Coating	90.4	114.0	104.5	98.4	165.8	138.6	94.8	170.3	139.8	86.9	127.1	110.8	90.4	127.1	112.2	89.5	165.8	135.0
09	FINISHES	103.4	132.7	118.1	104.2	165.1	134.8	109.5	165.5	137.6	100.1	134.0	117.1	98.8	134.1	116.5	101.6	157.9	129.9
COVERS	DIVS. 10 - 14, 25, 28, 41, 43, 44, 46	100.0	125.6	105.0	100.0	130.0	105.8	100.0	129.5	105.7	100.0	116.7	103.2	100.0	117.7	103.4	100.0	127.7	105.4
21, 22, 23	FIRE SUPPRESSION, PLUMBING & HVAC	92.4	128.4	105.3	92.7	165.2	118.7	92.7	180.1	124.0	92.3	128.4	105.2	99.9	128.4	110.1	99.8	138.0	113.5
26, 27, 3370	ELECTRICAL, COMMUNICATIONS & UTIL.	86.0	109.0	96.0	99.2	174.5	131.8	91.9	125.7	106.5	85.8	117.1	99.4	85.5	107.5	95.1	95.2	135.3	112.6
MF2018	WEIGHTED AVERAGE	100.5	124.5	109.3	97.7	152.4	117.9	100.4	148.3	118.1	96.6	125.8	107.4	100.0	124.3	108.9	104.7	138.0	117.0

City Cost Indexes

		CALIFORNIA															COLORADO		
		SANTA ROSA			STOCKTON			SUSANVILLE			VALLEJO			VAN NUYS			ALAMOSA		
	DIVISION	954			952			961			945			913 - 916			811		
		MAT.	INST.	TOTAL	MAT.	INST.	TOTAL	MAT.	INST.	TOTAL	MAT.	INST.	TOTAL	MAT.	INST.	TOTAL	MAT.	INST.	TOTAL
015433	CONTRACTOR EQUIPMENT		95.2	95.2		94.7	94.7		94.7	94.7		95.1	95.1		93.7	93.7		89.2	89.2
0241, 31 - 34	SITE & INFRASTRUCTURE, DEMOLITION	112.3	99.0	103.6	114.1	99.1	104.3	141.5	99.1	113.8	103.5	107.0	105.8	129.5	101.2	111.1	131.3	81.7	98.9
0310	Concrete Forming & Accessories	93.8	167.3	150.9	93.2	157.2	142.9	88.0	155.2	140.2	101.4	167.2	152.5	97.5	138.9	129.7	99.9	68.7	75.6
0320	Concrete Reinforcing	88.6	134.3	101.2	91.1	133.4	102.8	88.1	133.4	100.7	90.5	134.2	102.6	101.2	132.7	109.9	101.8	63.4	91.2
0330	Cast-in-Place Concrete	118.3	130.5	122.6	105.0	129.2	113.6	119.6	129.2	123.0	95.2	131.3	108.0	94.3	126.6	105.8	90.2	69.2	82.7
03	CONCRETE	111.6	146.9	125.5	102.9	141.6	118.2	117.9	140.8	126.9	103.8	146.5	120.7	110.4	132.4	119.1	104.9	68.6	90.6
04	MASONRY	102.2	153.8	133.6	106.1	144.3	129.3	110.8	144.3	131.2	68.6	153.8	120.4	151.3	138.1	143.3	132.0	67.4	92.8
05	METALS	109.4	118.8	111.2	103.7	116.1	106.2	103.1	116.2	105.6	96.5	111.0	99.3	86.4	114.8	92.0	99.1	78.5	95.0
06	WOOD, PLASTICS & COMPOSITES	98.2	173.9	132.2	103.5	162.4	129.9	102.8	159.7	128.3	111.5	174.2	139.6	94.5	137.6	113.8	99.2	71.1	86.6
07	THERMAL & MOISTURE PROTECTION	91.4	153.8	113.6	93.4	137.7	109.2	97.4	139.5	112.4	91.1	154.0	113.5	112.6	129.5	118.6	99.9	66.9	88.2
08	OPENINGS	96.6	161.9	111.3	97.3	150.8	109.4	103.7	149.3	114.0	102.7	161.2	115.9	87.6	136.4	98.6	91.6	68.2	86.3
0920	Plaster & Gypsum Board	115.9	176.3	154.2	120.5	164.4	148.3	108.9	161.6	142.3	115.9	176.3	154.2	122.9	139.1	133.2	89.0	70.3	77.1
0950, 0980	Ceilings & Acoustic Treatment	105.3	176.3	145.1	109.9	164.4	140.4	115.4	161.6	141.3	108.4	176.3	146.5	94.5	139.1	119.5	105.3	70.3	85.7
0960	Flooring	94.2	133.7	104.1	92.1	133.9	102.6	71.2	119.0	83.2	113.9	143.2	121.3	90.6	118.3	97.5	110.5	79.6	102.7
0970, 0990	Wall Finishes & Painting/Coating	86.9	161.3	131.2	90.1	138.5	119.0	96.3	134.0	118.8	95.7	170.3	140.2	94.7	127.1	114.0	100.7	71.0	83.0
09	FINISHES	99.5	162.4	131.1	101.8	153.2	127.6	98.8	148.5	123.8	106.4	165.2	135.9	99.5	133.9	116.8	104.3	71.2	87.7
COVERS	DIVS. 10 - 14, 25, 28, 41, 43, 44, 46	100.0	128.5	105.5	100.0	125.7	105.0	100.0	127.1	105.3	100.0	129.0	105.6	100.0	116.2	103.1	100.0	84.9	97.1
21, 22, 23	FIRE SUPPRESSION, PLUMBING & HVAC	92.3	174.5	121.8	99.8	132.6	111.6	92.1	132.7	106.7	100.2	146.9	116.9	92.5	128.4	105.4	92.5	66.8	83.3
26, 27, 3370	ELECTRICAL, COMMUNICATIONS & UTIL.	85.9	120.9	101.1	91.1	112.2	100.3	93.5	120.8	105.3	89.9	125.0	105.1	109.0	134.5	120.1	92.6	56.3	76.9
MF2018	WEIGHTED AVERAGE	100.0	145.9	116.9	100.5	131.6	111.9	102.0	132.1	113.1	98.1	140.9	113.8	99.5	128.2	110.1	99.5	69.1	88.3

		COLORADO																	
		BOULDER			COLORADO SPRINGS			DENVER			DURANGO			FORT COLLINS			FORT MORGAN		
	DIVISION	803			808 - 809			800 - 802			813			805			807		
		MAT.	INST.	TOTAL	MAT.	INST.	TOTAL	MAT.	INST.	TOTAL	MAT.	INST.	TOTAL	MAT.	INST.	TOTAL	MAT.	INST.	TOTAL
015433	CONTRACTOR EQUIPMENT		90.0	90.0		88.2	88.2		94.7	94.7		89.2	89.2		90.0	90.0		90.0	90.0
0241, 31 - 34	SITE & INFRASTRUCTURE, DEMOLITION	92.5	87.8	89.5	97.5	83.4	88.3	101.3	94.4	96.8	125.4	81.7	96.9	105.8	87.4	93.8	94.2	86.8	89.4
0310	Concrete Forming & Accessories	99.9	71.6	77.9	90.3	68.5	73.4	99.3	68.2	75.5	106.3	68.4	76.9	97.8	68.6	75.2	100.4	68.3	75.5
0320	Concrete Reinforcing	97.1	69.1	89.3	96.5	68.8	88.9	100.8	69.0	92.0	101.8	63.4	91.2	97.1	65.9	88.5	97.2	63.4	87.9
0330	Cast-in-Place Concrete	97.8	75.1	89.7	100.4	71.1	90.0	101.7	73.2	91.6	103.7	69.1	91.4	110.4	71.0	96.4	95.9	68.3	86.1
03	CONCRETE	100.1	72.9	89.3	102.4	70.1	89.7	109.1	70.8	94.0	107.0	68.5	91.8	108.6	69.6	93.2	98.9	68.1	86.7
04	MASONRY	94.2	69.3	79.1	97.8	61.2	75.6	103.9	64.0	79.7	119.1	67.4	87.7	108.5	67.5	83.6	107.7	67.5	83.3
05	METALS	89.5	79.2	87.5	92.9	78.8	90.1	102.0	78.1	97.2	99.1	78.2	95.0	90.7	77.9	88.2	89.2	76.7	86.7
06	WOOD, PLASTICS & COMPOSITES	100.5	72.7	88.0	87.3	70.7	79.9	102.4	70.8	88.2	110.4	71.1	92.8	97.2	70.6	85.3	100.5	70.6	87.1
07	THERMAL & MOISTURE PROTECTION	97.9	72.9	89.0	98.7	68.6	88.0	97.4	72.3	88.5	99.9	66.9	88.2	98.1	70.4	88.3	97.9	68.1	87.3
08	OPENINGS	90.0	71.7	85.9	93.8	70.0	88.4	99.3	70.6	92.8	97.7	68.2	91.0	90.0	69.3	85.3	90.0	68.0	85.0
0920	Plaster & Gypsum Board	114.9	72.4	88.0	99.3	70.3	80.9	110.4	70.3	85.0	107.1	70.3	83.8	105.0	70.3	83.0	114.9	70.3	86.6
0950, 0980	Ceilings & Acoustic Treatment	97.6	72.4	83.5	111.7	70.3	88.5	114.5	70.3	89.7	105.3	70.3	85.7	97.6	70.3	82.3	97.6	70.3	82.3
0960	Flooring	119.9	79.6	109.8	110.4	79.6	102.7	116.5	79.6	107.2	114.2	79.6	105.5	116.8	79.6	107.5	120.2	79.6	110.1
0970, 0990	Wall Finishes & Painting/Coating	90.2	75.4	81.4	89.9	78.3	83.0	99.1	73.2	83.6	100.7	71.0	83.0	90.2	71.0	78.8	90.2	71.0	78.8
09	FINISHES	106.0	73.4	89.6	104.8	71.6	88.2	109.5	71.0	90.2	107.1	71.2	89.1	104.1	70.9	87.4	106.0	70.9	88.4
COVERS	DIVS. 10 - 14, 25, 28, 41, 43, 44, 46	100.0	85.3	97.2	100.0	84.1	96.9	100.0	84.1	96.9	100.0	84.9	97.1	100.0	84.0	96.9	100.0	84.0	96.9
21, 22, 23	FIRE SUPPRESSION, PLUMBING & HVAC	92.6	74.6	86.1	100.3	66.7	88.3	100.1	74.2	90.8	92.5	54.4	78.8	100.1	71.7	89.9	92.6	67.7	83.7
26, 27, 3370	ELECTRICAL, COMMUNICATIONS & UTIL.	96.8	79.8	89.4	98.3	70.0	86.1	99.4	80.0	91.0	92.3	49.4	73.7	96.8	76.9	88.2	97.3	69.5	85.3
MF2018	WEIGHTED AVERAGE	94.9	76.0	87.9	98.2	70.9	88.1	102.2	75.1	92.3	99.9	65.5	87.3	98.5	73.7	89.4	95.3	71.3	86.5

		COLORADO																	
		GLENWOOD SPRINGS			GOLDEN			GRAND JUNCTION			GREELEY			MONTROSE			PUEBLO		
	DIVISION	816			804			815			806			814			810		
		MAT.	INST.	TOTAL	MAT.	INST.	TOTAL	MAT.	INST.	TOTAL	MAT.	INST.	TOTAL	MAT.	INST.	TOTAL	MAT.	INST.	TOTAL
015433	CONTRACTOR EQUIPMENT		92.0	92.0		90.0	90.0		92.0	92.0		90.0	90.0		90.6	90.6		89.2	89.2
0241, 31 - 34	SITE & INFRASTRUCTURE, DEMOLITION	139.3	88.3	106.1	103.4	87.0	92.7	128.0	88.9	102.5	94.7	87.5	90.0	133.6	85.3	102.1	121.1	82.1	95.7
0310	Concrete Forming & Accessories	96.3	68.2	74.4	92.8	68.1	73.6	105.2	69.2	77.2	95.5	68.7	74.7	95.9	68.3	74.5	102.4	68.8	76.3
0320	Concrete Reinforcing	101.1	63.4	90.6	97.2	63.2	87.8	101.3	65.7	91.4	97.1	65.8	88.4	101.0	63.4	90.6	97.6	69.0	89.7
0330	Cast-in-Place Concrete	90.1	68.1	82.3	96.0	70.4	86.9	99.8	71.6	89.8	92.2	71.0	84.7	90.1	68.6	82.5	89.5	71.6	83.1
03	CONCRETE	108.5	68.0	92.5	106.9	68.7	91.8	104.2	70.1	90.7	96.1	69.6	85.6	101.7	68.3	88.5	95.9	70.5	85.9
04	MASONRY	104.1	67.4	81.8	110.5	64.0	82.2	139.9	65.7	94.8	102.2	67.5	81.1	111.5	67.4	84.7	100.5	63.8	78.2
05	METALS	98.7	77.8	94.6	89.4	76.6	86.9	100.4	78.9	96.2	90.6	78.0	88.1	97.6	78.0	93.7	102.9	80.6	98.5
06	WOOD, PLASTICS & COMPOSITES	93.6	70.8	83.4	90.3	70.8	81.5	108.7	70.8	91.7	93.9	70.6	83.5	94.1	70.9	83.7	102.6	71.1	88.5
07	THERMAL & MOISTURE PROTECTION	99.8	66.9	88.1	98.6	68.5	87.9	99.2	69.0	88.4	97.6	70.4	87.9	99.9	66.9	88.1	98.8	68.1	87.9
08	OPENINGS	96.7	68.1	90.2	90.0	68.0	85.0	97.3	69.3	91.0	90.0	69.3	85.3	97.8	68.2	91.1	93.0	70.2	87.9
0920	Plaster & Gypsum Board	122.4	70.3	89.4	100.4	70.3	81.3	141.0	70.3	96.2	103.1	70.3	82.3	87.8	70.3	76.7	95.5	70.3	79.5
0950, 0980	Ceilings & Acoustic Treatment	104.4	70.3	85.3	97.6	70.3	82.3	104.4	70.3	85.3	97.6	70.3	82.3	105.3	70.3	85.7	115.3	70.3	90.1
0960	Flooring	109.8	79.6	102.3	114.8	79.6	106.0	113.6	79.6	105.1	115.8	79.6	106.7	112.3	79.6	104.1	111.3	79.6	103.4
0970, 0990	Wall Finishes & Painting/Coating	100.7	71.0	83.0	90.2	71.0	78.8	100.7	71.0	83.0	90.2	71.0	78.8	100.7	71.0	83.0	100.7	71.0	83.0
09	FINISHES	108.8	71.0	89.8	103.5	70.6	87.0	110.8	71.4	91.0	103.0	70.9	86.9	104.7	71.1	87.9	106.6	71.1	88.7
COVERS	DIVS. 10 - 14, 25, 28, 41, 43, 44, 46	100.0	84.3	97.0	100.0	83.7	96.9	100.0	84.8	97.1	100.0	84.0	96.9	100.0	84.6	97.0	100.0	84.8	97.0
21, 22, 23	FIRE SUPPRESSION, PLUMBING & HVAC	92.5	54.4	78.8	92.6	67.3	83.5	100.0	71.3	89.7	100.1	71.7	89.9	92.5	54.4	78.8	100.0	67.6	88.4
26, 27, 3370	ELECTRICAL, COMMUNICATIONS & UTIL.	91.0	49.4	73.0	97.3	71.7	86.2	92.2	54.0	75.6	96.8	76.9	88.2	92.2	49.4	73.6	92.6	62.8	79.7
MF2018	WEIGHTED AVERAGE	99.5	65.9	87.1	96.4	71.2	87.1	102.6	70.5	90.8	96.4	73.7	88.0	98.5	65.7	86.5	99.8	70.4	89.0

City Cost Indexes

		COLORADO			CONNECTICUT															
	DIVISION	SALIDA			BRIDGEPORT			BRISTOL			HARTFORD			MERIDEN			NEW BRITAIN		
		812			066			060			061			064			060		
		MAT.	INST.	TOTAL	MAT.	INST.	TOTAL	MAT.	INST.	TOTAL	MAT.	INST.	TOTAL	MAT.	INST.	TOTAL	MAT.	INST.	TOTAL
015433	CONTRACTOR EQUIPMENT		90.6	90.6		93.0	93.0		93.0	93.0		97.4	97.4		93.3	93.3		93.0	93.0
0241, 31 - 34	SITE & INFRASTRUCTURE, DEMOLITION	125.1	85.0	99.0	100.2	93.5	95.8	99.5	93.5	95.6	96.9	101.1	99.6	94.4	94.1	94.2	99.6	93.5	95.6
0310	Concrete Forming & Accessories	105.2	68.6	76.7	103.5	112.3	110.4	103.5	114.6	112.1	104.5	114.8	112.5	103.1	114.5	112.0	104.1	114.6	112.3
0320	Concrete Reinforcing	100.8	63.4	90.5	103.8	139.9	113.8	103.8	139.9	113.8	99.0	139.9	110.3	103.8	139.9	113.8	103.8	139.9	113.8
0330	Cast-in-Place Concrete	103.3	68.7	91.0	81.6	124.8	97.0	76.5	124.8	93.6	77.9	126.4	95.2	73.6	124.7	91.8	77.7	124.8	94.4
03	CONCRETE	103.1	68.4	89.4	96.6	120.9	106.2	94.5	121.9	105.3	95.0	122.5	105.9	93.2	121.9	104.5	95.0	121.9	105.6
04	MASONRY	140.4	67.4	96.1	121.0	128.9	125.8	112.5	128.9	122.4	116.1	129.0	123.9	112.2	128.9	122.3	114.7	128.9	123.3
05	METALS	97.2	78.3	93.4	98.4	116.0	101.8	98.4	115.9	101.8	101.6	114.1	104.1	95.3	115.8	99.4	94.4	115.9	98.6
06	WOOD, PLASTICS & COMPOSITES	104.3	70.9	89.4	110.5	109.2	109.9	110.5	112.4	111.4	102.0	112.6	106.7	110.5	112.4	111.4	110.5	112.4	111.4
07	THERMAL & MOISTURE PROTECTION	99.2	66.9	87.7	96.7	118.4	104.4	96.8	116.7	103.9	101.6	119.1	107.8	96.8	116.7	103.9	96.8	116.7	103.9
08	OPENINGS	91.6	68.2	86.3	95.8	117.0	100.6	95.8	118.3	100.9	97.6	118.4	102.3	97.7	118.8	102.5	95.8	118.3	100.9
0920	Plaster & Gypsum Board	88.0	70.3	76.8	130.8	109.5	117.3	130.8	112.8	119.3	119.8	112.8	115.3	134.2	112.8	120.6	130.8	112.8	119.3
0950, 0980	Ceilings & Acoustic Treatment	105.3	70.3	85.7	95.0	109.5	103.1	95.0	112.8	104.9	96.3	112.8	105.5	105.4	112.8	109.5	95.0	112.8	104.9
0960	Flooring	116.1	79.6	107.0	94.2	121.9	101.1	94.2	121.9	101.1	102.3	125.0	108.0	94.2	111.5	98.5	94.2	121.9	101.1
0970, 0990	Wall Finishes & Painting/Coating	100.7	71.0	83.0	91.3	126.9	112.6	91.3	126.9	112.6	99.1	126.9	115.7	91.3	126.9	112.6	91.3	126.9	112.6
09	FINISHES	105.4	71.1	88.0	99.0	115.3	107.2	99.1	117.1	108.1	102.3	117.8	110.1	102.3	115.3	108.9	99.1	117.1	108.1
COVERS	DIVS. 10 - 14, 25, 28, 41, 43, 44, 46	100.0	84.6	97.0	100.0	110.9	102.1	100.0	111.3	102.2	100.0	111.7	102.3	100.0	111.2	102.2	100.0	111.3	102.2
21, 22, 23	FIRE SUPPRESSION, PLUMBING & HVAC	92.5	67.8	83.6	100.2	117.5	106.4	100.2	117.5	106.4	100.1	117.5	106.3	92.6	117.5	101.5	100.2	117.5	106.4
26, 27, 3370	ELECTRICAL, COMMUNICATIONS & UTIL.	92.3	56.3	76.7	96.6	101.3	98.6	96.6	103.3	99.5	99.9	105.1	102.1	96.5	94.2	95.5	96.6	103.3	99.5
MF2018	WEIGHTED AVERAGE	99.1	69.5	88.2	99.3	114.2	104.8	98.7	114.9	104.7	100.3	115.8	106.0	96.5	113.4	102.7	98.0	114.9	104.2

		CONNECTICUT																	
	DIVISION	NEW HAVEN			NEW LONDON			NORWALK			STAMFORD			WATERBURY			WILLIMANTIC		
		065			063			068			069			067			062		
		MAT.	INST.	TOTAL	MAT.	INST.	TOTAL	MAT.	INST.	TOTAL	MAT.	INST.	TOTAL	MAT.	INST.	TOTAL	MAT.	INST.	TOTAL
015433	CONTRACTOR EQUIPMENT		93.3	93.3		93.3	93.3		93.0	93.0		93.0	93.0		93.0	93.0		93.0	93.0
0241, 31 - 34	SITE & INFRASTRUCTURE, DEMOLITION	99.5	94.0	95.9	90.2	94.0	92.6	100.0	93.4	95.7	100.5	93.4	95.8	99.9	93.5	95.7	100.0	93.2	95.6
0310	Concrete Forming & Accessories	103.1	114.5	112.0	103.1	114.4	111.9	103.5	112.3	110.3	103.4	112.3	110.3	103.5	114.6	112.1	103.4	114.3	111.9
0320	Concrete Reinforcing	103.8	139.9	113.8	81.4	139.9	97.6	103.8	139.8	113.8	103.8	139.8	113.8	103.8	139.9	113.8	103.8	139.9	113.8
0330	Cast-in-Place Concrete	79.1	122.1	94.3	67.4	122.0	86.8	80.3	123.2	95.5	81.6	123.2	96.4	81.6	124.8	97.0	76.2	118.5	91.2
03	CONCRETE	106.9	120.9	112.4	82.4	120.8	97.6	96.0	120.3	105.6	96.6	120.3	105.9	96.6	121.9	106.6	94.3	119.6	104.3
04	MASONRY	112.7	128.9	122.5	111.0	128.9	121.8	112.0	127.1	121.2	113.0	127.1	121.5	113.0	128.9	122.6	112.3	128.9	122.4
05	METALS	94.6	115.8	98.8	94.3	115.7	98.5	98.4	115.9	101.8	98.4	115.9	101.8	98.4	115.9	101.8	98.1	115.6	101.6
06	WOOD, PLASTICS & COMPOSITES	110.5	112.4	111.4	110.5	112.4	111.4	110.5	109.2	109.9	110.5	109.2	109.9	110.5	112.4	111.4	110.5	112.4	111.4
07	THERMAL & MOISTURE PROTECTION	96.9	116.3	103.8	96.7	116.4	103.7	96.9	117.7	104.3	96.8	117.7	104.2	96.8	116.7	103.9	97.0	115.6	103.6
08	OPENINGS	95.8	118.8	101.0	98.3	116.5	102.4	95.8	117.0	100.6	95.8	117.0	100.6	95.8	118.8	101.0	98.3	118.8	102.9
0920	Plaster & Gypsum Board	130.8	112.8	119.3	130.8	112.8	119.3	130.8	109.5	117.3	130.8	109.5	117.3	130.8	112.8	119.3	130.8	112.8	119.3
0950, 0980	Ceilings & Acoustic Treatment	95.0	112.8	104.9	94.5	112.8	104.7	95.0	109.5	103.1	95.0	109.5	103.1	95.0	112.8	104.9	94.5	112.8	104.7
0960	Flooring	94.2	121.9	101.1	94.2	113.7	99.1	94.2	121.9	101.1	94.2	121.9	101.1	94.2	121.9	101.1	94.2	108.5	97.8
0970, 0990	Wall Finishes & Painting/Coating	91.3	122.0	109.6	91.3	118.3	107.4	91.3	126.9	112.6	91.3	126.9	112.6	91.3	126.9	112.6	91.3	126.9	112.6
09	FINISHES	99.1	116.9	107.9	98.5	114.8	106.7	99.1	115.3	107.2	99.1	115.3	107.2	99.0	117.1	108.1	99.0	114.8	106.9
COVERS	DIVS. 10 - 14, 25, 28, 41, 43, 44, 46	100.0	111.3	102.2	100.0	111.2	102.2	100.0	110.9	102.1	100.0	110.9	102.1	100.0	111.3	102.2	100.0	111.2	102.2
21, 22, 23	FIRE SUPPRESSION, PLUMBING & HVAC	100.2	117.5	106.4	92.6	117.4	101.5	100.2	117.5	106.4	100.2	117.5	106.4	100.2	117.5	106.4	100.2	117.4	106.3
26, 27, 3370	ELECTRICAL, COMMUNICATIONS & UTIL.	96.5	101.7	98.7	95.0	96.1	95.5	96.6	101.3	98.6	96.6	104.1	99.8	96.3	101.7	98.6	96.6	99.0	97.6
MF2018	WEIGHTED AVERAGE	99.4	114.5	104.9	94.4	113.4	101.4	98.9	113.9	104.4	99.0	114.3	104.6	98.9	114.7	104.7	98.8	113.6	104.3

		D.C.			DELAWARE									FLORIDA					
	DIVISION	WASHINGTON			DOVER			NEWARK			WILMINGTON			DAYTONA BEACH			FORT LAUDERDALE		
		200 - 205			199			197			198			321			333		
		MAT.	INST.	TOTAL	MAT.	INST.	TOTAL	MAT.	INST.	TOTAL	MAT.	INST.	TOTAL	MAT.	INST.	TOTAL	MAT.	INST.	TOTAL
015433	CONTRACTOR EQUIPMENT		104.8	104.8		113.6	113.6		113.7	113.7		113.8	113.8		96.1	96.1		90.1	90.1
0241, 31 - 34	SITE & INFRASTRUCTURE, DEMOLITION	111.7	99.1	103.5	111.9	103.6	106.5	109.7	103.0	105.3	107.6	104.7	105.7	127.6	81.5	97.5	105.8	71.5	83.4
0310	Concrete Forming & Accessories	99.1	74.2	79.8	104.2	95.1	97.2	99.4	94.8	95.8	104.2	95.4	97.4	99.0	60.8	69.3	94.3	60.1	67.7
0320	Concrete Reinforcing	100.4	89.8	97.5	98.7	114.5	103.1	97.6	114.5	102.3	98.5	114.6	103.0	90.5	58.2	81.5	89.3	60.9	81.5
0330	Cast-in-Place Concrete	129.2	79.9	111.7	119.7	104.9	114.5	99.8	102.5	100.7	116.4	105.1	112.3	90.2	66.2	81.7	92.9	62.7	82.2
03	CONCRETE	105.6	79.7	95.4	102.0	102.9	102.4	93.8	102.1	97.1	100.6	103.1	101.6	89.5	64.0	79.4	90.7	63.0	79.8
04	MASONRY	108.1	87.7	95.7	106.2	100.9	103.0	103.4	100.1	101.8	106.0	100.9	102.9	87.1	61.9	71.8	101.3	56.6	74.1
05	METALS	102.3	95.3	100.9	101.1	119.5	104.7	102.6	122.8	106.6	102.7	119.8	106.1	107.4	86.8	103.4	104.6	88.8	101.5
06	WOOD, PLASTICS & COMPOSITES	97.0	72.6	86.0	101.5	92.2	97.4	97.0	91.9	94.7	101.5	92.2	97.4	96.0	59.0	79.4	82.7	60.2	72.6
07	THERMAL & MOISTURE PROTECTION	101.8	87.4	96.6	103.2	111.7	106.2	106.2	110.0	107.5	102.9	111.7	106.0	92.2	65.9	82.8	94.4	59.1	81.8
08	OPENINGS	104.7	75.6	98.2	98.1	104.1	99.5	95.2	103.9	97.1	98.1	104.1	99.5	93.6	58.0	85.5	96.1	59.3	87.8
0920	Plaster & Gypsum Board	109.8	71.8	85.7	125.6	91.9	104.2	121.9	91.9	102.8	125.6	91.9	104.2	92.7	58.4	70.9	111.6	59.7	78.7
0950, 0980	Ceilings & Acoustic Treatment	96.8	71.8	82.8	110.0	91.9	99.8	108.1	91.9	99.0	110.0	91.9	99.8	73.1	58.4	64.9	88.2	59.7	72.2
0960	Flooring	97.6	74.4	91.8	105.5	109.5	106.5	96.6	109.5	99.8	105.8	109.5	106.8	102.8	57.3	91.4	107.1	61.4	95.6
0970, 0990	Wall Finishes & Painting/Coating	94.9	68.7	79.3	99.1	116.8	109.6	89.0	116.8	105.5	99.1	116.8	109.6	102.6	57.9	75.7	92.6	57.3	71.5
09	FINISHES	99.9	72.6	86.2	108.1	99.0	103.5	100.9	98.7	99.8	108.5	99.0	103.7	93.5	59.2	76.3	99.3	59.5	79.3
COVERS	DIVS. 10 - 14, 25, 28, 41, 43, 44, 46	100.0	95.6	99.2	100.0	94.5	98.9	100.0	93.7	98.8	100.0	107.5	101.5	100.0	82.0	96.5	100.0	82.2	96.5
21, 22, 23	FIRE SUPPRESSION, PLUMBING & HVAC	100.0	93.1	97.5	99.9	117.6	106.3	100.3	117.5	106.5	100.0	117.6	106.3	99.9	75.6	91.2	99.9	67.1	88.1
26, 27, 3370	ELECTRICAL, COMMUNICATIONS & UTIL.	99.9	98.9	99.5	101.3	106.2	103.4	100.3	106.2	102.9	100.1	106.2	102.7	97.2	59.6	80.9	95.4	69.2	84.1
MF2018	WEIGHTED AVERAGE	102.2	88.6	97.2	101.7	107.3	103.7	100.1	107.3	102.8	101.7	107.8	103.9	98.9	68.8	87.9	98.9	67.0	87.1

City Cost Indexes

FLORIDA

DIVISION		FORT MYERS 339,341			GAINESVILLE 326,344			JACKSONVILLE 320,322			LAKELAND 338			MELBOURNE 329			MIAMI 330 - 332,340		
		MAT.	INST.	TOTAL	MAT.	INST.	TOTAL	MAT.	INST.	TOTAL	MAT.	INST.	TOTAL	MAT.	INST.	TOTAL	MAT.	INST.	TOTAL
015433	CONTRACTOR EQUIPMENT		96.1	96.1		96.1	96.1		96.1	96.1		96.1	96.1		96.1	96.1		96.3	96.3
0241, 31 - 34	SITE & INFRASTRUCTURE, DEMOLITION	117.1	81.8	94.1	134.0	81.7	99.9	127.6	81.2	97.3	119.0	81.7	94.7	135.3	81.5	100.2	108.1	83.4	92.0
0310	Concrete Forming & Accessories	89.5	61.6	67.8	93.4	62.2	69.2	98.8	63.3	71.2	85.5	63.8	68.7	94.8	63.6	70.5	103.3	62.6	71.7
0320	Concrete Reinforcing	90.3	73.5	85.7	95.9	60.8	86.2	90.5	60.6	82.2	92.6	71.8	86.8	91.5	67.4	84.8	99.7	60.8	88.9
0330	Cast-in-Place Concrete	96.9	65.4	85.7	103.6	65.5	90.1	91.1	64.9	81.8	99.1	65.9	87.3	108.8	66.3	93.7	90.0	69.0	82.5
03	CONCRETE	91.4	66.7	81.7	99.0	64.8	85.5	89.8	65.0	80.0	93.0	67.6	82.9	99.0	66.8	86.3	93.5	66.0	82.6
04	MASONRY	96.9	56.6	72.4	96.7	60.2	74.5	86.8	56.9	68.7	117.3	60.3	82.7	80.2	61.9	69.1	109.5	61.2	80.2
05	METALS	106.3	92.9	103.7	105.9	88.2	102.4	106.1	86.5	102.2	106.1	92.4	103.4	114.9	90.3	110.0	104.6	85.0	100.7
06	WOOD, PLASTICS & COMPOSITES	79.0	60.7	70.8	88.5	61.6	76.4	96.0	63.4	81.4	73.6	64.2	69.4	90.7	62.4	78.0	98.2	60.6	81.3
07	THERMAL & MOISTURE PROTECTION	94.2	61.1	82.4	92.5	62.6	81.8	92.5	62.0	81.6	94.1	62.5	82.8	92.6	64.5	82.6	95.4	63.9	84.2
08	OPENINGS	97.4	62.5	89.5	93.2	60.0	85.7	93.6	61.0	86.2	97.4	64.0	89.8	93.0	62.0	86.0	98.3	59.5	89.5
0920	Plaster & Gypsum Board	105.8	60.1	76.8	89.0	61.0	71.3	92.7	62.9	73.8	102.9	63.8	78.1	89.0	61.9	71.8	102.2	59.7	75.2
0950, 0980	Ceilings & Acoustic Treatment	82.6	60.1	70.0	70.1	61.0	65.0	73.1	62.9	67.4	82.6	63.8	72.1	72.7	61.9	66.6	88.6	59.7	72.4
0960	Flooring	104.9	69.2	96.0	101.1	59.6	90.7	102.8	60.2	92.1	103.6	63.9	93.6	101.3	62.0	91.5	105.7	60.2	94.3
0970, 0990	Wall Finishes & Painting/Coating	97.2	61.7	76.0	102.0	61.1	77.6	102.0	61.1	77.6	97.2	61.7	76.0	102.0	79.8	88.8	99.1	57.3	74.2
09	FINISHES	98.7	62.6	80.6	92.8	61.2	76.9	93.6	62.4	77.9	98.0	63.4	80.6	93.2	64.5	78.8	99.4	60.9	80.1
COVERS	DIVS. 10 - 14, 25, 28, 41, 43, 44, 46	100.0	80.5	96.2	100.0	80.2	96.2	100.0	80.4	96.2	100.0	81.8	96.5	100.0	82.4	96.6	100.0	84.9	97.1
21, 22, 23	FIRE SUPPRESSION, PLUMBING & HVAC	95.8	57.7	82.1	95.6	64.2	84.3	99.9	63.8	87.0	95.8	57.2	81.9	99.9	75.9	91.3	99.9	64.2	87.1
26, 27, 3370	ELECTRICAL, COMMUNICATIONS & UTIL.	96.3	60.1	80.6	97.3	58.2	80.4	97.0	64.4	82.9	95.6	52.1	76.7	98.0	67.9	85.0	98.1	74.9	88.0
MF2018	WEIGHTED AVERAGE	98.6	66.0	86.6	99.2	66.5	87.2	98.7	67.0	87.0	99.4	65.4	86.9	101.6	71.6	90.6	100.2	69.1	88.8

FLORIDA

DIVISION		ORLANDO 327 - 328,347			PANAMA CITY 324			PENSACOLA 325			SARASOTA 342			ST. PETERSBURG 337			TALLAHASSEE 323		
		MAT.	INST.	TOTAL	MAT.	INST.	TOTAL	MAT.	INST.	TOTAL	MAT.	INST.	TOTAL	MAT.	INST.	TOTAL	MAT.	INST.	TOTAL
015433	CONTRACTOR EQUIPMENT		103.7	103.7		96.1	96.1		96.1	96.1		96.1	96.1		96.1	96.1		103.7	103.7
0241, 31 - 34	SITE & INFRASTRUCTURE, DEMOLITION	126.6	94.4	105.6	141.2	81.6	102.4	140.8	81.4	102.0	128.0	81.7	97.8	122.4	81.5	95.7	123.0	94.3	104.3
0310	Concrete Forming & Accessories	104.5	64.9	73.8	98.0	64.9	72.2	95.3	64.9	74.8	98.9	63.6	71.5	93.8	59.8	67.4	104.5	64.0	73.0
0320	Concrete Reinforcing	100.4	63.2	90.1	94.5	67.7	87.1	96.8	65.5	88.2	91.5	68.7	85.2	92.6	70.8	86.5	100.6	60.8	89.6
0330	Cast-in-Place Concrete	111.7	68.6	96.4	95.8	66.3	85.3	118.4	64.7	99.3	106.9	65.8	92.3	100.2	63.9	87.3	93.6	68.9	84.8
03	CONCRETE	102.7	67.3	88.8	97.0	67.5	85.4	106.0	68.3	91.2	95.8	66.9	84.4	94.5	64.9	82.8	96.3	66.6	84.6
04	MASONRY	94.0	62.0	74.5	90.3	60.3	72.1	114.0	59.2	80.7	86.6	60.3	70.6	165.0	57.3	99.6	82.5	60.1	68.9
05	METALS	105.3	85.6	101.4	106.6	90.3	103.4	107.7	89.0	104.0	105.1	90.6	102.3	107.0	91.0	103.8	104.4	84.5	100.5
06	WOOD, PLASTICS & COMPOSITES	99.4	64.6	83.8	94.5	64.6	81.1	93.0	71.2	83.3	95.1	64.2	81.3	84.6	59.0	73.1	99.2	63.7	83.3
07	THERMAL & MOISTURE PROTECTION	95.6	68.0	85.8	92.7	62.8	82.0	92.6	62.1	81.8	101.8	62.5	87.8	94.3	58.9	81.7	95.3	64.3	84.2
08	OPENINGS	98.3	62.2	90.2	91.9	63.3	85.5	91.9	66.4	86.1	98.4	62.9	90.4	96.4	60.9	88.4	98.4	61.2	90.0
0920	Plaster & Gypsum Board	103.9	63.8	78.5	91.6	64.2	74.2	105.4	71.0	83.6	97.1	63.8	76.0	108.9	58.4	76.9	104.8	62.9	78.2
0950, 0980	Ceilings & Acoustic Treatment	84.1	63.8	72.7	72.7	64.2	67.9	72.7	71.0	71.7	86.8	63.8	73.9	83.8	58.4	69.5	90.0	62.9	74.8
0960	Flooring	104.5	59.6	93.3	102.6	73.8	95.4	99.7	60.8	89.9	106.9	49.1	92.4	106.3	53.9	93.2	100.6	61.6	90.8
0970, 0990	Wall Finishes & Painting/Coating	99.1	83.4	89.7	102.0	61.1	77.6	102.0	61.1	77.6	101.1	61.7	77.6	97.2	61.1	75.7	101.2	61.1	77.3
09	FINISHES	99.9	65.8	82.8	94.7	65.7	80.1	95.3	66.9	81.0	100.3	60.8	80.5	100.0	58.5	79.2	100.0	63.1	81.4
COVERS	DIVS. 10 - 14, 25, 28, 41, 43, 44, 46	100.0	83.4	96.8	100.0	81.6	96.4	100.0	81.7	96.5	100.0	80.5	96.2	100.0	80.2	96.2	100.0	81.4	96.4
21, 22, 23	FIRE SUPPRESSION, PLUMBING & HVAC	100.1	55.7	84.2	99.9	64.4	87.2	99.9	61.3	86.0	99.6	53.2	83.0	99.9	55.5	84.0	100.0	64.3	87.2
26, 27, 3370	ELECTRICAL, COMMUNICATIONS & UTIL.	100.1	62.3	83.7	96.4	56.9	79.3	98.6	49.8	77.5	97.8	52.1	78.0	95.6	58.9	79.7	100.7	55.8	81.2
MF2018	WEIGHTED AVERAGE	101.7	67.5	89.1	100.0	67.7	88.1	102.5	66.3	89.1	100.4	63.9	87.0	102.8	64.3	88.6	100.2	67.5	88.2

FLORIDA / GEORGIA

DIVISION		TAMPA 335 - 336,346			WEST PALM BEACH 334,349			ALBANY 317,398			ATHENS 306			ATLANTA 300 - 303,399			AUGUSTA 308 - 309		
		MAT.	INST.	TOTAL	MAT.	INST.	TOTAL	MAT.	INST.	TOTAL	MAT.	INST.	TOTAL	MAT.	INST.	TOTAL	MAT.	INST.	TOTAL
015433	CONTRACTOR EQUIPMENT		96.1	96.1		90.1	90.1		90.9	90.9		89.4	89.4		97.5	97.5		89.4	89.4
0241, 31 - 34	SITE & INFRASTRUCTURE, DEMOLITION	122.8	81.9	96.1	100.7	71.5	81.6	116.4	74.1	88.8	136.8	86.7	104.1	134.8	97.8	110.7	129.0	87.4	101.9
0310	Concrete Forming & Accessories	96.9	64.9	72.1	98.6	59.9	68.3	94.1	68.7	74.4	96.9	39.8	52.5	103.2	75.2	81.4	98.1	71.0	77.0
0320	Concrete Reinforcing	89.3	71.8	84.5	91.8	51.7	80.7	92.3	71.6	86.5	91.9	56.7	82.2	100.3	70.4	92.0	92.1	68.4	85.6
0330	Cast-in-Place Concrete	97.9	67.5	87.1	88.3	62.5	79.2	90.9	67.3	82.5	125.9	66.2	104.7	129.9	71.5	109.2	118.9	69.3	101.3
03	CONCRETE	93.0	68.6	83.4	88.7	61.1	77.8	86.7	70.4	80.3	98.3	53.4	80.6	102.5	73.6	91.1	93.6	70.7	84.5
04	MASONRY	102.2	63.1	78.4	100.8	51.6	70.9	83.5	67.6	73.8	73.8	64.1	67.9	84.5	68.0	74.5	85.7	69.9	76.1
05	METALS	106.4	92.5	103.7	103.0	84.9	99.4	107.4	96.8	105.3	91.9	75.3	88.7	97.8	82.1	94.7	91.7	82.1	89.8
06	WOOD, PLASTICS & COMPOSITES	89.6	64.2	78.2	88.4	60.2	75.8	86.2	69.6	78.8	91.2	32.7	65.0	101.4	78.3	91.0	93.0	72.9	84.0
07	THERMAL & MOISTURE PROTECTION	94.6	63.8	83.6	94.2	58.6	81.5	104.8	66.9	91.3	91.6	61.6	80.9	92.3	72.1	85.1	91.5	70.8	84.1
08	OPENINGS	97.4	64.0	89.8	95.7	57.3	87.1	87.8	71.5	84.1	88.5	46.9	79.1	100.5	75.6	94.9	88.5	72.1	84.8
0920	Plaster & Gypsum Board	112.8	63.8	81.7	116.4	59.7	80.4	95.9	69.4	79.1	93.4	31.2	54.0	99.2	77.9	85.7	94.8	72.7	80.8
0950, 0980	Ceilings & Acoustic Treatment	88.2	63.8	74.5	82.6	59.7	69.8	73.6	69.4	71.3	92.5	31.2	58.1	85.0	77.9	81.0	93.5	72.7	81.8
0960	Flooring	107.1	63.9	96.3	108.3	49.1	93.5	105.8	86.6	96.0	92.2	66.8	85.9	97.6	70.2	90.7	92.3	72.2	87.3
0970, 0990	Wall Finishes & Painting/Coating	97.2	61.7	76.0	92.6	57.0	71.4	96.9	96.8	96.9	94.5	83.5	87.9	101.2	95.6	97.9	94.5	81.7	86.9
09	FINISHES	102.0	64.1	83.0	98.6	57.0	77.7	94.2	71.0	82.5	97.1	47.3	72.1	97.7	76.6	87.1	96.6	72.4	84.4
COVERS	DIVS. 10 - 14, 25, 28, 41, 43, 44, 46	100.0	81.5	96.4	100.0	82.1	96.5	100.0	84.3	97.0	100.0	79.7	96.1	100.0	86.1	97.3	100.0	84.8	97.1
21, 22, 23	FIRE SUPPRESSION, PLUMBING & HVAC	99.9	58.7	85.1	95.8	55.1	81.2	99.9	71.0	89.6	92.6	59.9	80.8	100.1	71.7	89.9	100.1	65.8	87.8
26, 27, 3370	ELECTRICAL, COMMUNICATIONS & UTIL.	94.9	64.4	81.7	96.2	60.0	80.5	97.0	57.4	79.9	99.8	56.9	81.2	100.1	69.6	86.9	100.1	64.6	84.7
MF2018	WEIGHTED AVERAGE	100.3	68.1	88.4	97.3	61.9	84.2	98.0	71.6	88.3	94.8	60.7	82.2	99.8	75.6	90.9	96.1	71.8	87.2

City Cost Indexes

GEORGIA

DIVISION		COLUMBUS 318-319			DALTON 307			GAINESVILLE 305			MACON 310-312			SAVANNAH 313-314			STATESBORO 304		
		MAT.	INST.	TOTAL	MAT.	INST.	TOTAL	MAT.	INST.	TOTAL	MAT.	INST.	TOTAL	MAT.	INST.	TOTAL	MAT.	INST.	TOTAL
015433	CONTRACTOR EQUIPMENT		90.9	90.9		102.8	102.8		89.4	89.4		99.4	99.4		98.2	98.2		92.0	92.0
0241, 31 - 34	SITE & INFRASTRUCTURE, DEMOLITION	116.3	74.5	89.0	136.7	91.2	107.1	135.2	86.6	103.5	118.1	87.2	98.0	118.4	86.6	97.7	138.6	74.1	96.6
0310	Concrete Forming & Accessories	94.0	70.0	75.4	87.9	58.6	65.1	101.4	37.8	52.0	93.9	70.0	75.3	101.7	70.4	77.4	82.2	68.6	71.7
0320	Concrete Reinforcing	92.9	71.8	87.1	91.6	54.4	81.3	91.8	56.7	82.1	94.1	71.8	87.9	100.1	68.3	91.3	91.4	63.6	83.7
0330	Cast-in-Place Concrete	90.6	70.0	83.3	122.3	64.8	101.9	132.3	65.8	108.7	89.4	68.2	81.9	91.8	70.6	84.3	125.6	65.5	104.3
03	CONCRETE	86.8	72.0	80.9	96.6	62.0	82.9	100.9	52.4	81.8	86.5	71.4	80.6	88.5	71.5	81.8	97.1	68.4	85.8
04	MASONRY	82.7	70.0	75.0	72.4	62.6	66.5	82.8	63.2	70.9	95.1	69.4	79.5	77.9	68.1	72.0	75.7	64.0	68.6
05	METALS	107.1	98.2	105.3	92.7	88.8	92.0	91.2	75.4	88.1	101.7	98.2	101.0	104.0	92.6	101.7	96.0	93.4	95.5
06	WOOD, PLASTICS & COMPOSITES	86.2	71.1	79.4	74.7	59.2	67.7	96.0	30.3	66.6	90.5	71.8	82.1	98.8	71.9	86.7	66.8	71.6	69.0
07	THERMAL & MOISTURE PROTECTION	104.7	69.1	92.0	93.4	63.1	82.6	91.6	60.9	80.7	103.3	69.7	91.4	101.9	70.3	90.6	92.0	63.5	81.9
08	OPENINGS	87.8	72.2	84.3	90.0	61.0	83.4	88.4	45.6	78.8	87.8	72.3	84.3	97.8	71.6	91.9	90.8	70.2	86.2
0920	Plaster & Gypsum Board	95.9	70.9	80.0	82.9	58.6	67.5	95.8	28.8	53.3	97.0	71.5	80.9	99.6	71.4	81.7	82.8	71.4	75.6
0950, 0980	Ceilings & Acoustic Treatment	73.6	70.9	72.1	101.5	58.6	77.5	92.5	28.8	56.8	70.5	71.5	71.1	90.4	71.4	79.7	99.7	71.4	83.8
0960	Flooring	105.8	72.2	97.4	92.4	66.8	86.0	93.6	66.8	86.8	83.3	66.8	79.1	99.6	69.4	92.1	112.2	66.8	100.8
0970, 0990	Wall Finishes & Painting/Coating	96.9	80.0	89.8	84.1	62.2	72.1	94.5	83.5	87.9	99.2	96.8	97.8	99.1	82.0	88.9	92.7	62.2	74.5
09	FINISHES	94.1	71.7	82.8	104.3	60.2	82.2	97.5	45.7	71.5	83.2	71.9	77.5	97.9	71.3	84.6	108.8	67.8	88.2
COVERS	DIVS. 10 - 14, 25, 28, 41, 43, 44, 46	100.0	84.5	97.0	100.0	76.2	95.4	100.0	79.3	96.0	100.0	84.2	96.9	100.0	85.4	97.2	100.0	83.8	96.9
21, 22, 23	FIRE SUPPRESSION, PLUMBING & HVAC	100.0	66.3	87.9	92.6	54.6	79.0	92.6	59.1	80.6	100.0	68.3	88.6	100.1	68.0	88.1	94.5	62.6	83.1
26, 27, 3370	ELECTRICAL, COMMUNICATIONS & UTIL.	96.8	68.1	84.3	112.5	55.4	87.8	99.8	65.4	84.9	94.3	58.1	78.6	99.1	59.8	82.1	101.2	58.6	82.8
MF2018	WEIGHTED AVERAGE	97.9	72.9	88.7	96.6	64.5	84.8	95.3	61.2	82.8	96.2	72.8	87.6	98.7	72.0	88.9	97.1	68.5	86.5

GEORGIA / HAWAII / IDAHO

DIVISION		VALDOSTA 316			WAYCROSS 315			HILO 967			HONOLULU 968			STATES & POSS., GUAM 969			BOISE 836-837		
		MAT.	INST.	TOTAL	MAT.	INST.	TOTAL	MAT.	INST.	TOTAL	MAT.	INST.	TOTAL	MAT.	INST.	TOTAL	MAT.	INST.	TOTAL
015433	CONTRACTOR EQUIPMENT		90.9	90.9		90.9	90.9		95.8	95.8		101.5	101.5		151.9	151.9		93.2	93.2
0241, 31 - 34	SITE & INFRASTRUCTURE, DEMOLITION	126.9	74.1	92.4	121.4	73.6	90.2	158.4	99.2	119.8	165.4	109.9	129.2	209.0	96.2	135.4	89.8	88.9	89.2
0310	Concrete Forming & Accessories	83.1	70.0	72.9	85.2	68.3	72.1	89.8	119.1	112.6	100.4	121.5	115.0	92.0	59.7	66.9	97.7	81.4	85.1
0320	Concrete Reinforcing	94.6	60.7	85.2	94.6	53.4	83.2	91.7	120.4	99.6	104.7	120.4	109.0	154.3	41.3	123.0	96.4	76.3	90.8
0330	Cast-in-Place Concrete	89.0	67.3	81.3	100.6	65.4	88.1	221.5	120.3	185.6	172.8	121.6	154.6	191.9	99.1	158.9	81.6	99.0	87.8
03	CONCRETE	89.3	69.1	81.3	92.7	66.2	82.3	152.3	119.0	139.1	144.2	119.3	134.4	156.5	71.2	122.8	93.0	86.9	90.6
04	MASONRY	87.6	70.3	77.1	88.5	64.0	73.6	140.7	119.3	127.7	135.1	119.5	125.6	208.8	45.9	109.8	127.7	84.6	101.5
05	METALS	105.7	92.5	103.1	104.8	84.3	100.8	111.0	106.2	110.0	125.4	104.0	121.2	141.4	79.4	129.2	106.0	82.2	101.3
06	WOOD, PLASTICS & COMPOSITES	71.7	71.6	71.6	73.8	71.6	72.8	104.6	119.4	111.2	123.8	119.4	121.8	116.8	59.9	91.3	95.6	79.6	88.4
07	THERMAL & MOISTURE PROTECTION	104.8	69.0	92.1	104.7	63.8	90.1	96.6	114.4	102.9	107.8	116.2	110.8	111.2	65.9	95.1	92.2	85.7	89.9
08	OPENINGS	84.6	69.4	81.2	84.8	65.4	80.5	101.4	118.8	105.2	112.3	118.3	113.7	106.0	49.8	93.4	92.0	74.9	88.1
0920	Plaster & Gypsum Board	86.8	71.4	77.0	86.8	71.4	77.0	110.9	120.0	116.7	142.8	120.0	128.3	239.6	49.7	119.1	99.1	79.2	86.5
0950, 0980	Ceilings & Acoustic Treatment	72.3	71.4	71.8	71.2	71.4	71.3	109.5	120.0	115.3	121.4	120.0	120.6	254.0	49.7	139.5	111.3	79.2	93.3
0960	Flooring	101.5	72.9	94.3	102.4	66.8	93.5	79.0	135.4	93.1	100.8	135.4	109.5	96.5	44.4	83.4	94.2	84.7	91.8
0970, 0990	Wall Finishes & Painting/Coating	96.9	86.9	90.9	96.9	62.2	76.2	91.4	128.8	113.7	104.7	128.8	119.1	96.3	36.9	60.9	92.1	61.4	73.8
09	FINISHES	92.2	72.3	82.2	91.8	67.8	79.7	99.8	123.6	111.7	115.1	123.6	119.4	187.1	54.8	120.7	99.0	79.9	89.4
COVERS	DIVS. 10 - 14, 25, 28, 41, 43, 44, 46	100.0	84.5	97.0	100.0	77.9	95.7	100.0	110.8	102.1	100.0	110.8	102.1	100.0	87.6	97.6	100.0	90.2	98.1
21, 22, 23	FIRE SUPPRESSION, PLUMBING & HVAC	100.0	70.7	89.5	95.5	57.1	81.7	99.7	106.8	102.2	99.7	106.8	102.3	101.7	49.6	83.0	100.2	74.1	90.8
26, 27, 3370	ELECTRICAL, COMMUNICATIONS & UTIL.	95.9	52.5	77.1	97.8	58.6	80.8	101.2	114.9	107.1	102.0	114.9	107.6	142.1	45.5	100.2	100.0	73.1	88.3
MF2018	WEIGHTED AVERAGE	97.7	70.7	87.8	97.1	67.8	85.6	111.8	113.9	112.3	116.5	114.1	115.6	134.9	60.4	107.5	100.3	80.3	93.0

IDAHO / ILLINOIS

DIVISION		COEUR D'ALENE 838			IDAHO FALLS 834			LEWISTON 835			POCATELLO 832			TWIN FALLS 833			BLOOMINGTON 617		
		MAT.	INST.	TOTAL	MAT.	INST.	TOTAL	MAT.	INST.	TOTAL	MAT.	INST.	TOTAL	MAT.	INST.	TOTAL	MAT.	INST.	TOTAL
015433	CONTRACTOR EQUIPMENT		88.7	88.7		93.2	93.2		88.7	88.7		93.2	93.2		93.2	93.2		98.1	98.1
0241, 31 - 34	SITE & INFRASTRUCTURE, DEMOLITION	90.4	85.9	87.5	90.5	89.0	89.5	99.2	84.4	89.6	91.1	88.9	89.7	97.3	88.4	91.5	86.6	91.5	89.8
0310	Concrete Forming & Accessories	99.5	82.0	85.9	90.9	77.2	80.2	105.2	81.7	87.0	97.9	80.8	84.6	99.1	76.7	81.7	85.3	115.5	108.8
0320	Concrete Reinforcing	101.3	97.0	100.1	97.6	74.1	91.1	101.3	96.9	100.1	96.6	76.3	91.0	97.8	73.0	91.0	98.5	102.7	99.6
0330	Cast-in-Place Concrete	88.2	81.3	85.8	77.7	94.6	83.7	91.7	82.8	88.6	83.9	98.8	89.2	86.1	94.0	88.9	88.3	110.9	96.3
03	CONCRETE	98.1	84.5	92.7	86.8	83.1	85.3	101.1	84.9	94.7	92.4	86.5	90.1	98.3	82.5	92.1	89.9	112.5	98.8
04	MASONRY	130.2	84.8	102.6	123.1	86.1	100.6	130.7	83.2	101.9	125.6	86.3	101.7	128.7	79.1	98.5	114.2	109.7	111.5
05	METALS	99.0	89.5	97.1	112.9	81.3	106.7	98.4	89.1	96.6	113.4	81.7	107.1	113.0	80.5	106.6	94.4	122.9	100.0
06	WOOD, PLASTICS & COMPOSITES	93.3	81.0	87.8	87.1	75.2	81.8	100.9	81.0	92.0	95.6	79.6	88.4	96.8	75.2	87.1	77.0	115.3	94.2
07	THERMAL & MOISTURE PROTECTION	136.7	80.9	116.8	91.1	78.3	86.5	137.1	79.8	116.7	91.6	75.5	85.9	92.2	81.3	88.4	101.3	107.3	103.5
08	OPENINGS	107.4	75.9	100.3	94.7	70.3	89.2	101.4	79.5	96.4	92.6	67.9	87.0	95.3	70.9	89.8	88.9	119.5	95.8
0920	Plaster & Gypsum Board	155.5	80.8	108.1	88.3	74.6	79.7	157.7	80.8	108.9	91.2	79.2	83.6	94.1	74.6	81.7	78.0	116.1	102.2
0950, 0980	Ceilings & Acoustic Treatment	131.0	80.8	102.9	107.2	74.6	88.9	131.0	80.8	102.9	115.3	79.2	95.1	110.8	74.6	90.5	89.8	116.1	104.6
0960	Flooring	136.5	90.1	124.8	95.2	76.2	90.4	138.8	74.7	122.7	97.6	74.7	91.9	98.5	79.7	93.8	90.7	124.5	99.2
0970, 0990	Wall Finishes & Painting/Coating	109.4	68.2	84.8	92.2	41.9	62.2	109.4	59.6	79.7	92.0	52.9	71.7	92.2	57.9	71.7	87.3	118.7	106.9
09	FINISHES	156.4	82.0	119.0	96.4	73.0	84.7	157.5	77.8	117.5	100.1	77.5	88.8	100.1	75.3	87.6	88.3	118.1	103.3
COVERS	DIVS. 10 - 14, 25, 28, 41, 43, 44, 46	100.0	97.5	99.5	100.0	89.1	97.9	100.0	97.5	99.5	100.0	90.1	98.1	100.0	88.8	97.8	100.0	105.0	101.0
21, 22, 23	FIRE SUPPRESSION, PLUMBING & HVAC	96.8	86.6	93.1	103.6	77.2	94.1	101.3	83.1	94.8	100.0	71.9	89.9	100.0	69.0	88.9	92.4	103.0	96.2
26, 27, 3370	ELECTRICAL, COMMUNICATIONS & UTIL.	84.2	78.3	81.7	83.9	67.9	77.0	83.3	81.2	82.4	95.2	67.9	83.4	84.6	70.1	78.3	92.5	95.7	93.9
MF2018	WEIGHTED AVERAGE	103.8	84.3	96.6	99.8	78.5	92.0	104.4	83.3	96.9	101.3	78.3	92.9	101.4	76.5	92.2	93.4	107.8	98.7

City Cost Indexes

ILLINOIS

DIVISION		CARBONDALE 629			CENTRALIA 628			CHAMPAIGN 618 - 619			CHICAGO 606 - 608			DECATUR 625			EAST ST. LOUIS 620 - 622		
		MAT.	INST.	TOTAL	MAT.	INST.	TOTAL	MAT.	INST.	TOTAL	MAT.	INST.	TOTAL	MAT.	INST.	TOTAL	MAT.	INST.	TOTAL
015433	CONTRACTOR EQUIPMENT		105.5	105.5		105.5	105.5		98.9	98.9		98.7	98.7		98.9	98.9		105.5	105.5
0241, 31 - 34	SITE & INFRASTRUCTURE, DEMOLITION	93.1	92.3	92.5	93.4	93.0	93.1	93.1	93.7	93.5	92.1	103.0	99.2	92.9	92.4	92.6	98.3	93.1	94.9
0310	Concrete Forming & Accessories	97.5	105.8	104.0	99.8	109.3	107.2	92.7	126.9	119.3	100.7	158.5	145.6	101.3	114.9	111.8	94.4	111.5	107.7
0320	Concrete Reinforcing	101.6	93.2	99.3	101.6	93.8	99.5	98.5	98.9	98.6	98.0	150.7	112.6	99.4	98.5	99.1	101.6	104.5	102.4
0330	Cast-in-Place Concrete	86.0	100.7	91.2	86.4	108.7	94.3	102.3	119.6	108.5	107.9	153.7	124.2	93.9	111.1	100.0	87.9	115.4	97.7
03	CONCRETE	85.3	103.3	92.4	85.8	107.8	94.5	99.6	119.9	107.6	101.3	154.8	122.4	92.9	111.4	100.2	86.3	113.1	96.9
04	MASONRY	98.7	110.2	105.7	98.8	116.9	109.8	138.3	133.9	135.6	107.2	163.8	141.6	93.4	119.2	109.1	99.0	120.3	112.0
05	METALS	98.9	123.5	103.7	98.9	126.1	104.3	94.4	120.6	99.6	98.1	145.2	107.4	104.5	119.0	107.4	100.0	131.8	106.3
06	WOOD, PLASTICS & COMPOSITES	97.8	103.5	100.4	101.6	108.3	104.6	86.0	126.3	104.1	98.4	157.7	125.0	102.1	114.1	107.5	93.8	108.3	100.3
07	THERMAL & MOISTURE PROTECTION	93.7	95.7	94.4	93.8	106.8	98.4	102.0	118.1	107.7	105.6	148.6	120.9	98.4	110.2	102.6	93.7	107.8	98.7
08	OPENINGS	87.9	107.9	92.4	87.9	110.5	93.0	89.4	121.9	96.8	99.2	168.1	114.7	98.8	115.2	102.5	88.0	117.3	94.6
0920	Plaster & Gypsum Board	84.2	104.0	96.8	85.6	109.0	100.4	80.0	127.5	110.1	83.7	159.5	131.8	89.2	114.9	105.5	83.0	109.0	99.5
0950, 0980	Ceilings & Acoustic Treatment	94.5	104.0	99.8	94.5	109.0	102.6	89.8	127.5	110.9	92.2	159.5	129.9	105.9	114.9	110.9	94.5	109.0	102.6
0960	Flooring	116.5	110.3	114.9	117.3	102.5	113.6	93.3	125.6	101.4	98.8	160.9	114.4	103.2	120.3	107.5	115.6	102.5	112.4
0970, 0990	Wall Finishes & Painting/Coating	101.3	102.5	102.0	101.3	108.4	105.5	87.9	125.6	110.4	99.1	161.8	136.5	94.2	104.7	100.4	101.3	110.8	107.0
09	FINISHES	96.2	106.3	101.3	96.7	108.1	102.4	89.9	127.6	108.8	94.1	160.1	127.2	97.4	115.4	106.5	95.9	109.6	102.8
COVERS	DIVS. 10 - 14, 25, 28, 41, 43, 44, 46	100.0	104.7	100.9	100.0	104.9	100.9	100.0	109.2	101.8	100.0	126.9	105.2	100.0	105.7	101.1	100.0	109.3	101.8
21, 22, 23	FIRE SUPPRESSION, PLUMBING & HVAC	92.4	99.8	95.1	92.4	88.2	90.9	92.4	106.2	97.3	99.9	134.6	112.4	100.0	95.6	98.4	99.9	95.3	98.3
26, 27, 3370	ELECTRICAL, COMMUNICATIONS & UTIL.	92.3	107.1	98.7	93.0	94.6	93.7	94.1	95.7	94.8	99.2	133.2	113.9	94.4	88.9	92.0	92.8	103.2	97.3
MF2018	WEIGHTED AVERAGE	93.8	105.2	98.0	94.0	103.3	97.4	96.0	113.7	102.6	99.4	143.7	115.7	98.8	105.4	101.2	95.9	108.2	100.5

ILLINOIS

DIVISION		EFFINGHAM 624			GALESBURG 614			JOLIET 604			KANKAKEE 609			LA SALLE 613			NORTH SUBURBAN 600 - 603		
		MAT.	INST.	TOTAL	MAT.	INST.	TOTAL	MAT.	INST.	TOTAL	MAT.	INST.	TOTAL	MAT.	INST.	TOTAL	MAT.	INST.	TOTAL
015433	CONTRACTOR EQUIPMENT		98.9	98.9		98.1	98.1		90.0	90.0		90.0	90.0		98.1	98.1		90.0	90.0
0241, 31 - 34	SITE & INFRASTRUCTURE, DEMOLITION	92.3	92.2	92.2	88.3	91.6	90.5	88.5	93.6	91.9	81.2	92.1	88.3	88.0	93.0	91.3	88.2	93.0	91.3
0310	Concrete Forming & Accessories	106.5	105.7	105.8	92.6	116.2	110.9	99.0	161.0	147.2	91.9	144.4	132.7	108.6	124.8	121.2	98.2	157.9	144.5
0320	Concrete Reinforcing	102.3	84.2	97.3	98.1	103.1	99.5	108.1	139.2	116.7	108.5	131.4	114.9	98.2	129.7	107.0	108.1	150.6	119.8
0330	Cast-in-Place Concrete	93.6	107.1	98.4	90.9	108.0	97.0	98.1	150.9	116.8	91.4	132.3	105.9	90.8	125.8	103.2	98.1	143.1	114.1
03	CONCRETE	94.1	103.4	97.7	92.4	111.8	100.0	97.7	153.0	119.5	93.0	137.4	110.5	93.7	126.8	106.7	97.7	150.7	118.6
04	MASONRY	102.6	107.8	105.8	114.4	121.9	118.9	106.2	163.1	140.8	102.8	145.4	128.7	114.4	132.7	125.5	103.3	163.5	139.9
05	METALS	101.1	110.6	103.0	94.4	122.8	100.0	90.3	139.3	100.0	90.3	130.8	98.3	94.5	141.2	103.7	91.3	142.2	101.4
06	WOOD, PLASTICS & COMPOSITES	105.5	103.3	104.5	85.8	115.3	99.0	90.6	161.7	122.5	82.0	143.8	109.7	105.8	121.7	112.9	89.6	157.3	120.0
07	THERMAL & MOISTURE PROTECTION	98.0	100.1	98.8	101.5	106.1	103.1	112.1	146.4	124.3	111.4	137.4	120.6	101.9	120.0	108.6	112.6	147.4	125.0
08	OPENINGS	94.5	104.9	96.8	88.9	115.2	94.8	93.4	166.6	109.9	86.9	154.6	102.2	88.9	131.2	98.5	93.5	167.9	110.3
0920	Plaster & Gypsum Board	87.1	103.7	97.7	80.0	116.2	102.9	78.3	164.0	132.7	77.9	145.5	120.8	87.7	122.7	109.9	82.7	159.5	131.4
0950, 0980	Ceilings & Acoustic Treatment	94.5	103.7	99.7	89.8	116.2	104.6	94.8	164.0	133.6	94.8	145.5	123.2	89.8	122.7	108.2	94.8	159.5	131.1
0960	Flooring	104.2	111.6	106.1	93.1	124.5	101.0	97.5	160.9	113.4	95.0	144.4	107.3	98.3	128.8	105.9	98.0	160.9	113.7
0970, 0990	Wall Finishes & Painting/Coating	94.2	106.3	101.4	87.9	95.4	92.3	88.1	161.8	132.0	88.1	129.4	112.7	87.9	129.4	112.6	90.2	161.8	132.9
09	FINISHES	94.4	107.1	100.8	89.4	116.3	102.9	91.8	162.2	127.2	90.7	143.5	117.2	92.0	125.5	108.8	92.6	159.8	126.4
COVERS	DIVS. 10 - 14, 25, 28, 41, 43, 44, 46	100.0	104.0	100.8	100.0	106.2	101.2	100.0	126.2	105.1	100.0	113.0	102.5	100.0	108.2	101.6	100.0	126.0	105.0
21, 22, 23	FIRE SUPPRESSION, PLUMBING & HVAC	92.5	95.9	93.7	92.4	100.6	95.3	99.9	134.3	112.2	92.4	126.9	104.8	92.4	127.6	105.0	99.8	135.1	112.5
26, 27, 3370	ELECTRICAL, COMMUNICATIONS & UTIL.	93.4	107.0	99.3	93.0	92.7	92.9	97.7	134.5	113.6	94.8	133.9	111.8	91.6	133.9	109.9	98.0	133.1	113.2
MF2018	WEIGHTED AVERAGE	96.2	103.0	98.7	93.9	107.6	99.0	96.4	142.3	113.3	92.9	132.1	107.3	94.3	126.4	106.1	96.6	142.0	113.2

ILLINOIS

DIVISION		PEORIA 615 - 616			QUINCY 623			ROCK ISLAND 612			ROCKFORD 610 - 611			SOUTH SUBURBAN 605			SPRINGFIELD 626 - 627		
		MAT.	INST.	TOTAL	MAT.	INST.	TOTAL	MAT.	INST.	TOTAL	MAT.	INST.	TOTAL	MAT.	INST.	TOTAL	MAT.	INST.	TOTAL
015433	CONTRACTOR EQUIPMENT		98.1	98.1		98.9	98.9		98.1	98.1		98.1	98.1		90.0	90.0		104.6	104.6
0241, 31 - 34	SITE & INFRASTRUCTURE, DEMOLITION	92.4	91.7	92.0	91.2	93.1	92.5	87.0	90.5	89.3	92.0	93.4	92.9	88.2	92.8	91.2	96.3	102.0	100.0
0310	Concrete Forming & Accessories	96.7	117.4	112.8	103.6	111.5	109.7	94.4	102.7	100.9	101.1	133.3	126.1	98.2	157.9	144.6	101.8	115.4	112.4
0320	Concrete Reinforcing	95.7	103.2	97.8	102.1	78.1	95.5	89.1	96.0	97.6	90.1	135.5	102.7	108.1	150.6	119.8	99.1	98.5	98.9
0330	Cast-in-Place Concrete	88.2	115.3	97.8	93.7	116.0	101.6	88.9	100.8	93.1	90.2	131.5	104.9	98.1	116.7	113.7	89.3	109.9	96.6
03	CONCRETE	90.1	114.9	99.9	93.7	108.1	99.4	90.9	101.9	95.2	89.9	133.6	107.1	97.7	153.2	119.6	91.6	111.0	99.3
04	MASONRY	113.3	123.1	119.2	136.3	121.9	127.5	114.2	105.1	108.7	88.7	145.5	123.2	103.3	163.5	139.8	109.1	119.9	115.7
05	METALS	97.5	123.6	102.7	101.1	111.1	103.1	94.5	116.3	98.8	97.5	144.0	106.7	91.3	142.1	101.3	102.0	116.5	104.9
06	WOOD, PLASTICS & COMPOSITES	96.5	115.3	104.9	101.9	108.9	105.1	88.0	101.8	94.2	96.4	130.5	111.7	89.6	157.3	120.0	99.9	114.4	106.4
07	THERMAL & MOISTURE PROTECTION	102.2	111.4	105.5	98.0	105.0	100.5	101.5	95.8	99.5	104.6	132.8	114.7	112.6	147.4	125.0	102.7	112.2	106.1
08	OPENINGS	93.9	119.5	99.7	95.1	105.9	97.5	88.9	105.7	92.7	93.9	140.2	104.3	93.5	167.9	110.3	98.6	115.4	102.4
0920	Plaster & Gypsum Board	86.1	116.2	105.2	85.6	109.6	100.8	80.0	102.2	94.1	86.1	131.8	115.1	82.7	159.5	131.4	90.2	114.9	105.9
0950, 0980	Ceilings & Acoustic Treatment	98.0	116.2	108.2	94.5	109.6	103.0	89.8	102.2	96.8	98.0	131.8	116.9	94.8	159.5	131.1	109.5	114.9	112.5
0960	Flooring	95.9	124.5	103.0	103.2	102.5	103.1	93.9	96.0	94.5	95.9	129.0	104.2	98.0	160.9	113.7	103.0	122.4	107.9
0970, 0990	Wall Finishes & Painting/Coating	87.9	129.4	112.6	94.2	108.4	102.7	87.9	95.4	92.3	87.9	140.0	119.0	90.2	161.8	132.9	99.1	107.5	104.1
09	FINISHES	93.3	120.3	106.8	93.9	109.7	101.8	89.6	100.0	95.2	93.3	133.3	113.3	92.6	159.8	126.4	101.3	116.6	109.0
COVERS	DIVS. 10 - 14, 25, 28, 41, 43, 44, 46	100.0	106.6	101.3	100.0	105.8	101.1	100.0	98.6	99.7	100.0	113.4	102.6	100.0	126.0	105.0	100.0	106.6	101.3
21, 22, 23	FIRE SUPPRESSION, PLUMBING & HVAC	99.9	99.9	99.9	92.5	95.0	93.4	92.4	97.0	94.0	100.1	118.6	106.7	99.8	135.1	112.5	100.0	99.7	99.9
26, 27, 3370	ELECTRICAL, COMMUNICATIONS & UTIL.	93.4	92.2	92.9	92.2	103.2	97.0	89.0	91.6	90.2	93.7	131.0	109.8	98.0	133.1	113.2	101.0	87.4	95.1
MF2018	WEIGHTED AVERAGE	96.9	108.8	101.3	97.3	105.1	100.1	93.3	99.9	95.7	96.0	128.6	108.0	96.6	142.3	113.4	99.8	106.8	102.4

City Cost Indexes

		\multicolumn{18}{c	}{INDIANA}
	DIVISION	\multicolumn{3}{c	}{ANDERSON 460}	\multicolumn{3}{c	}{BLOOMINGTON 474}	\multicolumn{3}{c	}{COLUMBUS 472}	\multicolumn{3}{c	}{EVANSVILLE 476 - 477}	\multicolumn{3}{c	}{FORT WAYNE 467 - 468}	\multicolumn{3}{c	}{GARY 463 - 464}
		MAT.	INST.	TOTAL	MAT.	INST.	TOTAL	MAT.	INST.	TOTAL	MAT.	INST.	TOTAL	MAT.	INST.	TOTAL	MAT.	INST.	TOTAL
015433	CONTRACTOR EQUIPMENT		92.4	92.4		81.1	81.1		81.1	81.1		106.9	106.9		92.4	92.4		92.4	92.4
0241, 31 - 34	SITE & INFRASTRUCTURE, DEMOLITION	93.0	86.1	88.5	80.6	84.7	83.3	74.7	84.3	81.0	84.9	109.7	101.1	94.4	85.6	88.7	93.5	88.8	90.4
0310	Concrete Forming & Accessories	93.1	74.5	78.7	100.8	78.7	83.6	94.5	74.9	79.2	93.6	78.9	82.2	91.5	78.2	81.2	93.2	102.5	100.4
0320	Concrete Reinforcing	100.3	79.3	94.5	91.6	82.1	88.9	92.0	80.0	88.7	100.2	93.9	98.4	100.3	76.8	93.8	100.3	106.0	101.9
0330	Cast-in-Place Concrete	89.4	72.4	83.3	96.9	74.1	88.8	96.5	70.1	87.1	92.6	81.8	88.8	95.0	71.5	86.6	93.4	103.8	97.1
03	CONCRETE	92.6	75.4	85.8	95.3	77.5	88.3	94.6	74.0	86.5	96.2	82.9	91.0	94.8	76.3	87.5	94.2	103.6	98.0
04	MASONRY	92.3	74.5	81.5	92.0	69.7	78.4	91.8	68.7	77.8	87.5	78.1	81.8	98.3	70.3	81.3	93.8	101.4	98.4
05	METALS	97.6	88.5	95.8	97.5	76.2	93.3	97.5	74.2	92.9	91.9	90.2	91.6	97.6	86.7	95.4	97.6	103.1	98.7
06	WOOD, PLASTICS & COMPOSITES	88.6	74.6	82.3	105.7	79.5	94.0	99.1	75.3	88.4	88.4	78.0	83.7	88.5	80.9	85.1	86.5	100.9	93.0
07	THERMAL & MOISTURE PROTECTION	110.5	71.8	96.7	97.3	74.5	89.2	96.8	72.0	87.9	101.4	80.7	94.0	110.3	75.6	97.9	109.3	97.1	105.0
08	OPENINGS	91.5	72.8	87.3	95.4	76.6	91.2	91.9	73.6	87.8	90.2	79.0	87.7	91.5	75.0	87.8	91.5	105.9	94.7
0920	Plaster & Gypsum Board	101.1	74.3	84.1	91.6	79.8	84.1	88.0	75.3	80.0	86.3	77.2	80.5	100.4	80.8	88.0	93.9	101.4	98.6
0950, 0980	Ceilings & Acoustic Treatment	93.8	74.3	82.9	80.9	79.8	80.2	80.9	75.3	77.8	83.4	77.2	79.9	93.8	80.8	86.5	93.8	101.4	98.0
0960	Flooring	98.4	71.3	91.6	99.7	76.8	94.0	95.7	76.8	90.9	94.9	71.3	89.0	98.4	72.1	91.8	98.4	101.0	99.0
0970, 0990	Wall Finishes & Painting/Coating	93.0	69.2	78.8	85.2	76.6	80.1	85.2	74.4	78.7	91.3	82.3	85.9	93.0	68.2	78.2	93.0	109.4	102.8
09	FINISHES	94.4	73.2	83.7	91.2	78.2	84.7	89.5	75.2	82.3	89.8	77.5	83.6	94.2	76.6	85.3	93.3	102.8	98.1
COVERS	DIVS. 10 - 14, 25, 28, 41, 43, 44, 46	100.0	88.7	97.8	100.0	88.8	97.8	100.0	88.1	97.7	100.0	89.4	97.9	100.0	90.0	98.1	100.0	96.7	99.4
21, 22, 23	FIRE SUPPRESSION, PLUMBING & HVAC	99.9	72.4	90.0	99.6	75.1	90.8	92.1	72.6	85.1	100.0	78.3	92.2	99.9	71.2	89.6	99.9	97.3	99.0
26, 27, 3370	ELECTRICAL, COMMUNICATIONS & UTIL.	83.5	78.6	81.3	100.7	82.7	92.9	100.2	80.5	91.7	94.6	80.0	88.3	84.6	79.3	82.3	94.3	99.9	96.7
MF2018	WEIGHTED AVERAGE	95.4	77.1	88.7	97.1	77.7	89.9	94.6	75.5	87.6	94.7	83.1	90.4	96.0	77.2	89.1	96.7	99.9	97.9

		\multicolumn{18}{c	}{INDIANA}
	DIVISION	\multicolumn{3}{c	}{INDIANAPOLIS 461 - 462}	\multicolumn{3}{c	}{KOKOMO 469}	\multicolumn{3}{c	}{LAFAYETTE 479}	\multicolumn{3}{c	}{LAWRENCEBURG 470}	\multicolumn{3}{c	}{MUNCIE 473}	\multicolumn{3}{c	}{NEW ALBANY 471}
		MAT.	INST.	TOTAL	MAT.	INST.	TOTAL	MAT.	INST.	TOTAL	MAT.	INST.	TOTAL	MAT.	INST.	TOTAL	MAT.	INST.	TOTAL
015433	CONTRACTOR EQUIPMENT		91.2	91.2		92.4	92.4		81.1	81.1		98.2	98.2		91.2	91.2		89.3	89.3
0241, 31 - 34	SITE & INFRASTRUCTURE, DEMOLITION	92.9	96.6	95.3	86.7	85.4	85.8	75.0	84.3	81.1	75.9	97.4	89.9	81.2	85.4	83.9	72.5	86.3	81.5
0310	Concrete Forming & Accessories	93.8	84.8	86.8	96.3	72.8	78.0	91.7	77.1	80.3	90.6	73.0	77.0	90.9	74.1	77.9	90.4	71.7	75.9
0320	Concrete Reinforcing	99.9	87.5	96.5	90.7	80.3	87.8	91.6	80.2	88.4	91.2	73.5	86.3	101.3	79.2	95.2	92.2	75.7	87.6
0330	Cast-in-Place Concrete	86.8	87.1	86.9	88.5	77.1	84.4	97.0	74.9	89.1	90.7	69.6	83.2	101.8	71.7	91.1	93.6	69.5	85.1
03	CONCRETE	96.7	85.6	92.3	88.7	76.4	83.9	94.6	76.7	87.5	89.3	72.7	82.8	95.9	75.0	87.6	93.4	72.2	85.0
04	MASONRY	104.8	80.4	90.0	91.8	71.4	79.4	96.6	71.6	81.4	76.3	68.6	71.6	93.9	74.6	82.2	83.1	66.1	72.8
05	METALS	98.7	78.2	94.7	93.2	87.6	92.1	95.3	74.8	91.3	92.8	84.3	91.1	99.3	88.5	97.2	94.3	80.6	91.6
06	WOOD, PLASTICS & COMPOSITES	89.7	85.0	87.6	91.6	72.1	82.9	95.6	78.1	87.7	86.3	73.2	80.4	95.6	74.2	86.0	89.2	72.5	81.7
07	THERMAL & MOISTURE PROTECTION	105.6	81.2	96.9	109.7	71.8	96.2	96.7	74.2	88.7	102.2	71.4	91.2	99.5	73.1	90.1	90.9	68.9	83.1
08	OPENINGS	99.3	81.4	95.2	87.1	71.8	83.7	90.7	75.2	87.2	91.8	71.0	87.1	88.8	72.6	85.2	89.9	68.9	85.1
0920	Plaster & Gypsum Board	87.7	84.5	85.7	105.8	71.7	84.2	84.9	78.3	80.7	71.8	73.1	72.6	86.3	74.3	78.7	83.4	72.3	76.3
0950, 0980	Ceilings & Acoustic Treatment	101.3	84.5	91.9	94.2	71.7	81.6	76.3	78.3	77.4	90.2	73.1	80.6	80.9	74.3	77.2	83.4	72.3	77.2
0960	Flooring	102.3	84.0	97.7	101.5	82.5	96.7	94.7	76.8	90.2	68.9	76.8	70.9	95.5	71.3	89.5	92.5	48.4	81.5
0970, 0990	Wall Finishes & Painting/Coating	97.1	81.3	87.7	93.0	62.7	75.0	85.2	76.7	80.2	85.6	67.0	74.5	85.2	69.2	75.7	91.3	60.1	72.7
09	FINISHES	98.0	84.4	91.2	96.0	73.3	84.6	87.5	77.1	82.3	81.6	73.2	77.4	88.9	72.9	80.9	88.9	66.0	77.4
COVERS	DIVS. 10 - 14, 25, 28, 41, 43, 44, 46	100.0	92.4	98.5	100.0	88.5	97.8	100.0	88.3	97.7	100.0	83.6	96.8	100.0	87.8	97.6	100.0	83.4	96.8
21, 22, 23	FIRE SUPPRESSION, PLUMBING & HVAC	99.9	80.2	92.8	92.4	72.7	85.3	92.1	73.5	85.4	93.3	69.6	84.8	99.6	72.3	89.8	92.4	72.4	85.2
26, 27, 3370	ELECTRICAL, COMMUNICATIONS & UTIL.	98.5	87.6	93.8	85.7	71.6	79.6	100.0	74.3	88.8	92.7	68.4	82.1	90.4	70.0	81.6	94.0	69.2	83.2
MF2018	WEIGHTED AVERAGE	99.0	84.2	93.5	92.1	75.8	86.1	94.0	75.9	87.4	91.3	74.3	85.1	95.8	75.7	88.4	92.3	72.4	85.0

		\multicolumn{9}{c	}{INDIANA}	\multicolumn{9}{c	}{IOWA}
	DIVISION	\multicolumn{3}{c	}{SOUTH BEND 465 - 466}	\multicolumn{3}{c	}{TERRE HAUTE 478}	\multicolumn{3}{c	}{WASHINGTON 475}	\multicolumn{3}{c	}{BURLINGTON 526}	\multicolumn{3}{c	}{CARROLL 514}	\multicolumn{3}{c	}{CEDAR RAPIDS 522 - 524}
		MAT.	INST.	TOTAL	MAT.	INST.	TOTAL	MAT.	INST.	TOTAL	MAT.	INST.	TOTAL	MAT.	INST.	TOTAL	MAT.	INST.	TOTAL
015433	CONTRACTOR EQUIPMENT		108.7	108.7		106.9	106.9		106.9	106.9		95.2	95.2		95.2	95.2		92.4	92.4
0241, 31 - 34	SITE & INFRASTRUCTURE, DEMOLITION	92.8	97.4	95.8	86.0	109.6	101.4	81.6	109.8	100.0	84.6	86.9	86.1	77.3	87.6	84.0	88.9	87.2	87.8
0310	Concrete Forming & Accessories	99.4	73.4	79.2	94.6	74.0	78.6	95.4	76.8	81.0	96.4	85.3	87.7	82.4	76.0	77.4	103.1	80.8	85.7
0320	Concrete Reinforcing	98.9	78.1	93.1	100.2	79.1	94.3	92.7	80.0	89.2	93.4	87.7	91.8	94.0	77.0	89.3	94.0	93.6	93.9
0330	Cast-in-Place Concrete	89.5	77.2	85.1	89.6	75.3	84.5	97.5	81.7	91.9	118.2	50.5	94.1	118.2	75.0	102.8	118.5	80.2	104.8
03	CONCRETE	99.7	77.0	90.7	98.0	75.9	89.3	101.3	79.5	92.7	103.3	74.2	91.8	101.9	76.7	92.0	103.8	83.6	95.8
04	MASONRY	92.1	70.9	79.2	95.2	70.9	80.5	87.6	73.6	79.1	107.6	64.8	81.6	108.8	65.2	82.3	113.3	77.8	91.7
05	METALS	101.3	98.2	100.7	92.5	84.3	90.9	85.6	85.2	85.5	88.0	93.9	89.1	88.0	90.6	88.5	90.8	98.6	92.3
06	WOOD, PLASTICS & COMPOSITES	96.7	72.6	85.9	91.3	73.8	83.4	91.6	76.0	84.6	94.1	89.0	91.8	76.3	80.2	78.0	103.1	80.4	92.9
07	THERMAL & MOISTURE PROTECTION	101.9	75.3	92.4	101.5	75.3	92.2	101.4	77.7	93.0	105.3	69.1	92.4	105.3	70.7	93.0	106.1	76.4	95.6
08	OPENINGS	98.4	72.1	92.5	90.6	72.1	86.5	88.0	75.9	85.3	91.1	86.8	90.2	95.2	76.3	90.9	95.6	82.6	92.6
0920	Plaster & Gypsum Board	91.0	71.8	78.9	86.3	72.8	77.7	86.4	75.2	79.3	100.0	89.1	93.0	95.6	80.0	85.7	106.5	80.3	89.9
0950, 0980	Ceilings & Acoustic Treatment	85.3	71.8	77.7	83.4	72.8	77.5	78.4	75.2	76.6	108.4	89.1	97.6	108.4	80.0	92.5	111.6	80.3	94.1
0960	Flooring	99.9	81.9	95.4	94.9	71.9	89.2	95.6	76.8	90.9	98.5	61.9	89.4	94.1	71.2	88.3	114.7	82.5	106.6
0970, 0990	Wall Finishes & Painting/Coating	99.1	77.8	86.4	91.3	73.8	80.8	91.3	80.7	85.0	93.6	75.2	82.6	95.2	75.2	82.6	95.8	67.4	78.9
09	FINISHES	93.6	75.1	84.3	89.8	73.3	81.5	88.9	77.0	82.9	98.9	80.9	89.9	96.0	75.4	85.7	105.6	79.6	92.5
COVERS	DIVS. 10 - 14, 25, 28, 41, 43, 44, 46	100.0	90.7	98.2	100.0	89.9	98.0	100.0	88.8	97.8	100.0	92.3	98.5	100.0	88.5	97.8	100.0	91.6	98.4
21, 22, 23	FIRE SUPPRESSION, PLUMBING & HVAC	99.8	71.6	89.7	100.0	73.7	90.5	92.2	75.4	86.4	92.5	75.3	86.4	92.5	69.9	84.4	100.1	79.6	92.7
26, 27, 3370	ELECTRICAL, COMMUNICATIONS & UTIL.	99.7	82.1	92.1	93.9	78.9	87.4	94.1	77.5	86.9	96.3	64.3	82.4	96.7	68.5	84.4	95.1	74.1	86.0
MF2018	WEIGHTED AVERAGE	99.1	79.4	91.9	95.4	78.7	89.2	92.0	80.4	87.7	94.9	76.9	88.3	94.6	75.2	87.5	98.4	82.0	92.4

City Cost Indexes

IOWA

DIVISION		COUNCIL BLUFFS 515			CRESTON 508			DAVENPORT 527 - 528			DECORAH 521			DES MOINES 500 - 503,509			DUBUQUE 520		
		MAT.	INST.	TOTAL	MAT.	INST.	TOTAL	MAT.	INST.	TOTAL	MAT.	INST.	TOTAL	MAT.	INST.	TOTAL	MAT.	INST.	TOTAL
015433	CONTRACTOR EQUIPMENT		91.9	91.9		95.2	95.2		95.2	95.2		95.2	95.2		101.2	101.2		91.4	91.4
0241, 31 - 34	SITE & INFRASTRUCTURE, DEMOLITION	89.6	84.6	86.3	81.4	88.5	86.0	88.5	90.4	89.8	83.6	86.7	85.6	88.0	99.2	95.3	87.1	84.8	85.6
0310	Concrete Forming & Accessories	81.5	72.3	74.3	81.0	78.5	79.1	102.4	94.4	96.2	93.6	65.1	71.5	102.1	89.1	92.0	83.2	78.2	79.3
0320	Concrete Reinforcing	95.9	82.4	92.2	89.3	77.1	85.9	94.0	94.1	94.0	93.4	76.5	88.7	98.4	99.0	98.5	92.7	76.1	88.1
0330	Cast-in-Place Concrete	123.2	84.1	109.3	121.3	78.1	106.0	114.1	91.4	106.0	115.0	69.5	98.8	103.4	92.8	99.6	116.0	79.6	103.1
03	CONCRETE	105.3	79.2	95.0	101.8	79.0	92.8	101.9	94.0	98.8	101.4	69.8	88.9	101.7	92.6	98.1	100.1	79.2	91.8
04	MASONRY	113.1	74.1	89.4	112.1	71.9	87.7	108.4	89.4	96.9	129.7	62.3	88.8	98.7	88.4	92.5	114.3	65.8	84.9
05	METALS	94.4	93.9	94.3	93.1	91.1	92.7	90.8	104.0	93.4	88.1	89.5	88.4	99.2	101.3	99.6	89.0	90.6	89.3
06	WOOD, PLASTICS & COMPOSITES	74.6	70.6	72.8	74.5	80.2	77.1	103.1	94.1	99.1	90.2	64.4	78.6	99.4	88.2	94.4	77.0	79.0	77.9
07	THERMAL & MOISTURE PROTECTION	105.4	71.4	93.3	110.0	73.7	97.1	105.7	88.0	99.4	105.4	62.7	90.2	102.4	87.1	96.9	105.6	72.2	93.7
08	OPENINGS	94.8	77.0	90.8	105.5	77.9	99.3	95.6	95.8	95.6	93.9	70.6	88.6	97.3	93.8	96.5	94.8	79.1	91.3
0920	Plaster & Gypsum Board	95.6	70.3	79.5	95.9	80.0	85.8	106.5	94.4	98.8	99.0	63.7	76.6	90.2	88.0	88.8	95.6	79.0	85.1
0950, 0980	Ceilings & Acoustic Treatment	108.4	70.3	87.0	99.7	80.0	88.7	111.6	94.4	101.9	108.4	63.7	83.3	104.2	88.0	95.1	108.4	79.0	91.9
0960	Flooring	93.4	80.1	90.0	90.4	61.9	83.2	100.4	85.0	96.5	98.6	61.9	89.4	102.4	89.8	99.3	107.5	67.0	97.4
0970, 0990	Wall Finishes & Painting/Coating	90.8	57.5	70.9	87.4	75.2	80.1	93.6	86.8	89.6	93.6	75.2	82.6	99.1	82.1	89.0	95.4	74.0	82.6
09	FINISHES	96.6	71.6	84.0	91.9	75.2	83.5	101.2	91.9	96.5	98.8	65.3	82.0	99.2	88.3	93.7	101.0	75.7	88.3
COVERS	DIVS. 10 - 14, 25, 28, 41, 43, 44, 46	100.0	89.5	98.0	100.0	90.7	98.2	100.0	95.6	99.1	100.0	88.1	97.7	100.0	94.8	99.0	100.0	90.6	98.2
21, 22, 23	FIRE SUPPRESSION, PLUMBING & HVAC	100.1	75.6	91.3	92.5	71.7	85.0	100.1	90.1	96.5	92.5	66.9	83.3	99.9	85.0	94.6	100.1	72.0	90.0
26, 27, 3370	ELECTRICAL, COMMUNICATIONS & UTIL.	97.8	81.6	90.8	90.2	68.5	80.8	92.7	81.5	87.8	95.1	42.1	72.1	99.5	89.6	95.2	97.0	71.2	85.8
MF2018	WEIGHTED AVERAGE	98.7	79.0	91.4	96.0	76.8	88.9	97.4	91.3	95.1	95.6	67.4	85.2	99.4	90.8	96.2	97.1	76.4	89.5

IOWA

DIVISION		FORT DODGE 505			MASON CITY 504			OTTUMWA 525			SHENANDOAH 516			SIBLEY 512			SIOUX CITY 510 - 511		
		MAT.	INST.	TOTAL	MAT.	INST.	TOTAL	MAT.	INST.	TOTAL	MAT.	INST.	TOTAL	MAT.	INST.	TOTAL	MAT.	INST.	TOTAL
015433	CONTRACTOR EQUIPMENT		95.2	95.2		95.2	95.2		91.4	91.4		91.9	91.9		95.2	95.2		95.2	95.2
0241, 31 - 34	SITE & INFRASTRUCTURE, DEMOLITION	86.0	85.7	85.8	86.1	86.6	86.4	83.9	82.4	83.0	85.1	84.2	84.5	91.2	86.6	88.2	96.2	88.6	91.3
0310	Concrete Forming & Accessories	81.6	70.7	73.1	86.3	64.7	69.5	91.2	79.0	81.7	83.5	70.0	73.0	84.1	34.5	45.6	103.1	70.9	78.0
0320	Concrete Reinforcing	89.3	76.4	85.7	89.2	76.5	85.6	93.4	87.9	91.8	95.9	77.0	90.7	95.9	76.4	90.5	94.0	92.2	93.5
0330	Cast-in-Place Concrete	113.8	38.9	87.2	113.8	65.2	96.6	118.9	58.8	97.6	119.1	75.6	103.7	116.7	51.1	93.4	117.4	82.8	105.1
03	CONCRETE	97.7	61.7	83.5	98.1	68.1	86.2	102.8	74.4	91.6	103.1	74.3	91.8	102.2	49.6	81.4	103.2	79.8	94.0
04	MASONRY	111.0	46.8	72.0	124.8	61.2	86.2	110.2	49.8	73.5	112.5	67.1	85.0	133.1	47.0	80.8	106.8	64.3	81.0
05	METALS	93.2	89.2	92.5	93.3	89.5	92.5	87.9	95.1	89.3	93.4	91.3	93.0	88.2	88.7	88.3	90.8	97.6	92.1
06	WOOD, PLASTICS & COMPOSITES	75.1	80.2	77.4	80.8	64.4	73.5	86.7	88.8	87.7	77.0	71.2	74.4	78.1	31.2	57.1	103.1	70.1	88.3
07	THERMAL & MOISTURE PROTECTION	109.5	58.5	91.3	109.2	63.3	92.8	105.8	63.1	90.6	104.9	65.8	90.9	105.1	49.6	85.3	105.7	67.2	92.0
08	OPENINGS	99.5	68.8	92.6	91.8	70.6	87.0	95.2	84.1	92.7	87.1	69.3	83.1	92.2	41.8	80.8	95.6	76.1	91.2
0920	Plaster & Gypsum Board	95.9	80.0	85.8	95.9	63.7	75.5	96.1	91.6	93.2	95.6	70.9	80.0	95.6	29.5	53.7	106.5	69.6	83.1
0950, 0980	Ceilings & Acoustic Treatment	99.7	80.0	88.7	99.7	63.7	79.5	108.4	89.1	97.6	108.4	70.9	87.4	108.4	29.5	64.2	111.6	69.6	88.0
0960	Flooring	91.8	61.9	84.3	93.5	61.9	85.6	109.9	61.9	97.9	93.9	66.2	87.0	94.8	61.9	86.6	100.5	67.0	92.1
0970, 0990	Wall Finishes & Painting/Coating	87.4	72.2	78.3	87.4	75.2	80.1	95.4	75.2	83.3	90.8	75.2	81.5	93.6	74.3	82.1	93.6	84.0	87.9
09	FINISHES	93.2	70.4	81.8	93.7	65.0	79.3	101.9	76.5	89.1	96.6	69.6	83.0	98.2	41.9	69.9	102.2	71.0	86.5
COVERS	DIVS. 10 - 14, 25, 28, 41, 43, 44, 46	100.0	84.7	97.0	100.0	87.7	97.6	100.0	86.2	97.3	100.0	87.4	97.6	100.0	79.5	96.0	100.0	89.2	97.9
21, 22, 23	FIRE SUPPRESSION, PLUMBING & HVAC	92.5	64.2	82.3	92.5	69.8	84.3	92.5	65.7	82.9	92.5	75.4	86.4	92.5	64.2	82.4	100.1	74.4	90.9
26, 27, 3370	ELECTRICAL, COMMUNICATIONS & UTIL.	93.3	61.8	79.6	92.9	42.1	70.9	96.2	63.2	81.9	95.1	69.8	84.1	95.1	42.0	72.1	95.1	68.5	83.6
MF2018	WEIGHTED AVERAGE	95.5	67.4	85.1	95.4	67.7	85.2	95.4	71.9	86.8	95.5	74.8	87.9	95.7	57.3	81.6	98.0	76.4	90.1

IOWA / KANSAS

DIVISION		SPENCER 513			WATERLOO 506 - 507			BELLEVILLE 669			COLBY 677			DODGE CITY 678			EMPORIA 668		
		MAT.	INST.	TOTAL	MAT.	INST.	TOTAL	MAT.	INST.	TOTAL	MAT.	INST.	TOTAL	MAT.	INST.	TOTAL	MAT.	INST.	TOTAL
015433	CONTRACTOR EQUIPMENT		95.2	95.2		95.2	95.2		99.6	99.6		99.6	99.6		99.6	99.6		98.1	98.1
0241, 31 - 34	SITE & INFRASTRUCTURE, DEMOLITION	91.3	85.5	87.5	93.6	88.3	90.1	97.4	87.2	90.7	92.1	87.6	89.2	97.3	87.9	91.2	92.0	85.0	87.4
0310	Concrete Forming & Accessories	91.0	34.2	46.9	99.5	66.0	73.5	97.2	50.1	60.6	103.9	55.7	66.4	95.7	57.3	65.9	87.2	63.6	68.8
0320	Concrete Reinforcing	95.9	76.3	90.5	89.9	76.4	86.2	101.9	93.9	99.7	110.5	93.9	105.9	107.8	93.7	103.9	100.5	94.0	98.7
0330	Cast-in-Place Concrete	116.7	60.1	96.6	122.0	80.5	107.2	106.0	77.3	95.8	101.7	79.5	93.8	103.5	83.6	96.4	102.5	79.6	94.3
03	CONCRETE	102.8	52.5	82.9	103.8	74.1	92.1	103.7	68.9	89.9	103.7	72.1	91.2	103.8	74.2	92.1	97.7	75.7	89.0
04	MASONRY	133.1	47.0	80.8	111.9	71.8	87.6	105.0	54.5	74.3	89.9	58.2	70.6	97.4	56.2	72.4	111.6	59.5	79.9
05	METALS	88.2	88.4	88.2	96.0	91.3	95.1	96.9	94.7	96.4	97.2	95.4	96.8	98.5	95.1	97.9	96.5	95.6	96.3
06	WOOD, PLASTICS & COMPOSITES	86.5	31.2	61.7	98.3	61.9	82.0	90.6	46.6	70.8	95.6	52.2	76.1	85.4	52.9	70.8	79.1	62.5	71.7
07	THERMAL & MOISTURE PROTECTION	105.9	50.1	86.0	109.5	73.0	96.5	99.9	57.3	84.7	104.3	59.4	88.3	104.3	63.1	89.6	98.3	67.6	87.4
08	OPENINGS	102.5	41.8	88.8	92.1	70.1	87.1	89.3	57.1	82.0	95.4	60.1	87.5	95.4	60.6	87.5	87.5	67.8	83.1
0920	Plaster & Gypsum Board	96.1	29.5	53.8	104.5	61.1	77.0	79.9	45.3	57.9	88.5	51.0	64.7	81.8	51.8	62.8	76.3	61.7	67.1
0950, 0980	Ceilings & Acoustic Treatment	108.4	29.5	64.2	102.4	61.1	79.3	87.3	45.3	63.7	83.6	51.0	65.3	83.6	51.8	65.8	87.3	61.7	73.0
0960	Flooring	96.9	61.9	88.1	98.0	75.0	92.3	92.7	61.2	84.8	84.3	61.2	78.5	81.7	62.4	76.9	88.9	61.2	82.0
0970, 0990	Wall Finishes & Painting/Coating	93.6	50.8	68.1	87.4	78.9	82.3	92.7	91.5	92.0	97.3	91.5	93.9	97.3	91.5	93.9	92.7	91.5	92.0
09	FINISHES	98.9	38.3	68.5	97.1	68.0	82.5	88.7	55.2	71.9	86.2	59.3	72.7	84.6	60.5	72.5	86.2	65.4	75.8
COVERS	DIVS. 10 - 14, 25, 28, 41, 43, 44, 46	100.0	79.5	96.0	100.0	89.3	97.9	100.0	75.0	95.2	100.0	76.8	95.5	100.0	80.5	96.2	100.0	76.6	95.5
21, 22, 23	FIRE SUPPRESSION, PLUMBING & HVAC	92.5	64.2	82.4	100.0	76.4	91.5	92.2	64.1	82.2	92.6	63.9	82.3	100.2	72.0	90.1	92.2	66.1	82.8
26, 27, 3370	ELECTRICAL, COMMUNICATIONS & UTIL.	95.9	42.0	72.6	91.2	59.3	77.4	97.0	55.8	79.1	99.0	60.4	82.3	97.5	65.8	83.8	95.5	59.6	79.9
MF2018	WEIGHTED AVERAGE	96.9	57.1	82.3	98.3	74.3	89.5	96.0	65.7	84.9	96.2	68.1	85.9	98.2	71.1	88.2	94.7	70.3	85.7

City Cost Indexes

KANSAS

DIVISION		FORT SCOTT 667			HAYS 676			HUTCHINSON 675			INDEPENDENCE 673			KANSAS CITY 660 - 662			LIBERAL 679		
		MAT.	INST.	TOTAL	MAT.	INST.	TOTAL	MAT.	INST.	TOTAL	MAT.	INST.	TOTAL	MAT.	INST.	TOTAL	MAT.	INST.	TOTAL
015433	CONTRACTOR EQUIPMENT		98.8	98.8		99.6	99.6		99.6	99.6		99.6	99.6		96.7	96.7		99.6	99.6
0241, 31 - 34	SITE & INFRASTRUCTURE, DEMOLITION	89.5	85.1	86.6	95.0	87.5	90.1	80.8	87.8	85.4	94.5	87.8	90.1	89.8	86.5	87.7	94.7	87.4	90.0
0310	Concrete Forming & Accessories	106.7	75.1	82.1	100.9	54.4	64.7	89.1	51.6	60.0	114.0	61.6	73.3	102.7	98.9	99.7	96.1	53.6	63.1
0320	Concrete Reinforcing	99.8	90.4	97.2	107.8	93.9	103.9	107.8	93.9	103.9	107.1	90.4	102.5	96.9	101.2	98.1	109.3	93.6	105.0
0330	Cast-in-Place Concrete	95.0	75.3	88.0	80.2	77.6	79.3	74.3	79.4	76.1	103.9	79.5	95.3	81.4	96.1	86.6	80.2	76.4	78.9
03	CONCRETE	94.9	78.8	88.5	96.4	70.8	86.3	83.9	70.2	78.5	105.4	74.1	93.1	88.2	98.7	92.3	97.7	70.0	86.8
04	MASONRY	115.0	50.6	75.9	96.4	54.7	71.0	90.3	58.1	70.8	87.1	58.1	69.5	113.3	96.8	103.3	95.2	48.3	66.7
05	METALS	96.5	94.1	96.0	96.6	95.4	96.4	96.4	95.0	96.1	96.3	94.2	95.9	106.4	104.4	106.0	97.0	94.7	96.5
06	WOOD, PLASTICS & COMPOSITES	103.9	82.1	94.2	91.9	52.2	74.1	78.6	46.8	64.3	109.0	59.8	87.0	99.2	98.8	99.0	86.0	52.2	70.8
07	THERMAL & MOISTURE PROTECTION	99.3	65.3	87.2	104.6	57.9	88.0	103.2	58.5	87.2	104.5	67.2	91.2	99.0	97.2	98.4	104.7	55.4	87.1
08	OPENINGS	87.5	77.8	85.4	95.4	60.1	87.4	95.4	57.2	86.7	93.5	63.6	86.8	88.3	97.3	90.3	95.4	60.1	87.5
0920	Plaster & Gypsum Board	83.1	81.9	82.3	86.1	51.0	63.9	80.8	45.5	58.4	97.7	58.9	73.1	77.2	99.1	91.1	82.3	51.0	62.4
0950, 0980	Ceilings & Acoustic Treatment	87.3	81.9	84.3	83.6	51.0	65.3	83.6	45.5	62.2	83.6	58.9	69.8	87.3	99.1	93.9	83.6	51.0	65.3
0960	Flooring	102.2	59.9	91.6	83.5	61.2	77.9	79.6	61.2	75.0	87.3	59.9	80.4	80.8	95.6	84.5	81.8	61.2	76.7
0970, 0990	Wall Finishes & Painting/Coating	94.2	68.8	79.1	97.3	91.5	93.9	97.3	91.5	93.9	97.3	91.5	93.9	100.6	105.3	103.4	97.3	91.5	93.9
09	FINISHES	91.3	72.8	82.0	86.0	58.5	72.2	82.7	56.2	69.4	88.4	64.1	76.2	86.2	99.0	92.6	85.2	58.0	71.5
COVERS	DIVS. 10 - 14, 25, 28, 41, 43, 44, 46	100.0	77.5	95.6	100.0	75.6	95.3	100.0	76.2	95.4	100.0	77.6	95.7	100.0	96.1	99.2	100.0	75.0	95.2
21, 22, 23	FIRE SUPPRESSION, PLUMBING & HVAC	92.2	60.6	80.9	92.6	61.6	81.5	92.6	63.9	82.3	92.6	63.3	82.1	99.7	103.5	101.1	92.6	62.3	81.8
26, 27, 3370	ELECTRICAL, COMMUNICATIONS & UTIL.	95.1	60.4	80.1	98.5	60.4	82.0	96.2	54.3	78.0	97.2	64.8	83.2	97.6	92.3	95.3	97.5	60.4	81.5
MF2018	WEIGHTED AVERAGE	95.0	70.2	85.9	95.5	66.9	84.9	92.7	66.3	83.0	96.1	69.8	86.5	97.9	98.0	98.0	95.4	66.1	84.6

KANSAS / KENTUCKY

DIVISION		SALINA 674			TOPEKA 664 - 666			WICHITA 670 - 672			ASHLAND 411 - 412			BOWLING GREEN 421 - 422			CAMPTON 413 - 414		
		MAT.	INST.	TOTAL	MAT.	INST.	TOTAL	MAT.	INST.	TOTAL	MAT.	INST.	TOTAL	MAT.	INST.	TOTAL	MAT.	INST.	TOTAL
015433	CONTRACTOR EQUIPMENT		99.6	99.6		104.6	104.6		104.7	104.7		95.4	95.4		89.3	89.3		94.8	94.8
0241, 31 - 34	SITE & INFRASTRUCTURE, DEMOLITION	90.5	87.5	88.5	93.0	96.6	95.4	89.7	97.0	94.5	98.5	76.1	83.9	75.8	86.5	82.8	79.5	86.8	84.2
0310	Concrete Forming & Accessories	91.5	58.1	65.6	98.8	64.2	71.9	101.0	55.6	65.7	85.3	81.2	82.1	86.4	77.7	79.6	88.1	73.8	77.0
0320	Concrete Reinforcing	107.1	93.8	103.4	98.5	95.2	97.6	99.5	97.4	98.9	92.9	86.0	91.0	90.8	74.7	86.4	91.7	83.5	89.4
0330	Cast-in-Place Concrete	89.8	80.2	86.4	90.2	85.5	88.5	84.1	76.4	81.3	85.2	86.4	85.6	84.5	65.5	77.8	94.3	62.8	83.1
03	CONCRETE	94.1	73.4	85.9	92.3	78.0	86.7	90.2	71.3	82.8	89.6	85.2	87.8	88.3	73.4	82.5	91.7	72.2	84.0
04	MASONRY	109.5	51.8	74.4	107.6	61.2	79.4	88.0	52.4	66.4	94.2	82.9	87.3	96.2	65.4	77.5	93.0	49.3	66.4
05	METALS	98.3	95.8	97.8	101.0	94.9	99.8	100.8	94.8	99.6	93.7	102.9	95.5	95.0	83.4	92.7	94.3	86.6	92.8
06	WOOD, PLASTICS & COMPOSITES	80.7	57.1	70.1	95.5	62.9	80.9	98.7	52.8	78.1	71.4	79.6	75.1	82.6	80.2	81.7	80.8	80.2	80.5
07	THERMAL & MOISTURE PROTECTION	103.7	58.7	87.7	101.9	79.7	94.0	101.6	60.3	86.9	93.3	80.0	88.6	90.9	73.4	84.6	101.5	60.9	87.0
08	OPENINGS	95.4	63.3	88.1	98.0	70.5	91.8	98.0	62.0	89.9	89.2	81.0	87.3	89.9	75.7	86.7	91.1	79.2	88.4
0920	Plaster & Gypsum Board	80.8	56.2	65.2	89.1	61.7	71.7	87.6	51.3	64.6	59.4	79.4	72.1	78.6	80.2	79.6	78.6	79.4	79.1
0950, 0980	Ceilings & Acoustic Treatment	83.6	56.2	68.2	106.8	61.7	81.5	101.8	51.3	73.5	80.9	79.4	80.0	83.4	80.2	81.6	83.4	79.4	81.2
0960	Flooring	80.6	62.4	76.0	95.1	62.4	86.9	91.2	66.4	85.0	73.1	72.8	73.1	90.8	56.6	82.3	92.9	57.6	84.1
0970, 0990	Wall Finishes & Painting/Coating	97.3	91.5	93.9	99.1	91.5	94.6	99.1	99.6	99.4	92.7	80.3	85.3	91.3	62.4	74.1	91.3	47.9	65.4
09	FINISHES	83.6	61.4	72.4	98.0	65.5	81.7	95.3	60.8	78.0	77.6	79.5	78.6	87.6	72.3	79.9	88.4	68.5	78.4
COVERS	DIVS. 10 - 14, 25, 28, 41, 43, 44, 46	100.0	85.1	97.1	100.0	81.2	96.4	100.0	85.7	97.2	100.0	78.8	95.9	100.0	88.3	97.7	100.0	86.6	97.4
21, 22, 23	FIRE SUPPRESSION, PLUMBING & HVAC	100.2	65.5	87.7	99.9	70.3	89.3	99.9	68.2	88.5	92.1	76.4	86.5	100.0	73.5	90.5	92.5	68.7	83.9
26, 27, 3370	ELECTRICAL, COMMUNICATIONS & UTIL.	97.4	71.6	86.2	99.5	66.5	85.2	99.5	71.6	87.4	91.8	78.6	86.1	94.3	70.7	84.1	93.0	78.5	86.7
MF2018	WEIGHTED AVERAGE	97.2	70.3	87.3	99.0	74.1	89.9	97.7	71.2	88.0	91.5	81.8	87.9	94.0	74.7	86.9	92.9	72.6	85.4

KENTUCKY

DIVISION		CORBIN 407 - 409			COVINGTON 410			ELIZABETHTOWN 427			FRANKFORT 406			HAZARD 417 - 418			HENDERSON 424		
		MAT.	INST.	TOTAL	MAT.	INST.	TOTAL	MAT.	INST.	TOTAL	MAT.	INST.	TOTAL	MAT.	INST.	TOTAL	MAT.	INST.	TOTAL
015433	CONTRACTOR EQUIPMENT		94.8	94.8		98.2	98.2		89.3	89.3		99.9	99.9		94.8	94.8		106.9	106.9
0241, 31 - 34	SITE & INFRASTRUCTURE, DEMOLITION	81.6	87.2	85.3	76.9	96.8	89.9	68.3	85.8	79.7	81.9	97.9	92.3	77.9	87.7	84.3	73.8	108.2	96.2
0310	Concrete Forming & Accessories	85.0	68.9	72.5	83.5	64.3	68.6	80.8	65.7	69.1	101.8	71.5	78.2	84.2	74.6	76.8	91.3	69.8	74.6
0320	Concrete Reinforcing	89.5	82.8	87.6	90.8	70.5	85.2	91.3	75.1	86.8	98.1	75.4	91.9	92.2	83.0	89.6	90.9	75.7	86.7
0330	Cast-in-Place Concrete	87.6	66.6	80.2	90.2	74.7	84.7	76.4	62.5	71.5	87.8	71.0	81.9	90.7	64.2	81.3	74.7	77.3	75.6
03	CONCRETE	83.6	71.2	78.7	89.9	70.1	82.1	82.1	67.1	76.2	89.4	72.5	82.8	89.2	73.0	82.8	85.7	74.1	81.1
04	MASONRY	100.0	54.0	72.1	107.0	64.8	81.4	80.2	55.7	65.4	96.8	66.9	78.7	91.4	51.1	66.9	99.3	70.9	82.1
05	METALS	97.7	85.7	95.3	92.8	84.7	91.2	94.2	83.0	92.0	100.8	81.7	97.0	94.3	86.5	92.8	85.3	83.6	85.0
06	WOOD, PLASTICS & COMPOSITES	71.8	70.5	71.2	77.3	62.1	70.5	76.3	67.2	72.2	98.6	70.5	86.0	76.7	80.2	78.3	85.6	68.9	78.1
07	THERMAL & MOISTURE PROTECTION	103.8	62.5	89.1	102.4	65.4	89.2	90.4	61.6	80.1	102.7	69.1	90.7	101.3	62.5	87.5	100.8	74.3	91.4
08	OPENINGS	91.4	63.9	85.2	92.7	66.7	86.8	89.9	66.2	84.5	98.4	72.5	92.6	91.4	79.1	88.6	88.4	71.1	84.5
0920	Plaster & Gypsum Board	88.3	69.4	76.3	67.9	61.6	63.9	76.9	66.6	70.5	96.6	69.4	79.3	76.9	79.4	78.5	81.8	67.8	72.9
0950, 0980	Ceilings & Acoustic Treatment	73.2	69.4	71.1	90.2	61.6	74.2	83.4	66.8	74.1	94.1	69.4	80.2	83.4	79.4	81.2	78.4	67.8	72.4
0960	Flooring	89.0	57.6	81.1	66.9	74.8	69.0	88.7	66.1	83.0	102.2	70.4	94.2	91.5	57.6	83.0	94.2	68.1	87.6
0970, 0990	Wall Finishes & Painting/Coating	87.7	55.1	68.2	85.6	63.2	72.2	91.3	60.9	73.0	99.1	81.5	88.6	91.3	47.9	65.4	91.3	77.1	82.8
09	FINISHES	83.8	65.4	74.6	80.7	65.5	73.1	86.5	64.6	75.5	97.4	72.3	84.8	87.6	69.0	78.3	87.3	70.3	78.7
COVERS	DIVS. 10 - 14, 25, 28, 41, 43, 44, 46	100.0	87.9	97.7	100.0	86.8	97.4	100.0	85.2	97.1	100.0	89.7	98.0	100.0	83.1	96.7	100.0	50.2	90.3
21, 22, 23	FIRE SUPPRESSION, PLUMBING & HVAC	92.8	66.7	83.4	93.3	68.2	84.3	92.7	70.1	84.6	100.1	72.8	90.3	92.5	69.7	84.3	92.7	71.3	85.0
26, 27, 3370	ELECTRICAL, COMMUNICATIONS & UTIL.	93.3	78.5	86.9	94.0	64.5	81.2	92.8	69.3	82.7	100.6	69.3	87.1	93.0	78.5	86.7	94.0	69.3	83.3
MF2018	WEIGHTED AVERAGE	92.7	71.4	84.9	92.6	71.4	84.8	90.3	69.9	82.8	98.2	74.8	89.6	92.4	73.1	85.3	90.2	74.6	84.5

City Cost Indexes

		KENTUCKY																	
	DIVISION	LEXINGTON			LOUISVILLE			OWENSBORO			PADUCAH			PIKEVILLE			SOMERSET		
		403 - 405			400 - 402			423			420			415 - 416			425 - 426		
		MAT.	INST.	TOTAL	MAT.	INST.	TOTAL	MAT.	INST.	TOTAL	MAT.	INST.	TOTAL	MAT.	INST.	TOTAL	MAT.	INST.	TOTAL
015433	CONTRACTOR EQUIPMENT		94.8	94.8		96.9	96.9		106.9	106.9		106.9	106.9		95.4	95.4		94.8	94.8
0241, 31 - 34	SITE & INFRASTRUCTURE, DEMOLITION	86.9	89.7	88.7	80.5	98.5	92.2	84.3	109.7	100.8	75.1	108.4	96.8	105.9	75.4	86.0	72.6	87.2	82.1
0310	Concrete Forming & Accessories	98.4	70.7	76.9	98.9	78.7	83.2	89.5	73.9	77.4	87.3	73.9	76.6	94.9	77.7	81.4	85.3	69.5	73.0
0320	Concrete Reinforcing	98.2	84.9	94.5	97.5	85.0	94.1	90.9	75.2	86.6	91.5	74.0	86.6	93.4	85.9	91.3	91.3	83.0	89.0
0330	Cast-in-Place Concrete	89.7	79.9	86.2	84.4	70.7	79.5	87.1	80.0	84.6	79.6	74.3	77.7	93.7	81.7	89.4	74.7	80.4	76.7
03	CONCRETE	87.8	77.1	83.6	87.6	77.3	83.5	94.8	76.9	87.7	89.1	74.5	83.3	100.0	81.9	92.8	78.8	76.3	77.8
04	MASONRY	98.6	67.4	79.7	96.4	69.4	80.0	91.7	75.2	81.7	94.9	71.3	80.6	91.1	75.0	81.3	86.4	57.0	68.5
05	METALS	100.6	88.0	98.1	101.6	86.0	98.5	86.8	85.5	86.5	83.8	84.0	83.9	93.6	102.7	95.4	94.2	86.3	92.7
06	WOOD, PLASTICS & COMPOSITES	90.1	68.8	80.6	94.6	80.6	88.3	83.0	72.9	78.5	80.1	74.0	77.4	83.8	79.6	81.9	77.4	70.5	74.3
07	THERMAL & MOISTURE PROTECTION	104.2	74.3	93.5	100.4	74.3	91.1	101.4	77.1	92.7	100.9	74.2	91.4	94.1	72.3	86.3	100.8	64.6	87.9
08	OPENINGS	91.5	72.8	87.3	98.2	76.8	93.4	88.4	74.7	85.3	87.7	73.5	84.5	89.7	78.0	87.1	90.6	69.9	85.9
0920	Plaster & Gypsum Board	100.4	67.7	79.7	96.6	80.2	86.2	80.2	71.9	74.9	79.2	73.0	75.3	64.0	79.4	73.8	76.9	69.4	72.2
0950, 0980	Ceilings & Acoustic Treatment	76.4	67.7	71.6	94.1	80.2	86.3	78.4	71.9	74.8	78.4	73.0	75.4	80.9	79.4	80.0	83.4	69.4	75.6
0960	Flooring	93.0	59.9	84.7	93.8	58.2	84.9	93.7	56.6	84.4	92.9	68.1	86.7	76.5	57.6	71.8	91.7	57.6	83.2
0970, 0990	Wall Finishes & Painting/Coating	87.7	75.1	80.2	94.9	66.1	77.8	91.3	84.6	87.3	91.3	65.0	75.6	92.7	81.5	86.0	91.3	60.5	73.0
09	FINISHES	87.6	68.4	78.0	94.3	73.5	83.9	87.3	71.3	79.3	86.7	71.7	79.1	79.9	74.5	77.2	87.2	66.1	76.6
COVERS	DIVS. 10 - 14, 25, 28, 41, 43, 44, 46	100.0	89.5	98.0	100.0	89.5	98.0	100.0	90.4	98.1	100.0	81.4	96.4	100.0	43.4	89.0	100.0	88.1	97.7
21, 22, 23	FIRE SUPPRESSION, PLUMBING & HVAC	100.3	72.6	90.4	100.0	76.7	91.6	100.0	73.5	90.5	92.7	70.3	84.7	92.1	73.9	85.6	92.7	66.5	83.3
26, 27, 3370	ELECTRICAL, COMMUNICATIONS & UTIL.	94.7	70.5	84.2	100.6	73.6	88.9	94.0	68.3	82.9	95.3	68.8	83.8	93.4	78.6	87.0	93.2	78.5	86.8
MF2018	WEIGHTED AVERAGE	96.2	75.2	88.5	97.7	78.2	90.5	93.1	77.7	87.5	90.1	75.8	84.9	93.3	77.8	87.6	90.8	72.8	84.1

		LOUISIANA																	
	DIVISION	ALEXANDRIA			BATON ROUGE			HAMMOND			LAFAYETTE			LAKE CHARLES			MONROE		
		713 - 714			707 - 708			704			705			706			712		
		MAT.	INST.	TOTAL	MAT.	INST.	TOTAL	MAT.	INST.	TOTAL	MAT.	INST.	TOTAL	MAT.	INST.	TOTAL	MAT.	INST.	TOTAL
015433	CONTRACTOR EQUIPMENT		88.4	88.4		95.2	95.2		87.3	87.3		87.3	87.3		86.8	86.8		88.4	88.4
0241, 31 - 34	SITE & INFRASTRUCTURE, DEMOLITION	99.8	84.9	90.1	102.2	96.3	98.3	96.9	84.4	88.8	101.2	84.6	90.4	101.8	84.0	90.2	99.8	84.8	90.0
0310	Concrete Forming & Accessories	81.9	57.8	63.1	99.2	67.6	74.7	78.3	51.6	57.5	96.9	61.9	69.7	97.0	65.2	72.3	81.4	57.3	62.7
0320	Concrete Reinforcing	97.3	50.7	84.4	98.7	50.8	85.5	93.7	48.9	81.3	95.1	48.9	82.3	95.1	50.7	82.8	96.2	50.7	83.6
0330	Cast-in-Place Concrete	78.2	64.5	73.3	87.8	67.7	80.6	83.1	63.3	76.0	82.7	64.9	76.4	87.0	65.8	79.5	78.2	63.8	73.0
03	CONCRETE	80.8	59.8	72.5	88.3	65.4	79.3	83.3	56.2	72.6	85.0	61.5	75.7	86.8	63.6	77.6	80.5	59.4	72.2
04	MASONRY	114.1	60.7	81.6	84.5	58.6	68.8	89.0	58.5	70.5	88.9	61.5	72.3	88.8	62.9	73.0	108.8	59.5	78.8
05	METALS	99.1	70.3	93.4	101.8	72.8	96.1	89.3	68.4	85.2	88.8	68.5	84.6	88.6	69.2	84.8	99.0	70.3	93.3
06	WOOD, PLASTICS & COMPOSITES	82.1	56.6	70.7	94.5	70.6	83.8	73.6	49.4	62.7	97.8	61.8	81.6	95.6	65.4	82.1	81.3	56.6	70.2
07	THERMAL & MOISTURE PROTECTION	101.9	62.2	87.7	97.6	64.7	85.9	96.9	59.6	83.6	97.4	63.1	85.2	97.3	64.1	85.5	101.8	61.7	87.5
08	OPENINGS	103.7	56.1	92.9	98.0	67.7	91.2	94.8	49.8	84.7	98.3	56.4	88.8	98.3	59.5	89.5	103.6	54.6	92.6
0920	Plaster & Gypsum Board	83.9	55.9	66.1	95.2	69.9	79.2	89.6	48.4	63.5	98.9	61.2	75.0	98.9	65.0	77.4	83.7	55.9	66.0
0950, 0980	Ceilings & Acoustic Treatment	105.0	55.9	77.5	95.0	69.9	80.9	92.4	48.4	67.7	88.3	61.2	73.1	88.8	65.0	75.5	105.0	55.9	77.5
0960	Flooring	92.0	63.4	84.8	99.6	63.4	90.6	92.7	63.4	85.4	99.4	63.4	90.4	99.4	63.4	90.4	91.8	63.4	84.7
0970, 0990	Wall Finishes & Painting/Coating	97.1	56.3	72.8	99.1	56.3	73.6	102.9	53.2	73.3	102.9	53.1	73.2	102.9	56.3	75.1	97.1	58.0	73.8
09	FINISHES	93.4	58.3	75.8	98.8	66.0	82.3	95.0	53.1	74.0	97.2	61.2	79.1	97.3	64.0	80.6	93.3	58.2	75.7
COVERS	DIVS. 10 - 14, 25, 28, 41, 43, 44, 46	100.0	77.9	95.7	100.0	84.6	97.0	100.0	81.6	96.4	100.0	83.9	96.9	100.0	84.7	97.0	100.0	77.5	95.6
21, 22, 23	FIRE SUPPRESSION, PLUMBING & HVAC	100.3	59.5	85.7	100.1	58.2	85.1	92.6	56.6	79.7	100.1	57.8	85.0	100.1	60.6	86.0	100.3	58.4	85.3
26, 27, 3370	ELECTRICAL, COMMUNICATIONS & UTIL.	92.8	50.8	74.6	100.7	54.8	80.8	96.3	62.0	81.4	96.9	56.8	79.5	96.6	61.1	81.2	93.7	54.1	76.6
MF2018	WEIGHTED AVERAGE	97.0	61.8	84.1	98.2	65.6	86.2	92.0	60.8	80.5	94.6	63.0	83.0	94.7	65.3	83.9	96.9	61.7	83.9

		LOUISIANA									MAINE								
	DIVISION	NEW ORLEANS			SHREVEPORT			THIBODAUX			AUGUSTA			BANGOR			BATH		
		700 - 701			710 - 711			703			043			044			045		
		MAT.	INST.	TOTAL	MAT.	INST.	TOTAL	MAT.	INST.	TOTAL	MAT.	INST.	TOTAL	MAT.	INST.	TOTAL	MAT.	INST.	TOTAL
015433	CONTRACTOR EQUIPMENT		91.1	91.1		96.9	96.9		87.3	87.3		98.6	98.6		93.0	93.0		93.0	93.0
0241, 31 - 34	SITE & INFRASTRUCTURE, DEMOLITION	101.6	96.5	98.3	102.0	97.6	99.1	99.0	84.4	89.5	89.0	102.1	97.5	90.0	91.3	90.9	84.9	89.7	88.0
0310	Concrete Forming & Accessories	100.7	69.5	76.4	102.3	59.1	68.8	89.3	58.9	65.7	101.8	74.6	80.7	95.7	77.0	81.2	90.8	74.2	77.9
0320	Concrete Reinforcing	99.2	70.8	91.4	98.7	49.9	85.2	93.7	48.9	81.3	99.0	80.5	93.9	84.5	80.7	83.5	83.7	80.3	82.7
0330	Cast-in-Place Concrete	80.3	71.9	77.3	80.9	66.6	75.8	89.3	63.0	79.9	74.4	106.5	85.8	58.8	110.2	77.0	58.8	105.3	75.3
03	CONCRETE	87.9	70.5	81.0	86.4	60.9	76.4	87.4	59.4	76.4	93.4	87.3	91.0	84.0	89.9	86.3	83.7	86.9	84.9
04	MASONRY	92.7	63.4	74.9	96.5	59.9	74.3	111.4	58.1	79.0	113.3	89.3	98.7	126.9	91.7	105.5	134.5	86.9	105.5
05	METALS	99.3	69.9	93.5	101.9	68.2	95.2	89.3	68.4	85.2	105.5	90.8	102.4	91.3	93.6	91.7	89.7	92.4	90.2
06	WOOD, PLASTICS & COMPOSITES	98.4	71.6	86.4	98.7	58.8	80.8	82.2	59.6	72.1	100.8	71.3	87.6	95.1	74.0	85.7	87.5	71.3	80.2
07	THERMAL & MOISTURE PROTECTION	95.1	68.7	85.7	99.4	63.7	86.7	97.1	60.5	84.0	82.4	95.7	87.2	89.5	99.2	93.0	89.4	93.6	90.9
08	OPENINGS	100.0	68.5	92.9	98.1	54.4	88.2	99.0	51.6	88.4	98.2	75.6	93.1	95.2	80.2	91.8	95.2	74.7	90.6
0920	Plaster & Gypsum Board	87.0	70.9	76.8	100.9	57.7	73.5	91.1	58.9	70.7	91.3	70.3	78.0	96.0	73.2	81.5	89.7	70.3	77.4
0950, 0980	Ceilings & Acoustic Treatment	85.5	70.9	77.3	119.2	57.7	84.7	92.4	58.9	73.6	108.2	70.3	87.0	77.3	73.2	75.0	77.3	70.3	73.4
0960	Flooring	102.8	68.6	94.3	99.2	63.4	90.3	97.1	62.9	88.5	107.7	103.1	106.6	99.3	103.1	100.2	97.8	99.1	98.1
0970, 0990	Wall Finishes & Painting/Coating	113.5	59.9	81.5	99.1	58.0	74.6	102.9	53.2	73.3	113.5	83.8	95.8	99.1	93.6	95.8	99.1	79.0	87.1
09	FINISHES	98.8	68.5	83.6	105.1	59.6	82.2	96.7	58.9	77.7	105.3	79.8	92.5	91.9	82.5	87.2	90.7	78.5	84.6
COVERS	DIVS. 10 - 14, 25, 28, 41, 43, 44, 46	100.0	85.3	97.2	100.0	78.7	95.9	100.0	82.5	96.6	100.0	95.0	99.0	100.0	99.9	100.0	100.0	90.9	98.2
21, 22, 23	FIRE SUPPRESSION, PLUMBING & HVAC	99.7	60.9	85.8	100.1	59.1	85.4	92.6	56.3	79.6	99.7	71.6	89.6	100.2	75.4	91.3	92.7	71.6	85.1
26, 27, 3370	ELECTRICAL, COMMUNICATIONS & UTIL.	104.5	67.7	88.5	101.3	60.7	83.7	95.6	62.0	81.0	104.3	72.5	90.5	100.0	65.5	85.1	98.9	72.5	87.5
MF2018	WEIGHTED AVERAGE	98.3	69.5	87.7	99.0	64.2	86.2	93.9	62.2	82.2	100.7	82.4	94.0	95.7	83.1	91.0	93.5	80.9	88.9

City Cost Indexes

		MAINE																	
	DIVISION	HOULTON			KITTERY			LEWISTON			MACHIAS			PORTLAND			ROCKLAND		
		047			039			042			046			040 - 041			048		
		MAT.	INST.	TOTAL	MAT.	INST.	TOTAL	MAT.	INST.	TOTAL	MAT.	INST.	TOTAL	MAT.	INST.	TOTAL	MAT.	INST.	TOTAL
015433	CONTRACTOR EQUIPMENT		93.0	93.0		93.0	93.0		93.0	93.0		93.0	93.0		95.9	95.9		93.0	93.0
0241, 31 - 34	SITE & INFRASTRUCTURE, DEMOLITION	86.4	89.7	88.6	75.5	89.7	84.8	88.8	91.3	90.5	85.8	89.7	88.4	89.5	97.7	94.8	83.3	89.7	87.5
0310	Concrete Forming & Accessories	100.3	74.1	80.0	91.8	74.3	78.2	102.2	77.0	82.6	96.7	74.1	79.2	104.7	77.7	83.7	98.0	74.2	79.5
0320	Concrete Reinforcing	84.5	80.3	83.4	84.5	80.3	83.3	103.9	80.7	97.5	84.5	80.3	83.4	97.8	80.9	93.1	84.5	80.3	83.4
0330	Cast-in-Place Concrete	58.8	104.3	74.9	58.9	105.3	75.4	60.0	110.2	77.8	58.8	105.3	75.3	71.1	111.5	85.4	60.0	105.3	76.1
03	CONCRETE	85.0	86.5	85.6	79.4	86.9	82.4	86.9	89.9	88.1	84.4	86.8	85.4	91.9	90.6	91.4	82.1	86.9	84.0
04	MASONRY	106.4	86.9	94.5	122.5	86.9	100.8	107.2	91.7	97.8	106.4	86.9	94.5	108.1	91.8	98.2	100.0	86.9	92.0
05	METALS	90.0	92.3	90.4	85.6	92.5	87.7	95.7	93.6	95.3	90.0	92.3	90.5	100.8	92.2	99.1	89.8	92.4	90.3
06	WOOD, PLASTICS & COMPOSITES	100.3	71.3	87.3	90.1	71.3	81.6	103.0	74.0	90.0	96.4	71.3	85.1	102.6	74.1	89.8	97.7	71.3	85.8
07	THERMAL & MOISTURE PROTECTION	89.6	93.6	91.0	95.3	93.6	94.7	89.4	99.2	92.9	89.6	93.6	91.0	101.2	100.7	101.0	89.3	93.6	90.8
08	OPENINGS	95.2	74.7	90.6	97.7	77.9	93.2	98.0	80.2	94.0	95.2	74.7	90.6	98.6	80.2	94.4	95.2	74.7	90.6
0920	Plaster & Gypsum Board	97.9	70.3	80.4	102.9	70.3	82.2	103.4	73.2	84.2	97.0	70.3	80.1	108.1	73.2	85.9	97.0	70.3	80.1
0950, 0980	Ceilings & Acoustic Treatment	77.3	70.3	73.4	88.2	70.3	78.2	90.9	73.2	81.0	77.3	70.3	73.4	86.8	73.2	79.2	77.3	70.3	73.4
0960	Flooring	100.5	99.1	100.1	97.1	99.1	97.6	101.8	103.1	102.1	99.8	99.1	99.6	102.5	166.4	118.5	100.1	99.1	99.8
0970, 0990	Wall Finishes & Painting/Coating	99.1	79.0	87.1	82.5	90.7	87.4	99.1	93.6	95.8	99.1	79.0	87.1	99.1	93.6	95.8	99.1	79.0	87.1
09	FINISHES	92.6	78.5	85.5	94.8	79.8	87.2	97.1	82.5	89.8	92.3	78.5	85.3	97.4	95.5	96.4	92.1	78.5	85.2
COVERS	DIVS. 10 - 14, 25, 28, 41, 43, 44, 46	100.0	88.0	97.7	100.0	90.9	98.2	100.0	99.9	100.0	100.0	88.1	97.7	100.0	100.0	100.0	100.0	90.9	98.2
21, 22, 23	FIRE SUPPRESSION, PLUMBING & HVAC	92.7	71.6	85.1	92.8	71.6	85.2	100.2	75.4	91.3	92.7	71.6	85.1	100.1	75.5	91.3	92.7	71.6	85.1
26, 27, 3370	ELECTRICAL, COMMUNICATIONS & UTIL.	101.1	72.5	88.7	100.3	72.5	88.3	101.1	74.8	89.7	101.1	72.5	88.7	101.4	74.8	89.9	101.0	72.5	88.7
MF2018	WEIGHTED AVERAGE	93.2	80.7	88.6	92.3	81.2	88.2	97.0	84.4	92.4	93.1	80.8	88.5	99.2	86.6	94.5	92.4	80.9	88.2

		MAINE			MARYLAND													
	DIVISION	WATERVILLE			ANNAPOLIS			BALTIMORE			COLLEGE PARK			CUMBERLAND			EASTON		
		049			214			210 - 212			207 - 208			215			216		
		MAT.	INST.	TOTAL	MAT.	INST.	TOTAL	MAT.	INST.	TOTAL	MAT.	INST.	TOTAL	MAT.	INST.	TOTAL	MAT.	INST.	TOTAL
015433	CONTRACTOR EQUIPMENT		93.0	93.0		107.1	107.1		105.3	105.3		104.4	104.4		100.8	100.8		100.8	100.8
0241, 31 - 34	SITE & INFRASTRUCTURE, DEMOLITION	86.1	89.7	88.5	109.6	97.1	101.4	110.6	98.5	102.7	105.5	89.4	95.0	98.2	87.2	91.1	104.8	85.6	92.3
0310	Concrete Forming & Accessories	90.2	74.1	77.7	103.0	70.3	77.7	102.9	74.9	81.2	82.5	69.4	72.3	93.3	76.3	80.1	91.2	67.3	72.6
0320	Concrete Reinforcing	84.5	80.3	83.4	98.2	88.7	95.6	100.4	90.6	97.7	97.7	97.0	97.6	87.5	84.7	86.7	86.8	78.2	84.4
0330	Cast-in-Place Concrete	58.8	105.3	75.3	103.7	74.5	93.3	111.4	77.8	99.4	136.4	70.3	112.9	86.0	82.0	84.6	95.6	61.0	83.3
03	CONCRETE	85.1	86.8	85.8	95.1	76.3	87.7	101.7	79.6	93.0	106.4	76.2	94.5	83.5	81.1	82.6	89.2	68.6	81.1
04	MASONRY	118.0	86.9	99.1	98.1	68.6	80.2	105.6	73.9	86.3	123.1	67.3	89.2	100.6	84.5	90.8	114.9	53.1	77.4
05	METALS	89.9	92.3	90.4	101.0	101.1	101.0	100.4	97.8	99.9	84.1	108.6	88.9	95.7	102.1	97.0	96.0	98.5	96.5
06	WOOD, PLASTICS & COMPOSITES	86.6	71.3	79.7	99.6	70.6	86.6	100.6	74.6	89.0	70.9	68.7	69.9	85.4	73.6	80.1	82.6	73.5	78.5
07	THERMAL & MOISTURE PROTECTION	89.5	93.6	91.0	107.6	78.8	97.3	102.8	82.4	95.5	101.3	74.5	91.7	101.6	76.8	92.8	101.8	67.4	89.5
08	OPENINGS	95.2	74.7	90.6	98.5	79.7	94.2	99.7	80.3	95.3	92.9	78.6	89.6	93.4	78.3	90.0	91.8	76.3	88.3
0920	Plaster & Gypsum Board	89.7	70.3	77.4	115.1	69.7	86.3	115.1	73.7	88.8	98.6	68.1	79.3	114.5	73.2	88.3	114.5	73.1	88.2
0950, 0980	Ceilings & Acoustic Treatment	77.3	70.3	73.4	96.8	69.7	81.6	96.8	73.7	83.8	98.3	68.1	81.4	101.8	73.2	85.8	101.8	73.1	85.7
0960	Flooring	97.6	99.1	98.0	108.4	71.2	99.1	96.0	75.3	90.8	92.5	70.3	86.9	96.0	88.5	94.1	95.3	67.8	88.4
0970, 0990	Wall Finishes & Painting/Coating	99.1	79.0	87.1	99.1	64.8	78.6	99.1	68.5	80.8	93.9	64.8	76.5	93.6	75.2	82.6	93.6	64.8	76.4
09	FINISHES	90.8	78.5	84.6	104.4	69.1	86.7	100.3	73.7	86.9	96.4	68.3	82.3	102.3	78.3	90.2	102.5	67.3	84.8
COVERS	DIVS. 10 - 14, 25, 28, 41, 43, 44, 46	100.0	87.9	97.7	100.0	87.5	97.6	100.0	89.6	98.0	100.0	77.5	95.6	100.0	90.6	98.2	100.0	79.1	95.9
21, 22, 23	FIRE SUPPRESSION, PLUMBING & HVAC	92.7	71.6	85.1	100.0	78.6	92.3	100.1	84.1	94.3	92.6	78.8	87.6	92.3	67.3	83.3	92.3	65.5	82.7
26, 27, 3370	ELECTRICAL, COMMUNICATIONS & UTIL.	101.1	72.5	88.7	100.0	82.1	92.3	100.0	87.0	94.4	100.3	98.9	99.7	99.5	75.9	89.2	99.2	55.5	80.3
MF2018	WEIGHTED AVERAGE	93.4	80.8	88.7	100.2	80.3	92.9	100.9	83.8	94.6	95.6	82.1	90.6	94.8	79.8	89.3	96.1	69.1	86.2

		MARYLAND																MASSACHUSETTS		
	DIVISION	ELKTON			HAGERSTOWN			SALISBURY			SILVER SPRING			WALDORF			BOSTON		
		219			217			218			209			206			020 - 022, 024		
		MAT.	INST.	TOTAL	MAT.	INST.	TOTAL	MAT.	INST.	TOTAL	MAT.	INST.	TOTAL	MAT.	INST.	TOTAL	MAT.	INST.	TOTAL
015433	CONTRACTOR EQUIPMENT		100.8	100.8		100.8	100.8		100.8	100.8		97.2	97.2		97.2	97.2		103.3	103.3
0241, 31 - 34	SITE & INFRASTRUCTURE, DEMOLITION	92.6	86.1	88.3	99.7	87.5	91.8	104.8	85.4	92.1	92.9	82.3	86.0	99.0	82.1	88.0	89.8	103.7	98.8
0310	Concrete Forming & Accessories	97.9	83.8	86.9	92.2	80.7	83.3	107.6	46.1	59.8	90.8	68.7	73.6	98.6	68.7	75.3	106.5	137.3	130.4
0320	Concrete Reinforcing	86.8	105.3	91.9	87.5	84.7	86.7	86.8	58.6	79.0	97.0	97.0	97.0	97.7	96.9	97.5	101.1	149.3	114.4
0330	Cast-in-Place Concrete	77.4	66.9	73.6	82.0	82.1	82.0	95.6	59.1	82.6	139.6	70.6	115.1	156.5	70.4	125.9	80.3	140.6	101.7
03	CONCRETE	78.3	82.8	80.1	80.9	83.2	81.8	90.6	55.0	76.5	106.2	75.8	94.2	115.9	75.7	100.0	96.7	139.9	113.7
04	MASONRY	100.1	60.5	76.0	106.2	84.5	93.0	114.0	50.0	75.1	122.4	67.6	89.1	105.7	67.5	82.5	121.3	144.5	135.4
05	METALS	96.0	109.3	98.6	95.8	102.5	97.1	96.0	90.0	94.8	89.0	104.9	92.2	89.0	104.4	92.1	98.7	132.8	105.4
06	WOOD, PLASTICS & COMPOSITES	91.4	91.9	91.7	84.3	79.1	81.9	105.4	46.9	79.1	78.5	68.1	73.8	86.7	68.1	78.3	104.9	136.7	119.1
07	THERMAL & MOISTURE PROTECTION	101.4	72.9	91.2	101.9	82.3	94.9	102.1	63.0	88.2	104.0	78.8	95.0	104.5	78.8	95.4	96.5	137.7	111.2
08	OPENINGS	91.8	93.6	92.2	91.8	81.3	89.4	92.0	56.2	84.0	84.9	78.2	83.4	85.5	78.2	83.8	98.6	143.4	108.7
0920	Plaster & Gypsum Board	117.9	92.1	101.5	114.5	78.9	91.9	130.2	45.6	76.6	108.2	68.1	82.8	111.1	68.1	83.8	123.5	137.7	132.5
0950, 0980	Ceilings & Acoustic Treatment	101.8	92.1	96.4	103.3	78.9	89.6	101.8	45.6	70.3	107.4	68.1	85.4	107.4	68.1	85.4	101.3	137.7	121.7
0960	Flooring	97.3	67.8	89.9	95.6	88.5	93.8	100.4	67.8	92.2	98.2	70.3	91.2	100.8	70.3	93.2	104.8	159.0	118.4
0970, 0990	Wall Finishes & Painting/Coating	93.6	64.8	76.4	93.6	67.2	77.8	93.6	64.8	76.4	100.6	64.8	79.2	100.6	64.8	79.2	99.1	156.1	133.1
09	FINISHES	102.7	79.9	91.3	102.3	80.6	91.4	106.2	50.8	78.4	96.7	67.7	82.8	99.5	67.8	83.6	104.2	143.9	124.1
COVERS	DIVS. 10 - 14, 25, 28, 41, 43, 44, 46	100.0	51.1	90.5	100.0	91.2	98.3	100.0	75.2	95.2	100.0	76.2	95.4	100.0	74.3	95.0	100.0	116.7	103.2
21, 22, 23	FIRE SUPPRESSION, PLUMBING & HVAC	92.3	70.8	84.6	99.9	83.9	94.1	92.3	63.7	82.0	92.6	79.2	87.8	92.6	79.1	87.8	100.2	133.0	111.9
26, 27, 3370	ELECTRICAL, COMMUNICATIONS & UTIL.	100.1	77.4	90.3	99.4	75.9	89.2	98.6	53.5	79.1	95.9	98.9	97.2	94.6	98.9	96.5	102.6	126.4	112.9
MF2018	WEIGHTED AVERAGE	94.2	78.8	88.5	96.3	84.3	91.9	96.7	62.0	83.9	95.5	81.2	90.2	96.3	81.1	90.7	100.3	133.3	112.5

City Cost Indexes

		MASSACHUSETTS																	
		BROCKTON			BUZZARDS BAY			FALL RIVER			FITCHBURG			FRAMINGHAM			GREENFIELD		
	DIVISION	023			025			027			014			017			013		
		MAT.	INST.	TOTAL	MAT.	INST.	TOTAL	MAT.	INST.	TOTAL	MAT.	INST.	TOTAL	MAT.	INST.	TOTAL	MAT.	INST.	TOTAL
015433	CONTRACTOR EQUIPMENT		96.0	96.0		96.0	96.0		96.8	96.8		93.0	93.0		94.5	94.5		93.0	93.0
0241, 31 - 34	SITE & INFRASTRUCTURE, DEMOLITION	88.1	94.3	92.2	77.1	94.0	88.1	87.4	94.4	92.0	79.1	93.6	88.6	76.7	93.1	87.4	82.3	92.2	88.7
0310	Concrete Forming & Accessories	98.0	115.4	111.5	95.7	114.6	110.4	98.0	115.1	111.3	94.9	108.2	105.2	103.2	115.3	112.6	93.0	111.8	107.6
0320	Concrete Reinforcing	98.5	135.8	108.9	79.0	114.2	88.7	98.5	114.3	102.9	81.3	127.9	94.2	81.3	135.6	96.3	83.5	113.8	91.9
0330	Cast-in-Place Concrete	69.1	125.5	89.2	57.5	125.2	81.5	66.9	125.7	87.8	63.2	125.1	85.2	63.2	125.3	85.3	64.9	111.2	81.4
03	CONCRETE	88.3	122.4	101.7	74.7	118.2	91.8	86.3	118.6	99.0	75.8	117.4	92.2	78.3	122.2	95.6	78.6	111.6	91.7
04	MASONRY	119.6	128.1	124.8	110.6	128.1	121.2	120.0	128.1	124.9	107.1	120.4	115.2	114.0	124.2	120.2	112.5	111.4	111.8
05	METALS	94.4	124.2	100.3	87.7	114.7	93.0	94.4	115.3	98.5	92.2	116.8	97.0	92.2	123.2	98.4	96.2	108.5	98.6
06	WOOD, PLASTICS & COMPOSITES	95.7	114.6	104.2	91.4	114.6	101.8	95.7	114.8	104.3	95.2	105.6	99.9	103.8	114.4	108.5	92.5	114.9	102.5
07	THERMAL & MOISTURE PROTECTION	93.5	119.4	102.7	92.5	116.3	101.0	93.3	116.2	101.5	92.6	112.4	99.7	92.8	117.2	101.5	92.6	103.1	96.4
08	OPENINGS	94.9	122.6	101.2	91.3	112.2	96.0	94.9	113.2	99.0	97.8	115.6	101.8	88.2	122.5	96.0	97.8	113.7	101.4
0920	Plaster & Gypsum Board	109.0	115.0	112.8	99.4	115.0	109.3	109.0	115.0	112.8	108.2	105.7	106.6	113.1	115.0	114.3	110.3	115.3	113.5
0950, 0980	Ceilings & Acoustic Treatment	104.8	115.0	110.5	86.1	115.0	102.3	104.8	115.0	110.5	85.4	105.7	96.8	85.4	115.0	102.0	97.2	115.3	107.4
0960	Flooring	102.9	149.0	114.5	100.5	149.0	112.7	101.5	149.0	113.5	96.7	149.0	109.8	97.6	149.0	110.5	96.0	128.3	104.1
0970, 0990	Wall Finishes & Painting/Coating	87.3	129.5	112.5	87.3	129.5	112.5	87.3	129.5	112.5	89.2	129.5	113.3	90.0	129.5	113.6	89.2	107.2	99.9
09	FINISHES	100.7	123.3	112.0	93.2	123.3	108.3	100.3	123.4	111.9	93.0	118.0	105.6	93.8	123.1	108.5	96.5	115.3	105.9
COVERS	DIVS. 10 - 14, 25, 28, 41, 43, 44, 46	100.0	110.7	102.1	100.0	110.7	102.1	100.0	111.1	102.2	100.0	99.8	100.0	100.0	110.2	102.0	100.0	103.4	100.7
21, 22, 23	FIRE SUPPRESSION, PLUMBING & HVAC	100.6	98.5	99.8	93.1	93.9	93.3	100.6	98.2	99.7	93.0	94.9	93.7	93.0	109.8	99.0	93.0	92.7	92.9
26, 27, 3370	ELECTRICAL, COMMUNICATIONS & UTIL.	101.6	92.3	97.6	100.0	89.2	95.3	101.1	93.6	97.8	100.5	92.7	97.1	98.7	110.7	103.9	100.5	93.9	97.6
MF2018	WEIGHTED AVERAGE	97.5	111.2	102.6	91.1	107.8	97.2	97.2	109.5	101.7	92.7	106.7	97.9	92.4	115.5	100.9	94.4	103.4	97.7

		MASSACHUSETTS																	
		HYANNIS			LAWRENCE			LOWELL			NEW BEDFORD			PITTSFIELD			SPRINGFIELD		
	DIVISION	026			019			018			027			012			010 - 011		
		MAT.	INST.	TOTAL	MAT.	INST.	TOTAL	MAT.	INST.	TOTAL	MAT.	INST.	TOTAL	MAT.	INST.	TOTAL	MAT.	INST.	TOTAL
015433	CONTRACTOR EQUIPMENT		96.0	96.0		95.1	95.1		93.0	93.0		96.8	96.8		93.0	93.0		93.0	93.0
0241, 31 - 34	SITE & INFRASTRUCTURE, DEMOLITION	85.0	94.2	91.0	89.6	93.7	92.3	88.8	94.0	92.2	86.4	94.4	91.6	89.5	92.3	91.3	89.1	92.6	91.4
0310	Concrete Forming & Accessories	89.3	115.0	109.3	104.6	115.8	113.3	100.7	117.6	113.8	98.0	115.2	111.4	100.7	100.1	100.3	101.0	113.0	110.3
0320	Concrete Reinforcing	79.0	114.3	88.8	100.5	133.5	109.7	101.4	133.3	110.2	98.5	114.2	102.9	82.9	110.6	90.6	101.4	113.8	104.9
0330	Cast-in-Place Concrete	63.1	125.4	85.2	73.1	125.5	91.7	66.5	128.2	88.4	58.9	125.8	82.7	72.5	109.5	85.7	69.2	112.9	84.7
03	CONCRETE	78.8	118.4	94.4	91.8	122.1	103.8	85.7	123.7	100.7	84.1	118.7	97.7	83.3	105.3	92.0	86.8	112.8	97.1
04	MASONRY	118.4	128.1	124.3	120.4	130.5	126.5	106.1	131.5	121.6	118.7	126.7	123.6	106.7	106.5	106.6	106.4	114.5	111.3
05	METALS	89.2	115.1	94.3	96.6	123.3	101.9	96.6	120.3	101.3	94.4	115.3	98.5	96.4	106.9	98.4	99.5	108.6	101.3
06	WOOD, PLASTICS & COMPOSITES	83.6	114.6	97.5	105.0	114.6	109.3	103.5	114.6	108.4	95.7	114.8	104.3	103.5	100.4	102.1	103.5	114.9	108.6
07	THERMAL & MOISTURE PROTECTION	92.9	118.6	102.0	93.2	120.1	102.8	93.0	121.1	103.0	93.3	115.8	101.3	93.1	99.7	95.4	93.0	115.7	101.0
08	OPENINGS	91.8	113.4	96.7	91.6	121.9	98.4	98.9	121.9	104.1	94.9	117.3	100.0	98.9	104.9	100.2	98.9	113.7	102.2
0920	Plaster & Gypsum Board	94.4	115.0	107.4	117.5	115.0	115.9	117.5	115.0	115.9	109.0	115.0	112.8	117.5	100.4	106.6	117.5	115.3	116.1
0950, 0980	Ceilings & Acoustic Treatment	91.2	115.0	104.5	97.7	115.0	107.4	97.7	115.0	107.4	104.8	115.0	110.5	97.7	100.4	99.2	97.7	115.3	107.6
0960	Flooring	98.3	149.0	111.0	98.5	149.0	111.2	98.5	149.0	111.2	101.5	149.0	113.5	98.7	123.4	104.9	97.9	128.3	105.5
0970, 0990	Wall Finishes & Painting/Coating	87.3	129.5	112.5	89.3	129.5	113.3	89.2	129.5	113.3	87.3	129.5	112.5	89.2	107.2	99.9	89.9	107.2	100.2
09	FINISHES	93.5	123.3	108.5	98.5	123.3	110.9	98.5	124.5	111.5	100.2	123.4	111.9	98.5	105.3	101.9	98.5	116.1	107.3
COVERS	DIVS. 10 - 14, 25, 28, 41, 43, 44, 46	100.0	110.7	102.1	100.0	110.7	102.1	100.0	112.3	102.4	100.0	111.1	102.2	100.0	101.1	100.2	100.0	104.4	100.9
21, 22, 23	FIRE SUPPRESSION, PLUMBING & HVAC	100.6	102.4	101.3	100.0	113.5	104.8	100.0	119.4	107.0	100.6	98.2	99.7	100.0	89.8	96.4	100.0	94.3	97.9
26, 27, 3370	ELECTRICAL, COMMUNICATIONS & UTIL.	100.8	93.5	97.6	100.0	116.1	107.0	100.2	115.0	106.6	102.5	95.4	99.4	100.2	93.9	97.5	100.3	95.1	98.0
MF2018	WEIGHTED AVERAGE	94.1	110.4	100.1	97.8	117.8	105.2	97.1	119.2	105.2	97.0	109.8	101.7	96.9	99.3	97.7	97.9	104.6	100.4

		MASSACHUSETTS			MICHIGAN														
		WORCESTER			ANN ARBOR			BATTLE CREEK			BAY CITY			DEARBORN			DETROIT		
	DIVISION	015 - 016			481			490			487			481			482		
		MAT.	INST.	TOTAL	MAT.	INST.	TOTAL	MAT.	INST.	TOTAL	MAT.	INST.	TOTAL	MAT.	INST.	TOTAL	MAT.	INST.	TOTAL
015433	CONTRACTOR EQUIPMENT		93.0	93.0		104.6	104.6		94.2	94.2		104.6	104.6		104.6	104.6		95.0	95.0
0241, 31 - 34	SITE & INFRASTRUCTURE, DEMOLITION	89.1	93.6	92.0	82.5	88.4	86.4	86.1	79.0	81.5	77.1	87.1	83.6	82.3	88.5	86.4	94.4	98.7	97.2
0310	Concrete Forming & Accessories	101.3	116.5	113.1	98.0	99.0	98.8	103.1	78.9	84.3	98.1	75.4	80.5	97.9	99.7	99.3	95.6	104.4	102.4
0320	Concrete Reinforcing	101.4	140.0	112.1	97.1	98.7	97.6	94.6	76.8	89.7	97.1	98.0	97.4	97.1	99.9	97.9	100.7	100.4	100.6
0330	Cast-in-Place Concrete	68.8	125.2	88.8	91.2	93.9	92.2	80.7	89.3	83.8	87.3	82.0	85.4	89.2	94.7	91.2	108.6	99.4	105.4
03	CONCRETE	86.7	123.3	101.1	88.9	98.2	92.5	84.9	82.1	83.8	87.2	83.2	85.6	88.0	99.0	92.4	98.8	101.4	99.8
04	MASONRY	106.1	126.7	118.6	104.1	94.0	98.0	100.8	74.0	84.5	103.6	78.6	88.4	103.9	116.0	111.3	108.0	97.3	101.5
05	METALS	99.6	122.5	104.1	95.0	113.9	98.7	101.5	81.9	97.7	95.6	110.1	98.5	95.1	115.7	99.1	95.8	92.5	95.2
06	WOOD, PLASTICS & COMPOSITES	104.1	116.3	109.6	93.3	100.5	96.5	98.6	78.5	89.6	93.3	74.3	84.8	93.3	100.5	96.5	92.3	106.7	98.8
07	THERMAL & MOISTURE PROTECTION	93.0	115.3	101.0	109.4	93.9	103.9	104.1	75.1	93.8	107.2	79.9	97.5	108.0	101.2	105.6	108.2	103.9	106.7
08	OPENINGS	98.9	124.7	104.7	91.3	96.0	92.4	84.5	73.6	82.1	91.3	78.6	88.4	91.3	96.0	92.4	98.6	101.3	99.2
0920	Plaster & Gypsum Board	117.5	116.7	117.0	103.5	100.4	101.5	86.2	75.1	79.1	103.5	73.5	84.5	103.5	100.4	101.5	109.5	107.0	107.9
0950, 0980	Ceilings & Acoustic Treatment	97.7	116.7	108.4	101.1	100.4	100.7	82.2	75.1	78.2	101.6	73.5	85.8	101.1	100.4	100.7	113.1	107.0	109.7
0960	Flooring	98.5	150.2	111.4	92.6	104.0	95.5	101.3	63.1	91.7	92.6	80.2	89.5	91.6	98.5	93.3	97.8	103.4	99.2
0970, 0990	Wall Finishes & Painting/Coating	89.2	129.5	113.3	86.1	93.7	90.6	88.7	67.7	76.2	86.1	76.9	80.6	86.1	92.0	89.6	99.1	95.5	97.0
09	FINISHES	98.5	124.5	111.5	97.3	99.5	98.4	90.7	74.5	82.6	97.1	75.7	86.3	97.0	98.7	97.8	103.8	103.7	103.8
COVERS	DIVS. 10 - 14, 25, 28, 41, 43, 44, 46	100.0	105.4	101.1	100.0	100.0	100.0	100.0	101.1	100.2	100.0	94.4	98.9	100.0	100.4	100.1	100.0	100.6	100.1
21, 22, 23	FIRE SUPPRESSION, PLUMBING & HVAC	100.0	99.2	99.7	100.2	88.7	96.1	99.9	76.2	91.4	100.2	78.6	92.5	100.2	97.2	99.1	100.1	100.2	100.1
26, 27, 3370	ELECTRICAL, COMMUNICATIONS & UTIL.	100.3	98.3	99.4	96.1	97.3	96.6	93.7	69.2	83.1	95.0	73.4	85.7	96.1	92.6	94.6	100.6	100.0	100.3
MF2018	WEIGHTED AVERAGE	97.9	111.9	103.1	96.2	96.4	96.3	95.7	77.0	88.8	95.8	82.2	90.8	96.1	100.1	97.5	99.5	99.9	99.7

649

City Cost Indexes

		MICHIGAN																
	DIVISION	FLINT 484 - 485			GAYLORD 497			GRAND RAPIDS 493,495			IRON MOUNTAIN 498 - 499			JACKSON 492			KALAMAZOO 491		
		MAT.	INST.	TOTAL	MAT.	INST.	TOTAL	MAT.	INST.	TOTAL	MAT.	INST.	TOTAL	MAT.	INST.	TOTAL	MAT.	INST.	TOTAL
015433	CONTRACTOR EQUIPMENT		104.6	104.6		100.9	100.9		99.4	99.4		89.7	89.7		100.9	100.9		94.2	94.2
0241, 31 - 34	SITE & INFRASTRUCTURE, DEMOLITION	75.3	87.4	83.2	82.8	76.8	78.9	85.1	91.0	89.0	85.2	84.8	84.9	94.4	78.4	84.0	86.3	79.0	81.6
0310	Concrete Forming & Accessories	101.4	83.8	87.7	101.6	67.3	74.9	100.7	75.0	80.8	95.1	71.4	76.7	97.9	74.8	80.0	103.1	79.2	84.5
0320	Concrete Reinforcing	97.1	98.3	97.5	88.4	83.4	87.0	98.7	76.8	92.7	87.6	76.3	84.4	85.8	97.9	89.1	94.6	75.5	89.4
0330	Cast-in-Place Concrete	91.8	84.7	89.3	80.6	72.0	77.5	84.9	86.4	85.5	95.4	62.3	83.7	80.5	85.5	82.2	82.4	89.4	84.9
03	CONCRETE	89.4	88.0	88.8	81.7	73.5	78.5	91.4	79.3	86.6	88.1	70.0	81.0	77.9	84.0	80.3	87.1	82.1	85.1
04	MASONRY	104.1	87.0	93.7	111.9	65.5	83.7	97.9	72.2	82.3	96.3	71.8	81.4	90.1	78.2	82.9	99.1	80.4	87.7
05	METALS	95.1	110.7	98.2	103.0	105.5	103.5	97.9	80.5	94.5	102.2	87.4	99.3	103.3	108.6	104.4	101.5	82.0	97.7
06	WOOD, PLASTICS & COMPOSITES	98.0	83.6	91.5	92.0	66.7	80.7	97.8	74.0	87.1	92.0	71.7	82.9	90.6	72.5	82.4	98.6	78.5	89.6
07	THERMAL & MOISTURE PROTECTION	107.5	85.1	99.5	102.7	67.1	90.0	105.7	69.8	92.9	106.0	67.1	92.2	102.1	79.6	94.1	104.1	77.1	94.5
08	OPENINGS	91.3	83.0	89.4	83.6	71.4	80.8	98.8	72.8	93.0	89.5	63.3	83.6	82.8	78.8	81.9	84.5	74.7	82.3
0920	Plaster & Gypsum Board	105.9	83.0	91.4	85.5	65.0	72.5	93.9	70.9	79.3	55.4	71.5	65.7	84.1	70.9	75.7	86.2	75.1	79.1
0950, 0980	Ceilings & Acoustic Treatment	101.1	83.0	91.0	79.9	65.0	71.6	90.9	70.9	79.7	80.6	71.5	75.5	79.9	70.9	74.9	82.2	75.1	78.2
0960	Flooring	92.6	85.2	90.8	93.2	76.7	89.1	103.9	82.6	98.6	117.8	81.5	108.7	92.2	70.4	86.8	101.3	70.7	93.7
0970, 0990	Wall Finishes & Painting/Coating	86.1	75.6	79.8	84.4	72.5	77.3	99.1	72.5	83.3	103.1	61.9	78.5	84.4	83.3	83.8	88.7	73.4	79.6
09	FINISHES	96.9	82.8	89.8	89.3	68.8	79.0	97.0	75.8	86.3	93.5	72.2	82.8	89.8	73.9	81.8	90.7	76.6	83.6
COVERS	DIVS. 10 - 14, 25, 28, 41, 43, 44, 46	100.0	96.6	99.3	100.0	93.5	98.7	100.0	99.2	99.8	100.0	91.9	98.4	100.0	96.3	99.3	100.0	101.1	100.2
21, 22, 23	FIRE SUPPRESSION, PLUMBING & HVAC	100.2	83.6	94.2	92.9	71.0	85.0	99.9	80.7	93.0	92.6	75.4	86.4	92.9	77.2	87.2	99.9	77.8	92.0
26, 27, 3370	ELECTRICAL, COMMUNICATIONS & UTIL.	96.1	88.9	93.0	92.9	67.9	82.1	99.3	79.9	90.9	96.9	71.8	86.0	94.9	91.7	93.5	93.4	76.6	86.1
MF2018	WEIGHTED AVERAGE	96.1	88.4	93.3	94.0	74.3	86.7	97.8	79.6	91.1	95.3	75.0	87.8	93.3	83.5	89.7	95.8	79.4	89.8

		MICHIGAN															MINNESOTA		
	DIVISION	LANSING 488 - 489			MUSKEGON 494			ROYAL OAK 480,483			SAGINAW 486			TRAVERSE CITY 496			BEMIDJI 566		
		MAT.	INST.	TOTAL	MAT.	INST.	TOTAL	MAT.	INST.	TOTAL	MAT.	INST.	TOTAL	MAT.	INST.	TOTAL	MAT.	INST.	TOTAL
015433	CONTRACTOR EQUIPMENT		109.0	109.0		94.2	94.2		87.3	87.3		104.6	104.6		89.7	89.7		94.2	94.2
0241, 31 - 34	SITE & INFRASTRUCTURE, DEMOLITION	89.5	99.0	95.6	84.7	79.0	81.0	80.5	87.1	84.8	78.0	87.1	84.0	74.8	83.9	80.7	82.0	91.0	87.9
0310	Concrete Forming & Accessories	100.6	78.6	83.5	103.6	78.1	83.8	93.6	97.9	96.9	98.0	79.8	83.9	95.1	65.8	72.3	86.7	88.6	88.1
0320	Concrete Reinforcing	99.6	98.1	99.2	95.5	77.2	90.4	88.0	94.0	89.7	97.1	98.0	97.4	88.9	72.0	84.3	95.9	103.8	98.1
0330	Cast-in-Place Concrete	100.6	84.5	94.9	80.5	88.1	83.2	79.8	88.7	83.0	90.1	82.0	87.2	74.4	73.5	74.1	112.1	96.0	106.4
03	CONCRETE	94.3	85.3	90.7	84.1	81.4	83.0	77.8	93.5	84.0	88.4	85.2	87.1	75.8	70.6	73.8	99.0	95.1	97.5
04	MASONRY	99.6	85.4	91.0	98.2	78.9	86.5	97.9	89.7	92.9	105.9	78.6	89.3	94.4	67.7	78.0	106.4	104.8	105.4
05	METALS	97.3	106.4	99.1	100.2	82.5	96.7	97.6	87.6	95.6	95.1	110.0	98.0	102.1	85.4	98.8	91.1	119.6	96.7
06	WOOD, PLASTICS & COMPOSITES	97.8	76.8	88.4	97.3	77.0	88.2	88.8	100.5	94.0	90.8	80.4	86.2	92.0	65.4	80.1	70.5	84.7	76.9
07	THERMAL & MOISTURE PROTECTION	105.2	82.9	97.3	103.2	71.7	92.0	105.8	90.9	100.5	108.1	80.5	98.3	105.2	66.9	91.5	107.1	91.1	101.4
08	OPENINGS	98.7	79.4	94.4	83.7	74.5	81.6	91.1	93.9	91.7	89.7	82.0	88.0	89.5	59.4	82.7	95.8	106.6	98.2
0920	Plaster & Gypsum Board	89.5	76.1	81.0	68.9	73.5	71.8	100.2	100.4	100.3	103.5	79.8	88.4	55.4	65.0	61.5	94.4	84.9	88.3
0950, 0980	Ceilings & Acoustic Treatment	102.2	76.1	87.6	82.2	73.5	77.3	100.3	100.4	100.3	101.1	79.8	89.2	80.6	65.0	71.9	119.3	84.9	100.0
0960	Flooring	93.9	82.6	91.1	100.2	82.6	95.8	90.4	95.5	91.7	92.6	80.2	89.5	117.8	76.7	107.5	96.3	107.4	99.0
0970, 0990	Wall Finishes & Painting/Coating	99.1	73.9	84.1	87.0	73.7	79.1	87.8	83.3	85.2	86.1	76.9	80.6	103.1	35.0	62.5	90.8	94.2	92.8
09	FINISHES	97.2	78.2	87.6	87.4	78.2	82.8	96.1	96.2	96.2	97.0	79.2	88.1	92.7	64.1	78.3	100.1	92.2	96.1
COVERS	DIVS. 10 - 14, 25, 28, 41, 43, 44, 46	100.0	95.8	99.2	100.0	100.9	100.2	100.0	99.6	99.9	100.0	95.1	99.1	100.0	90.7	98.2	100.0	98.8	99.8
21, 22, 23	FIRE SUPPRESSION, PLUMBING & HVAC	99.9	85.1	94.6	99.8	81.7	93.3	93.1	91.1	92.4	100.2	78.2	92.3	92.6	70.9	84.8	92.8	85.0	90.0
26, 27, 3370	ELECTRICAL, COMMUNICATIONS & UTIL.	99.3	87.4	94.1	94.0	73.1	84.9	97.2	91.8	94.9	95.0	80.8	88.8	94.5	67.9	82.9	100.4	79.8	91.4
MF2018	WEIGHTED AVERAGE	98.2	87.6	94.3	94.8	79.6	89.2	93.5	91.9	92.9	95.8	84.1	91.5	93.2	71.6	85.2	95.8	93.7	95.0

		MINNESOTA																	
	DIVISION	BRAINERD 564			DETROIT LAKES 565			DULUTH 556 - 558			MANKATO 560			MINNEAPOLIS 553 - 555			ROCHESTER 559		
		MAT.	INST.	TOTAL	MAT.	INST.	TOTAL	MAT.	INST.	TOTAL	MAT.	INST.	TOTAL	MAT.	INST.	TOTAL	MAT.	INST.	TOTAL
015433	CONTRACTOR EQUIPMENT		96.5	96.5		94.2	94.2		102.3	102.3		96.5	96.5		102.8	102.8		96.9	96.9
0241, 31 - 34	SITE & INFRASTRUCTURE, DEMOLITION	84.9	95.4	91.8	80.7	90.6	87.2	92.6	102.0	98.8	82.4	94.7	90.4	88.3	102.1	97.3	90.7	93.8	92.7
0310	Concrete Forming & Accessories	86.6	91.3	90.3	83.1	76.9	78.1	101.4	104.4	103.8	95.8	101.1	99.9	101.7	120.8	116.6	101.8	104.7	104.0
0320	Concrete Reinforcing	95.2	103.9	97.6	95.9	103.5	98.0	99.0	104.5	100.6	95.1	107.0	98.4	99.3	107.9	101.7	95.5	107.5	98.9
0330	Cast-in-Place Concrete	122.0	100.5	114.4	108.9	97.0	104.7	141.0	107.1	129.0	112.3	101.1	108.3	124.8	119.7	123.0	134.6	102.1	123.0
03	CONCRETE	102.7	97.9	100.6	96.7	90.0	94.1	120.3	106.2	114.7	98.9	103.1	100.6	114.5	118.6	116.1	110.3	105.3	108.3
04	MASONRY	133.3	113.0	121.0	131.9	102.3	113.9	112.8	118.3	116.1	120.9	107.8	113.0	109.4	123.6	118.0	109.2	115.3	112.9
05	METALS	91.9	119.6	97.4	91.0	118.2	96.4	98.4	120.2	102.7	91.8	121.2	97.6	96.9	123.8	102.2	95.9	124.0	101.4
06	WOOD, PLASTICS & COMPOSITES	82.8	84.6	83.6	66.8	67.6	67.1	98.8	102.4	100.4	94.8	99.9	97.1	98.8	119.6	108.1	100.6	103.4	101.8
07	THERMAL & MOISTURE PROTECTION	104.7	98.7	102.6	106.9	94.5	102.5	105.2	106.8	105.8	105.2	93.1	100.9	106.6	121.0	111.7	111.3	100.3	107.4
08	OPENINGS	83.2	106.5	88.5	95.7	97.1	96.0	98.4	113.2	101.7	87.6	115.2	93.8	98.9	127.9	105.5	95.3	117.9	100.4
0920	Plaster & Gypsum Board	79.1	84.9	82.8	93.9	67.2	76.9	91.2	102.8	98.6	83.5	100.6	94.4	88.3	120.3	108.6	94.6	104.1	100.6
0950, 0980	Ceilings & Acoustic Treatment	63.9	84.9	75.6	119.3	67.2	90.1	110.4	102.8	106.1	63.9	100.6	84.5	100.9	120.3	111.8	99.9	104.1	102.3
0960	Flooring	95.3	107.0	98.2	95.2	76.6	90.6	100.6	107.0	102.2	96.2	94.0	95.7	95.5	125.3	103.0	95.5	95.9	95.6
0970, 0990	Wall Finishes & Painting/Coating	84.8	94.2	90.4	90.8	94.2	92.8	99.1	114.7	108.4	96.6	98.4	97.7	99.1	129.3	117.1	89.3	103.3	97.7
09	FINISHES	82.5	93.8	88.2	99.6	77.4	88.5	101.2	106.1	103.7	83.9	100.1	92.0	96.7	122.5	109.7	94.9	103.2	99.1
COVERS	DIVS. 10 - 14, 25, 28, 41, 43, 44, 46	100.0	100.9	100.2	100.0	97.8	99.6	100.0	103.2	100.6	100.0	101.3	100.2	100.0	107.6	101.5	100.0	102.1	100.4
21, 22, 23	FIRE SUPPRESSION, PLUMBING & HVAC	91.8	88.7	90.7	92.8	86.4	90.5	99.9	98.3	99.3	91.8	90.3	91.3	100.0	116.6	105.9	100.0	100.0	100.0
26, 27, 3370	ELECTRICAL, COMMUNICATIONS & UTIL.	99.5	100.9	100.1	100.2	77.9	90.5	99.7	100.9	100.2	102.9	96.1	99.9	99.5	118.1	107.6	98.8	96.1	97.6
MF2018	WEIGHTED AVERAGE	94.9	99.5	96.6	96.3	90.2	94.1	102.4	106.1	103.8	94.8	100.6	97.0	100.9	118.4	107.4	99.9	104.7	101.7

City Cost Indexes

DIVISION		MINNESOTA																	MISSISSIPPI		
		SAINT PAUL			ST. CLOUD			THIEF RIVER FALLS			WILLMAR			WINDOM			BILOXI		
		550 - 551			563			567			562			561			395		
		MAT.	INST.	TOTAL	MAT.	INST.	TOTAL	MAT.	INST.	TOTAL	MAT.	INST.	TOTAL	MAT.	INST.	TOTAL	MAT.	INST.	TOTAL
015433	CONTRACTOR EQUIPMENT		102.2	102.2		96.5	96.5		94.2	94.2		96.5	96.5		96.5	96.5		96.7	96.7
0241, 31 - 34	SITE & INFRASTRUCTURE, DEMOLITION	90.7	102.8	98.6	84.8	96.1	92.2	81.4	90.6	87.4	80.9	95.0	90.1	76.4	93.9	87.8	111.8	82.8	92.9
0310	Concrete Forming & Accessories	96.8	118.9	113.9	83.6	115.4	108.3	87.5	88.2	88.1	83.3	97.0	93.9	88.1	76.6	79.2	101.2	65.3	73.3
0320	Concrete Reinforcing	99.8	107.8	102.0	95.2	107.5	98.6	96.1	103.5	98.1	94.9	107.3	98.4	94.9	105.8	98.0	87.4	60.9	80.1
0330	Cast-in-Place Concrete	141.5	119.7	133.8	107.5	115.1	110.2	111.2	89.3	103.4	109.2	110.2	109.6	94.5	78.8	88.9	128.8	65.8	106.4
03	CONCRETE	120.1	117.7	119.1	94.8	114.5	102.6	98.0	92.5	95.8	94.9	104.5	98.7	87.0	84.0	85.8	100.8	66.4	87.2
04	MASONRY	110.6	124.9	119.3	116.1	118.3	117.4	106.4	99.9	102.5	119.1	114.9	116.6	131.5	83.7	102.5	76.9	60.7	67.0
05	METALS	98.3	122.9	103.2	92.6	122.8	98.5	91.2	118.1	96.5	91.7	122.0	97.7	91.6	117.8	96.8	92.3	88.8	91.6
06	WOOD, PLASTICS & COMPOSITES	93.5	116.2	103.7	79.0	113.7	94.5	72.1	84.7	77.8	78.6	91.6	84.4	84.6	72.5	79.2	97.1	65.7	83.0
07	THERMAL & MOISTURE PROTECTION	105.1	119.7	110.3	104.8	113.3	107.8	107.9	91.2	102.0	104.7	104.4	104.6	104.7	76.5	94.6	102.1	61.2	87.5
08	OPENINGS	98.3	125.0	104.3	87.9	123.7	96.0	95.8	106.6	98.2	85.1	111.4	91.0	88.4	96.1	90.1	96.2	60.3	88.1
0920	Plaster & Gypsum Board	88.3	117.0	106.5	79.1	114.9	101.8	94.4	84.9	88.3	79.1	92.1	87.4	79.1	72.4	74.9	109.6	65.3	81.5
0950, 0980	Ceilings & Acoustic Treatment	102.4	117.0	110.6	63.9	114.9	92.5	119.3	84.9	100.0	63.9	92.1	79.7	63.9	72.4	68.7	85.0	65.3	74.0
0960	Flooring	100.9	120.8	105.9	92.3	88.1	91.3	95.9	76.6	91.1	93.9	90.2	93.0	95.9	76.6	91.1	101.7	60.4	91.3
0970, 0990	Wall Finishes & Painting/Coating	98.4	127.2	115.6	96.6	126.7	114.5	90.8	94.2	92.8	90.8	94.2	92.8	90.8	98.4	95.3	91.9	46.0	64.5
09	FINISHES	98.7	120.1	109.4	82.0	112.1	97.1	99.9	86.9	93.4	82.2	95.0	88.6	82.4	78.3	80.3	95.7	62.4	79.0
COVERS	DIVS. 10 - 14, 25, 28, 41, 43, 44, 46	100.0	107.5	101.5	100.0	105.2	101.0	100.0	98.8	99.8	100.0	101.6	100.3	100.0	95.6	99.2	100.0	82.1	96.5
21, 22, 23	FIRE SUPPRESSION, PLUMBING & HVAC	99.9	116.7	105.9	99.3	113.3	104.3	92.8	85.2	90.1	91.8	105.6	96.7	91.8	78.8	87.1	100.0	53.7	83.4
26, 27, 3370	ELECTRICAL, COMMUNICATIONS & UTIL.	99.5	118.1	107.6	99.5	118.1	107.6	99.1	77.9	89.9	99.5	92.8	96.6	102.9	96.1	99.9	98.8	51.9	78.5
MF2018	WEIGHTED AVERAGE	102.0	117.9	107.9	95.4	114.2	102.3	95.6	91.8	94.2	93.4	103.8	97.2	93.5	88.3	91.6	97.1	64.0	84.9

DIVISION		MISSISSIPPI																	
		CLARKSDALE			COLUMBUS			GREENVILLE			GREENWOOD			JACKSON			LAUREL		
		386			397			387			389			390 - 392			394		
		MAT.	INST.	TOTAL	MAT.	INST.	TOTAL	MAT.	INST.	TOTAL	MAT.	INST.	TOTAL	MAT.	INST.	TOTAL	MAT.	INST.	TOTAL
015433	CONTRACTOR EQUIPMENT		96.7	96.7		96.7	96.7		96.7	96.7		96.7	96.7		101.6	101.6		96.7	96.7
0241, 31 - 34	SITE & INFRASTRUCTURE, DEMOLITION	108.1	80.9	90.4	108.7	81.6	91.0	116.5	82.8	94.5	111.6	80.7	91.4	107.7	91.4	97.1	114.7	81.0	92.5
0310	Concrete Forming & Accessories	86.4	40.2	50.5	87.4	42.3	52.3	82.7	59.2	64.4	97.2	40.4	53.1	103.9	67.2	75.5	87.6	54.3	61.8
0320	Concrete Reinforcing	98.6	59.8	87.9	93.5	59.9	84.2	99.2	60.0	88.4	98.6	59.8	87.9	98.6	65.0	89.3	94.1	29.5	76.2
0330	Cast-in-Place Concrete	105.9	55.1	87.9	131.4	57.1	105.0	109.1	64.3	93.2	113.9	54.9	92.9	111.0	70.3	96.5	128.4	56.3	102.8
03	CONCRETE	95.3	51.0	77.8	102.5	52.7	82.8	99.2	63.0	84.9	100.9	51.0	81.2	98.6	69.4	87.1	103.6	52.6	83.5
04	MASONRY	87.0	47.0	62.7	96.2	49.5	67.9	126.1	61.2	86.7	87.7	46.9	63.0	82.0	64.2	71.2	92.9	49.5	66.5
05	METALS	95.5	84.1	93.2	88.6	86.4	88.2	96.5	88.4	94.9	95.5	83.9	93.2	98.1	87.8	96.1	88.7	73.7	85.8
06	WOOD, PLASTICS & COMPOSITES	78.3	40.4	61.3	77.9	41.2	61.4	73.7	57.1	66.3	93.6	40.4	69.8	101.9	67.6	86.5	79.5	58.6	70.1
07	THERMAL & MOISTURE PROTECTION	99.7	47.2	81.0	101.9	50.3	83.5	100.0	60.6	86.0	100.1	49.2	82.0	99.8	64.6	87.2	102.0	52.3	84.3
08	OPENINGS	95.6	43.7	83.9	95.9	44.1	84.2	95.4	53.4	85.9	95.6	43.7	83.9	98.3	60.3	89.7	93.6	47.0	83.1
0920	Plaster & Gypsum Board	88.8	39.3	57.4	96.9	40.0	60.8	87.9	56.4	67.9	101.4	39.3	62.0	94.9	66.9	77.1	96.9	58.0	72.2
0950, 0980	Ceilings & Acoustic Treatment	85.0	39.3	59.4	78.6	40.0	57.0	86.0	56.4	69.4	85.0	39.3	59.4	89.1	66.9	76.6	78.6	58.0	67.0
0960	Flooring	102.7	60.4	92.1	97.5	60.4	88.2	101.4	60.4	91.1	106.9	60.4	95.2	98.8	65.3	90.4	96.6	60.4	87.5
0970, 0990	Wall Finishes & Painting/Coating	96.5	41.7	63.8	91.9	41.7	61.9	96.5	54.5	71.5	96.5	41.7	63.8	99.1	54.5	72.5	91.9	41.7	61.9
09	FINISHES	94.6	43.8	69.1	91.1	44.8	67.9	95.0	58.5	76.6	97.9	43.8	70.7	96.2	65.7	80.9	91.4	55.1	73.1
COVERS	DIVS. 10 - 14, 25, 28, 41, 43, 44, 46	100.0	43.2	89.0	100.0	44.1	89.2	100.0	81.4	96.4	100.0	43.2	89.0	100.0	83.3	96.8	100.0	31.0	86.6
21, 22, 23	FIRE SUPPRESSION, PLUMBING & HVAC	96.3	46.1	78.3	95.8	47.9	78.6	100.1	54.1	83.6	96.3	46.5	78.5	100.1	59.7	85.6	95.9	42.8	76.9
26, 27, 3370	ELECTRICAL, COMMUNICATIONS & UTIL.	98.0	37.0	71.6	97.5	49.0	76.5	98.0	56.1	79.8	98.0	34.7	70.6	101.3	56.1	81.7	98.3	51.6	78.0
MF2018	WEIGHTED AVERAGE	96.2	51.3	79.7	95.6	54.4	80.4	99.4	63.3	86.1	97.3	51.0	80.3	98.7	67.8	87.3	95.7	53.7	80.2

DIVISION		MISSISSIPPI									MISSOURI								
		MCCOMB			MERIDIAN			TUPELO			BOWLING GREEN			CAPE GIRARDEAU			CHILLICOTHE		
		396			393			388			633			637			646		
		MAT.	INST.	TOTAL	MAT.	INST.	TOTAL	MAT.	INST.	TOTAL	MAT.	INST.	TOTAL	MAT.	INST.	TOTAL	MAT.	INST.	TOTAL
015433	CONTRACTOR EQUIPMENT		96.7	96.7		96.7	96.7		96.7	96.7		103.2	103.2		103.2	103.2		97.8	97.8
0241, 31 - 34	SITE & INFRASTRUCTURE, DEMOLITION	101.2	80.8	87.9	107.2	82.8	91.3	106.2	80.8	89.7	83.6	85.6	84.9	88.0	85.7	86.5	98.1	84.0	88.9
0310	Concrete Forming & Accessories	87.5	41.5	51.7	84.2	66.1	70.1	83.2	41.7	51.0	96.6	85.3	87.8	88.6	76.7	79.3	86.7	86.8	86.8
0320	Concrete Reinforcing	94.7	30.9	77.0	93.5	64.8	85.6	96.5	59.7	86.3	102.9	86.6	98.4	104.2	80.0	97.5	101.5	92.1	98.9
0330	Cast-in-Place Concrete	114.0	54.7	92.9	122.0	66.0	102.1	105.9	55.9	88.1	79.5	87.1	82.2	78.7	79.8	79.4	93.4	78.6	88.1
03	CONCRETE	93.6	46.4	75.0	97.2	67.5	85.5	94.5	51.9	77.7	90.0	87.8	89.1	89.2	80.6	85.8	95.5	85.9	91.7
04	MASONRY	96.4	46.5	66.1	76.4	60.9	67.0	115.4	48.0	74.4	106.6	88.2	95.4	104.1	75.3	86.6	101.7	83.0	90.4
05	METALS	88.9	72.8	85.7	89.7	90.4	89.9	95.3	83.7	93.0	85.8	111.3	90.8	86.8	107.8	91.0	81.2	104.8	85.9
06	WOOD, PLASTICS & COMPOSITES	77.9	42.6	62.1	74.1	66.3	70.6	74.5	41.2	59.5	95.4	85.7	91.0	85.3	74.9	80.6	84.7	88.0	86.2
07	THERMAL & MOISTURE PROTECTION	101.5	49.2	82.9	101.6	61.7	87.4	99.7	47.5	81.1	101.4	88.9	97.0	100.8	78.0	92.7	99.4	83.1	93.6
08	OPENINGS	96.0	37.5	82.8	95.7	62.6	88.2	95.6	46.6	84.6	93.1	89.0	92.2	93.1	73.4	88.7	85.6	87.1	85.9
0920	Plaster & Gypsum Board	96.9	41.5	61.7	96.9	66.0	77.3	87.9	40.0	57.5	79.1	85.8	83.3	78.7	74.6	76.1	74.0	87.8	82.8
0950, 0980	Ceilings & Acoustic Treatment	78.6	41.5	57.8	79.1	66.0	71.7	85.0	40.0	59.8	90.5	85.8	87.9	90.5	74.6	81.6	87.9	87.8	87.8
0960	Flooring	97.5	60.4	88.2	96.6	60.4	87.5	101.6	60.4	91.3	100.4	86.8	97.0	97.5	79.4	93.0	104.7	89.3	100.8
0970, 0990	Wall Finishes & Painting/Coating	91.9	41.7	61.9	91.9	53.5	69.0	96.5	40.2	62.9	95.0	94.4	94.7	95.0	71.6	81.0	93.0	91.7	92.2
09	FINISHES	90.5	45.0	67.6	90.7	63.7	77.1	94.2	44.6	69.3	93.9	86.3	90.1	92.9	75.9	84.4	94.8	88.0	91.4
COVERS	DIVS. 10 - 14, 25, 28, 41, 43, 44, 46	100.0	45.7	89.5	100.0	82.2	96.6	100.0	44.1	89.2	100.0	95.5	99.1	100.0	94.4	98.9	100.0	95.2	99.1
21, 22, 23	FIRE SUPPRESSION, PLUMBING & HVAC	95.8	45.6	77.8	100.0	58.0	84.9	96.4	47.4	78.9	92.4	89.4	91.3	99.9	92.7	97.3	92.5	89.8	91.5
26, 27, 3370	ELECTRICAL, COMMUNICATIONS & UTIL.	96.7	49.8	76.4	98.3	53.7	79.0	97.9	49.0	76.7	95.5	68.4	83.8	95.5	87.7	92.1	93.7	67.5	82.3
MF2018	WEIGHTED AVERAGE	94.2	51.3	78.4	95.3	65.8	84.4	97.0	53.7	81.1	92.4	87.5	90.6	94.0	85.9	91.0	91.3	86.0	89.4

City Cost Indexes

		MISSOURI																	
		COLUMBIA			FLAT RIVER			HANNIBAL			HARRISONVILLE			JEFFERSON CITY			JOPLIN		
DIVISION		652			636			634			647			650 - 651			648		
		MAT.	INST.	TOTAL	MAT.	INST.	TOTAL	MAT.	INST.	TOTAL	MAT.	INST.	TOTAL	MAT.	INST.	TOTAL	MAT.	INST.	TOTAL
015433	CONTRACTOR EQUIPMENT		105.5	105.5		103.2	103.2		103.2	103.2		97.8	97.8		112.0	112.0		100.8	100.8
0241, 31 - 34	SITE & INFRASTRUCTURE, DEMOLITION	88.2	90.1	89.4	85.6	85.3	85.4	81.7	85.4	84.1	91.2	85.0	87.1	89.0	101.2	97.0	102.7	88.4	93.4
0310	Concrete Forming & Accessories	84.6	83.3	83.6	104.1	80.0	85.4	94.9	75.0	79.4	83.6	89.8	88.4	101.5	80.3	85.0	98.7	71.4	77.5
0320	Concrete Reinforcing	94.9	99.7	96.2	104.2	92.3	100.9	102.3	86.6	98.0	101.3	99.5	100.8	99.1	96.4	98.4	104.9	96.6	102.6
0330	Cast-in-Place Concrete	78.2	83.4	80.1	82.1	82.6	82.3	75.3	85.3	78.8	95.6	90.8	93.9	83.0	86.2	84.2	101.1	71.4	90.6
03	CONCRETE	80.7	87.9	83.6	92.7	84.8	89.6	87.0	82.5	85.2	92.9	92.8	92.9	88.3	86.7	87.7	96.8	77.0	89.0
04	MASONRY	126.2	86.8	102.3	104.2	68.8	82.7	98.4	85.2	90.4	95.8	89.6	92.0	88.3	87.0	87.5	95.2	79.2	85.5
05	METALS	97.2	117.9	101.3	85.7	112.4	90.9	85.8	110.9	90.7	81.6	108.9	87.0	97.2	113.3	100.3	83.6	103.2	87.5
06	WOOD, PLASTICS & COMPOSITES	76.4	81.5	78.7	105.8	81.3	94.8	93.0	73.7	84.3	80.7	89.5	84.7	99.0	77.2	89.2	98.5	70.7	86.0
07	THERMAL & MOISTURE PROTECTION	95.3	85.3	91.7	101.6	81.6	94.5	101.2	83.8	95.0	98.8	90.3	95.8	100.6	86.7	95.6	98.8	76.8	91.0
08	OPENINGS	97.9	85.1	95.0	93.1	88.3	92.0	93.1	75.9	89.2	85.5	93.5	87.3	97.6	81.9	94.1	86.5	73.8	83.6
0920	Plaster & Gypsum Board	75.0	81.3	79.0	85.7	81.2	82.9	78.9	73.4	75.4	72.4	89.4	83.2	84.2	76.4	79.3	80.9	69.9	73.9
0950, 0980	Ceilings & Acoustic Treatment	88.6	81.3	84.5	90.5	81.2	85.3	90.5	73.4	80.9	87.9	89.4	88.7	95.4	76.4	84.8	89.2	69.9	78.4
0960	Flooring	96.5	99.0	97.2	103.3	75.7	96.4	99.8	86.8	96.5	99.1	90.2	96.9	100.4	96.1	99.3	133.8	67.1	117.1
0970, 0990	Wall Finishes & Painting/Coating	98.3	81.1	88.1	95.0	63.7	76.4	95.0	83.6	88.2	97.5	95.8	96.5	99.1	81.1	88.4	92.7	67.4	77.6
09	FINISHES	87.8	85.4	86.6	95.7	76.8	86.2	93.5	77.0	85.2	92.6	90.3	91.4	95.4	82.3	88.8	103.6	70.2	86.8
COVERS	DIVS. 10 - 14, 25, 28, 41, 43, 44, 46	100.0	94.7	99.0	100.0	89.2	97.9	100.0	93.3	98.7	100.0	96.5	99.3	100.0	96.6	99.3	100.0	92.2	98.5
21, 22, 23	FIRE SUPPRESSION, PLUMBING & HVAC	99.9	94.2	97.8	92.4	87.0	90.4	92.4	87.8	90.7	92.5	90.6	91.8	99.9	97.8	99.2	100.1	66.0	87.8
26, 27, 3370	ELECTRICAL, COMMUNICATIONS & UTIL.	92.9	80.9	87.7	97.9	87.7	93.4	94.9	68.4	83.4	97.0	90.1	94.0	97.9	80.9	90.5	92.5	69.1	82.4
MF2018	WEIGHTED AVERAGE	95.6	90.7	93.8	93.1	85.8	90.4	91.5	84.0	88.8	90.8	92.2	91.3	96.5	91.3	94.6	94.2	76.5	87.7

		MISSOURI																	
		KANSAS CITY			KIRKSVILLE			POPLAR BLUFF			ROLLA			SEDALIA			SIKESTON		
DIVISION		640 - 641			635			639			654 - 655			653			638		
		MAT.	INST.	TOTAL	MAT.	INST.	TOTAL	MAT.	INST.	TOTAL	MAT.	INST.	TOTAL	MAT.	INST.	TOTAL	MAT.	INST.	TOTAL
015433	CONTRACTOR EQUIPMENT		103.4	103.4		94.5	94.5		96.5	96.5		105.5	105.5		96.7	96.7		96.5	96.5
0241, 31 - 34	SITE & INFRASTRUCTURE, DEMOLITION	96.1	97.8	97.2	83.4	81.0	81.8	73.4	84.2	80.5	84.0	89.5	87.6	83.2	84.7	84.2	76.1	84.8	81.8
0310	Concrete Forming & Accessories	99.0	101.5	100.9	86.7	71.2	74.7	86.9	71.9	75.3	93.3	92.2	92.4	91.4	71.0	75.5	87.7	71.9	75.5
0320	Concrete Reinforcing	99.7	107.7	101.9	102.5	74.8	94.8	105.7	68.2	95.3	95.4	95.3	95.4	93.6	98.9	95.1	105.0	68.2	94.8
0330	Cast-in-Place Concrete	99.2	100.5	99.7	82.0	75.2	79.6	63.1	76.3	67.8	80.1	91.9	84.3	83.6	74.3	80.3	67.5	76.3	70.6
03	CONCRETE	96.6	102.6	99.0	100.4	74.7	90.2	82.4	74.2	79.2	82.5	94.1	87.1	91.4	78.4	86.3	85.1	74.2	80.8
04	MASONRY	101.4	98.6	99.7	110.3	76.4	89.7	102.3	66.7	80.7	102.6	83.4	90.9	108.4	73.5	87.2	102.0	66.7	80.6
05	METALS	97.0	109.7	99.5	86.2	96.1	88.2	86.7	93.0	87.9	96.5	115.4	100.2	97.5	106.6	99.3	87.6	93.0	88.6
06	WOOD, PLASTICS & COMPOSITES	96.7	102.0	99.0	79.2	69.5	74.8	77.9	72.6	75.5	86.2	94.0	89.7	81.0	69.7	75.9	79.9	72.6	76.6
07	THERMAL & MOISTURE PROTECTION	100.2	103.6	101.4	106.6	81.4	97.7	105.1	74.5	94.2	95.6	89.7	93.5	100.3	78.7	92.6	105.2	73.7	94.0
08	OPENINGS	100.6	101.5	100.8	98.1	71.5	92.1	99.0	68.2	92.0	97.9	90.7	96.2	103.8	78.8	98.2	99.0	68.2	92.0
0920	Plaster & Gypsum Board	82.0	102.0	94.7	73.0	69.1	70.5	73.6	72.3	72.8	76.4	94.2	87.7	71.8	69.1	70.1	76.0	72.3	73.7
0950, 0980	Ceilings & Acoustic Treatment	94.1	102.0	98.5	88.7	69.1	77.7	90.5	72.3	80.3	88.6	94.2	91.7	88.6	69.1	77.7	90.5	72.3	80.3
0960	Flooring	103.3	99.3	102.3	75.8	86.4	78.4	91.6	75.7	87.6	99.1	90.6	97.0	74.2	65.3	71.9	92.1	75.7	88.0
0970, 0990	Wall Finishes & Painting/Coating	99.1	109.2	105.1	90.6	69.6	78.1	89.9	59.6	71.8	98.3	87.2	91.7	98.3	91.7	94.4	89.9	59.6	71.8
09	FINISHES	96.5	102.0	99.3	89.9	73.2	81.5	91.6	70.7	81.1	88.8	91.3	90.1	84.7	71.3	78.0	92.2	71.0	81.6
COVERS	DIVS. 10 - 14, 25, 28, 41, 43, 44, 46	100.0	99.5	99.9	100.0	92.8	98.6	100.0	92.0	98.4	100.0	97.0	99.4	100.0	90.9	98.2	100.0	87.6	97.6
21, 22, 23	FIRE SUPPRESSION, PLUMBING & HVAC	99.8	101.3	100.4	92.4	87.3	90.6	92.4	85.3	89.9	92.3	95.5	93.5	92.3	85.3	89.8	92.4	85.3	89.9
26, 27, 3370	ELECTRICAL, COMMUNICATIONS & UTIL.	99.4	97.3	98.5	93.9	68.3	82.8	94.5	87.6	91.5	92.2	76.2	85.3	91.9	90.1	91.1	94.1	87.6	91.3
MF2018	WEIGHTED AVERAGE	98.6	101.2	99.6	93.8	79.5	88.5	91.4	80.1	87.2	93.1	91.8	92.6	94.8	83.5	90.7	92.0	80.0	87.6

		MISSOURI										MONTANA							
		SPRINGFIELD			ST. JOSEPH			ST. LOUIS			BILLINGS			BUTTE			GREAT FALLS		
DIVISION		656 - 658			644 - 645			630 - 631			590 - 591			597			594		
		MAT.	INST.	TOTAL	MAT.	INST.	TOTAL	MAT.	INST.	TOTAL	MAT.	INST.	TOTAL	MAT.	INST.	TOTAL	MAT.	INST.	TOTAL
015433	CONTRACTOR EQUIPMENT		98.8	98.8		97.8	97.8		107.6	107.6		94.4	94.4		94.2	94.2		94.2	94.2
0241, 31 - 34	SITE & INFRASTRUCTURE, DEMOLITION	88.1	88.8	88.6	97.8	83.6	88.5	93.6	99.1	97.2	85.5	89.4	88.0	88.0	88.6	88.4	91.0	88.9	89.6
0310	Concrete Forming & Accessories	100.5	77.4	82.6	97.5	89.9	91.6	101.4	102.6	102.4	100.9	68.0	75.4	86.2	65.3	69.9	101.0	65.4	73.4
0320	Concrete Reinforcing	90.9	99.3	93.3	98.3	102.4	99.4	100.1	103.8	101.1	91.0	80.3	88.1	98.9	79.6	93.6	91.2	80.0	88.1
0330	Cast-in-Place Concrete	85.0	76.5	82.0	93.9	95.0	94.3	88.9	103.6	94.1	126.3	71.2	106.7	139.1	67.2	113.5	147.0	68.9	119.2
03	CONCRETE	88.9	82.0	86.2	92.3	94.8	93.3	93.2	104.1	97.5	103.8	72.2	91.4	108.2	69.5	92.9	112.2	70.2	95.6
04	MASONRY	82.9	84.7	84.0	96.4	87.7	91.1	84.0	105.4	97.0	146.7	84.3	108.8	142.4	71.7	99.4	147.9	76.5	104.6
05	METALS	104.4	105.0	104.5	88.5	110.5	92.8	97.4	116.7	101.3	104.6	89.5	101.6	98.4	88.1	96.4	101.7	89.0	99.2
06	WOOD, PLASTICS & COMPOSITES	90.3	75.1	83.5	98.5	90.3	94.8	100.3	101.6	100.9	99.2	64.1	83.5	82.2	62.6	73.4	100.9	62.6	83.7
07	THERMAL & MOISTURE PROTECTION	99.0	77.9	91.5	99.2	87.8	95.1	101.1	103.3	101.9	101.8	72.9	91.5	101.5	65.6	88.7	102.1	68.5	90.1
08	OPENINGS	105.9	87.4	101.7	89.8	95.8	91.2	99.1	105.7	100.6	101.7	64.9	93.4	100.0	63.4	91.8	102.9	67.6	94.9
0920	Plaster & Gypsum Board	77.6	74.7	75.7	83.4	90.2	87.7	81.7	102.0	94.5	121.4	63.6	84.7	114.5	62.0	81.2	127.7	62.0	86.0
0950, 0980	Ceilings & Acoustic Treatment	88.6	74.7	80.8	96.9	90.2	93.2	87.2	102.0	95.5	108.1	63.6	83.2	111.4	62.0	83.7	113.7	62.0	84.7
0960	Flooring	96.0	73.4	90.3	108.7	93.7	104.9	102.0	96.8	100.7	95.5	77.5	91.0	94.9	74.6	89.8	99.9	72.3	93.0
0970, 0990	Wall Finishes & Painting/Coating	92.2	101.4	97.7	93.0	106.7	101.2	99.1	105.6	103.0	92.2	86.5	88.8	90.5	60.2	72.4	90.5	85.0	87.2
09	FINISHES	90.1	79.3	84.7	99.1	92.5	95.8	94.3	101.5	97.9	99.8	70.9	85.3	99.4	65.9	82.5	103.4	67.9	85.6
COVERS	DIVS. 10 - 14, 25, 28, 41, 43, 44, 46	100.0	94.1	98.8	100.0	96.1	99.2	100.0	101.3	100.3	100.0	94.4	98.9	100.0	93.3	98.7	100.0	93.0	98.7
21, 22, 23	FIRE SUPPRESSION, PLUMBING & HVAC	99.9	72.5	90.1	100.1	85.6	94.9	99.9	104.4	101.5	99.9	75.5	91.2	99.9	64.6	87.3	99.9	71.0	89.6
26, 27, 3370	ELECTRICAL, COMMUNICATIONS & UTIL.	94.2	67.8	82.8	97.1	74.0	87.1	99.2	102.8	100.8	95.1	72.9	85.5	98.3	65.2	83.9	94.6	67.8	83.0
MF2018	WEIGHTED AVERAGE	97.7	81.0	91.6	95.1	89.3	93.0	97.3	104.5	99.9	102.5	77.4	93.3	101.6	71.1	90.4	103.4	74.1	92.6

652

City Cost Indexes

MONTANA

DIVISION		HAVRE 595			HELENA 596			KALISPELL 599			MILES CITY 593			MISSOULA 598			WOLF POINT 592		
		MAT.	INST.	TOTAL	MAT.	INST.	TOTAL	MAT.	INST.	TOTAL	MAT.	INST.	TOTAL	MAT.	INST.	TOTAL	MAT.	INST.	TOTAL
015433	CONTRACTOR EQUIPMENT		94.2	94.2		101.0	101.0		94.2	94.2		94.2	94.2		94.2	94.2		94.2	94.2
0241, 31 - 34	SITE & INFRASTRUCTURE, DEMOLITION	89.4	88.0	88.5	83.2	99.3	93.7	77.5	88.2	84.5	81.8	88.1	85.9	75.8	88.2	83.9	93.0	88.1	89.8
0310	Concrete Forming & Accessories	78.2	63.8	67.0	103.5	65.0	73.6	90.0	64.8	70.4	99.0	64.0	71.8	90.0	65.2	70.7	90.5	64.0	69.9
0320	Concrete Reinforcing	99.7	80.3	94.3	101.3	80.2	95.4	101.5	81.9	96.1	99.1	80.4	93.9	100.6	81.7	95.3	100.5	80.4	95.0
0330	Cast-in-Place Concrete	149.8	65.2	119.7	107.1	68.5	93.4	120.7	66.3	101.4	132.2	65.3	108.4	102.4	66.9	89.8	148.1	64.3	118.3
03	CONCRETE	115.0	68.2	96.5	103.8	69.7	90.3	99.5	69.3	87.6	105.9	68.3	91.0	89.3	69.6	81.5	118.1	68.0	98.3
04	MASONRY	143.6	72.6	100.5	128.9	70.6	93.5	141.1	74.4	100.6	150.1	72.6	103.0	172.0	71.4	110.9	151.6	72.6	103.6
05	METALS	94.6	87.3	93.2	100.0	84.9	97.0	94.5	88.0	93.2	93.9	87.4	92.6	95.0	87.8	93.6	94.0	87.4	92.7
06	WOOD, PLASTICS & COMPOSITES	71.2	62.6	67.4	104.9	62.9	86.0	86.8	62.6	76.0	96.8	62.6	81.5	86.8	62.6	76.0	85.4	62.6	75.2
07	THERMAL & MOISTURE PROTECTION	101.7	59.9	86.8	103.0	66.7	90.1	101.2	66.5	88.8	101.5	61.1	87.1	100.9	67.6	89.0	102.2	61.0	87.5
08	OPENINGS	100.5	63.5	92.2	99.4	63.7	91.3	100.5	63.8	92.2	100.0	63.5	91.8	100.1	63.8	91.9	100.0	63.5	91.8
0920	Plaster & Gypsum Board	108.9	62.0	79.2	117.5	62.0	82.3	114.5	62.0	81.2	125.3	62.0	85.1	114.5	62.0	81.2	117.3	62.0	82.2
0950, 0980	Ceilings & Acoustic Treatment	111.4	62.0	83.7	115.4	62.0	85.5	111.4	62.0	83.7	106.0	62.0	81.3	111.4	62.0	83.7	106.0	62.0	81.3
0960	Flooring	93.3	81.4	90.3	106.4	74.6	98.4	96.3	81.4	92.5	99.9	81.4	95.2	96.3	74.6	90.8	97.2	81.4	93.3
0970, 0990	Wall Finishes & Painting/Coating	90.5	60.2	72.4	99.1	53.4	71.8	90.5	80.9	84.7	90.5	60.2	72.4	90.5	80.9	84.7	90.5	60.2	72.4
09	FINISHES	98.6	66.6	82.5	107.3	65.1	86.1	99.3	69.3	84.3	100.7	66.6	83.6	98.9	68.1	83.5	99.9	66.6	83.2
COVERS	DIVS. 10 - 14, 25, 28, 41, 43, 44, 46	100.0	79.7	96.1	100.0	87.1	97.5	100.0	80.3	96.2	100.0	79.7	96.1	100.0	86.7	97.4	100.0	79.7	96.1
21, 22, 23	FIRE SUPPRESSION, PLUMBING & HVAC	92.4	62.0	81.5	100.1	64.2	87.2	92.4	62.4	81.6	92.4	67.7	83.6	99.9	64.5	87.2	92.4	67.7	83.6
26, 27, 3370	ELECTRICAL, COMMUNICATIONS & UTIL.	94.6	61.6	80.3	101.2	65.5	85.7	96.7	60.6	81.1	94.6	66.3	82.3	97.2	63.9	82.8	94.6	66.3	82.3
MF2018	WEIGHTED AVERAGE	99.5	69.4	88.4	101.9	71.3	90.6	97.6	70.3	87.6	98.7	71.3	88.6	99.3	71.0	88.9	100.4	71.3	89.6

NEBRASKA

DIVISION		ALLIANCE 693			COLUMBUS 686			GRAND ISLAND 688			HASTINGS 689			LINCOLN 683 - 685			MCCOOK 690		
		MAT.	INST.	TOTAL	MAT.	INST.	TOTAL	MAT.	INST.	TOTAL	MAT.	INST.	TOTAL	MAT.	INST.	TOTAL	MAT.	INST.	TOTAL
015433	CONTRACTOR EQUIPMENT		92.1	92.1		98.1	98.1		98.1	98.1		98.1	98.1		104.1	104.1		98.1	98.1
0241, 31 - 34	SITE & INFRASTRUCTURE, DEMOLITION	92.5	90.8	91.4	91.9	85.8	87.9	98.8	86.7	90.9	94.5	85.8	88.8	91.0	97.0	94.9	91.4	85.8	87.8
0310	Concrete Forming & Accessories	89.6	50.3	59.1	101.0	68.1	75.4	100.5	77.8	82.9	104.5	65.8	74.5	100.3	70.2	76.9	95.3	50.8	60.7
0320	Concrete Reinforcing	110.9	78.4	101.9	100.5	77.1	94.0	99.9	78.4	94.0	99.9	68.3	91.2	98.6	78.7	93.1	106.2	68.5	95.8
0330	Cast-in-Place Concrete	97.4	74.7	89.4	97.8	74.7	89.6	103.5	73.1	92.7	103.5	67.8	90.8	81.9	79.3	81.0	105.3	67.7	91.9
03	CONCRETE	108.2	64.7	91.0	97.3	73.3	87.8	100.8	77.4	91.5	101.1	68.3	88.2	91.0	75.9	85.0	101.0	61.5	85.4
04	MASONRY	109.3	69.8	85.3	104.4	69.7	83.3	97.8	69.4	80.6	104.6	66.6	81.6	88.5	73.5	79.4	104.2	69.7	83.3
05	METALS	97.9	81.5	94.6	92.9	93.1	93.0	94.7	94.7	94.7	95.2	89.2	94.0	102.6	92.2	100.5	92.9	89.2	92.2
06	WOOD, PLASTICS & COMPOSITES	81.1	44.4	64.6	93.9	68.0	82.3	93.0	78.6	86.5	97.9	65.4	83.3	97.0	68.3	84.1	89.3	45.2	69.6
07	THERMAL & MOISTURE PROTECTION	105.6	68.0	92.2	105.5	72.1	93.6	105.7	75.7	95.0	105.7	69.6	92.9	101.1	75.3	91.9	101.9	68.2	89.9
08	OPENINGS	88.4	52.7	80.3	88.4	66.8	83.5	88.4	76.9	85.8	88.4	63.3	82.7	98.1	65.0	90.7	88.9	50.6	80.3
0920	Plaster & Gypsum Board	73.3	43.0	54.1	91.3	67.3	76.1	90.5	78.3	82.8	92.2	64.7	74.8	103.9	67.3	80.7	80.0	43.9	57.1
0950, 0980	Ceilings & Acoustic Treatment	92.0	43.0	64.6	88.8	67.3	76.8	88.8	78.3	82.9	88.8	64.7	75.3	115.4	67.3	88.5	89.8	43.9	64.1
0960	Flooring	97.2	78.2	92.4	87.3	78.2	85.0	87.1	70.7	83.0	88.1	72.8	84.2	100.1	77.5	94.4	93.8	78.2	89.9
0970, 0990	Wall Finishes & Painting/Coating	158.6	45.9	91.4	74.2	53.4	61.8	74.2	73.3	73.6	74.2	53.4	61.8	99.1	70.5	82.0	87.9	40.0	59.3
09	FINISHES	93.3	53.5	73.3	87.9	68.2	78.0	87.9	76.0	81.9	88.5	65.6	77.0	104.1	71.1	87.5	90.1	53.3	71.6
COVERS	DIVS. 10 - 14, 25, 28, 41, 43, 44, 46	100.0	84.2	96.9	100.0	86.9	97.5	100.0	89.3	97.9	100.0	86.6	97.4	100.0	88.9	97.8	100.0	84.4	97.0
21, 22, 23	FIRE SUPPRESSION, PLUMBING & HVAC	93.8	67.4	84.3	92.6	67.7	83.7	100.2	77.9	92.2	92.6	67.0	83.5	99.9	78.0	92.1	92.4	67.6	83.5
26, 27, 3370	ELECTRICAL, COMMUNICATIONS & UTIL.	90.2	58.4	76.4	91.3	72.5	83.1	90.6	61.1	77.8	90.3	70.7	81.8	99.7	61.1	82.9	91.2	58.5	77.0
MF2018	WEIGHTED AVERAGE	96.8	67.0	85.9	93.8	73.9	86.5	96.1	76.9	89.0	94.8	71.5	86.2	98.9	76.4	90.6	94.2	66.9	84.2

NEBRASKA / NEVADA

DIVISION		NORFOLK 687			NORTH PLATTE 691			OMAHA 680 - 681			VALENTINE 692			CARSON CITY 897			ELKO 898		
		MAT.	INST.	TOTAL	MAT.	INST.	TOTAL	MAT.	INST.	TOTAL	MAT.	INST.	TOTAL	MAT.	INST.	TOTAL	MAT.	INST.	TOTAL
015433	CONTRACTOR EQUIPMENT		88.9	88.9		98.1	98.1		96.2	96.2		91.9	91.9		98.2	98.2		93.2	93.2
0241, 31 - 34	SITE & INFRASTRUCTURE, DEMOLITION	76.6	85.0	82.1	95.8	85.7	89.2	86.7	97.1	93.5	79.4	89.9	86.3	85.6	97.0	93.1	71.1	87.5	81.8
0310	Concrete Forming & Accessories	86.4	67.2	71.5	98.3	69.0	75.6	101.0	76.5	82.0	86.1	48.6	56.9	102.0	79.6	84.6	105.8	87.0	91.2
0320	Concrete Reinforcing	100.6	59.7	89.3	105.7	73.3	96.7	100.0	79.1	94.2	106.3	59.6	93.3	101.9	110.9	104.4	102.9	85.0	97.9
0330	Cast-in-Place Concrete	98.4	65.2	86.6	105.3	63.1	90.3	80.9	81.8	81.2	92.9	50.0	77.7	88.8	80.8	86.0	83.2	66.5	77.3
03	CONCRETE	95.7	66.0	84.0	101.1	69.0	88.4	91.0	79.2	86.3	98.1	52.3	80.0	102.0	85.5	95.5	93.1	79.6	87.8
04	MASONRY	109.2	69.7	85.2	93.3	69.2	78.7	89.5	80.5	84.0	104.3	69.2	83.0	131.3	63.2	89.9	141.6	61.0	92.6
05	METALS	96.2	77.0	92.4	92.5	91.4	92.2	103.1	85.1	99.5	103.5	76.4	98.2	103.3	92.4	101.2	107.5	83.7	102.8
06	WOOD, PLASTICS & COMPOSITES	78.2	67.6	73.4	92.1	69.8	82.1	98.6	76.1	88.5	77.1	43.2	61.9	102.1	80.4	92.4	114.4	92.8	104.7
07	THERMAL & MOISTURE PROTECTION	104.4	70.2	92.2	101.8	71.9	91.1	104.0	81.8	96.1	101.3	66.3	88.9	97.6	77.7	90.5	94.2	66.1	84.2
08	OPENINGS	89.1	62.2	83.1	88.3	70.0	84.2	98.1	77.5	93.5	89.8	48.5	80.4	97.8	78.8	93.5	98.5	80.1	94.3
0920	Plaster & Gypsum Board	92.0	67.3	76.3	80.0	69.2	73.2	99.2	75.8	84.3	82.7	42.2	57.0	117.4	79.8	93.6	129.8	92.8	106.4
0950, 0980	Ceilings & Acoustic Treatment	102.0	67.3	82.6	89.8	69.2	78.3	103.3	75.8	87.9	105.0	42.2	69.8	108.8	79.8	92.5	103.7	92.8	97.6
0960	Flooring	113.5	78.2	104.6	94.7	70.7	88.7	100.1	90.0	97.5	124.7	78.2	113.1	101.0	60.1	90.7	98.5	60.1	88.9
0970, 0990	Wall Finishes & Painting/Coating	133.8	53.4	85.8	87.9	69.1	76.7	99.1	58.6	74.9	157.4	54.2	95.9	99.1	79.4	87.4	94.5	70.5	80.2
09	FINISHES	106.5	67.8	87.1	90.4	69.3	79.8	99.9	76.9	88.3	111.7	53.5	82.5	103.9	75.6	89.7	100.6	81.6	91.0
COVERS	DIVS. 10 - 14, 25, 28, 41, 43, 44, 46	100.0	86.0	97.3	100.0	86.9	97.5	100.0	89.0	97.9	100.0	83.1	96.7	100.0	99.8	100.0	100.0	81.3	96.4
21, 22, 23	FIRE SUPPRESSION, PLUMBING & HVAC	92.2	66.8	83.1	99.9	69.6	89.0	99.9	76.9	91.6	91.8	66.1	82.6	100.1	76.8	91.7	96.1	69.0	86.4
26, 27, 3370	ELECTRICAL, COMMUNICATIONS & UTIL.	90.6	72.4	82.7	90.4	61.1	77.7	99.5	82.6	92.2	88.7	58.5	75.6	99.9	85.1	93.5	95.8	78.6	88.3
MF2018	WEIGHTED AVERAGE	95.2	70.8	86.2	95.4	72.1	86.8	98.7	81.2	92.3	97.0	64.2	85.0	101.9	81.5	94.4	100.3	76.4	91.5

City Cost Indexes

DIVISION		NEVADA									NEW HAMPSHIRE								
		ELY			LAS VEGAS			RENO			CHARLESTON			CLAREMONT			CONCORD		
		893			889 - 891			894 - 895			036			037			032 - 033		
		MAT.	INST.	TOTAL	MAT.	INST.	TOTAL	MAT.	INST.	TOTAL	MAT.	INST.	TOTAL	MAT.	INST.	TOTAL	MAT.	INST.	TOTAL
015433	**CONTRACTOR EQUIPMENT**		93.2	93.2		93.2	93.2		93.2	93.2		93.0	93.0		93.0	93.0		97.1	97.1
0241, 31 - 34	**SITE & INFRASTRUCTURE, DEMOLITION**	76.1	88.5	84.2	80.5	92.9	88.6	77.8	89.2	85.2	77.0	91.2	86.2	72.6	91.2	84.7	88.1	101.3	96.7
0310	Concrete Forming & Accessories	97.4	91.7	93.0	98.7	108.4	106.2	94.0	79.6	82.8	89.0	78.1	80.5	96.1	78.1	82.1	104.6	91.5	94.4
0320	Concrete Reinforcing	101.7	85.2	97.1	94.1	125.2	102.7	96.2	123.1	103.6	84.5	86.6	85.1	84.5	86.6	85.1	97.6	87.1	94.7
0330	Cast-in-Place Concrete	89.3	86.8	88.4	86.5	109.4	94.6	94.5	78.6	88.8	70.4	105.6	82.9	64.7	105.6	79.2	85.7	113.3	95.5
03	**CONCRETE**	99.2	88.9	95.1	94.5	111.2	101.1	97.9	86.9	93.6	85.5	89.6	87.1	80.1	89.6	83.8	97.9	98.3	98.1
04	**MASONRY**	147.1	67.4	98.7	130.9	107.0	116.4	139.9	63.1	93.2	99.2	89.6	93.4	100.5	89.6	93.9	111.2	100.2	104.5
05	**METALS**	107.4	86.4	103.3	116.7	106.7	114.7	109.3	98.4	107.1	91.3	90.8	91.2	91.3	90.8	91.2	98.6	90.2	96.9
06	**WOOD, PLASTICS & COMPOSITES**	101.1	94.7	98.3	99.7	105.6	102.3	94.0	80.2	87.8	87.5	75.7	82.2	96.2	75.7	87.0	102.6	90.2	97.0
07	**THERMAL & MOISTURE PROTECTION**	94.5	82.7	90.3	103.5	102.2	103.1	94.1	75.4	87.4	94.9	96.8	95.6	94.8	96.8	95.5	97.8	107.1	101.1
08	**OPENINGS**	98.4	81.2	94.5	97.5	112.1	100.8	96.4	81.4	93.0	97.7	76.8	93.0	98.7	76.8	93.8	97.9	88.0	95.7
0920	Plaster & Gypsum Board	122.6	94.8	105.0	113.3	106.0	108.6	107.2	79.8	89.8	102.9	74.9	85.1	103.9	74.9	85.5	102.1	89.9	94.4
0950, 0980	Ceilings & Acoustic Treatment	103.7	94.8	98.7	111.8	106.0	108.5	107.7	79.8	92.1	88.2	74.9	80.7	88.2	74.9	80.7	82.7	89.9	86.8
0960	Flooring	96.9	60.1	87.7	88.7	104.7	92.7	94.8	60.1	86.1	95.8	101.3	97.2	98.0	101.3	98.8	103.1	105.4	103.7
0970, 0990	Wall Finishes & Painting/Coating	94.5	99.5	97.5	97.3	120.9	111.3	94.5	79.4	85.5	82.5	80.0	81.0	82.5	80.0	81.0	99.1	97.2	98.0
09	**FINISHES**	99.6	87.5	93.5	98.2	108.8	103.5	97.8	75.4	86.6	93.7	81.9	87.8	94.1	81.9	88.0	95.9	94.2	95.1
COVERS	**DIVS. 10 - 14, 25, 28, 41, 43, 44, 46**	100.0	63.4	92.9	100.0	106.1	101.2	100.0	99.3	99.9	100.0	79.4	96.0	100.0	79.4	96.0	100.0	106.3	101.2
21, 22, 23	**FIRE SUPPRESSION, PLUMBING & HVAC**	96.1	86.2	92.6	100.2	105.4	102.1	100.1	76.8	91.7	92.8	73.9	86.1	92.8	74.0	86.1	100.2	87.7	95.7
26, 27, 3370	**ELECTRICAL, COMMUNICATIONS & UTIL.**	96.1	82.8	90.3	101.9	107.8	104.5	96.1	85.1	91.3	101.0	67.0	86.3	101.0	67.0	86.3	101.6	74.7	90.0
MF2018	**WEIGHTED AVERAGE**	101.1	83.6	94.7	103.7	106.4	104.7	101.7	81.6	94.3	93.4	81.5	89.0	92.9	81.5	88.7	99.3	91.9	96.5

DIVISION		NEW HAMPSHIRE															NEW JERSEY		
		KEENE			LITTLETON			MANCHESTER			NASHUA			PORTSMOUTH			ATLANTIC CITY		
		034			035			031			030			038			082,084		
		MAT.	INST.	TOTAL	MAT.	INST.	TOTAL	MAT.	INST.	TOTAL	MAT.	INST.	TOTAL	MAT.	INST.	TOTAL	MAT.	INST.	TOTAL
015433	**CONTRACTOR EQUIPMENT**		93.0	93.0		93.0	93.0		97.4	97.4		93.0	93.0		93.0	93.0		90.8	90.8
0241, 31 - 34	**SITE & INFRASTRUCTURE, DEMOLITION**	82.4	91.2	88.1	72.8	90.3	84.2	85.6	101.3	95.8	87.6	92.0	90.5	82.2	92.6	89.0	87.6	95.5	92.7
0310	Concrete Forming & Accessories	94.4	78.3	81.9	108.4	72.8	80.8	104.6	91.9	94.8	104.2	91.7	94.5	90.7	90.3	90.4	115.4	140.6	135.0
0320	Concrete Reinforcing	84.5	86.6	85.1	85.2	86.6	85.6	99.5	87.2	96.1	105.5	87.1	100.4	84.5	87.1	85.2	76.5	134.6	92.6
0330	Cast-in-Place Concrete	70.7	105.7	83.1	63.5	97.8	75.7	80.8	115.6	93.2	67.0	114.4	83.8	63.5	113.5	81.3	65.4	132.9	89.4
03	**CONCRETE**	85.4	89.7	87.1	80.3	84.5	81.9	96.4	99.3	97.5	89.3	98.9	93.1	79.5	98.0	86.8	83.2	135.6	103.9
04	**MASONRY**	101.5	89.6	94.3	114.4	75.7	90.9	111.0	100.2	104.4	106.0	100.1	102.4	100.7	97.3	98.6	108.1	137.2	125.8
05	**METALS**	92.0	91.2	91.9	92.1	90.8	91.8	100.1	91.2	98.3	99.5	92.6	98.1	93.6	94.1	93.7	96.2	114.5	99.8
06	**WOOD, PLASTICS & COMPOSITES**	94.1	75.7	85.9	109.2	75.7	94.2	102.6	90.3	97.1	107.6	90.3	99.9	89.4	90.3	89.8	124.3	141.6	132.0
07	**THERMAL & MOISTURE PROTECTION**	95.5	96.9	96.0	95.0	90.6	93.4	100.6	107.3	103.0	95.9	105.8	99.4	95.3	101.5	97.5	99.9	132.8	111.6
08	**OPENINGS**	96.4	80.0	92.7	99.6	76.8	94.5	97.6	90.8	96.1	100.6	87.5	97.6	101.1	79.0	96.1	97.8	137.6	106.8
0920	Plaster & Gypsum Board	103.4	74.9	85.3	125.1	74.9	93.2	107.8	89.9	96.4	118.0	89.9	100.2	102.9	89.9	94.7	131.5	142.8	138.7
0950, 0980	Ceilings & Acoustic Treatment	88.2	74.9	80.7	88.2	74.9	80.7	100.9	89.9	94.7	101.5	89.9	95.0	88.8	89.9	89.4	102.3	142.8	125.0
0960	Flooring	97.7	101.3	98.6	107.3	101.3	105.8	103.1	110.7	105.0	101.0	103.3	101.6	96.0	103.3	97.8	104.3	152.0	116.3
0970, 0990	Wall Finishes & Painting/Coating	82.5	91.8	88.1	82.5	80.0	81.0	99.1	113.4	107.6	82.5	110.1	98.9	82.5	90.8	87.5	82.6	143.0	118.6
09	**FINISHES**	95.3	83.2	89.2	99.7	78.4	89.0	101.4	97.2	99.3	101.8	95.3	98.5	94.4	92.4	93.4	102.4	144.2	123.4
COVERS	**DIVS. 10 - 14, 25, 28, 41, 43, 44, 46**	100.0	84.9	97.1	100.0	85.7	97.2	100.0	106.5	101.3	100.0	106.5	101.3	100.0	105.5	101.1	100.0	114.9	102.9
21, 22, 23	**FIRE SUPPRESSION, PLUMBING & HVAC**	92.8	74.0	86.1	92.8	66.7	83.5	100.2	87.7	95.7	100.4	87.8	95.8	100.4	86.0	95.2	99.3	132.7	111.3
26, 27, 3370	**ELECTRICAL, COMMUNICATIONS & UTIL.**	101.0	67.0	86.3	101.5	43.8	76.5	101.6	76.6	90.8	102.2	76.6	91.1	101.2	71.7	88.4	93.1	134.1	110.9
MF2018	**WEIGHTED AVERAGE**	93.8	82.1	89.5	94.3	74.1	86.9	99.8	92.9	97.3	99.0	91.8	96.3	95.4	89.6	93.3	96.5	130.3	108.9

DIVISION		NEW JERSEY																	
		CAMDEN			DOVER			ELIZABETH			HACKENSACK			JERSEY CITY			LONG BRANCH		
		081			078			072			076			073			077		
		MAT.	INST.	TOTAL	MAT.	INST.	TOTAL	MAT.	INST.	TOTAL	MAT.	INST.	TOTAL	MAT.	INST.	TOTAL	MAT.	INST.	TOTAL
015433	**CONTRACTOR EQUIPMENT**		90.8	90.8		93.0	93.0		93.0	93.0		93.0	93.0		90.8	90.8		90.5	90.5
0241, 31 - 34	**SITE & INFRASTRUCTURE, DEMOLITION**	89.1	95.8	93.5	100.3	96.8	98.0	104.4	96.8	99.5	101.3	96.8	98.4	93.8	96.8	95.7	96.5	96.5	96.5
0310	Concrete Forming & Accessories	104.8	140.8	132.7	94.2	141.9	131.2	106.4	142.0	134.1	94.2	141.8	131.2	98.6	142.1	132.4	99.3	141.0	131.7
0320	Concrete Reinforcing	100.5	134.6	109.9	73.9	148.3	94.5	73.9	148.3	94.5	73.9	148.3	94.5	95.9	148.3	110.4	73.9	148.2	94.5
0330	Cast-in-Place Concrete	63.4	133.0	88.1	67.6	134.5	91.4	58.1	134.2	85.2	66.1	134.1	90.3	52.8	134.6	81.8	58.7	132.8	85.0
03	**CONCRETE**	86.9	135.6	106.2	80.9	139.2	103.9	79.4	139.1	103.0	79.7	139.0	103.1	80.9	139.1	103.8	80.5	138.0	103.2
04	**MASONRY**	97.2	137.2	121.5	95.2	139.0	121.8	111.7	139.0	128.3	99.3	139.0	123.4	89.1	139.0	119.4	104.2	137.2	124.2
05	**METALS**	104.0	114.6	106.1	94.2	122.6	99.8	95.7	122.7	101.0	94.3	122.5	99.9	102.1	120.0	105.6	94.3	119.6	99.3
06	**WOOD, PLASTICS & COMPOSITES**	109.1	141.6	123.7	91.2	141.6	113.8	108.0	141.6	123.0	91.2	141.6	113.8	92.4	141.6	114.5	93.6	141.6	115.1
07	**THERMAL & MOISTURE PROTECTION**	99.7	133.5	111.7	97.8	134.3	110.8	98.1	137.4	112.1	97.6	132.5	110.0	97.4	137.4	111.6	97.5	131.3	109.6
08	**OPENINGS**	99.6	137.6	108.2	100.4	139.3	109.2	98.8	139.3	107.9	98.1	139.3	107.4	96.4	139.3	106.1	92.9	139.3	103.4
0920	Plaster & Gypsum Board	128.0	142.8	137.4	119.7	142.8	134.4	129.6	142.8	138.0	119.7	142.8	134.4	126.0	142.8	136.7	122.2	142.8	135.3
0950, 0980	Ceilings & Acoustic Treatment	120.1	142.8	132.8	97.7	142.8	123.0	98.2	142.8	123.2	97.7	142.8	123.0	113.6	142.8	130.0	97.7	142.8	123.0
0960	Flooring	101.5	152.0	114.2	86.4	176.5	108.9	90.8	176.5	112.3	86.4	176.5	108.9	87.2	176.5	109.6	87.5	176.5	109.8
0970, 0990	Wall Finishes & Painting/Coating	82.6	143.0	118.6	81.8	140.9	117.0	81.8	140.9	117.0	81.8	140.9	117.0	81.9	140.9	117.1	81.9	143.0	118.3
09	**FINISHES**	105.8	144.2	125.1	95.7	148.2	122.1	99.0	148.8	124.0	95.6	148.2	122.0	100.9	148.9	125.0	96.6	148.4	122.6
COVERS	**DIVS. 10 - 14, 25, 28, 41, 43, 44, 46**	100.0	114.9	102.9	100.0	127.4	105.3	100.0	127.4	105.3	100.0	127.4	105.3	100.0	127.4	105.3	100.0	114.8	102.9
21, 22, 23	**FIRE SUPPRESSION, PLUMBING & HVAC**	99.9	132.9	111.7	99.3	134.8	112.0	99.9	133.9	112.1	99.3	134.8	112.0	99.9	134.9	112.4	99.3	132.8	111.3
26, 27, 3370	**ELECTRICAL, COMMUNICATIONS & UTIL.**	95.5	134.1	112.2	92.4	136.6	111.5	92.7	136.6	111.7	92.4	136.0	111.3	94.8	136.0	112.7	92.3	131.3	109.2
MF2018	**WEIGHTED AVERAGE**	98.9	130.4	110.5	94.9	133.7	109.1	96.2	133.6	110.0	94.7	133.5	109.0	96.6	133.5	110.2	94.5	131.4	108.1

City Cost Indexes

		NEW JERSEY																	
		NEW BRUNSWICK			NEWARK			PATERSON			POINT PLEASANT			SUMMIT			TRENTON		
DIVISION		088 - 089			070 - 071			074 - 075			087			079			085 - 086		
		MAT.	INST.	TOTAL	MAT.	INST.	TOTAL	MAT.	INST.	TOTAL	MAT.	INST.	TOTAL	MAT.	INST.	TOTAL	MAT.	INST.	TOTAL
015433	CONTRACTOR EQUIPMENT		90.5	90.5		98.0	98.0		93.0	93.0		90.5	90.5		93.0	93.0		96.1	96.1
0241, 31 - 34	SITE & INFRASTRUCTURE, DEMOLITION	97.4	96.7	96.9	107.4	104.5	105.5	103.4	96.8	99.1	98.5	96.1	96.9	102.2	96.8	98.7	88.5	105.5	99.6
0310	Concrete Forming & Accessories	108.5	142.0	134.5	99.0	142.3	132.7	96.2	142.0	131.7	101.8	126.7	121.1	96.9	141.8	131.8	103.6	140.9	132.5
0320	Concrete Reinforcing	77.4	148.3	97.0	99.7	148.3	113.1	95.9	148.3	110.4	77.4	147.6	96.8	73.9	148.3	94.5	100.0	134.7	109.6
0330	Cast-in-Place Concrete	80.8	133.9	99.7	76.5	136.3	97.7	67.2	134.2	91.0	80.8	123.7	96.1	56.2	134.1	83.9	77.4	133.9	97.5
03	CONCRETE	95.7	138.8	112.7	92.7	139.9	111.3	86.6	139.1	107.3	95.1	128.3	108.2	76.9	139.0	101.4	93.6	136.0	110.3
04	MASONRY	105.6	139.0	125.9	99.9	139.1	123.7	96.0	139.0	122.1	93.8	122.1	111.0	98.2	139.0	122.9	104.5	137.3	124.4
05	METALS	96.3	119.9	100.9	103.1	121.1	106.7	98.1	122.7	102.9	96.3	118.4	100.7	94.2	122.5	99.8	103.2	114.0	105.3
06	WOOD, PLASTICS & COMPOSITES	115.8	141.6	127.3	94.8	141.9	115.9	94.1	141.6	115.4	105.7	126.2	114.9	95.4	141.6	116.1	100.8	141.6	119.1
07	THERMAL & MOISTURE PROTECTION	100.1	136.6	113.1	100.4	138.9	114.1	97.9	132.5	110.2	100.1	121.6	107.8	98.1	137.4	112.1	101.2	134.8	113.2
08	OPENINGS	92.9	139.3	103.4	98.7	139.4	107.9	103.0	139.3	111.2	94.7	132.3	103.2	104.7	139.3	112.5	97.8	136.1	106.4
0920	Plaster & Gypsum Board	128.8	142.8	137.7	117.7	142.8	133.6	126.0	142.8	136.7	121.1	127.0	124.9	122.2	142.8	135.3	120.1	142.8	134.5
0950, 0980	Ceilings & Acoustic Treatment	102.3	142.8	125.0	114.0	142.8	130.2	113.6	142.8	130.0	102.3	127.0	116.1	97.7	142.8	123.0	113.5	142.8	130.0
0960	Flooring	102.6	176.5	121.6	104.1	176.5	122.7	87.2	176.5	109.6	100.6	152.0	113.5	87.5	176.5	109.8	106.4	176.5	124.0
0970, 0990	Wall Finishes & Painting/Coating	82.6	140.9	117.4	94.9	140.9	122.4	81.8	140.9	117.0	82.6	143.0	118.6	81.8	140.9	117.0	99.1	143.0	125.3
09	FINISHES	102.5	148.8	125.8	107.0	149.1	128.1	101.0	148.8	125.1	100.9	133.5	117.3	96.7	148.2	122.5	107.7	148.5	128.2
COVERS	DIVS. 10 - 14, 25, 28, 41, 43, 44, 46	100.0	127.3	105.3	100.0	128.1	105.4	100.0	127.4	105.3	100.0	99.5	99.9	100.0	127.4	105.3	100.0	114.9	102.9
21, 22, 23	FIRE SUPPRESSION, PLUMBING & HVAC	99.3	133.7	111.7	99.9	134.9	112.5	99.9	134.9	112.4	99.3	129.1	110.0	99.4	130.1	110.4	99.9	132.7	111.7
26, 27, 3370	ELECTRICAL, COMMUNICATIONS & UTIL.	93.5	134.1	111.1	100.3	136.0	115.8	94.8	136.6	112.9	93.1	131.3	109.7	92.7	136.6	111.7	100.2	126.7	111.7
MF2018	WEIGHTED AVERAGE	97.7	132.9	110.7	100.4	134.5	112.9	97.5	133.7	110.8	97.1	124.5	107.2	95.1	132.8	108.9	100.2	130.6	111.4

		NEW JERSEY			NEW MEXICO														
		VINELAND			ALBUQUERQUE			CARRIZOZO			CLOVIS			FARMINGTON			GALLUP		
DIVISION		080, 083			870 - 872			883			881			874			873		
		MAT.	INST.	TOTAL	MAT.	INST.	TOTAL	MAT.	INST.	TOTAL	MAT.	INST.	TOTAL	MAT.	INST.	TOTAL	MAT.	INST.	TOTAL
015433	CONTRACTOR EQUIPMENT		90.8	90.8		104.7	104.7		104.7	104.7		104.7	104.7		104.7	104.7		104.7	104.7
0241, 31 - 34	SITE & INFRASTRUCTURE, DEMOLITION	90.9	95.8	94.1	93.8	94.0	93.9	107.4	94.0	98.6	95.8	94.0	94.6	98.9	94.0	95.7	105.1	94.0	97.9
0310	Concrete Forming & Accessories	98.4	140.7	131.3	99.7	68.7	75.6	96.1	68.7	74.8	96.1	68.5	74.7	99.8	68.7	75.7	99.8	68.7	75.6
0320	Concrete Reinforcing	76.5	134.6	92.6	94.2	68.8	87.2	103.8	68.8	94.1	105.0	68.7	94.9	103.0	68.8	93.5	98.6	68.8	90.3
0330	Cast-in-Place Concrete	70.5	132.9	92.7	82.6	69.5	78.0	85.4	69.5	79.7	85.3	69.4	79.7	83.4	69.5	78.5	78.5	69.5	75.3
03	CONCRETE	85.9	135.6	105.5	90.2	70.3	82.4	107.9	70.3	93.0	99.2	70.2	87.7	94.3	70.3	84.8	98.2	70.3	87.2
04	MASONRY	96.1	137.2	121.1	101.6	60.1	76.4	109.6	60.1	79.6	109.7	60.1	79.6	107.1	60.1	78.6	99.0	60.1	75.4
05	METALS	96.1	114.5	99.8	105.8	91.0	102.9	101.2	91.0	99.2	100.8	90.9	98.9	102.5	91.0	100.2	101.6	91.0	99.6
06	WOOD, PLASTICS & COMPOSITES	101.4	141.6	119.4	102.2	70.0	87.8	95.6	70.0	84.1	95.6	70.0	84.1	102.4	70.0	87.9	102.4	70.0	87.9
07	THERMAL & MOISTURE PROTECTION	99.6	132.8	111.4	100.9	70.7	90.1	95.5	70.7	86.6	94.5	70.7	86.0	101.1	70.7	90.3	102.0	70.7	90.9
08	OPENINGS	94.3	137.6	104.0	97.9	67.8	91.1	91.6	67.8	86.3	91.8	67.8	86.4	100.2	67.8	92.9	100.2	67.8	92.9
0920	Plaster & Gypsum Board	118.5	142.8	133.9	99.4	69.1	80.2	88.0	69.1	76.0	88.0	69.1	76.0	90.1	69.1	76.8	90.1	69.1	76.8
0950, 0980	Ceilings & Acoustic Treatment	102.3	142.8	125.0	122.6	69.1	92.6	105.3	69.1	85.0	105.3	69.1	85.0	114.6	69.1	89.1	114.6	69.1	89.1
0960	Flooring	100.1	152.0	113.1	94.1	66.7	87.2	99.0	66.7	90.9	99.0	66.7	90.9	95.6	66.7	88.4	95.6	66.7	88.4
0970, 0990	Wall Finishes & Painting/Coating	82.6	143.0	118.6	94.1	51.0	68.4	92.2	51.0	67.6	92.2	51.0	67.6	88.2	51.0	66.0	88.2	51.0	66.0
09	FINISHES	99.7	144.2	122.1	101.6	66.5	83.9	98.9	66.5	82.6	97.8	66.5	82.1	98.6	66.5	82.4	99.7	66.5	83.0
COVERS	DIVS. 10 - 14, 25, 28, 41, 43, 44, 46	100.0	114.9	102.9	100.0	86.7	97.4	100.0	86.7	97.4	100.0	86.7	97.4	100.0	86.7	97.4	100.0	86.7	97.4
21, 22, 23	FIRE SUPPRESSION, PLUMBING & HVAC	99.3	132.7	111.3	100.3	67.8	88.6	95.4	67.8	85.5	95.4	67.5	85.4	100.2	67.8	88.6	95.5	67.8	85.6
26, 27, 3370	ELECTRICAL, COMMUNICATIONS & UTIL.	93.1	134.1	110.9	83.3	69.0	77.1	85.6	69.0	78.4	84.4	69.0	77.7	82.1	69.0	76.4	81.7	69.0	76.2
MF2018	WEIGHTED AVERAGE	95.7	130.4	108.5	98.2	72.3	88.7	98.3	72.3	88.7	96.6	72.2	87.6	98.2	72.3	88.6	97.4	72.3	88.1

		NEW MEXICO																	
		LAS CRUCES			LAS VEGAS			ROSWELL			SANTA FE			SOCORRO			TRUTH/CONSEQUENCES		
DIVISION		880			877			882			875			878			879		
		MAT.	INST.	TOTAL	MAT.	INST.	TOTAL	MAT.	INST.	TOTAL	MAT.	INST.	TOTAL	MAT.	INST.	TOTAL	MAT.	INST.	TOTAL
015433	CONTRACTOR EQUIPMENT		83.2	83.2		104.7	104.7		104.7	104.7		108.5	108.5		104.7	104.7		83.3	83.3
0241, 31 - 34	SITE & INFRASTRUCTURE, DEMOLITION	98.4	76.0	83.8	95.8	94.0	94.6	99.9	94.0	96.0	99.7	100.4	100.2	93.0	94.0	93.7	108.3	76.0	87.3
0310	Concrete Forming & Accessories	92.8	67.7	73.3	99.8	68.7	75.6	96.1	68.7	74.8	100.4	68.9	75.9	99.8	68.7	75.6	97.8	67.7	74.4
0320	Concrete Reinforcing	102.9	68.5	93.4	100.3	68.8	91.6	105.0	68.8	94.9	100.3	68.8	91.6	102.2	68.8	93.0	97.8	68.6	89.7
0330	Cast-in-Place Concrete	80.6	68.2	74.4	81.1	69.5	77.0	85.3	69.5	79.7	86.2	71.8	81.1	79.5	69.5	75.9	87.1	63.2	78.6
03	CONCRETE	82.7	67.3	76.6	92.0	70.3	83.4	99.8	70.3	88.2	97.0	71.0	86.8	91.5	70.3	83.1	86.3	67.3	78.8
04	MASONRY	105.0	57.8	76.3	99.3	60.1	75.5	121.0	60.1	84.0	95.8	60.3	74.2	99.2	60.1	75.5	95.4	59.9	73.8
05	METALS	99.1	83.9	96.1	101.3	91.0	99.3	102.1	91.0	99.9	100.0	88.5	97.7	101.7	91.0	99.6	100.6	84.1	97.3
06	WOOD, PLASTICS & COMPOSITES	86.3	69.1	78.6	102.4	70.0	87.9	95.6	70.0	84.1	98.7	70.3	85.9	102.4	70.0	87.9	95.6	69.1	83.7
07	THERMAL & MOISTURE PROTECTION	86.3	66.0	79.1	100.8	70.7	90.1	94.6	70.7	86.1	103.7	73.0	92.8	100.8	70.7	90.1	91.7	66.6	82.7
08	OPENINGS	87.2	67.3	82.7	97.0	67.8	90.4	91.6	67.8	86.2	98.4	67.9	91.5	96.8	67.8	90.3	90.1	67.3	84.9
0920	Plaster & Gypsum Board	86.8	69.1	75.6	90.1	69.1	76.8	88.0	69.1	76.0	95.3	69.1	78.7	90.1	69.1	76.8	93.1	69.1	77.9
0950, 0980	Ceilings & Acoustic Treatment	101.6	69.1	83.4	114.6	69.1	89.1	105.3	69.1	85.0	112.8	69.1	88.3	114.6	69.1	89.1	113.4	69.1	88.6
0960	Flooring	129.2	66.7	113.6	95.6	66.7	88.4	99.0	66.7	90.9	105.3	66.7	95.6	95.6	66.7	88.4	123.4	66.7	109.2
0970, 0990	Wall Finishes & Painting/Coating	80.6	51.0	62.9	88.2	51.0	66.0	92.2	51.0	67.6	99.1	51.0	70.4	88.2	51.0	66.0	80.6	51.0	62.9
09	FINISHES	109.2	65.6	87.3	98.4	66.5	82.4	97.9	66.5	82.1	104.0	66.6	85.2	98.4	66.5	82.3	111.8	65.8	88.7
COVERS	DIVS. 10 - 14, 25, 28, 41, 43, 44, 46	100.0	84.6	97.0	100.0	86.7	97.4	100.0	86.7	97.4	100.0	87.2	97.5	100.0	86.7	97.4	100.0	84.5	97.0
21, 22, 23	FIRE SUPPRESSION, PLUMBING & HVAC	100.7	67.6	88.8	95.5	67.8	85.6	100.0	67.8	88.5	100.1	67.9	88.6	95.5	67.8	85.6	94.4	67.6	84.8
26, 27, 3370	ELECTRICAL, COMMUNICATIONS & UTIL.	88.0	74.6	82.2	82.8	69.0	76.8	85.1	69.0	78.1	100.8	69.0	87.0	81.9	69.0	76.3	85.9	69.0	78.6
MF2018	WEIGHTED AVERAGE	95.8	70.0	86.3	96.0	72.3	87.3	98.6	72.3	88.9	99.8	72.8	89.9	95.9	72.3	87.2	95.5	69.4	85.9

City Cost Indexes

DIVISION		NEW MEXICO TUCUMCARI 884			NEW YORK ALBANY 120-122			NEW YORK BINGHAMTON 137-139			NEW YORK BRONX 104			NEW YORK BROOKLYN 112			NEW YORK BUFFALO 140-142		
		MAT.	INST.	TOTAL	MAT.	INST.	TOTAL	MAT.	INST.	TOTAL	MAT.	INST.	TOTAL	MAT.	INST.	TOTAL	MAT.	INST.	TOTAL
015433	CONTRACTOR EQUIPMENT		104.7	104.7		111.6	111.6		112.7	112.7		100.4	100.4		105.3	105.3		96.9	96.9
0241, 31-34	SITE & INFRASTRUCTURE, DEMOLITION	95.4	94.0	94.5	78.6	103.0	94.5	91.8	86.1	88.1	93.3	104.2	100.4	109.7	114.3	112.7	90.5	97.5	95.1
0310	Concrete Forming & Accessories	96.1	68.5	74.7	104.7	102.5	103.0	100.4	88.6	91.3	90.9	177.7	158.3	106.4	174.2	159.1	105.1	109.7	108.7
0320	Concrete Reinforcing	102.9	68.7	93.4	99.2	110.4	102.3	95.6	106.0	98.5	91.8	163.7	111.7	96.0	238.8	135.5	99.6	109.0	102.2
0330	Cast-in-Place Concrete	85.3	69.4	79.7	76.3	114.3	89.8	105.5	101.0	103.9	69.6	159.4	101.5	107.4	158.2	125.4	126.3	117.2	123.0
03	CONCRETE	98.3	70.2	87.2	92.9	108.9	99.2	95.4	98.2	96.5	76.7	168.4	112.9	104.1	178.3	133.4	121.3	111.9	117.6
04	MASONRY	121.0	60.1	84.0	115.4	115.2	115.3	109.4	99.5	103.4	86.5	181.9	144.5	121.5	181.9	158.2	117.1	119.3	118.5
05	METALS	100.8	90.9	98.9	99.2	120.3	103.4	91.3	131.6	99.2	83.8	164.7	99.8	97.4	173.2	112.4	97.0	103.8	98.3
06	WOOD, PLASTICS & COMPOSITES	95.6	70.0	84.1	103.2	98.4	101.0	103.5	85.3	95.3	103.1	175.8	135.7	107.7	170.5	135.8	102.6	108.0	105.0
07	THERMAL & MOISTURE PROTECTION	94.5	70.7	86.0	97.6	107.3	101.1	106.3	90.5	100.7	97.2	160.1	119.6	105.1	159.0	124.3	99.8	106.9	102.3
08	OPENINGS	91.6	67.8	86.2	97.9	100.6	98.5	91.0	91.2	91.0	94.7	184.5	115.0	88.7	186.7	110.8	100.1	104.5	101.1
0920	Plaster & Gypsum Board	88.0	69.1	76.0	104.0	98.2	100.3	122.7	84.8	98.7	98.7	178.2	149.1	115.9	173.0	152.1	111.6	108.2	109.5
0950, 0980	Ceilings & Acoustic Treatment	105.3	69.1	85.0	95.4	98.2	97.0	104.8	84.8	93.6	77.7	178.2	134.1	97.1	173.0	139.7	95.4	108.2	102.6
0960	Flooring	99.0	66.7	90.9	100.6	104.5	101.6	109.9	95.7	106.3	96.3	180.0	117.3	117.0	180.0	132.8	99.3	115.4	103.3
0970, 0990	Wall Finishes & Painting/Coating	92.2	51.0	67.6	99.1	98.7	98.9	87.1	96.3	92.6	100.0	161.9	136.9	113.0	161.9	142.2	99.1	108.7	104.8
09	FINISHES	97.8	66.5	82.0	98.4	101.8	100.1	101.9	89.9	95.8	93.2	177.0	135.3	111.5	173.9	142.8	98.7	111.0	104.9
COVERS	DIVS. 10-14, 25, 28, 41, 43, 44, 46	100.0	86.7	97.4	100.0	101.2	100.2	100.0	97.2	99.5	100.0	139.5	107.6	100.0	138.1	107.4	100.0	105.8	101.1
21, 22, 23	FIRE SUPPRESSION, PLUMBING & HVAC	95.4	67.5	85.4	100.2	107.1	102.7	100.9	95.5	98.9	100.2	169.2	124.9	99.8	169.4	124.7	100.2	98.5	99.6
26, 27, 3370	ELECTRICAL, COMMUNICATIONS & UTIL.	85.6	69.0	78.4	100.6	105.1	102.5	100.3	96.1	98.5	98.0	171.2	129.7	103.1	171.2	132.6	100.9	99.3	100.2
MF2018	WEIGHTED AVERAGE	97.0	72.2	87.9	98.8	107.5	102.0	97.5	97.8	97.6	91.8	165.6	119.0	101.4	168.1	126.0	102.4	105.4	103.5

DIVISION		NEW YORK ELMIRA 148-149			NEW YORK FAR ROCKAWAY 116			NEW YORK FLUSHING 113			NEW YORK GLENS FALLS 128			NEW YORK HICKSVILLE 115,117,118			NEW YORK JAMAICA 114		
		MAT.	INST.	TOTAL	MAT.	INST.	TOTAL	MAT.	INST.	TOTAL	MAT.	INST.	TOTAL	MAT.	INST.	TOTAL	MAT.	INST.	TOTAL
015433	CONTRACTOR EQUIPMENT		115.1	115.1		105.3	105.3		105.3	105.3		108.2	108.2		105.3	105.3		105.3	105.3
0241, 31-34	SITE & INFRASTRUCTURE, DEMOLITION	86.3	87.0	86.8	108.9	114.3	112.4	108.9	114.3	112.4	68.8	94.3	85.4	104.4	112.6	109.7	104.4	114.3	110.9
0310	Concrete Forming & Accessories	82.4	91.3	89.3	91.7	178.0	158.7	95.9	178.0	159.7	85.1	90.6	89.4	87.8	146.4	133.3	95.9	178.0	159.7
0320	Concrete Reinforcing	99.4	105.0	100.9	96.0	238.8	135.5	97.7	238.8	136.8	96.3	101.5	97.7	96.0	165.0	115.1	96.0	238.8	135.5
0330	Cast-in-Place Concrete	111.0	100.5	107.3	116.2	158.2	131.1	116.2	158.2	131.1	73.5	107.4	85.5	98.6	147.4	116.0	107.4	158.2	125.5
03	CONCRETE	104.1	99.2	102.2	108.6	180.0	136.8	109.4	180.0	137.3	81.7	99.8	88.8	96.8	149.3	117.5	103.2	180.0	133.5
04	MASONRY	109.4	100.2	103.8	124.6	181.9	159.4	118.0	181.9	156.8	120.5	107.8	112.8	114.5	164.6	144.9	124.0	181.9	159.2
05	METALS	90.7	133.4	99.1	97.5	173.2	112.4	97.5	173.2	112.4	93.3	118.0	98.1	98.9	143.0	107.6	97.5	173.2	112.4
06	WOOD, PLASTICS & COMPOSITES	76.2	89.3	82.0	87.0	175.6	126.7	93.0	175.6	130.0	84.4	87.2	85.7	82.7	143.7	110.1	93.0	175.6	130.0
07	THERMAL & MOISTURE PROTECTION	99.1	90.6	96.1	104.9	159.9	124.5	105.0	159.9	124.6	91.4	98.5	94.0	104.6	147.6	119.9	104.8	159.9	124.5
08	OPENINGS	93.6	93.1	93.5	87.5	189.5	110.5	87.5	189.5	110.5	92.0	89.7	91.5	87.8	153.9	102.7	87.5	189.5	110.5
0920	Plaster & Gypsum Board	107.7	89.1	95.9	97.1	178.2	148.6	101.5	178.2	150.2	86.5	87.0	86.8	96.6	145.4	127.6	101.5	178.2	150.2
0950, 0980	Ceilings & Acoustic Treatment	99.4	89.1	93.6	80.3	178.2	135.2	80.3	178.2	135.2	85.0	87.0	86.1	79.8	145.4	116.6	80.3	178.2	135.2
0960	Flooring	95.5	95.7	95.6	112.7	180.0	129.6	113.9	180.0	130.5	90.3	96.5	91.8	111.8	172.4	127.0	113.9	180.0	130.5
0970, 0990	Wall Finishes & Painting/Coating	94.3	86.9	89.9	113.0	161.9	142.2	113.0	161.9	142.2	89.8	101.7	96.9	113.0	161.9	142.2	113.0	161.9	142.2
09	FINISHES	96.1	91.1	93.6	103.6	176.8	140.4	104.5	176.8	140.8	88.8	92.1	90.5	102.4	152.4	127.5	104.2	176.8	140.7
COVERS	DIVS. 10-14, 25, 28, 41, 43, 44, 46	100.0	96.1	99.2	100.0	138.7	107.5	100.0	138.7	107.5	100.0	86.4	97.4	100.0	123.8	104.6	100.0	138.7	107.5
21, 22, 23	FIRE SUPPRESSION, PLUMBING & HVAC	92.8	91.3	92.3	92.0	169.4	119.7	92.0	169.4	119.7	92.7	101.0	95.7	99.8	149.6	117.7	92.0	169.4	119.7
26, 27, 3370	ELECTRICAL, COMMUNICATIONS & UTIL.	97.8	99.7	98.6	106.6	171.2	134.6	106.6	171.2	134.6	95.0	93.5	94.3	102.5	134.8	116.5	101.9	171.2	131.9
MF2018	WEIGHTED AVERAGE	95.6	98.2	96.5	99.8	169.0	125.3	99.8	169.0	125.3	92.3	99.2	94.9	99.4	145.1	116.2	98.6	169.0	124.5

DIVISION		NEW YORK JAMESTOWN 147			NEW YORK KINGSTON 124			NEW YORK LONG ISLAND CITY 111			NEW YORK MONTICELLO 127			NEW YORK MOUNT VERNON 105			NEW YORK NEW ROCHELLE 108		
		MAT.	INST.	TOTAL	MAT.	INST.	TOTAL	MAT.	INST.	TOTAL	MAT.	INST.	TOTAL	MAT.	INST.	TOTAL	MAT.	INST.	TOTAL
015433	CONTRACTOR EQUIPMENT		88.8	88.8		105.3	105.3		105.3	105.3		105.3	105.3		100.4	100.4		100.4	100.4
0241, 31-34	SITE & INFRASTRUCTURE, DEMOLITION	87.6	85.7	86.4	121.9	108.8	113.4	110.8	114.3	113.1	118.4	108.8	112.1	94.4	99.9	98.0	93.8	99.9	97.8
0310	Concrete Forming & Accessories	82.4	81.6	81.8	86.5	118.3	111.2	100.7	178.0	160.7	95.2	118.3	113.2	81.8	127.2	117.1	95.8	124.1	117.8
0320	Concrete Reinforcing	99.5	99.8	99.6	96.9	143.8	109.9	96.0	238.8	135.5	96.0	143.9	109.3	91.7	163.9	111.7	91.8	163.8	111.7
0330	Cast-in-Place Concrete	115.2	95.8	108.3	99.2	132.5	111.0	110.8	158.2	127.7	92.9	132.5	107.0	77.7	140.1	99.9	77.7	139.8	99.8
03	CONCRETE	107.1	90.1	100.3	98.4	127.6	109.9	105.9	180.0	135.2	94.7	127.6	107.7	82.1	138.9	104.5	82.4	137.4	104.1
04	MASONRY	118.6	94.2	103.8	139.4	139.9	139.7	118.3	181.9	156.9	132.2	139.9	136.9	91.9	146.7	125.2	91.9	146.7	125.2
05	METALS	88.7	97.0	90.3	99.5	127.7	105.0	97.4	173.2	112.4	99.4	127.9	105.0	83.6	163.0	99.2	83.9	162.3	99.3
06	WOOD, PLASTICS & COMPOSITES	74.9	78.2	76.4	86.0	112.4	97.8	100.4	175.6	134.1	96.2	112.4	103.5	93.0	120.0	105.1	111.1	116.6	113.6
07	THERMAL & MOISTURE PROTECTION	98.6	85.5	94.0	108.4	131.4	116.6	105.0	159.9	124.6	108.2	131.4	116.5	97.8	136.4	111.6	98.0	134.2	110.9
08	OPENINGS	93.4	84.3	91.4	94.6	131.8	103.0	87.5	189.5	110.5	90.7	131.8	100.0	94.7	157.7	108.9	94.8	155.8	108.6
0920	Plaster & Gypsum Board	92.5	77.7	83.1	85.0	113.1	102.8	108.5	178.2	152.7	85.7	113.1	103.1	92.7	120.7	110.4	110.1	117.1	114.6
0950, 0980	Ceilings & Acoustic Treatment	94.9	77.7	85.3	70.0	113.1	94.2	80.3	178.2	135.2	70.0	113.1	94.2	75.0	120.7	100.6	75.0	117.1	98.6
0960	Flooring	98.8	91.8	97.0	108.8	143.8	117.5	115.4	180.0	131.6	110.5	143.8	118.9	88.1	160.9	106.4	95.0	146.9	108.0
0970, 0990	Wall Finishes & Painting/Coating	96.0	89.4	92.1	117.2	116.3	116.6	113.0	161.9	142.2	117.2	109.6	112.7	98.3	161.9	136.2	98.3	161.9	136.2
09	FINISHES	94.0	83.5	88.7	99.3	122.0	110.7	105.7	176.8	141.4	99.7	121.2	110.5	89.8	135.6	112.8	94.0	130.8	112.5
COVERS	DIVS. 10-14, 25, 28, 41, 43, 44, 46	100.0	94.6	98.9	100.0	108.0	101.5	100.0	138.7	107.5	100.0	108.0	101.5	100.0	116.1	103.1	100.0	101.8	100.3
21, 22, 23	FIRE SUPPRESSION, PLUMBING & HVAC	92.6	84.1	89.6	92.4	120.9	102.7	99.8	169.4	124.7	92.4	124.8	104.0	92.5	142.2	110.3	92.5	141.9	110.2
26, 27, 3370	ELECTRICAL, COMMUNICATIONS & UTIL.	96.5	84.5	91.3	96.6	103.5	99.6	102.2	171.2	132.1	96.6	103.5	99.6	94.9	151.8	119.6	94.9	126.1	108.5
MF2018	WEIGHTED AVERAGE	95.5	87.5	92.6	99.3	121.3	107.4	100.8	169.0	125.9	98.3	122.0	107.0	90.3	140.7	108.9	90.9	135.5	107.3

City Cost Indexes

DIVISION		NEW YORK																	
		NEW YORK 100 - 102			NIAGARA FALLS 143			PLATTSBURGH 129			POUGHKEEPSIE 125 - 126			QUEENS 110			RIVERHEAD 119		
		MAT.	INST.	TOTAL	MAT.	INST.	TOTAL	MAT.	INST.	TOTAL	MAT.	INST.	TOTAL	MAT.	INST.	TOTAL	MAT.	INST.	TOTAL
015433	CONTRACTOR EQUIPMENT		102.4	102.4		88.8	88.8		92.0	92.0		105.3	105.3		105.3	105.3		105.3	105.3
0241, 31 - 34	SITE & INFRASTRUCTURE, DEMOLITION	101.6	107.8	105.6	89.1	86.6	87.5	101.5	91.7	95.1	119.3	108.0	111.9	106.7	114.3	111.7	105.0	112.6	110.0
0310	Concrete Forming & Accessories	99.4	177.9	160.4	82.4	102.4	97.9	91.9	82.7	84.7	86.5	151.7	137.1	88.0	178.0	157.9	92.9	147.0	135.0
0320	Concrete Reinforcing	100.8	165.3	118.7	98.1	100.5	98.8	99.2	100.5	99.6	96.9	144.0	109.9	97.7	238.8	136.8	97.9	230.0	134.4
0330	Cast-in-Place Concrete	80.6	161.7	109.4	119.2	112.7	116.9	89.8	91.6	90.4	96.1	122.9	105.6	102.0	158.2	122.0	100.3	147.8	117.2
03	CONCRETE	87.4	169.6	119.8	109.1	105.5	107.7	92.6	89.0	91.2	96.2	139.4	113.3	99.7	180.0	131.4	97.9	160.8	122.7
04	MASONRY	101.3	182.0	150.3	125.6	112.7	117.8	114.6	87.7	98.2	130.4	133.0	132.0	112.6	181.9	154.7	120.0	164.6	147.1
05	METALS	101.6	166.2	114.4	90.9	97.5	92.2	95.8	94.4	95.5	99.5	128.6	105.2	97.4	173.2	112.4	99.6	166.6	112.8
06	WOOD, PLASTICS & COMPOSITES	112.0	176.1	140.7	74.8	98.2	85.3	92.8	80.0	87.1	86.0	162.4	120.2	82.9	175.8	124.4	89.1	143.7	113.6
07	THERMAL & MOISTURE PROTECTION	101.5	162.6	123.2	98.7	98.6	98.7	104.6	87.1	98.4	108.3	132.6	117.0	104.6	159.9	124.3	106.0	149.0	121.3
08	OPENINGS	102.7	188.2	122.0	93.4	94.8	93.7	99.2	85.8	96.2	94.6	154.3	108.1	87.5	189.5	110.5	87.8	169.8	106.3
0920	Plaster & Gypsum Board	110.6	178.2	153.5	92.5	98.2	96.1	112.4	79.2	91.3	85.0	164.6	135.5	96.6	178.2	148.4	98.4	145.4	128.2
0950, 0980	Ceilings & Acoustic Treatment	101.5	178.2	144.5	94.9	98.2	96.8	97.7	79.2	87.3	70.0	164.6	123.1	80.3	178.2	135.2	80.7	145.4	117.0
0960	Flooring	96.5	177.3	116.8	98.8	100.4	99.2	116.5	94.1	110.9	108.8	142.1	117.1	111.8	180.0	128.9	112.7	172.4	127.7
0970, 0990	Wall Finishes & Painting/Coating	99.1	161.9	136.6	96.0	108.7	103.6	112.9	84.5	96.0	117.2	109.6	112.7	113.0	161.9	142.2	113.0	161.9	142.2
09	FINISHES	101.7	176.7	139.4	94.1	102.8	98.5	101.8	84.4	93.1	99.2	147.9	123.6	102.7	176.8	139.9	103.1	152.4	127.9
COVERS	DIVS. 10 - 14, 25, 28, 41, 43, 44, 46	100.0	139.6	107.7	100.0	101.7	100.3	100.0	82.8	96.7	100.0	117.9	103.5	100.0	138.7	107.5	100.0	123.8	104.6
21, 22, 23	FIRE SUPPRESSION, PLUMBING & HVAC	100.1	169.4	124.9	92.6	94.5	93.3	92.6	90.1	91.7	92.4	108.1	98.1	99.8	169.4	124.7	100.1	150.4	118.1
26, 27, 3370	ELECTRICAL, COMMUNICATIONS & UTIL.	101.2	176.5	133.8	95.8	88.0	92.4	88.8	81.7	85.7	96.6	107.9	101.5	102.5	171.2	132.2	103.3	135.0	117.1
MF2018	WEIGHTED AVERAGE	99.6	167.2	124.5	96.5	98.0	97.1	96.1	87.7	93.0	98.7	125.3	108.5	99.4	169.0	125.0	100.2	149.7	118.4

DIVISION		NEW YORK																	
		ROCHESTER 144 - 146			SCHENECTADY 123			STATEN ISLAND 103			SUFFERN 109			SYRACUSE 130 - 132			UTICA 133 - 135		
		MAT.	INST.	TOTAL	MAT.	INST.	TOTAL	MAT.	INST.	TOTAL	MAT.	INST.	TOTAL	MAT.	INST.	TOTAL	MAT.	INST.	TOTAL
015433	CONTRACTOR EQUIPMENT		111.6	111.6		108.2	108.2		100.4	100.4		100.4	100.4		108.2	108.2		108.2	108.2
0241, 31 - 34	SITE & INFRASTRUCTURE, DEMOLITION	83.7	100.0	94.3	80.1	95.9	90.4	101.3	104.2	103.2	91.6	97.6	95.5	90.6	94.8	93.4	74.0	94.5	87.4
0310	Concrete Forming & Accessories	101.1	96.3	97.4	105.1	102.3	102.9	81.2	174.1	153.4	89.5	127.3	118.9	99.7	90.8	92.8	100.4	89.9	92.2
0320	Concrete Reinforcing	99.6	105.1	101.1	95.3	110.4	99.4	91.8	194.2	120.1	91.8	136.3	104.1	96.6	106.2	99.2	96.6	105.1	98.9
0330	Cast-in-Place Concrete	106.6	104.2	105.7	88.7	112.2	97.1	77.7	159.4	106.8	75.4	125.7	93.3	97.9	105.0	100.4	89.5	104.8	94.9
03	CONCRETE	112.0	101.7	108.0	93.1	108.3	99.1	83.0	171.5	117.9	80.4	127.9	99.2	97.1	99.8	98.2	95.1	99.1	96.7
04	MASONRY	104.3	103.7	103.9	117.6	115.1	116.1	98.6	181.9	149.2	92.0	128.0	113.9	102.4	105.6	104.4	92.8	105.7	100.7
05	METALS	101.7	117.9	104.9	98.5	123.6	103.5	82.3	164.9	98.6	82.3	123.8	90.5	95.9	119.6	100.6	94.0	119.1	98.9
06	WOOD, PLASTICS & COMPOSITES	96.7	94.0	95.5	111.0	98.1	105.2	91.6	170.8	127.1	102.8	129.1	114.5	100.6	86.9	94.5	100.6	85.2	93.7
07	THERMAL & MOISTURE PROTECTION	98.6	98.8	98.6	92.9	105.6	97.4	97.4	159.6	119.6	97.8	127.7	108.5	101.4	96.2	99.6	92.3	96.2	93.7
08	OPENINGS	98.0	96.0	97.6	97.0	99.4	97.5	94.7	181.8	114.3	94.8	139.2	104.8	92.8	90.4	92.3	95.6	89.2	94.1
0920	Plaster & Gypsum Board	112.7	93.8	100.7	101.8	98.2	99.6	93.4	173.0	143.9	97.3	130.0	118.1	111.5	86.6	95.7	111.5	84.9	94.6
0950, 0980	Ceilings & Acoustic Treatment	95.4	93.8	94.5	97.2	98.2	97.8	77.7	173.0	131.1	75.0	130.0	105.8	104.8	86.6	94.6	104.8	84.9	93.6
0960	Flooring	103.1	103.0	103.1	95.7	104.5	97.9	92.2	180.0	114.2	91.3	153.7	106.9	96.1	95.4	95.9	93.6	95.5	94.1
0970, 0990	Wall Finishes & Painting/Coating	94.9	97.7	96.6	89.8	98.7	95.1	100.0	161.9	136.9	98.3	112.8	106.9	89.9	98.8	95.2	83.6	98.8	92.6
09	FINISHES	99.6	97.4	98.5	96.3	101.6	99.0	92.2	174.1	133.3	91.0	131.3	111.3	99.2	91.7	95.4	97.6	90.9	94.3
COVERS	DIVS. 10 - 14, 25, 28, 41, 43, 44, 46	100.0	101.4	100.3	100.0	100.7	100.1	100.0	138.8	107.5	100.0	102.1	100.4	100.0	98.0	99.6	100.0	94.3	98.9
21, 22, 23	FIRE SUPPRESSION, PLUMBING & HVAC	100.1	90.4	96.6	100.2	107.0	102.6	100.2	169.3	124.9	92.5	111.1	99.2	100.4	92.8	97.7	100.4	99.0	99.9
26, 27, 3370	ELECTRICAL, COMMUNICATIONS & UTIL.	100.6	92.3	97.0	97.3	105.1	100.7	98.0	171.2	129.7	98.5	102.0	100.0	100.0	102.5	101.1	96.9	102.5	99.3
MF2018	WEIGHTED AVERAGE	101.4	98.6	100.4	98.2	107.0	101.4	92.7	165.5	119.5	90.3	118.0	100.5	98.1	99.0	98.4	96.2	99.9	97.5

DIVISION		NEW YORK									NORTH CAROLINA								
		WATERTOWN 136			WHITE PLAINS 106			YONKERS 107			ASHEVILLE 287 - 288			CHARLOTTE 281 - 282			DURHAM 277		
		MAT.	INST.	TOTAL	MAT.	INST.	TOTAL	MAT.	INST.	TOTAL	MAT.	INST.	TOTAL	MAT.	INST.	TOTAL	MAT.	INST.	TOTAL
015433	CONTRACTOR EQUIPMENT		108.2	108.2		100.4	100.4		100.4	100.4		97.1	97.1		102.2	102.2		101.7	101.7
0241, 31 - 34	SITE & INFRASTRUCTURE, DEMOLITION	80.2	94.5	89.5	93.0	100.0	97.5	99.9	100.0	99.9	102.2	76.7	85.6	104.4	87.1	93.1	107.0	84.4	92.3
0310	Concrete Forming & Accessories	83.8	91.7	90.0	94.4	137.6	127.9	94.7	138.3	128.6	95.9	59.4	67.6	102.0	62.8	71.6	102.0	59.9	69.3
0320	Concrete Reinforcing	97.2	106.1	99.7	91.8	164.0	111.8	95.4	164.0	114.4	97.3	59.4	86.8	99.7	65.7	90.3	98.4	60.1	87.8
0330	Cast-in-Place Concrete	104.3	105.3	104.6	69.1	140.2	94.3	77.2	140.3	99.7	111.5	69.2	96.4	113.7	72.6	99.1	126.0	69.2	105.9
03	CONCRETE	104.7	100.3	103.0	76.7	143.7	103.1	83.1	144.1	107.1	92.8	64.6	81.7	95.2	68.2	84.5	101.0	64.9	86.7
04	MASONRY	94.2	106.8	101.8	91.6	146.7	125.1	95.2	146.7	126.5	79.6	61.3	68.5	81.3	63.6	70.5	82.6	61.3	69.7
05	METALS	94.0	119.3	99.0	83.8	163.4	99.5	93.7	163.7	107.5	99.7	87.7	97.3	101.0	87.3	98.3	115.1	88.0	109.7
06	WOOD, PLASTICS & COMPOSITES	78.4	87.6	82.5	108.8	133.5	119.9	108.7	134.2	120.1	96.9	57.4	79.2	98.8	60.8	81.7	101.5	57.9	82.0
07	THERMAL & MOISTURE PROTECTION	92.5	96.9	94.0	97.7	139.4	112.6	98.0	140.1	113.0	110.0	59.3	91.9	102.6	64.8	89.1	106.7	59.4	89.9
08	OPENINGS	95.6	92.3	94.8	94.8	165.2	110.7	98.0	165.6	113.2	88.7	56.3	81.4	98.7	61.4	90.3	96.7	56.8	87.7
0920	Plaster & Gypsum Board	98.5	87.4	91.4	102.2	134.6	122.7	111.0	135.3	126.4	107.8	56.1	75.0	102.3	59.5	75.1	102.8	56.7	73.6
0950, 0980	Ceilings & Acoustic Treatment	104.8	87.4	95.0	75.0	134.6	108.4	104.0	135.3	121.6	102.0	56.1	76.3	104.1	59.5	79.1	91.7	56.7	72.1
0960	Flooring	88.1	94.6	89.7	93.5	172.4	113.2	92.9	180.0	114.7	100.0	59.8	89.9	103.4	65.5	93.9	111.4	59.8	98.5
0970, 0990	Wall Finishes & Painting/Coating	83.6	96.7	91.4	98.3	161.9	136.2	98.3	161.9	136.2	103.1	50.7	71.9	99.1	64.4	78.4	102.8	50.7	71.8
09	FINISHES	94.7	92.2	93.4	91.9	146.0	119.1	101.3	147.9	124.7	102.0	58.2	80.0	102.8	63.1	82.8	100.7	58.5	79.5
COVERS	DIVS. 10 - 14, 25, 28, 41, 43, 44, 46	100.0	98.6	99.7	100.0	120.1	103.9	100.0	128.5	105.5	100.0	84.0	96.9	100.0	85.1	97.1	100.0	84.0	96.9
21, 22, 23	FIRE SUPPRESSION, PLUMBING & HVAC	100.4	87.0	95.6	100.3	142.4	115.4	100.3	142.5	115.4	100.9	60.2	86.3	100.1	62.7	86.7	101.0	60.2	86.4
26, 27, 3370	ELECTRICAL, COMMUNICATIONS & UTIL.	100.0	87.3	94.5	94.9	153.7	120.4	98.6	158.9	124.7	99.8	51.5	78.9	100.6	81.2	92.2	94.4	51.1	75.6
MF2018	WEIGHTED AVERAGE	97.5	95.9	96.9	91.7	143.7	110.8	96.3	145.1	114.2	98.0	63.8	85.4	99.3	71.1	88.9	102.5	64.5	88.5

City Cost Indexes

		NORTH CAROLINA																	
	DIVISION	ELIZABETH CITY			FAYETTEVILLE			GASTONIA			GREENSBORO			HICKORY			KINSTON		
		279			283			280			270,272 - 274			286			285		
		MAT.	INST.	TOTAL	MAT.	INST.	TOTAL	MAT.	INST.	TOTAL	MAT.	INST.	TOTAL	MAT.	INST.	TOTAL	MAT.	INST.	TOTAL
015433	CONTRACTOR EQUIPMENT		105.2	105.2		101.7	101.7		97.1	97.1		101.7	101.7		101.7	101.7		101.7	101.7
0241, 31 - 34	SITE & INFRASTRUCTURE, DEMOLITION	107.8	85.6	93.3	101.6	84.1	90.2	102.1	76.7	85.5	106.9	84.4	92.2	98.0	84.1	89.0	96.8	84.1	88.5
0310	Concrete Forming & Accessories	85.3	58.2	64.2	95.4	58.1	66.5	103.1	60.1	69.7	101.7	59.9	69.2	91.4	59.9	67.0	87.2	58.1	64.6
0320	Concrete Reinforcing	96.8	62.8	87.4	100.6	60.1	89.4	97.7	60.1	87.3	97.7	60.1	87.3	97.3	60.1	87.0	96.8	60.1	86.6
0330	Cast-in-Place Concrete	126.3	68.8	105.8	116.9	66.7	99.0	108.9	69.3	94.9	125.1	69.2	105.2	111.4	69.0	96.4	107.6	66.7	93.0
03	CONCRETE	99.8	64.5	85.9	95.4	63.3	82.7	92.1	65.1	81.5	100.4	64.9	86.4	92.4	64.9	81.5	89.9	63.3	79.4
04	MASONRY	92.9	56.7	70.9	83.7	56.8	67.3	84.8	61.3	70.6	81.9	61.3	69.4	70.1	61.2	64.7	76.0	56.8	64.3
05	METALS	100.7	89.9	98.6	118.8	88.0	112.7	100.6	88.2	98.2	106.3	88.0	102.7	99.8	87.4	97.3	98.7	88.0	96.6
06	WOOD, PLASTICS & COMPOSITES	79.9	57.7	70.0	95.1	57.9	78.5	107.3	57.9	85.2	101.2	57.9	81.8	89.7	57.9	75.4	85.2	57.9	73.0
07	THERMAL & MOISTURE PROTECTION	105.6	57.1	88.3	109.3	57.3	90.7	110.2	59.4	92.1	106.2	59.4	89.5	110.2	59.4	92.1	110.1	57.3	91.3
08	OPENINGS	94.0	57.2	85.7	88.8	56.8	81.6	91.9	56.8	84.0	96.7	56.8	87.7	88.8	56.8	81.6	88.9	56.8	81.6
0920	Plaster & Gypsum Board	94.2	55.9	69.9	111.5	56.7	76.7	116.4	56.7	78.5	103.4	56.7	73.8	107.8	56.7	75.4	108.4	56.7	75.6
0950, 0980	Ceilings & Acoustic Treatment	91.7	55.9	71.6	106.5	56.7	78.6	110.2	56.7	80.2	91.7	56.7	72.1	102.0	56.7	76.6	110.2	56.7	80.2
0960	Flooring	104.4	59.8	93.2	100.1	59.8	90.0	102.8	59.8	92.0	111.4	59.8	98.5	99.9	59.8	89.9	97.4	59.8	88.0
0970, 0990	Wall Finishes & Painting/Coating	102.8	50.7	71.8	103.1	50.7	71.9	103.1	50.7	71.9	102.8	50.7	71.8	103.1	50.7	71.9	103.1	50.7	71.9
09	FINISHES	97.8	57.3	77.5	103.7	57.4	80.4	106.1	58.5	82.2	100.8	58.5	79.6	102.1	58.5	80.2	103.5	57.4	80.3
COVERS	DIVS. 10 - 14, 25, 28, 41, 43, 44, 46	100.0	83.9	96.9	100.0	82.5	96.6	100.0	84.2	96.9	100.0	84.0	96.9	100.0	84.2	96.9	100.0	82.5	96.6
21, 22, 23	FIRE SUPPRESSION, PLUMBING & HVAC	93.3	58.0	80.7	100.7	57.8	85.3	100.9	60.2	86.3	100.8	60.2	86.3	93.4	60.2	81.5	93.4	57.8	80.6
26, 27, 3370	ELECTRICAL, COMMUNICATIONS & UTIL.	93.7	61.6	79.8	102.1	51.1	80.0	99.5	81.5	91.7	93.7	51.5	75.4	98.6	81.5	91.2	98.5	49.7	77.4
MF2018	WEIGHTED AVERAGE	97.2	65.0	85.4	102.9	63.0	88.2	98.9	68.2	87.6	100.4	64.5	87.2	95.7	68.2	85.7	95.4	62.8	83.4

		NORTH CAROLINA																NORTH DAKOTA		
	DIVISION	MURPHY			RALEIGH			ROCKY MOUNT			WILMINGTON			WINSTON-SALEM			BISMARCK		
		289			275 - 276			278			284			271			585		
		MAT.	INST.	TOTAL	MAT.	INST.	TOTAL	MAT.	INST.	TOTAL	MAT.	INST.	TOTAL	MAT.	INST.	TOTAL	MAT.	INST.	TOTAL
015433	CONTRACTOR EQUIPMENT		97.1	97.1		107.8	107.8		101.7	101.7		97.1	97.1		101.7	101.7		100.3	100.3
0241, 31 - 34	SITE & INFRASTRUCTURE, DEMOLITION	100.1	76.4	84.7	106.0	86.3	99.7	105.9	84.1	91.7	103.1	76.4	85.7	107.2	84.4	92.4	89.2	99.1	95.7
0310	Concrete Forming & Accessories	103.8	54.9	65.8	101.7	59.6	69.0	92.7	59.3	66.8	97.3	58.1	66.9	103.7	59.9	69.6	101.7	75.7	81.5
0320	Concrete Reinforcing	96.8	57.9	86.0	98.9	60.1	88.2	96.8	60.1	86.7	98.1	60.1	87.6	97.7	60.1	87.3	98.8	97.4	98.4
0330	Cast-in-Place Concrete	115.3	66.6	98.0	129.7	70.3	108.6	123.5	68.3	103.9	111.0	66.7	95.3	128.2	69.2	107.3	111.8	91.0	104.4
03	CONCRETE	95.3	61.4	81.9	101.6	65.0	87.1	100.0	64.3	85.9	92.9	63.3	81.2	101.8	64.9	87.3	106.1	85.3	97.9
04	MASONRY	72.5	56.8	62.9	83.1	60.3	69.3	73.4	60.1	65.3	70.8	56.8	62.3	82.2	61.3	69.5	103.4	82.6	90.7
05	METALS	97.7	87.2	95.6	99.8	84.8	96.9	99.9	87.2	97.3	99.4	88.0	97.2	103.8	88.0	100.7	102.1	92.3	100.2
06	WOOD, PLASTICS & COMPOSITES	108.3	53.6	83.8	97.8	58.1	80.0	89.6	57.9	75.4	98.9	57.9	80.5	101.2	57.9	81.8	102.1	70.9	88.1
07	THERMAL & MOISTURE PROTECTION	110.2	56.5	91.1	101.4	60.5	86.8	106.1	58.8	89.3	110.0	57.3	91.2	106.2	59.4	89.5	105.8	84.5	98.2
08	OPENINGS	88.7	53.9	80.9	98.7	56.9	89.2	93.4	56.8	85.1	88.9	56.8	81.6	96.7	56.8	87.7	98.2	80.9	94.3
0920	Plaster & Gypsum Board	113.8	52.2	74.8	98.9	56.7	72.1	95.4	56.7	70.9	109.9	56.7	76.2	103.4	56.7	73.8	108.6	70.2	84.3
0950, 0980	Ceilings & Acoustic Treatment	102.0	52.2	74.1	88.2	56.7	70.5	88.5	56.7	70.7	106.5	56.7	78.6	91.7	56.7	72.1	113.8	70.2	89.4
0960	Flooring	103.1	59.8	92.2	102.4	59.8	91.7	107.5	59.8	95.5	100.5	59.8	90.3	111.4	59.8	98.5	100.2	51.6	88.0
0970, 0990	Wall Finishes & Painting/Coating	103.1	50.7	71.9	99.1	50.7	70.3	102.8	50.7	71.8	103.1	50.7	71.9	102.8	50.7	71.8	98.4	58.6	74.7
09	FINISHES	103.9	54.8	79.3	98.0	58.4	78.1	98.2	58.2	78.1	103.6	57.4	80.4	100.8	58.5	79.6	104.1	69.8	86.9
COVERS	DIVS. 10 - 14, 25, 28, 41, 43, 44, 46	100.0	82.1	96.5	100.0	84.0	96.9	100.0	83.7	96.8	100.0	82.5	96.6	100.0	84.0	96.9	100.0	91.9	98.4
21, 22, 23	FIRE SUPPRESSION, PLUMBING & HVAC	93.4	57.8	80.6	100.1	59.6	85.6	93.3	59.6	81.2	100.9	57.8	85.5	100.8	60.2	86.3	100.0	76.6	91.6
26, 27, 3370	ELECTRICAL, COMMUNICATIONS & UTIL.	100.3	49.7	78.4	99.9	61.0	83.1	94.7	51.1	75.8	100.4	49.7	78.4	93.7	51.5	75.4	99.8	86.1	93.8
MF2018	WEIGHTED AVERAGE	96.2	61.4	83.4	99.4	64.8	86.7	96.4	64.0	84.5	97.8	62.2	84.7	100.0	64.5	87.0	101.4	82.9	94.6

		NORTH DAKOTA																	
	DIVISION	DEVILS LAKE			DICKINSON			FARGO			GRAND FORKS			JAMESTOWN			MINOT		
		583			586			580 - 581			582			584			587		
		MAT.	INST.	TOTAL	MAT.	INST.	TOTAL	MAT.	INST.	TOTAL	MAT.	INST.	TOTAL	MAT.	INST.	TOTAL	MAT.	INST.	TOTAL
015433	CONTRACTOR EQUIPMENT		94.2	94.2		94.2	94.2		100.6	100.6		94.2	94.2		94.2	94.2		94.2	94.2
0241, 31 - 34	SITE & INFRASTRUCTURE, DEMOLITION	89.1	88.6	88.8	93.4	88.5	90.2	89.2	99.2	95.7	94.4	89.2	91.0	88.3	88.6	88.5	92.9	89.3	90.5
0310	Concrete Forming & Accessories	105.5	65.2	74.2	93.1	65.1	71.4	101.7	66.0	73.9	97.8	71.7	77.5	95.0	65.2	71.8	92.6	65.4	71.5
0320	Concrete Reinforcing	102.1	97.3	100.8	103.1	97.2	101.5	99.0	97.9	98.7	100.5	97.4	99.7	102.7	97.8	101.3	104.1	97.2	102.2
0330	Cast-in-Place Concrete	131.2	74.6	111.1	118.7	74.5	103.0	108.6	91.6	102.5	118.7	80.6	105.1	129.6	74.6	110.1	118.7	74.9	103.1
03	CONCRETE	111.2	74.9	96.9	109.2	74.8	95.7	107.5	77.7	95.7	107.0	80.0	96.3	109.6	75.0	95.9	106.3	75.2	94.0
04	MASONRY	111.2	77.5	90.7	113.0	75.9	90.4	92.4	85.8	88.4	105.6	80.4	90.3	123.1	85.6	100.3	103.4	74.4	85.8
05	METALS	98.5	93.0	97.4	98.4	92.6	97.2	102.1	92.5	100.2	98.4	93.7	97.5	98.4	93.5	97.4	98.7	93.7	97.7
06	WOOD, PLASTICS & COMPOSITES	103.1	61.3	84.4	87.1	61.3	75.5	98.8	61.7	82.2	93.2	68.2	82.0	89.7	61.3	77.0	86.7	61.3	75.3
07	THERMAL & MOISTURE PROTECTION	105.7	76.0	95.1	106.0	77.5	95.8	101.4	81.2	94.2	105.8	79.0	96.2	105.4	78.7	95.9	105.5	77.7	95.6
08	OPENINGS	96.1	75.6	91.4	96.0	75.6	91.4	96.9	75.8	92.1	94.9	79.4	91.4	96.0	75.6	91.4	95.0	75.6	90.6
0920	Plaster & Gypsum Board	110.9	60.7	79.1	100.0	60.7	75.1	93.8	60.7	72.8	101.7	67.8	80.2	101.2	60.7	75.5	100.0	60.7	75.1
0950, 0980	Ceilings & Acoustic Treatment	105.8	60.7	80.5	105.8	60.7	80.5	113.6	60.7	83.9	105.8	67.8	84.5	105.8	60.7	80.5	105.8	60.7	80.5
0960	Flooring	101.1	51.6	88.6	96.2	51.6	85.0	100.4	51.6	88.2	97.5	51.6	86.0	96.7	51.6	85.4	96.0	51.6	84.8
0970, 0990	Wall Finishes & Painting/Coating	89.9	50.1	66.1	89.9	50.1	66.1	99.1	59.8	75.7	89.9	58.7	71.3	89.9	50.1	66.1	89.9	51.1	66.7
09	FINISHES	99.4	61.3	80.3	97.1	61.3	79.1	102.4	62.7	82.4	97.4	67.0	82.1	96.8	61.3	79.0	96.5	61.4	78.9
COVERS	DIVS. 10 - 14, 25, 28, 41, 43, 44, 46	100.0	77.9	95.7	100.0	77.9	95.7	100.0	88.6	97.8	100.0	85.3	97.2	100.0	77.9	95.7	100.0	87.8	97.6
21, 22, 23	FIRE SUPPRESSION, PLUMBING & HVAC	92.5	70.6	84.7	92.5	65.9	83.0	99.9	66.7	88.0	100.1	73.6	90.6	92.5	65.0	82.7	100.1	64.9	87.5
26, 27, 3370	ELECTRICAL, COMMUNICATIONS & UTIL.	93.3	64.8	80.9	97.7	64.5	83.3	99.6	61.8	83.2	95.1	64.6	81.9	93.3	60.8	79.2	96.7	65.2	83.1
MF2018	WEIGHTED AVERAGE	98.6	73.8	89.5	98.7	72.6	89.1	100.7	75.3	91.3	99.5	76.9	91.2	98.5	73.0	89.2	99.5	72.9	89.7

City Cost Indexes

		NORTH DAKOTA			OHIO													
		WILLISTON			AKRON			ATHENS			CANTON			CHILLICOTHE			CINCINNATI		
DIVISION		588			442 - 443			457			446 - 447			456			451 - 452		
		MAT.	INST.	TOTAL	MAT.	INST.	TOTAL	MAT.	INST.	TOTAL	MAT.	INST.	TOTAL	MAT.	INST.	TOTAL	MAT.	INST.	TOTAL
015433	CONTRACTOR EQUIPMENT		94.2	94.2		88.0	88.0		84.2	84.2		88.0	88.0		93.6	93.6		97.6	97.6
0241, 31 - 34	SITE & INFRASTRUCTURE, DEMOLITION	89.5	89.3	89.4	86.2	90.8	89.2	87.8	82.4	84.3	86.3	90.7	89.2	82.0	90.6	87.6	84.8	99.4	94.3
0310	Concrete Forming & Accessories	99.8	71.7	78.0	98.6	82.4	86.0	88.2	83.2	84.3	98.6	74.4	79.8	90.8	74.1	77.8	94.4	73.1	77.9
0320	Concrete Reinforcing	105.0	97.2	102.8	102.1	90.5	98.9	97.1	80.1	92.4	102.1	73.2	94.1	95.5	79.7	91.1	99.2	79.4	93.7
0330	Cast-in-Place Concrete	118.7	80.6	105.1	100.9	85.7	95.5	111.6	88.6	103.5	101.9	84.3	95.6	101.3	84.5	95.3	96.8	79.9	90.8
03	CONCRETE	107.7	80.0	96.8	96.6	84.7	91.9	103.4	84.4	95.9	97.0	77.6	89.3	98.5	79.3	91.0	97.4	76.9	89.3
04	MASONRY	99.1	77.2	85.8	96.4	88.9	91.8	60.0	89.5	77.9	97.0	81.0	87.3	65.2	81.5	75.1	69.1	81.9	76.9
05	METALS	98.6	93.5	97.6	91.4	82.3	89.6	95.8	78.7	92.4	91.4	75.3	88.2	89.2	86.9	88.7	97.6	82.5	94.6
06	WOOD, PLASTICS & COMPOSITES	95.4	68.2	83.2	98.9	81.3	91.0	77.0	81.2	78.9	99.4	72.5	87.3	87.2	70.8	79.9	91.4	70.9	82.2
07	THERMAL & MOISTURE PROTECTION	105.7	79.0	96.2	101.7	88.3	96.9	98.3	87.3	94.4	102.6	84.8	96.2	100.8	80.1	93.4	99.8	81.2	93.1
08	OPENINGS	96.1	79.4	92.3	101.5	82.2	97.1	93.5	76.7	89.7	95.7	69.6	89.8	84.9	70.7	81.7	99.0	71.5	92.8
0920	Plaster & Gypsum Board	101.7	67.8	80.2	85.8	80.8	82.7	84.4	80.7	82.1	87.5	71.7	77.5	87.7	70.5	76.8	84.8	70.2	75.5
0950, 0980	Ceilings & Acoustic Treatment	105.8	67.8	84.5	95.1	80.8	87.1	114.2	80.7	95.4	95.1	71.7	82.0	108.2	70.5	87.1	97.2	70.2	82.1
0960	Flooring	98.2	51.6	86.5	89.3	75.1	85.8	111.2	74.4	102.0	89.6	68.0	84.2	90.0	67.4	84.4	93.8	77.8	89.8
0970, 0990	Wall Finishes & Painting/Coating	89.9	56.4	69.9	95.0	86.6	90.0	102.6	82.9	90.9	95.0	72.1	81.4	99.7	79.2	87.5	99.1	71.6	82.7
09	FINISHES	97.5	66.9	82.1	92.2	81.5	86.8	99.9	81.3	90.6	92.5	72.2	82.3	96.6	72.5	84.5	94.0	73.3	83.6
COVERS	DIVS. 10 - 14, 25, 28, 41, 43, 44, 46	100.0	87.4	97.6	100.0	92.1	98.5	100.0	91.3	98.3	100.0	90.5	98.2	100.0	88.1	97.7	100.0	88.2	97.7
21, 22, 23	FIRE SUPPRESSION, PLUMBING & HVAC	92.5	70.5	84.6	100.0	86.4	95.1	92.6	79.2	87.8	100.0	76.3	91.5	93.3	83.1	89.6	100.0	77.0	91.8
26, 27, 3370	ELECTRICAL, COMMUNICATIONS & UTIL.	95.3	65.2	82.3	99.3	80.8	91.3	102.5	87.5	96.0	99.0	80.7	91.1	99.1	79.9	90.8	99.4	75.8	89.2
MF2018	WEIGHTED AVERAGE	97.8	76.0	89.8	96.8	85.0	92.4	95.5	83.1	90.9	96.4	78.5	89.8	92.5	81.0	88.3	96.9	79.3	90.4

		OHIO																
		CLEVELAND			COLUMBUS			DAYTON			HAMILTON			LIMA			LORAIN		
DIVISION		441			430 - 432			453 - 454			450			458			440		
		MAT.	INST.	TOTAL	MAT.	INST.	TOTAL	MAT.	INST.	TOTAL	MAT.	INST.	TOTAL	MAT.	INST.	TOTAL	MAT.	INST.	TOTAL
015433	CONTRACTOR EQUIPMENT		93.9	93.9		97.1	97.1		87.7	87.7		93.6	93.6		87.1	87.1		88.0	88.0
0241, 31 - 34	SITE & INFRASTRUCTURE, DEMOLITION	85.8	97.8	93.6	83.6	97.6	92.7	82.8	90.6	87.9	82.9	90.3	87.7	83.8	81.7	82.4	85.6	90.7	88.9
0310	Concrete Forming & Accessories	98.5	88.7	90.9	93.5	85.4	87.2	92.7	77.1	80.6	92.8	70.5	75.4	88.1	69.6	73.7	98.7	76.4	81.4
0320	Concrete Reinforcing	100.5	91.7	98.1	100.8	80.1	95.1	101.2	78.0	94.8	101.2	82.9	92.4	97.1	77.8	91.8	102.1	90.5	98.9
0330	Cast-in-Place Concrete	100.6	97.2	99.4	99.4	90.9	96.4	86.8	81.5	84.9	93.0	76.0	86.9	102.5	82.1	95.3	96.0	88.4	93.3
03	CONCRETE	95.8	91.8	94.2	94.5	86.3	91.3	92.2	78.9	86.9	94.8	73.0	86.2	97.4	75.8	88.9	94.6	82.9	90.0
04	MASONRY	100.8	98.2	99.2	76.0	89.0	83.9	64.2	77.3	72.2	64.6	73.2	69.8	77.4	70.4	73.2	93.3	87.9	90.0
05	METALS	97.6	85.0	95.1	97.6	81.8	94.5	91.1	78.2	88.6	91.0	83.0	89.4	95.8	80.4	92.8	92.0	82.2	90.1
06	WOOD, PLASTICS & COMPOSITES	96.3	86.3	91.8	90.7	85.0	88.1	90.7	77.2	84.7	89.9	70.1	81.0	76.9	68.2	73.0	98.9	74.4	87.9
07	THERMAL & MOISTURE PROTECTION	100.5	96.4	99.0	102.0	87.9	97.0	104.3	78.0	95.0	100.9	74.4	91.4	97.9	79.4	91.4	102.5	85.0	96.3
08	OPENINGS	98.9	85.2	95.8	98.6	78.8	94.1	91.9	74.6	88.0	89.6	69.3	85.1	93.5	68.4	87.8	95.7	78.4	91.8
0920	Plaster & Gypsum Board	85.6	85.9	85.8	87.8	84.4	85.6	88.9	77.1	81.4	88.9	69.7	76.7	84.4	67.3	73.6	85.8	73.7	78.2
0950, 0980	Ceilings & Acoustic Treatment	93.6	85.9	89.3	95.4	84.4	89.2	108.2	77.1	90.8	108.2	69.7	86.6	114.2	67.3	87.9	95.1	73.7	83.1
0960	Flooring	93.8	96.0	94.3	91.2	76.0	87.6	93.4	71.4	87.9	91.0	70.3	85.8	110.7	69.1	100.3	89.6	83.8	88.1
0970, 0990	Wall Finishes & Painting/Coating	99.1	86.6	91.6	94.9	78.0	84.8	99.7	68.5	81.1	99.7	63.4	78.0	102.6	68.0	81.9	95.0	84.9	89.0
09	FINISHES	93.2	89.5	91.4	92.8	82.9	87.9	97.6	75.0	86.2	96.8	69.4	83.1	99.5	68.6	83.9	92.3	78.2	85.2
COVERS	DIVS. 10 - 14, 25, 28, 41, 43, 44, 46	100.0	96.9	99.4	100.0	91.4	98.3	100.0	87.6	97.6	100.0	86.0	97.3	100.0	90.0	98.1	100.0	92.9	98.6
21, 22, 23	FIRE SUPPRESSION, PLUMBING & HVAC	100.0	91.5	97.0	100.0	90.8	96.7	101.0	78.6	93.0	100.8	67.4	88.8	92.6	82.5	89.0	100.0	76.7	91.6
26, 27, 3370	ELECTRICAL, COMMUNICATIONS & UTIL.	99.6	88.6	94.8	99.2	83.0	92.2	97.6	75.4	88.0	97.9	67.2	84.6	102.8	67.4	87.4	99.1	73.9	88.2
MF2018	WEIGHTED AVERAGE	98.0	91.4	95.6	96.8	87.0	93.2	94.5	78.6	88.6	94.4	73.1	86.6	95.3	75.6	88.1	96.0	80.9	90.5

		OHIO																
		MANSFIELD			MARION			SPRINGFIELD			STEUBENVILLE			TOLEDO			YOUNGSTOWN		
DIVISION		448 - 449			433			455			439			434 - 436			444 - 445		
		MAT.	INST.	TOTAL	MAT.	INST.	TOTAL	MAT.	INST.	TOTAL	MAT.	INST.	TOTAL	MAT.	INST.	TOTAL	MAT.	INST.	TOTAL
015433	CONTRACTOR EQUIPMENT		88.0	88.0		89.0	89.0		87.7	87.7		92.2	92.2		92.3	92.3		88.0	88.0
0241, 31 - 34	SITE & INFRASTRUCTURE, DEMOLITION	79.8	90.2	86.6	75.7	87.6	83.5	83.1	90.5	88.0	98.5	94.7	96.0	81.3	88.4	86.0	86.1	90.4	88.9
0310	Concrete Forming & Accessories	87.4	74.9	77.7	91.1	72.2	76.4	92.7	75.8	79.6	91.0	72.0	76.2	94.8	88.4	89.8	98.6	75.3	80.5
0320	Concrete Reinforcing	93.0	71.0	86.9	97.2	70.9	89.9	101.2	78.0	94.8	95.4	91.8	94.4	105.4	86.2	100.1	102.1	81.1	96.3
0330	Cast-in-Place Concrete	93.4	80.7	88.9	86.0	80.9	84.2	89.1	81.7	86.5	93.4	82.3	89.5	94.2	89.9	92.7	99.9	84.4	94.4
03	CONCRETE	88.6	76.2	83.7	84.7	75.3	81.0	93.1	78.3	87.3	87.7	79.0	84.3	92.1	88.6	90.8	96.2	79.4	89.6
04	MASONRY	95.3	80.1	86.1	79.0	80.9	80.2	64.2	77.7	72.4	70.8	82.1	77.7	83.8	90.1	87.6	96.6	83.6	88.7
05	METALS	92.6	74.7	89.0	92.9	77.1	89.8	91.1	78.1	88.6	90.4	82.7	88.9	93.4	88.1	92.4	91.5	78.3	88.9
06	WOOD, PLASTICS & COMPOSITES	83.6	74.4	79.5	84.0	70.5	78.0	91.6	75.3	84.3	79.1	69.5	74.8	88.6	89.4	89.0	98.9	73.6	87.5
07	THERMAL & MOISTURE PROTECTION	101.0	83.1	94.6	97.9	80.6	91.7	104.2	78.0	94.9	109.3	79.2	98.5	98.0	89.8	95.1	102.7	85.6	96.6
08	OPENINGS	96.5	70.3	90.6	87.5	68.1	83.1	90.1	73.7	86.4	87.5	72.9	84.2	89.9	84.2	88.6	95.7	78.4	91.8
0920	Plaster & Gypsum Board	78.3	73.7	75.4	87.1	69.8	76.1	88.9	75.1	80.1	83.5	68.3	73.8	89.0	89.3	89.2	85.8	72.9	77.6
0950, 0980	Ceilings & Acoustic Treatment	96.4	73.7	83.7	100.6	69.8	83.3	108.2	75.1	89.7	99.1	68.3	81.8	100.6	89.3	94.3	95.1	72.9	82.6
0960	Flooring	85.1	87.4	85.7	87.9	87.4	87.8	93.4	71.4	87.9	115.3	85.2	107.8	88.3	92.4	89.3	89.6	86.1	88.7
0970, 0990	Wall Finishes & Painting/Coating	95.0	69.1	79.6	96.8	69.1	80.3	99.7	77.4	90.7	110.3	77.4	90.7	96.8	82.0	87.9	95.0	75.3	83.2
09	FINISHES	90.1	76.3	83.2	93.7	74.3	83.9	97.6	73.9	85.7	109.1	74.1	91.5	94.3	88.6	91.4	92.4	76.7	84.5
COVERS	DIVS. 10 - 14, 25, 28, 41, 43, 44, 46	100.0	89.8	98.0	100.0	87.4	97.6	100.0	87.4	97.6	100.0	86.5	97.4	100.0	93.9	98.8	100.0	90.3	98.1
21, 22, 23	FIRE SUPPRESSION, PLUMBING & HVAC	92.5	75.2	86.3	92.5	83.7	89.3	101.0	76.5	92.2	93.2	82.2	89.3	100.0	91.7	97.0	100.0	79.8	92.8
26, 27, 3370	ELECTRICAL, COMMUNICATIONS & UTIL.	97.9	80.8	90.5	97.3	80.8	90.2	97.6	77.4	88.8	90.1	94.8	92.1	100.8	92.5	97.2	99.1	80.7	91.1
MF2018	WEIGHTED AVERAGE	93.3	78.4	87.8	91.6	79.6	87.2	94.5	78.2	88.5	92.4	83.1	89.0	95.2	90.0	93.3	96.3	80.9	90.6

City Cost Indexes

		OHIO			OKLAHOMA														
DIVISION		ZANESVILLE			ARDMORE			CLINTON			DURANT			ENID			GUYMON		
		437 - 438			734			736			747			737			739		
		MAT.	INST.	TOTAL	MAT.	INST.	TOTAL	MAT.	INST.	TOTAL	MAT.	INST.	TOTAL	MAT.	INST.	TOTAL	MAT.	INST.	TOTAL
015433	CONTRACTOR EQUIPMENT		89.0	89.0		79.3	79.3		78.5	78.5		78.5	78.5		78.5	78.5		78.5	78.5
0241, 31 - 34	SITE & INFRASTRUCTURE, DEMOLITION	77.5	87.5	84.0	93.2	88.5	90.1	94.4	87.2	89.7	91.8	86.9	88.6	99.2	87.2	91.4	98.2	86.4	90.5
0310	Concrete Forming & Accessories	88.2	71.2	75.0	89.2	52.3	60.5	87.6	52.3	60.2	84.4	50.5	58.1	91.6	52.6	61.3	94.8	50.4	60.3
0320	Concrete Reinforcing	96.6	83.1	92.9	88.3	65.1	81.9	88.8	65.1	82.2	96.0	57.2	85.3	88.3	65.1	81.9	88.8	56.8	80.0
0330	Cast-in-Place Concrete	90.6	79.5	86.7	83.7	70.2	78.9	80.9	70.2	77.1	81.1	67.8	76.4	80.9	73.7	78.3	80.9	67.2	76.0
03	CONCRETE	87.3	76.5	83.0	82.3	61.0	73.9	81.8	61.0	73.6	83.0	58.0	73.1	82.2	62.3	74.3	84.2	57.6	73.7
04	MASONRY	76.9	78.0	77.6	94.0	60.6	73.7	118.4	60.6	83.3	87.2	56.0	68.3	100.7	60.6	76.3	95.6	49.9	67.9
05	METALS	94.1	84.2	92.2	97.0	63.0	90.3	97.1	63.0	90.4	91.6	60.0	85.3	98.5	63.3	91.6	97.7	58.1	89.9
06	WOOD, PLASTICS & COMPOSITES	78.8	70.5	75.1	90.9	49.5	72.4	89.9	49.5	71.8	81.1	49.5	66.9	94.0	49.5	74.1	98.4	49.5	76.5
07	THERMAL & MOISTURE PROTECTION	97.9	77.2	90.5	103.5	62.3	88.8	103.6	62.3	88.9	97.9	60.1	84.4	103.7	62.3	89.0	104.0	56.1	87.0
08	OPENINGS	87.5	73.2	84.3	102.2	50.8	90.6	102.2	50.8	90.6	93.2	49.0	83.2	103.2	52.4	91.8	102.3	49.0	90.3
0920	Plaster & Gypsum Board	81.8	69.8	74.2	90.9	48.7	64.1	90.7	48.7	64.0	73.2	48.7	57.6	91.9	48.7	64.5	91.9	48.7	64.5
0950, 0980	Ceilings & Acoustic Treatment	100.6	69.8	83.3	101.9	48.7	72.1	101.9	48.7	72.1	83.6	48.7	64.0	101.9	48.7	72.1	101.9	48.7	72.1
0960	Flooring	86.7	67.4	81.9	94.7	51.3	83.8	93.9	51.3	83.2	96.0	46.3	83.6	95.1	69.2	88.6	96.3	51.3	85.0
0970, 0990	Wall Finishes & Painting/Coating	96.8	79.2	86.3	92.9	42.3	62.7	92.9	42.3	62.7	96.4	42.3	64.1	92.9	42.3	62.7	92.9	37.5	59.9
09	FINISHES	92.7	70.6	81.6	95.5	49.6	72.5	95.5	49.6	72.4	87.9	47.6	67.7	96.0	53.3	74.6	96.8	49.2	72.9
COVERS	DIVS. 10 - 14, 25, 28, 41, 43, 44, 46	100.0	86.5	97.4	100.0	78.2	95.8	100.0	78.2	95.8	100.0	76.8	95.5	100.0	78.2	95.8	100.0	76.8	95.5
21, 22, 23	FIRE SUPPRESSION, PLUMBING & HVAC	92.5	80.8	88.3	92.7	66.2	83.2	92.7	66.2	83.2	92.6	63.9	82.3	100.2	66.2	88.0	92.7	61.8	81.6
26, 27, 3370	ELECTRICAL, COMMUNICATIONS & UTIL.	97.7	79.9	90.0	92.8	70.8	83.3	93.4	70.8	83.6	96.3	61.6	81.3	93.4	70.8	83.6	94.2	58.4	78.7
MF2018	WEIGHTED AVERAGE	92.0	79.0	87.2	94.3	64.4	83.3	95.3	64.3	83.9	91.7	60.9	80.4	96.9	65.0	85.2	95.2	59.2	82.0

		OKLAHOMA																	
DIVISION		LAWTON			MCALESTER			MIAMI			MUSKOGEE			OKLAHOMA CITY			PONCA CITY		
		735			745			743			744			730 - 731			746		
		MAT.	INST.	TOTAL	MAT.	INST.	TOTAL	MAT.	INST.	TOTAL	MAT.	INST.	TOTAL	MAT.	INST.	TOTAL	MAT.	INST.	TOTAL
015433	CONTRACTOR EQUIPMENT		79.3	79.3		78.5	78.5		88.4	88.4		88.4	88.4		90.9	90.9		78.5	78.5
0241, 31 - 34	SITE & INFRASTRUCTURE, DEMOLITION	95.9	88.6	91.1	86.0	87.1	86.7	86.7	84.4	85.2	90.5	84.3	86.5	95.8	101.6	99.6	92.4	86.9	88.8
0310	Concrete Forming & Accessories	94.6	56.2	64.8	82.4	55.1	61.2	96.7	50.5	60.8	101.7	54.1	64.7	98.4	62.0	70.1	91.7	50.6	59.7
0320	Concrete Reinforcing	88.5	65.1	82.0	95.7	68.1	88.1	94.2	65.0	86.1	95.1	62.7	86.2	99.7	65.2	90.1	95.1	65.0	86.8
0330	Cast-in-Place Concrete	78.2	73.8	76.6	71.1	70.5	70.9	74.5	68.7	72.4	75.4	69.2	73.2	82.2	72.1	78.6	83.3	67.9	77.8
03	CONCRETE	79.8	64.0	73.6	76.2	62.8	71.0	79.8	60.5	72.2	81.4	61.9	73.7	87.7	66.1	79.2	84.7	59.4	74.7
04	MASONRY	95.6	60.6	74.3	103.4	57.9	75.8	90.0	56.5	69.6	103.7	57.7	75.7	94.7	58.0	72.4	81.9	56.4	66.4
05	METALS	103.1	63.3	95.2	91.5	64.2	86.1	91.5	76.5	88.5	92.9	75.6	89.5	97.2	65.5	91.0	91.5	62.9	85.8
06	WOOD, PLASTICS & COMPOSITES	97.2	54.4	78.0	78.3	54.5	67.6	96.5	49.6	75.5	102.2	53.5	80.4	94.7	63.5	80.7	90.7	49.5	72.2
07	THERMAL & MOISTURE PROTECTION	103.6	63.0	89.1	97.6	61.7	84.8	98.1	61.0	84.8	98.4	60.2	84.8	95.4	64.3	84.3	98.1	60.4	84.7
08	OPENINGS	104.5	55.1	93.3	93.2	55.4	84.7	93.2	50.9	83.6	94.2	52.5	84.8	98.0	60.1	89.4	93.2	50.8	83.6
0920	Plaster & Gypsum Board	97.0	53.7	69.6	73.0	53.8	60.8	79.5	48.7	59.9	84.5	52.7	64.3	96.7	62.7	75.2	78.0	48.7	59.4
0950, 0980	Ceilings & Acoustic Treatment	118.3	53.7	82.1	83.6	53.8	66.9	83.6	48.7	64.0	99.5	52.7	73.2	106.8	62.7	82.1	83.6	48.7	64.0
0960	Flooring	96.4	69.2	89.6	95.3	65.6	87.9	100.5	46.3	86.9	102.3	60.9	91.9	99.9	69.2	92.2	98.4	51.3	86.6
0970, 0990	Wall Finishes & Painting/Coating	92.9	42.3	62.7	96.4	46.2	66.4	96.4	37.5	61.3	96.4	37.5	61.3	99.1	42.3	65.2	96.4	42.3	64.1
09	FINISHES	101.0	56.2	78.5	87.1	55.3	71.1	89.4	47.1	68.2	95.0	52.7	73.7	101.5	60.9	81.1	89.4	49.5	69.3
COVERS	DIVS. 10 - 14, 25, 28, 41, 43, 44, 46	100.0	78.8	95.9	100.0	77.9	95.7	100.0	77.2	95.6	100.0	78.0	95.7	100.0	79.6	96.1	100.0	76.8	95.5
21, 22, 23	FIRE SUPPRESSION, PLUMBING & HVAC	100.2	66.2	88.0	92.6	60.8	81.2	92.6	57.3	79.9	100.1	60.6	86.0	100.1	64.9	87.5	92.6	57.3	79.9
26, 27, 3370	ELECTRICAL, COMMUNICATIONS & UTIL.	94.2	70.8	84.1	95.4	67.7	83.4	96.2	67.8	83.9	95.2	82.6	89.7	99.9	70.9	87.3	95.2	58.4	79.3
MF2018	WEIGHTED AVERAGE	97.9	65.9	86.1	91.2	63.7	81.1	91.5	62.1	80.7	94.8	65.9	84.2	97.4	67.9	86.5	91.8	59.8	80.0

		OKLAHOMA											OREGON					
DIVISION		POTEAU			SHAWNEE			TULSA			WOODWARD			BEND			EUGENE		
		749			748			740 - 741			738			977			974		
		MAT.	INST.	TOTAL	MAT.	INST.	TOTAL	MAT.	INST.	TOTAL	MAT.	INST.	TOTAL	MAT.	INST.	TOTAL	MAT.	INST.	TOTAL
015433	CONTRACTOR EQUIPMENT		87.3	87.3		78.5	78.5		88.4	88.4		78.5	78.5		94.9	94.9		94.9	94.9
0241, 31 - 34	SITE & INFRASTRUCTURE, DEMOLITION	75.7	82.6	80.2	94.8	87.0	89.7	95.8	84.5	88.5	94.8	87.2	89.9	122.1	94.6	104.1	114.0	94.6	101.3
0310	Concrete Forming & Accessories	89.4	50.6	59.2	84.3	50.6	58.1	101.6	55.1	65.5	87.8	56.7	63.6	100.0	99.3	99.5	96.3	99.5	98.8
0320	Concrete Reinforcing	96.2	65.1	87.6	95.1	59.1	85.1	95.3	65.1	87.0	88.3	65.1	81.9	88.4	112.6	95.1	91.8	112.6	97.5
0330	Cast-in-Place Concrete	74.5	68.7	72.5	85.9	67.9	79.5	82.1	71.4	78.3	80.9	71.2	77.4	133.1	100.6	121.6	128.9	100.7	118.9
03	CONCRETE	81.3	60.5	73.1	85.6	58.4	74.9	85.2	63.6	76.6	81.9	63.3	74.5	116.8	101.6	110.8	109.4	101.8	106.4
04	MASONRY	90.3	56.5	69.7	104.7	56.4	75.4	91.0	57.7	70.8	89.7	60.6	72.0	114.9	102.9	107.6	111.2	102.9	106.1
05	METALS	91.5	76.5	88.6	91.4	60.8	85.4	97.2	77.0	93.2	97.2	63.3	90.5	110.2	96.9	107.6	110.9	97.2	108.2
06	WOOD, PLASTICS & COMPOSITES	86.7	49.6	70.1	80.9	49.6	66.8	101.2	54.6	80.3	90.0	55.2	74.4	107.3	99.5	103.8	101.9	99.5	100.8
07	THERMAL & MOISTURE PROTECTION	98.1	60.9	84.9	98.1	58.7	84.0	98.4	63.4	85.9	103.7	63.1	89.2	95.3	99.9	97.0	94.6	101.7	97.2
08	OPENINGS	93.2	50.9	83.6	93.2	49.4	83.3	95.5	55.1	86.4	102.3	55.1	91.6	92.2	102.6	94.5	92.4	102.6	94.7
0920	Plaster & Gypsum Board	76.3	48.7	58.8	73.2	48.7	57.6	84.5	53.8	65.0	90.7	54.5	67.7	123.3	99.5	108.2	120.1	99.5	107.0
0950, 0980	Ceilings & Acoustic Treatment	83.6	48.7	64.0	83.6	48.7	64.0	99.5	53.8	73.9	101.9	54.5	75.3	94.5	99.5	97.3	94.5	99.5	97.3
0960	Flooring	97.9	46.3	84.9	96.0	51.3	84.8	101.4	60.1	91.1	93.9	65.9	86.9	106.9	101.7	105.6	105.8	101.7	104.8
0970, 0990	Wall Finishes & Painting/Coating	96.4	42.3	64.1	96.4	37.5	61.3	96.4	56.0	72.3	92.9	42.3	62.7	99.7	74.2	83.7	97.7	62.2	76.5
09	FINISHES	87.5	47.7	67.5	88.2	48.1	68.0	94.9	55.2	75.0	95.5	57.9	75.6	106.3	97.0	101.6	104.3	95.7	100.0
COVERS	DIVS. 10 - 14, 25, 28, 41, 43, 44, 46	100.0	77.1	95.6	100.0	76.9	95.5	100.0	78.2	95.8	100.0	78.8	95.9	100.0	101.9	100.4	100.0	101.9	100.4
21, 22, 23	FIRE SUPPRESSION, PLUMBING & HVAC	92.6	57.3	79.9	92.6	63.9	82.3	100.1	60.7	86.0	92.7	66.2	83.2	92.6	97.6	94.4	100.1	108.7	103.2
26, 27, 3370	ELECTRICAL, COMMUNICATIONS & UTIL.	95.3	67.8	83.4	96.3	70.8	85.3	96.3	64.7	82.6	94.1	70.8	84.0	93.5	91.5	92.6	92.8	91.5	92.2
MF2018	WEIGHTED AVERAGE	91.1	62.0	80.4	92.8	62.4	81.6	96.0	64.9	84.4	94.3	65.7	83.8	102.7	97.9	100.9	103.1	100.1	102.0

City Cost Indexes

		OREGON																	
	DIVISION	KLAMATH FALLS			MEDFORD			PENDLETON			PORTLAND			SALEM			VALE		
		976			975			978			970 - 972			973			979		
		MAT.	INST.	TOTAL	MAT.	INST.	TOTAL	MAT.	INST.	TOTAL	MAT.	INST.	TOTAL	MAT.	INST.	TOTAL	MAT.	INST.	TOTAL
015433	CONTRACTOR EQUIPMENT		94.9	94.9		94.9	94.9		92.7	92.7		94.9	94.9		99.4	99.4		92.7	92.7
0241, 31 - 34	SITE & INFRASTRUCTURE, DEMOLITION	126.7	94.5	105.7	122.6	94.5	104.3	121.0	88.7	99.9	116.3	94.6	102.1	109.3	101.7	104.3	107.2	88.6	95.1
0310	Concrete Forming & Accessories	92.6	99.0	97.5	91.5	99.1	97.4	94.8	99.1	98.2	97.7	99.7	99.2	96.0	99.7	98.9	101.8	97.9	98.8
0320	Concrete Reinforcing	88.4	112.5	95.1	89.9	112.5	96.2	88.8	112.5	95.4	92.6	112.6	98.1	98.6	112.6	102.5	86.6	112.3	93.7
0330	Cast-in-Place Concrete	133.1	92.1	118.5	133.1	100.5	121.5	134.0	92.5	119.3	132.5	100.8	121.2	121.8	102.7	115.0	105.4	92.7	100.9
03	CONCRETE	118.8	98.5	110.8	114.5	101.5	109.4	103.6	98.7	101.7	111.2	101.9	107.5	109.7	102.4	106.8	88.3	98.2	92.2
04	MASONRY	129.2	102.9	113.2	107.3	102.9	104.6	118.7	103.0	109.1	113.4	102.9	107.0	114.9	103.0	107.7	116.1	103.0	108.1
05	METALS	110.2	96.6	107.5	110.5	96.7	107.7	117.8	97.1	113.7	112.8	97.3	109.7	118.8	95.3	114.2	117.5	95.8	113.2
06	WOOD, PLASTICS & COMPOSITES	95.6	99.5	97.3	94.3	99.5	96.6	99.3	99.6	99.4	103.4	99.5	101.7	95.5	99.7	97.3	109.9	99.6	105.3
07	THERMAL & MOISTURE PROTECTION	95.4	95.1	95.3	95.1	94.5	94.9	90.8	92.0	91.2	94.6	100.5	96.7	91.3	101.8	95.0	90.4	88.4	89.7
08	OPENINGS	92.2	102.6	94.5	94.8	102.6	96.5	89.1	102.7	92.1	90.5	102.6	93.2	97.5	102.7	98.7	89.0	89.8	89.2
0920	Plaster & Gypsum Board	115.6	99.5	105.4	114.9	99.5	105.1	102.6	99.5	100.6	118.3	99.5	106.4	117.6	99.5	106.1	111.8	99.5	104.0
0950, 0980	Ceilings & Acoustic Treatment	105.4	99.5	102.1	108.4	99.5	103.4	72.5	99.5	87.6	96.5	99.5	98.2	115.0	99.5	106.3	72.5	99.5	87.6
0960	Flooring	104.8	101.7	104.0	104.4	101.7	103.7	71.1	101.7	78.8	103.0	101.7	102.7	105.8	101.7	104.8	72.6	101.7	79.9
0970, 0990	Wall Finishes & Painting/Coating	97.7	71.7	82.2	97.7	71.7	82.2	89.0	77.7	82.3	97.2	77.7	85.6	99.1	69.5	81.4	89.0	74.2	80.2
09	FINISHES	108.0	96.7	102.3	107.7	96.7	102.2	76.2	97.5	86.9	103.8	97.4	100.6	108.1	96.6	102.3	76.9	97.1	87.0
COVERS	DIVS. 10 - 14, 25, 28, 41, 43, 44, 46	100.0	101.8	100.4	100.0	101.8	100.4	100.0	99.9	100.0	100.0	102.0	100.4	100.0	102.4	100.5	100.0	102.0	100.4
21, 22, 23	FIRE SUPPRESSION, PLUMBING & HVAC	92.6	97.5	94.3	100.1	103.0	101.1	99.9	103.6	101.2	100.1	108.8	103.2	100.1	108.8	103.2	99.9	66.9	88.0
26, 27, 3370	ELECTRICAL, COMMUNICATIONS & UTIL.	92.9	79.5	87.1	94.5	79.5	88.0	86.5	86.2	86.4	93.5	115.4	103.0	100.9	91.5	96.8	86.5	60.6	75.3
MF2018	WEIGHTED AVERAGE	103.6	95.5	100.6	104.2	97.1	101.6	101.1	97.4	99.7	103.7	103.8	103.7	106.3	100.8	104.3	98.9	85.1	93.9

		PENNSYLVANIA																	
	DIVISION	ALLENTOWN			ALTOONA			BEDFORD			BRADFORD			BUTLER			CHAMBERSBURG		
		181			166			155			167			160			172		
		MAT.	INST.	TOTAL	MAT.	INST.	TOTAL	MAT.	INST.	TOTAL	MAT.	INST.	TOTAL	MAT.	INST.	TOTAL	MAT.	INST.	TOTAL
015433	CONTRACTOR EQUIPMENT		108.2	108.2		108.2	108.2		106.9	106.9		108.2	108.2		108.2	108.2		107.5	107.5
0241, 31 - 34	SITE & INFRASTRUCTURE, DEMOLITION	89.4	93.6	92.1	91.3	93.4	92.6	89.9	90.3	90.1	84.9	91.0	88.9	81.1	93.0	88.9	85.0	90.4	88.5
0310	Concrete Forming & Accessories	99.0	104.7	103.4	82.4	83.9	83.6	80.9	73.9	75.4	85.0	87.6	87.0	83.8	87.8	86.9	85.6	69.7	73.2
0320	Concrete Reinforcing	96.6	108.3	99.8	93.6	99.1	95.1	95.5	94.9	95.3	95.6	94.9	95.4	94.2	114.1	99.7	94.3	100.7	96.0
0330	Cast-in-Place Concrete	88.7	100.4	92.8	98.8	88.4	95.1	101.9	78.6	93.6	94.4	82.8	90.3	87.2	93.9	89.6	94.0	85.5	91.0
03	CONCRETE	92.6	104.8	97.4	88.9	89.5	89.1	98.7	80.7	91.6	93.6	88.4	91.5	82.5	95.8	87.7	95.7	82.4	90.5
04	MASONRY	97.3	95.0	95.9	100.0	86.9	92.0	97.9	72.3	82.3	97.7	73.8	83.2	101.9	89.7	94.5	100.5	71.3	82.8
05	METALS	95.1	119.3	99.9	90.2	112.3	94.5	92.4	107.7	95.4	92.5	107.3	95.4	89.9	117.9	95.4	92.8	112.1	96.6
06	WOOD, PLASTICS & COMPOSITES	99.8	105.6	102.4	75.3	82.3	78.4	71.4	74.2	72.7	81.2	91.8	86.0	77.1	85.3	80.8	79.5	68.7	74.6
07	THERMAL & MOISTURE PROTECTION	101.4	109.2	104.2	99.4	91.5	96.6	102.6	79.9	94.5	101.1	81.1	94.0	99.0	90.7	96.0	98.6	74.5	90.0
08	OPENINGS	92.8	104.4	95.4	86.6	85.4	86.3	91.2	80.0	88.8	93.0	88.8	92.0	86.6	94.6	88.4	87.2	73.8	84.2
0920	Plaster & Gypsum Board	107.7	105.9	106.5	96.0	81.9	87.1	108.8	73.6	86.5	96.8	91.7	93.6	96.0	85.0	89.0	102.5	67.8	80.5
0950, 0980	Ceilings & Acoustic Treatment	92.5	105.9	100.0	96.6	81.9	88.4	108.0	73.6	88.7	96.7	91.7	93.9	97.1	85.0	90.4	88.8	67.8	77.1
0960	Flooring	96.1	93.6	95.5	89.6	100.2	92.3	96.1	92.9	95.3	91.5	92.9	91.8	90.4	94.3	91.4	99.1	69.8	91.8
0970, 0990	Wall Finishes & Painting/Coating	89.9	109.8	101.8	85.6	107.1	98.4	92.3	93.9	93.2	89.9	93.9	92.2	85.6	94.3	90.8	91.6	89.5	90.3
09	FINISHES	95.4	103.1	99.2	93.2	88.7	90.9	101.0	78.3	89.9	93.7	89.6	91.6	93.1	89.1	91.1	93.9	71.1	82.4
COVERS	DIVS. 10 - 14, 25, 28, 41, 43, 44, 46	100.0	102.3	100.4	100.0	97.6	99.5	100.0	93.8	98.8	100.0	96.3	99.3	100.0	99.3	99.9	100.0	91.5	98.3
21, 22, 23	FIRE SUPPRESSION, PLUMBING & HVAC	100.4	113.6	105.2	99.8	85.4	94.6	92.8	76.0	86.7	92.9	81.4	88.8	92.2	89.0	91.1	92.8	80.6	88.5
26, 27, 3370	ELECTRICAL, COMMUNICATIONS & UTIL.	99.3	94.2	97.1	91.2	107.9	98.4	100.1	107.8	103.5	96.0	107.8	101.1	91.5	95.9	93.4	93.5	76.4	86.1
MF2018	WEIGHTED AVERAGE	96.8	104.4	99.6	93.5	93.3	93.4	95.4	86.0	92.0	94.0	90.4	92.6	90.8	94.5	92.2	93.6	81.5	89.1

		PENNSYLVANIA																	
	DIVISION	DOYLESTOWN			DUBOIS			ERIE			GREENSBURG			HARRISBURG			HAZLETON		
		189			158			164 - 165			156			170 - 171			182		
		MAT.	INST.	TOTAL	MAT.	INST.	TOTAL	MAT.	INST.	TOTAL	MAT.	INST.	TOTAL	MAT.	INST.	TOTAL	MAT.	INST.	TOTAL
015433	CONTRACTOR EQUIPMENT		89.3	89.3		106.9	106.9		108.2	108.2		106.9	106.9		111.3	111.3		108.2	108.2
0241, 31 - 34	SITE & INFRASTRUCTURE, DEMOLITION	96.8	81.9	87.1	93.2	90.6	91.5	89.0	93.1	91.7	86.8	92.3	90.4	90.3	100.3	96.8	80.8	91.9	88.1
0310	Concrete Forming & Accessories	81.6	114.7	107.3	80.4	76.2	77.2	98.0	88.4	90.5	87.6	83.0	84.0	98.9	90.9	92.7	79.2	80.5	80.2
0320	Concrete Reinforcing	93.2	135.3	104.9	94.8	107.1	98.2	95.6	107.8	98.9	94.8	113.9	100.1	98.2	114.6	102.7	93.7	101.4	95.9
0330	Cast-in-Place Concrete	83.7	117.6	95.8	98.2	88.8	94.9	97.1	89.8	94.5	94.5	93.6	94.2	92.7	101.8	95.9	83.7	87.2	84.9
03	CONCRETE	87.7	118.9	100.0	99.9	87.4	95.0	89.1	93.5	90.8	94.9	93.3	94.3	92.6	99.9	95.5	85.7	88.0	86.6
04	MASONRY	100.2	121.5	113.1	98.2	84.1	89.6	90.3	91.8	91.2	107.2	86.2	94.4	96.5	96.1	96.3	109.1	80.6	91.8
05	METALS	93.0	116.9	97.7	92.4	112.8	96.4	90.6	115.2	95.4	92.4	116.4	97.1	99.8	117.6	103.3	94.8	113.0	98.4
06	WOOD, PLASTICS & COMPOSITES	76.2	114.0	93.1	70.3	74.2	72.0	96.7	87.4	92.5	78.8	79.1	78.9	95.7	87.6	92.0	74.3	79.0	76.4
07	THERMAL & MOISTURE PROTECTION	98.2	117.9	105.2	102.9	86.6	97.1	99.9	91.7	97.0	102.6	88.7	97.6	102.3	109.3	104.8	100.6	90.3	96.9
08	OPENINGS	95.0	120.6	100.8	91.2	82.8	89.3	86.7	90.9	87.6	91.1	91.2	91.1	98.4	89.0	96.3	93.3	84.5	91.4
0920	Plaster & Gypsum Board	94.2	114.6	107.1	107.4	73.6	85.9	107.7	87.1	94.6	109.5	78.6	89.9	111.6	87.1	96.1	94.7	78.5	84.4
0950, 0980	Ceilings & Acoustic Treatment	91.7	114.6	104.5	108.0	73.6	88.7	92.5	87.1	89.5	108.0	78.6	91.5	96.8	87.1	91.4	93.0	78.5	84.9
0960	Flooring	80.8	124.8	91.8	95.9	92.9	95.2	92.6	101.4	94.8	98.9	69.8	91.6	107.7	95.6	104.7	89.1	80.0	86.8
0970, 0990	Wall Finishes & Painting/Coating	89.9	127.7	112.4	92.3	109.8	102.7	95.9	90.3	92.6	92.3	94.3	93.5	98.4	91.2	94.1	89.9	92.5	91.4
09	FINISHES	86.8	117.6	102.2	101.1	81.8	91.4	95.9	90.6	92.8	101.7	80.9	91.3	101.8	91.1	96.4	91.3	81.4	86.3
COVERS	DIVS. 10 - 14, 25, 28, 41, 43, 44, 46	100.0	112.8	102.5	100.0	95.5	99.1	100.0	98.7	99.8	100.0	98.6	99.7	100.0	98.9	99.8	100.0	97.0	99.4
21, 22, 23	FIRE SUPPRESSION, PLUMBING & HVAC	92.2	119.1	101.9	92.8	78.7	87.7	99.8	94.1	97.7	92.8	81.7	88.8	100.2	98.1	99.5	92.9	85.9	90.4
26, 27, 3370	ELECTRICAL, COMMUNICATIONS & UTIL.	94.8	117.8	104.8	100.4	107.8	103.6	92.3	88.9	90.8	100.4	107.9	103.6	100.3	91.0	96.3	96.4	80.1	89.4
MF2018	WEIGHTED AVERAGE	93.0	115.6	101.3	95.7	89.9	93.6	93.6	94.3	93.9	95.4	92.4	94.3	98.8	98.0	98.5	93.7	87.5	91.4

City Cost Indexes

DIVISION		PENNSYLVANIA																	
		INDIANA 157			JOHNSTOWN 159			KITTANNING 162			LANCASTER 175 - 176			LEHIGH VALLEY 180			MONTROSE 188		
		MAT.	INST.	TOTAL	MAT.	INST.	TOTAL	MAT.	INST.	TOTAL	MAT.	INST.	TOTAL	MAT.	INST.	TOTAL	MAT.	INST.	TOTAL
015433	CONTRACTOR EQUIPMENT		106.9	106.9		106.9	106.9		108.2	108.2		107.5	107.5		108.2	108.2		108.2	108.2
0241, 31 - 34	SITE & INFRASTRUCTURE, DEMOLITION	85.5	91.6	89.5	90.3	92.6	91.8	83.0	93.4	89.8	78.5	93.3	88.1	83.9	92.3	89.4	82.5	92.1	88.7
0310	Concrete Forming & Accessories	81.6	87.5	86.2	80.4	83.4	82.7	83.8	84.7	84.5	87.5	89.8	89.3	91.8	99.9	98.1	80.1	81.0	80.8
0320	Concrete Reinforcing	94.1	114.2	99.7	95.5	114.1	100.6	94.2	114.0	99.7	93.9	106.1	97.3	93.7	96.9	94.6	98.2	104.3	99.9
0330	Cast-in-Place Concrete	92.6	93.4	92.9	102.8	87.5	97.3	90.7	93.6	91.7	79.9	98.4	86.5	90.7	90.4	90.6	88.9	84.8	87.5
03	CONCRETE	92.6	95.4	93.7	99.5	91.4	96.3	84.6	94.2	88.4	86.2	97.1	90.5	91.3	97.1	93.6	90.4	87.8	89.4
04	MASONRY	95.6	91.9	93.3	96.5	83.8	88.8	104.5	87.6	94.3	107.0	90.0	96.7	97.3	86.9	91.0	97.2	82.4	88.2
05	METALS	92.5	116.3	97.2	92.5	116.5	97.2	90.0	116.9	95.3	92.8	119.2	98.0	94.7	112.4	98.2	92.6	113.7	96.7
06	WOOD, PLASTICS & COMPOSITES	72.3	85.3	78.1	70.3	82.3	75.7	77.1	81.1	78.9	83.0	87.3	85.0	89.3	102.1	95.0	75.2	79.0	76.9
07	THERMAL & MOISTURE PROTECTION	102.4	91.3	98.5	102.6	87.4	97.2	99.1	89.7	95.7	98.1	107.2	101.3	101.1	100.3	100.8	100.7	81.6	93.9
08	OPENINGS	91.2	90.6	91.0	91.2	88.9	90.6	86.6	92.3	87.9	87.2	87.1	87.2	93.3	96.6	94.1	90.3	83.2	88.7
0920	Plaster & Gypsum Board	109.1	85.0	93.8	107.4	81.9	91.2	96.0	80.6	86.2	106.8	87.1	94.3	97.3	102.3	100.5	95.8	78.5	84.8
0950, 0980	Ceilings & Acoustic Treatment	108.0	85.0	95.1	108.0	81.9	93.4	97.1	80.6	87.9	88.8	87.1	87.9	93.0	102.3	98.2	96.7	78.5	86.5
0960	Flooring	96.5	92.9	95.6	95.9	97.3	96.3	90.4	92.9	91.0	100.0	95.6	98.9	93.7	84.3	91.3	89.7	92.9	90.5
0970, 0990	Wall Finishes & Painting/Coating	92.3	109.8	102.7	92.3	107.1	101.1	85.6	109.8	100.0	91.6	83.5	86.8	89.9	89.7	89.8	89.9	92.5	91.4
09	FINISHES	100.9	90.3	95.5	100.8	87.8	94.2	93.2	87.8	90.5	94.2	89.5	91.8	93.3	96.0	94.7	92.8	83.6	88.2
COVERS	DIVS. 10 - 14, 25, 28, 41, 43, 44, 46	100.0	99.2	99.9	100.0	97.0	99.4	100.0	98.9	99.8	100.0	97.5	99.5	100.0	101.0	100.2	100.0	97.7	99.5
21, 22, 23	FIRE SUPPRESSION, PLUMBING & HVAC	92.8	80.9	88.5	92.8	84.8	89.9	92.2	85.7	89.9	92.8	96.9	94.3	92.9	105.6	97.4	92.9	85.2	90.1
26, 27, 3370	ELECTRICAL, COMMUNICATIONS & UTIL.	100.4	107.8	103.6	100.4	107.9	103.6	91.2	107.8	98.4	94.3	89.2	92.1	96.4	115.2	104.6	96.0	84.8	91.1
MF2018	WEIGHTED AVERAGE	94.6	94.4	94.5	95.5	93.4	94.7	91.2	94.7	92.5	92.6	95.7	93.8	94.2	101.6	96.9	93.2	88.3	91.4

DIVISION		PENNSYLVANIA																	
		NEW CASTLE 161			NORRISTOWN 194			OIL CITY 163			PHILADELPHIA 190 - 191			PITTSBURGH 150 - 152			POTTSVILLE 179		
		MAT.	INST.	TOTAL	MAT.	INST.	TOTAL	MAT.	INST.	TOTAL	MAT.	INST.	TOTAL	MAT.	INST.	TOTAL	MAT.	INST.	TOTAL
015433	CONTRACTOR EQUIPMENT		108.2	108.2		94.4	94.4		108.2	108.2		101.1	101.1		98.4	98.4		107.5	107.5
0241, 31 - 34	SITE & INFRASTRUCTURE, DEMOLITION	81.4	93.7	89.4	99.8	90.0	93.4	80.3	91.3	87.4	105.3	103.9	104.4	94.0	95.7	95.1	80.9	90.9	87.4
0310	Concrete Forming & Accessories	83.8	91.6	89.9	83.7	119.0	111.1	83.8	84.2	84.1	99.8	136.4	128.2	99.7	98.5	98.8	79.0	79.6	79.5
0320	Concrete Reinforcing	93.1	95.4	93.8	96.3	135.3	107.1	94.2	85.2	91.7	101.0	152.1	115.1	100.4	122.8	106.6	93.2	102.4	95.7
0330	Cast-in-Place Concrete	88.1	93.8	90.1	94.2	115.5	101.8	85.5	86.1	85.7	105.7	133.5	115.6	101.4	100.6	101.1	85.2	95.1	88.7
03	CONCRETE	82.6	94.3	87.2	88.6	120.2	101.1	81.5	86.6	83.5	99.3	137.0	114.2	101.1	103.3	102.0	88.7	90.5	89.4
04	MASONRY	101.5	92.5	96.0	110.3	118.1	115.1	101.0	79.9	88.2	96.9	134.1	119.5	90.5	100.4	96.5	100.7	78.9	87.4
05	METALS	90.0	111.4	94.2	97.5	116.8	101.3	90.0	109.1	93.8	100.9	123.8	105.4	100.8	107.6	102.1	93.1	113.8	97.1
06	WOOD, PLASTICS & COMPOSITES	77.1	90.5	83.1	77.4	121.6	97.2	77.1	85.3	80.8	97.0	136.2	114.6	96.9	98.5	97.6	71.4	77.3	74.0
07	THERMAL & MOISTURE PROTECTION	99.0	90.9	96.1	105.1	117.3	109.5	98.9	83.1	93.3	101.2	137.2	114.0	104.8	100.3	103.2	98.1	90.4	95.4
08	OPENINGS	86.6	93.6	88.1	90.1	124.8	97.9	86.6	87.2	86.7	99.0	139.9	108.2	99.1	104.6	100.3	87.2	84.3	86.6
0920	Plaster & Gypsum Board	96.0	90.3	92.4	104.2	122.5	115.8	96.0	85.0	89.0	121.1	137.3	131.3	114.7	98.4	104.3	98.6	76.7	84.7
0950, 0980	Ceilings & Acoustic Treatment	97.1	90.3	93.3	100.9	122.5	113.0	97.1	85.0	90.4	106.8	137.2	123.9	102.2	98.4	100.1	88.8	76.7	82.0
0960	Flooring	90.4	97.0	92.1	93.7	124.8	101.5	90.4	92.9	91.0	101.7	147.9	113.3	101.9	106.8	103.1	96.5	92.9	95.6
0970, 0990	Wall Finishes & Painting/Coating	85.6	101.9	95.3	90.0	127.7	112.5	85.6	109.8	100.0	98.4	188.7	152.2	98.4	109.6	105.2	91.6	92.5	92.1
09	FINISHES	93.1	93.5	93.3	95.4	121.2	108.3	93.0	88.4	90.7	105.4	144.0	124.8	102.2	100.7	101.4	92.2	82.3	87.3
COVERS	DIVS. 10 - 14, 25, 28, 41, 43, 44, 46	100.0	99.9	100.0	100.0	112.3	102.4	100.0	96.7	99.4	100.0	118.5	103.6	100.0	103.4	100.7	100.0	96.9	99.4
21, 22, 23	FIRE SUPPRESSION, PLUMBING & HVAC	92.2	92.4	92.3	92.6	117.3	101.4	92.2	84.7	89.5	100.2	141.7	115.0	100.2	99.5	100.0	92.8	86.1	90.4
26, 27, 3370	ELECTRICAL, COMMUNICATIONS & UTIL.	91.5	93.2	92.2	97.9	126.4	110.2	92.6	95.9	94.0	100.6	160.7	126.6	100.8	114.6	106.8	93.3	81.3	88.1
MF2018	WEIGHTED AVERAGE	90.9	95.0	92.4	95.4	117.6	103.6	90.8	89.7	90.4	100.5	137.6	114.2	100.1	103.2	101.3	92.4	88.0	90.8

DIVISION		PENNSYLVANIA																	
		READING 195 - 196			SCRANTON 184 - 185			STATE COLLEGE 168			STROUDSBURG 183			SUNBURY 178			UNIONTOWN 154		
		MAT.	INST.	TOTAL	MAT.	INST.	TOTAL	MAT.	INST.	TOTAL	MAT.	INST.	TOTAL	MAT.	INST.	TOTAL	MAT.	INST.	TOTAL
015433	CONTRACTOR EQUIPMENT		113.7	113.7		108.2	108.2		107.5	107.5		108.2	108.2		108.2	108.2		106.9	106.9
0241, 31 - 34	SITE & INFRASTRUCTURE, DEMOLITION	106.9	102.6	104.1	89.8	93.0	91.9	78.7	92.2	87.5	82.1	92.2	88.7	90.1	91.6	91.1	85.8	92.2	90.0
0310	Concrete Forming & Accessories	101.5	85.8	89.3	99.2	86.5	89.4	85.3	84.3	84.5	85.8	82.1	82.9	89.2	76.8	79.6	74.6	87.8	84.8
0320	Concrete Reinforcing	97.6	108.2	100.5	96.6	108.0	99.7	94.9	99.3	96.1	96.9	104.4	99.0	95.8	100.7	97.2	94.8	114.2	100.2
0330	Cast-in-Place Concrete	84.4	94.0	87.8	92.6	90.5	91.8	89.3	89.1	89.2	87.2	86.2	86.9	93.1	86.5	90.8	92.6	93.5	93.0
03	CONCRETE	87.6	94.0	90.2	94.2	93.1	93.7	93.3	90.0	92.0	89.4	88.8	89.2	92.6	86.0	90.0	92.2	95.5	93.5
04	MASONRY	100.0	88.4	93.0	97.7	90.1	93.1	102.3	88.8	94.1	94.5	86.7	89.8	100.1	72.9	83.6	108.6	91.9	98.4
05	METALS	97.9	119.1	102.1	97.1	117.3	101.1	92.3	112.9	96.3	93.4	114.1	98.6	92.7	112.7	96.7	92.2	116.8	97.1
06	WOOD, PLASTICS & COMPOSITES	100.5	82.8	92.6	99.8	84.8	93.1	83.4	82.3	82.9	82.2	79.0	80.8	80.6	77.3	79.1	62.9	85.3	72.9
07	THERMAL & MOISTURE PROTECTION	106.1	104.1	105.4	101.3	89.2	97.0	100.4	101.5	100.8	100.9	81.9	94.1	99.2	83.1	93.5	102.3	91.3	98.4
08	OPENINGS	94.9	91.8	94.2	92.8	88.9	91.9	90.2	85.4	89.1	93.4	85.7	91.6	87.3	81.5	86.0	91.1	91.6	91.2
0920	Plaster & Gypsum Board	115.7	82.5	94.7	111.5	84.4	94.3	97.2	81.9	87.5	95.4	78.5	84.7	97.3	76.7	84.3	103.5	85.0	91.8
0950, 0980	Ceilings & Acoustic Treatment	88.1	82.5	85.0	104.8	84.4	93.4	92.6	81.9	86.6	91.7	78.5	84.3	84.7	76.7	80.3	108.0	85.0	95.1
0960	Flooring	96.6	90.5	95.1	96.1	98.0	96.6	94.2	92.4	93.7	91.9	84.3	90.0	97.0	92.9	96.0	93.5	103.4	96.0
0970, 0990	Wall Finishes & Painting/Coating	89.0	103.5	97.6	89.9	103.5	98.0	89.9	107.1	100.1	89.9	92.5	91.4	91.6	92.5	92.1	92.3	101.9	98.0
09	FINISHES	94.6	87.2	90.9	99.1	89.9	94.5	92.7	87.6	90.1	91.0	82.8	87.4	92.2	80.8	86.5	99.2	91.2	95.2
COVERS	DIVS. 10 - 14, 25, 28, 41, 43, 44, 46	100.0	98.0	99.6	100.0	98.7	99.7	100.0	95.8	99.2	100.0	98.6	99.7	100.0	97.9	98.7	100.0	99.3	99.9
21, 22, 23	FIRE SUPPRESSION, PLUMBING & HVAC	100.4	111.2	104.3	100.4	94.8	98.4	92.9	94.8	93.6	92.9	88.0	91.1	92.8	78.5	87.7	92.8	85.7	90.2
26, 27, 3370	ELECTRICAL, COMMUNICATIONS & UTIL.	101.9	93.3	98.2	99.3	89.8	95.2	95.1	107.9	100.6	96.4	126.2	109.3	94.0	81.8	88.7	98.8	107.9	102.7
MF2018	WEIGHTED AVERAGE	97.9	99.3	98.4	97.7	94.3	96.5	93.5	95.6	94.3	93.7	95.4	94.4	93.2	84.6	90.0	94.6	95.7	95.0

City Cost Indexes

PENNSYLVANIA

DIVISION		WASHINGTON 153			WELLSBORO 169			WESTCHESTER 193			WILKES-BARRE 186-187			WILLIAMSPORT 177			YORK 173-174		
		MAT.	INST.	TOTAL	MAT.	INST.	TOTAL	MAT.	INST.	TOTAL	MAT.	INST.	TOTAL	MAT.	INST.	TOTAL	MAT.	INST.	TOTAL
015433	CONTRACTOR EQUIPMENT		106.9	106.9		108.2	108.2		94.4	94.4		108.2	108.2		108.2	108.2		107.5	107.5
0241, 31 - 34	SITE & INFRASTRUCTURE, DEMOLITION	85.9	93.0	90.5	87.5	91.6	90.2	105.7	90.9	96.1	80.1	92.7	88.3	82.7	92.8	89.3	85.0	93.3	90.4
0310	Concrete Forming & Accessories	81.8	93.7	91.0	84.3	76.3	78.0	91.0	114.5	109.2	88.9	84.9	85.8	85.9	82.2	83.0	82.4	86.4	85.5
0320	Concrete Reinforcing	94.8	114.5	100.2	94.9	104.2	97.4	95.5	135.3	106.5	95.6	110.3	99.6	95.1	110.1	99.2	95.8	110.1	99.8
0330	Cast-in-Place Concrete	92.6	94.1	93.2	93.6	80.5	88.9	104.4	117.4	109.0	83.7	88.8	85.5	78.8	87.5	81.9	85.6	98.4	90.1
03	CONCRETE	92.8	98.5	95.1	95.1	84.2	90.8	95.1	118.7	104.4	87.0	92.0	89.0	82.7	90.4	85.8	90.1	96.1	92.5
04	MASONRY	96.2	94.3	95.0	104.3	73.3	85.5	104.5	121.5	114.8	109.4	92.9	99.4	92.2	87.2	89.2	101.0	90.0	94.3
05	METALS	92.2	118.0	97.3	92.4	112.9	96.4	97.5	116.6	101.3	92.5	117.9	97.5	92.8	118.6	97.9	94.4	119.1	99.3
06	WOOD, PLASTICS & COMPOSITES	72.3	92.8	81.5	80.5	76.6	78.7	86.2	113.9	98.6	85.3	83.1	84.3	76.7	80.9	78.6	75.2	82.9	78.6
07	THERMAL & MOISTURE PROTECTION	102.4	93.4	99.2	101.4	77.1	92.7	105.6	113.8	108.5	100.7	90.0	96.9	98.6	87.6	94.7	98.2	104.5	100.4
08	OPENINGS	91.1	98.7	92.8	93.0	81.5	90.4	90.1	120.5	97.0	90.3	88.1	89.8	87.3	86.9	87.2	87.2	85.4	86.8
0920	Plaster & Gypsum Board	109.1	92.7	98.7	95.5	76.0	83.2	104.7	114.6	111.0	97.0	82.7	87.9	98.6	80.5	87.1	98.6	82.5	88.4
0950, 0980	Ceilings & Acoustic Treatment	108.0	92.7	99.4	92.6	76.0	83.3	100.9	114.6	108.6	96.7	82.7	88.8	88.8	80.5	84.2	87.8	82.5	84.8
0960	Flooring	96.6	103.4	98.3	91.2	92.9	91.6	96.0	124.8	103.2	92.6	98.0	93.9	96.1	88.6	94.2	97.7	95.6	97.2
0970, 0990	Wall Finishes & Painting/Coating	92.3	101.9	98.0	89.9	92.5	91.4	90.0	127.7	112.5	89.9	106.2	99.6	91.6	106.2	100.3	91.6	86.7	88.7
09	FINISHES	100.9	95.9	98.4	92.6	80.8	86.7	96.6	117.5	107.1	93.6	88.9	91.3	92.6	85.3	88.9	92.3	87.2	89.8
COVERS	DIVS. 10 - 14, 25, 28, 41, 43, 44, 46	100.0	100.1	100.0	100.0	92.9	98.6	100.0	112.6	102.4	100.0	98.1	99.6	100.0	94.9	99.0	100.0	97.0	99.4
21, 22, 23	FIRE SUPPRESSION, PLUMBING & HVAC	92.8	89.0	91.4	92.9	78.5	87.7	92.6	119.1	102.3	92.9	94.4	93.4	92.8	93.6	93.1	100.3	96.9	99.1
26, 27, 3370	ELECTRICAL, COMMUNICATIONS & UTIL.	100.1	107.9	103.5	96.0	84.8	91.1	97.8	117.8	106.5	96.4	85.1	91.5	94.2	78.7	87.5	94.3	79.2	87.7
MF2018	WEIGHTED AVERAGE	94.5	98.3	95.9	94.4	84.6	90.8	96.3	116.1	103.6	93.4	93.5	93.4	91.6	91.0	91.4	94.8	93.7	94.4

PUERTO RICO / RHODE ISLAND / SOUTH CAROLINA

DIVISION		PUERTO RICO SAN JUAN 009			RHODE ISLAND NEWPORT 028			RHODE ISLAND PROVIDENCE 029			SOUTH CAROLINA AIKEN 298			SOUTH CAROLINA BEAUFORT 299			SOUTH CAROLINA CHARLESTON 294		
		MAT.	INST.	TOTAL	MAT.	INST.	TOTAL	MAT.	INST.	TOTAL	MAT.	INST.	TOTAL	MAT.	INST.	TOTAL	MAT.	INST.	TOTAL
015433	CONTRACTOR EQUIPMENT		91.1	91.1		95.8	95.8		100.9	100.9		101.3	101.3		101.3	101.3		101.3	101.3
0241, 31 - 34	SITE & INFRASTRUCTURE, DEMOLITION	125.9	88.5	101.5	84.4	93.9	90.6	87.6	103.4	97.9	131.9	83.3	100.2	127.3	83.3	98.6	115.8	83.7	94.9
0310	Concrete Forming & Accessories	77.0	20.5	33.1	97.9	116.4	112.2	95.3	116.5	111.8	95.5	59.0	67.2	94.4	61.3	68.7	93.4	62.4	69.3
0320	Concrete Reinforcing	107.9	17.3	82.8	98.5	115.1	103.1	98.7	115.1	103.3	98.3	54.2	86.1	97.4	59.7	86.9	97.2	64.1	88.0
0330	Cast-in-Place Concrete	90.5	32.5	69.9	56.3	112.1	76.1	77.2	113.5	90.1	97.4	64.2	85.6	97.4	64.3	85.6	114.4	66.6	97.4
03	CONCRETE	97.7	25.5	69.2	83.0	114.5	95.4	93.9	114.9	102.2	95.8	61.8	82.4	94.1	63.8	82.1	95.1	65.9	83.6
04	MASONRY	121.2	22.1	61.0	112.4	118.9	116.4	124.6	119.0	121.2	82.6	53.9	65.2	98.1	53.9	71.3	99.8	64.8	78.6
05	METALS	104.0	43.2	92.0	94.4	112.6	98.0	99.2	110.4	101.4	98.0	85.7	95.6	98.0	87.7	96.0	100.4	91.3	98.6
06	WOOD, PLASTICS & COMPOSITES	81.2	19.6	53.5	95.6	115.4	104.5	93.5	115.5	103.4	93.1	60.8	78.6	91.2	63.7	78.9	89.6	63.7	78.0
07	THERMAL & MOISTURE PROTECTION	143.0	26.1	101.4	93.0	113.3	100.2	97.7	114.7	103.8	108.3	56.9	90.0	108.0	57.9	90.1	107.1	63.5	91.5
08	OPENINGS	159.8	18.0	127.8	94.9	116.2	99.7	97.4	116.3	101.7	92.7	56.7	84.6	92.7	59.5	85.2	96.1	61.9	88.4
0920	Plaster & Gypsum Board	156.5	17.2	68.1	106.5	115.8	112.4	120.0	115.8	117.3	101.5	59.6	74.9	109.0	62.6	79.6	109.2	62.6	79.6
0950, 0980	Ceilings & Acoustic Treatment	227.8	17.2	109.7	91.6	115.8	105.1	113.1	115.8	114.6	96.0	59.6	75.6	106.9	62.6	82.1	106.9	62.6	82.1
0960	Flooring	194.8	26.6	152.6	101.5	126.3	107.8	108.2	126.3	112.7	107.7	80.4	100.8	109.0	67.9	98.7	108.7	79.7	101.4
0970, 0990	Wall Finishes & Painting/Coating	200.1	20.6	93.1	87.3	114.6	103.6	98.4	114.6	108.1	94.3	58.7	73.1	94.3	50.5	68.2	94.3	66.0	77.4
09	FINISHES	197.7	21.5	109.2	96.4	118.4	107.5	107.9	118.5	113.2	103.5	62.9	83.1	107.4	61.6	84.4	105.2	66.0	85.5
COVERS	DIVS. 10 - 14, 25, 28, 41, 43, 44, 46	100.0	24.9	85.4	100.0	106.1	101.2	100.0	106.4	101.2	100.0	82.5	96.6	100.0	75.5	95.3	100.0	83.3	96.8
21, 22, 23	FIRE SUPPRESSION, PLUMBING & HVAC	117.6	17.3	81.6	100.6	110.9	104.3	100.2	110.9	104.0	93.0	49.8	77.5	93.0	54.9	79.4	100.5	57.7	85.2
26, 27, 3370	ELECTRICAL, COMMUNICATIONS & UTIL.	120.3	22.3	77.9	102.5	94.8	99.2	101.1	94.8	98.3	94.0	55.1	77.1	95.9	59.1	79.9	95.1	61.6	80.6
MF2018	WEIGHTED AVERAGE	121.3	28.7	87.2	96.3	109.9	101.3	100.1	110.6	104.0	96.8	61.8	84.0	97.6	63.7	85.1	99.6	67.6	87.8

SOUTH CAROLINA / SOUTH DAKOTA

DIVISION		COLUMBIA 290-292			FLORENCE 295			GREENVILLE 296			ROCK HILL 297			SPARTANBURG 293			ABERDEEN 574		
		MAT.	INST.	TOTAL	MAT.	INST.	TOTAL	MAT.	INST.	TOTAL	MAT.	INST.	TOTAL	MAT.	INST.	TOTAL	MAT.	INST.	TOTAL
015433	CONTRACTOR EQUIPMENT		106.4	106.4		101.3	101.3		101.3	101.3		101.3	101.3		101.3	101.3		94.2	94.2
0241, 31 - 34	SITE & INFRASTRUCTURE, DEMOLITION	115.4	96.0	102.7	124.8	83.2	97.7	120.1	83.5	96.3	114.4	83.3	94.1	119.9	83.5	96.2	89.1	88.8	88.9
0310	Concrete Forming & Accessories	97.1	57.3	66.2	80.6	57.2	62.5	93.0	57.4	65.3	91.0	58.8	66.0	96.0	57.4	66.0	96.9	64.0	71.4
0320	Concrete Reinforcing	99.9	63.9	90.0	96.7	64.0	87.7	96.7	58.1	86.0	97.5	58.9	86.8	96.7	60.6	86.7	97.7	70.0	90.1
0330	Cast-in-Place Concrete	115.8	66.3	98.2	97.4	66.1	86.3	97.4	66.6	86.4	97.4	63.8	85.4	97.4	66.6	86.4	125.0	75.6	107.5
03	CONCRETE	95.7	63.2	82.9	90.5	63.3	79.7	90.4	62.6	79.5	89.5	62.3	78.8	90.7	63.0	79.8	108.1	70.1	93.1
04	MASONRY	92.4	63.2	74.7	82.8	64.7	71.8	80.9	64.8	71.1	104.6	53.2	73.4	82.7	64.8	71.9	125.1	70.6	92.0
05	METALS	98.2	87.1	96.0	98.8	89.7	97.0	98.8	89.3	96.9	98.0	87.3	95.9	98.8	89.7	97.0	95.6	82.4	93.0
06	WOOD, PLASTICS & COMPOSITES	94.3	57.0	77.6	73.9	57.1	66.3	89.4	57.1	74.9	87.6	60.8	75.6	94.0	57.1	77.5	95.9	59.0	79.3
07	THERMAL & MOISTURE PROTECTION	103.4	63.4	89.2	107.3	62.8	91.5	107.3	62.8	91.5	107.2	52.4	87.7	107.4	62.8	91.5	103.6	71.1	92.0
08	OPENINGS	98.3	58.3	89.3	92.8	58.3	85.0	92.7	57.3	84.7	92.7	57.8	84.8	92.7	57.5	84.8	92.8	70.4	87.7
0920	Plaster & Gypsum Board	108.4	55.8	75.1	94.9	55.8	70.1	99.6	55.8	71.8	99.1	59.6	74.1	102.5	55.8	72.9	109.7	58.3	77.1
0950, 0980	Ceilings & Acoustic Treatment	108.6	55.8	79.0	98.8	55.8	74.7	96.0	55.8	73.5	96.0	59.6	75.6	96.0	55.8	73.5	104.3	58.3	78.5
0960	Flooring	102.4	75.1	95.6	101.2	75.1	94.7	106.7	75.1	98.8	105.8	67.9	96.3	107.9	75.1	99.7	93.1	65.0	86.0
0970, 0990	Wall Finishes & Painting/Coating	94.9	66.0	77.7	94.3	66.0	77.4	94.3	66.0	77.4	94.3	58.7	73.1	94.3	66.0	77.4	85.1	72.9	77.8
09	FINISHES	104.9	61.2	82.9	100.1	61.4	80.7	101.2	61.4	81.2	100.6	60.6	80.5	102.0	61.4	81.6	95.8	65.3	80.5
COVERS	DIVS. 10 - 14, 25, 28, 41, 43, 44, 46	100.0	82.5	96.6	100.0	82.6	96.6	100.0	82.7	96.6	100.0	82.4	96.6	100.0	82.7	96.6	100.0	80.9	96.3
21, 22, 23	FIRE SUPPRESSION, PLUMBING & HVAC	100.0	54.1	83.6	100.5	54.1	83.9	100.5	53.2	83.6	93.0	49.4	77.4	100.5	53.2	83.6	100.1	77.1	91.9
26, 27, 3370	ELECTRICAL, COMMUNICATIONS & UTIL.	100.2	55.9	81.0	94.0	55.9	77.5	95.1	78.7	88.0	95.1	80.7	88.9	95.1	78.7	88.0	92.9	67.2	81.8
MF2018	WEIGHTED AVERAGE	99.5	65.1	86.8	97.4	64.5	85.3	97.5	67.4	86.5	96.3	65.2	84.8	97.7	67.5	86.6	99.1	73.5	89.7

City Cost Indexes

		SOUTH DAKOTA																	
		MITCHELL			MOBRIDGE			PIERRE			RAPID CITY			SIOUX FALLS			WATERTOWN		
DIVISION		573			576			575			577			570 - 571			572		
		MAT.	INST.	TOTAL	MAT.	INST.	TOTAL	MAT.	INST.	TOTAL	MAT.	INST.	TOTAL	MAT.	INST.	TOTAL	MAT.	INST.	TOTAL
015433	CONTRACTOR EQUIPMENT		94.2	94.2		94.2	94.2		100.3	100.3		94.2	94.2		100.3	100.3		94.2	94.2
0241, 31 - 34	SITE & INFRASTRUCTURE, DEMOLITION	83.3	88.2	86.5	83.3	88.2	86.5	89.3	98.0	95.0	88.1	88.5	88.4	84.3	98.9	93.8	83.2	88.2	86.4
0310	Concrete Forming & Accessories	95.8	41.2	53.4	85.5	41.7	51.5	99.0	79.6	83.9	104.7	52.5	64.2	97.3	80.1	84.0	81.7	68.2	71.2
0320	Concrete Reinforcing	97.2	69.9	89.6	99.7	69.8	91.4	100.0	72.2	92.3	91.3	71.9	85.9	100.3	95.9	99.1	94.5	69.7	87.6
0330	Cast-in-Place Concrete	121.5	48.6	95.6	121.5	74.2	104.7	126.9	78.3	109.6	120.5	74.8	104.3	99.8	80.3	92.9	121.5	73.9	104.6
03	CONCRETE	105.8	50.4	83.9	105.6	59.5	87.4	112.0	78.2	98.6	104.7	64.9	89.0	100.7	83.3	93.8	103.9	71.3	91.1
04	MASONRY	110.9	69.8	85.9	119.4	65.6	86.7	111.9	74.3	89.1	118.5	68.3	88.0	113.9	75.5	90.6	147.9	66.4	98.4
05	METALS	94.6	81.2	92.0	94.7	81.6	92.1	99.5	79.8	95.6	97.9	81.3	94.6	98.8	90.4	97.2	94.6	81.0	91.9
06	WOOD, PLASTICS & COMPOSITES	94.6	30.7	66.0	80.5	30.5	58.1	100.0	79.2	90.6	101.8	43.7	75.7	94.3	79.0	87.4	75.5	67.4	71.9
07	THERMAL & MOISTURE PROTECTION	103.5	65.9	90.1	103.4	68.9	91.1	104.1	79.4	95.3	101.8	72.5	92.8	104.5	81.8	96.4	103.2	70.3	91.4
08	OPENINGS	91.9	54.8	83.6	94.3	54.7	85.4	97.0	82.5	93.7	96.1	62.9	88.6	97.6	87.4	95.3	91.9	57.2	84.1
0920	Plaster & Gypsum Board	107.7	29.2	57.9	101.2	29.0	55.4	108.2	78.7	89.5	109.8	42.5	67.1	99.2	78.5	86.1	98.3	67.0	78.4
0950, 0980	Ceilings & Acoustic Treatment	99.8	29.2	60.2	104.3	29.0	62.1	111.9	78.7	93.3	107.1	42.5	70.9	110.4	78.5	92.5	99.8	67.0	81.4
0960	Flooring	92.8	70.3	87.1	89.4	41.6	77.4	102.4	69.6	94.2	92.5	65.0	85.6	99.9	74.2	93.4	88.3	39.2	76.0
0970, 0990	Wall Finishes & Painting/Coating	85.1	72.9	77.8	85.1	72.9	77.8	99.1	114.6	108.4	85.1	114.6	102.7	94.9	114.6	106.7	85.1	72.9	77.8
09	FINISHES	94.1	48.0	71.0	93.5	44.0	68.6	103.9	82.8	93.3	96.3	60.8	78.5	101.2	82.6	91.8	91.5	65.2	78.3
COVERS	DIVS. 10 - 14, 25, 28, 41, 43, 44, 46	100.0	73.3	94.8	100.0	73.1	94.8	100.0	88.1	97.7	100.0	83.0	96.7	100.0	88.2	97.7	100.0	76.6	95.5
21, 22, 23	FIRE SUPPRESSION, PLUMBING & HVAC	92.6	44.2	75.2	92.6	68.4	83.9	100.1	70.3	89.4	100.1	69.4	89.1	100.0	70.6	89.5	92.6	47.0	76.2
26, 27, 3370	ELECTRICAL, COMMUNICATIONS & UTIL.	92.1	67.2	81.3	92.9	35.4	68.0	99.5	42.5	74.8	91.2	42.5	70.1	99.6	67.2	85.6	91.6	67.2	81.0
MF2018	WEIGHTED AVERAGE	96.0	60.0	82.8	96.4	61.1	83.4	101.6	73.9	91.4	99.1	66.3	87.1	99.9	79.6	92.4	96.8	66.0	85.5

		TENNESSEE																	
		CHATTANOOGA			COLUMBIA			COOKEVILLE			JACKSON			JOHNSON CITY			KNOXVILLE		
DIVISION		373 - 374			384			385			383			376			377 - 379		
		MAT.	INST.	TOTAL	MAT.	INST.	TOTAL	MAT.	INST.	TOTAL	MAT.	INST.	TOTAL	MAT.	INST.	TOTAL	MAT.	INST.	TOTAL
015433	CONTRACTOR EQUIPMENT		101.0	101.0		96.1	96.1		96.1	96.1		101.5	101.5		95.7	95.7		95.7	95.7
0241, 31 - 34	SITE & INFRASTRUCTURE, DEMOLITION	102.4	90.0	94.3	97.2	81.1	86.7	103.4	80.3	88.3	109.9	90.6	97.3	107.4	80.4	89.8	91.3	81.2	84.7
0310	Concrete Forming & Accessories	100.6	58.5	67.9	82.9	56.9	62.7	83.0	30.0	41.8	90.9	66.6	72.0	85.2	56.5	62.9	99.2	63.3	71.3
0320	Concrete Reinforcing	93.1	64.4	85.1	86.0	58.4	78.3	86.0	58.1	78.3	86.0	65.3	80.2	93.5	60.6	84.4	93.1	66.8	85.8
0330	Cast-in-Place Concrete	94.9	61.1	82.9	94.4	60.5	82.3	107.0	54.1	88.2	104.5	63.6	90.0	76.3	55.8	69.0	89.2	64.1	80.2
03	CONCRETE	94.8	62.2	81.9	90.7	60.2	78.6	98.8	45.8	77.9	92.7	66.9	82.5	100.8	58.8	84.2	92.6	65.8	82.0
04	MASONRY	96.3	53.5	70.3	104.9	50.0	71.5	101.1	35.5	61.3	105.5	55.6	75.2	108.2	41.3	67.5	74.7	55.5	63.1
05	METALS	96.3	88.1	94.7	95.5	85.0	93.4	95.6	84.3	93.4	99.2	87.9	96.9	92.1	86.3	91.0	96.3	88.9	94.8
06	WOOD, PLASTICS & COMPOSITES	99.9	59.0	81.5	68.0	57.6	63.4	68.3	26.9	49.8	82.5	67.7	75.9	73.1	61.4	67.9	91.1	64.1	79.0
07	THERMAL & MOISTURE PROTECTION	107.9	59.0	90.5	98.0	56.2	83.3	98.4	47.5	80.3	99.9	62.0	86.4	103.6	53.8	85.9	101.9	62.6	87.9
08	OPENINGS	98.4	57.8	89.2	91.7	48.4	81.9	91.7	32.3	78.3	98.1	61.7	89.9	95.3	58.5	87.0	92.8	57.6	84.9
0920	Plaster & Gypsum Board	77.4	58.4	65.3	84.1	57.0	66.9	84.1	25.4	46.9	87.5	67.4	74.7	84.6	60.9	69.6	93.2	63.6	74.4
0950, 0980	Ceilings & Acoustic Treatment	98.0	58.4	75.8	75.4	57.0	65.1	75.4	25.4	47.4	80.5	67.4	73.1	94.1	60.9	75.5	95.9	63.6	77.8
0960	Flooring	102.4	57.7	91.2	87.8	48.3	77.9	87.8	44.8	77.0	83.9	52.7	76.1	102.4	52.7	90.0	106.5	56.8	94.1
0970, 0990	Wall Finishes & Painting/Coating	95.2	52.9	70.0	86.7	50.2	64.9	86.7	50.2	64.9	89.4	56.5	69.8	92.0	52.9	68.7	92.0	54.5	69.6
09	FINISHES	96.2	57.4	76.7	88.9	54.3	71.5	89.4	32.8	61.0	88.0	63.1	75.5	99.2	55.4	77.2	93.9	61.0	77.3
COVERS	DIVS. 10 - 14, 25, 28, 41, 43, 44, 46	100.0	80.4	96.2	100.0	80.1	96.2	100.0	73.2	94.8	100.0	82.9	96.7	100.0	77.5	95.6	100.0	81.7	96.5
21, 22, 23	FIRE SUPPRESSION, PLUMBING & HVAC	100.2	53.6	83.5	94.4	66.2	84.3	94.4	60.4	82.2	100.1	63.0	86.8	100.0	50.1	82.1	100.0	62.7	86.6
26, 27, 3370	ELECTRICAL, COMMUNICATIONS & UTIL.	103.8	73.8	90.8	96.0	45.0	73.9	96.8	54.6	78.5	103.7	58.5	84.1	93.6	46.7	73.3	96.7	57.0	79.5
MF2018	WEIGHTED AVERAGE	98.8	65.4	86.5	94.5	61.5	82.3	95.7	53.8	80.3	98.6	67.2	87.1	97.6	57.8	82.9	95.7	65.6	84.6

		TENNESSEE									TEXAS								
		MCKENZIE			MEMPHIS			NASHVILLE			ABILENE			AMARILLO			AUSTIN		
DIVISION		382			375,380 - 381			370 - 372			795 - 796			790 - 791			786 - 787		
		MAT.	INST.	TOTAL	MAT.	INST.	TOTAL	MAT.	INST.	TOTAL	MAT.	INST.	TOTAL	MAT.	INST.	TOTAL	MAT.	INST.	TOTAL
015433	CONTRACTOR EQUIPMENT		96.1	96.1		97.2	97.2		103.4	103.4		88.4	88.4		95.3	95.3		95.6	95.6
0241, 31 - 34	SITE & INFRASTRUCTURE, DEMOLITION	102.9	80.5	88.3	90.3	90.1	90.2	100.2	97.6	98.5	95.4	84.5	88.3	95.5	94.8	95.0	90.8	94.2	93.0
0310	Concrete Forming & Accessories	92.1	32.0	45.4	100.2	67.6	74.9	101.2	71.0	77.7	100.8	58.5	67.9	102.4	53.3	64.2	97.6	53.3	63.2
0320	Concrete Reinforcing	86.1	58.9	78.6	100.1	70.0	91.7	101.0	68.3	92.0	98.9	49.7	85.3	99.2	48.5	85.1	99.6	47.7	85.2
0330	Cast-in-Place Concrete	104.7	55.1	87.1	92.0	69.1	83.8	86.9	70.4	81.0	77.3	64.2	72.6	75.5	70.2	73.6	83.8	66.5	77.7
03	CONCRETE	98.1	47.2	78.0	97.9	69.5	86.7	97.3	71.3	87.0	84.5	59.9	74.8	88.8	59.3	77.2	88.3	57.8	76.3
04	MASONRY	104.1	40.6	65.6	81.7	57.7	67.1	97.0	63.5	76.6	94.3	59.6	73.2	88.0	61.9	72.2	91.0	60.7	72.6
05	METALS	95.6	84.9	93.5	100.4	82.0	96.8	100.4	84.0	97.2	108.8	71.0	101.4	104.5	68.8	97.4	101.5	67.7	94.8
06	WOOD, PLASTICS & COMPOSITES	79.7	29.0	57.0	95.8	67.2	83.0	98.0	71.6	86.1	101.1	60.3	82.8	98.7	51.3	77.4	94.7	52.8	76.0
07	THERMAL & MOISTURE PROTECTION	98.5	48.4	80.6	106.1	66.4	91.9	105.3	69.2	92.5	96.5	61.6	84.1	93.1	63.7	82.6	90.9	64.3	81.4
08	OPENINGS	91.7	33.8	78.6	100.3	63.5	92.0	99.2	68.1	92.2	100.8	56.0	90.7	98.9	51.0	88.1	98.4	50.7	87.6
0920	Plaster & Gypsum Board	88.2	27.5	49.7	87.8	66.4	74.2	81.2	70.8	74.6	91.3	59.7	71.2	104.4	50.0	69.9	92.0	51.6	66.4
0950, 0980	Ceilings & Acoustic Treatment	75.4	27.5	48.5	111.8	66.4	86.3	86.8	70.8	77.8	105.1	59.7	79.6	101.4	50.0	72.6	98.2	51.6	72.1
0960	Flooring	89.9	48.3	79.5	103.1	55.3	91.1	108.4	64.1	97.3	96.3	66.9	88.9	98.6	64.9	90.2	103.9	64.3	94.0
0970, 0990	Wall Finishes & Painting/Coating	86.7	39.2	58.4	95.5	74.1	82.7	98.7	65.9	79.2	98.8	53.2	71.6	104.7	51.7	73.1	104.7	43.6	68.1
09	FINISHES	90.5	34.0	62.1	101.8	65.7	83.7	97.8	69.1	83.4	95.5	59.5	77.4	101.2	54.6	77.8	99.2	54.0	76.5
COVERS	DIVS. 10 - 14, 25, 28, 41, 43, 44, 46	100.0	73.9	94.9	100.0	84.3	97.0	100.0	84.9	97.1	100.0	79.1	95.9	100.0	80.1	96.1	100.0	80.4	96.2
21, 22, 23	FIRE SUPPRESSION, PLUMBING & HVAC	94.4	52.7	79.5	100.1	73.5	90.5	100.1	73.0	90.4	100.1	49.4	81.9	100.0	53.2	83.2	99.7	58.5	84.9
26, 27, 3370	ELECTRICAL, COMMUNICATIONS & UTIL.	96.7	49.3	76.1	99.2	63.9	83.9	104.0	64.2	86.8	97.4	51.0	77.3	100.8	58.3	82.3	98.4	56.0	80.1
MF2018	WEIGHTED AVERAGE	95.8	52.5	79.9	99.1	70.7	88.7	100.0	73.1	90.1	99.1	59.8	84.7	98.9	61.6	85.2	97.6	61.9	84.4

City Cost Indexes

TEXAS

DIVISION		BEAUMONT 776-777			BROWNWOOD 768			BRYAN 778			CHILDRESS 792			CORPUS CHRISTI 783-784			DALLAS 752-753		
		MAT.	INST.	TOTAL	MAT.	INST.	TOTAL	MAT.	INST.	TOTAL	MAT.	INST.	TOTAL	MAT.	INST.	TOTAL	MAT.	INST.	TOTAL
015433	CONTRACTOR EQUIPMENT		91.2	91.2		88.4	88.4		91.2	91.2		88.4	88.4		97.6	97.6		108.2	108.2
0241, 31-34	SITE & INFRASTRUCTURE, DEMOLITION	92.5	87.3	89.1	100.0	84.4	89.8	81.0	87.0	84.9	101.7	84.4	90.4	123.8	80.1	95.3	111.7	100.4	104.3
0310	Concrete Forming & Accessories	104.4	54.9	65.9	97.4	55.4	64.8	82.9	53.0	59.7	99.0	55.5	65.2	102.5	51.7	63.0	97.7	61.6	69.6
0320	Concrete Reinforcing	100.0	70.5	91.8	89.8	46.0	77.6	101.4	46.0	86.1	99.0	46.0	84.3	87.9	48.8	77.0	100.3	50.7	86.6
0330	Cast-in-Place Concrete	72.0	66.7	70.1	96.7	54.6	81.7	57.7	54.6	56.6	79.3	54.7	70.5	102.0	64.3	88.6	101.8	69.1	90.2
03	CONCRETE	85.4	62.7	76.4	90.4	54.5	76.3	74.2	53.5	66.0	90.4	54.6	76.3	91.9	57.6	78.4	95.9	63.7	83.2
04	MASONRY	94.9	60.8	74.2	116.2	54.8	78.9	126.2	54.6	82.7	97.4	54.4	71.2	81.1	57.9	67.0	112.3	57.9	79.3
05	METALS	93.4	79.1	90.6	100.0	68.9	93.8	92.8	69.0	88.1	105.4	69.0	98.3	95.8	83.5	93.4	101.2	79.7	96.9
06	WOOD, PLASTICS & COMPOSITES	106.5	54.0	82.9	101.2	57.4	81.6	72.9	53.9	64.4	100.3	57.4	81.1	113.1	51.5	85.5	95.3	63.4	81.0
07	THERMAL & MOISTURE PROTECTION	96.1	64.6	84.9	91.7	58.0	79.7	89.4	58.4	78.3	97.1	57.9	83.1	97.4	60.1	84.1	91.8	65.3	82.3
08	OPENINGS	86.5	58.5	80.2	98.5	52.5	88.1	87.4	50.7	79.1	96.0	52.5	86.2	96.0	49.4	85.5	98.1	59.1	89.3
0920	Plaster & Gypsum Board	97.0	53.3	69.3	81.5	56.7	65.7	81.7	53.2	63.6	89.4	56.7	68.6	95.1	50.5	66.8	93.9	62.1	73.7
0950, 0980	Ceilings & Acoustic Treatment	107.0	53.3	76.9	84.9	56.7	69.1	96.3	53.2	72.1	99.2	56.7	75.4	100.8	50.5	72.6	103.2	62.1	80.1
0960	Flooring	109.9	72.4	100.5	82.3	48.9	73.9	85.5	60.0	79.1	95.0	48.9	83.5	114.6	70.6	103.6	103.1	67.5	94.2
0970, 0990	Wall Finishes & Painting/Coating	94.2	55.5	71.1	91.8	45.9	64.4	91.5	51.0	67.4	98.8	45.9	67.3	112.4	42.5	70.7	104.7	52.2	73.4
09	FINISHES	97.6	57.5	77.4	84.0	53.1	68.5	84.9	53.6	69.2	94.6	53.1	73.7	103.7	53.7	78.6	102.2	61.6	81.8
COVERS	DIVS. 10-14, 25, 28, 41, 43, 44, 46	100.0	75.9	95.3	100.0	78.4	95.8	100.0	75.1	95.2	100.0	78.4	95.8	100.0	77.5	95.6	100.0	81.3	96.4
21, 22, 23	FIRE SUPPRESSION, PLUMBING & HVAC	99.7	63.6	86.8	92.2	44.8	75.2	92.2	59.2	80.3	92.6	48.8	76.9	99.8	57.0	84.4	100.0	60.2	85.7
26, 27, 3370	ELECTRICAL, COMMUNICATIONS & UTIL.	96.6	65.1	83.0	95.0	41.1	71.7	97.5	56.4	79.7	97.4	49.7	76.7	97.2	61.1	81.5	93.4	60.5	79.1
MF2018	WEIGHTED AVERAGE	94.6	66.0	84.1	95.7	54.9	80.7	91.2	60.0	79.7	97.3	56.9	82.4	97.6	61.9	84.5	99.5	66.4	87.3

TEXAS

DIVISION		DEL RIO 788			DENTON 762			EASTLAND 764			EL PASO 798-799,885			FORT WORTH 760-761			GALVESTON 775		
		MAT.	INST.	TOTAL	MAT.	INST.	TOTAL	MAT.	INST.	TOTAL	MAT.	INST.	TOTAL	MAT.	INST.	TOTAL	MAT.	INST.	TOTAL
015433	CONTRACTOR EQUIPMENT		88.2	88.2		96.7	96.7		88.4	88.4		95.4	95.4		96.9	96.9		102.5	102.5
0241, 31-34	SITE & INFRASTRUCTURE, DEMOLITION	105.5	82.7	90.6	100.2	79.3	86.6	102.3	84.4	90.6	91.4	94.7	93.6	98.9	97.2	97.8	106.1	85.8	92.9
0310	Concrete Forming & Accessories	98.7	46.7	58.3	105.7	55.7	66.9	98.4	55.4	65.0	103.1	58.4	68.4	98.0	59.3	67.9	92.3	50.8	60.1
0320	Concrete Reinforcing	88.2	42.7	75.6	90.6	46.4	78.4	89.9	46.0	77.8	100.7	49.9	86.6	99.6	49.7	85.8	101.1	53.6	87.9
0330	Cast-in-Place Concrete	109.8	54.0	90.0	74.8	55.6	68.0	102.2	54.6	85.3	68.4	66.6	67.7	87.0	66.1	79.5	76.6	55.5	69.1
03	CONCRETE	106.4	49.7	84.0	75.7	56.0	67.9	94.0	54.6	78.4	87.1	60.6	76.7	88.4	60.8	77.5	85.9	55.1	73.7
04	MASONRY	93.6	54.5	69.9	122.9	60.2	84.8	90.5	54.8	68.8	93.4	63.7	75.4	90.6	61.6	73.0	90.4	54.7	68.7
05	METALS	94.3	65.6	88.7	99.3	83.3	96.1	99.7	69.0	93.7	105.0	69.7	98.0	102.5	69.7	96.0	94.5	86.6	93.0
06	WOOD, PLASTICS & COMPOSITES	96.5	45.9	73.8	115.3	57.5	89.4	107.5	57.4	85.1	98.7	58.9	80.9	95.5	60.7	79.9	87.1	50.8	70.8
07	THERMAL & MOISTURE PROTECTION	94.8	56.9	81.3	89.8	60.3	79.3	92.0	58.0	79.9	98.3	64.9	86.4	88.8	65.5	80.5	88.8	58.7	78.1
08	OPENINGS	91.9	43.4	81.0	116.5	52.2	102.0	67.3	52.5	64.0	98.8	53.7	88.6	98.2	56.2	88.7	90.8	50.8	81.8
0920	Plaster & Gypsum Board	90.3	44.8	61.5	86.9	56.7	67.7	81.5	56.7	65.7	87.6	57.8	68.7	90.4	59.7	70.9	89.6	49.8	64.4
0950, 0980	Ceilings & Acoustic Treatment	95.2	44.8	67.0	89.9	56.7	71.3	84.9	56.7	69.1	105.8	57.8	78.9	98.2	59.7	76.6	102.2	49.8	72.9
0960	Flooring	96.4	48.9	84.5	77.3	48.9	70.2	104.9	48.9	90.9	98.6	75.6	92.9	104.1	69.0	95.3	98.8	60.0	89.1
0970, 0990	Wall Finishes & Painting/Coating	101.1	37.8	63.4	102.0	43.4	67.1	93.3	45.9	65.1	104.7	48.7	71.3	104.7	50.8	72.6	103.5	47.7	70.2
09	FINISHES	94.9	45.5	70.1	82.8	52.9	67.8	91.2	53.1	72.1	99.8	60.3	80.0	100.0	60.1	79.9	95.1	51.4	73.2
COVERS	DIVS. 10-14, 25, 28, 41, 43, 44, 46	100.0	72.8	94.7	100.0	78.7	95.9	100.0	78.4	95.8	100.0	81.2	96.4	100.0	80.1	96.1	100.0	75.1	95.2
21, 22, 23	FIRE SUPPRESSION, PLUMBING & HVAC	92.2	53.6	78.4	92.2	50.4	77.2	92.2	44.8	75.2	99.9	61.8	86.2	99.7	58.0	84.8	92.1	59.3	80.4
26, 27, 3370	ELECTRICAL, COMMUNICATIONS & UTIL.	98.3	53.3	78.8	97.9	52.2	78.1	94.9	52.2	76.4	100.0	47.5	77.2	94.8	55.3	77.7	97.9	56.5	80.0
MF2018	WEIGHTED AVERAGE	96.3	55.7	81.3	95.8	59.4	82.4	93.1	56.5	79.6	98.9	63.3	85.8	97.6	63.7	85.1	93.4	61.5	81.6

TEXAS

DIVISION		GIDDINGS 789			GREENVILLE 754			HOUSTON 770-772			HUNTSVILLE 773			LAREDO 780			LONGVIEW 756		
		MAT.	INST.	TOTAL	MAT.	INST.	TOTAL	MAT.	INST.	TOTAL	MAT.	INST.	TOTAL	MAT.	INST.	TOTAL	MAT.	INST.	TOTAL
015433	CONTRACTOR EQUIPMENT		88.2	88.2		97.2	97.2		100.9	100.9		91.2	91.2		88.2	88.2		89.4	89.4
0241, 31-34	SITE & INFRASTRUCTURE, DEMOLITION	94.0	83.0	86.8	98.8	81.8	87.7	108.7	94.0	99.1	94.0	87.0	89.5	92.5	83.3	86.5	96.1	87.2	90.3
0310	Concrete Forming & Accessories	96.4	46.9	57.9	87.3	52.6	60.3	98.2	59.7	68.3	90.8	49.4	58.6	98.8	52.1	62.5	82.9	55.6	61.7
0320	Concrete Reinforcing	88.6	43.5	76.1	101.0	46.4	85.8	99.7	52.1	86.5	101.6	45.9	86.2	88.2	48.8	77.3	100.6	45.7	85.4
0330	Cast-in-Place Concrete	93.0	54.3	79.3	104.2	55.6	87.0	71.3	69.8	70.7	79.3	54.6	70.5	78.6	65.0	73.8	121.3	54.6	97.6
03	CONCRETE	89.4	50.1	73.9	93.8	54.5	78.3	84.0	62.9	75.7	90.2	51.8	75.1	85.0	57.1	74.0	106.2	54.5	85.8
04	MASONRY	99.0	54.6	72.1	178.5	60.1	106.6	89.1	64.4	74.1	125.9	54.6	82.6	87.8	59.9	70.8	173.6	53.5	100.6
05	METALS	93.7	66.6	88.4	94.2	82.0	91.8	101.2	75.1	96.0	92.7	68.9	88.0	97.3	69.1	91.9	87.2	67.9	83.4
06	WOOD, PLASTICS & COMPOSITES	95.9	45.9	73.5	79.3	53.2	67.6	95.5	59.5	79.4	83.7	49.1	68.2	96.5	51.4	76.3	72.2	57.5	65.6
07	THERMAL & MOISTURE PROTECTION	95.1	57.5	81.7	90.9	59.3	79.6	90.2	69.0	82.7	90.3	57.9	78.8	94.1	62.6	82.9	92.2	57.2	79.7
08	OPENINGS	91.1	44.2	80.5	89.8	50.2	80.9	98.8	56.7	89.3	87.4	47.6	78.4	91.9	49.2	82.2	81.1	52.1	74.5
0920	Plaster & Gypsum Board	89.4	44.8	61.1	79.3	52.1	62.0	90.4	58.3	70.0	85.3	48.2	61.8	92.5	50.5	65.8	76.6	56.7	63.9
0950, 0980	Ceilings & Acoustic Treatment	95.2	44.8	67.0	95.8	52.1	71.3	98.2	58.3	75.8	96.3	48.2	69.4	102.0	50.5	73.1	87.2	56.7	70.1
0960	Flooring	97.8	48.9	85.5	94.7	48.9	83.2	103.1	74.9	96.0	88.2	48.9	78.4	96.2	64.3	88.2	100.0	48.9	87.2
0970, 0990	Wall Finishes & Painting/Coating	101.1	39.3	64.2	94.5	45.9	65.5	104.7	57.4	76.5	91.5	51.0	67.4	101.1	43.8	66.9	86.7	43.4	60.9
09	FINISHES	94.3	45.6	69.8	94.5	50.7	72.5	100.7	62.0	81.3	97.2	48.8	67.9	95.6	52.8	74.1	97.5	52.9	75.1
COVERS	DIVS. 10-14, 25, 28, 41, 43, 44, 46	100.0	78.3	95.8	100.0	78.4	95.8	100.0	82.5	96.6	100.0	74.6	95.1	100.0	77.7	95.7	100.0	78.6	95.8
21, 22, 23	FIRE SUPPRESSION, PLUMBING & HVAC	92.3	58.4	80.1	92.5	52.4	78.1	99.7	62.6	86.4	92.2	59.2	80.3	99.7	59.3	85.2	92.5	52.0	77.9
26, 27, 3370	ELECTRICAL, COMMUNICATIONS & UTIL.	96.4	49.5	76.1	91.7	52.2	74.6	99.4	64.2	84.1	97.5	52.6	78.0	98.4	55.7	79.9	90.6	45.3	71.0
MF2018	WEIGHTED AVERAGE	93.7	56.6	80.1	96.7	59.3	82.9	97.6	67.2	86.4	93.7	58.4	80.7	95.5	60.7	82.7	95.8	57.0	81.5

City Cost Indexes

TEXAS

DIVISION		LUBBOCK 793-794			LUFKIN 759			MCALLEN 785			MCKINNEY 750			MIDLAND 797			ODESSA 797		
		MAT.	INST.	TOTAL	MAT.	INST.	TOTAL	MAT.	INST.	TOTAL	MAT.	INST.	TOTAL	MAT.	INST.	TOTAL	MAT.	INST.	TOTAL
015433	CONTRACTOR EQUIPMENT		99.1	99.1		89.4	89.4		97.8	97.8		97.2	97.2		99.1	99.1		88.4	88.4
0241, 31-34	SITE & INFRASTRUCTURE, DEMOLITION	118.1	83.7	95.6	91.3	86.5	88.2	123.9	80.3	95.4	95.5	81.8	86.6	117.4	83.6	95.3	95.7	84.6	88.5
0310	Concrete Forming & Accessories	100.8	54.0	64.4	86.1	49.5	57.7	102.6	47.5	59.8	86.4	52.6	60.1	105.2	60.7	70.6	100.7	60.4	69.4
0320	Concrete Reinforcing	99.7	49.7	85.9	102.4	59.9	90.6	87.9	48.7	77.1	101.0	46.4	85.8	100.3	49.8	86.3	98.9	49.7	85.3
0330	Cast-in-Place Concrete	77.4	67.9	74.1	108.4	53.9	89.1	110.8	56.2	91.4	97.7	55.6	82.8	82.3	68.1	77.3	77.3	64.1	72.6
03	CONCRETE	83.8	60.1	74.5	99.9	53.8	81.7	97.7	52.8	80.0	89.8	54.5	75.9	87.2	63.2	77.7	84.5	60.7	75.1
04	MASONRY	93.9	62.6	74.9	132.3	54.5	85.0	92.9	59.1	72.4	192.1	60.1	112.0	108.8	60.9	79.7	94.3	60.8	74.0
05	METALS	112.4	84.8	107.0	94.4	71.0	89.8	94.2	82.9	91.9	94.1	82.0	91.7	110.6	85.0	105.5	108.0	71.0	100.7
06	WOOD, PLASTICS & COMPOSITES	103.2	52.3	80.4	78.8	49.3	65.6	111.1	46.0	81.9	78.0	53.2	66.9	109.0	62.1	88.0	101.1	62.0	83.6
07	THERMAL & MOISTURE PROTECTION	87.4	63.1	78.8	92.0	56.7	79.4	97.4	59.9	84.0	90.7	59.3	79.5	87.7	63.3	79.0	96.5	62.5	84.4
08	OPENINGS	108.6	52.9	96.0	61.0	51.3	58.8	95.3	44.8	83.9	89.8	50.2	80.9	109.9	57.7	98.1	100.8	57.6	91.1
0920	Plaster & Gypsum Board	91.7	51.4	66.1	74.3	48.2	57.8	96.3	44.8	63.7	79.3	52.1	62.0	91.6	61.4	72.5	91.3	61.4	72.3
0950, 0980	Ceilings & Acoustic Treatment	106.5	51.4	75.6	79.9	48.2	62.2	102.0	44.8	70.0	95.8	52.1	71.3	101.5	61.4	79.0	105.1	61.4	80.6
0960	Flooring	91.3	67.5	85.4	134.3	48.9	112.9	114.3	70.6	103.3	94.3	48.9	82.9	92.1	66.8	85.8	96.3	62.5	87.8
0970, 0990	Wall Finishes & Painting/Coating	109.9	51.7	75.2	86.7	45.9	62.4	112.4	37.8	67.9	94.5	45.9	65.5	109.9	52.7	75.8	98.8	52.7	71.3
09	FINISHES	98.5	55.7	77.0	105.2	48.7	76.8	104.4	50.3	77.3	94.1	50.7	72.3	97.8	61.0	79.3	95.5	60.0	77.7
COVERS	DIVS. 10-14, 25, 28, 41, 43, 44, 46	100.0	79.6	96.0	100.0	75.0	95.1	100.0	77.3	95.6	100.0	78.4	95.8	100.0	80.1	96.1	100.0	79.8	96.1
21, 22, 23	FIRE SUPPRESSION, PLUMBING & HVAC	99.5	50.2	81.8	92.5	52.4	78.1	92.3	44.8	75.2	92.5	54.4	78.8	92.0	53.5	78.2	100.1	48.5	81.6
26, 27, 3370	ELECTRICAL, COMMUNICATIONS & UTIL.	96.1	50.5	76.4	91.4	54.6	75.4	97.0	28.2	67.2	91.8	52.2	74.6	96.1	58.4	79.8	97.6	58.4	80.6
MF2018	WEIGHTED AVERAGE	100.7	60.8	86.0	93.9	57.8	80.6	96.7	53.4	80.8	96.6	59.6	83.0	99.7	63.9	86.5	99.0	61.1	85.0

TEXAS

DIVISION		PALESTINE 758			SAN ANGELO 769			SAN ANTONIO 781-782			TEMPLE 765			TEXARKANA 755			TYLER 757		
		MAT.	INST.	TOTAL	MAT.	INST.	TOTAL	MAT.	INST.	TOTAL	MAT.	INST.	TOTAL	MAT.	INST.	TOTAL	MAT.	INST.	TOTAL
015433	CONTRACTOR EQUIPMENT		89.4	89.4		88.4	88.4		94.9	94.9		88.4	88.4		89.4	89.4		89.4	89.4
0241, 31-34	SITE & INFRASTRUCTURE, DEMOLITION	96.1	87.2	90.3	96.8	84.4	88.7	90.7	94.5	93.2	87.2	83.8	85.0	86.7	87.4	87.1	95.3	87.3	90.1
0310	Concrete Forming & Accessories	76.9	55.5	60.3	97.8	47.5	58.7	97.7	55.8	65.1	101.5	46.8	59.0	94.1	59.2	67.0	87.9	56.2	63.3
0320	Concrete Reinforcing	99.9	45.9	84.9	89.7	50.9	79.0	101.5	50.3	87.3	89.8	45.7	77.6	99.7	49.5	85.8	100.6	49.2	86.3
0330	Cast-in-Place Concrete	99.1	54.6	83.3	91.2	65.6	82.1	74.9	70.3	73.2	74.7	54.0	67.4	99.8	64.1	87.1	119.1	55.4	96.5
03	CONCRETE	98.7	54.5	81.3	87.1	55.6	74.7	85.9	60.6	75.9	77.2	50.3	66.6	94.0	60.1	80.6	105.8	55.7	86.0
04	MASONRY	126.1	53.5	82.0	113.2	78.9	92.4	93.9	63.0	75.1	121.8	54.6	81.0	196.9	58.6	112.9	185.0	54.8	105.9
05	METALS	94.2	68.0	89.0	100.2	72.4	94.7	101.3	66.9	94.5	99.8	67.1	93.3	87.0	70.1	83.7	94.0	69.4	89.1
06	WOOD, PLASTICS & COMPOSITES	67.8	57.5	63.2	101.8	45.9	76.6	95.3	54.8	77.2	111.1	45.9	81.9	87.3	60.8	75.4	81.0	57.5	70.4
07	THERMAL & MOISTURE PROTECTION	92.4	56.9	79.7	91.5	64.7	81.9	90.9	67.1	82.4	91.1	56.6	78.8	91.9	62.2	81.3	92.3	59.3	80.5
08	OPENINGS	60.9	52.5	59.0	98.5	47.0	86.9	98.8	52.1	88.2	63.9	46.1	59.9	81.0	56.5	75.5	60.9	54.7	59.5
0920	Plaster & Gypsum Board	74.1	56.7	63.0	81.5	44.8	58.2	93.4	53.5	68.1	81.5	44.8	58.2	82.6	60.1	68.4	74.3	56.7	63.1
0950, 0980	Ceilings & Acoustic Treatment	79.9	56.7	66.9	84.9	44.8	62.5	91.4	53.5	70.2	84.9	44.8	62.5	87.2	60.1	72.0	79.9	56.7	66.9
0960	Flooring	128.2	48.9	108.3	82.4	48.9	74.0	103.1	73.6	95.7	106.1	48.9	91.7	105.6	64.0	95.1	135.9	48.9	114.1
0970, 0990	Wall Finishes & Painting/Coating	86.7	45.9	62.4	91.8	45.9	64.4	104.7	45.1	69.2	93.3	39.3	61.1	86.7	51.7	65.8	86.7	51.7	65.8
09	FINISHES	104.0	53.2	78.5	83.8	46.4	65.0	97.5	57.5	77.4	90.3	45.6	67.9	99.3	59.2	79.2	106.0	54.1	80.0
COVERS	DIVS. 10-14, 25, 28, 41, 43, 44, 46	100.0	78.6	95.8	100.0	78.3	95.8	100.0	79.8	96.1	100.0	77.2	95.6	100.0	79.4	96.0	100.0	79.0	95.9
21, 22, 23	FIRE SUPPRESSION, PLUMBING & HVAC	92.5	51.2	77.7	92.2	48.8	76.7	99.7	62.6	86.4	92.2	48.0	76.4	92.5	54.1	78.7	92.5	53.2	78.4
26, 27, 3370	ELECTRICAL, COMMUNICATIONS & UTIL.	89.1	43.1	69.2	97.4	48.6	76.3	99.7	59.7	82.4	95.7	46.3	74.3	91.3	54.7	75.4	90.6	47.9	72.1
MF2018	WEIGHTED AVERAGE	93.2	56.5	79.7	95.4	58.7	81.9	97.4	64.4	85.3	91.7	54.1	77.8	95.3	61.4	82.8	96.7	58.4	82.6

TEXAS / UTAH

DIVISION		VICTORIA 779			WACO 766-767			WAXAHACHIE 751			WHARTON 774			WICHITA FALLS 763			LOGAN (UTAH) 843		
		MAT.	INST.	TOTAL	MAT.	INST.	TOTAL	MAT.	INST.	TOTAL	MAT.	INST.	TOTAL	MAT.	INST.	TOTAL	MAT.	INST.	TOTAL
015433	CONTRACTOR EQUIPMENT		101.4	101.4		88.4	88.4		97.2	97.2		102.5	102.5		88.4	88.4		92.5	92.5
0241, 31-34	SITE & INFRASTRUCTURE, DEMOLITION	110.3	83.7	93.0	97.6	84.1	88.8	97.3	82.2	87.4	115.2	85.6	95.9	98.3	84.5	89.3	101.3	86.7	91.8
0310	Concrete Forming & Accessories	91.8	46.9	57.0	100.0	59.6	68.6	86.4	62.7	67.9	86.5	48.4	56.9	99.9	58.7	67.9	99.9	68.9	75.8
0320	Concrete Reinforcing	97.1	45.7	82.9	89.6	49.7	78.6	101.0	53.2	87.7	101.0	45.7	85.7	89.6	49.7	78.5	96.6	82.6	92.7
0330	Cast-in-Place Concrete	85.9	55.5	75.1	80.9	64.1	74.9	103.1	64.6	89.4	88.3	54.6	76.3	86.4	68.3	80.0	77.8	73.2	76.2
03	CONCRETE	90.4	52.0	75.2	81.8	60.3	73.3	92.9	63.4	81.3	93.6	52.3	77.3	84.1	61.4	75.1	98.3	73.4	88.5
04	MASONRY	105.4	54.7	74.6	88.7	59.9	71.2	179.2	62.8	108.5	91.4	54.6	69.0	89.2	58.4	70.5	110.9	60.9	80.5
05	METALS	92.9	83.5	91.0	102.9	70.0	96.4	94.2	85.4	92.4	94.5	83.0	92.3	102.8	71.1	96.6	104.5	83.6	100.4
06	WOOD, PLASTICS & COMPOSITES	89.9	45.9	70.2	108.7	61.4	87.5	78.0	64.5	71.9	79.2	47.9	65.2	108.7	60.3	87.0	90.0	69.1	80.6
07	THERMAL & MOISTURE PROTECTION	91.8	56.0	79.1	91.8	62.6	81.4	90.8	64.0	81.3	89.1	58.3	78.1	91.8	61.3	81.0	93.0	67.1	83.8
08	OPENINGS	90.7	46.3	80.7	74.6	57.6	70.8	89.8	60.5	83.2	90.8	47.4	81.0	74.6	56.0	70.4	87.6	70.5	83.7
0920	Plaster & Gypsum Board	85.5	44.8	59.7	81.8	60.9	68.5	80.1	63.8	69.8	84.8	46.9	60.7	81.8	59.7	67.7	88.6	68.4	75.8
0950, 0980	Ceilings & Acoustic Treatment	104.5	44.8	71.1	85.8	60.9	71.8	98.6	63.8	79.1	102.2	46.9	71.2	85.8	59.7	71.2	107.2	68.4	85.4
0960	Flooring	99.6	48.9	86.9	105.6	67.3	96.0	94.3	61.9	86.2	97.0	59.6	87.7	106.1	69.7	97.0	99.0	62.1	89.8
0970, 0990	Wall Finishes & Painting/Coating	103.7	51.0	72.3	93.3	54.8	70.4	94.5	56.5	71.8	103.5	49.5	71.3	95.1	50.7	68.6	92.2	60.2	73.1
09	FINISHES	94.1	47.0	70.4	90.9	60.5	75.6	95.2	61.8	78.4	94.7	49.8	72.2	91.2	59.8	75.4	98.9	66.4	82.6
COVERS	DIVS. 10-14, 25, 28, 41, 43, 44, 46	100.0	74.5	95.1	100.0	79.3	96.0	100.0	80.5	96.2	100.0	74.7	95.1	100.0	79.1	95.9	100.0	85.3	97.1
21, 22, 23	FIRE SUPPRESSION, PLUMBING & HVAC	92.2	59.2	80.4	99.7	59.4	85.3	92.5	63.3	82.0	92.1	55.8	79.1	99.7	54.7	83.6	100.0	72.0	90.0
26, 27, 3370	ELECTRICAL, COMMUNICATIONS & UTIL.	101.4	48.1	78.3	97.6	54.0	78.7	91.8	62.3	79.0	100.1	52.7	79.5	100.3	51.8	79.3	93.0	70.9	83.5
MF2018	WEIGHTED AVERAGE	94.6	58.5	81.3	94.7	62.5	82.9	96.6	66.9	85.7	94.7	59.1	81.6	95.3	61.2	82.7	99.1	72.6	89.3

City Cost Indexes

		UTAH											VERMONT					
		OGDEN			PRICE			PROVO			SALT LAKE CITY			BELLOWS FALLS			BENNINGTON		
DIVISION		842,844			845			846 - 847			840 - 841			051			052		
		MAT.	INST.	TOTAL	MAT.	INST.	TOTAL	MAT.	INST.	TOTAL	MAT.	INST.	TOTAL	MAT.	INST.	TOTAL	MAT.	INST.	TOTAL
015433	CONTRACTOR EQUIPMENT		92.5	92.5		91.7	91.7		91.7	91.7		92.5	92.5		93.0	93.0		93.0	93.0
0241, 31 - 34	SITE & INFRASTRUCTURE, DEMOLITION	90.3	86.7	87.9	97.0	84.3	88.7	97.8	85.3	89.7	90.0	86.6	87.8	82.7	91.5	88.4	82.2	91.5	88.2
0310	Concrete Forming & Accessories	99.9	68.9	75.8	102.7	59.8	69.4	101.9	68.9	76.2	102.2	68.9	76.3	101.7	92.8	94.8	98.6	92.6	94.0
0320	Concrete Reinforcing	96.4	82.6	92.6	103.7	80.4	97.3	104.6	82.5	98.5	98.8	82.5	94.3	80.2	78.2	79.6	80.2	78.2	79.6
0330	Cast-in-Place Concrete	79.0	73.2	77.0	77.9	68.0	74.4	77.9	73.2	76.2	86.3	73.2	81.7	71.1	110.7	85.1	71.1	110.6	85.1
03	CONCRETE	90.5	73.4	83.7	100.5	67.0	87.3	99.4	73.3	89.1	105.6	73.3	92.9	82.6	96.6	88.2	82.4	96.5	88.0
04	MASONRY	105.2	60.9	78.3	116.7	62.3	83.7	116.8	60.9	82.8	119.4	60.9	83.8	103.5	89.4	94.9	115.1	89.4	99.5
05	METALS	105.0	83.6	100.8	101.4	81.6	97.5	102.3	83.5	98.6	109.1	83.6	104.1	91.1	89.5	90.8	91.0	89.4	90.7
06	WOOD, PLASTICS & COMPOSITES	90.0	69.1	80.6	94.2	58.2	78.1	92.0	69.1	81.8	92.5	69.1	82.1	107.6	96.8	102.8	103.9	96.8	100.7
07	THERMAL & MOISTURE PROTECTION	92.1	67.1	83.2	94.3	63.0	83.2	94.4	67.1	84.7	98.6	67.1	87.4	90.1	83.8	87.9	90.0	83.8	87.8
08	OPENINGS	87.6	70.5	83.7	91.1	70.3	86.4	91.1	70.5	86.5	89.1	70.5	84.9	95.6	88.4	93.9	95.6	88.4	93.9
0920	Plaster & Gypsum Board	88.6	68.4	75.8	92.9	57.2	70.3	89.6	68.4	76.2	96.5	68.4	78.7	99.9	96.6	97.8	98.7	96.6	97.4
0950, 0980	Ceilings & Acoustic Treatment	107.2	68.4	85.4	107.2	57.2	79.1	107.2	68.4	85.4	103.1	68.4	83.7	72.8	96.6	86.2	72.8	96.6	86.2
0960	Flooring	96.5	62.1	87.9	99.8	50.2	87.3	99.7	62.1	90.2	100.3	62.1	90.7	91.2	109.2	95.7	90.5	109.2	95.2
0970, 0990	Wall Finishes & Painting/Coating	92.2	60.2	73.1	92.2	53.9	69.4	92.2	58.5	72.1	95.3	59.1	73.7	89.3	90.2	89.8	89.3	90.2	89.8
09	FINISHES	97.0	66.4	81.7	100.0	56.7	78.3	99.5	66.2	82.8	98.7	66.3	82.4	85.7	96.0	90.9	85.4	96.0	90.7
COVERS	DIVS. 10 - 14, 25, 28, 41, 43, 44, 46	100.0	85.3	97.1	100.0	83.8	96.9	100.0	85.2	97.1	100.0	85.3	97.1	100.0	98.9	99.8	100.0	98.8	99.8
21, 22, 23	FIRE SUPPRESSION, PLUMBING & HVAC	100.0	72.0	90.0	95.9	58.7	82.6	100.0	72.0	90.0	100.2	72.0	90.1	92.6	78.9	87.7	92.6	78.9	87.7
26, 27, 3370	ELECTRICAL, COMMUNICATIONS & UTIL.	93.6	70.9	83.8	95.6	61.2	80.7	93.2	66.2	81.5	96.5	68.7	84.5	101.6	70.8	88.2	101.6	48.5	78.6
MF2018	WEIGHTED AVERAGE	97.7	72.6	88.4	98.6	65.8	86.5	99.3	71.8	89.2	101.7	72.3	90.9	92.6	86.7	90.4	92.9	83.5	89.5

		VERMONT																	
		BRATTLEBORO			BURLINGTON			GUILDHALL			MONTPELIER			RUTLAND			ST. JOHNSBURY		
DIVISION		053			054			059			056			057			058		
		MAT.	INST.	TOTAL	MAT.	INST.	TOTAL	MAT.	INST.	TOTAL	MAT.	INST.	TOTAL	MAT.	INST.	TOTAL	MAT.	INST.	TOTAL
015433	CONTRACTOR EQUIPMENT		93.0	93.0		97.6	97.6		93.0	93.0		97.6	97.6		93.0	93.0		93.0	93.0
0241, 31 - 34	SITE & INFRASTRUCTURE, DEMOLITION	83.3	91.5	88.6	90.6	101.7	97.9	82.1	91.1	88.0	86.0	100.9	95.7	89.2	92.5	91.4	82.2	90.6	87.7
0310	Concrete Forming & Accessories	102.0	92.8	94.8	103.7	83.2	87.8	98.5	87.5	90.0	103.7	94.5	96.5	102.3	83.2	87.5	96.0	87.5	89.4
0320	Concrete Reinforcing	79.3	78.2	79.0	98.7	82.1	94.1	80.9	78.2	80.1	97.9	82.1	93.5	102.3	82.1	95.2	79.3	78.2	79.0
0330	Cast-in-Place Concrete	73.3	110.7	86.6	88.1	114.2	97.4	68.9	103.2	81.1	81.7	114.2	93.3	69.6	113.1	85.1	68.9	103.1	81.1
03	CONCRETE	84.0	96.6	89.0	99.2	94.1	97.2	80.7	91.6	85.0	96.4	99.1	97.5	88.0	93.8	90.3	80.1	91.6	84.6
04	MASONRY	114.9	89.4	99.4	117.0	94.0	103.0	115.3	76.2	91.6	113.3	94.0	101.6	94.2	93.9	94.0	145.4	76.2	103.4
05	METALS	91.0	89.5	90.7	99.8	88.9	97.6	91.1	89.2	90.7	97.8	88.7	96.0	98.6	90.9	97.1	91.1	89.2	90.7
06	WOOD, PLASTICS & COMPOSITES	108.1	96.8	103.0	102.5	81.5	93.1	101.8	96.8	99.6	102.5	96.8	99.9	108.3	81.5	96.3	94.7	96.8	95.6
07	THERMAL & MOISTURE PROTECTION	90.2	83.8	87.9	95.2	95.9	95.5	89.9	77.9	85.6	94.8	97.6	95.8	90.3	94.4	91.7	89.7	77.9	85.5
08	OPENINGS	95.6	88.6	94.0	97.8	82.0	94.2	95.6	89.6	94.2	98.0	90.5	96.3	98.2	82.0	94.6	95.6	89.6	94.2
0920	Plaster & Gypsum Board	99.9	96.6	97.8	107.9	80.9	90.8	110.0	96.6	101.5	107.9	96.6	100.8	100.5	80.9	88.0	113.4	96.6	102.8
0950, 0980	Ceilings & Acoustic Treatment	72.8	96.6	86.2	81.2	80.9	81.0	72.8	96.6	86.2	80.7	96.6	89.6	78.2	80.9	79.7	72.8	96.6	86.2
0960	Flooring	91.4	109.2	95.8	99.2	109.2	101.7	93.5	109.2	97.4	99.2	109.2	101.7	91.2	109.2	95.7	96.0	109.2	99.3
0970, 0990	Wall Finishes & Painting/Coating	89.3	90.2	89.8	104.7	97.6	100.5	89.3	97.6	94.2	104.7	97.6	100.5	89.3	97.6	94.2	89.3	97.6	94.2
09	FINISHES	85.9	96.0	91.0	95.1	89.0	92.0	87.7	93.5	90.6	95.0	97.9	96.5	87.4	89.0	88.2	88.9	93.5	91.2
COVERS	DIVS. 10 - 14, 25, 28, 41, 43, 44, 46	100.0	98.9	99.8	100.0	98.7	99.8	100.0	94.4	98.9	100.0	100.4	100.1	100.0	98.7	99.7	100.0	94.4	98.9
21, 22, 23	FIRE SUPPRESSION, PLUMBING & HVAC	92.6	78.9	87.7	99.9	66.5	87.9	92.6	57.2	79.9	92.5	66.5	83.2	100.1	66.5	88.1	92.6	57.2	79.9
26, 27, 3370	ELECTRICAL, COMMUNICATIONS & UTIL.	101.6	70.8	88.2	101.6	51.9	79.7	101.6	48.5	78.6	101.1	51.9	79.8	101.6	51.9	80.1	101.6	48.5	78.6
MF2018	WEIGHTED AVERAGE	93.2	86.7	90.8	99.7	81.3	92.9	92.9	76.4	86.8	97.1	83.7	92.1	96.7	80.7	90.8	94.0	76.3	87.5

		VERMONT			VIRGINIA														
		WHITE RIVER JCT.			ALEXANDRIA			ARLINGTON			BRISTOL			CHARLOTTESVILLE			CULPEPER		
DIVISION		050			223			222			242			229			227		
		MAT.	INST.	TOTAL	MAT.	INST.	TOTAL	MAT.	INST.	TOTAL	MAT.	INST.	TOTAL	MAT.	INST.	TOTAL	MAT.	INST.	TOTAL
015433	CONTRACTOR EQUIPMENT		93.0	93.0		102.8	102.8		101.7	101.7		101.7	101.7		105.3	105.3		101.7	101.7
0241, 31 - 34	SITE & INFRASTRUCTURE, DEMOLITION	85.1	90.7	88.7	120.0	85.7	97.6	129.9	83.7	99.8	112.6	83.7	93.8	116.5	85.5	96.3	114.8	83.3	94.3
0310	Concrete Forming & Accessories	95.5	87.9	89.6	94.2	68.8	74.4	92.2	59.1	66.5	87.6	56.2	63.2	85.8	57.9	64.1	82.4	64.9	68.8
0320	Concrete Reinforcing	80.2	78.2	79.6	82.6	88.0	84.1	93.2	85.4	91.0	93.4	66.3	85.9	92.8	67.7	85.8	93.2	87.8	91.7
0330	Cast-in-Place Concrete	73.3	103.8	84.1	116.7	73.4	101.3	113.5	73.5	99.3	113.1	48.3	90.1	117.7	71.0	101.1	116.2	71.4	100.3
03	CONCRETE	85.3	92.0	88.0	95.8	75.2	87.7	99.6	70.5	88.1	97.3	57.1	81.4	98.2	66.1	85.5	96.2	72.7	86.9
04	MASONRY	129.5	77.5	97.9	89.1	71.4	78.4	94.6	71.0	80.2	90.6	52.4	67.4	114.1	53.4	77.2	104.1	66.1	81.1
05	METALS	91.1	89.2	90.7	102.4	101.2	102.2	100.4	100.4	100.4	99.2	91.4	97.6	99.5	94.1	98.4	99.6	100.0	99.6
06	WOOD, PLASTICS & COMPOSITES	99.5	96.8	98.3	94.9	67.5	82.6	90.7	54.5	74.5	81.1	54.4	69.1	79.1	54.9	68.3	77.3	63.8	71.2
07	THERMAL & MOISTURE PROTECTION	90.2	78.4	86.0	103.4	75.9	93.6	105.1	74.5	94.2	104.5	58.5	88.1	104.1	66.1	90.6	104.2	73.0	93.1
08	OPENINGS	95.6	89.6	94.2	94.7	72.6	89.7	93.0	65.3	86.8	95.8	61.0	87.9	94.1	61.6	86.8	94.4	70.6	89.0
0920	Plaster & Gypsum Board	97.0	96.6	96.8	109.7	66.5	82.3	105.1	53.2	72.2	99.8	53.0	70.1	99.8	53.0	70.1	100.0	62.7	76.4
0950, 0980	Ceilings & Acoustic Treatment	72.8	96.6	86.2	102.0	66.5	82.1	98.8	53.2	73.2	97.9	53.0	72.8	97.9	53.0	72.8	98.8	62.7	78.6
0960	Flooring	89.8	109.2	94.7	105.7	70.7	96.9	104.4	73.4	96.6	101.5	51.7	89.0	100.2	51.7	88.1	100.2	66.7	91.8
0970, 0990	Wall Finishes & Painting/Coating	89.3	97.6	94.2	116.2	65.4	85.9	116.2	68.1	87.5	102.1	42.9	82.9	102.1	47.4	74.6	116.2	65.2	85.8
09	FINISHES	85.2	93.8	89.5	104.7	67.9	86.3	104.1	61.2	82.6	100.8	56.5	78.6	100.5	55.3	77.8	101.1	64.3	82.6
COVERS	DIVS. 10 - 14, 25, 28, 41, 43, 44, 46	100.0	94.8	99.0	100.0	87.8	97.6	100.0	86.3	97.3	100.0	81.6	96.4	100.0	82.9	96.7	100.0	86.6	97.4
21, 22, 23	FIRE SUPPRESSION, PLUMBING & HVAC	92.6	57.9	80.2	100.4	81.4	93.6	100.4	83.3	94.3	92.9	47.3	76.5	92.9	66.8	83.5	92.9	78.6	87.7
26, 27, 3370	ELECTRICAL, COMMUNICATIONS & UTIL.	101.6	48.4	78.5	96.2	93.2	94.9	94.6	97.3	95.8	95.7	32.4	68.2	95.7	68.5	83.9	96.9	90.0	93.9
MF2018	WEIGHTED AVERAGE	93.9	76.7	87.5	99.7	81.2	92.9	100.1	79.9	92.6	97.1	57.2	82.4	98.1	68.2	87.1	97.6	78.3	90.5

City Cost Indexes

DIVISION		VIRGINIA																	
		FAIRFAX 220-221			FARMVILLE 239			FREDERICKSBURG 224-225			GRUNDY 246			HARRISONBURG 228			LYNCHBURG 245		
		MAT.	INST.	TOTAL	MAT.	INST.	TOTAL	MAT.	INST.	TOTAL	MAT.	INST.	TOTAL	MAT.	INST.	TOTAL	MAT.	INST.	TOTAL
015433	CONTRACTOR EQUIPMENT		101.7	101.7		105.3	105.3		101.7	101.7		101.7	101.7		101.7	101.7		101.7	101.7
0241, 31-34	SITE & INFRASTRUCTURE, DEMOLITION	125.5	83.8	98.3	113.2	84.4	94.4	114.4	83.2	94.1	110.5	82.4	92.2	122.4	83.6	97.1	111.1	84.0	93.4
0310	Concrete Forming & Accessories	85.9	61.6	67.0	102.9	57.0	67.3	85.9	59.7	65.5	91.3	55.3	63.3	81.3	58.2	63.3	87.6	57.5	64.2
0320	Concrete Reinforcing	93.2	88.1	91.8	90.1	61.2	82.1	93.9	72.9	88.1	92.1	39.8	77.6	93.2	75.9	88.4	92.8	66.6	85.5
0330	Cast-in-Place Concrete	113.5	74.5	99.6	117.4	80.3	104.2	115.3	69.5	99.0	113.1	48.4	90.1	113.5	72.7	99.0	113.1	71.7	98.4
03	CONCRETE	99.0	72.4	88.5	99.4	67.7	86.9	96.1	67.2	84.7	96.5	51.9	78.9	97.5	68.1	85.9	96.3	66.0	84.3
04	MASONRY	99.4	72.7	83.2	92.7	53.5	68.8	102.9	76.7	87.0	94.9	53.4	69.7	99.2	67.9	80.1	107.2	53.4	74.5
05	METALS	99.7	101.4	100.0	95.9	87.8	94.3	99.6	95.4	98.8	99.2	73.7	94.2	99.5	96.5	98.9	99.4	92.9	98.1
06	WOOD, PLASTICS & COMPOSITES	81.1	57.0	70.3	100.1	54.9	79.8	81.1	58.8	71.1	85.0	54.4	71.3	76.0	54.5	66.4	81.1	54.5	69.2
07	THERMAL & MOISTURE PROTECTION	104.8	76.6	94.7	99.6	65.9	87.6	104.3	74.7	93.7	104.5	56.0	87.2	104.6	75.0	94.0	104.3	65.9	90.6
08	OPENINGS	93.0	67.2	87.2	94.4	50.2	84.4	94.1	63.6	87.2	95.8	42.0	83.6	94.4	63.1	87.3	94.4	61.1	86.9
0920	Plaster & Gypsum Board	100.0	55.7	71.9	114.5	53.0	75.5	100.0	57.6	73.1	99.8	53.0	70.1	99.8	53.2	70.2	99.8	53.2	70.2
0950, 0980	Ceilings & Acoustic Treatment	98.8	55.7	74.6	99.7	53.0	73.6	98.8	57.6	75.7	97.9	53.0	72.8	97.9	53.2	72.8	97.9	53.2	72.8
0960	Flooring	101.7	75.8	95.2	103.4	51.7	90.4	101.7	64.8	92.5	102.6	51.7	89.8	100.0	72.2	93.0	101.5	51.7	89.0
0970, 0990	Wall Finishes & Painting/Coating	116.2	68.1	87.5	103.0	50.8	71.9	116.2	50.6	77.1	102.1	27.8	57.8	116.2	54.9	79.7	102.1	69.9	82.9
09	FINISHES	102.7	63.4	83.0	103.1	54.8	78.9	101.5	58.8	80.0	100.9	51.9	76.3	101.4	59.1	80.2	100.6	56.5	78.5
COVERS	DIVS. 10-14, 25, 28, 41, 43, 44, 46	100.0	87.1	97.5	100.0	79.2	96.0	100.0	70.2	94.2	100.0	77.9	95.7	100.0	81.8	96.5	100.0	81.6	96.4
21, 22, 23	FIRE SUPPRESSION, PLUMBING & HVAC	92.9	84.2	89.8	92.7	50.3	77.5	92.9	71.1	85.3	92.9	59.9	81.1	92.9	71.2	85.1	92.9	66.8	83.5
26, 27, 3370	ELECTRICAL, COMMUNICATIONS & UTIL.	96.2	95.9	96.1	92.0	64.6	80.1	94.7	97.3	95.8	95.7	64.6	82.2	95.8	72.4	85.6	96.2	60.3	80.7
MF2018	WEIGHTED AVERAGE	98.0	80.9	91.7	96.4	63.1	84.1	97.4	76.2	89.6	97.1	60.5	83.7	97.7	72.3	88.3	97.5	66.9	86.3

DIVISION		VIRGINIA																	
		NEWPORT NEWS 236			NORFOLK 233-235			PETERSBURG 238			PORTSMOUTH 237			PULASKI 243			RICHMOND 230-232		
		MAT.	INST.	TOTAL	MAT.	INST.	TOTAL	MAT.	INST.	TOTAL	MAT.	INST.	TOTAL	MAT.	INST.	TOTAL	MAT.	INST.	TOTAL
015433	CONTRACTOR EQUIPMENT		105.3	105.3		105.3	105.3		105.3	105.3		105.2	105.2		101.7	101.7		105.3	105.3
0241, 31-34	SITE & INFRASTRUCTURE, DEMOLITION	115.4	85.6	96.0	115.3	90.5	99.1	115.7	85.6	96.1	114.1	85.1	95.2	109.9	82.7	92.1	107.9	90.5	96.6
0310	Concrete Forming & Accessories	101.9	60.5	69.7	102.1	60.2	69.5	94.2	58.0	66.1	89.2	57.7	64.3	91.3	55.7	63.7	102.2	60.6	69.9
0320	Concrete Reinforcing	89.9	63.8	82.7	98.8	63.7	89.1	89.5	67.8	83.5	89.5	63.0	82.2	92.1	75.4	87.5	98.7	67.8	90.2
0330	Cast-in-Place Concrete	114.1	73.7	99.7	126.7	75.4	108.5	121.2	73.9	104.4	113.0	62.7	95.1	113.1	76.7	100.2	96.5	75.6	89.1
03	CONCRETE	97.2	67.5	85.5	104.6	67.7	90.1	101.0	67.1	87.6	95.5	62.0	82.3	96.5	68.2	85.3	92.1	68.7	82.9
04	MASONRY	90.2	54.0	68.2	90.4	54.1	68.3	99.2	55.2	72.4	94.3	52.6	69.0	86.5	50.3	64.5	90.5	55.3	69.1
05	METALS	98.8	92.5	97.6	100.1	88.6	97.8	96.0	94.3	95.6	97.7	91.5	96.5	99.2	92.6	97.9	100.3	90.5	98.4
06	WOOD, PLASTICS & COMPOSITES	98.4	58.8	80.6	98.8	58.5	80.7	87.2	54.9	72.8	82.3	54.9	70.1	85.0	54.4	71.3	98.8	58.5	80.7
07	THERMAL & MOISTURE PROTECTION	99.5	64.9	87.2	98.1	68.1	87.4	99.5	67.0	87.9	99.5	63.0	86.5	104.5	64.6	90.2	97.2	69.1	87.2
08	OPENINGS	94.6	62.3	87.3	98.5	62.6	90.4	94.1	61.6	86.8	94.7	60.0	86.9	95.8	52.8	86.1	98.3	63.5	90.5
0920	Plaster & Gypsum Board	117.2	57.0	79.0	111.8	57.0	77.0	106.8	53.0	72.7	108.8	53.0	73.4	99.8	53.0	70.1	108.6	57.0	75.9
0950, 0980	Ceilings & Acoustic Treatment	108.4	57.0	79.6	102.5	57.0	77.0	102.0	53.0	74.6	108.4	53.0	77.3	97.9	53.0	72.8	103.0	57.0	77.2
0960	Flooring	103.4	52.7	90.7	106.0	52.7	92.6	99.9	54.8	88.6	97.4	51.7	85.9	102.6	51.7	89.8	101.2	54.8	89.6
0970, 0990	Wall Finishes & Painting/Coating	103.0	54.1	73.8	104.7	54.9	75.0	103.0	56.0	75.0	103.0	54.9	74.3	102.1	42.9	66.8	104.7	56.0	75.7
09	FINISHES	105.6	57.5	81.5	105.0	57.5	81.1	101.7	55.9	78.8	102.7	55.0	78.8	100.9	52.7	76.7	103.3	58.0	80.5
COVERS	DIVS. 10-14, 25, 28, 41, 43, 44, 46	100.0	83.3	96.8	100.0	83.3	96.8	100.0	82.9	96.7	100.0	83.1	96.7	100.0	80.8	96.3	100.0	82.8	96.7
21, 22, 23	FIRE SUPPRESSION, PLUMBING & HVAC	100.2	62.6	86.7	99.7	62.1	86.2	92.7	66.9	83.4	100.2	62.2	86.6	92.9	60.3	81.2	99.7	66.8	87.9
26, 27, 3370	ELECTRICAL, COMMUNICATIONS & UTIL.	93.5	64.4	80.9	100.0	61.8	83.5	93.5	68.5	82.7	92.6	61.8	79.2	95.7	74.2	86.4	99.3	68.4	85.9
MF2018	WEIGHTED AVERAGE	98.7	67.2	87.1	100.7	66.9	88.3	96.8	68.7	86.5	97.9	65.2	85.9	96.8	66.5	85.7	98.8	69.4	88.0

DIVISION		VIRGINIA								WASHINGTON									
		ROANOKE 240-241			STAUNTON 244			WINCHESTER 226			CLARKSTON 994			EVERETT 982			OLYMPIA 985		
		MAT.	INST.	TOTAL	MAT.	INST.	TOTAL	MAT.	INST.	TOTAL	MAT.	INST.	TOTAL	MAT.	INST.	TOTAL	MAT.	INST.	TOTAL
015433	CONTRACTOR EQUIPMENT		101.7	101.7		105.3	105.3		101.7	101.7		88.6	88.6		96.9	96.9		99.6	99.6
0241, 31-34	SITE & INFRASTRUCTURE, DEMOLITION	113.5	84.0	94.3	113.3	84.2	94.3	121.2	83.3	96.5	108.8	82.8	91.9	107.9	101.4	103.7	109.4	105.0	106.5
0310	Concrete Forming & Accessories	98.7	57.8	66.9	90.9	57.0	64.6	84.0	60.3	65.6	83.6	58.5	64.1	116.4	103.9	106.7	100.4	103.1	102.5
0320	Concrete Reinforcing	93.1	66.7	85.8	92.8	65.3	85.2	92.6	72.0	86.9	77.0	96.2	82.3	93.3	114.3	99.1	100.0	113.8	103.8
0330	Cast-in-Place Concrete	128.5	80.4	111.4	117.7	80.2	104.4	113.5	59.0	94.2	97.8	76.1	90.1	111.7	110.2	111.2	98.4	111.0	102.9
03	CONCRETE	102.1	69.1	89.1	98.1	68.3	86.3	97.3	63.6	84.0	90.8	71.8	83.3	101.1	107.5	103.6	100.7	107.1	103.2
04	MASONRY	96.5	54.4	70.9	104.2	53.4	73.4	96.8	62.8	76.2	94.7	82.6	87.3	119.1	105.5	110.8	141.2	96.2	113.9
05	METALS	102.3	93.0	100.5	99.5	88.9	97.4	99.6	93.8	98.5	100.6	86.6	97.9	107.1	102.0	105.9	109.1	97.1	106.7
06	WOOD, PLASTICS & COMPOSITES	96.1	54.5	77.5	85.0	54.9	71.5	79.1	59.0	70.1	97.3	53.3	77.6	130.8	102.5	118.1	103.8	102.7	103.3
07	THERMAL & MOISTURE PROTECTION	104.3	67.6	91.2	104.1	65.9	90.5	104.7	69.8	92.2	84.3	74.4	80.8	99.8	106.7	102.3	96.9	105.4	99.9
08	OPENINGS	94.7	61.1	87.1	94.4	51.0	84.6	95.8	62.0	88.2	108.2	61.2	97.6	97.9	107.3	100.0	98.2	106.2	100.0
0920	Plaster & Gypsum Board	109.7	53.2	73.9	99.8	53.0	70.1	100.0	57.8	73.2	130.2	51.9	80.5	127.5	102.8	111.8	117.6	102.8	108.2
0950, 0980	Ceilings & Acoustic Treatment	102.8	53.2	74.6	97.9	53.0	72.8	98.8	57.8	75.8	86.6	51.9	67.1	98.7	102.8	101.0	106.2	102.8	104.3
0960	Flooring	105.7	53.2	92.6	102.1	51.7	89.5	101.2	66.7	92.6	82.7	69.4	79.4	99.8	101.6	100.2	100.3	86.0	96.7
0970, 0990	Wall Finishes & Painting/Coating	102.1	69.9	82.9	102.1	27.3	57.5	116.2	68.9	88.0	82.6	64.1	71.6	96.3	95.5	95.8	104.7	90.9	96.5
09	FINISHES	103.8	56.9	80.3	100.8	52.2	76.4	102.0	61.7	81.8	94.4	59.4	76.8	104.7	101.9	103.3	104.8	98.0	101.4
COVERS	DIVS. 10-14, 25, 28, 41, 43, 44, 46	100.0	81.8	96.5	100.0	79.2	96.0	100.0	74.0	95.0	100.0	92.5	98.5	100.0	102.2	100.4	100.0	102.2	100.4
21, 22, 23	FIRE SUPPRESSION, PLUMBING & HVAC	100.4	63.7	87.3	92.9	54.0	79.0	92.9	73.2	85.8	92.1	72.5	85.1	100.1	108.1	103.0	100.0	108.5	103.0
26, 27, 3370	ELECTRICAL, COMMUNICATIONS & UTIL.	95.7	55.2	78.1	95.1	74.9	86.4	95.0	81.7	89.2	83.4	85.1	84.2	104.1	103.5	103.8	100.9	101.3	101.1
MF2018	WEIGHTED AVERAGE	100.5	66.2	87.9	97.6	65.2	85.7	97.6	72.6	88.4	95.3	75.6	88.1	103.5	104.7	104.0	104.1	102.9	103.7

City Cost Indexes

		WASHINGTON																		
		RICHLAND			SEATTLE			SPOKANE			TACOMA			VANCOUVER			WENATCHEE		
DIVISION		993			980 - 981,987			990 - 992			983 - 984			986			988		
		MAT.	INST.	TOTAL	MAT.	INST.	TOTAL	MAT.	INST.	TOTAL	MAT.	INST.	TOTAL	MAT.	INST.	TOTAL	MAT.	INST.	TOTAL
015433	CONTRACTOR EQUIPMENT		88.6	88.6		99.2	99.2		88.6	88.6		96.9	96.9		93.7	93.7		96.9	96.9
0241, 31 - 34	SITE & INFRASTRUCTURE, DEMOLITION	113.9	83.9	94.4	113.0	103.0	106.5	113.7	83.9	94.2	111.3	101.1	104.7	122.7	89.8	101.3	118.6	98.6	105.6
0310	Concrete Forming & Accessories	83.7	82.7	82.9	104.7	108.4	107.5	89.2	82.3	83.9	105.5	103.1	103.6	105.3	95.7	97.9	107.1	74.9	82.0
0320	Concrete Reinforcing	73.8	96.3	80.1	99.5	119.4	105.0	74.3	96.9	80.6	92.6	114.3	98.6	93.1	114.2	98.9	93.1	86.2	91.2
0330	Cast-in-Place Concrete	98.0	84.3	93.1	117.8	112.0	115.8	101.9	84.1	95.6	114.9	109.1	112.8	128.3	99.9	118.2	117.3	84.1	105.5
03	CONCRETE	90.2	85.6	88.4	110.4	111.0	110.6	92.4	85.5	89.7	102.4	106.7	104.1	111.5	100.3	107.0	109.1	80.5	97.8
04	MASONRY	95.8	85.6	89.6	104.2	105.6	105.0	96.5	96.4	96.5	122.7	103.8	111.2	121.5	104.2	111.0	127.1	85.1	101.6
05	METALS	101.0	98.5	98.5	105.5	103.3	105.1	102.2	88.8	99.5	109.5	99.7	107.6	109.4	100.3	107.6	106.3	87.2	102.5
06	WOOD, PLASTICS & COMPOSITES	97.5	81.7	90.4	122.8	107.6	116.0	107.0	81.9	95.6	116.4	102.5	110.1	109.9	94.7	103.1	118.6	73.3	98.3
07	THERMAL & MOISTURE PROTECTION	92.6	84.2	89.6	99.7	110.0	103.4	91.3	84.8	89.0	99.7	106.9	102.3	99.9	100.7	100.2	99.3	79.9	92.4
08	OPENINGS	106.4	78.2	100.0	103.6	111.2	105.3	107.0	77.0	100.2	98.5	106.1	100.2	93.5	101.0	95.2	98.1	69.8	91.7
0920	Plaster & Gypsum Board	130.2	81.1	99.1	116.2	108.0	111.0	127.0	81.1	97.9	119.4	102.8	108.9	115.8	95.1	102.7	124.5	72.7	91.7
0950, 0980	Ceilings & Acoustic Treatment	89.6	81.1	84.9	100.7	108.0	104.8	87.6	81.1	84.0	103.2	102.8	103.0	95.8	95.1	95.4	94.0	72.7	82.1
0960	Flooring	82.8	77.1	81.4	92.2	103.4	95.0	81.0	93.9	84.3	95.1	95.2	95.1	100.3	98.7	99.9	97.0	69.4	90.1
0970, 0990	Wall Finishes & Painting/Coating	82.6	62.7	70.8	104.7	95.5	99.2	83.0	73.8	77.5	96.3	90.9	93.1	97.8	80.9	87.7	96.3	94.0	95.0
09	FINISHES	95.4	78.8	87.1	101.0	105.3	103.2	94.0	83.4	88.7	103.6	99.7	101.7	100.4	94.2	97.3	103.5	74.9	89.2
COVERS	DIVS. 10 - 14, 25, 28, 41, 43, 44, 46	100.0	97.3	99.5	100.0	103.2	100.6	100.0	97.2	99.5	100.0	101.7	100.3	100.0	95.4	99.1	100.0	94.8	99.0
21, 22, 23	FIRE SUPPRESSION, PLUMBING & HVAC	99.9	106.2	102.2	100.1	122.3	108.0	99.9	81.8	93.4	100.2	108.5	103.2	100.2	108.1	103.0	92.7	82.7	89.1
26, 27, 3370	ELECTRICAL, COMMUNICATIONS & UTIL.	79.7	97.9	87.6	100.9	126.4	112.0	81.0	80.1	80.6	104.0	101.3	102.9	113.5	100.9	108.1	104.5	84.1	95.7
MF2018	WEIGHTED AVERAGE	97.0	91.0	94.8	103.6	112.6	106.9	97.6	84.9	93.0	104.3	103.8	104.1	105.9	100.6	103.9	103.1	83.2	95.8

		WASHINGTON			WEST VIRGINIA														
		YAKIMA			BECKLEY			BLUEFIELD			BUCKHANNON			CHARLESTON			CLARKSBURG		
DIVISION		989			258 - 259			247 - 248			262			250 - 253			263 - 264		
		MAT.	INST.	TOTAL	MAT.	INST.	TOTAL	MAT.	INST.	TOTAL	MAT.	INST.	TOTAL	MAT.	INST.	TOTAL	MAT.	INST.	TOTAL
015433	CONTRACTOR EQUIPMENT		96.9	96.9		101.7	101.7		101.7	101.7		101.7	101.7		104.3	104.3		101.7	101.7
0241, 31 - 34	SITE & INFRASTRUCTURE, DEMOLITION	113.9	100.6	105.2	104.8	84.4	91.5	104.7	84.4	91.4	110.5	84.7	93.7	106.2	92.6	97.3	111.2	84.7	93.9
0310	Concrete Forming & Accessories	105.8	78.1	84.3	87.3	79.5	81.2	87.6	79.2	81.1	86.9	79.7	81.3	103.0	86.0	89.8	84.1	79.9	80.8
0320	Concrete Reinforcing	92.9	97.1	94.0	93.6	81.7	90.3	91.8	74.1	86.9	92.4	81.6	89.4	99.1	82.1	94.4	92.4	92.5	92.4
0330	Cast-in-Place Concrete	122.7	85.9	109.7	109.1	85.1	100.5	110.6	85.0	101.5	110.3	87.7	102.3	105.6	88.0	99.3	120.9	83.9	107.8
03	CONCRETE	106.8	84.4	97.9	92.2	83.1	88.6	93.4	81.1	88.8	95.1	84.2	90.8	94.2	86.9	91.3	99.1	84.7	93.4
04	MASONRY	115.3	96.8	104.1	85.2	80.3	82.2	87.7	80.3	83.2	97.9	86.0	90.7	83.3	86.2	85.1	100.9	86.0	91.9
05	METALS	107.0	92.7	104.1	99.2	100.9	99.5	99.5	98.1	99.2	99.7	101.2	100.0	97.9	98.6	98.1	99.7	105.0	100.7
06	WOOD, PLASTICS & COMPOSITES	116.9	73.3	97.4	84.8	79.4	82.4	83.3	79.4	81.5	82.3	77.0	79.9	99.4	86.2	93.5	78.1	77.0	77.6
07	THERMAL & MOISTURE PROTECTION	99.8	87.4	95.4	104.9	78.9	95.6	104.2	78.9	95.2	104.5	82.7	96.7	101.5	85.0	95.6	104.4	82.4	96.6
08	OPENINGS	98.1	84.0	94.9	97.7	76.6	92.9	96.2	74.8	91.4	96.2	75.2	91.5	97.9	80.3	93.9	96.2	79.9	92.6
0920	Plaster & Gypsum Board	118.7	72.7	89.6	90.2	78.8	83.0	97.8	78.8	85.7	99.0	76.4	84.7	102.3	85.7	91.8	96.4	76.4	83.7
0950, 0980	Ceilings & Acoustic Treatment	95.0	72.7	82.5	74.0	78.8	76.7	93.8	78.8	85.4	97.9	76.4	85.8	85.5	85.7	85.6	97.9	76.4	85.8
0960	Flooring	95.6	93.9	95.2	104.6	95.1	102.2	99.5	95.1	98.4	99.2	90.7	97.1	106.2	95.1	103.4	98.4	90.7	96.4
0970, 0990	Wall Finishes & Painting/Coating	96.3	73.8	82.9	101.9	81.9	89.9	102.1	79.8	88.8	102.1	85.5	92.2	104.7	87.9	94.7	102.1	85.5	92.2
09	FINISHES	101.7	78.8	90.2	92.5	82.7	87.6	98.2	82.5	90.3	99.9	82.0	90.9	99.1	87.9	93.5	99.2	82.0	90.6
COVERS	DIVS. 10 - 14, 25, 28, 41, 43, 44, 46	100.0	96.3	99.3	100.0	86.3	97.3	100.0	90.4	98.1	100.0	91.7	98.4	100.0	92.1	98.5	100.0	91.7	98.4
21, 22, 23	FIRE SUPPRESSION, PLUMBING & HVAC	100.2	107.3	102.7	92.7	87.1	90.7	92.9	75.6	86.7	92.9	89.7	91.7	99.7	88.9	95.8	92.9	89.9	91.8
26, 27, 3370	ELECTRICAL, COMMUNICATIONS & UTIL.	105.6	102.5	104.3	93.8	74.9	85.6	95.1	74.9	86.4	95.9	88.9	92.8	100.8	83.5	93.3	95.9	88.9	92.8
MF2018	WEIGHTED AVERAGE	104.0	94.7	100.6	95.4	83.9	91.2	96.2	81.0	90.6	97.2	87.2	93.5	98.2	88.3	94.5	97.7	87.9	94.1

		WEST VIRGINIA																	
		GASSAWAY			HUNTINGTON			LEWISBURG			MARTINSBURG			MORGANTOWN			PARKERSBURG		
DIVISION		266			255 - 257			249			254			265			261		
		MAT.	INST.	TOTAL	MAT.	INST.	TOTAL	MAT.	INST.	TOTAL	MAT.	INST.	TOTAL	MAT.	INST.	TOTAL	MAT.	INST.	TOTAL
015433	CONTRACTOR EQUIPMENT		101.7	101.7		101.7	101.7		101.7	101.7		101.7	101.7		101.7	101.7		101.7	101.7
0241, 31 - 34	SITE & INFRASTRUCTURE, DEMOLITION	108.1	84.7	92.8	112.3	85.6	94.9	119.7	84.4	96.7	108.4	84.6	92.9	105.5	85.8	92.7	116.6	85.8	96.5
0310	Concrete Forming & Accessories	86.3	80.4	81.7	101.2	83.1	87.1	84.5	79.3	80.5	87.4	72.2	75.6	84.5	80.3	81.2	89.3	86.3	87.0
0320	Concrete Reinforcing	92.4	82.3	89.6	94.9	85.1	92.2	92.4	74.1	87.3	93.6	85.4	91.3	92.4	92.5	92.4	91.8	81.5	88.9
0330	Cast-in-Place Concrete	115.5	87.6	105.6	118.9	89.8	108.6	110.7	85.0	101.6	114.3	80.9	102.4	110.3	92.7	104.0	112.7	88.1	104.0
03	CONCRETE	96.3	84.5	91.6	97.8	87.0	93.5	98.8	81.8	92.1	95.0	78.9	88.7	93.2	88.0	91.1	96.7	87.3	93.0
04	MASONRY	101.8	84.9	91.5	87.5	86.7	87.0	94.3	85.3	85.8	87.5	75.6	80.3	118.9	86.0	98.9	79.7	78.4	78.9
05	METALS	99.6	101.1	99.9	102.3	102.7	102.4	99.6	98.2	99.3	99.6	99.8	99.6	99.7	105.4	100.9	100.3	101.3	100.5
06	WOOD, PLASTICS & COMPOSITES	81.2	78.3	79.9	99.4	82.1	91.6	78.5	79.4	78.9	84.8	71.4	78.8	78.5	77.0	77.8	82.9	87.9	85.2
07	THERMAL & MOISTURE PROTECTION	104.2	83.0	96.7	105.2	82.5	97.1	105.0	78.9	95.7	105.1	72.5	93.5	104.2	83.7	96.9	104.5	81.7	96.4
08	OPENINGS	94.5	76.1	90.4	96.8	78.7	92.7	96.2	74.8	91.4	99.5	67.0	92.2	97.4	79.9	93.4	95.2	80.9	92.0
0920	Plaster & Gypsum Board	97.8	77.7	85.0	98.2	81.6	87.6	96.4	78.8	85.2	90.2	70.6	77.8	96.4	76.4	83.7	99.8	87.6	92.1
0950, 0980	Ceilings & Acoustic Treatment	97.9	77.7	86.6	74.0	81.6	78.2	97.9	78.8	87.2	74.0	70.6	72.1	97.9	76.4	85.8	97.9	87.6	92.1
0960	Flooring	99.1	95.1	98.1	111.2	94.3	106.9	98.5	95.1	97.7	104.6	88.6	100.6	98.5	90.7	96.6	101.8	94.2	99.9
0970, 0990	Wall Finishes & Painting/Coating	102.1	87.9	93.7	101.9	83.2	90.7	102.1	57.3	75.4	101.9	74.4	85.5	102.1	85.5	92.2	102.1	87.2	93.2
09	FINISHES	99.4	83.9	91.6	95.5	85.1	90.2	100.4	80.0	90.2	92.7	74.9	83.8	98.8	82.0	90.3	100.9	88.2	94.5
COVERS	DIVS. 10 - 14, 25, 28, 41, 43, 44, 46	100.0	91.8	98.4	100.0	91.8	98.4	100.0	90.4	98.1	100.0	89.0	97.9	100.0	91.7	98.4	100.0	91.4	98.3
21, 22, 23	FIRE SUPPRESSION, PLUMBING & HVAC	92.9	77.9	87.5	100.2	86.4	95.3	92.9	87.0	90.8	92.7	72.8	85.6	92.9	90.2	91.9	100.4	85.5	95.0
26, 27, 3370	ELECTRICAL, COMMUNICATIONS & UTIL.	95.9	83.5	90.5	95.9	83.0	90.3	93.8	74.9	85.6	97.0	68.4	84.6	96.0	88.9	92.9	95.9	84.4	90.9
MF2018	WEIGHTED AVERAGE	97.2	84.2	92.4	99.2	87.0	94.7	97.5	83.1	92.2	96.6	77.2	89.4	97.6	88.6	94.3	98.6	86.6	94.2

City Cost Indexes

DIVISION		WEST VIRGINIA									WISCONSIN								
		PETERSBURG 268			ROMNEY 267			WHEELING 260			BELOIT 535			EAU CLAIRE 547			GREEN BAY 541 - 543		
		MAT.	INST.	TOTAL	MAT.	INST.	TOTAL	MAT.	INST.	TOTAL	MAT.	INST.	TOTAL	MAT.	INST.	TOTAL	MAT.	INST.	TOTAL
015433	CONTRACTOR EQUIPMENT		101.7	101.7		101.7	101.7		101.7	101.7		95.4	95.4		96.2	96.2		94.2	94.2
0241, 31 - 34	SITE & INFRASTRUCTURE, DEMOLITION	104.9	85.5	92.3	107.7	85.5	93.2	117.2	85.6	96.6	85.3	96.0	92.3	86.2	95.3	92.1	88.6	91.7	90.6
0310	Concrete Forming & Accessories	88.1	81.1	82.7	83.6	81.0	81.6	91.4	79.4	82.1	95.4	87.7	89.4	98.2	92.8	94.0	110.6	102.7	104.5
0320	Concrete Reinforcing	91.8	82.3	89.2	92.4	85.7	90.5	91.2	92.4	91.6	100.2	138.6	110.8	91.8	109.2	96.6	90.7	106.2	95.0
0330	Cast-in-Place Concrete	110.3	87.6	102.2	115.5	80.0	102.9	112.7	89.8	104.6	89.9	91.6	90.5	110.0	99.3	106.2	113.8	99.0	108.5
03	CONCRETE	93.3	84.9	90.0	96.0	82.7	90.8	96.7	86.6	92.7	95.9	98.1	96.7	100.2	98.3	99.5	103.5	102.1	102.9
04	MASONRY	94.0	86.0	89.2	94.7	84.9	88.8	100.4	83.4	90.1	99.9	103.2	101.9	97.5	104.4	101.7	128.8	98.4	110.4
05	METALS	99.8	101.1	100.1	99.9	102.0	100.3	100.5	105.1	101.4	92.7	113.1	96.7	91.5	105.1	94.2	96.2	104.2	97.8
06	WOOD, PLASTICS & COMPOSITES	83.6	79.4	81.7	77.4	79.4	78.3	85.0	77.0	81.4	93.0	85.4	89.6	101.3	90.5	96.5	115.6	103.8	110.3
07	THERMAL & MOISTURE PROTECTION	104.3	78.1	95.0	104.4	77.7	94.9	104.7	81.1	96.3	102.0	87.8	96.9	104.7	99.9	103.0	107.0	99.3	104.3
08	OPENINGS	97.4	75.8	92.5	97.3	76.6	92.6	95.9	79.9	92.3	93.9	101.5	95.6	99.8	92.4	98.2	95.4	103.3	97.2
0920	Plaster & Gypsum Board	99.0	78.8	86.2	95.9	78.8	85.1	99.6	76.8	84.9	82.0	85.6	84.3	97.2	90.8	93.2	95.5	104.5	101.2
0950, 0980	Ceilings & Acoustic Treatment	97.9	78.8	87.2	97.9	78.8	87.2	97.9	76.4	85.8	89.9	85.6	87.5	93.9	90.8	92.2	87.8	104.5	97.1
0960	Flooring	100.0	90.7	97.6	98.3	88.6	95.9	102.6	90.7	99.6	96.3	106.1	98.8	83.8	115.1	91.7	100.3	116.7	104.4
0970, 0990	Wall Finishes & Painting/Coating	102.1	85.5	92.2	102.1	85.5	92.2	102.1	85.5	92.2	97.2	92.0	94.1	85.4	79.5	81.9	92.9	117.9	107.8
09	FINISHES	99.6	83.3	91.4	98.9	82.9	90.9	101.1	81.6	91.3	92.0	90.8	91.4	89.5	95.1	92.3	93.4	107.3	100.4
COVERS	DIVS. 10 - 14, 25, 28, 41, 43, 44, 46	100.0	89.8	98.0	100.0	91.9	98.4	100.0	86.4	97.4	100.0	96.7	99.4	100.0	93.3	98.7	100.0	97.6	99.5
21, 22, 23	FIRE SUPPRESSION, PLUMBING & HVAC	92.9	78.4	87.7	92.9	78.1	87.6	100.4	89.1	96.3	99.7	86.2	94.9	100.0	85.9	94.9	100.3	92.6	97.6
26, 27, 3370	ELECTRICAL, COMMUNICATIONS & UTIL.	97.6	68.5	85.0	97.2	68.4	84.7	94.5	88.9	92.1	98.9	75.0	88.6	102.0	95.8	97.9	95.4	100.3	97.5
MF2018	WEIGHTED AVERAGE	96.9	82.2	91.5	97.2	81.8	91.6	99.4	87.6	95.0	96.3	92.8	95.0	96.9	95.8	96.5	99.5	99.3	99.4

DIVISION		WISCONSIN																	
		KENOSHA 531			LA CROSSE 546			LANCASTER 538			MADISON 537			MILWAUKEE 530,532			NEW RICHMOND 540		
		MAT.	INST.	TOTAL	MAT.	INST.	TOTAL	MAT.	INST.	TOTAL	MAT.	INST.	TOTAL	MAT.	INST.	TOTAL	MAT.	INST.	TOTAL
015433	CONTRACTOR EQUIPMENT		93.7	93.7		96.2	96.2		95.4	95.4		99.4	99.4		88.6	88.6		96.5	96.5
0241, 31 - 34	SITE & INFRASTRUCTURE, DEMOLITION	88.8	94.6	92.6	81.6	95.3	90.5	80.9	95.5	90.4	85.1	103.1	96.8	82.1	93.8	89.8	83.0	94.2	90.3
0310	Concrete Forming & Accessories	106.8	107.7	107.5	83.0	92.9	90.7	94.7	86.5	88.4	100.1	102.3	101.8	100.5	116.0	112.6	92.0	83.8	85.7
0320	Concrete Reinforcing	100.1	109.7	102.7	91.6	105.0	95.3	100.9	96.1	99.6	98.7	105.2	100.5	98.7	116.4	103.6	90.2	103.3	93.8
0330	Cast-in-Place Concrete	97.8	103.0	99.6	98.9	99.4	99.1	89.3	91.1	90.0	82.8	104.9	90.6	83.3	113.1	93.9	114.5	93.7	107.1
03	CONCRETE	100.0	106.2	102.5	92.0	97.6	94.2	95.6	90.2	93.5	96.4	103.5	99.2	96.7	114.1	103.5	98.4	91.3	95.6
04	MASONRY	97.9	108.9	104.6	96.4	99.0	98.0	100.0	103.2	101.9	114.4	103.0	107.5	88.6	119.7	107.5	123.0	103.3	111.0
05	METALS	94.7	103.9	96.5	91.4	103.5	93.8	89.3	97.1	90.9	97.4	99.6	97.9	96.9	98.8	97.3	93.4	101.6	95.0
06	WOOD, PLASTICS & COMPOSITES	106.2	107.8	106.9	81.6	90.5	85.6	91.9	85.4	89.0	98.9	101.7	100.1	98.9	114.2	105.7	88.7	81.8	85.6
07	THERMAL & MOISTURE PROTECTION	102.9	104.1	103.3	104.1	97.8	101.9	101.8	87.5	96.7	99.5	102.7	100.6	101.3	115.1	106.2	104.9	93.8	101.0
08	OPENINGS	88.2	107.0	92.5	99.8	90.5	97.7	90.2	83.3	88.6	98.7	102.4	99.6	100.1	113.4	103.1	85.4	81.8	84.6
0920	Plaster & Gypsum Board	74.3	108.7	96.1	92.1	91.3	91.3	79.6	85.6	83.4	86.4	102.1	96.3	86.4	114.8	104.4	79.2	82.0	81.0
0950, 0980	Ceilings & Acoustic Treatment	89.9	108.7	100.5	92.1	90.8	91.4	82.2	85.6	84.1	94.8	102.1	98.9	94.8	114.8	108.2	62.5	82.0	73.4
0960	Flooring	115.7	111.0	114.6	79.4	116.7	88.7	96.0	99.9	96.9	103.1	114.8	106.0	95.4	121.9	102.1	94.9	102.6	96.8
0970, 0990	Wall Finishes & Painting/Coating	107.2	114.2	111.4	85.4	117.5	104.5	97.2	86.8	91.0	104.7	97.7	100.5	104.7	124.7	116.6	96.6	72.6	82.3
09	FINISHES	97.4	109.5	103.5	86.7	99.6	93.2	89.5	88.7	89.1	96.5	104.4	100.5	95.9	118.3	107.1	82.6	85.8	84.2
COVERS	DIVS. 10 - 14, 25, 28, 41, 43, 44, 46	100.0	99.5	99.9	100.0	98.6	99.7	100.0	96.7	99.4	100.0	101.2	100.2	100.0	103.8	100.7	100.0	84.8	97.1
21, 22, 23	FIRE SUPPRESSION, PLUMBING & HVAC	99.9	96.5	98.7	100.0	85.8	94.9	92.2	80.2	87.9	99.7	95.2	98.1	99.7	109.6	103.2	91.8	79.9	87.5
26, 27, 3370	ELECTRICAL, COMMUNICATIONS & UTIL.	99.0	95.2	97.4	97.8	100.0	98.9	98.5	75.5	88.6	98.4	98.3	98.3	98.3	102.8	100.3	96.9	75.6	87.7
MF2018	WEIGHTED AVERAGE	97.4	101.9	99.0	95.3	95.9	95.5	93.2	88.0	91.3	98.6	100.5	99.3	97.6	109.9	101.9	94.2	87.7	91.8

DIVISION		WISCONSIN																	
		OSHKOSH 549			PORTAGE 539			RACINE 534			RHINELANDER 545			SUPERIOR 548			WAUSAU 544		
		MAT.	INST.	TOTAL	MAT.	INST.	TOTAL	MAT.	INST.	TOTAL	MAT.	INST.	TOTAL	MAT.	INST.	TOTAL	MAT.	INST.	TOTAL
015433	CONTRACTOR EQUIPMENT		94.2	94.2		95.4	95.4		95.4	95.4		94.2	94.2		96.5	96.5		94.2	94.2
0241, 31 - 34	SITE & INFRASTRUCTURE, DEMOLITION	79.1	90.7	86.6	75.0	96.3	88.9	85.2	97.8	93.4	87.3	90.3	89.2	80.6	93.9	89.3	76.2	91.3	86.0
0310	Concrete Forming & Accessories	91.2	87.1	88.0	86.3	87.2	87.0	95.8	107.7	105.0	88.5	86.0	86.6	89.7	80.7	82.7	90.6	88.7	89.1
0320	Concrete Reinforcing	90.8	99.4	93.2	101.0	96.3	99.7	100.2	109.7	102.8	90.9	96.4	92.4	90.2	112.5	96.4	90.9	105.2	94.9
0330	Cast-in-Place Concrete	105.5	90.7	100.2	76.8	89.9	81.4	88.2	102.7	93.3	119.6	89.5	108.9	107.9	89.9	101.5	98.3	84.7	93.5
03	CONCRETE	94.1	91.0	92.8	85.7	90.3	87.5	92.2	106.2	99.5	104.5	89.6	98.6	93.6	90.1	92.2	89.7	90.6	90.1
04	MASONRY	111.3	104.6	107.2	98.9	103.2	101.5	99.9	108.9	105.4	132.4	102.6	114.3	122.1	101.1	109.4	110.7	102.6	105.8
05	METALS	93.7	100.5	95.0	90.1	100.9	92.2	94.3	104.0	96.2	93.1	99.2	94.3	94.5	105.4	96.7	93.0	102.9	95.0
06	WOOD, PLASTICS & COMPOSITES	89.7	85.5	87.8	80.4	85.4	82.6	93.3	107.8	99.8	86.2	85.5	85.9	86.6	77.8	82.7	88.9	88.1	88.6
07	THERMAL & MOISTURE PROTECTION	106.1	80.1	96.8	101.3	93.3	98.5	102.1	104.3	102.9	106.7	78.5	96.7	104.6	88.9	99.0	105.9	89.3	100.0
08	OPENINGS	92.2	87.2	91.0	90.3	90.3	90.3	93.9	107.0	96.8	92.2	83.3	90.2	84.7	90.0	85.9	92.3	90.1	91.8
0920	Plaster & Gypsum Board	81.5	85.6	84.1	73.5	85.6	81.2	82.0	108.7	99.0	81.5	85.6	84.1	79.6	77.9	78.5	81.5	88.4	85.9
0950, 0980	Ceilings & Acoustic Treatment	87.8	85.6	86.6	87.7	85.6	86.5	89.9	108.7	100.5	87.8	85.6	86.6	63.9	77.9	71.7	87.8	88.4	88.1
0960	Flooring	93.9	102.8	96.2	93.1	102.6	95.4	96.3	111.0	100.0	93.5	102.6	95.8	96.3	110.2	99.8	93.9	102.6	96.1
0970, 0990	Wall Finishes & Painting/Coating	90.8	99.1	95.8	97.2	86.8	91.0	97.2	116.4	108.6	90.8	71.1	79.0	84.8	94.0	90.3	90.8	74.0	80.7
09	FINISHES	89.1	91.3	90.2	88.9	89.6	89.2	92.0	109.7	100.9	89.7	87.7	88.7	82.5	86.9	84.7	88.9	89.6	89.2
COVERS	DIVS. 10 - 14, 25, 28, 41, 43, 44, 46	100.0	95.2	99.1	100.0	96.8	99.4	100.0	99.5	99.9	100.0	94.5	98.9	100.0	83.7	96.8	100.0	94.8	99.0
21, 22, 23	FIRE SUPPRESSION, PLUMBING & HVAC	92.8	79.6	88.1	92.9	86.2	90.5	99.7	96.5	98.6	92.8	79.7	88.1	91.8	82.1	88.3	92.8	80.2	88.3
26, 27, 3370	ELECTRICAL, COMMUNICATIONS & UTIL.	97.2	75.0	87.6	100.9	83.7	93.4	99.0	92.3	96.1	96.8	69.5	85.0	99.4	87.7	94.4	97.8	69.5	85.5
MF2018	WEIGHTED AVERAGE	94.6	88.2	92.2	92.1	91.4	91.8	96.5	101.8	98.5	96.7	86.2	92.8	94.0	90.1	92.6	93.9	87.7	91.6

City Cost Indexes

		WYOMING																	
	DIVISION	CASPER			CHEYENNE			NEWCASTLE			RAWLINS			RIVERTON			ROCK SPRINGS		
		826			820			827			823			825			829 - 831		
		MAT.	INST.	TOTAL	MAT.	INST.	TOTAL	MAT.	INST.	TOTAL	MAT.	INST.	TOTAL	MAT.	INST.	TOTAL	MAT.	INST.	TOTAL
015433	CONTRACTOR EQUIPMENT		99.7	99.7		93.2	93.2		93.2	93.2		93.2	93.2		93.2	93.2		93.2	93.2
0241, 31 - 34	SITE & INFRASTRUCTURE, DEMOLITION	102.3	98.5	99.8	96.7	87.2	90.5	87.2	86.9	87.0	100.0	86.9	91.4	94.3	86.9	89.4	91.9	86.9	88.7
0310	Concrete Forming & Accessories	103.3	62.8	71.8	105.9	62.5	72.2	94.4	60.8	68.3	99.3	60.8	69.4	93.1	60.6	67.9	101.6	62.7	71.4
0320	Concrete Reinforcing	101.2	82.3	96.0	92.5	82.6	89.7	99.8	82.4	95.0	99.5	82.4	94.8	100.4	82.4	95.4	100.4	79.0	94.5
0330	Cast-in-Place Concrete	95.9	78.8	89.8	90.4	77.3	85.7	91.3	75.8	85.8	91.4	75.8	85.8	91.3	75.7	85.8	91.3	76.3	86.0
03	CONCRETE	102.3	72.3	90.4	96.1	71.8	86.5	96.9	70.5	86.5	107.8	70.5	93.0	103.4	70.4	90.4	97.7	71.0	87.1
04	MASONRY	91.2	64.4	75.0	93.0	68.3	78.0	90.2	64.0	74.2	90.1	64.0	74.2	90.2	64.0	74.3	142.3	59.1	91.8
05	METALS	105.3	79.7	100.2	107.3	82.2	102.3	103.3	81.8	99.1	103.4	81.8	99.1	103.5	81.6	99.2	104.2	80.3	99.5
06	WOOD, PLASTICS & COMPOSITES	102.9	59.7	83.5	104.1	59.1	83.9	90.1	58.3	75.8	95.7	58.3	78.9	88.5	58.3	75.0	101.1	60.6	82.9
07	THERMAL & MOISTURE PROTECTION	97.5	67.7	86.9	93.4	67.6	84.2	94.1	63.9	83.3	95.3	63.9	84.1	94.8	66.9	84.8	94.2	66.7	84.4
08	OPENINGS	97.9	65.6	90.6	96.0	65.3	89.0	99.4	62.9	91.2	99.2	62.9	91.0	99.3	62.9	91.1	99.7	64.6	91.8
0920	Plaster & Gypsum Board	111.2	58.4	77.7	98.6	58.0	72.9	95.8	57.3	71.4	95.8	57.3	71.4	95.8	57.3	71.4	112.0	59.6	78.7
0950, 0980	Ceilings & Acoustic Treatment	99.1	58.4	76.3	84.4	58.0	69.6	85.4	57.3	69.6	85.4	57.3	69.6	85.4	57.3	69.6	85.4	59.6	70.9
0960	Flooring	103.1	75.3	96.1	101.8	75.3	95.2	96.4	63.5	88.1	98.5	63.5	89.7	95.9	63.5	87.8	100.2	55.8	89.1
0970, 0990	Wall Finishes & Painting/Coating	104.7	56.4	75.9	103.7	56.4	75.5	99.9	69.6	81.9	99.9	69.6	81.9	99.9	53.7	72.4	99.9	71.0	82.7
09	FINISHES	102.4	63.8	83.0	96.8	63.4	80.0	92.4	61.3	76.8	94.2	61.3	77.7	93.0	59.6	76.2	95.7	61.5	78.6
COVERS	DIVS. 10 - 14, 25, 28, 41, 43, 44, 46	100.0	84.4	97.0	100.0	88.0	97.7	100.0	92.6	98.6	100.0	92.6	98.6	100.0	82.2	96.6	100.0	86.8	97.4
21, 22, 23	FIRE SUPPRESSION, PLUMBING & HVAC	99.9	71.9	89.9	100.2	77.8	92.2	96.0	74.5	88.3	96.0	74.5	88.3	96.0	74.4	88.3	100.1	75.0	91.1
26, 27, 3370	ELECTRICAL, COMMUNICATIONS & UTIL.	97.7	59.3	81.1	95.2	65.1	82.2	93.4	55.5	77.0	93.4	55.5	77.0	93.4	59.4	78.7	92.5	62.4	79.5
MF2018	WEIGHTED AVERAGE	100.8	71.1	89.9	99.6	72.8	89.7	97.2	69.8	87.1	99.0	69.8	88.3	98.2	69.8	87.8	100.8	70.3	89.6

		WYOMING												CANADA					
	DIVISION	SHERIDAN			WHEATLAND			WORLAND			YELLOWSTONE NAT'L PA			BARRIE, ONTARIO			BATHURST, NEW BRUNSWICK		
		828			822			824			821								
		MAT.	INST.	TOTAL	MAT.	INST.	TOTAL	MAT.	INST.	TOTAL	MAT.	INST.	TOTAL	MAT.	INST.	TOTAL	MAT.	INST.	TOTAL
015433	CONTRACTOR EQUIPMENT		93.2	93.2		93.2	93.2		93.2	93.2		93.2	93.2		97.9	97.9		98.6	98.6
0241, 31 - 34	SITE & INFRASTRUCTURE, DEMOLITION	94.5	87.2	89.7	91.1	86.9	88.3	88.5	86.9	87.4	88.6	86.9	87.5	122.1	90.8	101.7	116.5	87.8	97.8
0310	Concrete Forming & Accessories	103.7	61.7	71.1	96.6	60.5	68.6	96.7	60.8	68.8	96.7	60.7	68.7	124.9	77.5	88.1	91.1	54.6	62.8
0320	Concrete Reinforcing	100.4	82.4	95.4	99.8	81.7	94.8	100.4	82.4	95.4	102.1	79.4	95.8	151.8	81.2	132.3	70.2	53.8	65.6
0330	Cast-in-Place Concrete	94.4	77.2	88.3	95.3	75.7	88.3	91.3	75.8	85.8	91.3	75.7	85.8	165.1	77.7	134.1	115.6	53.8	93.6
03	CONCRETE	104.0	71.4	91.1	101.0	70.2	88.8	97.3	70.5	86.7	97.7	69.9	86.7	150.7	78.9	122.4	104.1	55.4	84.9
04	MASONRY	90.5	66.5	75.9	90.5	52.9	67.7	90.2	64.0	74.3	90.2	64.0	74.3	171.6	83.8	118.3	156.6	53.9	94.2
05	METALS	107.3	81.7	102.2	103.3	80.7	98.8	103.5	81.8	99.2	104.2	80.7	99.5	114.3	89.5	109.4	128.6	73.0	117.6
06	WOOD, PLASTICS & COMPOSITES	106.1	58.3	84.7	92.8	58.3	77.3	92.9	58.3	77.4	92.9	58.3	77.4	117.3	76.4	99.0	91.3	54.8	74.9
07	THERMAL & MOISTURE PROTECTION	95.4	67.0	85.3	94.3	60.8	82.4	94.1	63.9	83.3	93.8	63.9	83.1	113.9	80.1	101.9	118.3	54.4	95.6
08	OPENINGS	100.0	62.9	91.6	98.3	62.9	90.3	99.6	62.9	91.3	93.8	62.2	86.7	89.2	76.4	86.3	84.8	48.4	76.6
0920	Plaster & Gypsum Board	118.7	57.3	79.7	95.8	57.3	71.4	95.8	57.3	71.4	96.1	57.3	71.5	153.8	75.9	104.4	119.8	53.5	77.8
0950, 0980	Ceilings & Acoustic Treatment	87.4	57.3	70.5	85.4	57.3	69.6	85.4	57.3	69.6	86.3	57.3	70.0	92.9	75.9	83.3	91.7	53.5	70.3
0960	Flooring	100.6	54.0	88.9	97.4	63.5	88.9	97.4	63.5	88.9	97.4	63.5	88.9	120.7	81.5	110.9	95.7	38.7	81.4
0970, 0990	Wall Finishes & Painting/Coating	102.6	56.4	75.1	99.9	51.9	71.3	99.9	69.6	81.9	99.9	53.7	72.4	106.8	77.6	89.4	112.3	44.4	71.8
09	FINISHES	99.8	59.3	79.4	93.0	59.4	76.1	92.7	61.3	77.0	93.0	59.6	76.2	112.4	78.5	95.4	98.0	50.7	74.2
COVERS	DIVS. 10 - 14, 25, 28, 41, 43, 44, 46	100.0	83.7	96.9	100.0	82.9	96.7	100.0	92.7	98.6	100.0	92.7	98.6	139.3	60.6	124.0	131.1	54.1	116.2
21, 22, 23	FIRE SUPPRESSION, PLUMBING & HVAC	96.0	75.9	88.8	96.0	74.4	88.3	96.0	74.4	88.3	96.0	74.4	88.3	110.3	87.6	102.2	110.6	60.7	92.7
26, 27, 3370	ELECTRICAL, COMMUNICATIONS & UTIL.	95.3	59.4	79.7	93.4	59.4	78.7	93.4	59.4	78.7	92.9	59.4	78.4	124.9	76.9	104.1	137.5	51.8	100.4
MF2018	WEIGHTED AVERAGE	100.1	70.6	89.2	97.8	68.4	87.0	97.4	70.3	87.4	97.1	69.9	87.1	121.0	82.1	106.7	117.1	59.1	95.7

		CANADA																	
	DIVISION	BRANDON, MANITOBA			BRANTFORD, ONTARIO			BRIDGEWATER, NOVA SCOTIA			CALGARY, ALBERTA			CAP-DE-LA-MADELEINE, QUEBEC			CHARLESBOURG, QUEBEC		
		MAT.	INST.	TOTAL	MAT.	INST.	TOTAL	MAT.	INST.	TOTAL	MAT.	INST.	TOTAL	MAT.	INST.	TOTAL	MAT.	INST.	TOTAL
015433	CONTRACTOR EQUIPMENT		97.2	97.2		97.8	97.8		98.1	98.1		119.7	119.7		99.0	99.0		99.0	99.0
0241, 31 - 34	SITE & INFRASTRUCTURE, DEMOLITION	126.4	87.8	101.2	126.1	91.0	103.2	110.6	89.1	96.6	118.5	108.8	112.2	106.2	90.6	96.0	106.2	90.6	96.0
0310	Concrete Forming & Accessories	129.6	62.2	77.3	112.0	84.0	90.2	84.9	64.1	68.7	119.6	87.1	94.3	117.3	74.7	84.2	117.3	74.7	84.2
0320	Concrete Reinforcing	87.1	51.0	77.1	84.1	80.0	83.0	72.3	44.6	64.6	75.3	74.9	75.2	72.3	67.7	71.0	72.3	67.7	71.0
0330	Cast-in-Place Concrete	124.7	66.2	103.9	149.0	96.1	130.2	153.2	63.7	121.4	145.8	93.5	127.2	120.2	82.9	107.0	120.2	82.9	107.0
03	CONCRETE	131.8	62.8	104.5	134.4	88.1	116.1	132.5	61.7	104.6	183.8	88.1	146.0	119.9	77.1	103.0	119.9	77.1	103.0
04	MASONRY	219.9	56.9	120.9	172.2	87.6	120.8	167.4	61.5	103.1	230.3	80.8	139.5	167.6	71.6	109.3	167.6	71.6	109.3
05	METALS	143.1	75.9	129.9	128.1	90.0	120.6	126.9	75.1	116.7	154.9	95.9	143.2	125.4	83.8	117.2	125.4	83.8	117.2
06	WOOD, PLASTICS & COMPOSITES	135.6	63.1	103.1	114.0	82.9	100.1	82.0	63.8	73.9	103.2	87.2	96.0	125.8	74.8	102.9	125.8	74.8	102.9
07	THERMAL & MOISTURE PROTECTION	133.6	63.8	108.7	126.8	85.1	111.9	121.7	63.0	100.8	147.2	89.3	126.5	120.7	78.4	105.6	120.7	78.4	105.6
08	OPENINGS	100.3	56.5	90.4	88.0	81.8	86.6	83.7	57.9	77.9	91.0	77.1	87.9	89.6	68.3	84.8	89.6	68.3	84.8
0920	Plaster & Gypsum Board	100.6	61.9	76.1	117.8	82.6	95.5	114.7	62.8	81.8	120.5	86.0	98.6	146.5	74.0	100.5	146.5	74.0	100.5
0950, 0980	Ceilings & Acoustic Treatment	94.0	61.9	76.0	78.3	82.6	80.7	78.3	62.8	69.6	105.8	86.0	94.7	78.3	74.0	75.9	78.3	74.0	75.9
0960	Flooring	123.0	57.8	106.7	107.9	81.5	101.3	94.1	55.0	84.3	126.8	77.8	114.5	107.9	80.2	100.9	107.9	80.2	100.9
0970, 0990	Wall Finishes & Painting/Coating	118.1	50.1	77.5	110.9	85.2	95.6	110.9	54.9	77.5	111.0	94.5	101.2	110.9	77.4	90.9	110.9	77.4	90.9
09	FINISHES	109.7	60.0	84.9	99.3	83.9	91.6	94.3	61.7	77.9	119.9	86.7	103.3	102.6	76.3	89.4	102.6	76.3	89.4
COVERS	DIVS. 10 - 14, 25, 28, 41, 43, 44, 46	131.1	55.8	116.5	131.1	62.3	117.8	131.1	56.8	116.7	131.1	84.5	122.1	131.1	70.4	119.4	131.1	70.4	119.4
21, 22, 23	FIRE SUPPRESSION, PLUMBING & HVAC	117.2	73.8	101.7	110.5	90.2	103.2	110.5	74.5	97.6	109.8	81.1	99.5	110.2	78.9	99.0	110.2	78.9	99.0
26, 27, 3370	ELECTRICAL, COMMUNICATIONS & UTIL.	130.8	58.5	99.5	134.6	76.5	109.4	135.4	54.4	100.3	134.7	83.6	112.5	129.3	60.5	99.5	129.3	60.5	99.5
MF2018	WEIGHTED AVERAGE	130.0	66.3	106.6	122.0	85.5	108.5	119.8	66.5	100.2	137.9	86.9	119.1	118.6	75.6	102.8	118.6	75.6	102.8

City Cost Indexes

CANADA

DIVISION		CHARLOTTETOWN, PRINCE EDWARD ISLAND			CHICOUTIMI, QUEBEC			CORNER BROOK, NEWFOUNDLAND			CORNWALL, ONTARIO			DALHOUSIE, NEW BRUNSWICK			DARTMOUTH, NOVA SCOTIA		
		MAT.	INST.	TOTAL	MAT.	INST.	TOTAL	MAT.	INST.	TOTAL	MAT.	INST.	TOTAL	MAT.	INST.	TOTAL	MAT.	INST.	TOTAL
015433	CONTRACTOR EQUIPMENT		122.2	122.2		99.2	99.2		96.8	96.8		97.8	97.8		97.9	97.9		95.3	95.3
0241, 31 - 34	SITE & INFRASTRUCTURE, DEMOLITION	145.2	107.9	120.9	113.2	91.0	98.7	131.7	86.3	102.1	124.2	90.6	102.3	109.2	87.3	94.9	123.0	87.3	99.7
0310	Concrete Forming & Accessories	112.5	50.5	64.4	117.8	86.2	93.3	105.9	71.0	78.8	109.8	77.7	84.8	90.6	54.8	62.8	95.8	63.9	71.0
0320	Concrete Reinforcing	60.5	43.6	55.9	52.9	90.0	63.2	80.2	45.6	70.6	84.1	79.7	82.9	75.6	53.8	69.6	83.6	44.6	72.8
0330	Cast-in-Place Concrete	136.8	57.4	108.6	108.8	91.3	102.6	145.2	60.2	115.0	134.0	87.7	117.6	129.4	53.7	102.5	140.1	63.1	112.8
03	CONCRETE	121.8	53.6	94.9	96.4	89.0	93.4	169.1	63.7	127.5	128.0	82.2	109.9	138.6	55.4	105.8	147.6	61.4	113.6
04	MASONRY	167.4	51.6	97.1	158.1	85.9	114.2	215.3	69.6	126.8	170.9	80.3	115.9	172.1	53.9	100.3	229.0	61.5	127.3
05	METALS	147.7	78.4	134.0	128.5	91.5	121.2	143.6	73.4	129.8	127.9	88.8	120.2	119.3	72.8	110.1	144.0	73.7	130.2
06	WOOD, PLASTICS & COMPOSITES	110.2	50.1	83.3	125.4	86.9	108.2	113.8	76.7	97.2	112.2	77.1	96.5	94.1	54.8	76.5	102.1	63.7	84.9
07	THERMAL & MOISTURE PROTECTION	146.1	54.9	113.6	118.8	91.4	109.0	136.8	61.3	109.9	126.4	80.2	109.9	124.2	54.4	99.3	134.7	62.9	109.1
08	OPENINGS	92.5	43.5	81.4	88.2	73.3	84.9	105.7	62.7	96.0	89.6	76.1	86.5	88.5	48.4	79.5	92.5	57.8	84.7
0920	Plaster & Gypsum Board	154.2	47.7	86.7	147.0	86.6	108.7	129.8	76.1	95.8	171.2	76.6	111.2	125.7	53.5	79.9	126.8	62.8	86.2
0950, 0980	Ceilings & Acoustic Treatment	107.0	47.7	73.8	90.8	86.6	88.4	94.0	76.1	84.0	81.5	76.6	78.7	78.4	53.5	64.5	100.8	62.8	79.5
0960	Flooring	123.1	51.6	105.2	107.9	80.2	101.0	108.9	46.2	93.2	107.9	80.3	101.0	102.9	59.2	92.0	105.0	55.0	92.5
0970, 0990	Wall Finishes & Painting/Coating	112.9	36.9	67.6	112.3	98.3	104.0	117.9	52.3	78.8	110.9	79.3	92.1	114.6	44.4	72.7	117.9	54.9	80.4
09	FINISHES	125.3	49.6	87.3	104.8	87.4	96.0	109.6	65.8	87.6	107.2	78.5	92.8	101.0	54.8	77.8	108.8	61.6	85.1
COVERS	DIVS. 10 - 14, 25, 28, 41, 43, 44, 46	131.1	55.4	116.5	131.1	75.3	120.3	131.1	56.3	116.6	131.1	60.2	117.4	131.1	54.0	116.2	131.1	56.5	116.7
21, 22, 23	FIRE SUPPRESSION, PLUMBING & HVAC	117.1	55.4	94.9	110.6	77.3	98.7	117.2	61.7	97.3	110.2	88.3	102.4	111.1	60.7	93.0	117.2	74.4	101.9
26, 27, 3370	ELECTRICAL, COMMUNICATIONS & UTIL.	148.2	44.1	103.1	130.8	79.5	108.6	125.0	47.8	91.6	132.4	77.7	108.5	134.6	49.0	97.5	127.7	54.4	96.0
MF2018	WEIGHTED AVERAGE	130.7	58.1	104.0	116.5	84.0	104.6	134.3	64.4	108.5	121.4	82.3	107.1	120.2	59.1	97.7	131.0	66.1	107.2

CANADA

DIVISION		EDMONTON, ALBERTA			FORT MCMURRAY, ALBERTA			FREDERICTON, NEW BRUNSWICK			GATINEAU, QUEBEC			GRANBY, QUEBEC			HALIFAX, NOVA SCOTIA		
		MAT.	INST.	TOTAL	MAT.	INST.	TOTAL	MAT.	INST.	TOTAL	MAT.	INST.	TOTAL	MAT.	INST.	TOTAL	MAT.	INST.	TOTAL
015433	CONTRACTOR EQUIPMENT		120.6	120.6		99.4	99.4		121.9	121.9		99.0	99.0		99.0	99.0		119.5	119.5
0241, 31 - 34	SITE & INFRASTRUCTURE, DEMOLITION	124.6	110.3	115.3	129.8	91.5	104.8	150.0	108.6	123.0	106.0	90.6	95.9	106.4	90.6	96.1	114.2	108.2	110.3
0310	Concrete Forming & Accessories	112.2	86.5	92.2	110.4	82.3	88.5	112.5	55.9	68.6	117.3	74.6	84.1	117.3	74.5	84.1	112.5	81.3	88.2
0320	Concrete Reinforcing	73.3	74.9	73.7	78.2	74.8	77.2	58.7	54.1	57.4	76.2	67.7	73.8	76.2	67.7	73.8	60.7	73.2	64.2
0330	Cast-in-Place Concrete	163.8	93.5	138.8	198.0	87.4	158.7	155.3	80.0	128.5	118.6	82.9	105.9	122.5	82.9	108.4	143.9	76.4	119.9
03	CONCRETE	190.1	87.8	149.7	152.9	83.3	125.5	129.0	58.0	101.0	120.2	77.1	103.2	121.9	77.0	104.2	124.8	79.3	106.9
04	MASONRY	227.7	80.8	138.4	213.4	78.8	131.6	179.7	55.3	104.1	167.5	71.6	109.2	167.7	71.6	109.4	176.9	79.4	117.7
05	METALS	148.5	96.0	138.1	159.2	87.8	145.2	144.6	83.1	132.5	125.4	83.7	117.2	125.7	83.6	117.4	147.4	96.5	137.4
06	WOOD, PLASTICS & COMPOSITES	102.1	86.4	95.1	107.8	81.9	96.2	101.3	55.7	80.9	125.8	74.8	102.9	125.8	74.8	102.9	101.3	81.6	92.5
07	THERMAL & MOISTURE PROTECTION	147.0	89.2	126.4	135.0	84.4	117.0	146.1	56.7	114.3	120.7	78.4	105.6	120.9	77.0	105.3	149.6	82.2	125.6
08	OPENINGS	91.4	76.7	88.1	89.6	74.2	86.1	92.0	47.9	82.1	89.6	64.2	83.9	89.6	64.2	83.9	91.8	73.8	87.7
0920	Plaster & Gypsum Board	157.4	85.2	111.6	115.4	81.3	93.8	123.8	53.5	79.2	121.2	74.0	91.2	121.2	74.0	91.2	123.7	80.3	96.2
0950, 0980	Ceilings & Acoustic Treatment	100.3	85.2	91.8	85.1	81.3	83.0	99.4	53.5	73.7	78.3	74.0	75.9	78.3	74.0	75.9	100.9	80.3	89.4
0960	Flooring	127.5	77.8	115.0	107.9	77.8	100.3	121.5	61.8	106.6	107.9	80.2	100.9	107.9	80.2	100.9	116.3	74.8	105.9
0970, 0990	Wall Finishes & Painting/Coating	113.8	94.5	102.3	111.0	81.8	93.6	113.7	56.5	79.6	110.9	77.4	90.9	110.9	77.4	90.9	113.4	82.6	95.0
09	FINISHES	123.8	86.2	104.9	101.9	81.7	91.7	113.5	57.3	85.3	99.2	76.3	87.7	99.2	76.3	87.7	109.5	80.7	95.1
COVERS	DIVS. 10 - 14, 25, 28, 41, 43, 44, 46	131.1	85.5	122.3	131.1	82.9	121.8	131.1	55.9	116.6	131.1	70.4	119.4	131.1	70.4	119.4	131.1	63.9	118.1
21, 22, 23	FIRE SUPPRESSION, PLUMBING & HVAC	109.8	81.1	99.5	110.9	87.2	102.4	117.1	69.2	99.9	110.2	78.8	99.0	110.5	78.8	99.1	110.7	75.2	97.9
26, 27, 3370	ELECTRICAL, COMMUNICATIONS & UTIL.	134.8	83.6	112.6	125.1	71.9	102.0	148.5	64.7	112.1	129.3	60.5	99.5	130.9	60.5	100.4	114.4	81.0	99.9
MF2018	WEIGHTED AVERAGE	137.6	86.9	118.9	132.2	82.5	113.9	130.6	66.7	107.0	118.4	75.4	102.6	118.9	75.3	102.9	124.4	82.1	108.8

CANADA

DIVISION		HAMILTON, ONTARIO			HULL, QUEBEC			JOLIETTE, QUEBEC			KAMLOOPS, BRITISH COLUMBIA			KINGSTON, ONTARIO			KITCHENER, ONTARIO		
		MAT.	INST.	TOTAL	MAT.	INST.	TOTAL	MAT.	INST.	TOTAL	MAT.	INST.	TOTAL	MAT.	INST.	TOTAL	MAT.	INST.	TOTAL
015433	CONTRACTOR EQUIPMENT		118.0	118.0		99.0	99.0		99.0	99.0		101.6	101.6		99.7	99.7		100.9	100.9
0241, 31 - 34	SITE & INFRASTRUCTURE, DEMOLITION	118.6	107.9	111.6	105.9	90.6	95.9	106.5	90.6	96.1	127.3	93.6	105.3	124.2	93.9	104.4	106.6	96.8	100.2
0310	Concrete Forming & Accessories	118.8	89.0	95.7	117.3	74.6	84.1	117.3	74.7	84.2	105.7	77.5	83.8	110.0	77.7	84.9	103.5	84.7	88.9
0320	Concrete Reinforcing	73.8	96.8	80.2	76.2	67.7	73.8	72.3	67.7	71.0	56.4	70.9	60.4	84.1	79.7	82.9	50.7	96.5	63.4
0330	Cast-in-Place Concrete	151.6	100.5	133.5	118.6	82.9	105.9	123.5	82.9	109.1	106.9	86.8	99.8	134.0	87.7	117.6	141.2	93.6	124.3
03	CONCRETE	136.1	95.2	119.9	120.2	77.1	103.2	121.3	77.1	103.8	133.6	80.3	112.6	130.4	82.2	111.4	108.7	90.3	101.5
04	MASONRY	183.4	96.7	130.7	167.4	71.6	109.2	167.8	71.6	109.4	174.2	78.3	116.3	177.7	80.4	118.6	152.4	94.2	117.1
05	METALS	153.6	105.3	144.1	125.7	83.7	117.4	125.7	83.8	117.4	129.2	85.7	120.6	130.3	88.8	122.1	145.0	97.4	135.6
06	WOOD, PLASTICS & COMPOSITES	104.0	87.7	96.7	125.8	74.8	102.9	125.8	74.8	102.9	95.1	76.3	86.7	112.2	77.2	96.5	95.5	83.0	89.9
07	THERMAL & MOISTURE PROTECTION	146.8	97.7	129.3	120.7	78.4	105.7	120.7	78.4	105.7	136.7	76.1	115.1	126.4	81.3	110.3	127.2	93.8	115.3
08	OPENINGS	87.4	87.1	87.3	89.6	64.2	83.9	89.6	68.3	84.8	86.9	74.1	84.0	89.6	75.8	86.5	78.4	83.0	79.4
0920	Plaster & Gypsum Board	125.1	86.5	100.6	121.2	74.0	91.2	146.5	74.0	100.5	99.4	75.3	84.1	174.4	76.7	112.5	108.2	82.6	91.9
0950, 0980	Ceilings & Acoustic Treatment	106.9	86.5	95.5	78.3	74.0	75.9	78.3	74.0	75.9	78.3	75.3	76.6	91.9	76.7	83.4	82.5	82.6	82.5
0960	Flooring	121.0	87.1	112.5	107.9	80.2	100.9	107.9	80.2	100.9	108.5	45.9	92.8	107.9	80.3	101.0	95.2	87.2	93.2
0970, 0990	Wall Finishes & Painting/Coating	110.4	97.6	102.7	110.9	77.4	90.9	110.9	77.4	90.9	110.9	70.8	87.0	110.9	73.3	88.5	105.3	88.3	95.2
09	FINISHES	113.4	89.3	101.3	99.2	76.3	87.7	102.6	76.3	89.4	98.5	71.2	84.8	110.5	77.9	94.1	93.0	85.0	89.0
COVERS	DIVS. 10 - 14, 25, 28, 41, 43, 44, 46	131.1	85.8	122.4	131.1	70.4	119.4	131.1	70.4	119.4	131.1	78.5	120.9	131.1	60.2	117.4	131.1	82.8	121.8
21, 22, 23	FIRE SUPPRESSION, PLUMBING & HVAC	109.9	88.5	102.2	110.5	78.8	99.1	110.5	78.9	99.1	110.5	82.0	100.2	110.2	88.8	102.4	109.1	88.1	101.6
26, 27, 3370	ELECTRICAL, COMMUNICATIONS & UTIL.	135.2	98.2	119.2	134.0	60.5	102.1	130.9	60.5	100.4	136.4	68.8	107.1	132.4	76.2	108.1	136.2	96.1	118.8
MF2018	WEIGHTED AVERAGE	129.4	94.9	116.7	119.0	75.4	103.0	119.1	75.6	103.1	122.4	78.8	106.3	122.7	82.4	107.9	119.8	91.0	109.2

City Cost Indexes

CANADA

DIVISION		LAVAL, QUEBEC			LETHBRIDGE, ALBERTA			LLOYDMINSTER, ALBERTA			LONDON, ONTARIO			MEDICINE HAT, ALBERTA			MONCTON, NEW BRUNSWICK		
		MAT.	INST.	TOTAL	MAT.	INST.	TOTAL	MAT.	INST.	TOTAL	MAT.	INST.	TOTAL	MAT.	INST.	TOTAL	MAT.	INST.	TOTAL
015433	CONTRACTOR EQUIPMENT		99.0	99.0		99.4	99.4		99.4	99.4		118.6	118.6		99.4	99.4		98.6	98.6
0241, 31 - 34	SITE & INFRASTRUCTURE, DEMOLITION	106.4	90.6	96.1	122.7	92.0	102.7	122.4	91.5	102.2	120.2	107.4	111.8	121.3	91.5	101.9	116.0	90.0	99.1
0310	Concrete Forming & Accessories	117.5	75.2	84.6	111.3	82.3	88.8	109.6	73.6	81.6	119.2	85.3	92.9	111.3	73.6	82.0	91.1	61.7	68.3
0320	Concrete Reinforcing	76.2	68.4	74.0	78.2	74.8	77.2	78.2	74.7	77.2	73.4	95.7	79.6	78.2	74.7	77.2	70.2	65.4	68.8
0330	Cast-in-Place Concrete	122.5	83.5	108.7	148.4	87.4	126.7	137.7	84.1	118.6	151.7	98.7	132.9	137.7	84.1	118.6	111.3	65.4	95.0
03	CONCRETE	121.9	77.7	104.4	132.6	83.4	113.1	128.0	78.3	108.4	136.1	92.7	119.0	128.1	78.2	108.4	102.3	64.9	87.6
04	MASONRY	167.8	72.3	109.8	186.0	78.8	120.9	167.7	73.0	110.2	190.8	95.1	132.7	167.6	73.0	110.1	156.2	71.3	104.6
05	METALS	125.5	84.0	117.3	149.9	87.9	137.6	129.1	87.7	120.9	152.0	105.9	142.9	129.3	87.7	121.1	128.6	85.8	120.1
06	WOOD, PLASTICS & COMPOSITES	125.8	75.4	103.2	111.4	81.9	98.2	107.8	73.2	92.3	104.0	83.3	94.7	111.4	73.2	94.3	91.3	59.2	76.9
07	THERMAL & MOISTURE PROTECTION	122.5	78.8	106.9	132.8	84.4	115.6	129.7	80.4	112.1	147.1	95.4	128.7	135.2	80.4	115.6	121.9	68.1	102.7
08	OPENINGS	89.6	64.8	84.0	89.6	74.2	86.1	89.6	69.4	85.0	88.0	83.7	87.0	89.6	69.4	85.0	84.8	56.9	78.5
0920	Plaster & Gypsum Board	121.2	74.7	91.7	108.8	81.3	91.3	103.8	72.3	83.8	125.1	82.0	97.8	106.7	72.3	84.9	119.8	58.0	80.6
0950, 0980	Ceilings & Acoustic Treatment	78.3	74.7	76.3	85.1	81.3	83.0	78.3	72.3	74.9	78.3	82.0	80.4	78.3	72.3	74.9	91.7	58.0	72.8
0960	Flooring	107.9	81.1	101.1	107.9	77.8	100.3	107.9	77.8	100.3	100.9	87.2	97.5	107.9	77.8	100.3	95.7	60.5	86.9
0970, 0990	Wall Finishes & Painting/Coating	110.9	78.1	91.3	110.8	89.3	98.0	111.0	69.5	86.3	113.0	94.6	102.0	110.8	69.5	86.2	112.3	74.2	89.6
09	FINISHES	99.2	76.9	88.0	100.2	82.5	91.3	97.8	73.8	85.8	107.7	86.2	96.9	98.1	73.8	85.9	98.0	62.3	80.0
COVERS	DIVS. 10 - 14, 25, 28, 41, 43, 44, 46	131.1	71.0	119.5	131.1	81.8	121.6	131.1	80.1	121.3	131.1	85.0	122.2	131.1	79.0	121.0	131.1	57.1	116.8
21, 22, 23	FIRE SUPPRESSION, PLUMBING & HVAC	109.3	79.6	98.7	110.7	84.2	101.2	110.2	84.2	100.9	109.9	86.6	101.5	110.5	81.2	100.0	110.6	75.3	97.9
26, 27, 3370	ELECTRICAL, COMMUNICATIONS & UTIL.	131.1	61.0	100.7	129.0	71.9	104.3	124.0	71.9	101.4	134.9	95.9	118.0	124.0	71.9	101.4	138.9	85.2	115.6
MF2018	WEIGHTED AVERAGE	118.7	75.9	103.0	126.7	82.0	110.3	120.0	79.1	104.9	128.9	93.0	115.7	120.3	78.4	104.9	117.1	73.6	101.1

CANADA

DIVISION		MONTREAL, QUEBEC			MOOSE JAW, SASKATCHEWAN			NEW GLASGOW, NOVA SCOTIA			NEWCASTLE, NEW BRUNSWICK			NORTH BAY, ONTARIO			OSHAWA, ONTARIO		
		MAT.	INST.	TOTAL	MAT.	INST.	TOTAL	MAT.	INST.	TOTAL	MAT.	INST.	TOTAL	MAT.	INST.	TOTAL	MAT.	INST.	TOTAL
015433	CONTRACTOR EQUIPMENT		120.6	120.6		96.5	96.5		95.3	95.3		98.6	98.6		95.2	95.2		100.9	100.9
0241, 31 - 34	SITE & INFRASTRUCTURE, DEMOLITION	129.1	107.0	114.7	122.1	86.6	98.9	115.6	87.3	97.1	116.5	87.8	97.8	128.3	88.5	102.3	116.5	96.9	103.7
0310	Concrete Forming & Accessories	113.1	87.2	93.0	94.7	51.5	61.2	95.7	63.9	71.0	91.1	54.8	62.9	130.1	75.3	87.6	108.5	87.8	92.4
0320	Concrete Reinforcing	61.6	90.2	69.5	55.2	57.4	55.8	80.2	44.6	70.3	70.2	53.8	65.6	94.2	79.3	90.0	80.3	98.9	85.4
0330	Cast-in-Place Concrete	117.7	96.2	110.0	133.6	60.6	107.6	140.1	63.1	112.8	115.6	53.9	93.6	135.0	75.5	113.8	163.4	102.7	141.8
03	CONCRETE	111.2	91.7	103.5	111.6	56.9	90.0	146.7	61.4	113.0	104.1	55.5	84.9	148.7	76.7	120.3	132.2	95.3	117.6
04	MASONRY	173.4	86.1	120.4	165.8	52.9	97.2	214.9	61.5	121.7	156.6	53.9	94.2	221.5	76.8	133.6	156.4	97.4	120.6
05	METALS	164.9	101.5	152.4	124.2	73.9	114.3	140.6	73.7	127.4	128.5	73.2	117.6	141.9	87.2	131.1	134.1	98.6	127.1
06	WOOD, PLASTICS & COMPOSITES	99.5	87.8	94.3	92.2	50.4	73.4	102.1	63.7	84.9	91.3	54.8	74.9	138.3	75.8	110.3	102.7	86.4	95.4
07	THERMAL & MOISTURE PROTECTION	144.5	93.6	126.4	120.0	55.9	97.2	134.7	62.9	109.1	121.9	54.4	97.9	140.4	76.9	117.8	127.9	98.3	117.4
08	OPENINGS	88.6	75.6	85.6	86.1	48.5	77.6	92.5	57.8	84.7	84.8	48.4	76.6	98.4	73.8	92.9	82.5	86.4	83.4
0920	Plaster & Gypsum Board	122.8	86.6	99.8	97.6	49.0	66.8	124.7	62.8	85.4	119.8	53.5	77.8	122.4	75.3	92.6	112.7	86.1	95.9
0950, 0980	Ceilings & Acoustic Treatment	113.2	86.6	98.3	78.3	49.0	61.9	94.0	62.8	76.5	91.7	53.5	70.3	94.0	75.3	83.5	79.3	86.1	83.1
0960	Flooring	103.2	83.0	98.2	100.2	50.1	87.7	105.0	55.0	92.5	95.7	59.2	86.6	123.0	80.3	112.3	97.4	89.2	95.3
0970, 0990	Wall Finishes & Painting/Coating	119.3	98.3	106.8	110.9	56.5	78.5	117.9	54.9	80.4	112.3	44.4	71.8	117.9	78.7	94.6	105.3	101.3	102.9
09	FINISHES	110.2	88.5	99.3	94.6	51.5	73.0	106.6	61.6	84.0	98.0	54.8	76.3	112.3	76.9	94.6	93.8	89.1	91.5
COVERS	DIVS. 10 - 14, 25, 28, 41, 43, 44, 46	131.1	77.4	120.7	131.1	53.6	116.1	131.1	56.5	116.7	131.1	54.1	116.2	131.1	58.8	117.1	131.1	83.5	121.9
21, 22, 23	FIRE SUPPRESSION, PLUMBING & HVAC	109.2	77.6	97.9	110.2	65.9	94.3	117.2	74.4	101.9	110.6	60.7	92.7	117.2	86.5	106.2	109.1	84.4	100.3
26, 27, 3370	ELECTRICAL, COMMUNICATIONS & UTIL.	148.0	79.5	118.3	136.4	52.3	99.9	125.8	54.4	94.9	137.2	51.8	100.2	130.0	77.3	107.1	136.6	97.3	119.5
MF2018	WEIGHTED AVERAGE	129.7	87.0	114.0	117.3	60.4	96.3	129.1	66.1	105.9	117.2	59.6	96.0	132.0	80.1	112.9	121.1	92.4	110.6

CANADA

DIVISION		OTTAWA, ONTARIO			OWEN SOUND, ONTARIO			PETERBOROUGH, ONTARIO			PORTAGE LA PRAIRIE, MANITOBA			PRINCE ALBERT, SASKATCHEWAN			PRINCE GEORGE, BRITISH COLUMBIA		
		MAT.	INST.	TOTAL	MAT.	INST.	TOTAL	MAT.	INST.	TOTAL	MAT.	INST.	TOTAL	MAT.	INST.	TOTAL	MAT.	INST.	TOTAL
015433	CONTRACTOR EQUIPMENT		120.2	120.2		97.9	97.9		97.8	97.8		99.8	99.8		96.5	96.5		101.6	101.6
0241, 31 - 34	SITE & INFRASTRUCTURE, DEMOLITION	119.6	108.0	112.0	122.1	90.7	101.6	126.1	90.5	102.9	123.0	89.5	101.2	118.6	86.7	97.8	130.6	93.6	106.5
0310	Concrete Forming & Accessories	113.1	89.6	94.8	124.9	74.2	85.5	112.0	76.4	84.3	111.5	62.0	73.0	94.7	51.4	61.0	100.4	73.1	79.2
0320	Concrete Reinforcing	65.6	95.7	73.9	151.8	81.2	132.3	84.1	79.8	82.9	78.2	51.0	70.7	57.6	57.4	57.6	56.4	70.9	60.4
0330	Cast-in-Place Concrete	137.9	101.9	125.1	165.1	72.6	132.2	149.0	77.4	123.6	137.7	66.2	112.3	121.0	60.5	99.5	134.0	86.9	117.3
03	CONCRETE	127.8	95.9	115.2	150.7	75.6	121.0	134.4	78.0	112.2	120.4	62.7	97.7	107.1	56.8	87.2	144.4	78.3	118.3
04	MASONRY	189.2	96.0	132.6	171.6	81.7	117.0	172.2	82.6	117.8	170.7	56.1	101.0	164.8	52.9	96.9	176.7	78.8	117.2
05	METALS	153.6	107.3	144.5	114.3	89.3	109.3	128.1	89.0	120.4	129.3	77.2	119.0	124.2	73.8	114.3	129.2	85.8	120.6
06	WOOD, PLASTICS & COMPOSITES	93.8	88.8	91.6	117.3	73.1	97.5	114.0	74.7	96.4	111.4	63.2	89.8	92.2	50.4	73.4	95.1	70.1	83.9
07	THERMAL & MOISTURE PROTECTION	147.2	97.2	129.4	113.9	77.7	101.0	126.8	82.0	110.8	120.7	63.5	100.3	119.9	54.9	96.8	131.8	75.4	111.7
08	OPENINGS	87.8	86.7	87.5	89.2	73.3	85.6	88.0	75.5	85.2	89.6	56.6	82.2	85.2	48.5	76.9	86.9	70.7	83.3
0920	Plaster & Gypsum Board	125.1	87.5	101.3	153.8	72.4	102.2	117.8	74.2	90.1	106.4	61.9	78.2	97.6	49.0	66.8	99.4	69.0	80.1
0950, 0980	Ceilings & Acoustic Treatment	106.9	87.5	96.1	92.9	72.4	81.4	78.3	74.2	76.0	78.3	61.9	69.1	78.3	49.0	61.9	78.3	69.0	73.1
0960	Flooring	100.9	83.1	96.4	120.7	81.5	110.9	107.9	80.3	101.0	107.9	57.8	95.3	100.2	50.1	87.7	104.3	62.9	94.0
0970, 0990	Wall Finishes & Painting/Coating	113.5	89.8	99.3	106.8	77.6	89.4	110.9	80.7	92.9	111.0	50.1	74.7	110.9	48.2	73.5	110.9	70.8	87.0
09	FINISHES	107.8	88.3	98.0	112.4	76.0	94.1	99.3	77.6	88.4	98.0	60.3	79.1	94.6	50.6	72.5	97.3	70.5	83.8
COVERS	DIVS. 10 - 14, 25, 28, 41, 43, 44, 46	131.1	84.1	122.0	139.3	59.5	123.8	131.1	60.4	117.4	131.1	55.8	116.5	131.1	53.6	116.1	131.1	77.8	120.8
21, 22, 23	FIRE SUPPRESSION, PLUMBING & HVAC	109.9	87.3	101.8	110.3	86.5	101.8	110.5	89.7	103.0	110.5	73.4	97.2	110.5	59.3	92.0	110.5	82.0	100.3
26, 27, 3370	ELECTRICAL, COMMUNICATIONS & UTIL.	135.2	96.5	118.5	127.1	76.2	105.1	134.6	76.9	109.6	135.7	50.7	98.8	136.4	52.3	99.9	134.2	68.8	105.9
MF2018	WEIGHTED AVERAGE	128.2	94.4	115.7	121.3	80.5	106.3	122.0	82.1	107.3	120.4	65.2	100.1	116.5	58.9	95.3	123.4	78.2	106.7

City Cost Indexes

CANADA

	DIVISION	QUEBEC CITY, QUEBEC			RED DEER, ALBERTA			REGINA, SASKATCHEWAN			RIMOUSKI, QUEBEC			ROUYN-NORANDA, QUEBEC			SAINT HYACINTHE, QUEBEC		
		MAT.	INST.	TOTAL	MAT.	INST.	TOTAL	MAT.	INST.	TOTAL	MAT.	INST.	TOTAL	MAT.	INST.	TOTAL	MAT.	INST.	TOTAL
015433	CONTRACTOR EQUIPMENT		122.1	122.1		99.4	99.4		127.3	127.3		99.0	99.0		99.0	99.0		99.0	99.0
0241, 31 - 34	SITE & INFRASTRUCTURE, DEMOLITION	129.6	107.3	115.1	121.3	91.5	101.9	138.5	118.0	125.1	106.1	90.8	96.2	105.9	90.6	95.9	106.4	90.6	96.1
0310	Concrete Forming & Accessories	113.0	87.4	93.1	119.0	73.6	83.7	120.1	83.4	91.6	117.3	86.2	93.2	117.3	74.6	84.1	117.3	74.6	84.1
0320	Concrete Reinforcing	62.6	90.2	70.3	78.2	74.7	77.2	71.7	79.8	73.9	54.5	90.0	64.3	76.2	67.7	73.8	76.2	67.7	73.8
0330	Cast-in-Place Concrete	117.6	96.4	110.1	137.7	84.1	118.6	176.1	92.3	146.3	124.8	91.2	112.8	118.6	82.9	105.9	122.5	82.9	108.5
03	CONCRETE	111.5	92.0	103.8	128.8	78.2	108.8	180.3	86.9	143.5	117.2	89.0	106.0	120.2	77.1	103.2	121.9	77.1	104.2
04	MASONRY	183.9	86.1	124.5	167.6	73.0	110.1	220.1	78.6	134.1	166.8	85.9	117.7	167.4	71.6	109.2	167.7	71.6	109.3
05	METALS	164.9	103.3	152.8	129.3	87.7	121.1	153.7	98.3	142.8	125.2	91.4	118.5	125.7	83.7	117.4	125.7	83.7	117.4
06	WOOD, PLASTICS & COMPOSITES	100.2	87.8	94.7	111.4	73.2	94.3	122.3	83.9	105.1	125.8	86.9	108.4	125.8	74.8	102.9	125.8	74.8	102.9
07	THERMAL & MOISTURE PROTECTION	143.5	93.7	125.7	143.0	80.4	120.7	147.2	79.3	123.0	120.9	91.3	110.4	120.9	78.4	105.7	122.5	78.4	106.8
08	OPENINGS	89.5	82.4	87.9	89.6	69.4	85.0	93.0	72.8	88.4	89.1	73.3	85.6	89.6	64.2	83.9	89.6	64.2	83.9
0920	Plaster & Gypsum Board	118.5	86.6	98.2	106.7	72.3	84.9	134.9	82.6	101.7	146.4	86.6	108.4	121.0	74.0	91.2	121.0	74.0	91.2
0950, 0980	Ceilings & Acoustic Treatment	107.5	86.6	95.8	78.3	72.3	74.9	113.8	82.6	96.3	77.8	86.6	82.7	77.8	74.0	75.7	77.8	74.0	75.7
0960	Flooring	102.9	83.0	97.9	111.0	77.8	102.7	122.7	87.2	113.8	109.0	80.2	101.8	107.9	80.2	100.9	107.9	80.2	100.9
0970, 0990	Wall Finishes & Painting/Coating	120.3	98.3	107.2	110.8	69.5	86.2	113.5	79.1	93.0	114.1	98.3	104.7	110.9	77.4	90.9	110.9	77.4	90.9
09	FINISHES	108.1	88.5	98.3	99.0	73.8	86.4	118.4	84.4	101.3	103.0	87.4	95.1	99.0	76.3	87.6	99.0	76.3	87.6
COVERS	DIVS. 10 - 14, 25, 28, 41, 43, 44, 46	131.1	77.4	120.7	131.1	79.0	121.0	131.1	65.0	118.3	131.1	75.3	120.3	131.1	70.4	119.4	131.1	70.4	119.4
21, 22, 23	FIRE SUPPRESSION, PLUMBING & HVAC	108.9	77.6	97.7	110.5	81.2	100.0	109.8	78.2	98.5	110.5	77.3	98.6	110.5	78.8	99.1	106.2	78.8	96.4
26, 27, 3370	ELECTRICAL, COMMUNICATIONS & UTIL.	148.0	79.6	118.3	124.0	71.9	101.4	134.4	81.5	111.5	130.9	79.5	108.6	130.9	60.5	100.4	131.4	60.5	100.7
MF2018	WEIGHTED AVERAGE	130.0	87.5	114.4	120.7	78.4	105.1	137.5	85.1	118.2	118.5	84.0	105.8	118.7	75.4	102.8	118.1	75.4	102.4

CANADA

	DIVISION	SAINT JOHN, NEW BRUNSWICK			SARNIA, ONTARIO			SASKATOON, SASKATCHEWAN			SAULT STE MARIE, ONTARIO			SHERBROOKE, QUEBEC			SOREL, QUEBEC		
		MAT.	INST.	TOTAL	MAT.	INST.	TOTAL	MAT.	INST.	TOTAL	MAT.	INST.	TOTAL	MAT.	INST.	TOTAL	MAT.	INST.	TOTAL
015433	CONTRACTOR EQUIPMENT		98.6	98.6		97.8	97.8		96.1	96.1		97.8	97.8		99.0	99.0		99.0	99.0
0241, 31 - 34	SITE & INFRASTRUCTURE, DEMOLITION	116.6	90.0	99.3	124.4	90.6	102.4	119.3	89.4	99.8	115.2	90.2	98.9	106.5	90.6	96.1	106.5	90.6	96.1
0310	Concrete Forming & Accessories	109.8	65.7	75.5	110.7	82.6	88.9	94.6	82.3	85.0	100.2	82.6	86.5	117.3	74.6	84.1	117.3	74.7	84.2
0320	Concrete Reinforcing	70.2	65.4	68.8	61.2	81.1	66.7	60.1	79.6	65.5	54.0	80.1	61.2	76.2	67.7	73.8	72.3	67.7	71.0
0330	Cast-in-Place Concrete	113.9	65.4	96.6	137.5	89.0	120.3	132.9	86.1	116.3	123.5	76.3	106.7	122.5	82.9	108.5	123.5	82.9	109.1
03	CONCRETE	105.1	66.7	90.0	123.6	85.1	108.4	121.5	83.6	106.5	107.6	80.6	97.0	121.9	77.1	104.2	121.3	77.1	103.8
04	MASONRY	175.6	71.3	112.2	183.2	85.0	123.5	180.4	78.3	118.4	167.9	87.8	119.3	167.8	71.6	109.4	167.8	71.6	109.4
05	METALS	128.5	85.8	120.0	128.1	89.3	120.4	120.4	86.6	113.7	127.3	92.9	120.5	125.4	83.7	117.2	125.7	83.8	117.4
06	WOOD, PLASTICS & COMPOSITES	114.4	64.6	92.1	113.0	82.0	99.1	94.7	82.9	89.4	99.7	84.7	93.0	125.8	74.8	102.9	125.8	74.8	102.9
07	THERMAL & MOISTURE PROTECTION	122.3	68.3	103.1	126.8	85.2	112.0	122.2	76.0	105.8	125.8	82.4	110.4	120.7	78.4	105.6	120.9	78.4	105.7
08	OPENINGS	84.8	58.9	78.9	91.1	78.9	88.3	88.3	72.2	84.6	83.1	81.9	82.8	89.6	64.2	83.9	89.6	68.3	84.8
0920	Plaster & Gypsum Board	138.8	63.6	91.1	140.0	81.6	103.0	115.1	82.6	94.5	107.6	84.5	92.9	121.0	74.0	91.2	146.4	74.0	100.5
0950, 0980	Ceilings & Acoustic Treatment	95.4	63.6	77.6	82.8	81.6	82.2	92.9	82.6	87.1	78.3	84.5	81.7	77.8	74.0	75.7	77.8	74.0	75.7
0960	Flooring	104.7	60.5	93.6	107.9	87.8	102.8	106.5	87.2	101.7	102.4	84.9	98.1	107.9	80.2	100.9	107.9	80.2	100.9
0970, 0990	Wall Finishes & Painting/Coating	112.3	74.2	89.6	110.9	91.2	99.2	114.6	79.1	93.4	110.9	84.6	95.2	110.9	77.4	90.9	110.9	77.4	90.9
09	FINISHES	104.2	65.4	84.7	103.5	84.8	94.1	105.1	83.6	94.3	95.7	83.7	89.7	99.0	76.3	87.6	102.4	76.3	89.3
COVERS	DIVS. 10 - 14, 25, 28, 41, 43, 44, 46	131.1	58.0	117.0	131.1	61.6	117.7	131.1	63.0	117.9	131.1	80.8	121.4	131.1	70.4	119.4	131.1	70.4	119.4
21, 22, 23	FIRE SUPPRESSION, PLUMBING & HVAC	110.6	75.3	97.9	110.5	95.1	104.9	109.5	77.9	98.2	110.5	85.2	101.4	110.2	78.8	99.0	110.5	78.9	99.1
26, 27, 3370	ELECTRICAL, COMMUNICATIONS & UTIL.	140.2	85.2	116.4	141.8	78.8	114.5	135.8	81.4	112.2	138.6	77.3	112.0	130.8	60.5	100.4	130.9	60.5	100.4
MF2018	WEIGHTED AVERAGE	119.0	74.5	102.6	122.4	86.0	109.0	118.9	81.0	105.0	117.7	84.3	105.4	118.8	75.4	102.8	119.1	75.6	103.1

CANADA

	DIVISION	ST CATHARINES, ONTARIO			ST JEROME, QUEBEC			ST JOHN'S, NEWFOUNDLAND			SUDBURY, ONTARIO			SUMMERSIDE, PRINCE EDWARD ISLAND			SYDNEY, NOVA SCOTIA		
		MAT.	INST.	TOTAL	MAT.	INST.	TOTAL	MAT.	INST.	TOTAL	MAT.	INST.	TOTAL	MAT.	INST.	TOTAL	MAT.	INST.	TOTAL
015433	CONTRACTOR EQUIPMENT		99.1	99.1		99.0	99.0		122.4	122.4		99.1	99.1		95.3	95.3		95.3	95.3
0241, 31 - 34	SITE & INFRASTRUCTURE, DEMOLITION	106.2	93.8	98.1	105.9	90.6	95.9	116.2	112.3	113.7	106.3	93.5	97.9	124.1	84.9	98.6	111.6	87.3	95.7
0310	Concrete Forming & Accessories	101.5	89.7	92.3	117.3	74.6	84.1	112.3	79.5	86.8	97.5	85.5	88.2	96.0	49.5	59.9	95.7	63.9	71.0
0320	Concrete Reinforcing	51.1	96.6	63.7	76.2	67.7	73.8	120.0	77.6	108.2	51.5	93.3	63.1	79.0	43.4	69.1	80.2	44.6	70.3
0330	Cast-in-Place Concrete	134.9	95.1	120.7	118.6	82.9	105.9	136.7	94.9	121.8	136.0	92.0	120.4	133.0	51.8	104.2	108.1	63.1	92.1
03	CONCRETE	106.0	93.1	101.0	120.2	77.1	103.2	141.0	85.7	119.1	106.3	89.6	99.7	157.6	50.5	115.3	133.5	61.4	105.0
04	MASONRY	151.8	96.4	118.1	167.4	71.6	109.2	195.1	85.1	128.3	151.8	93.2	116.2	213.9	51.5	115.3	212.0	61.5	120.6
05	METALS	134.0	97.4	126.8	125.7	83.7	117.4	142.4	96.0	133.2	133.5	96.2	126.1	140.6	67.5	126.2	140.6	73.7	127.4
06	WOOD, PLASTICS & COMPOSITES	93.1	89.3	91.4	125.8	74.8	102.9	102.0	77.6	91.0	88.8	84.8	87.0	102.7	49.1	78.7	102.1	63.7	84.9
07	THERMAL & MOISTURE PROTECTION	127.2	96.7	116.4	120.9	78.4	105.7	146.2	88.8	125.7	125.3	92.2	113.5	134.4	53.2	105.3	134.7	62.9	109.1
08	OPENINGS	77.7	86.8	79.8	89.6	64.2	83.9	91.7	69.4	86.7	78.3	82.3	79.2	102.2	42.9	88.8	92.5	57.8	84.7
0920	Plaster & Gypsum Board	102.6	89.1	94.0	121.0	74.0	91.2	146.5	76.1	101.8	100.7	84.5	90.4	125.9	47.7	76.3	124.7	62.8	85.4
0950, 0980	Ceilings & Acoustic Treatment	79.3	89.1	84.8	77.8	74.0	75.7	111.3	76.1	91.6	75.1	84.5	80.4	94.0	47.7	68.1	94.0	62.8	76.5
0960	Flooring	94.3	84.3	91.8	107.9	80.2	100.9	119.5	47.9	101.6	92.9	84.9	90.9	105.0	51.6	91.6	105.0	55.0	92.5
0970, 0990	Wall Finishes & Painting/Coating	105.3	97.6	100.7	110.9	77.4	90.9	115.3	91.6	101.2	105.3	89.2	95.7	117.9	36.9	69.6	117.9	54.9	80.4
09	FINISHES	91.1	89.6	90.3	99.0	76.3	87.6	116.8	74.7	95.7	89.3	85.5	87.4	107.4	48.8	78.1	106.6	61.6	84.0
COVERS	DIVS. 10 - 14, 25, 28, 41, 43, 44, 46	131.1	64.7	118.3	131.1	70.4	119.4	131.1	63.4	118.0	131.1	82.7	121.8	131.1	53.0	116.0	131.1	56.5	116.7
21, 22, 23	FIRE SUPPRESSION, PLUMBING & HVAC	109.1	87.3	101.3	110.5	78.8	99.1	109.6	78.1	98.3	109.9	85.4	100.8	117.2	55.1	95.0	117.2	74.4	101.9
26, 27, 3370	ELECTRICAL, COMMUNICATIONS & UTIL.	140.3	96.8	121.4	132.4	60.5	101.2	150.1	72.4	116.5	135.9	96.9	119.0	123.6	44.0	89.1	125.8	54.4	94.9
MF2018	WEIGHTED AVERAGE	117.3	91.6	107.8	118.9	75.4	102.9	130.0	82.4	112.5	116.6	90.0	106.8	131.2	54.5	103.0	127.3	66.1	104.8

City Cost Indexes

CANADA

DIVISION		THUNDER BAY, ONTARIO			TIMMINS, ONTARIO			TORONTO, ONTARIO			TROIS RIVIERES, QUEBEC			TRURO, NOVA SCOTIA			VANCOUVER, BRITISH COLUMBIA		
		MAT.	INST.	TOTAL	MAT.	INST.	TOTAL	MAT.	INST.	TOTAL	MAT.	INST.	TOTAL	MAT.	INST.	TOTAL	MAT.	INST.	TOTAL
015433	CONTRACTOR EQUIPMENT		99.1	99.1		97.8	97.8		118.9	118.9		96.2	96.2		98.1	98.1		135.4	135.4
0241, 31 - 34	SITE & INFRASTRUCTURE, DEMOLITION	110.9	93.6	99.6	126.1	90.2	102.7	117.7	108.1	111.4	111.6	88.7	96.6	110.8	89.1	96.7	122.0	122.1	122.1
0310	Concrete Forming & Accessories	108.5	87.7	92.3	112.0	75.4	83.6	112.7	98.6	101.8	137.2	74.5	88.5	84.9	64.1	68.7	118.1	85.6	92.8
0320	Concrete Reinforcing	45.7	96.2	59.7	84.1	79.3	82.8	65.5	99.2	74.8	80.2	67.7	76.7	72.3	44.6	64.6	71.9	89.3	76.7
0330	Cast-in-Place Concrete	148.5	94.5	129.3	149.0	76.0	123.1	137.8	111.6	128.5	111.9	82.3	101.4	154.8	63.7	122.4	142.1	96.9	126.1
03	CONCRETE	114.2	91.9	105.4	134.4	77.0	111.8	127.7	103.9	118.3	136.1	76.8	112.7	133.2	61.8	105.0	135.7	91.5	118.3
04	MASONRY	152.6	94.7	117.4	172.2	76.9	114.3	185.6	104.2	136.2	216.0	71.6	128.3	167.6	61.5	103.1	183.7	89.2	126.3
05	METALS	134.0	96.5	126.6	128.1	88.5	120.3	149.5	108.4	141.4	139.3	82.3	128.1	126.9	75.2	116.7	151.5	108.9	143.1
06	WOOD, PLASTICS & COMPOSITES	102.7	87.1	95.7	114.0	75.9	96.9	93.8	97.0	95.2	152.2	74.6	117.4	82.0	63.8	73.9	120.1	84.7	104.2
07	THERMAL & MOISTURE PROTECTION	127.5	93.7	115.4	126.8	77.0	109.0	147.1	105.5	132.3	133.8	78.2	114.0	121.7	63.0	100.8	147.4	87.4	126.0
08	OPENINGS	77.1	85.1	78.9	88.0	73.9	84.8	87.1	94.6	88.7	100.3	68.2	93.1	83.7	57.9	77.9	93.1	82.6	90.8
0920	Plaster & Gypsum Board	127.3	86.9	101.7	117.8	75.3	90.9	126.9	96.1	107.4	150.6	74.0	102.0	114.7	62.8	81.8	133.3	83.1	101.4
0950, 0980	Ceilings & Acoustic Treatment	75.2	86.9	81.8	78.3	75.3	76.6	113.8	96.1	103.9	92.6	74.0	82.2	78.3	62.8	69.6	113.8	83.1	96.6
0960	Flooring	97.4	90.3	95.6	107.9	80.3	101.0	120.8	92.5	113.7	123.0	80.2	112.3	94.1	55.0	84.3	112.5	81.2	104.7
0970, 0990	Wall Finishes & Painting/Coating	105.3	90.1	96.3	110.9	78.7	91.7	109.7	101.3	104.7	117.9	77.4	93.8	110.9	54.9	77.5	109.2	91.8	98.8
09	FINISHES	94.5	88.3	91.4	99.3	77.0	88.1	115.3	97.7	106.5	115.1	76.2	95.5	94.3	61.7	77.9	114.5	85.2	99.8
COVERS	DIVS. 10 - 14, 25, 28, 41, 43, 44, 46	131.1	64.2	118.2	131.1	59.1	117.2	131.1	88.7	122.9	131.1	70.1	119.3	131.1	56.8	116.7	131.1	83.6	121.9
21, 22, 23	FIRE SUPPRESSION, PLUMBING & HVAC	109.1	86.5	101.0	110.5	86.5	101.9	109.9	97.6	105.5	117.2	78.8	103.4	110.5	74.5	97.6	109.9	84.1	100.6
26, 27, 3370	ELECTRICAL, COMMUNICATIONS & UTIL.	136.2	96.0	118.8	138.6	77.3	112.0	134.9	98.4	119.1	126.5	60.5	97.9	130.0	54.4	97.3	135.1	75.4	109.3
MF2018	WEIGHTED AVERAGE	118.2	90.6	108.1	122.4	80.4	106.9	127.5	100.9	117.7	129.3	75.2	109.4	119.3	66.5	99.9	129.7	89.8	115.0

CANADA

DIVISION		VICTORIA, BRITISH COLUMBIA			WHITEHORSE, YUKON			WINDSOR, ONTARIO			WINNIPEG, MANITOBA			YARMOUTH, NOVA SCOTIA			YELLOWKNIFE, NWT		
		MAT.	INST.	TOTAL	MAT.	INST.	TOTAL	MAT.	INST.	TOTAL	MAT.	INST.	TOTAL	MAT.	INST.	TOTAL	MAT.	INST.	TOTAL
015433	CONTRACTOR EQUIPMENT		103.8	103.8		130.8	130.8		99.1	99.1		125.6	125.6		95.3	95.3		123.8	123.8
0241, 31 - 34	SITE & INFRASTRUCTURE, DEMOLITION	129.7	97.9	109.0	134.3	117.0	123.0	103.6	93.8	97.2	125.5	114.3	118.2	115.4	87.3	97.1	147.3	113.1	125.0
0310	Concrete Forming & Accessories	100.0	82.7	86.6	115.3	53.7	67.5	108.6	86.1	91.1	112.6	60.9	72.5	95.7	63.9	71.0	121.5	71.7	82.8
0320	Concrete Reinforcing	58.8	89.1	67.2	84.8	59.2	77.7	50.1	95.5	62.6	69.0	56.1	65.4	80.2	44.6	70.3	74.7	61.6	71.0
0330	Cast-in-Place Concrete	137.7	91.2	121.2	178.6	69.2	139.8	138.2	96.0	123.2	172.0	69.3	135.5	138.7	63.1	111.8	199.5	84.5	158.6
03	CONCRETE	163.9	87.2	133.6	178.8	62.0	132.7	107.7	91.6	101.4	149.4	64.6	115.9	146.1	61.4	112.7	171.7	75.7	133.8
04	MASONRY	183.3	89.0	126.0	260.7	54.6	135.5	152.0	95.7	117.8	211.8	60.3	119.7	214.7	61.5	121.7	246.4	64.8	136.0
05	METALS	122.9	92.0	116.8	152.6	87.3	139.7	134.0	96.9	126.7	153.3	85.3	139.9	140.6	73.7	127.4	154.5	89.1	141.6
06	WOOD, PLASTICS & COMPOSITES	99.0	82.0	91.4	110.2	52.6	84.4	102.7	84.6	94.6	109.9	61.7	88.3	102.1	63.7	84.9	117.1	73.1	97.4
07	THERMAL & MOISTURE PROTECTION	132.4	82.7	114.7	150.0	60.6	118.1	127.3	94.0	115.4	147.6	65.9	118.5	134.7	62.9	109.1	152.0	75.0	124.6
08	OPENINGS	89.6	77.4	86.8	103.1	50.2	91.2	77.0	84.1	78.6	94.0	55.6	85.3	92.5	57.8	84.7	94.6	62.1	87.2
0920	Plaster & Gypsum Board	108.3	81.2	91.1	159.5	50.1	90.1	113.0	84.3	94.8	134.9	59.6	87.1	124.7	62.8	85.4	162.8	71.3	104.8
0950, 0980	Ceilings & Acoustic Treatment	78.0	81.2	79.8	131.2	50.1	85.7	75.2	84.3	80.3	113.8	59.6	83.4	94.0	62.8	76.5	129.0	71.3	96.7
0960	Flooring	110.7	62.9	98.7	125.5	51.5	107.0	97.4	87.9	95.0	140.4	62.8	120.9	105.0	55.0	92.5	120.8	77.4	109.9
0970, 0990	Wall Finishes & Painting/Coating	114.6	91.8	101.0	121.1	49.2	78.2	105.3	91.0	96.8	109.4	48.6	73.2	117.9	54.9	80.4	125.1	70.4	92.4
09	FINISHES	102.7	80.2	91.4	135.5	52.6	93.9	92.3	86.7	89.5	123.2	60.3	91.6	106.6	61.6	84.0	132.6	72.1	102.2
COVERS	DIVS. 10 - 14, 25, 28, 41, 43, 44, 46	131.1	60.8	117.5	131.1	56.9	116.8	131.1	64.2	118.2	131.1	59.1	117.2	131.1	56.5	116.7	131.1	59.9	117.3
21, 22, 23	FIRE SUPPRESSION, PLUMBING & HVAC	111.1	81.7	100.6	117.7	67.1	99.6	109.1	88.0	101.6	110.0	59.5	91.9	117.2	74.4	101.9	118.2	83.0	105.6
26, 27, 3370	ELECTRICAL, COMMUNICATIONS & UTIL.	133.4	76.1	108.6	166.0	53.0	117.0	147.7	96.7	125.6	135.2	58.1	101.8	125.8	54.4	94.9	157.1	71.9	120.2
MF2018	WEIGHTED AVERAGE	125.3	83.6	110.0	145.7	65.7	116.3	118.3	90.8	108.2	133.5	66.9	109.0	129.0	66.1	105.9	143.4	78.2	119.4

Location Factors - Commercial

Costs shown in RSMeans cost data publications are based on national averages for materials and installation. To adjust these costs to a specific location, simply multiply the base cost by the factor and divide by 100 for that city. The data is arranged alphabetically by state and postal zip code numbers. For a city not listed, use the factor for a nearby city with similar economic characteristics.

STATE/ZIP	CITY	MAT.	INST.	TOTAL
ALABAMA				
350-352	Birmingham	100.6	70.5	89.5
354	Tuscaloosa	99.3	69.6	88.4
355	Jasper	100.6	67.2	88.3
356	Decatur	99.3	66.7	87.3
357-358	Huntsville	99.3	71.6	89.1
359	Gadsden	100.2	69.5	88.9
360-361	Montgomery	99.8	70.6	89.0
362	Anniston	99.2	64.0	86.3
363	Dothan	97.8	71.5	88.1
364	Evergreen	97.3	65.0	85.4
365-366	Mobile	99.4	67.8	87.8
367	Selma	97.5	68.3	86.7
368	Phenix City	98.0	67.8	86.9
369	Butler	97.5	66.7	86.2
ALASKA				
995-996	Anchorage	116.6	109.2	113.9
997	Fairbanks	116.2	109.6	113.8
998	Juneau	116.1	109.2	113.5
999	Ketchikan	124.5	109.8	119.1
ARIZONA				
850,853	Phoenix	100.4	73.7	90.6
851,852	Mesa/Tempe	97.1	71.5	87.7
855	Globe	96.3	70.2	86.7
856-857	Tucson	95.9	72.1	87.1
859	Show Low	96.6	70.3	86.9
860	Flagstaff	100.3	71.7	89.8
863	Prescott	98.4	70.9	88.3
864	Kingman	96.2	69.8	86.5
865	Chambers	96.2	70.2	86.6
ARKANSAS				
716	Pine Bluff	98.5	61.8	85.0
717	Camden	95.9	61.2	83.1
718	Texarkana	96.7	62.3	84.1
719	Hot Springs	95.1	60.6	82.4
720-722	Little Rock	97.4	63.4	84.9
723	West Memphis	94.0	65.3	83.4
724	Jonesboro	95.4	64.2	83.9
725	Batesville	92.6	60.4	80.7
726	Harrison	93.9	59.6	81.3
727	Fayetteville	91.9	61.4	80.6
728	Russellville	92.9	59.5	80.6
729	Fort Smith	96.4	61.1	83.4
CALIFORNIA				
900-902	Los Angeles	102.9	130.2	112.9
903-905	Inglewood	94.6	128.5	107.0
906-908	Long Beach	96.1	128.5	108.0
910-912	Pasadena	96.8	128.2	108.4
913-916	Van Nuys	99.5	128.2	110.1
917-918	Alhambra	100.4	128.2	110.6
919-921	San Diego	103.7	123.3	110.9
922	Palm Springs	97.1	125.9	107.7
923-924	San Bernardino	94.8	125.2	106.0
925	Riverside	99.6	126.0	109.3
926-927	Santa Ana	96.6	125.8	107.4
928	Anaheim	99.9	125.8	109.4
930	Oxnard	100.6	124.8	109.5
931	Santa Barbara	100.0	124.3	108.9
932-933	Bakersfield	102.0	124.3	110.2
934	San Luis Obispo	100.5	124.5	109.3
935	Mojave	97.8	123.9	107.4
936-938	Fresno	100.7	129.9	111.4
939	Salinas	101.3	137.9	114.7
940-941	San Francisco	105.4	160.2	125.6
942,956-958	Sacramento	97.6	132.2	110.3
943	Palo Alto	95.8	153.9	117.2
944	San Mateo	97.7	152.4	117.9
945	Vallejo	98.1	140.9	113.8
946	Oakland	100.5	151.3	119.2
947	Berkeley	99.5	151.3	118.6
948	Richmond	98.5	145.5	115.8
949	San Rafael	100.4	148.3	118.1
950	Santa Cruz	104.7	138.0	117.0

STATE/ZIP	CITY	MAT.	INST.	TOTAL
CALIFORNIA (CONT'D)				
951	San Jose	102.2	153.9	121.3
952	Stockton	100.5	131.6	111.9
953	Modesto	100.3	130.8	111.5
954	Santa Rosa	100.0	145.9	116.9
955	Eureka	101.7	134.0	113.6
959	Marysville	101.1	131.6	112.3
960	Redding	103.9	131.4	114.0
961	Susanville	102.0	132.1	113.1
COLORADO				
800-802	Denver	102.2	75.1	92.3
803	Boulder	94.9	76.0	87.9
804	Golden	96.4	71.2	87.1
805	Fort Collins	98.5	73.7	89.4
806	Greeley	96.4	73.7	88.0
807	Fort Morgan	95.3	71.3	86.5
808-809	Colorado Springs	98.2	70.9	88.1
810	Pueblo	99.8	70.4	89.0
811	Alamosa	99.5	69.1	88.3
812	Salida	99.1	69.5	88.2
813	Durango	99.9	65.5	87.3
814	Montrose	98.5	65.7	86.5
815	Grand Junction	102.6	70.5	90.8
816	Glenwood Springs	99.5	65.9	87.1
CONNECTICUT				
060	New Britain	98.0	114.9	104.2
061	Hartford	100.3	115.8	106.0
062	Willimantic	98.8	113.6	104.3
063	New London	94.4	113.4	101.4
064	Meriden	96.5	113.4	102.7
065	New Haven	99.4	114.5	104.9
066	Bridgeport	99.3	114.2	104.8
067	Waterbury	98.9	114.7	104.7
068	Norwalk	98.9	113.9	104.4
069	Stamford	99.0	114.3	104.6
D.C.				
200-205	Washington	102.2	88.6	97.2
DELAWARE				
197	Newark	100.1	107.3	102.8
198	Wilmington	101.7	107.8	103.9
199	Dover	101.7	107.3	103.7
FLORIDA				
320,322	Jacksonville	98.7	67.0	87.0
321	Daytona Beach	98.9	68.8	87.9
323	Tallahassee	100.2	67.5	88.2
324	Panama City	100.0	67.7	88.1
325	Pensacola	102.5	66.3	89.1
326,344	Gainesville	99.2	66.5	87.2
327-328,347	Orlando	101.7	67.5	89.1
329	Melbourne	101.6	71.6	90.6
330-332,340	Miami	100.2	69.1	88.8
333	Fort Lauderdale	98.9	67.0	87.1
334,349	West Palm Beach	97.3	61.6	84.2
335-336,346	Tampa	100.3	68.1	88.4
337	St. Petersburg	102.8	64.3	88.6
338	Lakeland	99.4	65.4	86.9
339,341	Fort Myers	98.6	66.0	86.6
342	Sarasota	100.4	63.9	87.0
GEORGIA				
300-303,399	Atlanta	99.8	75.6	90.9
304	Statesboro	97.1	68.5	86.5
305	Gainesville	95.3	61.2	82.8
306	Athens	94.8	60.7	82.2
307	Dalton	96.6	64.5	84.8
308-309	Augusta	96.1	71.8	87.2
310-312	Macon	96.2	72.8	87.6
313-314	Savannah	98.7	72.0	88.9
315	Waycross	97.1	65.8	85.6
316	Valdosta	97.7	70.7	87.8
317,398	Albany	98.0	71.6	88.3
318-319	Columbus	97.9	72.9	88.7

For customer support on your Plumbing Costs with RSMeans data, call 800.448.8182.

Location Factors - Commercial

STATE/ZIP	CITY	MAT.	INST.	TOTAL
HAWAII				
967	Hilo	111.8	113.3	112.3
968	Honolulu	116.5	114.1	115.6
STATES & POSS.				
969	Guam	134.9	60.4	107.5
IDAHO				
832	Pocatello	101.3	78.3	92.9
833	Twin Falls	101.4	76.5	92.2
834	Idaho Falls	99.8	78.5	92.0
835	Lewiston	104.8	83.3	96.9
836-837	Boise	100.3	80.3	93.0
838	Coeur d'Alene	103.8	84.3	96.6
ILLINOIS				
600-603	North Suburban	96.6	142.0	113.3
604	Joliet	96.4	142.3	113.3
605	South Suburban	96.6	142.3	113.4
606-608	Chicago	99.4	143.7	115.7
609	Kankakee	92.9	132.1	107.3
610-611	Rockford	96.0	128.6	108.0
612	Rock Island	93.3	99.9	95.7
613	La Salle	94.3	126.4	106.1
614	Galesburg	93.9	107.6	99.0
615-616	Peoria	96.9	108.8	101.3
617	Bloomington	93.4	107.8	98.7
618-619	Champaign	96.0	113.7	102.6
620-622	East St. Louis	95.9	108.2	100.5
623	Quincy	97.3	105.1	100.1
624	Effingham	96.2	103.0	98.7
625	Decatur	98.8	105.4	101.2
626-627	Springfield	99.8	106.8	102.4
628	Centralia	94.0	103.3	97.4
629	Carbondale	93.8	105.2	98.0
INDIANA				
460	Anderson	95.4	77.1	88.7
461-462	Indianapolis	99.0	84.2	93.5
463-464	Gary	96.7	99.9	97.9
465-466	South Bend	99.1	79.4	91.9
467-468	Fort Wayne	96.0	77.2	89.1
469	Kokomo	92.1	75.8	86.1
470	Lawrenceburg	91.3	74.3	85.1
471	New Albany	92.3	72.4	85.0
472	Columbus	94.6	75.5	87.6
473	Muncie	95.8	75.7	88.4
474	Bloomington	97.1	77.7	89.9
475	Washington	92.0	80.4	87.7
476-477	Evansville	94.7	83.1	90.4
478	Terre Haute	95.4	78.7	89.2
479	Lafayette	94.0	75.9	87.4
IOWA				
500-503,509	Des Moines	99.4	90.8	96.2
504	Mason City	95.4	67.7	85.2
505	Fort Dodge	95.5	67.4	85.1
506-507	Waterloo	98.3	74.3	89.5
508	Creston	96.0	76.8	88.9
510-511	Sioux City	98.0	76.4	90.1
512	Sibley	95.7	57.3	81.6
513	Spencer	96.9	57.1	82.3
514	Carroll	94.6	75.2	87.5
515	Council Bluffs	98.7	79.0	91.4
516	Shenandoah	95.5	74.8	87.9
520	Dubuque	97.1	76.4	89.5
521	Decorah	95.6	67.4	85.2
522-524	Cedar Rapids	98.4	82.0	92.4
525	Ottumwa	95.4	71.9	86.8
526	Burlington	94.9	76.9	88.3
527-528	Davenport	97.4	91.3	95.1
KANSAS				
660-662	Kansas City	97.9	98.0	98.0
664-666	Topeka	99.0	74.1	89.9
667	Fort Scott	95.0	70.2	85.9
668	Emporia	94.7	70.3	85.7
669	Belleville	96.0	65.7	84.9
670-672	Wichita	97.7	71.2	88.0
673	Independence	96.1	69.8	86.5
674	Salina	97.2	70.3	87.3
675	Hutchinson	92.7	66.3	83.0
676	Hays	95.5	66.9	84.9
677	Colby	96.2	68.1	85.9

STATE/ZIP	CITY	MAT.	INST.	TOTAL
KANSAS (CONT'D)				
678	Dodge City	98.2	71.1	88.2
679	Liberal	95.4	66.1	84.6
KENTUCKY				
400-402	Louisville	97.7	78.2	90.5
403-405	Lexington	96.2	75.2	88.5
406	Frankfort	98.2	74.8	89.6
407-409	Corbin	92.7	71.4	84.9
410	Covington	92.6	71.4	84.8
411-412	Ashland	91.5	81.8	87.9
413-414	Campton	92.9	72.6	85.4
415-416	Pikeville	93.3	77.8	87.6
417-418	Hazard	92.4	73.1	85.3
420	Paducah	90.1	75.8	84.9
421-422	Bowling Green	94.0	74.7	86.9
423	Owensboro	93.1	77.7	87.5
424	Henderson	90.2	74.6	84.5
425-426	Somerset	90.8	72.8	84.1
427	Elizabethtown	90.3	69.9	82.8
LOUISIANA				
700-701	New Orleans	98.3	69.5	87.7
703	Thibodaux	93.9	62.2	82.2
704	Hammond	92.0	60.8	80.5
705	Lafayette	94.6	63.0	83.0
706	Lake Charles	94.7	65.3	83.9
707-708	Baton Rouge	98.2	65.6	86.2
710-711	Shreveport	99.0	64.1	86.2
712	Monroe	96.9	61.7	83.9
713-714	Alexandria	97.0	61.8	84.1
MAINE				
039	Kittery	92.3	81.2	88.2
040-041	Portland	99.2	86.6	94.5
042	Lewiston	97.0	84.4	92.4
043	Augusta	100.7	82.4	94.0
044	Bangor	95.7	83.1	91.0
045	Bath	93.5	80.9	88.9
046	Machias	93.1	80.8	88.5
047	Houlton	93.2	80.7	88.6
048	Rockland	92.4	80.9	88.2
049	Waterville	93.4	80.8	88.7
MARYLAND				
206	Waldorf	96.3	81.1	90.7
207-208	College Park	95.6	82.1	90.6
209	Silver Spring	95.5	81.2	90.2
210-212	Baltimore	100.9	83.8	94.6
214	Annapolis	100.2	80.3	92.9
215	Cumberland	94.8	79.8	89.3
216	Easton	96.1	69.1	86.2
217	Hagerstown	96.3	84.3	91.9
218	Salisbury	96.7	62.0	83.9
219	Elkton	94.2	78.8	88.5
MASSACHUSETTS				
010-011	Springfield	97.9	104.6	100.4
012	Pittsfield	96.9	99.3	97.7
013	Greenfield	94.4	103.4	97.7
014	Fitchburg	92.7	106.7	97.9
015-016	Worcester	97.9	111.9	103.1
017	Framingham	92.4	115.5	100.9
018	Lowell	97.1	119.2	105.2
019	Lawrence	97.8	117.8	105.2
020-022, 024	Boston	100.3	133.3	112.5
023	Brockton	97.5	111.2	102.6
025	Buzzards Bay	91.1	107.8	97.2
026	Hyannis	94.1	110.4	100.1
027	New Bedford	97.0	109.8	101.7
MICHIGAN				
480,483	Royal Oak	93.5	91.9	92.9
481	Ann Arbor	96.2	96.4	96.3
482	Detroit	99.5	99.9	99.7
484-485	Flint	96.1	88.4	93.3
486	Saginaw	95.8	84.1	91.5
487	Bay City	95.8	82.2	90.8
488-489	Lansing	98.2	87.6	94.3
490	Battle Creek	95.7	77.0	88.8
491	Kalamazoo	95.8	79.4	89.8
492	Jackson	93.3	83.5	89.7
493,495	Grand Rapids	97.8	79.6	91.1
494	Muskegon	94.8	79.6	89.2

For customer support on your Plumbing Costs with RSMeans data, call 800.448.8182.

Location Factors - Commercial

STATE/ZIP	CITY	MAT.	INST.	TOTAL
MICHIGAN (CONT'D)				
496	Traverse City	93.2	71.6	85.2
497	Gaylord	94.0	74.3	86.7
498-499	Iron Mountain	95.3	75.0	87.8
MINNESOTA				
550-551	Saint Paul	102.0	117.9	107.9
553-555	Minneapolis	100.9	118.4	107.4
556-558	Duluth	102.4	106.1	103.8
559	Rochester	99.9	104.7	101.7
560	Mankato	94.8	100.6	97.0
561	Windom	93.5	88.3	91.6
562	Willmar	93.4	103.8	97.2
563	St. Cloud	95.4	114.2	102.3
564	Brainerd	94.9	99.5	96.6
565	Detroit Lakes	96.3	90.2	94.1
566	Bemidji	95.8	93.7	95.0
567	Thief River Falls	95.6	91.8	94.2
MISSISSIPPI				
386	Clarksdale	96.2	51.3	79.7
387	Greenville	99.4	63.3	86.1
388	Tupelo	97.0	53.7	81.1
389	Greenwood	97.3	51.0	80.3
390-392	Jackson	98.7	67.8	87.3
393	Meridian	95.3	65.8	84.4
394	Laurel	95.7	53.7	80.2
395	Biloxi	97.1	64.0	84.9
396	McComb	94.2	51.3	78.4
397	Columbus	95.6	54.4	80.4
MISSOURI				
630-631	St. Louis	97.3	104.5	99.9
633	Bowling Green	92.4	87.5	90.6
634	Hannibal	91.5	84.0	88.8
635	Kirksville	93.8	79.5	88.5
636	Flat River	93.1	85.8	90.4
637	Cape Girardeau	94.0	85.9	91.0
638	Sikeston	92.0	80.0	87.6
639	Poplar Bluff	91.4	80.1	87.2
640-641	Kansas City	98.6	101.2	99.6
644-645	St. Joseph	95.1	89.3	93.0
646	Chillicothe	91.3	86.0	89.4
647	Harrisonville	90.8	92.2	91.3
648	Joplin	94.2	76.5	87.7
650-651	Jefferson City	96.5	91.3	94.6
652	Columbia	95.6	90.7	93.8
653	Sedalia	94.8	83.5	90.7
654-655	Rolla	93.1	91.8	92.6
656-658	Springfield	97.7	81.0	91.6
MONTANA				
590-591	Billings	102.5	77.4	93.3
592	Wolf Point	100.4	71.3	89.6
593	Miles City	98.7	71.3	88.6
594	Great Falls	103.4	74.1	92.6
595	Havre	99.5	69.4	88.4
596	Helena	101.9	71.3	90.6
597	Butte	101.6	71.1	90.4
598	Missoula	99.3	71.0	88.9
599	Kalispell	97.6	70.3	87.6
NEBRASKA				
680-681	Omaha	98.7	81.2	92.3
683-685	Lincoln	98.9	76.4	90.6
686	Columbus	93.8	73.9	86.5
687	Norfolk	95.2	70.8	86.2
688	Grand Island	96.1	76.9	89.0
689	Hastings	94.8	71.5	86.2
690	McCook	94.2	66.9	84.2
691	North Platte	95.4	72.1	86.8
692	Valentine	97.0	64.2	85.0
693	Alliance	96.8	67.0	85.9
NEVADA				
889-891	Las Vegas	103.7	106.4	104.7
893	Ely	101.1	83.6	94.7
894-895	Reno	101.7	81.6	94.3
897	Carson City	101.9	81.5	94.4
898	Elko	100.3	76.4	91.5
NEW HAMPSHIRE				
030	Nashua	99.0	91.8	96.3
031	Manchester	99.8	92.9	97.3

STATE/ZIP	CITY	MAT.	INST.	TOTAL
NEW HAMPSHIRE (CONT'D)				
032-033	Concord	99.3	91.9	96.5
034	Keene	93.8	82.1	89.5
035	Littleton	94.3	74.1	86.9
036	Charleston	93.4	81.5	89.0
037	Claremont	92.9	81.5	88.7
038	Portsmouth	95.4	89.6	93.3
NEW JERSEY				
070-071	Newark	100.4	134.5	112.9
072	Elizabeth	96.2	133.6	110.0
073	Jersey City	96.6	133.5	110.2
074-075	Paterson	97.5	133.7	110.8
076	Hackensack	94.7	133.5	109.0
077	Long Branch	94.5	131.4	108.1
078	Dover	94.9	133.7	109.1
079	Summit	95.1	132.7	108.9
080,083	Vineland	95.7	130.4	108.5
081	Camden	98.9	130.4	110.5
082,084	Atlantic City	96.5	130.3	108.9
085-086	Trenton	100.2	130.6	111.4
087	Point Pleasant	97.1	124.5	107.2
088-089	New Brunswick	97.7	132.9	110.7
NEW MEXICO				
870-872	Albuquerque	98.2	72.3	88.7
873	Gallup	97.4	72.3	88.1
874	Farmington	98.2	72.3	88.6
875	Santa Fe	99.8	72.8	89.9
877	Las Vegas	96.0	72.3	87.3
878	Socorro	95.9	72.3	87.2
879	Truth/Consequences	95.5	69.4	85.9
880	Las Cruces	95.8	70.0	86.3
881	Clovis	96.6	72.2	87.6
882	Roswell	98.6	72.3	88.9
883	Carrizozo	98.3	72.3	88.7
884	Tucumcari	97.0	72.2	87.9
NEW YORK				
100-102	New York	99.6	167.2	124.5
103	Staten Island	92.7	165.5	119.5
104	Bronx	91.8	165.6	119.0
105	Mount Vernon	90.3	140.7	108.9
106	White Plains	91.7	143.7	110.8
107	Yonkers	96.3	145.1	114.2
108	New Rochelle	90.9	135.5	107.3
109	Suffern	90.3	118.0	100.5
110	Queens	99.4	169.0	125.0
111	Long Island City	100.8	169.0	125.9
112	Brooklyn	101.4	168.1	126.0
113	Flushing	99.8	169.0	125.3
114	Jamaica	98.6	169.0	124.5
115,117,118	Hicksville	99.4	145.1	116.2
116	Far Rockaway	99.8	169.0	125.3
119	Riverhead	100.2	149.7	118.4
120-122	Albany	98.8	107.5	102.0
123	Schenectady	98.2	107.0	101.4
124	Kingston	99.3	121.3	107.4
125-126	Poughkeepsie	98.7	125.3	108.5
127	Monticello	98.3	122.0	107.0
128	Glens Falls	92.3	99.2	94.9
129	Plattsburgh	96.1	87.7	93.0
130-132	Syracuse	98.1	99.0	98.4
133-135	Utica	96.2	99.9	97.5
136	Watertown	97.5	95.9	96.9
137-139	Binghamton	97.5	97.8	97.6
140-142	Buffalo	102.4	105.4	103.5
143	Niagara Falls	96.5	98.0	97.1
144-146	Rochester	101.4	98.6	100.4
147	Jamestown	95.5	87.5	92.6
148-149	Elmira	95.6	98.2	96.5
NORTH CAROLINA				
270,272-274	Greensboro	100.4	64.5	87.2
271	Winston-Salem	100.0	64.5	87.0
275-276	Raleigh	99.4	64.8	86.7
277	Durham	102.5	64.5	88.5
278	Rocky Mount	96.4	64.0	84.5
279	Elizabeth City	97.2	65.0	85.4
280	Gastonia	98.9	68.2	87.6
281-282	Charlotte	99.3	71.1	88.9
283	Fayetteville	102.9	63.0	88.2
284	Wilmington	97.8	62.2	84.7
285	Kinston	95.4	62.8	83.4

For customer support on your Plumbing Costs with RSMeans data, call 800.448.8182.

Location Factors - Commercial

STATE/ZIP	CITY	MAT.	INST.	TOTAL
NORTH CAROLINA (CONT'D)				
286	Hickory	95.7	68.7	85.7
287-288	Asheville	98.0	63.8	85.4
289	Murphy	96.2	61.4	83.4
NORTH DAKOTA				
580-581	Fargo	100.7	75.3	91.3
582	Grand Forks	99.5	76.9	91.2
583	Devils Lake	98.6	73.8	89.5
584	Jamestown	98.5	73.0	89.2
585	Bismarck	101.4	82.9	94.6
586	Dickinson	98.7	72.6	89.1
587	Minot	99.5	72.9	89.7
588	Williston	97.8	76.0	89.8
OHIO				
430-432	Columbus	96.8	87.0	93.2
433	Marion	91.6	79.6	87.2
434-436	Toledo	95.2	90.0	93.3
437-438	Zanesville	92.0	79.0	87.2
439	Steubenville	92.4	83.1	89.0
440	Lorain	96.0	80.9	90.5
441	Cleveland	98.0	91.4	95.6
442-443	Akron	96.8	85.0	92.4
444-445	Youngstown	96.3	80.9	90.6
446-447	Canton	96.4	78.5	89.8
448-449	Mansfield	93.3	78.4	87.8
450	Hamilton	94.4	73.1	86.6
451-452	Cincinnati	96.9	79.3	90.4
453-454	Dayton	94.5	78.6	88.6
455	Springfield	94.5	78.2	88.5
456	Chillicothe	92.5	81.0	88.3
457	Athens	95.5	83.1	90.9
458	Lima	95.3	75.6	88.1
OKLAHOMA				
730-731	Oklahoma City	97.4	67.9	86.5
734	Ardmore	94.3	64.4	83.3
735	Lawton	97.9	65.9	86.1
736	Clinton	95.3	64.3	83.9
737	Enid	96.9	65.0	85.2
738	Woodward	94.3	65.7	83.8
739	Guymon	95.2	59.2	82.0
740-741	Tulsa	96.0	64.4	84.4
743	Miami	91.5	62.1	80.7
744	Muskogee	94.8	65.9	84.2
745	McAlester	91.2	63.7	81.1
746	Ponca City	91.8	59.8	80.0
747	Durant	91.7	60.9	80.4
748	Shawnee	92.8	62.4	81.6
749	Poteau	91.1	62.0	80.4
OREGON				
970-972	Portland	103.7	103.8	103.7
973	Salem	106.3	100.8	104.3
974	Eugene	103.1	100.1	102.0
975	Medford	104.2	97.1	101.6
976	Klamath Falls	103.6	95.5	100.6
977	Bend	102.7	97.9	100.9
978	Pendleton	101.1	97.4	99.7
979	Vale	98.9	85.1	93.9
PENNSYLVANIA				
150-152	Pittsburgh	100.1	103.2	101.3
153	Washington	94.5	98.3	95.9
154	Uniontown	94.6	95.7	95.0
155	Bedford	95.4	86.0	92.0
156	Greensburg	95.4	92.4	94.3
157	Indiana	94.6	94.4	94.5
158	Dubois	95.7	89.9	93.6
159	Johnstown	95.5	93.4	94.7
160	Butler	90.8	94.5	92.2
161	New Castle	90.9	95.0	92.4
162	Kittanning	91.2	94.7	92.5
163	Oil City	90.8	89.7	90.4
164-165	Erie	93.6	94.3	93.9
166	Altoona	93.5	93.3	93.4
167	Bradford	94.0	90.4	92.6
168	State College	93.5	95.6	94.3
169	Wellsboro	94.4	84.6	90.8
170-171	Harrisburg	98.8	98.0	98.5
172	Chambersburg	93.6	81.5	89.1
173-174	York	94.8	93.7	94.4
175-176	Lancaster	92.6	95.7	93.8

STATE/ZIP	CITY	MAT.	INST.	TOTAL
PENNSYLVANIA (CONT'D)				
177	Williamsport	91.6	91.0	91.4
178	Sunbury	93.2	84.6	90.0
179	Pottsville	92.4	88.0	90.8
180	Lehigh Valley	94.2	101.6	96.9
181	Allentown	96.8	104.4	99.6
182	Hazleton	93.7	87.5	91.4
183	Stroudsburg	93.7	95.4	94.4
184-185	Scranton	97.7	94.3	96.5
186-187	Wilkes-Barre	93.4	93.5	93.4
188	Montrose	93.2	88.3	91.4
189	Doylestown	93.0	115.6	101.3
190-191	Philadelphia	100.5	137.6	114.2
193	Westchester	96.3	116.1	103.6
194	Norristown	95.4	117.6	103.6
195-196	Reading	97.9	99.3	98.4
PUERTO RICO				
009	San Juan	121.3	28.7	87.2
RHODE ISLAND				
028	Newport	96.3	109.9	101.3
029	Providence	100.1	110.6	104.0
SOUTH CAROLINA				
290-292	Columbia	99.5	65.1	86.8
293	Spartanburg	97.7	67.5	86.6
294	Charleston	99.6	67.5	87.8
295	Florence	97.4	64.5	85.3
296	Greenville	97.5	67.4	86.5
297	Rock Hill	96.3	65.2	84.8
298	Aiken	96.8	61.8	84.0
299	Beaufort	97.6	63.7	85.1
SOUTH DAKOTA				
570-571	Sioux Falls	99.9	79.6	92.4
572	Watertown	96.8	66.0	85.5
573	Mitchell	96.0	60.0	82.8
574	Aberdeen	99.1	73.5	89.7
575	Pierre	101.6	73.9	91.4
576	Mobridge	96.4	61.1	83.4
577	Rapid City	99.1	66.3	87.1
TENNESSEE				
370-372	Nashville	100.0	73.1	90.1
373-374	Chattanooga	98.8	65.4	86.5
375,380-381	Memphis	99.1	70.7	88.7
376	Johnson City	97.6	57.8	82.9
377-379	Knoxville	95.7	65.6	84.6
382	McKenzie	95.8	52.5	79.9
383	Jackson	98.6	67.2	87.1
384	Columbia	94.5	61.5	82.3
385	Cookeville	95.7	53.8	80.3
TEXAS				
750	McKinney	96.6	59.6	83.0
751	Waxahachie	96.6	66.9	85.7
752-753	Dallas	99.5	66.4	87.3
754	Greenville	96.7	59.2	82.9
755	Texarkana	95.3	61.4	82.8
756	Longview	95.8	57.0	81.5
757	Tyler	96.7	58.4	82.6
758	Palestine	93.2	56.5	79.7
759	Lufkin	93.9	57.8	80.6
760-761	Fort Worth	97.6	63.7	85.1
762	Denton	95.8	59.4	82.4
763	Wichita Falls	95.3	61.2	82.7
764	Eastland	93.1	56.5	79.6
765	Temple	91.7	54.1	77.8
766-767	Waco	94.7	62.5	82.9
768	Brownwood	95.7	54.9	80.7
769	San Angelo	95.4	58.7	81.9
770-772	Houston	97.6	67.2	86.4
773	Huntsville	93.7	58.4	80.7
774	Wharton	94.7	59.1	81.6
775	Galveston	93.4	61.5	81.6
776-777	Beaumont	94.6	66.0	84.1
778	Bryan	91.2	60.0	79.7
779	Victoria	94.6	58.5	81.3
780	Laredo	95.5	60.7	82.7
781-782	San Antonio	97.4	64.4	85.3
783-784	Corpus Christi	97.6	61.9	84.5
785	McAllen	96.7	53.4	80.8
786-787	Austin	97.6	61.9	84.4

Location Factors - Commercial

STATE/ZIP	CITY	MAT.	INST.	TOTAL
TEXAS (CONT'D)				
788	Del Rio	96.3	55.7	81.3
789	Giddings	93.7	56.6	80.1
790-791	Amarillo	98.9	61.6	85.2
792	Childress	97.3	56.9	82.4
793-794	Lubbock	100.7	60.8	86.0
795-796	Abilene	99.1	59.8	84.7
797	Midland	99.7	63.9	86.5
798-799,885	El Paso	98.9	63.3	85.8
UTAH				
840-841	Salt Lake City	101.7	72.3	90.9
842,844	Ogden	97.7	72.6	88.4
843	Logan	99.1	72.6	89.3
845	Price	98.6	65.8	86.5
846-847	Provo	99.3	71.8	89.2
VERMONT				
050	White River Jct.	93.9	76.7	87.5
051	Bellows Falls	92.6	86.7	90.4
052	Bennington	92.9	83.5	89.5
053	Brattleboro	93.2	86.7	90.8
054	Burlington	99.7	81.3	92.9
056	Montpelier	97.1	83.7	92.1
057	Rutland	96.7	80.7	90.8
058	St. Johnsbury	94.0	76.3	87.5
059	Guildhall	92.9	76.4	86.8
VIRGINIA				
220-221	Fairfax	98.0	80.9	91.7
222	Arlington	100.1	79.9	92.6
223	Alexandria	99.7	81.2	92.9
224-225	Fredericksburg	97.4	76.2	89.6
226	Winchester	97.6	72.6	88.4
227	Culpeper	97.6	78.3	90.5
228	Harrisonburg	97.7	72.3	88.3
229	Charlottesville	98.1	68.2	87.1
230-232	Richmond	98.8	69.4	88.0
233-235	Norfolk	100.7	66.9	88.3
236	Newport News	98.7	67.2	87.1
237	Portsmouth	97.9	65.2	85.9
238	Petersburg	96.8	68.7	86.5
239	Farmville	96.4	63.1	84.1
240-241	Roanoke	100.5	66.2	87.9
242	Bristol	97.1	57.2	82.4
243	Pulaski	96.8	66.5	85.7
244	Staunton	97.6	65.2	85.7
245	Lynchburg	97.5	66.9	86.3
246	Grundy	97.1	60.5	83.7
WASHINGTON				
980-981,987	Seattle	103.6	112.6	106.9
982	Everett	103.5	104.7	104.0
983-984	Tacoma	104.3	103.8	104.1
985	Olympia	104.1	102.9	103.7
986	Vancouver	105.9	100.6	103.9
988	Wenatchee	103.1	83.2	95.8
989	Yakima	104.0	94.7	100.6
990-992	Spokane	97.6	84.9	93.0
993	Richland	97.0	91.0	94.8
994	Clarkston	95.3	75.6	88.1
WEST VIRGINIA				
247-248	Bluefield	96.2	81.0	90.6
249	Lewisburg	97.5	83.1	92.2
250-253	Charleston	98.2	88.3	94.5
254	Martinsburg	96.6	77.2	89.4
255-257	Huntington	99.2	87.0	94.7
258-259	Beckley	95.4	83.9	91.2
260	Wheeling	99.4	87.6	95.0
261	Parkersburg	98.6	86.6	94.2
262	Buckhannon	97.2	87.2	93.5
263-264	Clarksburg	97.7	87.9	94.1
265	Morgantown	97.6	88.6	94.3
266	Gassaway	97.2	84.2	92.4
267	Romney	97.2	81.8	91.6
268	Petersburg	96.9	82.2	91.5
WISCONSIN				
530,532	Milwaukee	97.6	109.3	101.9
531	Kenosha	97.4	101.9	99.0
534	Racine	96.5	101.8	98.5
535	Beloit	96.3	92.8	95.0
537	Madison	98.6	100.5	99.3

STATE/ZIP	CITY	MAT.	INST.	TOTAL
WISCONSIN (CONT'D)				
538	Lancaster	93.2	88.0	91.3
539	Portage	92.1	91.4	91.8
540	New Richmond	94.2	87.7	91.8
541-543	Green Bay	99.5	99.3	99.4
544	Wausau	93.9	87.7	91.6
545	Rhinelander	96.7	86.2	92.8
546	La Crosse	95.3	95.9	95.5
547	Eau Claire	96.9	95.8	96.5
548	Superior	94.0	90.1	92.6
549	Oshkosh	94.6	88.2	92.2
WYOMING				
820	Cheyenne	99.6	72.8	89.7
821	Yellowstone Nat'l Park	97.1	69.9	87.1
822	Wheatland	97.8	68.4	87.0
823	Rawlins	99.0	69.8	88.3
824	Worland	97.4	70.3	87.4
825	Riverton	98.2	69.8	87.8
826	Casper	100.8	71.1	89.9
827	Newcastle	97.2	69.8	87.1
828	Sheridan	100.1	70.6	89.2
829-831	Rock Springs	100.8	70.3	89.6
CANADIAN FACTORS (reflect Canadian currency)				
ALBERTA				
	Calgary	137.9	86.9	119.1
	Edmonton	137.6	86.9	118.9
	Fort McMurray	132.2	82.5	113.9
	Lethbridge	126.7	82.0	110.3
	Lloydminster	120.0	79.1	104.9
	Medicine Hat	120.3	78.4	104.9
	Red Deer	120.7	78.4	105.1
BRITISH COLUMBIA				
	Kamloops	122.4	78.8	106.3
	Prince George	123.4	78.2	106.7
	Vancouver	129.7	89.8	115.0
	Victoria	125.3	83.6	110.0
MANITOBA				
	Brandon	130.0	66.3	106.6
	Portage la Prairie	120.4	65.3	100.1
	Winnipeg	133.5	66.9	109.0
NEW BRUNSWICK				
	Bathurst	117.1	59.1	95.7
	Dalhousie	120.2	59.1	97.7
	Fredericton	130.6	66.7	107.0
	Moncton	117.1	73.6	101.1
	Newcastle	117.2	59.6	96.0
	St. John	119.0	74.5	102.6
NEWFOUNDLAND				
	Corner Brook	134.3	64.4	108.5
	St. Johns	130.0	82.4	112.5
NORTHWEST TERRITORIES				
	Yellowknife	143.4	78.2	119.4
NOVA SCOTIA				
	Bridgewater	119.8	66.5	100.2
	Dartmouth	131.0	66.1	107.2
	Halifax	124.4	82.1	108.8
	New Glasgow	129.1	66.1	105.9
	Sydney	127.3	66.1	104.8
	Truro	119.3	66.5	99.9
	Yarmouth	129.0	66.1	105.9
ONTARIO				
	Barrie	121.0	82.1	106.7
	Brantford	122.0	85.5	108.5
	Cornwall	121.4	82.3	107.1
	Hamilton	129.4	94.9	116.7
	Kingston	122.7	82.4	107.9
	Kitchener	119.8	91.0	109.2
	London	128.9	93.0	115.7
	North Bay	132.0	80.1	112.9
	Oshawa	121.1	92.4	110.6
	Ottawa	128.2	94.4	115.7
	Owen Sound	121.3	80.5	106.3
	Peterborough	122.0	82.1	107.3
	Sarnia	122.4	86.0	109.0

Location Factors - Commercial

STATE/ZIP	CITY	MAT.	INST.	TOTAL
ONTARIO (CONT'D)				
	Sault Ste. Marie	117.7	84.3	105.4
	St. Catharines	117.3	91.6	107.8
	Sudbury	116.6	90.0	106.8
	Thunder Bay	118.2	90.6	108.1
	Timmins	122.4	80.4	106.9
	Toronto	127.5	100.9	117.7
	Windsor	118.3	90.8	108.2
PRINCE EDWARD ISLAND				
	Charlottetown	130.7	58.1	104.0
	Summerside	131.2	54.5	103.0
QUEBEC				
	Cap-de-la-Madeleine	118.6	75.6	102.8
	Charlesbourg	118.6	75.6	102.8
	Chicoutimi	116.5	84.0	104.6
	Gatineau	118.4	75.4	102.6
	Granby	118.9	75.3	102.9
	Hull	119.0	75.4	103.0
	Joliette	119.1	75.6	103.1
	Laval	118.7	75.9	103.0
	Montreal	129.7	87.0	114.0
	Quebec City	130.0	87.5	114.4
	Rimouski	118.5	84.0	105.8
	Rouyn-Noranda	118.7	75.4	102.8
	Saint-Hyacinthe	118.1	75.4	102.4
	Sherbrooke	118.8	75.4	102.8
	Sorel	119.1	75.6	103.1
	Saint-Jerome	118.9	75.4	102.9
	Trois-Rivieres	129.3	75.2	109.4
SASKATCHEWAN				
	Moose Jaw	117.3	60.4	96.3
	Prince Albert	116.5	58.9	95.3
	Regina	137.5	85.1	118.2
	Saskatoon	118.9	81.0	105.0
YUKON				
	Whitehorse	145.7	65.7	116.3

General Requirements — R0111 Summary of Work

R011105-05 Tips for Accurate Estimating

1. Use computer applications or pre-printed forms for orderly sequence of dimensions and locations. Keep track of phone conversations by recording (with permission) or note taking on computer applications or pre-printed forms.
2. Use only the front side if pre-printed forms are necessary. Label all pre-printed forms with the same convention.
3. Be consistent in listing dimensions: For example, length x width x height. This helps in rechecking to ensure that, the total length of partitions is appropriate for the building area.
4. Use printed (rather than measured) dimensions where given.
5. Add up multiple printed dimensions for a single entry where possible.
6. Measure all other dimensions carefully.
7. Use each set of dimensions to calculate multiple related quantities.
8. Convert foot and inch measurements to decimal feet when listing. Memorize decimal equivalents to .01 parts of a foot (1/8" equals approximately .01').
9. Do not "round off" quantities until the final summary.
10. Mark drawings with different colors as items are taken off.
11. Keep similar items together, different items separate.
12. Identify location and drawing numbers to aid in future checking for completeness.
13. Measure or list everything on the drawings or mentioned in the specifications.
14. It may be necessary to list items not called for to make the job complete.
15. Be alert for: Notes on plans such as N.T.S. (not to scale); changes in scale throughout the drawings; reduced size drawings; discrepancies between the specifications and the drawings.
16. Develop a consistent pattern of performing an estimate. For example:
    a. Start the quantity takeoff at the lower floor and move to the next higher floor.
    b. Proceed from the main section of the building to the wings.
    c. Proceed from south to north or vice versa, clockwise or counterclockwise.
    d. Take off floor plan quantities first, elevations next, then detail drawings.
17. List all gross dimensions that can be either used again for different quantities, or used as a rough check of other quantities for verification (exterior perimeter, gross floor area, individual floor areas, etc.).
18. Utilize design symmetry or repetition (repetitive floors, repetitive wings, symmetrical design around a center line, similar room layouts, etc.). Note: Extreme caution is needed here so as not to omit or duplicate an area.
19. Do not convert units until the final total is obtained. For instance, when estimating concrete work, keep all units to the nearest cubic foot, then summarize and convert to cubic yards.
20. When figuring alternatives, it is best to total all items involved in the basic system, then total all items involved in the alternates. Therefore you work with positive numbers in all cases. When adds and deducts are used, it is often confusing whether to add or subtract a portion of an item; especially on a complicated or involved alternate.

R011105-10 Unit Gross Area Requirements

The figures in the table below indicate typical ranges in square feet as a function of the "occupant" unit. This table is best used in the preliminary design stages to help determine the probable size requirement for the total project.

Building Type	Unit	Gross Area in S.F. 1/4	Gross Area in S.F. Median	Gross Area in S.F. 3/4
Apartments	Unit	660	860	1,100
Auditorium & Play Theaters	Seat	18	25	38
Bowling Alleys	Lane		940	
Churches & Synagogues	Seat	20	28	39
Dormitories	Bed	200	230	275
Fraternity & Sorority Houses	Bed	220	315	370
Garages, Parking	Car	325	355	385
Hospitals	Bed	685	850	1,075
Hotels	Rental Unit	475	600	710
Housing for the elderly	Unit	515	635	755
Housing, Public	Unit	700	875	1,030
Ice Skating Rinks	Total	27,000	30,000	36,000
Motels	Rental Unit	360	465	620
Nursing Homes	Bed	290	350	450
Restaurants	Seat	23	29	39
Schools, Elementary	Pupil	65	77	90
Junior High & Middle		85	110	129
Senior High		102	130	145
Vocational		110	135	195
Shooting Ranges	Point		450	
Theaters & Movies	Seat		15	

General Requirements — R0111 Summary of Work

R011105-20 Floor Area Ratios

Table below lists commonly used gross to net area and net to gross area ratios expressed in % for various building types.

Building Type	Gross to Net Ratio	Net to Gross Ratio	Building Type	Gross to Net Ratio	Net to Gross Ratio
Apartment	156	64	School Buildings (campus type)		
Bank	140	72	Administrative	150	67
Church	142	70	Auditorium	142	70
Courthouse	162	61	Biology	161	62
Department Store	123	81	Chemistry	170	59
Garage	118	85	Classroom	152	66
Hospital	183	55	Dining Hall	138	72
Hotel	158	63	Dormitory	154	65
Laboratory	171	58	Engineering	164	61
Library	132	76	Fraternity	160	63
Office	135	75	Gymnasium	142	70
Restaurant	141	70	Science	167	60
Warehouse	108	93	Service	120	83
			Student Union	172	59

The gross area of a building is the total floor area based on outside dimensions.

The net area of a building is the usable floor area for the function intended and excludes such items as stairways, corridors and mechanical rooms. In the case of a commercial building, it might be considered as the "leasable area."

General Requirements — R0111 Summary of Work

R011105-30 Occupancy Determinations

Function of Space	SF/Person Required
Accessory storage areas, mechanical equipment rooms	300
Agriculture Building	300
Aircraft Hangars	500
Airport Terminal	
Baggage claim	20
Baggage handling	300
Concourse	100
Waiting areas	15
Assembly	
Gaming floors (keno, slots, etc.)	11
Exhibit Gallery and Museum	30
Assembly w/ fixed seats	load determined by seat number
Assembly w/o fixed seats	
Concentrated (chairs only-not fixed)	7
Standing space	5
Unconcentrated (tables and chairs)	15
Bowling centers, allow 5 persons for each lane including 15 feet of runway, and for additional areas	7
Business areas	100
Courtrooms-other than fixed seating areas	40
Day care	35
Dormitories	50
Educational	
Classroom areas	20
Shops and other vocational room areas	50
Exercise rooms	50
Fabrication and Manufacturing areas where hazardous materials are used	200
Industrial areas	100
Institutional areas	
Inpatient treatment areas	240
Outpatient areas	100
Sleeping areas	120
Kitchens commercial	200
Library	
Reading rooms	50
Stack area	100
Mercantile	
Areas on other floors	60
Basement and grade floor areas	30
Storage, stock, shipping areas	300
Parking garages	200
Residential	200
Skating rinks, swimming pools	
Rink and pool	50
Decks	15
Stages and platforms	15
Warehouses	500

Excerpted from the 2012 *International Building Code,* Copyright 2011. Washington, D.C.: International Code Council. Reproduced with permission. All rights reserved. www.ICCSAFE.org

General Requirements — R0111 Summary of Work

R011105-40 Weather Data and Design Conditions

City	Latitude (1) 0	Latitude (1) 1'	Winter Temperatures (1) Med. of Annual Extremes	Winter Temperatures (1) 99%	Winter Temperatures (1) 97½%	Winter Degree Days (2)	Summer (Design Dry Bulb) Temperatures and Relative Humidity 1%	Summer (Design Dry Bulb) Temperatures and Relative Humidity 2½%	Summer (Design Dry Bulb) Temperatures and Relative Humidity 5%
UNITED STATES									
Albuquerque, NM	35	0	5.1	12	16	4,400	96/61	94/61	92/61
Atlanta, GA	33	4	11.9	17	22	3,000	94/74	92/74	90/73
Baltimore, MD	39	2	7	14	17	4,600	94/75	91/75	89/74
Birmingham, AL	33	3	13	17	21	2,600	96/74	94/75	92/74
Bismarck, ND	46	5	-32	-23	-19	8,800	95/68	91/68	88/67
Boise, ID	43	3	1	3	10	5,800	96/65	94/64	91/64
Boston, MA	42	2	-1	6	9	5,600	91/73	88/71	85/70
Burlington, VT	44	3	-17	-12	-7	8,200	88/72	85/70	82/69
Charleston, WV	38	2	3	7	11	4,400	92/74	90/73	87/72
Charlotte, NC	35	1	13	18	22	3,200	95/74	93/74	91/74
Casper, WY	42	5	-21	-11	-5	7,400	92/58	90/57	87/57
Chicago, IL	41	5	-8	-3	2	6,600	94/75	91/74	88/73
Cincinnati, OH	39	1	0	1	6	4,400	92/73	90/72	88/72
Cleveland, OH	41	2	-3	1	5	6,400	91/73	88/72	86/71
Columbia, SC	34	0	16	20	24	2,400	97/76	95/75	93/75
Dallas, TX	32	5	14	18	22	2,400	102/75	100/75	97/75
Denver, CO	39	5	-10	-5	1	6,200	93/59	91/59	89/59
Des Moines, IA	41	3	-14	-10	-5	6,600	94/75	91/74	88/73
Detroit, MI	42	2	-3	3	6	6,200	91/73	88/72	86/71
Great Falls, MT	47	3	-25	-21	-15	7,800	91/60	88/60	85/59
Hartford, CT	41	5	-4	3	7	6,200	91/74	88/73	85/72
Houston, TX	29	5	24	28	33	1,400	97/77	95/77	93/77
Indianapolis, IN	39	4	-7	-2	2	5,600	92/74	90/74	87/73
Jackson, MS	32	2	16	21	25	2,200	97/76	95/76	93/76
Kansas City, MO	39	1	-4	2	6	4,800	99/75	96/74	93/74
Las Vegas, NV	36	1	18	25	28	2,800	108/66	106/65	104/65
Lexington, KY	38	0	-1	3	8	4,600	93/73	91/73	88/72
Little Rock, AR	34	4	11	15	20	3,200	99/76	96/77	94/77
Los Angeles, CA	34	0	36	41	43	2,000	93/70	89/70	86/69
Memphis, TN	35	0	10	13	18	3,200	98/77	95/76	93/76
Miami, FL	25	5	39	44	47	200	91/77	90/77	89/77
Milwaukee, WI	43	0	-11	-8	-4	7,600	90/74	87/73	84/71
Minneapolis, MN	44	5	-22	-16	-12	8,400	92/75	89/73	86/71
New Orleans, LA	30	0	28	29	33	1,400	93/78	92/77	90/77
New York, NY	40	5	6	11	15	5,000	92/74	89/73	87/72
Norfolk, VA	36	5	15	20	22	3,400	93/77	91/76	89/76
Oklahoma City, OK	35	2	4	9	13	3,200	100/74	97/74	95/73
Omaha, NE	41	2	-13	-8	-3	6,600	94/76	91/75	88/74
Philadelphia, PA	39	5	6	10	14	4,400	93/75	90/74	87/72
Phoenix, AZ	33	3	27	31	34	1,800	109/71	107/71	105/71
Pittsburgh, PA	40	3	-1	3	7	6,000	91/72	88/71	86/70
Portland, ME	43	4	-10	-6	-1	7,600	87/72	84/71	81/69
Portland, OR	45	4	18	17	23	4,600	89/68	85/67	81/65
Portsmouth, NH	43	1	-8	-2	2	7,200	89/73	85/71	83/70
Providence, RI	41	4	-1	5	9	6,000	89/73	86/72	83/70
Rochester, NY	43	1	-5	1	5	6,800	91/73	88/71	85/70
Salt Lake City, UT	40	5	0	3	8	6,000	97/62	95/62	92/61
San Francisco, CA	37	5	36	38	40	3,000	74/63	71/62	69/61
Seattle, WA	47	4	22	22	27	5,200	85/68	82/66	78/65
Sioux Falls, SD	43	4	-21	-15	-11	7,800	94/73	91/72	88/71
St. Louis, MO	38	4	-3	3	8	5,000	98/75	94/75	91/75
Tampa, FL	28	0	32	36	40	680	92/77	91/77	90/76
Trenton, NJ	40	1	4	11	14	5,000	91/75	88/74	85/73
Washington, DC	38	5	7	14	17	4,200	93/75	91/74	89/74
Wichita, KS	37	4	-3	3	7	4,600	101/72	98/73	96/73
Wilmington, DE	39	4	5	10	14	5,000	92/74	89/74	87/73
ALASKA									
Anchorage	61	1	-29	-23	-18	10,800	71/59	68/58	66/56
Fairbanks	64	5	-59	-51	-47	14,280	82/62	78/60	75/59
CANADA									
Edmonton, Alta.	53	3	-30	-29	-25	11,000	85/66	82/65	79/63
Halifax, N.S.	44	4	-4	1	5	8,000	79/66	76/65	74/64
Montreal, Que.	45	3	-20	-16	-10	9,000	88/73	85/72	83/71
Saskatoon, Sask.	52	1	-35	-35	-31	11,000	89/68	86/66	83/65
St. John's, N.F.	47	4	1	3	7	8,600	77/66	75/65	73/64
Saint John, N.B.	45	2	-15	-12	-8	8,200	80/67	77/65	75/64
Toronto, Ont.	43	4	-10	-5	-1	7,000	90/73	87/72	85/71
Vancouver, B.C.	49	1	13	15	19	6,000	79/67	77/66	74/65
Winnipeg, Man.	49	5	-31	-30	-27	10,800	89/73	86/71	84/70

(1) Handbook of Fundamentals, ASHRAE, Inc., NY 1989
(2) Local Climatological Annual Survey, USDC Env. Science Services Administration, Asheville, NC

General Requirements — R0111 Summary of Work

R011105-50 Metric Conversion Factors

Description: This table is primarily for converting customary U.S. units in the left hand column to SI metric units in the right hand column. In addition, conversion factors for some commonly encountered Canadian and non-SI metric units are included.

	If You Know		Multiply By		To Find
Length	Inches	x	25.4[a]	=	Millimeters
	Feet	x	0.3048[a]	=	Meters
	Yards	x	0.9144[a]	=	Meters
	Miles (statute)	x	1.609	=	Kilometers
Area	Square inches	x	645.2	=	Square millimeters
	Square feet	x	0.0929	=	Square meters
	Square yards	x	0.8361	=	Square meters
Volume (Capacity)	Cubic inches	x	16,387	=	Cubic millimeters
	Cubic feet	x	0.02832	=	Cubic meters
	Cubic yards	x	0.7646	=	Cubic meters
	Gallons (U.S. liquids)[b]	x	0.003785	=	Cubic meters[c]
	Gallons (Canadian liquid)[b]	x	0.004546	=	Cubic meters[c]
	Ounces (U.S. liquid)[b]	x	29.57	=	Milliliters[c, d]
	Quarts (U.S. liquid)[b]	x	0.9464	=	Liters[c, d]
	Gallons (U.S. liquid)[b]	x	3.785	=	Liters[c, d]
Force	Kilograms force[d]	x	9.807	=	Newtons
	Pounds force	x	4.448	=	Newtons
	Pounds force	x	0.4536	=	Kilograms force[d]
	Kips	x	4448	=	Newtons
	Kips	x	453.6	=	Kilograms force[d]
Pressure, Stress, Strength (Force per unit area)	Kilograms force per square centimeter[d]	x	0.09807	=	Megapascals
	Pounds force per square inch (psi)	x	0.006895	=	Megapascals
	Kips per square inch	x	6.895	=	Megapascals
	Pounds force per square inch (psi)	x	0.07031	=	Kilograms force per square centimeter[d]
	Pounds force per square foot	x	47.88	=	Pascals
	Pounds force per square foot	x	4.882	=	Kilograms force per square meter[d]
Flow	Cubic feet per minute	x	0.4719	=	Liters per second
	Gallons per minute	x	0.0631	=	Liters per second
	Gallons per hour	x	1.05	=	Milliliters per second
Bending Moment Or Torque	Inch-pounds force	x	0.01152	=	Meter-kilograms force[d]
	Inch-pounds force	x	0.1130	=	Newton-meters
	Foot-pounds force	x	0.1383	=	Meter-kilograms force[d]
	Foot-pounds force	x	1.356	=	Newton-meters
	Meter-kilograms force[d]	x	9.807	=	Newton-meters
Mass	Ounces (avoirdupois)	x	28.35	=	Grams
	Pounds (avoirdupois)	x	0.4536	=	Kilograms
	Tons (metric)	x	1000	=	Kilograms
	Tons, short (2000 pounds)	x	907.2	=	Kilograms
	Tons, short (2000 pounds)	x	0.9072	=	Megagrams[e]
Mass per Unit Volume	Pounds mass per cubic foot	x	16.02	=	Kilograms per cubic meter
	Pounds mass per cubic yard	x	0.5933	=	Kilograms per cubic meter
	Pounds mass per gallon (U.S. liquid)[b]	x	119.8	=	Kilograms per cubic meter
	Pounds mass per gallon (Canadian liquid)[b]	x	99.78	=	Kilograms per cubic meter
Temperature	Degrees Fahrenheit	(F-32)/1.8		=	Degrees Celsius
	Degrees Fahrenheit	(F+459.67)/1.8		=	Degrees Kelvin
	Degrees Celsius	C+273.15		=	Degrees Kelvin

[a] The factor given is exact
[b] One U.S. gallon = 0.8327 Canadian gallon
[c] 1 liter = 1000 milliliters = 1000 cubic centimeters
    1 cubic decimeter = 0.001 cubic meter
[d] Metric but not SI unit
[e] Called "tonne" in England and "metric ton" in other metric countries

General Requirements   R0111 Summary of Work

R011105-60 Weights and Measures

Measures of Length
1 Mile = 1760 Yards = 5280 Feet
1 Yard = 3 Feet = 36 inches
1 Foot = 12 Inches
1 Mil = 0.001 Inch
1 Fathom = 2 Yards = 6 Feet
1 Rod = 5.5 Yards = 16.5 Feet
1 Hand = 4 Inches
1 Span = 9 Inches
1 Micro-inch = One Millionth Inch or 0.000001 Inch
1 Micron = One Millionth Meter + 0.00003937 Inch

Surveyor's Measure
1 Mile = 8 Furlongs = 80 Chains
1 Furlong = 10 Chains = 220 Yards
1 Chain = 4 Rods = 22 Yards = 66 Feet = 100 Links
1 Link = 7.92 Inches

Square Measure
1 Square Mile = 640 Acres = 6400 Square Chains
1 Acre = 10 Square Chains = 4840 Square Yards = 43,560 Sq. Ft.
1 Square Chain = 16 Square Rods = 484 Square Yards = 4356 Sq. Ft.
1 Square Rod = 30.25 Square Yards = 272.25 Square Feet = 625 Square Lines
1 Square Yard = 9 Square Feet
1 Square Foot = 144 Square Inches
An Acre equals a Square 208.7 Feet per Side

Cubic Measure
1 Cubic Yard = 27 Cubic Feet
1 Cubic Foot = 1728 Cubic Inches
1 Cord of Wood = 4 x 4 x 8 Feet = 128 Cubic Feet
1 Perch of Masonry = 16½ x 1½ x 1 Foot = 24.75 Cubic Feet

Avoirdupois or Commercial Weight
1 Gross or Long Ton = 2240 Pounds
1 Net or Short Ton = 2000 Pounds
1 Pound = 16 Ounces = 7000 Grains
1 Ounce = 16 Drachms = 437.5 Grains
1 Stone = 14 Pounds

Power
1 British Thermal Unit per Hour = 0.2931 Watts
1 Ton (Refrigeration) = 3.517 Kilowatts
1 Horsepower (Boiler) = 9.81 Kilowatts
1 Horsepower (550 ft-lb/s) = 0.746 Kilowatts

Shipping Measure
For Measuring Internal Capacity of a Vessel:
    1 Register Ton = 100 Cubic Feet

For Measurement of Cargo:
    Approximately 40 Cubic Feet of Merchandise is considered a Shipping Ton, unless that bulk would weigh more than 2000 Pounds, in which case Freight Charge may be based upon weight.

40 Cubic Feet = 32.143 U.S. Bushels = 31.16 Imp. Bushels

Liquid Measure
1 Imperial Gallon = 1.2009 U.S. Gallon = 277.42 Cu. In.
1 Cubic Foot = 7.48 U.S. Gallons

General Requirements — R0111 Summary of Work

R011110-30 Engineering Fees

Typical **Structural Engineering Fees** based on type of construction and total project size. These fees are included in Architectural Fees.

Type of Construction	Total Project Size (in thousands of dollars)			
	$500	$500-$1,000	$1,000-$5,000	Over $5000
Industrial buildings, factories & warehouses	Technical payroll times 2.0 to 2.5	1.60%	1.25%	1.00%
Hotels, apartments, offices, dormitories, hospitals, public buildings, food stores		2.00%	1.70%	1.20%
Museums, banks, churches and cathedrals		2.00%	1.75%	1.25%
Thin shells, prestressed concrete, earthquake resistive		2.00%	1.75%	1.50%
Parking ramps, auditoriums, stadiums, convention halls, hangars & boiler houses		2.50%	2.00%	1.75%
Special buildings, major alterations, underpinning & future expansion	▼	Add to above 0.5%	Add to above 0.5%	Add to above 0.5%

For complex reinforced concrete or unusually complicated structures, add 20% to 50%.

Typical **Mechanical and Electrical Engineering Fees** are based on the size of the subcontract. The fee structure for both is shown below. These fees are included in Architectural Fees.

	Subcontract Size							
Type of Construction	$25,000	$50,000	$100,000	$225,000	$350,000	$500,000	$750,000	$1,000,000
Simple structures	6.4%	5.7%	4.8%	4.5%	4.4%	4.3%	4.2%	4.1%
Intermediate structures	8.0	7.3	6.5	5.6	5.1	5.0	4.9	4.8
Complex structures	10.1	9.0	9.0	8.0	7.5	7.5	7.0	7.0

For renovations, add 15% to 25% to applicable fee.

General Requirements — R0121 Allowances

R012153-10 Repair and Remodeling

Cost figures are based on new construction utilizing the most cost-effective combination of labor, equipment and material with the work scheduled in proper sequence to allow the various trades to accomplish their work in an efficient manner.

The costs for repair and remodeling work must be modified due to the following factors that may be present in any given repair and remodeling project.

1. Equipment usage curtailment due to the physical limitations of the project, with only hand-operated equipment being used.
2. Increased requirement for shoring and bracing to hold up the building while structural changes are being made and to allow for temporary storage of construction materials on above-grade floors.
3. Material handling becomes more costly due to having to move within the confines of an enclosed building. For multi-story construction, low capacity elevators and stairwells may be the only access to the upper floors.
4. Large amount of cutting and patching and attempting to match the existing construction is required. It is often more economical to remove entire walls rather than create many new door and window openings. This sort of trade-off has to be carefully analyzed.
5. Cost of protection of completed work is increased since the usual sequence of construction usually cannot be accomplished.
6. Economies of scale usually associated with new construction may not be present. If small quantities of components must be custom fabricated due to job requirements, unit costs will naturally increase. Also, if only small work areas are available at a given time, job scheduling between trades becomes difficult and subcontractor quotations may reflect the excessive start-up and shut-down phases of the job.
7. Work may have to be done on other than normal shifts and may have to be done around an existing production facility which has to stay in production during the course of the repair and remodeling.
8. Dust and noise protection of adjoining non-construction areas can involve substantial special protection and alter usual construction methods.
9. Job may be delayed due to unexpected conditions discovered during demolition or removal. These delays ultimately increase construction costs.
10. Piping and ductwork runs may not be as simple as for new construction. Wiring may have to be snaked through walls and floors.
11. Matching "existing construction" may be impossible because materials may no longer be manufactured. Substitutions may be expensive.
12. Weather protection of existing structure requires additional temporary structures to protect building at openings.
13. On small projects, because of local conditions, it may be necessary to pay a tradesman for a minimum of four hours for a task that is completed in one hour.

All of the above areas can contribute to increased costs for a repair and remodeling project. Each of the above factors should be considered in the planning, bidding and construction stage in order to minimize the increased costs associated with repair and remodeling jobs.

General Requirements   R0121 Allowances

R012153-60   Security Factors

Contractors entering, working in, and exiting secure facilities often lose productive time during a normal workday. The recommended allowances in this section are intended to provide for the loss of productivity by increasing labor costs. Note that different costs are associated with searches upon entry only and searches upon entry and exit. Time spent in a queue is unpredictable and not part of these allowances. Contractors should plan ahead for this situation.

Security checkpoints are designed to reflect the level of security required to gain access or egress. An extreme example is when contractors, along with any materials, tools, equipment, and vehicles, must be physically searched and have all materials, tools, equipment, and vehicles inventoried and documented prior to both entry and exit.

Physical searches without going through the documentation process represent the next level and take up less time.

Electronic searches—passing through a detector or x-ray machine with no documentation of materials, tools, equipment, and vehicles—take less time than physical searches.

Visual searches of materials, tools, equipment, and vehicles represent the next level of security.

Finally, access by means of an ID card or displayed sticker takes the least amount of time.

Another consideration is if the searches described above are performed each and every day, or if they are performed only on the first day with access granted by ID card or displayed sticker for the remainder of the project. The figures for this situation have been calculated to represent the initial check-in as described and subsequent entry by ID card or displayed sticker for up to 20 days on site. For the situation described above, where the time period is beyond 20 days, the impact on labor cost is negligible.

There are situations where tradespeople must be accompanied by an escort and observed during the work day. The loss of freedom of movement will slow down productivity for the tradesperson. Costs for the observer have not been included. Those costs are normally born by the owner.

R012153-65   Infectious Disease Precautions

Contractors entering and working on job sites may be required to take precautions to prevent the spread of infectious diseases. Those precautions will reduce the amount of productive time during a normal workday. The recommended allowances in this section are intended to provide for the loss of productive time by increasing labor costs.

The estimator should be aware that one, many or none of these precautions apply to the line items in an estimate. Job site requirements and sound judgement must be applied.

Labor cost implications are based upon:

Temperature checks	Once per day
Donning/doffing masks and gloves	Four times per day (2 times each)
Washing hands (additional over normal)	Eight times per day
Informational meetings	Once per day
Maintaining social distance	Throughout the day
Disinfecting tools or equipment	Throughout the day

General Requirements — R0129 Payment Procedures

R012909-80 Sales Tax by State

State sales tax on materials is tabulated below (5 states have no sales tax). Many states allow local jurisdictions, such as a county or city, to levy additional sales tax.

Some projects may be sales tax exempt, particularly those constructed with public funds.

State	Tax (%)	State	Tax (%)	State	Tax (%)	State	Tax (%)
Alabama	4	Illinois	6.25	Montana	0	Rhode Island	7
Alaska	0	Indiana	7	Nebraska	5.5	South Carolina	6
Arizona	5.6	Iowa	6	Nevada	6.85	South Dakota	4.5
Arkansas	6.5	Kansas	6.5	New Hampshire	0	Tennessee	7
California	7.25	Kentucky	6	New Jersey	6.625	Texas	6.25
Colorado	2.9	Louisiana	4.45	New Mexico	5.125	Utah	6.10
Connecticut	6.35	Maine	5.5	New York	4	Vermont	6
Delaware	0	Maryland	6	North Carolina	4.75	Virginia	5.3
District of Columbia	6	Massachusetts	6.25	North Dakota	5	Washington	6.5
Florida	6	Michigan	6	Ohio	5.75	West Virginia	6
Georgia	4	Minnesota	6.875	Oklahoma	4.5	Wisconsin	5
Hawaii	4	Mississippi	7	Oregon	0	Wyoming	4
Idaho	6	Missouri	4.225	Pennsylvania	6	Average	5.11 %

Sales Tax by Province (Canada)

GST - a value-added tax, which the government imposes on most goods and services provided in or imported into Canada. PST - a retail sales tax, which five of the provinces impose on the prices of most goods and some services. QST - a value-added tax, similar to the federal GST, which Quebec imposes. HST - Three provinces have combined their retail sales taxes with the federal GST into one harmonized tax.

Province	PST (%)	QST (%)	GST (%)	HST (%)
Alberta	0	0	5	0
British Columbia	7	0	5	0
Manitoba	7	0	5	0
New Brunswick	0	0	0	15
Newfoundland	0	0	0	15
Northwest Territories	0	0	5	0
Nova Scotia	0	0	0	15
Ontario	0	0	0	13
Prince Edward Island	0	0	0	15
Quebec	9.975	0	5	0
Saskatchewan	6	0	5	0
Yukon	0	0	5	0

General Requirements — R0129 Payment Procedures

R012909-85 Unemployment Taxes and Social Security Taxes

State unemployment tax rates vary not only from state to state, but also with the experience rating of the contractor. The federal unemployment tax rate is 6.2% of the first $7,000 of wages. This is reduced by a credit of up to 5.4% for timely payment to the state. The minimum federal unemployment tax is 0.6% after all credits.

Social security (FICA) for 2023 is estimated at time of publication to be 7.65% of wages up to $147,000.

R012909-86 Unemployment Tax by State

Information is from the U.S. Department of Labor, state unemployment tax rates.

State	Tax (%)	State	Tax (%)	State	Tax (%)	State	Tax (%)
Alabama	6.10	Illinois	7.625	Montana	6.30	Rhode Island	9.80
Alaska	5.4	Indiana	7.4	Nebraska	5.4	South Carolina	5.46
Arizona	20.93	Iowa	7.5	Nevada	5.4	South Dakota	9.3
Arkansas	14.2	Kansas	7.6	New Hampshire	8.5	Tennessee	10.0
California	6.2	Kentucky	9.5	New Jersey	5.8	Texas	6.3
Colorado	10.39	Louisiana	6.2	New Mexico	6.4	Utah	7.3
Connecticut	6.8	Maine	6.16	New York	9.9	Vermont	6.5
Delaware	8.20	Maryland	10.50	North Carolina	5.76	Virginia	6.43
District of Columbia	7.6	Massachusetts	14.37	North Dakota	9.69	Washington	6.02
Florida	5.4	Michigan	10.3	Ohio	10.2	West Virginia	8.5
Georgia	8.1	Minnesota	9.5	Oklahoma	7.5	Wisconsin	8.5
Hawaii	5.8	Mississippi	5.6	Oregon	5.4	Wyoming	8.5
Idaho	5.4	Missouri	6.75	Pennsylvania	9.93	Median	7.50%

R012909-90 Overtime

One way to improve the completion date of a project or eliminate negative float from a schedule is to compress activity duration times. This can be achieved by increasing the crew size or working overtime with the proposed crew.

To determine the costs of working overtime to compress activity duration times, consider the following examples. Below is an overtime efficiency and cost chart based on a five, six, or seven day week with an eight through twelve hour day. Payroll percentage increases for time and one half and double times are shown for the various working days.

Days per Week	Hours per Day	Production Efficiency					Payroll Cost Factors	
		1st Week	2nd Week	3rd Week	4th Week	Average 4 Weeks	@ 1-1/2 Times	@ 2 Times
5	8	100%	100%	100%	100%	100%	1.000	1.000
	9	100	100	95	90	96	1.056	1.111
	10	100	95	90	85	93	1.100	1.200
	11	95	90	75	65	81	1.136	1.273
	12	90	85	70	60	76	1.167	1.333
6	8	100	100	95	90	96	1.083	1.167
	9	100	95	90	85	93	1.130	1.259
	10	95	90	85	80	88	1.167	1.333
	11	95	85	70	65	79	1.197	1.394
	12	90	80	65	60	74	1.222	1.444
7	8	100	95	85	75	89	1.143	1.286
	9	95	90	80	70	84	1.183	1.365
	10	90	85	75	65	79	1.214	1.429
	11	85	80	65	60	73	1.240	1.481
	12	85	75	60	55	69	1.262	1.524

General Requirements — R0131 Project Management & Coordination

R013113-40 Builder's Risk Insurance

Builder's risk insurance is insurance on a building during construction. Premiums are paid by the owner or the contractor. Blasting, collapse and underground insurance would raise total insurance costs.

R013113-50 General Contractor's Overhead

There are two distinct types of overhead on a construction project: Project overhead and main office overhead. Project overhead includes those costs at a construction site not directly associated with the installation of construction materials. Examples of project overhead costs include the following:
1. Superintendent
2. Construction office and storage trailers
3. Temporary sanitary facilities
4. Temporary utilities
5. Security fencing
6. Photographs
7. Cleanup
8. Performance and payment bonds

The above project overhead items are also referred to as general requirements and therefore are estimated in Division 1. Division 1 is the first division listed in the CSI MasterFormat but it is usually the last division estimated. The sum of the costs in Divisions 1 through 49 is referred to as the sum of the direct costs.

All construction projects also include indirect costs. The primary components of indirect costs are the contractor's main office overhead and profit. The amount of the main office overhead expense varies depending on the following:
1. Owner's compensation
2. Project managers' and estimators' wages
3. Clerical support wages
4. Office rent and utilities
5. Corporate legal and accounting costs
6. Advertising
7. Automobile expenses
8. Association dues
9. Travel and entertainment expenses

These costs are usually calculated as a percentage of annual sales volume. This percentage can range from 35% for a small contractor doing less than $500,000 to 5% for a large contractor with sales in excess of $100 million.

R013113-55 Installing Contractor's Overhead

Installing contractors (subcontractors) also incur costs for general requirements and main office overhead.

Included within the total incl. overhead and profit costs is a percent mark-up for overhead that includes:
1. Compensation and benefits for office staff and project managers
2. Office rent, utilities, business equipment, and maintenance
3. Corporate legal and accounting costs
4. Advertising
5. Vehicle expenses (for office staff and project managers)
6. Association dues
7. Travel, entertainment
8. Insurance
9. Small tools and equipment

General Requirements — R0131 Project Management & Coordination

R013113-60 Workers' Compensation Insurance Rates by Trade

The table below tabulates the national averages for Workers' Compensation insurance rates by trade and type of building. The average "Insurance Rate" is multiplied by the "% of Building Cost" for each trade. This produces the "Workers' Compensation Cost" by % of total labor cost, to be added for each trade by building type to determine the weighted average Workers' Compensation rate for the building types analyzed.

Trade	Insurance Rate (% Labor Cost) Range	Insurance Rate Average	% of Building Cost Office Bldgs.	Schools & Apts.	Mfg.	Workers' Compensation Office Bldgs.	Schools & Apts.	Mfg.
Excavation, Grading, etc.	1.9 % to 14.7%	8.3	4.8%	4.9%	4.5%	0.40%	0.41%	0.37%
Piles & Foundations	2.1 to 32.0	17.0	7.1	5.2	8.7	1.21	0.88	1.48
Concrete	2.6 to 26.5	14.5	5.0	14.8	3.7	0.73	2.15	0.54
Masonry	2.9 to 48.0	25.5	6.9	7.5	1.9	1.76	1.91	0.48
Structural Steel	2.3 to 30.9	16.6	10.7	3.9	17.6	1.78	0.65	2.92
Miscellaneous & Ornamental Metals	2.2 to 22.6	12.4	2.8	4.0	3.6	0.35	0.50	0.45
Carpentry & Millwork	2.7 to 25.2	14.0	3.7	4.0	0.5	0.52	0.56	0.07
Metal or Composition Siding	3.2 to 129.7	66.4	2.3	0.3	4.3	1.53	0.20	2.86
Roofing	4.0 to 101.9	52.9	2.3	2.6	3.1	1.22	1.38	1.64
Doors & Hardware	2.5 to 26.3	14.4	0.9	1.4	0.4	0.13	0.20	0.06
Sash & Glazing	3.1 to 18.1	10.6	3.5	4.0	1.0	0.37	0.42	0.11
Lath & Plaster	1.2 to 32.4	16.8	3.3	6.9	0.8	0.55	1.16	0.13
Tile, Marble & Floors	1.7 to 19.5	10.6	2.6	3.0	0.5	0.28	0.32	0.05
Acoustical Ceilings	1.4 to 18.3	9.9	2.4	0.2	0.3	0.24	0.02	0.03
Painting	2.1 to 35.8	18.9	1.5	1.6	1.6	0.28	0.30	0.30
Interior Partitions	2.7 to 26.8	14.7	3.9	4.3	4.4	0.57	0.63	0.65
Miscellaneous Items	1.3 to 97.7	49.5	5.2	3.7	9.7	2.57	1.83	4.80
Elevators	1.2 to 8.3	4.8	2.1	1.1	2.2	0.10	0.05	0.11
Sprinklers	1.5 to 13.2	7.3	0.5	—	2.0	0.04	—	0.15
Plumbing	1.3 to 12.6	6.9	4.9	7.2	5.2	0.34	0.50	0.36
Heat., Vent., Air Conditioning	2.1 to 14.7	8.4	13.5	11.0	12.9	1.13	0.92	1.08
Electrical	1.4 to 9.5	5.5	10.1	8.4	11.1	0.56	0.46	0.61
Total	1.2 % to 129.7%	65.4	100.0%	100.0%	100.0%	16.66%	15.45%	19.25%
	Overall Weighted Average	17.12%						

Workers' Compensation Insurance Rates by States

The table below lists the weighted average Workers' Compensation base rate for each state with a factor comparing this with the national average of 8.4%.

State	Weighted Average	Factor	State	Weighted Average	Factor	State	Weighted Average	Factor
Alabama	21.1%	251	Kentucky	21.0%	250	North Dakota	7.6%	90
Alaska	13.3	158	Louisiana	31.3	373	Ohio	7.8	93
Arizona	11.6	138	Maine	14.9	177	Oklahoma	14.3	170
Arkansas	8.4	100	Maryland	15.8	188	Oregon	12.5	149
California	35.8	426	Massachusetts	16.1	192	Pennsylvania	34.9	415
Colorado	7.2	86	Michigan	9.0	107	Rhode Island	14.7	175
Connecticut	23.9	285	Minnesota	22.7	270	South Carolina	31.6	376
Delaware	15.9	189	Mississippi	15.1	180	South Dakota	13.3	158
District of Columbia	12.8	152	Missouri	23.1	275	Tennessee	9.6	114
Florida	13.4	160	Montana	14.6	174	Texas	5.7	68
Georgia	55.3	658	Nebraska	18.1	215	Utah	7.9	94
Hawaii	16.8	200	Nevada	13.5	161	Vermont	15.6	186
Idaho	14.2	169	New Hampshire	14.9	177	Virginia	10.4	124
Illinois	34.5	411	New Jersey	23.2	276	Washington	11.8	140
Indiana	5.8	69	New Mexico	23.7	282	West Virginia	6.6	79
Iowa	17.2	205	New York	28.2	336	Wisconsin	17.1	204
Kansas	10.3	123	North Carolina	20.8	248	Wyoming	8.4	100
			Weighted Average for U.S. is	17.1% of payroll = 100%				

The weighted average skilled worker rate for 35 trades is 17.12%. For bidding purposes, apply the full value of Workers' Compensation directly to total labor costs, or if labor is 38%, materials 42% and overhead and profit 20% of total cost, carry 38/80 x 17.12% = 8.13% of cost (before overhead and profit) into overhead. Rates vary not only from state to state but also with the experience rating of the contractor.

Rates are the most current available at the time of publication.

General Requirements — R0131 Project Management & Coordination

R013113-80 Performance Bond

This table shows the cost of a Performance Bond for a construction job scheduled to be completed in 12 months. Add 1% of the premium cost per month for jobs requiring more than 12 months to complete. The rates are "standard" rates offered to contractors that the bonding company considers financially sound and capable of doing the work. Preferred rates are offered by some bonding companies based upon financial strength of the contractor. Actual rates vary from contractor to contractor and from bonding company to bonding company. Contractors should prequalify through a bonding agency before submitting a bid on a contract that requires a bond.

Contract Amount	Building Construction Class B Projects	Highways & Bridges Class A New Construction	Class A-1 Highway Resurfacing
First $ 100,000 bid	$25.00 per M	$15.00 per M	$9.40 per M
Next 400,000 bid	$ 2,500 plus $15.00 per M	$ 1,500 plus $10.00 per M	$ 940 plus $7.20 per M
Next 2,000,000 bid	8,500 plus 10.00 per M	5,500 plus 7.00 per M	3,820 plus 5.00 per M
Next 2,500,000 bid	28,500 plus 7.50 per M	19,500 plus 5.50 per M	15,820 plus 4.50 per M
Next 2,500,000 bid	47,250 plus 7.00 per M	33,250 plus 5.00 per M	28,320 plus 4.50 per M
Over 7,500,000 bid	64,750 plus 6.00 per M	45,750 plus 4.50 per M	39,570 plus 4.00 per M

General Requirements — R0154 Construction Aids

R015423-10 Steel Tubular Scaffolding

On new construction, tubular scaffolding is efficient up to 60' high or five stories. Above this it is usually better to use a hung scaffolding if construction permits. Swing scaffolding operations may interfere with tenants. In this case, the tubular is more practical at all heights.

In repairing or cleaning the front of an existing building the cost of tubular scaffolding per S.F. of building front increases as the height increases above the first tier. The first tier cost is relatively high due to leveling and alignment.

The minimum efficient crew for erecting and dismantling is three workers. They can set up and remove 18 frame sections per day up to 5 stories high. For 6 to 12 stories high, a crew of four is most efficient. Use two or more on top and two on the bottom for handing up or hoisting. They can also set up and remove 18 frame sections per day. At 7' horizontal spacing, this will run about 800 S.F. per day of erecting and dismantling. Time for placing and removing planks must be added to the above. A crew of three can place and remove 72 planks per day up to 5 stories. For over 5 stories, a crew of four can place and remove 80 planks per day.

The table below shows the number of pieces required to erect tubular steel scaffolding for 1000 S.F. of building frontage. This area is made up of a scaffolding system that is 12 frames (11 bays) long by 2 frames high.

For jobs under twenty-five frames, add 50% to rental cost. Rental rates will be lower for jobs over three months duration. Large quantities for long periods can reduce rental rates by 20%.

Description of Component	Number of Pieces for 1000 S.F. of Building Front	Unit
5' Wide Standard Frame, 6'-4" High	24	Ea.
Leveling Jack & Plate	24	
Cross Brace	44	
Side Arm Bracket, 21"	12	
Guardrail Post	12	
Guardrail, 7' section	22	
Stairway Section	2	
Stairway Starter Bar	1	
Stairway Inside Handrail	2	
Stairway Outside Handrail	2	
Walk-Thru Frame Guardrail	2	

Scaffolding is often used as falsework over 15' high during construction of cast-in-place concrete beams and slabs. Two foot wide scaffolding is generally used for heavy beam construction. The span between frames depends upon the load to be carried with a maximum span of 5'.

Heavy duty shoring frames with a capacity of 10,000#/leg can be spaced up to 10' O.C. depending upon form support design and loading.

Scaffolding used as horizontal shoring requires less than half the material required with conventional shoring.

On new construction, erection is done by carpenters.

Rolling towers supporting horizontal shores can reduce labor and speed the job. For maintenance work, catwalks with spans up to 70' can be supported by the rolling towers.

General Requirements   R0154 Construction Aids

R015433-10   Contractor Equipment

Rental Rates shown elsewhere in the data set pertain to late model high quality machines in excellent working condition, rented from equipment dealers. Rental rates from contractors may be substantially lower than the rental rates from equipment dealers depending upon economic conditions; for older, less productive machines, reduce rates by a maximum of 15%. Any overtime must be added to the base rates. For shift work, rates are lower. Usual rule of thumb is 150% of one shift rate for two shifts; 200% for three shifts.

For periods of less than one week, operated equipment is usually more economical to rent than renting bare equipment and hiring an operator.

Costs to move equipment to a job site (mobilization) or from a job site (demobilization) are not included in rental rates, nor in any Equipment costs on any Unit Price line items or crew listings. These costs can be found elsewhere. If a piece of equipment is already at a job site, it is not appropriate to utilize mob/demob costs in an estimate again.

Rental rates vary throughout the country with larger cities generally having lower rates. Lease plans for new equipment are available for periods in excess of six months with a percentage of payments applying toward purchase.

Rental rates can also be treated as reimbursement costs for contractor-owned equipment. Owned equipment costs include depreciation, loan payments, interest, taxes, insurance, storage, and major repairs.

Monthly rental rates vary from 2% to 5% of the cost of the equipment depending on the anticipated life of the equipment and its wearing parts. Weekly rates are about 1/3 the monthly rates and daily rental rates are about 1/3 the weekly rates.

The hourly operating costs for each piece of equipment include costs to the user such as fuel, oil, lubrication, normal expendables for the equipment, and a percentage of the mechanic's wages chargeable to maintenance. The hourly operating costs listed do not include the operator's wages.

The daily cost for equipment used in the standard crews is figured by dividing the weekly rate by five, then adding eight times the hourly operating cost to give the total daily equipment cost, not including the operator. This figure is in the right hand column of the Equipment listings under Equipment Cost/Day.

Pile Driving rates shown for the pile hammer and extractor do not include leads, cranes, boilers or compressors. Vibratory pile driving requires an added field specialist during set-up and pile driving operation for the electric model. The hydraulic model requires a field specialist for set-up only. Up to 125 reuses of sheet piling are possible using vibratory drivers. For normal conditions, crane capacity for hammer type and size is as follows.

Crane Capacity	Hammer Type and Size		
	Air or Steam	Diesel	Vibratory
25 ton	to 8,750 ft.-lb.		70 H.P.
40 ton	15,000 ft.-lb.	to 32,000 ft.-lb.	170 H.P.
60 ton	25,000 ft.-lb.		300 H.P.
100 ton		112,000 ft.-lb.	

Cranes should be specified for the job by size, building and site characteristics, availability, performance characteristics, and duration of time required.

Backhoes & Shovels rent for about the same as equivalent size cranes but maintenance and operating expenses are higher. The crane operator's rate must be adjusted for high boom heights. Average adjustments: for 150' boom add 2% per hour; over 185', add 4% per hour; over 210', add 6% per hour; over 250', add 8% per hour and over 295', add 12% per hour.

Tower Cranes of the climbing or static type have jibs from 50' to 200' and capacities at maximum reach range from 4,000 to 14,000 pounds. Lifting capacities increase up to maximum load as the hook radius decreases.

Typical rental rates, based on purchase price, are about 2% to 3% per month.

Erection and dismantling run between 500 and 2000 labor hours. Climbing operation takes 10 labor hours per 20' climb. Crane dead time is about 5 hours per 40' climb. If crane is bolted to side of the building add cost of ties and extra mast sections. Climbing cranes have from 80' to 180' of mast while static cranes have 80' to 800' of mast.

Truck Cranes can be converted to tower cranes by using tower attachments. Mast heights over 400' have been used.

A single 100' high material **Hoist and Tower** can be erected and dismantled in about 400 labor hours; a double 100' high hoist and tower in about 600 labor hours. Erection times for additional heights are 3 and 4 labor hours per vertical foot respectively up to 150', and 4 to 5 labor hours per vertical foot over 150' high. A 40' high portable Buck hoist takes about 160 labor hours to erect and dismantle. Additional heights take 2 labor hours per vertical foot to 80' and 3 labor hours per vertical foot for the next 100'. Most material hoists do not meet local code requirements for carrying personnel.

A 150' high **Personnel Hoist** requires about 500 to 800 labor hours to erect and dismantle. Budget erection time at 5 labor hours per vertical foot for all trades. Local code requirements or labor scarcity requiring overtime can add up to 50% to any of the above erection costs.

Earthmoving Equipment: The selection of earthmoving equipment depends upon the type and quantity of material, moisture content, haul distance, haul road, time available, and equipment available. Short haul cut and fill operations may require dozers only, while another operation may require excavators, a fleet of trucks, and spreading and compaction equipment. Stockpiled material and granular material are easily excavated with front end loaders. Scrapers are most economically used with hauls between 300' and 1-1/2 miles if adequate haul roads can be maintained. Shovels are often used for blasted rock and any material where a vertical face of 8' or more can be excavated. Special conditions may dictate the use of draglines, clamshells, or backhoes. Spreading and compaction equipment must be matched to the soil characteristics, the compaction required and the rate the fill is being supplied.

R015433-15   Heavy Lifting

Hydraulic Climbing Jacks

The use of hydraulic heavy lift systems is an alternative to conventional type crane equipment. The lifting, lowering, pushing, or pulling mechanism is a hydraulic climbing jack moving on a square steel jackrod from 1-5/8" to 4" square, or a steel cable. The jackrod or cable can be vertical or horizontal, stationary or movable, depending on the individual application. When the jackrod is stationary, the climbing jack will climb the rod and push or pull the load along with itself. When the climbing jack is stationary, the jackrod is movable with the load attached to the end and the climbing jack will lift or lower the jackrod with the attached load. The heavy lift system is normally operated by a single control lever located at the hydraulic pump.

The system is flexible in that one or more climbing jacks can be applied wherever a load support point is required, and the rate of lift synchronized.

Economic benefits have been demonstrated on projects such as: erection of ground assembled roofs and floors, complete bridge spans, girders and trusses, towers, chimney liners and steel vessels, storage tanks, and heavy machinery. Other uses are raising and lowering offshore work platforms, caissons, tunnel sections and pipelines.

General Requirements — R0154 Construction Aids

R015436-50 Mobilization

Costs to move rented construction equipment to a job site from an equipment dealer's or contractor's yard (mobilization) or off the job site (demobilization) are not included in the rental or operating rates, nor in the equipment cost on a unit price line or in a crew listing. These costs can be found consolidated in the Mobilization section of the data and elsewhere in particular site work sections. If a piece of equipment is already on the job site, it is not appropriate to include mob/demob costs in a new estimate that requires use of that equipment. The following table identifies approximate sizes of rented construction equipment that would be hauled on a towed trailer. Because this listing is not all-encompassing, the user can infer as to what size trailer might be required for a piece of equipment not listed.

3-ton Trailer	20-ton Trailer	40-ton Trailer	50-ton Trailer
20 H.P. Excavator	110 H.P. Excavator	200 H.P. Excavator	270 H.P. Excavator
50 H.P. Skid Steer	165 H.P. Dozer	300 H.P. Dozer	Small Crawler Crane
35 H.P. Roller	150 H.P. Roller	400 H.P. Scraper	500 H.P. Scraper
40 H.P. Trencher	Backhoe	450 H.P. Art. Dump Truck	500 H.P. Art. Dump Truck

Existing Conditions — R0241 Demolition

R024119-10 Demolition Defined

Whole Building Demolition - Demolition of the whole building with no concern for any particular building element, component, or material type being demolished. This type of demolition is accomplished with large pieces of construction equipment that break up the structure, load it into trucks and haul it to a disposal site, but disposal or dump fees are not included. Demolition of below-grade foundation elements, such as footings, foundation walls, grade beams, slabs on grade, etc., is not included. Certain mechanical equipment containing flammable liquids or ozone-depleting refrigerants, electric lighting elements, communication equipment components, and other building elements may contain hazardous waste, and must be removed, either selectively or carefully, as hazardous waste before the building can be demolished.

Foundation Demolition - Demolition of below-grade foundation footings, foundation walls, grade beams, and slabs on grade. This type of demolition is accomplished by hand or pneumatic hand tools, and does not include saw cutting, or handling, loading, hauling, or disposal of the debris.

Gutting - Removal of building interior finishes and electrical/mechanical systems down to the load-bearing and sub-floor elements of the rough building frame, with no concern for any particular building element, component, or material type being demolished. This type of demolition is accomplished by hand or pneumatic hand tools, and includes loading into trucks, but not hauling, disposal or dump fees, scaffolding, or shoring. Certain mechanical equipment containing flammable liquids or ozone-depleting refrigerants, electric lighting elements, communication equipment components, and other building elements may contain hazardous waste, and must be removed, either selectively or carefully, as hazardous waste, before the building is gutted.

Selective Demolition - Demolition of a selected building element, component, or finish, with some concern for surrounding or adjacent elements, components, or finishes (see the first Subdivision (s) at the beginning of appropriate Divisions). This type of demolition is accomplished by hand or pneumatic hand tools, and does not include handling, loading, storing, hauling, or disposal of the debris, scaffolding, or shoring. "Gutting" methods may be used in order to save time, but damage that is caused to surrounding or adjacent elements, components, or finishes may have to be repaired at a later time.

Careful Removal - Removal of a piece of service equipment, building element or component, or material type, with great concern for both the removed item and surrounding or adjacent elements, components or finishes. The purpose of careful removal may be to protect the removed item for later re-use, preserve a higher salvage value of the removed item, or replace an item while taking care to protect surrounding or adjacent elements, components, connections, or finishes from cosmetic and/or structural damage. An approximation of the time required to perform this type of removal is 1/3 to 1/2 the time it would take to install a new item of like kind (see Reference Number R220105-10). This type of removal is accomplished by hand or pneumatic hand tools, and does not include loading, hauling, or storing the removed item, scaffolding, shoring, or lifting equipment.

Cutout Demolition - Demolition of a small quantity of floor, wall, roof, or other assembly, with concern for the appearance and structural integrity of the surrounding materials. This type of demolition is accomplished by hand or pneumatic hand tools, and does not include saw cutting, handling, loading, hauling, or disposal of debris, scaffolding, or shoring.

Rubbish Handling - Work activities that involve handling, loading or hauling of debris. Generally, the cost of rubbish handling must be added to the cost of all types of demolition, with the exception of whole building demolition.

Minor Site Demolition - Demolition of site elements outside the footprint of a building. This type of demolition is accomplished by hand or pneumatic hand tools, or with larger pieces of construction equipment, and may include loading a removed item onto a truck (check the Crew for equipment used). It does not include saw cutting, hauling or disposal of debris, and, sometimes, handling or loading.

R024119-20 Dumpsters

Dumpster rental costs on construction sites are presented in two ways.

The cost per week rental includes the delivery of the dumpster; its pulling or emptying once per week, and its final removal. The assumption is made that the dumpster contractor could choose to empty a dumpster by simply bringing in an empty unit and removing the full one. These costs also include the disposal of the materials in the dumpster.

The Alternate Pricing can be used when actual planned conditions are not approximated by the weekly numbers. For example, these lines can be used when a dumpster is needed for 4 weeks and will need to be emptied 2 or 3 times per week. Conversely the Alternate Pricing lines can be used when a dumpster will be rented for several weeks or months but needs to be emptied only a few times over this period.

Existing Conditions — R0265 Underground Storage Tank Removal

R026510-20 Underground Storage Tank Removal

Underground Storage Tank Removal can be divided into two categories: Non-Leaking and Leaking. Prior to removing an underground storage tank, tests should be made, with the proper authorities present, to determine whether a tank has been leaking or the surrounding soil has been contaminated.

To safely remove Liquid Underground Storage Tanks:
1. Excavate to the top of the tank.
2. Disconnect all piping.
3. Open all tank vents and access ports.
4. Remove all liquids and/or sludge.
5. Purge the tank with an inert gas.
6. Provide access to the inside of the tank and clean out the interior using proper personal protective equipment (PPE).
7. Excavate soil surrounding the tank using proper PPE for on-site personnel.
8. Pull and properly dispose of the tank.
9. Clean up the site of all contaminated material.
10. Install new tanks or close the excavation.

Existing Conditions — R0282 Asbestos Remediation

R028213-20 Asbestos Removal Process

Asbestos removal is accomplished by a specialty contractor who understands the federal and state regulations regarding the handling and disposal of the material. The process of asbestos removal is divided into many individual steps. An accurate estimate can be calculated only after all the steps have been priced.

The steps are generally as follows:
1. Obtain an asbestos abatement plan from an industrial hygienist.
2. Monitor the air quality in and around the removal area and along the path of travel between the removal area and transport area. This establishes the background contamination.
3. Construct a two part decontamination chamber at entrance to removal area.
4. Install a HEPA filter to create a negative pressure in the removal area.
5. Install wall, floor and ceiling protection as required by the plan, usually 2 layers of fireproof 6 mil polyethylene.
6. Industrial hygienist visually inspects work area to verify compliance with plan.
7. Provide temporary supports for conduit and piping affected by the removal process.
8. Proceed with asbestos removal and bagging process. Monitor air quality as described in Step #2. Discontinue operations when contaminate levels exceed applicable standards.
9. Document the legal disposal of materials in accordance with EPA standards.
10. Thoroughly clean removal area including all ledges, crevices and surfaces.
11. Post abatement inspection by industrial hygienist to verify plan compliance.
12. Provide a certificate from a licensed industrial hygienist attesting that contaminate levels are within acceptable standards before returning area to regular use.

Concrete — R0330 Cast-In-Place Concrete

R033053-60 Maximum Depth of Frost Penetration in Inches

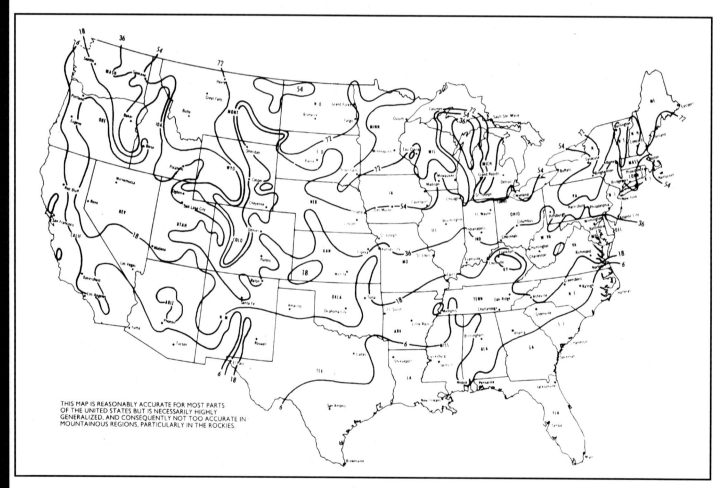

THIS MAP IS REASONABLY ACCURATE FOR MOST PARTS OF THE UNITED STATES BUT IS NECESSARILY HIGHLY GENERALIZED, AND CONSEQUENTLY NOT TOO ACCURATE IN MOUNTAINOUS REGIONS, PARTICULARLY IN THE ROCKIES.

Metals

R0505 Common Work Results for Metals

R050521-20 Welded Structural Steel

Usual weight reductions with welded design run 10% to 20% compared with bolted or riveted connections. This amounts to about the same total cost compared with bolted structures since field welding is more expensive than bolts. For normal spans of 18' to 24' figure 6 to 7 connections per ton.

Trusses — For welded trusses add 4% to weight of main members for connections. Up to 15% less steel can be expected in a welded truss compared to one that is shop bolted. Cost of erection is the same whether shop bolted or welded.

General — Typical electrodes for structural steel welding are E6010, E6011, E60T and E70T. Typical buildings vary between 2# to 8# of weld rod per ton of steel. Buildings utilizing continuous design require about three times as much welding as conventional welded structures. In estimating field erection by welding, it is best to use the average linear feet of weld per ton to arrive at the welding cost per ton. The type, size and position of the weld will have a direct bearing on the cost per linear foot. A typical field welder will deposit 1.8# to 2# of weld rod per hour manually. Using semiautomatic methods can increase production by as much as 50% to 75%.

Special Construction

R1311 Swimming Pools

R131113-20 Swimming Pools

Pool prices given per square foot of surface area include pool structure, filter and chlorination equipment, pumps, related piping, ladders/steps, maintenance kit, skimmer and vacuum system. Decks and electrical service to equipment are not included.

Residential in-ground pool construction can be divided into two categories: vinyl lined and gunite. Vinyl lined pool walls are constructed of different materials including wood, concrete, plastic or metal. The bottom is often graded with sand over which the vinyl liner is installed. Vermiculite or soil cement bottoms may be substituted for an added cost.

Gunite pool construction is used both in residential and municipal installations. These structures are steel reinforced for strength and finished with a white cement limestone plaster.

Municipal pools will have a higher cost because plumbing codes require more expensive materials, chlorination equipment and higher filtration rates.

Municipal pools greater than 1,800 S.F. require gutter systems to control waves. This gutter may be formed into the concrete wall. Often a vinyl/stainless steel gutter or gutter/wall system is specified, which will raise the pool cost.

Competition pools usually require tile bottoms and sides with contrasting lane striping, which will also raise the pool cost.

Fire Suppression

R2112 Fire-Suppression Standpipes

R211226-10 Standpipe Systems

The basis for standpipe system design is National Fire Protection Association NFPA 14. However, the authority having jurisdiction should be consulted for special conditions, local requirements, and approval.

Standpipe systems, properly designed and maintained, are an effective and valuable time saving aid for extinguishing fires, especially in the upper stories of tall buildings, the interior of large commercial or industrial malls, or other areas where construction features or access make the laying of temporary hose lines time consuming and/or hazardous. Standpipes are frequently installed with automatic sprinkler systems for maximum protection.

There are three general classes of service for standpipe systems:
Class I A system with 2-1/2" (65 mm) hose connections for Fire Department use and those trained in handling heavy fire streams.
Class II A system with either 1-1/2" (40 mm) hose stations for use by trained personnel or a hose connection for the fire department's use.
Class III A system with 1-1/2" (40 mm) hose stations for trained personnel and 2-1/2" (65 mm) hose connections for fire department use.

Standpipe systems are also classified by the way water is supplied to the system. The following are the types of systems:
Automatic Dry Standpipe A system containing air or nitrogen under pressure, with a water supply capable of meeting water demands at all times. Opening of a valve allows the air/nitrogen to dissipate, releasing the pressurized dry valve's clapper to open and fill the system with water.
Automatic Wet Standpipe A system containing water with a water supply capable of meeting system demands at all times. Open a valve or connection and water will immediately flow.
Combination Standpipe A system that supplies both sprinkler systems and fire department/hose connections. Manual operation of approved remote control devices located at each hose station.
Manual Dry Standpipe A system not containing water. Water is manually pumped into the system by means of a fire department connection attached to a water supply.
Semiautomatic Dry Standpipe A system with an attached water supply held back at a valve which requires remote activation to open and allow flow of water into the system.
Wet Standpipe A system containing water at all times.

Reprinted with permission from NFPA 14-2013, *Installation of Standpipe and Hose Systems*, Copyright © 2013, National Fire Protection Association, Quincy, MA. This reprinted material is not the complete and official position of the NFPA on the referenced subject, which is represented only by the standard in its entirety.

Fire Suppression
R2112 Fire-Suppression Standpipes

R211226-20 NFPA 14 Basic Standpipe Design

Class	Design-Use	Pipe Size Minimums	Water Supply Minimums
Class I	2 1/2" hose connection on each floor All areas within 150' of an exit in every exit stairway Fire Department Trained Personnel	Height to 100', 4" dia. Heights above 100', 6" dia. (275' max. except with pressure regulators 400' max.)	For each standpipe riser 500 GPM flow For common supply pipe allow 500 GPM for first standpipe plus 250 GPM for each additional standpipe (2500 GPM max. total) 30 min. duration 65 PSI at 500 GPM
Class II	1 1/2" hose connection with hose on each floor All areas within 130' of hose connection measured along path of hose travel Occupant personnel	Height to 50', 2" dia. Height above 50', 2 1/2" dia.	For each standpipe riser 100 GPM flow For multiple riser common supply pipe 100 GPM 300 min. duration, 65 PSI at 100 GPM
Class III	Both of above. Class I valved connections will meet Class III with additional 2 1/2" by 1 1/2" adapter and 1 1/2" hose.	Same as Class I	Same as Class I

*Note: Where 2 or more standpipes are installed in the same building or section of building they shall be interconnected at the bottom.

Combined Systems

Combined systems are systems where the risers supply both automatic sprinklers and 2-1/2" hose connection outlets for fire department use. In such a system the sprinkler spacing pattern shall be in accordance with NFPA 13 while the risers and supply piping will be sized in accordance with NFPA 14. When the building is completely sprinklered the risers may be sized by hydraulic calculation. The minimum size riser for buildings not completely sprinklered is 6".

The minimum water supply of a completely sprinklered, light hazard, high-rise occupancy building will be 500 GPM while the supply required for other types of completely sprinklered high-rise buildings is 1000 GPM.

General System Requirements

1. Approved valves will be provided at the riser for controlling branch lines to hose outlets.
2. A hose valve will be provided at each outlet for attachment of hose.
3. Where pressure at any standpipe outlet exceeds 100 PSI a pressure reducer must be installed to limit the pressure to 100 PSI. Note that the pressure head due to gravity in 100' of riser is 43.4 PSI. This must be overcome by city pressure, fire pumps, or gravity tanks to provide adequate pressure at the top of the riser.
4. Each hose valve on a wet system having linen hose shall have an automatic drip connection to prevent valve leakage from entering the hose.
5. Each riser will have a valve to isolate it from the rest of the system.
6. One or more fire department connections as an auxiliary supply shall be provided for each Class I or Class III standpipe system. In buildings having two or more zones, a connection will be provided for each zone.
7. There will be no shutoff valve in the fire department connection, but a check valve will be located in the line before it joins the system.
8. All hose connections street side will be identified on a cast plate or fitting as to purpose.

Reprinted with permission from NFPA 14-2013, *Installation of Standpipe and Hose Systems*, Copyright © 2013, National Fire Protection Association, Quincy, MA. This reprinted material is not the complete and official position of the NFPA on the referenced subject, which is represented only by the standard in its entirety.

Fire Suppression — R2113 Fire-Suppression Sprinkler Systems

R211313-10 Sprinkler Systems (Automatic)

Sprinkler systems may be classified by type as follows:
1. **Wet Pipe System.** A system employing automatic sprinklers attached to a piping system containing water and connected to a water supply so that water discharges immediately from sprinklers opened by a fire.
2. **Dry Pipe System.** A system employing automatic sprinklers attached to a piping system containing air under pressure, the release of which as from the opening of sprinklers permits the water pressure to open a valve known as a "dry pipe valve". The water then flows into the piping system and out the opened sprinklers.
3. **Pre-Action System.** A system employing automatic sprinklers attached to a piping system containing air that may or may not be under pressure, with a supplemental heat responsive system of generally more sensitive characteristics than the automatic sprinklers themselves, installed in the same areas as the sprinklers; actuation of the heat responsive system, as from a fire, opens a valve which permits water to flow into the sprinkler piping system and to be discharged from any sprinklers which may be open.
4. **Deluge System.** A system employing open sprinklers attached to a piping system connected to a water supply through a valve which is opened by the operation of a heat responsive system installed in the same areas as the sprinklers. When this valve opens, water flows into the piping system and discharges from all sprinklers attached thereto.
5. **Combined Dry Pipe and Pre-Action Sprinkler System.** A system employing automatic sprinklers attached to a piping system containing air under pressure with a supplemental heat responsive system of generally more sensitive characteristics than the automatic sprinklers themselves, installed in the same areas as the sprinklers; operation of the heat responsive system, as from a fire, actuates tripping devices which open dry pipe valves simultaneously and without loss of air pressure in the system. Operation of the heat responsive system also opens approved air exhaust valves at the end of the feed main which facilitates the filling of the system with water which usually precedes the opening of sprinklers. The heat responsive system also serves as an automatic fire alarm system.
6. **Limited Water Supply System.** A system employing automatic sprinklers and conforming to these standards but supplied by a pressure tank of limited capacity.
7. **Chemical Systems.** Systems using halon, carbon dioxide, dry chemical or high expansion foam as selected for special requirements. Agent may extinguish flames by chemically inhibiting flame propagation, suffocate flames by excluding oxygen, interrupting chemical action of oxygen uniting with fuel or sealing and cooling the combustion center.
8. **Firecycle System.** Firecycle is a fixed fire protection sprinkler system utilizing water as its extinguishing agent. It is a time delayed, recycling, preaction type which automatically shuts the water off when heat is reduced below the detector operating temperature and turns the water back on when that temperature is exceeded. The system senses a fire condition through a closed circuit electrical detector system which controls water flow to the fire automatically. Batteries supply up to 90 hour emergency power supply for system operation. The piping system is dry (until water is required) and is monitored with pressurized air. Should any leak in the system piping occur, an alarm will sound, but water will not enter the system until heat is sensed by a firecycle detector.

Area coverage sprinkler systems may be laid out and fed from the supply in any one of several patterns as shown below. It is desirable, if possible, to utilize a central feed and achieve a shorter flow path from the riser to the furthest sprinkler. This permits use of the smallest sizes of pipe possible with resulting savings.

Reprinted with permission from NFPA 13-2013, *Installation of Sprinkler Systems*, Copyright © 2012, National Fire Protection Association, Quincy, MA. This reprinted material is not the complete and official position of the NFPA on the referenced subject, which is represented only by the standard in its entirety.

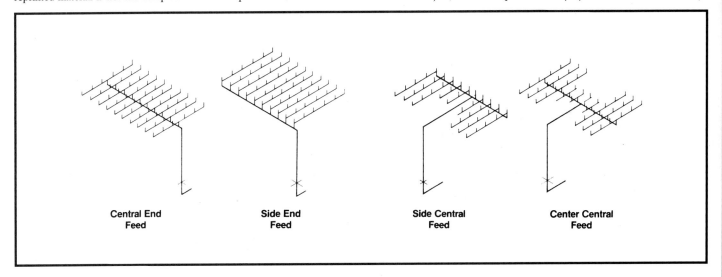

Central End Feed Side End Feed Side Central Feed Center Central Feed

Fire Suppression

R2113 Fire-Suppression Sprinkler Systems

R211313-20 System Classification

System Classification

Rules for installation of sprinkler systems vary depending on the classification of occupancy falling into one of three categories as follows:

Light Hazard Occupancy

The protection area allotted per sprinkler should not exceed 225 S.F., with the maximum distance between lines and sprinklers on lines being 15'. The sprinklers do not need to be staggered. Branch lines should not exceed eight sprinklers on either side of a cross main. Each large area requiring more than 100 sprinklers and without a sub-dividing partition should be supplied by feed mains or risers sized for ordinary hazard occupancy.
Maximum system area = 52,000 S.F.

Included in this group are:

Churches
Clubs
Educational
Hospitals
Institutional
Libraries
(except large stack rooms)
Museums

Nursing Homes
Offices
Residential
Restaurants
Theaters and Auditoriums
(except stages and prosceniums)
Unused Attics

Ordinary Hazard Occupancy

The protection area allotted per sprinkler shall not exceed 130 S.F. of noncombustible ceiling and 130 S.F. of combustible ceiling. The maximum allowable distance between sprinkler lines and sprinklers on line is 15'. Sprinklers shall be staggered if the distance between heads exceeds 12'. Branch lines should not exceed eight sprinklers on either side of a cross main.
Maximum system area = 52,000 S.F.

Included in this group are:

Group 1
Automotive Parking and Showrooms
Bakeries
Beverage manufacturing
Canneries
Dairy Products Manufacturing/Processing
Electronic Plans
Glass and Glass Products Manufacturing
Laundries
Restaurant Service Areas

Group 2
Cereal Mills
Chemical Plants—Ordinary
Confectionery Products
Distilleries
Dry Cleaners
Feed Mills
Horse Stables
Leather Goods Manufacturing
Libraries—Large Stack Room Areas
Machine Shops
Metal Working
Mercantile
Paper and Pulp Mills
Paper Process Plants
Piers and Wharves
Post Offices
Printing and Publishing
Repair Garages
Stages
Textile Manufacturing
Tire Manufacturing
Tobacco Products Manufacturing
Wood Machining
Wood Product Assembly

Extra Hazard Occupancy

The protection area allotted per sprinkler shall not exceed 100 S.F. of noncombustible ceiling and 100 S.F. of combustible ceiling. The maximum allowable distance between lines and between sprinklers on lines is 12'. Sprinklers on alternate lines shall be staggered if the distance between sprinklers on lines exceeds 8'. Branch lines should not exceed six sprinklers on either side of a cross main.
Maximum system area:
  Design by pipe schedule = 25,000 S.F.
  Design by hydraulic calculation = 40,000 S.F.

Included in this group are:

Group 1
Aircraft hangars
Combustible Hydraulic Fluid Use Area
Die Casting
Metal Extruding
Plywood/Particle Board Manufacturing
Printing (inks with flash points < 100 degrees F
Rubber Reclaiming, Compounding, Drying, Milling, Vulcanizing
Saw Mills
Textile Picking, Opening, Blending, Garnetting, Carding, Combing of Cotton, Synthetics, Wood Shoddy, or Burlap
Upholstering with Plastic Foams

Group 2
Asphalt Saturating
Flammable Liquids Spraying
Flow Coating
Manufactured/Modular Home Building Assemblies (where finished enclosure is present and has combustible interiors)
Open Oil Quenching
Plastics Processing
Solvent Cleaning
Varnish and Paint Dipping

Reprinted with permission from NFPA 13-2013, *Installation of Sprinkler Systems*, Copyright © 2012, National Fire Protection Association, Quincy, MA. This reprinted material is not the complete and official position of the NFPA on the referenced subject, which is represented only by the standard in its entirety.

Fire Suppression — R2113 Fire-Suppression Sprinkler Systems

R211313-40   Adjustment for Sprinkler/Standpipe Installations

Quality/Complexity Multiplier (For all installations)

Economy installation, add	0 to 5%
Good quality, medium complexity, add	5 to 15%
Above average quality and complexity, add	15 to 25%

Plumbing — R2201 Operation & Maintenance of Plumbing

R220102-20   Labor Adjustment Factors

Labor Adjustment Factors are provided for Divisions 21, 22, and 23 to assist the mechanical estimator account for the various complexities and special conditions of any particular project. While a single percentage has been entered on each line of Division 22 01 02.20, it should be understood that these are just suggested midpoints of ranges of values commonly used by mechanical estimators. They may be increased or decreased depending on the severity of the special conditions.

The group for "existing occupied buildings" has been the subject of requests for explanation. Actually there are two stages to this group: buildings that are existing and "finished" but unoccupied, and those that also are occupied. Buildings that are "finished" may result in higher labor costs due to the workers having to be more careful not to damage finished walls, ceilings, floors, etc. and may necessitate special protective coverings and barriers. Also corridor bends and doorways may not accommodate long pieces of pipe or larger pieces of equipment. Work above an already hung ceiling can be very time consuming. The addition of occupants may force the work to be done on premium time (nights and/or weekends), eliminate the possible use of some preferred tools such as pneumatic drivers, powder charged drivers etc. The estimator should evaluate the access to the work area and just how the work is going to be accomplished to arrive at an increase in labor costs over "normal" new construction productivity.

R220105-10   Demolition (Selective vs. Removal for Replacement)

Demolition can be divided into two basic categories.

One type of demolition involves the removal of material with no concern for its replacement. The labor-hours to estimate this work are found under "Selective Demolition" in the Fire Protection, Plumbing and HVAC Divisions. It is selective in that individual items or all the material installed as a system or trade grouping such as plumbing or heating systems are removed. This may be accomplished by the easiest way possible, such as sawing, torch cutting, or sledge hammering as well as simple unbolting.

The second type of demolition is the removal of some items for repair or replacement. This removal may involve careful draining, opening of unions, disconnecting and tagging electrical connections, capping pipes/ducts to prevent entry of debris or leakage of the material contained as well as transporting the item away from its in-place location to a truck/dumpster. An approximation of the time required to accomplish this type of demolition is to use half of the time indicated as necessary to install a new unit. For example: installation of a new pump might be listed as requiring 6 labor-hours so if we had to estimate the removal of the old pump we would allow an additional 3 hours for a total of 9 hours. That is, the complete replacement of a defective pump with a new pump would be estimated to take 9 labor-hours.

Plumbing
R2205 Common Work Results for Plumbing

R220523-80 Valve Materials

VALVE MATERIALS

Bronze:
Bronze is one of the oldest materials used to make valves. It is most commonly used in hot and cold water systems and other non-corrosive services. It is often used as a seating surface in larger iron body valves to ensure tight closure.

Carbon Steel:
Carbon steel is a high strength material. Therefore, valves made from this metal are used in higher pressure services, such as steam lines up to 600 psi at 850°F. Many steel valves are available with butt-weld ends for economy and are generally used in high pressure steam service as well as other higher pressure non-corrosive services.

Forged Steel:
Valves from tough carbon steel are used in service up to 2000 psi and temperatures up to 1000°F in Gate, Globe and Check valves.

Iron:
Valves are normally used in medium to large pipe lines to control non-corrosive fluid and gases, where pressures do not exceed 250 psi at 450° or 500 psi cold water, oil or gas.

Stainless Steel:
Developed steel alloys can be used in over 90% corrosive services.

Plastic PVC:
This is used in a great variety of valves generally in high corrosive service with lower temperatures and pressures.

VALVE SERVICE PRESSURES

Pressure ratings on valves provide an indication of the safe operating pressure for a valve at some elevated temperature. This temperature is dependent upon the materials used and the fabrication of the valve. When specific data is not available, a good "rule-of-thumb" to follow is the temperature of saturated steam on the primary rating indicated on the valve body. Example: The valve has the number 150S printed on the side indicating 150 psi and hence, a maximum operating temperature of 367°F (temperature of saturated steam and 150 psi).

DEFINITIONS

1. "WOG" – Water, oil, gas (cold working pressures).
2. "SWP" – Steam working pressure.
3. 100% area (full port) – means the area through the valve is equal to or greater than the area of standard pipe.
4. "Standard Opening" – means that the area through the valve is less than the area of standard pipe and therefore these valves should be used only where restriction of flow is unimportant.
5. "Round Port" – means the valve has a full round opening through the plug and body, of the same size and area as standard pipe.
6. "Rectangular Port" – valves have rectangular shaped ports through the plug body. The area of the port is either equal to 100% of the area of standard pipe, or restricted (standard opening). In either case it is clearly marked.
7. "ANSI" – American National Standards Institute.

R220523-90 Valve Selection Considerations

INTRODUCTION: In any piping application, valve performance is critical. Valves should be selected to give the best performance at the lowest cost.

The following is a list of performance characteristics generally expected of valves.
1. Stopping flow or starting it.
2. Throttling flow (Modulation).
3. Flow direction changing.
4. Checking backflow (Permitting flow in only one direction).
5. Relieving or regulating pressure.

In order to properly select the right valve, some facts must be determined.

A. What liquid or gas will flow through the valve?
B. Does the fluid contain suspended particles?
C. Does the fluid remain in liquid form at all times?
D. Which metals does fluid corrode?
E. What are the pressure and temperature limits? (As temperature and pressure rise, so will the price of the valve.)
F. Is there constant line pressure?
G. Is the valve merely an on-off valve?
H. Will checking of backflow be required?
I. Will the valve operate frequently or infrequently?

Valves are classified by design type into such classifications as Gate, Globe, Angle, Check, Ball, Butterfly and Plug. They are also classified by end connection, stem, pressure restrictions and material such as bronze, cast iron, etc. Each valve has a specific use. A quality valve used correctly will provide a lifetime of trouble-free service, but a high quality valve installed in the wrong service may require frequent attention.

R2205 Common Work Results for Plumbing

STEM TYPES
(OS & Y)—Rising Stem-Outside Screw and Yoke

Offers a visual indication of whether the valve is open or closed. Recommended where high temperatures, corrosives, and solids in the line might cause damage to inside-valve stem threads. The stem threads are engaged by the yoke bushing so the stem rises through the hand wheel as it is turned.

(R.S.)—Rising Stem-Inside Screw

Adequate clearance for operation must be provided because both the hand wheel and the stem rise.
The valve wedge position is indicated by the position of the stem and hand wheel.

(N.R.S.)—Non-Rising Stem-Inside Screw

A minimum clearance is required for operating this type of valve. Excessive wear or damage to stem threads inside the valve may be caused by heat, corrosion, and solids. Because the hand wheel and stem do not rise, wedge position cannot be visually determined.

VALVE TYPES
Gate Valves

Provide full flow, minute pressure drop, minimum turbulence and minimum fluid trapped in the line.
They are normally used where operation is infrequent.

Globe Valves

Globe valves are designed for throttling and/or frequent operation with positive shut-off. Particular attention must be paid to the several types of seating materials available to avoid unnecessary wear. The seats must be compatible with the fluid in service and may be composition or metal. The configuration of the Globe valve opening causes turbulence which results in increased resistance. Most bronze Globe valves are rising stem-inside screw, but they are also available on O.S. & Y.

Angle Valves

The fundamental difference between the Angle valve and the Globe valve is the fluid flow through the Angle valve. It makes a 90° turn and offers less resistance to flow than the Globe valve while replacing an elbow. An Angle valve thus reduces the number of joints and installation time.

Plumbing — R2205 Common Work Results for Plumbing

Check Valves

Check valves are designed to prevent backflow by automatically seating when the direction of fluid is reversed.
Swing Check valves are generally installed with Gate-valves, as they provide comparable full flow. Usually recommended for lines where flow velocities are low and should not be used on lines with pulsating flow. Recommended for horizontal installation, or in vertical lines only where flow is upward.

Lift Check Valves

These are commonly used with Globe and Angle valves since they have similar diaphragm seating arrangements and are recommended for preventing backflow of steam, air, gas and water, and on vapor lines with high flow velocities. For horizontal lines, horizontal lift checks should be used and vertical lift checks for vertical lines.

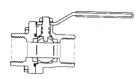

Ball Valves

Ball valves are light and easily installed, yet because of modern elastomeric seats, provide tight closure. Flow is controlled by rotating up to 90° a drilled ball which fits tightly against resilient seals. This ball seats with flow in either direction, and valve handle indicates the degree of opening. Recommended for frequent operation readily adaptable to automation, ideal for installation where space is limited.

Butterfly Valves

Butterfly valves provide bubble-tight closure with excellent throttling characteristics. They can be used for full-open, closed and for throttling applications.

The Butterfly valve consists of a disc within the valve body which is controlled by a shaft. In its closed position, the valve disc seals against a resilient seat. The disc position throughout the full 90° rotation is visually indicated by the position of the operator.

A Butterfly valve is only a fraction of the weight of a Gate valve and requires no gaskets between flanges in most cases. Recommended for frequent operation and adaptable to automation where space is limited.

Wafer and Lug type bodies when installed between two pipe flanges, can be easily removed from the line. The pressure of the bolted flanges holds the valve in place.
Locating lugs makes installation easier.

Plug Valves

Lubricated plug valves, because of the wide range of service to which they are adapted, may be classified as all purpose valves. They can be safely used at all pressure and vacuums, and at all temperatures up to the limits of available lubricants. They are the most satisfactory valves for the handling of gritty suspensions and many other destructive, erosive, corrosive and chemical solutions.

Plumbing — R2211 Facility Water Distribution

R221113-40 Plumbing Approximations for Quick Estimating

Water Control
Water Meter; Backflow Preventer, ... 10 to 15% of Fixtures
Shock Absorbers; Vacuum Breakers;
Mixer.

Pipe And Fittings .... 30 to 60% of Fixtures

> **Note:** Lower percentage for compact buildings or larger buildings with plumbing in one area.
> Larger percentage for large buildings with plumbing spread out.
> In extreme cases pipe may be more than 100% of fixtures.
> Percentages **do not** include special purpose or process piping.

Plumbing Labor
1 & 2 Story Residential .... Rough-in Labor = 80% of Materials
Apartment Buildings .... Rough-in Labor = 90 to 100% of Materials
Labor for handling and placing fixtures is approximately 25 to 30% of fixtures

Quality/Complexity Multiplier (for all installations)
Economy installation, add .... 0 to 5%
Good quality, medium complexity, add .... 5 to 15%
Above average quality and complexity, add .... 15 to 25%

R221113-50 Pipe Material Considerations

1. Malleable fittings should be used for gas service.
2. Malleable fittings are used where there are stresses/strains due to expansion and vibration.
3. Cast fittings may be broken as an aid to disassembling heating lines frozen by long use, temperature and minerals.
4. A cast iron pipe is extensively used for underground and submerged service.
5. Type M (light wall) copper tubing is available in hard temper only and is used for nonpressure and less severe applications than K and L.
6. Type L (medium wall) copper tubing, available hard or soft for interior service.
7. Type K (heavy wall) copper tubing, available in hard or soft temper for use where conditions are severe. For underground and interior service.
8. Hard drawn tubing requires fewer hangers or supports but should not be bent. Silver brazed fittings are recommended, but soft solder is normally used.
9. Type DMV (very light wall) copper tubing designed for drainage, waste and vent plus other non-critical pressure services.

Domestic/Imported Pipe and Fittings Costs

The prices shown in this publication for steel/cast iron pipe and steel, cast iron, and malleable iron fittings are based on domestic production sold at the normal trade discounts. The above listed items of foreign manufacture may be available at prices 1/3 to 1/2 of those shown. Some imported items after minor machining or finishing operations are being sold as domestic to further complicate the system.

Caution: Most pipe prices in this data set also include a coupling and pipe hangers which for the larger sizes can add significantly to the per foot cost and should be taken into account when comparing "book cost" with the quoted supplier's cost.

Plumbing

R2211 Facility Water Distribution

R221113-70 Piping to 10' High

When taking off pipe, it is important to identify the different material types and joining procedures, as well as distances between supports and components required for proper support.

During the takeoff, measure through all fittings. Do not subtract the lengths of the fittings, valves, or strainers, etc. This added length plus the final rounding of the totals will compensate for nipples and waste.

When rounding off totals always increase the actual amount to correspond with manufacturer's shipping lengths.

A. Both red brass and yellow brass pipe are normally furnished in 12' lengths, plain end. The Unit Price section includes in the linear foot costs two field threads and one coupling per 10' length. A carbon steel clevis type hanger assembly every 10' is also prorated into the linear foot costs, including both material and labor.

B. Cast iron soil pipe is furnished in either 5' or 10' lengths. For pricing purposes, the Unit Price section features 10' lengths with a joint and a carbon steel clevis hanger assembly every 5' prorated into the per foot costs of both material and labor.

Three methods of joining are considered: lead and oakum poured joints or push-on gasket type joints for the bell and spigot pipe and a joint clamp for the no-hub soil pipe. The labor and material costs for each of these individual joining procedures are also prorated into the linear costs per foot.

C. Copper tubing covers types K, L, M, and DWV which are furnished in 20' lengths. Means pricing data is based on a tubing cut each length and a coupling and two soft soldered joints every 10'. A carbon steel, clevis type hanger assembly every 10' is also prorated into the per foot costs. The prices for refrigeration tubing are for materials only. Labor for full lengths may be based on the type L labor but short cut measures in tight areas can increase the installation labor-hours from 20 to 40%.

D. Corrosion-resistant piping does not lend itself to one particular standard of hanging or support assembly due to its diversity of application and placement. The several varieties of corrosion-resistant piping do not include any material or labor costs for hanger assemblies (See the Unit Price section for appropriate selection).

E. Glass pipe is furnished in standard lengths either 5' or 10' long, beaded on one end. Special orders for diverse lengths beaded on both ends are also available. For pricing purposes, R.S. Means features 10' lengths with a coupling and a carbon steel band hanger assembly every 10' prorated into the per foot linear costs.

Glass pipe is also available with conical ends and standard lengths ranging from 6" through 3' in 6" increments, then up to 10' in 12" increments. Special lengths can be customized for particular installation requirements.

For pricing purposes, Means has based the labor and material pricing on 10' lengths. Included in these costs per linear foot are the prorated costs for a flanged assembly every 10' consisting of two flanges, a gasket, two insertable seals, and the required number of bolts and nuts. A carbon steel band hanger assembly based on 10' center lines has also been prorated into the costs per foot for labor and materials.

F. Plastic pipe of several compositions and joining methods are considered. Fiberglass reinforced pipe (FRP) is priced, based on 10' lengths (20' lengths are also available), with coupling and epoxy joints every 10'. FRP is furnished in both "General Service" and "High Strength." A carbon steel clevis hanger assembly, 3 every 10', is built into the prorated labor and material costs on a per foot basis.

The PVC and CPVC pipe schedules 40, 80 and 120, plus SDR ratings are all based on 20' lengths with a coupling installed every 10', as well as a carbon steel clevis hanger assembly every 3'. The PVC and ABS type DWV piping is based on 10' lengths with solvent weld couplings every 10', and with carbon steel clevis hanger assemblies, 3 for every 10'. The rest of the plastic piping in this section is based on flexible 100' coils and does not include any coupling or supports.

This section ends with PVC drain and sewer piping based on 10' lengths with bell and spigot ends and O-ring type, push-on joints.

G. Stainless steel piping includes both weld end and threaded piping, both in the type 304 and 316 specification and in the following schedules, 5, 10, 40, 80, and 160. Although this piping is usually furnished in 20' lengths, this cost grouping has a joint (either heli-arc butt-welded or threads and coupling) every 10'. A carbon steel clevis type hanger assembly is also included at 10' intervals and prorated into the linear foot costs.

H. Carbon steel pipe includes both black and galvanized. This section encompasses schedules 40 (standard) and 80 (extra heavy).

Several common methods of joining steel pipe — such as thread and coupled, butt welded, and flanged (150 lb. weld neck flanges) are also included.

For estimating purposes, it is assumed that the piping is purchased in 20' lengths and that a compatible joint is made up every 10'. These joints are prorated into the labor and material costs per linear foot. The following hanger and support assemblies every 10' are also included: carbon steel clevis for the T & C pipe, and single rod roll type for both the welded and flanged piping. All of these hangers are oversized to accommodate pipe insulation 3/4" thick through 5" pipe size and 1-1/2" thick from 6" through 12" pipe size.

I. Grooved joint steel pipe is priced both black and galvanized, in schedules 10, 40, and 80, furnished in 20' lengths. This section describes two joining methods: cut groove and roll groove. The schedule 10 piping is roll-grooved, while the heavier schedules are cut-grooved. The labor and material costs are prorated into per linear foot prices, including a coupled joint every 10', as well as a carbon steel clevis hanger assembly.

Notes:

The pipe hanger assemblies mentioned in the preceding paragraphs include the described hanger; appropriately sized steel, box-type insert and nut; plus 18" of threaded hanger rod.

C clamps are used when the pipe is to be supported from steel shapes rather than anchored in the slab. C clamps are slightly less costly than inserts. However, to save time in estimating, it is advisable to use the given line number cost, rather than substituting a C clamp for the insert.

Add to piping labor for elevated installation:

Height	%	Height	%
10' to 14.5' high	10%	30' to 34.5' high	40%
15' to 19.5' high	20%	35' to 39.5' high	50%
20' to 24.5' high	25%	40' and higher	55%
25' to 29.5' high	35%		

When using the percentage adds for elevated piping installations as shown above, bear in mind that the given heights are for the pipe supports, even though the insert, anchor, or clamp may be several feet higher than the pipe itself.

An allowance has been included in the piping installation time for testing and minor tightening of leaking joints, fittings, stuffing boxes, packing glands, etc. For extraordinary test requirements such as x-rays, prolonged pressure or demonstration tests, a percentage of the piping labor, based on the estimator's experience, must be added to the labor total. A testing service specializing in weld x-rays should be consulted for pricing if it is an estimate requirement. Equipment installation time includes start-up with associated adjustments.

Plumbing — R2213 Facility Sanitary Sewerage

R221316-10 Drainage Fixture Units for Fixtures and Groups

Fixture Type	Drainage Fixture Unit Value as Load Factors	Minimum Size of Trap (inches)
Automatic Clothes Washer, commercial (Note A)	3.0	2.0
Automatic Clothes Washer, residential	2.0	2.0
Full Bathroom Group w/bathtub or shower stall (1.6 gpf WC)	5.0	-
Full Bathroom Group w/bathtub or shower stall (WC flushing greater than 1.6 gpf) (Note D)	6.0	-
Bathtub (with or without overhead shower)	2.0	1.5
Bidet	1.0	1.25
Drinking Fountain	0.5	1025
Dishwasher, domestic	2.0	1.5
Emergency floor drains	0.0	2
Floor drains	2.0	2
Kitchen sinks, domestic	2.0	1.5
Lavatory	1.0	1.25
Shower (5.7 gpm or less flow rate)	2.0	1.5
Shower (5.7 gpm - 12.3 gpm flow rate)	3.0	2
Shower (12.3 gpm - 25.8 gpm flow rate)	5.0	3
Shower (25.8 gpm to 55.6 gpm flow rate)	6.0	4
Service Sink	2.0	1.5
Urinal	4.0	Note C
Urinal (1.0 gpf or less)	2.0	Note C
Urinal (nonwater supplied)	0.5	Note C
Water closet, flushometer tank, public or private	4.0	Note C
Water closet, private (1.6 gpf)	3.0	Note C
Water closet, private (flushing greater than 1.6 gpf)	4.0	Note C
Water closet, public (1.6 gpf)	4.0	Note C
Water closet, public (flushing greater than 1.6 gpf)	6.0	Note C

Notes:
A. A showerhead over a bathtub or whirlpool tub attachment does not increase the drainage fixture unit value.
B. Trap size shall be consistent with the fixture outlet size.
C. For fixtures added to a bathroom group, add the DFU value to those additional fixtures to the bathroom group fixture count.

Excerpted from the 2012 *International Plumbing Code,* Copyright 2011. Washington, D.C.: International Code Council. Reproduced with permission. All rights reserved. www.ICCSAFE.org

R221316-15 Drainage Fixture Units for Fixture Drains or Traps

Fixture Drain or Trap Size (inches)	Drainage Fixture Unit Value
1.25	1.0
1.5	2.0
2.0	3.0
2.5	4.0
3.0	5.0
4.0	6.0

Notes:
Drainage Fixture Unit values designate the relative load weight or different kinds of fixtures that shall be employed in estimating the total load carried by a soil or waste pipe.

Excerpted from the 2012 *International Plumbing Code,* Copyright 2011. Washington, D.C.: International Code Council. Reproduced with permission. All rights reserved. www.ICCSAFE.org

Plumbing — R2213 Facility Sanitary Sewerage

R221316-20 Allowable Fixture Units (d.f.u.) for Branches and Stacks

Pipe Diam.	Horiz. Branch (not incl. drains)	Stack Size for 3 Stories or 3 Levels	Stack size for Over 3 levels	Maximum for 1 Story building Stack
1-1/2"	3	4	8	2
2"	6	10	24	6
2-1/2"	12	20	42	9
3"	20*	48*	72*	20*
4"	160	240	500	90
5"	360	540	1100	200
6"	620	960	1900	350
8"	1400	2200	3600	600
10"	2500	3800	5600	1000
12"	3900	6000	8400	1500
15"	7000			

*Not more than two water closets or bathroom groups within each branch interval nor more than six water closets or bathroom groups on the stack.

Stacks sized for the total may be reduced as load decreases at each story to a minimum diameter of 1/2 the maximum diameter.

Plumbing — R2240 Plumbing Fixtures

R224000-10 Water Consumption Rates

Fixture Type	Water Supply Fixture Unit Value		
	Hot Water	Cold Water	Combined
Bathtub	1.0	1.0	1.4
Clothes Washer	1.0	1.0	1.4
Dishwasher	1.4	0.0	1.4
Kitchen Sink	1.0	1.0	1.4
Laundry Tub	1.0	1.0	1.4
Lavatory	0.5	0.5	0.7
Shower Stall	1.0	1.0	1.4
Water Closet (tank type)	0.0	2.2	2.2
Full Bath Group			
w/bathtub or shower stall	1.5	2.7	3.6
Half Bath Group			
w/W.C. and Lavatory	0.5	2.5	2.6
Kitchen Group			
w/Dishwasher and Sink	1.9	1.0	2.5
Laundry Group			
w/Clothes Washer and Laundry Tub	1.8	1.8	2.5
Hose bibb (sillcock)	0.0	2.5	2.5

Notes:
Typically, WSFU = 1GPM

Supply loads in the building water-distribution system shall be determined by total load on the pipe being sized, in terms of water supply fixture units (WSFU) and gallons per minute (GPM) flow rates. For fixtures not listed, choose a WSFU value of a fixture with similar flow characteristics. Water Fixture Supply Units determined the required water supply to fixtures and their service systems. Fixture units are equal to (1) cubic foot of water drained in a 1-1/4" pipe per minute. It is not a flow rate unit but a design factor.

Excerpted from the 2012 *International Plumbing Code*, Copyright 2011. Washington, D.C.: International Code Council. Reproduced with permission. All rights reserved. www.ICCSAFE.org

Plumbing — R2240 Plumbing Fixtures

R224000-20 Fixture Demands in Gallons per Fixture per Hour

Table below is based on 140°F final temperature except for dishwashers in public places (*) where 180°F water is mandatory.

Supply Systems for Flush Tanks			Supply Systems for Flushometer Valves		
Load	Demand		Load	Demand	
WSFU	GPM	CU. FT.	WSFU	GPM	CU. FT.
1.0	3.0	0.041040	-	-	-
2.0	5.0	0.068400	-	-	-
3.0	6.5	0.868920	-	-	-
4.0	8.0	1.069440	-	-	-
5.0	9.4	1.256592	5.0	15	2.0052
6.0	10.7	1.430376	6.0	17.4	2.326032
7.0	11.8	1.577424	7.0	19.8	2.646364
8.0	12.8	1.711104	8.0	22.2	2.967696
9.0	13.7	1.831416	9.0	24.6	3.288528
10.0	14.6	1.951728	10.0	27	3.60936
11.0	15.4	2.058672	11.0	27.8	3.716304
12.0	16.0	2.138880	12.0	28.6	3.823248
13.0	16.5	2.205720	13.0	29.4	3.930192
14.0	17.0	2.272560	14.0	30.2	4.037136
15.0	17.5	2.339400	15.0	31	4.14408
16.0	18.0	2.906240	16.0	31.8	4.241024
17.0	18.4	2.459712	17.0	32.6	4.357968
18.0	18.8	2.513184	18.0	33.4	4.464912
19.0	19.2	2.566656	19.0	34.2	4.571856
20.0	19.6	2.620218	20.0	35.0	4.678800
25.0	21.5	2.874120	25.0	38.0	5.079840
30.0	23.3	3.114744	30.0	42.0	5.611356
35.0	24.9	3.328632	35.0	44.0	5.881920
40.0	26.3	3.515784	40.0	46.0	6.149280
45.0	27.7	3.702936	45.0	48.0	6.416640
50.0	29.1	3.890088	50.0	50.0	6.684000

Notes:
When designing a plumbing system that utilizes fixtures other than, or in addition to, water closets, use the data provided in the Supply Systems for Flush Tanks section of the above table.

To obtain the probable maximum demand, multiply the total demands for the fixtures (gal./fixture/hour) by the demand factor. The heater should have a heating capacity in gallons per hour equal to this maximum. The storage tank should have a capacity in gallons equal to the probable maximum demand multiplied by the storage capacity factor.

Excerpted from the 2012 *International Residential Code,* Copyright 2011. Washington, D.C.: International Code Council. Reproduced with permission. All rights reserved. www.ICCSAFE.org

Plumbing — R2240 Plumbing Fixtures

R224000-30 Minimum Plumbing Fixture Requirements

Classification	Occupancy	Description	Water Closet Male	Water Closet Female	Lavatories Male	Lavatories Female	Bathtubs/Showers	Drinking Fountains	Other
Assembly	A-1	Theaters and other buildings for the performing arts and motion pictures	1:125	1:65	1:200			1:500	1 Service Sink
	A-2	Nightclubs, bars, taverns dance halls	1:40		1:75			1:500	1 Service Sink
		Restaurants, banquet halls, food courts	1:75		1:200			1:500	1 Service Sink
	A-3	Auditorium w/o permanent seating, art galleries, exhibition halls, museums, lecture halls, libraries, arcades & gymnasiums	1:125	1:65	1:200			1:500	1 Service Sink
		Passenger terminals and transportation facilities	1:500		1:750			1:1000	1 Service Sink
		Places of worship and other religious services	1:150	1:75	1:200			1:1000	1 Service Sink
	A-4	Indoor sporting events and activities, coliseums, arenas, skating rinks, pools, and tennis courts	1:75 for the first 1500, then 1:120 for the remainder	1:40 for the first 1520, then 1:60 for the remainder	1:200	1:150		1:1000	1 Service Sink
	A-5	Outdoor sporting events and activities, stadiums, amusement parks, bleachers, grandstands	1:75 for the first 1500, then 1:120 for the remainder	1:40 for the first 1520, then 1:60 for the remainder	1:200	1:150		1:1000	1 Service Sink
Business	B	Buildings for the transaction of business, professional services, other services involving merchandise, office buildings, banks, light industrial	1:25 for the first 50, then 1:50 for the remainder		1:40 for the first 80, then 1:80 for the remainder			1:100	1 Service Sink
Educational	E	Educational Facilities	1:50		1:50			1:100	1 Service Sink
Factory and industrial	F-1 and F-2	Structures in which occupants are engaged in work fabricating, assembly or processing of products or materials	1:100		1:100		See International Plumbing Code	1:400	1 Service Sink
Institutional	I-1	Residential Care	1:10		1:10		1:8	1:100	
	I-2	Hospitals, ambulatory nursing home care recipient	1 per room		1 per room		1:15	1:100	1 Service Sink
		Employees, other than residential care	1:25		1:35			1:100	
		Visitors, other than residential care	1:75		1:100			1:500	
	I-3	Prisons	1 per cell		1 per cell		1:15	1:100	1 Service Sink
		Reformatories, detention and correction centers	1:15		1:15		1:15	1:100	1 Service Sink
		Employees	1:25		1:35			1:100	
	I-4	Adult and child day care	1:15		1:15		1	1:100	1 Service Sink
Mercantile	M	Retail stores, service stations, shops, salesrooms, markets and shopping centers	1:500		1:750			1:1000	1 Service Sink
Residential	R-1	Hotels, Motels, boarding houses (transient)	1 per sleeping unit		1 per sleeping unit		1 per sleeping unit		1 Service Sink
	R-2	Dormitories, fraternities, sororities and boarding houses (not transient)	1:10		1:10		1:8	1:100	1 Service Sink
		Apartment House	1 per dwelling unit		1 per dwelling unit		1 per dwelling unit		1 Kitchen sink per dwelling; 1 clothes washer connection per 20 dwellings
	R-3	1 and 2 Family Dwellings	1 per dwelling unit		1:10		1 per dwelling unit		1 Kitchen sink per dwelling; 1 clothes washer connection per dwelling
	R-3	Congregate living facilities w/<16 people	1:10		1:10		1:8	1:100	1 Service Sink
	R-4	Congregate living facilities w/<16 people	1:10		1:10		1:8	1:100	1 Service Sink
Storage	S-1 and S-2	Structures for the storage of good, warehouses, storehouses and freight depots, low and moderate hazard	1:100		1:100		See International Plumbing Code	1:1000	1 Service Sink

Table 2902.1

Excerpted from the 2012 *International Building Code*, Copyright 2011. Washington, D.C.: International Code Council. Reproduced with permission. All rights reserved. www.ICCSAFE.org

Heating, Ventilating & A.C.   R2305 Common Work Results for HVAC

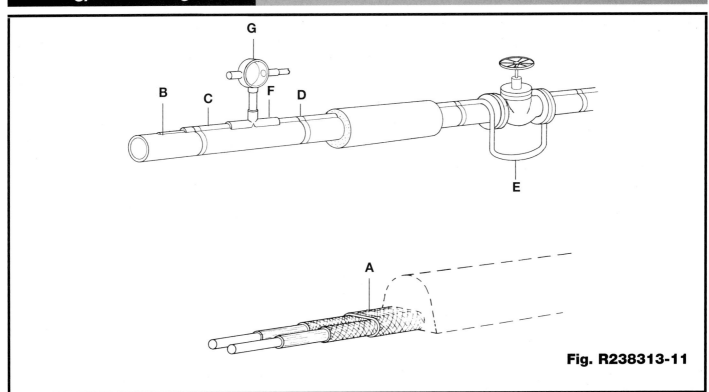

Fig. R238313-11

R230500-10   Subcontractors

On the unit cost pages of the R.S. Means Cost Data data set, the last column is entitled "Total Incl. O&P". This is normally the cost of the installing contractor. In the HVAC Division, this is the cost of the mechanical contractor. If the particular work being estimated is to be performed by a sub to the mechanical contractor, the mechanical's profit and handling charge (usually 10%) is added to the total of the last column.

Heating, Ventilating & A.C.   R2356 Solar Energy Heating Equipment

R235616-60   Solar Heating (Space and Hot Water)

Collectors should face as close to due South as possible, but variations of up to 20 degrees on either side of true South are acceptable. Local climate and collector type may influence the choice between east or west deviations. Obviously they should be located so they are not shaded from the sun's rays. Incline collectors at a slope of latitude minus 5 degrees for domestic hot water and latitude plus 15 degrees for space heating.

Flat plate collectors consist of a number of components as follows: Insulation to reduce heat loss through the bottom and sides of the collector. The enclosure which contains all the components in this assembly is usually weatherproof and prevents dust, wind and water from coming in contact with the absorber plate. The cover plate usually consists of one or more layers of a variety of glass or plastic and reduces the reradiation by creating an air space which traps the heat between the cover and the absorber plates.

The absorber plate must have a good thermal bond with the fluid passages. The absorber plate is usually metallic and treated with a surface coating which improves absorptivity. Black or dark paints or selective coatings are used for this purpose, and the design of this passage and plate combination helps determine a solar system's effectiveness.

Heat transfer fluid passage tubes are attached above and below or integral with an absorber plate for the purpose of transferring thermal energy from the absorber plate to a heat transfer medium. The heat exchanger is a device for transferring thermal energy from one fluid to another.

Piping and storage tanks should be well insulated to minimize heat losses.

Size domestic water heating storage tanks to hold 20 gallons of water per user, minimum, plus 10 gallons per dishwasher or washing machine. For domestic water heating an optimum collector size is approximately 3/4 square foot of area per gallon of water storage. For space heating of residences and small commercial applications the collector is commonly sized between 30% and 50% of the internal floor area. For space heating of large commercial applications, collector areas less than 30% of the internal floor area can still provide significant heat reductions.

A supplementary heat source is recommended for Northern states for December through February.

The solar energy transmission per square foot of collector surface varies greatly with the material used. Initial cost, heat transmittance and useful life are obviously interrelated.

Heating, Ventilating & A.C. R2383 Radiant Heating Units

R238313-10 Heat Trace Systems

Before you can determine the cost of a HEAT TRACE installation, the method of attachment must be established. There are (4) common methods:
1. Cable is simply attached to the pipe with polyester tape every 12′.
2. Cable is attached with a continuous cover of 2″ wide aluminum tape.
3. Cable is attached with factory extruded heat transfer cement and covered with metallic raceway with clips every 10′.
4. Cable is attached between layers of pipe insulation using either clips or polyester tape.

Example: Components for method 3 must include:
A. Heat trace cable by voltage and watts per linear foot.
B. Heat transfer cement, 1 gallon per 60 linear feet of cover.
C. Metallic raceway by size and type.
D. Raceway clips by size of pipe.

When taking off linear foot lengths of cable add the following for each valve in the system. (E)

In all of the above methods each component of the system must be priced individually.

SCREWED OR WELDED VALVE:
1/2″	=	6″
3/4″	=	9″
1″	=	1′ -0″
1-1/2″	=	1′ -6″
2″	=	2′
2-1/2″	=	2′ -6″
3″	=	2′ -6″
4″	=	4′ -0″
6″	=	7′ -0″
8″	=	9′ -6″
10″	=	12′ -6″
12″	=	15′ -0″
14″	=	18′ -0″
16″	=	21′ -6″
18″	=	25′ -6″
20″	=	28′ -6″
24″	=	34′ -0″
30″	=	40′ -0″

FLANGED VALVE:
1/2″	=	1′ -0″
3/4″	=	1′ -6″
1″	=	2′ -0″
1-1/2″	=	2′ -6″
2″	=	2′ -6″
2-1/2″	=	3′ -0″
3″	=	3′ -6″
4″	=	4′ -0″
6″	=	8′ -0″
8″	=	11′ -0″
10″	=	14′ -0″
12″	=	16′ -6″
14″	=	19′ -6″
16″	=	23′ -0″
18″	=	27′ -0″
20″	=	30′ -0″
24″	=	36′ -0″
30″	=	42′ -0″

BUTTERFLY VALVES:
1/2″	=	0′
3/4″	=	0′
1″	=	1′ -0″
1-1/2″	=	1′ -6″
2″	=	2′ -0″
2-1/2″	=	2′ -6″
3″	=	2′ -6″
4″	=	3′ -0″
6″	=	3′ -6″
8″	=	4′ -0″
10″	=	4′ -0″
12″	=	5′ -0″
14″	=	5′ -6″
16″	=	6′ -0″
18″	=	6′ -6″
20″	=	7′ -0″
24″	=	8′ -0″
30″	=	10′ -0″

Heating, Ventilating & A.C. R2383 Radiant Heating Units

R238313-10 Heat Trace Systems (cont.)

Add the following quantities of heat transfer cement to linear foot totals for each valve:

Nominal Valve Size	Gallons of Cement per Valve
1/2"	0.14
3/4"	0.21
1"	0.29
1-1/2"	0.36
2"	0.43
2-1/2"	0.70
3"	0.71
4"	1.00
6"	1.43
8"	1.48
10"	1.50
12"	1.60
14"	1.75
16"	2.00
18"	2.25
20"	2.50
24"	3.00
30"	3.75

The following must be added to the list of components to accurately price HEAT TRACE systems:
1. Expediter fitting and clamp fasteners (F)
2. Junction box and nipple connected to expediter fitting (G)
3. Field installed terminal blocks within junction box
4. Ground lugs
5. Piping from power source to expediter fitting
6. Controls
7. Thermostats
8. Branch wiring
9. Cable splices
10. End of cable terminations
11. Branch piping fittings and boxes

Deduct the following percentages from labor if cable lengths in the same area exceed:

150' to 250'   10%   351' to 500'   20%
251' to 350'   15%   Over 500'   25%

Add the following percentages to labor for elevated installations:

15' to 20' high   10%   31' to 35' high   40%
21' to 25' high   20%   36' to 40' high   50%
26' to 30' high   30%   Over 40' high   60%

R238313-20 Spiral-Wrapped Heat Trace Cable (Pitch Table)

In order to increase the amount of heat, occasionally heat trace cable is wrapped in a spiral fashion around a pipe; increasing the number of feet of heater cable per linear foot of pipe.

Engineers first determine the heat loss per foot of pipe (based on the insulating material, its thickness, and the temperature differential across it). A ratio is then calculated by the formula:

$$\text{Feet of Heat Trace per Foot of Pipe} = \frac{\text{Watts/Foot of Heat Loss}}{\text{Watts/Foot of the Cable}}$$

The linear distance between wraps (pitch) is then taken from a chart or table. Generally, the pitch is listed on a drawing leaving the estimator to calculate the total length of heat tape required. An approximation may be taken from this table.

Feet of Heat Trace Per Foot of Pipe

Pitch In Inches	\multicolumn{15}{c}{Nominal Pipe Size in Inches}														
	1	1¼	1½	2	2½	3	4	6	8	10	12	14	16	18	20	24
3.5	1.80															
4	1.65															
5	1.46	1.60	1.80													
6	1.34	1.45	1.55	1.75												
7	1.25	1.35	1.43	1.57	1.75											
8	1.20	1.28	1.34	1.45	1.60	1.80										
9	1.16	1.23	1.28	1.37	1.51	1.68										
10	1.13	1.19	1.24	1.32	1.44	1.57	1.82									
15	1.06	1.08	1.10	1.15	1.21	1.29	1.42	1.78								
20	1.04	1.05	1.06	1.08	1.13	1.17	1.25	1.49	1.73							
25		1.04	1.04	1.04	1.06	1.08	1.11	1.33	1.51	1.72						
30					1.04	1.05	1.07	1.24	1.37	1.54	1.70	1.80				
35						1.06	1.05	1.17	1.28	1.42	1.54	1.64	1.78			
40							1.05	1.14	1.22	1.33	1.44	1.52	1.64	1.75		
50								1.09	1.15	1.22	1.29	1.35	1.44	1.53	1.64	1.83
60								1.06	1.11	1.16	1.21	1.25	1.31	1.39	1.46	1.62
70								1.05	1.08	1.12	1.17	1.19	1.24	1.30	1.35	1.47
80									1.06	1.09	1.13	1.15	1.19	1.24	1.28	1.38
90									1.04	1.06	1.10	1.13	1.16	1.19	1.23	1.32
100										1.05	1.08	1.10	1.13	1.15	1.19	1.23

Note: Common practice would normally limit the lower end of the table to 5% of additional heat and above 80% an engineer would likely opt for two (2) parallel cables.

Electrical

R2605 Common Work Results for Electrical

R260519-90 Wire

Wire quantities are taken off by either measuring each cable run or by extending the conduit and raceway quantities times the number of conductors in the raceway. Ten percent should be added for waste and tie-ins. Keep in mind that the unit of measure of wire is C.L.F. not L.F. as in raceways so the formula would read:

$$\frac{\text{(L.F. Raceway} \times \text{No. of Conductors)} \times 1.10}{100} = \text{C.L.F.}$$

Price per C.L.F. of wire includes:
1. Setting up wire coils or spools on racks
2. Attaching wire to pull in means
3. Measuring and cutting wire
4. Pulling wire into a raceway
5. Identifying and tagging

Price does not include:
1. Connections to breakers, panelboards, or equipment
2. Splices

Job Conditions: Productivity is based on new construction to a height of 15' using rolling staging in an unobstructed area. Material staging is assumed to be within 100' of work being performed.

Economy of Scale: If more than three wires at a time are being pulled, deduct the following percentages from the labor of that grouping:

4-5 wires	25%
6-10 wires	30%
11-15 wires	35%
over 15	40%

If a wire pull is less than 100' in length and is interrupted several times by boxes, lighting outlets, etc., it may be necessary to add the following lengths to each wire being pulled:

Junction box to junction box	2 L.F.
Lighting panel to junction box	6 L.F.
Distribution panel to sub panel	8 L.F.
Switchboard to distribution panel	12 L.F.
Switchboard to motor control center	20 L.F.
Switchboard to cable tray	40 L.F.

Measure of Drops and Riser: It is important when taking off wire quantities to include the wire for drops to electrical equipment. If heights of electrical equipment are not clearly stated, use the following guide:

	Bottom A.F.F.	Top A.F.F.	Inside Cabinet
Safety switch to 100A	5'	6'	2'
Safety switch 400 to 600A	4'	6'	3'
100A panel 12 to 30 circuit	4'	6'	3'
42 circuit panel	3'	6'	4'
Switch box	3'	3'6"	1'
Switchgear	0'	8'	8'
Motor control centers	0'	8'	8'
Transformers - wall mount	4'	8'	2'
Transformers - floor mount	0'	12'	4'

Earthwork

R3123 Excavation & Fill

R312316-45 Excavating Equipment

The table below lists theoretical hourly production in C.Y./hr. bank measure for some typical excavation equipment. Figures assume 50 minute hours, 83% job efficiency, 100% operator efficiency, 90° swing and properly sized hauling units, which must be modified for adverse digging and loading conditions. Actual production costs in the front of the data set average about 50% of the theoretical values listed here.

Equipment	Soil Type	B.C.Y. Weight	% Swell	1 C.Y.	1-1/2 C.Y.	2 C.Y.	2-1/2 C.Y.	3 C.Y.	3-1/2 C.Y.	4 C.Y.
Hydraulic Excavator "Backhoe" 15' Deep Cut	Moist loam, sandy clay	3400 lb.	40%	165	195	200	275	330	385	440
	Sand and gravel	3100	18	140	170	225	240	285	330	380
	Common earth	2800	30	150	180	230	250	300	350	400
	Clay, hard, dense	3000	33	120	140	190	200	240	260	320
Power Shovel Optimum Cut (Ft.)	Moist loam, sandy clay	3400	40	170 (6.0)	245 (7.0)	295 (7.8)	335 (8.4)	385 (8.8)	435 (9.1)	475 (9.4)
	Sand and gravel	3100	18	165 (6.0)	225 (7.0)	275 (7.8)	325 (8.4)	375 (8.8)	420 (9.1)	460 (9.4)
	Common earth	2800	30	145 (7.8)	200 (9.2)	250 (10.2)	295 (11.2)	335 (12.1)	375 (13.0)	425 (13.8)
	Clay, hard, dense	3000	33	120 (9.0)	175 (10.7)	220 (12.2)	255 (13.3)	300 (14.2)	335 (15.1)	375 (16.0)
Drag Line Optimum Cut (Ft.)	Moist loam, sandy clay	3400	40	130 (6.6)	180 (7.4)	220 (8.0)	250 (8.5)	290 (9.0)	325 (9.5)	385 (10.0)
	Sand and gravel	3100	18	130 (6.6)	175 (7.4)	210 (8.0)	245 (8.5)	280 (9.0)	315 (9.5)	375 (10.0)
	Common earth	2800	30	110 (8.0)	160 (9.0)	190 (9.9)	220 (10.5)	250 (11.0)	280 (11.5)	310 (12.0)
	Clay, hard, dense	3000	33	90 (9.3)	130 (10.7)	160 (11.8)	190 (12.3)	225 (12.8)	250 (13.3)	280 (12.0)

Equipment	Soil Type	B.C.Y. Weight	% Swell	Wheel Loaders				Track Loaders		
				3 C.Y.	4 C.Y.	6 C.Y.	8 C.Y.	2-1/4 C.Y.	3 C.Y.	4 C.Y.
Loading Tractors	Moist loam, sandy clay	3400	40	260	340	510	690	135	180	250
	Sand and gravel	3100	18	245	320	480	650	130	170	235
	Common earth	2800	30	230	300	460	620	120	155	220
	Clay, hard, dense	3000	33	200	270	415	560	110	145	200
	Rock, well-blasted	4000	50	180	245	380	520	100	130	180

Earthwork

R3123 Excavation & Fill

R312319-90 Wellpoints

A single stage wellpoint system is usually limited to dewatering an average 15' depth below normal ground water level. Multi-stage systems are employed for greater depth with the pumping equipment installed only at the lowest header level. Ejectors with unlimited lift capacity can be economical when two or more stages of wellpoints can be replaced or when horizontal clearance is restricted, such as in deep trenches or tunneling projects, and where low water flows are expected. Wellpoints are usually spaced on 2-1/2' to 10' centers along a header pipe. Wellpoint spacing, header size, and pump size are all determined by the expected flow as dictated by soil conditions.

In almost all soils encountered in wellpoint dewatering, the wellpoints may be jetted into place. Cemented soils and stiff clays may require sand wicks about 12" in diameter around each wellpoint to increase efficiency and eliminate weeping into the excavation. These sand wicks require 1/2 to 3 C.Y. of washed filter sand and are installed by using a 12" diameter steel casing and hole puncher jetted into the ground 2' deeper than the wellpoint. Rock may require predrilled holes.

Labor required for the complete installation and removal of a single stage wellpoint system is in the range of 3/4 to 2 labor-hours per linear foot of header, depending upon jetting conditions, wellpoint spacing, etc.

Continuous pumping is necessary except in some free draining soil where temporary flooding is permissible (as in trenches which are backfilled after each day's work). Good practice requires provision of a stand-by pump during the continuous pumping operation.

Systems for continuous trenching below the water table should be installed three to four times the length of expected daily progress to ensure uninterrupted digging, and header pipe size should not be changed during the job.

For pervious free draining soils, deep wells in place of wellpoints may be economical because of lower installation and maintenance costs. Daily production ranges between two to three wells per day, for 25' to 40' depths, to one well per day for depths over 50'.

Detailed analysis and estimating for any dewatering problem is available at no cost from wellpoint manufacturers. Major firms will quote "sufficient equipment" quotes or their affiliates will offer lump sum proposals to cover complete dewatering responsibility.

Description for 200' System with 8" Header		Quantities
Equipment & Material	Wellpoints 25' long, 2" diameter @ 5' O.C.	40 Each
	Header pipe, 8" diameter	200 L.F.
	Discharge pipe, 8" diameter	100 L.F.
	8" valves	3 Each
	Combination jetting & wellpoint pump (standby)	1 Each
	Wellpoint pump, 8" diameter	1 Each
	Transportation to and from site	1 Day
	Fuel for 30 days x 60 gal./day	1800 Gallons
	Lubricants for 30 days x 16 lbs./day	480 Lbs.
	Sand for points	40 C.Y.
Labor	Technician to supervise installation	1 Week
	Labor for installation and removal of system	300 Labor-hours
	4 Operators straight time 40 hrs./wk. for 4.33 wks.	693 Hrs.
	4 Operators overtime 2 hrs./wk. for 4.33 wks.	35 Hrs.

Earthwork — R3141 Shoring

R314116-40 Wood Sheet Piling

Wood sheet piling may be used for depths to 20' where there is no ground water. If moderate ground water is encountered Tongue & Groove sheeting will help to keep it out. When considerable ground water is present, steel sheeting must be used.

For estimating purposes on trench excavation, sizes are as follows:

Depth	Sheeting	Wales	Braces	B.F. per S.F.
To 8'	3 x 12's	6 x 8's, 2 line	6 x 8's, @ 10'	4.0 @ 8'
8' x 12'	3 x 12's	10 x 10's, 2 line	10 x 10's, @ 9'	5.0 average
12' to 20'	3 x 12's	12 x 12's, 3 line	12 x 12's, @ 8'	7.0 average

Sheeting to be toed in at least 2' depending upon soil conditions. A five person crew with an air compressor and sheeting driver can drive and brace 440 SF/day at 8' deep, 360 SF/day at 12' deep, and 320 SF/day at 16' deep.

For normal soils, piling can be pulled in 1/3 the time to install. Pulling difficulty increases with the time in the ground. Production can be increased by high pressure jetting.

R314116-45 Steel Sheet Piling

Limiting weights are 22 to 38#/S.F. of wall surface with 27#/S.F. average for usual types and sizes. (Weights of piles themselves are from 30.7#/L.F. to 57#/L.F. but they are 15" to 21" wide.) Lightweight sections 12" to 28" wide from 3 ga. to 12 ga. thick are also available for shallow excavations. Piles may be driven two at a time with an impact or vibratory hammer (use vibratory to pull) hung from a crane without leads. A reasonable estimate of the life of steel sheet piling is 10 uses with up to 125 uses possible if a vibratory hammer is used. Used piling costs from 50% to 80% of new piling depending on location and market conditions. Sheet piling and H piles can be rented for about 30% of the delivered mill price for the first month and 5% per month thereafter. Allow 1 labor-hour per pile for cleaning and trimming after driving. These costs increase with depth and hydrostatic head. Vibratory drivers are faster in wet granular soils and are excellent for pile extraction. Pulling difficulty increases with the time in the ground and may cost more than driving. It is often economical to abandon the sheet piling, especially if it can be used as the outer wall form. Allow about 1/3 additional length or more for toeing into ground. Add bracing, waler and strut costs. Waler costs can equal the cost per ton of sheeting.

Utilities — R3311 Water Utility Distribution Piping

R331113-80 Piping Designations

There are several systems currently in use to describe pipe and fittings. The following paragraphs will help to identify and clarify classifications of piping systems used for water distribution.

Piping may be classified by schedule. Piping schedules include 5S, 10S, 10, 20, 30, Standard, 40, 60, Extra Strong, 80, 100, 120, 140, 160 and Double Extra Strong. These schedules are dependent upon the pipe wall thickness. The wall thickness of a particular schedule may vary with pipe size.

Ductile iron pipe for water distribution is classified by Pressure Classes such as Class 150, 200, 250, 300 and 350. These classes are actually the rated water working pressure of the pipe in pounds per square inch (psi). The pipe in these pressure classes is designed to withstand the rated water working pressure plus a surge allowance of 100 psi.

The American Water Works Association (AWWA) provides standards for various types of **plastic pipe.** C-900 is the specification for polyvinyl chloride (PVC) piping used for water distribution in sizes ranging from 4" through 12". C-901 is the specification for polyethylene (PE) pressure pipe, tubing and fittings used for water distribution in sizes ranging from 1/2" through 3". C-905 is the specification for PVC piping sizes 14" and greater.

PVC pressure-rated pipe is identified using the standard dimensional ratio (SDR) method. This method is defined by the American Society for Testing and Materials (ASTM) Standard D 2241. This pipe is available in SDR numbers 64, 41, 32.5, 26, 21, 17, and 13.5. Pipe with an SDR of 64 will have the thinnest wall while pipe with an SDR of 13.5 will have the thickest wall. When the pressure rating (PR) of a pipe is given in psi, it is based on a line supplying water at 73 degrees F.

The National Sanitation Foundation (NSF) seal of approval is applied to products that can be used with potable water. These products have been tested to ANSI/NSF Standard 14.

Valves and strainers are classified by American National Standards Institute (ANSI) Classes. These Classes are 125, 150, 200, 250, 300, 400, 600, 900, 1500 and 2500. Within each class there is an operating pressure range dependent upon temperature. Design parameters should be compared to the appropriate material dependent, pressure-temperature rating chart for accurate valve selection.

Change Orders

Change Order Considerations

A change order is a written document usually prepared by the design professional and signed by the owner, the architect/engineer, and the contractor. A change order states the agreement of the parties to: an addition, deletion, or revision in the work; an adjustment in the contract sum, if any; or an adjustment in the contract time, if any. Change orders, or "extras", in the construction process occur after execution of the construction contract and impact architects/engineers, contractors, and owners.

Change orders that are properly recognized and managed can ensure orderly, professional, and profitable progress for everyone involved in the project. There are many causes for change orders and change order requests. In all cases, change orders or change order requests should be addressed promptly and in a precise and prescribed manner. The following paragraphs include information regarding change order pricing and procedures.

The Causes of Change Orders

Reasons for issuing change orders include:

- Unforeseen field conditions that require a change in the work
- Correction of design discrepancies, errors, or omissions in the contract documents
- Owner-requested changes, either by design criteria, scope of work, or project objectives
- Completion date changes for reasons unrelated to the construction process
- Changes in building code interpretations, or other public authority requirements that require a change in the work
- Changes in availability of existing or new materials and products

Procedures

Properly written contract documents must include the correct change order procedures for all parties—owners, design professionals, and contractors—to follow in order to avoid costly delays and litigation.

Being "in the right" is not always a sufficient or acceptable defense. The contract provisions requiring notification and documentation must be adhered to within a defined or reasonable time frame.

The appropriate method of handling change orders is by a written proposal and acceptance by all parties involved. Prior to starting work on a project, all parties should identify their authorized agents who may sign and accept change orders, as well as any limits placed on their authority.

Time may be a critical factor when the need for a change arises. For such cases, the contractor might be directed to proceed on a "time and materials" basis, rather than wait for all paperwork to be processed—a delay that could impede progress. In this situation, the contractor must still follow the prescribed change order procedures including, but not limited to, notification and documentation.

Lack of documentation can be very costly, especially if legal judgments are to be made, and if certain field personnel are no longer available. For time and material change orders, the contractor should keep accurate daily records of all labor and material allocated to the change.

Owners or awarding authorities who do considerable and continual building construction (such as the federal government) realize the inevitability of change orders for numerous reasons, both predictable and unpredictable. As a result, the federal government, the American Institute of Architects (AIA), the Engineers Joint Contract Documents Committee (EJCDC), and other contractor, legal, and technical organizations have developed standards and procedures to be followed by all parties to achieve contract continuance and timely completion, while being financially fair to all concerned.

Pricing Change Orders

When pricing change orders, regardless of their cause, the most significant factor is when the change occurs. The need for a change may be perceived in the field or requested by the architect/engineer *before* any of the actual installation has begun, or may evolve or appear *during* construction when the item of work in question is partially installed. In the latter cases, the original sequence of construction is disrupted, along with all contiguous and supporting systems. Change orders cause the greatest impact when they occur *after* the installation has been completed and must be uncovered, or even replaced. Post-completion changes may be caused by necessary design changes, product failure, or changes in the owner's requirements that are not discovered until the building or the systems begin to function.

Specified procedures of notification and record keeping must be adhered to and enforced regardless of the stage of construction: *before*, *during*, or *after* installation. Some bidding documents anticipate change orders by requiring that unit prices including overhead and profit percentages—for additional as well as deductible changes—be listed. Generally these unit prices do not fully take into account the ripple effect, or impact on other trades, and should be used for general guidance only.

When pricing change orders, it is important to classify the time frame in which the change occurs. There are two basic time frames for change orders: *pre-installation change orders*, which occur before the start of construction, and *post-installation change orders*, which involve reworking after the original installation. Change orders that occur between these stages may be priced according to the extent of work completed using a combination of techniques developed for pricing *pre-* and *post-installation* changes.

Factors To Consider When Pricing Change Orders

As an estimator begins to prepare a change order, the following questions should be reviewed to determine their impact on the final price.

General

- *Is the change order work* pre-installation *or* post-installation?

  Change order work costs vary according to how much of the installation has been completed. Once workers have the project scoped in their minds, even though they have not started, it can be difficult to refocus. Consequently they may spend more than the normal amount of time understanding the change. Also, modifications to work in place, such as trimming or refitting, usually take more time than was initially estimated. The greater the amount of work in place, the more reluctant workers are to change it. Psychologically they may resent the change and as a result the rework takes longer than normal. Post-installation change order estimates must include demolition of existing work as required to accomplish the change. If the work is performed at a later time, additional obstacles, such as building finishes, may be present which must be protected. Regardless of whether the change occurs pre-installation or post-installation, attempt to isolate the identifiable factors and price them separately. For example, add shipping costs that may be required pre-installation or any demolition required post-installation. Then analyze the potential impact on productivity of psychological and/or learning curve factors and adjust the output rates accordingly. One approach is to break down the typical workday into segments and quantify the impact on each segment.

Change Order Installation Efficiency

The labor-hours expressed (for new construction) are based on average installation time, using an efficiency level. For change order situations, adjustments to this efficiency level should reflect the daily labor-hour allocation for that particular occurrence.

- *Will the change substantially delay the original completion date?*

  A significant change in the project may cause the original completion date to be extended. The extended schedule may subject the contractor to new wage rates dictated by relevant labor contracts. Project supervision and other project overhead must also be extended beyond the original completion date. The schedule extension may also put installation into a new weather season. For example, underground piping scheduled for October installation was delayed until January. As a result, frost penetrated the trench area, thereby changing the degree of difficulty of the task. Changes and delays may have a ripple effect throughout the project. This effect must be analyzed and negotiated with the owner.

- *What is the net effect of a deduct change order?*

  In most cases, change orders resulting in a deduction or credit reflect only bare costs. The contractor may retain the overhead and profit based on the original bid.

Materials

- *Will you have to pay more or less for the new material, required by the change order, than you paid for the original purchase?*

  The same material prices or discounts will usually apply to materials purchased for change orders as new construction. In some instances, however, the contractor may forfeit the advantages of competitive pricing for change orders. Consider the following example:

  A contractor purchased over $20,000 worth of fan coil units for an installation and obtained the maximum discount. Some time later it was determined the project required an additional matching unit. The contractor has to purchase this unit from the original supplier to ensure a match. The supplier at this time may not discount the unit because of the small quantity, and he is no longer in a competitive situation. The impact of quantity on purchase can add between 0% and 25% to material prices and/or subcontractor quotes.

- *If materials have been ordered or delivered to the job site, will they be subject to a cancellation charge or restocking fee?*

  Check with the supplier to determine if ordered materials are subject to a cancellation charge. Delivered materials not used as a result of a change order may be subject to a restocking fee if returned to the supplier. Common restocking charges run between 20% and 40%. Also, delivery charges to return the goods to the supplier must be added.

Labor

- *How efficient is the existing crew at the actual installation?*

  Is the same crew that performed the initial work going to do the change order? Possibly the change consists of the installation of a unit identical to one already installed; therefore, the change should take less time. Be sure to consider this potential productivity increase and modify the productivity rates accordingly.

- *If the crew size is increased, what impact will that have on supervision requirements?*

  Under most bargaining agreements or management practices, there is a point at which a working foreperson is replaced by a nonworking foreperson. This replacement increases project overhead by adding a nonproductive worker. If additional workers are added to accelerate the project or to perform changes while maintaining the schedule, be sure to add additional supervision time if warranted. Calculate the hours involved and the additional cost directly if possible.

- *What are the other impacts of increased crew size?*

  The larger the crew, the greater the potential for productivity to decrease. Some of the factors that cause this productivity loss are: overcrowding (producing restrictive conditions in the working space) and possibly a shortage of any special tools and equipment required. Such factors affect not only the crew working on the elements directly involved in the change order, but other crews whose movements may also be hampered. As the crew increases, check its basic composition for changes by the addition or deletion of apprentices or nonworking foreperson, and quantify the potential effects of equipment shortages or other logistical factors.

- *As new crews, unfamiliar with the project, are brought onto the site, how long will it take them to become oriented to the project requirements?*

  The orientation time for a new crew to become 100% effective varies with the site and type of project. Orientation is easiest at a new construction site and most difficult at existing, very restrictive renovation sites. The type of work also affects orientation time. When all elements of the work are exposed, such as concrete or masonry work, orientation is decreased. When the work is concealed or less visible, such as existing electrical systems, orientation takes longer. Usually orientation can be accomplished in one day or less. Costs for added orientation should be itemized and added to the total estimated cost.

- *How much actual production can be gained by working overtime?*

  Short term overtime can be used effectively to accomplish more work in a day. However, as overtime is scheduled to run beyond several weeks, studies have shown marked decreases in output. The following chart shows the effect of long term overtime on worker efficiency. If the anticipated change requires extended overtime to keep the job on schedule, these factors can be used as a guide to predict the impact on time and cost. Add project overhead, particularly supervision, that may also be incurred.

Days per Week	Hours per Day	Production Efficiency					Payroll Cost Factors	
		1st Week	2nd Week	3rd Week	4th Week	Average 4 Weeks	@ 1-1/2 Times	@ 2 Times
5	8	100%	100%	100%	100%	100%	100%	100%
	9	100	100	95	90	96	1.056	1.111
	10	100	95	90	85	93	1.100	1.200
	11	95	90	75	65	81	1.136	1.273
	12	90	85	70	60	76	1.167	1.333
6	8	100	100	95	90	96	1.083	1.167
	9	100	95	90	85	93	1.130	1.259
	10	95	90	85	80	88	1.167	1.333
	11	95	85	70	65	79	1.197	1.394
	12	90	80	65	60	74	1.222	1.444
7	8	100	95	85	75	89	1.143	1.286
	9	95	90	80	70	84	1.183	1.365
	10	90	85	75	65	79	1.214	1.429
	11	85	80	65	60	73	1.240	1.481
	12	85	75	60	55	69	1.262	1.524

Effects of Overtime

Caution: Under many labor agreements, Sundays and holidays are paid at a higher premium than the normal overtime rate.

The use of long-term overtime is counterproductive on almost any construction job; that is, the longer the period of overtime, the lower the actual production rate. Numerous studies have been conducted, and while they have resulted in slightly different numbers, all reach the same conclusion. The figure above tabulates the effects of overtime work on efficiency.

As illustrated, there can be a difference between the *actual* payroll cost per hour and the *effective* cost per hour for overtime work. This is due to the reduced production efficiency with the increase in weekly hours beyond 40. This difference between actual and effective cost results from overtime work over a prolonged period. Short-term overtime work does not result in as great a reduction in efficiency and, in such cases, effective cost may not vary significantly from the actual payroll cost. As the total hours per week are increased on a regular basis, more time is lost due to fatigue, lowered morale, and an increased accident rate.

As an example, assume a project where workers are working 6 days a week, 10 hours per day. From the figure above (based on productivity studies), the average effective productive hours over a 4-week period are:

$$0.875 \times 60 = 52.5$$

Depending upon the locale and day of week, overtime hours may be paid at time and a half or double time. For time and a half, the overall (average) *actual* payroll cost (including regular and overtime hours) is determined as follows:

$$\frac{40 \text{ reg. hrs.} + (20 \text{ overtime hrs.} \times 1.5)}{60 \text{ hrs.}} = 1.167$$

Based on 60 hours, the payroll cost per hour will be 116.7% of the normal rate at 40 hours per week. However, because the effective production (efficiency) for 60 hours is reduced to the equivalent of 52.5 hours, the effective cost of overtime is calculated as follows:

For time and a half:

$$\frac{40 \text{ reg. hrs.} + (20 \text{ overtime hrs.} \times 1.5)}{52.5 \text{ hrs.}} = 1.33$$

The installed cost will be 133% of the normal rate (for labor).

Thus, when figuring overtime, the actual cost per unit of work will be higher than the apparent overtime payroll dollar increase, due to the reduced productivity of the longer work week. These efficiency calculations are true only for those cost factors determined by hours worked. Costs that are applied weekly or monthly, such as equipment rentals, will not be similarly affected.

Equipment

- *What equipment is required to complete the change order?*

Change orders may require extending the rental period of equipment already on the job site, or the addition of special equipment brought in to accomplish the change work. In either case, the additional rental charges and operator labor charges must be added.

Summary

The preceding considerations and others you deem appropriate should be analyzed and applied to a change order estimate. The impact of each should be quantified and listed on the estimate to form an audit trail.

Change orders that are properly identified, documented, and managed help to ensure the orderly, professional, and profitable progress of the work. They also minimize potential claims or disputes at the end of the project.

Project Costs

Back by customer demand!
You asked and we listened. For customer convenience and estimating ease, we have made the 2023 Project Costs available for download at **RSMeans.com/2023books**. You will also find sample estimates, an RSMeans data overview video, and a book registration form to receive quarterly data updates throughout 2023.

Estimating Tips
- The cost figures available in the download were derived from hundreds of projects contained in the RSMeans database of completed construction projects. They include the contractor's overhead and profit. The figures have been adjusted to January of the current year.
- These projects were located throughout the U.S. and reflect a tremendous variation in square foot (S.F.) costs. This is due to differences, not only in labor and material costs, but also in individual owners' requirements. For instance, a bank in a large city would have different features than one in a rural area. This is true of all the different types of buildings analyzed. Therefore, caution should be exercised when using these Project Costs. For example, for courthouses, costs in the database are local courthouse costs and will not apply to the larger, more elaborate federal courthouses.
- None of the figures "go with" any others. All individual cost items were computed and tabulated separately. Thus, the sum of the median figures for plumbing, HVAC, and electrical will not normally total up to the total mechanical and electrical costs arrived at by separate analysis and tabulation of the projects.
- Each building was analyzed as to total and component costs and percentages. The figures were arranged in ascending order with the results tabulated as shown. The 1/4 column shows that 25% of the projects had lower costs and 75% had higher. The 3/4 column shows that 75% of the projects had lower costs and 25% had higher. The median column shows that 50% of the projects had lower costs and 50% had higher.
- Project Costs are useful in the conceptual stage when no details are available. As soon as details become available in the project design, the square foot approach should be discontinued and the project should be priced as to its particular components. When more precision is required, or for estimating the replacement cost of specific buildings, the current edition of *Square Foot Costs with RSMeans data* should be used.
- In using the figures in this section, it is recommended that the median column be used for preliminary figures if no additional information is available. The median figures, when multiplied by the total city construction cost index figures (see City Cost Indexes) and then multiplied by the project size modifier at the end of this section, should present a fairly accurate base figure, which would then have to be adjusted in view of the estimator's experience, local economic conditions, code requirements, and the owner's particular requirements. There is no need to factor in the percentage figures, as these should remain constant from city to city.
- The editors of this data would greatly appreciate receiving cost figures on one or more of your recent projects, which would then be included in the averages for next year. All cost figures received will be kept confidential, except that they will be averaged with other similar projects to arrive at square foot cost figures for next year.

See the website above for details and the discount available for submitting one or more of your projects.

Same Data. Simplified.

Enjoy the convenience and efficiency of accessing your costs anywhere:
- **Skip the multiplier** by setting your location
- **Quickly search,** edit, favorite and share costs
- **Stay on top of price changes** with automatic updates

Discover more at rsmeans.com/online

No part of this cost data may be reproduced, stored in a retrieval system, or transmitted in any form or by any means without prior written permission of Gordian.

50 17 | Project Costs

50 17 00 | Project Costs

			UNIT	UNIT COSTS 1/4	MEDIAN	3/4	% OF TOTAL 1/4	MEDIAN	3/4	
01	0000	**Auto Sales with Repair**	S.F.							01
	0100	Architectural		146	163	176	58%	64%	67%	
	0200	Plumbing		12.20	12.75	17.05	4.84%	5.20%	6.80%	
	0300	Mechanical		16.30	22	24	6.40%	8.70%	10.15%	
	0400	Electrical		25	31	39	9.05%	11.70%	15.90%	
	0500	Total Project Costs		244	255	262				
02	0000	**Banking Institutions**	S.F.							02
	0100	Architectural		220	270	330	59%	65%	69%	
	0200	Plumbing		8.85	12.35	17.15	2.12%	3.39%	4.19%	
	0300	Mechanical		17.60	24.50	28.50	4.41%	5.10%	10.75%	
	0400	Electrical		43	52	80	10.45%	13.05%	15.90%	
	0500	Total Project Costs		365	410	505				
03	0000	**Courthouse**	S.F.							03
	0100	Architectural		116	228	320	54.50%	58.50%	61%	
	0200	Plumbing		4.38	16.30	16.30	2.07%	3.13%	3.13%	
	0300	Mechanical		27.50	32.50	32.50	6.25%	12.95%	12.95%	
	0400	Electrical		35	40	40	7.65%	16.60%	16.60%	
	0500	Total Project Costs		211	390	520				
04	0000	**Data Centers**	S.F.							04
	0100	Architectural		262	262	262	68%	68%	68%	
	0200	Plumbing		14.35	14.35	14.35	3.71%	3.71%	3.71%	
	0300	Mechanical		36.50	36.50	36.50	9.45%	9.45%	9.45%	
	0400	Electrical		34.50	34.50	34.50	9%	9%	9%	
	0500	Total Project Costs		385	385	385				
05	0000	**Detention Centers**	S.F.							05
	0100	Architectural		243	256	272	52%	53%	60.50%	
	0200	Plumbing		25.50	31	37.50	5.15%	7.10%	7.25%	
	0300	Mechanical		32.50	46.50	55.50	7.55%	9.50%	13.80%	
	0400	Electrical		53.50	63	82	10.90%	14.85%	17.95%	
	0500	Total Project Costs		410	435	510				
06	0000	**Fire Stations**	S.F.							06
	0100	Architectural		141	180	284	46%	54.50%	61.50%	
	0200	Plumbing		14.75	19.70	25.50	4.67%	5.60%	6.35%	
	0300	Mechanical		22	31	42	6.10%	8.25%	10.20%	
	0400	Electrical		33.50	41	57.50	10.75%	12.55%	14.95%	
	0500	Total Project Costs		292	350	465				
07	0000	**Gymnasium**	S.F.							07
	0100	Architectural		121	160	160	57%	64.50%	64.50%	
	0200	Plumbing		2.97	9.75	9.75	1.58%	3.48%	3.48%	
	0300	Mechanical		4.56	41	41	2.42%	14.65%	14.65%	
	0400	Electrical		14.95	29	29	7.95%	10.35%	10.35%	
	0500	Total Project Costs		189	280	280				
08	0000	**Hospitals**	S.F.							08
	0100	Architectural		147	242	263	41.50%	47.50%	48%	
	0200	Plumbing		10.80	44.50	53	6%	7.65%	10.35%	
	0300	Mechanical		65	80.50	105	12.55%	17.95%	23.50%	
	0400	Electrical		32.50	73.50	84.50	10.95%	14.10%	16.85%	
	0500	Total Project Costs		345	520	555				
09	0000	**Industrial Buildings**	S.F.							09
	0100	Architectural		80.50	158	320	52%	56%	82%	
	0200	Plumbing		2.32	6.30	18.20	1.57%	2.11%	6.30%	
	0300	Mechanical		6.60	12.55	60	4.77%	5.55%	14.80%	
	0400	Electrical		10.10	11.50	96	7.85%	13.55%	16.20%	
	0500	Total Project Costs		119	181	595				
10	0000	**Medical Clinics & Offices**	S.F.							10
	0100	Architectural		134	166	218	48.50%	54%	62%	
	0200	Plumbing		12.30	18.55	30.50	4.50%	6.65%	8.75%	
	0300	Mechanical		19.90	30.50	54.50	7.80%	10.85%	15.75%	
	0400	Electrical		27	33.50	51	8.90%	11.20%	13.85%	
	0500	Total Project Costs		231	305	400				

50 17 | Project Costs

50 17 00 | Project Costs

			UNIT	UNIT COSTS			% OF TOTAL		
				1/4	MEDIAN	3/4	1/4	MEDIAN	3/4
11	0000	**Mixed Use**	S.F.						
	0100	Architectural		151	209	285	45.50%	52.50%	61.50%
	0200	Plumbing		8.55	15.55	16.55	3.31%	3.47%	4.18%
	0300	Mechanical		22.50	49	65	6.10%	13.60%	17.05%
	0400	Electrical		30	50.50	72.50	8.60%	11.65%	15.65%
	0500	Total Project Costs		264	460	470			
12	0000	**Multi-Family Housing**	S.F.						
	0100	Architectural		105	143	233	54.50%	62%	69%
	0200	Plumbing		9.40	15.15	20.50	5.25%	6.65%	8%
	0300	Mechanical		9.65	13	37	4.41%	6.05%	10.25%
	0400	Electrical		12.70	21.50	31	5.65%	7.90%	10.25%
	0500	Total Project Costs		174	286	370			
13	0000	**Nursing Home & Assisted Living**	S.F.						
	0100	Architectural		99	143	162	51.50%	55.50%	63.50%
	0200	Plumbing		10.60	15.95	19	6.25%	7.40%	9.20%
	0300	Mechanical		8.70	12.85	25	4.04%	6.70%	9.55%
	0400	Electrical		14.60	25.50	33.50	7.25%	11%	13.10%
	0500	Total Project Costs		174	224	296			
14	0000	**Office Buildings**	S.F.						
	0100	Architectural		130	177	244	54.50%	61%	69%
	0200	Plumbing		7	11	20.50	2.70%	3.78%	5.20%
	0300	Mechanical		13.70	23.50	36	5.55%	8.15%	11.10%
	0400	Electrical		18.35	30	48	7.80%	10.10%	12.90%
	0500	Total Project Costs		221	292	400			
15	0000	**Parking Garage**	S.F.						
	0100	Architectural		43.50	53	55.50	70%	79%	88%
	0200	Plumbing		1.43	1.50	2.80	2.05%	2.70%	2.83%
	0300	Mechanical		1.11	1.71	6.50	2.11%	3.62%	3.81%
	0400	Electrical		3.81	4.19	8.75	5.30%	6.35%	7.95%
	0500	Total Project Costs		53	64.50	70			
16	0000	**Parking Garage/Mixed Use**	S.F.						
	0100	Architectural		141	154	157	61%	62%	65.50%
	0200	Plumbing		4.52	5.95	9.10	2.47%	2.72%	3.66%
	0300	Mechanical		19.35	22	31.50	7.80%	13.10%	13.60%
	0400	Electrical		20.50	29	30	8.20%	12.65%	18.15%
	0500	Total Project Costs		230	240	248			
17	0000	**Police Stations**	S.F.						
	0100	Architectural		159	225	277	49%	61%	61.50%
	0200	Plumbing		21	25.50	25.50	5.05%	5.55%	7.70%
	0300	Mechanical		47.50	66.50	69	12.35%	14.55%	16.55%
	0400	Electrical		36	41.50	61.50	9.15%	12.10%	14%
	0500	Total Project Costs		298	415	455			
18	0000	**Police/Fire**	S.F.						
	0100	Architectural		155	155	475	55.50%	66%	68%
	0200	Plumbing		12.40	12.85	47.50	5.45%	5.50%	5.55%
	0300	Mechanical		19	30	109	8.35%	12.70%	12.80%
	0400	Electrical		21.50	27.50	124	9.50%	11.75%	14.55%
	0500	Total Project Costs		228	235	855			
19	0000	**Public Assembly Buildings**	S.F.						
	0100	Architectural		158	206	320	56.50%	61%	64%
	0200	Plumbing		8.35	12.25	18.10	2.63%	3.36%	4.39%
	0300	Mechanical		17.60	30.50	48.50	6.45%	8.75%	12.45%
	0400	Electrical		26	35	56	8.60%	10.70%	12.80%
	0500	Total Project Costs		254	340	505			
20	0000	**Recreational**	S.F.						
	0100	Architectural		152	230	325	49.50%	59%	64.50%
	0200	Plumbing		11.35	18.30	30	3.08%	4.67%	7.40%
	0300	Mechanical		18.10	27.50	41	5.15%	6.65%	11.35%
	0400	Electrical		22	37.50	54.50	7.10%	8.95%	10.80%
	0500	Total Project Costs		270	390	610			

For customer support on your Plumbing Costs with RSMeans data, call 800.448.8182.

50 17 | Project Costs

50 17 00 | Project Costs

			UNIT	UNIT COSTS			% OF TOTAL		
				1/4	MEDIAN	3/4	1/4	MEDIAN	3/4
21	0000	**Restaurants**	S.F.						
	0100	Architectural		172	270	340	57.50%	60%	63.50%
	0200	Plumbing		18.95	38	50	7.35%	7.70%	8.75%
	0300	Mechanical		20.50	27	51	6.50%	8.15%	11.15%
	0400	Electrical		20.50	33	66	6.75%	10.30%	11.60%
	0500	Total Project Costs		285	470	570			
22	0000	**Retail**	S.F.						
	0100	Architectural		77	120	248	54.50%	60%	64.50%
	0200	Plumbing		9.60	13.40	16.65	4.18%	5.45%	8.45%
	0300	Mechanical		9	12.75	23.50	4.98%	6.15%	7.05%
	0400	Electrical		14.30	29	43	7.90%	11.25%	12.45%
	0500	Total Project Costs		117	208	400			
23	0000	**Schools**	S.F.						
	0100	Architectural		133	169	226	50.50%	55.50%	60.50%
	0200	Plumbing		10.60	14.55	21	3.66%	4.57%	6.95%
	0300	Mechanical		25	36	52.50	8.90%	11.95%	14.55%
	0400	Electrical		25	34.50	44.50	9.45%	11.25%	13.30%
	0500	Total Project Costs		242	310	415			
24	0000	**University, College & Private School Classroom & Admin Buildings**	S.F.						
	0100	Architectural		172	224	272	50%	53.50%	58.50%
	0200	Plumbing		11.75	16.10	29.50	3.04%	4.30%	6.35%
	0300	Mechanical		34	51.50	66	9.20%	11.40%	14.40%
	0400	Electrical		28.50	41	53.50	7.70%	9.95%	12.55%
	0500	Total Project Costs		297	415	540			
25	0000	**University, College & Private School Dormitories**	S.F.						
	0100	Architectural		111	195	207	53%	61.50%	68%
	0200	Plumbing		14.65	21	24	6.35%	6.65%	8.95%
	0300	Mechanical		6.60	28	44.50	4.13%	9%	11.80%
	0400	Electrical		7.80	27	41.50	4.75%	7.35%	10.60%
	0500	Total Project Costs		164	310	370			
26	0000	**University, College & Private School Science, Eng. & Lab Buildings**	S.F.						
	0100	Architectural		191	226	335	48%	54.50%	58%
	0200	Plumbing		13.15	19.90	33.50	3.29%	3.77%	5%
	0300	Mechanical		50.50	94	96.50	11.70%	19.40%	23.50%
	0400	Electrical		39.50	51.50	53	9%	12.05%	13.15%
	0500	Total Project Costs		400	430	585			
27	0000	**University, College & Private School Student Union Buildings**	S.F.						
	0100	Architectural		151	395	395	54.50%	54.50%	59.50%
	0200	Plumbing		23	23	34	3.13%	4.27%	11.45%
	0300	Mechanical		43.50	70	70	9.60%	9.60%	14.55%
	0400	Electrical		38	66	66	9.05%	12.80%	13.15%
	0500	Total Project Costs		297	730	730			
28	0000	**Warehouses**	S.F.						
	0100	Architectural		65	98.50	180	60.50%	67%	71.50%
	0200	Plumbing		3.37	7.20	13.90	2.82%	3.72%	5%
	0300	Mechanical		3.99	22.50	35.50	4.56%	8.15%	10.70%
	0400	Electrical		8.40	27	45.50	7.75%	10.10%	18.30%
	0500	Total Project Costs		96.50	154	310			

Square Foot Project Size Modifier

One factor that affects the S.F. cost of a particular building is the size. In general, for buildings built to the same specifications in the same locality, the larger building will have the lower S.F. cost. This is due mainly to the decreasing contribution of the exterior walls plus the economy of scale usually achievable in larger buildings. The Area Conversion Scale shown below will give a factor to convert costs for the typical size building to an adjusted cost for the particular project.

The Square Foot Base Size lists the median costs, most typical project size in our accumulated data, and the range in size of the projects.

The Size Factor for your project is determined by dividing your project area in S.F. by the typical project size for the particular Building Type. With this factor, enter the Area Conversion Scale at the appropriate Size Factor and determine the appropriate Cost Multiplier for your building size.

Example: Determine the cost per S.F. for a 107,200 S.F. Multi-family housing.

$$\frac{\text{Proposed building area} = 107{,}200 \text{ S.F.}}{\text{Typical size from below} = 53{,}600 \text{ S.F.}} = 2.00$$

Enter Area Conversion Scale at 2.0, intersect curve, read horizontally the appropriate cost multiplier of .94. Size adjusted cost becomes .94 x $286.00 = $268.84 based on national average costs.

Note: For Size Factors less than .50, the Cost Multiplier is 1.1
For Size Factors greater than 3.5, the Cost Multiplier is .90

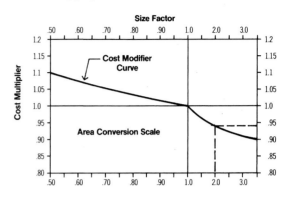

System	Median Cost (Total Project Costs)	Typical Size Gross S.F. (Median of Projects)	Typical Range (Low – High) (Projects)
Auto Sales with Repair	$255.00	24,900	4,700 – 29,300
Banking Institutions	410.00	9,300	3,300 – 38,100
Courthouse	390.00	56,000	24,700 – 70,500
Data Centers	385.00	14,400	14,400 – 14,400
Detention Centers	435.00	37,800	12,300 – 183,330
Fire Stations	350.00	12,400	6,300 – 49,600
Gymnasium	280.00	52,400	22,800 – 82,000
Hospitals	520.00	73,300	12,700 – 410,300
Industrial Buildings	181.00	21,100	5,100 – 200,600
Medical Clinics & Offices	305.00	24,200	2,300 – 327,000
Mixed Use	460.00	31,800	7,200 – 188,900
Multi-Family Housing	286.00	53,600	2,500 – 1,161,500
Nursing Home & Assisted Living	224.00	38,700	1,500 – 242,600
Office Buildings	292.00	21,000	1,100 – 930,000
Parking Garage	64.50	151,800	99,900 – 287,000
Parking Garage/Mixed Use	240.00	254,200	5,300 – 318,000
Police Stations	415.00	25,200	12,700 – 88,600
Police/Fire	235.00	44,300	8,600 – 50,300
Public Assembly Buildings	340.00	20,800	2,200 – 235,300
Recreational	390.00	27,700	1,000 – 223,800
Restaurants	470.00	5,900	2,100 – 42,000
Retail	208.00	26,000	4,000 – 84,300
Schools	310.00	69,400	1,300 – 410,800
University, College & Private School Classroom & Admin Buildings	415.00	48,300	2,400 – 196,200
University, College & Private School Dormitories	310.00	39,200	1,500 – 126,900
University, College & Private School Science, Eng. & Lab Buildings	430.00	60,000	5,300 – 117,600
University, College & Private School Student Union Buildings	730.00	48,700	42,100 – 50,000
Warehouses	154.00	10,900	600 – 303,800

Abbreviations

A	Area Square Feet; Ampere	Brk., brk	Brick	Csc	Cosecant
AAFES	Army and Air Force Exchange Service	brkt	Bracket	C.S.F.	Hundred Square Feet
ABS	Acrylonitrile Butadiene Stryrene; Asbestos Bonded Steel	Brs.	Brass	CSI	Construction Specifications Institute
A.C., AC	Alternating Current; Air-Conditioning; Asbestos Cement; Plywood Grade A & C	Brz.	Bronze	CT	Current Transformer
		Bsn.	Basin	CTS	Copper Tube Size
		Btr.	Better	Cu	Copper, Cubic
		BTU	British Thermal Unit	Cu. Ft.	Cubic Foot
		BTUH	BTU per Hour	cw	Continuous Wave
ACI	American Concrete Institute	Bu.	Bushels	C.W.	Cool White; Cold Water
ACR	Air Conditioning Refrigeration	BUR	Built-up Roofing	Cwt.	100 Pounds
ADA	Americans with Disabilities Act	BX	Interlocked Armored Cable	C.W.X.	Cool White Deluxe
AD	Plywood, Grade A & D	°C	Degree Centigrade	C.Y.	Cubic Yard (27 cubic feet)
Addit.	Additional	c	Conductivity, Copper Sweat	C.Y./Hr.	Cubic Yard per Hour
Adh.	Adhesive	C	Hundred; Centigrade	Cyl.	Cylinder
Adj.	Adjustable	C/C	Center to Center, Cedar on Cedar	d	Penny (nail size)
af	Audio-frequency	C-C	Center to Center	D	Deep; Depth; Discharge
AFFF	Aqueous Film Forming Foam	Cab	Cabinet	Dis., Disch.	Discharge
AFUE	Annual Fuel Utilization Efficiency	Cair.	Air Tool Laborer	Db	Decibel
AGA	American Gas Association	Cal.	Caliper	Dbl.	Double
Agg.	Aggregate	Calc	Calculated	DC	Direct Current
A.H., Ah	Ampere Hours	Cap.	Capacity	DDC	Direct Digital Control
A hr.	Ampere-hour	Carp.	Carpenter	Demob.	Demobilization
A.H.U., AHU	Air Handling Unit	C.B.	Circuit Breaker	d.f.t.	Dry Film Thickness
A.I.A.	American Institute of Architects	C.C.A.	Chromate Copper Arsenate	d.f.u.	Drainage Fixture Units
AIC	Ampere Interrupting Capacity	C.C.F.	Hundred Cubic Feet	D.H.	Double Hung
Allow.	Allowance	cd	Candela	DHW	Domestic Hot Water
alt., alt	Alternate	cd/sf	Candela per Square Foot	DI	Ductile Iron
Alum.	Aluminum	CD	Grade of Plywood Face & Back	Diag.	Diagonal
a.m.	Ante Meridiem	CDX	Plywood, Grade C & D, exterior glue	Diam., Dia	Diameter
Amp.	Ampere			Distrib.	Distribution
Anod.	Anodized	Cefi.	Cement Finisher	Div.	Division
ANSI	American National Standards Institute	Cem.	Cement	Dk.	Deck
		CF	Hundred Feet	D.L.	Dead Load; Diesel
APA	American Plywood Association	C.F.	Cubic Feet	DLH	Deep Long Span Bar Joist
Approx.	Approximate	CFM	Cubic Feet per Minute	dlx	Deluxe
Apt.	Apartment	CFRP	Carbon Fiber Reinforced Plastic	Do.	Ditto
Asb.	Asbestos	c.g.	Center of Gravity	DOP	Dioctyl Phthalate Penetration Test (Air Filters)
A.S.B.C.	American Standard Building Code	CHW	Chilled Water; Commercial Hot Water		
Asbe.	Asbestos Worker	C.I., CI	Cast Iron	Dp., dp	Depth
ASCE	American Society of Civil Engineers	C.I.P., CIP	Cast in Place	D.P.S.T.	Double Pole, Single Throw
A.S.H.R.A.E.	American Society of Heating, Refrig. & AC Engineers	Circ.	Circuit	Dr.	Drive
		C.L.	Carload Lot	DR	Dimension Ratio
ASME	American Society of Mechanical Engineers	CL	Chain Link	Drink.	Drinking
		Clab.	Common Laborer	D.S.	Double Strength
ASTM	American Society for Testing and Materials	Clam	Common Maintenance Laborer	D.S.A.	Double Strength A Grade
		C.L.F.	Hundred Linear Feet	D.S.B.	Double Strength B Grade
Attchmt.	Attachment	CLF	Current Limiting Fuse	Dty.	Duty
Avg., Ave.	Average	CLP	Cross Linked Polyethylene	DWV	Drain Waste Vent
AWG	American Wire Gauge	cm	Centimeter	DX	Deluxe White, Direct Expansion
AWWA	American Water Works Assoc.	CMP	Corr. Metal Pipe	dyn	Dyne
Bbl.	Barrel	CMU	Concrete Masonry Unit	e	Eccentricity
B&B, BB	Grade B and Better; Balled & Burlapped	CN	Change Notice	E	Equipment Only; East; Emissivity
		Col.	Column	Ea.	Each
B&S	Bell and Spigot	CO$_2$	Carbon Dioxide	EB	Encased Burial
B&W.	Black and White	Comb.	Combination	Econ.	Economy
b.c.c.	Body-centered Cubic	comm.	Commercial, Communication	E.C.Y	Embankment Cubic Yards
B.C.Y.	Bank Cubic Yards	Compr.	Compressor	EDP	Electronic Data Processing
BE	Bevel End	Conc.	Concrete	EIFS	Exterior Insulation Finish System
B.F.	Board Feet	Cont., cont	Continuous; Continued, Container	E.D.R.	Equiv. Direct Radiation
Bg. cem.	Bag of Cement	Corkbd.	Cork Board	Eq.	Equation
BHP	Boiler Horsepower; Brake Horsepower	Corr.	Corrugated	EL	Elevation
		Cos	Cosine	Elec.	Electrician; Electrical
B.I.	Black Iron	Cot	Cotangent	Elev.	Elevator; Elevating
bidir.	bidirectional	Cov.	Cover	EMT	Electrical Metallic Conduit; Thin Wall Conduit
Bit., Bitum.	Bituminous	C/P	Cedar on Paneling		
Bit., Conc.	Bituminous Concrete	CPA	Control Point Adjustment	Eng.	Engine, Engineered
Bk.	Backed	Cplg.	Coupling	EPDM	Ethylene Propylene Diene Monomer
Bkrs.	Breakers	CPM	Critical Path Method		
Bldg., bldg	Building	CPVC	Chlorinated Polyvinyl Chloride	EPS	Expanded Polystyrene
Blk.	Block	C.Pr.	Hundred Pair	Eqhv.	Equip. Oper., Heavy
Bm.	Beam	CRC	Cold Rolled Channel	Eqlt.	Equip. Oper., Light
Boil.	Boilermaker	Creos.	Creosote	Eqmd.	Equip. Oper., Medium
bpm	Blows per Minute	Crpt.	Carpet & Linoleum Layer	Eqmm.	Equip. Oper., Master Mechanic
BR	Bedroom	CRT	Cathode-ray Tube	Eqol.	Equip. Oper., Oilers
Brg., brng.	Bearing	CS	Carbon Steel, Constant Shear Bar Joist	Equip.	Equipment
Brhe.	Bricklayer Helper			ERW	Electric Resistance Welded
Bric.	Bricklayer				

Abbreviations

E.S.	Energy Saver	H	High Henry	Lath.	Lather
Est.	Estimated	HC	High Capacity	Lav.	Lavatory
esu	Electrostatic Units	H.D., HD	Heavy Duty; High Density	lb.; #	Pound
E.W.	Each Way	H.D.O.	High Density Overlaid	L.B., LB	Load Bearing; L Conduit Body
EWT	Entering Water Temperature	HDPE	High Density Polyethylene Plastic	L. & E.	Labor & Equipment
Excav.	Excavation	Hdr.	Header	lb./hr.	Pounds per Hour
excl	Excluding	Hdwe.	Hardware	lb./L.F.	Pounds per Linear Foot
Exp., exp	Expansion, Exposure	H.I.D., HID	High Intensity Discharge	lbf/sq.in.	Pound-force per Square Inch
Ext., ext	Exterior; Extension	Help.	Helper Average	L.C.L.	Less than Carload Lot
Extru.	Extrusion	HEPA	High Efficiency Particulate Air Filter	L.C.Y.	Loose Cubic Yard
f.	Fiber Stress	Hg	Mercury	Ld.	Load
F	Fahrenheit; Female; Fill	HIC	High Interrupting Capacity	LE	Lead Equivalent
Fab., fab	Fabricated; Fabric	HM	Hollow Metal	LED	Light Emitting Diode
FBGS	Fiberglass	HMWPE	High Molecular Weight Polyethylene	L.F.	Linear Foot
F.C.	Footcandles			L.F. Hdr	Linear Feet of Header
f.c.c.	Face-centered Cubic	HO	High Output	L.F. Nose	Linear Foot of Stair Nosing
f'c.	Compressive Stress in Concrete; Extreme Compressive Stress	Horiz.	Horizontal	L.F. Rsr	Linear Foot of Stair Riser
		H.P., HP	Horsepower; High Pressure	Lg.	Long; Length; Large
F.E.	Front End	H.P.F.	High Power Factor	L & H	Light and Heat
FEP	Fluorinated Ethylene Propylene (Teflon)	Hr.	Hour	LH	Long Span Bar Joist
		Hrs./Day	Hours per Day	L.H.	Labor Hours
F.G.	Flat Grain	HSC	High Short Circuit	L.L., LL	Live Load
F.H.A.	Federal Housing Administration	Ht.	Height	L.L.D.	Lamp Lumen Depreciation
Fig.	Figure	Htg.	Heating	lm	Lumen
Fin.	Finished	Htrs.	Heaters	lm/sf	Lumen per Square Foot
FIPS	Female Iron Pipe Size	HVAC	Heating, Ventilation & Air-Conditioning	lm/W	Lumen per Watt
Fixt.	Fixture			LOA	Length Over All
FJP	Finger jointed and primed	Hvy.	Heavy	log	Logarithm
Fl. Oz.	Fluid Ounces	HW	Hot Water	L-O-L	Lateralolet
Flr.	Floor	Hyd.; Hydr.	Hydraulic	long.	Longitude
Flrs.	Floors	Hz	Hertz (cycles)	L.P., LP	Liquefied Petroleum; Low Pressure
FM	Frequency Modulation; Factory Mutual	I.	Moment of Inertia	L.P.F.	Low Power Factor
		IBC	International Building Code	LR	Long Radius
Fmg.	Framing	I.C.	Interrupting Capacity	L.S.	Lump Sum
FM/UL	Factory Mutual/Underwriters Labs	ID	Inside Diameter	Lt.	Light
Fdn.	Foundation	I.D.	Inside Dimension; Identification	Lt. Ga.	Light Gauge
FNPT	Female National Pipe Thread	I.F.	Inside Frosted	L.T.L.	Less than Truckload Lot
Fori.	Foreman, Inside	I.M.C.	Intermediate Metal Conduit	Lt. Wt.	Lightweight
Foro.	Foreman, Outside	In.	Inch	L.V.	Low Voltage
Fount.	Fountain	Incan.	Incandescent	M	Thousand; Material; Male; Light Wall Copper Tubing
fpm	Feet per Minute	Incl.	Included; Including		
FPT	Female Pipe Thread	Int.	Interior	M^2CA	Meters Squared Contact Area
Fr	Frame	Inst.	Installation	m/hr.; M.H.	Man-hour
F.R.	Fire Rating	Insul., insul	Insulation/Insulated	mA	Milliampere
FRK	Foil Reinforced Kraft	I.P.	Iron Pipe	Mach.	Machine
FSK	Foil/Scrim/Kraft	I.P.S., IPS	Iron Pipe Size	Mag. Str.	Magnetic Starter
FRP	Fiberglass Reinforced Plastic	IPT	Iron Pipe Threaded	Maint.	Maintenance
FS	Forged Steel	I.W.	Indirect Waste	Marb.	Marble Setter
FSC	Cast Body; Cast Switch Box	J	Joule	Mat; Mat'l.	Material
Ft., ft	Foot; Feet	J.I.C.	Joint Industrial Council	Max.	Maximum
Ftng.	Fitting	K	Thousand; Thousand Pounds; Heavy Wall Copper Tubing, Kelvin	MBF	Thousand Board Feet
Ftg.	Footing			MBH	Thousand BTU's per hr.
Ft lb.	Foot Pound	K.A.H.	Thousand Amp. Hours	MC	Metal Clad Cable
Furn.	Furniture	kcmil	Thousand Circular Mils	MCC	Motor Control Center
FVNR	Full Voltage Non-Reversing	KD	Knock Down	M.C.F.	Thousand Cubic Feet
FVR	Full Voltage Reversing	K.D.A.T.	Kiln Dried After Treatment	MCFM	Thousand Cubic Feet per Minute
FXM	Female by Male	kg	Kilogram	M.C.M.	Thousand Circular Mils
Fy.	Minimum Yield Stress of Steel	kG	Kilogauss	MCP	Motor Circuit Protector
g	Gram	kgf	Kilogram Force	MD	Medium Duty
G	Gauss	kHz	Kilohertz	MDF	Medium-density fibreboard
Ga.	Gauge	Kip	1000 Pounds	M.D.O.	Medium Density Overlaid
Gal., gal.	Gallon	KJ	Kilojoule	Med.	Medium
Galv., galv	Galvanized	K.L.	Effective Length Factor	MF	Thousand Feet
GC/MS	Gas Chromatograph/Mass Spectrometer	K.L.F.	Kips per Linear Foot	M.F.B.M.	Thousand Feet Board Measure
		Km	Kilometer	Mfg.	Manufacturing
Gen.	General	KO	Knock Out	Mfrs.	Manufacturers
GFI	Ground Fault Interrupter	K.S.F.	Kips per Square Foot	mg	Milligram
GFRC	Glass Fiber Reinforced Concrete	K.S.I.	Kips per Square Inch	MGD	Million Gallons per Day
Glaz.	Glazier	kV	Kilovolt	MGPH	Million Gallons per Hour
GPD	Gallons per Day	kVA	Kilovolt Ampere	MH, M.H.	Manhole; Metal Halide; Man-Hour
gpf	Gallon per Flush	kVAR	Kilovar (Reactance)	MHz	Megahertz
GPH	Gallons per Hour	KW	Kilowatt	Mi.	Mile
gpm, GPM	Gallons per Minute	KWh	Kilowatt-hour	MI	Malleable Iron; Mineral Insulated
GR	Grade	L	Labor Only; Length; Long; Medium Wall Copper Tubing	MIPS	Male Iron Pipe Size
Gran.	Granular			mj	Mechanical Joint
Grnd.	Ground	Lab.	Labor	m	Meter
GVW	Gross Vehicle Weight	lat	Latitude	mm	Millimeter
GWB	Gypsum Wall Board			Mill.	Millwright
				Min., min.	Minimum, Minute

Abbreviations

Misc.	Miscellaneous	PCM	Phase Contrast Microscopy	SBS	Styrene Butadiere Styrene
ml	Milliliter, Mainline	PDCA	Painting and Decorating Contractors of America	SC	Screw Cover
M.L.F.	Thousand Linear Feet			SCFM	Standard Cubic Feet per Minute
Mo.	Month	P.E., PE	Professional Engineer; Porcelain Enamel; Polyethylene; Plain End	Scaf.	Scaffold
Mobil.	Mobilization			Sch., Sched.	Schedule
Mog.	Mogul Base			S.C.R.	Modular Brick
MPH	Miles per Hour	P.E.C.I.	Porcelain Enamel on Cast Iron	S.D.	Sound Deadening
MPT	Male Pipe Thread	Perf.	Perforated	SDR	Standard Dimension Ratio
MRGWB	Moisture Resistant Gypsum Wallboard	PEX	Cross Linked Polyethylene	S.E.	Surfaced Edge
		Ph.	Phase	Sel.	Select
MRT	Mile Round Trip	P.I.	Pressure Injected	SER, SEU	Service Entrance Cable
ms	Millisecond	Pile.	Pile Driver	S.F.	Square Foot
M.S.F.	Thousand Square Feet	Pkg.	Package	S.F.C.A.	Square Foot Contact Area
Mstz.	Mosaic & Terrazzo Worker	Pl.	Plate	S.F. Flr.	Square Foot of Floor
M.S.Y.	Thousand Square Yards	Plah.	Plasterer Helper	S.F.G.	Square Foot of Ground
Mtd., mtd., mtd	Mounted	Plas.	Plasterer	S.F. Hor.	Square Foot Horizontal
Mthe.	Mosaic & Terrazzo Helper	plf	Pounds Per Linear Foot	SFR	Square Feet of Radiation
Mtng.	Mounting	Pluh.	Plumber Helper	S.F. Shlf.	Square Foot of Shelf
Mult.	Multi; Multiply	Plum.	Plumber	S4S	Surface 4 Sides
MUTCD	Manual on Uniform Traffic Control Devices	Ply.	Plywood	Shee.	Sheet Metal Worker
		p.m.	Post Meridiem	Sin.	Sine
M.V.A.	Million Volt Amperes	Pntd.	Painted	Skwk.	Skilled Worker
M.V.A.R.	Million Volt Amperes Reactance	Pord.	Painter, Ordinary	SL	Saran Lined
MV	Megavolt	pp	Pages	S.L.	Slimline
MW	Megawatt	PP, PPL	Polypropylene	Sldr.	Solder
MXM	Male by Male	P.P.M.	Parts per Million	SLH	Super Long Span Bar Joist
MYD	Thousand Yards	Pr.	Pair	S.N.	Solid Neutral
N	Natural; North	P.E.S.B.	Pre-engineered Steel Building	SO	Stranded with oil resistant inside insulation
nA	Nanoampere	Prefab.	Prefabricated		
NA	Not Available; Not Applicable	Prefin.	Prefinished	S-O-L	Socketolet
N.B.C.	National Building Code	Prop.	Propelled	sp	Standpipe
NC	Normally Closed	PSF, psf	Pounds per Square Foot	S.P.	Static Pressure; Single Pole; Self-Propelled
NEMA	National Electrical Manufacturers Assoc.	PSI, psi	Pounds per Square Inch		
		PSIG	Pounds per Square Inch Gauge	Spri.	Sprinkler Installer
NEHB	Bolted Circuit Breaker to 600V.	PSP	Plastic Sewer Pipe	spwg	Static Pressure Water Gauge
NFPA	National Fire Protection Association	Pspr.	Painter, Spray	S.P.D.T.	Single Pole, Double Throw
NLB	Non-Load-Bearing	Psst.	Painter, Structural Steel	SPF	Spruce Pine Fir; Sprayed Polyurethane Foam
NM	Non-Metallic Cable	P.T.	Potential Transformer		
nm	Nanometer	P. & T.	Pressure & Temperature	S.P.S.T.	Single Pole, Single Throw
No.	Number	Ptd.	Painted	SPT	Standard Pipe Thread
NO	Normally Open	Ptns.	Partitions	Sq.	Square; 100 Square Feet
N.O.C.	Not Otherwise Classified	Pu	Ultimate Load	Sq. Hd.	Square Head
Nose.	Nosing	PVC	Polyvinyl Chloride	Sq. In.	Square Inch
NPT	National Pipe Thread	Pvmt.	Pavement	S.S.	Single Strength; Stainless Steel
NQOD	Combination Plug-on/Bolt on Circuit Breaker to 240V.	PRV	Pressure Relief Valve	S.S.B.	Single Strength B Grade
		Pwr.	Power	sst, ss	Stainless Steel
N.R.C., NRC	Noise Reduction Coefficient/ Nuclear Regulator Commission	Q	Quantity Heat Flow	Sswk.	Structural Steel Worker
		Qt.	Quart	Sswl.	Structural Steel Welder
N.R.S.	Non Rising Stem	Quan., Qty.	Quantity	St.; Stl.	Steel
ns	Nanosecond	Q.C.	Quick Coupling	STC	Sound Transmission Coefficient
NTP	Notice to Proceed	r	Radius of Gyration	Std.	Standard
nW	Nanowatt	R	Resistance	Stg.	Staging
OB	Opposing Blade	R.C.P.	Reinforced Concrete Pipe	STK	Select Tight Knot
OC	On Center	Rect.	Rectangle	STP	Standard Temperature & Pressure
OD	Outside Diameter	recpt.	Receptacle	Stpi.	Steamfitter, Pipefitter
O.D.	Outside Dimension	Reg.	Regular	Str.	Strength; Starter; Straight
ODS	Overhead Distribution System	Reinf.	Reinforced	Strd.	Stranded
O.G.	Ogee	Req'd.	Required	Struct.	Structural
O.H.	Overhead	Res.	Resistant	Sty.	Story
O&P	Overhead and Profit	Resi.	Residential	Subj.	Subject
Oper.	Operator	RF	Radio Frequency	Subs.	Subcontractors
Opng.	Opening	RFID	Radio-frequency Identification	Surf.	Surface
Orna.	Ornamental	Rgh.	Rough	Sw.	Switch
OSB	Oriented Strand Board	RGS	Rigid Galvanized Steel	Swbd.	Switchboard
OS&Y	Outside Screw and Yoke	RHW	Rubber, Heat & Water Resistant; Residential Hot Water	S.Y.	Square Yard
OSHA	Occupational Safety and Health Act			Syn.	Synthetic
		rms	Root Mean Square	S.Y.P.	Southern Yellow Pine
Ovhd.	Overhead	Rnd.	Round	Sys.	System
OWG	Oil, Water or Gas	Rodm.	Rodman	t.	Thickness
Oz.	Ounce	Rofc.	Roofer, Composition	T	Temperature; Ton
P.	Pole; Applied Load; Projection	Rofp.	Roofer, Precast	Tan	Tangent
p.	Page	Rohe.	Roofer Helpers (Composition)	T.C.	Terra Cotta
Pape.	Paperhanger	Rots.	Roofer, Tile & Slate	T & C	Threaded and Coupled
P.A.P.R.	Powered Air Purifying Respirator	R.O.W.	Right of Way	T.D.	Temperature Difference
PAR	Parabolic Reflector	RPM	Revolutions per Minute	TDD	Telecommunications Device for the Deaf
P.B., PB	Push Button	R.S.	Rapid Start		
Pc., Pcs.	Piece, Pieces	Rsr	Riser	T.E.M.	Transmission Electron Microscopy
P.C.	Portland Cement; Power Connector	RT	Round Trip	temp	Temperature, Tempered, Temporary
P.C.F.	Pounds per Cubic Foot	S.	Suction; Single Entrance; South	TFFN	Nylon Jacketed Wire

Abbreviations

TFE	Tetrafluoroethylene (Teflon)	U.L., UL	Underwriters Laboratory	w/	With
T. & G.	Tongue & Groove; Tar & Gravel	Uld.	Unloading	W.C., WC	Water Column; Water Closet
Th., Thk.	Thick	Unfin.	Unfinished	W.F.	Wide Flange
Thn.	Thin	UPS	Uninterruptible Power Supply	W.G.	Water Gauge
Thrded	Threaded	URD	Underground Residential Distribution	Wldg.	Welding
Tilf.	Tile Layer, Floor	US	United States	W. Mile	Wire Mile
Tilh.	Tile Layer, Helper	USGBC	U.S. Green Building Council	W-O-L	Weldolet
THHN	Nylon Jacketed Wire	USP	United States Primed	W.R.	Water Resistant
THW.	Insulated Strand Wire	UTMCD	Uniform Traffic Manual For Control Devices	Wrck.	Wrecker
THWN	Nylon Jacketed Wire			WSFU	Water Supply Fixture Unit
T.L., TL	Truckload	UTP	Unshielded Twisted Pair	W.S.P.	Water, Steam, Petroleum
T.M.	Track Mounted	V	Volt	WT., Wt.	Weight
Tot.	Total	VA	Volt Amperes	WWF	Welded Wire Fabric
T-O-L	Threadolet	VAT	Vinyl Asbestos Tile	XFER	Transfer
tmpd	Tempered	V.C.T.	Vinyl Composition Tile	XFMR	Transformer
TPO	Thermoplastic Polyolefin	VAV	Variable Air Volume	XHD	Extra Heavy Duty
T.S.	Trigger Start	VC	Veneer Core	XHHW	Cross-Linked Polyethylene Wire
Tr.	Trade	VDC	Volts Direct Current	XLPE	Insulation
Transf.	Transformer	Vent.	Ventilation	XLP	Cross-linked Polyethylene
Trhv.	Truck Driver, Heavy	Vert.	Vertical	Xport	Transport
Trlr	Trailer	V.F.	Vinyl Faced	Y	Wye
Trlt.	Truck Driver, Light	V.G.	Vertical Grain	yd	Yard
TTY	Teletypewriter	VHF	Very High Frequency	yr	Year
TV	Television	VHO	Very High Output	Δ	Delta
T.W.	Thermoplastic Water Resistant Wire	Vib.	Vibrating	%	Percent
		VLF	Vertical Linear Foot	~	Approximately
UCI	Uniform Construction Index	VOC	Volatile Organic Compound	Ø	Phase; diameter
UF	Underground Feeder	Vol.	Volume	@	At
UGND	Underground Feeder	VRP	Vinyl Reinforced Polyester	#	Pound; Number
UHF	Ultra High Frequency	W	Wire; Watt; Wide; West	<	Less Than
U.I.	United Inch			>	Greater Than
				Z	Zone

Index

A

Entry	Page
Abandon catch basin	22
Abatement asbestos	26
equipment asbestos	25
ABC extinguisher portable	67
extinguisher wheeled	67
Aboveground storage tank concrete	340
ABS DWV pipe	222
Absorber shock	256
vibration	129
A/C packaged terminal	366
removal fan-coil	323
removal rooftop	324
removal thru-the-wall	324
removal window	324
Accelerator sprinkler system	101
Access road and parking area	16
Accessory bathroom	64, 65
compressor	286
fuel oil	335
polypropylene	238
toilet	64
Acid resistant drain	279
resistant pipe	316
Acoustical sealant	55
ACR tubing copper	155
ADA compliant drinking fountain	307
compliant fixture support	302
compliant lavatory	305
compliant shower	296, 305
compliant water cooler	308
Adapter fire hose swivel	97
polybutylene	237
Adjustment factor	8
factor labor	108
for sprinkler/standpipe installations	703
Aeration sewage	468
Aerator	309
Aerial survey	22
After cooler medical	313
Aggregate spreader	584, 591
Air automatic vent	341
balancing	329
cock	341
compressor	286, 587
compressor dental	75
compressor medical	313
compressor package	286
compressor portable	587
compressor removal	109
compressor sprinkler system	101
conditioner cooling & heating	366
conditioner direct expansion	368
conditioner general	322
conditioner maintenance	19
conditioner packaged term.	366
conditioner portable	366
conditioner receptacle	380
conditioner removal	322
conditioner thru-wall	366
conditioner window	366
conditioner wiring	383
conditioning ventilating	366
control	340
curtain removal	322
deaerator	340
dryer system	313
eliminator	340
filter regulator lubricator	286
filter removal	322
filtration	25
gap fitting	256
hose	588
line coupler	286
purging scoop	340
quality	72
sampling	25
scoop	340
Air scrubber	588
Air separator	340
spade	588
unit removal make-up	323
vent automatic	341
vent convector or baseboard	368
Airless sprayer	25
Air-source heat pump	367
Alarm device	387
dry	88
fire	100
panel and device	387
panel module	312
residential	382
standpipe	100
system medical	312
transducer medical	312
valve sprinkler	88
vent	335
water motor	100
All fuel chimney	356, 358
service jacket insulation	133, 138
Alteration fee	8
Aluminum flashing	50, 278
insulation jacketing	146
pipe	433, 434
rivet	44
salvage	110
weld rod	45
Anchor bolt	33
chemical	38, 42
epoxy	38, 42
expansion	42
hollow wall	42
lead screw	43
machinery	35
metal nailing	42
nailing	42
nylon nailing	42
pipe conduit casing	457
plastic screw	43
screw	42
toggle bolt	42
wedge	43
Angle valve bronze	111
valve plastic	116
Anti-freeze inhibited	349
Anti-siphon device	256
Appliance	71
plumbing	287, 289, 308, 309
residential	71, 382
Arch culvert oval	436
Architectural fee	8
Area clean-up	27
Articulating boom lift	587
Asbestos abatement	26
abatement equipment	25
area decontamination	27
demolition	27
disposal	28
encapsulation	28
remediation plan/method	25
removal	26
removal process	698
Asphalt distributor	588
paver	590
paving	406
plant portable	591
Asphaltic binder	406
concrete	406
concrete paving	406
pavement	406
wearing course	406
Aspirator dental	75
Atomizer water	25
Attachment ripper	591
Attachments skidsteer	587
Auger earth	584
Auto park drain	278
Automatic fire-suppression	103
flush	302
washing machine	71
Automotive equipment	70
exhaust system	529
lift	86
spray painting booth	70
Autopsy equipment	76
Autoscrub machine	588
Axe fire	98

B

Entry	Page
B and S pipe gasket	270
Backer rod	54
Backfill	393
trench	391
Backflow preventer	255
preventer removal	109
preventer solar	364
Backhoe	585
bucket	586
extension	591
trenching	560, 562, 564
Backwater drainage control	431
sewer valve	431
valve	283
Bag disposable	25, 30
glove	26
Balance valve circuit setter	341
Balancing air	329
hydronic	347
water	330
Ball check valve	117
check valve plastic	117
valve brass	324
valve bronze	111, 112
valve for medical gas	312
valve grooved joint	203
valve plastic	116
valve polypropylene	117
valve slow close	99
wrecking	591
Baptistry	76
Bar front	82
grab	64
towel	64
tub	64
Barber chair	70
equipment	70
Barge construction	594
Barometric damper	353
Barrels flasher	588
reflectorized	588
Barricade	17
flasher	588
tape	17
Barrier and enclosure	16
dust	16
separation	26, 28, 29
slipform paver	592
Base cabinet	78
sink	78
stabilizer	592
vanity	78
Baseboard heat	368
heat electric	370
heater electric	370
removal hydronic	323
Baseplate scaffold	14
shoring	14
Basket type strainer	344
Bath hospital	305
paraffin	75
perineal	305
redwood	81
spa	81
steam	82
whirlpool	75, 81
Bathroom	295
accessory	64, 65
exhaust fan	350
faucet	297
five fixture	496
fixture	292, 293, 295, 296
four fixture	495
heater & fan	350
soaking	295
system	494-496
three fixture	494
two fixture	493
Bathtub	488
bar	64
enclosure	66
removal	109
residential	295
Beam attachment welded	119
clamp	119
flange clip	128
Bedding pipe	393
Bedpan cleanser	305
Bell & spigot pipe	261
signal	387
Bellow expansion joint	342
Bibb hose	341
Bidet	292
removal	109
rough-in	293
Bimodal MDPE, ASTM D2513	439
Binder asphaltic	406
Bituminous coating	412
paver	589
Blaster shot	590
Blind flange	186
structural bolt	45
Block manhole	418
manhole/catch basin	579
Blood bank refrigeration	74
Blowdown removal boiler	322
Blower insulation	589
Board insulation	331
mineral wool	331
Boat work	594
Boiler	359
blowdown removal	322
condensing	359
cut off low water	332
demolition	322
drain	341
electric	359
electric steam	359
gas fired	360
gas pulse	359
general	108
hot water	359, 360
insulation	332
oil-fired	360
removal	322
steam	360
steam electric	528
Bolt & gasket set	185
anchor	33

Index

blind structural 45
Bond performance 11, 694
Boom lift articulating 587
    lift telescoping 587
Booster system water pressure .. 260
Booth painting 70
Borer horizontal 592
Boring horizontal 417
    machine horizontal 584
    service 417
Borosilicate pipe 314
Borrow fill 393
    loading and/or spreading 393
Bottled water cooler 309
Boundary and survey marker 22
Bowl toilet 292
Box Buffalo 419
    distribution 432
    flow leveler distribution 432
    storage 13
    trench 591
    utility 419
Brace cross 46
Bracing shoring 14
Bracket pipe 119
    scaffold 14
Braided bronze hose 250
    steel hose 250
Brass pipe 151
    pipe fitting 152
    salvage 110
    valve 111
Break glass station 387
Breaker air gap vacuum 256
    pavement 588
    vacuum 256
Breeching insulation 332
Brick cart 588
    catch basin 418
    manhole 418
Bridge sidewalk 15
Bronze angle valve 111
    ball valve 112
    body strainer 346
    butterfly valve 112
    globe valve 113
    swing check valve 112
    valve 111
Bronze/brass valve 324
Broom finish concrete 38
    sidewalk 590
Brush chipper 585
    cutter 585, 586
Bubbler 307
    drinking 308
Bucket backhoe 586
    clamshell 585
    concrete 584
    dragline 585
    excavator 591
    pavement 591
Buffalo box 419
Buggy concrete 584
Builder's risk insurance 692
Building permit 12
    portable 13
    sprinkler 102
    temporary 13
Built-in range 71
    shower 296
Bulldozer 586
Bull float concrete 584
Buncher feller 585
Bunk house trailer 13
Burner gas conversion 361
    gun type 361

oil 361
    residential 361
Butt fusion machine 588
Butterfly valve 325, 428
    valve bronze 112
    valve grooved joint 204
Butyl caulking 55
    rubber 54
Bypass pipe 416

C

Cabinet base 78
    convector heater 372
    fire equipment 66, 98
    hardboard 78
    heater electric 372
    hose rack 66
    hotel 65
    kitchen 78
    medicine 65
    shower 65
    unit heater 372
    valve 67
Cable hanger 128
    jack 594
    pulling 591
    tensioning 591
    trailer 591
Cable/wire puller 591
Calcium silicate insulated system . 457
    silicate insulation 332, 457
    silicate pipe covering 135
Cap HDPE piping 426
    vent 277, 335
Car tram 591
Carbon dioxide extinguisher 103
Carrier and support removal 109
    fixture support 302
    pipe 120, 124
Carrier/support fixture 302
Cart brick 588
    concrete 584
    mounted extinguisher 67
Cartridge style water filter 288
Casework custom 78
Casing anchor pipe conduit 457
Cast in place concrete 36, 37
    iron cleanout 131
    iron fitting 184, 262
    iron manhole cover 437
    iron pipe 261
    iron pipe fitting 173, 262
    iron pipe gasket 270
    iron radiator 368
    iron trap 275
    iron vent cap 277
Caster scaffold 14
Cast-iron weld rod 45
Catch basin 437
    basin and manhole 580
    basin brick 418
    basin cleaner 591
    basin precast 418
    basin removal 22
    basin vacuum 591
    basin/manhole 579
Cathodic protection 83
Catwalk scaffold 15
Caulking 55
    lead 262
    oakum 262
    polyurethane 55
    sealant 54
Ceiling fan 349

heater 72
Cell equipment 76
    prison 82
Cellular glass insulation 134
Cement liner 416
Central station AHU removal .. 322
    vacuum 76
    vacuum unit 464
Centrifugal in-line motor 259
    pump 258, 590
Chain fall hoist 593
    hoist 462
    link fence 17
    saw 590
    trencher 391, 587
Chair barber 70
    dental 75
    hydraulic 75
    pipe support 124
Chamber decontamination 26, 28
    infiltration 433
Channel steel 122
Charge disposal 28
    powder 44
Check lift valve 115
    swing valve 112
    valve 88, 429
    valve ball 117
    valve flanged cast iron 429
    valve grooved joint 204
    valve silent 114, 327
    valve stainless steel 328
    valve wafer 115, 327
Checkered plate 46
    plate cover 46
    plate platform 46
Chemical anchor 38, 42
    dilution tank 319
    dry extinguisher 67
    spreader 591
    storage tank 319
    toilet 590
    water closet 468
Chemical-waste dilution tank ... 319
Chilled water pipe underground . 455
Chiller remote water 309
    removal water 324
Chimney all fuel 356, 358
    all fuel vent 358
    positive pressure 356, 358
    prefabricated metal 356
    vent 353
    vent fitting 358
    vent oval 355
Chipper brush 585
    log 586
    stump 586
Chipping hammer 588
Chloride accelerator concrete ... 37
Chlorination system 309
Church equipment 76
CI acid resistant drain 279
    roof drain system 518
Circuit setter 341
Circular saw 590
Circulating pump 348
Clamp beam 119
    pipe 119, 412
    pipe repair 413
    ring 422
    riser 120
    valve 116
Clamshell bucket 585
Classroom sink 300
    sink rough-in 300
Clean control joint 33

ductwork 19
    tank 24
Cleaner catch basin 591
    crack 592
    steam 590
Cleaning & disposal equipment .. 73
    duct 19
    internal pipe 415
    up 18
Cleanout and drain removal 109
    cast iron 131
    floor 130
    pipe 130
    polypropylene 132
    PVC 132
    tee 131
    wall type 131
Cleanouts 419
Clean-up area 27
Clevis pipe hanger 121
Climbing crane 592
    hydraulic jack 594
Clinic service sink 305
Clock timer 382
Closet water 292, 299
Clothes dryer commercial 70
Coat hook 64
Coating bituminous 412
    epoxy 412
    polyethylene 412
Cock air 341
    drain and specialty 341
    gas 111
    gauge 341
    pet 341
CO_2 extinguisher 67
    fire extinguishing system 103
Cold mix paver 592
Collection sewage/drainage 435
    system dust 464
Collector solar energy system ... 363
Combination ball valve 324
    device 379
Comfort station 82
Command dog 18
Commercial dishwasher 73
    gas water heater 290
    lavatory 300
    oil-fired water heater 291
    sink 300
    toilet accessory 64
    water heater 289, 291
    water heater electric 289
    water-heater 501-503
Commissioning 19
Compact fill 393
Compactor earth 585
    landfill 586
Companion flange 186
Compartment toilet 62
Compensation workers' 11
Compliant drinking
    fountain ADA 307
    fixture support ADA 302
    lavatory ADA 305
    shower ADA 296, 305
    water cooler ADA 308
Component control 333, 334
Component/DDC system
    control 332
Compressed air equipment
    automotive 70
Compression joint fitting 160
    seal 53
    tank 343
Compressor accessory 286

Index

air . . . 286, 587
air package . . . 286
reciprocating . . . 286
reciprocating hermetic . . . 286
removal air . . . 109
removal refrigerant . . . 324
Computer room unit removal . . . 322
Concrete asphaltic . . . 406
broom finish . . . 38
bucket . . . 584
buggy . . . 584
bull float . . . 584
cart . . . 584
cast in place . . . 36, 37
catch basin . . . 418
chloride accelerator . . . 37
conveyer . . . 584
core drilling . . . 39
direct chute . . . 37
distribution box . . . 432
drill . . . 376
drilling . . . 39
equipment rental . . . 584
fiber reinforcing . . . 37
float finish . . . 38
floor edger . . . 584
floor grinder . . . 584
hand trowel finish . . . 38
hole cutting . . . 377
hole drilling . . . 376
impact drilling . . . 39
insert hanger . . . 120
lance . . . 589
machine trowel finish . . . 38
manhole . . . 418
mixer . . . 584
non-chloride accelerator . . . 37
paver . . . 590
pipe . . . 435
pipe removal . . . 22
placement footing . . . 37
placing . . . 37
pump . . . 584
ready mix . . . 37
reinforcing . . . 35
retarder . . . 37
saw . . . 584
septic tank . . . 431
short load . . . 37
spreader . . . 590
tank aboveground storage . . . 340
trowel . . . 584
truck . . . 584
truck holding . . . 37
utility vault . . . 419
vibrator . . . 584
water reducer . . . 37
water storage tank . . . 430
winter . . . 37
Condensate meter rem. steam . . . 324
removal pump . . . 349
Condenser removal . . . 322
Condensing boiler . . . 359
furnace . . . 361
unit removal . . . 322
Conditioner general air . . . 322
maintenance air . . . 19
portable air . . . 366
Conditioning ventilating air . . . 366
Conduit & fitting flexible . . . 378
fitting pipe . . . 456
pipe prefabricated . . . 458
prefabricated pipe . . . 455, 457
preinsulated pipe . . . 455
Connection fire-department . . . 95
motor . . . 378
standpipe . . . 95
storz type . . . 95
utility . . . 419
Connector flexible . . . 249
gas . . . 249
water copper tubing . . . 250
Construction barge . . . 594
management fee . . . 8
photography . . . 12
sump hole . . . 392
temporary . . . 16
time . . . 8, 689
Contained pipe . . . 245
Containment unit dust . . . 17, 29
Contaminated soil . . . 24
Contingency . . . 8
Contractor overhead . . . 18
Control & motor starter . . . 383
air . . . 340
component . . . 333, 334
component/DDC system . . . 332
DDC . . . 332
DDC system . . . 333
draft . . . 353
flow check . . . 344
hand-off-automatic . . . 384
joint . . . 32
joint clean . . . 33
joint sawn . . . 32
joint sealant . . . 33
pressure sprinkler . . . 101
station . . . 384
station stop-start . . . 384
system . . . 332
valve heating . . . 335, 344
water level . . . 332
Control-component . . . 335
Convector cabinet heater . . . 372
hydronic heating . . . 368
Cooking equipment . . . 73
range . . . 71
Cooler beverage . . . 73
removal evaporative . . . 323
water . . . 308
Cooling tower removal . . . 322
Copper ACR tubing . . . 155
drum trap . . . 276
DWV tubing . . . 154
fitting . . . 156
flashing . . . 50, 278
grooved joint . . . 164
pipe . . . 153, 426
rivet . . . 44
salvage . . . 110
tube . . . 153, 426
tube fitting . . . 156
tubing oxygen class . . . 154
Core drill . . . 584
drilling concrete . . . 39
Cornice drain . . . 283
Corrosion monitor . . . 89
resistance . . . 412
resistant fitting . . . 316
resistant lab equipment . . . 319
resistant pipe . . . 314, 315
resistant pipe fitting . . . 316
resistant trap . . . 276
Corrosion-resistant sink . . . 300
Corrugated metal pipe . . . 433, 434
pipe . . . 433
steel pipe . . . 433
Cost mark-up . . . 11
Countertop sink . . . 295
Coupler air line . . . 286
Coupling fire hose . . . 97
mechanical . . . 196
plastic . . . 234
polypropylene . . . 238
Course wearing . . . 406
Cover checkered plate . . . 46
manhole . . . 437
stair tread . . . 18
Covering calcium silicate pipe . . . 135
protection saddle . . . 125
CPVC pipe . . . 223
valve . . . 117
Crack cleaner . . . 592
filler . . . 592
Crane . . . 462
climbing . . . 592
crawler . . . 593
crew daily . . . 13
hydraulic . . . 462, 593
material handling . . . 462
tower . . . 13, 593
truck mounted . . . 593
Crawler crane . . . 593
drill rotary . . . 588
shovel . . . 586
Crew daily crane . . . 13
forklift . . . 13
Cross . . . 427
brace . . . 46
Crowbar fire . . . 98
Cubicle shower . . . 296
toilet . . . 63
Culvert end . . . 436
pipe . . . 436
reinforced . . . 435
Cup sink . . . 301, 486
Curb builder . . . 584
extruder . . . 585
prefabricated . . . 374
slipform paver . . . 592
Cured in place pipe liner . . . 416, 417
Curtain removal air . . . 322
rod . . . 64
Custom casework . . . 78
Cut in sleeve . . . 427
in valve . . . 427
off low water boiler . . . 332
pipe groove . . . 204
Cutter brush . . . 585, 586
Cutting and drilling . . . 376
steel pipe labor . . . 172
torch . . . 590

D

Daily crane crew . . . 13
Damper barometric . . . 353
Darkroom equipment . . . 71
DDC control . . . 332
Deaerator . . . 340
air . . . 340
Deck drain . . . 278
roof . . . 48
Decontamination asbestos area . . . 27
chamber . . . 26, 28
enclosure . . . 26-28
equipment . . . 25
Decorator device . . . 379
switch . . . 379
Deep seal trap . . . 276
Dehumidifier . . . 588
removal . . . 322
Dehydrator package sprinkler . . . 101
Delivery charge . . . 15
Deluge sprinkler . . . 536, 538
sprinkler monitoring panel . . . 103
valve assembly sprinkler . . . 103
Demo hydronic convector & radiator . . . 323
Demolish remove pavement and curb . . . 22
Demolition . . . 697
asbestos . . . 27
boiler . . . 322
furnace . . . 323
hammer . . . 585
HVAC . . . 322
mold contaminated area . . . 29
pavement . . . 22
plumbing . . . 109
site . . . 22
torch cutting . . . 23
Dental chair . . . 75
equipment . . . 75
metal interceptor . . . 281
office equipment . . . 75
Derrick crane guyed . . . 593
crane stiffleg . . . 593
Detection intrusion . . . 386
leak . . . 386
probe leak . . . 386
system . . . 386
Detector check valve . . . 429
meter water supply . . . 254
smoke . . . 386
temperature rise . . . 386
Detention equipment . . . 76
Detour sign . . . 17
Device alarm . . . 387
anti-siphon . . . 256
combination . . . 379
decorator . . . 379
GFI . . . 380
receptacle . . . 380
residential . . . 378
Dew point monitor . . . 313
Dewater . . . 392, 393
pumping . . . 392
Dewatering . . . 392, 718
equipment . . . 594
Diaphragm pump . . . 590
valve . . . 116
Dielectric union . . . 342
Diesel hammer . . . 586
tugboat . . . 594
Diffuser pump suction . . . 347
suction . . . 347
Dilution tank chemical . . . 319
tank chemical-waste . . . 319
Dimmer switch . . . 379
Direct chute concrete . . . 37
Directional drill horizontal . . . 592
Disc harrow . . . 585
Discharge hose . . . 589
Disease infectious . . . 9
Dishwasher commercial . . . 73
residential . . . 71
Dispenser hot water . . . 288
napkin . . . 64
soap . . . 64
towel . . . 64
Dispersion nozzle . . . 103
Disposable bag . . . 25, 30
Disposal asbestos . . . 28
charge . . . 28
field . . . 432
garbage . . . 71
Distiller water . . . 74
Distribution box . . . 432
box concrete . . . 432
box flow leveler . . . 432
box HDPE . . . 432
pipe water . . . 421, 423

Index

Distributor asphalt 588
Ditching 392
Diving stand 80
Dog command 18
Dome drain 283
Domestic hot water temp maint . 128
   hot-water 498-500
   water booster system 260
Door bell residential 381
   fire 387
   shower 65
Double wall pipe 241, 438
Dozer 586
Draft control 353
   damper vent 353
Dragline bucket 585
Drain 275, 283
   acid resistant 279
   boiler 341
   CI acid resistant 279
   deck 278
   dome 283
   expansion joint roof 283
   facility trench 284
   floor 279
   main 283
   pipe 392
   PVC acid resistant 279
   roof 283
   sanitary 278
   scupper 284
   sediment bucket 279
   shower 275
   terrace 283
   trap seal floor 280
   trench 284
Drainage control backwater 431
   field 432
   fitting 273
   fixture units 709, 710
   pipe 314, 315, 431, 435
   trap 275, 276
Draindown valve 365
Drainwater heat recovery 292
Drill concrete 376
   core 584
   main 426
   quarry 588
   steel 588
   tap main 426
   track 588
Drilling concrete 39
   concrete impact 39
   horizontal 417
   plaster 58
   rig 584
   steel 43
Drinking bubbler 308
   fountain 307, 308
   fountain deck rough-in 308
   fountain floor rough-in ... 308
   fountain support 302
   fountain wall rough-in 307
Drip irrigation 407
   irrigation subsurface 407
   pan elbow 275
Driver post 592
   sheeting 588
Drum trap copper 276
Dry alarm 88
   pipe sprinkler head 101
   standpipe riser 554
Dryer accessory washer 298
   commercial clothes 70
   hand 64
   industrial 70

receptacle 381
residential 71
system air 313
vent 71, 299
Dry-pipe sprinkler system 101
Dual flush flushometer ... 298, 302
   flush valve toilet 302
Duck tarpaulin 16
Duct cleaning 19
   insulation 331
Ductile iron fitting 421
   iron fitting mech joint ... 422
   iron grooved joint 90, 199, 203
   iron pipe 421
Ductless removal split 324
Ductwork clean 19
Dump charge 23
   truck 587
Dumpster 23
Dumpsters 697
Dump truck off highway 587
Duplex style strainer 345
Dust barrier 16
   collection system 464
   containment unit 17, 29
DWV pipe ABS 222
   PVC pipe 222, 431
   tubing copper 154

E

Earth auger 584
   compactor 585
   scraper 586
   vibrator 390
Earthquake shutoff gas 361
   valve gas 361
Earthwork equipment rental ... 584
Ecclesiastical equipment 76
Economizer shower-head water . 296
Edger concrete floor 584
Efficiency flush valve high .. 302
Effluent-filter septic system 432
Ejector pump 282
Elbow drip pan 275
   HDPE piping 425
   pipe 199
Electric baseboard heater 370
   boiler 359, 528
   boiler small hydronic 528
   cabinet heater 372
   commercial water heater .. 289
   fire pump 556
   generator 589
   heater 72
   heater removal 323
   heating 370
   hoist 462
   hot air heater 372
   pool heater 361
   unit heater 371
   water cooler 308
   water heater 289
   water heater residential . 289
   water heater tankless 288
   water-heater commercial .. 501
   water-heater residential . 498
Electrical fee 8
   installation drilling 376
   knockout 377
   laboratory 74
Electricity temporary 12
Electrofusion welded PP pipe . 317
Elevated installation add ... 108
   pipe add 108

Elevator fee 8
   sump pump 285
Eliminator air 340
Emergency equipment laboratory . 74
   eyewash 306
   shower 305
Employer liability 11
Emulsion sprayer 588
Encapsulation asbestos 28
   pipe 28
Enclosure bathtub 66
   decontamination 26-28
   shower 66
End culvert 436
Energy circulator air solar .. 363
   distribution pipe steam .. 457
   system air purger solar .. 364
   system air vent solar 364
   system balancing valve solar . 365
   system control valve solar 364
   system controller solar .. 364
   system expansion tank solar . 365
   system gauge pressure solar . 365
   system heat exchanger solar . 364
   system storage tank solar . 364
   system vacuum relief solar 365
Engine exhaust elimination ... 350
Engineering fee 8, 688
Entrainment eliminator 281
Entrance screen 62
Epoxy anchor 38, 42
   coating 412
   fiberglass wound pipe 315
   resin fitting 226
   welded wire 36
Equipment 70, 584
   automotive 70
   barber 70
   cell 76
   cleaning & disposal 73
   darkroom 71
   dental 75
   dental office 75
   detention 76
   ecclesiastical 76
   fire 556
   fire hose 96, 556
   fire-extinguishing 103
   foundation formwork 32
   hospital 74
   insulation 332
   insurance 11
   laboratory emergency 74
   laundry 70
   lubrication 70
   medical 74-76
   medical sterilizing 74
   pad 36
   refrigerated storage 73
   rental 584, 695, 696
   rental concrete 584
   rental earthwork 584
   rental general 587
   rental highway 591
   rental lifting 592
   rental marine 594
   rental wellpoint 594
   roof support 127
   safety eye/face 306
   swimming pool 80
Escutcheon 254
   plate 99, 100
   sprinkler 100
Estimate electrical heating .. 370
   plumbing 497
Estimating 682

Ethylene glycol 349
Evaporative cooler removal ... 323
Evaporator removal 323
Excavating equipment 717
   trench 390
   utility trench 391
Excavation 390
   hand 390, 392
   septic tank 432
   tractor 390
   trench 390, 391, 560-562, 564
Excavator bucket 591
   hydraulic 584
Excavator hydro 586
Exchanger heat 365
   removal heat 323
Exhaust elimination engine ... 350
   elimination garage 350
   hood 71
   system 351
   system removal 323
Expansion anchor 42
   joint 342
   joint bellow 342
   joint grooved joint 203
   joint roof drain 283
   shield 42
   tank 343
   tank steel 343
Extension backhoe 591
   ladder 589
Extinguisher cart mounted 67
   chemical dry 67
   CO_2 67
   fire 67, 103
   FM200 fire 103
   installation 67
   portable ABC 67
   pressurized fire 67
   standard 67
   wheeled ABC 67
Extra work 11
Extruder curb 585
Eye wash fountain 306
   wash portable 306
Eye/face wash safety equipment . 306
Eyewash emergency 306
   safety equipment 306

F

Fabric-backed flashing 50
Face wash fountain 305
Facility trench drain 284
Factor 8
   security 9
Fan bathroom exhaust 350
   ceiling 349
   paddle 382
   removal 323
   residential 382
   ventilation 382
   wiring 382
Fan-coil A/C removal 323
Faucet & fitting 297, 302, 305
   bathroom 297
   gooseneck 305
   laundry 297
   lavatory 297
   medical 305
F&C plate 254
Fee architectural 8
   engineering 8
Feller buncher 585
Fence chain link 17

Index

plywood 17
  temporary 17
  wire 17
Fiber reinforcing concrete 37
Fiberglass panel 16
  pipe covering 137
  rainwater storage tank 285
  tank 338
  trench drain 284
  underground storage tank ... 261
Field disposal 432
  drainage 432
  office 13
  personnel 10, 11
Fill 393
  borrow 393
  by borrow & utility bedding . 393
  gravel 393
Filler crack 592
  joint 54
Fillet welding 44
Film equipment 71
Filter iron removal 288
  oil 335
  rainwater 468
  removal air 322
  swimming pool 309
  water 288
Filtration air 25
  equipment 80
Finishing floor concrete 38
Fin-tube radiation
  apartment bldg 520
Fire alarm 100
  axe 98
  call pullbox 387
  crowbar 98
  door 387
  equipment cabinet 66, 98
  extinguisher 67, 103
  extinguisher portable ... 66, 67
  extinguishing ... 531, 532, 435, 535,
    537, 538, 540, 541, 543, 544,
    548, 550, 552, 554-557
  extinguishing system . 96, 97, 103,
    105
  horn 387
  hose 97
  hose adapter 96
  hose coupling 97
  hose equipment 96
  hose gate valve 99
  hose nipple 97
  hose nozzle 97
  hose rack 98
  hose reel 98
  hose storage cabinet 66
  hose storage house 98
  hose valve 99
  hose wye 100
  hydrant 430, 575
  hydrant building 95
  hydrant remove 22
  protection 66
  protection system
    classification 702
  pump 104, 105
  retardant pipe 316
  sprinkler head 101
  suppression 557
  suppression valve 91
  tool 98
  valve hydrant 99
Fire-department connection 95
Fire-extinguishing equipment ... 103
Firestop wood 48

Firestopping 52
Fire-suppression automatic 103
  grooved joint 90, 92
  hose reel 98
  pipe fitting 93
  plastic pipe 93
Fitting adapter pipe 158
  cast iron 184, 262
  cast iron pipe 173, 262
  compression joint 160
  copper 156
  copper pipe 156, 166
  corrosion resistant 316
  drainage 273
  drainage special pipe 273
  ductile iron 421
  DWV pipe 231
  epoxy resin 226
  flanged 185
  flanged cast iron pipe 184
  flare joint 161
  flexible gas pipe 336
  forged steel pipe 191
  galvanized 274
  gas vent 353
  glass 314
  grooved joint 165, 197
  grooved joint pipe 90, 199
  grooved unit 164, 201
  HDPE 242
  insert pipe 237
  malleable iron 177
  malleable iron pipe ... 178, 194
  mechanical joint pipe 194
  monoflow 344
  pipe 184, 273, 423, 455, 457
  pipe conduit 456
  plastic 231
  plastic pipe 93
  polybutylene pipe 236
  polypropylene 238, 317
  PVC 228, 424
  PVC pipe 238
  refrigeration 161
  removal piping 109
  stainless steel 212
  stainless steel pipe 212
  steel 173, 184
  steel carbon pipe 187
  steel pipe 187
  tube 206
  vent chimney 353, 358
  weld 190
  weld joint pipe 191
  welded steel pipe 195
Fixture bathroom . 292, 293, 295, 296
  carrier/support 302
  institution 306
  plumbing . 280, 281, 288, 292, 294,
    301, 307, 348, 421
  prison 306
  removal 109
  removal prison 110
  residential 381
Flange blind 186
  clip beam 128
  companion 186
  gasket 185
  grooved joint 202
  PVC 236
  slip on escutcheon 254
  stainless steel 217
  steel 193, 202
  steel weld-on 193
  threaded 186
Flanged fitting 185

pipe 170
Flare joint fitting 161
Flasher barrels 588
  barricade 588
Flashing 50
  aluminum 50, 278
  copper 50, 278
  fabric-backed 50
  galvanized 278
  laminated sheet 50
  lead 278
  masonry 50
  mastic-backed 50
  neoprene 278
  paperbacked 50
  plastic sheet 51
  PVC 51
  sheet metal 50
  stainless 50
  vent 277
  vent chimney 354, 359
Flatbed truck 587, 591
  truck crane 592
Flexible conduit & fitting 378
  connector 249
  gas pipe fitting 336
  metal hose 250
  sprinkler connector 100
Float finish concrete 38
  valve 343
Floater equipment 11
Floodlight trailer 589
  tripod 588
Floor cleaning 18
  cleanout 130
  concrete finishing 38
  drain 279
  drain removal 109
  drain trap seal 280
  heating radiant 369
  heating removal radiant ... 323
  receptor 279
  sander 590
  scupper 284
Flow check control 344
  fitting hydronic 344
  meter 348
Flue chimney metal 353
  prefab metal 353
  shutter damper removal .. 323
Fluid heat transfer 364
Flush automatic 302
  flushometer dual 298, 302
  high efficiency toilet (HET) ... 302
  valve 302
FM200 fire extinguisher 103
  fire suppression 557
  system 557
Foam core DWV ABS pipe ... 222
  core DWV PVC pipe 222
  pipe covering 140
  rubber pipe covering 140
  spray rig 589
Foam-water system component .. 103
Folding door shower 65
Food service equipment 73
Foot valve 118
  valve oil 335
Footing concrete placement 37
  formwork continuous 32
  formwork spread 32
  reinforcing 35
  spread 36
Forklift 589
  crew 13
Formwork continuous footing ... 32

equipment foundation 32
  slab edge 32
  slab haunch 37
  slab on grade 32
  slab thickened edge 37
  slab trench 32
  slab turndown 37
  sleeve 32
  spread footing 32
Foundation mat 36
  mat concrete placement ... 38
Fountain 81
  drinking 307, 308
  eye wash 306
  face wash 305
  indoor 81
  lighting 310
  outdoor 81
  pump 309
  wash 301
  water pump 309
  yard 81
Frame scaffold 14
Framing lightweight 46
  lightweight angle 46
  lightweight channel 46
  miscellaneous wood 48
  pipe support 46
  slotted channel 46
  wood 48
Freezer 73
Frost penetration 698
Fuel oil gauge 335
  oil pump 337
  oil pump & motor set 337
  oil specialty 335
  oil valve 335
  tank 338
Fume elimination welding ... 352
  hood removal weld 323
Furnace condensing 361
  demolition 323
Fused pipe 425
Fusible oil valve 335
Fusion machine butt 588
  welded pipe fitting 317

G

Galley septic 432
Galvanized fitting 274
  flashing 278
  pipe fitting 275
  welded wire 36
Gantry crane 462
Gap fitting air 256
Garage exhaust elimination ... 350
  exhaust system 529
  ventilation 350
Garbage disposal 71
Gas cock 111
  connector 249
  conversion burner 361
  earthquake valve 361
  fired boiler 360
  fired infrared heater 362
  fired water-heater commercial . 502
  fired water-heater residential .. 499
  meter 335
  meter residential 335
  pipe 439
  piping flexible (CSST) ... 335
  piping medical 311
  pressure regulator 252
  pulse combustion 359

Index

regulator 252
safety valve 361
station tank 338
stop valve 111
tubing (CSST) 335
vent 353
vent fitting 353
water heater commercial 290
water heater instantaneous 290
water heater residential 290
water heater tankless 290
Gasket & bolt set 185
B and S pipe 270
cast iron pipe 270
flange 186
joint 53
joint pipe 262
joint pipe fitting 266
neoprene 53
toilet 298
Gasoline piping 438
Gate box 428
valve 325, 328, 429
valve grooved joint 204
valve soldered 112
Gauge cock 341
fuel oil 335
pressure 334
pressure/vacuum 334
vacuum 334
General air conditioner 322
boiler 108
contractor's overhead 692
equipment rental 587
fill 393
maintenance 19
Generator electric 589
steam 74
GFI receptacle 380
Gland seal pipe conduit 455
Glass door shower 65
filler 308
fitting 314
insulation cellular 134
lined water heater 72
mirror 64
P trap 276
pipe 109, 314
pipe fitting 314
pipe removal 109
process supply pipe 314
shower stall 65
Glassware sterilizer 74
washer 74
Globe valve 326, 328
valve bronze 113
Glove bag 26
Glycol ethylene 349
propylene 349
Gooseneck faucet 305
Grab bar 64
Gradall 585
Grader motorized 585
Grading 399
Gravel fill 393
pack well 419
Grease interceptor 280
trap 280
Grille painting 58
Grinder concrete floor 584
pump/sewage ejector removal 109
system pump 281
Grit removal and handling equipment 468
Groove cut labor steel 205
roll labor steel 205
Grooved joint check valve 204
joint copper 164
joint ductile iron 199, 203
joint fire-suppression 90, 92
joint fitting 165, 197
joint flange 202
joint pipe 197
joint plug valve 204
joint reducer 164
joint strainer 203
joint suction diffuser 203
joint valve 91
reducer 201
unit fitting 164, 201
Ground box hydrant 257
hydrant removal 109
post hydrant 258
Group shower 301
wash fountain 301, 489
Grout pump 590
Guard service 18
snow 51
sprinkler head 101
Guardrail scaffold 14
temporary 17
Guide pipe 121
Gun type burner 361
Guyed derrick crane 593

H

Hair interceptor 280
Hammer chipping 588
demolition 585
diesel 586
drill rotary 588
hydraulic 585, 589
pile 585
vibratory 586
Hammermill 591
Hand dryer 64
excavation 390, 392
hole 419
trowel finish concrete 38
Handicap tub shower 295
Handling material 18, 462
Hand-off-automatic control 384
Hanger & support pipe 119
assembly pipe 123
cable 128
clevis 121
pipe 119
plastic pipe 127
rod coupling 123
rod pipe 123
rod socket 126
roll 124
split ring 122
trapeze 124
U-bolt pipe 126
U-hook 127
vibration absorbing 129
Hanger/support removal pipe 109
Hanging lintel 46
Hardboard cabinet 78
Harrow disc 585
Hat and coat strip 64
Hauling 394
cycle 394
Haunch slab 37
Hazardous waste cleanup 24
waste disposal 24
HDPE distribution box 432
fitting 242
infiltration chamber 433
pipe 241
pipe dual wall 245
pipe liner 416
piping 425
piping cap 426
piping elbow 425
piping tee 426
Head sprinkler 100
Header pipe wellpoint 594
Heat baseboard 368
electric baseboard 370
exchanger 365
exchanger plate-type 365
exchanger removal 323
exchanger shell-type 366
pipe 366
pump 367
pump air-source 367
pump removal 323
pump residential 383
pump water heater 367
pump water-source 367
recovery drainwater 292
recovery package removal 323
therapy 75
trace system 370
transfer fluid 364
transfer package 291
Heater & fan bathroom 350
cabinet convector 372
ceiling mount unit 372
electric 72
electric hot air 372
gas fired infrared 362
gas residential water 290
gas water 290
infrared 362
infrared quartz 371
quartz 371
removal electric 323
removal space 324
sauna 82
space 589
swimming pool 360
swimming pool solar 525
terminal 362
tubular infrared 362
vertical discharge 372
wall mounted 372
water 72, 383
water residential electric 289
Heating 335
& ventilating unit removal 323
control valve 344
electric 370
estimate electrical 370
fin-tube residential 520
hot water solar 507
hydronic 359, 360, 368
industrial 359
insulation 133, 136, 137, 332
kettle 592
panel radiant 371
solar 363
solar-energy 515, 525
steam-to-water 365
Heavy duty shoring 14
lifting 695
Helicopter 593
High efficiency flush valve 302
efficiency toilet (HET) flush 302
efficiency urinal 302
impact pipe 220
pressure HDPE, ASTM D2513 446
Highway equipment rental 591
Hoist 462
chain 462
chain fall 593
electric 462
overhead 462
personnel 593
tower 593
Holding tank 468
Hole cutting electrical 377
drilling electrical 376
Hollow wall anchor 42
Hood and ventilation equip. 352
exhaust 71
fire protection 352
range 71
Hook coat 64
robe 64
type pipe outlet 196
Horizontal borer 592
boring 417
boring machine 584
directional drill 592
drilling 417
Horn fire 387
Hose & hydrant house 98
adapter fire 96
air 588
bibb 341
bibb sillcock 298
braided bronze 250
braided stainless steel 250
braided steel 250
discharge 589
equipment 96
fire 97
metal flexible 250
nozzle 98
rack 98
rack cabinet 66
reel fire 98
reel fire-suppression 98
suction 589
valve cabinet 67
water 589
Hospital bath 305
equipment 74
sink 305
type valve 329
water closet 304
whirlpool 305
Hot air heater electric 372
tub 81
water boiler 359, 360
water dispenser 288
water dispenser removal 109
water heating 359, 368
water temp maint domestic 128
water-steam exchange 291
water-water exchange 366
Hotel cabinet 65
Hot-water commercial 501-503
heating forced 520
solar-energy 505, 507, 509, 511, 513, 517, 523
system 498, 500-503
House fire hose storage 98
hose & hydrant 98
safety flood shut-off 115
Hubbard tank 75
Humidifier 72
removal 323
HVAC demolition 322
equipment insulation 332
piping specialty 250, 252, 281, 332, 343, 345, 347
Hydrant building fire 95
fire 430

Index

ground box ... 257
ground post ... 258
removal ... 22
removal ground ... 109
removal wall ... 109
remove fire ... 22
screw type valve ... 99
tool ... 98
wall ... 257
water ... 257
Hydraulic chair ... 75
crane ... 462, 593
excavator ... 584
hammer ... 585, 589
jack ... 594
jack climbing ... 594
jacking ... 695
lift ... 86
pressure test ... 330
Hydro excavator ... 586
Hydrocumulator ... 260
Hydromulcher ... 592
Hydronic balancing ... 347
baseboard removal ... 323
convector & radiator demo ... 323
energy underground ... 457
flow fitting ... 344
heating ... 359, 360, 368
heating control valve ... 344
heating convector ... 368
unit heater removal ... 323

I

Ice machine ... 73
Icemaker ... 71, 73
Impact sprinkler ... 409
wrench ... 588
In place pipe liner cured ... 416, 417
Indicator thermoflo ... 347
valve post ... 430
Indoor fountain ... 81
water storage tank ... 261
Induced draft fan removal ... 323
Industrial dryer ... 70
heating ... 359
safety fixture ... 305
safety fixture removal ... 109
Inert gas ... 24
Infectious disease ... 9
disease precautions ... 689
Infiltration chamber ... 433
chamber HDPE ... 433
Infrared heater ... 362
heater gas fired ... 362
heater tubular ... 362
quartz heater ... 371
Insert fitting PVC ... 238
hanger concrete ... 120
Inspection internal pipe ... 415
Installation add elevated ... 108
extinguisher ... 67
Instantaneous gas water heater ... 290
water heater ... 288
Institution fixture ... 306
Insulated protector ADA ... 132
Insulation ... 137
all service jacket ... 133, 138
blower ... 589
board ... 331
boiler ... 332
breeching ... 332
calcium silicate ... 332
duct ... 331
equipment ... 332

heating ... 133, 136, 137, 332
HVAC equipment ... 332
jacket stainless-steel ... 150
jacketing ... 142
jacketing aluminum ... 146
jacketing protective ... 142
pipe ... 132
polyethylene ... 140, 331
polyolefin ... 141
removal ... 26
vaporproof ... 134, 141
water heater ... 132
Insurance ... 11, 692
builder risk ... 11
equipment ... 11
public liability ... 11
Intake filter medical ... 311
Interceptor ... 280
drain oil ... 279
grease ... 280
hair ... 280
lint ... 280
metal recovery ... 281
oil ... 281
sand ... 281
Internal cleaning pipe ... 415
Interval timer ... 379
Intrusion detection ... 386
system ... 386
Invert manhole ... 437
Iron alloy mechanical joint pipe ... 315
body valve ... 325
removal filter ... 288
Irrigation drip ... 407
system sprinkler ... 407

J

J hook clamp w/nail ... 128
Jack cable ... 594
hydraulic ... 594
Jacketing insulation ... 142
Jackhammer ... 588
Jacking ... 417
Jet water system ... 421
Job condition ... 10
Jockey pump fire ... 105
Joint control ... 32
expansion ... 342
filler ... 54
gasket ... 53
grooved joint expansion ... 203
push-on ... 421
restraint ... 422, 425
sealer ... 53, 54

K

Kettle ... 73
heating ... 592
tar ... 590, 592
Kitchen cabinet ... 78
equipment ... 73
equipment fee ... 8
sink ... 295, 484
sink faucet ... 297
sink residential ... 295
unit commercial ... 72
Knee action mixing valve ... 305
Knockout electrical ... 377

L

Label pipe & valve ... 130
Labor adjustment factor ... 108
modifier ... 108
pipe cutting steel ... 172
pipe groove roll ... 205
pipe threading st steel ... 211
pipe threading steel ... 171
pipe weld stainless steel ... 211
pipe weld steel ... 172
Laboratory safety equipment ... 74
sink ... 73, 74, 300, 486
Ladder extension ... 589
rolling ... 15
towel ... 65
Lag screw ... 44
screw shield ... 42
Laminated sheet flashing ... 50
Lance concrete ... 589
Landfill compactor ... 586
Landscape fee ... 8
Laser level ... 589
Latex caulking ... 54
Laundry equipment ... 70
faucet ... 297
sink ... 296, 485
Lavatory ... 482
commercial ... 300
faucet ... 297
pedestal type ... 294
prison/institution ... 306
removal ... 109
residential ... 293
sink ... 293
support ... 302
system battery mount ... 483
vanity top ... 293
wall hung ... 294
Lawn mower ... 589
sprinkler ... 569
Leaching field ... 577
field chamber ... 432
pit ... 432
Lead caulking ... 262
flashing ... 50, 278
salvage ... 110
screw anchor ... 43
Leader line wye ... 100
Leads pile ... 585
Leak detection ... 386
detection probe ... 386
detection tank ... 386
Level laser ... 589
Leveling jack shoring ... 14
Liability employer ... 11
insurance ... 692
Lift automotive ... 86
hydraulic ... 86
scissor ... 462, 587
Lifting equipment rental ... 592
Light dental ... 75
stand ... 25
temporary ... 12
tower ... 589
underwater ... 80
Lighting fountain ... 310
outlet ... 381
residential ... 381
temporary ... 12
Lightning suppressor ... 378
Lightweight angle framing ... 46
channel framing ... 46
framing ... 46
Line remover traffic ... 592
Lined valve ... 115

Liner cement ... 416
pipe ... 416
Link seal pipe ... 253
Lint interceptor ... 280
Lintel hanging ... 46
Loader skidsteer ... 587
tractor ... 586
vacuum ... 25
wheeled ... 586
windrow ... 592
Locking receptacle ... 381
Locomotive tunnel ... 592
Log chipper ... 586
skidder ... 586
Low bed trailer ... 592
Lubricated plug valve ... 327
Lubrication equipment ... 70
Lubricator air filter regulator ... 286

M

Machine autoscrub ... 588
screw ... 44
trowel finish concrete ... 38
welding ... 591
Machinery anchor ... 35
Magnetic motor starter ... 383
Main drain ... 283
Maintenance cable temperature ... 128
general ... 19
mechanical ... 19
Make-up air unit removal ... 323
Malleable iron fitting ... 177
iron pipe fitting ... 177
Management fee construction ... 8
Manhole ... 418
brick ... 418
concrete ... 418
cover ... 437
frame and cover ... 437
invert ... 437
raise ... 437
removal ... 22
step ... 418
Manifold medical gas ... 313
roof fire valve ... 95
Marble screen ... 63
shower stall ... 65
sink ... 482
Marine equipment rental ... 594
Marker boundary and survey ... 22
pipe ... 130
Mark-up cost ... 11
Mason scaffold ... 13
Masonry flashing ... 50
manhole ... 418
saw ... 590
Mastic-backed flashing ... 50
Mat concrete placement
foundation ... 38
foundation ... 36
Material handling ... 18, 462
Mechanical ... 703
coupling ... 196
equipment demolition ... 323
fee ... 8
maintenance ... 19
roof support ... 127
tee ... 197
Medical after cooler ... 313
air compressor ... 313
alarm system ... 312
alarm transducer ... 312
clean copper tubing ... 153
equipment ... 74-76

738

For customer support on your Plumbing Costs with RSMeans data, call 800.448.8182.

Index

faucet 305
  gas manifold 313
  gas piping 311
  gas specialty removal 109
  intake filter 311
  nitrogen or oxygen 311
  sterilizer 74
  sterilizing equipment 74
  vacuum pump 310
  vacuum system 310
Medicine cabinet 65
Metal flexible hose 250
  flue chimney 353
  interceptor dental 281
  nailing anchor 42
  pipe 434
  pipe removal 109
  recovery interceptor 281
  support assembly 58
  toilet partition 62
  valve removal 110
Meter 335
  flow 348
  gas 335
  venturi flow 347
  water supply 254
  water supply detector 254
  water supply domestic 254
Metric conversion factors 686
Microtunneling 417, 418
Mineral wool board 331
  wool pipe covering 132
Minor site demolition 22
Mirror 64
  glass 64
Miscellaneous painting 58
  pump 259
Mixer concrete 584
  mortar 584, 589
  plaster 589
  road 592
Mixing shower valve 296
  valve 251, 298
  valve shower 296
Mobilization or demobilization . . . 15
Modification to cost 10
Modifier labor 108
Module alarm panel 312
  tub-shower 295
Moil point 588
Mold abatement work area 28
  contaminated area demolition . . 29
Monitor corrosion 89
  dew point 313
Monoflow fitting 344
  tee fitting 344
Monument survey 22
Mop holder strip 64
  sink 301
Mortar mixer 584, 589
Mortuary equipment 76
Motor centrifugal in-line 259
  connection 378
  starter 383
  starter & control 383
  starter enclosed & heated 383
  starter magnetic 383
  starter w/circuit protector 383
  starter w/fused switch 384
Motorized grader 585
  zone valve 335
Mount vibration absorbing 129
Mounting board plywood 48
Mower lawn 589
Muck car tunnel 592
Mud pump 584

trailer 592
Mulcher power 586
Multicycle valve package on-off . . 102
Mylar tarpaulin 16

N

Nailer pneumatic 588, 589
  wood 48
Nailing anchor 42
Napkin dispenser 64
Needle valve 118
Neoprene flashing 278
  gasket 53
Nipple fire hose 97
  pipe 177
Nitrogen or oxygen medical 311
No hub pipe 262
  hub pipe fitting 271
Non-chloride accelerator conc. . . . 37
Nondestructive pipe testing 330
Nonfusible oil valve 335
Nozzle dispersion 103
  fire hose 97
  fog 98
  playpipe 98
Nut threaded 123
Nylon nailing anchor 42

O

Oakum caulking 262
Observation well 419
Off highway dump truck 587
Office & storage space 13
  field 13
  trailer 13
Oil burner 361
  filter 335
  fired boiler 360
  fired water-heater commercial . 503
  fired water-heater residential . . 500
  interceptor 281
  interceptor drain 279
  shut-off valve 335
  specialty fuel 335
  valve fuel 335
Oil-fired boiler 360
  water heater 291
  water heater commercial 291
  water heater residential 291
Oil/water separator 469
Omitted work 11
On-off multicycle sprinkler 540
  multicycle valve package 102
Opening roof frame 46
Operating room equipment 75
OSHA testing 27
Outdoor fountain 81
Outlet lighting 381
Oval arch culvert 436
  chimney vent 355
Oven 71, 73
Overhaul 23
Overhead & profit 11
  contractor 18, 692
  hoist 462
Overtime 10, 11
Oxygen lance cutting 24
  vaporizer 311

P

P trap 276
  trap glass 276
  trap running 275
Packaged terminal A/C removal . 324
  terminal air conditioner 366
Packaging waste 28
Pad equipment 36
  prefabricated 374
  vibration absorbing 129
Paddle fan 382
Paint & coating 58
  interior miscellaneous 58
  sprayer 589
  striper 592
Painting booth 70
  grille 58
  miscellaneous 58
  pipe 58
  swimming pool 80
Panel and device alarm 387
  board residential 378
  fiberglass 16
  radiant heat 371
Paperbacked flashing 50
Paperholder 64
Paraffin bath 75
Parking lot paving 406
Partition shower 65
  toilet 62, 63
  toilet stone 63
Patient care equipment 75
Pavement asphaltic 406
  breaker 588
  bucket 591
  demolition 22
  planer 592
  profiler 592
  replacement 406
  widener 592
Paver asphalt 590
  bituminous 589
  cold mix 592
  concrete 590
  roof 51
  shoulder 592
Paving asphalt 406
  asphaltic concrete 406
  parking lot 406
Pedestal type lavatory 294
Perforated aluminum pipe 433
  pipe 433
  PVC pipe 433
Performance bond 11, 694
Perineal bath 305
Permit building 12
Personal respirator 25
Personnel field 10, 11
  hoist 593
Pet cock 341
Pete's plug 253
PEX pipe 225
  tubing 225, 369
  tubing fitting 369
Photography 12
  construction 12
  time lapse 12
Pickup truck 591
Pick-up vacuum 584
Pigtail steam syphon 341
Pilaster toilet partition 63
Pile driving 695, 696
  hammer 585
  leads 585
Piling sheet 719

Pin powder 44
Pipe & fitting 119, 303
  & fitting backflow preventer . . 255
  & fitting backwater valve 283
  & fitting borosilicate 314
  & fitting brass 111, 153
  & fitting bronze 114
  & fitting carbon steel 187
  & fitting cast iron 131, 263
  & fitting copper . 153, 154, 156, 166
  & fitting corrosion resistant . . . 317
  & fitting drain 283
  & fitting DWV 231
  & fitting faucet 297
  & fitting grooved joint 198
  & fitting hydrant 257
  & fitting iron body 326
  & fitting malleable iron 178
  & fitting polypropylene . . 117, 316
  & fitting PVC 220
  & fitting sanitary drain 278
  & fitting semi-steel 328
  & fitting stainless steel . . . 207, 213, 328
  & fitting steel 168
  & fitting steel cast iron 176
  & fitting trap 276
  & fitting turbine water meter . . 255
  & valve label 130
  acid resistant 316
  add elevated 108
  aluminum 433, 434
  and fittings 707
  bedding 393, 566, 567
  bedding trench 392
  bracket 119
  brass 151
  bursting 416
Pipe bypass 416
Pipe carrier 120, 124
  cast iron 261
  clamp 119, 412
  clamp plastic 127
  cleaning internal 415
  cleanout 130
  concrete 435
  conduit gland seal 455
  conduit prefabricated . . . 455, 457
  conduit preinsulated 455
  conduit system 455, 458
  contained 245
  copper 153, 426
  corrosion resistant 315
  corrugated 433
  corrugated metal 433, 434
  covering 132
  covering calcium silicate 135
  covering fiberglass 137
  covering foam 140
  covering mineral wool 132
  CPVC 223
  culvert 436
  cutting steel labor 172
  double wall 241, 438
  drain 392
  drainage 314, 315, 431, 435
  dual wall HDPE 245
  ductile iron 421
  DWV PVC 222, 431
  elbow 199
  encapsulation 28
  epoxy fiberglass wound 315
  fire retardant 316
  fire-suppression plastic 93
  fitting 184, 273, 423, 455, 457
  fitting adapter 158

Index

Entry	Page
fitting brass	152
fitting cast iron	173, 262
fitting copper	156, 166
fitting corrosion resistant	316
fitting drainage special	273
fitting DWV	231
fitting fire-suppression	93
fitting flanged cast iron	184
fitting forged steel	191
fitting galvanized	275
fitting gasket joint	266
fitting glass	314
fitting grooved joint	90, 199
fitting insert	237
fitting malleable iron	178, 194
fitting mechanical joint	194
fitting no hub	270
fitting pitched	273
fitting plastic	93, 226, 234, 235, 422
fitting polybutylene	236
fitting polypropylene	238
fitting PVC	238
fitting soil	262
fitting stainless steel	212
fitting steel	173, 187
fitting steel carbon	187
fitting weld joint	191
fitting weld steel	187
fitting welded steel	195
flanged	170
foam core DWV ABS	222
foam core DWV PVC	222
freezing	413
fused	425
gas	439
glass	109, 314
groove cut	204
groove roll labor	205
grooved joint	197
guide	121
hanger	119
hanger & support	119
hanger assembly	123
hanger clevis	121
hanger plastic	127
hanger rod	123
hanger strap	126
hanger U-bolt	126
hanger/support removal	109
HDPE	241
heat	366
high impact	220
inspection internal	415
insulation	132
insulation removal	26
internal cleaning	415
iron alloy mechanical joint	315
liner	416
liner HDPE	416
lining	416
link seal	253
marker	130
metal	434
nipple	177
nipple steel	177
no hub	262
painting	58
perforated aluminum	433
PEX	225
plastic	93, 220, 223
plastic FRP	220
polyethylene	422, 439
polypropylene	225, 316
prefabricated	455, 457
preinsulated	455, 457
pressed joint	165
process pressure	314
proxylene	316
PVC	220, 423, 431
PVC pressure	221
reinforced concrete	436
relay	392
removal	22
removal glass	109
removal metal	109
removal plastic	110
repair	412
repair clamp	413
residential PVC	224
ring hanger	121
rodding	415
roll single	124
roof support	127
seal	253
sewage	431, 434, 435
sewage collection PVC	431
shock absorber	257
single hub	261
sleeve	253
sleeve plastic	32
sleeve sheet metal	32
sleeve steel	32
soil	261
stainless steel	207
steam	459
steel	168, 434
subdrainage	433
subdrainage plastic	433
support	119
support chair	124
support framing	46
support saddle	124
tee	199
testing	330
testing nondestructive	330
threading st steel labor	211
threading steel labor	171
water	421
water distribution	426
weld joint	169, 207
weld stainless steel labor	211
weld steel labor	172
wrapping	412
X-ray	330
Pipe bursting	416
Piping designations	719
Piping excavation	560, 562, 564
fitting removal	109
flexible (CSST) gas	335
gas service polyethylene	439
gasoline	438
HDPE	425
specialty HVAC	250, 252, 281, 332, 343, 345, 347
storm drainage	434
to 10' high	708
Pit leaching	432
sump	392
Pitch pocket	51
Pitched pipe fitting	273
Placing concrete	37
Plan remediation	25
Planer pavement	592
Plank scaffolding	14
Plant screening	586
Plant-mix asphalt paving	406
Plaster drilling	58
mixer	589
Plastic angle valve	116
ball check valve	117
ball valve	116
coupling	234
fitting	231
FRP pipe	220
pipe	93, 220, 223
pipe clamp	127
pipe fire-suppression	93
pipe fitting	226, 234, 235, 422
pipe hanger	127
pipe polyethylene	241
pipe removal	110
pipe weld	244
screw anchor	43
sheet flashing	51
toilet partition	63
trap	277
trench drain	284
valve	116
valve removal	111
vent cap	278
Plastic-laminate toilet compartment	62
Plate checkered	46
escutcheon	99, 100
F&C	254
roadway	592
Plate-type heat exchanger	365
Platform checkered plate	46
trailer	590
Playpipe fire hose	98
Plow vibrator	587
Plug Pete's	253
pressure/temperature safety	253
p/t	253
p/t probe	253
valve	327
valve grooved joint	204
Plumbing	255
appliance	287, 289, 308, 309
approximations for quick estimating	707
demolition	109
fixture	280, 281, 288, 292, 294, 301, 307, 348, 421, 484, 491
fixture removal	109
fixture requirements	712
laboratory	74
system estimate	497
Plywood fence	17
mounting board	48
sheathing roof & wall	48
sidewalk	18
Pneumatic nailer	588, 589
Pocket pitch	51
Point moil	588
of use water heater	288
Polybutylene adapter	237
Polyethylene coating	412
insulation	140, 331
pipe	422, 439, 569, 572
plastic pipe	241
septic tank	432
tarpaulin	16
Polymer trench drain	284
Polyolefin insulation	141
Polypropylene accessory	238
cleanout	132
coupling	238
fitting	238, 317
pipe	225, 316
pipe fitting	238
shower	296
sink	300
tool	240
trap	277
tubing	225
valve	117
Polysulfide caulking	55
Polyurethane caulking	55
Polyvinyl tarpaulin	16
Pool concrete side/vinyl lined	568
filtration swimming	309
gunite shell	568
heater electric	361
heater swimming	361
swimming	80
Porcelain enamel sink	482
Portable air compressor	587
asphalt plant	591
building	13
eye wash	306
fire extinguisher	66, 67
Positive pressure chimney	356, 358
Post driver	592
indicator valve	430
Potable water softener	287
water treatment	287
Potable-water storage	261
storage tank	261
Powder actuated tool	44
charge	44
pin	44
Power mulcher	586
temporary	12
trowel	584
Preaction valve cabinet	102
Precast catch basin	418
receptor	65
septic tank	431
Prefab metal flue	353
Prefabricated comfort station	82
metal chimney	356
pad	374
pipe	455, 457
Preinsulated pipe	455, 457
Pressed joint pipe	165
Pressure & temperature measurement	253
booster package water	260
booster pump	260
booster system water	260
gauge	334
pipe	222
pipe process	314
pipe PVC	221
reducing valve steam	252
reducing valve water	114
regulator	252
regulator gas	252
regulator oil	252
relief valve	114
restricting valve	100
switch well water	421
test	330
test hydraulic	330
valve relief	114
washer	590
Pressure/temperature safety plug	253
Pressure/vacuum gauge	334
Pressurized fire extinguisher	67
Preventer backflow	255
removal backflow	109
Primer trap	277
Prison cell	82
fixture	306
fixture removal	110
toilet	76
Prison/institution lavatory	306
shower	307
sink	307
Probe plug p/t	253
Process supply pipe glass	314

Index

Product piping 438
Profiler pavement 592
Project overhead 11
sign 18
Promenade drain 278
Property line survey 22
Propylene glycol 349
Protection fire 66
winter 16
worker 25
Protective insulation jacketing 142
Protector ADA insulated 132
Proxylene pipe 316
P/t plug 253
P&T relief valve 114
PTAC unit 366
Pulse boiler gas 359
combustion gas 359
Pump 348, 419
and motor set 337
centrifugal 258, 590
circulating 348
concrete 584
condensate removal 349
contractor 392
diaphragm 590
fire 104, 105
fire jockey 105
fountain 309
fuel oil 337
general utility 258
grinder system 281
grout 590
heat 367
in-line centrifugal 348
medical vacuum 310
miscellaneous 259
mud 584
operator 393
pressure booster 260
removal 110
removal heat 323
rotary 259
sewage ejector 282
shallow well 421
shotcrete 584
submersible 285, 419, 590
sump 72, 284
trash 590
turbine 259
vacuum 310
water 348, 419, 590
water supply well 421
wellpoint 594
Pumping 392
dewater 392
Push-on joint 421
Putlog scaffold 15
PVC acid resistant drain 279
cleanout 132
fitting 228, 424
flange 236
flashing 51
insert fitting 238
pipe 220, 423, 431, 569, 572
pipe perforated 433
pipe residential 224
roof drain system 518
trap 277
union 236
valve 116
well casing 420

Q

Quarry drill 588
Quartz heater 371

R

Raceway 376, 377
Rack hose 98
Radiant floor heating 369
floor heating removal 323
heating panel 371
Radiator air vent 341
cast iron 368
supply valve 344
valve 344
Rainwater filter 468
storage tank fiberglass 285
Raise manhole 437
manhole frame 437
Rake tractor 586
Rammer/tamper 585
Ramp temporary 16
Range cooking 71
hood 71
receptacle 381
Ready mix concrete 37, 688
Receptacle air conditioner 381
device 380
dryer 381
GFI 380
locking 381
range 381
telephone 381
television 381
waste 65
weatherproof 380
Receptor & interceptor removal 110
floor 279
precast 65
shower 65, 280, 296, 301
terrazzo 65
Reciprocating compressor 286
hermetic compressor 286
Recirculating chemical toilet 468
Recovery package removal heat 323
Reducer grooved 201
grooved joint 164
Reducing tee 174
Redwood bath 81
tub 81
Reflectorized barrels 588
Refrigerant compressor removal 324
removal 324
Refrigerated storage equipment 73
Refrigeration blood bank 74
fitting 161
tubing 155
Refrigerator compartment cooler 309
Regulator gas 252
lubricator air filter 286
oil pressure 252
pressure 252
Reinforced concrete pipe 436
culvert 435
Reinforcing concrete 35
footing 35
Relay pipe 392
Release emergency sprinkler 100
Relief valve P&T 114
valve self-closing 114
valve temperature 114
vent removal 324
Relining sewer 416
Remediation plan 25
plan/method asbestos 25
Removal air conditioner 322
asbestos 26
bathtub 109
bidet 109
boiler 322
catch basin 22
concrete pipe 22
condenser 322
dehumidifier 322
evaporator 323
fan 323
fixture 109
heating & ventilating unit 323
humidifier 323
hydrant 22
insulation 26
lavatory 109
pipe 22
pipe insulation 26
plumbing fixture 109
pump 110
refrigerant 324
shower 109
sidewalk 22
sink 109
solar heating system 110
sprinkler system 110
steel pipe 22
tank 24
urinal 109
utility line 22
ventilator 324
wash fountain 109
water closet 109
water fountain 109
water heater 110
water softener 111
whirlpool/hot tub 109
Rental equipment 584
Repair pipe 412
Replacement pavement 406
Residential alarm 382
appliance 71, 382
application 378
bathtub 295
burner 361
device 378
dishwasher 71
door bell 381
dryer 71
fan 382
fin-tube heating 520
fixture 381
gas meter 335
gas water heater 290
heat pump 383
kitchen sink 295
lavatory 293
lighting 381
oil-fired water heater 291
panel board 378
pool 568
PVC pipe 224
roof jack 350
service 378
sink 295
smoke detector 382
sprinkler 101
switch 378
transition 350
wall cap 350
wash bowl 293
washer 71
water heater 72, 291, 383, 499
water heater electric 289
water-heater 498, 500
wiring 378, 382
Resistance corrosion 412
Resistant trap corrosion 276
Respirator 25
personal 25
Retarder concrete 37
Rigid joint sealant 55
Ring clamp 422
hanger pipe 121
Ripper attachment 591
Riser clamp 120
pipe wellpoint 594
standpipe 552, 555
Rivet 44
aluminum 44
copper 44
stainless 45
steel 45
tool 45
Road mixer 592
sweeper 592
temporary 16
Roadway plate 592
Robe hook 64
Rock trencher 587
Rod backer 54
coupling hanger 123
curtain 64
pipe hanger 123
socket 126
threaded 123
tie 46
weld 45
Roll hanger 124
Roller sheepsfoot 586
tandem 586
vibratory 586
Rolling ladder 15
tower scaffold 15
Roof drain 283
drain removal 109
drain system 518, 519
fire valve manifold 95
flashing vent chimney 359
frame opening 46
jack residential 350
paver 51
paver and support 51
sheathing 48
support equipment 127
support mechanical 127
support pipe 127
Rooftop A/C removal 324
Room unit removal computer 322
Rotary crawler drill 588
hammer drill 588
pump 259
Rototiller 586
Rough-in bidet 293
classroom sink 300
drinking fountain deck 308
drinking fountain floor 308
drinking fountain wall 307
sink corrosion resistant 301
sink countertop 295
sink cup 301
sink raised deck 295
sink service floor 301
sink service wall 301
tub 296
Rubber pipe insulation 140
Rubbish handling 23
Running trap 275

Index

S

S trap 276
Saddle covering protection 125
   pipe support 124
Safety equipment laboratory 74
   eye/face equipment 306
   fixture industrial 305
   fixture removal industrial 109
   flood shut-off house 115
   plug pressure/temperature 253
   shower 305
   shut-off flood whole house ... 115
   valve gas 361
   water and gas shut-off 115
Salamander 590
Sales tax 10, 690, 691
Sampling air 25
Sand backfill 566
   interceptor 281
Sandblasting equipment 590
Sander floor 590
Sanitary drain 278
   tee 271
Sauna 81
Saw chain 590
   circular 590
   concrete 584
   masonry 590
Sawn control joint 32
Scaffold baseplate 14
   bracket 14
   caster 14
   catwalk 15
   frame 14
   guardrail 14
   mason 13
   putlog 15
   rolling tower 15
   specialty 15
   stairway 14
   wood plank 14
Scaffolding 694
   plank 14
   tubular 13
Scissor lift 462, 587
Scoop air 340
   air purging 340
Scraper earth 586
Screed, gas engine,
   8HP vibrating 584
Screen entrance 62
   urinal 63
Screening plant 586
Screw anchor 42
   lag 44
   machine 44
Scrub station 75
Scrubber air 588
Scupper drain 284
   floor 284
Seal compression 53
   floor drain trap 280
   pipe 253
Sealant acoustical 55
   caulking 54
   control joint 33
   rigid joint 55
   tape 55
Sealer joint 53, 54
Seat toilet 293
   water closet 293
Secondary treatment plant 468
Security factor 9
   shower 307
Sediment bucket drain 279

strainer trap 277
   strainer Y valve 118
Seismic fire extinguishing 545
   wet pipe system 548, 549
Self-closing relief valve 114
Self-contained single
   pkg A/C rmvl 324
Semi-steel valve 327
Separation barrier 26, 28, 29
Separator 281
   air 340
   oil/water 469
Septic galley 432
   system 431, 577
Septic system, 1000
gallon, (5) 4" 578
Septic system chamber 433
   system effluent-filter 432
   tank 431, 577
   tank concrete 431
   tank polyethylene 432
   tank precast 431
   trench 577
Service boring 417
   residential 378
   sink 301, 487
   sink clinic 305
   sink faucet 302
   station equipment 70
   tap 573
Setter circuit 341
Sewage aeration 468
   collection PVC pipe 431
   collection valve 431
   collection vent 431
   ejector pump 282
   municipal waste water 468
   pipe 431, 434, 435
   treatment plant 468
Sewage/drainage collection 435
Sewer relining 416
   valve backwater 431
Sheathing 48
   roof 48
   roof & wall plywood 48
   wall 48
Sheepsfoot roller 586
Sheet metal flashing 50
   piling 719
Sheeting driver 588
   wood 392, 719
Shelf bathroom 64
Shell-type heat exchanger 366
Shield expansion 42
   lag screw 42
Shift work 10
Shock absorber 256
   absorber pipe 257
Shoring base plate 14
   bracing 14
   heavy duty 14
   leveling jack 14
   slab 15
Short load concrete 37
Shot blaster 590
Shotcrete pump 584
Shoulder paver 592
Shovel crawler 586
Shower arm 296
   built-in 296
   by-pass valve 297
   cabinet 65
   cubicle 296
   door 65
   drain 275
   emergency 305

enclosure 66
glass door 65
group 301
partition 65
polypropylene 296
prison/institution 307
receptor 65, 280, 296, 301
removal 109
safety 305
security 307
spray 298
stall 296
surround 66
system 490
Shower-head water economizer . 296
Shower/tub control set 298
Shower-tub valve spout set 298
Shut-off flood whole
house safety 115
Shutoff gas earthquake 361
Shut-off safety water and gas .. 115
   valve oil 335
   water heater safety 115
Shutter damper removal flue .. 323
Sidewalk bridge 15
   broom 590
   removal 22
   temporary 18
Sign 18
   detour 17
   project 18
Signal bell 387
Silent check valve 114, 327
Silicone 54
   caulking 55
Sillcock hose bibb 298
Simplex style strainer 344
Single hub pipe 261
   pipe roll 124
   pkg A/C rmvl self-contained .. 324
Sink barber 70
   base 78
   classroom 300
   commercial 300
   corrosion resistant rough-in .. 301
   corrosion-resistant 300
   countertop 295
   countertop rough-in 295
   cup 301
   cup rough-in 301
   faucet kitchen 297
   hospital 305
   kitchen 295
   laboratory 73, 74, 300
   laundry 296
   lavatory 293
   mop 301
   polypropylene 300
   prison/institution 307
   raised deck rough-in 295
   removal 109
   residential 295
   service 301
   service floor rough-in 301
   service wall rough-in 301
   slop 301
   stainless steel 300
   support 303
   waste treatment 280
Site demolition 22
   improvement 407
   irrigation 569, 572
   utility 566
Sitework manhole 579
Skidder log 586
Skidsteer attachments 587

loader 587
Slab edge formwork 32
   haunch 37
   haunch formwork 37
   on grade 36
   on grade formwork 32
   shoring 15
   thickened edge 37
   thickened edge formwork ... 37
   trench formwork 32
   turndown 37
   turndown formwork 37
Sleeve 253, 427
   and tap 422
   cut in 427
   formwork 32
   pipe 253
   plastic pipe 32
   sheet metal pipe 32
   steel pipe 32
   wall 254
Sliding door shower 65
   mirror 65
Slip on escutcheon flange 254
Slipform paver barrier 592
   paver curb 592
Slop sink 301
Slotted channel framing 46
   pipe 436
Slow close ball valve 99
Smoke detector 386
   vent chimney 353
Snow guard 51
Snubber valve 341
Soaking bathroom 295
   tub 295
Soap dispenser 64
   holder 65
Socket hanger rod 126
Socket-o-let 193
Softener water 287
Soil decontamination 24
   pipe 261
Solar air to water heat exchange . 527
   backflow preventer 364
   closed loop add-on hot water . 505
   closed loop hot water system . 517
   closed loop space/hot water . 523
   drain back hot water 506
   draindown hot-water 509
   energy 364
   energy circulator air 363
   energy system . 505, 511, 513, 517,
                         523
   energy system air purger 364
   energy system air vent 364
   energy sys. balancing valve ... 365
   energy system collector 363
   energy system control valve ... 364
   energy system controller 364
   energy system expansion tank . 365
   energy sys. gauge pressure ... 365
   energy system heat exchanger 364
   energy system storage tank ... 364
   energy system thermometer ... 365
   energy system vacuum relief .. 365
   heating 363, 713
   heating system 363
   heating system removal 110
   hot water 515
   recirculation hot water 511
   swimming pool heater 525
   system solenoid valve 365
Solar-energy pool heater 525
   water-heater 515
Solder 153

Index

Source heat pump water 367
Spa bath 81
Space heater 589
   heater removal 324
   office & storage 13
Spade air 588
   tree 587
Specialty 64
   piping HVAC .. 250, 281, 342, 345, 347
   scaffold 15
Split ductless removal 324
   ring hanger 122
Spotter 399
Spray painting booth automotive .. 70
   rig foam 589
   shower 298
   substrate 27
Sprayer airless 25
   emulsion 588
   paint 589
Spread footing 36
   footing formwork 32
Spreader aggregate 584, 591
   chemical 591
   concrete 590
Sprinkler ball valve 99
   cabinet 100
   connector flexible 100
   control pressure 101
   dehydrator package 101
   deluge system 537, 538
   dry pipe 530
   dry pipe system 530, 532
   escutcheon 100
   floor control valve 88
   head 100
   head guard 101
   head wrench 101
   irrigation system 407
   line tester 95
   monitoring panel deluge 103
   on-off multicycle system . 540, 541
   preaction system 533
   quantities 703
   release emergency 100
   residential 101
   system 100, 701
   system accelerator 101
   system dry-pipe 101
   system removal 110
   trim valve 99
   underground 407
   valve 88, 101
   wet-pipe system 543, 544, 548, 550
Stabilizer base 592
Stainless flashing 50
   rivet 45
   screen 62
   steel fitting 212
   steel flange 217
   steel globe valve 329
   steel pipe 207
   steel shelf 64
   steel sink 300, 482, 484
   steel tubing 205, 206
   steel valve 328
   weld rod 45
Stainless-steel insulation jacket ... 150
Stair temporary protection 18
Stairway scaffold 14
Stall shower 296
   toilet 62, 63
   type urinal 299
   urinal 299, 300
Standard extinguisher 67

Standpipe alarm 100
   connection 95
   equipment 556
   systems 699
Starter board & switch 384
   motor 383
Station AHU removal central 322
   control 384
   hospital 75
Steam bath 82
   bath residential 82
   boiler 360
   boiler electric 359
   cleaner 590
   condensate meter removal 324
   energy distribution pipe 457
   jacketed kettle 73
   pipe 459
   pipe underground 455
   pressure reducing valve 252
   radiator valve 344
   syphon pigtail 341
Steam-to-water heating 365
Steel channel 122
   drill 588
   drilling 43
   expansion tank 343
   fitting 173, 184
   flange 193, 202
   pipe 168, 434
   pipe corrugated 433
   pipe fitting 173, 187
   pipe labor cutting 172
   pipe nipple 177
   pipe removal 22
   rivet 45
   roof drain system 518
   salvage 110
   sink 482, 484
   tank 343
   tank aboveground 339
   underground storage tank 337
   weld rod 45
   well casing 420
   well screen 420
Step manhole 418
Sterilizer barber 70
   dental 75
   glassware 74
   medical 74
Stiffleg derrick crane 593
Stone toilet compartment 63
Stop valve 298
   water supply 298
Stop-start control station 384
Storage box 13
   potable-water 261
   tank 338
   tank chemical 319
   tank concrete aboveground ... 340
   tank fiberglass rainwater 285
   tank fiberglass underground .. 261
   tank potable-water 261
   tank steel underground 337
   tank underground 338
Storm drainage manhole frame .. 418
   drainage piping 434
   drainage system 519
Storz type connection 95
Strainer basket type 344
   bronze body 346
   duplex style 345
   grooved joint 203
   simplex style 344
   Y type bronze body 346
   Y type iron body 346

Strap pipe hanger 126
Strapless outlet 196, 197
Strap-on T outlet 202
Strip footing 36
Striper paint 592
Structural fee 8
   welding 44
Stump chipper 586
Subcontractor O&P 11
Subcontractors 713
Subdrainage pipe 433
   plastic pipe 433
   system 433
Submersible pump 285, 419, 590
   sump pump 285
Subsurface drip irrigation 407
Suction diffuser 347
   diffuser grooved joint 203
   diffuser pump 347
   hose 589
Sump hole construction 392
   pit 392
   pump 72, 284
   pump elevator 285
   pump submersible 285
Supply copper pipe water 426
   ductile iron pipe water 421
   HDPE water 425
   polyethylene pipe water 422
Support carrier fixture 302
   drinking fountain 302
   framing pipe 46
   lavatory 302
   pipe 119
   sink 303
   urinal 303
   water closet 303
   water cooler 304
Suppression valve fire 91
Suppressor lightning 378
Surfactant 27
Surround shower 66
   tub 66
Survey aerial 22
   monument 22
   property line 22
   topographic 22
Sweeper road 592
Swimming pool 80
   pool equipment 80
   pool filter 309
   pool filtration 309
   pool heater 361
   pool painting 80
   pool residential 568
   pools 699
Swing check valve 112, 326
   check valve bronze 112
Switch decorator 379
   dimmer 379
   residential 378
   tamper 101
   well water pressure 421
Switchboard electric 384
Swivel adapter fire hose 97
System boiler steam 528
   chamber septic 433
   component foam-water 103
   control 332
   deluge sprinkler 537, 538
   drinking fountain 491
   dry pipe sprinkler 530-532
   exhaust 351
   fire extinguishing . 96, 97, 103, 105

   fire sprinkler 531, 532, 534, 535, 537, 538, 540, 541, 543, 544, 548, 550
   FM200 fire suppression 557
   grinder pump 281
   heat trace 370
   on-off multicycle sprinkler . 539-541
   pipe conduit 455, 458
   plumbing estimate 497
   preaction sprinkler 533-535
   removal exhaust 323
   riser dry standpipe 555
   septic 431
   sitework catch basin 579
   sitework swimming pool 568
   sitework trenching .. 560, 562, 564
   solar-energy 511, 525
   solenoid valve solar 365
   sprinkler 100, 101, 103
   standpipe riser dry 554, 555
   standpipe riser wet 552
   storm drainage 518
   subdrainage 433
   wet pipe sprinkler 542-544

T

T outlet strap-on 202
Tag valve 130
Tamper 390, 588
   switch 101
Tandem roller 586
Tank aboveground steel 339
   aboveground storage conc. ... 340
   chemical-waste dilution 319
   clean 24
   compression 343
   darkroom 71
   disposal 24
   expansion 343
   fiberglass 338
   fiberglass rainwater storage ... 285
   fiberglass underground storage 261
   holding 468
   horizontal aboveground 339
   Hubbard 75
   leak detection 386
   potable-water storage 261
   removal 24
   septic 431
   steel 343
   steel underground storage ... 337
   storage 338
   water 338, 430, 591
   water heater storage 261
   water htr liquid container 110
   water storage solar 365
Tankless electric water heater 288
   gas water heater 290
Tank/wtr htr liquid ctnr removal . 110
Tap and sleeve 422
Tape barricade 17
   sealant 55
   underground 419
Tapping cross and sleeve 426
   main 426
   valve 427
Tar kettle 590, 592
Tarpaulin 16
   duck 16
   Mylar 16
   polyethylene 16
   polyvinyl 16
Tax 10

743

Index

sales ... 10
  Social Security ... 10
  unemployment ... 10
Taxes ... 691
Tee cleanout ... 131
  fitting monoflow ... 344
  HDPE piping ... 426
  mechanical ... 197
  pipe ... 199
  reducing ... 174
Telephone receptacle ... 381
Telescoping boom lift ... 587
Television receptacle ... 381
Temperature maintenance cable ... 128
  relief valve ... 114
  rise detector ... 386
Tempering valve ... 115
  valve water ... 115, 251
Temporary barricade ... 17
  building ... 13
  construction ... 12, 16
  electricity ... 12
  facility ... 17
  fence ... 17
  guardrail ... 17
  light ... 12
  lighting ... 12
  power ... 12
  ramp ... 16
  road ... 16
  toilet ... 590
  utility ... 12
Terminal A/C packaged ... 366
  A/C removal packaged ... 324
  air conditioner packaged ... 366
  heater ... 362
Terne coated flashing ... 50
Terrace drain ... 283
Terrazzo receptor ... 65
Test pressure ... 330
  well ... 419
Tester sprinkler line ... 95
Testing OSHA ... 27
  pipe ... 330
Thermoflo indicator ... 347
Thermometer ... 334
  solar energy system ... 365
  well ... 197
Thermostat contactor
combination ... 371
  integral ... 370
  wire ... 383
Thermosyphon hot-water ... 513
Thickened edge slab ... 37
Threaded flange ... 186
  nut ... 123
  rod ... 123
Threading labor st steel ... 211
  labor steel ... 171
Thread-o-let ... 192
Thru-the-wall A/C removal ... 324
Thru-wall air conditioner ... 366
Tie rod ... 46
Time lapse photography ... 12
Timer clock ... 382
  interval ... 379
Toggle-bolt anchor ... 42
Toilet ... 468
  accessory ... 64
  accessory commercial ... 64
  bowl ... 292
  chemical ... 590
  compartment ... 62
  compartment plastic-laminate ... 62
  compartment stone ... 63
  dual flush valve ... 302

gasket ... 298
  partition ... 62, 63
  prison ... 76
  seat ... 293
  stall ... 62, 63
  stone partition ... 63
  temporary ... 590
Tool fire ... 98
  hydrant ... 98
  polypropylene ... 240
  powder actuated ... 44
  rivet ... 45
Topographical survey ... 22
Torch cutting ... 590
  cutting demolition ... 23
Towel bar ... 64
  dispenser ... 64
Tower crane ... 13, 593, 695, 696
  hoist ... 593
  light ... 589
  removal cooling ... 322
Track drill ... 588
Tractor loader ... 586
  rake ... 586
  truck ... 591
Traffic line remover ... 592
Trailer bunk house ... 13
  floodlight ... 589
  low bed ... 592
  mud ... 592
  office ... 13
  platform ... 590
  truck ... 590
  water ... 591
Tram car ... 591
Transition residential ... 350
Transparent pipe ... 314
Trap cast iron ... 275
  deep seal ... 276
  drainage ... 275, 276
  grease ... 280
  plastic ... 277
  polypropylene ... 277
  primer ... 277
  PVC ... 277
  seal floor drain ... 280
  sediment strainer ... 277
Trapeze hanger ... 124
Trash pump ... 590
Treatment plant secondary ... 468
  plant sewage ... 468
  potable water ... 287
  salt water ... 287
Tree spade ... 587
Trench backfill ... 391, 566, 567
  box ... 591
  disposal field ... 432
  drain ... 284
  drain fiberglass ... 284
  drain plastic ... 284
  drain polymer ... 284
  excavating ... 390
  excavation ... 390, 391
  utility ... 391
Trencher chain ... 391, 587
  rock ... 587
  wheel ... 587
Trenching ... 392, 561
  common earth ... 560, 561
  loam & sandy clay ... 562, 563
  sand & gravel ... 564, 565
Tripod floodlight ... 588
Trowel concrete ... 584
  power ... 584
Truck concrete ... 584
  crane flatbed ... 592

dump ... 587
  flatbed ... 587, 591
  holding concrete ... 37
  mounted crane ... 593
  pickup ... 591
  tractor ... 591
  trailer ... 590
  vacuum ... 591
  winch ... 591
Tub bar ... 64
  hot ... 81
  redwood ... 81
  rough-in ... 296
  shower handicap ... 295
  soaking ... 295
  surround ... 66
Tube copper ... 153, 426
  fitting ... 206
  fitting copper ... 156
Tubing copper ... 153
  (CSST) gas ... 335
  fitting PEX ... 369
  oxygen class copper ... 154
  PEX ... 225, 369
  polypropylene ... 225
  refrigeration ... 155
  stainless steel ... 205, 206
Tub-shower module ... 295
Tubular scaffolding ... 13
Tugboat diesel ... 594
Tumbler holder ... 65
Tunnel locomotive ... 592
  muck car ... 592
  ventilator ... 592
Turbine pump ... 259
  water meter ... 255
Turnbuckle ... 123
Turndown slab ... 37
TV inspection sewer pipeline ... 415

U

U-bolt pipe hanger ... 126
U-hook hanger ... 127
Underdrain ... 418
Underground chilled water pipe ... 455
  hydronic energy ... 457
  piping ... 566
  sprinkler ... 407
  steam pipe ... 455
  storage tank ... 338
  storage tank fiberglass ... 261
  storage tank removal ... 697
  storage tank steel ... 337
  tape ... 419
Underwater light ... 80
Unemployment tax ... 10
Union dielectric ... 342
  PVC ... 236
Unit commercial kitchen ... 72
  gross area requirements ... 682
  heater cabinet ... 372
  heater electric ... 371
  heater removal hydronic ... 323
  removal condensing ... 322
  removal valance ... 323
Urinal ... 299
  high efficiency ... 302
  removal ... 109
  screen ... 63
  stall ... 299, 300
  stall type ... 299
  support ... 303
  system ... 480
  system battery mount ... 481

wall hung ... 299
  waterless ... 300
  watersaving ... 299
Utensil washer medical ... 74
  washer-sanitizer ... 74
Utility accessory ... 419
  box ... 419
  connection ... 419
  excavation ... 560, 562, 564
  line removal ... 22
  structure ... 579
  temporary ... 12
  trench ... 391
  trench excavating ... 391

V

Vacuum breaker ... 256
  breaker air gap ... 256
  catch basin ... 591
  central ... 76
  cleaning ... 76
  gauge ... 334
  loader ... 25
  pick-up ... 584
  pump ... 310
  pump medical ... 310
  system medical ... 310
  truck ... 591
  unit central ... 464
  wet/dry removal ... 591
Valance unit removal ... 323
Valve ... 324, 429
  assembly dry pipe sprinkler ... 102
  assembly sprinkler deluge ... 103
  backwater ... 283
  balancing & shut-off ... 344
  ball check ... 117
  box ... 428
  brass ... 111
  brass ball ... 324
  bronze ... 111
  bronze angle ... 111
  bronze butterfly ... 112
  bronze/brass ... 324
  butterfly ... 325, 428
  cabinet ... 67
  cap fire ... 99
  check ... 88, 429
  check lift ... 115
  circuit setter balance ... 341
  clamp ... 116
  control solar energy system ... 364
  CPVC ... 117
  cut in ... 427
  diaphragm ... 116
  draindown ... 365
  fire hose ... 99
  fire suppression ... 91
  float ... 343
  flush ... 302
  foot ... 118
  foot oil ... 335
  for medical gas ball ... 312
  fusible oil ... 335
  gas stop ... 111
  gate ... 325, 328, 429
  gauge zone ... 312
  globe ... 326, 328
  grooved joint ... 91
  grooved joint butterfly ... 204
  grooved joint gate ... 204
  heating control ... 344
  hospital type ... 329
  hot water radiator ... 344

744

Index

hydrant fire 99
hydrant screw type 99
iron body 325
lined 115
lubricated plug 327
materials 704-706
mixing 251, 298
mixing shower 296
motorized zone 335
needle 118
nonfusible oil 335
oil shut-off 335
plastic 116
plastic angle 116
plug 327
polypropylene 117
polypropylene ball 117
PVC 116
radiator 344
radiator supply 344
relief pressure 114
removal metal 110
removal plastic 111
selection considerations 704
semi-steel 327
sewage collection 431
shower by-pass 297
shower mixing 296
slow close ball 99
snubber 341
soldered gate 112
spout set shower-tub 298
sprinkler 88, 101
sprinkler alarm 88
sprinkler ball 99
sprinkler floor control 88
sprinkler trim 99
stainless steel 328
stainless steel globe 329
steam radiator 344
stop 298
swing check 112, 326
tag 130
tapping 427
tempering 115
washing machine 298
water pressure 114
water supply 298
water tempering 251
water utility distribution .. 428
with box zone 312
Y sediment strainer 118
Y-check 118
Valves grooved joint 91
Vanity base 78
  top lavatory 293, 482
Vaporizer oxygen 311
Vaporproof insulation ... 134, 141
Vent air automatic 341
  alarm 335
  automatic air 341
  cap 277, 335
  cap cast iron 277
  cap plastic 278
  chimney 353
  chimney all fuel 358
  chimney fitting 353, 358
  chimney flashing 354, 359
  chimney prefabricated rem. . 324
  convector or baseboard air . 368
  draft damper 353
  dryer 71, 299
  flashing 277
  flashing and cap removal .. 111
  gas 353
  metal chimney 353

radiator air 341
  removal relief 324
  sewage collection 431
Ventilation equipment
  and hood 352
  fan 382
  garage 350
Ventilator removal 324
  tunnel 592
Venturi flow meter 347
Vertical discharge heater ... 372
Vibrating screed,
  gas engine, 8HP 584
Vibration absorber 129
  absorbing hanger 129
  absorbing mount 129
  absorbing pad 129
Vibrator concrete 584
  earth 390
  plow 587
Vibratory hammer 586
  roller 586
Vitreous china lavatory 482
Vitreous-china service sink . 487

W

Wafer check valve 115, 327
Wall cap residential 350
  heater 72
  hung lavatory 294
  hung urinal 299
  hydrant 257
  hydrant removal 109
  sheathing 48
  sleeve 254
  type cleanout 131
Wash bowl residential 293
  fountain 301
  fountain group 301
  fountain removal 109
  safety equipment eye/face . 306
Washer 122
  and extractor 70
  commercial 70
  dryer accessory 298
  pressure 590
  residential 71
Washer-sanitizer utensil 74
Washing machine automatic ... 71
  machine valve 298
Waste cleanup hazardous 24
  disposal hazardous 24
  packaging 28
  receptacle 65
  treatment sink 280
Wastewater treatment system . 468
Watchman service 18
Water atomizer 25
  balancing 330
  booster system domestic ... 260
  bubbler 491
  chiller remote 309
  chiller removal 324
  closet 292, 299
  closet chemical 468
  closet healthcare 304
  closet hospital 304
  closet removal 109
  closet seat 293
  closet support 303, 304
  cooler 308, 492
  cooler bottled 309
  cooler electric 308
  cooler support 304

copper tubing connector 250
dispenser hot 288
distiller 74
distribution pipe 421, 423, 426
filter 288
filter commercial removal .. 111
filter dirt and rust 288
flow indicator 88
fountain removal 109
hammer arrester 256
heater 72, 383
heater commercial 289, 291
heater electric 289
heater gas 290
heater gas residential 290
heater heat pump 367
heater instantaneous 288
heater insulation 132
heater oil-fired 291
heater point of use 288
heater removal 110
heater residential 72, 291, 383
heater residential electric 289
heater safety shut-off 115
heater storage tank 261
heater under the sink 289
heater wrap kit 132
heating hot 359, 368
hose 589
hydrant 257
level control 332
meter turbine 255
motor alarm 100
pipe 421
pressure booster package ... 260
pressure booster system 260
pressure reducing valve 114
pressure relief valve 114
pressure switch well 421
pressure valve 114
pump 348, 419, 590
pump fire 105
pump fountain 309
pumping 392
purification 288
reducer concrete 37
service lead free 573
softener 287
softener potable 287
softener removal 111
source heat pump 367
storage solar tank 365
storage tank indoor 261
supply copper pipe 426
supply detector meter 254
supply domestic meter 254
supply ductile iron pipe ... 421
supply HDPE 425
supply meter 254
supply polyethylene pipe ... 422
supply PVC pipe 423
supply stop 298
supply valve 298
supply well pump 421
tank 338, 430, 591
tempering valve 115, 251
trailer 591
treatment 468
treatment potable 288
treatment salt 287
utility distribution valve . 428
well 419
Water-closet 479
  battery mount 479
  system 478
Water-heater electric .. 498, 501

gas-fired 499, 502
oil-fired 500, 503
solar-energy ... 507, 509, 511, 513, 517, 523
Waterless urinal 300
Watersaving urinal 299
Water-source heat pump 367
Water-water exchange hot ... 366
Wearing course 406
Weather data and design
  conditions 685
Weatherproof receptacle 380
Wedge anchor 43
Weights and measures 687
Weld fitting 190
  fume hood removal 323
  joint pipe 169, 207
  plastic pipe 244
  rod 45
  rod aluminum 45
  rod cast-iron 45
  rod stainless 45
  rod steel 45
Welded beam attachment 119
  structural steel 699
  wire epoxy 36
  wire fabric 36
  wire galvanized 36
Welding fillet 44
  fume elimination 352
  labor stainless-steel 211
  labor steel 172
  machine 591
  structural 44
Weld-O-Let 193
Weld-on flange steel 193
Well 392
  & accessory 419
  casing PVC 420
  casing steel 420
  gravel pack 419
  pump 419
  pump shallow 421
  screen steel 420
  thermometer 197
  water 419
  water pressure switch 421
Wellpoint 393
  discharge pipe 594
  equipment rental 594
  header pipe 594
  pump 594
  riser pipe 594
Wellpoints 718
Wet sprinkler seismic
  component 545-547
  sprinkler system 545
  standpipe riser 552
Wet/dry vacuum 591
Wheel trencher 587
Wheelbarrow 591
Wheeled loader 586
Whirlpool bath 75, 81
  hospital 305
Whirlpool/hot tub removal .. 109
Widener pavement 592
Winch truck 591
Window A/C removal 324
  air conditioner 366
Windrow loader 592
Winter concrete 37
  protection 16
Wire 716
  fence 17
  thermostat 383
Wiring air conditioner 383

745

Index

fan 382
   residential 378, 382
Wood firestop 48
   framing 48
   framing miscellaneous 48
   nailer 48
   plank scaffold 14
   sheet piling 719
   sheeting 392, 719
Work boat 594
   extra 11
Worker protection 25
Workers' compensation 11, 693
Wrapping pipe 412
Wrecking ball 591
Wrench impact 588
   sprinkler head 101
Wye fire hose 100

X

X-ray pipe 330

Y

Y sediment strainer valve 118
   type bronze body strainer 346
   type iron body strainer 346
Yard fountain 81
Y-check valve 118

Z

Zone valve gauge 312
   valve with box 312

Notes

Notes

Notes

Division Notes

	CREW	DAILY OUTPUT	LABOR-HOURS	UNIT	BARE COSTS				TOTAL INCL O&P
					MAT.	LABOR	EQUIP.	TOTAL	

Division Notes

	CREW	DAILY OUTPUT	LABOR-HOURS	UNIT	BARE COSTS				TOTAL INCL O&P
					MAT.	LABOR	EQUIP.	TOTAL	

Division Notes

	CREW	DAILY OUTPUT	LABOR-HOURS	UNIT	BARE COSTS				TOTAL INCL O&P
					MAT.	LABOR	EQUIP.	TOTAL	

Division Notes

	CREW	DAILY OUTPUT	LABOR-HOURS	UNIT	BARE COSTS MAT.	LABOR	EQUIP.	TOTAL	TOTAL INCL O&P

2023 Training Class Options
A tradition of excellence in construction cost information and services since 1942

Virtual classes offered monthly. Call for the schedule. ☏ 877.620.6245

Gordian offers training classes in a variety of formats—eLearning training modules, instructor-led classes, on-site training, and virtual training classes, as well as custom solutions. Please visit our website at rsmeans.com/products/training/seminars for our current schedule of class offerings.

Training classes that are offered in one or more of our formats are: Building Systems and the Construction Process; Construction Cost Estimating: Concepts & Practice; Introduction to Estimating; Scope of Work for Facilities Estimating; Facilities Construction Estimating; Fundamentals to Construction Cost Estimating; Maintenance & Repair Estimating for Facilities; Mechanical & Electrical Estimating; RSMeans CostWorks CD; and RSMeans Data Online Training.

Registration Information

How to register

By Phone
Register by phone at 877.620.6245

Online
Register online at rsmeans.com/products/services/training

Note: Purchase orders or credits cards are required to register.

Instructor-led Government Pricing

All federal government employees save off the regular seminar price. Other promotional discounts cannot be combined with the government discount. Call 781.422.5115 for government pricing.

If you have any questions or you would like to register for any class or purchase a training module, call us at 877.620.6245.

Construction Cost Estimating: Concepts and Practice

This one- or two-day introductory course to improve estimating skills and effectiveness starts with the details of interpreting bid documents and ends with the summary of the estimate and bid submission.

Topics include:
- Using plans and specifications to create estimates
- The takeoff process — deriving all tasks with correct quantities
- Summarizing the estimate to arrive at the final number
- Formulas for area and cubic measure, adding waste and adjusting productivity to specific projects
- Evaluating subcontractors' proposals and prices
- Adding insurance and bonds
- Understanding how labor costs are calculated
- Submitting bids and proposals

Who should attend: project managers, architects, engineers, owners' representatives, contractors, and anyone responsible for budgeting or estimating construction projects.

Fundamentals to Construction Cost Estimating

This self-paced course focuses on unit price estimating for facilities renovation, repair, and remodeling. Combining hands-on skill building with a discussion of best estimating practices and real-life problems, this informative online course will boost your estimating skills, bring you up to date with key concepts, and provide tips and guidelines that can save you time and help you avoid costly estimating oversights and errors.

Topics include:
- The three phases of estimating
- Bid document review
- How to perform quantity takeoffs
- How to price the work

Who should attend: facilities professionals and anyone involved in facilities planning, design, and construction.

For novice estimators, this course can serve as a primer to Facilities Construction Estimating Self-Paced Training or the following live training courses: Facilities Construction Estimating, Mechanical & Electrical Estimating, Assessing Scope of Work for Facilities Estimating, or Maintenance & Repair Estimating.

Mechanical & Electrical Estimating

This two-day course teaches attendees how to prepare more accurate and complete mechanical/electrical estimates, avoid the pitfalls of omission and double-counting, and understand the composition and rationale within the RSMeans data mechanical/electrical database.

Topics include:
- The unique way mechanical and electrical systems are interrelated
- M&E estimates — conceptual, planning, budgeting, and bidding stages
- Order of magnitude, square foot, assemblies, and unit price estimating
- Comparative cost analysis of equipment and design alternatives

Who should attend: architects, engineers, facilities managers, mechanical and electrical contractors, and others who need a highly reliable method for developing, understanding, and evaluating mechanical and electrical contracts.

Facilities Construction Estimating

In this two-day course, professionals working in facilities management can get help with their daily challenges to establish budgets for all phases of a project.

Topics include:
- Determining the full scope of a project
- Understanding of RSMeans data and what is included in prices
- Identifying appropriate factors to be included in your estimate
- Creative solutions to estimating issues
- Organizing estimates for presentation and discussion
- Special estimating techniques for repair/remodel and maintenance projects
- Appropriate use of contingency, city cost indexes, and reference notes
- Techniques to get to the correct estimate quickly

Who should attend: facility managers, engineers, contractors, facility tradespeople, planners, and project managers.

Assessing Scope of Work for Facilities Construction Estimating

This two-day practical training program addresses the vital importance of understanding the scope of projects in order to produce accurate cost estimates for facilities repair and remodeling.

Topics include:
- Discussions of site visits, plans/specs, record drawings of facilities, and site-specific lists
- Review of CSI divisions, including means, methods, materials, and the challenges of scoping each topic
- Exercises in scope identification and scope writing for accurate estimating of projects
- Hands-on exercises that require scope, takeoff, and pricing

Who should attend: corporate and government estimators, planners, facility managers, and others who need to produce accurate project estimates.

CostWorks CD Self-Paced Training Course

This self-paced course helps users become more familiar with the functionality of the CD. Each menu, icon, screen, and function found in the program is explained in depth. Time is devoted to hands-on estimating exercises.

Topics include:
- Searching the database using all navigation methods
- Exporting RSMeans data to your preferred spreadsheet format
- Viewing crews, assembly components, and much more
- Automatically regionalizing the database

This training session requires users to bring a laptop computer to class and to follow along using a purchased copy of RSMeans data CostWorks CD.

When you register for this course you will receive an outline for your laptop requirements.

Maintenance & Repair Estimating for Facilities

This two-day course teaches attendees how to plan, budget, and estimate the cost of ongoing and preventive maintenance and repair for existing buildings and grounds.

Topics include:
- The most financially favorable maintenance, repair, and replacement scheduling and estimating
- Preventive planning and facilities upgrading
- Determining both in-house and contract-out service costs
- Annual, asset-protecting M&R plan

Who should attend: facility managers, maintenance supervisors, buildings and grounds superintendents, plant managers, planners, estimators, and others involved in facilities planning and budgeting.

RSMeans Data Online Training

Construction estimating is vital to the decision-making process at each state of every project. Our online solution works the way you do. It's systematic, flexible, and intuitive. In this self-paced course you will see how you can estimate any phase of any project faster and better.

Topics include:
- Customizing our online estimating solution
- Making the most of RSMeans data "Circle Reference" numbers
- How to integrate your cost data
- Generating reports, exporting estimates to MS Excel, sharing, collaborating, and more

Also offered as a self-paced or on-site training program!

RSMeans data Training Cancellation Policy

Virtual Training (Individual)
If you are unable to attend a training class, a colleague may substitute at any time before the session starts by notifying the training registrar at 781.422.5115 or your sales representative. Gordian is not responsible for sending duplicate materials to the substitute colleague.

If you are unable to find a substitute and cancel fewer than ten (10) business days prior to the training class, you will either forfeit the registration fee or be allowed to apply your registration fee to the same class only once within the same calendar year. No-shows will forfeit their registration fees and no rescheduling is permitted. In the unfortunate circumstance that Gordian must cancel your event, Gordian will work with you to reschedule your attendance in the same training class at a later date or will fully refund your registration fee.

Any on-demand (self-paced) training modules are not eligible for cancellation, substitution, transfer, return, or refund.

Virtual Training (Private Group)
If you provide notice more than ten (10) business days prior to the training class, Gordian will work to reschedule your event. If you cancel your event fewer than ten (10) business days prior to the training class, you are responsible for paying for the trainer's time for the cancelled training, as well as the full cost of materials and shipping. In the unfortunate circumstance that Gordian must cancel your event, Gordian will work with you to reschedule your attendance in the same training class at a later date or will fully refund your registration fee.

Public Training Events (Individual)
If you are unable to attend a training conference, a colleague may substitute no fewer than ten (10) business days before the session starts by notifying the training registrar at 781.422.5115 or your sales representative. Gordian is not responsible for sending duplicate materials to the substitute colleague.

If you are unable to find a substitute and cancel fewer than ten (10) business days prior to the conference, you will forfeit the registration fee. No-shows will forfeit their registration fees and no rescheduling is permitted. In the unfortunate circumstance that Gordian must cancel your event, Gordian will fully refund your registration fee.

On-Site Training (Private Group)
If you provide notice more than ten (10) business days prior to the training class, Gordian will work with you to reschedule your event, but you are responsible for rescheduling fees associated with the trainer's time, airfare, and lodging. If you cancel fewer than ten (10) business days before your event, you are responsible for the full cost of the event. In the unfortunate event that Gordian must cancel your event, Gordian will work with you to reschedule your attendance at a later date or will fully refund your registration fee.

AACE Approved Courses
The AACE recognizes .1 CEUs per hour of training attended for all of Gordian's virtual training courses.

AIA Continuing Education
We are registered with the AIA Continuing Education System (AIA/CES) and are committed to developing quality learning activities in accordance with the CES criteria. Many seminars meet the AIA/CES criteria for Quality Level 2. AIA members may receive 14 learning units (LUs) for each two-day course.

Daily Course Schedule
The first day of each seminar session begins at 8:30 a.m. and ends at 4:30 p.m. The second day begins at 8:00 a.m. and ends at 4:00 p.m. Participants are urged to bring a hand-held calculator since many actual problems will be worked out in each session.

Continental Breakfast
Your registration includes the cost of a continental breakfast and a morning and afternoon refreshment break. These informal segments allow you to discuss topics of mutual interest with other seminar attendees. You are free to make your own lunch and dinner arrangements.

Hotel/Transportation Arrangements
We arrange to hold a block of rooms at most host hotels. To take advantage of special group rates when making your reservation, be sure to mention that you are attending the Gordian RSMeans data seminar. You are, of course, free to stay at the lodging place of your choice. Hotel reservations and transportation arrangements should be made directly by seminar attendees.

Important
Class sizes are limited, so please register as soon as possible.